THIRTY-FIFTH EDITION

KOVELS'
ANTIQUES
& COLLECTIBLES

PRICE LIST

FOR THE 2003 MARKET
ILLUSTRATED

THREE RIVERS PRESS
NEW YORK

THE CROWN PUBLISHING GROUP

Copyright © 2003 by Ralph and Terry Kovel

All rights reserved. No part of this book may be reproduced or transmitted
in any form or by any means, electronic or mechanical, including photocopying,
recording, or by any information storage and retrieval system,
without permission in writing from the publisher.

Published by Three Rivers Press, New York, New York.
Member of the Crown Publishing Group, a division of Random House, Inc.

www.randomhouse.com

THREE RIVERS PRESS and the Tugboat design are registered trademarks
of Random House, Inc.

Printed in the United States of America

Library of Congress Catalog Card Number: 83-643618

ISBN 0-609-80982-2

10 9 8 7 6 5 4 3 2 1

THIRTY-FIFTH EDITION

BOOKS BY RALPH AND TERRY KOVEL

American Country Furniture, 1780–1875

A Directory of American Silver, Pewter, and Silver Plate

Kovels' Advertising Collectibles Price List

Kovels' American Art Pottery:
The Collector's Guide to Makers, Marks, and Factory Histories

Kovels' American Silver Marks, 1650 to the Present

Kovels' Antiques & Collectibles Fix-It Source Book

Kovels' Bid, Buy, and Sell Online

Kovels' Book of Antique Labels

Kovels' Bottles Price List

Kovels' Collector's Guide to American Art Pottery

Kovels' Collectors' Source Book

Kovels' Depression Glass & Dinnerware Price List

Kovels' Dictionary of Marks—Pottery & Porcelain

Kovels' Guide to Selling, Buying, and Fixing
Your Antiques and Collectibles

Kovels' Guide to Selling Your Antiques & Collectibles

Kovels' Illustrated Price Guide to Royal Doulton

Kovels' Know Your Antiques

Kovels' Know Your Collectibles

Kovels' New Dictionary of Marks—Pottery & Porcelain

Kovels' Organizer for Collectors

Kovels' Price Guide for Collector Plates, Figurines,
Paperweights, and Other Limited Editions

Kovels' Quick Tips—799 Helpful Hints
on How to Care for Your Collectibles

Kovels' Yellow Pages: A Collector's Directory

The Label Made Me Buy It: From Aunt Jemima to Zonkers—
The Best-Dressed Boxes, Bottles and Cans from the Past

INTRODUCTION

This is the 35th year *Kovels' Antiques & Collectibles Price List* has been published. And the book is still being written by the original authors, Ralph and Terry Kovel. It has changed from a book with no illustrations and typewriter-style letters to this edition with hundreds of pictures and logos, about 50,000 prices, and dozens of tips about care. For this milestone anniversary edition, we have included a very special 16-page full-color insert, *Flea Market Finds,* which includes photographs and prices of unusual flea market buys from the past year.

READ THIS BEFORE YOU USE THIS BOOK—IT WILL HELP

This is a book for the average collector. All year we check prices, visit shops, shows, and flea markets, read hundreds of publications and catalogs, check online computer services and the Internet, and decide what antiques and collectibles are of most interest. We concentrate on the average pieces in any category. Sometimes one or two high-priced pieces are included in a category so you will realize that some of the rarities are quite valuable. For example, this year a very special collection of cast-iron toys sold at auction for exceptionally high prices. A few of these prices have been included.

Examples of furniture, silver, Tiffany, or art pottery may sell for more than $50,000; we list a few of those examples. The highest price in this book is $126,750 for a Hubley toy motorcycle van, "Say It with Flowers." The lowest price is $0.75 for a medical license. Most pieces we list cost less than $10,000. We even list the weird and the wonderful. This year you can find prices for a dressing stand with a money section and a mirror adorned with blue lights for $2,500 (it was used in a 1920s bordello); and an 18-inch piece of barbed wire from the Pine Ridge Indian Reservation for $5.50. If you search, you will find a lighter advertising Uncle Sam Cereal, a natural laxative, for $63; an advertising print for a cabinetmaker and undertaker for $115; and a judicial wig with a ponytail for $1,150. The smallest object is a half-inch button for $3. The largest is a Renaissance Revival breakfront bookcase, 110 inches by 90 inches, for $8,625.

Prices are up in some categories. Arts and Crafts and Art Pottery continue to rise in price. Especially active are Marblehead and Grueby pottery. A 12-inch-square Grueby tile with seven-color artwork auctioned for $73,700. Nippon is selling for very high prices because it is so popular with Japanese buyers. Ruby overlay glass is selling well and is pricey. There is continued interest in garden antiques of all kinds, from old flowerpots to large fountains. California-made pottery of the 1950s and Western and farm collectibles are popular in certain regions. Anything glass or pottery that is marked Czechoslovakia sells quickly.

The antiques malls that had been springing up all over the country seem to be doing less business. Some now offer items they also list on the Internet. Many have closed. Auctions and sales on the Internet are also influencing prices. A survey showed that Internet auction prices are still dropping; eBay prices are down 11 percent this year. The number of pieces listed that actually sold fell 24 percent from last year. Approximately 45 percent of serious buyers of antiques now use computers (and most of the new users are more than sixty years old). This percentage is increasing each year. The online market is international and getting larger. This has changed the pricing of some collectibles. Objects that are known in most of the world, such as pens, cigarette lighters, toys, Royal Doulton pottery, and ordinary '50s furniture, are selling at the same or slightly lower prices than last year. Only exceptional pieces are going for the extraordinary prices reported in the news media.

Each year categories are added or omitted to make it easier for you to find your antiques. New categories this year are Doll Clothes, Stone, and Royal Hickman.

The book is kept at about 800 pages because it is written to go with you to sales. We try to have a balanced format—not too many glass, pottery, or collectible items, a variety of furniture from the 18th through the 20th centuries, not too many items that sell for more than $5,000. The prices are *from* the American market *for* the American market. Few European sales are reported. We take the editorial privilege of not including any prices that seem to result from "auction fever." The computer-generated index is so complete it amazes us. Use it often. An internal alphabetical index is also included. For example, there is a category for Celluloid. Most items made of celluloid will be found there, but if there is a toy made of celluloid, it will be listed under Toy and also indexed under Celluloid. There are also cross-references in the listings and in the paragraphs. But some searching must be done. For example, Barbie dolls are found in the Doll category; there is no Barbie category. And when you look at "doll, Barbie," you will see a note that tells you that Barbie is under "doll, Mattel, Barbie" because most dolls are listed by maker. We differentiate between doll furniture made to a scale suitable for display of dolls and dollhouse furniture made in the small scale meant for a dollhouse.

All pictures and prices are new every year, except pictures that are pattern examples shown in Depression Glass and Pressed Glass. Photographs have been computer-enhanced to make them as crisp as possible. Antiques pictured are items offered for sale, not museum pieces. We hate to waste space, so whenever computer-generated spaces appear, we fill them with tips about care of collections, security, and other useful information. These tips are set in special type, so they will not be confused with the prices. Leaf through the book and learn how to wash porcelains, store textiles, guard against theft, and much more. We use new tips every year. Don't discard this book when it is time to buy a new one next year. Old Kovels' price books should be saved for future reference, and for tax and appraisal information.

The prices in this book are reports of the general antiques market. Each year every price in the book is new. We do not estimate or "update" prices. Prices are actual asking prices, although a buyer may have negotiated a price to a lower figure. No price is an estimate. We do not pay dealers and writers to estimate prices. Experience has shown that a collector of one type of antique is prejudiced in favor of that item, so those estimated prices are usually high or low, but rarely a true report. If a price range is given, it is because at least two identical items were offered for sale at different times. The computer prints the high and low figures. Price ranges are found only in categories like Pressed Glass, where identical items can be identified. If the price listed in this book is from an auction, it includes the buyer's premium, but like all the prices, it does not include sales tax. Some prices in *Kovels' Antiques & Collectibles Price List* may seem high and some may seem low because of regional variations. But each price is one you could have paid for the object somewhere in the United States.

If you are selling your collection, do not expect to get retail value unless you are a dealer. Wholesale prices for antiques are usually 50 percent less than retail. Remember, the antiques dealer must make a profit or go out of business. Internet auction prices are less predictable. Because of the international audience and "auction fever," prices often are higher or lower than retail.

THE RECORD PRICES HYPE

The media loves to report record prices, amazing auctions, high-priced discoveries, and events that really have little to do with the antiques and collectibles market familiar to the average collector. Over the past year, front-page stories told of a Chinese vase deaccessioned by a museum that was valued at $1,200, then for $1.45 million after it was auctioned in Hong Kong; and a Shaker stool that was found in storage after 30 years that sold for $2,100. Great stories, but—like winning the lottery—not likely to happen to everyone. So enjoy studying the auction records, but remember that these are the prices for the rarest and best.

RECORD-SETTING PRICES

ADVERTISING

Pub jug: $4,919 (£3,410) for a Barnsley Brewery jug made by Royal Doulton, 1906, 6 inches high.

CLOCKS AND WATCHES

Horner clock: $106,400 for a highly carved Horner mahogany grandfather clock with carved figures and nine-tube Westminster chime movement, 10 feet tall.

Any wristwatch: $1,911,770 for a yellow gold Patek Philippe wristwatch reference 1591 with a perpetual calendar, moon phases combined with indirect center seconds, and a screw-back case.

Stainless steel wristwatch: $1,129,500 for a stainless steel Patek Philippe gentleman's wristwatch with single-button chronograph, vertical registers, and pulsometer, c. 1926.

FURNITURE

American Windsor furniture: $138,000 for a sack-back Windsor chair with black painted finish and arm terminals carved as stylized hands.

Wooton desk: $123,200 for a Renaissance Revival Wooton desk, carved walnut, inlaid satinwood and ebony, with a gallery mounted with Trafalgar lion and crowns of royalty on either end, opens to drawers and pigeonholes, 73 x 42 x 30 inches.

Picture frame by Stanford White: $43,700 for an 1890s applied ornament and gilded frame designed by architect Stanford White, with raised grill, 24 x 32 inches; frame width, 8½ inches.

Wallace Nutting secretary: $36,750 for a No. 733 mahogany block-front, nine-shell Chippendale secretary, copied from one made by the Goddard-Townsend family, 104 inches.

Greene & Greene chiffonier: $311,000 for a Honduras mahogany chiffonier designed by Charles and Henry Greene, with five interior adjustable shelves, each door inlaid with mother-of-pearl; wood and metal "tree of life" design; fitted on the reverse with a full-length mirror, c. 1908, 69¼ x 55¼ x 25 inches.

LAMPS AND LIGHTING

Tiffany wisteria floor lamp: $324,800 for a Tiffany winter white and blue wisteria floor lamp, 24-inch-diameter shade.

Handel leaded lamp: $40,250 for a Handel leaded glass globe lamp mounted on a hollow bronze-type figure of Atlas, 54 inches tall with an 18-inch-diameter globe.

MISCELLANEOUS

Best Actress Oscar: $578,000 for the Oscar Bette Davis received as Best Actress for the Warner Brothers movie *Jezebel* in 1938.

Military belt: $32,380 for a military belt with an oval lead-filled brass plate bearing the Arkansas coat of arms in relief, c. 1861.

PEZ candy container space gun: $6,262 for a plastic PEZ space gun, bronzed-gold color with rocket ship and planetary symbols on the handle, dating from the late 1950s to early '60s, 5 inches.

Confederate military item: $54,625 for a Confederate officer's sword, forged by Alexandre Henri Dufilho, a New Orleans sword maker.

Fabergé Winter egg: $9,570,000 for the "Winter" Russian Imperial Easter egg produced by Carl Fabergé, decorated with 3,000 diamonds, including rose-cut diamonds; contained within the egg is a "surprise"—a basket of delicate spring flowers symbolizing the rebirth and seasonal change associated with Easter.

First typewriter: $84,000 for the first typewriter that was produced in a series, the 1867 Malling Hansen Writing Ball.

Parade saddle: $375,000 for the Roy Rogers McCabe parade saddle created during the Depression and designed with 31 artist-carved gold and silver scenes. Containing 1,400 ounces of sterling, 156 ounces of gold, and more than 500 Czechoslovakian rubies.

PAPER

Sainte-Marie-des-fleurs poster: $2,760 for the Paul Berthon Art Nouveau poster "Sainte-Marie-des-fleurs" advertising a novel by René Boylesve; depicting the image of a woman caressing flowers, 1898, 23¾ x 16¼ inches.

Le Livre de Magda poster: $2,300 for the Paul Berthon Art Nouveau poster "Le Livre de Magda" advertising a book of poetry with the image of a young woman with flowing blond hair, white doves, and flowering plants against a green and orange sky, 1898, 25¼ x 17⅞ inches.

Nectar: $4,600 for Plate 14 from *Documents Décoratifs*, called "Nectar," by Alphonse Mucha, a sensuous image advertising a mythical product; used as an instructional example of advertising techniques for art students, matted and framed, 15⅛ x 6½ inches.

Mucha poster: $47,150 for a complete set of Alphonse Mucha's "The Times of the Day, Paris," 1899.

Single comic book: $350,000 for the "Pay Copy" of Marvel Comics No. 1, with notations on pages and cover regarding payments to the creator of each story inside, cover date for Marvel Comics No. 1, October–November 1939.

POTTERY AND PORCELAIN

Wemyss pottery: $24,040 for a Wemyss pottery pig, in a seated position with black sponged marking on a shaded pink and white body, 18 inches long, c. 1900, printed retailer's mark for Thomas Goode & Co., impressed "Wemyss Ware R.H.&S." (A 6½-inch-long Wemyss pottery piglet in a sleeping position and painted with thistles sold for $18,210 at the same sale.)

Mocha ware: $50,600 for a baluster-form mocha ware jug with ocher, rust, and brown bands and dipped fans in marbled white, brown, and rust slip, c. 1810, 9½ inches.

Head vase: $4,000 for a 14-inch lady-head vase with pearl earrings, green outfit, and bow in hair, marked "Relpo #1982" (only four are known).

Korean porcelain jar: $1,200,000 for a Korean blue and white porcelain dragon-decorated jar, inverted pear shape, short neck, 19 inches high.

SPORTS

Kelson salmon fly: $2,750 for a full-dressed Gut Eyed Salmon Fly by George M. Kelson, tied on a 10/0 hook, 3¾ inches; professionally framed in an 8 ½-x-10-inch deep-walnut frame with three mats, 1880.

Baseball bat: $577,610 for Shoeless Joe Jackson's baseball bat, "Black Betsy."

Mickey Mantle baseball card: $275,000 for a Mickey Mantle mint 1952 Topps card.

TOYS, DOLLS, AND GAMES

Boy Robbing Bird's Nest mechanical bank: $34,720 for the J. & E. Stevens Co. cast-iron mechanical bank, "Boy Robbing Bird's Nest." Place the coin on tree limb, press the lever, and the limb falls against the tree, depositing the coin, c. 1906.

Automotive cast-iron toy: $126,750 for a Hubley cast-iron clockwork "Say It with Flowers" van drawn by an Indian motorcycle with driver, turquoise paint and gold trim, black roof and flower decals, c. 1932, 10¾ inches.

Albert Marque doll: $215,000 for an Albert Marque French bisque doll with socket head, portraying an older child; blue glass paperweight inset eyes, painted lashes, brush stroked and feathered brows, closed mouth, and original red mohair wig in bobbed cut, wearing original Margaine-Lacroix costume, 1916, 22 inches.

Schmitt & Fils doll: $48,000 for a French bisque Bebe made by Schmitt & Fils, with brown glass inset eyes, brush-stroked multifeathered brows, closed mouth, blond mohair wig, composition and wooden eight-loose-ball-jointed body, wearing antique undergarments and a gown of teal and ivory silk satin with matching bonnet, 19th century, 31 inches.

A NOTE TO COLLECTORS

You already know that this is a great overall price guide for all sorts of antiques and collectibles. Each entry is current, every picture is new, all prices are accurate.

But in the collecting world, things change quickly. Important sales produce new record prices. Fakes appear. Rarities are discovered. To keep up with these developments, read *Kovels on Antiques and Collectibles,* a monthly newsletter with up-to-date information on the world of collecting. It is filled with color photographs, about forty to an issue. The newsletter reports prices, trends, auction results, Internet sales, and other pertinent news for collectors *as it happens.* For a free sample of *Kovels on Antiques and Collectibles,* fill out and mail the postage-paid postcard at the back of this book. We also have a FREE informational website that gives pricing information, lists of important publications and sources for collectors, and excerpts from our newsletter. Visit www.kovels.com to learn more.

KEEP READING—
HOW TO USE THIS BOOK

There are a few rules for using this book. Each listing is arranged in the following manner: CATEGORY (such as Pressed Glass or Furniture), OBJECT (such as vase), DESCRIPTION (as much information as possible about size, age, color, and pattern). Some types of glass, pottery, and silver are exceptions to this rule. These are listed CATEGORY, PATTERN, OBJECT, DESCRIPTION. All items are presumed to be in good condition and undamaged, unless otherwise noted. If a maker's name is easily recognized, like Gustav Stickley, we try to include it near the beginning of the entry. If the maker is obscure, the name may be at the end. Because the descriptions are part of actual reports, we do not edit to make everything consistent in each category. We try to edit enough to be sure that two items are not actually two descriptions of the same piece.

Several special categories were formed to make the most sensible listing possible. For instance, "Tool" includes special equipment because the casual collector might not know the proper name for an "adze." Many of the glass entries are in special categories: Glass-Art, Glass-Blown, Glass-Contemporary, Glass-Midcentury, and Glass-Venetian. Major glass factories are still listed under the factory names, and well-known types of glass, such as cut, pressed, Depression, Carnival, etc., can be found in their own categories. The silver listings are also a bit different. You will find silver flatware in either Silver Flatware Plated or Silver Flatware Sterling. You will also find a section for Silver Plate, which includes coffeepots, trays, and other plated pieces. Solid or sterling silver is listed by country, so look for Silver-American, Silver-English, etc. Silver jewelry is listed under jewelry. Most pottery or porcelain is listed by factory name, such as Weller; or by item, such as Calendar Plate; or in sections like Dinnerware or Kitchen; or in a special section, Pottery-Art, Pottery-Contemporary, Pottery-Midcentury, etc.

Sometimes we make arbitrary decisions based on the number of entries or the amount of interest in a subject. Fishing has its own category, but hunting is part of the larger category called Sports. We have eliminated all guns except toys. It is not legal to sell weapons without a special license, so guns are not part of the general antiques market. Airguns, BB guns, rocket guns, and others are listed in the "Toy" section. Several idiosyncrasies of style appear because the book is printed by computer. Everything is listed according to the computer alphabetizing system. This means words such as "Mt." are alphabetized as "M-T," not as "M-O-U-N-T." All numerals are before all letters; thus "2" comes before "A." A quick glance will make this clear, as it is consistent throughout the book.

We made several editorial decisions. A bowl is a "bowl" and not a "dish," unless it is a special dish, such as a pickle dish. A butter dish is a "butter." A salt dish is called a "salt" to differentiate it from a saltshaker. It is always "sugar and creamer," never "creamer and sugar." Political collectors often refer to "pinbacks," the round celluloid or tin pins that are decorated with candidates' names and faces. The word "button" is sometimes used in this book instead of the word "pinback." Of course, the word "button" is also used when referring to the fasteners used on clothing. Where one dimension is given, it is the height; or if the object is round, the dimension is the diameter. The height of a picture is listed before width. Glass is clear unless a color is indicated.

Every entry is listed alphabetically, but the problem of language remains. Some antiques terms, such as "Sheffield" or "Pratt," have two meanings. Be sure to read the paragraph headings to know the meaning used. All category headings are based on the language of the average person at an average show, and we use terms like "mud figures" even if not technically correct.

This book does *not* include price listings of fine art paintings, antiquities, stamps, coins, or most types of books. *Big Little Books* and similar children's books *are* included. Comic books are *not* listed, but original comic art and cels *are* listed in their own categories.

All photographs in *Kovels' Antiques & Collectibles Price List* are listed with the prices asked by the seller. "Illus" (illustrated nearby) is part of the description if a photo is shown.

There have been misinformed comments about how this book is written. We *do* use the computer. It alphabetizes, ranges prices, sets type, and does other time-consuming jobs. Because of the computer, the book can be produced quickly. The last entries are added in June; the book is available in October. This is six months faster than would be possible any other way. But it is human help that finds prices and checks accuracy. We read everything at least three times, sometimes more. We edit from more than 60,000 entries to the 50,000 entries found here. We correct spelling, remove incorrect data, write category headings, and decide on new categories. We sometimes make errors. Information in the paragraphs is reviewed and updated each year. This year more than fifty corrections and additions were made in the category paragraphs.

Prices are reports from all parts of the United States, Canada, and Europe, translated to U.S. dollars at the rate of exchange prevalent at the time of the sale. The average rate of exchange between June 2001 and June 2002 was $0.65 U.S. to $1 Canadian. Prices are from auctions, shops, Internet sales, and shows. Every price is checked for accuracy, but we are not responsible for errors.

We cannot answer your letters asking for specific price information. But please write if you have any requests for categories to be included in future editions or any corrections to information in the paragraphs or prices.

When you see us at the shows and flea markets, please stop and say hello. Don't be surprised if we ask for your suggestions for the next edition of *Kovels' Antiques & Collectibles Price List.* Or you can write to us at P.O. Box 22200-K, Beachwood, Ohio 44122 or visit us at our website: www.kovels.com.

RALPH and TERRY KOVEL
July 2002

ACKNOWLEDGMENTS

We give special thanks to those who helped us with pictures and deeds: 20th Century Art & Design; Allard Auctions, Inc.; Andre Ammelounx; Auction Team Köln; Auctions Unlimited, Inc.; Be-Hold, Larry Gottheim; Bill Bertoia Auctions; Christie's; Cincinnati Art Galleries; Collectors Auction Services; Conestoga Auction Co.; Cottone Auctions; Craftsman Auctions; David Rago Auctions, Inc.; DeFina Auctions; Fontaine's Auction Gallery; Garth's Auctions, Inc.; Gary Metz's Muddy River Trading Co.; Gene Harris Antique Auction Center, Inc.; Glass-Works Auctions; Green Valley Auctions, Inc.; Ingrid O'Neil; Jackson's International Auctioneers & Appraisers; James D. Julia, Inc.; Jay Brown; Ken Farmer Auctions; Lang's Sporting Collectables, Inc.; Leland's Auctions; Los Angeles Modern Auctions; Mastronet; McMasters; New Orleans Auction Galleries, Inc.; Pacific Glass Auctions; Phillips; Randy Inman Auctions; Replacements, Ltd.; Robert C. Eldred Co., Inc.; Skinner, Inc.; Smith & Jones, Inc.; Smith House Toys; Sotheby's; Strawser Auction Group, Theriault's; Treadway Gallery, Inc.; Vicki & Bruce Waasdorp Auctions; William Doyle Galleries; Wm. Morford; York Town Auction Inc.

To the others in the antiques trade who knowingly or unknowingly contributed to this book, we say "thank you": A Touch of Glass Ltd.; American Pottery Auction; American Social History & Social Movement; American Toys; Anderson Auction; Annetta Bosselman; Antique Cane Auction; Antique Cowboy, David Denton; Antique Toy & Train Auction; ARK Antiques Catalog; Arthur Auctioneering; Automobilia Auction; Autopia Advertising Action; Barbara Balin; Bill Boyd; Bill Egleston Inc.; Bob Brady; Bruce Forster; Buffalo Bay Auction Co.; Butterfields; C & K Collectibles; Carlton Antique Toys; Charles Toberman; Charlton Hall; Cheryl Peterson; Collection Liquidation Auction; Collectors Sales & Services; D. Tuttle; Danese Theisen; Darcia Antiques; Dave Hudson; David R. Geiger Antiques; David Troffer; Decorative Art Auction; Delmer H. Youngen; Diane Gentile; Dick's Antiques; Donn Moberg; DuMouchelle's Art Galleries Co.; EAC Gallery; Early American Glass; Early Auction Co.; Edward Burczy; Eugene Philbrick; Fern Martin; Fink's Off The Wall Auctions; Flip Side Auction; Flomaton Antique Auction; Fran's Fancy Finds; Frank H. Boos Gallery; Gisela Antiques; Glass International; Gloria Greenberg Antiques; Gordon Phifer; Green River; Gurley's Toys; Gus Knapp; Gus Kokimos; Hart's; Hays & Associates; Helen & Bob Rarey; Herbet Allgood; Hesse Galleries; Hodge Podge Antiques; Hoosier Peddler; Howard L. Bell; Jack Herbert; Joe & Joan Baldini; John Finch; Joy Luke; JR's Antiques; Ken Chane; Keystone Toy Trader; Kinzua County Antiques; L. H. Selman, Ltd..; Leona Parsley; Linda & Co.; Lynn Geyer's; Mannio's; Marcia Petrella; Maritime Antiques Auction; Martines' Antiques; Mary Seufer; Mary Tupta Antiques; Mayer Gold; Mostly Heisey, Rhoda Curley; Naomi & Wally Bernstein; Nell Hitt; Only Mint; Paul Efron Antiques; PF Reed; R. Goldberg; Richard Keat; Robert Hildreth;

Robert S. Brink; Robert W. Dyke; Roger K. Smith; Ron Farley; Ron Oser Enterprise; Ron Smith; Rona & Dick Taylor; Russ Cochran's Comic Art Auction; Ryan Coup; Serge Agadjanian; Slater's Americana; Sloan's Auction Galleries; Snow Hill Antiques; Steenburgh; Steve & Cathy Sawchuck's; Sussex Antique Toy Shop; Sweeney's Emporium; Team's Tiffany Treasures; Ted Kromer; Temple's Antiques; Thee Merchants; Thomas Hill Ecollection; Thomaston Place Auction Galleries; Tom Sage, Jr.; Tom Snook; Tony Murland; Trader Fred's Toys of Yore; Truax & Company; Utopia Advertising Auction; Village Antiques; W. Fagan & Co., Inc.; Wacky Wicker Workers; Wayne & Phyllis Hilt; Weschler's; Wicker's Antiques; William Adorjan; William J. Jenack Estate Appraisers & Auctioneers; Woody's Auction Services; Yesterday's South, Inc.

We can't do this huge job alone. It takes the help of many people. Change is inevitable, and this book has survived several changes in technology and staff. To those at Crown who have adapted to each change we say, "Thank you." Dorothy Harris, our editor, again successfully shepherded the book through all its birth pangs and then added her special touch. Linda Loewenthal, Cindy Berman, Karen Minster, John Sharp, and David Tran at Crown and Merri Ann Morrell at Precision Graphics worked through the computer mysteries, forced the data to behave, and created perfect, printed pages, clear photographs, and an index. Benjamin Margalit and George Merlis took many of the pictures that show the details and style of the antiques and collectibles. Every year the technology we use changes so that *Kovels' Antiques and Collectibles Price List* stays up-to-date. Our staff keeps learning new ways to get quicker price information and better pictures. This means a lot of extra work and we want to thank all of those who toil with us daily. Thank you to Carmie Amata, Debbie Bedell, Kitty Busher, Grace DeFrancisco, Marcia Goldberg, Evelyn Hayes, Katie Karrick, Fran Keesey, Liz Lillis, Heidi Makela, Eleanore Melzak, Sara Puliafico, Geoffrey Regensburger, Lisa Russo, Nancy Saada, June Smith, Cherrie Smrekar, Edie Smrekar, Katie Smrekar, and Virginia Warner. And to Karen Kneisley, who works with all the photos and also hunts down and proofs prices, we give special appreciation. But it is Gay Hunter who keeps track of all of us at Crown and at Kovels, who pushes each person to keep on schedule, who reads and rereads the copy, and who chases each correction or addition to the 500 paragraphs, manages the spelling list, and double-checks the other minutiae that make this book consistent and accurate. She also seems to be able to solve our problems and smile even when a deadline is looming and we are behind. It amazes us that this is the thirty-fifth time we have finished the price book. Much has changed in the book, but the hard work of everyone has made each one a reality.

A. WALTER made pate-de-verre glass under contract at the Daum glassworks from 1908 to 1914. He started his own firm in Nancy, France, in 1919. Pieces made before 1914 are signed *Daum, Nancy* with a cross. After 1919 the signature is *A. Walter Nancy*.

Ashtray, Burnt Orange, Brown, 6 3/4 In.	7200.00
Dish, Lobster, Brown, 3 1/2 In.	1265.00
Figurine, Seal, Green, L. Mercier, 7 1/2 In.	863.00
Paperweight, Bumblebee On Rounded Base, Signed, 1 1/2 In.	863.00
Paperweight, Butterfly, Green Base, 4 x 3 1/4 x 1 1/2 In.	3000.00
Paperweight, Green Frog On Circular Base, Signed, 1 1/2 In.	3220.00
Plaque, Madame Rabutin DeSevigne Center Medallion, Square, 5 1/4 In.	1250.00
Vase, Birds On Flowering Branches, Blue, Green, Signed, 6 1/4 In.	4313.00
Vase, Distant Landscape, Summer Trees, Grasses Around Signature, 5 In.	1232.00
Vase, Pink, Green Floral Bank, Pink Mottled Ground, Handles, Signed, 6 In.	1610.00

ABC plates, or children's alphabet plates, were most popular from 1780 to 1860, but are still being made. The letters on the plate were meant as teaching aids for children learning to read. The plates were made of pottery, porcelain, metal, or glass. Mugs and other items were also made with alphabet decorations.

Plate, 3 Children & Dog, Children's Rhyme, Embossed, Staffordshire, c.1840, 6 In.	125.00
Plate, 3 Girls & Dog, Embossed Alphabet	42.00
Plate, Ben Franklin, Value Of Money, 5 In.	110.00
Plate, Calendar, Clock, 7 1/2 In.	450.00
Plate, Cat & Mouse, Enamel, Elsmore & Son, England, c.1887, 7 1/8 In.	182.00
Plate, Clock, Amber Glass, Late 1900s, 7 In.	75.00
Plate, Clock-Time, Staffordshire, 6 1/4 In.	425.00
Plate, Dr. Franklin Maxim, Staffordshire, 8 1/4 In.	395.00
Plate, Girl On Bicycle, Flowers, Deep Blue, C.A. & Sons, England, 7 1/4 In.	160.00
Plate, Horses, Alphabet Rim, Staffordshire, 5 In.	67.00
Plate, Jack & Jill Rhyme, White, Blue, Lord Nelson	29.00
Plate, Kitten & Puppy, Victorian Motto, Forget Me Not, Think Of Me, Germany, 7 In.	20.00
Plate, Kittens In Yarn, Tin, Ohio Art, Bryan, Oh., 4 1/4 In.	76.00
Plate, Kittens Jumping Rope, Sign Language, H. Aynsley & Co., c.1880, 6 3/8 In.	370.00
Plate, Mary Had A Little Lamb, Tin, 19th Century, 8 In.	65.00
Plate, Scrolled Numbers, Alphabet, Flowers, 10 Animals, Raised Rim, England, 8 1/8 In.	42.00
Plate, The Walk, Jockey On Horseback, Transfer, 5 1/8 In.	165.00
Plate, Tom Thumb, Tin, 3 In.	103.00
Plate, Who Killed Cock Robin, Verse, Tin, 7 3/4 In.	50.00
Plate, Woman Holding Rake, 2 Children, Transfer, 6 In.	110.00

ABINGDON POTTERY was established in 1908 by Raymond E. Bidwell as the Abingdon Sanitary Manufacturing Company. The company started making art pottery in 1934. The factory ceased production of art pottery in 1950.

Bookends, Horse Head, Weighted, Sealed, 6 x 3 1/2 In.	65.00
Cookie Jar, Hobbyhorse	110.00
Cookie Jar, Jack-In-The-Box	260.00
Cookie Jar, Little Bo Peep	160.00
Cookie Jar, Little Ol' Lady, Maroon	160.00
Cookie Jar, Mother Goose	310.00
Figurine, Swordfish, Turquoise, White, Black, 1948-1949, 4 1/2 x 4 1/4 In.	82.00
Jam Pot, Fruit Shape Lids, Underplate, Turquoise, Marked, 4 Piece	86.00
Planter, Daffodil, Figural, Yellow	67.00
Planter, Pooch, Pink, 4 In.	67.00
Planter, Sleeping Man, Under Cactus, 1940	44.00
Shelf, Cherub, Marked, 7 1/2 In.	95.00
Vase, Baluster, Coral Embossed, Flower, Scroll Handles, 3 1/2 In.	55.00
Vase, Double Cornucopia, Yellow, 8 1/2 In.	35.00
Vase, Japanese Woman Kneeling, Blinds, Bamboo, 5 x 5 In.	85.00
Vase, Riding Boot, Figural, Green, 1947, 7 In.	85.00

Vase, White, 10 3/4 In. 20.00
Wall Pocket, Flower Shape, Stem, Leaves, Signed, 9 In., Pair 145.00

ADAMS china was made by William Adams and Sons of Staffordshire, England. The firm was founded in 1769 and became part of the Wedgwood Group in 1966. The name "Adams" appeared on various items through 1998. All types of tablewares and useful wares were made. Other pieces of Adams may be found listed under Flow Blue and Tea Leaf Ironstone.

ADAMS
ENGLAND

Bowl, Vegetable, Rose, Impressed Adams, 8 3/4 x 11 In. 1100.00
Coffeepot, Dome Top, Rose, Shaped Spout, Handle Impressed Adams, 10 3/4 In. 4950.00
Pitcher, Jasperware, Early 19th Century, 6 1/4 x 5 x 7 In. 575.00
Pitcher, Rose, Shell Spout, Shaped Handle, 8 In. 935.00
Plate, Rose, Beaded Edge, Impressed, 10 1/2 In., 6 Piece 743.00
Plate, Rose, Impressed, 8 1/2 In., 4 Piece 358.00
Plate, Rose, Impressed, 9 1/2 In., 4 Piece 468.00
Platter, Fairy Villas, Scalloped Rim, 22 x 17 In. 375.00
Platter, Rose, Impressed Mark, 9 x 11 In. 688.00
Teapot, 3 People, Tudor Style Cottages, Dark Blue Transfer, 7 1/4 In. 467.00

ADVERTISING containers and products sold in the old country store are now all collectibles. These stores, with the crackers in a barrel and a potbellied stove, are a symbol of an earlier, less hectic time. Listed here are many of the advertising items. Other similar pieces may be found under the product name, such as Planters Peanuts. We have tried to list items in the logical places, so large store fixtures will be found under the Architectural category, enameled tin dishes under Graniteware, paper items in the Paper category, etc. Store fixtures, cases, and other items that have no advertising as part of the decoration are listed in the Store category.

Ashtray, Griswold No. 00, Skillet Shape, Griswold Emblem, Square, 9 In. 40.00
Ashtray, Hamm's Beer, Ceramic 110.00
Ashtray, Molders Union 30.00
Ashtray, Old Judge Coffee, Tin Lithograph, 2 3/4 x 2 3/4 In. 56.00
Ashtray, S.G. Gray, Carriages, Ottawa, Ill., Iron, Woman & Fan Shape, 6 1/2 In. 230.00
Bag, Flour, Cloth, Belgrade Flour Mill Co., Uncle Sam, 1941, 36 x 18 In. 40.00
Banner, Cascarets, Bowel Troubles, Black Boy Eating Watermelon, 27 x 44 In. 3250.00
Banner, Levi's America's Finest Overall Since 1850, Blue Denim, 30 x 76 In. 2196.00
Banner, Mayo's Cock Of The Walk Plug Tobacco, Oilcloth, 30 x 18 In. 170.00
Banner, Old Honesty Plug Tobacco, St. Bernard Dog, Oilcloth, 50 x 17 1/2 In. 345.00
Banner, P.F. Flyers, Play Your Best, Be A Winner, Bob Cousy, 1950s, 9 x 34 In. 528.00
Banner, Philco, Pre World War II, 2 Sides 165.00
Banner, Smith Brothers Cough Drops, Cloth, 14 x 27 In. 105.00
Banner, Stetson Hats, Stylized For Young Men, 1920s, 15 1/2 x 20 In. 375.00
Banner, Wrangler Western Wear, Champion Cowboys, Denim, 1960s, 45 x 74 In. 67.00
Barrel, Putnams Whiskey, Wooden, 4 Rusted Bands, 7 x 10 In. 60.00

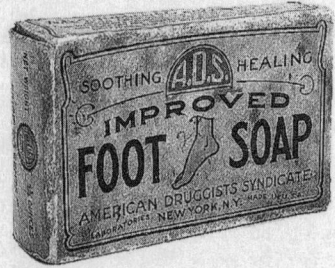

Advertising, Box, American Druggists, Improved Foot Soap, Contents, 4 1/4 In.

Advertising, Box, Assorted Hair Pins, Peacock, Gold Ink, 2 3/4 In.

Advertising, Box, Joke, Simpson's Cigars, Sit Down & Smoke, Little Chair, 1 In.

Advertising, Box, Parachute Powder, Dry Lubricant For Plastic Chutes, 3 1/4 In.

Billhook, Breakfast Cheer, Campbell Wood's Co. Coffee, Celluloid, 7 In.	135.00
Billhook, Hoppe Private Ambulance, Celluloid, 2 x 2 3/4 In.	100.00
Bin, Boardman & Sons, Coffee, Tea, 19 1/2 x 13 5/8 In.	610.00
Bin, Honest Scrap, Cat & Dog, Product, Hinged Lid, Tin, 18 x 12 In.	4400.00
Bin, Princess Coffee, Indian Princess, Hinged Lid, Peace Pipe, 23 1/2 x 11 3/4 In.	805.00
Bin, Sure Shot Chewing Tobacco, Indian, Bow & Arrow, 7 x 15 x 10 In.	855.00
Bin, Sure Shot Chewing Tobacco, Indian, Tin Lithograph, 15 1/4 x 8 x 10 In.	490.00
Bin, Tea, Bean & Co., Roll Front Door, Panel Of Victorian Woman, 12 1/2 x 19 In.	690.00
Bin, Tobacco, Jn. J. Bagley & Co., Game Bird Picture, Tin	450.00
Blotter, Ink, Meyer Radio Service, Castro & Diamond, San Francisco, 1930s	4.50
Blotter, Nestle's, Cherub Hugging Stork, Celluloid, 1910, 3 x 7 3/4 In.	60.00
Books may be included in the Paper category.	
Bottles are listed in their own category.	
Bottle Openers are listed in their own category.	
Box, see also Box category.	
Box, American Ace Tea, World War I Biplane, Cardboard, 3 1/4 x 2 1/2 In.	206.00
Box, American Druggists, Improved Foot Soap, Contents, 4 1/4 In. *Illus*	5.00
Box, Andrew Jergen's & Co., Uncle Sam, Wooden, 1870, 10 5/8 x 15 x 9 In.	115.00
Box, Assorted Hair Pins, Peacock, Gold Ink, 2 3/4 In. *Illus*	10.00
Box, Baker's Caracas Chocolate Tablets, Cardboard, 2 x 1 5/8 In.	165.00
Box, California Poppy Brand Oranges, Label, Lithograph, c.1888, 11 x 10 1/2 In.	525.00
Box, Cereal, Quaker Oats With Aunt Jemima's Old Plantation Pancakes, 7 x 4 In.	96.00
Box, Cigar, Rosewood, Silver Mounted, Mosaic Inlaid Lid, Porcelain, 4 1/2 x 10 In.	200.00
Box, Cigar, U.S. President William McKinley, Wood, 7 1/2 x 7 3/4 In.	85.00
Box, Cigarette, Princess, Colored Cigarettes, Wood, 1954	45.00
Box, Cobbler's Nails, Comical Black Man, Cardboard, 2 x 1 1/4 In.	95.00
Box, Crane's, Chocolate, Garden Of Allah, By Parrish, 1918, 11 x 5 In.	305.00
Box, Elizabeth Park Oats, Floral Garden, Cardboard, 7 1/2 x 4 1/4 In.	100.00
Box, Evenrude Motors, Outboard Marine & Mfg. Co., 1940s, 15 x 47 x 20 In.	85.00
Box, Fairbanks Floating Soap, Stenciled 2 Sides, Fairy Sitting On Rose	70.00
Box, Fairy Seeds, Seed Packs & Box, Wood, 12 x 7 x 4 In.	358.00
Box, Good Malden Coffee, Sears & Roebuck, 5 Lb., 10 1/2 In.	57.00
Box, Hindoo Spice, Wood, Detroit, Mich. Spice Co., 14 1/4 x 7 1/2 x 3 1/2 In.	72.00
Box, Hoyt's Candy, Boxcar Shape, Buffalo Peanuts, 18 1/2 In.	120.00
Box, Humphrey's Veterinary, Walnut, Divided Interior, Labels, Hardware, c.1900, 9 3/4 In.	336.00
Box, Joke, Simpson's Cigars, Sit Down & Smoke, Little Chair, 1 In. *Illus*	20.00
Box, Langcraft Electric Powered Outboard Motor, For LM-110 Model	11.00
Box, Parachute Powder, Dry Lubricant For Plastic Chutes, 3 1/4 In. *Illus*	10.00
Box, Shipping, Nigger Head Oysters, Auchinbauch Canning Co., Wood, 11 x 13 In.	775.00
Bread Box, Schepp's Coconut, Monkey Juggling Coconuts, Tin Lithograph, 1890s	200.00
Bread Box, Tin, Home Comet, Calumet, Square, c.1890, 12 In.	22.00
Broom Holder, Little Polly Brooms, Tin Lithograph, 6 1/4 x 2 1/2 In.	242.00
Broom Holder, Wilbur's Cocoa, Die Cut Tin Lithograph, 6 1/2 x 2 1/2 In.	495.00
Cabinet, Diamond Dyes, Blond Fairy, Philadelphia, 31 x 24 x 10 In.	1485.00
Cabinet, Diamond Dyes, Court Jester, Double Sliding Doors, 21 x 10 x 27 In.	810.00
Cabinet, Diamond Dyes, Evolution Of Women, 29 x 22 x 10 In.	550.00
Cabinet, Diamond Dyes, Governess, Embossed Tin Front, Wood, 30 x 22 x 10 In.	900.00
Cabinet, Diamond Dyes, Maypole, Front Door, Tin Sign, Wood, 30 x 22 x 10 In.	750.00

Cabinet, Display, Salerno, Baker Holding Coat Of Arms, Wood, 10 1/2 x 21 In. 150.00
Cabinet, Dr. Daniels' Veterinary Medicines, Wood, 19 x 27 x 7 In. 3000.00
Cabinet, Dr. Daniels', Embossed Tin Lithograph, Oak Case, 28 1/2 x 19 1/2 In. 468.00
Cabinet, Hanford's Balsam Of Myrrh, Oak, Glazed Door, 3 Shelves, 24 In. 425.00
Cabinet, Humphreys' Homeopathic Specifics, Cherrywood, 28 In. 1600.00
Cabinet, Humphreys' Specific Remedies, Oak, Glazed Top, 4 Drawers, 24 In. 1500.00
Cabinet, Lorillard Tin Tag Tobacco, Glass Door, Countertop, c.1800, 33 x 32 In. 2587.00
Cabinet, Munyon's Homeopathic Remedies, Oak, Tin Price List, 24 In. 290.00
Cabinet, P. Lorillard Tobacco, Inlaid Top, Reverse Etched Doors, 34 1/2 x 44 1/2 In. 5460.00
Cabinet, Putnam Dye, Gen. Putnam Picture, Tin Lithograph, 1920s, 19 x 14 In. 200.00
Cabinet, Spool, 4 Drawer, Willimatic Soft Finish Spool Cotton 6 Cord, 15 x 24 In. 281.00
Cabinet, Spool, Clark's Mile End Spool Cotton, Oak, 6 Drawers, 22 x 25 x 17 1/2 In. . . . 690.00
Cabinet, Spool, Clark's O.N.T. Spool Cotton, 6 Drawers . . . . .1350.00 to 1540.00
Cabinet, Spool, Clark's O.N.T. Spool Cotton, Walnut, 2 Drawers, 22 x 7 x 15 In. 402.00
Cabinet, Spool, Corticelli, 9 Drawers, Silk Thread, Oak 3300.00
Cabinet, Spool, Corticelli, 13 Drawers, Silk Thread, Oak 1210.00
Cabinet, Spool, Corticelli, 30 Drawers, Silk Thread, Oak 1430.00
Cabinet, Spool, Corticelli, Glass Front Top Drawers, Oak, 21 x 18 x 15 In. 460.00
Cabinet, Spool, Dorcas, 7 Drawers, Oak 2750.00
Cabinet, Spool, J. & P. Coats', 4 Drawers 470.00
Cabinet, Spool, J. & P. Coats', 6 Drawers 1265.00
Cabinet, Spool, J. & P. Coats', Lift Lid, 4 Drawers, Metal Pulls, 29 x 20 In. 250.00
Cabinet, Spool, J. & P. Coats', Oak, Lid, Register, 6 Drawers, 20 x 32 x 25 In. 605.00
Cabinet, Spool, J. & P. Coats', Original Spools, 2 Sliding Glass Doors, 23 x 10 In. 159.00
Cabinet, Spool, Kerr & Co.'s Dollar Brand, 6 Drawers, Oak 880.00
Cabinet, Spool, Pine, 12 Drawers, 2 Paneled Doors, Porcelain Knobs, 21 1/2 x 17 In. 200.00
Cabinet, Spool, Pine, Glass Front Drawers, 19th Century, 20 x 20 x 14 1/2 In. 635.00
Cabinet, Spool, Walnut, 3 Drawers, Brass Knobs, Some Label On Back, 11 x 18 In. 230.00
Cabinet, Vaseline, Tin, Back Door Access, 16 In. 100.00
Calendars are listed in their own category.
Can, Asset Cigar, Tin Lithograph, 5 1/2 x 4 1/2 In. 130.00
Can, Cigar, Cy Young 6710.00
Can, Home Run Cigar 3080.00
Can, Sky Ranger Aviation Motor Oil, Airplane, Flight Tested, White, Qt., 5 x 4 In. 160.00
Canisters, see introductory paragraph to Tins in this category.
Cards are listed in the Card category as card, advertising.
Case, Display, Curtiss Candy & Gum, Chicago, Ill., 48 x 153 x 72 In. 100.00
Case, Display, Doctor West's Toothbrush, Glass Slant Front, 9 x 13 x 7 In., 2 Piece 287.00
Case, Display, Eveready Battery, Tin Lithograph, c.1929, 16 1/2 x 9 1/4 In. 287.00
Case, Display, Keen Kutter Shears & Scissors, Etched Glass, Revolving, 31 In. 1150.00
Case, Display, Morse's Patent Straight Lip Drills, Mahogany, Doors, 14 x 28 x 8 In. 275.00
Case, Display, Poppers Cigar, Glass Slant Front Lid, 20th Century, 10 In. 170.00
Case, Display, Umbrella, F.C. Jougeson, Curved Glass Lift Top, Oak Trim, 48 In. 920.00
Case, Display, Zeno Gum, Oak, Glass Shelves, 18 x 10 1/4 x 8 In. . . . . .630.00 to 1595.00
Chair, P.B. Gravely Tobacco Co., Folding, Wood, 32 x 16 In. 145.00
Change Receiver, see also Tip Tray in this category.
Change Receiver, Miller High Life, 1950s, 5 1/2 x 4 In. 8.00
Change Receiver, Schlitz & Erlanger, Pair 28.00
Checkerboard, Hires Root Beer, Cover With Happy Boy, Square, 10 In. 200.00
Checkerboard, Hires Root Beer, Lithograph Covered, Folding, 12 x 6 In. 336.00
Cigar Cutter, Artie Cigars, Man, Sitting On Building, Smoking, Cast Iron 3190.00
Cigar Cutter, El Commercio Havana Cigars, Cast Iron, 1906, 9 In. 660.00
Cigar Cutter, My Friends Drink Hamm's Beer, Iron 345.00
Cigar Cutter, Rocky Ford, Cast Iron, Match Scratcher, Color Paper Indian Logo 660.00
Cigar Cutter, Yankee, Union Shield, Dispenses Matches, Cast Iron, 1900, 7 In. 750.00
Clocks are listed in their own category.
Coaster, Gretz Beer, 1940s, 4 In. 8.00
Coaster, Helbs, 1930s, 4 In. 11.00
Crock, Heinz, Apricot Preserves, 6 1/2 x 6 3/4 In. 965.00
Crock, Heinz, Cherry Preserves, Keystone Label, Stoneware, 1883, 5 3/4 x 4 3/4 In. 28.00
Crock, Heinz, Grape Jelly, Covered, Bail Handle, 9 1/2 In. 1050.00
Crock, Heinz, Keystone Pickling & Preserving Works, Pittsburgh, U.S.A., 1/2 Gal 675.00
Crock, Heinz, Preserves, Stoneware, Marked 1901, 7 1/2 x 4 1/2 In. 46.00

Cup, Armour's Vigoral, Pink Transfer Carnation On Outside, 3 1/2 In., 8 Piece 121.00
Cup & Saucer, Hills Brothers Tea & Coffee, Altenburg China, 5 In. 247.00
Decal, 7-Up, Die Cut, Dry Mount, 1971 . . . .   176.00
Dispenser, Bromo Seltzer, Inverted Bottle, Aluminum Base, 1930s, 15 1/2 In. . . . . .92.00 to 144.00
Dispenser, Cardinal Cherry Syrup, No Pump, 9 1/2 x 8 1/2 In., Pair 7700.00
Dispenser, Cherry Smash, Ceramic, 1900, 9 x 10 1/2 In. 1725.00
Dispenser, Daggett's Orangeade, Glass Bowl Top, Reverse Painted Base, 14 1/2 In. 460.00
Dispenser, Drink Ver-Ba, Ceramic, Vase Shape, 1918, 15 x 7 1/2 In. 1897.00
Dispenser, Fowler's Cherry Smash Syrup, Cluster Of Cherries, c.1900, 14 In. 1725.00
Dispenser, Grape Crush Syrup, Barrel Form, 10 In. 2300.00
Dispenser, Green's Muscadine Punch, Ceramic, Barrel, 1910, 8 1/2 x 12 In. 575.00
Dispenser, Hires Munimaker Marble Syrup, Clear Globe, 1909, 17 x 34 1/2 In. 3450.00
Dispenser, Hires Root Beer, Ceramic, Hourglass Shape, 14 x 7 In. 460.00
Dispenser, Howel's Orange Julep, 5 Cents, Ceramic, 14 x 9 In. 1495.00
Dispenser, Howel's Orange Julep, Orange Field, 1900, 14 In. 1810.00
Dispenser, Howel's Orange Julep, Orange, Porcelain, 15 In. 920.00
Dispenser, Lash's Syrup, Green Depression Glass, Black Base, 12 x 6 1/2 In. 150.00
Dispenser, Liggett's Root Beer Syrup, Side Dispenser, Oak Barrel, 13 In. 517.00
Dispenser, Maxwell House Iced Tea, Cover, Ceramic, Barrel, 9 x 12 In. 150.00
Dispenser, Mission-Real Fruit Juice, Lime Green Glass, 1950, 7 x 12 1/2 In. 60.00
Dispenser, Soap, Wall, Atlantic Refining, 6 In. 55.00
Dispenser, Victory Orange Punch, Trophy Shape, Metal, 32 x 51 In. 1380.00
Dispenser, Ward's Lemon Crush, Cherry Pump, Yellow Ground, 1920, 13 In. 1705.00
Dispenser, Ward's Orange Crush Syrup, 13 In. 1400.00
Display, 30 Cigars, Lady Liberty Holding Sword & Shield, Crown On Head, 19 In. 504.00
Display, Adam's Gum, Delicious Remedy For Indigestion & Dyspepsia, 1890s 625.00
Display, Barrus Mustard, 21 x 10 1/2 x 5 In. 132.00
Display, Budweiser, Clydesdales & Wagon, 1970, 23 In. 373.00
Display, Canada Dry, Die Cut, Cardboard, Signed, Armitage, Countertop, 28 In. 25.00
Display, Chesterfield Cigarettes, Martin & Lewis As Sailors, 1950, 30 x 60 In. 300.00
Display, Dingman Soap, Cardboard Lithograph, Countertop, Die Cut, Stand-Up 440.00
Display, Dutch Boy Paint, Uncle Sam, Cutout, 1918, 48 3/8 x 25 In. 400.00
Display, Ever-Ready Safety Razor, Cardboard, 3 Panels, 1920, 57 x 34 In. 149.00
Display, Folger & Co., Tea Bin, Tin Lithograph, Water & Import Ship 850.00
Display, Hartford Fire Ins. Co., Fire Wagon & Village, Oak Case, 19 x 58 In. 345.00
Display, Kotex, Nurse, Instructions, Counter Rack, 14 1/2 In. 200.00
Display, Lee Overalls, Figural, Boy Wearing Bib Overalls, Cardboard, 12 In. 138.00
Display, Life Saver, 3 Tiers, Tin, 10 Different Flavors Across Front, 30 x 14 In. 45.00
Display, Mazda Light Bulb, Art By Maxfield Parrish 440.00
Display, OshKosh B'Gosh, World's Best Overall, Cutout, 45 x 27 In. 345.00
Display, PEZ, Plastic, Red, 6 Dispenser Slots, Raised Name, 3 1/4 x 8 x 1/2 In. 24.00
Display, Red Goose Shoe, 2-Face Clown Head, Papier-Mache, 16 In. 258.00
Display, Remington, Different Nitro Club Boxes, 2 Shipping Crates, 32 1/4 In. 2100.00
Display, Smart Gum, True Blue Gum Co., Cardboard, 3 1/2 x 6 x 4 1/4 In. 265.00
Display, Smith Brothers Chewing Gum, 17 Original Packs 6050.00
Display, Splendid Furniture Finish, Wood, Tin Sign, 15 x 19 3/4 x 8 3/4 In. 578.00
Display, Tanlac Tonic, Nature's Medicine, Cardboard, 1930s, 51 x 33 In. 412.00
Display, Uncle Sam's High Grade Roasted Coffee, Tin, 1880, 22 x 12 1/2 In. 460.00
Display, Wheary Trunks, 3-D, Reverse Painted Glass, Light-Up, Frame, 13 x 16 In. 115.00
Display, Yucatan Gum, Tin, Hld. Beach Co., 1917, 6 1/2 x 6 x 4 3/4 In. 290.00
Dolls are listed in their own category.
Door Pull, Log Cabin Bread, Bakelite, Box, 1940s, 29 x 10 In. 300.00
Door Push, Chesterfield Cigarettes, Porcelain, 4 x 9 In. 578.00
Door Push, Duke's Mixture, Roll Of Fame, 5 1/4 x 8 In. 468.00
Door Push, Ex-Lax, Porcelain, 8 x 4 In. 358.00
Door Push, Hires, Metal, 13 1/2 x 2 5/8 In. 220.00
Door Push, Orange Crush, Porcelain, 1940s, 9 1/2 In. 413.00
Door Push, Orange Crush, Tin, 5 Cents, 1930s, 9 In. 523.00
Door Push, Rainbow Is Good Bread, Steel, 26 1/2 In. 230.00
Door Push, Stegmaier Brewing Co., Beer Bottle & Cone Top Can, 3 3/8 x 8 1/4 In. 85.00
Door Push, Sweet Heart Products, Porcelain, Die Cut, 5 x 5 In. 357.00
Door Push, Vicks, Porcelain, Product Box, 1930s 358.00
Door Push, Vicks, Vaporub Salve, Porcelain, Embossed, 6 1/2 x 3 3/4 In. 660.00

Fans are listed in their own category.

Figure, Bear, Fehr's Beer, Chalkware, 9 x 16 In.	45.00
Figure, Camp Lingerie, Woman, Composition, Wearing Lace-Up Bra, Girdle, 30 In.	500.00
Figure, Clinic Shoes, Nurse In Uniform, Cape, Walking, 22 In.	127.00
Figure, General Electric, Radio Man, Jointed Wood, Leather Chinstrap, 18 1/2 In.	920.00
Figure, Heinz 57 Tomato-Head, Rubber, Red Head, Green Leaf, Top Hat, 1940s	135.00
Figure, Lolli-Pop, Chief Watta Pop Brand, 9 1/2 x 9 1/2 In.	478.00
Figure, Nipper, RCA Victor, Papier-Mache, 36 In.	1550.00
Figure, OTC Medical Supports, Doctor, Holding Truss, Plaster, 25 x 19 In.	115.00
Figure, Q, Nestle's Quik Bunny, Bendable, Brown, Cream, Blue Q, 1980s, 6 In.	8.00
Figure, Reddy Kilowatt, Plastic, Luminous Gloves & Boots, c.1944, 5 In.	140.00
Figure, Wrigley's Gum, Arrow, Celluloid Face, Green, 1920s, 13 In.	495.00
Flyer, Bonnie Beach Resort, Lake Tahoe, Description & Rates, 1940s, 4 x 7 In.	9.00
Glass, Allen's Red Tame Cherry	25.00
Glass, Cascade Ginger Ale	35.00
Glass, Drink Moxie, Etched	45.00
Glass, Hiram Walker	5.00
Glass, Johnny Walker	5.00
Glass, Moxie Nerve Food, Etched	165.00
Glass, Walker's Bourbon, Gold Rim	15.00
Hat, GR Motorcoach Co., Die Cut Wing & Shield, 2 1/4 In.	145.00
Hat, McDonald's, Manager, Red Paper Headband, White Mesh Interior, 1954	35.00
Hat, Schlitz Beer, Straw, 1960s	4.00
Ice Box, Moxie, Lift Top, Pine, Lithograph, Grain Painted, 26 x 24 x 18 In.	345.00
Jar, Heinz, Pickle, Display, Glass, Ground Stopper, 9 1/2 x 5 In.	660.00
Jar, Horlick's Malted Milk, Reverse On Glass, 9 1/2 In.	420.00
Jar, Horlick's Malted Milk, Soda Fountain Display, Glass, Embossed Enameled Blue	330.00
Jug, Fine Prepared Mustard, James Marden, Rochester, 6 In. . . . .*Illus*	75.00
Jug, Shaker Brand Ketchup, Portland, Me., Gal.	165.00
Keg, Powder, Dupont, Metal, Green Paint, 25 Lb., 11 1/2 In.	55.00
Keg, Powder, Lafin & Rand, Metal, Orange Rifle 3F, 25 Lb., 11 3/4 x 9 1/2 In.	230.00
Key Chain, Nic-Nac Novelties, Cardboard Display, Airplanes, 11 x 7 1/2 In.	38.00
Key Fob, Washington's 200th Birthday, Brass, 1 1/4 In.	77.00
Kick Plate, Wishing Well Orange, Porcelain, 12 1/4 x 29 1/4 In.	155.00
Label, Beer, Free State Beer, 12 Oz.	5.00
Label, Beer, Peter Special Dark Beer, 1940s, 12 Oz.	27.00
Label, Beer, Phoenix Bock Beer, 1940s, 12 Oz.	18.00
Label, Beer, Tahoe, 1930s, 12 Oz.	33.00
Label, Cigar, American Citizen, George Washington, Eagle, Inner	5.00
Label, Cigar, Angel Brand, Cherub, Santa, 1900s	18.00
Label, Cigar, Dolly Madison, Brunette In Red Gown, 4 3/4 x 6 3/8 In.	3.50
Label, Cigar, Peaceful Henry, Winking Man, Smoking, Inner	9.00
Label, Cigar, Royal Opera, Romantic Couple, Castle, Outer, 4 1/2 x 4 1/2 In.	7.00
Label, Citrus, Basket Lemons, Blue Background, 12 1/2 x 8 3/4 In.	2.00
Label, Citrus, California Dream Oranges, Peacocks, Castle, Gilt, 11 x 11 In.	18.00
Label, Citrus, California Poppy Brand Oranges, Lithograph, 11 x 10 1/2 In.	525.00
Label, Citrus, Full O' Juice, Peeled Orange, Glass Of Juice, Lavender, 11 x 11 In.	2.00
Label, Citrus, Galleon Lemons, Sailing High Seas, c.1937, 12 1/2 x 8 3/4 In.	6.00
Label, Citrus, King David Oranges, King With White Beard, 11 x 11 In.	7.00
Label, Citrus, Mammy Brand, Mammy Holding Orange, 1950s, 3 1/2 x 8 1/2 In.	13.00
Label, Citrus, Orbit Oranges, Meteor In Shape Of Orange, Starry Skies, 11 x 11 In.	10.00
Label, Citrus, Sea Bird Lemons, Sea Gull, Yellow Letters, Blue, 12 1/2 x 8 3/4 In.	4.00
Label, Cosmetics, Queen Beauty Toilet Soap, Woman, Peacock, River, 8 1/4 x 14 In.	3.00
Label, Food, Black Joe Juice Grapes, Smiling Black Man, 4 1/4 x 13 In.	13.00
Label, Food, Don't Cry Sweet Potatoes, Black Youth Shooting Dice, 9 x 9 In.	5.00
Label, Food, Honest John, Man In Overalls Holding Crate Of Yams, 9 x 9 In.	6.00
Label, Food, Red Rooster Asparagus, Crowing Rooster, Red, Yellow, Navy, 7 x 9 In.	3.00
Label, Fruit, A Plus Pears, American Girl Athlete, 10 3/4 x 7 1/4 In.	2.00
Label, Fruit, American Eagle Grapes, Bald Eagle, Spread Wings, 13 x 4 In.	2.00
Label, Fruit, Apple Kids, 2 Boys Dragging Huge Apple Up Hill, 10 1/2 x 9 In.	4.00
Label, Fruit, Boy Blue Pears, Boy Blowing Horn, 10 3/4 x 7 1/4 In.	3.00
Label, Fruit, Eatmor, Boy In Overalls, Straw Hat, Holding Bitten Apple, 10 1/2 x 9 In. . . .	6.00
Label, Fruit, Gloria Apples, Ship, Sea, Sea Gull, Green Apples, 10 1/4 x 10 1/4 In.	8.00

**Never wash a tobacco "felt."
The small flannel flags and
pictures that were packed
with cigarettes in the early
1900s lose value if washed.**

Advertising, Jug, Fine
Prepared Mustard, James
Marden, Rochester, 6 In.

Advertising, Pennant, Pure
Gold Lemons, Mutual Orange
Distributors, Cal., 10 1/2 In.

Label, Fruit, Golden West, Bay, Ships Framed By Grapes & Plums, 13 x 4 In.	2.00
Label, Fruit, K O Pears, Boxing Glove Delivering Knockout Punch, 10 3/4 x 7 1/4 In.	8.00
Label, Fruit, Monmouth Cranberries, Revolutionary War Scene, 7 x 10 In.	2.00
Label, Fruit, Snomaid, Woman Throwing Snowball, Red Apple, 1935, 10 1/2 x 9 In.	20.00
Label, Fruit, Valley Home, Purple Plums On Aqua, 7 x 9 In.	1.00
Label, Fruit, White Swan Apples, Mama Swan & Cygnets, 8 1/4 x 11 In.	7.00
Label, Hotel, Albert Pike, View, 1930s, 3 1/2 In.	10.00
Label, Hotel, Antler's, Open All Year, Blue & White, 1930s, 2 3/4 In.	10.00
Label, Hotel, Brown Palace, One Of America's Hotel Aristocrats, 1930s, 3 1/4 In.	12.00
Label, Hotel, Del Monge, Cypress Point, 1930s, 3 3/4 In.	11.00
Label, Hotel, Fred Harvey, Red Ground, White Lettering, c.1930, 3 x 3 1/4 In.	11.00
Label, Hotel, Grunewald, Yellow Lettering, 4 1/8 In.	45.00
Label, Hotel, Monte Vista, Flagstaff, Green & White, c.1930, 4 1/2 x 2 In.	11.00
Label, Hotel, Santa Barbara Biltmore, Rose & Ivory, 1930s	11.00
Label, Hotel, Seminole, Image Of Seminole Indian, Oval, 1930, 5 1/4 x 4 In.	15.00
Label, Hotel, Senator, Pictures Hotel, 1930s	9.00
Label, Medicine, Extract Witch Hazel, 3 x 4 1/4 In.	1.00
Label, Milk, Clover Farm, Evaporated Milk, Cow, Clover Blossom, 2 1/4 x 8 In.	1.50
Label, Tobacco, Black Oak, Early American Military Parade, 12 1/2 x 6 1/2 In.	357.00
Lamps are listed in the Lamp category.	
License Tag, Mountain Dew, Tin, 1960s, 6 x 12 In.	60.00
Lunch Boxes are listed in their own category.	
Matchbook, Broadmoor Hotel, Catering To Gentile Clientele, 1940s	47.00
Matchbook, Manners Big Boy, Figural, Sandwich, Phone Number, 1960s	10.00
Megaphone, Dr Pepper, Heavy Paper, Metal Ring At Top, c.1950	385.00
Menu, Coor's Beer, 1940s, 6 1/2 x 9 7/8 In.	4.00
Menu, Del Tahquitz Hotel, Breakfast, Lunch & Pool, Floral Front, 7 x 10 In.	20.00
Menu, Edgewater Beach Hotel, Marine Dining Room, 9-15-1939	19.00
Menu, Fox Head 400 Beer, 1930s, 7 1/2 x 10 1/8 In.	11.00
Menu, Hotel Jayhawk, Kansas Statehouse, Jayhawk Logo, 1945, 8 1/2 x 12 In.	19.00
Menu Board, Squirt, Embossed Tin, 1950, 27 1/2 x 19 1/2 In.	165.00
Milk Can, Lid, Corrugated Steel, Geo. D. Ellis & Sons Inc., 5 Gallons Liquid, 25 In.	100.00

Advertising mirrors of all sizes are listed here. Advertising pocket mirrors range in size from 1 1/2 to 5 inches in diameter. Most of these mirrors were given away as advertising promotions and include the name
of the company in the design.

Mirror, Anderson Soups, Old Man Eating Bowl Of Soup, Celluloid, 1 3/4 In.	210.00
Mirror, Arrow Root, Pocket	95.00
Mirror, Aurora Beer, Pocket	33.00
Mirror, Ballantine Beer, Smoked Glass, 20 x 30 In.	33.00
Mirror, Beeman's Pepsin Gum, Celluloid, 2 1/8 In.	176.00
Mirror, Cantrihum Overalls, Brattleboro, Vt., Celluloid, Boxcar, 1 3/4 x 2 3/4 In.	154.00
Mirror, Cascarets, Pocket	125.00
Mirror, Charles Child's Buggy & Harness, Celluloid, 1 3/4 In.	165.00

Mirror, Cherry Brand, Fine Chocolates & Bon Bons, Gold Handle & Rim 100.00
Mirror, Cinzano, Pocket 45.00
Mirror, Emmett Cigars, Nude Woman, Celluloid, 2 3/4 x 1 3/4 In. 291.00
Mirror, Frisco Line, Train On Scenic Route, Celluloid, 2 1/8 In. 176.00
Mirror, Granola Digestives, Pocket 75.00
Mirror, H.P. Hood, Dairy Products, Celluloid, Cow In Center, 1 3/4 x 2 3/4 In. 198.00
Mirror, Highland Brand Canned Goods, Scottie In Kilt, Playing Bagpipes, Pocket 135.00
Mirror, Hires Root Beer, Foaming Mug Of Root Beer, Pocket, 1908, 3 In. 1300.00
Mirror, Hudson Fulton Celebration, 1909, 1 3/4 In. 187.00
Mirror, Humphrey's Witch Hazel Oil, Beveled, 11 x 9 In. 170.00
Mirror, Jamestown Expo, Skeleton Talking Into Wall Phone, Celluloid, 2 1/4 In. 256.00
Mirror, King Arthur Flour, Trademark Logo, Celluloid, 2 1/8 In. 132.00
Mirror, Lexington Autos, Roadster, Celluloid, 1 3/4 x 2 3/4 In. 440.00
Mirror, Lifebuoy Soap, Pocket 45.00
Mirror, Newbro's Hair Tonic, Celluloid, 2 3/4 x 2 In. 146.00
Mirror, Old Bridgeport Whiskey, Barrel Shape, Celluloid, 1 3/4 x 2 1/4 In. 104.00
Mirror, Providence Fenders, Train Conductor Looking At Fender Contraption, 2 In. 605.00
Mirror, Randall's Grape Juice, Celluloid, Round, 1 3/4 In. 118.00
Mirror, Statler Hotel, Celluloid, 2 7/8 x 1 3/4 In. 168.00
Mirror, Turkish Bath Oil, Hand Tinted Photo, Celluloid, 2 3/4 x 1 3/4 In. 206.00
Mirror, Watertown Daily Newspaper, Uncle Sam, Celluloid, 2 1/8 In. 232.00
Mirror, Wells Fargo & Co., Express, Crossed Flags, Frame, 1800s, 58 x 58 In. 1725.00
Mirror, Zymole Trokeys Gum, Celluloid, 2 3/4 x 1 3/4 In. 1980.00
Mug, Choo Choo Cherry, Red, Face, Hat, Plastic, 1969, 3 In. 10.00
Mug, Dad's Root Beer, Glass, 1950s, 5 1/4 In. 9.00
Mug, Goofy Grape, Purple, Green Hat, Eyes, Teeth, Plastic, 1969, 3 In. 7.00
Mug, Hires Root Beer, Little Boy With Bib, Mettlach, 5 In. 287.00
Mug, Nestle's Quik Rabbit, Embossed, Ears As Handles, Plastic, 1970s, 4 In. 10.00
Nodder, Big Boy, 1998, 7 1/2 In. 20.00
Pack, Cigarette, Camel, Contents, 1959 . . . . 20.00
Pack, Cigarette, Lucky Strike, Contents, 1959 . . . . 20.00
Pack, Cigarette, Tarreyton, Full, 1953 . . . . 25.00
Pack, Gum, Sweet 16, Wrigley, Trademark Girl, 1 3/8 x 1 1/4 In. 25.00
Pail, Buffalo Brand Peanut Butter, Tin Lithograph, Handle, Lb., 4 In. 190.00
Pail, Bunny Peanut Butter, Tin Lithograph, Rabbits & Animals, 12 Oz. 476.00
Pail, Dixie Kid Tobacco, Black Kid, Tin, 8 x 5 1/4 x 4 In. 468.00
Pail, Dixie Kid Tobacco, Bred In Old Kentucky, Tin Lithograph, Clasp Lock, 8 x 5 In. 165.00
Pail, Dixie Kid Tobacco, White Kid, Tin, 8 x 4 1/4 x 3 3/4 In. 2210.00
Pail, Dixie Queen Tobacco, 4 1/4 x 7 7/8 x 5 1/4 In. 165.00
Pail, Gail & Ax Tobacco, Sailor On Lid, Tin Lithograph, 4 3/4 x 7 1/2 In. 183.00
Pail, Green Turtle Cigars, Turtle Smoking, Tin Lithograph, 5 1/4 x 4 3/8 In. 210.00
Pail, Jolly Time Popcorn, Children, Tin Lithograph, 1920, 4 1/2 x 3 3/8 In. 426.00
Pail, Monarch Popcorn, Color Lithograph, Kids Popping Corn, 1920s, 3 3/4 x 3 In. 413.00
Pail, Morris Supreme Peanut Butter, Children At Seashore, Lb. 440.00
Pail, Mosemann's Peanut Butter, Tin Lithograph, Bail Handle, Lancaster, Pa., Lb. 33.00
Pail, Navy Tobacco, Gail & Ax, Silver Graphics, 7 1/2 x 4 1/2 x 4 3/4 In. 715.00
Pail, North Pole Tobacco, North Pole In Middle, 6 x 4 x 6 In. 385.00
Pail, Pickwick Peanut, 9 1/4 x 8 In. 153.00
Pail, Red Riding Hood Candy, Nursery Rhyme Images, 3 x 2 7/8 In. 715.00
Pail, Sweet Girl Peanut Butter, Bail Handle 750.00
Pail, Virginia's Pride Peanut Butter, Tin Lithograph, Yellow, 3 5/8 x 3 1/2 In. 334.00
Pail, Yorkshire Farm Peanut Butter, Children At Maypole, 3 1/4 x 3 1/2 In. 825.00
Panel, Glass, Lakeside Club Bouquet, People Sitting, Table, Frame, 18 1/2 x 21 In. 3300.00
Pencil, Ellsworth & Thayer, Makers Of Sheepskin Products, German Silver 35.00
Pencil, John Deere 7.50
Pencil, Mechanical, Neuweiler's Ale & Beer, 1940s 22.00
Pencil, Mutual Oil Co., Kansas City, Missouri, Nickel Plated Metal 6.00
Pencil, Poth's Beer, Christmas, 1930s 11.00
Pennant, Pure Gold Lemons, Mutual Orange Distributors, Cal., 10 1/2 In. . . . . *Illus* 7.50
Pin, Muhammad Ali For St. John's Toothpaste, Boxing Mr. Toothdecay, 1974 . . . . 450.00
Pin, Nabisco, Inner Seal In Logo, Celluloid, 1 In. 9.00
Pin, Wonder Woman Sensation Comics, Yellow & Red, 1942, 1 1/4 In. 1090.00
Pitcher, Myers, Importers Of Foreign & Domestic Liquors, c.1840, 9 1/4 In. 1500.00

Plaque, Indian Head, Plaster, Hanger Mountings, Tobacco Promo, 9 1/2 In. 10.00
Platter, Crawford Cooking Ranges, Oval 175.00
Pot Scraper, Mt. Penn Stove Co., Tin Lithograph, 2 7/8 x 3 3/8 In. 151.00
Pot Scraper, Sharples Cream Separator, Woman With Pail 225.00
Pouch, Tobacco, Old King Cole, 1920s 255.00
Rain Gauge, John Deere, Tin, Glass Tube, 1940, 5 In. 65.00
Record, Burger King, Red Skelton, Cardboard, Pledge Of Allegiance, 1969 . . . . 17.00
Salt & Pepper Shakers are listed in their own category.
Scales are listed in their own category.
Shaker, Jell-O, Yellow, Plastic, Peter Max Enterprises Inc., 1972, 7 1/4 In. 20.00
Sign, 7-Up, 2 Sides, Hanging, Fold-Out, 3-Dimensional, 1950s, 10 x 17 In. 230.00
Sign, 7-Up, Double Button, 1950s, 22 x 24 In. 935.00
Sign, 7-Up, Embossed, Pictures Bottle, Fresh Up, 1962, 48 x 18 In. 660.00
Sign, 7-Up, Embossed, Tin, Red Ground, White Lettering, 1947, 13 3/4 x 18 In. 210.00
Sign, A.J. Friend Bootmaker & Repairer, Tin, Wood, 19th Century 13 1/2 x 26 In. 822.00
Sign, Academy Parlor, Pocket Billiards, Reverse Painted, Illuminated, 32 In. 2300.00
Sign, Aces Up Soda, 3 7/8 x 10 In. 137.00
Sign, Advance Rumley, Power Farming Machinery, Cardboard, 15 x 21 In. 230.00
Sign, Ajax Heavies, 4 Geese, Box Of 12-Gauge Ajax Heavies Shells, 32 x 22 In. 2205.00
Sign, Ambulance, Wood, Arched Panel, Painted, Gilt Letters, 6 1/2 x 48 1/2 In. 1035.00
Sign, American Agricultural Chemical Co., Porcelain, 2 Sides, 25 x 18 In. 80.00
Sign, American Clover Blossom Co., Black & White, Frame, 1890, 16 x 20 In. 46.00
Sign, American Insurance Company, Newark, N.J., Dark Blue, England, 14 In. 155.00
Sign, American Lady Corsets, Pink & White Dress, Hat, Paper, Frame, 34 x 23 In. 440.00
Sign, Anamosa Ice Cream, Cardboard, Die Cut, Easel Back, 16 x 28 In. 93.00
Sign, Andy Pepsodent, Andy Holding Tube Of Pepsodent, Die Cut, 1930, 54 In. 950.00
Sign, Anheuser-Busch, Budweiser, Girl In Red Dress, 38 x 24 In. 1150.00
Sign, Anheuser-Busch, Custer's Last Fight, Cardboard, Wood Frame, 1897, 44 In. 610.00
Sign, Anheuser-Busch, Custer's Last Fight, Frame, 1930s, 46 x 36 In. 862.00
Sign, Ansell's, The Robin Hood, Tin, Oak Frame, 50 x 35 1/2 In. 660.00
Sign, Anvil, Tin, Late 19th Century, 16 x 11 x 30 1/2 In. 862.00
Sign, Apothecary, Mortar & Pestle, Figural, Copper, Jewels, Light-Up, 1900, 32 In. 2185.00
Sign, Apothecary, Mortar & Pestle, Figural, Iron Brackets For Hanging, 40 x 19 In. 3055.00
Sign, Appleby & Wallace Composition Roofers, Wood, Painted, 18 x 38 In. 259.00
Sign, Arden Fine Ice Cream, Wood & Masonite, 12 x 7 3/8 In. 160.00
Sign, Arden Ice Cream, Porcelain, Oval, 36 x 48 In. 440.00
Sign, Armour's Star Ham & Bacon, Boy Selling Ham To Lady, Tin, 1901, 21 In. 523.00
Sign, Armstrong Linoleum, Tin Over Cardboard, Gold Lettering, 34 x 10 In. 45.00
Sign, Arthurettes Cigars, Gentleman Loaded Down With Cigars, 11 x 15 In. 315.00
Sign, Ask For Free's Pure Rye, Rich & Mellow, Glass, Reverse Painted, 17 x 21 In. 1128.00
Sign, Athlophoros Rheumatism & Neuralgia Cure, Chromolithograph, 32 x 21 In. 650.00
Sign, Atlantic Beer, Man With Tray, Tin, Embossed, Frame, 17 x 22 3/4 In. 300.00
Sign, Atwater Kent Radio, Paper, c.1924 . . . . 230.00
Sign, Aultman Taylor, Tin Lithograph, Embossed, 1900, 13 1/2 x 19 1/2 In. 710.00
Sign, Ayer's Cathartic Pills, Putti Pouring Pills On Dish, Lithograph, 13 x 10 In. 300.00
Sign, Ayer's Cathartic Pills, Safe, Pleasant & Reliable, 1890, 27 x 13 In. 690.00
Sign, Ayer's Cherry Pectoral, Little Girl Holding Cherries & Bottle, 13 x 10 In. 250.00
Sign, Ayer's Hair Vigor, Glass, Reverse Painted, 15 x 13 In. 1600.00
Sign, Ayer's Hair Vigor, Long Haired Lady, Knapp Co., N.Y., 1896, 18 x 13 In. 400.00
Sign, Ayer's Hair Vigor, Young Lady With Flowing Hair By River, Tin, 22 x 16 In. 1000.00
Sign, Ayer's Sarsaparilla, Bottle Within Wreath, Chromolithograph, 13 x 10 In. 350.00
Sign, Ayer's, The Old Folks At Home, Seated Elderly Couple, Die Cut, 10 In. 130.00
Sign, Babbit's Soap, Paper, Matted, Frame, 21 x 35 1/2 In. 215.00
Sign, Baker's Vegetable Horse & Cattle Powder, Tin Lithograph, 28 x 32 In. 2800.00
Sign, Bar, On Suspended Gilded Sphere, Wrought Iron Hook, 18 In. 3738.00
Sign, Barker's Liniment, Dandy, Elegant Ladies, Farm, Car, By Hayes, 20 x 15 In. 600.00
Sign, Barnum & Bailey Circus, Evetta The Lady Clown, c.1895, 14 x 11 In. 105.00
Sign, Bartholomay Brewing Co., Girl, Riding Wheel, Wings, Frame, 45 x 35 In. 330.00
Sign, Beech-Nut Tobacco, Image Of Package, Tin, 17 1/2 x 13 1/2 In. 86.00
Sign, Beer, Neon, Polychrome, Metal, Painted, 24 x 14 x 5 5/8 In. 460.00
Sign, Belar Cigars, Tin Lithograph, Stepped Frame, Hanging, 10 x 7 1/2 In. 45.00
Sign, Ben Hur Five Cent Cigar, Chariot, Tin, Wood Frame, 25 1/2 x 17 1/4 In. 345.00
Sign, Berghoff Beer, Tin Over Cardboard, String Hung, 13 x 21 In. 70.00

Sign, Bergner & Engel Brewing, Paper On Cardboard, Frame, 13 x 16 In. 115.00
Sign, Best Food Co., American Artworks, Tin, 1910 . . . . 1100.00
Sign, Bijou Cigars, Young Woman Standing On Dock With Ocean, 1900, 15 In. 495.00
Sign, Bill Lynch Circus, Aerial View, 29 x 43 1/4 In. 77.00
Sign, Blue Jay Corn Plasters, Tin Lithograph, Man, 1930s, 14 x 4 In. 495.00
Sign, Bohemian Beer, Blinking Light-Up, 1940s, 14 In. 385.00
Sign, Bookseller, Wood, Cutout, 14 x 18 In. 1230.00
Sign, Boot, Giltwood, 19th Century, 16 3/4 x 32 x 2 3/4 In. 690.00
Sign, Boot, Giltwood, 19th Century, Full Body, 15 3/4 x 26 In. 920.00
Sign, Borden Milk, Elsie Emblem, Tin, Self-Framed, 17 1/2 x 17 1/2 In. 120.00
Sign, Boschee's German Syrup, Green's August Flower, Laboratory, Linen, 26 In. 375.00
Sign, Boschee's German Syrup, Green's August Flower, Woman, Easel, Tin, 30 In. 1000.00
Sign, Bottle, Wood, Painted, 19th Century, 35 3/8 x 9 In. 805.00
Sign, Bromo-Seltzer, Monochromatic, 14 3/4 x 12 1/2 In. 150.00
Sign, Brookfield Rye, Seminude Woman Holding Bottle, Tin Frame, 33 x 23 In. 2750.00
Sign, Brown's Vermifuge Comfits, Worm Lozenges, Board, Mom & Child, 13 In. 150.00
Sign, Buckeye Cultivators, We Sell Buckeye Cultivators, Flange, 18 1/2 x 9 In. 50.00
Sign, Budweiser Girl, Standing, Matted, Frame 1300.00
Sign, Budweiser, Horses & Stagecoach, Frame, 28 1/2 x 42 In. 82.00
Sign, Buffalo Brewing Co., Tin, Indian Drum, American Bison, 17 1/2 In. 3507.00
Sign, Bull Durham Smoking Tobacco, Tin Lithograph, Convex, Frame, 36 x 36 In. 3565.00
Sign, Bull Durham, A Royal Victor, Bullfight Scene, Frame, 33 1/2 x 51 1/2 In. 385.00
Sign, Bull Durham, Bull At Top, Cardboard, 2 Sides, c.1915, 8 1/2 x 11 In. 160.00
Sign, Burson Hose Co., Saratoga Springs, Light-Up, c.1920 . . . . 550.00
Sign, Butcher Shop, Figure Finial, Saw, Knife & Cleaver, Cast Iron, 19 x 24 In. 940.00
Sign, Butcher Shop, Split Pig, Molded Plaster, Painted 336.00
Sign, C.C. Coburn Stationers, News Agent, 2 Sides, Book Form, 27 x 20 1/2 In. 2415.00
Sign, Camera, Box Style, Full Relief, Sheet Iron, Molded, Painted, 11 x 7 x 17 In. 2530.00
Sign, Campbell's Soup, Porcelain, Curved, 1930s, 14 x 23 In. 743.00
Sign, Campbell's, Amos 'n' Andy, Chicken Soups, CBS Radio, 1940, 15 x 20 In. 60.00
Sign, Carling's Ale, 9 Pints Of The Law, Tin Lithograph, 18 1/2 x 12 In. 23.00
Sign, Carnation Fresh Milk, Porcelain, 14 1/4 x 15 In. 467.00
Sign, Carpenter Bros. Drugs, Leaded Glass, 2 Sides, Electrified, 63 x 28 In. 575.00
Sign, Carter's, Tin, Embossed, Self-Framed, 18 1/2 x 25 1/4 In. 935.00
Sign, Case Machine Co., Eagle, On Earth, Neon, Porcelain, 2 Sides, 72 x 40 In. 1610.00
Sign, Cat's Paw, Large Red Shoe, 8 Sides, Electrified, Telesigns-Chicago, 19 In. 488.00
Sign, Centlivre Tonic, Cardboard, 12 x 22 In. 65.00
Sign, Central Hudson Line, Couple On Boat, Lithograph, 1920, 28 x 44 In. 1093.00
Sign, Central Hudson Line, Man & Woman On Ship, Shoreline, 30 x 46 In. 275.00
Sign, Charles Denby Cigars, Black Bellhop, Chromolithograph, 56 In. 242.00
Sign, Charles Denby Cigars, Black Uniformed Man, Cardboard, 1940s, 9 x 15 In. 158.00
Sign, Cherry Blush Soda, Tin Over Cardboard, Beveled, 6 1/2 x 9 1/4 In. 770.00
Sign, Cherry Smash, Tin Over Cardboard, Button & Menu, 1930s, 9 x 14 In. 220.00
Sign, Cherry-Cheer Soda, Cardboard Lithograph, 1920s, 11 x 7 In. 144.00
Sign, Chesterfield, Buy Chesterfield Here, King-Size Packs, Red, Tin, 12 x 16 In. 105.00
Sign, Chocolate Cream Plug Tobacco, Woman With Handkerchief & Fan, 26 1/2 In. 517.00
Sign, Chocolate Menier, Girl Writing On Wall, 14 x 18 1/2 In. 33.00
Sign, Choctaw, American Indian, Red & White Background, 10 x 10 In. 236.00
Sign, Cigar, Dark Red Ground, Light-Up, Tin, Frame, 24 x 8 x 3 3/4 In. 390.00
Sign, Cigar, The Old Reliable Peg Top, Burnt Orange Ground, Frame, 48 x 14 In. 140.00
Sign, Clean Towel, Complete Linen Service, Porcelain, 52 x 33 In. 1540.00
Sign, Cobbler, Black Painted Iron Base, Early 20th Century, 23 1/2 x 13 In. 1763.00
Sign, Cobbler, Boot Form, Arched Foot, Wrought Iron Eyelet, 19 x 14 1/2 In. 4465.00
Sign, Cobbler, Polychrome, Mid 19th Century, 13 5/8 x 78 1/4 x 2 1/8 In. 4945.00
Sign, Coburger Curled Corner, Woman With 6 Mugs, Tin, 17 x 21 In. 357.00
Sign, Cognac Jacquet, Peacock, Laid On Linen, Bouchet, 44 x 61 In. 575.00
Sign, Columbia Yarns, Draped Miss Liberty, Tin, 23 3/4 x 17 1/2 In. 4312.00
Sign, Columbian Fruit Chewing Gum, Girl, Dogs, Easel Back, Frame, 11 1/2 x 8 In. 385.00
Sign, Columbian Rope, Fisherman, In Slicker, Paper, 30 x 49 In. 345.00
Sign, Consolidated Tours, Porcelain, 2 Sides, 22 1/2 x 19 In. 302.00
Sign, Continental Insurance, Soldiers, Tin, Self-Framed, 30 x 20 In. 690.00
Sign, Cook's Champagne, Bottle Of Champagne In Middle, Wood, Frame, 24 In. 121.00
Sign, Cooks Imperial, Tin, Self-Framed, 24 x 20 In. 275.00

Sign, Cooper, Barrel Form, 5-Point Compass Star, Wood, 30 x 14 1/2 In. 7050.00
Sign, Copper, Hammered, The British Gallery, A.A. Simpson, London, 24 x 28 In. 1495.00
Sign, Corticelli Spool Silk, Stages Of Silkworm, Tin, 16 x 11 1/4 In. 345.00
Sign, Cow Brand Baking Soda, Hunting Dog, Oilcloth, 21 1/2 x 30 1/2 In. 220.00
Sign, Cream Top Bottles, It Whips, Milk Bottle, Wood, Turned, Painted, 39 x 15 In. 719.00
Sign, Crossman's Seeds, Paper, Large Melons, Couple Embracing, 23 1/2 In. 2990.00
Sign, Cuckoo Rye Whiskey, Tin Lithograph, Bottle, Corkscrew, c.1905, 21 3/4 x 16 In. . . . 220.00
Sign, Cunard Line, Tin Lithograph, Oak Frame, 29 x 39 In. 800.00
Sign, D.M. Ferry Flower Seeds, Floral, Spider Web, 2 3/4 x 1 3/4 In. 393.00
Sign, D.S. Rickaby, Cabinetmaker & Undertaker, Frame, 1870s, 21 x 21 In. 115.00
Sign, Dan Patch Tobacco, Lithograph, Rooster, Goat, 1904, 24 x 24 In. 660.00
Sign, Dan Patch, Jockey & List Of Accomplishments, Frame, 1904, 29 x 22 In. 242.00
Sign, Dan Patch, Jockey Scene, Dan Patch In Speed Exhibition, Frame, 32 In. 550.00
Sign, Davis Soap, Paper Lithograph Poster, 20 x 13 3/4 In. 231.00
Sign, Davis' Pain Killer, People, Forest, Celebrating, Tin, 21 x 27 In. 2500.00
Sign, De Laval Cream Separator, Yellow Lettering, Black Ground, 8 1/4 In. 175.00
Sign, De Laval, Metal, 14 1/2 x 14 In. 73.00
Sign, Deacon's Plug Tobacco, Horse Race, 22 1/2 x 17 1/4 In. 1750.00
Sign, Dead Shot, Smokeless Black, Man With Dog, Shooting Ducks, 19 x 27 In. 495.00
Sign, Deer, Half-Round, Midwestern Store, Wood, 48 In. 2600.00
Sign, Dentist, Tooth Shape, Carved, Painted, Wood, 8 1/4 x 18 1/2 In. 2990.00
Sign, Derby Tobacco, Race Horse & Jockey, Cardboard, Frame, 22 1/2 x 27 1/4 In. 2310.00
Sign, Detroit Brewing Co., Young Lady Sipping From Glass Of Beer, 1911, 19 In. 205.00
Sign, Devilish Good Cigars, Embossed, Chain Hung, 9 7/8 x 13 3/4 In. 385.00
Sign, Dixie Boy, Paper, Frame, Portugal, 17 1/2 x 27 1/2 In. 127.00
Sign, Dixon Crucible Co., Young Girl, 1898, 20 x 10 1/8 In. 159.00
Sign, Dontophile, French Dental Cream, Red Letters, Tin Lithograph, 18 1/2 x 7 In. 209.00
Sign, Double Barrel Shotgun, Carved, Polychrome, 20th Century, 9 x 52 In. 1955.00
Sign, Douglas Hewitt & Co., Family Making Whiskey, Frame, 23 1/2 x 17 In. 805.00
Sign, Dr Pepper Bottling Co., Triangle, Red Ground, 1940, 21 x 12 In. 1573.00
Sign, Dr Pepper, Drink A Bite To Eat, Aluminum, Round, 1940s, 10 In. 215.00
Sign, Dr Pepper, Frame, Tin, 13 3/8 x 23 1/8 In. 25.00
Sign, Dr Pepper, Madalon Mason, Cardboard, String, 5 1/4 x 6 1/2 In. 1320.00
Sign, Dr. A.C. Daniel's Horse & Dog Medicines, Tin, 28 x 17 1/2 In. 80.00
Sign, Dr. Bell's Anti-Pain, Suffers Under Apple Tree, Graphic Arts, 49 x 34 In. 800.00
Sign, Dr. Chase's Nerve Food, Thermometer, Sheet Metal, Enamel, c.1915, 39 x 8 In. 805.00
Sign, Dr. Drake's German Croup Remedy, Portrait Of Lady, Tin, 1904, 19 x 13 In. 250.00
Sign, Dr. Hailes Ole Injun Tonic, Cardboard, 13 1/2 x 20 1/2 In. 50.00
Sign, Dr. Harter's Wild Cherry Bitters, Frame, 1898, 30 x 14 1/2 In. 1100.00
Sign, Dr. Jayne's Alternative, Blood Purifier, Glass, Reverse Painted, 12 x 14 In. 500.00
Sign, Dr. Jayne's Family Medicines, Martha Washington, 1900, 20 In. 330.00
Sign, Dr. Jayne's Family Medicines, The Flemish Bride, Tin, 19 x 15 In. 400.00
Sign, Dr. M.M. Townsend's Remedy, Frostburg, Md., Cardboard, 1900, 5 x 9 In. 45.00
Sign, Dr. Pierce's Golden Medical Discovery Used By 1st Americans, 39 x 27 In. 1495.00
Sign, Dr. Pierce's Little Giant Cathartic Pills, Paper, 1870s, 28 x 21 In. 3410.00
Sign, Dr. Radway's Remedies, Paper, Uncle Sam, Distributing Remedies, 26 x 36 In. 460.00
Sign, Dr. Siegert's Bitters, Pictures Bottle, Framed Under Glass, 1890s, 12 x 16 In. 605.00
Sign, Dr. Stanley's African Pine Cure, Paper Lithograph, 20 x 15 1/2 In. 1018.00
Sign, Dragon Storage Batteries, Tin, Wood Frame 302.00
Sign, Drink Grape Ola, It's Real Grape, Tin, Embossed, 1920s, 14 x 20 In. 550.00
Sign, Drink Moxie, White Lettering On Red, Tin, Cardboard Stand-Up, 9 x 6 In. 45.00
Sign, Drink Squeeze, Embossed Tin, 2 On Bench, 10 x 28 In. 259.00
Sign, Drug Store, Mortar & Pestle, Copper, Corner Type, 60 x 36 In. 600.00
Sign, Drug Store, Mortar & Pestle, Figural, Porcelain, On Steel, Neon, 23 x 25 In. 290.00
Sign, Druggist, Mortar & Pestle, Tin, Molded, Painted, 20 In. 2240.00
Sign, Drugs, Scrolled Corners, Tin & Wood, 28 1/4 x 54 In. 1725.00
Sign, Dueber Watch, 2 Women Selecting Pocket Watches, Marble Top, 22 x 28 In. 1380.00
Sign, Duke's Cross Cut Cigarettes, Victorian Woman, 16 1/2 x 9 1/2 In. 115.00
Sign, Dunlop, Promotes Various Golf Products, Tin, 38 x 13 1/2 In. 1375.00
Sign, Dunn's Eureka Liniment, Speed Sustainer, Horse Head, Wood, 13 x 33 In. 935.00
Sign, Duo Alarms Crownex, Alarm Clock Picture, Porcelain, 16 x 9 In. 69.00
Sign, Dupont Powder, Hunting Dog On Point, Frame, 1898, 28 1/2 x 24 In. 632.00
Sign, Durham Tobacco, Man On Bicycle, Paper, Frame, 17 x 21 1/2 In. 440.00

Sign, Dutch Masters Cigars, Canvas, Crazing, Gilt Shadow Box Frame, 21 x 29 In. 220.00
Sign, Dyer Packing, Canned Food, Tin Lithograph Over Cardboard, 11 x 8 In. 358.00
Sign, Eagle Tavern, Tin, Stone, Iron Stand, 1830, 17 1/2 x 33 In. 2115.00
Sign, Early Times Distillery, Plaster, Frame, 46 x 37 In. .... *Illus* 750.00
Sign, Edgeworth Extra High Grade Tobacco, 2 Smiling Men, Tin, 11 1/4 x 27 1/4 In. 368.00
Sign, Edwards Wire Rope, 2 Sides Cardboard, Giant Spool, 29 3/4 x 27 In. 400.00
Sign, El Macco Cigars, Image Of Couple Sharing Moment, 20 1/4 x 24 In. 568.00
Sign, Enameline, Young Girl With Puppy In Front Of Tree, Frame, 19 x 28 In. 303.00
Sign, Eskimo Pie, Porcelain, 6 1/2 x 36 In. 215.00
Sign, Esso, Girl, Thin Tin, 1960s, 16 In. 193.00
Sign, Evinrude Outboards, Motor & Boat Images, Tin, 14 1/2 x 25 1/2 In. 650.00
Sign, Exide Battery Service, Arrow, A.F. Knight, Die Cut Tin, 4 7/8 x 19 1/2 In. 35.00
Sign, ExLax, Chocolated Laxative, Tin, 1900s, 12 x 23 1/2 In. 80.00
Sign, Eye Glasses Repaired, Illuminated, Reverse Painted, 17 x 14 In. 12500.00
Sign, Firestone Tires, Most Miles Per Dollar, Cardboard, Trifold, 1920s, 30 x 60 In. 900.00
Sign, Firestone Tires, Name Across Middle, Die Cut Flange, 1930s, 15 x 26 In. 2420.00
Sign, Fish, Carved, Painted, Gray, Wood, Tin, 20th Century, 14 x 47 In. 2300.00
Sign, Fish, Painted, Sheet Metal, 20th Century, 46 1/2 x 8 1/2 x 12 5/8 In. 1955.00
Sign, Floor Coverings Upstairs, Black, Gold, Pointing Hand, Wood, 49 x 13 In. 440.00
Sign, Florsheim Shoe, 2 Sides, Engraved Gilt Letters, Scrolled Bracket, 23 x 13 In. 110.00
Sign, Florsheim Shoe, Deco, Circular, Glass Front, Silver Lettering, Mounted, 9 1/2 In. .. 70.00
Sign, Ford Motorcraft, Embossed, Aluminum, Frame, 24 x 36 In. 20.00
Sign, Fore 'n Aft Smoking Tobacco, Cardboard, c.1908, 30 1/2 x 12 1/4 In. 345.00
Sign, Fox Run Lodge, Copper Fox In Flight, Copper, 2 Sides, 21 x 27 1/2 In. 5880.00
Sign, Fred J. Kramer, Optician, Spectacles, Banner, Optical, Zinc, 13 1/2 x 41 In. 2090.00
Sign, Fresh Eggs, Painted, Oval Cutout, Wood, 20th Century, 17 x 11 1/2 x 16 In. 431.00
Sign, Fried Chicken In A Bag 35 Cents, Wood, 1925, 60 In. 595.00
Sign, Full Weight Cigars, Gumpert Bros., Tin Lithograph, 31 1/4 x 23 In. 3740.00
Sign, G.F. German Fir Cough Cure, Linen, Girl & Cat, 1908, 22 x 17 In. 350.00
Sign, G.G. Green, Cardboard, Frame, 41 1/2 x 30 1/2 In. 175.00
Sign, Gail & Ax Tobacco, Navy Tobacco, Now In New Pocket Pouches, 42 In. 560.00
Sign, Gawel Jewelers, Gruen Watch Time, Metal, Electric, Round, 15 In. 120.00
Sign, Genasco Roofing, St. Louis, Mo., Tin, Embossed, 27 1/2 x 19 3/4 In. 50.00
Sign, Genesee Beer, Original Artwork, Die Cut, 73 x 19 In. 220.00
Sign, George Potter Cigars, Image Of George Potter Smoking Cigars, 18 In. 45.00
Sign, Giltwood, Optician, Spectacles, Mid 19th Century, 96 x 70 x 1 7/8 In. 2070.00
Sign, Give A Bicycle, Santa In Sky, Family Christmas Scene, Frame, 29 x 15 In. 300.00
Sign, Gold Dust, Busy Cleaner, 10 x 15 In. 86.00
Sign, Gold Metal Flour, 1920s, 12 x 60 In. 1155.00
Sign, Gold Seal Champagne, Urbana Wine Co., Colonial Man, 10 3/4 x 14 1/2 In. 60.00
Sign, Gold Seal, Man Holding Glass, Tin, Frame, 15 x 19 In. 495.00
Sign, Gold Seal, Tin, Self-Framed, 15 1/2 x 19 In. 145.00
Sign, Grand Rapids Brewing Co., Game Hanging, Crazing, Gilt Frame, 25 x 13 In. 275.00
Sign, Grape-Nuts, Girl With Dog, Tin, Frame, 30 x 20 In. .... *Illus* 2100.00
Sign, Grapette, Bottle, Tin, Embossed, 1940s, 14 x 39 In. 1045.00

Advertising, Sign, Early
Times Distillery, Plaster,
Frame, 46 x 37 In.

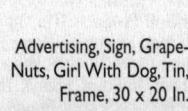

Advertising, Sign, Grape-
Nuts, Girl With Dog, Tin,
Frame, 30 x 20 In.

Sign, Great Western Champagne, Tin, Frame, 14 1/2 x 20 In. 250.00
Sign, Green River Whiskey, Man Standing Beside His Swayback Horse, 15 In. 120.00
Sign, Greyhound Lines, 2 Sides, Oval, 1940s, 20 x 36 In. 578.00
Sign, Grocer, Giltwood, Iron Mounts, Late 19th Century, 9 x 66 1/2 In. 2415.00
Sign, Hail Insurance On Growing Crops, Embossed, Green, Wood Frame, 22 In. 65.00
Sign, Hair Restorative, Painted, Wood, Late 19th Century, 55 1/4 x 20 In. 920.00
Sign, Hall's Hair Renewer, 3 Young Ladies, Tin, 14 x 11 In. 350.00
Sign, Hartford Fire Insurance Co., Man's Portrait, Shadowbox Frame, 27 x 20 In. 220.00
Sign, Hartshorn's Cough Balsam, Mother, Daughter, Torn Bag, 27 x 14 In. 550.00
Sign, Hartshorn's Root Beer, Black Boy Serving, 27 x 14 In. 750.00
Sign, Harvester Cigars, Young Lady & Product, Tin, Frame, 9 x 13 In. 180.00
Sign, Hasterlik Bros., Whiskey, 2 Cowboys, Tin, Frame, 31 x 43 1/4 In. 7150.00
Sign, Hawken Pianos, RCA, Nipper Listening To My Master's Voice, Tin, 28 In. 385.00
Sign, Health & Rest, Alma Spa, Alma, Michigan, Oak Frame, 17 x 22 5/8 In. 275.00
Sign, Heinz Ketchup, Pickle At Bottom Right Corner, Cardboard, 1908, 21 In. 145.00
Sign, Helmar Cigarettes, Young Woman Holding Cigarette Pack, Tin, 22 x 28 In. 385.00
Sign, Hercules Gunpowder, Black Man & Son Hunting, 1920, 19 1/2 x 13 1/2 In. 93.00
Sign, Hermans Seafood, Cod Center, Fresh Maine On Fish, Wood, 27 x 75 In. 400.00
Sign, Hires Root Beer, Chromolithograph, Flapper, Tin, Embossed, 14 x 19 1/2 In. 200.00
Sign, Hires Root Beer, Image Of Boy Holding Mug Of Root Beer, 20 In. 935.00
Sign, Hires Root Beer, Tin Lithograph Over Cardboard, Beveled, 6 x 8 3/8 In. 660.00
Sign, Hires Root Beer, Tin, Self-Framed, Oval, May 21, 1907, 20 x 24 In. 980.00
Sign, Hires, Pretty Girl, Tin Over Cardboard, 1920s, 6 1/2 x 9 In. 470.00
Sign, Hoffman House Pure Rye, Satyr, 4 Nymphs, Stream, Tin, 20 x 14 In. 120.00
Sign, Hohenadal Brewing, Die Cut Glass, 13 x 20 1/2 In. 45.00
Sign, Honest Scrap, Cat & Dog Separated By Product, 30 x 22 In. 1980.00
Sign, Hood's Sarsaparilla, Baby Playing With Blocks, Tin, 42 x 29 In. 800.00
Sign, Horse's Head, Harness Maker, Molded Zinc, 24 x 11 x 20 In. 2240.00
Sign, Horse's Head, Tin, Copper Repaint, 14 1/2 In. 522.00
Sign, Hostetter's Stomach Bitters, Safety First, St. George, Dragon, Celluloid, 6 In. 100.00
Sign, Hostetter's Stomach Bitters, St. George, Dragon, Metal, Embossed, 17 x 14 In. 400.00
Sign, Howell's Root Beer, Bottle Form, Die Cut, 30 x 9 In. 165.00
Sign, Ice Cream Cone, Figural, Painted Sheet Metal, Neon, 68 x 24 x 9 In. 149.00
Sign, Ice Cream Cone, Sheet Metal, Molded, Painted, 29 1/2 In. 1725.00
Sign, Ice Cream, Die Cut Porcelain, 2 Sides, Electrified Border, 72 x 38 In. 2860.00
Sign, IGA, Colorful Folk Art Style Eagle, Porcelain, 12 1/2 x 12 1/2 In. 220.00
Sign, Illinois Farm Supply Co., Light-Up, Convex Glass, 44 In. 630.00
Sign, Imperial Club Cigars, 5 Cents Cigars, Black Ground, 13 3/4 x 10 In. 120.00
Sign, International Marine Paints & Varnishes, Boats, Porcelain, 12 x 18 In. 1375.00
Sign, International Milk & Cream, Molded Cow's Head, Aluminum, 1920, 14 In. 630.00
Sign, International Stock Food, Young Girl With 14 Month Pig, Round, 1912, 15 In. 80.00
Sign, Invincible Motor Insurance, Tin Lithograph, 9 1/2 x 20 In. 240.00
Sign, J. & P. Coats' Spool Cotton, Cardboard, Sparrow Weaving Nest, 23 x 17 In. 400.00
Sign, J.C. Logan Hardware, Painted, 19th Century, 38 x 25 1/4 In. 1495.00
Sign, J.I. Case Threshing Machine Co., Tractor, Tin Lithograph, 20 x 13 1/2 In. 6500.00
Sign, J.J. Kelley, Horse Shoeing, Horseshoe, Blue Paint, White Letters, 34 x 31 In. 3450.00
Sign, J.R. Anderson Jeweler, Iron & Zinc, Pocket Watch Form, 2 Sides, 39 1/2 In. 730.00
Sign, Jacob Hoffman Brewing Co., Glass Of Beer, Frame, 34 x 24 1/2 In. 165.00
Sign, Jacob Hoffman Brewing Co., Wire Grate, Cast Iron Finials, 30 x 68 In. 1495.00
Sign, Jacobsen's Brown Beauties Cigar, Woman, Baseball Scene, Frame, 14 x 19 In. 480.00
Sign, James Pepper, Whiskey, Ms. Liberty, Flag Over Bottle, Tin, 45 x 33 In. 5170.00
Sign, Japp's Hair, Tin, Cardboard, Self-Framed, 13 1/4 x 9 1/4 In. 275.00
Sign, Jeddo-Highland Anthracite, Tin, Coal Image At Top, 18 x 24 In. 45.00
Sign, Jewel Stove, Porcelain, Curved Front, 18 1/2 x 20 In. 300.00
Sign, Jeweler, Watches, Father Time, Tin, Cast Iron, 29 1/2 x 24 x 2 In. 2185.00
Sign, Johnson & Johnson Red Cross Cotton, Plantation, Tin, 1894, 22 x 23 In. 350.00
Sign, Johnson's Anodyne Liniment, Pretty Woman Holding Bottle, 40 x 30 In. 400.00
Sign, K & B Coffee, Testimony Of Satisfied Customer, Tin, 31 1/2 x 72 In. 575.00
Sign, Keen Kutter, Scissors, Wood, Carved, Painted, Silver, Black, 21 x 77 x 3 In. 980.00
Sign, Keen Kutter, W.M. Bennett Hardware Gibbers, Ark., Tin, 26 x 10 In. 115.00
Sign, Kellogg's Corn Flakes, Campfire Girl Fixing Cereal, 1920s, 28 x 30 In. 810.00
Sign, Kendall's Spavin Cure, Family, Horse, Tin, 29 x 24 In. 700.00
Sign, Kendall's Spavin Cure, Woman, Horse, Frame, 28 1/2 x 21 1/2 In. 800.00

Sign, Key, Locksmith's Sign, Cast Iron, Painted, Red, c.1880, 30 In. 3750.00
Sign, Key, Red Paint, Wood, Early 20th Century, 13 3/4 x 51 3/8 In. 575.00
Sign, Key, Sheet Iron, Putty Painted, 19th Century, 35 1/2 x 48 1/2 In. 460.00
Sign, Kickapoo Joy Juice, Cardboard, 1965, 8 1/2 x 11 In. 170.00
Sign, Kingsbury, Die Cut, Easel Back, 14 1/2 x 17 In. 55.00
Sign, Kirk's Flake Soap, Curved Porcelain, Mounting Brackets, 20 x 14 In. 750.00
Sign, Kirk's Flake White Soap, Scruffy Man Writing Letter, 32 x 24 In. 300.00
Sign, Kis-Me Gum, 3 Girls, Die Cut, Cardboard, Matted, Frame, 12 x 16 In. 330.00
Sign, Kis-Me Gum, Kis-Me Co., Louisville, Cutout Girl, Cushion, Easel Back, 10 x 8 In. . 360.00
Sign, Kodak Film Developing & Printing, Porcelain, 2 Sides, 14 x 20 In. 740.00
Sign, Kodak, Showing Package, Iron & Chain Bracket, 7 x 17 In. 825.00
Sign, Kohler's Antidote, Seated Lady, Letter Of Praise, Tin, 45 x 31 In. 300.00
Sign, Korbel Champagne, Tin Lithograph Over Cardboard, c.1915, 13 x 19 In. 275.00
Sign, Korbel, California Champagne, Girl Holding Grapes On Vine, 19 x 13 In. 395.00
Sign, Korry Krome Sole Leather, Tin Lithograph, 9 1/2 x 19 1/2 In. 190.00
Sign, La Preferencia Cigar, Draped Victorian Woman, Cardboard, 35 1/2 x 25 In. 2530.00
Sign, Lager Beer, Bergner & Engel Brw'g Co., Painted, Wood, 30 x 60 In. 1725.00
Sign, Lash's Bitters, Tin Lithograph, 6 3/8 x 9 1/4 In. 190.00
Sign, Lawrence Barrett Cigar, Lawrence & Light Factory Over Spray, Round, 31 In. 770.00
Sign, Lee Union-All-Overalls, Union Made, Porcelain, Metal Frame, 60 x 36 In. 460.00
Sign, Lemon Soda, Porcelain, Convex, 13 x 19 1/2 In. 280.00
Sign, Lime Cola, Celluloid Over Cardboard, String Hung, Round, 9 In. 410.00
Sign, Locksmith, Crossed Keys, Padlock, Sheet Iron, Painted, Gilt, 33 x 40 In. 750.00
Sign, Locksmith, Key, Red Paint, 31 In. 950.00
Sign, Locksmith, Padlock, Zinc, Black Paint, Gilt Escutcheon, 37 x 27 1/2 In. 1495.00
Sign, Lubri-Gas, Correct Motor Fuel, Tin, 27 3/4 x 19 1/4 In. 800.00
Sign, Lucky Lager, Revolving Beer Can, Easel Back, 14 x 18 In. 38.00
Sign, M. Musser, Adamstown, Pa., Black, Mustard, Wood, 20 1/2 x 57 1/2 In. 495.00
Sign, Mail Pouch Chewing Tobacco, Cardboard, Easel Back, 21 x 14 In. 33.00
Sign, Mangum Radiators, Sales & Service, Porcelain, 16 x 24 In. 720.00
Sign, Marie Tempest Cigars, Profile Of Woman In Front, 16 x 22 In. 2090.00
Sign, Marlboro Cigarettes, Marlboro Cowboy, 1989, 5 x 16 x 62 In. 100.00
Sign, Mary F. Bergmann, Electrical Shoppe, Tin, Gold Letters, 18 x 29 In. 650.00
Sign, Mastercraft Pipe, Painted, Composition, 20th Century, 9 3/4 x 36 In. 175.00
Sign, Mavis Chocolate Beverage, Cardboard, 1920s, 29 1/2 x 18 1/2 In. 360.00
Sign, Mavis Chocolate Drink, Flange, Tin, 12 1/2 x 9 1/2 In. 200.00
Sign, Max J. Egge, Pocket Watch, Gilt Frame, Letters, Black Paint, 49 x 35 In. 1610.00
Sign, Maytag Appliances, Porcelain, 2 Sides, 28 x 70 In. 180.00
Sign, McLean's Liver & Kidney Balm, Chromolithograph, 27 1/2 x 21 1/2 In. 400.00
Sign, Meadville Pure Rye, Angel & Horn, Tin, Gilt Frame, 33 1/2 x 43 1/2 In. 3630.00
Sign, Meat Market, Gray Ground, Shadowed Letters, Wood, 15 3/4 x 43 In. 4465.00
Sign, Mechanical Haying Machine, Indiana Mfg. Co., Frame, 19 x 12 1/2 In. 110.00
Sign, Mello Ice Cream, 2 Sides, Metal Flange, 1957, 18 x 12 In. 115.00
Sign, Metz Brewing Co., Light-Up, Metal Frame, 10 x 25 1/2 In. 33.00
Sign, Millinery, Brass, Early 20th Century, 30 x 18 1/4 In. 460.00
Sign, Mishawaka Ball-Band Footrest, Tin Lithograph, 12 x 17 3/4 In. 80.00
Sign, Model Tobacco, Man Dressed As Cigar Store Indian, Cardboard, 22 x 9 In. 38.00
Sign, Monkey Brand Soap, Winged Monkey, Tin, 27 1/2 x 19 3/4 In. 290.00
Sign, Morland's Pub, Perched Falcon, Tin, Painted, Ebonized Frame, 48 x 36 In. 575.00
Sign, Morrell Hams, Cardboard, c.1940, 18 x 9 In. 50.00
Sign, Morton Salt, What's A Potato Without Morton's, Potato, 1940s, 18 x 36 In. 185.00
Sign, Mortuary, Turned, Painted, Gilded, 19th Century, 46 1/2 In. 1840.00
Sign, Mother's Oats, Our Boy, Holding Leopard Rug, Paper, Frame, 1906, 25 x 18 In. . . . 330.00
Sign, Mother's Oats, Our Boy, Matted, Oak Frame, 1906, 16 x 22 In. 200.00
Sign, Moxie, Cardboard, Embossed Letters, Raised Filigree, 21 1/2 x 15 In. 3960.00
Sign, Moxie, Drink Moxie, Red Ground, White Lettering, Flange, Tin, 18 x 9 In. 250.00
Sign, Munsingwear Clothes, Old Woman & 2 Children, Canvas, Frame, 36 x 28 In. 635.00
Sign, Murine, Cardboard, 16 x 29 In. 470.00
Sign, National Fire Ins. Co. Of Hartford, Tin, Wood Frame, 12 x 21 In. 80.00
Sign, NBC Crackers & Milk, Cardboard, Plexiglas, 10 3/4 x 22 3/4 In. 300.00
Sign, Neuweilers Ale, Reverse Painting On Glass, Wood, Stand-Up, 1950s, 8 x 8 In. 68.00
Sign, None Such Mince Meat, Indian Chief, Merrel & Soule, 19 1/2 x 27 1/2 In. 2300.00
Sign, North Carolina, State Seal, Wood Frame, 1890s, 20 1/2 x 26 In. 230.00

Sign, NuGrape Soda, Die Cut, Tin, 17 x 5 In. 120.00
Sign, O'Brien's Fine Candies, Little Boy & Girl, Frame, 6 In. 110.00
Sign, Oceanic Oysters R In Season, Tin Over Cardboard, 9 1/4 x 13 3/4 In. 33.00
Sign, Oh Boy Chewing Gum, Tin Lithograph, 1920s, 15 1/2 x 7 3/8 In. 515.00
Sign, Oh Boy Gum, Young Boy & Elf, Tin, 7 x 15 In. 290.00
Sign, Oildag Makes Motor Boat Run Like Velvet, Border, Frame, 23 x 14 3/4 In. 165.00
Sign, Old English Wax, Metal, Crackled, 7 x 11 In. 160.00
Sign, Old North State Tobacco, Tobacco That Is Tobacco, Oak Frame, 30 x 20 In. 130.00
Sign, Old Overholt Rye, Fly Fisherman, In Stream, Canvas, Frame, 1913, 33 x 20 In. 495.00
Sign, Optician, Brass, Metal, Glass, Early 1900s, 14 1/4 x 27 1/2 x 1 3/4 In. 2990.00
Sign, Optician, Human Eye & Eyebrow, Reverse Painted Glass, 15 x 19 In. 230.00
Sign, Optician, Metal, Lithograph Eyes, In Neon Spectacles, 11 x 28 In. 805.00
Sign, Optician, Wrought Iron, Cobalt Blue & Red Glass Lenses, France, 8 x 23 In. 920.00
Sign, Optometrist, Copper, Silver Foil, Early 20th Century, 7 3/4 x 52 In. 1725.00
Sign, Optometrist, Spectacles, Tin, Blue & Red Lenses, 2 Sides, 18 In. 2465.00
Sign, Orange Crush, Feel Fresh, Bottle, Crushy, 1940s, 17 x 47 In. 1155.00
Sign, Orange Crush, Refreshment For Workers & Fighters, WW II, 1944, 7 x 10 In. 110.00
Sign, Orange Crush, Refuse Substitutes, Tin, Dated 11-32, 27 1/2 x 10 In. 630.00
Sign, Orange Crush, School Girl, Holding Bottle, Die Cut, 1930s, 18 x 20 In. 520.00
Sign, Owens Pink Mixture, Little Girl, Babies Love It, 54 x 41 In. 650.00
Sign, Pabst Blue Ribbon Beer, Tin, 1940s, 9 x 22 In. 55.00
Sign, Palmist, Hand, Wood, Gilt, 20 x 10 In. 7840.00
Sign, Pangburn's Chocolates, Perky Cowgirl, 3-D Cardboard, 21 x 14 1/4 In. 175.00
Sign, Park Brewing, Pheasant, Mallard, Beer Bottles, Tin Lithograph, Round, 24 In. 825.00
Sign, Patton's Sun-Proof Paint, Sun With Human Face, Tin, 18 3/4 In. 460.00
Sign, Pawn Shop, Copper, Wood, 3-Arm Hanger, 3 Suspended Spheres, 12 In. 635.00
Sign, Pawn Shop, Gilded Wood, Iron, Late 19th Century, 27 1/8 x 34 In. 1090.00
Sign, Pawnbroker's, Copper & Iron, Bracket Hanger, 19th Century, 42 x 28 In. 4955.00
Sign, Pawnee Bill, Wild West Show, Hagerstown, N.D., c.1893, 20 x 14 In. 633.00
Sign, Peerless Amber, Metal, Light-Up, 1960s, 11 x 12 In. 95.00
Sign, Peerless Beer, Plastic, 1950s, 12 x 16 In. 33.00
Sign, Perfection Cigarettes, Fashionable Woman, Hat, Frame, 24 x 30 1/2 In. 690.00
Sign, Perfection Kerosene, Tin, Lamp Both Sides, 17 3/4 x 14 In. 520.00
Sign, Perry Davis' Vegetable Pain Killer, Tin, 21 1/2 x 27 1/4 In. 1500.00
Sign, Peter's Weatherbird Shoes, Wood Frame, 30 1/4 x 21 1/2 In. 690.00
Sign, Peterborough Canoe Co., Paddle Shape, Peterborough, Canada, Decal, 12 In. 66.00
Sign, Pharmacist, Mortar, Pestle, Metal, Early 20th Century, 39 1/2 x 32 In. 1150.00
Sign, Phez Juice, Tin Lithograph, 1920, 9 x 6 1/2 In. 575.00
Sign, Pickwick Ale, Men In Tavern, Toasting With Mugs, 22 x 28 In. 690.00
Sign, Piedmont Cigarettes, Blue Ground Porcelain, 2 Sides, 11 1/2 x 11 1/2 In. 100.00
Sign, Pilsner Lion Brewery, Glass, Wood Frame, 14 x 15 1/2 In. 255.00
Sign, Pocket Watch, Black Numbers & Hands, Wood, Iron Hanging Loop, 17 In. 825.00
Sign, Pocket Watch, Fraekorn, Owner, Zinc & Copper, 30 3/4 In. 4935.00
Sign, Pocket Watch, Gilded Zinc, Roman Numerals, Molded Crown, 13 1/2 In. 3760.00
Sign, Pocket Watch, Sheet Metal, Paint, Gilt, 30 x 21 In. 2070.00
Sign, Pompeian Beauty Night Cream, Paper, Roll Down, 1925, 27 In. 155.00
Sign, Portis Felt Hat, Bunny Soft Firma-Felt Hats, Top, Bottom Hangers, 1950, 49 1/2 In. .. 115.00
Sign, Post Toasties Cereal, Norman Rockwell, Boy & Girl, 29 1/2 x 25 1/2 In. 385.00
Sign, Post Toasties, Girl & Dog, Cardboard, 1909, 16 1/2 x 23 1/2 In. 420.00
Sign, Postmaster Smokers Tobacco, 2 For 5 Cents, 5 In. 38.00
Sign, Prince Albert, Tin Lithograph, Chief Joseph, 28 x 22 In. 1255.00
Sign, Quilts, Pine Plank, Checkered Ground, 8 3/8 x 25 1/8 In. 275.00
Sign, Raven Run Premium Anthracite, Tin, 18 x 24 In. 90.00
Sign, Razor, Painted, Green, Early 20th Century, 3 x 15 1/2 In. 259.00
Sign, RCA Victor Radios, Neon, Metal Frame, 14 x 40 1/4 In. 55.00
Sign, RCA Victor Television, Changes Color, Red, Green & Blue, 1950s, 16 x 15 In. 310.00
Sign, Red Goose Shoes, Red Duck In Center, Yellow Ground, 12 x 17 1/4 In. 165.00
Sign, Red Seal Dry Battery, Curved Decoration, 14 1/2 x 34 1/4 In. 800.00
Sign, Reid's Ice Cream, Celluloid Over Cardboard, Hanging, 1930s 140.00
Sign, Remington UMC, Arms & Ammunition, Tin, Frame, 31 x 13 In. 230.00
Sign, Remington, Man & Hunting Dog, Frame, 16 x 21 1/4 In. 95.00
Sign, Renault Champagne, Mirror, Art Deco, 24 In. 90.00
Sign, Restaurant, Lunch, Family Dinners, Reverse Gilt Lettering Frame, 17 x 30 In. 840.00

Advertising card collectors should be careful how the cards are displayed. Don't use the photo albums with plastic envelopes and a sticky cardboard backing (sometimes called "magnetic" albums). The cards will stick and the backs will be ruined.

Advertising, Sign, Sharples
Separator Co., Tin,
Self-Framed, 29 x 28 In.

Sign, Restaurant, Spoon, Fork, Cast Metal, 19th Century, 4 x 20 7/8 In., 2 Piece 750.00
Sign, Rice's Seeds, Jovial Fellow Lifting Large Turnip, 1890, 20 x 28 In. 815.00
Sign, Ritz Crackers, Die Cut, Cardboard, 23 x 12 In. 66.00
Sign, Rooster, Pine, Painted, Carved, Grooved, Early 20th Century, 28 x 22 In. 1920.00
Sign, Rose Exterminator Co., Owl Logo, Porcelain, 11 1/4 x 18 3/4 In. 150.00
Sign, Rose Valley Whiskey, Pat. Oct. 10th, 1905, H.D. Beach Co., 22 1/4 In. 425.00
Sign, Royal Crown Cola, Barbara Stanwyck, Holding Tray, Cardboard, 11 x 28 In. 66.00
Sign, Royal Crown Cola, Take Home A Carton, Red Lettering, 23 x 15 3/4 In. 578.00
Sign, Royal Crown, Cardboard, Wood Frame, U.O. Colson Co., Paris, Ill., 12 1/4 In. 25.00
Sign, S.B. Goff's Valuable Medicines, Herb Bitters, Cardboard, 1880, 11 x 16 In. 200.00
Sign, S.H. Knapp, Black-Smith, Low Relief Black Letters, Wood, 20 x 106 In. 3335.00
Sign, San Diego Transit System, Bus Stop, 12 1/2 x 16 In. 155.00
Sign, Satin Skin Powder, 42 x 28 In. 28.00
Sign, Satin Skin Powder, Paper, 28 x 43 In. 120.00
Sign, Savoy Beer, 3 Old Men On Fishing Trip, Tin, 19 3/4 x 15 3/4 In. 660.00
Sign, Schlitz Beer, Man In Tuxedo, 1972 Reprint, Frame, 26 1/2 x 20 1/2 In. 55.00
Sign, Sharples Separator Co., Tin, Self-Framed, 29 x 28 In. .... *Illus* 2700.00
Sign, Shell, Raised Relief Letters, Shell Form, 1940s 1100.00
Sign, Shoe, Woman's, Wood, 1870s, 25 x 19 x 5 In. 3600.00
Sign, Smith Ice Co. Pure Ice, Children In Lilac Filled Sailboat, 1907, 6 3/4 x 9 In. 105.00
Sign, Snider's Tomato Catsup, Tin Lithograph, 1930s, 16 3/4 x 11 In. ....525.00 to 990.00
Sign, Sooner Or Later You Will Buy A De Laval, Over 2,500,000 In Use, 42 In. 770.00
Sign, Southern Brewing Company, Reverse Painted Glass, Light-Up, 14 x 8 In. 1320.00
Sign, Spear Head Chewing Tobacco, Porcelain, 6 x 14 In. 250.00
Sign, Spears Gasoline, Restrooms, Porcelain, 2 Sides, 30 In. 175.00
Sign, Special Ice Cream, McBride Bros. & Kobbe, Porcelain On Metal, 30 x 14 In. 260.00
Sign, Squirt Soda, Boy Holding Bottle, Frame, 35 1/2 x 35 1/2 In. 330.00
Sign, Starcraft Metal Boats, Marine Graphics, 17 3/8 x 23 3/8 In. 120.00
Sign, Stauffer Bros., 5 Cent Cigar, Tin Lithograph, 2 Sides, 9 1/4 x 18 1/4 In. 240.00
Sign, Stetson Hats, Wood Grain Design, Wood Frame, 8 1/2 x 21 1/4 In. 355.00
Sign, Stewart Stoves, Porcelain, 2 Sides, 12 x 24 In. 635.00
Sign, Stollwreck, Porcelain On Metal, Cobalt Blue & White, 9 1/2 x 2 1/2 In. 200.00
Sign, Stone Hill Wine Co., Wine Allegory & Nude Women, Tin, 1910, 23 In. 630.00
Sign, Straight Razor, Wood, Painted, Iron, 19th Century, 4 1/2 x 29 x 1 In. 375.00
Sign, Straiton & Storm's Owl 5 Cents Cigar, 1901, 14 x 10 1/2 In. 850.00
Sign, Stubby Soda, Made In 5 Delicious Flavors, Tin, 2 Sides, 17 3/4 x 14 In. 140.00
Sign, Sun Maid Vineyard, Metal, Girl Holding Basket Of Grapes, 27 1/2 x 19 In. 525.00
Sign, Sunbeam Bread, Energy Packed, Girl On Left, 12 x 30 In., 1958 .... 1100.00
Sign, Sunbeam Bread, Energy Packed, Tin, Embossed, 1953, 19 x 55 In. 690.00
Sign, Sunroy D-X Products, Porcelain, 6 1/2 x 6 1/2 In. 1650.00
Sign, Sweet-Orr Overalls, Tug Of War Scene, Porcelain, 72 1/2 x 28 3/4 In. 460.00
Sign, T-N-T Popcorn, Black Ground, Yellow Embossed, 1950, 8 x 15 3/4 In. 56.00
Sign, Taco Bell, Bullwinkle's Crunch Club, Die Cut Cardboard, Easel, 12 x 16 In. 35.00
Sign, Teakettle, Inscribed Senior Both Sides, Metal, Early 20th Century, 21 In. 800.00

Sign, Tech Beer, Hunting Dog, Self-Framed, 26 1/2 x 18 1/2 In. 410.00
Sign, Templeton's Rheumatic Capsules, Keep Pain Away, Cardboard, 1900s, 21 In. 40.00
Sign, Terre Haute Brewing, Champagne Velvet, Factory, Frame, 24 1/2 x 51 In. 220.00
Sign, Texaco Fire Engine With Purchase, Cardboard, Framed Under Glass, 34 1/2 In. 220.00
Sign, Texas & Southwestern Rattle Raisers, Snakes, Porcelain, 20 x 12 In. 55.00
Sign, Tingley's Inn, Liberty Unbound, Wrought Iron, Polychrome, 36 x 24 In. 2300.00
Sign, Tobacconist, Cigars & Tobacco, Painted Wood, 8 1/4 x 42 x 1 In. 3335.00
Sign, Tomatoes, Wood, 2 Sides, 5 1/4 x 27 In. 250.00
Sign, Toothbrush, Pro-Phylactic Co., Painted, 20th Century, 3 x 47 1/4 In. 980.00
Sign, Totem Tobacco, Tobacco Tin, 20 1/4 x 18 1/4 In. 250.00
Sign, True Fruit, Tin, Self-Framed, 37 1/2 x 25 1/2 In. 385.00
Sign, Tuft's Arctic Soda Water, Island Tribe, Paper, 18 3/4 x 12 1/4 In. 1035.00
Sign, Tydol Triple X, Winter Front, Cardboard, 12 x 19 1/2 In. 415.00
Sign, United States Lines, America Welcomes You, Laid On Linen, 24 x 38 In. 460.00
Sign, Utica Club, West End Brewery, Cardboard Lithograph, 8 1/4 x 13 1/4 In. 495.00
Sign, Van Houten's Cocoa, Peasant Girl, Basket, Gilt Frame, 45 1/2 x 31 In. 660.00
Sign, Velvet Pipe Tobacco, Fireside, Father, Son, Grandfather, Tin, 27 3/4 In. 345.00
Sign, Veuve Amiot, Laid On Linen, 30 x 40 In. 400.00
Sign, Victrol Phonographs, Tin, Early 1900s, 40 x 31 In. 575.00
Sign, Vough's Drugstore, Remember Pearl Harbor, Plywood, 1942, 19 x 26 In. 300.00
Sign, Waitt & Bond Blackstone Cigars, Smoked From Coast To Coast, 35 x 12 In. 290.00
Sign, Walter's Keg Beer, Cardboard, 1950s, 14 x 22 In. 17.00
Sign, Ware Hotel, Flowers Either End, Tin, 33 x 57 In. 1485.00
Sign, Warner's Safe Nervine, Woman Slaying Tiger, 30 x 23 In. 1600.00
Sign, Watches, Jewelry, Clocks, Pocket Watch Form, Arabic Seconds, 26 x 20 In. 1410.00
Sign, Watchmaker, Chain & Fob, Painted, Gilded Zinc, 2 Sides, 26 x 19 In. 1230.00
Sign, Watchmaker, Painted, Wood, Iron, 19th Century, 32 x 22 In. 1725.00
Sign, Watchmaker, Sheet Metal, 2 Sides, 23 1/2 x 14 In. 5150.00
Sign, Waterman's Fountain Pen, Cardboard, Die Cut, 10 1/4 x 13 In. 300.00
Sign, Waterman's Ideal Fountain Pen, Cardboard Cutout, 19 x 10 In. 150.00
Sign, Weatherized Weatherbird Shoes, Rooster, Red, Black, Porcelain, 25 x 16 In. 1700.00
Sign, Weber Wagon, Wagon Picture, Chas. S. Culver, Ogee Frame, 26 x 20 In. 115.00
Sign, Welch's Grape Juice, Cardboard Lithograph, c.1910, 36 x 21 1/2 In. 5500.00
Sign, Welch's, Soda Fountain Scene, Cardboard, Matted, Frame, 29 1/4 x 14 1/2 In. 5500.00
Sign, Weona, Mustard Letters, White Ground, 8 1/2 x 49 In. 230.00
Sign, Western Farms Milk, Tin Over Cardboard, Beveled, 4 1/2 x 13 1/2 In. 360.00
Sign, Westland Ice Cream, Light-Up Clock, White Ground, Covington, Ky., 8 In. 90.00
Sign, Weyman's Honest Weight Tobacco, Gaucho On Horse, 3 1/2 x 16 3/4 In. 290.00
Sign, Wheeler Bro's, Pianos & Organs, c.1870, 15 1/4 x 172 x 1 3/4 In. 230.00
Sign, Whistle Orange Soda, Cardboard, 1951, 23 x 33 In. 425.00
Sign, Whistle Pop, Woman In Bathing Suit, Paper, Frame, 20 1/2 x 28 1/2 In. 250.00
Sign, Winchester Fishing Tackle, 3-Panel Fishing Display, 1920s, 30 x 42 In. 2420.00
Sign, Winchester Guns & Ammunition, Hunter, P.R. Goodwin, 1932, 37 x 33 In. 3850.00
Sign, Winchester Self-Loading Shotguns, Easel Back, 1911, 20 1/2 x 12 1/2 In. 2750.00
Sign, Wings Cigarettes, Die Cut Airplane, Cardboard, 10 x 12 1/2 In. 770.00
Sign, Wonder Bread, Mickey Mantle, Stan Musial, Cardboard, 10 x 14 In. 2515.00
Sign, Wrigley's Chewing Gum, Porcelain, 1930s, 36 x 14 In. 2530.00
Sign, Wrigley's Doublemint Gum, Red Ground, Tin, 1930, 13 x 6 In. 860.00
Sign, Wrigley's Juicy Fruit Gum, Frame, 24 1/4 x 14 3/8 In. 38.00
Sign, Wrigley's, Trademark Kid, Easel Back, 1930s, 30 x 18 In. 330.00
Sign, Wurzburger Beer, Plastic, Blue Ground, White Lettering, 13 3/4 x 5 In. 11.00
Sign, Wyandotte, Lithographed Tin, Self-Framed, 39 x 28 In. 4950.00
Sign, Yale Key, Pressed Tin, 2 Sides, Silver & Black Paint, 12 x 32 In. 345.00
Sign, Yellow Kid 5 Cent Cigars, 15 x 5 In. 1735.00
Sign, Young Girl On Fur Rug, Cat, Fan Behind, Easel Back, Frame, 6 1/2 x 9 3/4 In. 470.00
Sign, Zu Zu Ginger Snap, Paper, 20 x 26 In. 95.00
Soap, Uncle Sam In Every Home, Molded Uncle Sam, Box, 1890, 3 3/4 In. 115.00
Stickpin, Dutch Cleaning Woman, Figural, Enameled, 5 In. 145.00
Stove Plate, Indian Doe-Wah-Jack, Round Oak Stoves, 9 In. 110.00
Stringholder, Quom Custard Powder, Fox Hunt Graphic, 4 x 3 3/4 In. 250.00
Tap Knob, Blitz Weinhard, Wood, 1960s 12.00
Tap Knob, Chief Oshkosh Beer, Celluloid 14.00

Tap Knob, Hacker's Ale, 1940s 13.00
Tap Knob, Yotoc Beer, Celluloid, 1940s 12.00
Thermometers are listed in their own category.

Advertising tin cans or canisters were first used commercially in the United States in 1819 and were called *tins*. The English language is sometimes confusing. Today the word *tin* is used by most collectors to describe many types of containers, including food tins, biscuit boxes, roly poly tobacco containers, gunpowder cans, talcum powder sprinkle-top cans, cigarette flat-fifty tins, and more. Beer Cans are listed in their own category. Things made of undecorated tin are listed under Tinware.

Tin, 3 Honeys Condom, Disease Preventors Only Along Bottom, 1 5/8 x 1/4 In. 55.00
Tin, All American Cigars, American Statesmen, Tin Lithograph, 5 3/8 x 4 7/8 In. 745.00
Tin, American Girl, Tobacco, Flat, Pocket, 2 7/8 x 4 1/2 x 3/4 In. 385.00
Tin, An Eye For A Good Cigar, Grinning Black Man, 1920s, 6 In. 235.00
Tin, Armours Aluminum Oats, Cardboard, Chicago, 7 Oz., Pair 100.00
Tin, Autobacco, Tobacco, Man Driver, Tin Lithograph, Pocket, 4 3/8 x 3 7/8 In. 3850.00
Tin, Baby Mine Talc, Zanol, Baby, Toys, Tin Lithograph, 5 1/8 x 2 1/4 x 1 1/2 In. 175.00
Tin, Bambino Tobacco, Babe Ruth Silhouette, Metal, 1920s 1580.00
Tin, Beech-Nut Coffee, Key Opener On Lid, 1950s, Lb. 25.00
Tin, Beech-Nut Gum, Peppermint, Hinged Lid, Tin Lithograph, 3 3/4 x 5 1/4 In. 220.00
Tin, Ben-Hur Coffee, 10 1/2 x 11 1/2 In. 265.00
Tin, Birds Nest, MacFarlane & Lang, Biscuit 448.00
Tin, Black Cat Cigarette, Yellow Ground, Black Cat, 6 x 8 In. 11.00
Tin, Brighton Blend Coffee, Woman Sipping Coffee, 6 x 4 3/8 In. 360.00
Tin, Brown Betty Coffee, Brown Betty Profile Facing Sideways, Lb. 215.00
Tin, Bunny Peanut Butter, Character Images, Tin Lithograph, Bail Handle, 12 Oz. 1155.00
Tin, Camp Fire Coffee, Blue Ribbon Products, Pry Lid, 1930s, 2 1/2 Lb. 690.00
Tin, Carter's, Ink Eraser Product, Tin Lithograph, 2 x 3 x 1 7/8 In. 415.00
Tin, Checkers Tobacco, Weisert Bros., 4 1/2 x 3 x 7/8 In. . . . . *Illus* 688.00
Tin, Circus Wagon, Chad Valley, 6 1/2 x 5 1/2 In. . . . . 245.00 to 325.00
Tin, City Club Crushed Cubes, Burley Tobacco Co., 4 1/2 x 3 x 7/8 In. . . . . *Illus* 550.00
Tin, Clark's Teaberry Gum, Tin Lithograph, 6 3/4 x 2 1/2 In. 370.00
Tin, Columbia, Allspice, 3 x 2 1/4 x 1 1/4 In. 265.00
Tin, Comfort Talc, Lithograph, Nurse In Uniform, Baby, 1890s, 4 x 2 1/2 In. 620.00
Tin, Continental Cubes Tobacco, Pocket Tins On 5 Surfaces, 5 x 5 In. 520.00
Tin, Corona Gum, Hinged Lid, Banana Flavored Chewing Gum, 1 x 3 x 3/8 In. 325.00
Tin, Corona, Athlete Banana Chewing Gum, Tin Lithograph, Hinged Lid, 1 x 3 1/4 In. . . . 325.00
Tin, Crescent Salted Peanuts, Wilkes Barre Can Co., Philadelphia, 8 x 9 1/2 In. 136.00
Tin, Crispo, Lithographed Design, 1900, 5 In. 50.00

Advertising, Tin, Checkers
Tobacco, Weisert Bros.,
4 1/2 x 3 x 7/8 In.

Advertising, Tin, City Club
Crushed Cubes, Burley Tobacco
Co., 4 1/2 x 3 x 7/8 In.

Advertising, Tin, Ensign Cut
Tobacco, University Of Missouri
Flag, 4 1/2 x 3 x 7/8 In.

Advertising, Tin, Forest City,
Formosa Blend Tea, Conant,
Patrick, Label, 4 In.

Advertising, Tin, French's
Imported Paprika, Red, Green
Gold Lithograph, 3 1/4 In.

Advertising, Tin,
Hunter Cigars

Tin, Daisee Spice, Child In Flower Field, 3 x 2 1/4 x 1 1/4 In. 165.00
Tin, Dan Patch Cut Plug Tobacco, 3 1/4 In. 110.00
Tin, Dash Cigars, Jockey On Racehorse, Tin Lithograph, 3 1/4 x 3 1/2 In. 80.00
Tin, Dean's Peacock's Condom, Peacock Bird, 1 5/8 x 2 1/8 In.   110.00
Tin, Dixie Jumbo's Peanuts, Black Boy, Peanut Mouth, 8 3/4 In. 270.00
Tin, Dr. David Roberts Gall Balm, Waukesha, Wis., U.S.A., Contents, 1 3/4 In. 39.00
Tin, Dr. David Roberts Germocide, Veterinary Co., Waukesha, Wis., 6 1/2 In. 45.00
Tin, DuPont Smokeless Powder, Dogs, Guns On Label, Delaware, 7 x 6 In. 110.00
Tin, Egg-O, Baking Powder 75.00
Tin, Enck Cough Drops, W.C.E. Brand, Tin Lithograph, 2 1/2 x 1 5/8 In. 165.00
Tin, Ensign Cut Tobacco, University Of Missouri Flag, 4 1/2 x 3 x 7/8 In. . . . . *Illus*   990.00
Tin, Fairy Flake Baking Powder 150.00
Tin, Flagstaff Coffee, Sealed, 5 In. 165.00
Tin, Flying A Household Oil, Plastic Spout & Cap, 4 Oz. 33.00
Tin, Forest City, Formosa Blend Tea, Conant, Patrick, Label, 4 In. . . . . *Illus*   75.00
Tin, Fowler Coffee, Tin Lithograph, Pilgrim, Key Wind, Lb. 330.00
Tin, Franklin Coffee, Ben Franklin On Front, Canister, Small Top, 3 Lb. 2970.00
Tin, French's Imported Paprika, Red, Green Gold Lithograph, 3 1/4 In. . . . . *Illus*   15.00
Tin, Gibsons Baking Powder 75.00
Tin, Glossola Shoe Polish, Red Ground, White Letters, Eclipse Blacking Co., 3 In. 75.00
Tin, Gold Dust, Paper, Orange & Black, 10 Oz., 9 In. 46.00
Tin, Gold Medal Tobacco, Tin Lithograph, Square, 3 1/4 x 4 1/2 In. 275.00
Tin, Golden Pheasant Coffee, Bird On Front, Screw Lid, 1/2 Lb.   250.00
Tin, Good Cheer Cigar, Pop Lid, 5 1/2 In. 80.00
Tin, Good Wishbone Coffee, Gilt Lid, 4 Lb., 8 In. 80.00
Tin, Grand Order Cigars, Tin Lithograph, 37 1/2 x 13 In. 126.00
Tin, Heart's Delight Coffee, Tin Lithograph, Lb., 6 In. 85.00
Tin, Hercules Military Rifle Powder, 5 3/4 x 3 3/4 In. 40.00
Tin, Hiawatha Tobacco, American Indian, Tin Lithograph, 3 x 5 In. 115.00
Tin, Hiawatha Tobacco, Daniel Scotten Co., Detroit, Mi., 5 x 3 x 2 In. 110.00
Tin, Hills Bros. Coffee, Trademark Man, Tin Lithograph, 1920, 8 1/8 x 5 1/8 In. 115.00
Tin, Hoadley's Lime Fruit, Somers Bros. Lithographers, 7 3/4 x 5 1/8 x 5 1/8 In. 965.00
Tin, Honey Moon Tobacco, 10 Cents, Pocket 99.00
Tin, Horrocks & Ibbotson Very Best Split Shot, Round, 1 1/8 In.   80.00
Tin, Hunter Cigars . . . . *Illus*   390.00
Tin, Huntley & Palmers, Book Shape, Biscuit, Leather Band, 6 3/8 x 6 1/4 In. 144.00
Tin, Huntley & Palmers, Fire Scene, Biscuit 280.00
Tin, Huntley & Palmers, Straw Creel, Biscuit 505.00
Tin, Huntley & Palmers, Toby Shape, Biscuit 280.00
Tin, Iron Club Baking Powder 85.00
Tin, J.G. Dills, Cigar, Natural Leaf, Red, White & Black 17.00

Tin, J.G. Dills, Cigar, Woman Lounging, Yellow & Black 17.00
Tin, Jacob & Co., Biscuit, Oriental Cabinet, England, 5 1/2 x 6 3/4 In. 300.00
Tin, Jam Boy Coffee, Child Eating Jam Covered Bread, Tin Lithograph, 6 1/4 x 4 In. 496.00
Tin, Jergens Talc, Miss Dainty Talcum, 4 5/8 x 2 1/2 x 1 3/8 In. 242.00
Tin, Kamels Condom, Aaronoff Co., Mideastern Image, Tin, 1 5/8 x 2 1/8 In. 250.00
Tin, Kamo Rolled Oats, Paxton & Gallagher, Omaha, Neb. 210.00
Tin, Kar-A-Van Coffee Co., Toledo, Red & White, Camel Logo, 28 In. 55.00
Tin, Kennebec Cigar, American Can Co., 8 1/2 x 4 1/2 x 2 1/2 In. 39.00
Tin, Kentucky Club Tobacco, Pocket 25.00
Tin, King Edward Pocket Tobacco, Canada, 4 1/2 x 3 7/8 In. 825.00
Tin, Land O' Lakes Powdered Milk, Indian Maiden Holding Can, 1940s, 4 In. 150.00
Tin, Le Transparent Condom, Young's Rubber Co., 1 7/8 x 1 5/8 In. 165.00
Tin, Log Cabin Syrup, 100th Anniversary, 1887-1987 .... 60.00
Tin, Lux Liquid Detergent, Art Linkletter On Front, 1950s, 8 In., Qt. 20.00
Tin, Luzianne Coffee, Mammy Holding Signs, Scene On Reverse, 2 Lb. 68.00
Tin, Machwitz Coffee, 3 Big-Eyed Black Boys, Germany, 5 1/4 x 9 In. ....85.00 to 135.00
Tin, Manor House Coffee, McLaughlin Co., 6 1/4 x 4 1/4 In. 55.00
Tin, Maryland Club, Pocket Tobacco, Marburg Bros., Flat Top, 4 x 3 1/4 x 1 In. 580.00
Tin, Master Mason Pocket Tobacco, Tin Lithograph, Canada, 4 1/2 x 3 7/8 In. 1265.00
Tin, Mennen Talc, Seated Baby, Tin Lithograph, 1890s, 4 x 1 3/4 In. 175.00
Tin, Merrill's Foot Powder, Edwin Merrill Co., 3 1/2 x 1 1/4 In. 231.00
Tin, Mohawk Gun & Reel Lubricant, Plastic Spout & Cap, 3 Oz. 308.00
Tin, Monarch Peanut Butter, Teenie Weenie, Lid & Bail Handle, Lb., 4 In. 80.00
Tin, Monogram Coffee, Lb., 6 In. 150.00
Tin, Moses Cough Drops, Hoadley Co., 5 Lb., 8 x 6 x 4 In. 264.00
Tin, Mothers Worm Syrup, Gooch Quack Remedies, 6 7/8 x 2 1/4 In. 1650.00
Tin, Nebraska Blossom, Heacock Cigar Co., Woman, Cowboy Hat, 5 1/4 x 5 1/2 In. 1155.00
Tin, Negro Head Brand Oysters, 3 1/4 In. 182.00
Tin, Nigger Shoe Polish, Stork Carries Black Baby, Round, 1920s, 3 In. ....175.00 to 340.00
Tin, Niggerhead Shrimp, Multicolored Lithograph, 4 In. 420.00
Tin, Nutrine Candy, Tin Lithograph, 14 x 10 In. 139.00
Tin, Old Briar Tobacco, Gilt Lettering, 5 x 3 x 3 In. 11.00
Tin, Old Scotch Coffee, Scotsman Playing Bagpipe, Tin Lithograph, 6 x 4 1/4 In. 551.00
Tin, Old Squire Tobacco, Blue, Vertical, Canada, 4 3/8 x 3 x 7/8 In. 1155.00
Tin, Optimus Condom, Robert Pierce Inc., 1 5/8 x 2 1/8 In. 244.00
Tin, Orcico Cigar, 2 For 5 Cents, Indian Head Picture, 6 x 6 x 4 In. 120.00
Tin, Palmy Days Tobacco, Vertical, Gold Letters, 4 1/2 x 3 1/2 x 1 In. 330.00
Tin, Parker Tooth Powder, Painless Parker, Tin Lithograph, 3 7/8 x 2 1/4 In. 269.00
Tin, Paul Jones, Continental Tobacco Co., 4 1/2 x 3 7/8 In. ....*Illus* 3190.00
Tin, Pedro Smoking Tobacco, Yellow, Black & Red Writing, 4 1/2 x 4 1/2 x 5 3/4 In. 240.00
Tin, Penn's Cigar, Yellow Ground, Red & Black Lettering 6.00
Tin, Pickaninny Polish, Smiling Face, Twice The Shine, Half The Time, 4 In. 58.00

Advertising, Tin, Paul Jones,
Continental Tobacco Co.,
4 1/2 x 3 x 7/8 In.

**You can remove rust
from a tin by using an
ink eraser. If you can't
find an old one, use
the type that comes
on a ball-point pen.**

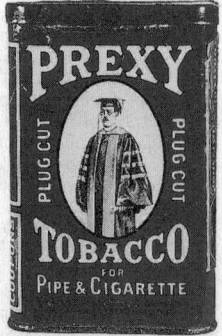

Advertising, Tin, Prexy
Tobacco, B. Payn's Sons,
4 1/2 x 3 x 7/8 In.

Advertising, Tin,
Trout Line, P.
Lorillard Co.,
33/4 x 3 1/4
x 1 1/8 In.

Advertising, Tin, Waltham Main Springs,
For Watches, Louis C. Kreger, 3 x 5 In.

Tin, Planter Novola Peanut Oil, Blue Label, Red Border, 5 Gal.	225.00
Tin, Polarine Cup Grease, 5 Lb.	165.00
Tin, Police Foot Powder, Uniformed Officer, Tin Lithograph, 4 5/8 x 2 x 1 3/4 In.	798.00
Tin, Powerlube Lubricant No. 3, Grease, Lb.	187.00
Tin, Prexy Tobacco, B. Payn's Sons, 4 1/2 x 3 x 7/8 In. ....*Illus*	2970.00
Tin, Queen's Taste Coffee, Girl With Tray, Yellow Ground, 5 7/8 x 4 1/4 In.	82.00
Tin, Reading Biscuit Company, Brass Plating, Applied Medallion, 11 x 10 In.	155.00
Tin, Red Goose Pencil, Tin Lithograph, Hinged Lid, 2 1/8 x 7 3/4 In.	143.00
Tin, Red Indian V-XX Lubricant, Grease, Logo, Lb.	187.00
Tin, Red Turkey Spice, Gobbler, Lithograph, 3 1/8 x 2 1/4 In.	168.00
Tin, Repose Chipped Plug Pocket Tobacco, Lithograph, Vertical, 4 x 3 x 7/8 In.	990.00
Tin, Revelation Smoking Mixture Pipe Tobacco, Philip Morris, 1926, 2 In.	90.00
Tin, Rex Brake Wafer, Man Working On Car Wheel, Lithograph, 2 1/8 x 1 1/4 In.	144.00
Tin, Romeo's Condom, Killian Mfg.Co., Yellow Ground, 1 5/8 x 2 1/8 In.	220.00
Tin, Saf-T-Way Condoms, Gotham Rubber Co., Black & White, 1 5/8 x 2 1/8 In.	165.00
Tin, Sailor's Pride, Bland Tobacco Co., Canister, Small Top, 6 1/4 x 4 7/8 In.	715.00
Tin, Santinola Shoe Polish, Black Man Shines Shoes, 1920s, 2 1/4 In.	40.00
Tin, Sears Roasted Coffee, Amber & Black, 1910, 25 Lb., 16 In.	100.00
Tin, Shoe Polish, L. Liechner Negro Black Shoe Polish, Germany, 3 1/4 In.	121.00
Tin, Signal Outboard Motor, Reverse Text, Stoplight Logo, Qt.	330.00
Tin, Silver Bell Condoms, Tiger Skin Rubber Co., 1 5/8 x 2 1/8 In.	330.00
Tin, Slave Master, Tobacco, Slave, Ship's Captain, 4 3/4 In.	179.00
Tin, Spalding & Merrick, Pocket Tobacco, Lithograph, 2 3/8 x 3 3/4 x 5/8 In.	250.00
Tin, Squibb Talc, Baby In Tub, 4 1/4 In.	227.00
Tin, Squirrel Peanut Butter, Canada, 3 3/4 x 3 In.	209.00
Tin, Strong Heart Coffee, Chas. Hewitt Co., Indian, Lithograph, Lb.	825.00
Tin, Summer Girl Cocoa, Cardboard, 1920s, 7 x 3 3/4 x 2 1/2 In.	275.00
Tin, Sunny South Sweet Milk Chocolate Peanuts, Smiling Black Girl, 7 3/4 In.	303.00
Tin, Swans Down Coffee, Swimming Swan, Pry Lid, Lb.	264.00
Tin, Sweet Clover, Pocket Tobacco, Flat, 2 3/8 x 3 3/4 x 5/8 In.	99.00
Tin, Sweet Cuba Fine Cut Tobacco, Yellow, Black Lettering, 8 In.	138.00
Tin, Sykes Talc, Young Children Front, Nurse On Back, 4 1/4 In.	160.00
Tin, Teenie Weenie Peanut Butter, Lilliputians, 1926, 14 1/2 x 12 1/2 In.	1035.00
Tin, Tobacco Girl, Girl & Leaf Trademark, Liberty Can Co., 5 1/2 x 6 1/4 x 4 1/4 In.	580.00
Tin, Tom Thumb Crescent Cracker, Blue & Silver Lithograph, 2 Lb. 8 Oz., 7 In.	57.00
Tin, Trout Line, P. Lorillard Co., 3 3/4 x 3 1/4 x 1 1/8 In. ....*Illus*	853.00
Tin, Trout Line, Pocket Tobacco, Fisherman, Vertical, 3 3/4 x 3 3/4 x 1 1/4 In.	578.00
Tin, Turkey Coffee, Wild Turkey On Both Sides, 3 Lb.	825.00
Tin, Tuxedo Tobacco, Man In Tuxedo, Flip Top, 4 1/4 x 2 7/8 x 3/4 In.	300.00
Tin, Uncle Sam Shoe Polish, 3 1/2 x 1 1/4 In.	74.00
Tin, Union Leader, Cigar, Cut Plug, Gilt Design	17.00
Tin, Unity Mixture, Pocket Tobacco, Lithograph, Vertical, 2 3/4 x 3 1/2 x 1 In.	1265.00
Tin, Vienna, Baking Powder	165.00
Tin, Violet Talc, Young Girl, Lithograph, 4 x 1 3/4 In.	145.00
Tin, Waltham Main Springs, For Watches, Louis C. Kreger, 3 x 5 In. ....*Illus*	15.00
Tin, Watkins Talc, Couple Both Sides, Box, 5 1/2 In.	290.00
Tin, Welcome Guest Coffee, Black Butler Holding Service Set, Lithograph, Lb.	715.00
Tin, Yankee Boy Tobacco, Lithograph, Vertical, 4 x 3 1/2 x 3 3/8 In.	990.00

Tin, Yellow Cab Cigars, Lithograph, 5 1/2 x 2 1/2 In. 1320.00
Tin, Zeno Gum, Slide Lid, Armour & Co., 1 x 3 1/4 In. 111.00

Advertising tip trays are decorated metal trays less than 5 inches in
diameter. They were placed on the table or counter to hold either the
bill or the coins that were left as a tip. Change receivers could be made
of glass, plastic, or metal. They were kept on the counter near the cash
register and held the money passed back and forth by the cashier.
Related items may be listed in the Advertising category under Change
Receivers.

Tip Tray, Admiral Dewey & Battleship, Lithograph, Round, 5 3/4 In. 55.00
Tip Tray, American Line Cruise Ship, Lithograph, Round, 4 1/4 In. 80.00
Tip Tray, Bartholomay Beers, Ales & Porter, Woman On Wheel, 4 3/8 In. 198.00
Tip Tray, Day & Night Tobacco, Tin Lithograph, Round, 5 1/2 In. 265.00
Tip Tray, Eye-Fix, Cherub Putting Eye Drops In Woman's Eye, 4 1/4 In. 275.00
Tip Tray, Frost Fence, 3 White Horse Heads, Tin, Petal-Shape Flange, 4 1/8 In. 80.00
Tip Tray, Incandescent Light & Stove Co., Tin Lithograph, 4 1/4 In. 80.00
Tip Tray, King's, Full Bottle & Glass, Woman Carrying Tray, 6 x 4 3/8 In. 730.00
Tip Tray, Koppitz-Melchers 50.00
Tip Tray, Moxie, 6 In. 360.00
Tip Tray, Mr. Tomas Brand 5 Cent Cigar, Black Cat, 4 1/4 In. 220.00
Tip Tray, Muehlebach Brewery, Tin Lithograph, 5 1/8 In. 85.00
Tip Tray, National Brewing Co., Man On Horse, Round 250.00
Tip Tray, Red Raven Mineral Water, Tin Lithograph, 4 1/4 In. 385.00
Tip Tray, Ruhstaller Lager, Woman, Steins, 4 3/8 In. 220.00
Tip Tray, S & H Green Stamps, 4 1/4 In. 60.00
Tip Tray, Success Manure Spreader, Kemp & Burpee Co., Syracuse, 3 x 4 3/4 In. 523.00
Tip Tray, Turborg Breweries, Black Boy Carrying Beer Tray, Ceramic, 5 In. 509.00
Tip Tray, White Top Champagne Co., Tin Lithograph, 4 1/4 In. 80.00
Tobacco Bin, Old English Curve Cut Pipe Tobacco, 13 x 8 In. 410.00
Tobacco Cutter, Ambrosia Brand, Cast Iron, 16 x 9 In. 210.00
Tobacco Cutter, Brown's Mule 105.00
Tobacco Cutter, Cherry, Shield Escutcheon, Serrated Base, 11 x 8 x 3 In. 275.00
Tobacco Cutter, Empire Plug 30.00
Tool, All-In-One, Clark Bars Are Great, Black Cast Iron, 7 In. ....*Illus* 15.00
Tray, Tip, see Tip Trays in this category.
Tray, Anheuser-Busch Brewing Association, 12 1/2 x 15 In. 115.00
Tray, Anheuser-Busch, Team Of Horses, With Bevo Wagon, 1910, 13 x 10 1/2 In. 115.00
Tray, Beer Drivers Union, 14th Anniversary, Dogs, Stable, 1908, 10 x 13 1/2 In. 195.00
Tray, Bernhardt, Herman Bernhardt Co., N.Y., Round, 4 1/4 In. 165.00
Tray, Big Jo, Tin Lithograph, Round, 4 1/4 In. 230.00
Tray, Budweiser, Early Wharf Scene, 1914, 17 1/2 x 13 In. 110.00
Tray, Cunningham Ice Cream, Factory, 15 1/4 x 18 1/2 In. 220.00
Tray, Diamond State Brewery, Tin Lithograph, Round, 12 In. 130.00
Tray, Edelweiss Beer, Young Beauty, Metal, Lithograph, 1913, 13 In. 126.00
Tray, Falstaff Brewing, Cavaliers, Tin Lithograph, 1920, 24 In. 60.00
Tray, Famous Narragansett Banquet Ale, Porcelain, 9 x 3 1/2 In. 170.00
Tray, Fan Tan Gum, Oriental Beauty, Tin Lithograph, 13 x 10 1/2 In. 126.00
Tray, Hick's Capudine Liquid, Cherubs Around, Package, Tin, 9 3/4 In. 150.00
Tray, Hires Root Beer, Young Woman, Tin, 13 1/4 In. 140.00
Tray, Hires, Girl In Center, Haskell Coffin, 1920s, 13 1/4 x 10 1/4 In. 330.00
Tray, Howertown Dairy Co., Tin Lithograph, 13 1/4 x 13 1/4 In. 222.00

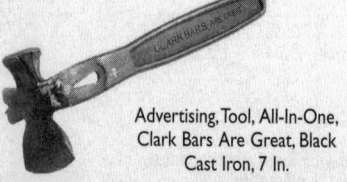

Advertising, Tool, All-In-One,
Clark Bars Are Great, Black
Cast Iron, 7 In.

**After cleaning your stuffed
moose head, polish the hair with
a wad of nylon stocking.**

Tray, Jersey Creme, Profile Of Girls, 12 In. 200.00
Tray, Moxie Beverage, Woman In Flowers, Tin Lithograph, Round, 6 In. 310.00
Tray, Niagara Ginger Ale, Niagara Falls, Tin Lithograph, 10 1/2 x 13 1/4 In. 110.00
Tray, NuGrape Soda, Woman With Bottle, 10 1/2 x 13 1/4 In. 120.00
Tray, Pure Springs Beer, Tin Lithograph, 10 1/2 In. 50.00
Tray, Rainier Beer, Seattle Brewer, Tin Lithograph, 13 1/4 x 10 1/4 In. 300.00
Tray, Rainier Pale Beer, 9 1/4 In. 100.00
Tray, Red Raven Splits, Crab & Rabbit Scene, Rectangular 150.00
Tray, Red Ribbon Beer, Mathie Brewing, Bear Drinking Beer, 13 1/4 x 13 1/4 In. 300.00
Tray, Robinson's Beer, Bustling Factory, Tin Lithograph, 12 In. 330.00
Tray, Schaller Brewery, Woman & Solar Eclipse, Tin Lithograph, Round, 13 In. 579.00
Tray, Soo Line, Montana Success, Soo Line Route, Tin, 10 1/2 x 15 In. 201.00
Tray, Standard Brewing Co., Mankato, Minn., 12 In. 410.00
Tray, Velvet Ice Cream, Children With Mom, 10 1/2 x 13 1/4 In. 630.00
Tray, Zipp's Cherri-O, Bird Sipping Beverage Through Straw, 12 In. ....650.00 to 750.00
Trophy, Green River Soda, Embossed Lettering, 9 1/2 x 14 In. 130.00
Umbrella, Dr. Daniels' Horse Colic Cure, 66 In. 575.00
Umbrella, Talbots, Men's Furnishings 1575.00
Whistle, Hand Holding Bottle, Embossed, 1930s, 7 x 10 In. 1050.00

AGATA glass was made by Joseph Locke of the New England Glass
Company of Cambridge, Massachusetts, after 1885. A metallic stain
was applied to New England Peachblow and the mottled design characteristic of agata appeared.

Bowl, Pink To Dark Pink, Scalloped Edge, 2 3/8 x 5 3/8 In. 1265.00
Cruet, Pink To White, Gold & Black Staining, 6 In. 865.00
Finger Bowl, Peachblow, Ruffled Rim, 5 1/4 In. 460.00
Vase, Ivory To Pink, Pinched Waist, 4 Sides, 6 In. 1045.00
Vase, Peachblow, Satin, 3 1/2 In. 2185.00
Vase, Pink To Rose, Ruffled Rim, Pinched Waist, 4 3/4 In. 1290.00
Vase, Pouch Shape, Crimped, Pinched Waist, 4 5/8 x 3 1/2 In. 1875.00

AKRO AGATE glass was made in Clarksburg, West Virginia, from 1932
to 1951. Before that time, the firm made children's glass marbles,
which are listed in this book in the Marble category. Most of the glass
is marked with a crow flying through the letter *A*.

Apothecary Jar, Cover, Opaque Blue, Label 175.00
Apothecary Jar, Cover, White, Label 45.00
Bell, Opaque Turquoise, 5 1/4 In. 85.00
Bell, Opaque Yellow, 5 1/4 In. 700.00
Bell, Pumpkin, 5 1/4 In. 900.00
Bowl, Cereal, Interior Panel, Lemonade & Oxblood, Marbleized, 3 3/8 In. 85.00
Bowl, Cereal, Interior Panel, Opaque Green, 3 3/8 In. 20.00
Bowl, Cereal, Interior Panel, Opaque Pink, 3 3/8 In. 27.00
Bowl, Cereal, Octagonal, Lemonade & Oxblood, Marbleized, 3 3/8 In. ....75.00 to 95.00
Bowl, Cereal, Octagonal, White, 3 3/8 In. 16.00
Bowl, Cereal, Stacked Disc, Interior Panel, Opaque Green, 3 3/8 In. 49.00
Cigarette Jar, Cover, Lime Green 125.00
Cornucopia, Pink, 3 1/4 In. 40.00
Creamer, Interior Panel, Creamer, Transparent Green, 1 1/4 In. 28.00
Creamer, Interior Panel, Opaque Blue, 1 1/4 In. 40.00
Creamer, Interior Panel, Opaque Yellow, Darts, 1 3/8 In. 40.00
Creamer, Interior Panel, Oxblood, Marbleized, 1 1/4 In. 50.00
Creamer, Interior Panel, Transparent Amber, 1 1/4 In. 39.00
Creamer, Miss America, White, Marbleized, Decal, 1 3/8 In. 125.00
Creamer, Octagonal, Opaque Dark Blue, Open Handle, 1 1/2 In. 29.00
Creamer, Octagonal, White, Closed Handle, 1 1/2 In. 16.00
Creamer, Stacked Disc, Interior Panel, Opaque Dark Blue, 1 3/8 In. 35.00
Creamer, Stacked Disc, Interior Panel, Transparent Blue, 1 3/8 In. 65.00
Creamer, Stacked Disc, Opaque Pink, 1 3/8 In. 25.00
Creamer, Stippled Band, Transparent Green, 1 1/2 In. 68.00
Cup, Concentric Ring, Opaque Blue, 1 1/4 In. 19.00
Cup, Concentric Ring, Opaque Green, 1 1/4 In. 9.00

Cup, Concentric Ring, Opaque Lavender, 1 1/4 In. 70.00
Cup, Concentric Ring, Opaque Yellow, 1 1/4 In. 15.00
Cup, Concentric Ring, Pumpkin, 1 1/4 In. 39.00
Cup, Concentric Ring, Transparent Green, 1 3/8 In. 15.00
Cup, Interior Panel, Opaque Pink, 1 1/4 In. 28.00
Cup, Interior Panel, Pumpkin, 1 3/8 In. 39.00
Cup, Octagonal, Opaque Blue, Closed Handle, 1 1/4 In. 23.00
Cup, Octagonal, Opaque Dark Blue, Closed Handle, 1 1/2 In. 15.00
Cup, Octagonal, Opaque Green, Closed Handle, 1 1/2 In. 9.00
Cup, Octagonal, Opaque Light Blue, Closed Handle, 1 1/4 In. 78.00
Cup, Octagonal, Pumpkin, Open Handle, 1 1/2 In. 35.00
Cup, Stacked Disc, Interior Panel, Pumpkin, 1 3/8 In. 39.00
Cup, Stacked Disc, Opaque Blue, 1 1/4 In. 23.00
Cup, Stacked Disc, Opaque Dark Blue, 1 1/4 In. 16.00
Cup, Stacked Disc, Opaque Green, 1 1/4 In. 8.00
Cup, Stippled Band, Transparent Cobalt, 1 1/2 In. 44.00
Cup, Stippled Band, Transparent Topaz, 1 1/4 In. ....16.00 to 21.00
Flowerpot, Banded Dart, Opaque Green, 2 1/2 In. 45.00
Flowerpot, Banded Dart, Orange, Marbleized, 5 1/2 In. 125.00
Flowerpot, Combo, Ribbed Top, Band Dart, Opaque Green, 5 In. 250.00
Flowerpot, Graduated Dart, Black, Scalloped, 4 In. 285.00
Flowerpot, Graduated Dart, Opaque Royal Blue, 4 In. 55.00
Flowerpot, Graduated Dart, Pumpkin, 5 1/4 In. 80.00
Flowerpot, Graduated Dart, Yellow, Flared, 3 In. 235.00
Flowerpot, Ribbed Top, Black, 1 3/4 In. 185.00
Flowerpot, Ribbed Top, Blue, 3 1/2 In. 28.00
Flowerpot, Ribbed Top, Lavender, Marbleized, 2 1/4 In. 125.00
Flowerpot, Ribbed Top, Orange, Marbleized, 4 In. 20.00
Flowerpot, Ribbed Top, Oxblood, 3 1/2 In. 85.00
Flowerpot, Ribbed Top, Oxblood, Marbleized, 1 3/4 In. 42.00
Flowerpot, Ribbed Top, Thumb, Black, 1 1/4 In. 165.00
Flowerpot, Ribbed Top, Thumb, Pumpkin, 1 1/4 In. 125.00
Flowerpot, Ribbed Top, Thumb, Turquoise, 1 1/4 In. 65.00
Flowerpot, Ribs & Flutes, Pumpkin, Scalloped Edge, 3 3/4 In. 285.00
Flowerpot, Wide Band Ribbed Top, Turquoise, 4 3/8 In. 75.00
Jar, Mortar & Pestle Cover, Blue, Enameled 45.00
Jar, Mortar & Pestle Cover, White, Enameled 25.00
Jardiniere, Graduated Dart, Orange, Marbleized, Square, 4 In. 95.00
Jardiniere, Graduated Dart, Pumpkin, Square, 5 In. 85.00
Jardiniere, Graduated Dart, Royal Blue, Square, 5 In. 125.00
Jardiniere, Narrow Ledge, Dark Forest Green, 4 1/2 In. 275.00
Jardiniere, Narrow Ledge, Pumpkin, 4 1/2 In. 135.00
Milk Bottle Cover, Yellow, 2 3/8 In. 1000.00
Pitcher, Water, Interior Panel, Transparent Topaz, 2 7/8 In. 43.00
Pitcher, Water, Octagonal, Blue, Marbleized, 2 7/8 In. 50.00
Pitcher, Water, Stacked Disc, Opaque Green, 2 7/8 In. 26.00
Planter, Rectangular, Black, 8 In. 750.00
Planter, Rectangular, Turquoise, 8 In. 85.00
Plate, Concentric Ring, Opaque Green, 4 1/4 In. 16.00
Plate, Concentric Ring, Transparent Cobalt, 3 1/4 In. 38.00
Plate, Interior Panel, Blue, Marbleized, 4 1/4 In. 32.00
Plate, Interior Panel, Opaque Yellow, 4 1/4 In. 16.00
Plate, Octagonal, Opaque Blue, 3 3/8 In. 15.00
Plate, Octagonal, Opaque Green, 3 3/8 In. ....5.00 to 10.00
Plate, Octagonal, Opaque Light Blue, 3 3/8 In. ....75.00 to 78.00
Plate, Raised Daisy, Opaque Blue, 3 1/8 In. 28.00
Plate, Stacked Disc, Opaque Blue, 3 1/4 In. 12.00
Plate, Stacked Disc, Opaque Light Blue, 3 1/4 In. 68.00
Plate, Stacked Disc, Transparent Green, 3 1/4 In. 12.00
Plate, Stippled Band, Transparent Cobalt, 4 1/4 In. 28.00
Plate, Stippled Band, Transparent Topaz, 4 1/4 In. ....8.00 to 13.00
Powder Jar, Cover, Apple, Ivory 450.00
Powder Jar, Cover, Apple, Opaque Green 425.00

Powder Jar, Cover, Colonial Lady, Blue 150.00
Powder Jar, Cover, Colonial Lady, Opaque Royal Blue 750.00
Powder Jar, Cover, Ribbed, White, Enameled 35.00
Powder Jar, Cover, Scotty Dog, Blue, Marbleized 165.00
Powder Jar, Scotty Dog, Clear 325.00
Saucer, Concentric Ring, White, 2 3/4 In. 4.00
Saucer, Interior Panel, Green, Marbleized, 2 3/4 In. 12.00
Saucer, Interior Panel, Opaque Blue, 2 3/4 In. 14.00
Saucer, Interior Panel, Pumpkin, 2 3/4 In. 15.00
Saucer, Miss America, Orange, Marbleized, 3 1/4 In. 155.00
Saucer, Miss America, White, 3 1/4 In. 22.00
Saucer, Octagonal, Opaque Blue, 2 3/4 In. 9.00
Saucer, Stacked Disc, Opaque Blue, 2 3/4 In. 45.00
Saucer, Stippled Band, Transparent Topaz, 2 3/4 In. 8.00
Shaving Mug, Black, Ring Handle 72.00
Sugar, Cover, Stippled Band, Interior Panel, Transparent Topaz, 1 1/2 In. 68.00
Sugar, Interior Panel, Opaque Dark Blue, Darts, 1 3/8 In. 43.00
Sugar, Interior Panel, Opaque Pink, 1 1/4 In. 38.00
Sugar, Stacked Disc, White, 1 1/4 In. 18.00
Teapot, Cover, Miss America, White, Decal, 2 5/8 In. 320.00
Tumbler, Octagonal, Pumpkin, 2 In. 32.00
Tumbler, Stacked Disc, Opaque Pink, 2 In. 10.00
Tumbler, Stippled Band, Transparent Green, 1 3/4 In. 12.00
Urn, Beaded Top, White, 3 1/4 In. 38.00
Vase, Graduated Dart, Black, Scalloped Top, 3-Footed, 6 In. 1200.00
Vase, Graduated Dart, Green, Marbleized, Scalloped Top, 3-Footed, 6 In. ... 125.00
Vase, Graduated Dart, Opaque Yellow, 8 3/4 In. 350.00
Vase, Graduated Dart, Opaque Yellow, Tab Handle, 6 In. 175.00
Vase, Hand, Orange, Burgundy, Red, Pumpkin & Green 38.00
Vase, Ribs & Flutes, Opaque Green, 8 In. 240.00
Vase, Ribs & Flutes, Opaque Yellow, 8 In. 325.00

ALABASTER is a very soft form of gypsum, a stone that resembles marble. It was often carved into vases or statues in Victorian times. There are alabaster carvings being made even today. Because the alabaster is very porous, it will dissolve if kept in water, so do not use alabaster vases for flowers.

Bowl, Yellow Tint, Carved, Footed, Italy, Late 19th Century, 6 x 8 1/2 In. 105.00
Bust, Art Nouveau Woman, 12 1/4 x 13 1/2 In. 715.00
Bust, Beauty, Lace Headdress & Bodice, Early 20th Century, 17 1/4 In. 460.00
Bust, Female Bacchante, Crowned, Grapevine Drapery, Firenze, 15 1/2 In. 400.00
Bust, Indian Princess, Lily Stem Base, Art Nouveau, Early 20th Century, 14 1/2 In. 518.00
Bust, Napoleon, 11 3/4 In. 545.00
Bust, Serene Woman In Wimple, Signed, 19th Century, 11 In. 380.00
Bust, Smiling Young Woman, Long Flowing Hair, Giursto Viti, 13 1/2 x 11 In. 345.00
Bust, Woman, With Long Braided Hair, 21 In. 865.00
Bust, Young Boy, 8 In. 96.00
Figurine, Girl Wearing Bonnet, Reading Book, 9 In. 107.00
Figurine, Girl, Crying, Holding Dead Bird, Stepped Pedestal, 14 In. 115.00
Figurine, Girl, Sunbonnet, Bow At Waist, Marble Base, A. Ciprianni, 28 1/2 In. 990.00
Figurine, Grand Tour, Boar, Seated, Marble Plinth, Italy, 19th Century, 7 x 4 In. 489.00
Figurine, Head Of Zeus, Ebonized Wood Plinth, 4 1/2 x 8 1/2 In. 690.00
Figurine, Rabbit, Reclining, White, Rests On Rectangular Base, 6 x 5 x 9 In. 2185.00
Figurine, Woman, Seated On Bench, Holding Flowers, Marble Base, 16 1/2 In. 660.00
Group, Allegorical, Woman Astride Bronze Eagle, 40 In. 2415.00
Group, Arab, On Resting Camel, 17 In. 690.00
Inkwell & Quill Holder, Enameled Flowers, 1837 .... 185.00
Lamp, Electric, Nude Woman, Seated On Rocky Grotto, Green Paint, 14 3/8 In. 220.00
Lamp, Electric, Renaissance Style, Carved, Dome Shade, Flowers, 66 In. 4406.00
Lamp, Female Nude Standing By Column, 31 In. 1150.00
Lamp, Oil, Grand Tour, Lion Masks, Rear Legs, Italy, 19th Century, 3 3/8 x 7 In. 104.00
Lamp, Sue Et Mare, Silver, Bronze, 1925, 18 In. 4800.00
Lamp, Urn Shape, Carved Classical Figures, 19 In. 935.00

Pedestal, Column, Black, White, Square Canted Corners, Octagonal Base, 39 x 11 In. . . . 460.00
Pedestal, Column, Round Top, Spiral Shaft, Leaves, Vines, Octagonal Base, 26 x 10 In. . . 405.00
Pedestal, Column, Variegated, Spiral Cut, Lathe-Cut Rings, 39 1/2 x 10 x 10 In. 575.00
Pedestal, Stepped Column, Lathe-Cut Ring, Octagonal Base, 1800s, 32 x 11 In. 795.00
Urn, Acanthus Leaf & Bacchus, 24 In., Pair 1870.00
Urn, Cylindrical, Bronze Lion Head Handles, Italy, Late 19th Century, 10 1/2 In. 635.00
Urn, Figural, Maiden's Head, Pedestal, Art Nouveau, 92 In. 3808.00
Vase, Garniture, Gilt Bronze Mount, Mid 1800s, 11 1/2 x 6 1/2 x 6 5/8 In., Pair 1465.00

ALEXANDRITE is a name with many meanings. It is a form of the mineral chrysoberyl that changes from green to red under artificial light. A man-made version of this mineral is sold in Mexico today. It changes from deep purple to aquamarine blue under artificial light. The Alexandrite listed here is glass made in the late nineteenth and twentieth centuries. Thomas Webb & Sons sold their transparent glass shaded from yellow to rose to blue under the name Alexandrite. Stevens and Williams had a cased Alexandrite of yellow, rose, and blue. A. Douglas Nash Corporation made an amethyst-colored Alexandrite. Several American glass companies of the 1920s made a glass that changed color under electric lights and this was also called Alexandrite.

Plate, Honeycomb, Ruffled Edge, 5 1/2 In. 952.00
Vase, Ball Base, Petal Rim, Flared, D'Agostino, 6 1/2 In. 31.00
Vase, Trumpet, 9 1/2 In. 60.00

ALUMINUM was more expensive than gold or silver until the 1850s. Chemists learned how to refine bauxite to get aluminum. Jewelry and other small objects were made of the valuable metal until 1914, when an inexpensive smelting process was invented. The aluminum collected today dates from the 1930s through the 1950s. Hand-hammered pieces are the most popular.

Bowl, Art Deco, Bronze, Flowers, Handles, Kensington, 6 5/8 x 2 1/2 In. 20.00
Bowl, Chip & Dip, Beaded, Serrated Rim, 2-Strand Dip Holder, Buenilum, 4 x 9 In. 23.00
Bowl, Cover, Divider, Bamboo, Everlast, 10 1/2 In. 36.00
Bowl, Half Round, Nambe, Stamped No. 647, 5 x 7 1/4 In. 58.00
Compote, Flaring, Spherical Lucite Shaft, Lurelle Guild, Kensington, 13 1/2 In. 58.00
Dish, Cover, Anchor, Arm, Hammer, Handle, Leaves, Vine, Everlast, 7 x 2 3/4 In. 23.00
Figure, Seated Black Man, Cast, 12 In. 184.00
Party Set, Bowl, Cover, 6 Dividers, 19 In. 27.00
Plate, Butterflies, Flowers, Branches, Scalloped Edge, Arthur Armour, 12 1/4 In. 46.00
Platter Set, Zodiac Symbols, Kensington, 18 In., 12 Piece 630.00
Serving Set, Red, Green, c.1950, 9 Piece 20.00
Spaghetti Set, Pot, Cover, Cheese Shaker, Reed Handles, Russel Wright, 8 In., 3 Piece . . 1900.00
Tray, Berries & Leaves, Handle, Wendell August, Grove City, Pa., 13 3/4 x 13 1/4 In. 75.00
Tray, Colonial Ladies, Farberware, 16 1/2 In. 36.00
Tray, Condiment, Glass Inserts, No. 462, Rodney Kent, 12 x 5 1/2 In. 42.00
Tray, Serving, Flowers, Scalloped Rim, Wendell August, No. 523, 18 In. 24.00
Tray, Serving, Pinecone, Hammered, Everlast, 14 In. 25.00
Tray, Shells, Lobster Handle, Bruce Fox, 10 1/2 x 10 1/2 In. 103.00
Washboard, Wavy Scrubbing Area, Impressed Fani Moser, 15 x 11 In. 630.00
Wastebasket, Pinecones, Wendell August Forge, 11 In. 210.00

AMBER, see Jewelry category.

AMBER GLASS is the name of any glassware with the proper yellow-brown shading. It was a popular color just after the Civil War and many pressed glass pieces were made of amber glass. Depression glass of the 1930s–1950s was also made in shades of amber glass. Other pieces may be found in the Depression Glass, Pressed Glass, and other glass categories. All types are being reproduced.

Box, Hinged Cover, Enameled Flowers, 3 1/2 x 2 1/4 In. 275.00
Box, Hinged Cover, Gold Branch, Flower & Leaves At Top, 3 1/4 x 6 1/2 In. 225.00
Box, Hinged Cover, Gold Enameled Flowers, Silver Leaves, 3 1/2 x 4 In. 195.00
Box, Hinged Cover, White Enameled Star, Flowers, 3 1/2 x 4 In. 165.00
Cruet, Enameled Flowers, Green Leaves, White Butterfly, Hollow Stopper, 9 In. 165.00

Decanter, Wine, Optic, Pewter Mounting, Pewter Stopper 245.00
Night-Light, Clear Candle Cup, Brass Holder, 9 1/2 In. 225.00
Pitcher, Enameled Sprays, Teal Leaves, Large Bird, 11 1/2 In. 195.00
Salt, Controlled Threading, Opalescent Interior, Scalloped Edge, 6 1/2 In. 35.00
Vase, Enameled House & Snow Scene, Brass Feet, 10 1/4 In. 155.00
Vase, Inverted Thumbprint, Enameled Flowers, Blue Butterfly, 7 1/2 In., Pair 255.00

AMBERETTE pieces are listed in the Pressed Glass category under the pattern name Amberette.

AMBERINA is a two-toned glassware made from 1883 to about 1900. It was patented by Joseph Locke of the New England Glass Company, but was also made by other companies. The glass shades from red to amber. Similar pieces of glass may be found in the Baccarat and Plated Amberina categories. Glass shaded from blue to amber is called *Blue Amberina* or *Bluerina*.

Bowl, Daisy & Button, Boat Shape, Serrated Rim, 10 x 8 1/4 In. 392.00
Bowl, Diamond-Quilted, 2 5/8 x 4 1/4 In. 50.00
Bowl, Diamond-Quilted, 5 In. 224.00
Bowl, Melon Ribbed, Scalloped Rim, Concave Polished Base, 9 x 6 1/4 x 2 3/4 In. 445.00
Bowl, Ruffled, Edge Enameled, 8 In. 127.00
Celery Vase, Reverse Swirl, Ball Shape, Applied Rigaree Rim, 4 x 4 1/2 In. 70.00
Celery Vase, Scalloped Edge, 7 x 3 1/2 In. 175.00
Cheese Dish, Cover, Daisy & Button, Round Knob, 7 x 5 In. 144.00
Cheese Dish, Cover, Enameled Flowers, 7 1/2 x 7 1/4 In. 115.00
Creamer, Amber Applied Handle, 4 1/2 In. 40.00
Cruet, Amber Handle, Ball Stopper, 7 In. 258.00
Cruet, Amber Handle, Cut Stopper, 9 In. 225.00
Cruet, Baby Thumbprint, 7 1/4 In. 150.00
Cruet, Diamond-Quilted, Amber Squared Handle, Amber Stopper, 4 In. 475.00
Cruet, Swirl, Faceted Stopper, Amber Handle, 6 In. 535.00
Decanter, Diamond-Quilted, Faceted Amber Stopper, 12 1/2 In. 259.00
Decanter Set, Cordials, Thumbprint, 9 1/4-In. Decanter, 13 Piece 150.00
Finger Bowl, Inverted Thumbprint, 2 3/4 x 5 1/8 In. 40.00
Finger Bowl, Melon Ribbed, 2 1/2 x 5 In. ....40.00 to 60.00
Finger Bowl, Ruffled Edge, 2 1/2 x 5 1/2 In. 40.00
Finger Bowl, Underplate, Thumbprint, 4 1/2 In. 80.00
Pitcher, Diamond-Quilted, Amber Handle, 6 3/4 In. 672.00
Pitcher, Inverted Thumbprint, Square Mouth, Applied Reeded Handle, 5 3/4 In. 450.00
Pitcher, Swirl, Amber Handle, 9 1/8 In. 210.00
Pitcher, Thumbprint, 6 1/2 In. 140.00
Pitcher, Water, Inverted Thumbprint, Applied Handle, 7 1/4 In. 144.00
Pitcher, Water, Inverted Thumbprint, Applied Reeded Handle, 8 In. 210.00
Punch Cup, Diamond-Quilted, Amber Reeded Handle, 2 1/2 x 2 3/8 In. 30.00
Toothpick, Diamond-Quilted, 2 1/2 x 2 In. ....140.00 to 375.00
Tumbler, Reverse Thumbprint, 1880s, 3 3/4 In. 95.00
Vase, Applied Amber Rigaree At Neck, Dimpled Sides, 9 In. 978.00
Vase, Bud, Trumpet, 5 x 2 1/2 In. 110.00
Vase, Bud, Trumpet, Footed, Ruffled Edge, 6 In. 385.00
Vase, Coin Spot, Flared Ruffled Edge, 7 1/4 In. 121.00
Vase, Jack-In-The-Pulpit, Folded Top, Ribbed, 8 In. 475.00
Vase, Jack-In-The-Pulpit, Fuchsia To Amber, 7 In. 180.00
Vase, Jack-In-The-Pulpit, Swirl, Applied Amber Rigaree, 11 In. 400.00

AMERICAN DINNERWARE, see Dinnerware.

AMERICAN ENCAUSTIC TILING COMPANY was founded in Zanesville, Ohio, in 1875. The company planned to make a variety of tiles to compete with the English tiles that were selling in the United States for use in fireplaces and other architectural designs. The first glazed tiles were made in 1880, embossed tiles in 1881, faience tiles in the 1920s. The firm closed in 1935 and reopened in 1937 as the Shawnee Pottery.

Tile, Female Silhouette, Green High Glaze, Arts & Crafts Oak Frame, 9 1/2 In. 334.00
Tile, Henry VIII & Anne Boleyn, Ivory, 6 x 6 In., Pair 110.00

Tile, Oriental Women, Oak Frame, 9 x 3 In. 400.00
Tile, Stylized Pea Pod, Organic Swirls, Green Glaze, 6 In. 69.00
Tile, Trivet, Stylized Swirled Pattern, Metal Base 35.00

AMETHYST GLASS is any of the many glasswares made in the dark purple color of the gemstone called amethyst. Included in this category are many pieces made in the nineteenth and twentieth centuries. Very dark pieces are called *black amethyst* and are listed under that heading.

Basket, Ruffled Edge, Blenko, 6 1/2 x 7 1/2 In. 68.00
Candlestick, Hexagon Base, 19th Century, 7 3/4 In. 635.00
Cocktail Shaker, Black Enameled, Frolicking Woman, Art Deco, Signed, 12 x 3 In. 402.00
Figurine, Bird, Long Tail, Venetian Style, 10 1/2 x 5 In., Pair 100.00
Goblet, Silver, Gilt, Engraved, Paneled, Baluster Stem, Scalloped Foot, 6 In., Pair 632.00
Jar, Sweetmeat, Domed Cover, Ball Finial, Engraved Grapevine, 14 1/4 In. 460.00
Pitcher, 3-Piece Mold, 9 1/4 x 7 3/4 In. 50.00
Vase, Gold Enameled Flowers, Leaves & Trim, Blue Dots, 4 1/2 x 3 1/2 In. 99.00
Vase, Tapering Sides, Base, Controlled Bubble, c.1960, 6 1/2 In. 28.00
Water Set, Silver Enameled Scrolls, Buildings, 10 1/4-In. Pitcher, 6 Piece 550.00
Wine, Trumpet Bowl, Cone Foot, England, c.1820, 4 1/4 In. 155.00

AMPHORA pieces are listed in the Teplitz category.

ANDIRONS and related fireplace items are included in the Fireplace category.

ANIMAL TROPHIES, such as stuffed animals, rugs made of animal skins, and other similar collectibles made from animal, fish, or bird parts, are listed in this category. Collectors should be aware of the endangered species laws that make it illegal to buy and sell some of these items. Any eagle feathers, many types of pelts or rugs (such as leopard), ivory, and many forms of tortoiseshell can be confiscated by the government. Related trophies may be found in the Fishing category. Ivory items may be found in the Scrimshaw or Ivory categories.

American Buffalo Head, Curly Horns 797.00
Antelope Head, Pronghorn, 33 In. 86.00
Buffalo Horn, Mounted 50.00
Caribou Head 750.00
Pheasant, Ring Neck, Black Lacquer Stand, 16 1/4 x 25 In. 288.00
Rattlesnake, Coiled, Painted Plaster Stand, 31 x 12 In. 66.00
Rug, Bear Skin, Full Body, 60 In. 431.00

ANIMATION ART collectibles include cels that are painted drawings on celluloid needed to make animated cartoons shown in movie theaters or on TV. Hundreds of cels were made, then photographed in sequence to make a cartoon showing moving figures. Early examples made by the Walt Disney Studios are popular with collectors today. Original sketches used by the artists are also listed here. Modern animated cartoons are made using computer-generated pictures. Some of these are being produced as cels to be sold to collectors. Other cartoon art is listed in Comic Art and Disneyana.

Cel, 2 Pink Panthers Pushing Rock With Pizza Box, 8 x 10 In. 86.00
Cel, Beauty & The Beast, Dancing In The Ballroom, 1991, 17 x 23 In. 1425.00
Cel, Chipmunks, Alvin, Simon, Theodore, Dressed As Cowboys, 5 1/2 x 7 3/4 In. 75.00
Cel, Flintstones, Modern Stone Age Family, 10 x 17 In. 495.00
Cel, Jetsons, Jane, Judy, Robot, On Air Motion Movers, 3 1/2 x 6 1/2 In. 70.00
Cel, Peter Pan, Captain Hook, 18 x 22 In. 975.00
Cel, The Adventures Of Raggedy Ann & Andy, 6 1/4 In. 75.00

APPLE PEELERS are listed in the Kitchen category under Peeler, Apple.

ARCHITECTURAL antiques include a variety of collectibles, usually very large, that have been removed from buildings. Hardware, backbars, doors, paneling, and even old bathtubs are now wanted by collectors. Pieces of the Victorian, Art Nouveau, and Art Deco styles are in greatest demand.

Altar Back, Sunburst, Giltwood, Eagle, Leafy Branch, France, 19th Century, 46 In. 980.00

Arch, Wood, Inscribed Thomas Clark, Church Warden, c.1720, 28 x 42 1/2 In. 4465.00
Balustrade Post, Cobalt Glaze, Wired As Lamp, 19th Century, 31 x 6 3/4 x 6 3/4 In. 288.00
Bathtub, Faucet, Shower Spray, Brass, Porcelain, 8 1/2 x 9 1/2 x 6 In. 310.00
Bathtub, Galvanized Sheet Metal, Oak Rim, Cast Iron Support Frame, 60 In. 595.00
Bracket, Parcel Gilt, Painted, Carved, Cherub, Continental, 19th Century, 18 1/2 In. 860.00
Bracket, Wall, Carved, Painted, Blackamoor, Italy, Early 19th Century, 16 1/2 In. 545.00
Brick, Incised 1768 . . . . 85.00
Cabinet, Mahogany, Hotel Key Stand, Divided Compartment, c.1900, 47 x 67 In. 615.00
Chimney Piece, Polychrome, Gold Banding, Staffordshire, 9 In. 275.00
Chimney Stack, Eagle, Walter Smith Jr., Superior Clay, Uhrichsville, Ohio 850.00
Chimney Stack, Square Top, Terra-Cotta, 26 x 12 x 12 In. 110.00
Chimney Stack, Square Top, Terra-Cotta, 28 x 13 x 13 In., Pair 225.00
Chimney Stack, Terra-Cotta, Baluster Shape, Mark, Boston, c.1880, 43 1/2 x 12 In. 345.00
Chimney Stack, Terra-Cotta, Crown Top, 34 x 13 1/2 In., Pair 280.00
Column, Figural, Mahogany, Male Caryatid, Bacchus Head Supports, 53 In., Pair 1960.00
Column, Tin, Tapered & Fluted, Flaking Paint, 80 x 13 In., Pair 310.00
Corbel, Horse Head, Cast Zinc, Painted Brown, 1870s, 32 x 26 1/2 In. 3288.00
Corbel, Horse Head, Flared Nostrils, J.W. Fiske, 31 x 25 1/2 In. 9400.00
Corbel, Pigeon Head, Weathered White, Gray, Blue, Green Paint, 21 x 20 In. 1725.00
Corbel, Wood, Carved, Painted, Red, White, 38 x 30 x 6 In., 6 Pairs 1680.00
Cross, Tin, Mid 1800s, 74 In. 1200.00
Door, Barn, Red Paint Traces, Window, Knocker, Strap Hinges, 1800s, 78 x 31 In. 88.00
Door, Hook, Brass, 5 x 2 3/4 In., Pair 450.00
Door, Leaded Glass Half Moons, Seascape, Wood, 48 x 22 1/2 In., Pair 25.00
Door, Leaded Glass, Beveled Glass Inserts, Wood Frame, 78 x 28 In. 1435.00
Door, Louis XV, Green Paint, Gilt, Foliate Scroll, Cartouches, 97 In., Pair 5060.00
Door, Temple, Pierced Iron Hardware, c.1700, 75 x 20 1/2 In., Pair 2900.00
Door Handle, Walter Gropius & Adolf Meyer, Nickel Plate, 9 1/8 x 1 1/2 In., Pair 1495.00
Door Knocker, Eagle, Bronze, 19th Century 145.00
Door Knocker, Figural, Face, Acanthus, Wings, Cream Paint, Iron, 21 x 8 1/2 In. 633.00
Door Knocker, Scrolled Backplate, Iron, New England, Early 1800s, 6 1/2 In. 295.00
Door Knocker, Snake, Iron, Brass Eyes, Coiled Tail, Wood Base, 8 1/4 In. 5175.00
Door Knocker, Steel, Shell Handle, Medieval Style, Continental, 11 x 14 In. 460.00
Door Latch, Head With Horns & Human Features, Africa, 10 In. 200.00
Doorknob, Doggie, Face & Paws Reach Out From Center, Bronze, 1870 . . . . 8500.00
Downspout, Copper, Embossed Design, Large, Pair 6050.00
Eagle, Cast Zinc, Outstretched Wings, Painted Silver, Bronze Patina, 28 x 46 In. 2070.00
Fence, Iron, Hand Forged, Ornate Design, Continental, 60 In. 500.00
Fence, Widow's Walk, Forged Iron, Victorian, 30 1/2 x 24 3/4 In., Pair 280.00
Finial, Acorn, Wood, White Paint, 19th Century, 9 3/4 In., Pair 375.00
Finial, Flame, Metal, 4 Radiating Gothic Scrolled Corbels, Wood Base, 69 x 27 In. 546.00
Finial, Star & Crescent, Copper, Verdigris, Ring & Baluster Base, 31 In., Pair 4140.00
Gate, Art Deco, Iron, Scroll Panels, 27 x 39 In., Pair 460.00
Gate, Security, Iron, Geometric, 20th Century, 75 x 30 In. 390.00
Gate, Spiral, Applied Florals, 3 Cast Iron Balls, Rectangular Frame, 32 x 39 In. 120.00
Gate, War Of 1812 Cap, Rifles, Swords, Bugle, Stars, Iron, Painted, 45 x 77 In. 5875.00
Head, Female, Wood, Gilt Coating, c.1820, 9 1/2 x 4 In. 245.00
Hitching Post, Clenched Fists On Top, 43 In., Pair 6500.00
Hitching Post, Horsehead, c.1860, 67 In., Pair 3600.00
Hitching Post, Iron, Tan, Brown, Black, Green Collar, 45 In. 2530.00
Hitching Post, Tapered Tree Trunk, Grapevines & Stars, Top Ring, 70 In. 600.00
Hitching Post, Youth Wearing Loose Garments, Cast Iron, Black Painted, 46 In. 1840.00
Hitching Post Finial, Iron, Horsehead, Acanthus Leaves Around Base, 13 In. 440.00
Key Box, Hotel, Ornate Cast Iron Front, Black Paint, Wooden Box Back 1265.00
Lamp Fixture, Cast Iron, Fierce Wolf-Type Animal, 50 x 20 In., Pair 345.00
Mailbox, Brass, Allegorical Relief, France, Late 1800s, 10 1/2 x 3 x 15 1/2 In. 520.00
Mantel, Acanthus, Wood, 19th Century, 49 1/4 x 58 In. 1300.00
Mantel, Arts & Crafts, Mahogany, Beveled Mirror, 72 1/2 x 52 1/2 x 9 In. 390.00
Mantel, Carved Scrolling, Leaf & Fruit, Molded Plinth, 55 1/2 x 80 1/2 In. 1008.00
Mantel, Carved, Oval Centerpiece On Tablet, Shelf, York County, 38 x 45 In. 880.00
Mantel, Classical, Stepped Cornice, Gadroon Molding, Gilding, 28 1/2 x 42 In. 195.00
Mantel, Country, Wide Shelf, Molding, Plain Pilasters, 76 x 59 In. 55.00
Mantel, Federal, Shelf, Reeded Pilasters, Gray Over Red Paint, 57 x 62 1/2 In. 250.00

Mantel, Federal, Shelf, Reeded, Plain Panels, Pilasters, Painted, 56 x 61 1/2 In. 715.00
Mantel, Louis XV Style, Gilt, Marble, 49 1/2 x 74 1/2 x 18 In. 35250.00
Mantel, Louis XV Style, Marble, Carved Leaf Frieze, 46 x 70 x 11 In. 14400.00
Mantel, Louis XVI Style, Black Veined Marble, 1915, 43 x 62 In. 6800.00
Mantel, Louis XVI Style, White Carved Marble, France, c.1900, 43 x 57 x 15 In. 4830.00
Mantel, Marble, Carved, France, c.1900, 42 x 55 x 15 1/2 In. 6038.00
Mantel, Pine, Red Paint, Reeded Capitals, 1800s, 77 x 103 In. 130.00
Mantel, Pine, Shelf, Ogee Molding, Pilasters, Painted, Faux Marble, 54 x 56 1/2 In. 110.00
Mantel, Poplar, Step Molding, Raised Corner Blocks, 64 x 55 In. 220.00
Mantel, Tripartite Backboard, Paneled Frame, 87 3/4 x 69 3/4 In. 2230.00
Mantel, Victorian, Pierced Brackets, Raised Panels, Fluted Pilaster, 49 x 60 In. 110.00
Mantel, Victorian, Pine, Painted, Columns, England, c.1875, 50 x 51 x 11 1/4 In. 225.00
Mirror, Overmantel, Classical, Gilt Gesso, Egg & Dart Mold, 1855, 33 In. 1265.00
Mirror, Overmantel, Louis Philippe, Gilt Composition, 19th Century, 85 x 45 In. 1610.00
Mirror, Overmantel, Napoleon III, Carved, Cenotaph Shape, 64 1/2 x 44 In. 1150.00
Mirror, Overmantel, Napoleon III, Giltwood, Carved, Cenotaph Shape, 53 x 38 In. 1150.00
Mirror, Overmantel, Napoleon III, Louis XVI Style, Giltwood, Carved, 75 x 44 In. 3680.00
Overmantel, Turned Spindles, 2 Supported Shelves, 19 x 52 1/2 In. 28.00
Overmantel Mirror, Arched Plate, Scroll Frame, 40 3/4 x 58 In. 230.00
Overmantel Mirror, Classical, Egg & Dart Mold, Gilt Gesso, 1855, 33 In. 1265.00
Overmantel Mirror, George III, Gilt, c.1800, 50 1/4 x 60 1/4 In. 2300.00
Overmantel Mirror, George III, Giltwood, Molded Frame, 18th Century, 69 In. 4830.00
Overmantel Mirror, Gilt Molding, Dome Top, 44 x 54 In. 100.00
Overmantel Mirror, Gothic Arch Crown, 3 Panels, Rope-Twist Columns, 1890, 65 In. ... 1230.00
Overmantel Mirror, Louis Philippe, Gilt Composition, 19th Century, 85 x 45 In. 1610.00
Overmantel Mirror, Napoleon III, Carved, Cenotaph Shape, 64 1/2 x 44 In. 1150.00
Overmantel Mirror, Napoleon III, Carved, Giltwood, Louis XVI Style, 75 x 44 In. 3680.00
Overmantel Mirror, Napoleon III, Giltwood, Carved, Cenotaph Shape, 53 x 38 In. 1150.00
Overmantel Mirror, Neoclassical, Gilt, Gesso, Wood, 1825-1830, 23 3/4 x 49 3/4 In. 2185.00
Overmantel Mirror, Urn, Bellflower & Shell, 3 Panels, c.1840, 68 In. 2910.00
Panel, Art Deco, Glass, Woman's Form, With Tree, France, 19 x 18 In. 517.00
Panel, Cast Iron, Art Nouveau, Scrolls, Flowers, 39 1/2 x 23 1/2 In. 400.00
Panel, Marquetry, Tunbridge Ware, Inlaid, Figures In Boat, c.1900 .... 225.00
Panel, Marquetry, Tunbridge Ware, Inlaid, Village Landscape, c.1900 .... 225.00
Pediment, Georgian, Exterior Door, Dentil & Pulvinated Moldings, 43 x 85 In. 1035.00
Pediment, Wood, Carved, Triangular, Late 19th Century, 19 1/2 x 78 In. 920.00
Post Cap, Horse Head, Flowing Mane, Pineapple, Stepped Base, Iron, 10 1/2 In., Pair ... 635.00
Roof Finial, Flag & Directionals, Zinc, Flower Petals At Center, 46 1/2 In. 1320.00
Shutters, Gothic, Louvered, Painted, Hinged, Mid 19th Century, 87 x 37 1/2 In. 345.00
Shutters, Pine, Double Panel, Pegged Construction, 71 x 16 3/4 In. 110.00
Sink, Porcelain, Flowers, Oval, Cheryl Wagner Design, 8 1/2 x 19 1/4 x 15 In. 1008.00
Spire, Oak, Carved, Gothic, Hexagonal, Quatrefoils, 65 1/4 In. 575.00
Windmill, Flint & Walling Manufacturing Co., Kendallville, Ind., U.S.A., Steel, c.1900 .. 1400.00

AREQUIPA POTTERY was produced from 1911 to 1918 by the patients
of the Arequipa Sanatorium in Marin County, north of San Francisco.
The patients were trained by Frederick Hürten Rhead, who had worked
at the Roseville Pottery.

Bowl, Pink, Yellow, Green Matte Glaze, Squeezebag Flowers, Rolled-In Rim, 7 In. 4600.00
Tile, Bird Of Paradise, Flowers, Vines, 6 x 6 1/2 In., 4 Piece 12650.00
Vase, Gourd Shape, Green Matte Glaze, Painted Mark, California 1912, 6 x 5 In. 748.00

**Moving your own belongings? Be careful about insurance. Rental
trucks or your car may have coverage for antiques that is too low.
Your homeowner's policy probably does not cover damage from poor
packing. Check with your agent before you move!**

ARGY-ROUSSEAU, see G. Argy-Rousseau category.

ARITA is a port in Japan. Porcelain was made there from about 1616. Many types of decorations were used, including the popular Imari designs, which are listed under Imari in this book.

Charger, Polychrome, Diaper Pattern, Flowers, Cranes, c.1912, 24 In.	1840.00
Sake Bottle, 3 Friends, Pine, Bamboo, Gray, Blue Underglaze, 11 1/4 In.	287.00
Umbrella Stand, Blue, White Design, Dragon Relief, 1911, 24 In.	690.00
Vase, Blue, White Roundels, Fruit, Birds, Flowers, 19th Century, 49 In.	460.00

ART DECO, or Art Moderne, a style started at the Paris Exposition of 1925, is characterized by linear, geometric designs. All types of furniture and decorative arts, jewelry, book bindings, and even games were designed in this style. Additional items may be found in the Furniture category or in various glass and pottery categories, etc.

Ashtray, Polished Chrome Plate, Two Pelicans Mounted In Center, 5 1/2 In.	22.00
Cocktail Set, Cobalt Glass, Stainless Steel, c.1940, 7 Piece	201.00
Cocktail Set, Stainless Steel, Evercraft, 1930-1940, 8 Piece	288.00
Dresser Set, Ivorene, c.1930, 12 Piece	173.00
Powder Jars, Glass, Green, c.1930, 6 & 9 In., 2 Piece	173.00
Vase, Ceramic, Chartreuse Glaze, Flared Top, Leaves On Front, Late 1940s, 8 In.	50.00
Vase, Pottery, Orange, Marked York P 282, 10 In.	250.00

ART GLASS, see Glass-Art category.

ART NOUVEAU is a style of design that was at its most popular from 1895 to 1905. Famous designers, including Rene Lalique and Emile Galle, produced furniture, glass, silver, metalwork, and buildings in the new style. Ladies with long flowing hair and elongated bodies were among the more easily recognized design elements. Copies of this style are being made today. Many modern pieces of jewelry can be found. Additional Art Nouveau pieces may be found in Furniture or in various glass categories.

Humidor, Brass, Copper, Hinged Lid, Enameled, Brass Handle, 6 x 10 x 5 In.	500.00
Plate, Birds, Flowers, Aesthetic Movement, Late 19th Century, 9 3/8 In., 9 Piece	144.00
Vase, Female Profile In Medallion, 2 Landscapes, Painted, 1900s, 8 In.	144.00

ART POTTERY, see Pottery-Art.

ARTHUR OSBORNE plaques are found in the Ivorex category.

AURENE glass was made by Frederick Carder of New York about 1904. It is an iridescent gold, blue, green, or red glass, usually marked *Aurene* or *Steuben*.

AURENE

Basket, Gold, Steuben	1650.00
Bowl, Blue, Applied Foot, 3 3/4 x 9 In.	920.00
Bowl, Blue, Calcite Interior, 4 3/4 In.	1035.00
Bowl, Blue, Rolled Over Rim, 3 Disc Footed, Signed, 10 In.	1345.00
Bowl, Gold, Calcite Interior, Cupped Rim, Early 20th Century, 10 In.	376.00
Bowl, Gold, Calcite Interior, Signed, 10 In.	330.00
Bowl, Gold, Flared Rim, 3 3/4 x 8 In.	1150.00
Candlestick, Gold, Applied Stem, Signed, No. 6384, 3 3/4 In, Pair	1438.00
Candlestick, Gold, Applied Wrap-Around Leaf On Stem, Signed, 12 1/4 In.	3623.00
Candlestick, Gold, Twisted Stem, Bulbous Socket, 6 In.	440.00
Candlestick, Gold, Twisted Stem, Tulip Shaped Cup, Signed, 8 In., Pair	1540.00
Chalice, Blue, Pulled Heart & Trailing Vine, Signed, 10 In.	3450.00
Compote, Blue, Calcite Interior, 7 x 3 In.	805.00
Plate, Gold, Acid-Cut Back, Label, 8 1/4 In.	288.00
Salt, Blue, Paneled, 1 3/4 x 1 1/8 In.	88.00
Salt, Blue, Ribbed, Pinched Rim, Footed, 1 1/2 x 2 1/4 In.	345.00
Shade, Gold, Green Pulled Feather, 3 1/2 x 5 1/2 In.	430.00
Shade, Gold, Intaglio Carvings, Signed, 4 1/4 In.	224.00
Shade, Ribbed, Gold, 4 1/2 x 2 1/4 In., Pair	287.00
Toothpick, Gold, Floral Rim, Bulbous, 1 7/8 x 2 7/16 In.	210.00
Vase, Blue, Calcite Interior, Flared Ruffled Edge, 4 1/2 In.	863.00

Vase, Blue, Flared Rim, Carder, 1915, 4 In. 860.00
Vase, Blue, Stick, Signed, No. 2556, 10 1/4 In. 540.00
Vase, Blue, Tree Trunk, 3 Prongs, Signed, No. 24, 6 1/4 In. ....1400.00 to 1500.00
Vase, Blue, White Pulled Leaf & Vine, 10 In. 4950.00
Vase, Bud, Blue, Signed 350.00
Vase, Gold, 4 Pinched Recesses, 7 7/8 In. 488.00
Vase, Gold, Flared Rim, Carder, Early 20th Century, 9 1/2 In. 980.00
Vase, Gold, Satin, Signed, 4 1/4 x 3 In. 470.00
Vase, Gold, Silver Blue Accents, Flared, 3 1/8 In. 137.00
Vase, Green Pulled Heart & Trailing Vine, On Gold, Signed, 5 In. 3808.00

AUSTRIA is a collecting term that covers pieces made by a wide variety of factories. They are listed in this book in categories such as Royal Dux, or Porcelain.

AUTO parts and accessories are collectors' items today. Gas pump globes and license plates are part of this specialty. Prices are determined by age, rarity, and condition. Signs and packaging related to automobiles may also be found in the Advertising category. Lalique hood ornaments will be listed in the Lalique category.

Ashtray, Michelin Man, White Man, Bakelite, Black Base, 1930s 110.00
Banner, Jaguar, Showroom, Fringed Bottom, Square, 45 In. 413.00
Blotter, Touring Car, 6 x 3 In. 154.00
Bottle, Standard Oil Company, Electric Cycle Oil, Paper Label, Late 1800s, 5 3/8 In. 440.00
Can, Grease, Texaco, Red & Green, Lb., 3 1/2 In. 126.00
Can, Paste Wax, GM Blue Coral, Pontiac Indian Head 25.00
Catalog, Rolls-Royce, Coachwork, Barker, Late 1920s 2035.00
Clock, Chalmer's, Brass, Black Dial, 1912, 3 In. 46.00
Gas Pump, Cities Service, Wayne 861, Clockface, Restored 2900.00
Gas Pump, Hayes Visible 1450.00
Gas Pump, Sinclair, Clear Vision, 4 Sides, Restored 1550.00
Gas Pump, Sinclair, Hayes 2 In 1, Clockface, Restored, 1930 .... 3150.00
Gas Pump, Sinclair, National Simplex, Green, Restored 5800.00
Gas Pump, Texaco, Bennett 150, Clockface, Restored 2850.00
Gas Pump, Texaco, Tokheim 870, Clockface, Restored 2850.00
Gas Pump, Wayne 60 .... 1150.00
Gas Pump Globe, Adams Oil Co., 19 In., 3 Piece 2530.00
Gas Pump Globe, Atlantic Gas, Blue Lettering, White Ground, 13 1/2 In. 350.00
Gas Pump Globe, Barnsdall Motor Fuel, Red Lettering, White Ground, 13 1/2 In. 235.00
Gas Pump Globe, Big West Gasoline, 13 1/2 In. 1595.00
Gas Pump Globe, Blue Sunoco, 49.9 Per Gallon, 1940s 1000.00
Gas Pump Globe, Deep Rock, Yellow Ground, 13 1/2 In. 130.00
Gas Pump Globe, Eagle, White Milk Glass, 20 In. 373.00
Gas Pump Globe, Esso 513.00
Gas Pump Globe, Ethyl Mobilgas 575.00
Gas Pump Globe, Federal Super Gasoline, Single, 15 In. 55.00
Gas Pump Globe, Flying A Diesel Fuel 990.00
Gas Pump Globe, Gilmore Blue-Green Gasoline, 15 In. 6600.00
Gas Pump Globe, Marathon Diesel Fuel, Blue Lettering, White Ground, 13 1/2 In. 145.00
Gas Pump Globe, Marathon Regular Mile-Make, White Ground, 13 1/2 In. 150.00
Gas Pump Globe, Mobilgas Aircraft, 13 1/2 In. 1787.00
Gas Pump Globe, Mobiloil Gargoyle, Embossed, 14 x 17 x 6 3/4 In. 1900.00
Gas Pump Globe, Multipower, Gas, Red Lettering, White Ground, Metal, 15 In. 230.00
Gas Pump Globe, Shell, Milk Glass, Shell Each Side, 18 In. 316.00
Gas Pump Globe, Skelly Keotane, Red Lettering, White Ground, 13 1/2 In. 160.00
Gas Pump Globe, Skelly Supreme, Red Lettering, White Ground, 13 1/2 In. 160.00
Gas Pump Globe, Texaco Fire Chief, 29.9 Per Gallon, 1940s 1000.00
Gas Pump Globe, White Crown Gasoline, 16 1/2 In. 235.00
Gas Pump Globe, White Eagle, White, Blunt Nose, 1932, 21 x 6 1/2 In. 1800.00
Headlight Lamp, Brass, Westchester No. 8, Beveled Glass Lens, Red Bull's-Eye, 12 In. ... 57.00
Headlight Lamp, Ford Motor Lamp No. 2, Beveled Glass Lens, 11 In., Pair 80.00
Headlight Lamp, Lucifer Nickel & Black Carbide, Pair 207.00
Headlight Lamp, Molded Glass Lens, Tin, 9 1/2 In., Pair 80.00
Hood Ornament, Mercury, Outstretched Arms, Brass, Chrome Plated, 7 In. 192.00
Hood Ornament, Open-Winged Bird, Brass, Chrome Plated, 5 1/2 In. 157.00

Hood Ornament, Red Goose Shoes, Cast Iron, Arcade, 4 1/4 In. 200.00
Hood Ornament, Sphinx, Seated, Armstrong Siddley, 3 1/2 In. 180.00
Lamp, Brass, 2 Beveled Glass Lenses, Red Bull's-Eye, Marked Solar, 11 1/2 In. 69.00
Lamp, Brass, 2 Beveled Glass Lenses, Red Bull's-Eye, Tin, 15 In. 126.00
Lamp, Buggy, Beveled Glass Lenses, 19th Century, 12 In. 23.00
Lamp, Dietz, Beveled Lenses, Red Bull's-Eyes, Tin, 11 In. 46.00
License Plate, Connecticut, 1916, Porcelain 40.00
License Plate, Connecticut, 1940 . . . . 1265.00
License Plate, Connecticut, Motorcycle, No. 9, 1937 . . . . 1045.00
License Plate, Indiana, 1915 . . . . 40.00
License Plate, Maine, 1914, White On Blue 170.00
License Plate, Michigan, 1914 . . . . 72.00
License Plate, Mountaineer, Bronze, Red Enameled Ground, Mounting Lugs, 21 x 11 In. . . 1092.00
License Plate, New Jersey, 1909, Porcelain On Iron, 13 x 6 In. 138.00
License Plate, New Jersey, 1912, Porcelain 70.00
License Plate, Pennsylvania, 1914, Dealer's 96.00
License Plate Attachment, Cave Of Mounds, Aluminum, 5 1/2 x 10 In. 77.00
License Plate Attachment, Cave Of Winds, Tin, 5 3/4 x 6 1/4 In. 93.00
License Plate Attachment, Dr Pepper, Tin, 1940, 10 In. 810.00
License Plate Attachment, Harold's Club, Reno, 14 In. 140.00
License Plate Attachment, Peacock Ice Cream, Cleveland Indians, Tin, 1950s, 9 7/8 In. . . 220.00
License Plate Attachment, Penzoil, We Are For Safety, Tin, 5 x 5 3/4 In. 375.00
License Plate Attachment, Pfister Hybrid, Tin, 6 In. 71.00
License Plate Attachment, Pure Oil Co., Drive Safely, Tin, 9 1/2 In. 160.00
License Plate Attachment, Ski Oregon, Tin, 1942, 5 x 12 In. 93.00
Mirror, Visor, Shell Del Fio Service, Cafe, 3 1/2 x 10 In. 33.00
Oil Can, Aero Mobiloil, Red Band, Tin, Qt. 275.00
Oil Can, Aero Motor Oil, Christenson Oil Co., Portland, Ore., Qt., 5 1/2 x 4 In. 55.00
Oil Can, Amelie Sub-Zero Motor, 1947, Qt. 120.00
Oil Can, Aroway Motor Oil, Red, Green Ground, Metal, 2 Gal., 11 1/2 x 8 1/2 In. 50.00
Oil Can, Cities Service Koolmotor Oil, Clover Logos, Qt. 55.00
Oil Can, En-Ar-Co Penn Motor, National Refining Co., Metal, Qt., 5 1/2 x 4 In. 30.00
Oil Can, Esso Unexcelled Motor Oil, Qt. 35.00
Oil Can, Fleet Motor Oil, Vehicle Graphics, Qt. 190.00
Oil Can, Gargoyle Mobiloil A, Qt. 240.00
Oil Can, Havoline Medium Motor Oil, 11 1/4 In., Gal. 55.00
Oil Can, HPX Motor Oil, Opened At Top, Metal, J.D. Street & Co., St. Louis, Mo., Qt. . . . 10.00
Oil Can, Indian Motorcycle Co., Red Lettering, Metal, Qt., 5 1/2 x 4 In. 160.00
Oil Can, Pennzoil Motor Oil, Red Bell Logo, Qt. 40.00
Oil Can, Pep Boys Motor Oil, Pure As Gold, Manny, Moe & Jack, Metal, 2 Gal., 11 In. . . 55.00
Oil Can, Pep Boys Western Motor Oil, Manny, Moe & Jack, Metal, 2 Gal., 11 3/4 In. . . . 120.00
Oil Can, Phillips Motor Oil, Qt. 175.00
Oil Can, Polarine Transmission Oil, 10 3/8 In., Gal. 220.00
Oil Can, Prestone, Pictures 1950s Indy Race Cars, 10 Oz. 28.00
Oil Can, Pure As Gold Motor Oil, Manny, Moe & Jack, Metal, 2 Gal., 11 1/2 x 5 In. 75.00
Oil Can, Rajah Motor Oil, Qt. 425.00
Oil Can, Shell Handy Oil, Lead Spout & Cap, 3 1/2 In. 230.00
Oil Can, Sinclair Opaline Motor Oil F Medium, Green, White, Tin, 1/2 Gal., 6 x 8 In. 200.00
Oil Can, Sunoco Household Oil, Lead Spout & Screw Cap, 4 Oz. 45.00
Oil Can, Texaco Harness Oil, Tin, 6 x 4 1/4 In. 99.00
Oil Can, Texaco Marine Motor Oil, Ships At Sea, White, Green Top & Bottom, Qt. 380.00
Oil Can, Texaco Motor Oil, Easy Spout, 15 In., 1/2 Gal. 630.00
Oil Can, Texaco Motor Oil, Logo With Black T, Handy Grip, Tin, 1/2 Gal., 7 x 8 In. 160.00
Oil Can, Texaco Motor Oil, Tin Lithograph, Green Ground, 6 3/4 x 3 3/4 In. 239.00
Oil Can, Zerolene Waterproof Grease, 3 1/2 x 2 In., 1/2 Lb. 95.00
Padlock, Union 76, Brass, 3 In. 88.00
Pennant, Speedway, Indiana, Indy 500 . . . . 300.00
Pin, Overland Cars, Oklahoma Motor Co., Celluloid, 1 In. 60.00
Plaque, BF Goodrich, Hercules, 15 Year Award, 13 1/2 x 9 In. 88.00
Platter, Standard Oil Co., Shenango China, Oval, 13 5/8 In. 192.00
Poster, Exide Batteries, Let Exide See You Home, 1930s, 30 x 20 1/4 In. 70.00
Poster, Jenatzy On Mercedes, Full Color, Mounted On Board, c.1903 . . . . 605.00
Poster, Wayne Gas Pumps, Paper, 32 3/4 x 22 In. 220.00

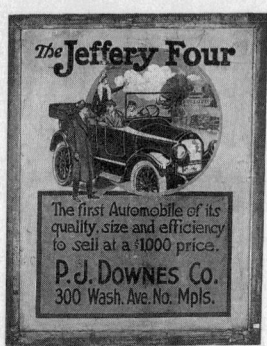

Auto, Advertising,
Sign, Jeffrey Four,
Automobile, Oil
On Canvas, Frame,
45 1/2 x 37 1/2 In.

Auto, Radiator Cover,
Boyce MotoMeter,
Thermometer,
Patented, 1913-1918

Rack, Display, Mazda Automotive Bulbs, Metal, Countertop, 15 1/2 x 24 1/2 In. 220.00
Rack, Display, Standard Oil Co., Indiana, 3 Shelves, Metal 395.00
Radiator Cover, Boyce MotoMeter, Thermometer, Patented, 1913-1918 . . . . *Illus* 60.00
Sign, Atlantic Refining Automobile Gasoline For Sale, Porcelain, 30 x 20 In. 55.00
Sign, Atlantic White Flash Gasoline, Porcelain, Red Ground, 1950s, 17 x 13 In. 140.00
Sign, Atlantic White Flash, Porcelain, Pump, 17 x 13 In. 180.00
Sign, Auto-Lite Spark Plugs, Emblem, 23 1/4 x 11 1/4 In. 260.00
Sign, Bonded Pennzoil Dealer, Porcelain, 2 Sides, 29 1/2 In. 175.00
Sign, Buick Quick Service, Porcelain, 2 Sides, 16 x 26 In. 577.00
Sign, Champion Spark Plugs, Painted Metal, 12 x 26 In. 258.00
Sign, Champion Spark Plugs, Tin, Emblem, 1920s, 14 3/4 x 51 1/2 In. 675.00
Sign, Chrysler Plymouth Service, 2 Sides, 1930s, 42 In. 1650.00
Sign, Cities Service, National Charge Cards, Tin, 12 x 20 In. 220.00
Sign, Columbus Shock Absorbers, Tin, 12 1/2 x 19 In. 55.00
Sign, Dayton Cub Tires, Bear Cub With Pail, Die Cut, 10 1/4 x 20 1/2 In. 99.00
Sign, De Soto & Plymouth Service, 1930s, 42 In. 968.00
Sign, Delco Batteries, 2 Sides, Tin, 17 1/2 x 23 1/4 In. 444.00
Sign, Delco Battery, Die Cut, Metal, 23 x 17 1/2 In. 198.00
Sign, Esso, Gasoline Girl, Tin, 5 1/4 x 16 In. 143.00
Sign, Gargoyle Mobiloil, Certified Service, Porcelain, 24 In. 580.00
Sign, Goodyear Tires Protect Our Good Name, Tin, Self-Framed, 7 x 21 In. 165.00
Sign, Goodyear, Tire Form, Name Across Middle, Germany, 1930s, 22 x 34 In. 1485.00
Sign, Grizzly Gasoline, Tin, 2 Sides, 24 x 36 In. 2255.00
Sign, Havoline Oil, No Smoking, Tin, Embossed, 9 1/4 x 18 1/4 In. 375.00
Sign, Jeffrey Four, Automobile, Oil On Canvas, Frame, 45 1/2 x 37 1/2 In. . . . . *Illus* 550.00
Sign, Kelly Springfield Tires, Lotta Miles, Cardboard, 21 x 27 3/4 In. 770.00
Sign, Kelly Springfield Tires, Porcelain, 2 Sides, 1920s, 28 x 40 In. 1700.00
Sign, Lion Head Motor Oil, Tin, Donaldson Art Sign Co., Covington, Ky., 11 In. 2500.00
Sign, Michelin Tire, Yellowing Lettering, Dark Blue Ground, Wood Frame, 72 In. 450.00
Sign, Michelin, Porcelain, 2 Sides, 25 1/2 x 25 1/2 In. 495.00
Sign, Mobilgas 5-Point Shield, Porcelain, 12 1/4 x 12 In. 203.00
Sign, Motorola Car Radio, Tin, 2 Sides, 20 x 28 In. 110.00
Sign, Oakland Pontiac Sales & Service, Porcelain, 2 Sides, 23 3/4 x 35 1/2 In. 632.00
Sign, Oilzum Motor Oil, Non Chatter Oilzum For Ford Cars, 6 x 16 In. 720.00
Sign, Oldsmobile Service, 2 Sides, Round, 1940s, 42 In. 1265.00
Sign, Packard Vehicles, Die Cut, Enamel, Wood Backing, 92 x 90 1/2 In. 1430.00
Sign, Pennzoil, Safe Lubrication, Porcelain, 2 Sides, Oval, 18 x 31 In. 120.00
Sign, Polarine, Perfect Motor Oil, Tin, 18 x 14 In. 190.00
Sign, Pontiac, Die Cut 1 Side, 1950s, 30 x 30 In. 660.00
Sign, Powerlube Motor Oil, Porcelain, 2 Sides, 28 x 20 In. 2860.00
Sign, Pump Plate, Douglas Gasoline, Porcelain, 12 x 18 In. 255.00
Sign, Pump Plate, EZ Serve Gasoline, Porcelain, 14 x 18 In. 70.00
Sign, Pump Plate, Fighter Ethyl Gasoline, Painted Steel, 10 x 10 In. 850.00
Sign, Pump Plate, Sunoco, Arrow, Porcelain, Blue, 22 1/4 x 18 1/2 In. 265.00
Sign, Pump Plate, Texaco Fire Chief, Dated 3-1-63, 12 x 18 In. 90.00
Sign, Puritan Motor & Tractor Oils, Keystone Cop, 35 1/2 x 11 1/4 In. 960.00

Sign, Quaker State Oil, White Lettering, Dark Green Ground, 9 3/4 x 13 3/4 In.	110.00
Sign, Rambler Parts & Service, Porcelain, 2 Sides, 1950s, 42 In.	530.00
Sign, Route 66, Die Cut Aluminum, 24 x 24 In.	1045.00
Sign, Shell Oil Co., Patrons Refrain From Smoking, Porcelain, 18 x 12 In.	330.00
Sign, Shell Oil, 2 Sides, 1938, 48 In.	1155.00
Sign, Skelly Tacolene Motor Oil, Porcelain, Enameled, 2 Holes, 2 Sides, 30 In.	195.00
Sign, Sky Chief Gasoline, Porcelain, 1940, 8 x 12 In.	190.00
Sign, Socony Motor Oil, Curved Porcelain, Pump, 15 x 15 In.	1070.00
Sign, Standard Oil Red Crown Gasoline, Cardboard, Metal Rim, 42 x 12 In.	190.00
Sign, Studebaker, Sales & Service, 1940s, 48 In.	800.00
Sign, Sunoco Motor Oil, Diamond Flange, 1930s, 26 x 36 In.	1265.00
Sign, Texaco Motor Oil, Paper Lithograph, 1939, 23 3/4 x 30 1/4 In.	745.00
Sign, Texaco, Porcelain, 96 In.	300.00
Sign, Tidewater Assoc. Oil Co., Porcelain, 7 7/8 x 11 3/8 In.	800.00
Sign, Union 76 Of California, No Trespassing, Porcelain, 8 x 24 In.	410.00
Sign, Union 76 Tires, Tin, 2 Sides, 48 x 13 In.	120.00
Sign, Union 76, No Smoking, Stop Your Motor, Porcelain, 15 x 11 3/4 In.	550.00
Sign, Valiant, Authorized Dealer, Round, 40 In.	475.00
Sign, Valvoline Motor Oils, Side-Cut Tin, 18 3/8 x 9 1/2 In.	300.00
Sign, Valvoline Oil, Green & Yellow, Round, 30 In.	150.00
Sign, Weed Chains Gasoline Price Dial, Rotating Dial, Tin, Wood, 1920, 24 x 17 In.	2035.00
Sign, Wolf's Head Motor Oil, Tin, Dated 7-39, 23 x 30 In.	470.00
Sign, Wolf's Head Oil, Vertical, 12 x 84 In.	250.00
Sign, Yale Tires, Tin, Wood Frame, 26 x 50 In.	475.00
Sign, Zerolene Oil, Porcelain, 2 Sides, 31 3/4 x 31 3/4 In.	275.00
Spark Plug, Chain O' Spark	65.00
Speedometer, Cadillac, Nickel Plated Brass, Lighted Dial, 60 Mph., 1910, 4 In.	46.00
Sugar, Sinclair Oil Co., Walker China, 6 In.	200.00
Tin, Farmer's Ride High Grade Oil, 4 Oz.	190.00
Tin, Nourse Heavy Duty, Landscape Scene Around Can, Qt.	120.00
Tin, Primer, Gasoline, Black Lettering, 19th Century, 9 In.	11.00
Travel Bassinet, Kozekar, Fits Pierce Arrow, Red Velvet, Metal Frame, c.1917	55.00

AUTUMN LEAF pattern china was made for the Jewel Tea Company beginning in 1933. Hall China Company of East Liverpool, Ohio, Crooksville China Company of Crooksville, Ohio, Harker Potteries of Chester, West Virginia, and Paden City Pottery, Paden City, West Virginia, made dishes with this design. Autumn Leaf has remained popular and was made by Hall China Company until 1978. Some other pieces in the Autumn Leaf pattern are still being made. For more information, see *Kovels' Depression Glass & Dinnerware Price List.*

Casserole, Cover, 8 1/2 In.	35.00
Compote, Footed Pedestal	525.00
Jug, Tilt	35.00

AVON bottles are listed in the Bottle category under Avon.

AZALEA dinnerware was made for Larkin Company customers from 1918 to 1941. Larkin, the soap company, was in Buffalo, New York. The dishes were made by Noritake China Company of Japan. Each piece of the white china was decorated with pink azaleas.

Celery Dish, Closed Handles, Red Mark, 10 In.	203.00
Coffeepot, After Dinner, 6 5/8 In.	561.00
Cup, After Dinner, 6 Piece	300.00
Eggcup	53.00
Jam Jar, Underplate, Ladle, 3 Piece	180.00
Mayonnaise Set, 3 Piece	25.00
Relish, 2 Sections, Loop Handle	280.00
Relish, 4 Sections, 10 In.	105.00
Sandwich Server, Handle, 9 3/4 In.	115.00
Snack Set, 8 3/4 In., 2 Piece	36.00
Spoon Holder, Red M Mark	39.00
Sugar & Creamer, Green	20.00

Sugar & Creamer, Red Mark 34.00
Syrup Set, Red M Mark, 3 Piece 51.00
Tile, Tea, 6 1/8 In. 41.00

BACCARAT glass was made in France by La Compagnie des Cristalleries de Baccarat, located 150 miles from Paris. The factory was
started in 1765. The firm went bankrupt and began operating again
about 1822. Cane and millefiori paperweights were made during the
1860 to 1880 period. The firm is still working near Paris making
paperweights and glasswares.

Bottle, Wine, Zipper Cut Rose Teinte, Zipper Stopper, 10 In. 165.00
Box, Hinged Lid, Entwined Ribbon, Beaded Border, Putto, Reclining On Snail, 7 In. 747.00
Carafe, Cut Diagonal Swirls, Rose Teinte, 10 In. 252.00
Decanter, 8 Sides, Parcel Gilt, Air Bubble Stopper, Gilt Trim, Footed, c.1900, 8 1/4 In. .. 230.00
Decanter, Hunter On Horseback, Flat Sides, Animals, Scalloped Mouth, 11 5/8 In., Pair .. 520.00
Decanter, Notch Cut, Acid Signature, 10 In. 600.00
Decanter, Panel Cut, Acid Signature, 10 1/2 In. 265.00
Decanter, Ringed Neck, Broad Waist, Wafer Stopper, 1930s, 10 1/2 In. 550.00
Decanter, Tapered Mallet, Acid Signature, 12 1/4 In. 365.00
Figurine, Bear, Seated, 9 In. 170.00
Goblet, Tranquility Pattern, 9 1/2 In., 6 Piece 1335.00
Lamp, Banquet, Cherubs, Clouds, Milk Glass, Hoof Feet, Electrified, 23 In. 1150.00
Mustard, Cover, Paneled, Scalloped, Spoon, Signed, 4 1/2 In. 190.00
Paperweight, Bridal Bouquet, Millefiori Tufted, Animal Silhouette, Star-Cut Pontil 1380.00
Paperweight, Butterfly, Amethyst Latticinio Body, Star-Cut Base 2415.00
Paperweight, Clematis, Faceted, 1850, 2 In. 865.00
Paperweight, Clematis, White, Red Blossoms, Blue, White Millefiori Border, 3 In. 2185.00
Paperweight, Floral, Alternating Green, White Millefiori Canes 2300.00
Paperweight, Floral, Mauve Edged White Anemones, Stardust Cane Stamens 690.00
Paperweight, Garland, Millefiori Canes, Cinquefoil 400.00
Paperweight, Garland, White Stardust Canes, Red, White Canes 1380.00
Paperweight, Millefiori, Concentric Rings In Red, Blue, White, Signed, No. 004 .... 175.00
Paperweight, Millefiori, Dupont Concentric, White, Blue, Green, Yellow, Red, 2 1/8 In. ... 110.00
Paperweight, Millefiori, Looped Garland, Upset Muslin Ground, Signed, 1973, 3 1/4 In. . 200.00
Paperweight, Millefiori, Silhouette Canes, Signed, 1847, 2 In. 1955.00
Paperweight, Multicolored Millefiori Carpet, France, 1968, 1 7/8 x 3 In. 430.00
Paperweight, Pansy, Green Leaves, Stem, Bud, Star-Cut Base, 2 1/2 In. 560.00
Paperweight, Pansy, Purple Petals, Purple Stardust Stamens 520.00
Paperweight, Pelican, Monkey, Dog, Rooster, Canes, France, 1848, 1 7/8 x 3 In. 2530.00
Paperweight, Pink Pompon With Leaves, Marked, France, 1992, 2 1/4 x 3 In. 805.00
Paperweight, Purple Double Clematis, Red & White Garland, Center, Stardust Cane, 2 In. 785.00
Paperweight, Red & White Primrose, Green Leaves, Center, Stardust Cane, 3 1/4 In. 1230.00
Paperweight, Squirrel Silhouette, Gridel Canes, Millefiori Rings, Signed, 1972 .... 316.00
Paperweight, Squirrel Silhouettes, Signed, 1972 .... 402.00
Paperweight, Sulphide, Cameo, Queen Victoria, Ruby Ground, Diamond Cut Sides 920.00
Paperweight Set, Sulphide, F.D. Roosevelt, Churchill, Wilson, T. Roosevelt, 4 Piece 230.00
Pitcher, Rose Teinte, Clear Handle, 9 1/4 In. ....275.00 to 295.00
Tumbler, Equinox Pattern, 5 In., 6 Piece 565.00
Vase, Cranberry, Satin, 1915, 6 In. 250.00
Vase, Flattened Oval, Engraved, 7 In. 150.00
Vase, Spill, Cut Scrolling Vines, Low Foot, 1900s, 6 In. 230.00
Vase, Vertical Tapered Flutes On Body, Rolled Rim, 20th Century, 9 3/4 In. 145.00

BADGES have been used since before the Civil War. Collectors search
for examples of all types, including law enforcement and company
identification badges. Well-known prison or law enforcement badges
are most desirable. Most are made of nickel or brass. Many recent
reproductions have been made.

Anti Horse Thief, Member, Metal Bar Pin, Assn. Logo, Black & White, 1 1/2 In. 190.00
Arden Dairy, Curved & Die Cut, Hat, 1 1/2 x 4 1/4 In. 300.00
Bus Driver, Star Bus Line, Chromed Metal, Cloisonne Enameling, 1950s, 2 3/4 In. 50.00
Cap, Bentley, Winged Logo 225.00
Cap, Truck Driver, Millo Oil Co., Chromed Metal, 2 3/4 x 2 3/4 In. 315.00

Captain's Hat, Mobil, 6 7/8 In. 465.00
Chauffeur, Arizona, Bronze, 1933, 2 In. 110.00
Colorado Sheriffs & Peace Officers Assn., Name Tag, Ribbon, Holster & Revolver, 1939 . 125.00
Colorado Sheriffs & Peace Officers Assn., Name Tag, Ribbon, Leather Chaps, 1949 ..... 80.00
Constable, Oval, 2 3/8 x 1 1/2 In. 140.00
Deputy Constable, Bexar County, Texas Seal Center, 1 1/2 x 2 In. 95.00
Deputy Constable, Santa Clara County, 2 3/4 x 3 1/8 In. 350.00
Deputy Constable, Texas Shield, Name In Eagle's Beak, Bexar County, 1 1/2 x 2 In. 95.00
Deputy Sheriff, 5-Point Star, Ball Tips, Saches-Lawler, 2 x 2 In. 250.00
Deputy Sheriff, 6-Point Star, Ball Tips, 2 1/4 x 2 1/2 In. 190.00
Deputy Sheriff, 6-Point Star, Ball Tips, Nickel Over Brass, 2 1/8 x 2 1/2 In. 210.00
Deputy Sheriff, 6-Point Star, Ed Jones, 1950s, 2 3/4 x 3 1/8 In. 225.00
Deputy Sheriff, Brown County Nebraska, Eagle Top, Reese, 1 3/4 x 2 1/8 In. 250.00
Deputy Sheriff, Cook County, Banners, 6-Point Star 245.00
Deputy Sheriff, Kent County, Cutout Star, 1 1/2 x 1 3/4 In. 190.00
Deputy Sheriff, San Mateo Co., 7-Point Star, Gold Filled, Irvine & Jachens, 2 In. 245.00
Employee, Rexall Drug Store, Metal, Inlaid Cloisonne, Train Shape, Employee Name 385.00
Employee, Sunoco, Inlaid Cloisonne Enamel, 1 7/8 x 3 In. 116.00
Employee, Union Pacific Porter, Chicago, Burlington & Quincy Railroad, Marked, Pair .. 23.00
Firefighting, New Bedford 41, Eng. 2, Custom Die 80.00
Firefighting, Rutland Fire Dept. 12, Custom Die, Marked Sterling 230.00
Firefighting, Steamer 1, East Brookfield, Hand Stamped, Octagonal, C Catch Pin 86.00
Game License, Michigan Resident, Pinback, Celluloid, 1929 .... 55.00
Guard, 2 Pitchfork Dingbats Around Title, 1890s, 2 1/8 x 1 3/8 In. 135.00
Guard, Ford, Hat Type, 1950s 16.00
Guard, Struck At Angle On Shield, 1 5/8 x 1 7/8 In. 150.00
Highway Patrol, 7-Point Star, Copper On Sterling, California, Irvine & Jachens 390.00
Highway Patrol, 7-Point Star, Surround Of Flowers, Copper 390.00
Marseilles Marchal, Shield, Eagle Top, 2 Banners, 1 3/4 x 2 1/4 In. 240.00
Officer, Special, 5-Point Star, Ball Tips, 2 5/8 In. 110.00
Peace Officer, Bronze Shield, Name Plate, Ribbon, Denver, 1930 .... 75.00
Photograph, ID, Clasp Pin, Texas Co., Amarillo, 2 In. 240.00
Police, 6-Point Star, 2 1/8 x 2 3/8 In. 130.00
Police, Chief Surgeon, State Of New York, 5-Point Stars, Gilt Eagle, 2 1/4 x 2 1/2 In. 223.00
Police, Chief, Gold Wash On Brass, Embossed Wreath, 2 3/4 x 1 1/2 In. 150.00
Police, Chief, Hat, 3 7/8 x 1 5/8 In. 200.00
Police, Fort Worth, Panther Over Shield, Fire Black Enamel, 2 1/8 x 2 7/8 In. 550.00
Police, Fort Worth, Texas, Star Center, Crouching Panther Over Shield, 2 1/8 In. 550.00
Police, New York State Detective, Eagle Crest, Black Enamel Lettering, 1880, 3 x 2 In. ... 110.00
Police, Special, 1921, Kansas City, Circle Star, 2 1/4 In. 95.00
Police, Special, 6-Point Star, Ball Tips, Columbia Stamp Wks., 2 1/4 x 2 1/12 In. 110.00
Police, Special, 6-Point Star, Ball Tips, German Silver, Ed Jones, 3 x 3 3/8 In. 220.00
Police, Special, 6-Point Star, Ball Tips, Iron Cross & Scroll, W.S. Darely & Co. 105.00
Police, Special, Circle Star, 2 1/4 In. 155.00
Police, Vancouver, 2 5/8 In. 350.00
Police, Vancouver, Circle Star, 5 Soldered Balls, 2 5/8 In. 270.00
Police, Vancouver, Circle, Star Center, 5/8 In. 350.00
Santa Fe Porter, Nickel Plated, Hat, 3 3/4 x 2 1/4 In. 135.00
Sheriff, Outstanding, Event, Name Plate, Ribbon, Leather Cowboy Hat, 1940 .... 150.00
Shield, Constable, Cutout Star, Montgomery County, Brass, 1 3/4 x 2 1/8 In. 225.00
Southern Prison Co., S.A. Tex, 1 1/8 In. 110.00
Warden, State Of New Hampshire, Forest First Service, Shield, Pinback 225.00

BANKS of metal have been made since 1868. There are still banks, mechanical banks, and registering banks (those that show the total money deposited on the face of the bank). Many old iron or tin banks have been reproduced since the 1950s in iron or plastic. Some old reproductions marked Book of Knowledge or John Wright, or Capron are listed. Pottery, glass, and plastic banks are also listed here. Mickey Mouse and other Disneyana banks are listed in Disneyana. We have added the M-numbers based on *The Penny Bank Book: Collected Still Banks* by Andy and Susan Moore.

Alpine Gentleman, Papier-Mache, 11 In. 65.00

Andy Gump, General Thrift Products, Cast Metal, 1920s, M 219, 5 3/4 In. 460.00
Aunt Jemima, With Spoon, Cast Iron, Gold Trim, M 168, 5 1/2 In. 103.00
Baby In Egg, Cast Metal, M 261, 7 In. 69.00
Baseball, Compliments Of Atlantic Dealer, Philadelphia Athletics, Tin, Chein, 4 1/4 In. . . 154.00
Bear, Begging, Cast Iron, A.C. Williams, c.1910, 5 3/8 In. 104.00
Bear With Honey Pot, Cast Iron, Hubley, M 717, 7 In. . . . . .330.00 to 402.00
Black Boy's Head In Alligator's Mouth, Slot On Gator's Back, Ceramic, 6 1/2 In. 190.00
Boat, Steamboat, Cast Iron, A.C. Williams, 1912, M 1459, 7 3/4 In. 150.00
Book, Simple Simon, Tin Lithograph, Kirchof, 1930s 110.00
Boy, Amish, Black Overalls, Blue Shirt, John Wright, 1970, 5 In. 65.00
Boy, Black, 2 Faces, Cast Iron, A.C. Williams, M 83, 4 1/8 In. 275.00
Buffalo, Cast Iron, A.C. Williams, M 560, 3 1/8 x 4 3/8 In. 77.00
Buffalo, Cast Iron, Brown Paint Body, Gray Ears, Hooves, 8 In. 44.00
Building, Skyscraper, Cast Iron, A.C. Williams, 1900s, M 1240, 5 1/2 In. 195.00
Bull, Cast Iron, John Wright, 1960s 95.00
Bull, On Base, Cast Iron, M 537, 5 7/8 In. 192.00
California Raisins, Plastic, Sunmaid Brand 65.00
Car, Limousine, Green, Driver, Coin Trap, Cast Iron, Arcade, M 1482, 8 In. 1375.00
Car, Yellow Cab, Cast Iron, Rubber Tires, Driver, 4 x 8 x 3 1/4 In. 880.00
Car, Yellow Cab, Driver, Coin Trap, Cast Iron, Zaumstein, Letters On Roof, Arcade, 8 In. . 467.00
Car, Yellow Cab, Driver, Iron Wheels, Cast Iron, Arcade, 8 In. 3080.00
Casper, American Bisque, 8 1/2 In. 210.00
Chiclets Gum, Machine, Hasbro, 1960s, 10 In. 55.00
Clown, Cast Iron, A.C. Williams, c.1908, M 211, 6 In. .110.00 to 209.00
Cottage, Blue & Green Sponge, Staffordshire, 3 3/4 In. 220.00
Counting House, Combination Dial, Clock Type, Cast Iron, 19th Century, 6 1/2 x 5 x 6 In. 230.00
Cupola, Cast Iron, Maroon, Brown Roof, Stencils, Vermong/Stevens, M 1145, 5 1/2 In. . . 403.00
Cupola, Red, Brown Roof, Gilt Stencils, Blue & White Trim, 5 1/2 In. 748.00
Dime, Piggy, Cardboard, Die Cut Pig, Slots For 10 Dimes, 1924, 5 x 6 In. 12.50
Dog, Boston Terrier, Cast Iron, 5 1/4 In. 34.00
Dog, Boxer, Cast Iron, Hubley, 1920s, M 357, 4 1/2 In. 165.00
Dog, Bull Terrier, Cast Iron, John Wright, 1960s 85.00
Dog, Puppo, With Bee, Cast Iron, Hubley, M 416, 4 3/4 In. 92.00
Duck, On Tub, Iron, Save For Rainy Day, Hat, Umbrella, Barrel, Hubley, M 615, 5 3/8 In. . 350.00
Electrolux Vacuum Cleaner, Model G, Plastic, 1950s, 5 1/2 In. 55.00
Fisherman, Bobbing Head, Composition, Hair, Cigarette, Pole, 3 1/2 x 4 x 7 In. 18.00
General Sheridan, Cast Iron, Arcade, 5 3/4 In. 57.00
Graf Zepplin, Cast Iron, A.C. Williams, 1920s, M 1428, 6 1/4 In. 172.00
Grandpa Dukes, Tin Lithograph, Germany, 1800s, M 275, 2 1/8 In. 247.00
Hen, Cast Iron, Yellow & Red, M 549, 6 In. 165.00
House, Leo Hanson Plaque, 2 Windows & Door Open, Tin, 7 x 5 1/2 In. 110.00
Indian Chief, Cast Iron, John Wright, 1960s 65.00
Kitty, Seated, Cast Iron, Hubley, 1930s, 4 In. . . . . .92.00 to 150.00
Liberty Bell, Glass, Opaque White, Embossed, 1776 Liberty, 4 1/4 x 4 In. 70.00
Lilliput, Yellow Ground, Red Roof, Cast Iron, J. & E. Stevens, Patent 1875, 4 1/4 In. 302.00
Lion, Cast Iron, John Wright, 1960s 65.00
Little Folks Cash Register, Tin Lithograph, 3 1/8 x 4 3/8 In. 104.00
Log Cabin Syrup Tin, Children Playing On One Side, 1960s 48.00
Magilla Gorilla, Plastic Book, Ideal For Hanna-Barbera, 1 x 4 1/4 x 6 In. 28.00
Mammy, With Hands On Hips, Cast Iron, Hubley, 1914 . . . . 295.00

Mechanical banks were first made about 1870. Any bank with moving
parts is considered mechanical. The metal banks made before World
War I are the most desirable. Copies and new designs of mechanical
banks have been made in metal or plastic since the 1920s. The condition of the paint on the old banks is important. Worn paint can lower a
price by 90%.

Mechanical, Acrobat, Cast Iron, J. & E. Stevens, 1883 . . . . 5600.00
Mechanical, Afghanistan, Russian Bear, British Lion, At Herat Gates, Cast Iron, 4 In. 550.00
Mechanical, Artillery, Painted Cast Iron, 1892, 8 In. 850.00
Mechanical, Artillery, Red Coat, Cast Iron, J. & E. Stevens, 8 In. 1700.00
Mechanical, Artillery, Union Soldier, Bronze Plated Iron, J. & E. Stevens, 1892, 8 In. 1350.00

Bank, Mechanical, Boy Scout Camp,
Cast Iron, J. & E. Stevens, 1912

Bank, Mechanical, Girl
Skipping Rope, Cast Iron,
J. & E. Stevens, 1890

Mechanical, Bad Accident, Black Man, Cart, Iron, J. & E. Stevens, 1888, 10 In. .2090.00 to 3472.00
Mechanical, Baseball, Cast Iron, 1960s 150.00
Mechanical, Bear & Tree Stump, Cast Iron, Judd Mfg., 1870s 672.00
Mechanical, Bill E. Grin, Cast Iron, 1950 .... 650.00
Mechanical, Boy & Bulldog, Black With Gold Washed Dog, Judd 1600.00
Mechanical, Boy On Trapeze, Cast Iron, J. Barton & Smith ....975.00 to 2750.00
Mechanical, Boy Scout Camp, Cast Iron, J. & E. Stevens, 1912 .... *Illus* 9500.00
Mechanical, Boys Stealing Watermelons, Iron, Kyser & Rex, 1885, 6 1/2 In. ....2070.00 to 2650.00
Mechanical, Bulldog, Painted Cast Iron, J. & E. Stevens, c.1880, 8 In. 1200.00
Mechanical, Bulldog, Savings Bank, East Iron, Clockwork, Ives, Blakeslee & Co., 1878 .. 6048.00
Mechanical, Butting Goat, Tree Stump, Cast Iron, Judd Mfg., 1887 .... 784.00
Mechanical, Cabin, Green, Man Kicks Coin, Cast Iron, J. & E. Stevens, 1885 .... 550.00
Mechanical, Cat & Mouse, Black & White Cat, J. & E. Stevens, c.1891, 5 1/2 In. 850.00
Mechanical, Cat & Mouse, Book Of Knowledge, Cast Iron, 8 In. 143.00
Mechanical, Cat & Mouse, Type 2, Cast Iron, J. & E. Stevens, 1891 .... 3080.00
Mechanical, Cat Sailboat, Cast Iron 1250.00
Mechanical, Chief Big Moon, Indian, Teepee, Red Base, J. & E. Stevens, 1899, 10 In. 4200.00
Mechanical, Circus Ticket Collector, Cast Iron, Judd Mfg. Co. 1232.00
Mechanical, Clown In Pony Cart, Iron, Shepard Hardware, 1888, 7 1/2 In. .....2700.00 to 6440.00
Mechanical, Clown On Globe, Cast Iron, J. & E. Stevens, 1890 ....1100.00 to 2400.00
Mechanical, Clown, Tin Lithograph, Chein 125.00
Mechanical, Darktown Battery, 3 Baseball Players, Cast Iron, Stevens, 1888, 9 3/4 In. 3738.00
Mechanical, Dentist, Blue Base, Cast Iron, J. & E. Stevens, 1880, 9 3/4 In. 5463.00
Mechanical, Dentist, Cast Iron, Book Of Knowledge 150.00
Mechanical, Dinah, Original Paint, Cast Iron, Wooden Base, 6 3/8 In. ....110.00 to 475.00
Mechanical, Dog On Turntable, Coin Goes On Dish, Crank Turns, Judd Mfg., 1895 ..... 595.00
Mechanical, Dog, Begging, Tin, Japan, 6 In. 46.00
Mechanical, Eagle & Eaglets, Cast Iron, Green Grass, J. & E. Stevens, 6 3/4 In. 350.00
Mechanical, Eagle & Eaglets, Cast Iron, J. & E. Stevens, Charles M. Henn 660.00
Mechanical, Eagle & Eaglets, Grass, Bellows, J. & E. Stevens, 1883, 6 3/4 In. ..1035.00 to 1092.00
Mechanical, Elephant, Howdah, Cast Iron, Slot Behind Head, Pull Tail, Hubley, 5 1/2 In. .. 999.00
Mechanical, Elephant, Howdah, Pull Tail, Cast Iron, Hubley, 1934 ....350.00 to 550.00
Mechanical, Elephant, Pull Tail, Cast Iron, 1960 .... 95.00
Mechanical, Fisherman's Luck, Cast Iron, Richards Toys 1275.00
Mechanical, Frog, On Round Lattice Base, Cast Iron, J. & E. Stevens, 1872 .... 1456.00
Mechanical, Frogs, Cast Iron, 1970s 125.00
Mechanical, Frogs, Cast Iron, J. & E. Stevens, 1882 .... 4500.00
Mechanical, Girl Skipping Rope, Cast Iron, J. & E. Stevens, 1890 .... *Illus* 8960.00
Mechanical, Happy Hippo, Tin, Built-In Key, Yone, 1960s, 2 3/4 x 6 1/2 x 2 In. 35.00
Mechanical, Hen & Chick, Cast Iron, J. & E. Stevens, 1901 .... 1792.00
Mechanical, Hoop-La, Cast Iron, Clown & Dog, John Harper, 1897, 8 1/4 In. 100.00
Mechanical, Horse Race, Type 2, Cast Iron, J. & E. Stevens, 1871 .... *Illus* 3360.00
Mechanical, House, Bowing Man In Cupola, Cast Iron, C.C. Johnson 495.00
Mechanical, Humpty Dumpty, Arm, Tongue, Eyes Move, Shepard Hardware, 1882 ...... 1232.00
Mechanical, I Always Did 'Spise A Mule, Boy, Bench, J. & E. Stevens, 1897 ...1000.00 to 2500.00
Mechanical, Indian & Bear, Cast Iron, J. & E. Stevens, 1880 ....1100.00 to 3500.00
Mechanical, Jolly Nigger, Cast Iron, Shepard Hardware, 1882 .... 750.00

Bank, Mechanical, Horse Race, Type 2, Cast Iron, J. & E. Stevens, 1871

Bank, Mechanical, Milking Cow, Cast Iron, J. & E. Stevens, 1888

Mechanical, Jolly Nigger, Made In England, Cast Iron, 6 1/4 In. 385.00
Mechanical, Jolly Nigger, Red Coat, Cast Iron, Beacon Product, 19th Century, 5 1/2 In. . . 650.00
Mechanical, Jonah & The Whale, Cast Iron, Shepard Hardware, 1890 . . . . .1700.00 to 3640.00
Mechanical, Las Vegas Jackpot, Cast Metal, 1950s 65.00
Mechanical, Lion & Monkeys, Cast Iron, Kyser & Rex, 1883, 8 3/4 In. . . . . .172.00 to 750.00
Mechanical, Magician, Painted, Cast Iron, J. & E. Stevens, 1901, 8 In. . . . . .1430.00 to 4200.00
Mechanical, Magie, Coin On Table, Tin, Germany 375.00
Mechanical, Mammy & Child, Yellow Dress, Cast Iron, Kyser & Rex, 1994 . . . .8500.00 to 8960.00
Mechanical, Marilyn Monroe, Marilyn's Dress Blows Up 150.00
Mechanical, Mason, Brick Layer, Hod Carrier, Shepard Hardware, 1887, 7 1/2 In.1045.00 to 4600.00
Mechanical, Merry-Go-Round, Cast Iron, 1960s 175.00
Mechanical, Milking Cow, Cast Iron, J. & E. Stevens, 1888 . . . . *Illus* 6720.00
Mechanical, Monkey, Coin In Slot, Monkey Tips Hat, Chein, 5 1/2 In. . . . . .40.00 to 180.00
Mechanical, Monkey, Jumping Monkey, Green Base, Hubley, 1925, 9 In. 173.00
Mechanical, Monkey, Tips Hat, Tin, Chein, Gene Bosch, 1960s 235.00
Mechanical, Mule Entering Barn, Cast Iron, J. & E. Stevens, 1880 . . . . 850.00
Mechanical, NAACP, Dollar In Back, Raises Arms, 15 In. 189.00
Mechanical, New Creedmoor, J. & E. Stevens, 1877, 10 In. 700.00
Mechanical, Nodding Scotsman, Cast Iron, 1950 . . . . 375.00
Mechanical, Novelty, House, Cast Iron, J. & E. Stevens, 1872, 4 1/4 In. . . . . *Illus* 1600.00
Mechanical, Organ Bank, Monkey, Cast Iron, Kyser & Rex, 1882, 5 1/4 In. 517.00
Mechanical, Organ Grinder & Bear, Cast Iron, Kyser & Rex, 1882, 7 In. 4542.00
Mechanical, Organ, Cat & Dog, Cast Iron, Kyser & Rex, 1882 . . . . .800.00 to 1150.00
Mechanical, Owl, Slot In Book, Cast Iron, Kilgore Mfg., 1926 . . . . 825.00
Mechanical, Owl, Turns Head, Cast Iron, J. & E. Stevens, 1880 . . . . 500.00
Mechanical, Paddy & The Pig, Cast Iron, Book Of Knowledge, 1960s 125.00
Mechanical, Paddy & The Pig, Cast Iron, J. & E. Stevens, 1882, 7 1/4 In. 650.00
Mechanical, Penny Pineapple Hawaii, Painted Cast Iron, 8 1/2 In. 180.00
Mechanical, Piano, Conversion, Cast Iron 2800.00
Mechanical, Pineapple, Anniversary Of Hawaii, Cast Iron, 4 1/4 In. 200.00

Bank, Mechanical, Novelty, House, Cast Iron, J. & E. Stevens, 1872, 4 1/4 In.

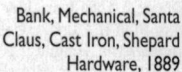

Bank, Mechanical, Santa Claus, Cast Iron, Shepard Hardware, 1889

Mechanical, Pump & Bucket, Cast Iron, Register, Dime, 1892 . . . . 1925.00
Mechanical, Punch & Judy, Cast Iron, Painted, 1960s, 7 1/2 In. . . . . .350.00 to 575.00
Mechanical, Punch & Judy, Cast Iron, Shepard Hardware, 1884 . . . . 2240.00
Mechanical, Punch & Judy, Small Letters, Cast Iron, Shepard Hardware, 1884, 7 1/4 In. . . . 600.00
Mechanical, Rabbit, In Cabbage, Ears Moving, Cast Iron, Kilgore, 1925 . . . . 230.00
Mechanical, Race Horse, Cast Iron, 1960s 325.00
Mechanical, Rocket Ship, Cast Metal, 1950s 175.00
Mechanical, Santa Claus, Cast Iron, Shepard Hardware, 1889 . . . . *Illus* 2200.00
Mechanical, Second National Duck, Tin Lithograph, Chein, 1950s 250.00
Mechanical, Sparky Savings Bank, Battery Operated, Box, 1930s 125.00
Mechanical, Speaking Dog, Sitting Girl, Shepard Hardware, 1885, 7 In. . . . . *Illus* 1610.00
Mechanical, Stump Speaker, Cast Iron, Shepard Hardware, 1886, 9 1/2 In. . . . . *Illus* 2809.00
Mechanical, Tammany, Cast Iron, Brown Trousers, J. & E. Stevens, 1873 . . . . .412.00 to 750.00
Mechanical, Tammany, Cast Iron, Gray Trousers, J. & E. Stevens, 1873 . . . . .374.00 to 675.00
Mechanical, Teddy & The Bear, Cast Iron, J. & E. Stevens, 1907, 10 In. . . . . . . .1430.00 to 4200.00
Mechanical, Teddy & The Bear, Gray Tree, Cast Iron, J. & E. Stevens, 10 In. 600.00
Mechanical, Toad On Stump, Cast Iron, J. & E. Stevens, 1886 . . . . .1120.00 to 1350.00
Mechanical, Trick Dog, Clown & Hoop, Barrel, 6-Part Base, Iron, Hubley, 1888, 8 1/2 In. . . 288.00
Mechanical, Trick Pony, Cast Iron, 1970s 125.00
Mechanical, Trick Pony, Original Patina, Iron, Shepard Hardware, 7 1/4 In. . . . .1495.00 to 1680.00
Mechanical, Tweety & Sylvester, Plastic, Talking, Moving Arms, 3 1/2 x 7 3/4 x 8 In. 48.00
Mechanical, Uncle Bugs, Looks Like Uncle Sam, Cast Iron, Box, 10 In. 690.00
Mechanical, Uncle Remus, Chicken Thief, In Coop, Book Of Knowledge, 1952, 5 3/4 In. . . 319.00
Mechanical, Uncle Sam & Arab, Barrel Between, Cast Iron, John Wright, 1975, 11 In. . . . 230.00
Mechanical, Uncle Sam, Cast Iron, Shepard Hardware, 1886 . . . . .2650.00 to 5600.00
Mechanical, Uncle Sam, Eagle On Base, Book Of Knowledge, Cast Iron, 1932, 11 In. . . . 120.00
Merry-Go-Round, Grey Iron, 5 In. 115.00
Minstrel, Place Coin On Chest, Tips Hat, Tin Lithograph, Levely Co., 1909, 7 In. 1064.00
Minstrel, Tongue Sticks Out, Swallows Money, Eyes Roll, Tin Lithograph, 7 In. 719.00
Mutt & Jeff, Cast Iron, A.C. Williams, 5 In. 6.00
North Pole, Ice Cream Freezer, Cast Iron 650.00
Pelican, Japanned Finish, Rabbit In Mouth, Trenton Lock & Hardware, 1878 . . . . 700.00
Pig, Cast Iron, Deckers Iowana, 2 In. 69.00
Pig, Seated, Cast Iron, A.C. Willliams, 1910, 3 In. 95.00
Pig, Wise, Cast Iron, Hubley, M 609, 1930s, 6 5/8 In. 275.00
Pigeon On Stump, Chalkware, Early 20th Century, 9 1/2 In. 165.00
Piggy, Cream Clay, Green & Brown Sponging, 6 In. 66.00
Prancing Horse, Cast Iron, 1930s, 8 In. 75.00
Rabbit, Seated, Cast Iron, Brown, John Wright, 1960 . . . . 65.00
Radio, Cast Iron, Kenton, 4 1/4 In. 115.00
Radio, Majestic, Die Cast, Cast Iron, Arcade, 1930 . . . . 38.00
Red Goose School Shoes, Cast Iron, Red, Gold, Arcade, M 628, 1920 . . . . 225.00
Reindeer, Small, Cast Iron, A.C. Williams, c.1935, M 736, 6 1/4 x 4 7/8 In. 104.00
Royal Safe Deposit Bank, Opens With Inserted Card 210.00

Bank, Mechanical, Speaking
Dog, Sitting Girl, Shepard
Hardware, 1885, 7 In.

Bank, Mechanical, Stump
Speaker, Cast Iron,
Shepard Hardware,
1886, 9 1/2 In.

Safe, Ideal Security, 5 1/2 In.	50.00
Safe, Young America, Cast Iron, Kyser & Rex, 1882, M 881, 4 1/2 In.	200.00
Santa Claus, Picks Up Phone, Rings, Nodding Head, Hang Up Coin Drops, S. & E., 8 In.	402.00
Savings, Home Town, Original Box, Marx	517.00
Scottish Man, Tin, 7 In.	150.00
Sharecropper, Black, Cast Iron, A.C. Williams, 1901, M 173, 5 1/2 In. ....175.00 to 375.00	
Sheep, Cast Iron, John Wright, M 600, 1960s	65.00
Solar System, Sun & Planets, Metal, Astro Mfg., 1950, 10 In.	275.00
Songbird On Stump, Cast Iron, A.C. Williams, c.1912, M 664, 4 3/4 In.	467.00
Stage Coach, Tin Lithograph, 3 x 3 1/2 In.	9020.00
State, Cast Iron, 4 In.	69.00
State, Cast Iron, 9 In.	34.00
Statue Of Liberty, Copper Toned White Metal, 1960	65.00
Steam Locomotive, Cast Metal, Silver Plated, 1960	65.00
Tank, World War I, Cast Iron, Camouflage Paint, 9 1/2 In.	160.00
Thing, From Addams Family, Plastic, Battery Operated, Box, 1964, 4 1/2 x 3 1/2 In.	65.00
Three Little Pigs, Tin Lithograph, Chein, 1930s, 3 In.	375.00
Three Wise Monkeys, Cast Iron, A.C. Williams, 1910, M 743, 3 1/4 In.	375.00
Tom & Jerry, Tin Lithograph	25.00
Top Hat, Star On Top, 4 1/2 In.	75.00
Treasure Chest, Cast Metal, 1960s	55.00
Truck, Coca-Cola, Chevy, Cast Metal, Ertl Toys, 1923	75.00
Uncle Sam, Top Hat, Pottery, Olive Green, 1908, 4 1/2 In.	57.00
Woolworth Building, Gold, Cast Iron, Kenton, M 1041, 8 In.	92.00
World, Tin Lithograph, Ohio Art, 5 In.	25.00

BANKO, Korean ware, and Sumida are terms that are often confusing. We use the names in the way most often used by antiques dealers and collectors. Korean ware is now called *Sumida Gawa* or *Sumida* and is listed in this book in the Sumida category. Banko is a group of rustic Japanese wares made in the nineteenth and twentieth centuries. Some pieces are made of mosaics of colored clay, some are fanciful teapots. Redware and other materials were also used.

Tea Set, Cups, Saucers, Creamer, Sugar, Teapot, Lids, Butterflies & Floral, 13 Piece	155.00
Teapot, Good Luck Symbol, Carved Design, 1 1/2 In.	36.00
Teapot, Green, Blue, Olive Millefiori, 3 In. ....*Illus*	65.00
Teapot, Oriental Man, Hands Spout, Pigtail Lifts Cover 7 1/2 x 5 1/2 In.	225.00

BARBED WIRE was first patented in 1867. Collectors want eighteen-inch samples.

Ingraham, 1892, 18 In.	23.00
Pattison Cross Wrap, Single Strand, 18 In.	10.00
Pine Ridge Indian Reservation, 18 In.	5.50
Smith Hanging Loop, 1897, 18 In.	21.00

Lock your doors and windows. In 65 percent to 82 percent of all home burglaries, the burglar enters through a door. Most often the doors were unlocked.

Banko, Teapot, Green, Blue, Olive Millefiori, 3 In.

Barber, Pole,
Porcelain, Leaded
Glass, Koken,
35 x 11 In.

Barber, Pole, Wood,
Tin, Wall Mount,
Wind Power, 25 In.

To prevent rust, don't store or display beer cans in a damp room. A deteriorating but collectible can is best left as is, although slight dents may be popped out.

BARBER collectibles range from the popular red and white striped pole that used to be found in front of every shop to the small scissors and tools of the trade. Barber chairs are wanted, especially the older models with elaborate iron trim.

Cabinet, Oak, Marble Top, 2 Front Panels Contain Copper Tins, 40 x 24 In.	550.00
Pole, Black & White, Gold Finial, 99 1/2 In.	1600.00
Pole, Black & White, Painted, Gold Painted Acorn Finial, 99 1/2 In.	1880.00
Pole, Giltwood, Polychrome, Turned, Ball Finial, Painted, Mid 19th Century, 85 x 13 In. .	460.00
Pole, Porcelain, Leaded Glass, Koken, 35 x 11 In. . . . . *Illus*	800.00
Pole, Porcelain, Metal, Electrified, 10 x 42 In.	1100.00
Pole, Red & White Stripes, Ball Finial, 82 In.	1200.00
Pole, Red & White Stripes, Painted, Spherical Ends, 19th Century, 36 In.	2350.00
Pole, Red, White & Blue Swirled Paint, Wall Mounted, Turned, Ball Finial, 48 In.	220.00
Pole, Stripes, Painted, Ring & Reel Turned Midsection, Ball Finial, 67 3/4 In.	1410.00
Pole, Wood, Half Round, Turned, Painted, Gilt Ball Finial, 53 1/4 x 11 1/2 In.	1955.00
Pole, Wood, Tin, Wall Mount, Wind Power, 25 In. . . . . *Illus*	450.00
Sign, Scissors, Iron, 60 In.	3025.00
Sign, Straight Razor, Wood, Carved, Painted, Incised Letters, 39 x 58 In.	460.00

BAROMETERS are used to forecast the weather. Antique barometers with elaborate wooden cases and brass trim are the most desirable. Mercury column barometers are also popular with collectors. It is difficult to find someone to repair a broken one, so be sure your barometer is in working condition.

A. Marinone, Top Silver Plated Gauge, Medallion Base, Mahogany, 37 1/2 In.	1320.00
Aneroid, Bell Flower Over Thermometer, Oak, 19th Century, 31 1/2 In.	345.00
Aneroid, C.L. Malmsjo, Enamel Bezel, Acorn Finial, 21 1/2 In.	287.00
Banjo, Arts & Crafts, Mahogany, Brass, 13 x 34 In.	230.00
Banjo, Clock, Mahogany, Satinwood Stringing, c.1800, 48 x 14 1/2 x 3 1/2 In.	1610.00
Banjo, Mahogany, Hydrometer, Mirror With Thermometer In Center, 38 In.	230.00
Black Forest, Tabletop, Birds, Leaves, With Thermometer, c.1885, 13 In.	224.00
Black Forest, Walnut, Game, Wolf Head, 28 In.	504.00
D.E. Lent, Mahogany Case, Applied Ripple Carving, Silver Metal Dial, 37 In.	1320.00
French Provincial, Painted, Parcel Gilt, Circular Dial, Signed, Paris, 41 x 17 In.	5100.00
G. Arzoni, Canterbury, Banded Inlay, Convex Mirror, Ivory Knob, 37 1/2 In.	275.00
G. Terza, Mahogany Over Pine, Shell Medallion Inlays, 38 In.	385.00
Georgian Style, Thermometer, Inlaid Mahogany, Broken Arch Crown, Mirror, 37 1/2 In. .	112.00
Hemingway, Walnut Case, Silver Metal Dial, Signed, Auburn, N.Y., 40 x 8 In.	1100.00
Holosteric, Apps, London, Drum Shape, Gilt Bronze Wreath, 7 In.	980.00
Holosteric, Brass, Beveled Glass, Wall Mount, 7 x 2 In.	336.00
J. Hicks, London, Drum, Oak Case	250.00
Marine, Gimbal, Rosewood, Ivory Scales, Screw Mount For Bulkhead	2310.00
Oak, Carved Leaves & Budding Flowers, Early 20th Century, 35 In.	385.00

Oak, Carved, Fruit, Flowers, 39 In.	616.00
Oak, Figural Crest, Flower Carving, 26 In.	448.00
Oak, Hanging, Carved, Birds, Game, Nuts, Fruits, Leaves, Tassels, 36 In.	1960.00
Oak, Leaf, Berry Carving, 28 In.	336.00
Oak, Thermometer, Scrolls & Foliage, Enameled Dial, 36 In.	187.00
Rainier Beer, Plastic Case, Instruction To Set, 12 1/2 In.	45.00
Rosewood, Marquetry, Banjo Shape, Black Enamel, Charles X, 40 x 12 1/4 In.	2185.00
Rosewood, Timby's, Patent Nov. 3rd, 1857, 39 x 4 In.	950.00
Stick, B. Pionchetti & Son, Mahogany, Glazed Door, c.1800, 40 In.	1265.00
Stick, Charles Wilder, N.H., Mahogany, Adjustable Scale, 1860, 38 In.	3105.00
Stick, Lent & Tower, Walnut Case, Original Finish, Silver Dial, 1850, 37 In.	1210.00
Stick, Mahogany, Brass, Spencer Browning & Co., London, 37 In.	2185.00
Stick, Oak, Richard, Ryde, I.W., Engraved Dial, Victorian, 38 x 7 1/2 x 1 3/4 In.	1035.00
Stick, Richard Spear, Carved, Inlaid Mahogany, c.1800, 38 In.	1265.00
Stick, Roach & Warner, Mahogany, Thermometer, 1890s, 37 1/4 In.	2990.00
Stick, W. Harris & Co., Mahogany, Silvered Brass, c.1800, 4 1/2 x 2 1/4 x 37 In.	1840.00
Storm, Admiral Fitzroy, Mahogany Case	2700.00
Thermometer, Banjo, Mahogany Inlay, Flowers, Circular, c.1800, 37 In.	575.00
Wheel, A. Torone, Shell & Bellflower Inlay, Thermometer, 37 1/2 In.	690.00
Wheel, C.A. Canti, Mahogany, Hygrometer, Thermometer, c.1800, 38 In.	1093.00
Wheel, Dolland, Mahogany, Thermometer, Line Inlay, London, 36 1/2 In.	1840.00
Wheel, F. Prandi & Co., Urn Finial, Convex Mirror, Scroll Pediment, c.1850, 50 In.	1725.00
Wheel, J. Poltil, Mahogany, Inlaid Patera Roundel, Thermometer, 38 1/2 In.	920.00
Wheel, Louis A. Smith, New York, c.1840	5500.00
Wheel, P. Galetti, Sheraton Style, Brass Urn, Shells, Bat Wing Roundel, Scotland, 40 In.	575.00
Wheel, Rosewood, Onion Top Cornice, Hygrometer Dial, Mirror, 1840s, 40 In.	345.00
Wooden Frame, Carved, Diamond Shape, 1910, 10 1/2 x 10 1/2 In.	325.00

BASEBALL collectibles are in the Sports category, except for baseball cards, which are listed under Baseball in the Card category.

BASKETS of all types are popular with collectors. American Indian, Japanese, African, Shaker, and many other kinds of baskets can be found. Of course, baskets are still being made, so the collector must learn to tell the age and style of the basket to determine the value.

Berry, Stave & Wire Construction, 2 Swing Handles, 3 3/8 x 4 1/2 In.	385.00
Bowl, Coiled, Interlocking Diamonds, 15 1/2 In.	575.00
Buttocks, 12 Ribs, Splint, Eye Of God Design, Handle, 8 1/4 In.	66.00
Buttocks, 18 Ribs, Wide Rim, Center Band, Bentwood Handle, 3 1/2 In.	165.00
Buttocks, 18 Wide Ribs, Center Band, Over-Weaving, Bentwood Handle, 6 1/2 x 7 1/2 In.	110.00
Buttocks, 26 Ribs, Weaving On Center Band, Bentwood Handle, 4 1/2 x 6 In.	330.00
Buttocks, 34 Ribs, Hickory Splint, Bentwood Handle, 8 1/2 x 14 In.	302.00
Buttocks, 38 Ribs, Splint, Bentwood Handle, 2 5/8 x 4 7/8 In.	550.00
Buttocks, 54 Ribs, Bentwood Handle, 5 1/4 In.	577.00
Buttocks, Half, 11 Ribs, Arched Handles, 23 In.	55.00
Buttocks, Half, Splint, Brown Paint, Bentwood Handle, 5 x 8 In.	192.00
Buttocks, Splint, Handle, 1/8-In. Splints, 3 1/2 x 4 x 4 In.	112.00
Buttocks, Splint, Red Splints, 5 3/4 x 5 1/2 x 6 1/2 In.	168.00
Buttocks, Splint, Southern, Miniature, 2 3/4 In.	295.00
Buttocks, Woven, God's-Eye Handle, High Sides, c.1900, Large	750.00
Cheese, Maine, Large	850.00
Coil, Circular, Straw, Coil Lid, 13 x 19 In.	44.00
Coil, Flat Bottom, Flared Sides, Butterflies, California, 14 x 29 1/2 In.	3740.00
Gathering, Splint, Natural, Round, Woven Foot Base, Bentwood Handle, 17 1/2 x 16 In.	110.00
Gathering, Splint, Round, Tapered Sides, Bentwood Handle, Stained, 15 x 15 1/2 In.	82.00
Gathering, Splint, Wood Handles, Bottle Bottom, 14 3/4 x 19 In.	220.00
Gathering, Wrapped Rim, 2 Bentwood Handles, 10 x 24 1/2 In.	220.00
Gourd, Painted Flowers & Leaves, Black Ground, Cutout Handle, Shaped Rim, 6 3/4 In.	230.00
Key, Tooled, Black Paint, 19th Century, 6 x 7 3/4 x 5 In.	5640.00
Laundry, Hawkeye, Patented, Burlington Basket Co., Iowa, 1938, 23 1/2 x 18 1/2 In.	77.00
Melon, Splint, 12 Ribs, Wide Bentwood Handle, 2 x 3 1/2 In.	104.00
Melon, Splint, 20 Ribs, Painted Interior, 14 x 13 In.	110.00
Melon, Splint, 26 Ribs, Arched Handle, 12 1/2 x 9 In.	110.00
Melon, Splint, 52 Ribs, Handle, 12 In.	154.00

Nantucket, Berry, Brass Plate On Handle, 1920, 7 1/2 In. 2800.00
Nantucket, Carved Swing Handle, Ferdinand Sylvaro, 7 3/4 x 11 1/2 In. 1725.00
Nantucket, Carved Swing Handle, Scribed Wooden Base, 10 3/4 In. 1610.00
Nantucket, Cover, Carved Swing Handle, Turned Checkerboard Finial, 1973, 6 In. 690.00
Nantucket, Lightship, Circular, Tapered Rounded Sides, Swing Handle, 10 In. 470.00
Nantucket, Oval, Swing Handle, Ferdinand Sylvaro, Label & Address, 5 x 9 x 6 1/2 In. ... 1553.00
Nantucket, Purse, c.1950 .... 4312.00
Nantucket, Round, Carved Wooden Swing Handle, Turned, 19th Century, 6 x 5 In. 2990.00
Nantucket, Swing Handle, 6 x 5 In. 2200.00
Nantucket, Swing Handle, Concentric Circles, 1945, 13 x 10 1/2 In. 2070.00
Picking, Round, Wire Bail Handle, Wooden Bottom, Grip, 9 1/2 x 15 In. 242.00
Picnic, Splint, Center Handle, Hinged, Rectangular, New England, 12 x 21 1/2 x 13 In. .. 66.00
Splint, 41 Ribs, Swing Handle, Bottle Bottom, 8 7/8 In. 469.00
Splint, Applied Bottom Frames, Rectangular, 17 1/2 x 12 x 10 In. 154.00
Splint, Barrel, Wooden Side Handles, 26 x 16 In. 82.00
Splint, Bentwood Handle, 7 x 7 1/4 & 7 1/2 In., Pair 82.00
Splint, Bentwood Swivel Handle, 8 x 11 1/2 In. 275.00
Splint, Checkerboard Weave, Swing Handle, Shaped & Arched Bottom, 9 x 10 In. 275.00
Splint, Cover, Woven, Round, Painted, 19th Century, 12 3/4 x 16 3/4 x 12 1/2 In. 374.00
Splint, Cover, XX & Dot Flowers, Dark & Light Brown, 8 x 11 In. 385.00
Splint, Field, Rectangular, End Handles, 14 x 32 x 20 1/2 In. 83.00
Splint, Green, Red, Orange, Wood Handle, 12 1/2 x 14 In. 100.00
Splint, Hanging, 3 Compartments, Decorative Loops, 41 x 26 In. 110.00
Splint, Hanging, Stepped Crest, Curlicues, Blue, Green & Yellow Bands, 10 1/2 x 11 In. . 165.00
Splint, Heart-Shaped Ears, 4 Turned Ring Bottom, c.1900, 8 1/2 In. 2800.00
Splint, Kick-Up Base, Wrapped Rim, Round, Green Paint, Bentwood Handle, 17 x 10 In. . 192.00
Splint, Oak, Fixed Handle, 16 x 10 In. 275.00
Splint, Oak, Fixed Handle, Patina, 13 1/2 x 8 1/2 In. 132.00
Splint, Oak, Fixed Handle, Squared Off, Rounded Double Rim Band, 8 x 14 x 9 1/2 In. .. 77.00
Splint, Polychrome, Carved Handle, 19th Century, 5 3/4 x 7 3/4 x 11 3/4 In. 402.00
Splint, Rectangular Base, Oval Top, 5 1/2 x 13 3/4 In. 60.00
Splint, Red, Brown, Blue Striped Splints, Brown Paint, Handle, 13 x 14 In. 517.00
Splint, Round, 2 Side Handles, 5 x 9 In. 264.00
Splint, Square Base, Shallow Lid, 18 x 18 3/4 x 21 1/2 In. 110.00
Splint, Wide Ribs, 2 Blue Bands, Wrapped Rim, 2 Bent Splint Handles, 7 1/2 x 3 In. 275.00
Splint, Wooden Sides, Rectangular, 19th Century, 3 x 14 1/2 x 47 In. 374.00
Splint, Work, Cover, 19th Century, 17 x 14 In. 172.00
Splint, Work, Handle, 17 1/2 x 16 In. 172.00
Splint Bamboo, Tapered Square Body, Splint Handle, Japan, 14 1/2 In. 52.00
Storage, Elm, Painted Calligraphy On Lid, Red, Green Lacquer, 18 x 16 In. 103.00
Sweetgrass, Round, 19th Century, 1 1/2 x 2 1/2 In. 431.00
Tray, Center Star, Twirling Ray Bands, Polychrome, Chemhuevi, Mary Snyder, 13 1/2 In. . 7050.00
Twig, Magazine, Bentwood Horseshoe Handle, 16 x 18 1/2 In. 75.00
Utility, Alternating Wide, Narrow Bands, Notched Handles, 21 x 16 In. 1380.00
Vine, Ribbed, Twisted Vine Handle, Rim, American, 11 1/4 x 18 1/2 x 22 In. 115.00

BATCHELDER products are made from California clay. Ernest
Batchelder established a tile studio in Pasadena, California, in 1909
and expanded until 1916. Then he built a larger factory with a new
partner. The Batchelder-Wilson Company made all types of architectural tiles, garden pots, and bookends. The plant closed in 1932. In
1936 Batchelder opened Batchelder Ceramics, also in Pasadena, and
made bowls, vases, and earthenware pots. He retired in 1951 and died
in 1957. Pieces are marked *Batchelder Pasadena* or *Batchelder Los
Angeles*.

BATCHELDER
LOS ANGELES

Tile, Birds, Leaves & Grapes, Blue, Brown Matte Glaze, 11 1/2 In. 748.00
Tile, Bucolic Landscape, Blue Engobe, Mahogany Molding, 7 1/2 In. 460.00
Tile, Bunny, Frolicking, Medium Blue Matte Glaze, 3 7/8 In. 180.00
Tile, Flowers, Blue, Brown Matte Glaze, Arts & Crafts Oak Frame, 5 1/2 x 8 1/2 In. 430.00
Tile, Hunt Scene, Mustard Yellow Glaze, Hunter & His Dog, 3 7/8 In. 160.00
Tile, Knights, On Horseback, Medieval Village, Green, Brown, 13 x 8 1/4 In. 1610.00
Tile, Lion, Ferocious, Pale Gray, Blue Matte Glaze, 3 7/8 In. 150.00
Tile, Pine Trees, Landscape, Blue & Gold Matte Glaze, 6 In. 690.00

BATMAN and Robin are characters from a comic strip by Bob Kane that started in 1939. In 1966, the characters became part of a popular television series. There have been radio and movie serials that featured the pair. The first full-length movie was made in 1989. The third movie was made in 1995.

Batmobile, Corgi, 1966	1742.00
Batmobile, On Card, 1964, 6 In.	290.00
Batmobile, With Launcher, On Card, 1970s, 6 In.	110.00
Book, Alphabet, Die Cut, Golden Press, 1966, 8 x 8 In.	5.00
Bowl & Mug Set, Ceramic, Glazed, White, Washington Pottery, England	30.00
Button, Batman & Robin Society Member, 3 In.	15.00
Coloring Book, Color By Number, 40 Pages, 11 1/4 x 13 1/2 In.	30.00
Comic Book, No. 13, Featuring Jerry Robinson Cover, 1942	1500.00
Comic Strip, Carmine Infantino, Sunday, 3/11/90, 14 x 20 In.	530.00
Costume, Cape, Full Face Mask, c.1966	15.00
Cup, Batman & Robin, Melmac, c.1966, 3 1/2 In.	40.00
Figure, Rubber, String Loop On Top, Hong Kong, 5 1/2 In.	20.00
Game, Cape Crusader & Robin, Board, 1966	405.00
Lunch Box, Plastic, Batman & Joker, Canadian Thermos Products, 8 x 9 1/2 x 5 In.	25.00
Model Kit, Penguin, Box, Aurora, 1967, 5 x 13 In.	255.00
Mug, Glass, White, 2 Black Portraits, 3 In.	12.00
Night-Light, Riddler, Box, 4 x 7 3/4 In.	85.00
Pen, Ballpoint, Robin Image, England, 6 1/4 In.	28.00
Pencil, Black, Yellow, Name, Symbol, 7 1/2 In.	10.00
Poster, Batman Swinging On Rope Over Gotham, Facsimile Signature, 11 x 14 In.	12.00
Poster, Joker, Red & White Target Behind, 11 x 14 In.	18.00
Puzzle, Frame Tray, Batman Rescues Robin From Joker, 11 1/2 x 14 1/2 In.	25.00
Sign, Display, Wallets, Die Cut, Cardboard, 5 3/4 x 15 3/4 In.	45.00
Towel, Beach, 1970s	25.00
Toy, Bike Siren, Figural, Plastic, Metal Handlebar Attachment, 5 1/2 In.	24.00
Toy, Official Batman Bat Chute, Yellow Parachute, 1966, 8 x 10 x 3/4 In.	35.00
Toy, Water Gun, Figural, Plastic, Durham Industries, 1970s, 6 In.	35.00

BAUER pottery is a California-made ware. J.A. Bauer moved his Kentucky pottery to Los Angeles, California, in 1909. The company made art pottery after 1912 and dinnerwares marked *Bauer* after 1929. The factory went out of business in 1962.

Florist Ware, Planter, Art Deco, Burgundy, Oval, 13 x 6 In.	30.00
Florist Ware, Planter, Swirl, Chartreuse, Signed, 5 x 6 In.	22.00
Florist Ware, Planter, Window Box, White Glaze, 11 5/8 x 6 5/8 In.	10.00
Florist Ware, Planter, Yellow, 7 x 12 In.	458.00
Florist Ware, Vase, Fan, Orange, Red Glaze, Matt Carlton, 4 In.	200.00
Florist Ware, Vase, Lotus, Ivory Glaze, Signed, 14 In.	150.00
Florist Ware, Vase, Oil Jar, Fred Johnson, Light Blue, 9 In.	88.00
Florist Ware, Vase, Ruffled, Wavy Rim, White Glaze, Matt Carlton, 6 In.	167.00
Florist Ware, Vase, Twist Handle, Red, Orange Glaze, Matt Carlton, 10 In.	711.00
Flowerpot, Burgundy Swirl, 7 1/4 In.	68.00
La Linda, Cup & Saucer, Rose	20.00
La Linda, Cup & Saucer, Turquoise	20.00
La Linda, Cup & Saucer, Yellow	20.00
La Linda, Plate, Burgundy, 6 In.	8.00
La Linda, Plate, Burgundy, 10 In.	17.00
La Linda, Plate, Rose, 6 In.	6.00
La Linda, Plate, Rose, 10 In.	15.00
La Linda, Plate, Turquoise, 6 In.	6.00
La Linda, Plate, Turquoise, 10 In.	15.00
La Linda, Plate, Yellow, 6 In.	6.00
La Linda, Plate, Yellow, 10 In.	15.00
Plainware, Butter, Black, 4 1/2 In.	55.00
Plainware, Butter, Red Orange, 4 1/2 In.	45.00
Ring, Bowl, Vegetable, Oval, 9 In.	125.00
Ring, Plate, Gray, 9 In.	45.00
Ring, Plate, Jade Green, 9 In.	45.00

Ring, Plate, Yellow, 9 In. 38.00

BAVARIA is a region in Europe where many types of porcelain were made. In the nineteenth century, the mark often included the word *Bavaria*. After 1871, the words *Bavaria, Germany*, were used. Listed here are pieces that include the name *Bavaria* in some form, but major porcelain makers, such as Rosenthal, are listed in their own categories.

Bowl, Grapes & Leaves, 4 1/2 x 10 In. 66.00
Cup, Mustache, Painted Flowers, Stems, Handle, 3 3/4 x 4 3/4 In. 29.00
Dish, Flower, Buttercup, Leaf Shape, Yellow, Vera Lister, 7 1/4 x 6 In. 65.00
Dresser Box, Cover, Rose, Cobalt Blue Border, Gold Trim, Lindner, 4 In. 32.00
Pitcher, Peach & Branch, Hand Painted, 6 x 7 x 9 1/2 In. 95.00
Plate, Forget-Me-Nots, Gold Trim, 6 In. 25.00
Plate, Roses, Handles, Hortense, Square, Signed, c.1904 . . . . 51.00
Tea Caddy, Victorian Courtship Panels, Frame, Gold Leaf, Fragonard, 6 1/4 x 3 3/4 In. . . . 40.00
Vase, White, Gold, Flowers, Gold Trim, 6 In. 15.50

BEADED BAGS are included in the Purse category.

BEATLES collectors search for any items picturing the four members of the famous music group or any of their recordings. Because these items are so new, the condition is very important and top prices are paid only for items in mint condition. The Beatles first appeared on American network television in 1964. The group disbanded in 1971. Ringo Starr and Paul McCartney are still performing. John Lennon died in 1980. George Harrison died in 2001.

Album, Magical Mystery Tour 10.00
Balloon, Orange, United Industries, Conn., 1964 . . . . 61.00
Christmas Ornament, Blown Glass 102.00
Cuff Links, Display Card, Press Initial Corp, 1964 . . . . 125.00
Display, Countertop, Group In Collarless Suits, Orange, Yellow, 1963, 18 In x 9 In. 4100.00
Doll, Bobbing Heads, Ceramic, Japan, 1864, 4 Piece 395.00
Doll, Drums, Guitars, Cases, 1997, 8 In. 705.00
Doll, Ringo Starr, Vinyl, Gold Accent On The Drum, Remco 75.00
Game, Flip Your Wig, 1960s 46.00
Lunch Box, Brunch Bag, Shoulder Strap, Zipper, Light Blue, 1965 . . . . 500.00
Lunch Box, Metal, Sticker, Instructions, Aladdin, 1965 . . . . 518.00
Lunch Box, Signatures, Air Flite, Locking Device, Vinyl, Black, NEMS 762.00
Model Kit, George Harrison, Instructions, Box, Revell, 1964 . . . . 350.00
Phonograph, 4 Speeds, Blue, Model No. 84 1000, 1964, 17 1/2 x 10 x 6 In. 2100.00
Photograph, Mahogany Frame, Autographed, 1964, 23 x 28 In. 899.00
Plate, Sgt. Pepper, 25th Anniversary Edition, China, Apple Core Ltd., 1982, 8 In. 30.00
Program, 1st American Tour, Autographed Above Each Picture, Philadelphia, 1964 . . . . . 10454.00
Record Carrying Case, 45 RPM, NEMS 260.00
Songbook, Revolver, Copyright 1966 . . . . 26.00
Songbook, Sgt. Pepper's Lonely Hearts Club Band, Charles Hansen, 1967 . . . . 33.00
Stick-Ons, Yellow Submarine, Vinyl, Dal Mfg. Corp., Copyright KFS-Suba, 1968 . . . . 60.00
Telephone, Double-Decker Bus Shape, Headlights & Billboard Light Up, Box 75.00
Thermos, Band Image, Portraits On Either Side, 6 1/2 In. 110.00
Toy, Car, Ford, Figures Of Beatles, Box, Rico, 1964, 19 In. 1525.00

BEEHIVE, Austria, or Beehive, Vienna, are terms used in English-speaking countries to refer to the many types of decorated porcelain bearing a mark that looks like a beehive. The mark is actually a shield, viewed upside down. It was first used in 1744 by the Royal Porcelain Manufactory of Vienna. The firm made porcelains, called *Royal Vienna* by collectors, until it closed in 1864. Many other German, Austrian, and Japanese factories have reproduced Royal Vienna wares, complete with the original shield or *beehive* mark. This listing includes the expensive, original Royal Vienna porcelains and many other types of beehive porcelain. The Royal Vienna pieces include that name in the description.

Coffee Service, Mythological Vignettes, c.1900, 13 Piece 4800.00
Cup & Saucer, Maiden & Cupid, Gold Interior, Signed, 4 x 6 1/2 In. 90.00

Cup & Saucer, Painted Figural Decoration, Red & Gold Ground 430.00
Figurine, Royal Vienna, Black Woman Holding Butterfly, 19th Century, 3 1/4 In. 700.00
Plate, Disarming Of Love, 9 3/4 In. 345.00
Plate, Rembrandt, Fur Coat & Cap, Artist, 9 1/2 In. 630.00
Plate, Victorian Woman, Burgundy & Gold Rim, 9 1/2 In. 505.00
Urn, Applied Flowers, Hand Painted, Pierced Lid & Base, Royal Vienna, 8 3/4 In. 650.00
Vase, 2 Women Sitting On Garden Bench With Cherub, 7 1/2 x 12 3/4 In. 1035.00
Vase, On Stand, Classic Reserve, Maroon, Pink Ground, Gilt Trim, 14 1/2 In., Pair 3740.00
Vase, Woman Feeding Chicks, Bronze Finish, 4 1/2 In. 1125.00
Vase, Yellow & Lavender Ground, Red Border, 8 1/2 In. 575.00

BEER BOTTLES are listed in the Bottle category under Beer.

BEER CANS are a twentieth-century idea. Beer was sold in kegs or
returnable bottles until 1934. The first patent for a can was issued to
the American Can Company in September of that year; and Gotfried
Kruger Brewing Company, Newark, New Jersey, was the first to use
the can. The cone-top can was first made in 1935, the aluminum pop-
top in 1962. Collectors should look for cans in good condition, with no
dents or rust. Serious collectors prefer cans that have been opened
from the bottom.

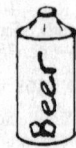

Budweiser, Flat Top, 1950s 22.00
Dutch Lunch Brand Beer, Keglined Flat Top, Grace Brothers Brewing Co., 12 Oz. 165.00
Falstaff, Cone Top, 6 In. 34.00
Fitzgerald, Cone Top, Fitzgerald Bros. Brewers, 7 1/2 In., Qt. 335.00
Hanley's Extra Pale Ale, Crowntainer, James Hanley Co, Providence, R.I., 12 Oz. 277.00
Henninger, Henninger Brewery, Frankfurt, Germany 30.00
Iroquois Indian Head Beer, Cone Top, Iroquois Beverage Corp, Buffalo, N.Y., 12 Oz. . . . 2010.00
Lucky Lager, Flat Top, 1950s 18.00
National Brewing Co., Baltimore, Md., Colt Beer 6.00
Rheingold Scotch Ale, Cone Top, Liebmann Breweries, Inc., N.Y., Qt. 22.00
Schlitz, Cone Top, 5 1/2 In. 15.50

BELL collectors collect all types of bells. Favorites include glass bells,
figural bells, school bells, and cowbells. Bells have been made of
porcelain, china, or metal through the centuries.

Box Turtle, Cast Metal, Black Patina, c.1890, 6 1/8 In. 259.00
Brass, Wood, Turned Handle, End Cap, Ebonized Clapper, 19th Century, 23 1/2 In. 402.00
Bronze, Chakra Finial, Java, 15th Century, 9 In. 977.00
Bronze, Ring Finial, Font Of Lotus Petals, Java, 16th Century, 7 1/4 In. 633.00
Call, Onyx Base, Brass Gallery & Bed, 8 Abalone Shells, 4 1/2 x 4 1/4 In. 132.00
Dinner, Arts & Crafts, Incised Byron Poem, Leather Strap, 21 x 12 3/4 x 6 1/4 In. 460.00
Dinner, Mission, Wooden Case, Wall 500.00
El Camino Real, Completed King's Highway, Iron, Brass, 1920s, 8 3/4 In. 175.00
Elephant Head, Tusks, Glass Eyes, Brass, c.1910, 6 1/2 In. 1150.00
Elizabethan Woman, Ivory Clapper Inside Of Skirt, 6 3/8 In. 805.00
Fenton, Velva Rose 35.00

Bell, Girl In Bonnet
With Flowers,
Brass, 3 In.

**Clean dirt and rust from an old iron
piece by spraying it with oven cleaner.
Put it in a sealed bag for an hour or
two, then rub the spray off with a
nylon scouring pad.**

Figure, Seated On Pillow, Umbrella, Gilt Metal, Onyx Base, 4 Ball Feet, c.1910, 5 3/4 In.	805.00
Girl In Bonnet With Flowers, Brass, 3 In. . . . . *Illus*	20.00
Gong, Bronze, Teardrop, Harry Bertoia, 1976, 15 1/2 x 9 In.	4025.00
Metal, Embossed, Meneelys' West, Troy, New York, c.1852	143.00
Rooster, Brass, Cast, Glass Eyes, Brown Patination, Early 20th Century, 5 In.	1090.00
School, Brass Ferrule, Wood Handle, 10 1/2 In.	92.00
School, Bronze, Turned Wood Handle, Original Clapper, 9 In.	52.00
School, Elkington & Co., No. 1157, Silver, 6 In.	73.00
Steeple, Cast Iron, On Stand, Thomaston, Maine, c.1860, 38 x 23 x 20 In.	784.00
Young Warrior Handle, Brass, 6 3/4 x 3 1/4 In.	115.00

BELLEEK china was made in Ireland, other European countries, and the United States. The glaze is creamy yellow and appears wet. The first Belleek was made in 1857. All pieces listed here are Irish Belleek. The mark changed through the years. The first mark, black, dates from 1863 to 1890. The second mark, black, dates from 1891 to 1926 and includes the words *Co. Fermanagh, Ireland*. The third mark, black, dates from 1926 to 1946 and has the words *Deanta in Eirinn*. The fourth mark, same as the third mark but green, dates from 1946 to 1955. The fifth mark, green, dates from 1955 to 1965 and has an R in a circle added in the upper right. The sixth mark, green, dates after 1965 and the words *Co. Fermanagh* have been omitted. The seventh mark, gold, was used from 1980 to 1993 and omits the words *Deanta in Eirinn*. The eighth mark, introduced in 1993, is similar to the second mark but is printed in blue. The word *Belleek* is now used only on the pieces made in Ireland even though earlier pieces from other countries were sometimes marked *Belleek*. These early pieces are listed by manufacturer, such as Ceramic Art Co., Haviland, Lenox, Ott & Brewer, and Willets.

Basket, 4-Strand Weave, Flowers, 2 Handles, c.1925, 9 1/8 In.	353.00
Biscuit Jar, Cover, Diamond, Gilt, 6th Mark	150.00
Bowl, Oak Leaf, 8th Mark, 8 In.	60.00
Bread Plate, Give Us This Day Our Daily Bread, Earthenware, 1st Mark	650.00
Bread Plate, Lace, Raised, Gilt, 2nd Mark, 10 In.	6500.00
Butter, Shamrock, 3rd Mark	50.00
Centerpiece, Floral & Basket Form, Black Mark, 12 In.	1725.00
Coffeepot, Shamrock, Gilt, 3rd Mark	300.00
Creamer, Echinus, 1st Mark	35.00
Creamer, Lotus, 4th Mark	35.00
Cup & Saucer, Harp Shamrock, 6th Mark	89.00
Cup & Saucer, Lily, Green & Gilt, 2nd Mark	250.00
Cup & Saucer, Neptune, 2nd Mark, 5 1/4 In.	110.00
Cup & Saucer, Shamrock, 2nd Mark, 2 In.	95.00
Cup & Saucer, Shamrock, Harp Handle, 3rd Mark, 5 In.	300.00
Cup & Saucer, Shell, 3rd Mark	110.00
Cup & Saucer, Thorn, Turquoise, Gilt, Impressed, 1st Mark	800.00
Cup & Saucer, Tridacna, 2nd Mark, Demitasse	70.00
Egg Tray, 6 Cups, 6th Mark	425.00
Figurine, Dog, Greyhound, Male & Female, Matte Finish, 6th Mark, Pair	425.00
Figurine, Dog, Terrier, 6th Mark	35.00
Figurine, Erin, Celtic Cross, 1st Mark	5500.00
Pitcher, Milk, Painted Flowers, Silver Handle, 2nd Mark, Large Size	400.00
Pitcher, Schumach Family History, Kriegshiem Coat Of Arms, Dec. 14, 1905	240.00
Plate, Shamrock, 3rd Mark, 7 In.	35.00
Plate, St. Luke, No. 615, 1st Mark	120.00
Plate, Sycamore Leaf, Pink, 5th Mark, 6 In.	15.00
Pot, Applied Flowers, 3rd Mark	175.00
Salt, Open, Shamrock, 6th Mark, 3 1/4 x 2 1/2 In.	50.00
Salt, Shamrock, 4th Mark	25.00
Spill, Corn, 6th Mark	45.00
Spill, Henshall, Pearl Finish, Applied Flowers, 5th Mark	100.00
Spill, Single Fish, 1st Mark	450.00
Sugar & Creamer, Harp Shamrock, 6th Mark	139.00

Sugar & Creamer, Ivy, 5th Mark	60.00
Tea Service, Basket Weave Molded Body, Ireland, 3rd Mark	400.00
Tea Set, Neptune, 2nd Mark, 12 Piece	1980.00
Tea Set, Teapot, 4 Cups & Saucers, Sugar & Creamer	1585.00
Teakettle, Tea-Making Directions Imprinted On Lid, 1st Mark, Large	450.00
Teapot, Tridacna, 4th Mark, Medium Size	150.00
Tree Topper, Angel, 8th Mark	60.00
Tree Topper, Cross, Gilt Star In Middle, 8th Mark	95.00
Trinket Box, Cherub, Cover, 6th Mark	75.00
Vase, Aberdeen, Flowers, Pearl, 6th Mark	285.00
Vase, Flowers, Basket, 1st Mark, 12 In.	1500.00
Vase, Rock Spill, Cornucopia Shape, Rock Formation, Ireland, 3rd Mark, 7 7/8 In., Pair . .	230.00
Vase, Tree Trunk, 6th Mark, 6 1/2 In.	300.00
Vase, Triple Fish, 6th Mark	1300.00

BENNINGTON ware was the product of two factories working in Bennington, Vermont. Both the Norton Company and the Lyman Fenton Company were out of business by 1896. The wares include brown and yellow mottled pottery, Parian, scroddled ware, stoneware, graniteware, yellowware, and Staffordshire-type vases. The name is also a generic term for mottled brownware of the type made in Bennington.

Bank, Uncle Sam, Brown & Blue Over Pink Tan, 4 3/8 In.	137.00
Batter Bowl, Brown, Cream, Orange, Green Glaze, Spout, Impressed Mark, 12 1/4 In. . . .	196.00
Bean Pot, Handle, Cover, 6 In.	45.00
Bottle, Coachman, Brown, Cream Glaze, 10 1/2 In.	863.00
Bottle, Flask, Book, Flint Enamel, Departed Spirits, G, 5 1/2 In.	385.00
Bottle, Flask, Book, Running Enameled Glaze, Impressed Departed Spirits G, 5 5/8 In. . .	935.00
Bowl, Rockingham Glaze, Flared, 13 1/2 In.	110.00
Bowl, Rockingham Glaze, Mark, 10 In.	45.00
Candlestick, Rockingham Glaze, 8 In.	275.00
Creamer, Cow, 6 3/4 In.	180.00
Cuspidor, Rockingham Glaze, Mustard To Brown, Lyman Fenton & Co., 9 3/4 In.	165.00
Dish, Ribbed, Cover, 7 In.	35.00
Dresser Box, Blue & White, Cherub Sleeping On Basket, Blue & White, 4 In.	300.00
Figurine, Cat, Seated, Flint Enamel Glazed, 19th Century, 14 x 12 1/2 In.	5500.00
Figurine, Lion, Flint Enamel, Clipped Mane, c.1849, 9 1/2 x 10 3/4 x 6 In.	3220.00
Inkwell, Lion's Head, Rockingham Glaze, 3 1/2 In.	190.00
Jar, Fitted Lid, Leaf Design, Dated 1862, 11 In.	1870.00
Lamp, Flint, Enamel, Blue, Square Base, Copper Font, Prisms, 14 1/2 In.	2530.00
Milk Boiler, Bulbous, Handle, 4 1/2 In.	85.00
Pitcher, Cascade, Waterfall Over Rocky Cliff, Tree Branch Handle, 9 3/8 In.	155.00
Pitcher, Embossed Stag & Boar, Northwind Spout, Hound Handle, 8 1/4 In.	250.00
Pitcher, Rockingham Glaze, 4 Petite Leaf-Stem Handles, 8 In.	150.00
Pitcher, Rockingham Glaze, Embossed Peacock, Tree, 8 1/4 In.	105.00
Pitcher, Toby, Dark Brown, Cream Glaze, Grape Cluster Handle, 7 In.	375.00
Pitcher, Toby, Rockingham Brown Glaze, Grape Cluster Handle, Flint Enamel, 6 In.	115.00
Plate, Serving, Rockingham, Shell Mold Rim, Square, 8 1/2 In.	60.00
Shaving Mug, Toby Philpots, Twig Handle, 3 1/2 In.	140.00
Snuff Jar, Toby, Rockingham, Enameled, 4 1/4 In.	920.00
Vase, Poppy, Parian, 1847-1858, 11 In.	345.00
Water Cooler, Column Shape, Mottled Brown Glaze, Acorn Knob, c.1850, 20 In.	2350.00

BERLIN, a German porcelain factory, was started in 1751 by Wilhelm Kaspar Wegely. In 1763, the factory was taken over by Frederick the Great and became the Royal Berlin Porcelain Manufactory. It is still in operation today. Pieces have been marked in a variety of ways.

Figurine, Woman & Eagle, Allegory Of Sight, 1765, 10 1/4 In.	265.00
Plaque, Cinderella, Feeding Doves, Giltwood Frame, Wagner, c.1890, 10 x 7 5/8 In.	4025.00
Plaque, Old Man Seated In Temple, Young Girl, Bird's-Eye Maple Frame, 22 x 17 1/2 In. .	130.00
Plaque, Rose De Mai, Society Woman, Wagner, 7 x 5 In.	2300.00
Plaque, Tavern Scene, Village In Background, Signed, 6 1/4 x 9 1/4 In.	2185.00
Plate, Mother's Day, 1971, Poodle, 4 Babies In Basket, 7 3/4 In.	35.00
Plate Set, Dinner, Peach, Blue Key Pattern Band, Mid 19th Century, 10 5/8 In., 6 Piece . .	138.00

BESWICK started making earthenware in Staffordshire, England, in 1936. The company is now part of Royal Doulton Tableware, Ltd. Figurines of animals, especially dogs and horses, Beatrix Potter animals, and other wares are still being made.

Animal, Boar, No. 1453A, 3 In.	20.00
Animal, Dog, Aberdeen Angus Bull, No. 1562, 4 1/2 In.	1700.00 to 1914.00
Animal, Dog, Bulldog, Bashford British Mascot, No. 965, 5 1/2 In.	70.00
Animal, Dog, Dalmatian, Arnoldene, No. 961, 5 3/4 In.	39.00
Animal, Dog, Doberman Pinscher, Annastock Lance, No. 2299, 5 3/4 In.	45.00
Animal, Dog, English Setter, Bayldone Baronet, No. 973, 5 1/2 In.	45.00
Animal, Dog, Great Dane, Ruler Of Oubourgh, No. 968, 7 In.	58.00
Animal, Donkey, No. 2267, 5 1/4 In.	19.00
Animal, Foal, No. 996, 3 1/4 In.	25.00
Animal, Foal, No. 1084, 4 1/4 In.	19.00
Animal, Hereford Bull, No. 1363A, 4 1/2 In.	80.00
Animal, Hereford Calf, No. 901B, 3 3/4 In.	100.00
Animal, Hereford Cow, No. 1360, 4 1/4 In.	64.00
Animal, Highland Cow, No. 1740, 5 1/4 In.	160.00
Animal, Horse, Arkle, Brown, No. 2065, 12 In.	115.00
Animal, Horse, Galloping, Palomino, No. 1374, 7 1/2 In.	213.00 to 240.00
Animal, Horse, Head Tucked, Leg Up, No. 1549, 7 1/2 In.	44.00
Animal, Lion, Facing Left, No. 2089, 5 1/2 In.	39.00
Animal, Sheep, Black-Faced, No. 1765, 3 1/4 In.	16.00
Animal, Shetland Pony, No. 1033, 5 3/4 In.	32.00
Animal, Shire Foal, No. 1053, 5 In.	25.00
Animal, Shire Mare, No. 818, 8 1/2 In.	64.00
Animal, Swish Tail Horse, No. 1182, 8 1/2 In.	50.00
Character Jug, Barnaby Rudge, No. 1121, 4 1/2 In.	47.00
Character Jug, Captain Cuttle, No. 1120, 4 1/2 In.	96.00
Character Jug, Jemima Puddle-Duck, No. 3088, 4 In.	225.00
Character Jug, Little Nell's Grandfather, No. 2031, 5 1/4 In.	35.00
Character Jug, Mr. Micawber, No. 310, 8 1/4 In.	44.00
Creamer, Mr. Micawber, No. 674, 3 1/4 In.	16.00
Creamer, Pecksniff, No. 1117	70.00
Creamer, Pickwick, No. 1119, 3 1/4 In.	16.00
Figurine, Appley Dapply, No. 2333, 3 In.	32.00
Figurine, Aunt Pettitoes, No. 2276, 3 3/4 In.	75.00
Figurine, Basil, DBH 14	176.00
Figurine, Benjamin Ate A Lettuce Leaf, No. 3317, 4 3/4 In.	42.00
Figurine, Benjamin Bunny Sat On Bank, Head Looks Down, No. 2803, 3 3/4 In.	125.00
Figurine, Catkin, DBH 12	80.00
Figurine, Chippy Hackee, No. 2627, 3C	110.00
Figurine, Cottontail, No. 2878, 3B, 3 3/4 In.	75.00
Figurine, Cousin Ribby, No. 2284, 3 1/2 In.	75.00
Figurine, Cowboy Snowman, D 56	176.00
Figurine, Flopsy, Mopsy & Cotton-Tail, No. 1274, 2 3/4 In.	25.00
Figurine, Foxy Whiskered Gentleman, No. 1277, 4 3/4 In.	25.00 to 300.00
Figurine, Gardener Rabbit, English Country Folk, No. 9155	65.00
Figurine, Gentleman Pig, No. 9149	75.00
Figurine, Goody Tiptoes, No. 1675	75.00 to 100.00
Figurine, Hunca Munca Sweeping, No. 2584, 3 1/2 In.	20.00 to 100.00
Figurine, Hunca Munca, No. 1198, 2 3/4 In.	21.00 to 85.00
Figurine, Jemima & Ducklings, No. 3786	80.00
Figurine, Jemima Puddle-Duck, No. 1092	175.00 to 225.00
Figurine, Jeremy Fisher, Catches A Fish, No. 3919, 3 In.	25.00 to 80.00
Figurine, Johnny Town-Mouse Eating Corn, No. 3031	48.00
Figurine, Johnny Town-Mouse, No. 1276, 3B Mark	90.00
Figurine, Kanga, Dark & Light Brown, Albert Hallman, England, No. 2217, 3 1/4 In.	50.00 to 57.00
Figurine, Lady Mouse, No. 1183	100.00
Figurine, Lady Pig, No. ECF8, 5 1/2 In.	75.00
Figurine, Lady Snowman, D 58	271.00
Figurine, Little Pig Robinson, No. 1104, 3 3/4 In.	80.00 to 128.00

Beswick, Figurine, Mrs. Rabbit &
Bunnies, No. 2543, 3 3/4 In.

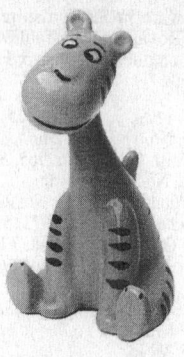

Beswick, Figurine, Tigger,
No. 2394, 3 In.

Beswick, Figurine, Winnie
The Pooh, Golden Brown &
Red, 1968-1990, No. 2193

Figurine, Little Pig Robinson, No. 1104/2 .... 375.00
Figurine, Mittens, Tom Kitten & Moppet, No. 3792 .... 195.00
Figurine, Mr. Alderman Ptolemy, No. 2424 .... 175.00
Figurine, Mr. Benjamin Bunny & Peter Rabbit, No. 2509, 4 In. 35.00
Figurine, Mr. Benjamin Bunny, No. 1940 .... 75.00
Figurine, Mr. Drake Puddle-Duck, No. 2628 .... 75.00
Figurine, Mr. Jeremy Fisher, No. 1157/1 .... 100.00
Figurine, Mr. Jeremy Fisher, No. 1157/2 .... 75.00
Figurine, Mrs. Rabbit & Bunnies, Blue Dress, White Apron, Chair, No. 2543, 3 3/4 In. 24.00
Figurine, Mrs. Rabbit & Bunnies, No. 2543, 3 3/4 In. .... *Illus* 24.00
Figurine, Mrs. Rabbit, No. 1200, 4 In. 21.00
Figurine, Mrs. Tiggy-Winkle, No. 1107, 3 1/4 In. 11.00
Figurine, Mrs. Tiggy-Winkle, No. 1107/1 .... 275.00
Figurine, Mrs. Tiggy-Winkle, No. 1107B 65.00
Figurine, Mrs. Tittlemouse, No. 1103 .... .75.00 to 195.00
Figurine, Old Mr. Brown, No. 1796, 3B 80.00
Figurine, Old Vole, DBH 13 .... 176.00
Figurine, Old Woman Who Lived In A Shoe, No. 1545, 2 1/2 In. 25.00
Figurine, Old Woman Who Lived In A Shoe, No. 1545, 2nd Mark 225.00
Figurine, Owl, Gold Label, No. 2216 .... 175.00
Figurine, Peter & Benjamin Picking Onions, No. 3930 .... 215.00
Figurine, Peter With Daffodils, No. 3597 .... 40.00
Figurine, Pied Piper, Man Playing Flute, Rats 400.00
Figurine, Pigling Bland, Lilac Jacket, No. 1365/2, 3B Mark 65.00
Figurine, Pigling Bland, No. 1365, 4 1/4 In. 20.00
Figurine, Pigling Bland, Purple Jacket, No. 1365 .... 500.00
Figurine, Rabbit, No. 2215, 3 1/4 In. 4.00
Figurine, Sir Isaac Newton, No. 2425, 3A Mark 525.00
Figurine, St. George, Guardian Saint Of England 650.00
Figurine, Store Stump Money Box, DBH 18, 3 In. 191.00
Figurine, Tabitha Twitchit, No. 1676, 3 1/2 In. 32.00
Figurine, Tigger, No. 2394, 3 In. .... *Illus* 74.00
Figurine, Timmie Willie From Johnny Town-Mouse, No. 1109, 2nd Mark 225.00
Figurine, Tom Kitten In Rookery, No. 3719 .... 36.00
Figurine, Tom Kitten, No. 1100, 3B Mark 90.00
Figurine, Tommy Brock, Spade Handle Out, Large Eye Patch, No. 1348 .... 650.00
Figurine, Winnie The Pooh, Golden Brown & Red, 1968-1990, No. 2193 .... *Illus* 57.00
Pepper Shaker, Sairey Gamp, No. 689, 2 1/2 In. 45.00
Pitcher, Robert Burns Bust, Floral On Reverse, Ivory, Stamped, 8 In. 165.00
Salt & Pepper, Laurel & Hardy, With Tray, 1930s, 4 x 3 In. 175.00
Saltshaker, Mr. Micawber, No. 690, 3 1/2 In. 45.00
Sugar, Pickwick, No. 1118 .... 70.00
Sugar, Tony Weller, No. 673, 2 3/4 In. 11.00

Teapot, Sam Weller, No. 1369, 6 1/4 In.	400.00
Vase, Trees, Deer, Owl, No. 678, Green, Burgundy, Yellow, 10 In.	57.00

BETTY BOOP, the cartoon figure, first appeared on the screen in 1931. Her face was modeled after the famous singer Helen Kane and her body after Mae West. In 1935, a comic strip was started. Her dog was named Bimbo. Although the Betty Boop cartoons ended by 1938, there was a revival of interest in the Betty Boop image in the 1980s and new pieces are being made.

Bimbo, Straw Stuffed Dog	550.00
Button, Celluloid, c.1931, 1 1/4 In.	850.00
Doll, Jointed, Wood & Composition, 12 In.	550.00
Handkerchiefs, Ribbon Tied To Each, Box, c.1931, 8 1/2 In.	1700.00
Jewelry Box, Cardboard, Satin Liner, Illustration Of Berry, 1932, 2 1/4 In.	250.00
Toy, Set, Fleisher Graphics, 7 Different Cartoons, c.1931, 23 Piece	5000.00

BICYCLES were invented in 1839. The first manufactured bicycle was made in 1861. Special ladies' bicycles were made after 1874. The modern safety bicycle was not produced until 1885. Collectors search for all types of bicycles and tricycles. Bicycle-related items are also listed here.

Columbia, Fire Arrow, Light Tank, Horn, Carrier, Black & White, 1960s	185.00
Elgin, Black Enamel, Gold Pinstripes, 26-In. Tubeless Tires, 19th Century	313.00
Firestone Speed Cruiser, Boy's, Orange, White Trim, 1950s-1960s, 30 x 72 In.	250.00
High Wheel, Butcher Cyclometer, England, 19th Century, 48-In. Front Wheel	5230.00
Huffy, Woman's, Yellow Submarine, 3-Speed, 1960s	2800.00
Iver Johnson, Leather Seat, Wooden Wheels, Decals, 71 In.	420.00
Pin, Hunter Arms Co.'s Bicycles, Trademark Dog, Celluloid, 7/8 In.	99.00
Schwinn, Apple Krate, Red, Banana Seat, 1960s	745.00
Sign, Michelin Bicycle Tires, Michelin Man On Bicycle, c.1962, 9 1/2 x 13 1/2 In.	150.00
Steel Wheels, Hard Rubber Tires, Leather Seat, Oak Frame, 58 In.	575.00
Tricycle, Tandem, Metal, Salmon Paint, Hard Rubber Tires, No Chain	110.00

BING & GRONDAHL is a famous Danish factory making fine porcelains from 1853 to the present. Underglaze blue decoration was started in 1886. The annual Christmas plate series was introduced in 1895. Dinnerwares, stoneware, and figurines are still being made today. The firm has used the initials B & G and a stylized castle as part of the mark since 1898.

Plate, Christmas, 1899, Church Bells Chiming In Christmas, 7 In.	475.00
Plate, Christmas, 1914, Chained Dog Getting Double Meal	125.00
Plate, Christmas, 1930, Arrival Of The Christmas Train	75.00
Vase, Harbor Scene, Sailing Ships, Steamship On Reverse, 17 In.	1100.00
Vase, Life-Size Birds, Nestled Among Leafy Branches, 16 In.	715.00

BINOCULARS of all types are wanted by collectors. Those made in the eighteenth and nineteenth centuries are favored by serious collectors. The small, attractive binoculars called *opera glasses* are listed in their own category.

Army & Navy, Day & Night, Brass, Enamel, Chevalier Paris, Expand To 7 In.	66.00
Bausch & Lomb, Brass, Victory Stereo 25 mm, 6 Power, Rochester, N.Y.	32.00
Carl Zeiss, 6 x 21, Marked	80.00
Carl Zeiss Jena, Telsexor, Marked	207.00
Feldstecher Zeiss, Marked Zeiss Karoly	27.00
Kendon, 6 x 30, Velvet Lined Case, Leather Strap, Japan	41.00
Leitz, Avioforte, Harrison & Co., 12 x 60, Montreal	585.00
Nikon Travel, 8 x 24, Focus Knob, Marked	36.00
U.S. Navy, Leather Case, No. 17912	36.00

BIRDCAGES are collected for use as homes for pet birds and as decorative objects of folk art. Elaborate wooden cages of the past centuries can still be found. The brass or wicker cages of the 1930s are popular with bird owners.

2 Tiers, Cupola, 2 Drawers, Birds On Peak, Tramp Art, 29 3/4 x 14 1/2 In.	1430.00

Bisque, Figurine, 2 Googlies,
Holding Wooden Brooms, 1915,
2 1/2 In. & 3 1/2 In.

Bisque, Figurine, Admiral
Peary, North Pole, Flag,
Hinged Mouth, 3 1/2 In.

Bisque, Figurine, Bride & Groom,
Sculpted Hair & Costumes,
1920, 7 In. & 7 1/2 In.

Bamboo, Wood, 35 In., Pair	1150.00
Church Form, Pine, Steeple, Peaked Roof, Tin Door, Wire Bars At Side, 23 x 18 1/2 In.	605.00
Etched Glass Panels, Base Steel Drawer, Domed Top, Hanging Ring, Inside Bell, 31 In.	275.00
Paddle Boat Shape, Victorian	2200.00
Pierced Metal, Wire, Painted, Victorian Style, Early 20th Century, 30 x 22 1/2 x 15 In.	690.00
Vanishing, Collapsible For Magic Trick, Instructions, Abbott's Magic Co., 5 x 4 1/2 In.	69.00
Wire, 3 Graduating Tiers, Small Diamond Panel Design, Victorian	2200.00
Wood, Architectural, Wire Screening, 2 Arched Doors, 17 x 10 3/4 x 30 In.	192.00
Wood, Greek Key Stamping, Ivory Spacer, Crown Finial, Chinese, 26 In.	110.00

BISQUE is an unglazed baked porcelain. Finished bisque has a slightly sandy texture with a dull finish. Some of it may be decorated with various colors. Bisque gained favor during the late Victorian era when thousands of bisque figurines were made. It is still being made. Additional bisque items may be listed under the factory name.

Basket, Rabbits On Cover, Eating Lettuce, Hand Painted, 2 Handles, 7 x 4 3/4 In.	385.00
Chicks On Basket Cover, Hatching From Eggs, 7 1/4 x 6 In.	770.00
Egg, Baby's Head, Emerging From Egg, Bare Bottom, 2 1/2 In.	275.00
Figurine, 2 Googlies, Holding Wooden Brooms, 1915, 2 1/2 In. & 3 1/2 In. .... *Illus*	275.00
Figurine, Admiral Peary, North Pole, Flag, Hinged Mouth, 3 1/2 In. .... *Illus*	1450.00
Figurine, Billiken, Sitting On Yellow Base, 6 In.	225.00
Figurine, Bride & Groom, Sculpted Hair & Costumes, 1920, 7 In. & 7 1/2 In. ...... *Illus*	880.00
Figurine, Bust, Boy & Girl, Reticulated Eyes, Molded Blond Curls, 9 1/2 In., Pair	450.00
Figurine, Child, Praying, White Nightgown, 1 3/4 x 3/4 In.	35.00
Figurine, Cupid, Blowing Gold Horn, Fasold & Starech, 5 In.	45.00
Figurine, Dignitary, Standing, Glazed, Kangxi, Chinese, Late 17th Century, 11 In.	5400.00
Figurine, Eagle, Standing On Pine Tree, Enameled, 1911, 8 1/4 In.	258.00
Figurine, Girl Holding Up Her Dress, Germany, c.1900, 8 1/4 In.	25.00
Figurine, Girl, Holding Seashell To Ear, Blue, Yellow Outfit, Bonnet, 10 1/2 In.	109.00
Figurine, Mother, Feeding Infant On Lap, Popov, Russia, Mid 19th Century, 6 1/8 In.	805.00
Figurine, Peasant, Dancing, Female, Raised Arm, Popov, Russia, c.1840, 6 1/4 In.	460.00
Figurine, Potter, Seated At Wheel, Ilonnilov Factory, Russia, Mid 19th Century, 5 In.	546.00
Figurine, Pug Dog, Seated On Pillow, Popov, Russia, Mid 19th Century, 1 1/2 x 2 1/4 In.	1035.00
Figurine, Scottish Girl, With Ball, Plaid Dress, Gold Trim, France, 10 x 4 1/4 In.	225.00
Figurine, Skater, Fallen, Woman, On Back, Pantaloons Showing, 4 In.	29.00
Figurine, Venus After Her Bath, Continental, White, 20th Century, 29 7/8 In.	575.00
Figurine, Woman, Diving, Rock Outcropping, Blue Bathing Suit, 17 1/2 In.	230.00
Figurine, Young Girl, Yellow Dress, Black Shoes, 1 x 3/4 In.	40.00
Group, Birds Nesting, 2 Chicks, Kornilov, Russia, c.1900, 4 1/2 In.	173.00
Mannequin Head, Woman, Topknot, Cobalt Blue Glass Inset Eyes, Germany, 1910, 11 In.	650.00
Vase, Jugendstil Design, 2 Handles, Royal Wettina, c.1905, 13 In.	288.00

BLACK memorabilia has become an important area of collecting since the 1970s. The best material dates from past centuries, but many recent items are also of interest. F & F is the mark used on plastic made by Fiedler & Fiedler Mold & Die Works, Inc. in the 1930s and 1940s. Objects that picture a black person may also be listed in this book under Advertising; Tins; Banks; Bottle Openers; Cookie Jars; Salt & Pepper; Sheet Music; Toys; etc.

Ashtray, Black Boy In Bathtub, 4 In.	70.00
Ashtray, Black Man, Big Lips, Chalkware, Prewar, 6 In.	120.00
Ashtray, Figural, Black Bass Player & Musical Notes, Ceramic, 1920s, 7 1/2 In.	334.00
Book, Little Black Sambo, Helen Bannerman, Platt & Munk Co., c.1935, 63 Pages	110.00
Brush, Clothes, Mammy	20.00
Bumper Sticker, Afro-American Automobile Ass'n., I Belong, Do You? 1968, 15 x 4 In.	17.00
Bust, Toussaint L'Overture, The Black Liberator Of Haiti, Carved Wood, Life Size	110.00
Cane, Figural, Man's Head, Glass Eyes, Ivory Teeth, Sculptured Features, 35 In.	4485.00
Card, Playing, Minstrels & Dancers, Cardboard, 14K Gold Edged, Plastic Box, 3 3/4 In.	40.00
Catalog, Everything For Your Minstrel Show, Songs, Skits, Props, Clothes, 44 Pages	110.00
Cigar Dispenser, Black Boy Holds Rings For Cigars, 2 Match Holders, c.1900, 5 1/2 In.	647.00
Cigarette Holder, Black Boy Peeps Out Of Huge Watermelon, Ceramic, 4 1/2 In.	133.00
Cigarette Holder, Black Man Screaming, Open Mouth Holds Cigarette, Bakelite, 4 1/2 In.	270.00
Condiment Set, Realistic Faces, Salt, Pepper, Mustard, Spoon, Ceramic, 7 1/4 In.	288.00
Cookie Jars are listed in the Cookie Jar category.	
Cup, Boy, Organ Grinder, Monkey, Majolica, 5 In.	120.00
Decanter, Comic Black Hobo On Barrel, Top Hat Stopper, Ceramic, 8 In.	40.00
Diploma, Charity Wilbur Scarbrough From Tuskegee, 1929, 20 x 16 In.	58.00
Doll, Child, Stockinet, Stitched Eyes, Mouth, Astrakhan Wig, 10 In.	518.00
Doll, Clown, Sad, Cloth, Hand Stitched, 2 Sides, Early 1900s, 6 1/2 In.	440.00
Doll, Lady, Stockinet, Embroidered Features, Red Stitch Mouth, Astrakhan Wig, 21 In.	2300.00
Doll, Mammy, Cloth, Hand Stitched, Layered Outfit, Apron, Bandana, c.1920, 5 1/2 In.	75.00
Doll, Man, Stockinet, Embroidered Features, Red Stitched Mouth, Astrakhan Wig, 21 In.	978.00
Doll, Muslin, Embroidered Eye Cuts, c.1940, 12 In.	550.00
Doll, Stockinet Head, Yarn Braids, Painted Eyes & Mouth, Cloths, Cloth, 16 In.	425.00
Earrings, Africa Shape, Nelson Mandella, Gold On Black	15.00
Figurine, Baby Fights Chicken Dinner, Chalkware, 1909, 11 In.	632.00
Figurine, Black Boys, Behind Fence, Eating Stolen Melons, Chalkware, 16 In.	220.00
Figurine, Chain Gang Black Man, Striped Clothes, Holding Chain, Pa., 1920s	475.00
Figurine, Jazz Band Musicians, Cast Iron, 2 1/2 In., 6 Piece	259.00
Figurine, Jazz Musician, Saxophone Player, Tuxedo, Pottery, 4 In.	77.00
Figurine, Jazz Musician, Spoons Player, Prewar, Pottery, 4 In.	88.00
Figurine, Man Sleeping, Woman Reading Bible, On Park Bench, 6 1/2 x 4 3/8 In.	8.00
Figurine, Slave, Headdress, Plaster, Black, Gold, A. Hacker, 1930s, 12 x 8 In., Pair	450.00
Figurine, Smiling Boy, Holds Knife, Carves Melon, Bisque, 1880s, 4 In.	277.00
Figurine, Uncle Tom & Eva, Staffordshire, 1880s, 11 In.	425.00
Figurine, Woman, Carrying Basket On Head, Wood, Polychrome, Decorated Skirt, 10 In.	460.00
Firecracker, Dixie Boy, Unopened Package Of 16, 3 1/4 In.	55.00
Humidor, Chalkware, Figural, Man, Watermelon, Painted, Late 19th Century, 12 In.	690.00
Humidor, Lifelike Slave Head, Terra-Cotta, Austria, 1880s, 6 1/2 In.	507.00
Humidor, Screaming Black Man, Terra-Cotta, Austria, c.1880, 7 In.	772.00
Jug, Milk, Auction This Day, Figures Of Slaves In Relief, Stoneware, Pewter Lid, 6 In.	1705.00
Jug, Uncle Tom & Eva, Slaves, Multicolored Decals, Wide Mouth, Stoneware, 3 x 3 In.	627.00
License Plate, Martin Luther King Image, In Memoriam, I Have A Dream, 11 3/4 x 6 In.	35.00
Man, Butler's Uniform, Cigarette Holder, Match, Ashtray, 34 1/2 In.	784.00
Man, Drunk, Moonshine Bottle As Pillow, Folk Art, 8 3/4 In.	70.00
Menu, Coon Chicken Inn, Smiling Face, 3 Restaurant Locations, 8 1/2 In.	80.00
Pencil Sharpener, Black Uncle Sam, Painted Cast Metal, 2 In.	110.00
Picture, Children Climbing Fence, Last One In's A Nigger, Black & White, 11 x 24 In.	85.00
Pie Bird, Chef In Yellow, Ceramic, 1940s, 4 In.	120.00
Pin, Black Girl Lifts Her Skirt, Painted Metal, c.1920, 3 1/2 In.	60.00
Pitcher, Servant Ringing Bell, Ceramic, Hand Painted, 5 In.	291.00
Placemat, Coon Chicken Inn, Map Of Base, Bellhop Face, 15 In.	97.00
Plate, Dinner, Black Boy Chases Chicken With Hatchet, Restaurant Chain, 9 In.	130.00
Plate, Uncle Remus, White Girl Sits In Lap, Story Tale Figures, 1920s, 6 1/4 In.	77.00
Platter, Nigger Head, Scalloped Edge, Black Man Head, 10 In.	97.00

Postcard, Dipping & Scraping Pine Trees, Turpentine Industry In The South, 1930s 21.00
Postcard, Negro Baptism, 'Down In Sunny Dixie, 1930s 21.00
Postcard, Pickin' Cotton, 'Down In Sunny Dixie, 1930s, 6 In. 21.00
Puppet, Finger, Mammy Holding White Baby, Hand Stitched, c.1920, 3 1/2 In. 60.00
Puppet, Minstrel, Hand Painted Cloth, Carved Wood, Banjo, Unused, Box, 14 In. 315.00
Puzzle, Sambo, Topsey, Mammy, Melons, Pigs, Marked Pickaninny, Cardboard, 10 In. 128.00
Shaker, Paprika, Aunt Jemima, Plastic, F & F, 1950s ....40.00 to 60.00
Shaving Mug, Close Shave, 2 Men Fighting With Razor, KPM, Germany, 3 1/2 In. 784.00
Shaving Mug, Fat Black Man's Face, I Am Not Greedy But I Like A Lot, 3 3/4 In. 80.00
Shaving Mug, Singing Black Minstrel, Double Level Top, Ceramic, 4 3/4 In. 337.00
Sheet Music, Best I Get Is Much Obliged To You, B.H. Burt, 1908, 13 x 10 3/4 In. 18.00
Smoke Stand, Ceramic, Hand Painted, Black Man Holds Tobacco Basket, 1880s, 7 In. ... 234.00
Spoon, Emerald Green Watermelon Bowl, Image Of Black Boy, Signed, 5 1/2 In. 368.00
Spoon Rest, Mammy, Head, Rockingham, 1940s, 8 In. 115.00
String Holder, Doll Shape, c.1890 .... 495.00
Toothpick Holder, Earthenware, Guitar Player, Harmonica Player, 2 x 1 1/4 In. 18.00
Wall Pocket, Black Boy Growing Out Of Pineapple, Ceramic, 6 3/4 In. 80.00
Whiskbroom, Mammy, Box, 7 In. 66.00
Window, Glass, Sign, Says No Colored 1500.00

BLACK AMETHYST glass appears black until it is held to the light, then
a dark purple can be seen. It has been made in many factories from
1860 to the present.

Biscuit Jar, 1920s 63.00
Bowl, Birds, Full Wingspan, Feathers, 3 x 7 1/2 In. 90.00
Box, Cover, Enameled Flowers, 2 1/2 In. 46.00
Decanter, 6 1/4 In. 200.00
Decanter, Bischoff Glass Co., 1950s, 16 In. 53.00
Sugar Shaker, Acorn, Gold Floral Trim, 5 In. 170.00
Tray, 2 Handles, Oval, 6 1/16 x 15 1/4 In. 36.00
Trinket Box, Clear Base, Art Deco, 1930s, 2 1/2 x 3 1/8 In. 30.00
Vase, 2 Handles, Urn Shape, c.1920, 1/2 x 5 In. 17.00
Vase, Flower Frog, 3-Footed, Smith, 5 In. 58.00

BLOWN GLASS, see Glass-Blown category.

BLUE GLASS, see Cobalt Blue category.

BLUE ONION, see Onion category.

BLUE WILLOW, see Willow category.

BOCH FRERES factory was founded in 1841 in La Louviere in eastern
Belgium. The wares resemble the work of Villeroy & Boch. The factory is still in business.

Box, Cover, Mauve & Blue Blossoms, Gilt Border, Canted Corners, Stamped, 3 x 5 In. 200.00
Box, Cover, Stylized Flowers, Turquoise, Sapphire Blue, Yellow, Black, 1 x 5 1/2 In. 287.00
Charger, Grazing Antelope At Center, Sapphire Blue, Green, Catteau, 14 In. 1150.00
Vase, Abstract Circle, Line, Triangles, Turquoise, Sapphire Blue, 12 In. 546.00
Vase, Bird Design, Green, Dark Brown Ground, Charles Catteau, 1930, 19 In. 12000.00
Vase, Blue Crackled Glaze, 3 Waves In Relief, Footed, Early 1900s, 8 1/2 In. 175.00
Vase, Central Band Of Irregular Ovals, Sapphire Blue, Green, Ivory, 9 3/4 In. 747.00
Vase, Flower Basket, 3 Stylized Flowers, Yellow, Orange, Sapphire Blue, 8 1/2 In. 400.00
Vase, Frieze Of Antelope Grazing, Sapphire Blue, Green, Catteau, 10 1/4 In. 1610.00
Vase, Frieze Of Antelope Grazing, Sapphire Blue, Green, Catteau, 13 1/4 In. 2415.00
Vase, Frieze Of Antelope Grazing, Sapphire Blue, Turquoise, Green, 1925, 9 In. 1265.00
Vase, Green Blossoms, Leaves, Turquoise Ground, Oval, c.1910, 11 3/8 In., Pair 920.00
Vase, Heart Shape, Flowers, Sapphire Blue, Blue, Green, Orange, 9 1/4 In. 805.00
Vase, Oval, Flaring Lip, 4 Grazing Deer, Fruit, Blue, Teal, Black, 1930, 12 In. 259.00
Vase, Sapphire Blue, Yellow, Light Blue, Marked, 9 1/2 In. 920.00
Vase, Scroll Design, Rolled Inward Rim, Brown, Turquoise, Pink, Ivory, 9 In. 545.00
Vase, Stylized Birds With Extended Wings, Sapphire Blue, Green, 11 1/2 In., Pair 920.00
Vase, Stylized Flowers, Pink, Sapphire Blue, Yellow Leaves, 12 In. 805.00
Vase, Stylized Moons, Lines, Turquoise, Yellow, Black, Ivory, 10 3/4 In. 460.00

Vase, Stylized Overlapping Arches, Ivory Glaze, Stepped Base, Stamped, 9 In. 200.00
Vase, Stylized Sunburst Flowers, Turquoise, Yellow, Sapphire Blue, 10 1/2 In. 575.00
Vase, Stylized Tulips & Flowers, Yellow Leaves, Sapphire Blue, Green, 10 1/2 In. 690.00
Vase, Stylized Yellow Blossoms, Leafy Vines, Yellow, Turquoise, Orange, 8 3/4 In. 690.00
Vase, Yellow Flowers, Yellow Blossoms, Burgundy Berries, Marked, 7 In. 920.00
Vase, Yellow, Black Repeating Bands, Purple, Pink Blossoms, 1925, 10 1/2 In. 430.00

BOEHM is the collector's name for the porcelains of Edward Marshall Boehm. In 1953 the Osso China Company was reorganized as Edward Marshall Boehm, Inc. The company is still working in England and New Jersey. In the early days of the factory, dishes were made, but the elaborate and lifelike bird figurines are the best-known ware. Edward Marshall Boehm, the founder, died in 1961, but the firm has continued to design and produce porcelain. Today, the firm makes both limited and unlimited editions of figurines and plates.

Figurine, Black Headed Grosbeak, 8 7/8 x 13 In. 137.00
Figurine, Magnolia With Azaleas, 5 3/4 x 10 In. 58.00
Figurine, Pelican, Bisque, 23 x 16 In. 4025.00
Group, Tropicana Rose, No. 44, 4 3/4 x 10 1/2 In. 70.00
Plate Set, Collector, Water Bird, Box, 10 7/8 In., 8 Piece 55.00
Sculpture, Blue Grosbeak, On Branch, No. 489, c.1967, 10 3/4 In. 288.00
Sculpture, Canada Goose, Painted Porcelain Base, Signed, Pair 850.00
Sculpture, Orchard Orioles, On Branch, No. 400-11, c.1970, 10 1/2 In. 316.00

BOHEMIAN GLASS, see Glass-Bohemian.

BONE DISHES were considered a necessary part of a table setting for the Victorian table. The crescent-shaped dish was kept at the edge of the dinner plate so the bones removed from the fish could be stored away from the uneaten food. Some bone dishes were made in more fanciful shapes and many resemble fish.

Apple Blossoms, Marked, Haviland & Co., Limoges, 6 x 3 In. 13.50
Brown & White, England, 1800s, 6 1/2 x 3 1/2 In. 25.00
Cobalt Blue, Gold Border, Marked, Stanley Pottery Co., England, 6 1/2 x 3 1/4 In. 46.00
Horse Drawn Chariot, Angel, Gold, Crescent Shape, Fornasetti Milano, Italy, 8 In. 105.00
Mason, Red, Pink, Crescent Shape, 8 1/4 In. 23.00
Peach Royal, Johnson Brothers, 6 x 3 1/2 In. 69.00

BOOKENDS have probably been used since books became inexpensive. Early libraries kept books in cupboards, not on open shelves. By the 1870s bookends appeared, especially homemade fret-carved wooden examples. Most bookends listed in this book date from the twentieth century. Bookends are also listed in other categories by manufacturer or material.

Abraham Lincoln, Bust, Cast Iron, Triangle Circle Insignia, c.1928, 5 1/4 In. 50.00
Anchor & Ship's Wheel, Brass, Die Cut, 6 In. 45.00
Arts & Crafts, Bronze, Medallion, Labyrinth, Chinese Style, England, 6 1/4 x 6 3/4 In. . . 259.00
Base, Slate, Black, L. Oudry, 1900s, 8 In. 645.00
Baseball Player, At Bat, Bronze, 6 In. 144.00
Camel, Cast Metal, Marble Base, c.1930, 6 In. 150.00
Camel, Ship Of The Desert, Polychrome, Cast Gray Metal, Ronson, c.1925, 7 1/2 In. 450.00
Dog, Scotty, Painted, Cast Iron, 6 In. 145.00
Dolly Dingle, Painted, Cast Iron, Grace Drayton Image, 5 In. 198.00
Eagle, 1976, Brass Plated, Colonial Virginia, 1968, 5 1/2 In. 35.00
Field Slaves, Praying, Church, Farmhouse, Egg Basket, 5 In. 192.00
Fox Head, Mahogany Backplate, Stepped Base, 6 5/8 x 4 3/8 In. 315.00
Gladiator, Man Fighting Beast, Cast Iron, Bronze, 5 1/2 In. 50.00
Gothic Church Window, Glass Insert, Painted Bronze Background, 6 1/4 In. . . . . *Illus* 155.00
Honeycomb, Cat's Heads, Cloisonne Panels, Blue & Green Flowers, 9 1/2 In. 50.00
Horse, Grazing, Bronze Finished Metal, 3 3/4 In. 45.00
Horse, Grazing, Saddled, Copper Finish, 5 1/2 x 4 1/2 In. 275.00
Horse, Rearing, Amber, L.E. Smith, 1940s, 8 x 5 3/4 In. 110.00
Horse Head, Thoroughbred, Iron, Littco, c.1928, 5 1/2 In. 90.00

For removing ink prices on matte-finished pottery try paste silver polish. It is a little abrasive and contains some cleaning chemicals that may help.

Bookends, Gothic Church Window, Glass Insert, Painted Bronze Background, 6 1/4 In.

Indian Chief, Bust Profile, Cast Iron, Copper Finish, 4 x 3 5/8 In.	175.00
Indian Chief, Full Headdress, Cast Iron, 4 3/4 In.	60.00
Jockey, Cast Metal, K & O, c.1932, 5 In.	175.00
Jockey, On Horse, Painted, Cast Iron, 5 In.	300.00
Lion & Tigress, Alfred Barye, Bronze, Early 20th Century, 10 1/4 In.	4500.00
Lion Family, White Glaze, Faience, Germany, 11 x 5 In.	175.00
Man's Profile In Front, Oscar Bach, Bronze, Hammered, Signed, 8 In.	1610.00
Medallion Of Katarina Elizabeth Goethe, 2 Columns, Bronze, E. Stelzer, 4 1/2 In.	115.00
Medieval Lord & Lady, On Horseback, Silver, India Paper Label, 7 1/4 In.	1045.00
Nude Maiden, Echo, Bronze, Armor Bronze Shop Mark, Ruhl, c.1925, 9 1/2 In.	500.00
Poor Man Showing Empty Pockets, JB Hirsch, c.1930, 6 In.	275.00
Poppy Pod, Inserts, Brass-Washed Copper, 5 1/4 x 5 1/4 In.	517.00
Sailing Ship, Bronze Finished Metal, Embossed Old Ironsides, 5 3/8 In.	40.00
Sailing Ship, Cast Iron, 5 In.	145.00
Scribe, Iron, Snead & Co., Jersey City, N.J., Patent Pending, c.1925, 4 1/4 In.	175.00
Shakespeare's House, Metal, Marked LV Ronson, 1923, 3 1/2 In.	50.00
Spanish Galleons, Cast Iron, Marked Verona, 5 1/4 In.	45.00
Squirrel, Eating, Cast Metal, Marble Base, Signed Frecourt, c.1930, 5 In.	175.00
The Thinker, Cast Iron, Painted Gold, 5 3/8 In.	45.00
Tiger, Gray, Iron, Judd, c.1925, 5 1/2 x 9 In.	300.00
Unicorn, Brass, Weighted, 7 1/2 In.	40.00
Washington, Promote Diffusion Of Knowledge, Bronze, Griffoul, G, 1915, 5 1/2 In.	300.00

BOOKMARKS were originally made of parchment, cloth, or leather. Soon woven silk ribbon, thin cardboard, celluloid, wood, silver, tortoiseshell, and metals were used. Examples made before 1850 are scarce, but there are many to be found dating before 1920.

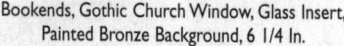

2 Girls, Flowers, Woodward's Fine Candies, c.1920	41.00
Abraham Lincoln, Metal, 1914, 4 1/2 In.	21.00
Carnegie Library, Heart Shape, Silver, Monogram, 1 3/8 In.	25.00
Douglas Room, Royal Palace Of Stirling, Lithograph, Wood, 4 1/4 In.	25.00
Flowers, Scrolling, Sterling Silver, Gorham, 2 x 2 In.	27.00
Haines Brothers Pianos, Sycamore, Oh., Kitten Climbing Up Dress	19.00
Holy Bible, Crosses, Beaded, Embroidered, Silk, Green, 36 x 3 1/4 In.	24.00
NASA Space Race, Blue, Mylar, Rocket Ship, Mark Your Place In Age Of Space	7.50
Oak Leaves, Handle, Gilt Metal, Banded Agate, 4 1/4 In.	35.00
Old Eagle Claw, Agate Marble, Rings, Bull's-Eye, Pike Peak, 3 3/4 In.	90.00
Sickle Form, Leaves, Beading On Stippled Ground, St. Petersburg, 1900, 3 In.	172.00

BOSSONS character wall masks, plaques, figurines, and other decorative pieces are made by W.H. Bossons, Limited of Congleton, England. The company was founded in 1946 and closed in 1996.

4 Seasons, Flowers, Marked, Cheshire, England	107.00
Chef, Stamped, England, 1969, 6 In.	72.00
Coronation Of Queen Elizabeth, Cameo Relief, Landmarks, 1953, 15 In.	212.00
Mozart, 1991, 7 In.	90.00

Old Salt, Marked, England, 1971	52.00
Rawhide, Cowboy In Hat With Pipe	65.00
Serbian, 5 1/2 In.	51.00
Sherlock Holmes, 6 1/2 In.	73.00
Sir Winston Churchill, 1966	870.00
Smuggler, Pirate, Eye Patch, 1964, 3 1/2 x 5 1/2 In.	51.00
Snake Charmer, Marked	46.00
Sydney Harbour Bridge Of Australia, 14 1/4 In.	258.00

BOSTON & SANDWICH CO. pieces may be found in the Lutz and Sandwich Glass categories.

BOTTLE collecting has become a major American hobby. There are several general categories of bottles, such as historic flasks, bitters, household, and figural. Pyro is the shortened form of the word *pyroglaze,* an enameled lettering used on bottles after the mid-1930s. This form of decoration is also called ACL or applied color label. For more bottle prices, see the book *Kovels' Bottles Price List* by Ralph and Terry Kovel.

18 Ribs, Swirled To Right, Midwestern, Globular, 6 In.	99.00
Apothecary, Mascotte, Ruby Stain, Ground Stopper, 24 In.	2300.00
Apothecary, Syr Limonis, Cobalt Blue, Label, Stopper, 9 x 3 1/2 In.	500.00

Avon started in 1886 as the California Perfume Company. It was not until 1929 that the name *Avon* was used. In 1939, it became Avon Products, Inc. Avon has made many figural bottles filled with cosmetic products. Ceramic, plastic, and glass bottles were made in limited editions.

Avon, American Schooner, 1972, 4 1/2 Oz.	10.00 to 14.00
Avon, Army Jeep, 1974, 4 Oz.	5.00 to 10.00
Avon, Bath Season, 1969, 3 Oz.	3.50 to 6.00
Avon, Blacksmith's Anvil, Black, 1972, 4 Oz.	9.00
Avon, Bowling Pin, 1960, 4 Oz.	10.00
Avon, Bridal Moments, 1976, 5 Oz.	10.00
Avon, Bucking Bronco, 1971, 6 Oz.	10.00
Avon, Buffalo Nickel, 1971, 5 Oz.	11.00
Avon, Car, Country Vendor, 1973	10.00
Avon, Car, Station Wagon, 1971, 6 Oz.	13.00
Avon, Car, Volkswagen, Blue, 1973, 4 Oz.	9.00
Avon, Cement Mixer, 1979, 3 Piece	14.00
Avon, Country Store, Coffee Mill, 1972, 5 Oz.	10.00
Avon, Courting Lamp, 1970, 5 Oz.	10.00
Avon, Daylight Shaving Time, 1968, 6 Oz.	15.00
Avon, Decanter, Cable Car, 1974, 4 Oz.	10.00 to 14.00
Avon, Firefighter 1910, 1975, 6 Oz.	9.00
Avon, Man's World, Globe, Plastic Stand, 1969, 6 Oz.	10.00 to 14.00
Avon, Potbelly Stove, Black, 1970, 5 Oz.	10.00
Avon, Remember When Gas Pump, 1976, 4 Oz.	10.00 to 16.00
Avon, Reo Depot Wagon, 1972, 5 Oz.	13.00
Avon, Snail, Perfume, 1968, 1/4 Oz.	10.00
Avon, Sniffy Skunk, 1978, 1 1/4 Oz.	6.00
Avon, Toy Soldier, 1964, 4 Oz.	12.00
Avon, Truck, Mail, Extra Special Male, 1979	5.00
Avon, Wagon, Reo Depot, 1973	12.00
Avon, Winnebago Motor Home, 1978, 5 Oz.	12.00
Barber, Acme Hair Vigor, Label Under Glass, 8 1/4 In.	1065.00
Barber, Amethyst, Hobnail, Rolled Lip, 7 5/8 In.	179.00
Barber, Amethyst, Mary Gregory Type, Ribs, Girl Walking, White Enamel, 7 1/4 In.	168.00
Barber, Amethyst, Ribs, Multicolored Enamel Flowers, Pontil, 7 7/8 In.	728.00
Barber, Amethyst, Ribs, Red & White Enamel Flowers & Dots, 6 7/8 In.	73.00
Barber, Bay Rum, Milk Glass, Label Under Glass, Woman Dancing, 10 In.	200.00
Barber, Bay Rum, White Camphor, Cabin, John W. Shaffer, Pewter Stopper, 10 In.	290.00
Barber, Bohemian Glass, Red, White Design, 8 3/4 x 3 1/2 In.	199.00

Barber, Brilliantine, Purple Amethyst, Multicolored & Gold Enamel, Metal Stopper, 3 In. 670.00
Barber, Bristol Type, Multicolored Painted Flowers, 7 1/2 In. 110.00
Barber, Chief, Indian Root & Herb Hair Tonic, Label Under Glass, Multicolored, 8 1/4 In. 2465.00
Barber, Cobalt Blue, Buck, Flowers, Hand Painted, Enameled, Open Pontil, 7 3/4 In. 470.00
Barber, Cobalt Blue, Mary Gregory Type, Tennis Player, White Enamel, 8 1/8 In. 225.00
Barber, Cobalt Blue, Ribs, Flowers, Multicolored Enamel, Rolled Lip, Pontil, 7 3/4 In. . . . 365.00
Barber, Cobalt Blue, Yellow, Orange, White Enamel, Mallet Shape, Pontil, 7 7/8 In. 78.00
Barber, Coin Spot, Mary Gregory Type, Cameo Decoration, 8 In. 336.00
Barber, Coin Spot, Turquoise Opalescent, Melon Sides, 7 In. 90.00
Barber, Coin Spot, Yellow Opalescent, Melon Sides, Ferns, 7 3/4 In. 123.00
Barber, Copper, Blue & Gold Design, Clear Glass Cover, Brass Foot, 7 In. 110.00
Barber, Cranberry, Opalescent, Applied Seaweed, Tapered, Stopper, 8 In. 297.00
Barber, Cranberry, Opalescent, Melon Ribs, Porcelain Stopper, 8 1/4 In. 255.00
Barber, Emerald Green, Ribs, Flowers, Dots, White, Orange Enamel, Pontil, 7 1/8 In. . . . 70.00
Barber, Enamel, Green, White, Orange Crosshatch, Blue Flowers, Stopper, 9 1/4 In., Pair . 165.00
Barber, Enamel, Green, White, Orange Crosshatch, White Flowers, Stopper, 9 1/4 In., Pair 190.00
Barber, Ess-Tee-Dee, Stops The Dandruff, Label Under Glass, Red, Green, Gold, 8 1/4 In. 1120.00
Barber, Glass, Emerald, Gold Floral, 8 x 4 In. 590.00
Barber, Grass Green, Mallet Shape, Yellow, White Enamel, 7 7/8 In. 112.00
Barber, Green, Frosted, Hobnail, Rolled Lip, 7 1/4 In. 70.00
Barber, Hair Tonic, Cut Glass, Greek Key & St. Louis Diamond, 11 In. 525.00
Barber, Koken's Heather Bloom, Label Under Glass, 8 3/8 In. 1790.00
Barber, Lime Green, Frosted, Ribs, Roses, Multicolored Enamel, Tooled Lip, Pontil, 8 In. 246.00
Barber, Milk Glass, Maroon, White, Gold, Silver Birds, Flowers, 8 5/8 In. 392.00
Barber, Osage Rub, Label Under Glass, Black, White, Gold, Tooled Mouth, 8 1/4 In. 900.00
Barber, Over The Top Hair Tonic, Label Under Glass, Black, Yellow, White, 7 7/8 In. . . . 952.00
Barber, Pink Amethyst, Art Nouveau Design, White, Gilt, Rolled Lip, Pontil, 7 3/4 In. . . . 112.00
Barber, Seaweed Pattern, Cranberry Opalescent, Porcelain Stopper, Tapered Neck, 10 In. . 450.00
Barber, Silver Horse Head, Buckle Neck, Cork Stopper, 5 3/4 In. 84.00
Barber, Turquoise Blue, Ribs, Flowers, Red & White Enamel, Tooled Lip, Pontil, 6 5/8 In. 56.00
Barber, Turquoise Opalescent, Hobnail, Pontil, 8 1/2 In. 56.00
Barber, Yellow, White Opalescent Leaf Design, 7 1/2 In. 127.00

Beam bottles were made to hold Kentucky Straight Bourbon, made by
the James B. Beam Distilling Company. The Beam series of ceramic
bottles began in 1953.

Beam, A-C Spark Plug, 1977 . . . . 35.00
Beam, Angelo's Delivery Truck, 1984 . . . . 75.00
Beam, Baseball, 100th Anniversary, 1969 . . . . 35.00
Beam, Bob Hope Desert Classic, 14th, 1973 . . . . .9.00 to 17.00
Beam, Box Car, 1983 . . . . 60.00
Beam, Boy's Town, 1973 . . . . 10.00
Beam, Cat, Siamese, 1967 . . . . 20.00
Beam, Cedars Of Lebanon, 1971 . . . . 7.00
Beam, Chevrolet, Corvette, 1978 Model, Black, 1984 . . . . 125.00
Beam, Collectors Edition, Vol. 1, Mardi Gras, 1966 . . . . 5.00
Beam, Collectors Edition, Vol. 4, The Judge, 1969 . . . . 5.00
Beam, Emmett Kelly, Willie The Clown, 1973 . . . . .25.00 to 35.00
Beam, Fox, Uncle Sam, 1971 . . . . 20.00
Beam, Harolds Club, Man In Barrel, No. 1, 1957 .385.00 to 400.00
Beam, Madame Butterfly, Opera, 1977 . . . . 245.00
Beam, Mark Anthony, 1962 . . . . 22.00
Beam, Mercedes Benz, 1974 Model, Red, 1986 . . . . .30.00 to 50.00
Beam, New Hampshire, Eagle, Regal China, 1971 . . . . 28.00
Beam, Ohio, State, 1966 . . . . .6.00 to 10.00
Beam, Political, Donkey, 1980, Superman 22.00
Beam, Poodle, Gray, 1970 . . . . 15.00
Beam, Shriners, Moila, Sword, 1972 . . . . 20.00
Beam, Sigma Nu Fraternity, Michigan, 1977 . . . . .9.00 to 15.00
Beam, Statue Of Liberty, 1975 . . . . .12.00 to 22.00
Beam, Telephone, 1897 Model, 1978 . . . . 30.00
Beam, Train, Casey Jones Caboose, 1989 . . . . 20.00
Beer, Angel's Brewery & Soda Works, Amber, Tooled Top, Qt. 165.00

Beer, C. Rothfuss & Co., Boston, Ma., Aqua, Porcelain Stopper, Pt. 45.00
Beer, C.A. Krueger Erie, Pa., Yellow, Tooled Top, Pt. 45.00
Beer, Cal Bottling Co., Amber, Tooled Top 35.00
Beer, Duke Ale, The Prince Of Pilsners, Amber, Label, 7 Oz. .... *Illus* 8.50
Beer, Fancy S In Circle, Green, Applied Top, Qt. 132.00
Beer, Frey & So., San Rafael, Amber, Porcelain Stopper 55.00
Beer, G.W. Hoxie's Premium Beer, Deep Blue Green, 6 5/8 In. 308.00
Beer, Glencoe Brewing Company, Glencoe, Minn., Amber, Uncle Sam, 1918, 9 1/4 In. ... 287.00
Beer, Gold Edge Bottling Works, J.F. Deininger Vallejo, Aqua 33.00
Beer, H.A. Peterson, Watsonville, Cal., Amber, Qt. 66.00
Beer, Honolulu Brewing Co., Blob Tooled Top, 1890, Qt. 77.00
Beer, J. Proll Bottling Works, US Lager SF, Cal., Amber, Porcelain Stopper 220.00
Beer, Johnson Liverpool, Compass, Green, Applied Top, Pt. 45.00
Beer, Jos. Schlitz, Amber, Applied Top, Bubbles, C & Co On Base 145.00
Beer, Mokelmule Hill, Amber, Crown Top, Qt. 99.00
Beer, National Bottling Co., Amber, Porcelain Stopper, Embossed Eagle 66.00
Beer, Primo, Cap 44.00
Beer, Richmond Bottling Works, Amber, Porcelain Stopper, 1/2 Pt. 22.00
Beer, Sierra Borrling Co., Amber, Porcelain Stopper, Qt. 440.00
Beer, Sunset Bottling Co., San Francisco, Cal., Gold Amber, Qt. 44.00
Beer, Wm. Schmiel, San Jose, California, Amber, Porcelain Stopper 55.00
Beer, Wreden's, Lager, Amber, Porcelain Stopper, Tooled Top, Qt. 44.00
Bininger, A.M. & Co., New York, Red, Amber, Applied Top 415.00
Bininger, A.M. & Co., Old Kentucky Bourbon, 1849 Reserve, Barrel, Amber, 8 1/8 In. ... 336.00
Bininger, A.M. & Co., Old Kentucky Reserve Bourbon, Barrel, Amber, 8 1/8 In. 728.00
Bininger, Clock, Regulator, Amber, Double Collar, Pontil, 6 In. 420.00
Bininger, Clock, Regulator, New York, Amber, Applied Top, Pontil 66.00
Bitters, B.T. 1865 S.C., Smiths Druid, Barrel, Yellow Amber, 9 1/2 In. 1792.00
Bitters, Banjo, Yellow Green, Bulbous Neck, Tapered Lip, 1860, 10 1/4 In. 7187.00
Bitters, Barrel, Strawberry Puce, Applied Mouth, 9 1/2 In. 476.00
Bitters, Barrel, Strawberry Puce, Applied Square Collar Mouth, c.1870, 9 3/8 In. 575.00
Bitters, Bourbon Whiskey, Cranberry Puce, Whittle Marks, Barrel 695.00
Bitters, Bourbon Whiskey, Strawberry Puce, Applied Mouth, Barrel, 9 1/2 In. 476.00
Bitters, Brown's Catalina, Cannon Shape, Deep Amber, Applied Mouth, 10 5/8 In. 896.00
Bitters, Brown's Celebrated Indian Herb, Blue Green, Tooled Mouth, 13 In. 1232.00
Bitters, Brown's Celebrated Indian Herb, Pat. 1868, 12 In. ....*Illus* 476.00
Bitters, Brown's Indian Queen, Patented 1867, Light Amber, Rolled Lip, 12 In. 770.00
Bitters, Brown's Indian Queen, Patented 1868, Yellow Amber, Rolled Lip, 12 In. 990.00
Bitters, Brown's Indian Queen, Patented February 11, 1868, Amber, 12 In. 715.00
Bitters, Bryant's Stomach, Lady's Leg, Olive Green, 8-Sided, 1875, 12 In. 5250.00
Bitters, Castilian, Golden Amber, Cannon Shape, Applied Mouth, 10 In. 1680.00
Bitters, Clark's Stomach, Golden Amber, Tooled Mouth, 9 In. 235.00

Bottle, Beer, Duke Ale,
The Prince Of Pilsners,
Amber, Label, 7 Oz.

Bottle, Bitters, Brown's
Celebrated Indian Herb,
Pat. 1868, 12 In.

Bottle, Bitters, Fish, W.H.
Ware, Clear, Pat. 1866,
11 1/2 In.

Bitters, Cunderango, Blue Green, Applied Lip, 1872-1880 .... 1210.00
Bitters, Curtis Cordial Calisaya Stomach, Tobacco Amber, Applied Band 330.00
Bitters, Davis Kidney & Liver, Best Invigorator & Cathartic, Golden Amber 295.00
Bitters, Dr. A.W. Coleman's Antidyspeptic & Tonic, Blue Green, Applied Mouth, 1860 .. 3200.00
Bitters, Dr. Bell's Golden Tonic, Figural Bell, Amber, Applied Mouth, c.1875, 10 1/8 In. . 8000.00
Bitters, Dr. Bishop's Wa-Hoo, Semi-Cabin, Red Amber, Applied Mouth, c.1875, 10 In. . . 900.00
Bitters, Dr. C.W. Roback's Stomach, Cincinnati, Oh., Golden Amber, Applied Top, 9 In. . 360.00
Bitters, Dr. Henley's O.K., Blue Aqua, Crude Top, 1869-1871 .... 5656.00
Bitters, Dr. Henley's Wild Grape Root IXL, Blue Green Aqua 2420.00
Bitters, Dr. Henley's Wild Grape Root IXL, Yellow Green 605.00
Bitters, Dr. Hoofland's Liver Complaint, Dyspepsia, Aqua, Pontil 77.00
Bitters, Dr. J. Hostetter's Stomach, Citron, Crude, Applied Top 180.00
Bitters, Dr. J. Hostetter's Stomach, Olive Amber, Crude, Applied Top 240.00
Bitters, Dr. Langley's Root & Herb, Boston, Light Green, Applied Square Collar, 8 1/2 In. 135.00
Bitters, Dr. Loew's Stomach, Emerald Green, Tooled Mouth, Label, 9 3/8 In. 1008.00
Bitters, Dr. Sperry's Female Strengthening, Waterbury, Ct., Blue Aqua, Label, 9 1/8 In. .. 530.00
Bitters, Drake's Plantation, 4 Log, Cherry Puce, 1860 .... 495.00
Bitters, Drake's Plantation, 4 Log, Deep Amber, 1860 .... 88.00
Bitters, Drake's Plantation, 4 Log, Yellow, Olive, 1860 .... 770.00
Bitters, Drake's Plantation, 5 Log, Deep Amber 385.00
Bitters, Drake's Plantation, 6 Log, Cabin, Pink, Copper, Puce, Tapered Lip, 1880, 10 In. . 290.00
Bitters, Drake's Plantation, 6 Log, Cabin, Puce, Sloping Collar, Patent 1862, 10 1/8 In. . 489.00
Bitters, Drake's Plantation, 6 Log, Golden Yellow Amber, 10 1/4 In. 90.00
Bitters, Drake's Plantation, 6 Log, Orange Amber, Bubbles, 1860 .... 66.00
Bitters, Drake's Plantation, 6 Log, Reddish Puce, Sloping Collar, 10 In. 213.00
Bitters, Drake's Plantation, 6 Log, Yellow, Olive Tone, Sloping Collar, 9 7/8 In. 1680.00
Bitters, E.F. Hall's, New Haven, Golden Amber, Applied Square Collar, c.1842 .... 265.00
Bitters, E.F. Hall's, New Haven, Yellow, Applied Square Collar, c.1843 .... 605.00
Bitters, E.G. Lyons & Co., Pastel Green, Backward N, Square Collar 5060.00
Bitters, Fish, Figural, Golden Amber, Red Tone, Applied Round Collar, 11 1/2 In. 280.00
Bitters, Fish, W.H. Ware, Clear, Pat. 1866, 11 1/2 In. ....*Illus* 1344.00
Bitters, Fish, W.H. Ware, Pat. 1866, Yellow Olive, Applied Mouth, 11 5/8 In. 1120.00
Bitters, Flora Temple Harness Trot, Copper Puce 375.00
Bitters, Geo. C. Hubble & Co., Semi-Cabin Shape, Amber 176.00
Bitters, Greeley's Bourbon Whiskey, Barrel, Grape Puce 605.00
Bitters, Greeley's Bourbon Whiskey, Barrel, Plum, Puce 500.00
Bitters, Greeley's Bourbon, Barrel, Chocolate, Puce 360.00
Bitters, Greeley's Bourbon, Barrel, Medium Olive Topaz, 9 1/4 In. 1000.00
Bitters, Greeley's Bourbon, Barrel, Smoky Topaz Puce, Applied Mouth, 9 1/4 In. 365.00
Bitters, H.H. Warner & Co., Tippecanoe, Gold Amber, Mushroom Lip, 9 In. 88.00
Bitters, Hibernia, Golden Amber, Applied Top, Bubbles, 1886-1890, Fifth 110.00
Bitters, Indian Maiden, Brown's Celebrated Indian Herb, Amber, Pat. 1867, 10 1/2 In. 99.00
Bitters, John Moffat, Price 1 Dollar, Phoenix, Root Beer Amber, OP, Rolled Lip, 5 1/2 In. . 1790.00
Bitters, John Root's, Buffalo, N.Y., Semi-Cabin, Blue Green, Applied Mouth, 10 1/4 In. . . 2240.00
Bitters, John Root, Emerald Green, Bubbles, Semi-Cabin, 10 In. 2640.00
Bitters, Ledlard's Stomach, Blue Green, Tapered Ring Lip, Pontil, 1865, 10 1/8 In. 3105.00
Bitters, Louis Taussig & Co., San Francisco, Ca., Amber, Applied Top, c.1880 .... 190.00
Bitters, Mishler's Herb, Dr. S.B. Hartman & Co., Yellow, Copper Tone, 8 3/4 In. 215.00
Bitters, National, Ear Of Corn, Golden Yellow, 12 1/2 In. 770.00
Bitters, National, Ear Of Corn, Red Amber, 12 1/2 In. 525.00
Bitters, Old Homestead Wild Cherry, Cabin, Amber, Sloping Collar, 9 3/4 In. 336.00
Bitters, Old Homestead, Wild Cherry, Cruse Tapered Applied Top 385.00
Bitters, Old Sachem & Wigwam Tonic, Barrel, Orange Amber, 9 1/2 In. 280.00
Bitters, Old Sachem Wigwam Tonic, Barrel, Apricot, Applied Square Collar 880.00
Bitters, Pineapple, Amber, Applied Top 154.00
Bitters, Pineapple, J.F.L. Capital, Amber, Applied Mouth, Pontil, 1875 .... 1800.00
Bitters, Red Jacket, Bennett Peters & Co., Root Beer Amber, Sloping Collar, 9 3/4 In. ... 215.00
Bitters, S.O. Richardson's Bitters, S. Reading, Ma., Aqua, Flared Lip, Pontil 165.00
Bitters, Sazerac Aromatic, Applied Band Top, PHD Monogram 385.00
Bitters, Sazerac Aromatic, Yellow Olive, PHD Monogram 1540.00
Bitters, Seward & Bentley, Buffalo, N.Y., Black Amethyst, Sloping Collar, 9 In. 6720.00
Bitters, Simon's Centennial, Bust Of G. Washington, Aqua, Double Collar, 21 In. 616.00
Bitters, Solomons' Strengthening & Invigorating, Sapphire Blue, Square, 9 3/4 In. 560.00

Bitters, Suffolk Philbrook & Tucker, Boston, Pig Shape, Golden Amber, Applied Mouth . 935.00
Bitters, Warner's Safe, Rochester, N.Y., Yellow Amber, 7 1/2 In. 896.00
Bitters, Wm. Allen's Congress, Emerald Green, Semi-Cabin, Applied Mouth, 10 1/4 In. . . . 2860.00
Bitters, Wm. Allen's Congress, Golden Amber 2640.00
Bitters, Wm. Allen's Congress, Semi-Cabin, Aqua, Bubbles 550.00
Black Glass, Bell Shape Mallet, Olive Green, Applied String Lip, Pontil, Belgium, 8 In. . . 100.00
Black Glass, Creme De Noyeaux, Painted Man & Woman, Continental, 11 1/2 In. 1900.00
Black Glass, I. Tucker X On Seal, Flattened Onion, Yellow Olive Amber, 6 3/4 In. 1900.00
Black Glass, James Oakes Bury 1771 On Seal, Cylindrical, Black Amber, 10 1/2 In. 1340.00
Black Glass, Mallet, R.K.B., Pontil, England, 1800-1820, 9 In. 365.00
Black Glass, Middle Temple & Horse On Seal, Cylindrical, Gray Olive Amber, 11 In. 100.00
Black Glass, Pancake Onion, Olive Green, Applied String Lip, Pontil, 5 3/4 In. 670.00
Cherry Nectar Syrup, Reverse Label Under Glass, 11 1/2 In. 2185.00
Coca-Cola bottles are listed in the Coca-Cola category.
Cordial, L.Q.C. Wishart's Pine Tree Tar, Phila, Patent 1859, Blue Green, 7 7/8 In. 260.00
Cordial, Lord Brougham Reform Flask, 7 In. 160.00
Cosmetic, A. Liddon, Deep Sapphire Blue, Vertical Fluted, Label, 7 3/4 In. 1065.00
Cosmetic, Buckingham Whisker Dye, Amber, Tooled Mouth, Label, Box, 5 In. 45.00
Cosmetic, Dr. Campbell's Hair Invigorator, Aurora, N.Y., Blue Aqua, Pontil, 6 1/2 In. 135.00
Cosmetic, Hall's Hair Renewer, Cobalt Blue, Glass Stopper, Label, 6 1/2 In. 135.00
Cosmetic, Lavender Bath Salts, Yardley's Old English, Label, Contents, 7 In. . . . . . . *Illus* 7.50
Cosmetic, Mary T. Goldman Co., Gray Hair Color Restorer, Box, 7 1/2 In. . . . . *Illus* 15.00
Cosmetic, R.P. Hall's Improved Preparation, Cobalt Blue, Indented Panels, 7 1/2 In. 390.00
Cure, Porter's Cure Of Pain, Cleveland, O., Blue Aqua, 6 1/2 In. 9.00
Cure, Warner's 3 Cities, 9 1/2 In. 32.00
Cure, Warner's Safe Cure, Light Amber Glass, 9 1/2 In. 25.00
Cure, Warner's Safe Cure, Olive Green Glass, 7 1/2 In. 86.00
Cure, Warner's Safe, Melbourne, Aus., London, Eng., Toronto, Red Amber, 9 5/8 In. 145.00
Decanter, 3-Piece Mold, Deep Olive Green, Applied Double Collar, Pontil, 8 3/8 In. 3360.00
Decanter, Amber, Cut Glass Panels, Mismatched Clear Faceted Stopper, 11 1/2 In. 165.00
Decanter, Blown, Clear, Flared Mouth, Pontil, Pressed Wheel Stopper, 10 In. 224.00
Decanter, Blown, Olive Green, Sheared Funnel Mouth, Keene, N.H., c.1816-1835, 7 In. . . 728.00
Decanter, Cut, Overlay, Amethyst To Clear, Star Cut Base, 19th Century, 7 3/4 In. 125.00
Decanter, English Pillar, Applied Ring, Pear Shape Stopper, Polished Pontil, 9 In. 330.00
Decanter, Figural, Clock, Clear, Frosted, Enamel Flowers, Metal Spigot, 9 1/4 In. 135.00
Decanter, Flared Lip, Pontil, Stopper, 1815, 8 3/4 In. 145.00
Decanter, Purple, Clear Etched Grape Design, Handles, Dutch, 9 In. 440.00
Decanter, Yellow Amber, Flash, Paneled, Etched, Stopper, 12 In. 55.00
Demijohn, Amber, Stoddard Type, Exterior Haze, 12 In. 44.00
Demijohn, Blue Green, 2-Piece Mold, Pontil, 19 3/4 In. 100.00
Demijohn, Dark Amber, Applied Collar, Residue, 19 1/2 In. 185.00

A dating tip for bottle collectors: The words "Federal Law forbids sale or re-use of this bottle" were used on liquor bottles from 1933 to 1964.

Bottle, Cosmetic, Lavender
Bath Salts, Yardley's Old
English, Label, Contents, 7 In.

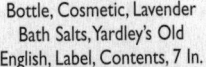

Bottle, Cosmetic, Mary T. Goldman
Co., Gray Hair Color Restorer,
Box, 7 1/2 In.

Demijohn, Deep Olive Green, Pontil, 1875-1895, 18 In. 95.00
Demijohn, Golden Amber, Applied Sloping Collar, 16 1/2 In. 410.00
Demijohn, Green, Bubbles, 12 In. 99.00
Demijohn, Pale Sapphire Blue, Applied Top, 15 In. 300.00
Demijohn, Yellow Olive, Applied Sloping Collar, Pontil, 15 In. 224.00
Drug, Brilliantine, Ruby Red, No Stopper, 4 In. 55.00
Ezra Brooks, New Hampshire, Old Man Of The Mountain, 1970 .... 28.00
Feeding, Pewter Top & Nipple, Blown Glass Well, 7 1/4 In. 900.00
Figural, Bear, Olive Green, 11 In. 50.00
Figural, Bellows, Cornflower Blue, Pontil, 1850, 10 In. 220.00
Figural, Bellows, Cranberry, White Rigaree Threading Neck, Clear Handles, 10 1/5 In. ... 220.00
Figural, Bellows, Sapphire Blue, Blown, Pontil, 1850, 8 7/8 In. 578.00
Figural, Book, Coming Thru The Rye, Pottery, Flask, Cobalt Blue Glaze, 5 In. 390.00
Figural, Cabin, Pink, Gasoline, Amber, Old Homestead, Sloping Collar, 1880, 9 5/8 In. 660.00
Figural, Cannon, Phalon & Son, Embossed Shield, Clear, 7 1/4 In. 179.00
Figural, Cannon, R. & G.A. Wright, Philada., Smoky Copper, Puce Tone, Label, 12 In. ... 616.00
Figural, Cannon, Shield, Crossed Flags, Embossed RF, Clear, Tooled Mouth, 12 1/2 In. .. 560.00
Figural, Double Cherub, Aottaoio Aspasia, Milk Glass, Mint Green, Painted, 9 3/4 In. 364.00
Figural, Mermaid, Pottery, Brown Glaze, Rockingham, Late 1800s 365.00
Figural, Monk, Clear, 1900-1930, 3 In. 125.00
Figural, Monkey Sitting On Barrel, Milk Glass, Geschutz, 1890-1915, 9 1/2 In. 1568.00
Figural, Moses, Poland Water, H. Ricker & Sons Proprietors, Label 55.00
Figural, Moses, Poland Water, H. Ricker & Sons Proprietors, Open Pontil 300.00
Figural, Negro Waiter, Clear Glass, Smooth Lip, Germany, 1885-1915, 14 3/8 In. 200.00
Figural, Pineapple, Golden Amber, Embossed, Applied Lip, Pontil, 1860, 8 3/4 In. 834.00
Figural, Shirt, Milk Glass, Ground Lip, Metal Screw Cap, 4 5/8 In. 112.00
Figural, Strawberry, Ground Lip, Ruby Red, 20th Century, 6 In. 505.00
Flask, 10 Diamond, Golden Yellow Amber, Sheared Lip, Pontil, 5 1/2 In. 1456.00
Flask, 16 Ribs, Vertical, Medium Cobalt Blue, Pontil, 5 1/2 In. 2352.00
Flask, 18 Ribs, Swirled To Right, Midwestern, Globular, 6 In. 99.00
Flask, 22 Vertical Ribs, Clear, Teardrop Shape, Pontil, 7 1/8 In. 90.00
Flask, A Little More Grape, Yellow, Green, Sheared Mouth, Open Pontil, 1850, 1/2 Pt. 8300.00
Flask, Agriculture, Blue Green Aqua, Sheared Mouth, Open Pontil, Embossed, 1840, Pt. ... 4900.00
Flask, Anchor & Sheaf Of Grain, Sapphire Blue, Double Collar, Qt. 2576.00
Flask, Anchor, Aqua, 1/2 Pt. 44.00
Flask, Arlington Bakersfield, Pumpkinseed, Amber, 1/2 Pt. 1210.00
Flask, B & F Co., New York, Bird Dogs, Birds & Rabbits On Reverse, Green, Pottery, Pt. 350.00
Flask, Baltimore, Liberty & Union, Olive, Sheared Lip, Pontil, Embossed, 1860, Pt. 6325.00
Flask, Book, Flint Enamel, Departed Spirits G, 5 1/2 In. 355.00
Flask, Broom, Blue Aqua, Tooled Top, 8 In. 88.00
Flask, Chestnut, 18 Vertical Ribs, Medium Sapphire Blue, Pontil, 6 3/4 In. 895.00
Flask, Chestnut, 24 Vertical Ribs, Medium Amber, Pontil, 4 3/4 In. 336.00
Flask, Chestnut, Blown, Yellow Olive Green, Pontil, 11 1/2 In. 725.00
Flask, Chestnut, Light Blue Green, Flattened, Pontil, 4 In. 215.00
Flask, Chestnut, Medium Olive Green, Applied Lip, Pontil, 5 1/2 In. 235.00
Flask, Chestnut, Midwestern, Amber, 24 Broken Ribs, Pontil, Tooled Mouth, 1820, 8 In. . 2690.00
Flask, Chestnut, Midwestern, Amber, 24 Broken Ribs, Swirled To Left, 1835, 4 5/8 In. 728.00
Flask, Chestnut, Midwestern, Red Amber, 24 Vertical Ribs, Tooled Mouth, 5 1/2 In. 212.00
Flask, Chestnut, Smoky Clear, Applied Neck Rings, Rigaree, Pinched Waist, 8 In. 245.00
Flask, Chestnut, Yellow Olive Green, Pinched Sides, Applied String Lip, 7 1/2 In. 785.00
Flask, Clasped Hands & Eagle, Aqua, Pt. 44.00
Flask, Clasped Hands & Eagle, Yellow Green, Applied Ring Mouth, Embossed, 1/2 Pt. 1095.00
Flask, Clear, Opalescent Looping, 8 1/4 In. 275.00
Flask, Continental, Oval, Flattened Back, Engraved Cartouche, 19th Century, 8 3/4 In. ... 115.00
Flask, Corn For The World, Medium Plum Puce, Sloping Collar, Qt. 2688.00
Flask, Cornucopia & Flask, Aqua, Open Pontil, 1/2 Pt. 121.00
Flask, Cornucopia & Urn, Ice Blue, Applied Double Collar, Pt. 280.00
Flask, Cornucopia & Urn, Olive Amber, Open Pontil, 1/2 Pt. ....66.00 to 88.00
Flask, Cornucopia & Urn, Olive Amber, Sheared Lip, Open Pontil ....80.00 to 99.00
Flask, Cornucopia, Medallion, Deep Aqua, Sheared, Rolled Mouth, Pontil, 1840, 1/2 Pt. .. 2415.00
Flask, Double Eagle, Aqua, Sheared Mouth, Open Pontil, Beaded, Embossed, 1840, Pt. .. 460.00
Flask, Double Eagle, Bennington Type Glaze, Mid 1800s 450.00

Flask, Double Eagle, Blue Green Aqua, Ribbed, Sheared Mouth, OP, 1860, 1/2 Pt. 604.00
Flask, Double Eagle, Ice Blue Aqua, Sheared Lip, Open Pontil, Qt. 202.00
Flask, Double Summer Tree, Aqua, Pt. 77.00
Flask, Eagle & Anchor, Golden Amber, Double Collar, Pt. 616.00
Flask, Eagle & Banner, Green, 14 Stars On Each Side, Pt. 1980.00
Flask, Eagle & Cornucopia, Aqua, Sheared Mouth, Open Pontil, Beaded, 1840, 1/2 Pt. ... 1150.00
Flask, Eagle & Flag, Coffin & Hay, Hammonton, Sheared Lip, Open Pontil 140.00
Flask, Eagle & Indian, Deep Aqua, 9 In. 143.00
Flask, Eagle & Shield, Louisville, Ky., Blue Aqua 69.00
Flask, Eagle & Stag, Emerald Green, Sheared Mouth, Pontil, Embossed, 1847, 1/2 Pt. ... 4313.00
Flask, Eagle, Concentric Ring, Yellow Green, Sheared Mouth, Pontil, Embossed, 1830, Pt. 4888.00
Flask, Eagle, Liberty, Red Amber, Collared Mouth, Wilmington Glass Co., 1872, Qt. 431.00
Flask, Eagle, Medallion, Aqua, Sheared Mouth, Open Pontil, Embossed, 1855, Pt. 1150.00
Flask, Fish Shape, Embossed, Screw Lid, Marked Towle Silver Plate, 6 In. 110.00
Flask, Flora Temple, Horse, Blue Green, Applied Ring Mouth, Embossed, 1880, Pt. 1438.00
Flask, For Pike's Peak, Prospector, Hunter, Topaz, Pontil, 1/2 Pt. 5040.00
Flask, George III Style, Enamel, Mold Blown, Pewter Stopper, Stenciled, 1900s, 8 In. . 115.00
Flask, Good Game, Stag & Tree, Aqua, Sheared Lip, OP, Coffin & Hay Mfg., 1847, Pt. .. 290.00
Flask, H. Brickwedel & Co., Applied Top, 1880-1883 .... 1870.00
Flask, Hallahan & Maccallum, Tooled Top, 1/2 Pt. 600.00
Flask, Henry Chapman & Co., 6 In. 121.00
Flask, Horse Pulling Cart & Eagle, Olive Green, Pontil, Pt. 784.00
Flask, Horseman & Hound, Yellow Green, Double Collared Mouth, c.1870, 1/2 Pt. 1093.00
Flask, Hunter & Fisherman, Calabash, Orange Amber 349.00
Flask, J.F. Cutter, Shield, Star, Roll Collar, 1870-1880 .... 1650.00
Flask, J.M. Ironey Wholesale Liquor, Pumpkinseed, Slug Plate, Bubbles, 1/2 Pt. 155.00
Flask, Jenny Lind, Aquamarine, Amber Striated Base, Applied Mouth, Pontil, 10 1/4 In. ... 310.00
Flask, Lafayette, Golden Honey, Yellow, Mint, Coventry Glass Works, 1825, 1/2 Pt. 920.00
Flask, Liberty, Eagle & Shield, Dark Amber, 1/2 Pt. 275.00
Flask, Liberty, Eagle & Shield, Dark Amber, Pt. 330.00
Flask, Liberty, Eagle & Shield, Dark Olive Green, Qt. 385.00
Flask, Masonic & Eagle, Wide Mouth, Rolled Collar, Pontil, Pt. 1100.00
Flask, Masonic Arch & Frigate, Yellow, Green, Sheared Mouth, OP, Embossed, 1830, Pt. . 865.00
Flask, Murdock & Cassel, Blue Green, Sheared Mouth, Open Pontil, Embossed, 1837, Pt. 4600.00
Flask, Pikes Peak, Applied Band, Smooth Base, Pt. 120.00
Flask, Pitkin, 16 Broken Ribs, Olive Green, Swirl To Right, Pontil, Tooled Mouth, 6 In. .. 500.00
Flask, Pitkin, 16 Swirled Ribs, Olive Green, Yellow, Sheared Lip, Pontil, 1815-1840 ..... 470.00
Flask, Pitkin, 24 Broken Ribs, Swirled To Left, Pontil, Tool Mouth, 7 In. 616.00
Flask, Pitkin, 30 Swirled Ribs, Yellow Amber, Sheared Mouth, Pontil, 1800s, 6 1/2 In. ... 770.00
Flask, Pitkin, 32 Broken Ribs, Blue Green, Swirl To Right, Pontil, Tooled Mouth 6 5/8 In. 785.00
Flask, Pocket, Midwestern, Oval, Ribs, Sheared Lip, Pontil, Bubbles, 7 In. 550.00
Flask, Prospector & Eagle, Aqua, Pt. 66.00
Flask, Purse, Pattern On Front & Back, Salt Glaze, 5 3/4 In. 64.00
Flask, Railroad, Eagle Olive Amber, Pt. 253.00
Flask, Scroll, Blue Aqua, Iron Pontil, Applied Mouth, Circles On Neck, 1855, Pt. 100.00
Flask, Scroll, Blue Aqua, Sheared Lip, Pontil, Pt. 280.00
Flask, Scroll, Cobalt Blue, Open Pontil, Tooled Lip, 1855, Pt. 3470.00
Flask, Scroll, Golden Amber, Sheared Mouth, Open Pontil, Embossed, 1860, 1/2 Pt. 835.00
Flask, Scroll, Golden Yellow Amber, Pontil, Sheared Lip, 1855, Pt. 560.00
Flask, Scroll, Light Apple Green, Iron Pontil, Sheared Lip, 1855, Pt. 140.00
Flask, Scroll, Lily, Brown, Rockingham, c.1860, Pt. 850.00
Flask, Scroll, Louisville Glassworks, Green Aqua, Pontil, Sheared Lip, 1845, Qt. 340.00
Flask, Scroll, Teal, Pontil, Sheared Lip, Embossed Circle, 1855, Pt. 840.00
Flask, Scroll, Yellow Green, Pontil, Applied Mouth, Bubbles, 1855, Qt. 950.00
Flask, Sheaf Of Barley, Amber, 1/2 Pt. 275.00
Flask, Sheaf Of Barley, Amber, Pt. 220.00
Flask, Sheaf Of Barley, Amber, Qt. 385.00
Flask, Sloop & Star, Bright Green, Sheared Mouth, Pontil, 1/2 Pt. 615.00
Flask, Sloop & Star, Green, Sheared Mouth, Open Pontil, Embossed, 1860, 1/2 Pt. 4600.00
Flask, Soldier & Dancer, Aqua, Sheared Mouth, Pontil, Pt. 179.00
Flask, Stag & Weeping Tree, 7 In. 165.00
Flask, Star & Sheaf Of Wheat, Deep Aqua, Open Pontil, Qt. 99.00

Flask, Success To The Railroad, Aqua, Sheared Mouth, Pontil, Pt. 840.00
Flask, Success To The Railroad, Golden Amber, Rough Lip, 6 3/4 In., Pt. 330.00
Flask, Success To The Railroad, Moss Green, Sheared Mouth, Pontil, Bubbles, 1850, Pt. . 980.00
Flask, Success To The Railroad, Yellow Amber, Sheared Mouth, 7 In. 200.00
Flask, Summer & Summer, Tree, Golden Yellow, Amber, Double Collar Mouth, 1860, Qt. 2645.00
Flask, Summer & Winter, Tree, Golden Amber, Applied Ring Lip, Bubbles, 1850, Pt. 2185.00
Flask, Summer & Winter, Tree, Variegated Citron, Double Collar, Pt. 420.00
Flask, Sunburst, Apple Green, Pontil, Tooled Mouth, 1825, Pt. 500.00
Flask, Sunburst, Blue Green, Pontil, Tooled Mouth, Bubbles, 1825, 1/2 Pt. 950.00
Flask, Sunburst, Green, Amber, Red, Sheared Lip, Open Pontil, Embossed, 1830, Pt. 10350.00
Flask, Sunburst, Medium Olive Green, Amber Tone, 1/2 Pt. 475.00
Flask, Sunburst, Olive, Sheared Lip, Pontil, 3/4 Pt. 3850.00
Flask, Sunburst, Pale Green, Pontil, Pt. 500.00
Flask, Sunburst, Red Puce, Pontil, Tooled Mouth, 1835, Pt. 6500.00
Flask, Sunburst, Yellow Amber, Sheared & Rolled Lip, Pontil, Pt. 840.00
Flask, Sunburst, Yellow Olive, Pontil, Sheared Lip, Bubbles, 1825, Pt. 750.00
Flask, Taylor & Ringgold, Rough & Ready, Light Amethyst, Pontil, Pt. 615.00
Flask, Tree & Sheaf Of Wheat, Aqua, Qt. 66.00
Flask, U.S.A Hospital, Olive Amber Qt. 550.00
Flask, Union, Clasped Hands & Eagle, Citron, Pt. 308.00
Flask, Union, Clasped Hands, Aqua, 1/2 Pt. 44.00
Flask, Washington & Eagle, Deep Blue Aqua, Pontil, Qt. 160.00
Flask, Washington & Eagle, Yellow, Green, Sheared Mouth, Open Pontil, 1840, Pt. 1668.00
Flask, Washington & Jackson, Yellow Green Amber, Sheared Lip, Pontil 230.00
Flask, Washington & Monument, Light To Medium Pink Amethyst, Pt. 450.00
Flask, Washington & Sheaf Of Wheat, Aqua, 1/2 Pt. 77.00
Flask, Washington & Taylor, Medium Blue Green, Open Pontil, Qt. 644.00
Flask, Washington & Taylor, Names Below Busts, Aquamarine, 7 In. 110.00
Flask, Washington & Taylor, Olive Green, Sheared Lip, Pontil, Embossed, 1860, 1/2 Pt. . . 5465.00
Flask, Washington & Taylor, Sheared Lip, Pontil, Bubbles, Pt. 120.00
Flask, Washington & Taylor, Turquoise Teal, Applied Top, Pontil, Qt. 825.00
Flask, Whiskey, Military, Presented By Capt. Wilson, 1892 For Attendance At Drills 290.00
Flask, Will You Take A Drink, Blue Green, Tooled Mouth, Embossed, 1890, 1/2 Pt. 776.00
Flask, Wormser Bros., Single Collar, 8 1/2 In. 230.00
Food, Atlantic Prepared Mustard, R.T. French Company, Label, 4 3/4 In. . . . . *Illus* 22.00
Food, Happy Time, Dutch Lunch Sauce, Nash-Underwood, Chicago, Label, 4 1/2 In. *Illus* 34.00
Food, Nash's Prepared Mustard, Lucky Joe Bank, Lip Label, 4 1/4 In. . . . . *Illus* 24.00
Food, Shriver's, Oyster Ketchup, Baltimore, Green, 7 1/2 In. 770.00
Food, Storage, Light Blue Green, Square, Wide Mouth, Flared Lip, 4 1/2 In. 134.00
Food, Storage, Olive Amber, Cylindrical, Wide Mouth, Flared Lip, 8 1/4 In. 364.00

Bottle, Food, Atlantic Prepared
Mustard, R.T. French Company,
Label, 4 3/4 In.

Bottle, Food, Happy Time, Dutch
Lunch Sauce, Nash-Underwood,
Chicago, Label, 4 1/2 In.

Bottle, Food, Nash's Prepared
Mustard, Lucky Joe Bank, Lip
Label, 4 1/4 In.

Bottle, Fruit Jar,
Good Housekeeping,
Embossed Aluminum
Lid, Qt.

You can date an old bottle from the spelling of the word "Pittsburgh." From 1891 to 1911 the h was removed by the U.S. Board of Geographic names. The old spelling was resumed because of complaints from those who lived in Pittsburg.

Food, Storage, Pale Apple Green, Wide Mouth, Flared Lip, 4 3/8 In.	263.00
Fruit Jar, Adams & Co., Aqua, Applied Collar, Embossed Glass Lid, Qt.	476.00
Fruit Jar, Atlas Easy Seal, Blue, Glass Lid, Wire Bail, Qt.	22.00
Fruit Jar, Atlas Easy Seal, Red Amber, Glass Lid, Iron Bail, Qt.	44.00
Fruit Jar, Banner, Reisd. Jan. 22d, 1867, Glass Lid, Aqua, 1/2 Gal.	145.00
Fruit Jar, BBGMCo., Cylindrical, Aqua, Zinc Band, Glass Lid, Midget Pt.	672.00
Fruit Jar, Beaver, Patd. Feb 12, 58, Zinc Screw Band, Midget Pt.	100.00
Fruit Jar, Dexter, Wreath Of Fruit & Vegetables, Aqua, Glass Lid, Midget Pt.	895.00
Fruit Jar, Fahnstock Albree & Co., Aqua, Pontil, Qt.	89.00
Fruit Jar, Gilberds Improved Star, Aqua, Glass Lid, Ground Lip, Pt.	785.00
Fruit Jar, Good Housekeeping, Embossed Aluminum Lid, Qt. .... *Illus*	7.00
Fruit Jar, Gray, Hemingray & Bros., 15 Vertical Flutes, Teal Green, Zinc Lid, Qt.	3585.00
Fruit Jar, H & S, Script, Aqua, Applied Mouth, Metal Yoke, Lid, Qt.	4200.00
Fruit Jar, Haines Improved, Cylindrical, Domed, Aqua, Glass Lid, 10 Oz.	755.00
Fruit Jar, Hero, Cylindrical, Sea Green, Zinc Lid & Screw Band, 1/2 Gal.	146.00
Fruit Jar, Independent, Pat. Oct. 24, 1882, Glass Screw Lid, Midget Pt.	100.00
Fruit Jar, M. Seller & Co., Blue Green, Cylindrical, Wax Sealer, Tin Lid, Qt.	896.00
Fruit Jar, Mason's Cross Patent Nov. 30th 1858, Citron, Zinc Screw Lid, Pt.	1232.00
Fruit Jar, Mason's Keystone, Pat'd Jan. 19, 1869, Aqua, Zinc Screw Lid, Midget Pt.	1456.00
Fruit Jar, Mason's Patent Nov. 30th 1858, SCA, Zinc Lid, Midget Pt.	90.00
Fruit Jar, Mason's Patent Nov. 30th, 1858, Christmas, Blue, Zinc Lid, Pt.	44.00
Fruit Jar, Mason's Patent Nov. 30th, 1858, Light Green, Ground Lip, Qt.	99.00
Fruit Jar, Mason's, GCCo, Patent Nov. 30th, 1858, Aqua, Yellow Striations, Zinc Lid, Pt.	1792.00
Fruit Jar, Mason's, Patent Nov. 30th 1858, Blue, Zinc Lid, 9 1/2 In.	198.00
Fruit Jar, Millville Atmospheric, Whitall's, June 18th, 1861, Aqua, Glass Lid, Pt.	560.00
Fruit Jar, Myer, Detroit, Mich., Cylindrical, Aqua, Ground Mouth, Qt.	476.00
Fruit Jar, NE Plus Air Tight, Bodine & Bros. Wms'town, N.J., Aqua, Glass Lid, 1/2 Gal.	1456.00
Fruit Jar, Ne Plus Ultra Air Tight, Bodine & Bros., Blue Aqua, 1/2 Gal.	1790.00
Fruit Jar, Owl, Milk Glass, Zinc Lid, Pt.	55.00
Fruit Jar, Potter & Bodine Air Tight, April 13th, 1858, Aqua, Wax Sealer, Pt.	1065.00
Fruit Jar, Puritan Trademark, Ship, Cylindrical, Aqua, Glass Lid, Iron Clamp, 1/2 Gal.	476.00
Fruit Jar, Safety Valve, Patd May 21, 1895, Grass Green, Metal Clamp, 1/2 Gal.	420.00
Fruit Jar, Safety, Yellow Amber, Embossed Glass Lid, Wire Closure, Qt.	246.00
Fruit Jar, Schaffer Jar, Rochester, Cylindrical, Aqua, Glass Lid, Metal & Wire Yoke, Pt.	672.00
Fruit Jar, Swayzee's, Improved Mason, Green, ABM, Qt.	88.00
Fruit Jar, Trademark Lightning, Amber, Glass Lid, Wire Bail, Qt.	55.00
Fruit Jar, Trademark Lightning, Citron, Glass Lid, Wire Bail, Qt.	66.00
Fruit Jar, Van Vliet Jar Of 1881, Pat. May 3, 1881, Aqua, Wire Yoke, Qt.	952.00
Fruit Jar, Wax Sealer, F.B. Co., Gold Amber, Qt.	61.00
Gin, Avon Hoboken & Co., Yellow Amber, 9 1/2 In.	44.00
Gin, Blankenheym & Nolet, Yellow, Green, Applied Top, 10 3/4 In.	66.00
Gin, Case, Seal & Top, Olive Green, Applied Top, A.V.R. Monogram	55.00
Gin, Case, T.J. Dunbar & Co., Boston, Olive Green, Yellow Tone, 9 1/2 In.	2576.00
Gin, Case, Yellow Amber, Olive Tone, Open Pontil, 9 1/2 In.	134.00
Gin, DBD, Olive Green, Embossed Star, Double Collar, Pontil	187.00

Gin, Erven L, Bols, Het Loots, Amsterdam, Olive Green, Pinched Waist, 10 In. 364.00
Gin, Inner Temple, Green Amber, Applied Seal, 10 In. 55.00
Gin, J.W. Arfmann, New York, Golden Amber, Strap Side, Tooled Mouth, 1/2 Pt. 146.00
Gin, London Jockey Club House, Jockey On Horse, Yellow Green, Double Collar, 10 In. . . 448.00
Ginger Beer, Gould's, Well At Carisbrooke Castle, 6 3/4 In. 48.00
Ginger Beer, Green Top, Crown Cork Closure, 9 In. 128.00
Ginger Beer, North & Randall, Blue Top, 6 1/2 In. 100.00
Ginger Beer, Sullivan's, Mustachioed Man, 8 1/4 In. 60.00
Ginger Beer, Walter Forbes & Co., Black Transfer, 9 In. 48.00
Ginger Beer, William Thomson, All White, Tan Lip, 8 1/2 In. 80.00
Gold Flowers & Leaves, 3-Petal Top, Bubble Stopper, Wafer Foot, 9 1/4 In. 125.00
Household, Ammonia, MNFD By The S.F. Gas Light Co., Aqua, 1/2 Gal., 10 1/2 In. 44.00
Household, Anchovy Paste, Jar, Stoneware, Wild Boar Scene, October 4, 1860, 4 In. 44.00
Household, Centaur Brand Pacific Vinegar & Pickle Works, Label, ABM, 7 In. 22.00
Household, Mustard, Barrel, Dark Olive Green, 4 In. 88.00
Household, Oil Of Spearmint, H.G. Hotchkiss, Lyons, N.Y., Cobalt Blue, Label 110.00
Household, Olive Oil, Preston & Merill, Boston, Gold Amber, 10 1/2 In. 66.00
Household, Winchester Crystal Cleaner, Embossed, Original Box 93.00
Ink, Barrel Teakettle Shape, Cobalt Blue, Ground Mouth, 2 1/4 In. 390.00
Ink, Blown, Globular, Yellow Olive, Sheared Mouth, Pontil, 2 In. 1345.00
Ink, Blown, Square, Yellow Green, Tooled Flared Mouth, Pontil, 2 In. 308.00
Ink, Brickett & Thayer, Pontil Base, Tooled Spout, Olive Amber, 1860, 9 3/4 In. 160.00
Ink, Carter, Cobalt Blue, Gothic Arch Pattern, 9 3/4 In. 121.00
Ink, Carters Cathedral, 6-Sided, Cobalt Blue, 1920-1930, 9 3/4 In. 110.00
Ink, Carters, Applied Mouth, Tooled Spout, Emerald Green, 1875-1885, 7 7/8 In. 100.00
Ink, Cone, Blue Green, Rolled Lip, Open Pontil, 1845-1855, 1 7/8 In. 365.00
Ink, Cylindrical, 7 Horizontal Rings, Light Yellow Olive, Disk Mouth, Pontil, 1 3/8 In. . . 6160.00
Ink, Cylindrical, 12 Vertical Flutes, Cobalt Blue, Ground Mouth, Sandwich, 1 5/8 In. . . . 672.00
Ink, Draper's Patent Jan 7th 1851, Pewter Screw Band, Lid, Glass Insert, 2 3/4 In. 168.00
Ink, Farley's, 8-Sided, Yellow Amber, Sheared Mouth, Pontil, Stoddard, 1 7/8 In. 950.00
Ink, Hall's Patent Simplex Hektograph, 19th Century 135.00
Ink, Harrison's Columbian, Cylindrical, Sapphire Blue, Inward Rolled Mouth, 2 1/8 In. . . 2128.00
Ink, Hohenthal Brothers & Co., Indelible Writing, Deep Olive Green, Master, 9 In. 1232.00
Ink, Igloo, Blue Green, 1875-1895, 5/8 In. 170.00
Ink, Igloo, Blue Green, Offset Neck, Ground Mouth, Label, 1860-1880, 2 In. 615.00
Ink, Igloo, G.M.W. & A.A.S., Aqua, Ground Lip, Indented Pen Rest On Dome, 1 3/8 In. . 50.00
Ink, Igloo, J. & I.E.M., Yellow Amber, 1870-1885, 1 3/4 In. 365.00
Ink, Igloo, Kirtland's W & H, Igloo, Domed, Yellow, Olive Tone, Sheared Mouth, 1 7/8 In. . . . 308.00
Ink, Leaf & Eye Teakettle Shape, Robin's-Egg Blue, Ground Mouth, 2 3/4 In. 500.00
Ink, Maynard & Noyes, Boston, Yellow Olive Amber, Flared Lip, 1840-1855, 5 5/8 In . . . 235.00
Ink, Perine Guyot, Cylindrical, Yellow Olive, Tooled Mouth, Pontil, France, c.1850, 2 In. . 168.00
Ink, Sandwich, Opalescent, 10 Panels, Multicolored Flowers, Base, 2 1/2 In. 365.00
Ink, Stafford's, Applied Mouth, Tooled Spout, Blue Green, 1875-1885, 9 5/8 In. 125.00
Ink, Teakettle, 6 Lobes, Acanthus Leaves, Opaque Lime Green, Ground Mouth, 2 1/2 In. . 475.00
Ink, Teakettle, 8-Sided, Cobalt Blue, Gold Flowers On Panels, Pontil, c.1890, 2 In. 500.00
Ink, Teakettle, 8-Sided, Corset Waist, Emerald Green, Ground Mouth, Brass Collar, 2 In. . 476.00
Ink, Teakettle, 8-Sided, Deep Opalescent Blue Milk Glass, Paneled Dome, 2 1/8 In. 364.00
Ink, Teakettle, 8-Sided, Sapphire Blue, Ground Mouth, 2 1/16 In. 280.00
Ink, Teakettle, Barrel, Cobalt Blue, 1875-1895, 2 1/4 In. 924.00
Ink, Teakettle, Benjamin Franklin, Cobalt Blue, Brass Collar, 4 1/2 In. 2016.00
Ink, Teakettle, Black Purple Amethyst, 1875-1895, 2 1/4 In. 235.00
Ink, Teakettle, Milk Glass, Polished Lip, c.1890, 2 1/8 In. 392.00
Ink, Teakettle, Square, Beveled Corners, Deep Amethyst, Ground Mouth, 1 5/8 In. 235.00
Ink, Umbrella, 8-Sided, Cornflower Blue, Tooled Mouth, 2 3/8 In. 672.00
Ink, Umbrella, 8-Sided, Deep Red Amber, Puce Tone, Tooled Lip, Pontil, 2 5/8 In. 308.00
Ink, Umbrella, 8-Sided, Grape Amethyst, Rolled Lip, 2 5/8 In. 1008.00
Ink, Umbrella, 8-Sided, Orange Amber, Inward Rolled Mouth, Pontil, 2 1/4 In. 1064.00
Ink, Umbrella, 8-Sided, Yellow Amber, Rolled Lip, Open Pontil, 1845-1860, 2 1/2 In. . . . 145.00
Ink, W.E. Bonney, Barrel, Aqua, Applied Sloping Collar, Pour Spout, Master 365.00
Jar, Fine Table Salt From J.T. Morton, London, Blue, Crude Applied Top, Pt. 175.00
Jar, Kis-Me Gum Co., Louisville, Ky., Glass Stopper, 1915-1930, 9 In. 50.00
Jar, Opium, Domed Cover, Lime Green, Square, Gold Painted Design, 12 In. 715.00
Jar, Storage, Blue Aqua, Blown, Pontil, Continental, 1830-1870, 3 3/4 In. 190.00

Jar, Storage, Yellow Green, Blown, Pontil, Continental, 1870, 9 1/4 In. 135.00
Jenny Lind, Aquamarine, Amber Striated Base, Applied Mouth, Pontil, 10 1/4 In. 308.00
Jug, Blown, Amber, Applied Mouth, Round Body, Pontil, Applied Handle, 6 In. 90.00
Liquor, Black Dude, Figural Body, 1920s, 3 3/4 In. 68.00
Log Cabin Hops & Buchu Remedy, Pat. Sept. 6, 1887, Amber, Blob Top, 10 1/8 In. 336.00
Magnus Root Beer Syrup, Reverse Label Under Glass, Testimonial, 10 1/2 In. 1840.00
Mason's, GCCo, Patent Nov. 30th, 1858, Aqua, Yellow Striations, Zinc Lid, Pt. 1792.00
Medicine, A.A. Cooley, Hartford, Con., Deep Olive Green, Oval, Open Pontil, 4 3/8 In. . .   392.00
Medicine, A.B. Stewart Druggist, Bodie, Ca., Monogram 550.00
Medicine, A.M. Cole Druggist, Virginia, Tooled Top 415.00
Medicine, Acute Indigestion, Dovetailed Box 59.00
Medicine, Bartine's Lotion, Blue Aqua, Pontil, 1845-1855, 6 1/2 In. 110.00
Medicine, Bedpan, Slipper, White, 3 1/2 In. 64.00
Medicine, Bludwine, Trademark, No Alcohol, For Your Health's Sake, 10 1/8 In. 179.00
Medicine, Boericke & Tafel Striturations, Amber, Applied Top, 7 1/2 In. 110.00
Medicine, Brant Indian Pulmonary Balsam, Medium Aqua, Applied Top 22.00
Medicine, C.A. Morris & Co., York, Pa., Aqua, Open Pontil, 1855, 5 In. 89.00
Medicine, Caswell Hazard & Co., Yellow Amber, 7 3/8 In. 106.00
Medicine, Clouds Cordial, Amber, Tapered Body, Applied Sloping Collar, Label, 10 In. . .   170.00
Medicine, Conner's Blood Remedy, Chattanooga, Tenn., Amber Tooled Mouth, 9 7/8 In. . .   125.00
Medicine, Crosse & Blackwell Meat Juice, 4 In. 80.00
Medicine, Dr. A. Atkinson, N.Y., Blue Aqua, Pontil, 7 3/4 In. 84.00
Medicine, Dr. Browder's Compound Syrup Of Indian Turnip, Aqua, OP, 7 In. 365.00
Medicine, Dr. D. Jane's Alterative, Aqua, Applied Top 22.00
Medicine, Dr. H. Van Fleck, Cornflower Blue, Cylindrical, OP, 8 1/8 In. 1792.00
Medicine, Dr. Irish's Indian Bone Ointment, Deep Blue Aqua, Tooled Mouth, 6 1/2 In. . . .   90.00
Medicine, Dr. J. Mcclintocks, Aqua, Flared Lip, 5 1/2 In. 55.00
Medicine, Dr. Mackenzie's Wild Cherry, Chicago, Clear, 8 3/8 In. 134.00
Medicine, Dr. Nywall's Family Medicine, Lundin & Co., Chicago, Il., Amber, 7 1/4 In. . .   29.00
Medicine, Dr. Robt B Folger's Olosanonian, New York, Aqua, OP, 7 1/2 In. 125.00
Medicine, Dr. Tobias, N.Y. Venetian Liniment, Aqua, 6 In. 15.00
Medicine, Dr. Warren's Expectorant, White & Hill, Nashua, N.H., OP, 6 1/2 In. 235.00
Medicine, E. Anthony, N.Y., Blue, Flared Lip, Pontil, 1850s 415.00
Medicine, E.S. Reed's Sons Apothecary, Milk Glass, Stopper, 4 5/8 In. 110.00
Medicine, Edwin J. Kuhns, Lansdale, Pa., Cobalt Blue, Cylindrical, 6 1/4 In. 160.00
Medicine, Emerald Green, 1835-1845, 7 1/4 In. 110.00
Medicine, Fountain Of Youth Hair Restorer, Cobalt Blue, Tooled Applied Top, 1870s 525.00
Medicine, G.C. Thaxter Druggist, Carson City, Aqua, Mortar & Pestle, 8 1/4 In. 1320.00
Medicine, G.W. Merchant Chemist, Lockport, N.Y., Blue Green, 5 5/8 In. 225.00
Medicine, G.W. Merchant, Lockport, N.Y., Citron, 5 1/8 In. 308.00
Medicine, Gottlieb Marshall & Co., Aqua, Embossed Dead Stuck Bug, Tooled Top 45.00
Medicine, Gun Wa's Chinese Remedy, Yellow Amber, Cleaned, 1875-1885, 8 In. 530.00
Medicine, H. Lake's Indian Specific, Aqua, Applied Ring Lip, Rectangular, 1850, 8 1/4 In.   1840.00
Medicine, H.T. Helmbold, Genuine Preparations, N.Y. & Phila., Milk Glass, 6 1/4 In. 590.00
Medicine, Handysides Health Food, Dark Olive Green Glass, 10 In. 46.00
Medicine, Henshaw & Edmands Druggists, Boston, Green, Flared Lip, Pontil, 10 1/2 In. . .   1540.00
Medicine, Herbal Magnetic Remedies, H.E. Kukgelmann & Co., N.Y., Aqua, 9 1/2 In. . . .   39.00
Medicine, Hunt's Liniment, E.E. Stanton, Singsing, N.Y., Aqua, Rectangular, 5 In. 29.00
Medicine, Hunts Remedy, Wm., E. Clarke Pharmacist, Providence, R.I., Aqua, 7 In. 15.00
Medicine, Inhaler, Bulbous, Marbled Body, 7 1/2 In. 48.00
Medicine, Inhaler, White Glaze, Butterfly & Flowers, 4 3/4 In.   223.00
Medicine, J.D. Doughty, Cincinnati, Apple Green, Open Pontil, 5 1/8 In. 500.00
Medicine, J.R. Nicols & Co., Chemist, Boston, Tooled Top, 9 In. 80.00
Medicine, J.W. Doran, Juneau, Alaska 300.00
Medicine, Kronkine, Clear, Embossed Dr. Clark Veterinary, Tooled Lip, 1900, 7 3/8 In. . . .   230.00
Medicine, L. Miller's Hair Invigorator, N.Y., Aqua, Oval, 5 1/2 In. 19.00
Medicine, L.Q.C. Whishart's Pine Tree Tar, Yellow Green, 1870, 9 5/8 In. 290.00
Medicine, Lynch & Clarks, New York, Dark Olive Amber, Pontil, Pt. 2016.00
Medicine, M.B. Robert's Vegetable Embrocation, Blue Green, Open Pontil, 5 1/2 In. 500.00
Medicine, M.B. Robert's Vegetable Embrocation, Emerald Green, Sloping Collar, 5 1/2 In.   112.00
Medicine, Measure, Black Transfer, January, 1877, Ceramic, 1 1/2 In. 16.00
Medicine, Measure, Ceramic, White Glaze, 1 1/2 In. 16.00
Medicine, Moore's Revealed MRR Remedy, Yellow Amber, Strap Sided, 8 7/8 In. 200.00

Medicine, Morton's Citrate Of Magnesia, Milwaukee, Cobalt Blue, 7 3/8 In. . . . . . .670.00 to 672.00
Medicine, Mrs. S.A. Allen's World's Hair Restorer, N.Y., Orange Amber, 7 In. 17.00
Medicine, Nelson Extract Of Roses & Rosemary H.P., Blue, Applied Top, Stopper 66.00
Medicine, Oldridge's Balm Of Columbia For Restoring Hair, Philadelphia, Aqua, 5 1/4 In. 79.00
Medicine, Opium, Clear, Red Poppies, c.1860 . . . . 10.00
Medicine, Peruvian Syrup, Blue Aqua, Cylindrical, 9 1/2 In. 100.00
Medicine, Prof. J.F. Tilton, Crown Of Science, Great Hair Producer, Sapphire, 6 3/4 In. . . 770.00
Medicine, Rheumatic Syrup, R.S. Co., Wolcott, N.Y., Amber, Double Collar, 10 In. 225.00
Medicine, Rushton & Aspinwall, Green, Applied, Tapered Collar, Pontil, 6 Oz. 6050.00
Medicine, S. Brechbill's Worm Medicine, Blue Aqua, Pontil, 4 In. 190.00
Medicine, Scurvy Ointment, 1 3/4 In. 70.00
Medicine, Selsus Skin Ointment, Box 16.00
Medicine, Stockton Drug Co., Stockton Ca., Green, Citrate, Crown Top 55.00
Medicine, Sun Drug Co., Los Angeles, Ca., Citrate Of Magnesia, Mortar & Pestle 120.00
Medicine, Swaim's Panacea, Philada., Deep Olive Green, Pontil, 7 7/8 In. 670.00
Medicine, Tenso Herbal Ointment, White Glaze, Black Transfer, 2 1/4 In. 48.00
Medicine, U.S.A. Hosp. Dept., Cobalt Blue, Cylindrical, 7 1/8 In. 246.00
Medicine, Vaughn's Vegetable Lithontriptic Mixture, Blue Aqua, Sloping Collar, 8 In. 146.00
Medicine, Warner's Diabetes Cure, Yellow Green, Tooled Top, 9 1/2 In. 550.00
Medicine, Wetherell's Cream Of Benzoin & Roses, Milk Glass, 1880-1895, 5 In. 246.00
Medicine, Wm. Radam's Microbe Killer Germ, Bacteria, Fungus Destroyer, Aqua, 10 In. . . 715.00
Medicine, Yellow Olive, Flared Lip, Open Pontil, 1835-1855, 5 In. 168.00
Milk, A Bottle Of Milk Is A Bottle Of Health, Embossed Side, 1/2 Qt. 25.00
Milk, Aaron B. Stoltzfoos, Bareville, Pa., Embossed, Round, Qt. 40.00
Milk, Aaron B. Stoltzfoos, Bareville, Pa., Round, 1/2 Pt. 40.00
Milk, Alta Crest Farms, Spencer, Mass., Yellow Green, ABM, 9 1/2 In. 670.00
Milk, Ben Jansing Farm Dairy, Licking Pike, Newport, Ky., Red, ACL, Tall, Round, Qt. . . 50.00
Milk, Beverly Farms, Chocolate Milk, Red ACL, 1/2 Pt. . . . . *Illus* 12.00
Milk, Blue Ridge Creamery, Luray, Va., Embossed, 1/2 Pt. 12.00
Milk, Burton's Place, S. Lake City, Utah, ACL, Square, Pt. 15.00
Milk, C.P. Beers, Russell, Pa., Embossed, 1/2 Pt. 15.00
Milk, Chestnut Farms Dairy, Washington D.C., Gill 10.00
Milk, Chocolate, Smiling Black Children, Lawrence Dairy Co., Qt., 9 1/2 In. 95.00
Milk, City Creamery Co., Bradford, Pa., Smoky Copper, ABM, 1/2 Pt. 336.00
Milk, Cloverleaf Dairy, Virginia, Green, ACL, Round, Pt. 10.00
Milk, Crater Lake Dairy Products, New Jersey, Girl & Dog, 1930 . . . . 35.00
Milk, D'Arbornne Dairy, Homer, La., ACL, Round, Pt. 25.00
Milk, Driggs Dairy Farm, Palmyro, Mich., ACL, Round, Qt. 50.00
Milk, E.F. Mayer, 1289 Hollenbeck St., N.H., Amber, 1934, Qt. 35.00
Milk, Equity, Sioux City, Iowa, Blue, ACL, Round, Qt. 35.00
Milk, Ethan-Allen, Essex Jct., Vermont, Amber, ACL, Square, Qt. 20.00
Milk, Farmers Dairy, Connellsville, Pa., ACL, Square, Qt. 15.00
Milk, Fernwood Dairy, G.W. Mattram, Auburn, Me., Green, ACL, Qt. 16.00
Milk, Harding Dairy, Magna, Utah, Round, Qt. 40.00
Milk, Hygienic Dairy Ltd., Honolulu, Round, 1941, Qt. 35.00
Milk, J.A. Scheetz, Steven, Pa., Embossed, Round, Qt. 35.00
Milk, J.J. March & Son, Hot Springs, S. Dak., Round, 1928, Qt. 40.00
Milk, J.R. Arnold, Valley Acres Farm, Hellam, Pa., Round, Qt. 80.00
Milk, Johnson's Dairy, Virginia, Minn., ACL, Round, 1/2 Pt. 20.00
Milk, Johnson's Farm Dairy, ACL, Square, Small Top, 1/2 Pt. 25.00
Milk, Joppe's Dairy, Grand Rapids, Mi., Embossed, 1/2 Pt. 15.00
Milk, Maplecrest Farm, Maynard, Green, ACL, Square, Qt. 15.00
Milk, Modern Dairy, T.A. Donovan, Cream Top, Mass. Seal, 1948, Qt. 20.00
Milk, Mortensen's Creamery, Red, ACL, Round, Qt. 30.00
Milk, Pleasant Dairy, Lewiston, Me., Red, ACL, Square, Qt. 22.00
Milk, Polk's Milk, Always Ahead, Gal. 95.00
Milk, Ray Stone, Landing, N.J., Round, Qt. 28.00
Milk, Rossley's Dairy, Leicester, Ma., Brown, ACL, Round, Qt. 22.00
Milk, Roy Stone, Landing, N.J., Embossed, Round, Qt. 28.00
Milk, Runnymede Farm, ACL, Square, 1/2 Pt. 20.00
Milk, Sanitary Dairy, Weed, Calif., Orange, ACL, Round, Tall, Qt. 50.00
Milk, Servalike Milk Dealers Assoc., Bay City, Vermont, Round, Qt. 25.00

Milk, Silver Hill Dairy, Portland, Oregon, Cop Top, Red, ACL, Qt. 100.00
Milk, Silverleaf Farms Dairy, Ironwood, Mich., ACL, Round, Pt. 20.00
Milk, Souder & Chick, Brunswick, Maryland, ACL, Squat, 1/2 Pt. 85.00
Milk, Starland Dairies, Savannah, Geo., ACL, Round, Qt. 30.00
Milk, Sterling Milk Company, Erie, Pa., Round, 1919, Qt. 20.00
Milk, Sunset Creamery, Roswell, N.M., ACL, Round, Qt. 45.00
Milk, Szep's Dairy, Bethelehem, Pa., ACL, Squat, 1/2 Pt. 8.00
Milk, T & M Dairy Ice Cream, Hits The Spot, Maroon, ACL, Tall, Round, Pt. 30.00
Milk, Universal Store Bottle, Ribbed, Round, Qt. 20.00
Milk, Weavers Quality Blue Ribbon Prod., Carwell, Mich., Round, Qt. 25.00
Milk, Westview, Black, ACL, Round, Qt. 25.00
Milk, Winona Dairy, Pringle's, Lebanon, N.H., Red, ACL, Qt. 20.00
Mineral Water, Artesian Spring Co., Ballston, N.Y., Yellow Olive, Pt. 112.00
Mineral Water, Boyd & Beard, B-Patent, Emerald Green, Sloping Collar, IP, 6 3/4 In. ... 90.00
Mineral Water, Bridgeton Glass Works, N.J., Blue Green, Metal Band Closure, 7 3/8 In. . 160.00
Mineral Water, Buffalo Lithia Water, Seated Woman, Orange Amber, 1/2 Gal. 1345.00
Mineral Water, Clarke & Co., New York, Deep Olive Green, Qt. 66.00
Mineral Water, Congress & Empire Spring Co., C, Saratoga, N.Y., Olive Green, Qt. 72.00
Mineral Water, Congress & Empire Spring Co., C, Saratoga, N.Y., Yellow Olive, Qt. 476.00
Mineral Water, Congress & Empire Spring Co., E, Saratoga, N.Y., Blue Green, Qt. 85.00
Mineral Water, E. Jenckes, Emerald Green, Block Mouth, Iron Pontil, 7 1/8 In. 235.00
Mineral Water, E.S. & H. Hart, Superior Soda Water, Teal Blue, 7 5/8 In. 200.00
Mineral Water, Excelsior Spring, Saratoga, N.Y., Red Amber, Pt. 106.00
Mineral Water, F. Schrader, Scranton, Pa., S, Emerald Green, Block Mouth, 7 1/8 In. 179.00
Mineral Water, G. Upp Jr., York, Pa., Emerald Green, Blob Top, IP, 7 1/4 In. 532.00
Mineral Water, G.A. Kohl, Lambertville, N.J., Blue Green, Sloping Double Collar, 7 In. . 235.00
Mineral Water, Gettysburg Katalysine Water, Yellow Green, Qt. 88.00
Mineral Water, H. Ingermann's, XXX Ale, Amber, Applied Mouth, Wire Closure, Qt. ... 125.00
Mineral Water, H.L. & J. W. Brown, Hartford, Ct., Emerald Green, Pontil, 7 1/8 In. 78.00
Mineral Water, Harrisburg Bottling Works, Yellow Olive, Applied Mouth, 8 1/2 In. 896.00
Mineral Water, Hawthorne Spring, Saratoga, N.Y., Emerald Green 33.00
Mineral Water, Highrock Congress Spring, C & W, Teal Blue, Double Collar, Pt. 224.00
Mineral Water, J. Cosgrove & Son, Cobalt Blue, Blob Top, Wire Closure, 7 1/2 In. 450.00
Mineral Water, J. Stouffer, Tannersville, Emerald Green, Blob Top, IP, 7 1/2 In. 392.00
Mineral Water, J. Wise, Allentown, Pa., Deep Cobalt Blue, Blob Top, 7 1/4 In. 168.00
Mineral Water, John H. Gardner & Son, Sharon Springs, N.Y., Blue Green, Pt. 202.00
Mineral Water, Ledlie, Trenton, N.J., Grass Green, Sloping Double Collar, 6 7/8 In. 56.00
Mineral Water, Meyer & Rotman, New York, Blue Green, Blob Top, IP, 7 1/4 In. 146.00
Mineral Water, Middletown Healing Springs, Grays & Clark, Yellow Amber, Qt. 90.00
Mineral Water, Oak Orchard Acid Springs, Yellow Amber, Qt. 89.00

Bottle, Milk, Beverly
Farms, Chocolate Milk,
Red ACL, 1/2 Pt.

Bottle, Pickle, Frank
Vogel Co., Gherkins,
Allegheny, Pa., Label, 7 In.

Bottle, Poison, Ceramic,
C2h5OH, Painted Devil, Skull,
Crossbones, 6 In.

Mineral Water, Pavilion United States, P, Saratoga, N.Y., Yellow Green, Pt. 190.00
Mineral Water, Rutherford's, Cincinnati, Cobalt Blue, 10-Sided, IP, 7 3/8 In. 476.00
Mineral Water, Saratoga Red Spring, Blue Green, Pt. 123.00
Mineral Water, Saratoga Spring, Olive Green, Pt. 168.00
Mineral Water, Star Spring Co,.Saratoga, N.Y., Amber, Pt. 134.00
Mineral Water, Swaim's Panacea, Philada, Yellow Olive, Pontil 990.00
Oil, Standard Oil Company, Electric Cycle Oil, Paper Label, Late 1800s, 5 3/8 In. 440.00
Pepper Sauce, Cathedral, 6-Sided, Blue Green, Double Collar, OP, 8 5/8 In. 300.00
Pepper Sauce, Cathedral, 8-Sided, Deep Forest Green, Double Collar, 9 In. 3024.00
Pepper Sauce, Cathedral, Blue Green, 6-Sided, Applied Lip, 1850, 8 3/4 In. 489.00
Pepper Sauce, Cathedral, Blue Green, 6-Sided, Applied Ring Lip, 1850, 9 In. 719.00
Perfume bottles are listed in their own category.
Pickle, Cathedral, 6-Sided, Rolled Lip, 13 1/2 In. 179.00
Pickle, Cathedral, Green, c.1850, 14 In. 400.00
Pickle, Cathedral, Light Blue Green, Rolled Lip, IP, 8 3/4 In. 224.00
Pickle, Cathedral, Medium Teal Blue, Green Tone, Rolled Lip, 11 7/8 In. 616.00
Pickle, Cathedral, R. & F. Atmore, Blue Aqua, Rolled Lip, Pontil, 11 1/2 In. 308.00
Pickle, Cathedral, Teal Blue, Rolled Lip, 11 7/8 In. 616.00
Pickle, Frank Vogel Co., Gherkins, Allegheny, Pa., Label, 7 In. .... *Illus* 35.00
Pickle, Goofus Glass, Cobalt Blue, Rose Design, Ground Lip, 1910, 15 1/4 In. 3360.00
Pickle, Goofus, Vase Shape, Flowers, Medium Topaz, 1880-1910, 15 In. 530.00
Pickle, Green, Applied Top, 11 In. 35.00
Pickle, Shaker Society Home Made Ripe Cucumber Pickles, Yellow Olive, 7 In. 450.00
Pickle, Skilton Foote & Co., Bunker Hill Pickles, Yellow Olive, 7 3/4 In. 235.00
Poison, 3-Sided, Tooled Mouth, 3 In. 168.00
Poison, 6-Sided, Green, Tooled Top 55.00
Poison, A.M. Bickford & Sons Ltd., Yellow Amber, Diamond Shape, 8 3/4 In. 110.00
Poison, Bowman's Drug Store, C.L.G. Co., Cobalt Blue, Irregular 6-Sided, 4 1/2 In. 134.00
Poison, Ceramic, C2H5OH, Painted Devil, Skull, Crossbones, 6 In. .... *Illus* 65.00
Poison, Cobalt Blue, Embossed Poison, Tooled Mouth, 5 1/4 In. ....123.00 to 125.00
Poison, Federation Francaise Druggists, Apple Green, 6-Sided, Skulls On Panels, 11 In. ... 840.00
Poison, Golden Yellow Amber, Tooled Lip, Mercury Bichloride Poison, Upjohn, 1890 ... 95.00
Poison, J.T.M. Co., Poison, Amber, Tooled Lip, 5 In. 530.00
Poison, Olive Green, Hobnail Pattern, Flask, Pontil, Sheared Lip, 5 5/8 In. 110.00
Poison, Owl Drug Co., 2-Winged Owl On Mortar & Pestle, Cobalt Blue, 1910, 4 In. 110.00
Poison, Owl Drug Co., Cobalt Blue, 9 3/4 In. 560.00
Poison, Owl Drug Co., Owl On Mortar & Pestle, Cobalt Blue, Triangular, Label, 9 1/2 In. 840.00
Poison, Ripley Co., New York, Citron, Tooled Top 22.00
Poison, Santonin, Skull & Crossbones, White Letters, Germany, 5 5/8 In. 840.00
Poison, Sharp & Dohme, Baltimore, Green Antiseptic Disks, Amber, Cork, 4 3/4 In. 235.00
Poison, Skull & Crossbones, Amber, Tooled Top, 2 1/2 In. 55.00
Poison, Strychnia, Poison, Oval, Outward Rolled Lip, 2 3/8 In. 125.00
Poison, Wm. Radam's Microbe Killer, Amber, Shield Shape Label, 10 1/4 In. 145.00
Powder Horn, Blown, Amber, Sheared Mouth, Tooled Neck, Applied Ring, 13 1/4 In. ... 670.00
Sake, Silver Overlay Of Poppies, White Blossom, Blue Leaves, 7 3/4 In. 440.00
Sarsaparilla, Dr. Townsend's, Albany, N.Y., Blue Green, Iron Pontil, 9 3/8 In. 840.00
Sarsaparilla, Dr. Townsend's, Albany, N.Y., Green, Tooled Top, M On Base 88.00
Sarsaparilla, Dr. Townsend's, Albany, N.Y., Moss Green, Double Layer Applied Top 130.00
Sarsaparilla, Dr. Townsend's, Albany, N.Y., Olive Green, Pontil, 9 1/2 In. 308.00
Sarsaparilla, Dr. Townsend's, Albany, N.Y., Peacock Teal, Applied Top 155.00
Scent, Cobalt Blue, Swirled Ribs, Applied Clear Rigaree, 3 1/4 In. 192.00
Scent, Cranberry, Enameled Flowers, Footed, 9 In. 99.00
Scent, Justice Perry, Purple, Flattened Globular, 1815, 1 7/8 In. 2420.00
Scent, Penslar, Green, Tooled Mouth, Stopper, Pinched Waist, 1890, 6 In. 85.00
Scent, Scallop Form, Black Amethyst, Pontil, Tooled Mouth, 1830, 2 1/2 In. 336.00
Scent, Scallop Form, Cobalt Blue, Sheared Mouth, 1870, 2 1/4 In. 156.00
Scent, Scallop Form, Sapphire Blue, Tooled Lip, 1859, 1 3/4 In. 308.00
Scent, Scrolled Silver Overlay, Red Glass, Stopper, c.1920, 3 3/8 In. 70.00
Scent, Sunburst, Amethyst, Pontil, Tooled Lip, 1830, 1 3/4 In. 365.00
Scent, Sunburst, Cobalt Blue, 18 Beads, Pontil, Tooled Lip, 1830, 2 7/8 In. 588.00
Scent, Sunburst, Cobalt Blue, 30 Beads, Pontil, 1830, 2 7/8 In. 560.00
Scent, Sunburst, Cobalt Blue, Pontil, Tooled Lip, 1830, 2 5/8 In. 670.00
Scent, Sunburst, Teal Green, Pontil, Tooled Lip, 1830, 2 In. 3080.00

Seal, EG, In Embossed Heart, Black Glass, Scarred Kick-Up, 9 1/8 In. 1456.00
Seal, H. Rickett's & Co., Glass Works Bristol, Black Glass, 12 1/2 In. 250.00
Seal, Middle Temple, Black Glass, Pontil, America, 1840-1860, 11 1/4 In. 210.00
Seal, R.I. Olborne, Mallet, Black Glass, England, 1735, 7 In. 3360.00
Snuff, 2 Fish, Lily, Tan & White, 2 3/8 In. 125.00
Snuff, 3-Color Overlay, Bubble Glass, Crickets, Plants, Chinese, 19th Century, 2 1/2 In. . . . 259.00
Snuff, A. Delpit No. 16, Golden Yellow Amber, Iron Pontil, Flared Lip, 1860, 4 1/4 In. 2016.00
Snuff, A. Delpit No. 16, St. Louis St., New Orleans, Gold Yellow, IP, 4 1/4 In. 2016.00
Snuff, A. Delpit No. 16, Yellow Olive Amber, Iron Pontil, Flared Lip, 1860, 4 3/4 In. 1344.00
Snuff, Adventurine, Blue, Carved, Boy Playing With A Butterfly, 2 In. 100.00
Snuff, Agate, 2 Swimming Fish, Orange & Brown, Tan Ground, 2 In. 125.00
Snuff, Agate, Cameo, Carved, Sage & Attendant, Seated On Rock, 19th Century, 2 1/4 In. 575.00
Snuff, Agate, Carved, Crouching Monkey Holding Peach, Chinese, 2 1/4 In. . . . . . . 144.00 to 145.00
Snuff, Agate, Carved, Man, Child With Bird, Mountain, Rectangular Shape, 3 1/8 In. 1250.00
Snuff, Agate, Dragons, Brown, White, Ochre, Chinese, 2 1/4 In. 460.00
Snuff, Agate, Insects, Bird, Vines, Black & Brown, 2 1/4 In. 600.00
Snuff, Agate, Interior Painted, Children, Coral Stopper, Chinese, 2 3/4 In. 115.00
Snuff, Agate, Lavender, Carved, Archaic Ribbed Vessel, Late 19th Century, 2 1/2 In. 145.00
Snuff, Agate, Orange, Red, Tan, 2 3/4 In. 150.00
Snuff, Amber, Carved, Fish, Water Plants, Etched Calligraphic Poem, Chinese, 3 In. 575.00
Snuff, Amethyst, Carved, Buddha Shape, Removable Hat, 2 1/2 In. 150.00
Snuff, Amethyst, White & Purple Design, 1 7/8 In. 100.00
Snuff, Aquamarine, Spade Shape, Relief Carving, Dragon, Pearl, Glass Stopper, 2 In. 575.00
Snuff, Black & White Jade, Carved Verso One Side, Lady Standing In Garden, 3 In. 300.00
Snuff, Blue Chalcedony, 2 3/8 In. 100.00
Snuff, Blue Chalcedony, Flower Design, 2 5/8 In. 250.00
Snuff, Blue Chalcedony, Inclusions, 2 1/4 In. 250.00
Snuff, Botswana Agate, Banding Pattern, 2 1/4 In. 100.00
Snuff, Botswana Agate, Carved, Horse 125.00
Snuff, Cameo Agate, Oval Shape, Red Carp, Gray Blue Ground, Agate Stopper, 2 In. 575.00
Snuff, Cameo Agate, Oval, Relief, Lui Hai, Frog, Brown On Tan Ground, 2 In. 345.00
Snuff, Carnelian Agate, Rooster, Jui Carving, Jadeite Stopper, 19th Century, 2 1/2 In. 259.00
Snuff, Chalcedony Agate, Flatted Oval, Man On Buffalo Back, Russet Parts, Chinese 690.00
Snuff, Chinese Calligraphy, Double Happiness, Yellow Ground, 2 3/4 In. 175.00
Snuff, Cinnabar, Lacquer, Miniature Vase Shape, 2 Reserve Panels, Chinese, 2 1/2 In. 69.00
Snuff, Cinnabar, Phoenix In Flight, Banana Leaves, 19th Century, 2 3/4 In. 173.00
Snuff, Cloisonne, Double Bottle, Light Blue, Indian Lotus Design, 2 3/4 In. 75.00
Snuff, Cloisonne, Enameled, Flattened Oval, Scholar's Symbols, Stopper, 1900s, 2 3/4 In. . 90.00
Snuff, Cloisonne, Seed Shape, Thousand Flowers Design, Blue Ground, 2 5/8 In. 185.00
Snuff, Coral, Fossilized, 2 3/8 In. 100.00
Snuff, Crystal, Black Rutiles, 2 1/2 In. 400.00
Snuff, Crystal, Golden Rutiles, 2 1/8 In. 450.00
Snuff, Crystal, Purple Gauze, 2 In. 750.00
Snuff, Deep Olive Green, Square, Tooled Mouth, 6 1/4 In. 392.00
Snuff, Enamel On Glass, Spade Shade, Celadon, Lapis Lazuli Stopper, 19th Century, 3 In. 375.00
Snuff, Fraserite, Carved, Dinosaur, 1 7/8 In. 75.00
Snuff, Glass, Chinese Characters, Opaque White Over Red, 2 3/4 In. 198.00
Snuff, Glass, Double Overlay, Lotus Flowers, Green & White Over Rose, 3 1/2 In. 130.00
Snuff, Glass, Double Overlay, White On Red, Children, Bats, Scroll, 2 1/2 In. 259.00
Snuff, Glass, Interior Painted Landscape & Figural, Su Quidong, 10th Century, 4 3/4 In. . . 230.00
Snuff, Glass, Lime Green Overlay, Stopper, Silver Spoon 115.00
Snuff, Glass, Overlay, Chinese Figures, Water Garden, Yellow Over White, 3 In. 230.00
Snuff, Glass, Red Overlay, Clear Ground, Flattened Oval, 19th Century, Chinese 545.00
Snuff, Glass, Swirled, Honey Amber, Chinese, 19th Century, 2 3/4 In. 115.00
Snuff, Glass, Temple Jar Shape, Polychrome Flower Design, Amethyst Stopper, 2 3/8 In. . 258.00
Snuff, Goldstone, Dark Green, Carved, Phoenix, 2 7/8 In. 100.00
Snuff, Hardstone, Button Finial, Sloping Shoulders, Carved Boy & Fish, 2 1/2 In. 45.00
Snuff, Howlite, Dragonfly, Flowering Plant, 2 3/4 In. 75.00
Snuff, Howlite, Horse, 3 1/8 In. 75.00
Snuff, Iron, Carved, Red Rooster, 2 In. 100.00
Snuff, Ivory, Carved As Squirrel, Bunch Of Grapes, 19th Century, 2 In. 230.00
Snuff, Ivory, Carved In The Round, Immortal Boy, Chinese, 19th Century, 4 In. 345.00
Snuff, Ivory, Erotic, Engraved, Polychrome Scenes, Men, Women, 20th Century, 3 1/4 In. . 185.00

Snuff, Ivory, Head & Shoulders Portrait, Bearded Dignitary, Court Costume, 2 1/4 In. 92.00
Snuff, Jade, Carved In Basket Form, Celadon Green, 18th Century, 2 1/4 In. 805.00
Snuff, Jade, Carved, Rabbit, 2 3/4 In. 150.00
Snuff, Jade, White, Cockerels, Calligraphy, Brown Parts, Flattened Rectangular, Chinese . 1270.00
Snuff, Jade, White, Flattened Oval, Chinese 1270.00
Snuff, Jadeite, Carved Figure, 2 3/4 In. 650.00
Snuff, Jadeite, Scenic View, Pine Tree, Bat, Clouds, 2 3/4 In. 650.00
Snuff, Jasper Agate, Flattened Rectangular, Incised Brocade Turban, Chinese 400.00
Snuff, Jasper, Pig, 2 1/2 In. 90.00
Snuff, Jasper, Red, 2 Frogs, Moth, Carved Lily Leaf, 2 In. 75.00
Snuff, Jasper, Red, Double Bottle, Carved, Elephant & Tall Grass, 2 In. 200.00
Snuff, Jasper, Red, Two Frogs, Moth, Carved Lily Leaf, 2 In. 75.00
Snuff, Jasper, Red, Two Horses, 2 1/4 In. 90.00
Snuff, Jasper, Red, White Fish, Tan Lily Leaf, 2 1/4 In. 175.00
Snuff, Lapis, Dark Blue, Carved, Quan Yin, Seated, 2 1/8 In. 225.00
Snuff, Lead Crystal, Painting Of 2 Asian Women, 3 1/4 In. 100.00
Snuff, Malachite, Phoenix Bird, 2 1/8 In. 150.00
Snuff, Milk Glass, Bok-Choy Cabbage, Green Leaves, Overlaid, Chinese, 2 1/2 In. 259.00
Snuff, Mongolian Silver, Dragon Panels, Turquoise Top, 2 3/4 In. 125.00
Snuff, Mother-Of-Pearl, Carved, Bird On Flowering Branch, 2 In. 150.00
Snuff, Mother-Of-Pearl, Carved, Two Dolphins, 2 1/8 In. 150.00
Snuff, Nephrite Jade, Pebble Shape, Red Skin Area, Coral Stopper, 18th Century, 2 1/2 In. 315.00
Snuff, Ocean Jasper, 1 7/8 In. 100.00
Snuff, Ocean Jasper, 2 1/4 In. 100.00
Snuff, Opal, Hawk Perched In Pine Tree, 2 1/8 In. 75.00
Snuff, Painted Agate, Children At Play, Ring Handles, Square, Chinese 1150.00
Snuff, Peking Glass, 5 Deer, Pine Tree, Crane, 2 5/8 In. 450.00
Snuff, Peking Glass, Green Overlay, Pink, White Ground, Chinese, 19th Century, 3 In. . . . 200.00
Snuff, Picture Jasper, Foo Dog, 2 3/8 In. 100.00
Snuff, Porcelain, Erotic, Spade Shape, Relief Figure Design, Porcelain Stopper, 2 3/4 In. . 200.00
Snuff, Porcelain, Lotus Plant, Green, Chinese, 19th Century, 2 3/4 In. 115.00
Snuff, Porcelain, Spade Shape, Figural Landscape, Mother-Of-Pearl Stopper, 2 In. 290.00
Snuff, Porcelain, Underglaze, Blue, Cylinder Shape, Dragon, Late 19th Century, 3 1/4 In. . 29.00
Snuff, Porcelain, Underglaze, Red, Blue, Figural Design, Landscape, Ivory Stopper, 3 In. . 210.00
Snuff, Puddingstone, Flattened Oval, Mask, Mock Ring Handles, Jade Stopper, 1 3/4 In. . . 138.00
Snuff, Pyrite, Gold, Carved, Buddha, Seated, 2 1/4 In. 80.00
Snuff, Quartz, 2 Black Rutiles, 2 1/8 In. 500.00
Snuff, Quartz, Carved, 2 Fish, Gold Rutiles, 2 3/4 In. 400.00
Snuff, Rock Crystal, 2 1/4 In. 150.00
Snuff, Ruby, Carved, Buddha Shape, Removable Hat, 2 1/4 In. 600.00
Snuff, Ryolite, Spring Of Coins, 2 1/2 In. 85.00
Snuff, Silver Plate, Enamel Nude, Marked, Alpaka, Brudro, c.1920, 2 1/4 In. 138.00
Snuff, Smoky Quartz, Carved In Shape Of Double Cicada, 2 3/8 In. 400.00
Snuff, Smoky Quartz, Carved, Shou-Lo Holding Peach Of Immortality, c.1920, 2 3/4 In. . 175.00
Snuff, Stone, Purple Gold, Carved, Dragon, 2 3/8 In. 100.00
Snuff, Tiger Iron, Giraffe, 2 1/2 In. 75.00
Snuff, Tiger Skin, Foo Dog, 2 1/4 In. 90.00
Snuff, Tiger-Eye Quartz, Lapis Stopper, Box, Chinese, 2 1/2 In. 90.00
Snuff, Tourmaline, Green, Carved, Buddha, 2 1/4 In. 1000.00
Snuff, Wood, Carved, Scenic View, 2 3/4 In. 75.00
Snuff, Zebra Stone, 2 1/4 In. 100.00
Soaky, Alvin, Upturned Red Baseball Cap, White Sweater, Holding Harmonica, 1963 . . . . 35.00
Soaky, Blabber Mouse, 1960s 55.00
Soaky, Mr. Magoo, Salesman's Sample 60.00
Soaky, Porky Pig, Salesman's Sample, 1960s 45.00
Soaky, Rocky & Bullwinkle, 1960s, Pair 65.00
Soaky, Top Cat, 1960s 70.00
Soaky, Tweety Bird, Salesman's Sample 45.00
Soda, Aqua, Ramroth Mineral Water, Troy, N.Y., Hutchinson, 1882 . . . . 7.00
Soda, Bay City, Star, Sapphire Blue 120.00
Soda, Boley & Co., Sac City, Ca., Graphite Pontil 242.00
Soda, Byars, N. Hoosick, N.Y., Hutchinson, 1882 . . . . 10.00

Soda, Carl Puck, Hoboken, N.J., Aqua, Hutchinson 8.00
Soda, Chase & Co., Stockton, Ca., Graphite Pontil 415.00
Soda, Dobler Brewery, Embossed Hand & Mug, Amber, Blob Top 10.00
Soda, E.S. Hart, Canton, Ct., Superior, Blue Aqua, Blob Top, Pontil, 7 5/8 In. 146.00
Soda, Eagle, Slug Plate, Green Teal, Graphite Pontil 230.00
Soda, Emerald Green, Yellow Tint, 8-Sided, Blob Top, IP, 7 1/2 In. 90.00
Soda, Erie Bottling Works, Utica, N.Y., Clear, Hutchinson 10.00
Soda, G.P. Morrill, Blue Teal 440.00
Soda, Grapefruit Sparkling Drink, Rampant Lion Within Shield, 7 In. 64.00
Soda, Green & Young, Schnectady, This Bottle Not To Be Sold, Aqua, Hutchinson 6.00
Soda, H. Sproat, Ice Blue, Torpedo Shape, Applied Sloping Collar, c.1850, 8 In. 1120.00
Soda, Hennessy & Nolan Ginger Ale, Aqua, Hutchinson, 1879 .... 10.00
Soda, Hennessy & Nolan, Albany, N.Y., Embossed Capital Building, Clear, Hutchinson .. 15.00
Soda, Hulschizer & Co., Premium, Slug Plate, Blue Green, 8-Sided, Blob Top, IP, 7 1/2 In. 900.00
Soda, Humboldt Artisan, Green Streak, Eureka, Ca. 55.00
Soda, John Mynderse, Schenectady, N.Y., Embossed Eagle, Clear, Hutchinson 12.00
Soda, King Syphon, Chrome Plated, Firm's Logo, N. Bel Geddes, 9 1/4 In., 3 Piece 1150.00
Soda, Koshist Bros., Nassau, N.Y., Amber, Blob Top 10.00
Soda, L & B, Blob Top, Graphite Pontil 120.00
Soda, M.B. & Co., M On Base, 1860, 7 1/4 In. 35.00
Soda, N. Richardson & Son, Trenton, N.J., Light Blue Green, Squat 17.00
Soda, N.C. Peterson, Laramie, Wy., Applied Top 100.00
Soda, Owen Casey Eagle Soda Works, Cobalt, Blob Top, Bubbles 198.00
Soda, Owen Casey Eagle Soda Works, Green Aqua, Blob Top 70.00
Soda, Owen Casey Eagle Soda Works, Green, Blob Top 130.00
Soda, Owen Casey Eagle Soda Works, Sapphire Blue, Blob Top 77.00
Soda, Owen Casey Eagle Soda Works, Steel Blue, Blob Top, Bubbles 176.00
Soda, Pacific Congress, Green Aqua, Big Top 35.00
Soda, Pacific Congress, Saratoga, Ca. 415.00
Soda, Pomroy & Hall, Blue Green, Mug Base, Blob Top, Pontil, 7 5/8 In. 1065.00
Soda, Sages Pacific Congress, Saratoga, Ca., Lime Green, Running Deer 825.00
Soda, Scout Hola Canadian Cola, White & Yellow Label, Quebec, 1926 .... 18.00
Soda, Seitz & Bro., Easton, Pa., Cobalt Blue, 8-Sided, Blob Top, Iron Pontil, 7 1/4 In. ... 530.00
Soda, Siphon, Plated Metal Top, Acid Etched, Blue Glass, 12 1/2 In. 11.00
Soda, Smith & Co., Charleston, Blue Green, 8-Sided, Applied Sloping Collar, 7 3/4 In. ... 728.00
Soda, Spring Bottling Works, Utica, N.Y., Clear, Hutchinson 9.00
Soda, Taylor & Son, Valparaiso, Chili, Teal, Graphite, Bubbles 275.00
Soda, Teal, Marked, ABM, Harry Slutz Philada, Hutchinson, Qt. 69.00
Tantalus, Cut Glass, Book Form, 6 Glasses, Leather Interior, England, 1800s, 15 x 11 In. . 690.00
Tantalus, Oak, Crystal, Silver, Hinged Top, 3 Decanters, Loop Handle, 1900, 13 x 5 In. ... 336.00
Target Ball, Amber, 3-Piece Mold, Diamond Mark 155.00
Target Ball, Blown, 3-Piece Mold, Yellow Amber, Sheared Mouth, 2 3/4 In. 78.00
Target Ball, Blown, 5-Piece Mold, Cobalt Blue, Sheared Mouth, 2 3/4 In. 175.00
Target Ball, Bogardus Glass Ball, Pat'd Apr 10, 1877, Yellow Amber, Diamond, 2 5/8 In. . 500.00
Target Ball, Bogardus Glass Ball, Pat'd Apr. 10, 1877, Amber, Hobnail, 2 5/8 In. 3920.00
Target Ball, Bogardus, Pat'd Apr. 10 1877, Backward 6, Lattice, Green, 2 5/8 In. 1064.00
Target Ball, Bogardus, Pat'd Apr. 10, 1877, Amber, Fishnet Design 540.00
Target Ball, Cobalt Blue, Allover Diamond, Sheared Mouth, 1880-1895, 2 3/4 In. 616.00
Target Ball, Cobalt Blue, Diamond, Man Shooting, 1880-1900, 2 5/8 In. 484.00
Target Ball, Copper Topaz, Allover Diamond, Blank Center Band, 2 5/8 In. 134.00
Target Ball, Dr. A. Frank, Charlottenburg Glashutten, Diamond, Yellow Olive, 2 5/8 In. .. 672.00
Target Ball, E.E. Eaton Guns & C., 53 State St., Chicago, Yellow Amber, 2 5/8 In. 4480.00
Target Ball, For Hockey's Patent Trap, Green Aqua, England, 2 3/8 In. 1008.00
Target Ball, G.O., Smoky Yellow Olive, 3-Piece Mold, 2 5/8 In. 560.00
Target Ball, Ira Paine's Filled Ball, Pat. Oct. 23, 1877, Amber, 3-Piece Mold 575.00
Target Ball, Ira Paine's Filled Ball, Pat. Oct. 23, 1877, Yellow Amber, 2 5/8 In. 475.00
Target Ball, Ira Paine's, Patd Oct 27th 1877, Straw Yellow, Amber Tone, 2 3/4 In. 180.00
Target Ball, Mauritz Widfors, Honey Amber, Scandinavian, 2 5/8 In. 670.00
Target Ball, W.W. Greener, St. Mary's Works, London, Diamond, Sapphire Blue, 2 5/8 In. 364.00
Tonic, Primley's Iron & Wahoo, Jones & Primley Co., Gold Amber, Cleaned, 9 1/2 In. ... 123.00
Tonic, Quinine, Manufactured By G.T.B. Chemical Co., Lexington, Ky., 9 In. 145.00
Tonic, Rohrer's Expectoral Wild Cherry, Lancaster, Pa., Gold Amber, 1875, 10 1/2 In. ... 336.00

Tonic, Rohrer's Expectoral Wild Cherry, Lancaster, Pa., Yellow Amber, IP, 10 1/2 In. 100.00
Vinegar, Maple Sap & Boiled Cider Vinegar, Cobalt Blue, Fluted Shoulders, 11 3/8 In. 840.00
Vinegar, Prairie King, Kansas, Label, 6 In. 60.00
Wax Sealer, 2-Piece Mold, Milk Bottle Shape, Aqua, Tin Lid, Iron Pontil, Qt. 123.00
Whiskey, AAA Old Valley, Embossed Cross, Single-Roll Top, Medium Amber, 1870 .... 1540.00
Whiskey, Backbar, Amber, Silver Overlay, Corn Stalk Decoration, 11 1/4 In. 336.00
Whiskey, Boulevard Bourbon Buneman Mercantile Co., Light Amber, Fifth 88.00
Whiskey, Buchanan's Absolutely Pure Malt, Cannon, Yellow Amber, 9 1/8 In. 532.00
Whiskey, Casey & Kabanaugh, Sacramento, Ca., Amber, Monogram 22.00
Whiskey, Chestnut Grove, Applied Band, Handle, Pontil, Labels, 1858, 9 In. 255.00
Whiskey, Chestnut Grove, C. Wharton On Seal, Amber, Ribs, Double Collar, 9 1/2 In. ... 335.00
Whiskey, Chestnut Grove, C.W. On Seal, Medium Amber, Applied Mouth, Handle, 9 In. . 134.00
Whiskey, Crescent Rye, Backbar, 9 1/4 In. 85.00
Whiskey, Embossed Eagle Liqueur Distilleries, Cincinnati, Yellow, Green, Squat, Qt. 59.00
Whiskey, Glen Lake Export Scotch, Jug, Cream, Black Transfer, Stoneware, 7 In. 390.00
Whiskey, Gold Medal Old No. 7, Jack Daniel's, Cork Stopper, 15 In. 22.00
Whiskey, Hudson Bay Company, Rye 88.00
Whiskey, James Gibb, San Francisco, Ca., Tooled Top, Amber, Qt. 200.00
Whiskey, Jk. F.T. & Co., Phila., Vertical Ribs, Medium Amber, Jug, Pontil, 7 1/4 In. 672.00
Whiskey, Lange & Bernecker, St. Louis, Mo., Amber, Applied Top 415.00
Whiskey, London Jockey Club House Gin, Horse & Rider, Applied Top 300.00
Whiskey, London Jockey Club House Gin, Horse & Rider, Light Green, Applied Top 770.00
Whiskey, London Jockey Club House Gin, Horse & Rider, Olive, Amber, Applied Top ... 165.00
Whiskey, M.G. Landsberg, Chicago, Embossed American Eagle, Amber, 1876, 11 In. 2350.00
Whiskey, Paul Jones, Backbar, Enamel Color, Backbar, 6 3/4 In. 245.00
Whiskey, Spruance Stanley & Co., San Francisco, Horseshoe, Star, Top, 1869, Fifth 55.00
Whiskey, Udolpho Wolfe Schiedam, Aromatic Schnapps, Amber, Applied Top, Pontil 210.00
Whiskey, Udolpho Wolfe Schiedam, Aromatic Schnapps, Applied Top, Graphite Pontil ... 66.00
Whiskey, Udolpho Wolfe Schiedam, Aromatic Schnapps, Yellow, Applied Top, Bubbles .. 100.00
Whiskey, Udolpho Wolfe's Schiedam, Aromatic Schnapps, Green 44.00
Whiskey, Udolpho Wolfe's Schiedam, Aromatic Schnapps, Green, Ambler, Applied Top .. 88.00
Whiskey, Udolpho Wolfe's Schiedam, Aromatic Schnapps, Yellow, Green, Puce 385.00
Whiskey, Voldner's Schiedam, Aromatic Schnapps, Lime, Applied Top, Graphite Pontil .. 198.00
Whiskey, Voldner's Schiedam, Aromatic Schnapps, Olive, Applied Top 77.00
Whiskey, Voldner's Schiedam, Aromatic Schnapps, Olive, Lime, Applied Top, Bubbles ... 99.00
Whiskey, Wildwood, Backbar, 9 1/4 In. 809.00
White Jade, Flattened Egg Shape, Ring Handle, Wooden Stand, Chinese, 14 In. 172.00
Wine, Black Glass, Deep Olive Amber, Onion, Applied String Lip, England, 7 In. 476.00
Wine, Dutch Onion, Applied String Collar, Dark Olive, Flared Top, 8 In. 154.00
Wine, Dutch Onion, Applied String Collar, Light Yellow, Olive 132.00
Wine, M. Russel, Deep Olive Amber, 8-Sided, England, 1755, 8 1/8 In. 1904.00
Wine, Melon Section, Gold Trim, Enameled Flowers, Green Leaves, 14 1/2 In. 175.00
Wine, Onion, Yellow Olive Green, Onion, Sheared Mouth, Magnum, 8 3/4 In. 2576.00

BOTTLE CAPS for milk bottles are the printed cardboard caps used during the past 85 years. Unusual mottoes, graphics, and caps from dairies that are out of business bring the highest prices.

Brookdale Farms, Creamed Cottage Cheese, 2 3/8 In. 3.00
US NTA, National Tuberculosis Assn., Christmas Seals, 1937 .... 15.00
US NTA, National Tuberculosis Assn., Christmas Seals, 1946 .... 5.00
US NTA, National Tuberculosis Assn., Christmas Seals, 1952 .... 1.00

BOTTLE OPENERS are needed to open many bottles. As soon as the commercial bottle was invented, the opener to be used with the new types of closures became a necessity. Many types of bottle openers can be found, most dating from the twentieth century. Collectors prize advertising and comic openers.

4-Eyed Man, Painted, Cast Iron, 3 3/4 In. 65.00
Bucktooth Boy, Cast Iron 105.00
Dog, Boston Terrier, Cast Iron, 9 In. 130.00
Drunk On Lamp Post, Bourbon Street, New Orleans 35.00
Fisherman, Painted, Cast Aluminum, 4 1/4 In. .... *Illus* 40.00

Bottle Opener,
Fisherman, Painted, Cast
Aluminum, 4 1/4 In.

Sweet Annie (*Artemisia annua*) is an herb that can help remove odors from antiques. Put fresh sprigs inside the drawer or box that needs deodorizing and in a few days the smell will be gone.

Goat, Seated, Cast Iron 46.00
Parrot, Colorful, Cast Iron, 4 In. 60.00

BOXES of all kinds are collected. They were made of thin strips of inlaid wood, metal, tortoiseshell, embroidery, or other material. Additional boxes may be listed in other sections, such as Advertising, Battersea, Ivory, Shaker, Tinware, and various Porcelain categories. Tea Caddies are listed in their own category.

Alms, Walnut, Initialed C.J. In Gold & Red, 4 3/4 x 6 1/2 In. 275.00
Apple, Walnut, Arched Top Sides, Narrow Compartment On Side, Lid, 4 3/4 x 12 1/4 In. .. 330.00
Arc De Triomphe, Bronzed Metal, Hinged Lid, Early 20th Century, 9 In. 575.00
Ballot, Top Hat Shape, Uncle Sam's, Deposit Tickets Here, Plastic, 1950, 15 x 15 In. 75.00
Band, Wallpaper Covered, Colored Diamonds, Lines, Scrolls, 3 1/8 x 5 1/4 In. 440.00
Band, Wallpaper Covered, Hannah Dais, Flowers, 10 1/2 In. 1485.00
Band, Wallpaper Covered, Oblong, Cover, 19th Century, 11 1/2 x 17 1/2 x 14 In. 1175.00
Band, Wallpaper Covered, Oblong, Cover, 19th Century, 9 1/2 x 14 1/2 x 11 1/4 In. 590.00
Band, Wallpaper Covered, Scrolled Floral, German Newspaper Interior Base, 3 1/2 x 2 In. 520.00
Bentwood, 1-Finger, Dark Green Paint, Iron Tacks, 5 1/4 x 3 3/8 In. 2420.00
Bentwood, 3-Finger, Lid, Iron Tacks, 9 1/8 In. 250.00
Bentwood, Black Ground, Polychrome House, Tree & Leaves, 1780s, 5 1/4 x 13 3/4 In. ... 1650.00
Bentwood, Design On Lid, Scandinavian, 18th Century, Small 450.00
Bentwood, Lid, Copper Finish, Oval, 5 1/2 x 4 1/8 x 2 1/8 In. 110.00
Bentwood, Old Green Paint, Oval, 5 3/4 x 4 1/4 x 2 3/16 In. 470.00
Bentwood, Oval Lid, Red Paint, Wooden Spring Latches Ends, Staples, 11 x 6 1/2 x 9 In. 220.00
Bentwood, Overlapping Seams, Vining Flowers On Lid, 4 3/4 x 9 In. 250.00
Bentwood, Reddish Brown Paint, Iron Tacks, 1 x 11 3/4 In. 495.00
Bible, Floral Lid, Walnut, Dark Finish, Vining Sides, Wire Nail, 16 3/4 x 12 x 6 In. 80.00
Bible, Jacobean, Oak, Carved, Stand, Linenfold Panel, Turned Legs, 21 x 19 x 15 In. 1265.00
Bible, William & Mary Style, Oak, Stand, Carved Frieze, Legs, c.1890, 22 x 21 x 14 In. .. 518.00
Bible, Wood & Hammered Copper, Slant Lid, Late 19th Century, 9 x 16 In. 123.00
Bird's-Eye Maple, Mahogany, Geometric Inlaid Lid, Applied Silver Heart, 5 x 12 In. 460.00
Blanket, Pine, Red, Mustard Grain Finish, Blue, White Wallpaper Interior, 37 x 15 In. ... 330.00
Bonnet, Formed, Orange Paper, Black & Gold Sunbursts, Metallic Gold Thread, 9 x 6 In. 855.00
Book Form, Gold Edges, Inlaid Hearts & Diamonds, Hidden Drawer, 9 3/4 In. 410.00
Book Form, Sprucegum, Inlaid Bands, Star & Crescent Moons, Slide Lid End, 5 3/4 In. .. 190.00
Brass Over Wood, Embossed Tavern Scene, Coat Of Arms, 36 x 15 x 20 In. 175.00
Bride's, Bentwood, 2 Hunters, Flowers Around Sides Of Lid, Laced Seams, 8 1/2 x 18 In. 440.00
Bride's, Bentwood, 2 Traveling Men On Lid, Tree, Laced Seams, 7 1/2 x 18 1/2 In. 410.00
Bride's, Bentwood, Rose Vining, German Verse Borders Lid, Laced Seams, 6 x 17 1/2 In. 715.00
Bride's, Overlapping Laced Scenes, Couple In Colonial Dress, 1796, 6 1/2 x 10 In. 495.00
Bride's, Scandinavian, Paint, Lithograph Center Panel, 6 x 18 1/2 x 11 In. 532.00
Bride's, Star On Cover, Black Ground, Tulips & Leaves, Wire Staples, 13 x 8 x 5 In. 1485.00
Burl, Cover, Scallop Feet, Molded Edge, Finial, 1900s, 9 1/4 x 7 In. 110.00
Burl, Hinged Lid, Mid 19th Century, 4 1/2 x 2 3/4 x 2 1/2 In. 115.00
Burl, Tambour Lid, Opens To 1 Drawer, Brass Pull, Bernard Harter, 2 5/8 x 4 5/8 In. 165.00
Camphorwood, Leather, Brass Bail Handles, Tea Paper Lining, Chinese, 3 x 31 In. 430.00

Candle, Cherry, Raised Panel Lid, Wrought Iron Strap Handles, 7 1/2 x 12 1/2 In.	190.00
Candle, Cylindrical, Tin, Scalloped Crest, Japanning, Loop On Back, 5 1/2 x 11 In.	165.00
Candle, Front Sliding Panel, Cutout Crest, Floral Carving On Front, 20 x 8 In.	165.00
Candle, Grain Painted, Dovetailed, Slide Lid, 3 Finger Pulls, Pine, 4 x 15 1/2 x 9 In.	825.00
Candle, Oak, Raised Panel Lid, Tombstone End, Extended Backboard With Hole, 19 In. . .	375.00
Candle, Pine, Dovetailed, Painted, Salmon, Double Slide Lid, Handle, 7 x 12 3/4 In.	3450.00
Candle, Pine, Incised Decoration, Slide Lid, 5 x 8 1/2 x 12 In.	259.00
Candle, Rectangular Storage Box, Faux Grain Painted, 16 1/2 x 12 In.	70.00
Candle, Slide Lid, Building & Landscape, Pegged Construction, Ivory Ground, 8 In.	300.00
Candle, Tin, Round, 2 Hanging Straps, Hinged Lid, Thumb Latch, 14 x 8 x 4 In.	105.00
Candle, Tin, Wall, Brown Paint, Cylindrical, 10 In.	165.00
Candle, Wall, Divided Interior, Gray Over Red Paint, 4 3/8 x 12 In.	520.00
Candle, Wall, Lollipop Crest, Oak, Inlaid Mahogany Heart, 19th Century, 21 In.	795.00
Candle, Wall, Pine, Poplar, Red Brown, Arched Crest, 14 x 6 5/8 x 10 5/8 In.	525.00
Candle, Wall, Poplar, Dovetailed Case, Slant Lid, 20th Century, 9 7/8 x 12 1/2 In.	250.00
Candle, Walnut, Slide Lids, Fixed Handles, 6 x 14 x 7 In.	275.00
Candle, Wooden, Cherry, Chip Carved, Brown, Early 19th Century, 19 1/2 x 5 In.	3000.00
Candle, Wooden, Hanging, Red	850.00
Capo-Di-Monte Style, Gilt Metal Mounted, Oval, 20th Century, 10 1/2 x 6 1/2 x 7 1/4 In.	150.00
Card, Mother-Of-Pearl, Quilted Diamond, Engraved, Partridge, Flower, 4 In.	166.00
Case, Scribe, Rosewood, Lacquer, Brass Inlay, Pen Tray, 2 Inkwells, c.1890, 10 x 5 x 6 In.	635.00
Casket, Ebony, Mahogany, Brass Mount, Bail Handles, Chubb & Son, 10 x 7 In.	690.00
Cellaret, Mahogany, Coffin Shape, Cover, Regency, 19th Century, 32 3/8 x 24 3/4 x 23 In.	1568.00
Chamfered Lid, Wood Paint, Black Sponge Painted Surface, 19th Century, 5 3/4 In.	800.00
Cherry, Slant Lid, Hinged, Scroll Carved Crest, 8 x 13 1/2 x 7 1/4 In.	1765.00
Chinese, Pig Skin, Courting Scene, Joy Symbol, Band Border, 18 x 11 x 6 In.	55.00
Cigarette, 14K Gold, Hammered, Multicolored Gold Band, Monogram, HRH, 3 In.	392.00
Cigarette, Rectangular, Black Enamel, Diamond, Cartier, London, 1936, 3 In.	405.00
Cinnabar Lacquer, Peach Shape, Carved Concubine In Garden, 4 1/2 In.	290.00
Coffer, Ebony, Rectangular, 5 Panels, Inlaid Flowers, Pietra Dura, Italy, 5 1/2 x 6 1/2 In. . .	1265.00
Collar & Cuff, Leatherized Exterior, Brass Shell Catch, Satin Lining, 5 1/2 x 7 1/2 In.	110.00
Curly Maple, Hinged Lid, Bent Wire Handle, Bernard Harter, 2 1/2 x 6 In.	165.00
Curly Maple, Raised Panel Lid, Ivory Handle, Bernard Harter, 2 3/8 x 5 1/8 In.	220.00
Cutlery, George III, Mahogany, Serpentine Sloped Lid, Divided Interior, 14 1/4 In.	1035.00
Cutlery, George III, Satinwood, Inlaid, Metal Lockplate & Handles, 1790, 24 x 9 3/4 In. . .	9000.00
Cutlery, Hinged Tulipwood Lid, Sloped, Star Inlaid Interior, Ring Handle, 1780, 14 3/4 In.	4800.00
Dark Mustard Finish, Light Yellow, Pink Tulips, 12 x 7 1/8 x 3 7/8 In.	770.00
Decanter, Napoleon III, Brass, Mother-Of-Pearl, Marquetry, 10 1/2 x 13 x 9 1/2 In.	1265.00
Decoupage, Cutouts Of Buildings, Animals, E Pluribus Unum, 5 1/4 x 11 In.	3850.00
Deed, Louis XIV, Walnut, Wrought Iron Mounted, Rectangular, 8 x 12 x 9 In.	2300.00
Desk, Ebonized Wood, Inlaid Interior, Bone, Elephant, Matara, 3 x 8 3/8 x 6 3/8 In.	793.00
Desk, Ebonized Wood, Inlaid, Quill, Bone, Slide Lid, c.1900, 2 1/8 x 8 3/4 x 4 1/2 In.	495.00
Desk, Lap, Mahogany, Brassbound, Secret Drawer, England, 8 1/2 x 20 1/2 x 12 In.	460.00
Desk, Mahogany, Satinwood Inlaid, Early 19th Century, 6 3/4 x 12 x 9 In.	690.00
Desk, Mahogany, Walnut, Mother-Of-Pearl, Cartouche, Escutcheon, 6 x 13 3/4 x 9 In. . . .	565.00
Desk, Quill Work, Bone Inlaid, Ebonized Wood, East Indian, 3 3/4 x 8 1/4 x 6 1/4 In.	290.00
Desk, Regency, Brass Mounted, Burgundy Leather, Early 19th Century, 4 x 10 x 7 In. . . .	405.00
Desk, Sorrento Marquetry, Polychromed, Square, c.1900, 2 1/2 x 6 7/8 x 6 3/4 In.	105.00
Desk, Tabletop, Pine, Lift Lid, 9 Compartments, Drawer, 15 x 27 x 19 In.	575.00
Ditty, Oak, Carved, Circles, Bird, Shellac Finish	80.00
Ditty, Pinwheel Carved, Scalloped Base, Scrubbed Salmon	825.00
Ditty, Whalebone, Copper Rivets, c.1850, 3 x 4 1/4 In.	2850.00
Document, Black Paint, Cut Nails, New England, 13 1/2 x 7 x 4 1/2 In.	110.00
Document, Bone Overlay, Bone Feet & Bindings, Floral Scrimshaw & Rabbits, 11 1/2 In.	110.00
Document, Dome Top, Floral, Brass Handle, Captain Whaley, Civil Ware, 9 In.	137.00
Document, Dome Top, Hinged, Burl Elm, Tray, Handles, Qing Dynasty, Chinese, 16 In. . . .	316.00
Document, Dome Top, Leather Covered, Metal Mounts, 16 x 8 1/2 x 9 In.	375.00
Document, Dome Top, Leather, Brass, Lock, Hasp, Handle, Lined, 1810, 10 x 6 x 4 In. . .	220.00
Document, Dome Top, Pine, Brass Bail Pull, Brass Hasp Lock, 5 3/4 x 13 In.	550.00
Document, Hide Covered, Brass Tacks, 12 x 7 x 5 In.	154.00
Document, Leather Covered, Tacks, Original Lining, 13 x 9 x 5 In.	120.00
Document, Leather, Brass Studding, 8 x 14 x 9 In.	130.00
Document, Leather, Maker Logo Interior, Early 1800s, 12 x 7 3/4 x 5 3/4 In.	165.00

Document, Lift Top, Early 18th Century, 28 1/2 x 17 x 27 In. 1150.00
Document, On Stand, Lift Top, Butterfly Hinges, Floral Frieze, 1700s, 28 x 17 x 27 In. . . . 1150.00
Document, Pine, Red Paint, Snipe Hinges, Wallpaper Lining, 18th Century, 5 x 13 In. . . . 250.00
Document, Red Wash, Leather & Hinges Hasp, George Hart, Oct. 23, 1824, 12 x 6 x 7 In. 385.00
Document, Rosewood Veneer, Brass Escutcheon, Lid Medallion, 8 In. 55.00
Document, Rosewood, Bird's-Eye Maple Parquetry, Victorian, 5 x 11 x 8 In. 460.00
Document, Satinwood, Mahogany, Canted Lid, Banded, Lining, George III, 7 x 12 In. . . . 660.00
Document, Tulips, Other Flowers, 19th Century 1210.00
Document, Wooden, Brown Over Yellow, Hinged Section, G.C. Lilley, 19 x 11 In. 385.00
Dog & Child On Lid, France Rails On Base, Bisque, 4 1/2 x 7 In. 110.00
Dome Top, Basswood, Dovetailed, Lock, c.1820-1830, 30 3/4 x 13 x 14 1/2 In. 2450.00
Dome Top, Burled Veneer, Brass Overlay, Handle, Continental, 9 x 4 1/2 x 6 1/2 In. 275.00
Dome Top, Decoupage, Urn, Flowers, Swag, Mustard Colored Ground, 4 x 7 x 10 In. 374.00
Dome Top, Dovetailed Sides, Square Nails, Initialed N.G., Iron Hasp Lock 14 1/4 x 27 In. 190.00
Dome Top, Fruitwood, Bone Inlay, Damask Lined, Footed, 1800s, 9 x 5 x 4 In. 170.00
Dome Top, Grain Paint, Swags, Birds, Basket, Flowers, Red, Yellow, Blue, 19 In. 630.00
Dome Top, Oak, Foliage On Lid, Covered Till & Lock, White Bonnet, 7 1/2 x 14 In. 55.00
Dome Top, Old Red Paint, Yellow Borders, Marbleized Red Paper Lining, 8 x 6 In. 300.00
Dome Top, Original Blue Paint, Star Design, Red, White, 5 1/2 x 3 7/8 x 4 3/4 In. 11500.00
Dome Top, Paper Covered, Snakelike Mottling, 11 x 19 x 12 1/2 In. 80.00
Dome Top, Pigskin, Blue Quilted Fabric, Japan, 5 1/2 x 16 x 5 In. 50.00
Dome Top, Pine, Blue Sky, White Ground, Wire Hinges, 4 1/4 x 2 1/2 x 2 5/8 In. 440.00
Dome Top, Pine, Dovetailed, Bun Feet, Chip Carved Fan & Star, Brass Hinges, 15 x 9 In. 55.00
Dome Top, Pine, Painted, Stylized Flowers, Leafy Vine, Leather Hinges On Lid, 7 x 12 In. 1610.00
Dome Top, White Pine, Green Paint, Yellow Leaves, Striping, c.1830, 18 x 29 x 16 1/2 In. 980.00
Dome Top, Yellow, Black Polka Dots, Salmon Ground, Green Interior, 5 1/4 In. 2300.00
Donut, Lid, Gold, Silver Roses, Handle, Wood, 9 1/8 x 5 In. 165.00
Dovetailed, Lid, Scrolled Feet, Butternut, Pine, 20 x 61 x 16 In. 110.00
Dragees, Louis XVI, Silver Gilt, Gold Mount, Tortoiseshell, Late 18th Century, 2 1/2 In. . 520.00
Dresser, Brass, Tortoiseshell Inlay, Serpentine Front, Sides, c.1880 . . . . 1230.00
Dresser, Mahogany, Traveling, Silver Plated Lids, Fold-Down Mirror, 7 7/8 In. 440.00
Dresser, Mother-Of-Pearl, Diamond Quilted, Mirrored Lid, 1830, 7 1/2 In. 865.00
Dresser, Porcelain, 2 Girls, Large Dog, White Base, Gilt Ribbon, England, 3 1/4 In. 55.00
Dresser, Silver, Tortoiseshell, Heart Form, Silver Harp & Ribbon Swags, 3 1/2 x 4 In. . . . 575.00
Dresser, White Goose, Figural, Tan Luster Base, Orange Branches, England, 5 x 4 1/2 In. . . . 110.00
Enamel, Silver, Stylized Flowers Cover, Art Deco, Round, 3 1/4 In. 980.00
Enamel On Copper, Bilston, c.1770, 1 1/2 x 2 3/4 In. 1095.00
Food, Bamboo, Lacquer, 3 Tiers, Animals, Flowers, Round, Chinese, 1800s, 25 x 16 In. . . 316.00
Game, Black Lacquer, Chinoiserie, Chamfered Corners, c.1850, 15 x 12 In. 840.00
Glass, Black, White Enamel, Brass Mounted, Late 19th Century, 5 1/2 In. 145.00
Glass, Gilt Metal Mounted, Oval, Frosted, c.1870, 7 In. 860.00
Glove, Kingwood, Brass Banded, Inlaid Bone, Hinged Fall Front, 3 1/4 x 10 1/2 x 4 In. . . 299.00
Glove, Rosewood, Inlaid Mother-Of-Pearl, Steel Bail Handle, Velvet, 3 x 10 x 4 In. 265.00
Group, Graduating Size, Covers, Painted, Oval, American, 19th Century, 7 Piece 3105.00
Gun, Mahogany, Brass Mounted, Oblong, Stand, Mid 19th Century, 21 1/2 x 26 x 10 In. . . 750.00
Hat, Tin, Painted, Serpentine Shaped, D.P. Wood, Maj. Gen. 6th Div., Handle, 17 x 17 In. 255.00
Hinged Lid, Silver Plate, Waved Band, Red Velvet Lining, Handles To Sides, 4 3/4 In. . . . 920.00
International Register, Metal, Glass Front, 9 In. 60.00
Iron Hinges, Copper Ring Handle, Stenciled Leaves, Hunter, 2 Deer, 3 3/4 x 10 In. 550.00
Jadeite, Face Cover, 2 Nude Women Standing Interior, 4 3/4 x 3 1/4 In. 1500.00
Jewelry, Allover White & Gold, Enameled Flower Center, Ormolu Feet, 4 x 4 In. 165.00
Jewelry, Bear, Glass Eyes, Switzerland, c.1910, 7 x 8 1/2 In. 460.00
Jewelry, Bird's-Eye Maple, Mother-Of-Pearl Inlay, Rosewood Banding, 12 In. 748.00
Jewelry, Brass Bands, Flowers & Diamond Pierced Design, Medallion On Lid, 7 x 4 In. . . 275.00
Jewelry, Casket, Regency, Rosewood, Sarcophagus, Gilt Bronze Handle, 6 x 10 1/4 x 7 In. 490.00
Jewelry, Diamond Quilted, Velvet Lined Interior, Bone Footed, 6 x 3 In. 230.00
Jewelry, Flowers, Scroll Relief, 8 x 10 x 12 In. 1175.00
Jewelry, Glass, Ruby Cut To Clear, Engraved Ship Pattern, 3 1/2 x 4 1/2 In. 168.00
Jewelry, Green Leather, Rectangular, Clipped Corners, Cartier, 13 1/2 x 8 1/2 In. 345.00
Jewelry, Lacquered, Recessed Panels, Double Lift Lids, Drawers, 13 x 9 x 6 3/4 In. 330.00
Jewelry, Mahogany, Inlaid, Oval Patera, 4 3/4 x 10 x 7 In. 105.00
Jewelry, Mother-Of-Pearl & Paper Flower, Beaded, Hinged Lid, Faille Lined, 1870, 8 In. . . 2415.00
Jewelry, Mother-Of-Pearl Inlay, Floral Paint, Black Lacquer, 2 x 9 In. 125.00

Jewelry, Multiple Woods, Zigzag Inlay, Velvet Lining, Mirror In Lid, 4 3/8 x 6 1/8 In. 110.00
Jewelry, Oak, Walnut, Parquetry, 3 Tiers, Compartmented, Bun Feet, 8 x 16 x 9 In. 730.00
Jewelry, Rosewood, Brass Scrolling, Bead Carved Edge, Regency, 5 x 10 In. 546.00
Jewelry, Rosewood, Coco Bola, Victorian, Mother-Of-Pearl Inlay, Carved, 6 x 12 x 9 In. . . 635.00
Jewelry, Rosewood, Gilt Brass, Marquetry Banded, Silk Lining, 4 5/8 x 9 x 6 3/8 In. 1335.00
Jewelry, Rosewood, Hinged Lid, Front, c.1840, 6 3/4 x 11 3/4 x 10 3/8 In. 200.00
Jewelry, Rosewood, Lined Interior, Bone Finial, 1820s, 4 1/4 x 10 3/4 In. 920.00
Jewelry, Rosewood, Mother-Of-Pearl Inlay, Casket Shape, Hinged, Regency, 7 x 12 x 9 In. 250.00
Jewelry, Rosewood, Mother-Of-Pearl Inlay, Hinged Lid, Fitted, Lift-Out Tray, 7 In. 476.00
Jewelry, Softwood, Stenciled Flower, Paper Lining, Mirror On Interior Cover 22.00
Jewelry, Tortoiseshell, Ivory, Painted Bird Medallion, Fitted, Carved Paw Feet, c.1890 . . . 616.00
Jewelry, Wood, Carved Leaf Design, Hinged Lid, Door, c.1910, 8 1/2 x 7 In. 345.00
Jewelry, Wood, Carved, Dragons, Hinged Lid, 2 Doors, 5 Drawers, 14 x 15 3/4 x 14 In. . . 2645.00
Knife, Birch, Painted Green, 15 1/4 x 9 3/4 x 5 1/2 In. 190.00
Knife, Curly Maple, Canted Sides, Divider, Curved Cutout Handle, 11 x 8 1/2 x 7 1/2 In. . 1320.00
Knife, Inlaid Mahogany, Hinged, Mid 19th Century, 4 1/4 x 9 1/4 x 10 1/2 In. 896.00
Knife, Mahogany Veneer, Wave Curve, 36 Cutouts Interior, England, 9 x 11 x 15 In. 825.00
Knife, Mahogany, Crossbanded, Inlaid, Yew & Holly Stars, Slant Lid, Bracket Feet, 16 In. 1610.00
Knife, Mahogany, Flame, Ebony Stringing, Slant Lid, George III, 14 x 9 x 10 In. 750.00
Knife, Mahogany, Inlaid, Hinged Lid, Interior Shell Inlay, 14 3/8 In. 375.00
Knife, Mahogany, Inlay, Ogee Front, Slope Lid, Ball Feet, 1800s, 17 x 15 x 11 In. 1150.00
Knife, Mahogany, Rosewood Banding, Brass Hardware, Bracket Feet, 16 1/4 In. 1455.00
Knife, Mahogany, Scalloped Front, Fan Inlaid On Lid, Divided Interior, 13 In. 220.00
Knife, Pine, Brown Grained, Handle Ends, Snake Heads, Inset Eyes, Square Nail, 12 In. . . 220.00
Knife, Pine, Mahogany Veneer, Scalloped Corners, 9 x 10 x 15 3/4 In. 550.00
Knife, Poplar, Brown Varnish, Alligatored, Canted Sides, New England, 14 x 8 x 4 In. . . . 85.00
Knife, Satinwood, Geometric Inlaid Edge, Bun Feet, 15 1/2 In. 1256.00
Knife, Satinwood, Inlaid Mahogany, Late 19th Century, 15 1/4 In., Pair 4370.00
Knife, Wooden, Wire Construction, Divider, Canted Sides, 2 5/8 x 14 In. 140.00
Lacquer, Brass Mounted, Parcel Gilt, Crimson, 19th Century, 2 x 12 1/2 x 7 In. 115.00
Lacquer, Gilt Metal Mounted, Flowerhead, Bamboo Trellis Pattern, 1800s, 7 x 8 x 8 In. . . 2040.00
Lacquer, Magic Carpet Design, Russia, 2 x 4 x 3 In. 65.00
Lady's, Leather, Tooled, Front Molded As Bound Books, Interior Shelves, 4 x 6 x 4 In. . . . 518.00
Leather, Brass Tack Borders, Brass Escutcheon, Floral Fabric, Mirror, 10 x 4 3/4 In. 330.00
Leather, Dome Top, Sheet Metal Latch, Hinged, Wallpaper Covered, Floral Stripe 805.00
Leather, Lid, Rosettes, Geometric Design, Brass Ring Handle, Footed, 15 In. 375.00
Leather Covered, Brass Tack Border, Brass Edges, End Handles, 19 x 9 3/4 In. 62.00
Letter, Black Lacquer Ground, Maki-E Decoration, Scrollwork, Japan, 5 1/2 x 1 3/4 In. . . 288.00
Letter, Brass Mounted, Sloped Lid, Brass Strapwork, 2 Handles, Fitted Interior, 15 1/4 In. 630.00
Letter, Mahogany, Serpentine Slanted Lid, Hinged Key Lock, Brass Feet, c.1810 . . . . 476.00
Letter, Rectangular, Divided Interior, 7 1/2 x 10 1/4 x 7 In. 575.00
Letter, Regency, Rosewood, Brass, Satinwood, Tooled Leather, Bun Feet, 5 x 10 In. 575.00
Letter, Regency, Slanted Lid, Stamped Asprey, Early 19th Century, 6 1/2 x 8 1/2 x 4 In. . . 1840.00
Letter, Satinwood, Seaweed Marquetry, 19th Century, 5 3/4 x 8 1/2 x 5 1/2 In. 575.00
Letter, Semicircular Mirror, Heart Cutout Finial, Decals, 18 x 8 1/2 In. 440.00
Letter, Tortoiseshell, Bone, Hinged, Paw Feet, c.1880, 3 1/4 x 8 x 6 In. 308.00
Letter, Walnut, Brass, Dome Top, Hinged, Fitted, England, c.1850, 9 x 4 3/4 In. 505.00
Letter, William IV, Rosewood, Tunbridge Inlay, Sarcophagus Shape, Bun Feet, 5 x 10 In. . 316.00
Lid, Gold Trim, Black Ground, Tommy Fay, Reinholds, Pa., 1898, 11 1/4 x 7 3/8 x 4 In. . . 360.00
Lid, Walnut, Lancaster County, Pennsylvania, Thistle Front, Sides, c.1840, 6 x 6 In. 3200.00
Lunch, Mahogany, Rectangular, Domed, Star & Diamond Inlay, Curved Handle, 9 x 5 In. . 750.00
Mahogany, Birch, Rectangular, Oval Inlay, Hinged Lid, Ball Feet, Inscribed, 6 x 11 x 8 In. 4115.00
Mahogany, Dresser Set, Traveling, Silver Plated Lids, Fold-Down Mirror, 7 7/8 In. 440.00
Mahogany, Hinged Lid, Recessed Brass Handles, Plaque, England, c.1890, 16 x 11 In. . . . 250.00
Mahogany, Lid, Shell Design, Brass Bail Handles, 9 1/4 x 11 1/2 In. 860.00
Mahogany, Marquetry, Inlaid, Cast Brass Handles, Hinged Lid, England, c.1840, 11 1/2 In. 420.00
Mahogany, Satinwood, 2 Brass Handles, Edwardian, Cover, 27 1/8 x 16 x 5 1/2 In. 980.00
Mahogany, Slide Lid, Chamfered Edges, 12 x 7 x 5 1/4 In. 165.00
Mahogany Flame Grained, Canvas Base, Alligatored Varnish, 10 x 5 1/2 x 5 In. 368.00
Maple, Slide Lid, Figured, Painted, Eagle, Scroll, c.1812, 1 3/4 x 5 x 8 In. 18800.00
Medallion, Commemoration, Wellington, British Victories, 19th Century, 1 7/8 In. 518.00
Metal, Enamel People On Balcony Scene Cover, Austria, 5 1/2 In. 978.00
Mirror, Rectangular Frame, Tan Ribbon On Box, 9 1/2 x 6 1/4 In. 1725.00

Box, Mother-Of-Pearl, Mahogany, Inlay,
Interior Compartments, Velvet, 11 x 7 In.

Do you have a large exposed window? Put up glass shelves and fill them with inexpensive, colorful bottles. A burglar would have to break all of it, with accompanying noise, to get in.

Mother-Of-Pearl, Mahogany, Inlay, Interior Compartments, Velvet, 11 x 7 In. . . . . . . *Illus*	690.00
Necessaire, Piano Form, Leather Cover, Music, 2 Perfume Bottles, 6 5/8 In.	546.00
Nesting, Cover, Wooden, Round, Compass Pinwheel, Chip Carved, c.1842, 4 Piece	4465.00
Oblong, Black Over Gilt Stencil Design, Bracket Feet, 24 1/2 x 3 3/4 x 4 In.	72.00
Ointment, Pressed Glass, Opalescent, Diamond & Beading, Pewter Lid, 1 x 2 1/4 In.	168.00
On Stand, Embossed Wheat & Cornucopia, Interior Lock, Short Divider, 20 1/4 In.	275.00
Paint, American Crayon Co., Tin Plate	8.50
Pantry, 2-Finger Joint, Green Paint, 19th Century	688.00
Pantry, Bentwood, Copper Tacks, Ink Initials S.H.B., Handle, 13 1/4 x 13 In.	220.00
Pantry, Bentwood, Cover, Wood Bail Handle, 13 x 10 3/4 In.	770.00
Pantry, Iron Tacks, Wooden Base Pegs, Bentwood, 2 3/4 x 7 In.	605.00
Pantry, Oak & Pine, Rosehead Nails On Lid, Cream Of Tartar, 18th Century, 7 In.	450.00
Pantry, Painted, Green, Red Star On Cover, 6 3/4 In.	110.00
Parchment Scroll, Painted Red, Chinese, 19th Century, 22 x 5 3/4 In.	575.00
Patch, Cloisonne, Pietra Dura, Table Form, Roman Ruins, Flowers, Italy, 1900s, 2 3/4 In.	550.00
Patch, Porcelain, Enamel, Courting Couple Scene, Flowers, Early 20th Century, 3 1/4 In. .	145.00
Patch, Silver, Pietra Dura, Oval, Flat Lid, Peasant Couple, Italy, c.1890, 3 1/4 In.	1380.00
Pencil, ABCs & Numbers, Paper Lithograph On Wood	15.00
Pencil, Robin Hood Shoes, Wood, Celluloid Sliding Top, 7-In. Ruler	15.00
Pencil, Scholar's Companion, Tin, Green, Gold Trim, Child's, 1800s, 6 1/2 In.	29.00
Pencil, Slide Lid, Mustard Panels, Dark Green Paint, 8 x 2 1/4 In.	550.00
Pencil, Uncle Sam, Paper On Wood, Ozark Pencil Co., 1918, 12 x 1 1/4 In.	52.00
Pencil, Wooden, Sliding Lid, Inlaid Slate, Francis Grant Turner, Portsmouth, N.H., 1839 . .	1210.00
People On Patios, 4 Brass Feet, Bamboo On Interior Of Lid, Brass Hinges, 4 x 6 1/2 In. . .	990.00
Pine, Chamfered Edge Lid, Black Graining, Wire Staple Hinges, 13 1/2 x 6 x 5 3/8 In. . . .	690.00
Pine, Cover, Landscape Scene, Verse Contained In Floral Wreath Design, 3 x 8 x 5 In. . . .	5750.00
Pine, Cover, Poplar, Original Red Paint, 12 x 6 1/4 x 5 3/4 In.	300.00
Pine, Faux Curly Maple, Brass Bail, Square Nails, Signed, 19 x 11 In.	495.00
Pine, Houses & Trees All Sides & Cover, Wooden Peg, 13 1/4 x 8 1/2 x 6 1/2 In.	410.00
Pine, Lock, Lid, Red, Dark Brown Graining, 12 1/4 x 10 x 3 1/2 In.	190.00
Pine, Newspaper Lining Dated 1768, Lock, Handle, England, 18th Century, 13 In.	350.00
Pine, Painted, Molded Edges, Turned Feet, Vines, Leaves, Tulips, 11 1/2 x 22 x 13 In. . . .	4600.00
Pine, Slant Lid, Blue, Yellow, Red Flowers, 1884, 4 3/4 x 3 1/4 x 2 3/8 In.	385.00
Pine, Slant Lid, Dovetailed Case, Beaded Edges, Interior Shelf, 6 3/4 x 17 In.	110.00
Pine, Slide Lid, Yellow Line Borders, Chamfered Lid, Square Nails, 11 x 6 7/8 x 4 In. . . .	220.00
Pipe, Cherry, Pierced Hanging Tab, Sloped Sides, 19th Century, 23 1/4 x 6 1/4 x 4 1/4 In.	3525.00
Pipe, Pine, Painted, Green, 16 x 6 In.	195.00
Pipe, Pine, Pierced Back, White Paint, 19th Century, 19 3/8 x 7 1/8 x 4 1/2 In.	489.00
Pipe, Pine, Red Finish, Dovetailed Drawer, 2 Compartments, 1813, 16 3/4 In.	1320.00
Pipe, Pine, Square Nails, Dovetailed Drawer, Brass Pull, Bernie Harter, 18 In.	330.00
Pipe, Wall, Mahogany, Line Inlay, Slant Lid, Scalloped Crest With Heart, 20 3/4 In.	220.00
Pipe, Wall, Pine, Dovetailed Drawer, Wood Peg Construction, 17 In.	330.00
Poplar, Brown Over Yellow Vinegar, Wrought Iron & Brass Hasp Lock, 24 x 12 x 10 In. .	550.00
Poplar, Slide Lid, Comb Design, Eagle 1 Side, Square Nails, 18 x 9 x 12 In.	300.00
Porcelain, Bowtie Shape, 2 Lids, Reserves, Floral Gilt Ground, Germany, 6 1/2 In.	690.00
Pyrographic Rose & Vine Decoration, Flared Sides, Hinged Lid, Arts & Crafts, 14 In. . . .	120.00
Rectangular, Hinged Lid, Kite Escutcheon, Coin Slot Opening, Ball Feet, 10 x 17 In.	940.00
Rosewood, 2 Sections, Painted Canton Enamel Interior, Late 19th Century, 5 x 8 1/4 In. . .	58.00

Rosewood, Brass Bound, Victorian, Scrolling, Hinged, 22 x 20 1/2 x 12 In. 1035.00
Rosewood, Floral Inlay, Line Inlay, Keyhole, 10 3/4 x 7 1/2 In. 22.00
Saffronwood, Cover, Cylindrical, Turned, Pink, Floral Die Cuts, Lehnware, 5 In. 880.00
Saffronwood, Floral Decal, Blue Finial, Pedestal Base, Cover, 3 1/4 In. 550.00
Salt, Pine, Painted, Red, Compass Star Incision, Square Nails, c.1810, 13 x 13 x 7 In. 2150.00
Salt, Wooden, Chip Carved, Melon Knob On Lid, England, c.1635, 7 In. 1450.00
Salt, Wooden, Wall, Softwood, Dovetailed, Arched Back, 4-Compartment Drawer 415.00
Salve, White Comb, Screw Lid, Pottery, Signed, 1 1/2 x 3 1/4 In. 2310.00
Silk, Lacquer, Red, Orange, Scalloped Rectangular Panels, Mahogany, 26 x 12 x 7 In. . . . 110.00
Silver, Embossed, 18 Lohan, Attributes, Early 20th Century, 9 1/2 In. 3000.00
Silver, Hinged Lid, Repousse Peasant Scenes, Continental, c.1880, 1 1/2 x 3 x 2 In. 345.00
Silver Gilt, Hinged Lid, Repousse, Peasant Scene, Dutch, 5 3/4 In. 316.00
Slide Lid, Geometric Design, Ivory Paint, Yellow Veneer, 6 3/8 x 3 x 1 7/8 In. 220.00
Slide Lid, Inlaid, Tapering Sides, Arched End, Heart Carving, c.1850, 2 1/2 x 2 1/2 x 8 In. 4465.00
Softwood, Bombe Shape, Applied Picture Frame Molding, 10 1/2 x 6 1/2 In. 70.00
Softwood, Bombe, Slide Lid, 7 In. 35.00
Softwood, Red, Green, Blue Flowers & Leaves, 11 x 6 1/2 In. 149.00
Specimen, Inlaid Stones, Rectangular, Cover, Lock, Key, Late 19th Century, 3 x 11 x 4 In. 250.00
Storage, Black Paint, Gold, Red Striping, Initials, Late 19th Century, 4 1/2 x 9 1/4 x 5 In. 316.00
Storage, Black, Red Grain Paint, Yellow Geometric Linear Border, 7 x 23 1/2 x 17 In. . . . 4025.00
Storage, Flowers, Leaves, Oriental, Repainted, 29 1/2 x 20 1/2 x 20 In. 165.00
Storage, Hinged Lid, Pine, Rectangular Shape, Black, White, Gray Smoke Design, 8 In. . 575.00
Storage, Lid, Bentwood, Brown Finish, Steel Tacks, Bail Handle, 11 1/2 x 6 1/2 In. 190.00
Storage, Lid, Bird's-Eye Maple, Mahogany Veneer, Silver Heart, 5 x 12 x 7 In. . . . . *Illus* 460.00
Storage, Lift Top, Turned Feet, 1850s, 17 1/4 x 62 x 17 1/4 In. 88.00
Storage, Oak, Carved, Molded Edge, Chip Carved Edges, Cover, 12 1/2 x 30 x 17 In. . . . 385.00
Storage, Overhanging Lid, Pine, Grain Painted, Mid 19th Century, 7 3/8 x 11 x 7 3/4 In. 430.00
Storage, Pine, 6-Board, Rosehead Nails, 1800, 13 1/2 x 26 x 15 In. 130.00
Storage, Pine, Scrollwork, Green, Yellow, Red, Blue, Black Enameled, 1830 . . . . 4600.00
Storage, Pine, Wall Mounted, New England, Early 19th Century, 8 1/2 x 14 1/2 x 3 5/8 In. 345.00
Storage, Satinwood, Mahogany, Grapevine Brass Handle, Compartments, 4 x 12 x 9 In. . . 1585.00
Strong, Cast Iron, Lift Top, Yellow, White, 6 1/2 x 15 x 8 In. 58.00
Strong, Iron, Oval Top, Original Rat Hole, No Key, Early 1800s, 25 x 17 x 15 In. 275.00
Strong, Steel, Brass, Engraved, Red Velvet Interior, Handles, c.1900, 5 1/2 x 7 In. 3000.00
Stud, Campaign Style, Edwardian, Brass Inlaid, Mahogany, Square, 4 1/2 x 8 x 8 In. 230.00
Sweetmeat Coffer, Gold & Black Lacquer, Giltwood, 4 1/2 x 15 x 12 1/4 In. 1495.00
Tantalus, Napoleon III, Boulle, Marquetry, Late 19th Century, 10 1/4 x 13 1/8 x 10 1/4 In. 575.00
Tartanware, Prince Charlie, Egg Form, Ivory Finial, Bands Of Gilt Linework, 3 1/4 In. . . 290.00
Tea, 2 Compartments, Diamond Quilted, Square Covers, Bone Finials, 3 3/4 In. 575.00
Tea, Burl, Double Section, Brass Inlay, Fitted Interior, Mixing Bowl, 1830s, 7 1/2 In. 690.00
Tea, Inlaid & Banded Mahogany, 2 Compartments, Mahogany Covers, 4 3/4 x 7 1/2 In. . . 865.00
Tea, Mahogany, 2 Reserves Of Seashells, Interior Covers Of Satinwood, 6 3/4 In. 1265.00
Tea, Mahogany, Ivory Escutcheon, Satinwood Interior, 1780s, 5 In. 546.00
Tea, Mahogany, Oak, Brass Mounted, Bracket Feet, 19th Century, 5 1/2 x 9 x 5 3/4 In. . . 305.00
Tea, Rosewood, Interior Rosewood Cover, Ivory Finial, Velvet Lined, 1840s, 4 1/4 In. . . . 1150.00
Tea, Walnut, Figural Marquetry, Dancing Peasant Couple On Lid, Gleaner Sides, 4 1/2 In. 575.00
Teak, Lift Top, Stepped Interior, Brass Hinges, Drawer, Locking, 19 x 24 x 16 In. 260.00
Tiger Maple, Mitered Construction, Bird's-Eye Maple Back, Sides, 13 1/2 x 7 1/4 In. 110.00
Tiger Maple & Marble, Hinged Lid, Marble Interior, 20th Century, 6 x 4 1/4 In. 345.00
Tin, Oval, Flower Engraved Lid, 2 Hearts, Initials JL, Eagle On Reverse, 4 x 2 1/2 In. . . . 410.00
Tinder, Tin, Candle Socket On Lid, Finger Ring Base, Oversize Striker, Round, 4 In. 410.00
Tobacco, Abalone Shell, Wood Cover, Ivory Ojime, Gourd Shape, 19th Century 115.00
Tobacco, Brass, Hinged Lid, Octagonal, 4 2/3 In. 80.00
Tobacco, Copper Body, Brass Lid & Bottom, Scenes Of Revelry, Dutch, 1 3/8 x 6 1/2 In. . 110.00
Tobacco, Iron & Lead, Admiral Nelson Relief Portrait, British Symbols In Relief, 1800s . . 450.00
Tobacco, Lid, Iron, Chained Slave Kneeling, Humanity, England, c.1770, 3 x 5 In. 2200.00
Tobacco, Prussians Over Austrian Army Victory On Lid, 1770s, 2 x 6 1/2 In. 170.00
Tobacco, Wooden, Inlay, Square, Pierced Bronze Brazier, Passion Flower, Asian, 8 1/2 In. 488.00
Toiletry, Wooden, Floral Inlay, Compartment Interior, Chinese, 1800-1900, 12 x 9 x 7 In. . 520.00
Tortoiseshell, Carved, Figures In Landscape, Chinese, c.1850, 4 In. 345.00
Tortoiseshell, Mahogany, Marquetry, Drawer, India, 19th Century, 8 x 14 x 9 In. 630.00
Tortoiseshell, Maison Giroux, Gilt Ormolu Base, Enamel Medallion, c.1865, 3 In. 525.00
Traveling, Mahogany, Base Drawer, Brass Pull, Inner Fold-Away Mirror, 4 1/2 x 11 In. . . . 140.00

Box, Storage, Lid, Bird's-Eye Maple, Mahogany
Veneer, Silver Heart, 5 x 12 x 7 In.

Box, Writing, Walnut, Brass Frame, Interior
Compartments, 11 1/2 x 8 1/2 In.

Treasure, Silk Brocade Covered, Embroidered, Peking Knot Stitch, Flowers, Fruit, 20 In. . .   166.00
Treasure, Wakahula, Maori, Solid Wood, Shells, Late 1900s, 18 x 4 x 5 1/2 In. 1500.00
Trinket, Pine, Hinged Lid, Red Paint, Wallpaper Lining, 18th Century, 6 In. 495.00
Trinket, Softwood, Log Cabin, Hinged Roof, Home Sweet Home, Hot Springs, N.C., 5 In. . .   275.00
Tulip & Heart Design, Mustard, Red, White, Gray, Turned Black Feet, 21 x 10 3/4 In. 1870.00
Vanity, Traveling, Mirror In Folding Top, Teak, Side Swings Out With Drawers, 8 In. 230.00
Wall, Horizontal Slide Lid, Pine, Red Paint, Pierced Arched Back, 16 x 9 In. 489.00
Wall, Mustard Paint, New England, 19th Century, 27 3/4 x 13 3/4 x 6 1/2 In. 5462.00
Wall, Pine, Red Repaint, Banner, Rose & Square Nail Heads, G. Myers, 1881, 21 In. 275.00
Wall, Taper, Pine, Red Paint, Pierced, 19th Century, 11 3/4 x 2 1/4 In. 3335.00
Walnut, Dovetailed, Slide Lid, 6 x 10 1/2 x 6 1/4 In. 110.00
Watercolor, Children At Play On Labels, Molded Tublets With Horseheads 44.00
Wedding, Lacquer, Chinoiserie, 4 Parts, Japanese, Divided Compartments, 1870, 17 In. . .   420.00
Wood, Black Forest, Lift Top, Mountain Goat Pediment, 14 x 5 x 10 In. 450.00
Wood, Brass, Iron Clasp, Side Handles, Embossed Simulated Straps, 31 x 17 3/4 x 19 In. .   22.00
Wood, Rosewood, Walnut, Inlaid Step-Up Interior, Fruit, Flowers, 14 x 13 x 19 In. 2016.00
Wood, Saffron, Bone Finial, 3 3/4 In. 140.00
Wood, School Girl, Bird's-Eye Maple, Painted, Flowers, Leaves, 4 x 11 x 8 In. 645.00
Wood, Slide Lid, Made From 1 Block, TWB 1847 In Mother-Of-Pearl, 5 x 2 x 2 In. 520.00
Wood, Temptation Of St. Anthony, Early 20th Century 1870.00
Wood, Wall, Painted, Winter Scene, Girl Feeding Sheep, c.1930, 12 x 18 In. 275.00
Work, Dome Top, Rosewood, Ireland, William IV, 7 1/2 x 14 1/2 x 12 In. 635.00
Work, Quill Work, Bone Inlaid, Ebonized Wood, East Indian, 4 1/2 x 10 1/4 x 7 1/4 In. . .   316.00
Writing, Brass, Rosewood, Leather Lined Writing Surface, 7 1/2 x 20 x 10 1/2 In. 1095.00
Writing, Calamander Wood, Compartments, Removable Tray, Pocket, 13 1/2 x 9 3/4 In. . .   430.00
Writing, Gilt Leather Inset, Fitted Interiors, 5 3/4 x 15 1/2 In. 180.00
Writing, Hinged Lid, Ebonized, Inlaid, Divided, Brass Bail Handle, c.1890, 11 1/2 In. 395.00
Writing, Hinged Lid, English Burl Walnut, Brass Bound, c.1870, 6 x 15 3/4 x 9 1/2 In. . .   252.00
Writing, Hinged Lid, Leather, Mahogany Banded, England, 5 1/2 x 15 5/8 x 9 3/4 In. 170.00
Writing, Hinged Lid, Mahogany, Marquetry, Mother-Of-Pearl, England, c.1890, 12 x 9 In.   180.00
Writing, Hinged Lid, Mahogany, Tooled Leather, 5 1/2 x 15 5/8 x 9 3/4 In. 190.00
Writing, Hinged Silver Inlay Lid, Rosewood, Fitted Interiors, 5 x 16 In. 260.00
Writing, Oak, Inlaid Bands, Velvet Interior, 4 1/2 x 13 1/2 x 8 3/4 In. 125.00
Writing, Rosewood, Brass Corners, Center Plate, Fitted Interior, Felt Writing Surface 165.00
Writing, Rosewood, Brass Inlaid Cartouche, Fitted Interior, Inset Handles, c.1850, 12 In. .   336.00
Writing, Rosewood, Mother-Of-Pearl Inlay, Late 19th Century, 3 3/4 x 14 x 9 5/8 In. 415.00
Writing, Slant Top, Inset Panel, Green Paint, Initial HB, 1765, 7 3/4 x 13 In. 200.00
Writing, Walnut, Brass Frame, Interior Compartments, 11 1/2 x 8 1/2 In. . . . .*Illus*   920.00
Writing, Walnut, Brass Nameplate, Escutcheon, Gilt Incised Leather, 5 1/2 x 12 x 9 In. . .   365.00
Writing, Walnut, Painted Fleur-De-Lis Design, Engraved Bronze Plate, 6 1/2 x 11 In. 920.00
Writing, Wood, Leather Covered, Fitted Interior, 5 3/4 x 15 1/2 In. 310.00
Writing Utensils, Gold Lacquer, Black, Leaves, Inkstone, Japan, 9 1/2 x 8 7/8 In. 1095.00

BOY SCOUT collectibles include any material related to scouting,
including patches, manuals, and uniforms. The Boy Scout movement
in the United States started in 1910. The first Jamboree was held in
1937. Girl Scout items are listed under their own heading.

Bulletin, Monthly Issue, May 1938, 16 Pages 10.00

Boy Scout, Patch, Air Force One, National
Capital Area Council, Embroidered, 5 In.

**Lemon oil is a good polish for
brass inside the house. After
polishing brass kept outdoors,
use a thin coat of paste wax to
protect the shine.**

Calendar, Rockwell Print, A Scout Is Reverent, 1954	5.00
Catalogue, Equipment, Self-Mailer, 1950	5.00
Hatchet, Metal Head, Wooden Handle, Marked, Collins, 14 In.	20.00
Hatchet, Steel, Black Matte Paint, Wooden Handle, Marked, Bridgeport, 13 In.	24.00
Jacket, Sea Explores, Canvas, Patch, 1950s	15.00
Knife, Sheath, Remington, Leather Handle, Stamped Boy Scouts Of America, 4-In. Blade	22.00
Manual, Jamboree, Washington, 1935, 4 1/2 x 7 In.	14.00
Patch, Air Force One, National Capital Area Council, Embroidered, 5 In. *Illus*	25.00
Poster, Boy Scout, S.A. Bonds, 3rd Liberty Loan, Leyendecker, 30 x 20 In.	440.00
Rocks & Minerals Kit, 1930s	5.00
Wall Plaque, Oath, Official Emblem, Wooden, 1940s, 3 1/2 x 5 1/2 In.	5.00
Whittling Kit, Deluxe, Manual, Knives, Wooden Box, 1945	75.00

BRADLEY & HUBBARD is a name found on many metal objects. Walter
Hubbard and his brother-in-law, Nathaniel Lyman Bradley, started
making cast iron clocks, tables, frames, andirons, lamps, chandeliers,
sconces, and sewing birds in 1854 in Meriden, Connecticut. The company became Bradley & Hubbard Manufacturing Company in 1875.
Charles Parker Company bought the firm in 1940. Their lamps are
especially prized by collectors.

Andirons, Diamond Design, Arts & Crafts, 20 3/4 In.	440.00
Candlestick, Square Pedestal Form, Brass & Green, Marked, 9 3/4 In., Pair	115.00
Lamp, 8-Panel Shade, Yellow, Green, 4-Armed Spider, 19 3/4 In.	1150.00
Lamp, Butterflies On Panel Shade, Square Standard, Signed, 24 In.	3454.00
Lamp, Gone With The Wind, Oil, Replaced Shade, 1880s	395.00
Lamp, Gone With The Wind, Pale Green Shade, Handles, 23 In.	520.00
Lamp, Hanging, Iron, Horse, Hook, Smoke Bell, Font, 1877	625.00
Lamp, Leaded Glass, Brown, Caramel, Border, Lion-Paw Base, 16 In.	1790.00
Lamp, Leaded Shade, Brown, Caramel Repeating Geometric Designs, 20 In.	2520.00
Lamp, Oil, Metal, Girl Playing Pipe, Glass Globe Shade, 20 In.	605.00
Lamp, Overlay Shade, 6 Sides, 3-Owl Base, Glass Eyes, Signed B&H, 6 In.	1680.00
Lamp, Parlor, Medallions Of Women, Mushroom Shade, Signed, 19 In.	365.00
Lamp, Slag Glass Shade, 1910, 24 In.	1300.00

BRASS has been used for decorative pieces and useful tablewares since
ancient times. It is an alloy of copper, zinc, and other metals. Additional brass items may be found under Bell, Candlestick, Tool, or
Trivet.

Basket, Wire, Footed, Rope Twist Handle, 13 1/4 x 12 1/2 In.	55.00
Bed Warmer, Copper Rivets, Engraved, Turned Maple Handle, 44 In.	360.00
Bed Warmer, Engraved Brass Lid, Copper Basin, Turned Wood Handle, 41 In.	144.00
Bed Warmer, Engraved Cover, Tulip Basket, Pierced, Scrolling, Turned Handles, 41 In.	275.00
Bed Warmer, Punched Circles & Stars Cover, Engraved Leaves, Turned Handles, 45 In.	85.00
Bed Warmer, Round Cover, Pierced, Adam & Eve In Relief, Tree, Snake, Animal, 43 In.	4025.00
Book Slide, Self-Closing, Jeweled Enamel Mounted, Gilt, England, c.1891, 14 7/8 In.	980.00
Bowl, On Stand, Raised Characters, Round, Footed, Handles, Oriental, 8 3/4 x 9 In.	80.00
Bowl, Shaving, Cow, Bird's Nest Scene, Winged Cherub In Key, Leaf Border, 9 1/2 In.	39.00
Bowl, Shaving, Hammered, Cutout For Chin, Hanging Loop, 4 3/4 x 11 3/4 In.	215.00
Bucket, 19th Century, 13 1/2 x 9 In.	90.00
Bucket, Figural Handles, Southeast Asia, 21 x 23 In.	144.00

Cachepot, Lion Head Handles, Scrolling Feet, Late 19th Century, 10 x 11 3/4 In. 448.00
Case, Crackled Enamel, Foil Ground, Gilt Ink Signature Inside Lip, 4 In. 305.00
Coal Bin, Arts & Crafts, Hammered, Ceramic Cabochons, Finial, England, 16 x 18 In. . . . 2070.00
Cocktail Set, Shaker, 6 Cups, Tray, Reichenbach, Chase, 1938, 11 3/4 In. 460.00
Cocktail Shaker, Folke Arstrom, Firm's Mark, Stockholm, 8 1/2 In. 2300.00
Dish, Repousse, Adam & Eve, Garden Of Eden, Holland, 18th Century, 16 In. 395.00
Door Knocker, Stylized Dolphin, 19th Century, 5 1/2 In. 375.00
Eagle, Adjustable Wings, Stamped, Gilt, New York, c.1891, Pair 545.00
Ewer, Continental, 13 In., Pair 545.00
Figurine, Eagle, Perched On Ball, Spread Wings, Soapstone Base, 14 x 9 1/2 In. 205.00
Figurine, Man Seated In Armchair, Reading Amadis De Gaule, Books At Feet, 8 In. 357.00
Figurine, Napoleon, Column Base, Plinth, Fruitwood, Miniature, c.1890, 14 In. 115.00
Figurine, Queen Elizabeth II, Bust, Rectangular Plinth, Numbered, 1900s, 8 1/4 In. 75.00
Figurine, Recumbent Lion, Steel Rectangular Base, c.1890, 10 3/4 In., Pair 460.00
Frame, Gilt, Taupe Silk Moire, 1st Empire Style, c.1900, 9 1/2 x 6 7/8 In., Pair 635.00
Funnel, Wine, Dovetail Construction, 18th Century 160.00
Group, 3 Stylized Nudes, Supporting Ball, Nickel Over Brass, Mid 1800s, 24 In. 1090.00
Group, Nickel, 3 Stylized Nudes, Supporting Ball, Mid 19th Century, 24 In. 1090.00
Helmet, Roman Style, Sapeure Pompiers De Paris, 10 1/2 x 12 In. 110.00
Humidor, Oak, Prince Of Wales Plumed, Motto, Back Drawer, 10 x 12 In. 8400.00
Incense Burner, Neoclassical Style, Pierced Leaf Cast Lid, 4 1/4 In., Pair 144.00
Jamb Hooks, 2 Sections, Belted Urn Finials, Late 18th Century, 4 1/2 x 4 In., Pair 460.00
Jardiniere, Baroque Wine Cistern, Paw Foot, c.1900, 8 x 20 In. 546.00
Jardiniere, Flared, 3 Crouching Oriental Figure Footed, Mounting Holes, 20 x 13 In. 275.00
Jardiniere, Oval, Embossed, Liner, Beaded Rim, Lion Mask Handles, Paw Feet, 19 x 8 In. . 635.00
Jardiniere, Paw Footed, Baroque Style, Lion Mask Handles, Edwardian, 7 1/4 x 14 In. . . . 635.00
Letter Holder, 3 Tiers, Crest, Facing Lions, Winged Griffin, Faces, Handles, 15 x 9 In. . . 330.00
Letter Holder, Cast, Stamped, Victorian, 7 1/2 x 10 x 6 In. 44.00
Lifeboat Binnacle, Compass, 9 In. 140.00
Lifeboat Binnacle, Plath Compass, Side Light, 11 In. 316.00
Magnifying Glass, Round, Wooden Handle, 8 1/4 x 4 In. 80.00
Mirror, Plateau, Shaped, Footed, 2 Handles, France, 3 1/2 x 19 x 11 In. 200.00
Mitten Warmer, 2 Engraved Birds, Flower Branch, Turned Wooden Handle, 9 In. 80.00
Mitten Warmer, Falstaff Figure On Lid, Turned Wooden Handle, England, 9 In. 110.00
Mortar, 2 Handles, Flared Rim, 2-Sided Pestle, 4 1/2 In. 50.00
Pipe Tamper, Barmaid Holding Bottle & Glass, 18th Century 95.00
Pipe Tamper, Box On Tamper, Cribbage Board Lid, Inside Dominos & Dice, c.1800, 2 In. . 675.00
Pipe Tamper, Cast, 19th Century, 3 1/4 In. 85.00
Pitcher, Chromium Plated, Normandie, P. Muller-Munk, Stamped Revere, 1935 . . . . 4025.00
Planter, Lion Heads With Ring Handles, Kinney Mfg. Co., 14 x 11 1/2 In. 230.00
Planter, Tabletop, Etched Design, Lion Head Handles, 6 x 13 In. 336.00
Planter, Tabletop, Oval, Scrolling Feet, c.1865, 6 1/4 In. 380.00
Planter Set, Polished, Lacquered, Graduated, Oval, 11 To 15 In., 3 Piece 220.00
Speaking Trumpet, Engraved D. Patten, 13 1/2 x 3 1/2 In. 785.00
Tantalus, Georgian, Square, Paw Feet, Early 19th Century, 10 1/2 x 8 1/2 x 8 1/2 In. 1265.00
Tieback, Curtain, Bell Flower Crest, Floral Medallion Center, 1870s, 17 In., Pair 450.00
Tieback, Curtain, Ribbon & Bellflower Crest, Floral Medallion, 1880s, 17 In., Pair 475.00
Tieback, Ribbon Crest Over Floral Medallion, Fluted Body, 17 In., Pair 290.00
Tinderbox & Candleholder, Inside Damper & Striker, 18th Century 495.00
Trophy, Tankard, Fowler Cup, Inlaid Walnut, Runner Up Prize, Sept. 17 1910, 5 1/2 In. . . 66.00
Vase, Cover, Cornucopia, Red Glass, Dragon Type Handle, 18 1/2 In. 3165.00
Wall Pocket, Hammered, Semicircular, Pierced, Scroll Crest, England, 9 1/2 x 6 In. 300.00
Whistle, Steam, Single Chime, Lever Control, 9 1/2 x 2 1/4 In. 290.00
Whistle, Steam, Single Chime, Lever Control, 12 x 2 1/4 In. 260.00
Whistle, Steam, Single Chime, Lever Control, Crane, 9 x 3 1/2 In. 316.00
Whistle, Steam, Triple Chime, Crosby Steam, Gage & Valve Co., Boston, 1877, 12 In. . . . 718.00
Wine Server, Barrel, Glass, Railroad Frame, 18 In. 1840.00

BRASTOFF, see Sascha Brastoff category.

BREAD PLATE, see various silver categories, porcelain factories, and pressed glass patterns.

BRIDE'S BASKETS OR BRIDE'S BOWLS were usually one-of-a-kind novelties made in American and European glass factories. They were especially popular about 1880 when the decorated basket was often given as a wedding gift. Cut glass baskets were popular after 1890. All bride's baskets lost favor about 1905. Bride's baskets and bride's bowls may also be found in other glass sections. Check the index at the back of the book.

BRIDE'S BASKET, Blue Hobnail Body, Frosted Clear Handle, 5 x 3 In. 130.00
   Cranberry, Enameled, Daisies, Silver Plated Holder, Signed, 10 In. 690.00
   Dark Purple Over White, Yellow Enameled, Ruffled Edge, 3 1/4 x 11 1/2 In. 180.00
   Peachblow, Clear Rigaree Rim, Silver Plated Holder, 10 1/2 x 11 In. 413.00
   Pink Over White, Gold Enameled Flowers, 13 In. 600.00
   Red, Yellow, White Spatter Over Peach, Gold Enameled Leaves, 8 In. 750.00
   Silver, Reticulated Swing Handle, 7 x 8 In. 140.00
   White, Blue Cased Interior, Blue Thorn Handle, Square, 5 1/2 x 6 In. 40.00
   White, Turquoise Rigaree Rim, Violet Bellflowers On Random Stems, 4 x 10 1/2 In. 196.00
   White, Yellow Casing, Amber Thorn Handle, Feather Feet, 10 x 8 In. 130.00
   White Over Light Blue, Multicolored Enameled Leaves, 1/4 x 8 In. 500.00
   White Over Pink, 10 1/2 In. 275.00
   Yellow Body, Twisted Ribs, Crimped Rim, Thorn Handle, 8 x 6 1/4 In. 210.00
BRIDE'S BOWL, Amethyst, Scalloped, Enameled Lacy Foliage, Satin, 10 3/4 In. 195.00
   Blue, Drape, Satin Ruffled Edge, Silver Plated Stand, 5 1/2 x 10 In. 165.00
   Blue, Enameled Yellow Flowers & Leaves, Dots On Ruffles, 11 In. 295.00
   Blue, Gold Enameled Flowers & Leaves, Satin Base Ring, Blue, 9 1/2 In. 165.00
   Blue, Ruffled Edge, Enameled Flowers, Satin, 3 x 9 1/2 In. 165.00
   Blue, Ruffled, Enameled Gold Flowers & Leaves, Satin, 3 x 9 1/2 In. 175.00
   Blue Over White, Enameled White Flowers, Green Leaves, 3 1/2 In. 225.00
   Cranberry Opalescent, Lattice, Ruffled Edge, 4 x 7 In. 240.00
   Enameled Flowers, Apricot Over Cream, Yellow Dots, Scissor-Cut Rim, 3 x 9 1/2 In. . . . 165.00
   Mother-Of-Pearl, Diamond Quilted, Apricot, White, Satin, 8 1/4 In. 287.00
   Peach Over White, Enameled Flowers, Scalloped, Satin, 14 x 12 In. 495.00
   Peachblow, Gold Enameled Fruit, Silver Plated Holder, 11 x 11 In. 173.00
   Pink Over Apricot, Enameled Purple Wisteria, 5 1/2 x 10 In. 920.00
   Pink Over White, Enameled Flowers, 9 1/2 x 10 In. 230.00
   Pink Over White, Ruffled Edge, Silver Plated Holder, 11 1/2 In. 425.00
   Pink Swirled Ribs Over Yellow, Silver Plated Holder, Signed, Wilcox, 8 In. 230.00
   Purple & White Flowers, Satin, Scalloped, 3 1/2 x 10 3/4 In. 195.00
   Shaded Deep Pink Over White, Enameled Flowers, Clear Rigaree Rim, 8 x 10 3/4 In. . . . 165.00
   White, Gold Enameled Flowers, Pink Ruffled Edge, Silver Plated Holder, 11 x 11 In. 230.00
   White Over Pink, Enameled Flowers, Leaves, Branches, Handles, 11 1/4 In. 425.00
   White Spatter Over Cranberry, Signed, Derby Silver Co., 14 x 11 1/2 In. 115.00

BRISTOL glass was made in Bristol, England, after the 1700s. The Bristol glass most often seen today is a Victorian, lightweight opaque glass that is often blue. Some of the glass was decorated with enamels.

   Creamer, French Couple, Pastoral, Handle, Metal Rim, 7 1/4 x 4 1/4 In. 25.00
   Ewer, White, Birds, Art Nouveau, Gold, c.1900, 17 In. 61.00
   Sugar, French Couple, Pastoral, Handle, Metal Rim, 7 1/4 x 4 1/4 In. 25.00
   Vase, Bulbous, Light Green, Enameled Branches, Birds, 16 In. 69.00
   Vase, Celadon, Asian Scenes, Enameled, 10 1/2 In., Pair 51.00
   Vase, Enameled Lilies, Tan, 13 In. 31.00
   Vase, Moon Flask Shape, Swallows In Flight, Garlands, 1880s, 13 3/8 In., Pair 230.00
   Vase, Winter Cottage, Daisies Border, Celadon, 12 1/2 In. 115.00

BRITANNIA, see Pewter category.

BRONZE is an alloy of copper, tin, and other metals. It is used to make figurines, lamps, and other decorative objects. Bronze lamps are listed in the Lamp category. Pieces listed here date from the eighteenth, nineteenth, and twentieth centuries.

   Ashtray, Bach, Oscar, Red Glass Liner, Signed, 6 1/2 In. 138.00
   Bowl, E.F. Caldwell & Co., Neoclassical Figures, Ball Feet, Cover, Signed, Pair 8400.00
   Bowl, E.T. Hurley, Fish, Stylized Spiral Ribs, Patina, 5 1/2 In. Diam. 1093.00

Bowl, Offering, Patina, Malachite, Java, Footed, 15th Century, 7 1/4 In. 115.00
Bowl, Oriental Designs, Raised Character Signature, 18 x 12 x 7 1/2 In. 220.00
Bowl, Rosewood Lid, Footed, Overlapping Lily Pad Base, 19th Century, 5 x 5 1/4 In. 275.00
Box, Hinged Cove, Round, Vine & Leaf, Handle, Japan, 16 1/4 In. 146.00
Bust, Ajax, Helmeted, Beard, Gilt Toga, Parcel Gilt Socle, 20th Century, 16 1/4 In. 862.00
Bust, Bacchus & Bacchante, Ionic Columnar Standard, 18 In., Pair 1150.00
Bust, Carrier-Belleuse, Rembrandt, Marble Plinth, 20 1/2 In. 2300.00
Bust, Classical Man & Woman, Black, Red Marble Base, 8 In., Pair 1955.00
Bust, Classical Woman, Upswept Hair, c.1880, 6 In. 224.00
Bust, Diana, Elaborate Coiffure & Diadem, 19th Century, 14 In. 705.00
Bust, Dog, Marble Base, Continental, 14 In. 840.00
Bust, Fairbanks, Avard, Tennyson, Gold Brown Patina, Wood Base, 1969, 26 In. 1080.00
Bust, Godet, Henri, Water Nymph, Emerging From Bulrushes, Early 20th Century, 16 In. . . 2645.00
Bust, Gruber, Jakob, Bust Of Woman, Elaborate Floral Bonnet, 12 x 13 In. 770.00
Bust, Hippocrates, Greek Classical, Travertine Base, Naples, c.1915, 16 x 9 x 6 1/2 In. . . . 1792.00
Bust, Houdon, Jean-Antoine, Goddess Diana, Crescent Moon Ornament, 26 In. 1210.00
Bust, Mercury, Brown & Parcel Gilt Patina, Square Base, 20th Century, 11 1/2 In. 403.00
Bust, Napoleon, Marble Base, Nannani & Goldscheider Foundry, 1913, 19 In. 1360.00
Bust, Pinedo, Emile, Lord Byron, Red Marble & Wood Base, 23 1/2 In. 860.00
Bust, Vanderstrader, Woman, Ivory Face, Dore Patina, Marble Pedestal, 9 In. 863.00
Bust, William Shakespeare, Waisted Socle, 18 In. 1150.00
Bust, Woman, Laurel-Leaf Crown, Flute Waisted Socle, 19 1/2 In. 1380.00
Bust, Woman, Renaissance Clothes, Crown, Waisted Socle, Square Base, 13 In. 690.00
Bust, Young Child, Stone Base, 20th Century, 12 1/2 In. 630.00
Censer, Deer Finial, Pierced Top, Bamboo Designs, 19th Century, 12 x 10 1/2 In. 615.00
Censer, Foo Dog Finial, Pierced Cover, Squat Body, Handles, c.1900, 7 In., Pair 336.00
Censer, Foo Dog Finial, Pierced Work Top, Chinese, c.1900, 10 1/2 In. 160.00
Censer, Green Patina, India, 18th Century, 7 In. 518.00
Censer Cover, Lotus Blossom Shape, 19th Century, 3 3/4 In. 28.00
Compote, Bach, Oscar, Birds On Neck, Cutout Design Base, 12 x 8 1/2 In. 690.00
Compote, Bach, Oscar, Original Silver Patina, 12 x 8 1/2 In. 690.00
Crucifix, Russian Orthodox, Mounted On Velvet, 18th Century, 8 3/4 x 6 1/2 In. 110.00
Desk Set, Sterling Silver, Heintz, 6 Piece 1093.00
Dice, Egg Shape, Squared Sides, Bells Inside, India, 19th Century, 2 1/4 In., Pair 86.00
Fountain, Flowers, Bowl, 20th Century, 34 In. 115.00
Fountain, Nude Nymph, 2 Pan Figures On Rim, Pump 3025.00
Fremiet, Emmanuel, Goat, Standing, 7 x 11 In. 1870.00
Garniture Set, Louis XVI, Cupid, Flowers, Blue Ground, Enamel, Candlestick, 3 Piece . . 3185.00
Garniture Set, Napoleon III, Patinated, Slate, Marble, Morning Glory, 11 In., Pair 805.00
Humidor, Gilt, Velvet, E.F. Caldwell & Co., Early 20th Century, 16 1/2 In. 4800.00
Incense Burner, Garuda Bird, Spread Wings, Chinese, c.1800, 10 1/4 x 7 In. 225.00
Incense Burner, Square, Apocryphal Xuande, Mark, 19th Century, 6 x 5 1/2 In. 605.00
Incense Burner, Turtle & Dragon Medallions, Bronze, Signed Gruschwitz, 14 1/2 In. 495.00
Inkwell, Yatate, Classical Shape, Silver Inlay On Handle, 19th Century 140.00
Inkwell, Yatate, Classical Shape, Silver Wire Inlay, Greek Key, Landscape, 19th Century . 160.00
Inkwell, Yatate, Cylinder Shape, Dowel-Like Handle, 19th Century 69.00
Inkwell, Yatate, Geometric Handle Cutouts, Basket Shape, 19th Century 69.00
Inkwell, Yatate, Hinged Lid, Dragon, Silver Inlay, Handle, Half Wheel, 19th Century 265.00
Inkwell, Yatate, Landscape, Mokko Shape, Square Slanted Handle, 19th Century 105.00
Inkwell, Yatate, Molded Dragon, Bowed Handle, Ridged Back, 19th Century 115.00
Inkwell, Yatate, Pistol Shape, Karakusa Engraving, 19th Century 833.00
Inkwell, Yatate, Shishi Mask Shape, Cutouts In Handle, 19th Century 195.00
Inkwell, Yatate, Silver Inlay, Classical Shape, Landscape With Seashells, 19th Century . . . 170.00
Inkwell, Yatate, Stylized Dragon Shape, Engraved Flower, 19th Century 126.00
Jardiniere, Engrand, George, 3 Women & 1 Monkey, Heads, Signed, 27 In. 2300.00
Jardiniere, Gilt Bronze Swags, Cylinder Cage Base, 42 In., Pair 15600.00
Master Salt, Charles X, Gilt, Gothic Detail, Tripod Base, Mid 19th Century, 5 1/2 In. 575.00
Medallion, Commemorative, Colonial & Indian Reception At Guild Hall, 1886, 3 In. 69.00
Mirror, Louis XVI Style, Gilt, Cobalt Blue Enamel, Young Girl Portrait, Hand, 9 3/4 In. . . 195.00
Paperweight, Deity Ebisu & Large Fish, 19th Century, 3 1/2 In. 86.00
Peacock, Enameled, Champleve, 14 In. 690.00
Planter, Detailed Serpent Handles, 8 x 16 In., Pair 560.00
Plaque, Autumn Beauty, Figural Reclining Woman, Neoclassical, Gilt, 1900s, 26 In. 2300.00

Plaque, Builders, Browning Co., Cleveland, Ohio, 1917, 4 x 7 In. 11.00
Plaque, Builders, General Motors Diesel Locomotive, 16 x 5 x 1/4 In. . . . . .80.00 to 125.00
Plaque, Charles Carroll Of Carrollton, Oak Frame, Charles Hogboom, 18 x 16 In. 1610.00
Plaque, Cotton Belt Route, Black Ground, 12 In. 977.00
Plaque, Declaration Of Independence, International Exh., Phila., 1876, 15 x 10 In. 1020.00
Plaque, Gentleman Portrait, Marble Socle, France, 13 In. 374.00
Plaque, George Washington, Giltwood Frame, Signed, 1820-1840 . . . . 3450.00
Plaque, Hunters, Near Ruins, Birds & Fruit Rim, Oval, 18 1/2 x 20 3/4 In. 220.00
Plaque, Louis Philippe, Mirrored, Gilt, Round, Troubadour Style, 11 1/2 In. 1093.00
Plaque, Relief Cityscape, Marked Nurnberg, 12 In. 165.00
Plaque, Sculpted, Lustered, Patina, Harry Bertoia, 1972, 8 3/4 x 16 1/2 In. 2300.00
Plaque, Shiva & Four Attendants, High Relief, Oval, India, 19th Century, 3 1/4 In. 316.00
Plaque, Soo Line, Name, Walnut Ground 115.00
Sconce, Ribbon & Leaf Design, 3 Branches, 12 x 17 In. 862.00
Sculpture, 2 Children Playing With Donkey, Marble Base, 6 In. 545.00
Sculpture, America, Allegorical, Patinated, Terra-Cotta, Mid 19th Century, 49 1/2 In. 6325.00
Sculpture, Anfrie, Charles, Soldier, Raised Pistol, Tattered Flag, Title Plaque, 11 1/2 In. . . 630.00
Sculpture, Archer, Kneeling, Patinated, Art Deco, c.1900 . . . . 2645.00
Sculpture, Ascending Lion, Marble Base, 18 In. 560.00
Sculpture, Athena & Ares, Plumed Helmet, Black Onyx Base, 14 1/4 In. 220.00
Sculpture, Bacchante, Standing, Vine-Draped Staff, Marble Base, 12 In. 633.00
Sculpture, Badger, 3 1/4 In. 325.00
Sculpture, Baily, Woman, Fancy Dress, Ivory, Onyx Base, 8 In. 749.00
Sculpture, Ball, Thomas, Daniel Webster, Brown Patina, 1853, 30 In. 5100.00
Sculpture, Barbedienne, Ferdinand, Kneeling Venus, Wood Base, 11 1/2 In. 460.00
Sculpture, Barbedienne, Ferdinand, Standing Figure Adjusting Sandal, 27 In. 4885.00
Sculpture, Barbedienne, Ferdinand, Walking Lion, Marble Base, 15 1/4 In. 2350.00
Sculpture, Barillot, Drummer, Standing, Medieval Clothes, Ivory, Onyx Base, 10 In. 865.00
Sculpture, Barye, Alfred, Basset Hound, Dark Brown Patina, 9 1/2 In. 1320.00
Sculpture, Barye, Alfred, Group Of Dogs, Green Patina, 10 3/4 In. 1320.00
Sculpture, Barye, Alfred, Lion, Standing, 15 In. 2200.00
Sculpture, Barye, Alfred, Mastiff, Seated, Dead Rats Between Paws, 4 3/8 In. 805.00
Sculpture, Barye, Alfred, Tartar Manchu, Early 20th Century, 20 1/2 In. 3000.00
Sculpture, Barye, Antoine-Louis, Bear, Lying On Back, Signed, 4 x 5 In. 488.00
Sculpture, Barye, Antoine-Louis, Bull, Rearing, Oval Sloped Base, 8 1/2 x 11 1/2 In. 6325.00
Sculpture, Barye, Antoine-Louis, Camel, Green Patina, Inscribed, 8 In. 3600.00
Sculpture, Barye, Antoine-Louis, Elephant, Brown Patina, Early 20th Century, 15 In. 1680.00
Sculpture, Barye, Antoine-Louis, Lioness, Wood Base, 11 In. 252.00
Sculpture, Barye, Antoine-Louis, Panther Attacking Stag, Black Patina, 11 In. 3000.00
Sculpture, Barye, Antoine-Louis, Panther Of India, Signed, 7 1/4 In. 1610.00
Sculpture, Barye, Antoine-Louis, Panther Of Tunisia, Marble Base, Signed, 7 1/2 In. 690.00
Sculpture, Barye, Antoine-Louis, Rearing Bull, 8 1/2 In. 5500.00
Sculpture, Barye, Antoine-Louis, Reclining Panther, Signed, 10 1/2 In. 1725.00
Sculpture, Barye, Antoine-Louis, Standing Jaguar, Signed, 8 In. 978.00
Sculpture, Barye, Antoine-Louis, Walking Lion, 9 In. 8400.00
Sculpture, Barye, Antoine-Louis, Walking Tiger & Lion, 7 1/2 In., Pair 9600.00
Sculpture, Barye, Antoine-Louis, Water Buffalo, 5 1/2 In. 5000.00
Sculpture, Barye, Antoine-Louis, Water Buffalo, Standing, 5 3/4 x 9 In. 5750.00
Sculpture, Barye, Arab Mounted On Camel, Green, Brown Patina, 9 In. 3600.00
Sculpture, Barye, Bear Attacked By Hounds, Green, Brown, 14 In. 12000.00
Sculpture, Barye, Bear, Seated, Green, Brown Patina, 8 In. 12000.00
Sculpture, Barye, Bringing Down Stag, Green Brown Patina, 38 In. 4500.00
Sculpture, Barye, Bull With Tiger, Black Patina, 10 1/4 In. 4500.00
Sculpture, Barye, Eagle With Outspread Wings, Open Beak, 13 In. 8400.00
Sculpture, Barye, Gaston De Foix, Black Patina, 14 In. 6000.00
Sculpture, Barye, Horse Attacked By Lion, Dark Green Patina, 16 In. 8400.00
Sculpture, Barye, Jaguar Devouring Hare, Black Patina, 21 In. 3000.00
Sculpture, Barye, Lion & Serpent, Black Green Patina, 15 In. 9000.00
Sculpture, Barye, Minerva, Brown Patina, 20th Century, 12 In. 6600.00
Sculpture, Barye, Nereid, Gold Brown Patina, 12 In. 9600.00
Sculpture, Barye, Ostrich, Gold Brown Patina, 8 In. 1080.00
Sculpture, Barye, Panther Attacking Prey, Dark Brown Patina, 18 In. 7200.00
Sculpture, Barye, Panther Attacking Stag, Green Patina, 13 1/2 In. . . . . .7800.00 to 8400.00

Sculpture, Barye, Reclining Panther, Early 20th Century, 7 1/2 In. 840.00
Sculpture, Barye, Theseus Slaying The Centaur, Green, Brown, 30 In. 24900.00
Sculpture, Barye, Tiger Devouring Gavial, Signed, Dated, 11 In. 2070.00
Sculpture, Bassett, Carroll, Horse, Brown Patina, Signed, 1930, 6 x 8 7/8 In. 460.00
Sculpture, Bear, Holding Cub, c.1940, 2 1/2 In. 385.00
Sculpture, Bear, Walking Grizzly, Incised Coat, 19 3/4 x 11 1/2 In. 336.00
Sculpture, Beetz, Elisa, Girl, Standing, Hooded Cape, Signed, Foundry Mark, 17 1/2 In. .. 2420.00
Sculpture, Benkei Stealing Bell From Dodoji Temple, Meiji Period, 10 x 7 In. 575.00
Sculpture, Bergman, Child, Clown Costume, Ivory Hands & Head, Onyx Base, 6 3/4 In. . 920.00
Sculpture, Bergman, Moroccan Street Performer, Animals, Cold Painted, 9 In. 2070.00
Sculpture, Birds, Brown Patina, Late 19th Century, 10 1/4 In. 3300.00
Sculpture, Bissell, Georges Edwin, Abraham Lincoln, Brown Patina, 16 1/2 In. 4200.00
Sculpture, Black Minstrels, Comic Garb, Playing Banjo, 1890s, 6 3/4 In. 490.00
Sculpture, Boar, Dark Brown Patina, Impressed Seal, Japan, 8 1/2 In. 2530.00
Sculpture, Bodhisttava, Seated, Lotus Leaf Throne, Semiprecious Stones, Base, 7 7/8 In. .. 1045.00
Sculpture, Bologna, Giovanni, Da, Mercury, Marble Base, 19 In. 460.00
Sculpture, Bonheur, Isidore Jules, Angry Bull, 13 3/4 In. 2700.00
Sculpture, Bonheur, Isidore Jules, Bull & Drover, Brown Patina, 10 3/8 x 21 x 6 5/8 In. .. 4600.00
Sculpture, Bonheur, Isidore Jules, Bull, Charging, Mid Stride, Head Down, 9 3/4 In. 1840.00
Sculpture, Bonheur, Isidore Jules, Bull, Standing, Head Raised, Oval Base, 5 x 7 3/4 In. . 920.00
Sculpture, Bonheur, Isidore Jules, Bull, Walking Up Rocky Grade, 12 1/4 x 13 3/4 In. ... 2070.00
Sculpture, Bonheur, Isidore Jules, Equestrian Group, Brown Patina, 20th Century, 24 In. . 4200.00
Sculpture, Bonheur, Isidore Jules, Jockey On Horseback, Marble Base, 25 x 24 In. 785.00
Sculpture, Bonheur, Isidore Jules, Jockey On Horseback, Marble Base, 29 x 29 1/2 In. ... 1560.00
Sculpture, Bonheur, Isidore Jules, Men On Horseback, Late 19th Century, 15 In. 9000.00
Sculpture, Bonheur, Isidore Jules, Standing Bull, Ovoid Base, 15 x 22 In. 3740.00
Sculpture, Bonheur, Ram & Ewe, Early 20th Century, 14 In. 3900.00
Sculpture, Bonheur, Rosa, Bull, Recumbent, Egg Shaped Base, 5 3/4 x 11 3/8 In. 3105.00
Sculpture, Bonheur, Rosa, Bull, Standing, Egg Shaped Base, 6 1/4 x 12 5/8 In. 2875.00
Sculpture, Bonheur, Rosa, Bull, Standing, Head Raised, Oblong Base, 6 x 8 1/2 In. 1840.00
Sculpture, Boreas, Rape Of Oreithyia, Naked Girl Held Firmly In His Arms, 39 In. 5400.00
Sculpture, Bouret, Eutrope, Woman, Renaissance Clothes, Napoleon III, Marble, 20 In. ... 2300.00
Sculpture, Bousquet, Robert, Tiger & Snake, Marble Base, 17 1/2 In. 750.00
Sculpture, Bousquet, Stag, Stone Base, 18 x 15 In. 550.00
Sculpture, Boy With Goat, Marble Base, Early 20th Century, 39 1/2 In. 9600.00
Sculpture, Boy With Pigs, 4 x 6 3/4 In. 375.00
Sculpture, Boy, With Turtle, Wooden Base, Early 20th Century, 6 In. 287.00
Sculpture, Buddha Head, Curled Hair, Top Piece Cast Separately, 5 5/8 In. 165.00
Sculpture, Buddha, Holding Alms Bowl, Standing On 4-Tier Lotus Base, Thailand, 57 In. .. 660.00
Sculpture, Buddha, Seated On Lotus Leaf Throne, Beaded Headdress, Base, 6 In. 330.00
Sculpture, Buddha, Seated, Chinese, 2 3/4 In. 57.00
Sculpture, Buddha, Standing With Raised Palms, 4-Tier Lotus Base, Thailand, 26 1/2 In. .. 184.00
Sculpture, Bulio, Woman, Putti With Grapes, Shaped Marble Base, 25 In. 3360.00
Sculpture, Bull At Pasture, Oval Naturalistic Base, Early 1900s, 2 3/4 x 4 3/4 x 2 In. 345.00
Sculpture, Bull Terriers, Standing, Rectangular Base, 1900s, 16 x 15 5/8 In. 400.00
Sculpture, Bull, About To Charge, Lowered Head, Raised Foreleg, 3 x 3 7/8 In. 690.00
Sculpture, Bull, Ivory Horns, Standing, Early 20th Century, 2 3/4 x 4 In. 345.00
Sculpture, Bull, Prize Winning Sign, Patina, Christofle & Cie., 14 x 15 1/2 x 6 3/8 In. ... 920.00
Sculpture, Bull, Renaissance Style, Raised Foreleg, Marble Base, 5 1/2 x 4 1/2 x 2 1/2 In. 375.00
Sculpture, Bull, Standing Nandi, Leaf Engraving, India, 19th Century, 5 1/2 In. 290.00
Sculpture, Bull, Standing, 1800-1700 B.C., 2 1/2 x 2 1/4 In. 545.00
Sculpture, Bulldog Pup, 12 In. 430.00
Sculpture, Caesar Augustus, Standing, 1 Outstretched Arm, Cherub Support, 38 1/2 In. ... 4310.00
Sculpture, Cain, Auguste, Bull, 21 1/2 In. 9600.00
Sculpture, Cain, Stalking Heron, Lily Pad, Unsuspecting Frog, 9 x 6 3/4 In. 345.00
Sculpture, Cartier, 2 Dogs, Marble Base, 13 x 8 x 20 In. 1064.00
Sculpture, Castells Capurro, E., Horses, Galloping, Wood Base, 10 1/2 x 25 3/4 In. 785.00
Sculpture, Cat, Chimney Sweep, 2 1/2 In. 476.00
Sculpture, Cat, Maid, 2 1/2 In. 336.00
Sculpture, Celestial Deities, 2 Figures, Bali, 19th Century, 6 In. 489.00
Sculpture, Charging Stag, Signed SE 93, 13 x 10 x 22 In. 1680.00
Sculpture, Cherub Playing Hornpipe, Doves Perched On Column, 9 In. 230.00
Sculpture, Chiparus, Demetre H., Dancer, Onyx Base, 21 1/4 In. 9000.00

Sculpture, Chiparus, Demetre H., Dancers, Costumed, Marble, Gilt, 24 1/2 x 16 In. 28000.00
Sculpture, Chiparus, Demetre H., Dancing Woman, Marble Base, 17 In. 560.00
Sculpture, Chipmunk, Cold Painted, Austria, 20th Century, 1 3/8 In. 115.00
Sculpture, Classical Women, Fruit, Amulet, Patinated, Slate, Marble Plinth, 14 In., Pair .. 1380.00
Sculpture, Clesinger, John-Baptiste, Brahman Bull, Standing, 11 5/8 In. 1495.00
Sculpture, Colinet, Exotic Dancer, Leg Raised, Holding Dress, Marble Base, 25 1/2 In. .. 5175.00
Sculpture, Colinet, Kneeling Female, Arms High, Marble Stepped Pedestal, 17 1/2 In. 5750.00
Sculpture, Colinet, Nude Female, Juggling, 20 1/2 In. 4370.00
Sculpture, Curts, T., Indian, Onyx Base, 20th Century, 22 In. 7800.00
Sculpture, Dakini, India, 19th Century, 5 1/2 In. 140.00
Sculpture, Dallin, Cyrus, Paul Revere, Brown Patina, 1861, 37 In. 16800.00
Sculpture, Dancing Faun, Italy, 6 In. 80.00
Sculpture, Dancing Faun, Mid 19th Century, 30 In. 730.00
Sculpture, Dancing Woman, Art Nouveau, Ivory Base 3335.00
Sculpture, David, Marble Plinth, 13 5/8 In. 160.00
Sculpture, De Taverna, F.P., Boy, Standing, Hands In Pockets, 1890, 11 In. 1380.00
Sculpture, Delabrierre, Edward, Grouse, 12 1/4 In. 6600.00
Sculpture, Delaigue, Victor Constantin, Dante's Inferno, Carved Stone Base, 18 In. 785.00
Sculpture, Descomps, Joseph Emanuel, Nude Female, Seated, Early 1900s, 16 x 24 In. .. 1610.00
Sculpture, Diana, Holding Arrow, 42 In. 2588.00
Sculpture, Dionysus, Holding Bunch Of Grapes, Kneeling Goat, 14 1/2 In. 690.00
Sculpture, Dog & Cat, Playing, Malachite Base, 11 1/2 In. 1380.00
Sculpture, Dog With Long-Tailed Pheasant In Mouth, 16 x 25 In. 460.00
Sculpture, Dog, Peony Sprig In Mouth, Japan, 19th Century, 9 x 10 1/2 In. 460.00
Sculpture, Dog, Standing, West Africa, 13 In. 170.00
Sculpture, Droust, C., Inventor, With Compass & Vice, Signed, 23 In. 1790.00
Sculpture, Dubucand, A., Warrior On Horseback, Shooting Arrow, 1881, 19 In. 2415.00
Sculpture, Dubucand, Alfred, Equestrian, Middle Eastern Man On Horseback, 31 In. 11400.00
Sculpture, Dying Gaul, Male Nude Figure Lying Down, Head Bent, 22 In. 1150.00
Sculpture, Eagle Perched On Rock, Marble Base, 7 1/4 In. 545.00
Sculpture, Eagle, Bennett, Chris, Mustang Foundries, Texas, Mid 20th Century 9500.00
Sculpture, Eagle, Spread Wings, Olive-Branch Wreath, Verdigris, 27 1/2 x 21 1/2 In. 3220.00
Sculpture, Egyptian Ruler, Standing, Gilt, Red Marble Base, Late 1800s, 13 In. 4025.00
Sculpture, Elephant Of Senegal, Marble Base, Signed, 8 1/4 In. 4110.00
Sculpture, Elephant Rearing, Trumpeting, Round Marble Base, 9 x 4 In. 560.00
Sculpture, Elephant, Ivory Tusks, 2 Tigers Attacking, Hollow, Brown Patina 200.00
Sculpture, Emperor Napoleon, Standing, Patinated, Late 1800s, 9 1/2 x 2 1/2 x 2 1/2 In. .. 460.00
Sculpture, Faguays, Pierre Le, Man, Wings, Rocky Ledge, Marble Base, 18 1/4 In. 1725.00
Sculpture, Fairy, Beneath Toadstool, Playing Flute, 1930s, 3 3/4 In. 315.00
Sculpture, Fauginet, Jacques-Auguste, Horse, 1841 .... 3000.00
Sculpture, Faun, Reclining, On Lion Skin, 8 In. 575.00
Sculpture, Faun, Square Marble Base, 13 In. 633.00
Sculpture, Female, Nude, Headless, Armless, Patinated, c.1900, 52 In. 2185.00
Sculpture, Fisherman, Standing, Basket On Back, Japan, Meiji Period, Signed, 19 In. 600.00
Sculpture, Foo Lion, Gilt, Tang Dynasty, Chinese, 3/4 In. 345.00
Sculpture, Fratin, Christophe, Greyhound With Hare, Gold, Brown Patina, 34 In. 11400.00
Sculpture, Fratin, Christophe, Tiger, Standing, 20 In. 1870.00
Sculpture, Frishmuth, Harriet, Nude Female Stretching, 1918, 20 In. 11500.00
Sculpture, Froment, Meurice, Seminude Woman, Tempted By Devil, Signed, 35 In. 11200.00
Sculpture, Gaudez, Adrien-Etienne, Mozart, Brown Patina, 18 1/2 In. 1560.00
Sculpture, Gauquie, Henri, Hunter, With Lion, 2 Colors, Signed, c.1885, 20 In. 1960.00
Sculpture, Girl Standing On Chair, Spelter, 13 1/2 In. 935.00
Sculpture, Gladiator, Lunging, Sienna Marble Base, Early 20th Century, 10 1/2 In. 375.00
Sculpture, God, Standing Male With Raised Hands, Square Base, 12 In. 805.00
Sculpture, Godchaux, Roger, Elephant, 9 In. 6000.00
Sculpture, Gorilla, Green Patina, Signed, 20th Century, 10 x 8 1/2 In. 575.00
Sculpture, Gorilla, On All 4 Legs, Green Patina, 10 x 8 1/2 In. 575.00
Sculpture, Gratchev, Alexei, Cossack On Horseback, Brown Patina, 16 1/2 In. 5100.00
Sculpture, Gratchev, Alexei, Falconers, Brown Patina, Late 19th Century, 18 In. 13200.00
Sculpture, Greyhound, Recumbent, Black Lacquer, Oval Wooden Base, 6 In. 500.00
Sculpture, Greyhounds, Brown Patina, Continental, 48 In., Pair 14400.00
Sculpture, Gueyton, Mozart, Brown Patina, 25 In. 3300.00
Sculpture, Hare, Standing, Polychrome, Vienna, Late 19th Century, 4 In. 520.00

Sculpture, Harlequin, Ivory, Art Deco, c.1920, 9 5/8 In. 920.00
Sculpture, Hartwig, Josef, Owl, c.1922, 6 3/8 x 3 In. 5175.00
Sculpture, Hebert, Pierre-Emile, Woman, Seminude, With Flowers, Signed, 25 In. 2070.00
Sculpture, Heigler, Deer, Doe, Fawn, Woodland Setting, Signed, 20 In. 560.00
Sculpture, Henies, H., Stallion, Rectangular Marble Base, 14 In. 6900.00
Sculpture, Hercules, Draped In Lion Skin, Club At Side, Leaning On Pedestal, 28 In. 4370.00
Sculpture, Hercules, Draped In Skin, Marble Base, 1930s, 13 In. 630.00
Sculpture, Holand, C., Man, Standing, Arm At Waist, Marble Base, 12 In. 375.00
Sculpture, Hollister, Antoinette, B., Pan, Looking Downward At A Bird, 49 In. 9600.00
Sculpture, Horse, In Full Stride, Marble Base, Continental, 25 x 24 In. 420.00
Sculpture, Horse, With Colt, Marble Base, Signed, Gorham Co., 11 1/2 x 7 x 18 In. 3360.00
Sculpture, Horses Of Marly, After Guillaume Coustou, 21 x 21 1/2 x 24 1/4 In., Pair 6038.00
Sculpture, Hottot, J., Victorian Woman On Rock, Holding Binoculars, Signed, 22 1/2 In. . 560.00
Sculpture, Humphriss, Charles, Indian On Horse, 16 In. 1320.00
Sculpture, Indian On Horseback, Brown Patina, 20th Century, 8 1/2 In. 4500.00
Sculpture, Jaguar Devouring Hare, Dark Brown Patina, 20th Century, 21 In. 1680.00
Sculpture, Joan Of Arc, Armor, Holding Sword, Ivory Face, Marble Plinth, 17 5/8 In. 690.00
Sculpture, Kabuki Dancer, Removable Gilt Fan & Mask, 1930s, 12 1/2 In. 275.00
Sculpture, Kauba, Carl, Bringing In The Kill, 20th Century, 14 3/4 In. 5700.00
Sculpture, Kauba, Carl, How-Kola, 20th Century, 24 In. 22600.00
Sculpture, Kauba, Carl, Indian Attack, Marble Base, 20th Century, 26 In. . . . . .9000.00 to 12000.00
Sculpture, Kauba, Carl, Indian Chief Grasping Fellow Warrior, 25 In. 15600.00
Sculpture, Kauba, Carl, Indian Chief, Marble Plinth, 31 1/2 In. 3600.00
Sculpture, Kauba, Carl, Indian On Horseback, 20th Century, 12 In. 3300.00
Sculpture, Kneeling Woman, Signed, 13 In. 1288.00
Sculpture, Knight, Charles R., Prince, Kneeling, Offering Slipper, Signed 575.00
Sculpture, Kossowski, Henryk, Jr., Female Harvester, Ivory Face & Arms, 1908, 13 In. . . 1265.00
Sculpture, Krishna, Licking Feet, India, 18th Century, 6 1/2 In. 290.00
Sculpture, Krishna, Playing Flute, Red Ochre Surface, India, 3 3/4 x 4 1/4 In. 520.00
Sculpture, Krodmo, Th., Horse, Copper Brown Patina, Signed, 15 x 17 x 6 1/4 In. 1345.00
Sculpture, Ladd, Anna Coleman, St. Elizabeth Of Hunrary, 22 In. 1380.00
Sculpture, Lambert-Ruck, Jean, 2 Shepherds, 14 1/2 In. 8400.00
Sculpture, Lanceray, Eugene, Boy Driving With 3 Girls In Cart, Black, 24 In. 9000.00
Sculpture, Lanceray, Eugene, Crawling Warrior, Russia, 8 In. 770.00
Sculpture, Lanceray, Eugene, Man On Horseback, Dark Brown Patina, 17 1/2 In. 4200.00
Sculpture, Lanceray, Eugene, Oxen, Drawing Cart, Driver, Marble Base, 20 In. 635.00
Sculpture, Laurel, P., Nude & Goat, Stone Base, c.1910, 18 x 13 In. 2700.00
Sculpture, Le Trevail, Blacksmith, With Anvil, c.1885, 31 In. 3360.00
Sculpture, Levasseur, Diana, With Bow, 28 In. 3080.00
Sculpture, Levy, Charles, Miner, 22 In. 1980.00
Sculpture, Lieberich, Nicholai, Farmer, On Horseback, 18 In. 3450.00
Sculpture, Lieberich, Nicholai, Group Of Cossacks & Dogs, Brown, 17 In. 7800.00
Sculpture, Lions Attacking Turtle, Signed, 18 1/2 In. 999.00
Sculpture, Louis XIV On Horseback, Black Patina, Late 19th Century, 43 1/2 In. 18000.00
Sculpture, Mahisasura Mardini, Detachable Halo, Nepal, 18th Century, 10 3/4 In. 860.00
Sculpture, Man & Boy, Early 20th Century, 47 In. 7200.00
Sculpture, Man Attacked By Bear, Marble Plinth, 16 In. 10200.00
Sculpture, Manvel, David, Late For Lunch, 14 1/2 In. 560.00
Sculpture, Marin, J., Winged Victory, 2 Figures, Marble Base, 32 In. 2745.00
Sculpture, Masson, Clovis, Lioness & Cub, Marble Base, 20 In. 575.00
Sculpture, Masson, Jules-Edmond, Pheasant, Gold, Brown Patina, 22 In. 2160.00
Sculpture, Medusa & Persius, 31 In. 1400.00
Sculpture, Mene, Pierre-Jules, 3 Terriers Hunting, Brown Marble Base, 14 1/4 In. 1955.00
Sculpture, Mene, Pierre-Jules, Bull, Standing, Naturalistic Base, 9 1/4 In. 4310.00
Sculpture, Mene, Pierre-Jules, Jockey On Horse, 14 In. 3630.00
Sculpture, Mene, Pierre-Jules, Pointer, Walking, Head Turned, 1 Paw Raised, 9 In. 750.00
Sculpture, Mene, Pierre-Jules, Retriever, 13 In. 1650.00
Sculpture, Mercie, Marius-Jean, Antonin, Gloria Victus, Gilt, Brown Patina, 36 In. 18000.00
Sculpture, Mercury, Brown Patina, 64 1/2 In. 1380.00
Sculpture, Minerva, Seated, Spear, Dagger, Parcel Gilt, 8-Sided Wood Base, 10 x 5 In. . . . 431.00
Sculpture, Moigniez, Jules, Bird Feeding Her Young, Gold, Brown Patina, 19 In. 3600.00
Sculpture, Moigniez, Jules, Horses & Hounds, Brown Patina, 20th Century, 17 In. 1560.00
Sculpture, Moigniez, Jules, Pointer With Pheasant, 16 1/2 In. 7200.00

Sculpture, Moigniez, Jules, Snipes Hunting Lizard, Dark Brown, 10 In., 3 Piece 2040.00
Sculpture, Monk, Seated, Double Lotus Throne, Late Ming Dynasty, Chinese, 5 1/2 In. . . 400.00
Sculpture, Monkey, Seated On Ball, Square Metal Base, Japan, 9 In. 575.00
Sculpture, Moor Carrying Satchel, Climbing Steps, Cold Painted, Vienna, 1800s, 5 1/2 In. 230.00
Sculpture, Moose, 4 In. 465.00
Sculpture, Moreau, L., Putto, Hatching Ducklings, Alabaster Egg, Marble, Signed, 8 In. . . . 1840.00
Sculpture, Moreau, Mathurin, Woman Holding Torch, 33 In. 4800.00
Sculpture, Moreau, Mathurin, Woman, Bird, Colombe, Revolving Base, c.1880, 26 In. 3190.00
Sculpture, Moreau, Mathurin, Women In Classical Dress, Marble Base, 21 In. 1380.00
Sculpture, Moreau, Seminude Woman, Bird, Grapes, 2 Colors, Signed, 35 In. 3080.00
Sculpture, Mythological Woman, Cherubs Around Base, Gold Polish, 35 3/4 In. 2530.00
Sculpture, Napoleon On Horseback, Gilt Bronze Stepped Base, 30 In. 10800.00
Sculpture, Narcissus, 24 In. 575.00
Sculpture, Narcissus, Circular Base, 24 In. 920.00
Sculpture, Nelson, Anton, Man Laborer, Base, Signed, Foundry Mark, 28 In. 805.00
Sculpture, Nine Songbirds On Limb, Patinated, Austria, 13 x 4 x 2 In. 2016.00
Sculpture, Noel, Tony, Gladiator, Signed, 22 In. 1175.00
Sculpture, Nubian Princess, Short Socle, Marble Base, 7 1/2 In. 402.00
Sculpture, Nude, Gilt, Art Deco Ashtray, Inscribed Au Revoir, 13 1/2 x 6 3/4 In. 805.00
Sculpture, Nun In Robes & Wimple, Ivory Face & Hands, France, c.1890, 17 In. 1265.00
Sculpture, Nymph, Nude, Pouring Out Cup, Vines & Cattails Base, 22 5/8 In. 1150.00
Sculpture, Orloff, Chana, Maternity, Mother & Child, 24 1/2 In. 7480.00
Sculpture, Parrot On Tree, 52 In. 520.00
Sculpture, Partially Nude Woman, Raising Bowl, Gilt, French Inscribed Title, 20 In. 1093.00
Sculpture, Pautrot, Ferdinand, Grouse, Naturalistic, Oak Stalks, Ovoid Base, 13 3/4 In. . . 920.00
Sculpture, Pautrot, Ferdinand, Pheasants, Dark Brown Patina, 13 1/4 In. 3300.00
Sculpture, Pautrot, Ferdinand, Setter & Bird, 8 1/2 In. 770.00
Sculpture, Pautrot, Ferdinand, Setter, Duck In Mouth, 12 1/2 In. 3000.00
Sculpture, Peyrol, Bull, Standing, Oval Base, 4 5/8 x 3 x 1 5/8 In. 1090.00
Sculpture, Pheasant & Lizard, Brown Patina, Early 20th Century, 28 In. 5400.00
Sculpture, Philipp, Woman Skier, Marble Base, Signed, 14 x 3 x 12 In. 1625.00
Sculpture, Picault, Emile-Louis, Honor Patria, Soldier, Sword, Signed, c.1880, 31 In. 5320.00
Sculpture, Picault, Emile-Louis, Napoleon, Marble Base, 9 In. 575.00
Sculpture, Picault, Emile-Louis, Seated Nude, At Well, Art Nouveau, Marble Base, 27 In. 4425.00
Sculpture, Plagnet, Leaping Antelope, Art Deco, Black Marble Base, Signed, 11 x 23 In. . 615.00
Sculpture, Posen, Leonid, Vladimirovitch, Bull, Brown Patina, 11 1/2 In. 1440.00
Sculpture, Proctor, A.P., Hound, Worrying Stick On Ground, Marble Plinth, 8 3/4 In. 2875.00
Sculpture, Ram's Head, Black Patina, 1900s, 5 1/2 x 7 In. 315.00
Sculpture, Rama, 8-Armed God Holding Bow, Lotus Throne, Square Base, 5 1/2 In. 430.00
Sculpture, Rama, Drawn Bow, Pointed Headdress, 37 In. 230.00
Sculpture, Rearing Bull, Attacked By Jaguar, Oblong Base, 8 1/2 x 11 In. 4025.00
Sculpture, Reclining Nude Woman, Patina, Continental, 19th Century, 10 x 24 In. 1790.00
Sculpture, Riviere, Maurice G., Sibling Rivalry, Green Marble Base, 27 In. 3680.00
Sculpture, Rolle, Christmas Day, Crying Boy, Drum, Horse, 21 In. 2875.00
Sculpture, Roman Chariot, Armored Driver, 2 Galloping Horses, Marble Base, 11 x 6 In. . 360.00
Sculpture, Roman Warrior, Sitting Pensively, Wearing Military Dress, 17 In. 920.00
Sculpture, Russell, Charles Marion, Pack Mule, Signed, 5 In. 520.00
Sculpture, Russell, Charles Marion, Stag, Wooden Base, 6 In. 750.00
Sculpture, Russell, Charles, Marion, Snake Priest, Zappo Foundry, 1929, 4 x 8 x 4 In. . . . 12500.00
Sculpture, Satyr & Fauns, Seated Female Feeding Grapes To Children, 12 In. 750.00
Sculpture, Satyr With Pipes, France, Signed, 26 In. 1035.00
Sculpture, Schwatenberg, S., Nude Man With Fencing Foil, Marble Plinth, 9 1/4 In. 575.00
Sculpture, Showgirl In Costume, 27 In. 825.00
Sculpture, Signoret-Ledieu, Lucie, Girl, Smelling Flower, Brown Patina, 26 1/2 In. 7200.00
Sculpture, Simard, Marie-Louise, Horse, Damascened, c.1925, 15 1/2 In. 17625.00
Sculpture, Skull, Human, Chinese, c.1900, 5 1/2 In. 1720.00
Sculpture, Soldier, Lighting Pipe, Inscribed 1810, Signed, 21 1/2 In. 1150.00
Sculpture, Soldier, Malachite Base, 6 1/2 In. 260.00
Sculpture, Soldier, Pack, Rifle, Filling Pipe, France, 1800s, 28 1/2 In. 2875.00
Sculpture, Soldier, Standing, Patinated, Malachite Base, Russia, 20th Century, 6 1/2 In. . . 259.00
Sculpture, Squirrel, Seated On Oval Plinth, 1908, 7 3/4 In. 2300.00
Sculpture, Stella, Etienne-Alexandre, Seasons, Allegorical, 37 In., 2 Piece 12000.00
Sculpture, Stella, Etienne-Alexandre, Woman Beside Putto, Brown Patina, c.1892, 36 In. . 4140.00

Sculpture, Stolo, Woman, Signed, 14 1/2 In. 460.00
Sculpture, Sykes, Charles, Spirit Of Ecstasy, Marble Base, 22 1/2 In. 1120.00
Sculpture, Szceblewski, V., Boy, Whistling, Signed, 22 In. 690.00
Sculpture, Tiger, Burlwood Base, Meiji Period, 22 In. 1150.00
Sculpture, Tissot, A., Monkey Begging, Silver Patina, Variegated Marble Plinth, 10 In. ... 315.00
Sculpture, Troubetzkoy, Paul, Boys With Wolf, 1915, 11 1/2 x 17 3/8 In. 9600.00
Sculpture, Truffot, Emile Louis, Fox & Pheasant, Late 19th Century, 23 In. 7200.00
Sculpture, Venus, Crouching, Nude, Rectangular Base, Late 19th Century, 11 1/2 In. 575.00
Sculpture, Venus, Kneeling Figure Fabric To Her Bosom, 5 In. 345.00
Sculpture, Vidal, Louis, Wary Bull, Head Lowered, Black Socle, 13 1/2 x 17 3/4 In. 1495.00
Sculpture, Villains, E., Rebecca At The Well, Hands On Jug, Marble Base, Signed, 8 In. .. 575.00
Sculpture, Vonnoh, Bessie, Potter, Young Girl, Brown Patina, 60 In. 64000.00
Sculpture, Walker, George, Black Man In Top Hat, Playing Cards, 32 12 In. 1176.00
Sculpture, Wandschneider, Wilhelm, World War I German Soldier, 13 In. 990.00
Sculpture, Warrior Repairing His Armor, 31 In. 3470.00
Sculpture, Warrior, Oriental, Traditional Hair Style, Footed, Lotus Design Base, 18 In. 165.00
Sculpture, Whippet, Seated, 1878, 7 1/2 In. 336.00
Sculpture, Winged Bull Of Nineveh, Human Face, Early 20th Century, 6 3/4 In. 460.00
Sculpture, Woerffel, C.F., Steer, Head Lowered, Standing By Fence, 12 1/4 In. 1495.00
Sculpture, Wolfers, Philippe, 2 Dancing Girls, Marble Base, 7 1/4 In. 1265.00
Sculpture, Wolff, Franz, Pig, 7 In. 7800.00
Sculpture, Woman Holding Mirror, Ivory, Cold Painted, Early 20th Century, 9 1/4 In. 2415.00
Sculpture, Woman Reading Book, Seated, Onyx Base, 14 1/4 x 15 In. 935.00
Sculpture, Woman, Standing, Diaphanous Gown, Art Nouveau, 24 In. 489.00
Sculpture, Young Man, Removing Thorn, Foot, Late 1800s, 11 1/2 x 8 In. 550.00
Sculpture, Young Woman In Diving Position, Circular Base, 20th Century, 23 In. 690.00
Sculpture, Zach, Bruno, Male Laborer, Standing With Scythe, Marble Base, 16 In. 545.00
Sculpture, Zach, Bruno, Sower, Standing, Oval Black Marble Base, 15 3/4 In. 690.00
Seal, Desktop, Bison, Front Legs Kneeling, Iron Base, 3 1/2 x 2 3/4 In. 325.00
Smoking Stand, Bach, Oscar, Signed, 36 In. 980.00
Stand, Putto Holding Grapevine Plateau & Base, Dore, Late 1800s, 9 3/4 In. 460.00
Tray, Card, Hammered, Comedy & Tragedy Masks, Gorham, Stamped, 9 1/2 In. 575.00
Tray, Offering, Conch Shell, Stylized Flowers, Java, 20 In. 980.00
Tray, Offering, Horn Of Plenty, Green Patina, Java, 18 3/4 In. 550.00
Urn, Bulbous, Flanges, Buddha, Emblems, Sino Tibetan, c.1900, 7 x 8 In. 115.00
Urn, Flying Birds, Blossoms, Japan, Meiji Period, 19 1/2 In., 3 Sections 259.00
Urn, Leafy Vines, Patinated, 2 Angular Handles, Continental, 1800s, 10 1/8 In. 430.00
Urn, Neoclassical, 8 Sides, Domed Foot, Square Base, India, 15 In. 375.00
Urn, Ormolu, Rust Color, Mottled, Leaf Handles, Lion Heads, Paw Feet, 25 In. 1150.00
Urn, Patinated, 2 Handles, Continental, Mid 19th Century, 10 1/8 In., Pair 920.00
Vase, Baluster Shape, Cast Relief Dragon, Japan, c.1926, 18 In. 400.00
Vase, Bird Decoration, Silver Overlay, Signed Silver Crest, Early 20th Century, 9 In., Pair 290.00
Vase, Birds, Branches, Relief Carving, c.1860, 24 In., Pair 896.00
Vase, Cheret, Joseph, Frogs, Children Hanging From Branches, Gilt, 15 In. 2300.00
Vase, Dragons, Oriental Design, Greek Key Top & Base, 18 3/4 In., Pair 660.00
Vase, Flared Bowl, Wave Base, Flared Bowl, Japan, 19th Century, 12 In. Diam. 1265.00
Vase, Flowers, Sterling Overlay, Mark, Pat. Aug. 27, 1912, 7 3/4 In. 230.00
Vase, Oriental, Relief Designs, Raised Rim, Cylinder, c.1800, 12 1/2 In. 165.00
Vase, Women Masks, Goblet Shape, Classical Revival, Handles, Round Base, 6 3/4 In. 489.00
Wall Pocket, Gourd Shape, Japan, Late 19th Century, 13 1/2 x 5 x 4 1/2 In. 390.00

BROWNIES were first drawn in 1883 by Palmer Cox. They are charac-
terized by large round eyes, downturned mouths, and skinny legs.
Toys, books, dinnerware, and other objects were made with the
Brownies as part of the design.

Doll, Brownie With Saxophone, Striped Pants, In Glass Case, Schoenhut, 36 In. 9900.00
Doll, Brownie With Tambourine, Pinstriped Jacket, Bowtie, Hat, Schoenhut, 36 In. 7700.00
Doll, Brownie, Pink Jacket, Beige Pants, Bowtie, Schoenhut, 36 In. 9350.00
Illustration, Brownies At Waterloo, On Horses, Palmer Cox, 1899, 9 x 7 3/4 In. 1870.00
Trade Card, Band Marching For Estey 25.00
Trade Card, Giant Cigar, Brownies Around, Besse, Besse & Co., New Haven, Ct. 18.00
Trade Card, Mechanical, Cottolene, Revolving Wheel Projects 6 Different Scenes 50.00
Trade Card, Playing With Giant Baseball, Judgement 18.00

BRUSH Pottery was started in 1925. George Brush first worked in 1901 in Zanesville, Ohio. He started his own pottery in 1907, but it burned to the ground soon after. In 1909 he became manager of the J.W. McCoy Pottery. In 1911, Brush and J.W. McCoy formed the Brush-McCoy Pottery Co. After a series of name changes, the company became The Brush Pottery in 1925. It closed in 1982. Collectors favor the figural cookie jars made by this company. Because there was a company named Brush-McCoy, there is great confusion between Brush and Nelson McCoy pieces. See McCoy category for more information.

MARK

Cookie Jar, Balloon Boy	400.00
Cookie Jar, Bear, Smiling	50.00
Cookie Jar, Chick & Nest	.80.00 to 240.00
Cookie Jar, Cinderella's Pumpkin Coach	120.00
Cookie Jar, Circus Horse	150.00
Cookie Jar, Clown, Bust	60.00
Cookie Jar, Clown, Green Bow	140.00
Cookie Jar, Covered Wagon	170.00
Cookie Jar, Cow, Cat Finial	200.00
Cookie Jar, Dog With Basket	210.00
Cookie Jar, Donkey & Cart	200.00
Cookie Jar, Granny, Green Dress	100.00
Cookie Jar, Happy Bunny	80.00
Cookie Jar, Hippo, Sitting	160.00
Cookie Jar, Hobby Horse	60.00
Cookie Jar, Humpty Dumpty	90.00
Cookie Jar, Laughing Hippo	400.00
Cookie Jar, Little Girl, Wearing Blue Dress, Blue Wings	375.00
Cookie Jar, Panda Bear	110.00
Cookie Jar, Peter Pan	.180.00 to 230.00
Cookie Jar, Pig, Formal, Green, Pink Vest	.140.00 to 160.00
Cookie Jar, Piggy, Sitting	110.00
Cookie Jar, Puppy Police	200.00
Cookie Jar, Raggedy Ann	200.00
Cookie Jar, Squirrel On Log	140.00
Cookie Jar, Squirrel, With Top Hat	130.00
Mug, Little Boy Blue	.60.00 to 400.00
Planter, Little Bo Peep	225.00
Vase, Spread, Turquoise, 5 Flutes, Art Deco, Late 1940s	125.00

BRUSH MCCOY, see Brush category and related pieces in McCoy category.

BUCK ROGERS was the first American science fiction comic strip. It started in 1929 and continued until 1967. Buck has also appeared in comic books, movies, and, in the 1980s, a television series. Any memorabilia connected with the character Buck Rogers is collectible.

Book, Color & Activity, Unused, 8 x 10 3/4 In., 60 Pages	14.00
Book, Paint, Full Color Cover, 1935, 11 x 14 In., 96 Pages	495.00
Book, Whitman Better Little, Buck Rogers In The War With The Planet Venus	78.00
Book, Whitman Big Big, Adventures Of Buck Rogers	120.00
Comic Strip, Printed October 17, 1937	25.00
Gun, Space, Gold	650.00
Helmet, Lightning Bolt, Goodyear	450.00
Map, Solar System, Cocomalt, 1933, 18 1/4 x 25 1/4 In.	590.00
Membership Card, Satellite Pioneers, 2 1/4 x 3 3/4 In.	48.00
Photograph, Radio Dixie Cup Premium	100.00
Photograph, Radio Portrayer, Matthew Crowley, 1936, 8 x 10 In.	85.00
Popgun, Cocomalt Cardboard, 1934, 5 x 10 In.	50.00
Popgun, Space, Buck Rogers Picture On Grip, Pressed Steel, 1930s, 9 1/2 In.	218.00
Punch-O-Bag, Morton's Salt Premium, 1935	50.00
Retail Display, Bubb-A-Loons, Tube, Pipe, Plastic Substance, Imperial Toy Corp.	8.00
Rocket Fighter, Pressed Steel, Rubber Tires, Wyandotte, 1936, 6 In.	175.00
Rocket Ship, Tin, Windup, Box, Marx, 12 In.	1080.00
Space Ranger Kit	200.00

Spaceship, Secret Bomb Sight, Launcher, Morton's Salt Premium, 1942 . . . . 70.00
Starship, Fighter Corgi, Die Cast Metal, Retractable Wings, 2 1/2 In. 15.00
Tablet, Lined, Glossy Cover, Kellogg Co. Premium, 1933, 6 x 8 In., 32 Pages 235.00
Toy, Helmet, Lightning Bolt, 1935, 9 1/2 In. 500.00
Watch, Buck & Wilma On Face, Lightening Bolt Hands, 2 In. 525.00

BUFFALO POTTERY was made in Buffalo, New York, after 1902. The
company was established by the Larkin Company, famous manufacturers of soap. The wares are marked with a picture of a buffalo and
the date of manufacture. Deldare ware is the most famous pottery
made at the factory. It has either a khaki-colored or green background
with hand-painted transfer designs.

BUFFALO POTTERY, Child's Set, Mary, Little Lamb, Warming Dish, Bowl, Mug, Saucer 55.00
Pitcher, Cinderella, c.1908, 4 x 5 In. 138.00
Pitcher, Pilgrim, Signed, 1907, 9 In. 402.00
Plate, Dr. Syntax Presenting A Floral Offering, 1911, 6 1/4 In. 300.00
Plate, George Washington, Chesapeake & Ohio RR, 1907, 10 1/2 In. 660.00
Plate, Misfortune At Tulip Hall, Emerald, 8 1/4 In. . . . . .330.00 to 415.00
Plate, Roosevelt Bears, Scallop, 1907, 7 1/4 In. 468.00
Plate, Ship, Ruby Red Orange Glaze, Abino, c.1912, 6 1/4 In. 165.00
Plate, Windmill & Boat Scene, Orange Glaze Cloud Banks, Abino, 1913, 6 In. 275.00
Plate, Windmill, Abino, c.1912, 8 1/4 In. 468.00
Punch Set, Tom & Jerry, Colorido, 6 1/2 x 11 In. 248.00
Sugar, Cover, Nautical, Abino, Harris & Stuart, c.1912, 4 1/2 In. 605.00
Tea Set, Stand, Silver Overlay, Traveling In Ye Olden Days, 6 In. 247.00
Teapot, Argyle, Tea Ball & Chain Attached To Cover, 6 3/4 In. 240.00
Tray, Card, Windmill, Boat, Abino, c.1912, 8 In. 275.00
Tray, Steam Ship, Abino, c.1912, 14 In. 410.00
Vase, Pinched Waist, Windmill, Boat, Abino, Harris, c.1912, 13 x 5 1/4 In. 410.00
BUFFALO POTTERY DELDARE, Bowl, Fallowfield Hunt, Breakfast At Three Pigeons, 5 x 14 In. 3190.00
Bowl, Fallowfield Hunt, The Death, Hunter Chase Scene, 3 3/4 In. 715.00
Bowl, Fern, Dr. Syntax Reading Tour, Butterflies, Flowers, Emerald, 8 In. 715.00
Bowl, Fruit, Ye Village Tavern, Gentlemen Gathered, 3 x 9 1/4 In. 385.00
Candlestick, Village Scene, House & Landscape, 5 In. 495.00
Candlestick, Village Scene, Signed, 1909, 9 1/8 In. 175.00
Chop Plate, Fallowfield Hunt, The Start, Hunting Dogs, 13 1/2 In. 330.00
Creamer, Fallowfield Hunt, Breaking Cover, Riders & Dogs, 2 x 4 In. 495.00
Cup, Shaving, Ye Razor, Gentleman Sitting In Chair, 1909, 6 In. 1430.00
Cup & Saucer, Bouillon, Fallowfield Hunt, Rider Scene, 1909, 2 In. 935.00
Cup & Saucer, Ye Olden Days, Gentleman Strolling, 6 In., 4 Piece 660.00
Humidor, Sailing Scene, There Was An Old Sailor, 1909, 7 1/4 x 6 In. 1100.00
Humidor, Ye Lion Inn, 7 x 6 1/2 In. 660.00
Matchbox Holder, Ashtray, Scenes Of Village Life, 3 & 6 In., Pair 715.00
Mug, Breaking Cover, Hunt Scene, Gentleman & Lady Riding, 3 In. 357.00
Mug, Dr. Syntax Made Free Of Cellar, Emerald, 4 1/2 In. 165.00
Mug, Fallowfield Hunt, 2 1/2 x 2 3/4 In. 880.00
Mug, Fallowfield Hunt, Breakfast At Three Pigeons, 4 1/2 x 5 In. 220.00
Mug, Fallowfield Hunt, Riders On Horseback, 1908, 4 1/2 In. 137.00
Pitcher, Dr. Syntax Amused With Pat In Pond, Emerald, 1911, 7 x 6 In. 1045.00
Pitcher, Dr. Syntax Bound To Tree, Emerald, 1911, 8 In. 715.00
Pitcher, Fallowfield Hunt, 1909, 6 In. 440.00
Pitcher, Fallowfield Hunt, Breaking Cover, 9 In. . . . . .660.00 to 800.00
Pitcher, Fallowfield Hunt, The Start, Rougeware, 9 1/4 In. 605.00
Pitcher, This Amazed Me, Gentlemen In Conversation, 1909, 9 In. 330.00
Pitcher, To Spare An Old Broken Soldier, 8 x 7 In. . . . . .302.00 to 316.00
Plaque, Dr. Syntax Sells Grizzle, Syntax Selling Horse, Emerald, 13 In. 1430.00
Plaque, Friday, Friars Eating Fish 1914, 13 In. . . . . .2310.00 to 2800.00
Plaque, Thursday, Friars Fishing In Pond, 1917, 13 In. . . . . .2200.00 to 4125.00
Plate, Calendar, 1910, Elves In Different Seasons Of Year, 9 1/2 In. 1540.00
Plate, Dr. Syntax Disputing His Bill, Emerald, 1909, 9 1/4 In. 220.00
Plate, Dr. Syntax Making A Discovery, Arched Border, Emerald, 10 In. 935.00
Plate, Dr. Syntax Pursued By A Bull, Emerald, 1911, 9 In. 935.00
Plate, Dr. Syntax Soliloquizing, Emerald, 7 1/4 In. 220.00

Plate, Dr. Syntax Star Gazing, Dr. Syntax & Woman, Emerald, 9 1/4 In. 825.00
Plate, Fallowfield Hunt, Breaking Cover, Riders On Horseback, 7 In. 110.00
Plate, Fallowfield Hunt, Rider Being Thrown From Horse, 6 1/4 In. 137.00
Plate, Fallowfield Hunt, The Death, Capture Of A Fox, 1908, 8 In. 220.00
Plate, Wall, Peacock On Fence, Cascading Plumage, Emerald, 12 In. 4675.00
Plate, Yankee Doodle, c.1909, 10 In. ....1980.00 to 2090.00
Plate, Ye Olden Times, Gentlemen Are Gathered, 9 1/4 In. 88.00
Plate, Ye Town Crier, Crier Announcing The Towns, 8 1/4 In. 88.00
Plate, Ye Village Gossips, Gentlemen Are Gathered, 1924, 10 In. 110.00
Relish Tray, Ye Olden Times, Oblong, 2 x 12 In. 525.00
Soup, Dish, Fallowfield Hunt, Breaking Cover, 2 x 9 In. 468.00
Soup, Dish, Ye Village Street, 2 Gentlemen Strolling, 1908, 9 In. 247.00
Tankard, Dancing Mice & Owl, Emerald, 12 1/4 In. 4950.00
Tankard, Fallowfield Hunt, Hunt Supper, c.1908, 12 1/4 x 6 1/2 In. 1430.00
Tankard, Fallowfield Hunt, The Hunt Supper, 12 In. 690.00
Tray, Card, Fallowfield Hunt, Breakfast At Three Pigeons, 1909, 8 In. 385.00
Tray, Heirlooms, Ladies Gathered Around Table, 1908, 14 In. 357.00
Tray, Ye Olden Times, Gentlemen Along Boardwalk, 1908, 12 In. 495.00
Wall Plaque, Ye Lion Inn, 13 In. 190.00

BUNNYKINS, see Royal Doulton category.

BURMESE GLASS was developed by Frederick Shirley at the Mt. Washington Glass Works in New Bedford, Massachusetts, in 1885. It is a two-toned glass, shading from peach to yellow. Some pieces have a pattern mold design. A few Burmese pieces were decorated with pictures or applied glass flowers of colored Burmese glass. Other factories made similar glass also called *Burmese*. Related items may be listed in the Fenton category, the Gunderson category and under Webb Burmese.

Biscuit Jar, Gold Enameled Acorns, Silver Plated Rim, 7 1/4 x 5 In. 600.00
Bowl, 6-Sided Rim, 2 3/8 x 2 1/2 In. 295.00
Bowl, Diamond-Quilted, Folded In Sides, Applied Decoration At Rim, 6 1/2 In. 600.00
Bowl, Square Top, Enameled, 4 In. 630.00
Bowl, White Enameled Honeysuckle, Butterfly, 1 3/4 x 3 In. 1175.00
Creamer, Crimped Spout, Reeded Handle, Paper Label, 4 1/2 In. 125.00
Fairy Lamp, Flowers, Gilt Metal Stand, 7 1/2 In. 1495.00
Figurine, Rose, 12 Leaves, Petals On Wired Stem, 9 x 1 1/2 In. 2240.00
Hat, Enameled Bumblebee Attracted To Flowering Stands, 3 In. 125.00
Rose Bowl, Applied Flowers, Crimped Top, 3 In. 345.00
Rose Bowl, Enameled Grape & Leaf, 6-Sided Rim, 3 1/4 In. 290.00
Shade, Swirled, Ribs, 5 3/4 x 8 1/2 In., Pair 440.00
Sherbet, Footed, 2 1/2 x 2 7/8 In. 325.00
Toothpick, Diamond-Quilted, Square Rim, 2 In. 575.00
Toothpick, Ruffled Edge & Foot, 4 In. 110.00
Toothpick, Square Rim, Glossy, 2 1/2 In. 259.00
Tumbler, Enameled, Clump Of Daisies, 3 3/4 In. 374.00
Tumbler, Juice, Tapered, 3 3/4 In. 275.00
Vase, Bulbous, Enameled Persian-Style Decoration, 11 1/2 In. 1438.00
Vase, Crimped, Ruffled Edge, 6 1/2 In. 80.00
Vase, Enameled Diving Dragonfly, White Orchids, Green Stems, 5 In. 280.00
Vase, Globular, Tall Neck, Enameled Leaves, 7 1/2 In., Pair 1115.00
Vase, Jack-In-The-Pulpit, Signed, Label, 4 1/2 In. 140.00
Vase, Lily, 10 In. 600.00
Vase, Ruffled Edge, Applied Ruffled Foot, 4 1/2 In. 190.00
Vase, Teardrop Shape, Enameled Flower Spray, 8 1/4 In. 920.00

BUSTER BROWN, the comic strip, first appeared in color in 1902. Buster and his dog, Tige, remained a popular comic and soon became even more famous as the emblem for a shoe company, a textile firm, and others. The strip was discontinued in 1920, but some of the advertising is still in use.

Button, Brownbilt Club, Buster Brown & Tige, Celluloid, 1 In. 16.00

> **To remove the brown deposits found in old vinegar cruets, fill the cruets with diluted ammonia for a few hours, then rinse.**

Buster Brown, Dispenser,
Helium, Painted, Mouth
Inflates Balloons, 36 In.

Button, Buster Brown Comedies Club Member, Buster, Tige, Lithograph, 7/8 In. 187.00
Calendar, 1902, Top & Bottom Metal Strips, Full Pad, Matted, Frame, 17 x 28 In. 770.00
Dispenser, Helium, Painted, Mouth Inflates Balloons, 36 In. . . . . *Illus* 550.00
Display, Figural, Buster & Tige, Wooden Shelves, 68 1/2, 2 Piece 410.00
Game, Pin The Tail, Oilcloth, In Wooden Frame, 21 1/2 x 33 1/2 In. 1155.00
Hobbyhorse, On Frame, Buster & Tige Picture, 36 x 28 In. 287.00
Pin, Celluloid, Pin, Buster & Tige, 1901-1910, 2 In. 310.00
Pocket Knife, Brown Bilt Shoe Premium, Ivory Celluloid, Black Text, 3 3/4 In. 45.00
Sign, Golden Sheaf Bakery, Buster Brown Bread, Dog Tige, Tin, 19 x 27 1/4 In. . . . 275.00 to 575.00
Toy, Bell Ringer, Buster Brown & Tige, Cast Iron, Steel Wheels, 7 In. 2970.00

BUTTER CHIPS, or butter pats, were small individual dishes for butter.
They were the height of fashion from 1880 to 1910. Earlier as well as
later examples are known.

Dahlia, 2 Heads, Blue, Black, 3 In. 20.00
Flowers, Blue, Green Leaves, 2 Outer Gold Bands, Scalloped, 3 1/2 In. 15.00
Flowers, Greens, Scalloped, Alfred Meakin Frankfort, Crown, 3 1/4 In. 12.00
Horse Drawn Car, Blue, White, Flowers On Edge, Lamberton China, 3 3/8 In. 50.00
Pansy, Figural, Black & White, 3 In. 18.00
Rose, Large Center Flower, Gold Design Scalloped Around Edge, 3 1/8 In. 18.00
Rose, Pink, Gold, Black, Yellow, Green, Johnson Bros., Crown, 3 In. 12.00
Roses, Dainty Pink Flowers, Green Leaves, Embossed Edge, Haviland, 3 1/8 In. 14.00
Victorian, Blue-Green & Gold Flower-Leaf Motif, Scalloped, 3 In. 25.00

BUTTER MOLDS are listed in the Kitchen category under Mold, Butter.

BUTTON collecting has been popular since the nineteenth century. Buttons have been known throughout the centuries, and there are millions
of styles. Gold, silver, or precious stones were used for the best buttons, but most were made of natural materials, like bone or shell, or
from inexpensive metals. Only a few types are listed for comparison.

Bakelite, Ball Shape, Black, 5/8 In. 3.25
Bakelite, Butterscotch, Log Shape, Fat, Carved Top, Carved Out Self Shank, 1 1/8 In. . . . 7.00
Bakelite, Butterscotch, Marbled, Triangular, Rounded Sides, 1 3/8 In. 5.00
Bakelite, Butterscotch, Round, Fish-Like Carving On Each Side, 1 1/8 In. 9.00
Bakelite, Butterscotch, Round, Scalloped Edge, 1 1/4 In. 5.00
Bakelite, Carved Edge Design, Dark Brown, Sew Through, 1 1/8 In. 7.00
Bakelite, Carved Open Design, Brown, Metal Shank, 1 7/16 In. 7.50
Bakelite, Carved Surface Design, Brown, Drilled Out Self Shank, 1 3/4 In. 20.00
Bakelite, Cylinder Shape, Dark Apple Juice, Embedded Confetti, Self Shank, 1 In. 5.00
Bakelite, Gear Shape, Dark Green, 1/2 In. 3.00
Bakelite, Log Shape, Apple Juice, Pink Tint, Embedded Confetti, 1 In. 5.00
Bakelite, Molded Openwork, Medium Brown, 1 1/16 In. 3.00
Bronze, Revolutionary War, Embossed 2 B P, 3/4 In. 516.00
Butterscotch, Marbled, Round, Carved, 1 1/8 In. 5.00
Celluloid, Glow Bubble, Domed, Iridescent Green, Metal Loop Shank, 1 1/8 In. 6.25
Celluloid, Knot Shape, Gold, Half Loop Shank, 1 In. 4.00
Celluloid, Knot Shape, Purple, Half Loop Shank, 1 In. 4.50
Celluloid, Knot Shape, Tan, Braided Center, Celluloid Half Loop Shank, 1 1/4 In. 4.50

Celluloid, Oval, Tight Top, French Ivory-Like Top, 1 3/8 In. 3.50
Celluloid, Polo Player, 1 11/16 In. 12.50
Celluloid, Round, Etched Lines, 4 Rhinestones, 1 1/4 In. 5.00
Celluloid, Round, Tight Top, French Ivory-Like, Metal Loop Shank, 1 In. 4.50
Celluloid, Round, Tight Top, Green, Art Deco, Domed Metal Hump Shank, 11/16 In. 2.65
Celluloid, Round, Tight Top, Red, Art Deco, Metal Loop Shank, 7/16 In. 3.25
Celluloid, Sailing Ship, Sew Through, 1 5/16 In. 8.00
Celluloid, Spaghetti Knot, Green, Celluloid Half Loop Shank, 1 1/16 In. 3.75
Glass, Black Painted Screen Back, Molded & Painted Flowers, 3/4 In. 4.50
Glass, Slag, Green, Blue, White, Gold, Brown Streaks, 11/16 In. 12.00
Glass, Slag, Yellow, Molded Triangle Shape Edging, 3/4 In. 8.50
Milk Glass, Hand Painted Flowers, Gold Rim, 3/8 In. 3.00
Milk Glass, Molded & Painted Fruit Basket, 13/16 In. 8.50
Muppet, 1980, Henson Asso. Inc., Miss Piggy, Fozzie, Rowlf, Kermit, Set Of 4 .... 20.00
Paperweight, Glass, Ball Shape, Green & White Stripes, 1/2 In. 8.50
Paperweight, Glass, Floating Blue & White Spots, Metal Shank, 1/2 In. 8.00

BUTTONHOOKS have been a popular collectible in England for many
years but are now gaining the attention of American collectors. The
buttonhooks were made to help fasten the many buttons of the old-
fashioned high-button shoes and other items of apparel.

Faceted Stone, Hallmark, 2 In. 52.00
Silver, Fruit, 3 1/4 In. 43.00
Silver, With Shoehorn, Art Nouveau, Flowers, Hallmark, England, c.1900 .... 32.00
Steel, With Shoehorn, Stamped, Case, c.1826 .... 56.00
Sterling Silver, Art Nouveau Woman, Lily, Marked, 925 Sterling Fine, c.1900, 8 In. 60.00
Sterling Silver, Engraved, A.W. Hare, 8 x 1 1/4 x 5/16 In. 160.00
Sterling Silver, Lion & Crown, Handle, Mother-Of-Pearl, CWF, 1902, 3 1/2 In. 52.00

BYBEE POTTERY was started in 1845 and is still working. The Lexington, Kentucky, firm makes pottery that is sold at the factory. Pieces are
marked with the name or with the name enclosed by the outline of the
state of Kentucky.

Cookie Jar, Cover, Blue Matte Glaze, Stamped, Cornelisons, 8 1/2 x 8 In. 100.00
Creamer & Sugar, Cover, Green Spongeware 13.00
Cruet, Vinegar, White, Signed, Dated 77 .... 25.00
Cuspidor, Fluted, Leaves, Sponging On Edges, 5 x 7 In. 21.50
Pitcher, Cover, Flowers, Pink, Spongeware, 9 1/4 In. 28.00
Pitcher, Yellow, Squat, 4 3/4 x 6 1/2 In., Qt. 15.50
Platter, Blue, 8 1/2 x 5 In. 26.00
Punch Bowl, Fluted, Pink, Blue, Spongeware, 13 Piece, 14 x 6 1/4 In., Gal. ... 61.00
Vase, 2-Tone Metallic Green, 2 Handles, Urn Shape, 6 x 4 3/4 In. 188.00
Vase, Arts & Crafts, Delft Blue, 2 Handles, 27 Seldon Bybee, 5 In. 75.00

CALENDARS made to hang on the wall or to be displayed on a desk top
have been popular since the last quarter of the nineteenth century.
Many were printed with advertising as part of the artwork and were
given away as premiums. Calendars with guns, gunpowder, or Coca-
Cola advertising are most prized.

1898, F.W. Devoe & C.T. Raynolds Co., 12 1/2 x 9 1/2 In. 57.00
1902, Chicago, Milwaukee & St. Paul Railroad, 6 Sheets, 10 x 12 3/4 In. 517.00
1903, Chicago, Milwaukee & St. Paul Railway, Women, Frame, 34 x 18 In. 317.00
1905, Christian Herald Bible House, Young Girls, Songbirds, 14 x 32 In. 165.00
1905, Metropolitan Life Ins. Co., Children Scene, Roses, 25 x 7 In. 210.00
1911, Worcester Merchant, Crosscut Tree Trunk, Cardboard, 15 1/2 In. 83.00
1914, Springfield Breweries, Victorian Woman, C. Ward Traver, 20 x 30 1/2 In. 575.00
1916, De Laval Cream Separator, Children, Wm. Phillips & Son, 12 x 24 In. 745.00
1918, J. Lopresty & Co., Bakery, Art Nouveau Style, Boston, Framed, 19 x 14 In. 241.00
1918, Uncle Sam, Holding Banner, Merry Christmas, Frame, 12 1/2 x 9 1/2 In. ... 46.00
1919, Edison Mazda, Spirit Of The Night, Woman, Attendants, 20 x 9 3/8 In. 13200.00
1920, Pershing Standing Over Lafayette's Tomb, Cardboard 38.00
1920, Winchester, Duck Hunting Scene, Frame, 19 1/2 x 38 In. 980.00
1922, New York Central, Travel Through 1830-1920 Pictures, Frame, 18 x 30 In. 264.00

1923, Edison Mazda, Lampseller Of Baghdad, 38 x 18 1/2 In. 4290.00
1924, Edison Mazda, Venetian Lamplighter, 19 1/8 x 8 1/2 In. 413.00
1924, Edison Mazda, Venetian Lamplighter, Pocket, Parrish, 3 3/4 x 2 1/4 In. 175.00
1924, Orange Crush, Matted, Framed, Under Glass 825.00
1927, Circe's Palace, Gift Box, Maxfield Parrish, 5 x 3 3/4 In. 70.00
1927, Daily Worker Order Form, Revolutionary Dates, 8 1/2 x 16 In. 25.00
1927, Edison Mazda, Reveries, 2 Women By Pool, 40 3/4 x 21 3/4 In. 1155.00
1928, Edison Mazda, Contentment, 2 Women On Sunlit Ledge, 40 1/2 x 21 In. 1018.00
1930, Ecstasy, Maxfield Parrish, 8 1/2 x 13 In. 1935.00
1930, Edison Mazda, Ecstasy, 20 3/4 x 10 In. 688.00
1930, Edison Mazda, Ecstasy, Pocket, Maxfield Parrish, 3 3/4 x 2 1/4 In. 165.00
1930, Fine Soo Line, Lake Louise, Alberta, R. Atkinson Fox, Frame, 34 x 29 In. 230.00
1931, Edison Mazda, Waterfall, 2 Girls Overlooking Waterfall, 40 3/4 x 21 In. 1925.00
1932, Edison Mazda, Solitude, Girl On Rocks, Sunlit Canyon, 19 1/8 x 8 1/2 In. 798.00
1933, Edison Mazda, Sunrise, Women On Balcony, Sunlit Canyon, 22 1/2 x 12 In. 495.00
1934, Northwestern Natl Insurance, Italian Garden, Vicobello, Maxfield Parrish 495.00
1935, Thinking Of You, Portrait Of Blond Woman, Teheichel, 7 x 14 In. 18.00
1936, American League, Against War & Fascism, 9 1/2 x 16 1/2 In. 380.00
1936, Communist Party, Earl Browder Picture.7 1/4 x 11 In. 76.00
1937, B & B, Twilight, Executive, 22 1/2 x 16 1/2 In. 660.00
1937, Ford Motor Co., Thrifty Twin, Scotty Dogs 28.00
1938, B & B, The Glen, Executive, 22 1/2 x 16 1/2 In. 495.00
1938, Edison Mazda, Egyptian Priestess, Victor Keppler, 19 1/8 x 8 1/2 In. 413.00
1939, Budweiser Beer, Art Deco Pinup, 5 1/2 x 12 In. 12.00
1940, Great Falls, 24 x 49 In. 445.00
1942, Burlington Railroad, Silver King, 24 1/4 x 18 In. 82.00
1942, Maas & Steffen Fur Company, 26 1/4 x 13 1/2 In. 344.00
1942, Pennsylvania Railroad, 28 1/2 x 29 In. 82.00
1942, Thomas Murphy Co., Thy Woods & Templed Hills, Salesman's Sample 578.00
1943, A Perfect Day, Maxfield Parrish, 11 x 16 In. 255.00
1943, Our Country! Right Or Wrong Our Country, Remember Pearl Harbor 55.00
1945, Happy Moments, Girl With Terrier Puppy, Jules Erbit, 10 x 19 In. 45.00
1946, Fairest Flower, Zoe Mozert, 10 x 17 1/2 In. 75.00
1946, Sinclair Gasoline, Full Pad, 33 1/2 x 16 In. 110.00
1946, Skelly Gasoline, 16 x 32 12 In. 55.00
1947, All American Girl, Blond Ice Skater, Red Outfit, Buell, 9 1/2 x 15 1/2 In. 28.00
1949, B & B, Village Church, Executive, 33 3/8 x 16 3/4 In. 176.00
1952, Ballantine, The Best In 1952, Woman Holding Beer, 14 x 20 In. 35.00
1952, Monthly Glamour Girl, Spiral Bound, Thompson, 8 3/4 x 12 1/4 In. 38.00
1952, Russell Crowther Trucking Co., Easel Back Or Wall Mount, 5 1/2 In. 82.00
1953, TWA, 2-Sided Pages, 24 x 16 In. 33.00
1954, Lincoln Way Sales & Service, Marilyn Monroe, Nude, Abbottstown, Pa. 83.00
1954, Old Glen Mill, Cardboard, Maxfield Parrish, 7 1/2 x 5 1/4 In. 140.00
1957, The Shake Down, Frahm, 10 x 16 3/4 In. 45.00
1958, Grapette, 16 x 33 In. 240.00
1958, It's A Date, Zoe Mozert, 16 x 23 1/2 In. 45.00
1960, Sheltering Oaks, Maxfield Parrish, 10 3/4 x 6 In. 70.00
1961, Casino, Harold's Opera House, 14 x 17 In. 78.00
1965, Lee's Variety Store, Locke Mills, Maine, Full Pad, 10 x 17 In. 165.00
1968, Horlacher Brewing Co., Metal Bands Top & Bottom, 16 x 34 In. 46.00
1970, Playboy Playmate 15.00
1974, Playboy Playmate 12.00
1976, Playboy Playmate 10.00
1993, Playboy Playmate 5.00
Perpetual, De Laval, Tin Lithograph, Easel Back, 1910-1920, 5 1/2 x 7 In. 1375.00

CALENDAR PLATES were very popular in the United States from 1906
to 1929. Since then, plates have been made every year. A calendar and
the name of a store, a picture of flowers, a girl, or a scene were featured on the plate.

1908, Plymouth Rock, Money Saved At Price's Store, Scalloped Edge, 9 In. 65.00
1908, Tiger Kitten, Souvenir Of Weston, Vt., Scalloped Edge, 9 In. 43.00
1909, E.D. Lanoue General Merchandise, Fruit, Ashkum, Ill., 7 5/8 In. 65.00

1909, Flying Bird, 1909 Sash In Beak, Souvenir Of Centralia, Ill., 8 1/4 In. 58.00
1909, Portrait Of Young Woman, Purple Ribbed Border, 4 Seasons, 8 7/8 In. 50.00
1909, Red Rose, Green Rim Fades To White, Calendars Around Edge, 8 1/4 In. 25.00
1909, Rose & Grape Cluster, Holly, B J Blakely Advertisement, 7 5/8 In. 32.00
1910, F.E. Curtis Jeweler, Cherubs Ringing Bell, Kemmerer, Wyo., 7 1/4 In. 127.00
1913, Carnation & McNichol, Boy Under Arbor, Months On Pillars, 7 1/4 In. 76.00
1917, Okeene Cash Store, World War II, Flags, Okeene, Tex, 8 3/8 In. 51.00
1920, Victory, Banner, Spread Eagle, Globe, Flags, 9 In. 46.00
1929, Flowers, Appreciation Of Patronage, Bert Smith, Exeter, Mo., 6 1/2 In. 40.00
1929, Roses, Ribbons & Bows Join Calendars, 12 Sides, 7 In. 44.00
1951, Country Scene In Center, 6 Calendars Each Side, Red Lettering, 10 1/4 In. 35.00
1952, Dutch Mill & Sailboats In Center, Floral Edge, Gold Printing, 10 In. 15.00
1953, Circle Of Calendars, Zodiac Signs, Center 1953 Zodiac Medallion, 9 In. 15.00
1955, Floral Wreath, Floral Rim, Clear Edge, 10 In. 15.00
1957, Circle Of Gold Dots, Zodiac Signs Below Each Month, 10 In. 15.00
1958, Flowers In Center, 6 Calendars Each Side Around Rim 35.00
1961, Cottage, Arched Bridge Over Stream, Staffordshire, 9 In. 19.00
1962, Floral, Figural Pattern Around Scalloped Edge, 9 In. 15.00
1963, 2 Vertical Rows Of Calendars, Sports Activities In Corners, 10 1/4 In. 15.00
1964, New Jersey Commemorative, State Map, Capital Dome, 10 1/8 In. 28.00
1965, Rooster Weathervane In Center, Script Writing, Floral Rim, 10 1/4 In. 18.00
1974, Blue, White, Alfred Meakin, 9 In. 15.50
1976, Currier & Ives, Royal China, 10 In. 26.00
1986, Garden Birds, Wedgwood 21.00

CAMARK POTTERY started in 1924 in Camden, Arkansas. Jack Carnes
founded the firm and made many types of glazes and wares. The company was bought by Mary Daniel. Production was halted in 1983.

Basket, Iris, Blue, Impressed Mark, U.S.A., 9 1/2 In. 82.00
Bowl, Fruit, Square Foot, Purple, Scalloped Edge, 7 x 8 1/2 In. 65.00
Bowl, Pansy Arranger, Top, Purple Violet, 2 3/4 x 4 In. 46.00
Candlestick, Blue Flowers, Paper Label, 6 In., Pair 57.00
Console, Fish, Green, 2 Candleholders, 3 Piece 19.00
Ewer, Pastel Blue, Spiral Design On Body & Handle, No. 134, 6 3/4 In. 39.00
Ewer, Pink Iris, Impressed Mark, 14 x 5 1/2 In. 62.00
Planter, Swan, Green 23.00
Vase, Burnt Orange, 2 Handles, Impressed Mark, 4 3/4 In. 49.00
Vase, Festoon Of Roses, 9 1/4 In. 115.00
Vase, Mauve, Green Matte, 8 1/2 x 9 1/4 In. 66.00
Vase, Multicolored Green Drip Glaze, Impressed Mark, 18 1/2 In. 2530.00
Vase, Pink Morning Glory, Yellow, Green, Impressed Mark, 8 1/4 x 7 1/2 In. 76.00
Vase, Rust, Orange, Yellow, Bulbous, 8 7/8 In. 180.00
Wall Pocket, Seahorse, Green, 7 5/8 In. 65.00

CAMBRIDGE GLASS Company was founded in 1901 in Cambridge,
Ohio. The company closed in 1954, reopened briefly, and closed again
in 1958. The firm made all types of glass. Their early wares included
heavy pressed glass with the mark *Near Cut*. Later wares included
Crown Tuscan, etched stemware, and clear and colored glass. The firm
used a C in a triangle mark after 1920. Some Cambridge patterns may
be included in the Depression Glass category.

Apple Blossom, Candlestick, Peach-Blo, 5 3/4 In. 55.00
Bashful Charlotte, Flower Frog, 6 1/2 In. 50.00
Caprice, Bowl, Crimped, 9 1/2 In. 21.00
Caprice, Bowl, Footed, Peach-Blo, 5 1/4 x 12 In. 150.00
Caprice, Bowl, Moonlight Blue, Footed, 10 1/2 In. 55.00
Caprice, Candlestick, 2-Light, Pair 37.00
Caprice, Candlestick, 3-Light, 6 In., Pair 60.00
Caprice, Candlestick, Moonlight Blue, 7 In., Pair 160.00
Caprice, Compote, Footed, 7 In. 30.00
Caprice, Cup & Saucer, La Rosa, Footed, 6 Oz. 30.00
Caprice, Dish, Mayonnaise, Underplate, Moonlight Blue 25.00
Caprice, Goblet, 10 Oz., 7 3/4 In. 12.00

Caprice, Ice Bucket 60.00
Caprice, Pitcher, Moonlight Blue, Ball Shape, 8 Oz., 8 1/2 In. 227.00
Caprice, Plate, Luncheon, 8 1/2 In. 28.00
Caprice, Plate, Moonlight Blue, 8 1/2 In. 13.00
Caprice, Platter, Moonlight Blue, Alpine, 14 In. 65.00
Caprice, Sugar 10.00
Caprice, Tumbler, Blown, Crystal, 10 Oz. 20.00
Caprice, Tumbler, Blue, 9 Oz., 5 In. 35.00
Caprice, Tumbler, Blue, Footed, 10 Oz. 40.00
Caprice, Tumbler, Footed, 12 Oz. 25.00
Caprice, Tumbler, Footed, Moonlight Blue, 9 Oz. 140.00
Caprice, Tumbler, Juice, Footed, Moonlight Blue, 5 Oz. 55.00
Caprice, Vase, Amber, 4 1/2 In. 65.00
Caprice, Water Set, Moonlight Blue, 7 Piece 500.00
Carmen, Candlestick, 2-Light, Keyhole 145.00
Chantilly, Plate, Salad, 8 In. 20.00
Cleo, Sandwich Server, Center Handle, Willow Blue, 11 In. 35.00
Crown Tuscan, Box, Candy, Cover, Marked, 6 In. 40.00
Crown Tuscan, Candlestick, 2-Light, 6 In., Pair 75.00
Crown Tuscan, Vase, Ball Shape, Gold Encrusted, Chintz Etch, Marked, 5 In. 210.00
Daisy, Basket, Arched Foot, Near Cut Mark, 7 1/2 In. 75.00
Daisy, Creamer & Spooner, Near Cut, Mark 45.00
Decagon, Console, 11 In. 150.00
Decagon, Cup & Saucer, Moonlight Blue 16.00
Decagon, Plate, Moonlight Blue, 7 1/2 In. 14.00
Decagon, Sugar & Creamer, Moonlight Blue 30.00
Draped Lady, Flower Frog, Amber, 13 In. 450.00
Draped Lady, Flower Frog, Emerald, 11 In. 700.00
Ebony, Bowl, Cambridge Square, 12 1/2 In. 50.00
Ebony, Decanter, Ball Shape, Crystal Handle & Stopper, Label, 32 Oz. 55.00
Ebony, Urn, Gold Trim 145.00
Ebony, Vase, Trumpet, Footed, 9 1/2 In. 95.00
Everglade, Vase, Oval, 6 In. 450.00
Georgian, Basket, Smoke Handle ....65.00 to 80.00
Georgian, Tumbler, Moonlight Blue, 9 Oz., 6 Piece 75.00
Helio, Bowl, Gold Rim, Ebony Foot, 8 In. 75.00
Helio, Candy Jar, Cover 150.00
Helio, Vase, Sweet Pea, Gold Rim 60.00
Honeycomb, Compote, Rubina, 5 In. 350.00
Imperial Hunt Scene, Tumbler, Iced Tea, Footed, Emerald, 12 Oz. 60.00
Jenny Lind, Bowl, Crimped, 4 1/2 x 11 In. 95.00
Marjorie, Vase, Near Cut Mark, 11 1/2 In. 65.00
Martha Washington, Vase, Fan, Milk Glass, 8 1/2 In. 45.00
Mt. Vernon, Candlestick, Royal Blue, 4 In., Pair 140.00
Mt. Vernon, Cordial, 1 Oz. 12.00
Mt. Vernon, Cordial, Milk Glass, 1 Oz. 40.00
Mt. Vernon, Decanter, Stopper, 8 3/4 In. 50.00
No. 687, Candlestick, Amber, c.1924-1930 .... 15.00
No. 1307, Candlestick, 3-Light 20.00
Nude, Brandy, Forest Green, 1 Oz. 175.00
Nude, Brandy, Moonlight Blue, 1 Oz. 450.00
Nude, Brandy, Optic Bowl, 1 Oz. 170.00
Nude, Brandy, Optic Bowl, Heather Bloom, 1 Oz. 295.00
Nude, Champagne, Carmen, 6 Oz. 115.00
Nude, Cocktail, Amethyst, 3 Oz. 125.00
Nude, Cocktail, Carmen, 3 Oz. 199.00
Nude, Cocktail, Clear Bowl & Foot, Ebony, Stem, 3 0z. 80.00
Nude, Cocktail, Mandarin Gold, 3 Oz. 125.00
Nude, Cocktail, Smoke, 3 Oz. 295.00
Nude, Compote, Amethyst Bowl, Farberware Base 65.00
Nude, Goblet, Forest Green, 9 Oz. 175.00
Oakwood, Vase, Handle, 10 1/2 In. 130.00
Portia, Vase, Bud, Gold Encrusted, Pair 75.00

Primrose, Nut Tray, Blue Enamel Border, Center Handle, 9 In. 25.00
Rose Lady, Flower Frog, Scalloped Base, Ivory, 9 1/2 In. 510.00
Rose Point, Bonbon, 7 In. 145.00
Rose Point, Bottle, Oil, 6 Oz. 145.00
Rose Point, Cocktail, Royal Blue, 5 Oz. 70.00
Rose Point, Mustard, Cover, 3 Oz. 90.00
Rose Point, Relish, 3 Sections, Handles, 8 In. 45.00
Rose Point, Relish, 5 Sections, 12 In. 65.00
Rose Point, Relish, 7 In. 90.00
Rose Point, Salt & Pepper, Individual 40.00
Rose Point, Sugar & Creamer 50.00
Rose Point, Vase, Keyhole, 10 In. 195.00
Roselyn, Torte Plate, 14 In. 25.00
Shell, Bowl, Forest Green, 10 In. 90.00
Sign, Advertising, Frosted Ground, Clear Letters, Oval 210.00
Stackaway, Ashtray Set, Blue, Emerald, Amethyst, Amber, Clear, 5 Piece 45.00
Swan, Milk Glass, 8 1/2 In. 105.00
Tally-Ho, Ball Vase, Amethyst 30.00
Tally-Ho, Ice Pail, Frosted Interior, Forest Green, Handle 89.00
Thistle, Bowl, Emerald Green, Marked, 9 In. 75.00
Tuxedo, Tumbler, Carmen Foot, 8 Oz. 9.00
Wheat Sheaf, Bottle, Cologne, Stopper, Near Cut Mark 45.00

CAMEO GLASS was made in much the same manner as a cameo in jewelry. Parts of the top layer of glass were cut away to reveal a different-
colored glass beneath. The most famous cameo glass was made during
the nineteenth century. Signed cameo glass pieces are listed under the
glasswork's name, such as Daum or Galle.

Biscuit Jar, Flowers, White, Blue, Bail Handle, Silver Plated Mount, 6 In. 748.00
Bowl, Pink Flowers & Swirls, Yellow Ground, Burgun & Schverer, 1900, 8 In. 4800.00
Box, Sterling Silver Lid, Mountain Landscape, 3 Sides, Lamartine, 3 In. 460.00
Goblet, Flowers, Strawberries, Satin, Ground, Paneled Stem, Gold Bands, 6 3/4 In. 110.00
Lamp, Forest Scene, Lake Against Distant Shore, Signed, Arsall, 15 In. 1008.00
Vase, Brown Enameled People, Yellow Ground, Burgun & Schverer, 3 7/8 In. 3000.00
Vase, Brown Leaves, Gold Ground, Burgun & Schverer, 1895, 7 3/4 In. 6600.00
Vase, Continuous Venetian Scene, Yellow & Orange Ground, Signed, 8 In. 975.00
Vase, Cranberry Flowers, Teal Ground, Signed TSV, 6 In. 140.00
Vase, Cut White Bands & Branches, Cranberry Branches On Neck, 6 1/4 In. 525.00
Vase, Flowers & Leaves, Gold Ground, Squat, Burgun & Schverer, 1895, 5 5/8 In. 6600.00
Vase, Flowers Growing From Base To Rim, Prussian Blue, 4 1/2 In. 1065.00
Vase, Gray Flowers Design, Orange, Flared Lip, England, Signed, 1900, 6 In. 4200.00
Vase, Gray Leaves, Yellow Gold Ground, Bulbous, England, 1900, 5 In. 2760.00
Vase, Gray, Russet Orange, Flowers, Tapered, Oval, France, c.1900, 3 1/2 In. 375.00
Vase, Holly, Satin Clear Ground, Gold Enameled Lines, Honesdale, 9 5/8 In. 495.00
Vase, Honeysuckle, Chartreuse Ground, Signed, 4 1/4 In. 616.00
Vase, Hunter In Village, Distant Forest, Lake Scene, Green Sky, Michel, 8 1/4 In. 364.00
Vase, Landscape With Trees, Enameled, Satin, Signed, Lamartine, 6 1/2 In. 980.00
Vase, Landscape, Heart Shape, Circular Foot, Gray, Peach, Green, 1910, 12 In. 196.00
Vase, Lavender Flowers, Leaves, Straight Sides, Burgun & Schverer, 1895, 3 3/4 In. 7200.00
Vase, Leaves, Purple Ground, Small Mouth, Burgun & Schverer, 1895, 5 1/4 In. 3900.00
Vase, Leaves, Purple, Flared Lip, Silver Mount, Burgun & Schverer, 1896, 7 In. 6600.00
Vase, Morning Glory Blossom, Leafy Vine, White Cut To Yellow, 9 In. 865.00
Vase, Mountain Landscape, House, Green & Brown, Signed, Michel, France, 8 In. 1035.00
Vase, Orange Anemone, Yellow Ground, England, 1900, 8 In. 3000.00
Vase, Peaches & Leaves, White Ground, Pink Interior, Enameled Signature, 9 In. 1540.00
Vase, Pink Enameled Flowers, Gray, Small Mouth, Burgun & Schverer, 5 1/8 In. 8400.00
Vase, Purple Flowers, Satin Indigo To White Ground, Conical, 4 7/8 In. 440.00
Vase, Purple Garden Of Flowers, Citron Ground, Signed, 3 3/4 In. 336.00
Vase, Purple, Green & Red Continuous Landscape, Baluster, 3 Sections, 12 In. 1035.00
Vase, Red Poppies, Iridescent Ground, Gold Enameled, Egg Shape, Signed, 6 In. 855.00
Vase, Red, White Carved Flowers, Leaves, 5 In. 2150.00
Vase, Ruby Carved Trees, Rose Colored Ground, 3 3/4 In. 780.00
Vase, Satin Violet Blossoms, Lavender Ground, Inscribed, Pantin, 5 In. 520.00

A glass vase or bowl can be cleaned with a damp cloth. Try not to put the glass in a sink filled with water. Hitting the glass on a faucet or the sink is a common cause of breakage.

Campbell Kids, Doll, Boy,
Printed Fabric, 10 1/4 In.

Vase, Spruce Stand Over Lake, Rocky Mountains, P. Nicolas, 5 1/2 In. 1345.00
Vase, Stems, Green Shading, Gray, Bottle Shape, Christian Meisenthal, 1895, 9 In. 3000.00
Vase, Stylized Flowers, Mottled, Yellow Ground, Flared Neck, 10 In. 630.00
Vase, Trailing Vines, Flowers, Satin Ground, Signed, Foussin, 14 3/8 In. 489.00
Vase, White Flowers & Fern Fronds, Opaque Pink Ground, England, 3 3/4 In. 770.00
Vase, White On Blue, Rose Blossom, Leafy Stem, 4 1/2 In. 920.00

CAMPAIGN memorabilia is listed in the Political category.

CAMPBELL KIDS were first used as part of an advertisement for the Campbell Soup Company in 1906. The kids were created by Grace Drayton, a popular illustrator of the day. The kids were used in magazine and newspaper ads until about 1951. They were presented again in 1966; and in 1983, they were redesigned with a slimmer, more contemporary appearance.

Bank, Cast Iron, Gold, A.C. Williams, c.1920, 3 5/16 In. 144.00
Bell Set, Fenton, Set Of 6 . . . . 180.00
Doll, Boy, Printed Fabric, 10 1/4 In. . . . . *Illus* 100.00
Doll, Chef & Flagman, 1994, Pair 150.00
Doll, Girl, Molded Hair, Old Red Plaid Dress, Composition, 12 In. 70.00
Doll, Petite, American Character, 1928 . . . . 400.00
Salt & Pepper, 4 In. 24.00

CANDELABRUM refers to a candleholder with more than one arm to hold many candles; a candlestick is designed to hold one candle. The eccentricity of the English language makes the plural of candelabrum into candelabra.

2-Light, Brass, Attached Handle & Snuffer, Pineapple Finial, 7 1/2 In. 242.00
2-Light, Brass, Shell & Scroll Base, Gothic Lions & Serpents, 12 In., Pair 220.00
2-Light, Bronze, Leaf Scroll Arms, Louis XVI, Marie Antoinette, 13 In., Pair 1840.00
2-Light, Bronze, Louis XVI, Leaf Arms, Round Base, Electrified, 18 In., Pair 1380.00
2-Light, Patinated, Gilt Bronze, Figural, Continental, 19th Century, 17 1/2 In., Pair 920.00
2-Light, Pulpit, Silvered Brass, Copper Shield, 16 7/8 In. 285.00
2-Light, Silver Plate, Fluted Scroll Branches, Raised Leaf & Bellflower, 9 In., Pair 805.00
2-Light, Silver, Stylized Leaf Supports, Signed Servin, Mexico, 8 1/2 In., Pair 520.00
3-Light, Brass, Louis XIV, Square, Marquetry, Scroll Footed, 18 1/4 In. 200.00
3-Light, Bronze, Charles X, Ormolu, Figural, Kneeling Woman, c.1820, 21 In. 1265.00
3-Light, Bronze, Patinated, Gilt, Louis Philippe, 20 In., Pair 2530.00
3-Light, Bronze, Scrolled Branches, Candle Nozzles, Bud Finial, 11 3/4 In. 2300.00
3-Light, Candlestick Pair, Gilt Bronze, Glass Prisms, 19th Century, 3 Piece 290.00
3-Light, Center Candle Cup, 2 Lower Cups, Silver Plate, Floral & Scroll, 18 1/4 In. 115.00
3-Light, Gilt Bronze, Glass, Continental, Early 19th Century, 17 1/4 In., Pair 1380.00
3-Light, Gilt, Blue Enamel, Scrolled Branches, 15 1/2 x 7 In., Pair 230.00
3-Light, Glass, Molded, Central Baluster Standard, 2 Scrolling Arms, 15 In., Pair 220.00
3-Light, Louis XVI, White Marble, Acanthus Cast Candle, 25 In., Pair 8400.00
3-Light, Parcel Gilt, S-Shape Arms, Bobeche, Prisms, Continental, 20 x 15 In. 880.00

3-Light, Serpent Scrolled Branch, Acorn Finial, 14 1/4 x 4 1/2 x 10 1/2 In. 1955.00
3-Light, Silver Plate, Baluster Stem, Oval Base, 1920s 125.00
3-Light, Silver Plate, Gadrooned, Fluted, Thistle-Form Nozzles, c.1800, 17 In., Pair 3165.00
3-Light, Silver Plate, Rococo Style, Baluster Shape Stem, Arms, 21 1/2 In., Pair 259.00
3-Light, Silver Plate, Scrolled Branches, Stork Center, Griffin Head, 1870s, 24 In. 980.00
3-Light, Silver Plate, Sheffield, 16 1/2 In., Pair 633.00
3-Light, Silver Plate, Turned Stem, Bobeche, Sheffied, c.1890, 13 3/4 In. 146.00
3-Light, Silver, Short Stem, Urn Finial, Campana Sconces, France, 7 1/8 In., Pair 3900.00
3-Light, Sterling Silver, Baluster, Round Base, Frank Whiting & Co., 14 In. 385.00
3-Light, Sterling Silver, Frank Whiting, 15 In., Pair 410.00
3-Light, Sterling Silver, Urn Holders, Glass Inserts, Pair 500.00
4-Light, Alabaster & Metal, Scrolled Standard, Cherub, 19 3/4 In., Pair 575.00
4-Light, Brass, Monkey Form, Plinth Base, c.1890, 25 In. 2875.00
4-Light, Bronze, 2 Female Figures, Raised On Square, Oval Base, 38 In., Pair 7800.00
4-Light, Bronze, Bears & Monkeys, Musical Instruments, Slate Base, 21 1/2 In. 880.00
4-Light, Bronze, Gilt, Classical Maiden, Wooden Base, Electrified, 36 In., Pair 1725.00
4-Light, Bronze, Louis XVI, Scroll Arms, Ram's Heads, 18 1/2 In., Pair 2300.00
4-Light, Bronze, Neo-Grecque, 2 Handles, Marble, R. Barbedienne, 24 In., Pair 2530.00
4-Light, Gilt, Patinated Bronze, Winged Maidens, Empire Style, 27 In., Pair 2820.00
4-Light, Gilt, Patinated Metal, Wheat Sheaves, Finial, Continental, 39 In., Pair 259.00
4-Light, Porcelain, Gilt Bronze, Napoleon III, Mid 19th Century, 31 In., Pair 3910.00
4-Light, Reeded Standard, Footed, Scrolling Arms, Italy, 19th Century, 20 1/2 In. 315.00
4-Light, Repousse, Chased, Black, Starr & Frost, N.Y., c.1890, 13 3/4 In. 5875.00
4-Light, Silver Plate, Acanthus Border, Sheffield, Boulton, c.1830, 29 In., Pair. 5400.00
4-Light, Silver Plate, Raised Leaf, Swag & Ram's Head, Square Base, 1868, 17 In. 170.00
4-Light, Sterling Silver, Scrolled Branches, Griffins On Plinth, Electrified, 26 1/2 In. 6615.00
4-Light, Sterling Silver, Vase Shape, Standard, Leaves, Yellow Ground, Electrified, 20 In. . . 3160.00
5-Light, Bronze, Cobalt Blue Porcelain, Urn Shape Base, Ram Heads, 21 In., Pair 1120.00
5-Light, Bronze, Louis XVI, Bacchus Form, Purple Marble Base, 33 In., Pair 5175.00
5-Light, Flower, Scroll Border, Theodore B. Starr, c.1910, 18 7/8 In., Pair 11165.00
5-Light, Gilt Brass, Continental, Early 20th Century, 17 1/4 In., Pair 460.00
5-Light, Gilt Bronze, Porcelain, Signed Dessart, England, 19th Century, 25 1/2 In. 1610.00
5-Light, Gilt Metal, Putti Standard, Porcelain Panel Insert, Victorian, 22 In., Pair 315.00
5-Light, Louis XV, Gilt Bronze, Figural, Cupid, Holding Ewer, 23 In. 920.00
5-Light, Silver Plate, Allover Ram's Head, Swag & Leaf, 1862, 23 In., Pair 2185.00
5-Light, Silver Plate, Flat Leaf Sconce, Cornucopia Arms, 1870s, 25 1/4 In., Pair 2760.00
5-Light, Silver Plate, Late 19th Century, 19 In., 2 Piece 1008.00
5-Light, Silver Plate, Leaf Arms & Base, Cupid On Standard, 27 In. 1610.00
5-Light, Silver Plate, Scrolled Branches, Urn Form Nozzles, 1870s, 15 x 7 1/2 In. 575.00
5-Light, Silver Plate, Scrolling Leaf Arms, Lion Rampart, c.1890, 27 In. 280.00
5-Light, Silver Plate, Vine Arms, Candle Shades, Reticulated, 26 In. 315.00
5-Light, Sterling Silver, Convertible, Gorham, 20th Century, 16 In. 1725.00
5-Light, Sterling Silver, Marked, Preisner, No. 724 . . . . 90.00
5-Light, Sterling Silver, Ram's Heads, Walker & Hall, England, 1900, 18 In., Pair 6000.00
5-Light, Victorian, Gilt Metal, Putti Standards, Porcelain Inserts, 22 In. 315.00
6 Light, Gilt Bronze, Napoleon III, Rococo Style, Putti, 33 1/2 In., Pair 3220.00
6-Light, Bronze Dore, Louis XIV Style, 19th Century, 31 In. 785.00
6-Light, Bronze, Gilt, Metal, Glass Drip Pans, Glass Pendants, 36 In., Pair 7800.00
6-Light, Bronze, Neoclassical Style, Early 20th Century, 35 In. 1035.00
6-Light, Gilt Brass, Napoleon III, Black Slate, Neo Grecque Style, 24 In., Pair 3220.00
6-Light, Gilt Bronze, Louis XV, Cupid Shape, Marble Base, 21 In., Pair 1265.00
7-Light, Bronze, Louis XV, 29 1/2 In., Pair 1035.00
7-Light, Bronze, Scrolled Arm, Tiered Base, c.1860, 28 In. 4032.00
7-Light, Oak, Copper Holders, Charles Rohlf, Branded, 6 1/2 x 10 1/4 In. 1095.00
8-Light, Bronze, Napoleon III, Cupid, Seated, Scrolled Feet, 30 In., Pair 5400.00
10-Light, Gilt Bronze, Rococo Style, Dogs, Birds, Napoleon III, 30 x 18 x 12 In. 12075.00
Bronze, Double Overlay Glass, Blue To White To Clear, 20 1/2 In., Pair 405.00
Bronze Color, Bird Feeding Chicks, Snails, Foliage, Auguste Nicholas Cain, 20 In. 865.00
Garniture, 3-Light, Silver Plate, Candlesticks, Reed & Barton, 3 Piece 170.00
Garniture, 3-Light, Silver Plate, Gilded, Candlestick Pair, Reed & Barton, 3 Piece 172.00
Garniture, Silver Plate, Centerpiece, Pierced, 3 Compotes, 18 In. & 7 In., 4 Piece 1300.00
Gilt, Patinated Bronze, Figural, Signed Clodion, Late 19th Century, 44 1/2 In. 31800.00
Gilt Brass, Intertwined Dolphins On Column, Double Sockets, 10 1/4 In. 110.00

Girandole, 3-Light, Brass, Marble Base, Priscilla & John, 15 In., Pair 105.00
Girandole, 3-Light, Bronze, Crystal, Marble, Late 19th Century, 18 1/2 x 16 In. 310.00
Girandole, 3-Light, Gilt Bronze, Indians, Man, Child, 1848, 17 1/2 In., Pair 1200.00
Girandole, 3-Light, Gilt Bronze, Prism Draped, Rococo Style, Mid 1800s, 17 In. 400.00
Girandole, 4-Light, Gilt Bronze, Cut Glass, Louis XVI, c.1900, 26 3/4 x 15 3/4 In. 1495.00
Girandole, 4-Light, Silvered Brass, Louis XIV Style, Late 19th Century, 21 1/2 In. 690.00
Girandole, 5-Light, Brass, 4 Arms, Bowed Font, Prisms, Marble Base, 18 x 15 In., Pair .. 635.00
Girandole, 6-Light, Gilt Bronze, Glass, Louis XV Style, 20th Century, 36 1/2 In. 920.00
Girandole, 6-Light, Gilt Metal, Cut Glass Finial, Continental, Late 1800s, 40 In., Pair 1495.00
Girandole, Brass, Faceted Cut Glass Chains, Drops, Ivory Marble Base, 12 In. 490.00
Girandole, Gilt Brass, Marble, Starr, Fellows & Co., 14 1/2 x 6 1/2 x 3 1/2 In., Pair 315.00
Italian Renaissance Style, 19th Century, 15 x 21 In., Pair 290.00
Parcel Gilt Bronze, Louis XVI Style, Late 19th Century, 21 3/4 In. 635.00
Porcelain, Woman Holding Lute, Floral, Germany, 20 1/2 In. 240.00
Silver, Neoclassical, Fluted Column, Garland, Pad Feet, Mexico, 33 In., Pair 4200.00
Silver, Outscrolling Arms, Medallion Center, A. Frisch, Norway, 7 3/4 In. 403.00
Silver, Plain Branches, 2 Sconces, A. Dragsted, Denmark, 4 1/2 In., Pair 345.00
Silver, Stylized Leaf Supports, 2 Candle Cups, Stamp Mark, Mexico, 8 In. 450.00
Silver Plate, 4 Flying Buttress Arches, Griffin On Each, 1870, 27 1/2 In., Pair 8338.00
Silver Plate, Convertible, Waisted Sconces, Knopped Stems, England, 17 1/2 In. 230.00
Silver Plate, Gadrooned Standards, Sheffield, c.1800, 11 1/2 x 9 1/2 In., 4 Piece 865.00
Silver Plate, Tapered Square Columns, Urn Shaped Sockets, S.H. & S.B. 605.00
Silvered & Parcel Gilt Bronze, Scrolled Arms, Urn Finial, 19 In., Pair 258.00

CANDLESTICKS were made of brass, pewter, glass, sterling silver, plated silver, and all types of pottery and porcelain. The earliest candlesticks, dating from the sixteenth century, held the candle on a pricket (sharp pointed spike). These lost favor because in times of strife the large church candlesticks with prickets became formidable weapons, so the socket was mandated. Candlesticks changed in style through the centuries, and designs range from classic to rococo to Art Nouveau to Art Deco.

Altar, French Gilt Bronze, Pricket, Gothic Style, Mid 1800s, 40 x 8 x 8 In. 3680.00
Beaded Ormolu Nozzles, Marble Columns, Chains, Suspending Acorns, 8 In., Pair 345.00
Black Lacquer, Gilt Decoration, Chinese, 1910, 14 In., Pair 252.00
Blown Glass, Yellow Olive, Inverted Lily Pad Rim, Star Prunts, 7 In., Pair 2530.00
Brass, 6-Sided Base, Lithophane Shield, Openwork, Seascape, 10 1/2 In. 300.00
Brass, Alpha, Removable Bobeche At Top, Jarvie, Signed, 11 In., Pair 850.00
Brass, Baluster Form Shaft, Mid Drip Pan, Continental, 9 x 6 7/8 In., Pair 2185.00
Brass, Baluster Shape, Hexagonal Base, Push-Up, 19th Century, 9 In., Pair 175.00
Brass, Beehive Style, Octagonal, Push-Up, 19th Century, 10 In. 220.00
Brass, Beehive, 10 In., Pair 160.00
Brass, Beehive, Push-Up, 19th Century, 8 3/4 In., Pair 175.00
Brass, Beehive, Push-Up, 19th Century, 10 3/4 In., Pair 470.00
Brass, Beehive, Push-Up, Stamped England, Registry Number, 11 In. 115.00
Brass, Bradley & Hubbard, 7 1/4 In. 80.00
Brass, Brass Baluster, Push-Up, Mid 19th Century, 11 In., Pair 115.00
Brass, Cast, Petal Shape, Shell Decoration, 18th Century, 8 1/4 In., Pair 1430.00
Brass, Chamberstick, On Gimbals, 18th Century, 8 1/2 In. 226.00
Brass, Classical, Push-Up, England, 1800, 7 In., Pair 110.00
Brass, Cylindrical Stem, Applied Druid Figures, Early 20th Century, 5 3/4 In., Pair 230.00
Brass, Dish Beneath Column, Holes In Candle Socket, Sapstan, 4 3/4 In. 880.00
Brass, Ecclesiastical, Acanthus Leaves, Grapes & Lambs, 17 1/2 In., Pair 55.00
Brass, Extractor, Cylindrical, Round Tiered Foot, 1800s, 7 5/8 In., Pair 115.00
Brass, Figural Male, Ring Handle, Gilt, Original Douter, c.1850-1870, 4 In. 175.00
Brass, Figural, Dog, Cup Shaped Sconce, 3 Seated Hounds, Chain, 7 1/2 In., Pair 630.00
Brass, Figural, Marble Base, Cut Glass Prisms, 15 In., Pair 302.00
Brass, Flared, Rolled Rim, Handle, 7 1/4 x 1 3/4 In., Pair 80.00
Brass, French Style, Round, Embossed Shaft, Octagon Top, 20th Century, 10 In., Pair 58.00
Brass, Gilt Lacquered, Tripodal, Louis Philippe Style, 12 In., Pair 400.00
Brass, Magnum Diamond Knops, Push-Up, Georgian, Mid 19th Century, 11 1/4 In. 115.00
Brass, Mid Drip, 17th Century, 7 1/2 In., Pair 7500.00
Brass, Mid Drip, Netherlands, Mid 17th Century, 8 x 4 In. 750.00

Brass, Monkey, Standing, Dressed In Livery, Oval Sconces, 20th Century, 6 1/2 In. 400.00 to 460.00
Brass, Notched Edge Drip Pan, Signed, 19th Century, 18 1/2 In. 115.00
Brass, Octagonal Base, Paneled Baluster Stems & Socket, 7 3/4 In., Pair 770.00
Brass, Oval, England, 1875, 6 In., Pair 375.00
Brass, Parrot Perch Shape, Miniature, Dutch, 6 1/4 In., Pair 230.00
Brass, Pricket, Tripod Base, England, 18th Century, 22 In., Pair 730.00
Brass, Push-Up, 19th Century, 5 In., Pair 138.00
Brass, Queen Anne, Scalloped Base, 8 In. 250.00
Brass, Rectangular, Pan, Push-Up, 5 x 7 x 6 In., Pair 259.00
Brass, Restauration, Chased, Detachable Bobeche, Early 19th Century, 9 1/4 In., Pair 978.00
Brass, Ring Turned Baluster Shaft, Square Pan Base, Continental, 5 5/8 In. 230.00
Brass, Ring Turned Shaft, Square Pan Base, Continental, 17th Century, 4 3/4 In. 750.00
Brass, Round Base, Finger Loop, Push-Up, 4 3/4 In. 110.00
Brass, Round Bases, Push-Up, 9 1/4 In., Pair 165.00
Brass, Round Stepped Base, Square Tapered Columns, Classical, 13 In., Pair 110.00
Brass, Scalloped Petal Base, Pierced Stem, Scalloped Socket, 8 1/4 In., Pair 140.00
Brass, Scrolled Base, Petal Sockets, 8 1/2 In., Pair 220.00
Brass, Seamed Construction, France, c.1730, 9 In. 495.00
Brass, Spring Load, Handle, Blown Glass Etched Shades, 18 In., Pair 220.00
Brass, Spring Load, Push-Up Slide, Ruffled Edge Shade, Tapered, 14 In. 55.00
Brass, Square Base, Panel Stem, 7 1/4 In. 220.00
Brass, Square Bases, Raised Circles, Tapered Stems, Facets, 6 1/8 In., Pair 192.00
Brass, Sword Hilt, Bulbous Sconce, Short Blade, Eagle, c.1900, 11 5/8 In., Pair 374.00
Brass, Triangle Base, Baluster Form Shaft, 17th Century, 9 In. 460.00
Brass, Turned Base, Push-Up, Tooled Rings, 6 3/4 In. 165.00
Brass, Wired As Lamps, Marble Base, 25 In., Pair 1450.00
Brass & Silver Plate, Border Of Palmettes, 3 Stylized Feet, 10 1/2 In., Pair 1725.00
Brass & Silver Plate, Stylized Palmettes, Fluted Columns, 1855, 12 In., Pair 635.00
Bronze, Acanthus Leaf Shaft, Tripod Base, Hairy Paw Feet, 10 3/4 In. 1955.00
Bronze, Continental, Renaissance Revival Style, Tulip Shape Sconce, 13 1/8 In. 460.00
Bronze, Continental, Renaissance Revival Style, Tulip Shape Sconce, 15 In. 690.00
Bronze, Crane, Gilt, Patinated Bronze, Japanese Style, 26 1/2 In., Pair 1495.00
Bronze, Enamel, Scrolling Handles, 8 1/2 In., Pair 290.00
Bronze, Louis XVI, 3 Cupids Standard, Gilt, Round Base, 8 In., Pair 865.00
Bronze, Louis XVI, Gilt, Fluted Standard, Beaded Circular Base, 9 1/2 In., Pair 430.00
Bronze, Louis XVI, Gilt, Fluted Standard, Beaded Circular Base, 11 In., Pair 575.00
Bronze, Renaissance Style, Floral Standard, Tripod Lions Base, 13 In., Pair 920.00
Bronze & Marble, Oriental Figurine, Marble Base, Chain Swags, 1830s, 12 In., Pair 2400.00
Carved Bone & Scrimshaw, c.1900, 12 In., Pair 225.00
Copper, Art Nouveau, Female Figure Shape, Gilt, 1905, 12 In., Pair 1120.00
Copper, Hammered, Arts & Crafts, 7 In., Pair 375.00
Copper, Hammered, Original Patina, 7 1/2 In. 525.00
Cut Glass, Anglo-Irish Style, 8 1/2 In. 405.00
Cut Glass, Anglo-Irish Style, c.1900, 7 In., Pair 489.00
Cut Glass, Light Green, Floral Sprays, 12 In., Pair 805.00
Cut Glass, Parcel Gilt, Continental, Fluted, Stepped Foot, Enamel, 9 1/2 In., 6 Piece 460.00
English Chromium, Open Barley Twist, Traditional, 8 In., Pair 69.00
Faience, Flower Base, 8 Lobes, France, Late 19th Century, 9 1/2 In. 375.00
Faience, Tulip Shape Sconce, Flowerhead Pierced Foot, Enameling, 9 1/8 In. 115.00
French Parcel Gilt Bronze, Marble, Late 19th Century, 11 5/8 In., Pair 920.00
Gilt, Patinated Bronze, Reeds, Leaf Bands, Charles X, 10 3/4 x 4 3/4 In., Pair 1095.00
Gilt Brass, Engine Turned, Restauration, Early 19th Century, 9 1/2 In., Pair 1380.00
Gilt Bronze, Spiral Flower Holder, Bracket Feet, Louis XV Style, 12 7/8 In., Pair 805.00
Giltwood, Altar, Cylindrical, Ribbed, Flower Shape Candle Cups, 3 Legs, 31 In., Pair ... 1095.00
Giltwood, Altar, Pricket, Baroque Standard, Italy, 32 1/2 In., 4 Piece 2070.00
Giltwood, Altar, Pricket, Turned, Acanthine Standard, Circular Base, 49 In., Pair 1265.00
Giltwood, Altar, Tole Drip Pan, Italy, Mid 19th Century, 31 In., Pair 1095.00
Glass, Blown Socket, Pressed Base, Pewter Insert, Pittsburgh Glass, 7 3/4 In., Pair 670.00
Glass, Blown, Round Base, Wafer Stem, Swirl Collar, 8 1/2 In., Pair 1540.00
Glass, Blue Opalescent Top, Clambroth Dolphin Base, 9 3/4 In. 750.00
Glass, Blue, Crystal, Bobeches, Prisms, Ground Pontil, 10 3/4 In., Pair 275.00
Glass, Clambroth, Hexagonal, 3 Knops, 7 In., Pair 160.00
Glass, Clambroth, Hexagonal, Single Construction, 6 3/4 In. 190.00

Glass, Dolphin, Bright Canary, 6-Sided Base, 6 3/4 In., Pair 1120.00
Glass, Double-Step Dolphin, Clambroth Base, Blue Translucent Top, Wafer, 9 3/4 In. 475.00
Glass, Fiery Opalescent, Petal Socket, Hollow Hexagonal Stem & Base, 8 In. 375.00
Glass, Petal & Loop, Canary, Sandwich, c.1850-1865, 7 In., Pair 145.00
Glass, Sandwich Style, Hexagonal, Canary Yellow, 9 1/4 In. 316.00
Iron, Adjustable, Arched Tripod Legs, Penny Feet, Stamped JM, Contemporary, 28 In. 210.00
Iron, Forged, Arts & Crafts, Flared Scalloped Rims, Triangle Shaft, 18 In. 130.00
Iron, Forged, Spiral, Top Finger Hold, Curled Push-Up Lift, Wood Base, 7 1/2 In. 165.00
Iron, Hog Scraper, Brass Wedding Band, Octagonal Base, Dousing Cone, 1700s, 8 In. 950.00
Iron, Hog Scraper, Signed Shaw, 19th Century, 7 1/4 In. 195.00
Iron, Pricket, 3 Legs, Ring Guard, Japan, 10 1/2 In. 28.00
Lacquer, Black & Gold, Cloud & Crane Design, 11 1/2 In. 160.00
Marble, Patinated Bronze, Paw Feet, Charles X, 10 1/2 x 4 x 4 In., Pair 1380.00
Marble Base, Urn Form, Brown Paint, Paw Feet, 15 In., Pair 660.00
Neoclassical, Louis Philippe, Pewter, Brass, Mid 19th Century, 10 1/4 In., Pair 489.00
Oak, Barley Twist & Brass, Twisted Stem, c.1870, 24 3/4 In., Pair 280.00
Parcel Gilt Bronze, Marble, Louis XVI Style, Late 19th Century, 14 1/2 In., Pair 865.00
Pewter, Henry Hopper, New York, c.1847, 12 In. 635.00
Pine, Turned, Black Paint, Tin Saucer, 19th Century, 26 1/2 x 6 1/2 In., Pair 920.00
Porcelain, Figure, Flowers, Putti Standards, France, 12 In., Pair 635.00
Porcelain, Knopped Form, Gilt, Jeweled, Cobalt Blue Ground, 10 1/2 In., Pair 1955.00
Porcelain, Putti, Holding Cornucopia, R. Block, Paris, 12 In., Pair 640.00
Porcelain, Temple, Bats In Clouds, Deer, Blue & White, 19th Century, 7 1/4 In., Pair 1560.00
Pres-Cut Glass, Hexagonal Sconce, Trapped Bubble Stem, 9 1/8 In., 5 Piece 490.00
Silver, 2 Prickets, Swings, Phoenix Shape, Carved Flames, Wings, 1770s, 19 In., Pair 2015.00
Silver, 6 Sides, Removable Bobeche, 1934 Inscription, Chinese, 8 1/4 In., Pair 1380.00
Silver, Dwarf, Neoclassical, Column Shape, London, c.1895, 4 In., Pair 546.00
Silver, E. Coker, Gadrooned Borders, England, 1766, 10 1/2 In., Pair 4800.00
Silver, Fluted & Paneled Stems, Urn Mark, Italy, 1780s, 9 5/8 In., Pair 4200.00
Silver, George II, Rococo, Gabriel Sleath, Francis Crump, 1754, 10 1/2 In., Pair 4200.00
Silver, George III, Detachable Nozzle, John Parsons & Co., 1788, 12 In., 4 Piece 4700.00
Silver, George IV, Rococo Flowers, Detachable Nozzle, J. & T. Settle, 1825, 9 In. 5700.00
Silver, Leaf Bobeche, Knopped Stem, 4 Feet, Russia, 1920s, 12 1/2 In., Pair 1150.00
Silver, Robert Makepeace & Richard Carter, 1776, 5 1/2 In., Pair 2350.00
Silver, Spring, Filigree & Mica Shade, Gorham, 10 1/4 In., Pair 130.00
Silver, Swag & Floral, Raised Reticulated Base, 11 In., Pair 2300.00
Silver Plate, Allover Geometric & Leaf, Column Standard, 1908, 5 7/8 In., Pair 170.00
Silver Plate, Bobeche, Notch Borders, Leaf Handle, Round, Snuffer, 1845, 6 In. 85.00
Silver Plate, Chamber, Octagonal, Acanthus Scrolls, Thumb Handle, c.1840, 4 1/4 In. 201.00
Silver Plate, Chamber, Round, Leaves, Snuffer, Bobeche, c.1845, 6 In. 86.00
Silver Plate, Chamber, Snuffer, Marked, Sheffield, 1834-1835 .... 40.00
Silver Plate, Chased Vintage On Bobeches, Wafers & Base, Signed, 9 1/4 In., Pair 140.00
Silver Plate, Corinthian Capital, Fluted Stem, Square Base, 1920s, 12 3/4 In. 784.00
Silver Plate, Corinthian Column Shape, Early 20th Century, 11 3/4 In., 4 Piece 1265.00
Silver Plate, Flower & Scroll Base, Removable Bobeche, 11 1/4 In., Pair 248.00
Silver Plate, Gadroon Bobeche, Column, Swag, Mid 19th Century, 6 1/4 In., Pair 230.00
Silver Plate, Leafage Standard, Gadroon Edge, Sheffield, 9 7/8 In., Pair 1955.00
Silver Plate, Queen Anne, Domed Circle, Canted Square Feet, 13 In., Pair 1265.00
Silver Plate, Raised Leaf Design, 1899, 4 5/8 In., Pair 172.00
Silver Plate, Rectangular, Shell & Scroll Border, Detachable Bobeche, 2 x 5 In. 86.00
Silver Plate, Removable Bobeches, Early 20th Century, 10 3/4 In., Pair 290.00
Silver Plate, Rococo Style, Baluster Shape Stem, Shell, 15 1/2 In., Pair 291.00
Silver Plate, Round, Columnar Shape, Geometric, Flowers, c.1908, Pair 172.00
Silver Plate, Sheffield, Flute Sconce, A. Goodman & Co., c.1800, 12 1/2 In., 4 Piece 4600.00
Silver Plate, Swag Design, Square Base, Sheffield, 12 x 5 In., Pair 560.00
Sterling Silver, 6 Sides, Chased, Floral, Scroll, Goldman Silversmiths, 11 1/2 In., Pair 259.00
Sterling Silver, Acanthus Scrolls, Dolphin Heads, Continental, 13 1/2 In., Pair 800.00
Sterling Silver, Bigelow, Kennard & Co., Embossed, Early 1900s, 7 In., Pair 172.00
Sterling Silver, Chamber, Bobeche, Snuffer, Scissors, London, 1790, 4 In., 4 Piece 2415.00
Sterling Silver, Chamber, Engraved Crest, John Carter, London, 1775, 3 x 5 In., Pair 1725.00
Sterling Silver, Chamber, Reed Urn, Chased, England, c.1840, 5 1/2 In., Pair 2415.00
Sterling Silver, Chamber, Snuffer, Beaded Edge, Eagle, London, c.1797, 4 x 6 In. 615.00
Sterling Silver, Chamber, Thistle Nozzle, Floral Drip Pan, WA, Chinese, 1880s, 5 In. 747.00

Sterling Silver, Columnar Stem, 2 Ribbed Bands, Fan Rosettes, 10 In., Pair 165.00
Sterling Silver, Columns, Corinthian, E. Coker, England, 1760, 12 In., 4 Piece 3900.00
Sterling Silver, Fluted Baluster, William Cafe, George II, England, 9 In., Pair 3450.00
Sterling Silver, Gadroon Border, Gorham, 9 1/2 In., Pair 450.00
Sterling Silver, Gadroon Border, Mark M With Sword, 4 x 4 In., Pair 56.00
Sterling Silver, George III Style, Crichton & Co., London, 1913, 11 1/2 In., Pair 4500.00
Sterling Silver, Gorham, Gadroon Rim, Bobeche, Round, 9 1/4 In., Pair 1035.00
Sterling Silver, Knopped Stem, Russia, 20th Century, 14 1/4 In., Pair 400.00
Sterling Silver, Leaf Decoration, Shaped Stepped Base, London, 1770, 10 In., Pair 4140.00
Sterling Silver, Oval Foot, Fluted Column, Gorham Mfg. Co., 11 3/4 In., 4 Piece 4465.00
Sterling Silver, Putto Kneeling Supports Conical Plinth, Continental, 10 1/2 In. 316.00
Sterling Silver, Scroll Handles, Detachable Nozzles, England, 1850, 5 In., 4 Piece 4800.00
Sterling Silver, Spreading Circular Base, 6 In., 4 Piece 1150.00
Sterling Silver, Taper, Baroque, Leaves, Garrard, George V, England, 5 In., Pair 690.00
Sterling Silver, Tapered Column, Stepped Base, Urn Socket, Gorham, 18 In., Pair 3080.00
Tin, Hog Scraper, 11 3/4 In., Pair 385.00
Tin, Hog Scraper, Wedding Band, Initials, Push-Up, 12 In. 480.00
Wood, Gilt, Gesso, Inverted Vase Shape, Scroll, Leaves, 3-Sided Base, 20 In., Pair 1095.00
Wood, Traveling, Put Together In Ball Form, England, c.1840, 4 In. Diam., Pair 470.00
Wrought Iron, 2-Light, Square Center Column, Tripod Base, 13 In. 275.00
Wrought Iron, Baluster Stem & Socket, Tripod Feet, 6 3/8 In. 220.00
Wrought Iron, Pricket, Rope Twist, 19th Century, 9 1/4 x 6 1/4 In., Pair 495.00

CANDLEWICK items may be listed in the Imperial and Pressed Glass categories.

CANDY CONTAINERS have been popular since the late Victorian era.
Collectors have long favored the glass containers, but now all types,
including tin and papier-mache, are collected. Probably the earliest
glass container sold commercially was the Liberty Bell made in 1876
for sale at the Centennial Exposition. Thousands of designs were made
until the cost became too high in the 1960s. By the late 1970s, reproductions were being made and sold without the candy. Containers
listed here are glass unless otherwise described. A Belsnickle is a nineteenth-century figure of Father Christmas.

Airplane, Spirit Of Goodwill, Victory Glass Co., c.1920, 4 5/16 In. 136.00
Alarm Clock 202.00
Barney Google, Riding Spark Plug, Sheared Lip, 1925, 5 In. 710.00
Belsnickle, Orange Robe, Gold Glitter, Black Boots, Feather Tree, 8 In. 330.00
Belsnickle, Yellow Robe, Applied Beads, Black Boots, Feather Tree, 7 3/4 In. 360.00
Boat, Model Cruiser, 4 1/2 In. 40.00
Boat, Remember The Maine, 7 In. .... *Illus* 45.00
Bunny, 1940s, 6 1/2 In. 55.00
Bunny, Long Eared, Wax Over Papier-Mache, Glass Eyes 675.00
Cannon, 2 Wheels 250.00
Cannon, Cobalt Blue, Metal Carriage, ABM, 4 1/4 In. 784.00
Car, 4 Doors, Square 1025.00
Car, Amos 'n' Andy, Open Air Taxi ....300.00 to 500.00
Car, Limousine, Pat. Apld. For, Slide Roof Closure, 2 3/8 In. 225.00
Car, Limousine, With Trunk, 4 13/16 In. 85.00
Car, Station Wagon, J.H. Millstein Co., 4 7/8 In. 35.00
Cat, Black, On Pumpkin, Germany, 1900-1915 .... 995.00
Cat, Black, Pressed Paper, 5 In. 85.00
Cat, On Pumpkin, Plaster & Pressed Paper, 6 In. 150.00
Cat, Paperboard, Tin, 7 In. 65.00
Cat's Head, Paper, 3 1/2 In. 415.00
Chicken, On Oblong Basket, Victory Glass Co., c.1930, 3 x 2 7/8 x 1 5/8 In. 30.00
Child, Bisque, c.1915 .... 795.00
Clock, Showing 11 O'Clock, Ruby Flash, 3 1/4 In. 588.00
Coach, 2 Footmen, Wooden, Gesso, Cloth Body Men, 18 1/2 x 9 3/4 In. 375.00
Dog, Bulldog, Round Base, Victory Glass Co., c.1930, 4 In. 56.00
Dog, Fur, White, Glass Inset Eyes, c.1900, 8 In. 475.00
Dog, Scotty, Head Up, J.C. Crosetti Co., 3 1/4 In. 50.00
Dog, Shaggy, Bisque, Intaglio Eyes, Easter Egg In Paws, 1915, 5 1/2 In. 325.00

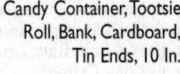

Candy Container, Boat, Remember The Maine, 7 In.

Candy Container, Dog,
With Top Hat, 4 1/8 In.

Candy Container, Tootsie
Roll, Bank, Cardboard,
Tin Ends, 10 In.

Dog, Sitting, Smile Damn You Smile, Clear, 4 1/4 In.	235.00
Dog, With Top Hat, 4 1/8 In. ....*Illus*	10.00
Doughboy, Glass	80.00
Easter Bunny, Bunny On Top Of Pressed Paper Box	45.00
Easter M&M's, Cardboard Tube, Plastic Figural Stopper, 9 1/4 In.	15.00
Elephant, GOP	160.00
Elf, West Germany	38.00
Fanny Farmer Candy, Uncle Sam, Hat Cover, Cylinder Type, 1944, 10 5/8 In.	11.00
Fat Boy On Drum, Clear, 1915-1920, 4 3/8 In.	130.00
Felix On Circus Tub	1660.00
Fire Engine, Fire Department In Circle, 5 In.	55.00
Fire Engine, Ladder Truck, Tin Closure	40.00
Fire Engine, Little Boiler	100.00
Fire Engine, Stough, c.1914, 5 1/8 In.	85.00
Fire Engine, V.G. Co., Little Boiler, Tin Closure	25.00
Flossie Fisher's Bed, Tin, No Glass, 3 3/4 In.	1810.00
Foxy Grandpa On Pig, Composition, Painted, Removable Pig Head, 5 x 6 In.	688.00
Ghost, Pressed Paper, 5 In.	85.00
Gun, Small Revolver, 4 1/2 In.	35.00
Halloween, Train, 3 Pumpkin Faces, Removable End	150.00
Helicopter, 2 Blades	150.00
Helicopter, Candy, Paper, T.H. Stough, 5 In.	250.00
Horn, 3 Valves, Closure	30.00
Horn, Clarinet, Closure, Candy	10.00
Horn, T.H. Stough, Candy, c.1960, 4 11/16 In. ....10.00 to 30.00	
Horn, Trumpet, Clear, No Paint, 5 1/2 In.	45.00
House, Front Dormer, Chimney, 2 1/2 In.	150.00
Jack-O'-Lantern, Open Top	25.00
Jeep, All American Willys, 1940s, 1 1/2 x 4 1/4 x 2 In.	28.00
Keystone Cop, Egg Crate Material, Painted Features, 12 In.	120.00
Kiddies Drinking Mug. T.H. Stough, Jeannette, Pa., 3 7/16 In.	35.00
Lamp, Hobnail, T.H. Stough, c.1940	348.00
Lantern, Stough's No. 81, c.1957, 4 1/2 In.	40.00
Locomotive, 999, Man In Window, Cambridge Glass Co., c.1916, 4 1/2 In.	100.00
Locomotive, Man In Window	175.00
Locomotive 1028	50.00
Monkey, Hear, See & Speak No Evil	355.00
Monkey Lamp, Closure, Contents	20.00
Mule, Pulling 2-Wheeled Barrel, With Driver, Closure	32.00
Nurser, Baby Dear, Closure, Contents	10.00
PEZ, Mickey Mouse, Yellow Stem, Removable Nose, 4 In.	14.00
PEZ, Santa Claus, Full-Bodied	125.00
Pickwick Character On Pig, Composition, Painted, Bobbing Ears, 6 1/2 In.	910.00
Pig, On Book, Composition, 2 3/4 In.	190.00
Pumpkin, Pressed Paper, 5 In.	85.00
Pumpkin Head, 6 In.	50.00

Pumpkin Man, Composition Arms, Attached By Wire, 6 In. 200.00
Rabbit, Eating Carrot, T.H. Stough, c.1947, 4 3/8 In. 40.00
Rabbit, Fleece Cloth Covering, Fur Tail, c.1900 .... 595.00
Rabbit, Forepaws Next To Body, Victory Glass Co., 5 In. 97.00
Rabbit, Gold Trim, 5 1/3 In. 128.00
Rabbit, Seated On Haunches, Glass Eyes, 1880s 695.00
Rabbit, Seated, Mica Flecks, 6 1/2 In. 28.00
Rabbit, With Wheelbarrow 28.00
Reclining Woman, Pewter, Art Nouveau Style, Signed Kayserzinn, 8 x 6 In. 106.00
Rocking Horse, Tin Closure 50.00
Rooster, On Stump, Papier-Mache & Wood, 9 3/4 In., Pair 1155.00
Rooster, Tin Tail Feathers, Papier-Mache, 8 1/4 In. 374.00
Santa Claus, Belsnickle, Papier-Mache, Late 20th Century, 6 In., Pair 12.00
Santa Claus, Belsnickle, Papier-Mache, Late 20th Century, 11 In. 23.00
Santa Claus, Brown Suit, Blue Trousers, Riding Reindeer, Velvet, 9 x 8 In. 980.00
Santa Claus, Leaving Chimney 95.00
Santa Claus, Leaving Chimney, Victory Glass Co., c.1930, 5 In. 77.00
Santa Claus, On Skis, Plastic, Marked Rosbro Plastic, 4 1/2 In. ....18.00 to 20.00
Santa Claus, Papier-Mache, Robe, Feather Tree, E.G. Billings, R.I., 14 1/2 In. 1210.00
Santa Claus, Walking, Germany, 8 In. 695.00
Snow White & 5 Dwarfs 274.00
Snowman, Round Body, Spring Neck, Top Hat, 2 Sections, 10 1/2 In. 29.00
Soldier, Doughboy, 6 In. 272.00
Spirit Of Goodwill, Paint, Closure 30.00
Stagecoach, Milk Glass, Tin Seat 204.00
Suitcase, Tin Closure 15.00
Telephone, Lynne Type, Raised Dial, 4 3/4 In. 40.00
Tootsie Roll, Bank, Cardboard, Tin Ends, 10 In. .... *Illus* 10.00
Turkey, Composition, With 6 Baby Turkeys, 7 In. 250.00
Turkey, Standing, Germany, 10 In. 1550.00
Uncle Sam, By Barrel 50.00
Village, 2-Story House, Tin, 3 1/8 In. 35.00
Village, Confectionery, Tin, 2 7/8 In. 35.00
World Globe On Stand 50.00

CANES and walking sticks were used by every well-dressed man in the
nineteenth century, but by World War I the style had changed. Today
canes are used by few but the infirm. Collectors prize old canes made
with special features, like hidden swords, whiskey flasks, or risqué pictures seen through peepholes. Examples with solid gold heads or made
from exotic materials, such as walrus vertebrae, are among the higher-
priced canes.

Allover Carved, Man's Head Handle, E.D. Coriell, 1931, 44 In. 2640.00
Amber & White Threading, 4 Sides, Twist At Handle & End, Glass, 35 In. 55.00
Balloon Shape Handle, Geometric Inlay, Stripes, Letters N, S, Masonic Calipers, 33 In. ... 110.00
Bird Handle, Bead Eye, Burned Polka Dots, Folk Art, 32 1/2 In. 55.00
Bone, Scrimshaw Handle, Spread Winged Eagle, 1864, 34 1/4 In. 1300.00
Brass, Dickens Character, Molded Brass Handle, Malacca Shaft, 2 x 39 1/4 In. 400.00
Carved, Animals, People, Low Relief, Brass Tack Eyes, Animal Head Handle, 35 In. 220.00
Carved, Bark Texture, Vine Relief, Tin Ferrule, Applied Animal Head, 36 In. 165.00
Carved, Flat, Sword Shape, Black People, Animals, Rounded Handle, 31 1/2 In. 715.00
Carved, Painted, Grinning Head, White Teeth, Late 19th Century, 35 1/2 In. 940.00
Carved, Painted, Leaves, Snake, Man's Head Tip, J. Goeller, Late 19th Century, 33 1/2 In. 59.00
Carved Bird Handle, Whistle In Tail, 32 1/4 In. 495.00
Carved Root, Abraham Lincoln, Men In Canoes, Animals, Handle, 34 In. 605.00
Crop, Copper Dog's Head, Braided Leather Shaft 287.00
Dog's Head, Carved, Bared Teeth, Spike Collar, Pennsylvania Germany, 1870, 34 In. 545.00
Dog's Head Terminal, Walnut, Hearts, Flowers, Eagle, Stars, Mid 19th Century, 32 In. ... 1200.00
Dove, Shamrocks, Heart & Acorn, French Prisoner Of War, 38 In. 137.00
Eagle Clutching Lyre, Ivory Handle, Stylized A, Sterling Band, 1905, 34 1/2 In. 168.00
Eagle Over Mermaid, Folk Art 1650.00
Ebonized Wood, Whalebone L-Shape Handle, Carved Shield, 35 1/2 In. 110.00
Ebony, Pug, Glass Eyes, Posing On Tufted Pillow, Silver Collar, Brass Ferrule, 36 In. 900.00

Enamel, Pale Pink, Swirl Design, Silver Ring Separator, 1905, 2 1/2 x 35 3/4 In. 800.00
Faux Bamboo, Ivory Handle, Black Man's Head, Stand-Up Collar, Bowtie, 35 1/4 In. 805.00
Fist Handle, Rattlesnake, 35 In. 302.00
G.A.R. Veteran's, Gold, Ebony Shaft, White Metal, Iron Ferrule, 1890, 36 In. 400.00
Gadget, Measuring, Malacca Shaft, Brass, Iron Ferrule, Sterling Collar, 1894, 36 In. 300.00
Glass, Aqua, Twisted Handle & End, 48 In. 60.00
Glass, Blown, 1800s 121.00
Glass, Blown, Spiral Stripes, 61 1/2 In. 247.00
Glass, Clear, White Stripe, Twisted Handle & End, 24 1/2 In. 28.00
Gold, Bloodstone, Rubies, Gold, Silver Overlay, Green Tone, 2 3/4 x 36 In. 1200.00
Gold, Enamel Peacock, Royal Blue Ground, Gold, Green, Red, Black Shaft, 1900, 36 In. . .   3300.00
Gold, Large Grecian Keys, C-Scroll Design, Tortoiseshell Veneer Shaft, 1840, 34 1/2 In. . .   2100.00
Gold, Presentation, Large Shaped Handle, Gold, Gray, White Ground, 1875, 36 In. 4750.00
Gold, Royal Blue, 4 Teardrops Handle, Black Enameled Hardwood Shaft, 35 3/4 In. 1400.00
Gold Head, Turquoise Carved Shaft, 34 In. 450.00
Hardwood Shaft, In God We Trust, Shields, Arrows, Crosses, 1893, 34 In. 2000.00
Horse Head Handle, Ivory, Wood Stick, 3 1/2 In. 230.00
Human Bust, Carved Bird Handle, 36 In. 110.00
Ivory, 2 Horses, T Handle, Large Horse With Glass Eyes, 1890, 37 In. 1000.00
Ivory, 3 Monkeys, 2 Screaming Monkeys, 1885, 37 1/8 In. 325.00
Ivory, Albatross, Nautical, Horn Collar, Brass Ferrule, 1850, 33 2/3 In. 1800.00
Ivory, Basket Of Flowers, Woven Basket, Roses, Daisies, Blond Malacca Shaft, 36 In. 1400.00
Ivory, Carved Male Lion, Perched On Ledge Surveying Scene Below, 1897 . . . .   1500.00
Ivory, Carved, Pair Of Monkeys, Japan, Late 19th Century, 3 1/4 In. 175.00
Ivory, Cat Head, Gold Plated Collar, 1900, 1 2/3 x 37 In. 200.00
Ivory, Chinese Lady, L Handle, Beautifully Robed Lady, 1880, 36 In. 900.00
Ivory, Claw & Ball, Blond Tortoiseshell Talons, 1885, 36 In. 1600.00
Ivory, Coat Of Arms, Long Bunch Of Grapes With Vines, 1850, 3 1/3 x 36 1/2 In. 1600.00
Ivory, Cupid, Long Bow Between Folded Hands, 1880, 36 In. 450.00
Ivory, Duck, Segmented Ivory Shaft, Fish, Frog, 34 1/4 In. 1900.00
Ivory, Eagle & Snake, Death To Traitors, 36 In. 1300.00
Ivory, Eagle, Broad Winged Insect, Horn Ferrule, 1890, 33 In. 325.00
Ivory, Eagle, Yellow Patina, Sterling Collar, 1896, 3 x 36 In. 750.00
Ivory, Female, Standing Nude, Malacca Shaft, 1878, 37 In. 3800.00
Ivory, Full-Bodied Setter, Glass Eyes, 1890, 4 1/2 x 35 In. 1500.00
Ivory, Half Crook Of Bulldog, Glass Eyes, 1917, 4 x 36 In. 450.00
Ivory, Horse, Diamond Eyes, Open Mouth, 1880, 35 1/4 In. 3200.00
Ivory, Lady Liberty, Lady With Tresses Hanging Down, 34 In. 350.00
Ivory, Male Lion & Wild Boar, 40 In. 1500.00
Ivory, Man With Empty Cornucopia, Hippo Handle, Large Horn, Ivory Ferrule, 1880 . . . .   950.00
Ivory, Man's Head Marked With Various Sections, 1850, 34 1/2 In. 3000.00
Ivory, Mother Goose, Glass Eyes, Frilled Bonnet, Open Mouth, 1880, 35 1/2 In. 1200.00
Ivory, Mouse, Brown Glass Eyes, 1899, 1 1/2 x 36 In. 2000.00
Ivory, Mr. Punch, Wearing Stocking Cap With Bell, 37 In. 1800.00
Ivory, Nautical, Captains Ashore, Ball, In Enclosed Hand, Whalebone, 38 In. 4250.00
Ivory, Nautical, Carved Whalebone, 1850, 32 In. 1900.00
Ivory, Nautical, White Whalebone Shaft, 1850, 33 1/2 x 1 1/4 In.   1800.00
Ivory, Nude, Maiden Filling Jug, 1880, 35 3/4 In. 2850.00
Ivory, Rabbit's Head, Amber Glass Eyes, Honey Shaft, 35 In. 1700.00
Ivory, Rose, Brass, Iron Ferrule, 1 2/3 x 35 1/2 In. 450.00
Ivory, Shaft, Dark Brown Exotic Hardwood, 3 3/4 x 37 In. 275.00
Ivory, Shakespeare, Malacca Shaft, Ferns, 1890, 4 x 35 In. 1000.00
Ivory, Shore Bird & Frog, Long Pointed Bill Biting Frog Trying To Escape, 37 In. 2800.00
Ivory, Skull, All Its Teeth, Horn Ferrule, 1890, 2 1/2 x 36 In. 1700.00
Ivory, Songbird, Perched Among Branches, Glass Eyes, 37 In. 800.00
Ivory, Spaniel Dog, Tiny Porcelain Eyes, Malacca Shaft, 35 In. 200.00
Ivory, Tortoiseshell Inlay, Black, White Tones, 1920, 35 In. 1800.00
Ivory, Twisted Silver Cable Inlay, 4 3/4 x 35 1/2 In. 650.00
Ivory, Winking Bald Man, Fat Man With Wry Smile, 34 3/4 In. 350.00
Ivory, Woman & Her Tambourine, Mahogany Shaft, 36 In. 500.00
Ivory, Young Lad, Silver, White Metal, 1886, 36 1/3 In. 750.00
Leather, Horn Handle, Prison Made, 1900s, 35 1/2 In. 60.00
Mahogany, Harmonica, Dark Metal Ferrule, 1890, 1 3/4 x 36 In. 2200.00

Porcelain, 2 Lovers On Each Side, 3 Small Balls, Silver, Dark Cherrywood, 1893, 34 In. . 850.00
Porcelain, Cockerel, Young Male Bird With Orange Combs, Germany, 1860, 37 In. 1600.00
Porcelain, Orange, Yellow, Pink Blossom T Handle, Malacca Shaft, 5 1/2 x 37 1/4 In. ... 1200.00
Porcelain, Painted Cobalt Blue, Ball Handle, Silver Collar, Tan Hardwood Shaft, 35 In. .. 900.00
Porcelain, Pale Blue Handle, Raised Bisque Design, Meissen, 1860, 35 3/4 In. 750.00
Porcelain, Woman, Black Ribbon In Her Hair, Black Ruffled Collar, 1880, 37 In. 1000.00
Raised Carved Snakes & Turtles, 37 In. 165.00
Relic, Royal Savage, Sunk At St. Johns, Que., White Metal Ferrule, 1894, 33 1/2 In. 1200.00
Remington Dog, Gun,.32 Caliber, 1876 .... 8525.00
Rhino Horn, Brown Shaft, Brass, Iron Ferrule, England, 1880 .... 700.00
Rhinoceros, Carved, Black Obsidian, Gold Gilt Collar, Horn Ferrule, 1900, 2 x 37 In. ... 3900.00
Scotch Guardsman, With High Black Helmet, 1900, 6 x 37 1/2 In. 600.00
Serpent, Carved, Green, 5 Men Climbing, Alligator, 32 In. 880.00
Shark Vertebrae, Metal Ferrule, Sterling Silver Shape & Decorated Knob, 35 In. 230.00
Silver, Faces, Inscribed, Sackenville, c.1860, 34 1/4 In. 672.00
Silver, Peacock, Faceted Sapphires, Single Small Diamond, 1904, 1 7/8 x 34 3/4 In. 3900.00
Silver, Spider, Garnet Body, Silver Knob Handle, Dark Red Tone, 1 1/4 x 35 3/4 In. 3900.00
Snake, Twining Around Branch, Devouring Man's Head, 1914-1917, 33 In. 247.00
Sterling Silver Top, Snake Wood Shaft, 35 In. 112.00
Tortoiseshell, Carved, Silver Enamels, Twisted Shape, Daisy, Beetle, 35 3/4 In. 750.00
Walking Stick, 14K Yellow Gold Handle, Wood Shaft, 36 1/2 In. 402.00
Walking Stick, 14K Yellow Gold Handle, Zebra Wood Shaft, Box, 38 In. 488.00
Walking Stick, 8 Flower & Geometric Panels, Silver Handle, Wood Shaft, 35 3/4 In. 315.00
Walking Stick, Bird, Monkey, Puppy, Carved Ivory Handle, Rosewood Shaft, 1911 ..... 315.00
Walking Stick, Brass Dog Head Handle, Wrist Strap, Iron, 19 1/2 In. 115.00
Walking Stick, Carved Vegetable Ivory, Vinaigrette Knob, Cedar Shaft 69.00
Walking Stick, Carved, Spiral Banners, Horse Head, Axes & Crosses, Red, 39 In. 110.00
Walking Stick, Cedar, Fish & Snake Handle, Snake Body Continues Down Shaft, 38 In. .. 143.00
Walking Stick, Ebonized Shaft, Whale Tooth Knot Shape Handle, c.1850, 39 In. 880.00
Walking Stick, Ebony, Cherry, Bone, Antler Handle 193.00
Walking Stick, Ebony, Ivory Mounted, Standing Elephant Grip, c.1900, 35 3/4 In. 546.00
Walking Stick, Flowers, Knob Handle, Rosewood Shaft, Leaves, 36 In. 287.00
Walking Stick, Fox Hunting Horn Handle, Brass, Wood Shaft, England 259.00
Walking Stick, Gadget, Concealed Inkwell, Nib Pen, Early 20th Century 201.00
Walking Stick, Gadget, Fishing Pole, Telescoping Shaft, Reel, c.1920 .... 316.00
Walking Stick, Gadget, Pocket Watch Holder Knob, Watch, Nickel Plated Brass 259.00
Walking Stick, Gadget, Political Parade Torch, Nickel Plated Brass, Hickory Shaft 259.00
Walking Stick, Gold Club, Early 20th Century, 36 3/4 In. 460.00
Walking Stick, Gold Filled Knob, Chased Floral, Leaf, Ebony Shaft, Bone Tip, 35 3/4 In. .. 230.00
Walking Stick, Hand Holding Cigar Top, Coiling Snake, Shenandoah Valley, 37 1/2 In. .. 2975.00
Walking Stick, Island Wood, Whale Ivory Knob, 3 Baleen Dividers, Metal Ferrule, 35 In. 193.00
Walking Stick, Ivory & Brass Jockey's Cap, Faux Bamboo Stick, 3 3/8 In. 345.00
Walking Stick, Maiden Head, Crooked Silver Plated Handle, Ebony Shaft, 37 In. 316.00
Walking Stick, Rosewood, Ivory Grip, 1900, 35 In. 173.00
Walking Stick, Rosewood, Silver & Mother-Of-Pearl Knob Top, Engraved Fish & Shells . 660.00
Walking Stick, Silver Handle, Brass Ferrule, Gorham, 1890, 3 1/3 x 33 In. 300.00
Walking Stick, Silver Handle, Inset Mother-Of-Pearl, Wood Shaft, Bamboo Case, 35 In. .. 170.00
Walking Stick, Silver Knob Handle, Ebony Shaft, 36 1/2 In. 260.00
Walking Stick, Sterling Silver Handle, Open Reveals Lighter, Wood Shaft, 1929, 36 In. ... 975.00
Walking Stick, Sunday Stick, Golf Putter L-Shaped Knob, Brass, Hickory Shaft, England . 230.00
Walking Stick, Whalebone, Silvered Band, Late 19th Century 403.00
Whalebone, Carved Feather Handle 415.00
Whalebone, Carved Whale's Tail, Crook Whalebone Handle, 1850, 5 x 36 3/4 In. 1000.00
Whalebone, Clenched Fist Handle, Reeded Spiral Shaft, 31 1/4 In. 1840.00
Whalebone, Dove Handle, Tapered Shaft, 13 1/4 In. 1265.00
Whalebone, Metal Spacer, 31 In. 330.00
Whalebone, Rosewood, Turks Head Knot Top, Baleen Spacers, Brass Tip, 35 1/4 In. 575.00
Whalesbone, 3 Baleen Dividers, Ivory Handle, Mother Of Pearl Inlay 403.00
White Enamel, Flowers, Large Pink Apple Blossoms, Green Leaves, 1890, 35 3/4 In. 1600.00
Woman, Carved, Natural Finish, 35 In. 1210.00
Woman, Topless, Carved, Ralph Buckwalter 825.00
Wood, Acrobat, Jester, Performing, Smiling Moon Face, 1884, 37 1/8 x 1 1/4 In. 1500.00

Wood, Carved Hand With Sleeve, Relief Frog, Acorn Knob Top, 36 In. 460.00
Wood, Cat, Burnt Orange Eyes, Large Ears, Conifer Wood Handle, 1900, 36 In. 3400.00
Wood, Horse Handle, Folk Art, c.1900, 36 1/4 In. 2850.00
Wood, Stick, Farm Implements Advertising, 35 In. 22.00
Wood, Whimsy, Ball, Painted, Red, c.1900, 37 In. 325.00

CANEWARE is a tan-colored, unglazed stoneware that was first developed by Josiah Wedgwood about 1770. It has been made by many companies since that time and is often used for cooking or serving utensils.

    Custard Cup, Basketwork, Neoclassical Border, Buff, c.1780, 3 In. 185.00
    Dish, Game & Rabbit, Grape Vines, Josiah Wedgwood, 10 1/2 x 8 In. 795.00

CANTON CHINA is a blue-and-white ware made near the city of Canton, in China, from about 1785 to 1895. It is hand decorated with Chinese scenes. Canton is part of the group of porcelains known today as Chinese Export Porcelain.

    Bowl, 12-Sides, Lahore, Burslem, T. Phillips & Sons, 5 x 13 In. 756.00
    Bowl, Lobe Shape, Orange Peel Glaze, 10 x 8 1/4 In. 330.00
    Bowl, Oval, 16 In. 980.00
    Bowl, Scalloped, 9 x 2 1/4 In. 520.00
    Bowl, Vegetable, Cover, Footed, Boar Head Handles, Leaf Finial, 8 x 11 In. 358.00
    Bowl, Vegetable, Cover, Orange Peel Glaze, Fruit Finial, 8 x 9 x 5 In. 190.00
    Bowl, Vegetable, Pagodas, Boats, Bridge Scene, 2 In. 110.00
    Candlestick, 2nd Period, 7 1/2 In., Pair 690.00
    Carafe, Village Scene, Egg Shape, Long Neck, 7 5/8 In. 690.00
    Container, Cover, Round, 2 Bail Handles, Flat Wafer Finial, 6 3/4 x 3 1/4 In. 990.00
    Creamer, 3 In. 90.00
    Creamer, Bull Nose Spout, Flared Rim, Orange Peel Glaze, 3 3/4 In. 220.00
    Creamer, Helmet Shape, Oriental Design, Crosses, Molded Swirls, Handle, Footed, 4 In. . 580.00
    Dish, Cover, Diamond Shape, Scalloped Edge, Orange Peel Glaze, 9 1/2 x 3 1/4 In. 220.00
    Dish, Deep, Oval, 11 In. 230.00
    Dish, Deep, Scalloped Edge, 9 In. 414.00
    Dish, Leaf Form, c.1840, 8 1/2 x 6 1/2 In. 330.00
    Dish, Shrimp, Porcelain, 19th Century, 10 1/4 x 9 1/2 In. 520.00
    Ginger Jar, Mounted As Lamp, 19th Century, 7 In. 172.00
    Hot Plate, Cover, 9 In. 460.00
    Jardiniere, Undertray, Hexagonal, Riverscapes, 1900s, 11 1/4 In., Pair 1035.00
    Pitcher, High Handle, Molded Fan End, Sloped Spout, Orange Peel Glaze, 6 In. 880.00
    Pitcher, Landscape Design, 19th Century, 6 1/2 In. 105.00
    Platter, Bridge, Pagodas, Island, Orange Peel Glaze, 14 x 17 1/2 In. 495.00
    Platter, Flared Rim, 13 1/2 x 10 In. 176.00
    Platter, Octagonal, 11 3/4 In. 259.00
    Platter, Octagonal, 12 1/4 x 9 3/8 In. 330.00
    Platter, Octagonal, 13 x 16 In. 330.00
    Platter, Octagonal, 19th Century, 11 3/4 x 14 3/4 In. 400.00
    Platter, Octagonal, Orange Peel Glaze, 12 1/2 x 9 3/4 In. 220.00
    Platter, Pagoda, Bridge & Canal Scene, Geometric Line Borders, 15 In. 797.00
    Punch Bowl, Porcelain, 15 1/2 In. 345.00
    Sauceboat, Undertray, 2 Handles, 7 3/4 In. 259.00
    Saucer, Enamel, European Subject, 18th Century, 8 5/8 In. 960.00
    Serving Dish, Cover, Egg Shape, Scallop Sides, 2 Intertwined Handles, 11 x 4 1/4 In. . . . 990.00
    Serving Dish, Short Foot Ring, c.1820, 9 7/8 x 8 1/2 In. 425.00
    Serving Dish, Short Foot Ring, Lozenge Form, c.1820, 9 7/8 In. 425.00
    Serving Dish, Square, Lobed Corners, Orange Peel Glaze, 8 1/2 x 8 1/2 x 1 3/4 In. 440.00
    Sugar, Cover, 2 Intertwined Handles, Applied Ends, Fruit Finial, 3 7/8 x 4 1/2 In. 520.00
    Teapot, 5 In. 385.00
    Teapot, Censer Form 1800.00
    Teapot, Oriental Scene, Canister Shape, Reeded Handle, Fruit Finial, 5 1/2 In. 910.00
    Teapot, Tapered, Intertwined Handle, Fruit Finial, 6 3/4 In. 580.00
    Tureen, Cover, Square, Hog's Head Handle, Octagonal Undertray, c.1790, 8 In. 920.00
    Tureen, Riverscapes, 19th Century, 9 x 13 In., Pair 1410.00

Tureen, Soup, Cover, Boar's Head Handles, 19th Century, 12 1/2 In. 1100.00
Tureen, Soup, Octagonal Form, Rabbit's Head Handles, Foo Lion Finial, 1870s, 12 1/4 In. . 520.00
Vase, Alternating Panels Of Oriental Figures, Court Scene, Flowers & Bird, 16 1/2 In. . . . 420.00
Vase, Cover, Porcelain, Stout, Panels, Gold Ground, Flowers, 25 In. 960.00
Vase, Cylindrical, 8 3/4 In. 1035.00
Warming Dish, High Base, Fruit Finial, Lid, 9 3/8 x 5 In. 660.00
Water Bottle, 9 In. 200.00
Water Bottle, Spout, 19th Century, 9 In. 1610.00

CAPO-DI-MONTE porcelain was first made in Naples, Italy, from 1743
to 1759. The factory moved near Madrid, Spain, reopened in 1771, and
worked to 1834. Since that time, the Doccia factory of Italy acquired
the molds and is using the crown and N mark. Societe Richard Ceram-
ica is a modern-day firm often referred to as Ginori or Capo-di-Monte.
This company uses the crown and N mark.

Bowl, Children Playing In Woods, Handles, Signed, 8 1/2 x 22 In. 60.00
Box, Allegorical Scenes, Rectangular, 10 In. 690.00
Box, Domed Lid, Cherubs, Flower Baskets, Interior Floral Sprigs, 8 x 4 1/4 In. 488.00
Candlestick, White Luster, Pink Roses, Green Leaves, 10 1/2 In., Pair 80.00
Chandelier, 6-Light, Applied Flowers, Gold Trim, Cobalt Medallions, 24 In. 300.00
Dresser Box, Bronze Fittings, Lion Mask Catch, 9 x 6 1/4 In. 230.00
Ewer, Earth & Water, Late 19th Century, 17 1/4 In., Pair 920.00
Figurine, Boy Eating Watermelon, Crown N, 7 In. 66.00
Figurine, Courting Couple, Metal Base, 10 1/4 x 9 1/2 In. 115.00
Figurine, Group, Man Warming Hands By Fire, Dog At Side, Crown N, 14 1/2 In. 330.00
Figurine, Nude, Draped, Beside Column, Crown N, 7 In. 137.00
Figurine, Shepherd, Playing Bagpipes, Sheep, Dog, Crown N, 7 1/4 In. 137.00
Mirror, Hand, Porcelain & Gilt Metal, Beveled Glass, 15 1/2 In. 97.00
Planter, Band Of Nude Nymphs, Stand, 20th Century, 44 3/4 In. 345.00
Stein, Cherubs Around Body, Nude Woman With Wings Handle, Lid, 1 Liter 790.00
Stein, Cover, Raised Figures, c.1890, 14 In. 336.00
Tray, Lady & Gentleman Conversing In Landscape Scene, 1759, 11 In. 3900.00
Urn, 2 Sections, Trefoil Base, Snake, Knights On Horses, Cover, 12 In., Pair 316.00
Urn, Lion Mask Side Handles, Pedestal Base, 8 1/2 In. 86.00
Vase, Gilt Bronze, Champleve Enamel Mount, 7 3/4 In., Pair 230.00

CAPTAIN MARVEL was introduced in February 1940 in Whiz comic
books. An orphan named Billy Batson met the wizard, Shazam, and
whenever he said the magic word he was transformed into a superhero.
A movie serial was released in 1940. The comic was discontinued in
1954. A second Captain Marvel appeared in 1966, a third in 1967.
Only the original was transformed by shouting *Shazam.*

Booklet, Punch-Out, 3 Figures, Paper, 1945, 12 x 9 1/2 In. 15.00
Car, Racing, Windup, Tin, Lithograph, Red, 4 In. 168.00
Patch, Wow, 1946 . . . . 60.00
Pennant, Red, White, Fawcett Pub, 1946, 14 1/2 In. 95.00
Pin, Captain Marvel Club, Shazam, Canada 40.00
Pin, Junior, c.1946 . . . . 35.00
Toy, Action, Ski Jump, Cardboard, Reed & Associates, Inc., Chicago, Il. 15.00
Wristwatch, Guarantee, Marvel Watchband, Original Packaging, 1938 . . . . 690.00

CAPTAIN MIDNIGHT began as a radio show in September 1940. The
first comic book appeared in July 1941. Captain Midnight was really
the aviator Captain Albright, who was to defeat the Nazis. A movie serial was made in 1942 and a comic strip was published for a short time.
The comic book Captain Midnight ended his career in 1948. The radio
premiums are the prized collector memorabilia today.

MJC-10 Plane Detector, Cardboard Tube, Peep Hole, 1942, 1 1/2 x 6 In. 165.00
Mug, Ovaltine, Plastic, Decal, 5 In. 65.00
Record, Longines, Premium By Longines Symphonette, 1970 . . . . 65.00
Record, Mysterious Radio Signals, Album Cover, 1940s, 33 1/3 RPM 24.00
Secret Squadron Manual, Envelope, 1947, 4 1/2 x 25 In., 16 Pages 95.00

CARAMEL SLAG, see Imperial Glass category.

CARDS listed here include advertising cards (often called trade cards), greeting cards, baseball cards, playing cards, and others. Color pictures were rare in the nineteenth century, so companies gave away colorful cards with pictures of children, flowers, products, or related scenes that promoted the company name. These were often collected and stored in albums. Baseball cards also date from the nineteenth century when they were used by tobacco companies as giveaways. Gum cards were started in 1933, but it was not until after World War II that the bubble gum cards favored today were produced. Today over 1,000 cards are issued each year by the gum companies. Related items may be found in the Postcard and Movie categories.

Advertising, American Central Insurance Co., Black & White, Red Lettering, 1912	39.00
Advertising, American Machine Co.'s Ice Cream Freezers, Rip Van Winkle	25.00
Advertising, Arbuckle Bros. Coffee, 3 Scenes Of Black People, 1893, 3 x 5 In.	175.00
Advertising, Chicago Daily News, Newsboy With Paper, Black & White	35.00
Advertising, Crown Jewel, Uncle Sam, Stove, 1876	165.00
Advertising, De Company, Bath House	70.00
Advertising, Donaldson Steam Lithographic Printers, Children & Umbrellas, April 1878	70.00
Advertising, Donk Bros. & Co. Coal, St. Louis, Tommy Knockers	125.00
Advertising, Florida Water Perfume, Water Sprites, 1878	15.00
Advertising, Great Family Wine & Bottling Co., Pixie Riding Snail	5.00
Advertising, Kellogg Cereal, Wild Bill Hickok, Breakfast Charts, 1950s, 8 x 10 In.	20.00
Advertising, Keystone Spool Silk, Columbia Image, 1877	880.00
Advertising, Lang's Pure Beer, Now Don't Drink It All, Flower Fairy, Butterfly	75.00
Advertising, Liebig Extract Of Beef, Gnome King's Birthday	15.00
Advertising, National Light Oil, Uncle Sam In Chair On Top Of World	80.00
Advertising, Perry's Proprietary Preparations, Map Of U.S.A, Blue, 1776/1876	99.00
Advertising, Pope Manufacturing Co., Woman & Bicycle	110.00
Advertising, Puzzle, Schlitz Brewing Co., Envelope, Dated 1899, 12 Piece	195.00
Advertising, Runkel Brothers Cocoa, Uncle Sam & Columbia Drinking Cocoa	35.00
Advertising, Stop-Look-Listen, Recruitment, California, 1920s, 5 1/2 x 3 1/2 In.	15.00
Advertising, Thomson Glove Fitting Corset, Woman, With Fairies	25.00
Advertising, Trick Pony Toy Savings Bank, Mechanical, New York News Co., 5 x 3 In.	57.00
Advertising, Wheeler & Wilson Sewing Machines, Fairy Fencing With Mosquito	6.00
Advertising, Wm. H. Schilly & Bros., Syracuse, N.Y., Fairy On Dolphin	6.00
Baseball, Babe Ruth, No. 144 .... *Illus*	41781.00
Baseball, Bob Feller, Topps, No. 88, 1952	2925.00
Baseball, Buck Weaver, T4 Obak Premium, Chicago Black Sox, Penciled 86	8639.00
Baseball, Frank Frisch, Goudey, No. 49, 1933	3141.00
Baseball, George Blaeholder, Goudey, No. 16, 1933	2338.00
Baseball, Ken Griffey Jr., Rookie, Fleer, 1989	15.00
Baseball, Leo Durocher, No. 147 .... *Illus*	1064.00
Baseball, Lou Gehrig, Goudey, No. 61, 1934	3545.00

Card, Baseball, Babe Ruth, No. 144

Card, Baseball, Leo Durocher, No. 147

Card, Baseball, Mel Ott, No. 127

Card, Greeting,
Valentine, Child's,
Box Of 25, 7 1/4 In.

Card, Baseball, Napolean
Larry Lajoie, No. 106

Baseball, Mel Ott, No. 127	*Illus*	1931.00
Baseball, Napolean Larry Lajoie, No. 106,	*Illus*	50556.00
Baseball, Pee Wee Reese, Topps, No. 333, 1952		9992.00
Baseball, Ted Williams, Rookie, Play Ball, No. 92, 1939		4145.00
Baseball, Watson Clark, Goudey, No. 17, 1933		2830.00
Football, Doak Walker, Bowman, No. 1, 1950		2310.00
Greeting, Valentine, Child's, Box Of 25, 7 1/4 In.	*Illus*	25.00
Greeting, Valentine, Winged Angel, Heart Body, Verse, Date 1824, 9 1/4 x 7 1/2 In.		1210.00
Hockey, Gordie Howe, Parkhurst, No. 88, 1952		1433.00
Movie Stars, Lucille Ball, Clark Gable, John Wayne, Etc., 2 1/8 x 1 1/8 In.		65.00
Playing, Civil War, Red, White & Blue Numbers, Face Theme, American Card Co.		800.00
Playing, Dr Pepper, Logo, Girl Holding Bottle, Box, c.1946		385.00
Playing, Edison Mazda, Maxfield Parrish, Box, 1920s		149.00
Playing, Faro, Spread Eagle, Revenue Stamp, 1898		525.00
Playing, History Of The Pack & Explanations, Many Secrets, Magic, Benham, W. Gurney		69.00
Playing, Jersey Whiskey, Yellow & Red Box, c.1900		45.00
Playing, Man From U.N.C.L.E., Robert Vaughn, Ed-U-Cards Mfg., Co., 1965		25.00
Playing, Mapes, 2 Decks, Red & Blue		56.00
Playing, Nevada Club, 2 Decks, Brown Box		6.00
Playing, No Revoke, Gold Edges, S.F. Hanzel, 1920s		250.00
Playing, Rock Island Railroad, Uncut Pair, Frame		57.00
Playing, Standard Oil, Box, 1930s		28.00
Playing, Standard Oil, Logo, 1930s, Box		45.00
Topps, Partridge Family, Unopened, Wax Box, 1971		615.00

CARDER, see Aurene and Steuben categories.

CARLSBAD is a mark found on china made by several factories in Germany, Austria, and Bavaria. Many pieces were exported to the United States. Most of the pieces available today were made after 1891.

Biscuit Jar, Bunches Of For-Get-Me-Nots, Brass Fittings, 7 In.	125.00
Condensed Milk Cover, Underplate, Flowers, Cobalt Blue, Gold Borders, Marked, 5 In.	95.00
Figurine, Girl Holding Umbrella, Blue, White, Green, c.1900, 5 1/2 In.	20.00
Plate, Oyster, 5 Wells, Flowers, c.1880, 8 3/4 In.	110.00
Platter, Fish, Marked, 1900, 21 x 9 x 1 1/2 In.	81.00
Vase, Botanical Form, Tendrils, White Glazed Top, Gilt Trim, Crazing, Marked, 9 In.	110.00

CARLTON WARE was made at the Carlton Works of Stoke-on-Trent, England, beginning about 1890. The firm traded as Wiltshaw & Robinson until 1957. It was renamed Carlton Ware Ltd. in 1958. The company went bankrupt in 1995, but the name is still in use.

Bowl, Green & Black Tree, Luster Handles & Foot, 7 1/8 x 12 1/4 In.	295.00
Bowl, Hollyhocks, Mottled Orange Luster, Pedestal, 3 x 7 1/4 In.	345.00
Chinese Bird, Dark Blue Luster, 6 In.	495.00
Dish, Spider Web, Spider Between Flowers & Leaves, Bottom, Butterfly, 6 1/2 In.	110.00
Flower Holder, Hardbell Flowers, Blue Ground, Marked, 2 1/2 x 10 In.	395.00

Humidor, Butterfly On Cover, Art Nouveau Bird, Tree, Enameled, Marbleized, Divider ..   70.00
Humidor, Oriental Birds, Gold & Dot Trim, Brass Closure & Finial, 4 1/4 In. 295.00
Jar, Cover, Foo Dog Finial, Flowers, Branches, Blue Mottled Ground, 9 In. ......325.00 to 350.00
Jar, Cover, Oriental Man & Woman, Fans, Gold Base Bands, 9 In. ....395.00 to 425.00
Vase, Cover, Oriental Scenes, Woman & Man In Boat, 7 3/8 In..................... 245.00
Vase, Oriental Scenes, Small Boats, Mother-Of-Pearl Interior, 11 In. 345.00

CARNIVAL GLASS was an inexpensive, iridescent, pressed glass made
from about 1907 to about 1925. More than 1,000 different patterns are
known. Carnival glass is currently being reproduced. Additional pieces
may be found in the Northwood category.

Acanthus, Bowl, Deep, Amethyst, 8 1/2 In. 175.00
Acanthus, Bowl, Deep, Green, 8 1/2 In. ....125.00 to 135.00
Acanthus, Bowl, Deep, Smoke, 8 1/2 In. 110.00
Acanthus, Plate, Marigold, 10 In. ....100.00 to 275.00
Acorn, Bowl, Marigold, 7 1/2 In. 75.00
Acorn, Bowl, Moonstone, 7 In. 150.00
Acorn, Bowl, Red, 7 In. 285.00
Acorn Burrs, Berry Set, Amethyst, 5 Piece 145.00
Acorn Burrs, Butter, Cover, Green 310.00
Acorn Burrs, Creamer, Green 130.00
Acorn Burrs, Pitcher, Amethyst 750.00
Acorn Burrs & Bark pattern is listed here as Acorn Burrs.
Apple Blossom Twigs, Bowl, Amethyst, 8 In............................. 550.00
Apple Blossom Twigs, Bowl, Blue, 8 In. 155.00
Apple Blossom Twigs, Bowl, Low, Ruffled Edge, White, 8 In. 130.00
Apple Blossom Twigs, Plate, Blue, 8 1/2 In. 450.00
Apple Tree, Pitcher, Marigold 135.00
Apple Tree, Pitcher, White 800.00
Apple Tree, Water Set, Marigold, 5 Piece 250.00
April Showers, Vase, 11 In. 125.00
April Showers, Vase, Amethyst Opalescent, 10 In. 700.00
April Showers, Vase, White, 10 In. 275.00
Arched Flute, Toothpick, Amethyst 250.00
Arched Flute, Toothpick, Ice Blue 250.00
August Flowers, Lamp Shade, Amethyst 120.00
Autumn Acorns, Plate, Green, 8 1/2 In. 950.00
Banded Diamonds, Pitcher, Marigold, Australian 1100.00
Banded Diamonds, Tumbler, Amethyst, Australia 150.00
Banded Drape, Pitcher, Enameled Forget-Me-Nots, Green 450.00
Banded Drape, Pitcher, Enameled Iris, Marigold 175.00
Banded Medallion & Teardrop pattern is listed here as Beaded Bull's-Eye.
Battenburg Lace No. I pattern is listed here as Hearts & Flowers.
Beaded Acanthus, Pitcher, Milk, Marigold 125.00
Beaded Bull's-Eye, Vase, Amethyst, 10 In................................. 250.00
Beaded Bull's-Eye, Vase, Amethyst, 11 In. 135.00
Beaded Bull's-Eye, Vase, Marigold, Swung, 10 3/4 In. ....*Illus*   50.00

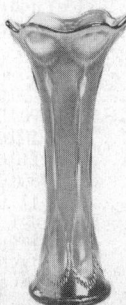

Carnival Glass, Beaded
Bull's-Eye, Vase, Marigold,
Swung, 10 3/4 In.

**To remove a sticky label, try heating
it with a hair dryer to soften the
adhesive. Any remaining glue could be
removed with isopropyl alcohol or
Goo Gone. If the silver is discolored,
clean it with silver polish.**

Beaded Cable, Rose Bowl, Amethyst Opalescent 250.00
Beaded Cable, Rose Bowl, Marigold 110.00
Beaded Medallion & Teardrop pattern is listed here as Beaded Bull's-Eye.
Bellflower, Bowl, Tricornered, Crimped, Amethyst, 7 In. . . . . .115.00 to 245.00
Big Basketweave, Vase, Amethyst, 9 In. 150.00
Big Basketweave, Vase, Amethyst, 10 In. 350.00
Big Basketweave, Vase, Ice Blue, 10 In. 600.00
Bird & Grapes, Wall Pocket, Marigold 140.00
Birds & Cherries, Bonbon, Amethyst 35.00
Birds & Cherries, Bowl, Crimped, Blue, 9 1/2 In. 650.00
Birds On Bough pattern is listed here as Birds & Cherries.
Blackberry, Water Set, Marigold, 7 Piece 1000.00
Blackberry & Checkerboard pattern is listed here as Blackberry Block.
Blackberry A pattern is listed here as Blackberry.
Blackberry B pattern is listed here as Blackberry Spray.
Blackberry Block, Pitcher, Blue 1300.00
Blackberry Block, Water Set, Marigold, 5 Piece 600.00
Blackberry Rays, Compote, Marigold 155.00
Blackberry Spray, Hat, Amethyst Opalescent 155.00
Blackberry Wreath, Bowl, Red, 10 In. 275.00
Blossomtime, Compote, Marigold 225.00
Blueberry, Tumbler, Amethyst 150.00
Boggy Bayou, Vase, Green, 11 In. 120.00
Butterfly & Berry, Bowl, Marigold, 9 In. 195.00
Butterfly & Grape pattern is listed here as Butterfly & Berry.
Cherry, Banana Boat, Cherry, Amethyst, 12 1/2 In. 403.00
Cherry, Bowl, Footed, Marigold, 8 3/4 In. 220.00
Cherry, Bowl, Ice Cream, Amethyst, 2 1/4 In. 294.00
Christmas, Compote, Amethyst 4000.00
Christmas Cactus pattern is listed here as Thistle.
Christmas Rose & Poppy pattern is listed here as Six-Petals.
Chrysanthemum, Bowl, Marigold, 8 x 2 1/2 In. 130.00
Chrysanthemum Wreath pattern is listed here as Ten Mums.
Cobblestones, Bowl, Amethyst, 9 In. 295.00
Constitution pattern is listed here as God & Home.
Dahlia, Water Set, Marigold, 5 Piece 1600.00
Daisy & Drape, Vase, White 300.00
Daisy Band & Drape pattern is listed here as Daisy & Drape.
Dragon & Lotus, Bowl, Blue, 8 1/2 x 2 1/2 In. 300.00
Dragon & Lotus, Bowl, Marigold, 9 In. 95.00
Dragon & Lotus, Dish, Marigold, 8 7/8 x 2 3/8 In. 173.00
Dragon & Lotus, Plate, Blue, 9 1/2 In. 1600.00
Dragon & Strawberry, Bowl, Footed, Blue, 9 In. 1700.00
Egyptian Band pattern is listed here as Round-Up.
Fan & Arch pattern is listed here as Persian Garden.
Fantasy pattern is listed here as Question Marks.
Farmyard, Bowl, Ruffled Edge, Amethyst, 10 In. . . . . .2200.00 to 2600.00
Field Thistle, Plate, Marigold, 9 1/2 In. 300.00
Fine Cut & Roses, Bowl, Amethyst 199.00
Fishscale & Beads, Basket, Aqua Opalescent, 9 1/2 In. 240.00
Floral & Diamond Point pattern is listed here as Fine Cut & Roses.
Fluffy Bird pattern is listed here as Peacock.
Four Flowers, Bowl, Peach, Opalescent, 6 1/2 In. 90.00
Gay Nineties, Tumbler, Amethyst 700.00
God & Home, Water Set, Blue, 7 Piece 2100.00
Grape & Cable, Bowl, Flat, Lime Green, 9 In. 210.00
Grape & Cable, Bowl, Footed, Blue, 8 In. 300.00
Grape & Cable, Bowl, Footed, Green, 11 x 5 In. 173.00
Grape & Cable, Bowl, Ice Cream, White 495.00
Grape & Cable, Candlestick, 4 x 4 1/2 In. 125.00
Grape & Cable, Hat, Green, 6 5/8 x 3 In. 125.00
Grape & Cable, Hatpin Holder, Green, 6 3/4 x 2 1/2 In. 395.00
Grape & Cable, Plate, Blue Stippled 3500.00

Grape & Cable, Plate, Sapphire, 7 In. 1300.00
Grape & Cable, Punch Bowl, Base, Marigold 403.00
Grape & Cable, Sweetmeat, Amethyst 325.00
Grape & Cable, Sweetmeat, Cover, Amethyst, 5 x 8 1/2 In. 230.00
Grape & Cable, Water Set, Amethyst, 7 Piece 316.00
Grape & Cable With Thumbprint, Cracker Jar, Marigold 275.00
Grape & Leaf, Powder Jar, Blue 130.00
Grape & Leaf, Punch Bowl, Blue, 7 In. 195.00
Grape & Leaf, Punch Bowl, Green, 7 In. 165.00
Grape & Peacock, Bowl, Blue, 9 In. 192.00
Grape Arbor, Hat, Green, Footed 325.00
Grape Arbor, Pitcher, Straight Sides, White 500.00
Grape Delight, Bowl, Marigold, 5 In. 100.00
Grapevine Diamonds pattern is listed here as Grapevine Lattice.
Grapevine Lattice, Plate, Marigold, 7 1/4 In. 275.00
Greek Key, Pitcher, Green 800.00
Hearts & Flowers, Bowl, Ruffled Edge, White 225.00
Heron & Rushes pattern is listed here as Stork & Rushes.
Hobnail pattern is listed in this book as its own category.
Hobstar, Compote, 8 x 6 1/2 In. 95.00
Hobstar & Feather, Rose Bowl, Green 4250.00
Intaglio pattern is listed here as Hobstar & Feather.
Inverted Strawberry, Pitcher, Tumbler, Marigold, 2 Piece 850.00
Irish Lace pattern is listed here as Louisa.
Jewels & Drapery, Vase, Blue, 11 In. 225.00
Kittens, Toothpick, Marigold 175.00
Lattice & Grape, Water Set, Marigold, 6 Piece 250.00
Lattice & Grapevine pattern is listed here as Lattice & Grape.
Leaf & Beads, Bowl, Amethyst, 4 In. 175.00
Leaf Chain, Plate, White, 9 1/4 In. 236.00
Leaf Medallion pattern is listed here as Leaf Chain.
Lined Lattice, Vase, Marigold, 9 In. 145.00
Lion, Bowl, Marigold, Ruffled Edge, 7 1/2 In. 99.00
Louisa, Nut Bowl, 3-Footed, Marigold, 4 5/8 In. 150.00
Melinda pattern is listed here as Wishbone.
Morning Glory, Vase, Funeral, Marigold, 17 In. 340.00
Oak Leaf & Acorn pattern is listed here as Acorn.
Ohio Star, Vase, Swung, Amethyst, 16 In. 18000.00
Orange Tree, Bowl, Blue, 9 In. 159.00
Orange Tree, Bowl, Crimped, Marigold, 10 1/2 In. 225.00
Orange Tree, Bowl, Royal Blue, 9 1/2 In. 200.00
Pansy, Bowl, Ruffled Edge, Amethyst, 9 In. 275.00
Peacock, Bowl, Beaded Edge, Amethyst, 9 1/2 In. 95.00
Peacock, Plate, Ribbed, Ice Green 550.00
Peacock & Grape, Bowl, Amethyst, 7 3/4 In. 90.00
Peacock & Grape, Bowl, Blue, 8 3/4 In. 150.00
Peacock & Grape, Bowl, Marigold, 8 In. 225.00
Peacock & Grape, Bowl, Marigold, 9 In. 210.00
Peacock & Urn, Bowl, Cobalt Blue, 8 3/4 In. 173.00
Peacock At The Fountain, Pitcher, Water, White 750.00
Peacock Eye & Grape pattern is listed here as Vineyard.
Peacock On Fence pattern is listed here as Peacock.
Pebbles, Bonbon, Green 100.00
Perfection, Pitcher, Purple 3350.00
Persian Garden, Bowl, White, 11 In. 325.00
Persian Medallion, Bowl, Ice Cream, White, 6 In. 165.00
Persian Medallion, Compote, Amethyst, Large 350.00
Persian Medallion, Compote, Blue, 6 1/2 In. 80.00
Persian Medallion, Compote, Blue, Large 200.00
Question Marks, Cake Plate, Peach Opalescent, Ruffled Edge, Footed 155.00
Ribbon Tie, Bowl, Amethyst, 9 1/4 In. 115.00
Ribbon Tie, Bowl, Marigold, 9 1/4 In. 190.00
Round-Up, Plate, Marigold, 9 In. 300.00

S-Repeat, Punch Set, Amethyst, Bowl, Base, 12 Cups 5300.00
Singing Bird, Water Set, Marigold, 7 Piece 585.00
Six Petals, Bowl, Peach, Opalescent, 7 1/2 In. 125.00
Spiralex, Vase, Amethyst, 9 x 3 x 4 In. 105.00
Stag & Holly, Bowl, 3-Footed, Ruffled Edge, Marigold, 10 1/2 In. 66.00
Stag & Holly, Bowl, Green, 10 In. 260.00
Stag & Holly, Bowl, Marigold, 7 3/4 In. 159.00
Stag & Holly, Chop Plate, Marigold, 13 In. 1200.00
Star Medallion, Pitcher, Milk, Marigold, 6 1/4 In. 80.00
Star Of David, Bowl, Green, 8 3/4 In. 150.00
Stippled Leaf & Beads pattern is listed here as Leaf & Beads.
Stippled Posy & Pods pattern is listed here as Four Flowers.
Stork & Rushes, Bowl, Amethyst, 8 1/4 x 3 3/4 In. 145.00
Strawberry pattern is listed here as Wild Strawberry.
Sunflower, Bowl, Ice Blue, 8 1/2 In. 1600.00
Ten Mums, Water Set, Blue, 7 Piece 1400.00
Thistle, Bowl, Amethyst, 8 1/2 In. 225.00
Thistle, Bowl, Marigold, 8 In. 95.00
Tree Trunk, Vase, Amethyst, 10 In. 185.00
Vineyard, Pitcher, Marigold, 9 1/4 In. 202.00
Vintage Leaf, Bowl, Marigold, 8 In. 95.00
Wide Panel, Epergne, White 1700.00
Wild Strawberry, Bowl, Green, 9 In. 160.00
Wishbone, Bowl, Amethyst, 2 1/2 x 9 1/2 In. 195.00

CAROUSEL or merry-go-round figures were first carved in the United
States in 1867 by Gustav Dentzel. Collectors discovered the charm of
the hand-carved figures in the 1970s, and they were soon classed as
folk art. Most desirable are the figures other than horses, such as pigs,
camels, lions, or dogs. A jumper is a figure that was made to move up
and down on a pole; a stander was placed in a stationary position.

Animals, Zoo, Wood, Mirror Center Pole, Canvas Top, Lights, Composition, c.1920 ..... 94.00
Chicken, Wood, Carved, Herschell-Spillman, c.1915, 53 3/4 x 45 In. 2300.00
Dog, Wood, Painted, Smiling Face, Short Legs, Padded Saddle Seat, Iron Grip, 46 In. 220.00
Goat, Wood, Brown Paint, Green Glass Eyes, Horsehair Chin, Wood Base, 31 x 35 In. 1610.00
Horse, Black Mane, Carved Straps & Saddle, Plaid Blanket, Looff, 1876, 90 In. 2750.00
Horse, Brass Pole, Polychrome Over Gesso, Turn Of The Century 2950.00
Horse, Carved, Fluted Fringe, Horsehair Tail, Stein & Goldstein, 52 In. 4400.00
Horse, Carved, Glass Jewels, Eagle Head Saddle, Horsehair Tail, Heyn, 50 In. 3300.00
Horse, Carved, Polychrome, Iron, Glass, Open Mouth, 19th Century, 43 x 59 In......... 4888.00
Horse, Child's, Metal, c.1900 .... 400.00
Horse, Jumper, 2 Faces, Michael On Neck, Savage, England, 1885, 72 x 45 In. 5060.00
Horse, Jumper, Carved, Painted, Open Mouth, Late 19th Century, 40 x 50 In. 470.00
Horse, Jumper, Carved, White, Gray Mane, U.S. Flag Under Saddle, c.1915, 62 In. 1850.00
Horse, Jumper, Inside Row, Glass Eyes, Carved Mane, Horsehair Tail, 39 x 44 In. 6050.00
Horse, Jumper, Stein & Goldstein, c.1918, 75 1/2 x 64 x 24 In. 21850.00
Horse, Jumping, Inside, Carved Saddle Blanket, Steel Pole, C.W. Parker, 62 In. 5500.00
Horse, Painted, Carved, Brooklyn, N.Y., c.1890, 53 x 40 In. 3800.00
Horse, Pine, Full-Bodied, White Paint, Carved Flowing Mane, Glass Eyes, 48 In. 1495.00
Horse, Pine, Full-Bodied, Yellow Paint, Carved Flowing Mane, Saddle, 58 In. 8050.00
Horse, Running, Ben On Neck Beside Mane, England 6950.00
Horse, Running, Wood, Carved, Painted, 60 In. 1960.00
Horse, Trotting, Carved, Rolled Scroll Saddle, Looff, 58 x 58 In. 4313.00
Panel, Chariot, Carved End, Pan & Nymph, Herschell-Spillman 6295.00
Pig, Dentzel, c.1905, 30 x 50 x 11 1/2 In. 11500.00

**Ordinary beer is great for cleaning a gilded mirror frame.
Just pour it on a soft rag, rub gently, and dry.**

Pig, Running, Carved, Limonaire Freres 2750.00
Rooster, Running, Carved Feathers, 2 Seats, England, 53 In. 3850.00
Rounding Board, Pastoral Scene, Flowers On Reverse, c.1915, 44 x 96 In. 920.00
Woody Woodpecker, Carved, Painted, Display Stand, 1950s, 32 In. 575.00

CARRIAGE means several things, so this category lists baby carriages, buggies for adults, horse-drawn sleighs, and even strollers. Doll-sized carriages are listed in the Toy category.

Baby Buggy, Upholstered Seat, 46 In. 546.00
Baby Buggy, Wicker, Twin Seats, Rolled Edges, Heywood, Victorian, 54 x 58 x 22 In. ... 2520.00
Boardwalk, Wicker, Victorian 625.00
Goat Cart, Slot Body, Wooden Spoke Wheels, Red Paint, Long Handle, Iron Brake Pedal 303.00
Horse Drawn, 2 Wheels, Hide Cover, Worn Paint, 20th Century, 37 x 53 In. 1380.00
Pedal Cart, Rubber Tires, Upholstered, Restored, 1900s, 26 x 18 x 23 In. 467.00
Pram, Wicker & Wrought Iron, c.1890, 35 x 40 In. 180.00
Push, Fringe On Top, Stenciled Wooden Body, Leather Top, 1860s, 45 x 55 In. 1525.00
Sleigh, Cutter, Red, Upholstered Seat, Pony Drawn, c.1920 .... 800.00
Stroller, Wicker, Withrow Manufacturing Co., Cincinnati, Ohio, 1902 .... 350.00
Wagon, Express, Red, White & Blue Painted, Large Rear Back Wheels, 1869 .... 1450.00
Wagon, Farm, Paris Mfg. Co., South Paris, Maine, Red Paint, 36 x 18 In. 1310.00
Wicker, Chiffon Canopy, Wood Wheels, Horsehair Mattress, 1930s, 47 x 46 x 24 In. 168.00

CASH REGISTERS were invented in 1884 because an eye on the cash was a necessity in stores of the nineteenth century, too. John and James Ritty invented a large model that resembled a clock and kept a record of the dollars and cents exchanged in the store. John Patterson improved the cash register with a paper roll to record the money. By the early 1900s, elaborate brass registers were made. About World War I, the fancy case was exchanged for the more modern types.

National, 15-Key 517.00
National, For Joseph Cuozzo, Wilmington, Del., Model 313, Polished 550.00
National, Model 216, $1.00 .... 1100.00
National, Model 250, $1.00 .... 825.00
National, Model 312, Embossed Scrollwork, Milk Glass Drawer, 20 In. 715.00
National, Model 313, $1.00 .... 550.00
National, Model 313, Brass, Special Edition, c.1884 .... 330.00
National, Model 313, Milk Glass Drawer Shelf, Flower, Geometric Design 550.00
National, Model 336, Brass, Embossed, Oak, Milk Glass Drawer, Shelf, 18 x 17 In. 225.00
National, Model 416, Nickel Plate Brass, Marble Shelf, 18 1/2 x 19 x 15 In. 480.00
National, Model 441B, Embossed, N Loop Handle, Marble Shelf, 21 x 18 In. 366.00
National, Nickel Plated Drawer Front, Brass, Porcelain, 21 In. 688.00
National, No. 442, Brass, Flower Case, Oak Drawer, 28 In. 603.00

CASTOR JARS for pickles are glass jars about six inches in height, held in special metal holders. They became a popular dinner table accessory about 1890. Each jar had a top that was usually silver or silver plate. The frame, also of a silver metal, had a handle that arched above the jar and a hook that held a pair of tongs. By 1900, the pickle castor was out of fashion. Many examples found today have reproduced glass jars in old holders. Additional pickle castors may be found in the various Glass categories.

Pickle, Clear Insert, Meridian Silver Plate Co., 1880, 9 In. 262.00
Pickle, Cobalt Blue, Silver-Plated Frame 225.00
Pickle, Daisy & Button Variant, Center Band, 11 In. 200.00
Pickle, Daisy & Button, Blue, Birds, Hands, Tongs, 5 x 11 In. 300.00
Pickle, Daisy & Button, With V Ornament, Blue, Meriden Frame, 11 1/2 In. 210.00
Pickle, Egyptian, Rockford Silver Plate Co., 11 In. 134.00
Pickle, Green, Flowers, Acorn Finial, Fleur-De-Lis, Pairpoint Mfg. Co. 117.00
Pickle, Inverted Thumbprint, Cranberry, 11 In. 850.00
Pickle, Inverted Thumbprint, Cranberry, Enameled Flowers, 13 In. 500.00
Pickle, Inverted Thumbprint, Cranberry, Gold & White Enameled Flowers, Gilt, 11 In. ... 325.00
Pickle, Inverted Thumbprint, Cranberry, Handles, 7 In. 275.00
Pickle, Panel With Diamond Point, Band At Top, Cherub On Handle, 12 In. 350.00

Pickle, Paneled Sprig, Cranberry, Enameled Flowers, 9 In. 600.00
Pickle, Rippled Coin Spot, Branch & Plums, Amberina, Meriden Holder, 13 3/4 In. 1960.00
Pickle, Spattered, Enameled Cosmos Flowers, Basket Weave Frame, 8 In. 588.00

CASTOR SETS holding just salt and pepper castors were used in the seventeenth century. The sugar castor, mustard pot, spice dredger, bottles
for vinegar and oil, and other spice holders became popular by the
eighteenth century. These sets were usually made of sterling silver. The
American Victorian castor set, the type most collected today, was made
of silver plated Britannia metal. Colored glass bottles were introduced
after the Civil War. The sets were out of fashion by World War I. Be
careful when buying sets with colored bottles; many are reproductions.
Other castor sets may be listed in various porcelain and glass categories in this book.

2 Bottles, Daisy & Button, Blue, Meridan Frame, 10 In. 675.00
2 Shakers, 2 Bottles, Treen, Black Walnut, Domed Base, Ring Top, 12 In. 247.00
3 Bottles, Silver, Rope Supports, Gorham, 1848, 8 1/2 In. 345.00
4 Cruets, Cranberry Glass, England 1395.00
5 Bottles, Cut Glass, Silver Plated Holder, Reticulated Frame, 11 In. 330.00
5 Bottles, Silver Plated Tops, Pairpoint Holder, 16 In. 345.00
5 Bottles, Vaseline, Silver Plate, Stand, c.1880, 15 In. 633.00
6 Bottles, Blown, R. Brothers, Silver Plated Frame, 9 1/2 x 7 x 5 In. 130.00
6 Bottles, Gadroon Edge, 8 x 6 1/2 In. 300.00
Salt & Pepper, Mustard Pot, Tapered Cylinders, Slanted Top, Tray, Silver, Denmark 2415.00

CATALOGS are listed in the Paper category.

CAUGHLEY porcelain was made in England from 1772 to 1814. Caughley porcelains are very similar in appearance to those made at the
Worcester factory. See the Salopian category for related items.

Cup & Saucer, Fluted, Scallop Edge, Cobalt Blue, Gold Trim 260.00
Dish, Leaf, Blue Willow, Marked, c.1780 . . . . 150.00
Saucer, Oriental, Pagodas, Islands, Figures, Gardens 62.00
Tea Bowl, Pagoda, Man In Doorway, 2 Figures Crossing Bridge, 3 In. 38.00

CAULDON Limited worked in Staffordshire, Great Britain, and went
through many name changes. John Ridgway made porcelain at
Cauldon Place, Hanley, until 1855. The firm of John Ridgway, Bates
and Co. of Cauldon Place worked from 1856 to 1859. It became Bates,
Brown-Westhead, Moore and Co. from 1859 to 1862. Brown-Westhead, Moore and Co. worked from 1862 to 1904. About 1890, this firm
started using the words *Cauldon* or *Cauldon ware* as part of the mark.
Cauldon Ltd. worked from 1905 to 1920, Cauldon Potteries from 1920
to 1962. Related items may be found in the Indian Tree category.

Plate, Bird In Center, Gold Border, 9 1/2 In. 44.00
Platter, Peonies, Leaves, Rectangular, 20th Century, 19 3/8 In. 40.00
Punch Bowl, Footed, 20th Century, 17 7/8 In. 460.00

CELADON is the name of a velvet-textured green-gray glaze used by
Chinese, Japanese, Korean, and other factories. The name refers both
to the glaze and to pieces covered with the glaze. It is still being made.

Bowl, Cut Corner, Famille Rose, 19th Century, 4 5/8 x 9 7/8 In. 575.00
Bowl, Famille Rose Border, Window Scene, 2 People Reading, 3 1/2 x 12 In. 360.00
Bowl, Ribbed, 3 Unglazed Fish In Center, 21 1/2 In. 520.00
Charger, Cavetto Incised, Radiating Lines, Porcelain, Ming Dynasty, 11 1/2 In. 370.00
Charger, Fluted Edge, Sunburst Center, Ming Dynasty, 12 3/4 In. 1265.00
Charger, Scalloped Rim, Fluted, Sloping Side, Stoneware, 2 1/2 x 18 1/4 In. 3920.00
Dish, Birds, Butterflies, Flowers, Fruit, Famille Rose, 16 In. 1720.00
Figurine, Woman, Standing, Glazed Bisque, 26 1/2 In. 315.00
Jar, 2 Foo Lions, Copper Red & Blue, Egg Shape, Qing Dynasty, 8 In. 80.00
Lamp Base, Urn, Crackled, Entwined Dragons, Chinese Export, 22 1/2 In. 9600.00
Vase, Gilt Bronze, Oval, Flared Neck, Lion Ring Handles, Louis XVI Style, 22 3/4 In. . . . 1175.00
Vase, Sleeve, Leaves, Zhejiang Province, 14 In. 990.00

When cleaning hairbrushes backed
with celluloid, don't plunge the
brushes in a sink full of water. If
water collects between the brush and
the plastic, it will cause damage.
Never keep in direct sunlight.
Celluloid is flammable.

Celluloid, Doll,
Grandma With Suitcase
& Umbrella, Painted,
Japan, 4 In.

CELLULOID is a trademark for a plastic developed in 1868 by John W.
Hyatt. Celluloid Manufacturing Company, the Celluloid Novelty Company, Celluloid Fancy Goods Company, and American Xylonite Company all used Celluloid to make jewelry, games, sewing equipment,
false teeth, and piano keys. Eventually, the Hyatt Company became the
American Celluloid and Chemical Manufacturing Company, the
Celanese Corporation. The name *Celluloid* was often used to identify
any similar plastic. Celluloid toys are listed under Toys.

Cigarette Holder, 1920s, 8 In.	20.00
Comb, Red Stones, Brass Trim, Porcelain Portrait, 1890, 4 x 3 In.	60.00
Doll, Grandma With Suitcase & Umbrella, Painted, Japan, 4 In. *Illus*	50.00
Dresser Set, French Ivory, Satin Lined Case, 3 Piece	100.00
Dresser Set, Pearlized Yellow, Butterscotch, Black Trim, 1930s, 11 Piece	245.00
Figurine, Policeman, Movable Arms, Silver Whistle, Japan, 1930s, 6 In.	30.00

CELS are listed in this book in the Animation Art category.

CERAMIC ART COMPANY of Trenton, New Jersey, was established in
1889 by J. Coxon and W. Lenox and was an early producer of American Belleek porcelain. It became Lenox, Inc. in 1906. Do not confuse
this ware with the pottery made by the Ceramic Arts Studio of Madison, Wisconsin.

Liquid Dispenser, Barrel, Set In Top Cover, Spigot, Blue Band, Rum, Gin, 11 In., Pair	920.00
Pitcher, Grapes, Hand Painted, Belleek	525.00

CERAMIC ARTS STUDIO was founded about 1940 in Madison, Wisconsin, by Lawrence Rabbett and Ruben Sand. Their most popular products were expensive molded figurines. The pottery closed in 1955. Do
not confuse these products with those of the Ceramic Art Co. of Trenton, New Jersey.

Figurine, Adonis & Aphrodite, 9 In. & 7 3/4 In., Pair	300.00
Figurine, Balky & Frisky, Black, 1950s, 3 3/4 In., Pair.	82.00
Figurine, Comedy & Tragedy, Gray, Blue Masks, 10 x 3 In., Pair	313.00
Figurine, Little Bo Peep & Sheep, 5 1/2 In. & 4 1/2 In., Pair	20.00
Plaque, Manchu & Lotus, Lantern Man & Woman, 8 In.	100.00
Salt & Pepper, Clown & Dog, 4 In. & 2 1/2 In.	60.00
Salt & Pepper, Hindu Boys, 4 1/2 In.	70.00
Salt & Pepper, Suzette On Pillow, 3 1/4 x 2 3/4 In.	115.00
Salt & Pepper Shaker, Washington Monument, U.S. Capitol, Gold Trim, 4 In.	15.00
Shelf Sitter, Boy Fishing, Pole & Hook, 4 3/4 In.	45.00
Vase, Bud, Lu-Tang, 3 Bamboo Stalks, 7 In.	27.00

CHALKWARE is really plaster of Paris decorated with watercolors. One
type was molded from Staffordshire and other porcelain models and
painted and sold as inexpensive decorations in the nineteenth century.
Figures of plaster, made from about 1910 to 1940 for use as prizes at
carnivals, are also known as chalkware. Kewpie dolls made of chalkware will be found in their own category.

Bank, Apple, Painted, Red & Yellow, 3 1/4 In.	182.00

Bank, Fruit, Watermelon, Grapes, Quince, 20th Century 1175.00
Bank, Peach, Painted, Ivory & Red, 2 1/2 In. 193.00
Bust, Beatrix 495.00
Bust, Black Hawk 1430.00
Bust, George Washington, Officer's Uniform, Fort Wayne, 35 In. 2200.00
Bust, Hiawatha 165.00
Bust, Indian Chief 193.00
Bust, Indian, War Bonnet, 1900-1910 .... 192.00
Bust, Sam, Lord Wise, 1901 .... 550.00
Cat, Nodder, Crouching, c.1883, 4 x 6 3/4 x 3 1/2 In. 2820.00
Cat, Nodder, Crouching, Painted, Gray, Tan, 19th Century, 3 3/4 x 3 1/2 x 7 In. 1035.00
Cat, Seated, Black, Yellow, Scratch Whiskers, 19th Century, 10 1/2 x 5 In. 7638.00
Compote, Fruit, 20th Century, 18 1/2 In. 55.00
Figurine, Angel, Praying, Green Wings, Pedestal, 8 1/4 In. 440.00
Figurine, Baby, 2 Pistols, Holster, Navy Cap, Pedestal, Remember Pearl Harbor 125.00
Figurine, Basket Of Fruit, Polychrome, 10 1/2 In. 980.00
Figurine, Boy, Green, Shirt, Hat, Kerchief, 11 3/4 In. 14.50
Figurine, Bulldog, Yellow Hat, Pipe, 6 1/2 In. 6.50
Figurine, Cat, Curled Tail, Red Collar & Ears, Green Base, 5 1/2 In. 550.00
Figurine, Cat, Seated On Yellow Base, Black Spots, 6 1/2 In. 632.00
Figurine, Cat, Seated, Articulated Fur, Painted, Early 20th Century, 13 1/2 In. 3055.00
Figurine, Cat, Seated, Wrapped Tail, 20th Century, 6 1/4 x 4 x 3 In. 1880.00
Figurine, Cat, Seated, Yellow Eyes, Red Collar, 19th Century, 11 In., Pair 4900.00
Figurine, Dog, Pink, Black Ears, Mouth, Collar & Base, 6 1/2 In. 330.00
Figurine, Dog, Poodle, Seated, 19th Century, 5 1/4 x 2 1/4 x 4 In. 1295.00
Figurine, Dog, Tan, White, Glitter On Ears, 1930, 9 1/2 In. 11.50
Figurine, Fireman, Holding Fire Horn, 19th Century, 14 1/2 In. 7050.00
Figurine, George Washington, On Horseback, 19th Century, 12 1/2 x 10 x 4 1/2 In. 5875.00
Figurine, Girl & Lamb, Early 20th Century, 5 1/4 In. 275.00
Figurine, Greyhound, Recumbent, 19th Century, 7 1/2 x 10 1/2 In. 58.00
Figurine, Jiggs, Stamped I.C.C.S, 8 1/2 In. 51.00
Figurine, Lamb, Reclining On Molded Base, 4 1/8 In. 165.00
Figurine, Parrot, On Sphere, Green Wings, Black Beak, 19th Century, 8 3/4 In. 825.00
Figurine, Parrot, On Stump, Early 20th Century, 12 1/2 In. 300.00
Figurine, Pigeon, Red & Green Wings, Black Beak & Feet, Perch, 6 In. 1265.00
Figurine, Poodle, Black Tail, Muzzle & Collar, Black & Red Ears, 7 1/4 In. 470.00
Figurine, Poodle, Fur Shoulders & Ears, Green Blue Base, 6 7/8 In. 275.00
Figurine, Rabbit, Orange Ears & Mouth, Yellow Eyes, Green Base, 5 1/4 In. 467.00
Figurine, Rabbit, Seated, Painted, 5 1/2 x 2 3/4 x 3 3/4 In., Pair 3525.00
Figurine, Rabbit, White Spots & Ears, Black Eyes, Pink Mouth, 8 In. 275.00
Figurine, Ram, Recumbent, Painted Face, Dimpled, 4 In. 175.00
Figurine, Rooster, 19th Century, 5 1/4 In. 60.00
Figurine, Rooster, Yellow Body, 7 In. 340.00
Figurine, Sailor Girl, 9 1/2 In. 28.00
Figurine, Salamander, Bearded Sailor, Cigar, Red & Blue Sailor Suit, 15 In. 1045.00
Figurine, Squirrel, Eating Nut, 19th Century, 5 In. 495.00
Figurine, Squirrel, Raised Paws, 19th Century, 7 x 3 x 4 In., Pair 1765.00
Figurine, Squirrel, Seated, Eating Nut, White Body, 6 In. 360.00
Figurine, Stag, Reclining On Ribbed Base, Brown Spots & Collar, 8 3/4 In. 660.00
Figurine, Stag, Recumbent, Painted, c.1883, 10 x 8 1/2 x 3 3/4 In., Pair 1525.00
Figurine, Woman, Pantsuit, Beret, Red, Blue, 14 In. 76.00
Garniture, Fruit & Leaves, Red Brown, Yellow, White Base, 10 3/4 In. 1705.00
Garniture, Fruit, Leaves, Square Base, Painted, 14 In., Pair 3290.00
Garniture, Pineapple, Painted Green, Candlestick, Painted Yellow, Blue, Red, 11 In. 940.00
Garniture, Urn Shape, Rosette Decorated Sides, Fruit, Lovebirds, 11 1/2 In., Pair 4700.00
Garniture, Urn, Yellow Fruit & Kissing Birds, Natural White, 12 In. 4290.00
Lamp, Boy At Well, Green Frosted Glass Shade, Marked Ohio Statuary 65.00
Nodder, Pig, Painted, Early 20th Century, 3 1/2 x 8 x 3 In. 355.00
Plaque, Oriental Girl, 8 1/2 In. 5.00
Vase, Cornucopia, 2 Seated Dogs At Side, Late 19th Century, 6 1/2 In. 190.00
Wall Hanging, Portrait Of Indian Chief, Wood, 1904 .... 440.00

CHARLIE CHAPLIN, the famous comic and actor, lived from 1889 to 1977. He made his first movie in 1913. He did the movie *The Tramp* in 1915. The character of the Tramp has remained famous, and in the 1980s appeared in a series of television commercials for computers. Dolls, candy containers, and all sorts of memorabilia picture Charlie Chaplin. Pieces are being made even today.

Box, Handkerchief, Lid, Embossed, Wood, Brass Hinges, 6 x 6 In.	35.00
Candle, 15 In.	20.00
Card, Bridgewater Cookies, Ltd., 1932, 1 1/4 x 1 3/4 In.	8.50
Doll, Louis Amberg & Sons, N.Y., 1915	566.00
Figurine, Charlie The Tramp, Lladro, No. 5233, Box, 11 In.	775.00
Flip Movie, 50 Pages, 1915, 1 1/2 x 2 In.	15.50
Lobby Card, A Dog's Life, Charlie Chaplin, 1918, 11 x 14 In.	189.00
Pencil Sharpener, Figural Head, 1920s, 2 In.	26.00
Pencil Tin, Canco, Henry Clive, 2 x 8 In.	61.00
Photo, Newspaper Wire Service, 1924, 8 x 10 In.	42.00
Pin, Glass Stones, Rhinestones, Metal, Red, Black, Dominique, 4 1/4 x 2 1/2 In.	36.00
Postcard, Photo, Marked 481, Cinemagazine-Edition, Paris	15.00
Puppet, Amazing Dancing Charlie, Cardboard, Jointed Knees, Hips, c.1920, 13 In.	125.00
Sheet Music, Those Charlie Chaplin Feet, 1915	18.50
Toy, Little Tramp, Automaton, Bowler Hat, Coat, Cane In, Hand, 13 1/2 In.	105.00
Toy, Twirls Cane, Original Box, Schuco, 1920s	950.00
Toy, Windup, Metal, Plastic, Reliable Toys, Canada	182.00

CHARLIE McCARTHY was the ventriloquist's dummy used by Edgar Bergen from the 1930s. He was famous for his work in radio, movies, and television. The act was retired in the 1970s.

Car, Charlie Driving, Head Spins, Marx, 8 In.	180.00
Car, Whoopee Car Action, Tin, Windup, Marx, 7 In.	144.00
Dummy, Composition Head, Black Tuxedo, Top Hat, Effanbee, 21 In.	190.00
Dummy, Composition, Head Moves, Mouth Opens, Drawstring, 12 1/4 In.	95.00
Eggcup, Ceramic, Orange Luster, Japan, 1930s, 1 3/4 In.	75.00
Figure, Chalk, Seated, Orange Hair, Blue Coat, Brown Shoes, 7 1/4 In.	40.00
Lobby Card, Detective, Frame, 1939	150.00
Perfume Bottle, Figural, Glass, 1930s, 3 1/2 In.	30.00
Poster, Charlie McCarthy, Detective, 1939, Insert	546.00
Poster, Feudin' N Fussin', Vitaphone Re-release, Frame, 42 x 26 In.	460.00
Stock Certificate, Pan Am Airways, To Edgar Bergen, Signed	275.00

CHELSEA porcelain was made in the Chelsea area of London from about 1745 to 1784. Some pieces made from 1770 to 1784 may include the letter *D* for *Derby* in the mark. Ceramic designs were borrowed from the Meissen models of the day. Pieces were made of soft paste. The gold anchor was used as the mark but it has been copied by many other factories. Recent copies of Chelsea have been made from the original molds. Do not confuse Chelsea porcelain with Chelsea Grape, a white pottery with luster grape decoration.

Bonbonniere, Agate Cover, Cupid Shape, Painted Flower Sprigs Interior, 1760, 2 In.	2880.00
Box, Cover, Russet Apple Shape, Turquoise & Puce Caterpillar Knob, 1755, 4 In.	8400.00
Box, Patch, Painted Bird Cover, Basket Shape, Marque De Mon Estime, 1760, 1 1/8 In.	780.00
Candlestick, Seated Rabbit, Scrolling Base, Back Handle, c.1770, 9 1/2 In., Pair	3600.00
Dish, Double Leaf, Anchor Mark, 1752, 8 & 3 3/4 In., Pair	2880.00
Dish, Dragon, Silver Shape, Crenellated, Shell Each End, Kakiemon, 11 3/8 In., Pair	8400.00
Dish, Fruits & Vegetables, Scroll Handles, Signed, 1760, 10 1/2 In., Pair	2760.00
Dish, Vine Leaf, Purple Veining Over Fruit, c.1760, 7 In., Pair	2400.00
Figurine, Gardeners, Continental, Late 19th Century, 8 5/8 In., Pair	431.00
Plate, Botanical, Spray, Flower Sprigs, Ladybird, Hans Sloane, 8 3/8 In.	2880.00
Plate, Bouquet, Rocaille Molded Rims, c.1770, 8 3/4 In., 2 Piece	288.00
Plate, Exotic Bird, Flowers, Mazarine Blue Rim, Gilt Scroll, 1760, 8 3/8 In., Pair	2280.00
Plate, Flower Spray, Trellis Molded Rim, Warren Hastings, 1755, 9 1/2 In.	1680.00
Plate, Leaf Shape, Crazing, 1755, 2 3/4 x 9 In.	1870.00

Plate Set, Exotic Bird, Green, Gold, Gold Anchor Mark, 9 1/2 In., 12 Piece 1553.00
Sauceboat, Strawberry Leaf, Flowers, Handle, Footed, Red Anchor, 7 1/2 In., Pair 4560.00
Soup, Dish, Strawberry, Flower Spray, Red Anchor Mark, 1755, 9 1/8 In., Pair 3840.00
Sprig, Cup, Handleless 9.50
Tea Bowl, Saucer, Figures & Buildings, Riverbank, Flowers, 1752, 2 & 4 3/4 In. 7800.00
Tea Bowl, Saucer, Lady In Pavilion, 8 Sides, Kakiemon, 1752, 1 15/16 & 4 3/4 In. 8050.00
Wine Cooler, Fruiting Grapevine, Handles, Front & Rear Flowers, c.1755, 8 1/4 In., Pair . 5100.00

CHELSEA GRAPE pattern was made before 1840. A small bunch of
grapes in a raised design, colored with purple or blue luster, is on the
border of the white plate. Most of the pieces are unmarked. The pattern is sometimes called *Aynsley* or *Grandmother*. Chelsea Sprig is
similar but has a sprig of flowers instead of the bunch of grapes.
Chelsea Thistle has a raised thistle pattern. Do not confuse these
Chelsea patterns with Chelsea Keramic Art Works, which can be found
in the Dedham category, or with Chelsea porcelain, the preceding
category.

Cup & Saucer, Gothic Pattern 45.00
Plate, Gold, 9 5/8 In. 15.50
Sugar, Octagonal 75.00
CHELSEA SPRIG, Cake Plate, 8 3/4 In. 22.00
Cup & Saucer 26.00
Plate, 6 1/2 In. 8.00

CHINESE EXPORT porcelain comprises all the many kinds of porcelain
made in China for export to America and Europe in the eighteenth,
nineteenth, and twentieth centuries. Other pieces may be listed in this
book under Canton, Celadon, Nanking, and Rose Medallion.

Basin, Armorial, Scroll Rim, c.1752, 3 x 14 1/4 In. 1345.00
Basin, Arms Of Tuite Impaling Stafford, c.1752, 14 1/4 In. 1200.00
Basket, Fruit, Undertray, Chromed Frets & Borders, 1840s, 3 1/2 x 9 In. 1095.00
Basket, Interior Peonies, Fenced Garden, Famille Rose, Handles, c.1750, 10 In. 1560.00
Basket, Reticulated, Willow Pattern, Blue, Rope Handles, 6 1/2 In. 230.00
Bottle, Slender Neck, Bulbous, Fish, Lotus Blossoms, 19th Century, 11 In., Pair 3600.00
Bough Pot, Cover, Octagonal, Court Scenes, Famille Rose, c.1820, 9 In., Pair 4830.00
Bough Pot, Leaf Handles, Polychrome Landscape, 1860s, 9 5/8 In. 3220.00
Bowl, Armorial, Blue & White, Early 18th Century, 10 In. 5060.00
Bowl, Armorial, Lions, Flowers, Blue Shields, 4 x 10 3/8 In. 375.00
Bowl, Armorial, Octagonal Rim, Shell, Bird, Flowers, c.1752, 1 1/2 x 8 3/4 In. 135.00
Bowl, Center, Oblong, Scroll Handles, Footed, 1736-1795, 6 1/2 x 12 1/2 In. 920.00
Bowl, Children Playing, Turquoise, Famille Rose, c.1800, 7 3/4 In., Pair 489.00
Bowl, Deep Cavetto, Flowering Enamels, Court Scene, Famille Rose, 6 1/2 In. 260.00
Bowl, Fruit, Stand, Flowers, Butterfly, Bok Choy Leaves, Famille Rose, 10 In. 1250.00
Bowl, Gilt Bronze, 2 Gargoyle Handles, Famille Rose, 11 1/2 x 13 In. 2530.00
Bowl, Hundred Flowers, Turquoise Interior, Famille Rose, c.1910, 7 3/4 In. 287.00
Bowl, Hunters, Horses, Fox, Scrolls, 4 1/2 x 11 In. 635.00
Bowl, Landscape, Painted Coat Of Arms, Motto, c.1810, 10 In. 1920.00
Bowl, Salad, Cut Corner, Famille Rose, 19th Century, 5 x 9 1/2 In. 374.00
Bowl, Scalloped Rim, Leaf Feet, Bronze Mounted, Imari, 6 x 10 1/2 In. 1230.00
Bowl, Serving, Square, Scalloped Edge, Blue & White, 2 1/2 x 10 x 10 In. 55.00
Bowl, Square, Cut Corners, Rose Medallion, 9 1/2 In. 1610.00
Bowl, Thousand Butterflies, 16 In. 1485.00
Bowl, Tobacco Leaf, c.1780, 6 1/2 In., 6 Piece 5400.00
Bowl, Tobacco Leaf, c.1800, 9 1/4 In. 2300.00
Bowl, Western Hunt Scene, 13 7/8 In. 6325.00
Box, Cover, Butterflies, Leaves, Compartmented, Famille Rose, 8 In. 530.00
Box, Cover, Duck Shape, Aubergine, Manganese & Yellow, 1830s, 5 1/4 In. 2400.00
Brush Holder, Stand, Polychrome Enamels, Early 20th Century, 11 x 5 In. 105.00
Cachepot, 8-Sided, Dragon Decoration, Wan-Li 405.00
Candlestick, Dragon Shape Handle, Famille Rose, c.1775, 5 In. 3900.00
Candlestick, Elephant Shape, Sconce On Back, Famille Rose, 6 1/2 In. 2160.00
Case, Calling Card, Carved Figures, Flower Border, Inscribed MES, 4 1/2 x 3 In. 345.00
Chamber Pot, 3 Sprays Of Peony & Prunus, Famille Rose, c.1750, 8 In. 960.00

Chamber Pot, Cover, Figural Reserves, Orange Borders, 8 1/2 x 9 1/2 In. 55.00
Charger, Armorial, Diaper Border, Van Wesck, c.1735, 14 1/8 In. 3000.00
Charger, Birds, Butterflies, Fruit, Famille Rose, Late 19th Century, 13 1/4 In. 345.00
Charger, Cavetto & Raised Rim, Rounded Foot, Famille Rose, 14 3/4 In., Pair 2300.00
Charger, Center Arms Of Van Herzeele, Gilt Spearhead Rim, c.1740, 14 1/4 In. 960.00
Charger, Central Reserve, Peacocks, Blue & White, 18th Century, 21 In. 6600.00
Charger, Flowers, Leaves, Gazebo, Egrets, Blue & White, 19th Century, 14 In. 400.00
Charger, Leaf, Shell & Scroll, Center Landscape, c.1780, 13 1/4 In. 3200.00
Charger, Leaf, Shell, Scrolls, Landscape Scene With Figures, c.1780, 13 1/4 In. 3585.00
Charger, Phoenixes, Flowers, Famille Vert, c.1700, 15 1/4 In. 3600.00
Charger, Scrolling Flower Border, Center Flowers, Famille Rose, c.1820, 12 1/2 In. 240.00
Coffeepot, Armorial, Lighthouse, Tapering, Twig Handle, c.1780, 8 In. 280.00
Coffeepot, Entwined Strap Handle, Famille Rose, c.1800, 8 3/4 In. 290.00
Creamer, Armorial, Classical Shape, Eagle Crest, c.1790, 4 1/2 In. 336.00
Creamer, Cover, Enamel, Coastal Scene, Church, Pear Shape, 5 In. 920.00
Creamer, Cover, Enamel, Tall Ships At Sea, 5 In. 2530.00
Creamer, Cover, Mandarin Scene, c.1750-1775, 5 1/4 In. 330.00
Creamer, Helmet Shape Jug, Painted Spread Wing Eagle, c.1800, 5 1/2 In. 575.00
Creamer, Helmet Shape, Polychrome Enameled Flowers, Scrolls, 5 In. 125.00
Creamer, Helmet Shape, Twig Handle, Pedestal Base, Late 19th Century, 5 3/8 In. 180.00
Cup & Saucer, Cupid & Psyche, Handleless, Polychrome & Grisaille, c.1750 . . . .   330.00
Custard Cup, Cover, Wyvern Crest, Dread Shame Motto, Late 1700s, 3 3/8 In., Pair 960.00
Dessert Service, Green Fitzhugh, 19th Century, 20 Piece 1232.00
Dessert Service, Sacred Birds & Butterfly, Red, Gilt, 19th Century, 6 Piece 1320.00
Dish, Enamel Gold Lacquer, Leafy Rim, 1830s, 11 x 8 In. 2070.00
Dish, Enamel, Peonies, Flower Border, 9 In. 140.00
Dish, Figural Decoration, Kidney Shape, Famille Rose, 11 In., Pair 920.00
Dish, Flower Medallion, Scenic Panel, Blue & White, Foliate Rim, 8 1/2 In. 130.00
Dish, Fluted, Flower Basket, Famille Vert, c.1722, Pair 2160.00
Dish, Landscape & Flowers, Oval Finial On Domed Lid, Quatrefoil Shape, 12 In. 520.00
Dish, Lappets, Lion Dog, Famille Verte, 8 1/4 In. 3000.00
Dish, Left Facing Eagle, Banner, E Pluribus Unum, Fitzhugh, Brown, Square, 9 In. 345.00
Dish, Saucer, Enamel, Famille Rose, Early 19th Century, 5 3/4 In., Pair 315.00
Dish, Vegetable, Fluted Rim, Oval, 8 1/2 x 7 3/4 In. 290.00
Dish, Vegetable, Oval, 8 1/2 x 7 3/4 In. 290.00
Dish Set, Scenic Landscape, Blue & White, 19th Century, 5 1/4 In. 85.00
Figurine, Cockerel, Brown Stump, Early 19th Century, 12 1/4 In., Pair 6900.00
Figurine, Crane, Wooden Roost, Polychrome Enameled, 16 In., Pair 546.00
Figurine, Crane, Wooden Roost, Turquoise Glaze, 17 1/2 In., Pair 635.00
Figurine, Glazed Biscuit, Fish Scale Pattern Costume, c.1722, 17 In. 6600.00
Figurine, Hawk, Penciled Feathers, Famille Rose, Rockwork, c.1900, 10 In. 345.00
Figurine, Hound, Seated, Bow Tied Collar, c.1780, 9 3/8 In.   4800.00
Figurine, Phoenix Bird Perched On Floral Base, 1930s, 16 1/4 In., Pair 9920.00
Figurine, Phoenix Bird, Left & Right, Famille Rose, 23 In., Pair 6330.00
Figurine, Phoenix Bird, On Rock, Ling-Chi Fungus, Famille Rose, 28 In., Pair 2900.00
Figurine, Rooster, Blanc-De-Chine, Before Rocky Mound, 1800s, 17 1/2 In. 1800.00
Figurine, Wrestling Boys, Holding Vase, Famille Rose, 16 In., Pair 430.00
Flask, Detachable Head Cover, Cat Form, Tail Handle, Late 19th Century, 10 In. 960.00
Garniture, Vase, Cover, Blue & White, c.1700, 19 1/4 In., 5 Piece 18000.00
Ginger Jar, Cover, Officials In Garden, Blue & White, 19th Century 60.00
Ginger Jar, Cover, Scroll Design, Blue & White, Lid, 17 In. 396.00
Ginger Jar, Wooden Cover, Flowers, Butterflies, Turquoise Glaze, Stand, 9 In., Pair 1150.00
Headrest, Rectangular Shape, Occupational Pursuits, Blue & White, Pair 1020.00
Jar, Cover, Barrel Shape, Leaves, Raised Foot, Blue Underglaze, 5 3/4 In., Pair 145.00
Jar, Cover, Dragon In Clouds, Baluster Shape, Blue & White, 25 In., Pair 4800.00
Jar, Cover, Flower Meander, Blue & White, c.1700, 7 1/4 In.   1560.00
Jar, Cover, Kylin Shape, Blue & White, 18th Century, 16 1/2 In. 8400.00
Jar, Domed Lid, Finials, Birds, Branches, Famille Rose, 1920s, 19 In., Pair 488.00
Jar, Domed Lid, Spire Finial, Famille Rose, 18 In., Pair 978.00
Jardiniere, Bird & Flowering Branches, Famille Verte, 10 In.   316.00
Jardiniere, Green Flowering Branches, Pink, Late 19th Century, 14 x 16 1/2 In. 110.00
Jardiniere, Landscape, Rounded, Tapered, Blue & White, 14 x 16 In. 345.00
Jardiniere, Ruffled Rim, Leaf Handles, Flower & Fruit Design, 12 x 19 x 9 In. 200.00

Jug, 2 Dogs Under Spout, Bird On Birdbath, Helmet Shape, c.1780, 5 1/2 In. 1800.00
Jug, Cider, Barrel Shape, Gilt, Entwined Handle, Cobalt Blue, 8 1/2 In. 690.00
Jug, Cider, Cover, Loop Handle, Continuous Interior Scene, 1840s, 10 3/4 In. 3600.00
Jug, Cover, Armorial, Foo Dog Finial, c.1800, 12 In. 2070.00
Jug & Basin, Silver Cover, Lotus Pad & Blossoms, Shell Feet, 1750s, 11 In. 3000.00
Lamp, Magpies, Peonies, Famille Rose, 25 In., Pair 300.00
Milk Jug, Cover, Armorial, Continental, Scroll Border, Mid 18th Century, 4 1/8 In. 780.00
Milk Jug, Cover, Armorial, Falconer, Rope Twist Border, c.1745, 5 In. 1440.00
Mug, Armorial, Batten Arms, Twig Handle, Blue Enameled Bands, c.1790, 5 1/2 In. 730.00
Mug, Court & Garden Scenes, Famille Rose, 4 3/8 In. 265.00
Night-Light, Cat Shape, Seated, Tail Curled Over Haunches, 19th Century, 8 In. 7800.00
Pitcher, Polychrome, Gilt, Eagle, American Shield, Flowers, 4 In. 345.00
Plate, Armorial, 3 Bands, Octagonal, c.1800, 7 1/2 In. 450.00
Plate, Armorial, Arms Of Edmund William Gilbert, c.1820, 9 1/8 In., Pair 900.00
Plate, Armorial, Barton Arms, Flower Garland, c.1770, 9 In. 615.00
Plate, Armorial, Double Crest, Flower Garland, Gilt Bands, c.1790, 9 In., Pair 2350.00
Plate, Armorial, Famille Verte Band, Crest, c.1717, 8 7/8 In., Pair 3900.00
Plate, Armorial, Flower Spray Border, Arms, Edwards Family, 1760, 6 1/4 In., Pair 615.00
Plate, Armorial, Gibbon, Famille Rose Sprays, c.1727, 8 7/8 In. 1920.00
Plate, Armorial, Gilt Rim, c.1725, 9 In. 340.00
Plate, Armorial, Hamilton Quartering Arran & Douglas, c.1738, 9 1/8 In. 2160.00
Plate, Armorial, Michel, Spearhead Band, c.1755, 9 In. 3000.00
Plate, Armorial, Pigot, c.1745, 9 In. 2160.00
Plate, Armorial, Teissier Arms, Blue & Gilt Border, Motto, 9 1/2 In. 390.00
Plate, Arms Of Beckford Of Jamaica, Arms & Crest Rim, c.1755, 8 1/2 In., Pair 5100.00
Plate, Bird, Branches, Fish, Famille Verte, c.1700, 9 In., Pair 1920.00
Plate, Birds, Willow, Octagonal, Famille Verte, c.1700, 9 1/2 In., Pair 2520.00
Plate, Blue Fitzhugh, 8 3/4 In. 140.00
Plate, Cartouche, Vine, Scene, Farmers Playing Cards, c.1750, 10 1/2 In. 900.00
Plate, Center Arms Of Sealy, Fitzhugh Border, c.1785, 9 1/2 In., 4 Piece 3900.00
Plate, Deshima Island, Cow, 3 Figures, Early 18th Century, 7 1/4 In., Pair 840.00
Plate, European Scene, Farmers Playing Cards, c.1750, 10 1/2 In. 900.00
Plate, European Subject, Black Monochrome, 2 Plates, Mug, c.1810 . . . . 4200.00
Plate, Export, Butterfly, Passion Flower Border, Famille Rose, c.1830, 8 In., Pair 104.00
Plate, Flower, Bird, Butterfly, Famille Rose, 8 In., 12 Piece 358.00
Plate, Green Fitzhugh, 9 1/2 In. 275.00
Plate, Luncheon, Rock Formation, 19th Century, 9 In., 14 Piece 259.00
Plate, Parasol, Honeycomb Border, Imari Palette, c.1735, 9 1/4 In., Pair 2912.00
Plate, Pompadour, Crested, c.1745, 10 In. 6000.00
Plate, Women Opening Parasols, c.1735, 9 1/4 In., Pair 2600.00
Platter, Armorial, Coat Of Arms, c.1790, 1 1/4 x 14 3/4 x 12 In. 1680.00
Platter, Armorial, Octagonal, c.1790, 14 In. 1500.00
Platter, Center Arms Of Blunt, Dot Border, c.1785, 14 1/8 In., Pair 1920.00
Platter, Deer, Leaves, Floral Border, Blue & White, 18th Century, 11 In. 1210.00
Platter, Green, Fitzhugh, Oval, Late 19th Century, 16 1/2 In. 1150.00
Platter, Handles, Rectangular Shape, Famille Rose, 1 3/4 x 14 x 7 In. 633.00
Platter, Meat, Footed, Famille Rose, 16 1/2 In. 743.00
Platter, Tobacco Leaf, Oval, c.1780, 14 3/4 In. 7200.00
Pot, Chocolate, Flowers, Vines, Peacocks, Famille Rose, 18th Century, 9 1/2 In. 460.00
Pot, Cover, Port Scene, Sailing Ships, Cat Faces Either Side, 13 1/2 In. 165.00
Punch Bowl, Armorial, Chain, Campbell, Duke Of Argyll Arms, 3 3/4 x 9 1/4 In. 2688.00
Punch Bowl, Arms Of Campbell, Duke Of Argyll, c.1770, 9 In. 2400.00
Punch Bowl, Bearing Arms Of Flight, Motto, 1750, 11 In. 1900.00
Punch Bowl, Blue Highlight, Gilt, Enameled, c.1790, 15 3/8 In. 1440.00
Punch Bowl, Court Scenes, Landscapes, Footed, Famille Rose, c.1820, 11 1/4 In. 489.00
Punch Bowl, Figures, Landscape, Birds, Famille Rose, c.1775, 16 1/4 In. 5100.00
Punch Bowl, Gold Crosshatch Design, Green Rim, Wreath Banded Base, 20 In. 5750.00
Punch Bowl, Landscape, Figures, Koi In Kelp, c.1750, 4 1/4 x 10 1/4 In. 1960.00
Punch Bowl, Mandarin Pattern, Domestic Scenes, Famille Rose, 11 1/2 In. 330.00
Punch Bowl, Outdoor Court Scene, Famille Rose, 1796-1820, 15 1/8 In. 690.00
Punch Bowl, Overall Polychrome Flowers, Stand, Famille Rose, 4 3/8 x 11 1/8 In. 705.00
Punch Bowl, Painted Inside & Out, Butterflies, Famille Rose, 1850s, 19 In. 4200.00
Punch Bowl, Paneled Design, Lotus Blossoms, c.1790, 6 x 9 In. 532.00

Punch Bowl, Pierced Bronze Rim, Scrolling Design, Bronze Base, Footed, 17 In. 476.00
Punch Bowl, Rose Garland, Flower Baskets, Famille Rose, Gilt Border, 15 In. 4230.00
Punch Bowl, Sloped Sides, Ring Base, Famille Rose, 5 x 11 In. 705.00
Sauceboat, Undertray, Figures, Bird, Famille Verte, Mid 19th Century, 5 1/2 In. 230.00
Saucer, Armorial, Flower Rim, Bird's Head, Plums, c.1760 . . . . 190.00
Saucer, Crucifixion, Blue & White, c.1710, 5 In. 600.00
Saucer, Flute, Alternating Petals, Flowers, Famille Verte, c.1700, 10 3/8 In. 600.00
Soup, Dish, Famille Rose, 9 1/2 In., 12 Piece 385.00
Soup, Dish, Gilt In Hair & Hats, Famille Rose, 9 7/8 In., Pair 220.00
Soup, Dish, Hope Allegory, Elias Hesket Derby Service, c.1786, 9 In. 4800.00
Soup, Dish, Tobacco Leaf, Bird Perched In Leaves, Scalloped Edge, c.1775, 9 In. 355.00
Sugar, Cover, Floral Garlands, Arms Command, c.1770, 5 x 7 In. 2400.00
Sugar, Cover, Interwoven Handle, Green & Gilt, Hand Painted, 5 In. 60.00
Tankard, Enamel, Hanging Basket, Birds, Barrel Shape, 6 In. . . . . .600.00 to 978.00
Tankard, Polychrome Enamel, Dutch Village Scene, Gilt Border, 5 1/2 In. 1900.00
Tea Bowl & Saucer, Tobacco Leaf, c.1780, 4 3/4 In., Pair 2160.00
Tea Canister, Blue & White, Silver Metal Mounted, c.1880, 6 1/8 In. 1680.00
Tea Set, Famille Rose, 9 Piece 200.00
Teapot, Cover, Butterfly, Chrysanthemum, Famille Verte, c.1700, 4 In. 660.00
Teapot, Cover, Cream Jug, Crested, Bird Holding Branch, c.1795, 5 1/4 In. 900.00
Teapot, Cover, Porcelain, Enamel, Gift Bearer, Serpentine Spout, 6 1/4 In. 175.00
Teapot, Cover, Stand, Pear Shape, Chrysanthemums, c.1740, 5 1/8 In. 3000.00
Teapot, Dome Cover, Bulbous Peddle Shape Body, Flowers, Vines, c.1790, 6 In. 364.00
Teapot, Enamel, Figures, Landscape, 6 1/2 In. 1210.00
Teapot, Enamel, Interior Scene, Men, Women, 5 In. 635.00
Teapot, Family Figures On 2 Sides, Ball Form, 6 In. 172.00
Teapot, Flower Urns, Insects, Bulbous, 5 1/4 In. 230.00
Teapot, Flowers & Birds, Lobed Handle, White Paste Glaze, 1920s, 5 In. 145.00
Teapot, Oval, Twisted Branch Handle, American Eagle, c.1800 . . . . 1035.00
Teapot, Pear Shape, Crowns, Monograms, Marriage Crest, Famille Rose, 5 1/2 In. 635.00
Teapot, Tapered, Hand Painted, Dome Top, Blue & Gilt, Silver Spout, 10 In. 220.00
Tray, Spoon, 6 Sides, Polychrome Enamel, Ships Along Coast, 5 In. 635.00
Tureen, Blue & White, Underglaze, Late 19th Century, 9 x 14 x 8 3/4 In. 1150.00
Tureen, Cover, Blue & White, Oval, 2 Handles, c.1780, 14 In. 316.00
Tureen, Cover, Platter, Armorial, Vaultier Dit Beauregard, 18th Century, 11 In. 8400.00
Tureen, Dome Cover, Gilded Handles, Famille Rose, 8 1/2 x 12 In. 1730.00
Tureen, Lotus, Cabbage Leaves, Stand, Famille Rose, 12 In. 925.00
Tureen, Soup, Boar's Head Handles, Tray, c.1800, 8 1/2 In. 4100.00
Tureen, Soup, Canted Edges, Domed Top, Blue, Red Enamel, 8 1/2 In. 3000.00
Tureen, Soup, Cover, Arms Of Erskine Impaling Elphinstone, c.1795, 13 1/2 In. 4800.00
Tureen, Soup, Cover, Undertray, Leaf Design, Foo Dog Finial, 1800s, 8 x 15 In. 2530.00
Tureen, Soup, Side Panels Of Peonies, 1765, 12 In., Pair 7800.00
Tureen, Underplate, Cover, Fruit Finial, c.1790, 9 1/2 x 14 x 9 1/2 In. 1900.00
Tureen, Undertray, Gilt Branch Handles, Pod Finial, Cover, 15 In. 1980.00
Urn, 8 Sides, Splayed Foot, Polychrome Enamel, Famille Rose, 25 In., Pair 3220.00
Urn, Chinese Heroes & Flowers, Birds, Polychrome Enameled, 25 1/2 In., Pair 3220.00
Urn, Cover, Double Gourd Shape, Famille Verte, Late 19th Century, 26 In. 3220.00
Urn, Cover, Shield Shape Body, Landscape In Cartouche, c.1810, 26 1/2 In. 8400.00
Urn, Dome Cover, Phoenix, Peonies, Famille Rose, 20th Century, 18 In., Pair 460.00
Urn, Scenic Panels, Famille Verte, Late 19th Century, 22 3/4 In., Pair 1300.00
Vase, 2 Bronze Winged Gargoyles, Court Scenes, Famille Rose, 18 In., Pair 1495.00
Vase, 9 Peaches, Bottle Form, Famille Rose, 19th Century, 20 In. 88.00
Vase, Armorial, Crest & Flowers, Twisted Body, Unglazed Foot, 1920s, 10 In. 70.00
Vase, Baluster Shape, Scalloped Edge, Gilt, Famille Rose, c.1900, 22 3/4 In., Pair 1725.00
Vase, Birds & Flowers, Moonflask Shape, Famille Jaune, 13 In., Pair 805.00
Vase, Bottle Shape, Lamp Mounted, Famille Verte, 14 1/2 In., Pair 3360.00
Vase, Bulbous, Garlic Shape, Kylin Handle, c.1850, 16 1/4 In., Pair 2070.00
Vase, Court Scene, Beaker Shape, Fluted, Gilt Base, Famille Rose, 25 In. 1035.00
Vase, Court Scene, Pavilion, Famille Rose, Oval, 18th Century, 17 1/2 In. 1093.00
Vase, Cover, 4-Toed Dragon, Foo Dog Handles, 17 In., Pair 633.00
Vase, Cover, Baluster Shape, Oriental Figures, c.1775, 11 1/2 In. 9600.00
Vase, Dome Cover, Flowering Branches, Famille Verte, 19th Century, 19 In. 575.00
Vase, Dome Cover, Foo Dog Finials, Gilt Handles, 20 In., Pair 2530.00

Vase, Flowering Branches, Yellow Ground, Cobalt Blue, Mounted As Lamps, 12 In. 259.00
Vase, Flowers & Bat, Turquoise, Egg Shape, Famille Rose, Qing Dynasty, 12 In. 184.00
Vase, Flowers, En Grisaille, Cylindrical, Flared Mouth, 6 In., Pair 920.00
Vase, Flowers, Underglaze Blue, 1920s, 17 1/4 In. 1395.00
Vase, Foo Dog Handles, Mandarin Court Scenes, Famille Rose, 23 1/2 In., Pair 1725.00
Vase, Half Shape, Turquoise, 15 1/2 x 9 1/4 In., Pair 1320.00
Vase, Lamp Mounted, Famille Rose, 16 3/4 In., Pair 9600.00
Vase, Lobed Cylinder, Flowers, Famille Rose, Mid 19th Century, 11 1/2 In. 1150.00
Vase, Oval Shape, Calligraphy, Famille Verte, Early 20th Century, 22 3/4 In. 489.00
Vase, People Overall, Foo Dog Handles, Gecko, Famille Rose, 35 1/2 In. 4543.00
Vase, Pheasant, Handles, Famille Rose, 1800s, 7 5/8 In., Pair 2990.00
Vase, Phoenix Birds, Landscape, Baluster, Late 19th Century, 9 In., Pair 288.00
Vase, Polychrome Enameled Landscape, White Paste Glaze, 1870s, 20 In. 115.00
Vase, Rouleau, Garden Terrace Scene, Famille Verte, c.1700, 17 1/2 In. 5400.00
Vase, Scalloped Rim, Foo Dog Handles, Famille Rose, Late 19th Century, 14 In. 308.00
Vase, Splayed Rim, Enameled Scroll, Unglazed Foot, 1820s, 14 In., Pair 748.00
Vase, Tapering, Oval, 2 Handles, Famille Rose, 19th Century, 18 1/4 In., Pair 288.00
Vase, Terrace Scenes, Lamp Mounted, Famille Rose, 12 1/2 In., Pair 4560.00
Vase, Tobacco Leaf, Trumpet Shape, Famille Rose, c.1780, 10 In. 5100.00
Vase, Wall, Boy Figure, Flowers, Famille Rose, 1780s, 6 1/2 In., Pair 2280.00
Vase, Water Hydra Relief, Court Scene, Famille Rose, 35 In., Pair 8625.00

CHINTZ is the name of a group of china patterns featuring an overall
design of flowers and leaves. The design became popular with English
makers about 1928. A few pieces are still being made. The best known
are designs by Royal Winton, James Kent Ltd., Crown Ducal, and
Shelley. Crown Ducal and Shelley are listed in their own sections.

Evesham, Compote, Royal Winton, 6 1/2 x 2 7/8 In. 280.00
Floral, Cup & Saucer, Bone China, Radfords Bone China Fenton, 2 1/4 In. 30.00
Floral, Sugar & Creamer, Gold Trim, James Kent, Ltd. Co., 2 1/2 In. 65.00
Fondeville, Cup & Saucer, Simpsons' Potters, Ltd., Cobridge, 4 3/8 In. 165.00
Pansy, Teapot, Bone China, 4 3/4 In. 50.00
Pekin, Dessert Set, Maroon Ground, Oriental Scene, Grimwades, 7-In. Plate, 3 Piece 110.00
Pitcher, Matt White Glaze, Gold Trim, Flowers, Art Deco Design, Royal Winton, 8 In. 75.00
Plate, Cake, Flowers, Green Leaves, Royal Albert, 9 1/2 In. 110.00
Rosina, Cup & Saucer, Scalloped, Gold, 4 & 5 1/4 In. 30.00
Somerset, Royal Winton, 5 3/4 x 3 1/2 In. 325.00
Summertime, Plate, Royal Winton, 6 1/4 In. 70.00

CHOCOLATE GLASS, sometimes mistakenly called caramel slag, was
made by the Indiana Tumbler and Goblet Company of Greentown,
Indiana, from 1900 to 1903. It was also made at other National Glass
Company factories. Fenton Art Glass Co. also made chocolate glass
from about 1907 to 1915. More recent pieces have been made by
Imperial and others.

Austrian, Creamer, 3 1/4 In. . . . . *Illus* 170.00
Austrian, Spooner, Child's, 3 In. 390.00

**"Never invest your money in anything
that eats or needs repainting." Wise
words from Billy Rose, a successful
showman and art collector.**

Chocolate Glass,
Austrian, Creamer,
3 1/4 In.

Cactus, Creamer, Cover 78.00
Cactus, Creamer, Greentown, 5 In. 34.00
Cactus, Mug, 3 1/2 In. 40.00
Cactus, Salt & Pepper, 3 1/4 In. 120.00
Cactus, Tumbler, 4 In. 29.00
Chrysanthemum Leaf, Nappy 400.00
Cruet, Stopper, c.1880, 5 1/2 In. 113.00
Dish, Hen On Nest, 5 1/2 In. 400.00
Dolphin, Cover 395.00
Geneva, Bowl, 4-Footed, 9 1/4 In. 69.00
Geneva, Creamer 120.00
Leaf Bracket, Butter, Cover, 7 1/4 In. .... .69.00 to 143.00
Leaf Bracket, Nappy, 5 1/2 In. 35.00
Leaf Bracket, Spooner, 4 In. 29.00

CHRISTMAS collectibles include not only Christmas trees and ornaments listed below, but also Santa Claus figures, special dishes, and even games and wrapping paper. A Belsnickle is a nineteenth-century figure of Father Christmas. A kugel is an early, heavy ornament made of thick blown glass, lined with zinc or lead, and often covered with colored wax. Christmas cards are listed in this section under Greeting Card. Christmas collectibles may also be listed in the Candy Container category. Christmas trees are listed in the section that follows.

Ad, Gold Medal Flour, Santa, Black & White, Ladies Home Journal, Dec. 1916 .... 15.00
Bell, Avon Heavenly Notes, Blue Porcelain, Angel Handle, Box, 1992, 5 1/2 In. 20.00
Bell, Garland Of Greetings, Red, Green Porcelain, Teddy Bear Handle, 1991, 4 In. 20.00
Bell, Mistletoe, Porcelain, Box, 1989, 5 1/2 In. 20.00
Bell, Porcelain, Box, 1987, 4 3/4 In. 15.00
Bell, Porcelain, Wood Handle, Box, 1985 .... 15.00
Bell, Waiting For Santa, Porcelain, Box, 1990, 5 1/2 In. 20.00
Bell, White Porcelain, Gold Trim, Box, 1986, 5 In. 15.00
Belsnickle, Composition Face, Wrinkle Lines, Cotton Hat, Beard, Coat, Russia, 12 In. ... 85.00
Belsnickle, Composition, Blue Coat, Moss Tree, 10 1/2 In. 250.00
Belsnickle, Holding Basket, Tree, Composition, Felt, Rabbit Fur, Wood Base, 12 In. 2310.00
Belsnickle, Papier-Mache, Smiling Mouth, Cane, Holding Tree, 16 In. 95.00
Belsnickle, Papier-Mache, White, Mica On Coat, Feather Tree, 7 3/4 In. 440.00
Belsnickle, Papier-Mache, Yellow, Gold Piping, Holding Tree, 10 In. 715.00
Belsnickle, Santa Claus, Magenta Coat, Germany, c.1895 .... 595.00
Blocks, ABC, Mr. Kris Kringle, McLoughlin Bros., 1890s 225.00
Book, Night Before Christmas, Whitman, 1940 .... 18.00
Book, Santa Claus & The Little Lost Kitten, Fuzzy Wuzzy Book, Whitman, 1952 .... 30.00
Book, Santa Claus, Fuzzy Wuzzy Book, By Eileen Vaughan, Whitman, 1947 .... 15.00
Book, Talking To Santa Claus, W.B. Conkey Co., Hardback, 1898 .... 30.00
Candleholder, Cast Iron, Hubley, 4 In. 99.00
Clicker, Tin Lithograph, Santa At Chimney Base, Sack Of Toys, 1930, 2 In. 75.00
Display, Store, Santa Claus, Animated 285.00

Christmas, Doll, Santa Claus, Printed Fabric, Thomas Nast, 15 In.

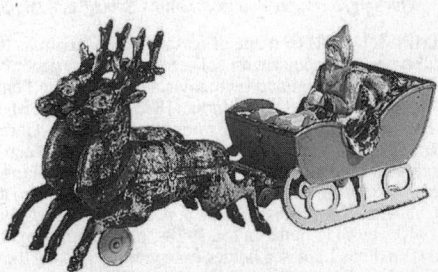

Christmas, Toy, Sleigh, Santa, Cast Iron, Kyser & Rex, c.1885, 13 In.

Doll, Santa Claus, Printed Fabric, Thomas Nast, 15 In. . . . . *Illus* 165.00
Elf Band Figures, Conductor, Instruments, Cardboard, Crepe Paper, Germany, 2 1/2 In. . . 86.00
Figure, Choir Singer, Boy, 1950s, Pair 275.00
Figure, Santa Claus, Cotton Batting, Scrap Face, Feather Tree, Dresden Stars, 8 In. 45.00
Figure, Santa Claus, Cotton Outfit, Composition Boots & Face, Paper Belt, 6 In. 34.00
Figure, Santa On Sled, Candy Cane Runners, Red Flocked Clothing, Napco, 9 In. 25.00
Figure, Santa, Clay Faced, Cotton Beard, Holding Ski Poles, Occupied Japan, 6 In. 95.00
Gift Tags, Paper, 1940s 1.00
Greeting Card, Disney Characters, 1948 Calendar Paper, 7 x 8 In. 115.00
Greeting Card, Houdini, In Christmas Stocking, 4 1/2 x 4 In. 1840.00
Greeting Card, To Be Cut Out & Sent, By Saalfield, 1946 . . . . 15.00
Greeting Card Booklet, Embossed, c.1930 . . . . 12.00
Handkerchief, Linen, Embroidered Santa Claus, c.1940, 6 1/2 In. 12.00
Mask, Papier-Mache, Streamer Trim, Cotton Bears, 1900s 65.00
Mold, Cake, Santa Claus, Hello Kiddies On Front, Cast Iron, Griswold, 12 In. 300.00
Nodder, Candy Box, Composition, Fur Beard, Flocked Clothes, West Germany, 9 In. 90.00
Paper Doll, Betty Bonnet's Christmas Party, Sheet With Santa Outfit, 1916 . . . . 22.00
Paperweight, Santa By Building Titled Santa Claus Land, Indiana, 3 In. 60.00
Planter, Santa's Sleigh, Santa Driver & Celluloid Reindeer, 1940, 12 In. 125.00
Planter, Singing Girl Holding Santa Head, Spaghetti Trim, Lefton, Japan, 4 In. 19.00
Plates that are limited editions are listed in the Collector Plate category or in the correct
factory listing.
Postcard, Santa & Elflike Brownie, Stecher Litho, Postmarked 1916 . . . . 10.00
Puzzle, Santa's Workshop, Heavy Cardboard, Lowe, 1940s 7.00
Record, I Saw Mommy Kissing Santa Claus, Peter Pan, 1950s 12.00
Roly Poly, Santa Claus, Original Box, 1910, 4 1/4 In. 350.00
Roly Poly, Santa Claus, Papier-Mache, Blue Base, Germany, Late 20th Century, 4 In. 29.00
Salt & Pepper Shaker, Mr. & Mrs. Santa, Marked Napco, Japan, 1950s, 4 In. 20.00
Sheet Music, Have Yourself A Merry Little Christmas, Judy Garland, 1944 . . . . 45.00
Sheet Music, Santa Claus Is Coming To Town, 1934 . . . . 4.00
Sign, Santa Bust Inside Wreath, Silk Screen, Mat, Frame, 27 x 36 In. 44.00
Spoon, Sterling Silver, Full Figure Of Santa, Marked Mayer Bros., 5 In. 115.00
Stocking, Santa Claus, Baby With Halo, Merry Christmas, Printed Cloth, 24 In. 495.00
Toy, Child On Sleigh, Venetian Dew, Composition Face, Hair Wig, Wooden Sleigh, 6 In. . . 62.00
Toy, Happy Santa, Rolls Along, Head Turns, Playing Drum, Battery, Cragstan, 12 In. 105.00
Toy, Noisemaker, Santa On Chimney, Toy Bag, Squeaker, Cardboard, 8 In. 30.00
Toy, Santa Claus & Sleigh, 2 Reindeer, Painted, Cast Iron, Hubley, 16 In. 2750.00
Toy, Santa Claus, Battery Operated, 5 Actions, Japan, 12 In. 195.00
Toy, Santa Claus, Felt Outfit, Composition Face, Fur Beard, Brush Tree, Squeak, 6 In. . . . 169.00
Toy, Santa Claus, Jack-In-The-Box, Wood, Red & White, Brick Chimney, 1938, 24 In. 1400.00
Toy, Santa Claus, Lead Pendulum Nodder, Windup, Celluloid, 7 In. 450.00
Toy, Santa Claus, Sleigh, 2 Reindeer, Tin Litho, Spring Motor, Strauss, Box, 11 In. 1700.00
Toy, Santa Claus, Windup, Alps, Japan, Box 125.00
Toy, Santa, Walking, Composition, Cloth Dressed, Lead Feet, 7 1/2 In. 525.00
Toy, Sleigh, Santa, Cast Iron, Kyser & Rex, c.1885, 13 In. . . . . *Illus* 15600.00
Toy, Tin, Celluloid Head, Santa, Rocks Back & Forth, Ringing Bell, Windup, Japan, 6 In. . 145.00
Toy, View Master, Santa Head, Look Through Eye, 8 Shots, Night Before Christmas, 4 In. . 55.00
Whirligig, Reindeer Pop In & Out As Santa Spins, Bells Ring, 1930s, 6 1/4 In. 100.00

CHRISTMAS TREES made of feathers and Christmas tree decorations of
all types are popular with collectors. The first decorated Christmas tree
in America is claimed by many states, including Pennsylvania (1747),
Massachusetts (1832), Illinois (1833), Ohio (1838), and Iowa (1845).
The first glass ornaments were imported from Germany about 1860.
Dresden ornaments were made about 100 years ago of paper and tinsel. Manufacturers in the United States were making ornaments in the
early 1870s. Electric lights were first used on a Christmas tree in 1882.
Character light bulbs became popular in the 1920s, bubble lights in the
1940s, twinkle bulbs in the 1950s, plastic bulbs by 1955. In this book
a Christmas light is a holder for a candle used on the tree. Other forms
of lighting include light bulbs. Other Christmas memorabilia is listed
in the preceding section.

Fence, 7 Sections, Gate, Painted, Cast Iron, 74 In. 440.00

Fence, 8 Sections, Fleur-De-Lis Tops, Green Paint, 11 3/4 In. 165.00
Fence, 8 Sections, Gate & Posts, Gothic Style, Cast Iron, Makes 28-In. Square 440.00
Fence, 14 Sections, Plumes At Top, 2 Gates, 11 5/8 In. 495.00
Fence, 26 Jointed Wooden Sections, Picket Gate, Silver Paint 55.00
Fence, Metal & Wood, Painted, Gate, Makes 45-In. Square 165.00
Light, Cobalt Blue, England, c.1910, 3 1/2 In. 165.00
Light, Coin Spot, Yellow, Amber Tone, Raised Foot, 4 1/8 In. 179.00
Light, Corset Waist, Horizontal Ribs, Medium Apple Green, 4 1/4 In. 179.00
Light, Diamond & Broken Rib, Aqua & Crystal, England, c.1890, 2 3/4 In. 90.00
Light, Diamond Pattern, Clear, Cranberry Red Flashing, 3 5/8 In. 56.00
Light, Diamond Quilted, Amber, Blue, White, Puce, Green, 3 1/2 In., 6 Piece 82.00
Light, Diamond, Crown Inside Shield, Chicago Lamp Candle Co., c.1910, 3 7/8 In. 192.00
Light, Diamond, Overall, Tin Chimney, Houchin Mfg. Co., 2 7/8 In. 160.00
Light, Diamond, Yellow Amber, c.1910, 3 1/2 In. 180.00
Light, Diamond, Yellowish Green, England, c.1890, 3 5/8 In. 100.00
Light, Golden Yellow Amber, Wire Handle, Tin Collar, c.1890, 3 In. 100.00
Light, Grape Cluster, Blue Aqua, England, c.1910, 4 In. 56.00
Light, Harlequin, Milk Glass, 3 1/2 In. 155.00
Light, Harlequin, Teal Green, c.1890, 3 5/8 In. 150.00
Light, King George, Cornflower Blue, Ground Rim, c.1900, 4 1/8 In. 235.00
Light, Lantern, Chicago Lampcandle Co., c.1890, 4 3/8 In. 80.00
Light, Pineapple, Frosted Pink, England, c.1920, 3 1/8 In. 123.00
Light, Sunburst, Yellow Green, G Inside Star, Ground Rim, 3 7/8 In. 67.00
Light, Tulip, Bluish Aqua, c.1890, 3 1/2 In. 110.00
Light Bulb, Santa Claus, Full Figured, Embossed Tree In Hand, 5 1/2 In. 12.00
Light Bulb, Snow-Covered House 5.00
Ornament, Angel, Treetop, Paper, Dresden, 1880s 495.00
Ornament, Asian Man, Standing, Cotton Batting, 1880-1914 .... 45.00
Ornament, Baby Head Rattle, 2 Sides, Happy-Sad Face, Wire Wrapped, 6 1/2 In. 168.00
Ornament, Baby In Bed, Wax Figure, Wire Bed, Cotton & Silk, Sebnitz, 3 1/4 In. 413.00
Ornament, Boat, Naval, Cardboard, Cotton Smoke, 1880-1914, 5 1/2 In. 650.00
Ornament, Boy, Bisque Head, Cotton Body, Candy Container Snowball, 1880 .... 550.00
Ornament, Candy Containter, Shoe, Dresden, Paper, Silver Gilt, Silk Bag 380.00
Ornament, Clip-On, Santa, Holding Embossed Tree, Black Moustache, 6 1/2 In. 73.00
Ornament, Clown, With Cane, Cotton Batting, 1880-1914 .... 43.00
Ornament, Dog, Front Paws Out, Tail Up, Cotton Batting, 1880-1914 .... 42.00
Ornament, Dog, Greyhound, 3-D, Applied Tail, Ears, Painted, Dresden, 3 1/2 In. 62.00
Ornament, Dog, Spaniel, Sitting, 3-D, Applied Collar, Painted, Dresden, 2 3/4 In. 50.00
Ornament, Doll Head, Blown Glass, Glass Eyes, Painted, Germany 130.00
Ornament, Double Balloon Form, Scrap Angel On Shaft, Wire Wrap, 6 1/4 In. 56.00
Ornament, Glass, Hand Painted, 2 Sides, 2 Faces, Father Christmas, Pre-Santa Image ... 147.00
Ornament, Kugel, Sapphire Blue, Brass Hanger, 4 1/2 In. 110.00
Ornament, Little Red Riding Hood, Gold Hood, 2 3/4 In. 6.00
Ornament, Man In The Moon, Wax Face, Wire & Metal Mesh, Sebnitz, 2 1/4 In. 715.00
Ornament, Man, With Cane, Standing, Cotton Batting, 1880-1914 .... 50.00

Christmas Tree, Stand, Santa Figure,
Molded Trees, Painted, Cast Iron, Germany

**Dust Christmas ornaments after
removing them from the tree. Do
not store them with the dust.
Wrap each ornament individually
in paper.**

Ornament, Mickey Mouse Santa, Crystal, Swarovski 80.00
Ornament, Pig, Standing, Cotton Batting, 1880-1914 .... 350.00
Ornament, Santa At Chimney, Mold-Blown Glass, Germany, 3 In. 150.00
Ornament, Santa In Airplane, Tinsel, Wire Wings, Blown Glass, Germany, 1950s 25.00
Ornament, Santa With Bag Of Toys, Blown Glass, 1940s, 3 In. 45.00
Ornament, Slipper, Woman's, Silk, Candy Container, Wedding Favor, 1920s, 4 In. 200.00
Ornament, Spaniel, Seated, Blown Glass, White, Black Eyes, 1930, 4 In. 70.00
Ornament, Spirit Of St. Louis, Glass, Cardboard Propeller, Metal Wheels, 5 In. 309.00
Ornament, Treetop, Angel, Spun Glass 85.00
Ornament, Uncle Sam Figures, Cardboard Cutout, Box, 1918, 4 Piece 29.00
Ornament, Violin, Pressed Cardboard, 1880-1914 .... 40.00
Platform, 6 Tiers, Turned Columns, Fencing, Animal Figures, 27 x 27 x 40 In. 440.00
Stand, Green, Bold White & Red Paint, Leaves, 9 3/4 x 9 3/4 In. 82.00
Stand, House Shape, Chimney, Sheet Metal, Painted, Red, White, 13 x 11 x 10 In. 121.00
Stand, Musical, Cast Iron, Tin, Wood Base, Painted, 4 Christmas Carols, 11 In. 275.00
Stand, Old Green & Gold, Shooting Stars, 5 1/2 x 11 1/4 In. 55.00
Stand, Round Tiered Middle, Square Short Table, Gallery, Red & Green, 1870 .... 1450.00
Stand, Santa Figure, Molded Trees, Painted, Cast Iron, Germany .... *Illus* 950.00
Stand, Tree Stump Base, St. Nicholas, Basket On Back, Cast Iron, 9 1/2 x 6 1/2 In. 330.00

CHROME items in the Art Deco style became popular in the 1930s. Collectors are most interested in high-style pieces made by the Connecticut firms of Chase Brass and Copper Company, and Manning Bowman.

Candlestick, Chase, Bugle, Cobalt Blue Glass, 2 3/4 In., Pair 185.00
Candlestick, Revere, Norman Bel Geddes, 3 In., Pair 288.00
Cocktail Set, Art Deco, Stainless Steel, Chase, 1930-1940, 11 Piece 374.00
Cocktail Set, Blue Moon, H.F. Reichenbach, 1935, 12 In. 1150.00
Cocktail Set, Shaker, 6 Cups & Tray, Manning Bowman, 13 In. 4025.00
Cocktail Set, Zeppelin Form, Shaker, Glasses, 9 Parts, Germany, 9 1/2 In. 2015.00
Coffee Set, Pot, Sugar, Tray, Cup & Saucer, Art Deco, Manning Bowman 489.00
Coffeepot, Tray, Handled, Bakelite, Manning Bowman, 15 In. 115.00
Ice Bucket, Penguin Design, Art Deco 35.00
Magazine Rack, Bakelite, Revere, 17 1/2 In. 58.00
Smoking Stand, Propeller Airplane, Cobalt Blue Glass, Art Deco, c.1930 .... 1610.00
Tray, Art Deco, Reverse Painted Glass, 12 x 28 In. 1610.00
Tray, Norman Bel Geddes, 14 1/2 In. 104.00
Tray, Round, Bakelite Handles, Mark Bruce Hunt, 11 In. 75.00

CIGAR STORE FIGURES of carved wood or cast iron were used as advertisements in front of the Victorian cigar store. The carved figures are now collected as folk art. They range in size from counter type, about three feet, to over eight feet high.

Indian, Headdress, Leaning On Barrel & Boxes, Painted, 19th Century, 36 In. 10000.00
Indian, Princess, Full-Length, Feathered Headdress, 62 In. 4300.00
Indian, Squaw, Warrior, Holding Tobacco Bundle, 20th Century, Pair 8225.00

CINNABAR is a vermilion or red lacquer. Pieces are made with tens to hundreds of thicknesses of the lacquer that is later carved. Most cinnabar was made in the Orient.

Box, 2 Figures On Bridge, Garden, 15 x 11 In. 141.00
Box, Deep Red, Carved, Landscapes, Flowers, Cover, Chinese, 5 In. 489.00
Box, Lid, Lovebirds, Flowers, Wood, c.1900, 8 1/2 In. 99.00
Incense Dish, Carved, Diaper Pattern, Bats, Lotus, Flattened Rim, 19th Century, 6 In. 144.00

CIVIL WAR mementos are important collectors' items. Most of the pieces are military items used from 1861 to 1865. Be sure to avoid any explosive munitions.

Banner, No Compromise With Traitors, Linen, Wooden Rods, 46 x 35 In. 6600.00
Bayonet, Bowie, Brass Guard, Leather Sheath, 19 3/4 In. 2895.00
Belt Plate, For Officer's Sword, Brass Eagle, Applied Nickel Silver Wreath, 19 1/2 In. 330.00
Bottle, Ink, Traveling, Brown Ironstone, 3 In. 45.00
Box, Flags Of The Confederacy, Richmond, Va., 1860s 55.00

Buckle Die, Confederate, S.C., Steel, Stamped, 5 1/2 x 5 1/2 In. 110.00
Button, Made From Bullet, 1 Central Hole, Lead, 1 1/2 In. 15.00
Canteen, Blue Cloth Covering, Pewter Spout, Tan Strap, 8 In. 550.00
Canteen, Confederate, Cedar, Folk Art, 7 1/2 x 2 1/2 In. 8338.00
Canteen, Reunion, Blue Felt, Hand Sewn V.S., Horse, Flowers, Leaves, Stopper 385.00
Cards, Playing, Red, White & Blue, No Numbers, American Card Company 800.00
Cartridge Box, Cross Leather Belt, With Brass U.S. Eagle Plates, 8 x 7 In. 605.00
Cartridge Box, Metal Insert, US Embossed On Flap, Ord. Inspection Stamp 193.00
Cartridge Box, Tin Inserts 489.00
Cartridge Pouch, Leather, Burnside's Brass Case Lead Ball 90.00
Coat, 5th Regiment, Maryland, 30 Brass Buttons, Medium 1295.00
Ditty Bag, Confederate, Canvas, Stenciled, 16 x 16 In. 5175.00
Drum, Painted Battle Scene, Marked Co. E 87th O.V.I., 12 x 28 In. 410.00
Drum, Snare, Eagle, Shield, Flags, D.C.B., Painted, Red, White, Blue, Gold, 14 x 18 In. . . 1150.00
Fife, Brass Ends, Nickel, Silver & Pewter Mouth Piece, 15 1/2 In. 165.00
Flag, 5-4-5 Configuration, Presented To Major Lennard, Mustered Out In 1865 .... 7000.00
Flag, Confederate, Reunion, Hand Sewn, 1910-1930, 29 x 23 In. 1485.00
Hatband, Confederate Secession, Card, On Cloth, 1860, 26 x 4 1/4 In. 3900.00
Knife, Carl Schlieper, Sheath, Box 92.00
Knife, Folding, 2 Blades, Wooden Scale Grips, Shield Shape Escutcheon 35.00
Leg Irons, Justin, Mo., 20 1/2 In. 148.00
Leg Irons, Locking, Connecting Chain, c.1860, 21 x 5 In. 390.00
Map, Battle Of Manassas, Black & White, 4 1/2 x 9 In. 15.00
Map, Central States, Olney's School Geography, 1844 .... 200.00
Map, Europe, Hand Colored, Olney's School Geography, 1844, 12 x 18 In. 95.00
Map, Suffolk, Virginia, Pen, Pencil, Chalk, David B. Philips, 8 x 10 In. 495.00
Map, Western Territories, 1844, 12 x 18 In. 200.00
Plaque, Metal, CAS 5th Alabama Dragoons, Crossed Rifles, Co. B CSA, 1863 .... 49.00
Portrait, Oil On Canvas, Captain John J Wizman, 34 x 27 In. 2470.00
Powder Horn, Carved In Relief, Double Headed Bird, Christian Symbols 430.00
Powder Horn, Cow, Carved, Plug, Brass Stud Hanger, Wooden Stopper, 10 In. 2290.00
Powder Horn, Scrimshaw, Dome Wood Plug, Wooden Pegs, Carved Nozzle, 17 In. 978.00
Powder Tester, Flintlock, Walnut Grip, Conrad George Kirschner, Mich., 5 3/4 In. 247.00
Rattle, Warning, Naval, Oak, 12 In. 173.00
Ribbon, Washington Brotherhood, Silk, Black With Gold Printing, Beads, Tassels 300.00
Saber, Confederate States, Wire Wrapped Grip, Bronze Hilt, Scabbard, c.1860, 42 1/2 In. . . 420.00
Saddle Holster, Percussion Pistol, Black Leather 400.00
Spurs, Officer's, Silver, Germany, 1860s, 2 1/4 In. 121.00
Surgeon's Kit, Mahogany Case, Gemrig 8030.00
Sword, Field Officer, Oval Blade, Folding Counter Guard, Ames, 29 3/4 In. 430.00
Sword, Musician's, Ames Mfg., Chicopee, Mass., 1862, 28-In. Blade 412.00
Sword, U.S. Army, Scabbard, Mansfield & Lamb, Leather Handle, c.1864 .... 448.00
Sword, Wooden Handle, Brass Hilt, Scabbard, Import, 1861 .... 412.00
Syringe, Pewter, Wood, 1860s, 2 x 13 In. 35.00
Torch, Wood Handle, Hurrah For Lincoln, c.1864, 23 1/2 In. 990.00

CKAW, see Dedham category.

CLARICE CLIFF was a designer who worked in several English factories after the 1920s, including A.J. Wilkinson Ltd., Wilkinson's Royal Staffordshire Pottery, Newport Pottery, and Foley Pottery. She is best known for her brightly colored Art Deco designs, including the "Bizarre" line. She died in 1972. Reproductions have been made by Wedgwood.

Alpine, Isis, Jug, Trees & House, Orange, Orange, Yellow Accents, 12 In. 1980.00
Autumn, Bizarre, Compote, Pastels, 3 x 5 In. 795.00
Autumn, Bizarre, Plate, Balloon Trees, House, Red Hillside, Scalloped Edge, 6 In. . . . *Illus* 523.00
Autumn, Bizarre, Vase, Orange, 6 In. 1150.00
Autumn, Plate, Deep Blue, Green, Yellow Balloon Trees, 9 In. 412.00
Brookfields, Biarritz, Bowl, Square, 8 1/4 In. 870.00
Brookfields, Bizarre, Jardiniere, 8 x 9 In. 2050.00
Brookfields, Bizarre, Trees & House, Tea Set, Pot, Creamer, Sugar 4200.00
Broth, Fantasque, Plate, Multicolored Flowers, Circle Abstracts, Green, Orange, 7 In. 302.00

Clarice Cliff, Autumn, Bizarre, Plate, Balloon Trees, House, Red Hillside, Scalloped Edge, 6 In.

Clarice Cliff, Delecia Citrus, Bizarre, Bowl, Oranges, Lemons, Flambe Drip Glaze, 4 x 9 In.

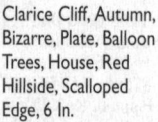

Clarice Cliff, Star, Plate, Red, Blue, Yellow Geometrics, Scalloped Edge, 5 1/2 In.

Clarice Cliff, Nasturtium, Inspiration, Vase, Blue, Pink Mottling, Aqua Ground, 7 In.

Chintz, Bizarre, Blue, Coffee Set, Tankard Pot, Creamer, Sugar, 6 Cups & Saucers	6240.00
Chintz, Bizarre, Bowl, Black, Orange, Tan, White Glaze, 2 1/4 x 7 In.	330.00
Chintz, Blue, Bizarre, Plate, Abstract Flowers, 6 3/4 In.	605.00
Crocus, Biscuit Barrel, Wicker Handle, Cream Background, 6 In.	350.00
Crocus, Bizarre, Jardiniere, 7 x 8 1/2 In.	880.00
Crocus, Bizarre, Vase, 6 In.	580.00
Delecia Citrus, Bizarre, Bowl, Oranges, Lemons, Flambe Drip Glaze, 4 x 9 In. ...... *Illus*	495.00
Delecia Citrus, Bowl, Orange, Bright Yellow Lemons, Green Leaves, 4 x 8 In.	440.00
Feathers & Leaves, Fantasque, Pitcher, Orange, Black, Yellow, 7 x 5 1/2 In.	880.00
Inspiration, Bizarre, Bowl, Painted Landscape, Marked, 5 1/2 In.	460.00
Limberlost, Bizarre, Salt & Pepper, Lighthouse, 3 1/4 In.	495.00
Melon, Bizarre, Vase, Pastels, 12 In.	2370.00
Nasturtium, Bizarre, Plate, Flowers, Red, Orange, Yellow, 7 In.	248.00
Nasturtium, Inspiration, Vase, Blue, Pink Mottling, Aqua Ground, 7 In. .... *Illus*	990.00
Petunia, Isis, Jug, Brown, Yellow Cafe-Au-Lait Ground, 9 3/4 x 8 In.	1650.00
Pie Bird, Black Bird, Newport	115.00
Pine Grove, Bizarre, Vase, Cylindrical, 5 x 2 1/2 In.	770.00
Pine Grove, Bizarre, Wall Plaque, Stylized Green, Blue Pines, Swirling Center, 10 In.	495.00
Raffia, Bowl, Indiana, Light Green Interior, 6 1/4 In.	400.00
Red Roofs, Fantasque, Clog, Black, Stylized Green Trees, 5 1/3 In.	467.00
Rhodanthe, Bizarre, Shaker, Bonjour Shape, 5 In.	665.00
Secrets, Bizarre, Honey Pot, Fly Finial, 3 x 3 In.	468.00
Star, Plate, Red, Blue, Yellow Geometrics, Scalloped Edge, 5 1/2 In. .... *Illus*	413.00
Viscaria, Biarritz, Sandwich Set, Large Plate, 7 Piece	1450.00

CLEWELL ware was made in limited quantities by Charles Walter Clewell of Canton, Ohio, from 1902 to 1955. Pottery was covered with a thin coating of bronze, then treated to make the bronze turn different colors. Pieces covered with copper, brass, or silver were also made. Mr. Clewell's secret formula for blue patinated bronze was burned when he died in 1965.

Lamp Base, Copper Clad, Original Patina, 15 In.	920.00

Vase, Bronze, Green, Brown Original Patina, 9 In.	863.00
Vase, Copper Clad, Bulbous, Red Brown Shading, Verdigris Patina, Inscribed, 9 x 12 In.	1610.00
Vase, Copper Clad, Deep Orange Original Patina, Green, Blue, 5 3/4 In.	978.00
Vase, Copper Clad, Large Shouldered Form, Original Patina, 11 1/2 In.	2875.00
Vase, Copper Clad, Lue, Green Patina, 6 3/4 In.	550.00
Vase, Copper Clad, Patina, 5 In.	253.00
Vase, Copper Clad, Patina, 6 1/2 In.	430.00
Vase, Copper Clad, Patina, 15 In.	2415.00
Vase, Copper Clad, Range, Deep Red, Green, Blue Patina, 4 1/4 In.	1280.00
Vase, Copper Clad, Verdigris Patina, Impressed Mark, 4 1/2 x 4 1/2 In.	518.00
Vase, Copper Clad, Verdigris Patina, Oval, Signed, 11 x 7 1/2 In.	1725.00
Vase, Copper Clad, Verdigris Patina, Tall Baluster, 11 x 5 In.	978.00

CLEWS pottery was made by George Clews & Co. of Brownhills Pottery, Tunstall, England, from 18906 to 1961. Additional pieces may be listed in the Flow Blue category.

Bowl, Sugar, Landing Of General Lafayette, Castle Garden, August 16, 1824	605.00
Creamer, City Hall, New York, Rose Border	220.00
Cup Plate, States, Building Center, Blue, 6 In.	550.00
Gravy, Underplate, Landing Of General Lafayette At Castle Garden	2475.00
Plate, America & Independence, Washington Portrait, States Border, Blue, 10 1/2 In.	467.00
Plate, America Holding Washington Portrait, States Border, 10 1/2 In.	110.00
Plate, Barrington Hall, Blue Transfer, 8 3/4 In.	154.00
Plate, Landing Of General Lafayette At Castle Garden, New York, 1824, 7 3/4 In.	220.00
Plate, Landing Of General Lafayette At Castle Garden, New York, 1824, 8 7/8 In.	.345.00 to 360.00
Plate, Landing Of General Lafayette At Castle Garden, New York, 1824, 9 In.	805.00
Plate, Landing Of General Lafayette At Castle Garden, New York, 1824, 10 In.	280.00
Plate, Landing Of General Lafayette, Blue Transfer, 10 In.	385.00
Plate, Playing At Draught's, Signed, 10 In.	392.00
Platter, Castle Ruins, Church, 19 In.	805.00
Platter, Doctor Syntax, Advertisement For A Wife, 15 In.	532.00
Platter, Landing Of General Lafayette At Castle Garden, 16 August, 1824	2200.00
Platter, Landing Of General Lafayette At Castle Garden, August, 1824	2200.00
Platter, Landing Of General Lafayette At Castle Garden, New York, 1824, 21 1/2	6500.00
Saucer, Landing Of General Lafayettte At Castle Garden, New York, 1824, 5 3/4 In.	275.00
Sugar, Landing Of General Lafayette At Castle Garden, New York, 1824	625.00
Undertray, St. Catherine's Hill, Near Guildford, Dark Blue, 11 1/4 In.	1120.00

CLIFTON POTTERY was founded by William Long in Clifton, New Jersey, in 1905. He worked there until 1908 making a line called *Crystal Patina*. Clifton Pottery made art pottery. Another firm, Chesapeake Pottery, sold majolica marked *Clifton ware*.

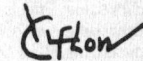

Vase, Black, Tan, Red American Indian Design, Signed, Arizona, 7 1/2 In.	196.00
Vase, Crystal Patina Glaze, Green & Mirrored Caramel Glaze, Round, Signed, 1906, 5 In.	575.00
Vase, Gourd, Crystal Patina Glaze, 1906, 5 In.	500.00
Vase, Green, Khaki Crystalline Glaze, Signed, 1906, 11 In.	1380.00
Vase, Indian Ware, Shumodovi, Arizona, Adobe Pattern, Ivory, Black, 3 1/4 x 5 1/2 In.	259.00
Vase, Tirrube, Bottle Shape, White Nasturtium, Stamped, 8 1/2 x 5 1/4 In.	375.00
Vase, Tirrube, White Wild Rose, Flaring, Stamped, 6 x 3 1/4 In.	230.00
Vase, Tirrube, Yellow & Orange Nasturtium, Terra-Cotta Ground, Marked, 12 x 8 In.	805.00

CLOCKS of all types have always been popular with collectors. The eighteenth-century tall case, or grandfather's clock, was designed to house a works with a long pendulum. In 1816, Eli Terry patented a new, smaller works for a clock, and the case became smaller. The clock could be kept on a shelf instead of on the floor. By 1840, coiled springs were used and even smaller clocks were made. Battery-powered electric clocks were made in the 1870s. A garniture set can include a clock and other objects displayed on a mantel.

Abbott, Samuel, Mirror, Pine Case, Painted Iron Dial, 8-Day, 1820, 31 In.	.1760.00 to 3850.00
Advertising, 3 Revolving Drums, Seth Thomas, Oak, c.1885, 68 In.	*Illus* 20900.00
Advertising, 7-Up, Case, Metal Dial, Center Logo, Square Wood, 15 1/2 x 15 1/2 In.	155.00
Advertising, 7-Up, You Like It-It Likes You, Plastic, Light-Up, Wood Frame, 15 x 15 In.	105.00

Clock, Advertising,
3 Revolving Drums,
Seth Thomas, Oak,
c.1885, 68 In.

Clock, Ansonia,
Regulator, Cherry, Lyre
Pendulum, Roman
Numerals, c.1893, 88 In.

Put your clock on the wall or on a level floor and move it as little as possible.

Advertising, Bulova Correct Time, Wooden Frame, Square, 17 x 17 In.	29.00
Advertising, Cliquot Club, Telechron, Light-Up, 1940s, 15 In.	495.00
Advertising, Corticelli Spool Silk Is The Best, In All Colors	580.00
Advertising, Double Cuckoo, Game Birds, Bone Numerals & Hands, 24 x 18 In.	280.00
Advertising, Dr Pepper, Neon, Square, 1940s, 16 In.	855.00
Advertising, Duffy's Pure Malt Whiskey, Wood Case, Glass Panel, New Haven Clock Co.	1375.00
Advertising, Elgin Watches, Piper's Jewelry, Electric, 15-In. Diam.	29.00
Advertising, Fisk Tires Time To Re-Tire, Desk, Adjuster Knob, Little Boy Logo, 6 1/4 In.	190.00
Advertising, Garfield Tea & Syrup, Wood Case, Single Train, Seth Thomas, 27 In.	1500.00
Advertising, Garfield Tea, Wooden, 18 x 27 1/2 In.	550.00
Advertising, General Electric, Bakelite Casing, Brass Stand, 1927, 6 In.	60.00
Advertising, Gibbons Beer-Ale, Telechron, Electric, Bakelite Case, 25 1/2 In.	100.00
Advertising, Gruen Watches, On Dial, Octagon, Second Hand, 15 1/2 In.	60.00
Advertising, Iroquois Breweries, Light-Up, Double Bubble, 16 In.	770.00
Advertising, Jaeger Watches, Front Winding, 8-Day	160.00
Advertising, Michelin Tires, Logo Face, Brass Hands & Numerals	190.00
Advertising, Mobil Pegasus, Light-Up, 15 In.	470.00
Advertising, Motorola Radio Home & Car, Neon Spinner, Second Sweep Arm, 21 1/2 In.	550.00
Advertising, Nature's Remedy, Vegetable Laxative, Pendulum, Gilbert, 16 x 31 In.	690.00
Advertising, Piper-Heidsieck Cigars, Iron, Copper Wash, 14 1/4 x 12 1/2 In.	1725.00
Advertising, Price's Milk, Glo-Dial Neon, Chrome Plated Case, 14 1/2 In.	520.00
Advertising, Quaker State Motor Oil, Plastic Face, Dualite, 16 1/2 In.	130.00
Advertising, RCA Sales & Service, Electric	45.00
Advertising, Royal Crown Cola, Light-Up, Pam Clock Co., New Rochelle, N.Y., 14 In.	190.00
Advertising, Schaefer Beer, Plastic & Metal, Light-Up, 1950s, 9 In.	25.00
Advertising, School, Corticelli, Oak, Sessions	660.00
Advertising, Shell Gasoline, White Field, Light-Up, New Rochelle, N.Y., 15 1/2 In.	275.00
Advertising, Sinclair Gas, Neon, Round	750.00
Advertising, Winchester, Pocket Watch Shape, Windup, 13-In. Diam.	85.00
Alarm, Searchlight, Windup, Battery, Bells & Light, Electric, 1910, 8 In.	70.00
Alarm, Windup, Oak Battery Base With Bells, Battery Operated, 1900, 8 1/2 In.	35.00
Ansonia, Art & Commerce Set, Porcelain Dial, Double Statue, 2 Side Pitchers, 3 Piece	1870.00
Ansonia, Chickadee, Porcelain, Cobalt Blue, Flowers, 6 x 6 In.	200.00
Ansonia, Crystal Palace, Brass Movement, Paper Dial, 8-Day, 1880, 16 1/2 x 14 In.	495.00
Ansonia, Crystal Palace, Walnut Platform, 8-Day, 1880, 16 1/2 x 14 In.	960.00
Ansonia, Gilded Metal, Glass Panel, Mercury Pendulum, Time & Strike, 15 1/2 In.	715.00
Ansonia, Gilt Design, Porcelain Case, 14 1/2 In.	316.00
Ansonia, Gingerbread, Walnut, Pendulum, Key, 19 x 11 1/2 In.	125.00
Ansonia, Girl Swinging From Tree Branch, Swinging Arm, 8 x 7 In.	1100.00
Ansonia, Gloria, Swinging Arm, 27 In.	1300.00
Ansonia, Hamlet, Macbeth, 14 x 16 In.	700.00
Ansonia, Juno, Swinging Arm, 28 In.	3500.00
Ansonia, Mantel, Black Iron Case, Classical Form, Gilt Ormolu, Portrait Ornament, 8-Day	110.00
Ansonia, Mantel, Enamel Face, Gilt Lion-Mask Handle, Black Marble Case, 10 3/8 In.	255.00
Ansonia, Mantel, Shakespeare's Macbeth, Brass & Porcelain Dial, 14 1/2 x 15 In.	335.00

Ansonia, Pagoda, Crescent Moon Finial, 10 In. 200.00
Ansonia, Regulator, Cherry, Lyre Pendulum, Roman Numerals, c.1893, 88 In. ...... *Illus* 15400.00
Ansonia, Regulator, Wall, Carved Oak Case, Time & Strike, 19th Century, 25 In. 170.00
Ansonia, Shelf, Ogee, Mahogany Veneer, Painted Metal Dial, 8-Day, Alarm, 30 1/2 In. 165.00
Ansonia, Wall, Aesthetic Movement, Ebonized Wood Case, 8-Day, 1870, 34 x 14 In. 2310.00
Art Deco, Square, Gold Hands, Brass, Black Marble Base, Tiffany & Co., 5 3/4 In. 260.00
Balloon, George III, Satinwood, Olivewood, Mahogany, Conch Shell Pattern, 14 In. 230.00
Banjo, Chelsea, Bigelow Kennard & Co., Mahogany, Ship's Bell Strike, 32 1/2 In. 715.00
Banjo, Dunning, J., Mahogany Case, Painted Iron Dial, Wood, Signed, 1820, 50 In. 6325.00
Banjo, E. Howard & Co., Rosewood Grained Case, Painted Metal Dial, 1860, 29 In. 2090.00
Banjo, Eaton, S., Mahogany, Weight Driven, Reverse Painting On Throat & Door, 34 In. . 4100.00
Banjo, Federal, Giltwood, Eglomise Glass Panels, Perry's Victory, 38 x 10 In. 3290.00
Banjo, Federal, Mahogany, Gilt Gesso, White Painted Dial, 1825, 43 In. 2070.00
Banjo, Federal, Mahogany, Painted Iron Dial, Crossbanded Veneer Case, 1805, 30 In. 1380.00
Banjo, Gilbert, Winstead, Conn., On Dial, Flowers, Eagle On Top 175.00
Banjo, Lyre, Classical, Mahogany, Carved, c.1830, 38 In. 1610.00
Banjo, Lyre, Mahogany Case, Painted Iron Dial, 8-Day, 1820, 38 x 11 In. 12650.00
Banjo, Lyre, Mahogany Case, Painted Iron Dial, 8-Day, 1830, 40 x 12 1/2 In. 9625.00
Banjo, Mahogany Case, Bird's-Eye Maple Panels, Painted Iron Dial, 8-Day, 1820, 35 In. . 9075.00
Banjo, Mahogany Veneer, Brass Bezel, Acorn Finial, 8-Day, 33 In. 2185.00
Banjo, Mahogany, Stamped HT, c.1820 .... 1380.00
Banjo, New Haven, Mahogany, Eagle Finial, Glass Door, Ship, Time & Strike, 44 In. 440.00
Banjo, Painted Tablet, Perry's Victory On Lake Erie, Tiffany & Co., 32 In. 670.00
Banjo, Reverse Painting, Ship 1265.00
Banjo, Seth Thomas, Reverse Painted Nautical Scene Lower Section, 31 In. 250.00
Banjo, Waltham, Federal Style, Eglomise, c.1900, 4 x 10 1/2 x 3 1/2 In. 1120.00
Banjo, Waterbury, Reverse Panel, Mt. Vernon, Enamel Dial, Eagle Finial, 41 In. 1495.00
Banjo, Whiting, Samuel, Reverse Painted Tablets, c.1825 .... 1700.00
Banjo, Willard, Simon, Gilt Molding, Brass Frets, Margaret Watts Painted Tablets, 33 In. . 1760.00
Banjo, Willard, White Painted Dial, Patriotic Eglomise Panels, Eagle, Mahogany, 33 In. .. 2016.00
Barometer, Turned Column Supports, Walnut, Foliage Base, 38 In. 310.00
Barraud, Bracket, Painted Face 2000.00
Bartholomew, G.W., Mantel, Empire, Mahogany, Stenciled, Conn., 34 x 17 x 5 In. 280.00
Baseball, Metal, White, 9 In. 90.00
Bigelow, Kennard & Co., Carriage, Brass, Repeat Mechanism, Alarm Dial 1035.00
Birdcage, Brass, Chrome Base, Brass Hanger, Japan, 3 1/4 In. 90.00
Birge & Fuller, Mahogany, Reverse Painting, 30-Hour, Time & Strike, 25 x 12 In. .. *Illus* 2530.00
Black, Starr & Frost, Regulator, Molded Brass Case, Glazed Sides, Porcelain Dial, 8 In. . 230.00
Black Forest, Angel Head, Leaf Design, 22 x 13 In. 415.00
Black Forest, Carved Fish, Guns, 8-Day, Brass Movement, 31 x 20 In. 770.00
Black Forest, Grape & Vine Carving, Shaped Case, Double Weights, 42 In. 3640.00
Black Forest, Mantel, 3 Birds, Woodland Carvings, 23 In. 1176.00

Clock, Birge & Fuller, Mahogany, Reverse Painting, 30-Hour, Time & Strike, 25 x 12 In.

Clock, Brace, Rodney, Mahogany, Carved, Wood Dial, 30-Hour, Time & Strike, 36 x 17 In.

Clock, Brown, J.C., Beehive Ripple, Reverse Painting, 8-Day, Time & Strike, 19 x 10 In.

Black Forest, Mantel, 4 Deer, Glass Eyes, Carved Rocky Ledges, 35 x 22 In. 4480.00
Black Forest, Mantel, 6 Birds, Chicks In Nest, Leaves, Branches, 27 In. 3080.00
Black Forest, Mantel, Carved, Stag, Mountain Goats, Woodland Scene, 34 In. 1680.00
Black Forest, Walnut, Carved, Birds On Tree, Germany, 1850s 3000.00
Black Forest, Walnut, Eagle, Antelope, Evergreens, 8-Day, Glass Dial, 47 x 12 In. 2640.00
Black Forest, Weight Driven, Game, Branch, Acorn Carvings, Deer's-Head Crest, 49 In. .   3920.00
Black Man, With Banjo, Blinking Eye, Cast Iron, Painted, c.1880, 16 In. . . . . . .1800.00 to 2800.00
Black Man Smiles, Eyes Move, Second-Hand Movement, Germany, 4 1/2 In. 273.00
Boardman & Wells, Mahogany, Tiger Maple Veneer, Classical, c.1825 . . . .   520.00
Boardman & Wells, Reverse Painting, Fairytale Scene, Double Weights, 32 x 16 In. 500.00
Boston Clock Co., Mantel, Greek Temple Form, c.1890, 18 1/2 In. 365.00
Boston Clock Co., Temple, Mahogany, Chiming, Ionic Columns, 1880s.16 3/8 In. 630.00
Bowen, George, Walnut, Brass Movement, Peaked, Arched Top, Applied Rosette 165.00
Brace, Rodney, Floral Bouquet Crest, Reverse Painting, Building, 36 x 18 In. 900.00
Brace, Rodney, Mahogany, Carved, Wood Dial, 30-Hour, Time & Strike, 36 x 17 In. . *Illus*   2090.00
Bracket, Boulle Style Case, France, 19th Century, 21 1/2 x 10 In.   575.00
Bracket, Chiming, Brass Loop Handle, Signed, Bracket Feet, 15 x 10 In. 1840.00
Bracket, Dome Crown, Beveled Door, Shaped Base, Early 20th Century, 15 In. 365.00
Bracket, George III, Mahogany Inlay, Satinwood, Brass Ball Feet, 13 1/2 In. 546.00
Bracket, Glazed Beveled Door, Oak, Early 20th Century, 15 In. 365.00
Bracket, Louis XV, Gilt Bronze, Boulle Marquetry, 19th Century, 13 3/8 In. 316.00
Bracket, Mahogany Case, Gilt Bronze Trim, Westminster Strike, Mid 19th Century, 28 In.   6800.00
Brass, Champleve, Enamel, Gilt, France, Early 20th Century 920.00
Brass, Garland Decoration, Inlaid Marble, 8-Day, Germany, 15 x 9 In. 200.00
Brass, Louis XVI, Table, Domed Cornice, Husk Garland Design, Cherub Head, 28 In. . . .   1955.00
Brass, Mystery, Classical Woman Figure, Raised Arm Holds Clock, 1950s, 30 1/4 In. . . .   470.00
Bright & Sons, Bracket, Oak, Carved, Triple Fusee Movement, Scarborough, 22 x 15 In. .   990.00
Bristol Brass & Clock Co., Shelf, Painted, Abalone, 8-Day, Cast Iron, 20 1/2 In. 248.00
British United Clock Co., Desk, Brass, Punched Frame, Electric, 4 x 6 In. 259.00
Bronze, Caesar, 8-Day, 1/2-Hour Strike, Applied Ormolu, Marble Base, 24 x 18 In. 935.00
Bronze, Gallery, Openwork Detail, Marble Dial, 21 x 32 In. 1680.00
Bronze, Gilt, Champleve, France, Early 20th Century, 15 1/4 In. 1150.00
Bronze, Gilt, Glass, Garniture, Electrified, Early 20th Century, 14 1/2 In., 3 Piece 7200.00
Bronze, Gilt, Louis XVI, Garniture, Marble, Late 19th Century, 3 Piece 21450.00
Bronze, Gilt, Renaissance Revival, Strapwork Scroll Dial, Cherubs, 3 1/2 x 4 5/8 In. 750.00
Bronze, Louis XV, Champleve, Barrel Shape, Cupid, Dolphin's Head Tripod Base, 8 In. . . .   1380.00
Bronze, Louis XV, Enamel, Gilt, Fountain Shape, Cupid, Drinking From Vase, 12 In. 1840.00
Bronze, Maidenhead Claw Feet, Porcelain Dial, Garniture, 18 In., 3 Piece 560.00
Bronze, Patinated, Gilt, Napoleon III, Garniture, 19th Century, 24 1/2 In., 3 Piece 18000.00
Bronze, Patinated, Gilt, Napoleon III, Garniture, Signed, 31 1/2 In. 19150.00
Bronze, Rococo, Putti, Signed, Paris, Garniture, 6 x 31 In., 3 Piece 11760.00
Bronzed Metal, Cherubs, Marble, Garniture, 16 x 8 x 22 In., 3 Piece 950.00
Bronzed Metal, Dancing Pan & Lyre, Garniture, c.1885, 25 In., 3 Piece 1625.00
Bronzed Metal, Marble, Cherub, Birds, Signed Le Vent, Garniture, 15 1/2 In., 3 Piece . . .   785.00
Bronzed Metal, Onyx, Winged Cherub, Scroll, Garniture, c.1875, 13 In., 3 Piece 730.00
Bronzed Metal, Reclining Woman, Urns, Green Marble Base, Moreau, Sculpture, 25 In. .   896.00
Bronzed Metal, Seated Woman, Cherub With Grapes, Garniture, 15 In., 3 Piece 840.00
Bronzed Metal, Seated Woman, Cupid, Onyx Base, Garniture, 16 x 6 x 21 In., 3 Piece . . .   950.00
Bronzed Metal, Woman Holding Globe, Marble Base, 25 x 26 In.   1456.00
Bronzed Metal, Woman Playing Harp, Marble Base, Garniture, 14 x 6 x 18 In., 3 Piece . .   670.00
Bronzed Metal, Woman, Pedestal, Cupid, Marble Base, Garniture, 19 x 7 x 14 In., 3 Piece   950.00
Brown, J.C., Beehive Ripple, Reverse Painting, 8-Day, Time & Strike, 19 x 10 In. . . *Illus*   1650.00
Brown, J.C., Beehive, Mahogany, Floral Tablet, Painted, 8-Day, 18 3/4 In. 1760.00
Caldwell & Co., Carriage, Brass, Double Dial, Beveled Glass, Embossed, Phil., 4 3/4 In. . .   170.00
Calendar, Gingerbread, Oak, Time & Strike, 8-Day, 22 1/2 x 14 1/2 In. 175.00
Calendar, Rosewood, Brass, 8-Day, Bristol, Conn., 1865, 32 In. 2070.00
Carriage, 8-Day, Molded Brass Case, Glazed Sides, Top, Marked H & H, France, 4 5/8 In.   176.00
Carriage, Alarm, Repeating, Roman Numerals, Brass Housing, Woman's, 7 1/8 In. 345.00
Carriage, Brass, Beveled Glass, Embossed Leaf Design, Double Dial, Key, 4 1/2 In. 345.00
Carriage, Brass, Beveled Glass, Swing Handle, Bracket Feet, 3 x 4 3/4 In. 230.00
Carriage, Brass, Cloisonne, Continental, Late 19th Century, 6 1/2 x 4 1/2 x 4 In. 375.00
Carriage, Brass, Cupid Design, Enameled, France, 3 1/2 In. 1093.00
Carriage, Brass, Embossed Design, Double Dial, Key, Signed D.H., 5 1/4 In. 290.00

Bright sunlight will damage antiques by fading colors or drying wood. There are several brands of film that can be applied to your window to cut UV rays, heat, and glare. 3M and Vista window film are the best known.

Clock, Carriage,
Original Carry Case,
Tiffany & Co.,
France, 4 7/8 In.

Carriage, Brass, Rectangular, Beveled Glass, Swing Handle, Bracket Feet, 3 x 4 3/4 In. . . . 230.00
Carriage, Brass, Seconds Dial, Beveled Glass Panels, Early 20th Century, 5 3/4 In. 345.00
Carriage, Brass, Silvered Inset Dial, Embossed Border, Beveled Glass, Key, 4 3/4 In. 230.00
Carriage, Bronze, Boat & Shore Scenes On Sides, Porcelain, 5 In. 1265.00
Carriage, Enamel, Couples, Putti, Doves, Roman Numerals, Germany, 5 In. 3335.00
Carriage, Gilt Filigree Dial, Black Lacquer Case, Gilt Ormolu, England, 30 In. 5175.00
Carriage, Half Strike Repeater, Enamel Dial, Seconds Dial, Tiffany & Co., 7 x 3 3/8 In. . . 920.00
Carriage, Louis XVI, Gilt Bronze, Square, Flat Leaves, 5 1/2 In. 430.00
Carriage, Name On Dial, All Around Beveled Glass, White Dial, Tiffany & Co., 4 3/4 In. . . 345.00
Carriage, Original Carry Case, Tiffany & Co., France, 4 7/8 In. . . . . *Illus* 660.00
Carriage, White Enameled Dial, Roman Numerals, Tree With Silk Flowers, 28 In. 6000.00
Cartel, Enameled Numerals, Female Head, Flanked By Floral Swags, 30 In. 1840.00
Cartel, Oak, Fruit, Flower Carvings, 23 In. 670.00
Charles X, Slate, Ormolu Roman Numerals, Raised On Scrolled Feet, 1825, 17 In. 750.00
Clarke, W.B., Wall, Walnut, Carved Leaves Base, England, c.1860, 28 In. 420.00
Cowell & Hubbard, Mantel, Oval Beveled Case, Brass & Cloisonne, 1920s, 10 1/2 In. . . . 575.00
Crane, Aaron, Shelf, Ebonized Wood Case, Paper Dial, 1850, 21 1/4 x 13 In. 1200.00
Crane, Aaron, Shelf, Rosewood Case, Paper Dial, 30-Day, 1850, 29 1/2 x 12 In. 5500.00
Curtis & Clark, Mahogany, Iron Dial, 8-Day, Time & Strike, 22 1/2 x 12 1/2 In. . . . . *Illus* 23100.00
DeRespinis, Lucia, Brass, Wood, Enameled Metal, 1957, 22 5/8 In. 1610.00
Desk, Cloisonne, Inlaid, Crystal, Winged Griffins, Claw Feet, 5 1/2 x 3 x 4 1/2 In. 1008.00
Desk, Fan Shape, Chrysanthemums, Silver, Gold, Japan, Early 20th Century, 7 1/8 In. . . . 1150.00
Desk, Silver Plate, Arched Case, 4 Bun Feet, 6 3/4 In. 200.00
Dreyfuss, Henry, Ben Bolt, Desk, Bakelite, Numbers, Ball Feet, Westclox, 1932, 5 x 4 In. . 69.00
Dutton, David, Wooden Works, Time & Strike, Alarm, 1830 . . . . 255.00
Edwardian, Figure 8, Walnut, Inlaid, Reverse-Painted Lower Table, 1800s 478.00
Eli & Samuel Terry, Mantel, Federal, Mahogany Pillar, House & Lake Scene, 31 In. 4600.00
Eli Terry, Mahogany, Inlaid Birch, Finials, Wood Dial, 30-Hour, 30 x 17 1/2 In. . . . . *Illus* 8250.00
Eli Terry, Pillar & Scroll, Mahogany, Reverse Painted House, Wooden Works, 29 1/4 In. . . 1650.00
Eli Terry, Pillar, Paw Feet, Gilded Columns, Triple Crest, Reverse Painting On Door 1000.00
Eli Terry, Shelf, Mahogany Case, Carved Paw Feet, Half Columns, Wooden Dial, 30 In. . . 495.00
Eli Terry, Shelf, Mahogany Case, Quarter Columns, Fruit Crest, 1830, 32 1/2 x 16 In. . . . 2530.00
Eli Terry, Triple-Arched Crest, Reverse Painting, Landscape On Door, Wood Dial, 29 In. . 1000.00
Eli Terry & Sons, Mantel, Federal, Mahogany Pillar, Scroll, 1825, 30 x 17 x 4 3/4 In. 1610.00
Eli Terry & Sons, Mantel, Federal, Mahogany, Pillar & Scroll, c.1825 . . . . 1840.00
Empire, Napoleon Plaque, 1860 . . . . 1700.00
Enamel, Allegorical Scenes, Building Shape, Vienna, 11 In. 2645.00
Forestville, Empire, 30-Hour, Repainted Face, 34 3/4 x 20 x 6 3/4 In. 99.00
Fournier, A., 2-Train, Tin Pendulum, Wall, Enamel Dial, Tin Surround, 43 1/2 In. 460.00
French, Double Figural, Swing Arm, Amour Et Printemps, 42 In. 4760.00
French, Open Escapement, Pagoda-Shaped Crown, c.1900, 15 In. 336.00
French, Walnut, Barometer, Turned Column Supports, Leaf Carved Base, c.1890, 38 In. . . 308.00
French, Walnut, Ornate Headboard, Beveled Glass Door, 15-Day, 43 In. 715.00
French Design, Oriental Urn Shape, Dragon Handles, Decorated Porcelain Dial 385.00
French Empire, Black Onyx, 2 Urns, Grecian Scene, 16 x 22 x 6 1/2 In. 550.00
Frost, Jonathan, Mantel, Time & Strike, Mahogany Case, Ogee, 1843, 27 x 15 In. 225.00
General Electric, Wall, Checkerboard Dial, Red Hands, Peter Max, 9 In. 200.00

Gilbert, Calendar, Hanging, Walnut Case, Paper Dial, Winston, Conn., 1870, 28 1/2 In. .. 1430.00
Gilbert, Gingerbread, Oak, 8-Day, Time & Strike, Pressed Grapes, Vines, 23 x 15 In. 165.00
Gilbert, Mantel, Wood Case, Painted Black, Flowers, Birds, Time & Strike, 15 In. 385.00
Gilbert, Regulator, Pinwheel, 8-Day, Gridiron Pendulum, Cherry ....*Illus* 16500.00
Gilbert, Steeple, Painted Roses On Door, 15 x 9 In............................... 90.00
Gilt Metal, Marble, Garniture, 7-Light Candelabra, Imps, Garland, Paw Feet, 24 1/2 In. .. 520.00
Giltwood, Painted Portico, Guilloche & Bread Carving, 2 Putto Draftsmen, 20 In. 630.00
Glass, Ball Shape, Red & Clear Jewels On Rim, 3 3/4 In. 690.00
Gustav Becker Works, Regulator, Vienna, Walnut, Porthole Case, 8-Day, c.1885, 45 In. .. 990.00
Hallcraft Corp., Torsion, Brass Case, Glass Cover, Etched Flowers, Germany, 9 In. 120.00
Hodges, Erastus, Shelf, Pillar & Splat, 30-Hour, Wood Torrington Movement, 26 In. 415.00
Hoffman, Andre, Mantel, Man & Woman, Rococo Base, Bronze, Glass Dome, 15 x 18 In. 1725.00
Holman, Salem, Shelf, Wooden Works, Painted Dial, Split Columns, Label, 34 In. 288.00
Horwitt, N.G., Wall, Enameled Face, Trim, Hands, Model 4628, Label, 1970, 12 In. 165.00
Howard, E., Astronomical, Burled Walnut, Mercury Pendulum, c.1873, 96 In. ......*Illus* 77000.00
Howard, E., Regulator, Railroad, No. 89, Oak, c.1890, 65 In. 2750.00
Howard Miller, Brass Ball, Spokes, Wooden Spheres, 24 In. 575.00
Howard Miller, Cork, Black, Orange Hands, 11 1/2 In. 374.00
Howard Miller, Desk, Chronopak, Walnut, Black Dial, White Hands, 7 x 6 In. 230.00
Howard Miller, Portable, Brass, Enameled Hands, Plexiglas Face, No. 4760, 6 1/2 x 4 In. .. 575.00
Howard Miller, Starburst, G. Nelson, 18 1/2 In. 460.00
Howard Miller, Wall, Ceramic, Rings Of Green, Blue & Gray, Meridian, 13 3/4 In. 115.00
Imhoff, Brass, Reticulated Doors, 15-Jewel, Key Wind, Knob Feet, Swiss, 5 x 4 x 2 In. .. 135.00
Incline Rolling, Cylinder, Marble Base, Engraved Days Of Week, Brass Plaque 7000.00
Ingraham, Regulator B, Octagon Top, School, Time Only, 8-Day, c.1903 .... 495.00
Ingraham & Co., Mantel, Walnut, Glass Door, Gold Flowers, Pendulum, 16 x 9 In. 60.00
Ithaca, Farmer's, No. 10, Double Dial, 26 x 12 In. 575.00
Ithaca, Regulator, Wall, Walnut Case, Paper Dial, 8-Day, 1880, 51 1/2 x 25 1/2 In. 3190.00
Ithaca, Wall, Calendar, Rosewood Case, 8-Day, 1870, 28 1/2 x 15 1/2 In. ......1150.00 to 1430.00
Ives, C. & L.C., Foliage Crest, Reverse-Painted Landscape, Dial Lifts, Escapement, 38 In. 900.00
Ives, Joseph, Mahogany, Reverse Painting, Wood Dial, 30-Hour, 24 x 14 In. ....*Illus* 16500.00
Ives & Lewis, Shelf, Mahogany, Case, Painted Wooden Dial, Pilaster Columns, 35 In. ... 2090.00
Japy Freres, Gilt Brass, Copper Case, Fish Scale, Garniture Set, 5-Light Candelabra 275.00
Japy Freres, Mantel, Renaissance Revival, Brass, Gilt, Dome Top, Handles, 18 In. 575.00
Jerome, C. & N., Shelf, Wood Dial, Columns, Splat, Mirrored Panel, 33 1/2 In. 195.00
Jerome, C., Shelf, Mahogany, Columns, Reverse Painted, New Haven, Conn., 26 In. 210.00
Jerome, Chauncey, Shelf, Painted Panel, New Haven, Conn., Mid 19th Century 330.00
Jerome, Chauncey, Wall, Rosewood, Piecrust Trim, Fusee Movement, 22 x 17 In........ 1125.00
Jerome & Co., Wall, Mahogany Veneer, Eglomise, 8-Day, Ogee, c.1830, 30 x 16 x 4 In. .. 130.00
Jones, Abner, Shelf, Mahogany Acanthus Base, Fruit, Pineapple Columns, 47 In. 3850.00
Jones, Abner, Shelf, Mahogany Case, 4 Drawers, Metal Dial, Sheration Feet, 1830, 54 In. 5225.00
Jugendstil, Wall, Cutout Top, Brass Details, German, 30 x 14 x 7 In.................. 920.00

Clock, Curtis & Clark, Mahogany,
Iron Dial, 8-Day, Time & Strike,
22 1/2 x 12 1/2 In.

Clock, Eli Terry, Mahogany,
Inlaid Birch, Finials, Wood Dial,
30-Hour, 30 x 17 1/2 In.

Clock, Gilbert, Regulator,
Pinwheel, 8-Day, Gridiron
Pendulum, Cherry

Junghans, Black Man With Top Hat, Turning Eyes, Germany, 9 1/2 In. 728.00
Junghans, Child Figure, Swinging Arm, 13 In. 785.00
Junghans, Regulator, Spring Wind, Carved, Pendulum, Vienna, 34 x 14 In. 240.00
Kaiser, Joseph, Bracket, Fusee Movement, Ebonized Wood, Brass, London, 23 x 19 In. . . 2640.00
King, John, Mantel, Regency, Mahogany, Brass Inlay, London, 20 x 14 In. 1095.00
Lantern, Wall, Single Strike, Weight Driven, 1790-1820 . . . . 2400.00
LeCoultre & Cie, Atmos, Presentation Plaque, 9 1/4 In. 248.00
LeCoultre Co., Desk, Quartz, Brass Dial & Hands, Square, Switzerland, 1950s, 7 In. 105.00
Lenzkirch, Mantel, Bronze Mounted, Oak, 24 In. 2240.00
LeRoy, Mantel, Lyre, Paris, 1800s, 21 In. 6050.00
Liberty & Co., Mantel, Oak, Copper Face, Slag Glass Window, Bell Top, Germany, 14 In. 1840.00
Liberty & Co., Pewter, Enameled, 4 1/4 In. 805.00
Litchfield Mfg. Co., Wall, Papier-Mache, Eagle & Flags Top, Pat. 1852, 20 In. 2875.00
Lux, Cape Cod Lighthouse, Light, 11 x 9 In. 70.00
Lux, Cuckoo, Small Crossed Rifles, 30-Hour, 16 x 10 In. 50.00
Lux, Moving Eye, Smiling Black Man, Chalkware, 8 1/2 In. 600.00
Lyre, Art, Signed Leroy, Paris, 1800s, 21 In. 6050.00
Lyre, Enamel Face, Flower Garlands, Ribbon-Tied Branches, 12 1/2 In. 1380.00
Lyre, Mahogany, 8-Day, Mother-Of-Pearl Inset, Eagle Finial, 32 In. 1485.00
Mahogany Veneer, Pillar & Scroll, Brass Urn Finials, Painted Wood Dial, 30 1/2 In. 1430.00
Mantel, 2 Draped Children, Flowers On Case, Late 19th Century, 13 In. 920.00
Mantel, Aesthetic Movement, Garniture, Gilt, Marble, 27 In., 3 Piece 3640.00
Mantel, Animal Heads & Urns, Shell & Urn Crest, 24 1/4 In. 165.00
Mantel, Armillary Sphere, Bronze, Shield Form Base, D'Aureville, 1820s, 16 1/2 In. 1955.00
Mantel, Art Deco, Onyx, Patinated Metal, c.1930, 24 5/8 In. 633.00
Mantel, Arts & Crafts, Time & Strike, 12 x 19 In. 144.00
Mantel, Arts & Crafts, Walnut Case, Light Wood Face, Dutch, 11 1/2 In. 1610.00
Mantel, Atlas, Ormolu, Atlas, White Enamel Dial, France, 20th Century, 14 In. 750.00
Mantel, Balloon Form, Tortoiseshell, Silver Plate Banding, Enamel Dial, 9 1/8 In. 920.00
Mantel, Black Marble, Bronze Hunting Dog By P.J. Mene On Top 750.00
Mantel, Black Marble, Scroll Top, Bronze Mounts, Figural Columns 110.00
Mantel, Black Marble, Temple Form, Porcelain Bezel, Chiming, 1880s, 16 1/2 In. 230.00
Mantel, Black Onyx, Gilt, Brass Fittings, Molded Crest, 4 Columns, 19 1/2 In. 440.00
Mantel, Brass, Tortoiseshell, Time & Strike, Continental, 19th Century, 8 1/2 x 5 1/2 In. . . 1380.00
Mantel, Brass, Tortoiseshell, Time & Strike, Roman Numerals, 8 1/2 x 5 1/2 In. 1380.00
Mantel, Bronze, Empire Style, Ram Heads, Hoof Feet, 2-Urn Candelabra, c.1860, 10 In. . . 1680.00
Mantel, Bronze, Gothic Case, Floral Carving, 22 In. 560.00
Mantel, Bronze, Gothic, 20 In. 728.00
Mantel, Bronze, Marble, Louis XVI, Allegorical, Lovebirds, Garniture Set, Urns, 3 Piece . 4025.00
Mantel, Bronze, Rococo, Neptune, Putti, Sea Serpents, Cattails, 29 In. 3304.00
Mantel, Bronze, Urn, Flame, Seated Figures, France, 26 In. 12880.00
Mantel, Bronze, Verdigris Patina, Alabaster, Signed, Albert Cheuret, 1925, 8 3/8 In. 6000.00
Mantel, Bronzed Metal, 2 Women Holding Terrestrial Globe, Marble Base, 33 In. 670.00
Mantel, Bronzed Metal, Marble, Maidens, Cupids, 2 Urns, 29 In. 1175.00
Mantel, Caldwell & Co., Round, Verde Antico Marble, Bronze, Ormolu, 15 x 4 In. 4935.00
Mantel, Cast Metal, 2 Standing Cupids In Front Of Mirrored Panels, 15 In. 525.00
Mantel, Chariot, Bronze, Figure, Clock In Wheel, Marble Base 1650.00
Mantel, Charles X, Gilt Bronze, Marble, Patinated Bronze, 20 x 13 3/4 x 6 In. 1955.00
Mantel, Charles X, Gilt Bronze, Patina, Belisarius, 19th Century, 20 3/4 x 14 1/2 x 5 In. . . 2990.00
Mantel, Charles X, Gilt Bronze, Portico Shape, Mid 19th Century, 20 x 9 1/2 In. 1955.00
Mantel, Charles X, Gilt, Rosewood, Muse & Winged Horse, 24 x 8 x 4 In. 2300.00
Mantel, Cherub, 2-Train, Half Hour Strike, Enamel Dial, Late 19th Century, 22 In. 990.00
Mantel, Children, Doll, Black Marble Base, 19 In. 1790.00
Mantel, Chinese Man Riding Elephant, France, 15 In. 898.00
Mantel, Enameled Face, Cherub Holding Basket Of Fruit, Marble Base, Key, 18 In. 275.00
Mantel, Faux Marble, Time & Strike, 11 x 14 In. 100.00
Mantel, Figured Fruitwood Veneer, Serpentine Sides, Pendulum, Tiffany & Co., 13 In. . . . 250.00
Mantel, French Empire, Gilt Bronze, Man With Mandolin, 16 1/2 In. 1176.00
Mantel, French Empire, Gilt Bronze, Woman, Goat, 17 In. 1000.00
Mantel, French Empire, Lyre, Dore Bronze Mountings, c.1850, 27 In. 2800.00
Mantel, French Rococo, Dore Bronze, Bacchus Head, Dolphins, Claw Feet, 15 1/2 In. . . . 1345.00
Mantel, Gilt Bronze, Continental, Mid 19th Century, 15 x 18 In. 1725.00
Mantel, Gilt Bronze, Time & Strike, Avian Form, Continental, 4 1/4 x 7 1/4 In. 290.00

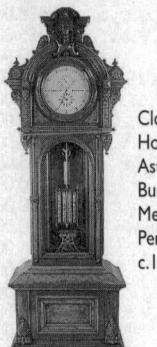

Clock,
Howard, E.,
Astronomical,
Burled Walnut,
Mercury
Pendulum,
c.1873, 96 In.

Clock, Ives, Joseph, Mahogany,
Reverse Painting, Wood Dial,
30-Hour, 24 x 14 In.

Clock, New Haven, Saxon,
Open Escapement

Mantel, Gilt Highlights, Enameled Floral Dial, Plinth & Scroll Feet, Paris, 16 x 9 1/2 In. . . 2070.00
Mantel, Gilt Metal, Floral Porcelain Dial, Urn Finial, 1880s, 13 1/4 In. 575.00
Mantel, Gilt Metal, Onyx, Woman Fishing, Boat, Dolphin Heads, Claw Feet, 22 In. 1000.00
Mantel, Gilt, Bronze, Patinated, Verde Antico, Marble, Louise XVI Style, 9 x 9 x 4 1/2 In. . 1495.00
Mantel, Gilt, Eglomise Portrait Of Lady, 3 Tier Facade, c.1830, 34 1/2 In. 590.00
Mantel, Gothic, Walnut, Mansard Roof, 3-Wind 1/4-Hour Chime, 23 x 11 x 14 In. 1230.00
Mantel, Half Striking, 2 Griffins, Putto Mask, 1820s, 17 In. 280.00
Mantel, Japy Freres, Temple Form, Glazed Sides, Floral Swag Under Dial, 5 1/4 In. 1265.00
Mantel, Key Wind, Painted Panel, 8-Day 196.00
Mantel, Liberty, Pewter Body, Copper Face, Mother-Of-Pearl, 10 In. 6325.00
Mantel, Lion Head Top, Irises, Green, Gold, Pendulum, Key, 12 x 11 1/2 In. 520.00
Mantel, Louis Philippe, Gilt Bronze, Mahogany, Portico Shape, 19 1/2 x 10 In. 800.00
Mantel, Louis Philippe, Lyre, Gilt Bronze, Dome, 19th Century, 27 1/2 x 14 1/2 x 5 In. . . 5290.00
Mantel, Louis XV, Gilt Bronze, Drum Case, 17 In. 3450.00
Mantel, Louis XV, Gilt Bronze, Late 19th Century, 16 1/2 In. 2400.00
Mantel, Louis XV, White Enamel, Blue Roman Numerals, Scrolled Feet, 13 1/2 In. 860.00
Mantel, Louis XVI, Bronze, Flat Leaf Metal Bezel, White Metal Case, 13 1/2 In. 290.00
Mantel, Louis XVI, Gilt Bronze, Enamel Dial, Floral Garlands, 16 x 9 1/4 x 4 1/2 In. 1090.00
Mantel, Louis XVI, Gilt Bronze, Marble, 19th Century, 26 1/2 x 23 3/4 x 10 1/2 In. 5100.00
Mantel, Louis XVI, Marble Mounted, Raised On Columns, 15 1/2 In. 2185.00
Mantel, Man, Holding Violin, Bow, Pendulum, Onyx Base, A. Moreau, Sculpture, 28 In. . . 660.00
Mantel, Marble, Black Case, 2 Floral Bands, Victorian, 14 1/2 In. 530.00
Mantel, Mercury Pendulum, Side Lights, Enamel Face, Tiffany & Co., c.1920 . . . . 365.00
Mantel, Mottled Green Marble, Gold Numerals, 8-Day, 1920s 2500.00
Mantel, Non-Chiming, Corniced Case, 2 Plinth Supports, 1930s, 6 1/2 In. 690.00
Mantel, Oak, Carved, Elk Crest, Lion-Head Feet, 26 In. 1230.00
Mantel, Opaline Glass, Mask & Scroll Design, 1800s, 7 1/2 x 6 1/2 x 12 In. 230.00
Mantel, Ormolu & Marble, Round Face, Bronze Brackets, Bud Feet, 16 x 22 In. 2115.00
Mantel, Paix & Progress, Scrolling Floral Legs, c.1880, 30 x 16 In. 810.00
Mantel, Porcelain Dials, Bronze Swags Base, 4 Leaf Feet, 1820s, 31 1/2 In. 4600.00
Mantel, Porcelain, Bronze, 4 Classical Figures, c.1860, 17 In. 4928.00
Mantel, Porcelain, Cherubs, Pink, White, Scalloped Base, Key, Tiffany & Co., 12 x 13 In. . 1265.00
Mantel, Porcelain, Floral Bouquets, Late 19th Century, 25 In. 2700.00
Mantel, Porcelain, Flowers, 4 Seasons Cupids, Germany, 19 In. 1723.00
Mantel, Prowling Lion, Rocky Ledge, 21 x 8 x 26 In. 1008.00
Mantel, Renaissance Revival, Dome, Gilt, Plinth Feet, c.1890, 27 x 11 x 7 In. 805.00
Mantel, Rococo, Bronze, Gilt, Enamel Dial, Beveled Glass Case, Oval, 20 In. 1725.00
Mantel, Rococo, Bronze, Woman Portrait, Urn Pediment, 28 In. 1736.00
Mantel, Rococo, Carved Wood, Gilt, Scenic Porcelain Plaque, 19 In. 730.00
Mantel, Rococo, Gilt Bronze, Figural Women, Ram Heads, 27 x 20 In. 3920.00
Mantel, Rococo, Gilt Bronze, Seated Cherubs, 22 x 19 In. 3750.00
Mantel, Rococo, Marble, Bronze, Urn Pediment, Flower Garlands, 23 In. 1344.00
Mantel, Sevres Panels, Angel Each Side, Gilt Bronze, Tiffany & Co., 12 x 25 In. 5500.00

Mantel, Steam Hammer, Industrial, France, 18 In. 5600.00
Mantel, Swinging Arm, Marble Base, France, 29 In. 2240.00
Mantel, Tambour, Oak, Keyless Rim Wind, 8-Day, 12 1/2 In. 70.00
Mantel, Temple Form, Ebonized, Gilt Metal, Plinth Base, Footed, France, 1844, 17 In. 400.00
Mantel, Temple, Empire Revival, Alabaster, Ormolu Mounted, 15 5/8 In. 230.00
Mantel, Time & Strike Alarm, 16 1/2 x 9 In. 200.00
Mantel, Time & Strike, Reverse-Painted Washington, Eglomise Panel, 27 x 16 In. 225.00
Mantel, Tortoiseshell & Silver, Sloped Cornice, Enamel Dial, 1907, 8 5/8 x 4 5/8 In. 920.00
Mantel, Victorian, Gilt Bronze, Rectangular Cornice, Paw Feet, 28 x 16 x 12 In. 5520.00
Mantel, Walnut, Gilt, Bronze, Stylized Lions Holding Shields, Signed, 32 1/2 In. 7200.00
Mantel, Walnut, Tulipwood Inlay, Gilt, Bronze Dial, Draped Plinth Base, 1900, 43 In. 6600.00
Mantel, White Enamel Numerals, Rectangular Beveled Glass, Bracket Feet, 9 In. 260.00
Maranville, Gilbert, Calendar, Carved Walnut, Painted Metal Dial, 8-Day, 1870, 34 In. ... 1700.00
Marti, Bracket, Boulle Style, Cupid Finial, Later Giltwood Shelf, 21 x 10 In. 575.00
Marti, S., Mantel, Half Striking, Beveled Glass Sides, Paw Feet, 1920s, 12 1/4 In. 430.00
Marti, S., Mantel, Porcelain Pillars, Enameled Face, Urn Finial, Cast Brass, 13 3/4 In. ... 190.00
Merriman & Ives, Shelf, Mahogany Case, Fluted Pilaster Columns, 1820, 36 In. 770.00
Mirror, Pine, Mahogany Veneer Case, Painted Iron Dial, 8-Day, 1820, 30 x 14 In. 2090.00
Mitchell & Adkins, Triple Arched Crest, Reverse Painting, Church, 2 Weights, 16 x 32 In. 425.00
Morbier, Embossed Peacocks, Birds, Fruit, Floral, Time & Strike, Pendulum, 58 x 13 In. . 240.00
Morbier, Enamel Urn, Flowers & Face, Pendulum, 59 x 12 In. 300.00
Mougin, Mantel, Porcelain, Flowers, 8-Day, Time & Strike, Gilt Dial, 10 1/2 In. 336.00
Munger, Asa, Shelf, Ironing Board Top, Mahogany Case, 8-Day, 1830, 37 1/4 In. 2530.00
Munger, Asa, Shelf, Mahogany Case, 8-Day, Brass Movement, 1830, 38 1/2 In. 6325.00
Nelson, G., 12 Natural Birch Balls, Brass Center, 23 In. 2415.00
Nelson, G., Ball, Painted Wood, Enameled Metal, Label, 1950, 13 In. 3680.00
Nelson, G., Ceramic Starburst, Model 7546, Slate Black Ground, White Hands, 13 In. ... 220.00
Nelson, G., Snowflake, Thin Brass Pieces, Wood Trim, Windup, c.1959, 24 In. 4800.00
Nelson, G., Wall, Brass Disk Face, Wood Dial, 13 1/2 In. 275.00
New Haven, Arts & Crafts, Brass Hands, Keyed Tenons, Label, 22 x 14 In. 375.00
New Haven, Columbia, Cherry, 30-Day, Double Spring, c.1890, 49 x 14 In. 1650.00
New Haven, Mantel, Arts & Crafts, Time & Strike, Early 20th Century, 12 x 5 1/4 x 19 In. 144.00
New Haven, Mantel, Metal, Painted Black, Time & Strike 300.00
New Haven, Mantel, Porcelain, Mary & Lambs On Face, Flowers, 9 x 6 In. 160.00
New Haven, Oak, Brass Hinges & Latch, Gold Numerals, Paper Label, 13 1/2 In. 190.00
New Haven, Regulator, Jeweler's, No. 8, Burled Walnut, Lyre Pendulum, 74 In. 8800.00
New Haven, Regulator, No. 1, Walnut, Time & Calendar Dial 415.00
New Haven, Saxon, Open Escapement .... *Illus* 578.00
New Haven, Wall, Oak Case, c.1900 .... 170.00
Onken, Oscar, Mantel, 8-Sided Metal Dial, Recessed Base With Stretcher, 19 x 9 x 6 In. ... 375.00
Petit, Mantel, Gilt Metal, Porcelain, Courting Couple, 11 3/8 x 11 In. 315.00
Phinney-Walker, Catskill Aqueduct, Cement, Keyless, c.1939, 10 x 12 1/2 In. 750.00
Pond & Barnes, Double Door, Reverse Painting, Squirrel, Double Weight Driven, 27 In. . 300.00
Pratt & Frost, Shelf, Wooden Movement, Painted Dial, Mirror Bottom, Label, 35 In. 230.00
Proud, J., Bracket, Inverted Bell Top, Hourly Chime, Silvered Bezel, 19 In. 2990.00
Regulator, Bronze, Crystal, Gold Dore, Claw Feet, Signed, Garniture, 18 1/2 In., 3 Piece . 1345.00
Regulator, Bronze, Marble Crystal, Beveled Glass, Bird Pediment, 22 In. 2130.00
Regulator, Bronzed Metal, Onyx Crystal, Curved Beveled Glass, Flower Face, 20 In. 1345.00
Regulator, Cloisonne-Style Enamel, Gilt Brass Case, Full Columns, Urn Finial, 16 1/2 In. 385.00
Regulator, Crystal, Brass, Rhinestone, Pendulum, France, 8 1/2 x 5 1/4 x 4 1/4 In. 390.00
Regulator, Crystal, Gilt Brass Case, Scrolled Top, Base, Acanthus, Porcelain Dial, 14 In. . 440.00
Regulator, Eclipse, Wall, Calendar, Wood, Octagonal Top, Pendulum 400.00
Regulator, No. 2, Crystal, Blue Porcelain Top, Base, Gilt, Open Escapement, 8-Day 220.00
Regulator, Softwood, Round Dial Surround, Long Drop, 21 1/2 In. 195.00
Regulator, Vienna, Carved, Shell Crest, Figural Columns, Spread Wing Eagle, 56 In. 1320.00
Regulator, Vienna, Double Weight, Jenny Lind Crest, 50 In. 1230.00
Regulator, Vienna, Enamel Dial, Time & Strike, Late 19th Century, 16 1/2 x 7 1/2 x 49 In. 460.00
Regulator, Vienna, Figural Brass Mounts, Double Weight, 54 In. 1960.00
Regulator, Vienna, Mahogany, 8-Day, 1 Weight, 38 x 13 1/2 In. 200.00
Regulator, Vienna, Mahogany, Turned Columns, 8-Day, Porcelain Dial, 30 In. 165.00
Regulator, Vienna, Maple, 8-Day, Time & Strike, c.1880, 52 x 16 In. 825.00
Regulator, Vienna, Maple, Serpentine Case, 8-Day, Time & Strike, c.1865, 35 x 14 In. 2310.00
Regulator, Vienna, Oak, Carved, Horse Pediment 560.00

Regulator, Vienna, Time & Strike, Enameled Dial, Roman Numerals, 16 1/2 x 49 In. 460.00
Regulator, Vienna, Walnut, Arched Crown, Finial, Glazed Panels, c.1890, 28 In. 215.00
Regulator, Wall, 8-Day, Time & Strike, Mahogany Case, Brass-Cased Columns, 32 In. . . . 280.00
Regulator, Wall, 8-Day, Time & Strike, Mahogany Case, Half Columns, 43 In. 335.00
Regulator, Wall, Mahogany, Painted Dial, Octagonal Case, 1850s, 28 In. 8400.00
Regulator, Wall, Walnut, Enameled Dial, Brass Pendulum, 1880s, 26 1/2 In. 290.00
Regulator, Walnut, Arched Pediment, Female Mask, Brass Dial, 1870s, 40 In. 290.00
Regulator, Walnut, Carved Foliate Acorn & Geometrics, 37 1/2 In. 400.00
Regulator, Walnut, Enamel Dial, Roman Numerals, 1870s, 30 In. 920.00
Regulator, Walnut, Figural Pendulum, Urn Pediment, Gustav Becker, Vienna, 43 In. 950.00
Regulator, Walnut, Horse Pediment, Glazed Door, c.1890, 43 x 16 In. 310.00
Regulator, Walnut, Jeweler's, 1 Weight, Incised Flowers, Eastlake Case, 97 In. 7475.00
Regulator, Walnut, Pediment Above Brass & Enamel Dial, Glazed Door, 1880s, 32 In. 315.00
Regulator, Walnut, Weight Driven, Allover Pierced Carving, 47 In. 5040.00
Regulator, Wooden Rearing Horse Top, Black Lacquer, Pendulum, Victorian, 35 x 14 In. . . 275.00
Rohde, G., Desk, Burled Wood, Painted Steel, Glass, Chrome, Herman Miller, 1936, 7 In. . 2300.00
Rohde, G., Z-Shape Chrome Bar, Glass Face, Acid-Etched Numerals, 12 1/4 In. . . . 1150.00
Royal Bonn, La Layon, Porcelain, Multicolored, Embossed Flowers, 14 x 15 In. 2200.00
Royal Bonn, Mantel, France, Porcelain, Green, Lavender, Pink, 13 x 9 In. 1300.00
Royal Bonn, Mantel, La Clairmont, Porcelain, Roses, Ansonia Works, 11 x 11 In. 900.00
Royal Bonn, Mantel, La Nord, Porcelain, Light To Dark Green, Iris, 12 x 13 In. 1100.00
Royal Bonn, Mantel, La Talma, Porcelain, Red, Flowers, Ansonia Works, 12 x 14 In. 1000.00
Royal Bonn, Mantel, Porcelain, Blue, Yellow, Brown, Ansonia, 14 In. . . . . *Illus* 1400.00
Royal Bonn, Mantel, Porcelain, Embossed Griffins, Ansonia Works, 11 x 13 In. 1000.00
Royal Bonn, Mantel, Porcelain, Green, Pink, Ansonia, 11 In. . . . . *Illus* 450.00
Sandoz-Vuille, Desk, Ball Shape, Green Marble, Pedestal, Silver Dial, 4 1/2 x 5 1/2 In. . . . 280.00
Sawin, J., Shelf, Mahogany Case, Acorn Finial, Ball Feet, Alarm, Boston, 38 In. 4400.00
School, Oak, Simulated Mahogany, Repainted Dial & Face 190.00
Schumann & Sons, Mantel, Church Shape, Gothic Revival, Onyx, Metal, 29 x 12 x 7 In. . 7650.00
Schumannn & Sons, Gothic Revival, Onyx, Gilt Metal 7640.00
Sessions, Regulator, Carved Oak Case, Calendar, Pendulum, Key, 36 x 17 In. 460.00
Sessions, Regulator, Drop, Oak, Octagon, 26 1/2 In. 385.00
Seth Thomas, Calendar, Double Dial, Carved Walnut, Burl Case, 8-Day, 1876, 35 In. 3300.00
Seth Thomas, Calendar, Double Dial, Walnut Case, Ebonized Trim, 8-Day, 1875, 24 In. . . 1155.00
Seth Thomas, Double Decker, Reverse Paintings, Ship, Floral Basket, 8-Day, 31 x 17 In. . . 400.00
Seth Thomas, Empire No. 31, Regulator, Glass Columns, Porcelain Dial, 23 In. 1570.00
Seth Thomas, Empire No. 32, Regulator, Crystal, Glass Columns, Porcelain Dial, 20 In. . . 1510.00
Seth Thomas, Empire, Mahogany Veneer, Painted, Plymouth Hollow, c.1835, 25 In. 345.00
Seth Thomas, Mahogany, 20th Century, 9 x 5 1/2 x 11 In. 76.00
Seth Thomas, Mahogany, Camelback, Time & Strike, 19 1/2 In. 70.00
Seth Thomas, Mantel, Adamantine Case, Senora Chime, c.1910, 15 x 14 In. 525.00
Seth Thomas, Mantel, Arch Top, Time & Sonora Chime, 18 1/2 In. 800.00
Seth Thomas, Mantel, Mahogany Veneer, Reverse Painted Snipe, 34-Hour, 1850, 15 In. . . 925.00
Seth Thomas, Mantel, Pillar & Scroll, Reverse-Painted Building, 1801, 30 1/4 In. 1045.00
Seth Thomas, Mantel, Pillar, Mahogany Flame Veneer, Rose Medallion, 29 In. 1375.00
Seth Thomas, Maple, Pillar & Scroll, Reverse Painted Door, Wooden Works, 31 In. 2420.00
Seth Thomas, Parlor, Rosewood Veneer, Arched Crest, Round Face, Tablet 138.00
Seth Thomas, Rosewood Case, Reverse Paintings, Eagle, Geometrics, 8-Day, 31 x 19 In. . . 800.00
Seth Thomas, School, Oak, 8 In. 260.00
Seth Thomas, School, Oak, Octagon, 8-Day Time & Strike, 23 1/2 In. 330.00
Seth Thomas, School, Octagon, Mahogany, Time & Calendar, 16 x 4 1/2 x 24 In. 260.00
Seth Thomas, Shelf, Mahogany Veneer, Ogee Cornice, 8-Day, Stepped Base, 16 In. 255.00
Seth Thomas, Shelf, Renaissance Revival, Time & Strike, Level In Base, 24 x 14 In. 230.00
Seth Thomas, Ship Wheel Shape, Brass, Mahogany Base, 8-Day, Key Wind, 8 3/4 In. . . . 365.00
Seth Thomas, Ship, Brass Case, 1-Day Lever, 30-Hour, 6 1/4 In. 120.00
Seth Thomas, Ship, Brass Case, Painted Tin Dial, 8-Day, 7 In. 140.00
Seth Thomas, Ship, Metal Case, Brass Face Ring, Painted Tin Dial, 8-Day, 7 1/4 In. 305.00
Seth Thomas, Tall Case, No. 34, Mahogany, 8-Day, Moon Phase Dial, 93 x 24 In. 3300.00
Seth Thomas, Tall Case, Regulator, No. 2, Oak, Round Bezel, Bombe Drop, 8-Day, 37 In. . 660.00
Seth Thomas, Tall Case, Weight Driven, Bonnet Top, Shell Carvings, Claw Feet, 94 In. . . 3640.00
Seth Thomas, Wall, Calendar, Burl Walnut Case, 8-Day, 1860, 40 x 19 In. 1100.00
Seth Thomas, Wall, Calendar, Burl Walnut Case, Painted Metal Dial, 1870, 51 In. 7700.00
Seth Thomas, Wall, Calendar, Double Dial, Mahogany Case, Applied Rosettes, 26 In. 770.00

Seth Thomas, Wall, Regulator, Rosewood Veneer Case, Painted Metal Dial, 41 In. 4125.00
Seth Thomas, Wall, Rosewood, 8-Day, 19th Century, 32 1/2 In. 400.00
Seth Thomas, Wall, Time & Strike, Late 19th Century, 26 3/4 In. 290.00
Shelf, 2 Rouge Columns, 8 Lapis Lazuli Panels, Ebonized Wood, Glass Door, 23 1/4 In. ... 860.00
Shelf, Alabaster, Egyptian & Classical, Spelter Figures, 15 1/2 x 14 x 6 3/4 In. 265.00
Shelf, Bronze, Time & Strike, 8-Day, Domed Glass, Mahogany Base, 17 In. 2520.00
Shelf, Empire, Mahogany, Reverse Painted, Crest, Paw Feet, Pendulum, 27 x 17 In. 550.00
Shelf, Federal, Pillar, Mahogany Scroll, Wooden Painted Dial, 1825, 31 In. 3740.00
Shelf, Glass Dome, Fruitwood Base, Brass Face, France, Signed Bulle, 10 1/2 In. 110.00
Shelf, Inlaid Cherry, Curly Maple Case, Painted Iron Dial, 8-Day, 1830, 42 x 14 In. 6325.00
Shelf, J.C. Brown, Acorn, Rosewood Case, Painted Metal Dial, 8-Day, 1840, 19 In. 7975.00
Shelf, Mahogany Case, Green, Blue Painted Interior, Wood Dial, 1815, 38 x 12 In. 12650.00
Shelf, Mahogany Scroll, Zinc Painted Dial, Molded Base, Ball Feet, 24 x 13 x 4 In. 1725.00
Shelf, Mahogany, Double Cornucopia Crest, Ionic Capitals, Paw Feet, 31 In. 7500.00
Shelf, Mahogany, Inlaid, Waisted Case, Brass, Ormolu, Ebonized, Porcelain, 16 In. 110.00
Shelf, Mahogany, Mixed Woods, Time & Strike, Inlay Door, Germany, 17 x 23 In. 265.00
Shelf, Oak, 8-Day, Top Spool Gallery, Incised Carved Case Accent, Molded Base, 19 In. . 100.00
Shelf, Regulator, Vienna, Rosewood Case, Porcelain Dial, Brass Dial Ring, 36 In. 195.00
Shelf, Rosewood, Mahogany Case, Brass Inlay, Eagle Talon Base, 1823, 47 x 25 In. 15400.00
Shelf, Silver Urn, Brass Snake, Marble Base, 9 In. 600.00
Shelf, Steeple, Mahogany Veneer, 19th Century, 19 1/2 In. 290.00
Ship, Chelsea, Mahogany Stand, Bells, Face 5 1/2 In. 575.00
Silver, Engraved Flower Scrolls, Japan, 1868, 6 In. 630.00
Skeleton, Brass, Arch Form, Chimes, Chapter Ring, Marble Base, England, c.1850, 18 In. 805.00
Skeleton, Brass, Silver Dial, Fusee Movement, 8-Day, Ebonized Base, 8 x 5 In. 1210.00
Skeleton, Brass, Silver Dial, Fusee Movement, 8-Day, Marble Base, 14 x 7 1/2 In. 1045.00
Skeleton, Brass, Silver Dial, Fusee Movement, 8-Day, Rosewood Base, 13 x 7 In. 2310.00
Skeleton, Brass, Silver Dial, Fusee Movement, 8-Day, Wood Base, 19th Century, 12 In. ... 935.00
Skeleton, Brass, Time & Strike, Fusee Movement, Marble Base, 13 1/4 x 7 x 4 3/4 In. 770.00
Skeleton, Fusee Movement, Time Only, 10 1/2 x 5 1/2 In. 330.00
Skeleton, Silvered Metal, Pierced Chapter Ring, Bun Feet, England, 19th Century, 15 In. . 980.00
Skeleton, Wood Base, Glass Dome, England, 17 x 12 In. 1550.00
Smith & Goodrich, Shelf, Ogee, Mahogany Veneer, Cornucopia & Lyre, 30-Hour 120.00
Soldier Dressed For Battle, Swing Arm, Germany, 13 In. 150.00
Starr, Theodore B., Mantel, Brass, Japy Freres Movement, France, 10 3/4 x 6 x 5 In. 400.00
Streeter, E.W., Carriage, Brass, Repeating, London, 20th Century, 6 5/8 In. 470.00
Table, Mahogany, 2-Train, Dome Case, Handle, Signed, 1800s, 19 In. 1410.00
Tall Case, 2 Walnut Boxes, Brass Rods, Pyramid Shape, Rivet Markers, Key, 67 x 12 In. . 430.00
Tall Case, 30-Hour, English Oak Case, 2 Winding Arbors, c.1840 .... 1495.00
Tall Case, 8-Day, Weight Driven, White Painted Dial, Inlay, Andrew Robertson, c.1810 .. 11500.00
Tall Case, Aesthetic, Black, Gold Rosettes, Oval Bevel Glass, Enamel, Brass Dial, 66 In. . 4480.00
Tall Case, Art Deco, Mahogany Burl Veneer, 8-Day, Brass Movement, 55 x 10 x 7 1/2 In. 450.00

Clock, Royal Bonn, Mantel,
Porcelain, Blue, Yellow, Brown,
Ansonia, 14 In.

Clock, Royal Bonn, Mantel,
Porcelain, Green, Pink,
Ansonia, 11 In.

Clock, Tall Case, E. Howard
& Co., Burl Walnut,
Astronomical, No. 47, 96 In.

Tall Case, Arts & Crafts, Dark Mahogany, Cabinet Below, 18 x 13 x 76 In. 185.00
Tall Case, Best, Samuel, Cherry, Scalloped Corners, Urn Finial, 1803, 99 In. 9900.00
Tall Case, Black Forest, Owls, On Branches, Winged Eagle Pediment 16800.00
Tall Case, Brass Face, Time & Strike, 8-Day, Germany, 82 1/2 In. 310.00
Tall Case, Broken Arch Pediment, Shell Inlay, Ogee, Rocking Ship Face 4400.00
Tall Case, Bronze Mounts, Pendulum, Miniature, 19 In. 1290.00
Tall Case, Cherry, Broken Arch Top, Painted Dial, Brass, 85 x 18 In. 3335.00
Tall Case, Cherry, Broken Arch Top, Wooden Works, New England, 1780, 87 x 17 In. . . . 3800.00
Tall Case, Cherry, Federal, Birds & Flowers On Dial 3737.00
Tall Case, Cherry, Molded Pediment, Reeded Columns, 1830-1840, 88 1/2 x 18 In. 5750.00
Tall Case, Cherry, Walnut, 8-Day, Time & Strike, Moon Phase, American 2860.00
Tall Case, Chippendale, 18th Century, Pennsylvania 7760.00
Tall Case, Chippendale, Arched Door, Swan's-Neck Crest, Pa., Late 18th Century, 96 In. . 7765.00
Tall Case, Chippendale, Mahogany, Bonnet, Swan's-Neck Broken Arch, 96 x 23 x 11 In. . 5290.00
Tall Case, Chippendale, Mahogany, Red, White & Blue Dial, 8-Day, Newburyport, 57 In. . 3640.00
Tall Case, Chippendale, Tiger Maple, Roman, Arabic Numerals, 96 3/4 x 19 1/2 In. 3220.00
Tall Case, Chippendale, Walnut, Basket Of Flowers, Roman Numerals, 94 In. 2300.00
Tall Case, Dominy, Cherry, 1790 . . . . 8800.00
Tall Case, E. Howard & Co., Burl Walnut, Astronomical, No. 47, 96 In. . . . . *Illus* 77000.00
Tall Case, Eberman, Jos., Cherry, Broken Arch Top, 8-Day, Lancaster, 96 x 19 x 11 In. . . . 8525.00
Tall Case, Elm, Parcel Gilt, Inlay, Ebonized, Classical, Holland, Early 1900s, 111 In. 9200.00
Tall Case, Embossed Gilded Brass Pendulum, 1870s, 89 In. 1150.00
Tall Case, Erlvh, J., Mahogany, Panel Door, Sedgefield, England, 1830s, 92 x 21 In. 2690.00
Tall Case, Farquharson, A., Mahogany, Steel Face, Date & Seconds Dial, 89 In. 2760.00
Tall Case, Federal, Birch, Swan's Neck, Tombstone Door, Turned Columns, 1820, 87 In. . 8050.00
Tall Case, Federal, Cherry, Inlaid, Columned Door, Early 19th Century, 88 1/2 In. 5465.00
Tall Case, Federal, Inlaid Cherry, 3 Brass Finials, Conn., c.1810, 95 1/2 In. 12925.00
Tall Case, Federal, Inlaid Cherry, Pennsylvania, Early 19th Century 5460.00
Tall Case, Federal, Mahogany, Tiger Maple, Ogee Feet, 1840, 91 In. 9775.00
Tall Case, Flowers, Sailing Ships Scene, Windmill, Brass Works, Miniature 100.00
Tall Case, George III, Elm, Fruitwood, Brass Face, c.1800, 99 x 20 3/4 x 10 In. 2875.00
Tall Case, George III, Inlaid Mahogany, Glazed Door, 89 x 19 x 9 In. 7475.00
Tall Case, Gordon, P., Walnut, Silver Ring Dial, Seconds, Calendar, Hour Strike, 108 In. . . 6000.00
Tall Case, Hoadley, S., Bonnet Top, Spindle Supports, Long Door, Bracket Feet, 89 In. . . . 2465.00
Tall Case, Hoadley, S., Bonnet Top, Wooden Works 3850.00
Tall Case, Hoadley, S., Pine, Quarter Columns, Wooden Works, Floral On Face, 90 In. . . . 2090.00
Tall Case, Hoadley, S., Wooden, Fretwork Top, Plymouth 2475.00
Tall Case, Hoadley, Silas, Grain Painted, Little House Painting Face, Brass Urn Finial . . . 2585.00
Tall Case, Inlaid Oak, Mahogany, Swan's-Neck Crest, Mid 19th Century, 87 In. 3335.00
Tall Case, Jones, Jacob, Butternut Finish, Brass Dial, Birds & Spandrels, 79 In. 14850.00
Tall Case, Leaded Glass Door, Shelves, 83 x 33 In. 1200.00
Tall Case, Leavenworth, W., Rose In Arch, Gold Wreath & Branches, 16 1/2 In. 140.00
Tall Case, Lister, Thomas, Oak, Brass Dial, Time & Strike, Calendar, 1740, 7 In. 1430.00
Tall Case, Mahogany, Ball Finials, Pierced Fretwork Crown, Wooden Dial, c.1780 . . . . . . 8960.00
Tall Case, Mahogany, Brass Works, Phases Of The Moon, 3 Ball & Eagle Finials 5500.00
Tall Case, Mahogany, Carved Pediment, England, 91 x 10 x 20 In. 3024.00
Tall Case, Mahogany, Domed, Beaded, Inlaid, Painted Face, Plinth Base, 90 x 21 In. 5020.00
Tall Case, Mahogany, Glazed & Arched Panel Door, England, 1840s, 89 In. 1460.00
Tall Case, Mahogany, Molded Waist & Door, Glass Panel, Brass Finials, 87 1/2 In. 2100.00
Tall Case, Mahogany, Painted Dial, Free-Standing Columns, 1850s, 81 In. 3000.00
Tall Case, Mahogany, Satinwood Inlay, Swan Pediment, Moon Phase Dial 1570.00
Tall Case, Oak, Arched Panel Door, Carved Door, Mask Heads, Brass Dial, c.1890, 91 In. 1790.00
Tall Case, Oak, Cornice, Beveled Panels, Carved Medallion, Plinth Base, c.1910, 84 In. . . 575.00
Tall Case, Oak, Mahogany Veneer, Fan Inlays, Beaded Door, 83 In. 2970.00
Tall Case, Ober, Henry, Federal, Cherry, Castle Top, Plinths, 8-Day, Elizabethtown, 96 In. 5500.00
Tall Case, Ocsar Onken Co., Mahogany, Brass Bracket Feet, Glass Door, 94 1/2 In. 2090.00
Tall Case, Olivewood Over Pine, Stepped Base, Brass Works & Weights, 84 1/2 In. 770.00
Tall Case, Painted, Broken Arch Top, Wood Finials, 30-Hour, 89 x In. 2640.00
Tall Case, Painted, Tombstone Door, Bombay Throat, Tapered Pedestal, 1700s, 72 In. 1570.00
Tall Case, Pine, Painted, Molded Door, New England, c.1820, 81 x 19 1/2 x 11 1/2 In. . . . 1955.00
Tall Case, Read & Watson, Cherry, 30-Hour, Strike, Wooden Works, 89 1/2 In. 2200.00
Tall Case, Reeded Columns, Fretwork, Brass Finials, Church In Arch, 92 1/4 In. 6875.00
Tall Case, Regency, Drum Head, Scotland, Mid 19th Century, 76 x 20 1/4 x 10 In. 5060.00

Tall Case, Regency, Mahogany, Scotland, Early 19th Century, 86 x 18 1/4 x 8 1/2 In. 5175.00
Tall Case, Revere, Ash, 8-Day, Moon Phase Dial, Westminster Strike, 72 x 18 In. 1870.00
Tall Case, Rococo, Walnut, 3 Weights, Cartouche, Engraved, Pendulum, 93 In. 3360.00
Tall Case, Rococo, Walnut, Atlas Supporting Celestial Globe, Holland, 120 In. 6600.00
Tall Case, Sanford, E., Federal, Grain Painted, Plymouth, Conn., 82 x 18 1/2 x 9 3/4 In. ... 3520.00
Tall Case, Schofield, Joseph, Mahogany, 1785 .... 2475.00
Tall Case, Schwartz, Peter, Queen Anne, Walnut, 30-Hour, Arched Dial, York, 118 In. 745.00
Tall Case, Sheraton, Mahogany, Swan Neck, 8-Day Movement, 97 x 21 1/2 x 9 In. 6325.00
Tall Case, Shop Of The Crafters, Mahogany Veneer, Roman Numerals, 85 x 13 In. 8000.00
Tall Case, Storr, Marmaduke, Brass Face, Man In Moon Dial, Mahogany, 90 In. 3850.00
Tall Case, Thompson, A. & J., Oak, Brass & Steel Face, Chime, Quarter Strike 1840.00
Tall Case, Tiger Maple, Carved, Brass Movement, Kutztown, Pa., 19th Century, 101 In. ...10925.00
Tall Case, Todd, J.W., Mahogany, Broken Arch Top, Stepped Waist, Glasgow, 84 In. 2970.00
Tall Case, Walnut, 8-Day, Arched Door, Painted Dial, Moon Calendar, c.1815, 96 In. 8500.00
Tall Case, Walnut, Burled Panels, Calendar, 104 x 15 x 22 In. 7840.00
Tall Case, Walnut, Enamel Dial, Black Chapters, Basket Of Flowers, Brass, 1850s, 99 In. . 1840.00
Tall Case, Walnut, Inlaid Tiger Maple, 8-Day, Tombstone Door, Crossbanded Base, 92 In. . 2185.00
Tall Case, Walnut, Tombstone Door, Hood, North Carolina, c.1810, 92 x 19 1/2 x 11 In. .. 8580.00
Tall Case, Watson, L., Cherry, Mahogany Band Under Hood, 1809, 96 In. 2035.00
Tall Case, Whiting, R., Grained Design Over Red Base Coat, Wire Hinges, 1835, 85 In. .. 1650.00
Tall Case, Whiting, R., Painted Dial, Broken Arch Pediment, Connecticut, 83 In. 2760.00
Tall Case, Wilson, James, Cherry, Late 18th Century, 94 In. 4600.00
Tall Case, Wingate, Frederick, Grained Bird's-Eye Maple, Reeded Columns, Painted Face 7700.00
Tall Case, Woolley Codnor, Oak, Brass Dial, Inscribed, 74 In. 575.00
Terry, Eli, Shelf, Mahogany Case, Reverse Painted Scene In Door, Strikes Hour 3895.00
Terry, Eli, Shelf, Painted Face, Lion Claw Feet, Wooden Works, c.1825, 30 1/2 In. 135.00
Terry & Andrews, Shelf, Beehive, Rosewood Veneer, Painted Dial, Bristol, Conn. 415.00
Terry & Andrews, Steeple On Steeple, Walnut, Roman Numerals, 8-Day, 26 x 13 In. 1025.00
Terry & Andrews, Steeple, Walnut Veneer, Reverse Painted Tablet 405.00
Terry & Sons, Pillar & Scroll, Brass Finials, Reverse Painted, 29 x 17 1/2 In. 1438.00
Tiffany clocks that are part of desk sets made by Louis Comfort Tiffany are listed in the
Tiffany category. Clocks sold by the store, Tiffany & Co., are listed here.
Time Recording Co., Oak, International Time Clock, Oak, Endicott, N.Y., 47 In. 440.00
Travel, Gilt Silver, Enamel Landscape, Onyx Base, Case, Continental, Late 1800s 1265.00
Travel, Silver & Tortoiseshell, Nickel Case, 8-Day, c.1910, 4 3/8 x 3 3/4 In. 290.00
Travel, Sterling Silver & Enamel, Roses, 20th Century, 2 1/2 In. 145.00
Travel, Van Cleef & Arpels, 18K Gold, Goldtone Dial, Square 1150.00
Travel, Van Cleef & Arpels, Metal, Domed Cylinder, 20 Diamonds, Inscribed, 1935 ..... 290.00
Turquoise & Blue Enamel, Copper Dial, Tudric, c.1906, 6 3/16 In. 3105.00
Union Mfg. Co., Shelf, Empire, Mahogany, Reverse Painted, Conn., 26 x 15 1/2 In. 172.00
United Clock Co., Our Uncle Sam, Roosevelt, North Atlantic Treaty, 1944, 11 x 13 In. ... 316.00
Vincenti & Cie., Mantel, Dome Top, Finials, Rectangular, 1860s, 12 1/2 In. 150.00
Vincenti & Cie., Regulator, Molded Brass, Oval Case, 8-Day, Porcelain Dial, 9 In. 360.00
Wag-On-Wall, Cherry, Quarter Columns, Weights, Pendulum, 98 In. 2750.00
Wag-On-Wall, Mahogany, Roman Numerals, 19th Century, 60 In. 575.00
Wall, Arts & Crafts, Brass Face, Repousse, Pendulum, England, 11 x 13 x 8 In. 865.00
Wall, Bronze, Lion, Ram's Heads, 30 In. 1400.00
Wall, Carved Oak, Beveled Glass Door, Westminster Chime, 48 In. 840.00
Wall, Carved Walnut, Floral Gilt Metal Dial, Stylized Florets, Spain, 39 x 10 In. 490.00
Wall, Empire Style, Gilt Bronze, Sunburst Shape, Tiffany & Co., 24 In. 920.00
Wall, Giltwood, Porcelain Face, Carved Thistle, Ribbon Bowknot Finial, 18 x 8 In. 600.00
Wall, Gothic, Full Standing Griffins, Cherubs, Maidenheads, 30 In. 1400.00
Wall, Half Strike, Reverse Painting, Ebonized Case, 1880s, 15 1/8 In. 260.00
Wall, Metal Scrollwork, Flying Bird, Nest On Crest, Chain Hanger, Electric, 24 In. 140.00
Wall, Napoleon III, Black & Gold, Carved, Wood, Late 19th Century, 22 1/2 x 19 In. 920.00
Wall, Scalloped, Ebonized Wood Frame, Mother-Of-Pearl Inlay, Paper Dial, 24 In. 103.00
Wall, Walnut, Carved, Winged Maidens, Gilt Caryatids, 50 x 28 In. 4200.00
Wall, Walnut, Gothic, Westminster Chime, Signed H. Rouge, 50 In. 1680.00
Wall, Walnut, Time & Strike, Spring Wind, Germany 110.00
Wall, Walnut, Turned Column Supports, Enamel Face, Barometer, Vienna, c.1890, 36 In. . 250.00
Waterbury, Carriage, Bracket Feet, 2 x 2 In. 80.00
Waterbury, Carriage, Brass, Beveled Glass, Roman Numerals, Alarm, 4 x 3 In. 60.00
Waterbury, Carriage, Brass, Rectangular, Swing Handle, Beveled Glass, 2 x 2 1/2 In. 170.00

Waterbury, Carriage, Rectangular, Swing Handle, Beveled Glass, 2 x 2 1/2 In. 175.00
Waterbury, Mantel, Porcelain, Urn Shape, Sailboat Scene, 2 Handles, 14 x 11 In. 550.00
Waterbury, Porcelain, Scene, 2 Women In Field, 18 x 15 In., 2 Piece 700.00
Waterbury, Shelf, Beehive, Painted Metal Dial, Reverse Painted, 30-Hour 130.00
Waterbury, Steeple, 8-Day, Chimes, 1880s, 19 In. 230.00
Waterbury, Wall, Augusta, Oak, 8-Day Time & Strike, 51 In. 360.00
Watson, L., Mantel, Stenciled Gold Leaves, Baskets Of Fruit Corners, 1809, 35 3/4 In. . . 495.00
Weber, K.E.M., Aluminum, Elliptical, Bakelite Stand, Flip Numbers, 1934, 4 x 7 In. 430.00
Welch, Beehive, Rosewood, 18 x 11 In. 175.00
Welch, Calendar, Wall, Rosewood Case, Painted Metal Dial, 8-Day, 1870, 32 1/2 In. 1485.00
Welch, E.N., Beehive, Rosewood, 8-Day, Metal Dial, 18 In. 195.00
Welch, E.N., Ogee, 8-Day, Mahogany Veneer, Eagle Tablet, Metal Dial 110.00
Welch, Mantel, Patti, Rosewood, 8-Day, Time & Strike, c.1875, 18 x 12 1/4 In. 1870.00
Welch, School, Rosewood Case, Painted Metal Dial, 8-Day, 1870, 25 In. 250.00
Welch, Shelf, Beehive, Mahogany, Reverse Painted Bottom Tablet, Label, 19 In. 200.00
Welch, Wall, Calendar, Astronomical, Rosewood, Paper Dial, 1870, 30 x 17 In. 6600.00
Welch Spring & Co., Calendar, Double Dial, Walnut Case, 1870, 31 x 20 In. 2695.00
White Onyx, Portico Shape, Gilt Ormolu, Dial, Vincenti & Cie Movement, Tiffany & Co. 1760.00
Willard, Aaron, Shelf, Fretwork Crest, Bell-Form Dial, Mahogany, c.1810 . . . . 8500.00

CLOISONNE enamel was developed during the tenth century. A glass enamel was applied between small ribbons of metal on a metal base. Most cloisonne is Chinese or Japanese. Pieces marked *China* are twentieth-century examples.

Bowl, Finial Cover, Pink & White Mums, Black Ground, Chinese, 6 4/3/4 In. 50.00
Bowl, Indian Lotus, Chinese Characters, Blue, Green, Red, Yellow Ground, Chinese, 8 In. 350.00
Bowl, Melon Ribbed, Cover, Polychrome, Black Ground, Phoenix, 6 x 3 1/4 In., Pair 495.00
Bowl, Multicolored Flowers, Vines, Yellow Ground, Chinese, 9 x 4 In. 250.00
Bowl, Petal Rim, Mums & Bird, Blue Ground, Chinese, 15 x 5 1/2 In. 350.00
Box, Cover, Peach Form, On 3 Leaves, Shou Medallions, Light Green, Chinese, 6 1/2 In. . 145.00
Box, Oval, Phoenix, Flower, 2 1/2 In. 600.00
Box, Rectangular, Bracket Feet, Butterfly, Flowers, Blue Ground, 4 3/4 In. 460.00
Charger, Water Lilies, Ducks On Border, Center Duck, Birds & Insects, 12 In. 190.00
Ewer, Dragon, Bulbous Body, Shaped Spout, Early 20th Century, 11 1/4 In. 375.00
Figurine, Korean Warrior, Colored Enamel On Coat, Dagger In Belt, Arrows, 16 1/4 In. . . 360.00
Figurine, Rooster, Green Feathers, Red & Blue Tail Feathers, Chinese, 7 In. 500.00
Figurine, Woman, Multicolored Chrysanthemums On Robe, 15 3/4 In. 192.00
Garniture Set, Flowers, Foo Dog, Gilt Bronze Mounted, 3 Piece 3450.00
Ginger Jar, Finial Cover, Mums, Black Ground, Chinese, 6 3/4 In. 40.00
Incense Burner, Bird Shape, Bat Design, Blue, 6 1/2 In., Pair 460.00
Incense Burner, Oriental Cartouches, Flowers & Bats, Legs Of Monsters, 9 In. 40.00
Incense Burner, Quail Shape, Cover In Bird's Back, Chinese, 1800, 5 In., Pair 2760.00
Jar, Cover, Allover Flowers, Blue Shades, Light Blue Ground, Chinese, 5 1/4 In. 40.00
Jar, Cover, Inverted Pear Shape, Flower, Butterfly 127.00
Jar, Cover, Round, Mythical Animals, Japan, Meiji Period, Late 1800s, 8 In. 259.00
Jar, Domed Cover, Coiling Dragon, Dragons On Sides, Chinese, 8 3/8 In. 170.00
Jardiniere, Aventurine, Polychrome, Animal, Leaves, Flower Reserves, 8 In. 240.00
Jardiniere, Black, Blue Interior, 12 In., Pair 4500.00
Ornament, Mythical Dragon, 20th Century, Pair 230.00
Plate, Crane & Millet Reverse, Grapes, Butterfly Border, 1911, 11 1/2 In. 690.00
Plate, Dragon & Phoenix Design, Clouds, Blue Ground, Chinese, 15 In. 1000.00
Plate, Ducks, Fish, Pedestal, Fluted, Chinese, 15 3/4 x 11 3/4 x 4 1/2 In. 750.00
Plate, Indian Lotus, Light Blue Ground, Pedestal, 6 1/4 x 3 1/2 In. 75.00
Plate, Petal, 6 Cranes, Cherry Blossoms, Flowers, Blue Rim, Chinese, 15 In. 500.00
Plate, Pheasants, Flowering Outcropping, Blues & Purple, Chinese, 14 7/8 In. 350.00
Plate, Polychrome Flowers, Tang Dynasty Horse, Green Saddle, 9 7/8 In. 165.00
Scepter, 3 Plaques Inset In Wooden Carved Frame, Early 20th Century, 22 In. 115.00
Teapot, Peonies, Insects, Black Ground, Chinese, 6 x 4 1/2 In. 100.00
Tray, Brocade, Rooster & Hen, Square, 1911, 10 1/2 In. 2530.00
Vase, 2 Enameled Scenes, Yellow Ground, Light Green Swirls, 4 1/2 In. 225.00
Vase, 5-Clawed Dragon, Red Ground, Early 20th Century, 6 1/8 In., Pair 115.00
Vase, 6 Dragons, Multicolored Accents, 4 1/4 In. 800.00
Vase, 18 Lohans Scene, 4 In. 150.00

Vase, 37 Figure Center Band, Allover Blue, Ring Handles, 12 In. 55.00
Vase, Allover Peonies & Mums, Multicolored Birds, Black Ground, Chinese, 12 In. 125.00
Vase, Baluster Shape, Waisted Neck, Cobalt Blue Ground, Wood Stand, 12 In., Pair 1265.00
Vase, Baluster Shape, Wisteria, Chrysanthemum, Blue Ground, 7 1/4 In. 430.00
Vase, Bamboo Edged Panels, Cranes & Flowers, Silver Mounts, 2 7/8 In. 470.00
Vase, Bats & Scrolling Leaves, Japan, c.1900, 15 In. 145.00
Vase, Bird, Chrysanthemum, Mustard Ground, Japan, Late 1800s, 7 1/4 In. 460.00
Vase, Birds, Flowers, Branches, 5 In. 33.00
Vase, Black Ground, 13 Crested Cranes, Silvered Base, Japan, 19th Century, 8 1/2 In. 144.00
Vase, Butterflies & Flowers, Black Ground, 1911, 6 In. 460.00
Vase, Circular Roses, Green Dragon, Silver Rim At Top, Suzuki Mark, 7 1/2 In. 395.00
Vase, Cover, Free-Form Flowers, Amber, Brown & Dark Green, 6 1/2 In., Pair 55.00
Vase, Domed Cover, Butterfly, Flower, Gold, Namikawa Ysuyuki, 4 1/2 In. 9200.00
Vase, Dragon, Midnight Blue Ground, 1911, 6 In. 316.00
Vase, Enameled Flowers, Green Vines, Yellow Ground, 4 In. 225.00
Vase, Flowering Vine, Black Ground, 19th Century, 4 In., Pair 230.00
Vase, Formalized Lotus Scrolls, 19th Century, 17 In., Pair 690.00
Vase, Horses, Pink Ground, 1911, 3 In. 630.00
Vase, Lotus Flowers, Dark Blue Ground, Chinese, 12 In. 225.00
Vase, Multicolored Flowers Lower Base, Blues & Greens, Chinese, 12 In. 225.00
Vase, Multicolored Flowers, Red Birds, Dark Blue Ground, Chinese, 12 1/4 In. 175.00
Vase, Oval, Bulbous, Bird, Branches, Flowers, Blue Enamel, Mocha Ground, 14 In. 900.00
Vase, Pear Shape, Chrysanthemum, Leaf Ground, 4 3/4 In. 230.00
Vase, Pear Shape, Floral Medallion, Olive Green Matte Ground, 10 1/4 In. 860.00
Vase, Phoenix, Butterfly, Dragon, Japan, Early 20th Century, 10 In. 690.00
Vase, Red, White & Green Flowers, Brass Trim, 13 3/4 x 5 1/2 In. 310.00
Vase, Roses, Red Foil Ground, Silver Base & Rim, Suzuki, 7 1/2 In. 395.00
Vase, Sage, On Dragon, Dark Blue Speckled Gold Neck, Flattened Oval, Japan, 12 In. ... 2190.00
Vase, Square, Red, Flowers, Birds, 9 In. 225.00
Vase, Taito, Pilgrim Flask Shape, Bird, Flower, Meiji Period, 8 1/2 In. 170.00
Vase, Taito, Seed Shape, Flower, Meiji Period, 8 In. 69.00
Vase, Turquoise, Green, Signed Ando, 10 3/4 In. 1380.00
Wine Pot, Cover, Dragons, Black Ground, Reservoir Interior, Chinese, 4 1/4 In. 150.00
Wine Pot, Cover, Multicolored Lotus, White Ground, Handle, Oblong, Chinese, 8 In. 400.00
Wine Pot, Enamel, Oval, Flowers, 4 1/2 In. 126.00

CLOTHING of all types is listed in this category. Dresses, hats, shoes,
underwear, and more are found here. Other textiles are to be found in
the Coverlet, Movie, Quilt, Textile, and World War I and II categories.

Apron, Cotton, Embroidered Flowers, Potholder Pocket, 20 1/2 x 24 1/2 In. 6.00
Apron, Half, Be Nice To Me I've Had A Bad Day, Terry Cloth, Cotton, 15 3/4 x 19 1/4 In. 8.00
Apron, Half, Crocheted, 13 x 18 In. 14.00
Apron, Half, Handkerchief, 16 1/2 x 29 In. 8.00
Apron, Silk, Embroidered, England, c.1720 .... 695.00
Apron, Silk, Embroidered, Queen Anne, Green, Red, Metallic Threads, c.1710 .... 1200.00
Bag, Evening, Blue Cabochon Snaps, Silver Oval Link Chain, 7 x 7 In. 168.00
Bathing Suit, Man's, 100% Wool, Moana Hotel, c.1930s 1600.00
Belt, Silk, Embroidered, Yellow, Bats & Flowering Branches, Late Qing, Chinese 115.00
Belt, Sterling Silver, Pierced Linked Plaques, Lozenge Shaped Buckle, England 431.00
Bobby Hat, Wreath Marked CPD, Tan Felt, Brass Finial, Brass Band, England, 1890s 275.00
Bonnet, Homespun Linen, Red, Green Silk, Metallic Embroidery, 1700s, Infant's 395.00
Boots, Lace Up, Voyagers, 10 In. 60.00
Boots, Riding, Leather, Wooden Boot Forms, England, 20th Century 118.00
Burnoose, Embroidery, Arts & Crafts, Silk, Pink & Cream, Liberty Of London, 1911 .... 770.00
Caftan, Embroidery, Metallic, Floral & Scalloped Center Front, Morocco, 1930s 288.00
Cap, Police, Double Eagle 207.00
Cape, Beaver, Sheared, Short 56.00
Cape, Mink, Natural Brown, Styled For Esther Parker 56.00
Cape, Stenciled, Red Lining, Gallenga, 1930s 4313.00
Chemise, Allover Silver Bugle Beads, Tied Bow & Streamers, V-Neck, Lanvin, 1929 .... 6900.00
Coat, Art Deco, Lame, Tan & Gold, Block Design, Velvet Lining, France, 1920s, Size 6 .. 1093.00
Coat, Denim, Indigo, 4 Breast Pockets, Wrangler, Size 34 .... 43.00
Coat, Embroidered, Knee Length, Shawl Fur Collar, Fur Lined, Chinese, 1920s 1495.00

Clothing, Hat, Love Letter, Linen Covered,
Printed Hearts & Messages, Bes-Ben

Clothing, Hat, Casino, Silk Printed,
Chips & Playing Cards, Bes-Ben

Clothing, Hat, Pillbox, Penguin, Black, Bes-Ben

Coat, Evening, Felted Wool, Pin Tucked Top, Lace Trimmed Sleeves & Bodice, Worth ... 3450.00
Coat, Mink, 3/4 Sleeves, Collar, Flap Pockets, 3 Buttons, Marilyn Monroe Owned 15000.00
Coat, Mink, Natural Brown, Paul Disjarden's Furs, Lewiston, 3/4 Length 336.00
Coat, Mink, Natural Gray Female, Murphy's, Lewiston, 1/2 Length 336.00
Coat, Raccoon, Murphy's, Lewiston, Full-Length 616.00
Coat, Silk, Dark Blue, Embroidered, Gold Floral & Vase, Chinese 825.00
Coat, Wool, Ranch Mink Collar, 1950s 150.00
Coat, Wool, Red & Black Plaid, 2 Slot Pockets, 5 Plastic Buttons, Penn-Rich, 1940s 55.00
Dress, Beaded, Chiffon, Multiple Beaded Tiers, Front Tier At Low Waist, 1920s, Size 4 .. 860.00
Dress, Chemise, Raspberry Velvet, Allover Floral, Embroidered Beads, 1910, Size 6 ..... 863.00
Dress, Chemise, Sleeveless, Low Waist, Beaded Band, Allover Floral, 1920s, Size 6 ..... 805.00
Dress, Chemise, Sleeveless, Sequins At Center & Sides, Bottom Loops, 1920s, Size 6 ... 3160.00
Dress, Chemise, White Chiffon, Allover Seed Pearls, Pointed Hemline, 1920s, Size 8 ... 1035.00
Dress, Cocktail, Black Faille, Tulip Shaped Skirt, Elbow Length Sleeves, Laurent, 1959 .. 1150.00
Dress, Cocktail, Random Placed Cut Bugle Beads, Over Blouse, Traina-Norell, c.1957 ... 2588.00
Dress, Court, Ivory Satin, Allover Flowers, Beaded Shoulder Trim, 1920s, Size 8 .... 9775.00
Dress, Evening, Black Crepe, Strapless, Sequined Band, Pearls & Beads, Adrian, Size 4 .. 6900.00
Dress, Evening, Cut Velvet, Tulle Bodice, Pearls, Bows At Shoulders, c.1910, Size 8 .... 805.00
Dress, Evening, Navy, Sequined, Full-Length, Bill Blass, 1970s 975.00
Dress, Flapper, Embroidered Flower Sprays, 1925-1929 .... 700.00
Dress, Garden Party, Embroidered, Pin Tucked Sleeves, France, Size 4 .... 978.00
Dress, Knit Sheath, Pink, V Back, Sequined Bodice To Hem, Balmain, 1960s, Size 6 .... 1035.00
Dress, Navy Blue, Silk, Sequined, c.1920 .... 3400.00
Dress, Sheath, Black Velvet, Strapless, Floor Length, Oscar De La Renta, 1960s 462.00
Dress, Train, Pingat Apple Design, E. Pingat, 60 Rue Louis Le Grande, Paris, c.1890 .... 4025.00
Dress, Tricot, Satin Buttons Down Side, Faux Button Holes, Chiffon Dickey, c.1915 ..... 870.00
Dress, Wedding, Satin, Beaded Medallions, Chiffon Top, Back Forms Into Train, Size 8 .. 690.00
Ensemble, Daytime, Wool, Velvet, Broadcloth, Madeleine Vionnet, c.1935, Size 4 ...... 4310.00
Gloves, Lace, Fingers Out, Ruffled Wrist, 1940s 45.00
Hat, Beaver, HB On Ornate Silver Band, Montreal 2530.00
Hat, Casino, Silk Printed, Chips & Playing Cards, Bes-Ben .... *Illus* 978.00
Hat, Cloche, Sequined, Black, 1940s 75.00
Hat, Love Letter, Linen Covered, Printed Hearts & Messages, Bes-Ben .... *Illus* 518.00
Hat, Pillbox, Penguin, Black, Bes-Ben .... *Illus* 518.00
Helmet, Dragoon Officer, Gilt, Comb, Plume, Leaf Chinstrap, France, c.1890, 11 In. 316.00
Jacket, Big Ben Chore, 4 Stitched Pockets, Brass Rivet Buttons, Wrangler, Size 34 ...... 40.00
Jacket, Biker, Leather, Wine Quilted Lining, Sears Hercules, 1950s, Size 44 .... 395.00
Jacket, Cotton, Ornate, Silver Plastic Buttons, India, Large 25.00
Jacket, Dark Blue House Denim, Open Front Pockets, Brass Button, Size 38 .... 55.00
Jacket, Denim, Big E-Mode, Metal Buttons, Levi, 1969, Medium 150.00
Jacket, Denim, Blue, 2 Breast Pockets, Sanforized Label, Lee, Medium 22.00
Jacket, Denim, Indigo Blue, 2 Pockets, Levi, Size 42 .... 21.00
Jacket, Embroidered Allover Peonies & Scorpions, Woman's, Late 19th Century 489.00
Jacket, Mink, Dark Brown, Bond Furs, Pasadena, Short 291.00
Jacket, Rider's, Leather, Black, Zippers, Brooks, 1960s, Large 238.00
Jacket, Warm-Up, Blue Nylon, 3 White Stripes On Shoulders, Adidas, Medium 20.00
Jacket, Windbreaker, White Body, Mesh Lining, Adidas, Small 245.00

Jeans, Indigo Denim, Casey Jones, Orange Stitching, 1950s, 30 x 30 In. 140.00
Kerchief, Polychrome Embroidered Border, Ties, c.1750 .... 250.00
Kimono, Silk, Beige, Embroidered Phoenix, Flowering Branches, Japan 375.00
Kimono, Silk, Blue, Embroidered & Painted Prunus Blossoms, Japan 185.00
Pants, Cotton, Gray, Lined Waist, Old Hickory, 34 x 32 In. 27.00
Pants, Wool, Plaid, Tapered To Laced Calf, L.L. Bean, 1898 .... 575.00
Robe, Brocade, Red & Gold, Allover Flowering Branches, Gold Buttons, Turkey 460.00
Robe, Ceremonial, Silk, Multicolored Flowers & Bird Design, Japan 115.00
Robe, Dragon, Brocade Of Dragons, Purple Ground, 20th Century 546.00
Robe, Embroidered, Mandarin Imperial Court, Dragons, Clouds, Bats, 46 3/4 In. 2750.00
Robe, Poncho, Embroidered, Stripes, Africa, 44 In. 230.00
Robe, Silk Gauze, Embroidered, Large & Small Cranes, Red Silk Gauze, Chinese, 1920s . 1495.00
Robe, Silk, Coral, Embroidered, Sprays Of Flowers, Black Border, Chinese 489.00
Robe, Silk, Dark Blue, Velvet Rondels, Calligraphy, Chinese 2530.00
Robe, Silk, Red, Wan Character Frets, Double Sleeves, Gold Ground, 19th Century 3740.00
Robe, Winter, Dark Blue Ground, Rabbit Fur Lining, Late 19th Century 230.00
Robe & Petticoat, Lace, Silk, Flowers, Woven Silver Metallic Accents, c.1750 .... 2900.00
Sarong, Double Ikat, Russet, Blue, Flowers, Geometric, Indonesian, 1880s, 79 x 19 In. ... 460.00
Scarf, Gold Crowns & Arabesques, Navy Blue Ground, Red Border, Hermes, 1960s 115.00
Scarf, Western Scenes, Horses & Cowboys, 26 x 26 In. 45.00
Scarf, White, Silk, Zodiac Symbols, Names On Border, Peter Max, 1960s, 26 1/2 In. 40.00
Scarf, Zodiac Signs, Yellow Ground, Peter Max Copyright, 1970, 26 x 12 In. 40.00
Shawl, Paisley, Black Center, 64 x 69 In. 55.00
Shawl, Paisley, Black Center, Colonnaded Edges, 60 x 120 In. 66.00
Shawl, Paisley, Green Center, Design Radiated To Corners, 66 x 72 In. 55.00
Shawl, Paisley, Late 19th Century, 56 x 108 In. 230.00
Shawl, Paisley, Wool, Embroidered Scrolls, 19th Century, 62 1/2 x 59 1/2 In. 200.00
Shawl, Scrolling Florals, Kashmir, 19th Century, 66 x 66 In. 345.00
Shirt, Field, Secret Service, Cotton, Dark Blue Collar, 4 Flap Pockets, Medium 30.00
Shirt, Fireman's, Red Wool, Abalone Buttons, Leather Number 1 .... 1500.00
Shirt, Fireman's, Red Wool, Leather Number, Abalone Buttons, Mid 19th Century 695.00
Shirt, Green, Blue, Tan, Woven Leather Buttons, 1950s, Medium, Pair 34.00
Shirt, Hawaiian, White Pineapple Design, Blue Cotton, 1980s, Large 22.00
Shoe, Basketball, BF Goodrich PF, White Canvas, 1950s, Size 9 .... 138.00
Shoes, High Top, Leather, Lace-Up, 17 Eyelets, High Heels, c.1910, 9 In. 80.00
Shoes, Penny Loafers, Black Leather, G. H. Bass, 1960s 40.00
Shoes, Sport, Gray Suede Trim, White Nylon, Nike, 1981, 7 1/2 In. 48.00
Skirt, Poodle, Gray Felt, Pink & Black Poodle, Sequin Collar, Chain, 1950s, Small 40.00
Snowsuit, Child's, Rose Beige, Talon Zipper, Tie Belt, Knit Cuffs, 1940s, Size 1 .... 40.00
Socks, Buster Brown, With Label, Box, 1910 .... 280.00
Stockings, Crewelwork, Red, Green, Brown, White, 1830s, Small, Pair 255.00
Suit, Dinner, Short Coat Dress, Slim Skirt, Shoulder Loops, Pearl Buttons, Adrian, Size 8 . 2070.00
Suit, Man's, Black Velvet Jacket, Plaid Kilt, Leather Belt, Tasseled Sporran, Scotland 485.00
Suit, Tweed, Checkerboard Wool, Caped Jacket, Straight Skirt, Jaques Fath, 1950s 2185.00
Sweater, Cardigan, Wool, High School Letter, Gold, 1950, Medium 55.00
Sweater, Navy Blue, Pink, White Flowers, Catalina, 1940s, Medium 27.00
Sweatshirt, Cotton, White, Pilgrim, 1960s, Size 36 .... 56.00
Top Hat, Silk, Hudson Bay Company, Winnipeg, Case, 14 1/4 x 20 In. 143.00
Top Hat, Silk, Leather Case, Burkhart, Cincinnati, Ohio 250.00
Top Hat, Straw, Band & Buckles, American, Early 19th Century 750.00
Uniform, Military Academy, Wool, Blue, Ivory, Silver Buttons, 1880s 56.00
Waistcoat, Man's, Silk, Embroidered, Flowers, Vines, Pockets, Late 18th Century 230.00
Wig, Judicial, Ponytails, Leather Case, Stand, Name In Gold, England, 1800s 1150.00

CLUTHRA glass is a two-layered glass with small air pockets that form
white spots. The Steuben Glass Works of Corning, New York, made it
in 1920. Kimball Glass Company of Vineland, New Jersey, made
Cluthra from about 1925. Victor Durand signed some pieces with his
name. Related items are listed in the Steuben category.

Vase, Green, Flared, Bulbous, Signed, 6 In. 196.00
Vase, Trumpet, Red, Yellow, White, Signed, 10 3/4 In. 660.00

COALPORT ware has been made by the Coalport Porcelain Works of England from 1795 to the present time. Early pieces were unmarked. About 1810–1825 the pieces were marked with the name *Coalport* in various forms. Later pieces also had the name *John Rose* in the mark. The crown mark has been used with variations since 1881. The date 1750 is printed in some marks, but it is not the date the factory started. Some pieces are listed in Indian Tree.

Bowl, Flowers, Paneled Border, c.1825, Pair	310.00
Bowl, Japan Pattern, Shell Shape, Footed, c.1825, 1 3/4 x 8 1/4 x 8 In., Pair	1456.00
Coffee Set, Pink Roses, Demitasse, 15 Piece	310.00
Dinner Service, Montreal Pattern, Stylized Star, Dolphin & Fruit Border, 1900s, 83 Piece	517.00
Luncheon Service, Wenham Pattern, 62 Piece	287.00
Luncheon Set, Flowers, Blue Beaded Edge, Tiffany & Co., 9 In., 6 Piece	336.00
Plate, Athlone, Blue Rim, Gilt Edge, 10 In, 12 Piece	840.00
Plate, Bengal Tiger, Gilt Rim, c.1850, 8 1/4 In., 4 Piece	1792.00
Plate, Bird, Flower Cartouches, Enamel, Gilt, Blue, 9 In.	2585.00
Plate, Desert, Mountain Lake, Cobalt Blue Ground, Gilt, Marked, 9 In., 12 Piece	575.00
Plate, Dinner, Gilt, White, Flowers, Arches, 20th Century, 10 1/4 In., 12 Piece	316.00
Plate, Oriental Flowers, Early 19th Century, 6 Piece	356.00
Plate, White, Raised Relief Scrolling On Edges, Divided By Flowers, 10 7/8 In.	25.00
Platter, Blue & White, Gold Rim, Incised Crown Mark, c.1850, 36 x 20 In.	375.00
Vase, Cover, Landscape Vignettes, Dark Blue, Ivory, Edward O. Ball, c.1900, 12 In.	529.00
Vase, Gilt, 2 Handles, Marked, 6 5/8 In.	235.00

COBALT BLUE glass was made using oxide of cobalt. The characteristic bright dark blue identifies it for the collector. Most cobalt glass found today was made after the Civil War. There was renewed interest in the dark blue glass in the late 1930s and dinnerwares were made.

Creamer, Diamond-Quilted, Applied Handle & Foot, 4 1/2 In.	330.00
Pitcher, Blown, Lily Pad, 8 1/2 In.	770.00
Salt & Pepper, Pear Shape, Pewter Tops	165.00
Sugar, Cover, 16 Swirled Ribs, Pontil, 1800, 5 7/8 In.	2860.00
Sugar, Cover, Engraved 1812 One Side, Initials On Other, England, 4 1/2 In.	1073.00
Sugar, Domed Cover, Spiral Finial, 1797, 7 1/8 In.	1430.00
Vase, Blown, Rolled Rim, Egg Shape, 9 3/8 In., Pair	1045.00

COCA-COLA was first served in 1886 in Atlanta, Georgia. It was advertised through signs, newspaper ads, coupons, bottles, trays, calendars, and even lamps and clocks. Collectors want anything with the word *Coca-Cola*, including a few rare products, like gum wrappers and cigar bands. The famous trademark was patented in 1893, the *Coke* mark in 1945. Many modern items and reproductions are being made.

Airplane Hanger Set, Separating Paper, 1943, 13 x 15 In., 20 Piece	660.00
Ashtray, 12 Languages, Porcelain, 12 1/2 In.	105.00
Ashtray, Pullmatch, Bottle Beneath Lampshade, 7 1/2 In.	4070.00
Booklet, Freckles & Friends, Whitman	20.00
Bookmark, Embossed Cardboard Color Lithograph, Opera Star, 5 3/8 x 2 3/8 In.	550.00

Coca-Cola, Bottle,
Kentucky Derby,
May 4, 1996,
ACL, 8 Oz.

Watch out for exploding antiques! Guns, shells, powder cans, nitrate movie film, and some chemicals left in old bottles or cans are dangerous. If you don't know about these items, contact your local police or fire department for help.

Bottle, Kentucky Derby, May 4, 1996, ACL, 8 Oz. . . . . *Illus*   6.00
Bottle, Syrup, Drink Coca-Cola, White ACL, Tooled Mouth, Tin Cap, 1915, 11 In. 550.00
Bottle, Syrup, White ACL, Tooled Mouth, Tin Cap, c.1915, 11 In. 550.00
Bottle Opener, Have A Coke, Drink Coca-Cola On Reverse, Loop Handle 5.00
Bottle Opener, Thirst Knows No Season, 1952 . . . .   4.00
Bottle Protector, 1933 . . . .   10.00
Box, Chewing Gum, 20 Packs, Graphics, c.1916 . . . .   1210.00
Box, Straw, Full & Unopened, 1930s 250.00
Calendar, 1899, Hilda Clark, Embossed, Framed Under Glass, Museum Mount 6600.00
Calendar, 1906, Juanita, 5 Cent Bottle, Complete Pad 17050.00
Calendar, 1907, Girl With Green Dress, Holding Glass 6050.00
Calendar, 1926, Girl With Tennis Racket, Flared Glass, Cardboard, Full Pad, 13 x 21 In. . .   880.00
Calendar, 1931, Barefoot Boy, Full Pad With December 1930 Strip 2310.00
Calendar, 1949, Seated Girl, Wearing Hat, Blue Dress, Drinking Coke, 21 In. 55.00
Carton, 6 Bottles, Miniature, 3 In. 125.00
Chalkboard, Menu, 2 Bottles At Bottom, Easel, 1952, 19 x 29 In. 305.00
Change Purse, Leather, Brass, Gold Lettering 195.00
Clock, Countertop, Fluorescent Light, 1950s 578.00
Clock, Drink Coca-Cola In Bottles, Glass, Metal, Plastic, Light-Up, 16 1/2 In. 350.00
Clock, Fishtail Coca-Cola Logo, Glass Lens, 1960s, 15 x 15 In. 253.00
Clock, Neon Spinner, Silhouette Girl Logo, c.1940, 18 In. 770.00
Clock, Neon, Square, c.1940, 15 In. 1760.00
Clock, Relieves Exhaustion, Baird, 1893-1896, 16 x 26 1/2 In. 6325.00
Clock, Selectoclock, Glass, Wooden Frame, 1939, 16 x 16 In. 200.00
Clock Radio, Cooler Shape, 1950 . . . .   3630.00
Coin-Operated Machine, Vendo V-81B, 1950s, 27 x 58 x 16 In. 3680.00
Cooler, Galvanized Steel, Progress Refrigerator Co., 1940s, 19 x 12 x 8 1/2 In. 170.00
Cooler, Galvanized Steel, Progress Refrigerator Co., 1950s, 19 x 14 x 9 In. 115.00
Dispenser, Cup, Coca-Cola On Side, Triangular Metal, 1950s, 26 In. 468.00
Dispenser, Fountain, Outboard Motor, 10 x 22 x 19 In. 170.00
Display, Countertop, Showing Santa Claus With Little Boy, Die Cut, 26 1/2 In. 35.00
Display, Regular Size Coca-Cola, 6-Bottle Carton, Cardboard, Die Cut, 11 3/4 In. 90.00
Doll, Buddy Lee, In Uniform, 13 1/4 In. 120.00
Door Bar, Porcelain, c.1950, 30 In. 1100.00
Door Pull, Aluminum, Bottle Shape, 1940s, 12 In. 525.00
Door Push, 1950s, 8 In., Pair 1650.00
Door Push, Iced Here, 1952 On Reverse, 31 1/2 In. 150.00
Fan, Mountain Scene, Cardboard, 7 x 10 1/2 In. 10.00
Flyer, Lillian Russell, Free Glass, 1904, 9 1/2 x 6 1/2 In. 110.00
Kick Plate, Drink Coca-Cola, Porcelain, 1920s, 10 x 30 In. 710.00
Label, Cigar, Hobbleskirt Bottle 126.00
Lamp, Figural Bottle, Milk Glass, Metal Base, Tin Cap, Late 1920s, 20 In. 14300.00
Lampshade, Frosted Glass, Tassel, 1930s 1320.00
Lantern, Revolving, Footed, 1960s, 20 In. 743.00
Matchbook Holder, Leather 358.00
Menu Board, Be Refreshed, Die Cut Tin, 1958, 17 3/4 x 26 In. 110.00
Menu Board, Frame, Tin, 27 1/2 x 19 In. 80.00
Mirror, Elaine, Turned Head, Pocket, 1916 . . . .   495.00
Mirror, Girl, Bandana Around Head, Pocket, 1908 . . . .   358.00
Mirror, Woman, Drinking, Pocket, 1913, 1 3/4 x 2 3/4 In. 115.00
Mobile, Cold Coke & Hot Food, Late 1950s, 14 x 13 In., 3 Piece 201.00
Notebook, Leather, 1904 . . . .   121.00
Pencil Holder, 75th Anniversary, Victorian Urn Shape, 7 In. 94.00
Pin, Service, 60 Year, 12 Diamond Chips, Cloisonne, 10K Gold, Box, 9/16 In. 1980.00
Scorekeeper, Baseball, 1930s, 20 x 30 In. 1100.00
Server Set, Box, 1932, 50 Piece 75.00
Sign, 2 Women, 1 Leaning On Counter With Elbow, Coke! Too, 1946, 16 In. 100.00
Sign, 3 People, Play Refreshed, Small, 1950 . . . .   743.00
Sign, Airplane Hanger, Curtiss Warhawk, Pursuit U.S. Army Air Force, 1944, 15 In. 61.00
Sign, Airplane Hanger, Douglas Havoc, U.S. Army Air Force, 1944, 13 x 15 In. 55.00
Sign, Airplane Hanger, Grumman Avenger, Torpedo Bomber U.S. Navy, 1944, 15 In. 58.00
Sign, Arrow, Ice Cold, Sold Here, 2 Sides, Diecut, 1927, 8 x 30 In. 880.00
Sign, Arrow, October 1953, 12 In. 1100.00

Sign, Bottle Handed To Girl With Tennis Racket, 1945 .... 440.00
Sign, Cafe, Drink Coca-Cola, Porcelain, 42 1/2 x 62 1/2 In. 1155.00
Sign, Cap, Pick Up 12, 12-Pack Pilaster, 1953 .... 1540.00
Sign, Cap, Serve Coke At Home, 6-Pack Pilaster, 1956 .... 770.00
Sign, Cap, Take Home A Carton Of Quality Refreshment, 6-Pack Pilaster, 1951 .... 1045.00
Sign, Coca-Cola In Bottles, Neon, 1939, 12 x 24 In. 6820.00
Sign, Coca-Cola, Cardboard, 1929, 33 x 20 In. 470.00
Sign, Coke For Me, Girl Getting Bottle, Cardboard, 1940s, 30 x 50 In. 75.00
Sign, Delicious & Refreshing, Fountain Service, Porcelain, 2 Sides, 1934, 60 x 42 In. 1080.00
Sign, Delicious Coca-Cola, Refreshes You Best, Red Ground, 12 In. 200.00
Sign, Drink Coca-Cola, Delicious Refreshing, Red Ground, Tin, 32 3/4 x 57 In. 350.00
Sign, Drink Coca-Cola, Fountain Service, Porcelain, 12 x 28 In. 600.00
Sign, Drink Coca-Cola, Fountain Service, Red Ground, Porcelain, 14 x 27 In. 1550.00
Sign, Drink Coca-Cola, Frame, Tin, 11 3/4 x 31 3/4 In. 165.00
Sign, Drink Coca-Cola, Porcelain, 1941, 25 1/4 x 26 1/4 In. 1000.00
Sign, Drink Coca-Cola, Wood Frame, Cardboard, Wood, Metal, 1950, 31 1/4 In. 85.00
Sign, Female Aviator, WWII Theme, Cardboard Lithograph, c.1940, 19 3/4 x 36 In. 2640.00
Sign, Girl In Boat, Wherever Thirst Goes, Cardboard, Horizontal, 1942 .... 743.00
Sign, Girl On Ping-Pong Table, Cardboard, String Hanger, 1938, 14 1/2 x 32 In. 688.00
Sign, Girl On Ski Slope, So Delicious, Cardboard, 1950s 525.00
Sign, Hospitality, Man & 2 Women, Cardboard, Canada, 1948, 62 x 33 In. 290.00
Sign, Lady Holding Bottle, Paper, 1913, 18 x 24 In. 7700.00
Sign, Lady Sitting On Log With Ice Skates, Cardboard, 1940, 29 1/2 x 50 In. 990.00
Sign, Lillian Nordica, Raised Oval Edge, Cardboard, String, 1904, 8 1/4 x 10 1/2 In. 22000.00
Sign, Mother & Daughter, Summer Floral Setting, Cardboard, 1950, 62 x 33 In. 260.00
Sign, Now! King Size Too! Same Sparkling Refreshment, Lime Green, 20 In. 40.00
Sign, Official Soft Drink Of Summer, 3-Color Neon, 1989, 24 In. 715.00
Sign, Pause, Go Refreshed, Bell Fountain Glass, Celluloid, Round, 1950s, 9 In. 3410.00
Sign, Porcelain, Curb Service, Silhouette Waitress & Car, 36 x 52 In. 1725.00
Sign, Santa Drinking Coke, The Pause That Refreshes, 24 x 11 1/2 In. 40.00
Sign, School Zone, Drive Safely, 2 Sides, Plywood, 1956, 16 x 48 In. 1430.00
Sign, Sign Of Good Taste, Vertical, 1960, 18 x 54 In. 300.00
Sign, Slow School Zone, Drive Safely, Girl Running 750.00
Sign, Snowman With Bottle, Cardboard, String Hanger, Canada, 1941, 16 x 27 In. 248.00
Sign, Take A Case Home Today For $1.00, Hand Holding Bottle, 1949 .... 600.00
Sign, The Pause That Refreshes, Light-Up, Moving, c.1930, 12 x 20 In. 9020.00
Sign, Things Go Better With Coke, Ice Cold, Full Cup, 1960s, 28 x 20 In. 2200.00
Sign, Things Go Better, 1960s, 18 x 54 In. 385.00
Sign, Verbena Hanging Festoon, Cardboard, Ribbon Attaches Pieces, 1932, 5 Piece 2970.00
Sign, Village Blacksmith, Norman Rockwell, 1933 .... 715.00
Sign, Waitress With Couple At Counter, Frame, 1912 .... 1100.00
Sign, Waitress, Lunch Refreshed, Cardboard, 1948, 16 x 27 In. 1760.00
Stadium Backpack & Vendor, Premix, Strap, Cup Dispenser, 1950s 580.00
Stringholder, 2 Sides, Tin, 1940s 5170.00
Sundial, Bottle Forms Timer 4235.00
Thermometer, 3-D, Plastic, 14 3/4 x 5 1/2 x 3 In. 10.00
Thermometer, Die Cut Tin Bottle, 17 1/8 In. 70.00
Thermometer, Masonite, Thirst Knows No Season, Coke Bottle, 1940s, 7 x 17 In. 770.00
Thermometer, Tin, Button Sign On Top, 3 x 9 1/2 In. 230.00
Tip Tray, 1903, Hilda Clark, Round, 6 In. ....835.00 to 1000.00
Tip Tray, 1906, Juanita, Drinking, Round, 4 x 6 In. ....375.00 to 500.00
Tip Tray, 1907, Relieves Fatigue, Woman, Green Dress, Border, 4 1/4 In. ....316.00 to 770.00
Tip Tray, 1909, Exhibition Girl, St. Louis World's Fair, 4 1/4 x 6 In. 258.00
Tip Tray, 1910, Coca-Cola Girl, 4 1/4 x 6 In. ....258.00 to 360.00
Tip Tray, 1913, Hamilton King Girl, 4 1/4 x 6 In. 373.00
Tip Tray, 1914, Betty, 4 1/4 x 6 In. 172.00
Tip Tray, 1916, Elaine, 4 1/4 x 6 In. ....144.00 to 220.00
Toy, Dispenser, Battery Operated, Paper Label Box, 1950s 700.00
Toy, Santa Claus, 1950s, 16 In. 86.00
Toy, Truck, Buddy L, Whitewall Tires, Chrome Hubcaps, 15 In. 172.00
Toy, Truck, Delivery, Marx, 1950s, 13 1/2 In. 275.00
Toy, Truck, Delivery, Pressed Steel, Yellow, Red, 1950s, 12 In. 144.00
Toy, Truck, Tin Lithograph, Sanyo, Japan, 12 1/2 In. 375.00

Tray, 1906, Juanita, Oval, 10 1/2 x 13 1/4 In. 517.00
Tray, 1908, Topless Girl, Holding Bottle, 12 1/4 In. . . . . .3850.00 to 6500.00
Tray, 1910, Hamilton King Girl, Fashionable Hat, 10 1/2 x 13 1/4 In. 1150.00
Tray, 1916, Elaine, Yellow Dress, Holding Glass Of Coke, 8 1/2 x 19 In. 176.00
Tray, 1922, Summer Girl, Holding Glass Of Coke, 10 1/2 x 13 1/4 In. 412.00
Tray, 1927, Curb Service, Man Serving Couple In Car, 10 1/2 x 13 1/4 In. 523.00
Tray, 1929, Girl In Yellow Bathing Suit, 10 1/2 x 13 In. .285.00 to 725.00
Tray, 1930, Telephone Girl, 10 1/2 x 13 1/2 In. 220.00
Tray, 1931, Barefoot Boy, Straw Hat, Dog, 10 1/2 x 13 1/4 In. 275.00
Tray, 1934, Tarzan, O'Sullivan, Weissmuller, 10 1/2 x 13 3/4 In. . . . . .148.00 to 300.00
Tray, 1935, Madge Evans, MGM 200.00
Tray, 1936, Hostess, Girl In Long Dress, Drinking Coke, 10/12 x 13 1/4 In. 220.00
Tray, 1937, Running Girl On Beach, Bottles Of Coke, 10 1/2 x 13 1/4 In. . . . . .125.00 to 368.00
Tray, 1938, Girl In Yellow Hat, Yellow Dress, 10 1/2 x 13 1/4 In. 220.00
Tray, 1939, Springboard Girl, 13 1/4 x 10 1/2 In. . . . . .150.00 to 357.00
Tray, 1940, Sailor Girl, 10 1/2 x 13 3/4 In. . . . . .110.00 to 165.00
Tray, 1941, Skater Girl, 10 1/2 x 13 1/4 In. . . . . .230.00 to 357.00
Tray, 1942, 2 Girls At Car, 10 1/2 x 13 1/4 In. . . . . .150.00 to 209.00
Tray, 1953, Menu Girl, Sports Theme Borders, 10 1/2 x 13 1/4 In. . . . . .27.00 to 57.00
Tray, 1961, Pansy Garden, Glass Of Coca-Cola, In Flower Bed, 10 1/2 x 13 1/4 In. 11.00
Tray, Drink Coca-Cola, American Art Works Inc., Coshocton, Oh., 10 x 13 1/4 In. 155.00
Truck, Die Cast, Budgie, England, 1950s, 5 1/2 In. 95.00
Urn, Syrup, Spigot, Cover, Presentation Sign, 1970s 495.00
Wagon, Wooden Sides, Wheels, Handle, 1972, 18 1/4 x 8 In. 30.00
Watch Fob, Duster Girl, Celluloid, Metal, 1911 . . . . 1155.00
Whistle, Tin Lithograph, Hobbleskirt Bottle, The Pause That Refreshes, 1930s, 2 In. 230.00

COFFEE GRINDERS, or coffee mills, of home size were first made about
1894. They lost favor by the 1930s. Large floor-standing or counter-
model coffee grinders were used in the nineteenth-century country
store. The renewed interest in fresh-ground coffee has produced many
modern electric and hand grinders, and reproductions of the old styles
are being made.

Adams, Walnut Board, 4 Legs, Iron Hopper, Countertop, 1840, 15 1/2 In. 137.00
American Duplex, Coffeepot Shape, Knob, 29 In. 175.00
Bronsen-Walton Coffee, Mounted, Cavalry Soldiers, Old Glory, Cleveland, Oh. 154.00
Cast Iron, Steel, Red, Black Paint, Lion Heads On Flywheel, 23 In. 350.00
Cast Iron, X-Ray, Glass Box, Metal Cup 250.00
Dovetailed Case & Drawer, Cherry & Poplar, Pewter Mounted, 9 1/2 In. 1320.00
Enterprise, Decals, Blue On Side Wheels, Knob On Drawer, 13 In. 357.00
Enterprise, Home Size, Pat. Oct. 21, 1873 . . . . 125.00
Enterprise, No. 2, Original Paint, 8 3/4-In. Wheels 1000.00
Enterprise, No. 7, Decals, Red, 19 1/2 In. 1265.00
Enterprise, No. 12, Eagle Finial, Cast Iron, Painted, 35 x 25 In. 230.00
Enterprise, No. 16, Cast Brass Eagle Finial, 68 In. 345.00
Enterprise, Pat. 10/21/1873, Home Size, 8 In. 125.00
Landers, Frary & Clark, Cast Iron, Original Paint, Yellow Letters, 12 In. 440.00
Landers, Frary & Clark, No. 11, 1909, 12 In. 525.00
Lane Brothers, 36 In. 1210.00
Metal Top & Handle, Dovetailed Wooden Box, Drawer, Porcelain Knob, 8 In. 68.00
P.O. Wein, No. 0, Iron Top, Brass Hopper, Canted Sides, 5 3/4 In. 220.00
Sun Manufacturing, Tulip & Stars, Tin, Greenfield, Ohio, 12 In., Pair 440.00
Walnut, Branded, Dovetailed Case, Molded Top, Iron Fittings, 7 In. 319.00
Walnut, Small Drawer, Brass Pull, Iron Crank & Plates, 9 1/2 In. 605.00

COIN SPOT is a glass pattern that was named by the collectors for the
spots resembling coins, which are part of the glass. Colored, clear, and
opalescent glass was made with the spots. Many companies used the
design in the 1870–1890 period. It is so popular that reproductions are
still being made.

Finger Lamp, Cranberry Opalescent, Crimped Handle, 3 1/2 In. 650.00
Lamp, Blue, 16 In., Pair 275.00
Lampshade, Emerald Green, 4 In. 130.00

Sugar Shaker, Blue, 4 1/2 In. ....160.00 to 200.00
Sugar Shaker, Ring Neck, Blue, Green, 4 3/4 In. 130.00
Sugar Shaker, Ring Neck, Rubina, 4 1/2 In. 220.00
Sugar Shaker, Waisted, Cranberry, 4 1/2 In. 250.00
Sugar Shaker, Waisted, Green, 4 1/2 In. 160.00
Sugar Shaker, Waisted, White, 4 3/4 In. 90.00
Sugar Shaker, White, 4 3/4 In. ....80.00 to 90.00
Syrup, Blue, Bulbous, 4 3/4 In. 120.00
Syrup, Green, Bulbous, 6 1/2 In. 250.00
Syrup, Opalescent & Clear 140.00
Tumbler, Cranberry Opalescent, 3 3/4 In. 31.00
Vase, Cranberry Opalescent, Flared Ruffled Edge, 9 1/2 In. 45.00
Vase, Cranberry Opalescent, Ruffled Rim, 4 x 1 1/2 In. 30.00
Water Set, Opalescent, 7 Piece 175.00

COIN-OPERATED MACHINES of all types are collected. The vending
machine is an ancient invention dating back to 200 B.C. when holy
water was dispensed in a coin-operated vase. Smokers in seventeenth-
century England could buy tobacco from a coin-operated box. It was
not until after the Civil War that the technology made modern coin-
operated games and vending machines plentiful. Slot machines, arcade
games, and dispensers are all collected.

Arcade, Challenger, Pellet Pistol, 10 Shots, 1 Cent, No Key, 24 In. 373.00
Arcade, U.S. Marshal, Wooden, Chrome & Nickel Trim, 28 x 22 In. 517.00
Baseball, Wood, Metal, Glass, Munves, Chicago, 1930s, 25 x 20 In. 967.00
Bat-A-Ball, Penny, Wood, Glass, Metal, 1930s, 17 In. 1183.00
Billiards Practice, A.B.T. Mfg. Co., Mahogany, 25 x 15 x 10 In. 2242.00
Candy, Clawson Stick Candy, Cast Iron, 1 Cent, Pat. 1912, 15 1/2 In. 360.00
Candy, Mint, Diamond J, 3 Flavors, 5 Cent, 18 x 10 1/2 x 6 In. 138.00
Card, 1 Baseball Trading Card & Gum For 10 Cents, 13 x 13 x 6 In. 275.00
Cigar, Foxy Grandpa, 5 Cent, Glass Display, 22 x 10 x 7 1/2 In. 3300.00
Cigar, Trade Stimulator, Oak, Nickel Drop, 1897, 19 1/2 x 14 1/2 In. 2000.00
Cigarette, 1 Lucky Strike For 1 Cent, Cigavend, 15 x 16 x 11 In. 209.00
Cigarette, Columbia, Cast Metal, Wooden, 5 Cent, Not Working, 18 In. 345.00
Cigarette, Kazoo, 1 Cent, Dice, 3 Of A Kind Wins Cigarettes, 8 x 10 x 5 1/2 In. 176.00
Cigarette, Tic-Tac-Toe, Win Cigarettes, Daval Mfg., 9 1/2 x 10 In. 248.00
Collar Buttons, 1 Collar Button For 10 Cents, Zeno, 10 1/2 x 5 1/2 In. 578.00
Comb, 5 Cent, Lawrence Mfg. Co., 38 In. 77.00
Dice, Joker's Wild, 5 Cent, Star Amusement Co., 7 x 11 x 15 In. 121.00
Dispenser, Napkin, 2 Sides, Answer Box, Ask Question Pull Lever, Chrome 90.00
Football, Kicker & Catcher, Arcade, Wooden, 1 Cent, 18 In. 632.00
Fortune Teller, Arcade, Art Deco, Rotate Handle, 10 Cents, 77 In. 632.00
Fortune Teller, Card, Fortune For 10 Cents, 23 x 36 x 16 1/2 In. 165.00
Gambling, Bally Skipper, 3 Balls For 5 Cents, 11 x 7 x 19 In. 413.00

Coin-Operated Machine,
Pinball, Imo Horse Race,
Germany, 1935

Coin-Operated
Machine, Slot, Lucky
Dice, 1928

Grip Tester, 1 Cent, Holly Mfg. Co., 13 x 8 x 9 In. 165.00
Gum, Acorn Gumball Machine, 1 Cent, Clear Globe, Cast Iron, 14 1/2 In. 66.00
Gum, Adams, Chiclets & Dentyne, 1 Cent, 10 x 16 In. 431.00
Gum, Baseball Card, 1 Cent Each, Stand Up, Acorn, 1950s 1685.00
Gum, Brookside Gum Machine, Clear Glass Globe, Boston, Mass., 11 In. 35.00
Gum, Clear Glass Globe, Aluminum, 14 In. 390.00
Gum, Ford 1 Cent Gum Machine, Clear Globe, Aluminum Base, 11 In. 55.00
Gum, Master Gumball Machine, 1 Cent, Metal, Porcelain, 16 x 8 In. 170.00
Gum, Mills Automatic Gum Machine, 6 Column Dispenser, 1936, 16 In. 60.00
Gum, Pepsin, 1 Cent, Fleers, c.1898, 15 x 4 In. 1980.00
Gum, Yuchu Ball, Clear Square Globe, Paper Label, Yu-Chu Co., N.J., 1925 .... 160.00
Gumball, 10 Cents, Lucky Cat, Aluminum, Lu-Kat Novelty Co. 7475.00
Gumball, Shooting, Hunter Duck, 18 x 9 1/2 x 20 In. 220.00
Horse Race, Each Way, Play With Large Coins, England, 32 x 18 x 6 In. 330.00
Machine, U.S. Postage Stamp, Uncle Sam, Automatic Dispenser, 1945, 20 In. 57.00
Matches, Box Of Matches For 1 Cent, Kreme Mfg. Co., 14 x 10 x 7 In. 385.00
Matches Vending, 1 Cent, Cast Iron Front, Patent 1910, 14 x 10 1/2 In. 690.00
Nut, Peanut, Advance Machine Co. Big Mouth, Swivel Door, 1925 .... 90.00
Nut, Peanut, Columbus Vending, Model A, 1 Cent, Glass Globe, 16 In. 253.00
Nut, Peanut, Sun Nut Machine, Glass, Cast Aluminum, Los Angeles, 14 In. 45.00
Nut, Pistachio, Columbus Vending, Model M, 5 Cent, Lock & Key, 14 In. 220.00
Pencil, Vendex, Custom Imprinted, 5 Cent, 13 x 21 In. 248.00
Personality Tester, 12 Answers, 1 Lights Up, 1 Cent, 28 x 11 x 10 In. 308.00
Pinball, Good Luck Horse Race, 7 x 12 x 22 In. 495.00
Pinball, Imo Horse Race, Germany, 1935 .... *Illus* 1803.00
Pinball, Jiggers, Wooden, Glass, 1 Cent, 1930s, 16 x 38 x 33 In. 431.00
Pinball, Short Stop, Exhibit Supply Co., 1940, 62 x 53 In. 1612.00
Pinball, Wahoo, Metal, Wood, Glass, 5 Cent, 1930s, 17 x 41 x 32 In. 345.00
Poker, Dean Novelty Co., Penny Spins Reels, 8 x 9 In. 248.00
Skill, Zipper, 5 Balls For 1 Cent, Binks Ind., Win Gumball, 17 x 12 x 9 In. 248.00
Slot, Caille, Ben Hur, Countertop, Oak Cabinet, 20 x 15 1/2 In. 2530.00
Slot, Gambling, Lucky Dice, 1928 .... 3000.00
Slot, Hy-Lo, Caille, 1 Cent, Poker Reels, Lock, Patent 1895, 18 1/2 In. 5462.00
Slot, Jennings 25 Cent Sun Chief, Aluminum, Wood, 26 x 15 x 15 In. 1980.00
Slot, Jennings, Pay Off In Mints, Oak, 26 x 15 In. 1725.00
Slot, Lion Front, 5 Cent, 26 In. 1955.00
Slot, Lucky Dice, 1928 .... *Illus* 3004.00
Slot, Mills 25 Cent, Side Vendor, Aluminum, Wood, 19 x 26 x 15 In. 1980.00
Slot, Mills Novelty, Hightop Blue Bell, 25 Cent, 26 x 16 x 15 1/2 In. 1210.00
Slot, Mills, Black Beauty, Race Car, Aluminum, 24 x 16 x 17 In. 440.00
Slot, Mills, Jackpot-Vendor, Back Door Lock, c.1928, 26 x 16 In. 1035.00
Slot, Mills, Paneled Oak, Cast Iron Footed, 1900, 26 x 65 x 12 In. 11500.00
Slot, Mills, Poinsettia, Aluminum Panels, 1920, 15 1/2 x 21 x 15 In. 1840.00
Slot, One Arm Bandit, Mills 5 Cent, 1776 Model, Mills Novelty Co. 633.00
Slot, Pace Bantam 5 Cent, 3 Reel, 19 x 14 In. 1650.00
Slot, Pace, 5 Cent, Aluminum Slot, 24 x 14 3/4 In. 1955.00
Slot, Watling Twin Jackpot 1 Cent Gumball Vendor, 24 x 15 x 15 In. 1760.00
Slot Machine Stand, Cast Iron, Egyptian Style, 29 x 17 x 17 In. 302.00
Stamp, American Postmaster Machine, Key, 14 1/2 x 13 1/2 In. 35.00
Stamp, Northwestern Corp. Postage, Key, Morris, Ill., 14 3/8 In. 35.00
Stamp, Schermack Postage Machine, Embossed, 14 1/8 x 7 3/4 In. 60.00
Stamp, Schermack, Three 3 Cent Stamps For 10 Cents, 13 x 7 In. 130.00
Stamp, Sno-Master Postage Machine, Baltimore, Md., 14 x 6 x 5 1/4 In. 25.00
Stamp, U.S.A. Postage Stamps, White Ground, 14 3/8 x 8 3/4 x 8 1/4 In. 25.00
Stephens Magic Beer Barrel, Get Pretzel After Play, 11 1/2 x 13 x 8 In. 880.00
Strength Tester, International Mutoscope Reel Co., 83 1/2 x 16 In. 8625.00
Strength Tester, Shake Hands, Uncle Sam, 1908 Repro, 1990, 75 In. 3162.00
Target, 10 Shots For 1 Cent, Hit Moving Balls, 17 x 10 x 24 In. 220.00
Trade Stimulator, Whiz Ball Penny Machine 325.00
Vending, Hershey Candy Bars, Penny Countertop, 1930s 440.00
Vending, Silver King Hot Nut, 5 Cent, Flashing Red Glass Top, 15 1/2 In. 57.00
Vending, Toilet Paper, 1 Cent, Amer. Vending Machine Co., 21 x 8 x 9 In. 1100.00

COLLECTOR PLATES are modern plates produced in limited editions. Some may be found listed under the factory name, such as Bing & Grondahl, Royal Copenhagen, Royal Doulton, and Wedgwood.

Fitz & Floyd, Poire Bleu, Box, 7 1/2 In.	20.00
Gorham, Titian Madonna, 1978, 8 3/4 In.	25.00
Kearns, Norman Rockwell, Sweethearts, No. 758, 1976	18.00
Knowles, Norman Rockwell, Scotty Plays Santa, 1980	10.00
Konigszelt, Rapunzel, Bavaria, 1982, 7 3/4 In.	25.00
Konigszelt, Rumplestilzchen, Bavaria, Box, 1981, 7 3/4 In., Bradex No. 4953	30.00
Royal Devon, Norman Rockwell, Down Hill Daring, 1975	13.00
Royalwood, Norman Rockwell, Doctor & The Doll, 1977	10.00

COMIC ART, or cartoon art, is a relatively new field of collecting. Original comic strips, magazine covers, and even printed strips are collected. The first daily comic strip was printed in 1907. The paintings on celluloid used for movie cartoons are listed in this book under Animation Art.

Drawing, Bringing Up Father, Sunday Page, Pen & Ink, G., McManus, 1918, 22 x 16 In.	4675.00
Drawing, Krazy Kat, Sunday Page, George Herriman, Pen & Ink, 1920, 19 x 17 In.	7700.00
Drawing, Little Nemo, Sunday Page, Slumberland, Pen, Ink, McCay, 1909, 28 x 21 In.	22000.00
Drawing, Rose O'Neill, Black Woman Doing Laundry, Sept. 16, 1902, 20 x 14 In.	1430.00
Drawings, Popeye, Sequence Of 10, Popeye Skiing, Pencil, 1947, 4 x 5 1/2 In.	145.00
Strip, Blondie, Sunday Page, With Topper, Chic Young, Sept. 15, 1963, 15 x 17 In.	221.00
Strip, Flash Gordon, Sunday Page, Alex Raymond, Aug. 17, 1914, 13 x 16 In.	7150.00
Strip, Gasoline Alley, Skeezix	10.00
Strip, Henry, Carl Anderson, Ghosted By John Liney, Aug. 14, 1967, 5 1/2 x 20 In.	77.00
Strip, Joe Palooka, Ham Fisher, 4 Dailies, Dec. 5, 6, 7, 9, 1950, 6 x 20 In., 4 Strips	220.00
Strip, Li'l Abner, Al Capp, July 21, 1935	10.00
Strip, Li'l Abner, Al Capp, Nov. 27, 1951, 6 1/2 x 22 1/2 In.	467.00
Strip, Li'l Abner, Al Capp, Sunday Page, Aug. 15, 1954, 21 1/2 x 21 In.	440.00
Strip, Little Savage, George Evans, Classic Illustrated No. 137, Mar. 1957, 18 x 12 In.	144.00
Strip, Peanuts, Charles M. Schulz, Snoopy Contemplates, 2 Strips, 1964, 5 x 27 In.	12100.00
Strip, Peanuts, Sunday Page, Charles M. Schulz, Linus, January 14, 1962, 15 x 22 In.	12100.00
Strip, Peter Rabbit, Harrison Cady, Sunday Page, Aug. 22, 1920, 25 1/2 x 20 In.	1028.00
Strip, Terry & The Pirates, Milton Caniff, Apr. 10, 1941, 6 x 20 In.	660.00
Strip, Terry & The Pirates, Milton Caniff, Blue Wash, Dec. 14, 1938, 6 x 20 In.	467.00
Strip, Weird Science-Fantasy, No. 25, Marie Severin, 1974, 13 x 10 1/2 In.	1936.00

COMMEMORATIVE items have been made to honor members of royalty and those of great national fame. World's fairs and important historical events are also remembered with commemorative pieces. Related collectibles are listed in the Coronation and World's Fair categories.

Charger, Prince William V, Princess, Orange Tree, Creamware, c.1790, 16 In.	9600.00
Figurine, King Edward VII, Mounted On Horse, Staffordshire, 11 5/8 In.	145.00
Figurine, Queen Of England, Year Of Jubilee, Staffordshire, 1887, 16 5/8 In.	230.00

Commemorative, Plate, Diamond Jubilee, Queen Victoria, 1897, Johnson Bros., 10 In.

Commemorative, Tin, Prince Of Wales, Thorne's Extra Super Creme Toffee, 5 1/4 In.

Figurine, Victoria, Queen Of England, Albert, Prince, Staffordshire, 17 In., Pair 1650.00
Picture, George II, Reverse Lithograph, Frame, 18 x 14 In. 192.00
Plate, Diamond Jubilee, Queen Victoria, 1897, Johnson Bros., 10 In. .... *Illus* 100.00
Plate, House Of Orange, Princess Louise, Border, Creamware, c.1790, 12 In. 3300.00
Tin, Price Of Wales, Thorne's Extra Super Creme Toffee, 5 1/4 In. .... *Illus* 80.00

COMPACTS hold face powder. A woman did not powder her face in public until after World War I. By 1920, the beauty parlor, permanent waves, and cosmetics had become acceptable. A few companies sold cake face powder in a box with a mirror and a pad or puff. Soon the compact was designed by jewelers and made of gold, silver, and precious materials. Cosmetic companies began to sell powder in attractive compacts of less valuable metal or plastic. Collectors today search for Art Deco designs, commemorative compacts from world's fairs or political events, and unusual examples. Many were made with companion lipsticks and other fittings.

14K Gold, Lion Holding Sword, Flowering Vine Thumbpiece 460.00
18K Gold, Florentine Finish, Mirror, Powder, 2 1/4 x 2 1/4 In. 460.00
Army Hat Shape, Army Emblem, Plastic, Puff, Mirror, 1 1/2 x 3 1/4 In. 73.00
Bakelite, 3 1/4 x 2 7/8 In. 255.00
Cartier, Paris, Art Deco, Sterling Gilt, Lacquer, Coral Pear, Diamond, Emerald, 2 5/8 In. .. 2250.00
Crystal Lucite, Scalloped, Gold Metal, Puff, Ziegfeld Glorified Girl, 4 1/2 x 3 3/4 In. 150.00
Enamel, Stylized Gold Starbursts, Turquoise Iridescent, Leather Case, 18K Gold 1092.00
Estee, Ice Crystal, White Crystal 405.00
Henriette, Billiard 8 Ball Shape, Marked, 1940s 128.00
Hermes, Enamel, Brass, Gold Crest, Rhinestones, Box, 1949 .... 241.00
Hilda Terry, Jitterbug Lindy Dancers, Puff, Mirror, c.1950, 3 1/2 In. 102.00
Kigu, Woman In Swing 45.00
Kigu De Luxe Cherie, Lipstick, Marcasite, Black Enamel, Box 72.00
Marathon, Guilloche Enamel, Snowflake, Roses, Vines, Handbag Shape, 1920s, 3 1/4 In. . 347.00
Pygmalion Globe, Gold Plate, Brass, 1950, 2 In. 136.00
Richard Hudnut, Cornucopia, Blue Enamel 71.00
Schildkraut, Seed Pearl Design 55.00
Scrolled Flowers, Griffin Borders, 18K Gold 1265.00
Shagreen & Metal, Camera 373.00
Silver, Brass, Raised Vine, Lead, Eiffel Tower, Air Ship, Hot Air Balloon, Puff, 1 3/4 In. .. 110.00
Silver, Enamel, Couple, Stage Performance Cover, Art Deco, Rectangular 3 In. 1740.00
Silver, Pietra Dura Mounted, Hinged, Floral Cartouche, Malachite, 2 1/4 In. 316.00
Silver, Rectangular, Hinged Lid, Dove, Olive Branch, 1900s, 3 1/4 In. 200.00
Stratton, Enameled Pheasant & Flowers 50.00
Tiffany, 14K Gold, Ribbed Box, 3 Channel Set Rubies, Mirror, Powder Compartment 805.00
Volupte, Goldtone, Hand Shape 280.00
Volupte, Poodle In Box, Box, Felt Pouch, Square, 3 In. 98.00
Wadsworth, Bonbon, Velvet, Black, 1940s-1950s, 5 In. 152.00
Whiting & Davis, Mesh, Brass, 3 3/8 x 3 1/8 x 1/2 In. 810.00

CONSOLIDATED LAMP AND GLASS COMPANY of Coraopolis, Pennsylvania, was founded in 1894. The company made lamps, tablewares, and art glass. Collectors are particularly interested in the wares made after 1925, including black satin glass, Cosmos (listed in its own category in this book), Martele (which resembled Lalique), Ruba Rombic (1928–1932 Art Deco line), and colored glasswares. Some Consolidated pieces are very similar to those made by the Phoenix Glass Company. The colors are sometimes different. Consolidated made Martele glass in blue, crystal, green, pink, white, or custard glass with added fired-on color or a satin finish. The company closed for the final time in 1967.

Lamp, Dogwood, Blue, White Interior, 19 In. 110.00
Plate, Dancing Nudes, 8 1/2 In. 69.00
Vase, Flying Seagulls, Orange On Green, Satin, 10 In. 115.00
Vase, Ruba Rombic, Jungle Green, 6 In. 805.00

CONTEMPORARY GLASS, see Glass-Contemporary.

COOKBOOKS are collected for various reasons. Some are wanted for the recipes, some for investment, and some as examples of advertising. Cookbooks and recipe pamphlets are included in this category.

Art Of Cookery, Hannah Glasse, Cooking Colonial, c.1763	895.00
Betty Crocker, Dinner For Two, Hardcover, 200 Pages, 1958	6.00
Betty Crocker, For Boys & Girls, First Edition, 1957	60.00
Betty Crocker, Picture Cooky Book, 1948, 45 Pages	20.00
Cotton Belt Route, Die Cut Logo, 16 Pages, 1920, 4 In.	30.00
Davis Baking Powder, 1904	10.00
Gone With The Wind, Famous Southern Recipes, Scarlett At Tara, 48 Pages	35.00
Henkels Flour, Good Things To East, Commercial Milling Co., Detroit, 1934, 65 Pages	20.00
Pillsbury, Best Bake-Off Recipe Book, 1959	15.00

COOKIE JARS with brightly painted designs or amusing figural shapes became popular in the mid-1930s. Many companies made them and collectors search for cookie jars either by design or by maker's name. Listed here are examples by the less common makers. Major factories are listed under their own names in other categories of the book, such as Abingdon, Brush, Hull, McCoy, Red Wing, and Shawnee. See also the Disneyana category.

Barney Rubble, Standing, Certified International	20.00
Bear, Flasher, Black Cover, American Bisque	200.00 to 480.00
Bear, On Stump, California Originals, 15 In.	70.00
Bear, Sheriff, Brown, Twin Winton, 11 In.	55.00
Bear, Sleeping, Japan	35.00
Bear, White, Royal Ware, 11 1/4 In.	80.00
Bear, With Bow, American Bisque	48.00
Bear, With Bowtie, Treasure Craft	55.00
Bear, With Hat, American Bisque, 11 1/2 In.	40.00 to 150.00
Blackboard Boy, American Bisque, 12 1/2 In.	270.00
Blackboard Clown, Blue Top, American Bisque, 13 3/4 In.	110.00
Blackboard Girl, American Bisque, 13 In.	180.00
Blackboard Hobo, Blue, American Bisque, 14 In.	210.00
Candy Baby, Blue, Yellow, Candy Cane On Cover, American Bisque	60.00
Casper, American Bisque, 13 1/2 In.	425.00
Cat, Fluffy, American Bisque, 12 1/4 In.	60.00 to 120.00
Cat, On Quilted Base, American Bisque, 13 In.	40.00
Cheerleader, Flasher, American Bisque	260.00
Chef, National Silver, 10 1/4 In.	243.00
Chef, Standing, American Bisque, 12 In.	60.00
Churn Boy, American Bisque, 11 3/4 In.	130.00
Clown, Blue, Tan, American Bisque, 12 In.	30.00
Clown, Head, Crying, Cardinal China Co., 9 1/2 In.	30.00
Clown On Stage, Flasher, American Bisque, 9 3/4 In.	150.00
Dino, With Golf Clubs, American Bisque	400.00 to 600.00
Dino & Pebbles, Certified International	20.00
Dog On Quilted Base, American Bisque, 13 In.	60.00
Elephant, With Baseball Cap, American Bisque, 10 In.	40.00
Feed Sack, American Bisque, 1958, 9 1/2 In.	150.00
Fred & Dino, American Bisque, 12 1/2 In.	500.00 to 750.00
Fred Flintstone, Standing, Certified International	20.00
Fred Flintstone House, Certified International	20.00
French Chef, Cardinal China Co., 9 In.	20.00
Frog, Neal, Sears Roebuck	65.00 to 75.00
Frog, Pink & Green, Japan	35.00
Frog, Reclining, California Originals	75.00
Frog, With Bowtie, California Originals	75.00
Happy Clown, American Bisque, 11 In.	50.00
Hen, Brown, Fapco, 7 1/4 In.	100.00
Hound, Green, Doranne Of California, 12 1/4 In.	100.00
Jack-In-The-Box, American Bisque, 12 In.	50.00
Jug, Beige, Brown Top, Cork Stopper, Incised Lines, Monmouth, 12 In.	25.00

Kitten, On Beehive, American Bisque, 11 3/4 In. .... .75.00 to 105.00
Kittens, On Ball Of Yarn, Dark Green & Brown Yarn, American Bisque, 10 1/2 In. 90.00
Kittens, On Ball Of Yarn, Light Green Yarn, American Bisque, 9 1/2 In. 40.00
Koala Bear, California Originals 50.00
Lamb, With Flower Hat, American Bisque, 13 In. 80.00
Little Girl Head, Cardinal China Co., 8 In. 20.00
Little Girl Lamb, American Bisque, 10 1/2 In. 40.00
Mammy, National Silver, 9 1/2 In. ....155.00 to 245.00
Marilyn Monroe, Clay Art, 14 In. 95.00
Mother Goose, Doranne Of California 125.00
Owl, Collegiate, American Bisque, 11 1/2 In. 85.00
Owl, Graduate, Treasure Craft, 11 1/4 In. 30.00
Owl, Neon Colors, Japan, 10 1/2 In. 35.00
Owl, Winking, California Originals, 12 3/4 In. 35.00
Pelican, California Originals 80.00
Pennsylvania Dutch Boy, American Bisque, 11 1/2 In. 450.00
Pig, Pink, Brown Spots, Corncob Finial, 5 3/4 In. 35.00
Pig In A Poke, Green Poke, American Bisque, 12 1/2 In. 60.00
Poodle, Red, American Bisque, 10 1/2 In. 95.00
Puppy, In Basket, American Bisque 50.00
Puppy, Light Green, Japan 30.00
Raccoon, Cookie Bandit, Metlox 200.00
Road Hog, Pig On Motorcycle, Clay Art, 11 1/2 In. 95.00
Rooster, California Originals, 9 In. 45.00
Rubbles House, American Bisque, 10 In. 200.00
Santa, Black, Clay Art, 10 In. 75.00
Soldier, Cardinal China Co., 12 3/4 In. 210.00
Squirrel, On Pinecone, Metlox, 12 In. 95.00
Squirrel, Twin Winton 45.00
Tortoise & Hare, Flasher, American Bisque, 9 3/4 In. 250.00
Turtle, Brown, California Originals 35.00
Wilma, On The Telephone, American Bisque 250.00
Wizard Of Oz, Dorothy & Toto, Star Jars 195.00
Woody Woodpecker Head, 14 1/2 In. 375.00

COORS ware was made by a pottery in Golden, Colorado, owned by the Coors Beverage Company. Dishes and decorative wares were produced from the turn of the century until the pottery was destroyed by fire in the 1930s. The name *Coors* is marked on the back. The company is still in business making industrial porcelain. For more information, see *Kovels' Depression Glass & Dinnerware Price List*.

Casserole, Cover, 2 Handles, Floral, Marked, 8 1/4 In. 62.00
Egg Bowl, Shirred, Tab Handles, Maroon, 5 1/4 In. 17.00
Plate, Rosebud, Maroon, 9 In. 15.00
Platter, Rosebud, Maroon, Tab Handle, 13 In. 51.00
Salt & Pepper, Rosebud, Orange 28.00
Vase, Brown, Green, Ribbed, 2 Embossed Handles, c.1930, 5 In. 46.00
Vase, Light Green Matte, White, Tapered Bottom, Paneled Sides 50.00
Vase, Terra-Cotta, White Matte, Floral, Stamped, 8 1/2 x 22 1/4 In. 75.00

COPELAND pieces listed here are those that have a mark including the word Copeland used between 1847 and 1976. Marks include Copeland Spode and Copeland & Garrett. See also Copeland Spode and Royal Worcester.

Figurine, Cupid, Winged, Quiver Of Arrows, Late 19th Century, 12 x 8 1/4 In. 230.00
Figurine, Parian, Autumn Woman, Summer Man, Marked, c.1855, 9 1/2 In., 2 Piece 441.00
Figurine, Saved, Sir Edwin Landseer, 8 In. 522.00
Lazy Susan, Canton Pattern, Red & Pink, Crown Signed, 17 1/4 x 6 1/2 In. 192.00
Plate, Brompton, Cobalt Blue, 10 1/4 In., 8 Piece 258.00
Platter, Armorial, Enamel Rococo Crest, 21 In. 176.00
Platter, Castle Ruin, Rural Bridge, 13 x 17 In. 92.00
Platter, Lace Design Border, Landscape With Bride, England, 1880, 17 x 14 In. 185.00
Spode, Tureen, Cover, Gainsborough Pattern, Lemon On Top, 7 x 11 In. 132.00

Sugar, Bamboo, Basket Weave, 4 In.	110.00
Teapot, Cover, Stoneware, Cauliflower Mold, Marked, c.1840, 4 3/4 In.	176.00
Vase, Gilt Trim, Birds, Ribbon Handles, Pink Ground, c.1860, 10 1/4 In.	287.00
Wall Bracket, Brown & White, Pair	66.00

COPELAND SPODE appears on some pieces of nineteenth-century English porcelain. Josiah Spode established a pottery at Stoke-on-Trent, England, in 1770. In 1833, the firm was purchased by William Copeland and Thomas Garrett and the mark was changed. In 1847, Copeland became the sole owner and the mark changed again. W.T. Copeland & Sons continued until a 1976 merger when it became Royal Worcester Spode. Pieces are listed in this book under the name that appears in the mark. Copeland Spode, Copeland, and Royal Worcester have separate listings.

Coffeepot, India Tree	203.00
Dish, Cover, Blue, Footed, 9 1/2 In.	195.00
Game Set, Turkey Platter, 13 Piece	1700.00
Jug, Golf Scene, Blue, Tan, Glaze, Jasperware, Marked, 6 x 5 In.	1690.00
Plate, Black Specks, Quail Hunt Scenes, Tiger Hunt Center, 10 1/2 In., 8 Piece	247.00
Plate Set, Green Ground, Gold Rim, Flower Transfer Center, Dinner, Lunch, 22 Piece	460.00
Platter, Mayflower, 12 7/8 x 9 3/4 In.	153.00
Platter, Tower, Deep Blue, Marked, 19 1/4 x 14 3/4 In.	275.00
Tea Tile, Chelsea Garden Pattern, 5 3/4 x 1/2 In.	210.00
Teapot, Pink, Tower, 3 1/2 In.	325.00
Teapot, Reynolds Pattern, 10 1/2 x 7 1/4 In.	255.00
Tureen, Sauce, Reynolds Pattern, Fruits, Flowers, Stamped, 1940, 7 x 5 In.	185.00
Tureen, Soup, Cover, Soup, Florence Pattern, England, 9 x 14 1/2 x 8 1/2 In.	380.00

COPPER has been used to make utilitarian items, such as teakettles and cooking pans, since the days of the early American colonists. Copper became a popular metal with the Arts & Crafts makers of the early 1900s, and decorative pieces, like desk sets, were made. Other pieces of copper may be found in the Arts & Crafts, Bradley & Hubbard, Kitchen, and Roycroft categories.

Bed Warmer, Brass Lid, Geometric Design, Turned Wood Handle	175.00
Bed Warmer, Engraved Lid, Turned Maple Handle, 42 In.	225.00
Bed Warmer, Etched, Pierced, Turned Tiger Maple Handle, 45 In.	69.00
Bed Warmer, Incised Flowers, Brass Lid, Turned Wooden Shaft, 43 In.	86.00
Bed Warmer, Pierced Lid, Hearts, Seraphs, Wood Handle	101.00
Bed Warmer, Punched Star, Turned Handle, c.1830	235.00
Bed Warmer, Wooden Handle, Attached Lid, Punched Design, Marked IB, 46 In.	275.00
Bowl, Gilded, Ring Foot, Marie Zimmermann, 1915, 4 3/4 x 14 In.	3700.00
Bowl, Hammered, Flared Rim, Pedestal Base, Marie Zimmerman, 6 x 13 In.	2760.00
Bowl, Hammered, Lobed, Didrich, 10 In.	345.00
Bowl, Hammered, Old Mission Kopperkraft, 8 1/2 In.	275.00
Bowl, Raised Berries, Circles, Waves, Blue & Green Patina, Jauchens, 7 In.	575.00
Box, Cigarette, Circle & Line Design On Lid, Chase, 7 x 3 In.	185.00
Box, Cigarette, Circle & Line Design, Wood Insert, Horseman & Chase, 7 x 3 In.	196.00
Box, Cuff Link, Hammered, 3 Sides, Embossed, Leather Lined, Karl Kipp, 2 x 6 x 3 In.	2530.00
Box, Hammered, Cloisonne Panel Lid, Pink Flower, Scrolled Feet, Arts & Crafts, 2 x 4 In.	345.00
Box, Tobacco, Ships At Sea, Flowers On Reverse, England, 18th Century, 6 In.	295.00
Brazier, Cabriole Legs, Handle, c.1790	185.00
Brazier, Wooden Handle, Shaped Feet & Supports, Early 18th Century	395.00
Can, Water, Marked J.M., 19th Century, 12 In.	135.00
Cauldron, Dovetail Seams, 2 Riveted Handles, 19 1/2 x 23 In.	500.00
Chafing Dish, Cover, Water Basin, Hammered Brass, c.1904, 12 x 21 In.	1430.00
Chamberstick, Gustav Stickley, Original Patina, 8 1/2 In.	660.00
Chamberstick, Hammered, Riveted Handle, Original Patina, G. Stickley, 9 x 7 In.	520.00
Charger, Enameled, Cavalier Portrait, Ornate Clothes, Oak Frame, 16 In.	5230.00
Charger, Hammered, Repousse Poppy Pods, Arts & Crafts, England, 11 In.	635.00
Charger, Owl In Relief, Hammered, Embossed, Liberty Paper Label, 29 1/2 In.	3105.00
Chocolate Pot, Wood Handle, Dovetail Construction, France, c.1750	495.00
Coat Rack, Mirror, Uncle Sam, Our Nation's Pride, 4 Hooks, 1898, 18 x 18 In.	375.00

Desk Set, Hinged Inkwell, Riveted Base, Glass Insert, Perpetual Calendar, G. Stickley ... 545.00
Figure, Eagle, Outstretched Wings, On Ball, Stand, Gold Repaint, 23 1/2 x 36 1/2 In. 3630.00
Figurine, Dancing Deity, Vishnu Dwarf, India, 9th Century, 3 In. 1092.00
Figurine, Toad, Patinated, Otto Muller, 1906, 9 1/2 In. 185.00
Frame, Tooled, Embossed Intertwining Flowers, Etched Brass Underlayer, 6 In. 290.00
Humidor, Hammered, 4 Riveted Handles, Stylized Flowers, Arts & Crafts, England, 7 In. . 635.00
Humidor, Hammered, Arts & Crafts, 5 1/2 x 4 1/4 In. 90.00
Humidor, Hammered, Craftsman Studios, Laguna Beach, 7 x 6 In. 259.00
Inglenook Hood, Hammered, Embossed Glasgow Roses, England, 34 x 30 x 8 In. 1610.00
Jar, Hammered, Benedict, 7 In. 219.00
Jardiniere, Hammered, Chrysanthemums, Arts & Crafts, 6 3/4 x 9 1/2 In. 230.00
Jardiniere, Hammered, Original Patina, Stickley Brothers, 10 1/4 In. 1495.00
Jardiniere, Hammered, Rolled Rim, Stickley Brothers, 9 1/4 x 14 1/4 In. 1495.00
Jardiniere, Pedestal, Hammered, Original Patina, 42 In. 1050.00
Jug, Beer, Dovetail Construction, 18th Century 250.00
Jug, Water, Straight Neck, Domed Lid, Wrought Iron Handle, 20 In. 140.00
Kettle, Cover, Hudson Bay Company, Gal., 7 In. 440.00
Kettle, Dutch, Swing Handle, Mid 19th Century, 10 1/2 x 10 1/2 In. 115.00
Kettle, Water, Dovetailed, Cover, Acorn Finial, Brass & Copper Handle, 11 1/2 In. 110.00
Kettle, Wrought Iron Mount, Continental, Mid 19th Century, 10 3/4 x 18 In. 115.00
Kitchen Mold Set, Jelly, Fish, Rings, Some Engraved, 18th-19th Century, 18 Piece 865.00
Loving Cup, Folded Rim, 2 Handles, 4 3/4 In. 165.00
Measure, Ear Shape Handle, Crown Mark On Interior, Gal., 11 In. 275.00
Molds are listed in the Kitchen category.
Mug, Ale, Dovetailed, Engraved Broad Arrow, Military, 1760, Pt. 550.00
Mug, Ale, U-Shape Drum, Scrolled Handle, Repousse Design, England, c.1740, Qt. 595.00
Ornament, Gilt, Abalone Mounted Shell, France, Late 19th Century, 8 1/4 In. 345.00
Plaque, Embossed, Peas & Pods, Round, Stickley Bros., 14 In. 690.00
Plate, Hammered, Stylized Quatrefoil, Rolled Border To Rim, Karl Kipp, 9 3/4 In. 460.00
Plate, Silver Inlay, Beetles, Cattails, Square, Los Castillo, Mexico, 12 1/2 In. 290.00
Sconce, Wall, 4 Sides, Hammered, Flame Head, Rivets, Arts & Crafts, 11 x 4 1/2 In. 405.00
Sconce, Wall, Hammered, Tooled Petals, Arts & Crafts, 13 In. 1035.00
Stockpot, Dovetailed, Tinned, Spigot 750.00
Sugar & Creamer, Yellow Band, Pink Luster, Floral Decoration, 4 In. 95.00
Teakettle, Burner, White Porcelain Handles & Finial, 19th Century, 19 In. 65.00
Teakettle, Concave Strap Handle, Domed, Gooseneck Spout, c.1825, 10 x 6 1/2 In. 405.00
Teakettle, Domed Lid, Strap Swing Hand, Gooseneck Spout, G. Tryon, c.1800, 11 x 7 In. 1150.00
Teakettle, Dovetailed, Gooseneck Spout, Signed On Bail, C. Smith 138.00
Teakettle, Gooseneck, Dovetailed Body, Lid, Finial, A. Keeney, 19th Century, 10 In. 275.00
Teakettle, Gooseneck, Fixed Handle, Brass Supports, Brass Lid Finial 110.00
Teakettle, Gooseneck, Iron Swing Handle, 10 In. 66.00
Teakettle, Swing Handle, Burnished, Holland, Mid 19th Century, 14 3/4 In. 316.00
Teapot, Luster, Raised Cobalt Blue Decoration, 6 x 10 In. 190.00
Tray, Flared Flat Rim, Bronze Handles, Stickley, 18 In. 880.00
Tray, Hammered, 2 Handles, Benedict, 20 In. 489.00
Tray, Hammered, 2 Open Handles, Brown Patina, Gustav Stickley, 19 In. 185.00
Tray, Hammered, Raised, Arts & Crafts, 21 1/2 In. 460.00
Tray, Hammered, Riveted Handles, Gustav Stickley, 19 3/4 In. 1095.00
Trophy, Baluster Shape, Applied Silver Anchor, Handles, Cover, c.1910, 17 In. 1955.00
Umbrella Stand, Hammered, Knob, 6 Sides, Stickley Brothers, 26 1/2 x 10 1/2 In. 1150.00
Umbrella Stand, Iron, Flower Repousse, Ceramic Cabochons, Arts & Crafts, 31 x 29 In. . 375.00
Urn, Brass Washed, Rolled Rim, Swirling Lobed Base, 24 x 17 In. 345.00
Urn, Hammered, Spigot On Stand, Burner, Jos. Heinrichs, c.1907, 13 1/2 In. 550.00
Vase, 3 Swirling Handles, Stamped 235, 9 x 8 In. 430.00
Vase, Hammered, 3 Buttress Shape, Original Patina, Karl Kipp, 7 1/2 In. 2070.00
Vase, Hammered, 6 Sides, Scalloped Rim, Flared Foot, 26 x 12 In. 460.00
Vase, Hammered, Applied Brass Foot, Handles, Arts & Crafts, 13 In. 300.00
Vase, Hammered, Bulbous, Original Patina, Stickley Brothers, 10 In. 460.00
Vase, Hammered, Dark Patina, Tall, Flared, Rolled Rim, G. Stickley, 10 1/2 x 6 In. 2415.00
Vase, Hammered, Flared & Lobed Body, Die Stamped, Marie Zimmerman, 7 x 11 In. 489.00
Vase, Hammered, Flared Top, Bulbous Bottom, Stickley Bros., 16 In. 1900.00
Vase, Hammered, Flaring, Riveted Handles, Green Enameled Flower, Arts & Crafts, 10 In. 316.00
Vase, Hammered, Flowers, Irma Hixon, 8 In. 520.00

Vase, Hammered, Original Patina, Stickley Brothers, 8 1/2 In. 750.00
Vase, Hammered, Tapered Base, Wide Mouth, Incised Mark, Jarvie, 4 3/4 In. 1725.00
Vase, M. Zimmerman, 1916, 7 In. 3680.00
Wall Hanging, Applied Cutout, Dutch Girl With Cat, Limbert, 6 1/2 In. 350.00
Water Spout, Buffalo Head In Lotus Blossom, Inlaid Brass & Silver, 19th Century 86.00

COPPER LUSTER items are listed in the Luster category.

CORALENE glass was made by firing many small colored beads on the
outside of glassware. It was made in many patterns in the United States
and Europe in the 1880s. Reproductions are made today. Coralene-
decorated Japanese pottery is listed in the Japanese Coralene category.

Tumbler, Pink, White, Bellflowers & Daisies, 3 3/4 In. 172.00
Vase, Honey Amber, Band Of Green & White Leaves At Neck, 3 1/2 x 2 1/4 In. 135.00
Vase, Seaweed, Rose, White, Yellow, 7 1/2 In. 525.00
Vase, White, Canary Yellow, Satinized, Feathers, 9 In. 225.00

CORDEY China Company was founded by Boleslaw Cybis in 1942 in
Trenton, New Jersey. The firm produced gift shop items. In 1969 it was
acquired by the Lightron Corp. and operated as the Schiller Cordey
Co., manufacturers of lamps. About 1950 Boleslaw Cybis began making Cybis porcelains, which are listed in their own category in this
book.

Candy Box, Cover, Blue Bird, Roses, Leaves, Pink, Green, Gold, Marked 44.00
Candy Dish, Rose Blossom, Gold Scrolls, No. 6000, 5 In. 30.00
Clock, Birds, Flowers, Sessions Movement, Stamped 908, 11 x 8 In. 152.00
Figurine, Bluebird On Stump, 12 In. 32.00
Figurine, Cat, Persian, Ribbon, Bow, c.1940, 8 1/2 In. 100.00
Figurine, English Lady, In Bustled Dress, 14 In. 61.00
Figurine, Gentleman, 11 In. 36.00
Figurine, Victorian Lady, Flowers, No. 5005, 6 In. 41.00

CORKSCREWS have been needed since the first bottle was sealed with
a cork, probably in the seventeenth century. Today collectors search for
the early, unusual patented examples or the figural corkscrews of
recent years.

Black Baby, Naked, Grinning, Exaggerated Features, Cast Metal, 5 In. 177.00
Iron, Attached Horsehair Bristles, Turned Reeded Handle, 4 1/2 x 4 1/2 In. 11.00
Ivory, Sterling Silver End Caps, Ribbed Banding, Engraved, Monogram, c.1890, 5 In. . . . 201.00
Ivory, Tusk Handle, Cavorting Putto Vintners, 20th Century, 10 1/2 In. 546.00
Lady's Leg, Folding, Blue & White Celluloid Stockings, Germany, 2 1/2 In. 375.00
Lady's Leg, Folding, Multicolored Stockings, Silver High Button Shoes, Germany, 3 In. . . . 525.00
Lady's Leg, Striped Leggings, Button Shoes, Multicolored 525.00
Old Snifter, Opener, Turn Head Corkscrew Comes Out Of Back Coat, 5 1/2 In. 82.00
Publican's, Steel & Wood Plunger Handle, Brass, 15 3/4 In. 488.00
Uncle Sam, Bust, Cast Iron, Removable Hat, 1932, 2 7/8 x 1 7/8 In., 2 Piece 287.00

Coronation, Plate, Edward VII,
Queen Alexandra Coronation,
1901, 8 1/4 In.

Coronation, Plate,
George V Coronation,
1911, 7 3/4 In.

Coronation, Tin,
Edward VIII, 1936,
5 1/2 In.

CORONATION souvenirs have been made since the 1800s. Pottery, glass, tin, silver, and paper objects with a picture of the monarchs and date have been sold at many coronations. The pieces that mention King Edward VIII, the king who was never crowned, are not rare; collectors should be sure to check values before buying. Related pieces are found in the Commemorative category.

Pitcher, King Edward VII, Queen Alexandra, Staffordshire, 1909, 7 3/4 In.	390.00
Plate, Edward VII, Queen Alexandra Coronation, 1901, 8 1/4 In. . . . . *Illus*	65.00
Plate, George V Coronation, 1911, 7 3/4 In. . . . . *Illus*	58.00
Plate, King George V & Queen Mary, June 22, 1911	375.00
Tin, Edward VIII, 1936, 5 1/2 In. . . . . *Illus*	80.00
Vase, King Edward VII & Queen Alexandra, Medallions, Royal Doulton, 11 In.	115.00

COSMOS is a pressed milk glass pattern with colored flowers made from 1894 to 1915 by the Consolidated Lamp and Glass Company. Tablewares and lamps were made in this pattern. A few pieces were also made of clear glass with painted decorations. Other glass patterns are listed under Consolidated Lamp and also in various glass categories. In later years, Cosmos was also made by the Westmoreland Glass Company.

Jug, Syrup, Milk Glass	255.00
Lamp, Oil, Painted Design, Lattice Ground, 14 x 9 In.	175.00
Lampshade, Consolidated Glass Co., c.1890, 7 In.	135.00
Lampshade, Kerosene, Puffy Glass, 7 1/3 In.	100.00
Pitcher, Consolidated Glass & Lamp Co., 8 In.	225.00
Water Set, 7 Piece	565.00

COVERLETS were made of linen or wool during the nineteenth century. Most of the coverlets date from 1800 to the 1880s. There was a revival of hand weaving in the 1920s and new coverlets, especially geometric patterns, were made. The earliest coverlets were made on narrow looms, so two woven strips were joined together and a seam can be found. The weave structures of coverlets can include summer and winter, double weave, overshot, and others. Jacquard coverlets have elaborate pictorial patterns that are made on a special loom or with the use of a special attachment. Quilts are listed in this book in their own category.

Jacquard, 2 Shades Of Blue & Red, Alternating Stripes, Fringe, 90 x 80 In.	440.00
Jacquard, Blue, Red, Ivory Field, 2 Panel, Sarah Ann Eavey, c.1854, 79 x 66 In.	605.00
Jacquard, Blue, White, Signature In Corner Blocks, Figural Borders, 2 Panel	470.00
Jacquard, Center Medallion & Rosettes, Masonic Emblems, 1824, 101 x 81 In.	4465.00
Jacquard, Center Medallion, Eagles & Shields, Vintage Border, 76 x 84 In.	247.00
Jacquard, Center Medallion, Red & Gray Stripes, Fruit & Roses, 74 x 82 In.	110.00
Jacquard, Center Medallion, Red, Navy, Olive, Natural, Floral Corners, 68 x 82 In.	192.00
Jacquard, Diamond Border 2 Sides, Floral Other, J. Keagy, 74 x 86 In.	495.00
Jacquard, Diamond Grid, Floral, Red, Navy, Olive, Natural, F. Yearous, 1852, 73 x 90 In.	1265.00
Jacquard, Double Pine Tree Border, Red, White, Blue, 2 Panel, 78 x 70 In.	195.00
Jacquard, Double Weave, Geometric Design, Navy Blue, White Pine Trees, 90 In.	302.00
Jacquard, Double Weave, Rose Medallion, Stars, W. Buechel 1846, 72 x 80 In.	250.00
Jacquard, Floral Medallion, Leaf Borders, Beiderwand, 80 x 86 In.	192.00
Jacquard, Floral Medallion, Quail In Corners, Blue Stripes, Fringe, 80 x 86 In.	467.00
Jacquard, Floral Medallion, Turkeys, Flowers, Leaves, Red, Green, Blue, 94 x 82 In.	220.00
Jacquard, Floral Medallions, E Pluribus Unum Border, Hunter, 78 x 88 In.	825.00
Jacquard, Floral Medallions, Navy, Natural Floral Border, 84 In.	410.00
Jacquard, Floral Medallions, Sunbursts, Flower & Berry Border, 73 x 76 In.	247.00
Jacquard, Floral Medallions, Urns Of Flowers Border, J. Snyder, 72 x 79 In.	467.00
Jacquard, Floral, Colored Stripes, Star & Vining Borders, 1859, 73 x 90 In.	165.00
Jacquard, Floral, Stars, Blue, Red, 3 Borders, H. Schna Veley 1840, 80 x 94 In.	385.00
Jacquard, Flowers, Green, White, Brown, Weeping Willow Border, 1859, 37 x 86 In.	910.00
Jacquard, Ivory Cotton, Wool, D. Crous, 1824, 93 x 88 In.	6463.00
Jacquard, Leaves, Stars, Tulip Border, Eagle Corner, Samuel Graham, 1844, 72 x 86 In. . .	440.00
Jacquard, Octagonal Floral Medallions, Floral Border, 1856, 69 x 75 In.	440.00
Jacquard, Red, Green, Blue, White, 2 Panel, Fringe, Signed M. Hoke, 1839	165.00
Jacquard, Seaweed & Wheel Medallions, Navy Blue & Natural, 73 x 90 In.	165.00

Jacquard, Snowball, Pine Tree Border, 76 x 80 In. 385.00
Jacquard, Snowflake Medallions, Train In Corners, c.1850, 78 x 82 In. 7151.00
Jacquard, Snowflake, Navy, White, Floral Borders, 66 x 89 In., 2 Panel 220.00
Jacquard, Star Medallion Center, Baskets, Red, Blue, Green, White Ground, 67 x 81 In. . . . 165.00
Jacquard, Summer & Winter, Center Blocks, Pine Tree Border, 74 x 96 In. 220.00
Jacquard, Summer & Winter, Floral Medallions, Tulip Border, 74 x 90 In. 385.00
Jacquard, Summer & Winter, Star Medallions, Tulips, Basket Border, 80 x 80 In. 440.00
Jacquard, Urns Of Flowers, Buildings & Palm Tree Border, 68 x 80 In. 440.00
Medallions, Red, Blue, Green, White, 2 Panel, Martin Hoke, Penn., 1844, 90 x 92 In. 1100.00
Overshot, Blue, Red, Aqua, 72 x 78 In. 275.00
Overshot, Lover's Knot, Lodemia Hill Kincheloe, 90 x 99 In. 385.00
Overshot, Square Optical, Natural & Pale Gold, 72 x 92 In. 110.00
Summer & Winter, Navy Blue, White, Pine Tree Borders, 2 Panel, 70 x 79 In. 220.00
Swans In Corners, Flower In Field, Blue & White, 72 x 88 In. 86.00

COWAN POTTERY made art pottery and wares for florists. Guy Cowan made pottery in Rocky River, Ohio, a suburb of Cleveland, from 1913 to 1931. A stylized mark with the word *Cowan* was used on most pieces. A commercial, mass-produced line was marked *Lakeware*. Collectors today search for the Art Deco pieces by Guy Cowan, Viktor Schreckengost, Waylande Gregory, or Thelma Frazier Winter.

Bookends, Boy & Girl Kneeling, Ivory High Glaze, 6 1/2 In. 207.00
Bookends, Oriental Red Over Yellow Glaze, Bucking Horse, 9 1/4 In. 460.00
Bookends, Peacock Blue Glaze, Elephant, 4 1/2 In. 92.00
Decanter, Alice Through The Looking Glass, Queen, Red Glaze, W. Gregory, 12 In. 176.00
Decanter, Ivory Glaze, Seated Queen, Signed, Waylande Gregory, 10 1/4 In. . . . . .460.00 to 489.00
Decanter, King & Queen, Waylande Gregory, 11 In., Pair 2000.00
Figurine, Flamingo, Ivory High Glaze, 11 In. 265.00
Figurine, Heron, Primrose Glaze, Waylande Gregory, 13 1/2 In. 264.00
Figurine, Parchment Glaze, Russian Peasant Playing Tamborine, 9 In. 575.00
Flower Frog, Flamingo, Oriental Red, 12 1/4 In. 288.00
Humidor, Orange, Brown Mottled Matte Glaze, 8 In. 345.00
Vase, Cover, Yellow, Green Glaze, 6 x 3 In. 207.00
Vase, Deep Blue Glaze, 3 1/4 In. 115.00
Vase, Faceted, Flared, Mottled Plum Semimatte Glaze, 8 x 7 1/4 In. 201.00
Vase, Gunmetal Glaze Dripped Over Sea Green, Cylindrical, 12 1/2 In. 633.00
Vase, Light Blue, Deep Rose Glaze, 8 3/4 In. 220.00
Vase, Yellow, Green, Black High Glaze, Stylized Flowers, Impressed Mark, 9 In. 1265.00

CRACKER JACK, the molasses-flavored popcorn mixture, was first made in 1896 in Chicago, Illinois. A prize was added to each box in 1912. Collectors search for the old boxes, toys, and advertising materials. Many of the toys are unmarked.

Ambulance, Tin Lithograph, 1930s 61.00
Booklet, Fold-Out, Native People, 1940-1950s, 25 In. 80.00
Bulldog, Glass, 1930s 52.00
Button, Pinback, Victorian Lady, Label, 1 3/16 In. 107.00
Doll, Sailor Boy, Vogue Dolls, 1979, 16 In. 41.00
Game, Tiddledy Winks, Cardboard, Whitman Publishing Co., 1920s 36.00
Gun, Bolt, No. B-8100, Marked, Japan 78.00
Mirror, Advertising, Celluloid, Glass, Rueckheim Bros. & Eckstein, 1 5/8 In. 96.00
Mirror, Cracker Kid & His Dog, Celluloid, 2 3/4 x 2 In. 605.00
Sign, Store, Sailor & Dog Holding 3 Boxes, Cardboard, 10 In. 96.00
Toy, Flapper, Cardboard, Plastic, Square, c.1920, 1 In. 87.00
Toy, Rider On Motorbike, Metal, Green, 1 1/4 In. 28.00
Toy, Sad, Happy Baby, Pull Tab, Paper, Rueckheim Bros. & Eckstein, 2 x 3 1/2 In. 67.00
Toy, Toonerville Trolley, 1 3/8 In. 690.00
Tray, Advertising, 1 1/2 x 1 In. 80.00

CRACKLE GLASS was originally made by the Venetians, but most of the ware found today dates from the 1800s. The glass was heated, cooled, and refired so that many small lines appeared inside the glass. It was made in many factories in the United States and Europe.

Bowl, Deep Amber, Ribbed, Ground Pontil, 10 1/4 In. 173.00

Candy Jar, Cover, Amber, 7 1/2 In. 12.00
Pitcher, Enameled, Fish & Seaweed, 6 In. 115.00
Vase, Enameled, Lobster & Flowers, Scalloped Top, 5 1/4 In. 58.00

CRANBERRY GLASS is an almost transparent yellow-red glass. It resembles the color of cranberry juice. The glass has been made in Europe
and America since the Civil War. It is still being made, and reproductions can fool the unwary. Related glass items may be listed in other
categories, such as Northwood, Rubena Verde, etc.

Bell, Swirl, Opalescent Edge, Swirled Ribbed Clear Handle, 12 1/2 In. 115.00
Biscuit Jar, Silver Plated Cover, 8 In. 105.00
Biscuit Jar, Silver Plated Cover, Bear Finial, c.1890, 10 In. 710.00
Bowl, 4 Applied Green Feet, Enameled, Insects, Rolled Edge, 11 x 7 In. 345.00
Casket, Jewelry, Hinged, Brass Enclosure, 4 x 5 1/2 x 3 1/2 In.   161.00
Compote, Gold Greek Key Border, 9 x 8 In. 46.00
Compote, White Flowers, Gold & Black Flowers On Stem, 4 1/2 In. 185.00
Cruet, Inverted Thumbprint, Applied Reeded Handle, Faceted Stopper, 8 In. 56.00
Decanter, 3-Petal Mouth, Clear Stopper, 11 In. 175.00
Decanter, 8 Sides, Clear Stopper, 12 1/2 In. 127.00
Decanter, Cut Panels At Base, Clear Stopper, 7 In. 210.00
Decanter, Enameled Flower, Handle, Blown Stopper, 7 3/4 In. 145.00
Decanter, Wine, Cut Base & Stopper, 7 x 4 1/2 In. 195.00
Decanter, Wine, Enameled Flowers, Brown & Green Leaves, Ball Stopper, 9 1/2 In. 225.00
Decanter, Wine, Enameled Flowers, Green Leaves, Clear Cut Stopper, 10 1/4 In. 195.00
Decanter, Wine, Wheel Engraved Flowers, Clear Cut Stopper, 11 1/4 In. 175.00
Decanter, Wine, White Dots, Gold Bands, Clear Ball Stopper, 9 1/4 In. 165.00
Epergne, Ruffled Rim, 1 Horn, 9 1/4 In. 140.00
Ewer, White Threaded Collar, Applied Clear Handle, Wafer Foot, 10 1/2 In. 235.00
Jug, Whiskey, Ribbed Optic, Applied Clear Handle, Hollow Stopper, 8 In. 80.00
Pitcher, Water, Honeycomb, Applied Clear Reeded Handle, Pontil, 8 In. 212.00
Pitcher, Water, Inverted Thumbprint, Ruffled Edge, Applied Handle, 8 1/2 In. 175.00
Pitcher, Water, White & Gold Enameled, 9 3/4 In. 90.00
Powder Box, Cover, White & Gold Enameled, 6 1/2 In. 385.00
Shade, Gold Band, White Drape, 5 1/2 x 7 In. 195.00
Sugar Shaker, Argus Swirl, 3 In. 350.00
Sugar Shaker, England 295.00
Sugar Shaker, Raindrop . . . . .143.00 to 176.00
Vase, Gold & Pink Around White Medallion, Flower, 8 In. 175.00
Vase, Gold Overshot, Gold Flower, Leaves, 10 1/2 In. 175.00
Vase, Mary Gregory Style Children, Gold Trim, 8 In., Pair 230.00
Vase, Rigaree, Silver Plated Eagle's Head Mount, WWH & Co., 16 1/2 In. 187.00
Vase, Trumpet, Clear Lattice Basket Holder, 16 In. 230.00
Water Set, Inverted Thumbprint, Applied Clear Handle, Square Mouth, 7 Piece 201.00
Water Set, Thumbprint, Morgantown, 9 Piece 290.00

CREAMWARE, or queensware, was developed by Josiah Wedgwood
about 1765. It is a cream-colored earthenware that has been copied by
many factories. Similar wares may be listed under Pearlware and
Wedgwood.

Basket, Painted Ruins, Turquoise Trim, Shell Handles, Pedestal, 1810, 10 1/2 In., Pair . . .   1080.00
Bowl, Flaring, Pierced Strap, Gold Trim, Pale Green Ground, 9 In. 86.00
Bowl, Yellow, Beaded Arches, Footed, 1824-1831, 8 x 9 5/8 In. 588.00
Charger, Feather Edge, Black Scenic Transfer, c.1770, 14 In. 1200.00
Charger, Gray, Green, Ocher, Staffordshire, c.1770, 17 1/4 In. 1880.00
Cistern, Yellow Ground, Footed, Staffordshire, 19th Century, 13 In. 705.00
Coffeepot, Cover, Brown, Ocher Slip, Bellflower Swags, 1780, 10 1/4 In. 3737.00
Cup, Stag Head, Stirrup, 1765, 5 1/2 In. 3290.00
Cup, Stirrup, Fox Head, Early 19th Century, 4 1/2 In. 3760.00
Cup & Saucer, Brick Red Slip, Red Handle, 1780, 5 1/8 In. 287.00
Dish, Leaf Shape, Green, Yellow, Manganese, c.1760, 11 In. 4110.00
Dish, Leaf Shape, Green, Yellow, Manganese, c.1765, 7 1/4 In. 1880.00
Figurine, Cat, c.1765, 4 1/2 In. 4700.00
Figurine, Milkmaid, Seated, Milking Cow, c.1775, 6 3/4 In. 1175.00

Figurine, Nude Child, Astride Bear, 1700s, 5 1/4 In. 690.00
Figurine, Sheep, Reclining, Early 19th Century, 3 3/8 In. 1998.00
Figurine, Squirrel, c.1770, 7 1/8 In. 7050.00
Group, Woman, Dog, Bagpipes, Country Arbor, c.1820, 9 1/4 In. 470.00
Jug, Cream, Glaze, Fruits, Leaves, c.1770, 5 1/2 In. 1116.00
Mug, Butterfly Over Word Ale, Yellow Ground, c.1815, 5 In. 4110.00
Mug, Chestnut Brown Slip Field, Black Mocha Trees, 1795, 4 1/2 In. 977.00
Mug, Eagle, Shield, Yellow Ground, c.1812, 4 1/2 x 4 1/8 In. 4110.00
Mug, Lafayette, Washington, Eagle, Banner, Black Transfer, Leaf Handle, 2 1/2 In. 1380.00
Pitcher, Man & Woman, On Sides, Marked Under Spout, G. Sugdin, 9 1/2 In. ... 850.00
Pitcher, Ribs, Applied Entwined Lapped Rib Handles, 9 3/4 In. 489.00
Pitcher, War Of 1812, Naval Officer, 6 1/2 In. 2016.00
Plate, 8 Sides, England, 18th Century, 8 1/4 In., Pair 520.00
Plate, Blue Transfer, Chinese Pagoda, 8 1/4 In., Pair 195.00
Plate Set, Berried Branch, Leaf Surround, c.1770, 4 Piece 7638.00
Platter, Feather Edge, Wreath, 14 1/2 x 18 1/2 In. 431.00
Platter, Gray, Green, Manganese, c.1770 .... 2233.00
Stand, Yellow Ground, Oval, c.1815, 10 1/4 In. 410.00
Stand, Yellow Ground, Round, c.1815, 8 3/8 In. 940.00
Tankard, Cylindrical, c.1770, 5 1/4 In. 3055.00
Tea Canister, Cover, Green, Brown, Ocher, c.1779, 5 3/8 In. 3760.00
Teabowl & Saucer, Beaker, Alternating Brown, Green Stripes, c.1770 ...... 1000.00
Teapot, Cover, Chinese Figures, Landscape, c.1765, 5 In. 5460.00
Teapot, Cover, Flower Finial, Globular, c.1760, 4 3/4 In. 9400.00
Teapot, Cover, Gray, Yellow, Green, Globular, c.1750, 5 1/4 In. 6465.00
Teapot, Cover, Leaf & Berry Vine, Globular, c.1780, 4 5/8 In. 325.00
Teapot, Cover, Leaf, Exotic Bird, Globular, c.1775, 4 1/2 In. 470.00
Teapot, Cover, Tree Trunk Form, c.1775, 5 1/4 In. 490.00
Teapot, Cover, Yorkshire, Green, Pierced Ball Finial, Scroll Spout, c.1778, 6 3/8 In. 3290.00
Teapot, Face On Spout, Vase, Flowers, 9 In. 770.00
Teapot, Multicolored Chinoiserie, 18th Century, 8 1/4 In. 74.00
Wall Pocket, Cornucopia Shape, Masks, Branches, c.1770, 8 1/2 In., Pair ... 12925.00
Wall Pocket, Mask, Scrolls, Yellow, Blue, Manganese, c.1780, 10 1/4 In. 4700.00
Wash Basin, Blue, Gray, Pink Bands, Orange, White, Brown Cat's Eyes, 1820 .... 9775.00

CREDIT CARDS, credit tokens, metal charge plates, phone cards, and other similar collectibles that replace money are now part of the numismatic collecting hobby.

Joseph Horne Co., 2 1/2 x 1 1/4 In. 8.50
Montgomery Ward, 1964 .... 6.00
Standard Oil, January, 1971 .... 10.00
Standard Oil Sohio National, 1960 .... 15.00
Union Oil Co. Of California, Logo At Top, Text On Reverse, 1934, 3 3/4 In. 175.00

CROWN DERBY is the name given to porcelain made in Derby, England, from the 1770s to 1935. Pieces are marked with a crown and the letter *D* or the word *Derby*. The earliest pieces were made by the original Derby factory, while later pieces were made by the King Street Partnerships (1848–1935) or the Derby Crown Porcelain Co. (1876–1890). Derby Crown Porcelain Co. became Royal Crown Derby Co. Ltd. in 1890. It is now part of Royal Doulton Tableware Ltd.

Bowl, Serving, Cover, Blue Mikado, Footed, Gold Trim, Stamped, 10 In. 365.00
Coffeepot, Old Avesbury Pattern, 8 In. 74.00
Cup & Saucer, Butterflies, Birds, Flowers, Plants 72.00
Ewer, Leaves, Flowers, Cobalt Blue, England, 1890, 7 1/2 In. 660.00
Figurine, Dwarf Busker, Theatre Royal Haymarket, Marked, 7 3/4 In. 520.00
Marmalade, Cover, Underplate, Engraved, Red, Pheasant, 4 3/4 & 3 x 4 1/2 In. 232.00
Plate, Dinner, Butterflies, Birds, Flowers, Plants, 10 1/2 In. 180.00
Soup, Cream, Marked, England 39.00
Teapot, Blue Harebell, No. 4645, 5 In. 280.00
Teapot, Imari, Red, Blue, Gold, Marked, No. 1128, 7 x 10 In. 565.00
Vase, Cover, Flowers, Cream, Yellow Ground, Signed, 11 In. 285.00
Vase, Leaves, Gold Finish, Pink, Marked, 13 1/2 In. 175.00

Vase, Urn, Imari, Man Fishing In Boat, 2 Handles, 18th Century, 7 x 5 In., Pair 910.00

CROWN MILANO glass was made by Frederick Shirley at the Mt. Washington Glass Works about 1890. It had a plain biscuit color with a satin finish. It was decorated with flowers and often had large gold scrolls.

Biscuit Jar, Dandelions, 7 x 4 3/4 In.	575.00 to 700.00
Biscuit Jar, Enameled Gold Chrysanthemums, 9 In.	430.00
Bisquit Jar, Pink, White, Green, Gold, Flowers, Silver Plated Hardware, Signed, 8 In.	2070.00
Bride's Bowl, Square, Gold, Brown, Salmon, Flowers, Silver Plated Holder, 10 In.	575.00
Compote, Ruffled Edge, Gold Enamel Rose	825.00
Creamer, Melon Ribbed, Gold Flowers, Silver Handle, 4 1/2 In.	500.00
Dish, Sweetmeat, Swirl, Applied Gold Bead Flowers, Label, 6 3/4 In.	575.00
Ewer, Pillow Shape, Landscape, Sheep & Shepherd, Signed, 10 In.	4887.00
Fernery, Amethyst, Brown, Gold, Green, Flowers, Signed, 8 In.	1035.00
Sugar & Creamer, Enameled, Reeded Handles, 4 In.	1725.00
Sugar Shaker, Egg Shape, Enameled Blue Flowers, 4 1/2 In.	375.00
Vase, Mythical Creatures, Cherubs, Gold Medallions, 5 x 7 In.	1850.00
Vase, Triangular, 3 Applied Leaf Handles, 8 x 5 1/2 In.	1350.00

CROWN TUSCAN pattern is included in the Cambridge glass category.

CRUETS of glass or porcelain were made to hold vinegar, oil, and other condiments. They were especially popular during Victorian times and have been made in a variety of styles since the eighteenth century. Additional cruets may be found in the Castor Set category and also in various glass categories.

Amber Glass, Amber Handle, Enameled Flowers, Bubble Stopper, 8 5/8 In.	165.00
Amber Glass, Enameled Daisies, Leaves Around Body, Amber Handle, Ball Stopper, 8 In.	135.00
Aqua Glass, Amber Handle & Foot, 9 1/2 In.	125.00
Clear Glass, Enameled White Flowers, Strawberries, Handle, Blue Ball Stopper, 7 3/4 In.	165.00
Clear Glass, Enameled, Violets, 3 Petal Mouth, Green Handle, Bubble Stopper, 8 1/2 In.	145.00
Clear Glass, Wafer Stem, Blue Handle & Stopper, 9 1/2 In.	140.00
Cranberry Glass, Ribbed, Cut Stopper, 7 3/4 In.	77.00
Cranberry Glass, Thumbprint, Clear Reeded Handle, 5 7/8 In.	33.00
Sapphire Blue Glass, Enameled White Flowers & Leaves, Handle, 6 1/4 In.	115.00
Sapphire Blue Glass, Ribbed, Applied Handle, Stopper, Pittsburgh, 8 3/4 In.	978.00

CUP PLATES are small glass or china plates that held the cup while a diner of the mid-nineteenth century drank coffee or tea from the saucer. The most famous cup plates were made of glass at the Boston and Sandwich factory located in Sandwich, Massachusetts. There have been many new glass cup plates made in recent years for sale to gift shops or limited edition collectors. These are similar to the old plates but can be recognized as new.

Creamware, Coggle Wheel Edge, Yellow Slip, Orange Glaze, 4 3/4 In.	632.00
Creamware, Flowers & Leaves, 5 Colors, Leeds, 5 1/4 In.	440.00
Flow Blue, Central Pattern, Medallion Border, England, 3 3/8 In.	135.00
Ironstone, Animals, Dark Blue Transfer, Copeland Spode, 3 3/4 In.	280.00
Pressed Glass, 3 Stippled Hearts, 48 Scallops, Opalescent, 3 1/2 In.	112.00
Pressed Glass, 4 Pineapples, 8 Sides, Fiery Opal, 3 7/16 In.	532.00
Pressed Glass, 4 Snail Center, Diamond Point, Rope Border, 3 1/2 In.	952.00
Pressed Glass, 5-Point Star, 10 Sides, Amethyst, 3 3/16 In.	448.00
Pressed Glass, 6-Petal Medallion, 12 Quatrefoils, Bead & Reel Border, 3 3/16 In.	56.00
Pressed Glass, 6-Point Star, Bull's-Eye & Point Border, 3 1/2 In.	336.00
Pressed Glass, 12-Point Star, 15 Even Ridged Scallops, 3 9/16 In.	308.00
Pressed Glass, 12-Point Star, 24 Bull's-Eyes Divided By Rays, 3 3/16 In.	728.00
Pressed Glass, Cloudy, Flower & Leaves, Leaf Border, Plain Edge, 3 In.	336.00
Pressed Glass, Daisy, Rope Border, 24 Scallops & Points, Light Green, 2 7/8 In.	224.00
Pressed Glass, Daisy, Stippled Star Band, 62 Scallops, Light Green, 3 In.	190.00
Pressed Glass, Eagle, Lacy, 1832, 79 Scallops, Opalescent, 3 1/2 In.	252.00
Pressed Glass, Eagle, Plain Band, 24 Bull's-Eyes Between Points, 3 1/2 In.	308.00
Pressed Glass, Lacy, Quatrefoil, Lunettes, Stars, Rope Border, 3 1/2 In.	1064.00
Pressed Glass, Lacy, Rope Border, 10 Sides, Fiery Opal, 3 5/8 In.	78.00
Pressed Glass, Log Cabin, Ivy Border, 22 Uneven Scallops, 3 3/8 In.	1008.00

Pressed Glass, Lyre & Beehive, Stippled, 42 Dotted Scallops, 3 In.	56.00
Pressed Glass, Lyre, Serrated Stippled Band, 42 Even Scallops, 3 In.	280.00
Pressed Glass, Lyre, Stippled Bull's-Eye Band, 30 Even Scallops, 3 1/16 In.	952.00
Pressed Glass, Maid Of The Mist, Dotted Circle Border, Plain Rim, Green, 3 7/16 In.	504.00
Pressed Glass, Pinkish Tint, Eagle, Daisy & Leaf Border, 42 Even Scallops, 3 1/4 In.	213.00
Pressed Glass, Running Vine, 5 Bull's-Eyes, Twisted Rope, 72 Scallops, Green, 3 3/8 In.	1008.00
Pressed Glass, Sunburst Center & Border, 53 Scallops, Blue Green, 3 3/8 In.	728.00
Pressed Glass, Sunburst Medallion, Stippled, 56 Even Scallops, 3 9/16 In.	952.00
Pressed Glass, Swirled Opaque Blue, 5-Point Star, Flower Border, Plain Rim, 3 5/8 In.	952.00
Pressed Glass, Torch, 34 Bull's-Eyes, 10-Scallop Rope, 3 1/4 In.	392.00
Pressed Glass, Torch, 36 Bull's-Eyes, 24 Scallops & Points, 3 3/8 In.	180.00
Pressed Glass, Waffle Center, Bull's-Eye Border, 3 9/16 In.	168.00
Pressed Glass, Weasel, Bull's-Eye & Laurel Band, 27 Scallops & Points, 3 /14 In.	112.00
Spatterware, Dahlia, Red & Blue Flower, Green Sprigs, 5 In.	770.00
Spatterware, Peafowl, Red Border, 3 3/8 In.	44.00
Spatterware, Thistle, Red & Green, Rainbow Border, 3 3/8 In.	2200.00
Staffordshire, Sailboat, Dark Blue Transfer, Clews, 4 1/2 In.	90.00
Staffordshire, Syntax Drawing From Nature, Dark Blue, Clews, 3 1/2 In.	448.00
Staffordshire, Woodlands Near Philadelphia, Dark Blue Transfer, Stubbs, 3 1/8 In.	308.00

CURRIER & IVES made the famous American lithographs marked with their name from 1857 to 1907. The mark used on the print included the street address in New York City, and it is possible to date the year of the original issue from this information. Earlier prints were made by N. Currier and use that name from 1835 to 1847. Many reprints of the Currier or Currier & Ives prints have been made. Some collectors buy the insurance calendars that were based on the old prints. The words *large*, *small*, or *medium folio* refer to size. The original print sizes were very small (up to about 7 x 9 in.), small (8.8 x 12.8 in.), medium (9 x 14 in. to 14 x 20 in.), large (larger than 14 x 20 in.). Other sizes are probably later copies. Other prints by Currier & Ives may be listed in the Card category under Advertising and in the Sheet Music category. Currier & Ives dinnerware patterns may be found in the Adams or Dinnerware categories.

Admiral Porter's Fleet Running Rebel Blockade, Walnut Frame, 15 x 18 3/4 In.	247.00
American Country Life, October Afternoon, Frame, 25 1/8 x 31 5/8 In.	660.00
American Country Life, Pleasures Of Winter, Frame, 21 1/2 x 28 In.	1100.00
American Country Life, Summer Evenings, N. Currier, Gold Frame, 28 x 33 5/8 In.	1430.00
American Fruit Piece, Frame, 29 x 36 In.	1210.00
American Homestead, Autumn, Frame, 15 1/8 x 19 1/8 In.	357.00
American Homestead, Autumn, Gilt Lined Frame, 13 1/2 x 9 3/4 In.	220.00
American Homestead, Spring, Gilt Frame, 15 5/8 x 19 5/8 In.	330.00
American Homestead, Spring, Matted, Frame, 17 x 21 In.	380.00
American Homestead, Summer, Bird's-Eye, Maple Frame, 16 1/2 x 20 1/2 In.	302.00
American Homestead, Summer, Curly Maple Frame, 16 1/2 x 20 5/8 In.	192.00
American Homestead, Summer, Frame, 16 3/4 x 19 1/2 In.	110.00
American Homestead, Winter, Gilt Frame, 15 1/2 x 19 1/2 In.	55.00
American Homestead, Winter, Frame, 15 1/2 x 19 1/2 In.	495.00
American Winter Scene, Evening, N. Currier, c.1854, 20 3/4 x 26 3/4 In.	4500.00
Autumn Fruits, Bunch Of Grapes Uncolored, Shadow Box Frame, 18 3/4 x 25 In.	220.00
Battle Of Wilderness, Frame, 10 x 14 3/16 In.	220.00
Bombardment Of Fort Sumter, Shadow Box Frame, 15 3/4 x 17 5/8 In.	192.00
Bound Down The River, Matted, Frame, 16 3/4 x 20 3/8 In.	1100.00
Brunn Castle, Wormy Chestnut Frame, 29 1/4 x 34 1/4 In.	880.00
Bustin Record, Time Knocked Out, Signed, Frame, 14 1/2 x 18 1/2 In.	275.00
Camping In Woods, Good Time Coming, 18 3/4 x 27 1/2 In.	3220.00
Cares Of Family, Illinois Medical Infirmary, Charleston, Frame, 12 x 14 In.	220.00
Celebrated Trotting Team Edward & Swiveller, 25 5/8 x 39 1/4 In.	440.00
Chance For Both Barrels, c.1857, 23 1/2 x 31 3/8 In.	5100.00
Chappaqua Farm, Horace Greeley Home, Frame, 15 1/2 x 19 1/2 In.	220.00
City Of New Orleans, Grained Frame, 16 1/2 x 20 5/8 In.	550.00
Clipper Ship, Three Brothers, 11 1/4 x 14 In.	220.00
Crack Shots In Position, Signed, Gilt-Lined Frame, 16 3/4 x 19 5/8 In.	220.00

Crack Team At Smashing Gait, 25 x 32 1/4 In. 770.00
Darktown Race, Facing Flag, Beveled Frame, 16 x 20 In. 247.00
Darktown Tourists, Peerless Tobacco Header, 24 In. 323.00
Dead Broke, Horse Race Losers Come Home, 1886, 24 In. 277.00
Dead Game, Quail, Gilt Frame, 20 3/4 x 16 3/4 In. 165.00
Dutchman, Matted, Frame, 17 1/2 x 13 3/4 In. 385.00
Early Winter, 9 1/2 x 16 3/4 In. 4140.00
English Snipe, Cross Corner Frame, 17 x 20 In. 275.00
Express Train, Curly Maple Frame, 19 x 23 1/8 In. 2310.00
Express Train, N. Currier, 7 7/8 x 12 1/4 In. 1840.00
Fall Of Richmond, April 2nd, 1865, Gilt-Lined Frame, 12 1/2 x 15 1/2 In. 220.00
Falls Des Chats, Ottawa River, Canada, Gilt Frame, 18 3/4 x 22 3/4 In. 110.00
Farmer's Home Harvest, Frame, 28 x 34 In. 357.00
Farmer's Home Harvest, Gilt Frame, 26 1/2 x 19 3/4 In. 550.00
Flora Temple & Princess, Horse Racing, Frame, 30 3/4 x 37 1/2 In. 1110.00
Four Seasons Of Life, Middle Age, Black Frame, 24 1/4 x 31 3/4 In. 660.00
Fox-Hunting, The Death, Frame, 18 x 21 1/2 In. 440.00
Garden Orchard & Vine, Frame, 22 5/8 x 20 In. 385.00
General Francis Marion, Encampment In Swamp, Frame, 12 1/2 x 15 1/2 In. 192.00
George Washington, Martha Washington, Black, White, Frame, 17 3/4 x 13 In., Pair 165.00
Great West, Signed, Frame, 16 3/4 x 20 3/4 In. 220.00
High Bridge At Harlem, New York, N. Currier, Curly Maple Frame, 16 x 20 In. 165.00
Home In Wilderness, Bird's-Eye, Maple Frame, 9 11/16 x 20 1/2 In. 302.00
Home Of Evangeline, Chestnut Frame, 26 3/8 x 31 3/4 In. 880.00
Home On Mississippi, Horses, Buggies, Maple Frame, 17 1/4 x 20 1/4 In. 715.00
Home On Mississippi, Victorian Shadow Box Frame, 11 x 14 In. 275.00
Home Sweet Home, Frame, 26 x 34 In. 467.00
Hudson Near Anthony's Nose, c.1860, 18 3/8 x 22 1/2 In. 3600.00
In Northern Wilds, Trapping Beaver, Beveled Frame, 12 9/16 x 16 1/2 In. 440.00
Ingleside Winter, Family Carrying Firewood, Frame, 15 x 19 In. 220.00
Lake Memphremagog, Owl's Head, Curly Maple Frame, 16 1/8 x 20 1/8 In. 110.00
Lake Memphremagog, Owl's Head, Shepherd & Sheep, 11 1/4 x 16 In. 247.00
Lakes Of Killarney, Frame, Large Folio 316.00
Life In Woods, Returning To Camp, 18 3/4 x 27 1/2 In. 4600.00
Life Of Fireman, New Era Steam & Muscle, N. Currier, c.1861, 20 5/8 x 27 7/8 In. 3300.00
Life Of Fireman, No. 3517, Matted, Frame, 22 x 29 7/8 In. 100.00
Life Of Fireman, Now Then With Will, Shake Her Up Boys, N. Currier, 22 x 30 In. 1440.00
Life Of Fireman, Shake Her Up Boys, N. Currier, c.1854, 17 1/8 x 25 7/8 In. 1920.00
Life Of Fireman, The Race, Jump Her Boys, N. Currier, c.1854, 17 x 25 7/8 In. 1680.00
Life Of Fireman, The Ruins, N. Currier, c.1854, 21 5/8 x 29 3/4 In. 3300.00
Life Of Sportsman, Camping In Woods, Frame, 16 x 20 In. 275.00
Life Of Sportsman, Coming Into Camp, Frame, 10 x 12 In. 220.00
Life Of Sportsman, Coming Into Camp, Frame, 19 x 23 In. 385.00
Life Of Sportsman, Going Out, Curly Maple Frame, 16 x 20 1/8 In. 412.00
Little Manly, Seated Boy In Uniform, Frame, 16 1/4 x 12 1/4 In. 99.00
Little Snowbird, Foxing, Gilt Liner, Frame, 16 x 12 In. 247.00
Mansion Of Olden Time, 12 1/2 x 16 3/4 In. 110.00
Maple Sugaring, Early Spring, Curly Maple Frame, 16 x 20 In. 770.00
Meeting Of Waters, Frame, 11 3/4 x 15 3/4 In. 137.00
Memorial, Isaiah H. Hatton, N. Currier, c.1843, 13 1/4 x 9 1/4 In. 118.00
Midnight Race On Mississippi, Matted Frame, 16 x 20 In. 385.00
New England Home, Small Folio, Frame 138.00
New York From Brooklyn Heights, N. Currier, c.1849, 15 1/2 x 18 1/4 In. 3300.00
Old Farm House, Winter Scene, Horse Drawn Sleigh, 10 3/8 x 14 In. 220.00
Old Ford Bridge, Man Fishing, Frame, 15 x 19 In. 192.00
Old Homestead, Farmyard, Beaded Liner Frame, 18 3/8 x 22 3/8 In. 165.00
Old Homestead In Winter, 18 7/8 x 26 7/8 In. 1725.00
Old Mill In Summer, Gold-Lined Frame, 18 x 22 In. 165.00
On Point, c.1857, 21 3/4 x 29 3/8 In. 3300.00
Partridge Shooting, 12 3/4 x 20 1/4 In. 690.00
Popping The Question, Red Frame, 13 x 17 In. 137.00
Rabbit Hunt, All But Caught, Hunters, On Horseback, N. Currier, 11 3/4 x 15 1/2 In. 275.00
Racing, Grand California Filly, Wildflower, Signed, Frame, 15 x 19 In. 165.00

Racquet River, Adirondacks, Gilt Frame, 15 x 18 In.		272.00
River, Group Of Card Players, Signed, Frame, 29 1/2 x 29 1/2 In.		715.00
Roadside Mill, Man Fishing, 16 1/2 x 12 3/4 In.		132.00
Ruffed Grouse, Matted, Gold-Lined Frame, 15 7/8 x 20 In.		220.00
Sailor's Adieu, N. Currier, 12 x 8 1/2 In.		92.00
Sailor's Return, N. Currier, 12 x 8 1/2 In.		57.00
Sale Of Pet Lamb, Frame, Medium Folio		259.00
Salmon Fishing, 8 1/2 x 12 1/2 In.		1265.00
Scenery Of Catskills, Couples Overlooking Valley, Frame, 15 1/2 x 19 1/2 In.		275.00
Siege Of Vera Cruz, N. Currier, Frame, March 1847, 17 1/2 x 21 In.		423.00
Skating Scene, Moonlight, Frame, 10 1/4 x 14 In.		660.00
Sluice Gate, Boy, Ready To Lift Gate, Frame, 11 3/8 x 14 3/8 In.		412.00
Squall Off Cape Horn, Frame, 15 x 19 In.		440.00
Star Of The Road, N. Currier, 8 1/8 x 12 1/2 In.		402.00
Summer Fruits, Tinted Ground, 18 1/2 x 22 1/2 In.		440.00
Summer Ramble, Curly Maple Frame, 24 x 20 In.		412.00
Through To Pacific, Foreground Train, Gold Frame, 18 x 22 In.		660.00
Trial Of Patience, Gilt-Lined Frame, 23 1/2 x 19 1/2 In.		330.00
U.S. Dragoons, Hand Colored, Black Frame, 9 13/16 x 13 11/16 In.		220.00
Washington As Mason, 12 x 8 1/2 In.		57.00
Watchers, Boy With Dog, Walnut Frame, 16 3/4 x 12 3/4 In.		132.00
Wild Duck Shooting, On The Wing, Frame, 15 x 19 In.		247.00
Winter Past Time, N. Currier, 10 1/2 x 15 In.		2990.00
Woodcock Shooting, Hunter Under Tree, 2 Dogs, Walnut Frame, 15 x 19 In.		330.00
Woodcock Shooting, N. Currier, 13 1/4 x 20 In.		862.00
Wreck Of Atlantic, Gold Frame, 17 x 20 In.		137.00
Zachary Taylor, Center Oval, 11 Previous Presidents Around, 12 x 13 1/2 In.		32.00

CUSTARD GLASS is a slightly yellow opaque glass. It was first made in England in the 1880s and was first made in the United States in the 1890s. It has been reproduced. Additional pieces may be found in the Cambridge, Fenton, Heisey, and Northwood categories. Custard glass is called Ivorina Verde by Heisey and other companies.

Argonaut Shell, Butter, Cover, 6 In.		325.00
Argonaut Shell, Spooner, 4 3/4 In.		103.00
Beaded Swag, Goblet, Enameled, Rose		75.00
Chrysanthemum Sprig, Berry Set, 5 Piece		625.00
Inverted Fan & Feather, Toothpick, Gold Trim		495.00
Maize is its own category in this book.		
Ribbed Drape, Toothpick		250.00
Sugar, Alabama State Fair, 1912		50.00

CUT GLASS has been made since ancient times, but the large majority of the pieces now for sale date from the brilliant period of glass design, 1880 to 1905. These pieces have elaborate geometric designs with a deep miter cut. Modern cut glass with a similar appearance is being made in England, Ireland, and the Czech and Slovak republics. Chips and scratches are often difficult to notice but lower the value dramatically. A signature on the glass adds significantly to the value. Other cut glass pieces are listed under factory names.

Banana Boat, Hobstar & Fan, 11 x 6 1/2 In.		58.00
Basket, Hobstar, Dimpled Handle		300.00
Bonbon, Hobstar Foot, Pedestal, 2 1/2 x 6 1/2 In.		325.00
Bottle, Bitters, Notched At Neck, Silver Plated Stopper, Signed, Bergen, 7in.		395.00
Bottle, Tulips, Shoulder Panels, Faceted Stopper, J. Hoare & Co., 1853, 6 1/4 In.		385.00
Bowl, 16-Point Star, Signed, Clark, 10 In.		173.00
Bowl, Amethyst, Engraved Forest Scene & Deer, 3 x 9 1/2 In.		50.00
Bowl, Arabesque, Strais, 4 x 8 In.		565.00
Bowl, Boat Shape, Zipper Bands & Stars, Sawtooth, 4 1/4 x 7 1/4 x 11 In.		385.00
Bowl, Chain Of Fans At Rim, Chain Of Hobstars, Center Buttons, 4 x 9 In		495.00
Bowl, Domed Cover, Knop Finial, Concentric Stepped Bands, 18 x 10 In.		588.00
Bowl, Flared, Scalloped Rim, Sawtooth, Round, 9 1/4 x 4 In.		275.00
Bowl, Floral & Berry, Hawkes, Gorham Sterling Silver Rim, 11 x 4 In.		978.00

Bowl, Hobstar & Cane, 5 x 10 In. 810.00
Bowl, Hobstar & Star, c.1900, 3 3/4 x 10 3/4 In. 166.00
Bowl, Hobstar, Signed, J. Hoare Co., 7 In. 115.00
Bowl, Hobstars, Petticoat Foot, 32-Point Hobstar Base, 5 x 8 In. 425.00
Bowl, Ice Cream, Hobstar, 11 1/2 x 8 In. 69.00
Bowl, Parisian, 3 Sides Blown In & Out, Dorflinger, 5 x 9 In. 725.00
Bowl, Rocaille, C Scrolls, Bronze Stand, Serpentine Feet, 16 3/4 x 20 1/2 In. 862.00
Bowl, Royal, Allover, Hunt Glass Co., 2 1/2 x 9 In. 300.00
Bowl, Ruby To Clear, Floral & Hobstar, 9 In. 173.00
Bowl, Russian & Hobstar, Sterling Silver Rim With Grapes, 10 In. 489.00
Bowl, Russian, Buttons, Hobstar Base, 9 1/4 In. 288.00
Bowl, Strawberry & Fan, 9 In. 58.00
Bowl, Sunburst, Notched Rim, Flared Foot, Stand, Brilliant, 1901, 13 x 14 In. 1528.00
Bowl, Whipped Cream, Gelenta, Signed, Clark, 3 x 7 1/4 In. 250.00
Box, Allover Floral, Round, Silver Mount, 6 1/2 In. 518.00
Butter, Cover, Cut Knop, 5 x 4 1/2 In. 325.00
Candlestick, 6 Sides Notched Base, Teardrop Stem, 9 In. 375.00
Candlestick, Engraved Leaves, Exotic Flowers, J. Hoare, 10 In., Pair 195.00
Candlestick, Pinwheel Base, 7 1/2 In., Pair 295.00
Candlestick, Star Base, Cane Stem, 9 In., Pair 633.00
Candlestick, Strawberry-Diamond, Chain Of Diamonds At Top, 10 3/4 In., Pair 625.00
Candlestick, Teardrop Stem, Feathered Rayed Base, 6 In., Pair 310.00
Carafe, Sunburst & Hobstar, Full Hobstar Base, 8 x 5 3/4 In. 210.00
Carafe, Water, Russian, 8 In., Pair 345.00
Celery Vase, Roundels, Swag & Tassels, Applied Stem & Foot With Cut Star, 8 7/8 In. 110.00
Chalice, Blue To Opal To Clear, Geometric Design, Clear Stem & Foot, 11 3/8 In. 173.00
Champagne, Strawberry-Diamond & Fans, Pittsburgh, c.1820-1830, 4 1/2 In. 200.00
Charger, Floral & Leaf, Scalloped Edge, 13 3/4 In. 374.00
Cheese Dish, Center Hobstar, 16 Hobstars, Step Cut Handles, 9 In. 135.00
Cheese Dish, Cover, Venetian, 8 Sides, 6 1/2 In. 748.00
Coaster, Leaf & Flower Chain, Sterling Silver Rim, 1912, 5 1/2 In. 125.00
Cocktail Shaker, Blunt Diamonds, Sterling Silver Cover, Hawkes, 12 1/2 In. 316.00
Compote, Blue To Opal To Clear, Bracket Rim, Convex Sides, 9 x 11 In. 374.00
Compote, Chain Of 6 Hobstars, Prism Cut Center, Variety Cut Base, 14 1/2 In. 2025.00
Compote, Cover, Sawtooth Edge, Pyramid Finial, 12 x 6 In., Pair 504.00
Compote, Hobnail, Cut Foot, 11 1/4 x 7 In. 431.00
Compote, Starburst, Cane, Geometric Stem, Hobstar Foot, 9 x 12 In. 460.00
Compote, Strawberry-Diamond & Fan, Circular Foot, Star Cut, 10 3/8 x 10 1/4 In. 662.00
Cooler, Wine, Meriden, 6 x 6 1/2 In. 185.00
Cruet, Floral & Star, Stopper, Signet, 7 In. 88.00
Cruet, Royal, Triple Pouring Spouts, Hunt 185.00
Cruet, Swirl Cutting, 7 1/2 In. 115.00
Decanter, Baluster Shape, Daisy & Button, Diamond, Ball Stopper, 12 In., Pair 115.00
Decanter, Basket Weave, Stepped Neck, 10 x 4 In. 385.00
Decanter, Basket Weave, Sterling Silver Stopper With Wheat & Leaves, 9 In. 565.00
Decanter, Bell Shape, Graduated Steps, c.1900, 9 In. 224.00
Decanter, Blue To Clear, Flared, Teardrop Stopper, Early 1900s, 15 In. 175.00
Decanter, Cranberry To Clear, Paneled Base & Sides, Stopper, 11 1/8 In. 248.00
Decanter, Crosshatch, 17 Hobstars, Oval, 10 1/4 x 5 1/4 In. 525.00
Decanter, Emerald Green To Clear, Star & Teardrop Stopper, 8 1/4 In. 440.00
Decanter, Fluted Base, Honeycomb Design, Drape & Tassel, Stopper, 9 3/8 In. 440.00
Decanter, Fluted Base, Panel Neck, Etched Foliage Band, Stars, Stopper, 9 In. 330.00
Decanter, Green To Clear, Diamond Point Band, Stopper, 12 1/4 In. 330.00
Decanter, Hobstar & Fan, 6 1/2 In. 144.00
Decanter, Hobstars, Cane & Crosshatch, Neck Rings, 24-Point Hobstar Base, 12 1/2 In. . . . 1095.00
Decanter, Honeycomb, Narrow Neck, Stopper, 14 1/2 In. 395.00
Decanter, Knopped Spire Finial, Stopper, Continental, 14 1/4 In., Pair 288.00
Decanter, Mallet Shape, Star Base, Stopper, 8 3/4 In., Pair 259.00
Decanter, No. 100, Elmira Cut Glass Co., 11 1/4 In. 445.00
Decanter, Oculus, Panels, Star Base, Late 19th Century, 11 In., Pair 1380.00
Decanter, Ship's, Anglo-Irish Style, Cut Mushroom Stopper, c.1900, 9 In. 805.00
Decanter Set, Pineapple Diamond, Footed, Pierced, Silver Frame, Center Handle, 20 In. . . 460.00
Decanter Set, Silver Plated Tag, Sherry, Port, c.1900, 15 In., Pair 345.00

Decanter Set, Square Section, Crescent Tags, Curacao, Anisette, 8 In., Pair	345.00
Decanter Set, Whisky, Brandy, Hexagonal Spire Finial, 20th Century, 31 In., 2 Piece	920.00
Dish, Corinthian, Napoleon's Hat, 12 x 8 1/2 In.	850.00
Dish, Pickle, 10-Point Elongated Hobstar, 3 1/2 x 8 In.	145.00
Dish, Strawberry-Diamond, 24-Point Hobstar, 8 In.	385.00
Dish, Sweetmeat, Cover, Strawberry-Diamond & Notch, Footed, Ireland, 8 In.	173.00
Dish, Sweetmeat, Dome Cover, Ball & Spire Finial, Early 20th Century, 12 In., Pair	633.00
Dresser Set, Tray, Comb & Brush, Orca, Maple City, 6 x 11 In.	395.00
Finger Bowl, Cobalt, Band Of Panels, 4 1/4 x 3 1/4 In.	55.00
Finger Bowl, Under Plate, Engraved Grapes & Leaves, Emerald Green, 6 1/2 In.	235.00
Flask, Amethyst To Clear, Floral & Scroll, 5 x 4 1/4 In.	2185.00
Flower Frog, Chain & Hobstars, Crosshatch, 6 x 7 In.	650.00
Flowerpot, Chain Of Hobstars, Miters & Fans, 5 In.	150.00
Girandole, Lyre Shape, Demilune, Chains, Giltwood, 34 x 13 In., Pair	805.00
Goblet, Diamonds, Sunburst On Base, 4 7/8 In.	73.00
Goblet, Engraved, Stag, Cut Lens & Thumbprints, Serrated Foot, 5 1/4 In.	25.00
Goblet, Flower Band, 4 1/4 In.	73.00
Humidor, 24-Point Hobstars, Silver Plated Cover, 8 1/2 In.	815.00
Humidor, Strawberry & Fan, Sterling Silver Cover, 6 1/2 In.	518.00
Ice Bucket, Crosscut Diamonds & Hobstars, Tab Handles, 6 x 5 3/4 In.	290.00
Ice Bucket, Fluted, Sterling Silver Mounted, Bail Handle, Early 20th Century, 6 5/8 In.	316.00
Ice Bucket, Harvard, Rayed Base, 6 In.	375.00
Inkstand, Blue To Opal To Clear, 3-Piece Silver Stand, 5 1/2 x 9 In.	460.00
Inkwell, Coral Hinged Top, Diamonds, 4 x 3 In.	295.00
Jar, Cover, Diamond-Cut Finial, Oval, Oriental Medallions, Cane & Star Ground, 10 In.	260.00
Jar, Cover, Star, Square Base, Flint, 9 1/2 x 4 1/2 In.	78.00
Jar, Olive, Texel, Maple City, 6 1/4 In.	295.00
Jug, Garlands Of Flowers & Leaves, 7 1/2 x 4 1/2 In., 2 Piece	425.00
Jug, Whiskey, Pinwheel & Thumbprint, Notched Handle, Signed, Clark, 5 3/4 In.	70.00
Jug, Whiskey, Pinwheel, Fan, Strawberry-Diamond, Notched Handle, 7 1/2 In.	110.00
Lamp, Boudoir, Mushroom Shade, Hobstars, Pyramidal Stars, 15 In.	1100.00
Lamp, Mushroom Shade, Pinwheel, Prisms, 10 x 19 In.	1035.00
Lamp, Mushroom, Shade, Floral & Leaf, Hobstar Base, 18 In.	690.00
Lamp, Star & Fan, 12 x 21 In.	1208.00
Lamp, Star & Fan, Brilliant, 12 x 21 In.	1208.00
Mustard, Cover, Hobstars, Caning & Fans, Rayed Star Base, 4 1/2 x 2 In.	525.00
Mustard, Silver Cover, White To Clear, Gold Trim, 4 1/2 In.	137.00
Pitcher, Allover Diamond Point, 6 In.	115.00
Pitcher, Band Of Strawberry-Diamond, Serrated Rim, Applied Handle, 7 In.	750.00
Pitcher, Daisy & Button, 9 In.	88.00
Pitcher, Hobstar & Cane, Straight Sides, 12 In.	690.00
Pitcher, Hobstar, Cut Handle, Sterling Silver Rim, Embossed Cover, 12 In.	633.00
Pitcher, Ruby Flash, Engraved Floral, Scalloped Foot, Scroll Handle, 10 3/4 In.	330.00
Pitcher, Strawberry-Diamond, Bakewell, 8 In.	605.00
Pitcher, Sunburst, Chain Of Hobstars, 8 1/2 x 7 1/2 In.	395.00
Pitcher, Syrup, Cranberry To Clear, Coin Spot, Metal Spout, 1880s, 7 In.	395.00
Pitcher, Water, Hobstar, 9 In.	173.00
Plate, Engraved, Butterfly, Elk, Irving, 5 x 6 1/4 In.	425.00
Plate, Engraved, Thistle Center, Running Leaves & Wheat Border, 9 1/2 In.	275.00
Pokal, Cranberry To Clear, Scalloped Edge, Cover, 6 1/2 x 11 In., Pair	98.00
Pokal, Ruby To Clear, Gold Rim, Engraved Floral, 9 5/8 In.	440.00
Punch Bowl, Base, Allover Floral Engraving, 14 In.	1150.00
Punch Bowl, Base, Flowers, Early 20th Century, 14 In.	1150.00
Punch Bowl, Base, Harvard, 12 In.	770.00
Punch Bowl, Base, Hobstar & Russian, 10 x 10 3/4 In.	360.00
Punch Bowl, Base, Pinwheels, Canes, Signed, Clark, 10 1/4 x 10 3/4 In.	575.00
Punch Bowl, Blossoms, Leaves, Prop In Meet Me In St. Louis Movie, 14 x 15 In.	1035.00
Punch Bowl, Hobstar & Flash, Sawtooth Rim, Pedestal Base, Brilliant, 14 1/8 In.	633.00
Punch Bowl, Scalloped Sawtooth Rim, 14 x 11 1/2 In.	1000.00
Punch Bowl, Strawberry-Diamond & Star, Clark, 8 x 14 1/4 In.	1625.00
Punch Bowl, Sunburst, Hobstars, 8 1/4 x 10 1/2 In.	1095.00
Spooner, Bull's-Eye Handles, Pinwheels With Hobstars, 4 1/2 In.	250.00
Spooner, Corinthian, Straus, 5 1/2 x 5 In.	225.00

Sugar, Argus Swirl, Pink Satin Finish, Leaf Form Finial, 5 x 3 1/4 In. 80.00
Sugar, Domed Cover, Galleried, Floral, Bakewell Page & Bakewell, 1840, 7 1/2 In. 2970.00
Sugar & Creamer, Strawberry-Diamond & Fan, Square 295.00
Sugar Shaker, Strawberry-Diamond, 2-Piece Metal Cover, 6 1/2 In. 58.00
Syrup, Hobstars, Crosshatch, Prism, Stars, Fans & Caning, Rayed Base, 6 3/4 In. 325.00
Tankard, Blue Cut To Opal To Clear, Radial Cut Base, Cut Rim, Strap Handle, 5 1/2 In. . .   240.00
Tantalus Set, 3 Bottles, Whiskey, Brandy, Gin, Pierced Frame, Handle, 1878, 10 In. 230.00
Tazza, Engraved, Arched & Floral Panels, Sawtooth Edge, 7 In., Pair 2185.00
Tobacco Jar, Monogrammed, Sterling Silver Cover, 6 1/2 x 7 1/2 In. 748.00
Tray, Double Hobstars, Fans, Crosshatch & Strawberry-Diamond, 14 In. 530.00
Tray, Flashed Flowers, Thistle, Leaf Center, Fan Handles, 2 1/2 x 12 7/8 In. 25.00
Tray, Florence Hobstar, Meridan, 15 1/2 x 9 1/2 In. 895.00
Tray, Hobstar, Cane, Crosscut Diamond, 3 x 5 1/4 x 11 7/8 In. 60.00
Tray, Hobstar, Crosshatch, Flower, 6-Point Star, Notched Rim, 6 1/2 In. 60.00
Tray, Hobstar, Pyramidal Star, Strawberry-Diamond, 2 x 4 1/2 x 11 1/2 In. 60.00
Tray, Ice Cream, Alternating Fan & Cane With Intersecting Star, 10 x 17 1/2 In. 1050.00
Tray, Ice Cream, Harvard, Reverse Pinwheel, 1 3/4 x 8 1/2 x 12 In. 90.00
Tray, Ice Cream, Hobstar, 15 3/4 x 9 In. 258.00
Tray, Ice Cream, Hobstar, Beaded X, Strawberry-Diamond, 2 1/4 x 7 3/8 x 14 In. 60.00
Tray, Ice Cream, Hobstar, Cane, Strawberry-Diamond Fan, 2 1/4 x 7 3/4 x 14 In. 70.00
Tray, Ice Cream, Hobstar, Strawberry-Diamond, Cane & Fan, 2 1/4 x 8 x 13 3/4 In. 60.00
Tray, Ice Cream, Hobstar, Strawberry-Diamond, Notched Prism, 2 x 7 1/2 x 14 In. 90.00
Tray, Ice Cream, Sonoma, Dorflinger, 15 x 10 1/2 In. 1425.00
Tray, Ice Cream, Strawberry-Diamond, Large Star, 2 3/8 x 9 3/4 x 17 In. 150.00
Tray, Ice Cream, Strawberry-Diamond, Pyramidal Star, Fan, 2 x 7 1/2 x 14 In. 110.00
Tumbler, Blue To Opal To Clear, 8 Panels, Leaves & Berries, Footed, 6 7/8 In. 110.00
Vase, Amber To Clear, Trumpet, Swelled Faceted Foot, Medallion, 10 3/4 In. 115.00
Vase, Ball, Pinwheels, Hobstars, Crosshatch, Cane, 12 In. 1025.00
Vase, Bishops Hat, Lotus Flower, William Allen, 2 x 8 In. 450.00
Vase, Blue To Opal To Clear, Trumpet, Scalloped Rim, 9 7/8 In. 173.00
Vase, Canary To Clear, Swirls, Satin Ground, Honesdale, 6 In. 275.00
Vase, Chalice, Reverse Pinwheel, Notched Star & Fan, 9 1/2 x 6 In. 160.00
Vase, Daisy, 48-Point Star Base, Footed, 8 x 7 x 4 5/8 In. 90.00
Vase, Diamond Block, Star & Spiral, 9 1/2 x 6 1/2 In. 56.00
Vase, Diamond Cut, Fluted, Louis XVI Style, Ormolu Mount, 20th Century, 14 1/8 In. . . .   1265.00
Vase, Engraved, Singing Birds, Flowers, Green, Applied Foot, 11 1/2 x 6 1/2 In. 210.00
Vase, Fan & Floral, Late 19th Century, 10 1/4 In. 27.00
Vase, Flower & Thistle, Sawtooth Rim, 12 x 4 1/2 In. 56.00
Vase, Green To Clear, Trumpet, 14 1/2 In. 690.00
Vase, Harvard, 3 Horizontal Rings, 16 x 7 1/4 In. 350.00
Vase, Hobstar & Notched Prism, Step-Cut Neck, Flared Rim, 10 3/4 In. 385.00
Vase, Intaglio, Berry, Vine, Flower, 12 In. 288.00
Vase, Oculus & Hobstars, Flared, c.1900, 11 3/4 In. 230.00
Vase, Opal To Ruby, 10 Prisms, 10 In. 403.00
Vase, Pineapple, 8 1/4 In. 288.00
Vase, Star & Fan, Brilliant, 15 In. 518.00
Vase, Star & Fan, Flared, Scalloped Rim, 15 In. 518.00
Vase, Thistle, 12 x 8 In. 259.00
Vase, Trumpet, Harvard Variant, 11 1/4 In. 165.00
Vase, Trumpet, Hobstar, Fan, Strawberry-Diamond, 12 x 5 1/2 In.   50.00
Vase, Urns, Rectangular Diamond Point Reserves, Faceted Stem, 19th Century, 7 1/4 In. . .   288.00
Vase, Vertical Flutes, Hobstars, 17 In. 748.00
Vase, Violet, Diamond & Hobstar, 3 x 5 In. 350.00
Vase, Whirlwind No. 1144, Maple City, 10 x 8 In. 825.00
Vase, White, Red, Green Thread Design, 8 1/2 x 5 In. 130.00
Waste Bowl, Rayed Base, Paneled, Muddler, 4 5/8 x 3 1/2 In. 55.00
Water Set, Hobstar & Pinwheel, 9 x 4 In., 7 Piece 230.00

CUT VELVET is a special type of art glass, made with two layers of
blown glass, which shows a raised pattern. It usually had an acid finish or a texture like velvet. It was made by many glass factories during
the late Victorian years.

   Lamp, Rose Over White Diamond-Quilted, Original Glass Ball Shade, 17 In. 495.00

Vase, Pink Over White, 7 3/4 In. 165.00

CYBIS porcelain is a twentieth-century product. Boleslaw Cybis came to the United States from Poland in 1939. He started making porcelains in Long Island, New York, in 1940. He moved to Trenton, New Jersey, in 1942 as one of the founders of Cordey China Co. and started his own Cybis Porcelains about 1950. The firm is still working. See also Cordey.

CYBIS

Figurine, Moses Holding Tablets, No. 714, Wood Base, Signed, 19 1/2 In. 230.00
Figurine, Owl, Baby, 4 1/2 In. 28.00
Figurine, Snowy Egret, Amid Cattails, No. 12, 17 3/4 In. 287.00

CZECHOSLOVAKIA is a popular term with collectors. The name, first used as a mark after the country was formed in 1918, appears on glass and porcelain and other decorative items. Although Czechoslovakia split into Slovakia and the Czech Republic on January 1, 1993, the name continues to be used in some trademarks.

CZECHOSLOVAKIA GLASS

Figurine, Musician, Trumpet Player, Green Base, 1900s, 8 In. 450.00
Figurine, Rabbit, On Haunches, Verdigris, Jade Green, 1920s, 3 x 2 In. 150.00
Perfume Bottle, Geometric Fan Stopper, 7 In. 165.00
Planter, Elephant, Tree Trunk Base, 13 3/4 x 13 1/4 In. 605.00
Vase, Blue, Enameled Flowers, Gold Rim, Footed, 4 1/4 In. 300.00

CZECHOSLOVAKIA POTTERY

Canister, Sugar, Burgundy & Black, Art Deco, 4 1/2 In. 35.00
Chocolate Set, Blue & White, 15 Piece 55.00
Pitcher, Blown Out Fruit, Hand Painted, 8 3/8 In. 160.00
Vase, Bird, Flowers, Hand Painted, 6 In. 125.00
Vase, Iridescent Yellow, Slender, Angular Handles, 8 3/4 In. 65.00
Vase, Tree Trunk Shape, Robin Perched On Limb, 4 In. 25.00
Wall Pocket, Figural Parrot, Hand Painted, 7 1/2 In. 100.00

D'ARGENTAL is a mark used in France by the Compagnie des Cristalleries de St. Louis. The firm made multilayered, acid-cut cameo glass in the late nineteenth and twentieth centuries. D'Argental is the French name for the city of Munzthal, home of the glassworks. Later they made enameled etched glass.

Lamp, Deep Crimson Grape Clusters, Trailing Vines, 23 In. 4113.00
Vase, Castle, Forest Scene, Brown Over Gold, 10 1/2 x 4 1/2 In. 1250.00
Vase, Large Flowers, Yellow Over Red, Signed, 7 x 4 1/2 In. 750.00
Vase, Morning Glories, Amber, Red, Orange, Bulbous, Slender Neck, Cameo, 10 In. 430.00
Vase, Roses, Mottled Red Over Deep Yellow, Cameo, 14 In. 2185.00
Vase, Royal Blue Carved Leaves Grow From Base, Signed, 6 In. 560.00
Vase, Tall Trees By Castle, High Mountain, Sunshine Sky, Signed, 7 3/4 In. 1456.00

DANIEL BOONE, a pre–Revolutionary War folk hero, was a surveyor, trapper, and frontiersman. A television series, which ran from 1964 to 1970, was based on his life and starred Fess Parker. All types of Daniel Boone memorabilia are collected.

Book, Daniel Boone Wilderness Scout, Illustrated, 1960s, 8 x 22 In. 8.00
Box, Trail Blazers Club, Fess Parker, American Tradition Co., 1964 .... 48.00
Costume, Mask, Ben Cooper Co., 1960s, 14 Piece 20.00
Pencil Case, Daniel Boone With Rifle, American Trading Co., 1964, 3 x 8 In. 20.00
Tumbler, Covered Wagon, 1960s, 5 In. 27.00

DAUM, a glassworks in Nancy, France, was started by Jean Daum in 1875. The company, now called *Cristalleries de Nancy*, is still working. The *Daum Nancy* mark has been used in many variations. The name of the city and the artist are usually both included.

Bowl, Brown Leaves, Purple, Blue, Yellow & Green, Satin, 7 1/4 In. 920.00
Bowl, Cover, Flowers, Opaline, Signed, 1 1/2 In. 1090.00
Bowl, Cover, Forest Lake Scene, Gold Finial, Signed, 1 3/4 In. 1560.00

Bowl, Cover, Mottled Red & Cranberry, Foil Inclusions, 5 1/2 In. 805.00
Bowl, Grapes & Vines, Green Over Mottled Red, 3 Sides, Signed, 11 In. 1495.00
Bowl, Hoof & Thumbprint, Scattered Gold Foil, Wrought Iron Frame, Signed, 10 In. 2200.00
Bowl, Large Columbines, Yellow, Cameo, 3 x 8 In. 2645.00
Bowl, Leaves & Berries, Yellow Over Mottled Red, Signed, 5 1/2 In. 1335.00
Bowl, Orange Fruit, Brown Branch, Leaves, Blue Ground, 3 x 6 In. 2070.00
Bowl, Red Flowers, Green Leaves, Yellow On Brown, 5 1/2 In. 980.00
Bowl, Ships In Harbor, Red Over Mottled Yellow, Signed, 8 1/2 In. 2300.00
Bowl, Yellow Irises, Cameo, Signed, 3 1/2 In. 1035.00
Box, Cover, Light Amethyst, Thistle, Gold Trim, Cameo, Signed, 5 x 4 1/2 x 3 In. 978.00
Box, Cover, Rose Seed Pods & Leaves, Mottled Gray, 6 In. 3737.00
Centerpiece, Clear, Free-Form, 4 1/2 x 14 x 10 1/4 In. 290.00
Decanter, Grand Mariner, Signed, 8 1/2 In. 1176.00
Decanter, Landscape, Gold Trim, Cylindrical, Signed, 3 In. 1495.00
Eggcup, Winter Landscape, Mottled Yellow, Cameo, 3 3/4 In. 720.00
Flask, Violet Blossoms, Enameled, Tapered Cylinder, Silver Mount, c.1900, 5 5/8 In. 374.00
Inkwell, Reddish-Orange, Black, Floral & Leaf, Signed, Cameo, 5 x 4 In. 1955.00
Lamp, Cameo Shade, Wrought Iron, Edgar Brandt, 1920, 13 3/4 In. 4800.00
Lamp Base, Geometric, Blue, Cameo, Signed, 18 1/2 In. 403.00
Pitcher, Flowers, Pink, Gold Trim, Flattened Oval, Cameo, Signed, 3 1/2 In. 920.00
Rose Bowl, Poppies, Pale Cranberry, Cameo, Signed, 3 1/2 x 4 In. 800.00
Rose Bowl, Thistle, Opaline, Cameo, Signed, 3 In. 290.00
Salt, Bucket, Enameled Sail Boats, Tranquil Lake, Road, Signed, 1 1/4 x 13/4 In. 1008.00
Salt, Enameled Harbor Scene, Yellow, Signed, 1 3/4 In. 805.00
Salt, Enameled Landscape, Trees, Snow, Signed, 1 3/4 In. 1150.00
Salt, Enameled Sailing Ships Scene, Country Road, Opalescent, 1 3/8 In. 1018.00
Salt, Enameled Winter Scene, Orange, Signed, 1 3/4 In. 1790.00
Salt, Flowers, Yellow, Cameo, Signed, 1 3/4 In. 805.00
Salt, Holly Leaves, Red Berries, Citron, Cameo, Signed, 1 1/8 x 2 In. 1344.00
Sconce, Mottled Cameo Shade, Metal Bird Mount, Signed, 6 In. 1725.00
Sconce, Shell Pocket, 3 Mermaids, Amethyst, Pate-De-Verre 980.00
Vase, Algae & Fish, Etched, Enameled, Gold, Mount, c.1898, 10 1/2 In. 17625.00
Vase, Amethyst Trees, Air Infused Trunks Looming Night Time Sky, Signed, 11 1/2 In. . . 9520.00
Vase, Applied Carved Marquetries, Mottled Blue, Signed, 7 In. 4600.00
Vase, Applied Dragonfly, Grass Around Base, Blue Gray, Cameo, Signed, 1900, 5 7/8 In. . . 8400.00
Vase, Band Of Leaves, Flowers, Deep Blue Green, Cameo, c.1930, 11 1/2 In. 7050.00
Vase, Berried Branches, Pink, Cameo, Signed, 10 1/2 In. 920.00
Vase, Berries, Leaves, Vines, Pink Over Green, 7 1/2 In. 865.00
Vase, Black, Foil Inclusion, Blown Into Wrought Iron, Majorelle, Signed, 10 1/2 In. 1840.00
Vase, Blown, Citron, Foil Inclusions, Wrought Iron, Majorelle, 7 1/2 In. 1610.00
Vase, Blue Flowers, Green Stems, Mottled Ground, Cameo, Signed, 7 3/4 In. 3450.00
Vase, Blue, Clear V-Shaped Panel, 1940s, 11 1/2 x 6 In. 805.00
Vase, Bottle Shape, Attenuated Neck, Mottled Orange, Purple, c.1915, 13 1/2 In. 230.00
Vase, Butterfly, Pink Flowers, Green Leaves, On Green, Cameo, 4 In. 1380.00
Vase, Carved Blackberries, On Yellow & Orange, Cameo, Signed, 5 In. 1265.00
Vase, Carved Flowers, Yellow, Orange, On Pink, Cameo, Signed, 24 In. 4025.00
Vase, Carved Orchids, Applied Opaline Teardrops, On Green, Cameo, 11 In. 5175.00
Vase, Carved Pink Crocuses, Gold Enameled, Cameo, Signed, 1900, 5 3/8 In. 11400.00
Vase, Cascading Green Ivy, Dimpled Ground, Signed, 10 In. 3080.00
Vase, Clear, Trapped Bubbles, Applied Orange Circles, Oval, Art Deco, Signed, 4 In. 345.00
Vase, Dandelion, Opaline, Pink, Stems, Leaves, Marked, 10 In. 2185.00
Vase, Enameled Boats At Sea, Yellow, Mottled Orange, 2 In. 1150.00
Vase, Enameled Flowers, Shaded Blue, Signed, 1 1/2 In. 1090.00
Vase, Enameled Flying Storks, Lily Pond, 3 Applied Handles, Cameo, Signed, 6 1/2 In. . . 5750.00
Vase, Enameled Leaves, Stems, Berries, On Mottled Yellow, Cameo, 15 In. 980.00
Vase, Enameled Poppies, Gold Enameled, On Green, Cameo, 5 In. 690.00
Vase, Enameled Prairie Scene, Long Neck, Signed, 1900, 13 1/8 In. 16800.00
Vase, Enameled Prairie Scene, Mottled Pink & Green, Cameo, Signed, 8 In. 10580.00
Vase, Enameled Sailboats, Yellow Dawn Background, Square, Signed, 4 1/4 In. 865.00
Vase, Enameled Trees, Rocks, Hillsides, Blue, c.1905, 21 In. 12500.00
Vase, Enameled Windmill Scene, Boats, People, Flying Birds, Signed, 5 In. 980.00
Vase, Enameled Windmill, Forest, Birch Trees, Boats, 4 Sides, 5 3/4 x 4 3/8 In. 1485.00
Vase, Enameled Yellow Berries, Spruce Leaves, Signed, 5 x 7 In. 1782.00

Vase, Enameled Yellow, Green, Black Orchids, Cameo, Signed, 3 1/2 In. 1265.00
Vase, Flower, Gold Enameled, Cameo, Signed, 7 In. 460.00
Vase, Flowers, Green Leaves, Yellow On Mottled Brown, Cameo, 6 In. 1150.00
Vase, Flowers, Long Leafy Stems, Geometric Foot, Signed, 21 In. 5040.00
Vase, Flowers, On Amber, Cameo, Signed, 5 In. 2115.00
Vase, Flowers, On Purple & White, Square Panel, Signed, 3 3/4 In. 1380.00
Vase, Flowers, On White & Orange, Cameo, Signed, 1 1/2 In. 977.00
Vase, Gold & Black Leafy Vines, Enameled Landscape Scene, Cameo, Signed, 6 5/8 In. . . . 345.00
Vase, Grape Leaves & Clusters, On Chartreuse, Rolled, Signed, 10 In. 308.00
Vase, Gray, Yellow, Orange Streaks, Leaves, Branches, Cameo, c.1920, 11 7/8 In. 1495.00
Vase, Green, Brown, Red Berries, On Lemon Yellow, Tangerine, Cameo, 17 1/2 In. 5875.00
Vase, Green, Lion, Gold Enameled, Cylinder Shape, Cameo, Signed, 9 3/4 In. 822.00
Vase, Landscape Of Trees, Lake, Mountain Range, Birds, Cameo, Signed, 2 In. 978.00
Vase, Landscape Scene, Brown Trees, Yellow Sky, Signed, Cameo, 1900, 9 1/2 In. 4800.00
Vase, Landscape Scene, Trees, Amber, Green, On Yellow, Cameo, Signed, 15 In. 3738.00
Vase, Large Flowers, Gold Enameled, Cranberry& Green, Flared, Signed, 15 1/2 In. 4310.00
Vase, Leaves & Berries, On Red, Cameo, Signed, 4 In. 1265.00
Vase, Leaves & Flowers, Blue, Yellow, On Rose, Cameo, 20 In. 6050.00
Vase, Leaves, Mottled Yellow, Purple, Green, Cameo, 12 1/4 In. 1150.00
Vase, Maroon Wooded Lake Scene, On Mottled Pumpkin, 9 1/2 In. 3055.00
Vase, Mistletoe, Dimpled Ground, Gold Enameled, Cameo, Signed, 3 In. 490.00
Vase, Mushrooms & Toadstools, Gray, Yellow, Amber & Purple, 1900s, 5 1/2 In. 7475.00
Vase, Orange, Burgundy, Blown Into Wrought Iron, Majorelle, 14 1/2 In. 2875.00
Vase, Orchids, Green, Brown, On Mottled Yellow, Cameo, 8 In. 1495.00
Vase, Orchids, On Mottled Yellow & Green, Signed, 3 1/2 In. 1035.00
Vase, Pillow, Carved Roses, Cameo, Signed, 5 1/2 In. 1060.00
Vase, Pillow, Enameled Summer Landscape, Quatrefoil Rim, Signed, 4 x 7 In. 1265.00
Vase, Pillow, Fall Trees, Meadow, Mountain, Stream, Signed, 3 1/4 x 4 1/4 In. 2576.00
Vase, Pillow, Lilies Of The Valley, Dimpled Grount, Footed, Signed, 6 In. 3735.00
Vase, Pillow, Sweet Peas, Dimpled Ground, Signed, 1 1/2 x 2 1/4 In. 896.00
Vase, Pink Cyclamen, Mottled Yellow & White, Cameo, Signed, 10 In. 3105.00
Vase, Pink To Green, Flared, Pate-De-Verre, Signed, 12 In. 2875.00
Vase, Pink, Applied Columbines, 20th Century, 9 In. 1320.00
Vase, Pond Lilies, Leaves, Emerald Green, Amber, Cameo, 9 3/4 In. 5875.00
Vase, Purple Bunches Of Grapes, Vines & Leaves, Signed, 19 In. 8800.00
Vase, Red Berries, On Green, Cameo, 6 1/4 In. 1380.00
Vase, Red Flowers, On Brown & Yellow, Cameo, Signed, 5 In. 1265.00
Vase, Red Flowers, On Mottled Brown & Yellow, Cameo, Signed, 2 In. 865.00
Vase, Rose, Geometric & Ovoid, Cameo, Signed, 11 3/4 In. 345.00
Vase, Shore Birds, On Opaline, Handles, Signed, 2 In. 855.00
Vase, Smokey, Abstract Floral Pattern, France, 13 x 4 1/2 In. 460.00
Vase, Spring Green, Violets, Leaves, On Periwinkle, Cameo, 1910, 23 In. 7640.00
Vase, Stick, Stems Of Leafy Lilies-Of-The Valley, Martele Finish, Signed, 5 In. 2240.00
Vase, Summer Scene, Green Landscape, Pale Blue, On White, Cameo, 8 3/4 x 3 3/4 In. . . 3450.00
Vase, Thistle, Brown, Beige, Tan, Cameo, c.1910, 6 In. 895.00
Vase, Thistles, Gold Rim, Diamond Shape Rim, Waisted, 7 1/8 In. 330.00
Vase, Tulips 1 Side, Enamel Scene Of Fisherman Other, Double Handle, 11 In. 2805.00
Vase, Wheat & Orange Poppies, Purple Iris, Pink, Yellow Stripes, Cameo, 9 x 4 In. 8050.00
Vase, White Flowers, Reedy Stems, Footed, Cameo, Signed, 1900, 17 1/2 In. 8400.00
Vase, Winter Scene, Leafless Brown Trees, Mottled Orange, Cameo, 15 1/4 In. 1840.00
Vase, Wooded Lake Scene, Mountains In Distance, Lime Green, Cameo, 25 In. 5875.00
Vase, Yellow, Maroon Flowers, Carved Leaves, Cameo, Signed, 10 1/2 In. 1955.00

DAVENPORT pottery and porcelain were made at the Davenport factory
in Longport, Staffordshire, England, from 1793 to 1887. Earthenwares,
creamwares, porcelains, ironstone, and other ceramics were made.
Most of the pieces are marked with a form of the word *Davenport*.

DAVENPORT
LONGPORT
STAFFORDSHRE

Blue, Relish, Leaf, 6 1/4 In. 60.00
Plate, Oak Leaves, Anchor Mark, 1800s, 8 In. 675.00
Platter, Tree, Bird, Flower, 16 1/2 In. 403.00
Toby Jug, Man, Waistcoat, Green Trousers, Marked, c.1830, 9 3/8 In. 290.00
Tray, Imari Pattern, Rounded Corners, Handles, c.1875, 18 1/4 x 12 1/2 In. 1568.00

DAVY CROCKETT, the American frontiersman, was born in 1786 and died in 1836. The historical character gained new fame in 1954 when the Walt Disney television show ran a series of episodes featuring Fess Parker as Davy Crockett. Coonskin caps and buckskins became popular and hundreds of different Davy Crockett items were made.

Cookie Jar, American Bisque	150.00
Cookie Jar, Davy In The Woods, American Bisque	310.00
Cookie Jar, McCoy	370.00
Costume, Wild Frontier Playsuit, Box, 1950s	855.00
Doll, Windup, Walking, Hard Plastic, Rubber Head, 18 In.	88.00
Fabric Remnant, Action Scenes, Green, Tan, Blue, 16 x 30 In.	15.00
Flashlight, Key Chain, Plastic, Portrait, 1/2 x 3/4 x 3, 1950s	28.00
Mug, Brush	140.00
Night-Light, Head, Red Coonskin Cap, 1950s, 1 1/2 x 1 In.	20.00
Patch, Red, Smiling Davy, 1950s, 4 1/2 x 6 In.	15.00
Pin, Crossed Rifles, Coonskin Cap, Powder Horn, 1 1/2 x 2 1/8 In.	20.00
Toy, Indian Fighter Fur Hat, Fess Parker On Box, 1950s	965.00

DE VEZ was a signature used on cameo glass after 1910. E. S. Monot founded the glass company near Paris in 1851. The company changed names many times. Mt. Joye, another glass by this factory, is listed in its own category.

Lamp, Lake, Mountain, Tree Branches, Island House On Shade, Signed, 17 In.	5500.00
Rose Bowl, 4-Point Crimped Rim, Grape Leaves, Hanging Grapes, Signed, 3 x 4 1/2 In.	560.00
Vase, Amethyst Boats On Blue Lake, Hanging Flowers From Rim, Sky, Signed, 9 1/2 In.	728.00
Vase, Boats Sailing At Sunset, Distant Shoreline, Signed, 6 3/4 In.	952.00
Vase, Cabin On Island, Mountain Lake, Frosted, Etched, 7 7/8 In.	880.00
Vase, Flowers On White, Flared Neck, Globular, Signed, 16 In.	1150.00
Vase, Green Leaf & Acorn, Green Over Frosted Clear, Cameo Signature, 6 1/2 In.	425.00
Vase, Ponderosa Pine, Front Of Mountain, Lake Scene, Yellow & Blue Sky, Signed, 8 In.	1400.00
Vase, Red Mums, Amber Over Frosted Clear, Cameo Signature, 7 1/2 In.	400.00
Vase, Sailboats, Mountains, Yellow Flowers, Etched, 7 In.	625.00
Vase, Sailing Ship, Wooded Lakeshore, Pink, Magenta & Maroon, Etched, 7 7/8 In.	468.00
Vase, Sunflowers, Orange & Purple, Etched, 5 1/8 In.	468.00
Vase, Venice, Man In Gondola, Hanging Roses & Sailing Ships, 8 In.	725.00
Vase, Water Landscape, Purple On Yellow & Orange, Signed, 12 1/2 In.	2760.00

DECOYS are carved or turned wooden copies of birds, fish, or animals. The decoy was placed in the water or propped on the shore to lure flying birds to the pond for hunters. Some decoys are handmade; some are commercial products. Today there is a group of artists making modern decoys for display, not for use in a pond.

Black Duck, A.E. Crowell, East Harwich, Mass.	978.00
Black Duck, Ben Holmes, Stratford, Conn., 1885	4025.00
Black Duck, Ken Harris	907.00
Black Duck, Premier Grade, Mason, 1900, 18 1/2 x 6 x 7 In.	3275.00
Black-Bellied Plover, Flattie Form, Original Paint	115.00
Black-Bellied Plover, Mason	6325.00
Black-Bellied Plover, Mason, New England	6325.00
Blue-Winged Teal, Painted, St. Lawrence River, 1920, 8 1/2 x 4 1/2 In.	400.00
Blue-Winged Teal, Squatting, Metal Feet, Vergle Hodge, '79, 13 In.	110.00
Blue-Winged Teal, Standing, V. Hodge 1 Foot, Chas Moore On Other, 5 x 12 1/4 In.	360.00
Blue-Winged Teal Hen, Tyzzer Rig, Lower Bill Missing, Keyes Chadwick	1210.00
Bluebill, Brass Tag, E. Burkholder, York, Penn., 14 In.	55.00
Bluebill, Painted Feathers, Tom Godin, 15 In.	165.00
Bluebill Drake, Black, White, Gray Paint, Glass Eyes, Wendell Smith, 13 In.	248.00
Bluebill Drake, Glass Eyes, Shot Scars, Mason	248.00
Bluebill Drake, Turned Head, Fred Bradshaw, Ward Brothers, 1948, 12 x 8 In.	550.00
Brant, Challenge Grade, Speculum Paint Wing Design, 1900, 20 x 7 x 8 3/4 In.	2175.00
Brant, Dry Black & Gray Paint, Glass Eyes, 17 1/4 x 8 1/2 In.	110.00
Bufflehead, Glass Eyes, Painted, Hollow	83.00
Bufflehead Drake & Hen, Ben Schmidt, Detroit, Pair	13750.00

Canada Goose, A. Elmer Crowell, 18 x 42 1/2 In. 3200.00
Canada Goose, Brown & White Paint, Black Neck, Glass Eyes, R On Base, 22 x 12 In. . . 1815.00
Canada Goose, Brown Glass Eyes, BJ, 13 x 24 1/2 In. 275.00
Canada Goose, Hollow Carved, Alfred Gardner, Accord, Mass., Original Paint 520.00
Canada Goose, Hollow Carved, Bob Kerr, Smith's Falls, Ontario, August '85 . . . . 1320.00
Canada Goose, Hollow Carved, Johnson Family, N.J. 1980.00
Canada Goose, Hollow Carved, Virginia 990.00
Canada Goose, Old Black, Gray, White Paint, Glass Eyes, Harry Ackerman, 11 x 23 In. . . 440.00
Canada Goose, Slat, Painted Head, Elmer Crowell, 18 x 42 1/2 In. 3760.00
Canada Goose, Swimming Form, James Lapham, Dennisport, Mass. 200.00
Canvasback, Glass Eyes, Black, Gray & White Body, 16 In. 165.00
Canvasback, Hollow Carved, John McGloughlin, N.J. 1045.00
Canvasback, Madison Mitchell, Md., Pair 990.00
Canvasback, Original Paint, Incised Stan White, Northeast, Md. 100.00
Canvasback, Solid Body, Red & Black Head, Tack Eyes, Mason, 16 In. 275.00
Canvasback Drake, Glass Eyes, Stamped W.O.G.H., 8 1/2 x 14 1/2 In. 300.00
Canvasback Drake, Original Paint, Cast Iron Spike Weight, Alvirah Wright, Duck, N.C. . . 7425.00
Canvasback Drake, Original Paint, Marked Jake Mallery, Lancaster Co., Pa., 1950 . . . . . . 79.00
Canvasback Drake, Wisconsin, Oversized 165.00
Canvasback Drake & Hen, Painted, Dick Robinson, Bel Air, Md., 1985, 5 3/4 In., Pair . . . 68.00
Canvasback Drake & Hen, Signed, Madison Mitchell, c.1978, 16 1/2 In., Pair 578.00
Crow, Black Body, Glass Eyes, Wire Legs, Charles Perdew, c.1930, 34 3/4 x 14 In. 705.00 to 825.00
Crow, Carved, Black Paint, White Speckles, Wood, Early 20th Century, 12 In. 375.00
Dowitcher, Head Turned, Spread Wings, James Lapham 460.00
Duck, Glass Eyes, Painted, Tom Taber, 14 In. 95.00
Duck, Light & Dark Green, White & Black Feathers, Painted Eyes & Bill, 12 1/4 In. 55.00
Eider, Humpback, Paddle Tail, Curved Rocking Bottom, Nova Scotia 2860.00
Fish, Wood, Tin Mountings, 20th Century, 15 In. 137.00
Golden Plover, Original Bill, Tack Eyes, Original Paint With Wear 865.00
Goldeneye Drake, Glass Eyes, Black, White, Gray, Hennepin, Illinois, c.1940, 13 In. 220.00
Goldeneye Hen, Vermont 190.00
Goose, Carved, Gray, White, Black, Glass Eyes, 16 1/2 x 9 3/4 In. 110.00
Goose, High Head, Painted, Madison Mitchell, 25 In. 550.00
Goose, Long-Necked, Swivel Head, Glass Eyes, Pink Bill, 17 In. 1350.00
Goose, Painted, Signed, Madison Mitchell, c.1952, 22 1/2 In. 605.00
Goose, Pine, Slat Body, Carved Tail & Head, Glass Eyes, Mark Kluck, 19 x 25 In. 165.00
Goose, Sleeping, Black Wings, White Bill, 10 x 21 In. 770.00
Green-Winged Teal, Lloyd Johnson, N.J., Pair 330.00
Green-Winged Teal, Painted Eyes, Lead Keep Weight, Crisfield, Maryland, 13 1/2 In. 300.00
Green-Winged Teal Hen, Painted, Ontario, Canada, 1935, 10 x 5 In. 400.00
Hermit Thrush, Life Size, Oval Base 195.00
Laughing Gull, New England 259.00
Long-Billed Dowitcher, Iron Bill, Tack Eyes, J.M. Dodge Factory, 11 1/4 In. 470.00
Mallard, Madison Mitchell, Md., Pair 935.00
Mallard, Preening, Hollow Carved, John Updike, N.J. 3850.00
Mallard, Stamp On Bottom, Crowell, 10 1/2 In. 2900.00
Mallard, Tucked-In-Head, Glass Eyes, Fox, 1970, 13 1/2 In. 80.00
Mallard Drake, Arnold Melbye, Dennis, Mass., Oval Base 518.00
Mallard Drake, Carved, Crowell, 10 1/2 In. 2900.00
Mallard Drake, Hollow Carved, Ron Koch Stamp, Omro, Wisconsin 165.00
Mallard Drake & Hen, Original Paint, Incised Miles Hancock, 1967, 6 1/4 In., Pair 215.00
Mallard Hen, Brown Glass Eyes, Carved Wood, 7 x 16 In. 440.00
Mallard Hen, Tack Eyes, Turned Head, Mason Factory 276.00
Merganser, American, Original Paint, 1896 . . . . 3495.00
Merganser, Carved Wing Detail, Slotted-In Head, 18 1/2 In. 1825.00
Merganser, H. Conklin, Pair 685.00
Merganser, Hen, Mason, c.1915 . . . . 16500.00
Merganser Drake, James Lapham, Dennisport, Mass. 335.00
Merganser Hen, Dean Rig, New England 1210.00
Peregrine Falcon, Harold Gibbs, Miniature 1725.00
Pintail, Glass Eyes, Mason, c.1900, Pair 2800.00
Pintail, Madison Mitchell, Md., Pair 880.00
Pintail Drake, Glass Eyes, Cork Base, Stamped PB, 19 1/2 In. 80.00

Pintail Drake, Hollow, Painted, Mason, Premier, 18 x 6 1/2 In. 465.00
Pintail Hen, Glass Eyes, Initials, 1971, 16 1/2 In. 80.00
Pintail Hen, Jess Urie, Md. 1375.00
Plover, Black & White, Elongated Beak, 8 1/2 In. 470.00
Plover, Gray Spots, Rod Support, Early 20th Century, 10 In. 470.00
Red-Breasted Merganser, Balsa, Wildfowler Factory, N.Y., Pair 1540.00
Red-Breasted Merganser, Hollow Carved, Les Van Brunt 880.00
Red-Breasted Merganser, Hollow, Horsehair Crest, Coastal, Maine, 1935, 16 x 5 1/2 In. . . 445.00
Red-Breasted Merganser Drake, Painted, Nantucket Island, 1920, 7 1/2 x 7 In. 2125.00
Redhead Drake, James Lapham, Dennisport, Mass. 175.00
Ruffed Grouse, James Lapham, Dennisport, Mass., Oval Base 259.00
Scaup Drake, Glass Eyes, Painted, Mason, 1894, 12 x 6 In. 550.00
Seagull, Wire Legs, Yellow Orange Bill, Glass Eyes, Wood Carving, 12 1/2 x 16 In. 165.00
Shorebird, Brown, Gray & White Underside, Willet, 1910, 11 1/4 In. 190.00
Shorebird, Metal Spike Beak, Driftwood Mount, Signed, Roe Terry, c.1989, 13 1/2 In. ... 60.00
Shorebird, Painted, Glass Eyes, 15 x 13 x 6 In. 56.00
Shorebird, Root Head, Sapp-Madara Family, N.J. 5170.00
Shorebird, Wood Bill, Black & White, Initials P.H., 8 3/4 In. 55.00
Shoveler, Tom Christie 880.00
Surf Scoter, Mussel In Mouth, Old Repaint, 1925, 15 x 6 1/2 In. 875.00
Surf Scoter, Painted, Hollow, Coastal Maine, 1935, 15 x 5 1/4 x 4 1/2 In. 380.00
Swan, Hollow Carved, Hurley Conklin, N.J. 1870.00
Swan, Hollow Carved, Pete Person, Va. 1320.00
White-Winged Scoter, Keyes Chadwick, Mass., Tyzzer Rig 3630.00
Widgeon, Ward Brothers, c.1930 .... 9900.00
Wilson's Snipe, Dennisport, Mass., Oval Base 320.00
Wood Duck, Hollow Carved, Wildfowler Factory, N.J., Pair 220.00
Woodcock, Harold Gibbs, Miniature 860.00
Yellowlegs, John Henry Verity, New York 5225.00
Yellowlegs, New Jersey Snipe, Painted, c.1910, 9 x 9 x 2 In. 1600.00
Yellowlegs, Root Head, Separate Head, Metal Bill, 1920s, 10 1/4 In. 470.00
Yellowlegs, Split- Tailed White Throat & Breast, Rod Support, 9 3/4 In. 235.00
Yellowlegs, Turned Head, Split Tail, Original Paint 345.00
Yellowlegs, Upright, White Breast, Black Body, White Spots, Early 20th Century 470.00

DEDHAM Pottery was started in 1895. Chelsea Keramic Art Works was established in 1872 in Chelsea, Massachusetts, by members of the Robertson family. The factory closed in 1889 and was reorganized as the Chelsea Pottery U.S. in 1891. The firm used the marks *CKAW* and *CPUS*. It became the Dedham Pottery of Dedham, Massachusetts. The factory closed in 1943. It was famous for its crackleware dishes, which picture blue outlines of animals, flowers, and other natural motifs.

Azalea, Creamer, No. 13, 3 x 3 In. 275.00
Azalea, Plate, 8 In. 165.00
Azalea, Plate, Deep Blue, Leaves With Adorned Heavy Veining, 8 1/4 In. 190.00
Bird In Potted Orange Tree, Plate, Blue, 6 In. 660.00
Bird In Potted Orange Tree, Rice Bowl, 2 x 3 1/4 In. 1100.00
Butterfly, Plate, Blue, 8 1/2 In. 300.00
Butterfly, Plate, Deep Blue, Floral Panels Between Butterflies, 6 In. 357.00
Chick, Plate, Blue, 8 1/2 In. 880.00
Clover, Plate, Deep Blue, Repeating Clover Intertwined, 8 1/3 In. 1870.00
Crab, Dish, Pickle, 2 x 10 In. 935.00
Crab, Plate, 8 1/2 In., 4 Piece 2090.00
Crab, Plate, Breakfast, Blue Ink Stamp, 8 3/4 In. 375.00
Day Lily, Plate, Vivid White Lilies, Cobalt Blue Ground, 6 1/4 In. 1980.00
Duck, Cup & Saucer, Deep Blue, 2 1/2 x 4 1/2 x 6 In. 660.00
Duck, Nappy, No. 2, Flared Rim, 2 1/3 x 9 In. 330.00
Duck, Plate, Blue, Water Lilies, 10 In. 330.00
Duck, Plate, Deep Blue, Ducks Wading Along Pond, 6 In. 275.00
Duck, Plate, Deep Blue, Tufted Feather Design, 8 1/2 In. 330.00
Elephant, Dish, Child's, 8 In. 1870.00
Elephant, Plate, 8 1/2 In. 1045.00
Elephant, Plate, Blue, 6 1/4 In. 1650.00

Elephant, Plate, Cobalt Blue Ground, 7 1/2 In. 1540.00
Grape, Plate, Deep Blue, 8 1/2 In. 140.00
Grape, Plate, Deep Blue, Clusters Of Grapes, 6 In. 190.00
Horse Chestnut, Plate, 8 1/2 In. 275.00
Horse Chestnut, Plate, Bread & Butter, Impressed Rabbit, 6 In. 145.00
Horse Chestnut, Plate, Cobalt Blue Accents, Deep Blue, 6 In. 220.00
Horse Chestnut, Plate, Deep Blue, Stylized Flowers, 10 In. 360.00
Horse Chestnut, Sugar, No. 1, Creamer, No. 4, Blue, 4 x 3 1/2 In. 360.00
Iris, Plate, White, Cobalt Blue, Black, 6 In. 190.00
Lobster, Plate, Salad, Blue Ink Stamp, 2 Impressed Rabbits, 8 In. 290.00
Lobster, Platter, Blue, 18 In. 2420.00
Magnolia, Cup & Saucer, Blue, 2 3/8 In. 150.00
Magnolia, Plate, Bread & Butter, Blue Ink Stamp, 6 In. 115.00
Magnolia, Plate, Deep Blue, Maude Davenport, 6 In. 220.00
Magnolia, Plate, Deep Blue, Open Magnolias, Leaf Design, 5 3/4 In. 190.00
Magnolia, Plate, Signed Maude Davenport, 10 In. 275.00
Moth, Plate, 8 1/4 In. 300.00
Moth, Plate, Deep Blue, Dots, Stripe, Wave Design, 8 1/2 In. 550.00
Moth, Plate, Signed Maude Davenport, 6 In. 468.00
Mushroom, Plate, 8 1/2 In. 1430.00
Mushroom, Plate, Vertical Stripes, 10 In. 2090.00
Mushroom, Soup, Dish, Shallow, 1 1/2 x 8 1/2 In. 1540.00
Night & Morning, Creamer, 5 In. 520.00
Pineapple, Plate, Tendrils Drifting, 10 In. 825.00
Polar Bear, Bowl, Deep Black, 1 1/8 x 5 3/4 In. 770.00
Polar Bear, Eggcup, Double, 3 x 3 In. 715.00
Polar Bear, Plate, Mammoth Polar Bears On Edge, 8 1/2 In. 605.00
Pond Lily, Plate, 6 In. 275.00
Pond Lily, Plate, Blue, 10 In. 248.00
Pond Lily, Plate, Deep Blue, Marked, Maude Davenport, 8 1/2 In. 275.00
Pond Lily, Plate, Signed Maude Davenport, 6 In. 1430.00
Poppy, Bowl, Oriental Type, Sloping Poppies, Blue Ink Stamp, 3 3/4 In. 1035.00
Rabbit, Ashtray, Blue, 4 In. 190.00
Rabbit, Bacon Rasher, 10 In. 468.00
Rabbit, Bonbon, 3 1/4 x 5 In. 468.00
Rabbit, Bowl, 5 1/2 In. 300.00
Rabbit, Bowl, Deep Blue, 2 x 5 1/2 In. 250.00
Rabbit, Bowl, Panel, 2 1/2 x 4 In. 2640.00
Rabbit, Charger, Large Rabbits In Repeat, 12 In. 495.00
Rabbit, Compote, 2 Handles, 3 1/2 x 5 1/2 In. 358.00
Rabbit, Creamer, Leaf Handle & Spout, Blue Lines, Blue Rabbit Label 40.00
Rabbit, Creamer, No. 1, Spherical, 3 1/2 x 6 In. 140.00
Rabbit, Creamer, Trumpet Neck, No.8, Bulbous, White Ground, 3 1/2 x 3 In. 440.00
Rabbit, Cup & Saucer, 2 1/4 In. 150.00
Rabbit, Cup & Saucer, Blue, 3 x 6 1/4 In. 250.00
Rabbit, Cup & Saucer, Demitasse, 2 x 4 1/4 In. 195.00
Rabbit, Nappy, Deep Blue, 1 1/2 x 6 In. 247.00
Rabbit, Pitcher, c.1900, 3 1/4 In. 175.00
Rabbit, Pitcher, Deep Blue, 5 1/4 x 5 3/4 In. 360.00
Rabbit, Plate, 8 1/3 In. 140.00
Rabbit, Plate, Blue Ink Stamp, c.1900, 10 1/4 In. 145.00
Rabbit, Plate, Blue, 10 In. 330.00
Rabbit, Plate, Blue, 5 7/8 In. 50.00
Rabbit, Plate, Blue, 6 In. 220.00
Rabbit, Plate, Child's, Deep Blue, Band Of Rabbits, 1 x 7 1/2 In. 550.00
Rabbit, Plate, Clockwise, Impressed Mark, 8 1/2 In. 200.00
Rabbit, Sauce, 1 1/4 x 5 In. 825.00
Rabbit, Sugar, 3 x 4 In. 650.00
Rabbit, Tureen, 4 x 7 In. 660.00
Rabbit, Vase, Blue, Bulbous, 5 1/2 x 4 1/2 In. 605.00
Snowtree, Cup & Saucer, 2 1/4 x 6 In. 250.00
Snowtree, Plate, Blue, 10 1/4 In. 300.00
Snowtree, Plate, Stylized Trees Covered With Snow, Maude Davenport, 9 3/4 In. 495.00

Snowtree, Plate, Trees With Snow Coverings, Deep Blue, 6 In. 99.00
Swan, Bowl, Deep Blue, Broad Band Of Swans & Cattails, 3 x 7 In. 520.00
Swan, Bowl, No. 3, Blue, 3 1/4 x 7 In. 300.00
Swan, Pitcher, Band Of Swan & Cattail, 5 x 6 In. 605.00
Swan, Plate, Blue, 8 1/2 In. 605.00
Swan, Plate, Butter, Blue Ink Stamp, 4 3/8 In. 260.00
Swan, Tile, Deep Blue, Elegant Swans Circular Band, 4 3/4 In. 495.00
Tapestry Lion, Plate, Deep Blue, Raised Moon Design, 8 1/2 In. 1210.00
Turkey Plate, Blue, Signed Maude Davenport, 8 1/4 In. 385.00
Vase, Blue, Green Glaze, Gray, Brown Streaks, Marked, CKAW, 5 1/8 In. 460.00
Vase, Flambe, Brown, Green, H. Robertson, 8 x 4 In. 980.00
Vase, Heavy Brown, Blue Drip Glaze, 7 1/2 In. 430.00
Vase, Multicolored Green Glaze, Blue & White Cutback Poppies, Robertson, 10 In. 18400.00
Vase, Pillow, Landscape, Relief, Bee, Dragonfly, Butterfly, Blue Green, 10 x 7 1/4 In. 935.00
Wild Rose, Butter Pat, 3 1/4 In. 300.00
Wild Rose, Butter Pat, Rose Petal Rim, 3 1/2 In. 357.00

DEGUE is a signature acid-etched on pieces of French glass made in the early 1900s. Cameo, mold blown, and smooth glass with contrasting colored rims are the types most often found.

Vase, Light Purple Grapes, Yellow, Red, On Brown, Cameo, 8 1/2 In. 325.00

DELATTE glass is a French cameo glass made by Andre Delatte. It was first made in Nancy, France, in 1921. Lighting fixtures and opaque glassware in imitation of Bohemian opaline were made. There were many French cameo glass makers, so be sure to look in other appropriate categories.

Ewer, Silver Foil Inclusions, Tall Spout & Handle, Signed, 16 In. 1265.00
Vase, Brown & Beige Berried Branches, Footed, Signed, 10 In. 1035.00
Vase, Elongated Pinecones, Pine Needles, On Green, Signed, 9 1/2 In. 730.00
Vase, Pinecones & Branches, On Orange, 3 1/8 x 3 3/4 In. 270.00
Vase, Stylized Flowers, Blue, On Mottled Green, Signed, 11 In. 175.00

DELDARE, see Buffalo Pottery Deldare.

DELFT is a tin-glazed pottery that has been made since the seventeenth century. It is decorated with blue on white or with colored decorations. Most of the pieces sold today were made after 1891, and the name *Holland* appears with the Delft factory marks. The word *delft* also appears on pottery from other countries. Delft was made in England in the eighteenth century.

Bottle, Blue & White, Handle, Inscribed Sack 1649, 6 3/8 In. 9600.00
Bottle Vase, Blue & White, Dutch, c.1700, 12 In. 360.00
Bowl, Fruit, Flowers, Yellow, Green, Blue, Purple, 18th Century, 14 In. 605.00
Bowl, Polychrome, Oriental Style, Landscapes, Canary Yellow, Iron Red, Blue, 6 x 12 In. .. 3960.00
Chamber Pot, White, 17th Century, Child's 265.00
Charger, Bird, Tree, Flowers, Bee, Marked, 18th Century, 13 In. 1980.00
Charger, Blue, Green, Iron Red, Yellow Flowers, Zigzag Border, 13 3/4 In. 1540.00
Charger, Blue, Yellow, Orange, Red, Green, c.1730, 13 1/2 In. 1155.00
Charger, Center Urn Of Flowers, Leaf Border, 13 3/4 In. 550.00
Charger, Farmer Surveying Fields, Sponged Trees, White, 18th Century, 12 In. 1095.00
Charger, Floral Polychrome, Red Over Glaze, 12 In. 550.00
Charger, Floral Underglaze, Yellow Border, A J O B On Reverse, 14 In. 440.00
Charger, Flowers & Bird, England, 1750, 1 1/2 x 13 1/2 In. 2420.00
Charger, Flowers & Feather, Blue Mark, 14 In. 410.00
Charger, Flowers, Hearts, Polychrome, Signed, 18th Century, 13 In. 1540.00
Charger, Man & Woman, Riding Horse Drawn Sleigh, Scalloped, Signed, 15 1/4 In. 155.00
Charger, Stylized Butterflies, Urn Of Flowers, Fan Of Feathers, 13 5/8 In. 770.00
Clock Set, Painted Windmill Scenes, Footed Clock, Urns, 16 In., 3 Piece 1120.00
Dish, Adam & Eve, 13 In. 8050.00
Dish, Tulip Design, 13 In. 9775.00
Figure, Cow, Standing, Flowers, Blue On White, Dutch, 19th Century, 5 1/4 x 8 In. 615.00
Flower Brick, Blue & White, Painted Baskets Of Flowers, 18th Century, 8 1/4 In. 2280.00

Jar, 8 Sides, 11 1/2 x 8 3/4 In. 465.00
Jar, Apothecary, Blue & White, Winged Angel, c.1680, 4 1/8 In. 5100.00
Jar, Apothecary, Myrrhe, C. Boraginis, Signed BP, 18th Century, 8 In., Pair 2530.00
Jug, Bird & Flowers, White, Bulbous, Straight Neck, Applied Handle, 7 7/8 In. 605.00
Lamp Base, Blue & White, 8 Sides, Oriental Figural Landscape, 18th Century, 13 1/2 In. .. 690.00
Plaque, Harbor Scene, 18 x 21 1/2 In. 412.00
Plaque, Rembrandt's Portrait Of Cossack, Brown On White, Marked, Frame, 27 In. 138.00
Plate, Blue & White, Portrait Of Queen Anne, Flanked By Initials AR, c.1720, 9 In. 6600.00
Plate, Coronation Of William & Mary, 1689, 8 1/4 In. 4600.00
Plate, Flowering Branch Behind Fence, 9 In. 550.00
Plate, Soup, Blue & White, Flowers, Late 18th Century, 9 1/4 In., Pair 345.00
Platter, Chinoiserie, Blue, Cartouches, Landscapes, Flowers, 13 In. 380.00
Punch Bowl, Fashionably Dressed Ladies & Men In Garden Scene, c.1750, 14 In. 10800.00
Punch Bowl, Floral Urns, Wreath Panels, Bird & Flowers On Interior, 1700s, 14 In. 8400.00
Punch Bowl, Napoleon Portrait, Polychrome Design, 1793, 5 3/4 x 12 In. 635.00
Punch Bowl, Polychrome, Portrait Of Napoleon, Dated 1793, 5 3/4 x 12 In. 635.00
Puzzle Jug, Pierced Neck, Inscribed Verse, James Etherington, c.1750, 8 In. 7800.00
Salt, Sawtooth In Base, Bird In Leafy Top, 17th Century 695.00
Stein, Blue Flowers, Pewter Lid, Engraved, Dated 1800, 9 1/2 In. 460.00
Tea Caddy, 4 Panels, Man & Dog, Gentleman, Flowers On 2 Panels, c.1750, 3 3/4 In. 9000.00
Tea Caddy, Blue & White, Octagonal, Figures In 6 Of 8 Panels, c.1750, 3 3/4 In. 9600.00
Tile, Blue & White, Cherubs, Mid 17th Century, Pair 185.00
Tile, Blue & White, Man, Outstretched Arms, Holding Hat, c.1750, 5 1/8 In., Pair 5700.00
Tile Set, Noah & Ark, Mulberry, Floral Border, Wooden Frame, 5 In., 40 Piece 165.00
Vase, Cover, Floral, Oriental River Scene, Kylin Knop, Marked, c.1800, 15 In., Pair 3900.00
Vase, Farmhouse Scene, Twisted Rope Handles, Crimped Rim, c.1750, 6 3/4 In. 6600.00
Vase, Tobacco, Indian Flanked Reserve, 1750s, 11 1/4 In. 2300.00
Vase, Women, Surrounded By Flowers & Birds, Panels, Bristol, 15 7/8 In., Pair 440.00

DENTAL cabinets, chairs, equipment, and other related items are listed
here. Other objects may be found in the Medical category.

Cabinet, 1 Long & 2 Short Glass Doors, Drawers, Painted, Nickel Trim, 65 x 44 In. 862.00
Cabinet, Silver, Glass Door 775.00
Chair, Upholstered, C. Ash, London, 1880 .... 7193.00

DENVER is part of the mark on an American art pottery. William Long
of Steubenville, Ohio, founded the Lonhuda Pottery Company in 1892.
In 1900 he moved to Denver, Colorado, and organized the Denver
China and Pottery Company. This pottery, which used the mark *Den-*
ver, worked until 1905 when Long moved to New Jersey and founded
the Clifton Pottery. Long also worked for Weller Pottery, Roseville
Pottery, and American Encaustic Tiling Company.

DENVER
c T &.
P Co

Vase, Column Shape, Flared Rim, Green Semimatte Glaze, Stamped Denaura, 9 x 4 In. .. 1840.00

DEPRESSION GLASS was an inexpensive glass manufactured in large
quantities during the 1920s and early 1930s. It was made in many colors and patterns by dozens of factories in the United States. Most patterns were also made in clear glass, which the factories called *crystal.*
If no color is listed here, it is clear. The name *Depression glass* is a
modern one. For more descriptions, history, pictures, and prices of
Depression glass, see the book *Kovels' Depression Glass & Dinner-*
ware Price List.

Adam, Ashtray, Green, 4 1/2 In. 25.00
Adam, Ashtray, Pink, 4 1/2 In. 27.00
Adam, Berry Bowl, Green, 4 3/4 In. 22.00
Adam, Bowl, Cereal, Pink, 5 3/4 In. 65.00
Adam, Bowl, Cover, Pink, 9 In. ....75.00 to 80.00
Adam, Bowl, Pink, 7 3/4 In. 30.00
Adam, Bowl, Pink, Oval, 10 In. 35.00
Adam, Butter, Cover, Pink ....95.00 to 145.00
Adam, Cake Plate, Footed, 10 In. 30.00
Adam, Cake Plate, Pink, Footed, 10 In. 25.00
Adam, Candlestick, Pink, 4 In., Pair 125.00

Adam, Creamer, Green 25.00
Adam, Creamer, Pink 25.00
Adam, Cup & Saucer, Green ....30.00 to 33.00
Adam, Cup & Saucer, Pink 35.00
Adam, Pitcher, Pink, 32 Oz. 90.00
Adam, Plate, Dinner, Pink, Square, 9 In. ....35.00 to 45.00
Adam, Plate, Salad, Green, Square, 7 3/4 In. 20.00
Adam, Platter, Pink, 11 3/4 In. 30.00
Adam, Salt & Pepper, Pink 100.00
Adam, Saucer, Pink 8.00
Adam, Sherbet, Green, 3 In. 38.00
Adam, Sherbet, Pink, 3 In. 35.00
Adam, Sugar, Cover, Pink 50.00
Adam, Tumbler, Green, 4 1/2 In. 35.00
Adam, Tumbler, Pink, 4 1/2 In. ....35.00 to 37.00
Alice, Cup & Saucer, Jade-Ite 8.00
American, Bowl, Oval, 9 In. 25.00
American, Compote, Cover, 9 1/2 In. 45.00
American, Ice Tub, Underplate, 6 1/2 In. 85.00
American, Ladle 25.00
American Pioneer, Cup 6.00
American Pioneer, Cup & Saucer, Green 12.00
American Pioneer, Cup, Green 12.00
American Pioneer, Ice Bucket, Pink, 6 In. 75.00
American Pioneer, Saucer, Pink 5.00
American Sweetheart, Berry Bowl, Pink, 9 In. ....60.00 to 73.00
American Sweetheart, Bowl, Cereal, 6 In. 20.00
American Sweetheart, Bowl, Cereal, Monax, 6 In. 20.00
American Sweetheart, Bowl, Cereal, Pink, 6 In. ......18.00 to 19.00
American Sweetheart, Bowl, Vegetable, Monax, Oval, 11 In. ... 90.00
American Sweetheart, Bowl, Vegetable, Pink, Oval, 11 In. 70.00
American Sweetheart, Bread Plate, Pink, 6 In. 6.00
American Sweetheart, Chop Plate, Monax, 11 In. 20.00
American Sweetheart, Creamer, Monax 12.00
American Sweetheart, Cup & Saucer, Monax 14.00
American Sweetheart, Cup & Saucer, Pink 25.00
American Sweetheart, Plate, Dinner, Monax, 9 3/4 In. 30.00
American Sweetheart, Plate, Dinner, Pink, 9 3/4 In. ...40.00 to 42.00
American Sweetheart, Plate, Red, Drilled Hole Middle 85.00
American Sweetheart, Plate, Salad, Blue, 8 In. 180.00
American Sweetheart, Plate, Salad, Pink, 8 In. 12.00
American Sweetheart, Plate, Salad, Red, 8 In. ......105.00 to 130.00
American Sweetheart, Plate, Server, Monax, 15 1/2 In. 275.00
American Sweetheart, Platter, Monax, Oval, 13 In. ....75.00 to 145.00
American Sweetheart, Platter, Pink, Oval, 13 In. .....55.00 to 60.00
American Sweetheart, Salt & Pepper, Monax, Footed 525.00
American Sweetheart, Salt & Pepper, Pink, Footed 595.00
American Sweetheart, Salver, Pink, 12 In. 25.00
American Sweetheart, Sherbet, Monax, Footed, 4 3/4 In. 23.00
American Sweetheart, Sherbet, Pink, Footed, 3 3/4 In. 25.00
American Sweetheart, Sherbet, Pink, Footed, 4 1/2 In. 19.00
American Sweetheart, Soup, Cream, Pink, 4 1/2 In. 100.00
American Sweetheart, Soup, Dish, Pink, 9 1/2 In. .....55.00 to 80.00
American Sweetheart, Sugar, Cover, Monax 625.00
American Sweetheart, Tumbler, Pink, 5 Oz., 3 1/2 In. ..100.00 to 110.00
American Sweetheart, Tumbler, Water, Pink, 10 Oz., 4 3/4 In. .. 200.00
Anniversary, Butter, Cover 18.00
Apple Blossom pattern is listed here as Dogwood.
Aunt Polly, Dish, Pickle, Blue, Handles, Oval, 7 1/4 In. 45.00
Aunt Polly, Tumbler, Blue, Footed, 6 1/2 In. 60.00
Aurora, Cup & Saucer, Cobalt Blue ....24.00 to 25.00
Aurora, Plate, Cobalt Blue, 6 1/2 .... 13.00
Aurora, Tumbler, Cobalt Blue, 10 Oz., 4 3/4 In. .....20.00 to 24.00

Avocado, Creamer, Green, Footed 40.00
Avocado, Pitcher, Green, 64 Oz. 15.00
Avocado, Sherbet, Green ....65.00 to 75.00
Avocado, Sugar, Green 40.00
Ballerina pattern is listed here as Cameo.
Bamboo Optic, Bowl, Green, 4 1/4 In. 7.00
Bamboo Optic, Cup, Green 7.00
Bamboo Optic, Soup, Dish, Pink, 7 1/4 In. 95.00
Banded Rib pattern is listed here as Coronation.
Banded Rings pattern is listed here as Ring.
Basket pattern is listed here as No. 615.
Block pattern is listed here as Block Optic.
Block Optic, Bowl, Cereal, Green, 5 1/4 In. 15.00
Block Optic, Bowl, Cereal, Pink, 5 1/4 In. 75.00
Block Optic, Candlestick, Pink, 1 3/4 In., Pair 75.00
Block Optic, Candy Jar, Cover 14.00
Block Optic, Candy Jar, Cover, Green 60.00
Block Optic, Creamer, Pink, Footed 15.00
Block Optic, Creamer, Rope Top 25.00
Block Optic, Creamer, Yellow, Footed 15.00
Block Optic, Cup, Pink 15.00
Block Optic, Goblet, Pink, 9 Oz., 5 3/4 In. 30.00
Block Optic, Goblet, Yellow, 7 1/4 In. 35.00
Block Optic, Mug, Green 35.00
Block Optic, Pitcher, Green, 80 Oz., 8 In. 60.00
Block Optic, Pitcher, Green, Bulbous, 54 Oz., 7 5/8 In. 80.00
Block Optic, Plate, Dinner, Green, 9 In. 25.00
Block Optic, Plate, Dinner, Snowflake, Green, 9 In. 25.00
Block Optic, Plate, Luncheon, Green, 8 In. 8.00
Block Optic, Plate, Luncheon, Pink, 8 In. 6.00
Block Optic, Plate, Sandwich, Green, 10 1/4 In. 50.00
Block Optic, Plate, Sherbet, Green, 6 In. 4.00
Block Optic, Plate, Sherbet, Pink, 6 In. 4.00
Block Optic, Salt & Pepper, Green, Footed 45.00
Block Optic, Saucer, With Cup Ring, Pink, 6 1/4 In. 10.00
Block Optic, Sherbet, Green, 5 1/2 Oz., 3 1/4 In. ....4.00 to 6.60
Block Optic, Sherbet, Green, Cone 7.00
Block Optic, Sherbet, Pink, 6 Oz., 4 3/4 In. 15.00
Block Optic, Sugar, Pink, Cone ....15.00 to 44.00
Block Optic, Tumbler, Green, 5 Oz., 3 1/2 In. 26.00
Block Optic, Tumbler, Pink, 12 Oz., 4 7/8 In. 25.00
Block Optic, Tumbler, Whiskey, 1 Oz., 1 5/8 In. 42.00
Bouquet & Lattice pattern is listed here as Normandie.
Bubble, Berry Bowl, Blue, 8 3/8 In. ....17.00 to 18.00
Bubble, Bowl, Cereal, Blue, 5 1/4 In. ....14.00 to 15.00
Bubble, Bowl, Fruit, 4 1/2 In. 5.00
Bubble, Bread Plate, Blue, 6 3/4 In. 3.00
Bubble, Creamer 8.00
Bubble, Creamer, Blue ....35.00 to 45.00
Bubble, Cup 5.00
Bubble, Cup & Saucer 6.00
Bubble, Cup & Saucer, Blue ....7.00 to 25.00
Bubble, Cup, Forest Green 8.00
Bubble, Goblet, Cocktail, Forest Green, 4 1/2 Oz. 13.00
Bubble, Grill Plate, Blue, 9 3/8 In. 22.00
Bubble, Pitcher, Red, Ice Lip, 64 Oz. 60.00
Bubble, Plate, Dinner, Blue, 9 3/8 In. 12.00
Bubble, Platter, Blue, Oval, 12 In. ....11.00 to 16.00
Bubble, Soup, Dish, 7 3/4 In. 5.00
Bubble, Soup, Dish, Blue, 7 3/4 In. 15.00
Bubble, Sugar, Blue 25.00
Bubble, Tumbler, Iced Tea, Red, 12 Oz. 13.00

Bullseye pattern is listed here as Bubble.
Butterflies & Roses pattern is listed here as Flower Garden with Butterflies.
Buttons & Bows pattern is listed here as Holiday.
Cabbage Rose pattern is listed here as Sharon.
Cameo, Berry Bowl, Green, Master, 8 1/4 In. 39.00
Cameo, Berry Bowl, Pink, Master, 8 1/4 In. 125.00
Cameo, Bowl, Cereal, 5 1/2 In. 5.00
Cameo, Bowl, Cereal, Green, 5 1/2 In. .... 35.00 to 41.00
Cameo, Bowl, Cereal, Yellow, 5 1/2 In. 40.00
Cameo, Bowl, Vegetable, Green, Oval, 10 In. .... 34.00 to 55.00
Cameo, Bowl, Vegetable, Yellow, Oval, 10 In. 42.00
Cameo, Butter, Cover, Green .... 125.00 to 235.00
Cameo, Cake Plate, Green, 3-Footed, 10 In. 28.00
Cameo, Candlestick, Green, 4 In., Pair .... 55.00 to 60.00
Cameo, Candy Jar, Cover, Green, 4 In. 75.00
Cameo, Candy Jar, Cover, Green, 6 1/2 In. 215.00
Cameo, Compote, Mayonnaise, Green, 5 In. 42.00
Cameo, Console, 3-Footed, Green, 11 In. 90.00
Cameo, Cookie Jar, Cover, Green .... 62.00 to 65.00
Cameo, Creamer, Green, 3 1/4 In. 22.00
Cameo, Cup & Saucer, Green 22.00
Cameo, Cup & Saucer, Yellow 11.00
Cameo, Cup, Platinum Trim 6.00
Cameo, Decanter, Green, Frosted, Stopper, 10 In. 36.00
Cameo, Decanter, Green, Stopper 185.00
Cameo, Goblet, Green, 4 In. 85.00
Cameo, Goblet, Water, Green, 6 In. .... 67.00 to 75.00
Cameo, Goblet, Water, Pink, 6 In. 164.00
Cameo, Goblet, Wine, Pink, 3 1/2 In. 860.00
Cameo, Grill Plate, Yellow, Closed Handles, 10 1/2 In. 7.00
Cameo, Ice Bowl, Green, Tab Handles, 5 1/2 x 3 In. 225.00
Cameo, Jam Jar, Cover, Green, Closed Handles, 2 In. 196.00
Cameo, Pitcher, Green, 20 Oz., 5 3/4 In. 207.00
Cameo, Pitcher, Green, 36 Oz., 6 In. 56.00
Cameo, Pitcher, Jug Type, Green, 56 Oz., 8 1/2 In. 56.00
Cameo, Pitcher, Jug Type, Pink, 56 Oz., 8 1/2 In. 18.00
Cameo, Pitcher, Water, Green, 36 Oz., 6 In. 60.00
Cameo, Plate, Dinner, Yellow, 9 In. 30.00
Cameo, Plate, Luncheon, Green 8 In. .... 12.00 to 55.00
Cameo, Plate, Luncheon, Green, 10 1/2 In. 12.00
Cameo, Plate, Luncheon, Yellow, 8 In. 10.00
Cameo, Plate, Sherbet, 6 In. 2.00
Cameo, Plate, Sherbet, Green, 6 In. 6.00
Cameo, Plate, Sherbet, Yellow, 6 In. 4.00
Cameo, Platter, Green, Closed Handles, 10 1/2 In. 25.00
Cameo, Platter, Green, Closed Handles, 12 In. 20.00
Cameo, Relish, 3 Sections, Round, 7 1/2 In. 45.00
Cameo, Relish, Green, Divided, 3 Sections, Handles, 3-Footed, 7 1/4 In. 55.00
Cameo, Salt & Pepper, Green, Footed .... 73.00 to 75.00
Cameo, Salt & Pepper, Pink, Footed 1325.00
Cameo, Sandwich Server, Green, Center Handle 1495.00
Cameo, Saucer, With Cup Ring, Green 178.00
Cameo, Sherbet, Green, 4 7/8 In. 35.00
Cameo, Soup, Cream, Green, 4 3/4 In. 195.00
Cameo, Soup, Dish, Green, 9 In. .... 90.00 to 100.00
Cameo, Sugar & Creamer, Green .... 40.00 to 56.00
Cameo, Sugar & Creamer, Yellow 28.00
Cameo, Sugar, Green, 3 In. 25.00
Cameo, Sugar, Green, Open, 4 1/4 In. 29.00
Cameo, Tray, Domino, Green, 7 In. 22.00
Cameo, Tray, Domino, Pink, 7 In. 185.00
Cameo, Tumbler, Green, 9 Oz., 4 In. 35.00

Cameo, Tumbler, Green, 11 Oz., 5 In. 35.00
Cameo, Tumbler, Green, Footed, 10 Oz., 4 3/4 In. 85.00
Cameo, Tumbler, Green, Footed, 11 Oz., 5 3/4 In. ....75.00 to 87.00
Cameo, Tumbler, Green, Footed, 15 Oz., 6 3/8 In. 108.00
Cameo, Tumbler, Juice, Green, 5 Oz., 3 3/4 In. 83.00
Cameo, Tumbler, Juice, Green, Footed, 3 Oz. 75.00
Cameo, Tumbler, Pink, 10 Oz., 4 3/4 In. 150.00
Cameo, Vase, Green, 8 In. ....45.00 to 59.00
Cameo, Water Set, Green, 6 Tumblers, 7 Piece 250.00
Candlewick pattern is listed in the Imperial Glass category.
Caprice pattern is included in the Cambridge Glass category.
Cherry Blossom, Berry Bowl, Green, 4 3/4 In. 22.00
Cherry Blossom, Berry Bowl, Pink, Master, 8 1/2 In. 60.00
Cherry Blossom, Bowl, Cereal, Green, 5 3/4 In. ....47.00 to 60.00
Cherry Blossom, Bowl, Cereal, Pink, 5 3/4 In. 65.00
Cherry Blossom, Bowl, Cereal, Pink, 6 In. 40.00
Cherry Blossom, Bowl, Fruit, Green, 3-Footed, 10 1/2 In. 95.00
Cherry Blossom, Bowl, Fruit, Pink, 3-Footed, 10 1/2 In. 113.00
Cherry Blossom, Bowl, Vegetable, Green, Oval, 9 In. 55.00
Cherry Blossom, Bowl, Vegetable, Pink, Oval, 9 In. 55.00
Cherry Blossom, Butter, Cover, Pink 125.00
Cherry Blossom, Cake Plate, Green, 3-Footed, 10 1/4 In. 38.00
Cherry Blossom, Cake Plate, Pink, 3-Footed, 10 1/4 In. 55.00
Cherry Blossom, Coaster, Green ....15.00 to 17.00
Cherry Blossom, Creamer, Green 22.00
Cherry Blossom, Creamer, Pink 20.00
Cherry Blossom, Cup & Saucer, Pink ....28.00 to 32.00
Cherry Blossom, Cup, Delphite 20.00
Cherry Blossom, Grill Plate, Green, 9 In. ....33.00 to 35.00
Cherry Blossom, Grill Plate, Pink, 9 In. 33.00
Cherry Blossom, Mug, Green 350.00
Cherry Blossom, Pitcher, Cone, Green, Footed, 36 Oz., 8 In. 70.00
Cherry Blossom, Pitcher, Delphite, 42 Oz., 8 In. 60.00
Cherry Blossom, Pitcher, Green, 36 Oz., 6 3/4 In. 60.00
Cherry Blossom, Plate, Child's, Delphite, 6 In. ....13.00 to 15.00
Cherry Blossom, Plate, Dinner, Delphite, 9 In. 25.00
Cherry Blossom, Plate, Dinner, Green, 9 In. ....26.00 to 28.00
Cherry Blossom, Plate, Dinner, Pink, 9 In. 25.00
Cherry Blossom, Plate, Sherbet, Green, 6 In. 12.00
Cherry Blossom, Platter, Pink, Divided, Oval, 13 In. ....75.00 to 85.00
Cherry Blossom, Sandwich, Tray, Green, 10 1/2 In. 35.00
Cherry Blossom, Sherbet, Green ....20.00 to 22.00
Cherry Blossom, Sherbet, Pink 20.00
Cherry Blossom, Soup, Dish, Pink, 7 3/4 In. 100.00
Cherry Blossom, Sugar, Cover, Green 38.00
Cherry Blossom, Sugar, Cover, Pink 25.00
Cherry Blossom, Sugar, Delphite 20.00
Cherry Blossom, Tumbler, 12 Oz., 5 In. 75.00
Cherry Blossom, Tumbler, Pink, 4 Oz., 3 3/4 In. 20.00
Cherry Blossom, Tumbler, Pink, 9 Oz., 4 1/2 In. 20.00
Cherry Blossom, Tumbler, Pink, 12 Oz., 5 In. 90.00
Cherry Blossom, Tumbler, Pink, Round Footed, 9 Oz., 4 1/2 In. 45.00
Cherry Blossom, Tumbler, Pink, Scalloped Foot, 8 Oz., 4 1/2 In. 40.00
Chinex Classic, Plate, Dinner, Ivory, With Castle, Plain Edge, 9 3/4 In. 16.00
Chinex Classic, Plate, Sherbet, Ivory, With Castle, Plain Edge, 6 1/4 In. 8.00
Chinex Classic, Sherbet, Ivory, With Castle, Blue Trim 25.00
Christmas Candy, Creamer 10.00
Christmas Candy, Saucer, Teal 15.00
Christmas Candy, Sugar 10.00
Circle, Cup & Saucer, Green 6.00
Circle, Cup, Green 6.00
Circle, Plate, Luncheon, Green, 8 1/4 In. 6.00
Circle, Plate, Sherbet, Green, 6 In. 2.00

Circle, Sherbet, Green, 3 1/8 In. 4.00
Cloverleaf, Creamer, Black 23.00
Cloverleaf, Cup & Saucer, Pink 12.00
Cloverleaf, Grill Plate, Green, 10 1/4 In. 25.00
Cloverleaf, Saltshaker, Yellow 70.00
Cloverleaf, Saucer, Black 6.00
Cloverleaf, Sherbet, Green . . . . .10.00 to 12.00
Colonial, Berry Bowl, 9 In. 75.00
Colonial, Berry Bowl, Green, 4 1/2 In. 20.00
Colonial, Bowl, Vegetable, Pink, Oval, 10 In. 45.00
Colonial, Butter, Cover . . . . .20.00 to 40.00
Colonial, Butter, Cover, Green 55.00
Colonial, Cup 8.00
Colonial, Cup & Saucer, Pink 18.00
Colonial, Cup, Pink 10.00
Colonial, Goblet, Claret, Green, 4 Oz., 5 1/4 In. 25.00
Colonial, Goblet, Cocktail, Green, 3 Oz., 4 In. 25.00
Colonial, Goblet, Cordial, Green, 1 Oz., 3 3/4 In. 30.00
Colonial, Goblet, Wine, Green, 2 1/2 Oz., 4 1/2 In. 30.00
Colonial, Plate, Dinner, Pink, 10 In. 55.00
Colonial, Plate, Luncheon, 8 1/2 In. 6.00
Colonial, Plate, Sherbet, Green, 6 In. 9.00
Colonial, Plate, Sherbet, Pink, 6 In. 7.00
Colonial, Sherbet, 3 In. 9.00
Colonial, Sherbet, Green, 3 3/8 In. 12.00
Colonial, Soup, Cream, Green, 4 1/2 In. . . . . .75.00 to 85.00
Colonial, Soup, Cream, Pink, 4 1/2 In. 80.00
Colonial, Sugar, Cover 35.00
Colonial, Tumbler, Green, 5 Oz., 3 In. 25.00
Colonial, Tumbler, Green, 9 Oz., 4 In. 42.00
Colonial, Tumbler, Pink, 9 Oz., 4 In. 22.00
Colonial, Whiskey, Green, 1 1/2 Oz., 2 1/2 In. 16.00
Colonial, Whiskey, Pink, 1 1/2 Oz., 2 1/2 In. 15.00
Colonial Block, Butter, Cover 25.00
Colonial Block, Sherbet, Green 5.00
Colonial Block, Sherbet, Pink 8.00
Colonial Block, Sugar, Open, White 10.00
Colonial Fluted, Bowl, Cereal, Green, 6 In. 18.00
Colonial Fluted, Bowl, Green, 4 In. 12.00
Columbia, Bowl, Cereal, 5 In. 18.00
Columbia, Bowl, Ruffled, 10 1/2 In. 20.00
Columbia, Bowl, Salad, 8 1/2 In. 20.00
Columbia, Bread Plate, 6 In. 4.00
Columbia, Butter, Cover 20.00
Columbia, Chop Plate, 11 In. 30.00
Columbia, Cup & Saucer . . . . .10.00 to 12.00
Columbia, Plate, Snack 35.00

Depression Glass,
Columbia

Depression Glass,
Coronation

Depression Glass,
Cubist

Columbia, Soup, Dish, 8 In. 22.00
Coronation, Berry Bowl, Pink, 4 1/4 In. 13.00
Coronation, Berry Bowl, Pink, Handled, 8 In. 15.00
Cracked Ice, Sugar & Creamer, Cover, Pink 85.00
Cracked Ice, Sugar, Cover, Pink 25.00
Criss Cross, Butter, Cover, Green, 1/4 Lb. 35.00
Criss Cross, Reamer, Lemon, Green, Tab Handle 25.00
Criss Cross, Reamer, Lemon, Pink, Tab Handle 275.00
Criss Cross, Reamer, Orange, Green, Open Handle ....25.00 to 95.00
Criss Cross, Reamer, Orange, Pink, Open Handle 200.00
Cube pattern is listed here as Cubist.
Cubist, Bowl, Dessert, Green, 4 1/2 In. 9.00
Cubist, Butter, Pink, Cover 85.00
Cubist, Candy Jar, Green 35.00
Cubist, Pitcher, Pink, 45 Oz., 8 5/8 In. 250.00
Cubist, Plate, Sherbet, Pink, 6 In. 3.00
Cubist, Salt & Pepper, Green 35.00
Cubist, Salt & Pepper, Pink 35.00
Cubist, Sugar, Green 8.00
Daisy pattern is listed here as No. 620.
Dancing Girl pattern is listed here as Cameo.
Diamond pattern is listed here as Miss America.
Diana, Bowl, Cereal, 5 In. 7.00
Diana, Bowl, Cereal, Pink, 5 In. 7.50
Diana, Bowl, Salad, Pink, 9 In. 22.00
Diana, Candy Jar, Cover, Green 40.00
Diana, Candy Jar, Cover, Pink 32.00
Diana, Console, Amber, 11 In. 18.00
Diana, Console, Pink, 11 In. 45.00
Diana, Cup & Saucer, After Dinner 13.00
Diana, Plate, Dinner, Pink, 9 1/2 In. 20.00
Diana, Platter, Amber, Oval, 12 In. ....16.00 to 22.00
Diana, Saucer 2.00
Diana, Tumbler, Pink, 9 Oz., 4 1/8 In. 50.00
Dogwood, Berry Bowl, Pink, 8 In. 65.00
Dogwood, Bowl, Cereal, Green, 5 1/2 In. 33.00
Dogwood, Bowl, Cereal, Pink, 5 1/2 In. 33.00
Dogwood, Bowl, Fruit, Green, 10 1/4 In. 300.00
Dogwood, Bread Plate, Pink, 6 In. 9.00
Dogwood, Cake Plate, Footed, Green, 13 In. ....115.00 to 120.00
Dogwood, Cup & Saucer, Green 48.00
Dogwood, Cup & Saucer, Pink, Thick 24.00
Dogwood, Cup & Saucer, Pink, Thin 26.00
Dogwood, Cup, Green 40.00
Dogwood, Pitcher, Pink, Decorated, 80 Oz., 8 In. 275.00
Dogwood, Plate, Dinner, Pink, 9 1/4 In. ....40.00 to 45.00
Dogwood, Plate, Luncheon, Green, 8 In. 9.00
Dogwood, Plate, Luncheon, Pink, 8 In. ....8.00 to 9.00
Dogwood, Salver, Pink, 12 In. 35.00
Dogwood, Saucer, Pink 6.00
Dogwood, Sherbet, Pink, Footed ....37.00 to 40.00
Dogwood, Sugar & Creamer, Pink 45.00
Dogwood, Sugar, Pink, Thin, 2 1/2 In. 18.00
Dogwood, Tumbler, Pink, Decorated, 10 Oz., 4 In. 45.00
Dogwood, Tumbler, Pink, Decorated, 12 Oz., 5 In. 85.00
Doric, Berry Bowl, Green, 4 1/2 .... 11.00
Doric, Berry Bowl, Green, 8 1/4 In. 36.00
Doric, Bowl, Cereal, Green, 5 1/2 In. 50.00
Doric, Bowl, Cereal, Pink, 5 1/2 In. 85.00
Doric, Bowl, Vegetable, Pink, Oval, 9 In. 47.00
Doric, Butter, Cover, Pink 90.00
Doric, Cake Plate, Green, 10 In. 30.00
Doric, Candy Jar, Cover, Pink 46.00

Doric, Creamer, Green 20.00
Doric, Cup & Saucer, Pink 13.00
Doric, Plate, Dinner, Pink, 9 In. 17.00
Doric, Platter, Green, 12 In. 25.00
Doric, Relish, Pink, 4 x 8 In. 18.00
Doric, Saltshaker, Green 20.00
Doric, Sherbet, Green 17.00
Doric, Sugar, Cover, Green 35.00
Doric, Sugar, Cover, Pink 37.00
Doric, Tumbler, Pink, 9 Oz., 4 1/2 In. . . . . .35.00 to 75.00
Doric & Pansy, Bowl, Ultramarine, Handles, 9 In. 47.00
Doric & Pansy, Butter, Cover, Ultramarine 450.00
Doric & Pansy, Salt & Pepper, Ultramarine 600.00
Doric & Pansy, Sugar & Creamer, Ultramarine 250.00
Doric & Pansy, Sugar, Ultramarine 145.00
Double Shield pattern is listed here as Mt. Pleasant.
Dutch Rose pattern is listed here as Rosemary.
Early American Prescut, Egg Plate, 12 x 12 In. 65.00
Early American Rock Crystal pattern is listed here as Rock Crystal.
Fine Rib pattern is listed here as Homespun.
Fire-King, Ashtray, Jade-Ite, 4 1/4 In. 35.00
Fire-King, Bowl, Jade-Ite, Restaurant, 16 Oz. 40.00
Fire-King, Butter, 1/4 Lb. 60.00
Fire-King, Casserole, Cover, 1 Pt. 15.00
Fire-King, Custard Cup, 5 Oz. 2.25
Fire-King, Eggcup, Double, Jade-Ite, Restaurant 60.00
Fire-King, Mixing Bowl, Ivory, Red Dots, 2 Qt. 65.00
Fire-King, Pie Plate, Juice Saver, Sapphire Blue, 10 3/8 In. 110.00
Floragold, Bowl, Fruit, Ruffled, 12 In. 40.00
Floragold, Bowl, Salad, Deep, 9 1/2 In. 43.00
Floragold, Butter, Cover, Iridescent 50.00
Floragold, Candlestick, 2-Light, Pair 65.00
Floragold, Creamer 9.00
Floragold, Cup 5.00
Floragold, Pitcher, 64 Oz. 38.00
Floragold, Pitcher, Iridescent, 64 Oz. 36.00
Floragold, Plate, Dinner, 8 1/2 In. . . . . .38.00 to 45.00
Floragold, Plate, Dinner, Iridescent, 8 1/2 In. 40.00
Floragold, Platter, Amber, 13 1/2 In. 50.00
Floragold, Salt & Pepper 55.00
Floragold, Saucer 12.00
Floragold, Sugar, Cover 23.00
Floral, Berry Bowl, Green, 4 In. 22.00
Floral, Berry Bowl, Pink, 4 In. . . . . .20.00 to 22.00
Floral, Bowl, Vegetable, Cover, Green, 8 In. 49.00
Floral, Bowl, Vegetable, Cover, Pink, 8 In. 60.00

Depression Glass, Doric

Depression Glass,
Florentine No. 2

Floral, Bowl, Vegetable, Green, Oval, 9 In. 26.00
Floral, Bowl, Vegetable, Pink, Oval, 9 In. .... 20.00 to 25.00
Floral, Butter, Cover, Pink .... 110.00 to 125.00
Floral, Candlestick, Green, 4 In., Pair .... 100.00 to 110.00
Floral, Candlestick, Pink, 4 In. 40.00
Floral, Candlestick, Pink, 4 In., Pair 110.00
Floral, Candy Jar, Cover, Green 20.00
Floral, Coaster, Pink, 3 1/4 In. 15.00
Floral, Creamer, Green 20.00
Floral, Creamer, Pink 18.00
Floral, Cup & Saucer, Green .... 26.00 to 28.00
Floral, Cup & Saucer, Pink 28.00
Floral, Cup, Green 15.00
Floral, Cup, Pink 15.00
Floral, Grill Plate, Green, 9 In. 22.00
Floral, Pitcher, Green, 24 Oz., 5 1/2 In. .... 595.00 to 650.00
Floral, Pitcher, Green, Cone, Footed, 32 Oz., 8 In. 45.00
Floral, Pitcher, Pink, Cone, Footed, 32 Oz., 8 In. 35.00
Floral, Plate, Dinner, Pink, 9 In. .... 20.00 to 22.00
Floral, Plate, Salad, Green, 8 In. .... 15.00 to 18.00
Floral, Plate, Salad, Pink, 8 In. 15.00
Floral, Plate, Sherbet, Green, 6 In. 10.00
Floral, Plate, Sherbet, Pink, 6 In. 8.00
Floral, Platter, Green, Oval, 10 3/4 In. 25.00
Floral, Platter, Pink, Oval, 10 3/4 In. 22.00
Floral, Relish, Green, 2 Sections, Oval 25.00
Floral, Relish, Pink, 2 Sections 22.00
Floral, Relish, Pink, 2 Sections, Oval .... 19.00 to 22.00
Floral, Salt & Pepper, Green, Footed 55.00
Floral, Salt & Pepper, Pink, Footed 50.00
Floral, Sherbet, Green 20.00
Floral, Sherbet, Pink 20.00
Floral, Sugar, Cover, Green 24.00
Floral, Sugar, Cover, Pink 25.00
Floral, Tumbler, Lemonade, Green, Footed, 9 Oz., 5 1/4 In. 65.00
Floral, Tumbler, Water, Green, Footed, 4 3/4 In. 25.00
Floral, Tumbler, Water, Pink, Footed, 7 Oz., 4 3/4 In. 22.00
Floral & Diamond Band, Berry Bowl, Green, 4 1/2 In. 12.00
Floral & Diamond Band, Sherbet, Green 8.00
Floral & Diamond Band, Tumbler, Iced Tea, Pink, 5 In. 50.00
Floral & Diamond Band, Tumbler, Water, Green, 4 In. 25.00
Florentine No. 1, Berry Bowl, Yellow, 5 In. 22.00
Florentine No. 1, Berry Bowl, Yellow, 8 1/2 In. 35.00
Florentine No. 1, Bowl, Cereal, Pink, 6 In. 50.00
Florentine No. 1, Butter, Cover, Yellow 165.00
Florentine No. 1, Creamer 10.00
Florentine No. 1, Creamer, Green 12.00
Florentine No. 1, Creamer, Ruffled 20.00
Florentine No. 1, Creamer, Yellow 12.00
Florentine No. 1, Cup & Saucer 13.00
Florentine No. 1, Cup & Saucer, Yellow 16.00
Florentine No. 1, Grill Plate, Yellow, 10 In. 15.00
Florentine No. 1, Plate, Dinner, Yellow, 10 In. 6.00
Florentine No. 1, Plate, Green, 8 1/2 In. 10.00
Florentine No. 1, Plate, Sherbet, 6 In. 4.00
Florentine No. 1, Plate, Sherbet, Yellow, 6 In. 7.00
Florentine No. 1, Sherbet, Green 13.00
Florentine No. 1, Sherbet, Yellow 13.00
Florentine No. 1, Soup, Cream, 5 In. 13.00
Florentine No. 1, Soup, Cream, Yellow, 5 In. 22.00
Florentine No. 1, Tumbler, Yellow, Footed, 4 In. 17.00
Florentine No. 2, Bowl, Vegetable, Cover, Yellow, Oval, 9 In. .... 85.00 to 90.00
Florentine No. 2, Creamer, Amber 12.00

Florentine No. 2, Gravy Boat, Liner, Amber, 11 1/2 In. 105.00
Florentine No. 2, Plate, Dinner, Yellow, 10 In. 16.00
Florentine No. 2, Platter, Amber, 11 In. 25.00
Florentine No. 2, Relish, Yellow, 3 Sections, 10 In. 35.00
Florentine No. 2, Sugar & Creamer, Green 18.00
Flower Garden With Butterflies, Compote, Canary Yellow, 2 7/8 In. 40.00
Flower Garden With Butterflies, Plate, 8 In. 25.00
Flower Garden With Butterflies, Plate, Amber, 8 In. 25.00
Flower Rim pattern is listed here as Vitrock.
Forest Green, Bottle, Water, Glass Lid 85.00
Fortune, Bowl, Pink, Handle, 4 1/2 In. 15.00
Fortune, Candy Dish, Cover 28.00
Fruits, Cup, Green 10.00
Fruits, Tumbler, 4 In. 25.00
Georgian, Berry Bowl, Green, 7 1/2 In. 65.00
Georgian, Cup & Saucer, Green 13.00
Georgian, Plate, Luncheon, Green, 8 In. . . . . .10.00 to 12.00
Georgian, Plate, Sherbet, Green, 6 In. 7.00
Georgian, Saucer, Green 3.00
Georgian, Sherbet, Green 11.00
Georgian, Sugar, Cover, Footed, 3 In. 37.00
Georgian, Tumbler, Green, 9 Oz., 4 In. . . . . .80.00 to 85.00
Hairpin pattern is listed here as Newport.
Harp, Cake Stand, Ice Blue, 9 In. 45.00
Harp, Cup & Saucer 45.00
Heritage, Berry Bowl, 5 In. . . . . .8.00 to 16.00
Heritage, Berry Bowl, 10 1/2 In. 27.00
Heritage, Cup & Saucer 12.00
Heritage, Plate, Dinner, 9 1/4 In. 10.00
Heritage, Plate, Salad, 8 In. 18.00
Hex Optic pattern is listed here as Hexagon Optic.
Hexagon Optic, Ice Bucket, Green, Pouring Lip, Metal Handle 39.00
Hexagon Optic, Pitcher, Green, 48 Oz., 9 In. 295.00
Hobnail pattern is listed in the Hobnail category.
Holiday, Berry Bowl, Pink, 5 1/8 In. 13.50
Holiday, Butter, Cover, Pink 40.00
Holiday, Candlestick, Pink, 3 In., Pair . . . . .110.00 to 135.00
Holiday, Console, Pink, Footed, 10 3/4 In. . . . . .70.00 to 165.00
Holiday, Creamer, Pink 9.00
Holiday, Cup & Saucer, Pink 12.50
Holiday, Pitcher, Water, Pink, 52 Oz., 6 3/4 In. 45.00
Holiday, Plate, Dinner, Pink, 9 In. . . . . .17.00 to 25.00
Holiday, Platter, Oval, 11 3/8 In. 13.00
Holiday, Tumbler, Pink, Footed, 4 In. 54.00
Homespun, Butter, Cover 39.00
Homespun, Platter, Pink, Closed Handles, Oval, 13 In. 23.00
Honeycomb pattern is listed here as Hexagon Optic.
Horizontal Ribbed pattern is listed here as Manhattan.
Horseshoe pattern is listed here as No. 612.
Iris, Berry Bowl, Iridescent, 8 In. 25.00
Iris, Bowl, Cereal, 5 In. . . . . .125.00 to 140.00
Iris, Bowl, Salad, Iridescent, Ruffled, 9 1/2 In. 14.00
Iris, Bowl, Sauce, Iridescent, Ruffled, 5 In. 25.00
Iris, Butter, Cover, Iridescent 45.00
Iris, Candlestick, Iridescent, Pair 30.00
Iris, Candlestick, Pair 40.00
Iris, Candy Jar, Cover . . . . .185.00 to 205.00
Iris, Coaster . . . . .95.00 to 140.00
Iris, Cover, For Butter, Round 28.00
Iris, Cover, For Sugar, Iridescent 10.00
Iris, Cup & Saucer, Iridescent 27.00
Iris, Cup, Iridescent, After Dinner 38.00
Iris, Goblet, Water, 8 Oz., 5 3/4 In. 28.00

Iris, Goblet, Wine, 4 In. 16.00
Iris, Goblet, Wine, 4 Oz., 4 1/2 In. .... .28.00 to 30.00
Iris, Goblet, Wine, Iridescent, 4 Oz., 4 1/2 In. 28.00
Iris, Nut Set 130.00
Iris, Pitcher, Footed, 9 1/2 In. 65.00
Iris, Pitcher, Iridescent, Footed, 9 1/2 In. 45.00
Iris, Plate, Dinner, 9 In. 55.00
Iris, Plate, Dinner, Iridescent, 9 In. 45.00
Iris, Sandwich Server, Iridescent, 11 3/4 In. 35.00
Iris, Saucer 12.00
Iris, Sherbet, 4 In. 25.00
Iris, Sherbet, Iridescent, Footed, 2 1/2 In. 15.00
Iris, Soup, Dish, 7 1/2 In. 180.00
Iris, Soup, Dish, Iridescent, 7 1/2 In. 50.00
Iris, Sugar, Cover 25.00
Iris, Tumbler, 4 In. 160.00
Iris, Vase, Iridescent, 9 In. 20.00
Iris & Herringbone pattern is listed here as Iris.
Jadite, Refrigerator Jar, Cover, 4 x 4 In. 22.00
Jadite, Refrigerator Jar, Cover, Round, 5 3/4 In. 50.00
Jane-Ray, Bowl, Vegetable, Jade-Ite, 8 1/4 In. 43.00
Jane-Ray, Plate, Dinner, Jade-Ite, 9 1/8 In. ....8.00 to 15.00
Jane-Ray, Platter, Jade-Ite, 9 x 12 In. 44.00
Jane-Ray, Soup, Dish, Jade-Ite, 7 3/4 In. 25.00
Jane-Ray, Sugar & Creamer, Cover, Jade-Ite 48.00
Jane-Ray, Sugar, Cover, Jade-Ite 35.00
Janice, Celery Dish, Cobalt Blue, 11 In. 48.00
Janice, Cup & Saucer, Cobalt Blue 32.00
Jennyware, Bowl, Pink, 6 In. 30.00
Jennyware, Bowl, Pink, 8 1/4 In. 35.00
Jennyware, Reamer, Pink 130.00
Jennyware, Shaker, Pink 20.00
Jubilee, Creamer, Yellow 24.00
Jubilee, Cup & Saucer, Yellow 25.00
Jubilee, Cup, Yellow 15.00
Jubilee, Plate, 3-Footed, Yellow, 14 In. 210.00
Jubilee, Plate, Salad, Yellow, 7 In. 14.00
Jubilee, Sugar, Yellow ....18.00 to 24.00
Jubilee, Tumbler, Water, Yellow, 10 Oz., 6 In. 33.00
Knife & Fork pattern is listed here as Colonial.
Lake Como, Bowl, 6 In. 30.00
Lake Como, Bread Plate, 7 1/4 In. 20.00
Lake Como, Creamer 35.00
Lake Como, Cup & Saucer 45.00
Laurel, Berry Bowl, French Ivory, Red Trim, 5 In. 9.00
Laurel, Candlestick, French Ivory, 4 In. 15.00
Laurel, Cup, French Ivory 8.00
Laurel, Plate, Dinner, French Ivory, Red Trim, Child's 15.00
Laurel, Plate, Green, Scotty Dog, Child's 55.00
Lincoln Inn, Cup & Saucer, Red 25.00
Lincoln Inn, Goblet, Wine 19.00
Line 300 pattern is listed in the Paden City category as Peacock & Wild Rose.
Lorain pattern is listed here as No. 615.
Louisa pattern is listed here as Floragold.
Lovebirds pattern is listed here as Georgian.
Madrid, Butter, Cover, Amber 70.00
Madrid, Candlestick, Amber, 2 1/4 In. 13.00
Madrid, Candlestick, Amber, 2 1/4 In., Pair 55.00
Madrid, Candlestick, Pink, 2 1/4 In., Pair 24.00
Madrid, Console, Pink, Low, 11 In. 13.00
Madrid, Creamer, Amber, Footed ....10.00 to 22.00
Madrid, Creamer, Footed, 3 1/2 In. 10.00
Madrid, Pitcher, Blue, Square, 60 Oz., 8 In. 225.00

Madrid, Plate, Luncheon, Amber, 8 7/8 In. 10.00
Madrid, Plate, Sherbet, Amber, 6 In. 5.00
Madrid, Platter, Oval, 11 1/2 In. 16.00
Madrid, Sauce, Amber, 5 In. 7.00
Madrid, Saucer, Amber 4.00
Madrid, Sugar 30.00
Madrid, Tumbler, Amber, 12 Oz., 5 1/2 In. 22.00
Madrid, Tumbler, Iced Tea, Green, 5 3/8 In. 53.00
Manhattan, Berry Bowl, Pink, Handles, 5 7/8 In. 19.00
Manhattan, Candlestick, Crystal, 4 1/2 In. Square 55.00
Manhattan, Candy Dish, Pink, Footed, 6 1/4 In. 38.00
Manhattan, Compote, 5 3/4 In. 35.00
Manhattan, Creamer, Pink, Oval 22.00
Manhattan, Plate, Dinner, 10 1/4 In. 17.00
Manhattan, Plate, Salad, 8 1/2 In. 24.00
Manhattan, Sauce, Handles, 4 1/2 In. 7.00
Manhattan, Sugar & Creamer 18.00
Manhattan, Sugar, Pink 18.00
Manhattan, Tumbler, Footed, 10 Oz. 20.00
Manhattan, Tumbler, Pink, Footed, 10 Oz. . . . . .16.00 to 55.00
Manhattan, Vase, 8 In. 25.00
Many Windows pattern is listed here as Roulette.
Martha Washington pattern is included in the Cambridge Glass category.
Mayfair Federal, Cup & Saucer 18.00
Mayfair Federal, Tumbler, 9 Oz., 4 1/2 In. 30.00
Mayfair Open Rose, Bowl, Cereal, Pink, 5 1/2 In. 45.00
Mayfair Open Rose, Bowl, Fruit, Scalloped, Blue, 12 In. 70.00
Mayfair Open Rose, Bowl, Fruit, Scalloped, Pink, 12 In. 65.00
Mayfair Open Rose, Bowl, Vegetable, Blue, Oval, 9 1/2 In. 75.00
Mayfair Open Rose, Bowl, Vegetable, Cover, Pink, 10 In. 150.00
Mayfair Open Rose, Bowl, Vegetable, Pink, 10 In. 39.00
Mayfair Open Rose, Butter, Cover, Pink, 7 In. 75.00
Mayfair Open Rose, Cake Plate, Blue, Handles, 12 In. .75.00 to 95.00
Mayfair Open Rose, Cake Plate, Pink, Footed, 10 In. 20.00
Mayfair Open Rose, Cake Plate, Pink, Handles, 12 In. .55.00 to 60.00
Mayfair Open Rose, Candy Dish, Cover, Blue . . . . .300.00 to 350.00
Mayfair Open Rose, Cookie Jar, Cover 69.00
Mayfair Open Rose, Cookie Jar, Cover, Pink . . . . .47.00 to 55.00
Mayfair Open Rose, Creamer, Pink 35.00
Mayfair Open Rose, Cup, Blue . . . . .65.00 to 70.00
Mayfair Open Rose, Cup, Pink . . . . .15.00 to 25.00
Mayfair Open Rose, Decanter, Pink, Stopper 235.00
Mayfair Open Rose, Goblet, Cocktail, Pink, 3 Oz., 4 In. 100.00
Mayfair Open Rose, Goblet, Wine, Pink, 3 Oz., 4 1/2 In. . . . . .120.00 to 145.00
Mayfair Open Rose, Pitcher, Juice, Blue, 37 Oz., 6 In. 165.00
Mayfair Open Rose, Pitcher, Juice, Pink, 37 Oz., 6 In. 50.00
Mayfair Open Rose, Plate, Blue, 5 3/4 In. 35.00
Mayfair Open Rose, Plate, Dinner, 9 1/2 In. 12.00
Mayfair Open Rose, Plate, Dinner, Pink, 9 1/2 In. 65.00
Mayfair Open Rose, Plate, Dinner, Yellow, 9 1/2 In. 18.00
Mayfair Open Rose, Plate, Luncheon, Pink, 8 1/2 In. 40.00
Mayfair Open Rose, Plate, Sherbet, Blue, 6 1/2 In. 23.00
Mayfair Open Rose, Sandwich Server, Green, Center Handle 65.00
Mayfair Open Rose, Sandwich Server, Pink, Center Handle 60.00
Mayfair Open Rose, Sherbet, Underplate, Blue, 2 1/4 In., 2 Piece 235.00
Mayfair Open Rose, Soup, Cream, Pink, 5 In. 55.00
Mayfair Open Rose, Sugar & Creamer, Blue 170.00
Mayfair Open Rose, Sugar, Blue 85.00
Mayfair Open Rose, Sugar, Pink, Frosted 35.00
Mayfair Open Rose, Tumbler, Blue, Footed, 5 1/4 In. 175.00
Mayfair Open Rose, Tumbler, Iced Tea, Pink, Footed, 15 Oz., 6 1/2 In. . . . . .30.00 to 85.00
Mayfair Open Rose, Tumbler, Juice, Pink, Footed, 5 Oz., 3 1/2 In. 140.00
Mayfair Open Rose, Vase, Sweet Pea, Pink . . . . .175.00 to 239.00

Mayfair Open Rose, Whiskey, Pink, 1 1/2 Oz., 2 1/4 In. 125.00
Miss America, Bowl, Cereal, 6 1/4 In. 12.00
Miss America, Candy Jar, Cover, Pink, 11 1/2 In. ....165.00 to 190.00
Miss America, Celery Dish, Pink, 10 1/2 In. 39.00
Miss America, Coaster, 5 3/4 In. 15.00
Miss America, Cup & Saucer 17.00
Miss America, Cup & Saucer, Pink 35.00
Miss America, Cup, Pink 28.00
Miss America, Goblet, Juice, Pink, 5 Oz., 4 3/4 In. 100.00
Miss America, Goblet, Water, Pink, 10 Oz., 5 1/2 In. 55.00
Miss America, Goblet, Wine, 3 Oz., 4 3/4 In. 21.00
Miss America, Grill Plate, Pink, 10 1/4 In. 30.00
Miss America, Plate, Dinner, Pink, 10 1/4 In. 45.00
Miss America, Plate, Sherbet, 5 3/4 In. 7.00
Miss America, Plate, Sherbet, Ice Blue, 5 3/4 In. 50.00
Miss America, Platter, Pink, Oval, 12 1/4 In. ....40.00 to 50.00
Miss America, Relish, 4 Sections, 8 3/4 In. 25.00
Miss America, Relish, Pink, 4 Sections, 8 3/4 In. 33.00
Miss America, Sherbet, Pink 32.00
Miss America, Sugar 23.00
Miss America, Sugar & Creamer, Green 24.00
Miss America, Sugar, Pink 22.00
Miss America, Tumbler, Water, 10 Oz., 4 1/2 In. 36.00
Moderntone, Berry Bowl, Amethyst, 5 In. 25.00
Moderntone, Butter, Cover, Blue 100.00
Moderntone, Creamer, Blue ....12.00 to 15.00
Moderntone, Creamer, Yellow 5.00
Moderntone, Cup & Saucer, Amethyst 17.00
Moderntone, Cup & Saucer, Blue 17.00
Moderntone, Plate, Dinner, Blue, 8 7/8 In. ....21.00 to 22.00
Moderntone, Plate, Luncheon, Blue, 7 7/8 In. 13.00
Moderntone, Plate, Sherbet, Blue, 5 3/4 In. ....6.00 to 7.00
Moderntone, Platter, Blue, Oval, 11 In. 45.00
Moderntone, Soup, Cream, Amethyst, 5 In. 22.00
Moderntone, Sugar, Blue 12.00
Moderntone, Tumbler, Blue, 9 Oz. 38.00
Moderntone, Whiskey, Blue, 1 1/2 Oz. ....31.00 to 42.00
Moderntone Little Hostess Party, Cup, Blue 10.00
Moondrops pattern is listed in the New Martinsville category.
Moondrops, Ashtray, Red 32.00
Moondrops, Butter, Cover, Amber 275.00
Moondrops, Butter, Cover, Cobalt Blue 550.00
Moondrops, Console, 3-Footed, 12 In. 95.00
Moondrops, Cup, Red 12.00
Moondrops, Goblet, Water, Red, 9 Oz., 6 1/4 In. 35.00

Depression Glass,
Madrid

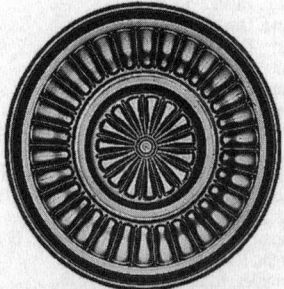

Depression Glass,
New Century

Depression Glass,
Normandie

Moondrops, Goblet, Wine, Red, 4 Oz., 4 In. 25.00
Moondrops, Plate, Luncheon, Red, 8 1/2 In. 20.00
Moondrops, Sherbet, Amber, 2 5/8 In. 11.00
Moonstone, Berry Bowl, 5 1/2 In. 10.00
Moonstone, Bowl, Crimped, 9 1/2 In. 25.00
Moonstone, Candlestick 10.00
Moonstone, Plate, 6 In. 7.00
Moonstone, Sherbet 7.00
Moonstone, Sugar 9.00
Moroccan Amethyst, Bowl, 8 Sides, 4 3/4 In. 10.00
Moroccan Amethyst, Bowl, Oval, 7 3/4 In. 16.00
Mt. Pleasant, Creamer, Black 20.00
Mt. Pleasant, Cup & Saucer, Blue 23.00
Mt. Pleasant, Cup, Blue 16.00
Mt. Pleasant, Plate, Black, Round, 8 In. 15.00
Mt. Pleasant, Saltshaker, Black 25.00
Mt. Pleasant, Saucer, Black, Round 5.00
Mt. Vernon pattern is included in the Cambridge Glass category.
Navarre, Relish, 3 Sections, 10 x 7 1/2 In. 47.00
Navarre, Sugar & Creamer, Footed, 3 5/8 In. 40.00
New Century, Plate, Dinner, 10 In. 55.00
New Century, Plate, Salad, Green, 8 1/2 In. 15.00
New Century, Saltshaker, Green 18.00
New Century, Tumbler, Amethyst, 5 Oz., 3 1/2 In. 15.00
New Century, Tumbler, Pink, 5 Oz., 3 1/2 In. 15.00
Newport, Bowl, Cereal, Platonite, Fired-On-Yellow, 6 1/2 In. 35.00
Newport, Cup & Saucer, Cobalt Blue 18.00
Newport, Cup & Saucer, Platonite, Fired-On-Green 19.00
Newport, Cup & Saucer, Platonite, Fired-On-Yellow 18.00
Newport, Soup, Cream, Pink, 4 3/4 In. 13.00
Newport, Sugar, Cobalt Blue 17.00
No. 601 pattern is listed here as Avocado.
No. 610, Bowl, Yellow, 8 1/2 In. 75.00
No. 612, Bowl, Cereal, Green, 6 1/2 In. 42.00
No. 612, Grill Plate, Green ....145.00 to 200.00
No. 615, Cup & Saucer, Yellow 21.00
No. 618, Plate, Salad, Amber, 8 3/4 In. 14.00
No. 618, Plate, Sherbet, 6 In. 7.00
No. 618, Plate, Sherbet, Amber, 6 In. 5.00
No. 618, Sherbet, Footed 18.00
No. 620, Bowl, Green, 7 3/8 In. 10.00
No. 620, Bowl, Vegetable, Amber, Oval, 10 In. 18.00
No. 620, Creamer, Footed 6.00
No. 620, Cup & Saucer 6.00
No. 620, Cup & Saucer, Amber 7.00
No. 620, Plate, Dinner, Green, 9 3/8 In. 8.00
No. 620, Plate, Green, 9 3/8 In. 7.00
No. 620, Plate, Sandwich, Amber, 11 1/2 In. 15.00
No. 620, Sugar, Amber 9.00
No. 620, Tumbler, Water, Amber, Footed, 9 Oz. 25.00
Normandie, Berry Bowl, Amber, 5 In. 10.00
Normandie, Berry Bowl, Amber, 8 1/2 In. ....22.00 to 35.00
Normandie, Berry Bowl, Iridescent, 5 In. 5.00
Normandie, Bowl, Vegetable, Oval, 10 1/4 In. 20.00
Normandie, Cup, Amber ....6.00 to 8.00
Normandie, Cup, Pink ....9.00 to 12.00
Normandie, Pitcher, Amber 85.00
Normandie, Plate, Amber, 6 In. 4.00
Normandie, Salt & Pepper, Amber 50.00
Normandie, Sugar & Creamer, Amber 15.00
Old Cafe, Plate, Dinner, Pink, 10 In. ....58.00 to 60.00
Old Colony, Bowl, Cereal, Pink, 6 3/8 In. 30.00
Old Colony, Bowl, Plain, 9 1/2 In. 55.00

Old Colony, Bowl, Ribbed, Pink, 9 1/2 In. 25.00
Old Colony, Butter, Cover, Pink 70.00
Old Colony, Compote, 7 1/2 In. 55.00
Old Colony, Grill Plate, 10 1/2 In. 40.00
Old Colony, Plate, Dinner, Pink, 10 1/2 In. 36.00
Old Colony, Plate, Luncheon, Pink, 8 1/4 In. 25.00
Old Colony, Plate, Salad, Pink, 7 1/4 In. ....28.00 to 30.00
Old Colony, Relish, Pink, 4 Sections, 13 In. 70.00
Old English, Tumbler, Green, Footed, 4 3/4 In. 28.00
Old Florentine pattern is listed here as Florentine No. 1.
Open Rose pattern is listed here as Mayfair Open Rose.
Optic Design pattern is listed here as Raindrops.
Ovide, Bowl, Cereal, White, Black Flowers, 5 1/2 In. 12.00
Ovide, Creamer, White, Black Flowers, 5 In. 30.00
Ovide, Sherbet, Green 3.00
Ovide, Sugar, Green 7.00
Panelled Aster pattern is listed here as Primo.
Parrot pattern is listed here as Sylvan.
Patrician, Berry Bowl, Golden Glo, 5 In. 13.00
Patrician, Berry Bowl, Golden Glo, 8 1/2 In. 46.00
Patrician, Bowl, Cereal, Green, 6 In. 30.00
Patrician, Butter, Cover Only, Green 60.00
Patrician, Butter, Cover, Green 170.00
Patrician, Cookie Jar, Cover, Golden Glo 90.00
Patrician, Creamer, Golden Glo, Footed ....12.00 to 15.00
Patrician, Creamer, Green, Footed 12.00
Patrician, Cup, Golden Glo 9.00
Patrician, Pitcher, Golden Glo, Handle, 8 In. 95.00
Patrician, Plate, Luncheon, Golden Glo, 9 In. 14.00
Patrician, Plate, Sherbet, Golden Glo, 6 In. 12.00
Patrician, Platter, Golden Glo, Oval, 11 1/2 In. ....30.00 to 40.00
Patrician, Saucer, Green 10.00
Patrician, Sherbet, Golden Glo 13.00
Patrician, Soup, Cream, Golden Glo, 4 3/4 In. ....17.00 to 22.00
Patrician, Sugar, Golden Glo ....15.00 to 22.00
Patrician, Tumbler, Golden Glo, 5 Oz., 4 In. 33.00
Patrician, Tumbler, Golden Glo, 9 Oz., 4 1/2 In. 30.00
Peacock & Wild Rose pattern is listed in the Paden City category.
Petal Swirl pattern is listed here as Swirl.
Petalware, Berry Bowl, Cremax, 9 In. 32.00
Petalware, Creamer, Monax, Red Flower 10.00
Petalware, Cup & Saucer, Pink 10.00
Petalware, Plate, Salad, Monax, Red Flower, 8 In. 10.00
Petalware, Plate, Salad, Pink, 8 In. 16.00
Petalware, Plate, Sherbet, Cobalt Blue, 6 In. 7.00
Petalware, Sherbet, Footed, 4 1/2 In. 20.00
Pineapple & Floral pattern is listed here as No. 618.
Pinwheel pattern is listed here as Sierra.
Pioneer, Vase, 7 7/8 In. 170.00
Poinsettia pattern is listed here as Floral.
Poppy No. 1 pattern is listed here as Florentine No. 1.
Poppy No. 2 pattern is listed here as Florentine No. 2.
Pretty Polly Party Dishes, see also the related pattern Doric & Pansy.
Primo, Coaster-Ashtray, Mandarin Yellow 8.00
Primo, Plate, Mandarin Yellow, 7 1/2 In. 10.00
Primo, Saucer, Green ....3.00 to 4.00
Primo, Tumbler, Water, Mandarin Yellow, 9 Oz., 5 3/4 In. 30.00
Princess, Bowl, Cereal, Green, 5 1/4 In. 35.00
Princess, Bowl, Hat Shape, Pink, 9 1/2 In. ....50.00 to 65.00
Princess, Cake Stand, Green, 10 In. 40.00
Princess, Candy Dish, Cover, Green 65.00
Princess, Cookie Jar, Cover, Pink 60.00
Princess, Cup & Saucer, Pink 28.00

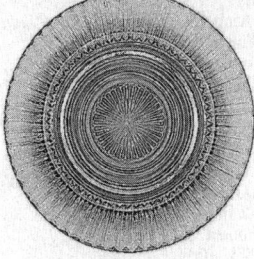

Depression Glass,
Princess

Depression Glass,
Queen Mary

Depression Glass,
Roulette

Princess, Cup, Apricot 6.00
Princess, Cup, Pink 13.00
Princess, Cup, Topaz 8.00
Princess, Grill Plate, Apricot, 9 1/2 In. 7.00
Princess, Pitcher, Green, 60 Oz., 8 In. 55.00
Princess, Platter, Green, Closed Handles, 12 In. 33.00
Princess, Sherbet, Green 23.00
Princess, Sherbet, Topaz, Footed 48.00
Princess, Tumbler, Green, Footed, 10 Oz., 5 1/2 In. 18.00
Princess, Tumbler, Iced Tea, Topaz, 13 Oz., 5 1/4 In. 60.00
Princess, Tumbler, Pink, Footed, 12 1/2 Oz., 6 1/2 In. 98.00
Prismatic Line pattern is listed here as Queen Mary.
Provincial pattern is listed here as Bubble.
Pyramid pattern is listed here as No. 610.
Queen Mary, Berry Bowl, Flared, 5 In. 7.00
Queen Mary, Berry Bowl, Pink, Flared, 5 In. 7.00
Queen Mary, Bowl, Pink, 2 Handles, 5 1/2 In. 15.00
Queen Mary, Candlestick, 2-Light, 4 1/2 In., Pair 20.00
Queen Mary, Candy Jar, Cover, Pink 90.00
Queen Mary, Creamer 6.00
Queen Mary, Cup, Pink 15.00
Queen Mary, Plate, Dinner, Pink, 9 1/2 In. 58.00
Queen Mary, Sugar & Creamer, Pink 35.00
Queen Mary, Tumbler, Footed, Pink, 10 Oz., 5 In. 65.00
Queen Mary, Tumbler, Water, Pink, 9 Oz., 4 In. 20.00
Raindrops, Cup & Saucer, Green 13.00
Ribbon, Berry Bowl, Green, Wide Bands, 8 In. 35.00
Ribbon, Saucer, Green 4.00
Ribbon, Sugar & Creamer, Green, Footed 30.00
Ring, Cocktail Shaker, 11 1/2 In. 95.00
Ring, Tumbler, 10 Oz., 4 3/4 In. 7.00
Ring, Tumbler, Footed, 5 Oz., 3 1/2 In. 9.00
Rock Crystal, Bowl, Amber, 5 In. 23.00
Rock Crystal, Cake Plate, Green, 11 In. 50.00
Rock Crystal, Creamer, Red 75.00
Rock Crystal, Finger Bowl, Red, 5 In. 60.00
Rock Crystal, Goblet, 3 Oz. 17.00
Rock Crystal, Goblet, Amber, 8 Oz. 26.00
Rock Crystal, Goblet, Cocktail, Red, Footed, 3 1/2 Oz. 40.00
Rock Crystal, Pitcher, Red, Tankard Type 1200.00
Rock Crystal, Plate, Amber, 7 1/2 In. 13.00
Romance, Sugar & Creamer 40.00
Romance, Tumbler, Water, Footed, 9 Oz., 5 1/2 In. 28.00
Rope pattern is listed here as Colonial Fluted.
Rose Cameo, Tumbler, Footed, 5 In. 25.00
Rosemary, Berry Bowl, Amber, 5 In. . . . . .6.00 to 7.00

Rosemary, Creamer, Amber 10.00
Rosemary, Cup & Saucer, Amber 13.00
Rosemary, Plate, Dinner, Amber, 9 1/2 In. 10.00
Rosemary, Soup, Cream, Amber, 5 In. 16.00
Roulette, Cup & Saucer, Green 11.00
Roulette, Cup, Green 8.00
Roulette, Pitcher, Pink, 64 Oz., 8 In. 45.00
Roulette, Tumbler, Iced Tea, Green, 12 Oz., 5 In. 33.00
Roulette, Tumbler, Water, Pink, 9 Oz., 4 1/8 In. 22.00
Round Robin, Underplate, Green, 6 In. 4.00
Roxana, Plate, Yellow, 5 1/2 In. 9.00
Roxana, Sherbet, Yellow, Footed 13.00
Royal Lace, Berry Bowl, Pink, 10 In. 35.00
Royal Lace, Bowl, Pink, 3-Footed, Rolled Edge 225.00
Royal Lace, Bowl, Vegetable, Cobalt Blue, Oval, 11 In. 75.00
Royal Lace, Butter, Cover, Pink 245.00
Royal Lace, Candlestick, Pink, Rolled Edge, Pair 110.00
Royal Lace, Cover, For Cookie Jar 15.00
Royal Lace, Creamer, Cobalt Blue, Footed . . . . .55.00 to 58.00
Royal Lace, Creamer, Footed 15.00
Royal Lace, Cup 10.00
Royal Lace, Cup & Saucer, Pink 33.00
Royal Lace, Cup, Cobalt Blue 40.00
Royal Lace, Cup, Green 20.00
Royal Lace, Cup, Pink 25.00
Royal Lace, Plate, Dinner, Cobalt Blue, 9 7/8 In. 55.00
Royal Lace, Plate, Sherbet, Cobalt Blue, 6 In. 18.00
Royal Lace, Plate, Sherbet, Green, 6 In. 11.00
Royal Lace, Salt & Pepper, Cobalt Blue 375.00
Royal Lace, Salt & Pepper, Green 128.00
Royal Lace, Saucer, Cobalt Blue 12.00
Royal Lace, Sherbet, Cobalt Blue, Footed 65.00
Royal Lace, Sherbet, Footed 10.00
Royal Lace, Soup, Cream, Cobalt Blue, 4 3/4 In. . . . . .47.00 to 50.00
Royal Lace, Tumbler, 9 Oz., 4 1/8 In. 12.00
Royal Lace, Tumbler, Water, Cobalt Blue, 9 Oz., 4 1/8 In. 55.00
Royal Ruby, Creamer, Footed 10.00
Royal Ruby, Cup, Square 7.00
Royal Ruby, Plate, Dinner, 9 In. 12.00
Royal Ruby, Sherbet 7.00
Royal Ruby, Sugar, Footed 10.00
Royal Ruby, Tumbler, Water, 4 In. 10.00
S Pattern, Cake Plate, Yellow, 13 In. 75.00
S Pattern, Creamer, Thin 6.00
S Pattern, Cup, Thick 4.00
S Pattern, Plate, 6 In. 3.00
S Pattern, Sugar, Thin 6.00
S Pattern, Tumbler, 4 In. 12.00
Sandwich Anchor Hocking, Bowl, 5 1/4 In. 18.00
Sandwich Anchor Hocking, Bowl, Cereal, Desert Gold, 6 1/2 In. 12.00
Sandwich Anchor Hocking, Butter, Cover 45.00
Sandwich Anchor Hocking, Cookie Jar, Cover, Desert Gold . . . . .37.00 to 55.00
Sandwich Anchor Hocking, Creamer 6.00
Sandwich Anchor Hocking, Creamer, Forest Green 30.00
Sandwich Anchor Hocking, Cup & Saucer 6.00
Sandwich Anchor Hocking, Plate, Dessert, Desert Gold, 7 In. 30.00
Sandwich Anchor Hocking, Plate, Dinner, Desert Gold, 9 In. . . . . .10.00 to 14.00
Sandwich Anchor Hocking, Plate, Dinner, Forest Green, 9 In. 125.00
Sandwich Anchor Hocking, Punch Bowl 55.00
Sandwich Anchor Hocking, Sandwich Server, Desert Gold, 12 In. 17.00
Sandwich Anchor Hocking, Saucer 4.00
Sandwich Anchor Hocking, Sugar, Forest Green 30.00
Sandwich Indiana, Cup 3.00

Sandwich Indiana, Sherbet 6.00
Sandwich Indiana, Sugar & Creamer 25.00
Saxon pattern is listed here as Coronation.
Sharon, Berry Bowl, 8 1/2 In. 25.00
Sharon, Berry Bowl, Amber, 5 In. 9.00
Sharon, Berry Bowl, Amber, 8 1/2 In. 6.00
Sharon, Berry Bowl, Green, 5 In. ....19.00 to 25.00
Sharon, Berry Bowl, Pink, 5 In. ....15.00 to 22.00
Sharon, Berry Bowl, Pink, 8 1/2 In. 40.00
Sharon, Bowl, Cereal, Pink, 6 In. 30.00
Sharon, Bowl, Fruit, Amber, 10 1/2 In. 55.00
Sharon, Bowl, Fruit, Green, 10 1/2 In. 45.00
Sharon, Bowl, Fruit, Pink, 10 1/2 In. 65.00
Sharon, Bowl, Vegetable, Amber, Oval, 9 1/2 In. 14.00
Sharon, Bowl, Vegetable, Green, Oval, 9 1/2 In. ....24.00 to 40.00
Sharon, Bread Plate, Green, 6 In. 9.00
Sharon, Butter, Cover, Amber ....45.00 to 55.00
Sharon, Butter, No Cover, Green 45.00
Sharon, Cake Plate, Pink, Footed, 11 1/2 In. 50.00
Sharon, Candy Jar, Cover 185.00
Sharon, Candy Jar, Cover, Amber 65.00
Sharon, Cover, For Butter, Amber, Round 32.00
Sharon, Creamer, Amber, Footed 15.00
Sharon, Creamer, Green, Footed 15.00
Sharon, Creamer, Pink, Footed 38.00
Sharon, Cup & Saucer, Amber 15.00
Sharon, Cup, Pink 22.00
Sharon, Plate, Dinner, Amber, 9 In. 15.00
Sharon, Plate, Dinner, Green, 9 In. ....25.00 to 45.00
Sharon, Plate, Dinner, Pink, 9 In. ....20.00 to 38.00
Sharon, Plate, Salad, Green, 7 1/2 In. 10.50
Sharon, Plate, Salad, Pink, 7 1/2 In. 32.00
Sharon, Platter, Amber, Oval, 12 1/2 In. 55.00
Sharon, Platter, Pink, Oval, 12 1/2 In. 55.00
Sharon, Salt & Pepper, Green 70.00
Sharon, Salt & Pepper, Pink 55.00
Sharon, Soup, Cream, Pink 50.00
Sharon, Sugar, Cover, Amber 35.00
Sharon, Sugar, Cover, Pink 45.00
Sharon, Sugar, Pink 38.00
Sharon, Tumbler, Amber, 9 Oz., 4 1/8 In. 30.00
Sharon, Tumbler, Amber, Thick, 12 Oz., 5 1/4 In. 62.00
Sharon, Tumbler, Pink, Thick, 12 Oz., 5 1/4 In. 155.00
Sharon, Tumbler, Pink, Thin, 12 Oz., 5 1/4 In. 35.00
Sharon, Tumbler, Water, Green, Thick, 9 Oz. 125.00
Shell Pink, Bowl, Gondola, 7 1/2 In. 35.00
Shell Pink, Vase, 7 In. 35.00
Sierra, Berry Bowl, Green, 8 1/2 In. 12.00
Sierra, Cup & Saucer, Pink 20.00
Sierra, Plate, Dinner, Pink, 9 In. 21.00
Sierra, Platter, Pink, Oval, 11 In. 55.00
Skol, Bowl, Capri Blue, 4 7/8 In. 8.00
Skol, Bowl, Capri Blue, 6 In. 12.00
Skol, Bowl, Capri Blue, 11 In. 25.00
Skol, Cup & Saucer, Capri Blue 6.00
Skol, Cup, Capri Blue 4.00
Skol, Tumbler, Capri Blue, 5 In. 10.00
Spiral Flutes pattern is listed in the Duncan & Miller category as Swirl.
Spoke pattern is listed here as Patrician.
Star, Pitcher, Crystal, 85 Oz. 18.00
Starlight, Creamer 10.00
Starlight, Plate, Dinner, 9 1/2 In. 18.00
Starlight, Sugar 10.00

Depression Glass, Sharon   Depression Glass, Sylvan

Stars & Stripes, Plate, Eagle Center, 8 In.	15.00
Stippled Rose Band pattern is listed here as S Pattern.	
Sunburst, Cup & Saucer	10.00
Swirl, Berry Bowl, Pink, 5 1/4 In.	10.00 to 15.00
Swirl, Berry Bowl, Ultramarine, 5 1/4 In.	13.00
Swirl, Bowl, Cereal, Ultramarine	18.00
Swirl, Bowl, Salad, Ultramarine, 9 In.	35.00
Swirl, Bowl, Ultramarine, 3-Toed, 2 5/8 x 5 1/2 In.	40.00
Swirl, Bowl, Ultramarine, Footed, Closed Handles, 10 In.	45.00
Swirl, Butter, Cover, Ultramarine	295.00 to 375.00
Swirl, Creamer, Delphite, Footed	15.00
Swirl, Creamer, Ultramarine, Footed	16.00 to 18.00
Swirl, Cup, Ultramarine	17.00
Swirl, Plate, Dinner, Ultramarine, 9 1/4 In.	20.00
Swirl, Salt & Pepper, Ultramarine	45.00
Swirl, Sherbet, Low, Ultramarine, Footed	25.00
Swirl, Sugar, Ultramarine	18.00
Swirl, Vase, Ultramarine, 8 1/2 In.	30.00
Sylvan, Bowl, Vegetable, Green, Oval, 10 In.	70.00
Sylvan, Butter, Bottom, Green	42.00
Sylvan, Creamer, Green, Footed	60.00
Sylvan, Cup & Saucer, Green	62.00
Sylvan, Cup, Green	20.00
Sylvan, Plate, Dinner, Amber, 9 In.	30.00
Sylvan, Plate, Salad, Green, 7 1/2 In.	40.00
Sylvan, Soup, Dish, Amber, 7 In.	40.00
Sylvan, Soup, Dish, Green, 7 In.	42.00
Sylvan, Sugar, Cover, Green	225.00
Tea Room, Bowl, Salad, Green, Deep, 8 3/4 In.	170.00
Tea Room, Ice Bucket, Green	68.00
Tea Room, Relish, Divided	10.00
Tea Room, Sugar & Creamer, Tray, Pink, Center Handle, 3 Piece	165.00
Thistle, Bowl, Pink, Rolled, 10 1/2 In.	60.00
Threading pattern is listed here as Old English.	
Turquoise Blue, Ashtray, 5 3/4 In.	26.00
Turquoise Blue, Bowl, Vegetable, 8 In.	30.00
Turquoise Blue, Creamer	12.50
Turquoise Blue, Mug	13.00
Turquoise Blue, Plate, Salad, 7 In.	20.00
Twisted Optic, Cup, Pink	5.00
Vertical Ribbed pattern is listed here as Queen Mary.	
Vitrock, Plate, Dinner, White, 9 In.	9.00
Waffle pattern is listed here as Waterford.	
Waterford, Cake Plate, Pink, Handles, 10 1/4 In.	35.00
Waterford, Goblet, 5 1/2 In.	16.00
Waterford, Sandwich Server, Pink, 13 3/4 In.	28.00
Waterford, Sugar & Creamer, Cover	14.00
Wild Rose pattern is listed here as Dogwood.	

Depression Glass, Waterford   Depression Glass, Windsor

Windsor, Berry Bowl, Pink, 8 1/2 In.	17.00
Windsor, Bowl, Cereal, Pink, 5 1/8 In.	25.00
Windsor, Bowl, Fruit, Pink, 12 1/2 In.	135.00
Windsor, Butter, Cover, Green	95.00
Windsor, Butter, Cover, Pink	60.00
Windsor, Candlestick, Pink, 3 In.	45.00
Windsor, Chop Plate, Green, 13 3/4 In.	38.00
Windsor, Chop Plate, Pink, 13 5/8 In.	45.00
Windsor, Creamer, Green	16.00
Windsor, Creamer, Pink	14.00
Windsor, Cup & Saucer, Green	10.00
Windsor, Pitcher, Pink, 52 Oz., 6 3/4 In.	30.00
Windsor, Plate, Dinner, Green, 9 In.	25.00
Windsor, Sandwich Server, Green, Open Handle, 10 1/4 In.	20.00
Windsor, Sandwich Server, Pink, Open Handle, 10 1/4 In.	45.00
Windsor, Sugar, Cover, Green	33.00
Windsor, Sugar, Cover, Pink	30.00
Windsor Diamond pattern is listed here as Windsor.	
Yvonne, Plate, Handle, Yellow, 12 In.	40.00

DERBY has been marked on porcelain made in the city of Derby, England, since about 1748. The original Derby factory closed in 1848, but others opened there and continued to produce quality porcelain. The Crown Derby mark began appearing on Derby wares in the 1770s.

Candlestick, Figural, Boy, Girl, Flowers Bocage, Pierced Scroll, c.1775, 6 5/8 In., Pair	600.00
Dish, Bloor, Cobalt Blue Ground, Topographical, Kidney Shape, c.1820, 10 1/4 In.	259.00
Dish, King's Pattern, Imari Design, Trees, Flowers, Oval, c.1825, 2 x 1 1/2 x 8 In., Pair	532.00
Dish, Sweetmeat, Imari Design, c.1810, 11 In.	157.00
Perfume Bottle, Cover, Enamel, Dragon, Flowers, 19th Century, 5 In.	118.00
Plate, Tree, Flowers, Blue, Red, Gilt, Imari, 19th Century, 8 3/4 In., 12 Piece	1116.00
Tankard, New Imari Design, c.1810, 5 In.	219.00
Urn, Pierced Rim Mounted By Mask, Gilt Paw Feet, 4 x 5 1/4 In., Pair	633.00
Vase, Allover Flowers, Gilt, 8 3/4 In.	863.00
Vase, Landscape, Ripton Near Derby, A View In Wales, 1820s, 8 3/4 In., Pair	1840.00

DICK TRACY, the comic strip, started in 1931. Tracy was also the hero of movies from 1937 to 1947 and again in 1990, and starred in a radio series in the 1940s and a television series in the 1950s. Memorabilia from all these activities are collected.

Badge, Dick Tracy Crimestoppers, Member Card, Bonnie Togs, 1940-1950, 2 x 4 In.	35.00
Badge, Operator 711 Private Eye, On Card, Japan, 1930s	12.00
Badge, Private Detective, Tin, Eagle, Silver Luster, On Car, Japan, 1950s	8.00
Badge, Sergeant, Transmittal Paper, Quaker Puffed Wheat, 1938, 4 x 7 1/2 In.	65.00
Book, Dick Tracy Junior Detective Kit, Punch-Out, Golden Press, 1962, 7 1/2 In.	35.00
Book, Dick Tracy's Secret Detective Methods & Magic Tricks, 1939, 5 x 7 1/2 In.	60.00
Booklet, Bankers Protective Appliance Corp, July 10, 1922	3.00
Buckle, Belt, Dick Tracy, Gold Luster Finish, Pyramid Belt Co., 1973, 2 1/2 x 2 3/4 In.	10.00
Camera, Face & Name On Lens, Bakelite, 1940s, 4 x 3 In.	145.00

Camera, Graphics, Black Metal, Seymore Products Co., Chicago, 1940s, 2 x 3 In.	35.00
Camera, Metal, Seymore Products Co., 2 x 3 x 5 In.	35.00
Camera, Snapshot, Black Metal, Seymore Products, 1940s, 2 x 3 x 5 In.	35.00
Cap Gun, Dick Tracy Snub Nose 38, Blister Pack, 1970s, 6 1/2 x 11 In.	30.00
Card, Gangster Rule In America, 12 Chapter Series, 1930s, 11 x 14 In.	24.00
Card, Jujitsu & Dick Tracy, Crimestopper Club Kit, 1961, 5 x 7 In.	12.00
Card, Merry Christmas From The Chester Goulds, 1974, 5 1/4 x 7 1/2 In.	55.00
Card, Tip-Top Bread, TV Show, 1952, 2 1/8 x 2 7/8 In., 3 Piece	24.00
Card, Valentine, Stand-Up, 1940s, 4 1/2 x 6 In.	20.00
Charm, Jujitsu, Figural, Pale Green, Rubber Loop, 1966	12.00
Commando Tommy Gun, Pop Pistol, Cardboard, 1940s, 5 x 10 In.	3.00
Display Kit, Dick Tracy 2 Way Wrist Radio, 1963, 2 1/2 x 8 1/2 x 23 1/2 In.	125.00
Favorite Funnies Printing Set, 6 Stamps, Superior Marking Equipment Co., 1941	58.00
Favorite Funnies Printing Set, Box, Early 1950s, 5 1/2 x 8 1/2 In.	58.00
Favorite Funnies Printing Set, Superior Marking Equipment Co., Box, Late 1940s	90.00
Figure, Junior Tracy, Plastic, Orange Hair, Marx, Germany, 1950s, 2 1/4 In.	18.00
Game, Calling All Cars, Police Chase, Parker Brothers, Box, 1930s	65.00
Game, Dick Tracy Detective, Whitman, Chester Gould Copyright, Box, 6 1/2 x 13 In. ...	75.00
Game, Dick Tracy Detective, Whitman, Famous Artists Syndicate, Box, 1937	30.00
Game, Spinner, Tracy Playing Pieces, Game Board, Box, 1933, 10 x 14 In.	247.00
Glass, Gravel Gertie, B.O. Plenty, Frosted White, Early 1950s, 5 In.	45.00
Glass, Vitamin Flintheart, Frosted White, Blue Painted Tracy, 1950-1960, 3 1/4 In.	45.00
Glass, Vitamin Flintheart, White Frosted, Late 1940s, 5 In.	45.00
Hairbrush, Dick Tracy Military Set, Oak, Wooden Black Grip, Pictures, 1940s	50.00
ID Card & Badge Holder, Rayline Detective Club, 1930s, 2 1/2 x 5 1/2 In.	20.00
Mug, Tracy Characters, Homer Laughlin, Early 1950s, 3 In.	100.00
Paper Doll, Baby Sparkle Plenty, Cardboard, Standup, Ideal, Book & Box, 1948	45.00
Phone Set, Dick Tracy Secret Service, Cardboard Paddle Grips, 1938, 3 x 7 1/2 In.	145.00
Pin, Dick Tracy, Sunday Post, Celluloid, 1950, 3 In.	35.00
Pistol, Clicker-Whistle, Special Police, Tin Lithograph, 1930s, 1 3/4 x 3 1/2 In.	15.00
Pistol, G-Man, Silver Luster, Pressed Steel, Late 1930s, 8 1/4 In.	15.00
Plate, Mugg & Tracy, Ceramic, Early 1950s, 9 x 9 In.	120.00
Police Station, Lithographed Strip Characters, Plastic Doors, Marx, 6 x 9 In.	550.00
Poster, Dick Tracy vs. Phanton Empire, Folded, Re-Issue 1952, 7 x 10 1/2 In.	95.00
Radio Set, 2-Way Electronic Wrist, Remco, Box, Late 1950s	25.00
Salt & Pepper, Alcatraz, China, Prison Inmates Caricature, 1960s, 4 1/2 In.	20.00
Siren Plane, Assembly Parts, Mailer, Quaker Cereals, 1938, 3 x 12 In.	165.00
Sketch, Portrait, Gould Autograph, 1970s, 8 1/2 x 11 In.	95.00
Song Booklet, Your Singing Cop, Safety Songs, Sgt. Wilburn Legree, 1946, 8 1/2 In.	15.00
Squad Car, Tin Lithograph, Friction, Battery Siren, Marx, 20 In.	325.00
Squad Car, Windup & Battery Operated, Comic Character, 1949, 11 In.	402.00
Sticker Sheet, Dick Tracy & Characters, C. Gould, 1970s, 1 1/2 x 3 1/4 In., 5 Piece	14.00
Target Set, Cardboard, Image Of Dick Tracy, Original Box, 17 In.	240.00
Toy, B.O. Plenty, Holding Sparkle Plenty, Clockwork, Marx, 8 1/2 In.	165.00
View-Master Kit, Gift Set, Warren Beatty As Dick Tracy, Disney, 1990	24.00
Wallet, Gang Busters, Brown Leather, Phillips H. Lord's, 1935, 3 1/4 x 4 1/4 In.	120.00
Wallet, Tracy Name & Picture, Black Vinyl, 1973	45.00
Wrapper, Dick Tracy Caramels, Waxed Paper, 1930s, 2 1/2 x 3 In.	65.00

DICKENS WARE pieces are listed in the Royal Doulton and Weller categories.

DINNERWARE used in the United States from the 1930s through the 1950s is listed here. Most was made in potteries in southern Ohio, West Virginia, and California. A few patterns were made in Japan, England, and other countries. Dishes were sold in gift shops and department stores, or were given away as premiums. Many of these patterns are listed in this book in their own categories, such as Autumn Leaf, Azalea, Coors, Fiesta, Franciscan, Hall, Harker, Harlequin, Red Wing, Riviera, Russel Wright, Vernon Kilns, Watt, and Willow. For more information, see *Kovels' Depression Glass & Dinnerware Price List*.

American Provincial, Cup, Homer Laughlin	5.00
Americana, Bowl, Vegetable, Oval, Homer Laughlin, 8 1/2 In.	32.00

Americana, Cup & Saucer, Homer Laughlin . . . . .25.00 to 39.00
Americana, Plate, Clipper Ship, Homer Laughlin, 7 In. 12.00
Americana, Plate, Home Sweet Home, Homer Laughlin, 10 In. 42.00
Americana, Platter, Homer Laughlin, 15 In. 140.00
Americana, Sauceboat, Homer Laughlin 27.00
Americana, Sauceboat, Underplate, Homer Laughlin 65.00
Americana, Soup, Coupe, Homer Laughlin 25.00
Americana, Dish, Homer Laughlin 95.00
California Ivy, Bowl, Vegetable, Round, Metlox, 9 In. 35.00
California Ivy, Creamer, Metlox 18.00
California Ivy, Cup & Saucer, Metlox 12.00
California Ivy, Gravy Boat, Metlox 40.00
California Ivy, Gravy Boat, Underplate, Metlox 35.00
California Ivy, Sugar, Cover, Metlox 25.00
California Provincial, Bowl, Fruit, Metlox, 6 In. 12.00
California Provincial, Butter, Cover, Metlox 30.00
California Provincial, Canister Set, Metlox, 4 Piece 225.00
California Provincial, Cup & Saucer, Metlox 13.00
California Provincial, Plate, Metlox, 10 In. 17.00
California Provincial, Platter, Oval, Metlox, 11 In. 39.00
California Provincial, Soup, Dish, Rim, Metlox, 8 In. 18.00
California Provincial, Sugar, Cover, Metlox 26.00
Carnival, Cup, Ivory, Homer Laughlin 7.00
Castle On The Lake, Bowl, Oval, Red, Johnson Brothers, 9 In. 12.00
Castle On The Lake, Platter, Oval, Pink, Johnson Brothers, 12 In. 12.00
Cavalier, Bowl, Fruit, Lily-Of-The-Valley Border, Homer Laughlin, 6 In. 3.50
Cavalier, Cup, Berkshire, Homer Laughlin 7.00
Cavalier, Plate, Square, Lily-Of-The-Valley Border, Homer Laughlin, 8 In. 8.00
Cavalier, Platter, Lily-Of-The-Valley Border, Homer Laughlin, 11 In. 17.00
Cavalier, Platter, Lily-Of-The-Valley Border, Homer Laughlin, 13 1/4 In. 19.00
Cavalier, Platter, Turkey, Gray Border, Homer Laughlin, 15 In. 35.00
Cavalier, Platter, Turkey, Teal Border, Homer Laughlin, 15 In. 35.00
Century, Plate, Ivory, Homer Laughlin, 8 3/4 In. 18.00
Century, Teapot, Ivory, Homer Laughlin 180.00
Cinnamon, Bowl, Cereal, Metlox, 6 1/2 In. 9.50
Cinnamon, Bowl, Vegetable, Metlox, 9 In. 25.00
Cinnamon, Creamer, Metlox 9.00
Cinnamon, Cup & Saucer, Metlox 9.00
Cinnamon, Plate, Metlox, 8 In. 8.50
Cinnamon, Plate, Metlox, 10 3/4 In. 12.00
Cinnamon, Platter, Oval, Metlox, 13 1/4 In. 25.00
Cinnamon, Salt & Pepper, Metlox 15.00
Cinnamon, Sugar, Cover, Metlox 13.00
Conchita, Bowl, Fruit, Swing Shape, Homer Laughlin 16.00
Conchita, Cup & Saucer, Swing Shape, Homer Laughlin 28.00
Conchita, Cup, Swing Shape, Homer Laughlin 22.00
Conchita, Plate, Swing Shape, Homer Laughlin, 6 In. 9.00
Conchita, Plate, Swing Shape, Homer Laughlin, 10 In. 44.00
Conchita, Shaker, Kitchen Kraft, Large, Homer Laughlin 70.00
Conchita, Soup, Dish, Swing Shape, Homer Laughlin 35.00
Currier & Ives, Ashtray, Blue, Royal China, 5 1/2 In. 18.00
Currier & Ives, Butter, Blue, Royal China, Lb. 40.00
Currier & Ives, Cake Plate, Blue, Royal China, 10 1/2 In. 30.00
Currier & Ives, Cup & Saucer, Blue, Royal China 5.25
Daisy Chain, Casserole, Homer Laughlin, 8 1/2 In. 38.00
Daisy Chain, Pie Plate, Homer Laughlin, 9 In. 45.00
Del Ray, Bowl, Fruit, Harmony House, 5 1/2 In. 10.00
Del Ray, Cup & Saucer, Harmony House 10.00
Del Ray, Plate, Harmony House, 10 In. 10.00
Del Ray, Platter, Harmony House 35.00
Del Ray, Sugar & Creamer, Harmony House 40.00
Dog Tooth Violet, Salt & Pepper, Footed, Blue Ridge 115.00

Dogwood, Bowl, Cereal, Homer Laughlin 12.00
Dogwood, Soup, Dish, Rim, Homer Laughlin 9.00
Early America, Bowl, Fruit, Homer Laughlin, 5 In. 22.00
Early America, Bowl, Vegetable, Oval, Homer Laughlin, 8 3/4 In. 65.00
Early America, Cup & Saucer, Homer Laughlin 40.00
Early America, Plate, Homer Laughlin, 6 In. 20.00
Early America, Plate, Homer Laughlin, 9 In. 42.00
Early America, Platter, Oval, Homer Laughlin, 11 In. 65.00
Early American Homes, Bowl, Monticello, Homer Laughlin, 7 In. 11.00
Early American Homes, Plate, Lincoln's Early Home, Homer Laughlin, 6 In. 9.00
Early American Homes, Plate, Mt. Vernon, Homer Laughlin, 9 In. 18.00
Early American Homes, Platter, Independence Hall, Homer Laughlin, 12 In. 45.00
Easter Parade, Sugar, Footed, Blue Ridge 58.00
Eggshell Cavalier, Platter, Turkey Decal, Teal Band, Homer Laughlin, 15 1/2 In. 55.00
Eggshell Georgian, Plate, Bombay, Homer Laughlin, 10 In. 12.00
Eggshell Georgian, Platter, Oval, Buddah, Homer Laughlin, 13 In. 25.00
Eggshell Georgian, Soup, Dish, Lug, Cotillion, Homer Laughlin 17.00
Eggshell Nautilus, Cup & Saucer, Silver Band, Homer Laughlin 9.00
Eggshell Nautilus, Plate, Silver Band, Homer Laughlin, 9 In. 8.00
Eggshell Nautilus, Soup, Cream, Rochelle, Homer Laughlin 16.00
Eggshell Nautilus, Sugar & Creamer, Buddah, Homer Laughlin 29.00
Eggshell Nautilus, Sugar & Creamer, Silver Band, Homer Laughlin 21.00
Epicure, Bowl, Cereal, Dawn Pink, Homer Laughlin, 5 1/2 In. 30.00
Epicure, Bowl, Cereal, Turquoise, Homer Laughlin, 5 1/2 In. 30.00
Epicure, Cup & Saucer, Charcoal Gray, Homer Laughlin 28.00
Epicure, Cup & Saucer, Snow White, Homer Laughlin 28.00
Epicure, Soup, Coupe, Charcoal Gray, Homer Laughlin, 8 In. 35.00
Epicure, Soup, Coupe, Dawn Pink, Homer Laughlin, 8 In. 35.00
Epicure, Soup, Coupe, Turquoise, Blue, Homer Laughlin, 8 In. 35.00
Freedom, Plate, Blue Ridge, 10 In. 22.00
Friendly Village, Plate, Stone Wall, Johnson Bros., 10 1/2 In. 35.00
Friendly Village, Plate, Sugar Maples, Johnson Bros., 6 1/4 In. 20.00
Friendly Village, Platter, Johnson Bros., 20 1/2 In. 275.00
Gigi, Bowl, Cereal, Metlox, 6 1/2 In. 9.50
Gigi, Coffeepot, Metlox 45.00
Gigi, Cup & Saucer, Metlox 9.00
Gigi, Plate, Metlox, 8 In. ....5.50 to 8.50
Gigi, Plate, Metlox, 10 3/4 In. 10.00
Gigi, Saltshaker, Metlox 9.00
Hacienda, Cup & Saucer, Homer Laughlin 22.00
Hacienda, Plate, Homer Laughlin, 6 1/4 In. 8.00
Hacienda, Soup, Coupe, Homer Laughlin 25.00
Homestead Provincial, Bowl, Fruit, Metlox, 6 In. 12.00
Homestead Provincial, Bowl, Vegetable, Cover, Metlox, 10 In. 90.00
Homestead Provincial, Canister Set, Metlox, 4 Piece 225.00
Homestead Provincial, Coaster, Metlox, 3 3/4 In. 16.00
Homestead Provincial, Cup & Saucer, Metlox 12.50
Homestead Provincial, Pepper Mill, Metlox 34.00
Homestead Provincial, Plate, Metlox, 6 3/8 In. 5.00
Homestead Provincial, Plate, Metlox, 10 In. 16.50
Homestead Provincial, Saltshaker, Hen, Metlox 17.00
Leaf, Relish, Rectangular, Taylor, Smith & Taylor 72.00
Liberty Blue, Cup & Saucer, Old North Church 12.00
Nova Leda, Salt & Pepper, Footed, Blue Ridge 89.00
Priscilla, Bowl, Fruit, Homer Laughlin, 5 In. 9.00
Priscilla, Bowl, Vegetable, Oval, Homer Laughlin 25.00
Priscilla, Bowl, Vegetable, Round, Homer Laughlin 25.00
Priscilla, Creamer, Homer Laughlin 20.00
Priscilla, Cup, Homer Laughlin 10.00
Priscilla, Plate, Homer Laughlin, 9 In. ....15.00 to 20.00
Priscilla, Soup, Dish, Homer Laughlin 15.00
Priscilla, Sugar, Cover, Homer Laughlin 25.00

Provincial Blue, Butter, Metlox	68.00
Provincial Blue, Dish, Hen On Nest, Cover, Large, Metlox	135.00
Provincial Blue, Dish, Hen On Nest, Cover, Small, Metlox	35.00
Provincial Blue, Mug, Large, Metlox	30.00
Provincial Blue, Pepper Mill, Metlox	45.00
Provincial Blue, Salt Mill, Metlox	45.00
Red Rooster, Ashtray, Metlox, 8 1/4 In.	35.00
Red Rooster, Bowl, Salad, Metlox, 8 1/4 In.	79.00
Red Rooster, Butter, Metlox	65.00
Red Rooster, Coffeepot, Metlox	98.00
Red Rooster, Cookie Jar, Metlox	90.00
Red Rooster, Dish, Hen On Nest, Cover, Medium, Metlox	98.00
Red Rooster, Dish, Hen On Nest, Cover, Small, Metlox	72.00
Red Rooster, Eggcup, Metlox	25.00
Red Rooster, Pitcher, Metlox	72.00
Red Rooster, Platter, Turkey, Metlox, 22 1/2 In.	249.00
Red Rooster, Relish, 3 Sections, Metlox	79.00
Red Rooster, Teapot, Metlox	78.00
Red Velvet, Plate, Blue Ridge, 10 In.	25.00
Rhythm, Bowl, Burgundy, Homer Laughlin, 5 1/4 In.	3.00
Rhythm, Cup & Saucer, Burgundy, Homer Laughlin	9.00
Rhythm, Cup & Saucer, Yellow, Homer Laughlin	9.00
Rhythm, Plate, Burgundy, Homer Laughlin, 10 In.	9.00
Rhythm, Plate, Dark Green, Homer Laughlin, 6 In.	5.00
Rose Marie, Candy Dish, Cover, Blue Ridge	160.00
Rose Marie, Salt & Pepper, Footed, Blue Ridge	90.00
Rose Marie, Sugar & Creamer, Footed, Blue Ridge	140.00
Rose Of Sharon, Salt & Pepper, Footed, Blue Ridge	35.00
Rose Of Sharon, Sugar & Creamer, Footed, Blue Ridge	140.00
Sculptured Daisy, Bowl, Vegetable, Cover, Metlox, Qt.	65.00
Sculptured Daisy, Coffeepot, Metlox	86.00
Sculptured Daisy, Cup & Saucer, Metlox	10.00
Sculptured Daisy, Plate, Metlox, 7 1/2 In.	8.00
Sculptured Daisy, Plate, Metlox, 10 1/2 In.	10.00
Sculptured Daisy, Salt & Pepper, Metlox	22.00
Ships, Marine Series, Box, Cigarette, Vernon Kilns	100.00
Skytone, Bowl, Vegetable, Round, Homer Laughlin, 7 1/2 In.	10.00
Skytone, Cup & Saucer, Homer Laughlin	6.50
Skytone, Cup, Homer Laughlin	4.00
Skytone, Gravy Boat, Attached Underplate, Homer Laughlin	16.50
Skytone, Plate, Homer Laughlin, 7 1/2 In.	7.00
Skytone, Plate, Homer Laughlin, 10 In.	10.00
Skytone, Salt & Pepper, Homer Laughlin	4.50 to 9.00
Skytone, Teapot, Homer Laughlin, 7 1/2 In.	45.00
Sweet Clover, Plate, Blue Ridge, 10 In.	22.00

DIONNE QUINTUPLETS were born in Canada on May 28, 1934. The publicity about their birth and their special status as wards of the Canadian government made them famous throughout the world. Visitors could watch the girls play; reporters interviewed the girls and the staff. Thousands of special dolls and souvenirs were made picturing the quints at different ages. Emilie died in 1954, Marie in 1970, and Yvonne in 2001. Annette and Cecile still live in Canada.

Book, We're 2 Years Old	20.00
Calendar, 1937	25.00
Doll, Composition, Socket Head, Sculpted, Painted Hair, c.1935, 8 In.	550.00
Doll, Madame Alexander, Composition, Bed, c.1935, 8 In., 5 Piece	1206.00
Doll, Toddler, Composition, Molded Hair, Painted Eyes, Tag, 7 1/2 In., 5 Piece	400.00
Paper Dolls, 1937	40.00
Picture, Baby, Frame, 1935	15.00
Platter, Inscribed, Born May 28, 1934, Maple Leaf, Porcelain, 11 In.	260.00
Poster, Quaker Oats, 1935, 14 1/2 x 31 1/2 In.	145.00

Dirk Van Erp, Lamp,
Copper, Mica Shade,
Orange, Wood
Chinese Base, 23 1/2 In.

Be careful removing a light
bulb from an old lamp with a
glass shade. The Tiffany lily-
shaped shades and others are
made so that the shade is held
in place by a screw-in bulb.

DIRK VAN ERP was born in 1860 and died in 1933. He opened his own studio in 1908 in Oakland, California. He moved his studio to San Francisco in 1909 and remained there until 1977. Van Erp made hammered copper accessories, including vases, desk sets, bookends, candlesticks, jardinieres, and trays, but he is best known for his lamps. The hammered copper lamps often had shades with mica panels.

Bookends, Repousse Stylized Flowers, Copper, 5 1/2 x 6 In.	2300.00
Bowl, Copper, Hammered, Closed-In Rim, Reddish Brown Patina, 2 1/2 x 8 1/2 In.	546.00
Chamberstick, Copper, Hammered, Closed Box Mark, 5 x 6 1/2 In.	1380.00
Chamberstick, Hammered, Closed Box Mark, 5 x 6 In.	1380.00
Inkwell, Copper, Hammered, Overhanging Top, Liner, Marked, 2 1/2 x 3 In.	518.00
Jardiniere, Bronze, Hammered, 2 Handles, 1920, 5 1/2 In.	7200.00
Jardiniere, Copper, Original Patina, 6 In.	1600.00
Lamp, Copper, Hammered, 3-Panel Shade, Mica, Single Socket, 11 In.	8000.00
Lamp, Copper, Hammered, Classical Base, Conical Shade, 4 Mica Panels, 17 1/2 In.	9200.00
Lamp, Copper, Hammered, Mica Shade, Original Patina, 19 x 25 In.	8050.00
Lamp, Copper, Hammered, Original Mica, 14 x 12 In.	13800.00
Lamp, Copper, Hammered, Riveted Arms, Mica, Vented Cap, 2 Sockets, 18 x 16 In.	13800.00
Lamp, Copper, Hammered, Shade, 15 1/2 x 16 In.	9200.00
Lamp, Copper, Hammered, Single Socket, 3 Paneled Shade, Marked, 11 x 11 In.	8000.00
Lamp, Copper, Mica Shade, Orange, Wood Chinese Base, 23 1/2 In.	*Illus* 31625.00
Tray, Copper, Hammered, 2 Raised Handles, 16 1/2 In.	715.00
Tray, Copper, Hammered, Embossed Handles, Marked, 13 1/2 In.	920.00
Tray, Copper, Hammered, Raised Handles, 13 1/2 In.	530.00
Vase, Copper, Hammered, 8 1/2 In.	1430.00
Vase, Copper, Hammered, Closed-In Rim, Dark Patina, Marked, 3 1/4 x 4 In.	2300.00
Vase, Copper, Hammered, Dark Patina, Oval, Closed-In Rim, 4 1/4 x 4 In.	978.00
Vase, Copper, Hammered, Mottled Patina, Oval, 7 x 5 1/2 In.	8050.00
Vase, Copper, Hammered, Original Patina, 4 1/2 In.	1035.00

DISNEYANA is a collector's term. Walt Disney and his company introduced many comic characters to the world. Collectors search for examples of the work of the Disney Studios and the many commercial products modeled after his characters, including Mickey Mouse and Donald Duck, and recent films, like *Beauty and the Beast* and *The Little Mermaid*.

Bank, Mickey Mouse, Beehive, Tin Lithograph, Holding Key & Honey Jar, c.1930, 3 In.	450.00
Bank, Mickey Mouse, Painted Composition, 6 1/2 In.	55.00
Bank, Mickey Mouse, Seated, Cast Metal, 1960	75.00
Bank, Mickey Mouse, Telephone, 1930s	135.00
Bell Toy, Mickey & Minnie Mouse Bell, Wood Pluto Pulling, Steel, 30 In.	230.00
Birthday Party Set, Disney Characters, Plastic, Best Plastics, 1950s, 13 x 21 In.	85.00
Biscuit Tin, Mickey Mouse, Topolino, Italy, 1930s, 5 x 8 1/2 In.	550.00
Biscuit Tin, Snow White, Switzerland, 1939, 7 x 4 In.	1580.00
Book, Donald Duck, First Appearance, Hardcover, 1936, 36 Pages	1760.00
Book, Ferdinand Story Book, Walt Disney Ent., 1938	50.00
Book, Mickey Mouse Comic Strip, No. 948, Whitman, 1932, 8 x 10 In.	180.00

Book, Snow White & Seven Dwarfs, Hardcover, 9 1/2 x 12 1/2 In. 55.00
Book, Walt Disney's Dumbo Songbook, 1941 .... 75.00
Camera, Donald Duck, Donald & Nephews, Plastic, Box, 4 1/2 In. 90.00
Camera, Donald Duck, Plastic, Herbert George Co., Box, 1940s, 5 In. 180.00
Carousel, Mickey Mouse, Donald Duck, Pluto, Goofy, Tin, Clockwork, Linemar, 7 In. 2530.00
Cel, see Animation Art category.
Chocolate Mold Set, Mickey, Minnie, Pluto, Donald Duck 170.00
Clock, Alarm, Bambi, Butterfly Ticks Seconds, Bayard, c.1960, 5 In. 360.00
Clock, Alarm, Donald Duck, Head Moves Ticking Seconds, Bayard, 1960, 5 In. 410.00
Clock, Alarm, Mickey Mouse, Waggling Head, Italy, 1930s, 5 In. 380.00
Clock, Alarm, Pinocchio, Jiminy Cricket Ticks Seconds, Bayard, c.1960, 5 In. 250.00
Clock, Alarm, Snow White, Seven Dwarfs, Ticks Seconds, Bayard, c.1970, 5 In. 300.00
Clock, Radio, Mickey Mouse, G.E. 115.00
Clock, Radio, Mickey Mouse, Plastic, General Electric, 11 In. 35.00
Condiment Set, Mickey & Minnie Mouse, Salt & Pepper, Mustard Pot, Handled Base ... 330.00
Costume, Mickey Mouse, With Mask, Box, 1940s 145.00
Costume, Mouseketeer, Original Box, 1950s 1200.00
Creamer, Donald Duck, Wade Heath, c.1935, 4 1/4 In. 500.00
Doll, Ferdinand The Bull, Straw Stuffed, 1938, 16 x 12 In. 230.00
Doll, Mickey Mouse, Brown & Black Velvet, Felt Ears, Applied Eyes, c.1940, 7 In. 489.00
Doll, Mickey Mouse, Cloth Swivel Head, Oilcloth, Pie Eyes, Knickerbocker, 11 In. 650.00
Doll, Mickey Mouse, Cloth, Composition Feet, Pie Eyes, Knickerbocker, 11 In. 750.00
Doll, Pinocchio, Composition Head, Wood Jointed Body, Box, Ideal, 7 1/2 In. 300.00
Doll, Pinocchio, Composition, Full Dress, Hat, Knickerbocker, 13 In. 360.00
Doll, Pinocchio, Wooden, Composition, Jointed, Ideal, c.1940, 11 In. 225.00
Drummer, Jazz, Tin Lithograph, Drumming Action, Walt E. Disney, 6 3/4 In. 1485.00
Figurine, Centaur, 10 In. .... *Illus* 1995.00
Figurine, Donald Duck, Seiberling, c.1930, 6 In. 340.00
Figurine, Dopey, Latex, Seiberling, 1940s, 5 1/2 In. 110.00
Figurine, Dumbo, Ceramic, Tag, 6 x 6 In. 70.00
Figurine, Geppetto, Bisque, Japan, 1939, 3 In. 85.00
Figurine, Happy, Latex, Seiberling, 1940s, 5 3/4 In. 110.00
Figurine, Mickey Mouse & Pluto, Silver, Walt Disney, 6 3/4 In. 165.00
Figurine, Mickey Mouse, Bisque, Name On Chest, 5 1/4 In. 230.00
Figurine, Mickey Mouse, Bisque, Painted, Movable Arms, Incised Base, 8 1/2 In. 935.00
Figurine, Mickey Mouse, Black Rubber, White Pie Eyes, Seiberling, 3 1/2 In. 60.00
Figurine, Mickey Mouse, Military Uniform, 4 1/2 In. 155.00
Figurine, Minnie Mouse, Celluloid, England, 2 1/2 In. 55.00
Figurine, Ostrich, 6 1/2 In. .... *Illus* 1020.00
Figurine, Pluto, Fun-E-Flex, 3 In. 225.00
Figurine, Pluto, Fun-E-Flex, 6 1/2 In. 425.00
Figurine, Sleepy, Latex, Seiberling, 1940s, 5 1/4 In. 110.00
Figurine, Snow White & Seven Dwarfs, Bisque, Prewar Japan, 8 Piece 375.00
Figurine, Three Hippos, 5 In. .... *Illus* 2130.00
Figurine, Thumper, Wade, 1 3/4 In. 3.00
Figurine, Trusty, Lady & The Tramp, Wade, 2 1/2 In. 16.00

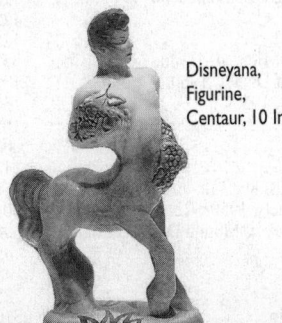

Disneyana,
Figurine,
Centaur, 10 In.

Disneyana, Figurine,
Ostrich, 6 1/2 In.

Disneyana,
Nodder,
Donald Duck,
Plastic,
5 1/8 In.

Disneyana, Figurine, Three Hippos, 5 In.

Game, Laram Pin Ball, On Card, 1930s, 10 1/2 In.	35.00
Game, Mickey Mouse, Circus, Tivoli Type, Box, Marks Bros., 20 x 9 In.	440.00
Game, Mickey Mouse, Coming Home, Board, Marks Bros., 20 x 8 1/2 In.	190.00
Game, Mickey Mouse, Helter Skelter Marble, Box, Chad Valley, 8 x 17 1/2 In.	316.00
Game, Mickey Mouse, Pin The Tail On, Envelope, Marks Bros., Mid 1930s, 18 x 22 In.	115.00
Game, Mickey Mouse, Ring Toss, Paper, Wood, England, 13 x 13 In.	145.00
Game, Mickey Mouse, Soldier Set, 8 Cardboard Figures, Wood Bases, Cork Gun, Marks	440.00
Game, Mickey Mouse, Soldier, 8 Stand-Up Soldiers, Pop Gun, Marks Bros., 8 x 18 In.	240.00
Glass, Milk, Mickey Mouse	130.00
Lunch Box, Mickey Mouse Club, Tin, Aladdin	65.00
Magazine, Mickey Mouse, Vol. 3 No. 3, Christmas Cover, Mickey Santa, 1938	400.00
Music Box, Mickey, Minnie & Pluto, Wood, Door, 10 In.	130.00
Mustard, With Salt & Pepper, Mickey Mouse, 1930s, 3 Piece	585.00
Napkin Ring, Mickey Mouse, Hand Painted, Celluloid, England, 1930s	265.00
Night-Light, Donald Duck, 1930s	495.00
Night-Light, Donald Duck, With Mickey & Pluto, 1930s, 3 3/4 In.	360.00
Nodder, Donald Duck, Plastic, 5 1/8 In. _Illus_	20.00
Noise Maker, Mickey Mouse, Horn & Ratchet Paper, Fiberboard, 7 In.	90.00
Pail, Mickey & Minnie Mouse, Pluto, Donald Duck In Wagon, Tin Lithograph, Gal.	1595.00
Pail, Mickey Mouse & Friends, Tin, 1940s	87.00
Pail, Mickey, Minnie, Porky & Donald Duck, Happynak No. 7, 1930s, 4 1/2 In.	251.00
Pail, Minnie Mouse & Felix, Paper Lithograph, Tin, Handle, Lids, 8 In.	1650.00
Pail, Snow White & Seven Dwarfs, Tin	20.00
Paint Set, Mickey Mouse Circus, Lionel, Box, 1930s	8350.00
Paperweight, Disneyworld 25th Anniversary, Swarovski	160.00
Paperweight, Mickey Mouse, Bisque Saxophone Player, 5 1/2 In.	99.00
Pencil Holder, Mickey Mouse, Composition, Painted, Dixon, 4 3/4 In.	99.00
Pencil Set, Mickey Mouse Club, Colored, Jolly Hobby Toys, 1950s, 9 x 5 In.	50.00
Perfume Bottle, Minnie Mouse, Ceramic, Removable Head, Tin Ears, 5 In.	275.00
Pin, Donald Duck, Donald In Rain Jacket, Norwich Knitting Co., 1935, 1 In.	375.00
Pitcher, Donald Duck, 6 In.	125.00
Planter, Bambi, 7 1/2 x 7 In.	125.00
Projector, Mickey & Friends, Movie Jecktor, 7 Paper Films, Box, 10 1/2 In.	357.00
Purse, Mickey Mouse As Uncle Sam, Leather, Beaded, Walt Disney, 1960, 8 x 9 In.	172.00
Roller Skates, Official Mouseketeer, Tin, Ball Bearing, Key, 1950s	50.00
Scissors, Donald Duck, Electric, WDP, 1950s, 5 3/4 In.	165.00
Scissors, Mickey Mouse, Tin Lithograph, 3 1/2 In.	200.00
Seeds, Flower, 10 Packets, 9 In.	11.00
Seesaw Parasol, Mickey & Minnie, Celluloid, Jointed, 1930s, 8 x 3 In.	1610.00
Sign, Donald Duck Cola, Die Cut, Cardboard, Disney Products, 1950s, 22 x 25 In.	605.00
Sled, Mickey Mouse Flyer, Wood & Metal, Steerable, Mickey & Minnie Decal, 33 In.	690.00
Soaky, Donald Duck, Salesman's Sample, 1960s	45.00
Soaky, Mickey Mouse, Salesman's Sample, 1960s	45.00
Soaky, Pinocchio, Salesman's Sample, 1960s	35.00
Stroller, Mickey Mouse & Betty Boop, Tin Lithograph, 10 In.	2310.00
Suitcase, Mickey Mouse, Red, Black, 6 x 9 In.	143.00

Disneyana, Toothbrush Holder, Donald Duck,
Ceramic, Double, 4 x 5 In.

The Mickey Mouse watch by
Ingersoll was made in 1933 with
Mickey wearing yellow gloves. The
word Ingersoll was on the watch
face. In 1934 "Made in the U.S.A."
was added, and in 1938 "c W.D.
Ent" was added.

Tea Set, Mickey Mouse, Sugar & Creamer, 4 Cups & Saucers, Japan, c.1935	553.00
Tea Set, Mickey Mouse, Tin Lithograph, Ohio Art	275.00
Thermometer, Mickey Mouse, Pluto, Tin Lithograph, 3 1/4 x 3 1/4 In.	209.00
Tie Rack, Mickey Mouse, Wood, 8 3/4 In.	150.00
Tin, Mickey, Minnie & Pluto, Candy, Switzerland, c.1932, 7 1/2 In.	695.00
Tin, Minnie Mouse, Tin Lithograph, Embossed Lid, 3 Sides, 5 In.	209.00
Toothbrush Holder, Donald Duck, Ceramic, Double, 4 x 5 In. . . . . *Illus*	336.00
Toothbrush Holder, Donald Duck, Walt E. Disney, 1930s, 5 In.	425.00
Toothbrush Holder, Mickey & Minnie Mouse, Hand Painted Bisque, 4 1/2 In. . . . . .175.00 to 295.00
Toothbrush Holder, Mickey & Minnie, Arms Around Bisque, 1930	275.00
Toothbrush Holder, Pluto, Bisque, Japan, 4 1/2 In.	90.00
Toy, Disney Characters, Drum, Tin Lithograph, Wooden Drumsticks, Ohio Art, 9 In.	230.00
Toy, Donald Duck & Goofy, Windup, Marx	590.00
Toy, Donald Duck & Pluto, Car, Red, White Tires, Sun Rubber, 6 1/4 In.	200.00
Toy, Donald Duck & Pluto, Handcar, Painted Tin, Composition, Lionel, 10 1/2 In.	375.00
Toy, Donald Duck, Acrobat, On Wire, Celluloid, Clockwork, Japan, c.1935, 5 In.	495.00
Toy, Donald Duck, Car Racer, Original Tires, Lindstrom, 4 In.	395.00
Toy, Donald Duck, Car, Convertible, Tin, Vinyl, Friction, Linemar, 6 In.	145.00
Toy, Donald Duck, Car, Dipsy, Box, Marx	750.00
Toy, Donald Duck, Car, Dipsy, Tin Lithograph, Linemar, 1950s . . . . .140.00 to 385.00
Toy, Donald Duck, Car, Fire Chief, Tin, Windup, Box, Linemar, 5 1/2 In.	2200.00
Toy, Donald Duck, Duet, Windup, Marx	485.00
Toy, Donald Duck, Fire Chief, Walks, Windup, Marx	95.00
Toy, Donald Duck, Friction, Tin Lithograph, Japan	300.00
Toy, Donald Duck, Handcar, Painted Tin, Composition, Mechanical, Lionel, 10 1/2 In. . . .	425.00
Toy, Donald Duck, Hopping, Tin, Mechanical, Linemar, 6 In.	210.00
Toy, Donald Duck, On Tricycle, Rolling, Fisher-Price, 1940s, 10 In.	300.00
Toy, Donald Duck, On Tricycle, Windup, Tin, Linemar, 1950s, 3 1/2 In.	525.00
Toy, Donald Duck, Paper, Wood, Plastic Feet, Quacks, Fisher-Price, 8 x 6 In. . . . . *Illus*	110.00
Toy, Donald Duck, Race Car, Tin, Celluloid Head	375.00
Toy, Donald Duck, Snow Shovel, Tin Lithograph, 1930s, 27 In.	370.00
Toy, Donald Duck, Tin, Clockwork, Schuco, 1930s	528.00
Toy, Donald Duck, Tricycle, Tin Lithograph, Plastic, Bell Revolves, Linemar, 4 In. .425.00 to 525.00
Toy, Donald Duck, Waddler, Tin Lithograph, Mechanical, Tail Moves, 5 In.	150.00
Toy, Donald Duck, Walker, Painted Composition, Mechanical, 11 In.	400.00
Toy, Donald Duck, Watering Can, Tin Lithograph, 3 x 5 3/4 x 2 1/4 In. . . . . *Illus*	193.00
Toy, Donald Duck, Whirling Tail, Tin, Windup, Linemar, 5 In.	207.00
Toy, Donald Duck, Xylophone, Litho Paper On Wood, Fisher-Price, 13 1/2 In.	180.00
Toy, Dumbo, Tin Lithograph, Clockwork, Marx, 3 1/2 In.	198.00
Toy, Ferdinand The Bull, Windup, Tin Lithograph	275.00
Toy, Ferris Wheel, Disney Characters, Tin, Windup, Chein, 17 In.	465.00
Toy, Goofy Dancing, Donald Plays Drums, Lithographed Base, Marx, 11 In.	402.00
Toy, Jiminy Cricket, Hopper, Windup, Linemar	595.00
Toy, Jiminy Cricket, Hops Around, Holding Umbrella, Box, Tin, Linemar, 6 In.	962.00
Toy, Ludwig Von Drake, Walking, Windup, Linemar, 5 3/4 In.	319.00
Toy, Mickey & Minnie Mouse, Acrobats, Celluloid, Box	2250.00

Toy, Mickey & Minnie Mouse, Barber, Japan, 1930 .... 1000.00
Toy, Mickey & Minnie Mouse, Handcar, Green, Clockwork, Steel, Lionel, 8 In. 660.00
Toy, Mickey & Minnie Mouse, Handcar, Original Box, Lionel, 9 In. 860.00
Toy, Mickey & Minnie Mouse, Marionettes, Wood, Cloth, 12 In. 55.00
Toy, Mickey & Minnie On Trapeze, Celluloid, Windup, 12 In. 440.00
Toy, Mickey & Pluto, Celluloid, Tin Lithograph, Mechanical, 19 In. 1100.00
Toy, Mickey Mouse Club Mouseketeers, Tambourine, Tin, Orange, Enamel, 6 1/4 In. 140.00
Toy, Mickey Mouse Club, Telephone, Talking, On Card, Hasbro, 1964, 12 x 5 In. . . .300.00 to 400.00
Toy, Mickey Mouse, Block Set, Walt Disney Enterprises, Halsam, Box, c.1935 .... 135.00
Toy, Mickey Mouse, Car, Dipsy, Windup, All Metal, Linemar 485.00
Toy, Mickey Mouse, Car, Motor, Erratic Action, Tin Lithograph, Marx, 5 1/2 In. 144.00
Toy, Mickey Mouse, Car, Racing, Tin, Celluloid, Windup, Occupied Japan, 3 In. 220.00
Toy, Mickey Mouse, Car, Racing, Tin, Rubber Tires, Wood Hubs, No Key, 4 In. 425.00
Toy, Mickey Mouse, Car, Tin Lithograph, Plastic, Mechanical, Marx, 5 1/2 In. 240.00
Toy, Mickey Mouse, Choo Choo, Paper Litho On Wood, Fisher Price, 9 In. 130.00
Toy, Mickey Mouse, Climbs String, Cardboard, Dolly Toy Co., Dayton, Ohio, 9 In. 248.00
Toy, Mickey Mouse, Drum, Tin Lithograph, Drumsticks, 6 In. 170.00
Toy, Mickey Mouse, Drummer, Plunger Action, Partial Box, Geo. Borgfeldt, 6 1/4 In. 2420.00
Toy, Mickey Mouse, Floor Sweeper, Tin Lithograph, Rolling Action, 1920s, 6 x 27 In. 200.00
Toy, Mickey Mouse, Flute, Tin Lithograph, Italy, 10 In. 175.00
Toy, Mickey Mouse, Globe Trotters Club, 1930s, 20 x 26 In. 795.00
Toy, Mickey Mouse, Handcar, In Bag, Santa, Tree, Motor, 10 1/2 In. .... .345.00 to 770.00
Toy, Mickey Mouse, Handcar, Minnie Pumping Car, Box, 1930s 2195.00
Toy, Mickey Mouse, Handcar, Tin, Composition, Mechanical, Lionel, 8 1/2 In. ....450.00 to 475.00
Toy, Mickey Mouse, Jack In The Box, Tin Lithograph 75.00
Toy, Mickey Mouse, Jazz Drummer, Tin Lithograph, Hand Action, Nifty, 6 3/4 In. 660.00
Toy, Mickey Mouse, Magician, Waves Wand, Drops Hat, Tin, Linemar, 10 In. 2090.00
Toy, Mickey Mouse, On Horse, Spring, Japan, 5 In. 605.00
Toy, Mickey Mouse, On Motorcycle, Windup, 3 1/2 In. 550.00
Toy, Mickey Mouse, On Rocking Horse, Celluloid, Wood Horse, Windup 1540.00
Toy, Mickey Mouse, On Scooter, Jointed Posable Figure, Wood, 1940s, 3 1/2 In. 195.00
Toy, Mickey Mouse, Organ Grinder, Crank, Minnie Dancing, Distler ....4935.00 to 5720.00
Toy, Mickey Mouse, Playing Xylophone, Windup, Tin, Linemar, 1950s, 6 1/2 In. . .250.00 to 625.00
Toy, Mickey Mouse, Playland, Box, WDP, 11 In. 4220.00
Toy, Mickey Mouse, Race Car, Tin Lithograph, Clockwork, 4 In. 275.00
Toy, Mickey Mouse, Rat Type Face, Wood, 1930, 5 1/2 In. 110.00
Toy, Mickey Mouse, Riding Pluto, Rocking Base, Celluloid, Clockwork, Japan, 8 In. 1760.00
Toy, Mickey Mouse, Robot, Plastic, Windup, Hong Kong, 9 1/2 In. 11.00
Toy, Mickey Mouse, Santa Car, Painted Tin, Mechanical, Lionel, 10 1/2 In. 700.00
Toy, Mickey Mouse, Squeeze, Wood, 1930s, 8 1/2 In. 30.00
Toy, Mickey Mouse, Tin Lithograph, Windup, Rogelio Sanchez, 6 In. 8800.00
Toy, Mickey Mouse, Tin, Plastic, Arcade Style, Box, 12 In. 11.00
Toy, Mickey Mouse, Top, Tin Lithograph, 9 1/2 In. 242.00
Toy, Mickey Mouse, Windup, Whirling Tail, Linemar, 5 1/2 In. 336.00
Toy, Mickey Mouse, Xylophone, Box, Marx 585.00
Toy, Minnie Mouse, Fun-E-Flex, Wood, Jointed, Cloth Dress, 5 In. 144.00

Disneyana, Toy,
Donald Duck, Paper,
Wood, Plastic Feet,
Quacks, Fisher-Price,
8 x 6 In.

Disneyana, Toy, Donald Duck, Watering Can,
Tin Lithograph, 3 x 5 3/4 x 2 1/4 In.

Toy, Minnie Mouse, In Rocker, Minnie Knitting, Tin, Windup, Linemar, 7 In. 385.00
Toy, Pinocchio, Acrobat, Metal Band, Rocking Platform, Windup, Marx, 1939 . . . . 425.00
Toy, Pinocchio, Acrobat, Tin Lithograph, Windup, 1930, 11 x 17 In. 213.00
Toy, Pinocchio, Bisque, Jointed, Crown Toy Co., 9 In. 350.00
Toy, Pinocchio, Cymbal Player, Windup, Rubber & Cloth, Box, 1960s, 11 In. 260.00
Toy, Pinocchio, Moving Pole, Whipping Into Somersault, Marx, 16 x 11 In. 500.00
Toy, Pinocchio, Tin Lithograph, Clockwork, Linemar, 5 1/2 In. 440.00
Toy, Pinocchio, Tin Lithograph, Eyes Move, Windup, Marx, 1939, 8 1/2 In. . . . . .350.00 to 375.00
Toy, Pinocchio, Walking, Swinging Arms, Tin, Windup, Linemar, 6 In. 926.00
Toy, Pluto, Band Leader, Tin, Windup, Linemar, 6 1/2 In. 66.00
Toy, Pluto, Drink Maker, Tin Lithograph, Mechanical, Linemar, 6 1/2 In. 130.00
Toy, Pluto, Drum Major, Moves Forward, Horn, Shakes, Windup, Linemar, Box, 6 In. 615.00
Toy, Pluto, Fire Hydrant, Walking, Windup, Japan 35.00
Toy, Pluto, Goofy, Jeep, Lithographed, Tin, Marx, 10 In. 275.00
Toy, Pluto, On Tricycle, Tin, Windup, Bell, Linemar, 3 1/2 In. 303.00
Toy, Pluto, Rollover, Tin, Windup, Marx, 9 In. 145.00
Toy, Pluto, Squeeze Bulb, Pluto Moves, Tin, Brevetti, 5 In. 95.00
Toy, Pluto, Tricycle, Peddles Trike, Tin & Celluloid, Linemar, 4 In. 480.00
Train, Mickey Mouse Meteor, 4 Pieces, Track, Marx, c.1947, 35 1/4 In. 553.00
Train Set, Mickey Mouse, Circus, Tin Lithograph, Clockwork, Track, 26 In. 1045.00
Umbrella, Mickey Mouse, 1930 . . . . 325.00
Watch, Donald Duck, 1939, 2 In. 470.00
Watch, Mickey Mouse On Face, Presentation Box, US Time, c.1955, 1 In. 550.00
Watch, Mickey Mouse, Ingersoll, Mickey's Picture Engraved On Back, 2 In. 517.00
Watch, Mickey Mouse, Kelton, 1946, 9 In. 200.00
Watch, Pocket, Mickey Mouse, Ingersoll, Box, 1934 . . . . 1235.00
Window, Mickey Mouse, Leaded Glass, 1979, 12 x 18 In. 27.00
Wristwatch, Donald Duck, Birthday Series, U.S. Time, Box, 1948, 4 1/4 In. 540.00
Wristwatch, Mickey Mouse, Ingersoll, Box, 1933, 6 1/4 In. 575.00
Wristwatch, Mickey Mouse, Red Band, Ingersoll 225.00
Wristwatch, Snow White, Box 75.00

DOCTOR, see Dental; Medical

DOLL entries are listed by marks printed or incised on the doll, if possible. If there are no marks, the doll is listed by the name of the subject or country or maker. Notice that Barbie is listed under Mattel. G.I. Joe figures are listed in the Toy section. Doll clothes and accessories are listed at the end of this section. The twentieth-century clothes listed here are in mint condition.

A.M., 15M, Bisque, Blue Set Eyes, Long Human-Hair Curls, Composition Body, 33 In. . . 405.00
A.M., 253, Bisque Head, Googly Eyes, Pert Smile, Papier-Mache, 6 In. 1300.00
A.M., 253, Bisque Socket Head, Mohair Wig, Googly, 5-Piece Composition Body, 6 In. . . 675.00
A.M., 323, Bisque Head, Closed Mouth, Mohair Wig, Googly, Composition, Dress, 13 In. . 475.00
A.M., 323, Girl, Blue Sleep Eyes, Googly, Closed Smile, Blond, White Dress, 9 In. 950.00
A.M., 351, Bisque Solid Dome Socket Head, Composition, Long Dress, Diaper, 22 In. . . . 300.00
A.M., 351, Brown Bisque, Sleep Eyes, Composition Body, Striped Dress, Socks, 13 In. . . . 275.00
A.M., 370, Bisque Shoulder Head, Blue Sleep Eyes, Jointed Kid Body, c.1900, 16 1/2 In. . 86.00
A.M., 370, Bisque Shoulder Head, Kid Body, 17 In. 70.00
A.M., 370, My Sweetheart, Bisque, Blond Wig, Sleep Eyes, Kid & Cloth Body, Tag, 17 In. . 50.00
A.M., 390, Bisque Head, Blue Sleep Eyes, Ash Blond Mohair Wig, 13 In. 200.00
A.M., 390, Bisque Head, Brown Sleep Eyes, Wood & Composition Body, 15 In. 115.00
A.M., 390, Bisque Socket Head, Light Blue Sleep Eyes, Blond Human Hair, 18 In. 290.00
A.M., 390, Bisque, Blond Mohair, Sleep Eyes, Teeth, Composition, Ball-Jointed, 19 In. . . . 70.00
A.M., 390, Bisque, Sleep Eyes, Open Mouth, Composition, Vintage Outfit, 23 1/2 In. 140.00
A.M., 992, Bisque, Sleep Eyes, 2 Teeth, Human Hair, Baby, Dress, Lace Trim, 22 In. 260.00
A.M., 1894, Bisque Socket Head, Blond Mohair, Teeth, Composition, Ball-Jointed, 20 In. . 120.00
A.M., 1904, Bisque Head, 4 Teeth, Mohair Curls, Composition, Jointed, Boy, Jacket, 16 In. 215.00
A.M., Bisque Head, Sleep Eyes, Painted Lashes, Teeth, Composition Body, 8 In. . . . . . *Illus* 310.00
A.M., Brown Bisque Socket Head, Painted Hair, Composition Body, Baby, 15 In. 275.00
A.M., Duchess, Bisque, Sleep Eyes, Blond Mohair Wig, Cloth Body, Vintage Dress, 20 In. 125.00
A.M., Fany, Bisque, Pouty, Painted Forelock Curl, Ball-Jointed Body, c.1912, 18 In. 9750.00
A.M., Just Me, Bisque, Painted, Side Sleep Eyes, 5-Piece Composition Body, 10 In. 900.00

Doll, A.M., Bisque Head, Sleep
Eyes, Painted Lashes, Teeth,
Composition Body, 8 In.

Doll, Advertising, Nauga,
Naugahyde, 10 1/2 In.

Doll, American Character, Toni,
Vinyl, Sleep Eyes, Rooted Hair,
Wedding Gown, 20 In.

A.M., Just Me, Bisque, Socket Head, Googly Sleep Eyes, c.1929, 10 In. 2800.00
A.M., Just Me, Painted Bisque, Blue Glass Sleep Eyes, Blond Mohair Wig, c.1930, 9 In. . . 1400.00
A.M., Lilly, Bisque, 4 Teeth, Sleep Eyes, Mohair Wig, Kid Body, 20 In. 135.00
A.M., My Dearie, c.1908, 22 In. 400.00
A.M., Nobbikid, Bisque, Socket Head, Brown Glass Eyes, Googly, c.1920, 7 In. 750.00
A.M., Painted Bisque Head, Wig, Composition Body, Early 1900s, 12 In. 235.00
A.M., Queen Louise, Bisque Head, Sleep Eyes, Teeth, Wood, Composition, Jointed, 21 In. 400.00
A.M., Queen Louise, Bisque Socket Head, Teeth, Human Hair, Wood, Composition, 29 In. 350.00
Adolph Menjou, Composition, Painted Eyes, 7 Teeth, 2-Piece Suit, 32 In. 725.00
Advertising, Nauga, Naugahyde, 10 1/2 In. . . . . *Illus* 200.00
Advertising, Sparkly, Seven-Up, Rubber & Cloth, 1970s, 18 In. 9.00
Alabama Baby, Cloth, Painted Hair, Stockings & Shoes, No Clothes, 11 In. 360.00
Alexander dolls are listed in this category under Madame Alexander.
Alice In Wonderland, Celluloid, Child's Body, Germany, 15 In. 230.00
Alt Beck & Gottschalck, 1367, Bisque, Wig, Composition, Eyelet Dress, Toddler, 24 In. . . 180.00
Alt Beck & Gottschalck, Bisque Shoulder Head, Cloth Body, Lady, Tiara, Dress, 19 In. . . 1350.00
Alt Beck & Gottschalck, Bisque, Brown Eyes, Blond Wig, Leather Arms, Boots, 16 In. . . 700.00
Alt Beck & Gottschalck, Bisque, Flirty Sleep Eyes, 2 Teeth, Wobbly Tongue, Baby, 25 In. 375.00
Alt Beck & Gottschalck, Bisque, Socket Head, Hip-Jointed, Toddler, c.1917, 17 In. 2300.00
Alt Beck & Gottschalck, Bisque, Socket Head, Teeth, Brunette Wig, Toddler, 18 In. 2400.00
Amberg, Newborn Babe, Bisque Head, Sleep Eyes, Closed Mouth, Cloth Body, 15 In. . . . 305.00
American Character, Toni, Vinyl, Sleep Eyes, Rooted Hair, Wedding Gown, 20 In. . . *Illus* 395.00
Ann Parker, Queen Elizabeth I, Molded Plastic, 11 1/2 In. 160.00
Annette Himstedt, Bastian, Vinyl, Cloth Body, Barefoot Children Collection, Boy, 26 In. 240.00
Annette Himstedt, Timi, Vinyl, Blond Hair, Cloth, American Heartland, 21 In. 270.00
Armand Marseille dolls are listed in this category under A.M.
Arranbee, Nancy Lee, Plastic Head, Nail Polish, Plaid Taffeta Dress, Skates, 20 In. 510.00
Arranbee, Nanette, Plastic Head, Sleep Eyes, Walker, Red Dress, Tag, Box, 21 In. 700.00
Automaton, 2 Gentlemen, Bisque Heads Turn, Offer Flowers, Germany, 1890s 2950.00
Automaton, Bebe With Mirror & Puff, Bisque, Lambert, France, c.1890, 18 In. 6000.00
Automaton, Butterfly Catcher, Bisque, Germany, 19 In. 2240.00
Automaton, Clown, Musical, Xylophone & Banjo Player, Bisque Heads, Pull Toy 1521.00
Automaton, Clown, Raises Limbs & Rings Bell When Keys Played, Bonnet, Early 1900 . 750.00
Automaton, Cook, Bisque, Comical Actions, Music, Roullet & Decamps, 1890, 18 In. . . . 3900.00
Automaton, Dancing, Man, Woman, France, 31 In., Pair 3920.00
Automaton, Lady With Lyre, Being Fanned, Papier-Mache Torso, 3 Tunes, c.1885 . . . . . . 5500.00
Automaton, Lambert, Russian Tea Server, Bisque, Velvet Covered Base, c.1895, 20 In. 7000.00
Automaton, Magician, Behind Table, With Cards, Porcelain, Zdenka, Continental, 8 In. . . 2300.00
Automaton, Monkey, Smoking Hookah, Musical, Animate, 27 In. 5750.00
Automaton, Orchestra, Character Faces, Intaglio Eyes, Germany, 17 x 16 x 3 In. . . . *Illus* 3500.00
Automaton, Rabbit, Emerges From Cabbage, Moves Ears, 1870s, 8 In. 546.00
Automaton, Twin Birds, Red, Yellow, Articulated, Roses, 10 x 6 In. 345.00
Automaton, Violin Player, Bisque, Torso Squeezed, Chimes, Bow Plays, 15 In. . . . . *Illus* 950.00

Doll, Automaton, Orchestra,
Character Faces, Intaglio Eyes,
Germany, 17 x 16 x 3 In.

Doll, Automaton, Woman,
Bisque, Brocade Dress,
Wooden Base, Lambert, 23 In.

Doll, Automaton, Violin Player,
Bisque, Torso Squeezed,
Chimes, Bow Plays, 15 In.

Automaton, Woman Winding Yarn, Turns Head, Wood Arms, Legs, Music, c.1885, 16 In.   2500.00
Automaton, Woman, Bisque, Brocade Dress, Wooden Base, Lambert, 23 In. . . . . *Illus*   2200.00
Automaton, Woman, Spinning Wheel, Bisque, Blond Wig, Set Eyes, Music, Box, 19 In. .   3400.00
Automaton, Yellow Kid Eating Ice Cream Cone, Licks, Rubs Tummy, Electric, 35 In. . . .   300.00
Averill, Bonnie Babe, Bisque Flange Head, Cloth Body, Long Dress, 20 In. 475.00
Averill, Bonnie Babe, Bisque Flange Head, Sleep Eyes, Painted Hair, Cloth Body, 17 In. . .   600.00
Averill, Bonnie Babe, Laughing Mouth, Teeth, Dimples, Molded Hair, c.1926, 13 1/2 In. . .   575.00
Baby Barry, Alfred E. Neuman, Vinyl, What Me Worry, 1961, 20 In. 2465.00
Bahr & Proschild, 144, Belton Indian, Bisque, Mohair Wig, 5-Piece Composition, 16 In. .   1300.00
Bahr & Proschild, 244, Indian, Bisque, Jointed, Mohair Wig, Skirt, Necklace, 11 In. 345.00
Bahr & Proschild, 567, Bisque, 2-Face, Molded Hair, Jointed, Toddler, 1911, 18 In. 4250.00
Bahr & Proschild, 585, Bisque, 2 Teeth, Human Hair, Composition Body, Baby, 25 In. . . .   425.00
Bahr & Proschild, 585, Bisque, 2 Upper Teeth, Clown Dress, Toddler, 16 In. 350.00
Bahr & Proschild, 604, Blond, Blue Sleep Eyes, 2 Teeth, Ball-Jointed, 15 In. 138.00
Bahr & Proschild, Bisque, Character, 5-Piece Composition, Bent-Leg Body, 9 In. 345.00
Bahr & Proschild, Bisque, Closed Mouth, Blond Wig, Wooden Jointed, Child, 20 In. 400.00
Barbie dolls are listed in this category under Mattel.
Barrois, Bisque, Swivel Neck, Blond Wig, Glass Eyes, Man, 29 In.   4100.00
Barrois, Fashion, Bisque Shoulder Plate, Closed Mouth, Blond Mohair, Kid Body, 17 In. . .   1200.00
Barrois, Fashion, Bisque Socket Head, Shoulder Plate, Kid Body, Short Dress, 18 In. 1300.00
Barrois, Fashion, Bisque, Swivel Head, Cobalt Blue Glass Eyes, Dehors Joints, 16 In. . . .   3100.00
Barrois, Fashion, Bisque, Swivel Head, Kid Body, Gusset Jointed Limbs, 1865, 34 In. . . .   4750.00
Barrois, Fashion, Gentleman, Bisque, Swivel Head, Cobalt Blue Glass Eyes, 13 In. 2600.00
Bathing Girl, Bisque, Seaside Poses, Blue, White Striped Swimsuits, c.1925, 5 In., Pair . .   650.00
Bathing Girl, Seated, Bisque, Leaning On Arms, 1 Piece, c.1915, 2 1/2 In. 650.00
Bawo & Dotter, Bisque, Brown Glass Sleep Eyes, Feathered Brows, 14 In. 5250.00
Bawo & Dotter, Bisque, Closed Mouth, Composition & Wood Jointed Body, 1912, 12 In.   8000.00
Bawo & Dotter, Bisque, Shoulder Head, Braids, Leather Boots, 1912, 16 In. 6500.00
Belton-Type, 183, Bisque Head, Closed Mouth, Human Hair, Jointed, 13 1/2 In. 431.00
Belton-Type, Bisque Head, Blue Paperweight Eyes, Closed Mouth, Jointed, 11 1/2 In. . . .   604.00
Belton-Type, Bisque Socket Head, Open-Close Mouth, Human Hair, Dress, 15 In. 1200.00
Bergmann dolls are also in this category under S & H and Simon & Halbig.
Bergmann, Bisque Socket Head, Sleep Eyes, Open Mouth, Jointed, Bride Gown, 23 In. . .   201.00
Bergmann, Bisque, Curls, Googly Eyes, Lours Wolfe, c.1920, 5 1/2 In. 300.00
Bergmann, Eleonore, Bisque, Mohair Wig, Jointed Composition Body, Pinafore, 25 In. . .   550.00
Bergner, Bisque, Multiface Character, Socket Head, Pull-String Crier, c.1910, 11 In. 1400.00
Bild-Lilli, Ash Blond, Blue Hair Tie, Peach Dress, Stand, 7 1/2 In. 1058.00
Bild-Lilli, Auburn, Forehead Curl, Hair Tie, Purple Fur Skirt, Germany, 11 1/2 In. 3055.00
Bild-Lilli, Blond, Black Ribbon Tie, Aqua Sheath, Pleated Peplum, Germany, 11 1/2 In. . .   2820.00
Bild-Lilli, Blond, Forehead Curl, High Neck Sweater, Orange Shorts, Germany, 7 1/2 In. . .   1175.00
Bild-Lilli, Blond, Forehead Curl, Plastic Hair Tie, White Skirt, Germany, 7 1/2 In. 1116.00
Bild-Lilli, Blond, Forehead Curl, White Tennis Dress, Germany, 11 1/2 In. 3055.00
Bild-Lilli, Brunette, Peach Hair Tie, White Satin Gown, Fur Stole, 11 1/2 In. 3525.00

Bild-Lilli, Hard Plastic, Coifed Ponytail, Original Box, c.1957, 11 In. 3000.00
Bild-Lilli, Redhead, Forehead Curl, Pink Gown, Stand, Tube, Cover, Germany, 11 1/2 In. . . 3819.00
Bild-Lilli, Yellow Hair, Black Hair Tie, Purple Top, Pedal Pushers, Germany, 11 In. 3525.00
Bisque, Asian Child, Swivel Head, Jointed Arms & Legs, c.1900, 5 1/2 In. 850.00
Bisque, Baby, Glass Eyes, With Rattle, Germany, c.1910, 3 1/2 In. 300.00
Bisque, Blond Sculpted Hair, Blue Headband, Painted Face, Blue Eyes, c.1870, 8 In. 575.00
Bisque, Blond Sculpted Hair, Hair Ribbon, Painted Face, Blue Eyes, c.1880, 24 In. 550.00
Bisque, Blue Glass Sleep Eyes, Googly, Germany, c.1920, 6 In. 550.00
Bisque, Blue Googly Eyes, Swivel Neck, Closed Mouth, Jointed, Boy, 5 In. 863.00
Bisque, Closed Mouth, Brown Glass Paperweight Inset Eyes, Bebe, c.1895, 21 In. 2300.00
Bisque, Closed Mouth, Human Hair, Jointed Composition Body, Dress, 16 In. 2200.00
Bisque, Closed Mouth, Mohair Curls, 5-Piece Body, Breeches, Tricorner Hat, Boy, 4 In. . . . 500.00
Bisque, Cobalt Blue Stationary Eyes, Open Mouth, Maroon Coat, 18 In. 288.00
Bisque, Glass Inset Eyes, Blond Sculpted Hair, Muslin Body, Germany, c.1880, 20 In. . . . 800.00
Bisque, Kestner Type, Blond Wig, Sleep Eyes, Open Mouth, Teeth, Jointed, Girl, 9 In. . . . 550.00
Bisque, Painted Eyes & Hair, Closed Mouth, Cloth Body, Tiara, Lace Dress, 24 In. 1900.00
Bisque, Painted Eyes & Hair, Closed Mouth, Lady, Antique Clothes, 18 1/2 In. 1125.00
Bisque, Painted Eyes & Hair, Cloth Body, China Lower Limbs, Lady, 17 1/2 In. 1225.00
Bisque, Painted Hair, Cloth Body, Lady, Antique Clothes, 21 1/2 In. 1450.00
Bisque, Set Eyes, Closed Mouth, Painted Curls, Cloth Body, Velvet Dress, 20 1/2 In. 1400.00
Bisque, Shoulder Head, Closed Mouth, Painted Hair, Cloth Body, Kid Arms, Dress, 19 In. 800.00
Bisque, Shoulder Head, Molded Painted Hair, Cloth Body, Satin Dress, 19 In. 1850.00
Bisque, Shoulder Head, Painted Eyes, Closed Mouth, Boy, Scottish Clothes, 15 In. 275.00
Bisque, Shoulder Head, Painted Eyes, Closed Mouth, Cloth Torso, 19 In. 450.00
Bisque, Shoulder Head, Painted Hair, Face, Muslin Body, Dollhouse Set, c.1890, 5 Piece . 1500.00
Bisque, Socket Head, Black Glass Enamel Inset Eyes, Asian Costume, c.1900, 15 In. 1000.00
Bisque, Socket Head, Blue Glass Sleep Eyes, Wedding Dress, c.1900, 21 In. 3250.00
Bisque, Socket Head, Intaglio Eyes, Painted Hair, 5-Piece Bent-Leg, Composition, 6 In. . . 155.00
Bisque, Socket Head, Intaglio Eyes, Painted Hair, Bent-Leg Composition Body, 8 In. 201.00
Bisque, Socket Head, Sleep Eyes, Jointed Composition, Trunk & Clothes, 13 In. 1750.00
Bisque, Socket Head, Sleep Eyes, Wig, Wood, Composition, Silk Dress, 28 In. 700.00
Bisque, Spiral Spring Attachment, Wooden Ball-Jointed Body, c.1885, 18 In. 1300.00
Bisque, Stiff Neck, Set Eyes, Replaced Human Hair, Jointed, Lace Dress, Bonnet, 8 In. . . . 315.00
Bisque, Swivel Head, Brown Stationary Eyes, Kid Body, Red Velvet Dress, 24 In. 316.00
Bisque, Swivel Head, Closed Mouth, Molded Hair, Kid Body, Clothes, 14 1/2 In. 3600.00
Bisque, Swivel Head, Human Hair, Kid Body, Floral Dress, Straw Hat, 18 In. 80.00
Bisque, Swivel Neck, Plump Face & Torso, Kid Body, Jointed, 1860, 18 In. 800.00
Bisque Head, Blond, Molded Scarf, Blue Eyes, Cloth Body, 12 In. 160.00
Bisque Head, Painted Eyes, Molded Wavy Hair, Cloth Body, White Snood, 1870, 13 In. . . 520.00
Black dolls are included in the Black category.
Borgfeldt, 258, Bisque, Blue Googly Eyes, 5-Piece Body, Sailor Suit, c.1925, 6 In. 1500.00
Borgfeldt, September Morn, Bisque, Naked Girl, Leaning, Sculpted Topknot, 1915, 5 In. . 1000.00

Doll, Bru Jne, 5, Bisque, Paperweight Eyes, Cream Satin Lace Dress, Child, 16 1/2 In.

Doll, Bru Jne, 8, Bisque, Kid Body, Paperweight Eyes, Velvet Dress, Child, 21 1/2 In.

Doll, Bru Jne, 8, Bisque, Kid Body, Paperweight Eyes, Velvet Dress, Child, 22 In.

Boudoir, Bride, Shoulder Head, Composition Limbs, Ivory Satin Gown, Hat, 1920s, 25 In.   115.00
Boudoir, Pierrot, Side-Glancing Eyes, Smile, Cloth Body, Silk Costume, Musical, 23 In. .   375.00
Bru Jne, 3, Bisque, Closed Mouth, Composition, Ball-Jointed, Gauntlet Arms, 14 In. 8050.00
Bru Jne, 5, Bisque Socket Head, Paperweight Eyes, Blond Mohair, Jointed, Bebe, 14 In. .   3100.00
Bru Jne, 5, Bisque, Paperweight Eyes, Cream Satin Lace Dress, Child, 16 1/2 In. . . . . *Illus* 18000.00
Bru Jne, 8, Bisque, Kid Body, Paperweight Eyes, Velvet Dress, Child, 21 1/2 In. . . . . *Illus* 19000.00
Bru Jne, 8, Bisque, Kid Body, Paperweight Eyes, Velvet Dress, Child, 22 In. . . . . *Illus* 23000.00
Bru Jne, Bebe Brevete, Bisque, Swivel Head, Blue Glass Inset Enamel Eyes, 21 In. 17500.00
Bru Jne, Bebe Bru, Bisque, Glass Paperweight Inset Eyes, Au Nain Bleu, c.1892, 29 In. . . 9750.00
Bru Jne, Bisque, Almond-Shape Brown Glass Enamel Eyes, Bebe, c.1883, 19 In. 17500.00
Bru Jne, Bisque, New Wig, Teeth, Composition, Walker Body, Jacket & Skirt, 22 In. 1250.00
Bru Jne, Bisque, Paperweight Eyes, Mohair Wig, Kid Body, Batiste Dress, 13 In. 3335.00
Bru Jne, Bisque, Tongue Tip, Dimpled Chin, Kid Body, Hinged Legs, c.1885, 15 In. 18500.00
Bru Jne, Fashion, Bisque, Swivel Head, Dehors Neck, Smiling, 14 In. 4500.00
Bru Jne, G, Fashion, Bisque, Glass Inset Eyes, Close Mouth, Smiling, c.1873, 18 In. 3000.00
Bruno Schmidt, 2042, Bisque, Jointed Toddler Body, 1910, 16 In. 2600.00
Buddy Lee, Plastic, Painted Side Eyes, Jointed, Phillips 66 Suit, 12 In. 285.00
Bye-Lo, Bisque Flange Head, Sleep Eyes, Cloth Body, Frog Legs, Original Dress, 13 In. . . .   300.00
Bye-Lo, Bisque Head, Blue Sleep Eyes, Cloth Body, Grace Putnam, c.1923, 14 In. 460.00
Bye-Lo, Bisque Head, Brown Eyes, Closed Mouth, Painted Hair, 1920, 12 In. 250.00
Bye-Lo, Bisque Head, Closed Mouth, Cloth Body, Celluloid Hands, Baby Dress, 11 In. . . .   225.00
Bye-Lo, Bisque Head, Cloth Body, Celluloid Hands & Legs, Baby Clothes, 11 In. 425.00
Bye-Lo, Bisque Head, Cloth Body, Celluloid Hands, White Dress, Knit Bonnet, 20 In. 600.00
Bye-Lo, Bisque Head, Sleep Eyes, Closed Mouth, Painted Hair, Baby Clothes, Cap, 8 In. . .   525.00
Bye-Lo, Bisque, Closed Mouth, Loop-Jointed Bent Arms & Legs, c.1923, 5 In. 1050.00
Bye-Lo, Bisque, Painted Hair, Jointed At Shoulders & Hips, 5 In. 400.00
Bye-Lo, Bisque, Sleep Eyes, Closed Mouth, Painted Hair, Cloth Body, Baby Dress, 14 In. . .   350.00
Bye-Lo, Bisque, Sleep Eyes, Painted Hair, Cloth Body, Celluloid Hands, Dress, 18 In. 300.00
Bye-Lo, Brown Sleep Eyes, Closed Mouth, Grace S. Putnam, 1920s, 13 In. 125.00
Bye-Lo, Dome Bisque Head, Sleep Eyes, Painted Face, Cloth Body, Putnam, 21 In. 600.00
Catterfelder Puppenfabrick, Bisque, Impish Smile, Character Baby, 9 In. 1000.00
Celluloid, Our Tiny Toddler, Painted Face, Knitted Romper, Boy, Box, 7 1/2 In. 45.00
Celluloid, Sailor, Cloth Body, Button, World War II, 1940s, 5 In.   30.00
Celluloid, Socket Head, Open-Close Mouth, Fully Jointed, Toddler, 2-Piece Suit, 16 In. . .   295.00
Chase, George Washington, All Cloth, Jointed Body, Painted Features, c.1900, 24 In. 6250.00
Chase, Molded Head, Painted, Blond Hair, Applied Ears, Cotton Sateen Body, 17 In. 230.00
Chase, Polly, Stockinet Head, Painted Face, Cloth Body, Baby Dress, 1912, 13 In. 325.00
Chase, Stockinet, Painted Molded Hair, Lace Dress, Shoes, Baby, 17 In. 475.00
China, Countess Dagmar, Painted Eyes & Hair, Cloth Body, Antique Dress, 15 In. 315.00
China, Downcast Eyes, Molded Blond Hair, Fabric Body, Original Court Dress, 19 In. 1725.00
China, Human Hair, Painted Eyes, Closed Mouth, Plaid Taffeta Dress, Hat, 19 In. 485.00
China, Molded Black Hair & Shirt, Cloth Body, Wooden Arms & Legs, Man, 18 1/2 In. . .   575.00
China, Painted Eyes, Molded Black Hair, Cloth Body, Leather Hands, Blouse, 22 In. 1600.00
China, Pink Luster, Shoulder Head, Painted Eyes, Closed Mouth, Cloth Body, 18 In. 200.00
China, Shoulder Head, Painted Black Hair & Eyes, Cloth Body, Satin Dress, 20 In. 1500.00
China, Shoulder Head, Painted Eyes, Cloth Body, Kid Arms, Germany, 19 In. 345.00
Cloth, Homespun, Bedpost Shape, Painted Brown Features, Early 19th Century, 10 In. 750.00
Cloth, Muslin, Ink Face, Stitched Joints, Dress, Leather Boots, c.1890, 16 In. 865.00
Cloth, Painted Features, Big Smile, Hair Bits Under Velvet Cap, Straw Stuffed, 12 In. 575.00
Cloth, Primitive, Molded, Oil-Painted Head, Inset Human Hair, Tan Faille Body, 19 In. . .   805.00
Composition, Ivory Dress, Silk Ribbon Trim, Undergarments, Accessories, 12 1/2 In. 250.00
Composition, Swivel Head, Brown Complexion, 3 Teeth, 5-Piece Body, Dress, 14 1/2 In. . .   275.00
Composition, Topsy Baby, 2 Teeth, Tufts Of Hair, Baby Dress, Diaper & Booties, 11 In. .   195.00
De Fuisseux, Domed Bisque Shoulder Head, Blue Paint Eyes, Muslin Body, 1910, 21 In. .   2200.00
Denamur, Bisque Head, Closed Mouth, Replaced Human Hair, Jumeau Body, Bebe, 14 In.   1200.00
DeWees Cochran, Latex, Blond Human Hair, Painted Eyes, Jacket, Skirt, Hat, 15 In. 160.00
Door Of Hope, Kindergarten Child, Wood Head & Hands, Embroidered Dress, 1920, 6 In.   1600.00
Dressel, 99, Shoulder Head, Open Mouth, Brown Mohair Wig, Kid Body, Boy, 15 In. 201.00
Dressel, 1348, Jutta, Bisque Head, Blue Sleep Eyes, Open Mouth, Mohair Curls, 20 In. . .   316.00
Dressel, Bisque Head, Sleep Eyes, Human Wig, Composition Teenage Body, Girl, 15 In. .   450.00
Effanbee, Candy Kid, Composition, Sleep Eyes, 5-Piece Toddler Body, Box, 12 In. 375.00
Effanbee, Composition Head, Flirty Eyes, Cloth Body, Slip, Dress, Cap, Baby, 25 In. 200.00
Effanbee, Composition, Painted Eyes, Closed Mouth, 2-Piece Suit, Boy, 17 In. 1960.00

Effanbee, Grumpy Cowboy, Composition, Pouty Mouth, Cloth Body, Felt Hat, 11 In. 475.00
Effanbee, Honey, Plastic, Socket Head, Blue Sleep Eyes, Blond, c.1950, 18 In. 990.00
Effanbee, Lovums, Composition, Sleep Eyes, 4 Teeth, Non-Working Crier, Box, 25 In. 675.00
Effanbee, Marilee, Composition, Sleep Eyes, Open Mouth, 4 Teeth, Ringlets, 1935, 29 In. 500.00
Effanbee, Patsy Ann, Composition, Sleep Eyes, 5-Piece Body, Organdy Dress, 19 In. 370.00
Effanbee, Patsy Ann, Plastic Head, Bent Right Arm, Sleep Eyes, Flowered Dress, 19 In. .. 500.00
Effanbee, Patsy Babyette Twins, Bisque, Closed Mouth, Matching Rompers, 8 1/2 In. 500.00
Effanbee, Patsy, Composition Head, Sleep Eyes, Bent Right Arm, Print Dress, 14 In. 185.00
Effanbee, Patsy, Composition Head, Sleep Eyes, Rosebud Mouth, 14 In. .... *Illus* 200.00
Effanbee, Patsy, Composition, Brown Eyes, Bobbed Hair, Lace Dress, 1930s, 13 In. 115.00
Effanbee, Patsyette, Composition, 5-Piece Body, Heart Tag, Extra Clothes In Box, 9 In. .. 550.00
Effanbee, Patsyette, Composition, Painted Hair, 5-Piece Body, Checked Dress, 9 In. 205.00
Effanbee, Plastic, Blue Eyes, Blue Taffeta Outfit, Straw Hat, Girl, 1950, 18 In. 300.00
Effanbee, Skippy, Composition Head, Blue Side-Glancing Eyes, 14 In. .... *Illus* 625.00
Effanbee, Skippy, Policeman's Uniform, 14 In. 1950.00
Ernst Heubach, 275, Bisque Shoulder Head, Strawberry Blond Mohair Wig, 18 In. 115.00
Ernst Heubach, 302.7, Bisque, Socket Head, Glass Eyes, Ball-Jointed, 28 In. 840.00
Ernst Heubach, 320, Bisque Head, Open Mouth, Pierced Nostrils, 15 1/2 In. 145.00
Ernst Heubach, 320, Bisque, Sleep Eyes, Teeth, Composition, Bent Limb, Baby, 8 In. ... 210.00
Ernst Heubach, 7604, Bisque Head, Composition Body, 8 In. 115.00
Ernst Heubach, 8727, Bisque Head, Composition Body, Boy, 10 In. 80.00
Fashion, Bisque, Glass Paperweight Inset Eyes, Candy Container Cart, c.1888, 12 In. ... 1500.00
Fashion, Bisque, Swivel Head, Kid Body, Velvet Clothes, Marked CD, France, 14 In. 2240.00
Fashion, Bisque, Swivel Head, Plump Face, Glass Inset Eyes, c.1867, 33 In. 5500.00
Fashion, Bisque, Swivel Head, Slanted Eyes, Maker's Mark, France, c.1865, 13 In. 7250.00
Fashion, Bisque, Swivel Neck Shoulder, Hair Wig, Paperweight Eyes, France, 26 In. 2300.00
Fashion, Bisque, Swivel Neck, Wooden Articulated, Costume, France, c.1860, 17 In. 7250.00
Fashion, Bisque, Wood Body, Swivel Head, France, c.1875, 18 In. 9000.00
Fleischmann & Bloedel, Eden Bebe, Bisque, Paperweight Eyes, Human Hair, 18 In. 460.00
Franz Schmidt, 1295, Bisque Head, Sleep Eyes, 2 Teeth, Composition, Toddler, 15 In. ... 675.00
Franz Schmidt, Bisque, Socket Head, Painted Hair, 2 Teeth, Romper Suit, 1915, 23 In. .. 2300.00
French, Bisque, Human Hair Wig, 4 Teeth, Wooden Adult Female Body, Jointed, 20 In. .. 225.00
French, Bisque, Mohair Wig, Paperweight Eyes, Teeth, Composition, Silk Dress, 20 In. .. 100.00
French, Bisque, Paperweight Eyes, Kid Body, Lady, Original Undergarments, 15 In. 2530.00
French, Bisque, Pouty Character, Socket Head, Brown Glass Sleep Eyes, c.1912, 19 In. .. 6250.00
French, Bisque, Shoulder Head, Swivel Neck, Blond Wig, Paperweight Eyes, 21 1/2 In. .. 15000.00
French, Bisque, Swivel Head, Oversized Eyes, Kid Body, Taffeta Suit, 14 In. 460.00
French, Bisque, Synthetic Wig, Dressed As Peasant, 13 1/2 In. 260.00
French, Bisque, Wig, Paperweight Eyes, Composition, Ball-Jointed, Skirt, Hat, 18 In. ... 1800.00
French, Papier-Mache, Shoulder Head, Glass Inset Eyes, Nun's Habit, c.1850, 22 In. 3000.00
French, Porcelain Shoulder Head, Blond Wig, Kid Body, Mitten Hands, c.1860, 14 In. ... 2600.00

Doll, Effanbee, Patsy,
Composition Head, Sleep Eyes,
Rosebud Mouth, 14 In.

Doll, Effanbee, Skippy,
Composition Head, Blue
Side-Glancing Eyes, 14 In.

Doll, Head, Painted Bisque,
Molded Green Hat, Cross
Necklace, 3 In.

Frozen Charlotte, China, Pink Tint, Painted Eyes & Hair, Nude, Boy, 11 1/2 In. 450.00
Fulper, Bisque Shoulder Head, Sleep Eyes, Brown Synthetic Braids, Cloth Body, 19 In. .. 85.00
G.I. Joe figures are listed in the Toy category.
Gans & Seyfarth, 120, Bisque, Blue Eyes, Open Mouth, Dressed, 21 In. 201.00
Gans & Seyfarth, Bisque, Open Mouth, Sleep Eyes, Original Dress, 21 In. 170.00
Gaultier, 5, Bisque Head, Enamel Eyes, Ball-Jointed, Straight Wrists, Bebe, 16 In. .. 3500.00
Gaultier, 5, Bisque, Swivel Head, Paperweight Eyes, Mohair Wig, c.1885, 16 In. 1870.00
Gaultier, 7, Bisque, Swivel Head, Kid Body, Antique Costume, 1870, 24 In. 5000.00
Gaultier, Bisque Head, Closed Mouth, Human Hair, Composition, Bebe, 24 In. 2450.00
Gaultier, Bisque Head, Paperweight Eyes, Mohair Wig, Cloth Body, 10 1/2 In. 1250.00
Gaultier, Bisque Head, Paperweight Eyes, Open-Close Mouth, Dress, Bebe, 26 1/2 In. ... 2000.00
Gaultier, Bisque Socket Head, Paperweight Eyes, Mohair Wig, Silk Dress, Bebe, 21 In. ... 2200.00
Gaultier, Bisque, Blond Wig, Bisque Upper Arms & Hands, c.1880, 12 In. 10750.00
Gaultier, Bisque, Glass Enamel Inset Eyes, Wooden, Articulated, c.1870, 15 In. 3800.00
Gaultier, Bisque, Kid Body, France, Bebe, c.1880, 19 In. 6000.00
Gaultier, Bisque, Paperweight Eyes, Wig, Jointed, Wood, Composition, Bebe, 24 In. 700.00
Gaultier, Bisque, Sculpted Boyish Hair, Painted Face, Blue Eyes, c.1860, 14 In. 40.00
Gaultier, Bisque, Swivel Head, Blue Glass Enamel Inset Eyes, Kid Body, c.1880, 14 In. ... 4750.00
Gaultier, Bisque, Swivel Head, Glass Eyes, Kid Body, Bebe, 22 In. 7750.00
Gaultier, Bisque, Tiny Tongue, Composition & Wood Jointed Body, c.1884, 20 In. 4500.00
Gebruder Heubach dolls are also in this category under Heubach.
Gebruder Heubach, 7067, Character, Smiling, c.1915, 4 In. 425.00
Gebruder Heubach, 7246, Bisque, Pouty, Downcast Eyes, c.1915, 25 In. 4600.00
Gebruder Heubach, 7911, Bisque Head, Glancing Eyes, Jointed, Boy, c.1910, 25 In. 5000.00
Gebruder Heubach, 8619, Stuck-Out Tongue, Blue Bonnet, c.1917, 12 In. 1400.00
Gebruder Heubach, Bisque, Brown Sleep Eyes, Closed Mouth, c.1912, 14 In. 1800.00
Gebruder Heubach, Bisque, Closed Mouth, Composition & Wood Body, 1917, 22 In. 3000.00
Gebruder Heubach, Bisque, Dolly Dimple, 4 Teeth, Kid Body, Organdy Dress, 17 1/2 In. 375.00
Gebruder Heubach, Bisque, Domed Socket Head, Closed Mouth, c.1915, 13 In. 750.00
Gebruder Heubach, Bisque, Googly, Sleep Eyes, Mohair Wig, 1-Strap Shoes, Dress, 7 In. 700.00
Gebruder Heubach, Bisque, Pouty, Glass Inset Eyes, Ball-Jointed Body, c.1914, 14 In. .. 1500.00
Gebruder Heubach, Brown Bisque, Muslin Jointed Body, Silk Costume, c.1910, 14 In. .. 5600.00
Gebruder Heubach, Brown Composition, Bent Limbs, Jointed Arms, Baby, c.1910, 13 In. 3000.00
Gebruder Heubach, Coquette, Bisque Head, Open-Close Mouth, Blond, Dress, 12 1/2 In. 1000.00
Gebruder Kuhnlenz, 44, Bisque Socket Head, Wig, Jointed Composition, Clothes, 20 In. . 275.00
Gebruder Kuhnlenz, 44-30, Bisque, Socket Head, Hair Wig, Paperweight Eyes, 22 In. ... 275.00
German, American School Boy, Bisque Head, Kid Body, Velvet Suit, 18 1/2 In. 375.00
German, Bisque Domed Head, Painted Eyes, 5-Piece Composition Body, Toddler, 12 In. . 275.00
German, Bisque Shoulder Head, Blond, Head Band, Painted Eyes, Kid Body, Dress, 8 In. 170.00
German, Bisque Socket Head, Composition, Jointed, Princess Outfit, 22 1/2 In. 190.00
German, Bisque, Ash Blond Mohair, Sleep Eyes, Composition, Ball-Jointed, Dress, 20 In. 250.00
German, Bisque, Blond Braids, Molded Features, Jointed, Blue Shoes, Knit Cape, 5 In. .. 35.00
German, Bisque, Blond Mohair, Kid, Cloth Body, Bisque Hands, Velvet Dress, Hat, 13 In. 60.00
German, Bisque, Blond Mohair, Set Eyes, Teeth, Kid Body, Satin Dress, 13 1/2 In. 50.00
German, Bisque, Blond Mohair, Sleep Eyes, Kid Body, Silk Floral Dress, 18 In. 90.00
German, Bisque, Blond Mohair, Sleep Eyes, Teeth, Composition, Ball-Jointed, 24 In. 160.00
German, Bisque, Blue Sleep Eyes, Synthetic Wig, 23 In. 210.00
German, Bisque, Brown Complexion, Mohair Wig, c.1890, 5 In. 350.00
German, Bisque, Brown, Wig, Sleep Eyes, Teeth, Composition, Jacket, Hat, Boy, 10 In. .. 65.00
German, Bisque, Flocked Hair, Painted Eyes, Open-Close Mouth, Baby, 5 1/4 In. 50.00
German, Bisque, Googly, Blond Bobbed Wig, 1-Strap Shoes, Blue Socks, c.1920, 5 In. .. 575.00
German, Bisque, Googly, Closed Mouth, Wood, Jointed Body, 1926, 12 In. 2800.00
German, Bisque, Googly, Painted Face, Box, c.1914, 6 In. 525.00
German, Bisque, Governess & Baby, Muslin Body, Pin-Jointed Limbs, c.1890, 7 In. 1000.00
German, Bisque, Mohair Wig, Sleep Eyes, Teeth, Composition, New Plaid Dress, 24 In. .. 150.00
German, Bisque, Shoulder Head, Cameo-Shape Face, Elongated Throat, c.1870, 4 1/2 In. . 850.00
German, Bisque, Shoulder Head, Elaborate Coiffure, Jewelry, 17 In. 725.00
German, Bisque, Shoulder Head, Molded Hair, Closed Mouth, Kid Body, Boy, 15 In. 425.00
German, Bisque, Shoulder Head, Wig, Set Eyes, Closed Mouth, Kid Body, Girl, 21 In. ... 275.00
German, Bisque, Side-Glancing Eyes, Molded Hair Wisps, Jointed, Toddler, 5 1/2 In. 30.00
German, Bisque, Sleep Eyes, Mohair Wig, 12 In. 172.00
German, Bisque, Sleep Eyes, Mohair Wig, Wood, Composition, Jointed, Redressed, 23 In. 250.00
German, Bisque, Sleep Eyes, Open Mouth, Mohair Wig, Composition, Child, 7 1/2 In. ... 250.00

German, Bisque, Socket Head, Fully Jointed Body, c.1895, 18 In. 700.00
German, Bisque, Socket Head, Mohair Wig, Sleep Eyes, Open Mouth, Teeth, Baby, 16 In.   650.00
German, Bisque, Swivel Head, Brown Glass Sleep Eyes, c.1890, 6 In. 500.00
German, Bisque, Wig, Sleep Eyes, Jointed, Molded Socks & Mary Janes, Dress, 4 In. . . .   70.00
German, China Shoulder Head & Hands, Molded Hair, Cloth Body, Dress, Lady, 16 In. . .   450.00
German, China Shoulder Head, Greiner-Style Hair, Cloth, Leather, Lady, 17 In. 600.00
German, China Shoulder Head, Molded Hair, Kid Body, Stitched Fingers, Lady, 16 In. . . .   650.00
German, China Shoulder Head, Molded Highland Mary Hair, Cloth Body, Dress, 16 In. . .   90.00
German, China, Black Molded Hair, Cloth Body, New Arms, Gown, Lace Trim, 16 In. 40.00
German, China, Shoulder Head, Black Hair, Painted Face, Crocheted Dress, 16 1/2 In. . . .   50.00
German, China, Shoulder Head, Covered-Wagon Hair Style, Painted Eyes, Lady, 25 In. . .   600.00
German, China, Shoulder Head, Molded Hair, Closed Mouth, Cloth Body, Girl, 11 1/2 In.   140.00
German, China, Shoulder Head, Molded Hair, Painted Eyes, Closed Mouth, Boy, 27 In. . .   270.00
German, China, Shoulder Head, Molded Hair, Painted Eyes, Cloth Body, 28 In. 375.00
German, China, Shoulder Head, Painted Eyes, Closed Mouth, Cloth Body, Girl, 19 In. . . .   525.00
German, China, Shoulder Head, Pink Luster, Painted Eyes, Closed Mouth, Boy, 26 In. . . .   350.00
German, Dolley Madison, China Head, Painted Eyes, Cloth Body, Velvet Dress, 21 In. . . .   350.00
German, Mary Jane, Flirty Sleep Eyes, 5-Piece Plastic Body, Walker, Pinafore, Tag, 16 In.   250.00
German, Parian Shoulder Head, Molded Hair, Snood, Painted Face, Cloth Body, 10 In. . . .   330.00
German, Porcelain Shoulder Head, Kid Body, Lady, c.1860, 24 In. 2900.00
German, Porcelain, Double Face, Young Girl & Aged Woman, Bonnet, c.1890, 11 In. 2300.00
German, Porcelain, Sculpted Black Curly Hair, Closed Mouth, c.1880, 36 In. 525.00
German, Socket Head, Composition, Ball-Jointed, Long-Waisted Dress, Lace Trim, 27 In.   375.00
German, Socket Head, Wig, Sleep Eyes, Open Mouth, Teeth, Composition, Girl, 13 In. . .   70.00
German, Tin Shoulder Head, Blond Molded Hair, Kid Body, Taffeta Dress, 17 In. 35.00
German, Wax, Molded Hair, Glass Eyes, Cloth Body, Wooden Arms, Legs, Dress, 23 In. . .   70.00
Gesland, Fashion, Bisque, Swivel Head, Blue Glass Enamel Inset Eyes, c.1880, 14 In. . . .   3900.00
Greiner, Papier-Mache Shoulder Head, Cloth Body, Striped Stockings, Dress, 16 In. 250.00
Greiner, Papier-Mache Shoulder Head, Molded Hair, Cloth Body, Kid Hands, 14 In. 170.00
Greiner-Style, China, Painted Eyes, Closed Mouth, Antique Dress, 11 1/2 In. 575.00
Guepratte, 9, Bebe Soleil, Bisque Head, Jointed Wood, Composition Body, Box, 23 In. . .   1400.00
Half Dolls are listed in the Pinchushion category.
Hamburger & Co., 17, Viola, Bisque Socket Head, 4 Teeth, Jointed, Composition, 22 In. .   300.00
Handwerck, 4, Bisque Head, Blue Sleep Eyes, Open Mouth, Auburn Curly Wig, 24 In. 430.00
Handwerck, 17, Bisque Socket Head, Human Hair, Jointed, Wood, Composition, 32 In. . .   1025.00
Handwerck, 99, Bisque, Sleep Eyes, Open Mouth, 4 Upper Teeth, Curly Wig, 28 In. 1000.00
Handwerck, 109, Bisque Head, Mohair Wig, Composition, Jointed, 17 1/2 In. 675.00
Handwerck, 109, Bisque, Set Eyes, Open Mouth, 4 Teeth, Jointed, Print Dress, 16 In. 220.00
Handwerck, Bisque, Brown Glass Sleep Eyes, Open Mouth, Child, c.1910, 24 In. 750.00
Handwerck, Bisque, Brown Sleep Eyes, Blond Mohair Wig, Original Dress, Box, 27 In. . . .   1600.00
Handwerck, Bisque, Sleep Eyes, Open Mouth, Human Hair Wig, Dressed, 18 In. 520.00
Handwerck, Bisque, Socket Head, Double Faced Googly, Jointed Body, 1915, 12 In. 2600.00
Handwerck, Brown Bisque Head, 4 Teeth, Mohair Wig, Dress, 19 In. 900.00
Handwerck, Brown Bisque Head, Teeth, Mohair Wig, Composition, 18 In. 350.00
Handwerck, Simon & Halbig Bisque Socket Head, Lace Dress, 21 In. 375.00
Hartmann, 28, Bisque Socket Head, Blue Sleep Eyes, Open Mouth, Mohair Wig, 20 In. . .   175.00
Hartmann, 29, Bisque Head, Sleep Eyes, Wood, Composition, Jointed, 23 In. 200.00
Hartmann, 315K, Bisque Head, Blue Glass Eyes, Open Mouth, Blond Mohair Wig, 30 In.   315.00
Head, Painted Bisque, Molded Green Hat, Cross Necklace, 3 In. . . . . *Illus*   30.00
Hertel Schwab, 126, Baby Skippy, Brown Sleep Eyes, Pursed Open Mouth, 9 3/4 In. 175.00
Hertel Schwab, 136, Bisque Head, Blue Flirty Eyes, Tin Eyelids, Blond Curls, 20 In. 175.00
Hertel Schwab, 136, Bisque Head, Blue Sleep Eyes, Open Mouth, 4 Teeth, 26 1/2 In. 175.00
Hertel Schwab, 141, Bisque Head, Intaglio Eyes, 2 Teeth, Composition, Romper, 16 In. . .   185.00
Hertel Schwab, 150, Bisque Head, Sleep Eyes, 4 Upper Teeth, Baby, Middy Dress, 26 In.   1300.00
Hertel Schwab, 157, Bisque Socket Head, Brown Sleep Eyes, Closed Mouth, 21 In. 3000.00
Hertel Schwab, 163, Bisque Socket Head, Watermelon-Slice Smile, c.1912, 10 In. 2800.00
Hertel Schwab, Bisque Head, Composition Body, 12 In. 80.00
Hertel Schwab, Bisque, Googly Eyes, Toddler Body, Antique Costume, 14 In. 5100.00
Hertel Schwab, Bisque, Jubilee Googly, Closed Mouth, Ball-Jointed, c.1920, 14 In. 6250.00
Hertel Schwab, Bisque, Jubilee Googly, Jointed Toddler Body, Costume, c.1914, 11 In. . .   3400.00
Hertel Schwab, Dome Bisque Head, Open-Close Mouth, Composition, Romper, 14 In. . . .   225.00
Heubach dolls are also in this category under Gebruder Heubach.
Heubach, 275, Bisque Head, Brown Sleep Eyes, Jointed Oilcloth Body, Legs, 21 In. 175.00

Heubach, 300, Brown Sleep Eyes, 2 Teeth, Movable Tongue, Human Hair, 10 In.	175.00
Heubach, 399, Bisque Socket Head, Sleep Eyes, Closed Mouth, Composition, 12 1/2 In.	350.00
Heubach, 399, Brown Bisque Head, Baby, Composition Body, Baby, 13 In.	275.00
Heubach, 760, Bisque, Pouty, Painted Eyes, Brush-Stroke Hair, 11 1/2 In.	230.00
Heubach, 6894, Bisque Socket Head, Blue Intaglio Eyes, Pouty Mouth, Boy, 16 1/2 In.	575.00
Heubach, 7246, Bisque Socket Head, Sleep Eyes, Pouty Mouth, Mohair Curls, 15 In.	1725.00
Heubach, Bisque, Blue Eyes, 5-Piece Bent-Limb Body, Baby, 15 In.	180.00
Heubach, Shoulder Head, Laughing, Molded Hair, Kid Body, Gray Knickers, Boy, 16 In.	460.00
Horsman, Bubble Betty, 1924, 22 In.	425.00
Horsman, Composition, Sleep Eyes, Mohair Wig, Organdy Dress, Toddler, 15 In.	65.00
Hush Puppy, From Shari Lewis, Squeaker, Gray, Jacket, 1962, Tarcher Production, 5 In.	25.00
Ideal, Deanna Durbin, Composition Head, Sleep Eyes, 5-Piece Body, 20 In. *Illus*	400.00
Ideal, Deanna Durbin, Composition, Green Sleep Eyes, Open Mouth, Human Hair, 21 In.	173.00
Ideal, Deanna Durbin, Composition, Sleep Eyes, Teeth, Human Hair, 5-Piece Body, 25 In.	400.00
Ideal, Lori Martin, Vinyl Head, Blue Sleep Eyes, Rooted Hair, Jeans, Boots, 38 In.	550.00
Ideal, Mary Hartline, Plastic, Sleep Eyes, 5-Piece Body, Heart On Dress, 15 In. *Illus*	300.00
Ideal, Snow White, Sleep Eyes, Mohair Wig, 5-Piece Composition Body, 13 In. *Illus*	300.00
Ideal, Soldier Flexy, Closed Smiling Mouth, Wood Torso, Khaki Uniform, 12 In.	125.00
Ideal, Toni, Plastic Head, Tagged Clothing, 21 In.	800.00
Ideal, Toni, Plastic, Sleep Eyes, 5-Piece Body, Dress, Purse, 1950s, 15 In. *Illus*	250.00
Ideal, Toni, Plastic, Sleep Eyes, 5-Piece Body, Embroidered Dress, 14 In. *Illus*	200.00
Ideal, Toni, Plastic, Sleep Eyes, Nylon Wig, Walker, Organdy Dress, Box, 14 1/2 In.	625.00
Ideal, Toni, Plastic, Sleep Eyes, Wig, Pique Dress, 15 In. *Illus*	235.00
Indian dolls are listed in the Indian category.	
J.D.K. also may be listed in this category under Kestner.	
Japanese, Bisque Head, Human Hair, Wood, Composition, Jointed, 18 In.	815.00
Japanese, Bisque, Human Hair, Sleep Eyes, Composition, Ball-Jointed, Redressed, 19 In.	45.00
Japanese, Bisque, Human Hair, Sleep Eyes, Teeth, Composition, Ball-Jointed, Coat, 14 In.	70.00
Japanese, Bisque, Molded Hair, 2 Faces, Sleeping & Frowning, Diaper, 7 In.	40.00
Japanese, Papier-Mache, Brown Glass Enamel Inset Eyes, Closed Mouth, c.1930, 16 In.	950.00
Japanese, Silk Head, Body, Painted, Kimono, Sedan Chair, Lady Reclining, 13 In.	58.00
Jumeau, 3, Bisque, Blue Glass Paperweight Inset Eyes, Bebe, c.1890, 12 In.	3900.00
Jumeau, 7, Bisque Head, Blue Paperweight Eyes, Brown Human Hair, Bebe, 17 In.	863.00
Jumeau, 7, Bisque, Socket Head, Spiral Threaded Eyes, Auburn Wig, c.1890, 16 In.	4000.00
Jumeau, 8, Bisque Head, Paperweight Eyes, Open Mouth, Auburn Human Hair, 21 In.	1093.00
Jumeau, 8, Bisque, Composition, Ball-Jointed, Straight Wrists, Child, 18 In.	1900.00
Jumeau, 8, Bisque, Socket Head, Paperweight Eyes, Bebe, c.1890, 19 In.	2500.00
Jumeau, 8, Bisque, Socket Head, Wooden Body, 6 Loose Ball Joints, 1878, 18 In.	6750.00
Jumeau, 8, Bisque, Socket Head, Wooden Fully Jointed Body, c.1888, 19 In.	4000.00
Jumeau, 8, Bisque, Wooden Body, Loose Ball-Jointed, Antique Costume, c.1878, 14 In.	5000.00
Jumeau, 8, Portrait, Bisque, Blond Animal Skin Wig, Composition, Redressed, 16 In.	650.00
Jumeau, 9, New Wig, Paperweight Eyes, Teeth, Composition, Ball-Jointed, Dress, 20 In.	850.00

Doll, Ideal, Deanna Durbin,
Composition Head, Sleep Eyes,
5-Piece Body, 20 In.

Doll, Ideal, Mary Hartline,
Plastic, Sleep Eyes, 5-Piece
Body, Heart On Dress, 15 In.

Doll, Ideal, Snow White, Sleep
Eyes, Mohair Wig, 5-Piece
Composition Body, 13 In.

Doll, Ideal, Toni, Plastic, Sleep
Eyes, 5-Piece Body, Dress, Purse,
1950s, 15 In.

Doll, Ideal, Toni, Plastic,
Sleep Eyes, 5-Piece Body,
Embroidered Dress, 14 In.

Doll, Ideal, Toni, Plastic,
Sleep Eyes, Wig, Pique Dress,
15 In.

Jumeau, 10, Bisque Socket Head, Human Hair, Jointed Wood & Composition, 22 In. 1300.00
Jumeau, 10, Paris Bebe, Bisque Socket Head, Paperweight Eyes, Box, c.1895, 22 In. 6500.00
Jumeau, 11, Bisque, Mohair Wig, Closed Mouth, Composition, Lace Dress, 24 1/2 In. . . . 5000.00
Jumeau, 11, Bisque, Sleep Eyes, Human Hair, Pull-String Mama Crier, 24 In. 3500.00
Jumeau, 12, Bisque Head, Open Mouth, Pierced Ears, Human-Hair Curls, Bebe, 24 In. . . . 863.00
Jumeau, 12, Bisque Socket Head, Human Hair, Jointed Wood & Composition, 26 In. 3000.00
Jumeau, 12, Bisque, Socket Head, Ball-Jointed Body, Plump Limbs, c.1885, 26 In. 7000.00
Jumeau, 12, Pressed Bisque Socket Head, Paperweight Eyes, Ball-Jointed, 22 In. 6750.00
Jumeau, 1907, Bisque, Paperweight Eyes, Open Mouth, Composition, Jointed, 23 In. 1800.00
Jumeau, 1907/15, Bisque, Set Eyes, Human Hair, Wood, Composition, Jointed, 32 In. . . . 1300.00
Jumeau, 1907/9, Bisque Socket Head, Teeth, Jointed Wood, Composition, Box, 20 In. . . . 850.00
Jumeau, Bisque Head, 6 Teeth, Mohair Wig, Composition, Dress, Clothes & Trunk, 15 In. . 2100.00
Jumeau, Bisque Socket Head, Amber Paperweight Eyes, Bebe, Dutch Costume, 21 In. . . . 8500.00
Jumeau, Bisque Socket Head, Jointed, Composition, Dress, 16 In. 1100.00
Jumeau, Bisque Socket Head, Paperweight Eyes, Replaced Human Hair, Jointed, 24 In. . . 1100.00
Jumeau, Bisque, Blond Mohair Wig, Jointed Wood & Composition, 21 1/2 In. 3300.00
Jumeau, Bisque, Blond Mohair, Paperweight Eyes, Composition Ball-Jointed, 19 In. 2100.00
Jumeau, Bisque, Blue Glass Sleep Eyes, Bebe, c.1896, 21 In. 4250.00
Jumeau, Bisque, Brown Complexion, Paperweight Eyes, Bebe, c.1895, 13 In. 2800.00
Jumeau, Bisque, Mohair Wig, Closed Mouth, Composition, Ball-Jointed, Shoes, 17 In. . . . 2700.00
Jumeau, Bisque, New Wig, Composition Ball-Jointed, Repainted Legs, Hands, 17 In. 800.00
Jumeau, Bisque, Paperweight Eyes, Auburn Wig, Jointed Body, Silk Dress, 16 1/2 In. . . . 2500.00
Jumeau, Bisque, Paperweight Eyes, Replaced Human Hair, Jointed, Bebe, 20 In. 1300.00
Jumeau, Bisque, Sleep Eyes, Human Hair Wig, Silk Dress, Bonnet, 17 In. 875.00
Jumeau, Bisque, Socket Head, Blond Wig, Original Costume, 1892, 26 In. 7000.00
Jumeau, Bisque, Socket Head, Blond Wig, Paperweight Eyes, Wood Body, 20 In. 3000.00
Jumeau, Bisque, Socket Head, Blue Glass Eyes, Bebe, c.1885, 18 In. 8250.00
Jumeau, Bisque, Socket Head, Brown Glass Enamel Eyes, c.1880, 25 In. 16000.00
Jumeau, Bisque, Socket Head, Fully Jointed Body, c.1896, 15 In. 3200.00
Jumeau, Bisque, Socket Head, Glass Enamel Inset Eyes, Bebe, c.1880, 21 In. 8500.00
Jumeau, Bisque, Socket Head, Paperweight Eyes, Jointed Body, Silk Dress, 1892, 22 In. . . 4500.00
Jumeau, Brown, Bisque Shoulder Head, Mohair Curls, Pink Kid Body, Clothes, 11 In. . . . 900.00
Jumeau, Brunette Mohair, Set Eyes, Teeth, Composition, Voice Box, Dress, 23 In. 700.00
Jumeau, Fashion, Bisque Head, Paperweight Eyes, Human Hair, Wood Body, 17 In. 4400.00
Jumeau, Fashion, Bisque Shoulder Head, Set Eyes, Mohair Wig, Kid Body, Suit, 19 In. . . . 1800.00
Jumeau, Fashion, Bisque Socket Head, Mohair Wig, Kid Body, Satin Dress, 10 1/2 In. . . . 1000.00
Jumeau, Fashion, Bisque, Blue Glass Enamel Eyes, Kid Body, c.1878, 11 In. 1900.00
Jumeau, Fashion, Bisque, Gray Eyes, Wig, Kid Body, Stitched Fingers, c.1880, 15 In. . . . 1200.00
Jumeau, Fashion, Bisque, Kid, Paperweight Eyes, Closed Mouth, Mohair Wig, 13 In. 1400.00
Jumeau, Fashion, Bisque, Mohair Wig, Set Eyes, Kid Body, Dressing Gown, 11 In. 750.00
Jumeau, Fashion, Bisque, Paperweight Eyes, Human Hair, Kid Body, Dress, 20 In. 1950.00
Jumeau, Fashion, Bisque, Swivel Head, Brown Glass Enamel Inset Eyes, c.1880, 3 In. . . . 950.00

Jumeau, Fashion, Bisque, Swivel Head, Kid Jointed Body, Mitten Hands, c.1880, 13 In. . . . 260.00
Jumeau, Fashion, Bisque, Swivel Neck, Blond Wig, Paperweight Eyes, 24 In. 2400.00
Jumeau, Great Ladies Series, Bisque Head, Mohair Wig, 5-Piece Composition Body, 9 In. . 475.00
Jumeau, Paris Bebe, Bisque Socket Head, Gray Paperweight Eyes, Jointed Wood, 18 In. . . 5000.00
Jumeau, Paris Bebe, Bisque, Closed Mouth, Blond Wig, Fully Jointed Body, 1892, 26 In. . . 7000.00
Jumeau, Portrait, Bisque Socket Head, Glass Enamel Eyes, Ball-Jointed, c.1880, 18 In. . . 6000.00
Jumeau, Portrait, Bisque Socket Head, Skin Wig, Jointed Wood & Composition, 13 In. . . . 1400.00
Jumeau, Premiere, Bisque, Blue Glass Enamel Inset Eyes, c.1880, 16 In. 5500.00
K * R, 18, Bisque, Closed Mouth, Socket Head, Glass Sleep Eyes, 30 In. 2600.00
K * R, 28, Bisque, Sleep Eyes, Open Mouth, Teeth, Mohair Wig, Baby Dress, 11 In. 345.00
K * R, 39, Bisque Socket Head, Sleep Eyes, Open Mouth, Composition, Child, 15 In. 365.00
K * R, 46, Bisque Head, Flirty Eyes, 4 Teeth, Human Hair, Composition, Girl, 17 1/2 In. . 700.00
K * R, 50, Bisque Socket Head, Brown Skin, Sleep Eyes, Open Mouth, Dress, Girl, 18 In. 1150.00
K * R, 62, Bisque Socket Head, Flirty Sleep Eyes, Wood, Composition Body, Girl, 28 In. . 425.00
K * R, 80, Bisque Socket Head, Sleep Eyes, Blond Mohair, Cutwork Costume, 31 In. 2000.00
K * R, 100, Bisque Socket Head, Open-Close Mouth, Composition, Baby, Dress, 14 In. . . 275.00
K * R, 100, Bisque, Dome Head, Painted Eyes, Open-Close Mouth, Baby, 19 In. 325.00
K * R, 100, Bisque, Molded Hair, Blue Eyes, Composition Body, Gown, c.1910, 11 In. . . 600.00
K * R, 100, Bisque, Molded Hair, Composition Bent-Limb Body, Baby Dress, 14 In. 300.00
K * R, 100, Bisque, Painted Eyes, Open-Close Mouth, Brown Socks, Shoes, 14 1/2 In. . . . 250.00
K * R, 100, Bisque Socket Head, Painted Blond Hair, Character, c.1909, 20 In. 1100.00
K * R, 101, Bisque, Mohair Braids, Painted Face, Composition, Straight Limbs, 8 1/2 In. . 525.00
K * R, 101, Bisque, Socket Head, Ball-Jointed Body, Antique Costume, c.1910, 15 In. . . . 3500.00
K * R, 101, Marie, Bisque, Glass Sleep Eyes, Socket Head, Mohair Wig, c.1912, 20 In. . . 12250.00
K * R, 101, Marie, Bisque, Socket Head, Painted Face, c.1912, 13 In. 1400.00
K * R, 107, Bisque, Pouty Lips, Solemn Boy, 5 Costumes, Trunk, 1910, 12 In. 1050.00
K * R, 114, Bisque Head, Blue Painted Eyes, Pouty, Mohair Coiled Braids, 8 1/2 In. . *Illus* 1175.00
K * R, 114, Bisque, Gretchen, Painted Features, Pouty Mouth, Dressed.17 In. 3450.00
K * R, 114, Gretchen, Bisque, Socket Head, Painted Face, c.1910, 25 In. 9500.00
K * R, 115, Bisque Socket Head, Sleep Eyes, Pouty, Jointed Toddler, c.1915, 16 In. 5700.00
K * R, 115A, Phillip, Bisque, Blue Glass Sleep Eyes, Brown Mohair Wig, c.1912, 19 In. . 3000.00
K * R, 115A, Phillip, Bisque, Socket Head, Sleep Eyes, Toddler Body, 1912, 16 1/2 In. . 4000.00
K * R, 116A, Bisque, Socket Head, Brown Glass Inset Eyes, Toddler, c.1915, 16 In. 1800.00
K * R, 116A, Brown Bisque Socket Head, Brown Eyes, Black Mohair Wig, Baby, 18 In. . 46.00
K * R, 117, Mein Liebling, Bisque, Socket Head, Blue Glass Eyes, c.1915, 15 In. 4100.00
K * R, 117N, Bisque Socket Head, Gray Flirty Sleep Eyes, Long Curls, Child, 27 1/2 In. . 4000.00
K * R, 121, Bisque, 2 Upper Teeth, Toddler, c.1920, 23 In. 2100.00
K * R, 121, Bisque, Socket Head, Blue Glass Sleep Eyes, Ball-Jointed, c.1915, 18 In. . . . 900.00
K * R, 121, Sleep Eyes, 2 Upper Teeth, Wobbly Tongue, Bent-Limb Body, Baby, 13 In. . . 400.00
K * R, 122, Bisque, Sleep Eyes, 2 Teeth, Replaced Human Hair, Baby Dress, 22 In. 500.00
K * R, 126, Bisque Head, Blue Glass Sleep Eyes, Bent-Limb Body, Character Baby, 10 In. 200.00
K * R, 126, Bisque Head, Brown Sleep Eyes, 2 Upper Teeth, Character Baby, 13 1/2 In. . . 430.00
K * R, 126, Bisque Head, Flirty Sleep Eyes, Mohair Wig, Composition, Baby, 15 In. 235.00
K * R, 126, Bisque Socket Head, 2 Teeth, Mohair Wig, Composition Body, Baby, 19 In. . . 400.00
K * R, 126, Bisque Socket Head, Sleep Eyes, Teeth, Composition, Baby Dress, 17 In. 375.00
K * R, 126, Bisque, Blue Glass Sleep Eyes, Open Mouth, Toddler, c.1920, 6 In. 750.00
K * R, 127, Bisque, Open Mouth, Tongue, Ball-Jointed Toddler, Costume, 1912, 16 In. . . . 1900.00
K * R, 128, Bisque Socket Head, Sleep Eyes, Open Mouth, Jointed Toddler Body, 18 In. . 3000.00
K * R, 128, Bisque, Sleep Eyes, Open Mouth, Mohair Wig, Maroon Wool Coat, 29 In. . . . 2900.00
K * R, 201, Bisque, Painted Features, Brown Wig, Kid Pin-Jointed Body, c.1910, 15 In. . . 1800.00
K * R, 403, Bisque, Socket Head, Glass Sleep Eyes, Blond Mohair Wig, c.1915, 23 In. . . . 500.00
K * R, 403, Bisque, Walker, Head Nods As She Walks, 5-Piece Composition Body, 21 In. 400.00
K * R, Bisque, 4 Upper Teeth, Girl, Underclothes, Socks, 1-Strap Shoe, 33 In. 1000.00
K * R, Bisque, Brown Complexion, Brown Glass Sleep Eyes, Open Mouth, c.1910, 14 In. 750.00
K * R, Bisque, Flirty Eyes, Ball-Jointed Toddler Body, Antique Costume, 1925, 16 In. . . . 1000.00
K * R, Bisque, Hinged Legs, Head Turns To Side, Child, 1915, 24 In. 1300.00
K * R, Bisque, Mein Liebling, Flirty Eyes, Ball-Jointed Toddler Body, c.1925, 16 In. 1000.00
K * R, Bisque, Mein Liebling, Sleep Eyes, Wooden Ball Jointed Body, c.1912, 23 In. 4800.00
K * R, Bisque, Peter, Socket Head, Painted Face, Mohair Wig, 15 In. 3000.00
K * R, Bisque, Sleep Eyes, Upper Teeth, Ball-Jointed Body, Boy, c.1915, 28 In. 2300.00
K * R, Gretchen, Bisque, Socket Head, Pouty Expression, Jointed Body, 1912, 15 In. 9000.00
K * R, Marie, Bisque, Downcast Pouty Lips, Closed Mouth, c.1909, 17 In. 3800.00
K * R, Mein Liebling, Bisque, Socket Head, Sleep Eyes, Jointed Body, Dress, 1912, 15 In. 6500.00

Doll, K * R, 114, Bisque Head,
Blue Painted Eyes, Pouty, Mohair
Coiled Braids, 8 1/2 In.

Doll, Kestner, 143, Bisque,
Brown Sleep Eyes, 4 Teeth,
Auburn Mohair Wig, 8 3/4 In.

Doll, Kestner, 8, Bisque Socket
Head, Sleep Eyes, Blond
Mohair Wig, Jointed, 13 In.

K * R, Peter, Bisque, Painted Features, Wooden Jointed, Sailor Outfit, 1909, 18 In. 3900.00
K * R, Peter, Bisque, Socket Head, Downcast Eyes, Pouty, Brunette Wig, 1910, 15 In. . . .   2800.00
K * R, Phillip, Bisque, Blond Painted Hair, Closed Mouth, c.1912, 15 In. 2400.00
K * R, Phillip, Bisque, Forelock Curl, Pouty, Ball-Jointed Body, c.1912, 15 In. 6250.00
Kathe Kruse, Cloth, Brown Hair, Green Eyes, Closed Mouth, Pouty Lips, 1915, 17 In. 3400.00
Kathe Kruse, Cloth, Brown Painted Eyes, Blond Human Hair, Girl, c.1940, 20 In. 1500.00
Kathe Kruse, Cloth, Jointed Legs, Red Cord Dress, 1927, 14 In.   2000.00
Kathe Kruse, Cloth, Oil-Painted Face, Germany, c.1922, 13 In. 2500.00
Kathe Kruse, Cloth, Pouty Expression, c.1940, 18 In. 2500.00
Kathe Kruse, Cloth, Swivel Head, Pouty Lips, Wig, Jointed Arms, Boy, 1935, 19 In. 1700.00
Kathe Kruse, German Child, Cloth Swivel Head, Muslin Body, c.1955, 19 In. 1200.00
Kathy Kruse, Cloth Head, Ball-Jointed Knees, Country Costume, 1911, 17 In. 3400.00
Kathy Kruse, Cloth, Painted Features, Curly Hair, Jointed Legs, Costume, 1915, 17 In. . .   2200.00
Kestner, 7, Bisque Head, Set Eyes, Human Hair, Kid Body, Ruffled Dress, 15 In. 425.00
Kestner, 8, Bisque Socket Head, Sleep Eyes, Blond Mohair Wig, Jointed, 13 In. . . . . *Illus*   2500.00
Kestner, 10, Bisque Socket Head, Human Hair, Wood & Composition Body, Dress, 15 In.   600.00
Kestner, 14, Bisque, Closed Mouth, Blue Eyes, Lamb's Wool Wig, 25 In. 1150.00
Kestner, 15, Bisque, Domed Socket Head, Painted Hair, Baby, c.1912, 20 In. 1000.00
Kestner, 128, Bisque, Closed Mouth, Socket Head, Blue Glass Inset Eyes, c.1895, 25 In. . .   2300.00
Kestner, 143, Bisque Head, Open Mouth, Molded Teeth, In Rocking Chair, 8 In. 865.00
Kestner, 143, Bisque, Brown Eyes, Open Mouth, Auburn Wig, White Dress, 8 3/4 In. 825.00
Kestner, 143, Bisque, Brown Sleep Eyes, 4 Teeth, Auburn Mohair Wig, 8 3/4 In. . . . *Illus*   825.00
Kestner, 143, Bisque, Socket Head, Blue Glass Sleep Eyes, Child, c.1915, 12 In. 550.00
Kestner, 143, Blue Sleep Eyes, 2 Upper Teeth, Blond Mohair Wig, 21 In. 1265.00
Kestner, 146, Bisque Socket Head, Brown Sleep Eyes, 4 Teeth, 32 In. 920.00
Kestner, 150, Bisque, 4 Upper Teeth, Mohair Wig, Jointed Shoulders, Lace Dress, 9 In. . .   300.00
Kestner, 150, Bisque, Sleep Eyes, Mohair Wig, Jointed Body, Baby Clothes, 10 In. 575.00
Kestner, 152, Bisque, Socket Head, Brown Glass Sleep Eyes, Open Mouth, c.1900, 14 In.   850.00
Kestner, 154, Bisque Head, Sleep Eyes, 4 Teeth, Human Hair, Kid Body, Dress, 15 In. . . .   375.00
Kestner, 154, Bisque, Sleep Eyes, 4 Teeth, Jointed Wood & Composition Arms, 22 1/2 In.   300.00
Kestner, 155, Bisque Socket Head, Jointed Body, Mohair Wig, Dress, Straw Hat, 24 In. . .   1500.00
Kestner, 161, Bisque, 4 Teeth, Ball-Jointed Body, Antique Clothing, c.1900, 16 In. 2000.00
Kestner, 164, Bisque, 4 Teeth, Blond Wig, Ball-Jointed Body, Dressed, c.1900, 14 In. 850.00
Kestner, 164, Bisque, 4 Teeth, Wooden Ball-Jointed Body, Child, c.1900, 24 In. 650.00
Kestner, 167, Bisque Socket Head, Brown Sleep Eyes, Open Mouth, Child, 16 In. 200.00
Kestner, 167, Bisque Socket Head, Inset Teeth, Brown Human Hair Wig, 20 In. 490.00
Kestner, 167, Bisque Socket Head, Sleep Eyes, 4 Upper Teeth, Wood, Composition, 20 In.   500.00
Kestner, 167, Bisque, Socket Head, Blue Glass Sleep Eyes, Mohair Wig, c.1910, 13 In. . .   1000.00
Kestner, 168, Bisque, 4 Teeth, Wooden Ball-Jointed Body, Child, 1915, 18 1/2 In. 700.00
Kestner, 169, Bisque, Socket Head, Loose Ball-Jointed Body, c.1890, 21 In. 2300.00
Kestner, 174, Bisque, Socket Head, Glass Sleep Eyes, c.1900, 23 In. 700.00
Kestner, 182, Bisque Socket Head, Blue Painted Eyes, Closed Mouth, 1910, 14 In. 3100.00

Kestner, 182, Bisque, Painted Eyes, Character, c.1915, 15 In. 2700.00
Kestner, 189, Bisque, Glass Sleep Eyes, Mohair Wig, Character, c.1912, 15 In. 4400.00
Kestner, 196, Bisque Socket Head, Fur Brows, Jointed, Wood, Composition, Dress, 25 In. 400.00
Kestner, 211, Bisque Head, Sleep Eyes, Mohair Wig, Composition, Toddler, 13 In. 675.00
Kestner, 211, Bisque Socket Head, Brown Sleep Eyes, Open Mouth, c.1915, 15 In. 600.00
Kestner, 220, Bisque Socket Head, Sleep Eyes, Open Mouth, Blond Mohair Wig, 21 In. .. 6250.00
Kestner, 220, Bisque, Brown Glass Sleep Eyes, Blond Human Hair Wig, Toddler, 20 In. .. 4700.00
Kestner, 241, Bisque, 4 Teeth, Ball-Jointed, Character, Antique Costume, 1912, 18 In. ... 1300.00
Kestner, 241, Bisque, Open Mouth, Brown Wig, Character, Antique Costume, 1912, 18 In. 6000.00
Kestner, 241, Bisque, Socket Head, Brown Glass Sleep Eyes, Character, c.1915, 30 In. ... 7000.00
Kestner, 243, Bisque Socket Head, Sleep Eyes, 2 Teeth, Chinese Baby, c.1912, 15 In. 6200.00
Kestner, 245, Hilda, Bisque, Brown Skin, Glass Sleep Eyes, Socket Head, c.1914, 18 In. . 4250.00
Kestner, 247, Bisque Socket Head, Sleep Eyes, Ball-Jointed, Toddler, c.1915, 16 In. 2900.00
Kestner, 247, Bisque Socket Head, Sleep Eyes, Composition Body, Baby Dress, 24 In. ... 600.00
Kestner, 247, Bisque Socket Head, Teeth, Mohair Wig, Composition, Toddler, 11 In. 2400.00
Kestner, 255, Bisque, 4 Teeth, Composition Body, Black Shoes, Bonnet, 8 3/4 In. 325.00
Kestner, 257, Bisque Socket Head, Upper Teeth, Composition Body, Baby, Dress, 20 In. . 500.00
Kestner, 260, Bisque, Brown Eyes, Open Mouth, Ecru Wool Dress, 21 In. 350.00
Kestner, 260, Bisque, Brown Sleep Eyes, Wooden, Jointed, Folklore Costume, 25 In. 1200.00
Kestner, 260, Bisque, Wooden Body, Jointed, Character, On Hobby Horse, c.1910, 26 In. . 4800.00
Kestner, Baby Jean, Bisque, Sleep Eyes, 2 Teeth, Composition Body, Baby Dress, 18 In. . 800.00
Kestner, Bisque Head, Blue Glass Eyes, Pouty Mouth, Molded Hair, Character, 14 In. ... 145.00
Kestner, Bisque Head, Pouty, Closed Mouth, Brown Glass Eyes, Composition, 16 1/2 In. . 460.00
Kestner, Bisque Head, Set Eyes, Closed Mouth, Human Hair, Kid & Cloth Body, 18 In. ... 550.00
Kestner, Bisque Socket Head, Brown Sleep Eyes, 2 Lower Teeth, Baby, c.1915, 25 In. ... 2400.00
Kestner, Bisque Socket Head, Set Eyes, Closed Mouth, Human Hair, Kid Body, 15 1/2 In. . 900.00
Kestner, Bisque, 3 Heads, Jointed Body, Laughing, Pouting, Chemise, Box, 1911, 11 In. . 9000.00
Kestner, Bisque, Brown Glass Sleep Eyes, Blond Mohair Wig, Child, c.1890, 9 In. 1500.00
Kestner, Bisque, Brown Glass Sleep Eyes, Closed Mouth, c.1885, 19 In. 1900.00
Kestner, Bisque, Brunette Wig, Wooden Ball-Jointed, Child, c.1890, 19 In. 2200.00
Kestner, Bisque, Closed Mouth, Character, Silk & Lace Dress, c.1912, 11 In. 1800.00
Kestner, Bisque, Closed Mouth, Paperweight Eyes, Original Shoes, 19 In. 2100.00
Kestner, Bisque, Dome Head, Blue Eyes, Open Mouth, Baby Gown, 17 In. 600.00
Kestner, Bisque, Shoulder Head, Blue Glass Eyes, Blond Mohair Wig, Kid Body, 14 In. ... 115.00
Kestner, Bisque, Sleep Eyes, Bent Limb Body, 2 Upper Teeth, Baby, 12 1/2 In. 288.00
Kestner, Bisque, Socket Head, 4 Teeth, Mohair Wig, Ball-Jointed Body, c.1900, 15 In. ... 800.00
Kestner, Bisque, Socket Head, Ball-Jointed Body, Child, c.1890, 21 In. 2200.00
Kestner, Bisque, Socket Head, Blue Glass Sleep Eyes, Mohair Wig, c.1890, 21 In. 3400.00
Kestner, Bisque, Socket Head, Dimple Lower Lip, 2 Teeth, Toddler Body, 1912, 15 In. ... 4800.00
Kestner, Bisque, Socket Head, Sleep Eyes, 4 Teeth, Bent-Limb Baby Body, c.1915, 10 In. 550.00
Kestner, Bisque, Turned Head, Set Eyes, Mohair Wig, Cloth, Kid Body, 11 In. 525.00
Kestner, Bisque, Wig, Wooden Body, Jointed, Child, Antique Costume, 1890, 30 In. 2600.00
Kestner, Brown Bisque, Swivel Neck, Astrakhan Wig, Jointed, Original Dress, 6 In. ... 374.00
Kestner, Hilda, Bisque, Sleep Eyes, 2 Teeth, Molded Hair, Christening Dress, 23 In. 3680.00
Kestner, Hilda, Bisque, Socket Head, Blue Glass Sleep Eyes, Toddler, c.1914, 23 In. 4000.00
Kestner, Hilda, Bisque, Socket Head, Sleep Eyes, 2 Teeth, Dress, Diaper, 1914, 16 In. ... 1600.00
Kestner, Hilda, Bisque, Socket Head, Sleep Eyes, Open Mouth, Baby Gown, 1814, 13 In. 2600.00
Kestner, Hilda, Bisque, Socket Head, Sleep Eyes, Open Mouth, Jointed Body, 14 In. 2500.00
Kestner, Hilda, Bisque, Socket Head, Sleep Eyes, Teeth, Dress, Pinafore, c.1914, 19 In. .. 3300.00
Kestner, Roberta, Bisque, Blue Sleep Eyes, Blond Wig, Kid Body, Wool Dress, 20 In. ... 310.00
Kewpie dolls are listed in the Kewpie category.
Kley & Hahn, 158, Bisque Head, Open-Close Mouth, 2 Teeth, Composition, Baby, 25 In. . 475.00
Kley & Hahn, 160, Bisque Socket Head, Sleep Eyes, Open Mouth, Baby Clothes, 11 In. .. 235.00
Kley & Hahn, 250, Bisque, Sleep Eyes, 4 Upper Teeth, Jointed Body, Underclothes, 25 In. 375.00
Kley & Hahn, 525, Bisque, Dome Head, Molded Hair, Composition, Baby, Dress, 11 In. .. 275.00
Kley & Hahn, 526, Bisque, Painted Features, Closed Mouth, Blond Wig, Character, 17 In. 4200.00
Kley & Hahn, 546, Bisque, Wooden Jointed Body, Bobbed Wig, Character, c.1915, 19 In. . 5600.00
Kley & Hahn, 548, Bisque, Socket Head, Blond Painted Head, c.1915, 27 In. 600.00
Kling, Bisque Shoulder Plate, Blond Wig, Muslin Body, Leather Arms, Child, 1885, 22 In. 800.00
Klumpe, Woman Doing Needlepoint, Paper Tag, 11 In. 400.00
Konig & Wernicke, 179, Bisque Socket Head, Human Hair, Composition, Toddler, 19 In. . 450.00
Konig & Wernicke, 1070, Bisque Socket Head, Blue Sleep Eyes, Scout Uniform, 22 In. ... 3500.00
Konig & Wernicke, Bisque, Open Mouth, 2 Teeth, Composition Body, Dress, 20 In. 650.00

Konig & Wernicke, Bisque, Socket Head, 4 Teeth, Brunette, Ball-Jointed, 1915, 28 In. . . .   650.00
Konig & Wernicke, Tommy Tucker, Bisque, Pouty, Jointed Body, 1912, 21 In. 2600.00
Leather, Oil-Painted Features, Painted Hair, Cloth Body, Leather Arms, c.1860, 12 In. . . .   863.00
Lenci, 110, Swivel Head, Painted Face, Blue Googly Eyes, c.1930, 18 In. 1800.00
Lenci, 150, Golfer, Felt Swivel Head, Cloth, Knickers, 1930, 17 In. 5200.00
Lenci, 1500, Golfer, Felt Swivel Head, Italian Cloth, Knickers, 1930, 17 In. 5200.00
Lenci, 300, Folklore Girl, Felt Swivel Head, Painted Face, Cloth, c.1930, 17 In. 1500.00
Lenci, 300, Tyrolean Boy, Swivel Head, Ringlet Curls, 17 In. 1300.00
Lenci, Aurelia, Felt, Blond Wig, Painted Molded Features, 14 In. 90.00
Lenci, Bellhop Winker, Black Felt Swivel Head, Muslin Torso, 1930, 11 1/2 In. 3100.00
Lenci, Black Felt Swivel Head, All Black Felt Body, Chubby Torso, c.1935, 15 In. 1500.00
Lenci, Black Felt Swivel Head, Googly Eyes, Felt Body, Organdy Skirt, 1928, 20 In. 3100.00
Lenci, Boy, Blue Suit, Cloth, Felt Swivel Head, Painted Face, c.1930, 17 In. 750.00
Lenci, Boy, Felt Swivel Head, Googly Eyes, Asian Costume, c.1930, 19 In. 4200.00
Lenci, Carlito Winker, Felt Swivel Head, Spanish Costume, c.1926, 11 1/2 In. 2200.00
Lenci, Clown, Felt Swivel Head, Red Hair, Painted Face, Cloth, c.1930, 18 In. 2700.00
Lenci, Felt 5-Piece Body, Googly Eyes, c.1930, 17 1/2 In. 2000.00
Lenci, Gentleman Dandy, Brown Googly Eyes, Cloth, c.1930, 23 In. 800.00
Lenci, Girl Skipping Rope, Felt Swivel Head, Cloth, c.1930, 23 In. 1300.00
Lenci, Girl, Felt Swivel Head, Closed Mouth, Organdy Dress, Ruffles, Felt Flowers, 14 In.   375.00
Lenci, Girl, Felt Swivel Head, Googly Eyes, Blond Braid, Folk Costume, c.1930, 19 In. . .   2100.00
Lenci, Girl, Felt Swivel Head, Mohair Wig, Cloth Body, Coat, Hat, 12 In. 400.00
Lenci, Girl, Felt Swivel Head, Painted Face, Cloth, Organdy Dress, c.1928, 23 In. 700.00
Lenci, Girl, Felt Swivel Head, Painted Face, Ringlet Curls, c.1930, 17 In. 900.00
Lenci, Girl, Felt Swivel Head, Painted Features, Pink Organdy Dress, 1930, 17 1/2 In. . . .   1700.00
Lenci, Golfer, Felt Swivel Head, Felt Body, Jointed Arms & Legs, 1925, 22 In. 4900.00
Lenci, Googly Girl, Felt Swivel Head, O-Shape Mouth, Glass Eyes, Cloth, 20 In. 2700.00
Lenci, Goose Girl, Felt Swivel Head, Felt Body, Jointed, 1940, 8 In. 800.00
Lenci, Italian Boy, Swivel Head, 5-Piece Felt Body, Jointed Arms, Legs, c.1930, 19 In. . . .   2300.00
Lenci, Italian Cowboy, Felt Swivel Head, Muslin Torso, Felt Costume, 1920s, 18 In. 2200.00
Lenci, Italian Girl, Felt Swivel Head, 5-Piece Felt Body, Folklore Dress, 1930, 19 In. 3100.00
Lenci, Italian Woman, Swivel Head, Elongated Felt Arms & Legs, c.1930, 27 1/2 In. 1700.00
Lenci, Little Drummer Boy, Googly, Pouty, Muslin Torso, Felt Limbs, c.1930, 17 In. 2600.00
Lenci, Mannequin, Swivel Head, Painted Features, Baby Body, 1930, 20 In. 3200.00
Lenci, Mascotte, Felt Head, Painted Eyes, Red Wig In Braids, Polka-Dot Dress, 8 In. 150.00
Lenci, Mimy, Felt Swivel Head, Googly, Bent Right Elbow, Adult Flapper, 1926, 30 In. . .   9000.00
Lenci, Mozart, Felt Swivel Head, Ponytail, Felt Costume, c.1926, 20 In. 4000.00
Lenci, Pajama Girl With Candlestick, Felt Swivel Head, Pouty, Jointed, 1930, 17 In. 1800.00
Lenci, Sailor, Felt Swivel Head, Closed Mouth, Blond Wig, Cloth, 17 In. 3000.00
Lenci, Sharpshooter, Felt Swivel Head, Italian Mountain Troop Uniform, 1930, 17 In. 5750.00
Lenci, Sheik, Felt Painted Face, Sideburns, Felt Body, c.1928, 30 In. 8500.00
Lenci, Snake Charmer, Hole For Wooden Pipe, Felt Body, Seated, 1925, 15 In. 2500.00
Lenci, Spanish Dancer, Felt Swivel Head, Bent Arms & Elbows, Skullcap, c.1925, 29 In. .   5400.00
Lenci, Sports Series, Felt Swivel Head, Side-Glancing Eyes, Blond Wig, 1930, 17 In. 3500.00
Lenci, Tirolese, Felt Swivel Head, Mohair Braids, Salon Lady, Italian Cloth, c.1930, 24 In.   1300.00
Lenci, Woman, Felt Swirl Head, Long Legs, Mohair Braids, Ethnic Costume, 26 In. 700.00
Lenci, Woman, Felt, Stitch-Jointed, Bent Knee, Teeth, Heels, Net Dress, 1930, 28 In. 8500.00
Limbach, Bisque Socket Head, Teeth, Human Hair, Composition, Character, 23 In. 625.00
Madame Alexander, Alice In Wonderland, Blue Eyes, Blond, Blue Dress, 1948, 18 In. 175.00
Madame Alexander, Alice In Wonderland, Blue Sleep Eyes, Blue Dress, Box, 14 In. 40.00
Madame Alexander, American Girl, Plastic, Sleep Eyes, Walker, Pinafore, Hat, 8 In. 285.00
Madame Alexander, Amy, Hard Plastic, Socket Head, Sleep Eyes, 1950s, 14 In. 275.00
Madame Alexander, Amy, Plastic Socket Head, Blue Sleep Eyes, c.1955, 12 In. 450.00
Madame Alexander, Amy, Plastic, Sleep Eyes, Blond Curls, 5-Piece Body, Dress, 14 In. . . .   550.00
Madame Alexander, Annabelle, Plastic, Blue Eyes, Red Skirt, Blue Sweater, 1951, 17 In. . .   850.00
Madame Alexander, Baby Clown, Plastic Head, Painted Features, Huggy Dog, 1955, 8 In.   750.00
Madame Alexander, Baby Genius, Composition Head, Muslin Body, c.1940, 11 In. 200.00
Madame Alexander, Beth, Plastic Socket Head, Sleep Eyes, Brown Hair, c.1960, 12 In. . . .   500.00
Madame Alexander, Cinderella, Hard Plastic, Socket Head, Sleep Eyes, 1950s, 20 In. 600.00
Madame Alexander, Cinderella, Plastic, Blue Eyes, Braids, Blue Satin Gown, 1950, 18 In.   250.00
Madame Alexander, Cinderella, Plastic, Sleep Eyes, Blond, Poor Outfit, 1950, 14 In. 800.00
Madame Alexander, Cissette, Hard Plastic Socket Head, Blond Hair, Box, c.1960, 10 In. . .   425.00
Madame Alexander, Coco Godey, Vinyl Head, Sleep Eyes, Jointed Body, 1966, 21 In. 500.00

Madame Alexander, Coco Lissy, Vinyl Head, Rooted Hair, Jointed Vinyl Body, 21 In. ... 600.00
Madame Alexander, Coco Melanie, Vinyl, Sleep Eyes, Jointed, Gown, 1966, 21 In. 525.00
Madame Alexander, Coco, Vinyl, Sleep Eyes, Jointed, Brocade Dress, 21 In. 425.00
Madame Alexander, Easter Girl, Plastic Head, Sleep Eyes, Prototype, c.1968, 8 In. 1100.00
Madame Alexander, Flowergirl, All Original, 14 In. 900.00
Madame Alexander, Glamour Girl, Hard Plastic Head & Body, Bouquet At Waist, 18 In. . 1900.00
Madame Alexander, Glamour Girl, Plastic, Jointed, Walker, Victorian Dress, 1953, 18 In. .. 2100.00
Madame Alexander, Good Fairy, Plastic, Blue Eyes, Blond, Gown, Crown, 1949, 14 In. ... 250.00
Madame Alexander, Jacqueline, Vinyl Head, Sleep Eyes, Plastic, Gown, 1961, 21 In. 450.00
Madame Alexander, Kathy Skater, 5-Piece Jointed Body, Braids, 18 In. 1500.00
Madame Alexander, Lissy Little Women, Plastic, Sleep Eyes, Dressed, 12 In., 5 Piece ... 550.00
Madame Alexander, Lissy, Hard Plastic Socket Head, Sleep Eyes, Box, c.1960, 12 In. ... 650.00
Madame Alexander, Lissy, Hard Plastic, Sleep Eyes, 1950s, 12 In. 1785.00
Madame Alexander, Lissy, Plastic, Jointed Body, Knee & Elbow Joints, 12 In. 1700.00
Madame Alexander, Little Women, Plastic, 5-Piece Body, Dress, 1950s, 14 In., 5 Piece .. 525.00
Madame Alexander, Madeline, Vinyl Head, Rooted Wig, Plastic, Nightgown, 17 In. 475.00
Madame Alexander, Maggie Mix-Up, Plastic Head, Straight Red Hair, Yellow Dress, 8 In. 275.00
Madame Alexander, Maggie, Plastic, Sleep Eyes, 5-Piece Body, Walker, Dress, 17 In. ... 700.00
Madame Alexander, Margaret O'Brien, Composition, Tagged Clothing, 1946, 21 In. 1150.00
Madame Alexander, Margaret O'Brien, Plastic Head, 5-Piece Jointed Body, 15 In. 1600.00
Madame Alexander, Mary Martin, Nell, South Pacific, Hard Plastic, Gown, 1948, 18 In. . 850.00
Madame Alexander, McGuffey Ana, Blond Braids, Sleep Eyes, Teeth, Tag, 15 In. 150.00
Madame Alexander, McGuffey Ana, Composition, 5-Piece Body, Plaid Dress, 16 In. 375.00
Madame Alexander, Pamela, Vinyl Head, Blue Sleep Eyes, Pink Tutu, 1963, 12 In. 600.00
Madame Alexander, Princess Margaret, 18 In. 750.00
Madame Alexander, Queen Elizabeth II, Coronation, Cissy Model, 1955, 21 In. 600.00
Madame Alexander, Quiz-Kins, Socket Head, Painted Hair, Hard Plastic, c.1958, 8 In. ... 225.00
Madame Alexander, Scarlett O'Hara, Black Wig, Curls, Composition, c.1940, 15 In. 1000.00
Madame Alexander, Scarlett O'Hara, Composition Head, Sleep Eyes, Wig, 17 In. 1050.00
Madame Alexander, Scarlett O'Hara, Plastic Head, Sleep Eyes, Brown Wig, 1960, 12 In. . 325.00
Madame Alexander, Sonja Henie, Composition Head, 6 Teeth, Skating Dress, 17 In. 625.00
Madame Alexander, Sonja Henie, Composition, Human Hair, 5-Piece Body, Box, 17 In. ... 750.00
Madame Alexander, Southern Belle, Socket Head, Composition Body, c.1910, 15 In. 1200.00
Madame Alexander, Susie Q & Bobby Q, Cloth, Mitten Hands, Blue Eyes, 13 In. 1600.00
Madame Alexander, Sweet Violet, Plastic, Walker, Dress, Hat Box, 1954, 18 In. 1700.00
Madame Alexander, Wendy, Bride, Plastic, Wig, 5-Piece Body, Box, 17 In. 550.00
Madame Alexander, Wendy, Plastic Socket Head, Eyes, Pajamas, Slippers, 1957, 8 In. ... 650.00
Madame Alexander, Wendy, Plastic Socket Head, Sleep Eyes, Floral Dress, c.1957, 8 In. . 425.00
Madame Alexander, Wendy-Kins, Bride, Socket Head, Sleep Eyes, Plastic, 1958, 8 In. ... 275.00
Madame Alexander, Wendy-Kins, Bridesmaid, Plastic Head, Sleep Eyes, c.1955, 8 In. ... 325.00
Madame Alexander, Wendy-Kins, Cap & Gown, Plastic Head, Sleep Eyes, c.1960, 8 In. ... 650.00
Madame Alexander, Wendy-Kins, Plastic Socket Head, Sleep Eyes, Organdy, c.1957, 8 In. 225.00
Madame Alexander, Wendy-Kins, Scarlett, Plastic Socket Head, Sleep Eyes, c.1968, 8 In. 275.00
Madame Alexander, Winnie Walker, Blue Eyes, Red Dress, Blue Coat, 1953, 15 In. 400.00
Mannequin, Kidskin Face, Painted Features, Black Silk Gown, c.1912, 14 In. 550.00
Marotte, Bisque Socket Head, Belton-Type, Mohair Curls, Jester's Hat, Musical, 14 In. .. 475.00
Mary Hoyer, Plastic, Sleep Eyes, 5-Piece Body, Knit Clothes, 1953, 14 In. .....*Illus* 335.00
Mattel, Allan, Painted Red Hair, Bendable Legs, Red Jacket, Blue Swim Trunks, Box ... 125.00
Mattel, Allan, Reddish Brown Hair, Blue Swim Trunks, Striped Jacket, c.1962, 12 In. ... 175.00
Mattel, Barbie, 35th Anniversary, Box 20.00
Mattel, Barbie, American Girl, Ash Blond, Beau Time, Bendable Legs 235.00
Mattel, Barbie, American Girl, Ash Blond, Blue Eyes, Bendable Legs, Box, c.1965, 11 In. 1900.00
Mattel, Barbie, American Girl, Ash Blond, Music Center Matinee 1293.00
Mattel, Barbie, American Girl, Ash Blond, Side Part, Booklet, Stand, Box .....1116.00 to 1763.00
Mattel, Barbie, American Girl, Ash Blond, Striped Swimsuit, Box 765.00
Mattel, Barbie, American Girl, Blond, American Airlines Stewardess, Japan 1645.00
Mattel, Barbie, American Girl, Blond, Blue Eyes, Bendable Legs, c.1965, 11 In. 475.00
Mattel, Barbie, American Girl, Blond, Geranium Lips, Swimsuit, Shoes, Stand, Box 2115.00
Mattel, Barbie, American Girl, Blond, Pink Lips, Midnight Blue Outfit, Fur Trim 355.00
Mattel, Barbie, American Girl, Bride, Ash Blond, Side Part, Red Lips 1765.00
Mattel, Barbie, American Girl, Brunette, Blue Eyes, Bendable Legs, c.1965, 11 In. 425.00
Mattel, Barbie, American Girl, Brunette, Midnight Gala, Stand 825.00
Mattel, Barbie, American Girl, Brunette, Red & White Kimono, Gold Obi, Purse 2235.00

Mattel, Barbie, American Girl, Brunette, Red Lips, Here Comes The Bride 1115.00
Mattel, Barbie, American Girl, Cinnamon Hair, Poodle Parade, Accessories 295.00
Mattel, Barbie, American Girl, Dark Blond, Bendable Legs, Swimsuit 350.00
Mattel, Barbie, American Girl, Red Hair, Blue Eyes, Bendable Legs, c.1965, 11 In. 475.00
Mattel, Barbie, Arabian Nights Ensemble, Brunette, Swirl Ponytail, Box, c.1964 .... 525.00
Mattel, Barbie, Blond, Lavender & White Kimono, Michigan Convention 1985 Ribbon .. 55.00
Mattel, Barbie, Blond, Swirl Ponytail, Blue Eyes, Red Swimsuit, Stand, Box, c.1964 .... 525.00
Mattel, Barbie, Blond, Swirl Ponytail, Solo In The Spotlight, Stand, Box 705.00
Mattel, Barbie, Bubble Cut, Ash Blond, Box, 1960s 375.00
Mattel, Barbie, Bubble Cut, Blond, Blue & Red Plaid Dress 85.00
Mattel, Barbie, Bubble Cut, Blond, Finger & Toe Paint, Red Swimsuit 65.00
Mattel, Barbie, Bubble Cut, Blond, Straight Leg, Red Swimsuit 95.00
Mattel, Barbie, Bubble Cut, Brunette, Gold Evening Sheath, Accessories 3590.00
Mattel, Barbie, Bubble Cut, Platinum Blond, Turquoise Eyes, Stand, Box, c.1961 .... 375.00
Mattel, Barbie, Bubble Cut, Titian Hair, Blue Eyes, Stand, Box, c.1961, 11 In. 290.00
Mattel, Barbie, Bubble Cut, Titian Hair, Eye Shadow, Red Nylon Swimsuit 75.00
Mattel, Barbie, Bubble Cut, Titian Hair, Straight Leg, Red Nylon Swimsuit, Box 105.00
Mattel, Barbie, Bubble Cut, Titian Hair, Striped Swimsuit, Stand, Booklet, Box 294.00
Mattel, Barbie, Color Magic, Blond, Gold 'n' Glamour, Box 940.00
Mattel, Barbie, Color Magic, Blond, Red Lips, Pretty As A Picture, Hat 411.00
Mattel, Barbie, Color Magic, Midnight, Hair Clip, Cobalt Blue Dress, Gold Belt, Bag ... 1469.00
Mattel, Barbie, Color Magic, Midnight, Ruby Hair, Bendable Legs, Box, c.1966 .... 2100.00
Mattel, Barbie, Color Magic, Red Hair 765.00
Mattel, Barbie, Color Magic, Scarlet Flame & Golden Blond Hair, Box, c.1966 .... 1600.00
Mattel, Barbie, Dream Wedding, Box 25.00
Mattel, Barbie, Eskimo, International Series, Box Date 1981 .... 65.00
Mattel, Barbie, Fashion Queen, Painted Hair, Gold & White Swimsuit, 3 Wigs, Box 300.00
Mattel, Barbie, Holiday, 1988, Box 300.00
Mattel, Barbie, Holiday, Black, 1993, Box 13.00
Mattel, Barbie, India, International Series, Box Date 1981 .... 50.00
Mattel, Barbie, Japanese, Brunette, Upswept Swirl Ponytail, Kimono, c.1964, 11 In. 350.00
Mattel, Barbie, Lemon Yellow Hair, Plastic Closet 675.00
Mattel, Barbie, Malibu, Blond, Blue Swimsuit, Plastic Sunglasses, Package Date 1970 ... 105.00
Mattel, Barbie, Marilyn Monroe, Seven Year Itch, Box 13.00
Mattel, Barbie, No. 1, Blond, Blue Eyes, Swimsuit, Stand, Box, c.1959, 11 In. 7000.00
Mattel, Barbie, No. 1, Blond, Ponytail, Black & White Swimsuit, Box 3200.00
Mattel, Barbie, No. 1, Blond, Ponytail, Striped Swimsuit 2820.00
Mattel, Barbie, No. 1, Brunette, Ponytail, 1959 .... 2200.00
Mattel, Barbie, No. 1, Brunette, Ponytail, Brown Eyes, Swimsuit, Stand, Box, 11 In. 7000.00
Mattel, Barbie, No. 1, Brunette, Striped Swimsuit, Sunglasses, Stand, Booklet, Box 4406.00
Mattel, Barbie, No. 2, Blond Hair, Ponytail, Black & White Striped Swimsuit 3800.00
Mattel, Barbie, No. 2, Blond, Ponytail 2585.00
Mattel, Barbie, No. 2, Blond, Ponytail, Striped Swimsuit 2235.00
Mattel, Barbie, No. 2, Blond, Ponytail, Striped Swimsuit, Booklet, Stand, Box 3055.00
Mattel, Barbie, No. 2, Blond, Ponytail, Striped Swimsuit, Stand, Box, 11 In. 6250.00
Mattel, Barbie, No. 2, Brunette, Ponytail, Striped Swimsuit, Stand, Booklet, Box 3525.00 to 3820.00
Mattel, Barbie, No. 2, Brunette, Ponytail, Striped Swimsuit, Stand, Box, 11 In. 6250.00
Mattel, Barbie, No. 3, Blond, Ponytail, Cameo Tutu, Ballet Shoes, Crown 355.00
Mattel, Barbie, No. 3, Blond, Ponytail, Mood For Music, Box 590.00
Mattel, Barbie, No. 3, Blond, Ponytail, Resort, Swimsuit, Box 1058.00
Mattel, Barbie, No. 3, Blond, Ponytail, Satin 'n' Rose 590.00
Mattel, Barbie, No. 3, Blond, Ponytail, Striped Swimsuit, Stand, Box, 11 In. 800.00
Mattel, Barbie, No. 3, Brunette, Ponytail, Striped Swimsuit, Stand, Box, 11 In. 650.00
Mattel, Barbie, No. 4, Black Hair, Ponytail, Black & White Striped Swimsuit, Stand 100.00
Mattel, Barbie, No. 4, Blond, Ponytail, Blue Eyes, Striped Swimsuit, 11 In. 300.00
Mattel, Barbie, No. 4, Brunette, Ponytail, Enchanted Evening 529.00
Mattel, Barbie, No. 4, Brunette, Ponytail, Sweater Girl 350.00
Mattel, Barbie, No. 4, Ponytail, Box, 1960s 475.00
Mattel, Barbie, No. 5, Blond, Ponytail, American Airlines Stewardess Outfit 145.00
Mattel, Barbie, No. 5, Blond, Ponytail, Red Leotard, Shoes, Stand, Booklet, Box 206.00
Mattel, Barbie, No. 5, Blond, Turquoise Eyes, Stand, Box, 1961, 11 In. 300.00
Mattel, Barbie, No. 5, Brunette, Blue Eyes, Stand, 1961, 11 In. 200.00
Mattel, Barbie, No. 6, Blond, Blue Eyes, Red Swimsuit, Blue Eyes, Stand, c.1962, 11 In. .. 150.00

Mattel, Barbie, No. 6, Blond, Blue Eyes, Red Swimsuit, Shoes, Stand, Box, c.1962, 11 In. 300.00
Mattel, Barbie, No. 6, Brunette, Blue Eyes, Swimsuit, Shoes, Stand, Box, 1962, 11 In. . . . 375.00
Mattel, Barbie, No. 6, Titian Hair, Ponytail, Registered Nurse, Accessories 880.00
Mattel, Barbie, No. 6, Titian Hair, Ponytail, Straight Leg, Pink & White Knit Swimsuit . . 55.00
Mattel, Barbie, Oriental, International Series, Box Date 1980 . . . . 40.00
Mattel, Barbie, Parisian, International Series, Box Date 1979 . . . . 40.00
Mattel, Barbie, Platinum Blond, Swirl Ponytail, Aqua Eyes, Red Swimsuit, 11 In. 450.00
Mattel, Barbie, Platinum Hair, Ponytail, Enchanted Evening, Pink Satin Gown 475.00
Mattel, Barbie, Platinum Swirl Hair, Box, Montgomery Ward Sticker, 1964 . . . . 2025.00
Mattel, Barbie, Romantic Interlude, Classique Collection, Box 20.00
Mattel, Barbie, Royal, International Series, Box Date 1979 . . . . 50.00
Mattel, Barbie, Soda Fountain Sweetheart, Coca-Cola, Box 65.00
Mattel, Barbie, Stand, Box, 1962 . . . . 385.00
Mattel, Barbie, Titian Hair, Ponytail, Sparkle Squares 646.00
Mattel, Barbie, Titian Hair, Swirl Ponytail, Riding In Park, Boots, Crop 470.00
Mattel, Barbie, Twist 'n Turn, Ash Blond, Dinner Dazzle 705.00
Mattel, Barbie, Twist 'n Turn, Blond, Bendable Legs, 2-Piece Vinyl Swimsuit 205.00
Mattel, Barbie, Twist 'n Turn, Blond, Pink Swimsuit, Bendable Legs, Japan 410.00
Mattel, Barbie, Twist 'n Turn, Brunette, Pink Velvet Coat, Fur Collar, Gloves, Japan 705.00
Mattel, Barbie, Yellow Hair, Bendable Legs, Diamond Pattern Swimsuit 300.00
Mattel, Brad, Molded Black Hair, Bendable Legs, Box, c.1970 . . . . 125.00
Mattel, Christie, Black Hair, Beige Lips, Bendable Arms & Legs 145.00
Mattel, Christie, Reddish Brown Hair, Brown Eyes, Talking, Box, c.1969, 11 In. 190.00
Mattel, Christie, Twist 'n Turn, Sticker, Box 380.00
Mattel, Francie, Auburn Hair, Bendable Legs, Sweet 'n' Swingin' 470.00
Mattel, Francie, Auburn Hair, Bendable Legs, Victorian Wedding Outfit 470.00
Mattel, Francie, Black, Dark Red Hair, Pink Lips, Printed Swimsuit 675.00
Mattel, Francie, Blond Flip, Bendable Legs, Black & White Houndstooth Suit 645.00
Mattel, Francie, Blond, Pink Lips, Rooted Eyelashes, Bendable Legs, Swimsuit 135.00
Mattel, Francie, Brown Hair, Bendable Legs, First Formal Outfit 646.00
Mattel, Francie, Brunette, Bendable Legs, Miss Teenage Beauty 470.00
Mattel, Francie, Brunette, Blue Kimono, Gold Lame Obi, Purse, Japan 1528.00
Mattel, Francie, Brunette, Red Flowered Kimono, Gold Lame Obi, Japan 1469.00
Mattel, Francie, Brunette, Tuckered Out, Curlers & Comb, Japan, Box 1175.00
Mattel, Francie, Dark Brown Hair, Bendable Legs, Orange Zip Vinyl Coat, Skirt 881.00
Mattel, Francie, Dark Brown Hair, Bendable Legs, Original Print Swimsuit 764.00
Mattel, Francie, Twist 'n Turn, Brown Eyes, Bendable Legs, Box, c.1967, 10 1/2 In. 1900.00
Mattel, Francie, Twist 'n Turn, Platinum Blond, Pink Lightning 410.00
Mattel, Julia, Twist 'n Turn, Brunette With Tint Of Red, Nurse Outfit, Box 200.00
Mattel, Julia, Twist 'n Turn, Red Hair, Bendable Legs, Nurse Outfit 125.00
Mattel, Ken, Blond, Painted Hair, Beige Lips, Red & White Striped Jacket, Red, Box 155.00
Mattel, Ken, Brown Hair, Blue Eyes, Doctor Outfit, 1962, 12 In. 375.00

Doll, Mary Hoyer, Plastic,
Sleep Eyes, 5-Piece Body,
Knit Clothes, 1953, 14 In.

Doll, Mattel, Ken, Play It
Cool, Brunette, Painted
Hair, Bendable Legs

Doll, Raggedy Ann,
Awake-Asleep, Applause,
12 1/2 In.

Mattel, Ken, Brunette Flocked Hair, Dreamboat Green Jacket, Green Pants, Straw Hat ... 90.00
Mattel, Ken, Brunette, Blue Eyes, Bendable Legs, Box, c.1965, 12 In. 500.00
Mattel, Ken, Brunette, Here Comes The Groom, Box 825.00
Mattel, Ken, Brunette, Painted Hair, Red & White Striped Jacket, Red Swim Trunks 50.00
Mattel, Ken, No. 1, Brunette, Red Swim Trunks, Stand, Box, 1960, 12 In. 250.00
Mattel, Ken, No. 2, Blond, Blue Eyes, Swim Trunks, Striped Jacket, Stand, Box, 12 In. .. 100.00
Mattel, Ken, Play It Cool, Brunette, Painted Hair, Bendable Legs .... *Illus* 125.00
Mattel, Midge, Blond Flip, Blue Eyes, 2-Piece Swimsuit, Stand, Box, c.1962, 11 In. 275.00
Mattel, Midge, Blond, Coral Lips, Orange Cotton Belle Dress 45.00
Mattel, Midge, Blond, Coral Lips, Painted Teeth 65.00
Mattel, Midge, Brunette Flip, Blue Eyes, 2-Piece Swimsuit, Stand, Box, c.1962, 11 In. ... 225.00
Mattel, Midge, Brunette, Orange Leotard, Straw Hat, Stand, Japan 1998.00
Mattel, Midge, Red Hair, Blue Eyes, Bendable Legs, Box, c.1965, 11 In. 475.00
Mattel, Midge, Red Painted Hair, Molded Head, Navy Blue Swimsuit, 3 Wigs 205.00
Mattel, Midge, Titian Flip, Blue Eyes, 2-Piece Swimsuit, Stand, Box, c.1962, 11 In. 175.00
Mattel, Midge, Titian Hair, Bendable Leg, Gold & Navy Blue Lame Sheath, Wire Stand . 185.00
Mattel, Midge, Titian Hair, Straight Leg, 2-Piece Chartreuse & Orange Swimsuit 45.00
Mattel, Mork, Talking Space Pack, Box, 16 In. 75.00
Mattel, Mrs. Beasley, Stuffed Cloth Body, White Polka-Dot Dress, 1967, 21 In. 45.00
Mattel, Mrs. Beasley, Vinyl Head, Blue Eyes, Blond Hair, Box, 1966, 20 In. 230.00
Mattel, P.J., Blond, Swingin' In Silver, Hair Ornaments, Beads, Boots 590.00
Mattel, Ricky, Red Molded Hair, Blue Eyes, Box, c.1966, 9 In. 150.00
Mattel, Ricky, Red Painted Hair, Tan Lips, Striped Jacket, Blue Swim Trunks, Box 85.00
Mattel, Scooter, Blond Hair, Brown Eyes, Bendable Legs, Box, c.1965, 9 In. 225.00
Mattel, Skipper, Ash Blond, Red & White Playsuit, Box, Japan 410.00
Mattel, Skipper, Blond, Bendable Arms & Legs 40.00
Mattel, Skipper, Blond, Blue Eyes, Red & White Romper, Box, c.1964, 9 In. 110.00
Mattel, Skipper, Blond, Junior Bridesmaid, Straight Legs, Pink Gown, Wire Stand 275.00
Mattel, Skipper, Blond, Malibu, Orange Swimsuit, Plastic Sunglasses, Box Date 1970 ... 90.00
Mattel, Skipper, Brunette, Blue Eyes, Red & White Romper, Box, c.1964, 9 In. 180.00
Mattel, Skipper, Red Hair, Blue Eyes, Bendable Legs, Box, c.1965, 9 In. 200.00
Mattel, Skipper, Titian Hair, Metal Headband, Straight Legs, Red & White Swimsuit 145.00
Mattel, Skipper, Titian Hair, Straight Leg, School Girl Outfit 65.00
Mattel, Skooter, Blond, Bendable Legs, Red & White Top, Denim Shorts, Box 125.00
Mattel, Skooter, Brunette, Ribbon Ties, Ship Ahoy Outfit, Blue Pleated Skirt 110.00
Mattel, Skooter, Titian Hair, Pink Lips, Straight Legs, Red & White Swimsuit, Box 105.00
Mattel, Stacey, Twist 'n Turn, Titian Hair, Painted Teeth, Floral Print Swimsuit 85.00
Mattel, Tiff, Pose 'n Play, Titian Hair, Bendable Arms & Legs, STOP Decal On Shirt 440.00
Mattel, Twiggy, Blond Hair, Blue Eyes, Bendable Legs, Mod Outfit, Box, c.1967, 10 In. . 300.00
Mattel, Yellowstone Kelley, Sports Set, Titian Hair, Bendable Legs, Red & White Shirt .. 575.00
Morgenthaler, Bisque, Socket Head, Human Hair Wig, Jointed Body, 19 In. 4000.00
Morimura, Bisque Head, Upper Teeth, Mohair Wig, Composition Body, Toddler, 13 In. ... 115.00
Morimura, Bisque Socket Head, 5-Piece Composition Body, 12 In. 70.00
Paper dolls are listed in their own category.
Papier-Mache, Enamel Eyes, Gusset Jointed Hips, Square Teeth, Nun's Habit, 15 In. 1150.00
Papier-Mache, Glass Eyes, Closed Mouth, Auburn Mohair Wig, Cloth Body, 1890, 10 In. . 115.00
Papier-Mache, Milliner's Model, Kid Body, Painted Hair, Original Dress, 12 1/2 In. 475.00
Papier-Mache, Milliner's Model, Kid Body, Wooden Arms & Legs, Silk Dress, 8 1/4 In. . 500.00
Papier-Mache, Milliner's Model, Painted Eyes & Curls, Original Dress, 12 1/2 In. 850.00
Papier-Mache, Milliner's Model, Painted Eyes, Kid Body, Wooden Arms, Legs, 11 In. ... 500.00
Papier-Mache, Mother Goose, Wrinkles, Painted Teeth, Muslin Body, c.1885, 21 In. 2700.00
Papier-Mache, Painted Face, Smiling, Baby, Crawling, Mechanical, R. Clay, 1871, 11 In. . 500.00
Papier-Mache, Shoulder Head, Painted Eyes & Hair, Kid Body, Dress, 9 3/4 In. 255.00
Papier-Mache, Solid Dome Head, Bellows In Midriff, Baby, c.1860, 27 In. 2800.00
Parsons-Jackson, Celluloid, Molded Hair, Face, Baby, Socks & Shoes, 11 1/2 In. 95.00
Petzold, Composition, Stockinet Body, Mitten Hands, Velvet Dress, 16 1/2 In. 275.00
Pincushion dolls are listed in their own category.
Porcelain, Enamel Eyes, Brunette Wig, Kid Body, Gusset-Jointed, 17 In. 875.00
Puppet, Hand, Chimpanzee, Steiff, Early 20th Century, Pair 230.00
Puppet, Ozwald, Paul Winchell's, Barwin Novelties, Box, 1950s 100.00
Puppet, Rabbit, Mohair, Steiff 75.00
Puppet, Smokey Bear, Vinyl, Cloth, Ideal, Mid 1960s, 9 In. 35.00
Puppet, Speedy Gonzalez, Soft Vinyl, Warner Bros., 9 1/2 In. 15.00

Puppet, Steve Zodiac, Fireball XL5, Pelham, Box, 1960s 1940.00
Raggedy Ann, Awake-Asleep, Applause, 12 1/2 In. .... *Illus* 650.00
Raggedy Ann, Georgene Novelties, 1950s, 15 In. 45.00
Raggedy Ann, Original Clothes, Marked Patented Sept. 7, 1915, Volland, 12 In. 2500.00
Raynal, Fashion, Felt Swivel Head, Painted Eyes, 5-Piece Cloth Body, Dress, Hat, 19 In. . 725.00
Recknagel, Bisque Socket Head, Open-Close Mouth, Character, Redressed, 9 In. 675.00
Recknagel, Solid Dome Socket Head, 2 Teeth, Blond, White Bonnet, Pink Dress, 12 In. ... 425.00
Remco, I Dream Of Jeannie, Posable, Screen Gems, Copyright 1977, 10 In. 80.00
Rohmer, Fashion, Bisque, Swivel Head, Painted Face, Blond Wool Wig, c.1860, 17 In. ... 4200.00
Rohmer, Fashion, Porcelain, Shoulder Head, Plump Face, c.1860, 17 In. 4250.00
Roullet Et Decamps, L'Intrepide Bebe, Bisque, Walking, Socket Head, c.1899, 22 In. ... 2000.00
S & H dolls are also listed here as Bergmann and Simon & Halbig.
S & H, 201, Bisque Head, Set Eyes, Teeth, Composition Body, Baby, Sailor Suit, 28 In. .. 700.00
S & H, 1079, Bisque, Socket Head, Brown Glass Sleep Eyes, Child, c.1900, 24 In. 600.00
S & H, 1079, Bisque, Socket Head, Brown Glass Sleep Eyes, Nun's Habit, c.1910, 17 In. . 500.00
S & H, 1909, Bisque, Sleep Eyes, Teeth, Wig, Wood, Composition, Jointed, 20 In. 195.00
S & H, Bisque, Domed Swivel Head, Shoulder Plate, Twill Body, Child, c.1880, 8 In. 2200.00
S.F.B.J., 226, Bisque, Socket Head, Glass Jewel Inset Eyes, Character, c.1912, 12 In. 1500.00
S.F.B.J., 22 D, Bisque Socket Head, Sleep Eyes, Open Mouth, Human Hair Wig, 19 In. ... 175.00
S.F.B.J., 226, Bisque Head, Jewel Eyes, Jointed Wood & Composition, Boy, 19 1/2 In. ... 1300.00
S.F.B.J., 226, Bisque Head, Jewel Eyes, Open-Close Mouth, Toddler, Sweater, 17 In. 1100.00
S.F.B.J., 301, Bisque Socket Head, Sleep Eyes, Wood & Composition Jointed, 11 In. 600.00
S.F.B.J., 301, Bisque, 4 Teeth, Walking, Kiss Throwing, 22 1/2 In. 525.00
S.F.B.J., 301, Bisque, Socket Head, Fleecy Wig, Papier-Mache Body, Clown, 1915, 15 In. . 1000.00
S.F.B.J., Bisque Head, 6 Teeth, Human Hair, Jumeau Body, Bebe, White Dress, 24 In. 1550.00
S.F.B.J., Bisque, Blond Mohair, Set Eyes, Teeth, Composition, Ball-Jointed, 19 In. 300.00
S.F.B.J., Bisque, Socket Head, 2 Upper Teeth, Antique Muslin Chemise, c.1912, 12 In. ... 2400.00
Sasha, Vinyl Socket Head, 5-Piece Body, Hip '60s, 1965, 16 In. 1500.00
Schmidt, 1899, Bisque, Shoulder Head, Sleep Eyes, Cloth Body, Red Wool Dress, 24 In. . 315.00
Schmidt, Bisque Socket Head, Blue Sleep Eyes, Closed Mouth, Character, c.1912, 21 In. 3250.00
Schmidt, Bisque, Composition & Wooden Jointed Toddler Body, 1912, 21 In. 2500.00
Schmidt, Bisque, Sleep Eyes, Open-Close Mouth, White Baby Dress, 14 In. 375.00
Schmidt, Bisque, Socket Head, Forelock, Ball-Jointed Toddler Body, c.1912, 23 In. 3750.00
Schmitt, 4, Bisque, New Wig, Composition, Ball-Jointed, Lace Dress, Hat, 23 1/2 In. 8000.00
Schoenau & Hoffmeister, Bisque Head, Composition, Masquerade, Box, 13 1/2 In. 525.00
Schoenau & Hoffmeister, Bisque, Human Hair Wig, Jointed Toddler Body, 1925, 25 In. ... 1400.00
Schoenhut, 300, Carved Socket Head, Spring-Jointed Body, Character Girl, 1917, 16 In. . 700.00
Schoenhut, 300, Wooden, Intaglio Eyes, Jointed, Human Hair, Girl, Redressed, 16 In. ... 300.00
Schoenhut, 301, Wooden Socket Head, Blue Intaglio Eyes, Spring-Jointed, 16 In. .... *Illus* 1900.00
Schoenhut, 308, Wooden, Intaglio Eyes, Mohair Wig, Girl, White Dress, 19 In. 450.00
Schoenhut, 308, Wooden, Socket Head, Blond Mohair Wig, Character Girl, c.1916, 19 In. 600.00
Schoenhut, 308C, Wood, Spring-Jointed Body, c.1916, 14 In. 1200.00
Schoenhut, Baby Face, Painted Features, Sticker On Back, 1911, 14 In. 200.00
Schoenhut, Carved Hair, Intaglio Eyes, Boy, 1911, 14 1/2 In. 402.00
Schoenhut, Miss Dolly, Wooden, Socket Head, Brown Painted Eyes, c.1915, 21 In. 600.00
Schoenhut, Wooden Head, Intaglio Eyes, Knit Union Suit, Socks, Shoes, 16 In. 900.00
Schoenhut, Wooden Head, Mohair Wig, Toddler's Body, Low-Waisted Dress, 11 In. 325.00
Schoenhut, Wooden Socket Head, Mohair Wig, Spring-Jointed Body, Girl, Dress, 14 In. . 275.00
Schoenhut, Wooden, Blond Mohair, Cotton Dress, Straw Hat, 17 In. 200.00
Schoenhut, Wooden, Carved Hair, Painted Brown Eyes, Girl, c.1912, 16 In. 800.00
Schoenhut, Wooden, Painted Face, Mohair Wig, Bent-Limb Body, Vintage Dress, 15 In. 420.00
Schoenhut, Wooden, Painted Hair & Face, Baby Dress, New Cap, 11 In. 250.00
Schoenhut, Wooden, Socket Head, Carved Blue Eyes, Character Girl, c.1912, 16 In. 500.00
Shackman, Miss Liberty, Bisque Head, Painted Eyes & Hair, Closed Mouth, Cloth, 18 In. 1650.00
Shirley Temple dolls are included in the Shirley Temple category.
Simon & Halbig dolls are also listed here under Bergmann and S & H.
Simon & Halbig, 126, 5-Piece Bent Limb Body, Baby, 12 In. 315.00
Simon & Halbig, 530, Bisque, Original Brown Wig, Period Clothes, 21 In. 258.00
Simon & Halbig, 607, Bisque Socket Head, Sleep Eyes, Blond Mohair Wig, 16 In. 2900.00
Simon & Halbig, 719, Bisque Socket Head, Brown Sleep Eyes, Jointed, 22 In. 1725.00
Simon & Halbig, 719, Bisque Socket Head, Glass Eyes, Mohair Wig, Child, 1890, 20 In. . 1800.00
Simon & Halbig, 719, Bisque Socket Head, Jointed, Mariner Suit, Child, 1895, 21 In. 1300.00
Simon & Halbig, 919, Bisque Socket Head, 4 Teeth, Jointed Body, c.1890, 20 In. 1900.00

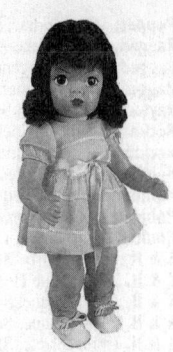

Doll, Schoenhut, 301, Wooden
Socket Head, Blue Intaglio Eyes,
Spring-Jointed, 16 In.

Doll, Simon & Halbig, 1159,
Bisque Head, Sleep Eyes,
Teeth, Blond Braids, 13 In.

Doll, Terri Lee, Plastic Head,
Saran Wig, 5-Piece Body,
Organdy Dress, 16 In.

Simon & Halbig, 920, Fashion, Bisque, Blue Glass Inset Eyes, c.1885, 20 In. 2300.00
Simon & Halbig, 929, Bisque, Modeled Face, Blond Mohair Wig, Child, c.1885, 23 In. . . .   1500.00
Simon & Halbig, 939, Bisque Socket Head, Mohair Wig, Jointed Composition, 17 In. 2700.00
Simon & Halbig, 939, Bisque, Socket Head, Open Mouth, Row Of Teeth, c.1890, 24 In. . . .   2100.00
Simon & Halbig, 949, Bisque Head, Pouty Mouth, Human Hair, Jointed, Dress, 32 In. . . .   2800.00
Simon & Halbig, 949, Bisque, Closed Mouth, Ball-Jointed Body, c.1890, 13 In. 1600.00
Simon & Halbig, 949, Bisque, Socket Head, Blue Glass Sleep Eyes, Child, c.1890, 14 In. .   1900.00
Simon & Halbig, 979, Bisque Head, Brown Glass Eyes, Tight Blond Mohair Curls, 9 In. .   635.00
Simon & Halbig, 1039, Bisque Head, 4 Teeth, Human Hair Wig, Dress, 23 1/2 In. 850.00
Simon & Halbig, 1039, Bisque Head, Brown Flirty Eyes, Open Mouth, Jointed, 22 In. . . .   575.00
Simon & Halbig, 1039, Bisque, Socket Head, Flirty Blue Glass Eyes, Child, c.1900, 22 In.   1200.00
Simon & Halbig, 1078, Blue Glass Sleep Eyes, Child, Scottish Costume, c.1900, 13 In. . . .   1000.00
Simon & Halbig, 1078, Blue Sleep Eyes, Open Mouth, Swiss Costume, 19 1/2 In. 345.00
Simon & Halbig, 1079, Bisque Socket Head, Teeth, Synthetic Wig, 5-Piece Body, 9 In. . . .   280.00
Simon & Halbig, 1129, Bisque Head, 4 Teeth, Mohair Wig, Oriental, Composition, 9 In. . . .   1275.00
Simon & Halbig, 1159, Bisque Head, Sleep Eyes, Teeth, Blond Braids, 13 In. . . . . . . *Illus*   1600.00
Simon & Halbig, 1159, Bisque, Blue Eyes, Silk Teddy, Stockings, High Heels, 13 In. 1600.00
Simon & Halbig, 1159, Fashion, Bisque, 4 Teeth, Ball-Jointed Body, c.1900, 19 In. 2000.00
Simon & Halbig, 1199, Bisque, Brown Eyes, Mohair Queue, Asian Child, Kimono, 18 In.   3400.00
Simon & Halbig, 1199, Bisque, Brown Side-Slanted Sleep Eyes, Asian Child, 1900, 15 In.   160.00
Simon & Halbig, 1249, Bisque Head, Blue Sleep Eyes, Brown Mohair Wig, 26 In. 748.00
Simon & Halbig, 1249, Bisque, Socket Head, Glass Sleep Eyes, Child, 14 In. 750.00
Simon & Halbig, 1249, Bisque, Socket Head, Teeth, Blond, Ball-Jointed, 1900, 22 In. 850.00
Simon & Halbig, 1279, Bisque, Sleep Eyes, 2 Upper Teeth, Period Mohair Wig, 21 In. . . .   1725.00
Simon & Halbig, 1279, Bisque, Socket Head, Brown Glass Sleep Eyes, c.1915, 18 In. . . .   1900.00
Simon & Halbig, 1299, Bisque Head, Brown Sleep Eyes, 2 Upper Teeth, Child, 18 In. . . .   635.00
Simon & Halbig, 1349, Bisque Socket Head, Sleep Eyes, Composition Body, 19 1/2 In. . .   370.00
Simon & Halbig, 1428, Bisque, Blue Glass Sleep Eyes, Character, c.1912, 13 In. 1500.00
Simon & Halbig, 1428, Bisque, Sleep Eyes, Bent-Limb Baby Body, Diaper, 14 1/2 In. . . .   800.00
Simon & Halbig, 1489, Bisque, Socket Head, Sleep Eyes, 2 Teeth, Baby, c.1915, 20 In. . . .   2500.00
Simon & Halbig, 1489, Erika, Bisque, Blue Glass Sleep Eyes, Toddler, c.1912, 21 In. 3600.00
Simon & Halbig, Bisque Head, Blue Sleep Eyes, Inset Teeth, Human Hair Wig, 26 In. 489.00
Simon & Halbig, Bisque Head, Blue Sleep Eyes, Open Mouth, Blond Mohair Wig, 21 In. .   345.00
Simon & Halbig, Bisque, Blond Hair, Handwerck Body, 21 In. 315.00
Simon & Halbig, Bisque, Glass Eyes, Blond Synthetic Wig, Kid Body, 16 In. 145.00
Simon & Halbig, Bisque, Oriental, Red & Gold Satin Costume, Sleep Eyes, 1910, 18 In. .   2100.00
Simon & Halbig, Bisque, Socket Head, Styled Wig, Lady, Sleep Eyes, 13 1/2 In. 950.00
Simon & Halbig, Bisque, Wooden Ball-Jointed Body, Asian Child, c.1910, 19 In. 1200.00
Simon & Halbig, Brown Bisque Head, Brown Eyes, Mohair Fleecy Wig, Child, 24 In. . . .   3300.00
Skeezix, Oilcloth, Yellow Hair, Blue & White Clothes, Black Shoes, c.1930, 13 1/2 In. 55.00
Sonneberg, 116, Bisque, Blue Glass Enamel Inset Eyes, Child, c.1885, 10 In. 2700.00
Sonneberg, 212, Bisque Socket Head, Sleep Eyes, Human Hair, Satin Dress, 15 In. 3700.00

Sonneberg, Closed Mouth, Blue Glass Spiral Threaded Eyes, Child, c.1885, 14 In. 1400.00
Sonneberg, Wax Shoulder Head, Cloth Body, Wooden Arms, Legs, Clothes, 17 In. 110.00
Steiff, Felt, Blond Mohair, Blue Eyes, Jointed, Gray Wool Overalls, Black Vest, 16 In. . . . 200.00
Steiner, Bisque Shoulder Head, Enamel Eyes, Key Wind, Original Gown, c.1867, 16 In. . . 5750.00
Steiner, Bisque, Blue Eyes, Socket Head, Lever Sleep Eyes, C Series, c.1885, 20 In. 5000.00
Steiner, Bisque, Blue Glass Paperweight Inset Eyes, Bebe, C Series, c.1885, 15 In. 4000.00
Steiner, Bisque, Blue Paperweight Eyes, Teeth, Mohair, Voice Box, Bebe, 18 In. 4888.00
Steiner, Bisque, Composition Body, Lever Sleep Eyes, Teeth, Human Hair, 18 In. 2900.00
Steiner, Bisque, Fringed Brows, Glass Paperweight Inset Eyes, Bebe, c.1889, 10 In. 3600.00
Steiner, Bisque, Glass Paperweight Inset Eyes, Closed Mouth, Bebe, c.1890, 18 In. 4750.00
Steiner, Bisque, Human Hair, Paperweight Eyes, Composition Ball-Jointed, 18 In. 1350.00
Steiner, Bisque, Paperweight Eyes, Boutique Label, c.1890, 21 In. 3900.00
Steiner, Bisque, Papier-Mache Fingers, Silk Dress, Underclothing, 16 1/2 In. 900.00
Steiner, Bisque, Size 2, Blue Glass Inset Eyes, Bebe, c.1890, 9 In. 2700.00
Steiner, Bisque, Socket Head, Blue Glass Inset Eyes, Bebe, France, c.1888, 22 In. 4000.00
Steiner, Bisque, Socket Head, Blue Glass Paperweight Inset Eyes, Bebe, 10 In. 4200.00
Steiner, Bisque, Socket Head, Closed Mouth, Blond Wig, Fully Jointed, c.1884, 18 In. . . . 6250.00
Steiner, Bisque, Socket Head, Closed Mouth, Straight Wrists, Jointed, c.1890, 16 In. 3800.00
Steiner, Bisque, Socket Head, Lever Eyes, 6 Teeth, Jointed, Mama Crier, 1890, 16 In. . . . 3000.00
Steiner, Bisque, Wooden Fully Jointed Body, Antique Costume, c.1899, 18 In. 8000.00
Steiner, Gigoteur, Bisque Dome Head, Replaced Wig, Mechanical, Dress & Hat, 16 In. . . 1900.00
Steiner, Gigoteur, Bisque, Glass Eyes, Teeth, Bebe, Sailor Dress, Key Wind, 1885, 18 In. . 2000.00
Swaine & Co., Bisque, Jointed Body, Sailor Costume, 1915, 17 In. 1800.00
Terri Lee, Connie Lynn, Plastic, Sleep Eyes, Skin Wig, Baby Clothes, Box, 18 In. 625.00
Terri Lee, Garden Party, Plastic, Closed Mouth, Synthetic Wig, 5-Piece Body, 1952, 16 In. 395.00
Terri Lee, Jerri Lee, Hard Plastic, Fleeced Hair, Brown Painted Eyes, c.1957, 16 In. 325.00
Terri Lee, Plastic Head, Painted Eyes, Closed Mouth, 5-Piece Body, Dress, 16 In. 425.00
Terri Lee, Plastic Head, Saran Wig, 5-Piece Body, Organdy Dress, 16 In. . . . . *Illus* 425.00
Terri Lee, Plastic Head, Synthetic Wig, 5-Piece Body, Long Formal, White Coat, 16 In. . . 475.00
Terri Lee, Plastic, Painted Eyes, Synthetic Wig, 5-Piece Body, Sunsuit, Hat, 16 In. 250.00
Terri Lee, Plastic, Platinum Hair, Curly Bangs, Painted Face, Box, c.1955, 16 In. 700.00
Terri Lee, Tiny Terri Lee, Hard Plastic, Socket Head, Sleep Eyes, Box, c.1958, 10 In. 300.00
Tete Jumeau, Bisque Socket Head, Ecru Dress, Lady, 20 In. 3100.00
Uncle Sam, Papier-Mache Head, Glass Eyes, Stockinet Body, Wool Jacket, 22 In. 1725.00
Unis, 60, Bisque Socket Head, Sleep Eyes, Mohair Wig, 5-Piece Composition, 9 1/2 In. . . 775.00
Ventriloquist Dummy, Painted, Applied Wool Hair, 20 x 7 1/2 In. 750.00
Vogue, Ginny, Braids, Hard Plastic Body, Box, 1955, 7 In. 375.00
Vogue, Ginny, Coronation Queen, Plastic Head, Sleep Eyes, 5-Piece Body, Crown, 7 In. . . 725.00
Vogue, Ginny, Plastic, Socket Head, Sleep Eyes, Auburn Braids, Ski Suit, c.1950, 8 In. . . . 150.00
Vogue, Ginny, Sweetheart, Plastic Head, Brown Sleep Eyes, Taffeta Dress, 1949, 8 In. . . . 655.00
Vogue, Toddles, Uncle Sam & Miss America, Composition, 7 1/2 In., Pair . . . . *Illus* 770.00
Wax, Closed Mouth, Ringlet Wig, Cloth Body, Papier-Mache Lower Arms & Legs, 11 In. 225.00
Wax, Downcast Pouty Expression, Child, Original Costume, c.1880, 22 In. 1200.00
Wax, Over Papier-Mache, Green Bonnet Over Mohair Curls, Cloth Body, 16 In. . . . 250.00
Wax, Shoulder Head, Blond, Cloth Body, Papier-Mache Arms & Legs, 16 In. 325.00
Wax, Shoulder Head, Glass Eyes, Cloth Body, Wax Arms & Legs, Blouse & Skirt, 20 In. . 350.00

Doll, Vogue, Toddles, Uncle Sam & Miss America,
Composition, 7 1/2 In., Pair

**Don't let anyone smoke near your
antique dolls. The nicotine residue
is harmful and the odor of the
smoke is objectionable.**

Wolfe, 152, Bisque Head, Sleep Eyes, Open Mouth, Bent-Limb Baby, 1920, 23 In. 575.00
Wooden, Abbess, Painted Features, Skull Cap, Articulated Body, c.1810, 5 In. 500.00
Wooden, Carved Head, Painted Eyes & Hair, Cloth Body, Print Dress, 20 In. 800.00
Wooden, Carved, Black Enamel Inset Eyes, Articulated Legs, c.1790, 16 In. 2200.00
DOLL CLOTHES, Barbie, American Airlines Stewardess Outfit, No. 984, Box, 1961-1964 . . . 120.00
Barbie, Apple Print Sheath, No. 917, Box, 1959 . . . . 420.00
Barbie, Benefit Performance, Red Tunic, Tulle Skirt, No. 1667, Box, 1967 . . . . 275.00
Barbie, Bride's Dream Outfit, Gown, Accessories, No. 947, Box, 1964 . . . . 230.00
Barbie, Busy Gal, Red Linen Suit, Accessories, No. 981, Box, c.1960 . . . . 150.00
Barbie, Campus Sweetheart, No. 1616, Box 264.00
Barbie, Commuter Set, Navy Knit Suit, Accessories, No. 916, Box, 1959 . . . . 303.00
Barbie, Debutante Ball Outfit, Box, 1966-1967 . . . . 1000.00
Barbie, Debutante Ball, No. 1666, Box 235.00
Barbie, Enchantment Evening, Pink Gown, Fur Stole, No. 983, Box, c.1961 . . . . 575.00
Barbie, Evening Enchantment, Red Chiffon Dress, Fur Trim, No. 1695, Box, 1967 . . . . . 250.00
Barbie, Fashion Luncheon, Pink Dress, Jacket, Accessories, No. 1656, Box, 1966 . . . . . . 1200.00
Barbie, Fraternity Dance Outfit, Fuchsia Chiffon Gown, No. 1638, Box, 1965 . . . . 175.00
Barbie, Fun n' Games, Rainbow Striped Dress, No. 1619, Box, 1965 . . . . 180.00
Barbie, Fun On Ice, Gold Pants, Sweater, Skates, No. 791, Box 75.00
Barbie, Garden Tea Party, Print Dress, Accessories, No. 1606, Box, 1964 . . . . 170.00
Barbie, Gay Parisienne, Navy Pindot Bubble Dress, No. 964, Box, 1959 . . . . 900.00
Barbie, Gold 'n' Glamour, Gold Woven Suit, Fur Trim, No. 1647, Box, 1965 . . . . 625.00
Barbie, Golden Evening, Knit Top, Long Skirt, No. 1610, Box, 1964 . . . . 225.00
Barbie, Golden Glory, Gold Damask Gown, Accessories, No. 1645, Box, 1965 . . . . 350.00
Barbie, Guinevere, Cobalt Velour Dress, Accessories, No. 0873, Box, 1964 . . . . 413.00
Barbie, Japanese Outfit, Red Kimono, No. 0821, Accessories, Box, 1964 . . . . 200.00
Barbie, Learns To Cook, Print Dress, Pots & Pans, No. 1634, Box, 1965 . . . . 605.00
Barbie, Midnight Blue, Pink Variation, No. 1617, Box 2820.00
Barbie, Miss Astronaut, No. 1641 . . . . 323.00
Barbie, Nighty Negligee Set, No. 965, Box, c.1960 . . . . 280.00
Barbie, Outdoor Art Show, Sheath Dress, Accessories, No. 1650, Box, 1967 . . . . 325.00
Barbie, Picnic, Denim Jeans, Checked Shirt, Accessories, No. 967, Box, c.1960 . . . . 450.00
Barbie, Plantation Belle, Organdy Dress, Accessories, No. 966, Box, c.1960 . . . . 230.00
Barbie, Red Flare, Red Velvet Coat, Hat, Accessories, No. 939, Box 135.00
Barbie, Roman Holiday, Dress, Striped Bodice & Jacket, No. 968, Box, 1959 . . . . 800.00
Barbie, Satin n' Rose, Bolero Jacket, Skirt, Accessories, No. 1611, Box 300.00
Barbie, Senior Prom Formal, Green Satin & Tulle Gown, No. 951, Box, 1964 . . . . 220.00
Barbie, Shimmering Magic, Silver Lame Dress, Satin Coat, No. 1664, Box, 1966 . . . . 500.00
Barbie, Skater's Waltz, Pink Body Suit, Skates, No. 1629, Box, 1965 . . . . 325.00
Barbie, Solo In The Spotlight, Black Gown, Accessories, No. 982, Box, 1962 . . . . 330.00
Barbie, Sophisticated Lady, Pink Taffeta Gown, Accessories, No. 993, Box, 1964 . . . . 150.00
Barbie, Sorbonne, Green Vest, Skirt, Striped Top, No. 1679, Box, 1967 . . . . 675.00
Barbie, Sweater Girl, Orange Sweater, Gray Skirt, No. 976, Box, c.1960 . . . . 350.00
Barbie, Wedding Day, No. 972, Box, 1959-1962 . . . . 170.00
Barbie, White Magic, White Satin Coat, Accessories, No. 1607, Box 275.00
Barbie, Winter Holiday, Leggings, Pullover, Parka, No. 975, 1959 . . . . 330.00
Case, Barbie, Perk Up, Red Vinyl, Zipper, 1964 . . . . 100.00
Ginny, Blue Flocked Robe, Nightgown, Slippers, No. 462, Box, 1955 . . . . 138.00
Ginny, Blue Organdy Dress, Lace, Accessories, No. 25, Box, 1953 . . . . 303.00
Ginny, Denim Shorts, Checked Shirt, Straw Hat, No. 670, Box, 1954 . . . . 303.00
Ginny, Dotted Raincoat, Umbrella, No. 6182, 1956 . . . . 77.00
Ginny, Floral Nightgown, No. 186, 1955 . . . . 44.00
Ginny, Gray Borgana Coat, Beret, Muff, No. 6186, Box, 1956 . . . . 77.00
Ginny, Green Velvet & Satin Dress, Accessories, No. 30, Box, 1952 . . . . 193.00
Ginny, Green Velvet Coat, Hat, Purse, No. 6183, 1956 . . . . 44.00
Ginny, Pink Cotton Sun Suit, Lace Trim, No. 127, Box 1954 . . . . 55.00
Ginny, Purple Velveteen Skating Costume, Accessories, No. 347, Box, 1956 . . . . 385.00
Ginny, Red Dress, Heart Lace Trim, Accessories, No. 6124, Box, 1956 . . . . 275.00
Ginny, Red Polka Dot Dress, Accessories, No. 132, Box, 1954 . . . . 440.00
Ginny, Tan Jodhpurs, Shirt, Riding Hat, Accessories, No. 6131, 1956 . . . . 77.00
Ginny, White Fur Coat, Beret, Muff, No. 6184, 1956 . . . . 99.00
Ken, Arabian Nights, Red Velvet Coat, Turban, No. 0774, Box, 1964 . . . . 225.00
Ken, Drum Major, No. 0775, Box, 1964-1965 . . . . 150.00

Ken, Graduation, Black Robe, Accessories, No. 795, Box, 1963-1964 .... 40.00
Ken, In Hawaii, Sarong, Accessories, No. 1404, Box, 1964 .... 130.00
Ken, In Mexico, Bolero Jacket, Sombrero, Accessories, No. 0778, Box, 1964 .... 300.00
Ken, In Switzerland, Lederhosen, Accessories, No. 0776, Box, 1964 .... 150.00
Ken, King Arthur, No. 0773, Box, 1964-1965 .... 300.00
Ken, Masquerade, Clown Suit, Accessories, No. 794, Box, 1963 .... 110.00
Ken, Prince Outfit, Green Brocade Jacket, Accessories, No. 0772, Box, 1964 .... 300.00
Ken, Sailor, No. 796, Box, 1963-1964 .... 130.00
Ken, Ski Champion, Black Pants, Red Jacket, Accessories, No. 798, Box, 1963 .... 190.00
Ken, Time For Tennis, No. 790, Box, 1962 .... 120.00
Ken, Tuxedo, No. 787, Box, 1961-1965 .... 250.00
Ken, Victory Dance, Blazer, Pants, Accessories, No. 1411, Box, 1964 .... 170.00
Skipper, Fancy Pants, Ruffled Pants, Vinyl Top, No. 1738, Box, 1970 .... 60.00
Skipper, Flower Girl, Yellow Dress, Floral Headband, No. 1904, Box, 1965 .... 110.00
Skipper, Lemon Fluff, Yellow Pajamas, No. 1749, Box, 1970 .... 90.00
Skipper, Rainy Day Checkers, Plaid Dress, Accessories, No. 1928, Box, 1966 .... 80.00
Skipper, Town Togs, Green Jumper, Jacket, Accessories, No. 1922, Box, 1966 .... 80.00
Skipper, Twice As Nice, Dress, Coat, Cap, No. 1735, Box, 1970 .... 70.00

DONALD DUCK items are included in the Disneyana category.

DOORSTOPS have been made in all types of designs. The vast majority of the doorstops sold today are cast iron and were made from about 1890 to 1930. Most of them are shaped like people, animals, flowers, or ships. Reproductions and newly designed examples are sold in gift shops.

2 Cats, Cast Iron, 7 In. 385.00
Basket Of Flowers, Painted, Polychrome Flowers, Marked B&H, 8 3/4 In. 220.00
Bear, Standing, With Honey, Cast Iron, 15 In. 2970.00
Bear, Standing, With Honey, Painted, Cast Iron, 15 1/2 In. 3630.00
Bellhop, Cast Iron, 9 In. 412.00
Bird, Cast Iron, 8 In. 297.00
Brick, 2 Frogs, Stark Brick Co., 7 3/4 x 4 3/4 In. 385.00
Burns Plows, Farmer Plowing Field, 2 Horses, Cast Iron, 11 1/2 In. 455.00
Cat, Black, Cast Iron, 9 1/2 In. 165.00
Cat, Cast Iron, 7 1/2 In. ....95.00 to 148.00
Cat, Cast Iron, 12 1/2 In. 176.00
Cat, Halloween, A.M. Greenblatt Studio, Cast Iron, 1927, 9 In. 715.00
Cat, Plaster, 1930s, 12 In. 95.00
Cat, Seated, Black, Green Eyes, 7 In. 488.00
Cat, Sitting, Cast Iron, 12 1/2 In. 302.00
Cat, Sitting, Hubley 325.00
Cat, White, Hubley 90.00
Clown, Cast Iron, 10 1/2 In. 605.00
Colonial Woman, With Fan, Marked WS, 9 1/2 In. 330.00
Cottage, Dark Green Roof, Painted, Cast Iron, Hubley, 8 In. 143.00
Cottage, With Fence, Cast Iron, 8 In. 302.00
Dog, 2 Scotty Dogs, 6 1/2 x 9 In. 115.00
Dog, Black & White Setter, Cast Iron, 8 3/4 x 15 3/4 In. 235.00
Dog, Boston Terrier, Black, White, Cast Iron, 9 3/4 In. ....75.00 to 150.00
Dog, Boxer, Full Figure, 10 1/2 x 10 1/2 In. 137.00
Dog, Bulldog, Cast Iron, 5 x 8 1/2 In. 57.00
Dog, Bulldog, Hubley, Cast Iron, 9 In. 385.00
Dog, Cocker Spaniel, Black, White, Cast Iron, 7 x 11 In. ....258.00 to 385.00
Dog, Fido, On Pillow, Cast Iron, 7 1/2 In. 412.00
Dog, German Shepherd, Cast Iron, 10 1/2 In. 330.00
Dog, Irish Setter, Full Figure, Cast Iron, 15 1/2 In. 275.00
Dog, Scotty, Black Paint, Cast Iron, 6 1/4 x 8 3/4 In. 172.00
Dog, Scotty, Black, 8 3/4 x 10 1/2 In. 155.00
Dog, Scotty, Cast Iron 9 In. 412.00
Dog, Setter, Cast Iron, 13 1/2 In. 302.00
Dog, Springer Spaniel, Cast Iron, 7 In. 275.00
Dog, Taylor Cook, Cast Iron, 1930, 7 1/2 In. 1100.00

Dog, Terrier, Cast Iron, 9 In. 247.00
Drum Major, Red & White Uniform, Cast Iron, 13 In. . . . . .143.00 to 275.00
Duck, With Beetle, Cast Iron, 10 1/2 In. 1320.00
Dutch Girl, Full Figured, Cast Iron, 4 x 2 In. 57.00
Dutch Girl With Water Pails, Cast Iron, 7 In. 184.00
Eagle, Spread Wings, On Rocky Perch, American Shield Front, 7 1/2 In. 330.00
Elephant, Cast Iron, 8 1/4 In. . . . . .132.00 to 175.00
Elf, Iron, c.1870, 10 In. 403.00
Fawn, Cast Iron, 10 In. 385.00
Flower Basket, Blue Bow, Wicker Basket, Cast Iron, 10 In. 121.00
Flower Basket, Girl, Bradley & Hubbard, Cast Iron, 11 In. 115.00
Flower Basket, Pink Bow, White Basket, Cast Iron, 10 In. 165.00
Flower Basket, Rope Handle, Cast Iron, 9 3/4 In. 187.00
Fox Head, Brown Paint, Cast Iron, 5 1/2 x 5 In. 413.00
Fruit & Flower Bowl, Painted, Cast Iron, 7 In. 55.00
George Washington, Painted, Cast Iron, 12 In. 60.00
Giraffe, Hubley, Cast Iron, 13 In. 3190.00
Giraffe, Stylized Figure, Brown Accents, Cast Iron, 16 1/2 In. 2415.00
Girl, Flowers, Cast Iron, 9 1/2 In. 1210.00
Girl, Holding Doll, Hubley, Cast Iron, 10 In. 345.00
Girl, Holding Flowers, Polychrome, Cast Iron, Early 1900s, 7 3/4 In. 245.00
Girl, Peasant, Holding Flowers, Painted, Cast Iron, 11 In. 275.00
Gnome, Marked Nick Bros., Inc., Reading, Penna., Cast Iron, 13 1/2 In. 303.00
Gnome, Standing, Cast Iron, 13 1/2 In. 154.00
Horse, Cast Iron, 8 In. 385.00
Horse, Cast Iron, 10 1/2 In. 187.00
Horse, Prancing, Cast Iron, c.1860 . . . . 1250.00
Humpty Dumpty, Painted, Cast Iron, 9 In. 3920.00
Kittens, In Basket, Cast Iron, 7 In. 247.00
Kittens, On Book, Cast Iron, Bradley & Hubbard, 5 In. 715.00
Lion, Flowing Mane, On Stepped, Scrolled Base, Black Paint, 15 x 10 x 2 1/2 In. 230.00
Lion, Gold Paint, Full Figure, Cast Iron, 6 1/2 In. 46.00
Lion, Splayed Feet, Cast Iron, 8 In. 247.00
Little Red Riding Hood, Wolf, National Foundry, Cast Iron, 7 x 5 In. 545.00
Owl, On Books, Eastern Specialty Co., Cast Iron, 9 1/2 In. 770.00
Panther, Cast Iron, 9 In. 357.00
Parrot, Bright Color Paint, Cast Iron, Early 1900s, 7 1/2 In. 250.00
Parrot, On Tree Stump, Cast Iron, 14 In. . . . . .200.00 to 247.00
Parrot, Red, Blue, Orange, Green, Black, Cast Iron, Late 1800s, 7 3/4 x 5 1/4 In. 350.00
Peacock, Cast Iron, 6 1/2 In. 302.00
Peacock, Cast Iron, 8 In. 357.00
Peacock, Fanned Tail Feathers, Polychrome, Cast Iron, Early 1900s 225.00
Peacock, Polychrome Paint, Cast Iron, Early 1900s 350.00
Penguin, Top Hat, Cast Iron, 10 In. 412.00
Pheasant, Hubley, Cast Iron, 9 In. 467.00
Pirate, Cast Iron, 7 In. 55.00
Quail, Cast Iron, 7 1/2 In. 605.00
Rabbit, Cast Iron, 12 In. 770.00
Rabbit, Cast Iron, Bradley & Hubbard, 15 In. 1595.00
Rabbit, Cast Iron, White Paint, 11 1/2 In. 302.00
Rabbit, Full Figure, White Paint, Cast Iron, 12 In. 525.00
Ram, Black Paint, Cast Iron, 7 x 9 1/2 In., Pair 345.00
Rooster, Cast Iron, 12 In. 495.00
Rumba Dancer, Cast Iron, 11 In. 742.00
Seahorse, Renaissance Style, Bronze, Late 19th Century, 11 1/4 In. 230.00
Skunk, Cast Iron, 8 In. 900.00
Soldier, Revolutionary War, Cast Iron, 14 In. . . . . .150.00 to 264.00
Soldier On Horse, Brass Plated Iron, 10 x 10 In. 69.00
Southern Bell, Carrying Hat & Flowers, Cast Iron, 11 1/2 In. 165.00
Squirrel, Black Paint, Bradley & Hubbard, Cast Iron, 10 3/4 In. 495.00
Squirrel, Bradley & Hubbard, 11 1/8 In. 550.00
Squirrel, Cast Iron, 6 1/2 In. 300.00
Squirrel, Cast Iron, 11 1/2 In. 1430.00

Squirrel, Half-Round Base, 6 3/4 In.	330.00
Squirrel, Sitting On Log, Bradley & Hubbard, 11 In.	110.00
Sunbonnet Girl, Cast Iron	325.00
Swallows, In Berries, Cast Iron, 8 1/2 In.	200.00 to 385.00
Tulips In Vase, White Vase, Painted, Cast Iron, 9 1/2 In.	220.00
Warrior, Painted, Bradley & Hubbard, Cast Iron, 13 In.	550.00
Whale, Cast Iron, 13 In.	242.00
Woman, Tropical Fruit, Cast Iron 11 1/2 In.	330.00

DORCHESTER POTTERY was founded by George Henderson in 1895 in Dorchester, Massachusetts. At first, the firm made utilitarian stoneware, but collectors are most interested in the line of decorated blue and white pottery that Dorchester made from 1940 until it went out of business in 1979.

**DORCHESTER
POTTERY WORKS
BOSTON, MASS.**

Bowl, Handles, Half Scroll, 3 x 7 1/4 In.	110.00
Bowl, Rooster With Details, Elephant In Satire Setting, 2 x 6 In., Pair	360.00
Candleholder, Half Scroll, Cobalt Blue, 2 x 5 In.	55.00
Casserole, Cover, Half Scroll, 5 1/2 x 7 In.	220.00
Casserole, Cover, Pinecone, 4 x 7 1/4 In.	165.00
Casserole, Half Scroll, 3 x 5 1/2 In.	80.00
Crock, Stylized Berry & Vine Design, Twirling Tendril, 9 3/4 x 7 In.	165.00
Dish, Blueberry, Ruffled, 1 1/2 x 6 1/2 In.	165.00
Jar, Colonial Lace, Sgraffito, 2 Handles, 5 1/4 x 5 In.	138.00
Perfume Bottle, Teardrop, Medium Blue, Cobalt Blue Glaze, 5 x 3 3/4 In.	330.00
Pitcher, Flowers, Sgraffito, 4 x 5 In.	165.00
Pitcher, Grape, Cobalt Blue, Vines, 6 1/2 x 6 1/2 In.	195.00
Pitcher, Pussy Willow, 4 1/4 x 6 In.	110.00
Pitcher, Rooster, Knesseth Denisons, 2 1/8 x 3 1/4 In.	55.00
Plate, Bird, Knesseth Denisons, 6 1/2 In.	90.00
Plate, Ship, Knesseth Denisons, 7 1/2 In.	275.00
Soap Dish, Half Scroll, 1 1/2 x 5 1/2 In.	165.00
Sugar, Dog, Jackie Burn Callder, 3 1/2 x 3 In.	110.00
Sugar & Creamer, Whale, 3 1/4 x 3 1/4 In.	99.00
Syrup, Full Scroll, 5 x 4 In., Pair	110.00

DOULTON pottery and porcelain were made by Doulton and Co. of Burslem, England, after 1882. The name *Royal Doulton* appeared on their wares after 1902. Other pottery by Doulton is listed under Royal Doulton.

Beaker, Cobalt Relief Leaf Band, White Berries, Silver Rim, 2 In.	150.00
Beaker, Green Cover, Tan Salt Glaze, Hunting Scene, Miniature, 1 3/4 In.	48.00
Biscuit Barrel, Sherry, Blue, Brown Filigree, Raised Letters, Signed, 11 x 8 In.	2990.00
Biscuit Jar, Floral Transfer, White Ground, Silver Cover, Handle, Burslem	80.00
Biscuit Jar, Flowers, Gold Trim, Flow Blue, Burslem, 6 1/2 In.	94.00
Biscuit Jar, Goats, Dog, Silver Plated Mount, Hannah Barlow, Lambeth, 1879, 5 7/8 In.	720.00
Biscuit Jar, Silver Plate, Cover, Stoneware, Hannah Barlow, Lambeth, 1879, 6 In.	3000.00
Bottle, Blue Cover, Tan Salt Glaze Bottom, Raised White Decoration, 3 1/2 In.	60.00
Bowl, Lions Against Basket Weave, Oval, Marshall & Roberts, Lambeth, 6 1/2 In.	440.00
Candlestick, Stoneware, Arthur B. Barlow, Lambeth, 1873, 11 1/4 In.	2040.00
Centerpiece, Art Nouveau Style, Stoneware, Frank Butler, Lambeth, c.1890, 22 1/2 In.	2160.00
Cheese Stand, Victorian Children Playing With Dog, Burslem, 2 1/4 In.	32.00
Clock Case, Shell Pediment, Stoneware, Lambeth, 1882, 12 1/4 In.	3600.00
Coffeepot, Cover, Stoneware, Lambeth, Arthur B. Barlow, 1875, 9 3/8 In.	1020.00
Creamer, Impressed Flowers, Cobalt Handle, Rim, 4 1/4 In.	90.00
Creamer, Salt Glaze, Man Seated On Barrel, Tree, Windmill, Silver Trim, 3 1/4 In.	50.00
Cup, Bread At Pleasure, Drink By Measure, 3 Handles, 6 In.	200.00
Dish, Oval, Cobalt Glaze, Brown & Yellow Flowers, Ruffled Rim, Holes, 2 1/2 x 4 In.	40.00
Ewer, Flowers, Leaves, Berries, Textured Yellow Body, Squat, Burslem, 7 1/2 In.	130.00
Ewer, Hounds, Fox, Stoneware, Hannah B. Barlow, Lambeth, 1875, 8 3/4 In.	960.00
Ewer, Leafy Neck, Stalk Handle, Stoneware, Frank A. Butler, Lambeth, 1890s, 19 In.	2040.00
Ewer, Pink & Yellow Flowers, Green & Mulberry Leaves, Burslem, 10 3/4 In.	120.00
Figurine, Frog, Canoeist, Stoneware, George Tinworth, Lambeth, c.1885, 5 In.	3360.00
Figurine, Nude Woman Mending Nets, White Glaze, Brown Speckles, 9 1/2 In.	3000.00

Figurine, Waning Of The Honeymoon, Stoneware, G. Tinworth, Lambeth, c.1890, 5 In. ... 3000.00
Inkstand, Ducks In Rushes, Flower, Wheat, Cobalt Spout, Foot, Hinged Lid, 6 In. 2200.00
Inkwell, Vertical Ribs, Incised Flowers, Leaves, Lambeth, 2 1/2 x 4 In. 180.00
Jar, Cover, Horses, Stoneware, Hannah Barlow, Lambeth, 1880s, 10 5/8 In. 1020.00
Jardiniere, Relief Flower Heads, Brown Border, Cobalt Rim, 3 Handles, Feet, 7 In. 220.00
Jug, Bellflower Relief On Neck & Shoulder, Reeded Handle, Lambeth, 4 1/2 In. 90.00
Jug, Horizontal Ribs, Flowers, Incised Branches, Buff Body, Swivel Cover, 7 In. 130.00
Jug, Incised Vertical Ribs, Flower Heads On Handle, Bulbous, Lambeth, 3 In. 40.00
Jug, Lend More Than Thou Owest, Ribbed, Paw Feet, 3 In. 90.00
Jug, Molded, Polychrome, Daisies, Blue, Green Leaves, Signed, 11 1/2 In. 58.00
Jug, Tan, Brown Glaze, Ribs, Relief Flower Bands, Silver Hinged Cover, Lambeth, 9 In. . 140.00
Jug, Those Who Have Money Are Troubled About It, 8 1/4 In. 160.00
Jug, Twixt The Cup & The Lip, There's Many A Slip, 6 3/4 In. 130.00
Match Holder, Beehive Shape, Basketweave, Applied Bees, Silver Rim, 2 In. 315.00
Menu Holder, School Board, Mouse Group, G. Tinworth, Lambeth, c.1886, 3 1/2 In. 2700.00
Mug, Good Measure, Heavens Treasure, Merry Meet, Merry Part, 5 1/4 In. 120.00
Mug, Rabbits, Stoneware, Hannah B. Barlow, Lambeth, 1879, 4 1/4 In. 2040.00
Mug, Sheep & Lambs, Blue, Buff, White Beaded Border, Leaves On Handle, 4 3/4 In. ... 500.00
Mustard Pot, Barrel Shape, Silver Plated Cover, Spoon, 2 1/2 In. 120.00
Pitcher, Flowers, Globular Form, Frank Butler, 7 3/4 In. 411.00
Pitcher, Isthmian Game, Green & Black Transfer, Bulbous, Burslem, 5 x 7 3/4 In. 126.00
Pitcher & Bowl, Watteau, Flow Blue 1000.00
Plaque, Terracotta, Barabbas, Peter, Frame, Late 19th Century, 12 3/4, 11 3/4 In., Pair ... 2700.00
Pot, Buff Body, Blue Berries, Circles, Leaves, Lambeth, 3 x 4 In. 90.00
Pot, Morning Glory, Cobalt Blue, White, Stoneware, Silver Handle, Burslem, 3 In. 145.00
Punch Bowl, Iris, Blue & White, 8 x 14 In. 316.00
Saltshaker, Stoneware, Betrayal, Crucifixion, G. Tinworth, Lambeth, c.1871, 4 In. 3000.00
Shaker, Bird Shape, Blue Glaze, Carved Features & Feathers, Lambeth, 4 3/4 In. 475.00
Sugar, Wilcome The Coming, Speed The Parting Guest, 3 1/2 In. 70.00
Table, Moorish Style, Stoneware, Lambeth, c.1900, 28 In. 9000.00
Tea Set, Floral Sprays, Vertical Ribs, Gilt Handles, Trim, 12 Piece 499.00
Teapot, Dame, Kingsware, The Cup That Cheers, Silver Mount Engraving, 6 1/2 In. 152.00
Tile, Stoneware, Frog, Ox, Snakes & Porcupine, c.1882, Lambeth, 5 3/4 In., Pair 3900.00
Tile, Wheelwright Shop, Terra-Cotta, Frame, Lambeth, c.1877, 7 1/2 x 7 3/4 In. 4500.00
Tobacco Jar, Cover, Scroll, Gilt Letters, Brown & Blue Bands, Lambeth, 5 1/4 In. 165.00
Tobacco Jar, Motto, Brown, Tan Salt Glaze, Cover, Lambeth, 6 In. 71.00
Tobacco Jar, Smoker In Skullcap, Silver Rim, 4 3/4 In. 64.00
Tobacco Jar, Stag Hunt Scene, Light & Dark Brown, Salt Glaze, Cover, 5 In. 70.00
Trivet, Salt Glaze, Applied White Toby, Hounds, Brown Trim, 6 1/4 In. 70.00
Vase, 2 Chrysanthemums, Ocher Leaves & Stems, Cobalt Border, 12 In. 225.00
Vase, 8 Sides, Chinese Dragon Handles, Francis Pope, Lambeth, 1870s, 11 In. 410.00
Vase, Bellflowers, Stoneware, Eliza Simmance, Lambeth, 1890s, 12 3/4 In., Pair 2160.00
Vase, Birds, Flowers, Oval, Harry Nixon, Flambe, 7 In. 940.00
Vase, Blue, Green & Yellow Glaze, Relief Flowers, Bulbous, 2 Handles, Lambeth, 5 In. ... 110.00
Vase, Bottle, Dragon, Stoneware, Francis C. Pope, 1922, 9 1/4 In. 660.00
Vase, Bottle, Quintuple, Stoneware, Frank A. Butler, Lambeth, 1878, 10 1/2 In. 1020.00
Vase, Brown, Green Salt Glaze, Handle To Rear, Lambeth, 6 In. 71.00
Vase, Bud, Bands Of Stars, Leaves, Berries, Mottled Ocher, Bulbous, 7 In. 110.00
Vase, Children, Flowers, Blue Ground, Flared Rim, Pedestal Foot, Lambeth, 5 In. 120.00
Vase, Commemorative, Queen Victoria, Stoneware, Lambeth, c.1887, 9 1/4 In. 2760.00
Vase, Cows, Landscape, Incised, Baluster, Hannah Barlow, 19 In. 978.00
Vase, Crowned Heads At Base, Stoneware, Mark V. Marshall, Lambeth, 1880, 12 1/4 In. . 2040.00
Vase, Deer In Landscape, Blue, Green, Brown On White, Triangles, Beads, 7 1/4 In. 525.00
Vase, Donkeys, Stoneware, Hannah B. Barlow, Lambeth, 1880s, 12 3/8 In. 840.00
Vase, Dragon At Neck, Lambeth, 1879, 10 5/8 In. 1200.00
Vase, Dragon, Stoneware, Mark V. Marshall, Lambeth, c.1900, 9 1/4 In. 5400.00
Vase, Dragons, Clouds, Stoneware, Lambeth, 1890s, 14 3/8 In. 2040.00
Vase, Faience, 4 Ladies, Billowing Dresses, Lambeth, c.1910, 16 In. 1560.00
Vase, Faience, Blackberries, Mary M. Arding, Lambeth, 1880s, 9 1/2 In. 1080.00
Vase, Faience, Fish Swimming, Waves, Lambeth, c.1900, 21 In. 4200.00
Vase, Faience, Magnolia, Blue Ground, No. 493, Helen A. Arding, Lambeth, 1880, 10 In. .. 720.00
Vase, Faience, Plums, Insects, Mary Butterton, Lambeth, 17 In. 420.00
Vase, Faience, White Apple Blossom, Ocher Shaded To Yellow, Flared Rim, 8 In. 375.00

Vase, Faience, White Flowers, Green & Brown Leaves, Cobalt Ground, 6 In. 120.00
Vase, Faience, Yellow Poppies, Turquoise Neck, Footed, Flared Rim, 8 In. 95.00
Vase, Fish, Seaweed, Stoneware, Eliz Simance, Lambeth, 1890s, 16 In. 2040.00
Vase, Flowers, Oval, Arthur Leslie Harradine, Lambeth, 10 In. 380.00
Vase, Glazed, Fleur-De-Lis, Stoneware, No. 564, Mark V. Marshall, 1907, 13 1/4 In. 1560.00
Vase, Gourd, Art Nouveau, Grapes, Leaves, Swirled Ribs, Mottled Green, 8 In. 60.00
Vase, Green, Mulberry, Blue, White Glaze, Incised Flowers, Beading, Lambeth, 6 In. 180.00
Vase, Horse, Stags, Hannah B. Barlow, Lambeth, 1890s, 16 1/8 In. 6600.00
Vase, Horses & Donkeys In Landscape, Brown & Blue On White, Stippled, 10 In. 625.00
Vase, Horses At Pasture, Brown Slip On White Ground, Blue & Olive Border, 9 In. 675.00
Vase, Horses, Incised, Scrolls, Green, Brown, Beige, Hannah Barlow, 16 In. 633.00
Vase, Impasto, Florence C. Roberts, Rosa Keen, Lambeth, 1884, 20 1/8 In. 1080.00
Vase, King & Queen, Coronation, Polychrome Medallions, Lambeth, 11 x 5 1/2 In. 345.00
Vase, Landscape, Running Deer, Hannah Barlow, 1873, 6 1/2 In. 705.00
Vase, Leaves, Seed Pod, Stoneware, Eliza Simmance, Lambeth, 1890s, 15 5/8 In. 1020.00
Vase, Painted, Flowers, D. Dewsberry, Burslem, c.1889, 25 3/4 In. 3000.00
Vase, Ponies, Stoneware, Hannah B. Barlow, Lambeth, 1880, Pair 1320.00
Vase, Ponies, Stoneware, N. 939, Hannah B. Barlow, Early 20th Century, 11 In. 720.00
Vase, Rabbit, Stoneware, Mark V. Marshall, Lambeth, 1880s, 8 In. 3240.00
Vase, Rembrandt Ware, Portrait, W. Nunn, Burslem, c.1910, 13 1/4 In. 510.00
Vase, Sheep Scene, Signed, Lambeth, 14 In. 1150.00
Vase, Sheep, Stoneware, Hannah B. Barlow, Lambeth, 1880s, 21 1/4 In. 1800.00
Vase, Spill, Mouse, Stoneware, G. Tinworth, Marked, Lambeth, c.1885, 3 1/2 In. 840.00
Vase, Stoneware, 2 Handles, Mark V. Marshall, Lambeth, 1890s, 10 1/2 In. 660.00
Vase, Stylized Trees, Stoneware, Frank A. Butler, Lambeth, 1890s, 16 1/2 In. 2160.00
Vase, Tube Lined, Flowers, Leaves, Stoneware, Frank Bulter, Lambeth, 1890s, 12 1/2 In. . . 1020.00
Vase, Tube Lined, Flowers, Seed Pods, Cell Pattern Ground, Lambeth, 1890s, 17 1/4 In. . . 3000.00
Vase, Tube Lined, Owl Masks, Stoneware, Mark V. Marshall, Lambeth, 1890s, 7 7/8 In. . . 1680.00
Vase, White Flowers, Rose, Yellow, Green Shading, Burslem, 9 In. 110.00
Vase, White, Stoneware, Harry Simeon, Lambeth, Early 20th Century, 18 3/4 In. 2160.00
Vase, Winged Fairies, Purple Ground, Stamped Doulton, Lambeth, England, 8 In. 1495.00
Vase, Wolves Among Leaves, Blue Slip, Buff Ground, Lambeth, 8 1/2 In. 350.00

DRESDEN china is any china made in the town of Dresden, Germany.
The most famous factory in Dresden is the Meissen factory. Figurines
of eighteenth-century ladies and gentlemen, animal groups, or cherubs
and other mythological subjects were popular. One special type of figurine was made with skirts of porcelain-dipped lace. Do not make the
mistake of thinking that all pieces marked *Dresden* are from the Meissen factory. The Meissen pieces usually have crossed swords marks,
and are listed under Meissen. Some recent porcelain from Ireland,
called *Irish Dresden*, is not included in this book.

Bowl, Applied Flowers, 4 Cherubs Support, Mid 20th Century, 5 1/2 x 13 In. 252.00
Bowl, Domed Lid, Alternating Flower Sprays, Blue Ground, 5 1/2 x 7 1/4 In. 145.00
Bowl, Pierced Body, Applied Flowers, Loop Handles, 20th Century, 4 x 11 1/2 In. 145.00
Chocolate Pot, Flowers, Gilt Urns, Feathered Handle, 1901-1930, 10 x 7 In. 95.00
Chocolate Pot, Flowers, Hand Painted, Gilt Rim, 5 3/4 x 8 1/2 In. 175.00
Clock, Figural, Encrusted With Flowers, Putti At Various Pursuits, 1900, 27 In. 7200.00
Compote, Dish, Footed, 6 In., 2 1/2 In., 2 Piece 300.00
Dessert Set, Painted Flowers, Reticulated, 8 1/2 In., 4 Piece 200.00
Figurine, 2 Women, Mischievous, 18th Century Dress, 11 In. 460.00
Figurine, 4 Horses Pulling Coach, Driver, Dogs, c.1945, 13 In. 750.00
Figurine, Allegorical, Figure Of Britannia With Lion At Her Feet, 14 In. 630.00
Figurine, Dog, Spaniel, Seated, Scratching Chin With Back Leg, 8 1/4 In. 520.00
Figurine, Lady & Men Playing Instruments, Dancing Couple, 20 x 10 x 10 In. 1200.00
Figurine, Woman In Pink Lace Dress, 5 3/4 In. 60.00
Inkstand, 2 Wells, Reticulated Lid, Berry Finial, Ivy Vines, Oval Stand, 1920s, 10 In. . . . 1092.00
Inkwell, Overall Gilt, Swan Form, 3 1/4 In. 175.00
Lamp, 4 Female Dancers, Silk Hand-Stitched Shade, Blue Mark, c.1900 . . . . 530.00
Plate, Floral Garlands, Center Floral Spray, c.1900, 10 In., 6 Piece 365.00
Plateau, Mirrored, 3 Tiers, Triangular Supports, 12 x 11 In. 115.00
Sugar, Domed Oval Cover, Flower Finial, Floral Bouquets, Early 20th Century, 4 In. 86.00
Teapot, Chinese Yi-Hsing, Black, Bamboo Design, Stoneware, 1930s, 6 In. 50.00

Teapot, Domed Cover, Serpentine Spout, Horizontal Ribbing Lower Half, 7 3/4 In. 40.00
Teapot, Gold, Purple Luster Glaze, 4 Women, 2 Men, 6 x 7 In. 450.00
Urn, Domed Cover, 2 Gilt Flying Loop Handles, Trumpet Foot, 14 1/2 In., Pair 690.00

DUNCAN & MILLER is a term used by collectors when referring to glass
made by the George A. Duncan and Sons Company or the Duncan and
Miller Glass Company. These companies worked from 1893 to 1955,
when the use of the name *Duncan* was discontinued and the firm
became part of the United States Glass Company. Early patterns may
be listed under Pressed Glass.

Canterbury, Sugar & Creamer 18.00
First Love, Candlestick, 2-Light, 6 In., Pair 210.00
Sandwich, Candlestick, Pair 45.00
Sandwich, Cruet, 6 1/2 In. 14.00
Sandwich, Plate, 8 In. 12.00
Shell & Tassel, Compote, 8 In. 75.00
Swirl, Compote, Green, 6 5/8 In. 24.00
Swirl, Cup & Saucer, Amber 25.00

DURAND art glass was made from 1924 to 1931. The Vineland Flint
Glass Works was established by Victor Durand and Victor Durand, Jr.,
in 1897. In 1924 Martin Bach, Jr., and other artisans from the Quezal
glassworks joined them at the Vineland, New Jersey, plant to make
Durand art glass.

Bowl, Deep Cranberry, White Pulled Feather, 1 3/4 x 7 In. 170.00
Bowl, Iridescent Blue, Purple Highlights, 6 In. 175.00
Candlestick, Cream, Gold Stripes, Gold Interior, Amber Foot, 10 In. 690.00
Candlestick, King Tut, Gold, Iridescent Blue, Signed, 10 In. 1035.00
Ginger Jar, Cover, Green Pulled Feather, Gold Iridescent, 7 1/2 In. 1840.00
Ginger Jar, Cover, King Tut, Green, Gold, Applied Amber, Signed, 9 In. 4025.00
Goblet, Red, White Pulled Feather, Amber Foot, Engraved Bowl, 5 1/2 In. 315.00
Lamp Base, Blue, White Pulled Feather, Amber, 12 1/2 In. 300.00
Plate, Transparent Blue, Scalloped Edge, 8 1/2 In. 115.00
Torchere, Green & Gold Pulled Heart, Trailing Vine, Leaf & Vine Shade, 21 1/2 In. 2016.00
Vase, Blue, Gold Pulled Feather, Gold Threading, Signed, 12 1/4 In. 1210.00
Vase, Flared Rim, Blue Iridescent, Gold Threading, Flared Rim, Oval, Signed, 8 In. 1265.00
Vase, Gold Iridescent, Gold Threading, 1925, 6 1/4 In. 575.00
Vase, Gold Iridescent, Wide Mouth, Signed, 6 In. 390.00
Vase, Gold, Blue Pulled Heart & Trailing Vine, Signed, 5 1/2 In. 1035.00
Vase, Green Pulled Feather, Amber Iridescent Ground, Signed, 16 1/2 In. 2990.00
Vase, Green Pulled Feather, Blue & White Gold Ground, Footed, 9 1/2 In. 5775.00
Vase, Green Pulled Swirls, Gold Oval, 7 In. 1265.00
Vase, Iridescent Blue, 10 1/2 In. 1265.00
Vase, Iridescent Cobalt Blue, Gold, Pulled Leaves & Vines, Marigold Interior, 11 In. 2415.00
Vase, Iridescent Gold Pulled Swirls, Signed, 6 In. 570.00
Vase, Iridescent Gold, Beehive, Signed, Numbered, 8 1/2 In. 978.00
Vase, Iridescent Gold, Blue, White Pulled Feather, Gold Threading, 12 In. 520.00
Vase, Iridescent Gold, Green Pulled Swirls, 12 In. 1610.00
Vase, Iridescent Gold, Woodland Scene, Cameo, Signed, 14 1/4 In. 4600.00
Vase, Iridescent Orange, White Pulled Feather, Green, Gold Threading, 9 1/2 In. 600.00
Vase, King Tut, Blue, Green Over Gold, 5 3/4 x 4 In. 1065.00
Vase, King Tut, Iridescent Blue, Orange, Gold Interior, 12 1/2 In. 1550.00
Vase, King Tut, Iridescent Orange, Blue, Gold Interior, 9 1/2 In. 1380.00
Vase, Light Pink Highlights, Gold Iridescent, Signed, 6 x 4 1/4 In. 550.00
Vase, Pulled Heart & Trailing Vine, Iridescent Peach, Signed, 1924, 8 In. 985.00
Vase, Trumpet, Iridescent Blue, Gold Foot, Signed, 10 In. 810.00

ELFINWARE is a mark found on Dresden-like porcelain that was sold in
dime stores and gift shops. Many pieces were decorated with raised
flowers. The mark was registered by Breslauer-Underberg, Inc., of
New York City in 1947. Pieces marked *Elfinware Made in Germany*
had been sold since 1945 by this importer.

Elfinware

Figurine, Shoe, High Heel, Forget-Me-Nots, 3 In. 75.00

Figurine, Shoe, High Heel, Green Trim, 3 1/2 x 1 1/4 In. 55.00
Figurine, Shoe, Oxford, Purple Flowers, Forget-Me-Nots, 4 In. 125.00
Figurine, Shoe, Pointed Elf-Like Toe, Flowers, 5 1/4 x 2 1/4 In. 175.00
Slipper, Blue Flowers At Edge, White Rose On Front, 1 1/2 x 3 1/4 In. 135.00

ELVIS PRESLEY, the well-known singer, lived from 1935 to 1977. He
became famous by 1956. Elvis appeared on television, starred in
twenty-seven movies, and performed in Las Vegas. Memorabilia from
any of the Presley shows, his records, and even memorials made after
his death are collected.

Photograph, Elvis, Performing, Candid, 5 x 4 In. 15.00
Record, Jailhouse Rock, 13 x 17 In. 575.00

ENAMELS listed here are made of glass particles and other materials
heated and fused to metal. In the eighteenth and nineteenth centuries,
workmen from Russia, France, England, and other countries made
small boxes and table pieces of enamel on metal. One form of English
enamel is called *Battersea* and is listed under that name. There was a
revival of interest in enameling in the 1930s and a new style evolved.
There is now renewed interest in the artistic enameled plaques, vases,
ashtrays, and jewelry. Enamels made since the 1930s are usually on
copper or steel, although silver was often used for jewelry. Graniteware is a separate category, and enameled metal kitchen pieces may be
included in the Kitchen category.

Bowl, Thistles, Low Undulating Form, 13 1/2 In. 345.00
Bowl, Underplate, Floral, Fox-Like Animal, Gilt, 4-In. Bowl, 7 3/4-In. Plate, 2 Piece 165.00
Box, Cover, Flower Design, Gilt, Cream Ground, Portrait Of Woman On Cover, 4 In. 345.00
Box, Flowers, Blue Ground, Round Ends, Rectangular, 13 In. 1840.00
Box, Ormolu, Champleve, Hinged Cover, France, Late 19th Century, 5 x 9 In. 430.00
Case, Gilt Metal Mounted, Baluster Shape, Landscape, Cover, Continental, 3 1/4 In. 375.00
Casket, Barrel Shape, Raised On 2 Satyrs, 5 3/4 In. 1150.00
Cigarette Case, Champleve Design, Engraved Russian Lettering, Marked 84, 2 5/8 x 4 In. 220.00
Dish, Rococo, Ormolu Mounted, Boat Shape, Couples, Cherubs, c.1850, 9 x 5 In. 1090.00
Dresser Set, Black & Red Stripes, Flared Sides, c.1930, 3 Piece 230.00
Ewer, Allegorical Scenes, 5 In. 520.00
Figurine, Coach, Hinged Cover, Woman Giving Billet Doux To Doves, 2 3/4 In. 860.00
Figurine, Sedan Chair, Pastoral Scenes, France, 4 In. 1495.00
Nef, Ship, Figural, Allegorical Scenes, Figures, Vienna, 6 In. 3200.00
Pin, Military, 8-Pointed Star, Cloud & Banner, Chinese, 3 1/4 In. 60.00
Placecard Holder Set, Polychrome Flowers, Box, c.1927, 12 Piece 345.00
Plaque, 3 Females, Whimsical Butterflies, Blue Ground, 20th Century, 14 1/2 x 24 In. 1093.00
Plaque, Venetian Style, Portrait, Girl, Colorful Hat, Dress, Ormolu Frame, 5 1/2 In. 290.00
Tazza, Allegorical Scenes, Figural Champleve, Handles, 3 In. 1150.00
Teaspoon, Shell & Putti Handle, Peacocks, Couples, Continental, 1800s, 5 3/8 In. 115.00
Tray, Rectangular, Rope Twist Border, Eagle Roundel, Russia, 12 1/8 x 9 3/8 In. 345.00
Urn, Aesthetic Movement, Ormolu Mounted, Carp In Water Grasses, Handles, 11 In., Pair 1610.00
Vase, Allegorical Scenes, Figural Handles, 7 1/2 In., Pair 3165.00
Vase, Champleve, Onyx, Late 19th Century, 16 In., Pair 5400.00
Vase, Continuous Landscape Of Deer Drinking At Forest Stream, Signed, 6 In. 315.00
Vase, Poppy Plant Design, Slate Blue Ground, Late 19th Century, 7 In. 345.00
Vase, Trumpet, Yellow, Pink & White Flowers, Gold Bands, Pedestal Base, 14 In. 185.00
Vase, Wisteria Design, Spherical, Signed, Camet, 3 In. 315.00
Wagon, Allegorical Scenes, Vienna, 11 In. 4025.00
Wagon, Boat Shape, Cupid & Bird, Allegorical Scenes, Vienna, 8 In. 1265.00

ESKIMO artifacts of all types are collected. Carvings of whale or walrus teeth are listed under Scrimshaw. Baskets are in the Basket category. All other types of Eskimo art are listed here.

Basket, Attu, Twined, Silk Thread, Cover, 1900, 7 1/4 x 1 3/4 In. 1870.00
Basket, Hooper Bay, Storage, Simple Line Design, Lid, c.1920, 8 x 11 In. 248.00
Basket, Inuit, Coiled Baleen, 2 Colors, Ivory Finial Of Seals, Eunice Hank, 4 1/4 In. 1380.00
Boots, Seal Skin, Thread Decorated, 14 x 11 x 6 In., Pair 115.00
Carving, Man, Full-Bodied, Mask, Wood Base, Whalebone, 6 1/2 x 3 x 1 1/2 In. 250.00

Carving, Soapstone, Inuit, Eskimo Paddling Kayak, Wood Paddle, Mid 1900s, 16 In. 546.00
Carving, Tribal Head, Legs, Mounted, Painted Base, Whalebone, 4 1/2 x 3 x 2 In. 280.00
Carving, Whalebone, 5 x 1 x 1/2 In. 170.00
Cribbage Board, Walrus Skull, 23 x 27 1/2 In. 1175.00
Doll, Painted Features, Carved Teeth, Covered In Fur, 11 In. 240.00
Figure, Swan, Nest, Inuit, Miniature 135.00
Goggles, Snow, Inuit, Carved Antler, Hollow Convex, 5 In. 865.00
Harpoon, Inuit, Wood & Bone, Wood Shaft, Bone Insets, Early 20th Century, 46 In. 230.00
Kayak, Man & Hunting Equipment, 20 In. 210.00
Kayak, Skin Covered, Wood Frame, Oars, Fishing Spear, 1 1/2 x 16 x 2 In. 336.00
Mask, Edward Kiolan, Nuniyak Island, 1975 . . . .   80.00
Mask, Inuit, Wood, Carved, Hollow Form, Oval, Pierced Eyes, Late 1800s, 6 1/4 In. 5462.00
Model, Umiak, Inuit, Sealskin & Wood, 3 Seats, Dark Patina, Late 1800s, 33 In. 920.00
Pouch, Shooting, Sealskin, Claws, Cat Skin Work, 10 1/2 x 11 In. 1485.00
Walrus Tusk, Cribbage Board, Hollowed Out End For Game Pieces, 20 x 23 In. 400.00

FABERGE was a firm of jewelers and goldsmiths founded in St. Petersburg, Russia, in 1842, by Gustav Faberge. Peter Carl Faberge, his son,
was jeweler to the Russian Imperial Court from about 1870 to 1914.
The rare Imperial Easter eggs, jewelry, and decorative items are very
expensive today.

ФАБЕРЖЕ

КФ

Ashtray, Copper, c.1914 . . . .   1265.00
Beaker, Silver & Cut Glass, Geometric Design, Silver Foot & Rim, c.1900, 4 In. 3600.00
Beaker, Silver, Marked, Stephan Wakewa, St. Petersburg, 1896, 2 7/8 In. 672.00
Beaker, Vodka, Gilt Silver, Enameled Vegetable Forms, 1910, 2 1/4 In. 3000.00
Box, Silver, Jeweled, Ribbon Tied Swags Of Leaves, 4 Diamonds, c.1900, 1 3/4 In. 7800.00
Cigarette Case, Chased Leaf Tips Border, Ruby Thumbpiece, c.1900, 3 3/8 In. 6000.00
Figurine, Elephant, Inturned Trunk, Diamond Eyes, Quartz, c.1900, 1 1/2 In. 9600.00
Figurine, Walrus, Ruby Eyes, Ivory Tusks, Resting With Head Up, 2 x 4 x 2 1/2 In. 5750.00
Page Knife, Silver Gilt, Enamel, Jade, Horse Head Finial, 9 3/4 In. 1568.00
Pin, Gold & Jeweled, Alternating Rubies & Diamonds, Case, c.1900, 2 1/4 In. 4800.00
Watch, Pendant, Imperial Peacock, Diamond, Sapphire, Enamel, Pearl, 26 In. 460.00

FAIENCE refers to tin-glazed earthenware, especially the wares made in
France, Germany, and Scandinavia. It is also correct to say that faience
is the same as majolica or Delft, although usually the term refers only
to the tin-glazed pottery of the three regions mentioned.

Bowl, Woman Carrying Cornucopiae, Sunburst, Green Spatter Leaves, 8 1/8 In. 385.00
Cachepot, Black & White Transfer Design, Scalloped, Lion Head Handles, 4 In., Pair . . .   335.00
Canister, Spaulding & Merick, Sunny Bank, Chicago, 9 In. 90.00
Charger, Green Bird Center, Green Vine & Red Berries Border, 11 In. 80.00
Charger, Polychrome Enamels, Italy, 20th Century, 18 3/4 x 20 In. 2585.00
Charger, Side Flowers, Scrolling Leaf Border, Coat Of Arms, France, 14 1/2 In. 112.00
Chocolate Pot, Cover, 3-Footed, Painted, Chinoiserie Scene, c.1720, 9 In. 3600.00
Cistern, Blue & White, Figural Galants Reserves, France, Mid 1700s, 7 x 16 1/2 In. 1380.00
Dish, Hen On Nest Cover, Egersund Pottery Factory, Norway, 7 1/2 In. 978.00
Figure, Seated Lion, White Body, Orange & Brown Glaze, France, 29 x 29 1/2 x 12 In. . .   400.00
Figurine, Boy & Girl, Holding Fruits & Vegetables, 5 3/4 x 4 In., Pair 860.00
Figurine, Nude Sitting In Waves, Gray, Green & Brown Glaze, 7 3/4 x 5 1/4 In. 110.00
Jar, Blue, Calligraphy, Animals, Long Neck, Handles, Oval, Moorish, 1900s, 30 In. 1610.00
Plate, Bouquet, Strasbourg, c.1770, 9 3/4 In. 145.00
Plate, Polychrome Design, Southern Germany, 18th Century 185.00
Plate, Polychrome, Verse, Southern Germany, 18th Century 374.00
Plate, Stylized Butterflies At Edge, Center Urn Of Flowers, Marked HH, 9 In. 412.00
Plate, Urn Of Flowers, 2 Birds On Branches, Marked HB, 8 1/2 In. 330.00
Stein, Building Scene, Pewter Lid, 3/4 Liter 254.00
Stein, Military Soldier, Horseback, Speaking To Seated Man, Pewter Lid, 1 1/2 Liter 173.00
Tankard, Flowers, Gold, Pewter Mounts, Schrezheim, c.1820 . . . .   575.00
Tankard, Leaping Horse, Tree, Pewter Mounts, Hannoversch, Muden, Mid 19th Century .   374.00
Tankard, Lovers Tryst, Polychrome, Pewter Mounts, Germany, Mid 18th Century 546.00
Tankard, Occupation, Tailor, Purple Glaze, Pewter Mounts, Salzburg, Mid 18th Century . .   374.00
Tankard, Polychrome, Hunter With Dog, Pewter Lid, Foot Rim, 18th Century, 7 7/8 In. . .   1092.00
Tureen, Soup, Ladle & Underplate, Blooming Tulips, Portugal, 11 x 15 In. 137.00

Fairing, Figurine, Siamese Twins, Chang & Eng, Germany, 3 3/8 In.

To dust small, fragile items like flower-decorated figurines, try blowing the dust away with a hand-held hair dryer set on low. For large, sturdy items, cover the end of the vacuum cleaner nozzle with an old nylon stocking, then vacuum.

Urn, Scenic Design, 2 Handles, Italy, 8 1/2 In., Pair	616.00
Vase, 4 Mermaids, Sea Creatures, Fish, Octopus, 11 7/8 In.	1200.00
Vase, Carp, Pierced Back For Flowers, 14 1/4 In.	150.00
Vase, Double Gourd, Pierced Neck, Gilded, Morning Glories, 19th Century, 22 In.	940.00
Vase, Mulberry, Cream, Footed, France, 18th Century Style, Exotic Bird, c.1900, 6 x 5 In.	92.00
Water Bottle, Long Neck, Flared Rim, Blue On White Oriental Design, 9 1/4 In.	83.00

FAIRINGS are small souvenir china boxes and figurines that were sold at country fairs during the nineteenth century. Most were made in Germany. Reproductions of fairings are being made, especially of the famous *twelve months of marriage* series.

Figurine, Siamese Twins, Chang & Eng, Germany, 3 3/8 In. *Illus*	100.00
Trinket Box, Acorn Finial Cover, Porcelain, Egg Shape, Flowers, Bluebird, Ormolu, 4 In.	165.00
Trinket Box, Baby On Cover, Baby & Polichinelle, 6 x 4 In.	325.00
Trinket Box, Bisque, Baby In Cradle, Lid	155.00
Trinket Box, Copper Luster, Tall Ship, Poem Inside Lid, Gray's Pottery, c.1935, 4 x 5 In.	70.00
Trinket Box, Dovetailed, Footed, Red, Yellow Design, Applied Flowers, Lehnware, 9 In.	2200.00
Trinket Box, Edwardian, Inlaid Satinwood, 24 x 13 1/2 x 12 1/4 In.	920.00
Trinket Box, Gilt Metal, Hinged Lid, Satin Interior, Oval Slate Base, c.1890, 4 1/2 In.	230.00
Trinket Box, Porcelain, Continental, Painted, Lady In Hat, Gilt Metal, Early 1900s, 4 In.	400.00

FAIRYLAND LUSTER pieces are included in the Wedgwood category.

FAMILLE ROSE, see Chinese Export category.

FANS have been used for cooling since the days of the ancients. By the eighteenth century, the fan was an accessory for the lady of fashion, and very elaborate and expensive fans were made. Sticks were made of ivory or wood, set with jewels or carved. The fans were made of painted silk or paper. Inexpensive paper fans printed with advertising were giveaways in the late nineteenth and early twentieth centuries. Electric fans were introduced in 1882.

Advertising, Guardian Angel, Kendall Motor Sales, Maquoketa, Iowa	25.00
Advertising, Kis-Me Chewing Gum, Paper, Wooden Handle, 15 x 10 In.	165.00
Bone, Carved, Evening, Silk, Giltwood, Framed, Polychrome, 14 3/4 x 23 3/4 In.	520.00
Boutique Label, Susse Freres, c.1860, 27 In., Pair	425.00
Electric, Galvin Electric, 4 Brass Blades, Wire Guard	84.00
Electric, General Electric, 4 Metal Blades, 12 In.	28.00
Electric, General Electric, 12-Inch Brass Blades, Oscillating, 17 In.	145.00
Electric, General Electric, Brass Cage, 12-Inch Blades, Ribbed Cast Iron Stand, 15 In.	546.00
Electric, General Electric, Oscillating, Brass Blades & Cage	45.00
Electric, General Electric, Table Top, Brass Blades, Wire Guard, 12 In.	85.00
Electric, Oscillating, Dark Brown Finish, Wire Cage, 1950, 13 In.	20.00
Electric, Robbins & Myers, 4 Brass Blades, Wire Guard, Felt Base	56.00
Electric, Western Electric, Hawthorn, Victor, Brass Blades, 12 In.	165.00
Electric, Westinghouse, 4 Metal Blades, Wire Guard, 10 In.	28.00

Electric, Westinghouse, Black, Whirlwind Model, 10 In.	25.00
Ivory, Carved, Kidskin Case, Scabbard Form, Ivory Link Chain, Belt Clip, 11 In.	920.00
Ivory, Cord Tied Posy Of Lilies Of The Valley, Late 19th Century, 7 3/4 In.	460.00
Ivory, Courting Scene, Lithograph, Julia M. Kibbe, France, 19 x 14 In.	410.00
Ivory, Figures In Garden, Harbor & Village Scene, Butterflies On Box	490.00
Ivory, Floral Carved, Tasseled Silk Cord, 9 1/4 In.	1380.00
Ivory, Folding, Landscape Scene, Children Watching Fireworks Display	375.00
Ivory, Gold Lacquer, Birds & Flowers, 19th Century, 11 1/2 In.	4025.00
Ivory, Silk, Painted Italian Courtyard Scene, Frame, 9 1/2 x 18 In.	220.00
Ivory, Silkwoman, Elaborate Dress, Hand Painted, Sequins, Frame, 15 1/2 x 24 In.	440.00
Lacquer, Black, Folding, Mandarins In Silk, Painted Ivory Faces, 19th Century	230.00
Lacquer, Gold & Silver Figures, Black, 4 Roses Interior	345.00
Lacquer Sticks, Court Figures, Painted, Silk, Giltwood Shadowbox, 20 In.	405.00
Mother-Of-Pearl Frame, Lithograph Scenes, Gold Floral Borders, Gilt Case, 21 x 14 In.	110.00
Paper, Black, Green & Purple Flowers, Lacquered Wood Base, Openwork, 8 x 12 In.	20.00
Paperboard, Watercolor, Stenciled, Gilt, Crescent Shape, 19th Century, 7 x 10 In., Pair	530.00
Paperboard, Watercolor, Stenciled, Gilt, Semicircular Shape, 16 1/2 x 11 3/4 In.	118.00
Silk, Black, Seed Pearl, Characters Beaded To Either Side, 19th Century, 12 In.	200.00
Silver Filigree & Gilt Stays, Birds & Flowers, Mandarins On Reverse, 19th Century	115.00
Wood Stays, Black Lacquer & Gold Figures In Garden, Paper, Lacquered Box, 10 1/2 In.	230.00

FAST FOOD COLLECTIBLES may be included in several categories, such as Advertising, Coca-Cola, Toy, etc.

FEDERZEICHNUNG is the very strange German name for a pattern of mother-of-pearl satin glass. The pattern had irregularly shaped sections of brown glass covered with a pattern of gold squiggle lines. It was first made in the late nineteenth century.

Vase, Air Trapped Octopus, Gold Tracery, 13 In.	1790.00

FENTON Art Glass Company, founded in Martins Ferry, Ohio, by Frank L. Fenton, is now located in Williamstown, West Virginia. It is noted for early carnival glass produced between 1907 and 1920. Some of these pieces are listed in the Carnival Glass category. Many other types of glass were also made. Spanish Lace in this section refers to the pattern made by Fenton.

Amber Snow Crest, Hat, 4 1/2 In.	45.00
Amber Snow Crest, Vase, 9 In.	35.00
Apple Blossom & Strawberry, Bowl, Honeycomb Design, 9 1/2 In.	60.00
Apple Blossom Crest, Ashtray	40.00
Apple Blossom Crest, Relish, Handles	95.00
Aqua Crest, Basket, 5 In.	140.00
Aqua Crest, Bowl, Salad, 10 In.	40.00
Aqua Crest, Vase, 8 1/2 In.	25.00
Aqua Crest, Vase, Round Top, 4 1/2 In.	40.00
Beatty Waffle, Basket, Green Opalescent, 1960, 7 In.	65.00
Black Rose, Bowl, 10 In.	75.00
Black Rose, Jug, Beaded Melon, 6 In.	50.00
Blue Ridge, Water Set, 1985, 5 Piece	200.00
Burmese, Hat, Flowers, Butterfly, FAGCA, 1982	145.00
Burmese, Pitcher, Enameled Maple Leaves	45.00
Burmese, Student Lamp, Enameled, 21 In.	275.00
Cactus, Basket, Milk Glass, 7 In.	25.00
Cactus, Bowl, Milk Glass, Rolled Sides, 9 x 6 1/2 In.	59.00
Cactus, Butter, Amber	15.00
Cactus, Cruet, Blue Opalescent	105.00
Cactus, Goblet, Aqua Opalescent	35.00
Cactus, Salt & Pepper, Topaz Opalescent	50.00
Coin Dot, Basket, Blue Opalescent, 7 In.	110.00
Coin Dot, Bowl, Cranberry Opalescent, 7 In.	65.00
Coin Dot, Bowl, Ruffled Edge, Amethyst, 8 In.	80.00
Coin Dot, Creamer, French Opalescent	25.00
Coin Dot, Hat, Blue Opalescent	35.00

Coin Dot, Pitcher, Aqua Opalescent, Squat 25.00
Coin Dot, Vase, French Opalescent, 5 1/2 In. 45.00
Coin Dot, Vase, Lime Green Opalescent, 7 In. 85.00
Colonial, Candy Box, Oval, Blue 25.00
Colonial, Candy Dish, Spring Green 20.00
Colonial, Salt & Pepper, Blue 40.00
Cornucopia, Vase, Azure Blue, 5 In. 225.00
Crystal Crest, Basket, Hat Shape 95.00
Crystal Crest, Vase, 6 In. 85.00
Crystal Crest, Vase, Hat Shape 35.00
Daisy & Button, Basket, Mulberry, 7 In. 75.00
Diamond Lace, Cruet, Topaz Opalescent, Clear Stopper, 8 1/2 In. 40.00
Diamond Lace, Epergne, 3 Horns, Milk Glass 40.00
Diamond Optic, Basket, Ruby Overlay, 7 In. 25.00
Diamond Optic, Vase, Pinch, Wild Rose, 7 1/2 In. 40.00
Diamond Optic, Water Set, Ruby Overlay, 5 Piece 145.00
Ebony Crest, Basket, 5 In. 75.00
Emerald Crest, Compote 45.00
Fairy Light, Lime Sherbet, Satin 35.00
Figurine, Alley Cat, Plum Slag, Satin 300.00
Figurine, Bear, Rosalene, Pink Roses 65.00
Figurine, Happiness Bird, Lavender, Satin 65.00
Figurine, Happiness Bird, Milk Glass, Satin 45.00
Figurine, Kissing Kids, Carnival Glass, 1981-1982, Pair 80.00
Figurine, Puddle Duck Set, With Hat, 6 Piece 240.00
Flame Crest, Basket, 2 1/2 In. 55.00
Georgian, Cup & Saucer, Ruby 75.00
Georgian, Plate, Salad, Ruby, 8 In. 65.00
Georgian, Salt & Pepper, Ruby, Plastic Lids, 4 In. 55.00
Georgian, Sherbet, Ruby 55.00
Georgian, Tumbler, Ruby, 8 1/2 Oz., 3 7/8 In. 15.00
Georgian, Tumbler, Ruby, Footed, 12 Oz., 6 In. 23.00
Georgian, Tumbler, Smoke Amethyst, 9 1/2 Oz., 4 1/4 In. 15.00
Gold Crest, Vase, Beaded Melon, 8 In. 20.00
Hanging Heart, Vase, Amethyst, 1981, 7 1/2 In. 95.00
Hobnail, Basket, Blue Opalescent, 4 1/2 In. 55.00
Hobnail, Basket, Cranberry Opalescent, 7 In. 70.00
Hobnail, Basket, French Opalescent, 5 1/2 In. 75.00
Hobnail, Bowl, Cranberry Opalescent, 10 In. 75.00
Hobnail, Bowl, Topaz Opalescent, 10 3/4 x 3 1/2 In. 85.00
Hobnail, Candleholder, Emerald Green Opalescent, 6 In., Pair 59.00
Hobnail, Candy Dish, Colonial Blue 10.00
Hobnail, Cruet, Blue Opalescent, Stopper 120.00
Hobnail, Cruet, Cranberry Opalescent, Stopper 165.00
Hobnail, Cruet, French Opalescent, Stopper 15.00
Hobnail, Epergne, Blue Opalescent, 3 Horns 65.00
Hobnail, Epergne, Milk Glass, 3 Horns 35.00
Hobnail, Lamp, Oil, Courting, Honey Amber 35.00
Hobnail, Lampshade, Metal Base, Honey Amber 45.00
Hobnail, Lavabo, Honey Amber, 3 Piece 55.00
Hobnail, Pitcher, French Opalescent, 80 Oz. 250.00
Hobnail, Pitcher, Juice, Blue Opalescent 95.00
Hobnail, Pitcher, Straight Sides, French Opalescent 275.00
Hobnail, Pitcher, Straight Sides, Green Opalescent 325.00
Hobnail, Pitcher, Water, Cranberry, Opalescent, 4-Corner, Applied Clear Handle, 8 In. . . . 60.00
Hobnail, Powder Box, Wooden Cover, French Opalescent 30.00
Hobnail, Tumbler, Blue Opalescent 15.00
Hobnail, Vase, Bud, Plum Opalescent, 8 In. 75.00
Hobnail, Water Set, Barrel Tumblers, Blue Opalescent, 80-Oz. Pitcher, 6 Piece 325.00
Honeycomb, Pitcher, Honey Amber, 1960s 83.00
No. 549, Candlestick, Jade Green, 8 1/2 In., Pair 45.00
Orange Tree, Mug, Persian Blue 48.00
Peach Crest, Basket, Hat, 5 In. 65.00

Peach Crest, Bowl, 13 In.	105.00
Peach Crest, Bowl, Shell Shape	60.00
Peach Crest, Epergne, 1 Horn	175.00
Peach Crest, Vase, 6 In.	45.00
Perfume Bottle, Cranberry	400.00
Plate, Mother's Day, Blue, Satin, 1974	10.00
Plate, Mother's Day, Red Carnival, 1979	35.00
Rib Optic, Small Basket, Green Overlay	30.00
Ribbed Pillar, Vase, Jamestown Blue, 5 In.	55.00
Rosalene, Flower Frog	59.00
Rosalene, Planter, Hexagonal	80.00
Rose Crest, Cornucopia	30.00
Rose Crest, Mayonnaise Set, 3 Piece	45.00
Rose Crest, Vase, Beaded Melon, 5 In.	30.00
Ruby Overlay, Salt & Pepper	55.00
Silver Crest, Basket, 11 In.	75.00
Silver Crest, Basket, 12 In.	35.00
Silver Crest, Basket, Enameled Violets In The Snow, 1970, 5 In.	55.00
Silver Crest, Bowl, 10 In.	65.00
Silver Crest, Bowl, Fruit, Footed, 11 In.	65.00
Silver Crest, Epergne, 1 Horn	195.00
Silver Crest, Plate, 8 1/2 In.	7.50
Silver Crest, Vase, 6 1/2 In.	25.00
Spanish Lace, Bell, Emerald Green Opalescent	59.00
Spanish Lace, Vase, Violets In The Snow	40.00
Teardrop, Cake Plate, Milk Glass	25.00
Teardrop, Candleholder, Milk Glass	10.00
Valencia, Ashtray, Colonial Blue	20.00
Valencia, Ashtray, Green Colonial	10.00
Vasa Murrhina, Basket, Handles, 10 In.	70.00
Vasa Murrhina, Bowl, Aventurine Green With Blue, 4 In.	20.00
Vasa Murrhina, Cream Pitcher, Autumn Orange	55.00
Vasa Murrhina, Pitcher, Melon, Ribbed Aventurine Green With Blue	185.00
Vasa Murrhina, Vase, Fan, Blue Mist	95.00
Vasa Murrhina, Vase, Melon Ribbed, Rose With Aventurine Green, 1985, 8 In.	75.00
Vasa Murrhina, Vase, Rose With Aventurine Green, 5 1/2 In.	65.00
Vasa Murrhina, Vase, Rose With Aventurine Green, 11 In.	125.00
Velva Rose, Compote	30.00
Velva Rose, Compote, Cover, 5 1/2 In.	125.00
Velva Rose, Epergne, 4 Horns	140.00 to 250.00
Wisteria, Candy Box, Knobby Bull's-Eye	45.00

FIESTA, the colorful dinnerware, was introduced in 1936 by the Homer Laughlin China Co., redesigned in 1969, and withdrawn in 1973. It was reissued again in 1986 in different colors and is still being made. The simple design was characterized by a band of concentric circles, beginning at the rim. Cups had full-circle handles until 1969, when partial-circle handles were made. Harlequin and Riviera were related wares. For more information about Fiesta, its colors and prices, see the book *Kovels' Depression Glass & Dinnerware Price List.*

Chartreuse, Bowl, Fruit, 4 3/4 In.	45.00
Chartreuse, Cup & Saucer	50.00
Chartreuse, Mug	40.00
Chartreuse, Nappy, 8 1/2 In.	45.00 to 50.00
Chartreuse, Plate, Deep, 8 1/4 In.	45.00
Chartreuse, Sauceboat	60.00
Cobalt Blue, Ashtray	45.00
Cobalt Blue, Candleholder, Bulb, Pair	99.00
Cobalt Blue, Carafe	275.00
Cobalt Blue, Casserole, Kitchen Kraft, Individual	205.00
Cobalt Blue, Chop Plate, 15 In.	60.00
Cobalt Blue, Coffeepot	295.00
Cobalt Blue, Creamer	32.00

Cobalt Blue, Cup & Saucer 42.50
Cobalt Blue, Cup & Saucer, After Dinner ....53.00 to 69.00
Cobalt Blue, Cup, Tea 35.00
Cobalt Blue, Eggcup 75.00
Cobalt Blue, Jug, Cover, Kitchen Kraft, Small 100.00
Cobalt Blue, Marmalade 297.00
Cobalt Blue, Mixing Bowl, No. 2 .... 135.00
Cobalt Blue, Mixing Bowl, No. 3 .... 30.00
Cobalt Blue, Mixing Bowl, No. 4 ....165.00 to 195.00
Cobalt Blue, Mixing Bowl, No. 5 ....36.00 to 61.00
Cobalt Blue, Mixing Bowl, No. 7 .... 138.00
Cobalt Blue, Mug 45.00
Cobalt Blue, Nappy, 8 1/2 In. ....25.00 to 40.00
Cobalt Blue, Plate, 6 In. ....7.50 to 20.00
Cobalt Blue, Plate, 9 In. ....20.00 to 30.00
Cobalt Blue, Plate, Deep, 8 1/4 In. 36.00
Cobalt Blue, Salt & Pepper, Kitchen Kraft 42.00
Cobalt Blue, Sauceboat 75.00
Cobalt Blue, Soup, Cream 80.00
Cobalt Blue, Spoon, Kitchen Kraft 140.00
Cobalt Blue, Spoon, Salad, Kitchen Kraft 90.00
Cobalt Blue, Stacking Unit, Kitchen Kraft 40.00
Cobalt Blue, Teapot, 8 Cup 225.00
Cobalt Blue, Tray, Figure 8 .... 80.00
Cobalt Blue, Tray, Utility ....25.00 to 40.00
Cobalt Blue, Tumbler, Juice 40.00
Cobalt Blue, Vase, Bud 125.00
Forest Green, Cup & Saucer 47.00
Forest Green, Mug, Tom & Jerry ....75.00 to 90.00
Forest Green, Plate, 10 In. 55.00
Forest Green, Vase, Bud 330.00
Gray, Ashtray 55.00
Gray, Cup & Saucer 45.00
Gray, Plate, 6 In. 7.00
Gray, Plate, Deep, 8 1/4 In. 55.00
Green, Cake Plate, Kitchen Kraft, 10 1/4 In. 65.00
Ivory, Ashtray 70.00
Ivory, Bowl, Fruit, 4 3/4 In. 32.00
Ivory, Bowl, Fruit, 5 1/2 In. ....20.00 to 30.00
Ivory, Carafe 275.00
Ivory, Casserole, French, Cover 3850.00
Ivory, Chop Plate, 13 In. ....50.00 to 55.00
Ivory, Chop Plate, 15 In. ....65.00 to 70.00
Ivory, Coffeepot, After Dinner 450.00
Ivory, Coffeepot, Cover 245.00
Ivory, Compote, 12 In. ....176.00 to 200.00
Ivory, Compote, Sweets 110.00
Ivory, Cup & Saucer 28.00
Ivory, Cup & Saucer, After Dinner 55.00
Ivory, Mixing Bowl, No. 5 ....175.00 to 205.00
Ivory, Mixing Bowl, No. 7 .... 455.00
Ivory, Nappy, 8 1/2 In. ....18.00 to 27.00
Ivory, Pitcher, Ice Lip 130.00
Ivory, Plate, 6 In. 8.00
Ivory, Plate, 9 In. 18.00
Ivory, Plate, 10 In. 20.00
Ivory, Plate, Deep, 8 1/4 In. ....45.00 to 56.00
Ivory, Plate, Dessert, 6 In. ....5.50 to 8.00
Ivory, Sauceboat 50.00
Ivory, Saucer 5.00
Ivory, Soup, Cream ....25.00 to 45.00
Ivory, Tray, Utility 30.00
Ivory, Vase, 8 In. ....550.00 to 700.00

Light Green, Ashtray 55.00
Light Green, Bowl, Fruit, 4 3/4 In. . . . . .50.00 to 95.00
Light Green, Bowl, Fruit, 5 1/2 In. . . . . .35.00 to 45.00
Light Green, Carafe 275.00
Light Green, Casserole, Kitchen Kraft, Individual 135.00
Light Green, Chop Plate, 13 In. 38.00
Light Green, Chop Plate, 15 In. . . . . .35.00 to 48.00
Light Green, Coffeepot 120.00
Light Green, Coffeepot, After Dinner 440.00
Light Green, Compote, 12 In. 160.00
Light Green, Compote, Sweets 90.00
Light Green, Cup & Saucer . . . . .30.00 to 42.00
Light Green, Cup & Saucer, After Dinner 66.00
Light Green, Eggcup 21.00
Light Green, Fork, Kitchen Kraft 115.00
Light Green, Jug, Cover, Kitchen Kraft, Large 230.00
Light Green, Mug 45.00
Light Green, Nappy, 8 1/2 In. . . . . .10.00 to 18.00
Light Green, Plate, 6 In. 6.00
Light Green, Plate, 9 In. . . . . .15.00 to 24.00
Light Green, Plate, 10 In. 32.00
Light Green, Plate, Deep, 8 1/4 In. 40.00
Light Green, Platter, Oval, Kitchen Kraft, 13 In. 60.00
Light Green, Salt & Pepper, Kitchen Kraft 65.00
Light Green, Sauceboat . . . . .22.00 to 45.00
Light Green, Stacking Unit, Kitchen Kraft 40.00
Light Green, Sugar, Cover 18.00
Light Green, Teapot, 8 Cup . . . . .100.00 to 180.00
Light Green, Tray, Utility 35.00
Light Green, Vase, 8 In. . . . . .400.00 to 485.00
Lilac, Butter, Cover, 1/4 Lb. . . . . .55.00 to 75.00
Lilac, Candleholder, Tripod, Pair 625.00
Lilac, Coffee Server, Cover 180.00
Lilac, Cup & Saucer, After Dinner 130.00
Lilac, Mug . . . . .20.00 to 35.00
Lilac, Pie Baker 80.00
Lilac, Pitcher, Disk, Large . . . . .60.00 to 100.00
Lilac, Pitcher, Disk, Miniature 80.00
Lilac, Pitcher, Disk, Small 110.00
Lilac, Pitcher, Juice, Miniature 65.00
Lilac, Teapot, Cover . . . . .110.00 to 140.00
Medium Green, Cup & Saucer . . . . .35.00 to 38.00
Medium Green, Plate, Salad, Individual . . . . .85.00 to 100.00
Plate, 1955, Monthly Calendar, Mantel Clocks In Center, Wheat Design Rim, 9 1/2 In. . . 48.00
Red, Ashtray 50.00
Red, Bowl, Fruit, 4 3/4 In. . . . . .40.00 to 60.00
Red, Bowl, Fruit, 5 1/2 In. 38.00
Red, Candleholder, Tripod, Pair 550.00
Red, Carafe . . . . .275.00 to 302.00
Red, Casserole, Kitchen Kraft, Individual 80.00
Red, Chop Plate, 15 In. . . . . .65.00 to 75.00
Red, Compote, 12 In. . . . . .170.00 to 187.00
Red, Compote, Sweets 150.00
Red, Cup & Saucer . . . . .30.00 to 45.00
Red, Cup & Saucer, After Dinner 65.00
Red, Jar, Cover, Kitchen Kraft, Large 300.00
Red, Mixing Bowl, No. 3 . . . . 140.00
Red, Mixing Bowl, No. 4 . . . . 155.00
Red, Mixing Bowl, No. 5 . . . . 200.00
Red, Mug 50.00
Red, Nappy, 8 1/2 In. . . . . .37.00 to 60.00
Red, Nappy, 9 1/2 In. . . . . .65.00 to 70.00
Red, Pitcher, Syrup 363.00

Red, Pitcher, Water, Ice Lip 121.00
Red, Plate, 6 In. 20.00
Red, Plate, 9 In. 25.00
Red, Plate, 10 In. 45.00
Red, Plate, Deep, 8 1/4 In. ....50.00 to 55.00
Red, Plate, Salad, Individual ....45.00 to 65.00
Red, Platter, Oval, 12 In. 60.00
Red, Sauceboat 65.00
Red, Soup, Cream 70.00
Red, Spoon, Kitchen Kraft 140.00
Red, Stacking Unit, Cover, Kitchen Kraft ....30.00 to 80.00
Red, Sugar 27.00
Red, Tumbler, Juice, 5 Oz. 40.00
Rose, Bowl, Fruit, 4 3/4 In. 55.00
Rose, Chop Plate, 15 In. 118.00
Rose, Cup & Saucer 48.00
Rose, Plate, 6 In. 20.00
Rose, Plate, 7 In. 14.00
Rose, Plate, 10 In. 30.00
Rose, Sauceboat 82.00
Turquoise, Ashtray ....35.00 to 60.00
Turquoise, Bowl, Fruit, 4 3/4 In. ....10.00 to 25.00
Turquoise, Bowl, Fruit, 5 1/2 In. 20.00
Turquoise, Carafe 300.00
Turquoise, Chop Plate, 13 In. ....22.00 to 40.00
Turquoise, Chop Plate, 15 In. 55.00
Turquoise, Compote, 12 In. 110.00
Turquoise, Compote, Sweets 70.00
Turquoise, Cup & Saucer 34.00
Turquoise, Cup & Saucer, After Dinner 55.00
Turquoise, Eggcup ....32.00 to 40.00
Turquoise, Jug, 2 Pt. 50.00
Turquoise, Mixing Bowl, No. 2 ....110.00 to 145.00
Turquoise, Mixing Bowl, No. 4 ....135.00 to 145.00
Turquoise, Mixing Bowl, No. 5 ....190.00 to 210.00
Turquoise, Mixing Bowl, No. 7 ....330.00 to 370.00
Turquoise, Mug 35.00
Turquoise, Nappy, 8 1/2 In. 20.00
Turquoise, Pitcher, Ice Lip 165.00
Turquoise, Plate, 6 In. ....7.00 to 15.00
Turquoise, Plate, 9 In. ....15.00 to 25.00
Turquoise, Plate, 10 In. ....30.00 to 55.00
Turquoise, Plate, Deep, 8 1/4 In. ....35.00 to 40.00
Turquoise, Platter, Oval, 12 In. 38.00
Turquoise, Sauceboat ....22.00 to 40.00
Turquoise, Saucer 3.75
Turquoise, Soup, Cream ....35.00 to 48.00
Turquoise, Sugar & Creamer 40.00
Turquoise, Teapot, 6 Cup ....90.00 to 165.00
Turquoise, Tray, Utility ....25.00 to 40.00
Turquoise, Vase, 8 In. ....550.00 to 605.00
Yellow, Ashtray ....25.00 to 35.00
Yellow, Bowl, Fruit, 4 3/4 In. ....10.00 to 25.00
Yellow, Bowl, Fruit, 5 1/2 In. 29.00
Yellow, Casserole, Kitchen Kraft, 8 1/2 In. 120.00
Yellow, Casserole, Kitchen Kraft, Individual 85.00
Yellow, Chop Plate, 13 In. 38.00
Yellow, Chop Plate, 15 In. 48.00
Yellow, Coffeepot, After Dinner 413.00
Yellow, Compote, 12 In. 100.00
Yellow, Compote, Sweets ....90.00 to 100.00
Yellow, Cup & Saucer 34.00
Yellow, Cup & Saucer, After Dinner ....40.00 to 65.00

Yellow, Eggcup 65.00
Yellow, Fork, Kitchen Kraft 130.00
Yellow, Jar, Cover, Kitchen Kraft, Large . . . . .275.00 to 310.00
Yellow, Jug, 2 Pt. . . . . .50.00 to 80.00
Yellow, Marmalade 295.00
Yellow, Mixing Bowl, No. 3 . . . . .120.00 to 155.00
Yellow, Mixing Bowl, No. 4 . . . . 135.00
Yellow, Mixing Bowl, No. 5 . . . . 150.00
Yellow, Mixing Bowl, No. 7 . . . . 90.00
Yellow, Mug . . . . .40.00 to 50.00
Yellow, Mustard . . . . .175.00 to 250.00
Yellow, Nappy, 8 1/2 In. . . . . .25.00 to 40.00
Yellow, Nappy, 9 1/2 In. . . . . .32.00 to 50.00
Yellow, Pie Plate, Kitchen Kraft, 10 In. 27.00
Yellow, Pitcher, Disk 100.00
Yellow, Plate, 6 In. . . . . .7.00 to 12.00
Yellow, Plate, 9 In. . . . . .12.00 to 18.00
Yellow, Plate, 10 In. . . . . .18.00 to 30.00
Yellow, Plate, Salad, Individual 50.00
Yellow, Platter, Oval, 12 In. 40.00
Yellow, Sauceboat . . . . .25.00 to 45.00
Yellow, Saucer 10.00
Yellow, Soup, Cream 35.00
Yellow, Stacking Unit, Kitchen Kraft 35.00
Yellow, Sugar . . . . .25.00 to 32.00
Yellow, Sugar & Creamer 35.00
Yellow, Syrup 385.00
Yellow, Teapot, 6 Cup . . . . .75.00 to 140.00
Yellow, Tray, Utility 35.00
Yellow, Tumbler, Juice 40.00
Yellow, Vase, 8 In. . . . . .425.00 to 550.00

FINCH, see Kay Finch category.

FINDLAY ONYX AND FLORADINE are two similar types of glass made by Dalzell, Gilmore and Leighton Co. of Findlay, Ohio, about 1889. Onyx is a patented yellowish white opaque glass with raised silver daisy decorations. A few rare pieces were made of rose, amber, orange, or purple glass. Floradine is made of cranberry-colored glass with an opalescent white raised floral pattern and a satin finish. The same molds were used for both types of glass.

Bowl, 2 x 2 1/4 In. 330.00
Butter, Platinum Design, 6 x 3 In. 1250.00
Spooner, 4 1/4 x 4 In. . . . . .137.00 to 165.00
Sugar Shaker, 5 3/4 In. 448.00
Syrup, 7 In. 476.00
Toothpick, Opal, Silver Infusion, 2 1/4 In. 564.00

FIREFIGHTING equipment and memorabilia of all types is wanted, from fire marks to uniforms to toy fire trucks. It is said that every little boy wanted to be a fireman or a train engineer 75 years ago and the collectors today reflect this interest.

Alarm, Bell Tower, Electro-Mechanical, Cast Iron Stand, Weight, Gamewell 4025.00
Alarm, Board, Slate, Wood Frame, Chalk Holder, 46 x 30 In. 115.00
Alarm, Pegboard, Wood Frame, Painted Markers, 33 x 31 In. 430.00
Alarm Box, Cast Iron, Pedestal, Gamewell, 84 In. 1095.00
Bell, Apparatus, Nickel, Acorn Finial, 12 In. 460.00
Bell, Hand Operated, 1860s 290.00
Belt, Parade, Black, White Cutout Letters, Allentown, Hose Around Buckle 90.00
Belt Buckle, Presented To W.A. Oliver, Pioneer Hose Co. No. 2 . . . . 1610.00
Box, Shipping, Dietz Lanterns, Wood, Black Stenciling, 20 In. 175.00
Box, Tool, Oak, Latrobe Fire Dept. No. 5, Sloping Lid, Latch, Seagrave, 24 In. 520.00
Bucket, Black Interior, Red Exterior, Leather Strap Handle, 13 1/4 In. 357.00

Bucket, Composition, Labeled B. F. F. D. 1, 11 1/2 In. 400.00
Bucket, Concord, Salmon, Black Banner, Gold Trim, M. Co. Bank, 13 1/2 In. 2645.00
Bucket, Eagle & Shield, Worn Paint, 19th Century, 11 In. 375.00
Bucket, Fiber, For Fire Only, Hayward, 12 In. 750.00
Bucket, Leather, Portsmouth, New Hampshire, 12 1/4 In. 13800.00
Bucket, Leather, Red Heart, Blue Ribbon, Jacob Jackson, 1818 .... 2250.00
Bucket, Leather, W. Crosby, Painted, 1821 .... 2200.00
Bucket, Leather, White Banner, Oval Cartouche, Keene, N.H., 19th Century, 13 In. 2070.00
Bucket, Leather, Wooden Band, Painted Black, S. Cornell, 19th Century, 14 1/4 In. 430.00
Bucket, Painted Leather, Herman Foster, Merrimac B L K 1380.00
Bucket, Thos. Barker, Hand Engine Fighting Fire, Enterprise Fire Club 1840 .... 805.00
Bucket, Worcester, Maroon, Black Rim, Gold Bands, Green Lettering, 12 In. 4600.00
Can, Steamer Oil, Brass, Stamped Ahrens Fire Engine Co., Cyclinder Plaque, 9 In. 635.00
Can, Steamer Oil, Brass, Stamped American Fire Engine Co., Lubricating Tag, 9 In. 489.00
Certificate, Boston Fire Dept., Thomas Quincy, 1836 .... 290.00
Certificate, Franklin Fire Co. 12, Frederick Colmire, By Queen Duval, 1867 .... 1380.00
Certificate, Philadelphia Assoc. For The Relief Of Disabled Firemen, 1861 .... 920.00
Extinguisher, Empire, Apparatus, Patented 1898, 21 In. 345.00
Extinguisher, Holloway, Apparatus, Chemical, American La France, 22 In. 750.00
Extinguisher, Mack, Apparatus, Foam, Hose & Shut Off Nozzle, 25 In. 375.00
Extinguisher, Sapfeu, Caluire, Extinctrice, Cobalt Blue, Stippled, 8 1/2 In. 728.00
Extinguisher, Sinclair's, London, Cobalt Blue, Diamond Pattern, Label, 7 1/2 In. 179.00
Extinguisher, Unic Extingtrice, 3 Circles, Amber, Vertical Ribs, 5 3/4 In. 235.00
Fire Alarm Box, Marked The Gamewell Fire Alarm Tel. Co., Iron, 12 In. 100.00
Fire Mark, Fire Assoc. Of Philadelphia, Cast Iron, 11 1/2 In. 230.00
Fire Mark, Fire Company, Germantown, Pennsylvania, Shaking Hands, Iron 1880.00
Fire Mark, Hydrant & Hose, Cast Iron, F.A. 85.00
Fire Mark, Iron, Snake & Flower, 19th Century, 10 3/4 In. 80.00
Fire Mark, Protector, Copper, England 430.00
Fire Mark, Raised Edged, Clasped Hands, Red, Green Paint, Iron, 1794, 10 x 9 In. 1380.00
Fire Mark, Steam Fire Engine, Cast Iron, Oval, Raised U.F. 345.00
Grenade, Grenade Extinctrice, Clear, France, 1880-1900, Pt., 5 1/2 In. 560.00
Grenade, Hayward Victory Grenade, Pale Aqua, Diamond, 7 1/4 In. 1568.00
Grenade, HNS, Yellow Amber, Qt., 7 1/4 In. 179.00
Grenade, Imperial Fire Extinguisher Co., Cobalt Blue, Horizontal Ribs, Label, 6 In.615.00 to 616.00
Grenade, System Labbe, Grenade Extincteur, Straw Yellow, France, 5 3/4 In. 224.00
Helmet, Chief, White Leather, Brookline, Ma., 8 Comb, Cairns, New Yorker 260.00
Helmet, Eagle, Black Leather, Eureka J C W, 8 Comb, Red Panels, Gold Eagle 1265.00
Helmet, High Eagle, Black Leather, Engine 1 OFD, 8 Comb 290.00
Helmet, Parade, 2 Maids Carrying Garland, Friendship, Top Hat Style, 5 1/2 In. 8855.00
Horn, Brass, Silver Plaque, Green Leather, Furst-Pless, Germany 55.00
Hose, Leather, Riveted, Couplings, Coiled, 29 In. 2300.00
House Gong, Brass, External Hammer, Trip Mechanism, Wooden, 17 x 13 3/4 In. 200.00
House Gong, Electro-Mechanical, Oak Case, Door, Rope Twist Molding, 17 In. 635.00
House Gong, Excelsior Gong, Glass Door, Gamewell, Wood Case, 15 3/4 In. 900.00
Ladder, Pompier, 12 Ft. 750.00
Lamp, 6 Sides, Ruby, Cobalt, Clear, Alternating Panels, Wheel Cut Vines, Excelsior 8625.00
Lamp, Engine, Ruby Glass Cut To Clear, Beveled Panels, Storm King 2, 21 In. 1840.00
Lamp, Engine, Side Mounted, Clear Lens, Finial, 17 1/2 In. 375.00
Lamp, Tin, Mica Window, Hinged Reflector Door, Chimney, Bracket, No. 4 .... 430.00
Lantern, Brass, Lift Up Cage, Clear Globe, Dietz 345.00
Lantern, Eclipse, Washington Hose Hook & Ladder, Brass, American LaFrance 1020.00
Lantern, Etched Glass Shields, Acorns, Leaves, Brass, Copper, c.1900, 17 In. 1920.00
Lantern, Green Over Clear Lens, Dewey Co., 19 1/2 In. 1610.00
Lantern, Metal, Painted Red, Clear Globe, Fixed Cage, Dewey Co., 13 1/2 In. 115.00
Lantern, Nickel, Lift Up Cage, Dietz 460.00
Lantern, Presentation, Nahant F. D., Brass, Fixed Cage, 11 1/2 In. 978.00
Lantern, Silvered Brass, Dietz 625.00
Lantern, Wristlet, Fixed Etched Globe, Excelsior 1, 13 In. 1495.00
Ledger, Americans Engine Co. No. VIII Journal, June 1854-March 1864 .... 230.00
Light Switch, Slate Base, Marked S. A. Stewart & Co., 10 x 5 In. 145.00
Match Safe, Raised Fire Engine Going To Fire, Home Insurance Co., Silver 635.00
Match Safe, Raised Relief Firemen, Home Insurance Co., Silver 375.00

Muffin Bell, Turned Wood Handle, Stamped Pat. Oct 27th 1863, 5 In. 489.00
Muffin Bell, Turned Wood Handle, Stamped Patented 1878, 5 1/2 In. 460.00
Noisemaker, Ratchet, Wood, 18th Century, Pair 179.00
Nozzle, Baker Stand Pipe, Brass, No. 3, 62 In. 315.00
Nozzle, Cellar, Brass, Gaandipson Mfg. Co., 7 3/4 x 2 1/2 In. 175.00
Nozzle, Cellar, Nickel, Elkhart Brass Mfg. Co., 6 x 1 1/2 In. 200.00
Nozzle, Controlling, Brass, Waldron, 8 x 1 3/4 In. 200.00
Nozzle, Piercing, Brass, Elkhart, Shut Off, 66 In. 240.00
Nozzle, Steamer, Brass, American Fire Engine Co., 26 In. 546.00
Photograph, Barnicoat Fire Society, 1890, 17 x 21 3/4 In. 230.00
Photograph, Chief's Car, City Of Brockton, 1930s, 12 x 16 In. 316.00
Photograph, Early Smith Hand-Operated Fire Engine, 9 1/2 x 14 In. 175.00
Photograph, Half-Plate Daguerreotype, 3 Men, Parade Dress, Union No. 2 Fire Co. 9200.00
Photograph, Ladder Co. No. 12 Boston, 13 3/8 x 15 In. 115.00
Shield, Presented To Veteran To Volunteer Firemen's Assoc., Hartford 2070.00
Shirt, Parade, Red Wool Bib, White Pearl Buttons 175.00
Time Stamp, Excelsior, Brass Case & Gears, Iron Base, Winding Key, Gamewell 405.00
Top Hat, Parade, Pressed Wool, Black, Gilt Lettering, Red Liner, 1848, 6 1/2 In. 2990.00
Top Hat, Parade, Pressed Wool, Friendship Fire Co. 5, 1848, 6 1/2 In. 2990.00
Trumpet, Nickeled, Red Cord, Tassels, 19 In. 548.00
Trumpet, Silver Plated, Chased, American, c.1880, 21 In. 4200.00
Walking Stick, Presented To President Of Nauaug Hose Co. No. 1, Scranton 489.00
Whistle, Steam, 3 Chamber, Domed, Acorn Final, Lunkenheimer, 2 1/2 x 10 3/4 In. 315.00
Whistle, Steam, Single Chamber, Brass, Morris, Toronto, 2 1/2 x 14 1/2 In. 290.00

FIREGLOW glass is attributed to the Boston and Sandwich Glass Company. The light-tan-colored glass appears reddish brown when held to the light. Most fireglow has an acid finish and enamel decoration, although it was also made with a satin finish.

Vase, Enameled Flowers, Ruffled Edge, 4 In. . . . . *Illus* 125.00

FIREPLACES were used to cook food and to heat the American home in past centuries. Many types of tools and equipment were used. Andirons held the logs in place, firebacks reflected the heat into the room, and tongs were used to move either fuel or food. Many types of spits and roasting jacks were made and may be listed in the Kitchen category.

Andirons, Arts & Crafts, Cutout Design, 20 In. 160.00
Andirons, Ball & Steeple Top, 18th Century, 17 In. 560.00
Andirons, Bell Metal, Cabriole Legs, Ball Feet, Urn Tops, Acorn Finials, 24 In. 1430.00
Andirons, Belle Epoque, Bronze Dore, Late 19th Century, 39 1/4 In. . . . . 1955.00 to 2070.00
Andirons, Brass & Iron Knife, Faceted Knob, 21 1/2 In. 750.00
Andirons, Brass & Iron, Baluster Shape, Ribbed, Faceted Shaft, Cabriole Legs, 23 In. 489.00
Andirons, Brass & Iron, Belted Lemon Tops, Cabriole Legs, 17 1/4 x 20 In. 750.00
Andirons, Brass & Iron, Cabriole Legs, Ball Feet, 23 x 10 x 20 1/2 In. 488.00
Andirons, Brass & Iron, Federal, Brass Urn Tops, Penny Feet, 18 1/2 x 16 In. 315.00

The best burglary protection is a dog. Inmates from three Ohio prisons were surveyed and said timed lights, dead-bolt locks, and alarms are deterrents; but the thing most avoided by a professional thief is a noisy dog.

Fireglow, Vase,
Enameled Flowers,
Ruffled Edge, 4 In.

Andirons, Brass & Iron, Federal, Row Of Beading, Ball Feet, 21 x 19 x 11 3/4 In. 690.00
Andirons, Brass & Iron, Knife Blade, Brass Shields, Penny Feet, 25 x 18 In. 1955.00
Andirons, Brass & Iron, Lemon Top, Pedestal Shafts, Cabriole Legs, 19 In. 690.00
Andirons, Brass & Iron, Spool Top, Cabriole Legs, Ball Feet, 14 1/2 In. 315.00
Andirons, Brass Urn Finials, Penny Feet, 20 1/2 In. 605.00
Andirons, Brass, Acorn Finial, Ring & Urn Turned Support, Ball Feet, c.1800s 1763.00
Andirons, Brass, Baker's, Fluted Column, Flower Rosette Finial, 10 In. 190.00
Andirons, Brass, Ball Tops, Cabriole Legs, Ball Feet, 16 In. 100.00
Andirons, Brass, Baluster Form, Scrolling Base, Half-Sphere Shaped Feet, 1800, 26 In. .. 1080.00
Andirons, Brass, Baluster Form, Scrolling Base, Sphere Shape Feet, 1800, 26 In. 1080.00
Andirons, Brass, Beaux Arts, Baluster Shape, Angular Support, Hoof Feet, 13 In. 315.00
Andirons, Brass, Belle Epoque, Continental, 19 3/4 In. 1150.00
Andirons, Brass, Cabriole Legs, Ball Feet, Acorn Tops, 17 1/2 In. 220.00
Andirons, Brass, Chip, Pendale, Lemon Top, 18th Century, 15 In. 450.00
Andirons, Brass, Chippendale, Spiral Finial, Turned Spiral Shaft, Claw Feet, 24 In. 5750.00
Andirons, Brass, Empire, Ball Tops, Cabriole Legs, Ball Feet, 16 1/2 In. 55.00
Andirons, Brass, Federal, Acorn Finials, Penny Feet, Early 19th Century, 19 In. 990.00
Andirons, Brass, Federal, Acorn, 20 1/2 In. 890.00
Andirons, Brass, Federal, Ball & Spire Finial, Ball Feet, c.1810, 19 1/2 In. 200.00
Andirons, Brass, Federal, Ball, 17 1/2 In. 460.00
Andirons, Brass, Federal, Column Shape, Urn Top, Lemon Finials, Cabriole Legs, 23 In. .. 60.00
Andirons, Brass, Federal, Knob Finial, Ball-Over-Ring, Baluster, Slipper Feet, 18 In. 705.00
Andirons, Brass, Federal, Urn Finials, Faceted Plinth, Cabriole Legs, Ball Feet, 20 In. ... 330.00
Andirons, Brass, George Washington, Uniform, 21 x 9 1/4 x 21 1/2 In. 200.00
Andirons, Brass, Guilloche Molded Urn, Husk Swag, 20th Century, 16 In. 260.00
Andirons, Brass, Lemon Finial, Log Stops, Cabriole Legs, Slipper Feet, 17 In. 360.00
Andirons, Brass, Louis XV, Continental, Paw Feet, 1800s 402.00
Andirons, Brass, Louis XVI Style, Chenet, Lyres, Pierced Shell, Leaf Guard, 30 In. 170.00
Andirons, Brass, Pierced Ball, Lion Head, Ring, 21 In. 290.00
Andirons, Brass, Plinth, Knife Blade, Brass Urn Form Finial, 21 1/2 In. 646.00
Andirons, Brass, Scalloped Cabriole Legs, Ball Feet, 21 1/2 In. 360.00
Andirons, Brass, Scrolled Cabriole Legs, Ball Top, Lacquer, Early 1900s, 18 In. 140.00
Andirons, Brass, Sphere Finial, Queen Anne Style, Late 19th Century, 18 In. 224.00
Andirons, Brass, Sunflower, 20 In. 750.00
Andirons, Brass, Turned Column Standards, Cabriole Legs, Ball Feet, 20 In. 400.00
Andirons, Brass, Urn Top, Tool Stand, 4 Tools, Victorian, 21 x 9 x 27 In. 590.00
Andirons, Bronze, Hounds, Gilt, France, 13 1/2 x 13 1/2 In. 1455.00
Andirons, Bronze, Hounds, Louis XV Style, Gilt, Ormolu, 19th Century, 19 x 17 In. 780.00
Andirons, Bronze, Hounds, Louis XVI, Column, Flower, Urns, Dore, 1880s, 17 x 17 In. ... 2645.00
Andirons, Bronze, Hounds, Napoleon III, Gilt, Wrought Iron, 11 3/4 x 10 In. 3910.00
Andirons, Bronze, Owl Heads, Talon Feet, 19th Century, 19 1/4 In. 230.00
Andirons, Bronze, Screen, Tool Holder, Arts & Crafts, 39-In. Holder, 5 Piece 33.00
Andirons, Cast Iron, Baseball Player, Painted, Early 20th Century, 20 x 6 1/2 In. 12000.00
Andirons, Cast Iron, Block Finial, Arts & Crafts, 16 In. 290.00
Andirons, Cast Iron, Brownie, Green Glass Eyes, 15 1/2 x 18 In. 920.00
Andirons, Cast Iron, Cat, Elongated Necks, Arched Feet, Early 1900s, 13 1/2 In. 2530.00
Andirons, Cast Iron, Coalbrookdale Co., 21 1/2 x 11 1/4 In. 3680.00
Andirons, Cast Iron, Dachshund Shape, 13 1/2 In. 145.00
Andirons, Cast Iron, Dolphins, American, Early 20th Century, 14 1/4 x 8 x 16 In. 720.00
Andirons, Cast Iron, Eagle Medallions, Snake Feet, Ring Finials, 15 In. 220.00
Andirons, Cast Iron, Empire, Federal, 1820 .... 450.00
Andirons, Cast Iron, George Washington, Mid 19th Century, 20 In. 110.00
Andirons, Cast Iron, Hessian Shape, 20 In. 175.00
Andirons, Cast Iron, Hessian Soldier, 20 x 9 1/2 x 19 In. 900.00
Andirons, Cast Iron, Horses, 1860s, 8 x 9 In. 290.00
Andirons, Cast Iron, Indian Brave Holding Tomahawk, 19 x 17 1/2 In. 2185.00
Andirons, Cast Iron, Musical Note, Chrome Plate Co., Nashville, 1925, 17 x 20 In. 1725.00
Andirons, Cast Iron, Owl Perched On Twig Base, Molded Glass Eyes, 15 3/8 In. 700.00
Andirons, Cast Iron, Owl, Black Repaint, Yellow Eyes, 15 1/2 In. 165.00
Andirons, Cast Iron, Owl, Half Round, Yellow Glass Eyes, 1887, 15 1/2 x 15 1/2 In. 700.00
Andirons, Cast Iron, Palm Frond, Stylized Scrolled Fronds, 20th Century, 22 x 11 In. 2185.00
Andirons, Cast Iron, Scrolled Feet, Splayed Legs, Tapered Columns, 1900s, 20 In. 55.00
Andirons, Cast Iron, Woman, Holding Torch, Black Paint, Gold Trim, 17 In. 190.00

Andirons, Chippendale, Ball & Claw Feet, Flaming Urn Finial, 32 x 13 x 22 In. 6720.00
Andirons, Chrome & Iron, Tubular Steel Shaft, Iron Feet, 22 1/2 x 7 x 18 In. 170.00
Andirons, Colonial Soldier 950.00
Andirons, Copper, Samuel Yellin, 32 x 14 x 24 In. 800.00
Andirons, Eagle Engraved Panels, Spread Wings, Acorn Finials, 20 x 10 1/4 In. 3850.00
Andirons, Eagle, Iron, Half Oval Fluted Bases, 12 1/2 In. 250.00
Andirons, Forged Iron, Ball Tops, Crooked Necks, Penny Feet, 17 In. 90.00
Andirons, Golf Bag 7500.00
Andirons, Hand Wrought, Anchor Shape, 19 1/4 In. 350.00
Andirons, Iron, Anchor Shape, 19 1/4 In. 350.00
Andirons, Iron, Ball & Twist Front, 1860s, 31 1/2 x 16 3/4 x 25 In. 784.00
Andirons, Iron, Bell Metal, Lemon Top, Ring Turned Round Shafts, Slipper Feet, 18 In. . . 748.00
Andirons, Iron, Owl, Rusty, 15 x 16 1/2 In. 297.00
Andirons, Jupiter, Thunderbolts, 19th Century, 31 1/2 In. 2070.00
Andirons, Metal, Federal, Bell Shaft, Double Urn, Acorn Finial, c.1820, 24 In. 1175.00
Andirons, Scrolled & Foliated Shape, Oriental Figure & Peacock, H. Vian, 1900, 10 In. . . 3910.00
Andirons, Serpentine Scroll Base & Feet, Basket Twist Columns, 23 1/2 In. 302.00
Andirons, Spit Hooks, 20 1/4 x 22 3/4 In. 785.00
Andirons, Urn & Spherule Finial, Scrolled Legs, 20 1/2 x 9 3/4 In. 230.00
Andirons, Wrought Iron, Anchor Shape, Turner, 24 x 13 1/2 x 29 In. 1500.00
Andirons, Wrought Iron, Anchor Shape, Turner, Isle Au Haut, Maine, 24 x 13 1/2 In. 3136.00
Andirons, Wrought Iron, Arched Bases, Penny Feet, 43 1/2 x 25 3/4 In. 330.00
Andirons, Wrought Iron, Baseball Shape, Penny Feet, Upright, 12 x 14 In. 165.00
Andirons, Wrought Iron, Brass Finial, Penny Feet, Turned Ball & Shaft, 17 x 16 In. 1925.00
Andirons, Wrought Iron, Goose Head, Curved Neck, Scrolled Legs, 18 In. 1880.00
Andirons, Wrought Iron, Gooseneck, Mid 19th Century, 15 1/2 x 15 1/2 In. 230.00
Andirons, Wrought Iron, Knife Blade, Gooseneck Polyhedron Finials, 18 1/2 x 17 In. 490.00
Andirons, Wrought Iron, Knife Blade, Penny Feet, Arched Base, Brass Finials, 20 In. 192.00
Andirons, Wrought Iron, No. 88, Ball Finials, Rings, Chain, G. Stickley, 20 In. 14900.00
Andirons, Wrought Iron, Serpentine Front, 11 In. 55.00
Andirons, Wrought, Iron, Woman's Torso, 19th Century, 12 In. 316.00
Bellows, Cast Iron, Lyre Form, Scrolled Frame, 1 Red, 1 Black, 12 1/2 In. 353.00
Bellows, Green Paint, Flowers, 16 1/2 x 7 In. 58.00
Bellows, Leather, Painted Scene, Studded Sides, 24 1/2 x 10 x 4 In. 1763.00
Bellows, Leather, Painted, Green Ground, Strawberries, Leaves, 22 In. 154.00
Bellows, Leather, Rose Maling, Red Ground, Green Edge, 18 3/8 In. 577.00
Bellows, Leather, Stenciled Fruit, Copper & Green, Brass Nozzle, 18 In. 110.00
Bellows, Painted Yellow House Inside Yellow Heart, Floral Border, c.1820 . . . . 1320.00
Bellows, Stenciled Strawberry Type Flowers, Striped Border, Brass Nozzle, 16 1/2 In. . . . 80.00
Bellows, Tortoiseshell & Brass, Scroll Inlay, Leather Panel, 1890s, 20 1/8 In. 575.00
Bellows, Turtle Back, Flowers & Foliage, Starburst At Hole, Brass Nozzle, 18 In. 357.00
Bellows, Turtle Back, Painted Crested Bird, On Branch, Brass Nozzle, 17 5/8 In. 385.00
Bellows, Turtle Back, Stenciled Flowers, Yellow, Green & Gold, Brass Nozzle, 17 In. 275.00
Bellows, Turtle, Painted Fruit, Brass Nozzle, Leather, 17 1/4 In. 110.00
Bellows, Turtle, Red Tulips, Green & Black Leaves, Brass Nozzle, 17 1/4 In. 220.00
Bellows, Yellow Ground, Stenciled Fruit Design, 19th Century, 17 In. 172.00
Bench, Openwork Slats, 6 Brass Legs, Tufted Vinyl Cushion, 29 5/8 x 9 1/4 In. 230.00
Bucket, Ash, Tole Painted, Fruit & Vine, Vented Cover, 2 Handles, c.1867, 11 x 12 1/2 In. 336.00
Chenet, Brass, Napoleon III, Patinated, Wrought Iron, 21 3/4 x 9 1/2 x 19 3/4 In., Pair . . . 1955.00
Chenet, Brass, Urn Design, 19th Century, 12 1/2 In., Pair 290.00
Coal Box, Brass, Square, Laurel Wreath & Urn Medallion, Federal, 19 x 14 x 14 In. 615.00
Coal Box, Mahogany, Slant Lid, Lift Top, Brass Handle, Scoop, 14 x 12 1/2 x 7 1/2 In. . . . 195.00
Coal Scuttle, Brass, 2 Cornucopia Handles, Neoclassical, 16 3/4 x 20 In. 375.00
Coal Scuttle, Hinged Lid, Loop Handle, Tin Liner, Late 19th Century, 16 x 13 5/8 In. 170.00
Coal Scuttle, Mahogany, Brass Handle, Metal Liner, c.1880, 13 x 13 In. 157.00
Coal Scuttle, Mahogany, Brass Handle, Slanted Hinged Lid, 19th Century, 13 x 19 In. . . . 168.00
Coal Scuttle, Mahogany, Brass Trim & Handle, Removable Shovel, 16 x 20 In. 80.00
Coal Scuttle, Serpentine Hinged Lid, Stylized Floral Front, Tin Liner, 19 3/4 x 16 In. 315.00
Coal Scuttle, Tole Painted, Scroll Handle, Sleigh Cover, Metal Insert, 23 x 10 x 8 In. 280.00
Crane, Wrought Iron, Round & Square Construction, 29 x 30 In. 275.00
Fan, Carved Wood 290.00
Fender, Brass & Wire, Brass Rim At The Top, Early 19th Century, 10 1/2 x 14 In. 750.00
Fender, Brass & Wire, Early 19th Century, 8 x 48 x 15 In. 630.00

Fender, Brass Mounted, Ring & Baluster Finials, Federal, c.1810, 14 1/2 x 53 In. 1765.00
Fender, Brass Upper Rim, Scrolling Wirework, c.1800, 16 1/4 x 41 3/4 x 14 1/4 In. 920.00
Fender, Brass, 2 Pierced Bands, Iron Frame, 15 x 46 1/2 In. 275.00
Fender, Brass, 6 Cherubs Holding Floral Swags, Clouds, 8 1/4 x 48 In. 385.00
Fender, Brass, Ball Finial Corners, Pierced, Early 1900s, 47 x 10 1/2 In. 165.00
Fender, Brass, Black Patinated Brass, Neo Grecque Style, 8 x 29 1/2 In. 430.00
Fender, Brass, Corner Pierced & Reeded Columns, Ball Finials, 32 1/4 In. 165.00
Fender, Brass, Empire, Paw Feet, Pierced Rope Twisted Apron, 57 x 14 x 8 In. 110.00
Fender, Brass, England, Turned Finials, 7 1/2 x 42 1/4 x 11 3/4 In. 160.00
Fender, Brass, Engraved & Pierced, Urn Shaped Finials, England, 58 In. 440.00
Fender, Brass, Floral Piercing, Lattice, Paw Feet, 43 5/8 In. 460.00
Fender, Brass, Frieze, Convex Band, Scrollwork, George IV, c.1825, 8 1/4 x 39 In. 405.00
Fender, Brass, Pierced Panel, 5 Paw Feet, 36 In. 190.00
Fender, Brass, Pierced, 9 x 47 x 12 In. 69.00
Fender, Brass, Seahorse & Scrolling, 11 1/2 x 55 1/4 In. 1080.00
Fender, Brass, Sphere Finial, England, Late 19th Century, 8 x 52 x 14 1/2 In. 560.00
Fender, Brass, Square, Sphere, England, Late 19th Century, 12 x 54 x 15 In. 560.00
Fender, Brass, Turned Finials, Open Work Line Shape, 46 1/2 x 14 1/2 x 12 In. 315.00
Fender, Brass, Vertical Wirework, Center Wire Scroll, 18 1/4 x 44 1/2 In. 1725.00
Fender, Brass, Wire, Finials, Brass Top Rail, c.1830, 14 3/4 x 48 1/2 x 15 In. 1380.00
Fender, Brass, Wire Mesh, Serpentine, 13 x 43 In. 520.00
Fender, Brass, Wire, Screen, 1840, 15 x 44 In. 1320.00
Fender, Brass, Wire, Scroll Design Center Band, Brass Rail, Federal, 41 x 9 x 12 In. 495.00
Fender, Brass, Wire, Urn Finials, Early 19th Century, 18 x 45 3/4 x 16 In. 690.00
Fender, Brass, Wirework, Curved End, Spiral & Swag, Federal, 15 1/2 x 43 x 21 In. 1175.00
Fender, Bronze, Gilt, France, 20th Century, 8 x 37 x 3 1/4 In. 1840.00
Fender, Bronze, Patinated Bronze, Louis XVI Style, France, 10 1/2 x 37 x 5 In. 1495.00
Fender, Bronze, Pedestal Mount, 2 Heraldic Lions Connected By Chain, 10 x 44 In. 1610.00
Fender, Bronze, Steel, Louis Philippe, Mid 19th Century, 8 x 42 x 3 In. 1955.00
Fender, Pierced & Engraved, Lions Amid Scrolling Leaves, 52 1/2 In. 375.00
Fender, Pierced & Ribbed Dividers, 6 Finials At Tops, 10 3/4 x 47 In. 220.00
Fender, Pierced Mid Section, Ogee Base, c.1860, 7 x 40 In. 728.00
Fender, Polished Steel, George III, 19th Century, 54 3/4 x 6 1/2 In. 230.00
Fender, Wrought Iron, Bronze Mounted, Gilt, Louis Philippe, 8 1/2 x 52 x 3 In. 1495.00
Fender, Wrought Iron, Scrolled, Upholstered Ends, Arts & Crafts, 69 x 23 x 24 In. 1430.00
Fireback, Cast Iron, Portrait Of Gentleman, Crowned Lion, 29 1/4 In. 345.00
Fireback, Cast Iron, Top Flanked By Dolphins, Shepherd With Flock, 33 x 21 1/2 In. 290.00
Fireback, Central Medallion, Bust Portrait, Lion, Inscription, 26 1/4 x 29 1/4 In. 345.00
Fireback, Iron, Tavern Scene, Attached Rack & Andirons, Continental, 24 x 12 In. 330.00
Firedog, Cast Iron, Lions Bearing Twisted Barsearly 20th Century, 15 In., Pair 690.00
Flue Cover, Plaster, Indian Design, 10 1/2 In. 16.00
Fork, Hand Forged, Brass Finial, 3 Tines, Black Paint, 1900s, 44 In. 55.00
Fork, Roasting, 2 Tines, Hanging Hook, Marked J.H. Sheirich, 9 3/4 In. 250.00
Grate, Coal, Cast Iron, George III, Serpentine, Brass Stand, Column Legs, 22 In. 315.00
Guard, Bronze, Trelliswork Grill, Sphinx Supporting Pedestal, 1840s, 10 x 38 In. 2530.00
Lighter Set, Copper, Arts & Crafts, Cape Cod Shop Pat. May 22nd, 1916, 3 Piece 180.00
Log Holder, Arts & Crafts, Slat Sides, 3 Cutouts, Copper Straps, 26 x 17 x 18 In. 475.00
Log Holder, Brass, Lions & Bird, Lion Paw Feet, 15 1/4 x 27 1/4 x 18 1/2 In. 120.00
Log Holder, L. & J.G. Stickley, Slat Sides, Cutout Handles, 20 x 20 x 19 In. 3335.00
Mantel is listed in the Architectural category.
Poker, Brass, Steel, 19th Century 150.00
Screen, 3 Hinged Panel, Heart Cutouts, Arts & Crafts, 14 x 32 In. 690.00
Screen, 6 Panel, Blue, White, Wood Frame, Late 19th Century 575.00
Screen, Brass, Iron, Neoclassical Style, Paw Feet, 19th Century, 42 x 13 x 16 In. 750.00
Screen, Brass, Iron, Paw Feet, Neoclassical, 1800s, 42 x 13 x 16 In. 747.00
Screen, Brass, Rosette & Bail Brasses At Top, Wire Waist, 30 1/4 x 43 In. 195.00
Screen, Canvas, Lifting Handle, Painted Floral Still Life, Trestle Supports, 36 x 36 In. . . . 545.00
Screen, Copper & Iron, Embossed Owl, Fruit, Whiplash Feet, Arts & Crafts, 32 x 18 In. . . 2185.00
Screen, Copper, Hammered, Ship, Riveted Border, Twisted Handle, 32 x 22 In. 288.00
Screen, Ebonized, Pierced Floral Carving Top, Floral Painting, Square, 1880 . . . . 180.00
Screen, Fan Shape, Louis XV, 20th Century, 30 1/2 x 40 In. 290.00
Screen, Federal Wirework, Brass, Swags, Scrollwork, c.1800 . . . . 1600.00
Screen, Gilt Bronze, Wire Mesh, Cheval Legs, Scroll Feet, 38 x 27 x 15 In. 4490.00

Screen, Half Round Crest, Ring Turned Frame, Scrolled Legs, 19th Century, 63 In. 590.00
Screen, Louis XIV, Giltwood, Late 19th Century, 48 1/2 x 30 1/4 In. 2400.00
Screen, Mahogany Stand, Cross Stitch Sampler, c.1842, 56 In. 863.00
Screen, Mahogany, Flower Needlework Panel, Snake Feet, 33 1/2 x 20 1/2 In. 94.00
Screen, Mahogany, Needlework Panel, Serpentine Crest, Arched Feet, 45 x 28 In. 220.00
Screen, Mahogany, Saber Legs, Velvet Panels, Continental, 41 x 24 In. 110.00
Screen, Mahogany, Theorem Insert, Acanthus Leaves, Urn Finials, 34 x 22 3/4 In. 247.00
Screen, Mahogany, Tortoise & Hare, Carved Monkey Corners, Gilt, 18th Century 3300.00
Screen, Ormolu, Needlework, Flowers, Louis XV, 20th Century, 32 1/2 x 25 In. 1150.00
Screen, Pole, Beech, Armorial Crests On Silk, 1859, 54 x 16 1/2 In., Pair 2070.00
Screen, Pole, Cherry, Floral Needlepoint Panel, Snake Feet, Turned Column, 54 3/4 In. . . 110.00
Screen, Pole, Chippendale, Needlepoint Panel, Tripod, 1900s, 16 x 24 In. 300.00
Screen, Pole, Gilt, Cabriole Legs, Arris Pad Feet, Queen Anne, 1770, 55 1/2 In. 5750.00
Screen, Pole, Gold & Amber Floral, Side Leaves, Framed Floral Fabric, 27 In. 880.00
Screen, Pole, Mahogany, Brass Candle Socket & Tapestry, 60 In. 110.00
Screen, Pole, Mahogany, Needlepoint Panel, Girl On Veranda, Urn Finial, 57 1/2 In. 357.00
Screen, Pole, Queen Anne, Mahogany, Needlework Screen, Snake Feet, 55 1/4 In. 6800.00
Screen, Pole, Regency, Rosewood, Floral Embroidered, 3 Scroll Feet, 48 x 14 In. 750.00
Screen, Pole, Satinwood, 3-Panel, Blue Silk Spandrels, Beveled Panel, 62 In. 1495.00
Screen, Pole, Satinwood, Painted Bellflowers, Stepped Plinth Base, 55 5/8 In. 345.00
Screen, Pole, Walnut & Mahogany, Adjustable, Upholstered, Flora On Silk, 67 In. 288.00
Screen, Polychromed & Parcel Gilt Tin, Napoleon III, 21 1/2 x 25 1/2 In. 575.00
Screen, Rosewood & Mahogany, Embroidered Silk, England 750.00
Screen, Satinwood, Fruit Basket Needlework, Circular, George III, 57 x 16 In. 1380.00
Screen, Scrolled Wire, Brass Rim, Serpentine, Finials, Early 19th Century, 14 x 55 In. . . . 2090.00
Screen, Victorian, Mahogany, Needlework, 19th Century, 53 x 33 x 17 In. 2760.00
Screen, Walnut, Brass, Embroidered, Victorian, Late 19th Century, 56 1/2 x 18 In. 575.00
Screen, Walnut, Domed Crest Above Arched Frieze, Needlework, Landscape, 44 1/2 In. . . 679.00
Screen, Walnut, Needlepoint Panel, Hunter On Rock, River & Town, Late 19th Century . . 247.00
Screen, Walnut, Pedestal Base, Adjustable, Renaissance Revival, 51 x 27 In. 1120.00
Screen, Wrought Iron, Acanthus Leaf, Arts & Crafts, 36 x 51 In. 200.00
Screen, Wrought Iron, Floral, Scrolled Ends, Arts & Crafts, 42 x 10 x 40 In. 720.00
Screen, Wrought Iron, Log Holder, Fire Tools & 32-In. Stand, Art Deco, 5 Piece 635.00
Shield, Painted, Winter Homestead Scene, Curved, Metal, Iron, c.1880, 45 x 24 x 8 In. . . . 560.00
Shovel, Brass, England, 1720, 13 In. 295.00
Shovel, Brass, Iron, Ball Top, Shaped Bowl, 34 x 7 x 2 In. 140.00
Stand, Kettle, Mid Georgian, Mahogany, Square, Outset Corners, 28 x 12 In. 1840.00
Surround, Carrara Marble, Carved, Inlaid, George III, c.1800, 48 1/4 x 68 1/4 In. 3565.00
Surround, Gilt & Patinated Putti, Musical Instruments, Stepped Base 4255.00
Surround, Oak, 6 Tier Shelf, Mirror, Carved Design, Victorian, 63 x 11 x 76 In. 862.00
Surround, Seated Brass Griffin, Joined By Leaf Bar, 1 Loop Handle, 16 x 29 1/2 In. 1725.00
Tongs, Brass, Beacon Finger Grip, 1890s, 8 1/2 In. 65.00
Tongs, Ember, Brass, Dutch, 18th Century, 10 3/8 In. 195.00
Tongs, Empire, Brass, Steel, 1820 . . . . 125.00
Tongs, Empire, Federal, 1820 . . . . 125.00
Tongs, Lemon Top, Bell Metal, Iron, 34 x 3 1/2 x 1 1/2 In. 112.00
Tongs, Wrought Iron, Log, 33 In. 224.00
Tongs, Wrought Iron, Penny Head, Round Shaft, Flared Grips, Square Handle, 29 In., Pair 28.00
Tongs, Wrought Iron, Round, Flat Oval Head To Square Head, Octagon Top Knob, 26 In. . 28.00
Tool Set, Brass & Iron, Tongs, Shaped Handles, 28 In., Pair 345.00
Tool Set, Tongs, Shovel, Brass, Iron, Ball Top, 29 x 3 x 1 1/4 In. 196.00
Tool Set, Wrought Iron, Tudor Style, Andirons, Holder, Shovel, Fork, Brass Caps, 5 Piece 2070.00
Tool Set, Wrought Iron, Tudor Style, Andirons, Tool Holder, Shovel, Fork, Brass Capped . 2070.00
Trammel, Forged, Colonial, 30 1/2 In. 72.00
Trammel, Wrought Iron, Sawtooth, 22 In. 198.00
Trammel, Wrought Iron, Square Shaft, Arched Legs, Penny Feet, 1700s, 58 x 25 In. 715.00

FISCHER porcelain was made in Herend, Hungary, by Moritz Fischer.
The factory was founded in 1839 and continued working into the
twentieth century. The wares are sometimes referred to as *Herend*
porcelain.

Bonbon, Queen Victoria, Cover, 5 1/2 In. 200.00
Bowl, Rothschild Baird, 10 In. 230.00

Cachepot, Fortuna, 6 1/2 In. 155.00
Dinnerware, Chinese Bouquet Pattern, 54 Piece 1100.00
Figurine, 2 Birds On Flowering Branches, 4 1/2 In. 160.00
Figurine, Peasants, Woodworker, Woman With Hoe, 20th Century, 12 3/4 In., 3 Piece 290.00
Figurine, Rabbit, White, Pink Eyes, Seated, Herend, 20th Century, 11 7/8 In., Pair 402.00
Figurine, Rooster, Overall Enamel Feather Detailing, Gold Accenting, 20th Century 345.00
Lamp, Birds On Branches, Dolphin Handles, Baluster Form, Hungary, 1900s, 17 In. 173.00
Plate, Gilt Reticulated Rim, Enamel, Gilt Monogram, Crown, c.1890, 8 3/8 In., 12 Piece . 1380.00
Plate Set, Dinner, Ozier Molded, Scattered Sprays, 20th Century, 10 3/4 In., 13 Piece ... 633.00
Tray, Queen Victoria, Oval, 12 1/2 In. 230.00
Tray, Queen Victoria, Square, 6 3/4 In. 200.00
Tureen, Undertray, Oval, Floral, Butterflies, Lemon Finial, Hungary, 1900s, 13 x 13 In. .. 690.00
Vase, Scroll & Floral, Gilt, Handles, Fluted Plinth, Herend, 10 1/2 In. 275.00

FISHING reels of brass or nickel were made in the United States by 1810. Bamboo fly rods were sold by 1860, often marked with the maker's name. Lures made of metal, or metal and wood, were made in the nineteenth century. Plastic lures were made by the 1930s. All fishing material is collected today and even equipment of the past thirty years is of interest if in good condition with original box.

Box, Tackle, Leather Over Wood .... *Illus* 1100.00
Box, Tackle, Wooden, Carved, Painted Fish, 7 x 23 x 7 In. 27.00
Box, Tackle, Wooden, Dovetailed, Metal Latch, 7 x 16 x 8 In. 77.00
Bucket, Bait, Hinged Lid, Metal, Wire Handle, Wooden Grasp, 10 1/2 x 15 In. 38.00
Bucket, Minnow, Collapsible Canvas, Bait Containers, 9 x 11 x 10 In. 70.00
Bucket, Minnow, Hinged Lid, Copper, Iron Handles, Insert, Davidson, Signed, 15 x 8 In. .. 275.00
Bucket, Minnow, Tin, Fish Design On Exterior, 10 Qt. 220.00
Canoe, Linkanoe, Canvas Cover, Breaks Into 10 Sections, 14 Ft. 6 In. 850.00
Catalog, Old Town Canoe Co., Color, 37 Pages, 1930 .... 110.00
Catalog, Old Town Canoe Co., Color, 37 Pages, 1931 .... 80.00
Creel, George Lawrence, Split Willow, Leather Trim, Portland, Ore., 1950, Size 15 .. *Illus* 9020.00
Creel, J.W. Elders, Handmade, Split Willow, Rogers, Arkansas, 1955, 17 x 8 In. 4070.00
Creel, Macmonies Hardware, Split Willow, Leather Trim, Zippered Lid, Model 80 ...... 2200.00
Creel, Ray Salminen, Split Willow, Leather Trim, Brass Tag, Acton, Mass. 550.00
Creel, Split Willow, Center Hole, Slanted Lid, 8 x 12 x 11 In. 80.00
Creel, Split Willow, Off-Center Hole, Metal Trim, Fish-Shaped Leather Latch, 5 x 10 In. . 66.00
Creel, Split Willow, Off-Center Hole, Metal Trim, Leather, Canvas, 5 1/2 x 10 x 6 In. 39.00
Creel, Thos. J. Conroy, Split Willow, Leather Harness, N.Y., 8 x 15 x 9 In. 880.00
Creel, Wicker, 13 x 7 1/2 In. 70.00
Creel, Wooden, White Cedar Slats, Trout On Lid & Front, Off-Center Hole, Leather Hinge 145.00
Drag Hook, Iron, 41 In. 50.00
Float, Minnow, Hartford, Wisc., Blue Paint, 28 x 8 In. 300.00
Fly, Carrie Stevens, Green Ghost Steamer, Upper Dam, Maine, Size 4 .... 415.00
Fly, Charles Akroyd, Gut-Eyed Salmon, Mounted, 7 x 8 In. Frame, Size 6 .... 880.00
Fly, George M. Kelson, Gut-Eyed Salmon, Mounted, Frame, 1880, 3 3/4 In. 2750.00
Fly, Jimmy Younger, Salmon, Full Dressed, 4 x 4 In. Frame 190.00
Fly, T.E. Pryce, Red Ranger 1650.00
Gaff Hook, Lead Body, Fish Shape, 2 Wrought Iron Barbed Hooks, 8 1/2 x 5 In. 60.00

Fishing, Box, Tackle, Leather Over Wood

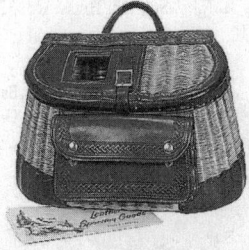

Fishing, Creel, George Lawrence, Split Willow,
Leather Trim, Portland, Ore., 1950, Size 15

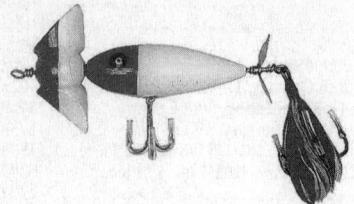

Fishing, Lure, Heddon,
Wooden Box, Flyer No. 150

Fishing, Lure, Bend Fishing
Tackle Co., Trout, Bend, Ore.

License, Pennsylvania, Resident's Citizen's License, 1942, 1 3/4 In.	20.00
Log Book, Whaling Bark, Samson, Long Island, Maps Of Trips, Leather Binding, 1816	1500.00
Lure, Bend Fishing Tackle Co., Trout, Bend, Ore. *Illus*	2970.00
Lure, Creek Chub, Baby Wiggle, Metallic Green	800.00
Lure, Heddon, Wooden Box, Flyer No. 150 *Illus*	935.00
Lure, Silver Shiner Special, Brass Lip	450.00
Lure, Yellow, Green Finish, Eger Baits Lure, No. 603, Box, 2 1/2 In.	22.00
Net, Folding, Brass & Aluminum, Triangular, 16-In. Handle	60.00
Net, Trout, Folding, Brass Latch, Rattan Wrapped Handle, Barnesfold Trademark, 24 In.	137.00
Reel, Abercrombie & Fitch Co., Salmon, Ivory Handle, Brass Foot, 1917, 4 1/2 In.	220.00
Reel, Abu Ambassadeur, Bait Casting, No. 2650	110.00
Reel, Abu Ambassadeur, Bait Casting, Red, No. 6000, Leather Case	110.00
Reel, Blue Grass, Bait Casting, German Silver, Jeweled, No. 4, 2 1/4 In.	330.00
Reel, Edward Vom Hofe, Casting, Maker's Leather Case	605.00
Reel, Edward Vom Hofe, Trout, Silver, Model 360, Size 2, 2 3/4 In.	5060.00
Reel, Edward Vom Hofe, Universal Star, Model 621, Hard Rubber Reel, 1902	485.00
Reel, Ernest Pflueger, Trout, No. 205, c.1897, 6 1/4 In.	990.00
Reel, Fin-Nor, Fly, Gold Anodized, No. 2, Marked Fin-Nor Since 1933, 3 1/8 In.	220.00
Reel, H.L. Leonard, Trout Fly, No. 44A *Illus*	2970.00
Reel, Hardy's, Trout, Featherweight, German Silver, Reversible Line Guide, 2 7/8 In.	250.00
Reel, Hardy's, Trout, Perfect, 2 7/8 In.	470.00
Reel, Hardy's, Trout, Perfect, Alnwick, England, Pat. No. 24245, 1917, 3 In.	715.00
Reel, Horton Mfg., Bait Casting, Blue Grass, No. 7 *Illus*	880.00
Reel, Julius Vom Hofe, Bait Casting, German Silver, Hard Rubber, Size 4, 2 1/8 In.	250.00
Reel, Julius Vom Hofe, Multiflying, Pat. Nov. 17, '85, Oct. 8, 1889, 2 3/4 In.	115.00
Reel, Meek, Bait Casting, Meek, German Silver, Jeweled, No. 3, 2 In.	2200.00
Reel, Meek, Trout, Agate Ring Line Guide, Click, No. 54, 2 7/8 In.	525.00
Reel, Meek, Trout, Anodized Finish, Click, No. 55, 3 1/8 In.	165.00
Reel, Nottingham, Brass, Walnut, 4 In.	138.00
Reel, Orvis, Fly, Magnalite Multiplier, England, 3 1/2 In.	305.00
Reel, Orvis, Salmon, Battenkill V, Adjustable Drag, England, 3 7/8 In.	80.00
Reel, Orvis, Trout Fly, Pat. 1874, Walnut Box *Illus*	1870.00
Reel, Orvis, Trout, England, 3 1/4 In.	220.00
Reel, Salmon, Aluminum Alloy, Ivory Handle, 4 In.	50.00
Reel, St. John, Salmon, Brass, No. 370, 3 7/8 In.	90.00

Fishing, Reel, Horton
Mfg., Bait Casting,
Blue Grass, No. 7

Fishing, Reel, Orvis, Trout Fly, Pat. 1874,
Walnut Box

Don't let dogs, cats, birds, or other pets roam your house. They may chew or scratch or even topple antiques. We once visited a collector whose cougar chewed a table leg while we talked.

Fishing, Reel, H.L. Leonard, Trout Fly, No. 44A

Reel, Thos. J. Conroy, Salmon, Aluminum Alloy, Brass, 4 3/8 In.	633.00
Reel, Winchester, Bait Casting, No. 4253, 1 7/8 In.	110.00
Rod, Edwards, Trout, Bristol, Model F 18-8, 8 Ft.	330.00
Rod, F.E. Thomas, Me-Special, 8 1/2 Ft.	415.00
Rod, Farlow & Co., Trout, 8 1/2 Ft., 3 Piece	275.00
Rod, Fenwick, Fly, Model FF107, 9 Ft.	70.00
Rod, Gene Edwards, 7 Ft., 2 Piece	275.00
Rod, H.L. Leonard, Fly, Tournament, Split Bamboo, Snake Glides, Mahogany Reel Seat	550.00
Rod, H.L. Leonard, Spinning, Graphite, 5 1/2 Ft., 2 Piece	330.00
Rod, H.L. Leonard, Trout, 7 1/2 Ft., 3 Piece	1100.00
Rod, H.L. Leonard, Trout, Model 37, 6 Ft.	1650.00
Rod, Hardy, Salmon, 9 Ft., 3 Piece	220.00
Rod, Orvis, Trout, 6 1/2 Ft., 2 Piece	330.00
Rod, Orvis, Trout, Impregnated Equinox, 8 Ft., 2 Piece	290.00
Rod, Payne, Salmon, Fly, Bamboo, 10 Ft., 3 Piece	520.00
Rod, Payne, Trout, Walnut, 9 Ft., 3 Piece	1760.00
Rod, Pezon & Michel, Trout, 8 1/2 Ft.	275.00
Rod, R.L. Winston, Trout, 8 Ft., 2 Piece	880.00
Rod, Thomas & Thomas, Trout, Caenis, 7 Ft., 2 Piece	1540.00
Rod, Winchester, Trout, USA 6030, 8 1/2 Ft.	215.00
Rod Case, Leather, Belt & Buckle Lid Latch, 2 x 42 In.	159.00
Scale, Hardy Bros., Nickel Silver, Brass, Hanging Ring, Hook, Alnwick, England, 15 Lb.	55.00
Trap, Orvis, Minnow, Perforated Metal Lid, Wire Harness, Manchester, Vt.	80.00

FLAGS are included in the Textile category.

FLASH GORDON appeared in the Sunday comics in 1934. The daily strip started in 1940. The hero was also in comic books from 1930 to 1970, in books from 1936, in movies from 1938, on the radio in the 1930s and 1940s, and on television from 1953 to 1954. All sorts of memorabilia are collected, but the ray guns and rocket ships are the most popular.

Comic Strip, Mac Raboy, Sunday, 10/4/64, 13 x 19 1/2 In.	385.00
Compass, Wrist, Vinyl Strap, Esquire Novelty Co., c.1951, 8 1/4 In.	60.00
Magazine, Look, No. 6, Buster Crabbe As Flash Gordon Cover, March 1938	75.00
Toy, Rocket Fighter, Tin Lithograph, Mechanical, Marx, 12 In.	230.00
Toy, Rocket, Mars, Pair Of Jet Planes, Red & Green, 2 1/2 In.	20.00
Toy, Starship, Tootsietoy, Die Cast Metal & Plastic, Green, White Wings, 5 In.	15.00

FLORENCE CERAMICS were made in Pasadena, California, from World War II to 1977. Florence Ward created many colorful figurines, boxes, candleholders, and other items for the gift shop trade. Each piece was marked with an ink stamp that included the name *Florence Ceramics Co.* The company was sold in 1964, and although the name remained the same the products were very different. Mugs, cups, and trays were made.

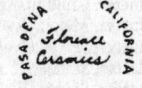

Figurine, Irene, Blue Dress, 6 In.	50.00
Figurine, Louis XVI & Marie Antoinette, 22K Gold Trim, 10 In., Pair	910.00
Figurine, Marilyn	310.00
Figurine, Peter	295.00

Figurine, Rhett Butler 380.00
Figurine, Scarlett 200.00
Figurine, Story Time 425.00

FLOW BLUE was made in England and other countries about 1830 to 1900. The dishes were printed with designs using a cobalt blue coloring. The color flowed from the design to the white body so that the finished piece has a smeared blue design. The dishes were usually made of ironstone china. More Flow Blue may be found under the name of the manufacturer.

Berry Bowl, Acadia, Royal Staffordshire, 5 1/2 In. 35.00
Berry Set, Flowers, Libertas Prussia, 8 Piece 66.00
Bowl, Cover, Pomeroy, Oval Finial, 5 1/4 x 11 1/2 In. 157.00
Bowl, Cover, Versailles, Applied Handles, Gilt Rim, Furnival, 8 In. 77.00
Bowl, Fruit, Abbey, c.1900, 7 1/2 In. 145.00
Bowl, Kin Shan, Paneled Sides, Scalloped Rim, 13 1/2 x 5 In. 300.00
Bowl, Vegetable, Cover, Matlock, Oval, F. Winkle, c.1890, 11 1/2 In. 175.00
Bowl, Vegetable, Cover, Pagoda, Gold Trim, Ashworth, 11 x 8 In. 365.00
Bowl, Vegetable, Cover, Touraine, Alcott, 4 1/2 x 11 1/2 In. 523.00
Butter, Cover, Touraine, Gilt, Liner, Stanley, 3 x 8 In. 297.00
Charger, Brush Stroke, 13 1/2 In. 247.00
Coffeepot, Brush Stroke, 9 In. 522.00
Coffeepot, Bulbous, Temple, 8 1/2 In. 1375.00
Coffeepot, Canova, Mayer, 11 In. 635.00
Coffeepot, Chapoo, 11 In. 3520.00
Coffeepot, Temple, Fluted, 9 3/4 In. 907.00
Compote, Canova, Handles, Open, Mayer, 6 1/2 x 10 In. 546.00
Compote, Cashmere, Pedestal 8750.00
Cuspidor 1800.00
Dinner Set, Hong Kong, Child's, 41 Piece 5700.00
Dish, Cover, Vegetable, Matlock, F. Winkle, c.1890, 7 x 11 1/2 In. 175.00
Dish, Vegetable, Cover, Canova, Mayer, 11 In. 259.00
Footbath, Batavia, Handles 3500.00
Gravy Boat, Touraine, Stanley, 4 x 8 1/2 In. 165.00
Jam Jar, Scinde, Attached Underplate 5000.00
Jar, Cover, Flowers, Gilt Trim, 2 Handles, Impressed Name, 14 x 15 In. 288.00
Jardiniere, Admiral Dewey, 2 Handles, Restored 5000.00
Jug, Hot Milk, Cover, Abbey, c.1900, 5 1/2 In. 105.00
Ladle, Soup, Oriental 1350.00
Mug, Oriental, Loop Handle, 5 In. 55.00
Mug, Singa, Cork, Edge & Malkin, 2 Handles, 2 Frogs 600.00
Pitcher, Chrysanthemum, Scalloped Rim, George Jones, 1880s 425.00
Pitcher, Milk, Landscape Scene, c.1875, 8 1/4 In. 202.00
Pitcher, Milk, Manila, 19th Century, 6 1/2 In. 316.00
Pitcher, Touraine, Stanley, 8 1/2 x 10 1/2 In. 715.00
Pitcher & Bowl, Adams, Eagle, Ornithology, Niagara Falls Ground 1195.00
Plate, Classical Garden Scene Center, Floral Border, c.1870, 12 1/2 In. 134.00
Plate, Salad, Marquis, W.H. Grindley, 8 In. 45.00
Plate, Salad, Touraine, Stanley, 7 1/2 In., 12 Piece 440.00
Plate, Touraine, A. Alcott, 9 3/4 In., 12 Piece 660.00
Plate, Vienna, New Wharf Pottery, 7 In. 35.00
Platter, Canoval, Mayer, 15 1/2 In. 330.00
Platter, Chinese Basket, Large Butterfly, James Mason, 14 x 17 3/4 In. 357.00
Platter, Crumlin, Myott, 17 1/2 In. 202.00
Platter, Meigh, Tivoli, 13 x 16 In. 88.00
Platter, Pelew, Oval, E. Challinor, 9 3/4 In. 192.00
Platter, Scinde, 12 x 15 In. 358.00
Platter, Scinde, Well & Tree, 18 In. 2900.00
Platter, Singanese, RH & Co., 12 x 15 3/4 In. 90.00
Platter, Swansea, Pagodas & Island, Seaside Center Scene, c.1810, 14 1/2 x 11 In. 234.00
Platter & Plate Set, Steers, Border, 13 Piece 2400.00
Platter Set, Turkey, Gilt Flowers, Vine Rim Design, 12 Plates, 13 Piece 605.00
Punch Cup, La Belle, Pedestal 475.00

Sauce Bowl, Touraine, Stanley, 12 Piece	385.00
Serving Dish, Shapoo, 7 x 10 In.	220.00
Soup, Dish, Touraine, Stanley, 7 1/2 In., 12 Piece	467.00
Sugar, Cover, Oriental Scenery, 8 Sides, Molded Handles, Finial, 8 1/2 In.	302.00
Sugar & Creamer, Canova, Mayer	345.00
Sugar & Creamer, Touraine, Stanley, 6 In.	357.00
Tea Set, Brush Stroke, 3 Piece	1200.00
Tea Set, Oriental Scene, Teapot, 4 Cup & Saucer, Child's, 12 Piece	410.00
Teapot, Abbey, George Jones & Sons, c.1900, 5 x 4 1/2 In.	115.00
Teapot, Cover, Oriental, 11 1/4 In.	165.00
Teapot, Leaf & Berry, Gilt Trim, 10 1/2 In.	518.00
Toilet, Paisley, Mercer	1500.00
Tureen, Cover, Peking, 11 In.	880.00
Tureen, Cover, Underplate, Cairo, M. Baker's & Kent	350.00
Tureen, Cover, Underplate, Peking, 7 In.	220.00
Tureen, Cover, Undertray, Ladle, Canova, Brown, 14 In.	1955.00
Tureen, Sauce, Scinde, 4 x 7 1/2 In.	137.00
Tureen, Soup, Cover, Ladle Cutout, Imperial PSL Empire II, 13 In.	99.00
Umbrella Stand, Floral	650.00
Undertray, Syrian, Brown, 19th Century, 14 1/2 In.	750.00
Urinal, Floral	350.00
Vase, Blue Iris, Gilt Ground, 6 Sides, English Mark, 9 1/4 In.	213.00
Vase, Iris, Gilt, 2 Handles, 7 1/2 In.	224.00

FLYING PHOENIX, see Phoenix Bird category.

FOLK ART is also listed in many categories of this book under the actual
name of the object. See categories such as Box, Cigar Store Figure,
Paper, Weather Vane, Wooden, etc.

Biplane, Beaded, World War I Type, France, 14 In.	2450.00
Bird House, Wooden, Tin, Pennsylvania Hex Design Barn, 28 1/2 x 32 1/2 x 21 1/2 In.	940.00
Bottle, Carved Winding Wheels, Center Column, Acorn Finial Turns & Wheels Spin	605.00
Bust, Man Wearing Hat & Coat, Sandstone, Carved, 24 x 14 x 9 In.	748.00
Carnival Doll, Knock Down, Cloth & Paint, Wooden Base, 1930s	95.00
Child's Head, Stone Carving, Incised Hair, Square Base, 19th Century, 9 x 6 x 6 1/2 In.	1410.00
Cradle, Rye Straw, Open Ends, Red Shaped Rockers, Lancaster Co., Pa., 13 x 7 In.	121.00
Diorama, Men Harvesting Cork, Made Of Cork, Frame, Tampa, Sicilian	1250.00
Eagle, Carved, Red Paint, Dots, Green Base, D & B S, 80, Pa., 16-In. Wingspan	220.00
Eagle, Spread Wings, Atop Post, Terra-Cotta, C. Peterson, c.1895, 87 In.	9200.00
Eagle, Spread Wings, Perched On Sphere, Carved Facial Features & Feathers, 33 In.	3290.00
Elephant, Carved, Pegged Wood, Painted, Tusks, Rope Tail, 28 x 18 1/4 In.	55.00
Farmer, Carved, Painted, Copper Rivets, Relief Face, Jointed, Converts To Game Table	275.00
Figure, Abraham Lincoln, Wood, Carved, Painted, Standing On Soapbox, 75 In.	7050.00
Figure, American Indian, Wood, Carved, Weathered, Silvio Zoratti, 1967, 19 1/2 In.	495.00
Figure, Colorado Gold Miner, Black Beard, Half Life Size	950.00
Figure, Comic Drunk Man, Sleeping With Moonshine Bottle As Pillow, 8 3/4 In.	66.00
Figure, Man & Woman, Dancing, Formal Dress, J.K. Hurst, Wood, Carved, 7 1/2 In.	165.00
Figure, Man, Holding Vase, Carved, Painted Wood, 20th Century	176.00
Figure, Man, Suit, Derby Hat, Painted Tie, Lips, Tack Buttons, Initialed HWC 1938, 9 In.	250.00
Frame, Applied Seashells, Square, Round Opening, 7 In.	345.00
Giraffe, Black On Yellow Spotted Body, 10 1/2 In.	98.00
Holder, Mailbox, Uncle Sam, Wood, Standing, Arms Out, 1918, 60 In. ....500.00 to	750.00
Horse, Jumping, Rider, Pine, Carved Bridle, Saddle, Blanket, 22 3/4 In.	1045.00
House, Hinged Top, 2 Fitted Sections, Lower Drawers, 14 x 9 In.	112.00
Lion, Terra-Cotta, Polychrome, Sandpaper Finish, c.1880, 14 1/2 x 11 1/2 In.	2350.00
Lioness, Pouncing, Wood, Metal Eyes, Silvio Zoratti, 1965, 9 x 28 In.	440.00
Man, Black Hair, Facial Accent, Jigger, Wood Jointed, 8 1/2 In.	90.00
Medicine Chest, Yellow & Green Diamond Center, Chrome, 1930s	250.00
Mirror, Carved Ship, Fish, Blue, Red, Green, Yellow, c.1900, 12 1/2 x 6 1/4 In.	575.00
Mirror, Hand, Wood, Carved, Buffalo Bill Handle, Acrobatic Men Around Frame, 13 In.	2300.00
Mirror, Shellwork	185.00
Model, Circus Wagon, Wood, Gesso, Removable Bar Covering, 15 1/2 x 7 1/4 In.	220.00
Panther, White & Black Eyes, Open Red Mouth, White Teeth, 7 1/2 x 14 1/2 In.	247.00
Pig, Black, White, Red Tongue, Applied Teeth, F.B.A., 9 1/2 x 21 1/2 In.	825.00

Plaque, Pine, Laminated Boards, Person Seated Beneath Trees, 11 3/8 x 13 In. 220.00
Rack, Utensil, 2 Carved Birds, 6 Wire Hooks At Base, 7 x 11 In. 330.00
Retablo, On Tin, Angel Wearing Armor, Feathered Crown, Cross & Orb, Frame, 15 1/4 In. 55.00
Retablo, San Antonio De Padua, Hand Painted, Tin Frame, 1850, 13 x 22 In. 495.00
Roundel, Shellwork 425.00
Salmon, Carved Scales, Painted, Articulated Fins & Tail, 19th Century, 42 1/2 In. 8225.00
Salt, Open, Pink Paint, Designs, Branches, Sawtooth Border, c.1880, 3 3/4 x 2 3/4 In. ... 4935.00
San Francisco Trolley, Bombay & Baghdad Streets, Wood, Metal Bumpers, 1920s 7950.00
Shelf, Hanging, Carved, Scrolls, Leafy Designs, 3 Tiers, 24 x 17 In. 750.00
Sign, Dealers In Horses, Horse, Buggy, Driver, Lead Man, 16 x 11 In. 5600.00
Slate, Whimsy, Red, Carved Foliate & Heart, Blade Ends, Stepped Base, 17 x 14 In. 1725.00
Sled, Black, Yellow, Swallow On Sides, Incised Carved JE Colby, Sept' 15th 1844 ...... 7500.00
Stag, Blue Gray Antlers, Underbody, 11 1/2 x 9 In. 88.00
Stag, Carved From 3 Pieces Of Wood, Applied Horns, Ears, Penna., 12 x 12 In. 220.00
Stand, Round, Silhouette, Black Cat, Extended Tail, Green Eyes, 23 x 9 1/4 In. 90.00
Table, Inlaid Whimsical Animals, Figures, Guilford, Ct., J.H. Norton, 1908 .... 1760.00
Tiger, Textured Fur, Nail Teeth, C. Peterson, c.1896, 30 x 63 In. 5175.00
Tip Tray, Bell Hop, c.1920 .... 1295.00
Toy, Steam Tractor, Wood, Brass Tacks, Flywheel, Iron Wheels, Painted, 25 1/2 In. 800.00
Toy, Uncle Sam, Wood, Carved, Acrobatic, Swing, Crank, Karl Gatzer, 16 In. 345.00
Tyrannosaurus Rex, Standing, Wood, Silvio Zoratti, 1967, 14 In. 440.00
Wall Pocket, Hearts Around Mirror, 2 Base Drawers, Made For Emma 420.00
Whirligig, American Indian In Canoe, Copper, Early 19th Century, 10 x 19 In. 595.00
Whirligig, Bathing Beauty In Cooked Pumpkin, Page Boy Hairdo, 9 In. 2090.00
Whirligig, Blacksmith, Pounding Hammer On Anvil, Pine, Metal, Huebbe, c.1945, 21 In. . 220.00
Whirligig, Chicken, Sheet Copper, Painted, White, Red, Yellow, Black, Stand, 20 x 21 In. . 230.00
Whirligig, Civil War Soldier, Full-Length, White Body, Coat, Kepi, 19th Century, 13 In. .. 2115.00
Whirligig, Cottage Birdhouse, Cream, Green, Yellow Trim, 20th Century, 13 x 18 In. 230.00
Whirligig, Covered Wagon, 2 Horses, Rider, Tin, Stenciled Base, 19 x 13 In. 80.00
Whirligig, Dancing Sam & Dan The Banjo Man, Box, 19 1/2 In. 1090.00
Whirligig, Duck, Wood, Painted Blue, White, Yellow, Rotating Wings, 28 3/4 In. 345.00
Whirligig, Ducks, Mallard Drake, Hen, Double Jointed, c.1930, Pair 2800.00
Whirligig, Farmer Milking Cow, Woman Churning Butter, Wooden, Metal, 16 In. 230.00
Whirligig, Lighthouse, Wood, Painted, Octagonal, Bird With Articulated Wings, 69 In. ... 940.00
Whirligig, Log Cabin, Flag, 3 Lumberjacks, 34 x 54 In. 4900.00
Whirligig, Man, Multicolored Propeller, R.A. Miller 595.00
Whirligig, Signalman, Semaphore Paddles, 13 In. 3200.00
Whirligig, Soldier, Orange Coat, Black Pants, Boots, Hat, Signed D & BS 80, 9 3/4 In. 110.00
Whirligig, Soldier, Revolutionary War, Painted, Red, Black, Hat, Leather Brim, 21 In. ... 6500.00
Whirligig, Trotting Horse, White, On Metal Stand, 28 1/4 x 21 x 28 1/2 In. 375.00
Whirligig, Uncle Sam, Wood, Carved, Painted, 1935, 17 3/4 x 13 In. 50.00
Whirligig, Uncle Sam, Wooden Swing Arms, Case, 1940, 15 x 4 3/4 In. 110.00

FOOT WARMERS solved the problem of cold feet in past generations.
Some warmers held charcoal, others held hot water. Pottery, tin, and
soapstone were the favored materials to conduct the heat. The warmer
was kept under the feet, then the legs and feet were tucked into a blanket, providing welcome warmth in a cold carriage or church.

Flint Enamel, Molded Face Below Spout, 11 1/2 In. 185.00
Oak & Walnut, Facing Birds, Berries & Plants, Bird & Grapes On Lid, 8 x 8 In. 550.00
Punched Tin, Circles & Hearts, Wooden Frame, Wire Bail Handle, 5 1/2 x 9 In. 247.00
Punched Tin, Circular Panels, Mortised Wooden Frame, Wire Bail Handle, 9 In. 165.00
Punched Tin, Fruitwood, Wood & Wire Bail Handle, 5 1/2 x 10 1/2 In. 66.00
Yew, Paneled Sides, Side Door, Brass Handle, 1887, 8 1/4 x 11 1/2 In. 357.00

FOOTBALL collectibles may be found in the Card and the Sports categories.

FOSTORIA glass was made in Fostoria, Ohio, from 1887 to 1891. The
factory was moved to Moundsville, West Virginia, and most of the
glass seen in shops today is a twentieth-century product. The company
was sold in 1983; new items will be easily identifiable, according to
the new owner, Lancaster Colony Corporation. Additional Fostoria
items may be listed in the Milk Glass category.

Alexis, Olive Tray 100.00

American, Ashtray, 3 In.	5.00
American, Bell	650.00
American, Bonbon, Amber	125.00
American, Bonbon, Blue	175.00
American, Bonbon, Ruby	125.00
American, Bottle, Cordial, Stopper	65.00
American, Bottle, Ketchup, Stopper	160.00
American, Bowl, Shrimp & Dip	400.00
American, Bowl, Trophy, Footed, 2 Handles, 8 In.	115.00
American, Bowl, Wedding, Cover, Large	850.00
American, Bowl, Wedding, Cover, Milk Glass, 6 1/2 In.	105.00
American, Box, Cosmetic, Round, 1 1/2 In.	750.00
American, Box, Hairpin	2000.00
American, Butter, Cover, Round	95.00
American, Cake Stand, Round, 10 In.	130.00
American, Candlestick, 2-Light, Bell Shape	125.00
American, Candlestick, Cone, Large	250.00
American, Candy Dish, 7 x 5 In.	450.00
American, Condiment Set, Cloverleaf Tray, 5 Piece	1000.00
American, Decanter Set, Cordial, Scotch, Rye, Gin, Frame, Lock	500.00
American, Dish, Banana Split	1200.00
American, Hair Receiver, Cover, Square, 3 In.	750.00 to 795.00
American, Jar, Sugar Cube, Silver-Plated Cover, Tongs	250.00
American, Marmalade, Cover, Spoon	125.00
American, Nappy, 7 In.	400.00
American, Perfume Bottle	100.00
American, Pitcher, Boudoir, Qt.	55.00
American, Relish, 3 Sections, Oval, 11 In.	40.00
American, Relish, 4 Sections, Square, 10 In.	150.00
American, Ring Tree	750.00
American, Stopper, Perfume	25.00
American, Tray, 5 Sections, Blue, Frame	324.00
American, Tray, Cloverleaf	250.00
American, Vase, Flared, 9 1/2 In.	250.00
American, Vase, Flared, 10 In.	90.00
American, Vase, Straight, 12 In.	150.00
American, Vase, Swung, 20 In.	400.00
American, Youth Set, Plate, Bowl, Mug	225.00
Arlington, Salt & Pepper, Milk Glass	30.00
Atlanta, Compote, 7 1/2 x 6 In.	45.00
Baroque, Bonbon, 3-Footed	18.00
Baroque, Candlestick, 1-Light, Topaz, 4 In., Pair	65.00
Baroque, Compote, Blue, 4 3/4 In.	35.00
Baroque, Mustard, Cover, Topaz	135.00
Baroque, Pitcher, Ice Lip, 44 Oz., 7 In.	125.00
Baroque, Sugar & Creamer, Topaz, Individual, 3 In.	50.00
Beacon, Relish, 4 Sections	10.00
Bell, Christmas, Red Flash	50.00
Bell, Horse Drawn Sleigh	20.00
Bell, Ice Skaters	20.00
Bell, Love Birds, Red Flash	65.00
Century, Pitcher, 16 Oz.	60.00
Century, Pitcher, 48 Oz.	125.00
Chintz, Bell, Dinner	125.00
Chintz, Candlestick, 5 1/2 In., Pair	75.00
Chintz, Plate, Cheese & Cracker, 11 In.	95.00
Coin, Bowl, Wedding, Cover	65.00
Coin, Box, Cigarette, Cover, Gold Coins	145.00
Coin, Lamp, Courting, Handle, Amber	110.00
Coin, Pitcher, 2 Qt.	95.00
Coin, Pitcher, Amber, 2 Qt.	55.00
Coin, Tumbler, Juice, 9 Oz., 3 3/8 In.	20.00
Coin, Urn, Cover, Footed, Amber	98.00

Colonial, Toothpick 38.00
Colony, Bowl, 3-Footed, 10 1/2 In. 20.00
Colony, Candlestick, 9 In. 50.00
Colony, Candy Dish, Cover, Milk Glass 33.00
Colony, Compote, Cover, 6 3/8 In. . . . . .35.00 to 42.00
Colony, Relish, 2 Sections, 7 1/4 In. 20.00
Fairfax, Bowl, Whip Cream, Azure 15.00
Fairfax, Cake Plate, Rose, 10 In. 25.00
Fairfax, Celery Dish, Orchid, 11 1/2 In. 35.00
Fairfax, Compote, Azure, 5 In. 32.00
Fairfax, Platter, Oval, Green, 15 In. 170.00
Fairfax, Sherbet, Yellow, 6 Oz., 4 1/4 In. 15.00
Fairfax, Sugar & Creamer, Azure 48.00
Flame, Candlestick, 3 In. 45.00
Flame, Candy Dish, Cover, Oval 35.00
Foster Block, Water Bottle 30.00
Fuchsia, Goblet, Cocktail 22.00
Fuchsia, Plate, Salad, 7 7/8 In. 15.00
Fuchsia, Sherbet, 5 3/8 In., Pair 30.00
Grape, Centerpiece, Orchid 90.00
Hartford, Salt & Pepper 47.00
Heather, Bowl, Footed, 10 3/4 In. 45.00
Hermitage, Mustard, Cover 45.00
Holly, Dish, Mayonnaise, Underplate, Ladle 60.00
Jamestown, Bowl, Azure, 4 1/2 In. 15.00
Jamestown, Bowl, Salad, Azure, 13 1/2 In. 65.00
Jamestown, Goblet, Pink, 9 1/2 Oz. 16.00
Jamestown, Plate, Azure, 8 In. 30.00
Jamestown, Sherbet, Azure 4.00
Jamestown, Tumbler, Ice Tea, Footed, Azure, 11 Oz. 18.00
Jamestown, Tumbler, Ice Tea, Pink, 12 Oz. 19.00
Jamestown, Tumbler, Juice, Footed, Azure, 5 Oz. 21.00
Jamestown, Wine, Pink, 4 Oz. 21.00
June, Candlestick, Topaz, Pair 45.00
June, Centerpiece, Mushroom, Crimped, 12 In. 95.00
June, Compote, Azure, 7 In. 145.00
June, Goblet, Water, 10 Oz., 8 1/4 In. 33.00
June, Goblet, Water, Azure, 10 Oz. 75.00
June, Gravy Boat 45.00
June, Plate, Breakfast, Azure, 8 3/4 In. 25.00
June, Plate, Rose, 7 1/2 In. 18.00
June, Sugar & Creamer 42.00
June, Tumbler, Water, Azure, 9 Oz. 50.00
June, Wine, Topaz, 3 Oz., 5 3/8 In. 50.00
Lafayette, Bonbon, Empire Green 40.00
Lafayette, Relish, 3 Sections, Handles 20.00
Lafayette, Relish, 3 Sections, Handles, Ruby 45.00
Mayfair, Relish, 4 Sections, Rose 17.00
Morning Glory, Bowl, 4-Footed, 10 In. 50.00
Navarre, Bell, Dinner, Blue . . . . .85.00 to 95.00
Navarre, Bowl, Flame, 12 1/2 In. 95.00
Navarre, Candlestick, 3-Light, 6 3/4 In., Pair 185.00
Navarre, Candlestick, 5 1/2 In., Pair 85.00
Navarre, Celery Dish, 11 In. 50.00
Navarre, Compote, Crown Footed, Topaz 50.00
Navarre, Dish, Mayonnaise, Underplate, 2 Sections 75.00
Navarre, Salt & Pepper, Footed . . . . .110.00 to 115.00
Navarre, Sauce, Underplate 165.00
Navarre, Vase, Gray, Trapped Bubble Design, Signed, Square, 8 In. 1035.00
Oakwood, Compote, Orchid, 8 In. 175.00
Pioneer, Sugar & Creamer, Ebony 12.00
Queen Anne, Compote, Amber 155.00
Romance, Cocktail, 3 1/2 Oz., 4 1/2 In. 20.00

Romance, Vase, Footed, 6 In.	125.00
Romance, Wine, 3 Oz., 5 In.	27.00
Rose, Vase, Optic, 6 1/4 In.	30.00
Sun Ray, Bowl, Iridescent, 9 1/4 In.	150.00
Sun Ray, Tumbler, 9 Oz., 5 1/2 In.	15.00
Sylvan, Sugar, Cover, Gold Flash	20.00
Trojan, Console, Topaz	30.00
Trojan, Ice Bucket, Topaz	110.00 to 120.00
Versailles, Bowl, Rose, 12 In.	75.00
Versailles, Celery Dish, Yellow, 11 1/2 In.	80.00
Versailles, Ice Bucket, Yellow	115.00
Versailles, Oyster, Cocktail, Azure, 5 Oz., 3 1/4 In.	50.00
Versailles, Relish, 2 Sections, Yellow, 8 1/2 In.	50.00
Vesper, Goblet, Amber, 9 Oz., 7 1/8 In.	25.00
Victoria, Bowl, Satin, 9 In.	80.00
Victoria, Celery Vase	75.00
Vogue, Toothpick	35.00
Willowmere, Plate Liner, 7 In.	10.00
Willowmere, Plate, Salad, 7 1/2 In.	16.00
Willowmere, Sherbet	17.00
Willowmere, Sugar	20.00
Windsor, Candy Dish, Cover, Topaz	35.00

FOVAL, see Fry category.

FRAMES are included in the Furniture category under Frame.

FRANCISCAN is a trademark that appears on pottery. Gladding, McBean and Company started in 1875. The company grew and acquired other potteries. They made sewer pipes, floor tiles, dinnerwares, and art pottery with a variety of trademarks. In 1934, dinnerware and art pottery were sold under the name Franciscan Ware. They made china and cream-colored, decorated earthenware. Desert Rose, Apple, El Patio, and Coronado were best-sellers. The company became Interpace Corporation and in 1979 was purchased by Josiah Wedgwood & Sons. The plant was closed in 1984 but a few of the patterns are still being made. For more information, see *Kovels' Depression Glass & Dinnerware Price List.*

Apple, Bowl, Cereal, 6 In.	25.00
Apple, Bowl, Salad, 10 In.	149.00
Apple, Bowl, Vegetable, Oval, Divided, 10 7/8 In.	72.00
Apple, Bowl, Vegetable, Round, 8 3/8 In.	33.00
Apple, Bowl, Vegetable, Round, 9 In.	55.00
Apple, Candlestick, 2 5/8 In.	145.00
Apple, Chop Plate, 14 In.	185.00
Apple, Creamer, 3 1/4 In.	22.00
Apple, Cup & Saucer	17.00
Apple, Mixing Bowl, Large, 8 In.	185.00
Apple, Plate, 8 In.	15.00
Apple, Plate, 9 5/8 In.	23.00
Apple, Plate, 10 5/8 In.	20.00
Apple, Plate, Steak, Oval, 11 In.	120.00
Apple, Platter, 12 1/2 In.	36.00
Apple, Platter, 19 1/4 In.	225.00
Apple, Saltshaker, Wooden Base, 5 1/2 In.	225.00
Apple, Sugar	22.00
Bountiful, Bowl, Cereal, 6 In.	24.00
Bountiful, Bowl, Fruit, 5 1/4 In.	20.00
Bountiful, Plate, 6 1/4 In.	14.00
Bountiful, Plate, 8 In.	18.00
Cafe Royal, Candlestick, 3 1/2 In., Pair	110.00
Cafe Royal, Napkin Ring	30.00
Coronado, Bowl, Cereal, Turquoise Matte, 6 1/4 In.	13.00

Coronado, Bowl, Fruit, Ivory Matte, 6 In. 12.00
Coronado, Bowl, Fruit, Turquoise Matte, 6 In. 12.00
Coronado, Bowl, Vegatable, Round, Turquoise Matte, 7 1/2 In. 22.00
Coronado, Bowl, Vegatable, Round, Ivory Matte, 7 1/2 In. 22.00
Coronado, Chop Plate, Coral Matte, 11 3/4 In. 25.00
Coronado, Chop Plate, Ivory Matte, 11 3/4 In. 25.00
Coronado, Creamer, Turquoise Matte 12.00
Coronado, Cup & Saucer, Coral Matte 12.00
Coronado, Cup & Saucer, Ivory Matte 12.00
Coronado, Cup & Saucer, Turquoise Matte 12.00
Coronado, Gravy Boat, Attached Underplate, Turquoise Matte 30.00
Coronado, Plate, Coral Matte, 6 1/4 In. 8.00
Coronado, Plate, Coral Matte, 8 In. 7.00
Coronado, Plate, Coral Matte, 9 1/4 In. 15.00
Coronado, Plate, Coral Matte, 10 3/8 In. 15.00
Coronado, Plate, Ivory Matte, 6 1/4 In. 8.50
Coronado, Plate, Ivory Matte, 9 1/4 In. 15.00
Coronado, Plate, Ivory Matte, 10 3/8 In. 18.00
Coronado, Plate, Turquoise Matte, 6 1/4 In. 8.50
Coronado, Plate, Turquoise Matte, 7 1/4 In. 9.00
Coronado, Plate, Turquoise Matte, 8 In. 12.00
Coronado, Plate, Turquoise Matte, 9 1/4 In. 15.00
Coronado, Plate, Turquoise Matte, 10 3/8 In. 18.00
Coronado, Relish, Oval, Turquoise Matte, 9 1/4 In. 30.00
Coronado, Salt & Pepper, Turquoise Matte 25.00
Coronado, Saucer, Turquoise Matte 2.00
Coronado, Soup, Cream, Underplate, Turquoise Matte 35.00
Coronado, Vase, Ivory Matte, 5 1/2 In. 175.00
Daisy, Mug, 5 1/4 In. 13.00
Desert Rose, Ashtray, 3 1/2 In. 20.00
Desert Rose, Bowl, Cereal, 6 In. ....14.00 to 16.00
Desert Rose, Bowl, Fruit, 5 1/4 In. 13.00
Desert Rose, Bowl, Salad, 10 In. ....100.00 to 115.00
Desert Rose, Bowl, Vegetable, 8 In. 32.00
Desert Rose, Bowl, Vegetable, 9 In. 40.00
Desert Rose, Bowl, Vegetable, Oval, Divided ....40.00 to 45.00
Desert Rose, Box, Cigarette 125.00
Desert Rose, Butter 37.00
Desert Rose, Butter, Cover 45.00
Desert Rose, Candlestick, Pair 135.00
Desert Rose, Casserole, Cover 80.00
Desert Rose, Chop Plate, 11 3/4 In. 80.00
Desert Rose, Chop Plate, 14 In. 175.00
Desert Rose, Compote, 8 In. 80.00
Desert Rose, Cookie Jar, Cover, 9 In. 295.00
Desert Rose, Creamer 20.00
Desert Rose, Cup & Saucer 15.00
Desert Rose, Dish, Heart Shape 125.00
Desert Rose, Eggcup, 3 1/2 In. ....30.00 to 35.00
Desert Rose, Ginger Jar, Lid, 2 3/4 In. 255.00
Desert Rose, Gravy Boat 30.00
Desert Rose, Grill Plate, Child's 195.00
Desert Rose, Jam Jar, Base Only 35.00
Desert Rose, Luncheon Set, Teapot, Oval Platter, 19 Piece 99.00
Desert Rose, Mug, 12 Oz. 50.00
Desert Rose, Napkin Ring ....53.00 to 65.00
Desert Rose, Pitcher, Milk, 6 1/4 In. ....70.00 to 95.00
Desert Rose, Pitcher, Water, 8 3/4 In. 125.00
Desert Rose, Plate, 6 3/8 In. 6.00
Desert Rose, Plate, 8 In. 18.00
Desert Rose, Plate, 9 1/2 In. 23.00
Desert Rose, Plate, 10 5/8 In. ....16.00 to 25.00
Desert Rose, Plate, Child's, 8 7/8 In. 65.00

Desert Rose, Plate, Salad, Crescent Shape	40.00
Desert Rose, Platter, 14 1/4 In.	60.00
Desert Rose, Relish, 3 Sections	70.00
Desert Rose, Relish, 10 7/8 In.	40.00
Desert Rose, Salt & Pepper	16.00
Desert Rose, Salt & Pepper Mill, Bulbous, 6 1/2 In.	425.00
Desert Rose, Salt & Pepper, Footed	79.00
Desert Rose, Soup, Cream, Cover	315.00
Desert Rose, Soup, Dish, 8 1/2 In.	28.00
Desert Rose, Sugar, Cover	27.00
Desert Rose, Syrup, 6 1/8 In.	92.00
Desert Rose, Teapot, Cover	.65.00 to 125.00
Desert Rose, Tumbler, Juice, 6 Oz.	48.00
El Patio, Bowl, Cereal, Turquoise Satin, 6 In.	12.00
El Patio, Bowl, Cereal, Yellow Satin, 6 In.	12.00
El Patio, Bowl, Fruit, Coral Satin, 5 1/4 In.	11.00
El Patio, Bowl, Fruit, Gray Satin, 5 1/4 In.	11.00
El Patio, Bowl, Fruit, Turquoise Satin, 5 1/4 In.	11.00
El Patio, Bowl, Fruit, Yellow Satin, 5 1/4 In.	11.00
El Patio, Bowl, Vegetable, Oval, Coral Satin, 9 1/4 In.	30.00
El Patio, Bowl, Vegetable, Oval, Gray Satin, 9 1/4 In.	30.00
El Patio, Bowl, Vegetable, Oval, Turquoise Satin, 9 1/4 In.	30.00
El Patio, Creamer, Gray Satin	9.00
El Patio, Cup & Saucer, Coral Gloss	13.00
El Patio, Cup & Saucer, Eggplant Gloss	28.00
El Patio, Cup & Saucer, Gray Satin	13.00
El Patio, Cup & Saucer, Turquoise Gloss	13.00
El Patio, Cup & Saucer, Turquoise Satin	13.00
El Patio, Cup & Saucer, Yellow Satin	13.00
El Patio, Cup, Coral Satin	10.00
El Patio, Cup, Gray Satin	10.00
El Patio, Cup, Turquoise Satin	10.00
El Patio, Plate, Coral Gloss, 8 In.	11.00
El Patio, Plate, Coral Satin, 6 1/2 In.	6.00
El Patio, Plate, Coral Satin, 8 In.	11.00
El Patio, Plate, Coral Satin, 10 1/2 In.	14.00
El Patio, Plate, Gray Satin, 6 1/2 In.	6.00
El Patio, Plate, Gray Satin, 10 1/2 In.	14.00
El Patio, Plate, Ivory Satin, 6 1/2 In.	6.00
El Patio, Plate, Turquoise Gloss, 10 1/2 In.	14.00
El Patio, Plate, Turquoise Satin, 6 1/2 In.	6.00
El Patio, Plate, Turquoise Satin, 8 In.	11.00
El Patio, Plate, Turquoise Satin, 10 1/2 In.	14.00
El Patio, Plate, Yellow Satin, 6 1/2 In.	6.00
El Patio, Plate, Yellow Satin, 10 1/2 In.	14.00
El Patio, Platter, Oval, Turquoise Satin, 11 3/4 In.	45.00
El Patio, Sugar, Cover, Coral Satin.	16.00
Forget-Me-Knot, Cup & Saucer	18.00
Forget-Me-Knot, Snack Tray, 8 1/2 In.	125.00
Fresh Fruit, Bowl, Cereal, 6 In.	24.00
Fresh Fruit, Bowl, Fruit, 5 1/4 In.	20.00
Fresh Fruit, Butter, Cover	75.00
Fresh Fruit, Cup	20.00
Fresh Fruit, Cup & Saucer	26.00
Fresh Fruit, Gravy Boat, Underplate	85.00
Fresh Fruit, Plate, 8 In.	25.00
Fresh Fruit, Plate, 10 3/4 In.	35.00
Ivy, Bowl, Fruit, 5 3/8 In.	9.00
Ivy, Pitcher, 8 In.	175.00
Ivy, Plate, 10 1/4 In.	28.00
Ivy, Platter, Oval, 13 1/8 In.	55.00
October, Baker, Rectangular, 13 3/4 In.	145.00
October, Baker, Square, 9 5/8 In.	120.00

October, Bowl, Cereal, 7 In.	12.00
October, Butter	45.00
October, Creamer	18.00
October, Cup & Saucer	10.00
October, Plate, 8 In.	10.00
October, Salt & Pepper	34.00
October, Sugar	18.00
Picnic, Pitcher, 7 1/8 In.	65.00
Wildflower, Chop Plate, 12 In.	300.00

FRANKART, Inc., New York, New York, mass-produced nude *dancing lady* lamps, ashtrays, and other decorative Art Deco items in the 1920s and 1930s. They were made of white lead composition and spray-painted. *Frankart Inc.* and the patent number and year were stamped on the base.

Ashstand, Hoop Girl, 31 In.	1500.00
Ashtray, Figural, Nude With Silver Enamel Finish, Signed, 6 1/4 x 9 3/4 In.	220.00
Lamp, Kneeling Woman, Pink Glass Ball Shade, 10 In.	875.00
Lamp, Seated Nymph, Holding 2 Crackle Glass Shades, Marked, 9 1/4 In.	1650.00
Lamp, Standing Nude Silhouette, Glass Disk Shade, Green Patina, 10 1/2 In.	670.00

FRANKOMA POTTERY was originally known as The Frank Potteries when John F. Frank opened shop in 1933. The factory is now working in Sapulpa, Oklahoma. Early wares were made from a light cream-colored clay from Ada, Oklahoma, but in 1956 the company switched to a red burning clay from Sapulpa. The firm makes dinnerwares, utilitarian and decorative kitchenwares, figurines, flowerpots, and limited edition and commemorative pieces.

Bookends, Rearing Horse, Onyx, Ada Clay, No. 420, 6 1/2 In.	90.00
Bowl, Dessert, Aztec, Desert Gold	6.00
Bowl, Leaf Shape, Prairie Green, Sapulpa Clay	20.00
Bowl, Salad, Matte Prairie Green, Sapulpa Clay, 1950-1951, 5 Qt.	100.00
Bowl, Vegetable, Lazybones, 2 Sections, Prairie Green, 11 In.	15.50
Canister Set, Scalloped Base, Desert Gold, Sapulpa, 4 Piece	50.00
Chip & Dip Set, Lazybones, Prairie Green, 12 In., 2 Piece	25.00
Egg Plate, Prairie Green, No. 814, 11 3/4 In.	70.00
Figurine, Dog, Collie, Onyx, 7 1/2 In.	200.00
Figurine, Elephant, Ada Clay, 3 1/2 In.	275.00
Figurine, Indian Chief's Head, Tan, 4 1/2 In.	180.00
Figurine, Leopard, Prancing, Onyx, Ada Clay, 1950-1954, 15 In.	250.00
Figurine, Swan, Tan, Ada Clay, 3 In.	50.00
Pitcher, Wagon Wheel, Prairie Green	50.00
Salt & Pepper, Bull, Dusty Rose, Ada Clay, 1942, 2 1/4 In.	260.00
Salt & Pepper, Lazybones, Sunflower Yellow	15.00
Salt & Pepper, Prairie Green, Ada Clay, 2 3/4 In.	195.00
Salt & Pepper, Teepee, Prairie Green	20.00
Trivet, Zodiac, Flame Glaze, 6 1/4 In.	15.00
Vase, Nautilus, Prairie Green, 3-Footed, No. 53	50.00
Vase, Scallop Top, Ribs, Verde Bronze, No. 79, 1934-1938, 7 In.	340.00
Vase, Tan Crystalline Glaze, Marked, 4 In.	10.00

FRATERNAL objects that are related to the many different fraternal organizations in the United States are listed in this category. The Elks, Masons, Odd Fellows, and others are included. Also included are service organizations, like the American Legion, Kiwanis, and Lions Club. Furniture is listed in the Furniture category. Shaving mugs decorated with fraternal crests are included in the Shaving Mug category.

Alhambra, Fez, Tan, Cream Tassel, Cloth, Rhinestones, Silver Sequins, Carrying Case	45.00
American Legion, Registration Packet, 36th National Convention, 1954	12.00
Eagles, Shaving Mug, Eagle & American Flag	110.00
Eastern Star, Pendant, 14K Gold, Raised Star, Intricate Enameling, 3/4 In.	95.00
Elks, Ring, Gold, High Relief, 10 3/4 In.	140.00
Elks, Tip Tray, 1907 Convention, Tin Lithograph, 4 1/4 In.	30.00

Elks, Watch Fob, Locket, Enameled, High Relief, Monogram On Reverse	95.00
Kiwanis, Necktie, Logo, Atlanta 1941, Peach Color, Textured	20.00
Knights Of Columbus, Cuff Links, 14K Gold, Art Deco Design, 3/4 In., Pair	95.00
Knights Of Columbus, Cuff Links, Goldstone, Red, White, Blue Enamel, 1 x 1/2 In.	30.00
Knights Of Pythias, Program, 93rd Annual Convention, 1960	4.00
Knights Of Pythius, Pendant, Goldstone, Enameled, Insignia, Victorian, 7/8 x 1 In.	50.00
Lions Club, Cuff Links, Red, Raised Insignia, 3/4 In., Pair	30.00
Lions Club, Lion, Traveling, Cast, Logo, Signed Barye, Uptown Baltimore, France	248.00
Loyal Order Of Moose, Souvenir Program, New Home Dedication, 1951	3.00
Masonic, Apron, Silk, Blue Band & Fringe, All Seeing Eye, Tools, 15 x 15 In.	55.00
Masonic, Apron, Silk, Symbols, Hand Painted, Square, 13 1/2 In.	660.00
Masonic, Cup & Saucer, Star Logo, Gold Trim	25.00
Masonic, Pendant, Bloodstone, Gold Crest, 9/16 x 5/8 In.	75.00
Masonic, Pitcher, Symbols, Woman With Children & Tools, Creamware, 8 5/8 In.	550.00
Masonic, Ring, Gold, Onyx, Emblem, Size 11	85.00
Masonic, Ring, Relief, Size 9	135.00
Masonic, Watch Fob, Locket, 7/8 In.	65.00
Odd Fellows, Doorstop, Crescent Moon, Stars, Bird, 3-Link Chain, Cast Iron, 7 x 6 In. . . .	250.00
Odd Fellows, Shaving Mug, Emblem, 3 3/4 In.	55.00
Phi Beta Kappa, Key, Presentation, Gold, Wriggle Work Border, c.1825, 2 In.	2820.00
Pythias Sisters, Supreme Constitution & Statutes, Revised Edition, 1958	10.00
Rotary International, Book, Proceedings, Hardbound, 25th Annual Convention, 1934 . . .	6.00

FRY GLASS was made by the H. C. Fry Glass Company of Rochester, Pennsylvania. The company, founded in 1901, first made cut glass and other types of fine glasswares. In 1922, they patented a heat-resistant glass called *Pearl Ovenglass*. For two years, 1926–1927, the company made Fry Foval, an opal ware decorated with colored trim. Reproductions of this glass have been made. Depression glass patterns made by Fry may be listed in the Depression Glass category. Some pieces of cut glass may also be included in the Cut Glass category.

FRY, Bowl, Clermont Cutting, Signed, 4 x 8 3/4 In.	295.00
Bowl, Interior, Enameled Gold & Blue Bands, Jade Pedestal, 4 x 8 In.	224.00
Candlestick, Alabaster Stem, Turquoise Diagonal Threading 10 1/2 In., 3 Piece	224.00
Lemonade Set, Heart Cutting, Pitcher, 6 Tumblers, 10 In.	385.00
FRY FOVAL, Candlestick, Cobalt Blue, Diagonal Threading, 2 Blue Wafers, 12 In., Pair	392.00
Coffeepot, Balled Finial, 9 1/2 In.	45.00
Coffeepot, Dripolator, Metal Handle, Silex, 11 1/4 In.	84.00

FULPER Pottery Company was incorporated in 1899 in Flemington, New Jersey. They made art pottery from 1910 to 1929. The firm had been making bottles, jugs, and housewares from 1805. Doll heads were made about 1928. The firm became Stangl Pottery in 1929. Fulper art pottery is admired for its attractive glazes and simple shapes.

Bowl, Blue, Ivory, Green Over Blue Matte Glaze, Effigy, Marked, 8 x 10 In.	805.00
Bowl, Cat's-Eye Flambe Interior, Mustard Matte Glaze Exterior, Footed, 3 3/4 x 8 In.	230.00
Bowl, Center, Green Crystallized Glaze, Footed, 4 x 11 3/4 In.	308.00
Bowl, Chinese Blue Glaze, Label, 8 1/2 x 2 1/4 In.	110.00
Bowl, Chinese Blue, Ivory Crystalline Interior, Footed, Racetrack Mark, 5 x 11 In.	375.00
Bowl, Copper Dust & Green Crystalline Glaze, Fish & Waves, Embossed, Marked, 11 In. .	920.00
Bowl, Copper, Brown Glaze, Embossed Stylized Maple Leaves, 3 1/2 x 8 1/8 In.	200.00
Bowl, Cucumber Green Crystalline Glaze, Mustard Matte, Squared Shoulder, 10 x 2 In. . .	173.00
Bowl, Green, Blue & Ivory Flambe Glaze, Peacock, Embossed Panels, Marked, 6 x 10 In.	546.00
Bowl, Green, Ivory Drip Glaze, Mustard Matte Glaze, 9 In.	173.00
Bowl, Mauve, Purple Matte Drip Glaze, Blue, Yellow, Green Interior, 9 1/2 In.	234.00
Bowl, Mottled Flambe Drip Glaze, Gray Body, 3 In.	92.00
Bowl, Multicolored Blue Interior, Pale Yellow, Cream, Tan Exterior, 9 In.	150.00
Bowl, Multicolored Emerald Green Glaze, Shell, Cream Petals, 3 3/4 x 11 1/2 In.	550.00
Candlestick, Multicolored Blue, Tan High Glaze, 3 Handles, 6 In.	230.00
Chandelier, Dome, Ivory & Blue Flambe, Blue Slag Insets, Bronze, Ink Mark, 6 x 17 In. .	7480.00
Cider Set, Brown Crystalline Matte Glaze, Tankard, 10 1/2 x 6 1/2 In., 5 Piece	518.00
Cider Set, Wisteria Blue Matte Glaze, Pitcher 10 1/2 x 8 In., 7 Piece	1380.00
Crock, Cover, Cobalt Blue Design, Incised Bands, Applied Ears, Marked, 12 In.	990.00

Don't soak dishes in chlorine bleach to remove a stain. It damages the glaze. Years ago we recommended this treatment, but more is known today. And never use Limeaway or other bathroom cleaners. They, too, ruin the glaze.

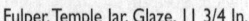

Fulper, Temple Jar, Glaze, 11 3/4 In.

Ewer, Turquoise Matte Crystalline Glaze Over Mirrored Green, 4 3/8 In.	230.00
Figurine, Cat, Yellow & Gunmetal Glaze, Stamped, 10 In.	920.00
Figurine, Ibis, Green & Blue Flambe Over Blue Matte Glaze, 5 1/2 x 10 1/2 In.	920.00
Flask, Pilgrim, Green, Black & Ivory Flambe Glaze, Ink Mark, 10 x 7 In.	575.00
Flower Frog, Froggie, Wisteria Glaze, 2 3/8 In.	115.00
Flower Frog, Green, c.1920, 7 In.	144.00
Flower Frog, Lily Pad, Medium Green Crystalline Glaze, 4 x 4 In.	80.00
Flower Frog, Mushroom Shape, 3 3/4 In., Pair	90.00
Jug, Blue Glaze, Singing Bird On Twig, c.1880, 2 Gal., 14 In.	330.00
Jug, Stoneware, Bathing Beauties, Cobalt Squeezebag, Stamped, 1890s, 13 x 8 1/2 In.	26450.00
Jug, Whimsical Cobalt Blue Flower, Stoneware, 11 In.	360.00
Lamp, 28 Leaded Glass Inserts, 16 1/2 x 17 In.	13850.00
Lamp, Crystalline Flambe Glaze, Cutout Geometric Design Shade, 16 1/2 x 14 In.	7480.00
Lamp, Parrot, Macaw, Purple Body, Green Stand, Electrified, 10 In., 2 Piece	850.00
Lamp, Tear Shape, Acorn Pulls, Cucumber Green Matte Glaze, 13 x 7 In.	920.00
Lamp Base, Oval, Purple, Blue Glaze, Racetrack Mark, 9 1/2 x 6 In.	375.00
Pitcher, Antique Verde Green, Panels, Handles, 4 x 5 In.	99.00
Pitcher, Colonial, Green, Gray Microcrystalline Glaze, Racetrack Mark, 6 1/4 x 6 1/4 In.	60.00
Temple, Jar, Black Mirror, Brown Glaze, Periwinkle Blue Flambe Ground, 11 In.	5250.00
Temple Jar, Glaze, 11 3/4 In. *Illus*	6037.00
Urn, Blue Green Flambe, Copper Dust Crystalline, Handles, Racetrack Mark, 8 x 7 In.	805.00
Urn, Chinese Blue Flambe Glaze, Short Rim, 4 Handles, 13 x 11 In.	1265.00
Urn, Grecian Shape, Cobalt Blue, Double Scrolled Handles, 11 In.	550.00
Urn, Indigo Blue Snowflake Crystalline Over Blue Flambe Glaze, 4 Ear Handles, 13 In.	4700.00
Urn, Mirrored Green Flambe Glaze, Nubbed Handles, Incised Mark, 11 1/2 x 8 1/2 In.	1495.00
Urn, Moss To Rose Flambe Glaze, Scrolled Handles, Racetrack Mark, 9 x 5 3/4 In.	230.00
Urn, Roman, Blue & Green Flambe Over Cobalt Matte, 2 Scroll Handles, 11 x 6 In.	316.00
Vase, 2-Tone Wisteria Blue Glaze, Twin Handles, 5 3/4 In.	200.00
Vase, Aqua & Olive Flambe Glaze, Bulbous, 2 Handles, Racetrack Mark, 8 1/2 x 8 In.	460.00
Vase, Black Glaze, Flambe Drip, 4 x 6 1/2 In.	300.00
Vase, Black Mirror Glaze, Brown, Ocher Flambe Glaze, 11 3/8 In.	2900.00
Vase, Black Mirror Glaze, Flared, 7 In.	489.00
Vase, Black Mirror Glaze, Flowing Copper Dust Glaze, 13 In.	1700.00
Vase, Black Mirror Glaze, Green Flemington Crystalline Glaze, 2 Handles, 2 7/8 In.	150.00
Vase, Black Mirror Glaze, Ivory Glossy Glaze, 11 3/8 In.	700.00
Vase, Black Mirror Glaze, Pedestal Form, Handles, 12 In.	750.00
Vase, Black Mirror Glaze, Silver, Cream, Yellow Flambe Glaze, 1916, 8 7/8 In.	500.00
Vase, Black Mirror Glaze, Tear Shape, Incised Racetrack Mark, 13 x 7 In.	865.00
Vase, Blue & Amber Crystalline Glaze, Gourd Shape, 2 Handles, Incised Mark, 7 1/2 In.	550.00
Vase, Blue & Green Mirror Glaze, Bulbous, Flared Rim, Racetrack Mark, 7 x 6 In.	290.00
Vase, Blue Crystalline Glaze, Baluster, Flared Rim, 8 x 5 1/2 In.	115.00
Vase, Blue Crystalline Glaze, Brown, 7 1/2 In.	690.00
Vase, Blue Crystalline Glaze, Green Matte Glaze, 12 In.	460.00
Vase, Blue Crystalline Matte Glaze, Periwinkle Flambe, Rolled Rim, 4 1/8 In.	260.00
Vase, Blue Drip Glaze, Blue, Green Matte Glaze, 9 1/2 In.	546.00
Vase, Blue Drip Over Green Glaze, 13 In.	345.00
Vase, Blue Flambe Glaze, Rust Ground, Flared Rim, 2 Handles, Stamp, 8 1/4 x 7 In.	635.00

Vase, Blue Green Glaze, Bubble In Body & Rim, 15 1/2 In. 805.00
Vase, Blue Matte Glaze, Purple, Brown Drip, 7 1/2 In. 250.00
Vase, Blue Snowflake Crystalline Glaze, 6 Sides, 7 5/8 In. 700.00
Vase, Blue Snowflake Crystalline Glaze, Glossy Green, 6 5/8 In. 345.00
Vase, Blue Snowflake Crystalline Glaze, Green, 10 1/2 In. 450.00
Vase, Blue, Brown Drip Crystalline Glaze, 6 In. 250.00
Vase, Blue, Brown Flambe Glaze, Banded Neck, San Francisco, 1915, 15 In. 2070.00
Vase, Blue, Gray Drip Glaze, Geometric Design Neck, 9 In. 550.00
Vase, Blue, Gray, Sand, Beige, Bulbous Shape, Signed, 7 In. 358.00
Vase, Blue, Green Crystalline Glaze, 2 Open Handles, 1915, 11 1/2 In. 4315.00
Vase, Blue, Green Flambe Glaze, Famille Rose, 6 5/8 In. 550.00
Vase, Blue, Green, Purple, 7 In. 495.00
Vase, Blue, Tan Crystalline Glaze, 5 In. 185.00
Vase, Brown, Yellow Flambe Glaze, Blue, 7 In. 288.00
Vase, Bud, Green Flambe Over Green Matte Glaze, 6 3/4 In. 150.00
Vase, Butterscotch Flambe Glaze, 12 In. 150.00
Vase, Butterscotch Flambe Glaze, Oval, Racetrack Mark, 6 x 3 3/4 In. 230.00
Vase, Butterscotch Glaze, 3 Handles, 6 1/2 In. 425.00
Vase, Cafe Au Lait Glaze, 2 Buttressed Handles, Ink Mark, 7 x 9 1/2 In. 750.00
Vase, Caramel, Blue, Brown High Glaze, 4 1/2 In. 184.00
Vase, Cat's-Eye Flambe Glaze, 11 1/2 In. 950.00
Vase, Cat's-Eye Flambe Glaze, Angular Buttressed Handles, 11 x 4 3/4 In. 690.00
Vase, Cat's-Eye Flambe Glaze, Cylindrical, 4 7/8 In. 275.00
Vase, Cat's-Eye Flambe Glaze, Orange, Handles, 8 In. 250.00
Vase, Cat's-Eye Flambe Glaze, Trumpet, 10 1/2 x 6 In. 80.00
Vase, Cat's-Eye Flambe Glaze, Trumpet, Bulbous Bottom, 10 5/8 In. 115.00
Vase, Charcoal, Brown, Yellow Drip Glaze, 3 3/4 In. 115.00
Vase, Chinese Blue Crystalline Flambe Glaze, Oval, Ink Mark, 12 x 4 1/2 In. 575.00
Vase, Chinese Blue Flambe Glaze, Applied Rose, 5 1/4 In. 100.00
Vase, Chinese Blue Flambe Glaze, Bullet Shape, 10 In. 2100.00
Vase, Chinese Blue Flambe Glaze, Green Flemington Flambe Glaze, 13 1/4 In. 1900.00
Vase, Chinese Blue Flambe Glaze, Handles, 7 7/8 In. 275.00
Vase, Copper Dust Crystalline Glaze, 2 Angular Handles, Marked, 4 3/4 x 5 3/4 In. 575.00
Vase, Copper Dust Crystalline Glaze, Classical Shape, Ink Mark, 12 x 7 In. 750.00
Vase, Copper Dust Crystalline Glaze, Corseted, Closed-In Rim, Raised Mark, 11 x 8 In. . . 10350.00
Vase, Copper Dust Crystalline Glaze, Handle, 11 3/4 In. 3500.00
Vase, Copper Dust Crystalline Glaze, Sloped Angular Handles, 9 1/2 In. 550.00
Vase, Copper Dust Crystallize Glaze, 2 Handles, 6 In. 605.00
Vase, Cream Flambe Glaze, Mustard Matte Glaze, 6 5/8 In. 500.00
Vase, Cream Ground, Signed, 7 Sides, 9 In. 200.00
Vase, Cream Matte Glaze, White, Lime Green Variegated Flambe Glaze, 11 1/2 In. 750.00
Vase, Cream, Olive Green, Bullet Shape, 10 In. 600.00
Vase, Cream, Yellow Flambe Glaze, Embossed Mushrooms, 9 7/8 In. 1400.00
Vase, Cucumber Green Crystalline Glaze, Bulbous, 3 Handles, Raised Mark, 6 x 8 1/2 In. . 1150.00
Vase, Cucumber Green Crystalline Glaze, Handles, 7 1/2 In. 635.00
Vase, Cucumber Green Matte Crystalline Glaze, Gourd Shape, 2 Handles, 6 3/4 In. 1035.00
Vase, Deep Blue Glaze, 4-Footed, 4 Handles, 2 3/4 x 5 In. 115.00
Vase, Edam, Leopard Skin Glaze, 5 1/2 In. 345.00
Vase, Elephant's Breath Flambe Glaze, Closed-In Rim, Ink Mark, 4 x 2 3/4 In. 315.00
Vase, Elephant's Breath Flambe Glaze, Ink Mark, 2 3/4 x 4 3/4 In. 489.00
Vase, Elephant's Breath Flambe, Leopard Skin Crystalline Glaze, 8 1/2 x 5 1/2 In. 1380.00
Vase, Elephant's Breath To Blue Crystalline Flambe Glaze, Closed-In Rim, 6 In. 315.00
Vase, Elephant's Breath, Leopard Skin Crystalline Flambe Glaze, Closed-In Rim, 8 x 5 In. . 2645.00
Vase, Flemington Green Flambe Glaze, 4 Sides, Coat Of Arms, Vasekraft, 8 In. 1035.00
Vase, Flemington Green Flambe Glaze, Bottle Shape, Ink Mark, 13 1/2 x 6 In. 980.00
Vase, Flemington Green Flambe Glaze, Buttressed Base, Ink Mark, 8 1/4 x 6 In. 490.00
Vase, Frothy Brown & Olive Flambe Glaze, Oval, Raised Racetrack Mark, 9 1/2 x 6 In. . . 920.00
Vase, Frothy Chinese Blue Flambe Glaze, Bullet Shape, Incised Racetrack, 10 1/2 In. 980.00
Vase, Global, Black Mirror Crystallize Glaze, Chinese Blue Flambe, 10 In. 1500.00
Vase, Glossy Blue Gray & Moss Flambe Glaze, Cattail, Ink Mark, 13 x 4 3/4 In. 4315.00
Vase, Gray, Caramel, Blue Drip Glaze, 7 In. 265.00
Vase, Gray, Lavender Blue Drip Glaze, Incised Geometric Design, 6 1/2 In. 300.00
Vase, Green Crystalline Glaze, Turquoise, Classical, 10 x 7 In. 290.00

Vase, Green Flambe Interior, Speckled Mustard Exterior, 6 x 7 1/4 In. 400.00
Vase, Green Flemington Drip Glaze, 5 1/8 In. 425.00
Vase, Green Glaze, Blue Matte Ground, Barrel Shape, 6 1/4 x 6 In. 170.00
Vase, Green Leopard Skin Glaze, 3 Handles, 6 1/2 In. 470.00
Vase, Green Matte Glaze, 5 7/8 In. 275.00
Vase, Green Multicolored Glaze, 3 Handles, Marked, 7 In. 250.00
Vase, Green, Blue & Red Glaze, 3 Handles, 6 1/2 In. 250.00
Vase, Green, Brown Metallic Glaze, 6 3/4 In. 490.00
Vase, Green, Brown, Caramel Glaze, 3 Handles, 6 1/2 In. 58.00
Vase, Green, Cream, Blue Flambe Matte Glaze, 8 In. 550.00
Vase, Green, Mauve, Blue Glossy Glaze, Rust Colored Crystals, Handles, 6 3/4 In. 325.00
Vase, Green, Teal Glossy Glaze, 16 1/2 In. 3300.00
Vase, Incised Cat's-Eye Glaze, Handles, 6 In. 290.00
Vase, Ivory Flambe Drip Glaze, Mustard Matte Ground, Ink Racetrack, 10 1/2 In. 800.00
Vase, Ivory Flambe Glaze, Blue Band, Stylized Peacock Feathers, Stamp, 6 x 10 In. 805.00
Vase, Ivory To Mirror Black Flambe Glaze, Incised Racetrack Mark, 9 1/2 x 6 In. 750.00
Vase, Ivory, Mahogany, Mirror Black Flambe Glaze, Ribbed, 2 Handles, 12 1/2 x 8 In. 230.00
Vase, Leopard Skin Crystalline Glaze, Milk Can Shape, 12 x 6 In. 920.00
Vase, Leopard Skin Crystalline Glaze, Racetrack Mark, 6 x 3 3/4 In. 345.00
Vase, Leopard Skin Crystalline Glaze, Trumpet, Flower Frog, 8 1/4 x 5 3/4 In. 370.00
Vase, Leopard Skin Crystalline Glaze, Trumpet, Scalloped Rim, 10 1/4 x 6 In. 1380.00
Vase, Leopard Skin Glaze, Handles, 8 7/8 In. 650.00
Vase, Leopard Skin Glaze, Oval, 8 1/4 In. 325.00
Vase, Light Blue Flambe Glaze, 3 Handled Form, 8 In. 400.00
Vase, Mauve Drip Over Maroon Glaze, 7 3/8 In. 375.00
Vase, Mirror Black Glaze, Blue, Rose Famille, Bulbous, Collared Neck, 7 1/2 x 7 1/2 In. .. 1495.00
Vase, Mirror Black Glaze, Green Glaze, Trumpet Shape, 11 1/4 x 7 In. 430.00
Vase, Moss To Rose Flambe Glaze, Bulbous, 2 Handles, 6 1/2 x 7 In. 260.00
Vase, Moss To Rose Flambe Glaze, Embossed Strap Neck, Incised Mark, 10 x 8 In. 370.00
Vase, Mouse Gray To Blue Flambe Glaze, Tapered, 2 Handles, Racetrack Mark, 10 x 7 In. 805.00
Vase, Multicolored Blue Crystalline Glaze, Handles, 9 In. 690.00
Vase, Multicolored Blue Crystalline Glaze, Red Matte Glaze, 9 In. 1840.00
Vase, Multicolored Blue Glaze, 6 1/2 In. 299.00
Vase, Multicolored Green Crystalline Glaze, 3 Handles, 8 In. 520.00
Vase, Multicolored Green Crystalline Glaze, 4 Buttressed Form, 8 In. 520.00
Vase, Multicolored Green Crystalline Glaze, Handles, 7 1/2 In. 299.00
Vase, Multicolored Green Flambe Glaze, Copper Dust Glaze, Open Handles, 9 1/2 In. ... 748.00
Vase, Multicolored Green Glaze, 11 1/2 In. 345.00
Vase, Multicolored Green, Blue Glaze, 11 In. 1600.00
Vase, Multicolored Ivory Matte Glaze, Red Matte Glaze, 11 1/2 In. 690.00
Vase, Oatmeal Flambe Glaze, Periwinkle Blue Glaze, 9 In. 400.00
Vase, Olive To Chinese Blue Flambe Glaze, Baluster, Ink Racetrack Mark, 9 x 5 1/2 In. .. 748.00
Vase, Olive, Dark Green Matte Glaze, 3 Angular Handles, 7 In. 170.00
Vase, Pink, Gray Crystalline Glaze, 8 1/2 In. 299.00
Vase, Purple, Green, Blue Drip, Rust, Yellow Glaze, 3 1/2 In. 440.00
Vase, Tapered Neck, Cat's-Eye Flambe Glaze, Bulbous, 2 Handles, 6 1/2 x 6 In. 635.00
Vase, Textured Leopard Skin Over Ivory Crystalline Glaze, 15 3/4 x 5 1/4 In. 1725.00
Vase, Umber, Blue Flambe Glaze, 5 5/8 In. 425.00
Vase, Under Blue & Green Mirror Glaze, Applied Salamander, Bottle Shape, 8 x 4 In. 550.00
Vase, Wisteria Glaze, 2 Gourd Shaped Handles, 7 1/2 x 6 In. 290.00
Vase, Wisteria Glaze, Classical Shape, Prunts At Shoulder, Racetrack Mark, 7 x 4 In. 489.00
Vase, Wisteria Glaze, Hexagonal, Racetrack Mark, 11 x 5 In. 345.00
Vase, Wisteria Glaze, Oval, Racetrack Mark, 6 3/4 x 4 In. 430.00

A glass vase or bowl can be cleaned with a damp cloth. Try not to put the glass in a sink filled with water. Hitting the glass on a faucet or the sink is a common cause of breakage.

Vase, Wisteria Matte Glaze, Squat, 2 Handles, Racetrack Mark, 5 3/4 x 7 1/2 In. 400.00
Wall Pocket, Blue Matte Glaze, 3 Pockets, Ink Mark, 11 1/2 In. 370.00

FURNITURE of all types is listed in this category. Examples dating from
the seventeenth century to the 1970s are included. Prices for furniture
vary in different parts of the country. Oak furniture is most expensive
in the West; large pieces over eight feet high are sold for the most
money in the South, where high ceilings are found in the old homes.
Condition is very important when determining prices. These are NOT
average prices but rather reports of unique sales. If the description
includes the word *style*, the piece resembles the old furniture style but
was made at a later time. It is not a period piece. Garden furniture is
listed in the Garden Furnishings category. Related items may be found
in the Architectural, Brass, and Store categories.

Aquarium, Iron Pedestal Base, Light-Up, Vaseline Bowl, 41 x 9 x 13 In. 1400.00
Armchairs are listed under Chair in this category.
Armoire, 2 Cupboard Doors, Bracket Feet, S-Scroll Spandrels, 1850s, 92 In. 2530.00
Armoire, Art Deco, Mahogany Veneer, 3 Drawers, 1930, 71 In. 1955.00
Armoire, Art Nouveau, Walnut, Carved Panel, Door, Beveled Mirror, 77 x 36 x 16 In. . . . 450.00
Armoire, Art Nouveau, Walnut, Carved, Drawer, Door, Beveled Mirror, 82 x 48 x 19 In. . . 560.00
Armoire, Arts & Crafts, Mirrored Door, Copper Panels, Stylized Flowers, 75 x 40 In. 1035.00
Armoire, Bird's-Eye Maple, Faux Bamboo, Door, c.1885, 88 x 21 x 37 In. 840.00
Armoire, Black Lacquer, Chinoiserie, Mirror, Long Drawer, c.1880, 19 x 42 In. 1790.00
Armoire, Classical, Mahogany Veneer, Deep Ogee Cornice, 19 x 60 x 90 In. 2200.00
Armoire, Country Pine, 2 Doors, France, 75 x 46 1/2 x 21 In. 1008.00
Armoire, Door, 2 Panels, Overhanging Cornice, Paw Feet, c.1825, 86 x 42 In. 2015.00
Armoire, Edwardian, Satinwood, Flat Cornice, Flowers, 2 Doors, 95 In. 10350.00
Armoire, Exotic Wood, Rectangular Top, Circular Iron Handles, 77 1/2 In. 2300.00
Armoire, French Provincial, Oak, Rectangular Top, Geometric Frieze, 88 In. 2415.00
Armoire, French Provincial, Regency Style, Oak, Carved, 100 x 62 1/2 x 26 3/4 In. 5290.00
Armoire, French Provincial, Walnut, Burl Panels, Shelf, 70 x 50 x 21 1/2 In. 1380.00
Armoire, Fruitwood, 2 Long Doors, Geometric Panels, Bun Feet, 1830s, 92 x 55 In. 5290.00
Armoire, Fruitwood, 2 Paneled Cupboard Doors, Scrolling Panels, 1860s, 85 In. 2990.00
Armoire, Guerin, Walnut, Arched Floral Crest Over Mirrored Door, Signed, 96 In. 1725.00
Armoire, Herter Bros., Walnut, Burl Panels, Roundels, Fitted Interior, 93 In. 8050.00
Armoire, Louis Philippe, Burl Walnut, Door, 19th Century, 64 1/2 x 41 1/2 x 20 In. 1495.00
Armoire, Louis XV, Bronze Mounts, Painted, Wire Mesh Inset Doors, 81 x 40 x 16 In. . . . 3900.00
Armoire, Louis XV, Chinoiserie, Painted, Arched Top, Panel Doors, 94 x 65 x 23 In. 8400.00
Armoire, Louis XV, Elm, 2 Paneled Doors, Mid 19th Century, 92 x 54 x 24 In. 2070.00
Armoire, Louis XV, Molded, Domed, 2 Paneled Doors, Scroll Toes, 101 x 55 x 26 In. . . . 5555.00
Armoire, Louis XV, Oak, Carved, Cabriole Legs, 65 1/2 x 24 1/2 x 92 In. 4125.00
Armoire, Louis XV, Oak, Rectangular Top, Floral Vine Top Border, 87 In. 3450.00
Armoire, Louis XV, Rectangular Top, Curved Cornice, France, 23 x 90 In. 690.00
Armoire, Louis XV, Rectangular Top, Stepped Band, France, 19th Century, 95 In. 1725.00
Armoire, Louis XV, Walnut, Arched Crest Rail, Cabriole Legs, France, 99 x 19 In. 1100.00
Armoire, Louis XV-XVI, Cherry, Elm, Molded Cornice, Scroll Feet, 24 x 80 In. 1150.00
Armoire, Louis XVI, Oak, Carved Frieze, Fluted Pilaster, Scroll Feet, 87 x 60 x 24 In. 2510.00
Armoire, Louis XVI, Oak, Rectangular Top, Curved Cornice, 86 1/2 In. 4025.00
Armoire, Mahogany, Arched Doors, Interior Shelves & Drawers, 81 1/2 In. 3136.00
Armoire, Mahogany, Paneled Doors Opening To Shelves, 74 In. 1610.00
Armoire, Neoclassical, Mahogany, Domed Cornice, Circular Panels, Italy, 78 In. 4140.00
Armoire, Painted, Parcel Gilt, 2 Doors, Continental, 78 x 60 1/4 x 25 1/4 In. 4025.00
Armoire, Pine, Frieze Shells, Paneled Doors, Flower Heads, 18th Century, 79 x 48 In. . . . 2415.00
Armoire, Renaissance Revival, Rosewood, 4 Doors, Pediment, Mirrors, 102 x 23 x 85 In. . . 3360.00
Armoire, Rococo, Figured Walnut Veneer, 2 Doors, Acanthus Leaf, 54 x 19 x 96 In. 935.00
Armoire, Tulipwood, Leaf & Mask Mounts, Putti Scene, Mirrored Doors, 102 In. 3105.00
Armoire, Victorian, Bamboo Turned, Mirrored Door, Lower Drawer, 83 x 38 In. 3525.00
Armoire, Victorian, Rosewood, Center Crest, Oval Mirrored Door, 113 x 22 x 54 In. 6720.00
Armoire, Victorian, Walnut, Double Door, Carved Pediment, 102 1/2 x 58 x 25 In. 1790.00
Armoire, Walnut, Carved Paneled Doors, Scrolled Feet, 89 x 64 In. 2415.00
Bar Cart, Tony Paul, Plywood, Black Painted Metal, Raymore, 1954, 33 In. 575.00
Bed, Art Deco, Brass, Sunburst Headboard, Side Rails, 1930s, 49 x 42 In. 420.00
Bed, Arts & Crafts, Paneled, Corbel Details, 53 x 42 x 79 In. 1495.00

Bed, Arts & Crafts, Vertical Slats, Inlaid Roses, Crown Molding, Scotland, 56 x 80 In. 2185.00
Bed, Birch, Oak, Pine, Pencil Post, Painted, c.1780, 84 x 54 x 78 In. 3600.00
Bed, Brass, Acorn Finials, 3 Spindles In Headboard & Footboard, c.1900, 54 In. 380.00
Bed, Brass, Open Headboard, Finial Rods, Posts, Footboard, 59 x 82 x 43 In. 1955.00
Bed, Cannonball Posts, Bunky Boards, c.1840, Pair 3250.00
Bed, Canopy, Arched, Federal, Mahogany, Turned Posts, 70 x 54 In. 4700.00
Bed, Canopy, Federal, Mahogany, Ring & Urn Turned Posts, 61 x 57 1/2 x 77 In. 6465.00
Bed, Canopy, Jacobean, Linenfold Design, Rope Twist, 70 x 84 In. Headboard 400.00
Bed, Canopy, Mahogany, Maple Mattress Frame, 1815, 89 In. 4700.00
Bed, Canopy, Maple, Pine, Turned, Tapered Posts, Turned Legs, 82 x 60 x 74 In. 440.00
Bed, Canopy, Sheraton, Mahogany, Spiral Posts, Urn Shape Base, 89 x 77 x 55 In. 2520.00
Bed, Canopy, Sheraton, Maple, Reeded Footboard Posts, Mattress, 73 x 60 x 82 In. 1000.00
Bed, Canopy, Tiger Maple, American, c.1830, 45 In. 1840.00
Bed, Christian Krass, Rosewood, Rectangular Headboard & Footboard, 1930s, 68 In. 1400.00
Bed, Classical, Rosewood, Grained, Stenciled, c.1850, 40 1/2 x 55 1/2 In. 520.00
Bed, Dark Mahogany, Central Integrated Plinth, Turned Feet, 1830s, 48 1/2 In. 977.00
Bed, Empire, Mahogany, Satinwood, France, 19th Century, 42 x 55 In. 1265.00
Bed, Feather Flame, Scrolled Headboard, Walnut Accents, Turned Feet, 46 x 74 x 51 In. . . . 3600.00
Bed, Four-Poster, Federal, Maple, 8-Sided Tall Posts, Arched Tester, 76 x 73 In. 920.00
Bed, Four-Poster, Federal, Tiger Maple, Turned, Carved, c.1815, 82 x 50 1/2 x 72 In. 1840.00
Bed, Four-Poster, Jacobean, Oak, Elongated Cabochons, Recessed Panels 2760.00
Bed, Four-Poster, Mahogany & Poplar, Paneled Headboard, 19th Century, 89 In. 1065.00
Bed, Four-Poster, Mahogany, Acanthus Leaf, Pineapple Finials, 95 1/2 In. 2200.00
Bed, Four-Poster, Mahogany, Pencil Posts, Finials, Scalloped Headboard, 89 In. 715.00
Bed, Four-Poster, Mahogany, Rice Grain Carving, 20th Century, 90 x 82 1/2 In. 730.00
Bed, Four-Poster, Pencil Posts On Headboard, Marlborough Feet, 82 1/2 x 58 In. 330.00
Bed, Four-Poster, Sheraton, Mahogany, Turned Post, Spindles, Child's, 70 x 34 x 69 In. . . . 2015.00
Bed, French Empire, Mahogany, Satinwood, Ormolu Mounts, 1800s, 42 x 55 In., Pair 1265.00
Bed, French Provincial, Rosewood, Kingswood, Carved Shell Crest, 62 x 62 x 81 In. 1570.00
Bed, G. Stickley, 10 Square Spindles, Casters, Branded Mark, Twin, 50 x 79 In. 2185.00
Bed, G. Stickley, No. 912, Mahogany, Paneled Headboard, 59 x 79 x 51 In. 4900.00
Bed, Half-Tester, Walnut, Chamfered Posts, 94 1/2 x 63 In. 2990.00
Bed, Herter Bros., Aesthetic Revival, Mahogany, c.1890, 67 1/2 In. 9400.00
Bed, Iron, Oval & Rounded Tubing, Scroll & Cross, Medallions, Full, 61 In. 550.00
Bed, Louis Philippe, Mahogany, Scrolled Ends, Ormolu Mounts, Block Feet, 44 x 77 In. . . . 1060.00
Bed, Low Post, Peaked Headboard, Molded Rails, Windsor Turned Leg 170.00
Bed, Mahogany, Bell Post, Rolling Pin Headboard, Footboard, 1830, 50 x 80 In. 730.00
Bed, Mahogany, Carved Scroll Crest, 8-Sided Posts, Urn Finials, 96 x 67 x 86 In. 2465.00
Bed, Mahogany, High Post, Flute, Carved, 81 x 58 In. 560.00
Bed, Mahogany, High Post, Pineapple & Swirling Leaves, Pineapple Finials, 83 In. 1210.00
Bed, Mahogany, Scroll Relief, 3/4 Size, 51 x 39 In. 115.00
Bed, Mahogany, Shell Carved Crest, Openwork, Scrolled Posts, Wood Rails 210.00
Bed, Mahogany, Single, Openworked Headboard, Footboard, Wood Rails, Pair 220.00
Bed, Maple, Fluted Posts, Shaped Headboard, Spade Feet, 83 In. 1800.00
Bed, Maple, Pine, Pencil Post, Painted, New England, c.1790, 80 x 72 x 53 In. 6000.00
Bed, Poplar, Spindle Turned, Beehive Posts, Acorn Finials, Arched Rail, 52 In. 1210.00
Bed, Rococo Revival, Rosewood, Carved, Leaf, Fruit, Mid 19th Century, 68 x 60 In. 8915.00
Bed, Rohde, Burl, Rounded Footboard, Ball Casters, 35 x 57 In. 460.00
Bed, Rope, Brown Flame Grain Painted, Ball Finials On Footboard, 72 In. 110.00
Bed, Rope, Cherry & Poplar, Pointed Finials, Broken Arch Headboard, 52 x 51 In. 275.00
Bed, Rope, Cherry, Ring-Turned Posts, Ball Finials, Paneled Headboard, 75 1/2 In. 275.00
Bed, Rope, Curly Maple, Cannonball Finials, Scroll Ends, 47 x 47 x 74 1/2 In. 605.00
Bed, Rope, High Post, Inverted Bell Finials, Peaked Headboard, 51 1/4 x 60 In. 825.00
Bed, Rope, Poplar, Red Paint, Mushroom Finials, 65 x 35 x 32 In. 520.00
Bed, Roycroft, Mahogany, Vertical Slats, Dovetailed Side Rails, 56 x 79 x 45 In. 1495.00
Bed, Sheraton, High Post, Walnut, Rolled Crest, Urn Finials, 77 x 55 1/2 x 83 In. 880.00
Bed, Sheraton, Pineapple Carved Posts, Rolling-Pin Head & Footboard, c.1835 . . . . 815.00
Bed, Sleigh, Mahogany, Carved, Laurel Wreaths, Early 19th Century, 54 x 60 In. 4750.00
Bed, Sleigh, Mahogany, S-Scrolled Ends, Side Panels, c.1850, 55 x 40 In. 375.00
Bed, Sleigh, Mahogany, Scrolled Head & Footboard, Block Feet, 19th Century, 82 In. 950.00
Bed, Sleigh, Mahogany, Scrolled Head & Footboard, c.1835, 46 1/2 x 53 In. 2125.00
Bed, Tester, 8-Sided Tall Posts, Paneled Headboard, Shell-Carved Crest, 114 1/2 In. 8050.00
Bed, Tester, Empire, Gothic, Mahogany, Panels, Carved, 108 x 86 x 90 In. 10925.00

Bed, Trundle, Turned Posts, Ball Finials, Child's 110.00
Bed, Trundle, Walnut, Turned Posts & Finials, Shaped Corners, 71 1/2 In. 110.00
Bed, Trundle, Wooden Wheels, c.1820, 66 x 42 In. 395.00
Bed, Victorian, Walnut, Floral Crest, Incised Medallion, Full, 89 x 63 In. 2520.00
Bed, Walnut, Flowers, Turned Posts, Rails, France, 58 In. 200.00
Bed, Walnut, Veneered, Slats, Rails, Twin 225.00
Bed, Wood, Spindled Headboard, Footboard & Rails, 56 x 40 In. 400.00
Bed Steps, Commode, 3 Tiers, Leather, Center Pullout Compartment, c.1850, 25 1/2 In. ... 785.00
Bed Steps, Commode, Mahogany, 3 Tiers, Leather Step, Hinged, 1850, 25 In. 785.00
Bed Steps, Mahogany, 3 Tiers, Pullout Slide, Leather, England, c.1860, 27 x 16 x 27 In. .. 728.00
Bed Steps, Pine, Gray Paint, Early 19th Century, 10 1/4 x 16 1/4 x 8 3/4 In. 633.00
Bed Steps, Regency, Mahogany, 3 Leather Treads, Early 1800s, 29 x 20 x 30 In. 4200.00
Bed Steps, Victorian, Mahogany, Leather Opening, Retractable, 18 x 16 In. 3000.00
Bed Steps, Walnut, Fabric On Inset Of Steps, 12 1/4 x 17 1/8 In. 660.00
Bed Steps, Walnut, Scalloped Front Apron, 3 Steps, Middle Slides Out, 28 1/4 In. 880.00
Bed Tray, Edwardian, Sheraton Style, Folding, c.1900, 10 x 25 x 15 In. 145.00
Bedroom Set, Aesthetic Revival, Mahogany, Raised Panels, Floral Carved Crests, 2 Piece 1400.00
Bedroom Set, Cottage, Black, Gold Trim, Washstand, Full Bed, 6 Piece 2750.00
Bedroom Set, Faux Bamboo, Marble Top, Princess Dresser, Commode, Queen Bed 4480.00
Bedroom Set, Herter Bros., Egyptian Revival, Ebonized, Gilt, 1870-1880 .... 17625.00
Bedroom Set, Louis XVI, Gilt Bronze, Pressed Glass, 20th Century, 3 Piece 7200.00
Bedroom Set, Mitchell & Rammelsperg, Rococo Revival, Mahogany, Ohio, 3 Piece 17250.00
Bedroom Set, Victorian, Carved Flowers, Berry Panels, Burled, 2 Piece 14000.00
Bedroom Set, Victorian, Oak, Carved, Flowers, Griffin Crest, Beveled Mirror, 2 Piece ... 7000.00
Bench, 10-Spindle Back, Bamboo Turnings, 35 x 47 3/4 In. 550.00
Bench, Amish, Poplar, Blue Paint, Rounded Front Corners, 47 1/2 x 16 x 32 In. 715.00
Bench, Bamboo, Saddle Seat, Canted Legs, 1880s, 22 x 12 1/2 In. 520.00
Bench, Beech, Butterfly Pattern, Stretcher Base, Chinese, 1900, 19 x 45 In. 784.00
Bench, Bucket, 2 Tiers, 41 x 13 1/2 x 36 In. 170.00
Bench, Bucket, Green Paint, Scrubbed Top, Mortised Legs, 55 x 14 x 18 In. 110.00
Bench, Bucket, Hardwood, 3 Graduated Shelves, 29 x 47 7/8 In. 440.00
Bench, Bucket, Pine, 1-Board Top, Shelf, 24 3/4 x 43 1/4 In. 165.00
Bench, Bucket, Pine, Blue Paint, Gallery Sides, Lower Shelf, Cutout Feet, 32 x 36 In. 165.00
Bench, Bucket, Pine, Bootjack Ends Mortised Through, 19 x 64 In. 165.00
Bench, Bucket, Pine, Cupboard, 2 Upper Doors, 2 Lower Doors, 60 1/4 x 36 1/2 In. 2750.00
Bench, Bucket, Pine, Dovetailed Case, Bootjack Ends, 2 Shelves, 48 x 32 In. 1100.00
Bench, Bucket, Pine, Painted, Late 18th Century, 24 x 31 x 9 1/2 In. 2185.00
Bench, Bucket, Pine, Poplar, Step Back, 2-Shelf Base, 11-In. Board Top, 41 In. 880.00
Bench, Bucket, Pine, Step-Down, 4 Shelves, C Ends, 47 3/4 In. 1980.00
Bench, Bucket, Poplar, Zinc-Covered Shelf, 2 Lower Shelves 3410.00
Bench, Bucket, Scalloped Gallery, Round Front Ends On Top, Shaped Front, 19 x 36 In. .. 110.00
Bench, Cane, Lacquer, Apron, Cloud Spandrels, Chinese, 1600-1700, 18 x 32 In. 690.00
Bench, Carved Wood, Vine-Pierced Panels, Lift Top, Oriental, Arms, 64 x 26 x 56 In. 1760.00
Bench, Child's, Abersal, Lancaster County, Pa., c.1930, 34 x 11 x 19 1/2 In. 595.00
Bench, Choir, Walnut, 2 Seats, Pierced Back, Hinged Seat, 1870s, 70 x 46 In. 2300.00
Bench, Deacon's, Pine, 19th Century, 73 x 26 1/2 In. 230.00
Bench, Deacon's, Sheraton, 1-Board Seat, Pa., 20 x 72 In. 1200.00
Bench, E. Wormley, Walnut, Bentwood Legs, Signed, 42 x 18 1/2 x 12 In. 800.00
Bench, Edwardian, Mahogany, Rectangular, Yellow Damask Upholstered, 19 In. 1265.00
Bench, Fir, Paneled Back, Cutout Slab Sides, Lift Seat, Oak Inside, 79 x 25 x 54 In. 7000.00
Bench, Folding Splayed Legs, Open Slat, 18 1/4 x 55 1/4 In. 110.00
Bench, G. Nakashima, Black Walnut, Slab Supports, 13 x 60 x 18 In. 4600.00
Bench, G. Nelson, Birch, Slats, Herman Miller, 1947, 14 x 72 In. 1610.00
Bench, G. Nelson, Blond Wood, Slatted, Ebonized Legs, 14 1/4 x 48 In. 7700.00
Bench, G. Nelson, Cane Top, Chrome Folding Legs, 48 x 14 In. 1265.00
Bench, G. Nelson, Ebonized, Slatted, 14 x 56 1/2 x 19 In. 545.00
Bench, G. Nelson, Plywood Risers, 6 1/2 x 72 1/4 In. 5550.00
Bench, G. Nelson, Steel, Painted, Cushions, Herman Miller, 74 1/2 x 25 1/2 In. 1150.00
Bench, G. Stickley, No. 224, Dark Mahogany, Original Finish 5000.00
Bench, George IV, Beech, Cane Seat, Reeded Legs, 16 x 36 x 18 In., Pair 9000.00
Bench, George IV, Mahogany, Olive Green Leather Seat, Reeded Legs, 20 In. 1955.00
Bench, George IV, Mahogany, Tufted Tan Leather Seat, Reeded Legs, 20 x 26 In. 2760.00
Bench, Gold, Copper, Silver Fruit Crest, Mustard Yellow Ground, 6 x 24 In. 825.00

Bench, Greene & Greene, Paneled Back, Cutout Slab Sides, 1905, 79 x 25 x 54 In. 7000.00
Bench, Hall, Arts & Crafts, Mahogany, Pierced Circular Design, 36 x 16 x 29 In. 1150.00
Bench, Hall, Arts & Crafts, Paneled Back, 72 x 29 x 54 In. 3100.00
Bench, Hall, Limbert, No. 81, Mahogany, Reversed Cutout, 14 x 16 x 45 In. 4025.00
Bench, Harness-Maker's, Pine, Brown Paint, 20 x 36 x 10 In. 145.00
Bench, Jumuwood, Horse-Hoof Feet, Beaded Edge Apron, 19 x 12 1/2 x 43 In. 430.00
Bench, Leather, Tufted Top & Sides, Brass Casters, 61 1/2 In. 3680.00
Bench, Leather, Tufted Top, Reeded Frieze & Legs, Brass-Cap Casters, 19 x 49 x 27 In. . . 2135.00
Bench, Light Brown, Morning Glory Stencil, 8 Legs, Plank Seat, Arms, Pa., 84 In. 1540.00
Bench, Log, Slat Seat & Back, Log Corner Braces On Legs, 32 1/2 x 44 1/2 In. 110.00
Bench, Louis XV Style, Upholstered, Gros & Petit Point, Cabriole Legs, 48 In. 1265.00
Bench, Mahogany, Acanthus On Aprons, Upholstered Slip Seat, 45 1/2 In. 275.00
Bench, Mahogany, Brown Leather, Brass Tack, Winged Paw Feet, 18 x 49 1/2 x 31 In. . . . 6615.00
Bench, Mahogany, Lift Seat, 16 x 48 x 36 In. 900.00
Bench, Mahogany, Scrolled Supports, Carved Petals At Edges, 1920s, 16 x 48 In. 360.00
Bench, Mahogany, Upholstered, Shaped Apron, Bobbin-Turned Legs, 15 x 48 In. 1265.00
Bench, Mammy's, Hand Painted Crest, Spindle Back, Plank Seat, Child Gate 880.00
Bench, Mammy's, Straight Crest, Spindle Back, Insert Gate To Hold Baby, 50 1/2 In. 110.00
Bench, Mortised, Beaded Apron, V-Cut Legs, 20 x 82 x 13 1/2 In. 80.00
Bench, Mortised, Storage Compartment, Shaped Legs, 18 x 57 x 11 In. 130.00
Bench, Oak, Pine & Yew, Doors Underneath, Wire Nails, 52 1/2 x 72 3/4 In. 1540.00
Bench, Oak, Plank Seat, Low Back, Rounded Sides, Flared Legs, 24 1/2 x 21 In., Pair . . . 8400.00
Bench, P. Evans, Chrome, Beige Suede Cushion, 17 x 25 1/2 x 19 1/2 In. 375.00
Bench, Painted, Yellow Line, Square Nails, Arched End Panels, 33 In. 275.00
Bench, Park, Softwood, 3-Slat Back, X Ends, 41 5/8 In. 140.00
Bench, Pencil-Post Legs, 18 1/2 x 38 In. 190.00
Bench, Piano, J.M. Young, Through Tenons & Pegged, Label, 20 x 38 In. 1610.00
Bench, Piano, Red Cushion, Carved Legs, Stretchers, 38 x 17 x 20 In. 615.00
Bench, Piano, Walnut, Burled Aprons On Aprons, Floral Inlay, Lift Top, 21 1/2 In. 250.00
Bench, Pine, 1-Board, Rope, Scalloped Legs & Aprons, 9 1/2 x 8 1/2 In. 335.00
Bench, Pine, Inset Panels, Lift Top, Shaped Arms, Square Feet, 45 1/2 x 18 x 40 In. 2090.00
Bench, Pine, Slat, Light Blue Paint, Bootjack Ends, 17 x 36 In. 90.00
Bench, Queen Anne, Walnut, Upholstered Seat, Cabriole Legs, 16 x 66 x 24 In. 8160.00
Bench, Railroad, Hardwood, Black Over Red Paint, 33 1/2 x 68 In. 330.00
Bench, Refectory, French Provincial, Chestnut, Plank Seat, 19 1/2 x 71 x 7 In., Pair 345.00
Bench, Robsjohn-Gibbings, Geometric Fabric, Original Finish, Signed, 14 In. 2530.00
Bench, Robsjohn-Gibbings, Red Pinstripe Upholstered, Tufted Cushion, 34 1/2 In. 880.00
Bench, Rosewood, Beaded Openwork Apron, Carved Flowers, Block Feet, 19 x 40 In. 345.00
Bench, Rounded Skirt, Bootjack Ends, Braces On Back, 18 1/2 x 71 In. 330.00
Bench, Sheraton, Figured Maple, Molded Rail, Mid 19th Century, 33 x 75 1/2 x 18 In. . . . 1610.00
Bench, Steel Case, Chrome, Vinyl, 1960s, 92 x 20 x 18 In. 400.00
Bench, Teak, Openwork Aprons, Covered Cushion, Scroll Feet, 20 x 45 In. 715.00
Bench, Trefoil Finials, Cutouts On Arms, Back Panel, 1880s, 50 x 30 In. 520.00
Bench, Tufted, Painted Cabriole Legs, 17 x 33 In. 60.00
Bench, Wagon, Turned Rings, Woven Splint Seat, Curved Arms, Tapered Legs 550.00
Bench, Walnut, Needlepoint Upholstered, Flowers At Top Of Feet, 16 x 46 In. 520.00
Bench, Walnut, Open Back, Arched Brackets, Cushion Seat, 1870s, 48 1/2 In. 2070.00
Bench, Water, Pine, 21 1/2 x 39 x 18 1/2 In. 1090.00
Bench, Water, Pine, Bootjack Ends, 20 x 46 3/4 In. 330.00
Bench, Water, Pine, Round Edges On Apron, Bootjack Ends, 20 1/2 x 63 In. 360.00
Bench, William & Mary Style, Beech, Twist Borders, Legs, 17 x 47 x 20 In. 1380.00
Bench, William IV, Mahogany, Tufted Leather Top, Reeded Circular Legs, 19 In. 1380.00
Bench, Windsor, Tablet Top, Crest Rail, 27 Rod Spindles, Mid 19th Century, 33 x 114 In. . . 315.00
Bench, Wrought Iron, Leather, Scrolled Ends, 28 x 70 In. 1905.00
Bidet, Chippendale, Cane Seat & Back, Floral Porcelain, Divided Top, 35 x 31 In. 825.00
Bidet, Mahogany, Mirror In Seat Cover, 18th Century 2500.00
Book Trough, Rose Valley, Gothic Revival, Carved Panels, 32 1/2 x 23 3/4 x 8 1/4 In. . . . 520.00
Bookcase, Arts & Crafts, 2 Doors, Leaded Glass, Inlaid Tulips, 52 x 46 In. 2645.00
Bookcase, Arts & Crafts, Center Glass Door, Narrow Side Doors, 48 x 13 x 55 In. 1495.00
Bookcase, Arts & Crafts, Oak, 2 Doors, Slag & Clear Glass, 4 Interior Shelves, 57 In. 460.00
Bookcase, Bamboo, Sea Grass Lined Top, 3 Open Shelves, 1880s, 36 In. 690.00
Bookcase, Black Japanned, Parcel Gilt, 3 Mullioned Doors, Shelves, 94 In. 9000.00
Bookcase, Burl Trim, 3 Doors, 3 Drawers In Base, Shell Pulls, 105 x 76 In. 7500.00

Bookcase, Chestnut, Tapered Shelves, Keyed Tenons, 53 x 38 In. 800.00
Bookcase, Chinese, Rosewood, 4 Shelves, Mid 19th Century, 67 x 34 1/2 x 13 In. 1265.00
Bookcase, Chippendale Style, Mahogany, 2 Glass Doors, 13 Panes, 52 x 45 x 13 In. 1045.00
Bookcase, Chippendale, Mahogany, Broken Pediment, Brass Screen Doors, 89 x 51 In. ... 460.00
Bookcase, Clipped Corner Gallery, Glass Panel Door, 2 Shelves, 56 x 28 x 13 1/2 In. 1035.00
Bookcase, Cornice, 6 Beaded-Edge Shelves, Cutout Feet, 78 x 54 In. 385.00
Bookcase, Edwardian, Mahogany, Inlaid, Glass Door, Mullions, 60 x 38 x 17 In., Pair ... 1150.00
Bookcase, Edwardian, Mahogany, String Inlay, 3 Glass Doors, Early 20th Century 1090.00
Bookcase, G. Stickley, Mahogany, 2 Doors, 56 x 43 x 13 In. 6000.00
Bookcase, G. Stickley, No. 544, Mahogany, 16 Panes, 62 x 12 x 56 In. 11000.00
Bookcase, G. Stickley, No. 703, Mahogany, 6 Adjustable Shelves, 58 In. 7480.00
Bookcase, G. Stickley, No. 715, Mahogany, 16 Panes, 36 x 56 In. 9200.00
Bookcase, G. Stickley, Oak, Rectangular Case, 3 Shelves, 1909, 56 3/8 In. 4700.00
Bookcase, George III, Gallery Top, Adjustable, England, 52 x 32 x 10 In. 4800.00
Bookcase, George III, Mahogany, 2 Astragal Glazed Doors, Top-Shaped Feet, 83 In. 4370.00
Bookcase, George III, Mahogany, 2 Glazed Doors, 5 Shelves, Ionic Columns, 83 In. 2760.00
Bookcase, George III, Mahogany, Pierced Pediment, Doors, Plinth, 95 x 60 x 20 In. 2910.00
Bookcase, George IV, Mahogany, Cross Braces, Open, Turned Legs, 72 x 15 In. 690.00
Bookcase, Globe-Wernicke, Stacked, Oak, 6 Sections, Cincinnati, 88 x 34 In. 825.00
Bookcase, Harden, 2 Sliding Doors, Inset Brass Handles, 3 Shelves, 44 x 15 x 56 In. 690.00
Bookcase, Harvey Ellis, Mahogany, 2 Doors, Paper Label, 58 x 42 In. 7475.00
Bookcase, L. & J.G. Stickley, 2 Doors, Through Tenons, Decal, 56 x 39 x 13 In. 5750.00
Bookcase, L. & J.G. Stickley, No. 638, Mahogany, 2 Doors, 6 Panes, 48 In. 5175.00
Bookcase, L. & J.G. Stickley, Oak, Glass-Paneled Door, Gallery Top, 55 x 30 In. 3740.00
Bookcase, Liberty, Gallery Top, Small Cabinet, Leaded Glass Door, 47 In. 3100.00
Bookcase, Liberty, Oak, Open, 3 Shelves, Gallery Top, c.1900, 47 x 36 In. 2645.00
Bookcase, Lifetime, 3 Doors, Faux Mullions, Gallery Top, 55 x 56 In. 2875.00
Bookcase, Lifetime, Drawer Over Door, Latticework Panes, Shelves, Label, 55 x 32 In. ... 2990.00
Bookcase, Lifetime, Mahogany, Dark Finish, 3 Doors, 54 x 55 In. 1750.00
Bookcase, Lifetime, Mahogany, Finish, 2 Doors, 45 x 42 x 12 In. 2000.00
Bookcase, Lifetime, Open, 3 Shelves, Gallery Top, 54 x 40 x 12 In. 520.00
Bookcase, Limbert, 2 Doors, 6 Open-End Shelves, 48 x 12 x 46 In. 2990.00
Bookcase, Limbert, 3 Doors, Divided Glass Panes, Copper, 9 Shelves, 56 x 14 x 50 In. .. 2645.00
Bookcase, Limbert, No. 222, Mahogany, 2 Doors, 38 x 14 x 51 In. 4600.00
Bookcase, Limbert, No. 327, Mahogany, Dark Finish, 1 Door, 37 x 16 x 50 In. 19550.00
Bookcase, Limbert, No. 340, Mahogany, 2 Divided Glass Panes, 32 x 11 x 46 In. 2070.00
Bookcase, Limbert, No. 358, 2 Doors, Copper Pulls, Splayed Legs, 48 x 14 x 57 In. 3750.00
Bookcase, Limbert, Oak, 2 Doors, 3 Adjustable Shelves, Copper Pulls, 57 x 40 1/2 In. ... 2760.00
Bookcase, Lundstrom, Arts & Crafts, Leaded Glass Doors, Shelves, 53 x 68 x 12 In. ... 2990.00
Bookcase, Mahogany, 2 Doors, 3 Shelves, Crisscross Front Panels, 46 x 49 x 13 In. 500.00
Bookcase, Mahogany, 2 Doors, Adjustable Shelves, 4 Base Drawers, 88 1/2 In. 450.00
Bookcase, Mahogany, 2 Glass Doors, Flower & Leaves Inlay, 64 x 53 In. 3055.00
Bookcase, Mahogany, 2 Glazed Doors, 2 Lower Doors, 1820s, 90 1/2 In. 5750.00
Bookcase, Mahogany, Figural Columns, Shaped Doors, c.1880, 66 x 16 x 52 In. 2520.00
Bookcase, Mahogany, Mullioned Glass Doors, Adjustable Shelves, 93 In. 9600.00
Bookcase, Mahogany, Sliding Door, Carved, c.1885, 52 x 18 x 61 In., Pair 3250.00
Bookcase, Mahogany, Victorian, 4 Narrow Doors, 19th Century, 57 x 12 1/2 In. 1380.00
Bookcase, Marcel Breuer, 3 Shelves, Ebonized Wood, Chrome, 48 x 10 x 48 In. 520.00
Bookcase, Oak, 2 Doors, Carved Door Panels, Beveled Mirrors, 90 x 18 x 56 In. 2800.00
Bookcase, Oak, 3 Glazed Leaded Glass Paneled Doors, 1900s, 61 x 13 1/2 x 63 In. 1380.00
Bookcase, Oak, 3 Sections, Sliding Glass Doors, Early 20th Century, 34 x 11 x 45 In. ... 460.00
Bookcase, Oak, 3 Sliding Doors, Reeded Pilasters, 68 1/2 x 72 1/2 x 15 In. 2760.00
Bookcase, Pine, 3 Shelves, Molded Cornice, Red Repaint, 29 x 9 1/2 x 39 3/4 In. 470.00
Bookcase, Pine, Dovetailed Case, 2 Drawers, Fitted Interior Locks, 27 1/4 In. 605.00
Bookcase, Regency, Mahogany, 2 Glazed Doors, 84 x 54 x 20 In. 1725.00
Bookcase, Regency, Mahogany, 3 Open Shelves, 42 x 36 x 14 In. 865.00
Bookcase, Regency, Mahogany, Broken Pediment, Bust, 98 x 56 1/2 x 19 In. 1495.00
Bookcase, Regency, Mahogany, Carved, Glazed, Lion-Paw Feet, 53 x 72 x 11 In. 3450.00
Bookcase, Regency, Oak, Carved Pediment, Doors, 93 x 88 1/2 x 17 1/2 In. 2760.00
Bookcase, Revolving, Burl Walnut, Inlaid, 2 Tiers, X-Brace, Casters, 18 1/2 x 31 In. 420.00
Bookcase, Revolving, Mahogany, 2 Divided Tiers, Casters, 31 x 18 1/2 In. 335.00
Bookcase, Revolving, Oak, 3 Tiers, Adjustable Bookrest, c.1880, 41 In. 785.00
Bookcase, Rococo Revival, Rosewood, Bonnet Top, Floral Crest, 124 x 66 x 25 In. 17250.00

Bookcase, Rococo Revival, Rosewood, Tracery, Drawers, 86 x 90 x 17 In. 5750.00
Bookcase, Rococo Style, Walnut, Carved, 2 Doors, Continental, 103 1/2 x 54 x 25 In. . . . 1095.00
Bookcase, Rosewood, 12 Open Compartments, 2 Sliding Doors, Shelves, 79 1/2 In. 295.00
Bookcase, Roycroft, Oak, 3 Open Shelves, Marked Ledwidge, 38 In. 4950.00
Bookcase, Stickley Bros., 2 Doors, 16 Panes, Faux Mullion, Metal Tag, 53 x 48 In. 3335.00
Bookcase, Stickley Bros., 2 Glass Doors, Slatted Gallery Top, Brass Tag, 50 x 35 In. 3740.00
Bookcase, Stickley Bros., Mahogany, Flowers, Leaded Glass, 60 In. 11500.00
Bookcase, Victorian, Carved Gothic Dividers On 2 Glass Doors, 2 Drawers, 120 In. 8960.00
Bookcase, Victorian, Rosewood, Mid 19th Century, 64 x 53 x 17 3/4 In. 1295.00
Bookcase, Victorian, Walnut, Carved Gallery, Columns, Burled Panels, 75 x 19 x 53 In. . . 2520.00
Bookcase, Victorian, Walnut, Carved Gallery, Glass Doors, 2 Drawers, 92 x 78 In. 6160.00
Bookcase, Walnut, 3 Sections, 4 Adjustable Shelves, 78 x 25 1/2 In. 385.00
Bookcase, Walnut, Carved Gallery, 2 Glass Doors, 2 Half Drawers, 74 x 48 In. 1430.00
Bookcase, Walnut, Pierced Cornice Set With Gargoyles, 92 In. 1495.00
Bookcase, William IV, Mahogany, Mullioned Doors, 2 Drawers, England, c.1818 . . . . 11500.00
Bookcase-Bench, McCobb, Mahogany, Planner Group, 60 x 18 1/2 x 39 In. 60.00
Bookcase-Cabinet, George III, Pine, Green Marbleized Columns, 96 x 109 In. 5175.00
Bookcase-Cabinet, Hanging, Gold Embossed, Glass Front Doors, c.1890 . . . . 1265.00
Bookcase-Cabinet, Limbert, No. 347, Mahogany, 1 Door, 2 Open Shelves, 17 x 47 In. . . . 4025.00
Bookcase-Cabinet, Mahogany, Upper Shelved Interior, Lower Door, 82 In. 800.00
Bookcase-Cabinet, Pine, Lacquer, Cracked-Ice Fretwork, 4 Drawers Over 2 Doors, 37 In. . 805.00
Bookcase-Cabinet, Victorian, Mahogany, 2 Gilt Arched Doors, 4 Shelves, 107 In. 2760.00
Bookcase-Cabinet, Walnut, 3 Open Shelves, Molded Cornice, Italy, 105 1/2 In. 14950.00
Bookcase-Cabinet, William IV, Mahogany, Rectangular Cornice, 91 1/2 In. 10065.00
Bookcase-Table, Mechanical, 5 Tiers, Tilts & Becomes Tabletop, c.1890 . . . . 730.00
Bookrack, G. Stickley, No. 74, Keyed Through Tenons, Lower Shelf, 30 x 34 In. 1380.00
Bookrack, G. Stickley, Revolving, Label, 9 1/2 x 13 In. 3392.00
Bookrack, Mahogany, Band Inlay, Acorn Cutouts, 15 x 8 3/4 x 7 3/8 In. 55.00
Bookstand, Barber Brothers, V Trough, 2 Shelves, Slab Sides, 28 x 9 x 28 In. 299.00
Bookstand, Bible, Walnut, 27 In. 160.00
Bookstand, Edwardian, Mahogany, Revolving, Square Top, c.1900, 12 1/2 x 12 In. 345.00
Bookstand, Encyclopedia, Slatted Sides, John Wanamaker Co., 29 1/2 x 29 1/2 In. 800.00
Bookstand, Federal, Mahogany, Tilt Top, Reeded Baluster Shaft, Bun Feet, 29 x 14 In. . . 825.00
Bookstand, Gothic Revival, Burl, Veneer, Arches, Trefoils, 13 1/2 x 5 3/4 In. 345.00
Bookstand, Liberty & Co., Mahogany, 4 Shelves, Slab Sides, 14 x 9 x 45 In. 1320.00
Bookstand, Light Wood Inlay, Fan, Revolving, 30 1/2 x 18 1/2 x 18 1/2 In. 420.00
Bookstand, Mahogany, Inlay, Revolving, 30 1/2 x 18 1/2 x 18 1/2 In. 310.00
Bookstand, Revolving, Square, Late 19th Century, 57 x 23 In. 620.00
Bookstand, Walnut, Inlay, Pierced Arch, Crest, Couple Dancing, c.1890, 11 x 14 5/8 In. . . 170.00
Bookstand, Wrought Iron, Open, Square Legs, Ball Feet, Continental, 12 x 15 x 12 In. . . . 460.00
Breakfront, Mahogany, Carved Lions' Heads, Mirrored Top, 90 x 23 x 90 In. 2800.00
Breakfront, Neoclassical Style, Mahogany, 19th Century, 98 x 76 x 25 In. 8050.00
Breakfront, Oak, Beveled Curio Cabinet, Carved Crest, 108 x 28 x 106 In. 2800.00
Breakfront, Walnut, 2 Sliding Glass Doors, Velvet Lining, Brass Frame, 65 In. 1595.00
Breakfront-Bookcase, 4 Divided Paneled Doors, 2 Short, 3 Long Drawers, 84 In. 2000.00
Breakfront-Bookcase, George III, Mahogany, 20th Century, 93 x 73 x 18 In. 3450.00
Breakfront-Bookcase, George III, Mahogany, 4 Astragal Glazed Doors, 89 In. 8060.00
Breakfront-Bookcase, George III, Mahogany, 6 Doors, 3 Drawers, 91 x 73 x 16 In. 3100.00
Breakfront-Bookcase, George III, Mahogany, 86 x 84 1/2 x 18 In. 4830.00
Breakfront-Bookcase, George III, Mahogany, Pine, 4 Panel Doors, 91 x 17 In. 2530.00
Breakfront-Bookcase, George III, Satinwood, Anthemion Frieze, 92 In. 26050.00
Breakfront-Bookcase, Georgian Style, Overall Gilt, Chinoiserie, 72 x 17 x 86 In. 1725.00
Breakfront-Bookcase, Mahogany, 2 Pairs Of Figured Doors, 1850s, 96 In. 6900.00
Breakfront-Bookcase, Mahogany, Glazed & Figured Doors, 1850s, 96 In. 7475.00
Breakfront-Bookcase, Renaissance Revival, Walnut, Burl, 3 Sections, 110 x 90 x 20 In. . . 8625.00
Buffet, Art Deco, Tulipwood, Marble Top, 20th Century, 39 1/2 x 113 x 20 1/4 In. 6325.00
Buffet, Cherry, Inlaid Stringing Accents, 2 Drawers, 2 Doors, 35 x 62 x 25 In. 1850.00
Buffet, Harvey Probber, Ash Veneer, 2 Sliding Doors, 2 Shelves, 36 3/4 x 42 In. 770.00
Buffet, Heywood-Wakefield, 3 Drawers, Shelves, c.1950, 48 x 19 x 32 1/2 In. 1265.00
Buffet, Louis XV, Fruitwood, Frieze Drawers, Doors, 40 x 57 x 19 In. 3740.00
Buffet, Louis XV, Oak, Carved Fruit, Mid 19th Century, 93 x 56 1/2 x 21 1/2 In. 4025.00
Buffet, Louis XV, Rectangular Top, 2 Field Panel Doors, Shaped Feet, 1700s 545.00
Buffet, McCobb, Mahogany, 2 Adjustable Shelves, 60 x 14 x 84 In. 2300.00

Buffet, Oak, 2 Doors, 2 Paneled Lower Doors, 1870s, 44 1/2 x 58 In. 3680.00
Buffet, Oak, Carved Women Supports, Cherub, Griffin Panels, 97 x 28 x 96 In. 11200.00
Buffet, Oak, Floral Basket Pediment, Side Cupboards, 2 Lower Doors, 1890s, 65 1/2 In. . . 1840.00
Bureau, Empire, Mahogany Veneer, Brass, 6 Drawers, 47 1/2 x 47 x 23 In. 750.00
Bureau, Federal, Cherry, Mahogany, Bowfront, 4 Drawers, Inlaid, 38 1/2 x 40 In. 2645.00
Bureau, Federal, Mahogany, String Inlay, Pigeonholes, Graduated Drawers, 44 x 46 In. . . 4115.00
Bureau, Fruitwood, Center Cupboard, Slant Front, Writing Surface, 44 x 23 1/2 In. 1035.00
Bureau, G. Stickley, No. 909, 2 Over 3 Drawers 2640.00
Bureau, Louis Philippe, Mahogany, Leather, 19th Century, 29 x 47 1/2 x 27 In. 1840.00
Bureau, Mahogany, 4 Drawers, Scrolled Backsplash, Oval Corners, 49 x 44 In. 805.00
Bureau, Mahogany, Ivory Escutcheons, Oval Brasses, Turned Feet, 39 x 43 x 19 In. 575.00
Bureau, Neoclassical, Mahogany Veneer, 3 Graduated Lower Drawers, 17 1/2 In. 1380.00
Bureau, Neoclassical, Mahogany, Rectangular Top, 3 Drawers, Gentleman's, 49 In. 575.00
Bureau, Neoclassical, Rectangular Top, 3 Graduated Drawers, Gentleman's, 52 In. 805.00
Bureau, Sheraton, Cherry, Tiger Maple Drawer Fronts, Ivory Inserts, Gentleman's 5500.00
Bureau-Bookcase, George III Style, Mahogany, Doors, 17 Panes, Sloped, 86 x 40 x 22 In. 3565.00
Bureau-Bookcase, Mahogany, Slant Front, Fitted Interior, Candle Rests, 95 In. 2645.00
Bureau-Bookcase, Mahogany, Upper Door, Interior Shelves, Drawers, 79 In. 1380.00
Bureau-Bookcase, Oak, Upper Drawers, Inside Shelves, Lower Drawers, 86 In. 1725.00
Bureau-Bookcase, Regency, Mahogany, Slant Front, 3 Graduated Drawers, 83 In. 2760.00
Cabinet, Arched Paneled Door, Shelves, 1 Over 2 Lower Drawers, 1930s, 63 In. 145.00
Cabinet, Art Nouveau, Oak, Carved, Continental, Early 20th Century, 78 x 79 x 32 In. 3740.00
Cabinet, Arts & Crafts, Mahogany, 4 Doors, 40 x 11 x 71 In. 3740.00
Cabinet, Arts & Crafts, Oak, Glass Doors, Shelves, c.1905, 59 x 39 In. 2250.00
Cabinet, Bar, Harvey Probber, Lift Top, 2 Doors, Brass Pulls, Shelves, 35 x 36 In. 295.00
Cabinet, Bar, Peter Hunt, Painted Design, 3 Side Drawers, 1 Door 2250.00
Cabinet, Baroque, Oak, Twist Supports, 3 Paneled Doors, 87 x 81 x 24 In. 920.00
Cabinet, Bedside, Chinese Style, Carved Birds, Dragons, Glass Door, 1800s, 45 In. 750.00
Cabinet, Black Lacquer, Drawer, Stretcher Legs, 9 Interior Compartments, 32 x 18 In. . . . 560.00
Cabinet, Black Lacquer, Top Doors, 2 Interior Doors, Foo Dog Finials, 74 In. 560.00
Cabinet, Burl, Marquetry, Ormolu Escutcheon, Angels, 55 x 52 In. 2585.00
Cabinet, Carved Oak, Continental, c.1860, 70 3/4 x 48 x 17 3/4 In. 2465.00
Cabinet, Carved Oak, Vitrine, Continental, c.1860, 66 x 29 x 22 In. 1680.00
Cabinet, Carved, Lacquered, Chinese, Late 19th Century, 63 x 96 3/4 x 20 1/4 In. 1955.00
Cabinet, Carved, Walnut, Italy, Early 18th Century, 9 x 10 3/4 x 8 1/2 In. 150.00
Cabinet, China, Arts & Crafts, 2 Doors, 8 Panes, Gallery, 68 x 42 x 15 1/2 In. 3100.00
Cabinet, China, Arts & Crafts, Mahogany, 2 Doors, 39 x 15 x 60 In. 1495.00
Cabinet, China, Bernhardt, Oriental Style, 2 Glazed & 2 Paneled Doors, 32 x 79 In. 345.00
Cabinet, China, Chippendale Style, Mahogany, 2 Glass Doors, Drawer, 80 x 37 In. 460.00
Cabinet, China, Crown Molding, 2 Paneled Doors, Inside Shelves, 2 Lower Doors, 71 In. 1100.00
Cabinet, China, G. Stickley, Backsplash, 12 Panes, Red Decal, 63 x 36 In. 6040.00
Cabinet, China, G. Stickley, Mahogany, 12 Panes, 36 x 15 x 63 In. 6900.00
Cabinet, China, G. Stickley, Mahogany, 2 Doors, 8 Panes, 36 x 14 x 56 In. 6000.00
Cabinet, China, G. Stickley, No. 815, Mahogany, 2 Doors, Gallery Top, 64 x 41 x 15 In. . . 6900.00
Cabinet, China, G. Stickley, No. 820, Mahogany, 12 Panes, 63 In. 5750.00
Cabinet, China, G. Stickley, Oak, Rectangular Case, 2 Doors, 1910, 64 1/2 In. 5300.00
Cabinet, China, L. & J.G. Stickley, 2 Doors, Glass Panes, Shelves, Marked, 55 x 48 In. . . 4025.00
Cabinet, China, Limbert, Door, Glass Panes, Extended Shelves, 58 x 45 x 16 In. . . . . *Illus* 7475.00
Cabinet, China, Limbert, Mahogany, Original Finish, 2 Doors, 58 x 48 x 15 1/2 In. 2700.00
Cabinet, China, Limbert, No. 473, 1 Door, 3 Divided Glass Panes, 45 x 16 x 58 In. 4500.00
Cabinet, China, Limbert, Plate Rail, 2 Doors, 62 1/2 x 46 In. 3450.00
Cabinet, China, Limbert, Plate Rail, Corbels, 2 Glass Panel Doors, 62 x 46 In. 5175.00
Cabinet, China, Limbert, Single Door, 3 Adjustable Shelves, Branded, 56 x 30 In. 2415.00
Cabinet, China, Mahogany, 2 Dovetailed Drawers, Mullion Dividers, 65 1/4 In. 1155.00
Cabinet, China, Mahogany, Bowfront, 3 Shelves, Claw & Ball Set, 52 x 39 x 17 In. 615.00
Cabinet, China, Oak, D-Shape, 2 Glass Sides, Large Glass Door 1795.00
Cabinet, China, Stickley Bros., No. 2017, Mahogany, Dark Finish, 2 Doors, 64 x 17 In. . . 3000.00
Cabinet, China, Stickley Bros., No. 8852, 2 Doors, 3 Shelves, Marked, 59 x 46 In. 2300.00
Cabinet, Chinoiserie, Black Lacquer Scene, Continental, 1800s, 32 x 19 x 12 In. 1680.00
Cabinet, Corner, Bird's-Eye & Tiger Maple, Convex Front, 2 Doors, 1 Drawer, 46 In. . . . 770.00
Cabinet, Corner, French Provincial, Gothic Style, Oak, 106 x 46 x 28 1/2 In., Pair 6900.00
Cabinet, Corner, Georgian, 1 Door, Shaped Shelves, 1780 . . . . 4200.00
Cabinet, Corner, Hanging, Arts & Crafts, Carved, Inlaid Door, Backsplash, 34 x 20 In. . . . 490.00

Furniture, Cabinet, China,
Limbert, Door, Glass
Panes, Extended Shelves,
58 x 45 x 16 In.

Furniture, Cabinet, Eames,
Shelves, Laminated Panels,
Steel Frame, 58 x 47 In.

Cabinet, Corner, Hanging, Blue Trim, Astral Door, Early 1800s, 27 x 15 x 47 In.	400.00
Cabinet, Corner, Hanging, George III, Mahogany, Late 1700s, 43 1/2 x 33 x 20 1/2 In.	1380.00
Cabinet, Corner, Hanging, George III, Oak, Late 18th Century, 47 1/2 x 35 x 20 In.	865.00
Cabinet, Corner, Hanging, Mahogany, 1 Door, Diamond Mullions, 42 x 28 In.	860.00
Cabinet, Corner, Hanging, Poplar, Paneled Door, Brass Pull, 25 3/4 x 26 In.	1210.00
Cabinet, Corner, Hanging, Walnut, Dentil Molding, Door, Shelves, 52 x 32 x 18 In.	1150.00
Cabinet, Corner, Louis Philippe, Mahogany, Mid 19th Century, 73 x 38 x 26 In.	2530.00
Cabinet, Corner, Louis XVI Style, Gilt Bronze Mounted, Marble Top, 68 x 27 In.	4700.00
Cabinet, Corner, Mahogany, Crown Over Panel Door, Bracket Feet, c.1850, 44 In.	950.00
Cabinet, Corner, Plastic, Modular, Shelves, Italy, 39 x 12 x 72 In.	980.00
Cabinet, Corner, Walnut & Cherry, 2 Base Doors, Glass Panels Top Doors, 82 1/4 In.	1870.00
Cabinet, Corner, Walnut, Glazed Panel Upper Doors, Drawer, 78 3/4 x 40 x 19 In.	1570.00
Cabinet, Corner, Walnut, Paneled Door, Interior Shelves, Continental, 50 x 21 In.	750.00
Cabinet, Cornice, 2 Panel Doors, 6 Shallow Drawers, 32 x 26 x 12 In.	550.00
Cabinet, Curio, 1 Door, Pane Of Glass & Inserts, Brass Gallery, 2 Shelves, 57 1/4 In.	550.00
Cabinet, Curio, Bird's-Eye Maple, 2 Shelves, Glass Door, c.1920, 42 In.	550.00
Cabinet, Curio, Chapman Mfg., Stripped Pine, Glazed Panel, 83 x 36 1/2 x 16 1/2 In.	615.00
Cabinet, Curio, Chinese, Rosewood, Standing, Late 19th Century, 31 1/2 x 31 1/2 x 9 In.	750.00
Cabinet, Curio, Edwardian, Walnut, Burl, Glass Door, Sides, Lighted, 63 x 23 x 14 In.	2240.00
Cabinet, Curio, Fleur-De-Lis, 4 Sides, Serpentine Glass Panels, 1 Shelf, 43 1/4 In.	770.00
Cabinet, Curio, French Provincial, Mahogany, Gilt, Rococo Scroll, Glass Panels, 58 In.	990.00
Cabinet, Curio, Gallery Top, Glass Doors, 2 Shelves, Faux Bamboo, 34 1/2 In.	200.00
Cabinet, Curio, George III Style, Mahogany, Stand, 94 x 44 x 16 1/2 In.	1065.00
Cabinet, Curio, Georgian Style, Dome Top, Glazed Panels, 94 x 29 In., Pair	4030.00
Cabinet, Curio, Hardwood, Floral Crown, Interior Shelves, Lower Doors, 82 1/2 In.	2576.00
Cabinet, Curio, Hekman, 4 Drawers, Engraved Pulls, Glass Panels Each Side, 84 In.	360.00
Cabinet, Curio, Oak, Bowfront, 3 Glass Doors, Carved Backsplash, 57 x 36 In.	1000.00
Cabinet, Curio, Oak, Mirror Back, Carved, Curved Glass, 3 Shelves, 58 x 17 x 52 In.	2072.00
Cabinet, Curio, Walnut, Burl, Marquetry, Paneled, Door, Brass, 42 1/2 In., Pair	1630.00
Cabinet, Curio, Walnut, Marquetry, Green Marble Top, Door, Dutch, 29 x 16 x 64 In.	730.00
Cabinet, Curio, Walnut, Marquetry, Marble Top, 52 3/4 x 22 x 14 1/2 In., Pair	1120.00
Cabinet, Display, Art Deco, Walnut Veneer, 3 Glass Shelves, 2 Doors, 1920s, 54 3/4 In.	435.00
Cabinet, Display, Eastlake, Mahogany, Carved, Mirror, c.1880, 78 x 44 x 12 In.	2300.00
Cabinet, Display, Gilt, Serpentine Glass All Sides, Floral, Bronze Bead, France, 37 In.	415.00
Cabinet, Display, Hanging, Walnut, Glazed Door, Shelves, Dutch, Late 1700s, 25 x 25 In.	800.00
Cabinet, Display, Mahogany, Arched Glass Door, Leaf Cast Mounts, 68 x 33 In.	1955.00
Cabinet, Dufrene, Ebene-De-Macassar, Maple, Marble Serpentine Top, 1925, 106 In.	6600.00
Cabinet, Dyer's, Painted, Decorated, Late 19th Century, 40 1/2 x 44 1/2 x 16 1/2 In.	6465.00
Cabinet, E. Wormley, Bifold Doors, Circular Pulls, 29 x 32 In.	790.00
Cabinet, E. Wormley, Mahogany, 2 Small Drawers, 30 x 24 In.	920.00
Cabinet, Eames, Birch Plywood, Herman Miller, 1950, 47 In.	6270.00
Cabinet, Eames, Shelves, Laminated Panels, Steel Frame, 58 x 47 In. .... *Illus*	9775.00
Cabinet, Eastlake, Walnut, Architect's, Fold-Out Easel, Dated 1876	1950.00
Cabinet, Edwardian, Polychromed, 2 Glazed Doors, c.1900, 38 x 43 1/4 x 12 1/2 In.	1035.00
Cabinet, Edwardian, Rosewood, Satinwood, c.1905, 43 3/4 x 25 1/2 x 17 1/2 In.	865.00
Cabinet, Empire, Mahogany, Bronze Mount, Cylinder, Marble, 32 x 17 In.	1150.00

Cabinet, Empire, Mahogany, Dentil, 10 Thin Over 6 Large Drawers, Half Columns, 35 In. 4290.00
Cabinet, Empire, Molded Top Over 2 Glass Doors, 2 Paneled Doors, 48 x 14 x 85 In. 1150.00
Cabinet, Filing, L. & J.G. Stickley, 2 Drawers, Rectangular Form, 31 x 21 In. 460.00
Cabinet, Filing, Oak, Crown Over Divided Doors, Document Section, 58 1/2 In. 560.00
Cabinet, Frank Lloyd Wright, Mahogany, Stacking, 2 Doors, 34 x 44 In. 8625.00
Cabinet, Fretwork, Drawer, 4 Doors, c.1890, 48 x 34 x 13 1/2 In. 500.00
Cabinet, Frieze, Sliding Doors, Brass Toe Caps, Casters, 31 2/3 In. 60.00
Cabinet, Fruitwood, Attenuated Pyramid, Gilt, Brass Inlay, 80 3/4 In. 980.00
Cabinet, Fruitwood, Upper Glazed Sections Over Drawer, 2 Doors, 81 In., Pair 2585.00
Cabinet, G. Nelson, Black Enamel, Steel Frame, Yellow, Olive Green, 29 In. 1725.00
Cabinet, G. Nelson, Walnut, 2 Sliding Glass Doors, Inner Shelf, 56 1/4 In. 1150.00
Cabinet, G. Nelson, White Enamel, Steel Frame, Orange, 33 x 30 In. 1150.00
Cabinet, George III Style, Mahogany, 2 Glazed Doors, 81 1/2 x 51 1/4 x 22 1/2 In. 1150.00
Cabinet, George III, Mahogany, 2 Doors, Drawer, Early 1900s, 13 5/8 x 12 x 9 In. 230.00
Cabinet, George III, Mahogany, 2 Sections, Molded Cornice, Glazed Doors, c.1800 ..... 3740.00
Cabinet, George III, Mahogany, Bowfront, Corner, Glazed Doors, 75 x 27 1/2 x 19 In. 2990.00
Cabinet, George IV, Mahogany, Projecting Molded Top, Melon Feet, 40 1/2 In. 5520.00
Cabinet, Gilt, Painted, 2 Doors, Symbols, Music, Art, Justice, Italy, 42 x 36 In. 1680.00
Cabinet, Glass Center, Porcelain Painting, Bronze Ormolu, 42 x 20 x 25 In. 1680.00
Cabinet, Gothic Revival, Mahogany, Spires, Arch-Shaped Panels, 115 x 25 x 39 In. 5320.00
Cabinet, Gothic Revival, Oak, 2 Doors, Tracery Apron, Plinth Base, 58 x 38 x 21 In. 860.00
Cabinet, Gothic Revival, Oak, Trapezoidal, Column Posts, 75 x 53 x 21 In. 630.00
Cabinet, Gothic Revival, Walnut, 3 Aligned Drawers, Molded Base, 14 1/2 In. 490.00
Cabinet, Hagan, Mahogany, 11 Drawers, Claw & Ball Feet, Signed, 48 x 23 x 39 In. 3920.00
Cabinet, Hanging, Arts & Crafts, Mahogany, Amber Glass, Hammered, 10 x 18 In. 240.00
Cabinet, Hanging, Arts & Crafts, Textured Green Glass Doors, Germany, 28 x 18 In. 290.00
Cabinet, Hanging, Cherry, Paneled, Painted, Mid 18th Century, 27 1/4 x 18 3/4 x 13 In. ... 8400.00
Cabinet, Hanging, Liberty, Overhanging Top, Stenciled Door Panel, Spring, 23 x 22 In. .. 1610.00
Cabinet, Hanging, Pine, 6 Glazed Panels, 19th Century, 40 x 32 x 9 In. 315.00
Cabinet, Hanging, Tooled Metal Door Panels, 21 x 31 In. 1265.00
Cabinet, Hardwood, 4 Lattice Doors, Chinese, 1800s, 66 x 41 x 21 In. 1725.00
Cabinet, Jacobean Style, Oak, Carved, Scroll Frieze, Gadrooned Legs, 32 x 29 x 20 In. .. 1600.00
Cabinet, Jacobean, Oak, 2 Paneled Doors, Shelves, Shaped Feet, 55 x 44 x 23 In. 1380.00
Cabinet, Jelly, Southern American Cherry, c.1850, 41 1/4 x 40 x 20 1/2 In. 500.00
Cabinet, Jewelry, Cherry, Lift-Up Mirror Door 2900.00
Cabinet, Jewelry, Mother-Of-Pearl, Black Lacquer, Scalloped-Edge Top, 11 In. 630.00
Cabinet, Lacquer, 2 Drawers, 2 Doors, Spandrels Sides, Chinese, 1800s, 31 x 42 In. 520.00
Cabinet, Lacquer, 2 Drawers, Extensive Landscape Design, Chinese, 72 x 56 In. 650.00
Cabinet, Lacquer, 2 Slat Panel Doors, 2 Drawers, Chinese, 1800s, 76 x 51 x 24 In. 1840.00
Cabinet, Lacquer, Red, Painted Children, 2 Doors, Chinese, 1700-1800, 74 x 44 In. 1600.00
Cabinet, Leaded Glass Doors, Mirrored Back, Splayed Legs, 35 x 15 x 53 In. 635.00
Cabinet, Liquor, 8 Sides, Interior Burner, Thermometer, Slots, Casters, 1910 .... 460.00
Cabinet, Liquor, Burl, Carved, 2 Doors, 2 Drawers, Interior Mirror, 62 x 29 In. 335.00
Cabinet, Liquor, Limbert, Pullout Copper Tray, 2 Doors With Pipe Racks, 36 x 29 In. 2185.00
Cabinet, Liquor, Oak, Iron Mounted, Glasses, 19th Century, 11 x 17 1/2 x 12 In. 1210.00
Cabinet, Louis Philippe, Walnut, Part Ebonized, 40 1/4 x 34 1/4 x 13 In. 1610.00
Cabinet, Louis XV, Gray, White Serpentine Marble Top, Splayed Legs, 35 1/2 In. 545.00
Cabinet, Louis XV, Mahogany, Marquetry, 3 Drawers, Rectangular, 28 x 11 In. 690.00
Cabinet, Louis XVI Style, Bombe, Parquetry, Bronze Mounts, France, 74 x 17 In. 5750.00
Cabinet, Louis XVI Style, Gilt Bronze Mounted, c.1900, 60 1/4 x 24 x 13 In. 7200.00
Cabinet, Louis XVI Style, Gilt Metal, Parquetry, Marble Top, 51 x 18 x 47 In. 460.00
Cabinet, Louis XVI Style, Walnut, Slate, Drawer, Paneled Doors, 34 x 44 x 20 In., Pair .. 3450.00
Cabinet, Louis XVI, Hardwoods, Marquetry, Veneer, Marble Top, 33 x 16 x 43 In. 2300.00
Cabinet, Louis XVI, Marquetry, Marble, 1 Allegorical Drawer, 60 x 48 x 19 In. 8050.00
Cabinet, Louis XVI, Serpentine Side, Mid 20th Century, 30 x 16 x 31 In. 259.00
Cabinet, Louis XVI, Serpentine Sides, 2 Doors, Floral Carved Glass Top, 30 x 31 In. 260.00
Cabinet, Magazine, G. Stickley, No. 72, Oak, 4 Shelves, H. Ellis, 42 x 22 In. 3525.00
Cabinet, Mahogany Inlay, Corner, England, 74 1/4 x 32 1/4 x 18 1/2 In. 840.00
Cabinet, Mahogany, 2 Banks Of 4 Drawers, 2 Cupboard Doors, Female Heads, 72 In. 4600.00
Cabinet, Mahogany, 4 Grilled Cupboard Doors, Ebonized Paw Feet, 37 x 60 x 13 In. 8915.00
Cabinet, Mahogany, Bowfront, 2 Doors Over 2 Drawers, New England, 40 x 35 x 17 In. .. 2640.00
Cabinet, Mahogany, Burl, 3 Drawers Over Doors, Outset Center, 38 x 62 In. 860.00
Cabinet, Mahogany, Chinese Man On Pediment, 2 Doors, 86 1/2 In. 1840.00

Cabinet, Mahogany, Glass Top & Sides, Bronze Mounts, 38 x 17 In. 770.00
Cabinet, Mahogany, Inlay, Drawer, Paneled Door, Square Legs, c.1890, 37 x 17 x 16 In. . . 259.00
Cabinet, Mahogany, Paneled Doors, 18 Interior Drawers, Ebony Pulls, 42 1/2 In. 1700.00
Cabinet, Mahogany, Pullout Base, 4 Glass Panes In Top, 67 3/4 In. 550.00
Cabinet, Mahogany, Shelves Over 3 Paneled Doors, 1880s, 86 In. 2185.00
Cabinet, Marble Top, Hinged Metal Doors, Interior Shelf, 32 In. 460.00
Cabinet, Marcel Coard, Art Deco, Mahogany, Ivory, Bronze, 1930, 37 1/2 In. 9000.00
Cabinet, Music, Arts & Crafts, Mahogany, Fruitwood & Mother-Of-Pearl Inlay, 42 In. . . . 2875.00
Cabinet, Music, G. Stickley, No. 70, Oak, Amber Panes, Paper Label, 47 1/2 In. 7475.00
Cabinet, Music, Incised Borders On Front & Lid, Divided Interior, 30 x 18 In. 140.00
Cabinet, Music, Mahogany, Glass Door, 48 x 24 1/2 In. 440.00
Cabinet, Music, Mahogany, Sliding Shelves, Beveled Mirror Back, 44 x 18 In. 302.00
Cabinet, Music, Rosewood, Woman Holding Banjo On Door, Skirt Drawer 3250.00
Cabinet, Music, Victorian, Mahogany, Gilt, Door, Marquetry Panel, 55 x 30 x 19 In. 4900.00
Cabinet, Oak, Divided Stained Glass Doors, Carved Panel Doors, c.1870, 91 1/2 In. 450.00
Cabinet, Oak, Door, Interior Shelf, Barley Twist Leg, Stretcher Base, 33 1/2 x 22 In. 170.00
Cabinet, Oak, Stained Glass, Leaded Glass Panels, Doors, c.1890, 88 1/2 In. 730.00
Cabinet, Oak, Upper Paneling, 2 Doors, 5 Lower Drawers, 59 x 57 In. 2250.00
Cabinet, Oriental, Elm, Rectangular, 4 Short Drawers, 2 Doors, 33 x 15 x 48 In. 580.00
Cabinet, Painted, 8 Sides, Brass Inlay, Mirror Base, France, 23 x 43 In. 2475.00
Cabinet, Panel Doors, Gilt Painted, Short Legs, Tibet, 1800s, 34 x 29 In. 460.00
Cabinet, Parcel Gilt, Crown Over Shelf, Marble Top Over Drawer, 1860s, 54 In. 980.00
Cabinet, Pine, Oak, Pair Of Glazed Doors, Cabriole Legs, 50 1/4 In. 2040.00
Cabinet, Raymond Loewy, DF2000, Molded Plastic Drawers, 41 x 22 x 49 1/2 In. 1955.00
Cabinet, Regency Style, Mahogany, Urn Knife Storage, 38 x 16 In. 1840.00
Cabinet, Regency, Black Japanned, Parcel Gilt, Shelf, 2 Doors, 72 x 37 In. 6000.00
Cabinet, Regency, Rosewood, 2 Silk-Lined Grille Doors, 1810, 34 x 36 x 13 In. 6600.00
Cabinet, Regency, Rosewood, Brass Inlay, Mirror, 3 Drawers, 2 Doors, 49 x 37 x 16 In. . . . 4830.00
Cabinet, Robsjohn-Gibbings, Light Walnut, Geometric Design, 70 1/4 In. 11750.00
Cabinet, Robsjohn-Gibbings, Mahogany, Original Finish, Signed, 35 x 31 In. 575.00
Cabinet, Rosewood, 4 Sliding Doors, 5 Drawers, Original Finish, 82 1/2 x 31 In. 2070.00
Cabinet, Scalloped Apron, Serpentine Panels, 2 Shelves, 1930s, 50 1/2 In. 1265.00
Cabinet, Shaker Style, Green Paint, Interior Shelves, 35 3/4 x 60 1/2 x 13 In. 470.00
Cabinet, Side-By-Side Paneled Doors, Inner Shelves, Arched Base, 57 x 56 In. 400.00
Cabinet, Smoking, Lakeside Craftshop, Mahogany, 2 Doors, 13 x 13 x 32 In. 375.00
Cabinet, Smoking, Mahogany, Carved Door, Original Dark Finish, 42 x 16 x 9 In. 400.00
Cabinet, Spanish Baroque, Pewter Inlay, Walnut, 34 3/4 x 43 x 26 In. 1725.00
Cabinet, Spanish Baroque, Walnut, 6 Doors, Late 1600s, 67 x 34 x 16 In. 1150.00
Cabinet, Spice, Pine, 8 Drawers, Dovetailed Case, 17 x 12 x 20 In. 430.00
Cabinet, Spice, Softwood, 12 Drawers, Dovetailed Case, Glass Knobs, 20 1/2 x 18 x 7 In. . 715.00
Cabinet, Spice, Softwood, 20 Drawers, Molded Top, Base, 18 x 27 In. 1100.00
Cabinet, Stereo, G. Nelson, Birch, Herman Miller, 57 x 18 1/2 x 24 In. 575.00
Cabinet, Stereo, G. Rohde, Burl Veneer, 3 Doors, Brass Pulls, 1940, 41 3/4 In. 330.00
Cabinet, Stickley, Paneled Door, Drawer, Wood Knob, Copper Hardware, 16 x 16 x 28 In. . 8000.00
Cabinet, Teak, 2 Top Drawers, 2 Lower Doors, Chinese Landscapes, 33 x 41 In. 1150.00
Cabinet, Teak, Red Paint, 2 Floral Paneled Doors, Scroll Legs, 40 x 11 In., Pair 920.00
Cabinet, Victorian, Beech, Brass Moldings, Columns, 41 In. 1955.00
Cabinet, Victorian, Mahogany, 3 Drawers, Plinth Base, Mid 1800s, 29 1/2 x 51 x 20 In. . . 690.00
Cabinet, Walnut, 2 Doors, Molded Cornice, Wire Rail, 13 3/8 x 4 3/4 x 16 In. 250.00
Cabinet, Walnut, 4 Doors, 16 Lower Drawers, 8 1/2 x 13 1/2 Ft. 5250.00
Cabinet, Walnut, Applied Geometric Moldings, Italy, 26 x 14 x 32 1/2 In., Pair 2300.00
Cabinet, Walnut, Burl, Dentil Crown, Panel Doors, Bracket Feet, Pair 1120.00
Cabinet, Walnut, Marquetry, Glass Doors, 3 Drawers, 1700s, 80 x 22 In. 10640.00
Cabinet, Walnut, Molded Cornice, Fluted Columns, Pad Feet, 91 1/2 In. 3000.00
Cabinet, Wedding, Flower & Fruit, 2 Shelves, Black Paint, 72 1/2 In. 1120.00
Cabinet-On-Stand, Black Lacquer, Coffer Top, Japan, 15 x 9 x 5 1/4 In. 225.00
Cabinet-On-Stand, Black Lacquer, Pierced Gallery, Chamfered Legs, 61 1/2 In. 4600.00
Cabinet-On-Stand, George III Style, Mahogany, Cabriole Legs, 40 x 48 x 25 1/2 In. 800.00
Cabinet-On-Stand, Jewelry, Rosewood, Traveling, Fitted, Mid 1800s, 11 x 11 x 16 In. . . . 520.00
Cabinet-On-Stand, Mahogany, Drawer & Door Side Columns, 1820s, 41 In., Pair 3900.00
Cabinet-On-Stand, Pine, Cornice, Glazed Door, Shelves, Italy, 1800s, 66 x 30 x 15 In. . . . 546.00
Cabinet-On-Stand, Rosewood, 2 Lower Doors, 3 Drawers, Shelf Stretcher, 56 In. 2415.00
Candlestand, Adjustable Top & Candleholder, Acorn Finial, 39 In. 1100.00

Candlestand, American Cherry, Tilt Top, Rectangular, c.1850, 27 1/4 x 18 x 14 1/2 In. 250.00
Candlestand, Black Paint, Snake Feet, 26 x 16 In. 1035.00
Candlestand, Cherry & Walnut, Tripod Base, Snake Feet, 26 1/2 x 16 In. 300.00
Candlestand, Cherry, 1-Board Tilt Top, Cabriole Legs, 26 In. 800.00
Candlestand, Cherry, Beveled Edge, Vase-Turned Standard, Queen Anne Legs, 26 In. ... 195.00
Candlestand, Cherry, Chestnut, Snake Feet, Connecticut, c.1780, 27 3/8 In. 1500.00
Candlestand, Cherry, Dish Top, Connecticut, c.1800 .... 1150.00
Candlestand, Cherry, Drawer, Connecticut, Late 18th Century, 15 1/2 x 17 1/2 In. 2875.00
Candlestand, Cherry, Rectangular Top, Black Paint, Connecticut, 26 x 17 In. 1840.00
Candlestand, Cherry, Round, Vase-Form Pedestal, Tripod Base, Pa., 27 1/2 x 17 In. 440.00
Candlestand, Cherry, Spider Legs, Oval Top 2450.00
Candlestand, Cherry, Square Top, Tripod, Early 19th Century, 28 x 16 1/2 x 17 1/2 In. 315.00
Candlestand, Cherry, Tilt Top, Birdcage Support, Tripod, 17 x 16 1/2 In. 875.00
Candlestand, Cherry, Tilt Top, Birdcage, Oval Fan Inlay, Cabriole Legs, 22 x 29 In. 770.00
Candlestand, Cherry, Tilt Top, Scalloped Bottom, Brass Latch, 28 3/4 In. 1375.00
Candlestand, Cherry, Tilt Top, Square 1-Board Top, Tripod Base, 28 x 17 3/4 In. 360.00
Candlestand, Cherry, Tray Top, Carved, Late 18th Century, 25 3/4 x 15 3/4 x 15 1/2 In. .. 2875.00
Candlestand, Cherry, Urn Shaft, 3 Arched Legs, c.1800, 28 x 17 1/4 In. 1265.00
Candlestand, Cherry, Vase-Turned Pedestal, Slipper Feet, 28 In. 460.00
Candlestand, Chippendale, Cherry, Birch, Cabriole Legs, Snake Feet, 14 x 25 1/2 In. 330.00
Candlestand, Chippendale, Cherry, Snake Feet, Square Top, 17 x 16 1/2 x 27 1/2 In. 550.00
Candlestand, Chippendale, Mahogany, Dish Top, Snake Feet, 25 1/2 In. 1430.00
Candlestand, Chippendale, Mahogany, Inlaid, Mass., c.1790, 27 x 20 In. 3000.00
Candlestand, Chippendale, Mahogany, Piecrust Top, Scrolled Feet, 18 x 24 In. 220.00
Candlestand, Chippendale, Mahogany, Scalloped Laminated Top, 20 x 16 x 25 In. 300.00
Candlestand, Chippendale, Mahogany, Tilt Top, 3 Cabriole Legs, Snake Feet, 16 x 27 In. .. 470.00
Candlestand, Chippendale, Tiger Maple, Circular Dish Top, 27 x 17 In. 1955.00
Candlestand, Chippendale, Walnut, Dish Top, 3 Cabriole Legs, 28 1/2 In. 4115.00
Candlestand, Chippendale, Walnut, Tilt Top, Urn Pedestal, Snake Feet, 17 x 27 In. 220.00
Candlestand, Dish Top, Downswept Legs, Snake Feet, c.1760, 26 1/4 In. 3300.00
Candlestand, Federal, Cherry, Birch, Tilt Top, Tapered Legs, 29 x 18 x 24 In. 260.00
Candlestand, Federal, Cherry, Circular Tilt Top, Scrolled Legs, Slipper Feet, 27 In. 200.00
Candlestand, Federal, Cherry, Oval Top, Urn Pedestal, Splayed Legs, Spade Feet, 29 In. . 1645.00
Candlestand, Federal, Cherry, Tilt Top, Serpentine Corners On Urn, 28 1/4 In. 750.00
Candlestand, Federal, Cherry, Tilt Top, Serpentine Corners, 27 x 17 x 18 In. 520.00
Candlestand, Federal, Cherry, Tilt Top, Tripod Base, Spade Feet, c.1820, 28 1/2 In. 405.00
Candlestand, Federal, Mahogany, Astragal Top, Urn Standard, Shoe Feet, 28 x 14 In. 590.00
Candlestand, Federal, Mahogany, Cabriole Legs, Snake Feet, c.1800, 36 3/4 x 17 In. 2645.00
Candlestand, Federal, Mahogany, Cloverleaf Tilt Top, c.1815, 29 x 26 x 17 In. 765.00
Candlestand, Federal, Mahogany, Figured, Tilt Top, c.1810, 28 3/4 x 17 x 25 In. 3900.00
Candlestand, Federal, Mahogany, Octagonal Top, Spade Feet, 27 x 14 x 15 In. 690.00
Candlestand, Federal, Mahogany, Tilt Top, c.1810, 29 x 16 3/4 x 25 1/2 In. 2875.00
Candlestand, Federal, Mahogany, Tilt Top, Pedestal, 29 1/2 x 28 1/2 x 19 1/2 In. 660.00
Candlestand, Federal, Mahogany, Turned, Leaf-Carved Standard, 3 Saber Legs, 27 In. ... 235.00
Candlestand, Federal, Maple, Dish Top, Tripod Curved Leg Base, 28 1/2 x 15 In. 2070.00
Candlestand, Federal, Maple, Early 19th Century, 25 1/4 x 19 1/2 In. 1840.00
Candlestand, Federal, Maple, Square Top, Vase & Ring Turned, Tripod Base, 27 In. 2415.00
Candlestand, Federal, Tiger Maple, Early 19th Century, 27 1/2 x 15 1/2 In. 1150.00
Candlestand, Federal, Wavy Birch, Tilt Top, Tripod Base, Spade Feet, 1810, 28 In. 2185.00
Candlestand, Fruitwood, Inlaid Diamond, Checkerboard Surround, 3 Spade Feet, 32 In. .. 3290.00
Candlestand, Hepplewhite Style, Mahogany, Oval, High Tripod Legs, 13 x 18 x 27 In. .. 192.00
Candlestand, Hepplewhite, Birch, 1 Drawer, Brass Pull, Tapered Legs, 20 x 16 x 28 In. .. 440.00
Candlestand, Hepplewhite, Bird's-Eye Maple Inlay, Octagon Shape, 3 Legs, 28 In. 1810.00
Candlestand, Hepplewhite, Cherry, Spider Base, Taper Legs, 16 x 16 x 28 In. 990.00
Candlestand, Hepplewhite, Cherry, Tilt Top, Tripod Legs, Early 1800s, 23 x 19 x 26 In. ... 345.00
Candlestand, Hepplewhite, Cherry, Tripod Base, Saber Legs, 16 x 16 1/2 x 28 1/4 In. ... 715.00
Candlestand, Hepplewhite, Mahogany, Pedestal, Tripod Base, 27 In. 505.00
Candlestand, Hepplewhite, Mahogany, Tilt Top, Pedestal Base, 29 x 22 1/2 x 22 In. 505.00
Candlestand, Hepplewhite, Maple, Red Wash, Quatrefoil Top, Column, 1800s, 22 x 16 In. 115.00
Candlestand, Hepplewhite, Maple, Square, Spider Base, 29 1/2 x 19 x 19 In. 450.00
Candlestand, Hepplewhite, Maple, Tripod, Early 19th Century, 22 x 16 x 28 In. 115.00
Candlestand, Mahogany, Birdcage, Vase-Turned Pedestal, 27 1/2 x 24 x 17 1/2 In. 1840.00
Candlestand, Mahogany, Center Top Medallion, Spade Feet, 28 1/2 x 22 1/2 In. 220.00

Candlestand, Mahogany, Dish Top, Pedestal, 3 Reeded Legs, 28 x 18 In. 195.00
Candlestand, Mahogany, Octagonal, Diamond Cut Apron, Pedestal, 3 Legs, 28 x 19 In. . . . 195.00
Candlestand, Mahogany, Oval Top, Double-Line Inlay, Vase-Form Pedestal, 29 x 28 In. . . . 70.00
Candlestand, Mahogany, Rings Under Top, Pierced Hearts, Shelf, 31 1/4 In. 250.00
Candlestand, Mahogany, Tilt Top, Down-Curving Legs, Ball Feet, c.1820, 28 In. 1200.00
Candlestand, Mahogany, Tilt Top, Flame Grained, 17 x 24 x 18 1/2 In. 110.00
Candlestand, Mahogany, Tilt Top, Snake Feet, 26 3/4 In. 250.00
Candlestand, Mahogany, Tilt Top, Vase & Urn Column, Spider Legs, c.1800, 28 In. 1550.00
Candlestand, Mahogany, Top Cloverleaf Inlay, 3 Scrolled Feet, 26 x 15 1/2 In. 375.00
Candlestand, Mahogany, Urn Columns, Tripod Base, Snake Feet, 26 3/8 In. 440.00
Candlestand, Mahogany, Wrought Iron Latch, Tripod Base, 30 1/4 In. 275.00
Candlestand, Maple & Walnut, Ring & Urn Turned Standard, Snake Feet, 25 1/2 In. 825.00
Candlestand, Maple, Dish Top, Tripod Woman's Legs 950.00
Candlestand, Maple, Round, Turned Post, Cabriole Leg, Mid 18th Century, 25 x 15 In. . . . 460.00
Candlestand, Mixed Wood, Round Top, Turned Pedestal, 27 1/2 x 18 3/4 In. 130.00
Candlestand, Octagonal Tilt Top, Vase-Form Pedestal, 3 Arched Tapered Legs, 29 In. 390.00
Candlestand, Queen Anne Style, Dish Top, Snake Feet, 1900s, 25 1/2 In. 170.00
Candlestand, Queen Anne, Cherry, Cabriole Tripod Base, Pad Feet, 26 In. 1725.00
Candlestand, Queen Anne, Cherry, Dish Top, Snake Feet, 25 1/2 In. 865.00
Candlestand, Queen Anne, Cherry, Square Top, Turned Column, 1780, 14 x 15 In. 825.00
Candlestand, Queen Anne, Mahogany, Dish Top, 18th Century, 28 1/2 x 25 1/2 In. 1380.00
Candlestand, Queen Anne, Mahogany, Dish Top, Urn Standard, Snake Feet, 30 In. 4700.00
Candlestand, Queen Anne, Square Top, Rounded Corners, Snake Feet, 28 x 17 In. 635.00
Candlestand, Queen Anne, Walnut, Dish Top, Slipper Feet, c.1760, 29 x 18 In. 2585.00
Candlestand, Regency, Mahogany, Tilt Top, Turned Shaft, Scrolled Legs 110.00
Candlestand, Sheraton, Mahogany, Cherry, Tilt Top, Tripod Base, 28 x 21 In. 290.00
Candlestand, Tilt Top, Octagonal Top, Scrolled Legs, Spade Feet, 28 x 24 In. 200.00
Candlestand, Victorian, Mahogany, Tilt Top, Oval, 3 Curved Legs, 29 x 24 In. 170.00
Candlestand, Walnut, Circular Top, Turned Shaft, Tripod Leg, Snake Feet, 26 1/2 x 24 In. 1850.00
Candlestand, Walnut, Dish Top, Urn Turned Shaft, Spider Legs, Centennial 165.00
Candlestand, Windsor, Pine, Gold, Dark Brown Paint, 16 x 16 3/4 x 27 1/2 In. 715.00
Canterbury, Divided Top Over 2 Drawers, Brass-Cap Casters, 22 1/2 x 19 In. 520.00
Canterbury, Mahogany & Walnut, 1 Drawer, 3 Compartments, 20 x 22 In. 935.00
Canterbury, Mahogany, 4 Top Compartments & Drawer, Finial Ends, 20 1/2 In. 440.00
Canterbury, Mahogany, Base Drawer, 4 Sections, Corner Finials, 19 x 19 1/2 In. 275.00
Canterbury, Mahogany, Drawer, Casters, 20th Century, 20 x 19 5/8 In. 800.00
Canterbury, Regency Style Mahogany, 4 Slotted Compartments, 22 x 19 x 15 In. . . . 259.00
Canterbury, Regency, Mahogany, 4 Compartments Over 2 Drawers, Casters, 22 x 19 In. . . 315.00
Canterbury, Regency, Mahogany, 4 Compartments, Shelf Stretcher, 20 x 17 x 15 In. 1150.00
Canterbury, Regency, Mahogany, 4 Slots, Drawer, Bulbous Legs, Casters, 23 x 19 In. 345.00
Canterbury, Regency, Mahogany, Bowed Divisions, 19th Century, 23 x 19 x 15 In. 2070.00
Canterbury, Rococo, Walnut, Molded Edges, Raised Panel, 26 x 19 x 20 In. 980.00
Canterbury, Sheraton Style, Mahogany, Dovetailed Drawer, Brass Casters, 20 x 14 In. 140.00
Canterbury, William IV, Mahogany, Rectangular Cross Brace, 16 3/4 x 14 In. 1610.00
Canterbury, William IV, Rosewood, X-Shaped Dividers, Drawer, c.1835, 19 x 20 x 16 In. 1955.00
Cart, Bar, Aero, Aluminum & Lucite, Removable Tray, c.1935, 33 1/2 In. 1380.00
Cart, Georgian Style, Mahogany, Fold-Down Ends, Shelf Stretcher, 35 x 49 In. 650.00
Cart, Serving, Brass, Tray Top, Rectangular, 32 x 33 x 20 In. 750.00
Cart, Serving, Scandinavian, Teak, Black Laminate, Taper Legs, 23 x 39 In. 490.00
Cassone, Baroque Style, Walnut, Caryatid Stiles, Hinged Lid, Italy, 24 x 68 x 20 In. 1090.00
Cassone, Walnut, Front Carved Caryatids, Intaglio Leaves, 17th Century, 22 x 64 In. 1035.00
Cellarette, Arts & Crafts, Mahogany, 1 Drawer, 2 Cabinet Doors, 30 x 15 x 36 In. 490.00
Cellarette, Gallery, Projecting Drawers Over Door, Rotating Wine Rack, 54 1/2 In. 1725.00
Cellarette, George III Style, Mahogany, Inlaid, 19th Century, 23 1/2 x 21 x 14 1/2 In. 1380.00
Cellarette, George III, Satinwood, Mahogany Inlay, Square Tapered Legs, 22 In. 1265.00
Cellarette, Georgian, Mahogany, Hinged Lid, Lift-Out Base, Late 1800s, 19 x 18 In. 330.00
Cellarette, Georgian, Mahogany, Stand, Molded Base, Casters, 16 x 27 1/2 In. 1495.00
Cellarette, Goodall, Lamb, Heighway, Cherry, Handle, c.1905, 30 x 20 1/4 x 16 1/4 In. . . 520.00
Cellarette, L. & J.G. Stickley, No. 23, Mahogany, Original Finish, 32 x 16 x 35 In. 9200.00
Cellarette, Limbert, No. 751, Mahogany, 1 Drawer, 25 x 17 x 36 In. 3220.00
Cellarette, Mahogany, 2 Brass Bands, Conforming Stand, Brass Casters, 25 In. 560.00
Cellarette, Mahogany, Canted Corners, Scrolled Feet, Velvet Lined, 23 x 34 x 22 In. 3700.00
Cellarette, Mahogany, Figural Head, Claw Feet, Reticulated Gallery, 45 x 21 x 18 In. 1680.00

Cellarette, Mahogany, Front & Side Panels, Lion Mask Handle, Lead Lined, 18 1/4 In. . . . 2990.00
Cellarette, Mahogany, Hinged Top, Tapered Case, Brass Ring Handles, c.1820, 19 In. 7800.00
Cellarette, Mahogany, Inlaid Molding, Handles, Stand, 27 1/2 x 22 x 14 1/2 In. 2090.00
Cellarette, William IV, Mahogany, Sarcophagus, Swags, Plinth Base, 22 x 28 In. 3910.00
Cellarette, William IV, Oak, Paneled, Molding, Ball Feet, Lead Lined, 25 x 35 x 23 In. . . 1850.00
Chair, 2 Shells On Crest Rail, 3 Banisters 6500.00
Chair, 3 Turned Spindles, Blue Paint, Pinstriping, Flowers, Crest, 13 1/2 In. 550.00
Chair, 9 Bamboo Spindles, Shaped Saddle Seat, Early 19th Century, Pair 2990.00
Chair, A. & P. Castiglioni, Mezzandro, Steel, Wood, Painted Steel Seat, 1957, 22 In. 230.00
Chair, Aalto, Blond Wood, Vinyl Upholstered Seat, Bentwood Legs, 29 In. 110.00
Chair, Acanthus Leaf-Carved Knees, Upholstered Slip Seat, 39 1/2 In. 140.00
Chair, Adam, Cane Seat, Painted, River Scene, Houses, Black, Gold Bands, Pair 880.00
Chair, Adirondack, Painted, Pair 518.00
Chair, Adjustable Backrest, Hinged Arms, Pullout Leg Rest, Cope's Patent, 45 In. 2760.00
Chair, Aluminum Frame, Upholstered Seat & Back, Swivel Base, Pair 275.00
Chair, Andre Deveche, Fruitwood, Velvet Upholstered & Arms, 1930, Pair 8700.00
Chair, Andre Sornay, Mahogany, Nail-Head Design, Leather Upholstered, Arms, 2 . . . . . . 7200.00
Chair, Arched Back, Arms, Blue & White Upholstery, Carved Footstool 200.00
Chair, Arched Padded Back, Carved Roses, Outscrolled Padded Arms, Pair 690.00
Chair, Arne Jacobsen, Egg, Fiberglass Shell, Aluminum, F. Hansen, 42 x 34 x 31 In. 1955.00
Chair, Arne Jacobsen, Egg, Red Leather, 1950s 11000.00
Chair, Arne Jacobsen, Egg, Vinyl, Aluminum, Fritz Hansen, c.1979, 36 x 28 x 42 In. 1955.00
Chair, Arne Jacobsen, Laminated Teak, Steel Legs, Arms, Marked FH, 28 In. 335.00
Chair, Arne Jacobsen, Swan, Wool, Fiberglass Shell, 29 x 30 In. 3450.00
Chair, Arrow Back, Cornucopia On Crest, Leaves On Back, 19th Century, 32 In. 935.00
Chair, Arrow Back, Yellow Pattern On Crest, Red & Black Graining, 32 1/2 In., Pair 120.00
Chair, Art Deco, Salon, Burl, U-Shape, France, 28 x 26 In., Pair 2185.00
Chair, Art Nouveau, Gilt, Carved, Arms, 39 In. 310.00
Chair, Art Nouveau, Swivel, Bronze Nude Crest, Tooled Leather Seat, Back, Arms, France 4315.00
Chair, Arts & Crafts, 3 Horizontal Slats, Saddle Seat, Swivel Base, 24 In. 250.00
Chair, Arts & Crafts, 8 Spindles, Leather Seat, Pegged, 1900s, 40 1/2 In., Pair 230.00
Chair, Arts & Crafts, Back Splat, Metal & Wood Inlay, Leather Seat, Arms, 43 In. 345.00
Chair, Arts & Crafts, Barrel, Cutout Gothic Window Back, Leather Seat, Arms, 41 In. . . . 1495.00
Chair, Arts & Crafts, Brace Back, Trapezoid Seat, 34 1/2 x 16 1/2 x 17 1/2 In. 115.00
Chair, Arts & Crafts, Curved Crest Rails, Vertical Back Slats, Leather Seats, 37 In. 285.00
Chair, Arts & Crafts, Mahogany, Central Vertical Slat, Arms, 18 x 18 In. 660.00
Chair, Arts & Crafts, Mahogany, Lift-Top Seat, 2 Vertical Slats, 33 x 29 In. 800.00
Chair, Arts & Crafts, Oak, 5 Back Slats, Leather Cushion, Flat Arms, 1900s, 39 In. 315.00
Chair, Arts & Crafts, Oak, Central Vertical Slats, Rush Seat, Arms, 21 x 16 x 34 In. 660.00
Chair, Arts & Crafts, Oak, Crest Rail Over 3 Vertical Back Slats, 44 x 17 x 20 In. 170.00
Chair, Arts & Crafts, Tapered Back Panel, Rosette, Cutout Handle, Rush Seat, England . . 200.00
Chair, Arts & Crafts, V-Back Form, 5 Vertical Slats, Leather Seat, Arms, 25 x 21 x 37 In. . 350.00
Chair, Arts & Crafts, Vertical Back Slats, Drop-In Vinyl Seat, 40 x 15 x 16 In. 230.00
Chair, Balloon Back, Morning Glories, Leaves On Crest & Splat, 33 In., Pair 715.00
Chair, Bamboo, 6-Spindle Back, Arms, Green Paint, 38 In. 330.00
Chair, Bamboo, 7-Spindle Back, Splayed Stretcher, 34 In. 220.00
Chair, Bamboo, Handle Top Rail, Trapezoid Backrest & Seat, c.1880 . . . . 420.00
Chair, Banister Back, 3 Half-Turned Slats, Scalloped Crest, Rush Seat, 42 1/2 In. 275.00
Chair, Banister Back, Black Paint, Rush Seat, Double Box Stretcher, 44 In. 253.00
Chair, Banister Back, Ring-Turned Front Posts, Upholstered Arms, 43 In. 1320.00
Chair, Banister Back, Rush Seat, Scrub Finish, 18th Century, 44 x 19 In. 170.00
Chair, Banister Back, Split Column, Painted Design, Stenciled, Scroll-Carved Arms 3850.00
Chair, Baronial Style, Mahogany, Domed Back, Padded Seat, Mid 19th Century, 56 In. . . . 1035.00
Chair, Baroque Style, Walnut, Leaf-Carved Arms, Upholstered, Stretchers, Turned Legs . . 920.00
Chair, Baroque, Beech, Carved, Upholstered, 45 x 30 x 19 1/2 In. 1265.00
Chair, Baroque, Carved Putti, Scroll Forms, Paw Feet, Arms, Italy, 53 In. 1035.00
Chair, Baroque, Italian Walnut, Leather, Arms, 52 3/4 In. 3220.00
Chair, Baroque, Walnut, Needlework Upholstery, Trumpet-Turned Legs 635.00
Chair, Barrel Back, Button Padded, Loose Cushion, Padded Arms, Pair 575.00
Chair, Beech, Cane Back, Cartouche Backrest, Leaf Arms, 18th Century 1150.00
Chair, Beech, Cane Backrest, Padded Arms, Flattened Legs 245.00
Chair, Beech, Carved Back Arches & Columns, Upholstered Seat, c.1890, Pair 310.00
Chair, Beech, Carved Frame, Needlework Tapestry Upholstery, 1880s 1680.00

Chair, Beech, Floral Crest, Padded Armrests, 1780s, 34 In., Pair 2300.00
Chair, Beech, Leaf Crest & Stiles, Slip Seat, 19th Century, Pair 2300.00
Chair, Beech, Medallion Back, Tapestry Upholstery, Arms, 38 In. 3220.00
Chair, Beech, Padded Top Rail, Trellis Splat, Out-Curved Arms, c.1900, 34 1/2 In., Pair .. 2300.00
Chair, Beech, Ribbon-Carved Back & Frame, Padded Back, Seat & Armrests, 1880s 560.00
Chair, Beech, Suede, Padded Armrests, Continental, Pair 1065.00
Chair, Beech, Tapestry Upholstery, Padded Armrests, Carved Crest, Pair 2130.00
Chair, Beech, Terminating Rosettes, Bow Seat, Square Legs, 38 In. 4600.00
Chair, Belter, Gilt Surface, Carved & Laminated, Arms, New Upholstered, c.1850 ...... 5980.00
Chair, Belter, Rosalie, Rococo Revival, Rosewood Laminate, Grapes Pattern, Arms, 43 In. 5060.00
Chair, Bergere, Louis XV Style, Carved Crest, Upholstered, Closed Arms, 33 In. 275.00
Chair, Bergere, Louis XV Style, Carved, Upholstered, Closed Arms, 35 1/2 In. 330.00
Chair, Bergere, Louis XV Style, Gilt, Carved, Velvet Upholstery, Closed Arms 440.00
Chair, Bergere, Louis XV Style, Giltwood, Floral-Carved Crest, Closed Arms, 36 In. 1265.00
Chair, Bergere, Louis XV, Beech, Serpentine Top Rail, Closed Arms, 40 In. 3600.00
Chair, Bergere, Louis XV, Walnut, Carved, Closed Arms, c.1740, Pair 3220.00
Chair, Bergere, Louis XVI Style, Beech, Carved, Closed Arms, Ottoman 1345.00
Chair, Bergere, Louis XVI Style, Gilt, Crest With Bow, Upholstered, Closed Arms, Pair .. 2760.00
Chair, Bergere, Mahogany, Columnar Supports, Loose Cushion, Closed Arms, 37 In. 1150.00
Chair, Bergere, Regency, Mahogany, Reed Carved, Cushioned Seat, Closed Arms, 34 In. .. 1035.00
Chair, Birch & Walnut, Corner, Pierced Splats, Crewel Upholstery, Arms, 36 In. 385.00
Chair, Bird's-Eye Maple, Top Rail Rosettes, Seat Rail, Scrolled Arms, 1820s, 36 In., Pair . 3220.00
Chair, Black Over Graining, Stenciled Medallion Crest, 5-Spindle Back, 32 1/4 In. 410.00
Chair, Black Paint, Scenic Back Splat, Rush Seat, Pillow Back, 33 In., Pair 200.00
Chair, Black Repaint, Scrolled Stiles & Crest Back, Gold, Cane Seat 165.00
Chair, Block Dividers On Legs, Rush Seat, Shaped Rear Stiles, 40 1/2 x 18 In. 990.00
Chair, Bowed Domed Crest, Ribbon Carving, Needlepoint, Padded Back, 1880s 489.00
Chair, British Colonial, Cane Seat & Back, Arms, India, Pair 9775.00
Chair, British Colonial, Rosewood, Reeded Arms, Early 19th Century 1150.00
Chair, Brown Paint, Concave Top Rail, Cane Backrest, Arms, c.1810, Pair 4800.00
Chair, C. Rohlfs, Oak, T-Shape Back, 1905, 32 In. 4115.00
Chair, Campechy, Sling Seat, Green Leather Upholstery, c.1900, 36 In., Pair 1840.00
Chair, Cane Back, Multicolored Design, Allegorical Medallion, Arms 2300.00
Chair, Carved, Arms, Needlepoint Upholstered, 20th Century, 16 x 35 In., Pair 495.00
Chair, Carved, Fruit & Flowers, Slip-In Seat, Lion-Carved Legs, Burma, 35 In. 750.00
Chair, Carved, Padouk Wood, Leaf Back, Bowfront, Slip Seat, India, c.1810 .... 1380.00
Chair, Charles Pollock, Executive, Brown Leather, Knoll, 1965 .... 400.00
Chair, Charles X, Rosewood, Pale Wood Inlay, Gothic Style, 37 1/2 In., Pair 9200.00
Chair, Cherry, Carved Wind God & Griffins, Spindle Splats, Cane Seat, Pair 410.00
Chair, Chinese Official's, Carved Openwork Back, Stretcher Base, 40 In., Pair 495.00
Chair, Chippendale Style, Cabriole Legs, Claw & Ball Feet 520.00
Chair, Chippendale Style, Centennial, Cutout Vase Back Splat, Loose Seat Cushion 155.00
Chair, Chippendale Style, Hardwoods, T-Head Nails, 1-Board Seat, England, 38 In. 140.00
Chair, Chippendale Style, Mahogany, Cutout Back Splat, Shell Skirt, 40 1/2 In., Pair 385.00
Chair, Chippendale Style, Mahogany, Front Cabriole Legs, Ball Feet, 45 x 18 1/2 In. 175.00
Chair, Chippendale Style, Mahogany, Gothic Back Splat, Horsehair Seat, Arms, 38 In. ... 360.00
Chair, Chippendale Style, Mahogany, Shell Carved Crest, Pierced Splat, Claw, Ball Feet .. 140.00
Chair, Chippendale Style, Maple, Crest Rail, Inverted Baluster Splat, Rush Seat, 39 In. ... 120.00
Chair, Chippendale Style, Wing, Carved Blind Fretwork, Straight Legs 110.00
Chair, Chippendale Style, Wing, Serpentine Crest, Stretcher Base, Upholstered 250.00
Chair, Chippendale, Cherry, Slipper, Stretcher Base, Back Splat, Crest, 36 In. 715.00
Chair, Chippendale, Mahogany, Arched Crest Rail, Pierced Splat, 36 In., Pair 4700.00
Chair, Chippendale, Mahogany, Carved Ears, Newport R.I., 18th Century 1035.00
Chair, Chippendale, Mahogany, Crest Rail, Upholstered, Claw Feet, 42 x 30 x 24 In. 1175.00
Chair, Chippendale, Mahogany, Pierced Back Splat, Dark Finish, Muslin Seat, 37 In. 2145.00
Chair, Chippendale, Mahogany, Pierced Back Splat, Rush Seat, Pair 575.00
Chair, Chippendale, Mahogany, Serpentine Crest Rail, Upholstered, Arms, 44 1/2 In. 4700.00
Chair, Chippendale, Mahogany, Serpentine Crest, Pierced Splat, Arms, 39 x 29 x 18 In. ... 1175.00
Chair, Chippendale, Mahogany, Serpentine Crest, Scrolled Arms, 39 In. 1295.00
Chair, Chippendale, Mahogany, Serpentine Crest, Scrolled Ears, c.1780, 37 In. 4935.00
Chair, Chippendale, Mahogany, Serpentine Crest, Slip Seat, Arms, 36 1/2 In. 305.00
Chair, Chippendale, Mahogany, Upholstered, New England, c.1780, 46 x 36 x 26 In. 6325.00
Chair, Chippendale, Mahogany, Upholstered, Seat Cushion, c.1780, 47 In. 12000.00

Furniture, Chair, Club, Mahogany, Tufted Barrel
Back, Cushioned Seat, Casters, Pair

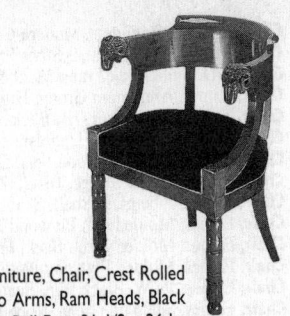

Furniture, Chair, Crest Rolled
To Arms, Ram Heads, Black
Seat, Ball Feet, 31 1/2 x 26 In.

Chair, Chippendale, Maple, Serpentine Crest, Rush Seat, c.1800, 41 x 16 1/2 x 21 In. 825.00
Chair, Chippendale, Walnut, Bowed Crest Rail, Scrolled Ears, Baluster Splat, 38 x 22 In. . 6325.00
Chair, Chippendale, Walnut, Carved Shell, Vase-Form Splat, Trapezoid Slip Seat, 39 In. . . 3760.00
Chair, Chippendale, Walnut, Serpentine Crest, Rush Slip Seat, Square Legs, 39 In., Pair . . 2070.00
Chair, Chippendale, Walnut, Serpentine Crest, Trapezoid Slip Seat, 40 In. 4600.00
Chair, Chippendale, Walnut, Shell Vase-Form Splat, Trapezoid Seat, Side, 41 In. 9775.00
Chair, Chippendale, Youth, Serpentine Back Slats, Molded Leg, Stretchers, 31 1/2 In. 115.00
Chair, Chrome, Brown Woven Leather Straps, Flat Bar Frame, Mid 1900s, 29 In. 200.00
Chair, Chrome, Leather Seat & Back Cushions, Canvas 495.00
Chair, Chrome, Wire, 1970s, 20 1/2 x 21 x 31 In. 80.00
Chair, Classical Style, Burl Veneer, Saber Leg, Carved & Pieced Crest Rail, Slip Seat 45.00
Chair, Claw Back, Rail Over Spindles, Plank Seat, c.1850 . . . . 179.00
Chair, Claw Back, Shaped Spindle, Plank Seat, c.1850, Child's 225.00
Chair, Club, Mahogany & Leather, Padded Back, Scrolled Arms, 20th Century, 35 In. 1095.00
Chair, Club, Mahogany, Barrel Back, Mid 19th Century, 33 1/2 In., Pair 5750.00
Chair, Club, Mahogany, Tufted Barrel Back, Cushioned Seat, Casters, Pair . . . . *Illus* 5750.00
Chair, Club, Regency, Mahogany, Downswept Back, Turned Legs, 33 In., Pair 6325.00
Chair, Club, William IV, Mahogany, Padded, Tufted, Mid 19th Century, 37 In. 2760.00
Chair, Constructivist, Czechoslovakia, c.1915, Pair 6500.00
Chair, Continuous Arm, H-Stretcher Base, Vase & Ring Legs, Upholstered Seat, 34 In. . . . 715.00
Chair, Corner, Cherry & Hickory, Rush Seat, Bamboo Turnings, 34 In. 1950.00
Chair, Corner, Chippendale, Mahogany, Chamfered Legs, Backrest, Handholds, 35 In. . . . 1870.00
Chair, Corner, English Provincial, Elm, Ash, U-Shape Arms, Slip Seat 1265.00
Chair, Corner, George III, Mahogany, U-Shaped Arms, Upholstered Slip Seat 1610.00
Chair, Corner, George III, Oak, Pierced Splats, Wood Seat, X-Stretcher, 32 1/2 In. 3700.00
Chair, Corner, Georgian Style, Vase-Form Splat, Upholstered Slip Seat 170.00
Chair, Corner, Georgian, Mahogany, Carved Flowers, Arms, 20th Century 750.00
Chair, Corner, Georgian, Open Vase Splat, Upholstered Slip Seat 230.00
Chair, Corner, Mahogany, Scrolling Out-Turned Hand Rests, Squared Legs, c.1780 . . . . . . 615.00
Chair, Corner, Mahogany, Shaped Arms, Openwork Splats, Rush Slip Seat 575.00
Chair, Corner, Mahogany, Shaped Back, 2 Vase-Form Splats, Pad Feet 2350.00
Chair, Corner, Mahogany, Slip Seat, Upholstered, Arm Supports, 22 3/4 In. 275.00
Chair, Corner, Pillow Back Crest, Painted Rush Seat, Pad Feet, Dark Brown, 29 In. 4025.00
Chair, Corner, Yew, England, 18th Century 520.00
Chair, Crest Rolled To Arms, Ram Heads, Black Seat, Ball Feet, 31 1/2 x 26 In. . . . *Illus* 4250.00
Chair, Crusade Scenes, Chip-Carved Edges, Face Finials, Rush Seat, 35 In., Pair 330.00
Chair, Cube, Arts & Crafts, Grand Rapids 5400.00
Chair, Cube, Lucite, Continuous-Form, Sunken Seat, 23 1/2 x 25 x 28 In. 430.00
Chair, Curly Maple, Cane Seat, Saber Legs, 31 3/4 In. 140.00
Chair, Curly Maple, Rear Saber Legs, Acanthus Leaves Splat, 32 1/2 In. 220.00
Chair, Curly Maple, Saber Leg, Cane Seat, Rolled Edge, Serpentine Posts, Crest, 32 In. . . 165.00
Chair, Curly Maple, Saber Leg, Cane Seat, Turned Front Stretcher, 17 x 32 In. 385.00
Chair, Curly Maple, Scrolled Rail, White Painted Seat, 19th Century, 33 In., Pair 225.00
Chair, Curved Padded Back, Incurved Button Seat, Arms 90.00
Chair, Deck, Teak, From Queen Elizabeth Ship, Folding, Pair 1400.00
Chair, Desk, Aalto, Birch, Red Laminate, Artek, 39 x 21 x 27 In. 690.00
Chair, Directoire, Mahogany, Bronze Dore Mounted, Arms, c.1795, Pair 1265.00

Chair, Dorothy Schindele, Modern Color Inc., 1950s, 17 x 20 x 30 In., Pair 175.00
Chair, Drawer Under Seat, 2 Steps Front, Gray Paint Under Yellow, Arms, 1890 . . . . 2250.00
Chair, E.D. Stone, Oak Frame, Seat & Back By Ozark Weavers, 1945, 35 1/2 In. 3910.00
Chair, Eames, Aluminum Group, High Back, Herman Miller, 22 1/2 x 30 x 41 1/2 In. 575.00
Chair, Eames, Aluminum, Tilt-Back, Upholstered, Casters, Arms, 1968, 34 In. 320.00
Chair, Eames, Aluminum, Upholstered, Coated Metal Arms, Herman Miller, 33 In. 200.00
Chair, Eames, Black Plywood Seat, Chrome Frame, 22 x 26 In. 310.00
Chair, Eames, DAX, Greige, Black, Zenith, Herman Miller, 25 x 24 x 31 In. 400.00
Chair, Eames, Fiberglass Shell, Seafoam Green, X-Base, Arms, Rope Edge, Label 745.00
Chair, Eames, Molded Ash Plywood Seat, 22 x 26 1/2 In. 1380.00
Chair, Eames, Molded Birch Back, Frame, 19 x 21 x 29 In. 575.00
Chair, Eames, Molded Plywood, Walnut Veneer, 1946, 28 In. 4600.00
Chair, Eames, PKW, Black Wire Seat, Swivel Base, 19 x 32 In. 3105.00
Chair, Eames, Seafoam Green, Rope Edge, Zenith Plastics, 1948, 24 In. 1150.00
Chair, Eames, Tilt Back Fiberglass Shell, Vinyl, Swivel Base, 27 In. 110.00
Chair, Eastlake, Carved, Pierced Crest, Upholstered, Late 19th Century, Pair 345.00
Chair, Ebonized, Fluted Stiles, Floral Crest, Upholstered Seat, Pair 290.00
Chair, Edwardian, Gilt Decorated, Ebonized, Arms, c.1900, 33 1/2 In., Pair 1380.00
Chair, Edwardian, Satinwood, Painted, Cane Seat & Back, Oval Plaque In Back, Pair 2350.00
Chair, Eero Saarinen, Womb, Tomato Red, Chrome Rod Legs, 36 x 39 x 37 In. 750.00
Chair, Egg, Rocker, Bent Beech, Cane, Antonio Volpe, 1910 . . . . 7800.00
Chair, Elm, Shaped Top Rail, Baluster Bask Splat, Pad Feet, c.1780 . . . . 785.00
Chair, Elm, Spindle Backrest, Shaped Arms 345.00
Chair, Empire Style, Mahogany, Checker Inlay Crest, Upholstered Seat, Paw Feet, Pair . . . 460.00
Chair, Empire Style, Mahogany, Upholstered, Carved, Padded Arms, Paw Feet, c.1890 . . . 480.00
Chair, Erich Dieckmann, Wood Frame, Plywood, Wicker Seat, Arms, c.1926, 30 1/4 In. . . 4600.00
Chair, Eugene Gaillard, Mahogany, Brass, Tooled Leather, Arms, 1905 . . . . 9600.00
Chair, Fan Splat, Brass Heraldic Shield, Saber Legs, Continental, Pair 2320.00
Chair, Fanback, 7 Spindles, Shield Seat, Shaped Crest, 36 1/8 In. 550.00
Chair, Faux Rosewood-Grained Frame, Carved, Serpentine, Scroll, Tufted, Upholstered . . 185.00
Chair, Federal, Mahogany Inlaid, Serpentine Crest, Upholstered, 46 1/2 In. 4900.00
Chair, Federal, Mahogany, Carved, Shaped Wings, c.1820, 48 In. 3290.00
Chair, Federal, Mahogany, Lyre Splat, Ring-Turned Slat, Molded Arms, 35 In. 1400.00
Chair, Federal, Shieldback, Carved, Fanned Splat, c.1810, 38 In. 10575.00
Chair, Finn Juhl, Chieftain, Walnut, Tan Leather, Original Finish, 38 x 36 In. 3220.00
Chair, Flemish, Open Arms With Lions' Heads, Upholstered Seat, Back, 44 x 18 In. 800.00
Chair, Folding, Elm, Horseshoe Back, Brass, Woven Suede Seats, Arms, Pair 300.00
Chair, French Empire Style, Mahogany, Upholstered, Scroll-Top Rail, Arms 190.00
Chair, French Provincial, Fruitwood, Restoration Style, Mid 19th Century, 37 In. 635.00
Chair, French Restauration, Mahogany, Trefoil Piercing, Early 19th Century, 34 In. 2070.00
Chair, French Restauration, Mahogany, Upholstered, Arms, Early 19th Century, 37 In. 2300.00
Chair, Fruitwood, Mother-Of-Pearl Inlay & Bone Marquetry, Arms, 19th Century 520.00
Chair, Fruitwood, Openwork Splat, Scrolled Arms, Slip Seat, Early 18th Century 1090.00
Chair, Fruitwood, Pierced Vertical Slat, Upholstered Seat, Pair 460.00
Chair, G. Hunzinger, Oak, Lollipop, Arms, c.1870 . . . . 880.00
Chair, G. Nakashima, Black Walnut, Maple, 4 Spindles, Sea Grass Seat, 1944, 26 In. 490.00
Chair, G. Nelson, Birch, Arms, Upholstered Seat, Back, Herman Miller, 1947, 31 1/2 In. . . 150.00
Chair, G. Nelson, Birch, Painted Steel, Cane Seat, Back, Herman Miller, 1948, 23 1/12 In. 1095.00
Chair, G. Nelson, Fiberglass, Flexible Back, Enamel, Chromed Steel, 1959, 30 In. 2350.00
Chair, G. Nelson, Pretzel, Laminated Birch Plywood Legs, 26 x 29 3/4 In. 2875.00
Chair, G. Rietveld, Zigzag, 1940s, 19 x 19 x 14 In. 1725.00
Chair, G. Stickley, 3 Slats, Notched Top Rail, Leather Seat, Arms, 43 In. 750.00
Chair, G. Stickley, 3 Vertical Slats, Leather Seat, Open Arms, Red Decal, 38 1/4 In. 690.00
Chair, G. Stickley, H-Back, Drop-In Seat, 17 x 16 x 40 In. 550.00
Chair, G. Stickley, H-Back, Drop-In Seat, Black Leather, 40 x 16 1/2 x 15 1/4 In. 490.00
Chair, G. Stickley, Ladder Back, Leather Seat, 34 x 15 x 17 In. 230.00
Chair, G. Stickley, Ladder Back, Woven Rush Seat, 36 x 17 x 17 In. 375.00
Chair, G. Stickley, Mahogany, Spindled, Signed, 32 1/2 x 16 x 17 In. 700.00
Chair, G. Stickley, Morris, Open Arms, New Leather Cushion, Eastwood Label, 39 In. 2875.00
Chair, G. Stickley, No. 64, Willow, Wicker, Mahogany, 32 x 31 x 27 In. 3600.00
Chair, G. Stickley, No. 314, Mahogany, Dark Brown Leather Seat, Arms, 39 In. 700.00
Chair, G. Stickley, No. 338, Mahogany, 3 Vertical Slats, Leather Seat, 16 In. 600.00
Chair, G. Stickley, No. 354, Mahogany, Original Brown Leather Seat, Side 1100.00

Furniture, Chair, Garden Tub, Formed
From Horseshoes, 39 1/2 In., Pair

If you buy an old chest with many
drawers of the same size, check to see if
the drawers slide freely. The drawers
may look the same, but they may be in
the wrong order. Try other positions
using clues like matching veneer,
number, or scratch marks.

Chair, G. Stickley, No. 356, Mahogany, Leather Back, Signed, 37 In.	800.00
Chair, G. Stickley, No. 367, Mahogany, Brown Leather Seat, Bow Arm, 37 In.	11000.00
Chair, G. Stickley, No. 369, Mahogany, Brown Leather Seat, 40 x 37 In.	8000.00
Chair, G. Stickley, No. 378, Mahogany, 9 Vertical Spindles, 17 x 16 x 40 In.	805.00
Chair, G. Stickley, No. 2608, Oak, 4 Back Slats, Leather Cushion, Decal, c.1902, 37 In.	575.00
Chair, G. Stickley, No. 2632, Horizontal Back Slats, 37 x 27 In.	690.00
Chair, G. Stickley, Oak, Beige Upholstered Seat, 4 Square Legs, 1909, 29 In.	4465.00
Chair, G. Stickley, Side & Back Spindles, Leather Cushion, Arms, Red Decal, 49 In.	4025.00
Chair, G. Stickley, Spindled Back & Sides, Leather Cushions, 29 x 26 x 27 In.	9775.00
Chair, G. Stickley, V-Back, 5 Vertical Slats, Leather Seat, Arms, 36 In.	1035.00
Chair, G. Stickley, Vertical Back Slats, Arms, 37 1/2 x 27 1/2 In.	860.00
Chair, G. Stickley, Vertical Back Slats, Open Arms, 39 x 26 1/2 x 23 In.	520.00
Chair, Garden Egg, Fiberglass, Upholstered Inside, Closes, 1968, 41 In.	2875.00
Chair, Garden Tub, Formed From Horseshoes, 39 1/2 In., Pair .... *Illus*	575.00
Chair, George II Style, Burl Walnut, Urn & Scroll Crest Rail, 20th Century, Pair	860.00
Chair, George II Style, Mahogany, Carved, Library, 19th Century	2875.00
Chair, George II Style, Mahogany, Carved, Library, Padded	750.00
Chair, George II Style, Walnut, Tapestry, Upholstered, Arms, c.1880	4256.00
Chair, George II, Curved Leaf Crest, Cabriole Legs, Arms, 37 1/2 In.	2760.00
Chair, George II, Mahogany, Carved, H-Stretcher, Mid 18th Century	345.00
Chair, George II, Mahogany, Carved, Open Splayed Back, H-Stretcher, 18th Century, Pair	1610.00
Chair, George II, Mahogany, Central Splat, Drop-End Upholstered Seat, Pair	6600.00
Chair, George II, Mahogany, Needlework, Serpentine Back, Cabriole Legs, 1700s	8400.00
Chair, George II, Mahogany, Rectangular Arch Back, Cabriole Legs, Wing	2160.00
Chair, George II, Mahogany, Serpentine Back, Bowfront Seat, Wing, Pair	18000.00
Chair, George II, Rosewood, Carved Leaf, Scroll, Leather Upholstered Seat, Pair	12000.00
Chair, George III Style, Black Japanned, Cane Back, Cushion, Arms, Early 1900s	1090.00
Chair, George III Style, Elm, Arched Open Back, Sheaf Splat	200.00
Chair, George III Style, Fruitwood, Chinoiserie, Pierced Back, Arms, 20th Century, Pair	1725.00
Chair, George III Style, Mahogany, Pagoda-Shape Rail, Leather, Arms, c.1890, Pair	615.00
Chair, George III Style, Mahogany, Pierced Urn Splat, Claw Feet, Arms, 20th Century	460.00
Chair, George III Style, Mahogany, Scrolled Headrest, Slatted Supports, Arms	230.00
Chair, George III Style, Walnut, Tufted Leather, Cabriole Legs, 20th Century	630.00
Chair, George III, Beech, Upholstered Seat, Shieldback, Arms, 1780, Pair	5760.00
Chair, George III, Black Japanned, Parcel Gilt, Cane Seat, Arms, 1800, Pair	9000.00
Chair, George III, Black Paint, Cane Seat, Loose Cushion, Open Arms, 1795, Pair	5700.00
Chair, George III, Giltwood, Beaded Oval Backrest, Serpentine Seat, Arms	8050.00
Chair, George III, Mahogany, Crest, Shieldback, Upholstered, Arms, 17 x 37 x 23 In.	3290.00
Chair, George III, Mahogany, Padded Back, Cushion, Wing, Late 18th Century, 43 In.	3450.00
Chair, George III, Mahogany, Pierced Palmette Back, Arms, Pair	6600.00
Chair, George III, Mahogany, Rectangular Backrest, Bowed Seat, Wing, Pair	7475.00
Chair, George III, Mahogany, Serpentine Seat, Brass Border, 1780, Pair	920.00
Chair, George III, Walnut, Wing, Claw & Ball Feet, 44 1/2 In.	4140.00
Chair, Georgian, Mahogany, Pierced Splat, Slip Seat, Straight Legs	220.00
Chair, Gerrit Rietveld, Zigzag, Elm, Van De Groenekan, c.1950, 29 7/8 In.	5750.00

Chair, Giltwood, Padded Back & Arms, Floral Upholstered, 1870s, 38 In., Pair 830.00
Chair, Giltwood, Scrolled Back, Straight Arms, Bowfront, c.1795 .... 1380.00
Chair, Giltwood, Scrolled, Leaf Supports, Marquetry Seat Rail, Arms, 51 In. 1550.00
Chair, Giltwood, Serpentine Cresting, Scrolled & Reeded Arms, 18th Century 2990.00
Chair, Gondola, Neoclassical, Rosewood, Russia, Early 19th Century, 34 1/2 In. 1380.00
Chair, Gothic Revival, Mahogany, Pierced Backrest, Victorian, 55 1/2 In. 630.00
Chair, Grasshopper, Bentwood Frame, Continuous Seat, Wool, 35 1/2 In. 1100.00
Chair, Grotto, Dolphin Arms, Scallop-Shell Seat, Late 19th Century 1725.00
Chair, H. Bertoia, Black Metal Tubular Base, 30 x 33 1/2 x 23 1/2 In. 115.00
Chair, H. Bertoia, Diamond, Tweed Seat Cover, Black Wire Frame, 30 3/4 In. 245.00
Chair, H. Bertoia, No. 422, Diamond Shape, Upholstered, Knoll, c.1955, 28 x 44 In. 460.00
Chair, H. Bertoia, Tall Back, Hickory Spindles, Plank Seat, 1970, 54 1/2 In. 550.00
Chair, Harden, Vertical Slats, Leather Drop-In Cushion, Arms, 41 x 28 x 24 1/2 In. 920.00
Chair, Hardwood, Dragon Posts, Pierced Crest, Continuous Arms, Paw Feet, 32 In. 275.00
Chair, Heart & Crown Cutout, Black Paint, Arms, Mid 18th Century, 47 1/2 In. 6900.00
Chair, Herter Bros., Aesthetic Revival, Walnut, Mid 19th Century, Pair 1150.00
Chair, Hickory, Plank Seat, Woven Rush Back, Arms, 41 x 30 In. 630.00
Chair, Horn, Back Cushion, Upholstered, Seats, Cowhide, 46 In., Pair 570.00
Chair, Hunzinger, Upholstered Seat & Back, Victorian, 32 x 23 In. 200.00
Chair, Inlaid Brass Heraldic Shield, Fan Splat, Continental, Pair 2300.00
Chair, Iron Frame, Leather Back, Brass Finials & Hand Rests, Brass Bun Feet 475.00
Chair, J.J. Young, Tall Back, Back Slats, Cushions, Arms, 48 x 27 x 24 In., Pair 1380.00
Chair, J.M. Young, No. 493, Mahogany, 5 Vertical Slats, Arms, 28 x 22 x 39 In. 1100.00
Chair, Jacobean Style, Carved Back, Plank Seat, Turned Legs, Stretchers, c.1890 .... 374.00
Chair, Jacobean Style, Carved Oak, Upholstered Seat, Late 19th Century, Pair 252.00
Chair, Jacobean Style, Mahogany, Cane Back, Seat, Open Arms, Stretcher, 1910, 50 In. .. 170.00
Chair, Jacobean Style, Mahogany, Open Arms, Spanish Feet, Cane Back, 1910, 47 In. 280.00
Chair, Jacobean Style, Walnut, Scroll Feet, Upholstered, Continental, 1900s, 52 In. 925.00
Chair, Jacobean, Oak, Carved, High Back, Late 17th Century, 50 1/2 In. 400.00
Chair, Jacobean, Walnut, Tapestry Upholstered, Open Arms, Stretchers 2530.00
Chair, Jean Pascaud, Mahogany, Upholstered, Bronze Sabots, Arms, 1935, Pair 7200.00
Chair, Joe Columbo, Elda, Padded Cocoa Leather, Fiberglass, Swivel Base, Italy, 1967 ... 3500.00
Chair, Joe Columbo, No. 4801, Lacquered Plywood, Arms, Kartell, c.1964, 23 1/8 In. 6325.00
Chair, Joe, Baseball Glove Form, Molded Urethane, Brown Leather, 1970 .... 4140.00
Chair, Josef Hoffman, Beech, Sitzmaschine, No. 670, c.1908, 43 3/4 In. 8970.00
Chair, Josef Hoffman, Thonet, Plywood, Beech, Oswald Haerdtl, c.1930, 30 In. 5750.00
Chair, Jules Leleu, Fruitwood, Upholstered, Arms, 1935, Pair 9600.00
Chair, L. & J.G. Stickley, Mahogany, 6 Vertical Slats, Arms, 28 x 24 x 38 In. 550.00
Chair, L. & J.G. Stickley, Mahogany, 8 Vertical Spindles, New Rush Seat, 36 In. 865.00
Chair, L. & J.G. Stickley, Mahogany, Burnt Orange Leather Seat, 40 In. 2450.00
Chair, L. & J.G. Stickley, Mahogany, Curved Slats, Brown Leather Seat, Arms, 32 In. ... 4888.00
Chair, L. & J.G. Stickley, Mahogany, Dark Brown Leather Seat, 37 x 15 In. 325.00
Chair, L. & J.G. Stickley, Mahogany, Slatted Sides, 40 x 28 1/2 x 25 In. 1500.00
Chair, L. & J.G. Stickley, Mahogany, Spindle Back, Upholstered Seat, 41 1/2 In. 430.00
Chair, L. & J.G. Stickley, Morris, Bow Arms, Slats, Upholstered, 38 x 34 x 41 3/4 In. 10350.00
Chair, L. & J.G. Stickley, Morris, Flat Arms, Vertical Slats, Tufted Leather, 43 In. 2415.00
Chair, L. & J.G. Stickley, Morris, Oak, Open Arms, 41 x 35 In. 1380.00
Chair, L. & J.G. Stickley, No. 330, Mahogany, 7 Spindles, Leather Seat, 16 x 37 In. 196.00
Chair, L. & J.G. Stickley, No. 332, Plank Seat, Paper Label 230.00
Chair, L. & J.G. Stickley, No. 350, 3 Horizontal Back Slats, Leather, 1910 .... 290.00
Chair, L. & J.G. Stickley, No. 412, Mahogany, Padded Arms, 35 x 39 x 40 In. 9200.00
Chair, L. & J.G. Stickley, No. 471, Mahogany, Leather Cushion, Signed, 32 x 40 In. 2645.00
Chair, L. & J.G. Stickley, No. 497, Mahogany, 5 Wide Slats, Open Arms, 31 In. 5225.00
Chair, Lacquered, Vase Splat, Slip-In Seat, Hoof Feet, 40 1/2 In., Pair 2760.00
Chair, Ladder Back, 3 Slats, Double Box Stretcher, Arms, Rush Seat, 42 In. 750.00
Chair, Ladder Back, 4 Slats, Arms, Rush Seat, Early 19th Century, 39 1/2 In. 115.00
Chair, Ladder Back, 4 Slats, Ball Finials, Rush Seat, 19th Century, Pair 635.00
Chair, Ladder Back, Arms, Acorn Finials, 6 Arched Slats, Turned Legs, Stretcher 330.00
Chair, Ladder Back, Cowhide Seat, Marble Falls, Texas, Feb. 5, 1939 .... 375.00
Chair, Ladder Back, Dark Green Paint, Woven Tape Seat, 20 1/2 x 38 In. 3850.00
Chair, Ladder Back, Finials, Rush Seat, Painted, New England, 41 1/2 In. 330.00
Chair, Ladder Back, Hardwood, Vase & Ring Arm Supports, Rush Seat, 46 1/2 In. 385.00
Chair, Ladder Back, Red Brown Refinish, Rush Seat, Turned Arms, 42 In. 140.00

Chair, Ladder Back, Splint Seat, 3 Arched Slats, Finials, Old Paint 77.00
Chair, Laminated Rosewood, C-Scroll Back, Needlepoint Seat, Victorian, 37 In. 825.00
Chair, Lawn, Painted, Wood, Rear Wheels, White, Blue Paint, 39 x 28 x 34 In., Pair 550.00
Chair, Leather, Padded Back, Cushion Seat, Arms, c.1900, 31 In., Pair 2300.00
Chair, Lescaze, Chromium Plated Steel, Leatherette, 1932, 29 In. 9200.00
Chair, Liberty & Co., Beech, Undulating Back Slats, Rush Seat, 37 1/4 x 19 x 16 In. 690.00
Chair, Library, William IV, Mahogany, Carving, Mid 19th Century, 42 1/2 In. 920.00
Chair, Limbert, 2 Vertical Back Slats, Leather Cushion, Open Arms, Branded, 42 In. 980.00
Chair, Limbert, Mahogany, Dark Brown Leather Seat, Arms, 36 x 29 x 22 1/2 In. 1000.00
Chair, Limbert, No. 519, Mahogany, Original Pegs, Spring Cushion, 32 x 37 In. 5175.00
Chair, Limbert, No. 818, Mahogany, Leather Cushion, Original Finish, 33 x 32 In. 4025.00
Chair, Limbert, No. 931, Mahogany, 3 Vertical Slats, Arms, 28 x 26 x 37 In. 690.00
Chair, Limbert, No. 1643, Mahogany, 5 Slats Under Each Arm, 30 x 39 In. 4320.00
Chair, Limbert, No. 1693, Mahogany, 4 Horizontal Splayed Legs, 31 x 39 In. 1095.00
Chair, Limbert, No. 500, Cafe, Mahogany, Angled Arms, 26 x 22 x 34 In. 5750.00
Chair, Limbert, Tan Rush Seat, 37 x 16 1/2 x 16 In. 450.00
Chair, Limbert, Wide Back Slat, Wooden Seat, 37 x 16 1/2 x 16 1/2 In. 230.00
Chair, Lolling, Chippendale Style, Mahogany, High Back, Serpentine Crest, Arms 50.00
Chair, Lolling, Chippendale Style, Serpentine Crest, Beaded Arm Supports, Upholstered .. 55.00
Chair, Lolling, Chippendale Style, Serpentine Crest, Leatherette Covering 55.00
Chair, Lolling, Mahogany, Acanthus Knees, Shaped Arms, Silk, 39 In., Pair 330.00
Chair, Lolling, Mahogany, Upholstered Trapezoid Seat, 1790s, 42 In. 7050.00
Chair, Lolling, Queen Anne, Mahogany, Bowed Seat, Upholstered, Arms, 42 In., Pair 440.00
Chair, Louis Majorelle, Carved Mahogany, Silk, Arms, Les Pins, 1900 .... 12000.00
Chair, Louis Majorelle, Carved Mahogany, Silk, Arms, Ombelle 7800.00
Chair, Louis Majorelle, Mahogany, Carved, Leather, c.1900, 29 3/4 In. 8225.00
Chair, Louis Majorelle, Stained Oak, Upholstered, Arms, 1900, Pair 8400.00
Chair, Louis Philippe, Rosewood, Ormolu Mounts, Scroll Arms, Green Silk, 40 In., Pair .. 4140.00
Chair, Louis XIII Style, Oak, Padded Back, Arms, c.1900, 35 In., Pair 575.00
Chair, Louis XIV Style, Giltwood, Upholstered, Leg Caps, Arms 4800.00
Chair, Louis XIV, Oak, Aubusson Upholstered, Leaf-Carved Scrolling Arms, Pair 1725.00
Chair, Louis XV Style, Beech, Floral Serpentine Seat, Padded Arms, 41 In., Pair 2530.00
Chair, Louis XV Style, Beech, Leaf-Carved Frame, Shaped Arms, Upholstered, c.1850 ... 865.00
Chair, Louis XV Style, Cartouche-Shaped Backrest, Scrolled Arms 490.00
Chair, Louis XV Style, Carved Floral Skirt, Gilt Paint, Pair 690.00
Chair, Louis XV Style, Gilt, Carved Scrolled Sides & Frame, Cabriole Legs, 34 In. 415.00
Chair, Louis XV Style, Giltwood, Arms, Late 19th Century, Pair 4830.00
Chair, Louis XV Style, Walnut, Arched Back, Scroll Arms 460.00
Chair, Louis XV Style, Walnut, Medallion, Carved, Stained, Arms, Pair 865.00
Chair, Louis XV Style, Walnut, Open Arms, Oval Backrest, Serpentine, Pair 490.00
Chair, Louis XV Style, Walnut, Ormolu Mounted, Early 20th Century, Pair 315.00
Chair, Louis XV, Beech, Carved, Scrolled Arms, Pair 4600.00
Chair, Louis XV, Beech, Serpentine Top Rail, Cabriole Legs, 37 In. 7800.00
Chair, Louis XV, Bleached Beech, Upholstered 720.00
Chair, Louis XV, Flower Heads Continuing To Form Padded Armrests, 38 In. 7800.00
Chair, Louis XV, Giltwood, Acanthine Frame, Cabriole Legs, 54 In. 2070.00
Chair, Louis XV, Giltwood, Serpentine Seat, Cabriole Legs, 19th Century, Pair 920.00
Chair, Louis XV, Giltwood, Shell Crest, Padded Arms, Cabriole Legs, 39 In., Pair 3680.00
Chair, Louis XV, Walnut, Carved, 2nd Quarter 18th Century 400.00
Chair, Louis XV, Walnut, Carved, Mid 18th Century 345.00
Chair, Louis XV, Walnut, Parcel Gilt, Shieldback, Early 20th Century, Pair 550.00
Chair, Louis XV, Walnut, Tapestry Upholstered, Pair 4025.00
Chair, Louis XVI Style, Beech, Cane, Upholstered, Padded Arms, Pair 785.00
Chair, Louis XVI Style, Carved Floral, Needlepoint Back, Seat & Armrests, 45 In. 230.00
Chair, Louis XVI Style, Carved Wood, Oval Back, Leaf Crest, Upholstered, Pair 4110.00
Chair, Louis XVI Style, Carved, Rectangular Back, Fluted Columns, Upholstered, Pair ... 800.00
Chair, Louis XVI Style, Gilt, Porcelain Panel Back, Silk, Early 1900s, 34 In. 275.00
Chair, Louis XVI Style, Giltwood, Beaded Backrests, Pierced Splat, c.1900, Pair 375.00
Chair, Louis XVI Style, Walnut, Cabriole Legs, Scalloped Apron, Upholstered, 35 In. 110.00
Chair, Lounge, Cast Metal, Floral Skirt, 12 x 84 1/2 In. 170.00
Chair, Lounge, E. & E. Laverne, Jonquil, Molded Plexiglas, Pad Seat, 1957, 29 In., Pair .. 3910.00
Chair, Lounge, Enameled Steel Base, Upholstered, Cantilevered Seat, 30 In. 465.00
Chair, Lounge, G. Nakashima, Walnut, Slat Back, Cushions, 30 x 25 In., Pair 2875.00

Chair, Lounge, Hickory, Branded, 33 x 54 In. 1955.00
Chair, Lounge, Knoll, Wool Upholstered, Bronze, 31 1/2 x 31 1/2 x 28 In. 300.00
Chair, Lounge, McCobb, Mahogany, Cane Back, Rubber Webbing, 34 In., Pair 980.00
Chair, Lounge, Paul Laszlo, Wool, Oak Legs, 31 x 32 x 28 In. 1495.00
Chair, Lounge, Robsjohn-Gibbings, Widdicomb, 24 1/2 x 34 x 32 1/2 In. 80.00
Chair, Lounge, W. Lescaze, Platted Rope Seat, 1937, 34 1/2 In. 2300.00
Chair, Mahogany, Arched Crest, Leather Padded Seat & Back, 1870s, 40 1/2 In., Pair 2760.00
Chair, Mahogany, Arched Top Rail, Continuing To Armrests, 1850s, 36 In., Pair 4140.00
Chair, Mahogany, Arms, Stuffed Seat, Early 19th Century, 32 1/2 In. 1380.00
Chair, Mahogany, Backrest Joined By Padded Arms, Drop-In Seat, 43 1/2 In. 2530.00
Chair, Mahogany, Barrel Back, Upholstered, Early 19th Century, 44 In. 7200.00
Chair, Mahogany, Button-Tufted Back, Padded Arms, 1880s, 40 1/2 In. 2070.00
Chair, Mahogany, Cane & Medallion Shaped Back, Cane Seat & Arms 11000.00
Chair, Mahogany, Cantilevered Seat, 1934 In., Pair 14100.00
Chair, Mahogany, Carved Acanthus Leaves, Upholstered Slip Seat, Arms, 36 In. 7425.00
Chair, Mahogany, Carved Flowers At Knees, Brocade Upholstered, 38 In. 467.00
Chair, Mahogany, Carved, Balloon Back, Upholstered, Pink, 50 x 30 In. 1045.00
Chair, Mahogany, Domed Top, Reeded Fan, Panel Seat, Top-Shaped Feet, 32 1/2 In. 1125.00
Chair, Mahogany, Flower & Bow Carved Splat, Needlepoint Seat, 38 x 23 1/2 x 21 In. 170.00
Chair, Mahogany, Inlaid Posts, Harp & Urn Splat, Mother-Of-Pearl Insert, 32 1/2 In. 80.00
Chair, Mahogany, Inlaid, Padded Back, 19th Century, Pair 1380.00
Chair, Mahogany, Ladder Back, Shaped Crest Rail, Stretchers, c.1810 .... 730.00
Chair, Mahogany, Leaf Over Splat, Drapery Swags, Floral Arms, 36 1/2 In. 6600.00
Chair, Mahogany, Leaf-Carved Knees, Crest & Posts, Pierced Splat, Label, 40 1/4 In. 360.00
Chair, Mahogany, Library, Rear Seat Rail, Pierced Splat, Bowed Seat Frame, 35 In. 800.00
Chair, Mahogany, Needlework Upholstered, Serpentine Top Rail, c.1760, Pair 7800.00
Chair, Mahogany, Notched Top Rail, 2 Horizontal Slats, Leather Seat, 39 In. 2415.00
Chair, Mahogany, Open Splat With Diamonds & Leaf Tips, Upholstered 2875.00
Chair, Mahogany, Padded Back, Joined By Dolphin-Carved Arms, 1820s, 35 In. 1610.00
Chair, Mahogany, Padded Back, Outcurved Arms, 19th Century, 34 1/2 In. 2300.00
Chair, Mahogany, Pedimented Top Rail, Curved Arms, Turned Legs, 37 In. 5750.00
Chair, Mahogany, Pierced & Carved Crest & Back, Shell Apron, Claw & Ball Feet 200.00
Chair, Mahogany, Pierced Back Splat, Molded Armrests, Square Legs, c.1810 .... 730.00
Chair, Mahogany, Pierced Back Splat, Molded Armrests, Upholstered Seat, c.1810 ...... 785.00
Chair, Mahogany, Pierced Back, Panel Seat, Baluster Legs, Victorian 1020.00
Chair, Mahogany, Pierced Splat, Leather, 1830s, 30 1/2 In. 2530.00
Chair, Mahogany, Planter's, Folding, Cane Seat & Back, 45 In. 175.00
Chair, Mahogany, Reeded Stiles, Scrolling Handrests, Curved Reeded Legs, c.1835 ..... 4790.00
Chair, Mahogany, Rose-Carved Knees & Apron, Scrolled Arms, Crewel Upholstered 385.00
Chair, Mahogany, Scroll-Top Stiles, Paneled Top Rail, c.1815, 30 In. 1380.00
Chair, Mahogany, Scrolled Arms, Cane Seat Folds Into Steps, 35 1/4 In. 1150.00
Chair, Mahogany, Scrolling Handrests, Molded Seat Rail, Pad Feet, c.1810 .... 672.00
Chair, Mahogany, Shaped Armrests, Scrolled Handholds, c.1750 .... 7200.00
Chair, Mahogany, Shaped Back, Pierced Back Splat, Out & Down Arms, Leaf Knees 172.00
Chair, Mahogany, Shaped Crest, Flaring Ears, Pierced Back Splat, Flaring Seat, Pair 86.00
Chair, Mahogany, Slipper, Punchwork Crest, Trapezoid Seat, 1755 .... 9600.00
Chair, Mahogany, Swivel, Leather Upholstered, Pair 420.00
Chair, Mahogany, Tapered Backrest, Painted Crest Of Eton College, 18th Century, Pair ... 3600.00
Chair, Mahogany, Teak Frames, Cane Seat, 25 1/2 x 29 x 21 In. 230.00
Chair, Mahogany, Trisected Back & Sides, Floral Crest, Cushion Seat, 1880s, 39 In. 863.00
Chair, Mahogany, Tufted Back, Padded Arms, Lotus-Carved Legs, 1830s, 42 In. 5290.00
Chair, Mahogany, Upholstered Barrel Back, Outscrolled Arms, Vase-Form Feet, 48 In. 3600.00
Chair, Mahogany, Upholstered Seat & Back, Shaped Arms, 40 In. 247.00
Chair, Mahogany, Writing, Flip Top, Ripple Molding, Shaped Apron, c.1854, 29 x 27 In. .. 2350.00
Chair, Majorelle, Mahogany, Upholstered, Arms, 1900 .... 5760.00
Chair, Maple & Walnut, Arched Crest, Pierced Splat, Outscrolled Arms, c.1745, 39 In. ... 1800.00
Chair, Maple & Walnut, Ogival Wings, Outscrolled Arms, Cushion Seat, 48 In. 8400.00
Chair, Maple, Banister Back, Arms, c.1780, 43 1/2 In. 2040.00
Chair, Maple, Cabriole Legs, Claw & Ball Feet, Portugal, 18th Century 980.00
Chair, Maple, Carved Crest Rail, Vase In Back Splat, Crewel Upholstered, 41 In. 920.00
Chair, Maple, Red Stain, Shaped Slats, Turned Arms, Legs, Rush Seat, Child's, 25 In. 690.00
Chair, Maple, Rush Seat, Spanish Feet, 39 In., Pair 3105.00
Chair, Maple, Serpentine Crest Rail, Trapezoid Rush Seat, 1790, 40 x 18 In. 490.00

Chair, Maple, Shaped Backrest, Continuous Arms, Rush Seat, 29 x 27 1/2 In. 230.00
Chair, Maple, Turned, Black Paint, Banister Back, Arms, Mid 18th Century, 42 1/2 In. . . . 1320.00
Chair, Maple, Urn-Form Splat, Rush Seat, Front Spanish Feet, 41 In. 300.00
Chair, Maple, Yoke Crests, Vase Splats, Rush Seat, Turned Feet, 38 In., Pair 860.00
Chair, Marcel Breuer, Chrome & Steel, Leather Seat & Arms, 28 1/2 x 31 In. 365.00
Chair, Marcel Breuer, Chrome Plated Steel Frame, Wood Armrests, c.1930, 33 3/4 In. 690.00
Chair, Marcel Breuer, No. B35, Chrome, Wood, Arms, Thonet, c.1930, 31 In. 7475.00
Chair, Marcel Breuer, No. B64, Chrome Tubular Steel, Arms, Thonet, c.1928, 31 In. 3680.00
Chair, Marcel Breuer, Wassily, Leather Seat, Back, Armrests, Chrome Frame, 30 In., Pair . 615.00
Chair, Marquise A La Reine, Louis XV Style, Walnut, Carved, Arched Back, Crest 520.00
Chair, Marquise, Louis XV, Painted, Gilt, Carved Shell Crest, Damask Upholstered, Pair . 1265.00
Chair, Mart Stam, Chrome-Plated Steel, Wood, Thonet, c.1935, 31 In. 2530.00
Chair, Martha Washington, Mahogany, Floral Upholstered, 38 1/2 In. 220.00
Chair, McCobb, Swivel, Leather, Aluminum Base, Casters, 34 x 28 x 19 In. 230.00
Chair, Medallion & Shaped Crest, Cane Seat, Silk Cushion, Saber Legs, 31 1/2 In., Pair . . 495.00
Chair, Michigan Chair Co., Mahogany, Cane Back, Signed, 17 x 18 x 38 In. 460.00
Chair, Mixed Woods, 7-Spindle Back, Shield Seat, Arched Crest, 39 In. 385.00
Chair, Mixed Woods, Fanback, 7-Spindle Back, 36 3/4 In. 660.00
Chair, Moroccan, Hardwood, Inlaid, Mother-Of-Pearl, Ivory, Arms, Pair 1150.00
Chair, Morris, 4 Vertical Arm Slats, Leather Cushion, Lifetime, 31 x 37 x 40 In. 2415.00
Chair, Morris, 4-Slat Adjustable Back, Square Legs, Coasters, 42 x 28 x 35 In. 795.00
Chair, Morris, Arts & Crafts, Oak, Curved Slats, Adjustable, Cushions, 1900s, 40 In. 920.00
Chair, Morris, Mahogany, Dark Finish, Spindles, Open Arms, 37 x 33 x 38 In. 2950.00
Chair, Morris, Oak, 3 Slats Under Each Arm, 4 Tapered Legs 1200.00
Chair, Morris, Oak, Through Tenons, Cushion Seat & Back, 30 In. 770.00
Chair, Morris, Quartersawn Oak, Adjustable Ladder Back, Loose Cushion, c.1925 . . . . . . 3680.00
Chair, Morris, Slat Sides, Upholstered, 40 x 33 1/2 In. 2645.00
Chair, N.G. Horwitt, Tubular Steel, Leatherette Seat, c.1930, 27 1/2 In. 7475.00
Chair, Napoleon III Style, Rectangular, Padded Back, Carved Arms, Pair 615.00
Chair, Napoleon III Style, Scroll Back, Slip Seat, Saber Legs, Slats, Pair 300.00
Chair, Napoleon III, Fruitwood, Bowfront, Cabriole Legs, Open Arms, c.1850, Pair 2300.00
Chair, Neoclassical, Mahogany, Gilt Metal Mounted, Lion Decoration, Austria, Pair 3000.00
Chair, Neoclassical, Painted, Parcel Gilt, Italy, c.1800 . . . . 690.00
Chair, Neogrecque, Canted, Scrolled Crest, Curule Base, Upholstered, 34 In., Pair 2585.00
Chair, Oak & Elm, Marquetry Backrest, Floral Filled Urns, Arms, Cane Seat, 1823, Pair . . 3300.00
Chair, Oak, Arms, Blue, Gray & White Upholstered Cushions, 43 x 24 x 32 In. 280.00
Chair, Oak, Carved Lion Head, Converts To Step Ladder, Victorian, 37 x 22 In. 4480.00
Chair, Oak, Ladder Back, Serpentine Slats, Plank Arms, Rush Seat, 19th Century 230.00
Chair, Oak, Pierced Back, Overall Floral & Scroll, Egg & Dart Border, 19th Century 100.00
Chair, Oak, Rectangular Backrest, Arched & Trefoils, Square Legs, 1870s, 41 1/2 In. 920.00
Chair, Oak, Savonarola, Leopard Head Arm Terminals, Brown Leather, 1880s, 30 1/2 In. . 750.00
Chair, Oak, Tapestry Upholstered, Acanthus Leaf Arms, Continental, 1900s, 42 In. 880.00
Chair, Old Hickory, Mahogany, 4-Spindle Back, 24 x 21 x 38 In. 175.00
Chair, Old Hickory, Mahogany, Spindled Bow Back, Arms, 25 x 21 x 36 In. 375.00
Chair, Old Hickory, Mahogany, Woven Splint Seat, Arms, Signed, 22 x 35 In. 520.00
Chair, Old Hickory, Mahogany, Woven Splint Seat, Original Finish, Arms, 36 In. 520.00
Chair, Opera, Brass Tubing, Upholstered, Medallion Back, 33 1/2 In., Pair 385.00
Chair, Otto Wagner, Beech, Plywood, Pierced Hole Back, c.1902, 31 3/4 In. 8970.00
Chair, Oval Back, Upholstered, 34 1/2 In. 80.00
Chair, Painted Lake & Woods Scene On Splat, Grained Seat, 31 x 16 In., Pair 2185.00
Chair, Paper Rush Seat, Shaped Arms, Ring Turned Legs, Ball Feet, 44 In. 440.00
Chair, Papier-Mache, Mother-Of-Pearl, Pierced Back, Drop-In Seat, 1800s, Pair 6000.00
Chair, Paul Follot, Art Deco, Giltwood, Arms, 1925, Pair 6000.00
Chair, Paulin, No. 437, Petal, Chromed Steel, Upholstered, 1959, 26 In. 1265.00
Chair, Paulin, No. 675, Steel, Black Leather Seat, Back, 1962, 34 3/4 In., Pair 4315.00
Chair, Peter Hvidt & O.M. Nielsen, Plywood, Padded Leather, Denmark, 1951, 31 In. . . . 345.00
Chair, Pierre Jeanneret, Scissor, Upholstered, Knoll, 23 x 31 x 29 In., Pair 2875.00
Chair, Pilgrim, High Back, Block & Turned 11220.00
Chair, Pine, Curved Crest Rail, Floral Band Apron, Chinese, c.1900, 42 In., Pair 900.00
Chair, Pine, Plank Seat, Stenciled Fruit Back Splat, Child's, 21 1/2 x 13 1/2 In. 140.00
Chair, Pine, Thumb Back, Plank Seat, 32 1/2 x 16 1/2 x 16 In., Pair 310.00
Chair, Plank Bottom, Shaped Seat, Faux Bamboo Spindle Back, c.1825, 36 In., Pair 330.00
Chair, Potty, Chippendale, Walnut, Shaped & Pierced Crest, Arms 535.00

Chair, Potty, Rabbit Ear, Black Paint, Gold Pinstriping, Child's, 21 In. 120.00
Chair, Potty, Walnut, Corner, Rolled Backrest, Scrolled Handrests 1870.00
Chair, Prairie School, Oak Park Masonic Lodge, E.E. Roberts, Arms, 25 x 24 x 37 In. . . . 635.00
Chair, Queen Anne Style, 4-Slat Back, Painted, Rush Seat, Scroll Arms, 41 In. 195.00
Chair, Queen Anne Style, Balloon Seat, Solid Splat, Cabriole Legs, Carved Knees, Arms . . 415.00
Chair, Queen Anne Style, Chinoiserie, Black Lacquered, Late 19th Century, 39 In., Pair . . 3910.00
Chair, Queen Anne Style, Chinoiserie, Gilt Figural Landscapes, Black Ground 300.00
Chair, Queen Anne Style, Japanned, Crest, Gilt Shell, Solid Splat, Cane Seat, Italy 275.00
Chair, Queen Anne Style, Mahogany, Bowed Crest Rail Back, Upholstered, 47 In. 17040.00
Chair, Queen Anne Style, Mahogany, Claw & Ball Feet, Shell-Carved Knees, 39 x 18 In. . 345.00
Chair, Queen Anne Style, Mahogany, Crest Over Pierced Splat, Padded Seat, Pair 260.00
Chair, Queen Anne Style, Mahogany, Padded Back, Seat, Arms, Late 19th Century, 38 In. 1840.00
Chair, Queen Anne Style, Mahogany, Pierced Splat, Claw & Ball Feet, c.1880, Pair 3136.00
Chair, Queen Anne Style, Mahogany, Slip Seat, Velvet, 1900s, 40 1/2 In., Pair 440.00
Chair, Queen Anne Style, Painted, Crest, Solid Splat, Leather Slip Seat, Cabriole Legs . . . 440.00
Chair, Queen Anne Style, Relief-Carved Legs, Eagle Heads, Claws, Upholstered, 47 In. . . 800.00
Chair, Queen Anne Style, Upholstered Seat, Pierced Vase Splat, Black Over Salmon Paint 450.00
Chair, Queen Anne, Carved Walnut, Serpentine Crest, 1760, 39 In., Pair 2870.00
Chair, Queen Anne, Grain Painted, Carved, Spanish Feet, Late 18th Century, 42 In. 1265.00
Chair, Queen Anne, Ladder Back, Black Over Red, Sausage, Splint Seat, Arms 385.00
Chair, Queen Anne, Ladder Back, Maple, 6 Slats, Shaped Arms, Rush Seat, 46 1/2 In. . . . 2820.00
Chair, Queen Anne, Mahogany, Yoke Crest Rail, Balloon Seat, 18th Century, Pair 4600.00
Chair, Queen Anne, Maple Finish, Rush Seat, 16 1/4 x 39 1/2 In. 220.00
Chair, Queen Anne, Maple, Carved, Spanish Feet, Arms, Late 18 Century, 41 In. 2645.00
Chair, Queen Anne, Maple, Molded Ears, Trapezoid Seat, Spanish Feet, 40 In. 3100.00
Chair, Queen Anne, Maple, Paper Rush Seat, Arched Crest, Spanish Feet, 40 1/2 In. 600.00
Chair, Queen Anne, Maple, Urn Slat, Rear Stiles, Turned Legs, Spanish Feet, 41 1/2 In. . . 550.00
Chair, Queen Anne, Mixed Woods, Stretchers, Rush Seat, Spanish Feet, 41 In. 360.00
Chair, Queen Anne, Oak, Yew, Replaced Paper Rush Seat, Arms, France, 42 In. 300.00
Chair, Queen Anne, Painted, Rush Seat, Oxbow Crest, Vase Splat 1600.00
Chair, Queen Anne, Turned Arm Supports, 3 Spindle Rows, Pad Feet 360.00
Chair, Queen Anne, Turned Rear Posts, Urn-Shaped Splat & Finials, 42 In. 330.00
Chair, Queen Anne, Walnut, Cabriole Legs, Square Feet, Pair 1200.00
Chair, Queen Anne, Walnut, Carved, Figured, c.1750, 39 1/2 In. 3600.00
Chair, Queen Anne, Walnut, Figured, Mass., c.1760, 38 In., Pair 4500.00
Chair, Queen Anne, Walnut, Roundabout, Mid 1700s, 32 1/2 x 17 1/2 x 29 1/2 In. 1955.00
Chair, Queen Anne, Walnut, Scrolled Arms, Valanced Seat, 4 Cabriole Legs, 31 In. 3100.00
Chair, Queen Anne, Walnut, Serpentine Crest, Vase Splat, Trapezoid Seat, 40 1/2 In. 7638.00
Chair, Queen Anne, Walnut, Vase Splat, Padded Disc Feet, c.1760, 40 1/2 In. 9400.00
Chair, Queen Anne, Yoke Back, Spanish Feet, England, Late 18th Century, 40 x 17 1/2 In. 230.00
Chair, R. Neutra, Mahogany, Bentwood & Steel, Leather Seat & Back, 1940 . . . . 2070.00
Chair, Ray Wilkes, Chicklet Foam, Upholstered Back, Seat & Sides, 27 1/2 In., Pair 295.00
Chair, Rear Posts, Vase Splat, Urn Finials, Paper Rush Seat, 44 In. 990.00
Chair, Rectangular Back, Rope Turned, Block Legs, Arms, 17th Century 230.00
Chair, Red Lacquer, Chinese, 19th Century, 34 x 17 1/2 x 15 In. . . . . *Illus* 1035.00
Chair, Red Lacquered, Shaped Rail & Back Splat, Shepherd's Crook Armrests, c.1900 . . . 660.00
Chair, Regency, Beech, Grain Painted, Serpentine Back, Early 19th Century, Pair 1035.00
Chair, Regency, Cane Seat, Black Paint, Trellis Back, Turned Legs, Arms, c.1810, Pair . . . 1495.00
Chair, Regency, Ebony Wood, Gilt Ball Finials, Flower Heads, Saber Legs 900.00
Chair, Regency, Mahogany, Floral Damask Gold Silk Slip Seats, Pair 920.00
Chair, Regency, Mahogany, Green Upholstered Trapezoid Slip Seat, Saber Legs 230.00
Chair, Regency, Mahogany, Horizontal Splat, Padded Seat, 32 In., Pair 8050.00
Chair, Regency, Mahogany, Inlaid, Carved, Shell Back, Upholstered, Arms, c.1800, Pair . . 4480.00
Chair, Regency, Mahogany, Painted, Shell-Carved Back, 1810, Pair 9000.00
Chair, Regency, Polychrome, Painted Crest, Cane Seat, 34 1/2 In., Pair 1150.00
Chair, Renaissance Revival, Rosewood, Upholstered, Arms, Mid 19th Century, 42 1/2 In. . 520.00
Chair, Renaissance Revival, Walnut, Arms, Victorian, 41 1/2 In. 715.00
Chair, Renaissance Revival, Walnut, Curle, Arms, Mid 19th Century, 48 1/2 In. 1610.00
Chair, Renaissance Revival, Walnut, Open Scrolling, Victorian, Pair 805.00
Chair, Ribbonback, Mahogany, Covered Seat, Arms, Centennial, 19 x 24 x 39 In. 340.00
Chair, Rocker, is listed under Rocker in this category.
Chair, Rococo Revival, Oak, Fountain Elms, Cornucopia, Ormolu, Arms, 44 1/2 In. 12650.00
Chair, Rococo Revival, Rosewood Laminate, Slipper, Carved Back, 42 In. 1380.00

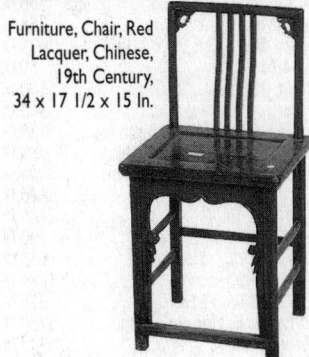

Furniture, Chair, Red Lacquer, Chinese, 19th Century, 34 x 17 1/2 x 15 In.

Furniture, Chair, Walnut, Spindle Back, Seat Rail, Burl Panel, Turned Legs, Casters, Pair

Chair, Rococo Revival, Rosewood, Leaf-Carved Crest, Pierced Stiles, 1850s 2415.00
Chair, Rosewood, Burl, Ebony Inlay, Medallions, Musical Instruments, 38 In., Pair 505.00
Chair, Rosewood, Foo Lion Splat, Arms, c.1900, 39 x 26 In. 430.00
Chair, Rosewood, Leaf Backrest, Upholstered, Slip Seat, Circular Legs, 1835, Pair 630.00
Chair, Rosewood, Leather Upholstered, Tufted Backrest, Padded Armrests, c.1820 ...... 5100.00
Chair, Rosewood, Ram's Head, On Stiles, Urn & Leaves Under Swag, 1880s, 30 In. 1035.00
Chair, Rosewood, Slipper, Downswept Back, Sides, Bulbous Legs, Casters, 30 In. 865.00
Chair, Rosewood, Slipper, Open Crest, Upholstered Back, Berlin Work, 41 In. 460.00
Chair, Roycroft, Single Back Slat, Swivel Base, Leather Seat, Marked, 41 In. 460.00
Chair, Roycroft, Single Broad Back Slat, Leather Seat, Arms, Marked, 40 3/4 In. 2300.00
Chair, Roycroft, Slipper, 2 Horizontal Back Slats, Tacked-On Leather Seat, 35 In. 2530.00
Chair, Rush Seat, Arched Crest, Bentwood Spindles, Acorn Finials, Continental, Pair 55.00
Chair, Rush Seat, Pierced Baluster Splat, Square Legs 345.00
Chair, Satinwood, Diamond Crest Rail, Center Rosette Splat, 34 In., Pair 4600.00
Chair, Satinwood, Pierced Back, Painted Urn & Flower, Tapered Legs, Pair 895.00
Chair, Satinwood, Scrolled Backrest, Reeded Slats, Upholstered Seat, Pair 805.00
Chair, Serpentine Top Over Vase Back Splat, Shepherd's Crook Arms, c.1730 .... 4800.00
Chair, Sheraton, Bamboo Turnings, Lyre Back, Rush Seat, 32 In. 405.00
Chair, Sheraton, Black, Gold Paint, Upholstered, c.1800 .... 200.00
Chair, Sheraton, Medallion Stretcher, Balloon Seat, Bowed Arms, 31 1/2 In. 165.00
Chair, Sheraton, Painted, Woven Balloon Seat, 36 x 17 1/2 x 15 1/2 In., Pair 336.00
Chair, Shield-Shaped Seat, Bamboo-Turned Base, 1870s, 20 3/4 In., Pair 605.00
Chair, Shop Of The Crafters, Mahogany, 4 Vertical Slats, Arms, 29 x 21 x 39 In. 1380.00
Chair, Simon Desanta, Flying Carpet, Rosenthal Einrichtung, 58 x 44 x 38 In. 1840.00
Chair, Slat Back, Painted, Arms, New England, Late 18th Century, 25 In. 345.00
Chair, Slat Back, Painted, New England, Late 18th Century, 31 1/4 In. 750.00
Chair, Slat Back, Painted, Rush Seat, Arms, Late 18th Century, 46 3/4 In. 2990.00
Chair, Spindle & Slat Back, Pillow Rest, Painted Design, Plank Seat, 1850, 34 In. 55.00
Chair, Splayed Legs, Saddle Seat, Carved Arms, Turned Supports, 37 In. 201.00
Chair, Splint Seat, Round Stiles, Turned Legs, Stretcher, Early 20th Century, 17 1/2 In. 59.00
Chair, Stickley Bros., 5 Back Slats, 19 x 18 x 34 In. 230.00
Chair, Stickley Bros., Mahogany, 3 Slats At Back, Original Finish, 31 x 36 In. 865.00
Chair, Stickley Bros., Mahogany, 8 Vertical Spindles, Arms, 26 x 23 x 38 In. 405.00
Chair, Stickley Bros., Mahogany, Solid Seat, 8 Spindles, 43 In. 345.00
Chair, Stickley Bros., No. 323, Mahogany, Reverse-Tapered Legs, Arms, 38 In. 1495.00
Chair, Stickley Bros., No. 354, Mahogany, Original Finish, 34 x 39 x 37 In. 2415.00
Chair, Stickley Bros., No. 501 1/2, Mahogany, 7 Vertical Slats, Arms, 30 x 44 In. 920.00
Chair, Stickley Bros., No. 841, Mahogany, Leather Seat, 16 x 29 In. 375.00
Chair, Straight Crest Rail, Bands Of Leaf Tips, Wreath Center, Late 19th Century 440.00
Chair, Swing-Out Leather-Covered Writing Surface 3300.00
Chair, T.E. Warren, Pinched Waist, Spring Steel, Tilts & Swivel, 41 In. 2185.00
Chair, Tapestry Upholstered, X-Form Seat, Seated Woman, Kneeling Man, 1680s 9600.00
Chair, Teak, 7 Contoured Back Slats, Angled Frame, Loose Seat, Arms, 32 1/4 In. 405.00
Chair, Teak, Ladder Back, Pinched Waist Back Slats, Leather, Denmark, 34 1/2 In. 80.00

Chair, Teak, Medallion Back, Pierced Carving, Apron, Arms, Oriental, 42 In. 360.00
Chair, Tete-A-Tete, Off-White Paint, Scroll Frame, Cane Back, Medallions, Pair 258.00
Chair, Thonet, Bentwood, Arms, Spring Mounted Pressed Wood Seat, 33 x 23 x 21 In. . . . 635.00
Chair, Tiger Maple Arms & Crest, Lyre Back, Balloon Seat, 34 In. 50.00
Chair, Tub, Faux Bamboo, Painted, Turned Spindles, Cane Seat, 1820s 5100.00
Chair, Tub, Louis XV Style, Gilt, Carved Wood, Leaves, Velvet 355.00
Chair, Tub, Mahogany, Padded Back Joined To Seat, Outscrolled Arms, 1870s, 27 In. 85.00
Chair, Tub, Oak, Barrel Back & Sides, Cane Seat, Top-Shaped Feet, 1830s, 30 1/2 In. . . . 980.00
Chair, Tubbs, Snowshoe, Woven Seat, Curved Arms, Wallingford, Vt., 23 x 23 x 35 In. . . . 1095.00
Chair, Tubular Anodized Aluminum, Oilcloth, Arms, 34 In. 8625.00
Chair, Twig, Bentwood Back, Slat Seat, Flared Rolled Arms, 44 1/2 In. 165.00
Chair, Twig, Bow Back, Circular Twig Arms, Rolled Seat, 32 3/4 In. 330.00
Chair, Unfolds Into 4-Step Ladder 255.00
Chair, V. Panton, Cone, Steel, Upholstered, F. Hansen, 1958, 23 In. 1380.00
Chair, V. Panton, Injected Plastic, Orange, Signed, 1974, 19 1/2 x 24 x 33 In. 375.00
Chair, V. Panton, Peacock, Chromed Steel Grid, Upholstered Discs, F. Hansen, 26 In. 5750.00
Chair, V. Panton, Yellow Injected Plastic, Signed, 19 1/2 x 24 x 33 In. 345.00
Chair, Van Der Rohe, Steel Frame, Cantilevered, Woven Cane Seat, Arms, 1920s 1440.00
Chair, Venetian, Painted, Upholstered, Crest, Scroll Arms, Cabriole Legs, c.1890, Pair . . . 1900.00
Chair, Victor Horta, Oak, Arms, Belgium, 1901, Pair 15600.00
Chair, Victorian, Mahogany, Cameo Back, Molded, Leaves, Pair 250.00
Chair, Victorian, Mahogany, Carved Crest, Upholstered, Arched Back, Cabriole Legs, Pair 880.00
Chair, Victorian, Mahogany, Carved, Casters, Padded Arms, c.1865, Pair 340.00
Chair, Victorian, Mahogany, Domed Back, Arms, Mid 19th Century, 33 In. 400.00
Chair, Victorian, Mahogany, Draped Gadroon, Carved Crest, Upholstered, 44 In., Pair . . . 360.00
Chair, Victorian, Mahogany, Molded Backrest, Scrolled Arms, Mid 19th Century, 36 In. . . 489.00
Chair, Victorian, Mahogany, Upholstered, Scrolling Armrests, c.1865, 42 In. 215.00
Chair, Victorian, Rosewood, Carved, Balloon Back, Upholstered, 39 x 18 x 19 In., Pair . . 335.00
Chair, Victorian, Upholstered, Fruit & Nut Carving, Crest, Knees, 17 1/2 In. 120.00
Chair, Victorian, Walnut, Balloon Back, Upholstered, Arms, 43 1/2 x 24 In. 340.00
Chair, Victorian, Walnut, Burl Veneer, Shaped Crests, Medallion, Upholstered, 6 Piece . . . 385.00
Chair, Victorian, Walnut, Carved Crest, Cartouche, Upholstered, Open Arms 525.00
Chair, Victorian, Walnut, Carved, Grape Clusters, Crest, Cabriole Leg, Upholstered, 34 In. 225.00
Chair, Victorian, Walnut, Spode Tile Inserts, Leather Seat, Late 1800s, Pair 440.00
Chair, W. Lescaze, Tubular Steel, Ebonized Wood, 1932, 34 In. 2300.00
Chair, W. Plattner, Gray Tweed Upholstered, Black Wire Base, 29 In., Pair 920.00
Chair, W. Whitely, Mahogany, Continuous Arms, Upholstered Seat, 28 1/2 In. 220.00
Chair, W.H. Gunlocke, Arched Crest, Continuous Arms, Vinyl Seat, 24 In., Pair 345.00
Chair, Wakefield Rattan Co., Wicker, Rolled Back, Ball Spirals, Victorian, 30 In. 480.00
Chair, Wallace Nutting, No. 390, Ladder Back, Arms, Script Brand 330.00
Chair, Wallace Nutting, No. 440, Windsor, Writing, Drawer Under Seat, Block Brand 2145.00
Chair, Wallace Nutting, No. 464, Carved, Arms, Script Brand 550.00
Chair, Wallace Nutting, No. 475, Flemish, Arms, Block Brand 1155.00
Chair, Wallace Nutting, Windsor, Bow Back, Arms, Block Brand 825.00
Chair, Walnut, Arched, Padded Back, Scrolled Arms, 19th Century, 46 1/2 In., Pair 4370.00
Chair, Walnut, Baluster Back Splat, Shepherd's Crook Armrests, 43 In., Pair 1680.00
Chair, Walnut, Baluster Back Splat, Turned Stretcher, Pair 448.00
Chair, Walnut, Carved & Pierced Gothic Back, Wheel Center, Padded Arms, c.1840 . . . . . 5175.00
Chair, Walnut, Carved Crest, Cabriole Legs, Arms, Victorian, 41 In. 220.00
Chair, Walnut, Fruit Crest, Floral Needlepoint & Petit Point Upholstered, Arms, 41 In. . . . 275.00
Chair, Walnut, Leaves & Rose On Crest, Simulated Leather, 43 1/2 In. 410.00
Chair, Walnut, Library, Upholstered, Scrolling Handrests, Claw & Ball Feet 365.00
Chair, Walnut, Marquetry, Slip Seat, Carved Knees, Claw & Ball Feet, 19 x 45 In. 345.00
Chair, Walnut, Molded Arms, Scrolled Handrests, Pierced Splat, 53 1/2 In. 300.00
Chair, Walnut, Padded Arched Seat & Back, Block Legs, Bun Feet, 1770s, 45 In., Pair . . . 1380.00
Chair, Walnut, Padded Back, Arms To Padded Seat, Barley-Twist Legs, 42 1/2 In. 1380.00
Chair, Walnut, Padded Back, Scrolling Arms, Front Stretcher, 1880s, 44 In. 1035.00
Chair, Walnut, Padded Seat & Back, Arms Joined At Seat, 1880s, 44 1/2 In. 865.00
Chair, Walnut, Scrolls & Shells On Arm Supports, Upholstered, 47 In. 660.00
Chair, Walnut, Shell-Carved Top Rail, Cane Seat & Back, X-Brace, 20th Century 1120.00
Chair, Walnut, Spindle Back, Seat Rail, Burl Panel, Turned Legs, Casters, Pair . . . . . *Illus* 1150.00
Chair, Walnut, Standing Lion, Shield Finials, Twisted Shaft Legs, Italy, 1900s 115.00
Chair, Walnut, Tall Backrest, Sloped Arms, Carved Handrests, 1930s, Pair 375.00

Chair, Walnut, Throne, Upholstered Back, Fluted Finials, Scrolling Arms 460.00
Chair, Walnut, Trumpet Legs, Corner Medallions, Button Back, 39 In. 220.00
Chair, Walnut, Upholstered Backrest, Padded Arms, X-Stretcher, 1880s 785.00
Chair, Walnut, Upholstered Backrest, Scrolled Arms, Hoof Feet 1150.00
Chair, Warren McArthur, Biltmore, Rubber Footpads, 21 x 24 x 32 In. 1150.00
Chair, Wegner, Papa Bear, Brown Wool, Teak Armrests, Dowel Legs, 39 In. 1380.00
Chair, Wegner, Swooping Contoured Frame, Upholstered, Dowel Legs, Arms, 40 In. 300.00
Chair, Wegner, Teak, Armrests, Cane-Wrapped Seat, Back, J. Hansen, 1949, 30 In. 1095.00
Chair, Wegner, Teak, Brown Wool Tweed, Dowel Legs, 39 x 35 1/2 x 28 In. 1380.00
Chair, Wegner, Upholstered Tweed Seat & Back, Sloped Armrests, Pair 600.00
Chair, Wegner, Valet, Denmark, 1940s 7500.00
Chair, Wendell Castle, Molar, Molded White Fiberglass, Black Plastic Trim, 35 In. 600.00
Chair, White Oak, Lollipop Back, Arm Supports, c.1870, 33 x 24 1/2 x 20 In. 880.00
Chair, Wicker, Green Paint, Magazine Rack Arms, 32 x 23 x 24 In., Pair 730.00
Chair, William & Mary, Roundabout, Salmon Paint, 31 3/4 In. 860.00
Chair, William IV Style, Mahogany, Circular Starburst Back, Reeded Legs, 33 1/2 In. 460.00
Chair, William IV Style, Mahogany, Shaped Back, Dish Seat, 19th Century, 37 In. 145.00
Chair, William IV, Mahogany, Balloon Back, 44 In. 3680.00
Chair, William IV, Mahogany, Concave Backrest, Reeded Legs, 30 In. 3220.00
Chair, William IV, Mahogany, Deeply Canted, Open Arms, Tufted, 32 In. 2990.00
Chair, William IV, Mahogany, Padded Back, Mid 19th Century, 37 1/2 In. 980.00
Chair, William IV, Mahogany, Paneled Crest, Scroll Arms, Upholstered, 42 In. 690.00
Chair, William IV, Oak, Arch Back, Carved, Tapered Legs, Top-Shaped Feet 265.00
Chair, William IV, Oak, Heraldic Emblem, Tapered Legs, Top-Shaped Feet, Pair . . . . *Illus* 1840.00
Chair, Windsor, 13 Spindles, Arms, Blue Paint, c.1810, 38 In. 3055.00
Chair, Windsor, Bamboo Turnings, 4 Spindles, Alligatored Brown Paint, Arms, 34 In. 385.00
Chair, Windsor, Bamboo Turnings, 6 Spindles, Center Splat, 19th Century 60.00
Chair, Windsor, Bamboo Turnings, 7 Spindles 140.00
Chair, Windsor, Bamboo Turnings, 7 Spindles, Sack Back, Pa. 990.00
Chair, Windsor, Bamboo Turnings, 7 Spindles, Stepped Crest, Painted Roses, 36 In., Pair . 1265.00
Chair, Windsor, Bamboo Turnings, Deep Brown Alligatored, Gutter Seat, Arms, 34 In. 550.00
Chair, Windsor, Bamboo Turnings, Medallion Crest, Arms 100.00
Chair, Windsor, Bamboo Turnings, Rabbit Ear, Stencil, Banded, New England, Pair 495.00
Chair, Windsor, Bamboo Turnings, Square Back, Arms, c.1810, 36 x 20 3/4 In. 315.00
Chair, Windsor, Bamboo Turnings, Straight Crest, Cutout Ends, Arms, Signed 165.00
Chair, Windsor, Birdcage, Bamboo Turnings, 7-Spindle Back, 33 In., Pair 715.00
Chair, Windsor, Birdcage, Splayed Bamboo-Turned Legs, 1810, 17 x 34 In. 385.00
Chair, Windsor, Bow Back, 6 Spindles, Black Paint, Child's, 29 In. 690.00
Chair, Windsor, Bow Back, 6 Spindles, H-Stretcher, 38 In. 990.00
Chair, Windsor, Bow Back, 6 Spindles, Plank Seat, Shaped Arms, 19th Century 385.00
Chair, Windsor, Bow Back, 7 Spindles, Bamboo Turned Legs, Shield Seat, 17 In. 360.00
Chair, Windsor, Bow Back, 7 Spindles, Black Paint, 37 1/2 In. 250.00
Chair, Windsor, Bow Back, 8 Spindles, Oak, Shield Shape, 36 In.   170.00
Chair, Windsor, Bow Back, 8 Spindles, Turned Legs, Pierced Splat, 45 In. 360.00
Chair, Windsor, Bow Back, 9 Spindles, Carved Knuckle Arms, Saddle Seat 440.00

Furniture, Chair, William IV, Oak, Heraldic
Emblem, Tapered Legs, Top-Shaped Feet, Pair

If you see any numbers or letters
on the frame of a wooden piece of
furniture, do not remove or erase
them. They may refer to a catalog,
and eventually you may be able to
attribute the piece to the proper
manufacturer.

Chair, Windsor, Bow Back, Arms, England, 45 1/4 In. 200.00
Chair, Windsor, Bow Back, Faux Marble Design On Seat & Arms, Oval Seat, 25 x 13 In. . 100.00
Chair, Windsor, Bow Back, Old Brown Paint, Red Wash, Turned Legs, Rush Seat, 27 In. . 385.00
Chair, Windsor, Bow Back, Painted, Philadelphia, c.1970, 38 In., Pair 6000.00
Chair, Windsor, Bow Back, Red Paint, c.1810, 34 1/4 In. 375.00
Chair, Windsor, Brace Back, 9 Spindles, Continuous Arm, Saddle Seat, Painted, 35 In. . . . 2185.00
Chair, Windsor, Brace Back, Robert Barrow, Vase & Ring Legs, Continuous Arm 220.00
Chair, Windsor, Brown Over Green, Bamboo-Turned Legs, Continuous Arm, 1900s, 35 In. 935.00
Chair, Windsor, Comb Back, 7 Spindles, Shaped Crest, Arms, 44 x 23 1/2 x 22 In. 4620.00
Chair, Windsor, Comb Back, Writing, D-Shape Seat, 2 Drawers, Blunt Arrow Feet, 47 In. . 935.00
Chair, Windsor, Drawer Under Writing Table, Arms, Connecticut, c.1780, 38 In. 2070.00
Chair, Windsor, Elm, Yew, Pierced Central Splat, Spindle, England, Pair 490.00
Chair, Windsor, English Elm, Hoop Back, Saddle Seat, Late 19th Century, 35 1/2 In. 173.00
Chair, Windsor, Fanback, 6 Spindles, Crest, Medallion Finials, 17 x 37 In. 300.00
Chair, Windsor, Fanback, 6 Spindles, Vase & Ring-Turned Legs, 36 In. 259.00
Chair, Windsor, Fanback, 7 Spindles, Shaped Crest, Shield Seat, 35 1/2 In., Pair. 825.00
Chair, Windsor, Fanback, 7 Spindles, Shaped Seat, Gutter, Back, 23 1/2 x 11 1/2 In. 330.00
Chair, Windsor, Fanback, 8 Spindles, Bamboo Turnings, Splayed Legs, 35 In. 230.00
Chair, Windsor, Fanback, 9 Spindles, Shaped Arms, Lobed Ears, Shaped Seat, 46 In. 4465.00
Chair, Windsor, Fanback, J. Mansfield, c.1780 . . . . 420.00
Chair, Windsor, Fanback, Laminated Bent Arms, Vinyl Seat & Back, c.1950, 31 x 25 In. . 315.00
Chair, Windsor, Fanback, Oak, Maple & Pine, Connecticut, c.1770 . . . . 2250.00
Chair, Windsor, Fanback, Painted, Serpentine Crest, Carved Ears, c.1780, 35 In. 1265.00
Chair, Windsor, Fanback, Red Paint, Bamboo Turnings, 17 1/2 x 35 1/2 In. 880.00
Chair, Windsor, Fanback, Red Paint, c.1790, 40 In. 860.00
Chair, Windsor, Fanback, Scrolled Crest, Carved Ears, Vase & Ring Legs 6075.00
Chair, Windsor, Hardwoods, 7 Spindles, Vase & Ring Legs, Shield Seat, 38 In. 190.00
Chair, Windsor, Leather Writing Surface, Silhouettes, 44 1/2 x 32 In. 3360.00
Chair, Windsor, Low Back, Writing Arm, c.1740 . . . . 2500.00
Chair, Windsor, Mahogany, 7 Spindles, Shield Seat, 17 1/2 x 34 In. 275.00
Chair, Windsor, Mahogany, Rod Back, Brown Paint, Arms, Late 18th Century, 36 In. 5875.00
Chair, Windsor, Mahogany, Spindles, Blue Over Black Paint, H-Stretcher, Arms 1430.00
Chair, Windsor, Oxbow, Yoke Shape Crest, Spindle Back, 18th Century, 26 1/4 In. 1880.00
Chair, Windsor, Plank Seat, Arrow Back, Painted, Arms, Pair 200.00
Chair, Windsor, Plank Seat, Stretcher Base, Arms, 43 1/2 x 24 In. 2690.00
Chair, Windsor, Sack Back, 7 Spindles, Black Paint, Shaped Seat, 36 In. 1380.00
Chair, Windsor, Sack Back, 7 Spindles, Painted, Saddle Seat, Arms, c.1780, 39 3/4 In. . . . 2645.00
Chair, Windsor, Sack Back, 9 Spindles, Green Paint, 1790s, 35 1/2 In. 3740.00
Chair, Windsor, Sack Back, Alligatored Black Paint Over Red, Arms, 13 1/2 In. 80.00
Chair, Windsor, Sack Back, Black Over Red Paint, 33 1/2 In. 1210.00
Chair, Windsor, Sack Back, Broad Saddle Seat, Continuous Arms, 33 x 24 In. 1500.00
Chair, Windsor, Sack Back, Green Paint, Connecticut, c.1780, 35 1/2 In. 3740.00
Chair, Windsor, Sack Back, J. Foster, Painted, c.1800, 37 3/4 In. . . . 235.00
Chair, Windsor, Sack Back, Oval Seat, Turned Legs, Scalloped Arms, Refinished, 38 In. . . . 410.00
Chair, Windsor, Sack Back, Painted, Arms 400.00
Chair, Windsor, Sack Back, Painted, New England, Late 18th Century, 35 1/2 In. 2185.00
Chair, Windsor, Sack Back, R.P. Scott, Bamboo Turned Base, Oval Seat, Arms, 36 1/2 In. 440.00
Chair, Windsor, Sack Back, Red Paint, New England, 1780-1790, 37 In. 2415.00
Chair, Windsor, Sack Back, Scalloped Handrests, Vase & Ring Turnings, 37 In. 1760.00
Chair, Windsor, Sack Back, Turned, Arms, New England, c.1800, 37 1/2 In. 1560.00
Chair, Windsor, Sack Back, Turned, Carved, Arms, Pennsylvania, c.1780, 35 In. 1800.00
Chair, Windsor, Sack Back, Vase & Ring Turned Legs, Oval Seat, Shaped Arms, 39 In. . . . 1045.00
Chair, Windsor, Shaped Back, Step-Down 825.00
Chair, Windsor, Shaped Backrest, Plank Seat, c.1830 . . . . 475.00
Chair, Windsor, Shaped Crest, 7 Spindles, Saddle Seat, Ringed Legs, Sponged Surface . . . 1265.00
Chair, Wing, Beech, Leaf-Carved Frame, Fluted Legs, Late 19th Century, Pair 460.00
Chair, Wing, Black Over Red, Flared Arms, Upholstered, Rush Seat, 50 In. 440.00
Chair, Wing, Carved Acanthus Leaves, Flowered Silk, 42 1/2 In. 440.00
Chair, Wing, Carved Claw & Ball Feet, Upholstered, Centennial, 44 1/2 In. 690.00
Chair, Wing, Carved Knees, Claw & Ball Feet, 45 x 32 In. 280.00
Chair, Wing, Chippendale Style, Mahogany, Claw & Ball Feet 60.00
Chair, Wing, Chippendale Style, Mahogany, Claw & Ball Feet, Outcurved Arms 290.00
Chair, Wing, Chippendale Style, Straight Crest, Scrolled Arms, Leatherette 300.00

Chair, Wing, Chippendale, Mahogany, Arms, 43 In. 2145.00
Chair, Wing, Chippendale, Mahogany, Red Leather, Pair 900.00
Chair, Wing, Chippendale, Mahogany, Rolled Arms, Arched Crest, 44 In., Pair 1760.00
Chair, Wing, Chippendale, Mahogany, Upholstered, Scrolled Arms, c.1780, 46 1/2 In. 2820.00
Chair, Wing, Down-Scrolling Fluted Arms, Scrolled Legs 70.00
Chair, Wing, French Provincial, Walnut, Molded Frame, 20th Century, 17 x 41 In. 110.00
Chair, Wing, George II Style, Walnut, Upholstered, Pillow, Arms, 20th Century 750.00
Chair, Wing, George III, Mahogany, Rose Diamond Upholstered, Arms, 1790 .... 1495.00
Chair, Wing, Georgian Style, Mahogany, Upholstered, Early 20th Century, 40 In. 475.00
Chair, Wing, Hepplewhite Style, Mahogany, Upholstered, 19th Century 980.00
Chair, Wing, Mahogany, Hoof Feet, Scalloped Apron, Upholstered, 47 3/4 In. 600.00
Chair, Wing, Mahogany, Leather Upholstered, Cushioned Seat 8400.00
Chair, Wing, Mahogany, Leather, Reeded Front & Flared Rear Legs, 42 In. 880.00
Chair, Wing, Mahogany, Scrolling Arms & Headrest, Upholstered, c.1900 .... 1900.00
Chair, Wing, Mahogany, Tapered Legs, Flared Arms, Upholstered, 42 1/2 In. 192.00
Chair, Wing, Queen Anne Style, Cabriole Legs, Green Leather, Brass Tacks, 42 In. 220.00
Chair, Wing, Queen Anne Style, Crewel Upholstered, Cabriole Legs, Pad Feet 303.00
Chair, Wing, Queen Anne Style, Kittinger, Mahogany, Scrolling Arms 400.00
Chair, Wing, Queen Anne Style, Mahogany, Hickory, Upholstered, Scroll Arms 385.00
Chair, Wing, Queen Anne Style, Mahogany, Upholstered, Serpentine, Arms, 46 In. 410.00
Chair, Wing, Scrolling Armrests, Crewel Upholstered, Pair 1790.00
Chair, Wing, Serpentine, Arched Crest, Upholstered, 43 In. 220.00
Chair, Wing, Sheraton, Cherry, Pine Frame, Turned Legs, 18 1/2 x 42 In. 220.00
Chair, Wing, Walnut, Upholstered Backrest, Outscrolled Arms 7200.00
Chair, Wright & Elwick, George II, Mahogany, Pierced Back, Serpentine Seat, Pair 7200.00
Chair, Yew, Dark Finish, 5-Slat Arched Back, Crest, Rush Seat, Continental, 37 In. 550.00
Chair, Yew, Ladder Back, Back Slats, Shaped Arms, Paper Rush Seat, 42 In. 110.00
Chair, Yoke Back, Arms, Spanish Feet 5175.00
Chair & Ottoman, Art Deco, Rattan, Bamboo, Upholstered 840.00
Chair & Ottoman, G. Nelson, Coconut, Steel Shell, Chrome Base, Green, 16 In. 4900.00
Chair & Ottoman, Leather, Wooden Legs, Brass Tacks, Contemporary, 33 In. 800.00
Chair & Ottoman, Lounge, W. Plattner, Knoll International, 41 x 36 x 39 In. 800.00
Chair & Ottoman, Peter Maly, Upholstered, 27 x 25 x 17 In., 4 .... 1150.00
Chair & Ottoman, Robsjohn-Gibbings, Slatted Back, Dowel Legs, Cushions, 30 1/2 In. ... 1650.00
Chair & Ottoman, Saarinen, Fiberglass Shell, Upholstered, 1959, 36 In. 1495.00
Chair & Ottoman, Saarinen, Womb, Boucle Upholstery, Metal Base 1200.00
Chair Set, Adam, Fruitwood, 5 Spindles, Crest, Painted Flowers, Upholstered, 4 .... 1650.00
Chair Set, Alexander Begge, Casalino, Plastic, 13 x 13 x 22 In., 6 .... 345.00
Chair Set, Arne Jacobsen, Ant, Rosewood, Steel, Plastic, F. Hansen, 1952, 29 In., 4 ..... 800.00
Chair Set, Arrow Back, Decorated, Crest, Cabbage Rose, Plank Seat, 6 .... 900.00
Chair Set, Art Deco, Mahogany, Rectangular Back, Upholstered, Flaring Arms, 4 .... 489.00
Chair Set, Art Nouveau, Walnut, Carved, c.1900, 8 .... 6325.00
Chair Set, Arts & Crafts, 3 Vertical Slats, Slip Seat, 18 x 17 x 39 In., 5 .... 690.00
Chair Set, Arts & Crafts, Mahogany, 2 Horizontal Slats, Wooden Seats, 37 In., 7 .... 1320.00
Chair Set, Arts & Crafts, Mahogany, 4 Vertical Slats, Leather Seats, 37 In., 3 .... 140.00
Chair Set, Ash & Hickory, 4 Half-Turned Back Posts, 1 Armchair, 5 Side, 19 In., 6 ..... 990.00
Chair Set, Balloon Back, Brown Paint, Fruit Stencils, c.1820, 6 .... 2900.00
Chair Set, Ballroom, Victorian, Gilt, Ebonized, Yellow Horsehair Upholstery, 12 .... 3820.00
Chair Set, Bamboo-Turned Legs & Rungs, Spindle Back, 34 1/4 In., 10 .... 880.00
Chair Set, Beech, Leaf-Carved Crest, Cane Back, Cushion Seat, 6 .... 4890.00
Chair Set, Biedermeier, Cherry Inlaid, Vase-Shaped Splats, Drop-In Seat, 4 .... 750.00
Chair Set, Black Repaint, Rose On Crest & Seat, Ball Turnings, Plank Seat, 18 In., 6 .... 660.00
Chair Set, Cane Back, Arched Crest Rail, Carved Flowers, Serpentine Seat, Cushion, 6 .. 630.00
Chair Set, Captain's, Arms, England, 6 .... 10350.00
Chair Set, Cherry, 5 Arches On Crest, Upholstered, 38 1/4 In., 6 .... 2310.00
Chair Set, Chinese Chippendale, Polychrome, Padded Seat, 41 In., 4 .... 1265.00
Chair Set, Chippendale Style, Mahogany, Carved, Arms, Cabriole Legs, c.1890, 10 ..... 6500.00
Chair Set, Chippendale, Mahogany, Pierced Vase Shape Splats, 37 In., 5 .... 5460.00
Chair Set, Chippendale, Mahogany, Upholstered Seat, 2 Scrolled Armchairs, 6 .... 1045.00
Chair Set, Curly Maple, Harp Splits, Scrolled Crests, Saber Legs, 33 3/4 In., 4 .... 1870.00
Chair Set, David Rowland, Stacking, Wire Waffle Seat & Back, Chrome Frame, 4 ...... 135.00
Chair Set, Eames, Black Wire Seat, Original Finish, 32 In., 4 .... 1380.00
Chair Set, Eames, DAR, Seafoam Green Fiberglass, 30 1/2 In., 4 .... 1495.00

Chair Set, Eames, DAX, Parchment Fiberglass Shell, 24 x 31 In., 4 .... 520.00
Chair Set, Eames, DCM, Molded Plastic, Orange Vinyl, c.1968, 30 In., 4 .... 115.00
Chair Set, Eames, DKX-2, Wire, Vinyl, Herman Miller, 19 x 21 x 32 1/2 In., 4 .... 345.00
Chair Set, Eames, DSX-1, Fiberglass Vinyl, Herman Miller, 18 x 21 x 31 In., 6 .... 210.00
Chair Set, Eames, Lounge, Aluminum Group, Blue Vinyl, Herman Miller, 4 .... 1840.00
Chair Set, Eames, Wire, Vinyl Seat, Black Tubular Legs, 32 In., 6 .... 495.00
Chair Set, Elm, Back Splats, Roundels Of Archaic Dragons, Chinese, 19th Century, 4 ... 1265.00
Chair Set, Empire, Mahogany, Saber Leg, Urn-Shaped Splats, Horsehair Seats, 33 In., 4 .. 450.00
Chair Set, Empire, Mahogany, Scroll Back, Upholstered, 2 Sphinx Armchairs, 4 .... 5175.00
Chair Set, Federal Style, Mahogany, Needlepoint Seat, 6 .... 1060.00
Chair Set, Federal, Mahogany, 5 Reeded Slats, Raked Rear Legs, 1800, 36 In., 4 ...... 1955.00
Chair Set, Federal, Mahogany, Figured Crest, Upholstered Slip Seat, Saber Legs, 6 ..... 715.00
Chair Set, Federal, Mahogany, Transitional, Mass., c.1790, 38 In., 4 .... 1920.00
Chair Set, Firehouse, Painted, D-Shape Seat, Odd Fellows Chain Link, 29 1/2 In., 4 ... 310.00
Chair Set, Flemington Iron Works, Iron Frame, Tall Back, Cutout Crest Rail, 51 In., 6 ... 990.00
Chair Set, Frank Lloyd Wright, Mahogany, Reupholstered Seat, Arms, 32 In., 6 .... 2070.00
Chair Set, Frank Lloyd Wright, White Cantilevered Seat, 20 x 22 x 32 In., 6 .... 2645.00
Chair Set, French Gothic Revival, Walnut, Crocket Finials, Arches, Padded Seat, 40 In., 6 1725.00
Chair Set, French Provincial, Beaded Lyre Back, Rosette, Rush Seats, Painted, 33 In., 4 .. 2700.00
Chair Set, French Provincial, Fruitwood, Rush Seat, Mid 19th Century, 8 .... 980.00
Chair Set, Fruitwood, Trapezoid Backrest, Upholstered Seat, 4 .... 1265.00
Chair Set, G. Stickley, Ladder Back, 3 Horizontal Slats, Leather Seats, 36 In., 4 ...... 6900.00
Chair Set, G. Stickley, Ladder Back, 3 Horizontal Slats, Leather Seats, Label, 36 In., 8 ... 5175.00
Chair Set, G. Stickley, Ladder Back, 3 Slats, Leather Seat, Tacks, 36 In., 4 .... 2185.00
Chair Set, G. Stickley, No. 306, Mahogany, Ladder Back, 25 x 17 x 36 In., 6 .... 5750.00
Chair Set, G. Stickley, No. 357, Leather Seat, Signed, 36 x 18 In., 4 .... 2760.00
Chair Set, G. Stickley, No. 370, Mahogany, Drop-In Seat, 1 Armchair, 36 In., 6 ...... 4025.00
Chair Set, George III Style, Mahogany, Ladder Back, 7 .... 1095.00
Chair Set, George III Style, Mahogany, Ribbonback, Carved Slats, 8 .... 3450.00
Chair Set, George III Style, Mahogany, Shieldback, 19th Century, 7 .... 1150.00
Chair Set, George III Style, Stained Birch, Open Back, Arched Crest, 6 .... 805.00
Chair Set, George III, Mahogany, Carved Flowers, Pierced Splat, Slip-In Seat, 8 ...... 7765.00
Chair Set, George III, Mahogany, Trapezoid Slip Seat, Tapered Legs, 4 .... 1035.00
Chair Set, Georgian Style, Mahogany, Pierced Rail, Slats, 6 .... 840.00
Chair Set, Georgian Style, Mahogany, Upholstered, 4 .... 650.00
Chair Set, Gothic Revival, Bowed Crest, Molded Uprights, Upholstered Seat, 38 In., 8 ... 3760.00
Chair Set, Gothic Revival, Oak, Carved Back, Figural Pediment, 50 In., 4 .... 1790.00
Chair Set, Gothic Revival, Oak, Padded Backrest, Oilcloth Seat, 1840s, 46 In., 4 ...... 4370.00
Chair Set, Grain Painted, Red, Black, 3 Curved Back Slats, Cane Seat, 33 In., 6 .... 230.00
Chair Set, H. Bertoia, Black Wire Grid Back, Vinyl, 30 In., 3 .... 265.00
Chair Set, H. Bertoia, White Wire, Yellow Seat Pad, 30 In., 6 .... 405.00
Chair Set, Half Spindles, Green, Flowers, Plank Seat, Branded J. Nees, 6 .... 495.00
Chair Set, Hans Olsen, Teak, Upholstered Seat & Back, Arms, Dowel Legs, 32 In., 4 .... 520.00
Chair Set, Hitchcock Style, Gilt Stencil, Plank Seat, Factory Mark, 4 .... 290.00
Chair Set, Hitchcock, Pillow Back, Gold Cornucopia Stencil, Rush Seat, 4 .... 1570.00
Chair Set, J. & J. Kohn, Bentwood, Cane Side, Strapwork Backrest, 8 .... 690.00
Chair Set, L. & J.G. Stickley, 5 Vertical Slats, Drop-In Seat Cushion, 38 In., 6 .... 4025.00
Chair Set, L. & J.G. Stickley, 5 Vertical Slats, Leather Cushion, Arms, 34 1/2 In., 4 ..... 3100.00
Chair Set, L. & J.G. Stickley, 6 Vertical Slats, Reupholstered Seats, Label, 37 In., 4 ..... 3335.00
Chair Set, Ladder Back, 3 Arched Slats, Rush Seats, Refinished, 35 In., 6 .... 365.00
Chair Set, Ladder Back, 3 Arched Slats, Rush Seats, Turned Finials, Late 1700s, 6 ...... 745.00
Chair Set, Ladder Back, 4 Arched Slats, Splint Seats, Turned Stretchers, 6 .... 250.00
Chair Set, Ladder Back, Fruitwood, Harlequin, Arms, England, 19th Century, 4 ...... 1840.00
Chair Set, Lancashire Style, Ladder Back, Beech, Rush Seat, 43 In., 10 .... 4600.00
Chair Set, Leaf & Floral Splat, Upholstered Seat, 1 Arm Chair, 6 .... 115.00
Chair Set, Limbert, No. 581, Ladder Back, 3 Horizontal Slats, 17 x 36 In., 6 .... 1840.00
Chair Set, Limbert, No. 911, Mahogany, Saddle Seat, 17 x 37 In., 6 .... 1430.00
Chair Set, Lolling, Kittinger, Mahogany, Slipper Feet, Leather, 42 In., 8 .... 3960.00
Chair Set, Louis XV Style, Oak, Serpentine Seat, Cabriole Legs, Stretchers, 8 .... 1150.00
Chair Set, Louis XV Style, Painted, Gilt, Carved, Upholstered, 2 Armchairs, 4 .... 3820.00
Chair Set, Louis XV Style, Polychrome, Parcel Gilt, Arms, c.1900, 37 In., 4 .... 5520.00
Chair Set, Mahogany, Carved Leaf Back, 6 .... 2300.00
Chair Set, Mahogany, Carved, Serpentine Front, 19th Century, 18 1/2 x 35 In., 4 .... 220.00

Chair Set, Mahogany, Crest, Over Fluted Splat, Padded Seat, 1870s, 38 In., 10 . . . . 7200.00
Chair Set, Mahogany, Northwind Heads, 6 . . . . 2745.00
Chair Set, Mahogany, Padded Leather Seat & Back, Arched Gallery, 37 3/4 In., 5 . . . . 2300.00
Chair Set, Mahogany, Pierced Interlace Backrest, 2 Armchairs, 8 . . . . 7800.00
Chair Set, Mahogany, Pierced Splats, Slip Seat, Silk, Late 19th Century, 6 . . . . 1980.00
Chair Set, Mahogany, Scalloped Top, Leather, 2 Armchairs, 37 In., 10 . . . . 2090.00
Chair Set, Mahogany, Scrolling Crest Rail, Padded Slip Seat, Saber Legs, 6 . . . . 1150.00
Chair Set, Mahogany, Shieldback, Centered Wheat Sheaf, Pierced Splat, 1870s, 12 . . . . . . 4830.00
Chair Set, Mahogany, Shieldback, Upholstered Seat, Spade Feet, 10 . . . . 3025.00
Chair Set, Maple & Kingwood, Button-Tufted Seat & Back, 1870s, 34 In., 5 . . . . 1150.00
Chair Set, Maple, New Cane Seat, 1860, 5 . . . . 385.00
Chair Set, Maple, Shaped Crest, Lyre-Shaped Splat, Cane Seat, 33 In., 9 . . . . 6465.00
Chair Set, Metal, Enameled Tractor Seat, Tubular Black Frame, Italy, 4 . . . . 345.00
Chair Set, Michigan Chair Co., Mahogany, 3 Vertical Slats, 18 x 17 x 37 In., 4 . . . . 460.00
Chair Set, Mission, Southwest, 8 . . . . 460.00
Chair Set, Modern Color Inc., Wrought Iron, Painted, Upholstered, 1951, 17 In., 4 . . . . . . 980.00
Chair Set, Napoleon III, Gilt, Polychrome, Gothic Style, 35 1/4 In., 4 . . . . 11500.00
Chair Set, Neoclassical, Mahogany, Arched Crest Rail, Trapezoid Slip Seat, 1830, 5 . . . . . 750.00
Chair Set, Neoclassical, Maple, Trapezoid Bowfront, Cane Seat, Saber Legs, 1820, 5 . . . . . 920.00
Chair Set, Neoclassical, Upholstered Seat, 2 Armchairs, 6 . . . . 6600.00
Chair Set, Otto Prutscher, Bent Beech, Stained, 1910, 3 . . . . 8400.00
Chair Set, Paine Furniture Co., Hepplewhite, Mahogany, Inlay, 1940s, 4 . . . . 995.00
Chair Set, Phyfe & Sons, Restoration, Mahogany, New York, 33 In., 6 . . . . 7200.00
Chair Set, Regency, Mahogany, Acanthine Splat, Padded Seat, 19th Century, 34 In. 1380.00
Chair Set, Regency, Scrolled Backrest, Upholstered Seat, 6 . . . . 2070.00
Chair Set, Risom, Walnut Frame, Green Leather Seat, Signed, 22 x 32 In., 4 . . . . 160.00
Chair Set, Rococo, Oak, Scrolled Crest, Back Splat, Round Seat, Curved Legs, 35 In., 8 . 6580.00
Chair Set, Rosewood, Graining, Stenciled, Gold Flowers, Rush Seat, 6 . . . . 180.00
Chair Set, Rosewood, Upholstered Seat, 1825, 4 . . . . 2000.00
Chair Set, Slat Back, Arched Stile, Rush Seat, 32 x 17 1/4 x 14 1/4 In., 6 . . . . 748.00
Chair Set, Teak, Curved Crest, Shaped Seat & Back, Woven Rope Seat, 1900s, 30 In., 8 . . 1610.00
Chair Set, Tub, Padded Seat & Back, Downswept Arms, Leather, 30 In., 3 . . . . 1380.00
Chair Set, Turned Front Stretcher, Urn Splats, Scalloped Crest, Paper Rush Seat, 6 . . . . . . 5060.00
Chair Set, Victorian, Grape Carved, Open Back, Upholstered, 34 In., 6 . . . . 690.00
Chair Set, Victorian, Salon, Marquetry, Upholstered Seat, 6 . . . . 6000.00
Chair Set, Walnut, Balloon Back, Carved Crests, Upholstered, 37 1/2 In., 4 . . . . 280.00
Chair Set, Walnut, Coat Of Arms Top Rail, Floral Splat, Padded Seat, 1890s, 4 . . . . 1450.00
Chair Set, Walnut, Leaf Crest & Seat Rail, Early 20th Century, 6 . . . . 2875.00
Chair Set, Windsor, 6 Spindles, H-Stretcher, Early 19th Century, 4 . . . . 5300.00
Chair Set, Windsor, Birdcage, Green & Black Paint, New England, 6 . . . . 8340.00
Chair Set, Windsor, Bow Back, 9 Spindles, 20th Century, 36 3/4 In., 4 . . . . 825.00
Chair Set, Windsor, Maple, Ash Rod, Bamboo-Turned Legs, 34 x 17 In., 6 . . . . 980.00
Chair-Table, Pine, Maple, Red Wash, New England, c.1800, 26 1/2 In. 2760.00
Chair-Table, Round, Painted, Turned Arm Supports, Dovetailed Drawer, 27 x 48 In. 3740.00
Chaise Longue, Beech, Faux Grained, Scrolled End, c.1850, 70 In. 2300.00
Chaise Longue, Chesterfield, Tufted Leather Cover, Adjustable Backrest, 62 In. 2990.00
Chaise Longue, Dark Beige Suede, Stitched Accents, 27 x 26 x 63 In. 145.00
Chaise Longue, E. Wormley, Bentwood, Reclining, Cane Back, 20 In. 1410.00
Chaise Longue, G. Nakashima, Slat Back, Rectangular Frame, Cushion, 33 x 77 In. 415.00
Chaise Longue, Louis XV, Beech, Carved Frame, Upholstered, 87 In. 940.00
Chaise Longue, Louis XVI, Beech, Cushion Seat, Fluted Legs, c.1790 . . . . 3740.00
Chaise Longue, Olivier Mourgue, Tubular Steel Frame, Purple, 65 x 25 In. 1150.00
Chaise Longue, Wicker, Brown, White Paint, Yellow Cushions, 54 x 32 1/2 x 29 In. 250.00
Chaise Longue, Wicker, Early 20th Century, 61 In. 85.00
Chaise Longue, Wicker, Willow, Drink & Magazine Holders In Arms, 19th Century 4500.00
Chamber Stand, Charles X, Walnut, Burl Walnut, 30 1/4 x 15 1/4 x 12 3/4 In. 1090.00
Chest, 2 Short Over 3 Long Drawers, Bracket Feet, 13 x 10 1/8 In. 185.00
Chest, 2 Short Over 3 Long Graduated Drawers, Spool Columns, c.1830, 22 x 24 3/4 In. . . 952.00
Chest, 2 Short, 3 Long Drawers, Bracket Feet, c.1850, 41 1/2 x 42 In. 1560.00
Chest, 2 Tombstone-Paneled Doors, British Sailor Picture, 1930 . . . . 1200.00
Chest, 4 Drawers, Black, Stenciled, 19th Century, 7 x 13 x 6 1/2 In. 315.00
Chest, 5 Drawers, Copper Pulls, Toeboard, 36 x 20 x 50 In. 2415.00
Chest, 5 Drawers, Walnut, Bun Feet, Molded Base, Wood Pulls, 1900s, 13 x 9 x 17 In. . . . 440.00

Chest, Acanthine Back Piece, 5 Drawers, Painted Florals, 1880s, 49 x 13 1/4 In. 1725.00
Chest, Bachelor's, Interior Labels, 4 Drawers, Batwing Brasses, 33 1/4 In., Pair. 1485.00
Chest, Bachelor's, Mahogany, 4 Drawers, Round Corners, Turned Feet, 1800s, 30 x 26 In.   920.00
Chest, Bachelor's, Mahogany, 4 Drawers, Dressing Slide, 3 Drawers, c.1780, 32 x 33 In. 4600.00
Chest, Baroque, Serpentine Front, Drawers, Floral Painted, Bun Feet, 33 x 43 x 24 In. . . . 10350.00
Chest, Biedermeier, 3 Graduated Drawers, Marlborough Legs, c.1830, 36 In. 2130.00
Chest, Biedermeier, Fruitwood, 3 Drawers, Figured Drawer Fronts, 38 x 31 x 17 In. 715.00
Chest, Biedermeier, Inlaid Mahogany, Frieze Drawer, 33 x 30 x 18 In. 3220.00
Chest, Biedermeier, Maple, Case Fitted With 2 Drawers, 31 x 36 In. 1725.00
Chest, Biedermeier, Walnut, 3 Drawers, Turned Legs, c.1835, 24 x 23 x 14 In. 1840.00
Chest, Birch, Brass Pulls, N.C., Late 18th Century, 76 3/4 x 42 1/2 x 23 In. . . . . *Illus* 66000.00
Chest, Birch, Red Washed, 4 Drawers, Bracket Base, c.1810, 33 1/2 x 39 In. 5175.00
Chest, Birch, Rope-Twist Pilasters, 6 Bonnet Drawers, 47 3/4 x 42 In. 495.00
Chest, Black Lacquer, Painted, Gilt Detail, Continental, 19th Century, 41 x 49 x 23 In. . . . 10200.00
Chest, Blanket, 2 Drawers, Hinged, Dovetailed, Painted, New England, 18 x 41 x 17 In. . . 110.00
Chest, Blanket, 2 Split Drawers, Inlaid Ivory Escutcheons, 2 Bail Handles, 33 x 50 In. . . . 345.00
Chest, Blanket, 6-Board, Dovetailed, Original Blue Paint, 38 x 18 x 26 In. 2300.00
Chest, Blanket, 6-Board, Grain Painted, Overhang Lift Top, Applied Molding, 10 x 16 In. 1035.00
Chest, Blanket, 6-Board, Orange Feather Graining, Black Trim, Pa., Marked., 1844 . . . . . 2145.00
Chest, Blanket, 6-Board, Red, White, Blue, Wavy Painting, Hinged Top, 15 x 38 In. 1725.00
Chest, Blanket, Alligatored Paint, Till, Hidden Drawer, Dovetailed Case, 22 x 44 1/4 In. . . 770.00
Chest, Blanket, B. Harter, Curly Maple, 3 Lower Case Drawers, 15 1/2 In. 1045.00
Chest, Blanket, Birch, Till, Drawer, Dovetailed, Brass, 14 x 21 3/4 In. 590.00
Chest, Blanket, Camphorwood, 33 x 16 1/2 x 15 In. 490.00
Chest, Blanket, Camphorwood, 6-Board, Chinese, 18 x 40 1/2 x 20 In. . . . . *Illus* 920.00
Chest, Blanket, Camphorwood, Brass, 1800s, 32 x 42 x 21 In. 800.00
Chest, Blanket, Camphorwood, Brassbound, Late 1800s, 40 1/2 x 18 1/2 x 19 1/2 In. 850.00
Chest, Blanket, Cherry, 3 Drawers, 1790, 10 In. 3165.00
Chest, Blanket, Cherry, Tapered, Scalloped, Star Design, 2-Board Top, 31 x 16 x 20 In. . . 300.00
Chest, Blanket, Chinese Chippendale, Teak, Floral, Pierced, 54 x 25 x 36 In. 4125.00
Chest, Blanket, Chippendale, Maple & Tiger Maple, 2 Drawers, 42 1/2 In. 5040.00
Chest, Blanket, Chippendale, Pine, Molded Hinged Cover, Bracket Feet, 26 In. 290.00
Chest, Blanket, Chippendale, Pine, Ogee Feet, Scrolled, Strap Hinges, 37 x 17 x 26 In. . . 1815.00
Chest, Blanket, Chippendale, Pine, Poplar, 18th Century, 20 x 43 1/2 x 19 In. 1650.00
Chest, Blanket, Chippendale, Softwood, Dovetailed, Straight Bracket Feet, Pa. 220.00
Chest, Blanket, Chippendale, Walnut, Inlaid, Drawers, c.1771, 30 x 51 3/4 x 23 In. 3740.00
Chest, Blanket, Chippendale, Walnut, Poplar, Bracket Feet, 45 x 21 1/2 x 27 In. 1870.00
Chest, Blanket, Decorated, Orange & Yellow Feathering, York County, Pa., 36 In. 715.00
Chest, Blanket, Dome Top, Bracket Feet, 22 x 29 In. 5500.00
Chest, Blanket, Dovetailed, Carved Bracket Feet, Lidded Till, 24 1/2 x 42 In. 520.00
Chest, Blanket, Dovetailed, Till, Green, Strap Hinges, 20 x 48 x 20 1/2 In. 250.00
Chest, Blanket, Dovetailed, Till, Turned Feet, 24 x 44 x 21 1/2 In. 900.00
Chest, Blanket, Dovetailed, Turned Feet, Brown Grain Painted, 24 x 42 x 18 In. 300.00
Chest, Blanket, Drawer, Red Paint, Molded Edges, Fan-Carved Shell, 32 x 37 1/2 x 16 In. 470.00
Chest, Blanket, Drawer, Wooden Knobs, 16 3/4 x 41 1/2 In. 200.00
Chest, Blanket, Edward Hall, 6-Board, Polychrome Hearts, 1839, 37 x 16 In. 290.00

Furniture, Chest, Birch,
Brass Pulls, N.C.,
Late 18th Century,
76 3/4 x 42 1/2 x 23 In.

Furniture, Chest, Blanket, Camphorwood,
6-Board, Chinese, 18 x 40 1/2 x 20 In.

Chest, Blanket, Feather Paint Over Red, Dovetailed & Pegged Construction, 10 In. 550.00
Chest, Blanket, Federal, Pine, Lift Top, Till, 2 Short Drawers, Ball Feet, 27 x 46 x 19 In. . .   1880.00
Chest, Blanket, Fishtail Strap Hinges, 2 Molded Lip Drawers, Bracket Base, Pa. 550.00
Chest, Blanket, G. Nelson, Birch, Square, Herman Miller, 1947, 22 1/2 x 24 x 24 In. 980.00
Chest, Blanket, G. Stickley, Mahogany, Dovetailed Sides, Lift Top, 17 x 36 x 22 In. 4000.00
Chest, Blanket, Grain Paint, High Turned Feet, 19th Century, 9 x 14 3/4 In. 3960.00
Chest, Blanket, Grain Painted, Lift Top, 39 1/2 x 18 x 16 In. 170.00
Chest, Blanket, Grain Painted, Molded Bracket Feet, 3 Drawers 470.00
Chest, Blanket, Green Paint, 6-Board, Mid 19th Century, 9 x 12 3/4 x 6 3/4 In. 2990.00
Chest, Blanket, Hinged Lid, 2 Lower Drawers, c.1890, 16 x 25 In. 1950.00
Chest, Blanket, Jacobean, English Oak, Lift Top, Iron, 15 1/2 x 46 1/2 x 15 1/2 In. 420.00
Chest, Blanket, Lift Top Cotter Pin Hinges, 2 False Drawers, 38 x 39 x 18 In. 140.00
Chest, Blanket, Lift Top, Square Corner Blocks, 18th Century, 22 x 40 1/2 In. 935.00
Chest, Blanket, Mixed Wood, Dovetailed, Arched Feet, 15 x 29 In. 80.00
Chest, Blanket, Molded Edge Top, Lidded Till, Dovetailed, Cedar Lined, 22 x 36 In. 145.00
Chest, Blanket, Moroccan, Inlaid, Simulated Mother-Of-Pearl, Ivory, 21 x 36 x 19 In. . . .   575.00
Chest, Blanket, Oak, 4 Inset Panels, Iron Hinges, Brown Interior, 25 1/2 x 46 In. 440.00
Chest, Blanket, Oak, Carved Front Panels, Stylized Bird, Leaf Panels, 28 x 51 In. 345.00
Chest, Blanket, Oak, Iron Straps & Bindings, Lift Top, 20th Century, 31 x 54 In. 1090.00
Chest, Blanket, Oak, Lift Top, Base Drawers, Till, Batwing Brass Pulls, 54 1/2 In. 1320.00
Chest, Blanket, Oak, Lifting Handles, Bracket Feet, 17 x 35 In. 170.00
Chest, Blanket, Oak, Mortise & Tenon, Square Legs, Inset Panels, England, 31 x 22 In. . . .   715.00
Chest, Blanket, Oak, Paneled Top & Front Panels, Block Feet, 35 x 39 In. 690.00
Chest, Blanket, Oak, Quartersawn, Relief Tulips, Till, 48 1/2 x 20 1/2 x 24 1/2 In. 935.00
Chest, Blanket, Painted Design, Covered Till, Drawer, Hinged Lid, 29 x 52 In. 1060.00
Chest, Blanket, Painted, 6 Drawers, Lift Top, Bracket Feet, 49 x 36 x 17 In. 3300.00
Chest, Blanket, Painted, Black, Brown, White Border, Arched Top, 20 x 50 x 21 In. 660.00
Chest, Blanket, Painted, Decorated, Hinged, 19th Century, 20 1/2 x 32 x 19 1/4 In. 2350.00
Chest, Blanket, Painted, Hinged, Interior Till, Turned Feet, 22 x 43 1/4 x 17 1/4 In. 560.00
Chest, Blanket, Painted, Yellow Grained, Strap Hinges, Ball Feet, 25 x 50 x 21 In. 250.00
Chest, Blanket, Pine, 2 Drawers, Snipe Hinges, 42 x 37 x 18 1/2 In. 750.00
Chest, Blanket, Pine, 2 False Drawers, 2 Bottom Drawers, 45 x 40 In. 1650.00
Chest, Blanket, Pine, 6-Board, Dentil Construction, c.1900, 15 x 37 x 15 In. 800.00
Chest, Blanket, Pine, 6-Board, Lift Top, Till, Interior Drawer, 24 x 47 x 17 In. 260.00
Chest, Blanket, Pine, Applied Molding, Turned Feet, Brass Escutcheon, 38 x 18 x 22 In. . .   410.00
Chest, Blanket, Pine, Black & White, Lidded Till, c.1830, 21 1/2 x 33 x 18 In. 6600.00
Chest, Blanket, Pine, Black Graining In Arches, Cutout Feet, 17 x 46 In. 110.00
Chest, Blanket, Pine, Black Ground, Yellow, Green Tree, 1847, 10 3/4 x 5 5/8 In. 2750.00
Chest, Blanket, Pine, Blue, Eagle, Pinwheels 690.00
Chest, Blanket, Pine, Cutout Ends Form Feet, Till, 21 x 40 In. 550.00
Chest, Blanket, Pine, Dovetailed Case, Till, AD 1824, 22 3/4 In.   660.00
Chest, Blanket, Pine, Dovetailed, Bracket Feet, 16 1/2 x 23 x 15 In. 209.00
Chest, Blanket, Pine, Floral Ground, 3 Panels, Platform Base, 9 3/4 x 19 3/4 In. 275.00
Chest, Blanket, Pine, Grain Painted, 4 Drawers, Round Knobs 6600.00
Chest, Blanket, Pine, Green Paint, 19th Century, 16 1/4 x 36 1/2 x 18 In. 460.00
Chest, Blanket, Pine, Hinged Lid, Short Drawer, Painted, c.1850, 19 1/2 In. 615.00
Chest, Blanket, Pine, Lift Top, Till, 2 Drawers, 1700s, 24 x 46 x 22 In. 500.00
Chest, Blanket, Pine, Molding, Panels, Strap Hinges, Bracket Feet, 48 x 22 1/2 x 22 In. . . .   250.00
Chest, Blanket, Pine, Mustard Grain Design, Red Brushed Borders 2200.00
Chest, Blanket, Pine, Painted, c.1800, 25 x 54 x 18 In. 520.00
Chest, Blanket, Pine, Poplar, Painted, c.1830, 18 x 25 1/2 x 13 3/4 In. 1680.00
Chest, Blanket, Pine, Rectangular Molded Edge, Bracket Feet, 32 1/2 In. 920.00
Chest, Blanket, Pine, Red & Yellow Paint, Bracket Feet, c.1850, 24 x 40 x 21 In. 9500.00
Chest, Blanket, Pine, Red Paint, New England, Early 18th Century, 33 x 38 In. 3450.00
Chest, Blanket, Pine, Red Stain, Bun Feet, 23 1/2 x 37 3/4 x 19 1/2 In. 225.00
Chest, Blanket, Pine, Runner Feet, Iron Strap Hinges, H.E., 1809, 45 x 22 x 21 In. 220.00
Chest, Blanket, Pine, Tulip Design, 3 Sections, 1879, 99 x 17 1/2 x 23 In. 1870.00
Chest, Blanket, Pine, Turned Feet, Molded Base, Strap Hinges, 34 x 18 x 19 3/4 In. 275.00
Chest, Blanket, Pine, Yellow, Red, Black Grained, Iron Hinges, Till, R.I., 45 x 24 In. 2200.00
Chest, Blanket, Poplar Top, Swirls Over Red Areas, Dovetailed Feet, 25 x 43 1/2 In. 1210.00
Chest, Blanket, Poplar, 1-Board Top, Wide Boards, Red Paint, 43 x 18 x 25 In. 625.00
Chest, Blanket, Poplar, Black Paint, Bracket Feet, 15 x 8 x 10 In. 440.00
Chest, Blanket, Poplar, Circles, Meandering Borders, Covered Till, 39 In. 825.00

Chest, Blanket, Poplar, Cyma Ends, T-Head Nails, Fitted Interior, 46 In. 1980.00
Chest, Blanket, Poplar, Fitted Interior, Covered Till, Lower Drawer, 21 In. 495.00
Chest, Blanket, Poplar, Flame Graining, Till, Secret Area Below, 25 x 43 In. 550.00
Chest, Blanket, Poplar, Geometric Design, Interior Till, 25 x 44 In. 1650.00
Chest, Blanket, Poplar, Iron Strap Hinges, 19th Century, 22 x 41 3/4 x 17 3/4 In. 1100.00
Chest, Blanket, Poplar, Painted Bow & Arrow, Black Feet, c.1850, 43 x 20 x 25 In. 3650.00
Chest, Blanket, Poplar, Painted, Dovetailed Case, Applied Bracket Feet, 22 x 36 x 19 In. . . 660.00
Chest, Blanket, Poplar, Painted, Dovetailed, Iron Hinges, Signed, 1795, 22 x 51 In. 9680.00
Chest, Blanket, Poplar, Polychrome, Painted, Long Island, c.1840, 40 x 44 x 19 1/2 In. . . . 8400.00
Chest, Blanket, Poplar, Red Graining, Bracket Feet, Dovetailed Case, Interior Till, 24 In. . . 660.00
Chest, Blanket, Poplar, Stenciled Leaves, Somerset County, 43 1/2 In. 825.00
Chest, Blanket, Poplar, Turned Legs, Inset Panels, Applied Molding, 38 x 19 x 24 In. 495.00
Chest, Blanket, Queen Anne, Maple, Birch, Lift Top, 2 Lip Drawers, 36 x 34 In. 1570.00
Chest, Blanket, Queen Anne, Painted, Flowers, Hearts, Hex Signs, Strap Hinges, Pa. 715.00
Chest, Blanket, Queen Anne, Softwood, Cotter Pin Hinge, New England, 36 x 42 x 17 In. . . 3300.00
Chest, Blanket, Red Paint, 1 Drawer, Thumbnail Molding, 19th Century 990.00
Chest, Blanket, Red Paint, Bracket Feet, Early 19th Century 110.00
Chest, Blanket, Red, Black Grain Painted, 6 Drawers, Inside Till, Hand-Forged Straps . . . 190.00
Chest, Blanket, Soap Hollow, 2 Drawers, 1842, 30 x 48 In. 5225.00
Chest, Blanket, Softwood, Dovetailed, Short Bracket Feet, Painted 210.00
Chest, Blanket, Softwood, Red Paint, Turned Feet, 19th Century, 8 1/2 x 14 In. 1155.00
Chest, Blanket, Sponged, Red, Yellow, & Black Trim, 3 Lower Drawers, 29 x 53 In. 1595.00
Chest, Blanket, Tiger Maple, Diamond Inlaid Key Escutcheon, 6 x 10 In. 1925.00
Chest, Blanket, Walnut, Figured Lid, Applied Molding, Bracket Feet, 14 x 7 In. 360.00
Chest, Blanket, Walnut, Hinged Lid, Opens To Storage & Drawer, c.1830, 31 1/2 In. 2015.00
Chest, Blanket, Walnut, Inlaid, Fan Pattern, 6-Board, Turned Feet, 19 x 33 1/2 x 15 In. . . . 315.00
Chest, Blanket, Walnut, Raised Front Panel, Tapered Feet, 15 1/2 x 26 12 In. 495.00
Chest, Blanket, Women, Horses, Leaf Designs, Hinged Lid, Stepped Base, 7 x 20 x 9 In. . . 590.00
Chest, Bombe, 3 Drawers, Claw & Ball Foot, Brass Hardware, 27 1/2 x 35 x 16 In. 310.00
Chest, Bombe, Dutch Style, Oak, 3 Drawers, Claw Foot, Brass Hardware, 26 x 29 x 16 In. . 365.00
Chest, Bombe, Oak, 3 Drawers, Ball Feet, Brass Hardware, 24 1/2 x 25 1/2 x 13 1/2 In. . . 390.00
Chest, Bombe, Oak, 3 Drawers, Claw & Ball Feet, Brass, 25 1/2 x 29 1/2 x 16 In. 310.00
Chest, Bowfront, Cherry, 4 Cock-Beaded Graduated Drawers, Ogee Feet, 33 In. 2990.00
Chest, Bowfront, Federal, Mahogany, 4 Graduated Drawers, Bracket Feet, 37 x 43 In. 3290.00
Chest, Bowfront, Mahogany, 2 Over 2 Drawers, Late 1700s, 32 x 41 In. 1100.00
Chest, Burl, Gilt Mounts, 2 Doors Open To 10 Drawers, Korea, 17 x 18 x 13 In. 100.00
Chest, Burled Veneers, 4 Drawers, Scalloped Aprons, Folding Server Top, 28 1/2 In. 660.00
Chest, Butler's, Drop Front, Cherry, False Drawer, 45 x 20 x 44 In. 470.00
Chest, Campaign, Mahogany, Early 20th Century, 36 x 19 1/2 x 40 1/2 In. 460.00
Chest, Campaign, Mahogany, Fold Down, 3 Graduated Drawers, 36 x 40 In. 460.00
Chest, Campaign, Mahogany, Tooled Top, Green Leather, Fold-Down, 3 Drawers 495.00
Chest, Camphorwood, Brass, Chinese Export, 18 x 40 x 19 In. 690.00
Chest, Cedar, Mahogany, Lift Top, False Drawers, Doors 190.00
Chest, Cedar, Scalloped Apron, Scroll Carving, 4 False Drawers, Lane, 32 x 45 In. 440.00
Chest, Cherry, 2 Drawers, Turned Feet, Bone Escutcheons, c.1840, 45 x 43 In. 670.00
Chest, Cherry, 4 Drawers, Dovetailed, Inlaid Top, c.1790, 35 x 38 x 22 In. 5200.00
Chest, Cherry, 8 Drawers, Dovetailed Case, Eagle Pulls, 41 3/4 x 20 1/2 In. 4400.00
Chest, Cherry, Banded Inlay Across Front, 4 Drawers, French Feet, 39 1/2 In. 2035.00
Chest, Cherry, Banded Inlay At Lower Case, Vining Goblet Inlay, 4 Drawers, 41 In. 5060.00
Chest, Cherry, Birch, 4 Drawers, Alligatored, 2-Board Top, New England, 39 x 36 In. . . . 1760.00
Chest, Cherry, Bird's-Eye Maple Drawer Fronts, Glass Knobs, Turned Feet 730.00
Chest, Cherry, Curly Maple, 6 Drawers, Walnut Pulls, 50 1/2 In. 1320.00
Chest, Cherry, Dovetailed Case, 4 Drawers, Claw & Ball Feet, Wood Pulls 5500.00
Chest, Cherry, Glass Knobs, 4 Drawers, Turned Legs, 17 x 14 1/2 x 9 In. 520.00
Chest, Cherry, Mahogany, Paneled, 3 Graduated Drawers, 35 1/2 x 42 x 18 In. 55.00
Chest, Cherry, Pine, Painted, Molded Crest, Early 1700s, 34 3/4 x 34 1/2 x 20 1/2 In. 4025.00
Chest, Cherry, Pyramid Form, 3 Graduated Drawers, c.1820 . . . . 9500.00
Chest, Cherry, Rectangular Top, Molded Edge, 3 Drawers, 1835, 54 x 23 In. 1840.00
Chest, Cherry, Scalloped Apron, 4 Drawers, Brass Pulls, Biscuit Corners, 40 1/2 In. 1650.00
Chest, Cherry, Serpentine, 4 Graduated Drawers, Bracket Feet, c.1760, 33 1/4 In. 12340.00
Chest, Cherry, String Inlay In Top Front, Oval Brasses, c.1815, 44 x 40 1/2 In. 2020.00
Chest, Cherry, Walnut, Turned Pilasters, Panels Over 4 Drawers, 51 3/4 In. 880.00
Chest, Chippendale Style, Mahogany Stain, Fan Inlay, 5 Drawers, 36 x 37 x 21 In. 670.00

Chest, Chippendale, Birch, 4 Drawers, Cock-Beaded Surround, c.1810, 35 x 39 In. 1495.00
Chest, Chippendale, Birch, 9 Drawers, 18th Century, 46 x 35 x 17 1/2 In. 1725.00
Chest, Chippendale, Block Front, Centennial, 37 x 20 x 33 In. 1150.00
Chest, Chippendale, Block Front, Molded Top Over 4 Shell Drawers, 37 x 33 In. 1150.00
Chest, Chippendale, Cherry, 2 Over 5 Drawers, Bracket Base, Cornice Molding, 51 In. . . . 4025.00
Chest, Chippendale, Cherry, 4 Drawers, 18th Century, 36 1/2 x 39 1/4 x 29 1/4 In. 1438.00
Chest, Chippendale, Cherry, 4 Drawers, Curly Maple Fronts, 39 x 38 In. 1325.00
Chest, Chippendale, Cherry, 4 Graduated Drawers, Bracket Feet, 38 x 19 x 40 In. 2200.00
Chest, Chippendale, Cherry, 4 Graduated Drawers, c.1780, 40 x 42 x 19 In. 1410.00
Chest, Chippendale, Cherry, 4 Graduated Drawers, c.1800, 33 x 41 x 20 In. 1880.00
Chest, Chippendale, Cherry, 4 Graduated Drawers, Ogee Feet, 40 x 29 x 39 In. 935.00
Chest, Chippendale, Cherry, Maple, 2 Over 4 Drawers, Center Pendant, 52 x 36 In. 2250.00
Chest, Chippendale, Cherry, Poplar, Bowfront, 4 Dovetailed Drawers 17160.00
Chest, Chippendale, Cherry, Rectangular Top, 3 Graduated Drawers, 35 3/4 In. 4310.00
Chest, Chippendale, Mahogany, 4 Inlaid Drawers, c.1800, 35 1/2 x 37 x 19 1/2 In. 4700.00
Chest, Chippendale, Mahogany, Carved, Pennsylvania, c.1800 . . . . 5000.00
Chest, Chippendale, Mahogany, Molded Edge, 1780-1800, 36 x 40 x 21 In. 7640.00
Chest, Chippendale, Maple, 3 Over 5 Graduated Drawers, Carved Fan, 49 x 37 In. 5290.00
Chest, Chippendale, Maple, Figured, 4 Drawers, c.1803, 35 1/2 x 39 x 19 1/2 In. 30550.00
Chest, Chippendale, Maple, Flat Molded Cornice, 6 Graduated Drawers, 53 x 37 In. 5000.00
Chest, Chippendale, Maple, Graduated Drawers, Beaded Apron, 42 x 41 x 17 In. 4200.00
Chest, Chippendale, Maple, Mass., c.1770, 52 x 39 3/4 x 21 3/4 In. 15600.00
Chest, Chippendale, Tiger Maple, 6 Graduated Drawers, 1790, 58 1/4 In. 11500.00
Chest, Chippendale, Walnut, 2 Short Over 3 Long Drawers, 1780, 38 x 34 x 20 In. 2900.00
Chest, Chippendale, Walnut, 2 Short Over 3 Long Drawers, c.1790, 33 1/4 x 35 1/4 In. 6465.00
Chest, Chippendale, Walnut, 3 Over 5 Drawers, 41 1/2 x 22 1/2 x 63 In. 4025.00
Chest, Chippendale, Walnut, 3 Over 5 Drawers, Philadelphia 2750.00
Chest, Chippendale, Walnut, 3 Over 5 Graduated Drawers, Brasses, 38 x 20 In. 3300.00
Chest, Chippendale, Walnut, 4 Graduated Drawers, 4 Ogee Feet, 33 x 38 x 19 In. 6900.00
Chest, Chippendale, Walnut, 5 Short Drawers Over 5 Long Drawers, 1784, 40 In. 13800.00
Chest, Chippendale, Walnut, 8 Drawers, Ogee Bracket Base, Reeded Corners, 33 In. 5040.00
Chest, Chippendale, Walnut, Carved, Molded Rectangular Top, Ball Feet, 37 In. 4310.00
Chest, Chippendale, Walnut, Figured, Philadelphia, c.1785 . . . . 4200.00
Chest, Chippendale, Walnut, Molded Cornice, 6 Drawers, 52 3/4 In. 2645.00
Chest, Chippendale, Wavy Birch, Cock-Beaded Overhanging Top, 4 Drawers, 34 In. 4315.00
Chest, Crossbanded Top, 2 Short, 3 Long Drawers, c.1830, 39 x 42 1/2 In. 1900.00
Chest, Curly Maple, 2 Over 3 Drawers, Walnut Pulls, 43 1/4 In. 2420.00
Chest, Curly Maple, 5 Dovetailed Drawers, Brass Pulls, 35 x 45 In. 385.00
Chest, Domed Top, Painted, Garlands, Blue Ground, c.1827, 25 1/2 x 25 1/4 x 15 In. 120.00
Chest, Dower, 3 Drawers, Bracket Base, Sponge Painted, Pa., c.1787 . . . . 1760.00
Chest, Dower, Blue Paint, Pink Flowers, Initials T.A.D., Continental, 1842 . . . . 495.00
Chest, Dower, Pine, Bun Feet, Wrought Iron Handles, 1804, 50 x 18 x 19 In. 770.00
Chest, Dower, Walnut, Lift Top, Till, 2 Drawers, String Inlay, Bracket Base, 25 In. 5000.00
Chest, Eastlake, Walnut, Marble Top, Incised Drawers, 31 1/2 x 45 1/2 x 21 In. 345.00
Chest, Empire, Cherry, Bird's-Eye Maple Veneer Drawers, Backsplash, 42 x 52 In. 1155.00
Chest, Empire, Cherry, Bird's-Eye Maple, 7 Drawers, Split Finials, 48 In. 550.00
Chest, Empire, Cherry, Tiger Maple Panels, Spiral-Turned Half Columns, Glass Knobs . . . 275.00
Chest, Empire, Mahogany, 2 Over 4 Drawers, Square Column Sides, Rolled Feet, 52 In. . . . 335.00
Chest, Empire, Mahogany, 4 Drawers, Ogee Molded Frame, Feet, 38 x 41 x 22 In. 165.00
Chest, Empire, Mahogany, Cherry, Step-Out Bonnet Drawer, 25 x 22 1/2 x 13 3/4 In. 3190.00
Chest, Empire, Mahogany, Gallery Top, 3 Set-Back Drawers, 48 x 43 x 20 In. 385.00
Chest, Empire, Mahogany, Line Inlay, 3 Drawers, 10 1/2 x 10 x 6 In. 750.00
Chest, Empire, Maple, 4 Drawers, Wood Pulls, Turned Feet, 43 x 21 3/4 x 47 In. 2035.00
Chest, Empire, Mixed Wood, Bow Top, Late 19th Century, 9 x 7 3/4 x 4 1/2 In. 340.00
Chest, Empire, Poplar, 4 Drawers, Block Feet, Turned Pulls, Child's, 23 x 14 x 25 In. 900.00
Chest, Empire, Tiger Maple, Walnut, 1 Large, 3 Graduated Drawers, 1845, 45 x 59 In. . . . 715.00
Chest, Faux Bamboo, 5 Drawers, Marble Top, Pair 7500.00
Chest, Faux Mahogany, Grain Painted, Hinged Top, 24 1/2 x 31 1/4 In. 590.00
Chest, Federal, Birch, Bird's-Eye Maple, Mahogany Veneer, 40 1/2 x 46 1/2 x 21 In. 8625.00
Chest, Federal, Cherry Inlay, Bowfront, c.1810, 41 x 42 x 21 1/2 In. 16450.00
Chest, Federal, Cherry Top, Cherry Inlay, String Inlaid Edge, 1806, 39 x 36 In. 4900.00
Chest, Federal, Cherry, 4 Drawers, Bowed Front, Bracket Feet, c.1800 . . . . 4310.00
Chest, Federal, Cherry, Bird's-Eye Maple, Cock-Beaded Drawers, Ball Feet, 41 In. 17250.00

Chest, Federal, Cherry, c.1780, 38 x 45 x 21 In. 4200.00
Chest, Federal, Cherry, Mahogany Veneer, 4 Graduated Drawers, 38 In. 1840.00
Chest, Federal, Cherry, Mahogany Veneer, Bowfront, 1810, 40 1/4 x 41 In. 3220.00
Chest, Federal, Cherry, Mahogany Veneer, Bowfront, 4 Cock-Beaded Drawers, 43 In. . . . 4025.00
Chest, Federal, Cherry, Mahogany, Inlaid, 2 Cupboard Doors, Drawer, 41 x 44 x 21 In. . . . 660.00
Chest, Federal, Cherry, Serpentine, 4 Graduated Drawers, 36 x 43 In. 10000.00
Chest, Federal, Cherry, Tiger Maple, Early 19th Century, 40 1/4 x 21 x 35 1/2 In. 6325.00
Chest, Federal, Mahogany Inlay, Bowfront, c.1820, 38 x 43 1/2 x 20 1/2 In. 4700.00
Chest, Federal, Mahogany Inlay, Rectangular Top, 4 Graduated Drawers, 35 In. 8625.00
Chest, Federal, Mahogany, Bowfront, Figured, c.1810, 38 x 41 x 21 In. 4200.00
Chest, Federal, Mahogany, Cherry, Bowfront, 4 Drawers, Escutcheons, 38 x 37 1/2 In. . . . 1980.00
Chest, Federal, Mahogany, Inlaid Veneered Edge, c.1810, 42 x 42 1/2 x 20 In. 1840.00
Chest, Federal, Mahogany, Inlay, Outset Corners, 3 Graduated Drawers, 45 x 46 In. 2350.00
Chest, Federal, Mahogany, Rectangular Hinged Top, French Feet, 11 x 8 In. 1495.00
Chest, Federal, Mahogany, Rectangular Top, 4 Graduated Drawers, 41 3/4 In. 2300.00
Chest, Federal, Mahogany, Serpentine Front, 4 Inlaid Drawers, 51 x 40 x 21 In. 605.00
Chest, Federal, Mahogany, Tiger Maple Inlay, 2 Over 3 Drawers, French Feet, 40 x 42 In. 4700.00
Chest, Federal, Maple, Cherry, Vermont, c.1810, 44 x 43 1/2 x 19 1/2 In. 3600.00
Chest, Federal, Maple, Flat Cornice, 5 Thumb-Molded Drawers, 1800, 53 x 20 In. 2990.00
Chest, Federal, Maple, Tiger Maple, Molded Overhanging Top, 4 Drawers, 36 x 40 In. . . . 1610.00
Chest, Federal, Poplar, Lift Top, 5 Drawers, 19th Century, 47 x 43 1/2 x 18 1/2 In. 10800.00
Chest, Federal, Red Paint, 2 Lower Drawers, New England, c.1810, 43 x 41 x 20 In. 1380.00
Chest, Federal, Tiger Maple, 4 Drawers, Ring-Turned Feet, c.1820, 43 x 40 x 20 In. 1840.00
Chest, Federal, Tiger Maple, Mahogany, 4 Graduated Drawers, 39 In. 4310.00
Chest, Federal, Walnut Inlay, 4 Long Drawers, 1800-1825, 38 x 38 x 21 1/2 In. 2585.00
Chest, Federal, Walnut, Serpentine Top, 4 Drawers, 4 Bracket Feet, 35 In. 9200.00
Chest, Florence Knoll, Birch, 3 Drawers, Knoll International, 36 x 18 x 28 In. 863.00
Chest, Frankl, Maple, Skyscraper, 5 Internal Drawers, 1980s, 67 1/2 In. 9775.00
Chest, French Pine, 3 Drawers, Spool-Turned Knobs, Bun Feet, 38 x 59 1/2 x 25 In. 448.00
Chest, French Provincial, Pogue, Maple, Courting Scene, Cincinnati, 52 x 19 x 34 In. 2090.00
Chest, French Restauration, Mahogany, Black Stone Top, 4 Drawers, 28 x 31 In., Pair . . . 2070.00
Chest, Fruitwood, 1 Projecting Drawer Over 3 Long, 1830s, 36 x 45 In. 3105.00
Chest, Fruitwood, Oak, 5 Drawers, Continental, 20th Century, 31 x 17 x 56 In. 330.00
Chest, G. Nakashima, Walnut, Short Drawers Over 3 Long, 32 x 36 In. 9775.00
Chest, G. Stickley, Mahogany, 2 Short Drawers Over 2 Long Drawers, 29 In. 9000.00
Chest, G. Stickley, No. 627, Oak, 2 Over 4 Drawers, Oval Hardware, 53 x 40 In. 8625.00
Chest, G. Stickley, No. 913, Mahogany, Dark Finish, 9 Drawers, 37 x 20 x 51 In. 12075.00
Chest, George II, Walnut, 2 Over 3 Drawers, 18th Century, 39 1/4 x 41 x 22 3/4 In. 3810.00
Chest, George II, Walnut, Inlaid, 5 Drawers, 18th Century, 38 1/2 x 39 x 22 1/2 In. 5150.00
Chest, George III Style, Mahogany, Bowfront, c.1840, 34 3/4 x 36 1/2 x 20 In. 2800.00
Chest, George III Style, Mahogany, Inlaid, Bowfront, c.1860, 46 x 40 1/2 x 19 1/2 In. 1120.00
Chest, George III Style, Walnut, Fruitwood, 20th Century, 8 3/4 x 7 3/4 x 4 3/4 In. 315.00
Chest, George III, 4 Long Drawers, Sleigh Feet, c.1810, 29 In. 4030.00
Chest, George III, Burl Walnut, Banded Inlaid Top, 35 1/2 x 43 x 21 In. 1610.00
Chest, George III, Mahogany Inlay, 3 Drawers, Bracket Feet, 38 x 36 x 18 In. 1380.00
Chest, George III, Mahogany, 2 Over 3 Long Drawers, c.1790, 41 x 38 x 20 In. 1955.00
Chest, George III, Mahogany, 2 Short, 3 Long Graduated Drawers, c.1810, 40 x 20 In. 1455.00
Chest, George III, Mahogany, 3 Graduated Drawers, Bracket Feet, 37 In. 1150.00
Chest, George III, Mahogany, 3 Graduated Drawers, Splayed Feet, 36 x 42 x 21 In. 2115.00
Chest, George III, Mahogany, 3 Long Drawers, 18th Century, 30 x 37 x 20 In. 2070.00
Chest, George III, Mahogany, 4 Drawers, Late 18th Century, 43 x 45 1/2 x 22 In. 1150.00
Chest, George III, Mahogany, 4 Graduated Drawers, c.1810, 40 x 43 x 21 In. 1065.00
Chest, George III, Mahogany, Banded Top, 2 Over 2 Graduated Drawers, 40 x 36 In. 1035.00
Chest, George III, Mahogany, Bowfront, 4 Drawers, 45 x 14 1/2 x 21 1/2 In. 2070.00
Chest, George III, Mahogany, Bowfront, Late 18th Century, 37 x 42 1/2 x 21 3/4 In. 2070.00
Chest, George III, Mahogany, Double, Late 18th Century, 40 x 74 x 22 1/2 In. 6040.00
Chest, George III, Mahogany, Ogee-Molded Top, 2 Over 3 Drawers, 42 x 45 In. 2185.00
Chest, George III, Mahogany, Rectangular Hinged Top, 3 Drawers, 44 In. 1150.00
Chest, George III, Mahogany, Rectangular Top, 3 Graduated Drawers, 39 1/2 In. 1840.00
Chest, George III, Rosewood, 5 Drawers, Late 18th Century, 39 x 38 1/4 x 19 3/4 In. 800.00
Chest, George IV, Mahogany Inlay, 6 Drawers, c.1840, 49 x 45 1/4 x 20 1/2 In. 1120.00
Chest, George IV, Mahogany, Beaded, Inlaid, Bowfront, 47 3/4 x 42 1/2 x 21 1/2 In. 2300.00
Chest, George IV, Mahogany, Bowfront, c.1825, 38 3/4 x 42 3/4 x 22 In. 1035.00

Chest, Georgian Style, Mahogany Inlay, Bowfront, c.1860, 41 1/2 x 43 1/2 x 21 In. 2464.00
Chest, Georgian Style, Mahogany Inlay, Bowfront, c.1840, 41 1/2 x 10 1/2 x 21 In. 1570.00
Chest, Georgian, Bowfront, Inlaid, 2 Short, 3 Long Drawers, Splay Feet, 1840, 40 x 20 In. 2240.00
Chest, Georgian, Mahogany, Drawers, Doors, Pedestal, c.1840, 38 x 22 1/2 x 12 5/8 In. .. 950.00
Chest, Georgian, Mahogany, Line-Inlaid Edge, 4 Drawers, 29 x 24 x 17 In. 1120.00
Chest, Georgian, Oak, 2 Over 3 Drawers, Mid 18th Century, 38 1/2 x 37 1/2 x 20 In. 1380.00
Chest, Georgian, Walnut, Crossbanded, Mid 18th Century, 42 x 41 x 22 In. 2185.00
Chest, Grain Painted, 3 Base Drawers, 2 Upper Drawers, 47 In. 440.00
Chest, Grain Painted, Red, Black, Hinged Top, 24 1/2 x 36 In. 5300.00
Chest, Grain Painted, Red, Gold, Rectangular Top, 1814, 39 1/2 x 40 x 17 3/4 In. 2300.00
Chest, Hardwood, 3 Drawers, Column Front, Spool-Turned Knobs, 11 x 15 x 10 3/4 In. .. 390.00
Chest, Hepplewhite, 4 Graduated Drawers, Beaded, Flared French Feet, 35 In. 2520.00
Chest, Hepplewhite, Cherry, 4 Graduated Drawers, Bowfront, Beaded, 38 1/2 In. 4480.00
Chest, Hepplewhite, Cherry, 9 Drawers, Molded Cornice, French Feet, 38 3/4 x 63 In. ... 7150.00
Chest, Hepplewhite, Cherry, Mahogany, 4 Drawers, 45 x 40 1/2 In. 1035.00
Chest, Hepplewhite, Cherry, Mahogany, 4 Drawers, Bracket Feet, 39 x 39 In. 2250.00
Chest, Hepplewhite, Curly Maple, Bowfront, 4 Drawers, 41 x 39 x 21 In. 2070.00
Chest, Hepplewhite, Mahogany, 4 Drawers, Apron, French Feet, 37 x 22 x 36 In. 4400.00
Chest, Hepplewhite, Mahogany, 4 Drawers, Bowfront, Beaded Edge, 36 x 35 x 18 In. ... 840.00
Chest, Hepplewhite, Mahogany, 4 Drawers, Diamond Pattern Inlay, Flared Feet, 38 In. ... 2520.00
Chest, Hepplewhite, Mahogany, 4 Graduated Drawers, French Feet, 41 x 19 x 37 In. 1870.00
Chest, Hepplewhite, Mahogany, 5 Drawers, Beaded Edge, 42 1/2 x 39 1/2 x 18 In. 840.00
Chest, Hepplewhite, Mahogany, Bowfront, 4 Drawers, Brass, 36 x 45 x 19 1/2 In. 360.00
Chest, Hepplewhite, Pine, Poplar, Mahogany Veneer, 4 Dovetailed Drawers 935.00
Chest, Hepplewhite, Walnut, Bowfront, Cock-Beaded Drawer, 38 x 38 1/2 x 19 In. 600.00
Chest, Hepplewhite, Walnut, Tiger Maple Drawer, Bail Handles, 23 x 18 x 11 In. 575.00
Chest, Herter, Walnut, Aesthetic Revival, 1870-1890, 46 1/2 x 32 1/2 x 19 1/4 In. 8815.00
Chest, Hinged Front, 2 Faux Drawers, Bracket Feet, 29 x 24 In. 500.00
Chest, Italian Neoclassical, Walnut, Parquetry, Early 1800s, 54 x 31 3/4 x 16 In. 3565.00
Chest, Jacobean Style, Oak, Frieze Drawer Over 4, Box Stretcher, 52 x 27 x 16 In. 3740.00
Chest, Jacobean, Oak, 3 Drawers, Geometric Pattern, Late 17th Century, 28 x 35 x 20 In. . 920.00
Chest, Jacobean, Oak, Carved, 3 Drawers, Paneled, Bracket Feet, 31 x 31 x 19 In. 1610.00
Chest, Jewel, Cherry, Shaped Wrought Iron Strap Hinges, 5 x 11 3/4 In. 360.00
Chest, Jewel, Fruitwood, Mother-Of-Pearl, Stars, Floral, Italy, 1800s, 24 x 30 x 36 In. ... 1265.00
Chest, Jewel, Mahogany Veneer, 4 Drawers, New England, 1825, 14 In. 1035.00
Chest, Jumuwood, Painted, Chinese, 28 1/2 x 39 x 25 In. 690.00
Chest, L. & J.G. Stickley, Mahogany, 69 x 38 x 18 In. 1850.00
Chest, Louis XV Style, Kingwood, Marble Top, Serpentine Front, 1890, 46 x 21 In. 2240.00
Chest, Louis XVI, Herringbone Inlay, 5 Drawers, Marble Top, 45 x 19 x 35 In. 2750.00
Chest, Mahogany Inlay, 2 Drawers, Late 19th Century, 30 x 31 x 17 1/4 In. 785.00
Chest, Mahogany Inlay, 5 Drawers, Flowers, Leaves & Scrolls, 49 x 38 In. 880.00
Chest, Mahogany, 2 Concealed Drawers Over 2 Short Drawers, 3 Long, 1830s, 47 In. ... 1840.00
Chest, Mahogany, 2 Over 2 Drawers, Line Inlay, Oval Brasses, 37 x 40 1/2 In. 1100.00
Chest, Mahogany, 2 Over 3 Drawers, Oval Brasses, 40 x 36 In. 1150.00
Chest, Mahogany, 2 Over 4 Drawers, 1 Stepped Out, Spiral-Carved Columns, 42 x 39 In. . 1035.00
Chest, Mahogany, 2 Short & 3 Long Drawers, Bracket Feet, 37 x 43 In. 2465.00
Chest, Mahogany, 2 Short, 3 Long Drawers, Bracket Feet, 44 x 40 In. 2240.00
Chest, Mahogany, 2 Short, 3 Long Drawers, Column Supports, c.1860, 46 1/2 In. 2016.00
Chest, Mahogany, 3 Drawers, Turned Wood Knobs, Ball Feet, 35 x 43 x 21 In. 450.00
Chest, Mahogany, 4 Graduated Drawers, Bracket Feet, c.1810, 30 x 25 1/2 In. 2240.00
Chest, Mahogany, 4 Graduated Drawers, Free-Standing Pilasters, 42 In. 660.00
Chest, Mahogany, 4 Raised Panel Drawers, Camphor Button Pulls, 15 x 13 3/4 In. 470.00
Chest, Mahogany, 5 Beaded Edge Drawers, Ogee Bracket Base, 41 x 48 x 22 In. 900.00
Chest, Mahogany, 5 Drawers, Beaded Edge, Bun Feet, 41 1/2 x 47 x 22 In. 840.00
Chest, Mahogany, 5 Drawers, Pullout Writing Surface, Brass, 31 1/2 x 30 x 17 In. 390.00
Chest, Mahogany, 6 Drawers, 1 Door, Folding Mirror, England, 42 x 23 x 35 In. 605.00
Chest, Mahogany, 6 Drawers, Stenciled Design, Swivel Mirror, 66 x 40 In. 5500.00
Chest, Mahogany, Block Front, Half-Round Columns, c.1860, 47 1/2 x 43 x 21 In. 1008.00
Chest, Mahogany, Bowfront, 2 Short, 3 Long Drawers, c.1840, 44 In. 1530.00
Chest, Mahogany, Bowfront, 2 Short, 3 Long Drawers, Scalloped Skirt, c.1860, 53 In. ... 1790.00
Chest, Mahogany, Bowfront, 3 Drawers, Lower Pullout Slide, c.1890, 54 In. 895.00
Chest, Mahogany, Bowfront, 3 Long Drawers, Splayed Feet, c.1840, 35 3/4 x 37 In. 390.00
Chest, Mahogany, Bowfront, 3 Over 4 Long Drawers, French Feet, 1790s, 44 In. 1175.00

Chest, Mahogany, Bowfront, 3 Short Drawers, Bracket Feet, c.1890, 30 1/2 In. 895.00
Chest, Mahogany, Bowfront, Floral Marquetry, 2 Lower, 4 Upper Drawers, 50 1/2 In. 770.00
Chest, Mahogany, Bowfront, Inlay, 2 Over 3 Drawers, Bracket Feet, 1850, 40 x 21 In. . . . 1680.00
Chest, Mahogany, Bowfront, Inlay, 2 Short, 3 Long Drawers, 1840, 20 x 40 In. 1120.00
Chest, Mahogany, Bowfront, Inlay, 2 Short, 3 Long Drawers, 1850, 40 x 21 In. 1680.00
Chest, Mahogany, Bowfront, Inlay, 3 Graduated Drawers, Splay Feet, c.1840, 43 In. 1630.00
Chest, Mahogany, Bowfront, Rope Twist, 4 Drawers, Brass Pulls, 36 3/4 In. 770.00
Chest, Mahogany, Brass Handles, Cabriole Legs, Pad Feet, 21 x 36 x 22 In. 795.00
Chest, Mahogany, Crossbanded Inlaid Top, 3 Long Drawers, c.1860, 46 1/2 In. 1232.00
Chest, Mahogany, Crossbanded, 2 Short, 3 Long Drawers, Bracket Feet, 1860, 45 In. 1565.00
Chest, Mahogany, Dovetailed, 3 Drawers, 1 On Top, 1800s, 16 x 15 x 9 In. 850.00
Chest, Mahogany, Fan Inlay Corners, 2 Short, 3 Long Drawers, c.1840, 43 x 42 1/2 In. . . . 1345.00
Chest, Mahogany, Federal, Inlaid, Reeded Edge, 4 Cock-Beaded Drawers, 41 x 42 In. 2530.00
Chest, Mahogany, Figural Panels Over 2 Small, 3 Large Drawers, 38 3/4 x 44 In. 330.00
Chest, Mahogany, Grained, 2 Short, 3 Long Drawers, c.1830, 40 In. 1790.00
Chest, Mahogany, Inlaid, Shaped Top Over 8 Long Drawers, 59 1/2 x 32 1/2 In. 615.00
Chest, Mahogany, Linenfold Inlay, 2 Short, 2 Long Drawers, 1870s, 32 In. 1230.00
Chest, Mahogany, Marble Top, 4 Drawers, Mirror Backsplash, 57 x 42 1/2 x 20 In. 390.00
Chest, Mahogany, Outset Corners, Fitted Case, 3 Drawers, 1800s, 45 In. 2350.00
Chest, Mahogany, Poplar, Pine, 4 Graduated Drawers, 39 x 43 In. 1790.00
Chest, Mahogany, Rectangular Top, 2 Short, 2 Long Drawers, c.1830, 35 x 34 1/2 In. 1345.00
Chest, Mahogany, Rectangular Top, 4 Drawers, c.1835, 42 x 43 x 18 3/4 In. 450.00
Chest, Mahogany, Serpentine Front, Graduated Drawers, Bracket Base, 37 x 38 In. 1090.00
Chest, Mahogany, Serpentine Front, Pullout Slide, 4 Drawers, 1930s, 33 x 33 In. 1055.00
Chest, Maple, 4 Dovetailed Drawers, Brass Pulls, Reeded Stiles, 41 1/2 In. 2035.00
Chest, Maple, 4 Graduated Drawers, Ogee Bracket Base, Brass Trim, 35 x 42 x 18 In. . . .   670.00
Chest, Maple, 6-Board, Vinegar Grain Painted, Red Brown, 22 3/4 x 41 In. 490.00
Chest, Maple, Birch, 4 Drawers, Framed Side Panels, Reeded Stiles, 41 x 42 In. 6600.00
Chest, Maple, Dovetailed Case, 2 Over 4 Drawers, 40 x 38 In. 3575.00
Chest, Maple, Dovetailed Case, Batwing Brasses, Bracket Feet, 58 1/2 In. 7700.00
Chest, Maple, Tiger Maple Drawer Fronts, Scrolled Feet 1230.00
Chest, Marquetry, Squares Between Legs, 2 Drawers, Leaf Pulls, 29 1/2 In. 1155.00
Chest, McCobb, Maple, Brass, 4 Drawers, Winchendon, 1948, 33 x 26 In. 1265.00
Chest, Mule, Mahogany, Top Opens To Void, 2 Pairs Of Short Drawers, 64 In. 4830.00
Chest, Mule, Pine, 2 Drawers, 2 False Fronts, Brass Pulls, 41 x 39 In. 660.00
Chest, Mule, Pine, Bootjack Ends, Base Drawer, Wooden Pulls, 35 x 38 In. 1320.00
Chest, Mule, Pine, Cream Band, Brown Leaves, Wood Knobs, 20th Century, 38 3/4 In. . . .   660.00
Chest, Mule, Pine, Red Paint, 2 Drawers, 3 False Fronts, 42 1/2 x 37 In. 2310.00
Chest, Mule, Pine, Scalloped Aprons, 2 False Fronts, Base Drawer, 3 Locks, 38 1/2 In. 880.00
Chest, Mule, Queen Anne, Pine, Brown Refinish, Faux 5 Drawers, 36 x 41 In. 1540.00
Chest, Napoleon III, Walnut, Marble Top, 4 Drawers, 19th Century, 37 x 48 x 22 In. 2875.00
Chest, Neoclassical, Mahogany Veneer, Rosewood Panel, Rectangular Top, 49 In. 1150.00
Chest, Neoclassical, Mahogany, 2 Short Over 1 Long Drawer, c.1840, 50 x 44 x 24 In. 330.00
Chest, Neoclassical, Mahogany, 5 Drawers, Mid 19th Century, 38 x 42 1/2 x 20 1/2 In. . . .   690.00
Chest, Neoclassical, Mahogany, Backsplash, Glass Pulls, 61 x 48 x 21 In. 1265.00
Chest, Neoclassical, Mahogany, Curly Maple, Drawer Opens To Desk, 44 x 43 x 22 In. . . . 1006.00

Furniture, Chest, Painted, 6-Board, Molding,
Feet, 10 1/2 x 15 3/4 x 8 1/4 In.

Furniture, Chest, Pine, 6-Board,
Mass., 1675-1710,
26 1/2 x 40 x 17 3/4 In.

Furniture, Chest, Pine, 6-Board, Painted, New
England, 23 1/2 x 40 1/2 x 17 1/2 In.

Furniture, Chest, Pine, Painted,
1875-1900, 21 3/4 x 43 x 30 5/8 In.

Chest, Neoclassical, Mahogany, Satinwood Inlaid, Marble Top, 32 x 47 x 20 In. 2300.00
Chest, Neoclassical, Mahogany, Silver, Dovetailed Sections, 27 x 32 x 28 1/2 In. 7475.00
Chest, Oak, Ash, 2 Short Over 3 Long Drawers, Fluted Pilasters, 1880s, 45 1/2 In. 1380.00
Chest, Oak, Domed Top, Dovetailed Case, Brass Lock, Pull, Dutch, 46 x 24 x 33 1/2 In. . . 385.00
Chest, Oak, Dovetailed Drawers & Case, 9 Drawers, Brass Pulls, 10 x 11 In. 385.00
Chest, Oak, Mahogany Veneer, 4 Drawers, Brass Pulls, 21 1/2 x 24 In. 220.00
Chest, On Stand, Queen Anne Style, Walnut, c.1900, 52 1/2 x 37 3/4 x 17 In. 1000.00
Chest, Oriental, Mahogany, Carved, Camphorwood Lining, Brass Lock, 19 x 35 x 18 In. . . 110.00
Chest, Painted, 6-Board, Molding, Feet, 10 1/2 x 15 3/4 x 8 1/4 In. . . . . *Illus* 1035.00
Chest, Painted, Green, Cream, Black Accents, Lidded Till Over 3 Drawers, 28 5/8 x 53 In. 4025.00
Chest, Pine, 2 Over 2 Drawers, Wooden Knobs, 34 x 35 In. 410.00
Chest, Pine, 2 Small Drawers, Green Panels, Brass Ring Pulls, 1889, 6 x 12 In. 690.00
Chest, Pine, 3 Beveled Front Drawers, Arched Apron, Wood Pulls, 11 x 13 3/4 In. 495.00
Chest, Pine, 3 Drawers, Porcelain Pulls, Backsplash, Bracket Base, 18 x 9 x 20 In. 470.00
Chest, Pine, 6-Board, Mass., 1675-1710, 26 1/2 x 40 x 17 3/4 In. . . . . *Illus* 4600.00
Chest, Pine, 6-Board, Painted, New England, 18th Century, 19 x 32 3/4 x 15 In. 1380.00
Chest, Pine, 6-Board, Painted, New England, 23 1/2 x 40 1/2 x 17 1/2 In. . . . . *Illus* 1955.00
Chest, Pine, 6-Board, Red Paint, Lift Top, Cutout Front Skirt, 23 1/2 x 44 In. 460.00
Chest, Pine, 6-Drawers, Molded Top Edge, Batwing Brasses, 45 x 38 x 18 In. 865.00
Chest, Pine, 9 Drawers, Bracket Feet, 19th Century, 48 x 26 x 12 In. 315.00
Chest, Pine, Black Paint, 3 Drawers, Scrolled Skirt, 34 1/2 x 27 1/2 In. 5465.00
Chest, Pine, Brown Paint, 4 Graduated Drawers, Applied Molding, 41 x 42 In. 575.00
Chest, Pine, Corner Posts, Lift-Out Section, Oval Brasses, 31 3/4 In. 935.00
Chest, Pine, Drawer, 2 Doors, Beaded Board Panels, 38 1/2 x 33 1/2 x 19 In. 1000.00
Chest, Pine, Hinged Lid, Molded Edge, Original Blue Paint, White, 17 In. 3565.00
Chest, Pine, Mahogany, Hinged Lid, Arched Feet, Sides, 1820-1830, 21 1/2 In. 2760.00
Chest, Pine, Painted, 1875-1900, 21 3/4 x 43 x 30 5/8 In. . . . . *Illus* 1840.00
Chest, Pine, Painted, 2 Drawers, Lift Top, 42 x 42 x 17 In. 4180.00
Chest, Pine, Painted, 3 Drawers, Backsplash, Scroll Legs, c.1840, 10 x 9 x 6 In. 975.00
Chest, Pine, Paneled Ends, Divided Top Drawer, 3 Lower Drawers, 26 x 19 1/2 In. 600.00
Chest, Pine, Scalloped Front Apron, 4 Drawers, Brass Pulls, 38 1/4 x 39 3/4 In. 1815.00
Chest, Pine, Stained, 2 Drawers, New England, 18th Century, 39 1/2 x 37 x 18 In. 690.00
Chest, Pine, Vinegar & Putty Painted, 6-Board, 19th Century, 14 1/4 x 36 x 17 3/4 In. 1840.00
Chest, Polychrome, Landscape, 3 Drawers, 19th Century, 31 1/2 x 28 x 18 In. 2530.00
Chest, Poplar, 4 Drawers, Brass Pulls, 35 1/2 x 32 1/2 In. 935.00
Chest, Poplar, 6 Drawers, 47 x 35 x 20 In. 495.00
Chest, Poplar, Lift Top Over Drawer, Applied Molding, Cutout Feet, 37 x 36 In. 1150.00
Chest, Queen Anne Style, Burl Walnut, Early 19th Century, 33 x 34 x 21 In. 2990.00
Chest, Queen Anne Style, Mahogany, 4 Drawers, Inset Leather Top, Bracket Feet 580.00
Chest, Queen Anne Style, Oyster Walnut, Satinwood Design, 38 1/2 x 41 x 22 In. 1840.00
Chest, Queen Anne Style, Walnut, Starburst Inlay, 2 Drawers, 38 1/2 x 40 x 21 In. 1380.00
Chest, Queen Anne, Burl Walnut, 2 Over 3 Graduated Drawers, 35 x 39 x 20 In. 1955.00
Chest, Queen Anne, Cedar, Lift Top, Mahogany, 36 1/2 x 17 x 34 In. 200.00
Chest, Queen Anne, Maple, 5 Drawers, New England, c.1760, 53 x 38 x 19 In. 3055.00
Chest, Queen Anne, Maple, Poplar, 5 Graduated Drawers, Cabriole Legs, 69 x 36 In. 5465.00
Chest, Queen Anne, Walnut, 2 Short Over 3 Long Drawers, 33 x 37 x 19 In. 2530.00
Chest, Queen Anne, Walnut, 3 Drawers, Early 18th Century, 37 x 37 3/4 x 22 3/4 In. 3220.00

Chest, Queen Anne, Walnut, 3 Over 2 Over 3 Drawers, Bracket Feet, Pa., 55 x 41 In.	5900.00
Chest, Red, White, Blue, 6-Board, 15 1/8 x 37 3/4 x 20 In. . . . . *Illus*	1725.00
Chest, Regency, Mahogany, 3 Graduated Drawers, 48 x 48 1/2 x 22 In.	980.00
Chest, Regency, Mahogany, 4 Drawers, Mid 19th Century, 41 x 49 1/2 x 23 3/4 In.	1380.00
Chest, Regency, Mahogany, Bowfront, 3 Graduated Drawers, Plinth Base, 38 In.	1380.00
Chest, Regency, Mahogany, Bowfront, Plinth Base, 40 1/2 x 43 x 21 In.	1725.00
Chest, Regency, Mahogany, Brass Band Inlay, 3 Drawers, Scalloped Skirt, 9 1/2 In.	250.00
Chest, Regency, Mahogany, Egyptian Caryatids, Projecting Ends, 35 x 47 x 22 1/2 In. . . .	1725.00
Chest, Rohde, Burl Walnut, Bowfront, 6 Drawers, 36 x 46 x 20 In.	920.00
Chest, Rosewood, Marble Top, Bronze Mounts, 7 Drawers, 53 x 13 x 23 In.	1400.00
Chest, Rupp Style, Black & Red Feathering, 4 Drawers, 40 x 19 1/2 x 49 In.	220.00
Chest, Rupp Style, Orange & Yellow Feathering, 4 Drawers, 40 x 19 x 49 In.	550.00
Chest, Scalloped Bracket Base, Divided Drawer Interiors, 17 3/4 x 11 In.	850.00
Chest, Shaker, Herb, Mahogany, 15 Drawers, Chamfered Edges, Molded Top, 72 x 12 In. . .	1060.00
Chest, Sheraton, Birch, 4 Drawers, Banded Inlay, Button Feet, Backsplash, Thistle Pulls . .	3300.00
Chest, Sheraton, Cherry, 2 Over 3 Drawers, Inlay, Tab Construction, 18 x 10 x 20 In.	1980.00
Chest, Sheraton, Cherry, 2 Over 3 Graduated Drawers, Feet, 42 x 20 x 45 1/2 In.	1320.00
Chest, Sheraton, Cherry, 4 Drawers, Turned Feet, 3-Board Top, 39 x 19 3/4 x 38 In.	1650.00
Chest, Sheraton, Cherry, 4 Drawers, Turned Legs, Beading, Escutcheons, 43 x 20 x 44 In.	1760.00
Chest, Sheraton, Cherry, Applied Edge, Paneled, 4 Drawers, 44 1/2 x 39 x 19 In.	880.00
Chest, Sheraton, Cherry, Gallery Top, 4 Cock-Beaded Drawers, 44 1/2 x 39 1/2 x 20 In. . .	1375.00
Chest, Sheraton, Cherry, Pine, Bowfront, Curly Maple Veneer Drawer, Gold Refinish	1760.00
Chest, Sheraton, Mahogany, Bowfront, 4 Drawers, New England, 1825, 42 x 43 In.	880.00
Chest, Sheraton, Mahogany, Cherry, Bowfront, Reeded Panels, 44 1/2 x 41 x 22 In.	1210.00
Chest, Sheraton, Mahogany, Figured Maple, 4 Drawers, Scallop Apron, 41 x 40 x 20 In. . .	1100.00
Chest, Sheraton, Pine, 5 Dovetailed Drawers, 54 x 21 3/8 x 43 In.	470.00
Chest, Sheraton, Softwood, 3 Dovetailed Drawers, Turned Legs, 12 3/4 x 13 3/4 In.	745.00
Chest, Softwood, 2 Drawers, Porcelain Knobs, Backsplash, Shelf, 16 x 12 In.	80.00
Chest, Spice, Butternut & Pine, 3 Drawers, Divided Interiors, 2-Door Top, 30 In.	165.00
Chest, Spice, Oak, Paneled Door, 8 Interior Drawers, 14 1/2 x 14 In.	4800.00
Chest, Spice, Step Back, Painted Labels, 15 Drawers, 10 1/2 In.	300.00
Chest, Spice, Walnut, 14 Bird's-Eye Maple Drawers, 19th Century, 17 1/2 In.	2475.00
Chest, Stickley Bros., 2 Over 4 Drawers, Backsplash, Brass Pulls, 40 x 38 In.	2875.00
Chest, Stickley Bros., Pivoting Mirror, 2 Over 4 Drawers, Metal Tag, 67 x 36 In.	2185.00
Chest, Sugar, Handles On Cover, Handles On Body, 32 1/2 In.	560.00
Chest, Teak, 4 Center Drawers, 2 Carved Doors, Chinese, 34 x 50 x 20 In.	345.00
Chest, Tiger Maple, 2 Stepped Over 4 Drawers, 50 x 40 1/2 x 19 In.	2185.00
Chest, Tiger Maple, c.1825, 46 x 45 In.	2645.00
Chest, Various Woods, Marquetry, Geometric, Wallpaper Lined, c.1900, 25 x 12 In.	2400.00
Chest, Victorian, Mahogany, Projecting Top, Mid 19th Century, 42 x 46 x 21 In.	920.00
Chest, Victorian, Mahogany, Serpentine, 4 Graduated Drawers, 44 x 22 x 37 In.	385.00
Chest, Victorian, Walnut, 2 Over 2 Large Drawers, Bracket Feet, 42 x 29 x 30 In.	200.00
Chest, Victorian, Walnut, Maple, 6 Drawers, Crest, Scallops, 40 x 20 x 46 In.	220.00
Chest, W. Nutting, Curly Maple, 4 Drawers, Bracket Feet, 37 x 38 x 19 In. . . . . *Illus*	5610.00
Chest, Walnut, 2 Over 3 Drawers, Spool Half Columns, c.1855, 25 x 18 x 13 1/2 In.	4180.00
Chest, Walnut, 2 Over 3 Graduated Drawers, 2 Secret Drawers, Lock, 48 In.	1980.00
Chest, Walnut, 3 Drawers, Domed Mirror, Plinth Base, 1800s, 42 x 29 In.	200.00
Chest, Walnut, 3 Long Drawers, Shield Drawer Pulls, Paw Feet, 37 x 36 In.	2415.00

Furniture, Chest, Red, White, Blue, 6-Board,
15 1/8 x 37 3/4 x 20 In.

Furniture, Chest,
W. Nutting, Curly
Maple, 4 Drawers,
Bracket Feet,
37 x 38 x 19 In.

Furniture, Chest, Walnut, Burl Veneer,
Carved, Glass Pulls, 13 1/2 x 14 1/4 In.

Furniture, Chest, Walnut, Inlaid, Yellow Pine,
North Carolina, 1795-1830, 46 x 42 x 20 In.

Chest, Walnut, 4 Drawers, Beveled Mirror, Glove Box, Brass Ring Pulls, 67 x 36 In. 480.00
Chest, Walnut, 4 Graduated Drawers, Carved Feet, Wood Knobs, 17 x 16 x 11 1/2 In. 460.00
Chest, Walnut, 4 Over 2 Side-By-Side Drawers, 1880s, 63 x 57 In. 950.00
Chest, Walnut, 4 Over 6 Drawers, Mushroom-Turned Knobs, 30 1/2 x 39 1/2 In. 1740.00
Chest, Walnut, 6 Dovetailed Drawers, Dust Shelves, 38 7/8 In. 3025.00
Chest, Walnut, 6 Drawers, Marquetry Top Drawer, Side Lock, 1880s, 61 1/2 In. 1345.00
Chest, Walnut, Bowfront, Carved, Marble Top, 3 Drawers, Swivel Mirror, 60 x 38 x 20 In.   530.00
Chest, Walnut, Burl Veneer, Carved, Glass Pulls, 13 1/2 x 14 1/4 In. . . . . *Illus*   3335.00
Chest, Walnut, Carved Columns, 7 Burled Drawers, Side Lock, 60 x 20 x 40 In. 2240.00
Chest, Walnut, Domed Top, Carved Scrolled, Fruit Vines, 28 x 21 1/2 In. 5700.00
Chest, Walnut, Inlaid Circles, 2 Short Over 3 Long Drawers, 33 1/2 In. 7200.00
Chest, Walnut, Inlaid, Yellow Pine, North Carolina, 1795-1830, 46 x 42 x 20 In. . . . . *Illus*   39600.00
Chest, Walnut, Marquetry, Mirror, 3 Over 4 Graduated Drawers, Bun Feet, 40 x 20 In. . . .   785.00
Chest, Walnut, Pine Backboard, 3 Drawers, 19th Century, 28 x 19 1/2 x 13 In. 6380.00
Chest, Walnut, Scalloped Apron, 4 Dovetailed Drawers, French Feet, 36 x 41 1/2 In. 1540.00
Chest, Walnut, Scalloped Aprons, 2 Over 4 Drawers, Brass Pulls, 54 1/2 In. 1650.00
Chest, Walnut, Serpentine Front, Flame Veneer, Dovetailed Drawers, 16 1/4 In. 470.00
Chest, Wellington, Mahogany, Inlaid, 6 Graduated Drawers, 42 1/2 x 18 x 15 In. 450.00
Chest, Wellington, Molded Edge, 7 Drawers, Pilasters, England, 43 x 17 x 20 In. 335.00
Chest, Wellington, Satinwood, Painted Flowers, 6 Short Graduated Drawers, 19 x 16 In. . .   840.00
Chest, White Pine, Blue Paint, 6-Board, Mid 19th Century, 17 1/2 x 35 1/3 x 15 In. 980.00
Chest, William & Mary Style, Boxwood, Oyster Burl Walnut, 37 x 44 1/2 x 24 In. 2185.00
Chest, William & Mary Style, Burl Walnut, 5 Drawers, 38 1/2 x 40 1/2 x 19 In. 2760.00
Chest, William & Mary, Burl Walnut, Inlaid Radiant Star, 2 Over 3 Drawers, 33 In. 2300.00
Chest, William IV, Mahogany, 4 Graduated Drawers, Doric Columns, 38 In. 1725.00
Chest, William IV, Mahogany, Bowfront, 2 Aligned Drawers, 54 1/2 x 20 1/2 In. 575.00
Chest, William IV, Mahogany, Bowfront, 3 Graduated Drawers, 51 x 47 x 21 In. 1095.00
Chest, William IV, Mahogany, Bowfront, Flame Veneer, 2 Over 3 Drawers, 44 x 52 In. . .   840.00
Chest, Wine, George III, Mahogany, Late 18th Century, 36 x 18 x 19 In. 750.00
Chest, Yellow Pine, 18th Century, 33 x 38 3/4 x 19 In. 5100.00
Chest-On-Chest, 2 Short Drawers, 3 Lower Drawers, Bracket Feet, 1780s, 72 x 42 1/2 In.   3680.00
Chest-On-Chest, Chippendale, Cherry, Quarter Columns, New Brasses, 1780, 70 In. 5230.00
Chest-On-Chest, Chippendale, Walnut, Figured, Pa., c.1780, 75 x 43 x 24 In. 13200.00
Chest-On-Chest, Egg & Dart Molding, 3 Short, 3 Long Drawers, 80 1/2 In. 7200.00
Chest-On-Chest, George III Style, Mahogany, 8 Drawers, c.1860, 72 3/4 x 45 x 21 In. . . .   2015.00
Chest-On-Chest, George III, Mahogany, 2 Cock-Beaded Aligned Drawers, 71 In. 2300.00
Chest-On-Chest, George III, Mahogany, 2 Short Over 6 Drawers, 1790 . . . .   7800.00
Chest-On-Chest, Georgian, Mahogany, 2 Over 3 Cock-Beaded Drawers, 68 x 47 x 21 In. .   2420.00
Chest-On-Chest, Mahogany, 4 Long Graduated Drawers, Early 20th Century, 50 In. 615.00
Chest-On-Chest, Mahogany, Burl, Serpentine, 4 Over 3 Drawers, Butler's Slide, 64 In. . . .   3910.00
Chest-On-Chest, Mahogany, Dentil Frieze, Ogee Feet, Continental, 76 In. 3000.00
Chest-On-Chest, Mahogany, Upper 2 Over 3 Long Drawers, Lower Drawers, 70 In. 1265.00
Chest-On-Chest, Pine, Red Paint, Early 19th Century, 38 3/4 x 42 x 20 In. 1955.00

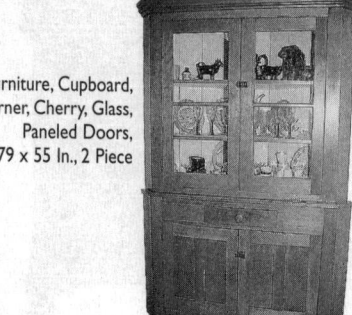

Furniture, Cupboard,
Corner, Cherry, Glass,
Paneled Doors,
79 x 55 In., 2 Piece

Furniture, Chest-On-Chest, Poplar,
New England, 37 x 86 x 18 In.

Chest-On-Chest, Pine, Red Paint, New England, 18th Century, 42 x 38 x 17 3/4 In. 1150.00
Chest-On-Chest, Poplar, New England, 37 x 86 x 18 In. . . . . *Illus* 1150.00
Chest-On-Chest, Poplar, Pine, Grain Painted, 19th Century, 37 x 38 1/2 x 17 1/2 In. 805.00
Chest-On-Chest, Queen Anne, Maple, 3 Over 3 Over 2 Graduated Drawers, 69 x 41 In. . . . 3525.00
Chest-On-Stand, Chinese, Lacquered, Pictorial Scenes, Brass Hasps, 36 x 26 1/2 In. 935.00
Chest-On-Stand, George III Style, 4 Drawers, 19th Century, 49 1/2 x 51 1/2 x 22 In. 1790.00
Chest-On-Stand, Mahogany, 2 Short Drawers, c.1890, 36 1/2 In. 730.00
Chest-On-Stand, Oriental, Low, Rectangular, Brass Handles, 18 x 39 3/4 x 22 1/2 In. 520.00
Chiffonnier, Art Deco, Bird's-Eye Maple, 3 Drawers, 2 Doors, Bakelite, Brass 335.00
Chiffonnier, Louis XV, Gilt Metal, 20th Century, 28 1/2 x 14 x 11 1/2 In. 460.00
Chiffonnier, Mahogany, 2 Doors, Multidrawer Interior, Brass Mounts, 53 x 26 x 38 In. . . . 1515.00
Coat Rack, Art Deco, Chrome Hangers, Marble Base, 68 1/2 In. 150.00
Coat Rack, J. & J. Kohn, Bent Beech, Stained, 1905, 80 x 27 In. 3300.00
Coat Rack, Mahogany, Fluted Column, Cabriole Legs, 3 Brass Hooks 99.00
Coat Rack, P. Derby & Co., Pyramid Shaft, 8 Hangers, Buttressed Base, 73 x 19 In. 145.00
Coat Rack, Painted Bronze, 5 Hooks, 1880s, 13 In. 465.00
Coat Rack, Wall, Twig, Bentwood Heart & Horseshoe, 5 Pegs, 20th Century, 34 x 20 In. . . 145.00
Coat Rack, Yogi Bear & Boo Boo, Die Cut, Height Marker, 47 1/2 In. 45.00
Coffer, Charles I, Oak, Paneled Front, Carved Leaves, Stile Legs, Cover, 20 x 39 x 17 In. . 1265.00
Coffer, Charles I, Wainscot, Floral, Scroll & Date 1660 Carving, 52 x 22 x 27 In. 345.00
Coffer, Ebony, Pewter, Inlaid Hard Stones, Late 19th Century, 1 1/2 x 3 3/4 x 3 In. 345.00
Coffer, English Mahogany, Hinged Cover, Early 20th Century, 8 1/2 x 14 x 10 1/2 In. 190.00
Coffer, George III, Mahogany, Handle, Divided Interior, 5 1/2 x 8 1/2 x 5 3/4 In. 489.00
Coffer, Mahogany, Cover, Brass Plaque, Early 20th Century, 9 x 13 3/4 x 10 1/2 In. 170.00
Coffer, Regency, Mahogany, Sarcophagus, Satin Lining, Gilt Paw Feet, 6 3/4 In. 635.00
Coffer, Renaissance Revival, Walnut, Brass, Strapwork, 8 1/2 x 13 1/2 x 9 3/4 In. 1495.00
Coffer, Rosehead & Square Nails, 3 Compartments, 25 x 73 In. 550.00
Commode, 1 Top Over 2 Side Drawers, Door, Towel Bar 235.00
Commode, Ash, Cushion Frieze Drawer, 1 Door, Block Feet, 1870s, 30 1/2 In., Pair 1840.00
Commode, Black Lacquered, 1 Lower Door, Oriental Landscape, 1880s, 33 x 40 In. 3450.00
Commode, Bombe, Painted, Figured Marble Top, 1770s, 37 1/2 x 35 1/2 In. 2070.00
Commode, Charles X, Walnut, Gray Marble Top, 3 Drawers, Bracket Feet, 37 1/2 In. 2990.00
Commode, Charles X, Walnut, Marble, 2 Over 3 Drawers, Mirror, Secret Drawer 6800.00
Commode, Chippendale, Maple, Shaped Arms, Cabriole Legs, 52 x 27 In. 1175.00
Commode, Elm, Ogee Frieze Drawer, Cupboard Door, Bracket Feet, 36 1/2 x 27 In. 1725.00
Commode, Empire, Elm, Charcoal Marble Top, Frieze Drawer, 35 1/2 In. 25.00
Commode, Empire, Mahogany, Lift Top, Drawer, 2 Doors, Bracket Feet, 29 x 26 In. 345.00
Commode, Empire, Mahogany, Marble, 2 Carved Maiden Doors, 39 x 49 x 24 In. 1725.00
Commode, Figured Veneers, Base Drawer, Cast Hardware, Marble Top, 32 1/2 In. 275.00
Commode, French Empire, Bronze Dore, Marble Top, c.1810, 35 x 51 x 23 In. 4025.00
Commode, French Restauration, Mahogany, Marble Top, 35 1/2 x 50 3/4 x 23 In. 1380.00
Commode, French Restauration, Mahogany, Marble Top, 4 Drawers, 36 x 48 In. 1610.00
Commode, French Restauration, Walnut, Drawers, 19th Century, 35 1/2 x 49 1/2 x 22 In. . 2760.00
Commode, French Restauration, Walnut, Marble Top, Mid 19th Century, 39 x 48 x 27 In. . 1495.00

Commode, Fruitwood, Marble Top, 4 Graduated Drawers, 1850s, 39 In. 1495.00
Commode, Fruitwood, Serpentine Top, 3 Drawers, Floral Frieze, 1780s, 34 1/2 In. 8625.00
Commode, George III, Mahogany, 2 Drawers, Square Legs, 32 x 16 In. 2300.00
Commode, George III, Mahogany, Galleried Tray Top, 2 Doors, 29 In. 1610.00
Commode, George III, Mahogany, Gallery Top, 30 x 16 x 14 In., Pair 1150.00
Commode, George III, Mahogany, Late 18th Century, 28 x 20 x 17 1/2 In. 865.00
Commode, Italian Walnut, Polychrome, 3 Long Drawers, 36 x 54 x 24 1/2 In. 4370.00
Commode, J. Widdicomb, Inlay, Drawer, Panel Doors, 3 Drawers, Art Deco, 44 x 33 In. . . 805.00
Commode, Louis Philippe, Walnut, Gray Marble Top, 40 x 48 1/2 x 22 In. 980.00
Commode, Louis Philippe, Walnut, Marble Top, Bun Feet, 36 x 51 x 23 In. 1725.00
Commode, Louis XV Style, Beech, 2 Drawers, 20th Century, 37 x 47 x 19 In. 775.00
Commode, Louis XV Style, Beech, 3 Drawers, 1900s, 35 x 46 x 22 In., Pair 1955.00
Commode, Louis XV Style, Bronze Mounted, Painted, 33 x 47 x 23 In. 10200.00
Commode, Louis XV Style, Kingwood, Marble Top, c.1900, 30 1/2 x 29 x 16 1/2 In. 980.00
Commode, Louis XV Style, Kingwood, Marble Top, Drawers, Bronze Sabots, 44 x 18 In. 1120.00
Commode, Louis XV Style, Tulipwood, c.1900, 35 1/2 x 37 x 19 1/2 In., Pair 13200.00
Commode, Louis XV, 3 Long Drawers, Mid 1700s, 36 x 53 x 27 In. 3740.00
Commode, Louis XV, Fruitwood, French Provincial, 15 x 21 3/4 x 11 3/4 In. 690.00
Commode, Louis XV, Gray Serpentine Marble Top, 2 Drawers, 34 1/2 x 18 In. 1955.00
Commode, Louis XV, Marquetry, 2 Drawers, Marble Top, 33 x 28 x 19 In., Pair 460.00
Commode, Louis XV, Serpentine Top, 3 Drawers 4025.00
Commode, Louis XV, Tulipwood, Bombe, 2 Deep Drawers, Splayed Legs, 34 In. 1100.00
Commode, Louis XV-XVI, Mahogany, Marquetry, 3 Drawers, 37 x 55 x 21 In. 4600.00
Commode, Louis XVI Style, Fruitwood, Planked Top, 34 x 41 3/4 x 22 In. 2070.00
Commode, Louis XVI Style, Kingwood, Marble Top, Bronze, 34 1/2 x 28 1/2 x 15 In. . . . 900.00
Commode, Louis XVI Style, Mahogany, Brass, Early 20th Century, 32 x 32 x 16 In. 1150.00
Commode, Louis XVI Style, Mahogany, Rectangular Marble Top, 2 Drawers, 36 In. 865.00
Commode, Louis XVI Style, Oak, 2 Long Drawers, Early 19th Century, 29 x 44 x 23 In. . . 690.00
Commode, Louis XVI Style, Porcelain, Gilt Bronze, 39 1/2 x 73 1/2 x 27 3/4 In. 23750.00
Commode, Louis XVI Style, Tulipwood, Ormolu, 20th Century, 36 x 52 1/2 x 22 1/2 In. . 4140.00
Commode, Louis XVI, Molded Rectangular Top, 2 Long Drawers, 33 x 24 In. 5750.00
Commode, Mahogany, Bed Steps, Hinged, Turned Legs, c.1850, 19 x 19 3/4 x 19 3/4 In. . 560.00
Commode, Mahogany, False Doors, 3 Drawers, Tambour Roll Front, England, 24 x 19 In. 770.00
Commode, Mahogany, Fossilized Top, Side Columns, 20th Century, 41 In. 1380.00
Commode, Mahogany, Marble Top, 2 Drawers, Stretcher Shelf, c.1900, 27 x 13 1/2 In. . . 430.00
Commode, Mahogany, Parquetry, Drawer, France, 30 x 21 In. 1570.00
Commode, Napoleon III, Marble Top, Tortoiseshell Frieze, 42 1/2 In., Pair 5980.00
Commode, Neoclassical, Fruitwood, Marble Top, 2 Drawers, 35 x 51 x 24 In., Pair 7475.00
Commode, Neoclassical, Gilt, Cream Paint, Rectangular Top, Italy, 36 x 72 x 23 In. 5290.00
Commode, Regency, Mahogany, Bed Step, 3 Green Upholstered Treads, 27 1/2 In. 630.00
Commode, Regency, Serpentine Gray Marble Top, 3 Drawers, 34 x 24 3/4 In. 9600.00
Commode, Rococo, Walnut, Serpentine Banded Top, 2 Ormolu Drawers, 30 In. 1725.00
Commode, Rosewood, Bombe, Serpentine White Marble Top, Bun Feet, 43 1/2 In. 1725.00
Commode, Star, Banded Inlay, 30 x 17 1/4 x 12 1/2 In. 1035.00
Commode, Walnut, Fitted Interior, Drawers, Pedestal Base, 43 x 55 x 23 In. 3450.00
Commode, Walnut, Frieze Drawer, 3 Central Drawers, Bun Feet, 35 1/2 In. 4390.00
Commode, Walnut, Marble Top, Ogee Frieze Drawer, Lower Drawers, 1840s, 37 1/2 In. . 2530.00
Commode, Wood, Serpentine Front, Boule Cartouche, Paneled Doors, 44 x 76 In. 2800.00
Console, Art Deco, Bronze, Painted, Marble, Cone-Shape Legs, 32 x 33 x 13 In. 865.00
Console, Art Deco, Wrought Iron, Marble Top, Stylized Leaf Standard, 35 x 34 In. 2590.00
Console, Art Deco, Wrought Iron, Painted, Marble, Scrolled Legs, 48 x 17 1/2 In. 520.00
Console, Art Deco, Wrought Iron, Parcel Gilt, Marble, 1925, 33 x 56 x 17 In. 3900.00
Console, Charles X, Mahogany, Inlaid, Twist Legs, 61 1/2 x 42 1/2 x 24 In. 1495.00
Console, Cherry, Bird's-Eye Maple Veneer Apron, c.1800, 29 1/2 x 35 x 17 In. 1955.00
Console, Empire, Mahogany, Bronze Mount, Rectangular, Mirror, 36 x 61 In., Pair 4900.00
Console, Frankl, Johnson Furniture Co., 39 3/4 x 20 x 29 1/2 In. 1265.00
Console, Frankl, Mahogany, Laminated Cork, c.1952, 71 1/4 In. 7760.00
Console, George III Style, Mahogany, Demilune, 19th Century, 29 x 47 x 22 1/2 In. 520.00
Console, Gilbert Poillerat, Wrought Iron, Parcel Gilt, Marble, 34 x 43 x 15 In. 9000.00
Console, Giltwood, Marble Top, Fluted Legs, 1840s, 33 x 43 1/2 In. 3900.00
Console, Giltwood, Marble Top, Pierced Frieze On C-Scroll Legs, 1880s, 36 x 56 In. . . . 2300.00
Console, Italian Rococo, Carved, 2-Color Marble Top, Hoof Feet, 37 x 22 x 44 In. 4200.00
Console, Jacobean Style, Oak, D-Shape, Foldover, Swing Leg, 33 x 16 1/2 x 29 In. 260.00

Console, Limbert, Mahogany, Cut Corner Top, 6-Leg Base, 66 x 21 x 29 In. 7480.00
Console, Louis Philippe, Mahogany, Marble Top, 37 1/2 x 44 1/2 x 18 In. 2530.00
Console, Louis XV, Giltwood, Marble Top, Leaf Frieze, 35 x 58 x 25 In. 3740.00
Console, Louis XVI, D-Shape Marble Top, Garland Apron, 35 1/2 x 18 In., Pair 2760.00
Console, Louis XVI, Gilt, D-Shape Marble Top, 36 x 58 1/2 x 22 In. 1265.00
Console, Louis XVI, Mahogany, Amboyna, Marble, 2 Shelves, 36 x 48 In. 8400.00
Console, Mahogany, Drawer, Urn-Shaped Legs, Maddox Tables, Jamestown, N.Y., 30 In. . . 110.00
Console, Mahogany, Frieze Drawer, Recessed Plinth, 37 3/4 x 37 x 17 In. 6900.00
Console, Mahogany, Inlaid, D-Shape, Tapered Legs, Spade Feet, c.1900, 80 x 20 In. 450.00
Console, Mahogany, Paneled Back, Scroll Supports, 2 Doors, 33 1/2 x 55 In. 4760.00
Console, Mahogany, Paneled Frieze, Joined To Lower Shelf, 1820s, 34 x 36 In. 3220.00
Console, Marble Top, Swag & Dolphin Relief Design, 33 x 68 In. 1955.00
Console, Marble, Bronze, 1928, 63 x 15 3/4 In. 12000.00
Console, Napoleon III, Walnut, Kingwood, Bronze Dore, 1 Drawer, 1890, 45 x 18 In. 3800.00
Console, Regency, Mahogany, Gray Variegated Marble Top, Rectangular, 36 In. 7200.00
Console, Rococo Revival, Rosewood, Scroll Carved Backsplash, 47 x 49 x 19 In. 3220.00
Console, Rococo, Beech, Onyx Top, Leaf Carved, 34 x 17 x 11 In., Pair 3740.00
Console, Rococo, Carved Wood, Dolphin Base, Marble, Rectangular, 47 In., Pair 9780.00
Console, Rosewood, Marble Top, Serpentine Front, 37 x 62 1/2 x 19 In. 900.00
Console, Walnut, Charcoal Marble Top, 1 Drawer, 2 Lower Shelves, 1850s, 34 In. 2990.00
Console, William IV, Walnut, Marble Top, 19th Century, 33 x 33 3/4 x 16 1/2 In. 1840.00
Console, Wrought Iron, Marble Top, Pierced, Scrolling Frieze, 42 x 17 In. 4406.00
Costumer, G. Stickley, Double, Hooks, Red Decal, 72 In. 1380.00
Costumer, Stickley Bros., Double Tapered Post, Copper Hooks, 17 x 20 x 69 In. 460.00
Cradle, Bentwood, Canopy, 80 x 57 x 24 In. 1000.00
Cradle, Bentwood, Rockers, Late 19th Century, 32 x 38 In. 85.00
Cradle, Charles X, Mahogany, Barrel Shape, Early 19th Century, 56 x 41 x 21 1/4 In. 5750.00
Cradle, Cherry, Heart Cutouts, Dovetailed, Canopy, 24 x 41 x 28 1/2 In. 360.00
Cradle, Dovetailed, Arched Headboard, Cutout Heart, Scrolled End Rockers, 22 x 38 In. . . 615.00
Cradle, Mahogany, Heart Cutout, Handles, Scrolled Terminals, 45 x 25 x 25 In. 300.00
Cradle, Pine, Grain Painted, Rocker, 27 x 42 In. 170.00
Cradle, S. Simmons, Curly Maple, Pierced Cutouts Form Handles, 20 x 41 In. 385.00
Cradle, Softwood, Hooded, Heart Cutout Handholds, Rockers, Scrolled Ends, Pa. 110.00
Cradle, Tiger Maple, Heart Cutouts, Shaped Ends, Pennsylvania 770.00
Cradle, Victorian, Walnut, Turned Supports, Burled Panel, Swinging 275.00
Cradle, Walnut, Dovetailed, Scalloped Heart Baseboard, 24 x 44 x 19 In. 770.00
Cradle, Walnut, Hooded, Dovetailed, Branded W. Weaver, 1876, 9 1/4 x 12 In. 145.00
Credenza, G. Nelson, Walnut Veneer, Masonite Sliding Doors, Steel Legs, 19 x 70 In. . . . 2875.00
Credenza, Porcelain Mounted, Ebonized, Parcel Gilt, Late 1800s, 43 x 72 x 18 In. 4600.00
Credenza, Robsjohn-Gibbings, Mahogany, Brass Legs, 3 Drawers, 32 1/2 In. 1035.00
Credenza, Tuscan Style, Oak, Carved, Drawers, Doors, c.1900, 11 3/8 x 17 x 7 1/2 In. . . . 375.00
Credenza, Walnut Veneer, 2 Sliding Doors, Shelves, Chrome Legs, 55 3/4 In. 715.00
Crib, Birch, Tall Tapered Posts, Urn Supports, 69 1/2 In. 220.00
Crib, Federal, Cherry, Column-Turned Posts, 4 Urn-Turned Finials, 40 x 48 In. 120.00
Crib, Tiger Maple, Turned Posts, Arched Ends, Rockers, c.1820, 35 x 35 1/2 In. 1200.00
Crib, Tiger Maple, Turned Posts, Cheese-Cutter Rockers, Arched Ends, 1820 . . . . 1200.00
Crib, Wallace Nutting, Walnut 1540.00
Cupboard, 3 Shelves, Door Below, H Hinges, 18th Century 3740.00
Cupboard, Arched Aprons, 2 Doors, Inset Panels, Interior Shelves, Inner Drawers, 72 In. . . 220.00
Cupboard, Art Deco, Etched Glass, Grain Painted, Coffee Grinder Attached To Door 945.00
Cupboard, Arts & Crafts, Oak, Step Back, Beveled Glass Panes, 77 x 40 In. 995.00
Cupboard, B. Harter, Pewter, Pine, Poplar, 1 Base Door, 3 Shelves, 80 In. 1210.00
Cupboard, Bonnet Top, 2 Sections, Bombay Front, Inlaid, Dutch, 93 x 20 x 50 In. 5040.00
Cupboard, Bowfront, Flame Veneer, 2 Doors, 3 Drawers, 4 Shelves, 46 In. 1760.00
Cupboard, Bracket Feet, Scalloped Apron, Panel Doors, Cornice, 39 x 17 x 76 In. 605.00
Cupboard, Charles II, Oak, Geometric Molded Door, Drawer, Ball Feet, 25 x 12 x 24 In. . . 1035.00
Cupboard, Charles X, Oak, Marble Top, Mid 19th Century, 41 x 45 1/2 x 23 In. 1265.00
Cupboard, Cherry, Blind Doors, Ebonized Trim, Red Wash, c.1860, 81 x 48 In. 4500.00
Cupboard, Cherry, Dovetailed Case, 4 Raised Panels On Door, Brass Lever, 39 In. 1375.00
Cupboard, Chimney, Mixed Woods, Open, 5 Shelves, 77 In. 770.00
Cupboard, Chimney, Pine, Polka Dots, Paneled Door, Shelves, Iron Latch, 75 1/2 In. 4070.00
Cupboard, Corner, 2 Sections, Marquetry, Dutch, 80 x 32 In. 2800.00
Cupboard, Corner, 4 Paneled Glazed Doors, Canted Corners, Red, Gray Paint, 20 In. 6325.00

Cupboard, Corner, Barrel Back, Arched Door, Leaded Glass Pane, 2 Shelves, 48 1/4 In. . . . 990.00
Cupboard, Corner, Barrel Back, Yellow Paint, 2 Over 2 Doors, 3 Shelves, 97 x 49 In. 8960.00
Cupboard, Corner, Cherry, 2 Base Paneled Doors, 1 Top Door, Wavy Glass, 84 1/4 In. . . . 6875.00
Cupboard, Corner, Cherry, Bracket Base, Panel Doors, Molded Cornice, 21 x 87 In. 10725.00
Cupboard, Corner, Cherry, Glass, Paneled Doors, 79 x 55 In., 2 Piece . . . . *Illus* 1320.00
Cupboard, Corner, Cherry, Mid 19th Century, 82 x 45 x 24 In. 1150.00
Cupboard, Corner, Cherry, Molded Cornice, Glazed, Paneled Doors, 32 x 80 In. 2415.00
Cupboard, Corner, Cherry, Mullioned Doors, Shelves, Fitted Interior, 87 In. 2300.00
Cupboard, Corner, Cherry, Pine, 1 Top Door, 2 Blind Base Doors, 1850, 42 x 84 In. 3300.00
Cupboard, Corner, Cherry, Pine, Rectangular Top, 2 Aligned Drawers, 90 In. 6325.00
Cupboard, Corner, Cherry, Shelf In 2-Door Base, Top Doors, Shelves, 83 1/2 In. 1925.00
Cupboard, Corner, Chestnut, Walnut, 12 Panes, Porringer Shelves, Ogee Bracket Feet . . . 2970.00
Cupboard, Corner, Chippendale, Cherry, 2 Sections, 3 Doors, Drawer, 88 x 47 In. 2820.00
Cupboard, Corner, Chippendale, Tiger Maple, 12 Pane Glass Door, 82 x 26 In. 3960.00
Cupboard, Corner, Chippendale, Walnut, c.1800, 84 x 52 In. 2760.00
Cupboard, Corner, Federal Style, Mahogany, 2 Sections, Charm Furniture Co. 880.00
Cupboard, Corner, Fielded Panels, 3 Shaped Shelves, H Hinges, 87 x 47 In. 1265.00
Cupboard, Corner, George III, Pine, Hanging, Arched Glazed Panel Door, 41 In. 2990.00
Cupboard, Corner, Hanging, Blue Painted Interior, Shaped Shelves, 23 3/4 In. 1900.00
Cupboard, Corner, Hanging, Georgian, Oak, Brass Mounted, Tiered, 41 x 24 1/2 x 17 In. . . 2070.00
Cupboard, Corner, Hanging, Mahogany, Blind Door, 3 Interior Shelves, 38 x 27 x 18 In. . 220.00
Cupboard, Corner, Hanging, Mahogany, Inlaid, Cornice, Glazed Door, 49 x 25 1/2 In. . . . 1210.00
Cupboard, Corner, Hanging, Oak, Blind Door, Stepped Cornice, 44 x 30 x 22 In. 385.00
Cupboard, Corner, Hanging, Oak, Raised Panel Door, 2 Shelves, 38 x 28 In. 495.00
Cupboard, Corner, Hanging, Pine, Open Shelf, Scrolled Crest, 41 x 20 In. 440.00
Cupboard, Corner, Mahogany, 2 Upper Doors, 8 Panes, 2 Lower Doors, 70 In. 375.00
Cupboard, Corner, Maple, 2 Base Doors, 6 Panes, Batwing Pulls, 75 In. 1980.00
Cupboard, Corner, Maple, 2 Base Raised Panel Doors, 2 Top Doors, 72 In. 1650.00
Cupboard, Corner, Painted, 2 Top Doors, 2 Base Doors, 81 3/4 x 45 1/2 In. 2640.00
Cupboard, Corner, Pine, 2 Glass Doors Over 2 Paneled Doors, 85 x 66 In. 4600.00
Cupboard, Corner, Pine, 9-Pane Door, Drawers, Wooden Knobs & Latch, 1920 . . . . 900.00
Cupboard, Corner, Pine, Continental, 18th Century 2990.00
Cupboard, Corner, Pine, Dentil Molding, Paneled Doors, 41 In. 660.00
Cupboard, Corner, Pine, Paneled Doors Top & Bottom, Rosehead & Square Nails, 77 In. . 2200.00
Cupboard, Corner, Pine, Paneled, c.1810, 90 x 46 1/2 x 26 In. 9600.00
Cupboard, Corner, Pine, Top Glass & Base Panel Doors, 18th Century 7280.00
Cupboard, Corner, Pine, Upper Paneled Doors, Upper Shelves, 81 In. 1045.00
Cupboard, Corner, Poplar, 2 Base Paneled Doors, Top Door, Shelves, 90 1/2 In. 5280.00
Cupboard, Corner, Poplar, 2 Paneled Doors Over 1 Door, Bracket Feet, 83 1/2 In. 450.00
Cupboard, Corner, Poplar, Arched Door, Pilasters, 2 Doors, 91 x 47 1/2 x 21 3/4 In. 700.00
Cupboard, Corner, Poplar, Mahogany, 12-Pane, 2 Drawers, 89 x 41 In. 6900.00
Cupboard, Corner, Poplar, Pine, 2 Paneled Doors Over 1 Drawer, 99 x 46 In. 450.00
Cupboard, Corner, Poplar, Pine, Mortise & Tenon Panels, Iron Latch, 36 In. 770.00
Cupboard, Corner, Queen Anne, Blue Green Paint, H Hinges, Mid 18th Century 28500.00
Cupboard, Corner, Softwood, 12-Pane Door, 2 Paneled Doors, 3 Drawers, 115 x 28 In. . . 2100.00
Cupboard, Corner, Softwood, 2 Over 2 Doors, Stepped Cornice, 91 x 34 In. 2200.00
Cupboard, Corner, Softwood, Blind Door, Frame Molding, Shelves, 78 1/2 x 50 x 32 In. . 660.00
Cupboard, Corner, Tiger Maple, Paneled Door, 20th Century, 20 x 9 1/2 In. 230.00
Cupboard, Corner, Walnut, 2 Panel Doors, 4 Serpentine Shelves, 87 x 18 In. 6325.00
Cupboard, Corner, Walnut, Pine, Bracket Feet, Scalloped Apron, 46 x 22 x 84 In. 4125.00
Cupboard, Crock, Pine, Step Back, 2 Upper & 2 Lower Doors, 1850s 3800.00
Cupboard, Curly Maple, Mellow Gold Finish, 5 Dovetailed Drawers, 44 In. 8525.00
Cupboard, Door, Square Nail Construction, Strap Hinges, 4 Shelves, 21 x 54 x 21 In. 45.00
Cupboard, Elm, Ash, Cushion Frieze Drawer Case, Paneled Door, 1880s, 35 In., Pair 1265.00
Cupboard, Federal, Cherry, Tiger Maple, 3 Cock-Beaded Drawers, 1820, 84 In. 3220.00
Cupboard, George III, Mahogany, Hanging, Early 19th Century, 36 x 38 x 11 In. 575.00
Cupboard, Hanging, Eastlake, Paneled Door, 2 Interior Shelves, 27 1/2 In. 220.00
Cupboard, Hanging, Oak, Walnut, Central Inlaid Door, Wide Cornice, 19th Century 2530.00
Cupboard, Hanging, Painted Flowers, Russia, c.1860, 30 x 12 x 39 In. 1250.00
Cupboard, Hanging, Pine, 2 Shelves, c.1900, 25 3/4 x 17 x 33 In. 360.00
Cupboard, Hanging, Pine, Cornice, Front Crest, Applied Moldings, 1 Shelf 495.00
Cupboard, Hanging, Pine, Glazed Door, Interior Shelves, 34 1/4 x 30 1/2 In. 3760.00
Cupboard, Hanging, Pine, Stepped Case, 3 Shelves, Arched Top, Finial, 18 x 8 x 31 In. . . . 715.00

Cupboard, Hanging, Queen Anne Style, Tiger Maple, Glass Door, 32 x 23 x 27 1/2 In. 1375.00
Cupboard, Hanging, Softwood, Stepped Cornice, Raised Panel Door, 40 x 27 In. 715.00
Cupboard, Hanging, Walnut, Paneled, Pa., c.1760, 35 1/2 x 32 x 13 1/2 In. 9600.00
Cupboard, Hanging, Walnut, Upper Shelf, 2 Drawers, 14 1/2 x 22 x 7 In. 385.00
Cupboard, Jelly, 2 Doors, 2 Inset Panels, Cast Iron Latches, 59 x 51 In. 1650.00
Cupboard, Jelly, 2 Doors, Brass Pulls, Curved Front Feet 3080.00
Cupboard, Jelly, Dry Mustard Paint, 2 Paneled Doors, 2 Drawers, 58 In. 3630.00
Cupboard, Jelly, Mustard Red Paint, 2 Doors, Worn & Flaking, 43 x 21 x 50 In. 605.00
Cupboard, Jelly, Pine, Door On Front, Brass Pulls, Interior Shelves, 53 1/2 In. 550.00
Cupboard, Jelly, Pine, Poplar, 2 Base Doors, 2 Drawers, Wood Pulls, 51 1/2 In. 715.00
Cupboard, Jelly, Poplar, 2 Drawers Over 2 Panel Doors, Backsplash, 44 x 19 x 50 In. 1870.00
Cupboard, Jelly, Poplar, Scalloped Aprons, 4 Shelves, Porcelain Pulls, 71 1/2 In. 1210.00
Cupboard, Limbert, Cloud-Lift Apron, 3 Small Panes, 1 Large Pane, 9 3/4 x 40 In. 7760.00
Cupboard, Louis XV Style, Rosewood, Marquetry, Glazed Door, France, 52 x 31 x 20 In. . . 2530.00
Cupboard, Mahogany, 1 Glass Door, Child's, 40 In. 180.00
Cupboard, Mahogany, Cylindrical Form, Shelved Interior, Pedestal, 29 In. 400.00
Cupboard, Mahogany, Dentil Crown, 2-Panel Door, Bracket Feet, c.1860, 24 x 22 In. 950.00
Cupboard, Mahogany, Hanging, Glass Doors, Shelves, Dentil Molding, 42 x 30 x 9 In. . . 220.00
Cupboard, Mahogany, Marble Top, Columns, Fitted Door, 28 1/2 x 15 1/2 In. 540.00
Cupboard, Mahogany, Marquetry On Sides, Tambour Front, Drawer, 1870s, 27 In. 805.00
Cupboard, Maroon Paint, 2 Doors, Early 20th Century, 24 1/2 x 11 1/2 x 8 1/2 In. 220.00
Cupboard, Mixed Woods, Open, 3 Open Shelves, Base Door, Latch, 73 x 39 In. 2200.00
Cupboard, Mortise & Tenon, Red Paint, 1840, 69 x 76 In., 2 Piece 1760.00
Cupboard, Oak, Broken Cornice, Gothic Arch Doors, 72 x 28 x 17 In. 1840.00
Cupboard, Oak, Griffin Support, Birds In Rush, Cattails, Griffin Crest, 99 x 23 x 55 In. . . 1680.00
Cupboard, Oak, Pegs & Shelves, 2 Doors Lower Section, 80 x 64 In. 2990.00
Cupboard, Oak, Raised Panel, Drawer, Brass Pull, Glass Inserts, 30 1/2 In. 275.00
Cupboard, Oak, Step Back, Carved Fruit, Nuts, Vine Pulls, 101 x 22 1/2 x 51 In. 1960.00
Cupboard, Oak, Step Back, Figural Carving, Lion, Wolf Head, 96 x 23 x 51 In. 1960.00
Cupboard, Open Hutch Under 2 Paneled Doors, Interior Plate Rack, 84 1/2 In. 5500.00
Cupboard, Pewter, Pine, 1 Door Base, 3 Shelves, Beaded Trim, Brass Pull, 80 In. 1155.00
Cupboard, Pewter, Pine, Interior Scalloped Shelves, 2 Doors, 72 x 57 In. 1870.00
Cupboard, Pewter, Pine, Step Back, Base Drawer, 3 Shelves, 77 3/4 In. 5025.00
Cupboard, Pewter, Poplar Boards Back, Center Drawer, Cutout Bracket Feet 600.00
Cupboard, Pewter, Walnut, 3 Shelves, Wood Pulls, 78 3/4 In. 1760.00
Cupboard, Pewter, Yellow Pine, Red Paint, 2 Drawers, Doors, 74 x 45 x 20 In. 5720.00
Cupboard, Pine, 2 Double-Arched Doors, 2 Lower Drawers, Doors, 1880s, 81 In. 920.00
Cupboard, Pine, Blue Paint, Square Nails, Board & Batten Door, 2 Shelves, 41 1/2 In. . . . 3090.00
Cupboard, Pine, Glazed, 2 Sections, Step Back, c.1835, 87 x 52 x 20 In. 3220.00
Cupboard, Pine, Painted, Paneled, 2 Sections, 18th Century, 82 x 72 x 53 In. 9600.00
Cupboard, Pine, Painted, Step Back, 3 Open Shelves, Doors, 77 x 46 x 18 In. 2000.00
Cupboard, Pine, Poplar, 2 Doors, 5 Interior Shelves, 78 1/2 x 52 1/2 In. 1650.00
Cupboard, Pine, Poplar, Step Back, Bracket Feet, 79 3/4 x 22 In. 1725.00
Cupboard, Pine, Poplar, Walnut, Pie Shelf, 2 Doors Top, 6 Panes Each, 89 In. 3575.00
Cupboard, Pine, Step Back, Glazed Paneled Doors Over 2 Drawers, c.1870, 83 In. 1325.00
Cupboard, Pine, Step Back, Scalloped Frieze, c.1850, 75 x 45 x 17 In. 1230.00
Cupboard, Pine, Tongue & Groove Board Door, 4 Shelves, Latch, 62 In. 440.00
Cupboard, Poplar, Grain Painted, 19th Century, 46 3/4 x 47 3/4 x 19 In. 1060.00
Cupboard, Queen Anne Style, Oak, Plinth Pedestal, Paneled Door, 36 x 23 x 23 In. 635.00
Cupboard, Queen Anne, Walnut, Panel Door, Scalloped Shelves, 1760, 30 x 39 In. 9300.00
Cupboard, Red & Black Grained Paint, 19 In. 1650.00
Cupboard, Regency, Mahogany, Oval Paneled Door, Brass Bands, 36 x 25 In., Pair 6615.00
Cupboard, Regency, Rosewood, 2 Grille Doors, 40 1/2 x 43 x 13 1/2 In. 4370.00
Cupboard, Shelf, 2 Glazed Doors, 3 Drawers, 20th Century, 21 x 14 In. 175.00
Cupboard, Softwood, Grain Painted, 3 Glass Paned Doors, Victorian, 49 x 84 In. 715.00
Cupboard, Step Back, 2 Doors Over 4 Drawers, Porcelain Pulls, Child's 495.00
Cupboard, Step Back, 2 Doors Top, Pie Shelf, 2 Drawers Over 2 Doors, Painted 275.00
Cupboard, Step Back, 2 Glass Doors Top, 2 Drawers & Paneled Doors Base, Painted 2750.00
Cupboard, Step Back, Oak, Ash, 2 Doors, 2 Drawers, Victorian, Child's, 57 x 33 In. 990.00
Cupboard, Step Back, Oak, Carved, Griffin Supports, Pierced Crest, 102 x 22 x 51 In. . . . 1680.00
Cupboard, Step Back, Pine, 2 Paneled Doors, Apple Green Paint, 73 x 39 x 14 In. 4260.00
Cupboard, Step Back, Pine, 2 Sliding Glass Doors Over Door & 3 Drawers, 90 x 60 In. . . 850.00
Cupboard, Step Back, Pine, 3 Upper Shelves, 2 Doors, 75 x 38 x 20 In. 275.00

Cupboard, Step Back, Pine, Cornice, Batten Door, Shelf, 83 x 39 x 20 In. 495.00
Cupboard, Step Back, Pine, Red Wash, 2 Doors Top, 1 Door Base, 36 x 70 In. 1540.00
Cupboard, Step Back, Poplar, 4 Doors, Shelves, Cast Iron Latches, 43 x 23 x 72 In. 1045.00
Cupboard, Step Back, Walnut, 2 Base Doors, Pie Shelf, Candle Drawers, 82 In. 5775.00
Cupboard, Step Back, Walnut, 2 Glass Doors, Panel Base, Molded Cornice, 49 x 90 In. . . 2310.00
Cupboard, Step Back, Walnut, 2 Paneled Doors, 2 Drawers, Pie Shelf, 85 In. 3500.00
Cupboard, W. Pease, Raised Panels, Cornice, Door, Shelves, Blue Paint, 61 x 48 x 16 In. . 1155.00
Cupboard, Walnut, 2 Glass Doors, Over Long Drawer, Folds To Writing Top, 91 In. 1045.00
Cupboard, Walnut, 2 Glass Doors, Shelves, N.C., c.1810, 95 1/2 x 54 x 23 In. 17600.00
Cupboard, Walnut, Blind Door, Half Columns, Drawer, c.1845, 77 x 42 In., 2 Piece 1455.00
Cupboard, Walnut, Piedmont, N.C., Early 19th Century, 89 1/4 x 54 x 21 In. 9350.00
Cupboard, Walnut, Poplar, Bracket Base, 4 Doors, 3 Shelves, 40 3/4 x 17 1/2 x 83 In. . . . 2200.00
Cupboard, Walnut, Satinwood, Rosewood & Elm Inlay, Hinged Front, 32 1/2 In. 1610.00
Cupboard, Window Sill, Batten Door, Bracket Feet, Shelf, Painted, 17 x 16 x 12 In. 825.00
D'Hauteur D'Appui, Napoleon III, 19th Century, 44 3/4 x 52 1/2 x 17 1/2 In. 2530.00
Daybed, Arts & Crafts, Trundle 1180.00
Daybed, Biedermeier, Birch, Panel Front Rail, c.1830, 40 x 77 In. 3360.00
Daybed, Brayton International, Ebonized Frame, Slip Cover, Metal Legs, 82 In. 245.00
Daybed, Cane, Boulle Inlaid Crest, Late 18th Century 2185.00
Daybed, G. Nelson, Birch Frame, Aluminum Hairpin Legs, 75 x 33 x 27 In. 2415.00
Daybed, G. Nelson, Birch Frame, White Wool Cushion, Hairpin Legs, 10 In. 2530.00
Daybed, Harvey Probber, Mahogany, Brass Fittings, 80 x 30 x 25 In. 805.00
Daybed, Henredon, Figured Walnut, Scrolling Head & Foot, 40 1/4 x 83 3/4 In. 1000.00
Daybed, Jacobean, Slanted Headrest, Upholstered, Late 17th Century, 76 In. 840.00
Daybed, Louis XV Style, Toile, Upholstered, 38 x 35 x 74 In. 4800.00
Daybed, Mahogany, Arched Crest Rails, Ball Finials, Hinged Lower Section, 62 In. 290.00
Daybed, Mahogany, Outscrolled Head & Footboard, 1820s, 35 x 69 In. 1095.00
Daybed, Mahogany, Scroll Crest, Spindled Back, Dark Red, Green, 72 x 37 In. 460.00
Daybed, Outscrolled Head & Footboard, Concave Rails, 1840s, 34 x 80 In. 2760.00
Daybed, Pine, Polychrome, Mid 19th Century, 32 1/2 x 74 1/2 x 24 In. 3220.00
Daybed, Robsjohn-Gibbings, Wood, Canvas, Upholstered, Widdicomb, 32 x 92 In. 5465.00
Daybed, Rosewood, Split Bamboo, Chinese, Mid 19th Century, 19 x 32 x 77 In. 1495.00
Daybed, Stickley, Sloping Sides, Mortised Ends, Tapered Legs, Cushion, 76 1/2 In. 1265.00
Daybed, Teak, Rear Shelf, Tweed Upholstered Cushions, Signed, 29 1/2 x 76 3/4 In. 805.00
Daybed, Van Der Rohe, Rosewood Frame, Steel Legs, Brown Leather, 79 x 39 In. 3450.00
Desk, Aesthetic Revival, Ebonized, Central Frieze Drawer, Leather Top, 29 1/2 x 23 In. . . 1725.00
Desk, Architect's, George III, Mahogany, 2 Slides, Drawer, c.1775, 32 x 36 x 23 In. 4310.00
Desk, Art Nouveau, Chestnut, Leather Insert, Early 20th Century, 31 x 55 x 33 1/2 In. . . . 4025.00
Desk, Arts & Crafts, Drawer, Slatted Bookcase Ends, 30 x 40 x 24 In. 315.00
Desk, Arts & Crafts, Drop Front, Applied Brass Straps, Shelf, 26 x 12 x 48 In. 375.00
Desk, Arts & Crafts, Drop Front, Pyramid Post, 4 Drawers, 42 1/2 x 37 1/2 x 20 In. 690.00
Desk, Arts & Crafts, Gull Gallery, Center Drawer, Side Cabinets, 38 x 42 x 22 In. 690.00
Desk, Arts & Crafts, Slatted Bookcase Ends, Copper Pulls, 29 1/2 x 17 x 28 In. 200.00
Desk, Ash, Planked Top Over Frieze, Side Drawer, 1880s, 32 x 41 3/4 In. 865.00
Desk, Attorney's, Mahogany, 2 Doors, 7 Drawers, c.1840, 49 1/2 x 53 x 25 3/4 In. 2800.00
Desk, Bonheur Du Jour, Tulipwood, Shelves, 2 Drawers, Bronze Mounted, 58 In. 4600.00
Desk, Bookkeeper's, Walnut, Slant Surface, Divided Side Drawer, 1868, 75 x 29 In. 340.00
Desk, British Colonial, Stand, Brass Bound, Lift Top, 35 x 21 x 14 In. 520.00
Desk, Burl Walnut, Tooled Leather Top, 5 Drawers, Claw & Ball Feet, 36 x 60 x 31 In. . . . 1725.00
Desk, Burl, Blue Leather Writing Surface, Ink Bottles, 6 x 13 3/4 x 9 In. 390.00
Desk, Butler's, Federal, Mahogany, Inlaid, Prospect Drawer, c.1810, 43 x 47 x 24 In. 2585.00
Desk, Butler's, Federal, Mahogany, Line Inlay, 1 Over 3 Graduated Drawers, 42 x 45 In. . 1295.00
Desk, Butler's, Mahogany, Shaped Top, Diamond-Cut Molded Edge, 22 x 27 x 24 In. 365.00
Desk, Butler's, Walnut, Step Back, Carved Pulls, Bookcase, Victorian, 100 x 20 x 53 In. . . 1400.00
Desk, Campaign, Colonial, Camphorwood, 3 Drawers, Brass Mounted, 32 x 51 x 23 In. . . 1495.00
Desk, Campaign, Georgian, Mahogany, 22 1/2 x 20 1/2 x 10 In. 920.00
Desk, Campaign, Mahogany, Camphor Lining, Hinged Lid, Brass Trim, England 415.00
Desk, Campaign, Regency, Mahogany, Brass Bound, 22 x 21 x 11 1/2 In. 920.00
Desk, Campaign, Regency, Mahogany, Early 1800s, 22 x 16 3/4 x 10 1/4 In. 1840.00
Desk, Campaign, William IV, Brass Mounted, Mahogany, 25 x 21 3/4 In. 635.00
Desk, Captain's, Mahogany, Splashguard, Folding Top, 2 Drawers, 37 x 31 x 19 In. 400.00
Desk, Carlton House, Mahogany, 2 Long, 2 Short Drawers, 41 In. 3450.00
Desk, Cherry, 2 Drawers, Leather Insert, Late 20th Century, 30 In. 1440.00

Desk, Chippendale, Birch, Oxbow, Slant Front, c.1780, 43 x 42 x 20 1/2 In. 4600.00
Desk, Chippendale, Slant Front, Cherry, 3 Graduated Drawers, Conn., 1780, 43 3/4 In. . . . 10925.00
Desk, Chippendale, Slant Front, Mahogany, 18th Century, 43 x 43 3/4 x 22 1/2 In. 1150.00
Desk, Chippendale, Slant Front, Mahogany, 4 Drawers, 39 x 20 5/8 x 42 1/2 In. 3575.00
Desk, Chippendale, Slant Front, Mahogany, 4 Graduated Drawers, 44 In. 3525.00
Desk, Chippendale, Slant Front, Mahogany, 9 Pigeonholes, 4 Long Drawers, 42 x 39 In. . . 4700.00
Desk, Chippendale, Slant Front, Mahogany, c.1780, 42 1/2 x 43 1/2 x 21 3/4 In. 5875.00
Desk, Chippendale, Slant Front, Mahogany, Dovetail, Ogee Feet, Beaded Drawers, 42 In. . 3640.00
Desk, Chippendale, Slant Front, Mahogany, Serpentine Interior, Claw & Ball Feet, 36 In. . 895.00
Desk, Chippendale, Slant Front, Maple, c.1780, 43 1/2 x 37 x 19 1/2 In. 12000.00
Desk, Chippendale, Slant Front, Maple, Dovetail, 4 Graduated Drawers, 40 x 36 In. 7000.00
Desk, Chippendale, Slant Front, Maple, Drawers, Pigeonholes, 41 x 18 x 36 In. 5175.00
Desk, Chippendale, Slant Front, Maple, Drawers, Pigeonholes, c.1780, 41 x 38 In. 5700.00
Desk, Chippendale, Slant Front, Maple, Tiger Maple, Dovetail, 13 Drawers, 42 In. 10080.00
Desk, Chippendale, Slant Front, Pine, Maple Finish, 6 Drawers, Bracket Feet, 41 In. 3575.00
Desk, Chippendale, Slant Front, Tiger Maple, 3 Graduated Drawers, 40 x 35 In. 5175.00
Desk, Chippendale, Slant Front, Walnut, 3 Drawers, Ogee Bracket Feet, 42 In. 4600.00
Desk, Chippendale, Slant Front, Walnut, Bracket Base, Late 18th Century 12000.00
Desk, Chippendale, Slant Front, Walnut, Fitted Top, 4 Drawers, Refinished, 1780, 41 In. . 1045.00
Desk, Chippendale, Walnut, Dovetailed, Door, 4 Graduated Drawers, 39 x 36 In. 2250.00
Desk, Clerk's, Walnut, Gallery Over Slant Surface, 3 Drawers, 19th Century, 55 In. 500.00
Desk, Cylinder, Marquetry, Bombay Front, Dutch, 44 x 23 x 48 In. 5040.00
Desk, Davenport, Burl Walnut, Mechanical Top, Dutch, Mid 19th Century 5175.00
Desk, Davenport, Leaf Scroll Gallery, Lift-Lid Writing Surface, Fitted Interior, 37 In. 3850.00
Desk, Davenport, Oak, Late 19th Century, 36 x 35 In. 2100.00
Desk, Davenport, Satinwood, Brass Gallery, Leather Surface, 5 Drawers, 21 x 17 In. 2420.00
Desk, Davenport, Walnut, 4 Side Drawers, Interior Drawers, Fan Supports, 37 1/2 In. 660.00
Desk, Davenport, Walnut, Leather Surface, Storage Area, 4 Side Drawers, 1870s, 37 In. . . 2185.00
Desk, Drop Front, Fruitwood, Satinwood, Rosewood, Carved, Panels, 56 x 23 x 53 In. . . . 1345.00
Desk, Drop Front, Mahogany, Glass Paneled Doors, Inner Shelves, 40 x 40 In. 400.00
Desk, Drop Front, Mahogany, Kneehole, Interior Drawers, Cubbyholes, 47 In. 2130.00
Desk, Drop Front, Oak, Bookcase Side, Letter Section, 7 Bowed Doors, 47 In. 225.00
Desk, Drop Front, Oak, Fitted Interior, Drawers, Pigeonholes, 1800, 37 1/2 In. 450.00
Desk, Dunbar, Walnut Veneer, Curved Form, Hinged Swing-Out Drawers, c.1950, 57 In. . 230.00
Desk, Ebene-De-Macassar, Kneehole, Bronze, France, 1925, 30 In. 6000.00
Desk, Edwardian Style, Satinwood, Decorated, Carlton House, 38 1/2 x 52 x 24 1/2 In. . . 3450.00
Desk, Edwardian, Satinwood, Painted Swags, 1 Drawer, Fitted, 1895, 29 x 30 x 18 In. . . . 1115.00
Desk, Edwardian, Satinwood, Painted, 20th Century, 37 1/2 x 47 3/4 x 24 1/2 In. 4370.00
Desk, Elizabethan Revival, Oak, Drawer, Wide Legs, 31 x 33 x 22 In. 1495.00
Desk, Elm, 2 Drawers, Chinese, Late 19th Century, 35 x 37 x 20 In. . . . . *Illus* 865.00
Desk, Emile-Jacques Ruhlmann, Oak, 1 Drawer, Leather Insert, 1930, 47 x 27 In. 7200.00
Desk, Ernest Boiceau, Sycamore, Mahogany, 1 Side Drawer, 1928, 53 x 24 In. 7200.00
Desk, Federal, Mahogany Inlay, Broken Pediment, Bookcase, 91 x 47 1/2 x 22 1/2 In. . . . 9400.00
Desk, Federal, Mahogany, 2 Sliding Tambour Doors, 4 Drawers, 47 x 41 In. 4115.00
Desk, Federal, Mahogany, Inlaid Columns, 3 Drawers, Bookcase, 83 x 42 In. 2235.00
Desk, Federal, Slant Front, Walnut, 12 Drawers, Maryland, c.1800, 45 x 40 x 20 In. 2300.00
Desk, Frank Lloyd Wright, Chair, Heritage Henredon, Taliesin Design, 52 x 20 x 28 In. . . 1150.00
Desk, G. Nakashima, Black Walnut, 2 Drawers, Tapered Plank Sides, 26 x 38 In. 7190.00
Desk, G. Nelson, Drop Front, Pullout, 3 Drawers, Satin Chrome Pulls, 40 In. 1150.00
Desk, G. Nelson, Home Office, Herman Miller, 54 x 28 x 41 In. 4025.00
Desk, G. Nelson, Original Forest Green Finish, Green Leather Top, 40 In. 11500.00
Desk, G. Nelson, Painted Wood, Laminate Top, Chromed Steel Swag Legs, 35 x 39 In. . . . 6900.00
Desk, G. Nelson, Swagged Legs, Wood, Plastic, Chromed Steel, Herman Miller, 39 x 28 In. 6900.00
Desk, G. Nelson, Walnut, Micarta Surface, Chromed Steel Legs, 1959, 34 In. 4600.00
Desk, G. Stickley, Drop Front, Gallery Top, 2 Lower Shelves, c.1903, 51 x 26 x 11 In. . . . 7480.00
Desk, G. Stickley, Drop Front, Inlaid, Cubbyholes, Harvey Ellis 8050.00
Desk, G. Stickley, Drop Front, Mahogany, 1 Drawer, Open Shelf, 47 In. 4400.00
Desk, G. Stickley, Drop Front, Oak, Interior Door, 1 Drawer, Signed, 44 1/2 In. 3220.00
Desk, G. Stickley, Full Gallery Top, 2 Doors, Slots, 2 Drawers, Red Decal, 40 x 41 In. . . . 2645.00
Desk, G. Stickley, Gallery Top, 2 Drawers, Tapered Legs, 38 x 22 In. 1150.00
Desk, G. Stickley, No. 453, Letter Slots, 2 Drawers Over Shelf, c.1902, 39 x 22 In. 1840.00
Desk, G. Stickley, No. 709, Mahogany, Leather Top, Signed, 29 x 24 In. 2300.00
Desk, G. Stickley, No. 720, Mahogany, 2 Drawers, Red Decal, 38 x 23 x 37 In. 1955.00

Desk, G. Stickley, No. 729, Drop Front, Gallery Top & Interior, 5 Drawers, 45 x 36 In. ... 3740.00
Desk, G. Stickley, No. 732, Drop Front, 4 Drawers, Craftsman Label, 43 x 32 In. 3220.00
Desk, G. Stickley, Paneled Slat Front, Drawer, Wood Knobs, 26 x 15 In. 2300.00
Desk, George I, Walnut, Kneehole, Parquetry, 31 1/4 x 29 1/2 x 18 3/4 In. 3740.00
Desk, George III, Mahogany, Drop Leaves, Drawer, 31 x 40 x 19 In. 400.00
Desk, George III, Mahogany, Early 19th Century, 32 1/2 x 52 x 20 1/2 In. 1840.00
Desk, George IV, Mahogany, Pedestal, Leather Top, 31 x 60 1/2 x 30 1/2 In. 4600.00
Desk, Georgian Style, Teak, Slant Front, Hinged Writing Surface, 41 2/3 x 36 x 16 In. ... 390.00
Desk, Grain Painted, Hinge, 3 Interior Drawers, 36 x 24 3/8 x 20 3/4 In. 4890.00
Desk, Harvey Probber, Walnut Veneer, 4 Locking Drawers, Chrome Frame, 78 In. 385.00
Desk, Hepplewhite, Bird's-Eye Maple, Mahogany, 2 Doors, 3 Drawers, 46 x 40 In. 3575.00
Desk, Hepplewhite, Tambour, Maddox, Inlaid, Fold Down, Drawers, 42 x 36 x 19 In. 495.00
Desk, Italian Rococo Revival, Walnut, Slant Front, Early 20th Century, 37 x 31 x 18 In. .. 1955.00
Desk, Jean Prouve, Steel, Wood, Chair, Child's, Ateliers, c.1948 .... 3680.00
Desk, Kimbal & Cabus, Ebonized, Minton Tiles, Cabinet, 61 x 15 x 42 In. 10100.00
Desk, L. & J.G. Stickley, Mahogany, 1 Drawer, 22 x 17 x 30 In. 1955.00
Desk, L. & J.G. Stickley, No. 500, Mahogany, 1 Drawer, 42 x 26 x 30 In. 863.00
Desk, L. & J.G. Stickley, No. 612, Mahogany, Kneehole, 8 Drawers, 60 x 45 In. 7150.00
Desk, L. & J.G. Stickley, No. 661, Drop Front, Signed, 44 1/2 x 42 In. 1670.00
Desk, L. & J.G. Stickley, Slant Front, Drawers, Original Wood Knobs, 45 x 21 x 42 In. .. 1265.00
Desk, Leather Inset Surface, 3 Short Drawers, Tapered Legs, Brass Casters, 31 x 48 In. .. 500.00
Desk, Lifetime, Drop Front, Mahogany, 43 x 38 x 18 In. 950.00
Desk, Limbert, 2 Drawers, Copper Pulls, Lower Shelf, Branded Mark, 29 x 48 x 30 In. 1840.00
Desk, Limbert, Ash, Overhanging Top, Letter Rack, 2 Open Shelves, 38 x 15 x 44 In. 2200.00
Desk, Limbert, Inset Top, Drawer, Bookcase Ends, 18 1/4 x 44 1/4 x 28 In. 920.00
Desk, Limbert, Mahogany, Drawer, Cutout Slab Sides, 37 x 14 x 40 In. 1265.00
Desk, Limbert, No. 602, Mahogany, 2 Open Shelves, 26 x 12 x 46 In. 2070.00
Desk, Louis Philippe Style, Mahogany, Brass Molding, 31 1/2 x 56 3/4 x 31 In. 3220.00
Desk, Louis XV, Mahogany, 2 Short Drawers, Rectangular Top, 37 1/2 In. 750.00
Desk, Louis XVI, Mahogany, Pierced Gallery, Bronze Mounted, 43 x 20 In. 4600.00
Desk, Mahogany, 5 Small Drawers, Kneehole, Pad Feet, 19th Century, 30 1/2 In. 2015.00
Desk, Mahogany, 6 Upper Drawers, Brass Gallery, Writing Surface, Drawer, 42 In. 1725.00
Desk, Mahogany, 7 Drawers, Kneehole, 30 x 46 x 21 1/2 In. 560.00
Desk, Mahogany, Broken Swan's-Neck Pediment, Glass Doors, Bookcase, 81 x 39 In. 940.00
Desk, Mahogany, Burl, Lift Top, 2 Drawers, 3 Interior Drawers, 34 x 30 x 19 In. 1790.00
Desk, Mahogany, Conforming Case, Long Drawer, 4 Short, 30 1/2 x 45 In. 2115.00
Desk, Mahogany, Cylinder, 3 Pedestal Drawers, 5 Pigeonholes, Leather Surface, 45 In. ... 880.00
Desk, Mahogany, Double Bowfront, 3 Drawers, Shaped Gallery, 31 x 48 In. 280.00
Desk, Mahogany, Kneehole, Block & Shell, 1860, 42 x 29 In. 1955.00
Desk, Mahogany, Leather Surface, 3 Drawers On Side, 2 Pedestals, 30 x 57 In. 2185.00
Desk, Mahogany, Leather Writing Surface, Frieze, 2 Drawers, 29 x 51 In. 1955.00
Desk, Mahogany, Overhanging Top, 5 Drawers, Brass Drop Pulls, 30 x 50 x 52 In. 920.00

Furniture, Desk, Elm, 2 Drawers, Chinese, Late
19th Century, 35 x 37 x 20 In.

Furniture, Desk, Sugar, Cherry, Iron Lock,
Kentucky, 19th Century, 43 x 45 3/4 x 24 In.

Desk, Mahogany, Pedestal, Leather Surface, 3 Drawers, 1880s, 32 x 60 In. 3740.00
Desk, Mahogany, Tooled Leather Top, 2 Drawers, 30 x 58 In. 630.00
Desk, Man On 1 Door, Woman On Other, Writing Surface, Drawers, 53 In. 1650.00
Desk, Marquetry, 5 Drawers, Bronze Mounts, Stamped Leather Top, 31 x 43 1/2 In. 2240.00
Desk, McCobb, Blond Finish, 5 Drawers, Brass Pulls, Winchendon, 53 x 26 In. 230.00
Desk, McCobb, Maple, Double Pedestal, Winchendon, 1948, 29 1/2 x 53 In. 750.00
Desk, McHugh, Long Center Drawer, Bookcase Sides, 2 Short Drawers, 30 x 48 In. 630.00
Desk, Mixed Woods, Carved Dragon's Heads, Top Drawers, Pagoda Top, 69 In. 1430.00
Desk, Norman Bel Geddes, Metal, Drawer, Simmons, 34 x 19 x 31 In. 69.00
Desk, Oak, 1 Drawer, Iron Strap Hinges, 2 Interior Drawers, 43 1/2 In. 770.00
Desk, Oak, Leather Surface, 2 Drawers, Paneled Legs, 1850s, 29 1/2 In. 2530.00
Desk, Oak, Mahogany, Flame Grain, 2 Parts, Continental, 55 x 32 1/4 x 53 In. 880.00
Desk, Partners, Carved, Dragons, Foo Dogs, Cabriole Legs, 2 Drawers, 59 x 42 In. 550.00
Desk, Partners, George III, Mahogany, Gilt Leather Top, 2 Pedestals, 71 x 40 In. 2800.00
Desk, Partners, George III, Mahogany, Gilt Tooled Top, Central Frieze, Door, 32 In. 5175.00
Desk, Partners, Mahogany, 18 Carved Drawers, Lion-Head Pulls, 31 x 48 x 30 In. 880.00
Desk, Partners, Mahogany, 9 Drawers, Column Front, Claw Feet, Fan Carved, 32 x 48 In. 670.00
Desk, Partners, Mahogany, Carved Acanthus, Pedestal, Claw Feet, 29 x 30 x 48 In. 1450.00
Desk, Partners, Mahogany, Leather Top, 2 Short & Center Drawer, c.1860, 59 1/2 In. 2910.00
Desk, Partners, Mahogany, Leather Top, 3 Pedestal, Drawers, Cupboard Doors, 31 In..... 9000.00
Desk, Partners, Mahogany, Pedestal, Gilt Brown Leather Writing Surface, 29 In........ 6040.00
Desk, Partners, Mahogany, Raised Panels, Safe, Carved Apron, c.1890, 30 x 54 x 72 In. .. 7840.00
Desk, Partners, Oak, Carved Faces On Doors, Hairy Paw Feet, 29 1/2 x 48 In. 2750.00
Desk, Pedestal, 4 Drawers, Opening To Bands Of Pigeonholes, Writing Slope 3000.00
Desk, Pine, 2 Wide Dovetailed Drawers, Scalloped Crest, 51 x 23 x 40 In. 715.00
Desk, Pine, Black Sponge, Red Ground, Dovetail, Signed, 1810, 23 x 15 In. 330.00
Desk, Pine, Gallery Top, Panel Sides, 5 Drawers On Each Side, 32 x 48 In. 400.00
Desk, Pine, Poplar, Blue Paint, Hinged Top, Well Over 2 Drawers, Child's, 33 x 25 In. ... 1035.00
Desk, Pine, Slant Front, Interior Well, 2 Drawers, Square Legs, c.1840, 34 x 61 In. 1150.00
Desk, Plantation, Cherry, Hinged Lift-Up Top, Fitted Interiors, Drawers, c.1850, 58 In. 1560.00
Desk, Plantation, Pine, Hinged Front, Storage Space, c.1800, 34 x 33 In. 895.00
Desk, Plantation, Pine, Slant Front, Inner Storage, c.1800, 34 x 33 In. 900.00
Desk, Plantation, Poplar, Pine, 3 Base Drawers, Fold-Out Writing Surface, 76 In. 9900.00
Desk, Queen Anne, Cherry, Slant Front, Bracket Base, 4 Drawers, New Hampshire, 35 In. 1430.00
Desk, Queen Anne, Slant Front, Fruitwood, 10 Pigeonholes, 4 Drawers, 40 x 34 x 19 In. . 1880.00
Desk, Queen Anne, Slant Front, Mahogany, Carved, Figured, c.1770, 42 x 39 x 23 In. ... 26050.00
Desk, Queen Anne, Slant Front, Walnut, New England, c.1780, 19 x 17 3/4 x 12 In. 14400.00
Desk, Queen Anne, Slant Front, Walnut, Serpentine Drawers, Bracket Feet, 41 In. 2530.00
Desk, Raymond Loewy, Formica, Red & White, 1968, 30 x 60 In. 2875.00
Desk, Rectangular Top, Over 1 Drawer, Flanked By 2 Drawers, 31 1/2 x 37 In. 1495.00
Desk, Red & Black Grained Paint, Yellow Interior, Foldover, 30 In.................... 3200.00
Desk, Regency Style, Mahogany, Ormolu Mounted, Leather, 2 Drawers, 30 x 59 x 29 In. . 4200.00
Desk, Regency, Burl-Banded Top, Drop Side, Over 2 Drawers, 33 x 26 x 29 In. 860.00
Desk, Regency, Rosewood, Pedestal, Leather Top, 5 Drawers, 29 x 52 x 31 In. 6600.00
Desk, Renaissance Revival, Walnut, Leather, Drawer, Ornate Carved Base, 36 x 22 In. ... 440.00
Desk, Renaissance Revival, Walnut, Rectangular Molded Top, Leaf Borders, 30 x 22 In. .. 630.00
Desk, Rococo, Chinoiserie, Red Lacquer, Slant Front, Continental, 42 x 36 x 22 In. 12000.00
Desk, Rococo, Walnut, Rectangular Crossbanded Top, Cabriole Legs, Italy, 31 In. 2300.00
Desk, Roll Top, Edwardian, Oak, Fitted Interior, Lower Drawers, High Top, 1900 .... 1015.00
Desk, Roll Top, English Oak, 4 Drawers, Casters, c.1800, 49 1/2 x 60 x 32 In. 1000.00
Desk, Roll Top, Golden Oak, Locking Petty Cash Drawer, c.1895 .... 6900.00
Desk, Roll Top, Oak, Derby Desk Co. 2300.00
Desk, Roll Top, S Roll, Walnut, Pigeonholes, Original Finish, Victorian 2750.00
Desk, Roll Top, S Roll, Walnut, Victorian 2750.00
Desk, Rosewood, Kneehole, 4 Drawers & Front Cabinet, Open Shelf, 29 x 60 In. 275.00
Desk, School, Lift Top, Partial Gallery, Paint Traces, H-Stretcher, 1850s, 34 x 24 In. 240.00
Desk, Schoolmaster's, Scrolled Gallery, Hinged Top, Blue Paint, 48 x 28 In. 1495.00
Desk, Schoolmaster's, Slant Front, Letter Section, 2 Drawers, 41 1/4 x 28 In. 600.00
Desk, Shaped Top, 7 Drawers, Flower & Serpent Inlays, Dutch, 32 x 44 x 21 In. 1150.00
Desk, Shelf, Bamboo Tripod Base, Putti, Gargoyles, Hinged Lid, 41 In. 4200.00
Desk, Sheraton, Slant Front, Birch, Cherry, 8 Dovetailed Drawers, 39 1/2 x 47 In. 1320.00
Desk, Shop Of The Crafters, No. 279, Mahogany, Splayed Legs, 46 In. 1380.00
Desk, Slant Front, Curly Maple, Drawer, Secret Drawer, 39 3/4 In. 4180.00

Desk, Slant Front, 1 Drawer, Floral Marquetry, Fitted Interior, Bronze Mounts, 35 In. 1380.00
Desk, Slant Front, 12 Interior Drawers, 8 Pigeonholes, Hidden Drawer, 41 1/2 In. 1900.00
Desk, Slant Front, Carved Figurals, Cabriole Legs, Victorian, 39 x 20 x 52 In. 3575.00
Desk, Slant Front, Cherry, Maple, New England, Early 18th Century, 34 1/2 x 34 1/2 In. . . . 3335.00
Desk, Slant Front, Fitted Interior, Drawers, Pigeonholes, Lower Drawer 560.00
Desk, Slant Front, Gumwood, Thumb-Molded Drawer, Turned Legs, 36 In. 5290.00
Desk, Slant Front, Mahogany, 5 Base Drawers, Marquetry, Flower Basket, 43 In. 825.00
Desk, Slant Front, Mahogany, 7 Drawers, 6 Pigeonholes, Center Door, 39 x 38 x 22 In. . . 690.00
Desk, Slant Front, Mahogany, Base Drawers, Interior Drawers, Pigeonholes, 43 1/2 In. . . . 1480.00
Desk, Slant Front, Mahogany, Brass, Hunt Scenes, Drawer, c.1890, 41 x 25 x 20 In. 1495.00
Desk, Slant Front, Mahogany, Divided Interior, 4 Drawers, Late 19th Century, 40 In. 1400.00
Desk, Slant Front, Mahogany, Ornately Carved, Continental 2495.00
Desk, Slant Front, Maple, 19th Century, 77 x 43 x 18 In. 920.00
Desk, Slant Front, Maple, 4 Graduated Drawers, Bracket Feet, 45 x 44 In. 3055.00
Desk, Slant Front, Pine, Drawer, Stretcher, Late 1700s, 42 1/2 x 29 3/4 x 19 In. 2415.00
Desk, Slant Front, Pine, Mortise & Tenon, Old Paint, 29 x 30 x 25 In. 715.00
Desk, Slant Front, Pine, Splashback, 1890, Child's 125.00
Desk, Slant Front, Poplar, 10 Interior Drawers, Ring Turned Feet, 39 x 23 x 44 In. 550.00
Desk, Slant Front, Serpentine Front, Bracket Base, 38 x 31 In. 115.00
Desk, Slant Front, Walnut, 10 Interior Drawers, 8 Pigeonholes, 1730s, 42 x 46 In. 5750.00
Desk, Slant Front, Walnut, 19th Century, 23 x 23 x 32 In. 230.00
Desk, Slant Front, Walnut, Fitted Interior, Frieze Drawer, Italian, 36 x 32 In. 500.00
Desk, Slant Front, Walnut, Fitted Interior, Wells, 3 Drawers, 18th Century 5750.00
Desk, Softwood, Low Gallery, Hinged Lift Top, Painted, Eagle, 32 x 22 x 29 In. 100.00
Desk, Spinet, Art Deco, Walnut, Pigeonhole Center, 1 Drawer Each Side End 220.00
Desk, Steel Frame, Laminate Top, 3 Drawers, Chrome Pulls, 29 1/2 x 47 1/2 In. 8825.00
Desk, Stickley Bros., Slatted Bookshelf, Lower Shelf, 30 x 44 x 28 In. 750.00
Desk, Sugar, Cherry, Iron Lock, Kentucky, 19th Century, 43 x 45 3/4 x 24 In. . . . . . . *Illus* 20900.00
Desk, Thomas Nisbet, Brunswick, Senate & Legislature, 1840s 6500.00
Desk, Tooled Leather Top, 6 Drawers, Brass Paw Feet, Pull Rings, 30 x 48 x 27 In. 3450.00
Desk, Victorian, Bird's-Eye Maple, 6 Drawers, Plinth, c.1870, 28 x 30 x 23 In. 690.00
Desk, Victorian, Walnut, Hinged Lid, Drawers, 19th Century, 34 x 21 x 21 In. 1230.00
Desk, Walnut Sides, White Laminate, Swagged Legs, Chrome Base, 34 x 39 x 28 In. 4315.00
Desk, Walnut Veneers, Inlay, 4 Drawers Each Side, Continental, 46 x 23 x 33 In. 300.00
Desk, Walnut, Fold-Out Surface, Upper Bookcase, Paned Doors, 1850s, 6 . . . . 6040.00
Desk, Walnut, Inset Leather Top, Tiger Maple Interior, 8 Drawers, 23 x 22 1/2 x 36 In. . . . 920.00
Desk, Walnut, Leather Inset Top, 5 Short Drawers, Pad Feet, 30 x 42 In. 450.00
Desk, Walnut, Leather Surface, 2 Drawers, Early 20th Century, 29 x 35 1/2 In. 335.00
Desk, Walnut, Leather Surface, 6 Short Drawers, Claw & Ball Feet, 30 1/2 In. 4030.00
Desk, Walnut, Leather Top, Pullout Surface, Cabriole Legs, Scrolled Toes, 30 x 45 In. 2070.00
Desk, William & Mary Style, Walnut, Marquetry, Pedestal, 1800s, 30 1/2 x 48 x 25 In. . . . 2070.00
Dinette Set, Formica Top, Gold & Black, Iron Base, 2 Leaves, 6 Chairs 400.00
Dining Chair Set, George II Style, Mahogany, Lion-Head Arms, c.1900, 27 1/2 In., 8 . . . . 4830.00
Dining Set, 6 Upholstered Chairs, Wrought Iron, Glass-Top Table, 60 x 36 x 29 In. 747.00
Dining Set, Charles Dudouyt, Oak, 2 Draw-Leaf, 1940, 129-In. Table, 7 Piece 7200.00
Dining Set, Harvest, 6 Ladder Back Chairs, Rush Seats, 7 Piece 425.00
Dining Set, Oriental Style, Extension Table, Yoke-Back Chairs, 2 Armchairs, 7 Piece 345.00
Dining Table, Drop Leaf, Mahogany, Gateleg, c.1800, 28 3/4 x 48 x 62 3/4 In. 500.00
Dresser, Arts & Crafts, 2 Drawers Over 1, Mirror, Glove Boxes, 64 x 43 In. 1725.00
Dresser, Arts & Crafts, Granite Top & Backsplash, Inlaid Frame, German, 43 x 42 In. 630.00
Dresser, Arts & Crafts, Mahogany, 4 Drawers, 36 x 21 x 63 In. 2530.00
Dresser, Charles II, Oak, Drawers, Cupboard, 17th Century, 32 x 75 3/4 x 19 1/2 In. 3100.00
Dresser, Cherry, 2 Parts, 3 Upper Shelves, 3 Lower Drawers, 80 1/2 x 67 In. 2875.00
Dresser, Compac Furniture Co., Mahogany, Mirror In Middle, 26 x 30 In. 1090.00
Dresser, Frank Lloyd Wright, Mahogany, 8 Drawers, 2 Doors, Henredon, 34 x 66 In. 4313.00
Dresser, G. Nelson, Mahogany, 4 Drawers, Black Enameled Knobs, 32 In. 2415.00
Dresser, G. Stickley, No. 911, Mahogany, Original Finish, 48 x 22 x 66 In. 4025.00
Dresser, Herter Bros., Mahogany, Aesthetic Revival, c.1890, 74 x 48 1/2 x 22 In. 11165.00
Dresser, Hinged Top, Brass Inlay, Divided & Lined Interior, 1880s, 13 1/4 In. 900.00
Dresser, L. & J.G. Stickley, Mirror, 2 Drawers Over 3, Decal, 69 x 38 In. 2760.00
Dresser, Leaf & Shell Carving, Bowed, Mirror Arms, Half Drawers, Marble Top, 9 Ft. 7500.00
Dresser, Mahogany, 4 Drawers, Brass Hardware, Carved Bracket Feet, 1930s, 38 In. 550.00
Dresser, Mahogany, Dovetailed Drawers, Brass Pulls, Locks, Pineapple Finials, 71 In. 1430.00

Dresser, Maple, 2 Over 2 Drawers, Serpentine Front, Beveled Mirror 630.00
Dresser, McCobb, Blond Finish, 6 Drawers, Dowel Legs, Winchendon, 34 x 48 In. 1095.00
Dresser, Meader & Co., Rosewood, Marble Top, Wishbone Mirror, Victorian 300.00
Dresser, Michigan Chair Co., Inset Top, Mirror, 2 Doors, Drawers, 49 x 32 x 24 In. 1840.00
Dresser, Oak, 3 Graduated Drawers, S-Supported Oval Mirror 695.00
Dresser, Oak, Cornice Over 2 Shelves, Lower Outset Doors, 18th Century, 85 1/2 In. 2300.00
Dresser, Oak, Cornice, Lancashire, England, 79 x 59 1/2 x 21 1/2 In. 1495.00
Dresser, Painted, Flowers, Mirror, 6 Drawers, Hatbox Compartment, 53 x 31 x 18 In. 3550.00
Dresser, Pewter, 3 Open Shelves, 3 Drawers, 2 Paneled Doors, England, 55 x 76 In. 1150.00
Dresser, Pewter, Pine, Red, Blue, Green Paint, Flat Top, Pa., 72 x 43 x 8 In. 13800.00
Dresser, Renaissance Revival, Walnut, Bird's-Eye Interior, Crest, 99 x 23 x 49 In. 950.00
Dresser, Walnut, Marble Top, 3 Dovetailed Drawers, Mirror, c.1870, 74 x 42 In. 532.00
Dresser, Welsh, Elm, 6 Drawers, 2 Doors, Shelves, Spice Drawers, 1700s, 72 x 60 In. ... 17500.00
Dresser, Welsh, Oak, Upper Section Shelves, Drawers, 19th Century, 82 x 77 x 20 In. ... 5750.00
Dresser, William & Mary, Triple, Rectangular, Bun Feet, 72 x 18 x 31 In. 750.00
Dry Sink, Blue Paint, Zinc Lined, 6 Drawers, Porcelain Knobs, 64 In. 2400.00
Dry Sink, Chestnut, High Back, Gallery Top, 2 Doors, Zinc Lined, 71 x 36 x 17 In. 715.00
Dry Sink, Mustard Paint, c.1840 .... 2850.00
Dry Sink, Pine, Metal Lined, Paneled Doors & Ends, 33 x 48 x 23 In. 400.00
Dry Sink, Pine, Paneled Doors, Drawer, 19th Century, 38 x 50 In. 860.00
Dry Sink, Poplar, 2 Paneled Base Doors, Drawer At Side, Top Shelf, 43 3/4 In. 880.00
Dry Sink, Poplar, 2 Paneled Doors In Base, Zinc Lined, 32 x 48 1/4 In. 1375.00
Dry Sink, Poplar, Cupboard, Mortise & Tenon, Raised Panels, 1860-1880, 86 x 42 In. ... 1895.00
Dry Sink, Softwood, 2 Drawers, Doors, Painted, Lancaster County, 45 1/2 x 43 x 20 In. ... 2530.00
Dry Sink, Walnut, 2 Paneled Doors, Drawer, Top Shelf, Iron Latch, 42 1/2 In. 1430.00
Dry Sink, Walnut, Maple, Square-Nail Construction, Inset Panels On Doors, 29 3/4 In. ... 825.00
Dumbwaiter, Chippendale, Mahogany, 3 Tiers, 42 x 17 1/2 In. 335.00
Dumbwaiter, George III, Mahogany, 3 Tiers, Scalloped, Cabriole Legs, 41 x 25 In. 2910.00
Dumbwaiter, Mahogany, 3 Graduated Tiers, Saber Legs, Casters, c.1790, 59 In. 1900.00
Dumbwaiter, Mahogany, 3 Tiers, Baluster Supports, Tripod Base, 43 In. 980.00
Dumbwaiter, Mahogany, 3 Tiers, Piecrust Edge, Carved Legs, Pad Feet, c.1890, 43 In. 530.00
Dumbwaiter, Mahogany, 4 Tiers, Late 18th Century, 56 In. 2185.00
Dumbwaiter, Rococo, Light Floral Marquetry, 3 Tiers, Double Line Borders, 41 In. 865.00
Easel, Beech, Mahogany, Stamped Chambon On Reverse, 19 x 16 In. 1380.00
Easel, Heraldic, Ax Finials, Knights In Armor, Claw & Ball Feet, Brass, 66 In. 365.00
Easel, Lyre Form, Scroll Top, Splayed Legs, England, 58 In. 520.00
Easel, Oak, Portfolio, Brass Mountings, 53 x 13 x 28 In. 840.00
Etagere, 3 Shelves, Inlaid, Late 19th Century, 22 x 14 x 46 In. 170.00
Etagere, Brass, Glass, 4 Graduated Round Shelves, Victorian, 66 In. 1380.00
Etagere, Chinese Export, Lacquered, Late 19th Century 4600.00
Etagere, Georgian, Marquetry, Open-Urn Pediment, Center Mirror, 54 x 97 In. 2185.00
Etagere, Japanese, Hardwood, Outscrolled Top, Shelves, c.1926, 86 x 60 x 21 In. 3450.00
Etagere, Louis XVI Style, Kingwood, Burr Yew, 29 1/4 x 15 3/4 In., Pair 2185.00
Etagere, Mahogany, Multisectioned, Beveled, Claw Feet, 55 x 15 x 56 In. 1960.00
Etagere, Mahogany, Pierced Sides, Brass Finger Pulls, Mahogany, 34 x 16 x 6 1/2 In. ... 168.00
Etagere, Oak, 3 Tiers, Gallery, Frieze, Casters, Victorian, 50 x 48 x 20 In. 5100.00
Etagere, Oak, Rectangular Top, Fluted Tapered Square Legs, 38 In. 1380.00
Etagere, Rococo, Metal, Gilt, 4 Shelves, Applied Leaves, 52 In. 550.00
Etagere, Rosewood, Bonnet Top, Carved Apron, Legs, J & J.W. Meeks, 105 x 21 x 70 In. . 19600.00
Etagere, Victorian, Mahogany, Columns, Mid 19th Century, 48 1/2 x 23 1/2 x 16 In. 1265.00
Etagere, Walnut, 2 Shelves, Fret-Carved Scroll Supports, 3 Drawers, 34 x 20 x 63 In. 460.00
Fainting Couch, Eastlake, Walnut, Folds To Daybed, Pencil Carved, 37 x 76 In. 230.00
Fainting Couch, Empire, Mahogany Veneer, Upholstered, Scroll Arms, 53 x 39 In. 1870.00
Fernery, Rosewood, Fruitwood, Flower Inlay, Brass Mounts, 29 x 27 x 17 In. 1120.00
Footstool, Art & Crafts, Mahogany, Original Leather Seat Cover, 18 x 14 x 16 In. 115.00
Footstool, Arts & Crafts, Black Leather Seat, Pyramid Posts, 10 x 17 x 11 1/2 In. 175.00
Footstool, Arts & Crafts, Drop-In Leather Seat, 12 x 18 x 12 In. 144.00
Footstool, Arts & Crafts, Vinyl Seat, 15 x 20 x 14 In. 200.00
Footstool, Beech, Beadwork Cushion, Bun Feet, 1820s, 4 x 10 3/4 In., Pair 865.00
Footstool, Birch, Ebonized Ball Feet, 1840s, 7 x 14 In. 920.00
Footstool, Black Velvet & Leopard Upholstered, Ball Feet 225.00
Footstool, Brown Graining Over Red, Hooked Cushion, 7 1/2 x 14 x 9 In. 140.50
Footstool, Carved Leaves On Legs, Top Floral Panels, Needlepoint Cover, 19 In. 275.00

Footstool, Cricket, Limbert, No. 200, Splayed Slab Legs, Original Finish, 18 x 7 In. 489.00
Footstool, Cricket, Limbert, No. 201 1/2, Mahogany, Leather Top, 20 x 12 In. 400.00
Footstool, Cricket, Limbert, No. 204 1/2, Mahogany, Rectangular Top, 18 x 9 In. 345.00
Footstool, Cricket, Limbert, Splayed Legs, 19 x 10 In. 105.00
Footstool, Cricket, Walnut, Brown Paint, Square Nails, Canted Legs, Apron, 14 x 6 In. . . 330.00
Footstool, Embroidered, Windmill, Fringed Apron, Turned Cherry Legs, 12 1/2 x 7 1/2 In. 66.00
Footstool, Frank Lloyd Wright, Plywood, Internal Section, 1950s, 18 In. 5750.00
Footstool, French Provincial, Needlepoint Upholstered, 21 x 15 x 13 In. 275.00
Footstool, G. Nakashima, Walnut, X-Plank Base, Cushion, Square, 18 1/2 In. 2530.00
Footstool, G. Stickley, Arched Sides, Cross Stretchers, Leather Seat, 17 x 20 In. 5750.00
Footstool, G. Stickley, Leather, Flared Feet, Red Decal, 12 x 12 x 5 In. 980.00
Footstool, G. Stickley, Leather, Tacks, Paper Label, 20 x 16 x 15 In. 650.00
Footstool, G. Stickley, No. 300, Mahogany, Leather Seat, 20 x 16 x 15 In. 635.00
Footstool, G. Stickley, No. 302, Mahogany, Leather Red Decal, 13 x 5 In. 750.00
Footstool, Jumuwood, Incurved Horse-Hoof Feet, 8 x 12 x 24 In. 145.00
Footstool, L. & J.G. Stickley, Mahogany, Original Finish, Signed, 19 x 14 x 18 In. 920.00
Footstool, L. & J.G. Stickley, No. 1292, Mahogany, 7 Vertical Spindles, 18 In. 1035.00
Footstool, L. & J.G. Stickley, Straight Rails, Leather-Covered Cushion, 38 x 17 In. 520.00
Footstool, Leather, Mahogany Stepped Base, Bun Feet, 8 x 13 x 13 In. 120.00
Footstool, Lifetime, Oak, Concave Stretchers, 14 x 18 x 12 In. 1210.00
Footstool, Limbert, No. 224, Mahogany, Leather Seat Rail, 18 x 12 x 13 In. 575.00
Footstool, Louis XV, Giltwood, Serpentine Padded Cushion, 6 1/2 In. 635.00
Footstool, Louis XV, Rosewood, Padded Top, Floral Carved Legs, 19 x 23 x 21 In. 1150.00
Footstool, Mahogany, Brass-Tacked Leather, Scroll Carving, 12 1/2 In., Pair 805.00
Footstool, Mahogany, Cabriole Legs, Paw Feet, Upholstered, 8 1/2 x 12 In. 110.00
Footstool, Mahogany, Framed, Floral Needlepoint Top 140.00
Footstool, Mahogany, Ogee Bracket Feet, 1840s, 12 x 22 In. 225.00
Footstool, Mahogany, Round, Floral Needlepoint, Hinged Top, Pair 495.00
Footstool, Maple, Needlepoint Over Cylinder, 19th Century, 11 x 14 In. 140.00
Footstool, Marquetry, 4 Cattle-Horn Feet, 12 x 16 In. 220.00
Footstool, Needlework Top, Black Ground, Houses, Trees, Cabriole Legs, 9 x 14 x 10 In. . 115.00
Footstool, Oak, Brown Leather Seat, 4 Legs 275.00
Footstool, Oak, Horseshoe Nails, 14 x 12 In. 175.00
Footstool, Oak, Plank Top, Splay Base, Turn Legs, Box Stretcher, England, 1700s, 12 In. 260.00
Footstool, Pine, Lift Top, Interior Compartment, Needlework Upholstered, 14 In. 300.00
Footstool, Quaker Mission Craft, Brown Leather Top, Decal, 16 1/2 x 18 x 15 In. 105.00
Footstool, Queen Anne Style, Cherry, Leather Top, 22 x 17 x 17 In. 165.00
Footstool, Red Paint, Blue & Yellow Geometric & Star, 5 3/4 x 9 In. 935.00
Footstool, Regency, Mahogany, Tan Upholstered Leather, 12 x 15 In., Pair 575.00
Footstool, Rope-Twist Legs & Frame, Upholstered, 17 x 23 In. 770.00
Footstool, Rosewood, Needlepoint Top, Dog On Red Pillow 630.00
Footstool, Roycroft, Mahogany, 4 Tapered Legs, Signed, 9 x 15 x 9 In. 550.00
Footstool, Roycroft, Mahogany, Brown Leather Top, Tapered Legs, 10 x 16 x 9 In. 748.00
Footstool, Rush Seat, Painted, Tulips & Berries, Turned Legs, Pa., 1800s, 11 x 12 In. 960.00
Footstool, Spread-Eagle Corners, Hoofed Feet, Tufted Gold Cushion, 8 x 13 In. 90.00
Footstool, Stenciled Fruit & Leaves, Black Stripes, Green Paint, 8 1/4 x 12 In. 250.00
Footstool, Tiger Maple, Scrolling, Needlepoint Seat Cover, 8 x 17 x 12 1/2 In. 56.00
Footstool, Van Der Rohe, Lacquered Steel Frame, Cane Seat, 1920s, 22 x 16 In., Pair . . . 575.00
Footstool, Walnut, Adjustable, Victorian 155.00
Footstool, Walnut, Dancing Figures On Needlepoint Cover, 17 1/2 x 22 In. 550.00
Footstool, Walnut, Hinged Top, Berries & Leaves, Victorian 495.00
Footstool, Walnut, Needlepoint Cover, Carved Skirt, Fluted Legs, 14 x 26 3/4 In. 170.00
Footstool, Walnut, Rose Needlepoint Cushion, Strawberries, 8 x 16 In. 170.00
Footstool, William & Mary Style, Walnut, Gros Point Upholstered, 17 In. 805.00
Footstool, William IV, Mahogany, Rectangular Frame, Paw Feet, 5 1/2 In. 460.00
Footstool, Windsor, Green Paint, Carved Stick Legs, 8 1/2 x 15 In. 110.00
Frame, Arts & Crafts, Pewter Finish, Stepped Cove, 27 1/2 x 55 1/2 In. 170.00
Frame, Arts & Crafts, Punchwork, Engraved Signature, FH, 20th Century, 23 x 29 In. . . . 6900.00
Frame, Barbizon, Applied Ornaments, Gold Paint, France, 19th Century, 26 x 30 1/4 In. . . 1140.00
Frame, Beaded & Braided Canvas, 39 1/2 x 29 1/2 In. 140.00
Frame, Beaded Oval Surround, Dogwood Flowers, Easel, 12 x 11 In. 86.00
Frame, Bird's-Eye Maple, Gilt Liner, 20 3/4 x 16 3/8 In. 440.00
Frame, Bronze Beaded Liner, Deep Cove, 19th Century, 48 x 39 In. 735.00

Frame, Bronze, Cold Painted, Austria, 9 5/8 In.	518.00
Frame, Bronze, Enamel, Flowers, Mirrors, Geissenhuiner, J.A., c.1885, 15 x 17 In.	5545.00
Frame, Cross Corner, Popsicle Stick Pieces, 14 1/2 In.	50.00
Frame, Double, Red Stones, Greek Key Border, Easel, 1880s, 3 7/8 In.	430.00
Frame, Empire Style, Gilt Brass, 3 Compartments, c.1900, 6 1/2 x 11 1/4 In.	800.00
Frame, Gesso, Gilt, Textured Liner, 22 x 32 In.	110.00
Frame, Gilt, Applied Composition, Continental, 19th Century, 24 x 26 In.	600.00
Frame, Gilt, Hand Carved, France, Late 18th Century, 46 x 62 In.	8050.00
Frame, Gilt, Islamic Patterned Cove, Applied Ornament, 1850s, 36 x 56 In.	12650.00
Frame, Louis XVI Style, Gilt Bronze, c.1900, 13 1/4 x 9 In., Pair	2300.00
Frame, Presentation, Oval Surround, 2 Doors, Initial At Top, 1870s, 7 1/2 x 8 In.	345.00
Frame, Shadowbox, Cherry, Carved Crest, Swirling Acanthus Leaves, 18 x 10 3/4 In.	220.00
Frame, Shadowbox, Mahogany, Round, 15 1/2 In.	30.00
Frame, Shadowbox, Walnut, Relief Bark, Gilt Inner Liner, 34 1/2 x 22 In.	165.00
Frame, Shallow Cove, Classical Theme, 35 1/2 x 27 1/2 In.	280.00
Frame, Stanford White, Gilt Applied Composition, Dutch Style, 12 x 17 In.	3100.00
Frame, Tabernacle, Carved Gilt, Continental, 18th Century, 14 x 24 In.	600.00
Frame, Wood, Brass Sheet, Stylized Water Lilies, Easel, 13 3/8 x 10 In.	290.00
Frame, Wrought Iron, Floral, Gilt, Beaded, Openwork Rose Branches, 1800s, 26 x 23 In.	635.00
Glider, Old Hickory, Mahogany, Woven Splint Seat, 52 x 32 x 34 In.	4600.00
Glider, Old Hickory, Indiana, 37 x 85 In.	540.00
Hall Stand, Art Nouveau, Oak, Mirror, Glove Box, Brass Rail, Hardware, 84 x 47 x 9 In.	390.00
Hall Stand, Black Forest, Full Standing Bear, Beveled Mirror, Glass Eyes, 74 In.	4480.00
Hall Stand, Edwardian, Oak, Bevel Mirror, Round, Barley Twist Legs, 73 x 22 x 10 In.	390.00
Hall Stand, George Hunzinger, Cherry, Mirror, Arms, c.1885, 51 x 20 x 85 In.	5600.00
Hall Stand, John Salerini, Wrought Iron, Marble, Early 1900s, 60 x 32 x 12 In.	990.00
Hall Stand, Metal, Mirror, Original Patina, 79 x 32 1/2 x 10 1/2 In.	600.00
Hall Stand, Oak, Slat Back, Glove Box, Brass, Round Bevel Mirror, 75 x 24 x 10 3/4 In.	450.00
Hall Stand, Victorian, Flowers, Scroll, Mirror Back, 1800s, 33 x 10 1/2 x 81 1/2 In.	490.00
Hall Stand, Victorian, Hat & Umbrella, Mirror Top, Marble, Drawer, Drip Pan, 81 In.	715.00
Hall Stand, Victorian, Relief Floral & Scroll, Mirror, 33 x 10 1/2 x 81 1/2 In.	490.00
Hall Tree, Arts & Crafts, Mahogany, Copper Heart Design, 48 x 15 x 77 In.	3220.00
Hall Tree, Arts & Crafts, Mahogany, Original Copper Hooks, 20 x 68 In.	310.00
Hall Tree, Bear Form, Cubs Climbing, Mother At Base, Hoof Feet, 86 In.	1175.00
Hall Tree, Cherry, Birch, Gold On Ball Finials, Spider Base, Urn Finial, 77 1/2 In.	2310.00
Hall Tree, Lift-Top Seat, Lion-Head Hooks	1850.00
Hall Tree, Limbert, No. 230, Mahogany, Revolving Hat Rack, 25 x 68 In.	335.00
Hall Tree, Maple, Faux Bamboo, 7 Pegs, 3 Leg Base, c.1890, 73 In.	825.00
Hall Tree, Rococo Revival, Walnut, Marble, Mid 19th Century, 107 x 55 x 17 In.	21850.00
Hall Tree, Walnut, Marble Top Over Drawer, Iron Drip Trays, Inlaid Birds, 104 In.	3100.00
Hat Rack, Victorian, Walnut, Carved, Lion Head, Shell, Scroll, 35 x 36 In.	1230.00
Hat Rack, Warren McArthur, Anodized Aluminum, 1930s, 67 In.	3680.00
Headboard, G. Nelson, Black Leather, Plank Legs, 56 In.	1540.00
Headboard, Louis XV Style, Mahogany, Burl, Ormolu Mounted, 60 x 64 In.	805.00
Headboard, McCobb, Cherry Finish, 7 Brass Spindles, Full, 38 1/2 x 53 In.	105.00
Headboard, Raymond Loewy, 2 Drawers, Molded Plastic, 62 x 16 x 21 In.	185.00
High Chair, Ash, Cherry, Ring-Turned Stiles, Spindles, Arms, Splint Seat, 35 In.	1035.00
High Chair, Blue, Arched Slats, Crest, Turned Legs, Splint Seat, Ball Finials, 18 x 34 In.	410.00
High Chair, Hardwood, Finial Posts, Arm Turnings, Splayed Legs, 34 x 17 1/2 In.	420.00
High Chair, Heywood Brothers, Wicker, Wheels, 37 1/3 In.	550.00
High Chair, Maple, Hickory, Ladder Back, Turned, Shaped Finials, 33 1/2 In.	1320.00
High Chair, Maple, Painted, Turned, New England, Early 18th Century, 37 In.	12650.00
High Chair, Sailboat Carving	240.00
High Chair, Slat Back, Yellow Paint, Back Legs Splay Outward	300.00
High Chair, Turned Legs, Plank Seat, Tapered Arms, Spindles, Crest, 24 x 36 In.	2310.00
High Chair, Twig, Bentwood Elements, Woven Seat, 34 In.	303.00
High Chair, Wallace Nutting, Lift Food Tray, New England Turnings	2310.00
High Chair, Wicker, Woven Backrest, Hinged Tray, Stretchers, Late 19th Century	78.00
High Chair, Windsor, Bamboo Turning, Red, Yellow, & Black Paint, 24 In.	330.00
High Chair, Windsor, Bamboo, Flared Crest, 3 Spindles, Anna Sargent, Marietta	187.00
High Chair, Windsor, Comb Back, 7 Spindles, Shaped Seat, Continuous Arm, 25 In.	2233.00
High Chair, Windsor, Maple, Pine, Stencil, Mid 19th Century, 33 1/2 x 17 1/2 x 14 In.	715.00
Highboy, Cherry, Chestnut, Scalloped Aprons, 2 Small, 3 Large Drawers, 77 1/4 In.	1320.00

Highboy, Chippendale, Maple, Graduated Drawers, Ball Feet, 71 x 38 x 19 In. 2300.00
Highboy, Chippendale, Maple, New England, 71 1/4 x 38 1/4 In. 2300.00
Highboy, Mahogany, 2 Sections, Lower 4 Long Drawers, 3 Short Drawers, 86 In. 690.00
Highboy, Mahogany, Flat Top, Cabriole Legs, Pad Feet, 1720-1740, 73 x 37 In. 9800.00
Highboy, Mahogany, Shell & Leaves, 9 Top Drawers, Claw & Ball Feet, 90 In. 1430.00
Highboy, Maple Veneer, Burl, 20th Century, 79 x 36 In. 560.00
Highboy, Queen Anne, Cherry, 6 Over 3 Drawers, Batwing Brass, 36 x 19 x 72 In. 6325.00
Highboy, Queen Anne, Curly Maple, Pine, 5 Graduated Drawers, 39 x 70 In. 2530.00
Highboy, Queen Anne, Mahogany, 2 Drawers, Fan Carved, Acorn Pendants, 64 In. 2295.00
Highboy, Queen Anne, Mahogany, 5 Graduated Drawers, Cabriole Legs, 72 In. 2300.00
Highboy, Queen Anne, Maple, 2 Sections, 1760-1790, 69 x 37 1/2 x 20 In. 18975.00
Highboy, Queen Anne, Maple, 5 Graduated Drawers, Scalloped Apron, 72 x 40 x 18 In. . . . 1980.00
Highboy, Queen Anne, Maple, Bonnet Top, Carved, c.1770, 74 x 42 x 19 1/2 In. 15600.00
Highboy, Queen Anne, Tiger Maple, R.I., Late 18th Century, 38 1/2 x 39 1/2 x 21 In. 3105.00
Highboy, Urn & Flame Finals, 3 Drawers Over 2 Drawers, Carved Knees, 63 1/2 In. 345.00
Highboy, Walnut, Flat Top, Scalloped Apron, 9 Drawers, c.1740, 67 x 38 In. 6800.00
Highboy, Walnut, Scalloped Apron, Drawer In Base, 7 Drawers In Top, 70 In. 4480.00
Highboy, William & Mary, Oak, 5 Drawers, Molded Posts, England, 39 x 20 x 65 In. 770.00
Highboy, William & Mary, Walnut, 3 Over 3 Drawers, Turned Legs, X-Stretcher, 64 In. . . . 3150.00
Hoosier Cabinet, Oak, Enamel Surface, Painted Interior, Maidsaver, 72 x 29 x 19 In. 1005.00
Hoosier Cabinet, Oak, Flour Sifter 1400.00
Hoosier Cabinet, White Paint, Red Knobs, 1950s 600.00
Humidor, French Provincial, Marble Top, Drawer, Door, Tapered Legs, 34 x 19 x 15 In. . . 225.00
Humidor, Oak, Marble Top, Liner, Drawer, Door, Shelf, 32 1/2 x 15 x 14 1/2 In. 225.00
Huntboard, Center Drawer, Mid 19th Century, 41 1/2 x 53 1/2 In. 560.00
Huntboard, Cherry, Shaped Backboard, 4 Short Drawers, Tapered Legs, 44 x 75 In. 1230.00
Huntboard, Federal, Cedar, 2 Inlaid Short Drawers, Square, Tapered Legs, 36 x 62 In. 6465.00
Huntboard, Mahogany, 4 Drawers, Tall Tapered Legs 415.00
Huntboard, Mahogany, Bowed Doors, Concave Doors, Trapezoid Tapered Legs, 36 In. . . . 5040.00
Huntboard, Mahogany, Ireland, Early 19th Century, 29 1/2 x 84 1/2 x 54 In. 4900.50
Huntboard, Maple, 2 Rows Of 3 Drawers, Kearneysville, W.V., 38 1/2 x 63 x 21 1/2 In. . . 1815.00
Hutch, Cherry, Oval Top, Compartment, Hinged Top, Shoe Feet, 27 x 40 In. 4025.00
Hutch, Peter Hunt, Painted, Flower, Star, 55 x 57 x 17 1/2 In. 920.00
Hutch, Pine, Red, Cyma-Curved Cutouts Ends, Compartment Base, 62 x 35 In. 2970.00
Hutch, Tudor Style, Oak Stained Panel Doors, Carved Masks, 47 x 76 In. 630.00
Hutch, Tudor Style, Oak, Early 20th Century, 47 x 18 x 76 In. 635.00
Kas, Amish, Poplar, Paneled Ends, 2 Doors, 8 Shelves, Divided Center, 93 1/4 In. 990.00
Kas, Baroque, Ebony, Inlaid Oak, Rosewood, Dutch, Early 18th Century, 61 x 64 x 26 In. 2875.00
Kas, Baroque, Rosewood, Rectangular Top, Bun Front Feet, 32 1/2 x 88 In. 1440.00
Kas, Cherry, 2 Raised Doors, 2 Short Drawers, Bun Feet, 77 x 67 In. 4935.00
Kas, Cherry, Rectangular Top, Stepped Cornice, Turned Turnip Feet, 1750 . . . . 3360.00
Kas, Chippendale, Gumwood, Rectangular Top, Ogee Bracket Feet, 1780 . . . . 8400.00
Kas, Walnut, Arched Doors, Double Raised Panels, 2 Drawers, 78 x 58 x 23 In. 2750.00
Kas, William & Mary, Cherry, Pine, Poplar, Rectangular Top, 1780, 26 x 77 In. 4025.00
Kas, William & Mary, Gumwood, Poplar, Rectangular Top, 1740, 55 x 78 In. 13800.00
Kas, William & Mary, Poplar, Rectangular Top, Stepped Cornice, 23 x 78 3/4 In. 5175.00
Ladder, Library, Brass Mounted, Folding, Late 19th Century, 77 1/2 In. 1380.00
Ladder, Library, Mahogany, 5 Rungs, Brass Treads, 62 In. 489.00
Ladder, Library, Mahogany, Folding, c.1900, 79 1/2 In. 2070.00
Ladder, Library, Regency Style, Mahogany, 4 Rungs, Brass Treads, 53 In. 345.00
Ladder, Library, Regency Style, Mahogany, Brass Mount Steps, 53 In. 315.00
Ladder, Library, Regency Style, Mahogany, Folding, 4 Rungs, 53 In. 316.00
Ladder, Library, Regency, Mahogany, Folding, 4 Rungs Brass Tread, 52 In. 375.00
Ladder, Library, Regency, Mahogany, Folding, 5 Rungs, 62 In. 575.00
Ladder, Regency, Pine, 10 Steps, Mid 19th Century, 109 x 19 In. 805.00
Lap, Mahogany, Brass, Stand, Late 19th Century, 19 1/4 x 15 7/8 x 9 7/8 In. 635.00
Lap Desk, Antler Ivory & Sandalwood Lined, Leather Writing Slide, 1880s, 11 3/4 In. 575.00
Lap Desk, Burl Walnut, Brass Bound, Hinged Lid, Leather Surface, c.1850, 14 x 9 In. . . . 259.00
Lap Desk, Burl Walnut, Mosaic Inserts, Brass Interior, 4 1/2 x 14 x 10 In. 635.00
Lap Desk, Fruitwood, Abalone, Gilt Banded, Velvet Surface, 5 1/2 x 13 x 8 3/4 In. 299.00
Lap Desk, George III, Mahogany, Compartments, Hinged Lid, Felt Surface, 14 x 9 In. . . . 200.00
Lap Desk, George IV, Mahogany, Brass Bound, Mid 19th Century, 12 1/2 x 9 3/4 In. 1265.00
Lap Desk, George IV, Rosewood, Inlaid, Mid 19th Century, 22 x 14 3/4 x 10 3/4 In. 1725.00

Lap Desk, Gray & Black Paint, Lift Top, 20 In. 175.00
Lap Desk, Mahogany, Brass Bail Handles, Hinged Lid, c.1860, 17 3/4 x 9 1/2 In. 196.00
Lap Desk, Mahogany, Brass Lock & Name Plate, Brass Bound, 5 3/4 In. 350.00
Lap Desk, Mahogany, Brass Plaque, Ivorine Ruler, Late Victorian, 8 x 17 7/8 x 12 In. 1265.00
Lap Desk, Mahogany, Folding, Brass Handles, Velvet Lined Insert, 7 x 17 In. 275.00
Lap Desk, Mahogany, Gilt, Green Leather Writing Surface, 24 x 20 3/4 x 10 In. 1035.00
Lap Desk, Mahogany, Lift Handles, Wells, Side Drawer, England, c.1890, 17 x 9 x 6 In. ... 175.00
Lap Desk, Mahogany, Marquetry, Lid, England, 19th Century, 17 x 11 1/2 In. 504.00
Lap Desk, Papier-Mache, Gilt, Floral, 2 Inkwells, Slope Lid, 2 Drawers, 14 x 17 x 8 In. ... 375.75
Lap Desk, Pine, Slant Front, 3/4 Lift Top, Compartment Interior, 15 x 25 In. 145.00
Lap Desk, Rosewood, Brass Bound, Leather & Gold Interior, Ink Bottle, 14 x 9 In. 310.00
Lap Desk, Rosewood, Brass Inlay, Velvet Writing Surface, 2 Wells, 10 1/2 x 16 In. 460.00
Lap Desk, Rosewood, Brass Mounted, Early 20th Century, 5 5/8 x 16 x 9 1/2 In. 259.00
Lap Desk, Rosewood, Inlaid Mother-Of-Pearl, Rose Velvet Surface, 6 x 16 x 9 1/2 In. ... 520.00
Lap Desk, Rosewood, Presentation Plaque, Leather Surface, 7 x 17 1/2 In. 1035.00
Lap Desk, Walnut, Incised, Drop Front, Fold-Out Compartments, 16 x 12 x 15 In. 840.00
Lectern, Fruitwood, Slanted Surface, Mid 19th Century, 37 x 25 1/2 x 16 In. 1150.00
Lectern, Regency Style, Mahogany, Leather Inset Bookrest, 20th Century, 45 In. 300.00
Library Steps, Mahogany, 4 Leather-Lined Steps, 18th Century, 36 1/2 In. 4200.00
Library Steps, Mahogany, D-Shape Side Rail, 78 3/4 x 13 1/2 In. 476.00
Library Steps, Pine, Rectangular Treads, Diagonal Braces, 1870s, 61 In. 575.00
Library Steps, Walnut, Leather Inset, Folding, 5 Tiers, Shoe-Form Supports, 42 In. 840.00
Linen Press, 2 Doors, Inset Flamed Panel, 2 Lower Short Drawers, 2 Long, 84 In. 3220.00
Linen Press, 2 Paneled Doors, 2 Short Drawers, 2 Long Drawers, 1780s, 81 1/2 In. 3910.00
Linen Press, 2 Paneled Doors, 2 Short Drawers, 2 Long Drawers, 88 In. 2300.00
Linen Press, 2 Paneled Doors, Flanked By Pilasters, 4 Lower Drawers, 1840s, 88 In. 2760.00
Linen Press, Chippendale, Oak, 18th Century, 68 x 36 x 20 1/2 In. 1625.00
Linen Press, George III Style, Mahogany, Molded Cornice, 84 x 47 3/4 x 25 In. 2300.00
Linen Press, George III, Mahogany, 2 Doors Over 4 Drawers, 80 x 54 In. 2760.00
Linen Press, George III, Mahogany, 2 Paneled Doors Over 3 Drawers, 81 x 51 In. 3220.00
Linen Press, George III, Mahogany, 2 Paneled Doors, Bracket Feet, 85 In. 3220.00
Linen Press, George III, Mahogany, Cornice, 2 Drawers, 79 x 49 1/2 x 24 1/2 In. 3450.00
Linen Press, George III, Mahogany, Cornice, Late 18th Century, 75 x 52 x 24 In. 3680.00
Linen Press, George III, Mahogany, Paneled Doors, Bracket Feet, 88 x 25 In. 3220.00
Linen Press, George III, Mahogany, Plain Frieze, 2 Graduated Drawers, 85 1/2 In. 2645.00
Linen Press, George III, Mahogany, Rectangular Molded Cornice, 82 x 24 In. 3680.00
Linen Press, George III, Mahogany, Rectangular Molded Cornice, 85 x 22 In. 2760.00
Linen Press, George III, Molded, Door, Compartments, Bracket Feet, 86 x 50 x 22 In. ... 2510.00
Linen Press, Georgian Style, Mahogany, Inlaid, 82 1/4 x 44 1/4 x 23 1/2 In. 1460.00
Linen Press, Gumwood, 2 Arched Panel Doors, 3 Base Drawers, 1770 .... 11500.00
Linen Press, Hepplewhite, Mahogany, 2 Sections, 3 Drawers, 74 x 34 3/4 x 21 3/4 In. ... 1120.00
Linen Press, Mahogany, 2 Paneled Doors, Lower Drawers, 85 1/2 In. 4025.00
Linen Press, Mahogany, 6 Short & 1 Long Drawer, 1810, 50 x 22 In. 5150.00
Linen Press, Mahogany, Central Swag Medallion, Lower Drawers, 1770s, 96 In. 8625.00
Linen Press, Mahogany, Classical Figures, Shelved Interior, c.1815, 76 3/4 In. 6460.00
Linen Press, Mahogany, Cornice Over Doors, 2 Short Over 2 Long Drawers, 72 In. 1610.00
Linen Press, Mahogany, Doors, 2 Short Over 2 Long Drawers, 1820s, 87 In. 2760.00
Linen Press, Mahogany, Egyptian Busts, Columns, 76 x 53 x 25 1/2 In. .... *Illus* 2990.00
Linen Press, Mahogany, Inlaid Frieze, Panel Doors, Lower 5 Drawers, 80 3/4 In. 2245.00
Linen Press, Mahogany, Molded Cornice, Bracket Feet, 76 x 43 x 22 In. .... *Illus* 2300.00
Linen Press, Mahogany, Overhanging Cornice, 2 Paneled Doors, 7 Drawers, 86 In. 3740.00
Linen Press, Mahogany, Pierced Crown, Linenfold Panel Doors, 93 x 42 1/2 In. 2015.00
Linen Press, Mahogany, Serpentine Cornice, 3 Drawers, 111 x 75 x 27 In. 13225.00
Linen Press, Mahogany, Top Inlaid Doors, Lower 3 Long Drawers, 1870s, 88 In. 2015.00
Linen Press, Neoclassical, Oak, Early 19th Century, 94 x 63 3/4 x 20 3/4 In. 3565.00
Linen Press, Oak, Mahogany Diamond String Inlay, c.1850 .... 880.00
Linen Press, Regency, Mahogany, 2 Flame Paneled Doors Over 4 Drawers, 84 x 53 In. .. 3680.00
Linen Press, Regency, Mahogany, 3 Graduated Drawers, 76 In. 2990.00
Linen Press, Regency, Mahogany, Doors, Early 19th Century, 80 1/2 x 44 x 22 1/2 In. ... 2185.00
Linen Press, Regency, Mahogany, Early 19th Century, 80 1/2 x 47 1/2 x 22 In. 6040.00
Linen Press, Regency, Mahogany, Molded Cornice, Reeded Feet, 91 x 24 In. 4140.00
Linen Press, Satinwood, Molded Cornice, Drawers, 85 x 50 x 23 1/2 In. .... *Illus* 2070.00
Linen Press, Walnut, Carved, Panel Door, Leaf Pulls, Scroll Feet, c.1860, 49 x 23 In. 5000.00

Furniture, Linen Press, Mahogany,
Egyptian Busts, Columns,
76 x 53 x 25 1/2 In.

Furniture, Linen Press,
Mahogany, Molded Cornice,
Bracket Feet, 76 x 43 x 22 In.

Furniture, Linen Press,
Satinwood, Molded Cornice,
Drawers, 85 x 50 x 23 1/2 In.

Linen Press, Yellow & White Pine, 2 Paneled Doors, Shelves, 66 x 51 In. 785.00
Love Seat, Carved Top Back Rail, Fruit, Leaves, Upholstered, 64 In. 690.00
Love Seat, Eastlake, Cherry, Pierced, 2-Heart Upholstered Back, Arms, Restored, 51 In. . . . 1895.00
Love Seat, Heywood Bros. & Co., Wicker, Red Cushions, 32 x 48 x 24 In. 1350.00
Love Seat, Mahogany, Late 19th Century, 27 x 35 3/4 In. 650.00
Love Seat, Mahogany, Upholstered, Child's, 27 x 36 3/4 In. 650.00
Love Seat, Victorian, Mahogany, Cameo Back, Flower Carved Crest, Gold Velvet 165.00
Love Seat, Walnut, Carved Columbus Head, c.1860 . . . . 1100.00
Love Seat, Walnut, Floral & Scrolled Carving, Upholstered, 83 x 40 In. 315.00
Lowboy, B. Harter, Cherry, 3 Dovetailed Bottom Drawers, 3 Top Drawers, 30 1/2 In. 3190.00
Lowboy, Cherry, 3 Drawers, Padded Feet, Pennsylvania House, 24 x 28 In. 165.00
Lowboy, Chippendale, Mahogany, Rectangular Gadroon Top, 3 Drawers, 29 In. 2300.00
Lowboy, Chippendale, Walnut, 3 Aligned Drawers, Claw & Ball Feet, 30 In. 4370.00
Lowboy, George III, Mahogany, Drawers, Cabriole Legs, 28 1/2 x 34 x 23 In. 1955.00
Lowboy, Pine, 2 Doors, Shelf, Diamond Panels, Painted, 18th Century, 40 x 43 In. 5040.00
Lowboy, Queen Anne Style, Oak, Thumb-Molded Top, Pad Feet, 27 x 34 x 19 In. 920.00
Lowboy, Queen Anne, Mahogany, Fan Carved, Acorn Drop Pendants, 32 x 35 In. 1230.00
Lowboy, Queen Anne, Oak, 3 Drawers, Shaped Apron, Pad Feet, 30 x 18 x 28 In. 460.00
Lowboy, Queen Anne, Walnut, Rectangular Top, 3-Frieze Drawer, Cabriole Legs, Pad Feet 1840.00
Lowboy, Thomasville, 33 x 38 In. 145.00
Mirror, Acorn Drops At Top, Filigree Basket Of Fruit, 2 Parts, 46 x 21 In. 690.00
Mirror, Adam Style, Carved Wood, Gesso, Gilt, c.1900, 36 x 16 In. 146.00
Mirror, Adam Style, Half Column Frame, Flower Decoration, 35 x 45 In. 140.00
Mirror, Adam Style, Wood Frame, Eagle Crest, Scrollwork, Late 1800s, 52 x 25 In. 825.00
Mirror, Aesthetic Revival, Pierced, Leafy Scrolled Crest Rail, 1890, 29 x 100 In. 660.00
Mirror, Arched Plate, Greek Key Incised Frame, Ribbon Crest, 1870s, 53 x 33 In. 2185.00
Mirror, Art Deco, Ebonized Wood, Antiqued, Mid 20th Century, 60 1/4 x 60 In. 230.00
Mirror, Art Nouveau, 2 Pinecone Shaped Fruits, Leaves, 1900, 27 x 41 In. 385.00
Mirror, Arts & Crafts, Hammered, Copper, Repousse, Original Patina, 24 x 36 In. 1210.00
Mirror, Arts & Crafts, Oak, Copper Panel, Tulips, Flower-Form Hooks, 41 x 26 In. 1495.00
Mirror, Arts & Crafts, Rectangular, Inlaid Frame, Green, Beige, 19 x 15 In. 45.00
Mirror, Baroque, Arched Plate Within Gilt Lead Border, Sweden, 41 x 28 In. 12000.00
Mirror, Baroque, Giltwood, Carved, Florentine, Early 18th Century, 48 x 42 In. 4140.00
Mirror, Baroque, Giltwood, Scalloped Frame, Leaves, Shell Pediment, 32 x 20 In. 860.00
Mirror, Baroque, Walnut, Carved Giltwood, 19th Century, 29 1/2 x 28 In. 635.00
Mirror, Beveled Arched Plate, Leaf Scroll, Shell At Top, 1830s, 80 1/2 x 48 1/2 In. 4150.00
Mirror, Beveled Glass, Openwork Scroll, Swinging Stand, 12 1/4 x 19 In. 110.00
Mirror, Beveled Plate, Paper Backing, 3-Fold, Hanging Chain, 10 In. 70.00
Mirror, Beveled Shield Plate, Pierced, Etched Crest, Etched Frame, 47 x 24 In. 925.00
Mirror, Biedermeier, Mahogany, Plain Frieze, Crest, Beveled Plate, 48 x 28 In. 1985.00
Mirror, Biedermeier, Mahogany, Scandinavia, Mid 19th Century, 62 x 26 1/2 In. 865.00

Mirror, Biedermeier, Walnut, Ogee Molding, Paneled Stiles, c.1830, 37 x 26 In. 345.00
Mirror, Black & Gold Paint, Reverse Painted, Buildings, 2 Parts, 19 In. 165.00
Mirror, Black Half Columns, Stencils, Flowers, Eglomise Panel, Landscape, 35 x 16 In. . . . 415.00
Mirror, Brass, Patinated, Embossed, Cushion Shape, 22 1/2 x 13 In., Pair 430.00
Mirror, Cartouche Form, Carved Scrolled Leaves, 30 3/4 In. 115.00
Mirror, Carved Tendrils & Eagle Heads, Gold & Red Paint, Oval, 18 x 62 In. 825.00
Mirror, Carved Wood, Gesso, Gilt, Continental, Late 19th Century, 54 x 58 In. 225.00
Mirror, Cast Iron, Eagle Crest, Lattice Borders, Oval, 15 1/2 x 11 In. 85.00
Mirror, Charles X Style, Giltwood, Carved, Gesso, 43 x 32 1/2 In. 1150.00
Mirror, Charles X, Giltwood, Cream Paint, Ogee Molded Frame, 48 1/4 In. 1380.00
Mirror, Cheval, Aesthetic Revival, Oak, Circles & Bars, 1890, 73 In. 2400.00
Mirror, Cheval, Beveled, Brass Attachments, 4 Carved Paw Feet, Oval, 32 x 23 x 70 In. . . . 980.00
Mirror, Cheval, Carved & Harp Form Frame, Scrolling Feet, 75 x 37 In. 560.00
Mirror, Cheval, Faux Bamboo, Pierced Crest, 19th Century, 30 1/2 x 71 In. 6325.00
Mirror, Cheval, Mahogany, Acanthus Leaf Legs, Pineapple Finial, 33 x 21 x 73 In. 1210.00
Mirror, Cheval, Mahogany, Carved & Fluted Side Supports, Claw Feet, 73 x 35 In. 605.00
Mirror, Cheval, Mahogany, Dental Crown, Beveled, Iron Finial, 1900, 25 1/2 x 20 In. . . . 450.00
Mirror, Cheval, Mahogany, Oval Plate, Leaves, Late 19th Century, 75 In. 630.00
Mirror, Cheval, Neoclassical, Mahogany, Columns, c.1900, 76 x 28 1/2 x 24 In. 1495.00
Mirror, Cheval, Neoclassical, Mahogany, Saber Legs, 19th Century, 72 x 38 1/2 x 22 In. . 4830.00
Mirror, Chinese Export, Black Lacquer, Parcel Gilt, Ogee Arch Crest, 56 x 31 In. 6600.00
Mirror, Chippendale Style, Mahogany, Crest, Spread-Wing Eagle, 30 x 16 In. 440.00
Mirror, Chippendale, Curly Maple, 26 x 17 1/2 In. 275.00
Mirror, Chippendale, Curly Maple, Rectangular, 21 x 45 In. 660.00
Mirror, Chippendale, Giltwood, Leaf Carved, C-Scroll, c.1890, 33 x 53 In. 1035.00
Mirror, Chippendale, Mahogany Veneer, Arched, Scrolled Crest, 39 1/2 In. 630.00
Mirror, Chippendale, Mahogany Veneer, Crest, Ears, 12 3/4 x 24 1/4 In. 275.00
Mirror, Chippendale, Mahogany Veneer, Giltwood, 18th Century, 31 In. 1095.00
Mirror, Chippendale, Mahogany Veneer, Giltwood, Rectangular Frame, 41 In. 920.00
Mirror, Chippendale, Mahogany Veneer, Giltwood, Shaped Crest, 37 1/2 x 19 In. 825.00
Mirror, Chippendale, Mahogany Veneer, Molded Rectangular Frame, 45 In. 3450.00
Mirror, Chippendale, Mahogany Veneer, Parcel Gilt, Scrolled Crest, 37 x 20 In. 862.00
Mirror, Chippendale, Mahogany, 18 x 10 3/4 In. 310.00
Mirror, Chippendale, Mahogany, 37 1/2 x 20 In. 195.00
Mirror, Chippendale, Mahogany, Arched Crest, Phoenix, 20 x 36 In. 4025.00
Mirror, Chippendale, Mahogany, Arched Pediment, 1803, 32 3/4 x 45 In. 12650.00
Mirror, Chippendale, Mahogany, Gilt Urn & Flower Spray On Scrolled Crest, 52 In. 1725.00
Mirror, Chippendale, Mahogany, Giltwood, Incised Leafy Vines, 31 1/2 x 17 In. 1150.00
Mirror, Chippendale, Mahogany, Giltwood, Pierced Crest, Parcel Gilt Liner, 55 In. 8625.00
Mirror, Chippendale, Mahogany, Parcel Gilt, c.1780, 46 In. 14100.00
Mirror, Chippendale, Mahogany, Parcel Gilt, Inlaid, 45 x 22 In. 825.00
Mirror, Chippendale, Mahogany, Pierced Base, Gilt Leaves, Phoenix, 44 x 22 In. 7050.00
Mirror, Chippendale, Mahogany, Pierced Pediment, Gilt Phoenix, 36 x 20 In. 1295.00
Mirror, Chippendale, Mahogany, Pine, Molded Liner, 19 3/4 x 11 1/2 In. 550.00
Mirror, Chippendale, Mahogany, Scroll, Top Crest, 17 x 11 3/4 In. 550.00
Mirror, Chippendale, Mahogany, Scrolled Crest, 44 x 21 1/2 In. 980.00
Mirror, Chippendale, Mahogany, Scrolled Crest, Leaf Ears, Refinished, 13 x 23 3/4 In. . . . 1210.00
Mirror, Chippendale, Mahogany, Veneer, New England, Late 18th Century, 25 x 14 1/2 In. 635.00
Mirror, Chippendale, Scrolled Crest, Pierced Gilt Flowers, 18th Century, 22 x 14 In. 400.00
Mirror, Chippendale, Walnut Veneer, Carved, Parcel Gilt, Scrolled Crest 1380.00
Mirror, Chippendale, Walnut, Crest, Scroll Corners, Liner, 11 1/2 x 18 In. 300.00
Mirror, Chippendale, Walnut, Gilt Gesso, Phoenix Carved Crest, 44 x 23 In. 705.00
Mirror, Chippendale, Walnut, Giltwood, Ornate Crest, 1770, 45 In. 6900.00
Mirror, Circular Plate, Applied Metal Clockface, c.1900, 59 3/4 In. 2645.00
Mirror, Convex, 2 Candle Sockets, Glass Bobeches, Frame, Eagle Finial, 37 In. 880.00
Mirror, Convex, Giltwood, Molded Ball Frame, Winged-Eagle Top, 81 x 83 In. 5060.00
Mirror, Convex, Giltwood, Round Plate, Wreath Of Fruit & Leaves, 29 3/4 In. 2760.00
Mirror, Convex, Giltwood, Spread-Wing Eagle Finial, Leafy Scrolls, 48 x 29 x 4 In. 3760.00
Mirror, Convex, Spread-Wing Eagle Finial, Leaves On Base, 1880s, 33 In. 165.00
Mirror, Courting, Harbor Scene On Panel, Beveled Glass, 32 x 22 1/2 In. 5400.00
Mirror, Courting, Marbleized, Eglomise Panels, Stepped Crest, 17 x 11 1/2 In. 1705.00
Mirror, Courting, Molded, Rectangular Frame, Stag, Leaping, 11 x 18 In. 3738.00
Mirror, Courting, Pine, Mahogany, Reverse Painted, Roses, White Ground, 16 x 11 In. 1430.00

Mirror, Directoire Style, Giltwood, Carved, Sunburst, Italy, c.1900, 30 In. 920.00
Mirror, Dressing, Beveled, Columns, Cast Metal Jesters, 10 1/4 x 18 1/2 In. 100.00
Mirror, Dressing, Brass, 3 Flower Lights, Painted, Flowers & Leaves, Round, 24 In. 750.00
Mirror, Dressing, Cloisonne, Cherub, Floral Swag, 10 1/2 x 7 3/8 In. 860.00
Mirror, Dressing, Floral, 3 Panels, 76 x 32 In. 2300.00
Mirror, Dressing, George III, Drop Front, 6 Drawers, Japanned, 28 x 12 In. 2070.00
Mirror, Dressing, George III, Mahogany, Satinwood, 3 Drawers, c.1790, 30 x 20 x 8 In. . . 1380.00
Mirror, Dressing, Giltwood, Leaf-Carved Frame, Center Shell, Easel, 14 x 12 In. 265.00
Mirror, Dressing, Hepplewhite, Mahogany, Bowfront, 2 Drawers, Line Inlay, 19 x 19 In. . . 220.00
Mirror, Dressing, Mahogany Veneer, Ball Feet, 16 x 14 1/2 x 11 In. 70.00
Mirror, Dressing, Mahogany Veneer, Canted Turned Supports, 3 Drawers, 25 x 23 In. 140.00
Mirror, Dressing, Mahogany, Arched, Candle Arms, 1875, 30 3/4 In. 430.00
Mirror, Dressing, Mahogany, Inlaid, Drawer, Adjustable, 16 x 14 x 6 1/2 In. 210.00
Mirror, Dressing, Mahogany, Tilting Frame, Drawer, 20 x 14 3/4 In. 120.00
Mirror, Dressing, Neoclassical, Mahogany, Scroll Supports, c.1829, 23 x 21 x 7 1/2 In. . . . 1880.00
Mirror, Dressing, Renaissance Revival, Gilt Bronze, Enamel, Jewels, 17 x 14 1/2 In. 920.00
Mirror, Dressing, Sterling Silver, Beveled, Swallows In Flight, Easel, 19 1/2 In. 1495.00
Mirror, Dressing, Walnut, Inlaid, Bowed Front, Drawer, 4 Gold Flowers, 19 x 13 In. 175.00
Mirror, Dressing, Wood, Carved, Violin Form, Cupids, Victorian, 29 In. 980.00
Mirror, Eastlake, Walnut, 1860, 31 1/2 x 19 In. 200.00
Mirror, Eastlake, Walnut, Burl, Arch Top, Bust Medallion, 95 x 56 In. 2310.00
Mirror, Eastlake, Walnut, Dome Shape, Shield At Top, c.1875, 74 x 65 In. 560.00
Mirror, Ebonized, Chinoiserie, Arched Crest, Beveled Plate, Oriental, 40 1/2 x 25 In. 630.00
Mirror, Edwardian, Bull's-Eye, Black Lacquer, Parcel Gilt, 19 In., Pair 4140.00
Mirror, Edwardian, Gilt Composition, Oval, c.1900, 45 x 22 In. 690.00
Mirror, Edwardian, Lacquered, Trumeau, Chinoiserie, 56 x 28 In. 1150.00
Mirror, Edwardian, Marquetry, Scrolled Vines, Crossbanded Stiles, 68 In. 860.00
Mirror, Edwardian, Patinated Brass, Reticulated, Easel, 25 1/2 x 21 1/2 In. 175.00
Mirror, Eglomise Panel, Half Column, Corner Blocks, Boy With Hoop, 31 x 15 1/2 In. . . . 740.00
Mirror, Empire Style, Mahogany, Convex, Carved Eagle, Scroll, 19th Century, 35 In. 1320.00
Mirror, Empire, Gold Gilt, Rosette Corner Blocks, Spool Frame, 34 x 23 In. 195.00
Mirror, Federal Style, Gilt Frame, Transfer On Tablet, Beveled, 46 1/2 x 22 1/2 In. 165.00
Mirror, Federal Style, Gilt Gesso Floral, Eagle Crest & Leaves, 34 In. 230.00
Mirror, Federal, Architectural Top, Early 19th Century, 45 x 14 In. 3740.00
Mirror, Federal, Architectural Top, Painted Panel, Fruit, Flowers, 28 1/2 x 16 1/2 In. 3960.00
Mirror, Federal, Eagle, Striped Medallion, Reverse Painted, Reeded Pilasters, 39 In. 385.00
Mirror, Federal, Eglomise, Painted, Rosettes, Reverse Painted, 20 1/2 x 12 In. 940.00
Mirror, Federal, Flame Urn Crest, Ram's Head, Early 1900s, 36 x 48 In. 170.00
Mirror, Federal, Gilt & Eglomise, Reverse Painted, Mass., 1805-1815 . . . . 1955.00
Mirror, Federal, Gilt Gesso, Woman With A Spyglass, Portland, Me., 1825 . . . . 920.00
Mirror, Federal, Giltwood, Applied Spherules, 1810-1820, 13 1/2 In. 1510.00
Mirror, Federal, Giltwood, Eglomise Panel, Nautical Design, 33 x 15 1/2 In. 2130.00
Mirror, Federal, Giltwood, Eglomise, Acorns, Early 19th Century, 41 In. 1150.00
Mirror, Federal, Giltwood, Eglomise, Early 19th Century, 40 1/2 x 23 In. 1090.00
Mirror, Federal, Giltwood, Eglomise, Reverse-Painted Ship, 24 1/2 In. 520.00
Mirror, Federal, Giltwood, Flat Overhanging Cornice, Reeded Pilasters, 58 In. 1265.00
Mirror, Federal, Giltwood, Marbleized Border, 1815, 21 x 32 1/4 In. 2530.00
Mirror, Federal, Mahogany Veneer, Basket Of Flowers, Diamond Lattice, 47 In. 1840.00
Mirror, Federal, Mahogany Veneer, Molded Cornice, 1820, 40 3/4 x 22 In. 630.00
Mirror, Federal, Mahogany Veneer, Reeded Columns, 35 x 17 1/2 In. 2185.00
Mirror, Federal, Mahogany, 2 Sections, Reverse Painted, Ormolu, 32 1/4 x 18 In. 360.00
Mirror, Federal, Mahogany, Gilt, Rosette Terminals, 1800, 20 x 51 In. 9775.00
Mirror, Federal, Mahogany, Inlaid, Scrolled Veneer Pendant, 47 3/4 In. 630.00
Mirror, Federal, Painted, Cornice, Fluted Half Columns, York County, 21 1/2 x 13 1/2 In. . . 44.00
Mirror, Flemish Style, Red Polychrome, Gilt Highlights, Mid 1900s, 28 x 57 In. 750.00
Mirror, Floral Medallion, Urn & Leaves Crest, 62 1/2 x 3 In. 5060.00
Mirror, Fruitwood, Cresting Set With Fossil Stone, c.1900, 35 x 38 In. 2300.00
Mirror, G. Nakashima, Walnut, Widdicomb, c.1958, 52 x 4 x 43 In. 240.00
Mirror, G. Stickley, Ash, Rectangular, Beveled Glass, Hooks, 48 x 29 In. 1265.00
Mirror, G. Stickley, Mahogany, 23 x 29 In. 1500.00
Mirror, G. Stickley, No. 68, Signed, 28 x 42 In. 3500.00
Mirror, George II Style, Oak, Parcel Gilt, Arched, Cheval Stand, 25 x 23 x 9 In. 175.00
Mirror, George III Style, Celadon, Parcel Gilt, Oval, 45 x 30 In. 4800.00

Mirror, George III Style, Giltwood, Leaf, Floral, Scrolling, 42 x 21 1/2 In., Pair 8050.00
Mirror, George III Style, Yew, Parcel Gilt, 20th Century, 50 1/2 x 26 1/2 In. 1265.00
Mirror, Georgian, Giltwood, Gadroon Carved, Oval, 25 x 21 1/2 In. 405.00
Mirror, Georgian, Walnut, Serpentine Border, Ogee, 42 x 22 In. 1495.00
Mirror, Gesso, Carved Fruit, Flowers, Victorian, 45 x 35 1/2 In. 110.00
Mirror, Gesso, Gilt, Fisherman On River Bank, Column Supports, c.1830, 31 1/4 In. 950.00
Mirror, Gesso, Gilt, Matched Corners, Matching Liner, Victorian, 22 1/2 x 36 In. 250.00
Mirror, Gesso, Gilt, Shells, Velvet Lined, 29 3/4 x 35 1/2 In. 190.00
Mirror, Gesso, Gold Leaf, Arch Top, Openwork Pediment, Victorian, 47 x 26 In. 70.00
Mirror, Gilt Bronze, Double Face, Marble Base, 1840s, 14 In. 1610.00
Mirror, Gilt Bronze, Marble, Palmettes, Pineapple, Round, Frame, 2 Sides, 11 1/2 In. 115.00
Mirror, Gilt Finish, Applied Gesso Beading, Victorian, 34 x 30 In., Pair 550.00
Mirror, Gilt Gesso, Half Turned, Rosettes At Corners, 17 1/2 x 24 In. 165.00
Mirror, Gilt Phoenix, Scrolled Top & Bottom, 46 x 24 In. 1870.00
Mirror, Gilt Scroll, Leaf & Floral, 38 x 32 In. 170.00
Mirror, Gilt, Bird, Scroll & Leaf Design, Continental, Early 1900s, 27 x 48 In. 400.00
Mirror, Gilt, Carved, Trumeau, Continental Style, 64 x 36 In. 310.00
Mirror, Gilt, Chip Carved, 8 Sides, 24 Inserts, Contemporary, 18 x 27 In. 145.00
Mirror, Gilt, Gesso, Reticulated Acanthus Leaves, 31 x 27 In. 310.00
Mirror, Gilt, Gesso, Wood, New England, 1830-1850, 37 x 18 1/2 In. 1035.00
Mirror, Gilt, Molded Crown & Base, Reeded Pilasters, Beveled, 60 x 42 1/2 In. 560.00
Mirror, Gilt, Oval, 32 x 24 In. 85.00
Mirror, Giltwood, Acorn Finials, 28 1/2 x 46 x 5 In. 800.00
Mirror, Giltwood, Arched Top, Leaf-Carved Frame, 1780s, 54 x 28 In. 4025.00
Mirror, Giltwood, Asymmetrical Crest, Pierced Scrollwork, 1860s, 52 In., Pair 5060.00
Mirror, Giltwood, Bull's-Eye, Sunburst Form, 1830s, 34 1/2 In. 3450.00
Mirror, Giltwood, Carved & Turned, Mid 1800s, 32 x 19 In. 860.00
Mirror, Giltwood, Carved Pierced Leaves & Cranes, Ebonized, 20 x 37 In. 125.00
Mirror, Giltwood, Carved, Azeglio Pancani, New York, 33 x 24 In. 990.00
Mirror, Giltwood, Carved, Black Lacquer, Bull's-Eye, George VI, 14 In. 200.00
Mirror, Giltwood, Convex, 3-Ray Sunburst, Italy, 30 1/2 In. 2530.00
Mirror, Giltwood, Egg & Dart, Scrolling Candle Arms, Incised Leaves, 60 In. 2400.00
Mirror, Giltwood, Eglomise, Reverse Painted, c.1880, 30 1/2 x 18 In. 500.00
Mirror, Giltwood, Eglomise, Seascape, Scrolled Acanthus, 39 x 21 In. 3290.00
Mirror, Giltwood, Engraved Maiden, 31 1/2 x 23 In. 4495.00
Mirror, Giltwood, Floral Urn On Crest, Flowers, Oval, 47 3/4 x 21 1/2 In. 520.00
Mirror, Giltwood, Gold, Silver Threads, Textile Frame, Octagonal, 48 x 35 1/4 In. 375.00
Mirror, Giltwood, Half-Round Plate, Acanthus Leaves, 31 x 21 In. 175.00
Mirror, Giltwood, Leaf Lyre, George III, 42 x 21 In. 1150.00
Mirror, Giltwood, Mirrored Panels, Urn Crest, 1780 . . . . 9000.00
Mirror, Giltwood, Panel Borders, Rectangular, 1780, 57 x 37 In. 9000.00
Mirror, Giltwood, Rectangular Plate, Scroll & Leaf, 1870s, 51 x 27 1/2 In. 3680.00
Mirror, Giltwood, Red Painted, Acanthus Scrolls, 20th Century, 30 x 26 1/2 In. 1035.00
Mirror, Giltwood, Shells, Volute Border, Bird Design, Continental, 78 In. 5520.00
Mirror, Giltwood, Trumeau, Figure & Landscape Scene, George III, 57 x 37 1/2 In. 1725.00
Mirror, Giltwood, Trumeau, Urn Draped In Leaf Swags, 1820s, 71 3/4 x 25 1/2 In. 570.00
Mirror, Girandole, Carved, Seated Stag, Acanthus, 41 x 14 1/2 In. 8050.00
Mirror, Girandole, Gilt, Gesso, Wood, England, 19th Century, 28 In. 980.00
Mirror, Girandole, Giltwood, Brass Mounted, George II, 63 x 33 In., Pair 36800.00
Mirror, Gold Leaf, Flowers, Gesso, 37 x 32 In. 285.00
Mirror, Gold Leaf, Gesso, Cut Velvet Liner, Acanthus Leaf Decoration, 33 x 29 1/2 In. 390.00
Mirror, Gold Leaf, Lemon Gold Interior, 27 1/2 x 23 In. 275.00
Mirror, Gothic Revival, Mahogany, Open Fretwork Frieze, c.1860, 38 x 49 x 4 In. 375.00
Mirror, Green Clover Border, Salmon Ground, 12 x 14 In. 300.00
Mirror, Hepplewhite, Mahogany, Scrolled Crest, c.1810, 39 x 21 In. 3450.00
Mirror, Italian Baroque Style, Giltwood, Octagonal, Double Border, 47 x 33 In. 3300.00
Mirror, Italian Rococo Style, Giltwood, 19th Century, 38 3/4 x 21 In., Pair 1725.00
Mirror, Italian Rococo Style, Giltwood, 19th Century, 43 x 30 3/4 In. 865.00
Mirror, Ivory, Beveled, Order Of Garter, Easel, 29 3/4 x 20 1/2 In. 1092.00
Mirror, Jade Inlay, Enamel, Silver Base, Chinese, Early 20th Century, 11 In. 345.00
Mirror, Japanned, Candlestick Arms, c.1770, 44 1/2 x 24 1/2 In. 12925.00
Mirror, L. & J.G. Stickley, Hanging, 3 Sections, Signed, 24 1/2 x 55 1/2 In. 1725.00
Mirror, Louis Majorelle, Mahogany, Ombelle Flower, c.1905, 70 x 46 3/4 In. 11163.00

Mirror, Louis XV, Giltwood, Galant & His Consort, Scrolled Frame, 24 1/2 In. 2070.00
Mirror, Louis XVI Style, Giltwood, 60 1/2 x 39 1/2 In. 5290.00
Mirror, Louis XVI, Trumeau, Late 18th Century, 63 1/2 x 28 In. 2300.00
Mirror, Louis XVI, Trumeau, Pediment, c.1850, 81 x 48 1/2 In. 1680.00
Mirror, Mahogany, Brass Candleholders At Base, 45 1/2 x 24 1/2 In. 715.00
Mirror, Mahogany, Carved Crest, Inner Lining, 21 In. 750.00
Mirror, Mahogany, Eagle, Outstretched Wings, Husk Swags, 1830s, 40 In. 1955.00
Mirror, Mahogany, Fretwork Across Top, Beaded Frame, 20th Century, 24 x 42 1/2 In. 110.00
Mirror, Mahogany, Gilt Floral, Shell & Scroll, Flowering Urn Finial, 49 x 24 In. 315.00
Mirror, Mahogany, Giltwood, Urn Finial, Swan Crest, c.1890, 50 In. 520.00
Mirror, Mahogany, Outset Cornice, Whalebone Spherules, Reeded Columns, 29 In. 978.00
Mirror, Mahogany, Phoenix Pediment, Carved Leaf Frame, c.1770, 53 In. 3808.00
Mirror, Mahogany, Rectangular Plate, Molded Shell Pendant, George III, 61 In. 1495.00
Mirror, Mahogany, Rosewood Inlay, Sawtooth, Shields, Horse, c.1876, 13 x 15 In. 2700.00
Mirror, Mahogany, Scalloped Frame, Shell On Crest, Gold Paint Liner, 32 x 17 In. 275.00
Mirror, Mahogany, Scalloped Top, Surround Over Scrolled Base, 25 x 10 In. 646.00
Mirror, Mahogany, Scalloped-Corner Frame, Brass Hook, 14 1/2 x 10 3/4 In. 55.00
Mirror, Mahogany, Scrolled Pediment, Borders, Gold Carved Eagle Finial, 48 In. 500.00
Mirror, Mahogany, Scrolled Top, Eagle, 19th Century, 40 x 20 In. 550.00
Mirror, Mahogany, Scrolled Top, Rectangular Plate, Scrolled Ears, 1780s, 26 1/2 In. 765.00
Mirror, Mahogany, Swan's-Neck Crest, Spread-Winged Phoenix, 1750s, 73 In. 5400.00
Mirror, Mahogany, Swing-Frame, Turned Supports, 3 Drawers, George III, 24 x 20 x 9 In. . 750.00
Mirror, Mahogany, Teardrop Cornice, Rope Twist Half Pilasters, 2 Parts, 56 x 32 In. 770.00
Mirror, Maple, Figured, Molded Frame, Applied Ivory, 22 1/2 x 18 1/2 In. 5640.00
Mirror, Mutton Fat Jade, Dragon & Salamander, Phoenix & Flowers On Back, 8 In. 690.00
Mirror, Napoleon III, Giltwood, Arched Plate, Beaded, Molded Frame, 44 In. 545.00
Mirror, Napoleon III, Giltwood, Arched Plate, Molded Frame, 58 x 44 In. 1150.00
Mirror, Napoleon III, Giltwood, Arched, Carved, Louis XVI Style, 83 1/2 x 53 In. 4140.00
Mirror, Napoleon III, Giltwood, Arched, Molded Frame, Mid 19th Century, 55 x 40 In. . . 1150.00
Mirror, Napoleon III, Giltwood, Bead Covered, 60 1/4 x 40 1/2 In. 1265.00
Mirror, Napoleon III, Giltwood, Carved, Gesso, 58 1/2 x 41 In. 2185.00
Mirror, Napoleon III, Giltwood, Carved, Plaster, Oval, Rococo Style, 66 x 43 In. 1610.00
Mirror, Napoleon III, Giltwood, Cluster Of Grapes, Leaves, Mantel, 89 x 8 In. 4600.00
Mirror, Napoleon III, Giltwood, Floral Garland, Molded Frame, 46 3/4 x 36 In. 1035.00
Mirror, Napoleon III, Giltwood, Floral Porcelain Plaques, 77 x 36 In. 10800.00
Mirror, Napoleon III, Giltwood, Gothic, Arch, Mid 19th Century, 60 x 37 In. 1840.00
Mirror, Napoleon III, Giltwood, Incised, Bead Carved, 61 x 43 1/2 In. 1380.00
Mirror, Napoleon III, Giltwood, Late 19th Century, 55 1/2 x 39 1/2 In. 920.00
Mirror, Napoleon III, Giltwood, Molded Beaded Frame, Leaf Design, 50 In. 575.00
Mirror, Napoleon III, Giltwood, Molded Frame, 19th Century, 46 1/2 x 33 In. 865.00
Mirror, Napoleon III, Giltwood, Plaster, Convex, Carved, Oval, 26 1/2 x 21 In. 750.00
Mirror, Napoleon III, Giltwood, Rectangular Plate, Molded Frame, 46 1/2 In. 1495.00
Mirror, Napoleon III, Giltwood, Ring-Molded Frame, Flowers, 56 x 40 In. 1495.00
Mirror, Napoleon III, Giltwood, Ring-Molded Frame, Garlands, 51 1/2 In. 1150.00
Mirror, Napoleon III, Silvered Wood, Carved, Leaves, Scrolls, 32 x 24 In. 520.00
Mirror, Neoclassical, Ebonized Giltwood, Italy, Late 19th Century, 52 x 43 1/2 In. 2760.00
Mirror, Neoclassical, Giltwood, Beaded, Ribbon Frame, Fluted Columns, 39 1/2 In. 690.00
Mirror, Neoclassical, Giltwood, Convex, Spread-Wing Eagle, 19th Century, 46 1/4 In. . . . 4700.00
Mirror, Neoclassical, Giltwood, Cornice, c.1830, 42 1/2 x 26 1/2 In. 430.00
Mirror, Neoclassical, Giltwood, Early 20th Century, 37 1/2 x 17 1/2 In. 690.00
Mirror, Neoclassical, Giltwood, Guilloche Frame, Leaf Scrolls, 58 1/2 In. 690.00
Mirror, Neoclassical, Giltwood, Leaf-Tip Border, Cove-Molded Frame, 47 1/2 In. 550.00
Mirror, Neoclassical, Giltwood, Projecting Cornice, Carved Frieze, 41 x 24 In. 1116.00
Mirror, Neoclassical, Mahogany, Carved Giltwood, 19th Century, 47 In. 850.00
Mirror, Neoclassical, Mahogany, Carved, Balusters, c.1835, 40 1/2 x 22 In. 460.00
Mirror, Neoclassical, Mahogany, Convex Molded Frame, Bun Feet, 28 In. 145.00
Mirror, Neoclassical, Narrow, Rectangular Frame, Leaf Band Border, 1840, 32 In. 580.00
Mirror, Neoclassical, Ogee Frame, Parcel Gilt Band, Late 19th Century, 30 x 21 3/4 In. . . 310.00
Mirror, Neoclassical, Pine, Gilt, Beveled Plate, 52 1/2 In. 2070.00
Mirror, Neoclassical, Pine, Gilt, Frieze Drawer, Reeded Frame, 51 x 49 In. 2760.00
Mirror, Neoclassical, Red Velvet Ground, 1900, 23 3/4 x 19 3/4 In. 170.00
Mirror, Neoclassical, Tiger Maple, Molded Frame, 1840s, 35 x 23 In. 1035.00
Mirror, Oak, Fluted Bands, Stenciled J. Postel, c.1900, 38 1/2 x 27 1/2 In. 145.00

Mirror, Overhanging Cornice, Man & Women In Landscape Scene, 1850, 31 In. 460.00
Mirror, Parcel Gilt, Painted Floral Frame, Oval, Late 1700s, 31 x 23 In. 5040.00
Mirror, Pier, Arched Plate, Shell Frame, 1870s, 69 x 41 In. 2530.00
Mirror, Pier, Biedermeier, Cherry, c.1815, 44 x 20 In. 865.00
Mirror, Pier, Double Arched, Pierced, Leaves, 45 x 30 In. 460.00
Mirror, Pier, Eastlake, Walnut, Shaped Cornice, Fluted, Veneered Frame, 111 x 27 In. 195.00
Mirror, Pier, Empire, Mahogany, Arched Plate, Gilt Bronze, 81 In. 2530.00
Mirror, Pier, Federal, Mahogany, Carved Crest, Shelf, Cornucopias, 107 In. 4600.00
Mirror, Pier, George II Style, Gilt, Late 19th Century, 49 1/4 x 32 In. 1495.00
Mirror, Pier, Gilt Frame, Arched Top, 82 In. 415.00
Mirror, Pier, Gilt, Flower Cartouche, Cupid, Victorian, 89 x 99 x 28 In. 550.00
Mirror, Pier, Giltwood, Arched Plate, Birds & Trailing Leaves, 1870s, 81 x 48 In. 3680.00
Mirror, Pier, Giltwood, Arched Plate, Flowers, Spiral-Carved Frame, 90 x 53 In. 4600.00
Mirror, Pier, Giltwood, Arched Plate, Leaf Frame, 1870s, 69 1/2 x 49 1/2 In. 1610.00
Mirror, Pier, Giltwood, Arched Plate, Ringed & Fluted Frame, 70 1/2 x 51 In. 1495.00
Mirror, Pier, Giltwood, Carved, High Relief Eagle, Spiral Columns, 61 x 30 In. 1725.00
Mirror, Pier, Giltwood, Overhanging Crest, Lions' Masks, 1820s, 27 1/2 x 42 In. 1150.00
Mirror, Pier, Giltwood, Pierced Cartouche, 1870s, 70 x 43 In. 1150.00
Mirror, Pier, Iron Frame Set With Tiles, Diamond Deign, Iron Easel, 53 3/4 In. 193.00
Mirror, Pier, Louis XVI Style, Giltwood, Beveled, Serpentine Top, c.1900, 60 x 44 In. 1610.00
Mirror, Pier, Louis XVI, Giltwood, Polychrome, Carved, Pierced Crest, 57 x 34 1/2 In. . . . 4370.00
Mirror, Pier, Maple, Faux Bamboo, Pierced Geometric Top, Swivels, 76 1/2 In. 2350.00
Mirror, Pier, Napoleon III, Giltwood, Plaster, Renaissance Revival, 115 1/2 x 41 In. 1725.00
Mirror, Pier, Neoclassical, Gilt, Italy, 44 x 18 In. 1265.00
Mirror, Pier, Neoclassical, Gilt, Rectangular Cornice, Cream Paint, 70 3/4 In. 1725.00
Mirror, Pier, Neoclassical, Giltwood, Reeded Pilasters, 34 1/2 x 62 In. 2300.00
Mirror, Pier, Queen Anne, Gilt Gesso, Arched, Mirror Borders, 1705, 73 x 39 In. 8400.00
Mirror, Pier, Queen Anne, Gilt Gesso, Arched, Mirror Borders, 76 x 34 In., 2 Piece 9000.00
Mirror, Pier, Rococo Revival, Gold Paint, Wood & Glass, Victorian, 85 x 35 In. 336.00
Mirror, Pier, Rococo, Giltwood, Gilt Flowers, Beveled, Sweden, 51 x 22 1/2 In. 4485.00
Mirror, Pier, Shield & Crown Over Frame, Marble Top Bracket, c.1865, 82 x 32 1/2 In. . . . 1900.00
Mirror, Pier, Walnut, Carved, Beveled, Victorian, 74 x 43 In. 560.00
Mirror, Pier, Walnut, Slanted Side Mirrors, Side Columns, 97 1/2 x 34 In. 1345.00
Mirror, Pine, Church Surrounded By Trees, Green, Gold, Black Ground, 19 x 10 In. 140.00
Mirror, Pine, Figured Mahogany Veneer, Scalloped Crest, 23 x 11 3/4 In. 715.00
Mirror, Pine, Mahogany Veneer, Stepped Moldings, Flowers At Side, 48 1/2 In. 825.00
Mirror, Pine, Mahogany Veneer, Stepped Sides, Gilt Floral Rosettes, 44 x 23 In. 660.00
Mirror, Pine, Reverse-Painted House & Trees, Half Pilasters, 2 Part, 29 1/2 In. 190.00
Mirror, Prince Of Wales Plume, Crown & Gilt Frame, c.1800, 47 1/2 x 24 In. 2015.00
Mirror, Queen Anne Style, Giltwood, 19th Century, 38 3/4 x 22 1/2 In., Pair 980.00
Mirror, Queen Anne Style, Japanned Design, 58 1/2 x 24 In. 190.00
Mirror, Queen Anne Style, Oriental Decoration, Red, Gold, Black, Scalloped, 40 x 24 In. . . 1380.00
Mirror, Queen Anne Style, Walnut, Cushion-Molded Frame, 33 x 22 1/2 In. 1095.00
Mirror, Queen Anne Style, Walnut, Gilt, Late 19th Century, 27 1/2 x 16 1/2 In. 200.00
Mirror, Queen Anne, Black Paint, Beaded, Shaped Frame, Beveled Glass, 23 x 13 In. 2185.00
Mirror, Queen Anne, Mahogany, Carved Birds On Crest, 42 x 17 In. 5750.00
Mirror, Queen Anne, Mahogany, Pierced Crest, Shell, Feather, 22 In. 600.00
Mirror, Queen Anne, Mahogany, Tombstone Top, Beaded, Gilt, Ogee Frame, 25 In. 900.00
Mirror, Queen Anne, Walnut Veneer, Giltwood, Leaves, England, 1770, 35 3/4 In. 1035.00
Mirror, Queen Anne, Walnut, 2 Parts, Scalloped, Arch Crest, 43 3/4 x 18 3/4 In. 1100.00
Mirror, Queen Anne, Walnut, Giltwood, Cutout Crest, Incised Star, 39 x 17 In. 2380.00
Mirror, Queen Anne, Walnut, Veneer, Parcel Gilt, Crest, 35 x 14 1/2 In. 1410.00
Mirror, Queen Anne, White Pine, Parcel Gilt, Painted, c.1770, 24 x 13 In. 16100.00
Mirror, Regency Style, Giltwood, 22 x 9 In., Pair 400.00
Mirror, Regency Style, Giltwood, Convex, Ebonized, Round, 48 x 30 x 10 In. 3450.00
Mirror, Regency Style, Giltwood, Convex, Gesso, Eagle, Scrolling, 39 In. 1955.00
Mirror, Regency Style, Gold Leaf, Urn & Garland Crest, Wreath, Swag Drop, 50 x 20 In. . . 275.00
Mirror, Regency, Carved Giltwood, Ebonized, England, 37 1/2 x 23 1/2 In. 2760.00
Mirror, Regency, Ebonized, Carved Giltwood, Bull's-Eye, 32 x 22 1/2 In. 920.00
Mirror, Regency, Ebonized, Carved Giltwood, Bull's-Eye, 42 x 36 In. 1610.00
Mirror, Regency, Giltwood, Black Lacquer, Bull's-Eye, Carved, 39 x 25 x 15 In. 1610.00
Mirror, Regency, Giltwood, Convex, Eagle & Tassel Crest, Early 19th Century, 25 In. 4025.00
Mirror, Regency, Giltwood, Convex, Ebonized, 2 Candle Arms, 1810, 44 In. 8400.00

Mirror, Regency, Giltwood, Convex, Winged Eagle, 26 x 14 1/2 In., Pair 1380.00
Mirror, Regency, Giltwood, Double Border, Shell, Scroll Design, 54 x 29 In. 13200.00
Mirror, Regency, Giltwood, Ebonized, Bull's-Eye, 40 x 26 1/2 x 6 1/2 In. 8910.00
Mirror, Regency, Giltwood, Ebonized, Bull's-Eye, Early 1800s, 38 x 27 3/4 In. 2070.00
Mirror, Removable Candle Brackets, Scrolled Brass Vining, 13 1/8 In. 250.00
Mirror, Renaissance Revival, Gilt, Mantel, 82 x 60 In. 3640.00
Mirror, Renaissance Revival, Giltwood, Husk Swags, Marble Shelf, 56 x 79 In. 3335.00
Mirror, Renaissance Revival, Giltwood, Molded Plaster, Anthemion, Columns, 99 x 73 In. 120.00
Mirror, Renaissance Revival, Giltwood, Molded Plaster, c.1870, 150 x 36 x 14 In., Pair . . 235.00
Mirror, Renaissance Revival, Walnut, Burled Panels, Shelf, 62 x 36 In. 1960.00
Mirror, Renaissance Revival, Walnut, Shadowbox Frame, 1870, 24 x 48 In. 560.00
Mirror, Reverse Engraved Roman Soldier, 1880s, 37 1/2 x 20 In. 1610.00
Mirror, Reverse Painted Church, Corner Rosettes, 20 x 10 5/8 In. 275.00
Mirror, Reverse Painted Church, Mahogany Veneer, 20 1/2 x 11 1/4 In. 140.00
Mirror, Reverse Painted Upper Panel, 19th Century, 20 3/4 x 11 1/4 In. 85.00
Mirror, Reverse Painted, Ribbon Of Leaves, 2 Parts, 24 1/4 In. 440.00
Mirror, Robert Adam Style, Giltwood, Early 19th Century, 48 x 23 In. 2875.00
Mirror, Robsjohn-Gibbings, Mahogany, Brass Trim, Signed, 34 In. 460.00
Mirror, Rococo Style, Etched, Framed, Scrolled, Venetian, 56 In. 400.00
Mirror, Rococo Style, Gesso On Wood, Phoenix Crest, Serpentine Leaf Frame, 36 x 43 In. 99.00
Mirror, Rococo Style, Giltwood, Late 19th Century, 20 1/2 x 46 1/2 In. 1610.00
Mirror, Rococo, Composition, Gilt Finish, Floral Relief, Arched Crest, 39 x 52 In. 110.00
Mirror, Rococo, Composition, Scrollwork, Gilt Finish, 50 x 32 In. 195.00
Mirror, Rococo, Giltwood, Leaves, Pagoda Crest, 52 x 29 In. 935.00
Mirror, Rococo, Giltwood, Pair Of C-Scrolls, Grapevine, 43 In. 1380.00
Mirror, Rococo, Wood, Gilt, Pierced Leaf Frame, Rectangular, 50 x 40 In. 2300.00
Mirror, Rosettes, Reverse Painted Ship On River, 20th Century, 9 1/2 x 5 In. 360.00
Mirror, Rosewood Veneer, Gilt, 19th Century, 38 x 44 1/2 In. 920.00
Mirror, Rosewood, Satinwood, Marquetry, Ball Feet, Victorian, 16 1/2 In. 170.00
Mirror, Shaving, Bird's-Eye Maple, Hand Dovetailed, c.1890 . . . . 1495.00
Mirror, Shaving, Blue Paint, Drawer, 22 In. 85.00
Mirror, Shaving, Curly Maple, 2 Base Drawers, Brass Pulls 550.00
Mirror, Shaving, Jugendstil, 28 x 18 In. 490.00
Mirror, Shaving, Mahogany Veneer, Serpentine Front, 3 Drawers, Brass Pulls, 22 In. 190.00
Mirror, Shaving, Mahogany, 2 Drawers In Base, Ebony Inlay, Oval, 20 x 14 In. 420.00
Mirror, Shaving, Mahogany, 27 In. 9775.00
Mirror, Shaving, Mahogany, 3 Drawers, Octagonal Frame, 25 x 22 1/2 In. 190.00
Mirror, Shaving, Mahogany, Bowfront Case, 1 Drawer, 17 5/8 x 12 1/2 In. 400.00
Mirror, Shaving, Mahogany, Bowfront Case, 3 Drawers, Brass Finials, 23 In. 110.00
Mirror, Shaving, Mahogany, Rectangular Molded Frame, George III, 23 In. 1095.00
Mirror, Shaving, Pine, Bowfront, 2 Drawers, Pierced Crest & Uprights, 25 In. 300.00
Mirror, Shaving, Pine, Mahogany Veneer, Pine, Brass Pulls, Acorn Finials 220.00
Mirror, Shaving, William IV, Mahogany, Spiral-Carved Swing Stand, 29 x 29 In. 175.00
Mirror, Shaving, Wood, Lift Top, Wallpaper Interior, 6 x 6 7/8 x 1 1/2 In. 192.00
Mirror, Sheraton, Gilt, Actress On Upper Tablet, 35 x 15 1/2 In. 490.00
Mirror, Sheraton, Gilt, Grain Painted, Reverse Painted Tablet, 27 x 13 1/2 In. 315.00
Mirror, Sheraton, Mahogany Veneer, Reverse Painted Fruit, 29 1/2 x 14 In. 290.00
Mirror, Sheraton, Mahogany Veneer, Reverse Painted, 26 x 13 1/2 In. 315.00
Mirror, Sheraton, Tiger Maple Veneer, Eglomise Plate, Brass, 28 x 13 1/2 In. 935.00
Mirror, Shield, Urn Of Flowers, 6 Portrait Roundels, 42 3/4 In. 345.00
Mirror, Stickley Bros., Mahogany, Rectangular, 36 x 30 In. 980.00
Mirror, Tiger Maple, c.1830, 19 x 16 In. 460.00
Mirror, Tortoiseshell, Arched Plate, Dutch, 52 x 59 1/2 In. 1265.00
Mirror, Veneer, Molded, Painted, 19th Century, 27 x 18 1/2 In. 1265.00
Mirror, Wallace Nutting, No. 2889, Pine, Scallop Molding, Crest, 16 x 16 In. 690.00
Mirror, Walnut, Arched Top Over Frame, 2 Parts, 19th Century, 33 In. 345.00
Mirror, Walnut, Beveled, Molded Frame & Base, 1920s, 65 x 38 1/2 In. 390.00
Mirror, Walnut, Carved Acanthus Leaves, Victorian, Mantel, 72 x 63 In. 660.00
Mirror, Walnut, Carved Birds, Leaves, Grapes, Victorian, Mantel, 1860, 79 x 75 In. 2875.00
Mirror, Walnut, Carved Leaves & Fruit, 19 1/2 x 24 In. 330.00
Mirror, Walnut, Carved Pediment & Finials, 41 x 24 In. 1495.00
Mirror, Walnut, Dragon Clutching Crescent Moon, 31 x 31 In. 1725.00
Mirror, Walnut, Dragon Clutching Mirror, 3 Claws, Intertwined Tail, 42 In. 860.00

Mirror, Walnut, Flame Veneer, Scalloped Base & Top, 20th Century, 21 1/2 In. 110.00
Mirror, Walnut, Parcel Gilt, Pierced, Fretted Crest, Bird, Pendant, George II, 31 x 17 In. . . . 750.00
Mirror, Walnut, Parcel Gilt, Rectangular Swan's Neck, George III, 66 In., Pair 5175.00
Mirror, Walnut, Ripple Carved, Serpentine Edges, 32 x 20 1/2 In. 250.00
Mirror, Walnut, Serpent-Head Supports, 1830s, 25 In. 1400.00
Mirror, Walnut, Swan's-Neck Crest, Gadrooned Frame, George II, 40 In., Pair 1560.00
Mirror, William IV, Convex, Circular Plate, Vines, Leaves Frame, 19 In. 920.00
Mirror, William IV, Giltwood, Carved, 3 Sections, 24 x 64 In. 1840.00
Mirror, Wood, Gesso, Gilt, Carved, Scrolling Leaf-Form Pediment, c.1870, 47 x 33 In. . . . 1680.00
Mirror, Wood, Gesso, Gilt, Continental, 54 1/4 x 32 1/2 In. 475.00
Mirror, Wood, Oval, 23 1/4 x 27 1/2 In. 60.00
Mirror, Wood, Silvered, Carved, Shagreen, 3 Parts, Grotesque Animals, 33 x 40 In. 2585.00
Office Suite, Art Deco, Limed Oak, Gray Pattern Upholstered, 1935, 4 Piece 8400.00
Ottoman, Arne Jacobsen, Egg, Black Leather, Aluminum, Fiberglass, F. Hansen, 1950 . . . 1495.00
Ottoman, Empire Style, Mahogany, Scrolled Feet, Needlepoint Upholstered 70.00
Ottoman, Frank Lloyd Wright, Mahogany, Green Tufted Fabric, 27 x 27 x 16 In. 1610.00
Ottoman, Leather, Hinged Tufted Seat, Molded Plinth, 17 x 74 x 30 In. 9600.00
Ottoman, Mahogany, Zebra Skin, Hinged Lid, Storage, Bun Feet, 19 x 49 x 18 In. 4485.00
Ottoman, Victorian, Mahogany, Leather, Late 19th Century, 16 x 19 1/2 x 19 1/2 In. 1035.00
Ottoman, Wegner, Teak, Dark Brown, Upholstered, 16 x 27 1/2 x 16 In. 550.00
Overmantel, see Architectural category.
Parlor Set, Art Deco, Wood Frame, Scrolled, Velvet, France, 5 Piece 4600.00
Parlor Set, Georgian Style, Mahogany, Pierced Design, Settee, 2 Armchairs, 3 Piece 8810.00
Parlor Set, Gilt Leaf Finish, Roses, Tulips & Leaves, Wreath Crests, 7 Piece 2145.00
Parlor Set, Giltwood, Polychrome, Italy, Mid 19th Century, 5 Piece 6325.00
Parlor Set, Louis XVI Style, Giltwood, Settee, 2 Armchairs, 67 In. 10200.00
Parlor Set, Mahogany, Carved Maiden Busts, Serpents Crests, Upholstered, 6 Piece 6160.00
Parlor Set, Original Finish, 3 Vertical Slats, 75 x 27 x 40 In., 3 Piece 2530.00
Parlor Set, Renaissance Revival, Walnut, Burled Trim, 7 Piece 1456.00
Parlor Set, Rosewood, Flower Crest, Scroll Open Arms, Tufted, Roux, 2 Piece 13225.00
Parlor Set, Walnut, Grape-Carved Crest, Double Camelback Sofa, 1870, 3 Piece 1915.00
Pedestal, Adam Style, Mahogany, Ogee Top, c.1840, 47 x 23 1/2 x 22 1/2 In., Pair 3250.00
Pedestal, Arts & Crafts, Mahogany, Octagonal Top, Rectangular Cutouts, 35 In. 865.00
Pedestal, Arts & Crafts, Stained Glass Panels, Tulips, c.1910, 12 1/2 x 11 x 38 In. 805.00
Pedestal, G. Stickley, Circular Top, 4 Legs, Crossed Shoe Feet, 36 x 14 In. 2530.00
Pedestal, Gilt Bronze, Onyx, 49 3/8 In. 3000.00
Pedestal, Giltwood, Acanthine Supports, Scroll Toes, 41 3/4 x 16 3/4 In., Pair 2116.00
Pedestal, Joseph Hoffmann, Beech, 3 Round Standards, Triangular Base, 43 In. 1725.00
Pedestal, L. & J.G. Stickley, No. 27, Square Top, Long Corbels, 14 x 14 x 48 In. 7480.00
Pedestal, Limbert, No. 244, Mahogany, Circular Top, Arched Legs, 16 x 26 In. 3450.00
Pedestal, Louis XV Style, Tulipwood, 19th Century, 52 3/4 x 18 1/2 x 15 In. 19150.00
Pedestal, Louis XVI Style, Egyptian Marble, Late 1800s, 47 x 16 x 14 In. 1955.00
Pedestal, Mahogany, Circular Top, Ribbed Standard, 3 Winged Legs, Paw Feet, 49 In. . . . 530.00
Pedestal, Marble, Bronze Capital & Base, Bronze Feet, 1830s, 39 3/4 In. 2760.00
Pedestal, Marble, Doric Column, Italy, 43 x 8 x 8 In. 1035.00
Pedestal, Neoclassical, Marble, Carved, Octagonal Top, Late 19th Century, 40 In. 390.00
Pedestal, Neoclassical, Rectangular Top, Gadrooned, Rope-Twist Border, 42 In. 1725.00
Pedestal, Oak, Mahogany, Geometric Inlaid Top, Continental, 36 x 15 In. 431.00
Pedestal, Onyx, Green, Gilt-Bronze Mount, Round Standard, Square Base, 42 In. 460.00
Pedestal, Onyx, Round, Cylinder Post, Ring Turnings, Octagonal Base, 31 x 9 In. 230.00
Pedestal, Onyx, Square Top & Base, 39 1/2 x 14 1/2 In. 615.00
Pedestal, Onyx, White, Gilt Bronze Mounted, Spreading Square Standard, 45 In. 1610.00
Pedestal, Prairie School, Oak Park Masonic Lodge, E.E. Roberts, 14 x 14 x 33 In. 1495.00
Pedestal, Regency, Mahogany, Frieze Drawer, Top-Shaped Feet, 46 1/2 x 23 In. 1265.00
Pedestal, Renaissance Revival, Ebonized, Carved, Revolving Top, 39 x 15 In. 1960.00
Pedestal, Renaissance Revival, Walnut, Carved, 39 x 16 x 16 In. 2295.00
Pedestal, Rosewood, Open-Mouthed Griffin, Scrolled Panels, 1870s, 42 1/2 In., Pair 8340.00
Pedestal, Victorian, Painted, Octagonal, 19 x 14 3/4 x 14 3/4 In. 340.00
Pedestal, Walnut, Central Fluted Column, Small Side Columns, 1880s, 31 In. 1380.00
Pedestal, Walnut, Paneled Frieze, Square Top, Tapered Shaft, Continental, 39 In. 805.00
Pie Safe, 12 Punched Tin Panels, 2 Drawers, Turned Legs, Painted, c.1840, 62 x 41 In. . . . 9500.00
Pie Safe, 12 Punched Tin Panels, Pots Of Flowers, Base Drawer, 54 1/2 x 38 In. 2310.00
Pie Safe, 3 Screened Panels, 1 On Side, Wood Door Latch, 42 In. 495.00

Pie Safe, Cherry, 4 Pillars & Arches Each Door, 2 Top Drawers, 46 1/2 In. 3300.00
Pie Safe, Hardwoods, 2 Punched Doors, Compass Star, Drawers, 45 In. 1430.00
Pie Safe, Pine, Yellow Paint, Mortise & Tenon, 6 Open Panels, 1860, 68 x 48 In. 990.00
Pie Safe, Plank Gallery, 2 Punched Galvanized Tin Panels, 71 x 47 In. 550.00
Pie Safe, Poplar, Dovetailed Drawer, 41 1/2 x 17 1/2 x 57 In. 1100.00
Pie Safe, Punched Tin Panels, Drawers Over 2 Doors, Painted, Virginia, 1820s, 42 In. 2750.00
Pie Safe, Walnut, 12 Punched Tin Panels, 2 Drawers, Pinwheels & Columns, 63 1/2 In. . . 2200.00
Pie Safe, Walnut, 2 Doors, Original Finish, Turned Legs, Va. 4200.00
Pie Safe, Walnut, 3 Drawers, 2 Panel Doors, Punched Tin, 56 1/2 x 58 1/2 In. 3520.00
Pie Safe, Walnut, 8 Punched Hearts & Stars Panels, 2 Doors 5100.00
Pie Safe, Walnut, Pierced Tin Panels On Sides & Door, Mid 1800s, 59 In. 2995.00
Pie Safe, Walnut, Poplar, Punched Tin Panels, 2 Drawers, Doors, 48 1/2 x 53 x 19 In. 3190.00
Pie Safe, Walnut, Punched Tin Panels, 2 Doors, Stars, Masonic Compass, 73 1/2 In. 2860.00
Pie Safe, Walnut, Tin, Tennessee, Mid 19th Century, 56 1/2 x 58 1/2 x 19 1/2 In. . . . *Illus* 3520.00
Pie Safe, Yellow Pine, 12 Punched Tin Panels, 2 Doors, Blue Paint 3100.00
Planter, Twig, Split Log Facing, Rectangular Center Panel, Handles, 27 x 27 In. 330.00
Rack, Arts & Crafts, Canted, Vertical Slats, Shelf, 30 x 16 x 35 In. 575.00
Rack, Baker's, Victorian, Wrought Iron, Brass, Late 19th Century, 78 In., Pair 3680.00
Rack, Drying, Curly Maple, 2 Rows On 3 Bars, Shoe Feet, 48 In. 300.00
Rack, Herb, Blue Repaint Over Gray, Scalloped Top & Base, Wire Nails, 36 x 7 x 4 In. . . . 220.00
Rack, Herb, Pine, Folding, Accordion Action, 20 x 16 In. 80.00
Rack, Herb, Pine, Green Paint, 3 Sections, Middle Crossbars, 49 x 32 In. 220.00
Rack, Magazine, Cast Iron, Nude Woman Ends, Scrollwork, 22 In. 145.00
Rack, Magazine, Hanging, Acanthus Crest, Fleur-De-Lis, Mercury Bust, 1880s, 21 1/2 In. 230.00
Rack, Magazine, Jean Royere, Gilt Metal, Lacquered Wood, c.1955, 20 In. 5980.00
Rack, Magazine, L. & J.G. Stickley, 4 Shelves, Open Sides, Decal, 45 x 21 In. 2415.00
Rack, Magazine, Lakeside Crafters, Cutout Back, 3 Graduated Troughs 575.00
Rack, Magazine, Mahogany Finish, Thonet, 22 x 18 x 10 1/2 In. 1450.00
Rack, Magazine, Tapered Legs, Mahogany Base, 2 Sections, Brass Inserts, 33 1/2 In. 275.00
Rack, Music, G. Stickley, 4 Shelves, Backsplash, Tapered Posts, 39 x 22 x 15 In. 4315.00
Rack, Pipe, Shaped Drawer, Triangular, Canted Sides, 18 x 5 1/8 In. 385.00
Rack, Quilt, Birch, Mortised, Shoe Feet, Refinished, 27 1/2 x 34 In. 85.00
Rack, Quilt, Cherry, H-Shaped Base, Mortised Posts, 33 x 13 1/2 x 32 1/2 In. 110.00
Rack, Quilt, Gold Brown Finish, Arched Top Ends, Shoe Feet, 26 x 31 1/2 In. 330.00
Rack, Quilt, Lime Paint Over White, 3-Fold, 3 Cross Pieces, 71 x 63 In. 660.00
Rack, Quilt, Oak, Tapered Posts, Turned Crossbar, Chamfered Shoe Feet, 60 x 24 In. 220.00
Rack, Quilt, Pine, 3-Fold, 60 x 26 1/2 In. 410.00
Recamier, Aesthetic Revival, Inlaid Mahogany, Herter Bros., c.1890, 76 In. 10575.00
Recamier, Beech, Carved Frame & Skirt, c.1920, 80 In. 850.00
Recamier, Mahogany, Frame Outscrolled 1 End, Inscrolled Other, 1830s, 81 In. 4140.00
Recamier, Mahogany, Gadroon & Acanthus On Crest, Carved Fruit, 1830 . . . . 7760.00
Recamier, Mahogany, Waterleaf Carved Back, Scrolled Ends, Convex Seat Rail, 1825 . . . . 6900.00
Recamier, Neoclassical, Mahogany Veneer, Upholstered, 1825-1835, 33 x 73 x 23 In. 1035.00
Recamier, Regency, Parcel Gilt, Ebonized, Cane Seat, Cushion & Back, 41 In. 1840.00
Recamier, Renaissance Revival, Walnut, Upholstered, Tufted, Ogee Mold, 72 In. 375.00
Rocker, Adirondack, Bentwood Frame, Slats, 38 1/2 x 22 1/2 x 30 In. 200.00
Rocker, Arts & Crafts, Mahogany, Woven Seat & Back, Willow Arms, 31 x 33 In. 635.00
Rocker, Arts & Crafts, Oak, Early 20th Century, 48 x 21 x 66 In. 290.00
Rocker, Arts & Crafts, Open Arms, Corbels, Back Slats, Leather Seat, 33 1/2 x 26 x 31 In. 230.00
Rocker, Balloon Back, Original Paint, Lancaster County, Pa., c.1835 . . . . 1850.00
Rocker, Bamboo Turnings, Windsor, 9 Spindles, Continuous Arm, Converted, 1810 . . . . . 145.00
Rocker, Boston, Painted, Stencils, Gold Stripe, Cane Seat, Spool-Turned Legs, 42 In. 110.00
Rocker, Carved Roses, Leaves, Brocade Upholstered 220.00
Rocker, Comb Back, 5-Spindle Back, Stenciled Fruit, Bamboo Turned Legs, 44 1/4 In. . . . 935.00
Rocker, Curly Maple, Slipper, Cane Seat, Back, 19th Century 145.00
Rocker, Dark Green, Gold Foliate, Red Border, Pa., 17 x 42 In. 220.00
Rocker, Federal Style, Ebonized, Gilt Stencil, 7-Spindle Back, 44 x 23 x 20 In. 59.00
Rocker, Fruit & Floral Stencil, Shaped Spindles & Armrests, Plank Seat, c.1850 . . . . 225.00
Rocker, G. Stickley, 5 Vertical Slats, Leather Cushion, Open Arms, Decal, 37 x 27 In. 1150.00
Rocker, G. Stickley, Mahogany, 5 Vertical Slats, 4 Horizontal Slats, 38 In. 1380.00
Rocker, G. Stickley, No. 311 1/2, Mahogany, 5 Slats, 26 x 28 x 35 In. 690.00
Rocker, G. Stickley, No. 317, Mahogany, 5 Vertical Slats, 27 x 28 x 39 In. 920.00
Rocker, G. Stickley, No. 323, Mahogany, 5 Wide Slats, 29 x 31 x 40 In. 1725.00

Furniture, Pie Safe, Walnut, Tin, Tennessee,
Mid 19th Century, 56 1/2 x 58 1/2 x 19 1/2 In.

Furniture, Rocker, Limbert,
Slat Back, Curved Rail,
Covered Cushion,
38 x 25 x 29 In.

Rocker, G. Stickley, No. 359, Mahogany, 9 Vertical Spindles, 18 x 34 In. 490.00
Rocker, G. Stickley, No. 375, Mahogany, 11 Vertical Spindles, 45 In. 4600.00
Rocker, G. Stickley, No. 2607, Oak, 4 Back Slats, Leather Cushion, c.1902, 34 In. 575.00
Rocker, G. Stickley, Oak, Arms, Leather Seat, 33 x 26 In. 390.00
Rocker, G. Stickley, Oak, High Back, Arms, 43 x 27 1/4 x 28 In. 250.00
Rocker, G. Stickley, Oak, Leather Seat, 34 1/2 x 26 1/4 x 23 In., Pair 280.00
Rocker, G. Stickley, Spindled Back, Paddle Arms, Slatted Seat Support, 36 x 32 x 36 In. . 1495.00
Rocker, Gilt, Stencil Decoration, Red Paint, Pa., 1830-1840, 30 x 15 1/2 In. 230.00
Rocker, Gold Stenciled Urn, Fruit & Flowers On Crest, Scrolled Arms, 40 In. 220.00
Rocker, Grapes, Acorns & Leaves, Green Ground, Scrolled Arms, 41 In. 550.00
Rocker, Half-Arrow Back, Stenciled Floral Crest, 40 3/4 In. 110.00
Rocker, Harden, Mahogany, 5 Vertical Slats, Original Finish, 30 x 32 x 38 In. 1095.00
Rocker, Harden, Mahogany, Dark Brown Leather Seat, Wavy Arms, 36 x 24 In. 1850.00
Rocker, Harden, Wavy Arms & Back, Side Vertical Slats, 38 x 27 1/2 x 31 1/2 In. 430.00
Rocker, Herman Miller, Molded Fiberglass, Steel Rod Base, Birch Runners, Arms, 26 In. . 440.00
Rocker, Heywood Bros. Co., Wicker, Natural, Cane Seat & Back, Arms, 37 In. 145.00
Rocker, Heywood-Wakefield, 2 Back Slats, Spindled Sides, Saddle Seat, 36 x 28 x 32 In. . 230.00
Rocker, Hickory, Spindled Sides, 36 x 25 In. 460.00
Rocker, Hickory, Woven Reed Back Panel, Branded, 33 x 23 In. 1035.00
Rocker, Hunzinger, Walnut, Ivory Flower Upholstered, 31 x 23 1/2 x 33 In. 225.00
Rocker, Jacques Adnet, Leather, Metal, Hermes, c.1950, 35 1/2 In. 8970.00
Rocker, L. & J.G. Stickley, 6 Vertical Slats, Drop-In Cushion, Open Arms, Label, 40 In. . . 1725.00
Rocker, L. & J.G. Stickley, Back Slats, Corbels, Leather Cushion, 36 x 28 x 27 In. 805.00
Rocker, L. & J.G. Stickley, Mahogany, 6 Vertical Slats, Original Finish, 28 x 26 In. 700.00
Rocker, L. & J.G. Stickley, No. 336, Mahogany, 4 Vertical Slats, 26 x 27 x 39 In. 865.00
Rocker, L. & J.G. Stickley, No. 401, Bent Arms, 5 Vertical Slats, 33 x 36 x 39 In. 4500.00
Rocker, L. & J.G. Stickley, No. 409, Mahogany, 4 Vertical Slats, 28 x 30 In. 5175.00
Rocker, L. & J.G. Stickley, No. 427, Leather Seat, Bow Arms, 38 x 31 In. 5750.00
Rocker, L. & J.G. Stickley, No. 436, Mahogany, 6 Vertical Slats, 28 x 40 In. 1380.00
Rocker, L. & J.G. Stickley, No. 437, Mahogany, 6 Vertical Slats, 28 x 38 In. 1840.00
Rocker, L. & J.G. Stickley, Oak, 4 Vertical Slats, Leather Cushion Seat, 33 In. 470.00
Rocker, L. & J.G. Stickley, Oak, Vertical Slats, Arms, 1918, 34 In. 630.00
Rocker, L. & J.G. Stickley, Sewing, Mahogany, 4 Slats, Rush Seat, 17 x 30 In. 345.00
Rocker, Ladder Back, 3 Slats, Rush Seat, Flower Decoration, Yellow Striping 45.00
Rocker, Ladder Back, Finials, 3 Arched Slats, Flat Arms, Box Stretcher, 21 In. 190.00
Rocker, Ladder Back, Rush Seat, Turned Stretchers, Arms 150.00
Rocker, Laminated Cardboard 1495.00
Rocker, Lifetime, No. 688 1/2, Mahogany, Original Finish, Signed, 28 x 30 1/2 In. 3105.00
Rocker, Limbert, Cane Back Panel, Fabric Drop-In Spring Seat Cushion, 32 x 28 In. 550.00
Rocker, Limbert, Dark Mahogany Finish, Dark Brown Leather Seat, Arms, 36 In. 3250.00
Rocker, Limbert, Dark Mahogany, 42 x 29 x 21 In. 1450.00
Rocker, Limbert, No. 588, Mahogany, 5 Vertical Slats, Recovered Cushion, 38 In. 690.00
Rocker, Limbert, No. 644 1/2, Mahogany, 4 Vertical Slats Back, 29 x 36 In. 400.00
Rocker, Limbert, No. 822, Mahogany, 4 Vertical Slats, Mahogany, 22 x 30 x 32 In. 600.00
Rocker, Limbert, No. 826, Mahogany, 5 Vertical Slats, Original Finish, 27 x 40 In. 575.00

Rocker, Limbert, Slat Back, Curved Rail, Covered Cushion, 38 x 25 x 29 In. . . . . *Illus* 690.00
Rocker, Louis Cyr Type, Round Posts, Cane Seat & Back, Arms, Oversize 600.00
Rocker, Mahogany, Carved Crest, Leaf-Carved Arm Supports, Upholstered, 41 In. 225.00
Rocker, Mahogany, Pierced Concave Back, Leaves, Dolphin Heads, 1880s, 39 1/2 In. 2185.00
Rocker, Maple, Banister Back, Shaped Splat, Turned Front Stretcher 200.00
Rocker, Morris, L. & J.G. Stickley, Drop-In Seat, Arms, 39 1/2 x 29 1/2 x 34 3/4 In. 1380.00
Rocker, Morris, Stickley Bros., Open Arm, Drop-In Cushion, 39 x 30 x 34 1/2 In. 1840.00
Rocker, Needlepoint Seat, Back Beatrix Potter Mouse, Open Arms, Child's 30.00
Rocker, Oak, Leather Seat, Arms, 36 x 26 In. 250.00
Rocker, Oak, Lion Heads, Floral Upholstered Back, Seat, 42 1/2 x 22 1/2 x 24 In. 250.00
Rocker, Oak, Shaped Press-Carved Crest, Lyre Splat, Cane Seat 35.00
Rocker, Oak, Slat Back, Rounded Open Arms, Child's, 23 In. 90.00
Rocker, Old Hickory, Mahogany, Rustic Twig Design, Original Finish, 35 In. 375.00
Rocker, Old Hickory, Mahogany, Woven Splint Seat, 22 x 35 In. 520.00
Rocker, Painted, Connecticut River Valley, Arms, 1780 . . . . 3250.00
Rocker, Plail Furniture Co., Barrel Shape, Vertical Slates, Cushion, 46 x 21 x 32 In. 3335.00
Rocker, Plank Bottom, Berry & Fruit Crest, Cheese-Cutter Rockers 39.00
Rocker, Plank Seat, Child's 170.00
Rocker, Plank Seat, High Back, Shaped Crest, Olive Grain Painted, Stenciling 35.00
Rocker, Plank Seat, Shaped Crest, Vase Splat, Painted, 22 1/2 In. 176.00
Rocker, Platform, Beech, Iron, Rattan, Late 20th Century 805.00
Rocker, Platform, Walnut, Line Carving, Upholstered Seat, Back, Victorian, 30 In. 345.00
Rocker, Platform, Wicker, Crosshatch, Open Arms, Victorian, c.1800, 40 In. 230.00
Rocker, Rush Seat, Back Spindles, Arm Supports, 38 In. 60.00
Rocker, Sewing, Binghamton, Vertical Slats, Drop-In Seat, 40 1/2 x 19 x 17 3/4 In. 345.00
Rocker, Sewing, G. Stickley, Chestnut, Leather Seat, Carved Orb Rail, 34 x 19 1/2 In. . . . 1265.00
Rocker, Sewing, L. & J.G. Stickley, Back Slat, Spindles, Crest Rail, 33 1/2 x 18 x 23 In. . . 175.00
Rocker, Shaker Style, Tape Seat, 19th Century 160.00
Rocker, Shaker, Back Slat, Arms, Label, Mt. Lebanon, 1875 . . . . 1050.00
Rocker, Shaker, Maple, Tape Seat, New Lebanon, c.1880, 17 1/2 x 42 1/2 In. 860.00
Rocker, Shaker, No. 0, Child's, New Lebanon, Early 20th Century, 24 In. 940.00
Rocker, Shaker, No. 4, Tape Seat & Back, Label, Mt. Lebanon, 35 In. 220.00
Rocker, Shaker, No. 6, Label, Mt. Lebanon 975.00
Rocker, Shaker, No. 6, Rush Seat 440.00
Rocker, Shaker, No. 7, Red & Black Woven Seat, Stretcher Base, 40 1/2 In. 950.00
Rocker, Shaker, No. 7, Red & Green Woven Seat 935.00
Rocker, Shaker, No. 7, Shawl Bar, Arms, Mt. Lebanon 850.00
Rocker, Shaker, Original Dark Finish, Olive Green Tape Seat, Red Stripe, 33 In. 300.00
Rocker, Shaped Crest, Wide Splat, Scrolled Arms, Painted, Pa. 22.00
Rocker, Shop Of The Crafters, Mahogany, Open Arm, 37 x 33 x 26 In., Pair 2000.00
Rocker, Simulated Rosewood, Painted, High Back, Stenciled, New England 195.00
Rocker, Stickley Bros., Ladder Back, Seat Cushion, Open Arms, 33 1/2 x 28 1/2 In. 1035.00
Rocker, Stickley Bros., Mahogany, Dark Brown Leather Seat, 35 x 25 x 20 In. 1760.00
Rocker, Stickley, Oak, V Back, Leather Seat, Arms, 33 x 26 1/4 x 23 In. 225.00
Rocker, Thonet, Bentwood, Cane Seat & Back, Partial Label, 24 In. 190.00
Rocker, Thonet, Bentwood, Mahogany, Arms, Cane Seat, 40 x 21 x 16 In. 310.00
Rocker, Twig, Bentwood Arms, 4 Slats, Bent-Twig Seat, 42 In. 550.00
Rocker, Twig, Bentwood Back, Split Log Seat, Log Arms, 39 1/2 In. 330.00
Rocker, Twig, Bentwood Crest, Arms, Splayed Wing Back, Colored Dots, 24 x 10 1/4 In. . . 220.00
Rocker, Twig, Blue Paint, Bentwood Crest & Arms, 11 1/2 In. 100.00
Rocker, Twig, Bow Back, 11 Spindles, Word Baby On Seat, Stripes, 19 In. 320.00
Rocker, Walnut Arms, Stenciled Fruit On Crest, Bamboo-Turned Legs, 42 3/4 In. 385.00
Rocker, Wegner, Beech, Woven Rope Seat, Denmark, 1944, 42 x 25 In. 520.00
Rocker, Wicker, Brown, Child's 60.00
Rocker, Windsor, Arched Crest, 13 Tall Spindles, Plank Seat, Turned Arms, 48 In. 290.00
Rocker, Windsor, Bamboo Turnings, 7 Spindles, Crest, Black, Yellow Trim, Arms, 31 In. . . 275.00
Rocker, Windsor, Bamboo Turnings, Slat Back, Arms, Early 19th Century 259.00
Rocker, Windsor, Birdcage, 7 Spindles, Bamboo Turnings, Serpentine Arms, 1806, 44 In. . 935.00
Rocker, Windsor, Elm, Yew, Spindle Backrest, England, 19th Century 750.00
Rocker, Windsor, Sack Back, D-Shape Saddle Seat, Converted, 1800, 35 In. 240.00
Screen, 2-Panel, Mahogany, Pierced Fretwork, Silk Panels, Continental, 41 In. 110.00
Screen, 2-Panel, Silk, Birds In Flight, Branches, Magnolias, Japan, 61 3/4 x 34 In. 635.00
Screen, 3-Panel, Arts & Crafts, Leather Over Wood, 24 x 66 In. 1500.00

Screen, 3-Panel, Arts & Crafts, Mahogany, Japanned Leather, Stenciled, 67 In. 520.00
Screen, 3-Panel, Arts & Crafts, Oak, Grid Top, Cutout Fern Center, 68 In. 1035.00
Screen, 3-Panel, Canvas Cover, Cascading Blooms, 69 In. 55.00
Screen, 3-Panel, Canvas, Arch Top, Floral & Figure Cartouches, c.1890, 73 In. 375.00
Screen, 3-Panel, Carved, Inlaid, Mother-Of-Pearl, Abalone, Taj Mahal, 73 1/2 x 73 In. . . .   960.00
Screen, 3-Panel, Cloth Cover, Cherubs, Urns Of Fruit, Scroll Feet, 79 1/2 In. 770.00
Screen, 3-Panel, Decoupage Scrape, Victorian Life Scenes, c.1890, 66 3/4 x 81 In. 560.00
Screen, 3-Panel, Mahogany, Fabric Panels, Mid 19th Century, 78 1/2 x 84 In. 2300.00
Screen, 3-Panel, Mahogany, Hinged, 64 x 54 In. 260.00
Screen, 3-Panel, Pagoda, Willow Trees, Brass Tacks, 68 x 51 In.   55.00
Screen, 3-Panel, Silk Cover, Gold & Blue Flowers, 81 x 63 In. 1265.00
Screen, 3-Panel, Spindle Dividers, Scalloped Apron, Center Diamond Panel, 71 In. 140.00
Screen, 4-Panel, Art Deco, Lacquered, Gold-Leaf Lobster, Squares Top Band, 58 x 72 In. . .   150.00
Screen, 4-Panel, Bookshelves Transfer, Reversible, Piero Fornasetti, 1950, 48 In. 9000.00
Screen, 4-Panel, Ducks In Winter Pond Landscape, Japan, 18 1/2 x 53 In. 230.00
Screen, 4-Panel, Enameled Frame, Painted, Working Figures, Japan, 29 x 85 In. 220.00
Screen, 4-Panel, Kesi, Wood, Carved Warriors, Horses, Chinese, 1800s, 74 In. 865.00
Screen, 4-Panel, Louis XVI Style, Giltwood, Needlepoint Tapestry, 70 1/2 x 82 In. 1840.00
Screen, 4-Panel, Needlework, Elizabethan Figures, 1880s, 78 In. 4500.00
Screen, 4-Panel, Painted Canvas, House Scenes, 19th Century, 69 In. 2415.00
Screen, 4-Panel, Rococo Revival, Mirror, Painted, 96 In. 3175.00
Screen, 4-Panel, Trompe L'Oeil, Books On Shelf, Inkwell, Spectacles, 72 x 64 In. 275.00
Screen, 4-Panel, Wood, Polychrome, Parcel Gilt, Crimson Lacquer, 65 3/4 x 64 In. 115.00
Screen, 5-Panel, Louis XV, Gilt, Carved Ribbon Crest, Landscape, 69 x 85 In. 1840.00
Screen, 5-Panel, Wallpaper, Polychrome, Stag Hunt, 66 1/2 x 97 1/2 In. 2760.00
Screen, 6-Panel, Coromandel, Birds, Flowers, Leaves, Chinese, c.1860, 70 x 80 In. 1570.00
Screen, 6-Panel, Eames, Plywood, Canvas Hinges, 1952, 67 In. 2760.00
Screen, 6-Panel, Folding, Kano School, Landscape Scene, Marked, 69 x 150 In. 2415.00
Screen, 6-Panel, Lacquered, Allover Landscape & Figural, Chinese, 96 x 72 In. 230.00
Screen, 7-Panel, Grape Cluster, Leaf & Vine Cutout, 66 x 168 In. 1440.00
Screen, 7-Panel, Palace Garden, Women & Boys, Famille Verte, 18th Century, 66 In. 3600.00
Screen, 8-Panel, Eames, Herman Miller, c.1950, 100 x 68 1/2 In. 3450.00
Screen, 8-Panel, Precious Things, Boys At Play, Lake, Bamboo Reverse, 96 x 144 In. 2380.00
Screen, 9-Panel, Rosewood, Reverse Painted Scenes, Mirror Back, Chinese, 120 x 120 In. .   3360.00
Screen, Aubusson Tapestry, Acanthine Crest, Scrolled Toes, 1880s, 49 x 30 In. 1725.00
Screen, Black Lacquer, Papier-Mache, Chinoiserie Figures, 1830s, 55 1/2 In, Pair 4500.00
Screen, Brass Frame, Center Grotesque Mask, 16 Beveled Panel, 1880s, 36 x 25 In. 345.00
Screen, Figural Landscape, Gold On Black, Floral Roundels, 84 x 128 In. 690.00
Screen, Leaded Cameo Glass, Acid-Etched Trees, Wood Frame, Jacques Gruber, 44 In. 6900.00
Screen, Mahogany, Cabriole Legs, Scroll, Feet, Chippendale, 54 In. 440.00
Screen, Mahogany, Needlepoint Panel Of Gentleman, 56 1/2 In. 250.00
Screen, Mahogany, Needlework, Tripod Base, 1800s 345.00
Screen, Mahogany, Spiral Urn Pole, Needlepoint Screen, Chippendale, 60 In. 3920.00
Screen, Needlepoint, Faux Walnut, Baroque, 19th Century, 57 x 39 In. 1495.00
Screen, Needlework, Flowers, Bow, Ring & Urn Shaft, Mahogany Stand, 62 In. 3738.00
Screen, Pole, Mahogany, Girl With Dog, Needlepoint, Carved Tripod Base, 64 In. 2310.00
Seat, Wagon, Hickory, Pine, Woven Ash Splint, Herringbone, c.1840, 36 In. 1150.00
Secretary, Aesthetic Period, Mahogany, 2 Sections, Cabinet Top, 84 x 42 x 17 In. 990.00
Secretary, Burl Walnut, Slant Front, Fitted Interior, Drawers, 29 1/2 In. 1790.00
Secretary, C. Braakman, Drop-Front, Wood, Locking, 2 Doors, 51 1/2 In. 600.00
Secretary, C. Briggs, Glazed Mullioned Doors, Slanted Writing Surface, 55 x 36 In. 1200.00
Secretary, Century Furniture Co., Serpentine, Floral Painted, 2 Piece, 37 x 79 In. 2750.00
Secretary, Cherry, Slant Front, Broken Pediment, 18th Century, 88 x 38 x 21 In. 18400.00
Secretary, Chippendale, Maple, Bracket Feet, 2 Doors Over 4 Drawers, 42 x 20 x 85 In. . .   8250.00
Secretary, Drop Front, Biedermeier, Fruitwood, Fitted Interior, c.1820, 60 In. 2645.00
Secretary, Drop Front, Biedermeier, Mahogany, 3 Drawers, Stepped Top, 59 x 42 In. 2640.00
Secretary, Drop Front, Inlaid Lyre, Musical Designs, 60 x 39 In. 9900.00
Secretary, Drop Front, Louis XV, 4 Drawers, Flowers, Bronze, 48 x 18 In. 980.00
Secretary, Drop Front, Mahogany, Bird's-Eye Maple Interior, 57 In. 1630.00
Secretary, Drop Front, Mahogany, Drawer, Fitted Interior, Cabinet Doors, 55 x 38 In. 1610.00
Secretary, Drop Front, Walnut, Burl Walnut Veneers, Bird's-Eye Maple Interior, 86 In. . . .   6500.00
Secretary, Dutch, Walnut, Bombe Slant Front, 3 Drawers, 84 x 43 1/2 x 20 In. 2015.00
Secretary, Empire, Mahogany Veneer, 2 Sections, Molded Cornice, 79 x 44 1/2 In. 1150.00

Secretary, Empire, Mahogany, 2 Sections, 5 Drawers, 2 Doors, 79 3/4 x 42 x 20 In. 1345.00
Secretary, Empire, Mahogany, Slant Front, 2 Sections, 82 x 42 x 21 In. 670.00
Secretary, Federal, Mahogany Inlay, c.1810, 51 3/4 x 41 x 18 1/4 In. 8815.00
Secretary, Federal, Mahogany, Butler's Desk, Fitted Interior, 41 x 83 1/2 x 21 In. 4070.00
Secretary, Georgian, Mahogany, Slant Front, 3 Long & 1 Apron Drawer, 39 x 20 In. 5775.00
Secretary, Glass Paneled Door, Urn Finials, Slant Front, Fitted Interior, 72 1/2 In. 460.00
Secretary, Hepplewhite, Mahogany, Veneer, Line Inlay, Folding Surface, 35 x 57 In. 2530.00
Secretary, Mahogany, Flame Birch, Fold-Down Surface, 4 Base Drawers, 83 1/2 In. 7475.00
Secretary, Mahogany, Late 18th Century, 94 1/2 x 49 1/2 x 20 In. 6325.00
Secretary, Mahogany, Oak, Interior Drawers, Center Door, 42 1/2 In. 5225.00
Secretary, Mahogany, Tucker, Wine Drawer, 3 Long Drawers, c.1830 . . . . 3360.00
Secretary, Neoclassical, Yellow Pine, 2 Glass Top Drawers, 4-Drawer Base 4675.00
Secretary, Pine, Alligatored Red Brown, Chamfered Corner, 40 x 22 In. 7425.00
Secretary, Queen Anne Style, Walnut, Mirrored Door, 79 1/2 x 24 1/2 x 19 1/2 In. 5520.00
Secretary, Queen Anne Style, Walnut, Slant Front, 2 Mirrored Doors, 76 x 36 x 20 In. . . . 2070.00
Secretary, Rococo, Rosewood, 3 Graduated Shelves, Fitted Interior, 71 1/2 In. 4370.00
Secretary, Tambour, 2 Part, Lift-Top Storage Area, 2 Lower Drawers, 45 1/2 In. 1150.00
Secretary, Tambour, Door, Lower Drawers, Pigeonholes, 47 1/2 In. 575.00
Secretary, Venetian Style, Mirror, Slant Front, Scrolls, Figures, 82 x 36 x 16 In. 3450.00
Secretary, Walnut, 9 Bottom Drawers, Double Doors, c.1760 . . . . 9500.00
Secretary, Walnut, Paneled Doors, Cubbyholes, c.1880 . . . . 1495.00
Secretary, Wooton, Renaissance Revival, Burl Panels, 3 Hinges, 75 x 29 x 44 In. 8960.00
Secretary-Bookcase, 2 Glazed Doors, Shelves, Writing Surface, Fitted Interior, 82 In. . . . 410.00
Secretary-Bookcase, 3 Doors, Slant Front, Pigeonholes, 3 Drawers, 104 In. 200.00
Secretary-Bookcase, Campaign, Tombstone Doors, 4 Drawers, Anglo-Indian, 77 In. 8050.00
Secretary-Bookcase, Cornice Over 2 Arched Doors, Writing Surface, 1850s, 86 In. 2760.00
Secretary-Bookcase, Eastlake, Walnut, 3 Drawers, Slant Front, c.1875, 102 x 43 x 22 In. . 1380.00
Secretary-Bookcase, Federal, Mahogany, 2 Sections, 1810-1820, 73 x 38 x 19 In. 7640.00
Secretary-Bookcase, George III Style, Mahogany, 89 1/2 x 39 1/2 x 20 In. 1840.00
Secretary-Bookcase, George III, Mahogany, 2 Astragal Doors, 87 x 42 x 21 In. 3910.00
Secretary-Bookcase, George III, Mahogany, 2 Doors, 18th Century, 85 x 41 x 21 In. 4370.00
Secretary-Bookcase, George III, Mahogany, Inlaid, Pigeonholes, Paneled, 36 x 19 In. . . . 1568.00
Secretary-Bookcase, George IV, Mahogany, 2 Astragal Glazed Doors, 84 In. 13800.00
Secretary-Bookcase, Mahogany, 2 Doors, Pigeonholes, Leather Surface, 1810, 98 In. 7840.00
Secretary-Bookcase, Mahogany, 2 Glazed Doors, Butler's Desk, Fitted Interior, 81 In. . . . 800.00
Secretary-Bookcase, Mahogany, Gothic Doors, Bird's-Eye Maple Shelves, 93 1/2 In. 4880.00
Secretary-Bookcase, Mahogany, Inlaid Frieze, Pigeonholes, Doors, c.1900, 42 x 20 In. . . 2575.00
Secretary-Bookcase, Mahogany, Late 18th Century, 85 x 36 x 21 1/2 In. 3450.00
Secretary-Bookcase, Mahogany, Slant Front, Fitted Interior, 3 Drawers, 77 In. 280.00
Secretary-Bookcase, Neoclassical, Mahogany Veneer, Bird's-Eye Maple, c.1840 . . . . 2300.00
Secretary-Bookcase, Renaissance Revival, Walnut, 1 Drawer, 84 x 68 x 22 In. 4315.00
Secretary-Bookcase, Rosewood, Continental, 19th Century, 89 1/2 x 48 x 21 1/2 In. 7475.00
Secretary-Bookcase, Rosewood, Upper Glazed Doors, Fold-Out Surface, 99 1/2 In. 5060.00
Secretary-Bookcase, Sheraton, Mahogany, 3 Sections, Mullioned Doors, 81 In. 5060.00
Secretary-Bookcase, Upper Doors, Lower Drawer, Writing Surface, 79 1/2 In. 3450.00
Secretary-Bookcase, Walnut, 2 Doors Top, 6 Drawers, Victorian, 83 x 43 x 20 In. 1320.00
Server, Aesthetic Style, Butternut, Marble Top, Minton Tile Backsplash, 46 x 42 x 21 In. . 900.00
Server, Arts & Crafts, 2-V Backsplash, 2 Drawers Over Bottom Shelf, 45 x 42 In. 1150.00
Server, Arts & Crafts, Canted Corners, Mirror, Arch, 1915, 38 In. 1365.00
Server, Arts & Crafts, Inlaid Backsplash, Stretcher, 1 Drawer, England, 38 x 36 In. 1090.00
Server, Arts & Crafts, Oak, 1 Long & 2 Short Drawers Over 2 Doors, 35 x 54 x 24 In. . . . 345.00
Server, Arts & Crafts, Oak, Backsplash, Single Drawer, Lower Shelf, 36 In. 1265.00
Server, Bernhardt, Oriental Style, Pullout Shelf, 2 Drawers, 2 Doors, 48 x 36 In. 290.00
Server, Cherry, 3 Drawers, Fan Carved, 38 1/2 x 40 x 19 In. 1495.00
Server, Cherry, Curly Maple Facade, 2-Panel Base Doors, Backsplash, 60 1/2 In. 1705.00
Server, Chinese, 5 Dovetailed Drawers, Relief Panel Fronts, Square Legs, 50 x 25 In. 220.00
Server, Edwardian, Cherry, 3 Drawers, 2 Doors, Carved Panels, Mirror, 79 x 54 x 21 In. . . 728.00
Server, Edwardian, Oak, Mirror Back, Recessed Panel, Painted, 59 x 51 1/2 x 18 1/2 In. . . 785.00
Server, Federal, Mahogany, Shelf, Casters, c.1820, 34 1/2 x 34 /12 x 18 In. 8225.00
Server, G. Stickley, No. 802, Mahogany, 2 Drawers, 42 x 18 x 38 In. 3335.00
Server, G. Stickley, No. 819, Mahogany, 3 Drawers, 1 Full Drawer, 39 In. 4315.00
Server, Gallery, Openworked Support, Linen Board, 4 Drawers, Maslow Freen, N.Y. 495.00
Server, George III, Mahogany, Central Drawer, 34 3/4 x 23 In. 6615.00

Server, Hepplewhite Style, Mahogany, Bowfront, Backsplash, Marble, 39 x 36 x 20 In. 390.00
Server, L. & J.G. Stickley, Backsplash, Arched Apron, 2 Lower Shelves, 38 x 40 In. 3105.00
Server, Lifetime, 3 Half Drawers, 60 x 22 x 40 In. 2300.00
Server, Limbert, No. 410, 2 Drawers, Cutout Backsplash, Lower Shelf, 47 x 44 In. 2185.00
Server, Limbert, No. 413, Mahogany, 1 Drawer, 2 Lower Shelves, 42 x 19 x 41 In. 3220.00
Server, Limbert, Plate Rail, Corbels, 2 Short Drawers Over Long Drawer, 42 x 42 In. 3450.00
Server, Limbert, Plate Rail, Drawers, Lower Shelf, Copper Pulls, Branded, 40 x 40 In. 2185.00
Server, Mahogany, 2 Drawers Over Cupboard Doors, Recessed Doors, 31 x 58 In. 865.00
Server, Mahogany, 2 Tiers, Scalloped, Shelf, Bronze, France, 34 x 21 In. 175.00
Server, Mahogany, 3 Drawers, Inlaid Panels, Spade Feet, c.1780 . . . . 9600.00
Server, Mahogany, Backsplash, 4 Short Drawers, Paneled Doors, c.1830, 49 In. 2350.00
Server, Mahogany, Bowfront, 2 Drawers, Door, Spade Feet, c.1830, 35 x 42 In. 1630.00
Server, Mahogany, Graduated Shelves, Drawers, Doors, 19th Century, 46 x 20 x 71 In. 345.00
Server, Mahogany, Marble Top, 1 Drawer, Acanthus Leaf Carvings, Batwing Brasses 520.00
Server, Mahogany, Serpentine Top & Sides, Square Legs, 74 In. 7200.00
Server, Mahogany, Swivel Flat Top, 1 Drawer, 31 x 36 x 18 In. 150.00
Server, Mixed Woods, Marble Top, Open Shelf, Sunray On Side Doors, 20th Century 1155.00
Server, Napoleon III, Walnut, 2-Shelf Top, 2 Drawers & 2 Doors Base, 1850 . . . . 4800.00
Server, Neoclassical, Mahogany, Drop Leaf, 2 Drawers, Banded, 36 x 24 In. 605.00
Server, Oak, Walnut Veneer, Carving, 2 Paneled Doors, France, 48 x 23 x 37 In. 1155.00
Server, Pine, Bird's-Eye & Tiger Maple Graining, Splashguard, Drawer, 34 x 31 x 17 In. . . 175.00
Server, Pine, Stained, 5 Drawers, 6 Legs, England, 19th Century, 30 1/2 x 47 x 22 In. 575.00
Server, Queen Anne, Walnut, 3 Drawers, Flip-Down Door, Claw Feet, 29 x 60 In. 335.00
Server, Stickley Bros., Mahogany, Rectangular Top, Tapered Legs, 36 In. 1150.00
Server, Stickley Bros., No. 8613, Mahogany, 1 Drawer, Signed, 54 x 46 In. 2875.00
Server, Stickley Bros., No. 8701, Mahogany, Rectangular Top, 36 x 37 In. 1095.00
Server, Walnut, Marble Top, Backsplash, 2 Drawers, Victorian, Doors, 46 x 41 x 21 In. 1120.00
Server, Walnut, X-Stretcher, Continental, Early 20th Century, 33 x 82 x 23 In. 730.00
Settee, Adirondack, Double Seat, Splayed Arms, Continuing To Feet, 1920, 35 1/2 In. . . . 750.00
Settee, Anglo-Indian Style, Walnut, Cushion Seat, Scroll Arms, 20th Century, 31 x 54 In. 920.00
Settee, Arched Crest, Painted, Plank Seat, 26 1/2 x 26 x 9 In. 5300.00
Settee, Arne Jacobsen, Aluminum, Fiberglass, Upholstered, F. Hansen, 29 1/2 In. 3795.00
Settee, Arts & Crafts, Drop Arm, 11 Slats, Drop-In Cushions, 56 x 24 x 37 In. 400.00
Settee, Bamboo, Turned & Chamfered Spindles, Box Stretcher, 78 x 33 In. 1015.00
Settee, Biedermeier, Columns Over Square Legs, Rectangular, 66 In. 1610.00
Settee, D. Kendall, Phoenix, Carved Flowers On Crest Rail & Posts, 38 x 57 In. 2185.00
Settee, Double Rush Seat, Black Paint, Gold Stenciled Decoration 290.00
Settee, Empire, Mahogany, Scroll Back, Upholstered, Sphinx Scroll Arms 2070.00
Settee, Empire, Oak, Mahogany Veneer, Semicurved Arms, Upholstered, 64 In. 550.00
Settee, Floral Medallions, Acanthus-Leaf Arms, Upholstered, Cushion Seat, 32 3/4 In. 1155.00
Settee, Floral Panels, Bowed Apron, Reeded Arms, Upholstered, 37 x 53 In. 440.00
Settee, French Provincial, Fruitwood, Triple Chairback, Early 19th Century, 77 1/2 In. . . . 546.00
Settee, George III, Walnut, 5 Fluted Pilasters, White Painted Shell, Tufted 8500.00
Settee, Georgian, Lion Form, Open Arm, Upholstered Seat & Back, Paw Feet, 46 In. 575.00
Settee, Gothic Revival, Maple, Blue Paint, Philadelphia, 1845-1860, 72 In. 3900.00
Settee, Gustav Siegal, Bent Beech, Stained, Bronze, J. & J. Kohn, 1900, 48 In. 5400.00
Settee, Hitchcock Style, Spindle Back, Scroll Arms, Black Paint, Gold Stenciling, 33 In. . . 420.00
Settee, Jens Risom, Wooden Base, Tapered Legs, Upholstered, 1951, 30 x 55 In. 1095.00
Settee, Ladder Back, Turned Arms, Finials, Arched Slats, Splint Seat, 36 x 21 x 32 In. 550.00
Settee, Leather Seat, Signed, 36 x 63 In. 1495.00
Settee, Lifetime, Vertical Slats, Drop-In Seat, Leather, 30 x 61 x 28 In. 3105.00
Settee, Limbert, No. 1957, Mahogany, Dark Brown Saddle Seat, 38 x 51 x 21 In. 2250.00
Settee, Louis XIV Style, Parcel Gilt, Scrolled Arms, Upholstered, 50 x 31 x 87 In., Pair . . 5175.00
Settee, Louis XV, Carved Flowers, Damask Upholstered, 79 In. 865.00
Settee, Louis XV, Wood, Gilt, Carved Flowers, 72 In. 865.00
Settee, Louis XVI Style, Giltwood, Padded Back, Late 19th Century, 39 x 52 x 21 In. 1150.00
Settee, Louis XVI, Gold Repaint, Barrel Back, Carved Front Swags, 5 Legs, 53 In. 1430.00
Settee, Mahogany, Carved Skirt, Scrolled Arms, Late 19th Century, 28 x 84 In. 1570.00
Settee, Mahogany, Double Chairback, Carved, Claw & Ball Feet, 40 x 45 x 20 In. 960.00
Settee, Mahogany, Double Chairback, Serpentine Rail, Strapwork Splat, 60 In. 7200.00
Settee, Mahogany, Double Chairback, Shepherd's Crook Armrests, 48 1/2 In. 4480.00
Settee, Mahogany, Top Leaves, Scrolled Arms, Pierced Splats, Slip Seat, Upholstered . . . 385.00
Settee, Maple, Double Back, Turned Stiles, Arched Slats, Oak Splint Seat, 31 x 33 In. 1060.00

Settee, Neoclassical, Maple, Fiddleback, Open Scroll Arms, Cane Seat, 30 x 70 In. 3470.00
Settee, Neoclassical, Wood Lyre, Green, Brocade Silk, 31 In. 750.00
Settee, Old Hickory, No. 120, Original Finish, Cane Back, 36 x 80 x 22 In. 1250.00
Settee, Padded Back Joined To Seat, Outscrolled Arms, Upholstered, 36 x 68 In. 2530.00
Settee, Painted, Shaped Crest, 3 Wide Splats, Plank Seat, Yellow, Leaves, 34 x 78 In. 3740.00
Settee, Plank Bottom, Scrolled Arms, Turned Legs, 77 In. 70.00
Settee, Quarter Round, Upholstered Backrest, Kidney Form, Cushion, 1950s, 64 In. 1790.00
Settee, Queen Anne Style, Burl, Double Back, Shaped Crest Rail, 20th Century, 47 In. 950.00
Settee, Queen Anne, Walnut, Upholstered, Rolled Arm, 6 Legs, 38 x 59 x 27 In. 2090.00
Settee, Renaissance Revival, Walnut, Bronze Medallion, Carved Crest, 43 x 24 x 54 In. ... 895.00
Settee, Renaissance Revival, Walnut, Carved, Burled Trim, Upholstered, 42 x 57 In. 840.00
Settee, Rococo, Mahogany, Triple Back, Scrolled Carved Crest, 75 In. 580.00
Settee, Rosewood, Serpentine Crest, Canted Back, Upholstered, 35 x 65 In. 2350.00
Settee, Scrolled Returns, Crewel Upholstered, Padded Drake Feet 2090.00
Settee, Splint Seat, Red Paint, Arms, Tennessee 2450.00
Settee, Vertical Back & Underarm Slats, Drop Arm, 40 x 53 In. 1670.00
Settee, Victorian, Medallion Back, Concave Front, Carved, Down-Filled Cushions 1295.00
Settee, Victorian, Walnut, Finger Carved, Flower & Scroll Crest, 34 x 58 In. 390.00
Settee, Walnut, Ribbon-Carved Crest, Outscrolled Arms, Padded Seat, 37 x 62 1/2 In. ... 2300.00
Settee, Wicker, Double Fanback, Velvet Cushion, c.1890, 40 1/2 x 41 1/2 x 17 1/2 In. ... 1790.00
Settee, William IV, Mahogany, Scrolled Crest, Scrolled Arms, 19th Century, 38 In. 1840.00
Settee, Windsor, Central Horizontal Splat, Ring-Turned Legs, 35 x 21 x 71 In. 1725.00
Settee, Wing, George II Style, Giltwood, 48 1/2 In. 690.00
Settee, Wing, William & Mary, Block & Spindle Turning, 55 In. 575.00
Settle, Arts & Crafts, Broad Back, Side Slats, Drop-In Seat, 39 x 72 x 32 In. 2875.00
Settle, Arts & Crafts, Even Arm, 15 Flats, Notched Top Rail, Leather Seat, 80 In. 2875.00
Settle, Arts & Crafts, Mahogany, Leather Cushion, 84 x 29 x 36 In. 2875.00
Settle, Arts & Crafts, Oak, 15 Vertical Slats, Pegged Tenons, Drop Arms, 37 x 69 In. 1150.00
Settle, Arts & Crafts, Oak, Even Arm, Crest Rail, 9 Vertical Slats, 3 On Sides, 65 In. 2645.00
Settle, Chestnut, Curved Seat & Back, 1810 .... 3400.00
Settle, Curly Maple & Poplar, Arm Spindles, 4 Back Spindles, 36 In. 770.00
Settle, Drop Arm, Cushion Seat, 36 1/2 x 82 x 30 In. 2400.00
Settle, G. Stickley, No. 205, Mahogany, 5 Back Slats, Red Decal, 30 In. 2760.00
Settle, G. Stickley, No. 208, Vertical Slats, New Leather Cover, Decal, 29 x 76 In. 6900.00
Settle, G. Stickley, No. 212, Mahogany, Blue Leather Seat, 36 x 24 In. 2100.00
Settle, G. Stickley, Oak, 8 Wide Back Slats, 29 x 32 In. 5175.00
Settle, Green, Stenciled Fruit Back, Plank Seat, Figure-8 Arms, 8 Turned Legs, 73 In. ... 1430.00
Settle, Hardwood, Stenciled Crest Rail & Stretchers, Fruits & Deer, 76 1/2 In. 1870.00
Settle, Hickory, 1 Hinged Drop Arm, 35 x 79 In. 1840.00
Settle, J.M. Young, Dark Mahogany, Upholstered, 35 x 82 x 31 In. 2250.00
Settle, L. & J.G. Stickley, Drop Arms, Vertical Slats, Leather Cushion, 77 x 30 x 36 In. .. 2415.00
Settle, L. & J.G. Stickley, Mahogany, Brown Leather Seat, 37 x 72 x 22 1/2 In. 2350.00
Settle, L. & J.G. Stickley, No. 214, Mahogany, 22 Curved Slats, 62 x 28 x 33 In. 6900.00
Settle, L. & J.G. Stickley, No. 222, Oak, Brown Leather, 38 3/4 In. 11750.00
Settle, L. & J.G. Stickley, No. 261, Leather Seat, Drop Arm, 38 x 64 In. 2012.00
Settle, L. & J.G. Stickley, No. 281, Mahogany, 16 Back Slats, 76 x 31 x 34 In. 1265.00
Settle, L. & J.G. Stickley, Open Arm, Cloud-Lift Crest Rail, Horizontal Slats, 36 x 53 In. . 1265.00
Settle, L. & J.G. Stickley, V-Crest Rail, Spring Seat, Open Arms, Red Decal, 38 x 76 In. . 4150.00
Settle, Limbert, Mahogany, Even Arm, Original Finish, 36 x 73 x 30 In. 3250.00
Settle, Limbert, No. 649 1/2, Mahogany, 14 Vertical Slats, Leather Seat, 41 In. 2760.00
Settle, Limbert, Shaped Drop Arms, Branded, 40 x 63 In. 1495.00
Settle, Pine, Arrow Back, 23 Spindles, 77 3/4 In. 1100.00
Settle, Pine, London, England, 1850, 49 x 58 x 17 In. 1850.00
Settle, Pine, Painted, Child's, New England, 19th Century, 29 3/4 x 40 x 14 1/2 In. 9600.00
Settle, Pine, Rail Over Paneled Back, Seat Over Storage Compartment, 73 1/2 In. 630.00
Settle, Poplar, Pine, Arrow Back, Plank Seat, Refinished, 1850, 31 x 97 In. 165.00
Settle, Poplar, Straight Back & Sides, Worn Paint, Even Arms, 1860, 93 x 28 In. 100.00
Settle, Shop Of The Crafters, Mahogany, Light Tan Cushion Seat, 37 x 73 x 30 In. 1750.00
Settle, Spindle Back, Plank Seat, Black Paint, 1860, 30 x 78 x 20 In. 285.00
Settle, Stickley & Brandt Co., Mahogany, Light Brown Leather Seat, 39 x 84 x 32 In. 4750.00
Settle, Triple Chairback, Arms, 19th Century 1435.00
Shelf, Blue Gray Paint, Lovebirds, Cutout Tulip, Backsplash, Box, 27 1/2 In. 300.00
Shelf, Comb, Pine, Relief Scroll & Leaves, Star On Pocket, Pierced Trim, 10 5/8 In. 140.00

Shelf, Corner, Hanging, Victorian, Mahogany, 2 Open Shelves, 20 In. 400.00
Shelf, Giltwood, Carved, Monkey Mask, Bracket, 15 1/2 x 11 1/2 In. 575.00
Shelf, Hanging, 3 Shelves, Bird's-Head Finials, 20th Century, 22 x 19 In. 190.00
Shelf, Hanging, 4 Tiers, Late 18th Century, 35 x 36 1/2 In. 2160.00
Shelf, Hanging, Carved, Eagle On Branch, Acorns, Oak Leaves, 22 x 21 In., Pair 4730.00
Shelf, Hanging, Grain Painted, 19th Century, 8 1/2 x 25 1/2 x 5 1/2 In. 130.00
Shelf, Hanging, Mahogany, Fretwork, 2 Open Shelves, 19th Century, 26 1/2 In. 7200.00
Shelf, Hanging, Mahogany, Open Fret Ends, 2 Drawers, Bair Furniture, Hanover 130.00
Shelf, Hanging, Mahogany, Pagoda Shape, Late 19th Century, 8 x 7 1/2 x 24 In. 805.00
Shelf, Hanging, Mahogany, Whale's Tail Sides, 4 Shelves, 33 x 26 In. 840.00
Shelf, Hanging, Oak, Dovetailed, Scalloped Molding, 29 x 32 In. 85.00
Shelf, Hanging, Pine, 3 Shelves, Curved Top, Shaped Ends, 21 1/2 x 6 x 28 In. 165.00
Shelf, Hanging, Pine, Scalloped Ends, 2 Shelves, 20 x 5 7/8 x 23 3/4 In. 110.00
Shelf, Hanging, Poplar, Cherry, Red Paint, Early 19th Century, 14 3/4 x 18 x 4 3/4 In. ... 1035.00
Shelf, Hanging, Red Paint, Arched Molded Cornice, 71 x 38 x 7 3/4 In. 3290.00
Shelf, Hanging, Scalloped Support, Utensil Slots, 23 1/2 x 20 In. 385.00
Shelf, Hanging, Scrolled Form, Dovetailed, Plate Rails, c.1830, 26 x 39 1/2 In. 2300.00
Shelf, Hanging, Walnut, Mirror, Pierced, 19th Century, 22 1/2 x 11 x 7 3/4 In. 460.00
Shelf, Mahogany, Acorn Finials, Brass Thistle Mounts, 34 1/2 x 34 x 6 In. 196.00
Shelf, Mahogany, Whale Ends, Early 19th Century, 31 1/2 x 32 1/2 x 9 In. 1380.00
Shelf, Neoclassical, Giltwood, Bracket, c.1900, 11 1/2 x 6 1/2 x 5 1/2 In., Pair 800.00
Shelf, Neoclassical, Giltwood, Carved, Bracket, 19th Century, 7 1/2 x 7 1/2 x 7 1/2 In. ... 115.00
Shelf, Oak, Carved, Lion's Head, Brass, Iron Hardware, 10 x 35 1/4 x 4 In. 224.00
Shelf, Oak, Lion's Head, Beveled Mirror Back, Brass Hardware, 16 x 38 x 6 In. 224.00
Shelf, Pine, Pewter, Scalloped Ends, Plate Rests, 3 Shelves, 31 1/2 In. 110.00
Shelf, Pine, Pierced Perimeter, Bowed Top, Green & Cream, 9 x 56 In. 1610.00
Shelf, Rococo Revival, Style, Giltwood, Bracket, Italy, Late 19th Century, 13 x 15 x 9 In. .. 750.00
Shelf, Walnut, 3 Tiers, Turned Legs & Supports, Scroll-Cut Galleries, 39 x 19 x 50 In. ... 358.00
Shelf, Walnut, Carved, Eagle, Fruit, 26 In. 715.00
Shelf Bracket, Beech, Parcel Gilt, c.1900, 16 1/2 x 15 x 7 1/4 In., Pair 1035.00
Sideboard, Art Deco, Ebony & Ivory Inlay, 3 Center Shelves, 2 Doors, 43 x 54 x 16 In. .. 920.00
Sideboard, Art Deco, Zebrawood, Flowers, Early 20th Century, 66 x 20 x 37 1/2 In. 1725.00
Sideboard, Arts & Crafts, Mahogany, 2 Drawers, 2 Cabinets, 54 x 23 x 75 In. 3105.00
Sideboard, Backsplash, Center Cutlery Drawer, Side Drawers, 1840s, 49 1/2 In. 1725.00
Sideboard, Carved, Open Top, England, Late 19th Century 1150.00
Sideboard, Charak Modern, Lacquered, Door, 2 Drawers, Decal, c.1950, 39 x 60 In. 1725.00
Sideboard, Charles Dudouyt, Oak, Rosewood, 2 Side Doors, 1940 .... 6000.00
Sideboard, Cherry, 3 Central Drawers, 2 Doors, 6 Legs, Tenn., c.1850, 43 x 63 x 20 In. .. 4290.00
Sideboard, Cherry, 3 Drawers Over 2 Doors, 4 Footed Front, 2 Rear, c.1830, 49 x 60 In. .. 2520.00
Sideboard, Cherry, 3 Drawers Over 2 Doors, 6 Legs, 60 1/4 In. 3400.00
Sideboard, Cherry, Corner, 2 Paneled Base Doors, 2 Drawers, Initialed N.E., 50 In. 6600.00
Sideboard, Eastlake, Walnut, 2 Shelves, Marble Top, 2 Over 1 Long Drawer, 75 In. 800.00
Sideboard, Empire, Mahogany, Carved, Baltimore, 2nd Quarter 19th Century 2530.00
Sideboard, Federal Style, Mahogany, Serpentine, 3 Drawers, 4 Doors, 67 x 39 x 25 In. ... 1430.00
Sideboard, Federal Style, Pine, Green Paint, 39 x 49 1/2 x 19 1/2 In. 635.00
Sideboard, Federal, Mahogany, Inlaid, c.1800, 42 1/2 x 61 x 24 In. 9600.00
Sideboard, Federal, Mahogany, Inlaid, Serpentine, c.1800, 39 3/4 x 67 x 26 1/2 In. ... 10800.00
Sideboard, Federal, Mahogany, Kidney-Shaped Top, 4 Doors, Square Legs, 38 x 72 In. .. 3525.00
Sideboard, Federal, Mahogany, Line Inlay, 3 Drawers Over Doors, Tapered Legs, 42 In. ... 6465.00
Sideboard, Federal, Mahogany, Rectangular Top, Turned Tapered Legs, 1815, 56 In. 1955.00
Sideboard, Federal, Mahogany, Satinwood Inlay, Rectangular Top, 41 In. 26450.00
Sideboard, Federal, Mahogany, Serpentine, Inlaid, 3 Doors, 2 Drawers, 37 x 66 In. 5875.00
Sideboard, Federal, Maple, Figured, Kentucky, c.1825 .... 11000.00
Sideboard, Frank Lloyd Wright, Mahogany, Recessed Handles, 86 x 20 x 46 In. 2990.00
Sideboard, French Provincial, Oak, 3 Drawers, Doors, 42 x 75 x 22 1/2 In. 670.00
Sideboard, G. Nelson, Rosewood Veneer, 3 Drawers, 80 x 18 1/2 x 32 In. 3335.00
Sideboard, G. Stickley, Mahogany, 1 Long Drawer, 4 Legs 3500.00
Sideboard, G. Stickley, Mahogany, 2 Doors, 3 Drawers, 56 x 22 x 50 In. 4900.00
Sideboard, G. Stickley, Plate Rail, 4 Drawers, 2 Doors, Strap Hinges, Label, 50 x 70 In. .. 8625.00
Sideboard, George III Style, Mahogany, Bowed Front, c.1890, 36 1/2 x 66 x 24 In. 1345.00
Sideboard, George III Style, Mahogany, Bowed, 19th Century, 39 x 67 x 26 1/2 In. 2464.00
Sideboard, George III, Mahogany, Rectangular Banded Top, Fluted Legs, 38 In. 2760.00
Sideboard, George III, Mahogany, Rectangular Top, 3 Frieze Drawers, 36 x 21 In. 9200.00

Sideboard, George III, Mahogany, Satinwood, Serpentine Top, Tapered Legs, 34 In. 2990.00
Sideboard, George III, Mahogany, Serpentine Top, 1 Central Drawer, 35 1/2 In. 6900.00
Sideboard, George IV, Mahogany, Rail, 19th Century, 42 x 74 1/2 x 30 1/2 In. 11500.00
Sideboard, Hepplewhite Style, Inlaid Mahogany, Serpentine, 37 x 69 x 26 1/2 In. 1095.00
Sideboard, Hepplewhite, Cherry, Pine, Inlay, 3 Drawers, 4 Doors, c.1825, 46 x 73 In. 3080.00
Sideboard, Hepplewhite, Gallery, 3 Side Drawers, Center Door, 1830, 55 In. 4675.00
Sideboard, Hepplewhite, Mahogany, Inlaid, Serpentine, 39 3/4 x 68 x 23 In. 3640.00
Sideboard, Hepplewhite, Mahogany, Satinwood Inlay, 5 Drawers, 35 1/2 x 70 x 24 In. ... 3640.00
Sideboard, Hepplewhite, Mahogany, Serpentine, 2 Side Doors, 72 x 22 x 37 In. 2420.00
Sideboard, L. & J.G. Stickley, 3 Center Drawers, 2 Doors, Long Drawer, 44 x 48 In. 4600.00
Sideboard, L. & J.G. Stickley, 4 Drawers, 2 Cabinet Doors, Copper, 72 x 25 x 50 In. 8625.00
Sideboard, L. & J.G. Stickley, Mahogany, 4 Drawers, Original Finish, 72 x 62 In. 7480.00
Sideboard, L. & J.G. Stickley, No. 731, Original Finish, 49 1/2 x 72 x 25 In. 6500.00
Sideboard, L. & J.G. Stickley, No. 734, Backsplash, 2 Cupboards, 1912, 44 In. 2070.00
Sideboard, L. & J.G. Stickley, No. 735, Strap Hinges, 46 1/2 x 56 In. 1840.00
Sideboard, Limbert, 2 Over 2 Drawers, Side Cabinets, Linen Drawer, 46 x 66 In. 3450.00
Sideboard, Limbert, 2 Over 3 Drawers Flanked By 2 Doors, Long Drawer, 57 x 60 In. 4315.00
Sideboard, Limbert, Backsplash, Open Shelf Over Drawer, 51 x 60 In. 5465.00
Sideboard, Limbert, Copper Hardware, Plate Rail, 54 x 21 x 42 In. 2185.00
Sideboard, Limbert, Extended Top, Corbels, Mirrored Back, 57 x 60 x 23 In. ...... *Illus* 9200.00
Sideboard, Limbert, No. 421, Mahogany, Overhanging Top, Green Finish, 57 In. 5175.00
Sideboard, Limbert, No. 451, Mahogany, 2 Drawers, Original Finish, 60 x 57 In. 9200.00
Sideboard, Limbert, No. 1456 3/4, Oak, Arched, Mirrored Backsplash, 52 x 22 x 54 In. .. 3820.00
Sideboard, Limbert, No. 1456, Oak, Mirrored Back, 12-Panel Door 3820.00
Sideboard, Limbert, Oak, Early 20th Century, 52 1/2 x 22 x 54 In. 3220.00
Sideboard, Mahogany Patina, 52 x 60 x 19 1/2 In. 600.00
Sideboard, Mahogany Veneer, 2 Drawers, 2 Doors, Half Columns, Paw Feet, 1800s ... 3575.00
Sideboard, Mahogany Veneer, 3 Woven-Wood Sliding Doors, Brass Strips, 62 3/4 In. 1700.00
Sideboard, Mahogany, 1 Long Drawer, Flanked By Short Drawers, 36 3/4 In. 690.00
Sideboard, Mahogany, 2 Long, 1 Short Drawer, Wine Drawer, c.1810, 37 In. 4930.00
Sideboard, Mahogany, 3 Center Drawers, Drawer Over Door, 1880s, 42 In. 2185.00
Sideboard, Mahogany, 3 Drawers, 4 Doors, Curved Front, Spade Feet, 42 x 61 x 23 In. .. 1290.00
Sideboard, Mahogany, 4 Paneled Doors, 3 Drawers, Gallery, 46 1/2 x 68 In. 1815.00
Sideboard, Mahogany, Beehive-Turned Legs, 19th Century, 45 1/2 In. 2760.00
Sideboard, Mahogany, Bowfront, 2 Drawers, Wine Drawer, Door, c.1810, 37 1/2 In. 7280.00
Sideboard, Mahogany, Bowfront, 2 Long Drawers, 2 Lined Wine Drawers, 72 In. 2350.00
Sideboard, Mahogany, Bowfront, Top Over Long Drawer, 2 Doors, 35 x 55 1/2 In. 1630.00
Sideboard, Mahogany, Crest, Mirror Backsplash, 2 Doors, c.1900, 16 x 39 1/4 In. 575.00
Sideboard, Mahogany, Fitted Case, Cutlery Drawer, Spade Feet, 1770s, 35 1/2 In. 3910.00
Sideboard, Mahogany, Inlaid Bowfront, 2 Doors, Spade Feet, c.1840, 48 In. 2015.00
Sideboard, Mahogany, Inlay At Drawers & Doors, Shelf At Back, 82 1/2 In. 2310.00
Sideboard, Mahogany, Raised On Leaf Legs, Carved Paw Feet, 52 x 59 x 24 In. 5750.00
Sideboard, Mahogany, Serpentine, c.1805, 39 1/2 x 74 x 31 1/2 In. 34100.00
Sideboard, Marble Top, Deer-Head Pediment, 2 Drawers, 2 Doors, c.1870, 81 In. 2910.00
Sideboard, McComb, Leather-Covered Sliding Doors, Shelves, 35 3/4 x 66 In. 220.00
Sideboard, Mission, Oak, 2 Center Drawers, 2 Doors, 72 x 22 x 38 In. 825.00
Sideboard, Oak, Fish-Carved Trim, Fruit At Drawer 650.00
Sideboard, Oak, Recessed Center, 2 Drawers Over Doors, Garlands, 1880s, 94 In. 3680.00
Sideboard, Open Bottom, 2 Upper Doors, Paneled, Carved Figures, 55 In. 2130.00
Sideboard, P. Laverne, Bronze Panels, 6 Brass Doors, 3 Cabinets, 28 3/4 x 78 In. 3740.00
Sideboard, Padouk Wood, 3 Drawers, Stringing & Leaves, 1840s, 31 In. 9775.00
Sideboard, Pierre Cardin, Chrome, Brushed, Glass Top, 4 Drawers, 30 x 74 x 19 In. 690.00
Sideboard, Pine, Scalloped Aprons, 2 Base Doors, 3 Drawers At Top, 20 1/2 x 6 In. 580.00
Sideboard, Regency, Bowfront, Mahogany, Banded Top, Reeded Pilasters, 38 In. 1725.00
Sideboard, Regency, Mahogany, Brass Gallery, Stepped Front, 69 x 37 x 21 In. 2475.00
Sideboard, Regency, Mahogany, Ebonized, Bowed, Brass, 1810, 37 x 55 x 28 In. 8400.00
Sideboard, Regency, Mahogany, Ebonized, Concave Front, 2 Drawers, 85 In. 9600.00
Sideboard, Regency, Mahogany, Inlaid, Drawer, 2 Doors, Spade Feet, c.1840, 47 x 21 In.. 3140.00
Sideboard, Regency, Mahogany, Pedestal, Shell Back, 19th Century, 47 x 61 x 25 In. 2530.00
Sideboard, Renaissance Revival, Burl Oak, Projecting Top, 38 x 71 3/4 x 24 1/2 In. 1380.00
Sideboard, Rosewood, 4 Drawers, Sliding Doors, Shelves, Warming Tray, 78 1/4 In. 275.00
Sideboard, Rosewood, Drawers, 3 Cabinets, Trestle Leg, Herman Miller, 32 x 80 x 18 In. 2875.00
Sideboard, Rosewood, Flower Marquetry, 43 x 73 1/2 x 17 1/2 In. 952.00

Furniture, Sideboard,
Limbert, Extended
Top, Corbels,
Mirrored Back,
57 x 60 x 23 In.

Furniture, Sideboard, Walnut, Inlaid, Pine, Brass,
N.C., 1800-1820, 41 1/2 x 56 1/2 x 20 1/2 In.

Sideboard, Serpentine Front, Long Drawer, 2 Doors, Spade Feet, 58 3/4 In. 1792.00
Sideboard, Stickley Bros., 2 Short Over 2 Long Drawers, 2 Paneled Doors, 46 x 66 In. . . 4600.00
Sideboard, Stickley, Plate Rail, 3 Drawers, 2 Cabinets, Copper Pulls, 44 x 48 x 20 In. . . . 2760.00
Sideboard, Tiger Maple, Cherry, Bowfront, 2 Drawers Over 2 Doors, 45 x 40 In. 6900.00
Sideboard, Victorian, Mahogany, Beveled Mirrors, Curio Cabinet, 92 x 22 x 72 In. 3360.00
Sideboard, Victorian, Oak, Curved Side Doors, Fish, Game, Lion Crest, 103 x 25 x 82 In. . 560.00
Sideboard, Walnut Veneer, Center Drawers, 2 Sliding Doors, Pullout Tray, 77 1/4 In. 1175.00
Sideboard, Walnut, 4 Banded Inlay Drawers, Sheaves Of Wheat Brasses, 98 1/4 In. 385.00
Sideboard, Walnut, Carved, Cupboard Top, Panel Doors, 19th Century, 89 x 57 x 21 In. . . 840.00
Sideboard, Walnut, Inlaid, Pine, Brass, N.C., 1800-1820, 41 1/2 x 56 1/2 x 20 1/2 In. *Illus* 39600.00
Silver Chest, Hardwood Veneers, Base Drawer, Drop Front, Drawers, 40 In. 550.00
Silver Chest, Walnut, 2 Drawers, Tiffany & Co., 1937, 22 x 14 x 13 In. 275.00
Sofa, Beech, Upholstered, Cane, Carved, Continental, c.1900, 91 In. 1120.00
Sofa, Biedermeier Style, Blond Wood, Mid 19th Century, 36 x 74 1/2 x 26 3/4 In. 2300.00
Sofa, Birch Legs, Upholstered, Florence Knoll, 1950, 30 x 90 In. 3220.00
Sofa, Camelback, Chippendale Style, Mahogany Base, Rolled Arms, Upholstered, 80 In. . 275.00
Sofa, Camelback, Chippendale Style, Mahogany, Carved, Claw & Ball Feet, Upholstered . 275.00
Sofa, Camelback, Chippendale, Mahogany, Blind Fretwork, Carved Legs, Upholstered . . . 165.00
Sofa, Camelback, George III Style, Mahogany, 61 1/2 In. 1150.00
Sofa, Camelback, George III Style, Mahogany, Upholstered, 20th Century, 31 x 65 In. . . . 460.00
Sofa, Camelback, George III, Mahogany, Upholstered, Tapered Legs, 34 x 80 In. 5750.00
Sofa, Camelback, Hickory Chair Co., George III Style, Mahogany, 35 In., Pair 1100.00
Sofa, Camelback, Mahogany Legs & Stretchers, Upholstered, 81 1/2 In. 1045.00
Sofa, Camelback, Reed Arms, Legs, Early 20th Century, 73 In. 635.00
Sofa, Camelback, Upholstered, Claw & Ball Feet, 72 In. 630.00
Sofa, Chesterfield, Mahogany, Leather, Button-Padded, Victorian, 27 x 79 x 32 In. 635.00
Sofa, Chinese Chippendale Style, Mahogany, Early 20th Century, 85 x 31 x 35 In. 220.00
Sofa, Chinese Chippendale Style, Upholstered, 20th Century, 49 x 33 In., Pair 615.00
Sofa, E. Wormley, Mahogany Base, Velvet, Dunbar, 81 x 30 In. 2875.00
Sofa, E. Wormley, Mahogany, Upholstered, Dunbar, 89 x 33 x 27 1/2 In. 750.00
Sofa, Empire, Mahogany, Flame Veneer Panels, Serpentine Arms, Upholstered, 89 In. 3410.00
Sofa, Empire, Walnut, Arched Padded Back, Outcurved Padded Arms, 73 1/2 In. 690.00
Sofa, Empire, Walnut, Carved Lyre Frame, Horsehair Upholstered, Swan Arms, 66 In. 1100.00
Sofa, Federal Style, Mahogany, Philadelphia, 36 x 75 x 24 1/2 In. 590.00
Sofa, Federal, Mahogany, Leaf-Carved Reeded Legs, 34 x 75 1/2 x 15 In. 3105.00
Sofa, Federal, Reeded Top, Scrolled Arms, Paw Feet, c.1890, 64 In. 1680.00
Sofa, Folke Ohlsson, Tweed Upholstered Frame, 8 Loose Cushions, 28 x 73 In. 465.00
Sofa, French Provincial, Carved, Gold Brocade Fabric, 35 x 52 In., Pair 1320.00
Sofa, French Provincial, Down Cushions, Upholstered, Silk, 34 x 46 In. 1840.00
Sofa, Fruit Carved, Scrolled Back & Crest, Rolled Arms, 1825 . . . . 4890.00
Sofa, G. Nakashima, Walnut, Spindle Back, Tapered Dowel Legs, 72 x 30 In. 3335.00
Sofa, G. Nelson, Marshmallow, Upholstered, Vinyl, 1956, 52 In. 12925.00
Sofa, G. Nelson, Marshmallow, Wool, 53 x 31 x 33 In. 20700.00
Sofa, G. Nelson, Sling, 6 Leather Cushions, Tubular Chrome, 30 x 86 x 31 In. . .2645.00 to 6235.00
Sofa, George III, Mahogany, Padded Arms, Loose Cushion, c.1760, 72 In. 1840.00
Sofa, Green Striped, Silk, Upholstered, Milo Baughman, 27 x 84 x 34 In. 1495.00
Sofa, Harvey Probber, Silk, Tufted Back Cushion, Even Arm, 103 In. 3100.00

Sofa, John Jeliff, Renaissance Revival, Walnut, Upholstered, c.1870, 43 x 32 x 78 In. 7000.00
Sofa, Jules Leleu, Art Deco, Scalloped Back, Velvet, 77 In. 575.00
Sofa, Louis XV Style, Carved, Scrolled Arms, Cabriole Legs, Velvet, 78 In. 330.00
Sofa, Louis XV, Fruitwood, Mid 19th Century, 36 x 80 1/2 x 28 1/2 In. 5290.00
Sofa, Louis XVI, Beech, Curved Back, Scrolled Arms, 54 In. 865.00
Sofa, Mahogany Flame, Swan's-Neck Arms, Shell Crest, Upholstered, 1800s 700.00
Sofa, Mahogany, Brocade Upholstered, Tapered Legs, 38 x 78 In. 250.00
Sofa, Mahogany, Cornucopia Arms, Paw Feet, Upholstered, c.1825 . . . . 5460.00
Sofa, Mahogany, Cornucopia Carving At Arms, Paw Feet, c.1890, 80 In. 560.00
Sofa, Mahogany, Down & Feather Cushions, Square Legs, Brocade Upholstered, 73 In. . . . 880.00
Sofa, Mahogany, Eagle Decoration, Damask Upholstery, c.1825, 84 In. 3800.00
Sofa, Mahogany, Floral Rail, Padded Arms, Leaf-Carved Feet, c.1840, 86 In. 2350.00
Sofa, Mahogany, Leaf-Carved Scroll Ends, Seat Rail, Paw Feet, 38 1/2 In. 3910.00
Sofa, Mahogany, Stepped-Down Back, Cast Eagles On Feet, 1850s, 31 x 95 In. 3585.00
Sofa, Mahogany, Tablet Crest, Floral Bud Ends, Paw Feet, 32 1/2 x 75 In. 565.00
Sofa, Mahogany, Upholstered, Padded Seat, Top-Shaped Feet, c.1900, 78 In. 1150.00
Sofa, McCobb, 3 Seat Cushions, Tapered Dowel Legs, Upholstered, 28 x 80 In. 575.00
Sofa, Morrison & Hannah, Enamel Frame, Sling Seats, Upholstered, Knoll, 28 x 79 In. . . . 375.00
Sofa, Neoclassical, Mahogany Veneer, Leaf Design, Dolphin Legs, 33 1/2 In. 1380.00
Sofa, Neoclassical, Mahogany, Carved, Figured, Philadelphia, c.1830, 87 In. 3600.00
Sofa, Neoclassical, Mahogany, Rounded Crest Rail, Light Blue Velvet Backrest, 36 In. . . . 1265.00
Sofa, Neoclassical, Mahogany, Scrolled Back, Swan's Neck Arms, 1850s, 65 x 25 In. 660.00
Sofa, Neoclassical, Mahogany, Scrolled Crest Rail, Paw Feet, 34 1/2 In. 800.00
Sofa, Neoclassical, Mahogany, Upholstered, Carved Hairy Paw Feet 990.00
Sofa, Peter Maly, Swing, Upholstered, 64 x 32 In. 1495.00
Sofa, Peterhvidt & Orla Neilsen, Teak, Upholstered, France & Son, 50 x 30 x 28 In. 575.00
Sofa, Red Leather, Button-Upholstered Back, Cushion Seat, c.1900, 27 x 74 In. 545.00
Sofa, Regency, Rosewood, Plain Frieze, Lotus Legs, 19th Century, 30 In. 2530.00
Sofa, Renaissance Revival, Rosewood, Inlaid, Upholstered, c.1870, 72 In. 1265.00
Sofa, Rococo Revival, Rosewood Laminate, Pierce-Carved Frame, 49 1/2 x 76 x 34 In. . . . 7765.00
Sofa, Rococo Revival, Walnut, Serpentine Crest, Damask Upholstered, 75 In. 920.00
Sofa, Rococo, Rosewood, Asymmetrical Leaf-Carved Crest, Cabriole Legs, 47 In. 4140.00
Sofa, Shaped Button-Tufted Back, 3 Cushions, Scrolling Arms, 75 In. 60.00
Sofa, Sheraton Style, 3-Panel Back, Scroll Arms, Upholstered, 8 Legs, 35 x 77 x 31 In. . . 835.00
Sofa, Sheraton, Rosewood, Upholstered, 6 Reeded Legs, Arms, 36 x 73 x 20 In. 670.00
Sofa, Tapestry Seat & Back, Figural & Hunt Scene, Open Arms, 74 In. 2875.00
Sofa, Teak, Vertical Backsplash, Arms, 6 Loose Cushions, Upholstered, Tag, 75 1/2 In. . . . 400.00
Sofa, Tufted Leather, Rolled Armrests, Early 20th Century, 76 In. 6720.00
Sofa, Victorian, Carved Walnut, Cabriole Legs, Velvet, Button Back, 77 In. 660.00
Sofa, Victorian, Rosewood, Floral Urn Crests, Upholstered, 45 x 32 x 62 In. 4200.00
Sofa, Victorian, Rosewood, High Back, Carved Crest, Tufted, Upholstery, 44 x 62 x 27 In. 900.00
Sofa, Victorian, Walnut, Serpentine Rose-Carved Crest, 63 In. 165.00
Sofa, Walnut End-Table Arms, Crimson Velour, Herman Miller, 27 x 120 1/2 x 32 In. 3000.00
Sofa, Walnut Veneer Panels, Incised Bronze, Gilt, Curule Base, 44 x 71 x 27 In. 2070.00
Sofa, Walnut, 3 Back Sections, Finger-Carved Throughout, c.1860, 37 x 60 In. 36.00
Sofa, Walnut, Cameo Back, Flower & Grape Cluster Crest, Upholstered, 42 x 66 x 25 In. . 1790.00
Sofa, Walnut, Center Floral Shell, Padded Back Joined By Armrests, 1770s, 72 In. 2990.00
Sofa, Walnut, Mahogany Veneer, Poplar, Scrolled Arm Supports, 34 x 71 x 26 In. 1650.00
Sofa, Walnut, Medallion Back, Crest, Burl Panels, 63 x 24 x 34 In. 250.00
Stand, Adirondack, Birch, Stretcher, Polychrome Bird, 30 1/2 x 14 1/2 x 14 3/4 In. 1380.00
Stand, Aesthetic Revival, Ebonized, Gilt Incised Design, 19th Century, Pair 550.00
Stand, Art Deco, Walnut, Drawer, Shelf Over 3 Shelves, c.1930, 27 x 28 In., Pair 690.00
Stand, Arts & Crafts, Hammered Brass, Round Top, Shelf, 27 x 18 In. 175.00
Stand, Bamboo, Rattan, Octagonal Top, Shelf, 28 x 19 x 19 In. 110.00
Stand, Birch, Mahogany, Drawer, Turned & Reeded Legs, Ball Feet, 28 In. 3290.00
Stand, Birch, Poplar, Drawer, Walnut Pull, Pegged Legs, 28 In. 1210.00
Stand, Birch, Yellow Pine, Georgia, Early 19th Century, 28 3/4 x 30 1/2 x 19 1/2 In. 825.00
Stand, Burl Panels, Marble Top, Shaped Skirt, Molded Edge, 30 x 32 1/2 x 23 1/2 In. . . . 1035.00
Stand, Carved Pedestal, Boy In Rushes, Swan, Dolphins, Cattails, 36 In. 2800.00
Stand, Carved Pedestal, Climbing Cupid, Flower Garlands, Winged Griffin, 62 In. 5320.00
Stand, Cherry, 2 Graduated Cock-Beaded Drawers, Ball Feet, 18 3/4 x 18 1/2 In. 770.00
Stand, Cherry, Circular Top, Black Paint, 3 Legs, 26 x 18 In. 750.00
Stand, Cherry, Dovetailed Drawer, Burl Knobs, 29 x 21 3/4 In. 990.00

Stand, Cherry, Dovetailed Drawer, Carved Basket & Leaves, 2-Board Top, 29 1/2 In. 1760.00
Stand, Cherry, Dovetailed Drawer, Wood Pulls, Pegged Construction, 26 1/4 x 24 In. 165.00
Stand, Cherry, Drawer, Rectangular Top, 28 1/2 x 22 In. 115.00
Stand, Cherry, Drawer, Sandwich Glass Knob, 27 1/2 In. 290.00
Stand, Cherry, Drawer, Tall Turned Legs, 20 x 19 1/2 x 29 3/4 In. 300.00
Stand, Cherry, Fitted Dovetailed Drawer, Wooden Pulls, 27 x 18 1/2 In. 935.00
Stand, Cherry, Inlaid, New England, Early 19th Century, 26 1/2 x 18 3/4 x 11 3/4 In. 2530.00
Stand, Cherry, Maple, 4 Blocks, Turned Legs, New England, 26 x 18 In. 860.00
Stand, Cherry, Painted, New England, Early 19th Century, 27 1/2 x 10 x 10 In. 5750.00
Stand, Cherry, Round Top, Swing Leg, 4 Legs, 29 1/2 In. 550.00
Stand, Cherry, Turned Legs 220.00
Stand, Chinese, Carved, Rouge Marble Top, Early 20th Century, 18 x 14 x 32 In. 400.00
Stand, Chippendale, Pine, Drawer, Chamfered Splayed Legs, Painted, 28 x 16 x 19 In. .. 3300.00
Stand, Corner, Fruitwood, 2 Shelves, Tambour Front, Shaped Crest, France, 32 x 21 In. .. 225.00
Stand, Corner, Hepplewhite, Mahogany, String Inlay, High Splash, Drawer, 48 In. 1230.00
Stand, Corner, Regency Style, Mahogany, Inlaid, Basin, Center Shelf, Drawer, 34 x 24 In. 230.00
Stand, Curly Maple, 2 Drawers, Floral Brass Pulls, 27 x 18 3/4 In. 1100.00
Stand, Curly Maple, Dovetailed Drawer, Brass Pull, 27 3/4 x 17 3/4 In. 880.00
Stand, Curly Maple, Drawer, Splayed Legs, Turned Finial, 27 3/4 In. 385.00
Stand, Curly Maple, Drawer, Walnut Pull, Old Beebe, 1767, 27 1/4 In. 2090.00
Stand, Curly Maple, Fitted Drawer, Wooden Pull, 28 3/4 In. 935.00
Stand, Curly Maple, Pegged Construction, Drawer, Splayed Legs, 26 3/4 In. 605.00
Stand, Curly Maple, Raised Ring Cuffs On Legs, Turned Pulls, 20th Century 470.00
Stand, Drink, L. & J.G. Stickley, Mahogany, Copper Top, Original Patina, 28 In. 1300.00
Stand, Drink, L. & J.G. Stickley, No. 587, Mahogany, Square Top, 16 x 27 In. 690.00
Stand, Drink, L. & J.G. Stickley, Round, Copper Top, Red Decal, 28 x 18 In. 7475.00
Stand, Drink, Stickley Bros., Round Copper Top, Arched Aprons, Flared Legs, 28 x 18 In. 3000.00
Stand, E. Wormley, Mahogany, Drawer, 16 x 13 x 25 In. 800.00
Stand, Eastlake, Pattern Stone Top, Reeded Frame, Splayed Legs, 16 x 12 x 34 In. 220.00
Stand, Empire Style, Gilt Bronze, Onyx, Early 20th Century, 26 In. 430.00
Stand, Empire, Cherry, Bowfront, 2 Drawers, Rope-Twist Legs, 22 x 21 1/2 x 30 In. 880.00
Stand, Empire, Cherry, Bowfront, 2 Veneer Drawers, 3-Board Top, 24 x 24 In. 550.00
Stand, Empire, Mahogany, Poplar Veneer, Late 19th Century, 28 x 21 3/4 x 17 1/2 In. ... 315.00
Stand, Empire, Marble Top, Pedestal, Fluted Sides, Octagonal Foot, 1800s, 30 x 16 In. .. 980.00
Stand, Faux Mahogany, Red & Gold, 2 Drawers, Pedestal, Platform Base, 29 In. 690.00
Stand, Federal, Cherry, Drawer, Rectangular Top, 4 Tapered Legs, 27 3/4 In. 980.00
Stand, Federal, Cherry, Rectangular Top, Frieze Drawer, Ball Feet, 29 In. 260.00
Stand, Federal, Cherry, Tilt Top, Ring & Urn Turned Pedestal, Spade Feet, 27 In. 2350.00
Stand, Federal, Mahogany Veneer, Drawer, Rectangular Top, 2 Drawers, 28 In. 1090.00
Stand, Federal, Maple, Birch, Drawer, Overhanging Top, Tapered Legs, 28 x 17 In. 550.00
Stand, Federal, Pine, Drawer, Square Tray Top, 4 Tapered Legs, 29 1/2 x 19 In. 490.00
Stand, Federal, Pine, Maple, Stained, New England, 1800-1810, 26 x 19 x 16 1/2 In. 490.00
Stand, Federal, Walnut, Overhanging Top, Drawer, Square Tapered Legs, 29 x 18 In. 550.00
Stand, Fern, Art Deco, Wrought Iron, Scroll Form, Marble Top, 1900s, 39 In. 690.00
Stand, Fern, Black Forest, Nude Woman Shaft, Late 1800s, 43 In., Pair 1900.00
Stand, Fern, Brass, Marble Insert, Cabriole Legs, Openwork Shelf, Scrolled Feet, 29 In. .. 85.00
Stand, Fern, Carved Leaves, Reeded, Continental, Late 19th Century, 61 In. 460.00
Stand, Fern, George III, Mahogany, Leaf Tilt Top, Leaf Pad Feet, 44 1/2 x 9 In., Pair 1955.00
Stand, Fern, Gesso, Gold Paint, Marble, Cabriole Legs, Shelf, Continental, 19 x 19 In. 440.00
Stand, Fern, Incised Flowers, 5 Cabriole Legs Attached To Base, Label, 36 x 11 In. 80.00
Stand, Fern, Mahogany, Acanthus Leaf-Carved Legs, Tripod Base, 37 3/4 In. 300.00
Stand, Fern, Mahogany, Leaf Carved, Quatrefoil Base, Continental, 1800s, 61 In. 460.00
Stand, Fern, Pine, Short Spider Base, 4 Raised & Chamfered Rings, 33 In. 90.00
Stand, Fern, Teak, Leaf Carvings, Pierced Blossoms, 8 Sides, 35 1/2 In. 250.00
Stand, Fern, Teak, Soapstone Insert, Dragons' Faces, Berries On Apron, Paw Feet, 32 In. . 385.00
Stand, Fern, Wrought Iron, Scroll Form, Art Pottery Tile Top, Early 1900s, 29 In. 460.00
Stand, Floral & Leaf Design, Gold, Dark Red Paint, 21 1/2 x 19 1/4 x 30 In. 495.00
Stand, Folio Display, Stretcher Base, Hinged Front Panel, 39 In. 330.00
Stand, Folio, Display, Rosewood, Curtis & Richardson, 1850s, 50 x 48 x 35 In. 8400.00
Stand, French Provincial, Walnut, Marble, Drawer, Door, Cabriole Legs, 35 x 17 x 15 In. . 390.00
Stand, French Provincial, Walnut, Marble, Drawer, Door, Cabriole Legs, 36 x 16 x 17 In. .. 365.00
Stand, G. Nakashima, Laurel Veneer, Widdicomb, c.1958, 22 x 21 x 21 In., Pair 805.00
Stand, G. Nelson, Edge, Herman Miller, 17 1/2 x 18 1/2 x 23 1/2 In. 2185.00

Stand, George II, Mahogany, Dish Top, Urn, 3 Scroll Legs, 22 x 11 1/2 In.	3000.00
Stand, George III, Mahogany, 3/4 Gallery Top Shelf, Drawers, 30 x 22 In.	8400.00
Stand, George III, Mahogany, Bowfront, Gallery, 2 Base Drawers, 1790, 38 x 29 In.	7800.00
Stand, George III, Mahogany, Elm, Circular Mahogany Top, 27 x 20 In.	545.00
Stand, George III, Mahogany, Sliding Tray, Cup Rest, c.1800, 29 x 18 x 18 In.	1265.00
Stand, Graining, Drawer, Straight Tapered Legs, 30 x 18 1/2 x 18 In.	220.00
Stand, Handcraft, Drawer, Signed, 29 x 24 x 16 In.	1100.00
Stand, Hardwood, Bird's Head On Cabriole Legs, Claw Feet, Chinese, 20 x 20 x 30 In. . .	230.00
Stand, Hepplewhite, Cherry Finish, Curly Maple Veneer, 22 1/2 x 21 x 29 In.	165.00
Stand, Hepplewhite, Cherry, Drawer, Tapered Legs, 26 x 18 x 18 1/2 In.	1495.00
Stand, Hepplewhite, Cherry, Drawer, Wood Pull, 1-Board Top, 27 3/4 x 19 1/2 In.	385.00
Stand, Hepplewhite, Mahogany, Drawer, 2-Board Top, Tapered Legs, 19 x 15 x 29 In. . . .	300.00
Stand, Hepplewhite, Walnut, Drawer, Tapered Legs, 1-Board Top, 17 x 17 x 28 In.	600.00
Stand, Herter Bros., Aesthetic Revival, Mahogany, c.1880, 28 1/2 x 18 x 18 In.	10575.00
Stand, Herter Bros., Rosewood, Inlaid, Marble Top, Gold Incising, 31 x 18 x 18 In.	7840.00
Stand, Hickory, Shelf, 28 x 24 In.	800.00
Stand, Jacobean, Oak, 4 Long Drawers, Twist Legs, Stretchers, c.1690, 47 x 37 x 22 In. . .	1610.00
Stand, Jeremiah Stahl, Drawer, Painted, Soap Hollow, 30 In.	3850.00
Stand, Joshua Jones, Renaissance Revival, Walnut, 31 1/2 x 20 x 17 1/2 In.	1495.00
Stand, Kettle, Mahogany, Tray Top, Candle Slide, Marlborough Legs, 29 x 12 x 12 In. . . .	1035.00
Stand, L. & J.G. Stickley, No. 573, Mahogany, Round, Signed Handcraft, 29 In.	1200.00
Stand, L. & J.G. Stickley, No. 574, Mahogany, 29 1/8 In.	800.00
Stand, Lifetime, Dark Mahogany, Oval, 30 x 22 In.	1500.00
Stand, Louis Philippe, Mahogany, Marble, 29 1/2 x 15 x 13 1/4 In.	1955.00
Stand, Louis XV Style, Ormolu, Burl Walnut, Early 20th Century, 45 x 12 1/2 In.	800.00
Stand, Louis XVI Style, Marquetry, Ormolu, Round, France, 30 x 20 In.	980.00
Stand, Louis XVI Style, Tulipwood, Parquet, Round Top, Drawer, 1800s, 29 x 24 In.	1265.00
Stand, Luggage, Arts & Crafts, Slatted Top Over 4 Tapered Legs, Spindle Sides, 19 In. . .	475.00
Stand, Luggage, Mahogany, Slatted Top, Holland & Sons, 19th Century, Pair	8400.00
Stand, Luggage, Stickley Bros., Slatted Top, Tapered Legs, Vertical Spindles, 19 In.	475.00
Stand, Luggage, William IV, Mahogany, Slatted Top, H-Stretcher, 17 x 30 x 17 3/4 In. . . .	635.00
Stand, Magazine, 3 Shelves, Cutout Handles, 28 x 17 In.	260.00
Stand, Magazine, 4 Shelves, Slatted Sides, 40 x 16 In.	345.00
Stand, Magazine, Arts & Crafts, Mahogany, 3 Shelves, 27 x 13 x 36 In.	100.00
Stand, Magazine, Arts & Crafts, Mahogany, Dark Finish, Rectangular Top, 15 x 46 In. . . .	865.00
Stand, Magazine, Arts & Crafts, Mahogany, Peaked Spindles, 21 x 12 x 36 In.	175.00
Stand, Magazine, Arts & Crafts, Vertical Slats, 5 Tiers, Branded CPM, 50 x 18 In.	2415.00
Stand, Magazine, E. Wormley, Walnut, Triangular Walnut Top, 24 x 22 In.	978.00
Stand, Magazine, G. Stickley, 3 Shelves, Arched Aprons, Harvey Ellis, 42 x 21 In.	2300.00
Stand, Magazine, G. Stickley, 4 Shelves, D-Shape Handles, Red Decal, 40 x 14 In.	2185.00
Stand, Magazine, G. Stickley, Beveled Overhanging Top, 3 Shelves, 35 x 15 In.	2300.00
Stand, Magazine, G. Stickley, Mahogany, 3 Shelves, Rectangular Top, 42 In.	5175.00
Stand, Magazine, G. Stickley, Mahogany, Square Top, Splayed Sides, 44 In.	3335.00
Stand, Magazine, G. Stickley, No. 72, Mahogany, Signed, 42 x 13 In.	2500.00
Stand, Magazine, G. Stickley, No. 79, Mahogany, 4 Shelves, 14 x 10 x 40 In.	3000.00
Stand, Magazine, L. & J.G. Stickley, No. 46, Mahogany, 3 Vertical Slats, Signed	1495.00
Stand, Magazine, L. & J.G. Stickley, Slat Ends, Arched Apron, 4 Shelves, 42 x 21 In. . . .	1265.00
Stand, Magazine, L. & J.G. Stickley, Slat Ends, Decal, 30 x 36 x 12 In.	3000.00
Stand, Magazine, Limbert, 3 Tiers, Original Finish, 18 x 15 x 29 In.	1035.00
Stand, Magazine, Limbert, 4 Open Shelves, Slat Sides, Branded, 42 x 20 In.	2185.00
Stand, Magazine, Limbert, 5 Shelves, Cutouts, Flared Sides, Branded, 40 x 23 In.	3450.00
Stand, Magazine, Limbert, Cutout Sides, 4 Shelves, 37 x 16 1/2 In.	920.00
Stand, Magazine, Limbert, Mahogany, Dark Finish, Cutout Sides, 37 x 20 x 14 In.	900.00
Stand, Magazine, Limbert, No. 801, Oak, 30 x 11 x 29 In.	1600.00
Stand, Magazine, Mahogany, 4 Shelves, 19 x 10 x 36 In.	345.00
Stand, Magazine, Mahogany, 4 Splayed Legs, 30 x 20 x 12 In.	350.00
Stand, Magazine, Old Hickory, Woven Cane, U-Shaped Handle, 23 1/2 x 22 x 15 In.	1035.00
Stand, Magazine, Plastic, Molded, Recessed Handle, 4 Sections, Kartell, 15 1/2 In.	290.00
Stand, Magazine, Revere, Chrome, Flexible Sides, Bakelite Handle, 17 1/2 x 12 In.	355.00
Stand, Magazine, Round Cutouts, 43 x 18 x 12 In.	1100.00
Stand, Magazine, Roycroft, No. 087, Mahogany, Rectangular Top, 33 x 39 In.	10350.00
Stand, Magazine, Square Top, 3 Shelves, 14 x 14 x 36 In.	400.00
Stand, Magazine, Stickley Bros., 4 Shelves, Paper Label, 40 x 26 In.	1440.00

Stand, Magazine, Tobey, Splayed Sides, Carved, Leather, 3 Shelves, 13 x 13 x 44 In. 2415.00
Stand, Magazine, Twig, Arched Side Handles, 30 x 21 1/2 In. 80.00
Stand, Mahogany, 3 Drawers, Bag Drawer, Column Legs, Stretcher Base, 28 x 19 In. 2530.00
Stand, Mahogany, 3 Drawers, Cabriole Leg, Brass Hardware, 29 1/2 x 21 1/2 In. 110.00
Stand, Mahogany, 3 Drawers, Drop Leaves, Turned Half Columns, 29 x 19 x 19 In. 1045.00
Stand, Mahogany, 3 Legs, Medallion In Tapered Feet, Candle Slide, 26 1/2 In. 275.00
Stand, Mahogany, Barley-Twist Spindles, Round Base, Cast-Iron Claw Feet, 32 x 12 In. . . 450.00
Stand, Mahogany, Basin, England, Late 18th Century, 32 1/2 x 14 1/2 x 14 1/2 In. 800.00
Stand, Mahogany, Burl, Bowfront, Shaped Backsplash, 3 Drawers, Shelf, 37 x 19 In. 1120.00
Stand, Mahogany, Drawer, Tall Tapered Legs, Pair 300.00
Stand, Mahogany, Drop Leaf, End Drawer, Brass Pull, 23 x 13 5/8 In. 440.00
Stand, Mahogany, England, c.1800, 32 x 14 x 14 In. 375.00
Stand, Mahogany, Folding, Spider Legs, 3 Platforms, 20th Century, 33 1/2 In. 165.00
Stand, Mahogany, Henkel-Harris, 2 Drawers, Brass Bail Pulls, 28 1/2 In. 300.00
Stand, Mahogany, Inset Leather Top, Tripod Pedestal Base, 29 1/2 x 48 In. 230.00
Stand, Mahogany, Lemieux & Olivier, Drawer, Lower Shelf, Turned Legs, N.H. 90.00
Stand, Mahogany, Scalloped At Knees, Center Shell, Drawer, 27 1/2 In. 330.00
Stand, Maple, Mahogany Banded, 2 Drawers, Backsplash 4700.00
Stand, Maple, Tiger Maple, Drawer, Tapered Legs 385.00
Stand, Marble Pedestal, Round Top, Rope-Turned Post, 26 In. 110.00
Stand, McCobb, Planner Group, Maple, Drawer, Shelf, Winchendon, 23 x 22 x 15 In. . . . 175.00
Stand, Michigan Chair Co., Dark Oak, 4 Narrow Legs, 24 3/4 x 14 x 30 In. 345.00
Stand, Michigan Chair Co., Mahogany, Rectangular Top, 20 x 15 x 30 In. 1093.00
Stand, Music, Cabinet Top, 5 Shelves, 40 x 20 In. 1150.00
Stand, Music, Mahogany Finish, Floral, Lyre On Back, Adjustable, 1890, 55 In., Pair 645.00
Stand, Music, Mahogany, Pierced & Scrolled Fretwork, 35 x 22 x 13 In. 345.00
Stand, Music, Regency Style, Mahogany, Tripod Base, 45 In. 1175.00
Stand, Norman Bel Geddes, Green Metal, Shelf, 16 x 16 x 27 1/2 In., Pair 70.00
Stand, Oak, Recessed Panel Door, Spool-Turned Legs, 27 1/2 x 16 x 15 In. 225.00
Stand, Onondaga Shops, No. 512, Mahogany, 28 x 24 In. 1500.00
Stand, Onyx, Brass, Square, Pierced Frame, Pierced Shelf, Applied Feet, 31 x 13 1/2 In. . 145.00
Stand, Oriental Style, Rosewood, Carved, Marble Top, Curved Legs, Skirt, 30 x 11 In. . . . 345.00
Stand, Oriental, Rosewood, Marble Top, Carved, Claw & Ball Feet, 18 x 16 In. 320.00
Stand, Oriental, Rosewood, Marble Top, Rose Insert, Claw & Ball Feet, 33 x 23 In. 690.00
Stand, Oriental, Rosewood, Pierced Heart Carving, Shelf, 30 x 12 In. 345.00
Stand, Oriental, Teak, Leaf Carved Apron, Polished Stone Inset, 23 x 18 In. 330.00
Stand, Oriental, Teak, Open Carved Leaf Apron, Polished Stone Inset, 19 x 10 In. 220.00
Stand, Overhanging Top, Reeded Balusters, Drawer, Added Shelf, 1850 . . . . 150.00
Stand, Painted, Beaded Apron, Drawer, Straight Tapered Legs, 28 1/2 x 22 x 22 1/2 In. . . 110.00
Stand, Painted, Octagonal Pedestal, Flat Base, 8 Braces, Red, Green, 31 1/2 x 19 1/2 In. . . 190.00
Stand, Pine, 3 Tiers, Brackets, Semicircular, Feet, Casters, 42 x 22 x 27 In. 250.00
Stand, Pine, Drawer, Rectangular Tray, 4 Tapered Legs, 26 1/2 x 17 1/2 In. 750.00
Stand, Pine, Drawer, Wood Pull, Ring-Turned Legs, Tapered Feet, 28 3/4 x 22 In. 495.00
Stand, Pine, Drawer, Wood Pulls, Turned Legs, 21 1/2 x 16 x 29 In. 440.00
Stand, Pine, Green Paint, 4 Tapered Legs, 19th Century, 30 3/4 x 8 1/2 In. 230.00
Stand, Pine, Stepped, 3 Shelves, Scalloped Trim, 28 x 40 1/2 In. 250.00
Stand, Pine, Yellow Paint, Drawer, Square Tapered Legs, 27 1/2 x 16 1/2 In. 1955.00
Stand, Plant, 3 Stepped Tiers, Bentwood Crest, Gray Paint, Late 19th Century, 65 In. 1725.00
Stand, Plant, 4 Tiers, Crisscross Back Support, 41 x 42 In. 450.00
Stand, Plant, Art Deco, Iron, 18 1/2 x 18 1/2 x 20 In. 260.00
Stand, Plant, Art Deco, Iron, Scroll, Glass Insert Top, 18 1/2 x 18 1/2 x 20 In. 259.00
Stand, Plant, Arts & Crafts, 2 Tiers, Pyramid Posts, 28 x 12 In. 145.00
Stand, Plant, Black Forest, Standing Bear, Glass Eyes, 36 In. 2070.00
Stand, Plant, Brass, Cast Base With Round Onyx Inset, 29 x 14 In. 1430.00
Stand, Plant, Corner, Hanging, Pine, Brown, 5 Bowed Shelves, 51 x 47 In. 220.00
Stand, Plant, Double, Black Forest, Bear, Glass Eyes, 51 In. 2800.00
Stand, Plant, Empire, Square Verdigris Marble Top, Square Base, France, 31 In. 980.00
Stand, Plant, G. Stickley, Mahogany, Grueby Tile Top, 24 In. 6000.00
Stand, Plant, G. Stickley, Mahogany, Original Finish, 22 x 17 In. 3500.00
Stand, Plant, G. Stickley, Rail, Arched Apron, Arched Stretchers, 30 x 12 x 13 In. 2300.00
Stand, Plant, L. & J.G. Stickley, Oak, Signed, 24 x 12 In. 1610.00
Stand, Plant, Limbert, No. 239, Mahogany, Octagonal Top, 18 x 28 In. 1495.00
Stand, Plant, Limbert, No. 251, Mahogany, Flared Slab Sides, 17 x 24 In. 1840.00

Stand, Plant, Mahogany, 2 Drawers, Center Shelf, Tripod Base, Snake Feet, 33 In. 190.00
Stand, Plant, Mahogany, Drawer, Center Shelf, Tripod Base, Snake Feet, 31 1/2 In. 100.00
Stand, Plant, Napoleon III, Marquetry, Rectangular Center, 35 x 33 x 16 In. 2875.00
Stand, Plant, Pink Marble Top, Carved, Oriental, 22 x 32 In. 660.00
Stand, Plant, Poplar, Weathered, 3 Tiers, Square Nails, 36 x 23 x 21 1/2 In. 165.00
Stand, Plant, Thonet, Bentwood, Round Top, Urn & Flower Design, Impressed, 30 In. ... 200.00
Stand, Plant, Tripod Stick Construction, 3 Platforms, Green Point, 55 x 24 In. 310.00
Stand, Plant, Twig, Bentwood Crown, Square Base, 24 In. 80.00
Stand, Plant, Wire, 2 Tiers, Lattice Pattern, Splayed Legs, Oval, 1950s, 26 x 21 x 44 In. ... 400.00
Stand, Red, Black Grain Painted, Gold Floral Stencils, Drawer, Turned Legs 440.00
Stand, Regency, Mahogany, 5 Graduated Shelves, Turned Feet, 1900s, 54 x 15 In. 1610.00
Stand, Rosewood Veneer, Hinged Turtle Top, Plaque, Mother-Of-Pearl, 15 x 12 x 33 In. ... 385.00
Stand, Rosewood, Marble Cloverleaf Top, Pink Marble Insert, 32 x 4 In. 290.00
Stand, Rosewood, Marquetry, Kidney Shape, Brass, 20 x 26 x 16 In. 225.00
Stand, Rosewood, Pink Marble Top, Openwork Carving, Stretcher Base, Chinese 130.00
Stand, Shaving, Beveled Mirror, Adjustable, Inlaid Top, Door, 19th Century, 59 In. 480.00
Stand, Shaving, Eastlake, Walnut, Pedestal Base, Drawer, 38 x 18 In. 200.00
Stand, Shaving, Georgian, Mahogany, Early 19th Century, 26 1/2 x 23 1/4 x 9 In. 400.00
Stand, Shaving, Inlaid, Swing Mirror, Drawer 250.00
Stand, Shaving, Mahogany, 3 Short Drawers, Platform Base, Bun Feet, c.1825, 23 In. ... 395.00
Stand, Shaving, Mahogany, Cabinet, 4 Drawers, Ball Feet, 28 In. 840.00
Stand, Shaving, Mahogany, Framed Mirror, 3 Drawers, Platform Base, c.1820, 24 In. ... 365.00
Stand, Shaving, Mahogany, Oval Frame, 3 Drawers, Platform Base, Bun Feet, 23 In. 390.00
Stand, Shaving, Rectangular Frame, England, c.1860, 14 1/2 In. 195.00
Stand, Sheraton, Birch, Drawer, 2-Board Top, Biscuit Corner, Turned Legs, 18 x 29 In. .. 410.00
Stand, Sheraton, Cherry, 2 Drawers, Biscuit Corners, 1-Board Top, Beaded, 18 x 18 In. .. 715.00
Stand, Sheraton, Cherry, 3 Drawers, 2-Board Top, Turned Legs, 20 x 19 1/2 x 26 3/4 In. .. 80.00
Stand, Sheraton, Cherry, Drawer, Beaded Top, Spiral-Turned Legs, 18 1/2 x 28 In. 2420.00
Stand, Sheraton, Cherry, Pine, Drawer, Turned Legs, Beaded Edge, Glass Pull, 18 x 30 In. 880.00
Stand, Sheraton, Cherry, Tiger Maple, 2 Drawers, New Pulls, Turned Legs, 18 3/4 In. ... 770.00
Stand, Sheraton, Curly Maple, 2 Drawers, Brass Pulls, Turned Legs, 20 1/4 x 17 In. 770.00
Stand, Sheraton, Curly Maple, Drawer, 1-Board Scrubbed Top, 22 x 17 In. 1540.00
Stand, Sheraton, Drawer, Brass Pull, 29 1/2 x 17 x 17 In. 505.00
Stand, Sheraton, Mahogany, 2 Drawers, 29 x 22 3/4 x 17 In. 250.00
Stand, Sheraton, Mahogany, 2 Drawers, Molded Top, Carved Legs, 29 1/2 x 19 1/2 In. ... 490.00
Stand, Sheraton, Mahogany, 3 Drawers, Drop Leaf, Rope-Twist Legs, 29 x 18 x 9 In. 2130.00
Stand, Sheraton, Mahogany, Bird's-Eye Maple, 2 Drawers, Drop Leaf, 28 x 17 In. 1000.00
Stand, Sheraton, Mahogany, Cherry Veneer, 2 Drawers, Reeded Columns, 29 In. 275.00
Stand, Sheraton, Mahogany, Reeded, Casters, 2 Drawers, 1-Board Top, 23 x 30 In. 1100.00
Stand, Sheraton, Maple, Turned Legs, Drawer, 2-Board Top, 22 x 19 1/2 x 27 3/4 In. 300.00
Stand, Sheraton, Poplar, Cherry Finish, Brass Pull, Turned Feet, 15 x 16 x 26 In. 715.00
Stand, Sheraton, Tiger Maple, Drawer, c.1820, 29 1/2 x 20 1/2 x 16 1/2 In. 1035.00
Stand, Sheraton, Walnut, Drawer, Arrow Feet, 1860, 19 x 22 x 29 In. 360.00
Stand, Sheraton, Walnut, Turned Legs, Drawer, 27 x 17 1/2 x 19 1/2 In. 345.00
Stand, Smoking, Black Boy Between Vases, Shell Ashtray, 6 3/4 In. 140.00
Stand, Smoking, Black Forest, Figural Mounts, Gnomes, Tree-Trunk Base, 40 In. 2520.00
Stand, Smoking, Black Forest, Goat Crest, Leaf Carving, c.1880, 68 x 16 x 34 In. 2800.00
Stand, Smoking, Black Man Holds Cigars, Ashtray, 1880s, 6 3/4 In. 370.00
Stand, Smoking, Black Minstrel Plays Accordion, Strike On Side, 1890s, 5 In. 235.00
Stand, Smoking, Black Prancing Cakewalker, 1880s, 8 1/2 In. 445.00
Stand, Smoking, Black Woman Holds Matches, Cigars, Ashtray, 1880s, 6 1/4 In. 520.00
Stand, Smoking, Bronze, Figural Owls, Match Striker, Austria, c.1890, 5 x 6 In. 315.00
Stand, Smoking, Glass Shelves, Pullout Drawer, 1938, 24 1/2 In. 2530.00
Stand, Smoking, Lakeside Crafts Shops, Canted Legs, Paper Label, 28 x 11 In. 375.00
Stand, Smoking, Slate Top, Tobacco Container, Match & Pipe Holder, 20 1/2 In. 165.00
Stand, Softwood, Green Paint, Panel Sides, Box, Lift Top, Turned Shaft, 22 1/2 In. 70.00
Stand, Softwood, Square Top, Blue Green Paint, 28 1/2 In. 300.00
Stand, Stationery, Florentine, Gilt Tool, Leather, 3 Compartments, 6 1/2 x 11 x 4 1/2 In. ... 405.00
Stand, Stickley Bros., No. 081, Mahogany, Round, 4 Legs, 29 x 18 In. 600.00
Stand, Teak, Dragon Heads, Soapstone Insert, Chinese Label, 18 1/4 x 20 In. 275.00
Stand, Telephone, G. Stickley, No. 605, Mahogany, Square Top, 18 x 32 In. 750.00
Stand, Telephone, G. Stickley, No. 605, Original Finish, Square Top, 29 In. 1265.00
Stand, Telephone, Wrought Iron, Marble Top, Chair, 45 x 11 x 21 In. 560.00

Stand, Tiger Maple, 3 Drawers, Square Top, Turned Legs, 30 x 22 In. 1150.00
Stand, Tiger Maple, Turned Tapered Columns Over Frieze Drawer, 36 x 24 In. 4600.00
Stand, Tiger Maple, Walnut, Drawer, Drop Leaf, Turned Legs, 30 x 18 x 26 In. 470.00
Stand, Twig, Split-Log Apron, Log Base, 29 3/4 In. 220.00
Stand, Walnut Crotch Veneer, Beaded Tray Top, 2 Drawers, Turned Legs, 16 In. 715.00
Stand, Walnut, 2 Drawers In Apron, Candle Slides, Marble Top, Metal Gallery, 28 In. . . . 330.00
Stand, Walnut, 2 Drawers, Tenn., Early 19th Century, 30 x 18 3/4 x 20 3/4 In. 2640.00
Stand, Walnut, 4 Turned Column Supports, Bracket Base, Italy, 22 x 22 x 28 In. 2590.00
Stand, Walnut, Carved, Burl & Rosette Trim, 30 x 24 x 17 In. 195.00
Stand, Walnut, Gray Marble Top, 3 Drawers, 27 x 17 x 13 1/2 In. 575.00
Stand, Walnut, Marble Top, Carved, Urn-Turned Shaft, Victorian, 30 x 32 x 24 In. 1035.00
Stand, Walnut, Marble Top, Curved Gallery, Center Shelf, 31 1/2 In. 1610.00
Stand, Walnut, Marble Top, Drawer, Fruit-Carved Handle, Curved Legs, Victorian, 28 In. 195.00
Stand, Walnut, Marble Turtle Top, Skirted, Victorian, 29 1/2 x 33 1/2 x 24 1/2 In. 575.00
Stand, Walnut, Reddish Brown & Black, c.1840, 27 x 20 In. 1225.00
Stand, Walnut, Round, Pedestal Base, 4 Shaped Legs, Victorian, 21 x 13 In. 45.00
Stand, Windsor, Round Top, Ringed Support, 3 Turned & Swelled Legs, 25 In. 2820.00
Stand, Wood, Inset Rouge Marble Top, Carved, Floral Open Work, Chinese, 19 In. 85.00
Stand, Writing, George III, Mahogany Inlay, Late 18th Century, 46 1/2 In. 375.00
Stand, Yellow Pine, Drawer, Tapered Legs, Early 19th Century, 24 x 17 1/2 x 26 In. 290.00
Stool, Baroque, Walnut Trestle, Rectangular Seat, Scroll Feet, 19 1/2 In., Pair 1265.00
Stool, Baroque, Walnut, Round, X-Stretcher, Upholstered Top, 18 x 21 In., Pair 2530.00
Stool, Baroque, Walnut, Turned, Pierced, Spindle Colonnade, Stuffover Seat 405.00
Stool, Biedermeier, Walnut, Square, c.1825 . . . . 635.00
Stool, Bird's-Eye Maple, Thick Rectangular Seat, 3 Simple Chamfered Legs, 24 1/2 In. . . 70.00
Stool, Drafting, Adjustable Arm, Chrome Swivel Base, Upholstered, W. Germany, 36 In. . 240.00
Stool, Frank Gehry, Corrugated Cardboard, 1972, 15 1/4 x 17 In. 2530.00
Stool, Fruitwood, Carved, Needlework, Cabriole Legs, Scroll Toes, 16 x 17 1/2 x 16 In. . . 1060.00
Stool, G. Nelson, Vanity, Tubular Aluminum, Upholstered, 1950s, 20 3/4 In. 2350.00
Stool, G. Stickley, Tapered Legs, Branded Signature, 21 x 16 x 17 In. 2500.00
Stool, George II Style, Walnut, Needlepoint Seat, Hairy Paw Feet, 20th Century 460.00
Stool, George III Style, Walnut, Serpentine Seat, Upholstered, 20th Century 920.00
Stool, Gout, Victorian, Oak, Adjustable, Padded Top, Raised End, 14 x 21 x 17 In. 575.00
Stool, Green Paint, Round Tapered Legs, Stretcher Base, 33 x 21 1/2 In. 495.00
Stool, Henry II Style, Mahogany, Padded Top, Square Legs, 19 x 23 x 18 1/2 In. 1150.00
Stool, I. Noguchi, Walnut, Chrome Plated, Rocking, Knoll, 14 x 16 3/4 In. 5750.00
Stool, Indian Style, Gilt Metal, Embossed, 16 1/4 x 12 1/2 In., Pair 3300.00
Stool, Italian Rococo Style, Walnut, Carved, Grotto 920.00
Stool, Jacobean Style, Oak, Heart Cutout, 19th Century, 23 In. 550.00
Stool, Jacobean Style, Oak, Thumb-Molded Seat, Stretchers, 18 x 17 In. 635.00
Stool, Jacobean Style, Oak, Upholstered, Rope-Turned Leg, c.1900, 16 x 21 x 21 In. 250.00
Stool, Limbert, No. 61, Mahogany, Solid Seat, Original Finish, 12 x 15 x 24 In. 490.00
Stool, Louis Philippe, Mahogany, Upholstered, Square Tapered Legs, Casters, 13 In. 1840.00
Stool, Mahogany, Box-Form Cushion, Curule Base, 1830s, 17 1/2 x 16 In. 460.00
Stool, Mahogany, Padded Top Over Frieze, 1870s, 16 1/2 x 22 In. 920.00
Stool, Mahogany, Padded Top, Curule Base, 1880s, 17 1/2 x 20 In. 400.00
Stool, Mahogany, Padded, Tufted, Leather Top, Beehive Feet, 13 x 49 x 24 In. 1265.00
Stool, Mahogany, Serpentine Edges, Upholstered Top, Cabriole Legs, 15 x 20 In. 59.00
Stool, Mahogany, Slip Seat, Curule Base, c.1830, 19 In. 630.00
Stool, Mahogany, Slip Seat, Molded Rim, Shaped Apron, Cabriole Legs, 17 1/2 x 18 In. . . 1456.00
Stool, Mahogany, Stepped Base, Bun Feet, Sloping Leather-Covered Frame, 8 x 13 In. . . . 115.00
Stool, Mahogany, Upholstered Top, Carved Skirt, Cabriole Legs, Claw & Ball Feet, 20 In. 270.00
Stool, Napoleon III, Ebonized, Bronze, Aubusson Top, Round Legs, 23 In. 1265.00
Stool, Napoleon III, Giltwood, Roses, Rope-Twist Base, 15 In. 5060.00
Stool, Napoleon III, Giltwood, Upholstered, Mid 19th Century, 19 x 24 x 24 In. 3450.00
Stool, Oak, Leaf-Carved Frieze, England, 19th Century, 10 1/2 x 19 x 12 1/2 In. 316.00
Stool, Oak, Padded Leather Upholstered Top, Tapered Legs, England, 17 x 16 In. 460.00
Stool, Oak, Plank Top, Shaped Skirt, Box Stretcher, 21 x 11 1/4 In. 630.00
Stool, Oak, Stretcher Base, 1-Board Top, 19 x 19 1/2 In. 140.00
Stool, Organ, Upholstered Seat, Mahogany Pedestal Base, 21 x 14 x 14 In. 195.00
Stool, Oval Seat, Painted, Tapered Legs, 17 1/4 In. 195.00
Stool, P. Evans, Steel, Leather Cushion, Sculpted Geometric Forms, 18 1/2 x 18 In. 330.00
Stool, Padded Oval Seat, Leaf-Carved Apron, Cabriole Legs, 1870s, 8 1/2 x 14 In. 345.00

Stool, Padded Top, Scrolled Toes, 1890s, 8 x 9 In. 345.00
Stool, Painted, Cutout Plank Ends, Tole Decoration, 6 1/2 x 11 x 7 In. 55.00
Stool, Painted, Geometric Strapwork, Russia, 8 7/8 x 13 1/2 In. 115.00
Stool, Pencil-Post Legs, Mortised Through Top, 24 3/4 x 13 3/4 In. 410.00
Stool, Piano, Federal, Mahogany, c.1820, 20 x 13 In. 690.00
Stool, Piano, Federal, Mahogany, Upholstered, Wood Thread, Ball Feet, 22 x 13 1/2 In. . . 59.00
Stool, Piano, Federal, Mahogany, Wood Post, Reeded, Scrolled Legs, c.1815, 19 x 13 In. . 529.00
Stool, Piano, Mahogany, Dolphin Supporting Seat Back, Swivels, Paw Feet, 1820s 2300.00
Stool, Piano, Oak, Round, Upholstered, 4 Legs, Adjustable, W.D. Allison Co., 19 In. 85.00
Stool, Piano, Rosewood, Carved, Swivel Top, England, c.1880, 20 x 12 1/2 In. 110.00
Stool, Piano, Victorian, Scrimshaw Whale Vertebrae Seat, Wheels, Nova Scotia 500.00
Stool, Piano, Walnut, Cherry, Cloth Upholstered, Adjustable, 27 In. 275.00
Stool, Pine, Oval Top With Cutout Handhold, 21 x 15 In. 165.00
Stool, Queen Anne Style, Walnut, Pad Top, Cabriole Legs, c.1900, 19 1/2 x 24 x 18 In. . . 980.00
Stool, Rectangular, Female Figural Supports, Cherubs, 1870s, 19 x 19 In. 2530.00
Stool, Red Graining Over Base Coat, Round Seat, 6 1/2 x 13 3/4 In. 825.00
Stool, Red Paint, Tapered Legs, Vase & Ring Turnings, Oval Top, 15 1/2 x 20 In. 300.00
Stool, Regency Style, Mahogany, Padded Seat, Late 19th Century, 18 1/2 x 21 x 15 In. . . . 635.00
Stool, Regency, Bamboo Circular Legs, Leaf Reserves, Late 19th Century, 18 In. 690.00
Stool, Regency, Faux Rosewood, Padded, Tufted, Stretcher, 19 1/2 x 22 x 17 In. 865.00
Stool, Regency, Mahogany, Concave Seat, Upholstered, 13 1/2 x 20 1/2 x 12 In. 1725.00
Stool, Regency, Mahogany, Upholstered, Leather, Early 1800s, 15 x 51 1/2 x 23 1/2 In. . . 1840.00
Stool, Rosewood Veneers, Revolving, Adjustable, 22 x 18 In. 110.00
Stool, Rosewood, Upholstered, Serpentine Frame, Cabriole Legs, French Toes, 15 x 22 In. 316.00
Stool, Stickley, No. 398, Leather Sling Seat, Wide Arched Stretcher, 19 x 15 x 16 In. 1500.00
Stool, Stickley, Solid Top, Tapered Legs, Branded, Paper Label, 21 x 16 x 17 In. 2400.00
Stool, Tiger Maple, Square-Nail Construction, 18th Century, 7 1/2 x 14 In. 420.00
Stool, V. Kagan, Aluminum, Vinyl Upholstered, 1955, 13 3/4 In. 9200.00
Stool, Vanity, Mahogany, Oval Slip Seat, Dutch, 19th Century, 23 x 25 In. 375.00
Stool, Vanity, William & Mary Style, Walnut, Needlework Upholstered, 17 x 25 In. 1090.00
Stool, Wallace Nutting, No. 102, Windsor, Script Brand 220.00
Stool, Walnut Base, Yew Top, Pegged Construction, Oval Top, 18 x 15 In. 220.00
Stool, Walnut, Flame-Stitched Upholstered Seat, Early 18th Century 375.00
Stool, Walnut, Needlepoint Seat, Shell-Carved Knees, Claw & Ball Feet 220.00
Stool, Walnut, Needlework Cushion, Cabriole Legs, 19 In. 1090.00
Stool, Walnut, Padded Needlework Top, Curule Base, 1820s, 15 x 16 1/2 In. 1150.00
Stool, Walnut, Padded Seat, Cabriole Legs, 19 x 26 In. 280.00
Stool, Walnut, Upholstered Slip Seat, Molded Frame, Pad Feet, 17 x 22 1/2 In. 225.00
Stool, William & Mary Style, Walnut, Drop-In Seat 460.00
Stool, William & Mary, Mahogany, Trumpet Turnings, Serpentine X-Stretcher 70.00
Stool, William IV, Mahogany, Tufted Leather Upholstered Top, Reeded Legs, 19 In. 1380.00
Stool, Windsor, Black Paint, Tripod, Early 19th Century 150.00
Swing, Old Hickory, Mahogany, A-Frame, 9 Vertical Poles, Signed, 67 x 93 In. 1840.00
Swing, Porch, Arms, Child's, 16 x 30 In. 230.00
Swing, Porch, Wicker, White Paint, Flat Arms, Bar Harbor 672.00
Table, 4 Legs Connected To Center Pedestal, 6 Leaves, Pads, 48 In. 1440.00
Table, Adam Style, Mahogany, Demilune, X-Stretcher, 32 1/2 x 46 x 22 In. 980.00
Table, Adam Style, Mahogany, Serpentine Top, Fluted Legs, 34 1/2 x 51 1/2 x 26 In. 920.00
Table, Adam Style, Mahogany, Serpentine Top, Top-Shaped Feet, 34 x 51 x 26 In. 690.00
Table, Aesthetic Revival, Burl Elm, Ebonized, Concave Sides, 39 1/2 x 48 x 16 In. 1495.00
Table, Aesthetic Revival, Mahogany, Rectangular, Spindle Sides, 26 x 31 x 22 In. 2300.00
Table, Altar, Archaic Dragon Spandrels, 18th Century, 32 x 41 1/2 In. 2070.00
Table, Altar, Archaic Dragons On Spandrels & Side Panels, 35 x 100 In. 490.00
Table, Altar, Chicken-Wing Wood, Beaded Borders, 34 1/4 x 58 1/2 x 16 In. . . . . *Illus* 1955.00
Table, Altar, Elm, Mortised Construction, Chinese, Mid 19th Century, 32 x 77 In. 470.00
Table, Altar, Pierced Carvings, Molded Edges, Oriental, 93 x 17 x 36 1/2 In. 220.00
Table, Altar, Plank Top, Scroll & Leaf Supports, Trestle Legs, Chinese, 37 x 82 In. 5405.00
Table, Altar, Softwood, Red Lacquer, Peaches & Peonies Design, 38 In. 1380.00
Table, Amboyna, Lift Top, Leather-Lined Drawer, Pullout Surface, 1820s, 29 1/4 In. 7200.00
Table, Architect's, Mahogany, Leather Surface, Easel, Adjustable Surface, 30 In. 165.00
Table, Art Deco, Ebony, Mirror Top, Metal Rails, Shelf, c.1930, 26 x 25 In. 920.00
Table, Art Deco, Giltwood, Glass Top, Pedestal, c.1930, 29 3/4 x 32 1/4 x 22 In., Pair . . . 750.00
Table, Art Deco, Slate, Wrought Iron, 1930, 17 1/2 In. 7200.00

Furniture, Table, Altar, Chicken-Wing Wood,
Beaded Borders, 34 1/4 x 58 1/2 x 16 In.

Furniture, Table,
Biedermeier, Birch,
Inset Needlework
Panel, Turned Legs,
30 x 22 In.

Table, Art Deco, Wrought Iron, Mirror Top, Scrolled Frame & Legs, 1930s, 23 x 17 In. ... 375.00
Table, Art Deco, Zebrawood, Round Top, Smaller Base, 25 x 25 In. 1610.00
Table, Art Nouveau, Marquetry, Stylized Stem Legs, Shelf, 29 x 17 x 24 In., Pair 1265.00
Table, Art Nouveau, Marquetry, Tree, Rabbit Scene, 30 x 20 In. ....575.00 to 800.00
Table, Arts & Crafts, 16 Green Tiles, Square Top, 4 Legs, Rectangular, 36 x 28 In. 1100.00
Table, Arts & Crafts, Mahogany, Circular Top, 26 x 30 In. 290.00
Table, Arts & Crafts, Mahogany, Large Rectangular Top, Signed, 76 x 31 In. 8625.00
Table, Arts & Crafts, Oak Top, Original Finish, 30 x 29 In. 490.00
Table, Arts & Crafts, Oak, Pedestal, Early 20th Century, 34 1/2 x 21 1/2 In. 920.00
Table, Arts & Crafts, Oak, Shelf Stretcher, Strap Corbels, Square Legs, 30 x 36 In. 400.00
Table, Arts & Crafts, Pottery Tiles Set In Wrought-Iron Frame, Floral, 18 In. 325.00
Table, Arts & Crafts, Round Top, Carved Oak Trees, England, 28 3/4 x 24 In. 460.00
Table, Arts & Crafts, Walnut, Folding, Octagonal, Shelf, England, 43 x 21 x 31 In. 400.00
Table, Baker's, Possum-Belly Curved Drawer, 2 Breadboards, c.1860, 29 x 48 In. 695.00
Table, Bamboo, Inset Turquoise Tile Top, Anglo-Indian, 31 x 14 x 14 In. 490.00
Table, Bamboo, Rabbit Decoupage Designs, Lower Shelf, c.1870, 28 x 21 x 14 1/2 In. 750.00
Table, Bamboo, Rattan, Shelf, Octagonal Top, 28 1/2 x 22 x 22 In. 170.00
Table, Banquet Ends, George III, Mahogany, Inlaid, D-Shape, c.1850, 28 x 41 x 19 In. ... 2350.00
Table, Baroque, Fruitwood, Inset Top, Frieze Drawer, 30 x 18 x 23 In. 750.00
Table, Baroque, Oak, Rectangular Overhanging Top, 31 1/8 x 61 x 29 1/2 In. 6600.00
Table, Beech, Octagon Top, X-Form Base, 19th Century, 26 x 25 In. 490.00
Table, Bench, Pine, Mortised Seat, 27 3/4 x 47 x 35 In. 385.00
Table, Bentwood, Circular Top, Four Molded Legs, Austria, 30 x 36 In. 550.00
Table, Biedermeier, Birch, Inset Needlework Panel, Turned Legs, 30 x 22 In. ......*Illus* 2760.00
Table, Biedermeier, Birch, Top Opens, Faux Drawer, Saber Legs, 31 x 22 x 17 In. 5025.00
Table, Biedermeier, Fruitwood, Top Opens, Lift-Out Tray, Sections, 32 x 21 x 18 In. 1985.00
Table, Biedermeier, Walnut, Part Ebonized, c.1825, 29 3/4 x 18 1/2 In. 1150.00
Table, Birch, Marquetry, 19th Century, 28 3/4 x 35 3/4 x 17 In., Pair 5175.00
Table, Black Lacquered Wood, Chrome Curved Legs, 1929, 18 In. 2350.00
Table, Blackamoor, Breeches, Walking, Holding Tray, Late 19th Century, 59 1/2 In. 5750.00
Table, Blue Paint, D-Shape, Overhanging Top, 3 Square Tapered Legs, 27 x 40 In. 2185.00
Table, Brass, Pottery, Tile With Leaves, Pottery Pedestal, c.1875, 34 In. 8050.00
Table, Brooks, Mahogany, Cutout Sides, 45 x 29 In. 1495.00
Table, Brooks, Mahogany, Rectangular Cutouts, Octagonal Top, 36 x 30 In. 4315.00
Table, Brooks, Mahogany, Splayed Slab Cutout Sides, 17 x 24 In. 1300.00
Table, Brown Paint, Mid 19th Century, 32 1/2 x 54 1/4 x 12 3/4 In. 470.00
Table, Card, Cherry, Flame Veneer, Fluted Bands Over Feet, Rounded Corners, 29 3/4 In. .. 2860.00
Table, Card, Chippendale, Mahogany, Molded Edge, Hinged Leaf, 28 x 31 1/2 x 30 In. .. 2350.00
Table, Card, Edwardian, Mahogany, Inlaid, D-Shape, Early 1900s, 29 x 32 x 16 In....... 390.00
Table, Card, Empire, Mahogany, Pedestal Base, Ball Feet, 29 1/2 x 34 x 16 1/2 In. 505.00
Table, Card, Empire, Mahogany, Shaped Top, Drop Apron, Lyre Base, Scroll Feet, 1840 .. 169.00
Table, Card, Federal, Birch, Pine, Rectangular Overhanging Top, Red Paint, 28 In. 1495.00
Table, Card, Federal, Mahogany Veneer, Concave Center, 3 String Panels, 28 In. 5750.00
Table, Card, Federal, Mahogany Veneer, Elliptical Top, 1800, 29 In. 6900.00
Table, Card, Federal, Mahogany Veneer, New England, 1800, 29 x 38 x 19 In. 860.00
Table, Card, Federal, Mahogany Veneer, Reeded Edge, Legs, 29 1/2 x 17 1/2 In. 2645.00
Table, Card, Federal, Mahogany, Bird's-Eye Maple Veneer, 31 x 37 1/2 x 17 15/8 In. 7475.00

Table, Card, Federal, Mahogany, Carved, Trick Leg, Oval Top, c.1810, 29 x 37 x 19 In. . . 5640.00
Table, Card, Federal, Mahogany, Inlaid Leaf & Line, c.1810, 29 1/4 x 36 x 17 3/4 In. 3055.00
Table, Card, Federal, Mahogany, Inlaid Lines, Eagle, Urns, Square Legs, 30 x 36 In. 700.00
Table, Card, Federal, Mahogany, Inlaid, Bowed Front, c.1800, 28 x 35 1/2 x 16 3/4 In. 1610.00
Table, Card, Federal, Mahogany, Inlaid, Rounded Corners, 3-Panel Skirt, 29 3/4 In. 4900.00
Table, Card, Federal, Mahogany, Inlaid, Rounded Corners, Rectangular Top, 1810, 29 In. . 2100.00
Table, Card, Federal, Mahogany, Inlaid, Rounded Corners, Square Tapered Legs, 29 In. . . 6900.00
Table, Card, Federal, Mahogany, Inlaid, Serpentine Top, Rounded Corners, 29 x 36 In. . . . 1095.00
Table, Card, Federal, Mahogany, Raised On Square Tapered Legs, Spade Feet, 35 In. 345.00
Table, Card, Federal, Mahogany, Rectangular Hinged Top, Splayed Legs, 29 x 17 In. 1150.00
Table, Card, Federal, Red Paint, Overhanging Top, Square Tapered Legs, 30 x 41 In. 1610.00
Table, Card, George III, Mahogany, D-Shape, Leather Surface, 30 x 36 x 18 In. 2300.00
Table, Card, Georgian, Leather Inlaid Top, Cabriole Legs, 29 x 29 x 29 In. 575.00
Table, Card, Georgian, Mahogany, 27 1/2 x 13 In. . . . . *Illus* 1495.00
Table, Card, Georgian, Mahogany, Satinwood String Inlay, 30 x 20 In. 805.00
Table, Card, Hepplewhite Style, Mahogany, Satinwood, Floral Inlay, Serpentine, 30 In. . . . 785.00
Table, Card, Hepplewhite, Mahogany Veneer, Medallion Inlays, 34 x 17 x 30 In. 3300.00
Table, Card, Hepplewhite, Mahogany, Console, Line Inlay, 28 1/2 x 36 x 17 3/4 In. 2530.00
Table, Card, Hepplewhite, Mahogany, Drawer, Banded Inlay, 29 x 36 x 18 In. 2415.00
Table, Card, Hepplewhite, Mahogany, Inlay, Peg Feet, 36 x 17 1/2 x 29 In. 3025.00
Table, Card, Hepplewhite, Mahogany, Line Border Inlay, D-Shape, 36 x 18 x 30 In. 770.00
Table, Card, Mahogany Veneer, Rosewood Outline, Carved Paw Feet, 1830, 30 In. 1495.00
Table, Card, Mahogany, Burl Veneer Front, Swing Leg, Drawer, 29 x 35 In. 785.00
Table, Card, Mahogany, Burl, Beaded, Reeded Legs, Brass Hairy Paw Casters, 29 In. 2520.00
Table, Card, Mahogany, Console, Carved Leaves, Turned Legs, Brass Inlay, 1820s, 37 In. . 4400.00
Table, Card, Mahogany, Federal, Inlaid, Elliptical Front, Rounded Ends, 29 3/4 x 35 In. . . 2645.00
Table, Card, Mahogany, Felt Surface, Molded Cartouches, c.1830, 29 x 36 In. 950.00
Table, Card, Mahogany, Hepplewhite, Inlay On Lower Apron, Veneered Panels, 29 In. 1100.00
Table, Card, Mahogany, Overhanging Top, Tapered Legs, c.1810, 28 x 33 1/2 In. 2850.00
Table, Card, Mahogany, Pedestal Base, Scrolled Feet, 28 x 34 x 17 In. 225.00
Table, Card, Mahogany, Satinwood, Inlaid, Bowfront, Reeded Legs, 10 In. 1460.00
Table, Card, Mahogany, Shaped Aprons, Line Inlay, Border, 1930s, 28 3/4 In. 550.00
Table, Card, Mahogany, Sliding Back Leg, Wells For Chips, 29 3/4 x 29 In. 430.00
Table, Card, Mahogany, Urn Medallion, Opens To Dining Table, 3 Leaves, 38 1/2 In. 1045.00
Table, Card, Sheraton, Mahogany, Console, Serpentine Front, c.1830, 30 1/4 x 36 In. 1610.00
Table, Card, Sheraton, Mahogany, Diamond Inlay Border, Reeded Legs, 28 In. 1200.00
Table, Card, Sheraton, Mahogany, Serpentine Front, Reeded Leg, 28 In. 1960.00
Table, Card, Sheraton, Mahogany, Serpentine, Hinged, New England, 1810, 37 x 17 In. . . 1650.00
Table, Card, Walnut, Top Unfolds To Green Felt, Card Tray, Label, 29 3/4 x 35 In. 1610.00
Table, Cast Iron, Wood Top, Dolphin Base, 27 1/2 x 24 x 24 In. 320.00
Table, Center, Empire, Mahogany, Marble Top, Triangular Base, 28 x 36 In. 940.00
Table, Center, Galle, Rosewood, Inlaid, Shaped Top, Signed, 30 x 20 x 29 In. 3540.00
Table, Center, George II Style, Mahogany, Ireland, 31 3/4 x 50 x 26 1/4 In. 1265.00
Table, Center, Georgian Style, Mahogany, Oval, 29 1/2 x 49 1/2 x 30 3/4 In. 900.00
Table, Center, Louis XV Style, Walnut, Carved, Marble Top, c.1900, 29 x 32 x 20 In. 920.00
Table, Center, Louis XVI, Bronze, Rectangular Top, 8 Tapered Legs, 30 In. 20300.00
Table, Center, Mahogany, Molded Edge, Round, Pedestal, Cabriole Legs, 42 x 30 In. 195.00
Table, Center, Mahogany, Turtle Top, Fluted, Carved, Urn Pedestal, 56 x 42 In. 900.00
Table, Center, Marble, Circular Top, Flared Pedestal, Paneled Base, 35 In. 1150.00
Table, Center, Painted Chinoiserie, Tapered Turned Feet, c.1830, 27 x 34 In. 2760.00
Table, Center, Regency, Mahogany, Rosewood Banding, 28 x 54 In. 16675.00
Table, Center, Renaissance Revival, Fruitwood, Marble Top, 2 Seated Lions, 27 x 34 In. . . 530.00
Table, Center, Renaissance Revival, Lacquered, Inlaid, Victorian, 52 x 30 x 30 In. 4400.00
Table, Center, Rosewood, Ornately Carved, Turtle Marble Top, 48 x 33 In. 7150.00
Table, Center, Victorian, Burl Walnut, Round, Carving, Scroll Feet, 29 1/2 x 53 In. 3220.00
Table, Center, Victorian, Gilt, Marble Turtle Top, Carved Cherubs, Column, 31 x 46 In. . . 4130.00
Table, Center, Victorian, Scalloped Top & Skirt, Applied Carvings, 34 In. Diam. 3575.00
Table, Center, William IV, Mahogany, Circular Top, Reeded Bun Feet, 27 1/2 In. 1725.00
Table, Center, William IV, Mahogany, Oak, Acanthus Turned Stem, 29 1/2 In. 2200.00
Table, Center, William IV, Rosewood, Circular Top, Plinth, Paw Feet, 29 1/2 In. 3000.00
Table, Center, William IV, Rosewood, Tilted Circular Top, Bun Feet, 30 x 47 In. 2760.00
Table, Center, William IV, Walnut, Octagonal Top, Cabriole Legs, 28 3/4 In. 7765.00
Table, Chair, Butternut, Oval Tilt Top, Shoe Feet, Drawer Beneath, 28 x 53 x 39 In. 2875.00

Furniture, Table, Card, Georgian,
Mahogany, 27 1/2 x 13 In.

Furniture, Table, Console, George III, Japanned
Pine, 1740, 34 x 34 x 20 In.

Table, Charles II, Oak, 2-Board Top, Cleat Ends, Molded Frieze, Turned Legs, 30 x 25 In.   1955.00
Table, Charles X, Gilt Bronze, Round, Mid 19th Century, 30 In. 750.00
Table, Cherry, Barber Pole Inlay, Mortise & Tenon, Drawer, N.C., c.1930 ....   715.00
Table, Cherry, Inlaid Ivory Escutcheon, Drawer, Tapered Legs, 28 x 19 x 16 3/4 In. 6500.00
Table, Cherry, Rectangular Top, Molded Edge, Conn., 1750, 24 1/2 x 15 1/2 x 24 In. 19550.00
Table, Cherry, Red Stained, Cross-Stretcher Base, c.1810, 27 x 32 x 23 In. 690.00
Table, Cherry, Softwood, Drawer, Turned Legs, 29 x 35 1/2 x 20 In. 195.00
Table, Chippendale Style, Mahogany, Piecrust Top, Carved Turned Shaft 220.00
Table, Chippendale, Mahogany Finish, Carved Base, Cabriole Legs, 34 x 27 In. 1265.00
Table, Chippendale, Walnut, Notched Top, Carved Brush Feet, 29 1/2 x 28 x 17 In....... 5460.00
Table, Chrome, Glass, Cantilever, Travertine Marble Base, 1960s, 51 x 39 x 18 In. 575.00
Table, Cinnabar, Carved, Red Lacquer, Black Enamel, 19th Century, 28 x 17 x 13 In. 825.00
Table, Coffee, Art Deco, Blue Mirror Top, Rectangular Base 250.00
Table, Coffee, Brass, Chinese Landscape & Figures, Philip LaVerne, 17 1/2 x 47 In. 3105.00
Table, Coffee, Burl Walnut, Loop Top, Late 19th Century, 21 x 44 x 57 In. 575.00
Table, Coffee, Chinese, Lacquered, Black, Flowers, Cloisonne Insets, 16 x 50 x 19 In. ...   250.00
Table, Coffee, Chinese, Teak, 3 Drawers, Scrollwork, 64 x 13 x 13 In. 385.00
Table, Coffee, E. Wormley, Ash Frame, White Laminate Top, 88 x 15 In. 520.00
Table, Coffee, E. Wormley, Burled Wood Veneer, 54 x 27 x 13 1/2 In. 1725.00
Table, Coffee, E. Wormley, Mahogany, Travertine Top, Signed, 13 In. 1150.00
Table, Coffee, Eames, Oak Veneer, Round, Chrome, Herman Miller, 1966, 36 In. 220.00
Table, Coffee, Ebonized Wood, Black, 2 C-Section Forms, 1940s-1950s, 48 x 24 In. 920.00
Table, Coffee, Frank Lloyd Wright, Mahogany, Circular Slate Top, Cruciform Base 2990.00
Table, Coffee, Frankl, Johnson Furniture Co., 48 x 14 In. 1840.00
Table, Coffee, Free-Edge Top, Plank Support, Tapered Dowel Legs, 16 1/2 x 82 x 29 In. ..   865.00
Table, Coffee, G. Nakashima, Walnut, 2 Slab Supports, 60 x 23 x 16 In. 6900.00
Table, Coffee, G. Nelson, Green Linoleum Free-Form Top, 3 Steel Rod Legs, 16 x 46 In. . 7475.00
Table, Coffee, I. Noguchi, Black Laminated Birch Top, 1948, 15 3/4 In. 8225.00
Table, Coffee, Jumuwood, Relief, Mythical Figures, Drawer, 34 1/2 x 44 1/2 x 22 In. 1380.00
Table, Coffee, Laminate, Rubber, Steel Rod Legs, Herman Miller, 1962, 15 x 59 In. 400.00
Table, Coffee, Lotus, Rectangular Top, Widdicomb, 15 3/4 x 48 x 22 In. 315.00
Table, Coffee, Lucite, Round, c.1970, 25 1/2 x 16 In. 130.00
Table, Coffee, Mahogany Veneer, Free-Form Top, Walnut Legs, 15 x 70 In. 8860.00
Table, Coffee, Marble Top, Carved Skirt, Legs, Victorian, 18 x 37 In. 865.00
Table, Coffee, Max Kuehne, Green Decorated Gesso Top, Flowers, 15 x 51 x 20 In. 1380.00
Table, Coffee, McCobb, Mahogany, 30 x 30 x 16 In. 160.00
Table, Coffee, Oriental, Cloisonne, Black Lacquer, 20th Century, 49 x 24 x 18 1/2 In. 220.00
Table, Coffee, Oval Top, Floral Urn, Marquetry, Medallions, 18 1/2 x 39 1/4 In. 170.00
Table, Coffee, Peter Hvidt & Orla Neilsen, Teak, Rattan, Steel, 39 1/4 x 19 1/2 In. 300.00
Table, Coffee, Plate-Glass Top, Geometric Forms, Square, 42 In. 990.00
Table, Coffee, Robsjohn-Gibbings, Glass Top, Widdicomb, 55 x 31 x 19 In. 1840.00
Table, Coffee, Robsjohn-Gibbings, Mahogany, 4 Brass Legs, 28 x 16 In. 635.00
Table, Coffee, Robsjohn-Gibbings, Mahogany, Rectangular, 53 x 29 x 16 In. 920.00
Table, Coffee, Robsjohn-Gibbings, Mahogany, Widdicomb, 40 x 40 x 14 In. 310.00
Table, Coffee, Rosewood, Lower Shelf, Denmark, 16 1/2 x 29 3/4 In. 290.00
Table, Coffee, Rosewood, Tile-Inset Top, Cane Lower Shelf, 17 x 59 In. 440.00
Table, Coffee, Saarinen, Marble, White Enamel Pedestal Base, 16 x 36 In. 460.00

Table, Coffee, Van Der Rohe, Glass Top, Chrome & Steel X-Base, Square, 42 In. 550.00
Table, Coffee, Van Der Rohe, Plate-Glass Top, Chrome X Base, 40 In. 180.00
Table, Coffee, Wegner, Oak, Teak Veneer, Dowel Legs, 20 1/2 x 43 3/4 In. 80.00
Table, Coffee, White Marble Top, Gilt Metal Base, Turtle Form, 36 In. 60.00
Table, Coffee, Wrought Iron, Round Legs, Ring Turnings, 16 x 40 In. 110.00
Table, Conference, Eames, White Plastic Top, Black Trim, 29 In. 230.00
Table, Conference, Mahogany, Contemporary, Oval, Chromed Steel, 96 x 55 x 28 In. 170.00
Table, Console, Black Enamel, Carved, Cabriole Legs, Scrolled Crest, Marble Top, 60 In. 510.00
Table, Console, Empire Style, 3 Leaf Supports, France, 44 x 14 x 33 In. 375.00
Table, Console, George III Style, Mahogany, D-Shape, Tapered Legs, 32 x 45 x 18 In. . . . 750.00
Table, Console, George III Style, Mahogany, Inlaid, D-Shape, 32 x 45 x 18 In. 920.00
Table, Console, George III, Japanned Pine, 1740, 34 x 34 x 20 In. . . . . *Illus* 3105.00
Table, Console, Giltwood, Marble, Cabriole Legs, Continental, 35 x 64 x 24 In. 6600.00
Table, Console, Italian Baroque Style, Painted, 19th Century, 30 1/2 x 60 x 15 In. 1955.00
Table, Console, Louis XVI Style, Giltwood, Ebonized, Marble Top, 38 x 43 x 22 In., Pair 6040.00
Table, Console, Mahogany, Inverted Half-Circle Pedestal, Brass Paw Feet, 30 1/2 In. 615.00
Table, Console, Mahogany, Marble Top, Drawer In Case, 33 x 39 In. 1840.00
Table, Console, Neoclassical, Marble Top, Mahogany, Parcel Gilt, Italy, c.1800 . . . . 8340.00
Table, Console, Oriental, Black Lacquer, Ornately Carved, Foo Dog Feet, c.1840, 47 In. . . 3080.00
Table, Console, Walnut Top & Base, Fluted Column, 30 x 36 In. 355.00
Table, Console, Wrought Iron, Green Paint, Wall Mounted, 32 x 14 In. 145.00
Table, Curly Maple, Inlaid Checkerboard Top, 31 x 19 1/4 In. 220.00
Table, D-Shape, Cast Iron Baluster Legs, Marble Top, 33 1/2 x 37 x 16 1/2 In., Pair 5060.00
Table, Dinette, Saarinen, White Marble Top, Laminate Base, 28 1/2 x 36 In. 750.00
Table, Dining, Art Deco, Rosewood, 29 x 60 x 40 In. 3525.00
Table, Dining, Art Deco, Rosewood, Marble, Green Glass Top, France, 1940, 38 In. 8060.00
Table, Dining, Arts & Crafts Style, Southwest, Decorated, 2 Leaves, 78 x 40 x 30 In. 345.00
Table, Dining, Arts & Crafts, Split Pedestal, Round Top, 4 Leaves, 30 x 48 In. 2300.00
Table, Dining, Bair Furniture Co., Federal Style, Mahogany, Zigzag Inlay, 54 In. 360.00
Table, Dining, Birch, Drop Leaf, Square Legs, 29 x 42 In. 860.00
Table, Dining, Burl Walnut, 2 Pedestals, Leaf Knees, 20th Century, 29 x 88 In. 4310.00
Table, Dining, Cherry, Curly Maple Top & Leaves, Ball Feet, 30 In. 495.00
Table, Dining, Drop Leaf, Chippendale, Birch, New England, c.1800, 17 x 48 In. 1440.00
Table, Dining, Drop Leaf, Federal, Mahogany, Splayed Legs, Paw Feet, 27 x 53 In. 1645.00
Table, Dining, Drop Leaf, Louis Philippe, Mahogany, Brass Casters, 81 1/2 x 17 3/4 In. . . 3220.00
Table, Dining, Drop Leaf, Mahogany, 1880s, 28 x 37 1/2 In. 1380.00
Table, Dining, Drop Leaf, Mahogany, 19th Century, 30 x 60 In. 690.00
Table, Dining, Drop Leaf, Mahogany, Inlaid, Tapered Legs, c.1850, 50 x 128 In. 2128.00
Table, Dining, Drop Leaf, Mahogany, Shaped Corner Leaves, 29 1/2 x 47 3/4 In. 560.00
Table, Dining, Drop Leaf, Mid Georgian, Mahogany, c.1760, 28 x 46 x 41 In. 1840.00
Table, Dining, Drop Leaf, Neoclassical, Carved, Stenciled, c.1825, 28 x 94 x 48 In. 1380.00
Table, Dining, Drop Leaf, Queen Anne, Walnut, Maple, c.1760, 27 1/2 x 46 1/2 x 47 In. . . 3300.00
Table, Dining, Drop Leaf, Sheraton, Mahogany, Spiral-Carved Legs, 30 x 48 In. 635.00
Table, Dining, Drop Leaf, Teak, 2 Leaves, Gateleg, Denmark, 29 x 34 In. 605.00
Table, Dining, Drop Leaf, Wallace Nutting, Sheraton Style, Cherry, 29 x 48 x 22 1/2 In. . . 2300.00
Table, Dining, Drop Leaf, Widdicomb, Extension, 4 Leaves, 27 x 39 In. 115.00
Table, Dining, Drop Side, Walnut, 6 Legs, Porcelain Casters, 1850s, 39 x 28 x 29 In. 230.00
Table, Dining, Elizabethan Style, Cherry, 4-Board Top, 30 1/2 x 39 7/8 x 84 In. 1345.00
Table, Dining, Federal, Mahogany, 3 Sections, Reeded Legs, 29 x 54 x 115 In. 9400.00
Table, Dining, Federal, Mahogany, Bowed Ends, 6 Tapered Legs, 28 x 47 x 65 In. 1175.00
Table, Dining, Federal, Mahogany, Hinged Top, Bell Floral Inlay, 28 x 46 x 57 In. 2185.00
Table, Dining, Frank Lloyd Wright, Mahogany, Circular Top, 48 x 29 In. 3105.00
Table, Dining, G. Nakashima, Walnut, 1960, 29 x 60 x 36 In. 6900.00
Table, Dining, G. Nelson, Birch, Center Zinc Planter, Herman Miller, 73 x 40 In. 2530.00
Table, Dining, G. Nelson, Hard Plastic Top, Green, Black Base, 29 1/2 In. 460.00
Table, Dining, G. Nelson, Hard Plastic Top, White Rubber Trim, 78 x 29 In. 575.00
Table, Dining, G. Nelson, Walnut Veneer, Lazy Susan, Pedestal Base, 29 x 48 In. 880.00
Table, Dining, G. Stickley, Circular Top, Split Pedestal, 4 Leaves, 30 x 54 In. 5175.00
Table, Dining, G. Stickley, No. 625, Oak, Hexagonal Top, 29 1/2 x 48 In. 4145.00
Table, Dining, George II Style, Walnut, Pedestals, Saber Legs, Snake Feet, 48 x 102 In. . . 2690.00
Table, Dining, George III Style, Mahogany, 2 Pedestals, Extension, 30 x 83 x 39 In. 865.00
Table, Dining, George III Style, Mahogany, Inlaid, 3 Pedestals, 30 x 144 x 48 In. 3795.00
Table, Dining, George III Style, Mahogany, Inlaid, Twin Pedestals, 30 x 137 x 48 In. 1840.00

Be careful when polishing painted furniture. Use only a true wax or polish labeled safe for painted surfaces. Linseed oil and other products will darken the paint.

Furniture, Table, Dining, Limbert, Oval Top, Splayed Slab Sides, Cutouts, 29 x 45 x 30 In.

Table, Dining, George III, Mahogany, 2 Pedestals, 2 Leaves, 1900s, 30 x 78 x 38 In.	2645.00
Table, Dining, George III, Mahogany, 2 Ring-Turned Pedestals, 30 x 84 x 46 In.	2990.00
Table, Dining, George III, Mahogany, Claw & Ball Feet, 2 Leaves, 47 x 150 In.	2352.00
Table, Dining, George III, Mahogany, Reeded Edge, 4 Downswept Legs, 30 In.	6000.00
Table, Dining, George IV, Mahogany, Round, Carved, 3-Footed, Casters, 30 x 52 In.	6944.00
Table, Dining, Georgian Style, Extension, Early 20th Century, 65 x 46 x 29 In.	6325.00
Table, Dining, Georgian Style, Mahogany, Carved, Square Legs, Extension, 66 x 43 In.	998.00
Table, Dining, Georgian Style, Mahogany, Inlaid, c.1860, 28 1/2 x 66 In.	1232.00
Table, Dining, Georgian, Mahogany, D-Shape Top, 4 Leaves, 1800s, 179 x 42 In.	1725.00
Table, Dining, Glass, Polished Steel, Contemporary, 36 x 60 x 30 In.	170.00
Table, Dining, Hastings, Circular Top, Apron, Shoe Feet, Casters, Five 9-In. Leaves	1725.00
Table, Dining, I. Noguchi, Laminated Plywood, Circular Top, 1957, 28 In.	1175.00
Table, Dining, L. & J.G. Stickley, No. 713, Oak, 4 Leaves, 30 x 48 In.	2350.00
Table, Dining, L. & J.G. Stickley, Oak, Round, 2 Leaves, 29 x 48 In.	1495.00
Table, Dining, Limbert, Buttressed Pedestal, 2 12-In. Leaves, Branded, 28 x 48 In.	1725.00
Table, Dining, Limbert, No. 423, Mahogany, Circular Top, 4 Legs, 54 x 30 In.	4888.00
Table, Dining, Limbert, No. 1487, Mahogany, Circular Top, 54 x 29 In.	5750.00
Table, Dining, Limbert, Oval Top, Splayed Slab Sides, Cutouts, 29 x 45 x 30 In. . . . *Illus*	2990.00
Table, Dining, Louis XV Style, Scalloped Frieze, Cabriole Legs, 30 x 36 3/4 x 86 In.	5290.00
Table, Dining, Mahogany, 2 Pedestals, 3 Leaves, 54 In.	2035.00
Table, Dining, Mahogany, 2 Pedestals, Lion's Head Casters, c.1815, 30 x 72 3/4 In.	4928.00
Table, Dining, Mahogany, 2 Pedestals, Paw Casters, 29 1/2 x 48 In.	1530.00
Table, Dining, Mahogany, 2 Pedestals, Saber-Shaped Legs, Casters, 29 x 48 In.	3136.00
Table, Dining, Mahogany, 2 Pedestals, Vase-Form Standard, Brass Paws, 1870s, 69 In.	230.00
Table, Dining, Mahogany, 3 Pedestals, Brass Casters, 2 Leaves, c.1900, 29 x 45 In.	3584.00
Table, Dining, Mahogany, 4 Leaves, Padded Snake Feet, 20th Century, 66 In.	935.00
Table, Dining, Mahogany, D-Shape Top, Conforming Skirt, Swing Legs, 29 x 47 In.	3760.00
Table, Dining, Mahogany, Gadroon Edge, Leaf-Carved Knees, 1 Leaf, c.1890, 80 In.	1008.00
Table, Dining, Mahogany, Inlaid, Duncan Phyfe, 1920s, 29 x 10 x 46 3/4 In.	3080.00
Table, Dining, Mahogany, Narrow Apron, Legs Headed By Metal Rings, 45 1/2 In.	290.00
Table, Dining, Mahogany, Oval, 3 Parts, 1800, 102 In. Open	7188.00
Table, Dining, Mahogany, Plum Pudding, Tilt Top, Saber Legs, c.1820, 58 In.	6720.00
Table, Dining, Mahogany, Satinwood Crossbanded, 3 Parts, 155 In.	5175.00
Table, Dining, Marble, Oval, Contemporary, 43 x 60 x 30 In.	345.00
Table, Dining, McCobb, Mahogany, Directional, Brass, 2 Leaves, 72 x 40 x 29 In.	240.00
Table, Dining, Neoclassical, Mahogany, D-Shape Ends, c.1850, 28 x 46 x 154 In.	8815.00
Table, Dining, Neoclassical, Walnut, 2 Sections, Carved, c.1825, 29 1/2 x 47 x 21 In.	2300.00
Table, Dining, Parquetry Marble Top, Fluted Columnar Plinths Base, 29 1/4 In.	690.00
Table, Dining, Parquetry, Carved Frieze, Cabriole Legs, 30 x 75 x 44 In.	3045.00
Table, Dining, Regency Style, Mahogany, Oval, 3 Pedestals, 30 x 113 1/2 x 46 In.	2990.00
Table, Dining, Regency, Mahogany, Accordion Action, W. Wilkinson, 1810, 88 In. Open	9600.00
Table, Dining, Regency, Mahogany, Gateleg Trestle, 28 x 48 x 158 In.	11500.00
Table, Dining, Renaissance Revival, Walnut, Carved Pedestal Base, Round, 30 x 50 In.	2520.00
Table, Dining, Robsjohn-Gibbings, Light Walnut, 29 1/2 x 72 In.	3525.00
Table, Dining, Saarinen, Tulipwood, Laminate Top, Enameled Pedestal Base, 54 In.	770.00
Table, Dining, Sheraton Style, Mahogany, Inlaid, Double Pedestal, 29 3/4 x 48 In.	2465.00
Table, Dining, Stickley Bros., No. 2670, Mahogany, Circular Top, 48 x 30 In.	575.00
Table, Dining, Stickley, Circular Top, Split Pedestal, Shoe Feet, 30 x 54 In.	4600.00

Table, Dining, Tulipwood, Laminate Top, Enameled Pedestal Base, 29 x 42 In. 440.00
Table, Dining, Victorian, Mahogany, Inlaid, Satinwood Band, 29 1/2 x 65 x 57 In. 3910.00
Table, Dining, Walnut, 2 Leaves, Widdicomb, Label, 29 3/4 x 60 1/2 In. 1540.00
Table, Dining, Walnut, D-Shape Top, 4 Side Legs, 2 Leaves, 29 1/2 x 60 In. 990.00
Table, Dining, Walnut, Faceted Tapered Legs, Round, 1 Leaf, 48 In. 255.00
Table, Dining, William IV, Mahogany, Reeded Edge, Bun Feet, 29 1/2 x 90 In. 6350.00
Table, Dressing, Adam Style, Satinwood, Shield Mirror, Classical Scenes & Leaves 5750.00
Table, Dressing, Art Deco, African Bubinga Wood, Rosewood Trim, 1930, 15 x 36 In. . . . 1150.00
Table, Dressing, Biedermeier, Fruitwood, Rectangular Top, Frieze Drawer, 37 In. 1035.00
Table, Dressing, Cherry, Fitted Interior, Divided Compartments, 1870s, 27 In. 615.00
Table, Dressing, Federal, Satinwood, Mahogany, 2 Short Drawers, 37 In. 805.00
Table, Dressing, George III, Mahogany, Top Opens, Cupboard, Casters, 34 x 18 In. 1720.00
Table, Dressing, Grain Paint, Black, Red, Turned Legs, Scrolled Backsplash, 34 x 32 In. . 290.00
Table, Dressing, Mahogany, 1 Long Over 6 Short Drawers, 1760s, 32 In. 1495.00
Table, Dressing, Mahogany, 2 Short Over 1 Long Drawer, Ball Feet, 30 x 32 In. 705.00
Table, Dressing, Mahogany, Bowfront, Square, Fluted Standards, 22 x 20 1/2 In. 165.00
Table, Dressing, Mahogany, Drawers, Brass Pulls, Table Rock Furn. Co., 30 In. 220.00
Table, Dressing, Mahogany, Inlaid Bowfront, Oval Mirror, Swing Frame, 57 x 42 x 25 In. 1265.00
Table, Dressing, Mahogany, Kneehole, 1 Long, 6 Short Drawers, c.1760, 30 In. 1090.00
Table, Dressing, Mahogany, Leaf Crest, Drawer, Marble Top 5175.00
Table, Dressing, Mahogany, Marble Top, Stepped Cornice, Drawer, 1825, 98 In. 9775.00
Table, Dressing, Mahogany, Platform Base, 2 Drawers, 82 3/8 In. 1650.00
Table, Dressing, Maple, 2 Aligned Drawers, Reeded Edge, Tapered Legs, 33 1/2 In. 230.00
Table, Dressing, Marble Top, Band Of Stiff Leaf Tips, Mirror, Shelf, Late 1800s, 32 In. . . 230.00
Table, Dressing, N. Bel Geddes, Enameled & Chromium, Mirror, 1932, 30 In. 3680.00
Table, Dressing, Oak, Faux Center Drawers, 2 Drawers Each Side, 28 x 31 1/2 In. 200.00
Table, Dressing, Painted, Flowers, Instruments, Bowfront, Drawer, Mirror, 56 In. 6325.00
Table, Dressing, Painted, Stenciled, Gallery, Shelf, Drawer, 36 1/2 x 32 x 15 In. 4675.00
Table, Dressing, Pine, Backsplash, 33 x 32 x 16 In. 90.00
Table, Dressing, Queen Anne, Walnut, 1 Long Over 3 Short Drawers, 28 In. 4025.00
Table, Dressing, Queen Anne, Walnut, 1 Long Over 3 Short Drawers, 29 x 32 In. 9400.00
Table, Dressing, Queen Anne, Walnut, Carved, c.1750, 30 3/4 x 32 3/4 x 21 In. 8400.00
Table, Dressing, Regency, Mahogany, Bowfront, Crossband Top, 30 x 16 x 31 In. 550.00
Table, Dressing, Renaissance Revival, Walnut, Mirror Mounted, Scrolled Legs, 30 x 26 In. 375.00
Table, Dressing, Sheraton, Mahogany, Curly Maple Veneer Drawer, 36 x 19 x 29 In. 495.00
Table, Dressing, Sheraton, Pine, Floral, Drawer, Biscuit Corners, 36 x 17 x 38 In. 1210.00
Table, Dressing, Softwood, 2 Scratch Bead Drawers, New England, 64 x 35 x 19 In. 1100.00
Table, Dressing, Victorian, Walnut, Marble Top, 3 Drawers, 31 x 44 x 19 In. 410.00
Table, Drop Leaf, Birch, Drawer, New England, 19th Century, 30 x 17 x 36 In. 715.00
Table, Drop Leaf, Cherry, 1-Board Top, 46 3/4 In. 440.00
Table, Drop Leaf, Cherry, 1-Board Top, Turned Legs, 42 In. 330.00
Table, Drop Leaf, Cherry, 6 Wing Legs, Drawer, Ball Feet, 30 x 41 x 19 1/2 In. 140.00
Table, Drop Leaf, Cherry, Serpentine Top, Drawer, Marlborough Legs, 30 x 36 In. 8815.00
Table, Drop Leaf, Cherry, Tall Turned Legs, Brass Feet, 27 x 42 In. 120.00
Table, Drop Leaf, Chippendale, Cherry, X-Stretcher, 14-In. Leaves, 40 x 14 3/4 In. 275.00
Table, Drop Leaf, Chippendale, Mahogany, Serpentine Ends, 29 x 19 1/2 x 42 In. 940.00
Table, Drop Leaf, Drawer, 4 Saber Legs, c.1820, 27 3/4 x 42 In. 1400.00
Table, Drop Leaf, Edwardian, Mahogany, Drawers, c.1895, 29 x 31 x 21 In. 1380.00
Table, Drop Leaf, Edwardian, Painted Satinwood, 2 Drawers, 1895, 29 In. 8100.00
Table, Drop Leaf, Extension, Cherry, Turned Legs, 2-Board Top, 27 x 42 In. 825.00
Table, Drop Leaf, Federal, Mahogany Veneer, Reeded Swelled Legs, Ball Feet, 28 In. 805.00
Table, Drop Leaf, Federal, Mahogany, Concave End, Drawer, Fluted Arched Legs, 28 In. . . 4315.00
Table, Drop Leaf, Federal, Maple, Rectangular Top, 6 Tapered Legs, 30 x 45 In. 520.00
Table, Drop Leaf, Gateleg, Early 19th Century, 28 x 45 3/4 In. 1065.00
Table, Drop Leaf, George III, Mahogany, 6 Square Tapered Legs, Casters, 1800s 460.00
Table, Drop Leaf, George III, Mahogany, Early 19th Century, 28 x 40 x 58 In. 1035.00
Table, Drop Leaf, George III, Mahogany, Gateleg, c.1810, 27 3/4 x 45 x 47 1/2 In. 785.00
Table, Drop Leaf, George III, Mahogany, Gateleg, Oval Top, Pad Feet, c.1790, 30 x 27 In. 1000.00
Table, Drop Leaf, Grain Painted, Neoclassical, c.1840, 29 x 19 1/2 x 40 1/4 In. 920.00
Table, Drop Leaf, Hepplewhite, Cherry, Bowed Skirt, Drawer, 1800, 32 x 22 In. 880.00
Table, Drop Leaf, Hepplewhite, Cherry, Rule Joints, 1-Board Top, 42 x 18 x 29 1/4 In. . . . 220.00
Table, Drop Leaf, Hepplewhite, Cherry, Swing Leg, Square Edged Leaves, 29 x 36 In. . . . 900.00
Table, Drop Leaf, Hepplewhite, Flamed Apple Wood, c.1800, 30 x 42 x 16 In. 1035.00

Table, Drop Leaf, Hepplewhite, Mahogany, Inlaid, Swing Leg 500.00
Table, Drop Leaf, Hepplewhite, Walnut, Swing Leg, 30 1/2 x 45 x 17 In. 250.00
Table, Drop Leaf, L. & J.G. Stickley, Footed Base, Circular Top, 30 x 28 In. 690.00
Table, Drop Leaf, Lifetime, No. 902, Mahogany, 2 17-In. Leaves, 12 x 30 In. 690.00
Table, Drop Leaf, Louis XV Style, Fruitwood, Cabriole Legs, 30 x 56 x 39 In. 1725.00
Table, Drop Leaf, Mahogany, 2 Drawers, Lyre Base, Mass., 35 x 17 In. 430.00
Table, Drop Leaf, Mahogany, 28 x 27 x 14 In. 390.00
Table, Drop Leaf, Mahogany, 6 Legs, Swing Leg, Turned, Brass Casters, 28 x 45 x 22 In. . 285.00
Table, Drop Leaf, Mahogany, Acanthus Legs, Tapered Feet, 29 1/2 In. 430.00
Table, Drop Leaf, Mahogany, Brass Casters, 1770s, 29 1/4 In. 1840.00
Table, Drop Leaf, Mahogany, Brass Inlay, Carved, Neoclassical, c.1835, 27 x 54 x 38 In. . 690.00
Table, Drop Leaf, Mahogany, Carved Apron, Claw Feet, 29 1/2 x 35 In. 505.00
Table, Drop Leaf, Mahogany, Carved Legs, Brass Casters, Leaves, England, 37 x 21 In. ... 715.00
Table, Drop Leaf, Mahogany, Drawer, Carved Pedestal Base, 29 x 30 In. 495.00
Table, Drop Leaf, Mahogany, Drawer, Pineapple Columns, c.1835, 55 1/2 In. 4480.00
Table, Drop Leaf, Mahogany, Gateleg, Pad Feet, c.1810, 28 1/2 In. 840.00
Table, Drop Leaf, Mahogany, Gateleg, Pad Feet, c.1810, 28 x 45 x 46 In. 1790.00
Table, Drop Leaf, Mahogany, Gateleg, Tapered Legs, c.1790 .... 1460.00
Table, Drop Leaf, Mahogany, Late 18th Century, 28 1/2 x 36 x 18 In. 1610.00
Table, Drop Leaf, Mahogany, Leaves, Fluted Tapered Leg, Spade Feet, 21 1/2 In. 670.00
Table, Drop Leaf, Mahogany, Rectangular Top, 1830, 29 In. 805.00
Table, Drop Leaf, Mahogany, Scalloped Apron, Claw & Ball Feet, 1770, 18 1/2 x 52 In. . 9000.00
Table, Drop Leaf, Mahogany, Scalloped End Aprons, 2-Board Leaves, 48 In. 3025.00
Table, Drop Leaf, Mahogany, Shaped Corners, Cabriole Legs, Knuckled Feet, 55 x 45 In. . 960.00
Table, Drop Leaf, Mahogany, Swing Leg, Arched Aprons, Tapered Legs, 31 x 21 x 45 In. . 110.00
Table, Drop Leaf, Mahogany, Turned Pedestal, Paw Casters, Neoclassical, 29 x 46 In. ... 1880.00
Table, Drop Leaf, Maple, Dovetailed Drawer Ends, 1-Board Top, 27 x 36 1/2 In. 1100.00
Table, Drop Leaf, Maple, Scalloped & Shaped Aprons, 28 x 48 In. 990.00
Table, Drop Leaf, Maple, Swing Leg, Turned Legs, Oval, Child's, 18 x 21 x 29 In. 320.00
Table, Drop Leaf, McCobb, Blond Finish, Dowel Legs, Winchendon, 29 x 36 In. 520.00
Table, Drop Leaf, Mixed Hardwoods, 2 Drawers, Pressed Glass Pulls, 28 In. 440.00
Table, Drop Leaf, Oak, 1-Board Top, Pegged, Gateleg, England, 35 x 12 x 16 In. 880.00
Table, Drop Leaf, Oak, Baluster Supports, Gateleg, 30 x 21 In. 1265.00
Table, Drop Leaf, Queen Anne Style, Mahogany, Circular Legs, Pad Feet, 28 1/2 In. 805.00
Table, Drop Leaf, Queen Anne Style, Mahogany, Dovetail Corners, 19th Century, 39 In. .. 220.00
Table, Drop Leaf, Queen Anne Style, Mahogany, Pad Feet, 28 x 48 1/2 x 17 In. 865.00
Table, Drop Leaf, Queen Anne, Cherry, Mahogany, c.1790, 27 3/4 x 40 1/2 x 38 In. 4700.00
Table, Drop Leaf, Queen Anne, Mahogany, D-Shape Leaves, c.1760, 28 x 43 x 43 In. 14100.00
Table, Drop Leaf, Queen Anne, Maple, Cabriole Legs, Pad Feet, 28 x 45 In. 3740.00
Table, Drop Leaf, Queen Anne, Maple, Cabriole Legs, Padded Disc Feet, 28 x 47 In. 3055.00
Table, Drop Leaf, Queen Anne, Scrolling, Cabriole Legs, 1700s, 27x 30 1/4 x 14 3/4 In. .. 2530.00
Table, Drop Leaf, Renaissance Revival, Walnut, 20 Drawers, Mechanical, 30 x 13 x 36 In. 1510.00
Table, Drop Leaf, Rosewood, Drawer, Reeded Columns, 26 x 51 In. 4000.00
Table, Drop Leaf, Satinwood, 2 Frieze Drawers, Brass Casters, 28 1/2 In. 8050.00
Table, Drop Leaf, Sheraton, Birch, Red Top & Leaves, 36 1/4 x 10 x 28 3/4 In. 495.00
Table, Drop Leaf, Sheraton, Mahogany, Bird's-Eye Maple Veneer, 27 x 22 x 17 In. 805.00
Table, Drop Leaf, Sheraton, Mahogany, Drawer 1 End, Cut Down, 36 x 22 x 17 In. 330.00
Table, Drop Leaf, Sheraton, Mahogany, Reeded Legs, 48 x 86 In. 535.00
Table, Drop Leaf, Sheraton, Maple, Birch, Brown Paint, Scrub Top, 29 x 38 In. 225.00
Table, Drop Leaf, Sheraton, Maple, Graining On Leaves, Turned Legs 220.00
Table, Drop Leaf, Sheraton, Maple, Mahogany, Spiral-Turned Legs, 28 x 43 In. 2810.00
Table, Drop Leaf, Sheraton, Walnut, Beading, 1 Drawer, 36 x 20 x 29 1/2 In. 770.00
Table, Drop Leaf, Stickley Bros., No. 2817, Mahogany, 30 x 14 x 30 In. 635.00
Table, Drop Leaf, Tapered Legs, 19th Century, 47 x 15 1/2 x 27 In. 170.00
Table, Drop Leaf, Walnut, 21 1/2 x 16 x 27 1/2 In. 345.00
Table, Drop Leaf, Walnut, 6-Leg Base, c.1825, 28 1/2 x 48 In. 450.00
Table, Drop Leaf, Walnut, Serpentine Corners, 6 Turned Legs, 29 x 20 1/2 x 45 In. 220.00
Table, Drop Leaf, Walnut, Shell Carving At Knees, Claw & Ball Feet, 28 1/2 In. 880.00
Table, Drop Leaf, Walnut, Stepped Platform Stretcher, Triangular Leaves, 25 In. 1955.00
Table, Drop Leaf, William & Mary, Box Stretcher, Gateleg, Leaves, 29 x 42 x 49 In. 550.00
Table, Drop Leaf, William & Mary, Oak, Gateleg, 24 x 49 x 39 In. 1035.00
Table, Drop Leaf, William & Mary, Walnut, Turned Legs, 30 x 35 x 45 In. 1035.00
Table, Drum, Mahogany, Leather Top Over Drawers, Downswept Legs, 41 In. 345.00

Table, Drum, Neoclassical, Mahogany, 3 Drawers, Pedestal Shaft, 29 1/4 x 29 In. 8815.00
Table, Drum, Regency, Oak, Gilt Tooled Leather Top, 4 Drawers, 3 Bun Feet, 29 x 45 In. . . 5740.00
Table, E. Wormley, Mahogany, Round Top, 20 x 26 1/2 In. 750.00
Table, Eames, Plywood, Black Underframe, 1947, 15 1/2 In. 9200.00
Table, Eastlake Style, Marble Top, Rectangular, 28 1/2 x 28 x 20 1/2 In. 50.00
Table, Eastlake Style, White Marble, 30 x 23 x 17 In. 330.00
Table, Eastlake, Glass Beadwork Top, Angels & Cherubs, Ebonized, 3-Footed 715.00
Table, Ebonized, Center Flower Spray, Scalloped Apron, Cabriole Legs, 1850s, 29 In. . . . 1725.00
Table, Edwardian, Brass, Leather Inset, Late 19th Century, 21 x 12 1/4 In. 115.00
Table, Edwardian, Mahogany, Bowfront, c.1900, 35 1/2 x 37 x 20 In. 575.00
Table, Edwardian, Mahogany, Inlaid, Bowfront, c.1905, 30 x 35 x 19 In. 460.00
Table, Edwardian, Painted, Harbor Scene, Tapered Round Legs, 20 x 22 x 15 1/2 In. 2000.00
Table, Edwardian, Satinwood, Banded Top, Leaf Design, 1900, 30 x 22 In. 375.00
Table, Eileen Gray, E1027, 20 x 24 In. 575.00
Table, Elm, Dragon Roundels On Side Panels, Chinese, 19th Century, 19 x 55 In. 920.00
Table, Elm, Oval Top, Swinging Support, Trestle Ends, Plank Base, 29 x 47 x 36 In. 1985.00
Table, Elm, Paneled Top, Frieze Apron, Square, Chinese, 1700-1800, 28 x 13 In. 375.00
Table, Elm, Variegated Marble Top, Grooved Edge, Paneled Support, 1850s, 30 In. 4600.00
Table, Empire Style, Gilt Bronze, Marble Top, 3 Legs, X-Stretchers, 27 x 16 In. 7200.00
Table, Empire, Gilt Bronze, Marble Top, Shelf, 3 Reeded Scrolling Legs, 29 x 27 In. 7475.00
Table, Empire, Mahogany, 2 Drawers, Pedestal, Scrolled Feet, 28 x 18 x 15 1/2 In. 140.00
Table, Empire, Mahogany, Feather Grained, Ripple Molding, 30 x 25 x 41 In. 1400.00
Table, Empire, Mahogany, Gilt, Bronze, 2 Tiers, Tripod Base, 28 In. 375.00
Table, Empire, Mahogany, Rosewood, Drawers, Gilt Bronze Mount, 32 x 61 x 30 In. 1955.00
Table, Empire, Rosewood, Round Top, 1860s 2800.00
Table, English Regency Style, Mahogany, Baluster Pedestal, 30 x 36 x 36 In. 840.00
Table, Federal Style, Walnut, Drawer, Early 20th Century, 30 x 34 1/2 x 22 In. 1210.00
Table, Federal, Cherry, Rectangular Top, Frieze Drawer, Ball Feet, 28 In. 860.00
Table, Federal, Cherry, Tilt Top, Rectangular Top, Tripod Curved Legs, 28 1/4 In. 690.00
Table, Federal, Mahogany, 2 Drawers, Tapered Ring & Column Turned Legs, 28 x 25 In. . . 7640.00
Table, Federal, Mahogany, Rectangular Top, Tapered Inlaid Legs, 28 In. 1610.00
Table, Federal, Rectangular Rounded Edges, Frieze Drawer, 28 x 17 1/2 In. 1035.00
Table, Folding, Coach, Mahogany, Undercarriage, Sloped Surface, 27 x 22 x 18 In. 1380.00
Table, Frank Lloyd Wright, Hexagonal Top, Tri-Slab Base, Henredon, 19 x 19 x 17 In. . . . 600.00
Table, Frank Lloyd Wright, Mahogany, Drawer, Recessed Handle, 26 x 23 In. 920.00
Table, Frank Lloyd Wright, Mahogany, Hexagonal Top, Signed, 25 x 25 x 27 In. 800.00
Table, Frank Lloyd Wright, Mahogany, Paneled Top, Original Finish, 21 x 23 In. 920.00
Table, Frank Lloyd Wright, Mahogany, Paneled Top, Recessed Handle, 21 x 23 In. 1150.00
Table, Frank Lloyd Wright, Mahogany, Tri-Slab Base, Original Finish, 19 x 17 In. 805.00
Table, French Provincial, Beech, Marble Top, 21 x 25 x 17 In. 135.00
Table, French Provincial, Cherry, Early 19th Century, 29 1/2 x 35 3/4 In. 1725.00
Table, French Provincial, Fruitwood, Drawer, Hoof Feet, 29 x 28 x 28 In. 2300.00
Table, French Provincial, Fruitwood, Plank Oval Top, Square Legs, 28 x 43 x 32 In. 1125.00
Table, French Provincial, Mahogany, Marble Insert, Ormolu, Tripod, 21 x 30 In., Pair . . . 1100.00
Table, French Provincial, Marquetry, Marble Top, 2 Drawers, 30 x 23 1/2 x 16 In., Pair . . 575.00
Table, French Provincial, Oak, Plank Top, Box Stretcher, 27 x 30 x 21 In. 430.00
Table, French Provincial, Oak, Planked Top, 29 1/2 x 45 1/2 x 31 In. 805.00
Table, French Renaissance Style, Walnut, 2 Tiers, 30 1/4 x 35 1/2 x 20 1/4 In. 805.00
Table, G. Nelson, Mahogany, Walnut Drawer, White Laminate Top, 18 In. 300.00
Table, G. Stickley, Circular, Cross Stretchers, Mortised, Decal, 1902, 28 x 23 In. 5750.00
Table, G. Stickley, Drop Leaf, Mahogany, Rectangular Top, Gateleg, 42 x 30 In. 980.00
Table, G. Stickley, Drop Leaf, Mahogany, Straight Legs, 30 x 12 x 28 In. 635.00
Table, G. Stickley, Mahogany, Dark Finish, Round, Shoe Feet, 29 1/2 x 36 In. 2500.00
Table, G. Stickley, No. 411, Mahogany, Circular Top, 30 x 29 In. 5750.00
Table, G. Stickley, No. 424, Original Black Finish, Red Decal, 29 In. 2860.00
Table, G. Stickley, No. 440, Mahogany, Circular Top, 30 x 28 In. 3740.00
Table, G. Stickley, No. 607, Mahogany, Circular Top, 24 x 29 In. 1840.00
Table, G. Stickley, No. 644, Cross Stretchers, Eastwood Label, 29 x 30 In. 1955.00
Table, G. Stickley, No. 648, Mahogany, Circular Top, Signed, 30 In. 9200.00
Table, Galle, Marquetry, 3 Tiers, Floral Shelf, 33 x 26 In. 4020.00
Table, Game, Checkerboard, Mustard Paint, Tilt Top, Tripod, 31 x 15 In. 5750.00
Table, Game, Checkerboard, Painted, Red Border, 27 3/4 x 17 x 17 1/2 In. 2415.00
Table, Game, Cherry, Mahogany, Swivel Top, Mid 19th Century, 35 x 17 x 29 In. 290.00

Furniture, Table, Game, George III, Mahogany,
Suede Interior, Fret Legs, 29 x 36 In.

Furniture, Table, Game, Walnut, Felt Surface,
Carved Legs, Casters, 29 x 36 x 19 In.

Table, Game, Chippendale, Mahogany, Flip Top, c.1800, 28 1/2 x 34 1/2 x 18 1/2 In. 865.00
Table, Game, Federal, Inlaid, D-Shape, Hinged, Tapered Legs, 29 x 41 x 21 In. 1175.00
Table, Game, Federal, Mahogany, Carved, Figured, 29 x 36 x 18 3/4 In. 8400.00
Table, Game, Federal, Mahogany, Carved, Saber Legs, Hairy Paw Feet, 28 x 36 x 18 In. ... 3055.00
Table, Game, Federal, Mahogany, Flip Top, Carved, Reeded Legs, 30 x 36 In. 825.00
Table, Game, Federal, Mahogany, Hinged Top, Inlaid Oval Reserve, 28 x 36 In. 1880.00
Table, Game, Federal, Mahogany, Inlaid, D-Shape, Checkerboard, 31 x 36 x 18 In. 1115.00
Table, Game, Federal, Mahogany, Maple Inlay, Hinged Top, Serpentine Front, 28 x 34 In. 5640.00
Table, Game, Federal, Mahogany, Satinwood Inlaid, c.1810, 36 x 36 x 17 1/2 In. 9600.00
Table, Game, Federal, Mahogany, Trick Leg, c.1815, 29 x 36 1/2 x 18 1/2 In. 7800.00
Table, Game, Federal, Satinwood, Inlaid, Trick Leg, c.1815, 28 1/2 x 36 x 17 In. 5400.00
Table, Game, Floral Inlay, Floral Medallions, Flip Top, Drawer, 29 x 39 In. 5175.00
Table, Game, Frankl, Mahogany, White Cork Top, Johnson Furniture, 32 x 27 In. 240.00
Table, Game, Gateleg, Flip Top Enclosing Leather Surface, Spade Feet, 32 3/4 In. 920.00
Table, Game, George III, Mahogany, Serpentine Top, Cabriole Legs, 28 In. 3450.00
Table, Game, George III, Mahogany, Suede Interior, Fret Legs, 29 x 36 In. .... *Illus* 1495.00
Table, Game, George IV, Mahogany, Coromandel, Recessed Frieze, 29 1/2 In. 1380.00
Table, Game, Georgian Style, Needlepoint Panel, Flip Top, 34 x 17 x 29 1/2 In. 2760.00
Table, Game, Hepplewhite Style, Inlaid Satinwood, D-Shape, 30 x 36 x 18 In. 560.00
Table, Game, L. & J.G. Stickley, Mahogany, Original Finish, Signed, 48 x 29 In. 1840.00
Table, Game, L. & J.G. Stickley, No. 519, Mahogany, Original Finish, 30 In. 800.00
Table, Game, Liberty & Co., Mahogany, Flip Top, 4 Legs, Pad Feet, Signed, 30 In. 1380.00
Table, Game, Louis XV, Marquetry, Tooled Leather Top, Flip Top, 28 x 17 x 31 In. 230.00
Table, Game, Mahogany, Apron Drawer, Folding Top, Batwing Brass, 28 In. 550.00
Table, Game, Mahogany, Apron, Flip Top, Cyma Legs, Leaf Knees, 1850s, 35 3/4 In. 865.00
Table, Game, Mahogany, Checkerboard, Red, Yellow & Black, Shelf, 20 x 20 x 29 In. 165.00
Table, Game, Mahogany, Egg & Dart Border, Bead & Reel Edge, 1760, 28 3/4 In. 5100.00
Table, Game, Mahogany, Fan Inlay, Rear Drawer, Base Surface, 1870s, 31 In. 3450.00
Table, Game, Mahogany, Flame Veneer, Folding Top, Paw Feet, Brass Casters, 29 3/4 In. . 1045.00
Table, Game, Mahogany, Flip Top, Acanthus Carved Pedestal, Paw Feet, 30 In. 2530.00
Table, Game, Mahogany, Flip Top, Short Drawer, Tapered Legs, 1880s, 30 x 42 In. 310.00
Table, Game, Mahogany, Folding Top Over Long Drawer, c.1810, 29 x 36 In. 2900.00
Table, Game, Mahogany, Inlaid, D-Shape Top, 19th Century, 29 1/2 x 36 x 17 In. 785.00
Table, Game, Mahogany, Inlaid, Drawer, c.1820, 27 1/2 x 11 x 16 1/2 In. 730.00
Table, Game, Mahogany, Ivory Inlay, Tilt Top, Shelf, Victorian, 29 x 22 x 22 In. 390.00
Table, Game, Mahogany, Octagonal, Glass Top, Door, X-Stretcher, 30 x 30 1/2 In. 45.00
Table, Game, Mahogany, Serpentine Front, Inlaid Frieze, Square Legs, 30 In. 9600.00
Table, Game, Mahogany, Serpentine Front, Tapered Legs, c.1820, 29 1/2 In. 1345.00
Table, Game, Mahogany, Tooled Leather Top, Cabriole Legs, 28 x 33 In. 920.00
Table, Game, Marquetry, Mother-Of-Pearl, Flip Top, N. Africa, 32 x 33 x 17 In. 1150.00
Table, Game, Michigan Chair Co., Wide Cutout Legs, Hexagonal, 29 x 42 In. 1610.00
Table, Game, Napoleon III, Ebonized, Marquetry, Flip Top, 30 x 34 x 17 In. 1725.00
Table, Game, Napoleon III, Foldover, Late 19th Century, 30 3/4 x 27 3/4 x 16 In. 460.00
Table, Game, Opens To Playing Surface, Fitted Interior, Claw & Ball Feet, 28 1/2 In. 1570.00
Table, Game, Pineapple Column, Side Drawer, 30 x 40 1/2 In. 440.00
Table, Game, Queen Anne Style, Mahogany, Burl, 29 x 33 x 16 1/2 In. 1035.00
Table, Game, Queen Anne Style, Walnut, D-Shape, 28 1/2 x 33 x 16 5/8 In. 475.00
Table, Game, Regency, Mahogany, Paneled Standard, 19th Century, 29 x 36 x 18 In. 1035.00

Table, Game, Regency, Rosewood, Brass Inlay, Early 19th Century, 30 x 36 x 18 In. 4370.00
Table, Game, Renaissance Revival, Walnut, Tilt Top, Claw Foot Pedestal, 47 x 26 In. 1400.00
Table, Game, Rosewood, Brass Inlay, Square Pedestal, 4 Saber Legs, 31 x 36 In., Pair . . . 3360.00
Table, Game, Rosewood, Inlaid Checkerboard Top, Tripod Base, 29 x 18 In. 1380.00
Table, Game, Rosewood, Mahogany, Marquetry, Reversible, 1930, 28 1/2 In. 19150.00
Table, Game, Stickley Bros., Square Top, Cross Stretcher, 36 x 30 In. 1495.00
Table, Game, Walnut, Felt Surface, Carved Legs, Casters, 29 x 36 x 19 In. . . . . *Illus* 863.00
Table, Game, Walnut, Round Checkerboard Top, With Chess Set, 3 Legs 1540.00
Table, Game, Walnut, Seaweed Marquetry, Concave Front, Drawer, 30 In. 2875.00
Table, Gateleg, English Oak, Stretcher, Early 18th Century, 25 1/2 x 37 1/2 x 15 In. 805.00
Table, Gateleg, Jacobean, Full Drawer, Sausage-Turned Legs, England, 45 x 21 In. 3080.00
Table, Gateleg, Mahogany, Hinged Top, Maple, Drawer, 28 3/8 In. 1725.00
Table, Gateleg, Maple, Oval, Hinged Drawer, Turned Base, 1700s, 29 x 13 In. 4300.00
Table, Gateleg, Maple, Turned, Red Stain, Butterfly Legs, New England, 24 x 12 In. 2280.00
Table, Gateleg, Oak, Figured, Carved Top, Twisted Swing Legs, 29 x 35 1/2 x 19 In. 390.00
Table, Gateleg, William & Mary Style, Oak, Box Stretcher, D-Shape Leaves 750.00
Table, George II Style, Gray Paint, 18 1/2 x 32 3/4 x 17 In. 5100.00
Table, George II, Mahogany, Rectangular Top, Cabriole Legs, Side, 31 x 25 In. 5700.00
Table, George III Style, Mahogany, D-Shape, Square Tapered Legs, 29 x 47 x 19 In. 920.00
Table, George III Style, Mahogany, Frieze Drawer, c.1900, 36 x 44 1/4 x 18 3/4 In. 405.00
Table, George III Style, Mahogany, Inlaid, Flaming Urn, D-Shape, 29 x 35 x 18 In., Pair . 1380.00
Table, George III Style, Mahogany, Tripod, Piecrust Top, Early 1900s, 31 x 13 1/2 In. . . . 290.00
Table, George III, Mahogany, 3 Pedestals, Rounded Ends, 134 x 45 In. 7475.00
Table, George III, Mahogany, Bowfront, T Style, Marble Top, 29 x 35 x 19 In. 920.00
Table, George III, Mahogany, Burl, 1 Long & 2 Short Drawers, 28 x 32 x 18 In. 920.00
Table, George III, Mahogany, Canted Rectangular Top, 27 x 19 x 16 In. 200.00
Table, George III, Mahogany, D-Shape Top, Late 18th Century, 29 3/4 x 36 x 16 3/4 In. . . 920.00
Table, George III, Mahogany, D-Shape, 18th Century, 28 x 45 x 20 3/4 In., Pair 2070.00
Table, George III, Mahogany, D-Shape, Late 18th Century, 28 x 45 x 22 In., Pair 2300.00
Table, George III, Mahogany, Dish Top, Tripod, Late 18th Century, 28 x 23 3/4 In. 1610.00
Table, George III, Mahogany, Drawer, Square Legs, Reeded, 33 1/2 x 40 x 19 In. 1720.00
Table, George III, Mahogany, Molded Edge, 28 x 38 x 23 In. 1955.00
Table, George III, Mahogany, Rosewood, Sunburst Inlay, 32 x 45 x 18 In., Pair 2530.00
Table, George III, Mahogany, Scalloped Apron, Lower Drawer, 32 x 15 In., Pair 1325.00
Table, George III, Mahogany, Silver, Dish Top, Cabriole Legs, 29 x 42 x 27 In. 4140.00
Table, George III, Satinwood, Burnished Palmettes, Laurel Branches, 33 x 20 In. 15525.00
Table, George III, Satinwood, Octagonal Top, Floral Border, 1900, 28 1/4 In. 805.00
Table, George III, Satinwood, Tulipwood Crossbanded Top, Faux Drawer, 27 x 34 In. 8400.00
Table, George IV, Rosewood, Serpentine, Leaf Cabriole Legs, Scroll Feet, 52 In. 1725.00
Table, Georgian Revival, Mahogany, Marble Top, 37 x 47 x 20 1/2 In., Pair 13800.00
Table, Georgian Style, Mahogany, Bowfront, Late 19th Century, 30 x 36 x 19 In. 420.00
Table, Georgian, Mahogany, Inset Leather Top, 24 x 27 In., Pair 230.00
Table, Gillows, George III, Mahogany, Inlaid, D-Shape Leaf, Drawer, 29 x 28 In. 3600.00
Table, Gilt, Patinated Bronze, Cloisonne Inset, 37 1/2 x 21 In., Pair 22600.00
Table, Gilt, Patinated Bronze, Figural, 27 x 21 In. 8400.00
Table, Giltwood, Onyx Top, Leaf-Carved Center Shelves, Scroll Stretchers, 32 1/2 In. . . . 575.00
Table, Glass Top, Gilt Iron, Rectangular, Late 20th Century, 27 x 23 In. 230.00
Table, Gold Leaf Finish, Black Onyx Insert On Top, Griffin Supports, 32 x 23 In. 5830.00
Table, Gueridon, Empire Style, Gilt Bronze, Marble Top, 27 1/2 x 16 In., Pair 6900.00
Table, Gueridon, Empire Style, Gilt Bronze, Marble, Late 19th Century, 27 x 28 In. 5750.00
Table, Gueridon, Empire Style, Marble, Gilt Bronze, Round, Shelf, 29 1/2 x 31 In., Pair . . 5750.00
Table, Gueridon, Empire, Brass, Circular Charcoal Gray Marble Top, 1900, 29 In. 5520.00
Table, Gueridon, Gilt, Patinated Bronze, 34 1/4 x 18 In., Pair 19150.00
Table, Gueridon, Louis XVI, Chinoiserie, Pierced Brass Gallery, c.1900, 26 x 25 1/2 In. . . 2300.00
Table, Gueridon, Napoleon III, Beech, Onyx Top, Octagonal, 31 x 16 In. 575.00
Table, Gueridon, Napoleon III, Marble Top, Square, Late 19th Century, 32 1/2 x 11 1/2 In. 805.00
Table, Hall, Queen Anne, Mahogany, Rococo Aprons, Cabriole Legs, 1900s, 72 x 21 In. . . 470.00
Table, Hand-Painted Landscape, Courting Scenes, Roses, 30 x 28 In. 1980.00
Table, Handkerchief, Hepplewhite, Mahogany, Inlaid, 29 x 21 3/4 x 22 In. 840.00
Table, Handkerchief, Mahogany, Triangular Top, Drop Leaf, Swing Leg, 27 In. 550.00
Table, Harvest, Ash, 3-Board Top, Old Red Wash, 31 1/2 x 94 3/4 In. 660.00
Table, Harvest, Birch, Pine, Leaves, 1-Board Top, 20 x 66 In. 825.00
Table, Harvest, Cherry, Pegged Construction, Drawer, 30 x 78 1/2 In. 1680.00

Table, Harvest, French Provincial, Cherry, Drop Leaf, 60 1/2 x 83 In. 2350.00
Table, Harvest, French Provincial, Cherry, Shaped Skirt, 30 1/2 x 36 x 84 In. 1008.00
Table, Harvest, Pine, Rosehead Nails On Top, 6 Turned Legs, 29 3/4 x 26 3/4 In. 300.00
Table, Harvest, Pine, Sawbuck, Red Paint On Baseboards, 27 1/2 x 99 In. 1430.00
Table, Harvest, Walnut, 2 Dovetailed Drawers, 4-Board Top, 33 1/2 x 80 In. 880.00
Table, Hepplewhite, D-Shape, England, 1780 .... 2650.00
Table, Hepplewhite, Tiger Maple, Shaped Leaves, 36 x 16 In. 1460.00
Table, Hickory, Mahogany, Rustic, 32 x 60 x 30 In. 1350.00
Table, I. Noguchi, Triangular Glass Top, 2-Piece Birch Supports, 1950s, 50 In. 3220.00
Table, Ice Cream, Cast Iron, Square Glass Top, Bentwood Chairs, 5 Piece 1725.00
Table, Iron, Marble, Reeded Column, Tripod Legs, Late 1800s, 24 x 18 In. 520.00
Table, Iron, Mosaic, Greek-Key Bands, Gilt Paw Feet, 20th Century, 30 x 84 In. 805.00
Table, Irving & Sasson, Louis XV Style, Gilt, Metal, Marquetry, 31 x 21 In. .... *Illus* 2070.00
Table, Italian Neoclassical, Walnut, Parquetry, 19th Century 2300.00
Table, Jacobean Style, Mahogany, Early 1900s, 70 x 20 x 28 1/2 In. 290.00
Table, Jacobean, Oak, Ebonized, D-Shape Top, Frieze Drawer, c.1690, 31 x 46 x 25 In. .. 2645.00
Table, James Martin, Free-Edge Single Plank, Tapered Dowel Legs, 14 x 72 3/4 x 16 In. .. 489.00
Table, John Meeks, Rococo, Rosewood, White Turtle Top, Cutout Carving, 1840s 2420.00
Table, Josef Hoffman, Wood, White Paint, c.1905, 28 7/8 x 26 7/8 In. 8050.00
Table, Kidney Shape, 2 Tiers, Contemporary, 50 x 29 x 19 In. 230.00
Table, Kingwood, Marble Top, Brass Mounted, Cabriole Legs, 30 x 26 In., Pair 950.00
Table, Kingwood, Marble Top, Frieze, End Drawer, Candle Slide, 1880s, 33 3/4 In. 1380.00
Table, Kittinger, New England Style, Mahogany, Tray Top, Candle Slides 745.00
Table, Knoll, Wood Grain, Metal Frame, 66 x 32 x 29 1/4 In. 1489.00
Table, Knoxville, Mahogany, 4 Cutout Legs, 29 x 24 In. 1100.00
Table, L. & J.G. Stickley, Mahogany, Dark Finish, 28 x 30 In. 800.00
Table, L. & J.G. Stickley, No. 515, Octagonal, Shelf, Foot Base, 21 x 24 In. 1500.00
Table, L. & J.G. Stickley, No. 530, Oak, Drawer, 1915, 29 In. 860.00
Table, L. & J.G. Stickley, No. 608, Shelf, Handcraft Mark, 23 x 24 In. .... *Illus* 4025.00
Table, L. & J.G. Stickley, Round Top, Overhang, Cross Stretcher, 29 1/2 x 36 In. 2070.00
Table, L. & J.G. Stickley, Round, Lower Shelf, Cross Stretchers, 24 x 29 In. 1150.00
Table, Lacquer, Black, Riverscape Scene, Chinese, 1715, 36 x 22 In. 9600.00
Table, Lacquer, Prunus, Brown, Gold, Chrysanthemum, 20th Century, 12 x 32 x 26 In. ... 60.00
Table, Le Corbusier, P. Jeanneret, C. Perriand, c.1930, 27 3/4 x 48 1/8 x 32 1/2 In. 6670.00
Table, Library, Aesthetic Revival, Rosewood, Oak, Burled Walnut, 29 x 45 x 29 In. ..10575.00
Table, Library, Arts & Crafts, Drawer, Ring Pulls, Macmurdo Feet, 29 1/2 x 48 x 35 In. .. 1380.00
Table, Library, Arts & Crafts, Mahogany, Drawer, 42 x 30 In. 160.00
Table, Library, Arts & Crafts, Oak, Drawer, Shelf, Hammered Pulls, 1912, 30 In. 520.00
Table, Library, Arts & Crafts, Oak, Drawer, Side Shelves, 1900s, 40 x 26 In. 345.00
Table, Library, Arts & Crafts, Oak, Drawers, Middle Shelf, 1900s, 36 x 24 In. 345.00
Table, Library, Arts & Crafts, Oak, Oval, Drawer, Side Shelves, H.P. Robertson, 29 In. ... 920.00
Table, Library, Arts & Crafts, Trestle, Keyed-Through Lower Shelf, 95 x 42 In. 1955.00
Table, Library, Drawer, Pillar Supports, Shelf Stretcher, 29 x 38 In. 315.00
Table, Library, Drawer, Trestle Base, 30 x 68 In. 115.00

Furniture, Table, Irving & Sasson,
Louis XV Style, Gilt, Metal,
Marquetry, 31 x 21 In.

Furniture, Table, L & J.G. Stickley,
No. 608, Shelf, Handcraft Mark,
23 x 24 In.

Table, Library, Edwardian, Oak, Stretcher, Victorian, 29 x 38 x 23 In. 1035.00
Table, Library, Elm Top, Bentwood Legs, Bronze Feet, 1948, 30 x 108 In. 10925.00
Table, Library, Elm, Leather Insert, Working & False Drawers, 1825, 31 In. 4800.00
Table, Library, Empire, Mahogany, Scrolled Pedestal Ends, Bowtie Footrest Stretcher 220.00
Table, Library, Federal, Mahogany, Lobed Leaves, Splayed Legs, Brass Feet, 29 x 41 In. . . 50.00
Table, Library, G. Stickley, 2 Drawers, Iron Hardware, 54 x 32 x 30 In. 3105.00
Table, Library, G. Stickley, Mahogany, 3 Drawers, Red Decal, 54 x 32 x 30 In. 4600.00
Table, Library, G. Stickley, No. 401, Mahogany, Red Decal, Signed, 48 x 29 In. 1265.00
Table, Library, G. Stickley, No. 614, Mahogany, 2 Drawers, 48 x 30 In. 1725.00
Table, Library, G. Stickley, No. 615, Mahogany, Leather Top, 48 x 30 In. 3000.00
Table, Library, G. Stickley, No. 637, Oak, Shelf, 28 1/2 x 48 In. 1200.00
Table, Library, G. Stickley, No. 651, Mahogany, Original Leather Top, 30 In. 4025.00
Table, Library, G. Stickley, Tacked-On Leather Top, Keyed-Through Tenon, 29 x 48 In. . . 3450.00
Table, Library, George IV, Mahogany, Paw Casters, Early 19th Century, 29 1/2 x 47 In. . . 4370.00
Table, Library, Hepplewhite, Mahogany, Doors, Oval, 29 1/2 x 48 x 32 1/2 In. 1120.00
Table, Library, Jacobean Style, Oak, Stained, Carved, 30 1/2 x 56 1/2 x 35 In. 2300.00
Table, Library, Jacobean, Oak, Glass Top, Leaves, Marked 1641, 30 x 73 x 25 In. 635.00
Table, Library, L. & J.G. Stickley, 2 Divided Shelves, Vertical Slats, 27 x 27 In. 11500.00
Table, Library, L. & J.G. Stickley, 2 Drawers, Rectangular Top, Signed, 48 x 29 In. 1495.00
Table, Library, L. & J.G. Stickley, Mahogany, Slatted Legs, Lower Shelf, 29 x 50 In. 1955.00
Table, Library, L. & J.G. Stickley, No. 530, Mahogany, Rectangular Top, 29 In. 1495.00
Table, Library, L. & J.G. Stickley, No. 531, Mahogany, Rectangular Top, 29 In. 980.00
Table, Library, L. & J.G. Stickley, No. 822, Mahogany, 2 Drawers, 48 x 30 x 29 In. 2760.00
Table, Library, L. & J.G. Stickley, Trestle, Heart-Shaped Legs, Shelf, 40 x 24 In. 1955.00
Table, Library, L. & J.G. Stickley, Trestle, Keyed-Through Sides, Label, 72 x 45 In. 4320.00
Table, Library, Lifetime, 2 Arched Drawers, Corbels, Lower Shelf, 29 x 52 x 24 In. 2300.00
Table, Library, Limbert, Blind Drawer, Writing Board, 42 x 26 x 29 In. 2070.00
Table, Library, Limbert, Mahogany, Dark Finish, Rectangular Top, Leather Cover, 29 In. . . 2415.00
Table, Library, Limbert, Mahogany, Turtle Top, Drawer, 48 x 28 x 29 In. 2000.00
Table, Library, Limbert, No. 146, Cutout Sides, Lower Shelf, 44 x 29 1/2 In. 1725.00
Table, Library, Limbert, Oak, Square Ebony Inlay, Drawer, 29 x 42 x 26 In. 2070.00
Table, Library, Limbert, Oval, Cutout Stretchers, Flaring Legs, 28 x 47 In. 7475.00
Table, Library, Limbert, Oval, Overhanging Top, Mortised Lower Shelf, 29 x 45 In. 2070.00
Table, Library, Mahogany, Bookrest Top, Candle Slides, 1880s, 29 In. 1265.00
Table, Library, Mahogany, Drop Leaf, Drawer, Hairy Legs, Paw Feet, c.1825, 28 In. 2350.00
Table, Library, Mahogany, Original Finish, 4 Canted Legs, 29 x 28 In. 1250.00
Table, Library, Mahogany, Scrolled, Carved Skirt, Lower Shelf, Pad Feet, 30 x 66 x 42 In. 1430.00
Table, Library, Mahogany, Sliding Extension Ends Under Top, 31 1/2 In. 5280.00
Table, Library, Mahogany, Tooled Leather Top, Casters, England, 1830, 55 x 26 In. 9500.00
Table, Library, Oak, Carved Mosaic, Carved Top, Drawer, Shelf, 28 x 45 1/2 x 30 In. . . . 1870.00
Table, Library, Oak, Carved Skirt, Turned Legs, Stretcher, 29 x 23 x 42 In. 615.00
Table, Library, Oak, Drawer, Reeded Legs, Shelf Stretcher, 29 x 38 In. 170.00
Table, Library, Rectangular Top, 2 Blind Drawers, 36 x 24 x 29 In. 2070.00
Table, Library, Renaissance Revival, Mahogany, Frieze, c.1890, 30 x 78 x 30 In. 1155.00
Table, Library, Rosewood, Gadroon Carved, Inlaid, Round, 31 x 50 In. 8340.00
Table, Library, Rosewood, Rounded Corners, Dowel Legs, Foil Label, 29 3/4 x 78 3/4 In. 405.00
Table, Library, Stickley & Brandt Co., Oak, 2 Drawers, 30 x 48 In. 1090.00
Table, Library, Stickley Bros., Leather Top, 29 1/2 x 46 In. 1440.00
Table, Library, Stickley Bros., Overhanging Top, 3 Drawers, Brass, 30 x 60 x 36 In. 1725.00
Table, Library, Stickley, 2 Drawers, Spindled Sides, Lower Shelf, 29 x 48 x 30 In. 1095.00
Table, Library, Stickley, No. 404, Oak, Keyed Mortise, c.1903, 28 x 24 x 36 In. 1495.00
Table, Library, Victorian, Mahogany, Burl, Rosewood, 2 Drawers, 29 x 36 In. 660.00
Table, Library, Walnut, Leather Top, Drawer, Female Mask On Base, Hoof Feet, 54 In. . . . 4140.00
Table, Library, Walnut, Short Drawer, Acanthus Leaf Legs, c.1900, 39 1/2 In. 600.00
Table, Library, William IV, Mahogany, Mid 19th Century, 29 1/4 x 59 1/2 x 35 1/2 In. . . 3220.00
Table, Limbert, Flared Legs, Circular, 23 x 30 In. 650.00
Table, Limbert, Mahogany, Original Finish, 4 Splayed Legs, 38 x 29 In. 2875.00
Table, Limbert, No. 101, Mahogany, Octagonal Top, Splayed Legs, 30 x 30 In. 520.00
Table, Limbert, No. 117, Mahogany, Circular Top, 4 Splayed Legs, 36 x 29 In. 990.00
Table, Limbert, No. 146, Mahogany, Splayed Slab Sides, 45 x 30 x 29 In. 2990.00
Table, Limbert, No. 148, Mahogany, Circular Top, Splayed Legs, 30 x 29 In. 4315.00
Table, Limbert, No. 153, Mahogany, Turtle Top, Slab Sides, 48 x 30 In. 3738.00
Table, Limbert, Rounded Corners, Arch Apron, Shelf, Cutouts, 30 x 34 In. . . . . *Illus* 24150.00

Remove crayon marks from wooden furniture by rubbing mayonnaise on the marks. Rub with a damp cloth about five minutes later.

Furniture, Table, Limbert,
Rounded Corners, Arch Apron,
Shelf, Cutouts, 30 x 34 In.

Furniture, Table, Limbert,
Square Top, Cutout Plank Sides,
Inset Shelf, 29 1/2 x 20 In.

Table, Limbert, Square Top, Cutout Plank Sides, Inset Shelf, 29 1/2 x 20 In. . . . . *Illus* 4315.00
Table, Limbert, Square Top, Plank Sides, Lower Shelf, 29 x 20 x 20 In. 4315.00
Table, Lloyd Loom, Chromium Plated, Lacquered Wood, 1930s, 17 1/2 x 27 In. 3000.00
Table, Louis Philippe, Cherry, Shelf, Trestle, Mid 19th Century, 28 x 15 x 14 In. 630.00
Table, Louis Sognot, Wood, Chrome Steel, 1930, 30 x 11 3/4 In. 6000.00
Table, Louis XV Style, Fruitwood, Oval, Inset Marble, Cabriole Legs, 20 x 29 x 20 In. 805.00
Table, Louis XV Style, Gilt, Cherubs Border, Onyx Inset, 30 x 23 In. 440.00
Table, Louis XV Style, Mahogany, Kidney-Shape, Drawers, Cabriole Legs, 24 x 13 In. . . . 705.00
Table, Louis XV Style, Mahogany, Marble Top, Gilt Bronze Mounted, Round, 33 x 23 In. . . 980.00
Table, Louis XV Style, Marquetry, Flowers, Fold-Down, Cabriole Legs, 29 x 35 x 35 In. . . 690.00
Table, Louis XV Style, Painted, Marble Top, Leaf Frieze, 19 x 41 x 20 In. 860.00
Table, Louis XV Style, Tulipwood, Bronze, 19th Century, 27 1/2 x 12 x 9 1/2 In. 4800.00
Table, Louis XV Style, Walnut, 20th Century, 28 3/4 x 20 1/4 x 14 1/4 In. 1150.00
Table, Louis XV Style, Walnut, Drawer, 18th Century, 32 3/4 x 20 1/4 x 27 In. 880.00
Table, Louis XV, Circular Marquetry Top, 22 1/2 In. 690.00
Table, Louis XV, Kingwood, Gilt Writing Surface, 3 Drawers, 30 x 29 In. 5175.00
Table, Louis XV, Mahogany, Floral Inlay, Serpentine Shirt, 31 x 23 In. 440.00
Table, Louis XV, Mahogany, Kidney-Shaped Marble Top, Bronze, 21 x 11 In. 690.00
Table, Louis XV, Oval Marble Top, Drawer, 30 x 22 x 16 In., Pair 8625.00
Table, Louis XV, Walnut, Marble, Cabriole Legs, Round, 15 In., Pair 1380.00
Table, Louis XVI Style, Chinoiserie, 30 x 20 1/4 x 12 1/2 In., Pair 2875.00
Table, Louis XVI Style, Kingwood, Tulipwood, Leather, 29 x 23 3/4 x 17 1/2 In. 865.00
Table, Louis XVI Style, Malachite Veneer, Bronze Dore, 22 x 28 x 15 1/2 In. 4600.00
Table, Louis XVI Style, Marquetry, Bronze Dore Mounted, 31 x 37 x 23 1/4 In. 1380.00
Table, Louis XVI Style, Ormolu, Vitrine, Glass Panel Top, c.1900, 30 x 25 x 17 In. 4140.00
Table, Louis XVI Style, Sycamore, Maple, Bronze Dore, Drawers, Victorian, 29 x 55 In. . 4370.00
Table, Louis XVI Style, Tulipwood, Parquetry, 19th Century, 21 x 21 1/2 x 15 In. 575.00
Table, Louis XVI Style, Walnut, Carved, Rounded Corners, 29 3/4 x 36 x 21 3/4 In. 288.00
Table, Louis XVI Style, Walnut, Parcel Gilt, Marble Top, Carved, 36 1/3 x 81 x 23 In. . . . 2300.00
Table, Louis XVI, Cherry, Inlaid, c.1770, 23 x 17 x 12 In. 750.00
Table, Louis XVI, Mahogany, Inlaid, Brass, 18th Century, 29 x 19 x 12 3/4 In. 2300.00
Table, Louis XVI, Mahogany, Tan Marble Top, 27 1/2 x 25 3/4 In. 2760.00
Table, Louis XVI, Wrought Iron, Marble Top, Scroll & Leaf Design, 56 x 21 x 34 In. 920.00
Table, Mahogany, Banded Inlay On Apron, D-Shape, 24 x 49 In. 300.00
Table, Mahogany, Brown Leather Inset Top, 4 Drawers, 18th Century, 28 x 36 In. 2530.00
Table, Mahogany, Canton Fish-Strainer Mazarine Top, 1800s, 16 x 14 In. 1920.00
Table, Mahogany, Concave Sides, Painted Flower Frieze, Osborne Cottage, 36 1/2 In. . . . 7800.00
Table, Mahogany, Crossbanded, Tambour Cupboard, 29 x 20 In. 1035.00
Table, Mahogany, Dense Plum Pudding Top, Hexagonal Pedestal 2875.00
Table, Mahogany, Egg & Dart Frieze, Scrolled Toes, 1820s, 28 1/2 x 24 In. 3900.00
Table, Mahogany, Flame Veneer, Marble Top, 1920s, 33 x 48 In. 1320.00
Table, Mahogany, Fretwork Gallery, Tripod, Carved Flower Heads On Feet, 29 1/2 In. . . . 6000.00
Table, Mahogany, Inlaid, Bellflower Detail, 6 Legs, 3 Leaves, 30 x 48 In. 1650.00
Table, Mahogany, Inlaid, Leaded Glass, Brass, Grand Rapids, Mich., 25 x 21 In. 560.00

Table, Mahogany, Inlaid, Lift Top, Swing Leg, Paine Furniture, 30 3/4 x 36 x 18 In. 670.00
Table, Mahogany, Inlay, 2 Drawers, 29 3/4 x 18 x 15 In., Pair .... *Illus* 2645.00
Table, Mahogany, Inset Glazed Panel, Crossbanded Stretcher, 27 3/4 In. 345.00
Table, Mahogany, Leaf-Carved Pedestal, Paw Feet, 1880s, 29 1/2 In. 1495.00
Table, Mahogany, Leaf-Carved Tripod Base, 20th Century, 26 x 24 In. 460.00
Table, Mahogany, Marble Top, 3 Drawers, 3/4 Gallery, 29 x 24 In. 460.00
Table, Mahogany, Marble Top, Blind Fretwork Frieze, 33 x 58 1/4 In., Pair 3900.00
Table, Mahogany, Marble Top, Scrolling Legs, Paw Feet, Ormolu Mounts, 27 x 38 In. ... 2300.00
Table, Mahogany, Marquetry, Enameled Glass, Water Lily, 1900, 55 x 19 In. 4800.00
Table, Mahogany, Pierced Scrollwork Stretcher, Center Finial, 26 3/4 x 25 In. 660.00
Table, Mahogany, Rectangular Top, Central Drawer, 29 In. 5640.00
Table, Mahogany, Rosewood Banding, Liner Interior, 1820s, 28 1/2 x 36 In. 1150.00
Table, Mahogany, Round Top, Pedestal, c.1810, 27 x 24 1/8 In. 450.00
Table, Mahogany, Satinwood, Spider Gateleg, Ring-Turned Legs, 1780s, 28 1/2 In. 8400.00
Table, Mahogany, Small Side Drawer, Platform Base, Casters, c.1825, 28 x 21 In. 900.00
Table, Mahogany, Stenciled Flowers, Bellflowers & Leaves, Flared Legs, 28 x 26 In. 385.00
Table, Mahogany, Sunburst On Top, Brass Gallery, Bamboo-Turned Legs, 25 1/2 In. 495.00
Table, Mahogany, Tilt Top, Cabriole Leg Tripod, Pad Feet, 28 3/4 x 23 1/2 x 17 3/8 In. .. 1380.00
Table, Mahogany, Trestle Supports, Splayed Bases, 1820s, 27 x 35 1/2 In. 750.00
Table, Mahogany, Turned Pedestal, Reeded Saber Legs, Brass Paw Feet, 29 x 48 x 58 In. .. 620.00
Table, Maple, Black Paint, Drawer, Stretcher Base, Turned Feet, 13 3/4 x 9 1/2 In. 550.00
Table, Maple, Figured, 1 Over 2 Small Drawers, Shaped Cutout, 28 x 23 x 19 In. 525.00
Table, Marble Top, 2 Leaf-Carved Lower Doors, Carved Leaves, 25 1/2 In., Pair 400.00
Table, Marble Top, Bowfront, 3 Scrolling Legs, 34 x 36 In. 920.00
Table, Marcel Breuer, No. B18, Glass, Chrome Plated, Thonet, c.1928, 31 x 26 In. 6900.00
Table, Marquetry, Scroll, Ball & Tapered Foot Stretcher, Fluted Legs, 44 In. 1840.00
Table, Maurice Champion, Sycamore, Round, c.1946 .... 12500.00
Table, Metal, Marble, Bowfront, Continental, 20th Century, 38 1/2 x 57 1/2 x 13 In. 335.00
Table, Moroccan, Ebony, Mother-Of-Pearl, Inlaid, Octagonal, Pair 865.00
Table, Napoleon III Style, Ebonized, Late 19th Century, 29 1/2 x 22 3/4 x 18 3/4 In. 460.00
Table, Napoleon III, Ebonized, Gilt Bronze, Drawers, Tooled Leather Top, 56 x 26 In. ... 4315.00
Table, Napoleon III, Gilt Bronze, Porcelain Mounted, Late 19th Century, 31 1/2 In. 20300.00
Table, Neoclassical, Circular Black Marble Top, Paw Feet, 28 x 26 In. 1840.00
Table, Neoclassical, Mahogany, 2 Tiers, Gilt Bronze Mounted, 36 x 33 x 22 In. 3450.00
Table, Neoclassical, Mahogany, Mid 19th Century, 29 1/2 x 45 In. 2530.00
Table, Neoclassical, Mahogany, Ring-Turned Trestle Base, Sunderland, 1900, 23 In. 980.00
Table, Nesting, Aalto, Birch, Circular Top, 3 Laminated Legs, 17 x 13 In. 220.00
Table, Nesting, Edwardian Style, Satinwood, Trestle, 25 x 21 x 14 In., 3 Piece 1380.00
Table, Nesting, Galle, Cityscapes On 3, Floral On 4th, Signed, 29 x 23 In., 4 Piece 2300.00
Table, Nesting, Galle, Fruitwood, Sailboat, Shoreline, 26 In., 19 In., 14 In., 3 Piece 2000.00
Table, Nesting, Galle, Marquetry, Signed, 29 x 23 x 14 In., 3 Piece 2300.00
Table, Nesting, Mahogany Inlay, Faux Bamboo Supports, 24 x 19 x 13 In., 3 Piece 225.00
Table, Nesting, Mahogany, Marquetry, 20th Century, 29 In., 4 Piece 690.00
Table, Nesting, Mahogany, Saber Legs, Turned Stretchers, England, 27 In., 4 Piece 330.00
Table, Nesting, Marcel Breuer, Birch Veneer, c.1936, 14 5/8 x 18 x 24 In., 3 Piece 6325.00
Table, Nesting, Oak, Carved Sides, Front, Drawer, 20 x 18 1/2 In., 3 Piece 225.00
Table, Nesting, Oak, Shaped Side Aprons, Turned Legs, Stretcher Base, 3 Piece 225.00
Table, Nesting, William IV, Mahogany, Lacquered, Oriental Landscape, 30 In., 3 Piece ... 1840.00
Table, Oak, Drawer, Turned Legs, Claw & Ball Feet, Bronze Mounts, 29 x 28 x 50 In. 465.00
Table, Oak, Inset Leather Writing Surface, Square Legs, 1870s, 30 x 21 In. 920.00
Table, Oak, Stretcher Base, Open Rope-Twist Legs, Century Furniture, 27 1/2 x 24 In. ... 300.00
Table, Oak, Tapered Legs, Drawer, 1800s, 30 x 29 In. 1680.00
Table, Oak, Winged Griffin Supports, Carved Apron, 10 Leaves, Square, 54 In. 7840.00
Table, Old Hickory, Mahogany, Circular V-Board Top, 30 In. 550.00
Table, Old Hickory, Oak Top, Cross Stretchers, 3-Leg Base, 30 x 30 In. 550.00
Table, Oriental, Teak, Openworked Apron, Polished Stone Inset, 31 x 16 x 12 In. 220.00
Table, Painted, Flowers, Ribbons, Round, Pedestal Base, 3-Part Foot, 30 x 23 In., Pair ... 1095.00
Table, Parquetry, Round, Platform Stretcher, Continental, 29 3/4 x 17 7/8 In. 530.00
Table, Pembroke, Cherry, Band Inlay, Drawer, Brass Pull, 32 1/4 In. 825.00
Table, Pembroke, Cherry, Figured, Tapered Legs, 29 x 22 x 36 In. 120.00
Table, Pembroke, Chippendale Style, Mahogany, Serpentine Top, 29 x 39 x 19 In. 300.00
Table, Pembroke, Chippendale, Mahogany, Reeded Legs, Square Feet, 28 x 29 In. 3290.00
Table, Pembroke, Chippendale, Maple, Figured, c.1790, 28 x 20 x 30 In. 3600.00

Furniture, Table,
Mahogany, Inlay,
2 Drawers,
29 3/4 x 18 x 15 In.,
Pair

To remove a stain from a polished granite top, mix the center of some slices of white bread with 6% hydrogen peroxide. Put the paste on the stain overnight. Wash off the next day and the stain should be gone.

Table, Pembroke, Drop Leaf, George VI, Mahogany, c.1840, 29 1/2 x 33 x 20 In.	1120.00
Table, Pembroke, Drop Leaf, Georgian Style, Mahogany, c.1840, 28 3/4 x 16 x 4 In.	785.00
Table, Pembroke, Drop Leaf, Hepplewhite Style, Satinwood, Inlay, Drawer, 26 x 18 In. . .	920.00
Table, Pembroke, Drop Leaf, Mahogany, Drawer, Cabriole Legs, c.1780, 28 In.	8400.00
Table, Pembroke, Drop Leaf, Mahogany, Drawer, D-Shape Leaves, Brass Casters, 1810 . .	890.00
Table, Pembroke, Drop Leaf, Mahogany, Drawer, D-Shape Leaves, Brass Casters, 29 In. .	615.00
Table, Pembroke, Drop Leaf, Mahogany, Serpentine Top, Drawer, c.1900, 28 In.	660.00
Table, Pembroke, Drop Leaf, Tiger Maple, c.1840, 26 x 26 x 22 In.	1500.00
Table, Pembroke, Drop Leaf, William IV, Mahogany, Reeded Legs, 1830, 29 In.	1065.00
Table, Pembroke, Federal, Cherry, Oval Top, Drawer, Beaded Legs, 1800, 28 1/2 In.	980.00
Table, Pembroke, Federal, Mahogany Veneer, 1815-1820, 27 1/2 x 35 3/4 x 21 1/2 In. . . .	980.00
Table, Pembroke, Federal, Mahogany, Inlaid, c.1810, 28 1/2 x 35 x 33 1/3 In.	3300.00
Table, Pembroke, Federal, Mahogany, Line Inlay, Square Tapered Legs, 28 In.	4700.00
Table, Pembroke, Federal, Mahogany, Rectangular Top, Square Tapered Legs, 29 In.	600.00
Table, Pembroke, George III, Mahogany, 4 Splayed, Reeded Legs, 29 x 25 In.	2300.00
Table, Pembroke, George III, Mahogany, Chamfered Legs, 27 x 37 3/4 x 37 3/4 In.	1265.00
Table, Pembroke, George III, Mahogany, Oval Top, 26 3/4 x 38 1/2 x 30 In.	800.00
Table, Pembroke, George III, Mahogany, Pedestal, c.1840, 28 3/4 x 22 x 25 3/4 In.	1176.00
Table, Pembroke, George III, Mahogany, Reeded Edge, c.1800, 28 1/2 x 37 x 36 In.	2070.00
Table, Pembroke, George III, Mahogany, Rounded Corners, 27 1/2 x 40 x 28 3/4 In.	865.00
Table, Pembroke, George IV, Mahogany, Casters, c.1830, 28 x 21 1/2 x 30 In.	840.00
Table, Pembroke, George IV, Mahogany, Pedestal, c.1820, 27 x 44 x 39 In.	1725.00
Table, Pembroke, George IV, Mahogany, Rectangular Top, Turned Legs, 28 1/4 In.	690.00
Table, Pembroke, Hepplewhite, Cherry, Shaped Corners, Lipped Drawer, Tapered Legs . .	390.00
Table, Pembroke, Hepplewhite, Mahogany, Drawer, Leaves, England, 19 x 28 In.	715.00
Table, Pembroke, Hepplewhite, Mahogany, Tapered Legs, Drawer, 20 x 34 x 29 In.	880.00
Table, Pembroke, Kittinger, Hepplewhite, Mahogany, D-Shape Leaves, 30 x 19 In.	330.00
Table, Pembroke, Mahogany Veneer, Splayed Square Legs, 1795-1810, 28 In.	4900.00
Table, Pembroke, Mahogany, c.1830, 27 3/4 x 19 x 34 In.	1345.00
Table, Pembroke, Mahogany, Drawer, Brass Pull, Tapered Legs, 29 1/2 x 30 x 20 In.	770.00
Table, Pembroke, Mahogany, Drawer, Brass Pulls, 25 x 26 1/2 In.	410.00
Table, Pembroke, Mahogany, Drawer, D-Shape Leaves, 28 1/2 x 47 x 36 In.	5300.00
Table, Pembroke, Mahogany, Frieze, Short Drawers, Turned Legs, c.1830, 40 3/4 In.	785.00
Table, Pembroke, Mahogany, Line Inlay Around Leaves, Drawer, 28 1/2 In.	1750.00
Table, Pembroke, Mahogany, Marquetry, Leaves, Drawer, Bellflower, 1830s, 28 In.	4480.00
Table, Pembroke, Regency, Mahogany, Drawer, Bail Brass Pull, Tapered, Casters	550.00
Table, Pembroke, Sheraton, Cherry, Dovetailed Drawer, Turned Legs, 29 x 30 x 48 In. . . .	405.00
Table, Pembroke, Sheraton, Cherry, Shaped Leaves, Turned Legs, 35 x 18 1/2 In.	635.00
Table, Pembroke, Sheraton, Mahogany, Inlay, c.1830, 29 x 21 1/2 x 33 In.	1065.00
Table, Pembroke, Sheraton, Mahogany, Rope-Twist Legs, Brass Caps, Casters	770.00
Table, Pier, Chippendale, Mahogany, 1760-1780, 27 1/2 x 30 1/2 x 17 1/2 In.	6465.00
Table, Pier, Hepplewhite, Mahogany, Crossbanded, Rectangular, 1800, 42 x 19 In.	470.00
Table, Pier, Mahogany, Marble Top, Mirror Backplate, Paw Feet, c.1840, 33 x 36 x 17 In.	4465.00
Table, Pier, Neoclassical, Inlaid, Stencil, Gilt, Marble Top, 1840, 39 x 41 1/2 x 19 In. . . .	10000.00
Table, Pier, Neoclassical, Mahogany, Carved, 19th Century, 35 1/2 x 47 x 19 1/4 In.	5875.00
Table, Pine Top, 3 Drawers, Molded Lip, Wood Pulls, Turned Legs, 29 1/2 x 54 x 30 In. . .	770.00

Table, Pine Top, Drawer, X-Stretcher, Old Paint, New England, 29 x 25 x 25 In. 1870.00
Table, Pine Top, Pine, 2 Scratch-Beaded Drawers, Overhang, Red Paint, 28 x 60 x 38 In. . 990.00
Table, Pine, Drawer, Scalloped Apron, Stretcher Base, 28 1/4 x 43 x 23 In. 670.00
Table, Pine, Drawer, Shaped Apron, Stretcher Base, 29 x 58 1/2 x 29 In. 560.00
Table, Pine, Drawer, Tapered Legs, H-Stretcher, 27 x 45 1/2 x 33 1/2 In. 250.00
Table, Pine, Faux Tortoiseshell, Compass-Rays Border, Ebonized, 33 x 53 1/2 In. 2875.00
Table, Pine, Inset Red & White Top, Leaf Edge, Fluted Legs, Italy, 16 x 25 In. 545.00
Table, Pine, Maple, Drawer, Brass Rosette Knobs, Tapered Legs, 27 x 18 x 22 1/2 In. 280.00
Table, Pine, Maple, Original Red Paint, Turned Columnar Legs, 28 1/2 In. 2185.00
Table, Pine, Oriental Landscape, Scrolled Feet, 28 x 31 In. 1725.00
Table, Pine, Painted, Overhanging Top, D-Shape, 3 Beaded Square Legs, 29 x 40 In. 460.00
Table, Pine, Sawbuck Trestle, Iron Braces On Stretcher, 28 x 66 1/2 In. 440.00
Table, Pine, Trestle, 30 x 72 In. 785.00
Table, Poplar, Mortise & Tenon, Green Paint, 3-Board Top, 28 x 60 1/2 x 42 1/2 In. 660.00
Table, Poplar, Yellow Repaint, Gray Traces, 1-Board Top, Mortised, 39 x 15 x 26 In. 690.00
Table, Porch, Bamboo, Glass Top, 40 x 27 x 30 In. 145.00
Table, Pyrographic, Intersecting Shaped Legs, Folding, Hinged, 1900s, 25 x 24 In. 520.00
Table, Queen Anne Style, Burl Walnut Veneers, Plexiglas Top, 26 x 38 In. 145.00
Table, Queen Anne Style, Burl Walnut, Early 20th Century, 28 3/4 x 31 3/4 x 20 In. 225.00
Table, Queen Anne Style, Mahogany, Marble Top, Drawer, Turned Legs, 28 x 27 In. 1070.00
Table, Queen Anne Style, Walnut, Pad Feet, Early 20th Century, 30 3/4 x 36 x 22 In. 920.00
Table, Queen Anne, Cherry, Black Paint, Mid 18th Century, 26 1/2 x 29 1/2 x 30 3/4 In. . 8625.00
Table, Queen Anne, Tiger Maple, Molded Edge, Paneled Feet, 28 x 29 x 20 In. 20700.00
Table, Queen Anne, Walnut, Rectangular Top, 3 Thumb Drawers, 29 In. 2415.00
Table, Queen Anne, Walnut, Swing Legs, Cabriole Legs, Refinished, 1790, 54 x 44 In. . . . 1045.00
Table, Refectory, 1-Board Top, 3 Drawers, Stretcher Base, 31 x 90 x 25 In. 2600.00
Table, Refectory, Cherry, Round, Planked, 29 1/2 x 75 x 29 1/2 In. 1095.00
Table, Refectory, French Provincial, Cherry, Planked Top, 30 x 69 x 31 3/4 In. 2115.00
Table, Refectory, Louis Philippe, Fruitwood, Stretcher Shelf, 32 1/2 x 24 1/2 x 32 In. . . . 4370.00
Table, Refectory, Pine, Rectangular Top, Canted Lyre Supports, Spain, 30 x 31 In. 1035.00
Table, Refectory, Walnut, Plank Top, Early 18th Century, 107 x 27 In. 6325.00
Table, Regency, Bird's-Eye Maple, Trictrac, 4 Splayed Legs, 28 x 41 x 21 In. 2300.00
Table, Regency, Black Japanned, Parcel Gilt, Chinoiserie, Drawer, 1810, 36 In. 9600.00
Table, Regency, Mahogany, Crossbanded Edge, Pedestal, Round, c.1810, 30 x 21 In. 635.00
Table, Regency, Mahogany, Rosette Splashboard, 2 Frieze Drawers, 40 1/2 In. 2070.00
Table, Regency, Mahogany, Round Top, Molded Edge, 3-Part Base, 30 x 53 In. 2760.00
Table, Regency, Mahogany, Round, Triangular Base, Early 19th Century, 29 x 44 In. 1725.00
Table, Regency, Oak, Figured Band, Early 19th Century, 29 1/2 x 51 In. 8338.00
Table, Regency, Oak, Greek-Key Inlay, Tooled Leather Top, Splayed Legs, 30 x 34 In. . . . 1265.00
Table, Renaissance Revival, Fruitwood, Marquetry, Drawer, c.1875, 30 x 54 In. 2530.00
Table, Renaissance Revival, Walnut, Angular Leaves, Greek-Key Bands, 29 In. 1035.00
Table, Renaissance Revival, Walnut, Carved Panels, Square Pedestal, c.1890 . . . . 490.00
Table, Renaissance Revival, Walnut, Marble Top, 35 x 22 In. 1495.00
Table, Renaissance Revival, Walnut, Marble, Turtle Top, 29 1/2 x 26 x 37 In. 670.00
Table, Robsjohn-Gibbings, Mahogany, Widdicomb, 32 x 22 1/2 In. 300.00
Table, Robsjohn-Gibbings, Walnut, Sorrel Finish, 1952, 53 1/2 In. 4025.00
Table, Rococo Revival, Floral Marquetry, Round, Italy, 30 3/4 x 49 In. 3450.00
Table, Rococo Revival, Italian Giltwood, Marble Top, 28 1/2 x 27 In. 5520.00
Table, Rococo Revival, Rosewood, American, Mid 19th Century, 30 x 47 1/2 x 32 In. . . . 9200.00
Table, Rococo Revival, Walnut, Marquetry, Serpentine, 19th Century, 29x 28 x 14 1/2 In. . 805.00
Table, Rococo Revival, Walnut, Serpentine Marble Top, 28 1/2 x 30 x 16 In. 865.00
Table, Rococo, Gilt, Marble, Classical Mask Frieze, Claw Feet, 34 x 62 x 29 In. 8050.00
Table, Rococo, Painted, Porringer Top, Continental, 18th Century, 29 1/2 x 35 x 23 In. . . . 3105.00
Table, Rococo, Porcelain, Blue, Twisted Standard, Tripod, Germany, 25 x 18 In., Pair 2875.00
Table, Rose Tarlow, Black, Scarlet Lacquer, Pair Of Birds, 29 1/2 In. 8340.00
Table, Rosewood Veneer, Marble Top, Duck-Head Knees, c.1860, 30 x 35 In. 1065.00
Table, Rosewood, Banded, Raised Top, Turned Standard, 3-Part Base, 28 x 45 In. 4300.00
Table, Rosewood, Carved Leaves, Various Animals, Indo-Burmese, 28 x 54 In. 1035.00
Table, Rosewood, Cylindrical Standard, Scrolled Toes, 1820s, 47 In. 4600.00
Table, Rosewood, Figured Top, 3-Part Platform, Bun Feet, 1820s, 28 1/2 x 51 In. 4600.00
Table, Rosewood, Inset Royal Copenhagen Tiles, Denmark, 17 x 18 1/2 In. 355.00
Table, Rosewood, Marble Top, Carving, Chinese, Mid 19th Century, 31 1/4 x 16 x 12 In. . 316.00
Table, Rosewood, Marble Turtle Top, Dog On Cross Stretchers, 29 x 36 x 24 In. 1815.00

Table, S. Huneck, Dachshunds, Pair, On Hind Legs, 1990, 24 x 24 In. 290.00
Table, Satinwood, Banded Oval Top, Flowers, Wreath, Square Tapered Legs, 30 In. 2300.00
Table, Sawbuck, Oval Top, Square Nails In Base, 27 1/2 x 23 3/4 In. 550.00
Table, Sawbuck, Pine, 2-Board Top, Square-Head Nails, 26 x 72 In. 660.00
Table, Sawbuck, Pine, 4-Board Top, Breadboard Ends, Peaked Stretcher, 48 In. 440.00
Table, Sawbuck, Pine, 66 x 34 x 29 In. 495.00
Table, Sawbuck, Pine, Square-Nail Construction, Storage Well, 27 x 29 1/2 In. 990.00
Table, Sawbuck, Rosehead Nails, Dovetailed Stretcher Base, 18th Century 3800.00
Table, Scene Of Aesop's Fable, Fox & Crane, Inlaid Top, Carved Stretcher, 51 In. 4750.00
Table, Sewing, Arts & Crafts, Oak, Gallery, 24 x 48 x 34 In. 225.00
Table, Sewing, Cherry, Dovetailed Drawers, Turned Pulls, 28 1/2 x 55 In. 1760.00
Table, Sewing, Cherry, Drawer, 3-Board Top, Square Tapered Legs, Pa., 55 x 36 In. 1365.00
Table, Sewing, Cherry, Drawer, Brass Pull, 27 x 30 In. 990.00
Table, Sewing, Cherry, Mahogany, Fitted Drawer, 20 1/2 x 27 In. 3900.00
Table, Sewing, Cherry, Pegged Construction, 2-Board Top, 28 x 36 In. 410.00
Table, Sewing, Curly Maple, 2 Divided Drawers, Batwing Brasses, 28 1/2 In. 2530.00
Table, Sewing, Drop Leaf, Empire, Mahogany, 2 Drawers, Turned Legs 120.00
Table, Sewing, Drop Leaf, Grain Painted Red Orange, 2 Drawers, 29 x 16 In. 345.00
Table, Sewing, Drop Leaf, Sheraton, Tiger Maple Top, 2 Stained Mahogany Drawers 495.00
Table, Sewing, Drop Leaves, Turned Legs, Red 500.00
Table, Sewing, Egyptian Revival, Bird's-Eye Maple, Ebonized, Bronze, 25 x 20 x 27 In. . . 2240.00
Table, Sewing, Faux Marble Top, 2 Dovetailed Drawers, Wood Knobs, 1900s, 36 In. 55.00
Table, Sewing, Federal, Mahogany Veneer, Faux Bamboo, 3 Drawers, 28 In. 3740.00
Table, Sewing, Federal, Mahogany, Maple Veneer, 2 Drawers, Turned Feet, 29 In. 6325.00
Table, Sewing, Federal, Mahogany, Rectangular Top, 2 Graduated Drawers, 30 In. 630.00
Table, Sewing, Federal, Maple, Figured, 2 Drawers, 19th Century, 27 x 18 x 21 In. 1060.00
Table, Sewing, Federal, Maple, Figured, Early 19th Century, 29 x 20 x 19 In. 940.00
Table, Sewing, Federal, Maple, Pine, Birch, c.1825, 29 1/2 x 16 1/2 x 16 1/2 In. 400.00
Table, Sewing, Federal, Tiger Maple, Early 1800s, 17 3/4 x 27 1/2 x 16 3/4 In. 980.00
Table, Sewing, Federal, Tiger Maple, New England, 1800-1810, 29 1/2 x 20 x 15 3/4 In. . . 1955.00
Table, Sewing, George III, Medallion Painting Of Mother & Children, 27 In. 3450.00
Table, Sewing, Hepplewhite, Pine, 2 Large Drawers, 61 x 42 In. 605.00
Table, Sewing, Lift Top, Overall Gilt & Floral, 29 x 13 In. 1150.00
Table, Sewing, Louis Philippe, Fruitwood, 2 Drawers, Mid 1800s, 26 x 18 x 12 In. 690.00
Table, Sewing, Mahogany, 2 Divided Drawers, Rockingham Pulls, 29 In. 1760.00
Table, Sewing, Mahogany, 2 Drawers, Square Pedestal, Casters, 28 3/4 x 17 3/4 In. 355.00
Table, Sewing, Mahogany, 2 Short Drawers, Dragon-Carved Rail, c.1825, 29 In. 1665.00
Table, Sewing, Mahogany, Drop Leaf, Finials, 2 Drawers, Square Base, Scrolled Feet 145.00
Table, Sewing, Mahogany, Gallery Top, 2 Drawers, Shelf Stretcher, 27 x 19 In. 490.00
Table, Sewing, Mahogany, Lift Top, Adjustable Surface, 29 x 22 x 18 In. 3220.00
Table, Sewing, Mahogany, Octagonal Compartment On Top, Lift Top, Silk Cover, 30 In. . . 580.00
Table, Sewing, Mahogany, Scroll Feet, 28 1/2 x 20 1/2 x 19 In. 1150.00
Table, Sewing, Maple, 2 Drawers, Frieze, Brass Hardware, Button Feet, c.1815, 34 In. . . . 9000.00
Table, Sewing, Maple, Canted Corners, Straight Skirt, Tapered Legs, 28 x 21 In. 2875.00
Table, Sewing, Martha Washington, Mahogany, 3 Dovetailed Drawers, 29 x 27 In. 110.00
Table, Sewing, Napoleon III, Mahogany, Frieze Drawer, Stretcher, 30 x 31 x 17 In. 345.00
Table, Sewing, Neoclassical, Mahogany, Rectangular Hinged Top, 31 1/2 In. 375.00
Table, Sewing, Neoclassical, Mahogany, Stepped Base, 28 3/4 x 21 x 15 1/2 In. 430.00
Table, Sewing, Neoclassical, Mahogany, Walnut Panel, Drawer, Basket, 29 x 18 x 14 In. . . 275.00
Table, Sewing, Oak Base, Walnut Veneer Top, Arts & Crafts, Germany, 32 x 24 In. 460.00
Table, Sewing, Oak, Marble Top, Tiled Back, 2 Drawers, 44 x 48 In. 500.00
Table, Sewing, Pine, Drawer, Porcelain Pull, Tapered Legs, 47 1/2 x 35 x 29 1/4 In. 880.00
Table, Sewing, Pine, Robin's-Egg Blue Paint, Square Nails, Square Legs, 25 3/4 In. 940.00
Table, Sewing, Rococo Revival, Rosewood, Lift Top, Cabriole Legs, 32 x 21 x 16 In. 2300.00
Table, Sewing, Sheraton, Cherry, 2 Maple Front Drawers, 1830s 995.00
Table, Sewing, Sheraton, Lift Top, False Drawer Front, Distressed, 26 x 24 x 12 In. 330.00
Table, Sewing, Tiger Maple, 2 Drawers, Dark Finish 7150.00
Table, Sewing, Tiger Maple, Mid Atlantic, Early 19th Century, 27 1/2 x 17 3/4 In. 980.00
Table, Sewing, Walnut, 2 Drawers, Pegged Construction, 28 3/4 x 47 In. 440.00
Table, Sewing, Walnut, Drawer With Wooden Pull, 27 x 66 3/4 In. 440.00
Table, Sewing, Walnut, Mahogany Veneer, 2 Drawers, Turned Legs, 30 x 21 x 21 In. 165.00
Table, Sheraton, Satinwood Panel, Serpentine Front, 36 x 17 1/2 x 29 In. 5500.00
Table, Side, Art Deco, Round Mirror Top, Chrome Scroll Supports, 27 x 26 In. 1035.00

Table, Side, Federal, Mahogany, Lyre Base, 30 x 34 In. 440.00
Table, Side, G. Nelson, Birch, Leather Top, Herman Miller, 1947, 22 1/2 x 30 In. 575.00
Table, Side, G. Stickley, Mahogany, Poppy Top & Shelf, Reticulated Legs, 23 x 19 In. 4315.00
Table, Side, Galle, Art Nouveau, Inlaid Poppies, Scalloped Edge, Fluted Legs, 30 In. 2070.00
Table, Side, George III, Rosewood, Tulipwood, Inlaid, 2 Drawers, 30 x 19 3/4 In. 9000.00
Table, Side, Hepplewhite Style, Mahogany, Satinwood, Floral, Inlaid, 27 1/2 In., Pair 950.00
Table, Side, Hepplewhite Style, Walnut, Drawer, Legs, 29 1/2 x 28 x 20 In. 140.00
Table, Side, Limbert, Square Top, Rounded Corners, Cutout Plank Sides, Shelf, 29 In. 4315.00
Table, Side, Louis XV, Kingwood, Bronze Mounted, Drawer, 30 x 18 x 13 5/8 In., Pair . .   390.00
Table, Side, Louis XVI, Oval Marble Top, Marquetry Frieze, 26 x 17 x 13 In. 1495.00
Table, Side, Louis XVI, Oval Marble Top, Pierced Gallery, 1 Drawer, 29 x 23 x 17 In. 1495.00
Table, Side, Mahogany, Drawer, 29 x 15 x 15 In. 60.00
Table, Side, Mahogany, Drawer, Pedestal Base, 29 x 24 In. 250.00
Table, Side, Neoclassical, Bird's-Eye Maple, Splayed Feet, Round, 32 In., Pair 835.00
Table, Side, Neoclassical, Mahogany, Dish Top, Drawer, Square Legs, 28 x 21 In., Pair . .   1090.00
Table, Side, Oak, Round, 3 Legs, Carved Top, Leaves, 20 1/2 x 18 1/2 In. 170.00
Table, Side, Old Hickory, Circular Chamfered Board Top, 25 x 28 In. 1150.00
Table, Side, Queen Anne, Drawer, Pod Feet, 1700s, 26 x 16 x 26 In. 460.00
Table, Side, Queen Anne, Faux Drawer Front, Pod Feet, Late 1700s, 22 x 14 x 25 In. 345.00
Table, Side, Teak, Inlaid, Mother-Of-Pearl, Granite, Flowers, Barrel, 1870, 21 x 18 In. . . .   390.00
Table, Side, Victorian, Walnut, Marble Top, Burl Trim, 29 x 29 x 21 In. 280.00
Table, Side, Walnut, Slab Top, 2 Molded Drawers, Italy, 1900s, 40 x 17 x 32 In. 230.00
Table, Side, Wegner, Teak, Triangular Shape, 3 Legs, Carl Hansen, 1956, 17 1/2 In. 575.00
Table, Side, Wicker, White, Round Top, Lower Shelf, 4 Flaring Legs, 1910, 30 In. 210.00
Table, Side, William & Mary, Birch, Pine, Oval, Ring-Turned Legs, 24 x 33 In. 8050.00
Table, Side, William IV, Mahogany, Bowed Top, 2 Drawers, Splayed Legs, 36 In. 1495.00
Table, Side, William IV, Mahogany, Frieze Drawer, Rectangular Top, 32 1/2 In. 690.00
Table, Side, Windsor, Pine, Breadboard Ends, Turned Legs, New England, 20 x 29 In. . . .   2415.00
Table, Softwood, Pine Top, Drawer, 2-Board Top, Old Paint, 29 x 48 x 26 1/2 In. 1100.00
Table, Stickley Bros., Drawer, Lower Shelf, Wooden Knobs, 21 x 17 x 29 In. 1600.00
Table, Stickley Bros., No. 250, Circular Top, Lower Shelf, Paper Label, 24 x 30 In. 950.00
Table, Stickley Bros., Round Top, Tacked-On Leather, Square Shelf, 30 x 26 In. 1265.00
Table, Stickley, Octagonal Top, Lower Shelf, Shoe Base, 21 x 21 x 24 In. 1500.00
Table, Stickley, Pegged Construction, 29 1/4 x 96 x 23 3/4 In. . . . . *Illus* 11500.00
Table, Tavern, Black Paint, Vase & Ring Turned, Stretcher Base, Late 1700s 750.00
Table, Tavern, Cherry, Painted, Stretcher Base, Oval, 18th Century, 25 x 27 x 21 In. 3680.00
Table, Tavern, Curly Maple, Scalloped Aprons, Pad Feet, 20th Century, 26 1/2 In. 990.00
Table, Tavern, Dovetailed Drawer, Square Tapered Legs, 18th Century, 27 x 35 In. 400.00
Table, Tavern, Maple, Drawer, 26 x 41 1/2 x 24 1/2 In. 1150.00
Table, Tavern, Maple, Pine, Breadboard Ends, 27 1/2 x 46 3/4 In. 4125.00
Table, Tavern, Maple, Pine, Drawer, Stretcher Base, Turned Legs, 1700s, 25 x 32 In. 5175.00
Table, Tavern, Maple, Poplar, Drawer, 2-Board Top, Pegged, Refinished, 33 x 23 In. 495.00
Table, Tavern, Oak, Frieze Drawers, Turned Legs, 29 x 33 In. 575.00
Table, Tavern, Pine Top, Maple Base, Drawer, c.1760-1780, 27 x 46 3/4 x 28 In. 11500.00
Table, Tavern, Pine, Cherry Base, Baluster-Turned Legs, 1760-1780, 25 In. 1610.00
Table, Tavern, Pine, Maple, Oval Top, Splayed Legs, 18th Century, 24 x 25 x 33 In. 2300.00
Table, Tavern, Pine, Porringer Shape, 32 1/2 x 26 In. 1120.00
Table, Tavern, Queen Anne, Mahogany, Short Next To Long Drawer, 29 1/2 x 48 x 29 In. . .   5300.00
Table, Tavern, Queen Anne, Maple, 4-Board Top, Beaded Aprons, 36 x 23 In. 825.00
Table, Tavern, Queen Anne, Padded Disc Feet, 18th Century, 26 1/2 x 31 x 25 In. 1295.00
Table, Tavern, Queen Anne, Ring-Turned Cuffs, Rosehead Nails, 26 1/2 x 26 1/2 In. 1980.00
Table, Tavern, Red Wash, Drawer, Overhanging Top, American 880.00
Table, Tavern, Red, Drawer, Tapered Legs, Breadboard Top, Wood Knob, 27 In. 1380.00
Table, Tavern, Walnut, 2-Board Top, Long Drawer, Vase-Turned Legs, Stretchers, Pa. 660.00
Table, Tavern, William & Mary, Maple, Breadboard Top, Knob Feet, 15 x 25 In. 2530.00
Table, Tavern, William & Mary, Maple, Red Paint, 39 x 25 In. 3740.00
Table, Tavern, William & Mary, Walnut, Drawer, 18th Century, 25 x 22 1/2 x 31 In. 10800.00
Table, Tea, Arts & Crafts, Round Top, Apron, Lower Shelf, Cross Stretchers, 30 x 35 In. .   575.00
Table, Tea, Cherry, 2-Board Top, 18th Century, 26 1/2 x 36 1/4 x 27 1/2 In. 11550.00
Table, Tea, Chippendale, Mahogany, Dish Top, Birdcage Center, Tripod, 27 x 25 In. 690.00
Table, Tea, G. Stickley, No. 608, Mahogany, 26 x 24 In. 1500.00
Table, Tea, George I, Walnut, Foldover, Hinged Top, 29 x 34 x 32 In. 2185.00
Table, Tea, George II, Mahogany, Rectangular Dish Top, Ireland, 32 x 21 In. 9000.00

Table, Tea, George III, Mahogany, Foldover, c.1770, 29 3/4 x 35 3/4 x 17 3/4 In. 2645.00
Table, Tea, L. & J.G. Stickley, No. 608, Circular, Lower Shelf, 23 x 24 In. 4025.00
Table, Tea, L. & J.G. Stickley, Round, Overhang, Arched Stretchers, c.1910, 29 x 42 In. . . 1495.00
Table, Tea, Mahogany, 1-Board Top, Snake Feet Dovetailed Into Rings, 28 In. 715.00
Table, Tea, Mahogany, Acanthus Leaf Panels, England, 28 3/4 In. 660.00
Table, Tea, Mahogany, Candle Slides, Carved Shells, 20th Century, 25 1/2 In. 190.00
Table, Tea, Mahogany, Dish Top, Turned Pedestal, Tripod, Slipper Feet, 29 1/2 x 24 In. . . 980.00
Table, Tea, Mahogany, Padded Snake Feet, 27 In. 360.00
Table, Tea, Overhanging Breadboard Top, Square Tapered Legs, Button Feet, 26 x 31 In. . . 980.00
Table, Tea, Queen Anne, Mahogany, Tray Top, 27 3/4 x 28 x 19 1/8 In. 6325.00
Table, Tea, Queen Anne, Maple, Oval Top, Black Paint, Rhode Island, 26 x 30 x 25 In. . . . 1610.00
Table, Tea, Sectioned Interior, 3-Pyramid Standard, 1810s, 29 x 13 In. 9920.00
Table, Tea, Stickley Bros., Mahogany, Circular, Cross Stretcher, Tag, 28 x 41 In. 550.00
Table, Tea, Tilt Top, Cherry, Padded Snake Feet, 2-Board Scalloped Top, 28 In. 1430.00
Table, Tea, Tilt Top, Chippendale, Cherry, Birdcage Support, 3 Cabriole Legs, 29 In. 705.00
Table, Tea, Tilt Top, Chippendale, Mahogany, Birdcage Support, c.1780, 27 x 32 In. 8225.00
Table, Tea, Tilt Top, Chippendale, Mahogany, Dish Top, Tripod, 25 x 26 In. 275.00
Table, Tea, Tilt Top, Chippendale, Mahogany, Round, Pedestal, Early 1800s, 30 x 28 In. . . 345.00
Table, Tea, Tilt Top, Federal, Mahogany, Serpentine Top, Pad Feet, 28 1/2 In. 2070.00
Table, Tea, Tilt Top, Georgian, Walnut, Birdcage, Late 18th Century, 28 1/2 x 32 1/2 In. . . 5175.00
Table, Tea, Tilt Top, Lacquer, Floral & Gilt Design, 1860 . . . . 310.00
Table, Tea, Tilt Top, Mahogany, Cabriole Legs, Slipper Feet, 1750-1780, 28 x 33 In. 4700.00
Table, Tea, Tilt Top, Queen Anne, Cherry, Birdcage, Cabriole Legs, 27 1/2 In. 2240.00
Table, Tea, Tilt Top, Queen Anne, Mahogany, Birdcage Support, Pad Feet, 28 In. 460.00
Table, Tea, Tilt Top, Queen Anne, Walnut, Lancaster County, c.1760, 28 x 34 In. 2280.00
Table, Tea, Tilt Top, Walnut, Turned Center Post, 3 Snake Feet, 27 1/2 x 32 In. 460.00
Table, Teak, Floral Carving, Soapstone Insert, Round, Oriental, 21 x 23 In. 410.00
Table, Teak, Marble Top, Butterflies & Moths, Late 19th Century, 32 1/2 In. 630.00
Table, Teak, Original Finish, 71 x 23 x 18 In. 200.00
Table, Tiger Maple, Maple, Drawer, Tapered Legs, Brass Knob, 27 x 21 x 16 1/2 In. 280.00
Table, Tilt Top, Carved Scrolling Acanthus, 3 Scrolled Legs, 20th Century, 29 3/4 In. 1925.00
Table, Tilt Top, Chinoiserie, Red Lacquer, Gilt Birds, Landscape, 1880s 1230.00
Table, Tilt Top, Chippendale, Mahogany, Birdcage Support, c.1790, 27 x 32 In. 650.00
Table, Tilt Top, Chippendale, Mahogany, Birdcage, Turned Column, 19th Century, 28 In. . . 840.00
Table, Tilt Top, Chippendale, Mahogany, Carved, c.1780, 28 x 31 x 31 1/2 In. 2875.00
Table, Tilt Top, Chippendale, Mahogany, Molded Circular Top, 28 1/4 In. 4600.00
Table, Tilt Top, Chippendale, Mahogany, Serpentine Molded Top, Spade Feet, 28 In. 2070.00
Table, Tilt Top, Chippendale, Walnut, 1-Board Cherry Top, 3-Footed, 22 x 25 In. 1650.00
Table, Tilt Top, Federal, Mahogany, Cloverleaf, Urn & Ring Standard, 29 x 25 x 18 In. . . 765.00
Table, Tilt Top, Fruitwood, Tripod Base, 19th Century, 27 x 27 In. 430.00
Table, Tilt Top, George II, Mahogany, Gallery, Tripod, 24 In. Diam. 7200.00
Table, Tilt Top, George II, Mahogany, Pedestal, Mid 18th Century, 29 1/4 x 28 In. 980.00
Table, Tilt Top, George II, Mahogany, Serpentine, Urn Column, Cabriole Legs 5040.00
Table, Tilt Top, George III Style, Mahogany, Birdcage, Piecrust Edge, 30 1/2 x 31 5/8 In. . 530.00
Table, Tilt Top, George III Style, Mahogany, Tripod, 19th Century 980.00
Table, Tilt Top, George III, Mahogany, Birdcage, Round Top, c.1790, 27 1/2 x 31 In. 896.00
Table, Tilt Top, George III, Mahogany, Dish Top, Tripod, Cabriole Legs, 27 x 24 In. 1150.00

Furniture, Table, Stickley, Pegged
Construction, 29 1/4 x 96 x 23 3/4 In.

Furniture, Table, Walnut, Marble Top, Carved
Frieze, X-Stretcher, 29 x 31 x 21 In.

Table, Tilt Top, George III, Mahogany, Leaf-Carved Cabriole Legs, 28 1/2 x 26 In. 200.00
Table, Tilt Top, George III, Mahogany, Tripod, Pad Feet, 26 1/4 x 23 3/4 In. 690.00
Table, Tilt Top, George III, Oak, Tripod, Cabriole Legs, 27 1/2 x 30 3/4 In. 750.00
Table, Tilt Top, Georgian Revival, Mahogany, Carved, Pedestal, 31 x 31 3/4 x 31 3/4 In. . 690.00
Table, Tilt Top, Georgian, Mahogany, Birdcage, Snake & Pad Feet, c.1820, 28 1/2 In. 730.00
Table, Tilt Top, Georgian, Walnut, Molded, Carved, 27 x 20 1/2 In. 1090.00
Table, Tilt Top, Mahogany Top, Piecrust Top, Carved Knees, Slipper Feet, 29 In. Diam. . . 1400.00
Table, Tilt Top, Mahogany, 3 Legs, Pad Feet, Late 18th Century, 27 3/8 x 32 In. 1090.00
Table, Tilt Top, Mahogany, 3 Saber Legs, c.1830, 28 1/2 x 14 In. 420.00
Table, Tilt Top, Mahogany, Birdcage Support, 1700s, 32 In. Diam. 7200.00
Table, Tilt Top, Mahogany, Birdcage, Pad Feet, Rhode Island, 34-In. 1-Board Top 990.00
Table, Tilt Top, Mahogany, c.1780, 26 x 25 1/2 x 18 3/8 In. 616.00
Table, Tilt Top, Mahogany, Cabriole Legs, Pad Feet, 28 In. 690.00
Table, Tilt Top, Mahogany, Dish Top, Fluted Stem, Tripod, Pad Feet, 27 x 30 In. 870.00
Table, Tilt Top, Mahogany, Fluted Pedestal, 3 Legs, Claw & Ball Feet, c.1880 . . . . 390.00
Table, Tilt Top, Mahogany, Leaf-Carved Pedestal, Tripod Legs, 28 3/4 In. 2400.00
Table, Tilt Top, Mahogany, Piecrust Edge, Rope-Twist Center Post 115.00
Table, Tilt Top, Mahogany, Piecrust Top, Birdcage Support, Tripod Base, 27 In. 1150.00
Table, Tilt Top, Mahogany, Rotating Over Birdcage, Tripod, 28 In. 4200.00
Table, Tilt Top, Mahogany, Round Top, Carved, Claw & Ball Feet, 30 x 30 In. 950.00
Table, Tilt Top, Mahogany, Tripod Base, Birdcage, Snake Feet, 27 3/4 x 36 In. 990.00
Table, Tilt Top, Maple, Piecrust Top, Late 19th Century, 25 x 22 In. 179.00
Table, Tilt Top, Molded Edge, Square Base, Splayed Legs, Brass Paw Casters, 29 x 60 In. 2300.00
Table, Tilt Top, Napoleon III, Marquetry, Ebonized, Fluted, Scroll Base, 48 x 35 In. 1060.00
Table, Tilt Top, Papier-Mache, Napoleon III Scene 8200.00
Table, Tilt Top, Pine, 3-Board Top, Chair Base, Brown Paint, New England, 28 x 48 In. . . 7030.00
Table, Tilt Top, Renaissance Revival, Walnut, Inlaid, Octagonal Top, c.1880 . . . . 690.00
Table, Tilt Top, Tiger Maple, Rectangular Top, Shaped Corners, 3 Scrolled Legs, 29 In. . . 865.00
Table, Tilt Top, Victorian, Mahogany, Round, Turned Tripod Pedestal, 30 x 29 In. 85.00
Table, Tilt Top, Victorian, Papier-Mache, Painted Coastal Scene, Parcel Gilt, 29 x 30 In. . 8400.00
Table, Tilt Top, Victorian, Walnut, Round Top, 4 Leg Pedestal, 31 x 46 In. 2000.00
Table, Tilt Top, Walnut, Birch, Octagonal Top, Inlaid 8-Point Star, Arched Feet, 28 In. . . . 770.00
Table, Tilt Top, Walnut, Urn Column, Raised Rings, Snake Feet, 28 In. 330.00
Table, Tray, George III, Mahogany, Rectangular Inset Top, 18 3/4 x 27 In. 660.00
Table, Tray, Mahogany, 3/4 Gallery Sides, Folding X-Frame Base, 31 x 29 3/4 In. 375.00
Table, Tray, Mahogany, Brass, Oval, 2 Handles, Inlaid Flowers, 1880, 26 x 18 In. 335.00
Table, Tray, Mahogany, Glass, Claw & Ball Feet, 29 1/2 x 33 1/2 x 21 In. 530.00
Table, Tray, Mahogany, Parquet Inlay, 2 Silver Handles, Engraved, 1879, 30 x 21 In. 1790.00
Table, Tray, Mahogany, Raised Gallery, Handles, 19th Century, 28 x 18 1/4 x 27 In. 500.00
Table, Tray, Mahogany, Tapered Leg, 18th Century, 21 1/2 x 32 1/2 x 18 1/2 In. 365.00
Table, Tray, Papier-Mache, Flowering Peonies, Mid 19th Century, 19 x 32 In. 4500.00
Table, Tray, Victorian, Handles, Gallery, 19th Century, 31 In. 520.00
Table, Tray, Victorian, Mahogany, Gallery, 19th Century, 22 x 31 x 22 In. 1090.00
Table, Tray, Victorian, Mahogany, Handles, Bowed Front, 22 x 34 x 20 In. 750.00
Table, Tray, Walnut, Glass Tray, Carved Figures At Well, Legs With Masks, 22 In. 805.00
Table, Trestle, Cherry, Batons, Removable Pins, Late 19th Century, 29 x 77 x 40 In. 765.00
Table, Trestle, G. Stickley, Leather Top, Original Tacks, Mark, 48 x 30 In. 9500.00
Table, Trestle, G. Stickley, Stretcher Mortised Through Plank Sides, 15 x 9 In. 5750.00
Table, Trestle, George IV, Mahogany, 2 Leaves, 2 Drawers, 1820, 30 x 35 x 28 In. 6000.00
Table, Trestle, Iberian Baroque, Walnut, Wrought Iron Stretchers, 30 x 40 x 27 In. 3105.00
Table, Trestle, Italian Rocco Style, Walnut, 32 x 54 3/4 x 25 In. 635.00
Table, Trestle, Keyed Through Lower Shelf, J.M. Young, 30 x 48 x 28 In. 920.00
Table, Trestle, L. & J.G. Stickley, No. 599, Mahogany, 29 x 54 x 32 In. 2500.00
Table, Trestle, L. & J.G. Stickley, Sideways Stretchers, Mortised, 28 x 48 In. 2645.00
Table, Trestle, Mahogany, Signed, J.M.Young, 31 x 54 x 32 In. 2250.00
Table, Trestle, Maple, Pine, New England, 18th Century, 28 x 35 1/2 x 25 1/2 In. 1800.00
Table, Trestle, Oak, Urn Pedestals, Platform Stretcher, c.1910, 30 1/2 x 31 1/2 In. 225.00
Table, Trestle, Pine Top, 3-Board, Cast Iron Scroll Ends, 95 x 24 In. 275.00
Table, Trestle, Robert Thompson, Oak, Carved Mouse Climbing Leg, 28 x 60 x 33 In. 4600.00
Table, Tulipwood, Amboyna Geometric Border, Cabriole Legs, 30 In. 1495.00
Table, Turtle Top, Inlaid Flowers, Cabriole Legs, France, 34 x 23 In. 470.00
Table, Twig Base, Rectangular Top, Original Finish, 22 x 16 x 28 In. 235.00
Table, Twig, Bent Hickory, Square Top, Splayed Base, Scalloped Trim, 20 x 20 x 30 In. . . 580.00

Table, Twig, Gray Dots, Arched Sides With Picket Bands, 28 x 28 In. 1700.00
Table, Typewriter, Marcel Breuer, No. B21, Thonet, c.1928, 27 1/8 x 39 x 18 In. 6325.00
Table, Typewriter, Walnut, Enameled, Shelf, 1950s, 60 x 16 x 29 In. 175.00
Table, Van Der Rohe, No. MR515/H, Thonet, c.1932, 24 x 31 3/4 In. 3220.00
Table, Victorian, Ebonized, Scrolled Gilt Banding, Mid 19th Century, 29 x 33 1/2 In. 1095.00
Table, Victorian, Gilt, Polychrome, Mid 19th Century, 29 1/2 x 43 3/4 In. 2990.00
Table, Victorian, Mahogany, Marble Turtle Top, Carved, 29 x 44 x 31 In. 1150.00
Table, Victorian, Mahogany, Round Top, Leaf Carving, Mid 19th Century, 30 x 53 In. . . . 1265.00
Table, Victorian, Marble Top, Round, Flower-Carved Apron, 29 x 22 In. 105.00
Table, Victorian, Mother-Of-Pearl Inlay, Circular Top, 30 x 31 In. 2415.00
Table, Victorian, Rosewood, Marble Turtle Top, Shelf, Carved Dog, 35 1/2 x 23 x 29 In. . 980.00
Table, Victorian, Shaped Marble Top, Carved Apron, Finials, Center Post, 30 x 35 x 25 In. 1265.00
Table, Victorian, Walnut, Marble Top, Press-Carved Apron, Central Finial, 29 x 26 In. . . . 85.00
Table, Victorian, Walnut, Shaped Marble Top, Apron, Legs, Finial, 29 x 30 x 20 In. 330.00
Table, W. Plattner, Chrome-Plated Wire Base, 16 x 18 In. 805.00
Table, Wallace Nutting, Maple, Drop Leaf 1155.00
Table, Walnut Veneer, Triangular Top, Risom Label, 21 x 26 1/2 In. 70.00
Table, Walnut, 2 Drawers, 3-Board Top, Square Legs, Cabriole Feet, 63 x 35 x 30 In. 8800.00
Table, Walnut, Breadboard Top, Stretchers, Square Legs, 18 x 48 x 18 In. 1265.00
Table, Walnut, Burled Veneers, Drawer, Brass Ring Pull, Pad Feet, 24 1/2 In. 220.00
Table, Walnut, Drawer At Short End, Hoof Feet, Late 18th Century, 29 x 20 In. 2875.00
Table, Walnut, Figured Grain, Frieze With Short Drawer, Saber Legs, c.1860, 31 In. 950.00
Table, Walnut, Inlaid & Carved Flower Heads, Figural Supports, 31 x 29 In. 750.00
Table, Walnut, Marble Top, Carved Frieze, X-Stretcher, 29 x 31 x 21 In. . . . . *Illus* 1495.00
Table, Walnut, Marble Top, Carved Stretchers, Finial, 1870, 38 x 25 x 29 In. 3200.00
Table, Walnut, Marble Top, Heads Amid Grape Clusters At Knees, 1880s, 28 1/2 In. 3680.00
Table, Walnut, Marble Top, Round, Urn Pedestal, Scroll Legs, 41 x 30 1/2 In. 4600.00
Table, Walnut, Marble Top, Shaped Edge, Molded, Shaped Legs, 27 1/2 x 29 1/2 In. 110.00
Table, Walnut, Marquetry Panel Center, Polychromed Pedestal, 1880s, 28 In. 1725.00
Table, Walnut, Onyx Top, Carved Lion Masks, Paw Feet, 33 x 36 In. 1955.00
Table, Walnut, Overhanging Top, Dovetailed Drawer, Tall Turned Legs 440.00
Table, Walnut, Panels Of Stylized Bellflowers, Mask Headed Legs, 32 1/2 In. 2185.00
Table, Walnut, Segmented Top, Center Sunburst, Round Plinth, 20th Century, 65 In. 4370.00
Table, Walnut, Short Drawer, Platform Stretcher & Shelf, 1920, 30 In. 420.00
Table, Walnut, Slab Top, Molded Drawers, Italy, Early 20th Century, 40 x 17 x 32 In. 230.00
Table, Walnut, Slant Front, Hinged Lid, Figured, c.1800, 10 3/4 x 21 In. 600.00
Table, Walnut, Trestle Base, Melon-Turned Legs, 2 Supports, 1910, 31 x 48 In. 1265.00
Table, Walnut, Turned Feet, 1760, 28 1/4 x 35 x 26 3/4 In. 4600.00
Table, Walnut, Wide Board Top, Drawer, Channel Panels, 17th Century, 2 In. 1495.00
Table, Wegner, Rosewood, Square, Stainless Steel Legs, 19 x 33 x 33 In. 255.00
Table, White Marble Top, Oval, Pedestal Base, 29 x 31 x 24 In. 1210.00
Table, White Marble, Oval Top, Octagonal Pedestal, 18th Century, 20 x 16 x 29 In. 2990.00
Table, Wicker, Platform Stretcher Base, D-Shape Gallery Ends, c.1890, 27 x 34 In. 335.00
Table, Wicker, Shelf Stretcher Base, 28 1/2 x 32 x 22 1/2 In. 170.00
Table, Wicker, Shelf Stretcher, Trestle Base, Pair 345.00
Table, William & Mary, Curly Walnut, 3 Drawers, 1720-1750, 29 x 60 x 35 In. 25850.00
Table, William & Mary, Maple, Stretcher, Gateleg, c.1730, 26 3/4 x 50 x 42 In. 5875.00
Table, William & Mary, Oak, Rectangular Molded-Edge Top, Turned Legs, 26 In. 630.00
Table, William & Mary, Pine, Oak, Turned Legs, 30 x 19 1/2 x 28 In. 1070.00
Table, William IV Style, Mahogany, 19th Century, 28 1/2 x 37 3/4 x 62 1/2 In. 615.00
Table, William IV, Mahogany, 3/4 Gallery, 19th Century, 31 3/4 x 42 x 21 1/2 In. 3220.00
Table, William IV, Mahogany, Circular Variegated Green Marble Top, 39 In. 1150.00
Table, William IV, Mahogany, Marble, Mid 19th Century, 30 1/2 x 25 x 25 In. 5520.00
Table, William IV, Mahogany, Plain Frieze, Cylindrical Base, 28 In. 5750.00
Table, William IV, Mahogany, Raised Rectangular Top, 28 1/2 In. 980.00
Table, William IV, Mahogany, Sunburst, Round, Mid 19th Century, 29 1/2 x 48 In. 2530.00
Table, William IV, Rosewood, Papier-Mache, 3-Part Base, 26 x 16 In. . . . . *Illus* 1840.00
Table, Wine Tasting, French Provincial, Oak, Folding Top, 30 1/2 x 55 1/2 x 42 In. 635.00
Table, Wine Tasting, French Provincial, Oak, Round, Swinging Base, 28 1/2 x 35 In. 545.00
Table, Wine Tasting, French Provincial, Pine, Tilt Top, Swing Out Base, 26 x 48 x 38 In. . . 690.00
Table, Wine Tasting, Fruitwood, Hinged Top, Trestle Base, 1880s, 28 x 37 In. 750.00
Table, Wood, Carved, Flowers, Octagonal Top, 3 Dragon Legs, Bali, 29 x 28 x 19 In. 690.00
Table, Writing, G. Stickley, No. 459, Decal & Paper Label, 28 1/2 x 43 In. 1495.00

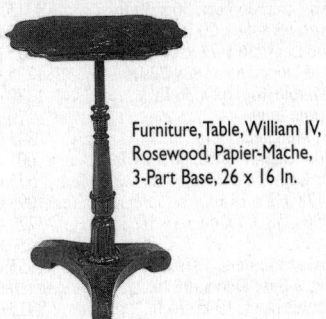

Furniture, Table, William IV,
Rosewood, Papier-Mache,
3-Part Base, 26 x 16 In.

Furniture, Vitrine, Louis XVI, Mahogany, 1880

Table, Writing, Regency, Mahogany, Early 19th Century, 29 x 47 1/2 x 29 1/2 In. 3680.00
Table, Writing, William IV, Mahogany, Gilt Tooled Leather, 29 x 54 x 27 1/2 In. 1380.00
Table, Writing, William IV, Mahogany, Tooled Green Leather Surface, 29 1/2 In. 5290.00
Table, Wrought Iron, Blue Mirrored Glass Top, Arrow & Diamond Legs, 28 1/2 In. 4025.00
Table, Wrought Iron, Gilt Bronze Mounted, Marble, Late 19th Century, 28 x 26 In. 3220.00
Table, Wrought Iron, Tile Top, 8 Mueller Tiles, Village, Birches, 20 x 25 x 13 In. 5750.00
Table, Wrought Iron, Tile Top, Flower & Birds, 19 1/2 x 16 1/2 x 16 1/2 In. 280.00
Table, Yew, 3 Downswept Legs, 3-Sided Plinth, Mid 19th Century, 48 In. 1495.00
Tabouret, G. Stickley, Mahogany, Round Top, Cross Stretchers, 18 x 20 In. 800.00
Tabouret, G. Stickley, No. 603, Mahogany, 20 In. 700.00
Tabouret, L. & J.G. Stickley, Legs Mortised Through Octagonal Top, 17 x 15 In. 750.00
Tabouret, L. & J.G. Stickley, No. 558, Mahogany, Signed, 17 x 15 In. 1300.00
Tabouret, Limbert, No. 211, Mahogany, Original Finish, Splayed Legs, 12 x 16 In. 240.00
Tabouret, Limbert, No. 251, Mahogany, Rectangular Cutouts, 17 x 24 In. 2415.00
Tabouret, Mahogany, Circular Top, Michigan Chair Co., 15 x 18 In. 750.00
Tabouret, Stickley Bros., No. 111, 3 Splayed Legs, Hexagonal Top, 18 x 19 In. 920.00
Tea Cart, Drop Leaf, Mahogany, Removable Glass Tray Top, 2 Shelves, 29 x 31 In. 150.00
Tea Cart, Mahogany, Brass Inlay, Glazed Panels, Shelf Stretcher, 29 1/2 In. 290.00
Tea Cart, Mahogany, Glass Tray, Spiral-Turned Supports 520.00
Tea Cart, Pine, Glass Tray Top, 28 1/2 In. 60.00
Tea Cart, Stickley Bros., Glass Tray Top, Handle, 28 x 17 x 29 In. 690.00
Tray On Stand, Harbor Scene, Oval, New Wooden Table Base, 21 x 29 x 20 In. 990.00
Tray On Stand, Regency Style, Tooled Leather, X-Stretcher, 1900s, 18 x 32 In. 300.00
Trolley, Mahogany, 3 Tiers, Molded Gallery, Casters, 45 1/2 x 42 x 16 1/2 In. 672.00
Trolley, Mahogany, 3 Tiers, Spherule Finials, Turned Legs, 47 x 42 x 17 In. 2645.00
Trolley, Rolo, Cees Braakman, No. PB 01, c.1950, 26 3/4 x 17 3/4 x 31 In. 4025.00
Trolley, William IV, Mahogany, Mid 19th Century, 50 x 47 1/2 x 22 In. 2300.00
Umbrella Stand, G. Stickley, Mahogany, Original Finish, 29 x 12 In. 250.00
Umbrella Stand, G. Stickley, Mahogany, Triple, 34 x 21 x 12 In. 750.00
Umbrella Stand, Lakeside Crafters, Dark Mahogany, Cylindrical, 25 1/2 x 10 In. 150.00
Umbrella Stand, Oak, Rectangular, 2 Open Sides, 2 Cutout Sides, 28 x 12 x 10 In. 90.00
Umbrella Stand, Oak, Slender Baluster Form, Pierced Lotus Panels, Liner, 23 3/8 In. 460.00
Umbrella Stand, Porcelain, Cobalt Blue Deer, Oriental, 1900s, 23 3/4 In. 190.00
Umbrella Stand, Stickley Bros., Mahogany, Flush Apron, 4-Footed, 34 In. 375.00
Vanity, G. Nelson, Hanging, Hinged Top, Interior Light & Mirror, 32 In. 175.00
Vanity, G. Nelson, Mahogany, 2 Drawers, Flip Top, 23 x 14 x 17 In. 2875.00
Vanity, G. Rohde, Mirror Between 2 Drum Cabinets, Bakelite Pulls, 66 In. 2070.00
Vanity, G. Stickley, Mahogany, Hinged Mirror, Rectangular Top, 34 x 53 In. 1725.00
Vanity, Hepplewhite Style, Cherry, Drawer Over Kneehole, 31 x 36 In. 220.00
Vanity, Hickory Twig, Mirror, Adirondack, 20th Century, 54 1/2 x 39 5/8 x 19 In. 1610.00
Vanity, Jacques Adnet, Chromium Plated, Mirror, 4 Drawers, 1930, 45 x 45 In. 4600.00
Vanity, Maple, Faux Bamboo Turned, 3 Shelves, c.1890, 55 x 31 x 22 3/4 In. 5640.00
Vanity, Napoleon III, Mahogany, Hinged Top, Marble, 4 Drawers, 38 x 31 x 19 In. 490.00
Vanity, Oak, Swing Mirror, Drawer, 29 x 57 In. 180.00
Vanity, Pedestal, Blue Lights Around Mirror, Money Section, 1920 .... 2500.00
Vanity, Rococo, Walnut, Carved Flowers, Kerosene Sconces, 75 x 20 x 44 In. 2800.00

Vanity, Roycroft, Drawer, Pivot Mirror, Tapered Legs, Mackmurdo Feet, 56 x 39 In. 4315.00
Vanity, Stickley Bros., No. 9035, 5 Drawers, Triple Mirror, 55 x 44 x 20 In. 2185.00
Vitrine, Bowed Door, Glass Sides, Bronze Trim, Cabriole Legs, 56 x 25 x 14 In. 695.00
Vitrine, Federal Style, Walnut, Parquetry, Cornice, Glazed Doors, 85 x 46 x 22 In. 1725.00
Vitrine, Louis XV Style, Vernis Martin, Figural Panel, Marble Top, 62 x 36 In. 1380.00
Vitrine, Louis XV Style, Walnut, Glass Top, Sides, Cabriole Legs 170.00
Vitrine, Louis XV, Horn Veneer, Serpentine, Gilt Bronze Mounted, 19 In. 345.00
Vitrine, Louis XV, Mahogany, Crest, Floral Inlay, Cabriole Legs, France, 60 x 21 In. 605.00
Vitrine, Louis XV, Metal Mount, Rectangular Top, Saber Legs, 56 x 27 x 14 In. 575.00
Vitrine, Louis XVI Style, Giltwood, D-Shape, 68 1/2 x 128 1/2 x 14 In. 1095.00
Vitrine, Louis XVI Style, Mahogany, Ormolu, Brass, 1900s, 58 3/4 x 44 x 14 1/2 In. 3220.00
Vitrine, Louis XVI, Mahogany, 1880 . . . . *Illus* 3450.00
Vitrine, Mahogany, 3 Doors, Arched Panels, Sphinx-Headed Pilasters, 1870s, 81 In. 1955.00
Vitrine, Mahogany, Painted Florals, Banding, Drop Front, 2 Base Doors, 66 In. 1210.00
Vitrine, Mahogany, Rectangular Case, Stylized Floral Center Door, 1905, 74 In. 8815.00
Vitrine, Regency, Mahogany, 2 Glazed Doors, Broken Pediment, Gilt Urn, 93 In. 1610.00
Vitrine, Regency, Satinwood, 2 Hinged Sections, 27 3/4 x 59 1/2 x 27 In. 3220.00
Vitrine, Tortoiseshell, Beveled Glass, Gilt Bronze Mount, 10 x 15 1/2 x 11 In. 2185.00
Vitrine, Victorian, Burl Walnut, Cornice, 2 Glazed Doors, 88 1/2 x 52 x 20 In. 2760.00
Vitrine, Victorian, Mahogany, Glazed Doors, 19th Century, 84 x 65 1/2 x 19 1/2 In. 2185.00
Vitrine, Walnut, Marquetry, Domed, Mid 19th Century, 83 x 54 1/2 x 13 3/4 In. 4830.00
Vitrine, William IV, Mahogany, Projecting Top, 3 Doors, Plinth Base, 82 x 79 In. 3440.00
Wardrobe, Aesthetic Style, Softwood, Painted, 2 Doors, Drawer, 81 x 46 x 21 In. 560.00
Wardrobe, Art Deco, Oak, Rectangular Top, 2 Doors, 1930, 23 3/4 x 77 1/2 In. 460.00
Wardrobe, Arts & Crafts, Oak, 4 Long Drawers Over 2 Open Shelves, 59 3/4 In. 14950.00
Wardrobe, Bamboo, Rattan, Drawer, Door, Brass Mounting, 67 1/2 x 35 x 19 In. 390.00
Wardrobe, Chippendale, Poplar, Mustard Yellow, Rectangular Top, 20 x 67 In. 2750.00
Wardrobe, Corner, Walnut, Poplar, Chestnut, Red Paint, 19th Century, 81 In. 3025.00
Wardrobe, Dark Red Paint, Dovetailed Drawer, 42 x 17 x 80 In. 2200.00
Wardrobe, George III, Mahogany, 2 Doors, Banded, 19th Century, 80 x 54 x 24 In. 865.00
Wardrobe, George III, Mahogany, Early 19th Century, 77 1/2 x 76 1/2 x 25 In. 2185.00
Wardrobe, Mahogany, Carved, Paneled Doors, Cornice, Footed, 86 x 48 x 22 In. 1150.00
Wardrobe, Mahogany, Paneled Doors, Bracket Feet, Late 19th Century, 78 In. 560.00
Wardrobe, Mahogany, Paneled Doors, Shelves 1 Side, Hanging Area Other, 80 In. 1840.00
Wardrobe, Maple, 2 Base Drawers, Top Paneled Doors, 84 In. 2090.00
Wardrobe, Mixed Woods, Scalloped Apron, Base Drawer, Beveled Mirror, 8 3/4 In. 360.00
Wardrobe, Pine, 6-Panel Cupboard Doors, 4 Shelves, Bracket Feet, 87 1/2 In. 1495.00
Wardrobe, Pine, Door, Original Red Paint, New England, 13 x 67 1/2 In. 4140.00
Wardrobe, Pine, Oak, Rosettes, Barley-Twist Columns, 18th Century, 81 1/2 In. 4000.00
Wardrobe, Pine, Paneled, Old Refinish, Red Paint Remnants, N.Y., c.1840 . . . . 3600.00
Wardrobe, Pine, Peaked Cornice, 2 Doors, Cast Iron Latch, Hooks, 81 x 48 In. 2090.00
Wardrobe, Pine, Poplar, 2 Paneled Doors, 2 Drawers, Wood Pulls, 79 1/2 In. 2640.00
Wardrobe, Pine, Poplar, Rectangular Thick Top, Brown Paint, 83 1/2 In. 525.00
Wardrobe, Pine, Rectangular Top, Rattail Iron Hinges, Canada, 18 x 50 x 76 In. 1870.00
Wardrobe, Poplar, 2 Paneled Doors, Divided Interior, Shelves, Hanging Area, 65 In. 880.00
Wardrobe, Poplar, Rectangular Top, 4 Shelves, Yellow Grain Painted, 80 In. 440.00
Wardrobe, Poplar, Rectangular Top, Brown Over Tan Wood Graining, 93 In. 990.00
Wardrobe, Poplar, Red Stain, Cupboard Doors, Recessed Panels, Drawer, 81 x 58 In. 1955.00
Wardrobe, Softwood, Painted, Cornice, Paneled Doors, Yellow, Red, 80 x 44 x 13 In. . . . 220.00
Wardrobe, Victorian, Bird's-Eye Maple, Faux Bamboo, 17 3/4 x 40 x 92 In. 3160.00
Wardrobe, Victorian, Pine, Original Blue Paint, White Porcelain Knob, 71 In. 520.00
Wardrobe, Victorian, Walnut, Molded Cornice, Bracket Feet, 17 3/4 x 73 In. 1650.00
Wardrobe, William IV, Mahogany, Central Door, Plinth Base, 83 x 86 x 19 In. 1840.00
Washstand, Cast Iron, Gothic Lancer Arch, Knight, France, 10 1/2 In. 920.00
Washstand, Cedar, c.1820, 35 1/2 x 27 x 18 In. 460.00
Washstand, Corner, Cherry, Bird's-Eye Maple, Drawer, c.1830, 37 x 27 In. 3500.00
Washstand, Corner, George III, Mahogany Inlay, Bowfront, Square Legs, 42 In. 575.00
Washstand, Corner, Mahogany, Bowfront, Lower Shelf, 1 Drawer, 38 x 21 1/2 In. 330.00
Washstand, Corner, Sheraton, Cherry, Bowfront, Drawer, 2 Doors, 28 x 19 x 50 In. 1320.00
Washstand, Dutch Marquetry, 2 Tiers, Kidney Form, Ormolu Mounts 430.00
Washstand, Eastlake, Walnut, 3 Drawers, Door, Victorian, 27 1/2 x 28 1/2 x 15 In. 165.00
Washstand, Edwardian, Marble Top, Large Center Mirror, 2 Small Side Mirrors 3750.00
Washstand, Federal, Maple, Rectangular Gallery Top, Ball Feet, 1820, 34 x 15 In. 430.00

Washstand, Hepplewhite, Pine, Brown & Red Paint, Square Legs, 26 3/4 x 18 In. 880.00
Washstand, Mahogany Veneer, Dovetailed Drawer, Brass Pulls, 37 3/4 In. 385.00
Washstand, Mahogany, Pitcher Well, Top Frame, Carved Center Scrolls, 32 1/2 In. 140.00
Washstand, Pine, Base Drawer, Eagle-Head Brass Pull, 37 1/2 x 14 In. 275.00
Washstand, Queen Anne, Mahogany, Turned Platform Base, Snake Feet, 11 x 36 In. 220.00
Washstand, Sheraton, Cherry, Bowfront, 3 Drawers, 2 False, Turned Legs, 24 x 38 In. ... 700.00
Washstand, Sheraton, Cherry, Dovetailed Gallery, Drawer, Vaseline Glass Knob 470.00
Washstand, Sheraton, Pine, Yellow Painted Chrome, Black Pinstripe, Drawer, 40 In. 3135.00
Washstand, Sheraton, Walnut, Pine Top, Gallery, Virginia, 19th Century, 27 x 27 In. 390.00
Washstand, Softwood, 2 Paneled Doors, Free-Standing Column Supports, Turned Legs .. 385.00
Washstand, Softwood, Lower Drawer, Turned Legs 180.00
Washstand, Softwood, Scroll Supports, Side Towel Racks, Drawer, Door 190.00
Washstand, Tiger Maple, c.1825, 36 1/2 x 16 3/4 In. 980.00
Washstand, Walnut, Marble Top, Soap Dish, 1 Long Over 2 Short Drawers, 39 x 36 In. .. 460.00
Washstand, Walnut, White Marble Top, 19th Century, 28 x 20 x 29 1/2 In. 115.00
Washstand, Walnut, White Marble Top, Drawer, Raised Turned Legs, 28 x 20 x 29 In. ... 115.00
Washstand, White Marble Top, Soap Stands, Drawer Over Doors, 1880s, 39 1/2 In. 980.00
Wastebasket, Arts & Crafts, Mahogany, Canted Sides, 4 Vertical Slats, 15 x 18 In. 635.00
Wastebasket, Stickley Bros., Mahogany, Original Finish, 18 x 14 In. 450.00
Whatnot Shelf, 3 Tiers, Faux Bamboo Supports, Lower Door, Shelves, 64 In. 2530.00
Whatnot Shelf, Corner, Bamboo, Mirrors In Frame, Shelves, 56 In. 230.00
Whatnot Shelf, Regency Style, Mahogany, 4 Shelves, 80 x 20 x 16 In. 430.00
Whatnot Shelf, Regency, Faux Rosewood, 3 Shelves, Turned Uprights, Casters, 58 In. ... 1725.00
Whatnot Shelf, Regency, Mahogany, 4 Shelves Over 6 Paneled Drawers, 80 x 20 In. 430.00
Whatnot Shelf, Walnut, 4 Tiers, Apron Drawer, 19th Century 1035.00
Whatnot Shelf, Walnut, Ink Graining, 5 Shelves, Mitchell, 30 x 11 x 58 In. 440.00
Window Seat, Arts & Crafts, Leather Drop-In Cushion, Slatted Sides, 27 x 14 x 17 In. ... 650.00
Window Seat, Arts & Crafts, Leather Drop-In Cushions, Notched Rail, 27 x 17 In. 650.00
Window Seat, Arts & Crafts, Oak, Grenfeld Rug Top, Boats, Icebergs, 13 x 51 x 16 In. .. 1010.00
Window Seat, Eastlake, Walnut, Incised Legs, Rounded End, Flowers, 14 x 60 x 20 In. .. 140.00
Window Seat, Louis XV, Scrolled, Padded Armrests, Cabriole Legs, 29 x 18 In. 1610.00
Window Seat, Louis XVI Style, Cane, Painted, Parcel Gilt 520.00
Window Seat, Louis XVI Style, Walnut, Padded Seat, Overscrolled Arms, Casters 520.00
Window Seat, Mahogany, Outscrolled Sides, Upholstered, c.1770, 24 x 38 In. 5100.00
Window Seat, Mahogany, Scrolled Arms & Slats, Needlepoint Seat 520.00
Wine Cooler, George III Style, Mahogany, Brass Bound, Oval, Pair 1725.00
Wine Cooler, George III, Mahogany, Sarcophagus, c.1800, 22 x 27 1/4 x 18 In. 2415.00
Wine Cooler, Mahogany, Door, Opening To 3 Drawers, 1870s, 36 1/2 In. 865.00
Wine Cooler, Regency, Mahogany, Oval Opening, Casters, 1810, 30 x 22 x 22 In. 4200.00

G. ARGY-ROUSSEAU is the impressed mark used on a variety of objects
in the Art Deco style. Gabriel Argy-Rousseau, born in 1885, was a
French glass artist. In 1921, he formed a partnership that made pate-
de-verre and other glass. He worked until 1952 and died in 1953.

G-ARGY-
ROUSSEAU

Ashtray, Medallion, Oval, Purple, Pate-De-Verre, Signed, 1923, 6 1/4 In. 1725.00
Bowl, Blue Poppies, White, Pate-De-Verre, Signed, 3 In. 5463.00
Bowl, Red Berries, Green Leafy Branches, White, Pate-De-Verre, Signed, 2 1/2 In. 3220.00
Bowl, Triangular Panels, Yellow Flowers, Purple Leaves, Pate-De-Verre, 3 1/2 In. 6325.00
Box, Cover, Cornflowers, Cobalt, Pate-De-Verre, 1920, 2 3/4 In. 3900.00
Box, Cover, Honesty, Leaves, Brown, Pate-De-Verre, 1920, 3 1/2 In. 3900.00
Box, Cover, Purple Flowers, White, Round, Pate-De-Verre, 2 3/4 In. 3450.00
Clock, Boudoir, Purple Daises, Brass Face, Pate-De-Verre, Signed 1400.00
Figurine, Woman Bathing, Pate-De-Verre, 1928, 10 1/4 In. 18000.00
Lamp, Exotic Leaves, Wrought Iron Frame, Pate-De-Verre, 1925, 11 3/4 In. 8400.00
Lamp Base, Birds Of Paradise, Pale Yellow, Pate-De-Verre, 1929, 5 1/2 In. 4800.00
Night-Light, Geometric, Iron, Pate-De-Verre, 1930, 6 3/4 In. 4200.00
Paperweight, Amber, Brown Interior, Pate-De-Verre, 1 3/4 x 2 1/4 In. 3000.00
Pendant, Rose Blossom, Pink, Brown, Round, Pate-De-Verre, c.1924, 2 In. 690.00
Pendant, White Flowers, Black Stamens, Signed, 2 x 1 1/2 In. 1065.00
Soup, Coupe, Ivy, Pate-De-Verre, 1919, 3 1/2 x 4 1/2 In. 4200.00
Soup, Coupe, Pumpkins, Pate-De-Verre, 1922, 3 3/4 x 4 3/8 In. 300.00
Vase, Brown Flowers, White, Cylindrical, Pate-De-Verre, Signed, 5 3/4 In. 3450.00
Vase, Circle Design, Gold, Brown, Handles, Pate-De-Verre, 1929, 9 In. 5400.00

Vase, Double Flowers, Pate-De-Verre, 1933, 5 In. 5400.00
Vase, Fauns & Nymphs, Pale White, Pate-De-Verre, 1923, 8 7/8 In. 8400.00
Vase, Flowered Medallions, Pate-De-Verre, 1925, 10 1/8 In. 13200.00
Vase, Flowers, Tragedy & Comedy, Gray, Pate-De-Verre, 1922, 10 1/8 In. 6600.00
Vase, Linear Design, Palmettes, Green, Pate-De-Verre, 1927, 7 In. 4500.00
Vase, Masks, Pale Yellow, Pate-De-Verre, 1914, 4 In. 9000.00
Vase, Masks, Purple, Pale Pink, Pate-De-Verre, 1914, 4 In. 13200.00
Vase, Parma Violets, Pale Pink, Pate-De-Verre, 1917, 5 7/8 In. ....3840.00 to 4200.00
Vase, Pink Flowered Branch, Purple, Pate-De-Verre, Signed, 5 1/2 In. 4900.00
Vase, Red Linear Design, Pink, Speckled Leaves, Pate-De-Verre, 6 1/2 In. 6000.00
Vase, Red Poppies, Pate-De-Verre, Signed, 5 3/4 In. 2530.00
Vase, Red Thistles, Purple, Pate-De-Verre, 1920, 6 In. 4800.00
Vase, Scarabs, Pate-De-Verre, 1922, 5 3/4 In. 4500.00
Vase, Thebes, Pale Yellow, Pate-De-Verre, 1924, 6 5/16 In. 3900.00
Vase, Trees In Bloom, Brown, Pale Purple, Pate-De-Verre, 1925, 6 In. 7200.00
Vase, White Dot Flowers, Palmettes, Pate-De-Verre, 1927, 7 In. 4800.00

GALLE was a designer who made glass, pottery, furniture, and other Art Nouveau items. Emile Galle founded his factory in France in 1874. After Galle's death in 1904, the firm continued to make glass and furniture until 1931. The name *Galle* was used as a mark, but it was often hidden in the design of the object. Galle glass is listed here. Pottery is in the next section. His furniture is listed in the Furniture category.

Bottle, Scent, Tropical Sunset, Ebony Spider Mums, Mushroom Stopper, Cameo, 4 1/4 In. 2990.00
Bowl, Boy Picking Fruit, Amber, Gold Highlights, 3 x 9 In. 345.00
Bowl, Light Pink To Gray, Pinched Edge, 4 Pulled Corners, Cameo, Signed, 7 1/2 In. 920.00
Bowl, Red, Yellow Flowers, Canoe Shape, Cameo, Signed, 9 1/2 In. 1410.00
Bowl, Thistles, Triangular, Signed, 7 In. 460.00
Box, Cover, Blue Flowers, On Peach, Oval, Cameo, Signed, 4 In. 630.00
Box, Cover, Landscape, Boat On Body Of Water, Cameo, Signed, 5 1/4 In. 980.00
Candle Lamp, Bees & Flowering Branches, Cameo, 11 In. 345.00
Compote, 6 Swimming Fish On Cover, Half-Circle Banded Rim, Signed, 4 1/2 In. 560.00
Cup & Saucer, Flowers, Amber & Red Mottled Ground, Signed, 2 1/4 In. 1495.00
Decanter, Amber, Flattened, Oval, Applied Buttons, Ribbed Mushroom Stopper, 9 1/2 In. 1610.00
Decanter, Enameled Peasants, Harvesting Grapes, Ribbed Stopper, Signed, 13 In. 336.00
Ewer, Enameled, Man Playing Bagpipe, Peasants, Round Handle, Signed, 8 x 6 In. 900.00
Ewer, Flowers, Rope Twist Handle, Cameo, Signed, 8 3/4 In. 1380.00
Inkwell, Flowers & Leaves, Matching Stopper, Cameo, Signed, 2 x 4 In. 900.00
Jug, Green, Lime Green, Apricot On Gray, 2 Handles, Cameo, 7 In. 1150.00
Lamp, Gold Yellow Mushroom Shade, Stepped Base, Cameo, Signed, 13 1/4 In. 825.00
Lamp Base, Wooded Lake Scene, On Moss Green, Cameo, 18 1/4 In. 2585.00
Powder Box, Scenic, Amethyst, Blue, Cameo, Signed, 5 3/4 In. 1035.00
Tray, Amber, Flowers & Buds, Pink, Cream, Red, Gold Enamel, Cameo, Signed, 4 1/4 In. . 115.00
Vase, Allover Green Leaves, Olive Green To Lemon Yellow, Cameo, 29 1/2 In. 2750.00
Vase, Amber Berries, Vines, On White & Burgundy, Oval, Cameo, Signed, 14 In. 1650.00
Vase, Amber, Mocha Trees, Chartreuse Leaves, Cameo, Signed, 11 1/2 In. 1150.00
Vase, Aqua, Periwinkle Morning Glory, Ribbed, Tricornered Rim, Signed, 7 3/4 In. ... 1380.00
Vase, Banjo, Amethyst Leaves, On Peach & Blue, Cameo, Signed, 5 1/2 In. 450.00
Vase, Banjo, Blossoms & Leaves, Brown, Flared, Cameo, Signed, 5 1/2 x 2 1/2 In. 450.00
Vase, Banjo, Branches, Leaves & Berries, Orange, Cameo, 5 1/2 x 2 1/2 In. 850.00
Vase, Banjo, Brown, Lavender Flowers, On Yellow, Green, Cameo, 6 3/4 In. 1090.00
Vase, Banjo, Green Pods, Leaves, Gray On Apricot, Cameo, 6 1/2 In. 1170.00
Vase, Berries & Leaves, Red Tones On Yellow, Cameo, 2 3/4 In. 300.00
Vase, Blossoming Clematis, Leaves, On Pale Yellow, Cameo, 20 3/8 In. 4115.00
Vase, Blown-Out Leaves, On Yellow, Cameo, 12 In. 10350.00
Vase, Brown Leaves, Berries, On Green, Cameo, 5 1/2 In. 630.00
Vase, Brown Pond Lilies, Cameo, 3 3/4 In. 345.00
Vase, Bud, Citron, Raspberry Primroses, Brown Leaves, Cameo, Signed, 4 In. 805.00
Vase, Burgundy, Deep Red Flowering Tiger Lilies, Leaves, Cameo, 20 1/4 In. 5875.00
Vase, Carved Pink Tulips, On Butterscotch, Cameo, Signed, 8 1/2 In. 1100.00
Vase, Clematis, Leaves, On Deep Yellow, Violet, Cameo, 23 1/2 In. 4700.00
Vase, Crimson, Burgundy Thorny Branches, Blossoming Roses, 7 3/8 In. 1880.00
Vase, Dangling Catkins, Olive Green On Peach, Chartreuse, Cameo, Signed, 3 1/2 In. 185.00

Vase, Dark Brown Flowers & Leaves, On Amber, Cameo, Signed, 5 In.	575.00
Vase, Dark Olive Ferns, Scalloped Rim, Cameo, 7 1/4 In.	385.00
Vase, Deep Purple Berries & Leaves, On Green, Cameo, Signed, 9 x 2 In.	980.00
Vase, Deep Red Bleeding Hearts, On Yellow Gray, Cameo, 9 1/2 x 3 1/2 In.	2300.00
Vase, Dense Wooded Lake Scene, Deep Caramel On Peach, Cameo, 17 3/4 In.	7050.00
Vase, Elaborate Blue, Purple Flowers, On Yellow, Cameo, 8 In.	2070.00
Vase, Enameled Thistles, On Pale Amber, Signed, 7 1/2 x 2 1/4 In.	805.00
Vase, Flower Pods, Blown-Out Leaves, Running Leaf & Vine Rim, Signed, 7 In.	5040.00
Vase, Flowers, Etched, Reverse Painted, Clover Shape, c.1900, 9 In.	9400.00
Vase, Flowers, On Green, Enameled, Cameo, Squared Flattened Oval, Signed, 6 In.	805.00
Vase, Four O'Clocks, On White, Cameo, 5 1/2 In.	440.00
Vase, Garden Of Delphiniums, Dark Blue Stems, Cameo, Signed, 12 1/2 In.	1460.00
Vase, Gentiana Flowers, Orange, Brown Footed Base, Cameo, Signed, 1900s, 6 3/8 In.	7200.00
Vase, Green Ferns & Leaves, On Peach, Cameo, 13 1/2 In.	3525.00
Vase, Green Flowers, On Light Pink, Oval, Signed, 3 1/4 In.	375.00 to 460.00
Vase, Green Tall Trees, Distant Horizon, Cameo, Signed, 9 1/2 In.	1630.00
Vase, Green Thistle Design, On Pink, Cameo, 3 1/2 In.	545.00
Vase, Hibiscus, Amber Yellow, Orange, Red, Cameo, Signed, 20th Century, 17 In.	8050.00
Vase, Hills & Lake Behind Large Trees, On Blue, Cameo, 16 In.	2875.00
Vase, Hollyhock, Pale Amber, Salmon, Maroon, Cameo, Signed, 17 In.	5750.00
Vase, Landscape, Trees Surrounding Body Of Water, Blue, Green, Brown, 13 In.	2300.00
Vase, Large Iris Design, Cameo, Signed, 9 1/4 x 4 In.	2530.00
Vase, Lavender Flowers, Frosted Ground, Tapering Form, Footed, Signed, 9 In.	690.00
Vase, Lavender Flowers, On White, Cylindrical, Cameo, Signed, 16 In.	2875.00
Vase, Lavender Flowers, Pink Mottled Ground, Signed, 4 In.	490.00
Vase, Leaves & Seed Pods, Translucent Green To Salmon, Cameo, Signed, 9 3/4 In.	460.00
Vase, Maple Leaf, Pod Design, Yellow, Amber Ground, Cameo, 6 1/2 In.	690.00
Vase, Maroon Flowers, On Yellow, Cameo, Signed, 9 1/4 In.	1610.00
Vase, Mountain Landscape, Brown On Yellow, Cameo, 7 3/4 In.	1060.00
Vase, Oak Tree Branches, Acorns, Cameo, Signed, 12 In.	1400.00
Vase, Olive Poppies, Lavender Blue Band, On Frosted Yellow, Cameo, 6 1/4 In.	880.00
Vase, Orange Leaves, Berries, On Pale Yellow, Cameo, 5 1/4 In.	745.00
Vase, Orange Wisteria On Frosted Ground, Signed, 4 In.	280.00
Vase, Orchid Blossoms, Brown On Amber, Tapered Oval, Cameo, Signed, 8 In.	805.00
Vase, Orchid, Orange, Green On Amber, Cameo, Signed, 20th Century, 14 In.	8625.00
Vase, Pendant Wisteria Branches, Leaves, White On Deep Purple, 18 1/8 In.	2350.00
Vase, Phlox, Orange, Deep Red On Amber, Cameo, Signed, 20th Century, 16 In.	8050.00
Vase, Pilgrim, Marine Scene, Cameo, Signed, 5 1/4 In.	3300.00
Vase, Pillow, Green, Purple Hyacinth, On Cream, Handles, Cameo, Signed, 11 1/2 In.	3850.00
Vase, Pink Flowers, On Amber, Cameo, Signed, 8 1/4 In.	860.00
Vase, Pink, Lavender Flowers, Cameo, Signed, 6 In.	970.00
Vase, Pink, Red Enameled Lilies, On Pale Amber, Signed, 12 x 5 In.	1265.00
Vase, Plum Clematis Blossoms, On Crimson Pink, Cameo, Signed, 9 3/4 In.	920.00
Vase, Plum Leaves, On Light Orange, Footed, Cameo, Signed, 1900-1925, 15 1/4 In.	8400.00
Vase, Pond Plant Life, Orange & Brown On Amber To Cream, Cameo, 3 3/8 In.	545.00
Vase, Prunus Blossoms, Aqua Blue, Brown On Frosted Yellow, 17 1/4 In.	4465.00
Vase, Purple Flower, On Shaded Yellow, Flared, 13 In.	1495.00
Vase, Purple Flowers, On Yellow, Cameo, Signed, 6 1/2 In.	750.00
Vase, Purple Flowers, On Yellow, Trumpet Shape, Cameo, Signed, 6 1/2 In.	540.00
Vase, Purple Orchids, On Deep Green, Cameo, 3 1/2 x 4 1/2 In.	1620.00
Vase, Red Flowers, On Frosted Yellow, Bulbous, Cupped Mouth, Signed, 9 In.	4315.00
Vase, Red, Flowers, Enameled, Gold, Applied Marqueties, Handles, c.1894, 10 In.	19975.00
Vase, Red, Orange, White, Flowers, Cameo, Signed, 5 In.	1090.00
Vase, Rio De Janeiro Scene, Orange, Deep Red On Cream, Cameo, Signed, 9 3/4 In.	4140.00
Vase, Roses, On Amber, Orange & Red, Oval, Cameo, Signed, 9 3/4 In.	460.00
Vase, Rust Marquetry, Lily Flower & Bud, On White, Cameo, Signed, 6 x 4 In.	1760.00
Vase, Scenic, Amethyst, Yellow, Green, Conical Shape, Cameo, c.1900, 7 In.	1344.00
Vase, Scenic, Brown Trees At Border Of Lake, Pale Yellow, Gray Ground, 8 In.	1610.00
Vase, Sinewy Flowers, Yellow Ground, Cameo, 3 3/4 x 2 5/8 In.	440.00
Vase, Stick, Light Green Fern, On Frosted Pink, Cameo, Signed, 12 1/4 In.	920.00
Vase, Stylized Chrysanthemums With Cabochon Centers, 23 5/8 In.	4935.00
Vase, Trees Surround Bridge, Distant Hills, Mountains, Yellow Sky, Signed, 6 In.	660.00
Vase, Trumpet, Auburn Orchids, On Citron, Signed, 4 1/2 In.	978.00

Vase, Trumpet, Vine, Brown, Pale Yellow, Trumpet Blossoms, Cameo, Signed, 21 In. 3450.00
Vase, Tulips, Leaves, Chartreuse, Chestnut Brown, Cameo, 14 3/8 In. 3290.00
Vase, Vertical Internal Bands, Leafy Flowering Stems, Signed, 8 1/4 In. 2300.00
Vase, Yellow Cranberries, Goblet Shape, Cameo, Signed, 8 In. 1035.00
Vase, Yellow Crocus, Brown Leaves, On Light Citron, Cameo, 8 1/2 In. 6900.00

GALLE POTTERY was made by Emile Galle, the famous French designer, after 1874. The pieces were marked with the initials *E. G.* impressed, *Em. Galle Faiencerie de Nancy*, or a version of his signature. Galle is best known for his glass, listed above.

Ewer, Dancing Couple, Paper Label, Signed, 8 In. 745.00
Ewer, Enameled, Signed, Galle, Nancy, 7 1/2 In. 1790.00
Ewer, Scene Of Wolf On Snowy Landscape, Signed, 11 In. 1150.00
Figurine, Rampant Lion, Castle Tower, Shield, Banner, Motto, Signed, 16 1/2 In. 1095.00
Figurine, Shepherd & Shepherdess, Painted Marks, 9 In. 230.00
Plaque, Fish Below Crown, Figures In Landscape, Signed, 11 In. 1150.00
Vase, Double Fish, Molded, Signed, 20th Century, 6 In. 1495.00
Vase, Enameled Flowers & Buds, Purple, Pink, Brown, Green, Handle, Signed, 6 3/8 In. . . 316.00
Vase, Floral & Diagonal Band, Gold Enameled, Handles, Signed, c.1900, 10 3/8 In. 345.00
Vase, Flowers, Egg Shape, Signed, 6 In. 1150.00
Vase, Wooded Lake Scene, Chestnut, Caramel Brown Glaze, 16 1/2 In. 8225.00

GAME collectors like all types of games. Of special interest are any board games or card games. Transogram and other company names are included in the description when known. Other games may be found listed under Card, Toy, or the name of the character or celebrity featured in the game.

A-Team, Parker Brothers, 1984 . . . . 20.00
Action Baseball, Pressman Toy Corp., Marbles, Board, 1965 . . . . 28.00
Amazing Dunninger Mind Reading, Hasbro, Board, 1967 . . . . 150.00
Amusing Game Of Kilkenny Cats, Parker Bros., Board, Spinner, Box, 1890 . . . . 316.00
Andy Gump, His Game, Board, 1924 . . . . 70.00
Animal Bingo, Baldwin, Box 125.00
Artists, Owens & Agar, Card, 1850s 350.00
As The World Turns, Parker Brothers, 1966 . . . . 70.00
Barney Miller, Parker Brothers, 1977 . . . . 12.00
Baseball, Great American Game, Tin Lithograph Field, Revolving Play Drum, 13 In. 86.00
Baseball Game, Wood Case, Philadelphia Game Mfg. Co., 1912, 19 x 13 x 2 In. 260.00
Basketelle Marbles, Marx Toys, 1950s 15.00
Battle Cry, Civil War, Board, Box, Milton Bradley, 1962 . . . . 50.00
Battle Line, Board, Soldiers, Tanks, Ideal, Box, 1964 . . . . 24.00
Beat The Clock, Clock, 40 Hilarious Stunts Booklet, Lowell Toy, 1954 . . . . 20.00
Black Sambo, Target, Tin Gun & Darts, Wyandotte, 23 x 14 In. 172.00
Board, 2 Sides, Black & White Paint, Initials M.B., Early 1800s, 14 x 11 In. 2175.00

Game, Board, Painted,
America, c.1910,
15 1/2 x 16 In.

Game, Board, Painted,
Child's Puzzle, 1890-1910,
18 1/2 x 12 In.

Game, Board, Painted, Squares
Numbered 1 To 32, N.Y.C.,
1870, 16 1/2 x 14 1/2 In.

Game, Board, Parcheesi, Green,
White, Black, Yellow, Geometric
Corners, 19 1/2 In.

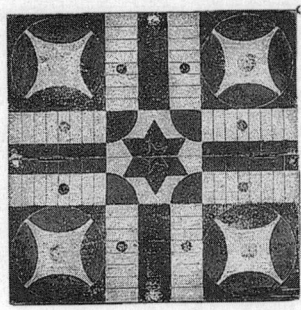

Game, Board, Parcheesi, Patriotic,
Folding, Late 19th Century,
17 3/4 x 18 In.

Board, Backgammon, Needlepoint, 35 3/4 x 29 In. 545.00
Board, Backgammon, Red, Black & White, Black & White Checkers, 14 x 17 In. 1380.00
Board, Black & Green Blocks, Orange Opposite Side, June 22, 1901, 17 x 18 In. 550.00
Board, Checkers & Backgammon, Mahogany, Cherry, Inlay, Folding, Pieces, 18 x 20 In. . 195.00
Board, Checkers & Chinese Checkers, Pine, Painted, c.1850, 17 x 25 In. 1680.00
Board, Checkers & Parcheesi, 18 1/2 x 18 3/4 In. 2090.00
Board, Checkers & Parcheesi, 22 x 36 In. 6037.00
Board, Checkers & Parcheesi, Cruciform, 19th Century, Square, 19 1/2 In. 5290.00
Board, Checkers & Parcheesi, Horse & Rider Design, Red & Yellow, 20 x 28 In. 750.00
Board, Checkers & Parcheesi, Stars At Corners, Faux Burl Wood, Red & Black, 22 In. ... 4600.00
Board, Chinese Checkers, Polychrome Painted, 20th Century, 24 1/4 In. 1090.00
Board, Chinese Checkers, Wood, Round, Polychrome Painted, Molded Rim, 19 1/2 In. .. 920.00
Board, Corner Pockets, American, First Quarter 20th Century, Square, 25 1/2 In. 3737.00
Board, Cribbage, Ivory, Floral Carving, Screw-Off Cap For Game Pieces, 7 In. 68.00
Board, Green Checkerboard & Line, Gallery, 12 3/4 x 20 5/8 In. 1210.00
Board, Ludo & Chinese Checkers, 1877, 14 1/2 x 14 1/4 In. 4700.00
Board, Marble, Arched Frame, Gutters, Polychrome Painted Diamond, 12 x 22 In. 978.00
Board, Mirrored, Walnut Frame, c.1900 .... 975.00
Board, Painted, America, c.1910, 15 1/2 x 16 In. .... *Illus* 4025.00
Board, Painted, Child's Puzzle, 1890-1910, 18 1/2 x 12 In. .... *Illus* 1495.00
Board, Painted, Squares Numbered 1 To 32, N.Y.C., 1870, 16 1/2 x 14 1/2 In. ...... *Illus* 4315.00
Board, Parcheesi, 21 3/4 x 28 3/4 In. 4750.00
Board, Parcheesi, Bird's-Eye Maple Over Mahogany, 22 x 15 In. 470.00
Board, Parcheesi, Green, White, Black, Yellow, Geometric Corners, 19 1/2 In. ..... *Illus* 2875.00
Board, Parcheesi, Multicolored, Mosaic Like Field, c.1890, 18 1/2 x 19 In. 4025.00
Board, Parcheesi, Painted, Green, Orange, Brown, Star Center, Applied Frame, 15 x 15 In. 1610.00
Board, Parcheesi, Painted, Polychrome, c.1880, 27 x 27 In. 4025.00
Board, Parcheesi, Patriotic, Folding, Late 19th Century, 17 3/4 x 18 In. .... *Illus* 4315.00
Board, Parcheesi, Pine, Stenciled Home, 19 3/8 x 19 In. 3575.00
Board, Parcheesi, Polychrome, Painted, Drawer, c.1920, 15 1/2 x 16 In. 1725.00
Board, Parcheesi, Polychrome, Painted, Early 20th Century, 15 x 18 In. 1955.00
Board, Penny Pitch, Painted, Wood, Red, White, Pinwheel, c.1900, 18 1/4 In. 3740.00
Board, Pine, Brass Spikes, Painted, Gilt Stencil, Gothic Arch Form, c.1880, 38 x 19 In. .. 5400.00
Board, Pine, Oak Trim, Square Nail Construction, Mustard & Black, 18 3/4 x 18 3/4 In. .. 1045.00
Board, Pine, Red & Yellowed Ivory Paint, Brown Ends, Gallery Edge, 14 3/4 x 28 In. ... 415.00
Board, Polychrome, Painted, 2 Sides, c.1880, 19 x 19 In. 8050.00
Board, Polychrome, Painted, Folding, 2 Sides, c.1880, 17 x 19 In. 250.00
Board, Polychrome, Painted, Folding, 2 Sides, Late 19th Century, 21 x 21 In. 1840.00
Board, Red & Black, Yellow Line Dividers, Gray, 14 3/4 x 15 In. 495.00
Board, Red & Mustard Paint, Black Line Dividers, 22 1/2 x 22 1/4 In. 440.00
Board, Spy vs. Spy, Mad's, 20 Tiles, 13 Plastic Bombs, Milton Bradley, 1986 .... 10.00
Board, Travel Theme, 8 1/2 x 12 1/2 In. .... *Illus* 15.00
Board, Wheel, Carnival, Painted, Revere Beach, Massachusetts, c.1915, 49 1/4 x 33 In. .. 750.00
Board, Wood, Brown & Tan Blocks, 2 Diamond Design, Sectioned, 27 x 19 1/4 In. 140.00

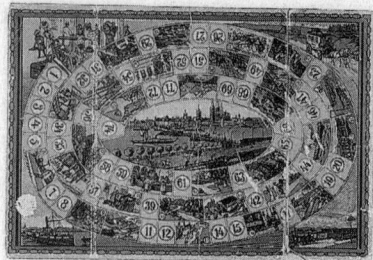

Game, Board, Travel Theme,
8 1/2 x 12 1/2 In.

Game, Checkerboard, Gilt, Molded Edge,
Saco, Maine, 19th Century, 18 3/4 x 20 In.

Board, Wood, Green & Black, Applied Trim, 32 Raised Blocks, 22 1/2 x 14 3/4 In. 385.00
Board, Wood, Painted, Bucking Bronco, Tractor, Dogs On Corners, 1920, 26 x 27 In. 2415.00
Board, Wood, Painted, Red & Yellow, Cutout Corner Pockets, Applied Frame, 25 x 25 In. 3740.00
Bobbsey Twins, Twins On Fame, Milton Bradley, Board, 1957 . . . . 90.00
Bowling, Ranger 30, With Pins 225.00
Candid Camera, Allen Funt On Cover, Lowell, Board, 1963 . . . . 75.00
Captain Kangaroo, Milton Bradley, Board, 1956 . . . . 60.00
Carpet Ball, Concentric Blue Circles, 3 1/8 In. 175.00
Carpet Ball, Swirled Red, Crossed Black Stripes, 2 1/2 In. 100.00
Carpet Ball, Yellow Crossed Stripes, 3 In. 200.00
Casper The Friendly Ghost, Milton Bradley, Board, 1959 . . . . 45.00
Checkerboard, Backgammon, Parcheesi, Painted Wood, Early 20th Century, 17 x 24 In. . . 1840.00
Checkerboard, Black & Orange Squares, Gilt, Scallop & Scroll Border, 19 x 20 In. 1840.00
Checkerboard, Drawer, c.1870, 29 In. 2070.00
Checkerboard, Folding, Painted, Geometric, Brass Latch, 12 x 11 1/2 In. 495.00
Checkerboard, Gilt, Molded Edge, Saco, Maine, 19th Century, 18 3/4 x 20 In. . . . . . *Illus* 5175.00
Checkerboard, Glass, Blue & White, Yellow & Green, Late 1800s, 14 3/4 x 14 3/4 In. . . . 230.00
Checkerboard, Gray Frame, Side Trays, White & Green, 18 1/2 x 28 1/2 In. 110.00
Checkerboard, Green Paint, Circle In Square Inlay, Frame, c.1890, 16 1/4 x 16 1/4 In. . . . 1725.00
Checkerboard, Lapboard, Incised, Painted, Measuring Tape, 19th Century, 20 x 35 3/4 In. 316.00
Checkerboard, Oak & Mahogany Squares, Sliding Lid Holds Checkers, 20 1/4 x 14 In. . . 330.00
Checkerboard, Oak, Painted, Black & Gilt Squares, 19 x 18 In. 1610.00
Checkerboard, Painted, Black & Red, Yellow Border, Fleur-De-Lis, 25 In. 745.00
Checkerboard, Painted, Black, Gray, Red Outline, Mid 19th Century, 13 3/4 x 14 In. 1035.00
Checkerboard, Painted, Drawer, c.1870, 17 x 29 In. 2070.00
Checkerboard, Painted, Red, Black, Gray Green Border, Mid 19th Century, 16 x 17 In. . . 1150.00
Checkerboard, Painted, Red, Green, Late 19th Century, 17 x 17 In. 1495.00
Checkerboard, Painted, Wood, Black, White, Blue, 19th Century, 14 x 18 In. 1150.00
Checkerboard, Pine, Butternut Scallops, Black Ground, 17 1/2 x 17 3/8 In. 1210.00
Checkerboard, Pine, Painted, Letters AC & L, 1856, 27 3/4 In. 3220.00
Checkerboard, Pine, Painted, Staggered Border, Breadboard Ends, c.1860, 22 x 19 In. . . . 3850.00
Checkerboard, Polychrome, Painted, Applied Frame, Early 20th Century, 19 x 24 1/2 In. . 1265.00
Checkerboard, Polychrome, Painted, c.1870, 18 1/2 x 18 1/2 In. 1840.00
Checkerboard, Red, Black Trim, Pots Of Flowers, 20th Century, 20 1/2 x 28 3/8 In. 525.00
Checkerboard, Wood, American, c.1890, 16 1/4 In. 1725.00
Checkerboard, Wood, Inlaid, 19th Century, 16 x 16 In. 230.00
Checkerboard, Wood, Painted, Mitered Frame, Pullout Drawer, 19 x 25 In. 1610.00
Checkerboard, Wood, Painted, Red, White, Blue, Red Frame, c.1876, 19 x 24 In. 2300.00
Checkers & Parcheesi, Corner Pockets, Capture & Attack, 28 3/4 In. 575.00
Chess Set, Oriental Pieces, Ivory, Brown, Fitted Box, Opens To Board, 24 x 24 In. 495.00
Chessboard, Faux Painted, Wooden, 2 Drawers, 2 Sets Of Chessman 690.00
Chicago's Great Blizzard, C.P. Marino, 1978 . . . . 85.00
Chit Chat, The Hugh Downs Game Of Conversation, Milton Bradley, 1963 . . . . 8.00
Cribbage, Bear Headed Form, Ivory Tusk, Seals, Walrus & Floral, 16 In. 1035.00
Cribbage, Ivory, Seated Figure, Top Knot, Threaded Knob, 5 Pegs, 7 1/4 In. 100.00
Croquet, 4 Mallets, 4 Balls, Brass Footed Wickets & Posts, Mahogany Box 375.00
Croquet, Ottawa, Ontario, c.1950 . . . . 190.00

Croquet Set, Wood, Colored Mallets, Poles, Balls, Daisy, Box, 31 In. 65.00
Dart Board, Cork On Plywood, Painted Baseball Diamond, c.1930, 22 x 22 In. 1380.00
Dart Board, Pine, Painted, Red, White, Blue, Midwest, c.1930, 18 1/4 x 19 1/4 In. 1840.00
Dating Game, Board, Cards, Money, Hasbro, 1968 . . . . .12.00 to 25.00
Dave Garroway's License Bingo, Tablet Of Game Sheets, Midwestern, 1958, 6 x 9 In. 15.00
Dexterity Puzzle, Cootie War, Time 110.00
District Messenger Boy, Spinner, 3 Figures, McLoughlin Bros., Board, 1886 . . . . 150.00
Doc Holiday Wild West, Transogram, Box, Board, 1960 . . . . 18.00
Dominoes, Bone & Ebony, Pine Slide Lid Box, 28 Pieces, Early 19th Century 495.00
Dominoes, Chip Carved Box, 2 Lidded Sections, Hold Dice, 31 Bone Dominoes, 8 In. 220.00
Dominoes, Ebony & Ivory, Dovetailed Box, Slide Lid, 18th Century 420.00
Dominoes, Wood, Inlay, Bone, Ebony, Box, 10 x 5 3/4 In. 80.00
Dr. Busby, Literary, Beige Cover, W. & S.B. Ives, Card, 1843 . . . . 450.00
Dr. Busby, Literary, Green Cover, W. & S.B. Ives, Card, 1843 . . . . 250.00
Elliot Ness & The Untouchables, Transogram, Board, 1961 . . . . 45.00
Emergency, Milton Bradley, Board, 1974 . . . . 12.00
Family Feud, Milton Bradley, Board, 1977 . . . . 8.00
Fantasy Island, Board, Cards, Markers, Ideal, 1978 . . . . 17.00
Fantasy Island, View Of Island, Columbia Pictures Television, Ideal, Board, 1978 . . . . . . 15.00
Football, Parker Bros., Popular Edition, Board, Spinner, Box 175.00
Fortune Telling, Circus On Lid, Donkey's Head Pointer, France, 1900, 10 x 8 1/2 In. 450.00
Fox & Geese, Pine, Flower Shape, Applied Tin Game Piece Holder, Board, 1930, 9 In. . . . 115.00
Game Of Characters, American, F.G. & O.F. Decker, c.1889 . . . . 50.00
Game Of Characters, Foreign, F.G. & O.F. Decker, c.1889 . . . . 50.00
Game Of Politics, Parker Bros., Board, Box, 1950, 17 x 19 3/4 In. 29.00
Goblin Ten Pin, 10 Lithograph Figures, 3 Balls, Original Box 550.00
Gong Show, Chuck Barris Productions, American Publishing, Board, 1977 . . . . 75.00
Great Cable Challenge, Showtime, 1980 . . . . 75.00
I'm Gary Moore & I've Got A Secret, Lowell Toy Co., 1956 . . . . 38.00
Improved Game Of Fish Pond, McLoughlin Bros., 1890 . . . . 150.00
Jack-Pot, Mechanical, Slot, Buffalo Toy, Box, 1920s 85.00
Jan Murray's Charge Account TV Word Game, Lowell Toy, Board, 1961 . . . . 15.00
Jeopardy, 4th Edition, 1964 . . . . 8.00
Jetsons, Rosey The Robot With Astro On Cover, Transogram, Board, 1962 . . . . 110.00
Jigsaw Puzzle, Addams Family Mystery, Cleopatra's Plight, Milton Bradley, 1965 . . . . . . 85.00
Jigsaw Puzzle, Adventures Of Robin Hood, Built-Rite, 1956 . . . . 8.00
Jigsaw Puzzle, Alien, Space Jockey, H.G. Toys, 1979, 10 x 14 In. 9.00
Jigsaw Puzzle, Anne Hathaway's Cottage, 106 Pieces, Bradley, Box, c.1910, 6 x 8 In. . . . 15.00
Jigsaw Puzzle, Ben Casey, Operating Room Scene, Bing Crosby Production, 1962 . . . . . . 10.00
Jigsaw Puzzle, Beverly Hillbillies, 1921 Rattletrap, Jaymar, 1963 . . . . 15.00
Jigsaw Puzzle, Big Boy, Double Cheeseburger, Blue Ground, 1960s, 6 1/2 x 9 1/2 In. 70.00
Jigsaw Puzzle, Boo Boogey Man, 3 Cannibals, 3 Missionaries, Box 126.00
Jigsaw Puzzle, Buck Jones Movie Cut Ups, 300 Pieces 20.00
Jigsaw Puzzle, Bugs Bunny, Licking Lollipop, 1960, 7 x 9 1/2 In. 10.00
Jigsaw Puzzle, Cheyenne, Milton Bradley, 1957, Set Of 3 . . . . 45.00
Jigsaw Puzzle, Dallas, J.R. Ewing, Lorimar Productions, 500 Pieces, 1980, 11 x 15 In. . . . 8.00
Jigsaw Puzzle, Decoys, Hunter Aiming Rifle, Ducks, Woodcraft, 150 Pieces, 1930s, 10 In. . 20.00
Jigsaw Puzzle, Game Of Patience, Wood Box, 8 1/2 x 10 1/2 In., Set Of 3 . . . . Illus 100.00
Jigsaw Puzzle, Good Dog, Boy Removing Splinter From Dog's Paw, 1930s, 10 In. 445.00
Jigsaw Puzzle, Hood's Sarsaparilla, Quack Medicines, Cardboard, 1890s, 10 x 15 In. 95.00
Jigsaw Puzzle, Horses, Haywagon Crossing Stream, J. Salmon, 500 Pieces, 1930s, 18 In. . 100.00
Jigsaw Puzzle, Huckleberry Hound, Painting Buoy, Whitman, 1960s, 7 x 9 In. 25.00
Jigsaw Puzzle, Illya Kuryakin, Milton Bradley, 1966 . . . . 25.00
Jigsaw Puzzle, Night Before Christmas, Milton Bradley, Boxed Set Of 3 . . . . 275.00
Jigsaw Puzzle, Painting, 2 Women, Bathing Feet, Box, Parker Bros., 1930s, 23 x 25 In. . . 375.00
Jigsaw Puzzle, Sliced Nations, Selchow & Righter, Part Of Box, 1881 . . . . 20.00
Jigsaw Puzzle, Sunset Scene, Rocky Shore, Tuck, Box, 499 Pieces, 1930s, 21 x 15 In. . . . 125.00
Jigsaw Puzzle, Tarzan Of The Apes, Johnny Weissmuller As Tarzan, 1932, 8 1/2 x 11 In. . 145.00
Jigsaw Puzzle, U.S., Paper On Wood, Hinged Oak Box, 60 Pieces, Milton Bradley 230.00
Jigsaw Puzzle, United States, With Uncle Sam, Wood Mount, Milton Bradley, 12 x 10 In. 115.00
Jigsaw Puzzle, United States, Wood, Parker Bros., c.1915, 20 x 12 1/2 In. 130.00
Jigsaw Puzzle, Wood Pieces, Woman In Garden, Title In 3 Languages, Box, 6 x 6 In. 110.00
Knockout Boxing, Northwestern Toys, Battery Operated, 1940-1950, 15 In. 285.00

Krazy Table Tennis, Oddly Shaped Bats, Net, Posts, Rules, 1930s 145.00
Kreskin's ESP, Board, Charts, Cards, Pendulum, Milton Bradley, 1966 ....8.00 to 14.00
Lincoln Highway & Checkers, Cards, Parker Bros., Board, 1925 .... 80.00
Loterie, Maison Simonne Loterie, Central Wheel On Inner Lid, Prizes, 14 x 10 In. 1000.00
Magic Circus Game, American Toys Co., Box 65.00
Mah-Jongg Set, Bone & Bamboo Tiles, Case, 6 1/4 x 9 1/4 In. 92.00
Mah-Jongg Set, Fruitwood, Figures & Flowers, 5 Drawers, Ivory & Bamboo Tiles, 10 In. . . 172.00
Manage Your Own Baseball Team, Built-Rite, 1950s 25.00
Marble, Runs Incline With Elephant & Whirligig, Windup, Box, Germany, 1950s 350.00
Military, Tri-Tactics, Board, Cardboard Pieces, Metal Stands, Box, 8 x 16 In. 5.00
Monday Morning Coach, James De Hart, Winston-Salem, N.C., Oil Cloth, Card, 1934 ... 86.00
Mother Goose, Target, Lithographed Paper, Nursery Rhyme Characters, Reed, 18 In. 440.00
Mr. Magoo, Secret Messages, Glasses, Standard Toykraft, Board, 1964, 18 x 18 In. 20.00
Munsters, Karo-Vue Productions, Card, 1964 .... 29.00
My Favorite Martian, Bill Bixby & Ray Walston, Transogram, Board, 1963 .... 110.00
Newlywed Game, 3rd Edition, Hasbro, Board, 1969 .... 45.00
No Time For Sergeants, Board, Spinner, Ideal, 1964 .... 30.00
No Time For Sergeants, Warner Bros. Pictures Inc., 1964 .... 30.00
North Atlantic Shipping, Trans Freight Lines, 1980 .... 75.00
Our Gang, 1930, Tipple-Topple, All-Fair Co. 635.00
Parcheesi & Backgammon, Folding, Painted, Red Ground, 18 x 18 In. 2300.00
Parlour Tennis, Paper Covered Battledores, Net, Posts, c.1900 .... 270.00
Penny Pitch, Painted, c.1900, 18 1/4 In. 3738.00
Phil Silver, Sgt. Bilko, You'll Never Get Rich, Gardner Games, 1955 .... 48.00
Pinball, Lucky Clown, Bagatelle, Die Cut Box, 1950s, 6 1/2 In. 30.00
Pinball, Wood, Painted, Applied Nail Track Pattern, c.1930, 14 x 28 1/2 In. 345.00
Ping-Pong, Box Top Labels, Faeries & Cobweb Graphics, Brass Posts, Box, J. Jacques ... 336.00
Pinhead Game Of Hide & Seek, Remco, 1959 .... 8.00
Pokerette Bogatelle, Tin, Glass, Wooden Frame, T. Conn, 1930s, 7 1/2 In. 75.00
Polo, Tin Lithograph, Cardboard, Push & Pull Activated, Carters, 24 In. 70.00
Pool, Table, Brunswick, Oak, Lockable Cue Rack, Decal, 60 x 35 1/2 In. 1550.00
Pop Za Ball Game Of Skill, Mattel 14.00
Press, Playing Card, Victorian, Oak, Brass, Crank, Trefoil Feet, 19th Century, 6 3/8 In. 172.00
Prospecting The Gold Rush, Selchow & Righter Co., Board, 1953 .... 10.00
Punchboard, Uncle Sam Wants You To Win! World Wide Inc., 1942, 3 1/2 x 2 1/8 In. ... 11.00
Puzzle, Gilbert Boxed Problem Puzzles, 6 Piece 18.00
Puzzle, Harry Houdini Official Magic, Houdini Wire Puzzle Co., 1926, 9 x 3 1/2 In. 1955.00
Puzzle, Indian, Pipe Stem, Wooden, 1850, 31 1/2 In. 960.00
Puzzle, Rootie Kazootie, Rootie & Polka Dottie Giving Poochie A Bath, 1950s 10.00
Puzzle, Sohio Oil Co., Box, 1933, 11 x 14 1/2 In. 75.00
Puzzle, Tally Ho, S. Lyman, c.1878 .... 445.00
Puzzle, Tip Top Bread, Envelope, 1952, 7 x 8 In. 45.00
Quick Draw McGraw, Private Eye, Milton Bradley, Board, 1960, 16 x 18 1/2 In. 10.00
Red Riding Hood, Parker Bros., Adventure Series, Board, Spinner, Box, 1895 .... 144.00
Ring Toss, Wood Backplate, Small Hooks, Printed Numbers, 4 Leather Rings, 16 In. 172.00
Ring Toss, Wood, White Paint, 9 Numbered Pegs, Hinged Easel Stand, 56 x 24 In. 460.00

Game, Jigsaw Puzzle, Game Of Patience,
Wood Box, 8 1/2 x 10 1/2 In., Set Of 3

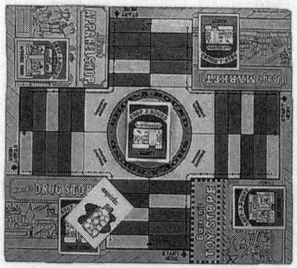

Game, Shop Around, Board, Pieces,
11 1/2 x 13 3/4 In.

Roulette, Toy Prizes, Wooden Box, Maroon Cover, France, c.1890, 11 x 8 In. 650.00
Roulette Table, Will & Finck, San Francisco, Victorian 11160.00
Roulette Wheel, Ten For One, Polychrome, Painted, Gilded, c.1890, 24 x 24 In. 3335.00
Round The World With Nellie Bly, Milton Bradley, Board, 1890 . . . .   50.00
Sambo, Lithographed Cardboard, Spinner, Pieces, 1945, 20 x 40 In. 180.00
Scores N Stripes, Bagatelle, Twin Level Tin Lithograph, Box, c.1953, 12 In. 100.00
Shooting Gallery, 8 Painted Birds, On Iron Rods, 1940s, 4 x 45 In. 345.00
Shooting Gallery, Target, Duck, Gaff Type, Brass, White Paint, 7 1/2 In. 104.00
Shooting Gallery, Target, Elephant, Cast Iron, White Paint, 9 1/2 In. 247.00
Shooting Gallery, Target, Holding Leaf, Head Retracts When Hit, Cast Iron, 19th Century 1880.00
Shooting Gallery, Target, Lion, Running, Cast Iron, White Paint, 12 1/2 In. 220.00
Shooting Gallery, Target, Mountain Goat, Leaping, Cast Iron, White Paint, 8 3/4 In. 148.00
Shooting Gallery, Target, Squirrel, Gaff Type, Brass, White Paint, 4 3/4 In. 82.00
Shooting Gallery, Target, Stag, Running, Cast Iron, Black Paint, 9 1/2 In. 220.00
Shop Around, Board, Pieces, 11 1/2 x 13 3/4 In. . . . . Illus   3.00
Skee Ball, Battery Operated, Marx-A-Scorebox, 1950s, 32 x 13 In. 150.00
Skittles, Wooden Pins & Ball, Cast Iron 2925.00
Solitaire, Pine, Round, Turned, Brown Stain, Board, Late 19th Century, 9 3/4 In. 35.00
Stop & Go, Shell Oil, Spinner, 80 Cards, Instructions, 1 Token, Comics, 1936, 10 In. 230.00
Super Spy, Milton Bradley, Board, 1971 . . . .   8.00
Swayze News Quiz, Board, Map, John Cameron Swayze Photo, Milton Bradley, 1954 . . .   15.00
Table Tennis, Vellum Battledores, Net, Metal Posts, Rules, Bussey, Xmas 1900 . . . .   304.00
Table Tennis, Whiff-Waff, Linen Covered Box, Wood Handles, Ball Tube, c.1900 . . . .   224.00
Table Tennis, Wooden Bats & Net Posts, Rules, Box 96.00
Target, Baseball, Official Dartball, Cork, Art Deco, 49 In. 1650.00
Target, Magic Circus, Tin Lithograph, American Toys Co., Box, 1950s, 11 x 11 In. 65.00
Tavern, Wood, Iron Frog, Wheel, Tin Holes, Feet, France, 15 1/2 x 20 1/4 x 29 1/2 In. . . .   578.00
Tic-Tac-Dough, TV Quiz Game, Transogram, 1950s 20.00
Token, Chip For Gambling Casino, Magician Names On Each, 7 Piece 150.00
Uncle Sam's Mail, Milton Bradley, Board, 1926, 16 1/4 x 15 In. 115.00
Wachter's Parlor Base Ball, Bagatelle, Board, 1888 . . . . 2970.00
Wheel, Gambling, Painted, Wood, Red, Blue, Yellow, 19th Century, 25 x 16 In. 2070.00
Wheel, Gambling, Polychrome, Painted, Early 20th Century, 28 1/4 x 23 3/4 In. 633.00
Wheel Of Fortune, H.C. Evans, 32 In. 2650.00
White Shadow Basketball, 1970s TV Show, Cadaco, Board, 1980 . . . .   95.00
Wyatt Earp, Life & Legend, Transogram, 1958 . . . .   70.00

GAME PLATES are plates of any make decorated with pictures of birds, animals, or fish. The game plates usually came in sets consisting of twelve dishes and a serving platter. These sets were most popular during the 1880s.

Bird, In Branches, Crescent, England, 1940s, 10 In. 40.00
Bird Set, Rose Border, Gold Trim, Bavaraia, 12 1/2 In.-Platter, 5 Piece 130.00
Fish, Floral Border, Marked, H & Co., 1878-1889, 8 3/8 In. 135.00
Pheasant, Flambeau, Limoges, 10 In. 100.00
Plate, Hunt Scene, Spode, 10 1/2 In., 12 Piece 231.00
Prairie Hen, Flambeau, Limoges, 12 In. 285.00
Quail, Hanging On Wall, Signed, Muville, Limoges, 1900-1012, 12 1/2 In. 300.00
Sandpiper, Gold Trim, Bavaria, 9 In. 40.00

GARDEN FURNISHINGS have been popular for centuries. The stone or metal statues, wire, iron, or rustic furniture, urns and fountains, sundials, and small figurines are included in this category. Many of the metal pieces have been made continuously for years.

Basin, Lead, Demilune, Classical Figures, Eagles, Grapevines, Dated 1738, 53 1/4 x 26 In. 1150.00
Bench, Branch & Leaf, Quatrefoil Feet, Green Paint, 33 x 50 1/2 In. 880.00
Bench, Camelback, Sunray & S-Scroll Frets, Bromwell Co., White Paint, 53 In. 1045.00
Bench, Cast Iron, Charcoal Enamel, Cabriole Legs, Openwork, Leaves, 45 x 41 In. 990.00
Bench, Cast Iron, Wood, Antiqued White Paint, 19 x 55 1/2 x 17 3/4 In. 1955.00
Bench, Hunting Dog Medallion, Leaves, Cast Iron, Victorian, 31 1/2 In. 635.00
Bench, Openwork Fern On Back & Legs, 31 x 43 1/2 In. 300.00
Bench, Passion Flower, Cast Iron, 1900, 33 x 17 1/2 x 26 In. 3450.00
Bench, Scrolling Splayed Legs, Floral Back & Arms, Cast Iron, c.1850, 80 In. 1200.00

Bench, Teak, Turned Front Legs, Scrolled Arm Supports, 3 Floral Panels, 58 1/2 In., Pair . 1100.00
Bench, Twig With Leaves, Cast Iron, Kramer Bros., 31 x 37 1/2 In. 715.00
Bench, Vintage Designs, Scrolled Seat, Cast Iron, 29 x 36 In., Pair 330.00
Birdbath, Lead, Figural, Girl Holding Shell, 2 Spigots, Rock Base, c.1895, 38 In. 520.00
Birdbath, Sailboat Sundial, Metal Stand 55.00
Birdhouse, 3-Peaked Gables, Arched Arcades, 3 Doors, Green, Wood & Wire, 30 1/4 In. . 517.00
Birdhouse, Georgian, Faux Chimneys, Windows, Door, Base Pan, Wood, Wire, 21 3/8 In. . 517.00
Chair, Gothic Arch, Molded Crest, Cast Iron, 1900, 36 In. 690.00
Chair, Intertwining Flowers, Foliage, Cabriole Legs, Arm, Cast Iron, 32 In. 1725.00
Chair, Urn Splat, Scrolled Rear Posts, Scrolled Arms, 28 1/4 In., Pair 3025.00
Chair & Bench, Openwork, Scrolled Seats, Cast Iron, Bench, 35 1/2 In. 350.00
Chair Set, Iron, Painted, Adams & Storrie, Philadelphia, 37 x 17 1/2 x 16 In., 4 Piece 2128.00
Dibbler, Yew, Boot Form Handle, Early 19th Century 165.00
Figure, Cupid, Standing, Holding Lyre, Lead, 40 In. 646.00
Figure, Deer, Standing, Cast Iron, J.W. Fiske, 61 In. 4950.00
Figure, Dog, Whippet, Lying Down, Iron, J.W. Fiske Iron Works, Pair 7150.00
Figure, Draped Nude, Sitting, Marble, 53 In. 6900.00
Figure, Gnome, Cast Iron, Early 1900s, 28 In. 315.00
Figure, Gnome, Watering Can, Painted, Incised, Cast Iron, 27 In. 3630.00
Figure, Male, Standing, Holding Flute, Female, Dancing, Lead, 60 In. 2400.00
Figure, Pan, Bronze, Bronze Base, 33 In. 560.00
Figure, Pan, Playing Pipes, Lead, 31 In. 2585.00
Figure, Rook, Cast Lead, 15 x 10 x 5 In. 560.00
Figure, Rooster, Iron, White Paint, 35 In. 776.00
Figure, Venus, Cast Iron, Rusted Finish, 35 In. 1725.00
Figure, Woman, Sandstone, 53 In. 2995.00
Figure, Woman, Sitting, Concrete, 1920s 2200.00
Figure, Woman, With Butterfly, Cast Zinc, J.W. Fiske, Late 1800s, 41 In. 5175.00
Font, Putti Formed Pedestal, Round Marble Pedestal Base, 43 1/2 In. 2352.00
Fountain, 2 Children Under Umbrella, Zinc, Fiske Brothers, 60 In. 4600.00
Fountain, 2 Graduated Bowls, Lobed Bottoms, Center Ivy Leaves, Cast Iron, 50 In. 687.00
Fountain, 3-Piece Center, Lion's Head On Column, Open Mouth, Cherub Finial, 63 In. . . 4125.00
Fountain, Figural, Cherub On Fish, Marble, 33 In. 3600.00
Fountain, Lion Head, Cast Iron 950.00
Fountain, Urn Shape, Iron, Horsehead Finials, Abendroth Brothers, 1940s, 48 x 63 In. . . . 5940.00
Fountain, Weeping Willow Trees, Lead Patina, 76 x 53 x 26 In. 6325.00
Horse Head, Zinc, Wall Mounted, Molded, Open Mouth, Flowing Man, 19 x 16 x 17 In. . 1650.00
Jardinere, Cartouche Of Birds & Flowers, Yellow Ground, 1880s, 24 In., Pair 2016.00
Lawn Jockey, Black Man, Red Jacket, Hat, Blue Pants, Black Boots, Concrete, 43 In. 50.00
Lawn Jockey, Cast Aluminum, Original Paint, Dark Brown, 19 In. 436.00
Ornament, Cast Stone, Bust, Acanthine Molded Pedestal, Socle Base, 53 x 19 In. 2508.00
Ornament, Lion, Concrete, 21 x 50 In. 495.00
Ornament, Rabbit, Sitting, Ears In Air, White Paint, Pink Highlights, Iron, 11 x 10 In. . . . 184.00
Ornament, Rooster, Cast Iron, White, 35 In. 776.00
Patio Set, 8 Chairs, 3 Benches, Brown Cushions, Sweden 568.00
Pedestal, Marble, Carved Leaves, 28 x 16 In., Pair 1495.00
Pedestal, Neoclassical, Variegated Stone, Circular Plinth, 44 x 34 In. 748.00
Planter, Carved Stone, 18 x 16 1/2 x 16 In. 187.00
Planter, Hourglass Shape, Case Fluting, Iron, 6 1/4 x 7 In. 39.00
Planter, Rococo Motif, Footed, Iron, 16 x 9 x 10 In., Pair 126.00
Seat, Blue & White, 4 Sides, Landscape Scenes, Chinese Export, 18 In., Pair 1495.00
Seat, Double Cash Symbols, Stylized Floral Border, Chinese Export, 19 In., Pair 3300.00
Seat, Floral Sprays, Objects, Blue & White, Porcelain, Qing Dynasty, Chinese, 18 In. 920.00
Seat, Oriental, Barrel Shape, Blue, White, Panels, Birds, Leaves, 20 1/4 In. 220.00
Seat, Pierced Hunting Dog Medallion, Planked Wooden Seat, Cast Iron, 29 1/2 In. 489.00
Seat, Porcelain, Rose Medallion, Hexagonal, Vignettes, Cantonese, 1880, 18 In., Pair 7245.00
Seat, Reticulated Center, 2 Borders, Blue, White, 19th Century, 19 In. 575.00
Seat, Sgraffito Carving, Celadon, Ming Dynasty, Sea Green, 17 In. 2530.00
Seat, Tree Trunk Form, Ivy & Blackberries, Majolica, 19 In. 990.00
Seat, Twig, Grapevines, Majolica, 18 1/2 In. 1100.00
Seat, Wood, Oriental, Inlaid Mother-Of-Pearl, Marble Top, 18 In. 302.00
Set, Settee, 2 Side Chairs, Shelf, Scrolling, Wrought Iron, 1880s, 4 Piece 375.00
Set, Vintage, White Paint, Table, Armchair, Bench, Side Chair 302.00

Sprinkler, Attached On Head, Cast Cement, c.1920, 14 1/4 x 10 1/2 In. 546.00
Sprinkler, Walking Tractor, Silver Painted Wheels, c.1950, 9 1/4 x 30 1/2 In. 230.00
Sprinkler, Yellow, Green & Red Paint, Cast Iron, 13 1/2 In. 660.00
Stool, Blue, White, Oriental, 19th Century, 11 x 21 1/2 In. 220.00
Sundial, Zodiac, Tilted Ring, 12 Carved Zodiac Signs, Late 19th Century, 15 1/2 In. 4700.00
Table, 3 Sections, Cast Stone, Pedestal Base, 23 x 20 In. 224.00
Table, Clay Tiles Top, Wrought Iron Base, Scrolled Legs & Stretcher, 29 x 70 In. 302.00
Table, Faux Mosaic, 3 Scrolling Supports, Tripod Base, Cast Metal, 27 1/2 x 36 In. 143.00
Table, Marble Top, Scroll Foot Base, Quatrefoil Cutouts, Cast Iron, c.1900, 31 x 27 In. . . 920.00
Table, Marble, Rectilinear Top, Square Columns At Each Corner, Italy, 35 1/2 In. 1003.00
Table, Wrought Iron, White Enamel Paint, Splayed Legs, 4-Section Tile Top, 16 x 20 In. . 143.00
Urn, Cast Iron, Dark Green Paint, 1870, 21 x 25 In., Pair 2415.00
Urn, Cast Iron, Dark Green Paint, 1875, 40 x 20 In., Pair 2070.00
Urn, Cast Iron, Dark Green Paint, Classical Design, Amphora, 29 x 24 In. 1035.00
Urn, Cast Iron, Dark Green Paint, Fluted Basin, 1890, 16 x 13 3/4 In. 230.00
Urn, Cast Iron, Dark Green Paint, U-Shape Handles, 1890, 21 x 16 1/2 In., Pair 1035.00
Urn, Cast Iron, Square Plinth, Round Bowl, Pair 247.00
Urn, Cherubs, Floral Garlands, Handles, Lion Heads, Serpents, 19 1/2 In. 440.00
Urn, Egg & Dart Lip, Concave Body, Plinth Base, Cast Iron, 1850s, 14 x 14 1/2 In., Pair . 748.00
Urn, Egg & Dart Lip, Figural Medallion, Laurel Wreath, Cast Iron, 23 1/2 x 19 In. 431.00
Urn, Full-Sized Cherubs Holding Urn On Shoulder, Cast Iron, 53 In., Pair 862.00
Urn, Lead, Handle, 18 In., Pair 345.00
Urn, Leaf Form Handles, Floral Garland, Rams' Heads, Cast Bronze, 32 x 20 In., Pair . . . 3360.00
Urn, Neoclassical, Campana Shape, 19th Century, 33 x 23 In. 978.00
Urn, Neoclassical, Marble, Campana Shape, 18 1/2 x 15 In. 403.00
Urn, Raised Base Panel, Cast Iron, Scrolled Leaf Handle, Signed Hay, 36 x 29 1/2 In. . . . 440.00
Urn, Relief, Vintage Motif, Iron, 11 1/2 In., Pair 259.00
Urn, Scroll Handles, Removable Interior Pot, Flared Rim, Iron, 34 In. 410.00
Urn, Terra-Cotta, Molded Lip, Fluted Standard, Applied Masque Handles, 56 In., Pair 1058.00
Urn, White Marble, Carved Scrollwork, Grapes, Masks, Leaves, 37 In., Pair 2875.00
Vase, Black Satin Painted Finish, Rectangular Pedestal Base, Cast Iron, 56 In., Pair 3680.00
Vase, Neoclassical Figural Design, Iron, 19th Century, 29 In. 616.00

GARDNER Porcelain Works was founded in Verbiki, outside Moscow, by the English-born Francis Gardner in 1766. The Gardner family retained ownership of the factory until 1891 and produced porcelain tablewares, figurines, and faience.   ГАРДНЕРЪ

Bisque, Match Box, Figural, Girl By Trunk, Seated Baby, c.1875, 5 3/4 In. 374.00
Figurine, 2 Boys At Well, Baskets Of Mushrooms, Mid 19th Century, 3 1/2 In. 747.00
Figurine, 2 Boys Playing With Eggs, Mid 19th Century, 5 1/2 In. 1035.00
Figurine, 2 Men Conversing, c.1860, 8 3/8 In. 920.00
Figurine, 2 Men Conversing, Signed, Mid 19th Century, 8 1/4 In. 1035.00
Figurine, Children, 1 Seated, 1 Playing Horn, Mid 19th Century, 4 3/4 In. 746.00

Gardner, Figurine, Jewish Man, From Dead Souls, c.1880, 8 1/4 In.

Gardner, Figurine, Man, Crossed Arms, Marked, 8 In.

Gardner, Figurine, Man, With Child, Marked, 1850, 11 1/4 In.

Gardner, Figurine, Woman,
Water Carrier, Blue Mark,
1820, 9 3/4 In.

Gardner, Group, 3 Drunken Men,
Holding Bottle, Accordion,
Marked, 1860, 10 In.

Gardner, Group, Drunken
Husband, Wife, Child,
1860, 9 1/4 In.

Figurine, Dancing Peasant, Holding Apron, Hand On Hip, Bisque, c.1860, 8 1/4 In. 546.00
Figurine, Dandy, Holding Egg Nest, Bisque, Mid 19th Century, 11 In. 863.00
Figurine, Fish Seller, Holding Basket, Net, Early 19th Century, 8 3/4 In. 1035.00
Figurine, Fisherman, Basket On Head, Early 19th Century, 8 1/2 In. 1150.00
Figurine, Girl, Dancing, c.1830, 5 1/4 In. 805.00
Figurine, Glazier, Holding Pallet, c.1840, 7 3/8 In. 1093.00
Figurine, Glazier, Holding Pallet, c.1845, 4 1/2 In. 1093.00
Figurine, Ice Breaker, Man With Ice Pick, Bisque, Mid 19th Century, 10 5/8 In. 978.00
Figurine, Jewish Man, From Dead Souls, c.1880, 8 1/4 In. . . . . *Illus* 920.00
Figurine, Jewish Man, Standing, Holding Umbrella, Bisque, c.1860, 9 In. 2300.00
Figurine, Maid, Holding Wooden Basket, Wreath, Late 19th Century, 8 In. 575.00
Figurine, Man & Woman, Elegant Dress, c.1820, 6 1/2 x 6 3/4 In. 1840.00
Figurine, Man, Crossed Arms, Marked, 8 In. . . . . *Illus* 920.00
Figurine, Man, Elderly, Seated, Wearing High Boots, Bisque, c.1860, 6 1/2 In. 575.00
Figurine, Man, Holding Broom, Early 19th Century, 6 5/8 In. 1150.00
Figurine, Man, Playing Accordion, Legs Crossed, Mid 19th Century, 7 In. 862.00
Figurine, Man, Seated, Playing Accordion, Signed, Mid 19th Century, 6 1/2 In. 862.00
Figurine, Man, With Child, Marked, 1850, 11 1/4 In. . . . . *Illus* 1150.00
Figurine, Man, With Kettle, Moujik, Wearing Apron, c.1830, 7 1/2 In. 1090.00
Figurine, Mother Feeding Infant On Lap, Bisque, Mid 19th Century, 6 1/2 In. 863.00
Figurine, Old Woman, Walking Stick, Basket, Mid 19th Century, 6 1/2 In. 747.00
Figurine, Old Woman, Wearing Shawl, Carrying Bundle, Signed, c.1860, 8 1/4 In. 805.00
Figurine, Peasant Boy, Pushing Wheelbarrow, Early 19th Century, 5 3/4 In. 1150.00
Figurine, Peasant Girl, Basket To Front, Signed, Early 19th Century, 7 3/8 In. 1035.00
Figurine, Peasant Man, Bearded, Seated By Tree Trunk, Bisque, c.1840, 5 1/2 In. 690.00
Figurine, Peasant Man, Dancing, Hands On Hips, Bisque, 19th Century, 9 1/2 In. 920.00
Figurine, Peasant Man, Drinking From Kovsh, Bisque, c.1860, 5 1/2 In. 690.00
Figurine, Peasant Man, Seated, Holding Child, Bisque, Mid 19th Century, 9 In. 920.00
Figurine, Peasant Woman, Carding, Bisque, Mid 19th Century, 5 In. . . . . 546.00 to 748.00
Figurine, Peasant Woman, Carrying Baby, Bisque, Mid 19th Century, 9 1/2 In. 460.00
Figurine, Peasant Woman, Carrying Baby, Signed, c.1860, 9 1/8 In. 633.00
Figurine, Peasant Woman, Child Playing Accordion, Mid 19th Century, 3 7/8 In. 633.00
Figurine, Peddler, Fur Trimmed Coat, Tray On Head, Bisque, c.1840, 8 In. 635.00
Figurine, Peddler, Fur Trimmed Coat, Tray On Head, Mid 19th Century, 7 1/2 In. 690.00
Figurine, Polish Couple, Holding Hands, Signed, 19th Century, 10 3/8 In. 1090.00
Figurine, Siberian Woman, Carrying Baby, Bisque, Late 19th Century, 9 1/2 In. 575.00
Figurine, Soldier, Holding Sword, Book, 19th Century, 8 In. 1092.00
Figurine, Tea & Pastry Vendor, Holding Tea Urn, Bisque, Mid 19th Century, 7 1/4 In. 633.00
Figurine, Tea Vendor, Holding Urn, Cup, c.1830, 9 1/2 In. 1265.00
Figurine, Tea Vendor, Rococo Base, Gardner, c.1825, 7 5/8 In. 920.00
Figurine, Tea Vendor, Standing, Holding Kettle, Russia, c.1840, 7 1/2 In. 1093.00
Figurine, Turk, Holding Can In Hand, Handkerchief In Other, Signed, 8 In. 1380.00

Figurine, Woman, Berry Baskets On Shoulder, Russia, Early 19th Century, 7 1/2 In. 1150.00
Figurine, Woman, Carrying Berry Baskets, c.1820, 7 3/8 In. 1035.00
Figurine, Woman, Holding Flower In Left Hand, Basket In Right, Signed, 7 In. 1495.00
Figurine, Woman, Water Carrier, Blue Mark, 1820, 9 3/4 In. .... *Illus* 6325.00
Group, 1 Child Standing, 1 Seated On Broken Cart Wheel, Bisque, c.1870, 5 In. 805.00
Group, 3 Drunken Men, Holding Bottle, Accordion, Marked, 1860, 10 In. .... *Illus* 2415.00
Group, 4 Children At Log-Framed Well, c.1860, 3 1/4 In. 1035.00
Group, Boy, Holding Crab, c.1840, 5 1/2 In. 978.00
Group, Drunken Husband, Wife, Child, 1860, 9 1/4 In. .... *Illus* 1035.00
Group, Uniformed Man & Cobbler, Bisque, c.1855, 7 1/4 In. 920.00
Inkwell, Porcelain, Figural, Peasant Man, Cover In Log Bundle Shape, 5 1/2 In. 920.00

GAUDY DUTCH pottery was made in England for America from about
1810 to 1820. It is a white earthenware with Imari-style decorations of
red, blue, green, yellow, and black. Only sixteen patterns of Gaudy
Dutch were made: Butterfly, Carnation, Dahlia, Double Rose, Dove,
Grape, Leaf, Oyster, Primrose, Single Rose, Strawflower, Sunflower,
Urn, War Bonnet, Zinnia, and No Name. Other similar wares are called
Gaudy Ironstone and *Gaudy Welsh*.

Coffeepot, Urn, Dome Top, 11 In. 2860.00
Creamer, Butterfly, Helmet Form, 4 7/8 In. 3300.00
Creamer, Carnation, 4 1/2 In. 660.00
Creamer, Leaf, 4 3/4 In. 4620.00
Cup, Carnation 130.00
Cup & Saucer, Butterfly 300.00
Cup & Saucer, Butterfly, Handleless 1870.00
Cup & Saucer, Carnation 440.00
Cup & Saucer, Double Rose, Handleless ....135.00 to 360.00
Cup & Saucer, Dove, Handleless 220.00
Cup & Saucer, Grape, Handle, Marked 960.00
Cup & Saucer, Grape, Handleless 220.00
Cup & Saucer, Oyster, Yellow Ground 605.00
Cup & Saucer, Single Rose ....220.00 to 330.00
Cup & Saucer, Single Rose, Handleless ....220.00 to 550.00
Cup & Saucer, Sunflower, Handleless 660.00
Cup & Saucer, Urn 110.00
Cup & Saucer, Urn, Handleless 605.00
Cup & Saucer, War Bonnet, Handleless 715.00
Cup Plate, War Bonnet, 4 1/4 In. 1650.00
Pitcher, Double Rose, Bulbous, Elaborate Handle, 4 3/4 In. 365.00
Pitcher, War Bonnet 2250.00
Plate, Butterfly, 4 In. 4750.00
Plate, Butterfly, 8 1/2 In. 1760.00
Plate, Butterfly, 9 7/8 In. 825.00
Plate, Butterfly, Marked, 8 1/4 In. 300.00
Plate, Carnation, 7 1/2 In. ....360.00 to 550.00
Plate, Carnation, 8 1/2 In. ....550.00 to 660.00
Plate, Double Rose, 9 3/4 In. 330.00
Plate, Double Rose, 10 In. 935.00
Plate, Dove, 6 1/2 In. 605.00
Plate, Dove, Impressed 5, 8 1/2 In. 360.00
Plate, Grape, 7 In. ....275.00 to 770.00
Plate, Grape, 8 1/4 In. 440.00
Plate, Oyster, 7 3/8 In. 220.00
Plate, Single Rose, 8 1/4 In. 550.00
Plate, Soup, Double Rose, 8 3/4 In. 660.00
Plate, Soup, Grape, 7 In. 495.00
Plate, Soup, War Bonnet, 8 1/2 In. 825.00
Plate, Strawflower, Impressed Riley, 10 In. 4290.00
Plate, Sunflower, 8 1/4 In. ....1320.00 to 1870.00
Plate, Sunflower, 9 3/4 In. ....3300.00 to 4867.00
Plate, Urn, 5 1/4 In. 1100.00
Plate, Urn, 10 In. 385.00

Plate, War Bonnet, 8 1/4 In. ....1825.00 to 2530.00
Plate, War Bonnet, Marked, 6 1/4 In. 910.00
Saucer, Carnation, Cobalt Blue, Orange, Green & Yellow, 5 1/2 In. 104.00
Soup, Dish, War Bonnet, 8 1/4 In. 580.00
Sugar, Cover, Grape, Handles, 5 1/2 In. 660.00
Sugar, War Bonnet, Marked, 5 1/2 In. 300.00
Teapot, Butterfly, 5 3/4 In. 1265.00
Teapot, Carnation, 5 3/4 In. 1980.00
Teapot, Double Rose, 6 1/4 In. 3190.00
Teapot, Oyster, 6 1/4 In. 300.00
Teapot, Single Rose 3750.00
Teapot, War Bonnet 1800.00
Toddy, War Bonnet, 5 1/8 In. 190.00
Waste Bowl, Carnation, 2 3/4 x 5 1/2 In. ....220.00 to 550.00

GAUDY IRONSTONE is the collector's name for the ironstone wares
with the bright patterns similar to Gaudy Dutch. It was made in
England for the American market. There may be other examples found
in the listing for Ironstone or under the name of the ceramic factory.

Charger, Rabbit Transfer, Frogs Between Rabbits, 13 In. 1100.00
Coffeepot, Pinwheel, Signed, 12 In. 834.00
Coffeepot, Urn, Paneled, Ring Handle, 9 In. 467.00
Creamer, Pagodas & Palm Trees, Face On Handle, 6 1/2 In. 93.00
Cup & Saucer, Primrose & Leaf 121.00
Cup & Saucer, Raised Surface, Cobalt Blue, Iron Red, 5 3/4 x 3 In. 99.00
Cup & Saucer, Seeing Eye, Handleless, 4 Piece 220.00
Cup Plate, Seeing Eye, Niagara Shape, Signed, 5 In., 3 Piece 385.00
Pitcher, Flowers, Serpent Handle, 11 In. 302.00
Pitcher, Flowers, Serpent Handle, Man's Head, Crazing, 6 1/4 In. 137.00
Pitcher, Paneled, Oriental Flowerpots, Figural Handle, Mason's, 8 1/4 In. 330.00
Pitcher, Pinwheel, 5 3/4 In. 143.00
Plate, Blackberry, Niagara Shape, E. Walley, 9 1/2 In. 104.00
Plate, Seeing Eye, Niagara Shape, E. Walley, 8 1/2 In. 110.00
Plate, Seeing Eye, Paneled, Marked Pearl White, 9 1/4 In. 95.00
Plate, Seeing Eye, Round, Niagara Shape, Signed, 6 1/2 In. 85.00
Plate, Soup, Seeing Eye, Niagara Shape, Signed E. Walley, 9 3/4 In. 330.00
Plate, Strawberry, Pink Flowers, Flow Blue Leaves, 12 Sides, 10 In. 247.00
Plate, Urn, Flow Blue, Pink & Red Flowers, Copper Luster, 8 1/2 In. 110.00
Platter, Pinwheel, Paneled, 10 1/4 x 13 1/4 In. 384.00
Platter, Scalloped Edge, Ashworth Bros. Hanley, 19 1/2 x 15 1/2 In. 345.00
Soup, Dish, Scalloped Rim, Center 5-Petal Flower, 10 1/2 In. 110.00
Soup, Dish, Seeing Eye, Marked Pearl White, 10 In. 440.00
Sugar, Cover, Pinwheel, Signed 14, 7 3/4 In. 165.00
Waste Bowl, Molded Rims, 3 5/8 x 5 1/4 In. 110.00
Waste Bowl, Seeing Eye, 3 3/4 x 5 1/4 In. 110.00

GAUDY WELSH is an Imari-decorated earthenware with red, blue,
green, and gold decorations. Most Gaudy Welsh was made in England
for the American market. It was made after 1820.

Bowl, Blue, Gold Flower, Green Leaves, Handles, 6 1/2 x 4 1/4 x 5 7/8 In. 275.00
Cup & Saucer, Bell Flower, Scalloped Top 22.00
Cup & Saucer, Blue Bands, Leaves, Handleless 137.00
Cup & Saucer, Cobalt Blue, Iron Red, Green, Blue Luster Highlights, 6 x 3 In. 248.00
Cup & Saucer, Grapevine, Oyster, 5 Piece 220.00
Cup & Saucer, Grapevine, Paneled Sides, Cobalt Blue, Iron Red, 6 x 3 In. 330.00
Cup & Saucer, Iron Red, Cobalt Blue, Green, Copper Luster, Mark, 6 x 3 In. 110.00
Mug, Cobalt Blue, Green, Orange, Pink Floral, 2 In. 357.00
Mug, Grapevine Variant, 3 3/4 In. 192.00
Mug, Oyster, Allerton, 1831, 3 In. 165.00
Pitcher, Cambrian Rose, Copper Luster, Handle, Diamond-Quilted Spout, 5 1/4 In. 275.00
Pitcher, Cobalt Blue, Iron Red, Green, Raised Flowers, 7 3/4 x 7 1/2 x 4 1/2 In. 440.00
Pitcher, Cream, Polychrome, Snake Handle, Floral, 5 In. 83.00
Pitcher, Cream, Rose Helmet, 5 In. 1375.00

Pitcher, Cream, Tar Baby, Bulbous, 3 1/2 In.	39.00
Pitcher, Green Flowers, Grapes, Cobalt Blue, Iron Red, Lavender, Handle, 8 In.	330.00
Pitcher, Milk, Polychrome, Snake Handle, Flowers & Leaves, 6 In.	110.00
Pitcher, Milk, Tar Baby, Bulbous, Loop Handle, 5 In.	72.00
Pitcher, Octagon, Raised Relief, Flowers, Blue, Red, Green, 7 1/2 x 7 1/2 x 5 1/2 In.	415.00
Pitcher & Bowl, Cobalt Blue, Iron Red, 4 x 1 1/4 x 4 In.	468.00
Pitcher & Bowl, Grapevine, Scalloped Edges, Miniature	220.00
Plate, Iron Red Flowers, Cobalt Blue, Green Copper Luster, Pair	330.00
Platter, Purple Roses, Green Leaves, Blue, Red Buds, 7 1/4 x 10 In.	110.00
Serving Bowl, Flowers, Marked Ashworth Bros. Hanley, 9 In.	99.00
Soup, Dish, Oyster, Teal Green & Luster, 10 1/4 In.	82.00
Sugar, Cover, Cobalt Blue Band, Orange & Green Flowers & Urns, 7 In.	165.00
Sugar, Raised Shell Handles, Iron Red, Blue, Yellow, Green, 5 1/2 x 6 1/4 x 5 In.	715.00
Tea Set, Tulip, Ribbed Handles & Finials In Serving Pieces, 7 Piece	440.00
Teapot, Columbine, Molded Feet, Handle, Spout & Finial, 8 In.	275.00
Teapot, Orange, Blue, Flowers, Octagonal, 8 1/2 x 9 x 5 1/2 In.	550.00
Teapot, Vine, Acanthus Leaves, Flower Finial, 7 In.	220.00
Tray, Tulip Variant, Molded Handles, 9 1/4 In.	137.00
Waste Bowl, Blue, Iron Red, Yellow, Green, Stepped Diamond, 2 3/4 x 5 1/2 In.	440.00
Waste Bowl, Orange & Green Flowers, 3 1/4 x 6 1/4 In.	55.00

GENE AUTRY was born in 1907. He began his career as the *Singing Cowboy* in 1928. His first movie appearance was in 1934, his last in 1958. His likeness and that of the Wonder Horse, Champion, were used on toys, books, lunch boxes, and advertisements.

Ashtray, Glass, Dark Green, Where A Friend Finds A Friend, 5 1/4 In.	65.00
Boot, Child's, Little Gents, 3 Buckles, Box, 1950	650.00
Boots, Rubber, 3 Buckles, Box	225.00
Box, For Youth, Cowboy Boots, Western Designs All Sides, Yellow & Blue	85.00
Box, Ranch Outfit	75.00
Card Set, Mule Train Movie Re-release, 8 Sepiatone Lobby Cards, 11 x 14 In.	30.00
Christmas Card, Personal, Imprinted Signature After Greeting, 5 1/4 x 7 3/4 In.	65.00
Coloring Book, Cowboy Adventures, Die Cut, 46 Pages, Merrill Publishing, 1941	45.00
Comic Book, Fawcett Vol. 1, No. 6, March 10, 1943	115.00
Comic Book, No. 8, Smiling Photo On Front, July-August 1947	45.00
Flip Book, Pocket Television Theater, Gene Autry Rides To The Rescue, 2 1/8 x 3 In.	60.00
Key Chain Card, Television, 3 1/4 x 5 1/2 In.	15.00
Lunch Box, Metal, Universal Industries, 1954	460.00
Movie Still, Autographed, Beyond The Purple Hills, 1950, 8 x 10 In.	65.00
Photograph, Black & White, Children's Hour Performance, 1950, 8 x 10 In.	12.00
Photograph, Black & White, Matted, Autograph, 11 x 14 In.	100.00
Portrait, Color, Glossy, World Championship Rodeo, Dates, Ticket Prices, 7 x 9 In.	25.00
Program, Melody Ranch, Black & White Photos, 16 Pages, 8 1/2 x 11 In.	35.00
Program, Traveling Performances, Early 1950s, 12 Pages, 8 1/2 x 11 In.	28.00
Song Folio, Gene & Champion On Cover, 52 Pages Of Words & Music	25.00
Tie Rack, Framed Photo, Late 1940s, 15 In.	78.00
View-Master Reel, No. 950, Sawyers Inc., 1950	9.00
Wallet, Inset Photo, Vinyl, Tan Cover, Brown Interior	75.00

GIBSON GIRL black-and-blue decorated plates were made in the early 1900s. Twenty-four different 10 1/2-inch plates were made by the Royal Doulton pottery at Lambeth, England. These pictured scenes from the book *A Widow and Her Friends* by Charles Dana Gibson. Another set of twelve 9-inch plates featuring pictures of the heads of Gibson Girls had all-blue decoration. Many other items also pictured the famous Gibson Girl.

Handkerchief, Silk, Box, 16 In.	30.00
Perfume Bottle, Figural, Milk Glass	100.00
Plate, Mrs. Diggs Is Alarmed, Royal Doulton, 1900, 10 1/2 In.	125.00
Plate, She Becomes A Trained Nurse, 10 1/2 In.	250.00
Plate, Subject Of More Hostile Criticism, Royal Doulton, 1900, 10 1/2 In.	125.00
Scrapbook, Original Girbon Girl, Ray Gilmore, c.1900	60.00
Tin, Cigarette, Manoli Gibson Girl, Germany, 1920s	35.00

GILLINDER pressed glass was first made by William T. Gillinder of Philadelphia in 1863. The company had a working factory on the grounds at the Centennial and made small, marked pieces of glass for sale as souvenirs. They made a variety of decorative glass pieces and tablewares.

GILLINDER

Saltshaker, Melon Ribbed, Satin, Green Enameled Flowers	30.00
Shoe, Bow, Frosted Top, Gillinder Centennial, 6 1/4 In.	15.00
Shoe, Ribbed, High Top, Hobnail, 4 1/2 In.	75.00
Sugar Shaker, Melon Ribbed, Pink Flowers, Green Leaves, Screw Cap, 3 1/2 In.	250.00

GIRL SCOUT collectors search for anything pertaining to the Girl Scouts, including uniforms, publications, and old cookie boxes. The Girl Scout movement started in 1912, two years after the Boy Scouts. It began under Juliette Gordon Low of Savannah, Georgia. The first Girl Scout cookies were sold in 1928.

Bookmark, Art Deco Girl, Brass	21.00
Catalog, Equipment, 1936, 10 x 7 1/2 In.	60.00
Compact, Green Enamel, Gold Logo, German Silver, 1940s-1950s	100.00
Doll, Brownie, Uniform, Raincoat, Boots, Virga, 8 In.	120.00
Doll, Cadette, Uniform, Box, Effanbee, 11 In.	305.00
First Aid Kit, Wartime Container, Johnson & Johnson, 1942, 5 1/4 x 11 1/2 In.	55.00
Medal, Badge Of Merit, Fabric Swag, Early 1900s, 2 1/2 In.	760.00
Pin, Hiker, Painted, Bakelite, 1950s	45.00
Sampler, Motto, Laws, Embroidered, Frame, 1940s, 128 x 22 In.	120.00
Sash, 18 Badges, 5 Pins, 1970s, 22 In.	45.00
Uniform, 35 Badges, Brownie Patch, 1938-1935	300.00
Uniform, Mariner, Middy Top, Pleated Skirt, Navy Blue, 1950s, 28 In.-Waist	360.00

GLASS-ART. Art glass means any of the many forms of glassware made during the late nineteenth or early twentieth century. These wares were expensive and production was limited. Art glass is not the typical commercial glass that was made in large quantities, and most of the art glass was produced by hand methods. Later twentieth-century glass is listed under Glass-Contemporary, Glass-Midcentury, or Glass-Venetian. Even more art glass may be found in categories such as Burmese, Cameo Glass, Tiffany, and other factory names.

Bowl, Iridescent Bronze Green, Loetz Type, 7 1/4 x 2 1/4 In.	140.00
Bowl, Iridescent Gold, Stretch Edge, Karl Weldmann, 1926-1936, 2 1/2 x 5 In.	275.00
Compote, Iridescent Gold, Amethyst Foot, Karl Weldmann, 1916-1936, 9 In.	795.00
Cruet, Diamond-Quilted, Enameled Flowers, Blue, Stopper, 5 In.	110.00
Epergne, 2 Bowls, Beveled Plateau, Flowers, Ring, Early 20th Century, 16 In.	518.00
Epergne, 4 Horns, Silver Plated Holder	115.00
Epergne, Shallow Bowl At Top, Stems Holding 6 Baskets, 12 1/2 In.	100.00
Goblet, Green, Swirled Ribs, Vertical Panels, Cobalt Blue Lines, 5 In.	55.00
Sugar & Creamer, Ivory, Silver Plated Stand, England, 19th Century	110.00
Sugar Shaker, Acorn, White To Pink, Gold Floral Trim, 5 In.	190.00
Syrup, Acorn, White To Pink, 6 1/2 In.	210.00
Vase, Art Deco, Relief Nudes, Blue, Flared, Cylindrical, 8 3/4 In.	633.00
Vase, Enameled Bellflowers, Austria, 1900, 7 1/2 In.	145.00
Vase, Gold Iridescent, Blue Interior, Flared, Cone Shape, 1900s, 4 In.	144.00
Vase, Opalescent Interior, Meandering Air Bubbles, Ruffled Edge, Signed, 6 5/8 In.	2090.00
Vase, Opaque Green, 9 7/8 In.	172.00
Vase, Pink Overlay, Acid Cut, Fern Frosted Background, Trapezoidal, 12 In.	748.00
Vase, Slender, Green, Vertical White Opalescent Stripes, Pink Rigaree, 8 In.	80.00
Vase, Trumpet, Yellow, White, Gold Flecks, Bell Foot, Scroll Handles, 25 1/2 In.	431.00
Vase, White To Rose, Blue & White Applied Flower Design, Thorn Handle, 11 In.	209.00
Vase, Yellow & Clear Stripes, White Dove, Clover, Bimini, Austria, 1900, 6 1/2 In.	40.00
Water Set, Cobalt Blue, Flowers & Cherries, Iridescent Stain, Pitcher, 6 Tumblers	141.00

GLASS-BLOWN was formed by forcing air through a rod into molten glass. Early glass and some forms of art glass were hand blown. Other types of glass were molded or pressed.

Amberina, Decanter, Bar, Polished Base, 9 3/4 x 3 3/8 In.	630.00

Apothecary Set, Jar, Cover, Blue, France, 7 Piece 1904.00
Basket, Overshot, Rolled Rim, Turned Up Sides, 4 3/4 x 8 1/4 x 10 1/2 In. 35.00
Beaker, Engraved Flowers, c.1900 .... 48.00
Bottle, Geometric, Cobalt Blue, Tam O'Shanter Stopper, 6 3/8 In. 150.00
Bowl, 18 Ribs, Green Aqua, Flared, Footed, 3 1/4 x 4 1/4 In. 448.00
Bowl, Amber, Rolled Rim, 2 x 6 1/8 In. 450.00
Bowl, Cobalt Blue, Flared Rim, Footed, Handles, 19th Century, 5 1/2 In. 402.00
Bowl, Cobalt Blue, Rolled Rim, Pontil, 2 1/4 x 5 1/2 In. 340.00
Bowl, Deep Olive Green, 1840-1860, 4 5/8 x 9 1/2 In. 840.00
Bowl, Grass Green, Flared, Ground Pontil, 8 1/2 x 3 3/4 In. 165.00
Bowl, Light Sapphire Blue, Flared, Rolled Rim, 3-Piece Mold, Pontil, 2 1/2 x 4 1/2 In. 896.00
Bowl, Overshot, Green To Clear, Ruffled & Crimped Rim, 3 1/4 x 11 In. 110.00
Chalice, Olive Amber To Burgundy Puce, Conical Bowl, Pedestal, 1860, 5 5/8 In. 550.00
Chalice, Overshot, Gold Rim, Hollow Ringed Stem, 7 7/8 In. 80.00
Cheese Cover, Amber, Rolled Rim, Applied Knop, Pontil, 1840, 4 1/2 In. 415.00
Compote, Engraved Floral, Dome Base, Pedestal, 9 x 6 3/8 In. 715.00
Compote, Flared, Banded, Gadrooned Edge, Pedestal, New England Glass, 4 1/8 In. 3850.00
Compote, Gray Aqua, Ogee Bowl, Pedestal, Pontil, 1830, 5 3/8 x 5 3/8 In. 5390.00
Compote, Opalescent White, Scalloped, Knop Pedestal, 1870, 6 1/2 x 8 3/8 In. 605.00
Compote, Rolled Rim, Domed Lid, Tapered Handle, 14 1/2 In. 495.00
Creamer, 12 Diamonds, Cobalt Blue, Applied Handle, Pontil, 3 In. 750.00
Creamer, Aqua, Slender Cylinder, Horizontal Band, 1850, 5 1/2 In. 550.00
Creamer, Banded Rim, Applied Rings, Pittsburgh, 4 3/4 In. 110.00
Creamer, Cobalt Blue, Applied Handle, Conical Foot, Pontil, 1860, 4 1/2 In. 550.00
Creamer, Cobalt Blue, Applied Handle, Pontil, 43 3/4 In. 400.00
Creamer, Cobalt Blue, Paneled, Reeded Body, Handle, 3-Piece Mold, 1840, 4 In. 2875.00
Creamer, Cobalt Blue, Reeded Body, Handle, 3-Piece Mold, 1825-1840, 4 In. 3105.00
Creamer, Knop Cover, 24 Ribs Swirled To Right, Deep Cobalt Blue, 1880, 3 In. 308.00
Decanter, Amethyst, Fluted, Applied Mouth & Ring, Tin & Cork Stopper, 12 In. 1456.00
Decanter, Amethyst, Spiral Neck, 19th Century, 11 1/8 x 3 3/8 In. 630.00
Decanter, Claret, Yellow, Overshot, Footed, Rope Handle, Stopper, 1870, 14 In. 750.00
Decanter, Cobalt Blue, Round Stopper, Early 20th Century, 9 3/4 In, Pair 402.00
Decanter, Dark Olive Green, Sunburst Design, Swirled Ribs, 6 3/4 x 3 1/2 In. 2875.00
Decanter, Flared Mouth, 3-Piece Mold, Pontil, 10 1/2 In. 215.00
Decanter, Geometric, 3 Applied Double Rigaree Neck Rings, Stopper, 10 1/4 In. 130.00
Decanter, Green, 19th Century, 15 In. 127.00
Decanter, Hooped, Pale Green, Ribbed Lower Body, 1820-1840, 8 5/8 In. 4600.00
Decanter, Ship's, Domed Stopper, Ringed Neck, 1930s, 9 In. 175.00
Decanter, Ship's, Emerald Tinted, Engraved, Anglo Irish, 10 x 7 In. 748.00
Decanter, Waffle Print Stopper, Silver-Plated Brandy Label, 9 1/2 In. 55.00
Epergne, Dolphin Footed, Single Horn, Anthemion & Dart, 21 3/4 x 11 3/4 In. 1265.00
Fernery, Overshot, Rolled Rim, Applied Feet & Lion Head Handles, 7 7/8 In. 50.00
Jar, Apothecary, Cover, Round Base, Pontil, Knop Finial, 15 In. 165.00
Jar, Applied Finial Cover, 2 Applied Rings, Bulbous Base, Footed, 14 In. 310.00
Jar, Cover, Green, Bulbous, Flat Base, Flared, 2 Applied Handles, 6 x 6 1/2 In. 385.00
Jar, Cover, Pale Yellow Green, 1830-1870, 9 1/4 x 4 5/8 In. 135.00
Jar, Sweetmeat, Cover, Applied Knop Finial, Trumpet Shape, Dip Mold, 16 In. 690.00
Jug, Child's, Rolled Rim, Concentric Circles Around Pontil, c.1830, 2 In. 120.00
Ladle, Toddy Lifter, Cut, Tapered Top Opening, Paneled Body, 19th Century, 5 In. 115.00
Loving Cup, Olive Amber, Bell Shape, 3 Handles, Pedestal, Stoddard, 1850, 6 In. 5720.00
Milk Pan, 12 Vertical Ribs, Blue, Indented Center, Midwestern Pattern, 5 In. 690.00
Milk Pan, Deep Amethyst, Rolled Rim, Bubble, 1822-1829, 8 1/2 In. 2000.00
Milk Pan, Pale Green, Rolled Rim, Pontil, 20 1/2 x 4 In. 965.00
Mug, Amethyst, Applied Curled Handle, 3 1/2 x 4 1/8 In. 1456.00
Mug, Engraved Floral Wreath, Ellery, 7 In. 110.00
Pastry Server, 2 Tiers, Overshot, Cranberry To Clear, 9 1/2 In. 60.00
Pitcher, Aqua, Tapering Cylindrical Neck, Strap Handle, Pontil, 7 1/2 In. 1980.00
Pitcher, Dark Blue, Blue, Beehive, Urn Shape, Spout, Clear Handle, 6 5/8 In. 2870.00
Pitcher, Engraved Woods Scene, Twist Handle, New England Glass Co., 9 In. 495.00
Pitcher, Olive Amber, Lily Pads, Wide Threaded Neck, Handle, Applied Foot, 8 5/8 In. ... 8050.00
Pitcher, Pale Aqua, Applied Thread, Trefoil Handle, 1860, 9 1/4 x 5 1/2 In. 2070.00
Plate, Amber, 16 Ribs, Folded Rim, Pontiled Base, 5 1/4 In. 1456.00
Powder Jar, Cover, Applied Green Snake, Overshot, Gold Rim, 3 1/2 In. 170.00

Puff Box, Applied Finial Cover, Underplate, Overshot, Gold Rim, 6 x 4 1/2 x 7 In. 90.00
Salt, 11 Ribs, Vertical, Amethyst, Double Ogee Bowl, 2 5/8 In. 1100.00
Salt, 12 Ribs, Swirled Left, Light Green, Double Ogee Bowl, Scalloped, 2 3/8 In. 1300.00
Salt, 16 Ribs, Swirled Right, Sapphire Blue, Ogee Bowl, Pontil, 2 5/8 In. 300.00
Salt, 16 Ribs, Vertical, Yellow Green, Urn Bowl, Pontil, 1830, 3 1/8 In. 550.00
Salt, 20 Ribs, Vertical, Sapphire Blue, Double Ogee Bowl, Pontil, 2 3/4 In. 300.00
Salt, 22 Ribs, Vertical, Swirled Left, Amethyst, Double Ogee Bowl, 2 1/4 In. 1300.00
Salt, 26 Ribs, Dark Cobalt Blue, Conical, Pedestal, 3 In. 413.00
Salt, Blue, Diamond Petal, Footed, Midwestern, 1770-1815, 2 3/4 In. 385.00
Salt, Lockport Blue, Flared Rim, Bowl Applied To Stem, Round Base, 2 1/4 x 2 3/4 In. .. 672.00
Salt, Master, Overshot, Cranberry Insert, Silver Plated Frame, Claw Feet, 2 x 5 In. 140.00
Sugar, Applied Finial Cover, Cobalt Blue, Tooled Stem, Rolled Rim, 7 1/2 In. 2240.00
Sugar, Cover, Footed, 3-Piece Mold, 1830, 7 In. 5770.00
Sugar, Overshot, Cranberry Insert, Silver Plated Frame, Cover, Bird Finial, 6 1/4 In. 160.00
Sugar Shaker, Clear, Brass Cap, Pontil, 4 1/2 In. 252.00
Tumbler, Flip, Diamond & Rib Bands, Light Amethyst, 5 3/4 In. 330.00
Tumbler, Flip, Engraved Crowned Shield, Lion, Floral Basket, 8 1/2 In. 275.00
Tumbler, Flip, Flowers, Paneled, 8 In. 192.00
Tumbler, Flip, Paneled Base, Crosshatch Ovals, Engraved Rim, 3-Piece Mold, 6 In. 330.00
Tumbler, Flip, Paneled Base, Engraved Rim, 3-Piece Mold, 6 In. 358.00
Tumbler, Flip, Rayed Base, Sunburst & Diamond Band, 3-Piece Mold, Pontil, 5 5/8 In. .. 525.00
Tumbler, Flip, Swag & Birds, Wide Top Fluting, 7 1/2 In. 220.00
Tumbler, Leaf Engraving, I.F. Miller, 4 3/4 In. 137.00
Tumbler, Whiskey, Green Aqua, Applied Foot, Rough Pontil, Vermont, 3 In. 224.00
Vase, 12 Panels, Rolled Rim, Pontil, 8 In. 1120.00
Vase, 12-Pillar Mold, Swirled To Right, Applied Foot, Scalloped Rim, 10 In. 246.00
Vase, Bud, Engraved Flowers, Early 19th Century, 4 1/4 In. 165.00
Vase, Cobalt Blue, Applied Rings, 19th Century, 8 In. 750.00
Vase, Cobalt Blue, Applied Rings, Flared, New England Glass, 1840, 11 1/4 In. 7700.00
Vase, Emerald Green, 2 Handles, Open Pontil, Congressville Glass, 8 1/4 In. 1800.00
Vase, Engraved Birds, Crosshatches, Round Base, 2 Handles, Folded Rim, 8 In. 275.00
Vase, Gallery Rim, Pillar Mold, Round Foot, Pittsburgh, 1840, 7 1/2 In. 2035.00
Vase, Hyacinth, Deep Ruby Red, Ribbed, Semi-Fluted Lip, 7 In. 448.00
Vase, Hyacinth, Golden Amber, Ground Rim, c.1880, 5 3/4 In. 448.00
Vase, Hyacinth, Lavender Blue, Egg Shape, Applied Funnel Foot, 1860, 8 1/2 In. 550.00
Vase, Hyacinth, Light Lavender Blue, Seed Bubbles, Egg Shape, 1860, 8 1/2 In. 220.00
Vase, Hyacinth, Medium Green, Swirls In Glass, Tooled Mouth, 7 7/8 In. 146.00
Vase, Hyacinth, Purple Amethyst, Tooled Mouth, c.1905, 5 3/4 In. 365.00
Vase, Opaque White, Cased In Clear, Clear Stem & Base, c.1850, 13 1/2 x 8 1/2 In. 670.00
Vase, Sapphire Blue, Flared, Ball Knop, Footed, New England Glass, 1840, 8 7/8 In. 1815.00
Vase, Smoke Blue, Flared Rim, Round Base, Knop Stem, Footed, 6 3/4 x 7 1/2 In. 275.00
Vase, Translucent Jade Green, Ball Body, Flared Mouth, 7 7/8 In. 50.00
Vase, Trumpet, Amethyst, Rolled & Folded Rim, Polished Pontil, 7 1/2 In., Pair 1460.00
Vase, Trumpet, Amethyst, Rolled Rim, 7 1/2 x 3 1/2 In. 1840.00
Vase, Trumpet, Ruby Overlay, Tooled Mouth, 12 x 4 1/4 In., Pair 1380.00
Vase, Witch's Ball Cover, Amber, Flared, Rolled, Folded Rim, Open Pontil, 12 1/4 In. 728.00
Wax Seal, Striped, Blue & White, Reads Geena, 2 1/8 In. 168.00
Wine, Amethyst, Engraved, Flared Rim, Round Base, Baluster Stem, 5 In. 110.00
Wine, Engraved Hunting Scene, Square Cut Base, Short Stem, 4 1/2 In. 385.00
Witch's Ball, Aqua, Decoupage, Flowers, Animals, Birds, Butterflies, 1900s, 6 1/2 In. ... 259.00
Witch's Ball, Blue, Clear, Blowpipe Mouth, Looping, Spherical, 1850, 3 7/8 In. 173.00
Witch's Ball, Golden Amber, Crackle Glass, Chain, 1900s, 3 1/2 In. 144.00
Witch's Ball, Red Amber, Blowpipe Mouth, Spherical, c.1900, 4 3/4 In. 144.00
Witch's Ball, Royal Purple, Tooled, Ground Mouth, Spherical, 1900s, 4 1/2 In. 144.00
Witch's Ball, Ruby Red, Blowpipe Mouth, Chain, Rectangular, 1900s, 4 1/4 In. 201.00
Witch's Ball, Swirled, Cobalt Blue, Blowpipe Mouth, Spherical, 1900s, 6 In. 173.00
Witch's Ball, Violet, Stand, Open Pontil, 12 In. 1230.00

GLASS-BOHEMIAN

Bohemian glass is an ornate overlay or flashed glass made during the Victorian era. It has been reproduced in Bohemia, which is now a part of the Czech Republic. Glass made from 1875 to 1900 is preferred by collectors.

Beaker, Amber Flashed, Medallions, Engraved Buildings, Waisted, 4 1/2 In. 290.00

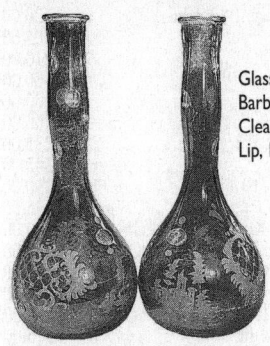

Glass-Bohemian, Bottle, Barber, Ruby Cut To Clear, Engraved, Rolled Lip, 1885-1925, Pair

Don't use gold- or silver-decorated glasses if the trim has turned chalky gray. This is a source of lead poisoning.

Beaker, Blue Cut To Clear, Enameled, Oval Reserves, Mid 19th Century, 4 3/4 In.	345.00
Beaker, Enameled, Ocher, Beige, Scrolling, Gold, Mid 19th Century, 5 In.	210.00
Beaker, Flared, Gold Enameled, Paneled, Medallions, Vines, 4 7/8 In.	160.00
Beaker, Ruby Flashed, Enameled, Flowers, Paneled, Mid 19th Century, 5 1/8 In.	489.00
Beaker, Ruby Flashed, Engraved Buildings, Thumbprints, Monogram, 5 1/8 In.	230.00
Beaker, Vaseline, Enameled Flowers, Silver Scrolls, Cobalt Rim, 4 3/4 In.	230.00
Bottle, Barber, Ruby Cut To Clear, Engraved, Rolled Lip, 1885-1925, Pair .... *Illus*	220.00
Bottle, Scent, Cruet Shape, Blue Overlay, Cut Glass, Teardrop Stopper, 9 In.	150.00
Bottle, Stopper, Yellow Cut To Clear, Grapevine, Silver Mount, 15 In.	145.00
Bowl, Black, Cut Geometrics, Lobmeyr, Urban Janke, Ludwig Heinrich, 4 In.	345.00
Bowl, Hooked Design, Bronze Green, White, Poschinger, 4 1/2 x 8 1/4 In.	325.00
Bowl, Intaglio Cut Glass, Scalloped Edge, 8 1/4 In.	75.00
Bowl, White Cut To Ruby, Lobed Edge, Late 19th Century, 8 1/8 In.	185.00
Decanter, Amber Cut To Clear Panels, Horses, Dogs & Deer, 15 1/4 In.	770.00
Decanter, Amethyst Cut To Clear, 15 1/2 In.	145.00
Decanter, Balus, Gold Grapevine, Handle, Baluster Stoppers, 1900, 9 3/4 In., Pair	325.00
Decanter, Blue Cut To Clear, Grape Leaves, c.1900, 11 In.	420.00
Decanter, Cobalt Blue, Enameled Magnolia, Shot Glass Stopper, 11 In.	230.00
Decanter, Cut Panels, Scene Of Deer In Wooded Field, Fence, 14 3/4 In.	225.00
Decanter, Ruby Cut To Clear, Scenic Stopper, c.1900, 16 In.	125.00
Decanter, Ruby Enamel, Diaper Cutting, Lozenge Shape, 16 1/2 In., Pair	219.00
Decanter Set, Ruby Cut To Clear, Animal Foot, 1900s, 4 Piece	225.00
Decanter Set, Ruby Flashed, Gold Enameled, c.1830, 12 In., 7 Piece	1150.00
Drinking Horn, Green, Historismus Enameled Crest, 1870s, 11 x 3 In.	195.00
Goblet, Clear, Faceted Knop Standard, Stag Hunt Scene, 10 1/2 In., Pair	575.00
Goblet, Enameled Floral, Green Stem, Frosted, Gilt Rim, Lobmeyr Type, 9 In.	110.00
Goblet, Flared, Enameled, Engraved, Paneled, Raised Reserve, 5 3/4 In.	259.00
Goblet, Geometric, Flowers, Amber, Blue, 6 3/4 In.	230.00
Goblet, White Over Pink, Gothic Tracery, Gold, Mid 19th Century, 5 1/2 In.	345.00
Humidor, Brass Scarabs Cover, Engraved, Benedict, Karnak Brass, 4 x 6 1/2 In.	110.00
Perfume Bottle, Red, Paneled, Scalloped Foot, Silver Flowers, Vines, 4 1/2 In.	259.00
Perfume Bottle, Scent, Blue Overlay, Starburst, Teardrop Stopper, 7 1/4 In.	150.00
Pitcher, Red Cut To Clear, Pinwheel & Fan, Thumbprint Borders, 10 In.	110.00
Pokal, Cover, Pink To Clear, Enameled Flowers, Grapes, Gilt, 13 In.	2310.00
Shade, Iridescent Green, Cone Shape, Dimpled, Early 1900s, 7 3/4 In., Pair	405.00
Syrup, Diamond-Quilted, Marbled Feathers, Loetz Type, 1900, 8 In.	375.00
Tumbler, Gold Enameled, Engraved Building & Church, Neuwelt, 1860, 3 1/2 In.	135.00
Vase, Amber Flashed, Engraved Forest Scenes, Panel-Cut Stems, 7 3/4 In., Pair	235.00
Vase, Amethyst Cut To Clear, Flowers, 7 1/2 In., Pair	288.00
Vase, Black Basalt, Carved Lilies, Tricornered Rim, Carl Goldberg, 8 1/2 In.	375.00
Vase, Blue Cut To Clear, Grape Clusters, 6 1/4 In.	60.00
Vase, Blue To Clear, Squares & Rectangles, Otto Prutscher, c.1910, 5 1/2 In.	460.00
Vase, Cased, Rose, Mauve, Green, Fluted Rim, 4 Applied Crystal Feet, 7 In.	85.00
Vase, Cobalt Blue, Swirled Oil Spot, Metal Collar, Loetz Type, 3 1/4 x 4 1/2 In.	95.00
Vase, Cobalt To Clear, Flared, Rectangles, Otto Prutscher, c.1910, 4 1/4 In.	230.00
Vase, Cover, Cranberry, Goblet Shape, Faceted Sides, 15 1/2 In.	575.00

Vase, Cranberry Cut To Clear, Floral & Diamond Cut, 20th Century, 14 3/4 In. 120.00
Vase, Cupids Flanking Cartouche, 15 In. 805.00
Vase, Emerald Green, Gold Iris, Wheel Cuttings, 10 1/4 In. 210.00
Vase, Engraved Landscape, Flared, Cylindrical, Early 20th Century, 10 1/2 In. 400.00
Vase, Flowers & Diamonds, Early 20th Century, 14 3/4 In. 200.00
Vase, Gilt Flowers, Twisted Shape, 6 3/4 In. 200.00
Vase, Goblet Shape, Continuous Scene, Deer In Forest, 13 1/2 In., Pair 2235.00
Vase, Green Flashed, Engraved, Cover, c.1850, 9 3/4 In., Pair 345.00
Vase, Green Iridescent, Rolled Inward Rim, Tapered Body, 1900s, 10 1/2 In. 290.00
Vase, Green, Enameled Poppy, Gold Rim, 1900, 8 1/4 In., Pair 175.00
Vase, Iridescent Bronze Green, Silver Threading, Collars, Pallme-Koenig, 5 In., Pair 350.00
Vase, Iridescent Purple, Green Base, Kralik, 1900, 11 3/4 In. 595.00
Vase, Iridescent Red, Blue Gold Pulled Wavy Band, Double Gourd, 9 In. 1150.00
Vase, Iridescent, Blue Gray Threading, Pallme-Koenig, 1900, 4 1/4 x 4 3/4 In. 195.00
Vase, Iridized Amber, Green, Pulled Wavy Band, 6 Sides, 1900s, 13 In. 259.00
Vase, Opaline, Bronze Mount, Scrollwork, Flowers, c.1900, 17 1/2 In. 375.00
Vase, Ruby Cut To Clear, Trumpet Shape, Late 19th Century, 8 1/2 In. 374.00

GLASS-CONTEMPORARY includes pieces by glass artists working after 1975. Many of these pieces are free-form, one-of-a-kind sculptures. Paperweights by contemporary artists are listed in the Paperweight category. Earlier studio glass may be found in Glass-Venetian.

Butter, Italian Burmese, 9 1/4 In. 81.00
Plate, Textured, Yellow, Green, Charcoal, Maurice Heaton, 7 In.   12.00
Vase, Clear, Red, Black Geometric, Cylindrical, F. Haida, 6 In. 230.00
Vase, Cover, Clear, White & Lavender Geometric, F. Haida, 1992, 7 In. 460.00
Vase, Gold Feather, Iridescent, 9 In. 75.00
Vase, Gold Iridescent, 5 In. 29.00
Vase, Heart & Vine, Gold Iridescence, Tiffany & Co., 5 1/2 In. 115.00
Vase, Multicolored Glass, Stags In Battle, Signed, Wm. Morris, 1988, 19 In. 12925.00
Vase, Opalescent, Enameled Purple Landscape, Frosted Ground, 3 In. 275.00
Vase, Trees With Blossoms, Gold Brown, White, Iridescent, 10 In. 29.00

GLASS-CUT, see Cut Glass category.

GLASS-DEPRESSION, see Depression Glass category.

GLASS-MIDCENTURY refers to art glass made from the 1950s to the 1980s. Some glass factories, such as Baccarat or Orrefors, are listed under their own categories. Earlier glass may be listed in the Glass-Art and Glass-Contemporary categories. Italian glass may be found in Glass-Venetian.

Bust, Woman, Green & Gold, Edris Eckhardt, Signed, 8 x 3 1/8 In. 660.00
Vase, Beak, Per Lutkin, Holmegaard, 1960, 18 In. 460.00
Vase, Bud, 6 Pulled Pink Flowers, Large Bubbles, Paperweight, 4 1/4 In. 44.00
Vase, Cut, Dark Blue, Round Foot, 8 Sides, Austria, 6 3/4 In. 268.00
Vase, Flared, Smokey, Holmegaard, 1959, 11 1/4 In. 58.00
Vase, Smoke Over Clear, Pulled Edge, Holmegaard, 1955, 9 In. . . . . *Illus*   350.00

Glass-Midcentury, Vase, Smoke
Over Clear, Pulled Edge,
Holmegaard, 1955, 9 In.

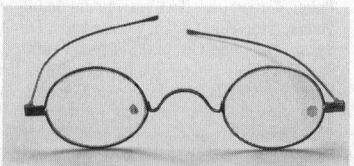

Glasses, Spectacles, Silver Wire, 1830s

GLASS-VENETIAN. Venetian glass has been made near Venice, Italy, since the thirteenth century. Thin, colored glass with applied decoration is favored, although many other types have been made. Collectors have recently become interested in the Art Deco and 1950s designs. Glass was made on the Venetian island of Murano from 1291. The output dwindled in the late seventeenth century but began to flourish again in the 1850s. Some of the old techniques of glassmaking were revived, and firms today make traditional designs and original modern glass. Since 1981, the name *Murano* may only be used on glass made on Murano Island. Other pieces of Italian glass may be found in the Glass-Contemporary and Glass-Midcentury categories of this book.

Bottle, Iridescent, Filligrana & Murrines, Bertil Vallien, 10 x 5 In.	115.00
Bowl, Millefiori Canes, Red Ground, 3 3/4 In.	172.00
Bowl, Oval, Bullicante, Venini, Murano, 1940s, 3 3/4 x 9 In.	575.00
Bowl, Pink, Gold Foil Interior, Acid Etched, Venini, Murano, 3 x 5 In.	115.00
Bowl, Pulegoso, White, Inlaid, D. Martens, Aureliano Toso, 1954, 6 3/4 In.	230.00
Bowl, Sommerso, Red Bands Exterior, Seguso, 2 1/2 x 5 3/4 In.	115.00
Compote, Painted Grapes, Gold Rim, Jewelling, 3-Footed, c.1910, 7 3/4 In.	690.00
Compote, Pink, Gold Flecks, Ribbed, 8 x 7 In.	220.00
Compote, Pink, Gold Flecks, Ribbed, Threading, Hollow Stem, 5 7/8 x 7 In.	190.00
Dish, Leaf Shape, Amethyst Canes, Venini, Murano, 3 1/4 x 10 In.	460.00
Figurine, 2 Seated Birds, 11 x 10 In.	60.00
Figurine, Chicken, Blue Satin, Applied Murrine Eyes, Millefiori Egg, 6 1/2 x 4 3/4 In.	104.00
Figurine, Man, Woman, Dancing, Blue Clothes, Gold Flakes, Murano, 11 In., Pair	275.00
Figurine, Ram, Clear Body, Black Details, Murano, 6 3/4 x 7 In.	200.00
Goblet, Topaz, Teal Berry Printie, Ribbed, Applied Rigaree, 9 1/2 In.	55.00
Hourglass, Cobalt Blue Top, Red Bottom, Acid Stamped, Venini, c.1957, 7 1/2 In.	750.00
Parfait, Ruby Trumpet Bowl, Internal Gold, 1950s, 5 5/8 In.	230.00
Pitcher, Amethyst, Applied Clear Handle, Venini, 8 1/4 x 6 1/4 In.	460.00
Vase, Black, White Swirl, Deep Purple, Blue, D. Martens, 1943, 8 In.	12000.00
Vase, Etched, Amphora Shape, Ormolu, Trefoil Base, Early 20th Century, 14 1/2 In.	805.00
Vase, Frammentato, Shards Of Canes, Red, Light Blue, White, 1955, 9 In.	4200.00
Vase, Incalmo, Paper Labels, Thomas Sterns, 1960, 11 5/8 In.	6610.00
Vase, Inciso, Gray, Acid Stamped, Venini, Label, 1956, 14 In.	2300.00
Vase, Irregular Draped Side, Gold Inclusions, Italy, 10 In.	35.00
Vase, Light Green Swirling Ribs, Gold Inclusions, Italy, 7 1/2 In.	92.00
Vase, Occhi, Wintergreen, White Murrines, Tobia Scarpa, 1960, 7 3/8 In.	1998.00
Vase, Periwinkle Blue, Red, Yellow, Navy Blue, D. Martens, 1950, 22 In.	8225.00
Vase, Pulegoso On Interior, Foil Label, Venini, 12 In.	700.00
Vase, Venini, Flared, Purple Iridescent, 5 In.	230.00
Wig Stand, Floral, Murano, Pink Rose, 6 1/4 x 3 5/8 In.	55.00

GLASSES for the eyes, or spectacles, were mentioned in a manuscript in 1289 and have been used ever since. The first eyeglasses with rigid side pieces were made in London in 1727. Bifocals were invented by Benjamin Franklin in 1785. Lorgnettes were popular in late Victorian times. Opera Glasses are listed in their own category.

Lorgnette, Diamond, Onyx, Navette Shape, Platinum Mount, Art Deco	2300.00
Lorgnette, Engraved, Flowers, Vines, Monogram, 14K Gold	690.00
Racing, Prewar, 2 Pair	215.00
Spectacles, Round Lenses, 12K Gold Filled Frames, Blue Fitted Snap Case, 1940	40.00
Spectacles, Silver Wire, 1830s	*Illus* 100.00
Sun, Orange Shade, Lime Green & Pink, Labeled Emilo Pucci, 1960s	210.00

GOEBEL is the mark used by W. Goebel Porzellanfabrik of Oeslau, Germany, now Rodental, Germany. Many types of figurines and dishes have been made. The firm is still working. The pieces marked *Goebel Hummel* are listed under Hummel in this book.

Goebel

Plaque, Boy Praying, Intaglio, Fancy Rim, 1978, 8 1/2 In.	20.00
Sugar & Creamer, Tray, Friar Tuck	105.00
Toothpick, Dutch Girl, 2 Sides	85.00

GOLDSCHEIDER has made porcelains in three places. The family left Vienna in 1938 and started factories in England and in Trenton, New Jersey. The New Jersey factory started in 1940 as Goldscheider-U.S.A. In 1941 it became Goldscheider-Everlast Corporation. From 1947 to 1953 it was Goldcrest Ceramics Corporation. In 1950 the Vienna plant was returned to Mr. Goldscheider, and the company continues in business. The Trenton, New Jersey, business, now called *Goldscheider of Vienna*, imports all of the pieces.

Bust, Woman Wearing Hat, Turquoise, Mottled Orange, Stamped, Early 1900s, 15 In. 431.00

GOLF, see Sports category.

GONDER Ceramic Arts, Inc., was opened by Lawton Gonder in 1941 in Zanesville, Ohio. Gonder made high-grade pottery decorated with flambe, drip, gold crackle, and Chinese crackle glazes. The factory closed in 1957. From 1946 to 1954, Gonder also operated the Elgee Pottery, which made ceramic lamp bases.

Figurine, Water Carrier, Oxblood High Glaze, 14 1/2 In. 65.00
Lamp, Acorn, White & Burgundy Speckled Glaze, 12 1/2 In. 60.00
Vase, 2 Openings, Tan To Red Drip Glaze, 12 1/2 In. 90.00
Vase, Conch Shell, Chartreuse & Brown Drip Glaze, Handle, 13 1/2 In. 70.00
Vase, Swan, Blue & Brown Speckled Glaze, 9 In. 45.00

GOOFUS GLASS was made from about 1900 to 1920 by many American factories. It was originally painted gold, red, green, bronze, pink, purple, or other bright colors. Many pieces are found today with flaking paint, and this lowers the value.

Bowl, Carnation & Elk, 9 1/2 In. 70.00
Charger, Painted Butterflies, 11 In. 100.00
Pickle Jar, Dogwood Flower, Red & Gold Paint, 12 1/2 In. 60.00
Salt & Pepper, Figural Grape Clusters, Celluloid Tops 30.00
Vase, Cockatoos, Floral Sprays, Orange, Burgundy & Gold Paint, 10 In. 60.00
Vase, Scrolls & Roses, Red, Green & Gold Paint, 13 In. 80.00

GOSS china has been made since 1858. English potter William Henry Goss first made it at the Falcon Pottery in Stoke-on-Trent. The factory name was changed to Goss China Company in 1934 when it was taken over by Cauldon Potteries. Production ceased in 1940. Goss china resembles Irish Belleek in both body and glaze. The company also made popular souvenir china, usually marked with local crests and names.

Bust, Sir Walter Scott, 5 1/4 In. 60.00
Cachepot, Cover, Applied Flower Finial, Green & Yellow Design, 3 In. 260.00
Figurine, Bunty, Girl In 1800s Style Dress & Bonnet, 6 In. 240.00
Figurine, Nurse, Crest, City Of Sheffield, England, 5 1/4 In. 100.00
Figurine, Parian, Classical Woman, Marked, c.1865, 12 1/2 x 13 1/4 In, 2 Piece 235.00
Mug, Crest, Australia, 2 Handles, 3 1/4 In. 90.00
Mug, Crest, Harvard University, Hand Painted Transfer, 5 1/4 In. 75.00

GOUDA, Holland, has been a pottery center since the seventeenth century. Two firms, the Zenith pottery, established in the eighteenth century, and the Zuid-Hollandsche pottery made the brightly colored art pottery marked *Gouda* from 1898 to about 1964. Other factories followed. Many pieces featured Art Nouveau or Art Deco designs. Pattern names in Dutch, listed here, seem strange to English-speaking collectors.

Basket, Monda, Curved, Cornelis A. Prins, c.1926, 7 1/2 x 4 1/2 In. 220.00
Bowl, Bird, Brown, Orange, Blue, Yellow Tail, Black Outline, 3 1/2 x 6 1/2 In. 360.00
Bowl, Bonzo, Circles Interior, Abstract Design On Rim, Blue, Orange, Rust, 1928, 3 In. . . 470.00
Bowl, Congola, Ribbon Handle, Center Purple Flower, 3 x 12 In. 300.00
Bowl, Costa, Blue, Rust, Ocher, Green Starburst, 1912, 4 1/2 In. 385.00
Bowl, Dahlia, Orange Flower, Mid 1920s, 2 x 11 1/2 In. 165.00
Bowl, Darla, Orange, Cobalt Blue Fanlike Shapes, Off-White, Yellow Dots, 1928, 6 In. . . . 250.00

Bowl, Desire, Scalloped Edge, Flowers, Yellow, Rust, Cobalt Blue, 2 1/4 x 9 In. 220.00
Bowl, Flowers, Yellow, Orange, Lilac, Green, Orange Bands, Black Border, 1920 . . . . 220.00
Bowl, Green, Yellow Sunflower, Green, Yellow, Brown Dragonfly, A. Prins, 2 1/2 In. 275.00
Bowl, Robur, Abstract Florals, Black Ground, c.1920, 5 In. 165.00
Bowl, Zonnebloer, Scalloped Rim, Sunflowers, Dots & Squiggles, Signed, c.1925, 12 In. . 880.00
Box, Rhodian, Abstract Arches, Mid 1920s, 3 x 5 In. 195.00
Candlestick, Flared, Drip Pan & Bulbed Cup, Art Nouveau, Marked, 18 In., Pair 430.00
Candlestick, Gandia, Early 1920s, 9 In., Pair 300.00
Candlestick, Gold Ovals, Black Borders, Swirls Down Column, Signed, 1925, 7 In., Pair . 470.00
Candlestick, Paris, Turquoise, Cobalt, Mustard, Rust Outline, Ocher Bands, 1928, 8 In. . . 330.00
Candlestick, Rhodian, Gold Green, Orange, Blue Vertical, Horizontal Bands, 14 In. 275.00
Candlestick, Vlist, c.1920, 14 x 6 In. 330.00
Candy Dish, Juliana Ivora Pattern, c.1920, 4 x 7 In. 165.00
Candy Dish, Metz, Arched Handle, Early 1930s, 3 x 7 1/4 In. 140.00
Candy Dish, Orchis, Orange, Rust, Blue, Yellow Flowers, Pale Green Field, 2 1/2 In. 165.00
Card Tray, Windmill, High Glaze, Pieter Woerlee, c.1910, 10 In. 250.00
Chalice, Golota, Stylized Blue, Orange Flowers, Ocher Design, 1929, 7 1/2 x 5 In. 385.00
Chalice, Romeo, Orange, Rust Flowers, Ocher Circle, Green Geometrics, 7 In. 440.00
Chamberstick, Veronic, Blue, Brown, Yellow, 7 1/4 x 4 1/4 In. 302.00
Charger, Yellow, Orange Flowers, Leaves, Green, Rust Geometric Band, 1929, 2 In. 880.00
Decanter, Turquoise, Lilac Rope Twists, Orange, Yellow Stylized Flowers, 6 1/2 In. 180.00
Decanter, Turquoise, Lilac Rope Twists, Orange, Yellow Stylized Flowers, 10 3/4 In. 180.00
Dish, Camellia, Handles, Daisy, Vines, 7 1/4 In. 77.00
Dish, Handled, Lanac, Cobalt Blue, Yellow Glaze, 7 In. 138.00
Figurine, Lamb, Iridized Gold & Gray Blue Base, Signed, 3 1/4 x 3 In. 145.00
Figurine, Lamb, Standing, Marked, 3 3/4 x 2 x 3 In. 165.00
Humidor, Rhodian, c.1918, 7 x 6 In. 300.00
Inkwell, Cover, Cobalt Blue, Lavender, Orange, Green, Ocher, 1926, 4 1/2 x 6 1/2 In. 357.00
Inkwell, Princess Ivora Pattern, Abstract Flowers, c.1926, 4 1/4 x 10 In. 385.00
Jar, Cover, Maryke, Early 1930s, 15 1/2 x 9 In. 550.00
Jardiniere, Carlos, Stylized Yellow, Blue, Brick Red Flowers, Ocher, White Ground, 5 In. 140.00
Lamp, Tapered Oval, Butterfly, Matte Glaze, AJK Holland, c.1920, 11 3/4 In. 290.00
Lantern, Open Chimneys, Orange, Blue, Mustard, Green, Electrified, 1912, 9 1/2 In. 385.00
Oil Jar, Maas, High Glaze, Bulbous Oil Chamber, c.1919, 7 1/4 x 4 1/4 In. 330.00
Pitcher, Damascus III, Green, Blue Thistles, Pink Crown, Green Borders, 8 1/4 In. 550.00
Pitcher, Distel, Lions, Late 1920s, 5 x 7 In. 110.00
Pitcher, Indus, Bulbous, 9 1/2 x 7 1/2 In. 275.00
Pitcher, Maas, Abstract Dot & Line Design, Brown, Orange, Green, Handles, 5 x 4 In. . . . 385.00
Pitcher, Maroon, Yellow, Black, Green Orchids, Black Bottom, 1920, 6 1/4 x 3 In. 605.00
Pitcher, Stylized Flower, Angled Handle, Green, Rust, Blue, Marked, c.1910, 10 In. 230.00
Planter, Egyptian, Phoenix Bird, c.1924, 3 1/4 x 11 In. 195.00
Planter, Modica, High Glaze, Violin Shape, 15 In. 190.00
Planter, Robert, Abstract, 1950s, 4 x 6 In. 110.00
Plate, Bird, Peacock, On Branch, Sunflowers, Black Border, Signed, c.1930, 8 1/2 In. . . . 990.00
Plate, Wall, Yellow, Orange, Ocher, Cobalt, Olive Swirl Around Middle, 1935, 2 x 13 In. . 360.00
Pot, Purple Pansies, Yellow, Green Centers, 3 Curved Feet, 1920, 4 x 6 In. 660.00
Shoe, Wall Hanging, Modica, 10 In. 138.00
Stand, Plant, Cobalt Blue, Orange, Yellow, Lilac, Brown, Black Border, 1928, 5 1/2 In. . . 935.00
Tazza, Nanette, Orange, Rust, Aqua, Lilac Petals, 6 1/2 In. 220.00
Tazza, Sonny, Blue, Green, Orange, Lilac, Yellow, Cream Ground, 5 1/2 x 9 In. 220.00
Tazza, Yellow, Blue Flowers, Cobalt Blue, Rust, Green Mottled Bands, 5 1/2 x 9 In. 220.00
Tobacco Jar, Collier, Vertical Abstract Design, Cobalt, Orange, Turquoise, 1925, 6 In. 330.00
Tray, Green Lined Edge, Stylized Yellow, Rust, Blue Flowers, 1 x 12 x 8 In. 250.00
Tray, Green, Purple, Orange Flowers, 1921, 16 1/2 x 12 In. 330.00
Tray, Marko, Brown, Cream, Blue, Yellow Swirl, Black Border, 15 1/2 In. 550.00
Tray, Turquoise, Lilac Rope Twists, Orange, Yellow Stylized Flowers, 1926, 1 x 13 In. . . . 600.00
Vase, Black Glaze, Lavender, Red, Green Flowers, Flattened Body, Long Neck, 4 In., Pair 460.00
Vase, Breetvelt, Swirling Abstract Cobalt Blue, Lavender, Pale Pink, Orange, 4 In. 360.00
Vase, Broad, High Glaze, Stylized Flowers, 12 x 12 In. 880.00
Vase, Corona, Flared, Tapered Body, c.1931, 11 x 6 In. 410.00
Vase, Country Scene, Tapered, Glossy Glaze, Natural Tones, Zuid, Holland, c.1910, 19 In. 1265.00
Vase, Crocus, Blue, Orange, Green, Rust, Lilac, Ocher Outline, Loop Handles, 1919, 7 In. 300.00
Vase, Dorian, 4 Handles, c.1926, 7 x 6 In. 525.00

Vase, Flowera, Vibrant Iris Style Flower, c.1929, 9 1/2 x 5 1/2 In. 275.00
Vase, Flowers & Leaves, Yellow, Green, Blue, Oval, Flared Rim, Marked, 11 In. 405.00
Vase, Francis, Green, Turquoise, Lilac, White, Black, Brown Border, 8 1/4 x 6 In. 550.00
Vase, Ice Skaters, Long Neck, Bulbous, Blue & Brown Glaze, Marked, 9 3/4 In. 175.00
Vase, Jack, Large Flowers, Signed Karel Van De Heuvel, c.1926, 10 In. 220.00
Vase, Large Yellow Abstracts, Green, Cobalt Blue, c.1901, 14 1/4 x 6 1/2 In. 520.00
Vase, Lilac Flowers, Orange, Green, Cobalt Blue, 6 1/4 x 6 In. 302.00
Vase, Lorona, Bulbous, Karel Van De Heuvel, 8 1/2 x 4 1/2 In. 468.00
Vase, Madlin, High Glaze, Purple, Magenta, Green, Brown, 24 x 7 1/2 In. 1650.00
Vase, Multicolored Flowers, 2 Handles, Signed, 11 In. 345.00
Vase, Orange Curlicues, Medium Green Ground, Black Border, 1924, 7 1/2 x 7 In. 410.00
Vase, Purple Flowers, Black Accents, Elongated Flowers, Brown, 1910, 13 In. 1100.00
Vase, Purple, Pink Irises, Greige Field, Cream Circle, Dots Design, 10 1/2 x 5 1/2 In. 770.00
Vase, Stylized Lilies, Leaves, Purple, Green, Yellow, Elongated Neck, Marked, 13 1/4 In. . 865.00
Vase, Stylized Orange, Rust, Blue, Green, Lilac Flowers, White Glaze, 1925, 17 In. 1760.00
Vase, Tulips, Leaves, Squat, Bulbed Neck, Arched Handles, Painted Distel, 7 3/4 In. 518.00

GRANITEWARE is an enameled tinware that has been used in the
kitchen from the late nineteenth century to the present. Earlier graniteware was green or turquoise blue, with white spatters. The later ware
was gray with white spatters. Reproductions are being made in all colors.

Coffee Roaster, Black & White, Screen Drum, Wood Handle, 8 3/4 x 5 1/4 In. 525.00
Dinner Carrier, Cream & Green, 5 Stacked Sections, Handle, 13 1/2 In. 225.00
Match Holder, Light Blue, Gold Band, Marked Allumettes, 7 1/2 x 5 7/8 In. 165.00
Pan, Lady Finger, Blue 275.00
Pan, Muffin, 6 Cup, 10 1/2 x 7 In. 65.00
Pan, Muffin, 12 Cup, Gray, 14 3/4 x 11 In. 65.00
Pitcher, Blue, 13 1/2 In. 175.00
Pitcher, Green, 15 In. 175.00
Platter, Stenciled Turkey, 1960, 17 1/2 In. . . . . *Illus* 45.00
Salt Box, Blue, Marked With Teapot, S, Wooden Lid, Poland, 9 1/4 In. 225.00
Teapot, Light Gray, Embossed Cover, Wrought Iron Range Co., St. Louis, No. 8 . . . . 200.00

GRUEBY Faience Company of Boston, Massachusetts, was incorporated in 1897 by William H. Grueby. Garden statuary, art pottery, and
architectural tiles were made until 1920. The company developed a
matte green glaze that was so popular it was copied by many other factories making a less expensive type of pottery. This eventually led to
the financial problems of the pottery.

Bowl, Blue Matte Glaze, Horizontal Lines, 9 1/4 In. 978.00
Bowl, Cover, Mustard Matte Glaze, 4 In. 575.00
Bowl, Lotus, Green Matte Glaze, Gloss Green Interior Glaze, Applied Leaves, 6 x 7 In. . . . 1610.00
Bowl, Vertical Ribs, Green Matte Glaze, Wilhelmina Post, 1 1/2 x 4 In. 450.00
Lamp, Green Matte Glaze, Carved Leaves, Bulbous, Bigelow & Kennard Shade, 29 In. . . 14950.00
Lamp, Vase Base, Green Matte Glaze, Bronze Mounts, Leaded Glass Shade, 20 x 11 In. . . 8625.00
Paperweight, Scarab, Veined, Blue Gray Matte Glaze, 3 3/4 x 2 3/4 In. 748.00
Tile, 8 Geese, Green Matte Glaze, 9 In. 11500.00

Graniteware, Platter, Stenciled Turkey,
1960, 17 1/2 In.

Gundersen, Goblet,
Burmese, 8 In.

Tile, Dark Green Sea Gulls & Waves, Green Matte Glaze, Oak Frame, 6 In. 2990.00
Tile, Diamond Shape Design, Caramel Matte Glaze, Blue, 3 In., Pair 192.00
Tile, Green Matte Glaze, Multicolored Brown Glaze, 3 In., Pair 690.00
Tile, Man On Bench, Blue Glaze, Red Clay Reverse, 6 In. 330.00
Tile, Mustard Matte Glaze, Burnt Orange Ground, Arts & Crafts Oak Frame, 6 In. 978.00
Tile, Pines, Landscape, Green & Blue, Cuenca, Square, 6 In. 3450.00
Tile, Ship Under Full Sail, 8 x 8 In. 1750.00
Tile, Tulip, Pink, Green Matte Ground, Tiffany Trivet Base, Marked MS, 6 In. 8625.00
Vase, 2-Tone Leathery Blue Matte Glaze, Squat, 3 3/4 x 3 1/4 In. 690.00
Vase, Applied & Carved Leaves, Green Matte Glaze, Faience Mark, 8 x 6 1/2 In. 4025.00
Vase, Applied Broad Leaves, Leathery Green Matte Glaze, Egg Shape, 23 x 9 In. 6900.00
Vase, Applied Leaves, Alternating Buds, Green Matte Glaze, 11 1/2 x 5 1/2 In. 5175.00
Vase, Applied Leaves, Alternating Buds, Green Matte Glaze, 13 x 13 1/2 In. 40250.00
Vase, Applied Leaves, Curdled Green Matte Glaze, 3 x 4 1/2 In. 4900.00
Vase, Applied Leaves, Full-Height Buds, Leathery Green Matte Glaze, 15 1/4 x 8 In. 10350.00
Vase, Applied Leaves, Green Matte Glaze, Signed, Ruth Ericson, 4 1/2 In. 3335.00
Vase, Applied Leaves, Multitone Yellow, Brown Matte Glaze, 9 In. 14900.00
Vase, Applied Leaves, Thick Green Glaze, 5 In. 2875.00
Vase, Broad Leaves, Cucumber Green Matte Glaze, Marie A. Seaman, 12 1/4 In. 9400.00
Vase, Bulbous, Applied Leaves & Buds, Tooled, Green Matte Glaze, 7 1/2 x 4 1/2 In. 2875.00
Vase, Bulbous, Blue Matte Glaze, 4 1/2 x 3 In. 489.00
Vase, Bulbous, Flared Neck, Leaves, Long Stem Buds, Green, Marked, 7 In. 1800.00
Vase, Bulbous, Leathery Ivory Matte Glaze, 15 1/4 x 10 In. 2415.00
Vase, Cerulean Blue Matte Glaze, Cobalt Speckles, 4 x 2 1/4 In. 550.00
Vase, Closed Shaped, Yellow Matte Glaze, 4 In. 1095.00
Vase, Cucumber Green Curdled Glaze, 2 3/4 x 2 1/4 In. 330.00
Vase, Curdled Ivory Matte Glaze, Ribbed Body, 8 x 3 3/4 In. 1100.00
Vase, Cut-Back Panel, Green Matte Glaze, Impressed Mark, 9 In. 4250.00
Vase, Dark Green Matte Glaze, 3 Vertical Molded Leaves, 7 1/2 In. 1840.00
Vase, Full-Height Leaves, 3-Lobed, Feathered Green Matte Glaze, 7 1/4 x 4 In. 4025.00
Vase, Full-Height Leaves, Yellow Buds, Oatmealy Green Matte Glaze, 12 x 6 1/2 In. 5750.00
Vase, Gourd Shape, Applied & Carved Leaves, Green Matte Ground, Marked, 8 x 4 In. .. 2070.00
Vase, Green Matte Glaze, 4 1/4 In. 635.00
Vase, Green Matte Glaze, Applied Leaves & Flowers, 3 Yellow Daffodils, 10 In. 13800.00
Vase, Green Matte Glaze, Applied Leaves, Long Stemmed Buds, 11 1/2 In. 4675.00
Vase, Green Matte Glaze, Applied Vertical Leaves, 8 In. 2070.00
Vase, Green Matte Glaze, Carved & Applied Tall Leaves, Egg Shape, 5 1/2 x 4 In. 2300.00
Vase, Green Matte Glaze, Carved, Applied Leaves, Signed, Wilhelmina Post, 8 In. 5750.00
Vase, Green Matte Glaze, Horizontal Lines, Marked, 2 In. 980.00
Vase, Green Matte Glaze, Marked, Annie V. Lingley, 6 In. 1495.00
Vase, Green Matte Glaze, Vertical Leaves, Marked 11 In. 8050.00
Vase, Leaf & Flowers, Mottled Green Glaze, 11 1/2 In. 5225.00
Vase, Leathery Green Matte Glaze, Applied Rows Of Leaves, Squat, 4 3/4 x 5 1/2 In. 2645.00
Vase, Leaves Alternating Buds, Green Matte Glaze, Marie Seaman, 9 x 4 1/4 In. 2070.00
Vase, Long Flared Neck, Molded Vertical Leaves, Stems, Buds, Green Matte, 7 In. 1800.00
Vase, Multitoned Green Matte Glaze, Applied Water Lilies, Marked, 10 In. 4025.00
Vase, Mustard Matte Glaze, 2 In. 1035.00
Vase, Oval, Green Glaze, Annie Lingley, 6 x 4 In. 3300.00
Vase, Pointy Leaves, Green Matte Glaze, Teardrop Shaped, Ruth Erickson, 6 3/4 x 4 In. .. 10350.00
Vase, Thick Textured Oatmeal Matte Glaze, Sculpted Vertical Ribs, 4 In. 2300.00
Vase, Trumpet, Cucumber Green Matte Glaze, Mahogany Interior, 7 1/2 In. 1870.00
Vase, Trumpet, Ribbed Design, Cerulean Blue Matte Glaze, 6 1/2 x 5 In. 1210.00
Vase, Vertical Ribs, Corseted Shoulder, Ocher Matte Glaze, Faience Mark, 9 1/2 x 5 In. .. 7480.00
Vase, Vertical Ribs, Gourd Shaped, Feathered Green Matte Glaze, 15 1/2 x 9 In. 5750.00
Vase, Volcanic Flowing Purple Matte Glaze, Circle Mark, 3 x 4 In. 883.00
Vase, Watermelon Shape, Curdled Dark Green Matte Glaze, Applied Leaves, 9 1/2 x 7 In. 5750.00

GUNDERSEN glass was made at the Gundersen-Pairpoint Glass Works
of New Bedford, Massachusetts, from 1952 to 1957. Gundersen
Peachblow is especially famous.

Bell, Burmese, Clear 3-Ball Handle, 7 1/2 In. 420.00
Cruet, Peachblow, White Reeded Handle, 7 3/4 In. 230.00
Cup & Saucer, Peachblow, Applied White Handle, 5 1/4 x 3 1/4 In. 58.00

Decanter, Peachblow, 12 In., Pair	345.00
Goblet, Burmese, 8 In. .... *Illus*	149.00
Goblet, Cream To Pink, 6 1/4 In.	168.00
Vase, Lily, Peachblow, Satin, 9 1/2 In.	58.00
Vase, Peachblow, Tricornered Rim, Tapered, 10 1/4 In.	120.00

GUNS that may be classed as toys, such as BB guns, air rifles, and cap guns, are listed in the Toy category.

GUSTAVSBERG ceramics factory was founded in 1827 near Stockholm, Sweden. It is best known to collectors for its twentieth-century art wares, especially a green stoneware with silver inlay called *Argenta*.

Gustafsberg

Bowl, Silver Griffin, Turquoise Matte Glaze, Signed, Argenta, 9 1/2 In.	250.00
Bowl, Yellow, Rust Glaze, Wilhelm Kage, 1950, 2 1/2 In.	374.00
Vase, Blue & Brown Matte Glaze, Incised Swirled Ribs, Chestnut Shape, 7 1/4 In.	575.00
Vase, Blue Glaze, Horizontal Ribs, Stepped Foot, Signed, Kage, 5 In.	500.00
Vase, Blue, Green Hare's-Fur Glaze, Berndt Friberg, 1964, 12 1/2 In.	1265.00
Vase, Double Gourd, Butterfly & Garden, Signed, Lindberg, 7 1/2 In.	225.00
Vase, Oxblood High Glaze, Signed, Friberg, 1942, 12 1/4 In.	700.00
Vase, Sgraffito Flowers & Feather, Turquoise Matte Glaze, Ekberg, 11 In.	305.00
Vase, Sgraffito Flowers, Yellow Matte Glaze, Signed, Ekberg, 12 3/4 In.	425.00

GUTTA-PERCHA was one of the first plastic materials. It was made from a mixture of resins from Malaysian trees. It was molded and used for daguerreotype cases, toilet articles, and picture frames in the nineteenth century.

Case, Relief Scroll, Flowers, 19th Century, 6 x 5 In.	287.00

HAEGER Potteries, Inc., Dundee, Illinois, started making commercial art wares in 1914. Early pieces were marked with the name *Haeger* written over an *H*. About 1938, the mark *Royal Haeger* was used in honor of Royal Hickman, a designer at the factory. The firm is still making florist wares and lamp bases. See also the Royal Hickman category.

Haeger

Bowl, No. R-371, 13 1/2 x 6 In.	8.00
Planter, Gray Donkey & Basket, 9 In.	35.00
Vase, Basket, Brown, 8 In.	24.00
Vase, Black Impala, No. 2707, 15 In.	175.00
Vase, Earth Wrap, 16 In.	92.00
Vase, Earth Wrap, Marigold Ground, Cylindrical, 7 1/8 In.	46.00
Vase, Orange Peel, Felt Covered Base, 12 1/2 In.	127.00
Vase, Orange Peel, Felt Pad, 7 1/4 In.	161.00
Vase, Peacock Glaze, Black Matte With Multicolored Drip, 15 1/2 In. .... *Illus*	110.00
Vase, Textured Orange Glaze, Chocolate Brown Underglaze, 10 In.	115.00

HALF-DOLL, see Pincushion Doll category.

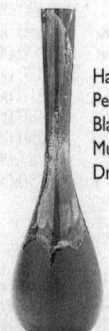

Haeger, Vase,
Peacock Glaze,
Black Matte With
Multicolored
Drip, 15 1/2 In.

Be careful where you put a fresh pumpkin or gourd. Put a plastic liner underneath them. A rotting pumpkin will permanently stain wood or marble.

Clean the silver decorations on Argentaware made by Gustavsberg with commercial silver polish.

HALL CHINA Company started in East Liverpool, Ohio, in 1903. The firm made many types of wares. Collectors search for the Hall teapots made from the 1920s to the 1950s. The dinnerwares of the same period, especially Autumn Leaf pattern, are also popular. The Hall China Company is still working. For more information, see *Kovels' Depression Glass & Dinnerware Price List*. Autumn Leaf pattern dishes are listed in their own category in this book.

HALL'S
SUPERIOR
QUALITY
KITCHENWARE

Blue Bouquet, Cruet	15.00
Cameo Rose, Platter, Oval, 15 1/2 In.	85.00
Heather Rose, Platter, Handles, 11 In.	22.00
Heather Rose, Sugar, Cover, 4 1/2 In.	15.50
Poppy, Jug, Ball	200.00
Poppy, Plate, Dinner, 10 In.	33.00
Red Poppy, Mixing Bowl, Large	35.00
Rose White, Bean Pot, 7 1/2 In.	120.00
Rose White, Salt & Pepper, 7 1/2 In.	70.00
Royal Rose, Saltshaker	30.00
Taverne, Coaster	40.00
Taverne, Gravy Boat	16.00
Taverne, Pie Server	30.00
Teapot, Donut, Chinese Red	355.00
Teapot, Pert, Rose White, 3 Cup	45.00
Tomorrow's Classic, Bowl, Vegetable, Fantasy, 9 3/4 In.	31.00
Tomorrow's Classic, Teapot, Fantasy	50.00

HALLOWEEN is an ancient holiday that has changed in the last 200 years. The jack-o'-lantern, witches on broomsticks, and orange decorations seem to be twentieth-century creations. Collectors started to become serious about collecting Halloween-related items in the late 1970s. The papier-mache decorations, now replaced by plastic, and old costumes are in demand.

Bag, Trick Or Treat, Plastic, 12 x 11 1/2 In.	*Illus*	6.00
Candy Container, Bisque & Paper, Germany, 7 In.		440.00
Candy Container, Jack-O'Lantern, Ball Shape, Paper Over Cardboard, 2 1/2 In.		66.00
Costume, Bionic Woman		50.00
Costume, Caesar, Planet Of The Apes		30.00
Costume, Dukes Of Hazzard, Ben Cooper, 1979		15.00
Costume, Heckle & Jeckle, Terrytoons Inc., 1950s, Pair		55.00
Costume, Shari Lewis Charlie Horse, Plastic, Halco, 1961		30.00
Doll, Witch, Black & Orange Costume, Hard Plastic, 7 In.		45.00
Goblin, Pressed Paper, 6 In.		150.00
Hat, Party, Paper, Black Cat, Witch, Pumpkin, Germany, 1910		68.00
Horn, Banana, Pressed Paper, 6 In.		85.00

Halloween, Bag, Trick Or Treat,
Plastic, 12 x 11 1/2 In.

Halloween, Wall Decoration,
Cats, Flocked, 12 1/4 In.

Halloween, Wall Decoration, Jack-
O'-Lantern, U.S.A., 8 1/2 x 12 In.

Horn, Pickle, Pressed Paper, 6 In.	85.00
House, Cat, String Tags, 3 1/2 In.	66.00
Jack-O'-Lantern, Paperboard, 4 1/2 In.	44.00
Jack-O'-Lantern, Paperboard, 5 1/2 In.	88.00
Jack-O'-Lantern, Tin, Pierced Features, Pole Mount, 19th Century, 9 In.	1092.00
Lantern, Black Cat, Tissue Paper Eyes & Mouth, Cat Fangs, 3 1/2 In.	150.00
Lantern, Clown, Pressed Paper	150.00
Lantern, Pressed Paper, 6 In.	150.00
Nodder, Tiger, Paper, 5 In.	22.00
Noisemaker, Gene Bosch, Chein	185.00
Wall Decoration, Cats, Flocked, 12 1/4 In. *Illus*	5.00
Wall Decoration, Jack-O'-Lantern, U.S.A., 8 1/2 x 12 In. *Illus*	5.00

HAMPSHIRE pottery was made in Keene, New Hampshire, between 1871 and 1923. Hampshire developed a line of colored glazed wares as early as 1883, including a Royal Worcester-type pink, olive green, blue, and mahogany. Pieces are marked with the printed mark or the impressed name *Hampshire Pottery* or *J.S.T. & Co., Keene, N.H.* Many pieces were marked with city names and sold as souvenirs.

Bowl, Blue Matte Glaze, Water Lilies, Squat, 2 1/4 x 5 1/2 In.	375.00
Bowl, Lotus Pads & Leaves, Smooth Green Matte Glaze, Signed, 2 3/4 x 10 In.	460.00
Bowl, Molded Leaves, Green Matte Glaze, 9 In.	430.00
Bowl, Water Lilies, Pads, Embossed, Smooth Green Glaze, 3 1/4 x 10 In.	405.00
Bowl, Water Lily Pads & Leaves, Signed, 3 x 10 In.	345.00
Candlestick, Handle, Gray Mottled, Aqua, Blue Glaze, 5 1/2 x 5 In.	410.00
Clock, Mantel, Green Matte Glaze, Elongated Body, Seth Thomas, 15 x 10 In.	2420.00
Inkwell, Pale Beige Matte Glaze, Dark Maroon Veining, 3 1/8 x 4 1/4 In.	330.00
Lamp, Green Matte Glaze, Flower Buds Design, Electrified, 14 x 8 In.	1100.00
Lamp, Green Matte Glaze, Leaded Shade, Squat, Signed, 15 1/2 In.	1200.00
Lamp, Green Matte Glaze, Pond Lily, 16 1/2 x 20 1/2 In.	3300.00
Lamp Base, Green Matte Glaze, Queen Anne Feet, Gray, 6 3/4 x 7 1/2 In.	470.00
Lamp Base, Green Matte Glaze, Yellow Glass Leaded Shade, Electrified, 15 In.	1610.00
Lamp Base, Hunter Green Glaze, Melon Style Base, 11 1/2 x 12 In.	1210.00
Vase, Blue Matte Glaze, Molded Geometric Design, 5 In.	460.00
Vase, Brown Matte Glaze, 4 1/2 In.	285.00
Vase, Brown, Lavender Glaze, 5 x 3 1/4 In.	520.00
Vase, Bulbous, Blue Matte Glaze, Rectangular Handles, Marked, 7 In.	748.00
Vase, Bulbous, Embossed, Ears Of Corn, 5 3/4 x 5 1/2 In.	430.00
Vase, Buttermilk Matte Glaze, Pale Yellow Leaves, Trumpet, 9 1/2 x 6 1/2 In.	1320.00
Vase, Cattails & Blades Of Grass, Melon Shape, Mustard Matte Glaze, 4 3/4 In.	605.00
Vase, Cylindrical, Green Matte Glaze, Inscribed, 4 5/8 In.	240.00
Vase, Dark Blue Matte Glaze, Applied Mushrooms, Squat, Marked, 6 In. Diam.	750.00
Vase, Embossed Lotus Buds, Mottled Green Glaze, Stamped, 7 x 5 In.	489.00
Vase, Embossed Rows Of Leaves, Yellow Matte Glaze, Stamped, 8 1/4 x 6 1/2 In.	635.00
Vase, Feathered Blue Gray Matte Glaze, Stamped, 9 x 4 1/2 In.	430.00
Vase, Green Matte Glaze, 4 1/4 In.	207.00
Vase, Green Matte Glaze, 6 x 6 1/4 In.	715.00
Vase, Green Matte Glaze, 8 In.	245.00
Vase, Green Matte Glaze, Blue Top, 7 In.	489.00
Vase, Green Matte Glaze, Flared Rim, 2 Handles, 15 x 15 1/2 In.	690.00
Vase, Green Matte Glaze, Handles, 4 1/2 x 4 In.	410.00
Vase, Green Matte Glaze, Molded Stems & Buds, Long Leaves, Marked, 7 In.	489.00
Vase, Green Matte Glaze, Molded Vertical Leaves, 11 In.	518.00
Vase, Green Matte Glaze, Molded Vertical Ribs, 3 1/2 In.	310.00
Vase, Green Matte Glaze, Oval, Raised Design, 2 Handles, Stamp, 7 x 4 In.	345.00
Vase, Green Matte Glaze, Vertical Molded Leaves, 3 In.	546.00
Vase, Hunter Green Matte Glaze, 9 3/4 x 8 In.	715.00
Vase, Leaves In Repeat, Green Matte Glaze, Oblong Panels, 8 x 7 1/2 In.	990.00
Vase, Lightning Bolt, Green Matte Glaze, 7 1/2 x 4 In.	605.00
Vase, Lily Pad, Inverted Rim, Tailing Stems, Green Matte Glaze, Cylindrical, 14 In.	1380.00
Vase, Molded Leaf Design, Multicolored Green Matte Glaze, 7 1/2 In.	935.00
Vase, Molded Leaves, Multicolored Brown Matte Glaze, 7 In.	550.00
Vase, Mustard, Ocher Matte Glaze, Ocher, Brown Leaves, Gourd, 3 3/4 In.	770.00

Vase, Navy Blue, Medium Blue Glaze, Mahogany Interior, 6 3/4 x 4 1/4 In. 605.00
Vase, Oval, Rounded Lip, Teal Blue Glaze, Early 20th Century, 7 1/2 In. 405.00
Vase, Pond Lily Pads, Green Matte Glaze, 8 x 5 1/2 In. 1210.00
Vase, Purple Wisteria Glaze, Pale Aqua Glaze, 7 x 3 1/2 In. 1210.00
Vase, Red Matte Glaze, 4 Broad Leaves Around Body, Incised Mark, 3 1/2 In. 805.00
Vase, Sea Green Variegated Design, Cerulean Blue Body, 8 1/4 x 4 In. 990.00
Vase, Swollen, Deep Black Matte Glaze, 8 In. 518.00
Vase, Tapered, Blue, Green Matte Glaze, Impressed Mark, 8 In. 748.00
Vase, Teal Matte Glaze, Dark Teal, Ivory Interior, 2 1/2 x 3 1/2 In. 550.00
Vase, Water Lily, Green Matte Glaze, 7 1/8 x 5 In. 770.00
Vase, White Mottled Glaze, Cobalt Blue Interior, 5 x 5 1/2 In. 770.00

HANDEL glass was made by Philip Handel working in Meriden, Connecticut, from 1885 and in New York City from 1893 to 1933. The firm made art glass and other types of lamps. Handel shades were made not only of leaded glass in a style reminiscent of Tiffany but also of reverse painted glass. Handel also made vases and other glass objects.

Chandelier, 5 Hanging Shades, Paneled Amber Glass, Brass Chain & Cap, 14 x 29 In. . . . 2000.00
Hanging Shade, 8 Curved Panels, Oak Leaves, 24 1/2 In. 5880.00
Hanging Shade, Ball Shape, Parrots, Brass Cap, Signed, 16 In. 1610.00
Hanging Shade, Metal Overlay, Diamonds, Garland, Caramel, Purple Slag, 24 In. 4590.00
Hanging Shade, Rose & Leaf Shade, 24 In. 5040.00
Humidor, Cover, Enameled, Indian Chiefs, 6 In. 700.00
Lamp, 2-Light, Domed Shades, Slag Glass, Bronze Base, 22 x 22 In. 1100.00
Lamp, 3-Light, Twilight, Shade, Striated Bronze Base, 28 In. 6040.00
Lamp, 4 Panels, Metal Overlay, Green & Yellow Slag Glass, Bronze Base, 61 In. 1840.00
Lamp, 5-Light, Yellow & Amber Slag Glass, Panels, Diamonds, Copper Base, 64 In. 9975.00
Lamp, 6 Fluted Panels, Metal Overlay, Adjustable Bronzed Metal Base, 6 x 14 In. 2300.00
Lamp, 6 Panels, Metal Overlay, Adjustable, Bronzed Metal Base, 14 In. . . . . *Illus* 2300.00
Lamp, 6 Panels, Palm Trees, Blue Moonlit Sky, Metal Woodland Base, Signed, 7 In. 4480.00
Lamp, 6 Panels, Pulled Feather, Cone Shade, Signed, 15 In. 1905.00
Lamp, 8 Panels, Green & Caramel Slag Glass, Bronzed Metal, 23 1/2 In. . . . . *Illus* 1840.00
Lamp, 8 Panels, Green Enamel, Tulips, Chrysanthemums, 17 In. 2800.00
Lamp, 8 Panels, Metal Overlay, Palm Trees, Bronzed Metal Base, 67 In. 7480.00
Lamp, 8 Panels, Metal Overlay, Sunset Palm Shade, Brickwork Design, Signed, 20 In. . . . 5600.00
Lamp, 9 Panels, Metal Overlay, Sunset Palm, Art Nouveau Base, 16 In. . . . . . . .4480.00 to 5040.00
Lamp, Autumn Scene, Reverse Painted, Greek Key Base, 1919, 23 In. 5875.00
Lamp, Bell-Shaped Harp, Domed Shade, Copper, 56 1/2 In. 1035.00
Lamp, Bird & Leaf Scene, Domed Shade, Little Boy Metal Base, Signed, 10 In. 1680.00
Lamp, Bird Of Paradise Border, Brass Base, Signed, 1919, 23 In. 10800.00
Lamp, Blossom Shaped Shade, Glass Panels, Bronze Base, Arched Pivot Arm, 14 In. 1265.00
Lamp, Blossoms, Oblong, Signed, 10 In. 3640.00
Lamp, Castle In Landscape, Signed, 18 In. 9350.00
Lamp, Ceiling, Ball Shape, Parrot Decoration, Verte Brass Fitter, Signed, 16 In. 1610.00
Lamp, Chipped Ice Shade, Cone Shape, Bronze, Fuel Canister Shape, Teroma, 22 1/4 In. . . 6325.00
Lamp, Chipped Ice Shade, Daffodils, Lush Green, 1924, 24 In. 16450.00
Lamp, Chipped Ice Shade, Virginia Creeper Shaped Bronzed Base, Stamped, 22 In. 3450.00

Handel, Lamp, 6 Panels,
Metal Overlay,
Adjustable, Bronzed
Metal Base, 14 In.

Handel, Lamp, 8 Panels,
Green & Caramel Slag Glass,
Bronzed Metal, 23 1/2 In.

Lamp, Daffodil, Bronze Base, 17 3/4 x 25 1/2 In. 7475.00
Lamp, Desk, 2 Peacocks, Flowering Branches, Brown Metal Base, Marked, 8 In. 1810.00
Lamp, Desk, 2-Light, Pyramidal, Caramel Slag Glass, Geometric, Bronze Base, 22 In. ... 1495.00
Lamp, Desk, Green Enameled Mosserine, Oblong Shade, Stripped Patina 1450.00
Lamp, Desk, Green Slag Glass, Original Patina, 12 In. 1000.00
Lamp, Desk, Landscape Scene, Trees, Rolling Hill, White Puffy Clouds, 14 In. 1150.00
Lamp, Desk, Landscape, Cloth Label, 12 1/2 In. 747.00
Lamp, Desk, Moonlit Forest Scene, Reverse Painted, Signed, 12 1/2 In. 3737.00
Lamp, Exotic Birds, Orange, Red, Black, Domed Shade, Bronze Base, 18 In. . .6720.00 to 14560.00
Lamp, Flowering Vines, Pink, Yellow, Green, Amber & White Ground, 1933, 28 In. 8050.00
Lamp, Flowers, Butterflies, Signed, 7 In. 3640.00
Lamp, Flowers, Hanging, 24 1/2 In. 4110.00
Lamp, Gold Berries, On Lime Green To Brown, Mushroom Shade, Metal Base, 19 In. 635.00
Lamp, Gold Daffodils, Leaves, Signed, 1911, 27 In. 5875.00
Lamp, Hanging Lantern, Bronze Base, Adjustable Arched Arm, 60 In. 500.00
Lamp, Hanging, Geometric Glass Shade, Hammered Copper, 15 x 4 3/4 In. 1725.00
Lamp, Harbor Scene, Etched, Umber, Gilt Spelter Base, 14 In. 1150.00
Lamp, Junglebird, Domed Shade, Bronzed, Metal Pierced Base, Signed, 7 In. 8970.00
Lamp, Landscape Scene, Paneled Shade, Bronze Metal Base, Signed, 18 x 24 1/2 In. 5465.00
Lamp, Landscape, 23 In. 3525.00
Lamp, Leaves, Red, Amber, Gold, Patinated Bronze Melon Shaped Base, 21 x 18 In. 4125.00
Lamp, Metal Overlay, Apple Blossom, Green Slag Glass, Brown Leaves, 27 x 65 In. 14560.00
Lamp, Metal Overlay, Cattails, Caramel Slag Glass, Bronze Base, 22 In. 5750.00
Lamp, Metal Overlay, Grapevine, Green Slag Glass, Domed Shade, 22 In. 1955.00
Lamp, Metal Overlay, Steuben Intarsia Glass, 1915, 76 In. 8640.00
Lamp, Night-Light, Goodnight Owls On Shade, Many A Time On Base, 7 In. 1900.00
Lamp, Olympic Rain Forest, Yellows & Golden Colors, Signed, 26 In. 10350.00
Lamp, Opal Glass Shade, Vine Border, Signed, 18 In. 4480.00
Lamp, Persian Carpet Border, Bronze Base, 24 In. 6325.00
Lamp, Piano, Scenic, 9 In. 1900.00
Lamp, Rose Blossom, Butterflies, Domed Shade, Signed, 18 In. 10080.00
Lamp, Roses, Leaves, Pink, Yellow, Green, Fluted Baluster Base, Acorn Pulls, 16 x 23 In. 2530.00
Lamp, Stained Band Of Pink Flowers Shade, Spreading 8-Sided Base, 18 1/2 In. 1840.00
Lamp, Steuben Shade, Green Iridescent Glass, Bronze Base, 57 1/2 x 13 In. 3105.00
Lamp, Sunset Scene, Bronze Tree Trunk Base, Signed, 24 In. 4945.00
Lamp, Tree Landscape, Flower Shaped Bronze Base, 20 In. 2760.00
Lamp, Trees Overlooking River, Signed, 18 In. ....5600.00 to 6160.00
Lamp, Twilight, 3-Color Sky, Trees, Bronze Striated Patina, Acorn Pulls, 28 1/2 In. 5940.00
Lamp, Wild Roses, Leafy Stems, Bronze Base, Signed, 14 1/2 In. 1960.00
Lamp, Windmills On Water, Signed, 15 In. 3080.00
Lamp, Winter Scene, Bronze Tree Trunk Base 5500.00
Lamp, Wisteria Shade, Ahart, Signed, 13 In. 7840.00
Lamp Base, Mermaid, Bronze 5320.00
Night-Light, Flowers, Domed Shade, Signed, 7 In. 2240.00
Sconce, Gas, 10 x 10 In. 520.00
Shade, Chrysanthemums, Metal Base, Signed, 3 In. 3360.00
Shade, Flower, Red, Orange, Green Ground, Bronzed Metal Cap, Signed, 18 In. 4200.00
Shade, Tulip Shape, Pink Slag Glass, Free-Form Petals, Green Leaves, Stamp, 10 1/2 In. . 770.00
Vase, Teroma, Mountain Lake, Birch In Foreground, Signed, Broggi, 8 In. 1210.00
Vase, Teroma, Palm Trees & Leaves, Signed, Palme, 10 In. 460.00
Vase, Teroma, Panoramic Landscape, 9 1/2 In. 1610.00

HARDWARE, see Architectural category.

HARKER Pottery Company was incorporated in 1890 in East Liverpool, Ohio. The Harker family had been making pottery in the area since 1840. The company made many types of pottery but by the Civil War was making quantities of yellowware from native clays. They also made Rockingham-type brown-glazed pottery and whiteware. The plant was moved to Chester, West Virginia, in 1931. Dinnerwares were made and sold nationally. In 1971 the company was sold to Jeannette Glass Company and all operations ceased in 1972. For more information, see *Kovels' Depression Glass & Dinnerware Price List.*

Chesterton, Platter, Avocado, Oval, 11 3/4 x 8 1/2 In. 16.00

Have an emergency plan for your collection. For storms with advance warning, arrange to move the collection to another location or at least pack it and move it to the safest part of the house.

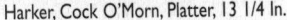

Harker, Cock O'Morn, Platter, 13 1/4 In.

Cock O'Morn, Platter, 13 1/4 In. .... *Illus*	25.00
Corinthian, Cake Plate, Teal	20.00
Corinthian, Salt & Pepper	20.00
Corinthian, Sugar, Cover	18.00
Persian Key, Soup, Dish	9.00
Springtime, Plate, Dinner, 10 In.	16.00
White Clover, Cup & Saucer, Meadow Green	15.00
White Clover, Plate, Bread & Butter, Meadow Green, 6 In.	5.00
White Clover, Plate, Dinner, Meadow Green, 10 In.	15.00
White Clover, Platter, Coral Sand, 11 In.	20.00

HARLEQUIN dinnerware was produced by the Homer Laughlin Company from 1938 to 1964, and sold without trademark by the F. W. Woolworth Co. It has a concentric ring design like Fiesta, but the rings are separated from the rim by a plain margin. Cup handles are triangular in shape. Seven different novelty animal figurines were introduced in 1939. For more information on Harlequin dinnerware, see *Kovels' Depression Glass & Dinnerware Price List.*

Forest Green, Bowl, Salad, Individual, 7 1/2 In.	42.00
Gray, Bowl, Salad, Individual, 7 1/2 In.	40.00
Gray, Cup	11.00
Gray, Gravy Boat	35.00
Gray, Plate, 7 In.	8.00
Gray, Plate, 9 In.	14.00
Green, Figurine, Duck	140.00
Light Green, Bowl, Salad, 7 1/2 In.	42.00
Maroon, Figurine, Duck	110.00
Maroon, Sugar, Cover	22.00
Maroon, Tumbler	62.00
Mauve Blue, Bowl, 36s, 6 1/2 In.	40.00
Mauve Blue, Figurine, Cat	240.00
Mauve Blue, Figurine, Donkey	240.00
Mauve Blue, Figurine, Penguin	60.00
Mauve Blue, Tumbler	53.00
Medium Green, Cup	45.00
Medium Green, Plate, 9 In.	38.00
Red, Pitcher, Ball, 22 Oz. .... 75.00 to 80.00
Red, Platter, 11 In.	25.00
Red, Saltshaker	15.00
Red, Tumbler	56.00
Rose, Bowl, Fruit, 5 1/2 In.	11.00
Rose, Bowl, Oatmeal, 36s, 6 1/2 In.	28.00
Rose, Cup	11.00
Rose, Cup & Saucer	15.00
Rose, Pitcher, Water	70.00
Rose, Plate, 10 In.	36.00
Rose, Platter, 11 In.	10.00

Rose, Soup, Dish 30.00
Rose, Tumbler 53.00
Spruce Green, Figurine, Cat 190.00
Spruce Green, Figurine, Donkey 190.00
Spruce Green, Figurine, Lamb 150.00
Turquoise, Bowl, Salad, 7 1/2 In. 28.00
Turquoise, Cup & Saucer 11.00
Turquoise, Plate, 7 In. 6.00
Turquoise, Plate, 9 In. 10.00
Turquoise, Plate, 10 In. 36.00
Turquoise, Platter, Oval, 13 In. 25.00
Turquoise, Saltshaker 10.00
White, Figurine, Duck, Gold Trim 30.00
White, Figurine, Penguin, Gold Trim 30.00
Yellow, Cup & Saucer 11.00
Yellow, Figurine, Cat 160.00
Yellow, Figurine, Donkey 210.00
Yellow, Figurine, Lamb .... 30.00 to 50.00
Yellow, Figurine, Penguin 210.00
Yellow, Platter, 11 In. 18.00
Yellow, Saltshaker 10.00
Yellow, Saucer 2.00
Yellow, Saucer, After Dinner 13.00
Yellow, Tumbler 47.00
Yellow, Tumbler, Water 75.00

HATPIN collectors search for pins popular from 1860 to 1920. The long pin, often over four inches, was used to hold the hat in place on the hair. The tops of the pins were made of all materials, from solid gold and real gemstones to ceramics and glass. Be careful to buy original hatpins and not recent pieces made by altering old buttons.

Amethyst, Tiny Pearl On Top, 6 1/2 In. 75.00
Carnival Glass, Bird Of Paradise 2000.00
Carnival Glass, Bird Of Paradise, Owl, Gold Beak, Blue 1600.00
Carnival Glass, Leaf & Veil 750.00
Carnival Glass, Strawberry, Amber 700.00
Carnival Glass, Top O' Morning 125.00
Carnival Glass, Waves, Green 120.00
Gem Set, Moonstone, Mine Cut, Spider, 14K Gold Mount 490.00
Gold, Sword Form, John Buford, Brigadier General, U.S.A. 1540.00
Porcelain, Round, Hand Painted, Scene, Flowers, 1-In. Round, 8 1/4 In. 85.00

HATPIN HOLDERS were needed when hatpins were fashionable from 1860 to 1920. The large, heavy hat required special long-shanked pins to hold it in place. The hatpin holder resembles a large saltshaker, but it often has no opening at the bottom as a shaker does. Hatpin holders were made of all types of ceramics and metal. Look for other pieces under the names of specific manufacturers.

Forget-Me-Nots, Attached Pin Dish, 4 x 4 1/2 In. 165.00
Multicolored Flowers Front & Back, Gold Trim, 5 In. 65.00
Porcelain, Cone Shape, Hanging 235.00
Roses, Beige & Yellow Ground, Yellow & Pink Roses, 5 1/4 In. 60.00

HAVILAND china has been made in Limoges, France, since 1842. The factory was started by the Haviland Brothers of New York City. Pieces are marked *H & Co.*, *Haviland & Co.*, or *Theodore Haviland*. It is possible to match existing sets of dishes through dealers who specialize in Haviland china. Other factories worked in the town of Limoges making a similar chinaware. These porcelains are listed in this book under Limoges.

HAVILAND & CO.

Ashtray, Horse Head 25.00
Chocolate Pot, Countess Pattern, 10 1/2 In. 450.00
Chocolate Pot, Gold Accents Around Handle, Marked, 1887, 8 In. 270.00

Chocolate Set, Mirabeau, 6 Tall Cups & Saucers, 10 Demitasse, Red Mark, 23 Piece 500.00
Fish Set, Painted, Shells, Seascape, Signed V.A. Barlett, 20 Piece 805.00
Pitcher, Pink Flowers, Green Branches, Early 1900s, 8 In. 450.00
Platter, Pink Blossoms, Gold Trim, Marked, c.1900, 14 1/2 x 9 1/2 In. 105.00
Teapot, Red Flowers, Green Fern, Gold Accents, c.1895, 7 1/2 x 4 1/4 x 4 1/2 In. 295.00
Tureen, Roses, Ivy, Gold Edges, Lid, 6 1/2 x 12 In. 360.00
Tureen, Soup, Cover, Pink Carnations, 1890s, 6 1/2 x 12 x 4 1/2 In. 625.00
Vase, Applied Flowers, Painted, Ernest Chaplet, 4 In. 25.00
Vase, Scenes Of Woman In Hat, Signed, 5 1/2 In. 265.00

HAWKES cut glass was made by T. G. Hawkes & Company of Corning, New York, founded in 1880. The firm cut glass blanks made at other glassworks until 1962. Many pieces are marked with the trademark, a trefoil ring enclosing a fleur-de-lis and two hawks. Cut glass by other manufacturers is listed under either the factory name or in the general Cut Glass category.

Bowl, Chrysanthemum Variant, 3 3/4 x 9 In. 445.00
Bowl, Hobstar Base, Lower Inside Crosscut Diamonds, 5 x 9 In. 875.00
Bowl, Holland Borders, Signed, 7 In. 275.00
Candy Dish, Alternating Hobstars & Crosscut Diamonds, 3 Sections, Signed 295.00
Champagne, Floral Cut & Leaf Pattern, Diamond Shapes, Signed, 8 Piece 670.00
Champagne, Iris, Signed, 6 Piece 725.00
Cocktail Shaker, Duck Flying, Sterling Silver Base, Rim & Lid, 12 1/2 In. 345.00
Compote, Allover Floral, Circular Pedestal Base, 7 1/2 x 7 In. 85.00
Compote, Floral Sprays, Crosscut Lappets, Garlands, Trumpet Foot, 5 5/8 x 8 In. 230.00
Decanter Set, Sherry, Hobstar & Fan, Signed, 4 3/4 In., 6 Piece 115.00
Dish, Dessert, Iris, Signed, 4 x 3 3/4 In., 4 Piece 1025.00
Dish, Mayonnaise, Underplate, Crosshatching Diamonds, Hobstars, Signed, 6 3/4 In. 395.00
Humidor, Brunswick, Signed, 7 3/4 In. 1175.00
Rose Bowl, Hobstar Base, Signed, 7 x 8 In. 775.00
Vase, Floral Swags, Medallions, Frosted, Signed, 1900s, 8 3/4 In. 69.00
Vase, Green To Clear, Fan, Signed, 7 1/2 In. 112.00
Vase, Venetian, 14 x 6 1/2 In. 875.00

HEAD VASES, generally showing a woman from the shoulders up, were used by florists primarily in the 1950s and 1960s. Made in a variety of sizes and often decorated with imitation jewelry and other lifelike accessories, the vases were manufactured in Japan and the U.S.A. Less elaborate examples were made as early as the 1930s. Religious themes, babies, and animals are also common subjects. Other head vases are listed under manufacturers' names and can be located through the index at the back of this book.

Blond Girl, Ponytail, Inarco No. E2783, 6 In. .... *Illus* 440.00
Cynthia, Off-Shoulder Dress, White Hat, Betty Lou Nichols, 6 3/4 In. 495.00

Head Vase, Blond Girl, Ponytail,
Inarco No. E2783, 6 In.

Head Vase, Lucille Ball, Mame,
Aqua Hat & Collar, Rubens, 11 In.

Head Vase, Marilyn Monroe, Earrings,
Relpo, Box & Label, 6 3/4 In.

Donna, Pink Dress, Betty Lou Nichols, 5 In. 275.00
Eggbert, Winking Eye, Mustache, Flat-Top Hat, Betty Lou Nichols, 8 1/2 In. 990.00
Flora Belle, Black Hair, Green, Yellow & Black Striped Dress, Betty Lou Nichols, 10 In. . 905.00
Green Bonnet, Pearl Dangle Earrings, Napco 450.00
Henrietta, 8 1/2 In. 660.00
Louisa, Betty Lou Nichols, 7 1/2 In. 625.00
Lucille Ball, Mame, Aqua Hat & Collar, Rubens, 11 In. ....*Illus* 495.00
Marilyn Monroe, Earrings, Relpo, Box & Label, 6 3/4 In. ....*Illus* 605.00
Mary Lou, Black High-Neck Dress, White Ruffle Collar, Betty Lou Nichols, 5 1/2 In. ... 175.00
Nellie, Pink Dress, Brown Hair, 6 In. 93.50
Planter, Flora Belle, Betty Lou Nichols, 11 In. 700.00
Valerie, Betty Lou Nichols, 7 3/4 In. 610.00
Woman, Applied Flowers, Applied Lashes, 6 In. 88.00
Woman, Black Hat, Band & Bow, Black Dress, White Collar, 7 In. 358.00
Woman, Blue Dress, 2 Hair Ribbons, Inarco, 7 In. 330.00
Woman, Blue Scalloped Brim Hat, Japan, 6 In. 50.00
Woman, Bow On Blue Dress, Large Lashes, Ardco, 6 1/2 In. 220.00
Woman, Green & White Dress, Hat, Brim Up, Necklace & Earrings, Relpo, 5 3/4 In. 155.00
Woman, Green Hat, White Band & Bow, Green Dress, Closed Eyes, 7 In. 358.00
Woman, Green, White Hat, Applied Lashes, Flowered Rim, Napco, 1959, 6 In. 88.00
Woman, Hat, With Bow, Light Blue, Applied Lashes, 5 1/2 In. 121.00
Woman, Large Lashes, Long Blond Hair, Velco, 7 In. 303.00
Woman, Madonna, White, Folding Hands, Brody, 6 1/4 In. 77.00
Woman, Pigtails, Green Dress, Earrings, Ruben, 5 1/2 In. 99.00
Woman, Pink Bow, Large Ruffled Collar, 5 In. 25.00
Woman, Pink Hair Bow, White Dress, 5 3/4 In. 303.00
Woman, Pink, White Ruffled Hat, Band & Flowers, Velco, 6 In. 50.00
Woman, Sleeveless Blue Dress, Blond Hair, Inarco, 6 In. 440.00
Woman, Tam Hat, Yellow Hair, Ruben, 5 1/2 In. 176.00
Woman, With Coat & Hat, Hand On Up-Turned Collar, Napco, 5 1/2 In. 175.00
Woman, Yellow Hat With Flowers, White, 6 3/4 In. 39.00

HEDI SCHOOP Art Creations, North Hollywood, California, started
about 1945 and was working until 1954. Schoop made ceramic figurines, lamps, planters, and tablewares.

*Hedi Schoop
S*

Figurine, Asian Couple, Navy Blue, White, Textured Hair, 12 In., Pair 45.00
Figurine, My Sister & I, Dutch Couple, Signed, Hedi Schoop, 1940s, 11 In., Pair 145.00
Figurine, Young China, Chinese Musicians, 1946 .... 145.00
Planter, Girl Holding Bouquet Of Flowers & Vase, 9 1/4 In. 110.00

HEINTZ ART Metal Shop made jewelry, copper, silver, and brass in
Buffalo, New York, from 1906 to 1935, when a new company name
was taken and the mark became *Silvercrest*. The most popular items
with collectors today are the copper desk sets and vases made with
applied silver designs.

Ashtray, Matchbox Holder, 4 x 8 In. 192.00
Bookends, Leaves, Silver On Bronze, 3 x 4 3/4 In., Pair 132.00
Candlestick, Silver On Bronze, 5 In. 287.00
Cup, Michigan State Fair, 10 In. 230.00
Humidor, Chain Link Cover, Silver On Bronze, Cedar Lining, 3 x 10 x 6 In. 316.00
Inkwell, Silver On Bronze, Verdigris Patina, 2 1/4 x 3 1/2 In. 184.00
Lamp, Bronze, Verdigris Patina, Squat, Sterling Floral Overlay, 15 1/2 In. 2875.00
Lamp, Desk, Geometric Bands, Silver On Bronze, 12 x 9 In. 950.00
Lamp, Flowers & Leaves, Bronze Shade, 3 Sections, Label, 9 In. 1265.00
Lamp, Flowers, Silver On Bronze, Stamped, 15 1/2 In. ....*Illus* 2875.00
Lamp, Flowers, Silver On Bronze, Verdigris Patina, 9 1/2 In. 1210.00
Lamp, Lilies, Silver On Bronze, Cutout Shade, Fabric Liner, 11 x 11 1/2 In. 3105.00
Letter Rack, Owls, Original Patina, Signed, 4 x 6 x 2 1/4 In. 224.00
Stringholder, Leaves, Silver On Bronze, Bell Shape, Stamp, 3 x 4 In. 546.00
Vase, Bird On Branch, Silver On Bronze, Stamped, 10 In. 374.00
Vase, Bud, Roses, Silver On Bronze, Die Stamped, 6 x 2 In. 518.00
Vase, Columbine, Silver On Bronze, 11 x 5 In. 550.00
Vase, Columbine, Silver On Bronze, Cylindrical, Verdigris, 10 x 4 In. 400.00

Heintz Art, Lamp,
Flowers, Silver On
Bronze, Stamped,
15 1/2 In.

**Keep a "mystery disaster" box.
If you find a piece of veneer, an
old screw, or even a porcelain
rose bud, put it into the box
until you are able to make the
necessary repairs.**

Vase, Daffodil, Silver On Bronze, 10 In.	575.00
Vase, Flowers, Silver On Bronze, 7 1/4 In.	430.00
Vase, Flowers, Silver On Bronze, Verdigris Patina, 7 1/2 x 3 1/4 In.	315.00
Vase, Freesia, Silver On Bronze, Cleaned Patina, 11 x 3 3/4 In.	300.00
Vase, Hollyhock, Silver On Bronze, Original Patina, Cylindrical, 9 In.	675.00
Vase, Leafy Branch, Silver On Bronze, Verdigris Patina, 11 1/2 x 3 1/2 In.	1265.00
Vase, Mistletoe, Silver On Bronze, Original Patina, 10 1/2 x 4 In.	300.00 to 400.00
Vase, Peacock, Silver On Bronze, Tapered, Peacock, 11 x 31 1/2 In.	545.00
Vase, Tobacco Flower, Silver On Bronze, Dark Verdigris Patina, 11 x 4 1/2 In.	550.00

HEISEY glass was made from 1896 to 1957 in Newark, Ohio, by A. H.
Heisey and Co., Inc. The Imperial Glass Company of Bellaire, Ohio,
bought some of the molds and the rights to the trademark. Some
Heisey patterns have been made by Imperial since 1960. After 1968,
they stopped using the *H* trademark. Heisey used romantic names for
colors, such as *Sahara*. Do not confuse color and pattern names. The
Custard Glass and Ruby Glass categories may also include some
Heisey pieces.

Acorn, Plate, Flamingo, 7 In.	18.00
Animal, Asiatic Pheasant	175.00
Animal, Bunny, Head Down, 2 1/2 In.	200.00
Animal, Chick, Head Up, 1 In.	70.00
Animal, Colt, Balking	130.00
Animal, Colt, Kicking	95.00
Animal, Colt, Standing	168.00
Animal, Cygnet	225.00
Animal, Elephant, Small	240.00
Animal, Goose, Wings Down	459.00
Animal, Hen	425.00
Animal, Mallard, Wings Up	120.00
Animal, Piglet, Sitting, 1 1/8 In.	85.00
Animal, Rabbit, Paperweight	130.00 to 190.00
Animal, Ringneck Pheasant	120.00
Animal, Rooster	425.00
Animal, Sow	700.00
Animal, Sparrow	95.00
Aristocrat, Candlestick, Gold Encrusted, 7 1/2 In., Pair	85.00
Athena, Nappy, 6 In.	30.00
Athena, Plate, 14 In.	10.00
Athena, Sugar & Creamer, Tray	180.00
Balda, Jug, Monticello Etch, 40 Oz.	125.00
Banded Flute, Ashtray, Matchbox Stand	75.00
Banded Flute, Goblet, 7 Oz.	35.00
Banded Flute, Matchbox, Cover	190.00
Banded Flute, Mug, Root Beer	45.00
Banded Flute, Nappy, Footed, 4 1/2 In.	12.00

Banded Flute, Punch Cup	10.00
Banded Flute, Tray, Round, 13 In.	90.00
Banded Flute, Water Set, Bottle, 7 Piece	200.00
Banded Picket, Basket, Flamingo	160.00
Barbara Fritchie, Brandy, 3/4 Oz.	65.00
Barbara Fritchie, Brandy, Alexandrite Bowl, Clear Foot, 3/4 Oz.	375.00
Beaded Panel & Sunburst, Butter, Cover	15.00
Beaded Panel & Sunburst, Pitcher, 1/2 Gal.	25.00
Beaded Panel & Sunburst, Salt	10.00
Beehive, Plate, 5 In.	10.00
Beehive, Plate, 10 In.	25.00
Beehive, Plate, Flamingo, 5 In.	18.00
Beehive, Plate, Flamingo, 8 In.	10.00
Brookville, Sherbet, Footed, Handle, 3 1/2 Oz.	30.00
Carcassone, Champagne, Cobalt Blue Bowl, Clear Stem & Foot	125.00
Carcassone, Cocktail, Cobalt Blue Bowl, Clear Stem & Foot, 3 Oz.	100.00
Carcassone, Sherbet, Alexandrite, 6 Oz.	135.00
Carcassone, Tumbler, Footed, Alexandrite, 8 Oz.	145.00
Charter Oak, Bowl, Flamingo, 4 1/4 In.	18.00
Charter Oak, Goblet, Flamingo, 8 Oz.	15.00
Christos, Decanter, Sahara	250.00
Coarse Rib, Plate, 7 In.	25.00
Coarse Rib, Plate, 14 In.	30.00
Coarse Rib, Plate, Flamingo, 4 1/2 In.	8.00
Coarse Rib, Plate, Flamingo, 7 1/2 In.	13.00
Coarse Rib, Plate, Moongleam, 14 In.	75.00
Coarse Rib, Punch Cup	10.00
Cobel, Cocktail Shaker, Duck & Cattail Cutting, Qt.	90.00
Cobel, Cocktail Shaker, Horsehead Stopper, 2 Qt.	200.00
Colonial, Syrup, Sanitary, Cover, 8 Oz.	38.00
Colonial, Syrup, Sanitary, Cover, 28 Oz.	52.00
Colonial, Wine, 4 1/4 In.	50.00
Coronation, Cocktail Shaker, Rooster Stopper	75.00
Coventry, Goblet, Zircon, 8 Oz.	165.00
Creole, Bowl, Grapefruit, Alexandrite	210.00
Creole, Cocktail, Alexandrite, 4 Oz.	100.00
Creole, Cordial, Alexandrite, 1 1/2 Oz.	300.00
Creole, Goblet, Alexandrite Bowl, Clear Stem & Foot, 11 Oz.	110.00
Criss Cross, Nappy, 8 In.	65.00
Crystolite, Ashtray, 3 1/4 In.	11.00
Crystolite, Box, Cigarette, Cover	42.00
Crystolite, Candlestick, 2-Light, Pair	100.00
Crystolite, Candlestick, Square, 4 In., Pair	30.00
Crystolite, Celery Dish, 12 In.	25.00
Crystolite, Cheese Stand, 5 1/2 In.	27.00
Crystolite, Coaster	12.00
Crystolite, Lamp, Silk Shade, 33 In.	750.00
Crystolite, Sherbet, 7 Oz.	10.00
Crystolite, Syrup, Metal Cover	25.00
Crystolite, Tray, Oval	45.00
Daisy & Leaves, Tumbler, 8 Oz.	85.00
Danish Princess, Goblet, Water, 8 In.	65.00
Diamond Point, Ashtray, Individual	30.00
Duplex, Bonbon, Handles, Flamingo, 8 In.	25.00
Duquesne, Tumbler, Footed, 10 Oz.	25.00
Electro, Lamp, Portable, Glass Harp, Silk Shade, 9 In.	350.00
Elizabeth, Candlestick, 10 In.	225.00
Empress, Bowl, Floral, Dolphin Footed, Sahara, 11 In.	95.00
Empress, Candy Box, Cover, Sahara, 6 In.	225.00
Empress, Celery Dish, Sahara, 13 In.	30.00
Empress, Compote, Sahara, 6 In.	45.00
Empress, Cup & Saucer, After Dinner, Sahara	85.00
Empress, Cup & Saucer, Sahara	32.00

Empress, Cup, Sahara	15.00
Empress, Dish, Mint, Moongleam, 6 In.	40.00
Empress, Dish, Pickle & Olive, Sahara, 7 In.	45.00
Empress, Ice Bucket, Tongs, Silver Overlay, Butterfly	75.00
Empress, Jug, Flamingo, 3 Pt.	200.00
Empress, Nut Cup, Sahara	15.00
Empress, Nut Dish	49.00
Empress, Plate, 8 1/2 In.	5.00
Empress, Plate, Old Colony Etch, Sahara, 8 In.	25.00
Empress, Plate, Sahara, 6 1/4 In.	10.00
Empress, Plate, Sahara, 8 In.	20.00
Empress, Plate, Sahara, 10 1/2 In.	110.00
Empress, Relish, 3 Sections, Sahara	35.00
Empress, Relish, 4 Sections, Gold Trim, 16 In.	25.00
Empress, Soup, Cream, Underplate	45.00
Empress Sahara, Creamer, Pink	50.00
Fancy Loop, Nappy, Emerald, Gold Trim, 4 1/2 In.	30.00
Fancy Loop, Plate, 9 In.	110.00
Fancy Loop, Punch Cup, Straight Sides, Footed	35.00
Fancy Loop, Toothpick	40.00
Fancy Loop, Tumbler	30.00
Fandango, Bonbon, 5 1/2 x 4 In.	25.00
Fandango, Punch Cup	10.00 to 16.00
Fandango, Salt	40.00
Fandango, Sugar	35.00
Fandango, Sugar & Creamer, Individual	50.00
Fandango, Toothpick	65.00 to 99.00
Fandango, Wine, 3 Oz.	40.00 to 90.00
Fern, Relish, 4 Sections	20.00
Flat Panel, Dish, Ice Cream Cone, Silver Overlay	75.00
Flat Panel, Humidor, Hollow Cover, Benson & Hedges, Pat. Dec. 25, '08, 6 x 9 1/2 In.	192.00
Flat Panel, Jar, Cover, Horseradish	20.00
Flat Panel, Puff Box, Butterfly Cutting On Cover	75.00
Flat Panel, Sherbet	5.00
Flat Panel, Vase, 12 In., Pair	105.00
Fluted Border, Plate, Moongleam, 8 In.	20.00
Gascony, Decanter, Sportsman Etch	450.00
Gibson Girl, Bowl, Flower Frog	20.00
Gibson Girl, Bowl, Flowers, Flower Frog, Chantilly Cut, 8 In.	20.00
Greek Key, Celery Dish, 9 In.	65.00
Greek Key, Celery Dish, Oval, 12 In.	65.00
Greek Key, Plate, 5 In.	20.00
Greek Key, Punch Bowl	80.00
Greek Key, Tumbler, Soda, Footed, Flared	40.00
Groove & Slash, Spooner	90.00
Half Circle, Sugar, Sahara	25.00
Ipswich, Champagne, Moongleam, 6 Oz.	45.00
Jack-Be-Nimble, Candlestick, Pair	50.00
Kathie, Plate, 8 In.	10.00
Kohinoor, Goblet, Zircon Bowl, Clear Stem & Foot, 9 Oz.	120.00
Lariat, Candy Box, Cover, Footed, 7 In.	95.00
Lariat, Candy Jar, Cover, Footed, 11 1/2 In.	40.00
Lariat, Cheese Dish, Cover	50.00
Lariat, Cheese Dish, Cover, Footed	125.00
Lariat, Coaster	11.00
Lariat, Plate, 10 1/2 In.	115.00
Lariat, Platter, Oval	60.00
Lariat, Punch Bowl, Underplate, 12 Cups	110.00
Lariat, Relish, 3 Sections, Round, 10 In.	45.00
Lariat, Sugar, Cover	20.00
Lariat, Tray, Handles, Round, 14 In.	50.00
Lariat, Vase, 7 In.	25.00 to 40.00
Legionnaire, Sherbet, Lily Cutting	5.00

Locket On Chain, Bowl, Footed, 8 In. 25.00
Lodestar, Nappy, Shallow, 7 In. 40.00
Medium Flat Panel, Cruet, Oil, Floral Cutting, 4 Oz. 20.00
Military Cap, Ashtray 15.00
Minuet Etch, Plate, Queen Ann, 7 In. 30.00
Minuet Etch, Plate, Toujours, 8 In. 20.00
Minuet Etch, Tumbler, Juice, Symphone, 5 Oz. 40.00
Narrow Flute, Cracker & Cheese Set, 2 Piece 25.00
Narrow Flute, Jug, 3 Pt. 45.00
Narrow Flute, Nut Dish, Flamingo, Oval 44.00
Narrow Flute, Pitcher, Qt. 135.00
Narrow Flute, Sugar, Domino, Moongleam 600.00
Narrow Flute, Sugar, Individual, Moongleam 25.00
New Era, Candlestick, 2-Light, Prisms, Pair 140.00
New Era, Cocktail, 3 1/2 Oz. 25.00
Oakwood, Tumbler, Soda, Fox Chase Etch, 5 Oz. 25.00
Octagon, Basket, 5 In. 752.00
Octagon, Candlestick, 1-Light, Blue & Gold Stain, 7 In. 60.00
Octagon, Dish, Mayonnaise, Footed, Ladle, Hawthorne 122.00
Octagon, Sugar & Creamer, Sahara 20.00
Old Dominion, Wine, Empress Etch, 3 Oz. 65.00
Old Glory, Goblet, Windsor Cutting, 9 Oz. 95.00
Old Sandwich, Bowl, Popcorn, Footed, Sahara 50.00
Old Sandwich, Candlestick, 2-Light, Sahara 625.00
Old Sandwich, Candlestick, Cobalt Blue, 6 In. 135.00
Old Sandwich, Cocktail, 3 Oz. 22.00
Old Sandwich, Mug, Beer, 12 Oz. 35.00
Old Sandwich, Oyster Cocktail, Sahara, 4 Oz. 95.00
Old Sandwich, Plate, Sahara, Square, 8 In. 20.00
Old Sandwich, Tumbler, Iced Tea, Footed, Flamingo 45.00
Old Sandwich, Wine, 2 1/2 Oz. 20.00
Old Williamsburg, Claret, 4 Oz. 65.00
Old Williamsburg, Cocktail, 3 Oz. 25.00
Orchid Etch, Bowl, Waverly, 10 In. 120.00
Orchid Etch, Butter, Cover, Waverly 215.00
Orchid Etch, Candlestick, 2-Light, Fern, Pair 250.00
Orchid Etch, Candlestick, 3-Light, Cascade, Pair 200.00
Orchid Etch, Candlestick, Mercury, Pair 70.00
Orchid Etch, Cordial, Tyrolean, Oz. 105.00
Orchid Etch, Decanter, Sherry, Oval, Silver Overlay Stopper, Pt. 150.00
Orchid Etch, Dish, Lemon, Queen Ann, 6 1/2 In. 400.00
Orchid Etch, Ice Bucket, Handles, Waverly ....450.00 to 495.00
Orchid Etch, Pitcher, Martini, Stirrer, Pt. 295.00
Orchid Etch, Pitcher, Water, Ice Lip, Gallagher Shape, 73 Oz. 550.00
Orchid Etch, Sherbet, Tyrolean, 5 Oz. 70.00
Park Lane, Cordial, Brian Cliff Cutting 70.00
Patrician, Candelabra, 3-Light, 21 In. 250.00
Peach Melba, Dish, Grapefruit 45.00
Peerless, Decanter, Stopper, Pt. 75.00
Petal, Creamer, Flamingo 15.00
Pillows, Rose Bowl, 6 1/2 In. 70.00
Pine Cone, Bowl, Limelight, 6 1/4 In. 50.00
Pineapple & Fan, Toothpick 85.00
Plain Panel, Cruet, Oil, Cutting, 6 Oz. 35.00
Plain Panel, Tumbler, 8 Oz. 75.00
Plantation, Ashtray 45.00
Plantation, Bowl, Flared, Label, 9 In. 300.00
Plantation, Bowl, Gardenia, Footed, 11 1/2 In. 180.00
Plantation, Bowl, Salad, 9 In. 225.00
Plantation, Candlestick, 2-Light, Pair 165.00
Plantation, Candy Dish, Cover 175.00
Plantation, Oyster Cocktail, 4 Oz. 100.00
Plantation, Pitcher, Ice Lip, 1/2 Gal. 400.00

Plantation, Plate, 7 In. 20.00
Plantation, Punch Cup 10.00
Plantation, Sugar & Creamer 80.00
Plantation, Sugar & Creamer, Ivy Etch 60.00
Plantation, Tumbler, Water, Footed, 8 Oz. 400.00
Plantation, Wine, 3 Oz. 55.00
Pleat & Panel, Creamer, Moongleam 10.00
Pleat & Panel, Cruet, Stopper, Moongleam 110.00
Pleat & Panel, Jam Jar, Cover, Flamigo, 4 3/4 In. 15.00
Pleat & Panel, Pitcher, Moongleam 175.00
Pleat & Panel, Plate, Flamingo, 14 In. 65.00
Pleat & Panel, Plate, Moongleam, 8 In. 25.00
Prince Of Wales, Nappy, 4 In. 5.00
Prince Of Wales, Spooner 140.00
Priscilla, Butter Chip 10.00
Priscilla, Mustard, Cover 20.00
Priscilla, Toothpick 10.00
Priscilla, Toothpick, Floral Cutting 80.00
Priscilla, Toothpick, Ruby Stain, Gold Trim 67.00
Priscilla, Vase, Violet, Flared, 4 In. 30.00
Prison Stripe, Spooner 120.00
Punty Band, Mug, Souvenir, Argyle, Wisconsin 20.00
Puritan, Bottle, French Dressing 5.00
Puritan, Box, Cigarette, Horsehead, Finial Cover, 9 1/2 In. 55.00
Puritan, Jug, Pt. 70.00
Queen Ann, Bowl, Floral, Footed, 11 1/2 In. 55.00
Queen Ann, Dish, Lemon, Cutting On Cover, Arberware Tray 30.00
Recessed Panel, Basket, 9 In. 160.00
Recessed Panel, Candy Jar, Turquoise Enameled Panels 85.00
Revere, Plate, West Point Crest Etch, 8 In. 10.00
Revere, Vase, Cloister Cutting, 7 1/2 In. 20.00
Rib & Panel, Candy Box, Cover, Oval 45.00
Rib & Panel, Plate, Cheese, Moongleam, 6 In. 25.00
Ridgeleigh, Ashtray, Zircon, Square, 2 In. . . . . .70.00 to 75.00
Ridgeleigh, Ice Tub, Handles, 6 1/2 In. 60.00
Ridgeleigh, Jam Jar, Cover, Spoon 10.00
Ridgeleigh, Vase, 3 1/2 In. 25.00
Rose Etch, Candlestick, Mercury, 3 In. 20.00
Rose Etch, Champagne, 6 Oz. 20.00
Rose Etch, Cup & Saucer, Waverly 65.00
Saturn, Candlestick, 2-Light, Limelight, 5 In. 500.00
Saturn, Plate, Paper Label, 10 In. 20.00
Spanish, Goblet, Cobalt Blue Bowl, Clear Stem & Foot, Pair 275.00
Stanhope, Candlestick, 2-Light, Prisms, Pair 450.00
Stanhope, Plate, 7 In. 10.00
Stanhope, Tumbler, Soda, Zircon Bowl & Foot, Clear Stem, 12 Oz. 140.00
Stanhope, Vase, 9 In. 130.00
Stanhope, Vase, Bakelite, Handle Knobs, 9 1/8 In. 920.00
Steele, Rose Bowl, Hawthorne 85.00
Steele, Rose Bowl, Sahara 85.00
Steeple Chase, Cocktail 25.00
Suez, Champagne, Sultana Stem, 6 Oz. 45.00
Sunburst, Ashtray, Bridge Club 10.00
Sunburst, Celery Dish, 12 In. 75.00
Sunburst, Jam Jar, Handle 25.00
Swirl & Raindrop, Bowl, Floral, Moongleam, 12 In. 25.00
Touraine, Punch Cup 5.00
Town & Country, Bowl, Dawn, 5 In. 75.00
Town & Country, Plate, Dawn, 14 In. 75.00
Town & Country, Plate, Paper Label, 14 In. 10.00
Tricorn, Candlestick, 3-Light 110.00
Trident, Candlestick, 2-Light, Sahara, Pair 90.00
Tudor, Bowl, Fruit, Moongleam, 10 In. 95.00

Tudor, Cocktail, Oyster, 4 Oz.	10.00
Tudor, Pitcher, Straight Sides, Footed, 3 Pt.	130.00
Tudor, Tumbler, 8 Oz.	30.00
Twentieth Century, Goblet, Soda, Dawn, 5 Oz.	30.00
Twentieth Century, Goblet, Soda, Sahara, 5 Oz.	30.00
Twist, Bonbon, Handles, Flamingo	30.00
Twist, Dish, Pickle, Moongleam, 7 In.	28.00
Twist, Jug, Flamingo, 3 Pt.	110.00
Twist, Plate, Marigold, 7 In.	20.00
Twist, Relish, Marigold, 10 In.	20.00
Twist, Sugar & Creamer, Moongleam	100.00
Universal, Cocktail, Tally Ho Etch, 3 1/2 Oz., Pair	60.00
Victorian, Candlestick, 2-Light, 10 In., Pair	75.00
Victorian, Goblet, 1 Ball, Sahara, 9 Oz.	55.00
Victorian, Goblet, 2 Ball, 9 Oz.	20.00
Victorian, Goblet, 4 1/2 In.	18.00
Wabash, Champagne, Mayflower Etch, Clear Bowl, Moongleam Stem & Foot, 5 1/2 In.	40.00
Wabash, Cocktail, Mayflower Etch, Clear Bowl, Moongleam Stem & Foot, 5 7/8 In.	35.00
Wabash, Goblet, Mayflower Etch, Clear Bowl, Moongleam Stem & Foot, 7 In.	48.00
Wabash, Sherbet, Mayflower Etch, Moongleam Green Stem, 3 3/4 In.	35.00
Waldorf Astoria, Toothpick	110.00
Warwick, Candlestick, 2-Light, Pair	30.00
Waverly, Dish, Jelly, Cover, Footed, 6 1/2 In.	55.00
Waverly, Jar, Cigarette, Cover, Seahorse Handles	245.00
Waverly, Relish, 2 Sections	10.00
Waverly, Relish, 3 Sections, Oval, 11 1/2 In.	15.00
Wellington, Candlestick, Moongleam, 10 In, Pair	800.00
Whaley, Tankard, Frontenac Etch, 54 Oz.	110.00
Whirlpool, Mustard, Cover	100.00
Whirlpool, Plate, 17 1/2 In.	10.00
Windsor, Candlestick, 7 In., Pair	80.00 to 130.00
Winged Scroll, Nappy, Emerald With Gold Trim, 4 In.	15.00
Yeoman, Bonbon, Bowtie, Handle, Moongleam, 4 In.	55.00
Yeoman, Goblet, Moongleam, 10 Oz.	30.00
Yeoman, Plate, Moonglo Cutting, 8 In.	25.00
Yeoman, Relish, 4 Sections, Round, 11 In.	10.00
Yeoman, Soup, Dish	85.00

HEREND, see Fischer category.

HEUBACH is the collector's name for Gebruder Heubach, a firm working in Lichten, Germany, from 1840 to 1925. It is best known for bisque dolls and doll heads, their principal products. They also manufactured bisque figurines, including piano babies, beginning in the 1880s, and glazed figurines in the 1900s. Piano Babies are listed in their own category. Dolls are included in the Doll category under *Gebruder Heubach* and *Heubach*. Another factory, Ernst Heubach, working in Koppelsdorf, Germany, also made porcelain and dolls. These will also be found in the Doll category under Heubach Koppelsdorf.

Figurine, Bicyclists, Boy & Girl, 13 In.	1695.00
Figurine, Dutch Girl, Seated, Blue & White Dress, Bisque, 6 1/2 In.	195.00
Figurine, Men & Woman, Bicyclists, Germany, c.1900, 14 x 15 In.	558.00

HISTORIC BLUE, see factory names, such as Adams, Clews, Ridgway, and Staffordshire.

HOBNAIL glass is a style of glass with bumps all over. Dozens of hobnail patterns and variants have been made. Clear, colored, and opalescent hobnail have been made and are being reproduced. Other pieces of hobnail may also be listed in the Duncan & Miller Fenton, and Francisware categories.

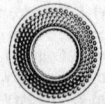

Banana Stand, Yellow	235.00
Barber Bottle, White, Lavender, Flared Lip, 8 In. .... *Illus*	175.00
Bowl, Vaseline, Footed, 2 1/2 x 5 1/2 In.	75.00

Hobnail, Barber Bottle, White,
Lavender, Flared Lip, 8 In.

Holt-Howard, Dish,
Cottage Cheese, Cover,
Cozy Kitten, Plaid Border,
1958, 4 1/4 In.

Creamer, Rose Opalescent, Applied Handle, 5 In.	100.00
Pitcher, Amethyst	1400.00
Pitcher, Milk, Rose Opalescent Satin, Reeded Handle, 6 In.	200.00
Pitcher, Water, Blue, Applied Handle, Open Pontil, 7 In.	70.00
Puff Box, Cover, Tray, Blue, Opalescent, Applied Finial, 6 In.	150.00

HOCHST, or Hoechst, porcelain was made in Germany from 1746 to 1796. It was marked with a six-spoke wheel. Be careful when buying Hochst; many other firms have used a very similar wheel-shaped mark.

Figurine, 3 Wrestling Cherubs, Oval Base, 7 1/2 In.	235.00

HOLLY AMBER, or golden agate, glass was made by the Indiana Tumbler and Goblet Company of Greentown, Indiana, from January 1, 1903, to June 13, 1903. It is a pressed glass pattern featuring holly leaves in the amber-shaded glass. The glass was made with shadings that range from creamy opalescent to brown-amber.

Bowl, 7 1/4 In.	420.00
Tumbler, Flared Rim, 4 x 3 In.	450.00

HOLT-HOWARD was an importer who started working in 1949 in Stamford, Connecticut. The company sold many types of table accessories, such as condiment jars, decanters, spoon holders, and saltshakers. The figures shown on some of his pieces had a cartoon-like quality. The company was bought out by General Housewares Corporation in 1969. Holt-Howard pieces are often marked with the name and the year or *HH* and the year stamped in black. The HH mark was used until 1974. There was also a black and silver label.

Beverage Set, Winking Santa, Pitcher, 6 Cups, 1960		60.00
Candleholder, 3-Light, Totem Pole Santa, 1958, 8 1/2 In.		22.00
Dish, Cottage Cheese, Cover, Cozy Kitten, Plaid Border, 1958, 4 1/4 In.	*Illus*	65.00
Letter Holder, Cozy Kitten		45.00
Salt & Pepper, Cozy Kitten, White, Pink & Blue Collar, 5 In.		70.00

HOPALONG CASSIDY was a character in a series of twenty-eight books written by Clarence E. Milford, first published in 1907. Movies and television shows were made based on the character. The best-known actor playing Hopalong Cassidy was William Lawrence Boyd. His first movie appearance was in 1919, but the first Hopalong Cassidy film was not until 1934. Sixty-six films were made. In 1948, William Boyd purchased the television rights to the movies, then later made fifty-two new programs. In the 1950s, Hopalong Cassidy and his horse, named *Topper*, were seen in comics, records, toys, and other products. Boyd died in 1972.

Badge, Paper	5.00
Badge, Star, Tin	35.00
Binoculars	85.00
Book & Records, Singing Bandit	65.00
Book Cover, Brown, Paper, Hoppy Photo & Signature, Bond Bread	20.00

Hopalong Cassidy, Boots,
Cowboy, Hoppy, Leather,
Elastic Pull Tabs, Acme

Hopalong Cassidy,
Game, Cardboard,
Punch-Out Pieces,
Hoppy Play
Money, 1950

Hopalong
Cassidy, Guitar,
Wooden,
Hoppy &
Topper, Box

Boots, Cowboy, Hoppy, Leather, Elastic Pull Tabs, Acme . . . . *Illus* 100.00
Bottle, Hair Trainer, Hoppy On Label, Contains White Liquid, 4 Oz., 5 In. 14.00
Button, Bank Teller, Savings Club Promotion, 3 In. 32.00
Camera, Flash, Box 45.00
Carrying Bag, Insulated, Silver Foil, Metallic Blue Outside, Dairylea Ice Cream 28.00
Catalog, Automatic Toy Co., 1950, 3 x 4 1/2 In., 16 Pages 20.00
Chaps, 1950s 175.00
Clock, Cuckoo, Animals, 8-Day, Lux, West Germany 190.00
Comic Book, Fawcett Vol. 4 No. 23, Sept. 1948 . . . . 48.00
Cup, Chow Set, Milk Glass 60.00
Cup, Hoppy, Name In Lasso, Cowboy Roping Steer, Ceramic, 2 3/4 x 3 In. 40.00
Dixie Cup, Photograph, Color 75.00
Figures, Hoppy & Topper Set, Plastic, Display Size 2 x 5 In., 5 1/2 In. 60.00
Figurine, Hoppy & Topper, Cast Metal, Tempo, England, Pair 125.00
Figurine, Hoppy, Lead, Painted, Timpo, England, 1950s, 2 1/4 In. 60.00
Flashlight 100.00
Frame, Picture, Leatherette 50.00
Game, Cardboard, Punch-Out Pieces, Hoppy Play Money, 1950 . . . . *Illus* 55.00
Game, Spelet Board, Spelling, Denmark 100.00
Glass, Hoppy Favorite, Black Picture, 8 Oz. 15.00
Gloves, Child's, Fringed 105.00
Guitar, Wooden, Hoppy & Topper, Box . . . . *Illus* 120.00
Home Movie, Hidden Gold Series 18.00
Hopalong-Aid Drink Packet, Glossy Waxed Paper, 3 1/2 x 5 In. 120.00
Jewelry Box, Gold & Brown, Lasso, Name Inside, Anson, 1 1/4 x 2 3/4 x 3 In. 40.00
Lamp, Motion, Photo Of Hoppy & Topper, Plastic, 1949 . . . . 825.00
Lid, Cottage Cheese, Puritan All Star, Waxed Cardboard, 1950s, 4 1/4 In. 20.00
Lunch Box, Metal, Aladdin, 1954 . . . . *Illus* 140.00
Lunch Box, Metal, Scalloped Decal, Aladdin, 1950 . . . . *Illus* 110.00

Hopalong Cassidy,
Lunch Box, Metal,
Aladdin, 1954

Hopalong Cassidy, Lunch Box,
Metal, Scalloped Decal,
Aladdin, 1950

Hopalong Cassidy, Toy,
Rocking Horse, Topper,
Hooves On Rockers

Milk Bottle, Hoppy On 2 Sides, Dairylea On 2 Sides, 8 1/2 In.	40.00
Mirror, Dr. West Dental Kit, Metal Frame, 4 x 6 In.	30.00
Movie Press Book, Mystery Man, 1944, 11 1/2 x 14 3/4 In.	20.00
Mug, Milk Glass, Black Lettering	45.00
Night-Light, Beige Glass, Pistol In Holder Shape, 10 In.	230.00
Night-Light, Glass Gun & Holster, Wall Mount, Aladdin, 10 In.	402.00
Pencil Case, Red Slipcase, Pencils, Crayons, Protractor, 1/4 x 4 3/8 x 8 1/8 In.	85.00
Photo, Hoppy, Full Color, Signature, 1950 Boyd Copyright, 8 x 10 In.	8.00
Picture, Bill Boyd, Reverse Shows Hopalong 20 Scenes, 1938, 8 x 10 In.	75.00
Picture, Hoppy & Signature, Jaeger's Butternut Bread, Red Imprint, 8 x 10 In.	30.00
Place Mat, Paper, Scenes All Around, 10 1/2 x 13 1/4 In.	25.00
Plate, Party, Paper, White, Colorful Hoppy & Topper, 8 1/2 In.	18.00
Poster, Foreign Movie Re-release, Helten Fra Nevada, 24 x 33 In.	35.00
Poster, Hoppy Sage Cologne, Attached Cologne Sample, Frame	20.00
Program, Leather Burners, Danish, Copenhagen, 1943, 8 Pages	20.00
Radio, Aluminum, Arvin	800.00
Skirt, Cowgirl's, Hoppy & Topper, Cotton Twill, Black, 18-In. Waist	45.00
Song Folio, 12 Songs From 8 Movies, 1940, 9 x 11 3/4 In., 48 Pages	40.00
Stationery, Hoppy, Topper, Western Boys & Girls, 25 Folded 4 x 5 Sheets	22.00
Sunglasses, White Plastic Frame, Green Lenses, Applied 6-Shooters	20.00
Toy, On Horse, Twirls Lasso, Rocking Platform, Windup, Marx, 1940s	375.00
Toy, Range Rider, Hopalong & Topper, Tin Lithograph, Marx, Box, 11 In.	495.00
Toy, Rocking Horse, Topper, Hooves On Rockers ...... *Illus*	130.00
Tumbler, Breakfast, Milk Glass	45.00
View-Master Reel, Envelope, No. 955, Sawyers Inc., 1950	10.00
Wallpaper, Smiling Hoppy, Twirling Rope, Topper, Chuck Wagon, 18 x 19 In.	60.00
Woodburning Set, Electrical Tool, Watercolors, Wood Plaques, 1950	60.00
Woodburning Set, Image Of William Boyd, Mag, American Toy, 1950	115.00
Wristwatch, Ingersoll, Printed Leather Band, Metal Buckle, 7 In.	833.00
Wristwatch, Original Band	110.00

HOWARD PIERCE has been working in Southern California since 1936. In 1945, he opened a pottery in Claremont. His contemporary-looking figurines are popular with collectors. Pieces are marked with his name. He stopped making pottery in 1991.

Howard Pierce

Figurine, Bear & Cub	50.00
Figurine, Dachshund, Brown, 9 1/2 In.	120.00
Figurine, Dolphin, Riding Wave, Tan, 9 1/2 In.	125.00

HOWDY DOODY and Buffalo Bob were the main characters in a children's series televised from 1947 to 1960. Howdy was a redheaded puppet. The series became popular with college students in the late 1970s when Buffalo Bob began to lecture on campuses.

Activity Book, Dot To Dot, Stickers, Cutouts, Whitman, 1953, 10 1/2 x 12 In.	14.00
Baby Bib, Die Cut Thin Vinyl, Kagran, 16 1/2 x 16 In.	40.00
Badge, Celluloid, Full Color On White, 1980s Revival Era	18.00
Bandanna, Cotton, Linen Weave, Red & White, Rope Trim, 19 1/2 x 20 In.	45.00
Bank, Pig Riding, Shawnee	290.00
Barrette, Figural, Plastic, Painted	25.00
Belt, Cowhide Leather, Silvered Brass Buckle, Tin Clip & Tip, 26 In.	65.00
Book, Golden, No. 475, Wild West, Buffalo Bob & Howdy Autograph, 1952	150.00
Book, Howdy Doody In The Wild West, Big Golden Book, Full Color, 32 Pages	20.00
Box, Kunkel's Howdy Doody Shoe Polish, 5 1/2 x 7 1/4 x 9 1/2 In.	70.00
Cake Decorations On Card, Plastic, Die Cut, 6 Candleholders, Name Plate Holder	40.00
Catalog, Merchandise, Buffalo Bob & Howdy Autograph, 1955	600.00
Comic Book, Jackpot Of Fun, Full Color, DCA Food Industries, 16 Pages	20.00
Comic Book, No. 1, Buffalo Bob & Howdy Autograph, 1949	600.00
Comic Book, No. 2, Buffalo Bob & Howdy Autograph, 1960	200.00
Costume, Indian Princess, Kagran, Box, c.1951-1956	50.00
Figure, Inflatable, Vinyl, Flattened 12 x 26 In.	40.00
Football, Leather, White, 8 In.	30.00
Game, Ball Rolling Target Game, Parker Bros.	95.00
Game, Electric Doodler, Harett-Gilmar & Kagran, c.1951-1956	75.00

Key Chain, 4-Piece Puzzle	18.00
Pencil, Wood, Topped By 3-D Plastic Head	24.00
Puppet, Rubber Head, Painted, Fabric Hand Cover, Late 1940s, 8 In.	30.00
Puzzle, Frame Tray, Clarabell, 11 3/8 x 15 x 7/8 In.	24.00
Sign, Fudge Bar, Glossy Paper, 9 x 12 In.	60.00
Toy, Acrobat, Composition Head, Arnold Toys, 10 In.	180.00
Toy, Band, Tin Lithograph, Mechanical, 8 In.	975.00
Toy, Band, Windup, Unique Art	1050.00
Toy, Cart, Tin Lithograph, Mechanical, Ny-Lint, 9 In.	325.00
Toy, Dancer, Piano, Doin' The Howdy Doody, Tin, Clockwork, Box, 6 1/2 In.	2200.00
Wallpaper Roll, Howdy & Friend, Circus Theme, 1948, 19 1/4 x 13 In.	195.00
Watch, Girls, Metal Case, Green Vinyl Wrist Straps, Eye Pupils Move	60.00

HULL pottery was made in Crooksville, Ohio, from 1905. Addis E. Hull bought the Acme Pottery Company and started making ceramic wares. In 1917, A. E. Hull Pottery began making art pottery as well as the commercial wares. For a short time, 1921 to 1929, the firm also sold pottery imported from Europe. The dinnerwares of the 1940s, including the Little Red Riding Hood line, the high gloss artwares of the 1950s, and the matte wares of the 1940s, are all popular with collectors. The firm officially closed in March 1986.

Bow Knot, Vase, Blue, 6 1/2 In.	230.00
Little Red Riding Hood, Bank, Standing	170.00
Little Red Riding Hood, Basket, Open	40.00
Little Red Riding Hood, Butter	218.00 to 380.00
Little Red Riding Hood, Canister, Coffee	400.00
Little Red Riding Hood, Cookie Jar, Poinsettia	425.00
Little Red Riding Hood, Cookie Jar, Poppy, Open	160.00 to 275.00
Little Red Riding Hood, Creamer, Crawling, 4 In.	50.00
Little Red Riding Hood, Creamer, Ruffled Skirt	150.00 to 355.00
Little Red Riding Hood, Creamer, Tab Handle	80.00
Little Red Riding Hood, Dresser Jar, Red Bow, 8 3/4 In.	450.00
Little Red Riding Hood, Grease Jar, Wolf, Yellow, 6 1/2 In.	550.00
Little Red Riding Hood, Jug, Batter, Poppy Design, 6 3/4 In.	125.00
Little Red Riding Hood, Mustard Pot, Spoon, 5 1/2 In.	275.00 to 390.00
Little Red Riding Hood, Pitcher, Milk, Poppy Design, 8 In.	130.00
Little Red Riding Hood, Planter, Hanging, Wall, 9 In.	150.00
Little Red Riding Hood, Salt & Pepper, Closed Poppy Decal	50.00
Little Red Riding Hood, Salt & Pepper, Open Poppy Decal, Large	82.00 to 150.00
Little Red Riding Hood, Salt & Pepper, Small	54.00 to 95.00
Little Red Riding Hood, Sugar, Cover	90.00
Little Red Riding Hood, Tea Set, Teapot, Sugar & Creamer, 3 Piece	1100.00
Little Red Riding Hood, Teapot	140.00 to 185.00
Magnolia, Sugar & Creamer, 3 3/4 In.	75.00
Twin Geese, Planter, 7 1/4 In.	25.00
Water Lily, Vase, Blue, Pink, 8 1/2 In.	150.00
Wildflower, Bowl, Hanging, Footed, 7 1/2 In.	311.00
Wildflower, Ewer, 8 1/2 In.	81.00
Wildflower, Vase, 6 1/2 In.	69.00
Woodland, Ewer, 6 1/2 In.	70.00

HUMMEL figurines, based on the drawings of the nun M.I. Hummel (Berta Hummel), are made by the W. Goebel Porzellanfabrik of Oeslau, Germany, now Rodenthal, Germany. They were first made in 1935. The *Crown* mark was used from 1935 to 1949. The company added the *bee* marks in 1950. The *full bee* with variations, was used from 1950 to 1959; *stylized bee,* 1957 to 1972; *three line mark,* 1964 to 1972; *last bee,* sometimes called *vee over gee,* 1972 to 1979. In 1979 the V bee symbol was removed from the mark. *U.S. Zone* was part of the mark from 1946 to 1948; *W. Germany,* was part of the mark from 1960 to 1990; The *Goebel, W. Germany* mark, called the *missing bee* mark, was used from 1979 to 1990; *Goebel, Germany* with the crown and WG, originally called the *new mark,* was used from 1991

through part of 1999. The newest version of the bee mark with the word *Goebel,* the *current mark* or *Goebel with full bee,* was adopted in 2000. A special *Year 2000* backstamp was also introduced. Porcelain figures inspired by Berta Hummel's drawings were introduced in 1997. These are marked BH followed by a number. They are made in the Far East, not Germany. Other decorative items and plates that feature Hummel drawings have been made by Schmid Brothers, Inc., since 1971.

Bell, Annual, 1978, Let's Sing	30.00
Bell, Annual, 1979, Farewell	25.00
Bell, Annual, 1980, Thoughtful	25.00
Bell, Annual, 1981, In Tune	30.00
Bell, Annual, 1982, She Loves Me	50.00
Bell, Annual, 1983, Knit One	50.00
Bell, Annual, 1984, Mountaineer	50.00
Bell, Annual, 1985, Sweet Song	50.00
Bell, Annual, 1986, Sing Along	75.00
Bell, Annual, 1988, Busy Student	75.00
Bell, Annual, 1989, Latest News	75.00
Bell, Annual, 1992, Whistler's Duet	80.00
Bell, Christmas, 1989, Ride Into Christmas	30.00
Candleholder, No. 440, Birthday Candle, New Mark	123.00
Clock, No. 441, Call To Worship, New Mark	680.00
Clock, No. 442, Chapel Time, New Mark	900.00
Figurine, No. 1, Puppy Love, New Mark	300.00
Figurine, No. 2/0, Little Fiddler, Vee Over Gee	80.00
Figurine, No. 3/1, Bookworm, New Mark	126.00
Figurine, No. 4, Little Fiddler, Full Bee	400.00
Figurine, No. 5, Strolling Along, Double Crown	518.00
Figurine, No. 5, Strolling Along, Stylized Bee	150.00
Figurine, No. 6/0, Sensitive Hunter, Crown Mark	518.00
Figurine, No. 8, Bookworm, Full Bee	170.00
Figurine, No. 9, Begging His Share, Stylized Bee	140.00
Figurine, No. 12/2/0, Chimney Sweep, Vee Over Gee	55.00
Figurine, No. 12/I, Chimney Sweep, Full Bee	270.00
Figurine, No. 15/0, Hear Ye, Hear Ye, Vee Over Gee	88.00
Figurine, No. 16/1, Little Hiker, Full Bee	80.00
Figurine, No. 16/1, Little Hiker, Stylized Bee	175.00
Figurine, No. 20, Prayer Before Battle, New Mark	110.00
Figurine, No. 21/I, Heavenly Angel, Double Crown	575.00
Figurine, No. 23/I, Adoration, Crown Mark	605.00
Figurine, No. 25, Angelic Sleep, Vee Over Gee	90.00
Figurine, No. 28/II, Wayside Devotion, Full Bee	263.00
Figurine, No. 28/II, Wayside Devotion, New Mark	485.00
Figurine, No. 42/0, Good Shepherd, Full Bee	575.00
Figurine, No. 43, March Winds, New Mark	100.00 to 185.00
Figurine, No. 47/2, Goose Girl, Double Crown, c.1935	805.00
Figurine, No. 49/0, Two Market, Crown Mark	518.00
Figurine, No. 50/0, Volunteers, New Mark	124.00 to 198.00
Figurine, No. 51/I, Village Boy, Vee Over Gee	128.00
Figurine, No. 52/1, Going To Grandmas, Full Bee	750.00
Figurine, No. 53, Joyful, Crown Mark	288.00
Figurine, No. 53, Joyful, Stylized Bee	190.00
Figurine, No. 56, Culprits, Crown Mark	690.00
Figurine, No. 56/A, Culprits, Vee Over Gee	120.00
Figurine, No. 57/0, Chick Girl, Crown Mark	275.00
Figurine, No. 57/0, Chick Girl, Full Bee	129.00
Figurine, No. 57/0, Chick Girl, Vee Over Gee	85.00
Figurine, No. 58/0, Playmates, Vee Over Gee	73.00
Figurine, No. 59, Skier, New Mark	132.00
Figurine, No. 59, Skier, Stylized Bee	300.00
Figurine, No. 65, Farewell, Crown Mark	575.00

Figurine, No. 66, Farm Boy, Double Crown 575.00
Figurine, No. 66, Farm Boy, New Mark 157.00
Figurine, No. 67, Doll Mother, Stylized Bee 160.00
Figurine, No. 70, Holy Child, New Mark 101.00
Figurine, No. 72, Spring Cheer, Stylized Bee 690.00
Figurine, No. 72, Spring Cheer, Vee Over Gee 90.00
Figurine, No. 73, Little Helper, Vee Over Gee 68.00
Figurine, No. 74, Little Gardener, Crown Mark . . . . .220.00 to 288.00
Figurine, No. 79, Globe Trotter, Crown Mark 403.00
Figurine, No. 79, Globe Trotter, New Mark 140.00
Figurine, No. 80, Little Scholar, Crown Mark 460.00
Figurine, No. 81/0, School Girl, Full Bee 160.00
Figurine, No. 82/0, School Boy, Stylized Bee 240.00
Figurine, No. 82/2/0, School Boy, Crown Mark 300.00
Figurine, No. 82/2/0, School Boy, Stylized Bee 110.00
Figurine, No. 84/V, Worship, Vee Over Gee 700.00
Figurine, No. 85, Serenade, Double Crown 805.00
Figurine, No. 86, Happiness, Crown Mark . . . . .217.00 to 345.00
Figurine, No. 87, For Father, Crown Mark 690.00
Figurine, No. 89/I, Little Cellist, Vee Over Gee 105.00
Figurine, No. 94/I, Surprise, Stylized Bee 425.00
Figurine, No. 94/I, Surprise, Vee Over Gee 350.00
Figurine, No. 95, Brother, New Mark 86.00
Figurine, No. 95, Brother, Vee Over Gee 250.00
Figurine, No. 97, Trumpet Boy, Stylized Bee 125.00
Figurine, No. 98, Sister, Stylized Bee 325.00
Figurine, No. 109, Happy Traveller, Vee Over Gee 65.00
Figurine, No. 110/0, Let's Sing, Vee Over Gee 160.00
Figurine, No. 111, Wayside Harmony, Crown Mark 575.00
Figurine, No. 111/3/0, Wayside Harmony, Crown Mark 345.00
Figurine, No. 119, Postman, Full Bee 123.00
Figurine, No. 124/I, Hello, Vee Over Gee 125.00
Figurine, No. 127, Doctor, Stylized Bee 225.00
Figurine, No. 129, Band Leader, Vee Over Gee 79.00
Figurine, No. 131, Street Singer, New Mark . . . . .132.00 to 235.00
Figurine, No. 132, Star Gazer, New Mark 250.00
Figurine, No. 133, Mother's Helper, Full Bee 150.00
Figurine, No. 135, Soloist, Full Bee 250.00
Figurine, No. 136/I, Friends, Three Line Mark 110.00
Figurine, No. 141/3/0, Apple Tree Girl, Full Bee 175.00
Figurine, No. 142/I, Vee Over Gee 97.00
Figurine, No. 142/X, Apple Tree Boy, Vee Over Gee 11500.00
Figurine, No. 143/1, Boots, Vee Over Gee 234.00
Figurine, No. 152/A0, Umbrella Boy, New Mark 700.00
Figurine, No. 152/B0, Umbrella Girl, New Mark 700.00
Figurine, No. 153/I, Auf Wiedersehen, New Mark 196.00
Figurine, No. 154/I, Waiter, Vee Over Gee 130.00
Figurine, No. 171, Little Sweeper, Vee Over Gee 68.00
Figurine, No. 172/0, Festival Harmony, New Mark 360.00
Figurine, No. 175, Mother's Darling, New Mark 143.00
Figurine, No. 176/0, Happy Birthday, Stylized Bee 160.00
Figurine, No. 178, Photographer, Full Bee 200.00
Figurine, No. 183, Forest Shrine, New Mark 360.00
Figurine, No. 184, Latest News, Full Bee 109.00
Figurine, No. 184, Latest News, Vee Over Gee 125.00
Figurine, No. 188, Celestial Musician, Vee Over Gee 115.00
Figurine, No. 195/I, Barnyard Hero, New Mark 206.00
Figurine, No. 196/0, Telling Her Secret, Full Bee 280.00
Figurine, No. 197 2/0, Be Patient, Full Bee 400.00
Figurine, No. 198 2/0, Home From Market, Three Line Mark 200.00
Figurine, No. 198/2/0, Home From Market, Vee Over Gee 70.00
Figurine, No. 199/0, Feeding Time, New Mark 240.00
Figurine, No. 200/I, Little Goat Herder, New Mark 155.00

Figurine, No. 203, Signs Of Spring, Full Bee 193.00
Figurine, No. 203/I, Signs Of Spring, New Mark 275.00
Figurine, No. 204, Weary Wanderer, New Mark 295.00
Figurine, No. 218/2/0, Birthday Serenade, Vee Over Gee 130.00
Figurine, No. 220, We Congratulate, New Mark 195.00
Figurine, No. 255, Stitch In Time, New Mark 190.00
Figurine, No. 256, Knitting Lesson, Three Line Mark 250.00
Figurine, No. 257, For Mother, Vee Over Gee 70.00
Figurine, No. 261, Angel Duet, Vee Over Gee 125.00
Figurine, No. 300, Bird Watcher, Vee Over Gee 125.00
Figurine, No. 305, Builder, Three Line Mark 206.00
Figurine, No. 306, Little Bookkeeper, Three Line Mark 148.00
Figurine, No. 308, Little Tailor, Vee Over Gee 95.00
Figurine, No. 321, Wash Day, New Mark 192.00
Figurine, No. 322, Little Pharmacist, Vee Over Gee 88.00
Figurine, No. 327, Run-A-Way, New Mark 295.00
Figurine, No. 328, Carnival, Three Line Mark ....98.00 to 280.00
Figurine, No. 331, Crossroads, Halt Sign On Ground, New Mark 375.00
Figurine, No. 331, Crossroads, Vee Over Gee 196.00
Figurine, No. 337, Cinderella, New Mark 187.00
Figurine, No. 340, Letter To Santa Claus, New Mark 385.00
Figurine, No. 344, Feathered Friends, New Mark 340.00
Figurine, No. 347, Adventure Bound, New Mark 2255.00
Figurine, No. 351, Botanist, New Mark 120.00
Figurine, No. 356, Gay Adventure, Vee Over Gee 85.00
Figurine, No. 361, Favorite Pet, Vee Over Gee 118.00
Figurine, No. 363, Big Housecleaning, New Mark ....190.00 to 335.00
Figurine, No. 366, Flying Angel, New Mark 155.00
Figurine, No. 377, Bashful, Vee Over Gee 75.00
Figurine, No. 378, Easter Greetings, New Mark 245.00
Figurine, No. 380, Daisies Don't Tell, New Mark ....110.00 to 192.00
Figurine, No. 381, Flower Vendor, Vee Over Gee 85.00
Figurine, No. 386, On Secret Path, New Mark 290.00
Figurine, No. 389, Girl With Sheet Of Music, New Mark 60.00
Figurine, No. 390, Boy With Accordion, New Mark 60.00
Figurine, No. 391, Girl With Trumpet, New Mark 60.00
Figurine, No. 394, Timid Little Sister, New Mark 289.00
Figurine, No. 396, Ride Into Christmas, New Mark 525.00
Figurine, No. 399, Valentine Joy, New Mark 115.00
Figurine, No. 406, Pleasant Journey, New Mark 950.00
Figurine, No. 421, It's Cold, New Mark ....105.00 to 220.00
Figurine, No. 422, What Now, New Mark 105.00
Figurine, No. 431, The Surprise, New Mark 105.00
Figurine, No. 471, Harmony In Four Parts, New Mark 1080.00
Figurine, No. 479, I Brought You A Gift, New Mark 75.00
Figurine, No. 482, One For You, One For Me, New Mark 71.00
Figurine, No. 548, Flower Girl, New Mark 75.00
Holy Water Font, No. 35/0, Good Shepherd, Double Crown 184.00
Plaque, No. 140, Mail Is Here, Vee Over Gee 123.00
Plaque, No. 180, Tuneful Goodnight, Vee Over Gee 112.00
Plaque, No. 187A, M.I. Hummel, Vee Over Gee 150.00
Plaque, No. 310, Searching Angel, Vee Over Gee 150.00
Plaque, No. 323, Merry Christmas, Vee Over Gee 150.00
Plate, Anniversary, 1975, Stormy Weather 100.00
Plate, Annual, 1972, Hear Ye, Hear Ye ....30.00 to 50.00
Plate, Annual, 1974, Goose Girl 35.00
Plate, Annual, 1975, Ride Into Christmas 50.00
Plate, Annual, 1976, Apple Tree Girl 40.00
Plate, Annual, 1978, Happy Pastime 25.00
Plate, Annual, 1979, Singing Lesson ....22.00 to 50.00
Plate, Annual, 1980, School Girl 100.00
Plate, Annual, 1985, Chick Girl 50.00
Plate, Annual, 1986, Playmates 125.00

HUTSCHENREUTHER Porcelain Company of Selb, Germany, was established in 1814 and is still working. The company makes fine quality porcelain dinnerwares and figurines. The mark has changed through the years, but the name and the lion insignia appear in most versions.

LORENZ
HUTSCHEN REUTER

GERMANY

Figurine, Ballet Dancers, White, Gilt, C. Werner, 9 In.	350.00
Figurine, Nude, Holding Flowers, Fawn, Label, Germany, US Zone, 9 1/4 In.	330.00
Plaque, Woman, Sheer Drape, Gilt Frame, Signed Wagner, c.1890, 12 x 10 In.	

ICONS, special, revered pictures of Jesus, Mary, or a saint, are usually Russian or Byzantine. The small icons collected today are made of wood and tin or precious metals. Many modern copies have been made in the old style and are being sold to tourists in Russia and Europe and at shops in the United States. Rare, old icons have sold for over $50,000.

Archangel Michael, Clouds, Sword In Right Hand, Scale & Figure, Greece, 27 1/2 In.	9000.00
Archangels Michael & Gabriel, Romania, 19 Century, 23 x 16 1/4 In.	635.00
Christ, Enthroned, Nun Saint Below, Shadowbox, Portugal, 22 1/2 x 18 1/2 In.	375.00
Christ, Nativity, St. Nicholas, Saints, 4 Panels, Russia, 19th Century, 21 1/2 x 17 1/2 In.	920.00
Court Scene, Triptych, Gothic Style Frame, Enamel & Carved Wood, 22 1/2 In.	1265.00
Kazan Mother Of God, Enameled Oklad, Russia, c.1900, 9 x 7 In.	2520.00
Life Of Christ, Central Scene, Smaller Scenes Surround, 17 x 14 In.	575.00
Madonna & Child, Chased Silver & Brass, Pierced Halos, Gilt Frame, Russia, 7 In.	358.00
Madonna & Child, Russia, 10 1/4 x 8 1/2 In.	520.00
Man, Writing On Tablet, Silver Overlay, Painted, Frame, 12 1/2 x 9 In.	230.00
Mother Of God, 4 Images, Chalk On Panel, Russia, 19th Century, 17 1/2 In.	390.00
Mother Of God, Joy For All Who Suffer, 19th Century, 14 1/4 x 11 1/2 In.	520.00
Mother Of God Of The Sign, Silver Oklad, Chalk On Wood, Mid 19th Century, 8 x 6 In.	108.00
Saint, Red Robes, Silver Halo, Gilt Frame, 6 3/4 In.	248.00
Saints Images, 4 Registers, 19 1/2 x 17 1/2 In.	345.00
St. George, Slaying Dragon, Princess, King, Queen In Tower, Curved Wood Panel, 12 In.	138.00
St. George, Slaying Dragon, Russia, 19th Century, 13 1/4 x 10 In.	460.00
St. George, Slaying Dragon, Russia, 19th Century, 23 x 19 In.	1150.00
St. Nicholas, 19 3/4 x 16 1/2 In.	690.00
St. Nicholas, 19th Century, 12 1/4 x 10 1/2 In.	258.00
St. Nicholas, As Bishop Delivering Blessing, Holding Book Of Gospels	575.00
St. Nicholas, Painted Face, Hands, Oil On Board, Brass Overlay, Russia, 9 x 10 1/2 In.	230.00
St. Nicholas, Russia, 19th Century, 15 1/2 x 12 1/2 In.	480.00
Trinity, Gilded Silver Riza, 10 x 12 In.	6160.00
Virgin Kazanskaya, Brass Pressed Into Border, Russia, 12 1/2 x 10 1/4 In.	200.00

IMARI porcelain was made in Japan and China beginning in the 17th century. In the 18th century and later, it was copied by porcelain factories in Germany, France, England, and the United States. It was especially popular in the 19th century and is still being made. Imari is characteristically decorated with stylized bamboo, floral, and geometric designs in orange, red, green, and blue. The name comes from the Japanese port of Imari, which exported the ware made nearby in a factory at Arita. *Imari* is now a general term for any pattern of this type.

Bottle, Gourd Form, Cobalt, Red & Gilt Flowers, Phoenix Birds & Dragons, 18 1/4 In.	330.00
Bowl, Bell Shape, Pinwheel Brocade, Late 19th Century, 9 3/4 In.	373.00
Bowl, Brocade Flowers, Metal Rim, Early 19th Century, 10 In.	69.00
Bowl, Center, Bronze Dore, Floral & Leaf Design, 2 Handles, Pedestal, c.1860, 13 In.	3248.00
Bowl, Central Reserve Design, 3 Schooners, Sailors, Flower Sprays, Nanban, 3 1/2 In.	747.00
Bowl, Cover, Blue & White, Red & Gold Overlay, 1900, 4 1/4 x 3 1/4 In.	100.00
Bowl, Cover, Crane & Flower Panels, Gold Leaves Between, 1860, 4 1/4 x 3 In.	150.00
Bowl, Cover, Garden Medallion, Blue & White, Gold & Red Accents, 5 1/4 x 4 In.	250.00
Bowl, Cover, Multicolored Scene, Fence, Pine & Willow Branches, 1860, 4 1/4 In.	200.00
Bowl, Decorated Interior, Outside Rim, 3 1/2 x 7 1/4 In.	28.00
Bowl, Dragons, Vertical, Tapering Sides, Flared Rim, Cobalt, Gold Border, 5 x 12 1/4 In.	302.00
Bowl, Figure Standing On Rock, Mt. Fuji Ground, Gold, Red, 1860, 8 1/4 x 3 1/4 In.	300.00
Bowl, Fish, Blue Birds, Flowers, Paneled Scenes, Footed, Teakwood Stand, 5 x 12 In.	863.00
Bowl, Flower Shape, Late 19th Century, 9 1/2 In.	69.00

Bowl, Grass & Flowers, 3 Petal Blue Center, Scalloped, 4 x 10 In. 173.00
Bowl, Lotus, Cranes, Flowers, Central Medallion, Scalloped, Ribbed, 4 3/4 x 9 1/2 In. . . . 490.00
Bowl, Scalloped, 4 x 8 1/4 In. 140.00
Censer, Polychrome, Lobed Body, Scroll Handles, c.1912, 8 In., Pair 1035.00
Charger, 2 Crane Reserves, 2 Landscapes, Center Bonsai Tree, 1870s, 25 In. 1955.00
Charger, 3 Medallions, Overlapping Circle Border, Early 1800s, 12 In. 220.00
Charger, 4 Large Flowering Plants, Blue Border, Lattice Design Between, 12 1/4 In. 330.00
Charger, Birds, Flowers, Serpent, Panels, Blue Border, 18 In. 575.00
Charger, Bowl, Flowers, Landscapes, Raised Rim, Panels, Late 19th Century, 3 x 12 In. . . 420.00
Charger, Central Medallion, Coiled Dragon, Flaming Pearl, c.1900, 22 In. 1150.00
Charger, Central Medallion, Flowers, Lotus, Red Ground, 19th Century, 18 In. 1095.00
Charger, Central Medallion, Peonies, Reserve Panels, Flowers, Birds, 20th Century, 18 In. 375.00
Charger, Central Medallions, Blossoming Trees, Birds, 10 Leaf Panels, 12 3/4 In., Pair . . . 520.00
Charger, Deer In Wood, Border Of Birds, 21 3/4 In. 1035.00
Charger, Fan Reserves, Floral Sprays, Alternating Cranes, Meiji, 18 1/2 In. 575.00
Charger, Figures, Birds, Flowers, Asymmetric Panel, Geometric, c.1880, 15 1/2 In. 215.00
Charger, Floral Panels Over Whirling Ground, 18 1/2 In. 330.00
Charger, Floral Spray, Medallions, Scalloped Reeded Rim, c.1860, 18 1/2 In. 840.00
Charger, Floral, Center Cartouche, Fan Shaped Panels, c.1860, 14 1/2 In. 310.00
Charger, Flowers, Birds, Blue, Rust, Red, Vignettes, Folding Stand, 24 1/2 In. 1095.00
Charger, Foo Dog & Phoenix, Yellow, Green, Blue & Red Border, c.1860, 27 x 4 1/2 In. . 1400.00
Charger, Geometric & Floral, Polychrome Panels, 18 In. 330.00
Charger, Gilt, Fan Shaped Panels, 19th Century, 18 In. 1150.00
Charger, Hoo-Birds In Well, 1870s, 12 3/8 In. 460.00
Charger, Landscape, Fruit, Alternating Medallions, Late 19th Century, 14 In. 224.00
Charger, Mountainous Scene, Medallion, Birds & Fans Reserves, 8 Sides, Meiji, 12 In. . . 230.00
Charger, Oriental Man At Table, Floral On Reverse, Paneled Borders, 18 1/2 In. 360.00
Charger, Pheasant Center, Red & Gold Polychrome Design, 6 Sections, 18 In. 330.00
Charger, Phoenix Bird & Bull, c.1880, 18 1/4 In. 1630.00
Charger, Scalloped, Reeded Rim, Body, Alternate Panels, c.1880, 12 In. 190.00
Charger, Sleeping Oriental Woman, Interior Medallion, Floral Rim, 15 5/8 In. 220.00
Charger, Tomato Red Pagoda, Dragons, Birds & Flowers, 15 3/4 In. 220.00
Chawan, Flame & Cloud, Early 19th Century, 4 In., Pair 230.00
Compote, Flowers & Waves, 2 Blue & 1 Pink Fish Interior, 1850, 5 1/4 x 4 1/4 In. 400.00
Compote, Sea Waves, Blue Carp Interior, Double Crimped Rim, 1860, 6 1/4 x 4 1/2 In. . . 500.00
Compote, Small Fish, 2 Blue Carp Swimming In Seaweed Interior, 1860, 6 x 4 1/2 In. . . . 400.00
Dish, Awabi Shell Shape, Butterfly, Paulownia Flower, Silver Lacquered, Early 1800s . . . 70.00
Dish, Blue & Iron Red Enamels, Floral Rim, Unglazed Foot, 1880s, 8 1/4 In., 4 Piece . . . 405.00
Dish, Scalloped, Reeded Body, Alternate Panels, Late 19th Century, 8 1/2 x 10 In., Pair . . 224.00
Dish Set, Chrysanthemum, Central Medallion, Leaves, Flowers, c.1926, 9 1/2 In. 345.00
Fishbowl, Floral Reserve, Everted Rim, Gilt, Meiji, 18 x 19 1/2 In., Pair 690.00
Ginger Jar, Domed Cover, Mushroom Finial, Landscapes, Vertical Ribs, 1900s, 12 In. . . . 316.00
Jar, Domed Cover, Dragon, Peonies, Bamboo, Cylindrical, Polychrome, c.1912, 12 3/4 In. . 430.00
Jar, Tomato Red Panels, Polychrome, Dog Finials, 7 1/2 In., Pair 825.00
Jardiniere, Deer, Floral, Egg Shape, Cobalt Cartouches, Leaves, c.1910, 8 1/2 x 10 In. . . . 460.00
Jardiniere, Garden Scenes, Bulbous, Medallions, Late 19th Century, 11 1/2 In. 2240.00
Jardiniere, Underglaze Blue, Lacquer Paint, Reserves Of Flowers, 1860s, 9 3/4 In. 865.00
Mug, Floral, Blue & Red Cartouches, Ear Handle, c.1800, 6 1/2 In. 290.00
Plate, 3 Scenic Panels, Blue & White, 1870, 15 1/4 In. 750.00
Plate, Basket With Bonsai Tree, Birds & Plants, Cut Corners, Square, 10 1/4 x 10 1/4 In. . 250.00
Plate, Blue Dragon Center, 3 Medallions, Gold Horse Borders, 1800, 9 3/4 In. 700.00
Plate, Chop, Orange Flowers, 4 Reserves, Bird, Branch, 2 Foo Dogs, 21 5/8 In. 660.00
Plate, Crossed Bamboo Sticks, Morning Glory Vine, Blue & White, 1830, 7 3/4 In. 1000.00
Plate, Fish Form, Enamel, 15 1/2 x 10 1/2 In. 390.00
Plate, Floral Panels, Scalloped Rim, 20th Century, 10 3/4 In., Pair 220.00
Plate, Flowering Tree, Blue Medallions Around Border, Square, 1860, 11 In. 750.00
Plate, Flowers, Leaves, Iron Red, Cobalt Blue, Cartouches, Gilt Vine Band, 11 In., Pair . . 805.00
Plate, Flowers, Tree, Bird, Rocks, Blue & White, 1870, 16 In. 600.00
Plate, Garden Scene Center, Diapering Rim, Square, 1860, 9 3/4 In. 750.00
Plate, Mums, Red & Gold, Blue Divides Mum Panels, 1820, 8 3/4 In. 500.00
Plate, Octagonal, Blue & Polychrome Enamel, 1870s, 12 1/2 In. 575.00
Plate, Pine, Bamboo, Plum Trees, Red & Gold Trim, 1860, 15 3/4 In. 1300.00
Plate, Raised Floral, Blue, White, Gilt, Square, 10 3/4 In. 175.00

Plate, Sweetmeat, Alternating Tree, Plant Reserves, c.1900, 8 5/8 x 8 1/2 In., Pair 115.00
Punch Bowl, Carnations & Mums, Pheasants, Gold Overglaze, Teak Base, 15 3/4 In. 440.00
Punch Bowl, Flower Center, Scalloped, 6 Cartouches, Cobalt Blue, 6 x 13 1/2 In. 690.00
Sake Cup Set, Butterfly, Flowers, Kirwood Box, 19th Century 138.00
Serving Dish, Shell Shape, Flowers, Meiji, c.1900, 10 In. 230.00
Tazza, Butterflies, Figures, Chrysanthemum Border, Flared Pedestal, 7 3/4 x 9 1/2 In. 138.00
Umbrella Stand, Cobalt Blue, Orange, 4 Floral Reserves, 24 1/2 In. 855.00
Urn, Cover, Alternating Panels, Traditional Colors, c.1880, 12 In. 190.00
Urn, Domed Cover, Foo Dog Finial, Oval Body, c.1900, 20 1/2 In. 896.00
Vase, Birds, Flower Reserves, Bulbous Base, Flared Trumpet Top, Scalloped, 26 In. 415.00
Vase, Chrysanthemums, Scalloped Body, Underglaze, Blue & Iron Red, 25 1/4 In., Pair .. 2530.00
Vase, Cranes, Other Birds, Cartouches, Oval, Pedestal Base, 1880, 15 3/4 In., Pair 616.00
Vase, Domed Cover, Painted Flowering Benches, Oval, 1840, 26 1/2 In. 1265.00
Vase, Dragon At Top, Red & Blue Panels, Bottle Form, 12 In. 330.00
Vase, Floral, Red, Orange & Dark Blue, Ribbed Base, 8 1/8 In., Pair 385.00
Vase, Flowers, Trees, Baluster Shape, Alternating Panels, c.1690, 19 In. 1792.00
Vase, Splayed & Leaf Rim, Ribbed Body, Unglazed Foot, Enamel, 1870s, 9 1/2 In. 805.00
Vase, Swimming Carps, Green Net, Waisted Neck, Oval, 37 1/2 In. 690.00

IMPERIAL GLASS Corporation was founded in Bellaire, Ohio, in 1901.
It became a subsidiary of Lenox, Inc., in 1973 and was sold to Arthur
R. Lorch in 1981. It was sold again in 1982, and went bankrupt in
1984. In 1985, the molds and some assets were sold. The Imperial
glass preferred by the collector is freehand art glass, carnival glass,
slag glass, stretch glass, and other top-quality tablewares. Tablewares
and animals are listed here. The others may be found in the appropriate sections.

Art Glass, Vase, Blue & Orange Pulled Stripes, Pinched Waist, 10 1/2 In. 840.00
Art Glass, Vase, Iridescent White Pulled Loops, 10 1/2 In. 345.00
Atterbury, Dish, Lion On Lacy Cover, Purple Slag 295.00
Beaded Block, Creamer, Iridescent 45.00
Beaded Block, Plate, Canary, Square, 7 3/4 In. 30.00
Candlewick, Ashtray, 6 In. 135.00
Candlewick, Bonbon, 7 1/2 In. 250.00
Candlewick, Bowl, Chip & Dip, 14 In. 675.00
Candlewick, Butter, Cover, 1/4 Lb. 45.00
Candlewick, Cake Plate, Birthday, 72 Candleholders, 14 In. 375.00
Candlewick, Dish, Cottage Cheese, 6 In. 50.00
Candlewick, Goblet, 10 Oz. 35.00
Candlewick, Pitcher, 80 Oz. 50.00
Candlewick, Relish, 4 Sections, Handles, 9 1/2 In. 30.00
Candlewick, Soup, Cream, 5 In. 50.00
Candlewick, Tumbler, Juice, 5 Oz. 8.00
Cape Cod, Cocktail, 3 1/2 Oz. 10.00
Cape Cod, Goblet, Water, 10 Oz. 15.00
Cape Cod, Sherbet, Tall, 6 Oz. 8.00
Cape Cod, Sugar, 3 1/2 In. 4.00
Cape Cod, Tumbler, Footed, 10 Oz., 6 In. 15.00
Cape Cod, Wine, 3 Oz. 8.00
Eagle, Compote, Cover, Purple Slag 195.00
Old Colony, Goblet, Amber, 6 1/2 In. 7.00
Waverly, Box, Chocolate, Cover, Carmel Slag 165.00
Windmill, Pitcher, Ruby Slag, 6 1/2 x 3 1/2 In. 105.00

INDIAN art from North America has attracted the collector for many
years. Each tribe has its own distinctive designs and techniques. Baskets, jewelry, pottery, and leatherwork are of greatest collector interest.
Eskimo art is listed in another category in this book.

Amulet, Sioux, Turtle, Black & White Beads, 4 1/2 In. 550.00
Apron, Great Lakes, Black Cloth, Beaded, Flowers, Berries, Brown Straps, 16 x 17 In. 805.00
Armband, Crow, Corrugated Brass, Tag, Crow Agency, August 22, 1888, 4 1/2 In., Pair .. 748.00
Baby Carrier, Plateau, 1950, 37 x 14 1/2 In. 242.00
Bag, Arapaho, Tobacco, Vertical Beaded Design Bands, 34 In. 9400.00

Bag, Bandolier, Ojibwa, Floral Shoulder Strap, Pony Bead & Wool Tassels, c.1900, 35 In.	920.00
Bag, Chippewa, Ojibwa, Twined, Horizontal Bands, Cloth Band Rim, Tassels, 1830s, 6 In.	300.00
Bag, Crow, Beaded, Carrying Strap, U-Shape, Fringe, c.1900, 8 1/2 In.	920.00
Bag, Crow, Mirror, Bilateral Floral, Fringe, c.1900, 15 In.	3740.00
Bag, Great Lakes, Bandolier, Beaded, Leaf Design, Beaded Fringe, Triangles, 11 In.	3163.00
Bag, Great Lakes, Bandolier, Beaded, Panel Of Angular Flowers, Geometric, 37 In.	3820.00
Bag, Hide, Beaded, Vertical Bands, Scalloped Border, Panels, Iron Bells, 8 1/2 x 6 1/4 In.	770.00
Bag, Iroquois, Beaded, Niagara Falls, Green Floral, White Bird, Cover, 5 1/2 In.	110.00
Bag, Iroquois, Flower Beadwork, Hanging White Beads, Velvet Backing, 7 x 7 In.	138.00
Bag, Nez Perce, Cornhusk, 1910	3500.00
Bag, Nez Perce, Cornhusk, Yarn Devices Front, Triangles Back, 22 In.	1725.00
Bag, Ojibwa, Tobacco, Beaded, Stylized Floral Panel, Red Hem Tape, 43 In.	2230.00
Bag, Plateau, Beaded Cloth, Early 1900s, 11 x 8 1/4 In.	2530.00
Bag, Plateau, Cornhusk, 3 Rows Of Triangles, Cloth Binding, Late 1800s, 21 1/2 x 17 In.	750.00
Bag, Plateau, Cornhusk, Polychrome, Geometric Designs, c.1900, 10 1/4 In.	920.00
Bag, Sioux, Beaded, 4 1/4 In.	215.00
Bag, Sioux, Tobacco, Beaded, Diamond, Triangle, Cross, 30 In.	1060.00
Bag, Sioux, Tobacco, Beaded, Vertical Bands, Diamond Design, 38 In.	2000.00
Bag, Ute, Deerskin Panels, Sinew Sewn, Beadwork, 15 x 20 In.	3300.00
Bag, Woodlands, Beadwork, Floral, Late 19th Century, 6 x 5 In.	290.00
Bag, Woodlands, Floral, Beaded, 8 x 9 In.	330.00
Band, Hat, Navajo, Sterling Silver, 1 Turquoise Stone, 1960s, 26 In.	75.00
Bank, Hopi, Gourd, Mudhead Shape, Signed Ted Puhuyesva, c.1885, 6 x 16 In.	35.00
Basket, Algonquin, Splint, Potato Stamped Design, Late 19th Century, 7 1/4 x 12 In.	480.00
Basket, Apache, Bowl, Coiled, Radiating Geometric Design, 2 7/8 x 13 1/4 In.	2070.00
Basket, Apache, Bowl, Coiled, Stepped Triangle Design, c.1940, 2 x 13 x 9 In.	190.00
Basket, Apache, Bowl, Radiating Interlocked Pattern, 11 1/4 In.	985.00
Basket, Apache, Coiled, Polychrome, Geometric Bands, 5 3/4 x 15 In.	3410.00
Basket, Apache, Round, 1935, 6 x 2 In.	275.00
Basket, Gift, Coiled, Geometric, Red Feather Tufts, Late 19th Century, 3 3/4 In.	1265.00
Basket, Hat, Makah, American Flags, 1920, 7 1/2 x 5 1/2 In.	1320.00
Basket, Havasupai, Twined, Overcast Rim, Found Grand Canyon, 1910, 4 1/4 x 9 In.	250.00
Basket, Hopi, Bowl, Series Of Horizontal Rings, Individual Corn Kernels, 2 x 3 1/2 In.	1290.00
Basket, Hopi, Coiled, Tapered, Polychrome, Kachina Faces, 7 x 10 In.	990.00
Basket, Hopi, Kachina Faces, Beaded Necklace, 7 x 9 In.	300.00
Basket, Hupa, Bowl, Half Twist Stitch, 1920s, 5 x 8 In.	450.00
Basket, Hupa, Bowl, Split Parallelogram, 1910, 5 x 3 1/4 In.	385.00
Basket, Hupa, Bowl, Utility, Stepped Geometric, Late 19th Century, 16 In.	860.00
Basket, Kawaiisu, Concentric Rings Encircled By 5-Pointed Star On Base, 7 In.	10575.00
Basket, Kawaiisu, Outlined Vertical Lightning Bands, 6 x 14 1/2 In.	7640.00
Basket, Kawaiisu, Raised Neck, Stepped Vertical Bands Of Sharp Serrates, 4 3/4 In.	4110.00
Basket, Kawaiisu, Round Body, Diagonal Zigzag Bands At Base, 5 1/4 In.	1760.00
Basket, Kawaiisu, Round Body, Grasshopper Stitch, Checkered Design, 5 1/2 In.	7050.00
Basket, Kawaiisu, Single Zigzag Design, Dark Colored Sides, 5 In.	3820.00
Basket, Kawaiisu, Steep Flared Sides, Repeated Series Of Serrated Panels, 5 1/2 In.	4110.00
Basket, Kawaiisu, Stepped, Outlined Diagonal Bands, Bracket Fern, 4 1/2 In.	2350.00
Basket, Kawaiisu, Woven Flared Sides, Abstract Butterfly Design, 6 5/8 In.	8225.00
Basket, Klickitat, Tall, Imbricated, Polychrome Geometric Designs, c.1930, 11 x 11 In.	1045.00
Basket, Maidu, Quail Top Knot, Chevron, Lightning & Cross, 1930, 11 1/2 x 2 1/4 In.	1540.00
Basket, Mission, Diegueno, Polychrome, 1890, 6 x 4 1/4 In.	660.00
Basket, Mission, Oblong, Coiled, Floating V Design, c.1910, 7 1/2 x 5 1/2 x 4 1/4 In.	275.00
Basket, Navajo, Wedding, 1900, 15 In.	990.00
Basket, Navajo, Wedding, Coiled, Stepped Triangles, Red Band, 1920s, 15 3/4 In.	260.00
Basket, Paiute, Baby Carrier, Wicker, Attached Cloth Doll, 18 In.	165.00
Basket, Panamint, Floating Diamond Lozenges Hook Design, 4 1/8 x 6 5/8 In.	2645.00
Basket, Panamint, Pair Of Checkered Zigzag Meanders Encircling Sides, 5 1/4 In.	3230.00
Basket, Panamint, Series Of Vines Hung With Blossoms Contrasting Colors, 4 In.	1645.00
Basket, Papago, Olla, Open Crosses, 1920, 13 x 16 In.	605.00
Basket, Pima, Child's, Burden, 1880, 14 x 8 In.	1650.00
Basket, Pima, Coiled, Deep Bowl, Fret Design, c.1920, 12 x 3 1/2 In.	550.00
Basket, Pima, Coiled, Horsehair, Squash Blossom Design, c.1995, 2 x 2 In.	145.00
Basket, Pima, Oval, Diamond, Sawtooth, 3 1/4 x 12 1/2 x 11 1/2 In.	1760.00
Basket, Pima, Round Bowl, 1935, 10 1/2 x 2 In.	220.00

Basket, Pomo, Bowl, Coiled, Round, Maze Pattern, Late 1800s, 5 1/2 In. 1150.00
Basket, Pomo, Bowl, Coiled, Zigzags, Shells & Beads, c.1900, 6 In. 345.00
Basket, Pomo, Coiled Bowl, Light & Dark Brown Checkerboard, c.1900, 3 x 1 In. 155.00
Basket, Pomo, Coiled, Flared, Triangle Pattern, Glass Beads, Late 1800s, 5 3/4 In. 345.00
Basket, Pomo, Coiled, Geometric, Flying Geese Design, 2 1/4 x 5 3/4 In. 195.00
Basket, Pomo, Coiled, Oval, Stylized Amphibian, Patina, 3 x 10 3/4 x 7 1/2 In. 2200.00
Basket, Pomo, Shoulder Bag, 1910, 8 1/2 x 4 In. 1430.00
Basket, Salish, Storage, Cover, 1900, 19 x 11 x 14 In. 1100.00
Basket, Salish, Twined, Bark Base, Half Twist Overlay Cedar, Bear Grass, 5 1/4 x 4 In. . . 214.00
Basket, Skokomish, Twined, Dog Designs, Rim Loops c.1935, 5 x 3 1/2 In. 575.00
Basket, Tulare-Yokut, Storage, 1920, 16 x 6 1/2 In. 4675.00
Basket, Yavapai, Oval Platter, 1930, 17 x 13 x 2 In. 770.00
Basket, Yokut, Rattlesnake, Coiled, Flared, Flat Bottom, Red, Black, 8 1/2 x 15 1/2 In. . . 2200.00
Belt, Concha, Silver, Oval With Starbursts, Turquoise Centers, 33 In. 260.00
Belt, Hopi, Concha, Silver With Gold Accents, 36 x 2 In. 385.00
Belt, Navajo, Concha, Silver, Discs, Turquoise & Stars, Links, Butterfly Buckle, 37 In. . . 805.00
Belt, Navajo, Concha, Sterling Silver, Oval Conchas, Leather Belt, Copper Hanks 470.00
Belt, Plains, Beaded Bars, c.1900, 23 1/2 In. 345.00
Belt Buckle, Navajo, Sterling Silver, 1 Turquoise Stone, 1970s, 3 x 3 1/2 In. 150.00
Belt Pouch, Allover Beaded Hide, 1930, 7 x 7 In. 495.00
Blanket, Navajo, Diamonds, Zigzags, Narrow Stripes, 73 x 53 In. 5580.00
Blanket, Navajo, Red, White, Gray, Black, Geometric, 51 x 93 In. 690.00
Blanket, Navajo, Saddle, Red, Black, White, Germantown, 1890-1900, 34 x 30 In. 1600.00
Blanket, Navajo, Serrated Diamonds, Brown, Black, Natural Field, 56 x 78 In. 2970.00
Blanket, Navajo, Wool, 3 Panels Of Zigzag Devices, Red Field, Child's, 52 x 32 In. 4600.00
Blanket, Osage, Friendship, Ribbon Applique, Stroud, Beads 4500.00
Blanket, Saddle, Navajo, Homespun, 31 x 26 In. 28.00
Blanket, Saddle, Navajo, Wool, Hand Carded, Double Twill, Red, Black, 31 x 50 In. 195.00
Blanket, Tlinget, Button, Beaded Eagle, Orange, Green, Child's 27.00
Bonnet, Quillwork, 2 Flying Birds, Star, Half Moon, Child's, 10 x 10 In. 920.00
Boots, Plains, Hide, Beaded, Green, Blue, Crescents At Toe, Leather Sole, 18 1/2 In. 1540.00
Bottle, Northwest Coast, Basket, 9 3/4 In. 275.00
Bottle, Sioux, Ink, Carters Ink In Beads, 2 1/4 In. 110.00
Bow, Central Plains, Ash, Tapered Hand Grip, Double Notch, Twisted Sinew String, 48 In. 750.00
Bow, Hupa, Ash, Painted Geometrics, Late 19th Century, 40 In. 1095.00
Bow, Santo Domingo, Pueblo, 46 In. 55.00
Bowl, Acoma, Stepped Terrace Design, Dotted Band Dividing Sections, 4 x 7 1/2 In. 190.00
Bowl, Apache, Coiled, 2 Bands Stepped Triangles, c.1900, 13 In. 550.00
Bowl, Dough, San Juan, 2-Tone Red, 1940s, 6 x 10 In. 275.00
Bowl, Dough, Santo Domingo, Pottery, 1920 . . . . 8750.00
Bowl, Dough, Zuni, Pottery, 1890 . . . . 8750.00
Bowl, Dough, Zuni, Volutes & Geometric Design, Feather Stepped, 5 x 11 In. 1410.00
Bowl, Hopi, Inward Curving Sides, Abstract Feathers, Early 20th Century, 10 In. 520.00
Bowl, Mimbres, Black On White, Crosshatched Designs, 5 1/2 x 10 1/2 In. 880.00
Bowl, Prehistoric Hopi, Sikyatki Pottery, Geometric Designs, 8 1/2 x 4 In. 440.00
Bowl, San Ildefonso, Gunmetal Finish, Marie & Julian, 3 In. 315.00
Bowl, Santa Clara, Form Of Circular Figures, Camilio Sunflower Tafoya, 1972, 3 3/4 In. . 1380.00
Bowl, Zia, Polychrome, Red & Black, Geometric Designs, Signed Lois Medina, 11 In. . . . 489.00
Box, Birchbark, Micmac, Quill Decorated, Domed, Mid 19th Century, 5 x 9 1/2 x 7 In. . . . 2420.00
Box, Work, Quillwork, Geometric Shapes, Rainbow Zigzags, Dome Top Lid, 4 x 6 x 5 In. 635.00
Bracelet, Navajo, 1 Oblong Turquoise Stone, 3 Wire Shank, 1930s, 2 In. 100.00
Bracelet, Navajo, Cluster, Sterling Silver & Turquoise, 1970s, 2 1/4 In. 130.00
Bracelet, Navajo, Cuff, Sterling, Kingman Turquoises, Signed A.P., 1 1/2 In. 130.00
Bracelet, Navajo, Hand Wrought Silver, 4-Row, Square Turquoise Stones, 2 x 7 In. 550.00
Bracelet, Navajo, Sand Cast, 5 Stones, 1 1/2 In. 190.00
Bracelet, Navajo, Silver, Channel Cut Turquoise Bands, Signed M. Silver, 1970s 60.00
Bracelet, Navajo, Silver, Turquoise, 19 Nevada Green Stones, Old Pawn, c.1950, 7 x 2 In. 305.00
Bracelet, Navajo, Silver, Turquoise, 3 Stones, Flower Blossom 160.00
Bracelet, Navajo, Silver, Turquoise, Cluster, Old Pawn, 20th Century, 1 1/2 x 6 In. 175.00
Bracelet, Navajo, Silver, Turquoise, Old Pawn, c.1930, 7 x 3 In. 525.00
Bracelet, Navajo, Sterling Silver, Castle Dome Turquoise, Signed H. Nez, 1 3/4 In. 165.00
Bracelet, Navajo, Twisted Wire, 11 Green Stones, Center Large Bead, Early 20th Century 2645.00
Bracelet, Silver, Inlaid Pinion Chip Turquoise & Coral, Stamped STC--, 2 1/4-In. Wide . . 80.00

Bracelet, Silver, Turquoise, 7 Stones, Monogram 185.00
Bracelet, Zuni, Silver, 2 Color Stone Inlay, Knife Wing Man, 1 3/4 In. 375.00
Bracelet, Zuni, Silver, Turquoise & Shell Inlay, Knife Wing Dancer, 8 x 1 3/4 In. 358.00
Breastplate, Plains Woodlands, Vertical Bone Panels, Silk Ribbon, 34 In. 587.00
Breastplate, Sioux, Pine Ridge, German Silver, Man's, 1900s 80.00
Cane, Central Plains, Twined Diamond Form Snakes, Late 19th Century, 31 In. 316.00
Cane, Iroquois, Human Head, Protruding Bird Head Handle, 1800s, 34 1/2 In. 575.00
Cane, Northwest Coast, Totemic Creatures, Late 19th Century, 36 1/2 In. 1380.00
Canteen, Acoma, Triple Lobe, Leno, 1980s, 5 x 14 In. 250.00
Canteen, Hopi, Bust Of Butterfly Mana Kachina, Face Paint, 7 x 6 3/4 In. 3525.00
Canteen, Hopi, Carrying Lugs, Stylized Feather Design, 5 In. 575.00
Canteen, Hopi, Pottery, Hump Back, Flat Bottom, 7 1/2 x 6 In. 358.00
Canteen, Navajo, Hand Hammered Silver, Stamped, 3 3/4 x 3 In. 358.00
Canteen, Santa Ana, Painted Design, 1940s, 7 x 7 In. 275.00
Case, Knife, Crow, Beaded, Sawtooth Pattern, Buffalo Calf, 1880s, 11 1/4 In. 3450.00
Case, Knife, Quills, Tin Cone, Fringe, 13 x 4 1/2 In. 660.00
Case, Sioux, Awl, 11 In. 80.00
Club, Northeast Coast, Carved Wood, Snake, Turtle, Heart, Human Face, 1800s, 33 In. 405.00
Club, Penobscot, Root, Chip Carved, Floral Handle, Head, Metal Stand, 27 In. 546.00
Club, Plains, Skull Cracker, Stone Head, Muslin Wrapped Wood Handle, 1900s, 25 In. 60.00
Club, Stone Head, Leather, Beaded, Tassels, 8 1/2 x 3 In. 225.00
Cradle, Seneca, Doll's, Muslin, Sun Shade, 1910, 19 1/2 x 8 1/2 x 7 1/2 In. 880.00
Cradle Cover, Orange & Red Quill Panel, Green & Purple Stepped Triangles, 27 In. 4315.00
Cradleboard, Leather Over Wood, Beaded, Red, White, Blue, Green, c.1900, 14 1/2 In. ... 250.00
Cradleboard, Mohawk, Wooden, 1811, 16 x 31 In. 352.00
Cradleboard, Osage, 1910, 10 1/2 x 42 In. 70.00
Cradleboard, Pueblo, Pine Plank Back, 1900s, 10 1/2 x 27 In. 200.00
Cradleboard, Sioux, Quilled, 1880 .... 7500.00
Crucifix, Southwest, Beadwork, White, 32 x 17 In. 1380.00
Cup, Horn, Canoe Shape, Cork Base, Leather Handle, 5 In. 30.00
Diorama, Hopi, Badger Kachina & Girl, Holding Melon, Mask, Kilt, Feathers, 11 In. 110.00
Dipper, Potlatch, Spruce, Northwest Coast, Late 19th Century, 17 1/2 x 5 1/2 In. 395.00
Doll, Apache, Man, Beaded, Hide, Fringe & Hawkbell, Late 1800s, 15 1/2 In. 1725.00
Doll, Apache, Painted Features, Black Mohair Wig, Blanket, Kid Clothing, 9 1/2 In. 200.00
Doll, Apache, Squaw With Papoose, Blanket, Box, 11 In. 375.00
Doll, Braided Human Hair, Beaded Leather Outfit, Fringe, Moccasins, c.1900, 12 1/2 In. . 440.00
Doll, Central Plains, Beaded, Muslin Body, Buckskin Dress, Late 1800s, 14 In. 1150.00
Doll, Cherokee, Cloth, Orange Dress, Bead & Shell Necklace, Painted Face, 15 In. 250.00
Doll, Hide, Beaded, Woman, Black Hair, White Beaded Highlights, 8 3/4 In. 110.00
Doll, Kiowa, Buckskin, Full Costume, 19 1/2 x 8 1/2 x 7 1/2 In. 2200.00
Doll, Northern Plains, Cloth & Hide, Beaded, Dress, Moccasins, Late 1800s, 15 1/2 In. .. 1150.00
Doll, Seminole, Cotton, Hide, Glass Beads, Early 1900s, 15 In. 800.00
Doll, Skookum, Bully Good, Blanket, Beads, Headdress, Box, c.1925, 24 In. 2200.00
Doll, Skookum, Man, Wearing Blanket, Feather Headdress, Store Model, 36 In. 805.00
Doll, Storyteller, Holding 3 Babies & Dog, Seferina Ortiz, 6 x 7 In. 950.00
Doll, Ute, Buckskin Dress, Beadwork, Bead & Painted Face, Female, 1880s, 18 In. 3105.00
Doll, Ute, Deerskin, Thread-Sewn, Beadwork, Horsehair Wig, Painted Face, c.1900, 17 In. 4750.00
Dress, Blackfoot, Beaded At Yoke, Contoured Stripe, Bugle Beads, 1920s, 45 In. 115.00
Dress, Buckskin, With Purse & Bone Necklace, Beaded 515.00
Dress, Cheyenne, Buckskin, Beaded, Fringe, Girl's, 1910, 30 x 41 In. 1045.00
Dress, Lakota, Child's, Trade Cloth, Calico Edged, Sequins, Bells, Ribbon, 1800s, 30 In. . 3738.00
Dress, Seminole, Cowrie Shells, Amber Glass Beads, Bright Colors, Cotton, 48 x 48 In. ... 415.00
Drum, Pueblo, Hide Heads & Beater, 1900s, 31 x 21 In. 350.00
Drum, Pueblo, Painted Cottonwood Body, Rawhide Covering, 8 7/8 x 9 In. 302.00
Drum, Wood, Leather, Double Heads, Painted, Taos, N.M., c.1920, 12 1/2 x 10 1/2 In. ... 963.00
Effigy, Owl, Zuni, Brown & Red On White, c.1910, 7 x 6 In. 600.00
Effigy, Southwest, Casa Grande, Buff Ground, Stylized Fish, 6 1/2 In. 50.00
Figure, Mermaid, Cochiti, Ivan Lewis, 1980s, 6 x 9 In. 700.00
Gloves, Embroidered, Flowers & Leaves On Back, Cuffs, Leather, Pair 145.00
Hat, Havasupai, Beaded Designs, 19th Century, 10 x 6 1/2 In. 550.00
Hat, Hopi, Brown Geometric Design, 3 x 7 In. 259.00
Hat, Hupa, Basketry, Tightly Twined, Geometric Pattern, c.1900, 6 3/4 In. 920.00
Hat, Nez Perce, Woman's, Twined, Cornhusk, Geometric Design, 19th Century, 6 x 7 In. .. 1320.00

Hat, Pima, Basketry, 1940s, 2 x 8 In. 400.00
Hat, Rain, Northwest Coast, Tomemic Masks, Cedar Bark, Cone Shape, 6 x 13 In. 2970.00
Headdress, Crow, Deer, Porcupine Hair Roach, Wooden Display Stand, c.1940, 13 x 3 In.   470.00
Horse Collar, Cloth, Red, Floral Beadwork, Tin Cone Danglers, c.1880, 44 x 9 In. 1850.00
Jar, Acoma, Allover Zigzag Sawtooth Bands, 5 5/8 x 8 3/4 In. 2350.00
Jar, Acoma, Black & White, Sarah Garcia, 11 x 8 1/4 In. 247.00
Jar, Acoma, Fine Line, Allover Fine Line Grid, 8-Pointed Stars, 5 3/4 x 7 1/4 In. 1880.00
Jar, Acoma, Ocher & Umber Diamonds Cover Body, Ocher Bottle Bottom, 9 x 10 1/2 In. . 1595.00
Jar, Acoma, Polychrome, Tapered Neck, Orange & Brown Slip, Early 1900s, 7 3/4 In. ... 405.00
Jar, Acoma, White Slip Body, Birds, Crosshatched Designs, 9 x 11 In. 1870.00
Jar, Acoma, X's Over Slip, Alternating With Squares, 8 x 10 In. 2365.00
Jar, Anasazi, Black Slip, Gray Ground, Bands In Geometric Designs, 5 1/4 In. 750.00
Jar, Hopi, Band Of Repeated Hooks & Scrolls, 5 5/8 x 6 3/4 In. 1530.00
Jar, Hopi, Bird Design, Orange, Signed, 4 3/4 In. 140.00
Jar, Hopi, Cone Form, Butterflies, Delaine Tootsie, 6 x 8 In. 145.00
Jar, Hopi, Globe Shape, 4 Wing & Scroll Designs, 4 3/4 x 6 3/8 In. 1290.00
Jar, Hopi, Globe Shape, Migration Of Opposing Wing Design, 6 3/4 In. 2645.00
Jar, Hopi, Nampeyo, Curvilinear Design, Lugs, 9 x 7 In. 2090.00
Jar, Hopi, Seed, Abstract Feathers, Polychrome, Red, Brown Slip On Cream, 1900s, 9 In. . 4025.00
Jar, Hopi, Tapered Neck, Polychrome, Black & White Slip, Brown Ground, 7 1/4 In. 230.00
Jar, Laguna, Red & Black On White, E. Cheromiah, 1970s, 9 x 10 In. 325.00
Jar, Maricopa, Pottery, Black, Buff & Red, 1910, 5 x 4 In. 145.00
Jar, San Ildefonso, Blackware, Flared, Marie & Julian Martinez, Signed, 1940, 2 3/4 In. ... 935.00
Jar, San Ildefonso, Blackware, Maria Poveka, 1970s, 3 1/4 In. 450.00
Jar, San Ildefonso, Blackware, Panel Of Repeated Negative Feathers, 6 x 6 3/8 In. 1760.00
Jar, San Ildefonso, Blackware, Repeated Feather Design, 3 Framing Bands, 7 3/8 In. 6460.00
Jar, San Ildefonso, Blackware, Sinuous Water Serpent, Feather Head Crest, 13 1/2 In. 2940.00
Jar, Santa Clara, Blackware, Charging Mountain Sheep & Buffalo, 8 In. 1057.00
Jar, Santa Clara, Blackware, Gunmetal Design, 6 1/8 In. 8225.00
Jar, Santa Clara, Blackware, Wedding, Sinuous Water Serpent Design, 13 1/2 In. 4400.00
Jar, Santa Clara, Globe Shape, Large Bucks Running, Belen Tapia, 8 In. 940.00
Jar, Santa Clara, Sgraffito, 6 Different Kachina Figures In A Row, 7 3/8 x 8 1/4 In. 2350.00
Jar, Santa Clara, Sgraffito, Black, Globe Shape, 2 Red Circular Cartouches, 2 x 4 In. 700.00
Jar, Santa Clara, Wedding, Globe Shape, Stirrup Handle, 8 1/4 x 5 1/2 In. 880.00
Jar, Santo Domingo, Globe Shape, 8-Pointed Stars, Split Feather Tips, 10 x 11 In. 2230.00
Jar, Seed, Santa Clara, Black On Black, Avenu, c.1950, 5 x 5 In. 190.00
Jar, Tesuque, Bean Dancer, 2 Pairs Of Deer, 2 Rosettes, Lid, 9 x 10 3/4 In. 1175.00
Jar, Washo, Seed, 1900, 12 x 13 In. 470.00
Jar, Zuni, Pottery, Oval, Rust, Cream, Black Deer, Geometric, c.1880, 5 x 6 In. 460.00
Kachina, Hand Carved Cottonwood Root, 8 In. 470.00
Kachina, Hemis Kachin Mana, Late 1920s 3500.00
Kachina, Hopi, Chief Mudhead, Rattle, Feather, Leather, 11-16-77, MG, KG, 13 1/4 In. ... 165.00
Kachina, Hopi, Horns, Red Body Paint, Kilt, Cape, Whips, Feathers, Hair, 14 1/2 In. 190.00
Kachina, Hopi, Mudhead, Feathers, Scarf, Kilt, Concha Belt, Rattle, Hualapai, 12 In. 137.00
Kachina, Hopi, Pachavu Hu, Bean Dancer, Sash, Kilt, Hair, Feather, Leather, 22 In. 220.00
Kachina, Hopi, Toho, Long Hair, Flat Face, Snout, Kilt, Horsehair, 12 1/2 In. 190.00
Kachina, Hopi, Wolf, Traditional Dress, 1960s, 1 In. 155.00
Kachina, White Buffalo, Fur, Black Horns, Kilt, Rattle, Bow, Wood Base, 25 1/2 In. 440.00
Kachina, Zuni, Carved Wood, Cloth, Polychrome, Horsehair Beard & Hair, 1940s, 15 In. . 1725.00
Kettle, Sioux, Feast, Brass, 10 1/2 x 16 In. 70.00
Knife, Beaded Sheath, Colored Beads, Brass Cones, 6 1/2 x 2 In. 400.00
Knife, Patch, Stag Handle, Bullet Starter, 8 In. 90.00
Leggings, Crow, Hide, Calico Lining, Floral, 1880s, 19 In. 920.00
Leggings, Great Lakes, Black Cloth, Beadwork Flowers, Red Trim, 31 In. 575.00
Leggings, Ojibwa, Velvet Panel, Multicolored Floral Beadwork, c.1900, 16 1/2 In. 345.00
Leggings, Quilled, 31 1/2 In., Pair 265.00
Leggings, Santee, Sioux, Beaded, 1930, 15 x 17 In. 1100.00
Mask, Cherokee, Wood, Carved, Hollow, 4 Teeth, 2 Horns, Intertwined Snake, 11 1/2 In. . 4600.00
Mask, Iroquois, False Face Society, Tin Eye Patches & Nose Tip, 11 3/4 In. 800.00
Mask, Iroquois, Wood, Hollow, Oval, Brown & Red, Pierced Eyes, 1900s, 10 In. 490.00
Mask, Northwest Coast, Raven, Wood, Beak, Chief Ben Andrews, Nootka, B.C., 29 In. ... 550.00
Mask, Northwest Coast, Wood, Hollow Form, Polychrome, Early 1900s, 14 1/2 In. 2645.00
Medicine Bag, Apache, Deerskin, Sacred Imagery Beadwork, Fringe, c.1865, 15 x 10 In. . 3800.00

Mitten, Chippewa, Beaded, Single, 13 1/2 In.	35.00
Moccasins, Apache, High-Top, Maltese Crosses Vamps, Cactus Kicker Toes, 24 In.	920.00
Moccasins, Arapaho, Attached Leggings, Silver Buttons, 1880s, 19 In.	9775.00
Moccasins, Beaded, Flowers, Glazed Cotton, Purple Ribbon, 12 In.	195.00
Moccasins, Central Plains, Beaded Hide, Geometrics, Red, Yellow, Green, c.1900, 10 In.	345.00
Moccasins, Central Plains, Buffalo Hide, Beaded, Geometric Designs, Late 1800s, 10 In.	520.00
Moccasins, Central Plains, Child's, Beaded, Purple, White, Blue, Gold, Red	520.00
Moccasins, Cheyenne, Sinew Sewn Beadwork, Hard Soles, 10 In.	1650.00
Moccasins, Cheyenne, Sinew Uppers, Rawhide Soles, c.1800, 9 1/2 In.	1150.00
Moccasins, Fur Trader, 18 In.	175.00
Moccasins, Hide, Beaded, Red Stepped Diamonds, Blue, White Field, 9 3/4 In.	990.00
Moccasins, Iroquois, Child's, 5 In.	140.00
Moccasins, Iroquois, Floral Beadwork, Cloth Vamps, Soft Hide Soles, 9 1/2 In.	230.00
Moccasins, Lakota, Hide Uppers, Hard Soles, Blue Ground, 19th Century, 10 In.	575.00
Moccasins, Leather, Beaded, Velvet Top & Sides, Woven Wool Binding & Lining	45.00
Moccasins, Micmac, Baby's, Hide Vamps & Cuffs, Floral Beadwork, 1850s, 3 1/2 In.	1265.00
Moccasins, Northern Plains, Child's, Beaded, Soft Hide Soles, 1880s, 5 1/2 In.	1095.00
Moccasins, Ojibwa, Soft Soles, Semicircular Purple Cloth Flap, Leaves, 9 1/2 In.	2230.00
Moccasins, Plains, Beaded, Orange Outline, Chevrons, 11 1/4 In.	220.00
Moccasins, Plains, Cheyenne, Beaded, White Bead Ground, Cloth Cuff, 1890, 10 1/4 In.	660.00
Moccasins, Plains, Violet Beadwork, 10 1/2 In.	80.00
Moccasins, Pueblo, Dance, Cloth & Hide With Trim, 1940s, 7 1/2 In.	290.00
Moccasins, Sioux, Beaded, Dark Green & White, 10 5/8 In.	825.00
Moccasins, Sioux, Beaded, End Tassels Of Tin Tobacco Container, 10 3/4 In.	1210.00
Moccasins, Sioux, Child's, Soft Hide Uppers, To Crazy Bull, 4 1/4 In.	575.00
Moccasins, Southern Plains, Geometric Beadwork, Red Ocher, Blue High Uppers	935.00
Moose Call, Birchbark, 16 1/4 In.	65.00
Necklace, Coral, Turquoise, White Shell, 20 Strand, 31 In.	385.00
Necklace, Hopi, Sterling, 2 Side Pieces, Pendant With Turquoise, 22 In.	155.00
Necklace, Navajo, 20 Squash Blossom, 3 Turquoise Stones, 18 In.	430.00
Necklace, Navajo, Silver, Turquoise, Flower Blossom	460.00
Necklace, Navajo, Squash Blossom, Sand Cast, 1940s, 26 In.	550.00
Necklace, Navajo, Sterling Silver, Turquoise, Box, 24 In.	165.00
Necklace, Pueblo, Coral & Turquoise, 3 Strand, Turquoise Pendant, c.1900, 13 In.	345.00
Necklace, Pueblo, Lone Mountain Turquoise, Kachina Pendant, c.1950, 26 In.	55.00
Necklace, Pueblo, Rolled Turquoise Beads, 2 Strand, Clasp, 1950s, 11 In.	175.00
Necklace, Santo Domingo, Heishi Turquoise, 2 Strand, Shell Spacers, 14 In.	550.00
Necklace, Sioux, Quill, Red & White, 3 7/8-In. Diam.	83.00
Necklace, Trade Bead, Large & Medium Amber Beads, Yellow To Dark Red	275.00
Necklace, Zuni, 6 Strand, Fetish, 28 In.	413.00
Needle Case, Iroquois, Mid 19th Century	28.00
Olla, Acoma, Polychrome Parrot, Sarah Garcia, 9 x 10 In.	225.00
Olla, Apache, Basket, High Shoulder Form, Red & Black Checkered, 1940s, 7 1/4 In.	977.00
Olla, Apache, Coiled, Flattened Shoulder, Diagonals, Diamonds, 21 3/4 x 20 In.	13200.00
Olla, Hopi, Stylized Connecting Medallions, 2 Birds, Late 19th Century, 8 1/2 In.	8050.00
Olla, Pima, Willow & Martynia, Allover Geometric Design, 9 7/8 x 8 In.	1650.00
Olla, Santo Domingo, Geometric Bands, Cream Ground, 11 In.	3737.00
Olla, Shipibo, Human Face, Geometric Designs, c.1940, 22 x 17 In.	220.00
Olla, Zia, Polychrome, Elizabeth Medina, 1980s, 9 x 10 In.	375.00
Olla, Zuni, Deer With Heart Lines, Black Bottom & Inner Neck, 1880s, 8 1/4 In.	2645.00
Olla, Zuni, Flared Neck, Paneled Body, Brown & Red Scrolls, c.1900, 7 1/2 In.	316.00
Painting, Kiowa, Dancer, Raised Shield, Signed Tsa-To-Ke, Frame, 12 1/2 x 11 1/8 In.	165.00
Painting, Oil On Board, Moonlight Campfire Scene, Signed Qewdeminon, 16 x 12 In.	463.00
Picture, Gouache, Making A Stand, By Rainbow Hand, 18 x 21 1/4 In.	55.00
Picture, Laguna, Pueblo Dancer, Gouache, Cardboard, Ca Chavez, 1924, 19 x 15 In.	192.00
Picture, Traditional Eagle Dancer, Gouache, Woody Big Bow, c.1960, 15 x 11 In.	55.00
Pin, Navajo, Silver, Turquoise, Figure 8 Shape, c.1940, 4 1/4 x 1 1/2 In.	55.00
Pipe, Bird's Head Mouth Piece, Wood & Stone, Late 19th Century, 13 In.	143.00
Pipe, Carved Bowl, Flat Sided Oval Stem, Burn Designs, 17 1/2 In.	1955.00
Pipe, Central Plains, Ash Stem, Elbow Form Bowl, Late 19th Century, 20 In.	862.00
Pipe Bag, Beaded, Geometric, Green, Black, Pink, Blue, White, Fringe, 21 In.	660.00
Pipe Bag, Beaded, Leaf & Diamond, Blue, Hide Fringe, 26 In.	920.00
Pipe Bag, Blackfoot, Hide, Beaded Panel, Fringe, 1910, 23 x 5 3/4 In.	605.00

Pipe Bag, Cheyenne, Beaded, Geometric, Hide Fringe, 24 In. 1668.00
Pipe Bag, Cree, Beaded Panel Front, 4-Leaf Clover Back, Quill Flap, 1880s, 30 In. 1840.00
Pipe Bag, Cree, Beaded Top & Sides, Floral On White Ground, 1880s, 31 In. 1725.00
Pipe Bag, Lakota, 3 Rows Of Beadwork, Hide, Tin Cone & Feathers, Late 1800s, 32 In. . 1265.00
Pipe Bag, Lakota, Buckskin Beaded Top, Cross & Diamond, Late 19th Century, 23 In. 2300.00
Pipe Bag, Plains, Beaded, Vivid Colors, 39 In. 1955.00
Pipe Bowl, Northern Style, With Beaver & Otter Bowl 852.00
Pipe Tomahawk, Hitched Horsehair, Stone Pipe Bowl & Blade, 1900s, 19 1/2 In. 690.00
Plate, Hopi, Bird Effigy, c.1920, 8 1/2 x 5 x 3 1/2 In. 935.00
Plate, San Ildefonso, Arched Feathers, Central Band Of Scrolls, 13 5/8 In. 2115.00
Pouch, Apache, Hide, Beaded, Geometric Designs, Tin Cone Dangles, Late 1800s, 5 In. ... 750.00
Pouch, Apache, Morning Star, Beaded Hide, Tin Cone Dangles, 1870s, 5 1/2 In. 520.00
Pouch, Leather, Cross Pattern, Beadwork, Red, White & Blue, Tassels, 5 x 3 In. 200.00
Pouch, Nez Perce, Beaded, 8 1/2 x 5 1/2 In. 130.00
Purse, Chippewa, Beaded, 4 1/2 x 4 1/2 In. 55.00
Purse, Micmac, Quill, Multicolored Zigzag Geometric, 5 1/2 x 6 1/4 In. 230.00
Purse, Sioux, Boy's, 1906, 8 x 5 3/4 In. 240.00
Purse, Sioux, Child's, 5 In. 85.00
Quirt, Woven Horsehair, Spiral Detail, 2 Leather Straps, Prison Made, 32 In. 250.00
Rattle, Blackfoot, Leather, Red Paint, 15 In. 27.00
Rattle, Blackfoot, Shaman's, 1880, 17 x 6 In. 825.00
Rattle, Carved, Bird Head, Human, Turkey, Painted Green & Red, 13 3/8 In. 1500.00
Rattle, Iroquois, Wood & Horn, 5 1/2 In. 25.00
Rug, Navajo, Alternating Brown, Natural Panels, Red Field, Stepped Borders, 48 x 60 In. . 2750.00
Rug, Navajo, American Flag, USA, S Woven Backward, 19 x 18 In. 630.00
Rug, Navajo, Black & White Diamonds, Blue, Green Border, Carded Yarn, 31 x 59 In. .. 275.00
Rug, Navajo, Black, White, Dark Brown Border, 60 x 42 In. 550.00
Rug, Navajo, Black, White, Gray, Sunrise, 34 x 55 In. 275.00
Rug, Navajo, Black, White, Tan, 50 x 65 In. 690.00
Rug, Navajo, Center Diamond, Lightning & Feather, 62 x 41 1/2 In. 1955.00
Rug, Navajo, Center Geometrics, Ivory Ground, Border Of Squares, 51 x 29 In. 375.00
Rug, Navajo, Crystal, c.1920, 64 x 40 In. ....*Illus* 1725.00
Rug, Navajo, Dazzler, 42 x 87 In. 535.00
Rug, Navajo, Diamond Bands, Black, Red, Orange, Brown, Gray, White, 31 x 46 In. 385.00
Rug, Navajo, Diamond Pattern, Red, White, Gray & Blue, 28 x 59 In. 365.00
Rug, Navajo, Diamonds, Black, Gray, Red, 1930s, 53 x 60 In. 275.00
Rug, Navajo, Diamonds, Brown, Cream, Red, Stepped Border, c.1930, 45 x 54 In. 1610.00
Rug, Navajo, Diamonds, Natural Field, Red, Brown, Concentric Borders, 72 x 52 In. 1650.00
Rug, Navajo, Eye Dazzler Style, Diamonds, Red Field, Black, Charcoal, Blue, 45 x 64 In. . 1650.00
Rug, Navajo, Feather & Diagonal Band, Orange, Black, Brown, Natural, Red, 34 x 58 In. . 220.00
Rug, Navajo, Geometric Designs, Vegetal Dye, c.1970, 59 x 32 In. 175.00
Rug, Navajo, Geometric Feather Pattern, Tan, Black & Brown, 36 x 63 In. 364.00
Rug, Navajo, Geometric, Black, White, Tan, Red, 20th Century, 41 x 65 In. 550.00
Rug, Navajo, Geometric, Brown, Red, White, Gray Ground, Fringe, c.1930, 36 x 64 In. .. 400.00
Rug, Navajo, Geometric, Red, Brown, Cream, 38 x 77 In. 495.00
Rug, Navajo, Geometric, Red, Brown, Tan Ground, c.1920, 45 x 54 In. 1955.00
Rug, Navajo, Gray, Mustard, Brown, Cream Ground, c.1920, 40 x 60 In. 489.00
Rug, Navajo, Gray, Natural, Black, Tan, 38 x 68 In. 220.00
Rug, Navajo, Gray, Tan, Natural White, 54 x 88 In. 960.00

Indian, Rug, Navajo, Crystal,
c.1920, 64 x 40 In.

Indian, Rug, Navajo, Rust, Black & White
Zigzags, 70 x 41 In.

Rug, Navajo, Light Tan, White, Dark Brown, 49 x 28 In. 400.00
Rug, Navajo, Red, Black, White, Brown Diamonds, 1930, 35 x 50 In. 900.00
Rug, Navajo, Red, White, Black Geometric Designs, 37 x 59 In. 600.00
Rug, Navajo, Red, White, Black, 45 x 32 In. 525.00
Rug, Navajo, Rust, Black & White Zigzags, 70 x 41 In. . . . . *Illus* 1495.00
Rug, Navajo, Serrated Diamond, Tan, Red, Natural, 45 x 78 In. 770.00
Rug, Navajo, Serrated Diamonds, Red, Black, White, Gray, 1930s, 51 x 80 In. 1210.00
Rug, Navajo, Shiprock, Terraced Diamonds, Brown, Gray, Black, 24 x 26 In. 300.00
Rug, Navajo, Stylized Bird, Beige Field, Hooked Borders, White, Black, 67 x 35 In. 1320.00
Rug, Navajo, Sun Symbols, Geometric Designs, Center Figure, c.1900, 55 x 79 In. 2640.00
Rug, Navajo, Sunrise, Terraced & Serrated, Gray, Brown, Red, Natural, 36 x 65 In. 880.00
Rug, Navajo, Tan, Red, White Geometric Shapes, Dark Brown Border, 1930, 60 x 37 In. . . 600.00
Rug, Navajo, Teec Nos Pos, Brown, Gray, Red, 45 x 64 In. 1150.00
Rug, Navajo, Teec Nos Pos, Crab Motifs, West Reservation Storm Pattern, 54 x 90 In. . . . 825.00
Rug, Navajo, Terraced Diamond, Brown, Gray, Natural, Red Border, 59 x 76 In. 495.00
Rug, Navajo, Terraced Ground, 2 Interior Red Crosses, Natural, 39 x 78 In. 715.00
Rug, Navajo, Transitional, Stripes, Red, Orange, Gray, c.1910, 33 x 53 In. 220.00
Rug, Navajo, Two Gray Hills, 3 Stripes Of Connected Diamonds, 67 1/2 x 40 1/4 In. 990.00
Rug, Navajo, Two Gray Hills, Serrated Diamond, Gray, Brown, Black, Border, 36 x 59 In. . 330.00
Rug, Navajo, White Border, Brown, Red, Tan, 51 x 36 In. 550.00
Rug, Navajo, Wide Ruins, Vegetal Dye, Gold, Pink, Black, Stepped Diamonds, 36 x 57 In. 275.00
Rug, Navajo, Yei, Dark Green Plant In Center, Geometric Shapes, 45 x 30 In. 500.00
Rug, Navajo, Yei, Red, Blue, Dark Green, 28 x 32 In. 400.00
Rug, Navajo, Zigzag Design, Brown & Gray On Cream Ground, 90 x 56 In. 450.00
Rug, Yei, 5 Figures, Mustard Ground, Gray Border, 37 x 48 In. 285.00
Rug, Yei, Corn Dancers, Holding Feathers, Red, Brown, 56 x 38 In. 770.00
Rug, Yei, Navajo, Brown Field, Stepped Hourglass Border, 53 x 81 In. 715.00
Saddle Blanket, Geometric Pattern, Gray, White & Tan, 25 x 41 In. 250.00
Sash, Assumption, Hand Woven, 1700-1800, 10 Ft. 660.00
Sash, Blackfoot, Beaded, Yellow Design, Turquoise Ground, 27 1/2 In. 165.00
Sash, Great Lakes, Woven, 92 In. 231.00
Sash, Sioux, Beaded, Red Diagonal Stripes, White Ground, 17 1/2 In. 145.00
Scraper, Hide, Forged, 6 1/2 x 3 1/2 In. 40.00
Sheath, Apache, Knife, Top Beaded Cross, Chevrons On Bottom, Fringe, 9 1/2 In. 1430.00
Sheath, Knife, Beaded, Geometric Shapes, Green, Blue & Red, Yellow Ground, 10 In. . . . 1000.00
Sheath, Knife, Lakota, Beaded 1 Side Hide, Beaded Fringe, c.1900, 8 1/2 In. 460.00
Sheath, Knife, Sioux, Child's, 4 1/4 In. 30.00
Shirt, Blackfoot, Man's, Beaded, Long Side Tail Hem, Trade Cloth Binding At Sleeves . . 165.00
Shirt, Man's, Buckskin, Bead, Hair, Shells, Fringe, Plexiglas Case, 32 1/2 x 36 1/2 In. . . . 1090.00
Snuffbox, Birch Bark, 3 x 2 1/2 In. 30.00
Snuffbox, Wooden, Cover, 3 x 1 5/8 x 1 5/8 In. 45.00
Tomahawk, Hand Forged, 9 1/4-In. Head, 17 1/2-In. Shaft 920.00
Tomahawk Head, Spear Point, Forged, 1870 . . . . 365.00
Totem Crest, Tlingit, Crosspiece For Full-Size Totem Pole, 1950s 4500.00
Totem Pole, Carved, Stacked Figures, Bird Head Top, Spread Wings, Painted, 16 In. 83.00
Totem Pole, Northwest Coast, Carved Wood, Frog, Bird, Sitka, Alaska, July 1901, 31 In. . 2415.00
Totem Pole, Raven God, Haida, North British Columbia, c.1920, 23 1/2 x 1 In. 770.00
Trade Beads, Blue Chevrons, 1800s, 12 1/2 In. 80.00
Trade Beads, Cornaline D'Aleppo, Pony Beads, 12 Long Strings, c.1850, 12 x 30 In. 110.00
Tray, Apache, 5-Pointed Stars Across The Base, 4 1/2 x 18 1/4 In. 3525.00
Tray, Apache, Center Star Within Spoked Band, Willow & Martynia, 10 1/8 In. 1100.00
Tray, Apache, Large Life Size Rosette Design, Dark Tondo, 5 1/4 x 20 1/2 In. 3525.00
Tray, Apache, Large Rosette Set With Small Crosses, 2 1/2 x 15 1/4 In. 2350.00
Tray, Apache, Panels Of Human & Animal Figures, 2 1/2 x 14 3/4 In. 3525.00
Tray, Apache, Red, Concentric Rosettes, Black Outlines, 3 3/4 x 12 3/4 In. 1762.00
Tray, Mono, Gambling, With Cup, Ida Bishop 4450.00
Tray, Papago, 1970s, 2 1/2 x 21 1/2 In. 200.00
Tray, Pima, 2 Bands Of Repeated Whirling Log Design, 6 1/4 x 18 3/4 In. 2645.00
Tray, Pima, 4-Arm Design, Fretted Bands, 5 1/2 x 22 1/4 In. 1410.00
Tray, Pima, Angular Box Scrolls, Whirling Logs, 6 1/2 x 22 In. 1760.00
Tray, Pima, Basketry, Human & Lizard, 1920s, 7 In. 350.00
Tray, Pima, Wide Dark Center, Hooked Meanders, Whirlwind Design, 6 x 16 In. 2115.00
Tray, Southwest, Woven, Geometric Star, Spirit Line, 2 Colors, 14 1/2 In. 99.00

Tray, Squash Blossom Design, Fretted Bands, 3 1/2 x 22 3/4 In. 3525.00
Vase, Acoma, Seated Figure, Early 20th Century, 6 1/2 In. 420.00
Vase, Hope, Parrot, Fawn, 1970s, 10 1/2 x 7 1/2 In. 500.00
Vase, San Ildefonso, Gunmetal Glaze, Signed, 3 1/4 x 6 3/4 In. 575.00
Vase, Santo Domingo, Wedding, Pottery, Margaret Tafoya, 20th Century 7500.00
Vase, Southwestern, Black, Urn Form, 20th Century, 10 1/2 In. 70.00
Vase, Southwestern, Bulbous, Black, Brown, 20th Century, 6 1/2 In. 100.00
Vase, Tembladera, Humanoid Head Protruding From Top, Red, Orange, 10 In. 2115.00
Vase, Wedding, A. Nahoonhoa, 1980s 275.00
Vase, Zia, Traditional Bird & Geometric Designs, Kathy Pino, c.1940, 7 x 9 In. 120.00
Vest, Central Plains, Lakota, Fully Beaded, White Ground, Late 19th Century, 21 In. 2300.00
Vest, Sioux, Beaded, Wool, Coarse Woven, Reinforced Edge 90.00
Vest, Sioux, Child's, Flags, 1880s 5500.00
War Shirt, Apache, Cutouts, Red, Ocher, 1870, 29 x 56 In. 3575.00
War Shirt, Gros Ventre, Beaded 11750.00
Weaving, Navajo, 2 Yei Woman, Bows & Arrows, Rainbow God, 30 x 40 In. 550.00
Weaving, Navajo, Germantown, Swastikas, Triangles, Diamonds, c.1920, 19 x 19 In. 330.00
Weaving, Navajo, Homespun Wool, Serrated Central Diamond, 55 x 39 In. 290.00
Weaving, Navajo, Pattern Both Ends, Rows Of Terraced Diamonds, 58 x 37 In. 3220.00
Weaving, Navajo, Pictorial, Bird, Blue, White Ground, Brown, Gray Borders, 18 x 19 In. . 220.00
Weaving, Navajo, Third Phase, Black, Brown, Gray, Red, Tassels, c.1900, 46 x 66 In. 880.00
Weaving, Navajo, Wool, Center Diamond & Arrows, Fringed, 42 1/2 x 33 In. 4025.00
Whetstone, Wooden Base 80.00
Yei Set, Navajo, 6 White Masked Yei Dancers, Phillip Woody, c.1985, 7 In. 120.00

INDIAN TREE is a china pattern that was popular during the last half of the nineteenth century. It was copied from earlier Indian textile patterns that were very similar. The pattern includes the crooked branch of a tree and a partial landscape with exotic flowers and leaves. Green, blue, pink, and orange were the favored colors used in the design.

Cup & Saucer, 8 Sides, Gold Trim, Coalport, After Dinner 65.00
Platter, John Haddock & Sons, 19 In. 55.00
Platter, W.T. Copeland & Sons, 13 In. 120.00
Soup, Cream, Edge Malkin & Co., Burslem, Staffordshire, 9 1/4 In. 70.00
Soup, Dish, Edge Malkin & Co., 1873-1903, 9 1/4 In. 65.00
Tea Set, Teapot, Sugar, Creamer, Washington Potteries 280.00

INKSTANDS were made to be placed on a desk. They held some type of container for ink, and possibly a sander, a pen tray, a pen, a holder for pounce, and even a candle to melt the sealing wax. Inkstands date to the eighteenth century and have been made of silver, copper, ceramics, and glass. Additional inkstands may be found in these and other related categories.

Alarm Clock, On Wood Base, 2 Cut Glass Inkwells, c.1880 . . . . 400.00
Art Nouveau, Double, Water Lilies, c.1910 . . . . 250.00
Brass, Female Figure Holding Apple, c.1890 . . . . 275.00
Brass, Gilt, Art Nouveau, 1900 . . . . 90.00
Brass, Griffins, 3 Velvet-Lined Sections, Shell Tray, 19th Century, 12 x 7 1/2 In. 1456.00
Brass, Marble, With Candleholder, 2 Glass Inserts, 10 7/8 x 5 1/2 x 4 3/8 In. 330.00
Bronze, 2 Pen Trays, Crystal Bottles, Lids, Short Drawer, Feet, 1870s, 7 1/4 In. 1176.00
Bronze, Art Nouveau, 2 Wells, Pen Tray, Raised Leaf, Berry, Signed, Louchet, 7 x 13 In. . 460.00
Bronze, Enamel, 2 Wells, Pen, 9 In. 288.00
Bronze, Fleur-De-Lis, Flowers Throughout, Mounted As Lamp, Late 19th Century, 23 In. . 805.00
Bronze, Horse Head, Horseshoe, Square Inkwell, Pen Tray, 12 3/8 In. 287.00
Bronze, Man Working On Anvil, Early 20th Century, 9 x 12 1/4 In. 450.00
Bronze, Napoleon III, Gilt, Venus At Toilette, Rectangular, 16 In. 3450.00
Bronze, Ogee Shape, Plinth Feet, 2 Inkwells, Cover, 10 3/4 In. 120.00
Carved Stone, Pair Of Mice, Baby Mice Nibbling Corn, 4 Wells, 1870s, 6 In. 345.00
Cast Iron, Victorian, 2 Glass Inkwells, Hinged Lids, Letter, Penholder, 9 x 9 In. 85.00
Gentleman & Seated Woman, Dog, Fitted Interior, 7 1/2 x 5 1/2 In. 400.00
Gilt Bronze, Marble Base, Mid 19th Century, 5 1/2 x 9 1/2 x 4 1/2 In. 2760.00
Gilt Bronze, Marble, 3 Lidded Inkwells, Sander, Charles X, 4 1/4 x 7 1/2 x 11 1/4 In. 980.00
Micro Mosaic Cover, Brass, Venezia, 2 1/4 x 10 x 7 In. 99.00

Flea Market Finds

Flea market shopping is one of the most popular recreational activities in the country. More people go to flea markets than to baseball games, concerts, or golf courses. So join family and friends or go alone, and have fun looking, shopping, meeting people, and perhaps finding a treasure. You'll get exercise walking the miles of booths, and at some markets you'll find unusual and tasty food.

Markets are found in every area. They range from general flea markets that sell socks and plants as well as crafts and collectibles, to the "true" antiques and collectibles flea markets. A collector wants a flea market that allows only dealers who sell antiques, collectibles, and related products like metal polish or books. Best are the special large flea markets advertised as "extravaganzas." These shows feature more than a thousand dealers for a weekend event. It's easy to find a good flea market; check antiques publications, your local paper, or dealers and collectors. Don't drive to a distant market unless you are sure it is a market for collectibles, not modern gift-shop pieces and clothing.

Arrive early, if possible, so you can see items as they are unpacked. If there is a map of the flea market, study it and plan your day. Some say it is best to "go to the left." Most

Noisemakers are always fun. Some are more costly than others. These papier-mâché whistles, a cucumber and a banana, 6 and 4 inches long, cost $85 each. They were made in the 1930s.

shoppers start by heading right, so booths on the right-hand side of the show will be crowded.

Dress for the market. Wear comfortable shoes and clothes suited to warm, cold, or wet weather. Use suntan lotion and a hat. Take sunglasses, money, and checks. Be sure your money is in a secure place, a fanny pack or a zippered shoulder bag. Carry a magnifying glass (to read marks), tape measure (to be sure the desk you want fits into your car), a magnet and a small knife (to check the type of metal), and batteries (to test old battery-operated toys or radios). Carry a large tote bag or a folding grocery cart. You will need it to carry purchases around the flea market. Wear a bright scarf so your friends can find you. Take a cell phone so you can call home to check a size or call your temporarily lost friends at the flea market. Take business cards to hand out to dealers who may have your type of collectible "back at the shop." Collect dealer cards.

This Coke souvenir of Super Bowl XXVIII, played in 1994 at the Georgia Dome in Atlanta, costs $4.

Buy it when you see it. If you don't, you may not be able to find your way back to the treasure you left behind. If you do get back, it may have been sold. If you want to match your silver pattern or dishes, take a sample with you. Examine pieces carefully for repairs, nicks, or other problems. If it seems too good to be true, it probably is—there are many fakes on the market today. Be sure the paper price sticker is not covering a chip or tear, and ask to have it removed if it is on paper or a gold-leaf frame. Check the number of pieces in a game. Ask if electrical items like toasters work. Test toys. Avoid fabrics with strong odors. Ask about baskets, sprinkling cans, sleds, painted chests, wooden bowls, and many other items that

Cowboy and Western memorabilia, including toys, are lassoing plenty of collectors. Girls' holster sets were usually made of white or light colors. This set from the 1950s, with cap guns, was marked $565.

look like American country pieces but may be imported from Europe or Asia. They should cost less than American pieces. Irradiated glass is found at most markets today. These dark purple or blue pieces are attractive, but they have lost their value as antiques.

Bargaining is expected at a flea market, but good manners are important. Don't insult the dealer or the collectible. Offer less than the asking price, then negotiate. Large items like dining room sets often sell for low prices at the end of the show because dealers don't want to haul them home. Rarities sell for almost full price any time during a show. Use cash. Credit cards are not generally accepted, and dealers hesitate to take a check from an unknown buyer.

If you really want a large, heavy item, you may be able to arrange to have it taken to your home. We once had a three-tier iron fountain delivered to our house about 40 miles away in exchange for dinner and a tip.

Pack your purchases in the car with care. You may want to take old blankets along if you plan to buy furniture. Glass and china should be wrapped in crumpled newspaper and put in bags or boxes so pieces do not bang together. Oil paintings should be carried flat, picture down, but protect the surface of the frame. Don't leave pieces in a hot car. Take a cord to tie down the trunk.

This is considered the earliest American car toy. The horseless carriage, made of painted tin and cast iron, was manufactured by James Fallows & Company about 1905. It's 9 inches long and was marked $1,400.

Once you return home, unpack your great buys; record a description, date, and price for each piece; and exchange stories about the day's events with friends and family. The best part of your day at a flea market often comes years later in memories prompted by the painting on your wall or the bracelet on your wrist.

We have visited twenty major flea markets this past year while working on *Flea Market Finds with the Kovels,* our weekly series on Home & Garden Television (HGTV). Pictured here are many of our "flea market finds"—some we bought, and others we longed for. Most are small enough to carry out of a show by hand.

Collectors used to shop only for ceramic salt and pepper shakers. Now plastic novelty shakers are beginning to sell—especially to baby boomers trying to recreate the look of their childhood homes. Here are two fun sets for the kitchen—a Westinghouse washer and dryer, $25, and a Mixmaster mixer, also $25. Both are about 3 inches high.

The Sleepy Eye Milling Company's advertising premiums and signs are the focus of a dedicated group of collectors. The company milled flour in Sleepy Eye, Minnesota. Its blue and white pottery premiums picturing the Indian chief, Sleepy Eye, were made by Weir Pottery Company and Western Stoneware Company, both of Monmouth, Illinois, and by the Minnesota Stoneware Company of Red Wing, Minnesota. This sign was one of two massive cast-iron signs that hung at the mill. It is more than 5 feet tall and shows the company's logo, the profile of Chief Sleepy Eye. It's rare to see something this pricey at a flea market. It was marked $24,000. Needless to say, we didn't buy this one.

The plastic blister wrap on this 1980 Matchbox Mayflower van has never been opened, making it prime pickings for a toy collector. It's a Mercedes container truck, introduced in 1977. Over the years, the truck appeared in different color combinations and with the names of different moving companies. This version, with a green cab and a green cargo area, is worth $25. Another version, with the German company name "Confern" on it, is worth $125.

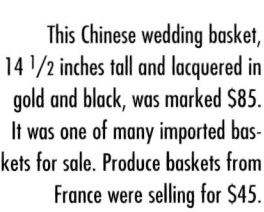

Walt Disney's Mickey Mouse is a perennial favorite with collectors. Here's a $15 Mickey made of painted hollow plastic. He was manufactured in Hong Kong in the 1950s or '60s and stands 5 3/4 inches tall.

This Chinese wedding basket, 14 1/2 inches tall and lacquered in gold and black, was marked $85. It was one of many imported baskets for sale. Produce baskets from France were selling for $45.

If you're looking for small and inexpensive collectible glass, try character glasses. Many were premiums at fast-food chains. Here are two glasses featuring the 1980 movie *The Empire Strikes Back*. They're 5 3/4 inches tall and sell for $5 to $10 apiece. Be sure the colors have not faded. *Star Wars* toys of all kinds are big sellers and have been since the movie series debuted in 1977.

Toy robots can be found at flea markets, but they're not inexpensive. A battery-operated Planet Robot made in 1955 by Yoshiya, a Japanese maker, copied Robby the Robot from the movie *Forbidden Planet*. A real Planet Robot sells for $600. This one (left) is a recent key-wind reproduction. The lithographed tin Spaceman (center) made by SY Toys of Japan around 1955, was selling for $650. Wind his key, and he'll walk forward while his arms move up and down and his loop antenna spins. The third Japanese space toy (right) is a Space Scooter from the 1950s. He's made of lithographed tin and plastic and sells for $595.

Toothpick holders are favorites with collectors who want to buy small antiques that are easy to display. Pictured is a Beveled Star pattern pressed glass toothpick holder manufactured by the Model Flint Glass Company about 1900. It's worth $120.

Here's a toy that's not easy to find at a flea market. It's a 1904–05 tin lithographed Lehmann windup motorcycle toy that sells for $1,800. It's called "Uncle on World Tour." The "uncle" raises and lowers his hat, while the man in back turns the parasol. Collectors can also shop for missing toy parts at flea markets.

Even a commonplace kitchen utensil, like this Pyrex mixing bowl, can be an example of high design. This 4-quart bowl is part of the Cinderella nesting set designed by architect Philip Johnson in 1958. The set came in a variety of fired-on solid colors, with and without fired-on decorations. Avocado green was introduced in the '60s. Pyrex kitchenware is very affordable right now. This bowl costs only $5.

The members of the 1970s rock group KISS were known for their outrageous makeup and costumes. Only one of their songs made the Top 10 hit list, but the group's fan club, the KISS Army, issued numerous collectibles, ranging from trading cards and belt buckles to dolls and lunch boxes. Sealed wax packs of trading cards, like this Series One set from 1978, sell for $7 to $10 each. A sealed box of packs goes for $60 to $70. Newer collectibles from the '90s fetch high prices, too.

The Peanuts collectibles you remember from your childhood are for sale at flea markets. This 1971 vinyl Peanuts lunch box, made by King Sealey Thermos, sells for $200 if the original thermos is inside. If the thermos is missing, the price drops to about $40. Look for other character lunch boxes, too.

This Jane-Ray Jade-ite covered sugar, 2 1/4 inches high, was made by Anchor Hocking Glass Corporation of Lancaster, Ohio, sometime between 1950 and the mid-'60s. It is worth $35 to $50. Jade-ite and other opaque green dinnerware and glassware can be found in abundance at flea markets. But an expert we spoke to warned collectors to be careful. Many pieces have been reproduced.

This Japanese lusterware bird pitcher originally sold about 1910 as a souvenir of Buffalo, New York. The only connection between the bird and Buffalo is the fact that the bird's breast is marked with the city's name. Today the small pitcher sells for $22.

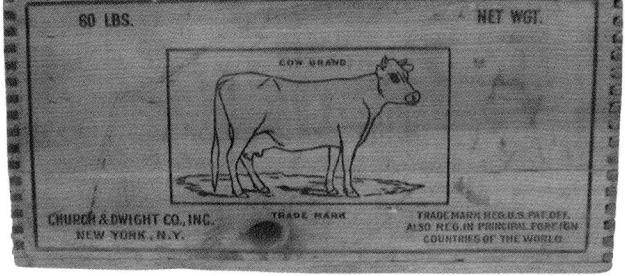

Wooden crates sell. This 24-by-18-inch crate was cleaned and lightly sanded to remove its rough edges. It once held Cow Brand aerated salt (saleratus). The brand was marketed by Church & Dwight Company, makers of Arm & Hammer baking soda and other household products. Why a cow? Because the salt was a leaven used with sour milk in baking. Collectors favor boxes with pictures of animals or well-known brand names, so this box costs $168.

Sometimes a flea market dealer has an unusual item. This 6-inch Chinese boy figurine was made by Gort China Company of Metuchen, New Jersey, a little-known company. It is signed "Wing Li 1954" and sells for $150. Eric and Walter Gort founded their company in 1944. For more than ten years, Gort made intricately detailed bone china figurines.

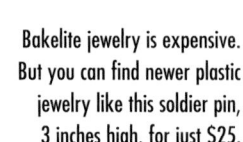

Bakelite jewelry is expensive. But you can find newer plastic jewelry like this soldier pin, 3 inches high, for just $25.

Within the past decade, we've seen more and more vintage lawn sprinklers at flea markets. They've been "discovered" by collectors. Some, like this cowboy-with-lariat sprinkler, are both clever and practical. He's made of iron and sprays water by swinging his lariat. The sprinkler sells for $1,895.

This George Washington candy container dates from 1940s Germany. The figure is papier-mâché and the round box is cardboard. The 8-inch container costs $125.

Electric percolators made of china can be found at most flea markets. This Royal Rochester coffee set in the Golden Pheasant pattern was made by Robeson Rochester Corporation of Rochester, New York. It includes a ceramic coffee percolator-urn, sugar, creamer, and syrup pitcher. The set sells for $175. We also saw some unusual all-china drip coffeepots made during World War II, when aluminum wasn't available for consumer products. Hall, Porcelier, and a few other American companies made about fifty different all-china coffeepots between 1943 and 1947.

Holiday collectibles can be found at flea markets all year long. The papier-mâché pumpkin-head Halloween figure, 6 inches tall, was marked $225; and the felt and wood Father Christmas, also 6 inches tall, was $175. They're both from the 1920s or '30s. Don't let reproductions of these holiday characters fool you.

A friend collects figural vases shaped like pretty ladies and uses them for dinner party decorations. Her table looks festive when the ladies "parade" down the center holding fresh flowers. We thought of her when we picked up this 9-inch Victorian girl vase for $30. The vase is marked "Relpo, 6447." Relpo stands for Reliable Glassware & Pottery Company, a Chicago import firm in business since 1950. The style of the mark indicates this vase was made in the 1960s.

This purple Hot Wheels hot rod is eye-catching, but that's not the most significant color on the toy. The red line on the tires is what's important to collectors. Hot Wheels used red-lined tires on these cars during the 1960s and '70s. Later hot rods had all-black tires. An early car sells for $35.

Sometimes we see dealers selling imported collectibles in wholesale quantities. These 18-inch European coffee grinders were part of a group of thirty at a booth stocked with an odd assortment of multiples, including sleds, graniteware bread boxes, and artillery baskets filled with empty shells. The wall-mounted coffee grinders were made for home use in the 1930s and '40s. The Art Deco–style grinder (center) was priced at $75. The Delft-style and D-E models were $125 each. D-E stands for Douwe-Eggbert, an old European coffee company now owned by the American company Sara Lee.

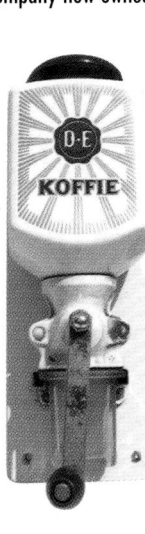

A dealer was selling this as a recent reproduction of the old Northwood glass pattern, Cherry and Cable. It's a footed tumbler made in the 1990s by Mosser Glass Inc. of Cambridge, Ohio. Mosser calls the pattern Large Cherry Thumbprint. Northwood made the pattern in crystal or carnival glass, not in green or opalescent colors. A reproduction lemonade set, including a pitcher and eight of these tumblers, sells for $250.

Colorful Blue Ridge dinnerware, made by Southern Potteries of Erwin, Tennessee, sells better in the South than in the North. We found this Nocturne pattern plate at a Florida show. Its decoration was hand-painted on the company's fluted Colonial shape. Price is $25.

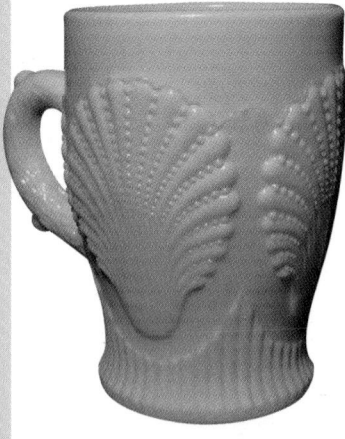

This 1969 custard glass reproduction of a Beaded Shell mug copies a pattern first made by Dugan Glass Company of Indiana, Pennsylvania, in the early 1900s. Original mugs in the pattern were made in several colors of carnival glass: amethyst, cobalt blue, marigold, purple, and white.
The reproduction, marketed by L.G. Wright Glass Company of New Martinsville, West Virginia, sells for $15. But it could fool the unsuspecting collector. It's marked with a poor copy of the Northwood mark, an underlined N in a circle.

We found this Silhouette pattern teapot by Crooksville China Company in a booth also displaying Taverne pattern serving pieces by Hall China Company. These two patterns are so similar that they have been confusing collectors since their introduction in the 1930s. The black decal on Silhouette pieces includes a dog under the table. Taverne's decal has no dog. Taverne pattern dinnerware to match Hall's serving pieces was made by Taylor, Smith and Taylor. This teapot is worth $25.

Pigeon Forge Pottery is a good seller at flea markets. The pottery worked in Pigeon Forge, Tennessee, from 1946 to 2000. Best are pieces signed by one of the individual artists. This Pigeon Forge sugar & creamer set was a bargain—priced $9. Neither piece was signed.

Couroc Company was founded in Monterey, California, in 1948. This Couroc tray, made of plastic and inlaid with aluminum and wood, is decorated with a clever mosaic of kitchen spices. It's 13 3/8 inches in diameter and sells for $35.

Lightning rod balls look out of place sitting on a dealer's table. This combination weather vane—lightning rod shows how the ball is attached. The rod goes through the center of a ribbed milk glass ball in this example. Because of the star finial and cutout directional indicators, this 32-inch weather vane costs $298. The dealer also had a variety of unattached lightning rod balls, like this 5-inch free-blown amber one, $280, and mold-blown onion opaque blue one, $175.

This Dutch girl doll captured our hearts because Terry had one when she was a little girl. The 8 1/2-inch "Mascotte" doll was made by the Italian company Lenci beginning in 1930. Most Mascottes are dressed in ethnic costumes. The dolls are made of felt with molded faces and painted expressions. This one was priced $450.

Peaked Cornice, Central Trefoil & Flowers, Engraved Border, 1870s, 9 1/4 In. 230.00
Porcelain, 3 Pumps, c.1850 . . . .   1400.00
Porcelain, Cylindrical, Floral Sprays, Doulton Lambeth, Silver Mounted, 1901, 3 In. 200.00
Porcelain, Sarcophagus, 2 Pots, Sacrifice To Hymen Medallion, Wedgwood, 6 7/8 In. 1495.00
Puma & Lion Form, 2 Wells, Rouge Marble & Slate Plinth, 1880s, 9 x 6 1/8 In. . . .   431.00
Recumbent Lion, 2 Wells, Leaf & Acanthus Border, Green Marble Base, 14 1/2 x 7 In. . . .   230.00
Rose Granite, Patinated, Bronze Mounted, Continental, 2 1/2 x 11 1/2 x 7 In. 200.00
Round, Beaded Border, Lift Top, Cut Glass Pot, Geometric Decoration, 1882, 8 1/2 In. . . .   172.00
Salt Glaze, 3 Quill Holes, Ink Well At Top, Grapes & Vines Around, 1 3/4 x 2 1/4 In. 103.00
Silver, Inkwell, Taper, 2 Stands, Cut Glass Wells, EJ & BW, England, 1847, 13 x 9 In. 575.00
Silver, Palmette, Acanthus Borders, 2 Cut Glass Wells, George Angell, 1865, 16 In. 3300.00
Silver Plate, 2 Wells, With Candleholder, Sheffield, 4 1/2 x 14 x 11 In. 210.00
Silver Plate, Blue Glass Ink Pot, Allover Pierced Rococo, Taper Holder, 1900, 5 1/2 In. . . .   200.00
Silver Plate, Buffalo, 2 Wells, Leaf Form Feet, 5 x 10 1/2 In. 250.00
Silver Plate, Egyptian Revival, Sphinx Shape, Center Handle, 2 Cut Glass Wells, 6 In. . . .   1230.00
Silver Plate, Rounded Rectangular Base, 2 Pen Trays, 1870, 7 x 8 x 10 1/2 In. 290.00
Silver Plate, Shell Form, Shell Footed, Frosted Glass, 1853, 9 1/2 In. 490.00
Silver Plate, Spread Winged Eagle, On Rock, 2 Bottles, Overall Floral & Leaf, 10 3/4 In. . .   210.00
Silver Plate, Triangular, Raised Edges, Copper Flowers, Hinged Lid, 1900, 8 In. 104.00
Stylized Shell Form, Bird On Branch, Removable Liner, Pen Supports, 12 In. 145.00
Vase-Form Cover, Matching Sander, 2 Sealing Wax Taper Holders, Pen Well, 7 In. 1095.00
Walnut, Ebonized, Crystal, Double, Continental, 19th Century, 5 x 13 x 9 1/2 In. 134.00
Wood, Pen Rest, 2 Birds On Top, Branch Held Pens, 2 Inks, Leaf Covers, 16 In. 970.00

INKWELLS, of course, held ink. Ready-made ink was first made about
1836 and was sold in bottles. The desk inkwell had a narrow hole so
the pen would not slip inside. Inkwells were made of many materials,
such as pottery, glass, pewter, and silver. Look in these categories for
more listings of inkwells.

2 Wells, 2 Children Studying Primer, Removable Top, Staffordshire, 1877 . . . .   120.00
Amber Glass, Amber Hinged Top, Round Indentations Each Side, 4 x 2 1/2 In. 295.00
Amber Hinged Top, Stippled, 4 x 2 1/2 In. 295.00
Bisque, Lion, Hand Painted, Aqua Base, England, 4 1/4 In. 137.00
Brass, Dog, Orb Inkwell, Glass Liner, 3 Seated Hounds Base, Chains, 4 5/8 x 4 1/4 In. . . .   375.00
Brass, Double, Hinged Lids, Glass Insert Cups, 7 1/2 x 4 In. 25.00
Brass, Yatate, Reeding, Lid, Bottom Coin Design, Lotus Blossom, Phoenix, 19th Century .   210.00
Bronze, Baker's Dog Head Form, Pen Tray, Glass Bottle, Patinated Spelter, 3 1/2 In. 345.00
Bronze, Black Pirate, Pull Bandana To Open At Neck, 5 1/2 In. 540.00
Bronze, Bulldog, Porcelain Insert, Glass Eyes, 5 1/2 x 7 In. 840.00
Bronze, Figural, Dickens' Character Bust, Painted, Austria, 3 x 3 1/2 In. 1792.00
Bronze, Figure Of Pan, Neoclassical, Gilt, Italy, 8 x 7 In. 400.00
Bronze, Indian Chief, Multicolored Patina, 4 x 6 x 7 In. 784.00
Bronze, Louis XVI Style, Cartouche, Floral, Dore, Late 19th Century, 4 1/2 x 9 x 8 In. . . .   1035.00
Bronze, Skirt Shape, Brush Holder, Scribe Set, Inlay, 19th Century 172.00
Bronzed Metal, Figural, Bull, 9 In. 140.00
Bust Of Soldier, Civil War Regiment, Shell Cap, c.1865, 5 1/2 In. 1219.00
Copper, Sloping Sides, Coral Cartouche On Cover, Potter Studio, 3 x 4 1/4 In. 402.00
Cordiform, Fountain, Green Mottled Glaze, Royal Doulton, c.1906, 2 3/4 In. 878.00
Cottage, 2 Windows, Tiled Roof, Pen Nib To Rear, 2 1/2 In. 160.00
Cut Glass, Brass Mounted, Rectangular, Button Base, Brass Lid, c.1900, 5 In. 115.00
Cut Glass, Green Hinged Top, Allover Design On Bottom, 3 3/4 In. 295.00
Cut Glass, Marble Encrier, Ormolu, Louis XVI Style, Late 19th Century, 7 x 13 1/4 In. . . .   1495.00
Cut Glass, Silver Mounted, Button Cut Base, England, c.1913, 7 1/2 x 6 In. 1265.00
Cut Glass, Swirl, Sterling Floral Repousse Base, Ball Shape Top, Gorham, 4 1/2 In. 670.00
Cut Glass Well, Chinese Silver Stand, Bamboo Pen Rest, Wang Hing, 1920s, 4 In. 316.00
Dover Crested, Colored Crest, 1 3/4 x 2 3/4 In. 48.00
Embossed Lid, Ormolu Base, 2 1/2 x 4 In. 34.00
Fence Form, 2 Urn Form Candle Sconces, Square Cut Wells, Plated Lids, 11 1/2 In. 170.00
Glass, 3-Piece Mold, Blown, Olive Amber, Coventry, Conn. Glass, 1 1/2 x 2 1/4 In. 165.00
Glass, 3-Piece Mold, Blown, Olive Amber, Coventry, Conn. Glass, 1 3/4 x 2 5/8 In. 275.00
Glass, 3-Piece Mold, Blown, Olive Green, Coventry, Conn. Glass, 1 3/4 x 2 5/8 In. 190.00
Glass, Amber, Hinged Top, Embossed Stipple Design, Square, 4 In. 295.00
Glass, Birdcage, 4 In. 81.00

Glass, Emerald Green, Urchin Form, Brass Hinged Top, Clear Glass Insert, 2 1/2 x 4 In. ... 230.00
Glass, Green Favrile, On Brass Base, Lion's Head Lid, Corner Lion Paws, 1977 .... 520.00
Glass, Round Ball Hinged Top, Embossed Ribs Resemble Bamboo, 4 3/4 x 2 1/2 In. 295.00
Glass, Sterling Silver Stopper, Flag, Star, Sanford's, 2 1/4 x 3 3/4 In. 125.00
Glass, Streaked, Marbleized, 4-Footed Stand, Metal Collar, Flame Finial, 6 In. 252.00
Iron, Yatate, Silver Inlay, Kettle Shape, Handle, Ball Shape, Early 19th Century 80.00
Malachite, Lid, Square Crystal Well, Stone Base, Pen Rest, 5 x 7 In. 840.00
Metal, Painted White, Head Of Joseph Jacques Cessaire, c.1918 .... 150.00
Milk Glass, Teakettle, Hand Painted Flowers, 2 Tiers, Brass Cap, 2 1/4 In. 160.00
Onyx Base, Champleve, c.1890 .... 200.00
Parade Helmet, English Cavalry, Regimental Badge, Horsehair Plume, 20 In. 375.00
Pewter, Glass Insert, 5 Surrounding Quill Holders, Round 50.00
Pony Finial, Sponge Painted, Kitt Rix, 5 1/4 In. 230.00
Porcelain, Kneeling Peasant Figure, Supporting Box & Cover, Gardner, 5 1/2 In. 865.00
Porcelain, Kutani, Squat, Bell Shape, Cartouches, Flowers, c.1920, 2 3/4 In. 67.00
Pottery, Boat Shape, Brown Glaze, McKearin Label, 3 1/4 In. 165.00
Pyramid, Thermometer On Pylon, Vaseline Glass Base, 1977 .... 52.00
Sewer Tile, Open Sided Square, Cone Form, Footed Base, 3 1/2 x 3 1/2 In. 80.00
Silver, Enameled Fishing Boat, Enameled Anchor On Side, England, 8 In. 575.00
Silver, Enameled Scenes, Lovers, Putti, Winged Women, Gilt, Continental, 10 x 6 In. 1980.00
Silver, Paperweight Style, Bulbous, Clear Glass, Hinged Silver Lid, G.J., 6 1/2 In. 290.00
Silver Metal, Eagle, Outstretched Wings, 6 In. 247.00
Silver Mounted, Octagon, Glass Liner, Whiplash Flower, Galt & Bros., c.1910, 5 1/4 In. .. 3290.00
Spaniel, Lying Down, Staffordshire, 19th Century 835.00
Sterling Silver Repose Top, Cut Glass, 4 Legs, 3 3/4 x 3 3/4 In. 750.00
Stoneware, Central Well, 3 Apertures For Pens, Brown Glaze, 19th Century, 2 3/4 In. 295.00
Stoneware, Stenciled Blue Empire, Other Word On 2 Sides, 1 3/8 In. 110.00
Swan, Staffordshire, 3 1/2 In. 99.00
Teakettle, Brown Glaze, 2 3/4 In. 16.00
Traveling, Bakelite, Green, Globe Shape, 3 Legs, Sanford Ink Co., Box, 2 3/4 In. 165.00
Traveling, Brass Holder, Leather Cover, Ink In Gold, 1 3/4 x 2 In. 95.00
Traveling, Glass Bottle, Screw-On Lid, Waterman, Inc., c.1900 .... 60.00
Traveling, Olive Wood, Screw-On Lid, c.1870 .... 575.00
Traveling, Silver, Monogrammed, Twist Lock Top, 1904 .... 450.00
Turtle Boy, Black Boy Rides Turtle, Glass Inserts, 1890, 5 1/2 In. 836.00
Turtle Boy, Boy Rides Turtle, Glass Well, 1890s, 5 1/2 In. 831.00
Wood, Glass Insert, Owl, Hinged Head, Yellow Glass Eyes, 3 1/2 In. 60.00
Yellowware, Circular, Embossed Face & Flower Design, Rockingham Glaze, 4 1/2 In. 80.00
Yellowware, Figural, Man's Head, Open Mouth, 3 In. 176.00
Yellowware, Shoe Form, Rockingham Glaze, 4 3/4 In. 95.00

INSULATORS of glass or pottery have been made for use on telegraph
or telephone poles since 1844. Thousands of different styles of insulators have been made. Most common are those of clear or aqua glass;
most desirable are the threadless types made from 1850 to 1870.

Armstrong, 51-C3, Red Amber, Smooth Base 12.00
Chicago Diamond, Embossed Shoulder, Blue 70.00
Gayner, No. 90, Light Aqua 7.00
H.G.Co., No. 7, Ice Green, Smooth Base 30.00
Hemingray, No. 21, Emerald Green, Amber Streaks 42.00
Hemingray, No. 21, Hemingray Blue, Teepee Style 6.00
Hemingray, No. 23, Hemingray Blue Aqua 18.00
Hemingray, No. 43, Hemingray Blue 8.00
Lynchburg, No. 36, Green ....10.00 to 15.00
Lynchburg, No. 38, Light Aqua 5.00
Maydwell, No. 16, Pink 26.00
Maydwell, No. 20, White, Milk Glass, Smooth Drip Points 16.00
McLaughlin, No. 9, Delft Blue, Smooth Base 10.00
Mclaughlin, No. 9, Emerald Green 20.00
McLaughlin, No. 10, Ice Lime 6.00
McLaughlin, No. 16, 7-Up Green, Bubbles 50.00
McLaughlin, No. 20, Light Cornflower Blue, Backward N 24.00

Pyrex, No. 661, Light Carnival, Smooth Base 75.00
Pyrex, No. 662, Carnival, Smooth Base 40.00
W. Brookfield, Cauvets, Aqua, Old Flat Style, 1870 .... 22.00
Whitall Tatum, No. 4, Blue Aqua, Smooth Base 5.00
Whitall Tatum, No. 4, Ice Aqua, Smooth Base 5.00
Whitall Tatum, No. 5, Light Aqua, Smooth Base 4.00
Whitall Tatum, No. 512U, Amber, Smooth Base 8.00

IRISH BELLEEK, see Belleek category.

IRON is a metal that has been used by man since prehistoric times. It is
a popular metal for tools and decorative items like doorstops that need
as much weight as possible. Items are listed here or under other appropriate headings, such as Bookends, Doorstop, Kitchen, Match Holder,
or Tool. The tool that is used for ironing clothes, an iron, is listed in the
Kitchen category under Iron and Sadiron.

Bell, Clapper, 2 Brackets, Jones & Hitchcock, Troy, N.Y., 1854 .... 220.00
Bench, Painted, Green, Wood Plank Seat, Back, Late 19th Century, 33 7/8 x 48 x 28 In. ... 575.00
Bill Holder, Atlantic Coast Line, 1915, 4 In. 46.00
Book Press, Black Enamel Finish, Brass Trim, Oval Nameplate, Castle Series, London .. 595.00
Boot Scraper, Black Paint Arched Shape, Light Brown Horse Over Boot Scrape, 17 In. ... 488.00
Boot Scraper, Granite Base, Scrolled Top 308.00
Boot Scraper, Inverted Sea Serpent Form, Mounted, Contemporary Base, 10 x 8 In. 83.00
Boot Scraper, Regency, Columnar Uprights, Rectangular Stone Plinth, 15 In. 1150.00
Bootjack, Naughty Nellie, 10 In. ....92.00 to 115.00
Bootjack, Pinwheel, Reticulated, England, 14 x 16 In. 448.00
Bootjack, Pistol Form, Boars Either Side, 9 1/4 In. 295.00
Candlestick, Cherub, Wall Mounted, 23 1/2 In., Pair 299.00
Crucifix, Church, Scrolled, 2 Supporting Angels Each Side, 49 In. 302.00
Cuspidor, Shell Form, Scrolled Leaf Feet, 4 3/4 x 13 In. 55.00
Doormat, Grid Of Connected Hearts, Late 19th Century, 29 1/2 x 18 In. 345.00
Dove, White Paint Traces, Early 19th Century, 8 x 12 x 9 1/2 In. 980.00
Drawer Bar, Flat Hourglass Shape Backplate, 10 x 4 In. 105.00
Eagle, Outstretched Wings, Gilt Painted, 19th Century, 13 1/2 In. 1955.00
Figure, Bird, Hinge & Scythe, Railroad Towplate Base, Marco, 12 x 23 In. 80.00
Figure, Bull Terrier Puppy, Standing, Black, White, c.1880, 4 1/4 x 6 In. 280.00
Figure, Bull Terrier, 9 1/2 x 10 In. 250.00
Figure, Dog, Whippet, Licking Paw, Gold Finish, Patina, Mene Style, 11 x 7 In. 86.00
Figure, Eagle, Spread Wings, Silver Paint, 30 3/4 x 9 3/4 In. 220.00
Figure, Greyhound, Lying Down, Hollow Body, Black Paint, 50 x 21 In. 1430.00
Figure, Greyhound, Lying Down, Late 19th Century, 7 x 16 In. 520.00
Figure, Hobo, Blackface, Painted, 5 5/8 In. 110.00
Figure, Nubian Child, Tole Peinte, Parcel Gilt, Black Paint, Tray, 32 In. 4370.00
Figure, Unicorn, Gold, Lying Down, Stepped Base, England, 27 1/2 In. 170.00
Figure, Venus, Crouching, Plinth Base, 36 In. 1150.00
Finial, Eagle, Spread Wings, 9 x 15 1/4 In. 165.00
Flint Striker, Medieval, England 160.00
Footman, Curved, Pierced Frieze, Trivet Shelf, Serpentine Legs, Pad Feet, 14 x 12 In. ... 170.00
Hasp, Closing, Attached Locking Pin, Marked 1808 M.I. EBY, Lancaster County, 23 In. ... 385.00
Heater, Gas, Louis XV Style, Ormolu Mounted, Painted, Early 1900s, 31 x 22 x 14 In. .. 1150.00
Hinge, Barn, Flat, Tapered Body, Round Head, Green Paint, 46 x 2 1/2 In., Pair 30.00
Hinge, Chest, Round Tulip Head, Tapered, Flat Ovals, Pointed Tulip, 20 x 4 1/2 In., Pair . 250.00
Hinge, Flat, Fine Scrolls, 22 x 4 1/2 In., Pair 300.00
Hinge, Ram's Horn, Beveled Curls, Original Pintels, 10 x 5 In. 910.00
Hitching Post, Clenched Fist, Holding Chain & Ring, 43 In., Pair 7638.00
Hitching Post, Finial, Horse Head, Mouth Pierced By 2 Rings, Late 19th Century, 8 In. .. 705.00
Hitching Post, Finial, Horse Head, Yellow Bridle, Musculature Nostrils & Mouth, 14 In. . 2233.00
Hitching Post, Finial, Napoleon's Head, Fringed Epaulets, 19th Century, 8 In. 4465.00
Hitching Post, Horse Head, Abstracted Head, Pronounced Ears, Fluted Column, 27 1/2 In. 705.00
Hitching Post, Horse Head, Curly Mane, Lion's Head Base, Late 19th Century, 35 1/2 In. 352.00
Hitching Post, Horse Head, Fluted Column, Late 19th Century, 44 1/4 In. 1645.00
Hitching Post, Leaf Molded Capital & Plinth, Late 19th Century, Black, 49 In. 1058.00

Hitching Post, Swan's Head, Feathered, 3-Part Ribbed Post, 19th Century, 52 1/2 In. 2115.00
Horse Stake, 13 7/8 In. 28.00
Horseshoe, Asymmetrical Upturned Ends, Front Half Nailed, Colonial America, 1780 ... 45.00
Jardiniere, Arches, Scrolls, Crosses, Ball Feet, Mid 1800s, 22 1/4 x 22 x 16 In., Pair 4140.00
Keys, Jail, 6 On Ring, 1800-1900 .... 70.00
Lamp Standard, Circular Base, Columnar Shaft, Relief, Grape Leaves, 18 In., Pair 529.00
Lavabo, Enamel, Squat, Urn Shape Basin, Shield Backsplash, 28 x 22 1/2 x 11 1/4 In. ... 748.00
Magazine Holder, Female Ends, Scrollwork, Mid 20th Century, 22 In. 145.00
Mailbox, Leaf & Urn Below Box, Horns Either Side, Man On Horseback, 46 In. 360.00
Mask, Noh, Realistic, Age Lines, Eye, Nose, Mouth Openings, Japan, 8 3/4 In. 230.00
Ornament, Pigeon, Black Paint, Early 20th Century, 12 1/2 x 14 1/2 In., Pair 230.00
Panel, Relief, Napoleon, 12 3/4 x 8 3/4 In. 115.00
Paperweight, Riverboat, Hubley, 4 1/2 In. 95.00
Pipe Tamper, Acorn Finial, England, 18th Century 95.00
Pipe Tongs, Heart Cutout In Handle, Pipe Tamper On Other Handle, 18th Century, 17 In. . 1600.00
Plant Stand, Curved Hoof Feet & Legs, Acorn Drop, Dish Top, 32 In. 360.00
Planter, Modeled Top Edge, c.1880, 33 x 13 3/4 x 14 1/2 In. 1190.00
Plaque, Lion Head, Open Mouth, Round Black Background, Painted Gold, 16 In. 225.00
Plate, Builders, American Locomotive Co., 1937, 14 x 7 1/2 In. 115.00
Plate, Builders, Baldwin-Lima, Embossed, Diesel, Red Enamel Paint, 14 x 7 In. 80.00
Plate, Builders, General Motors, Diesel, 15 1/2 x 5 1/4 In. 46.00
Plate, Builders, Vulcan Iron Works Builders, No. 4337, 1941, 9 1/4 In. 184.00
Pot, Witch's, Tapered Tripod Foot, Flared Mouth, Handle, 11 x 11 1/2 In. 70.00
Safe, Hinged Top Over Handled Structure, Block Feet, 19th Century, 22 x 28 1/2 In. 170.00
Safe, Wells Fargo, Flowers, Lattice Front, Iron Ring Handles, Interior Shelves, 22 In. ... 410.00
Sconce, Wall, Tinned, Circular, 1900s, 10 In., Pair 1800.00
Sculpture, Buzzard, Neck Ruffle, Eyes & Comb, Black Paint, 28 x 16 In. 275.00
Sculpture, Woman, Bare Breasted, Red Skirt, Steel Wool Hair, Screw Nose, 23 1/4 In. ... 55.00
Shutter Stay, Scroll Arm, Penny Head, Flat Body, 25 x 5 In. 209.00
Splint Holder, Conical Socket, Tripod Base, Penny Feet, Adjustable, 40 1/2 In. 605.00
Stove Plate, Floral, Heart & Walnut Design, 18th Century, 22 1/4 x 23 1/4 In. 440.00
Sugar Nippers, Petal Design, Spring, 18th Century, 8 7/8 In. 125.00
Sugar Nippers, Scalloped & Line Engraving, 9 1/2 In. 50.00
Thumb Latch, Tulip & Flame, Filed Tulip Head, Turned Handle, Penny Head, 11 x 3 In. . 190.00
Thumb Latch, Tulip Handle, Leaves, With Mounting Hardware, 11 x 3 In. 520.00
Ticket Register, Sequential Numbering, 4 Digits, 7 In. 35.00
Tobacco Cutter, Chaw, Save The Tags, Bracket Held Blade, 19 In. 375.00
Tobacco Cutter, Guillotine Type, Hand Operated, Voss, No. 6 .... 110.00
Umbrella Stand, Openwork Shaft, 2 Oval Holders, Shaped Tray, Claw Feet 56.00
Wall Pocket, Cherub, Painted White, Pair 69.00
Windmill Weight, 5-Pointed Star, Raised Numbers, Early 20th Century, 7 1/2 x 3 In. 920.00
Windmill Weight, Bull, Boss, Full-Bodied, Black, Tan Highlights, 13 x 13 3/4 x 4 In. ... 1495.00
Windmill Weight, Bull, Flat, Fairbury, Nebraska, Early 20th Century, 18 1/2 x 25 1/2 In. . 546.00
Windmill Weight, Bull, Flat, Painted, Black & White, 19 x 24 1/2 In. 489.00
Windmill Weight, Bull, Full-Bodied, Red Paint, Early 20th Century, 12 x 13 x 10 In. 1035.00
Windmill Weight, Bull, Red Paint, Original Base, 20th Century, 18 1/2 x 9 7/8 In. 1150.00
Windmill Weight, Bull, Red, White Highlights, 20th Century, 18 1/4 x 24 1/2 In. 862.50
Windmill Weight, Bull, Simpson Windmill Machine Company, 12 1/2 x 14 1/8 In. 1092.00
Windmill Weight, Eagle, Feathered Spread Wings, Holding Cornucopia, 14 1/2 In. 1998.00
Windmill Weight, Eagle, Feathered Spread Wings, Knuckled Talons, 1813, 21 In. 1410.00
Windmill Weight, Eagle, Holding Branch & Cornucopia, 1813, 18 1/4 In. 1410.00
Windmill Weight, Horse, Long Tail, Black Paint, Long Tail, 20th Century, 19 x 17 In. ... 1380.00
Windmill Weight, Horse, Long Tail, Short Base, Silver, 18 1/2 x 17 1/2 x 3 x 12 In. 920.00
Windmill Weight, Rooster, Articulated Comb, Eyes & Sawtooth Tail, 15 1/2 In. 940.00
Windmill Weight, Rooster, Elgin Wind Power & Pump Co., Ill., 16 x 16 1/2 In. 805.00
Windmill Weight, Rooster, Elgin Wind Power & Pump, 18 3/4 x 15 1/2 In. 1150.00
Windmill Weight, Rooster, Full Round, Rainbow Molded Tail, 20th Century, 24 3/4 In. .. 5640.00
Windmill Weight, Rooster, Hummer, Rectangular Base, White, Red, 13 In. 862.50
Windmill Weight, Rooster, Mogul, Elgin Wind Power & Pump Co., 18 3/4 x 20 In. 3105.00
Windmill Weight, Rooster, Orange Comb & Waddle, Early 20th Century, 23 In. 8813.00
Windmill Weight, Rooster, Rainbow Tail, White, Red, On Green Base, 19 x 18 1/2 In. ... 5750.00
Windmill Weight, Rooster, Rainbow Tail, White, Yellow, Black Base, 17 x 18 In. 2070.00

Windmill Weight, Rooster, Standing On Rectangular Base, Silver, Red, 16 x 9 x 4 In. 1495.00
Windmill Weight, Rooster, Standing, On Rectangular Base, 18 x 20 1/2 In. 5175.00
Windmill Weight, Rooster, White, Red, Raised Numbers On Tail, 15 1/2 x 16 x 4 In. 1495.00
Windmill Weight, Silver Paint, Bull Shape, Late 19th Century, 18 1/2 x 26 x 10 In. 1410.00
Windmill Weight, Squirrel, Elgin Wind Power & Pump, 15 1/2 x 13 1/2 In. 1955.00
Windmill Weight, Squirrel, Perched On Base, Brown, Gold, Green Paint, 19 x 5 x 9 In. ... 3737.50
Windmill Weight, W, On Rectangular Base, Early 20th Century, 16 1/2 x 11 x 9 In. 977.50
Windmill Weight, Warship, Monitor, Concrete, Blue Paint, 7 1/2 x 28 1/2 x 12 In. 1955.00

IRONSTONE china was first made in 1813. It gained its greatest popularity during the mid-nineteenth century. The heavy, durable, off-white pottery was made in white or was decorated with any of hundreds of patterns. Much flow blue pottery was made of ironstone. Some of the decorations were raised. Many pieces of ironstone are unmarked, but some English and American factories included the word *Ironstone* in their marks. Additional pieces may be listed in other categories, such as Chelsea Grape, Chelsea Sprig, Flow Blue, Gaudy Ironstone, Mason's Ironstone, Moss Rose, Staffordshire, and Tea Leaf Ironstone.

Bowl, Blue Leaf Rim, Red Stripes, Spatter Flowers, Tunstall, England, 9 5/8 In. 140.00
Bowl, Cobalt Blue, Transfer, Amhurst, Japan, 4 1/4 x 8 1/2 In. 440.00
Bowl, Flowers, Blue, Green Trim, Ring Footed Base, 19th Century, 4 1/2 x 9 1/2 In. 440.00
Bowl, Vegetable, Hawthorn, Signed, 7 x 9 In. 110.00
Centerpiece, Amherst, Imari Style, Pagoda, Relief Exterior, Japan, 6 x 11 In. 660.00
Coffeepot, Ceres Shape, Green Wheat, Elsmore & Forster, 9 1/2 In. 580.00
Coffeepot, Hawthorn, Signed, 9 1/4 In. 385.00
Creamer, Blue Snowflake, 4 1/2 In. 110.00
Creamer, Ceres Shape, Green Wheat, 6 1/4 In. 250.00
Creamer, Ceres Shape, Green Wheat, 7 1/4 In. 275.00
Creamer, Cuckoo, Castle Scene On Reverse, 3 1/4 In. 360.00
Creamer, Hawthorn, 5 3/4 In. 250.00
Cup Plate, Hawthorn, 4 1/4 In. 70.00
Figurine, Victorian Man & Woman Dancing, 6 3/4 x 5 x 3 1/2 In., Pair 112.00
Fish Set, Fish In Water, Green & Gold Rim, 7 Conforming Plates, 8 Piece 365.00
Gravy Boat, Green Wheat, Elsmore & Forster, 5 1/2 In. 248.00
Mug, Green Wheat, Elsmore & Forster, 3 1/2 In. 310.00
Mug, Straight Sides, Verse, Loop Handle, 3 3/4 In. 80.00
Pitcher, Blue Wash, Gold Trim, Bishop & Stonier, England, 7 In. 70.00
Pitcher, Scenic Design, A. Meakin, 7 In. 45.00
Pitcher, Wheat & Flowers, Johnson Bros., 8 x 8 1/2 x 5 1/2 In. 56.00
Plate, American Flag, Red Band Border, 9 In. 770.00
Plate, Blue Snowflake, 6 3/4 In. 385.00
Plate, Blue Snowflake, 8 3/4 In., 6 Piece 385.00
Plate, Dinner, Hawthorn, Signed, 10 1/4 In. 50.00
Plate, Luncheon, Hawthorn, 9 1/4 In., 4 Piece 95.00
Plate, Salad, Hawthorn, Signed, 8 1/4 In., 4 Piece 70.00
Platter, 2 Scenes, Sailboat, Bird & Forest, Impressed Mark, 18 1/2 In. 115.00
Platter, Advertising, Baker, Knowlton & Co., Stradling, N.Y., White, 13 3/4 x 20 In. 290.00
Platter, Blue Snowflake, 10 x 13 1/2 In. 580.00
Platter, Corn & Stalk, 20 x 14 3/4 In. 140.00
Platter, Fish, Cauldon, Blue Transfer, Sea Run Brown Trout, 19th Century, 19 In. 402.00
Platter, Gentlemen's Cabin, Boston Mails Series, 19th Century, 13 1/2 In. 230.00
Platter, Green Wheat, Oval, Elsmore & Forster, 12 1/2 In. 192.00
Platter, Hawthorn, Signed, 12 1/4 x 16 In. 110.00
Platter, Imari Design, 16 x 20 In. 880.00
Platter, Moss Rose, White, J. & G. Meakin, 16 x 11 1/2 In. 125.00
Punch Bowl, Brown Leaf Transfer, 8 1/2 x 16 1/2 In. 252.00
Punch Bowl, Hand Painted Floral, 19th Century, 7 x 16 1/2 In. 224.00
Relish, Ceres Shape, Green Wheat, Elsmore & Forster, 4 3/4 In. 209.00
Relish, Hawthorn, Signed, 5 x 6 In. 132.00
Sauceboat, White, Johnson Bros., 7 1/2 x 3 1/2 In. 75.00
Sugar, Cover, Blue Snowflake, 7 3/4 In. 385.00
Sugar, Cover, Ceres Shape, Green Wheat, Handles, Elsmore & Forster, 8 In. 358.00

Sugar, Cover, Hawthorn, Scrolled Handles, Signed, 7 1/4 In.	248.00
Tureen, Cover, Brown Transfer, Flowers, Colony, England, 12 5/8 x 7 In.	95.00
Tureen, Cover, Footed, White, Red Cliff, Ladle, 10 1/2 x 11 1/2 In.	195.00
Tureen, Cover, Leaf & Swag, 8 x 13 x 8 1/2 In.	112.00
Tureen, Soup, Acanthus Leaf, Double Handles, Fruit Finial, 13 x 16 In.	302.00
Vegetable Tureen, Sydenham Shape, T. & R. Boote, 8 1/2 In.	84.00
Wash Bowl, Pitcher, Hawthorn	330.00
Waste Bowl, Blue Snowflake, 3 1/2 x 5 3/4 In.	275.00
Waste Bowl, Green Wheat, Elsmore & Forster, 3 1/2 x 5 1/2 In.	193.00

IVORY from the tusk of an elephant is thought by many to be the only true ivory. To most collectors, the term *ivory* also includes such natural materials as walrus, hippopotamus, or whale teeth or tusks, and some of the vegetable materials that are of similar texture and density. Other ivory items may be found in the Scrimshaw and Netsuke categories. Collectors should be aware of the recent laws limiting the buying and selling of elephant ivory and scrimshaw.

3 Chicks, Wood Base, Engraved Beetle Signature, Chinese, 2 1/4 In.	110.00
Ball, Diptych, Carved, Taking Of Bologne, Continental, 20th Century, 2 1/2 x 2 3/8 In.	460.00
Boat, Dragon Shape, 12 Sailors, Rowing, 3 Flags, 6 3/4 In.	28.00
Bone, Figure, Man, Woman, Elaborate Dress, Chinese, c.1900, 13 In., Pair	123.00
Box, Cover, Liner, Incised Dragonfly, Spiral, Tiffany & Co., 4 In.	2300.00
Box, Cylindrical, Figural Landscape Painted On Cover, 2 In.	200.00
Bridge, Hippopotamus Tooth, Depicting Figures, Pavilions, Early 20th Century, 10 In.	65.00
Brushpot, Cylindrical, Relief Figural Design, Key Fret Carved Foot, c.1920, 6 In.	373.00
Bust, African Woman, Beaded Earrings & Necklace, Cherry Base, 5 1/4 In.	410.00
Charger, Oval, Bacchanalian Feast Scene, Border, Late 19th Century, 27 3/4 In.	30650.00
Cigarette Holder, Carved	40.00
Comb, With Cabochon, Rhinestones & Silver Colored Pique Point, c.1910, 4 x 3 In.	80.00
Crucifix, Carved, Mahogany, Baroque Style, Continental, Early 20th Century, 25 1/4 In.	1150.00
Diptych, Carved Nut, 2 Biblical Scenes Interior, Continental, Late 1800s, 2 In.	750.00
Dresser Set, Monogrammed, Powder Box, Combs, Brushes, 16 Piece	460.00
Figurine, Boar, Seated, Wearing Goggles, Walking Stick, Continental, 4 1/4 x 6 7/8 In.	1495.00
Figurine, Brushpot, Pavilion & Trees Scenes, Pierced, Chinese, 19th Century, 5 In.	2185.00
Figurine, Buddhist Saints, Chinese, Late 19th Century, 10 1/2 In., Pair	575.00
Figurine, Dancer, Agate Base, Samuel Lipchitz, 18 In.	5400.00
Figurine, Doctor's Lady, Caucasian Woman, Stands Nude, Wood Pedestal, 7 1/2 In.	330.00
Figurine, Ebisu, Holding Bamboo Pole, Reaching For Fish, 5 1/2 In.	718.00
Figurine, Elegant Lady, Trumpeting Cavalier, 6 & 7 1/2 In., Pair	825.00
Figurine, Elephant & Lions, 6 1/4 x 9 In.	115.00
Figurine, Elephant, Man Clinging To Trunk, Japan, 19th Century, 10 x 8 In., Pair	1380.00
Figurine, Fisherman, Lowering Fish In Basket, 5 In.	316.00
Figurine, Garden Lantern, Bird, Ivy, Monkeys, Stained, Signed, Japan, 6 1/2 In.	2645.00
Figurine, Geisha, Dancing, Mother-Of-Pearl On Kimono, 5 5/8 In.	520.00
Figurine, Goddess Kuan Yin, Chinese, 19th Century, 12 In.	230.00
Figurine, Immortal Lan Tsai Ho, With Her Basket Of Flowers, 12 In.	345.00
Figurine, Leopard, Walking, Tongue Handing Out, Late 19th Century, 8 1/4 In.	170.00
Figurine, Mahakala, Cape, Human Head Garland, Beaded Lotus Base, Tibet, 5 3/4 In.	3560.00
Figurine, Maiden, Standing Prunus, Musical Instrument, Wood Stand, 10 1/2 In.	145.00
Figurine, Maiden, Standing, Prunus Branch, Circular & Carved Wood Stand, 9 1/2 In.	57.00
Figurine, Man, Carved, Continental, Ebonized Wood Pedestal, 8 7/8 In., Pair	3737.00
Figurine, Man, With Cane, Black Beard, Flower In Hand, Wood Base, 6 3/4 In.	28.00
Figurine, Man, With Dove In Birdcage, 20th Century, 4 In.	170.00
Figurine, Noh Actor, Meiji Period, Japan, 8 1/2 In.	460.00
Figurine, Nude Woman, Standing, Marble Socle, Preiss, Germany, 9 7/8 In.	6000.00
Figurine, Oriental Woman With Lute, Wood Stand, 11 In.	300.00
Figurine, Pekineses On Pillow, Early 20th Century, 1 5/8 x 1 5/8 In.	287.00
Figurine, Poor Cleric, Tattered Cloak, Long Crucifix, Wood Socle, 1890s, 6 1/2 In.	430.00
Figurine, Priest, Black Robe, Holding Pomegranate, Late 19th Century, 5 3/8 In.	520.00
Figurine, Putto, Winged Boy In Drapery Apron, Carving Wood, Plinth Base, 4 1/2 In.	460.00
Figurine, Rakan With Small Boy & Dragon, Signed, Gyokutomo, 7 In.	230.00
Figurine, Sage, Carrying Gourd Bottle, 20th Century, 4 In.	170.00

Figurine, Scholar, Branch Of Magnolia Flowers, Chinese, 19th Century, 16 In. 375.00
Figurine, Standing Female, Flowers, Wood Base, Glass Dome, Chinese, 7 In. 200.00
Figurine, Tara, Standing On Lotus Pod, Early 20th Century, 7 1/4 In. 69.00
Figurine, Tortoise, Monkey, Rodents, Japan, c.1900, 2 1/4 x 3 1/2 In. 616.00
Figurine, Venus, Cupid, Continental, Ebonized Base, Late 19th Century, 13 1/2 In., Pair .. 4310.00
Figurine, Warrior, Bow & Arrows, Standing, Carved Native Wood Stand, 11 1/4 In. 200.00
Figurine, Woman & Man, Standing, 13 In. 230.00
Figurine, Woman, Blue Eyes, Pink Dress, Brass Oval Frame, 4 1/4 In. 176.00
Figurine, Woman, Flowers In Hair, Low Cut Dress, Dumot, Leather Case, 4 1/2 In. 330.00
Figurine, Woman, Holding Basket, Feeding Dove, Early 20th Century, 8 5/8 In. 980.00
Figurine, Woman, Nude, 6 1/4 In. 185.00
Figurine, Woman, With Chicken, 10 In. 170.00
Figurine, Woman, With Lacquered Hair, Chinese, 19th Century, 3 1/2 In. 115.00
Glove Stretcher, 6 5/8 In. 55.00
Group, Depicting 2 Meijin With Flowers, 19th Century, 4 1/2 In. 345.00
Group, Gentleman In Buggy, 2 Servants, 11 x 16 1/2 In. 1035.00
Group, Immortals, Carved, Etched, 20th Century, 3 3/4 x 4 1/2 In., 18 Piece 1840.00
Group, Lotus Pad, 2 Monkeys, Crab, Tortoise, Late 19th Century, 3 In. 345.00
Group, Man, Trimming Shears, Flowerpot, 5 In. 100.00
Group, Woman, Standing, Floral Bouquets, Wooden Base, Glass Dome, Chinese, 7 In. 207.00
Handle, Umbrella, Fair Scene, Musicians & People, Wearing Masks, Signed, 9 1/2 In. ... 192.00
Microscope, Field, 2 In. 460.00
Miniature, Picture, Actress, Wreath In Hair, Mask, Frame, Russia, c.1910, 3 1/2 In. 2185.00
Miniature, Portrait, Girl, Shawl, Gilt, Ebonized Frame, Signed, c.1890, 5 1/2 x 5 In. 402.00
Miniature, Portrait, Man In Uniform, Woman, 2 1/4 x 2 1/8 In., Pair 1380.00
Miniature, Portrait, Man In Wig, Blue Coat, Gilt Frame, c.1790, 3 3/8 In. 172.50
Miniature, Portrait, Matron, Seated, Lace Shawl, Frame, Signed Kittner, 1846, 4 x 3 In. .. 431.00
Miniature, Portrait, Officer, Oval, Reverse Set, Monogram, Frame, Signed, c.1850, 5 In. . 172.00
Miniature, Portrait, Woman, Hair Curls, Red Dress, Blue Ground, Round Frame, 2 3/4 In. 385.00
Miniature, Portrait, Woman, Renaissance Clothes, Onyx, Wolfratshausen, 8 In. 4313.00
Miniature, Portrait, Woman, Wig, Headband, Dress, Ermine Trim, Initials O.S., 1 3/4 In. . 248.00
Miniature, Portrait, Young Boy, Tree, Dog, Blue Ground, Round Frame, 2 3/4 In. 1100.00
Miniature, Portrait, Young Woman, Blue Eyes, Gold Oval Frame, c.1910, 3 3/4 x 2 3/4 In. 115.00
Miniature, Portrait, Young Woman, Red Dress, Engraved, Pieced Frame, Oval, 1 3/4 In. .. 220.00
Mirror, Dieppe Carved, Oval Mirror, Crest, Lions, Cherubs, Eagle, c.1890, 33 x 20 1/2 In. 1150.00
Okimono, 3 Snow Monkeys, Hear No Evil, See No Evil, Speak No Evil, 1 1/8 In. 70.00
Okimono, Man, Standing, Holding Sword, Japan, Meiji Period 403.00
Okimono, Round, Silver Beetles, Japan, 1 1/2 In. 374.00
Okimono, Warrior, Woman, 3 Oni, Large Bell, Signed Munetoshi, Late 19th Century 373.00
Panel, Rosewood, Greek Temple Shape, Victorian, Late 19th Century, 7 7/8 x 6 1/4 In. .. 252.00
Plaque, Painted, Sexual Positions, Red, Black Border, India, c.1900, 6 x 3 1/4 In., Pair ... 316.00
Puzzle Ball, Hanging, Chinese, 19th Century, 12 In. 115.00
Puzzle Ball, Imperial Figure Finial, Attendant & Toad, Bird & Basket Of Flowers, 15 In. . 1725.00
Ring, Round Sides, Flat Rectangular Top, Brown Circles, Congolise, 1800s 110.00
Scene, Open Gourd Shape, Figures, Sea Monsters, 20th Century, 5 3/4 x 10 In. 978.00
Seal, Rabbit Shape Resting On Rectangular Platform, Late 19th Century, 2 x 2 In. 145.00
Tongs, Salad, Ebony Bands, Decorative Dots, 10 1/2 In., Pair 66.00
Triptych, Mary, Queen Of Scots, Queen Elizabeth & Lord Darnley, Continental, 9 In. 2530.00
Tusk, Man On Skis Drawn By Reindeer, 6 3/4 In. 115.00
Urn, Intertwined Fighting Dragons, Wooden Base, 5 In. 82.00
Vase, Buddhist Saints, Japan, 19th Century, 5 1/2 In., Pair 230.00
Vase, Cover, Immortals, Flattened Oval, Qing Dynasty, Chinese, 9 In., Pair 980.00
Vase, Gourd, Lion Mask Handles, Figure In Mountain Landscape, 5 In. 115.00
Vase, Stork, Palm Tree, Openwork Trunk, Carved, 8 In. 55.00

JACK-IN-THE-PULPIT vases, oddly shaped like trumpets, resemble the
wild plant called jack-in-the-pulpit. The design originated in the late
Victorian years. Vases in the jack-in-the-pulpit shape were made of
ceramic or glass, and the complete list of page references can be found
in the index.

Vase, Green Diamond Quilted, Silver Flecks, 9 1/2 In. 67.00
Vase, Multicolored Enamel Flowers, Interior Yellow Flowers, 7 1/2 In. 145.00

JADE is the name for two different minerals, nephrite and jadeite. Nephrite is the mineral used for most early Oriental carvings. Jade is a very tough stone that is found in many colors from dark green to pale lavender. Jade carvings are still being made in the old styles, so collectors must be careful not to be fooled by recent pieces. Jade jewelry is found in this book under Jewelry.

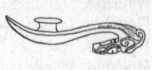

Bottle, White, Carved, Flattened Oval, Ring Handle, Chinese, 13 7/8 In.	170.00
Bowl, Translucent, Foot Ring, Late 19th Century, 5 1/2 In.	2645.00
Box, Pomander, Cover, Pierced, 8 Precious Emblems, Chinese, 18th Century, 6 In.	489.00
Ewer, Spinach Green, Engraved, Tao-Tich Masks, Dragon Handles, 12 x 13 In.	805.00
Figurine, Bird, Celadon, Fitted Stand, Chinese, Late 19th Century, Box, 8 In., Pair	690.00
Figurine, Elephant, Spinach, Chinese, 2 3/4 In.	100.00
Figurine, Fisherman, With Basket, Jumping Fish, 19th Century, 4 x 4 In.	315.00
Figurine, Foo Dog, Soo Chow, Carved, Reclining, 4 Puppies, Stand, 3 1/2 x 1 3/4 In.	440.00
Figurine, Foo Dog, Standing, Yellow Green, Carved, Chinese, Early 1800s, 3 x 2 3/4 In.	330.00
Figurine, Meirin, White, Loose Robe, Holding Scholar's Object, Chinese, 1900s, 7 In.	980.00
Figurine, Seated Woman, 2 Attendants, 3 1/2 In.	600.00
Figurine, Woman, Robe, Holding Gourd, Caramel, Stained, Wooden Base, 11 1/2 In.	80.00
Letter Opener, Cased, Gold, Semiprecious Stones, Encrusted Handle, 14K Gold, 7 3/4 In.	315.00
Plaque, Immortals In Landscape, Pale Celadon, Burlwood Frame, 4 3/4 x 8 1/4 In.	290.00
Screen, Celadon, Riverscape, Flowers On Reverse, Stand, Qing Dynasty, 12 In., Pair	1035.00
Vase, Buffalo, Relief Dragons, Gray Green, Green Mottling, Cover, 10 x 8 In.	290.00
Vase, Carved, Tao-Tich Masks, Olive Green, Cover, 5 1/4 In.	115.00
Vase, Spinach, Lappets, Oval, Thick Mouth & Handles, Chinese, 5 1/4 In.	8050.00
Water Dropper, Celadon, Creature, Open Mouth, Dragon, 3 In.	2185.00

JAPANESE WOODBLOCK PRINTS are listed in this book in the Print category under Japanese.

JASPERWARE can be made in different ways. Some pieces are made from a solid colored clay with applied raised designs of a contrasting colored clay. Other pieces are made entirely of one color clay with raised decorations that are glazed with a contrasting color. Additional pieces of jasperware may also be listed in the Wedgwood category or under various art potteries.

Cachepot, Underplate, Bell Shape, c.1900, 8 1/4 x 8 1/2 In.	310.00
Cheese Dome, Acorn Finial, Acanthus, Leaves, Putti, c.1900, 11 x 8 In.	145.00
Creamer, Figure Of Queen Each Side, Flowers Around Figures, 3 In.	55.00
Plaque, Art Nouveau Style, Woman, White, Flowing Hair, Flowers, Green, 13 x 10 In.	60.00
Plaque, Blue & White, Round, Psyche & Infant Cupid, Blue Ground, 7 1/2 x 8 In.	290.00

JEWELRY, whether made from gold and precious gems or plastic and colored glass, is popular with collectors. Values are determined by the intrinsic value of the stones and metal and by the skill of the craftsmen and designers. Victorian and older jewelry have been collected since the 1950s. More recent interests are Art Deco and Edwardian styles, Mexican and Danish silver jewelry, and beads of all kinds. Copies of almost all styles are being made. American Indian jewelry is listed in the Indian category.

Barrette, Ribbon Design, Green Gold, Edwardian, France, 18K Gold	201.00
Bracelet, 7 Amethysts, 18K Gold, 1900	1150.00
Bracelet, 12 Geometric Links, Platinum, Diamonds, 1935	1610.00
Bracelet, 27 Diamond Center Elliptical, Linked Diamonds, Platinum, 1930s, 6 3/8 In.	2148.00
Bracelet, 43 Sapphires, 282 Diamonds, Platinum, Art Deco, 7 1/2 In.	3140.00
Bracelet, Agate Barrel Link, 5 Links, Suspending Heart Form Lock	260.00
Bracelet, Angel, Slides With Rubies, Pearls, Opals, Art Nouveau, 14K Gold, 1910	2120.00
Bracelet, Baguette, Pave Diamonds Platinum, Boucher, 1945	375.00
Bracelet, Bakelite, Alternating Brown & Clear Bands, Etched, Rhinestones, 3/4-In. Wide	295.00
Bracelet, Bakelite, Bowtie, Cream & Black, 5/8-In. Wide	2820.00
Bracelet, Bakelite, Chain, Suspended Dog Related Items, 6 1/2 In.	645.00
Bracelet, Bakelite, Crosshatch, Inlaid, Multicolored, 7/8-In. Wide	7050.00
Bracelet, Bakelite, Cuff, 2 Serpents, Sphere In Center, 1 1/2-In. Wide	3525.00
Bracelet, Bakelite, Random Dots, Orange, Cream Dots, 1/2-In. Wide	1880.00

Bracelet, Bakelite, Spiky Multicolored Teeth 8910.00
Bracelet, Bangle, 9 Round Cut Garnets, Fitted Case, Kendall & Dent, England 545.00
Bracelet, Bangle, 11 Round Diamonds, Reticulated Mount, 14K Yellow Gold, c.1960 .... 690.00
Bracelet, Bangle, 15 Mine Cut Diamonds, 14K Gold 1490.00
Bracelet, Bangle, 38 Collet Diamonds, Black Enamel, 14K Gold, Victorian 630.00
Bracelet, Bangle, 62 Diamonds, 14K White Gold, Rose Pearl 990.00
Bracelet, Bangle, Applied Lion's Head, Diamond Eyes, Mouth, Victorian, 14K Gold 590.00
Bracelet, Bangle, Black Enamel Leaves, Diamonds, 14K Gold, Stamped KJG 920.00
Bracelet, Bangle, Black Tracery Enamel, Leaves 315.00
Bracelet, Bangle, Black Tracery Enamel, Scalloped Edge, 14K Gold, 1865, Pair 1095.00
Bracelet, Bangle, Graduated Opals, 15K Gold 1265.00
Bracelet, Bangle, Hinged, 12 Oval Sapphires, 3 Diamonds, 14K Yellow Gold 430.00
Bracelet, Bangle, Hinged, Hammered Finish, 22K Gold, Zolotas 2185.00
Bracelet, Bangle, Hinged, Latticework, Diamonds, Turquoise, Buccellati, 18K Gold, 1950 6670.00
Bracelet, Bangle, Openwork, 3 Square Cut Sapphires, Edwardian, 14K Gold 375.00
Bracelet, Bangle, Oval Buckle Plaque, Half Pearls, Blue Enamel, Victorian, 14K Gold ... 800.00
Bracelet, Bangle, Ribbed Design, Oval, 15K Gold 345.00
Bracelet, Bangle, Silver, Shadowbox Design, Inlaid, Mexico, 2 5/8-In. Wide 20.00
Bracelet, Bangle, Split Pearl Fleur-De-Lis, Turquoise Bead 488.00
Bracelet, Bangle, Turquoise, Pearl, 10K Gold 1095.00
Bracelet, Cameo, Lava, 11 Plaques, Pompeii, Classical Women Profiles, Victorian, 7 In. .. 520.00
Bracelet, Charm, 6 Hearts, Clover Shape Links, 14K Gold 375.00
Bracelet, Charm, 10 Gold & Silver Charms, Colored Stones, 14K Gold 175.00
Bracelet, Charm, Coin, 14K Gold 400.00
Bracelet, Charm, Embossed, 9K Gold, Coins, Trinkets 375.00
Bracelet, Charm, Malachite, Agate, 14K Gold 805.00
Bracelet, Citrine Link, Curb Links, 18K Gold 460.00
Bracelet, Coin, 5 Gold Sovereigns, Dated 1911, 1913 & 1917, 18K Gold, 8 In. 1150.00
Bracelet, Cuff, Engraved, Strapwork, Flowers, Sterling Silver, Signed, Georg Jensen 545.00
Bracelet, Cuff, Geometric Design, Yellow, Green, Red Enamel 745.00
Bracelet, Cuff, Gypsy, Applied Gold Cameos, 14K Gold 920.00
Bracelet, Cuff, Hinged Buckle, Lapis, Diamonds, Tiffany & Co., 18K Gold 3910.00
Bracelet, Cuff, Woven Wire Herringbone Design, 14K Gold 690.00
Bracelet, Diamond & Sapphire, 74 Beads, Art Deco, 7 In. 3795.00
Bracelet, Diamond Line, 32 Cut Diamonds, Art Deco, 7 1/4 In. 7475.00
Bracelet, Diamond, 16 Sapphires, 14K White Gold, Art Deco, 7 1/4 In. 1460.00
Bracelet, Diamond, Art Deco, 18K White Gold, 6 1/2 In. 2240.00
Bracelet, Diamond, Geometric Links, Art Deco, 17K White, Yellow Gold, 6 5/8 In. 1035.00
Bracelet, Diamond, Pearl, Signed, King, 18K Gold, 2 1/2-In. Wide 1725.00
Bracelet, Diamond, Ruby, Art Deco, Platinum Flexible Mount, 1920-1930, 7 x 1/4 In. ... 3910.00
Bracelet, Domed Links, Cabochon, Turquoise, Garnet, Renaissance Revival, 7 In. 230.00
Bracelet, Enamel, Cobalt Blue, Signed, Cartier, London, Polished, 18K Gold, 8 In. 1610.00
Bracelet, Figural, Dragon Head Terminals, Green, Yellow, Red, Brown, 18K Gold 575.00
Bracelet, Figure 8-Shape Links, Pouch, Signed, M. Buccellati, 18K Gold 1495.00
Bracelet, Flexible, Flower Engraved Links, Silver Tone, Hobe, 7 In. 200.00
Bracelet, Floral & Elliptical Links, 5 Button Pearls, Art Nouveau, 18K Gold, 7 1/2 In. ... 690.00
Bracelet, Geometric Links, Diamonds, Art Deco, Platinum, 6 3/4 In. 6170.00
Bracelet, Gold Plaques, Jade, Art Deco, Tiffany & Co., 7 1/2 In. .... *Illus* 4600.00
Bracelet, Gold Swirl, Pave Rosettes, Pennino, 1945 .... 490.00
Bracelet, Hinged Bangle, Emerald Cut Amethyst, Diamonds, 14K Gold Band, 1940 ..... 1150.00
Bracelet, Hinged Bangle, Lion's Head, Diamond In Mouth, Art Nouveau, 14K Gold 865.00
Bracelet, Intaglio Citrines, Carved Image Of 4 Seasons, Onyx, Diamonds, Art Deco 8520.00
Bracelet, Link, Buckle Closure, Silver, Signed, Hermes, 8 1/2 In. 690.00
Bracelet, Link, Diamond, Synthetic Blue Sapphire, Art Deco, c.1930, 7 In. 920.00
Bracelet, Link, Faux Rose Agates, Rubies, Art Nouveau, Silver Tone, 6 1/2 In. 69.00

Jewelry, Bracelet, Gold Plaques, Jade,
Art Deco, Tiffany & Co., 7 1/2 In.

Bracelet, Milled Edge, Florentine, Italy, 18K Gold 460.00
Bracelet, Moonstone, Links, Clusters, Bezel Set, Arts & Crafts, Zircon, 6 1/2 In. 750.00
Bracelet, Oval Carved Crystal Plaques, Diamond Centers, 14K White Gold, Art Deco ... 765.00
Bracelet, Serpentine, Bangle, Mottled Green, Russet, 3 Piece 115.00
Bracelet, Silver, Hollow Links, Retro Moderne, Mexico 1265.00
Bracelet, Silver, Link, Round Balls, Taxco, Mexico, 5 1/2 In. 140.00
Bracelet, Silver, Links, Center Plate, Mexico, 7 3/4 In. 185.00
Bracelet, Silver, Round Links, Etched, Mexico, 9 In. 69.00
Bracelet, Silver, Star & Geometric Line, Enamel, Hinged Plaques, Art Deco, 7 In. 499.00
Bracelet, Singa Heads, Cowry Shells, Bronze, Indonesia, 19th Century 170.00
Bracelet, Slide, Flexible, Turquoise Enamel Buckle, Victorian, 18K Gold 1380.00
Bracelet, Slide, Seed Pearls, Brickwork, Foxtail Fringe, Victorian, 14K Gold 345.00
Bracelet, Slide, Seed Pearls, Opals, 14K Gold 485.00
Bracelet, Snake Shape, 4 Ruby Eyes, 14K Yellow Gold 920.00
Bracelet, Sterling Silver, 6 Round Medallions, Classical Figure Profiles, 1900, 7 1/2 In. .. 470.00
Bracelet, Sterling Silver, Abstract Open Shape Links, Signed, Henning Koppel, 7 3/4 In. . 920.00
Bracelet, Sterling Silver, Cuff, Wide Abstract Design, Tiffany & Co., Italy, 1975 .... 460.00
Bracelet, Sterling Silver, Double Links, Toggle Clasp, 8 In. 260.00
Bracelet, Sterling Silver, Enamel, Rider On Reindeer, Cerulean Blue Ground 200.00
Bracelet, Sterling Silver, Floral, Rosette Links, Signed, Georg Jensen, Denmark, 18 In. ... 500.00
Bracelet, Sterling Silver, Link, Ternini, 8 In. 25.00
Bracelet, Sterling Silver, Tapered, Incised, Bow, Arrows, Antonio Pineda, Mexico, 1950s . 460.00
Bracelet, Sterling Silver, Tennis, Oval Sapphires, Rose Cut Diamonds, 1980s 470.00
Bracelet, Wide, Baguette, Pave Diamonds, Art Deco, 1940 .... 230.00
Bracelet, Winged Scarabs, Winged Snake, Egyptian Revival 980.00
Bracelet, Woven Wire, Box Clasp, Oval Plaque, Applied Bird, 14K Gold, Victorian 750.00
Buckle, Dragon Head, Inlaid Silver, 2 Characters On Reverse, Bronze, 5 In. 490.00
Buckle, Enamel, Silver Gilt, Clipped Corners, Bow & Swag, Edwardian 400.00
Buckle, Pierced Shape, Numerous Small Stones, Flowers Enamel, Silver 109.00
Buckle, Silver, Curved Rectangular, France, Late 1800s, 2 1/4 x 1 7/8 In., Pair 115.00
Buckle, Tsunami, Tidal Wave, Moonstone, 18K Gold, Nora Pearson, c.1980 .... 978.00
Chain, Watch, Silver, Wide Oval Trace Links, Victorian, 62 In. 172.00
Charm, Erotic, Silver, 1 In. 46.00
Cigar Cutter, Chased Flower Vine Design, 14K Gold 260.00
Cigarette Case, Basket Weave, Synthetic Sapphire Thumbpiece, 18K Gold, 3 x 5 In. 1495.00
Cigarette Case, Sterling Silver, Enamel, 4 Game Birds In Flight, 4 x 3 In. 520.00
Cigarette Case, Sterling Silver, Enamel, Jumping Sailfish In Sea, 4 x 3 In. 575.00
Cigarette Case, Sterling Silver, Enamel, Maiden In Sea, Shiebler, Art Nouveau, No. 47 .. 1998.00
Cigarette Case, Sterling Silver, Engraved Lines, Red Stone Cabochon Thumbpiece 400.00
Cigarette Case, Sterling Silver, Etched, Horse & Rider Jumping, 4 x 3 In. 290.00
Cigarette Holder, Square Ruby Tip, Sapphires, Box, Mellerio, Paris, 18K Gold 320.00
Clasp, Bird & Flower, Plaque Shape, Art Nouveau, 14K Gold 430.00
Clip, Citrine, Stylized Bow Knot, 14K Yellow, Rose Gold 515.00
Clip, Diamond, Modified Triangle Shape, Art Deco, Platinum 1380.00
Clip, Dress, Baguette, Pear Cut Emeralds, Coro, 1940, Pair 290.00
Clip, Dress, Coral & Onyx, Cartier, 18K Yellow Gold, Pair 920.00
Clip, Dress, Diamond, Ruby, Platinum Triangular Mount, Art Deco, c.1935, 2 x 1 1/2 In. .. 5290.00
Clip, Dress, Faceted, Pear Shape Diamonds, Eisenberg, Platinum, 1940 .... 260.00
Clip, Fish, Tropical, Blue, Green, Orange Enamel, Italy, 18K Gold 290.00
Clip, Platypus, Enamel, Orange, Yellow Guilloche, 18K Gold 258.00
Clip, Silver, Comical Face, Hammered & Incised, Kalo, Impressed Mark, 1 1/2 In. 518.00
Clip, Silver, Hammered, Triangle, Spiral At Top, Hammered Silver, Holland, 2 In. 92.00
Collar, Necklace, Flowers, Beaded, Slide Clasp, Arts & Crafts, 1908, 13 In. 3565.00
Comb, 4 Rhinestones, 3 Turquoise Pieces, Gold Decoration, 4 1/8 x 2 3/4 In. 48.00
Cuff Links, 3 Rhinestones In Handle, Derringer, 1 x 1 1/8 In. 17.00
Cuff Links, Anchor Shape, Rope Twist Accents, Russian Hallmark, 14K Gold 345.00
Cuff Links, Barbells, Sterling Silver, Tiffany & Co., 1 1/8 x 7/16 In. 110.00
Cuff Links, Blue Enamel, Octagonal, Engraved, Diamond, 14K Gold 230.00
Cuff Links, Bowling Ball & Pins, Sloan & Co., 14K Gold 175.00
Cuff Links, Button Form, Bead Medallion, Georg Jensen, 1 1/2 In. 150.00
Cuff Links, Chased Gold Lion's Heads, 18K Gold 1380.00
Cuff Links, Diamond, Ruby Cabochon, 18K Gold 5460.00
Cuff Links, Diamond, Yellow Gold Center, Engraved Platinum Edges 290.00

Cuff Links, Elliptical, Laurel & Ribbon, Art Nouveau, France, 18K Gold 290.00
Cuff Links, Hair, 14K Gold Pinwheel, 1 1/16 In. 325.00
Cuff Links, Horse Head, Diamonds, 14K Yellow Gold, Stone Eyes, 1 In. 300.00
Cuff Links, Ivory Elephants, Blankets Trimmed In Gold, 1 In. 125.00
Cuff Links, Mine Cut Diamond, Oval, Victorian, 14K & 18K Gold 86.00
Cuff Links, Mother-Of-Pearl, Cultured Pearl, France, 14K Yellow Gold 44.00
Cuff Links, Musical, Brahms Lullaby 50.00
Cuff Links, Oval, Chased Edges, Diamond, Victorian, 14K Gold 170.00
Cuff Links, Rectangular, Red & White Enameled Stripes, Allsopp-Steller, 14K Gold 145.00
Cuff Links, Round, Cobalt Blue Stripes, Richardson & Co., 14K Gold 175.00
Cuff Links, Sterling Silver, Circular, Concave, 2 Curved Lines, Georg Jensen, 3/4 In. 185.00
Cuff Links, Sterling Silver, Circular, Concave, 2 Lines, Georg Jensen, Denmark, 2 In. 160.00
Cuff Links, Sterling Silver, Enamel, 4 Vices, Women, Gambling, Horses, Liquor 130.00
Cuff Links, Sterling Silver, Grotesque Faces, Flexible Bar Links, Art Nouveau, Gorham . . 460.00
Cuff Links, Sterling Silver, Pierced Fish Shape, Antonio Pineda, Mexico 460.00
Cuff Links, Sterling Silver, Round, Horse Head Chased Top, Georg Jensen, 3 In. 250.00
Cuff Links, Sterling Silver, Sculptured Faces, Owlets, Garnet Eyes 110.00
Cuff Links, Tortoise, Hare, Frog, Bull, 14K Gold 1380.00
Cuff Links, Viking Ship At Sunrise, Norway, 1/2 x 1/4 In. 110.00
Earrings, 18K Gold Wire, Teardrop Shape, Platinum Setting, 11 Diamonds, Cartier 2415.00
Earrings, 2 Caliber Rubies, Signed, 18K Gold 690.00
Earrings, 3 Diamonds, Collet Set, Curved Mount, Platinum, 14K White Gold 575.00
Earrings, 3 Marquise Cut Diamonds, 18K Gold 690.00
Earrings, 4 Pearl Cruciform, Diamond Center, 14K White Gold 690.00
Earrings, Abstract Chased Design, Signed, 18K Gold 2185.00
Earrings, Black Pearl, With Jackets, 14K Yellow Gold 22.00
Earrings, Bracelet, Sterling Silver, Amethyst, Leaves, Flowerhead, Georg Jensen, 7 In. . . . 1495.00
Earrings, Central Baroque Pearl, Miriam Haskell, 1945 . . . . 315.00
Earrings, Citrine, Faceted, Rope Twist Gold Frame, 14K Gold 490.00
Earrings, Citrine, Scalloped Frame, Yellow Gold, Platinum 360.00
Earrings, Cluster, White Gold Bead Stamen, 14K White Gold 430.00
Earrings, Coral In Leaves, 18K Yellow Gold 1025.00
Earrings, Cornucopia Holding Bouquet Of Flowers, Platinum 805.00
Earrings, Cultured Pearl, Pave Diamonds 1380.00
Earrings, Dangle, Colorless Paste, Ribbon Tied Leaves, Screw Backs, c.1920s 315.00
Earrings, Diamond, Large Baroque Pearls, 18K Gold 1955.00
Earrings, Diamond, Sapphire, Art Deco Style, White Gold, 1 In. 250.00
Earrings, Diamonds, Baguette Cut, Spoke Wheel Shape, 18K Yellow Gold 4140.00
Earrings, Dome Shape, Bogoff, 1950 . . . . 290.00
Earrings, Double Hoops, Ribbed, Signed Bulgari, 18K Gold 920.00
Earrings, Emerald, Bead, Leafy Swag, Gold Mount 490.00
Earrings, Faceted, Square Cut Stones, Weiss, 1950 . . . . 260.00
Earrings, Flower Shape, Diamonds, Pearls, 14K White Gold, 1840s 560.00
Earrings, Flower, 4 Marquise Diamonds, 18K White Gold 1495.00
Earrings, Flowerhead, Heart Shape Moonstone Petals, Sapphire, 14K Gold, c.1940 . . . . . . 1090.00
Earrings, Garnet Cluster, 12 Garnets, 18K Gold 230.00
Earrings, Gold Leaves With Dangling Pearls, Gold Filigree, Miriam Haskell, 1945 . . . . . . 175.00
Earrings, Gold, Granulated Work, Carnelian, Southeast Asia, 18th Century, 1/2 In. 175.00
Earrings, Large Central Baroque Pearl, Gold Diamonds, 1950 . . . . 290.00
Earrings, Mabe, Pearl, Leaf Prongs, 14K Gold 520.00
Earrings, Man's Face, Flowing Hair, Serpent, Art Nouveau, 14K Gold 230.00
Earrings, Moonstone, Sapphire Terminals, Polished 14K Gold Scrolls 315.00
Earrings, Necklace, 3 Crescent Shape Gold, Diamonds, Miriam Haskell, 1945 . . . . 345.00
Earrings, Openwork Flower, Suspended Freshwater Pearls, Art Nouveau, 18K Gold 1880.00
Earrings, Pave Diamond, Marquise, 1950 . . . . 200.00
Earrings, Pave, Baguette Diamonds, Sterling Silver, 1945 . . . . 575.00
Earrings, Pearl, Diamond, 14K Yellow Gold 255.00
Earrings, Pearls, Round Circular Pave Diamond Tops, Platinum 860.00
Earrings, Pendant, Amethyst Tops, Graduated Collet Set Amethysts, 14K Gold 320.00
Earrings, Pendant, Angelskin Coral, Diamond, Collet Set 1035.00
Earrings, Pendant, Circular Cut Diamonds, 14K Gold 690.00
Earrings, Pendant, Diamond, Opal, Bezel Set, Melee Tops, Platinum Top 175.00
Earrings, Pendant, Diamond, Sapphire, Art Deco, Platinum, c.1910, 1 1/7 In. 1456.00

Earrings, Pendant, Diamonds, Sapphire, Art Deco, Platinum 1725.00
Earrings, Pendant, Floret Shape, Overlapping 18K Gold Wire Twists, Round Diamonds .. 345.00
Earrings, Pendant, Flower Head Shape, Collet Set Diamonds, Silver Topped Gold Mounts 690.00
Earrings, Pendant, Round Turquoise, Center Star & Rose Cut Diamond, Victorian 315.00
Earrings, Pendant, South Sea Pearls, 10 1/2 mm, 20 Small Diamonds, Gold, 14 In. 1900.00
Earrings, Peridot, Round Diamond, 18K Gold, Kim Klementis 750.00
Earrings, Pink Sapphire, 20 Bead, Collet Set Diamonds, Cathy Carmendy, 20K Gold 430.00
Earrings, Red Garnets, Pear Shape, Post & Friction, 14K Yellow Gold 49.00
Earrings, Rhinestone Clusters, Silver Tone, Faux Gray Topaz, Weiss 145.00
Earrings, Ribbed Design, Row Of Ivy Leaves, Signed, 18K Gold 690.00
Earrings, Rose Cut Diamonds, Blue Enamel, 14K Yellow Gold, 20th Century 260.00
Earrings, Round Banded Agates, 14K Gold 145.00
Earrings, Rows Of Baguette Cut Sapphire, 18K Gold 315.00
Earrings, Ruby, Diamond, Platinum Mount, c.1940 .... 1725.00
Earrings, Sapphires, Art Deco, 18K Yellow Gold, c.1920 .... 785.00
Earrings, Scrolling Shapes, Center Emerald Cut Emeralds, 3 Diamonds, c.1940 .... 1456.00
Earrings, Signed, Elsa Peretti, 18K Gold 805.00
Earrings, Silver Tone, Rhinestone, Fleur-De-Lis Setting, Penino 115.00
Earrings, Spray Design, Platinum 2070.00
Earrings, Sterling Silver, Bird On Branch, Heart Shape, Screw Type, Georg Jensen 130.00
Earrings, Sterling Silver, Hoop, Pierced Figures, Antonio Pineda, Mexico 115.00
Earrings, Sterling Silver, Leaf Shape, Green Enamel, Signed, Brian, 1 1/8 In. 65.00
Earrings, Sterling Silver, Open Heart, Bird, Branch, Screw Back, Georg Jensen, 1/2 In. .. 150.00
Earrings, Stud, Diamond, 14K Yellow Gold Mounting 345.00
Earrings, Stylized Organic Shape, Emeralds, 18K Gold 2760.00
Earrings, Sunburst Shanked By Trefoil Design, France, 18K Gold, c.1800 .... 315.00
Earrings, Swirling Leaf Shape, Diamond Set Petals, 18K Yellow Gold, c.1950 .... 1065.00
Earrings, Teardrop, White Figures Above Beaded Border, Wedgwood, 1 1/2 In. 460.00
Earrings, Tourmaline, Pink Cabochon, 14K Gold 545.00
Hatpins are listed in this book in the Hatpin category.
Lavaliere, Diamond, Synthetic Ruby, Pearl Chain, Edwardian, Continental, 20 1/2 In. 1955.00
Lavaliere, Pendant, Scrolled Openwork, Emerald, Diamonds, Pearl, Edwardian 1880.00
Lavaliere, Platinum, Diamonds, Sapphire, Openwork, Art Deco, Tiffany & Co., 16 1/4 In. 4370.00
Lavaliere, Plique-A-Jour, Green Enamel, Freshwater Pearl Drop, Jugendstil, Hallmark ... 1495.00
Lavaliere, Rose Cut Diamonds, Sapphire, 18K Gold 630.00
Lipstick Case, Engraved, Mirror, Buccellati, 18K Gold Thumbpiece, 2 3/4 x 3 1/4 In. 805.00
Locket, Black Enamel, Seed Pearl Design, Victorian, 14K Gold, 1 x 3/4 In. 315.00
Locket, Chain, Beading, Wire Twist, Seed Pearls, 14K Gold, 26 In. 690.00
Locket, Chain, Diamond, Shield Shape, Victorian, 18K Yellow Gold, c.1870 .... 4370.00
Locket, Circular, Garnet, Diamonds, Suspended Batons, Twisted 18K Gold Wire, 1880 ... 635.00
Locket, Enamel Cherub, Lyre, 18K Gold, Etruscan Revival 1035.00
Locket, Enamel Flowers, 2 Compartments, Engraved, 14K Gold, c.1880 .... 260.00
Locket, Filigree Octagon, Link Chain, Gold Plated Beads, 14K Yellow Gold 320.00
Locket, Heart Shape, 14K Gold, Pave Pearls, Seed Pearl & Link Chain, Edwardian, 28 In. 825.00
Locket, Leaves, Ruby, Diamond, 18K Gold Mount, Hallmarks France 1725.00
Locket, Mourning, Jet, Platinum & Diamond, Lady Waller, Died August 30th, 1878, 2 In. 770.00
Locket, Photograph, Grosgrain Ribbon, Victorian, 18K Gold, c.1876 .... 318.00
Locket, Platinum, 3 Circular Cut Diamonds, Green Enamel, Art Deco 920.00
Locket, Shakudo, Peacock, 15K Gold, c.1870 .... 1265.00
Minauderie, Gold, Black Enamel, Geometric, Lipstick, Compact, Art Deco 690.00
Money Clip, Crystal Jumping Horse & Rider, 24K Gold 1375.00
Necklace, 2 Black Onyx Stones, 2 Diamonds, 2 Seed Pearls, Victorian, 14K Gold, 1871 .. 1400.00
Necklace, 2 Cultured Pearls Strands, 14K Yellow Gold Clasp With Pearls & Rubies 980.00
Necklace, 19 Pearls, Spaced By Curb & Fancy Links, 18K Gold, c.1925 .... 460.00
Necklace, 23 Sapphires, Art Nouveau Style, 14K Gold, 16 In. 730.00
Necklace, 336 Baguette Diamonds, Graduated, Riviera 10800.00
Necklace, Agate, Light Blue Enamel Plaques, 14K Gold 550.00
Necklace, Amber & Blue Stones, Beads, Diamond Shape Earrings, Dior, 1960 .... 250.00
Necklace, Arts & Crafts, Sterling Silver, Blue-Green Enamel Pendant, 2 1/8 In. 460.00
Necklace, Chain, Beehive Shapes, Double Circular Sections, 14K Yellow Gold, 1880 .... 980.00
Necklace, Chain, Box Link, Circular Flower Balls, 14K Gold, c.1920 .... 748.00
Necklace, Chain, Diamond Encrusted Leopard Heads, Ruby Eyes, 14K Gold, 16 In. 3450.00

Necklace, Chain, Enameled Navette Shape Links, Plique-A-Jour, Art Nouveau, 14K Gold	575.00
Necklace, Chain, Flower & Leaf Beads, 28 Hollow Links, 18K Gold, c.1840	4890.00
Necklace, Chain, Link, Niello, Rose Gold Links, 42 In.	345.00
Necklace, Chain, Scarab, Turquoise, Scrolled Links, Art Nouveau, 14K Gold, 27 In.	1840.00
Necklace, Chain, Slide, Wire Twist Links, Moss Agate, Victorian, 18K Gold, 66 In.	1840.00
Necklace, Chain, Sterling Silver, Rope Twist Curb Links, Tiffany & Co., 16 In.	320.00
Necklace, Cherry Amber, 35 Graduated Beads, Elliptical, Box Clasp, 23 1/2 In.	230.00
Necklace, Choker, Double Rope Twist, Signed NM, 18K Gold, 16 In.	2990.00
Necklace, Chrysoberyl, Green, Yellow, 14K Gold	1150.00
Necklace, Coral Beads, Quartz, Sibyl Dunlop, 1920s	4000.00
Necklace, Coral Beads, Wire Twist Design, Gold Beads	1035.00
Necklace, Coral, Cherub Medallion, Roses, Floral Pendants, 14K Gold Chain, c.1900	1850.00
Necklace, Diamond, Textured, Flexible, Signed, Tiffany & Co., 18K Gold Link, 17 3/4 In.	630.00
Necklace, Enamel, Emerald Beads, Winged Sun Disc, Cobras, Egyptian Revival, c.1900 . .	10062.00
Necklace, Etruscan Revival, 14K Gold Beads, 16 In.	1150.00
Necklace, Faux Pearl, Flower Clasp, 8-Strand Pearl Cascade, Kenneth Jay Lane	430.00
Necklace, Floral Crystals, Black Centers & Beadwork Ground, Coppola E Toppo	1840.00
Necklace, Flower, Baroque Pearl Drops, 1950	259.00
Necklace, Fringe, Pear Shape Garnets, Etruscan Revival, 18K Gold Beads, 15 3/4 In.	4887.00
Necklace, Gilt Collar, Filigree Flowers & Foliage, Chanel, France	1093.00
Necklace, Gold Swirl Design, Pave Rosettes, Pennino, 1945	520.00
Necklace, Lalique, Feuilles De Lierre, Ivy Leaves, Opalescent Green, Silk Cord, 40 In. . . .	2990.00
Necklace, Large Diamonds At Neckline, Bogoff, 1945	520.00
Necklace, Mandarin Court, Carved Fruit Pits, Blue Peking Glass, Early 19th Century	345.00
Necklace, Medallion, Gold, Enamel, Round, Engraved, Arabic, Flowers, 3 In.	260.00
Necklace, Moonstone, Sapphire, Emerald, Curb Link Chain, 14K Gold, 1940s, 17 In.	2645.00
Necklace, Mother & Baby Elephants, Open Work Carving, Ivory Beads, 17 1/2 In.	66.00
Necklace, Nugget Pendant, 14K Yellow Gold	575.00
Necklace, Ojime Bead, 39 Various Beads, 19th Century	920.00
Necklace, Opal, Sapphire Beads, 14K White Gold, Diamond Box Clasp, 22 In.	490.00
Necklace, Oval Pendant, Pearls, Rubies, Garnet, Renaissance Revival Style	460.00
Necklace, Pearl Mesh Chain, Suspended Circular Brooch, Seed Pearls, Edwardian	10000.00
Necklace, Pendant, Aquamarine, Pearls, Triple Curb Link Chain, Arts & Crafts, 18 In. . . .	5875.00
Necklace, Pendant, Dahlia, Blue, Pate-De-Verre, Gilt Metal, Segmented Chain, 1930s	690.00
Necklace, Pendant, Sterling Silver, Carved, Turquoise, 19 1/2 In.	175.00
Necklace, Pierced Swag Shape Links, 4 Pearls, Art Nouveau, 17 In.	230.00
Necklace, Round, Geometric Links, Retro, 14K Pink Gold, Hallmark L.B., 16 In.	460.00
Necklace, Shell Cameo, Rosettes, Victorian, 14 In.	862.00
Necklace, Silver Florets, Shells, Pearls, Suspended Cross, Australia, 1890, 18 In.	1765.00
Necklace, Silver Tone, Faux Amethysts, Citrines, Faux Pearl Drops, Alice Caviness, 13 In.	460.00
Necklace, Silver, Navajo Pearls, Stamped, Graduated Beads, 17 In.	130.00
Necklace, Silver, Teardrop Center, Tapered Side Pieces, Leaves, Beads, Turquoise, 18 In. .	55.00
Necklace, Snake Shape, Cut Ruby Eyes, 18K Yellow Gold	517.00
Necklace, Spiral Mesh Link Flexible Rope, Tubular Shape, 18K Gold, c.1870, 17 1/2 In. . .	460.00
Necklace, Sterling Silver, Moonstone Pendants, Labradorite Links, Georg Jensen, 16 In. . .	7475.00
Necklace, Synthetic Ruby, Seed Pearl, Edwardian, 14K Yellow Gold, c.1900, 17 In.	635.00
Necklace, Thorn, Leaf Pendants, Seed Pearls, Art Nouveau, 18K Gold, 17 In.	1955.00
Necklace, Tubogas, Flexible White 18K Gold, Yellow Gold Studs, Pouch, Bulgari	2990.00
Necklace, Turquoise, Agate, Pearl, c.1880, 19 1/2 In.	575.00
Pendant, $20 Liberty Coin, Basketweave Mount With 6 Diamonds, America, 1927	405.00
Pendant, 3 Emeralds, 10 Diamonds, Pearl, Chain, Gold, George IV, c.1800	532.00
Pendant, Anemone, Pearl, Diamond, Enamel, Art Nouveau, 14K Gold . . . . *Illus*	1840.00
Pendant, Bow, Center Diamond, Small Diamond Surround, Edwardian, 1895	1955.00
Pendant, Bow, Rose Gold, Seed Pearls, Diamond, c.1860	315.00
Pendant, Brass, Scrolling Dragon, Borneo, 19th Century, 2 1/2 In.	58.00
Pendant, Cameo, Shell, 4 Women Bathers, Retractable Bail, Victorian	862.00
Pendant, Carved Coral, Flowerhead, Art Deco, 14K Gold Mount	375.00
Pendant, Chrysanthemum, Diamond, Freshwater Pearl Petals, Edwardian, 14K Gold	259.00
Pendant, Coin Silver, American Indian Dancer, Inlaid Stone Chips, Turquoise, 1 In.	45.00
Pendant, Diamond Center, Modern, 14K Yellow Gold.	220.00
Pendant, Gold Repousse, Peacock, Granulated Beads, India, 19th Century, 1 3/4 In.	115.00
Pendant, Goldfish, Emerald Eyes, Stamped Tiffany & Co., 18K Gold, 3 In.	920.00

Pendant, Jade, Carved, Arched Top, Dragon, Foo Dog, Lotus, 2 1/2 x 1 1/2 In. 575.00
Pendant, Jadeite, Deer, Chinese Characters, 19th Century, 2 1/4 x 1 1/2 In. 345.00
Pendant, Panther, Gold, 18K Gold Link Chain, Signed, Cartier 1840.00
Pendant, Pin, Black Opal, 14K Gold Chased, Engraved Leaves Frame, Arts & Crafts 375.00
Pendant, Puzzle, Unfolds Into Torso, Brass, Signed, M. Berrocal, 1973 . . . . 345.00
Pendant, Relief Sculpted Crab, 6 Sides, Marked 750, 18K Yellow Gold 460.00
Pendant, Rococo Scroll Design, Seed Pearls, Renaissance Revival 575.00
Pendant, Rose Cut Diamond Crown, Suspended Pear Shape Moonstone, Edwardian 2468.00
Pendant, Silver, Enamel, Square Plaque, Urn With Flowers, Art Deco 1725.00
Pendant, Snowflake, Obsidian, 14K Gold, c.1900 . . . . 260.00
Pendant, Sphinx Head, Carved Amethyst, 14K Gold Cap & Bail, Egyptian Revival 690.00
Pendant, Sterling Silver, Black Onyx, Gourd Mark, Taxco 450.00
Pendant, Sterling Silver, Bone, Bird Shape, Articulated Tail Feathers, Cipher 75.00
Pendant, Sterling Silver, Round, Bird, Wreath, Berries, Georg Jensen, c.1945, 1 1/4 In. . . 202.00
Pendant, Watch, 18K Yellow Gold, Diamond, Enamel, Open Face, Lady's, Tiffany, 1871 . 2300.00
Pendant, Woman's Profile, Emerald, Diamond, Pearls, Art Nouveau, 14K Gold 1725.00
Pin, 2 Sinuous Vines, Turquoise, Rectangular, Art Nouveau, 18K Gold 316.00
Pin, 3 Sections, Harbor Scenes, 14K Yellow Gold, Early 1900s 145.00
Pin, Agate, Moss, Oval Frames, Victorian, 14K Rose Gold 265.00
Pin, Amethyst, Pearl, Gold Bead Accents, Gilt, Dorrie Nossiter, England 1095.00
Pin, Aurora Borealis, Starburst Design, Rhinestones, Weiss, Gold Color Metal, 2 In. 35.00
Pin, Bakelite, Apple, 5 Leaves, Suspended From Bar, 2 In. 380.00
Pin, Bakelite, Atlas, 2 Suspended Globes, 2 In. 1175.00
Pin, Bakelite, Baseball Bat, Suspended Glove, Ball, 2 5/8 In. 1528.00
Pin, Bakelite, Bumblebee, 2 7/8 In. 4700.00
Pin, Bakelite, Cat, Pivoting Tail, 2 3/8 In. 4115.00
Pin, Bakelite, Courting Couple Under Apple Tree, Bakelite, 2 1/4 In. 6037.00
Pin, Bakelite, Cruise Ship, Suspended Suitcase, Fish, 2 1/2 In. 588.00
Pin, Bakelite, Dog & Soldier, Pivoting Arm & Rifle, Marble Red, 3 In. 2885.00
Pin, Bakelite, Dog, Googly-Eyed, Red, Holding Bone, 3 In. 8625.00
Pin, Bakelite, Dog, Green Scotty With White Scotty Center 75.00
Pin, Bakelite, Fish, Swirls, Elliptical, Reverse Carved, Painted, 3 7/8 In. 120.00
Pin, Bakelite, Flowers, Butterfly, Oval, Reverse Carved, 3 In. 120.00
Pin, Bakelite, Flying Fish, 3 1/2 In. 205.00
Pin, Bakelite, Frog Playing Guitar, Brown & Green, Rotating Arm, 3 In. 1725.00
Pin, Bakelite, Gavel, 3 In. 410.00
Pin, Bakelite, Giraffe, Butterscotch, Brown Spots, Leather Ears, 4 In. 2300.00
Pin, Bakelite, Log Suspending Tomato, Carrot, Radish, Potato, 3 Leaves, 1 7/8 In. 5175.00
Pin, Bakelite, Lozenge Shape Sections, Black, Orange, Green, Red, Yellow 646.00
Pin, Bakelite, Monkey, Googly-Eyed, Wearing Fez, 2 3/4 In. 6169.00
Pin, Bakelite, Monkey, Perched On Bar Pin, Rose Cut Diamond, 14K Gold 805.00
Pin, Bakelite, Native Carrying Bananas, 3 In. 705.00
Pin, Bakelite, Octopus, 2 3/4 In. 2115.00
Pin, Bakelite, Owl, 2 7/8 In. 530.00
Pin, Bakelite, Owl, Leather Ears, 2 5/8 In. 205.00
Pin, Bakelite, Peaches, Leaves, Suspended From Bar, Celluloid, 1 7/8 In. 440.00
Pin, Bakelite, Pistol, Suspended Cowboy Hat, Lasso, Saddle, 2 1/2 In. 265.00
Pin, Bakelite, Pygmy, Big Smile, Ring On Arms, Bone In Hair, 1920s 525.00
Pin, Bakelite, Rabbit, In Magician's Hat, 3 In. 880.00
Pin, Bakelite, Rabbit, Pivoting Arm, 2 7/8 In. 1998.00
Pin, Bakelite, Red Ribbon, Suspended Hearts, Balls, Letter, 2 1/4 In. 235.00
Pin, Bakelite, Soldier Courting, Apple Tree, 2 1/4 In. 6037.00
Pin, Bakelite, South American Figure On Horseback, 3 1/2 In. 235.00
Pin, Bakelite, Stars & Stripes, Suspended From Bar, Cream, Black, 3 In. 825.00
Pin, Bakelite, Sterling Silver, Beer Mug, 2 In. 175.00
Pin, Bakelite, Walrus, 2 1/4 In. 825.00
Pin, Bakelite, Wood, Bison, Pivoting Head, 3 1/4 In. 600.00
Pin, Bakelite, Wood, Cat, Looking In Fishbowl, Reverse Carved, Painted, 2 3/4 In. 765.00
Pin, Bakelite, Wood, Windmill, Suspended Clogs, 1 1/2 In. 150.00
Pin, Ballerina, Cultured Pearl Ball, 14K Gold, 1950 . . . . 345.00
Pin, Bar, 7 Square Cut Diamonds, 18K Gold, 8 Rubies, Cartier 690.00
Pin, Bar, 17 Mine Cut Diamonds, Silver Topped 14K Mount, Art Deco 1528.00

Jewelry, Pendant, Anemone, Pearl, Diamond, Enamel, Art Nouveau, 14K Gold

Jewelry, Pin, Flower, Pearl In Center, Coro, 1 1/2 In.

Jewelry, Pin, Pansy, Enameled, Seed Pearls, Diamond Center, Art Nouveau

Pin, Bar, Baroque Pearls, Rose Cut Diamonds, 14K Gold	750.00
Pin, Bar, Carved Moonstone Flanked By Diamond Stars, Edwardian	1000.00
Pin, Bar, Classical Warrior Moonstone Plaque, Diamonds, 14K Gold, C & Co.	2070.00
Pin, Bar, Diamond Center, 4 Smaller Diamonds, Platinum, 2 1/2 In.	450.00
Pin, Bar, Duck, Enamel Heads, Ruby Eyes, 5 Graduated Sizes, Platinum Bar, Art Deco	1725.00
Pin, Bar, Enamel Anemone, Pink, Green, Krementz & Co., 14K Gold	373.00
Pin, Bar, Interlocking Links, Pearl, Edwardian, 14K Gold	143.00
Pin, Bar, Platinum, 7 Diamonds, Art Deco	1380.00
Pin, Bar, Platinum, Diamond, Filigree Mount, Art Deco	1725.00
Pin, Bar, Platinum, Diamond, Silver Topped Gold Mount	635.00
Pin, Bar, Sterling Silver, Rectangular, Openwork, 3 Panels, Georg Jensen, Denmark, 2 In.	120.00
Pin, Bee Shape, Gold Wings, Sapphire Head & Body, 14K Yellow Gold	215.00
Pin, Bird, Cabochon Sapphire, Bead Set Diamond, Coral Branch, 18K Gold	2530.00
Pin, Bird, Ruby Eye, Paris, 18K Gold	750.00
Pin, Bloodstone, Diamond, Ruby, Flower Design, Victorian, 18K Gold	490.00
Pin, Blue Enamel Medallion, Gold Inlay Flowers, 10K Yellow Gold, 1850	730.00
Pin, Blue Enamel Medallion, Pink Border, Serpent Scene, 10K Pink Gold, 1850	620.00
Pin, Blue Enamel Medallion, White Gold Scrolling Flowers, 1850, 1 x 2 In.	450.00
Pin, Blue Enamel Shield Medallion, Crown Of Gold, Seed Pearls, 18K Gold	1290.00
Pin, Bow, Engraved, Pendant Foxtail Chain Tassel, 14K Yellow Gold, c.1880	460.00
Pin, Boxing Kangaroos, Aventurine, Signed, D. Viterbo, 18K Gold	315.00
Pin, Branches, Signed, 14K Gold, 1963	230.00
Pin, Bridled Horse's Head, Rose Gold Reins, 18K Yellow, 1910	575.00
Pin, Bug Shape, Ruby Eye, 6 Small Cut Diamonds, Enamel, 14K White Gold	460.00
Pin, Burmese Jadeite Plaque, Gold Frame, 14K Yellow Gold	690.00
Pin, Butterfly, Moonstone, Diamond, Garnet, Edwardian, 14K Gold	3565.00
Pin, Butterfly, Yellow Gold, Diamonds, Gold & Green Enamel	390.00
Pin, Cameo, Carnelian, Profile Of Classical Maiden, Greek Key Surround, Yellow Gold	290.00
Pin, Cameo, Lava, 2 Figures & Goose, Twisted Gold Border, 14K Gold, c.1890	730.00
Pin, Cameo, Shell, Classical Figure Wearing Laurel, Grape Leaf Headdress	200.00
Pin, Cameo, Shell, Diamond On Necklace, Diamond In Hair Pin, White Gold, 1880s	345.00
Pin, Cameo, Shell, Female Bust Profile, Gold Filled, 1 1/2 In.	130.00
Pin, Cameo, Shell, Profile Of Classical Male, Oval, 14K Gold	230.00
Pin, Cameo, Woman, Coral, High Relief, Yellow Gold Frame, Victorian, 2 In.	265.00
Pin, Carved Crystal Basket, Multicolored Gems, Onyx & Diamond Accents, Art Deco	6465.00
Pin, Carved Moonstone, Profile Of A Classical Figure, 18K Yellow Gold	1955.00
Pin, Center Diamond, With Leaf Surround, Guilloche Enamel, Edwardian, 18K Gold	575.00
Pin, Central Cabochon Emerald With Diamonds, 1945	490.00
Pin, Champleve Enamel Woman's Portrait, Diamond Headdress, Gold, c.1900	490.00
Pin, Chased Sailing Vessel Riding Ocean Swells, 1 3/4 In.	95.00
Pin, Circle, 4 Calibre Cut Sapphires, Platinum Mount, Signed, Yard	3105.00
Pin, Circle, Etched Crystal, 2 Platinum Diamond Set Plaques, Art Deco, Tiffany & Co.	3055.00
Pin, Circle, Lily Pad, Wire Twist, Green Sapphire, Tiffany & Co., 18K Gold	4113.00
Pin, Clover, Black, Green Enamel, Diamond, 14K Gold	400.00
Pin, Copper, Stylized Pre-Columbian Mask, Rebajes, 2 1/2 x 2 1/2 In.	330.00

Pin, Coral, Pearl, Daisy Shape, 14K Gold 230.00
Pin, Coral, Profile Of A Classical Figure & Lyre, Oval, 14K Gold 375.00
Pin, Cross, Large Central Turquoise, Filigree Gold, Miriam Haskell, 1945 .... 490.00
Pin, Demi Parure, Coral, 2 Bars, 3 Teardrop Pendants, Victorian, 14K Gold 316.00
Pin, Demi Parure, Ear Pendants, Coral Beads, Carved Rose, Amphorae, 14K Gold 546.00
Pin, Diamond, Art Deco, Platinum 3795.00
Pin, Diamond, Bow Rose Cut, Green Glass Grape Cluster, 14K Gold 1035.00
Pin, Diamond, Collet Set Cushion Diamonds, 14K Yellow Gold, 1820 .... 5400.00
Pin, Diamond, Crescent Shape, 21 Mine Cut Diamonds 1610.00
Pin, Diamond, Crescent Shape, Signed, Pickslay & Co., 18K Yellow Gold 22715.00
Pin, Diamond, Filigree Platinum, Reticulated Marquis Shape, Art Deco, 2 1/4 x 1 In. 2530.00
Pin, Diamond, Griffin With Prong Set Rose Cut Diamonds, 18K Yellow Gold 980.00
Pin, Diamond, Jockey On Horseback, Maroon Ground, 18K Gold, 1882 .... 860.00
Pin, Diamond, Openwork, Art Deco, 14K Yellow Gold, c.1935, 2 1/4 x 1 1/4 In. 546.00
Pin, Diamond, Openwork, Mine Cut Diamond, 18K Yellow Gold 5060.00
Pin, Diamond, Openwork, Platinum, c.1920 .... 2990.00
Pin, Diamond, Portrait Of Lady With Flowers In Hair, 18K Gold 980.00
Pin, Diamond, Rose Cut Diamond, Black Silk Ribbon, 18K Yellow Gold 230.00
Pin, Diamond, Rose Cut, Green Stone, Gold Mount 805.00
Pin, Diamond, Starburst Design, Mine Cut Diamonds, 14K White Gold, 19th Century ... 1380.00
Pin, Diamonds, Platinum Topped Yellow Gold Mount, Edwardian 4312.00
Pin, Double, Bow, Rhinestones, Green Pate-De-Verre, Center Teardrop Pendant 1380.00
Pin, Dragonfly, Green & Yellow Enamel, Art Nouveau, 14K Gold, 2 1/4 In. 260.00
Pin, Earrings, Gold Tone, Rhinestone Feathers, Ribbons, Oleg Cassini 98.00
Pin, Enamel Orange Blossom, Diamond Center, Green Vine, Pearl, Art Nouveau 1000.00
Pin, Enamel, Garnet, Pearl, Clara Flagg, Victorian, 14K Yellow Gold 805.00
Pin, Exotic Bird, Pink & Purple Enamel, Purple Tail, Hattie Carnegie, 5 3/4 In. 80.00
Pin, Eye, White & Black Enamel, Faux Flock Pupil, Rhinestones, Christian Dior 1380.00
Pin, Faux Ivory, Branch Coral, Abstract, Miriam Haskell, 3 In. 80.00
Pin, Figural, Astrological Goat Inside Crescent Moon, Textured, Boucher, 1 x 1 In. 45.00
Pin, Figural, Curved Leaf, Coppery Gold Rhinestones, Weiss, 2 1/2 x 1 1/4 In. 60.00
Pin, Florenza, Flower, Frosted Glass Petals, Signed, Gold Tone, 2 In. 69.00
Pin, Flower Head, Collet Set Cabochon Garnets, Knife Edge Bar Mounts, 18K Gold 690.00
Pin, Flower Ribbon Design, Mine Cut Diamonds, 22K Yellow Gold, 1860 .... 4025.00
Pin, Flower Shape, Diamond Inset Petals, Enamel Leaves, c.1950 .... 560.00
Pin, Flower, Pearl In Center, Coro, 1 1/2 In. .... *Illus* 45.00
Pin, Flower, Purple, White Iridescent Enamel, 14K Gold 345.00
Pin, Flower, Rock Crystal Petals, Diamonds, Ruby, 18K White Gold Mount 545.00
Pin, Flower, Wire Leaves, Round Diamonds, Van Cleef & Arpels, 18K Gold 1265.00
Pin, Flowers Filigree, Cabochon Ruby, 14K Gold, 1920 .... 225.00
Pin, Flowers, Gold Stems, Cutout Petals, Multicolored, Gold Centers, Kramer, 2 x 3 In. ... 50.00
Pin, Flowers, Gold, Moonstone, Aquamarine, Floral Spray 345.00
Pin, Foo Dog, Black Onyx, Full Cut Emerald, Diamonds 575.00
Pin, Frog, Pave Diamond Head, Cabochon Green Stone Eyes, 18K Gold 690.00
Pin, Front View Of Model T Ford, Rhinestones, Signed, JJ, 1 1/4 x 1 In. 13.00
Pin, Gold Plate, Swirl Design, Faceted Ovals In Garnet, Amethyst, Citrine, Coro, 3 x 4 In. . 85.00
Pin, Goldfish Shape, 2 Round Rubies, Sapphires & Emeralds, 14K White Gold 85.00
Pin, Goldtone, Round, Imitation Jade & Coral Oval Cabochons, Sarah Coventry, 2 In. ... 13.00
Pin, Golf, Brushed Gold Bag Design, Checkerboard Design, 14K Gold 290.00
Pin, Goose In Flight, Marked 925, SB, 2 3/8 x 2 In. 20.00
Pin, Grape Cluster & Vine Design, Beveled Edge Glass, Maggie Bewington 130.00
Pin, Griffin, Enamel, Green Guilloche Enamel Wings, 14K Gold 690.00
Pin, Heart Shape, Green, Blue Enamel Leaf, Flowers, 1 1/8 In. 125.00
Pin, Horse, Ruby Eye, Pave Diamonds, 14K Gold 440.00
Pin, Insect, Gold, Amethyst, Diamond, 18K Gold 1495.00
Pin, Insect, Mother-Of-Pearl Body, Red Stone Eyes, 18K Gold 3795.00
Pin, Insect, Turquoise & Pearl, Gold Legs & Wings, Pearl Head, 14K Gold, 1930 .... 280.00
Pin, Iris Shape, Pink Iridescent Enamel, Diamond Stamens, 14K Gold, Art Nouveau 2350.00
Pin, King Charles Spaniel, Rope Twist Oval Frame, 14K Gold 575.00
Pin, Kite Shape, Turquoise, Ornate Tassel, 14K Gold Frame, c.1860 .... 460.00
Pin, Laval, Apollo In Full Figure Holding Lyre, 14K Gold, 1825 .... 431.00
Pin, Leaf, Diamond Set Branch, Diamond Stem, Cluster, 18K White Gold Mount 575.00
Pin, Leaves, Rose Cut Diamond Silver Buds, Buccellati, 18K Gold 1495.00

Pin, Maltese Cross, Blue Rhinestones, 2-Color Crystals, Kramer, 2 1/4 x 2 1/4 In. 55.00
Pin, Memorial, Hand Tinted Photograph, Woven Hair Border, Rubies, Pearls, c.1910 . . . . 465.00
Pin, Micro Mosaic, Country Scene, Bridge, 19th Century, 2 1/2 x 2 In. 2760.00
Pin, Micro Mosaic, Oval Onyx Plaque, Roman Ruin, Victorian, 18K Gold Frame 700.00
Pin, Micro Mosaic, Reclining King Charles Spaniel Center, Gold Frame 860.00
Pin, Moonstone, Oval, Platinum, Arts & Crafts, Tiffany & Co., 18K Yellow Gold 4945.00
Pin, Moonstone, Sapphire Trefoil, Binder Brothers, Retro, 14K Gold 345.00
Pin, Mourning, Gold & Enamel, Glass Locket, Garnet Set Buckle, Victorian 256.00
Pin, Nature Design, Blue Foil, Gilt, 1920 . . . . 460.00
Pin, Nephrite Jade, Openwork, Blister Pearl, Arts & Crafts, 9K Gold 315.00
Pin, Oblong Openwork Plaque, 33 Diamonds, Art Deco, 18K White Gold 1295.00
Pin, Onyx, Oval, Flowing Bow, 14K Gold, Rose Cut Diamonds, 1860 . . . . 635.00
Pin, Open Fan, Alternating Stripes Of Gold & Lapis Glass, Marvella, 2 1/2 x 1 3/4 In. 25.00
Pin, Openwork Flower, Seed Pearl Petals, Diamond Center, Edwardian, 14K Gold 558.00
Pin, Orchid, 18K Yellow Gold, 1900, 1 1/4 x 2 In. 530.00
Pin, Oval Citrine, Greek Key Border, Pearls, Blue Enamel Fleur-De-Lis, 1880 . . . . 805.00
Pin, Oval Cut Amethyst, Seed Pearl Border, Suspended Amethyst & Pearls, 1900 . . . . 635.00
Pin, Pansy, Cobalt Blue Enamel, Art Nouveau, 14K Gold 440.00
Pin, Pansy, Diamond, 14K Gold 1440.00
Pin, Pansy, Enamel, Pink Opaque, 14K Gold 1150.00
Pin, Pansy, Enameled, Seed Pearls, Diamond Center, Art Nouveau . . . . *Illus* 1495.00
Pin, Pearl Drops, Floral Openwork, Victorian, 14K Yellow Gold 520.00
Pin, Pearl Orchid Center, Textured Gold Ground, Baroque 1265.00
Pin, Pendant, Seed Pearl, Early 20th Century, 14K Yellow Gold, 1 1/2 In. 560.00
Pin, Petals & Leaves, Yellow Gold, Pearls, Cranberry Enamel, Art Nouveau, c.1900 . . . . . 430.00
Pin, Photo, Baby's Face, Round, Victorian, 10K Gold, 1 1/4 x 1 1/4 In. 145.00
Pin, Pinched Sides, Flowers, George W. Frost, 1 1/2 x 2 1/2 In. 245.00
Pin, Portrait Of Marie Antoinette, France, 18K Yellow Gold Feather Frame 690.00
Pin, Portrait, Mother & Child, Hand Painted, Porcelain, Victorian, Gold Frame 850.00
Pin, Portrait, Oval, Engraved Frame, Double Sided Revolving Locket, 14K Gold, c.1885 . 170.00
Pin, Portrait, Woman, Headdress, Moonstone, Pearl, Gilt Frame, Flenret, 3 x 2 3/4 In. 490.00
Pin, Railroad Spike, Square Cut Emerald, Rose Cut Diamonds, Victorian 633.00
Pin, Reverse Intaglio Circular Shape, Bird In Flight, 18K Yellow Gold 690.00
Pin, Roman Ruins Within Goldstone Ground, 14K Gold 1035.00
Pin, Rose Cut Diamond, Flower Sprays 690.00
Pin, Rose Cut Diamonds, Bow Design 1265.00
Pin, Scarab, Egyptian, Plique-A-Jour, Silver, Turquoise, Faience 230.00
Pin, Scroll Filigree, Seed Pearls, Victorian, 14K Gold, 2 x 1/2 In. 435.00
Pin, Scroll, Sailor's Knot, 14K Gold, c.1878, 2 x 1 In. 350.00
Pin, Serrated Edges, Leaf Shape, Gilbert Oakes, 1 1/2 x 1 1/2 In. 1200.00
Pin, Shell Design, Amethyst, Turquoise, Pearl, Georgian 290.00
Pin, Shooting Star, Mine Cut Diamond, Black Enamel, Victorian, 14K Gold 575.00
Pin, Silver Accents, Skakudo Ground, Gold, Japan 260.00
Pin, Silver, Abstract Curves, Mexico, 1 7/8 x 2 1/2 In. 45.00
Pin, Single Cut Diamonds, 18K Gold, 1950 . . . . 575.00
Pin, Skeleton, Bones, Plastic, Spring For Neck, Metal Ring, Japan, 1955, 6 In. 70.00
Pin, Soldier Carrying Rifle, Defiant Fist, Plastic, Ivory, Brown, 1 1/4 x 2 1/2 In. 13.00
Pin, Spider, Clear Rhinestone, Large 45.00
Pin, Starburst, 14K Gold, 1900 . . . . 1725.00
Pin, Starburst, 18K Gold, Pearl & Mine Cut Diamonds, Edwardian 1265.00
Pin, Starfish, Beau Silver, Impressed Mark, Arts & Crafts, 1 1/2 In. 115.00
Pin, Starfish, Cultured Pearl, 18K Gold 4370.00
Pin, Sterling Silver, 14K Gold Washed, Flower Spray, Bow, Swirls, Hobe, 3 5/8 x 2 In. . . 125.00
Pin, Sterling Silver, 2 Leaping Dolphins, Marked Georg Jensen, 3 In. 160.00
Pin, Sterling Silver, 2 Leaping Dolphins, Signed, Georg Jensen, Denmark, 1 1/2 In. 185.00
Pin, Sterling Silver, 3-Petal Flower Blossom, Circular, Madeline Turner, 1 5/8 In. 95.00
Pin, Sterling Silver, Abstract Design, Blue Enamel Inlay, Signed HK, Georg Jensen 520.00
Pin, Sterling Silver, Abstract Grapevine, Georg Jensen 546.00
Pin, Sterling Silver, Abstract Shape, Curvilinear Line, Green & Pink Stones, 1950 . . . . . . 1115.00
Pin, Sterling Silver, Abstract, Chinese Character, Signed, Georg Jensen, 1 1/4 In. 320.00
Pin, Sterling Silver, Abstract, Chinese Character, Signed, Georg Jensen, 2 1/2 In 280.00
Pin, Sterling Silver, Bar, Marcasite, Hammered, Wire Twist Openwork, 1908 . . . . 764.00
Pin, Sterling Silver, Bird, Wheat, Square Openwork Mount, Signed Georg Jensen 200.00

Pin, Sterling Silver, Blossom & Leaf Sprig Design, England, Late 18th Century 1200.00
Pin, Sterling Silver, Chased Flower, Leaf Shape, Panis Gallery, 1 x 2 1/8 In. 165.00
Pin, Sterling Silver, Chased Thistle Design, Panis Gallery, 1 1/8 x 2 In. 165.00
Pin, Sterling Silver, Danish Flower, Cabochon Moonstone, Georg Jensen, 1 1/2 In. 300.00
Pin, Sterling Silver, Deer, Brushed Gold, Signed, BM Co., 1 1/4 x 3 In. 25.00
Pin, Sterling Silver, Floral, Bead Center, 3 Leaves At Base, Georg Jensen, 2 In. 180.00
Pin, Sterling Silver, Flower, Moonstone, Oval Base, Signed, Georg Jensen, 2 1/2 In. 260.00
Pin, Sterling Silver, Heart Pierced By Arrow, Signed, Beau, 2 x 3/4 In. 23.00
Pin, Sterling Silver, Heart, Thread Mold, 2 Leaping Dolphins, Branch, Georg Jensen, 3 In. 375.00
Pin, Sterling Silver, Oval Bead Medallion, Signed Georg Jensen, 1 3/8 In. 200.00
Pin, Sterling Silver, Oval, 8 Beads & 4 Leaves, Georg Jensen, 2 In. 180.00
Pin, Sterling Silver, Pagoda, Calibre Green Onyx, France 290.00
Pin, Sterling Silver, Plique-A-Jour Enamel, Abstract Shape, Openwork, Art Nouveau 880.00
Pin, Sterling Silver, Seahorse, Sterling Silver, Open Eyehole, Marked HG In Circle, 1 In. . 17.00
Pin, Sterling Silver, Stylized Center Dove, Within Raised Leafy Frame, Georg Jensen 315.00
Pin, Sterling Silver, Woman In Profile, Flowing Hair, Art Nouveau, Stamped No. 1273 . . . 235.00
Pin, Stick, Celtic Intertwined Design, Liberty, Impressed Mark, 1 3/4 In. 290.00
Pin, Stick, Hammered Sterling Silver Stem, Lapis, Cutout Setting, 3 1/4 In. 230.00
Pin, Stylized Insect Design, Green Verdigris, Carence Crafters, 1 1/2 x 2 1/4 In. 375.00
Pin, Stylized Ribbon, Bow, Ruby & Diamond Clusters, Retro, 14K Bicolor Gold 575.00
Pin, Sunburst, Diamond, Smaller Mine Cut Diamonds On Rays, 14K Gold, 1900 . . . . 460.00
Pin, Swallow, Enamel Cobalt Blue Wings, With Diamond Edge, Pearl Body 290.00
Pin, Swan, Opal, 14K Gold 490.00
Pin, Turtle, Speckled Green Glass Body, Signed Gerry's, 2 1/4 x 1 1/4 In. 18.00
Pin, Turtle, Studded With Rubies, Italy 750, 18K Yellow Gold 230.00
Pin, Turtle, Tiny Turquoise & 6 Cut Diamonds, .33 Carats 345.00
Pin, Violin, White Gold Strings, France, 18K Gold 1380.00
Pin, Watch, 14K Gold, Diamond, Enamel, Bow Shape, Ribbons, Tiffany, c.1899 . . . . 635.00
Pin, Yellow Gold, Enamel, Rectangular, Mountain Lake Landscape, Leather Box 690.00
Pin, Young Woman, Profile, Flowing Hair, Rope Twist Surround, 1920s, 3 In. 460.00
Pin & Earrings, 10 Brilliants, Abstract Design, 18K Gold Openwork, c.1965 . . . . 635.00
Pin & Earrings, Sterling Silver, Rod & Reel, Creel Earrings, Beau Sterling 275.00
Pin & Locket, Hinged, Rose Cut Diamond Pansy, 18K Gold 430.00
Ring, 3 Rows Of 18K Gold Beads, Chaumet, Box, Size 7 1/2 . . . . 920.00
Ring, 3 Textured Bands, White, Yellow, Rose Gold, Cartier, Man's, 18K Gold, Size 11 . . . 260.00
Ring, Amethyst, Ruby, Retro, 14K Gold 495.00
Ring, Archer's, White Jade, Black, Brown Markings, Brown Scroll Design, 18th Century . 172.00
Ring, Band, Diamond, Hexagonal, Tiffany & Co., 18K Gold, Size 4 3/4 In. 1380.00
Ring, Band, Graduated Pearls Set In Black Enamel Frames, Victorian, 18K Gold 290.00
Ring, Band, Onyx Segments, With Pearl, Victorian, Size 8 . . . . 130.00
Ring, Black Opal, Platinum, Art Deco, Marcus & Co., Size 4 . . . . 4715.00
Ring, Cabochon Sapphire, Openwork Shoulders, Diamonds, Art Deco, Size 5 3/4 In. 3055.00
Ring, Cameo, Profile Of Classical Woman, Vine, Scroll Design, 14K Gold 345.00
Ring, Circular Bezel Set Round Garnet, Seed Pearls, 14K Gold, Arts & Crafts, Size 6 3/4 . 3290.00
Ring, Citrine, Oval, Diamonds, Bezel Set, Man's, Tiffany & Co., 14K Gold, Size 8 1/2 In. 373.00
Ring, Cocktail, 12 Round Rubies, 6 European Cut Diamonds, 1940 . . . . 575.00
Ring, Cocktail, Platinum, Star Sapphire Cabochon, Diamonds On 2 Sides, 1940 . . . . 1840.00
Ring, Diamond Shape, Platinum, Sapphire, Diamonds, Openwork, Art Deco, Size 6 1/2 . . 860.00
Ring, Diamond, 2 Pearls, 18K Gold, c.1860, Size 4 3/4 . . . . 230.00
Ring, Diamond, Millegrain Enamel, Art Deco, 18K Gold Gallery & Shank, Size 4 1/4 . . . 920.00
Ring, Diamond, Platinum Topped, Edwardian, 14K Yellow Gold Mount, Size 7 3/4 . . . . . . 5750.00
Ring, Diamond, Platinum, X-Design, Schlumberg, 18K Gold, 1956 . . . . 4140.00
Ring, Dinner, Diamond, Art Deco, 14K White Gold 1725.00
Ring, Dinner, Diamond, Art Deco, 14K Yellow, White Gold, c.1935, 5 1/2 In. 748.00
Ring, Dinner, Diamond, Art Deco, Platinum Mount, c.1930, 3 1/2 In. 3220.00
Ring, Earrings, Coral, Ribbed Fruit, Leaves, Victorian, 14K Gold, 3 Piece 1265.00
Ring, Elongated Oval, Pink Pearl, 11 Mine Cut Diamonds, 14K Gold, Edwardian 558.00
Ring, Eternity Band, 18 Brilliant Cut Diamonds, Platinum, Tiffany & Co., Size 6 . . . . 4370.00
Ring, Eternity Band, Platinum, Diamond, Round, Tiffany & Co., Size 6 . . . . 4830.00
Ring, Eternity, 9 Brown Diamonds, 9 Colorless Diamonds, Platinum 2530.00
Ring, Eternity, 26 Cut Diamonds, Platinum, Size 7 . . . . 800.00
Ring, Eternity, Sapphire, Size 6 . . . . 290.00

Ring, Family Crest, Tiffany & Co., 18K Yellow Gold, Early 20th Century, 5 1/2 In. 632.00
Ring, Flower Shape, Pearl On Black Onyx Center, Black Enamel Leaves, Victorian 316.00
Ring, Geometric, Sterling Silver, 14K Gold Inclusions, Lobel, Impressed Mark, 3/4 In. ... 299.00
Ring, Intaglio, Carnelian, Seated Figure, Hope, Victorian, c.1860 .... 635.00
Ring, Jade, Oval, 18K Gold, 1940 .... 1725.00
Ring, Mourning, Enameled, Black & White, 18K Gold, 1780, Size 6 1/4 .... 345.00
Ring, Navette, Ruby, Diamond Floret, Rose Cut Diamond, 14K Gold 690.00
Ring, Opal, Rose Cut Diamonds, 18K White Gold 1035.00
Ring, Oval Turquoise, Flowers On Shoulders, Art Nouveau, 14K Gold Mount, 3 3/4 In. .. 176.00
Ring, Oval, Jade, Split Shoulders, Bullet Shape Diamond Baguettes, Art Deco, Size 6 .... 1763.00
Ring, Platinum Openwork, Bezel-Set Mine Cut Diamonds, Art Deco, Size 5 3/4 In. 1528.00
Ring, Platinum, 3 Diamonds, Oval Filigree, Art Deco, Size 6 .... 1265.00
Ring, Platinum, Diamond, Art Deco, Size 5 .... 1150.00
Ring, Platinum, Emerald, Diamond, Art Deco, Size 6 1/2 .... 4370.00
Ring, Posy, Brass, Love For Love, 18th Century 295.00
Ring, Ruby, Diamonds On 2 Sides, Platinum, Pierced, Art Deco, Size 2 1/4 .... 2990.00
Ring, Sapphire, 8 Diamonds, Filigree, Art Deco, 14K White Gold, 1920 .... 445.00
Ring, Sapphire, Diamond, Prong Set, Platinum Mount, c.1922, Size 4 3/4 .... 805.00
Ring, Scroll Design, 3 Stones, Diamonds, Bezel Set, Platinum, Art Deco 4945.00
Ring, Silver, 18K Gold Wash, Emerald, Diamond, Art Deco, c.1930 .... 900.00
Ring, Solitaire, Diamond, Brilliant Cut, Tiffany Mount, 14K Yellow Gold 3450.00
Ring, Solitaire, Diamond, Pierced Gallery, Platinum Mount, Tiffany & Co., Size 6 1/4 ... 1495.00
Ring, Sterling Silver, Moonstone, Oval Mount, Signed, Paloma Picasso, Size 6 1/2 ...... 635.00
Ring, Sterling Silver, Opal, Dragon Setting, Art Nouveau, 1 In. 375.00
Ring, Sugarloaf Sapphire, Platinum, Signed, S. Kind Sons, Size 7 .... 1265.00
Ring, Tiger Eye, Saddle Shape, Signed, Tiffany & Co., 18K Gold, Size 3 1/2 In. 575.00
Stickpin, Bat's Head, Round Garnet, Diamond, Man's, 14K Yellow Gold, c.1890 .... 230.00
Stickpin, Bee, 2 Rubies, 16 Diamonds, 18K Gold 302.00
Stickpin, Crescent Moonstone, 3 Diamonds, Platinum Mount 316.00
Stickpin, Eagle, Gold, 3/4 x 2 In. 13.00
Stickpin, Flower, Cabochon Sapphire, 14K Gold, Enamel Accents, Art Nouveau 230.00
Stickpin, Indian Head, Headdress, Quiver, Diamond, Art Nouveau, Krementz, 14K Gold . 287.00
Stickpin, Mine Cut Diamond Petals, Pearl Center, Platinum Topped, Edwardian 144.00
Stickpin, Pear Shape Diamond, Lavender, Ivory Pearls, Platinum, Edwardian, 18K Gold . 316.00
Stickpin, Peridot, Seed Pearl, Vine & Scroll, Signed Kuhn, Edwardian, 14K Gold 144.00
Stickpin, Pharaoh Bust, Jasper, Egyptian Revival, France, 18K Gold 690.00
Stickpin, Sapphire, Signed, 18K Gold 2300.00
Stickpin, Scarab, Blue Enamel, Stylized Birds, Egyptian Revival, 14K Gold 230.00
Tie Bar, 7 Crimped Collet Set Cabochon Rubies, Stamped Buccellati, 18K Gold 288.00
Tie Bar, Crystal Jumping Horse & Rider, 18K Gold 895.00
Tie Bar, Sterling Silver, Arrow Design, Openwork Top, Marked Georg Jensen, 1 1/12 In. .. 70.00
Tie Bar, Sterling Silver, Arrow, Openwork Along Sides, Georg Jensen, Denmark, 1 1/2 In. 80.00
Tie Bar, Sterling Silver, Rectangular, 2 Sets Of Beads, Medallion, Georg Jensen, 2 In. ... 140.00
Tie Bar, Sterling Silver, Slender Oval Shape, 2 Curved Lines, Georg Jensen, 2 1/2 In. 50.00
Watches are listed in their own category.
Wristwatches are listed in their own category.

JOHN ROGERS statues were made from 1859 to 1892. The originals were bronze, but the thousands of copies made by the Rogers factory were of painted plaster. Eighty different figures were created. Similar painted plaster figures were produced by some other factories. Rights to the figures were sold in 1893 and they were manufactured for several more years by the Rogers Statuette Co. Never repaint a Rogers figure because this lowers the value to collectors.

Group, Checkers Up At The Farm, 21 x 17 In. 390.00
Group, Coming To The Parson, 22 x 16 1/2 In. 196.00
Group, Elder's Daughter, 21 1/2 x 17 In. 280.00
Group, Fugitive's Story, 22 x 16 In. 560.00
Group, Is It So Nominated In The Bond, 23 x 19 1/2 In. 168.00
Group, Madam Your Mother Craves A Word With You, 19 x 19 In. 225.00
Group, Town Pump, 1880, 13 1/2 x 11 In. 390.00
Group, Weighing The Baby, 21 x 16 In. 110.00

Group, Why Don't You Speak For Yourself John, 22 x 17 In. 364.00
Group, Wrestlers, Terra-Cotta, 28 x 18 In. 616.00

JUDAICA is any memorabilia that refers to the Jews or the Jewish religion. Interests range from newspaper clippings that mention eighteenth-and nineteenth-century Jewish Americans to religious objects, such as menorahs or spice boxes. Age, condition, and the intrinsic value of the material, as well as the historic and artistic importance, determine the value.

Box, Charity, Figural Scenes, Silver, 3 In. 175.00
Box, Charity, General Israel Orphans Home For Girls, Hebrew & English, 1949, 4 3/4 In. . 316.00
Box, Charity, Mausoleum Shape, Silver, Continental, 5 In. 3165.00
Breast Plate, Crown Finial, Temple Columns, Festival Plaques, Sterling Silver, Russia ... 805.00
Breast Plate, Crown, Tablet, Candelabrum & Leaves, 20th Century, 14 In. 520.00
Calendar, Omer, Silver, Filigree, 5 In. 546.00
Candelabrum, 7-Light, Openwork Branch, Bronze, Poland, 19th Century, 14 In. 115.00
Candelabrum, Sabbath, 5-Light, Deer, Brass, 12 In. 230.00
Candlestick, Sabbath, Baluster Body, Silver Plate, Poland, 19th Century, 10 In., Pair 290.00
Candlestick, Sabbath, Square Base, Silver Plate, Poland, 1909, 12 1/2 In., Pair 460.00
Candlestick, Sabbath, Tulip Form Bobeche, Brass, Poland, 1880s, 10 1/4 In., Pair 200.00
Case, Scroll, Pierced Leaf Center, Sterling Silver, c.1900, 7 1/4 In. 200.00
Container, Charity, Barrel Form, Inscribed Tzedakah, In Hebrew, Silver Plate, 3 1/4 In. . . 460.00
Container, Charity, Columns, Star Of David, Wailing Wall, Top Slot, Hebrew Text, 7 In. . . 920.00
Contract, Marriage, Parchment, Hebrew Text, M. Beatricia To A. Nino, 1887, 27 In. 1725.00
Crown, Torah, Acorn Finial, Bells, Filigree, Silver, Continental, 1830s, 5 In. 2185.00
Cup, Kiddush, Beaker Form, Hebrew Inscription, Sterling Silver, Denmark, 3 1/2 In. 490.00
Cup, Kiddush, Figural Scenes, Silver, 7 In. 230.00
Cup, Kiddush, Inscribed Markus First, Sterling Silver, Russia, 1864, 2 3/4 In. 260.00
Dish, Bread, Silver, 2 Challahs, Leaves, Continental, 16 1/2 In. 750.00
Etrog, Box, Hinged Lid, Hebrew Inscription, Pewter, Late 19th Century, 4 1/2 In. 546.00
Etrog, Container, Oval, Hinged Domed Lid, 1934, 5 1/2 In. 230.00
Etrog, Container, Silver, Leaves, Continental, 5 1/2 In. 920.00
Finial, Half-Moon Form, Pendant Bells, Chased Leaves, Sterling Silver, Africa, 7 1/4 In. . . 290.00
Finial, Torah, Bells, Chased Leaves, Sterling Silver, Africa, 1880s, 9 In. 490.00
Gregger, Purim, Figural Scenes, Silver, Continental, 5 In. 1380.00
Holder, Matzoh, Men Holding Baskets, 3 Tiers, Silver Plate, 13 In. 2300.00
Lamp, Hanukkah, Backplate, Star Of David, 8 Oil Pans, Brass, Morocco, 12 In. 980.00
Lamp, Hanukkah, Bowed Well, Candelabrum, Sterling Silver, Russia, 1916, 9 1/2 In. 1265.00
Lamp, Hanukkah, Central Servant, Lions & Tablets, 8 Oil Fonts, 20th Century, 14 3/4 In. . 1380.00
Lamp, Hanukkah, Crown Finial, Star Of David, Oil Pitcher, Russia, 1880s, 11 In. 6496.00
Lamp, Hanukkah, Front Bank Of Oil Fonts, Bronze, Italy, 17th Century, 4 5/8 In. 630.00
Lamp, Hanukkah, Servant, 8 Oil Fonts, Bronze & Copper, Italy, 16th Century, 6 In. 230.00
Lamp, Hanukkah, U Form Branches, Candleholders, Brass, Jerusalem, 1920s, 9 1/4 In. 750.00
Lamp, Memorial, 5 Pottery Lamps, Drawer, Wood, Persia, 20th Century, 13 In. 860.00
Lamp, Memorial, Verse, Tapered Foot, Otto Natzler, 1950s, 5 1/4 In. 1840.00
Menorah, Eagle Finial, 9 Grapevine Branches, Silver, Continental, 1894, 25 In. 3105.00
Menorah, Hanukkah, Serpentine Bank Of Candleholders, Silver Plate, Poland, 11 1/2 In. . . 460.00
Menorah, Traveling, Silver, Continental, 2 1/2 In. 345.00
Mezuzah, Tablets, Etched, Brown, Sterling Silver, Poland, 5 1/2 In. 400.00
Plaque, Dancing Hasidim, Pottery, 18 x 12 In. 86.00
Plate, Passover, Figures Amid Leaves, Hebrew Text, Pewter, 19th Century, 15 In. 747.00
Plate, Purim, Center Scene, Haman Leading Mordechai, Hebrew Text, 9 1/4 In. 345.00
Pointer, Torah, Bone & Turquoise, Pointed Hand, N. Africa, 20th Century, 8 3/4 In. 460.00
Pointer, Torah, Crown Finial, Pointed Hand, Silver, Wood, Continental, 12 1/2 In. 345.00
Pointer, Torah, Mid Section Beading, Loop Chain, Sterling Silver, 1880s, 12 In. 200.00
Pointer, Torah, Silver Chain, 19th Century 1475.00
Postcard, European Synagogues, In Binder, Early 20th Century, 72 Piece 2185.00
Ring, Marriage, Hebrew Mozel Tov, Sterling Silver, 20th Century 287.00
Rug, Menorah, 7 Branches, Stylized Zion Lettering, Star Of David, Wool, 1914, 4 x 6 Ft. . 2645.00
Scroll, Esther, Brass Case, 13 In. 630.00
Scroll, Esther, Olive Wood Case, 18 In. 635.00
Scroll, Esther, Wood Tabernacle, 18 In. 175.00

Sculpture, Moses, Holding 10 Commandments, Glass, Base, H. Perlman, 25 In. 144.00
Spice Box, Tower, Filigree Sides, Silver, Continental, 11 1/4 In.   1035.00
Spice Box, Tower, Filigree Sides, Silver, Continental, 17 In. 3165.00
Spice Box, Tower, Pierced Figural Panels, Silver, Continental, 10 In. 2590.00
Spice Container, Animal Head Finial, Silver, Continental, 7 In. 230.00
Spice Container, Flag Shape, Brass, 9 1/2 In. 690.00
Spice Container, Floral Repousse Band, Silver, Continental, 4 1/2 In. 635.00
Spice Container, Flowers, Perched Bird, Pierced Base, Sterling Silver, Poland, 8 3/4 In. . .   345.00
Spice Container, Lion & Lamb, Silver, Continental, 7 1/4 In. 865.00
Spice Container, Open Mouth, 835 & Handarbeit, Sterling Silver, Germany, 7 1/4 In. 690.00
Spice Container, Silver, Knop, Standard, Ivory, Continental, 6 In.   374.00
Spice Container, Silver, Lion Heads Sides, Continental, 4 1/2 In.   259.00
Spice Container, Silver, Wood Handle, Continental, 5 In. 520.00
Spice Tower, Pendant Flags, 4-Footed, Sterling Silver, Germany, 10 1/2 In. 460.00

JUGTOWN Pottery refers to pottery made in North Carolina as far back as the 1750s. In 1915, Juliana and Jacques Busbee set up a training and sales organization for what they named *Jugtown Pottery*. In 1921, they built a shop at Jugtown, North Carolina, and hired Ben Owen as a potter in 1923. The Busbees moved the village store where the pottery was sold to New York City. Juliana Busbee sold the New York store in 1926 and moved into a log cabin near the Jugtown Pottery. The pottery closed in 1959. It reopened in 1960 and is still working near Seagrove, North Carolina.

Bowl, Chinese Blue Glaze, Red Highlights, 7 1/2 In. 470.00
Candlestick, Redware, Glazed, 12 In. 115.00
Jar, Oval, Flared Rim, Runny White Glaze, 9 1/2 In. 415.00
Jar, Oval, Tapered, Mottled Chinese Blue Glaze, Speckled Red Highlights, 6 1/2 In. 385.00
Jar, Oval, Tapered, Runny, Chinese Blue Glaze, Jade To Light Blue Shading, 6 In. 360.00
Jug, Face, Green Glaze, Matte Sand Glaze, Vernon Owens, Stamped, c.1993, 9 x 8 In. . . .   345.00
Jug, Oval, Raised Collar Rim, Chinese Blue Glaze, Blue & Red Highlights, Oval, 5 In. . . .   770.00
Pitcher, Frogskin Glaze, Mottled Yellow, Brown, Mark, 9 1/2 In. 195.00
Urn, 2 Applied Strap Handles, Frogskin Glaze, Medium To Pale Olive, 7 3/4 In. 165.00
Urn, Blue Glaze, 6 1/2 x 5 1/4 In. 805.00
Vase, Blue, Copper Red Reduction Glaze, Mark, Ben Owen, 10 In. 9460.00
Vase, Bulbous, Chinese Blue Glaze, 5 In. 546.00
Vase, Bulbous, Handles, Chinese Blue Crystalline Mottled Glaze, Stamped, 9 x 7 1/2 In. . .   2415.00
Vase, Bulbous, Tapered, Chinese Blue Glaze, 5 In. 635.00
Vase, Cabinet, Oval, Chinese Blue Crackled Gaze, 4 1/4 x 2 3/4 In. 145.00
Vase, Chinese Blue Glaze, 6 In. . . . . .748.00 to 805.00
Vase, Chinese Blue Glaze, Red Highlights, 4 1/4 In. 220.00
Vase, Chinese Blue Glaze, Red Highlights, Inverted Bell, 6 1/2 In. 660.00
Vase, Chinese Blue Glaze, Red, Purple Highlights, 9 In. 690.00
Vase, Egg, Black Ankle, Runny White Over Brown Glaze, Mark, 6 In. 523.00
Vase, Egg, Chinese Blue Glaze, Mottled Turquoise, Blue, Mark, 6 In. 880.00
Vase, Egg, Raised Rim, Mottled Chinese Blue Glaze, Red Highlights, 5 1/4 In. 495.00
Vase, Egg, Turquoise Glaze, Mark, 6 1/2 In. 413.00
Vase, Ridge Blue Glaze, Seagrove, North Carolina, Moore, 1982, 5 1/4 x 6 1/4 In. 201.00

JUKEBOXES play records. The first coin-operated phonograph was demonstrated in 1889. In 1906 the *Automatic Entertainer* appeared, the first coin-operated phonograph to offer several different selections of music. The first electrically powered jukebox was introduced in 1927. Collectors search for jukeboxes of all ages, especially those with flashing lights and unusual design and graphics.

AMI, Model 500, 1950s Selections, 78 RPM, Chicago, 1949, 64 In. 805.00
AMI, Model R-88, 200 Selections, 53 x 41 In. 460.00
Dance Hall Mirror Ball, Speaker Inside, Pla-Mor, 1939 . . . .   2910.00
Gabels Automatic Entertainer, Paneled Oak Case, 20 Records, 78 RPM, 36 x 18 In. 860.00
Seeburg, Classic, Mahogany Cabinet, 20-Disc Selector, 1939, 51 In. 1955.00
Wurlitzer, Arched Form, Chrome & Plastic Front, 59 In. 2232.00
Wurlitzer, Model 800, 3 Bubble Tubes, Plays 24 Selections, 78 RPM, 1940, 61 In. 6165.00

KATE GREENAWAY, who was a famous illustrator of children's books, drew pictures of children in high-waisted Empire dresses. She lived from 1846 to 1901. Her designs appear on china, glass, and other pieces. Figural napkin rings depicting the Greenaway children may also be found in the Napkin Ring category under Figural.

Figurine, Anna, Purple, White, No 2802	325.00
Figurine, Carrie, No. 2800	325.00
Figurine, James, No. 3013	850.00
Figurine, Sophie, Red, Green, No. 2833	325.00
Figurine, Tess, Green, 1978-1988, No. 2885	350.00
Sculpture, Lucy, No. 2863	275.00

KAY FINCH Ceramics were made in Corona Del Mar, California, from 1935 to 1963. The hand-decorated pieces often depicted whimsical animals and people. Pastel colors were used.

Dish, Shell, Speckled Brown, Low Gloss, 6 1/2 In.	35.00
Figurine, Godey Couple, Each Holding Bouquet Of Flowers, 9 In., Pair	150.00
Figurine, Owl, Tootsie, Pearl Gray, Brown Eyes & Tail, 3 3/4 In.	75.00

KAYSERZINN, see Pewter category.

KELVA glassware was made by the C. F. Monroe Company of Meriden, Connecticut, about 1904. It is a pale, pastel-painted glass decorated with flowers, designs, or scenes. Kelva resembles Nakara and Wave Crest, two other glasswares made by the same company.

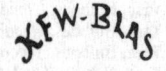

Box, Pink Enameled Floral, Scalloped, Satin Lining, Metal Hardware, Signed, 4 In.	405.00
Jewelry Box, Enameled Lily, Pink Satin Lining, Signed, 5 3/4 In.	630.00

KENTON HILLS Pottery in Erlanger, Kentucky, made art wares, including vases and figurines that resembled Rookwood, probably because so many of the original artists and workmen had worked at the Rookwood plant. Kenton Hills opened in 1939 and closed during World War II.

Ginger Jar, Cover, Danish Blue Glaze, Harold Bopp, 1940, 8 3/4 In.	250.00

KEW BLAS is the name used by the Union Glass Company of Somerville, Massachusetts. The name refers to an iridescent golden glass made from the 1890s to 1924. The iridescent glass was reminiscent of the Tiffany glass of the period.

Vase, Gold, Pink & Green Pulled Feather, 7 7/8 In.	990.00

KEWPIES, designed by Rose O'Neill, were first pictured in the *Ladies' Home Journal*. The figures, which are similar to pixies, were a success, and Kewpie dolls and figurines started appearing in 1911. Kewpie pictures and other items soon followed. Collectors search for all items that picture the little winged people.

Bisque, Blunderboo, Lying On Stomach, c.1915, 3 1/2 In.	350.00
Bisque, Brown Side-Glancing Googly Eyes, Jointed, Antique Dress, Kestner, 12 In.	7750.00
Bisque, Doodle Dog, Spotted, Seated, Blue Modeled Wings, c.1915, 2 1/2 In.	775.00
Bisque, Glass Eyes, Germany, c.1915, 6 In.	950.00
Bisque, Grenadier, Standing, Sailor Cap, Side-Glancing Eyes, Blue Wings, 1915, 4 In.	3400.00
Bisque, Holding Oversize Pen, Legs Sprawled, Topknot, Side-Glancing Eyes, 3 In.	475.00
Bisque, Hot Air Balloon Traveler, Rose O'Neill, c.1920, 4 1/2 In.	3800.00
Bisque, Painted Shoes, Socks, c.1915, 4 In.	450.00
Bisque, Pirate, White Flat-Top Hat, Pink Bowtie, Blue Knickers, 1915, 5 In.	850.00
Bisque, Pirate, White Top Hat, Pink Bowtie, Blue Knickers, O'Neill, 1915, 5 In.	850.00
Bisque, Side-Glancing Eyes, Jointed Shoulders, Knitted Dress, 10 In.	400.00
Bisque, Sitting, With Black Cat In Lap, Side-Glancing Eyes, 3 1/4 In.	375.00
Bisque, Soldier, Jointed Arms, Starfish Fingers, Blue Wings, O'Neill, 5 In.	575.00
Bisque, Soldier, Starfish Styled Fingers, Germany, c.1915, 5 In.	575.00
Bisque, Standing, Jointed Arms, Heart Label, O'Neill On Feet, c.1915, 6 In.	550.00
Bisque, With Flower, Seated, Extended Arms, Head Askance, Germany, c.1915, 3 In.	375.00

Bisque, With Pen, Seated, Sprawled Legs, Germany, 3 In. 475.00
Bottle, Scent, Hands Holding Lower Legs, Blue Eyes, 3 In. 230.00
Composition, Painted Tufts Of Hair, Blue Sunsuit, Socks, Cameo, 12 In. 175.00
Plastic, Hard, Jointed Arms, Irwin, 1950s, 6 1/2 In. 25.00
Plastic, Jointed Arms, 1950s, 6 1/2 In. 20.00
Scootles, Composition, Painted Face, Crazing, Redressed, Shoes, Cameo, 13 In. 70.00
Tea Service, Porcelain, Pink Edges, Transfer Designs, Rose O'Neill Wilson, c.1915, 5 In. . 650.00
Traveler With Doodle Dog, Spotted Dog, Label On Torso, c.1915, 3 1/2 In. 325.00

KIMBALL, see Cluthra category.

KING'S ROSE, see Soft Paste category.

KITCHEN utensils of all types, from eggbeaters to bowls, are collected today. Handmade wooden and metal items, like ladles and apple peelers, were made in the early nineteenth century. Mass-produced pieces, like iron apple peelers and graniteware, were made in the nineteenth century. Also included in this category are utensils used for other household chores, such as laundry and cleaning. Other kitchen wares are listed under manufacturers' names or under Advertising, Iron, Tool, or Wooden.

Baker's Table, Pine, 2-Board Top, Apron, Overhanging Breadboard, 27 x 44 x 27 In. 580.00
Basket, Egg, Hen Shape, Wire 11.00
Basket, Wire, Twisted, Openwork, Victorian Form, Footed Base, 2 Handles, 9 x 7 1/2 In. . 39.00
Berry Set, Sugar Shaker & Creamer, Hand Painted 80.00
Board, Cutting, Tiger Maple, Shaped Handle, 24 x 18 In. 137.00
Bowl, Burl, 7 x 2 3/4 In. 385.00
Bowl, Burl, 8 1/4 x 2 1/2 In. 330.00
Bowl, Burl, Ash, Scrubbed, Ring Rim, Turned, 14 5/8 x 3 3/4 In. 935.00
Bowl, Burl, Ash, Turned Foot, Flared Rim, 5 5/8 x 2 3/8 In. 410.00
Bowl, Burl, Ash, Turned Foot, Ring Around Rim, 16 1/2 x 5 1/8 In. 1650.00
Bowl, Burl, Brown Finish, Turned, Shallow Foot Base, 11 1/2 x 4 1/2 In. 1430.00
Bowl, Burl, Incised Line Around Base, 6 1/8 x 2 In. 385.00
Bowl, Burl, Raised Rim, 9 1/8 x 3 1/4 In. 495.00
Bowl, Burl, Raised Turned Rim, 11 3/4 x 4 3/4 In. 1100.00
Bowl, Chopping, Burl, Painted, Red Wash, 19th Century, 19 3/4 In. 460.00
Bowl, Griswold, No. 2, Slant Emblem 55.00
Bowl, Scotch, Griswold, No. 2, Miniature 425.00
Bowl, Scotch, Griswold, No. 3, Erie 40.00
Bowl, Turned Wood, Blue Painted, Scrubbed Interior, Raised Ring Rim, 12 1/2 x 3 In. ... 250.00
Bowl, Turned Wood, Red-Brown Wash, Hanging, 21 1/4 x 7 1/2 In. 770.00
Bowl, Wood, Red Paint, Scrubbed Interior, Raised Band Rim, 20 1/2 x 6 1/4 In. 630.00
Bowl, Yankee, Griswold, No. 4, Erie, Bail Handle 75.00
Box, Pantry, Bentwood, Double Staves On Base, 6 1/4 x 12 1/4 In. 440.00
Box, Pantry, Bentwood, Lapped Seams, Copper Tacks, K.F. Putnam, 6 3/4 x 3 In. 130.00
Box, Pantry, Bentwood, Stencil, Carved Stars, J. Burr, 1862, 3 x 6 3/4 In. 250.00
Box, Pantry, Lapped, Steel Tacks, Finial On Lid, 10 1/4 x 12 In. 630.00
Box, Pantry, Pine, Hickory Sides, Rose Nail Heads, 3 3/4 x 12 In. 220.00
Box, Pantry, Pine, Laced Seams, Pegged Construction, 4 x 9 1/2 In. 80.00
Box, Salt, Grain Painted, Interior Compartments, Hanging Hole, 8 In. 1375.00
Bread Box, Delft Style, Dutch Tiles, Bands, Villeroy & Boch, Transfer, 18 x 10 x 8 In. ... 2415.00
Broiler, Wrought Iron, Fireplace, Handle Flares & Splits Into 15 Sections, 19 x 31 In. 520.00
Bucket, Lard, Bail Handle, Tin, Marked Naphey's Phila. 1776-1876, 2 1/2 In. 55.00
Butter, Cover, Jadite, Lb. 99.00
Butter Mold, look under Mold, Butter in this category.
Butter Paddle, Burl, Stylized Bird Hook Handle, 9 In. 550.00
Butter Paddle, Cow, Carved, Circle Carved At Handle End, 12 In. 1540.00
Butter Paddle, Curly Maple, Figural Handle, 8 1/2 In. 110.00
Butter Paddle, Curly Maple, Hooked Handle, 9 5/8 In. 275.00
Butter Paddle, Curly Maple, Horse Head Handle, 8 1/4 In. 275.00
Butter Paddle, Maple, Bird Shaped Handle, 6 1/4 In. 110.00
Butter Stamp, Acorn & Leaves, 3 5/8 In. 110.00
Butter Stamp, Acorn & Leaves, Coggled Edge, 1-Piece Handle, 4 In. 385.00

Butter Stamp, Acorn & Leaves, Twist Border, 4 5/8 In. 137.00
Butter Stamp, Acorn & Thistle, Threaded Handle, 3 7/8 In. 137.00
Butter Stamp, Carved Flowers, Leaves, 3 In. 330.00
Butter Stamp, Cow, 1 Piece, Wood, 4 In. 770.00
Butter Stamp, Cow, 2 1/2 x 4 1/4 In. 1485.00
Butter Stamp, Cow, 4 3/8 In. 165.00
Butter Stamp, Cow, Flower, Coggled Edge, 4 1/4 In. 467.00
Butter Stamp, Cow, On Wavy Grass, 4 5/8 In. 110.00
Butter Stamp, Cow, Ring Hanger, 3 1/4 In. 192.00
Butter Stamp, Cow, Screw-In Handle, 4 3/8 In. 110.00
Butter Stamp, Cow, Standing At Fence, Rope-Twist Border, 4 1/4 In. 220.00
Butter Stamp, Cow, Threaded Handle, 4 1/8 In. 880.00
Butter Stamp, Crosshatched Heart, 1-Piece Handle, Tin, 2 1/2 In. 220.00
Butter Stamp, Double Heart, 5 1/4 In. 132.00
Butter Stamp, Double Tulip, Rectangular, 4 1/4 x 3 1/8 In. 1540.00
Butter Stamp, Eagle & Sun, Crosshatched, 4 5/8 In. 357.00
Butter Stamp, Eagle, On Branch, Wings Spread, 3 x 4 1/4 In. 300.00
Butter Stamp, Eagle, On Laurel Branch, Coggled Rim, 1-Piece Handle, 4 1/2 In. 577.00
Butter Stamp, Eagle, Shield & Arrows, Incised Border, 1-Piece Handle, 4 5/8 In. 192.00
Butter Stamp, Eagle, Shield, Laurel Leaves, 3 3/4 In. 190.00
Butter Stamp, Eagle, Shield, Leaf Border, 4 1/4 In. 360.00
Butter Stamp, Eagle, Star, 4 1/8 In. 385.00
Butter Stamp, Eagles, 2 Sides, Initials MS, Potted Flower On Reverse, 4 1/2 In. 925.00
Butter Stamp, Flowers, Wood, 4 1/2 In. 300.00
Butter Stamp, Geometric, Oak, England, 18th Century 165.00
Butter Stamp, Geometric, Star, Sunburst, Initials L.R.E. On Back, 3 7/8 In. 275.00
Butter Stamp, Heart & Leaves, Crosshatched, Half Round, Threaded Handle, 7 In. 660.00
Butter Stamp, Lollipop, Carved Leaves, Curly Maple, Coggled Edge, 8 3/4 In. 330.00
Butter Stamp, Lollipop, Quatrefoil Leaf, Hole In Handle, 3 5/8 In. 715.00
Butter Stamp, Lollipop, Starflower, Ridged Edges, 4 x 9 1/2 In. 660.00
Butter Stamp, Lollipop, Starflower, Sunrise & Initials BU On Reverse, 3 1/2 x 8 In. 385.00
Butter Stamp, Lollipop, Stylized Leaves & Bud, Coggled Double Rim, 3 3/4 x 7 1/2 In. .. 250.00
Butter Stamp, Lyre, Wood, 4 In. 95.00
Butter Stamp, Partridge, Threaded Handle, 4 1/8 In. 797.00
Butter Stamp, Pineapple, Coggled Rim, 1-Piece Handle, 4 1/2 In. 140.00
Butter Stamp, Pinwheel, Coggled Rim, Signed E.A., 1826, 3 3/4 In. 330.00
Butter Stamp, Pomegranate, 1866, 3 3/4 In. 110.00
Butter Stamp, Pomegranate, Inserted Handle, 3 1/2 In. 50.00
Butter Stamp, Prince Of Wales Feather Crest, 3 1/4 In. 110.00
Butter Stamp, Sheaf Of Wheat, 4 1/2 In. 140.00
Butter Stamp, Sheaf Of Wheat, Half Round, 6 7/8 In. ....190.00 to 300.00
Butter Stamp, Sheaf Of Wheat, Half Round, Inset Handle, 7 In. ....220.00 to 250.00
Butter Stamp, Sheaf Of Wheat, Threaded Handle, 3 3/8 In. 275.00
Butter Stamp, Sheaf Of Wheat, Turned Wood, 19th Century, 4 1/2 In. 285.00
Butter Stamp, Sheep, 2 3/8 x 4 1/8 In. 1815.00
Butter Stamp, Sheep, Rope-Twist Border, 2 3/4 In. 410.00
Butter Stamp, Star Flower Surrounded By Hearts, 4 1/2 In. 137.00
Butter Stamp, Strawberries, Leaves, Threaded Handle, 3 1/2 In. ....110.00 to 440.00
Butter Stamp, Stylized Eagle, Shield, Laurel Leaves 1922.00
Butter Stamp, Stylized Pomegranate, Coggled Rim, 1-Piece Handle, 4 1/2 In. 192.00
Butter Stamp, Stylized Thistle, 4 1/4 In. 104.00
Butter Stamp, Stylized Tulip, Notched Edge, 4 1/2 In. 137.00
Butter Stamp, Stylized Tulip, Rosettes, Turned Wood, 19th Century, 5 In. 468.00
Butter Stamp, Swan In Bell, Turned Handle, 4 1/2 x 5 3/4 In. 60.00
Butter Stamp, Swimming Swan, Incised Border Lines, 4 1/8 In. 357.00
Butter Stamp, Thistle, Carved, 4 1/2 In. 165.00
Butter Stamp, Thistle, Crosshatched, Half Round, Threaded Handle, 7 In. 460.00
Butter Stamp, Thistle, Rope Twist Border, 4 7/8 In. 105.00
Butter Stamp, Triple Tulip, Leaves, 1 x 5 1/8 In. 660.00
Butter Stamp, Tulip, Half Round, Threaded Handle, 7 In. 632.00
Butter Stamp, Tulip, Star, Geometric, 3/4 x 3 7/8 In. 385.00
Butter Stamp, Tulip, Stars, Notched Edge, 4 3/4 In. 302.00
Butter Stamp, Whistle, 3 1/4 In. 137.00

Cabbage Cutter, Maple, Heart Cutout, 25 5/8 In.	330.00
Cabbage Cutter, Tombstone Top, Heart Cutout, Reeded Edge, Walnut, 6 3/4 x 18 3/4 In.	110.00
Cabbage Cutter, Walnut, Heart Cutout, 19 1/2 x 10 In.	130.00
Cabbage Cutter, Walnut, Heart Cutout, 19 x 7 3/4 In.	55.00
Cabbage Cutter, Walnut, Steel Blade, Hanging Hole, Notched Edge, 22 In.	154.00
Cabbage Cutter, Wooden, 11 x 38 In.	16.00
Can Opener, Edlund, No. 3, Adjustable, Clamp, Crank	25.00
Canister, Coffee, Jadite, 40 Oz.	320.00
Canister, Cover, Sugar, Jadite, 4 1/4 x 4 1/4 x 5 In.	295.00
Canister, Cover, Tea, Jadite, 4 1/4 x 4 1/4 x 5 In.	265.00
Canister, Floral Lid, Jadite, 4 7/8 x 4 7/8 x 5 5/8 In.	80.00
Canister Set, Checkered Band, Pates, Cafe, Sucre, Tin, Early 20th Century, 3 Piece	120.00
Carrier, Cutlery, Drawer, G. Dickerman, 1858	1045.00
Case, Spoon, Sliding Lid, Chip Carved Design, With 3 Pewter Spoons, 12 1/2 In.	302.00
Casserole, Cover, Chrome, Griswold, No. 65	225.00
Casserole, Cover, Griswold, No. 69, Red & Cream	85.00
Cauldron, 3 Legs, Handle, Iron, 7 1/2 x 13 In.	184.00
Cherry Pitter, Table Clamp, New Standard No. 20, 12 In.	25.00
Cherry Pitter, Wood, Mechanized, 19th Century, 9 1/2 In.	440.00
Chopper, Chop-Ette, Bing Corp., New York, Stainless Steel, 7 x 5 In.	16.00
Chopper, Food, Cutout Heart, Wood, Brass, 10 3/4 In.	275.00
Chopper, Half Round, Wishbone Handle, Wood Knob, Black Paint, 8 In.	20.00
Chopper, Nut, Aluminum, Pink Wood Knob Top, 6 In.	12.00
Chopper, Rostfrei, Double Blade, Yellow Painted Handles, 5 1/4 x 1 3/8 In.	15.00
Chopping Block, Wood, Original Paint, Ironbound, 2 Hoops, 3 Turned Legs, 1860s	600.00
Churn, Box Shape, Gray Paint, 31 In.	69.00
Churn, Butter, Rocking, Wood	95.00
Churn, Cover, Dasher, Incised Ring, Wrought Iron Band, 11 x 4 3/4 In.	412.00
Churn, Dazey, Wood, Cast Iron Flywheel & Gears, Porcelain Knobs, 27 In.	175.00
Churn, Red Paint, 21 In.	230.00
Churn, Wood, E.H. Funk's Champion, Bracket Base, Grain Painted, 22 3/4 In.	1150.00
Churn, Wooden, Hand Crank, c.1860, 41 x 22 x 31 In.	995.00
Coffee Grinders are listed in their own category.	
Coffee Mill, Box Type, Drawer, Crank, Domed Hopper, c.1900	45.00
Coffee Mill, Side, Cast Iron, Crank, Sheet Metal Hopper, Brass Logo, P.S. & W. Co.	75.00
Coffee Mill, Table, Wood, Brass Label, France	85.00
Coffee Mill, Tin, Brown & Green Paint	85.00
Coffee Mill, Wall, Cast Iron, Hinged Lid, Favorite No. 7	160.00
Coffee Mill, Wall, Cast Iron, Upper Bean Canister, Iron Clip On Cup Below, 8 In.	160.00
Coffee Mill, Wall, Crystal, Glass Jar Bean Container, Screw-On Lid, Arcade, 17 In.	185.00
Coffee Mill, Wall, Wood, Dovetailed, Sliding Glass Window, Iron Clip On Cup, 15 In.	120.00
Coffee Set, Sunbeam, Art Deco Design, 14 1/2 In. Tray, 11 1/2 In. Pot, 5 Piece	350.00
Coffeepot, Copper, Fruitwood Handle, c.1900, 11 1/8 In.	230.00
Colander, Brass, Pierced, 2 Handles, 1850s, 4 1/4 x 10 In.	345.00
Colander, Footed, Ring, Tin, c.1930, 9 1/2 x 5 1/2 In.	65.00
Cookie Board, Man Wearing Hat, Horse, Wagon, 6 1/2 x 18 In.	250.00
Cookie Board, Soldier On Prancing Horse, Walnut, 5 1/2 x 4 In.	357.00
Cookie Cutter, Bearded Man With Hat, Carrying Book, Tin, 9 3/4 In.	935.00
Cookie Cutter, Bird On Branch, Oval, 5 1/4 In.	330.00
Cookie Cutter, Cat, Seated, 3 1/4 In.	20.00
Cookie Cutter, Deer, Long Ears, Tin, 7 5/8 In.	470.00
Cookie Cutter, Eagle, Crimped Tail & Wings, Tin, 6 In.	165.00
Cookie Cutter, Eagle, Punched Decoration At Finger Hole, Tin, 4 1/2 x 4 3/4 In.	248.00
Cookie Cutter, Eagle, Spread Wings, 6 x 6 1/2 In.	440.00
Cookie Cutter, Eagle, Spread Wings, Finger Hole, 4 1/2 x 4 3/4 In.	250.00
Cookie Cutter, Elephant, 3 1/4 x 4 1/4 In., Pair	330.00
Cookie Cutter, Elephant, Strap Handle, Tin, 4 5/8 In.	55.00
Cookie Cutter, Gingerbread Man, Mid 19th Century, 8 In.	295.00
Cookie Cutter, Horse, Tin, 4 x 4 1/4 In.	39.00
Cookie Cutter, Horseless Carriage, Early 20th Century	650.00
Cookie Cutter, Lovebirds, Shield & Bell, Folded Edge Handle, Tin, 3 1/2 x 5 1/2 In.	253.00
Cookie Cutter, Man In The Moon, 5 x 3/4 In.	935.00
Cookie Cutter, Man On Horseback, Tin, Folded Edge Handle, 7 1/2 x 5 1/2 In. . . . . . . *Illus*	358.00

Kitchen, Cookie Cutter, Man On
Horseback, Tin, Folded Edge
Handle, 7 1/2 x 5 1/2 In.

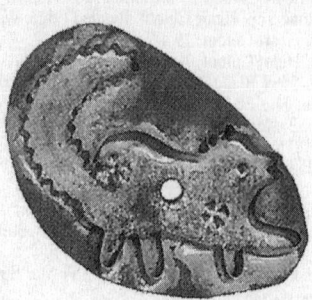

Kitchen, Cookie Cutter,
Squirrel, Tin,
4 x 5 In.

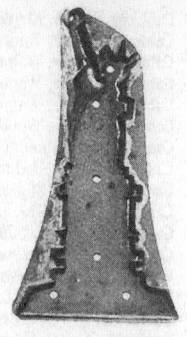

Kitchen, Cookie Cutter,
Statue Of Liberty,
Tin, 9 5/8 In.

Cookie Cutter, Man, Profile, Derby Hat, 6 1/2 x 2 5/8 In.	165.00
Cookie Cutter, Man, Top Hat, Long Coat, Tin, 7 3/4 In.	300.00
Cookie Cutter, Man, Top Hat, Oval Handle, Bakery Type, 7 5/8 In.	220.00
Cookie Cutter, Pig, Folded Edge Handle, Tin, 3 x 5 In.	60.00
Cookie Cutter, Rabbit, On Hind Legs, 4 1/2 x 2 1/2 In.	110.00
Cookie Cutter, Rabbit, Punched Rosette, Tin, 2 3/4 x 4 1/2 In.	105.00
Cookie Cutter, Razorback Boar, 3 1/4 x 5 1/4 In.	110.00
Cookie Cutter, Reindeer, Rack Of Antlers, Tin, Strap Handle, 6 7/8 In.	440.00
Cookie Cutter, Rooster, Rosettes, 4 x 4 1/2 In.	80.00
Cookie Cutter, Santa, Green Wood Knob	10.00
Cookie Cutter, Squirrel, Punched Rosette, 4 x 5 In.	195.00
Cookie Cutter, Squirrel, Running, Out-Stretched Tail, 3 x 5 1/2 In.	104.00
Cookie Cutter, Squirrel, Running, Raised Tail, 3 x 5 In.	145.00
Cookie Cutter, Squirrel, Tail Over Back, 4 x 5 In.	130.00
Cookie Cutter, Squirrel, Tin, 4 x 5 In. *Illus*	193.00
Cookie Cutter, Statue Of Liberty, Tin, 9 5/8 In. *Illus*	2475.00
Cookie Cutter, Teddy Bear, Strap Handle, 5 1/4 In.	27.00
Cookie Cutter, Tomahawk, Folded Edge Handle, Tin, 6 1/4 x 4 3/4 In.	72.00
Cookie Cutter, Turkey, Tin, 6 1/2 x 5 In.	1155.00
Cookie Cutter, Violin, Pierced Hole In Back Plate, 7 1/2 x 3 3/8 In.	192.00
Corn Holder, Machined Aluminum, Cylindrical, Hacker, c.1930, 6 Piece	207.00
Corn Sheller, Cast Iron	140.00
Crimper, Iron, Turned Handle, Ball Finial, 7 1/2 In.	100.00
Dipper, Wrought Iron, Brass, Copper Rivet, Punch Design, Scroll Hook, 18 In.	176.00
Dish, Burl, Striated Figured Rim, Crack, 6 x 1 1/2 In.	377.00
Dough Box, Blue Paint, 2-Board Top, Bootjack Ends, 30 x 38 x 21 In.	490.00
Dough Box, Pale Green Paint, Base, 4 Legs, 30 x 41 In.	2100.00
Dough Box, Pine, Smoke Grained, Handles, Late 19th Century, 11 1/4 x 25 x 13 1/2 In.	290.00
Drip Jar, Cover, Jadite, Aluminum Label	55.00
Dutch Oven, Cover, Hanging Handle, Iron, 12 In.	201.00
Dutch Oven, Griswold, No. 8, Erie, 3 Legs, Tite-Top	75.00
Dutch Oven, Griswold, No. 8, Erie, Cover	110.00
Dutch Oven, Griswold, No. 11, Erie, Tite-Top	170.00
Dutch Oven, Griswold, No. 13, Iron, Tite-Top	1000.00
Egg Basket, Wire, Collapsible	50.00
Egg Timer, Prayer Lady	95.00
Eggbeater, Archimedes Screw On Drill, Red Handle, England, 10 1/2 In.	15.00
Eggbeater, Cyclone, Iron, Tin, c.1902, 11 3/4 In.	75.00
Eggbeater, Dover, Cast Iron, Wood Handle, Patent 1870, 16 In.	431.00
Eggbeater, H.L. Co., Side Handle, 9 1/2 In.	395.00
Eggbeater, Hollister Coil Spr. Mfg., Twin Speed, Wood Handle, 12 In.	22.00
Eggbeater, Jaquette No. 3, Cast Iron, 12 In.	1200.00
Eggbeater, Taplin, Light Running, 10 1/2 In.	45.00

Eggbeater, Wire Mesh, Patent 1867 .... 55.00
Flue Cover, Mother & Father Seated At Table, Girl Playing With Cat, 8 x 6 3/4 In. 402.00
Fly Chaser, Spring Wound, Bamboo Pole, Feather End, Iron, 84 In. 11.00
Flycatcher, Deep Blue Aqua Glass, Embossed TUR, 5 In. 175.00
Flycatcher, Glass, Spherical, 3-Footed, Mid 19th Century, 7 1/2 In. 46.00
Food Chopper, Wrought Iron, Brass, Turned Wood, Semi-Circular Blade, 1800s, 11 In. ... 132.00
Fork, Folding, 2 Tines, Wood Panel Handle, Silver Pique Design, Hearts, 17th Century ... 295.00
Fork, Roasting, Wrought Iron, 2 Tines, Serpent Head, Turned Handle, Cutouts, 17 In. 248.00
Fork, Roasting, Wrought Iron, 2 Tines, Twisted Shaft, Double Turned Loop, 30 1/2 In. 55.00
Fork, Spatula Other End, Wrought Iron, 2 Tines, 20 In. 154.00
Grater, 2 Parts, 4 Grating Surfaces, Mincer, Stainless Steel, Plastic Handle, 5 3/4 In. 9.00
Grater, Flat, Stainless Steel, Wood Box, Sweden, 3 1/4 x 7 3/4 In. 13.00
Grater Set, Brass, Tin, Pierced Demilune, Handle, Early 20th Century, 4 Piece 230.00
Griddle, Cast & Wrought Iron, Handle, 3-Footed 120.00
Griddle, Griswold, No. 7, Handle, Stand, Pa., USA 60.00
Griddle, Griswold, No. 9, Handle 200.00
Griddle, Griswold, No. 10, Bail Handle, Block Erie, Pa., USA 145.00
Grill, Barbeque, Griswold, Legs 1000.00
Grill, Wrought Iron, Drip Pan, Heart Shape Handle, Penny Feet, 19 1/2 In. 385.00
Grill, Wrought Iron, Wavy Bars, 3 Penny Feet, 28 1/2 In. 345.00
Grinder, Meat, Enterprise Co., c.1880 .... 22.00
Grinder, Spice, Duplex, Tabletop Model, c.1880 .... 17.00
Grinder, Spice, Oak, Sawtooth Design, Initials WA, 17th Century 495.00
Hook, Kettle, Iron, Forged, Scroll On Shank, 11 In. 495.00
Hotplate, Everhot, McGraw-Edison Co. 7.00
Icebox, Maple, Door 595.00
Icebox, Paten's Wooden, Pine & Poplar, Zinc Lift Lid, Label, 28 x 28 In. 448.00
Icebox, Slate Shelves, Knobs, 1860 .... 750.00
Iron, Charcoal, Dragon, Cast Iron 800.00
Iron, Coal, Brass, Teardrop Shape, Pierced, Wood Handle, Latch Spring, 8 In. 110.00
Iron, Electric, Hot Point, Wooden Handle, c.1925 .... 5.60
Iron, Flat, Wrought Iron, 3 1/2 x 7 In. 86.00
Iron, Fluter, Cast Iron, 9 x 5 1/2 In. 66.00
Jar, Grease, Flowerpots, Red, Black, Cover, Anchor Hocking 50.00
Juicer, Cast Aluminum, Ebaloy, Inc., Rockford, Il., 12 x 2 1/2 In. 16.00
Juicer, Orange, Tin, Hand Crank, c.1920 .... 11.00
Kettle, Apple Butter, Copper, Bail Handle, 19th Century 325.00
Kettle, Elongated Gate, Iron, 7 1/2 In. 250.00
Kettle, Griswold, No. 6, Slant Logo, Erie, Flat Bottom 95.00
Kettle, Griswold, No. 7, Slant Logo, Erie, Flat Bottom 60.00
Kettle, Spigot, Hanging Handle, Iron, 13 In. 160.00
Ladle, Brass, Touchmark, Signed Richard Lee, New England, c.1800 .... 1200.00
Ladle, Flattened Handle, Punch Circle, Scrolled Hanging Hook, 9 In. 110.00
Ladle, Horn, Snake Handle, Head Extends Onto Back Of Bowl, 14 In. 770.00
Ladle, Twist Design, Line, Brass, Copper, 13 In. 106.00
Ladle, Wood, Carved Fluting On Ends & Handle, 7 3/4 In. 100.00
Lard Press, Wooden Lid, Liner, Round, 1870 .... 1850.00
Lazy Susan, Edwardian, Mahogany, Georgian Style, c.1900, 24 3/4 In. 105.00
Lobster Cracker, Red Paint, Lobster Claw Shape, 5 In. 10.00
Match Holders can be found in their own category.
Match Safes can be found in their own category.
Meat Tenderizer, Stoneware, Relief, Pat'd Dec. 25, 1877, Wood Handle, 9 1/2 In. 175.00
Meat Tenderizer, Wood, Hammer Shape, 10 1/2 In. 12.00
Mixer, Malt, Arnold Electric, White Porcelain Base, 17 1/2 In. 52.00
Mixer, Milk Shake, Gilchrist 22.00
Mixer, Milk Shake, Gilchrist, Patented April 17, 1923, 17 In. 29.00
Mixer, Milk Shake, Hamilton Beach, Soda Fountain, Marble Base, 20 In. 230.00
Mixer, Milk Shake, Handy Hannah, Cast Iron Base, Painted, 13 In. 75.00
Mixer, Milk Shake, Mix 'N Whip Master, 3 Heads, Racine Electric Prod., 20 In. 480.00
Mixing Bowl, Delphite, Horizontal Rib, c.1937, 9 3/4 In. 296.00
Mixing Bowl, Delphite, Vertical Ribs, 9 In. 175.00
Mixing Bowl, Folk Art, Blue Chicken, Federal Glass, 9 1/2 x 4 1/4 In. 15.00
Mixing Bowl, Ivory, Red Dots, Fire-King, 2 Qt. 65.00

Mixing Bowl, Jadite, Vertical Rim, 9 In. 55.00
Molds may also be found in the Pewter and Tinware categories.
Mold, Butter, Block Type, Snowflake & Flower, Finger Joint Construction 44.00
Mold, Butter, Cow, Farmer With Scythe, Hinged, Latteria Sociale, 3 x 10 1/2 x 7 In. 165.00
Mold, Cake, Fish, Robin's Egg Blue Paint 58.00
Mold, Cake, Lamb, Reclining, Griswold, Cast Iron, 7 x 10 1/2 In. 82.00
Mold, Cake, Rabbit, Griswold, 10 x 11 In. 143.00
Mold, Candle, see Tinware category.
Mold, Cheese, Heart Shape, Geometric Piercing, 3 Triangular Feet, Tin, 4 1/2 In. 210.00
Mold, Chocolate, Comic Character With Cigar, 6 1/4 In. 60.00
Mold, Cookie, Redware, Flowers, Swan, Wolf, People, Springerle, 5 x 3 In. 110.00
Mold, Cookie, Woman At Well, Man & Woman With Plant, 3 3/8 x 28 In. 247.00
Mold, Doughnut, Ace Clover Leaf, Cast Iron, Hinged, Long Handles 125.00
Mold, Food, Crystal & Rope Pattern, Copper, Marked 267, 4 x 4 1/2 In. 105.00
Mold, Food, Crystal Pattern, Copper, Brass Ring, Marked N99, 4 1/2 x 6 In. 176.00
Mold, Food, Fish Tail, Tin, Hanging Ring, 11 x 5 x 2 1/2 In. 195.00
Mold, Food, Grape Design, Marked, Yellowware, 7 1/2 In. 100.00
Mold, Food, Lion & Lioness, Yellowware, 9 x 10 x 4 1/2 In. 545.00
Mold, Food, Rabbit, Pottery, Orange Glaze, 12 1/2 In. 230.00
Mold, Food, Recumbent Ram, Pottery, Glazed Interior, Blue, Brown, 2 Piece, 9 x 12 In. ... 140.00
Mold, Food, Redware, Black Rim, 4 1/2 x 1 7/8 In. 190.00
Mold, Food, Redware, Black Rim, Raised Beaded Edge, 4 1/4 x 1 1/2 In. 275.00
Mold, Food, Sheaf Of Wheat Design, Yellowware, 5 1/2 x 4 In. 33.00
Mold, Food, Turk's Head, Redware, Manganese Splotching 20.00
Mold, Food, Turk's Head, Redware, Sponged Rim, Stamped 10, 9 1/4 In. 73.00
Mold, Food, Turk's Head, Redware, Swirl Pattern, Manganese Spatter, Sponging, 9 3/4 In. 78.00
Mold, Gelatin, Mottled Brown Glazed, Handle, Redware, 2 1/2 x 6 x 5 In. 220.00
Mold, Ice Cream, see Pewter category.
Mold, Jelly, Wagner, Aluminum, Round, 9 1/4 x 2 1/4 In. 245.00
Mold, Maple Sugar, Deep Heart, Smaller Heart With Cross, 8 3/4 x 6 1/2 In. 143.00
Mold, Pastry, Maple, Carved Flowers & Birds, 19th Century, 11 1/4 In. 412.00
Mold, Pastry, Wood, Castle, Fish, Swan, Flowers, 5 1/2 In. 71.00
Mortar & Pestle, Lignum Vitae, Turned 92.00
Noodle Cutter, Turned Wood Handle, Copper Head From Large U.S. Coin., 9 In. 88.00
Noodle Cutter, Turned Wood Handle, Head From Large 1837 U.S. Coin, 6 In. 143.00
Noodle Cutter, Wooden Head, Copper Wheel From Used Trade Token, 1800s, 7 In. 66.00
Noodle Cutter, Wrought Iron Wheel, Bowed & Tapered Handle, Marked 1826, 7 In. 198.00
Noodle Cutter, Wrought Iron, Round Handle, Openwork Brass Head, 7 In. 28.00
Pan, Bread, Griswold, No. 24, Erie 885.00
Pan, Bread, Griswold, No. 28, Erie 325.00
Pan, Bread, Ideal, Pat Aug 3, 1897, Blackened Tin, Hinged Lid, 13 x 5 x 3 1/2 In. 45.00
Pan, Bundt, Griswold, Frank Haye 285.00
Pan, Bundt, Griswold, Iron 1200.00
Pan, Corn Stick, Cast Iron, 6 Impressions, 6 x 12 In. 11.00
Pan, Corn Stick, Griswold, No. 22 .... 85.00
Pan, Corn Stick, Griswold, No. 272 .... 250.00
Pan, Egg, Poaching, 2 Handles, Copper, 1870s, 10 1/2 In. 345.00
Pan, Folded Rim, Deep Amber, 1850-1870, 3 3/8 x 9 5/8 In. 616.00
Pan, Muffin, French Roll, Griswold, No. 15 .... 160.00
Pan, Muffin, Gem, Favorite, Piqua Ware, No. 3 .... 240.00
Pan, Muffin, Gem, Griswold, No. 7 .... 195.00
Pan, Muffin, Gem, Griswold, No. 11 .... 75.00
Pan, Muffin, Gem, Griswold, No. 12 .... 250.00
Pan, Muffin, Gem, Griswold, No. 17 .... 135.00
Pan, Muffin, Golf Ball, Griswold, No. 19 .... 450.00
Pan, Muffin, Griswold, No. 16 .... 375.00
Pan, Muffin, No. 16 .... 200.00
Pan, Muffin, Turk's Head, Griswold, No. 140 ....145.00 to 200.00
Pan, Muffin, Wagner Ware, Little Gem, Open Frame, Aluminum, 12 Cup 135.00
Pan, Popover, Favorite, Piqua Ware, Solid Frame, 9 Cup 210.00
Pan, Popover, Griswold, No. 18 .... 100.00
Pan, Pudding, Ceramic, Grimwades, London, 1911 .... 245.00

Pan, Vienna Roll, Griswold, No. 4	685.00
Pan, Vienna Roll, Wagner Ware, Sidney, O., No. 1331	85.00
Pan, Wheat Stick, Griswold, No. 27	210.00
Pan, Wheat Stick, Griswold, No. 28	185.00
Pastry Blender, Wire, Steel, Red Handle, Androck, 5 1/2 x 4 In.	6.00
Peel, Pie, Heart Cutout In Blade, 19 1/4 In.	137.00
Peel, Wrought Iron, Ram's-Horn Handle, 35 1/2 In.	55.00
Peeler, Apple, Iron Blade, Walnut Platform, Crank, 9 1/4 x 13 3/4 In.	50.00
Peeler, Apple, White Mountain, Goodell Co., Antrim, N.H., 11 In. *Illus*	65.00
Peeler, Apple, White Mountain, Table Mount, Hand Crank, 1880-1900	28.00
Peeler, Potato, Hamlinite, Tin, Crimped Edge, Grit Stone, 4 1/2 x 2 1/2 In.	75.00
Pestle, Wood, Handle, 10 In.	22.00
Pie Bird, Roe's Rosebud, c.1900	125.00
Pie Crimper, Bird & Animals, Curly Maple, Early 19th Century, 9 In.	86.00
Pie Crimper, Brass Wheel, Forged Iron Shaft, Wood Handle, 6 3/4 In.	60.00
Pie Crimper, Nude Woman, Dolphins Head, Ivory, Carved, 7 1/2 In.	2588.00
Pie Crimper, Shaped Handle, Button Finial, Wrought Iron, 8 3/4 In.	165.00
Pie Crimper, Unicorn With Fish Tail, Carved Bone, 7 In.	220.00
Pie Lifter, Wire, Spring Action, 15 In.	20.00
Pie Server, Turquoise Handle, Ekco	6.00
Pot, Buldge, Griswold, No. 7, Erie	90.00
Pot, Copper, Dovetailed, Tin Lined, Handle, 9 1/4 In.	175.00
Pot Set, Copper, Wrought Iron, Graduated Sizes, 19th Century, 4 Piece	123.00
Pot Set, Copper, Wrought Iron, Graduated Sizes, Covers, 19th Century, 4 Piece	179.00
Potato Cooker, Iron, Impressed Handle, Wallace Nutting	2145.00
Potato Masher, 2 Spiral Heads, Wooden Handle, 10 x 3 3/4 In.	24.00
Rack, Dish, Wire, Hanging Utensil Holder, c.1900, 16 In.	90.00
Rack, Display, Griddle, Griswold	525.00
Rack, Meat, 3-Prong Hooks, Ring Hanger Top, Iron, 14 x 16 In.	385.00
Rack, Utensil, Hanging, Wrought Iron, Stepped Crest, Scrollwork, 5 Tools, 10 x 30 In.	192.00
Rack, Utensil, Hanging, Wrought Iron, Stepped Crest, Twisted Rods, 5 Tools, 21 x 13 In.	495.00
Rack, Utensil, Wrought Iron, Crescent Shape, Wall Mounted, 11 Hooks, 12 1/2 x 19 In.	308.00
Reamers are listed in their own category.	
Refrigerator Dish, Cover, Delphite, 4 x 8 In.	155.00
Refrigerator Dish, Cover, Jadite, 4 x 8 In.	50.00
Refrigerator Jar, Cover, Delphite, 32 Oz.	170.00
Roaster, Chestnut, Copper, Engraved, 18th Century, 42 x 11 In.	336.00
Roaster, Chestnut, Cylindrical Case, Iron, Wire Basket Insert, Trivet Stand, Handle, 11 In.	112.00
Roaster, Chestnut, Iron Pan & Handle, Scrolled Finial, Brass Lid & Finial, 47 In.	80.00
Roaster, Chestnut, Tin, Pierced Brass Lid, Iron Handle, Hook End, 22 1/2 In.	104.00
Roaster, Cover, Wagner, No. 9, Oval, Raised Letters	350.00
Roaster, Griswold, No. 5, Oval, With Trivet	495.00
Roaster, Griswold, No. 9, With Trivet, Oval	85.00
Roaster, Hearth, Iron & Tin, Handles, 19th Century, 22 1/4 In.	805.00
Roaster, Oval, Wagner, No. 6, Hammered Aluminum	55.00
Roaster, Wagner, Oval	250.00
Rolling Pin, Aluminum, 17 1/2 In.	15.00
Rolling Pin, Black Glass, Mountain, White Flecks Throughout, 15 1/2 In.	101.00
Rolling Pin, Cobalt Blue, Boat, Gypsy Green, 1860, 15 In.	115.00
Rolling Pin, Curly Maple, 16 1/2 In.	275.00
Rolling Pin, Glass, Cobalt Blue, 1890-1930, 28 In.	134.00
Rolling Pin, Glass, Cobalt Blue, Tooled Knob On End, 15 1/2 In.	123.00
Rolling Pin, Glass, Sapphire Blue, 15 In.	27.00
Rolling Pin, Wood, Ivory Handles, Scrimshaw Inscription, 19 1/2 In.	495.00
Salt & Pepper Shakers are listed in their own category.	
Saucepan, Brass, Iron Handle, Copper Rivets, c.1800, 6 In.	70.00
Saucepan, Cast Brass, Iron Handle, Copper Rivets, c.1800, 6 In.	70.00
Scale, Egg Grading, Zenith, Cast Iron, Blue & Red Paint, 8 In.	22.00
Scoop, Lard, Flat Blade, Signed H.T., 1819, 13 1/2 In.	71.00
Scoop, Sugar, Wagner Ware, Aluminum	25.00
Scraper, Dough, Steel, Heart Cutout, Tooled Edges, 4 In.	467.00
Shaker, Paprika, Delphite, Ribbed, Round	140.00

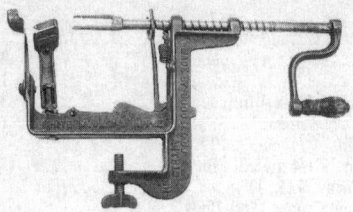

Kitchen, Peeler, Apple, White Mountain,
Goodell Co., Antrim, N.H., 11 In.

Kitchen, Sifter, Flour, Androck Hand-I-Sift,
Tin Lithograph, Wood Handle, 5 In.

Shaker, Pepper, Delphite, Square 125.00
Shaker, Pepper, Jadite, Square 50.00
Shaker, Salt, Delphite, Ribbed, Round 88.00
Sharpener, Knife, Hardwood Handle, Hanging Link, Winchester, No. 1561 . . . . 65.00
Sifter, Flour, Androck Hand-I-Sift, Tin Lithograph, Wood Handle, 5 In. . . . . *Illus* 25.00
Sifter, Flour, Crank On Top, 11 3/4 x 6 1/2 In. 35.00
Sifter, Flour, Handle, Crank Handle, 6 In. 42.00
Sifter, Tin, Black Wood Handle, Cover On Each End, Ernst Reich & Co., 6 3/4 x 9 In. 65.00
Skewer Hooks, Forged, Painted Shafts, Scrolled End, Iron, 6 1/2 In. 440.00
Skillet, Cover, Griswold, No. 3, High Domed Cover 210.00
Skillet, Griswold, Colonial Breakfast, Square, 3 Sections, 9 In. 60.00
Skillet, Griswold, No. 2, Slant, Smoke Ring, Erie, Pa., USA 500.00
Skillet, Griswold, No. 3, Large Block, Smooth Bottom 25.00
Skillet, Griswold, No. 3, Slant, Erie 45.00
Skillet, Griswold, No. 3, Smooth Bottom 100.00
Skillet, Griswold, No. 3, Square 250.00
Skillet, Griswold, No. 4, Large Block, Chrome 65.00
Skillet, Griswold, No. 4, Slant 150.00
Skillet, Griswold, No. 5, Slant 45.00
Skillet, Griswold, No. 6, Large, Block, Heat Ring 65.00
Skillet, Griswold, No. 6, Square 200.00
Skillet, Griswold, No. 7, Large Block, Smooth Bottom 35.00
Skillet, Griswold, No. 8, Erie 30.00
Skillet, Griswold, No. 9, Erie 50.00
Skillet, Griswold, No. 10, Erie 80.00
Skillet, Griswold, No. 10, Small Logo 45.00
Skillet, Griswold, No. 12, Erie 150.00
Skillet, Griswold, No. 12, Small Logo, Heat Ring 100.00
Skillet, Griswold, No. 107, Griddle 125.00
Skillet, Iron, Brass, Donut & Diamond, Long Handle, Footed, 18th Century 350.00
Skillet, Wagner, No. 1069, Cover, Drip Drop, Raised Letters 65.00
Skillet, Wagner, No. 1220, Square, 11 In. 30.00
Skillet Cover, Griswold, No. 6, Aluminum 40.00
Skillet Cover, Wagner, No. 9, Aluminum 30.00
Skimmer, Brass & Wrought Iron, Punched Star Design, Flat Handle, 1800s, 19 In. 83.00
Slaw Board, Single Blade, Heart Cutout On End, 22 In. 605.00
Slicer, Tomato, Red Handle, Ekco, 11 1/4 In. 8.00
Smoothing Board, Wood, Carved Geometric, Names, Scandinavian, 1745, 26 In. 1495.00
Smoothing Board, Wood, Carved Horse Handle, Figures, Scandinavian, 17 1/2 In. 2070.00
Smoothing Board, Wood, Relief Diamonds, Pinwheels, Hearts, Initialed E.I.D, 1829 . . . . 660.00
Spatula, Forged, Hanger, Iron, 16 In. 120.00
Spatula, Wrought Iron, Arched Blade, Hanging Hole, P.E. Will, 14 1/4 In. 38.00
Spatula, Wrought Iron, Bell Shape Blade, Hanging Hook, 17 3/4 In. 50.00
Spatula, Wrought Iron, Brass Blade, Scrolled Hanging Hook, 17 1/2 In. 38.00
Spatula, Wrought Iron, Inlaid Brass HB On Handle, 14 1/4 In. 61.00
Spatula, Wrought Iron, Painted Flowers, Hanging Hook, 13 3/4 In. 742.00
Spatula, Wrought Iron, Small Blade, Hanging Hole, Signed, D.K. Biehl, 13 1/4 In. 192.00
Spice Box, Hanging, Ash, Oak, 8 Drawers, Arched Crest, 16 7/8 x 11 In. 165.00
Spice Box, Pine, Slide Lid, 5 Compartments, 18th Century, 12 x 5 x 3 In. 1500.00

Spice Box, Slide Lid, Pine, Green Tulips, Red, White, Yellow, 7 1/4 x 2 1/2 x 5 1/2 In. . . .   550.00
Spice Box, Slide Lid, Poplar, Pine, Birch, Green Paint, 5 Sections, 14 x 7 1/2 x 4 3/4 In. . .   550.00
Spice Box, Square Nails, Original Apple Green Over Red Paint, c.1800, 10 1/2 In. 650.00
Spice Cabinet, Poplar, Oak, Arched Crest, 2 Pulls, 18 x 11 In. 358.00
Spice Cabinet, Walnut, Lift Top, 2 Over 3 Drawers, 11 x 20 1/2 In. 385.00
Spice Chest, 8 Drawers, 4 Rows Of 2 Drawers, Wall Mount, 17 x 10 x 5 In. 236.00
Spice Chest, Pine, 4 Drawers On Right Side, 6 Over 1 Drawer On Left Side, 13 1/4 In. . .   550.00
Spice Chest, Walnut, 12 Drawers, Brass Pulls, Inlaid Star In Door, B. Harter, 22 In. 3080.00
Spice Chest, Walnut, Maple, 12 Drawers, Wood Pulls, 17 x 20 In.   715.00
Spice Tower, Fruitwood, Turned, 19th Century, 8 x 3 3/4 In. 747.00
Spoon, Tasting, Brass Bowl, Wrought Iron Handle, Scrolled Hanging Hook, 8 3/4 In. 115.00
Spoon, Tasting, Fireplace, Wrought Iron Handle, Copper Rivets, Hanging Hook, 8 3/4 In. .   192.00
Spoon Rack, Cherry Wood, Cut Nail Construction, Early 1900s, 24 x 13 1/2 x 6 In. 440.00
Stand, Breadboard Lid, Lift Top, Drawer, Red Paint 410.00
Stand, Kettle, Brass, Wrought Iron Brace, Pierced, Stamped Bush, 1850, 8 1/2 x 11 In. . . .   220.00
Stove Plate, Tin Over Wood, Fireplace, Wabash Screen Door Co., Minneapolis 30.00
Strainer, Applewood, Punched 15 1/2 In. 2100.00
Strainer, Cheese, Pottery, Yellow, Albany Glaze, Handle, 7 x 10 In. 302.00
Strainer, Tin, Handle, 6 1/2 In. 45.00
Stringholder, Tin, Red Paint, Attaches To Wall With String 40.00
Sugar Ax, Forged Blade, Turned Wooden Handle, 10 1/2 In. 185.00
Sugar Nippers, Cast Iron, Leaf Designs, Stamped B. Smith, 9 1/2 In. 275.00
Sweeper, Carpet, Tin, Union, Providence, R.I., Paper Label, 42 In.   144.00
Table, Drawers, Cutting Board, Enamel Top, 1920s, 31 x 56 x 26 1/2 In. 450.00
Table, Drop Leaf, Butterscotch Paint, Black Trim, 19th Century 300.00
Table, Drop Leaf, Yellow Pine, Tapered Legs, Early 19th Century, 21 x 42 In. 290.00
Table, Enamel Top, Drawers, Cutting Board, 1920s, 31 x 56 x 26 In. 450.00
Teakettle, Copper, Fireplace, Swing Handle, 1870s, 13 1/4 In. 460.00
Teakettle, Copper, Gooseneck Spout, D. Bentley & Sons, 12 In. 770.00
Teakettle, Griswold, No. 9, Erie 250.00
Teakettle, Wagner, No. 212, Sidney, 1/2 Pt. 80.00
Teapot, Tin Cover, Square, Side Flanges, Paneled Spout, Iron, Bail Handle, 9 x 5 1/4 In. . .   80.00
Toaster, Heart Form Handle, Revolving Rack, Rope Twist Holders, Iron, 16 1/2 In. 308.00
Toaster, Hearth, Wrought Iron, Scroll Design, New England, 18th Century, 15 In. 258.00
Toaster, Porcelain, Wild Flower To Decal, Porcelier Mfg. Co., Breensburg, Pa., 1930 . . . .   1600.00
Toaster, Porcelain, Wire Frames To Hold Bread, Blue Willow, 1928 . . . .   2995.00
Toaster, Sunbeam, Model T-9, Art Deco, Chrome Plated, 1940, 9 x 9 x 4 In. 55.00
Towel Bar, Jadite, 15 In. 63.00
Tray, Spice, Red Oak, 18th Century, 15 In. 695.00
Trivet, see Trivet category.
Utensil Set, Wrought Iron Hooks & Rack, 19th Century, 6 x 10 In., 7 Piece 173.00
Waffle Iron, Dominion Electric, Double, Mini, 13 1/2 In. 6.00
Waffle Iron, Dominion Electric, Wood Handles, Gauge In Lid, 12 1/2 In. 6.00
Waffle Iron, Griswold, No. 18, Heart & Star 165.00
Waffle Iron, Hearts, Stars, Iron 150.00
Waffle Iron, Porcelain, Decal, Porcelier Mfg. Co., Greensburg, Pa., 1930s 1600.00
Waffle Iron, Square, Favorite 95.00
Waffle Iron, Wagner Ware, Square, Pat. Feb. 22, 1919 . . . .   710.00
Washboard, Aluminum, Wavy Scrubbing Area, Fani Moser On Front, 15 x 11 3/4 In. 632.00
Washboard, Cast Iron, 2 Rosettes On Arched Top, 21 1/2 x 12 In.   977.00
Washboard, Redware Board, Wood Frame, Child's, 13 3/8 x 6 5/8 In. 577.00
Washboard, Wood Frame, Pottery Insert, 25 x 12 1/4 In. 55.00
Washing Machine, Anchor Brand, No. 770, Hand Crank, Iron Stand 210.00
Washing Machine, Wringer, Full Size 225.00

KNIFE collectors usually specialize in a single type. In the 1960s, the United States government passed a law that required knife manufacturers to mark their knives with the country of origin. This seemed to encourage the collectors, and knife collecting became an interest of a large group of people. All types of knives are collected, from top quality twentieth-century examples to old bone- or pearl-handled knives in excellent condition.

Ames, Sheffield, Pearl Handle, 10 3/4 In. 360.00

Bowie, Bone & Sheffield Handle, Samuel Wragg, Sheffield, Leather Sheath, 1845, 10 In. . 10580.00
Bowie, Spearpoint, Sheffield, Ivory Handle, Mid 19th Century, 6-In Blade. 410.00
Bowie, Stag Handle & Scabbard, Holtzapffel, London, 1860, 12 1/2 In. 410.00
Buffalo Style, 14 3/4 In. 1155.00
Butcher, Russell, 17 1/2 In. 155.00
Butterfly, Brass Plastic Grip, Marked, Valor Miami USA, 4-In. Blade 75.00
Credit Card, Plastic Case, Disappearing Blade Into Grip, Edge-Tex, 2 1/4 x 1 3/4 In. 65.00
Crooked, Carved Burl Handle, 10 3/4 In. 140.00
Dirk, Brass Grip, Lion-Head Pommel, Horn Panels, 18th Century, 16 1/2 In. 1350.00
Diver, Combat, U.S. Navy Seals, M3 MOD 2V376, Original Box, 6-In. Blade 58.00
E.M. Dickenson, Sheffield, 10 1/2 In. 330.00
Folding, Bone Handle, Long Bolster, 9 In. 130.00
Folding, Draw, Greenlee, 17 7/8 In. 60.00
Folding, Horn Handle, 8 1/2 In. 110.00
Henry Bolsover, Sheffield, 14 In. 55.00
Horn Handle, 17 7/8 In. 220.00
Hunting, Antler Handle, Engraved Blade, 9 1/2 In. 145.00
Hunting, IXL-Hunters Companion, Ivory Handle, 11 3/4 In. 550.00
Hunting, Kinjal, Wooden Handle, 11 1/2-In. Blade 165.00
Lathan & Owen, Sheffield, 16 1/2 In. 35.00
Leather, Steel Handle, Osborne Co., N.J., 5 1/2 In. 20.00
Patch, Antler Grip, Rusted Blade, Colonial America, 4 1/4 In. 140.00
Pocket, Bone Handle, Shield, 2 Blades, Closed 3 1/2 In. 60.00
Pocket, Bone Scales, Striker, Blades, Screw, Tweezers, Toothpick, 3 1/2 In. 165.00
Pocket, Columbian Exposition, Uncle Sam 1 Side, Miss Liberty Other, 1893, 2 7/8 In. 155.00
Pocket, Parfleche Sheath, Lloyd One Star Rosebud, 1996 . . . . 16.00
Pocket, Staghorn Handle, Folding, 18th Century, Open 8 In. 195.00
Pushbutton, Pocket Clip, Open & Close Blade, 2 3/4 In. 20.00
Pushbutton, White Pearlescent Grips, 5-In. Blade 85.00
Skinning, Russell Green River, 10 1/2 In. 137.00
Slater Bros., Sheffield, Stag Handle, 1850s 440.00
Snow, J. Russel Co., To Cut Blocks Of Snow, 19 1/2 In. 1454.00
Survival, U.S. Navy Pilot, Type 4, Leather Sheath, 5-In. Blade 80.00
Trench, Stag Grip, Ball End Guard, Leather Sheath, Ulrich Solingen 65.00
Wilson, Sheffield, 9 1/2 In. 140.00

KNOWLES, TAYLOR & KNOWLES items may be found in the KTK and Lotus Ware
categories.

KOREAN WARE, see Sumida.

KOSTA, the oldest Swedish glass factory, was founded in 1742. During
the 1920s through the 1950s, many pieces of original design were
made at the factory. The firm is still working.

LU
KOSTA

Bowl, Clear, Controlled Interior Bubbles, Vicke Lindstrand, 4 x 12 1/2 In. 115.00
Bowl, Internal Threads, Vicke Lindstrand, 1955, 8 1/4 In. 173.00
Vase, Blue, Green, Signed, Vicke Lindstrand, 1952, 11 1/4 In., Pair 978.00

Kosta, Vase, Internal
Tree & Leaves,
1960s-1970s, 7 In.

To test the age of engraving on
glass, place a white handkerchief on
the inside. If the engraving is old,
the lines will usually show up
darker than the rest of the glass.
New engraving has a bright,
powder-like surface.

Vase, Clear Over Blue, Mottled Green, Signed, 1960, 5 1/2 In. 150.00
Vase, Clear Over Blue, Signed, 1950, 7 1/2 In. 489.00
Vase, Clear Over Purple, Blue, Signed, 1950, 7 1/2 In. 518.00
Vase, Controlled Bubbles, Clear Over Green, Signed, 1950, 6 1/4 In. 115.00
Vase, Internal Threads, Elliptical, Acid Etched, Vicke Lindstrand, 1955, 8 1/2 In. 518.00
Vase, Internal Tree & Leaves, 1960s-1970s, 7 In. . . . . *Illus* 1000.00
Vase, Small Boat, Fishing Net Design, 1966, 12 In. 121.00

KPM refers to Berlin porcelain, but the same initials were used alone
and in combination with other symbols by several German porcelain
makers. They include the Konigliche Porzellan Manufaktur of Berlin,
initials used in mark, 1823–1847; Meissen, 1723–1724 only; Krister
Porzellan Manufaktur in Waldenburg, after 1831; Kranichfelder Porzellan Manufaktur in Kranichfeld, after 1903; and the Kister Porzellan
Manufaktur in Scheibe, after 1838.

K.P.M

Dessert Set, Fruit Clusters, Leaves, Gilt Rim, Scroll Molded Edge, 7 1/2 In., 12 Piece . . . 1840.00
Figurine, Blanc De Chine, Boy, In Skates, Warming Hands, c.1900 . . . . 65.00
Figurine, Enameled Flower & Leaves, Man, Hat, Woman, Hat, Fan, Signed, 8 1/2 In., Pair 325.00
Figurine, Poet Being Crowned With Laurel, By Angel, Cherub, 20th Century, 13 In. 355.00
Lithophane, see also Lithophane category.
Plaque, Empress Louise, Giltwood Frame, Impressed, c.1890, 21 x 16 In. 3450.00
Plaque, German Officer, In Uniform, Paper Label, Early 19th Century, 6 In. 4310.00
Plaque, Landscape, Gilt Frame, Signed, 14 x 15 1/2 In. 2875.00
Plaque, Magdalene Penitent, 6 x 9 In. 1840.00
Plaque, Maiden, Butterfly, 12 1/2 x 9 7/8 In. 6040.00
Plaque, Nude, Red Cloak, Signed, 9 1/2 x 6 1/2 In. 4600.00
Plaque, Penitent Magdalene, Reclining With Book, Al Fresco, c.1900, 9 5/8 x 7 1/4 In. . . . 825.00
Plaque, Ruth, Late 19th Century, 12 3/4 x 7 7/8 In. 2300.00
Plaque, Shipwreck Scene, Signed, 7 1/2 x 9 3/4 In. 5175.00
Plaque, Sistine Madonna, Gilt Frame, c.1900, 11 x 18 In. 1765.00
Plaque, Victorian Gentleman, Giltwood Frame, 8 5/8 x 6 In. 259.00
Plaque, Wader In Lily Pond, Signed, 9 1/2 x 7 1/2 In. 5175.00
Plaque, Woman Holding Daisies, Signed, 9 x 6 1/2 In. 5175.00
Plaque, Woman, Empire Type Clothes, Gilt Frame, Impressed Mark, 6 x 3 3/4 In. 2530.00
Plaque, Woman, Profile, Provincial Bonnet, Shawl, Wood Frame, Oval, Signed, 11 In. . . . 895.00
Plaque, Woman, Reading, Signed, 7 1/2 x 10 In. 1610.00
Plaque, Woman, Seated, Partially Clad, 12 1/2 x 7 1/2 In. 9775.00
Plaque, Young Woman, Bearing Tray, Oval, Velvet Lined Frame, 10 5/8 x 8 1/2 In. 1090.00
Plate, Rustic House, 1 Near Sea, Other Forest, Gilt, Purple Borders, 10 1/4 In., Pair 230.00
Portrait, Memorial, Young Man, Oval Frame, Black, White, c.1900, 3 In. 265.00
Punch Bowl, Domed Lid, Dionysian Putto Finial, Bouquets & Sprigs, 1880s, 14 1/2 In. . . 2760.00

KTK are the initials of the Knowles, Taylor & Knowles Company of
East Liverpool, Ohio, founded by Isaac W. Knowles in 1853. The company made many types of utilitarian wares, hotel china, and dinnerwares. They made the fine bone china known as Lotus Ware from 1891
to 1896. The company merged with American Ceramic Corporation in
1928. It closed in 1934. Lotus Ware is listed in its own category in this
book.

**K.T.&K.
CHINA**

Bowl, Flower Floater, Peach, Gloss Glaze, Applied Ribbons, 12 1/2 x 7 In. 29.00
Cuspidor, Red Gold Spatter, Gilt, 8 1/2 x 7 1/2 In. 55.00
Gravy Boat, Bluebird, 3 1/2 x 8 In. 55.00
Plate, Presidential, Great Seal Of U.S., Blue Border, c.1898, 7 3/4 In. 11400.00
Vase, Nosegay, White, Ribbon & Bow, Pink & Yellow Dots, 4 1/4 In. 15.00

KU KLUX KLAN items are now collected because of their historic
importance. Literature, robes, and memorabilia are available. The Klan
was outlawed in 1869 and reemerged in 1915. It is still in existence, so
new material is found.

Belt Buckle, Klansmen Led By Knight Rider, 3 1/4 In. 105.00
Book, Catechism & Song Book, 1924 . . . . 35.00
Candy Dish, Ceramic, Knight Rider, Flaming Cross, Heart Shape, 5 1/2 In. 156.00
Cuspidor, Brass, Embossed Emblem, 11 In. 133.00

Flag, Parade, Used In Washington March, 1925, 18 In. 235.00
Knife, Metal, Celluloid, Orange, Brown, Duty & Honor, 2-In. Blade, 6 1/2 In. 116.00
Magazine, Nighthawk Weekly News, March 12, 1924, 11 1/2 x 8 In. 150.00
Paperweight, Klansman Flag, 1 Country, 1 Flag, 1 School, 3 3/4 In. 275.00
Patch, Cotton, Embroidered, Bible, Klansman, Burning Cross, New Jersey, 3 In. 20.00
Patch, Cotton, Embroidered, Hooded Alligator, Cross On Shoulders, Florida, 3 In. 35.00
Patch, Cotton, Embroidered, Hooded Klansman Over State Of Illinois, 3 3/4 In. 25.00
Plaque, Knight Rider On Rearing Horse, Flaming Cross, 1925, 9 In. 295.00
Plate, Knowles China, 14K Gold Imgae, School, Red White, Blue, 1925, 6 1/4 In. 120.00
Postcard, Schoolhouse Float Riders KKK Pageant Day, Miami, Fla., 1925, 5 1/2 In. 86.00
Poster, Recruiting, Cardboard, Early 1960s 105.00
Robe & Hood, Cross On Robe 155.00
Sheet Music, Our Mothers Of Liberty, Women Of The Klan, 1924 .... 70.00
Statue, Hand Painted Chalk, Black, Red, KKK Inscribed On Base, 8 In. 75.00
Statue, Painted Lead, Klansman Holding Fiery Cross, 3 1/4 In. 55.00
Taillight Insert, Embossed KKK Over Cross, Late 1920s Ford Assembly, 3 In. 156.00
Watch Fob, Brass, Inlaid Bakelite, Town Scene, Chain, c.1925, 12 In. 90.00

KUTANI ware is a Japanese porcelain made after the mid-seventeenth century. Most of the pieces found today are nineteenth-century. Collectors often use the term *kutani* to refer to just the later, colorful pieces decorated with red, gold, and black pictures of warriors, animals, and birds.

Bowl, Cover, Flowers, Scenes Of Japanese Women, Birds, Branches On Lid, 7 1/2 In. ... 3385.00
Cup, Saki, Crane, Gold Lacquer, Red Center, 1 1/4 x 2 1/2 In. 35.00
Dessert Set, Various Scenes, Rust, Black, Gilt, Late 19th Century, Service For 10 ...... 40.00
Figurine, Rooster, Standing, Gilt, Early 20th Century, 11 1/4 In. 145.00
Pitcher, 7 In. 35.00
Vase, Traveling Scholar, Pear Shape, Early 20th Century, 14 In. 170.00

L.G. WRIGHT Glass Company of New Martinsville, West Virginia, started selling glassware in 1937. Founder "Si" Wright contracted with Ohio and West Virginia glass factories to reproduce popular pressed glass patterns, like Rose & Snow, Baltimore Pear, and Three Face, and opalescent patterns, like Daisy & Fern and Swirl. Collectors can tell the difference between the original glasswares and L.G. Wright reproductions because of colors and differences in production techniques. Some L.G. Wright items are marked with an underlined W in a circle. Items that were made from old Northwood molds have an altered Northwood mark--an angled line was added to the N to make it look like a W. Collectors refer to this mark as "the wobbly W."

Daisy & Fern, Cruet, Parian Swirl Design, Blue Opalescent, Stopper, 6 In. 110.00
Daisy & Fern, Syrup, Blue Opalescent, Bulbous, 6 1/4 In. 190.00
Daisy & Fern, Syrup, White Opalescent, Bulbous, 6 In. 100.00
Fern, Lamp, Cranberry Opalescent 200.00
Fern, Vase, Pinch, Cranberry, 7 1/2 In. 35.00
Inverted Dot, Sugar & Creamer, Cranberry Opalescent 100.00
Moss Rose, Pitcher, Peachblow 350.00
Moss Rose, Vase, Peachblow, 9 In. 200.00
Puffed Roses, Rose Bowl, Honey Amber, Satin 45.00
Snowflake & Lattice, Tumbler Set, Cranberry Opalescent, 3 3/4 x 3 In., 4 Piece 198.00
Wild Rose, Goblet, Large 20.00

LACQUER is a type of varnish. Collectors are most interested in the Chinese and Japanese lacquer wares made from the Japanese varnish tree. Lacquer wares are made from wood with many coats of lacquer. Sometimes the piece is carved or decorated with ivory or metal inlay.

Box, Guri, Seal Paste, Round, Carved, Stylized Flowers, Japan, 3 In., Pair 200.00
Box, Lakeside Village Scene, Interior Sections, c.1890, 25 x 12 3/8 In. 460.00
Box, Louis XV, Gilt Metal Mounted, Red, Coffered Lid, Mid 18th Century, 4 x 11 x 8 In. . . 2400.00
Calligraphy Brushes, Cover, Carved, Cinnabar, Bats, Clouds, 11 1/4 In., Pair 259.00
Inkwell, Yatate, Guri, Classical Shape, Scroll Design, 19th Century 860.00
Jardiniere, Black, Oriental Decoration, Handles, Mid 19th Century, 37 1/2 x 31 x 13 In. ... 1265.00

Lamp, Candlestick, Gold Lacquer, Enamel Interior Scene, Wooden Stand, 27 In. 290.00
Mirror, Dressing, Allover Gilt Floral, Chinese, 21 x 10 x 20 In. 460.00
Panel, Applied Ivory Branches, Birds, Painted Mums, Overlay, 72 x 33 In., Pair 550.00
Shrine, Gilt, Pagoda Shape, Tiers, Japan, Early 20th Century, 22 3/4 x 14 1/2 x 11 1/2 In. . . 390.00
Tray, 2 Figures & Pagoda, Red Ground, Floral Border, 28 x 19 In. 385.00

LADY HEAD VASE, see Head Vase.

LALIQUE glass was made by Rene Lalique in Paris, France, between
the 1890s and his death in 1945. The glass was molded, pressed, and
engraved in Art Nouveau and Art Deco styles. Pieces were marked
with the signature *R. Lalique*. Lalique glass is still being made. Pieces
made after 1945 bear the mark *Lalique*. Jewelry made by Rene Lalique
is listed in the Jewelry category.

R.LALIQUE

Ashtray, Tabago, Clear, Frosted Glass, Molded, c.1928, 5 1/2 In. 230.00
Bowl, Campanules, Stylized Flowers, Signed, 12 In. 805.00
Bowl, Champs-Elysees, Stylized Leaves, Oval, 18 In. 747.00
Bowl, Coquilles No. 2, Shells, Opalescent, Molded, Engraved, 8 1/4 In. 575.00
Bowl, Flora-Bella, Clear & Opalescent Glass, Stenciled, c.1930, 15 1/2 In. 2990.00
Bowl, Marguerites, Daisies, 9 In. 630.00
Bowl, Martigues, Opalescent, Molded Fish, Signed, 14 In. 1762.00
Bowl, Nemours, Rosettes, Clear, Frosted Glass, Black Enamel Highlights, 9 3/4 In. 546.00
Bowl, Nemours, Rosettes, Clear, Frosted Glass, Sepia Patina, Brown Highlights, 10 In. . . . 920.00
Bowl, Ormeaux No. 1, Molded Elm Leaves, Blue Stain, 12 1/2 In. 517.00
Bowl, Poissons No. 1, Fish, Signed, 9 1/2 In. 630.00
Box, Cigarette, Fouad I, Portrait, Clear, Frosted Glass, Sepia Patina, Square, c.1924, 4 In. . 115.00
Box, Cover, Cerises, Cherries, Black Celluloid Base, Molded, c.1923, 2 3/4 In. 863.00
Box, Cover, Roger, Pheasants & Cabochons, Topaz Glass, Molded, c.1926, 5 1/4 In. 633.00
Ceiling Light, Soleil, Stylized Sunbursts, Signed, 12 In. 3220.00
Champagne, Ange, Box, Engraved, 8 In., 6 Piece 1150.00
Decanter, Selestat, Clear Glass, Applied Black Ring At Neck, Stopper, 11 In. 863.00
Decanter Set, Nippon, Clear Glass, Stenciled, 10 In., 7 Piece 1150.00
Door Handles, Faun, 16 3/4 In., Pair . . . . .1150.00 to 1495.00
Door Handles, Frolicking Satyr, Marc Lalique, 1962, 16 3/4 In. 3150.00
Door Handles, Soleil, 19 In., Pair 2300.00
Figurine, Aigle, Eagle, 9 In. 345.00
Figurine, Chat Assis, Sitting Cat, Clear, Frosted Glass, Engraved, c.1970, 8 1/4 In. 690.00
Figurine, Chat Couche, Reclining Cat, Clear, Frosted Glass, Engraved, c.1970, 9 1/4 In. . . . 575.00
Figurine, Coq De Jungle, Clear, Frosted Glass, Stenciled, Signed, c.1936, 16 In. 1265.00
Figurine, Danseuse, Dancer, Arms Up, Clear, Frosted Glass, c.1918, 9 1/2 In. 863.00
Figurine, Deux Danseuses, 2 Nudes Dancing, Frosted, Signed, 10 x 4 1/2 In. 926.00
Figurine, Grande Nue Socle Lierre, Female, Nude, Clear, Frosted Glass, Plinth, 14 In. 17250.00
Figurine, Gregoire, Toad, Crystal, Sitting, Inscribed, 3 In. 285.00
Figurine, Moyenne Voilee, Opalescent Glass, Blue Patina, Engraved, c.1912, 5 3/8 In. 5175.00
Figurine, Source De La Fontaine Calypso, Clear, Frosted Glass, Plinth, 27 In. 22000.00
Finger Bowl, Pouilly, Band Of Fish, Flared, Blue Patina, Acid Stamped, 1933, 5 In. 1035.00
Frame, Quatre Perruches, 4 Parakeets, Frosted, 1926, 4 1/4 In. 575.00
Goblet, Hagueneau, Wine, Stenciled, 7 1/2 In., 12 Piece 2300.00
Goblet, Reims, Water, Zigzag Frieze, Stenciled, 5 In., 10 Piece 1035.00
Hatpin, Feuilles, Leaves, Clear, Foil-Backed Glass, Silvered Metal Mount, 9 3/4 In. 1955.00
Hatpin, Scarabees, Beetles, Clear, Foil-Backed Glass, Silvered Metal Mount, 9 3/4 In. 1725.00
Hood Ornament, Coq Houdan, Rooster, Clear, Frosted Glass, Wheel Cut, 8 In. 4600.00
Hood Ornament, Coq Nain, Rooster In Crouched Position, 1928, 7 In. 1150.00
Hood Ornament, Pintade, Guinea-Fowl, Clear, Frosted, Chrome Collar, Molded, 6 In. . . . 4313.00
Hood Ornament, St. Christophe, Clear, Frosted Glass, Molded, 4 1/2 In. 690.00
Hood Ornament, Tete D'aigle, Eagle's Head, Clear, Frosted Glass, Engraved, 4 1/4 In. . . . 575.00
Hood Ornament, Tete D'Epervier, Sparrowhawk's Head, Opalescent Glass, 2 1/2 In. 2645.00
Hood Ornament, Victoire, Stylized Head, Amethyst Tinted Glass, 1938, 10 In. 19250.00
Jardiniere, Acanthes, Acanthus Leaves, Clear, Frosted, Sepia Patina, Wheel Cut, 18 In. . . 978.00
Lamp, Cariatides, Gray Glass, Dome Shade, 1920, 13 In. 18000.00
Mirror, Deux Oiseaux, Facing Peacocks, Signed, 1914, 6 1/4 In. 1150.00
Paperweight, Deux Aigles, Eagle Heads, c.1914, 4 In. 805.00
Paperweight, Deux Aigles, Eagle Heads, Deep Amber Glass, Wheel Cut, c.1914, 4 In. 690.00

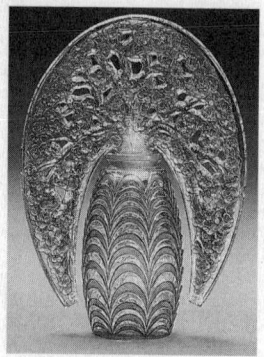

New security idea: Have one of the
neighbors park a second car in your
driveway. Your house will look occupied and
the car will be seen coming and going.

Lalique, Perfume Bottle,
Bouchon Fleurs De Pommiers,
Cascade Stopper, 5 1/2 In.

Paperweight, Perche, Fish, 6 1/4 In. 145.00
Pendant, Ange Et Colombe, Angel & Dove, Clear, Frosted, Gilt, Sepia Patina, 1 3/4 In. . . 575.00
Pendant, Gui, Mistletoe, Yellow Glass, Molded, c.1920, 2 In. 430.00
Perfume Bottle, Ambre Antique, Coty, Greek Maidens, Clear, Frosted, Sepia, 6 In. 1725.00
Perfume Bottle, Amphitrite, Shell, Clear, Frosted, Blue Patina, c.1920, 3 3/4 In. 2990.00
Perfume Bottle, Bouchon Fleurs De Pommiers, Cascade Stopper, 5 1/2 In. . . . . *Illus* 8625.00
Perfume Bottle, Camille, Ridged Fans, Clear, Frosted, Molded, c.1927, 2 1/4 In. 635.00
Perfume Bottle, Epines No. 4, Thorns, Clear, Frosted Glass, Gray Patina, 3 1/4 In. 460.00
Perfume Bottle, Fleurs Concave, Indented Flowers, Clear, Frosted, Blue Patina, 4 1/4 In. . 1150.00
Perfume Bottle, Je Reviens, Worth, Dark & Light Blue Glass, Display, 11 1/4 In. 575.00
Perfume Bottle, L'Air Du Temps, Nina Ricci, Entwined Birds Stopper, 1947, 3 In. 350.00
Perfume Bottle, L'Air Du Temps, Nina Ricci, Sealed With Contents, Display, 12 1/2 In. . . 978.00
Perfume Bottle, La Belle Saison, Houbigant, Radiating Leaves, 4 1/2 In. 1150.00
Perfume Bottle, Le Baiser Du Faune, Signed, Molinard, 1928, 5 3/4 In. 10800.00
Perfume Bottle, Palerme, Pearl Garland, Clear Glass, Molded, c.1926, 4 1/2 In. 635.00
Perfume Bottle, Pan, Satyr Masks, Clear, Frosted, Gray Patina, c.1920, 5 In. 1150.00
Perfume Bottle, Rosace Figurines, 4 Nymphs, Clear, Frosted, Figural Stopper, 4 1/2 In. . . 4025.00
Perfume Bottle, Roses D'Orsay, Clear, Frosted, c.1912, 4 In. 2415.00
Perfume Bottle, Telline, Scallop Shell, Clear, Frosted, Gray Patina, Engraved, 3 3/4 In. . . 805.00
Perfume Bottle, Tzigane, Corday, Spiral Zigzags, Clear, Frosted, Box, c.1938, 4 1/2 In. . . 520.00
Plate, Algues, Seaweed, Opalescent, Wheel Cut, 14 In. 750.00
Plate, Coquilles, Shells, Signed, 9 1/2 In. 430.00
Plate, Fleurons No. 2, Opalescent, Stenciled, 10 1/2 In. 375.00
Plate, Ondines, Water Nymphs, Opalescent, Wheel Cut, Engraved, c.1921, 11 In. 1840.00
Powder Box, Enfants, Children, Clear, Frosted, Sepia Patina, Engraved, 4 1/4 In. 460.00
Powder Box, Georgette, Dragonflies, Signed, 6 3/4 In. 1380.00
Powder Box, Helene, Greek Maidens, Clear, Frosted, Sepia Patina, c.1942, 4 1/2 In. 460.00
Vase, Aigrettes, Egrets & Reeds, Smoky Gray Glass, 1926, 9 1/8 In. 7200.00
Vase, Albert, Falcon Head Handles, Signed, 1925, 7 In. 1116.00
Vase, Albert, Falcon Head Handles, Topaz Glass, Wheel Cut, c.1925, 6 3/4 In. 1955.00
Vase, Alicante, Parakeet Design, Signed, 1927, 10 In. 9200.00
Vase, Amiens, Opalescent, Wheel Cut, c.1929, 7 1/4 In. 1840.00
Vase, Annecy, Clear Glass, Black Enameled Highlights, Stenciled, 6 In. 1610.00
Vase, Avallon, Birds & Grapes, Opalescent, Stenciled, c.1935, 5 1/4 In. 1725.00
Vase, Bandes De Roses, Rose Bands, Clear, Frosted, Sepia Patina, Molded, 9 1/2 In. 1840.00
Vase, Beautrellis, Cabochons, Topaz Glass, Wheel Cut, c.1927, 5 1/2 In. 1265.00
Vase, Biches, Doe, Clear, Frosted, Sepia Patina, Engraved, 6 1/2 In. 750.00
Vase, Birds & Archers, Amber, Molded, Frosted, 1921, 10 5/8 In. 6600.00
Vase, Borneo, Leaves, Clear, Frosted, Blue Enamel Highlights, Wheel Cut, 9 In. 2070.00
Vase, Borromee, Peacock Heads, Clear, Frosted, Sepia Patina, Engraved, c.1928, 9 In. . . . 2300.00
Vase, Bouchardon, Figural Female Handles, Clear, Frosted, Sepia Patina, c.1926, 5 In. . . . 2645.00
Vase, Camargue, Horse Medallions, Clear, Frosted, Sepia Patina, Engraved, 11 In. 4025.00
Vase, Ceylan, 8 Parrots, Opalescent Glass, Wheel Cut, c.1924, 9 1/2 In. 5775.00
Vase, Chamonix, Vertical Ridges, c.1933, 6 In. 805.00
Vase, Chamonix, Vertical Ridges, Opalescent Glass, Stenciled, c.1933, 6 In. 920.00

Vase, Coqs Et Plumes, Roosters, Clear, Frosted, 6 In. 805.00
Vase, Courges, Molded Squash, Turquoise Blue Glass, 1914, 7 1/2 In. 9600.00
Vase, Dahlias, Clear, Frosted, Sepia Patina, Black Highlights, Engraved, 5 In. 2645.00
Vase, Dampierre, Molded Birds, 4 3/4 In. 345.00
Vase, Danaides, Figures, Pouring Water From Jars, Molded Base, c.1926, 7 In. . .1320.00 to 3735.00
Vase, Davos, Bubble Clusters, Amber Glass, Engraved, c.1932, 11 1/2 In. 3738.00
Vase, Domremy, Thistle, Emerald Green Glass, 1926, 8 1/2 In. 7050.00
Vase, Domremy, Thistle, Opalescent Glass, Engraved, c.1926, 8 1/4 In. 865.00
Vase, Douze Figurines Avec Bouchon Figurine, Frosted, Stopper, c.1920, 11 1/2 In. 3450.00
Vase, Druides, Mistletoe, Opalescent, Green Patina, Molded, c.1924, 7 In. 1495.00
Vase, Ecailles, Scales, Deep Topaz Glass, Stenciled, c.1932, 9 3/4 In. 3450.00
Vase, Epicea, Spruce Fir, Clear, Frosted, Gray Patina, Molded, c.1923, 9 In. 980.00
Vase, Formose, Fish, Emerald Green Glass, c.1924, 6 1/2 In. 5170.00
Vase, Formose, Fish, Red, Orange, 1924, 6 3/4 In. 7200.00
Vase, Formose, Fish, Yellow Opalescent, Sepia Patina, Molded, c.1924, 6 1/2 In. 3220.00
Vase, Gobelet, 6 Figurines, Signed, 1912, 7 1/2 In. 1380.00
Vase, Grenade, M10-45, Black Glass, Stenciled, Engraved, c.1930, 4 3/4 In. 2530.00
Vase, Grenade, Sapphire Blue, Molded & Frosted, 1930, 4 5/8 In. 4800.00
Vase, Gui, Mistletoe, Teal Blue Glass, 1920, 6 7/8 In. 6000.00
Vase, Gui, Mistletoe, White Opalescent, Green Patina, Molded, c.1920, 6 3/4 In. 800.00
Vase, Honfleur, Leaf Handles, Clear, Frosted, Wheel Cut, Engraved, 5 1/2 In. 978.00
Vase, Languedoc, Leaves, Clear, Frosted, Sepia Patina, Engraved, c.1932, 8 3/4 In. 5750.00
Vase, Laurier, Laurel Leaves, Opalescent, Wheel Cut, Engraved, c.1922, 7 In. 1265.00
Vase, Lotus, Lotus Blossoms, Frosted Ground, Signed, 5 3/4 x 5 In. 700.00
Vase, Malesherbes, Leaves, Opalescent, Gray Patina, Stenciled, 9 1/4 In. 1610.00
Vase, Malines, Pointed Leaves, Clear, Frosted, Engraved, c.1924, 5 In. 750.00
Vase, Martinets, Clear Frosted, Engraved, c.1970, 9 1/2 In. 865.00
Vase, Moissac, Overlapping Leaves, Opalescent, Footed, c.1950, Stenciled, 5 1/2 In. 635.00
Vase, Myrrhis, Waving Leaves, Relief Pattern, 7 In. 750.00
Vase, Myrrhis, Waving Leaves, Topaz Glass, Molded, c.1926, 7 1/2 In. 1495.00
Vase, Ormeaux, Elm Leaves, Clear, Frosted, Engraved, c.1926, 6 1/2 In. . . . . .635.00 to 750.00
Vase, Ormeaux, Elm Leaves, Opalescent, Engraved, c.1926, 6 1/2 In. 489.00
Vase, Ornis, Bird Handles, Clear, Frosted, Gray Patina, Wheel Cut, c.1926, 7 1/2 In. 1725.00
Vase, Oursin, Sea Urchin, Clear, Frosted, c.1935, 7 1/4 In. . . . . .1150.00 to 1840.00
Vase, Perruches, Parakeets In Branches, Cased Opalescent, Blue Patina, 10 In. 6325.00
Vase, Perruches, Parakeets In Branches, Clear, Frosted, Molded, c.1919, 9 1/2 In. 2875.00
Vase, Pierrefonds, Spiraling Handles, Amber Glass, Signed, 1926, 6 1/8 In. 7200.00
Vase, Piriac, Medial Band Of Fish & Waves, 1930, 7 1/4 In. 1380.00
Vase, Plumes, Feathers, Cased Opalescent, Molded, Engraved, c.1920, 8 In. . . . . .977.00 to 1095.00
Vase, Poissons, Fish, Cased Red Glass, Molded, Engraved, c.1921, 9 In. 16415.00
Vase, Raisins, Grapes, Vines, Frosted, 1928, 7 In. 725.00
Vase, Rampillon, Relief Diamonds, Fleurettes, Opalescent, Blue Gray, Cut, 1927, 5 In. . . . 1095.00
Vase, Ronces, Bramble Thorns, Electric Blue Glass, 1921, 9 1/2 In. 1765.00
Vase, Ronces, Bramble Thorns, Signed, c.1921, 9 1/2 In. 2456.00
Vase, Royat, Molded Ribs & Projecting Nodules At Rim, 6 In. 1035.00
Vase, Saint-Marc, Horizontal Geometric Bands, c.1939, 6 3/4 In. 520.00
Vase, Sauterelles, Clear, Frosted, Blue & Green Patina, c.1912, 10 1/2 In. 4315.00
Vase, Sauterelles, Grasshoppers, Grass, Blue, Green Patina, c.1912, 10 In. . . . .4313.00 to 7475.00
Vase, St. Francois, Birds & Leaves, Clear, Opalescent, Stenciled, c.1930, 7 In. 2070.00
Vase, St. Tropez, Leaves & Berries, Opalescent, Stenciled, c.1937, 7 1/2 In. 1150.00
Vase, Tourbillons, Whirlwind, Clear, Black Enamel Highlights, Cut, c.1926, 8 In. 38500.00
Wine Cooler, St. Emilion, Clear, Frosted, Engraved, c.1942, 10 In. 1150.00

LAMPS of every type, from the early oil-burning Betty and Phoebe
lamps to the recent electric lamps with glass or beaded shades, interest
collectors. Fuels used in lamps changed through the years; whale oil
(1800–1840), camphene (1828), Argand (1830), lard (1833–1863), turpentine and alcohol (1840s), gas (1850–1879), kerosene (1860), and
electricity (1879) are the most common. Other lamps are listed by
manufacturer or type of material.

   Advertising, 7-Up, Bottle Attached To Base, 4 Logos, Silk Screened, Electric, 23 In. 105.00
   Advertising, McAvoy Malt, Frosted Globe, Decal, Boy & Dog, 11 1/2 In. 475.00
   Aladdin, B-25, Victoria, Ceramic, Gold Bands, Oil, 1947 . . . . 350.00

Aladdin, B-80, Beehive, Clear Crystal 50.00
Aladdin, B-81, Beehive, Green Crystal 135.00
Aladdin, B-83, Beehive, Ruby Crystal 750.00
Aladdin, B-85, Quilt, White Moonstone, 1937 .... 250.00
Aladdin, B-86, Quilt, Green Moonstone, 1937 .... 310.00
Aladdin, B-87, Vertique, Rose Moonstone, 1938 ....300.00 to 525.00
Aladdin, B-88, Vertique, Yellow Moonstone, 1938 .... 435.00
Aladdin, B-90, Quilt, White Moonstone Font, Black Foot, 1937 .... 400.00
Aladdin, B-91, Quilt, White Moonstone Font, Rose Foot, 1937 .... 275.00
Aladdin, B-92, Vertique, Green Moonstone, 1938 .... 500.00
Aladdin, B-93, Vertique, White Moonstone, 1938 .... 850.00
Aladdin, B-100, Corinthian, Clear Crystal, 1935 .... 75.00
Aladdin, B-110, Cathedral, White Moonstone 275.00
Aladdin, B-110, Corinthian, White Moonstone, 1935 .... 175.00
Aladdin, B-111, Cathedral, Green Moonstone, Jade 275.00
Aladdin, B-111, Corinthian, Green Moonstone, Apple-Green, 1935 .... 225.00
Aladdin, B-112, Corinthian, Rose Moonstone, 1935 .... 195.00
Aladdin, B-125, Corinthian, White Moonstone Font, Green Foot, 1935 .... 175.00
Aladdin, B-126, Corinthian, White Moonstone Font, Rose Foot, 1935 .... 225.00
Aladdin, No. 11 Burner, Nickel Plated Brass, Embossed, Frosted Shade, Electrified, 19 In. 175.00
Aladdin, Student, Brass, Green Shade, Stepped Base, Electrified, 24 In. 525.00
Alcohol, Silver Plate, Elephant, Rearing, 6 1/2 In. 1610.00
Argand, 2 Arms, Acanthus Leaf Finial, Prisms, Over Fluted Stem, Electrified, 24 1/2 In. . . 2115.00
Argand, Black, Complete Burner, Chimney, Shade, 14 1/4 x 9 1/2 In., Pair 1035.00
Argand, Brass, Clear & Frosted Shades, Single Arm, Urn Font, 16 3/4 In., Pair . . 3300.00
Argand, Brass, Fluted, Tapered, Reservoir, Hanging Prisms, Animal Feet, 18 1/2 In., Pair . 700.00
Argand, Brass, Single Arm, Urn Font, 16 3/4 In., Pair ....*Illus* 3300.00
Argand, Bright & Co., Urn Shape, Square Base, Electrified, 28 In. 55.00
Argand, Johnston Brookes & Co. Gilt, Cast Bronze, Cut Glass, Stamped, c.1830 .... 5175.00
Argand, Patinated Metal, Parcel Gilt Bronze, Center Urn, Masks, Late 1800s, 22 1/2 In. . . 575.00
Astral, Cornelius, Gilt, Damascene, Polished Fitter Shade, 1845 .... 1800.00
Astral, Cornelius, Lemon Gilt Bronze, Classical, Persian Design, 1845, 28 1/2 In., Pair . . . 2600.00
Astral, Gilt Bronze, George Washington, Column, Marble Plinth, Electrified, 1840, 30 In. 1600.00
Astral, Hanging, Brass, 3-Arm Ring 835.00
Astral, Lemon Gilt Bronze, Period Shade, Prisms, Electrified, 1830, 28 In. 1800.00
Astral, Solar, Hooper, Classical, 1845 .... 575.00
Betty, Brass, Rooster Finial, 1840, 9 1/2 In. 95.00
Betty, Copper, Twisted Wrought Iron Hanger & Pick, 4 1/2 x 8 1/2 In. 190.00
Betty, Double Wick Support, Wire Wick Pick, Marked D On Bottom, 5 x 5 3/8 In. 55.00
Betty, H. & R. Bokera, Iron, Wire Wick Pick Chain, Hanging Hook, 4 In. 105.00
Betty, Tin, Dish Foot, Ipswich, 9 1/4 In. 105.00
Betty, Tripod Base, Copper Disc, Column, Adjustable, Socket 1 Side, Lamp Other, 16 In. 360.00
Bouillotte, 3-Light, Ormolu, Gilt, Louis XVI Style, Tole Shade, 22 In. 1265.00
Bouillotte, 3-Light, Silver Plate, Louis XVI Style, Crimson Tole Shade, c.1900, 18 1/4 In. 750.00
Bradley & Hubbard lamps are included in the Bradley & Hubbard category.
Camphene, Morey & Ober, Bell Shape, 5 1/2 In. 260.00

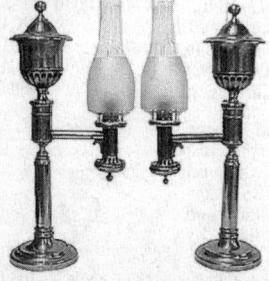

Lamp, Argand, Brass, Single Arm, Urn
Font, 16 3/4 In., Pair

Castor oil is good for dried-out
leather. Clean the leather with saddle
soap and water, dry, then rub in castor
oil with a soft cloth. It leaves a shiny
finish. Neat's-foot oil is also good, but
it leaves a dull appearance.

Candle, Hanging, Blown Glass Globe, Folded Rim, Pierced Ring, Smoke Bell, 7 x 12 In. . . 550.00
Ceiling Light, Bronze, Leaded Glass, Geometric Panels, Prairie School, 11 x 11 In. 2415.00
Chandelier, 1-Light, Shell Form Bowl, Dolphin Over Font, Leaf Chain Links, 24 In. 7475.00
Chandelier, 3-Light, Arched Wire Arms, Tapered Shaft, Bulbous Base, 19 x 20 In., Pair . . 4620.00
Chandelier, 3-Light, Brass, Red, Arts & Crafts, Mica Panels, Period Chain, 27 In. 2300.00
Chandelier, 3-Light, Fantastic Bird Arm, Urn Standard, 22 In. 2070.00
Chandelier, 3-Light, Tan Slag Glass, Painted Metal, c.1920, 15 In. 170.00
Chandelier, 3-Light, Wrought Iron, Bud & Leaf, Electrified, 19 In. 390.00
Chandelier, 4-Light, Brass, Art Nouveau, 3 Arms, Long Drop, Glass Prisms, 40 In. 1400.00
Chandelier, 4-Light, Brass, Art Nouveau, Flame-Shaped Citrine Glass Shades, 32 x 15 In. 3100.00
Chandelier, 4-Light, Brass, Glass Beads, Amethyst Teardrop, 18 In. 615.00
Chandelier, 4-Light, Brass, Hammered, Steuben Shades, 18 x 18 x 20 In., Pair 4310.00
Chandelier, 4-Light, Brass, Silvered, Louis XVI Style, Beaded Glass, c.1900, 22 x 16 In. . 1955.00
Chandelier, 4-Light, Bronze, Louis XV Style, Gilt, Beads, Prisms, 22 In. 410.00
Chandelier, 4-Light, Ceiling, Scrolling Arms, Steuben Shades, Amber, Signed, 5 x 24 In. . 1345.00
Chandelier, 4-Light, Crystal Beads, Pendants, Jewels, Scroll Arms, Chains, 26 In. 2185.00
Chandelier, 4-Light, Empire, Bronze, Gilt, Metal, Patinate, Swan Arms, 18 In. 1530.00
Chandelier, 4-Light, Gilt Bronze, Etruscan Style, Flame Globe, Victorian, 38 x 20 In. 2300.00
Chandelier, 4-Light, Leaf Holders, Pendant, Plumed Corona Support Chain, 40 In. 5750.00
Chandelier, 4-Light, Putto Joined By Antlers With Candleholders, Electrified, 33 In. 7200.00
Chandelier, 4-Light, Tole, Yellow, Electrified, 15 x 26 In. 860.00
Chandelier, 4-Light, Tubular Form, Fluted Bulb Holders, 15 x 21 In. 75.00
Chandelier, 5-Light, Brass, Arts & Crafts, 21 In. 520.00
Chandelier, 5-Light, Brass, Pressed Glass, Floral Bobeches, White Applied Flowers, 28 In. 978.00
Chandelier, 5-Light, Bronze Dore, St. Joseph Lily, Poppy Spray, c.1925, 21 x 27 In. 1265.00
Chandelier, 5-Light, Bronze, Art Nouveau, Mermaids, Ruffled White Glass Shades, 26 In. 4480.00
Chandelier, 5-Light, Bronze, Cut Glass Shades, 42 x 38 In. 1400.00
Chandelier, 5-Light, Cut Crystal, Sawtooth Dish, Bud Pendants, Bead Chains, 28 x 33 In. 2170.00
Chandelier, 5-Light, Gilded Plaster, Carved Wood, 22 In. 615.00
Chandelier, 5-Light, Gilt Metal, Empire Style, Faceted Glass Lustres, 20th Century, 25 In. 520.00
Chandelier, 5-Light, Gilt, Wrought Iron, Louis XVI Style, c.1900, 30 x 15 In. 635.00
Chandelier, 5-Light, Iron, Arts & Crafts, Iridescent Art Glass Shades 1320.00
Chandelier, 5-Light, Louis XVI Style, Blue Opaline Teardrop Pendants, 19 x 13 In. 920.00
Chandelier, 5-Light, Metal, Art Nouveau, Lunettes, Grillwork, Glass Liner, 28 x 20 In. . . . 230.00
Chandelier, 5-Light, Neoclassical, Prism Drops, 30 In. 690.00
Chandelier, 5-Light, Spelter Metal & Brass, Graduated Beads, 18 1/2 In. 490.00
Chandelier, 6-Light, Beaded Edged, Pink Raindrops, Chains, Electrified, c.1900, 31 In. . . 1840.00
Chandelier, 6-Light, Brass & Rock Crystal, Knopped Standard, 24 In. 2960.00
Chandelier, 6-Light, Brass, Baluster Shaft, Scroll Branches, 18th Century, 22 x 31 In. 1610.00
Chandelier, 6-Light, Brass, Beaded Glass Strings, Drop Prisms, Electrified, 29 x 36 In. . . 1765.00
Chandelier, 6-Light, Brass, Beaded, Amethyst Flower Drops, 21 In. 785.00
Chandelier, 6-Light, Brass, Beaded, Aqua Teardrops, 28 In. 2575.00
Chandelier, 6-Light, Brass, Cut Crystal, Blue Beads, 27 In. 3250.00
Chandelier, 6-Light, Brass, Flowering Branches, Made In Spain Label, 20 In. 230.00
Chandelier, 6-Light, Brass, Swan's-Head Arms, Faceted Bead Chains, Prisms, 32 In. 1955.00
Chandelier, 6-Light, Brass, Teardrop Pendants, Facet Cut Ruby Glass Chain, 27 x 19 In. . 1610.00
Chandelier, 6-Light, Bronze Dore, Rococo, Early 20th Century, 21 x 27 In. 1380.00
Chandelier, 6-Light, Bronze, Louis XV Style, Gilt, Birdcage Shape, Bird In Center, 19 In. 1290.00
Chandelier, 6-Light, Bronze, Rococo, Gilt, Beads, Pendants, 36 In. 3525.00
Chandelier, 6-Light, Crystal, Beaded Cage, Faceted Jewels, Electrified, 28 x 24 In. 1725.00
Chandelier, 6-Light, Flowerhead Bosses, Teardrop Crystals, 1880s, 38 In. 4025.00
Chandelier, 6-Light, Gilt Bronze, 18th Century Style, Cut Glass, Prisms, 18 x 25 1/2 In. . . 489.00
Chandelier, 6-Light, Gilt Bronze, Altar, Center Ruby Votive Shade, 1880s, 32 In. 750.00
Chandelier, 6-Light, Gilt Bronze, Crystal, Cobalt Blue, Early 19th Century, 29 x 24 In. . . 6325.00
Chandelier, 6-Light, Gilt Bronze, Faceted Based, Cobeille Shape, c.1900, 40 x 27 In. 4830.00
Chandelier, 6-Light, Metal & Crystal, Scrolling Arms, 6 Smaller Arms, Ball Drop, 24 In. . 1035.00
Chandelier, 6-Light, Neoclassical, Prism Drops, 25 In. 345.00
Chandelier, 6-Light, Ribbon-Tied Wreaths, Crystal Strands, 20th Century, 31 In. 1035.00
Chandelier, 6-Light, Rococo, Cut Glass, Drops & Pendants, 42 In. 805.00
Chandelier, 6-Light, Wrought Iron, Edgar Brandt, 34 x 22 In. 9600.00
Chandelier, 8-Light, 2 Tiers Of Candle Arms, Glass Prisms, 48 In. 2070.00
Chandelier, 8-Light, Brass, Circular Crystal Layers, 26 In. 550.00
Chandelier, 8-Light, Brass, Gilt, Pierced Circular Corona, Geometric Chain, 53 x 23 In. . . 865.00

Chandelier, 8-Light, Brass, Louis XVI Style, Faceted Drops, Prisms, 38 x 20 1/2 In. 1495.00
Chandelier, 8-Light, Brass, Prisms Frame, Early 20th Century, 30 x 29 In. 2990.00
Chandelier, 8-Light, Bronze Dore, Louis XIV Style, 34 3/4 x 33 3/4 In. 3450.00
Chandelier, 8-Light, Cage Form, Scrolled Arms, Prisms, Electrified, 32 In. 2875.00
Chandelier, 8-Light, Corona Supports Links Of Chain, Leaf Drip Pans, 45 In. 8625.00
Chandelier, 8-Light, Empire, Faceted Streamers, Prisms, 19th Century, 35 3/4 In. 4600.00
Chandelier, 8-Light, George I Style, Giltwood, Masks, Electrified, 31 x 35 In. 11400.00
Chandelier, 8-Light, Patinated Bronze, Louis XV Style, c.1900, 41 x 28 In. 6040.00
Chandelier, 8-Light, Plumed Corona Supporting Chain, Bud Finial, Drip Pans, 38 x 29 In. . 4600.00
Chandelier, 8-Light, Scrolling Arms, Disc Form Standard, 35 In. 2300.00
Chandelier, 10-Light, Bronze, Rococo, Gilt, Leaf Cast Arms, 25 In. 940.00
Chandelier, 12-Light, Bronze & Cloisonne, Glass Pendants, Late 19th Century, 26 In. . . . 2885.00
Chandelier, 12-Light, Bronze, Empire Style, Gilt, Cone Shape Standard, Leaf Arms, 28 In. 1150.00
Chandelier, 12-Light, Bronze, Gilt, Repousse Brass, Floral Tier, 44 x 38 In. 3220.00
Chandelier, 12-Light, Bronze, Louis XV, Knopped Standard, Scrolling Arms, 30 In. 1610.00
Chandelier, 12-Light, Bronze, Louis XVI, Gilt, Cut Glass, Beaded Pendants, 42 In. 9400.00
Chandelier, 12-Light, Gilt Brass, Empire Style, Glass, Roping, 44 x 36 In. 1955.00
Chandelier, 12-Light, Pewter, Louis XIV Style, c.1900, 29 x 28 In., Pair 3680.00
Chandelier, 12-Light, Tin, Arched Supports, Hang Chain 1485.00
Chandelier, 14-Light, Scroll Branches, Wax Pans, Cage Form, 32 x 35 In. 2990.00
Chandelier, 16-Light, Bronze, Rococo, Glass, Knopped Standard, Pendants, 32 In. 6330.00
Chandelier, 18-Light, Cut Glass, Louis XV Style, 20th Century, 44 x 30 In. 4140.00
Chandelier, 18-Light, Gilt Brass, Louis Philippe Style, Electrified, c.1900, 43 x 37 In. . . . 26450.00
Chandelier, 18-Light, Painted & Parcel Gilt, Acanthus Branches, 3 Tiers, 45 x 35 1/2 In. . 1150.00
Chandelier, 20-Light, Gilt Bronze, Louis XV, Various Glass Pendants, 48 x 32 In. 4600.00
Chandelier, 24-Light, Metal, Empire, Gilt, Beads, Pendants, 24 In. 590.00
Chandelier, Alabaster, Patinated Bronze, Bacchic Masks, 22 In. 2530.00
Chandelier, Billiards, Brunswick, Kan Tro 4115.00
Chandelier, Billiards, Wrought Iron, Art Deco, Green Stained Glass, 1910, 22 x 22 In. . . . 1500.00
Chandelier, Brass, Arts & Crafts, 5 Hanging Lanterns, Geometric Design, 36 x 18 In. 1955.00
Chandelier, Brass-Finished Iron, Slag Glass, Chain, Arts & Crafts, 14 x 24 In. 805.00
Chandelier, Bronze, Art Deco, Center Shade, 4 Cone-Shaped Frosted Glass Shades, 26 In. 2300.00
Chandelier, Bronzed Metal, Arts & Crafts, Riveted, Hammered, Stained Glass 23 x 57 In. 489.00
Chandelier, Gilt Brass, Porcelain Flower Heads, Songbird, c.1900, 27 3/4 x 18 In. 3450.00
Chandelier, Gilt Bronze, Beaded Cage, Crystal Jewels, Electrified, 30 In. 5060.00
Chandelier, Gilt Metal, Neoclassical, Basket Form, Prism Drops, 17 x 20 In. 290.00
Chandelier, Gilt Metal, Neoclassical, Prism Drops, Late 19th Century, 17 x 24 In. 345.00
Chandelier, Hammered Copper, Benedict, Mica Conical, 15 x 18 In. 1840.00
Chandelier, Metal & Slag Glass, Octagonal, Chain & Ceiling Cap, 16 x 34 In. 860.00
Chandelier, Metal Leaf Ceiling Mount, Frosted Glass, Paperclip Chains, 14 x 25 In. 575.00
Chandelier, Ormolu, Louis XVI Style, Enamel, Cut Glass, Early 20th Century, 34 x 18 In. 3220.00
Chandelier, Silvered Metal, Neoclassical, Prism Drops, Early 20th Century, 13 x 22 In. . . 115.00
Chandelier, Wrought Iron, Hammered, Amber Glass Panels, Arts & Crafts, 16 x 29 In. . . . 920.00
Electric, 2-Light, Green Cased Glass Shades, Bronze Base, 7 In. 2240.00
Electric, 2-Light, Painted Shade, Tree In Meadow, Gas Style, 34 In. 110.00
Electric, 2-Light, Teakwood, Hand Carved, Leaves, Flowers, Foo Dogs, 43 In., Pair 330.00
Electric, 3-Light, Aluminum, Enameled, Yellow, Green, Orange, 1955, 71 In. 185.00
Electric, 3-Light, Bronze, Cloisonne Animal Faces Base, Oriental, 74 In. 605.00
Electric, 3-Light, Chrome Spherical Fixtures, Black Metal Frame, Italy, 59 3/4 In. 520.00
Electric, 3-Light, Spelter & Brass, Newel Post, Woman Standing On Waves, Fish, 28 In. . 220.00
Electric, 4-Light, Green Onyx, Brass Base & Top, Floral Garlands, 28 1/2 In. 410.00
Electric, 4-Light, Newel Post, Boy Playing Violin, Beaded Glass, Onyx Base, 29 In. 825.00
Electric, 7-Light, Floral Sprouts, Coil Spring Surrounds Bulb, Chrome Base, 1960s, 63 In. 635.00
Electric, Aluminum, Flip-Up Light, Spun Shaft, 1950s, 55 In. 295.00
Electric, Archille & Pier Castiglioni, Arco, Marble Base, Stainless Arc, Flos, 78 x 95 In. . 1150.00
Electric, Architect, Tubular Steel, Metal, Ball & Socket Base, Aluminum, c.1930, 26 In. . . 2990.00
Electric, Arco, Swing Arm, Chrome Shaft, Hemispherical Shade, Slate Base, 86 x 84 In. . 863.00
Electric, Art Deco, Bell-Form Shade, Swirling & Feathered, J. Cleamimimu, 20 In. 950.00
Electric, Art Deco, Inverted Tulip Shade, Opaque Green Shaft, Iron Base, 21 1/2 In. 34.00
Electric, Art Deco, Iridescent Flashed Glass, Torchere Shade, Chrome Base, 14 In., Pair . . 290.00
Electric, Art Deco, Metal, Painted, Agate Glass, c.1930, 9 1/4 In. 230.00
Electric, Art Deco, Painted Isinglass Shade, Black & Green Hardstone Slabs, 22 In. 920.00
Electric, Art Deco, Saturn, Glass, Green, Crystal, Painted Heavenly Bodies, c.1930, 12 In. 633.00

Electric, Art Deco, Trefoil Etched Shade, Wrought Iron Tripod, Applied Rosettes, 19 In. . 920.00
Electric, Art Deco, White Paper Shade, Wrought Iron, Gilt, 1930, 70 x 22 In. 8400.00
Electric, Art Glass, Amethyst, Applied Green Berry Buttons Waist, Continental, 28 1/2 In. 635.00
Electric, Art Nouveau, Metal & Slag Glass Shade, Cast Flower-Form Base, 22 In. 605.00
Electric, Art Nouveau, Reclining Nude Woman, Embossed, Spherical Base, 22 1/2 In. . . . 330.00
Electric, Arteluce, Gray Metal Shade, Yellow, Marble Base, Italy, c.1940, 12 x 8 x 14 In. . 575.00
Electric, Arts & Crafts, 4 Hammered Brass Bands, Leaded Glass Shade, Base, 29 In. 690.00
Electric, Arts & Crafts, Caramel Slag Glass Shade, Metal Base, 22 In. 415.00
Electric, Arts & Crafts, Patinated Metal, Glass, Southwest, Early 1900s, 24 1/2 In. 805.00
Electric, Arts & Crafts, Pierced Candle Design Shade, Mica Ground, 14 x 10 x 16 In. . . . 1380.00
Electric, Arts & Crafts, Pierced Shade, Green Slag Glass, Shaft Base, Square, 19 In. 660.00
Electric, Azeglio Pancani, Wood, Hand Carved, With Postcard, 20 x 8 x 34 In. 330.00
Electric, Ball Standard, Scalloped Bowl, Hanging Drop Prisms, 35 1/2 In. 200.00
Electric, Bisque, Woman, Brass Base, 23 In. 55.00
Electric, Blackamoor, Gondolier, Parcel Gilt, Gesso, Painted, Early 20th Century, 31 In. . . 1265.00
Electric, Blackamoor, Painted, Purple, Green, Gold, Man, Woman, 31 1/2 In., Pair 615.00
Electric, Blanc De Chine, Figural, Quan Yin, Standing, Chinese, 31 In. 170.00
Electric, Bohemian Glass, Engraved, Landscape, Early 20th Century, 18 3/4 In., Pair . . . 2760.00
Electric, Boston Glass Works, Slag Glass Panels, Metal Overlay Shade, 1900s, 22 In. 750.00
Electric, Boudoir, Bell-Form Glass Shade, Painted Scene, Brass Base, 1900s, 13 In. 345.00
Electric, Boudoir, Geometric Design, Reverse Painted Shade, Metal Base, E.M., 18 1/2 In. 290.00
Electric, Boudoir, Steel, Black Shade, 10 In. 2070.00
Electric, Bowl, Filled With Fruit, Grapes, Blue Glass, Italy, 15 In. 1095.00
Electric, Brass, Amber Hammered Glass Shade, 6 Panels, Extended Arm, 51 In., Pair 1265.00
Electric, Brass, Apple Wood, Masks, Reeded Stem, Sphere, 20th Century, 54 In. 100.00
Electric, Brass, Art Deco, Etched Nude Female, Grapevines, France, c.1925, 21 In. 518.00
Electric, Brass, Blue Glass Font, Thumbprint, Marble Base, 12 1/2 In., Pair 210.00
Electric, Brass, Floral Font Top, Slag Paneled Shade, Scrolled Leaves, 14 x 21 In. 935.00
Electric, Brass, Frosted Glass, Inverted Baluster Shape, Prisms, 20th Century, 26 In. 345.00
Electric, Brass, Mica Shade, 8 Panels, 3 Legs, Early 20th Century, 24 In. 400.00
Electric, Brass, Parchment Shade, Column Form, 60 x 14 In. 390.00
Electric, Brass, Pierced Crescent & Star, Amber Beaded Tassel Shade 275.00
Electric, Bronze Neo-Egyptian Base, Beaded Basket Shade, c.1900, 28 In. 430.00
Electric, Bronze, 6 Slag Panels, Grillwork Shade, Flower, Vine, Metal Base, 24 x 19 In. . . . 635.00
Electric, Bronze, Applied Dragons & Medallions Around, Oriental, No Shade, 37 In. 410.00
Electric, Bronze, Brown Shade, Red Jewels On Apron, 15 x 27 In. 5040.00
Electric, Bronze, CT Foundry, Classic, Rocky Hill, Conn., Floor 1200.00
Electric, Bronze, Loie Fuller, Nude Woman, Hands Up, Late 19th Century, 14 1/2 In. 3900.00
Electric, Bronze, Louis XVI, Painted Metal Shade, Square Sections, Floral, Gilt, 29 In. . . 1035.00
Electric, Bronze, Nandi The Bull, On Throne, Lotus Form On Back, 11 1/2 In. 230.00
Electric, Bronze, Slag Glass Shade, Brown, White Panels, Petal-Form Base, 23 1/2 In. . . . 335.00
Electric, Bronze, Vines, Leaves, Flowers, 29 In. 1400.00
Electric, C. Eaton, Brass, Art Nouveau, Water Lily Shape, Abalone Shell Shade, 16 In. . . . 2070.00
Electric, Carved Wood, Figural, Quan Yin, Chinese, 33 In. 175.00
Electric, Cast Metal, Reverse Painted Autumn Scene, Marked A & R Co., 25 In. 920.00
Electric, Ceiling, Brass, Arts & Crafts, Flame-Shaped Opalescent Glass Shade, 11 In. 1265.00
Electric, Ceiling, Brass, Sputnik, 12 Radiating Arms, 19 x 18 In. 220.00
Electric, Ceiling, Circular Shade, Pleated Ivory Silk, 43 1/2 In. 180.00
Electric, Ceiling, Panton, Moon Pendant Light, Acrylic Rings, Chrome Shaft, 14 x 13 In. . 230.00
Electric, Ceiling, Samuel Yellin, Wrought Iron, Mica, Twist Design, 9 x 15 In. 5775.00
Electric, Ceiling, Tiffany Type, Leaded, Slag Panels, Floral, 20 In. 400.00
Electric, Celadon, Jar Shape, Carved Wood Base, Stone Finial, Lid, Chinese, 26 In. 330.00
Electric, Champleve Enamel, Leaves, Floral, Figures, Fringe Shade, Round Base, 62 In. . . 750.00
Electric, Christian Dell, Polo Popular, Tubular Steel, c.1929, 15 3/4 In. 518.00
Electric, Chrome & Glass, Flower Form, Contemporary, 77 In. 170.00
Electric, Cinnabar, Turned Wood Base, Chinese, 19th Century, 36 In. 550.00
Electric, Circular Glass Globe, Chrome Cylindrical Base, 1960s, 21 In. 185.00
Electric, Cloisonne, Blue, Green, Burgundy, Birds, Flowers, Goldstone, 34 In. 250.00
Electric, Cloisonne, Double Gourd, Patinated Copper, Chinese, 21 In., Pair 175.00
Electric, Cloisonne, Seed Shape, Fan Design, c.1900, 9 1/2 In. 145.00
Electric, Cloisonne, Urn, Blue Ground, Flowers, Carved Rosewood Stand, 18 1/2 x 9 In. . 290.00
Electric, Coach, Brass, Black Paint, Square Beveled Panel, Electrified, 27 In., Pair 1840.00
Electric, Contemporary Liting Inc., Spun Aluminum, Mushroom, Turquoise, 1950s, 11 In. 600.00

Electric, Copper, Art Nouveau, Domed Shade, Heart-Shaped Glass Inserts, 10 x 20 In. 1960.00
Electric, Copper, Arts & Crafts, Flared Legs, Mica Shade, Canister Base, 20 x 13 In. 1840.00
Electric, Copper, Hammered, Cutout Copper Shade, Mica Inserts, 21 x 18 1/2 In. 1955.00
Electric, Copper, Hammered, Shade, Original Patina, 13 In. 865.00
Electric, Copper, Shade, Conical, Riveted Base, 4 Battens, 1909, 23 In. 2820.00
Electric, Cornelius & Co., Brass, Rococo, Cut Glass Prisms, No Shade, 26 In. 630.00
Electric, Cranberry Cut To Clear, Flowers, Dots, Marble Bases, Bohemian, 20 In. 165.00
Electric, Decoupage, Faux Marble, Baluster Shape, Giltwood Base, 20 In., Pair 1800.00
Electric, Desk, Aluminum, Bakelite, Paper Label, 1939, 13 In. 4500.00
Electric, Desk, Brushed Aluminum Shade, Tubular Brass Shaft, 17 1/2 x 13 In. 110.00
Electric, Desk, Green Shade, Adjustable Brass Shaft, Circular Marble Base, 15 x 9 In. ... 220.00
Electric, Desk, Lightolier, Pivoting, Ivory Shade, Brass Shaft, Enameled Base, 16 x 16 In. 80.00
Electric, Desk, Polaroid Corp., Bakelite & Aluminum, Paper Label, 1939 .... 4600.00
Electric, Desk, Sergio Mazza, Mushroom Shade, Glass, Chrome Base, 1960, 11 x 15 In. . 145.00
Electric, Desk, Vico Magistretti, Eclese, Enamel, Red, White, Rotating Diffuser, 7 x 4 In. . 70.00
Electric, Desny, Nickeled Bronze, Adjustable, Square, Wall, 1926, 6 1/4 In. 7200.00
Electric, Duffner & Kimberly, French Renaissance, Base, 3 Legs, 19 In. 34820.00
Electric, Duffner & Kimberly, Leaded Glass, Shell-Shaped Shade, 25 x 70 In. 13440.00
Electric, Duffner & Kimberly, Leaded Shade, Green, Red, Yellow Designs, 16 In. 5600.00
Electric, Duffner & Kimberly, Leaded Shade, Ivy, Granite Glass, Cast Bronze Base, 17 In. 19360.00
Electric, Duffner & Kimberly, Leaded Shade, Red Blossoms, Green Leaves, 20 In. 8960.00
Electric, Edouard Wilfrid Buquet, Aluminum Shade, Metal Arm, Base, c.1927, 21 In. ... 4370.00
Electric, Egyptian Revival, Composition, Obelisk, Gilt, Marble, 20th Century, 19 In., Pair 575.00
Electric, Fred Flintstone, Hard Vinyl, Tin Base, 9 1/2 In. 65.00
Electric, Frederick Cooper, Classical, Brass, Turned Wooden Urn, No Shade, 39 In. 120.00
Electric, Frosted Cube Shade, Square Cork Base, 1960s, 12 3/4 In. 240.00
Electric, G. Grossman, Wrought Iron, Painted, Glass, Ralph O. Smith, 1951, 62 In. 635.00
Electric, G. Nakashima, Hickory & Fiberglass Shade, Free-Form Burl Walnut, 19 In. 4600.00
Electric, G. Nakashima, Oak Burl, Fiberglass, 1960s, 25 1/4 In. 5750.00
Electric, G. Stickley, Hammered Copper Harp, Bell-Shaped Shade, Footed Base, 57 In. . 4315.00
Electric, G. Stickley, Hammered Iron, Amber Glass Shade, Patina, 9 x 29 In. 3740.00
Electric, Garlanded Border, Ribbon-Tied Swags, Leaf Tips, 20th Century, 65 In. 515.00
Electric, Gilbert Watrous, Chromium Plated, 1950s, 22 In. 1840.00
Electric, Gilded Brass, 3 Cornucopia, Adjustable, 3 Dogs At Base, 27 In. 1100.00
Electric, Gilt Bronze, Loie Fuller, The Dance, After Raoul François Larche, 17 In. 1230.00
Electric, Gilt Floral & Sparrows, Brown & Mauve Ground, 16 x 10 In. 525.00
Electric, Ginger Jar, Cover, Carved Chinese Plinth, 9 3/4 In., Pair 400.00
Electric, Gorham, Caramel Wavy Shade, Fan Base, 16 In. 4200.00
Electric, Gorham, Leaded Domed Shade, Border, Leaves, Flowers, Bronzed Base, 17 In. . 8400.00
Electric, Gorham, Leaded Shade, Green Geometric, Tulip Border, 18 In. 2520.00
Electric, Hall, Brass, Etched Glass, Pierced Band, Cylinder Shape, 36 In. 615.00
Electric, Hall, Gilt Bronze, Shaped Dome Frame, Etched Glass Panels, 22 In. 365.00
Electric, Hall, Iron, Openwork Leaves, Opalescent Hobnail Shade, 46 1/2 In. 330.00
Electric, Hall, Scrolling Metal, 8-Sided Slag Glass, 24 In. 645.00
Electric, Hammered Copper, Conical Shade, 3 Mica Insets, 19 1/4 In. 1380.00
Electric, Hanging, 4 Frosted Panels, Square, 10 In. 57.00
Electric, Hanging, Art Deco, Molded, Amber, Clamshell Shape, 10 1/2 In. 210.00
Electric, Hanging, Brass Font, Double Angle, Milk Glass Shades, Electrified 350.00
Electric, Hanging, Brass, Etched Globe, Wreath & Horns Surround, 4 1/2-In. Shade 60.00
Electric, Hanging, Duffner & Kimberly, Green Ground, Fleur-De-Lis Border, 24 1/2 In. ... 5600.00
Electric, Hanging, Leaded Glass, Stylized Flowers, Caramel Geometric, 24 In. 2240.00
Electric, Hanging, Lightolier, Frosted Glass Shade, Brass Ceiling Cap, Label, 23 x 12 In. . 295.00
Electric, Hanging, Metal, Brass Washed, Caramel Slag Glass Shades, 3 1/2 x 4 3/4 In. 290.00
Electric, Hanging, Parrot On Perch, Bronze, 2-Light, Whimsical, Austria, 15 x 11 1/4 In. . 1725.00
Electric, Hanging, Poul Henningsen, Aluminum, Red Paint, Denmark, 1958, 19 3/4 In. 400.00
Electric, Hanging, Poul Henningsen, Charlotenborg, Louis Poulsen, 1958, 21 x 26 In. ... 1150.00
Electric, Hanging, Stained Glass Panels, Victorian 2850.00
Electric, Industrial Arts, Aluminum Framed Glass Inserts, Pyramid Plastic Base, 31 In. 330.00
Electric, Jacques Adnet, Leather, Textured Paper Shade, 1955, 27 1/2 In. 4800.00
Electric, Jefferson, Painted Shade, Abstract Design, Polished Bronzed Base, 16 In. 2240.00
Electric, Karl Trabert, No. 6580, Metal, Steel, Wood, Schanzenbach, c.1934, 16 1/2 In. .. 1035.00
Electric, L. & J.G. Stickley, Pyramid Wicker Shade, Mahogany Base, 23 x 14 In. 920.00
Electric, La Danse Des Nymphs, Bronze & Marble, Art Glass Shade, 23 In. 760.00

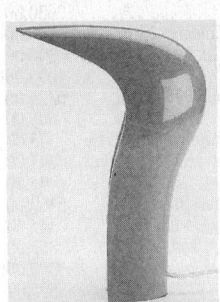

Lamp, Electric, Lampreti,
Chrome Orange Plastic,
Casati E Ponzio, 12 1/2 In.

Lamp, Electric, Moe-Bridges,
Reverse Painted Shade, Boats,
Bronzed Metal, 24 In.

Electric, Lampreti, Chrome Orange Plastic, Casati E Ponzio, 12 1/2 In. . . . . *Illus*	200.00
Electric, Laurel Lamp Co., Chrome Shaft, Mushroom Frosted Shade, Label, 60 x 12 In. . .	400.00
Electric, Laurel Lamp Co., Chrome, Domed Shade, Cylindrical, Label, 19 1/2 x 12 In.	165.00
Electric, Laurel Lamp Co., Pinched Waist, Enamel Base, Mushroom Shade, 16 x 12 In. . .	860.00
Electric, Laurel Lamp Co., White Glass Mushroom Shade, Round Wood Base, 12 In.	400.00
Electric, Laurel, Frosted Glass Mushroom Shade, Brushed Chrome Base, 60 In.	385.00
Electric, Laurel, Tulip Shape, Shade, Frosted Glass, Chrome Base, Lamp Co., 63 In.	230.00
Electric, Leaded Domed Shade, Apron & Fleur-De-Lis Designs, 18 In.	2520.00
Electric, Leaded Glass Shade, Caramel Slag Panels, Walnut Base, Early 1900s, 23 In. . . .	460.00
Electric, Leaded Glass, Continuous Apple Blossom Band, Caramel Brickwork, 18 In. . . .	3080.00
Electric, Leaded Glass, Pagoda Shade, 4 Arms, Yellow, Green, Red Slag, 17 1/2 x 12 In. .	520.00
Electric, Leaded Glass, Poinsettia, Urn Shape, Bronze Base	310.00
Electric, Leaded Glass, Tulip Shade, Rainbow Color Background	4950.00
Electric, Leaded Shade, Green, White Striated Glass, Continuous Flower Border, 19 In. . .	4200.00
Electric, Lightolier, Brass, Adjustable Glass Dome Shade, 20 1/2 x 20 In.	465.00
Electric, Lillian Palmer, Copper, Chinese Style, Mica Shade, 4 Panels, Handle, 21 x 18 In.	8250.00
Electric, Linen Shade, Flaring, Adjustable Height, Ball Feet & Finial, 55 1/2 In.	275.00
Electric, Louis Poulsen, Tiered Amber Glass Shade, Patinated Brass Stem, c.1933, 58 In. .	3450.00
Electric, Lumiere, 3-Light, Louis XV Style, Ormolu, Early 20th Century, 23 3/4 In., Pair	1035.00
Electric, Marble, Louis XV Style, Bronze Mount, Double Gourd Shape, 1900s, 41 In. . . .	1610.00
Electric, Marble, Overlay Glass, White Cut To Green, Gilt, Stepped Base, 25 In.	635.00
Electric, Marianne Brandt, No. 656, Opalescent Shade, c.1929, 7 3/4 x 8 5/8 In.	978.00
Electric, Mermaids, Fish, Starfish, Aqua, Orange, White, Iridescent Glazes, 22 1/4 In. . . .	375.00
Electric, Metal Shade, Acanthus Leaves & Shells Base, Flying Swan Arms	385.00
Electric, Metal, Glazed Panel, Pierced Dome Top, Stained Glass, 20th Century	225.00
Electric, Miller Lamp Co., Green Slag, Ivy, Berry Grillwork, Flower Base, 24 x 18 In. . . .	600.00
Electric, Miller, Student, Double, Original Shades, 32 In. . . . . .4290.00 to 5225.00
Electric, Mitchell, Bakelite, Bed, Radio	40.00
Electric, Moe-Bridges, Reverse Painted Shade, Boats, Bronzed Metal, 24 In. . . . . . . *Illus*	1150.00
Electric, National Cash Register, Slag Glass Shade, Blue, Purple, Bronze Base, 14 In. . . .	2800.00
Electric, Nelson, Bubble, Spun Fiber Over Metal Wire Frame, H. Miller, 1956, 38 In.	1093.00
Electric, Nessen, Bronze, Brushed Chrome, Swing Arm, Enamel Light Switch, 43 3/4 In. .	145.00
Electric, Night-Light, Cat, Irice	20.00
Electric, Night-Light, Owl, Porcelain, Glass Eyes, 20th Century, 8 3/4 In.	695.00
Electric, No. 502, Hammered Copper, Silk Lined Shade, Gustave Stickley, 16 x 19 In. . . .	690.00
Electric, Noguchi, Spherical Mulberry Paper Shade, Bamboo Shaft, 74 In.	1035.00
Electric, Noguchi, Spherical Mulberry Paper Shade, Weighted Metal Base, 74 In.	1400.00
Electric, Oak, Arts & Crafts, 4-Sided Base, Carmel Slag Glass Shade, 21 x 13 In.	980.00
Electric, Oak, Green, Cream, Brown Slag Glass Shade, 18 x 25 In.	1955.00
Electric, Old Mission Kopperkraft, Copper, Hammered, Mica Shade, 3 Panels, 12 In.	4025.00
Electric, Ormolu Mounted, Sevres, Urn, Woman, Mirror, Blue, Gilt, c.1900, 11 1/2 In. . . .	690.00
Electric, Overlay Metal Floral Design, Pale Green Glass Shade, 17 x 22 In.	1210.00
Electric, Panton, Ivory Plastic Pedestal Base, 29 x 22 In.	465.00
Electric, Panton, Panthella, Molded Plastic, Domed Shade, Flared Base, 1960, 28 In.	430.00
Electric, Parchment Shade, Black & Gold, 1950s, Pair	140.00
Electric, Parrot, On Turned Wooden Perch, Glass, Beaded, 18 In.	4315.00
Electric, Phoenix, Hillside Woodland Scene Shade, Interior Painted, 18 In.	2690.00

Electric, Pittsburgh, Winter Night Scene Shade, Interior Painted, 16 In. 2630.00
Electric, Porcelain, Peony, Blue & White, Baluster Shape, Wood Base, Chinese, 25 In. . . . 690.00
Electric, Porcelain, Urn, Blue Ground, Flowers, Continental, c.1900, 17 In. 390.00
Electric, Porcelain, Urn, Gilt, 35 In. 1095.00
Electric, Poul Henningsen, Opalescent Shade, Brass Shaft, Louis Poulsen, 1927, 17 In. . . 6325.00
Electric, Psychedelic, Hourglass Shape, 1960s, 22 x 40 In. 605.00
Electric, R. Sonneman, White Plastic Orb Shade, Chrome Shaft, Wood Base, 1960s, 56 In. 375.00
Electric, Robot, Chrome, 3-Way Nose Switch, Lights Head & Hands, Italy, c.1970, 30 In. 895.00
Electric, Robot, Metal, Silver Paint, Hinged Body, 1950-1960 . . . . 95.00
Electric, Seuss, Leaded Glass Shade, Flowers, Yellow, Orange, White, Brass Base, 23 In. . 5460.00
Electric, Silver Plate, Candlestick, Hugenot Style, Ivory Shade, France, 6 3/4 In., Pair . . . 345.00
Electric, Silver Plate, Candlestick, Louis XVI Style, Card Shade, France, 18 In., Pair 865.00
Electric, Silver Plate, Candlestick, Tole Shade, France, c.1900, 11 1/2 In. 490.00
Electric, Silver, Swag, Leaves, Shells, Paw Feet, 1909, 30 In. 805.00
Electric, Slag Glass Panel, Domed Shade, Ribbed Trefoil Base, Early 1900s, 19 In. 920.00
Electric, Slag Glass Panels, Dragonfly, Grillwork, Overlapping Leaves, Base, 23 x 18 In. . 800.00
Electric, Spelter Base, Stagecoach, Amber Globe, 13 In. 40.00
Electric, Spelter, Cast Tulips, Reverse Painted Glass Shade, 25 In. 770.00
Electric, Sportsman's Trophy, 4 Deer Hooves, 15 In. 200.00
Electric, Squirrel, Tail Forms Stem, Grapevines, Brass Ears, Paws & Pinecone, 8 3/4 In. . . 110.00
Electric, Stained Glass, Conical Shade With Dragonflies, Urn Base, 4-Footed, 21 In. 6900.00
Electric, Stemlite, Egg-Shape Shade, Smoky Quartz, Chrome Pedestal Base, 21 x 9 In. . . . 175.00
Electric, Student, Brass, Milk Glass Shade, Brass Reservoir, 20 1/8 In. 335.00
Electric, Student, Brass, Single Arm, White Cased Glass Shade, 20 1/2 In. 230.00
Electric, Tomi Parzinger, Gilt Metal, 1950s, 67 1/2 In., Pair 4025.00
Electric, Uncle Sam, Pledge Of Allegiance, Portable, Plastic, 1950, 7 7/8 x 4 3/8 In. 100.00
Electric, Urn, Enameled, Polychrome Poppies, Mums, Blue, Oriental, 26 1/2 In. 45.00
Electric, Urn, Faux Porphyry, 20th Century, 15 1/2 In., Pair 460.00
Electric, Vase, Applied Leaf Shapes, Cartouche, Romantic Scene, France, 1870s, 22 In. . . 250.00
Electric, Vase, Decalcomania, Chinese Figures, Mythical Animals, 15 In., Pair 9600.00
Electric, Von Nessen, Anywhere, Enameled Aluminum, Wood Switch, 14 In. 1840.00
Electric, Von Nessen, Enameled Shade, Brushed Steel, 14 1/2 x 20 In. 60.00
Electric, Von Nessen, Plastic Shade, Adjustable Arm, Chrome Pole & Base, 50 1/2 In. . . . 175.00
Electric, Von Nessen, Steel, 28 x 17 In., Pair 300.00
Electric, Von Nessen, White Glass Shade, Swing Arm, Brushed Chrome, 59 3/4 In. 135.00
Electric, WB Brown Co., Oak & Green Slag Glass, 23 In. 520.00
Electric, Wilkinson, Flower Shade, Red, Orange, Locking Mechanism Base, 20 In. 3360.00
Electric, Wilkinson, Geometric Shade, Leaded, Green, Pink & Green Flowers, 17 In. 2100.00
Electric, Wilkinson, Leaded Shade, Stylized, Locking Mechanism Base, 18 In. 3080.00
Electric, Wire Mesh Shade, Copper Column, Curled Wrought Iron Base, 70 In. 140.00
Electric, Wisteria Shade, Green Leaves, Bronze Base, 13 1/2 In. 4760.00
Electric, Woman, Feeding Birds, Ivory Face & Arms, Onyx Base, 1930s, 12 3/4 In. 1035.00
Electric, Wood & Slag Glass Shade, Caramel Glass, Column Base, 21 In. 750.00
Electric, Wood, Covered Jar Shape, Carved Base, Cinnabar Finials, 21 In. 176.00
Electric, Wood, Slag Glass Shade, Wood Tapered Column, 1922, 15 x 24 In. 104.00
Electric, Wood, Stack Of Books Shape, Painted, 16 In., Pair 1320.00
Electric, Wood, White Cut To Clear Glass, 2 Medallions, Gold Trim, 15 In. 250.00
Electric, Wrought Iron, Panel Shade, Scroll, Arrow Finial, 3-Footed, c.1920, 56 In., Pair . 800.00
Fairy, Blue Nailsea, Rubbed Base, Clarke Insert, Looped Shade, 6 x 7 In. 336.00
Fairy, Burmese Dome, Crystal Pyramid Cup, 3 3/4 In. 230.00
Fairy, Burmese Shade, Clarke Base, 5 In. 196.00
Fairy, Burmese Shade, Clarke Insert, Ruffled Burmese Base, 4 1/4 In. 390.00
Fairy, Burmese, Raspberry Punty Design, 4 3/8 In. 1380.00
Fairy, Crimped Top, Ruffled Bottom, Alternating Jewels, Blue Satin Glass, 5 1/2 In. 365.00
Fairy, Diamond Quilted, Satin, Blue, Pressed Glass Base, 4 In. 145.00
Fairy, Nailsea, Red, 5 1/2 x 6 In., 3 Piece 600.00
Fairy, Oak Leaves, Cream To Rose, 3 In. 450.00
Fairy, Pink To White Ruffled Edges, Flower-Petal Base, 6 x 7 7/8 In. 165.00
Fairy, Rainbow Mother-Of-Pearl, Ruffled, Crystal Insert, 8 In. 430.00
Fairy, Rose Nailsea Shade, Crystal Cricklite Base, 4 1/4 In. 230.00
Fairy, Satin Glass, Pink, Jeweled, Matching Base, 5 In. 345.00
Fat, Soapstone, Rectangular, Kudlik, Eskimo, 9 3/8 In. Long 99.00
Fluid, 2-Light, Messenger, Brass, Patinated, Urn Reservoir, Prisms, N.Y., c.1840, 18 In. . . 295.00

Fluid, 3-Piece Mold, Amethystine, Wafer Stem, Pressed Base, 6 In. 336.00
Fluid, Acanthus Leaf, 1840-1860, 11 In., Pair 315.00
Fluid, Amethyst Glass Font, Oval, Vesica Designs, Brass Column, Marble Base, 9 7/8 In. . 520.00
Fluid, Amethyst Glass, Oval, Punty Design, Fluted Columnar Standard, 10 5/8 In. 2530.00
Fluid, Blown Glass, Strawberry Diamonds, Fans, Brass Burners, Knop Stem, 13 In., Pair . 1150.00
Fluid, Blown Pink Glass, White Ribbons, White Threads, Circular Base, 10 1/4 x 5 1/4 In. 3220.00
Fluid, Blue & White Jar, Baluster, Foo Dog Rings, Chinese, Mid 19th Century, 27 In., Pair 1150.00
Fluid, Blue, White, Punty Design, Gilt Swags, Stepped Marble Base, 30 1/2 In. 4600.00
Fluid, Brass Font, Blue, White Latticinio Glass, Marble Base, 13 In. 260.00
Fluid, Brass, Bulbous Font, Baluster Shaft, Saucer Base, 5 1/2 In., Pair 99.00
Fluid, Brass, Engraved Chimney, 19th Century, 8 In. 90.00
Fluid, Cobalt Blue, Burning Peg, Brass Collar, 5 In., Pair 2127.00
Fluid, Cobalt Blue, White, Cut Overlay, Columnar Brass Standard, 1880, 11 In., Pair 4025.00
Fluid, Cobalt Blue, White, Oval Cut Design, Stepped Marble Base, 16 1/2 In. 12650.00
Fluid, Cobalt Blue, White, Oval Designs, Gilt Metal Trim, 16 1/4 In. 9775.00
Fluid, Conical Font, Blade Stem, Round Base, Tin & Cork Burner, 4 1/2 In. 476.00
Fluid, Cranberry Cut, White, Oval, Punty Design, Fluted Columnar Standard, 13 In. 1955.00
Fluid, Cranberry Star, Oval Design, Columnar Brass Standard, 1880, 12 1/2 In. 2070.00
Fluid, Cut Glass, Blue Cut To Clear Overlay, Gilt, Figural Base, 19th Century, 12 In. 1090.00
Fluid, Cut Glass, Cobalt Blue, White Overlay, Oval, Punty Design, 13 x 5 In. 1610.00
Fluid, Cut Glass, Cobalt Blue, White Overlay, Oval, Punty Design, 1860-1870, 13 5/8 In. . 1265.00
Fluid, Cut Glass, Cobalt Blue, White Overlay, Oval, Punty Design, 19th Century, 11 In. . . 1610.00
Fluid, Cut Glass, Cobalt Blue, White Overlay, Oval, Star, Vesica Design, 12 3/4 x 5 In. . . . 1090.00
Fluid, Cut Glass, Cobalt Blue, White Overlay, Oval, Star, Vesica, Punty Design, 13 x 5 In. 2300.00
Fluid, Cut Glass, Cobalt Blue, White Overlay, Star, Vesica Design, 13 x 5 In. 3220.00
Fluid, Cut Glass, Cobalt Blue, White Overlay, Stepped Marble Base, 12 x 4 1/2 In. 1090.00
Fluid, Cut Glass, Cranberry Cut To Clear Overlay, Brass Plinth, Marble Base, 1800s, 9 In. 633.00
Fluid, Cut Glass, Cranberry, White Overlay, Oval, Punty, Vesica Design, 17 In. 460.00
Fluid, Cut Glass, Emerald Green, Clear, Pressed Hexagonal Base, 11 In. 4890.00
Fluid, Cut Glass, Green Cut To White, Matching Column, 2-Step Marble Plinth, 12 1/2 In. 115.00
Fluid, Cut Glass, Green, Oval, Punty, Diamond Design, 13 3/16 In. 1090.00
Fluid, Cut Glass, Hobstar & Cane, Dome, Prisms, Matching Base, 5 x 14 In. 260.00
Fluid, Cut Glass, Hobstar & Fan, Mushroom, Prisms, Matching Base, 5 1/4 x 13 In. 345.00
Fluid, Cut Glass, Hobstar & Pinwheel, Mushroom, Attached Prisms, 13 In. 345.00
Fluid, Cut Glass, Opaque Blue Overlay, Punty Design, Stepped Marble Base, 13 In. 690.00
Fluid, Cut Glass, Opaque Ruby, White Overlay, Punty, Fluted Baroque Base, 13 3/4 In. . . 1150.00
Fluid, Cut Glass, Opaque White, Overlay, Oval, Punty Designs, 12 3/4 In. 1380.00
Fluid, Cut Glass, Pineapple & Hobstar, Prisms, 1920s, 24 x 12 In. 3850.00
Fluid, Cut Glass, Pink Opaque, White Overlay, Round Punty Design, 12 1/8 In. 470.00
Fluid, Cut Glass, Pink, White Overlay, Oval, Punty, Slash Design, 10 3/4 In. 550.00
Fluid, Cut Glass, Pink, White Overlay, Oval, Star Design, Stepped Marble Base, 12 1/4 In. 2070.00
Fluid, Cut Glass, Pink, White Overlay, Oval, Vesica, Star, Stepped Marble Base, 11 In. . . . 1955.00
Fluid, Cut Glass, Red Cut To Clear Overlay, Brass Column, 2-Step Marble Plinth, 11 In. . 405.00
Fluid, Cut Glass, Red Cut To Clear Overlay, Brass Pedestal, 2 Tier, Marble, 11 1/2 In. . . . 460.00
Fluid, Cut Glass, Red, White Overlay, Star, Vesica, Reeded Standard, 12 x 4 3/4 In. 860.00
Fluid, Cut Glass, Ruby To White, Double Cut Overlay, Punty, Gilt, c.1880, 13 x 5 In. 1380.00
Fluid, Cut Glass, Ruby, Floral, Vine Gilt Band, Oval, Punty Design, 14 3/8 In. 1035.00
Fluid, Cut Glass, Ruby, Pinwheel, Quatrefoil, Punty Design, 12 5/8 In. 1380.00
Fluid, Cut Glass, Spherical Shade, Column Shaft, Round Base, 27 In. 3290.00
Fluid, Cut Glass, Turquoise Blue, Overlay, Gilt Metal Trim, 16 1/8 In. 4025.00
Fluid, Cut Glass, White Opaque, Oval, Punty Design, Floral Gilt Band, 1870, 14 In. 520.00
Fluid, Cut Glass, White Opaque, Ruby, Punty, Vesica Design, 13 In. 1150.00
Fluid, Cut Glass, White To Blue, Overlay, Reeded Hexagon Standard, Gilt, 13 x 5 In. 1955.00
Fluid, Cut Glass, White To Clear, Overlay, Punty On Standard, Marble, c.1880, 16 x 5 In. . 4025.00
Fluid, Cut Glass, White To Green, Cut Overlay, Opaque Green, Marble Base, 21 x 7 In. . . 4310.00
Fluid, Cut Glass, White To Green, Overlay, Black Standard, Gilt, c.1880, 13 x 5 In. 6325.00
Fluid, Cut Glass, White, Green, Oval Designs, Stepped Marble Base, 16 1/4 In. 6900.00
Fluid, Engraved Glass Font, Pewter Collar, Square Base, 9 1/2 In., Pair 728.00
Fluid, Etched Camphor Shade, Pendant Prisms, Brass Column, Electrified, 21 In. 290.00
Fluid, Faceted Diamond Shade, Lavender Opaque Ribbed Stand, 13 5/8 In. 920.00
Fluid, Gilt Metal, Cut Overlay, Stepped Marble Base, 28 1/2 x 6 In. . . . . 1265.00 to 2415.00
Fluid, Gilt Metal, Cut Overlay, Stepped Marble Base, 33 1/4 x 6 1/4 In. 10350.00
Fluid, Horizontal Ribbed Glass, White Loop Swirl, Brass Standard, Brass Base, 11 In. . . . 860.00

Fluid, Opaque White Font, Gilt Leafy Scroll, Clambroth Baroque Base, 13 7/8 In. 460.00
Fluid, Owl, Opaque White Glass, Ball Shade, 8 In. 520.00
Fluid, Pressed Glass, Diamond Thumbprint, Ribbed Gilt Brass Standard, Marble, 13 In., Pair 1035.00
Fluid, Pressed Glass, Lime Green Font, Black Glass Base, 19th Century, 8 1/2 In. 315.00
Fluid, Pressed Glass, Moon & Star, 9 1/2 In. 375.00
Fluid, Pressed Loop, Amethyst Glass, Single Construction, New England Glass, 8 1/2 In. .. 390.00
Fluid, Pressed Loop, Canary Glass, Brass Collar, Marble Base, New England Glass, 9 In. .. 365.00
Fluid, Punty, Rib Design Font, Blue Opalescent Baroque Base, 13 In. 690.00
Fluid, Round Glass Font, Blade Stem, Round Base, Sheared Mouth, 4 1/4 In. 365.00
Fluid, Spar, Ebonized, Parcel Gilt, Columnar, Derbyshire, 16 1/4 In. 1680.00
Fluid, Swan, Yellow Green, Stepped Hexagonal Base, 9 5/8 In. 290.00
Fluid, White Gilt Quatrefoil, Oval, Star, Vesica Design, White Flute, 12 1/4 In. 630.00
Fluid, White Oval Designs, White Opalescent Standard, Marble Base, 12 In., Pair 575.00
Gas, Bronze, Floral Openwork, Grotesque Mask Footed, Originally Oil, Oriental, 73 In. ... 825.00
Gas, Colt, Brass, Glass Globe, 1 Clear, Other Blue Gray, 13 In., Pair 302.00
Gasolier, 3-Light, Cut Glass Bowl, Gilt Bronze, Chain Swags, 1880s, 36 In. 2300.00
Gasolier, 6-Light, French Restoration, Gilt Brass Mount, Tole, 25 1/2 x 24 1/2 In. 1840.00
Gasolier, 6-Light, Urn Tier, Branches, Cherubs Holding Shade, Electrified, 50 In. 2990.00
Grease, Bale Top With Hanger & Brass Ring, Rooster Finial, 23 In. 440.00
Grease, Bronze, Satyr's Head, Faux Verdigris Finish, 4 1/2 In. 90.00
Grease, Cast Iron, Twist Stem, Reservoir Top, Pan Base, 7 3/4 In. 110.00
Grease, Hanging, Wrought Iron, Tricornered, Twisted Post, Black Paint, 7 In. 250.00
Grease, Tin, Floral, Short Spout, Weighted Cone Base, 10 1/2 In. 100.00
Handel lamps are included in the Handel category.
Jacobsen, Enameled Metal, Adjustable Reflector, Label, 13 3/4 x 29 In. 520.00
Kerosene, Acanthus Leaf, Blue Opaque Glass, 26 1/2 In. 450.00
Kerosene, Acanthus Leaf, Clambroth, 6-Leaf Standard, Square Base, 10 x 4 In. ..750.00 to 1150.00
Kerosene, Angle, Cased Green Shade, Electrified, 20 In. 120.00
Kerosene, Artichoke, Ball Shade, Embossed Base, 16 In. 240.00
Kerosene, Artichoke, Ball Shade, Red Satin Glaze, Embossed Base, 16 In. 450.00
Kerosene, Banquet, Ball Shade, Brass, Molded, Painted Irises, Red, Blue, 27 1/2 In. 259.00
Kerosene, Banquet, Brass, Flow Blue, Ball Shade, Urn Shape, Pear, Black Ground, 28 In. .. 920.00
Kerosene, Banquet, Brass, Onyx, Floral & Scrolls, Reticulated, 20 In. 210.00
Kerosene, Banquet, Brass, Onyx, Reticulated Font, Dragonslayer, Electrified, 25 In. 310.00
Kerosene, Banquet, Convertible, Silver Plate, Cut Glass, Candlestick, 20th Century, 32 In. 345.00
Kerosene, Banquet, Cranberry Glass Font, Cut Panels, Glaze Pottery Stem, 21 In. 275.00
Kerosene, Banquet, Diamond, Double Wick Burner, 24 In. 375.00
Kerosene, Banquet, Dresden Type, Applied Decoration, Painted, 19th Century, 29 1/2 In. .. 145.00
Kerosene, Banquet, Filigree Font Frame, Open Handles, 25 In. 100.00
Kerosene, Banquet, Gilt, Blue, 16 1/2 In. 90.00
Kerosene, Banquet, Light Green Ground, Pink Flowers, 15 1/2 In. 130.00
Kerosene, Banquet, Medallions, Ornate Foot, 21 1/2 In. 120.00
Kerosene, Banquet, Onyx, Metal, Slag Panels, Ball Shade, Brass Grill, Zinc Base, 32 In. .. 405.00
Kerosene, Banquet, Pink & White Latticinio Font, Brass Column, Marble Base, 15 In. ... 375.00
Kerosene, Banquet, Porcelain, Flowers On Base, Column & Font, 31 In. 190.00
Kerosene, Banquet, Silver Plated Corinthian Column, Glass Font, Electrified, 34 In. 410.00
Kerosene, Banquet, White Metal, Brass, Marble Body, Gold, 29 In. 460.00
Kerosene, Banquet, White Metal, Cherub Stem, Brass Drop In Front, 31 In. 900.00
Kerosene, Banquet, White Metal, Red Ball Shade, 33 In. 225.00
Kerosene, Banquet, White Milk Glass, Flowers, Blue, Pink, Green, 28 In. 690.00
Kerosene, Betty, Brass, 9 3/4 In. ....*Illus* 120.00
Kerosene, Betty, Copper, Pine Stand, Iron Hanger & Wire Pick, 5 x 7 1/2 In. 250.00
Kerosene, Blown Glass, Hurricane, Column For Pillar Candle, Brass Ring, 23 3/8 In. 360.00
Kerosene, Blown Glass, Ruby Stained, Frosted, 8 1/2 In. 110.00
Kerosene, Blue Speckles, Ribbed Font, Green, Red Base, Pat Aug. 1885, 19th Century ... 770.00
Kerosene, Brass, Peach Opalescent Ribbed Shade, Enameled, Butterfly, Flowers, 24 In. ... 330.00
Kerosene, Brass, Plume & Atwood, Cranberry, Hornet Burner, c.1870, 10 In. ......*Illus* 110.00
Kerosene, Brass, Polished, Rayo, Milk Glass Shade, Branches, Painted Flowers 66.00
Kerosene, Brass, Roses, Leaves, Glass Font, Shade, Prisms, Electrified, 22 In. 470.00
Kerosene, Bristol Type, White, 2-Step Font, Bell-Shaped Stem, Circular Foot, 10 In. 25.00
Kerosene, Bristol Type, White, Painted, Blue, Orange, Yellow Flowers, Finger Loop, 4 In. 30.00
Kerosene, Bristol, Vase Shape, Brown, White Enamel Flower Garden Design, 18 1/2 In. ... 100.00
Kerosene, Bronze, 3-Light, Empire, Adjustable Green Tole Shade, 21 1/2 In. 1265.00

Lamp, Kerosene, Betty, Brass, 9 3/4 In.

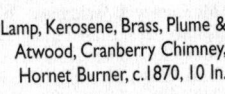

Old, clean cloth diapers are ideal for cleaning metal: very soft and lint free.

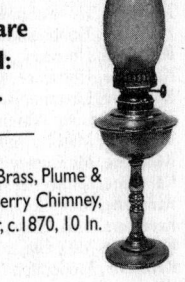

Lamp, Kerosene, Brass, Plume & Atwood, Cranberry Chimney, Hornet Burner, c.1870, 10 In.

Kerosene, Bronze, Bacchus, Swags, Snake Column, Marble Font, Electrified, 19 In., Pair	2640.00
Kerosene, Bronze, Ball Shade, Elephant Trunks, 3 Sections, Oriental, 46 In.	800.00
Kerosene, Bronze, Bulbous, Satyr's Head, Belt, Shield, 3-Footed, 8 In.	220.00
Kerosene, Bronze, Italian Neoclassical Style, 3-Part Base, 70 In.	1440.00
Kerosene, Bronze, White Linen Shade, Bamboo, Bird Relief, Japan, Meiji Period, 27 In.	950.00
Kerosene, Bronze, White Opaline Glass, Pendant, Pedestal, Early 1800s, 12 In.	400.00
Kerosene, Canary Glass, Yellow, Waisted Loop, Monument Base, 1840-1860, 10 x 3 In.	2990.00
Kerosene, Cast Iron, Painted, Flame Shade, Bacchante, Grapevines, Victorian, 91 In.	920.00
Kerosene, Clipper Ship, Brass, Hexagonal, 28 In.	400.00
Kerosene, Coach, Brass, 5 Panes, Eagle Finial, Mounting Bracket, 29 In., Pair	55.00
Kerosene, Coach, Old Black Paint, Green Lenses, 19th Century, 13 In., Pair	50.00
Kerosene, Cobalt Blue, Faceted Font, Hexagonal Tiered Standard, Mid 1800s, 9 x 4 In.	3100.00
Kerosene, Cobalt Blue, Fluted Brass Stem, Step Marble Foot, 18 1/2 In.	1090.00
Kerosene, Cranberry Cut, Gold Design, White Milk Glass Base, 12 1/2 In.	980.00
Kerosene, Cut Glass, Corn In Shield, Inverted, Applied Finger Loop, 3 In.	170.00
Kerosene, Cut Glass, Corn In Shield, Oval Band Base, 8 In.	170.00
Kerosene, Cut Glass, Corn, Footed, Applied Finger Loop, 4 3/4 In.	280.00
Kerosene, Cut Glass, Daisy & Bowknot, Cobalt Blue, 10 1/2 In.	65.00
Kerosene, Cut Glass, Diamond Band & Shield, Applied Finger Loop, 3 In.	65.00
Kerosene, Cut Glass, Green, Geometric Design Font, Step Marble Base, 20 1/4 In.	600.00
Kerosene, Cut Glass, White, Cranberry Windows, White Clambroth Base, 13 In.	575.00
Kerosene, Cut Glass, White, Fluted Brass Stem, Double-Step Marble Base, 11 In.	390.00
Kerosene, Dark Amber Glass, Amethyst Fonts, Plain Feet, 9 1/2 & 7 In., 3 Piece	460.00
Kerosene, Faience, White, Flowering Vines, 19th Century, 30 In.	3900.00
Kerosene, Finger, Pale Blue Clambroth, Clambroth Handle, 3 x 4 In.	920.00
Kerosene, Floral Glass Shade, Cherub Standard, Late 1800s, 31 In.	230.00
Kerosene, Flowers, Glass Shade, Cherub Standard, Early 20th Century, 31 In.	230.00
Kerosene, Gilt Bronze, Louis Philippe, Tole, Mid 19th Century, 21 In., Pair	2760.00
Kerosene, Gilt Bronze, Louis XV Style, Patinated, 19th Century, 15 1/2 In.	978.00
Kerosene, Gilt Bronze, Neoclassical, Corinthian Column, Marble, Stepped Base, 21 In.	1150.00
Kerosene, Gone With The Wind, Black Wrought Iron, Copper Metal Base, 21 In.	290.00
Kerosene, Gone With The Wind, Butterscotch Satin Glaze, Brass Base, 22 In.	100.00
Kerosene, Gone With The Wind, Embossed Grape, Vine, 24 In.	425.00
Kerosene, Gone With The Wind, Flowers, White Opaque, Green, Pink, Red, 22 In.	375.00
Kerosene, Gone With The Wind, Flowers, White, Light Brown Ground, 16 In.	50.00
Kerosene, Gone With The Wind, Milk Glass, Spider, Web, Flowers, 18 In.	230.00
Kerosene, Gone With The Wind, Molded Poppies, White, Purple, Pink, 22 In.	375.00
Kerosene, Gone With The Wind, Poppies, White Opaque, Green Glaze, 21 1/2 In.	150.00
Kerosene, Gone With The Wind, Red Roses, White, Ball Shade, Electrified, 26 In.	575.00
Kerosene, Gone With The Wind, Roses, White Opaque, Green Glaze, 23 In.	210.00
Kerosene, Gone With The Wind, Satin Glass, Blue, 19th Century, 24 In.	1095.00
Kerosene, Gone With The Wind, White Milk Glass, Flowers, Brown, Green, Gold, 31 In.	630.00
Kerosene, Gone With The Wind, White Milk Glass, Flowers, Rose, Green, Pink, 27 In.	460.00
Kerosene, Gone With The Wind, White Milk Glass, Fruit, Green, Pink, Blue, 27 In.	520.00
Kerosene, Gone With The Wind, White Milk Glass, Rose, Green, Yellow Ground, 26 In.	460.00
Kerosene, Gone With The Wind, White Opaque, Pink, 23 In.	225.00
Kerosene, Green & White Glass Shade, Gold Trim, Electrified, 20 x 12 1/2 In.	195.00

Kerosene, Hanging, Blue Hobnail Shade, White Opalescent, Red Brass Frame, 14 In. 1410.00
Kerosene, Hanging, Mother-Of-Pearl Satin Glass, Raspberry, White, Brass Frame, 14 In. . 1440.00
Kerosene, Hobbs Snowflake, Blue Opalescent, 9 1/2 In. ....400.00 to 700.00
Kerosene, Hobbs Snowflake, Cranberry Opalescent, 9 In. ....475.00 to 900.00
Kerosene, Hurricane, Blown, Cut, Engraved, Anglo-Irish Style, Early 20th Century, 15 In. 375.00
Kerosene, Hurricane, Wheel-Cut Bands Of Circles On Ends, 12 3/4 In., Pair 55.00
Kerosene, Laverite, Bronze, Art Nouveau, Red Marble Base, L. Gregoire, 44 In. 3640.00
Kerosene, Loop, Vaseline Glass, Hexagonal Standards, Bases, 8 & 8 1/2 In., Pair 800.00
Kerosene, Marble, Pink, Urn, Engraved Amber Pedestal, Open Top, Step Base, 18 In. 195.00
Kerosene, McKenney & Waterbury Co., Stained Glass Shade, Flowers, Bronze, 23 In. ... 575.00
Kerosene, Midwestern, Brass Fitting, Blue Base, 1880 .... 198.00
Kerosene, Milk Glass Shade, Embossed Flowers, Wheel Cut Font, Putti, 27 In. 132.00
Kerosene, Milk Glass, Blue, Flared & Fluted Base, 10 In. 280.00
Kerosene, Milk Glass, Flowers, Shade Ring, Prisms, Brass Base, Footed, Victorian, 28 In. 45.00
Kerosene, Moderator, Cherubim, Brass, Etched, Globe, Mahogany Base, 22 In. 750.00
Kerosene, Moderator, Gilt Bronze, Porcelain, Victorian, 26 1/2 x 5 1/2 x 7 1/2 In. 520.00
Kerosene, New England Glass Co., Green, Stem, Plain Round Foot, Signed, 8 1/2 In. 2070.00
Kerosene, Onyx, Brass, Scroll, Ball Shade, Caramel, Slag, Shell Base, 35 In. 345.00
Kerosene, Opaline Glass, Blue & White, 19th Century, 21 In. 635.00
Kerosene, Peg, Brass, Blue Swirl Mother-Of-Pearl Satin Glass Shade, 12 1/2 In. 165.00
Kerosene, Peg, Cased, Yellow, Ribbed, Brass Base, 21 1/2 In. 460.00
Kerosene, Pink Opalescent Shade, Embossed Frame, Openworked Bows, Ribbed, 14 In. . 440.00
Kerosene, Plume & Atwood, Hornet, Flashed Cranberry Chimney, Brass, c.1870, 10 In. ... 110.00
Kerosene, Porcelain, Blue, White, Rampant Dragons, Chinese, 19th Century, 26 In., Pair . 980.00
Kerosene, Porcelain, Urn Shape, Woman Picking Flowers, Brass Base, Victorian, 27 In. .. 44.00
Kerosene, Pressed Glass, Apple Blossom, Light Green Bands, 12 1/2 In. 25.00
Kerosene, Pressed Glass, Beaded Diamond & Rib Bands, Finger Loop, 3 1/2 In. 55.00
Kerosene, Pressed Glass, Bull's-Eye, Green, 10 In. 70.00
Kerosene, Pressed Glass, Bull's-Eye, Powder Blue Base, Gild On Font, 14 In. 320.00
Kerosene, Pressed Glass, Cabbage Rose, Applied Finger Loop, Ribbed Edge, 3 1/2 In. ... 120.00
Kerosene, Pressed Glass, Central Beaded Panel, Amber, 9 1/2 In. 70.00
Kerosene, Pressed Glass, Cherry, Brass Stem, Slate Base, 9 1/2 In. 80.00
Kerosene, Pressed Glass, Chilson, Footed, Finger Loop, 6 1/4 In. 45.00
Kerosene, Pressed Glass, Clarissa, Nickel Plated Collar, Round Wick Burner, 12 In. 260.00
Kerosene, Pressed Glass, Columbian Coin, Opaque White, Gilded Coins, 9 1/2 In. 30.00
Kerosene, Pressed Glass, Cord & Tassel, 6 1/2 In. 180.00
Kerosene, Pressed Glass, Daisy, Footed, Finger Loop, 5 1/4 In. ....85.00 to 140.00
Kerosene, Pressed Glass, Diamonds, Reversed Pattern, Finger Loop, 3 In. 60.00
Kerosene, Pressed Glass, Dome Shade, Flowers, 20 x 8 1/2 In. 225.00
Kerosene, Pressed Glass, Duncan, Rayed Panel, Hinge Burner, Finger Loop, 4 In. 100.00
Kerosene, Pressed Glass, Ellipse, Footed, Finger Loop, 5 1/4 In. 70.00
Kerosene, Pressed Glass, Empress, Clinched Collar, Footed, Finger Loop, 5 In. 50.00
Kerosene, Pressed Glass, Fish Scale, 7 In. 45.00
Kerosene, Pressed Glass, Fleur-De-Lis & Tassel, 7 1/4 In. 40.00
Kerosene, Pressed Glass, Gem, Collar Impressed April 13, 1875, Finger Loop, 3 1/2 In. .. 65.00
Kerosene, Pressed Glass, Greek Key, Shoulder Pattern, Footed, Finger Loop, 4 3/4 In. ... 85.00
Kerosene, Pressed Glass, Green, 9 3/4 In. 45.00
Kerosene, Pressed Glass, Heart, 8 In. 70.00
Kerosene, Pressed Glass, King's Crown, Crimped-Edge Chimney, 8 1/2 In. 140.00
Kerosene, Pressed Glass, Moon & Star, Ruby, Miniature, 7 1/2 In. 200.00
Kerosene, Pressed Glass, Pearl, Footed, Finger Lamp, 5 1/2 In. 45.00
Kerosene, Pressed Glass, Prince, Green, 8 1/4 In. 100.00
Kerosene, Pressed Glass, Ribbed Loop, Brass Connector, Green Base, 8 3/4 In. 110.00
Kerosene, Pressed Glass, Scroll, Opaque White, Brass Screw Connector, 10 1/2 In. 50.00
Kerosene, Pressed Glass, Shield With Star, Cobalt Font, Amethyst Base, 10 In. 375.00
Kerosene, Pressed Glass, Snowflake, Opalescent, Footed, Applied Finger Loop, 5 In. 600.00
Kerosene, Pressed Glass, Thumbprint, Blue, Vaseline Base, 11 In., Pair 335.00
Kerosene, Pressed Glass, Turkey Track, Footed, Finger Loop, 6 1/2 In. ....120.00 to 140.00
Kerosene, Pressed Glass, Versailles, Milk Glass, Fired-On Decoration, 8 1/2 In. 100.00
Kerosene, Pressed Glass, Vintage, Ruby Flashed, Brass Standard, Marble Base, 14 1/2 In. 400.00
Kerosene, Pressed Glass, Wheat In Shield, Footed, Applied Finger Loop, 3 1/2 In. .130.00 to 170.00
Kerosene, Pressed Glass, White Metal Figural Stem, Woman, Urn, Frosted Font, 12 In. .. 55.00
Kerosene, Rayo, Brass, Pink Satin Glass Shade, Lobed, Ruffled Top, White 90.00

Kerosene, Silvered Bronze, 1-Light, Parcel Gilt, Tole, Dolphin Base, 15 In. 750.00
Kerosene, Silvered Bronze, Louis XVI Style, 2-Light, Bouillotte, Tole, 1800s, 26 In. 3000.00
Kerosene, Spelter, Angel, Flowing Gown, Flowers, Foundry Mark, France, 18 x 50 In. . . . 770.00
Kerosene, Student, Adjustable Milk Glass Shade, 29 x 27 In. 365.00
Kerosene, Student, Brass, Double, Cased, Green, Glass Shades, 19th Century, 24 1/2 In. . . 575.00
Kerosene, Student, Enameled Shade, Ball Stem, Double, Cut Jade Finial, Chinese, 19 In. . 252.00
Kerosene, Student, Nickel Plate, Cased Green Glass Shade, 19th Century, 23 In. 115.00
Kerosene, Theodore Dick, Earthenware, Gilt Bronze Mount, c.1890, 22 In., Pair 5400.00
Kerosene, White Glass Shade, Acid-Etched Base, Stars, Cast Iron Bracket, Hanger 140.00
Kerosene, White Milk Glass Shade, Iron Bracket, Gold, 4 In. 460.00
Kerosene, Wrought Iron, Paper Shades, Pillar, Foliate & Scroll, Stepped Base, 9 x 33 In. . 1150.00
Lard, Kinnear, Rectangular Saucer Base, 1851, 13 3/4 In. 110.00
Lard, S.N. & H.C. Ufford, Boston, Saucer Base, 1851, 7 In. 155.00
Lard, Tole, Central Reservoir, Early 19th Century, 24 x 15 In., Pair 489.00
Oil, 2-Light, Cut & Etched Shades, Tubular Branches, 19th Century, 19 1/2 In. 1380.00
Oil, 2-Light, Cut & Etched Shades, Twin Scroll Handles, Electrified, 22 x 13 1/2 In. 2185.00
Oil, Amethyst Font, Milk Glass Base, 9 1/2 In., Pair 340.00
Oil, Barber's, Flemish Brass, Spout, Removable Font, 13 7/8 In. . . . . *Illus* 77.00
Oil, Bigler, Amethyst, Octagonal Concave Paneled Standard, 1840-1860, 9 1/2 In. 2185.00
Oil, Blown, Suspension, Domed Smoke Shade, Oval Globe, Brass Collar, 20 In. 980.00
Oil, Blown, Tooled Mouth, Glass Stem, 4 1/4 In. 615.00
Oil, Bohemian, Milk Glass, Cobalt Blue, 11 In., Pair 255.00
Oil, Brass Connector, Collar & Burner, Buckle Font, Ribbed Stem, Milk Glass Base, 11 In. 140.00
Oil, Brass, Blue & White Striped Crystal, Embossed Ribbing, Marble Base, 9 1/2 In. 2015.00
Oil, Brass, Floral Swags, Fluted Body, Electrified, 1870s, 24 In., Pair 420.00
Oil, Brass, Friction Primers Under Hinged Cover, Snake-Head Handles, 1867, 7 In. 66.00
Oil, Brass, Frosted To Clear Shade, Clear Font, Prisms, 12 In. 240.00
Oil, Bronze, Pink Cased Swirl Half Shade, Drop-In Oil Font, Duplex Burner, 10 In. 920.00
Oil, Capo-Di-Monte, Loop Handle, Late 19th Century, 4 1/2 In. 185.00
Oil, Carcel, Paris, Porcelain, Brass Leaf Stand, Polychrome, c.1850, 30 1/4 In., Pair 575.00
Oil, Carnival Glass, Zipper Loop, Marigold, Pearl Top Chimney, 7 1/2 In. 288.00
Oil, Coolidge Drape, Cobalt Blue, Tulip-Top Chimney, 10 In. 480.00
Oil, Copper & Brass Carbide, Brilliant Searchlight, Duluth, Pat. 1902, 7 In. 55.00
Oil, Cranberry Glass, Cut To Clear, Brass Holder, Wall Mount, 10 1/4 In. 345.00
Oil, Cranberry Glass, Cut To Clear, Clambroth Base, Gold Highlighting, 12 1/4 In. 460.00
Oil, Cranberry Glass, Optic Paneling, Brass Stem, Black Pottery Foot, 13 1/2 In. 175.00
Oil, Cranberry Glass, Rainspot, Dome Shade, Pair 440.00
Oil, Cresset, Wrought Iron, Tripod Base, Ram's-Horn Tabs, Crossed Center, 33 1/4 In. . . . 275.00
Oil, Cut Glass, Hearts & Stars, Clambroth Base, 10 1/2 In. 86.00
Oil, Cut Glass, Red Cut To White To Clear, Milk Glass Base, Pear-Shape Font, 10 1/2 In. . 1035.00
Oil, Cut Glass, Sheldon Swirl, Amber Font, Black Base, 8 1/2 In. 230.00
Oil, Cut Glass, White Cut To Clear, Ruffled, Brass Fittings, Marble Base, 21 1/2 In. 302.00
Oil, Domed Top, Urn Shape, Cartouche, Floral Still Life, Birds, Paris, 1840s, 19 1/2 In. . . 2350.00
Oil, E. Thomas & Williams, Ltd., Brass, Miner's, 6 In. 90.00
Oil, Gilt Bronze, Ceramic, 20th Century, 8 5/8 In. 460.00

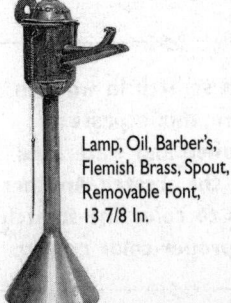

Lamp, Oil, Barber's,
Flemish Brass, Spout,
Removable Font,
13 7/8 In.

Lamp, Oil, Hanging,
Brass Candleholders,
Chain Supports,
Majolica Font, 52 In.

Lamp, Oil, Lucerna,
Brass, 3 Wicks,
Snuffer, Extinguisher,
Wick Pick, 7 1/4 In.

Oil, Glass, Owl & Shield, Dark Turquoise Blue, Lock-On Burner, 9-Panel Base, 8 1/2 In. . . 1035.00
Oil, Glass, Paneled, Hexagonal Base, Pewter Collar, Snuffer Cap, Burner, 8 1/2 In. 55.00
Oil, Glass, Petal Font, Dome Top, Baluster Stem, Brass Collar, Hexagonal Base, 9 5/8 In. . . 66.00
Oil, Gorham, Sterling Silver & Bronze 795.00
Oil, Hanging, Brass Candleholders, Chain Supports, Majolica Font, 52 In. . . . . *Illus* 825.00
Oil, Hobbs Snowflake, Blue Opalescent, Piecrust Chimney, Clear Foot, 8 1/4 In. 375.00
Oil, I. Smith, Pat'd. Aug. 8, 1854, Tin, 6 1/4 In. 390.00
Oil, Jensen, Amber, Opalescent Striped Font, Beaded Base, 7 1/4 In. 288.00
Oil, Kosmos-Brenner, Pink Satin Glass, Ribbed Swirl Shade, Ring, Embossed Base, 14 In. 300.00
Oil, Lace Maker's, Cut Glass, Amethyst, 10 3/4 In. 195.00
Oil, Lucerna, Brass, 3 Wicks, Snuffer, Extinguisher, Wick Pick, 7 1/4 In. . . . . *Illus* 44.00
Oil, Manhattan Brass Co., Brass Burner, Cranberry Glass, Applied Leaf Feet, 9 5/8 In. 130.00
Oil, Milk Glass, Diamond Point, Victor Burner, Column Chimney, 11 1/2 In. 116.00
Oil, Paneled Stem & Font, Brass Collar, Hexagonal Base, 10 1/2 In. 220.00
Oil, Peg, Blue Satin Glaze, 10 Panels, 8 In. 90.00
Oil, Peg, Blue Swirl Glaze, 14 3/4 In., Pair 375.00
Oil, Peg, Cranberry Ruffle-Top Shade, Applied Beads, Multicolored Enamel, 17 In. 375.00
Oil, Peg, Cranberry Shade, Cranberry Glaze, 16 1/2 In. 180.00
Oil, Peg, Cream Iridescent Shade, Amber Iridescent Glaze, 15 In., Pair 250.00
Oil, Peg, Embossed Drape, Amber, 6 1/2 In. 50.00
Oil, Peg, Pink Satin Glaze, Diamond, Prism, White Metal, 20 In. 350.00
Oil, Peg, Purple Flowers, Leaf, 6 1/2 In. 30.00
Oil, Peg, Silver Plate, Cut Glass, 12 1/2 In. 120.00
Oil, Peg, Sunset Orange Diamond, Mother-Of-Pearl Satin Glaze, 10 1/2 In. 150.00
Oil, Pewter, Pan Base, Applied Finger Loop Stem, Font, Double Brass Burner, 7 1/2 In. . . 165.00
Oil, Pressed Glass, Ceramic Corners, Blown Font, Brass Collar, Waterfall Base, 6 In. 115.00
Oil, Pressed Glass, Engraved, Floral, Rib Inside, Stepped Base, 7 3/4 In. 275.00
Oil, Pressed Glass, Gold & Brown Reverse Painted Stem, Milk Glass Foot, 10 In. 345.00
Oil, Pressed Glass, Lyre Font, Brass Collar, Hexagonal Base, 8 1/4 In. 155.00
Oil, Pressed Glass, Milton, Cobalt Blue, Finger, Flower Band, Applied Handle, 3 1/2 In. . . 403.00
Oil, Pressed Glass, Primrose, Clear Opalescent, Finger, Zero Burner & Chimney, 3 1/4 In. . 316.00
Oil, Pressed Glass, Teardrop Stem, Font, Brass Collar, Octagonal Concave Base, 10 3/4 In. 190.00
Oil, R.S. Merrill, Peg, Cranberry Glass, Brass Candlestick, Collar & Burner, 1866, 12 In. . 170.00
Oil, Red Satin Glass, Molded Raised Flowers, 10 1/2 In. 248.00
Oil, Ripley, Marriage, Clambroth Fonts 1700.00
Oil, Rumford, Brass, c.1790, 13 1/2 In., Pair . . . . *Illus* 2090.00
Oil, Rundbrenner, Amethyst Glass, Brass Candlestick, Marble Block Base, 11 1/4 In. 95.00
Oil, Silver, Figural, Kneeling Cherub, Holding Oil Font, Quatrefoil Base, 18 In. 345.00
Oil, Sinumbra, Milk Glass Shade, Faux Tortoiseshell Painted Column, 23 In. 1870.00
Oil, Sinumbra, Neoclassical, Electrified, 1840 . . . . 2400.00
Oil, Student, Brass, Yellow Satin Glass Shade, c.1875, 21 1/4 In. 495.00
Oil, Swan Top Of Standard, Mouth Supporting Ring, Rosettes On Plinth, 1820s, 11 In. . . . 2185.00
Organ, Brass, Adjustable, Hand-Painted Globe, Parker, Late 1800s, 64 In. 430.00
Pairpoint lamps are in the Pairpoint category.
Perfume, Metal, Blue Enamel Shade, Gold Birds, DeVilbiss, 8 1/2 In. 440.00
Perfume, Metal, Orange, Blue Reverse Painted Shade, DeVilbiss, 7 In. 467.00

Lamp, Oil, Rumford, Brass, c.1790, 13 1/2 In., Pair

To cover a scratch in wooden
furniture, mix a paste of
instant coffee and water and
rub it into the scratch. Another
quick fix is to color the scratch
with the proper color crayon.

Perfume, Metal, Orange, Blue Shade, Black Enamel Peacock, DeVilbiss, 7 In. 385.00
Rush, Iron, Candleholder, Twisted Arm, Counterweight, Wooden Bun Foot, Painted, 10 In. 165.00
Sconce, 1-Light, Anthemion, Cast Head Of Bearded Man, 11 In., Pair 520.00
Sconce, 1-Light, Brass, Cobra Shape, Shaped Flower Socket, 22 In., Pair 805.00
Sconce, 1-Light, Brass, Heart Shape, Scrolled Arm, Molded Backplate, 10 In., Pair 160.00
Sconce, 1-Light, Bronze, Swan, Electrified, 9 1/2 x 2 1/4 In. 1265.00
Sconce, 1-Light, Tin, Oval Backplate, Crimped, 14 3/8 In. 110.00
Sconce, 1-Light, Tin, Round Crimped Reflectors, Small Center Mirror, 8 3/4 In., Pair 2310.00
Sconce, 2-Light, Aesthetic Movement, Ebonized, Center Panel, Figural Scene, 28 In. 705.00
Sconce, 2-Light, Beveled Glass Mirror, Urn, Dolphin, 19 x 9 In., Pair 410.00
Sconce, 2-Light, Brass, Floral Frame, Putti, Beveled Mirrors, 18 1/2 In., Pair 145.00
Sconce, 2-Light, Bronze Dore, Louis XVI Style, Candle Arms, c.1900, 22 In., Pair 1732.00
Sconce, 2-Light, Bronze, Louis XV Style, Porcelain, Bow-Hung Basket, 18 In., Pair 1380.00
Sconce, 2-Light, Crystal Starburst, Rosette Terminals, Crystal Chains, c.1900, 20 In. Pair . 3910.00
Sconce, 2-Light, Gilt Brass, Regency Style, 19th Century, 16 x 9 1/2 In., Pair 1725.00
Sconce, 2-Light, Gilt Brass, Verdigris Patinated, Directoire Style, 11 1/2 x 9 x 3 In. 1035.00
Sconce, 2-Light, Gilt Bronze, Louis Philippe, Tulip-Shaped Nozzles, 6 3/4 x 3 In., Pair . . . 7507.00
Sconce, 2-Light, Gilt Bronze, Louis XV Style, Scrolling Leaf Arms, 18 1/2 In., Pair 380.00
Sconce, 2-Light, Gilt Bronze, Louis XVI Style, 20th Century, 26 3/4 In., Pair 430.00
Sconce, 2-Light, Gilt Bronze, Louis XVI Style, Draped Urn Shape, c.1900, 15 In., Pair . . . 345.00
Sconce, 2-Light, Gilt Bronze, Regency Style, Dolphin, Alligator, 19 x 9 3/4 x 7 In., Pair . . 980.00
Sconce, 2-Light, Gilt Bronze, Regency Style, Electrified, France, 17 x 10 1/2 In., Pair . . . 1495.00
Sconce, 2-Light, Gilt, Crystal, Wrought Iron, Rococo Style, 16 x 12 x 6 1/2 In., Pair 3450.00
Sconce, 2-Light, Gilt, Louis XVI Style, Napoleon III, 28 1/4 x 12 1/2 x 6 In., Pair 3450.00
Sconce, 2-Light, Giltwood, George III, Outspread Eagle, 36 x 12 1/2 In., 4 Piece 9600.00
Sconce, 2-Light, Leaf Wrapped Standard, Fruit Finial, Goat's Head, Birds, 25 In. 2070.00
Sconce, 2-Light, Mirrored, Reverse Painted Borders, Center Reverse Cherubs, 17 In., Pair 935.00
Sconce, 2-Light, Musician Within Trellis, Flowers, 16 In., Pair 6900.00
Sconce, 2-Light, Rococo, Cartouche, Mirror Back, Geometric, 23 In., 4 Piece 3450.00
Sconce, 2-Light, Wedgwood Inserts, Scrolled Arms, Ribbons, Leaves, 18 In., Pair 740.00
Sconce, 3-Light, Brass, Beveled Glass Mirror, 18 x 10 In., Pair 410.00
Sconce, 3-Light, Brass, Embossed Leaves, Repousse, Leaf-Shaped Bobeche, 14 In., Pair . 615.00
Sconce, 3-Light, Brass, Glass Prisms, Beveled Mirror, Man's Head, 17 In., Pair 110.00
Sconce, 3-Light, Brass, Repousse, Oval Plate, Embossed, Thistle Nozzles, 11 x 13 In. 860.00
Sconce, 3-Light, Brass, Ribbon & Acanthus Leaf Bracket, Electrified, 14 1/4 In., Pair 310.00
Sconce, 3-Light, Bronze, Arrow Shape, Medusa Medallion, c.1920, 30 x 13 In. 1120.00
Sconce, 3-Light, Bronze, Christopher Columbus Head, 31 x 32 x 18 In., Pair 250.00
Sconce, 3-Light, Bronze, Flames, Arrows, Eagle Wings On Back Plate, 1820s, 18 In., Pair 2430.00
Sconce, 3-Light, Bronze, Scroll & Leaf, c.1880, 6 x 12 In. 310.00
Sconce, 3-Light, Chinese Porcelain, Gilt Metal Mount, Famille Rose Plate, 20 In., Pair . . . 2000.00
Sconce, 3-Light, E. F. Caldwell, Bronze, Louis XVI, Gilt, Beads, Pendants, 27 In., 4 Piece 6900.00
Sconce, 3-Light, Gilt Bronze, Lion Mask Form, Urn Nozzles, 8 x 9 1/2 In. 1035.00
Sconce, 3-Light, Gilt Bronze, Louis XVI Style, Rock Crystal, 30 In., Pair 6600.00
Sconce, 3-Light, Gilt Bronze, Louis XVI Style, Scrolling Arms, Electrified, 20 In., Pair . . 765.00
Sconce, 3-Light, Gilt Bronze, Palms Of Victory, Electrified, c.1900, 18 x 14 In., 4 Piece . . 865.00
Sconce, 3-Light, Gilt Bronze, Socket With Detachable Bobeche, 22 x 14 1/2 In. 2760.00
Sconce, 3-Light, Gilt, Wrought Iron, Rococo, Acanthus Leaf, Electrified, 30 x 12 In., Pair 520.00
Sconce, 3-Light, Ormolu, Louis XVI Style, Urn, Lion's Head, Electrified, 29 x 20 In., Pair 9000.00
Sconce, 3-Light, Tiers Of Floral Bosses, Tiered Drops, Faceted Chains, Drip Pans, 16 In. . 400.00
Sconce, 3-Light, Upswept Branches, 1840s, 6 1/2 x 9 1/2 In. 2070.00
Sconce, 4-Light, Gilt Bronze, Louis XV Style, Female Mask, Ribbon Bow, 45 In., Pair . . . 825.00
Sconce, 4-Light, Gilt Bronze, Louis XVI Style, Bowknot, 50 1/2 x 16 1/2 In., Pair 1725.00
Sconce, 4-Light, Gilt Bronze, Louis XVI Style, Courting Lovers Scene, Electrified, 31 In. 2185.00
Sconce, 4-Light, Gilt Bronze, Putto, Mask, Restoration Style, 23 x 15 1/4 In., Pair 2990.00
Sconce, 5-Light, Brass, Torch-Shaped Wall Plate, 40 1/2 In., Pair 440.00
Sconce, 5-Light, Cut Glass, Louis XV, Ormolu, 20th Century, 20 In., Pair 4830.00
Sconce, 5-Light, Gilt Bronze, Rococo, Cupid, Cornucopia, Electrified, 24 In., Pair 2590.00
Sconce, 5-Light, Gilt, Empire Style, Flower Form, Husk Wall Plate, c.1875, 11 In., Pair . . 2185.00
Sconce, 5-Light, Neoclassical, Prism Drops, 25 In., Pair 800.00
Sconce, 6-Light, Gilt Bronze, Leaf Cast, Fluted, 27 1/2 In. 805.00
Sconce, 6-Light, Gilt, Neoclassical Style, Prism Drops, 48 In., Pair 3450.00
Sconce, 6-Light, Gilt, Neoclassical, Allover Design, Prism Drops, 48 In., Pair 3450.00
Sconce, 7-Light, Louis XVI Style, Figural, 40 In., Pair 7200.00

Sconce, 14-Light, Brass Wash, Wheat Sheaf, Branching Candle Fixtures, 1950s, 60 In. . . . 200.00
Sconce, Ballroom, Tin, Painted Star, Early 19th Century, Pair 1650.00
Sconce, Brass, Art Deco, Flowers, Electrified, 10 x 2 x 6 In. 56.00
Sconce, Brass, Arts & Crafts, Leaded Glass Shades, Embossed Poppies, 14 x 6 In., Pair . . 2530.00
Sconce, Brass, Flowers, 10 x 3 x 7 In., Pair 310.00
Sconce, Brass, Hurricane Shades, Smoke Guards, 19th Century, 25 x 7 1/4 In., Pair 1680.00
Sconce, Brass, Hurricane, Neoclassical, Mid 19th Century, 19 x 13 In., Pair 1725.00
Sconce, Brass, Iridescent Amber Hammered Handel Glass Shade, 10 x 11 In. 460.00
Sconce, Brass, Tolled Design, Signed Jarvie, 13 1/2 In. 900.00
Sconce, Bronze, Architectural, Neoclassical, Electrified, Early 1900s, 42 In., Pair 860.00
Sconce, Bronze, Art Deco, Diamond-Shaped Glass Inserts, c.1930, 14 In., Pair 865.00
Sconce, Bronze, Inverted Umbrella Shaped Shades, Beaded Chains, 12 In., 4 Piece 805.00
Sconce, Candle, Mirror, Crimped Drip Pan, 8 In., Pair 220.00
Sconce, Candle, Tin, Crimped Back Crest, Flowers, 12 7/8 In., Pair 200.00
Sconce, Ebonized Wood, Faux Marble, Neoclassical, Continental, 11 1/2 In., Pair 430.00
Sconce, G. Stickley, Hammered Copper, Double-Ribbon Frame, Curls, 6 1/2 In., Pair 1955.00
Sconce, Gilt Bronze, Louis XVI Style, 20th Century, 8 1/8 In., Pair 290.00
Sconce, Gilt Carved Wood, Hand Holding Torch, Painted, 30 In., Pair 645.00
Sconce, Nickeled Brass, Art Deco, Frosted Glass Shade, Curved Arm, Early 1900s, 16 In. . 69.00
Sconce, Painted, Mirrored, Candle Arms, Continental, 32 x 19 In., Pair 1058.00
Sconce, Panton, Polished Brass, Perforated Shade, Chrome Shaft, Label, 14 x 13 In. 230.00
Sconce, Pavel Tynel, Lightly Perforated Shade, 11 Reflectors, 16 1/2 x 12 3/4 In. 1235.00
Sconce, Tin, Crimped Top, 13 1/2 In. 170.00
Skater's, Tin, Glass Globe, Bail Handle, 7 1/4 In. 85.00
Tiffany lamps are listed in the Tiffany category.
Torchere, 3-Light, Brass, Gondola, 3 Putti, 6-Sided Glass Lantern, 57 x 31 In. 400.00
Torchere, 4-Light, Griffins' Heads Conjoined By Chains, Electrified, 1870s, 45 In. 2990.00
Torchere, 4-Light, Overall Scrolling Leaf, Tripod Base, Early 20th Century, 59 In. 315.00
Torchere, 6-Light, Wood, Carved, Bronzed, Parcel Gilt, Column, c.1900, 73 x 12 In. 1150.00
Torchere, Baluster, Rope-Twist Carving, Square Ogee Base, 1920s, 48 In., Pair 310.00
Torchere, Brass Shade, Fluted, Wood Standard, Brass Base, Contemporary, 62 3/4 In., Pair 430.00
Torchere, Brass, Hemispheric Shade, Laminated Wood Shaft, 65 In. 80.00
Torchere, Ebonized, Carved Shaft, Maiden, Round Base, 13 x 36 1/2 In. 935.00
Torchere, Empire, Fringed Silk Shade, Square Plinth, Electrified, 63 In. 2300.00
Torchere, Giltwood, Georgian, 18th Century, 49 1/2 x 6 1/2 In. 1150.00
Torchere, Mahogany, Reeded & Carved Column, Stepped Base, c.1900, 55 In., Pair 310.00
Torchere, Rope-Twist Carving, Square Ogee Base, 1920s, 48 In. 180.00
Torchere, William IV, Mahogany, Marble Top, Mid 19th Century, 51 x 18 In. 1955.00
Torchere, Wrought Iron, Parcel Gilt, Spiraling Roses, Leaves, Painted, Pricket, 58 In., Pair 1495.00
Whale Oil, 5-Light, Brass, Adjustable Shade, Scrolled Branches, Dish Foot, 22 In. 700.00
Whale Oil, 6-Panel Fonts, Nickel Plate Collar, 10 In., Pair 4310.00
Whale Oil, Amethyst Glass, Cut Flowers, 11 1/2 In. 230.00
Whale Oil, Amethyst Glass, Pewter Collar, Octagonal Standard, Square Base, 10 In. 2130.00
Whale Oil, Amethyst Glass, Pressed Hexagonal Base, 8 1/2 In. 345.00
Whale Oil, Amethyst Glass, Pressed Loop, Pewter Collar, Octagonal Standard, 8 In. 1380.00
Whale Oil, Amethyst Glass, Printie Block, Hexagonal Base, 8 1/4 In. 460.00
Whale Oil, Black Glass, Double Baluster Standard, Kerosene Converted, 1860, 11 3/4 In. . . 1815.00
Whale Oil, Blue, Clear Font, Brass Collar, 4 3/4 In., Pair 170.00
Whale Oil, Brass, Double Copper Burners, 8 1/2 In., Pair 1955.00
Whale Oil, Brass, Inverted Beehive Stem, 8 1/2 In., Pair 715.00
Whale Oil, Canary Glass, Blown, Eye & Scale, Pressed Hexagonal Base, 8 3/4 In. 460.00
Whale Oil, Canary Glass, Waisted Loop, Pewter Collar, Hexagonal Base, 9 In., Pair 1090.00
Whale Oil, Clear Font, Cup Plate Base, No Burner, 6 In. 1380.00
Whale Oil, Clear Font, Cut Stepped Feet, 7 1/4 In., Pair 240.00
Whale Oil, Clear Font, Free Blown, Wineglass Stem, 5 1/4 In. 2300.00
Whale Oil, Clear Font, Plain Step, Square Base, 7 5/8 In., Pair 290.00
Whale Oil, Clear Font, Single Bead Stem, 4 1/8 In., Pair 1090.00
Whale Oil, Clear Font, Spill-Proof Tops, Plain Feet, 4 1/4 In., Pair 1150.00
Whale Oil, Clear Font, Stepped Embossed Base, 7 5/8 In., Pair 430.00
Whale Oil, Clear Font, Wineglass Stem, Plain Feet, 3 1/4 In., Pair 490.00
Whale Oil, Clear Glass, Waisted Loop, Pewter Burner, Hexagonal Base, 11 In., Pair 520.00
Whale Oil, Clear Glass, Wineglass Stem, Plain Feet, 3 3/4 & 3 1/2 In., Pair 520.00

Whale Oil, Cobalt Blue Glass, 4-Printie Block, Hexagonal Base, 11 1/4 In. 2590.00
Whale Oil, Cobalt Blue Glass, Pewter Collar, Octagonal Standard, 10 1/4 In., Pair 1380.00
Whale Oil, Cobalt Blue Glass, Pressed Loop, Pewter Collar, 8 1/2 In. 3450.00
Whale Oil, Cobalt Blue Glass, Printie Block, Hexagonal Base, 8 3/4 In. 1725.00
Whale Oil, Crossman, West & Leonard, Pewter, 7 In. 250.00
Whale Oil, Crystal, Free-Blown Font, Ribbed Hollow Stem, Plain Base, 10 In. 2590.00
Whale Oil, Dark Cranberry Glass, Cut Overlay, Pressed Hexagonal Base, 10 3/4 In. 2300.00
Whale Oil, Deep Amethyst Glass, Pewter Collar, Hexagonal Standard, 8 1/4 In. 1380.00
Whale Oil, Emerald Green Glass, Cut Overlay Glass, Hexagonal Base, 10 1/4 In. 290.00
Whale Oil, Finger, Amethyst Glass, Handle, Plain Foot, 3 In., Pair 1150.00
Whale Oil, Finger, Amethyst Glass, Molded Loop Design, 3 1/4 In., Pair 345.00
Whale Oil, Finger, Cobalt Blue Glass, Pewter Collar, 3 1/4 In. 690.00
Whale Oil, Finger, Cobalt Blue Glass, Pewter Collar, 3 1/4 In., Pair 1380.00
Whale Oil, Finger, Conical Font, Applied Handle, Plain Feet, 2 7/8 In., Pair 460.00
Whale Oil, Finger, Dark Amethyst Glass, Pewter Collar, Handle, 3 1/4 In. 6040.00
Whale Oil, Finger, Medium Blue, Footed, Handle, 3 In., Pair 170.00
Whale Oil, Finger, Pewter Collar, Applied Loop Handle, 3 1/4 In., Pair 115.00
Whale Oil, Finger, Teal Green, Loop Handle, 3 1/4 In., Pair 575.00
Whale Oil, Finger, White Clambroth Glass, Pewter Collar, 3 1/4 In. 690.00
Whale Oil, Finger, White Opalescent Glass, Pewter Collar, 3 1/4 In. 1495.00
Whale Oil, Free-Blown Glass, Pewter Collar, Pressed Quatrefoil Base, 10 1/4 In., Pair . . . 575.00
Whale Oil, Free-Blown Glass, Pewter Collar, Pressed Quatrefoil Base, 10 In., Pair 400.00
Whale Oil, Frosted Swag, Tassel Design, Inverted Shade, 18 In., Pair 460.00
Whale Oil, Glass, Blown Font, 4 Step, Square Base, 4 3/8 In., Pair 460.00
Whale Oil, Glass, Clear, Faceted Sides, 10 In. 115.00
Whale Oil, Glass, Clear, Pewter Burner & Collar, 5 3/4 In. 440.00
Whale Oil, Glass, Free-Blown, Raised Square Base, 8 In., Pair 460.00
Whale Oil, Glass, Swag & Tassel, Quatrefoil Base, 16 In., Pair 805.00
Whale Oil, Globe Shape, Hollow Stem, 9 1/2 In., Pair 3622.00
Whale Oil, Honeycomb Font, Brass Collars, Clambroth Base, 10 1/2 In. 55.00
Whale Oil, Pear Shape, White Loopings, 8 1/4 In., Pair 290.00
Whale Oil, Peg, Cranberry Glass, Clear Font, Brass Stems, Marble Feet, 9 In., Pair 860.00
Whale Oil, Petticoat, Free-Blown Globe, 8 3/4 In., Pair 6500.00
Whale Oil, Pewter Collar, Stepped Square Base, 11 In., Pair 630.00
Whale Oil, Powder Blue Glass, Clear Glass Stem, 8 1/2 In., Pair 60.00
Whale Oil, Pressed Glass, Acanthus Leaf, 10 1/2 In. 390.00
Whale Oil, Pressed Glass, Bull's-Eye & Thumbprint, Pewter Collar, Hexagonal Base, 8 In. 330.00
Whale Oil, Pressed Glass, Cobalt Blue, Octagonal Standards, Square Base, 10 1/4 In., Pair 4310.00
Whale Oil, Pressed Glass, Loop, Teal Green Glass, Octagonal Standard, 8 1/2 In. 3450.00
Whale Oil, Pressed Glass, Moon & Star, Brass Double-Wick Burner, 11 1/4 In. 145.00
Whale Oil, Ruby, Clear Overlay, Brass Collar, 4 In. 575.00
Whale Oil, Samuel Davis, Tin, Patented May 6th, 1856, 7 1/4 In. 745.00
Whale Oil, Teal Blue Glass, Octagonal Standard, Square Base, 10 1/4 In. 2470.00
Whale Oil, Teal Green Glass, Free-Blown, 7 In. 3680.00
Whale Oil, Teal Green Glass, Pewter Collar, Octagonal Standard, Square Base, 8 In. 2415.00
Whale Oil, Teardrop Shape, 8 3/8 & 6 3/4 In., Pair 90.00
Whale Oil, Twin Tube, Embossed, Pewter Collar, Square Base, 5 1/4 In., Pair 490.00
Whale Oil, Urn Shape, Single Spout, 19th Century, 9 1/4 In. 125.00
Whale Oil, Wineglass Stem, Plain Feet, 3 1/2 & 3 3/4 In., Pair 520.00
Wrought Iron, Alabaster Shade, Leaf Design, Subes, 1925, 23 In. 3525.00
LAMPSHADE, Arts & Crafts, Caramel Slag Glass, Oak, For 4-Branch Base, 9 x 18 In. 175.00
Hanging, Ice Cream Parlor, Slag, Jeweled, Hinged Lower Section, 23 x 17 In. 860.00
Hurricane, Blown & Cut Glass, Leaves Spray, Folded Rim, 1860s, 22 In. 1610.00
Pressed Glass, Inverted Bell, Roses, Pierced Basket Weave Trumpet Stand, 32 In. 4800.00

LANTERNS are a special type of lighting device. They have a light
source, usually a candle, totally hidden inside the walls of the lantern.
Light is seen through holes or glass sections.

Arts & Crafts, Tan Slag Glass Panels, Metal Base, 11 In. 80.00
Barn, 4 Panes, Bentwood Handle, Tin Cover Over Top Vent, Wire Latch, 8 3/4 In. 825.00
Barn, Oak & Pine, Wooden Peg Construction, Wrought Iron Hardware, 14 1/2 In. 580.00
Barn, Pine, Wire Bail Handle, Copper Deflector Top, 14 In. 250.00

Barn, Scrolled Edging & Apron, Wire Hinges & Latch, Wooden, 12 In. 220.00
Brass, Fan Shape Reflector, Engraved Flowers, Bat Form Trim, Chinese, 27 x 8 In., Pair . 340.00
Brass, Fireman's, Red Globe, 19 In. 460.00
Brass, Pickwick, 2 Wick Tubes, 11 1/4 In. 140.00
Brass Ring, Wire Cage, Glass, Signed, A. French Patent September 25, 1866, 14 In. 260.00
Bronze, Arts & Crafts, Openwork Leaf & Vine, Blue & White Enamel Flowers, 28 In. . . . 505.00
Bronze, Japanese, Menacing Look, Flaming Ball Finial, Late 18th Century, 77 In. 550.00
Bronze, Oval Body, Round Feet, Baluster-Turned Stem, Relief Dragons, Japan, 18 In. . . . 345.00
Candle, 4 Glass Sides, Wire Hinges & Protectors, Ring Handle, 1855, 15 3/4 In. 525.00
Candle, Brass, Hinged Doors, Handles, Loop, Collapsible & Hinged Hood, 11 In., Pair . . . 330.00
Candle, Bronze, Pagoda, Round, Animals In Relief, Bells, Electrified 55.00
Candle, Hallway, 6 Etched Glass Panels, Black Tin Gothic Frame, 15 1/4 In. 315.00
Candle, Tin, Glass, Carrying Handle, Dome-Top Vent, 12 In. 143.00
Candle, Wooden, Blue Gray Paint, Hand Blown Glass Panes, Early 19th Century 2850.00
Carriage, Wooden, Ebonized, Silvered Metal, Gas Fittings, 19th Century, 30 1/2 In. 230.00
Coach, Brass, Beveled Glass Panes, Electric, 1900s, 16 1/2 In., Pair 80.00
Coach, Metal & Glass, Double Stepped Flue, Gas Light Control, J.V. Waldon, 20 In., Pair 1880.00
Coleman, Model 2200, Green Enameled Top, Glass Globe, Swing Handle, 1950 . . . . 30.00
Coleman, Model 2280, Green Enameled Top, Chrome Base, Swing Handle, 1948 . . . . 27.00
Double, Student, Tin, Brass, Cone Shape Shades, Adjustable Cups, Dish Base, 20 In. 375.00
Fireman's, King Fire Dept., Dietz, 19 In. 290.00
Gilt Bronze, 6 Sides, Leaf Corona, Beveled Glass Panes, Fruit & Shell Pendant, 42 In. . . . 1380.00
Gilt Bronze, Continental, Leaf Scrolled Branch, Beveled Glass Panes, 22 In., Pair 4140.00
Gilt Bronze, Gothic, Bronze, Pierced Chains, France, 19th Century, 40 x 8 In. 230.00
Glass Globe, 8-Sided, Tin Font, Star & Diamond Piercing, Brass Burner, 10 In. 330.00
Hall, Giltwood, Pendant, Italy, c.1900, 22 x 7 x 10 1/2 In. 3680.00
Hall, Louis XV, Bronze, 5 Sides, Serpentine Glass Panels, Hanging Ring, 28 x 17 In. 2990.00
Hall, Pear Shape, Frosted, Engraved, Brass Mounted, Chains, 25 In. 460.00
Hanging, 8 Sides, 3 Glass Panels, Ring Hanger, Brass, 30 x 9 In. 140.00
Hanging, Amethyst, Smoke Shade, 25 In. 1200.00
Hanging, Arts & Crafts, Copper, Octagonal, Hammered Glass Panels, 28 x 13 In. 805.00
Hanging, G. Nelson, No. 492, Crenellated Vinyl, Electric, 1966, 18 x 18 In. 300.00
Hanging, Gustav Stickley, Copper, Square Cutouts At Top Over Yellow Glass, 10 In. 4600.00
Hanging, Gustav Stickley, Wrought Iron, White Glass Panes, Vented Roof, 9 x 31 In. 1955.00
Hanging, Night-Light, Brass Fence & Pole, Ruby Jewel, Candle Cup, 12 In. 245.00
Kelly & Company, Rochester, N.Y., Etched General P.H. Sheridan, 12 In. 3795.00
Mixed Woods, Mortised Construction, 4 Panes, Wire Hinges, Bail Handle, 12 1/4 In. 154.00
Onion Globe, Tin Font, Base & Ring Handle, Wire Guards, 9 In. 385.00
Pierced Star & Diamonds, Glass Diamonds, Onion, 15 1/2 In. 290.00
Presentation, Brass, Nickel Plated, Etched Glass, Kelly & Co., c.1870, 12 In. 3300.00
Samuel Yellin, Wrought Iron, Mica, Floral Cutouts, Twisted Stems, 29 x 16 In. 4600.00
Ship's, Brass, Cobalt Blue Shades, 10 1/2 In., Pair 575.00
Ship's, Brass, Suspension Frame, Nunn & Co., London, 16 In. 430.00
Skater's, Brass Plate Base, Top, Adjustable Wick, Carry Ring, 4 1/2 In. 580.00
Skater's, Clear Globe, Wire Handle, 7 1/8 In. 110.00
Slag Glass Panels, Hammered Copper, 9 x 4 x 4 In. 345.00
Tin, Candle, 4 Glass Panels, 4 Sides, Ring Handle, 15 1/2 In. 275.00
Tin, Candle, 4 Sides, Ring Handle, Wire Hanger, 3 1/2 x 8 1/2 In. 250.00
Tin, Candle, Pierced, 20 In. 345.00
Tin, Candle, Rectangular, 3 Glazed Sides, Strap Work, 19th Century, 17 In. 460.00
Tin, Dome Top, 3 Glass Panes, Crimped Candle Socket, Reflector, Duntafil, 9 3/4 In. 410.00

**You can clean copper with lemon juice and salt or
with Worcestershire sauce.**

**You can clean aluminum with silver polishing cream.
It's good for the new aluminum wheels on your car, too.**

Tin, Hanging, Old Dark Green Paint, Embossed, 17 1/2 In. 410.00
Tin, Pierced, Conical Top, Star & Diamond, Fixed Globe, 19th Century, 16 1/2 In. 1955.00
Tin, Punched, 4 Diagonal Lines, Circular, Handle, 15 x 5 1/2 In. 200.00
Tin, Punched, Cone Top, Round Handle 275.00
Tin, Punched, Geometric, Circles & Slats, 23 x 9 In. 825.00
Tin, Punched, Rayed Circles, Ring Handle, Square, Chained Latch Door, 11 3/8 In. 825.00
Tin, Punched, Stars & Sunburst, Clear Glass, 4 Wire Guards, Square, 15 1/2 x 4 1/2 In. .. 200.00
Tin, Punched, Sunburst On Door, Circle & Stars, Handle, 14 x 6 In. 200.00
Wedding, Landscape Reserves, Chinese Export, 1880s, 13 5/8 In. 460.00
Wooden, Tin Top, Base, Glass, Hinged Door, Handle, 7 x 13 1/2 In. 440.00
Wrought Iron, 2 Tiered Roofover Cages, Arts & Crafts, 16 x 16 x 16 In. 175.00

LE VERRE FRANCAIS is one of the many types of cameo glass made in
France. The glass was made by the C. Schneider factory in Epinay-sur-
Seine from 1920 to 1933. It is a mottled glass, usually decorated with
floral designs, and bears the incised signature *Le Verre Francais*.

Ewer, Red Flowers, On Mottled Cream & Blue, Signed, 12 In. 1840.00
Lamp, Bleeding Hearts, On Blue, Bell Shape Shade, 18 1/2 In. 8625.00
Lamp, Stylized Flowers, On Yellow, Wrought Iron Base, Signed, 7 In. 975.00
Night-Light, Flowers On Mottled Ground, 8 In. 280.00
Shade, Thorny Branch, Roses & Leaves, On Frosted Pink, c.1921, 6 In. 250.00
Vase, Brown Hanging Fruit, On Mottled Orange, Purple Handles, 10 In. 2640.00
Vase, Butterflies, On Mottled Light Blue, Signed, Hegis, 7 1/2 In. 2700.00
Vase, Lavender Dahlias, On Pink Mottled, 17 In. 2400.00
Vase, Oak Tree, On Orange & Yellow, Signed, 12 In. 1344.00
Vase, On Mottled Yellow, Red Stylized Flowers, Oval, 11 3/4 In. 1955.00
Vase, Orchids, Yellow, On Mottled Blue, 10 In. 1725.00
Vase, Papillion, 1925, 18 3/4 In. 9600.00
Vase, Purple Flowers, On Mottled Orange, White, Signed, 16 In. 1150.00
Vase, Red Poppies, On Yellow, Signed, 10 1/4 In. 2495.00
Vase, Rose Flowers, On Mottled Yellow, 17 1/2 In. 2472.00
Vase, Stylized Chrysanthemum Blossoms, Aubergine, Lavender, 14 In. 999.00
Vase, Stylized Flowers, On Mottled Orange, White, Signed, 12 In. 1085.00
Vase, Stylized Flowers, On Mottled White, Signed, 4 In. 630.00
Vase, Stylized Flowers, On Mottled Yellow, Signed, 12 In. 975.00
Vase, Stylized Fruit & Foliage, On Cranberry, Footed, Signed, 17 In. 1150.00
Vase, Stylized Geometric Leaves, Gourd Shape, 8 In. 920.00
Vase, Stylized Landscape, Blue & Green, Signed, 4 In. 2530.00
Vase, Sunbursts Around Honeycomb, On Orange, Signed, 4 x 5 1/2 In. 448.00
Vase, Tall Mushrooms, On Mottled Red, Gray, 8 1/2 In. 2415.00

LEATHER is tanned animal hide and it has been used to make decorative and useful objects for centuries. Leather objects must be carefully
preserved with proper humidity and oiling or the leather will deterio-
rate and crack. This damage cannot be repaired.

Belt, Cowboy & Horse, Roping Steer, Embossed, 3 Buckles, Billets 295.00
Belt, Wreath Disc Marked Police, 2 Piece Interlock Buckle 150.00
Binding Group, Decorative, Mid 20th Century, 7 1/2 x 5 1/4 In., 9 Piece 144.00
Bucket, Shot, Coat Of Arms, Cloth Lining, Loop Handle, England, 29 In. 412.00
Chaps, Step In, Large Stitch, Leg Fringe, 33 In., Iron Belt Buckle 650.00
Cigarette Case, Blossoms, Embossed, Art Deco Dispenser, 3 x 2 1/4 x 1 In. 92.00
Figurine, Horse, Harness & Bridle, Glass Eyes, 37 x 38 In. 7500.00
Frame, Alligator, Brass Mounted, 7 3/4 x 6 1/4 In. 518.00
Hobbles, Horse, Rawhide, 18 In. 94.00
Hobbles & Lead, Braided, 2 Rings, 2 Balls, 8 Filigreed Silver Ferrels, 12-Ft. Rope 225.00
Holster, Embossed Rope Border, Double Loop, Iver Johnson, c.1900 .... 175.00
Holster, Single Action, Mexican Loop, Tooled, Holds Colt S.A., 7 1/2 In. 195.00
Holster, Single Action, Shelton-Payne, El Paso, Holds Colt, 5 1/2 In. 650.00
Holster, Whip Stitch, Trimmed At Muzzle, Frazier, Pueblo, Colo. 350.00
Liqueur Case, 4 Books, Leather Lined, 6 Square Decanters, 16 Beakers, 1860s, 10 1/4 In. . 322.00
Notepad, Inset Silver Plaque On Cover, Elephants, Trees 86.00
Saddle, Fleur-De-Lis Tooling, Wood Stirrups, Tin, W. Davis & Son, S.F., c.1905, 24 In. .. 770.00

LEEDS pottery was made at Leeds, Yorkshire, England, from 1774 to 1878. Most Leeds ware was not marked. Early Leeds pieces had distinctive twisted handles with a greenish glaze on part of the creamy ware. Later ware often had blue borders on the creamy pottery. A Chicago company named Leeds made many Disney-inspired figurines. They are listed in the Disneyana category.

LEEDS POTTERY.

Bowl, Blue & Yellow Flowers, Leaves, Vine Border, 3 3/4 x 12 1/2 In.	1073.00
Bowl, Blue, Green, Tan Flowers, Leaves, Chain Link Border, 5 x 11 1/4 In.	880.00
Bowl, Blue, Yellow, Green, Brown Interior, Brown Vine Border, 10 3/4 x 4 3/4 In.	660.00
Charger, Brown Swag, Cobalt Blue, Brown, Yellow Flowers, 14 3/8 In.	1870.00
Charger, Feather, Blue, Pagoda, Landscape, Oval, 12 1/2 In.	495.00
Charger, Feather, Blue, Yellow Body, Flowers, Scalloped Edge, Oval, 13 1/4 In.	715.00
Coffeepot, Dome Cover, 4 Colors, Blue Flowers & Leaves, 9 3/4 In.	3300.00
Coffeepot, Dome Cover, Oriental Scene, Blue, Brown, Green, Egg Shape, Handle, 9 In.	440.00
Creamer, Flowers, 4 Colors, Leaf Handle, 4 3/4 In.	440.00
Creamer, Flowers, 5 Colors, Buds, Leaves, 4 1/2 In.	130.00
Creamer, Green, Yellow, Tan, Embossed, Fluted, Beaded, 4 1/4 In.	770.00
Creamer, Pineapple, Embossed Oval Design, Fluted Base, 4 1/2 In.	825.00
Creamer, Tulips, Yellow, Brown, Green, Dark Brown Stripes On Rim	800.00
Cup & Saucer, Barn Scene, Rust, Fence & Trees	715.00
Cup & Saucer, Blue On White, Flowers & Leaves, Soft Paste, Handleless	70.00
Cup & Saucer, Blue, Green Flowers, Brown Stripes On Rim	137.00
Cup & Saucer, Flowers, Gold, Green, Brown Leaves, Handleless	275.00
Cup & Saucer, Green Grid, Orange Dots, Blue Circles	220.00
Cup & Saucer, Leaves & Drape Design, Soft Past, Handleless	28.00 to 30.00
Cup & Saucer, Peafowls, Blue, Gold, Yellow, Handleless	190.00
Cup & Saucer, Pearlware, Flowers, Blue, Yellow, Green Goldenrod, Handleless	220.00
Cup & Saucer, Sunflower, Yellow Flower	660.00
Cup & Saucer, Tan & Brown Sprig & Vines, Soft Paste, Handleless	70.00
Cup & Saucer, Wreath, Roses, Leaves	935.00
Mug, Flowers & Branches, 4 Colors, Straight Sides, Handle, 6 In.	520.00
Mug, Incised Bands, Mottled Drape, Straight Sides, Loop Handle, 6 In.	1430.00
Pepper Pot, Draped Floral Garlands, 3 Colors, 4 1/2 In.	120.00
Pitcher, Banded, Grape Leaves, Peacocks, 8 3/4 In.	550.00
Pitcher, Cover, Feather Edge, Cobalt Blue Flower Blossom, Pearlware, 7 x 13 In.	430.00
Pitcher, Cream, Flowers, Bulbous, 4 Colors, Soft Paste, 3 1/2 In.	220.00
Pitcher, Flowers, 4 Colors, 6 5/8 In.	495.00
Plate, 5 Colors, Blue Feather Edge, Vine Border, 8 Sides, 6 1/4 In.	2310.00
Plate, 5 Colors, Flowers, Leaves, 8 1/2 In.	880.00
Plate, 5 Colors, Flowers, Leaves, Vine Border, 8 In.	200.00
Plate, Blue Feather Edge, Cluster Of Strawberries	745.00
Plate, Blue Feather Edge, Flower Bud, Leaves, 8 1/4 In.	825.00
Plate, Blue Feather Edge, Flowers, 9 3/4 In.	385.00
Plate, Blue Feather Edge, Flowers, Soft Paste, 8 In.	175.00
Plate, Blue Feather Edge, Pansy, Embossed, Blue, Green Tan, 10 1/4 In.	1155.00
Plate, Chop Plate, Blue, Yellow Flowers, Green Leaves, White Ground, 14 1/4 In.	825.00
Plate, Green Feather Edge, American Eagle, 8 Sides, 5 In.	1760.00
Plate, Green Feather Edge, Flowers, Sprigs, 6 3/4 In.	525.00
Plate, Green Feather, Acorn, Flowers, Leaf & Fish Scale Border, 6 3/4 In.	935.00
Plate, Green Feather, Eagle & Shield, 8 In.	1045.00
Plate, Leaf & Acorn, Green & Yellow, 8 1/4 In.	140.00
Plate, Peacock, In Tree, Blue, Yellow, Black Spots, Green Rim, 9 In.	11705.00
Plate, Peafowl, Brown Border, Blue, Yellow, Tan, 8 Sides, 7 In.	1045.00
Plate, Peafowl, In Tree, Blue, Gold, Yellow, Green Leaves, 10 In.	660.00
Plate, Peafowl, Tree Shape, Yellow, Blue, Gold, Green Leaves, 7 In.	495.00
Plate, Rearing Horse, Blue Trim, Shell Edge, 9 1/2 In.	358.00
Plate, Rose, Brown Band Border, Pearlware, 10 In.	248.00
Plate, Tulip, Yellow, Brown, Green, Multicolored Flower Border, 7 1/4 In.	495.00
Platter, Blue Feather Edge, Impressed Best Goods, 12 1/2 x 15 1/4 In.	100.00
Platter, Green Feather Edge, 12 1/2 x 15 1/2 In.	60.00
Platter, Green Feather Edge, American Eagle, 8 5/8 x 11 3/4 In.	165.00
Sugar, Cover, Acorn Finial, 5 Colors, Flowers, Shell & Ring Handles, 6 In.	605.00
Sugar & Creamer, Blue Flowers, Buds, Tooled Handle, 2 1/2 In.	330.00

Tea Caddy, Dome Cover, Blue Flowers, Soft Paste, 5 3/4 In. 330.00
Teapot, Flowers & Leaves, 5 Colors, 6 1/2 In. 495.00
Teapot, Globular, Entwined Strap Handle, Creamware, c.1780, 3 1/2 In. 460.00
Vase, Blue Transfer, Oriental Scene, Scalloped Border, Pearlware, 8 x 4 1/2 x 3 1/4 In. 660.00
Waste Bowl, Green, Gold Leaves, 6 x 2 7/8 In. 110.00
Waste Bowl, Green, Gold, Mustard, Black Leaves, Blue Band, 4 1/4 x 3 In. 110.00

LEFTON is a mark found on pottery, porcelain, glass, and other wares imported by the Geo. Zoltan Lefton Company. The company began in 1941 and is still in business. It was restructured in 2002 and is now called the Lefton Company. The company mark has changed through the years; but because marks have been used for long periods of time, they are of little help in dating an object.

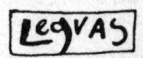

Bank, Lion's Head, Glasses, Stopper, 7 3/4 x 4 In. 25.00
Cookie Jar, White, Holly, No. 6054 .... 44.00
Cup & Saucer, White, Holly, No. 6067 .... 12.00
Dish, Happy Anniversary, No. 5510, Label, 6 x 4 In. 20.00
Dish, Sleigh, Green Holly, Label, 8 In. 26.00
Figurine, Clown, In Barrel, With Trick Dog, Label, 4 1/4 In. 20.00
Figurine, Panda, No. 01837, 6 1/2 x 3 1/4 In. 26.00
Head Vase, Woman, White Ruffled Hat, With Flowers, Yellow Dress, 6 In. 66.00
Head Vase, Woman, White, Yellow Hat, Pink Flowers, Yellow Dress, 6 1/2 In. 50.00
Head Vase, Woman, Yellow Straw Hat, Black Band, 6 In. 132.00
Music Box, You Light Up My Life, Label, 6 1/2 x 4 1/2 In. 34.00
Pincushion, Turtle, No. 02042, 3 x 2 x 2 3/4 In. 20.00
Planter, Christmas Boot, Label, 4 1/4 x 5 1/4 x 2 In. 18.00
Planter, Madonna With Child, 7 x 5 5/8 In. 70.00
Tidbit, Holly, Candy Cane Edge 40.00

LEGRAS was founded in 1864 by Auguste Legras at St. Denis, France. It is best known for cameo glass and enamel-decorated glass with Art Nouveau designs. Legras merged with Pantin in 1920 and became the Verreries et Cristalleries de St. Denis et de Pantin Reunies.

Bowl, Stylized Flowers, On Yellow & Orange, Signed, 6 In. 1093.00
Rose Bowl, Enameled Winter Scene, On Frosted Orange, 6 x 6 In. 392.00
Vase, Carmel, Etched Branches, Leaves, Brown & Green Enameled, Signed, 10 1/4 In. ... 316.00
Vase, Enameled Artichoke, Green & Cream Enameled Leaves & Fruit, Signed, 5 1/4 In. ... 336.00
Vase, Enameled Wooded Lake, Beached Skiff, Signed, 5 3/4 In. 1045.00
Vase, Leaves, On Rose, Cylindrical, Signed, 19 1/2 In. 865.00
Vase, Medallion Of Deer, On Mottled Ground, Signed, 9 1/2 In. 920.00
Vase, Trailing Leaves, Seed Pods, Enameled, Elongated Egg Shape, 1880, 8 In. 510.00

LENOX is the name of a porcelain maker. Walter Scott Lenox and Jonathan Cox founded the Ceramic Art Company in Trenton, New Jersey, in 1889. In 1906, Lenox left and started his own company called *Lenox*. The company makes a porcelain that is similar to Irish Belleek. The marks used by the firm have changed through the years and collectors prefer the earlier examples. Related pieces may also be listed in the Ceramic Art Co. category.

Bowl, President's Club, Box 30.00
Bowl, Windmill Border, 5 x 10 1/2 In. 88.00
Plate, Fish Underwater, Gold Rim, Morley, 9 1/4 In., Pair 70.00
Punch Set, Stylized Purple Grapes, Leaves, Gold Rim, Bowl, 11 Cups, 13 x 15 1/2 In. ... 575.00
Tea Set, Courtship Scene, Gold Scrolls & Handle, Belleek, 3 Piece, 7-In. Teapot 82.00
Teapot, Tea Strainer, Cover, Silver Overlay, Scrolling Handle, Signed, 6 In. 134.00

LETTER OPENERS have been used since the eighteenth century. Ivory and silver were favored by the well-to-do. In the late nineteenth century, the letter opener was popular as an advertising giveaway and many were made of metal or celluloid. Brass openers with figural handles were also popular.

Alligator, Brass, R.H. Stewart & Co., 7 In. 11.00
Buick Motor Cars, Brass, 9 1/4 In. 57.00

Medallion Of Napoleon, Silver Plated, 8 1/2 In. 86.00
New Orleans Great Northern Railroad, 8 1/4 In., Pair 69.00

LIBBEY Glass Company has made many types of glass since 1888, including the cut glass and tablewares that are collected today. The stemwares of the 1930s and 1940s are once again in style. The Toledo, Ohio, firm was purchased by Owens-Illinois in 1935 and is still working under the name *Libbey Incorporated*. Additional pieces may be listed under Amberina, Cut Glass, and Maize.

Bowl, Amberina, Rolled Rim, Signed, 9 1/2 In. 345.00
Bowl, Controlled Bubble, Pale Green Stretch, c.1930, 9 In. 130.00
Bowl, Hobstar, 8 In. 58.00
Bowl, Hobstar, Signed, 9 In. 121.00
Celery Dish, Wedgemere, Rolled Rim, 11 1/2 x 5 1/2 In. 960.00
Compote, Cut Glass, Rectangular Base, Etched Mark, 13 1/2 In. 460.00
Compote, Engraved Fuchsia Flowers, Twist Stem, Signed, 7 1/4 In. 60.00
Decanter, Harvard, 15 In. 395.00
Dish, Glenda, Signed, 1 3/4 x 8 In. 415.00
Punch Bowl, Stand, Repeating Sunburst Cartouches, Notched Rim, c.1901, 13 x 14 In. . . . 1528.00
Tazza, Hobstar Foot, Signed, 5 x 6 In. 450.00
Vase, Amberina, Honeycomb Quilting, 6-Sided Rim, 2 1/2 In. 550.00
Vase, Amberina, Wafer & Ribbed Knop On Foot, 7 7/8 In. 825.00
Vase, Engraved Orchid & Lily-Of-The Valley, Signed, 4 3/8 In. 165.00
Vase, Ferns & Flowers, Zipper Cut Neck, Rayed Star Base, 14 In. 1525.00
Vase, Flower-Form, Bulbous, Signed, 11 1/4 In., Pair 2128.00
Vase, Harvard, Blue Cut To Clear, 10 In. 1100.00
Vase, Harvard, Cranberry Cut To Clear, 12 In. 1200.00
Vase, Jack-In-The-Pulpit, 12 Optic Ribs, Amber, Signed, 5 In. 885.00
Vase, Ribbed, Footed, Signed, 11 In. 728.00
Vase, Star Block & Thistle Cutting, Signed, 14 x 5 In. 252.00

LIGHTERS for cigarettes and cigars are collectible. Cigarettes became popular in the late nineteenth century, and with the cigarette came matches and cigarette lighters. All types of lighters are collected, from solid gold to the first of the recent disposable lighters. Most examples found were made after 1940. Some lighters may be found in the Jewelry category in this book.

Chevrolet, You Will Never Be Behind The 8 Ball, Black Plastic Body, Table, 2 1/2 In. . . . 33.00
Cigar, Rice Ball, Pewter, Snuffer, 2 In. 35.00
Colt 45 Malt Liquor Tin Can With Lighter Inset In Top, Table, Japan 20.00
Dunhill, Nude, Art Deco, Chrome Figure, Black Bakelite Base, 5 In. 28.00
Dunhill, Sylph Ruler, Nickel Finish 125.00
Dunhill, Trench Type, Metal, Enamel, Box, 2 1/4 In. 26.00
Evans, Case, Lighter, Compact, Mirror, Rhinestone, Black, White Enamel, 4 x 2 1/2 In. . . . 50.00
Fighter Plane, Art Deco, Chrome, With Music Box 175.00
Gas, Cigar, Cigarette, Premier Cigarettes From Recompense, 10 x 7 x 21 In. 1180.00
Gillette Cricket, Clack, Blue, Red, Orange Flowers, Yellow Sun, 1970, 4 In. 20.00
Lillian Russell, 5 Cent Cigars, Kerosene Fired, 11 In. 1900.00
Milwaukee Rd. Railroad, Hadson & Warren, Box, Pair 46.00
Mobil, Slim Style, Pocket, Box, 2 1/8 In. 80.00
Olsher, Windmill Shaped, Art Deco, Chrome, 6 In. 82.00
Parker, Nude, Art Deco, Chrome Figure, Brown Bakelite Base, Box, 5 In. 50.00
Penguin, Mohawk Gasoline, Cloisonne, 2 1/4 In. 240.00
Phiney-Walker, Combination Table Lighter, Alarm Clock, Brass, 5 1/4 x 4 x 2 1/2 In. 35.00
Prince, Grand Piano Shape, Plastic, Japan, 4 x 2 3/4 x 3 1/2 In. 35.00
Richfield Oil Co., Slim Style, 2 1/8 In. 80.00
Ritepoint, Green Tinted Plastic, Visual Fuel Supply 20.00
Ronson, Brushed Aluminum Case, Box 26.00
Ronson, Capri, Black, Chrome, Violets, 1956 . . . . 45.00
Ronson, Octette Art Deco, Torch Tip, 3 5/8 x 3 3/4 x 2 1/2 In. 65.00
Ronson, Silver Finish, Crown Table, Box 31.00
Ronson, Vanguard, Chrome Finish, Black Enamel, Red Details, 2 1/4 In. 20.00

Rowenta, Pepsi Logo, Checkered Nickel Finish, Slim Line 39.00
Sankei, Cruise Ship Shaped, Chrome, Blue, White Enamel, 1 1/4 x 3 1/4 x 1/4 In. 32.00
Santa Fe Railroad, Pair 11.00
Sarome, Cruise Ship Shaped, Chrome, Red, Black Enamel, Hindu Swastika 22.00
Signal, Service Style, Aluminum, 2 1/4 In. 20.00
Soo Line, Warren & Warco, Original Box, Pair 23.00
Starlite, Polished Finish, Rhinestones, Clock Face, Japan 20.00
Texaco Marine Products, Slim Style, 2 1/8 In. 230.00
Thorens, Art Glass, Switzerland, 4 In. 62.00
Thorens, Brushed Finish, Cylinder, Switzerland, 1930s, 4 In. 62.00
Urn, Pewter, Felt Covered Bottom, 4 1/2 In. 25.00
Vulcan, Frisco & Illini Railroad Club, Box, Pair 17.00
Zippo, Big West Oil Co., Gift Box, Montana, 2 1/4 In. 120.00
Zippo, Camfield, Brushed Finish, 1950 .... 25.00
Zippo, Farmington Savings Bank, Brushed Aluminum, Black, Red Trim, Box 50.00
Zippo, Fixture Fashions Flora, Indiana, Green Enamel, Brushed Finish 70.00
Zippo, Green, Yellow, Red Logo, Brushed Finish, Table 37.00
Zippo, J.H. Hamlen & Sons, Inc., Brushed Finish 32.00
Zippo, Moeschl-Edwards Co., Black, Orange Enamel, Engraved Rolling Doors 63.00
Zippo, Red Emblem, Brushed Stainless Finish, 1972 .... 22.00
Zippo, Red, Blue Logo, Slim Line, Nickel Finish 30.00
Zippo, Uncle Sam Cereal, Natural Laxative, With Cereal Box, 1952, 2 1/4 x 1 1/2 In. 63.00

LIGHTNING ROD and lightning rod balls are collected. The glass balls
were at the center of the rod that was attached to the roof of a house or
barn to avoid lightning damage.

Cow, Weathervane, Delphite Blue Ball, 61 In. 180.00
Horse & Buggy, Weathervane, Bracket, Ground Wire, 21 1/2 In. 41.00
Pheasant, Weathervane, Black Paint, Robbins, 35 x 20 In. 60.00
LIGHTNING ROD BALL, Lavender, 10 Sides, Marked, Dodd & Struthers 15.00
Milk Glass, Blue, Paneled, Signed, The S Co., 4 1/2 In. 26.00
Plastic, Red, 4 1/2 In. 15.00

LIMOGES porcelain has been made in Limoges, France, since the mid-
nineteenth century. Fine porcelains were made by many factories,
including Haviland, Ahrenfeldt, Guerin, Pouyat, Elite, and others.
Modern porcelains are being made at Limoges and the word *Limoges*
as part of the mark is not an indication of age. Haviland, one of the
Limoges factories, is listed as a separate category in this book.

Bowl, Cover, Rose Garlands, Gilt Trim, Signed, 5 1/2 In. 55.00
Bowl, Gold Flowers, Rim, Bawo & Dotter, 1900-1914, 3 3/4 x 8 1/2 In. 144.00
Bowl, Porcelain, Overall Grapevine, Gilt, 15 x 6 1/2 In. 430.00
Box, Cover, Floral, Flow Blue, White, Green & Gold, Shell Shape, 1890s, 2 1/2 In. 200.00
Cachepot, Enamel, 3 Figural Panels, 1 Floral Panel, Bronze Mounts, 6 1/2 x 13 x 8 In. ... 5520.00
Cake Plate, Iris & Trees, Gold Rim, Open Handles, Signed T. Barid, Marked, 11 In. 40.00
Candlestick, Man & Woman, Supporting Urn, M. Redon, Signed, 1890, 9 In., Pair 728.00
Centerpiece, Allover Grapevine, Gilt Trim, 15 x 6 1/2 In. 430.00
Chocolate Set, Violet Pansies, Twig Shape Finials, 12 x 14-In. Tray, 14 Piece 895.00
Chop Plate, 3 Large Pansies, Gold Border, Duval, 12 3/4 In. 265.00
Dinner Service, C. Ahrenfeldt, Service For 12, Serving Pieces, 103 Piece 365.00
Ewer, Gold Flowers, Bawo & Dotter, c.1880, 9 1/4 In. 316.00
Ewer, Jean Pouyat, 1891-1932, 10 1/2 In. 175.00
Fish Set, 12 Plates, Ladle, Underplate, Platter, Fish Center, 13 Piece 1540.00
Fish Set, 12 Plates, Platter, Various Fish, Hand Painted, Signed, 13 Piece 1200.00
Jardiniere, Pink Roses, 2 Gilt Handles, Pedestal, 9 x 13 In. 360.00
Jardiniere, Tresseman & Vogt, 1892-1932, 8 3/4 x 11 In. 460.00
Mug, Shaving, Occupational, Sailing Ship, H.F. Bimmerman, 3 1/2 x 3 1/4 In. 575.00
Oyster Plate, 6 Oyster-Shaped Wells, Pink Glaze, Gilt Trim, c.1876, 6 Piece 245.00
Oyster Plate, Open Shells Resting On Sea Grass, Blue, Gilt Rim, 9 In., 18 Piece 4465.00
Pitcher, Birds & Flowers, Gilt, 6 Sides, 1900, 12 x 10 In. 240.00
Pitcher, Roses, Pink & White, Gilded Handle, 13 In. 220.00
Plaque, Pate-Sur-Pate, Venus & Cupids, 9 x 6 In., Pair 1955.00

Plate, Armorial, Gilt, Cream, 20th Century, 9 1/2 In, 4 Piece 185.00
Plate, Cavalier, Lepic, Signed, 1908-1920, 10 In. 325.00
Plate, Dessert, Queen's Rose, 9 1/2 In., 12 Piece 200.00
Plate, Dessert, Scalloped Rim, Green Husk Trim, Center Violets, 8 1/4 In. 200.00
Plate, Gilt, Flowers, 10 1/4 In., 12 Piece 230.00
Plate Set, Dessert, Green Band, Roses, Tray, Handles, Blakeman & Henderson, 13 Piece . 85.00
Plate Set, Dessert, Louis XVI, Putti, Gilded Lappet Border, 9 1/2 In., 12 Piece 690.00
Platter, Conifers & Rocky Ledge, Sailing Vessels, 1879, 11 In. 600.00
Platter, Oval, Floral, 20 In. 69.00
Punch Bowl, Gilt Design & Interior, Black Ground, Hessler, 10 1/2 In. 920.00
Punch Bowl, Grape & Vine, Green T & V Mark, c.1907, 6 3/4 x 16 In. 1380.00
Punch Bowl, Green, Red Berries, Gold Rim, Stand, Serpent Feet, Signed, 6 x 12 In. 920.00
Tankard, Grape Cluster, Painted, Blue, Red, Green, Mark, 14 In.................... 460.00
Teapot, Aladdin's Lamp Shape, Pink Flowers, Gold Handle, c.1890, 4 x 9 In. 95.00
Tobacco Jar, White Luster, Gold Trim, Monogram 13335.00
Tray, Dresser, Painted, Man, Woman, Sheep, Landscape, Pink Ground, Oval, 9 x 12 In. ... 69.00
Tureen, Underplate, Cover, Allover Floral, Gilt Trim, 13 x 11 In..................... 290.00
Vase, Art Nouveau, Jean Pouyat, 1891-1932, 7 In. 316.00
Vase, Floral, Gilt Fern Handles, 13 3/4 In. 275.00
Vase, Irises, Hand Painted, Cylinder, Tapered, Short Neck, Flared Rim, Marked, 14 In. ... 460.00
Vase, Landscape, Beer Drinking, Enamel, Sarlandie, 6 In. 316.00
Vase, Luster, Pink, Peacock, Flowers, Hand Painted, Blue Ground, Marked, 14 In. 290.00
Vase, Pillow, Bouquet Of Garden Flowers, 1880, 8 1/2 x 11 In. 350.00
Vase, Portrait, Gypsy Girl, Roses, Applied Gold Loop Handles, Ball Feet, 9 x 8 In. 375.00

LINDBERGH was a national hero. In 1927, Charles Lindbergh, the aviator, became the first man to make a nonstop solo flight across the Atlantic Ocean. In 1932, his son was kidnapped and murdered, and Lindbergh was again the center of public interest. He died in 1974. All types of Lindbergh memorabilia are collected.

Bank, Aluminum, Key Lock, Grannis & Tolton, 1930s, M124, 6 1/2 In. 295.00
Book, Lone Eagle 22.00
Pin, Airplane, Lucky Lindy Welcome, Spirit Of St. Louis, 1927 .... 85.00

LITHOPHANES are porcelain pictures made by casting clay in layers of various thicknesses. When a piece is held to the light, a picture of light and shadow is seen through it. Most lithophanes date from the 1825–1875 period. A few are still being made. Many lithophanes sold today were originally panels for lampshades.

Half Shade, French Countryside, Farm Buildings, 2 1/2 x 3 1/2 In. 235.00
Half Shade, Lovers On Bridge, 2 In Front, 2 Walking, 2 On Bridge, 2 3/4 x 5 1/4 In. 275.00
Lamp, 4 Portraits Of Beauties On Shade, Lithophane Panels In Base, c.1900, 13 In. 635.00
Lamp, Bronze, Erotic, Domed Shade, Female Bust Finial, 31 1/2 In. 2300.00
Panel, Courting Couple, Woman Bathing, KPM, 5 7/8 In., Pair 275.00
Shade, Grandmother Teaching Granddaughter To Sew, Hunter On Shade, 5 3/4 In. 190.00
Stein, Baseball Scene, Pitcher, Batter, Catcher, Porcelain, Pewter Lid, 1/2 Liter 2995.00
Stein, Character, Men Hunting, Dogs, Enameled, Porcelain, Pewter Lid, 1/2 Liter 360.00
Stein, Character, Monk, Barmaid In Cellar, Enameled, Porcelain, Pewter Lid, 1/2 Liter ... 267.00
Stein, Character, Munich Child, Porcelain Lid, 8 1/4 In., 1/2 Liter ....390.00 to 719.00
Stein, Germania Monument, National Denkmal A.D. Niederwald, 1/2 Liter 115.00
Stein, Men & Women Talking, Transfer, Enamel, Pewter Lid, Dog Finial, 1/2 Liter 120.00
Stein, Military, Trumpeter, 2 Sides, Porcelain, Thumblift, 10 In., 5 Liter 290.00
Stein, Monk, Young Girl, Schutzenliesl, Transfer, Enameled, Pewter Lid, 1/2 Liter 360.00
Stein, Occupational, Baker, Bakery, Porcelain, Darmstadt, 1907, 1/2 Liter 150.00
Stein, Occupational, Beer Wagon Driver, Pewter Lid, Horse Finial, 1/2 Liter 390.00
Stein, Occupational, Bellman, 2 Scenes, Pewter Lid, 1/2 Liter 725.00
Stein, Occupational, Butcher, Porcelain, Transfer, Enameled, Pewter Lid, 1/2 Liter 288.00
Stein, Occupational, Cabinetmaker, 3 Scenes, Porcelain, Pewter Lid, 1/2 Liter 515.00
Stein, Occupational, Furniture Maker, Porcelain, Pewter Lid, 1/2 Liter 485.00
Stein, Occupational, Landmann, Farming, Porcelain, Pewter Lid, 1/2 Liter 240.00
Stein, Porcelain Inlaid Lid, Blue Onion, 1/2 Liter 155.00
Stein, Wedding Scene, Bird, Flowers, Music, Transfer, Enamel, Pewter Lid, 1 Liter 230.00

LIVERPOOL, England, was the site of several pottery and porcelain factories from 1716 to 1785. Some earthenware was made with transfer decorations. Sadler and Green made print-decorated wares from 1756. Many of the pieces were made for the American market and feature patriotic emblems, such as eagles, flags, and other special-interest motifs. Liverpool pitchers are always called Liverpool jugs by collectors.

Bowl, Alnomac Ship Transfer, Historical Figures, Creamware, 1795, 12 In.	8050.00
Jug, American Officer Holding Sword, Foot On Lion, Flags, 10 1/2 In.	2015.00
Jug, Compass Rose, Ship, Success To Trade, Jack Spritsails Frolic, 10 In.	460.00
Jug, Eagle, Flag, Shield, E Pluribus Unum Banner, Masonic Emblems, Black Transfer	2070.00
Jug, Farmers Arms 1 Side, Farmer & Wife & Barnyard Other, 7 In.	550.00
Jug, Farmers Arms, In God Is Our Trust, Black Transfer, Creamware, 9 In.	800.00
Jug, Large Farmyard Scene, Farmer's Arms, Black Transfer, Creamware, 9 In.	750.00
Jug, Masonic Symbols 1 Side, 3-Masted Ship Other, 9 1/2 In.	2130.00
Jug, Obverse, Cooper's Arms, Black Transfer, Creamware, 19th Century, 9 In.	345.00
Jug, Obverse, Washington In Glory, America In Tears, Creamware, 9 1/4 In.	1725.00
Jug, Presentation, Masonic Scenes All Sides, Success To Delemere, 9 1/2 In.	880.00
Jug, Sailing Ship, Courtship Scene, Monogram, Red Accents, 9 1/4 In.	1150.00
Jug, Ship Flying American Flag, Washington On Reverse, 15 States, c.1796, 11 1/2 In.	2400.00
Jug, Ship, American Flag, Pastoral Scene On Reverse, Transfer, 9 3/4 In.	1035.00
Jug, Shipwright's Arms, Ship Caroline, American Flag, Black Transfer, 8 5/8 In.	220.00
Mug, Love & Obedience, Strap Handle, Creamware, Early 19th Century, 6 1/4 In.	260.00
Plate, View Of Vessel Flying American Flag, Birds At Rim, 10 In.	450.00

LLADRO is a Spanish porcelain. Juan, Jose, and Vicente Lladro opened a ceramics workshop in Almacera in 1951. They soon began making figurines in a distinctive, elongated style. In 1958 the factory moved to Tabernes Blanques, Spain. The company makes stoneware and porcelain figurines and vases in limited and unlimited editions. Dates given are first and last years of production.

LLADRÓ®

Ball, Christmas, No. 1603, 1988	80.00
Ball, Christmas, No. 5656, 1989	80.00
Ball, Christmas, No. 5730, 1990	100.00
Ball, Christmas, No. 5829, 1991	75.00
Ball, Christmas, No. 5913, 1992	50.00
Bell, Autumn, No. 7615, 1993	35.00
Bell, Christmas, No. 5525, 1988	40.00
Bell, Christmas, No. 5803, 1991	50.00
Bell, Christmas, No. 6010, 1993	50.00
Bell, Christmas, No. 6139, 1994	50.00
Bell, Spring, No. 7613, 1991	50.00
Bell, Summer, No. 7614, 1992	35.00
Bell, Winter, No. 7616, 1994	100.00
Clock, Pierrot, No. 5778, 8 In.	475.00
Figurine, Angel Tree Topper, No. 5719, 1991-Present	225.00
Figurine, Angelic Violinist, No. 6126, 1994, Retired	175.00
Figurine, Aranjuez Little Lady, No. 4879, 1974-1996	350.00
Figurine, At The Circus, No. 5052, 1979-1985, 13 In.	1200.00
Figurine, August Moon, No. 5122, 1982-1993	350.00
Figurine, Bashful Bather, No. 5455, 1988-Present	190.00
Figurine, Bedtime, No. 5347, 1986-1998	600.00
Figurine, Best Friend, Collectors Club, No. 7620, 1993-1994	320.00
Figurine, Billy Soccer Player, No. 5135, 1982-1983	800.00
Figurine, Bird Watcher Boy, No. 4730, 1970-1985	350.00
Figurine, Boy On Carousel Horse, No. 1470, 1985-Present	945.00
Figurine, Boy With Double Base, No. 4615, 1969-1979	475.00
Figurine, Boy With Guitar, No. 4614, 1969-1979	375.00
Figurine, Bugler, No. 5406, 1987-1990	400.00
Figurine, Cadet Captain, No. 5404, 1987-1990	400.00
Figurine, Can I Play? No. 7610, 1990-1991	475.00
Figurine, Cat Girl, Sitting With Tail Out, No. 5164, 1982-1985	500.00

Figurine, Drummer Boy, No. 5403, 1987-1990	450.00
Figurine, Flag Bearer, No. 5405, 1987-1990	450.00
Figurine, Flowers Of The Season, No. 1454, 1983-Present	2550.00
Figurine, Garden Classic, No. 7617, Limited Edition, 1991	800.00
Figurine, Girl On Carousel Horse, No. 1469, 1985-Present	945.00
Figurine, Girl Tennis Player, No. 4798, 1972-1981	400.00
Figurine, Girl With Bonnet, No. 1147, 1971-1985	300.00
Figurine, Girl With Doll, No. 1083, 1969-1985	300.00
Figurine, Girl With Flowers, No. 1088, 1969-1989	645.00
Figurine, Girl With Lamb, No. 1010, 1969-1993	300.00
Figurine, Girl With Lamb, No. 4584, 1969-1993, 10 1/2 In.	250.00
Figurine, Girl With Lilies, Sitting, No. 4972, 1977-1997	210.00
Figurine, Girl, Flowers In Pot, No. 5028, 1980-1985	800.00
Figurine, Girl, Putting On Slippers, No. 0000	450.00
Figurine, Good Bear, No. 1205, 1972-1989	150.00
Figurine, Goya Lady, No. 5125, 1982-1990	300.00
Figurine, Hamlet, No. 4729, 1970-1980	700.00
Figurine, Holy Shepherds, 3 Piece, No. 5809, 1991	175.00
Figurine, In The Meadow, Little Bunny, No. 1508, 1986-1991, 4 1/4 In.	250.00
Figurine, Lady Of The East, No. 1488, 1986-1993, 15 In.	945.00
Figurine, Lamplighter, No. 5205, 1984-Present	435.00
Figurine, Oriental Girl, No. 4840, 1973-1997	515.00
Figurine, Playful Kittens, No. 5232	300.00
Figurine, Puppy Love, No. 1127, 1971-1996	330.00
Figurine, Serene Moments Blue, No. 5550, 1989-1993	150.00
Figurine, Thursday's Child, No. 6018, 1993-1997	285.00
Figurine, Time To Sew, No. 5501, 1988-Present	110.00
Figurine, Wanderer, No. 5400, 1987-1998	265.00
Figurine, Wednesday's Child, No. 6015, 1993-1997	285.00
Figurine, Yachtsman, No. 5206, 1984-1994	300.00
Plate, Christmas, Caroling, No. 7006, 1971	200.00

LOCKE ART is a trademark found on glass of the early twentieth century. Joseph Locke worked at many English and American firms. He designed and etched his own glass in Pittsburgh, Pennsylvania, starting in the 1880s. Some pieces were marked *Joe Locke*, but most were marked with the words *Locke Art*. The mark is hidden in the pattern on the glass.

Bowl, Grape Pattern, Engraved, Signed, 4 7/8 x 2 1/2 In.	280.00
Pitcher, Woman Equestrian, Scroll Border Top, Loop Border Bottom, Signed, 7 1/2 In.	1400.00
Salt, Water Lily, Signed, 1 1/2 x 3 In.	150.00
Vase, Morning Glories, Ruffled Edge, Footed, Signed, 12 In.	1580.00
Vase, Poppy, Etched, Rolled Rim, Footed, Signed, 9 In.	130.00

LOETZ glass was made in many varieties. Johann Loetz bought a glassworks in Austria in 1840. He died in 1848 and his widow ran the company; then in 1879, his grandson took over. Most collectors recognize the iridescent gold glass similar to Tiffany, but many other types were made. The firm closed during World War II.

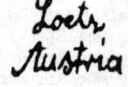

Bowl, Petal, Circular, Bulbous, Ruffled Edge, Blue & Purple Iridescent, 5 x 6 In.	600.00
Compote, Cover, Blue Oil Spot Foot & Bowl, Balled Stem, Blue Finial, 8 1/2 In.	708.00
Cup, Gold & Polychrome, Iridescent, Applied Handle, Incised, 3 3/4 In.	288.00
Lamp, Opal Bud Shape Shade, Bronze Flower Base, 18 In.	2875.00
Lamp, Opal Shade With Amber Spatter At Top, Silver Plated Bronze Root Base, 14 1/5 In.	3105.00
Lamp, Owl Shape, Applied Beak, Eyes, Metal Foot, 17 In.	3450.00
Lamp, Titania, Silver & Gray Stalagmites, Clear Cased, Gourd Shape, 8 In.	1630.00
Rose Bowl, Green, Amber Pulled Swirls, 4 1/4 In.	287.00
Rose Bowl, Pale Lavender, Gold, Blue Pulled Waves, Signed, 5 In.	1955.00
Vase, 3 Applied Teardrops, Signed, 6 5/8 In.	1045.00
Vase, Acorn, Iridescent Blue Green, Footed, 4 In.	115.00
Vase, Amber Pulled Swirls, 4-Sided Rim, 4 1/4 In.	290.00
Vase, Amber, Green & Blue Pulled Waves, Tapered, Pinched Bottom, 7 1/2 In.	700.00

Loetz, Vase, Iridescent,
Butterscotch, On Pearlized
Ground, 18 1/2 In.

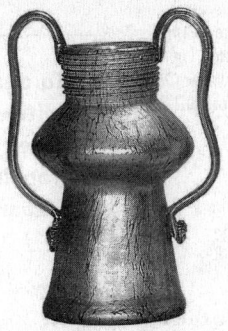

Loetz, Vase, Papillon, Green,
Iridescent Golden Blue Applied
Threading, 8 1/2 In.

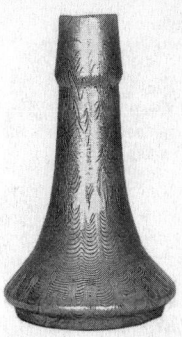

Loetz, Vase, Pulled Waves,
Blues, Greens, Copper, Topaz,
Magenta, Signed, 11 3/4 In.

Vase, Amber, Pink, Blue Iridescent, Applied Tendrils, 9 In. 1035.00
Vase, Amber, Pink, Green Iridescent, Loop Handle, 7 1/2 In. 720.00
Vase, Amethyst, Pulled Wood Grain, Iridescent, Ruffled Rim, 13 In. 500.00
Vase, Amethyst, Threaded Body, Pierced Rim, Pewter Pod Feet, 11 In. 500.00
Vase, Blue & Gold Iridescent Pulled Waves, On Clear Amber, Double Gourd, 5 1/4 In. 1840.00
Vase, Blue Iridescent Pulled Waves, On Olive Green, Signed, 5 x 4 In. 2130.00
Vase, Blue Iridescent, Goblet Shape, 9 1/2 In. 1410.00
Vase, Blue Iridescent, Pink Glass, Signed, 8 1/2 In. 1265.00
Vase, Blue Pulled Feathers, Angular Neck, 7 3/4 In. 336.00
Vase, Blue Pulled Feathers, On Gold Iridescent, Signed, 10 x 5 In. 3160.00
Vase, Blue Pulled Waves, On Gold Iridescent, Signed, 11 1/2 x 5 In. 3050.00
Vase, Blue Swirled Pulled Waves, Gold & Platinum Iridescent, Squat, 3 1/2 In. 690.00
Vase, Blue, Iridescent Green, Purple Drapes, Ruffled Edge, 10 1/2 In. 1090.00
Vase, Brown Iridescent, Tree Trunk Shape, 10 1/2 In. 690.00
Vase, Brown Stems, Leaves & Buds, On Yellow, Signed, 4 3/4 In. 390.00
Vase, Clear Crackle, Applied Amber Buttresses, Flared, 8 In. 860.00
Vase, Emerald Green Pulled Waves, Gold Iridescent, 11 1/2 x 5 In. 517.00
Vase, Flower Shape, Pulled Rim, Damascene Textured, 6 1/2 In. 3450.00
Vase, Gold, Oil Spots, Pink Combed, Dotted Iridescent Blue, Dimpled, 3 3/4 In. 2070.00
Vase, Green & Blue Pulled Waves, On Iridescent Gold, Cutout Silver Base, 10 In. 4315.00
Vase, Green & Gold, Oil Spot, Pulled Feathers, Rose Petals, On Lime Ground, 8 1/4 In. ... 3920.00
Vase, Green, Applied Decoration On Sides, Ground Pontil, 13 1/4 In. 345.00
Vase, Green, Red Rim, Flared, Ball Footed, 5 In. 345.00
Vase, Iridescent Blue, Gold, On Amber, Roll Rim, 10 In. 575.00
Vase, Iridescent Blue, Gourd Shape, 6 Applied Teardrops, 1900, 8 1/2 In. 980.00
Vase, Iridescent Blue, Pinched Sides & Top, Ground Pontil, 5 1/2 In. 460.00
Vase, Iridescent Blue, Squat, Rolled Rim, 2 Applied Ribbed Handles, 1900, 8 In. 750.00
Vase, Iridescent Gold, Pulled Feathers, 6 3/4 In. 345.00
Vase, Iridescent Pulled Waves, Blue, Tapering Cylinder, Triangular Neck, 10 In. 230.00
Vase, Iridescent, Butterscotch, On Pearlized Ground, 18 1/2 In. .... *Illus* 34500.00
Vase, Iridescent, Cobalt Trailing, On Amber, Squat, 4 Applied Loop Handles, 1900, 8 In. .. 1380.00
Vase, Iridescent, Damascene Texture, Signed, 7 1/2 In. 1400.00
Vase, Light Green, Applied Light Blue Handles & Discs, 5 3/4 In. 500.00
Vase, Mauve, Pink, Lavender, Green, Orange, Baluster, Trefoil Rim, 1900, 7 In. 2070.00
Vase, Octopus, Deep Brown, White Interior, 8 x 6 1/2 In. 2130.00
Vase, Oil Spot, Amber Iridescent, Handles, 7 1/4 In. 635.00
Vase, Oil Spot, Amber, Iridescent, Flared, Applied Handles, 7 1/4 In. 550.00
Vase, Oil Spot, Blue, Pulled Waves, On Iridescent Amber, Bulbous, 6 1/2 In. 2185.00
Vase, Oil Spot, Blue, Ruffled Edge, 7 In. 140.00
Vase, Oil Spot, Blue, Silver Overlay, 4 1/2 In. 225.00
Vase, Oil Spot, Highly Iridized Blue, 2 Applied Amber Buttresses, 10 In. 1500.00

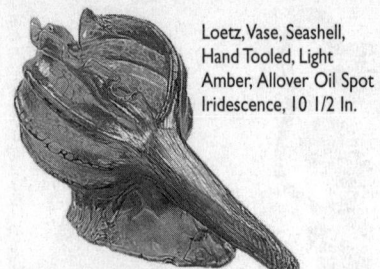

Loetz, Vase, Seashell,
Hand Tooled, Light
Amber, Allover Oil Spot
Iridescence, 10 1/2 In.

**To clean a stained enamel or
graniteware pan, fill the pan with
water, and add the peel of an
apple or a cut-up stalk of
rhubarb. Boil for ten minutes.**

Vase, Oil Spot, Leaves, Blue, Silver Overlay, 3 In.	980.00
Vase, Oil Spot, Pulled Waves, Blue, Rose, Gold, Purple, On Yellow, 3 Handles, 9 In.	9200.00
Vase, Oil Spot, Swirl, Pink, Satin, Ruffled & Crimped Rim, 5 In. Diam.	350.00
Vase, Oil Spots, On Green, Blue Iridescent, 7 1/4 In.	345.00
Vase, Orange Pulled Hearts & Vines, Signed, 9 In.	112.00
Vase, Pale Amethyst, Gold Pulled Feathers, Signed, 6 x 3 1/2 In.	2930.00
Vase, Paperweight, Clear Over Green, Ribbed, Silver Flowers, 6 In.	260.00
Vase, Paperweight, Lime Green Trailing, Tangerine Orange Ground, 10 3/8 In.	2820.00
Vase, Paperweight, Pulled Feathers, Clear Over Orange, 4 1/2 In.	3024.00
Vase, Papillion, Cobalt Blue, 3 3/4 In.	210.00
Vase, Papillon, Green, Iridescent Golden Blue Applied Threading, 8 1/2 In. ... *Illus*	403.00
Vase, Pink, Platinum Gold Pulled Trailings, 3 x 5 In.	518.00
Vase, Pulled Wave, Gold Iridescent, 12 1/2 x 6 In.	1725.00
Vase, Pulled Waves, Blues, Greens, Copper, Topaz, Magenta, Signed, 11 3/4 In. ... *Illus*	14950.00
Vase, Purple Iridescent, Green Iridescent Threading, 14 1/2 In.	200.00
Vase, Purple Pulled Stripes, Green Spots, Ruffled Rim, Urn Shape, 8 In.	250.00
Vase, Purple, Blue, Green Iridescence, Fluted, Crimped, 9 In.	600.00
Vase, Red To Gold Shaded, Textured Surface, Early 20th Century, 6 In.	112.00
Vase, Salmon Pink Iridescent, Reverse Wave Design, 6 1/4 x 3 1/2 In.	2070.00
Vase, Seashell, Hand Tooled, Light Amber, Allover Oil Spot Iridescence, 10 1/2 In. .. *Illus*	400.00
Vase, Sienna Branches Of Pine Needles, Acorns Around Sides, Signed, 8 1/2 In.	730.00
Vase, Silver Pulled Trailing, Iridescent, Applied Lily Pads, 1900, 8 3/4 In.	7640.00
Vase, Trumpet, Green, On Yellow Iridescent, Blue Pulled Feather, 5 In.	210.00
Vase, Trumpet, Pulled Waves, Metallic, Magenta, Topaz, Purple, Copper, Blue, 11 3/4 In.	14900.00
Vase, Umber & Amber Diagonal Pulled Waves, Ruffled Edge, 12 3/4 In.	390.00

LONE RANGER, a fictional character, was introduced on the radio in
1932. Over three thousand shows were produced before the series
ended in 1954. In 1938, the first Lone Ranger movie was made. Television shows were started in 1949 and are still seen on some stations.
The Lone Ranger appears on many products and was even the name of
a restaurant chain for several years.

Action Figure, Accessory Set, The Adventure Of The Tribal Powwow	48.00
Action Figure, Accessory Set, The Hidden Rattler Adventure	45.00
Action Figure, Accessory Set, The Lone Ranger Rides Again	25.00
Action Figure Set, Handcuffs, Keys, Badge, Glasses	17.00
Belt, Tonto & Ranger, Vinyl, Tan, Brass Buckle & Tip, Youth, 1 x 31 In.	115.00
Belt & Holster, Tonto, Cowhide, Indian Design	135.00
Card, Color Contest, General Mills Promotion, 1951, 3 x 5 In.	15.00
Colorforms Cartoon Kit	24.00
Comic Book, No. 3, Hi-Yo Silver, Dell, 78 Pages, 8 1/2 x 11 1/2 In.	135.00
Comic Book, No. 114, Clayton Moore Autograph	150.00
Comic Strip, Peace Patrol, Color, Nov. 1958, 10 x 12 1/2 In.	15.00
Costume, Vinyl, 1 Piece, Molded Plastic Mask	24.00
Costume, Vinyl, Black & Yellow, 1 Piece, Ben Cooper, 17 1/2 x 60 In.	24.00
Eggcup, Ceramic, White, England, 1961, 2 x 2 3/8 In.	40.00
Eyeglass Case, Holster Shape, Leather, Snap Fastener, 1950s, 3 1/3 x 6 1/2 In.	35.00
Figurine, Chalkware, Full Body, Hands On Holsters, 15 1/4 In.	75.00

Figurine, Chalkware, Lone Ranger On Horse	50.00
Football, Lone Ranger & Silver, Rubber, White, Black, Sun Rubber Co., 1950s, 9 In.	70.00
Glass, Lone Ranger, Plastic, Color, 4 3/8 In.	15.00
Guitar, Lone Ranger & Tonto, Jefferson Mfg., 1950s, 31 In.	15.00
Pencil, Mechanical, Plastic & Brass, Lone Ranger Figure Top, 1950s	75.00
Pencil, Mechanical, Plastic, Red, Brass Trim, Floating Figure, 5 1/2 In.	75.00
Pencil Case, Cardboard, Hinged Lid, Brass Snap, American Lead Pencil Co., 1938	75.00
Photograph, Black & White, Autograph, 8 x 10 In.	80.00
Picture, Black & White, Textured Paper, Dairy Co. Premium, 8 x 10 In.	38.00
Picture, Your Friend, Lone Ranger, Laminated On Plywood, 5 3/4 x 7 1/4 x 3/8 In.	45.00
Postcard, 1 Cent	25.00
Poster, Lone Ranger Wants You, Restaurant Franchise, 17 1/2 x 21 1/2	58.00
Poster, Tonto, Full Color, Wheaties Premium, 1957, 25 x 69 In.	95.00
Poster, Tonto, Life Size, White Ground, 25 x 69 In.	95.00
Puzzle, 4 Numbered Strips, Parker Bros., 1950	120.00
Puzzle Story, Lone Ranger & Tonto, 4 Panels, Parker, c.1940, 7 x 18 In.	148.00
Record, Legend Of The Lone Ranger, 1981	25.00
Target, Tin Lithograph, 2 Sides, Marx, 9 1/2 In.	40.00
Toothbrush Holder, Lone Ranger, On Rearing Horse, 1938	85.00
Toy, Bop, Inflatable, Soft Vinyl, Weighted Bottom, 4 1/2 x 14 1/2 In.	95.00
Toy, Clicker Pistol, Steel, Hollow, Black & Silver Enamel, Decal, 1940s, 8 In.	65.00
Toy, Horse, Rocking, Wood, 40 In.	650.00
Toy, Lone Ranger, On Silver, Twirling Lasso, Windup, Marx, 1938	295.00
Toy, Picture Printing Set, Stamper Kraft No. 4092, 1939	95.00
Toy, Rocking, Gun In Hand, Lasso Spins, Marx, 1938, 10 In.	1127.00
Wrist Cuffs, Cowhide Leather, Die Cut, Tan, Metal Snap Fasteners, Late 1930s	40.00
Wristwatch, Brown Vinyl Band, Yellow Face, Lone Ranger, Tonto, 1950s	20.00
Wristwatch, Die Cut Dial, Movable Hands, Moving Disc, With Pictures	20.00

LONGWY Workshop of Longwy, France, first made ceramic wares in 1798. The workshop is still in business. Most of the ceramic pieces found today are glazed with many colors to resemble cloisonne or other enameled metal. Many pieces were made with stylized figures and Art Deco designs. The factory used a variety of marks.

Bottle, Enameled, Carp, Cherry Blossoms, Pink, Blue, White, 8 1/2 x 4 In., Pair	115.00
Bowl, Flower Medallions, Ivory & Cobalt Ground, Ruffled Rim, Gilt Trim, 2 1/2 x 9 In.	105.00
Bowl, Flowers, Polychrome, Blue Ground, Almond Shape, Scalloped Rim, 2 x 11 In.	115.00
Bowl, Peacock Flower Interior, Striped Exterior, Abstract Flower Handles, 9 1/2 In.	161.00
Box, Ceramic, Stylized Flower Panels, Crackle Glaze, Signed, 3 x 3 In.	280.00
Candlestick, Dolphin Shaft, Enameled Flowers, Gilded, 9 1/4 In., Pair	145.00
Charger, Flowers, 3 Storks, Polychrome, Blue Ground, Green Ink Stamp, 14 1/4 In.	690.00
Charger, Phoenix, Flowers, Polychrome, Stamped Mark, 13 3/4 In.	460.00
Compote, 3 Stylized Flower Clusters, Yellow, Brown, Green, Ivory, 11 3/4 In.	290.00
Compote, Band Of Stylized Flowers, Blue, Green, Brown Leaves, 4 1/8 x 9 3/4 In.	230.00
Compote, Flowers, Flared, Faceted, Polychrome, Green Ink Stamp, 5 1/2 x 13 1/4 In.	430.00
Compote, Round, Octagonal Base, Repeat Flower Clusters, Yellow, Brown, Green, 12 In.	310.00
Flask, Wine, Donut Shape, Rope Handle, Stylized Birds, Flowers, Stamped, 11 1/2 In.	259.00
Girandole, 2-Light, Mirrored Plate, Tiles In Brass Frame, Acorn Nozzles, 17 x 9 7/8 In.	750.00
Inkstand, Birds, Flowers, 2 Ink Pots, Pen Tray, Stamp Box, 3 3/4 x 10 x 6 1/2 In.	230.00
Lamp Base, Bird, Flowers, Ivory & Blue Ground, Cylindrical, Wood Base, 6 x 4 In.	115.00
Plate, Enameled, Flowers, Polychrome, Impressed, 8 3/4 In.	175.00
Tea Set, Butterflies, Birds, Flowers, Aqua Ground, Polychrome, Stamped Mark, 7 Piece	230.00
Tray, Boat Scene, Flowers, Polychrome, Rectangular, 2 Handles, Stamped, 15 x 7 In.	259.00
Vase, Flowers, Flared, Scalloped Rim, Polychrome, Green Ink Stamp, 9 3/4 In.	405.00
Vase, Multicolored Incised Flowers, Impressed Mark, 5 1/2 In.	375.00

LONHUDA Pottery Company of Steubenville, Ohio, was organized in 1892 by William Long, W. H. Hunter, and Alfred Day. Brown underglaze slip-decorated pottery was made. The firm closed in 1896. The company used many marks; the earliest included the letters *LPCO*.

Mug, Berries On Branch, Signed, 4 1/2 In.	95.00
Tile, Dogwood, Brown Glaze, 5 1/2 x 6 In.	177.00

LOTUS WARE was made by the Knowles, Taylor & Knowles Company of East Liverpool, Ohio, from 1890 to 1900. Lotus Ware, a thin porcelain which resembles Belleek, was sometimes decorated outside the factory. Other types of ceramics that were made by the Knowles, Taylor & Knowles Company are listed under KTK.

Ewer, Green & Cream, Relief, Flowers, Gilt Rim, 6 In.	305.00
Vase, Pink & Green, Flowers, Applied Beading, Cutwork Handles, 6 In.	320.00
Vase, White, Ewer Shape, Twisted-Rope Handles, 9 x 5 In.	360.00

LOY-NEL-ART, see McCoy category.

LUNCH BOXES and lunch pails have been used to carry lunches to school or work since the nineteenth century. Today, most collectors want either early tobacco advertising boxes or children's lunch boxes made since the 1930s. These boxes are made of metal or plastic. Boxes listed here include the original Thermos bottle inside the box unless otherwise indicated. Movie, television, and cartoon characters may be found in their own categories.

LUNCH BOX, Alf, Canadian Flicker, Red Plastic, Canadian Thermos Products Ltd., 1988	10.00
Alvin & Chipmunks, Vinyl, King Seeley Thermos, 1963	80.00 to 110.00
American Museum Of Natural History, Dinosaur, Birthday Cake, Vinyl, 1960s	110.00
Archies, Metal, Aladdin, 1969	135.00
Backgammon, Vinyl, King Seeley Thermos, 1960s	20.00
Ballerina, Vinyl, Aladdin, 1962	120.00 to 135.00
Barbie, Midge, Black, Vinyl, Dome, King Seeley Thermos, 1964	60.00
Beany & Cecil, Brown Vinyl, King Seeley Thermos, 1963	145.00
Boston Red Sox, Vinyl, Ardee, 1960s	40.00 to 95.00
Cabbage Patch Kids, Metal, King Seeley Thermos, 1984	8.00
Captain Kangaroo, Vinyl, King Seeley Thermos, 1964	75.00 to 86.00
Carousel, Vinyl, Aladdin, 1962	155.00
Casper The Friendly Ghost, Vinyl, King Seeley Thermos, 1966	144.00
Cheerleaders, Vinyl, Prepac, 1960s	75.00
Corsage, Multicolored Flowers, Vinyl, King Seeley Thermos, 1970	30.00
Cowboy, Horse, Vinyl, Tan	75.00
Dogs, Yorkshire Terriers, Vinyl, Yellow, Ardee, 1960s	60.00
Dr. Seuss, Metal, Aladdin, 1970	115.00
Dukes Of Hazzard, Metal, Aladdin, 1980	35.00
Fess Parker, Vinyl, Aladdin, 1960s	58.00
Flintstones & Dino, Metal, Aladdin, 1962	86.00
Flying Nun, Metal, Aladdin, 1968	100.00 to 120.00
Football, Varsity, Laces, Needle Hole, Tin, Decoware, 1950s	90.00
Freihofer's Chocolate Chip Cookies, Vinyl, c.1960	50.00
Frontier Cabin, Vinyl, Bear Cubs At Rear Window, Ardee, 1960s	95.00
Girl & Poodle, Vinyl, Ardee, 1960s	65.00
Happy Days, The Fonz, Canadian Thermos Products Ltd., 1976	15.00
Happy Powwow, Vinyl, Children As Cowboys & Indians, Bayville, 1970s	65.00
Holiday Cruise, Vinyl, Travel Tags & Stickers, 1960s	65.00
How The West Was Won, Matt Dillon, Metal, King Seeley Thermos, 1979	65.00
It's About Time, Dome, Metal, Aladdin, 1967	230.00

Rub tartar-control toothpaste on your scratched snow dome paperweights. It will remove the smaller scratches.

Lunch Box, Mahogany, Inlaid Star, Diamond, Dome, Curved Handle

Jonathan Livingston Seagull, Metal, Aladdin, 1973	75.00
Junior Nurse, Vinyl, King Seeley Thermos, 1963	75.00 to 105.00
Kaboodle Kit, Girls Arm-In-Arm With Kits, Vinyl, Aladdin, 1960s	65.00
Kewtie Pie, Vinyl, Girl Watering Flowers, Aladdin, 1967	65.00
Knight In Armor, Metal, Universal Industries, 1959	575.00
Lassie, Metal, King Seeley Thermos, 1978	85.00
Mahogany, Inlaid Star, Diamond, Dome, Curved Handle	*Illus* 748.00
Mam'zelle, Vinyl, Aladdin, 1971	125.00
Mary Poppins, Metal, Aladdin, 1965	65.00
Munsters, King Seeley Thermos, 1965	550.00
National Football League, Photos Of Helmets Of American & National Teams, 1976	14.00
NFL, Helmets, King Seeley Thermos, 1976	15.00
Peter Pan, Plastic, Designed Like Peanut Butter Sandwich, Berby Foods Inc., 1974	40.00
Ponytail, Poodle, Vinyl, Gray Border, American Thermos, 1960s	70.00
Ponytail Eats 'n Treats, Girls On Seesaw, Vinyl, American Thermos, 1959	60.00
Ponytail Tidbit Kit, Girls Drinking, Vinyl, American Thermos, 1959	65.00
Psychedelic, Dome, Yellow, Pink, Red, Orange, Metal, Aladdin, 1969	75.00
Ringling Bros., Barnum & Bailey Circus, Vinyl, King Seeley Thermos, 1970	125.00
See America, Metal, Ohio Art, 1972	10.00
Sesame Street, Metal, King Seeley Thermos, 1980	15.00
Shari Lewis & Her Friends, Vinyl, Aladdin, 1963	100.00
Six Million Dollar Man, Metal, Aladdin, 1974	52.00
Smokey The Bear, Vinyl, King Seeley Thermos, 1965	115.00
Steve Canyon, Metal, Aladdin, 1959	85.00 to 115.00
Stewardess, Vinyl, Aladdin, 1962	100.00
Thermos, Boating, Motorboat Waterskiing, American Thermos Products, 1960	20.00
Truck, 18-Wheeler, Man & Boy In Cab Of Truck, Aladdin, 1978	20.00
Twiggy, Lavender, Vinyl, Zipper Top, Aladdin, 1967	115.00 to 170.00
Wagon Train, Metal, King Seeley Thermos, 1964	155.00
Woody Woodpecker, Metal, Aladdin, 1972	115.00
Wrangler, Cowboy On Horseback, Branding Marks, Vinyl, Aladdin, 1962	165.00
LUNCH BOX THERMOS, Chevrolet, America's Favorite, Dancing Baseball, Hotdog, 1976	40.00
Gentle Ben, Aladdin, 1968	15.00
Go Go, Dancing Couples, Aladdin, 1966	15.00
Laugh-In, Aladdin, 1968	32.00
Maxwell House Coffee, Orange, King Seeley Thermos, 1960s	15.00
NFL, Quarterback, Referee, Aladdin, 1964	20.00
Partridge Family, Metal, Label, 1971	55.00
Rat Patrol, Aladdin, 1967	65.00
Ringling Bros., Barnum & Bailey Circus, Metal, King Seeley Thermos	30.00
Space, Saturn & Allover Planets, England, 1950s	55.00
Trout Flies, Underwater Scene, Metal, American Thermos, 1950s	18.00

LUNEVILLE, a French faience factory, was established about 1730 by Jacques Chambrette. It is best known for its fine biscuit figures and groups and for large faience dogs and lions. The early pieces were unmarked. The firm was acquired by Keller and Guerin and is still working.

Bowl, Old Strasbourg, Tulips, Square, 10 In.	86.00
Box, Wild Roses, Pink, Lift-Off Lid, 8 x 6 x 2 1/2 In.	225.00
Cup & Saucer, Tulips, Fluted Details, Pink Rims	26.00
Muffiner, Country Bouquet, 9 1/2 In.	56.00
Plate, Violette, Gilt Trim, Signed, 8 1/8 In.	43.00
Teapot, White, Pink Flowers, Green Leaves, 6 In.	39.00

LUSTER glaze was meant to resemble copper, silver, or gold. It has been used since the sixteenth century. Some of the luster found today was made during the nineteenth century. The metallic glazes are applied over a glaze. The finished color depends on the combination of the clay color and the glaze. Blue, orange, gold, and pearlized luster decorations were used by Japanese and German firms in the early 1900s. Tea Leaf pieces have their own category.

Copper, Creamer, Quilted Spout, Sheepherder Scene, Blue Band, 4 1/4 In.	105.00

Copper, Creamer, Scrolled Handle, Basket Of Flowers On Band, 4 In. 120.00
Copper, Pepper Pot, Pink Leaves, Blue Berries, 4 1/8 In. 165.00
Copper, Pitcher, Blue Band, Red Transfer, 4 In. 155.00
Copper, Pitcher, Dolphin Handle, North Wind Spout, Basket Of Flowers, 7 3/4 In. 250.00 to 275.00
Copper, Pitcher, Figures, Polychrome, Banded, Blue, Pink, 8 1/2 In. 120.00
Copper, Pitcher, Green, Relief Decoration, Polychrome, 4 1/2 In. 50.00
Copper, Pitcher, Handle, Green Flowers, Footed, 7 3/8 In. 300.00
Copper, Pitcher, Light Blue Ground, Flowers, 5 x 5 1/2 In. 185.00
Copper, Pitcher, Man Playing Flute, Yellow Band, White, Beading, Enameled, 7 In. .. 250.00
Copper, Pitcher, Polychromed, Initials E.E., 7 In. 715.00
Copper, Pitcher, Relief Figures, Blue, 6 In. 250.00
Copper, Pitcher, Sprigged Blue Thistle Band, 6 In. 165.00
Copper, Pitcher, Strawberry Design, Ribbed, Scroll Handle, Fan Spout, Blue Band, 4 In. . 55.00
Copper, Pitcher, Transfer, Polychrome, 6 In. 300.00
Copper, Pitcher, Yellow Ground, 2 Scenes, Woman, Girl Playing Badminton, Doll 155.00
Copper, Pitcher, Yellow Ground, Cornwallis York Towne Surrender, Lafayette, 6 1/2 In. ... 396.00
Copper, Salt, Blue Band, Pink Leaves, Yellow Berries, 2 x 3 1/4 In. 110.00
Copper, Saltshaker, Blue Band, Orange & Luster Design, 4 1/2 In. 165.00
Fairyland luster is included in the Wedgwood category.
Peach, Pitcher, Milk, Black Stripe, Bird & Flowers, c.1910, 4 In. 18.00
Peach, Toast Rack, 4 Slots, Flower Baskets At Ends, c.1910, 7 In. 28.00
Peach & Blue, Sugar, Lake Scene 15.00
Peach & Pearl White, Pitcher, Milk, Village Scene, c.1910, 5 In. 20.00
Peach & Pearl White, Teapot, Cherry Blossom, White Lace Overlay, c.1910, 7 In. 40.00
Pink, Cup & Saucer, Handleless Cup 90.00
Pink, Figurine, 4 Women, 4 Seasons, Dixon, Austin & Co., Early 1800s, 8 In., 4 Piece ... 3850.00
Pink, Pitcher, Death Of Punch, c.1900, 5 In. 165.00
Pink, Pitcher, Figural, Matronly Woman, Orange, Blue, Coronet, England, 9 1/8 In. 99.00
Pink, Pitcher, Molded, 5 In. 358.00
Pink, Pitcher, Shell Molded, Hunt Scenes, Stone China D&B, 8 In. 330.00
Pink, Pitcher, Ship & Poem, 4 In. 330.00
Pink, Pitcher, Toby, 6 In. 495.00
Pink, Plaque, Retribution Steamer, 7 x 8 In. 550.00
Silver, Jug, Pineapple Diamond, Early 19th Century, 6 In. 250.00
Silver, Pitcher, Eagle Transfer, 16 Star American Flag, Success To U.S., 1812, 4 1/2 In. .. 4675.00
Silver, Toby Jug, Early 19th Century, 5 In. .... 325.00 to 425.00
Sunderland luster pieces are listed in the Sunderland category.
Tea Leaf luster pieces are listed in the Tea Leaf Ironstone category.
Yellow, Cup & Saucer, Rust Flowers, Blue Leaves, Handleless 800.00
Yellow, Cup Plate, Rust Flowers, Green Vine Border, 3 1/2 In. 415.00
Yellow, Pitcher, Flowers, Silver Decoration, 5 3/4 In. 360.00
Yellow, Plate, Toddy, Flowers & Leaves Center, Brown Border, 5 3/4 In. 165.00
Yellow, Vase, Flowers & Leaf, Brown & Rust Bands, 5 1/4 In. 385.00
Yellow, Waste Bowl, Mother & Child Scenes, Maroon Designs, 2 1/2 x 5 1/4 In. 250.00

LUSTRE ART GLASS Company was founded in Long Island, New York,
in 1920 by Conrad Vahlsing and Paul Frank. The company made lampshades and globes that are almost indistinguishable from those made
by Quezal. Most of the shades made by the company were unmarked.

Shade, Tulip, Gilt, White Pulled Feathers, Green Trim, 5 In. 255.00

LUSTRES are mantel decorations or pedestal vases with many hanging
glass prisms. The name really refers to the prisms, and it is proper to
refer to a single glass prism as a lustre. Either spelling, luster or lustre,
is correct.

Devil's Fire, Blue, Red, White, Green, Yellow, 7 1/2 In. 224.00
Parcel Gilt, Green, Polychromed, Albert Prisms, Bohemian, 12 1/2 x 6 1/2 In. 175.00
Pink Cased, White Enamel & Gilt Leaves, Double Rows Of Clear Prisms, 14 3/8 In. 770.00
Ruby, Enameled Flowers, Scalloped Top, 7 Small, 7 Large Prisms, 14 1/4 In., Pair 190.00
Trumpet Shape, Pillar Flutes & Lozenge Cuts, Cut Glass Drops, 11 1/2 In., Pair 690.00
Trumpet Shape, White Case, Cranberry Flash, Knop Stem, 1890, 13 In., Pair 750.00
White Cut To Emerald Green, Gilt Flowers, Cut Panels, 10 Prisms, 10 In., Pair 800.00

MAASTRICHT, Holland, was the city where Petrus Regout established the De Sphinx pottery in 1836. The firm was noted for its transfer-printed earthenware. Many factories in Maastricht are still making ceramics.

Pitcher, Timor Pattern, 5 1/4 In.	30.00
Plate, 1944 Liberation, Delft Blue, 8 In.	25.00
Sugar & Creamer, Balmoral Pattern, Red & White, 4 1/2 In.	30.00
Tureen, Undertray, Ladle, Acanthus Leaf, Ironstone, Petrus Regout & Co., 13 In.	123.00

MAIZE glass was made by W.L. Libbey & Son Company of Toledo, Ohio, after 1889. The glass resembled an ear of corn. The leaves were usually green, but some pieces were made with blue or red leaves. The kernels of corn were light yellow, white, or light green.

Butter, Husks Of Corn Outlined In Gold On Cover & Finial, 6 1/2 x 7 1/4 In.	1120.00
Tumbler, Green Corn Husks, 4 In.	980.00
Tumbler, Yellow Husks, c.1889, 4 In.	50.00

MAJOLICA is a general term for any pottery glazed with an opaque tin enamel that conceals the color of the clay body. It has been made since the fourteenth century. Today's collector is most likely to find Victorian majolica. The heavy, colorful ware is rarely marked. Some famous makers include Wedgwood; Minton; Griffen, Smith and Hill (marked *Etruscan*); and Chesapeake Pottery (marked *Avalon* or *Clifton*). Majolica made by Wedgwood is listed in the Wedgwood category.

Basket, Basket Weave & Flowers, Ribbon, Bow, 8 1/2 In.	440.00
Basket, Fruits, Turquoise, 9 In.	385.00
Basket, Grapevine, Arbor, Handle, 6 In.	60.00
Basket, Laced Basket Weave, Flowers, 10 In.	415.00
Biscuit Jar, Metal Collar Cover & Handle, 1870s	450.00
Bowl, Blue Exterior, Lavender Pink Interior, Shell Feet, 4 1/2 x 9 1/2 In.	55.00
Bowl, Daisy, Etruscan, c.1875, 9 In.	316.00
Bowl, Interior Shells & Seaweed, Stippled Ground, Green & Brown Glaze, 9 5/8 In.	300.00
Bowl, Leaf Design, 10 In.	230.00
Bowl, Maple Leaf, 10 1/4 In.	99.00
Bowl, Mottled, Oval, 2 White Dogs On Edge, 11 In.	1375.00
Bowl, Scallop Shell, 3 Snail Form Feet, 8 1/2 In.	259.00
Bowl, Shell, Seaweed, Waves, 9 1/2 In.	165.00
Bowl, Shell, Yellow, 3 Shell Feet, 9 1/2 In.	99.00
Butter Chip, Blackberry	140.00
Butter Chip, Butterfly, Turquoise Ground	137.00
Butter Chip, Daisy, Wheat, Ribbon, Bow	110.00
Butter Chip, Overlapping Leaf	35.00
Cachepot, Grapes & Leaves, Marked, Avalon Faience, 5 1/2 In. .... *Illus*	65.00
Cake Stand, Begonia Leaf Design, 9 1/4 In.	127.00
Cake Stand, Blue & Brown Grape Leaves, Pink Ground, Tree Trunk Base, 5 1/4 In.	470.00

Majolica, Cachepot, Grapes & Leaves, Marked, Avalon Faience, 5 1/2 In.

Majolica, Cheese Keeper, Basket Weave, Blackberry, Amber, Green, Blue, 10 1/2 In.

Majolica, Cheese Keeper, Lily & Fern, Green, Yellow, Etruscan, 11 In.

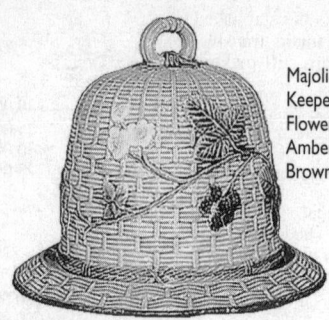

Majolica, Cheese Keeper, Rope, Leaf, Flowers, Mottled Amber, Green, Brown, 9 1/2 In.

Majolica, Cheese Keeper, Turquoise Dome Top, Green, Yellow, Cow Handle, 9 In.

Cake Stand, Bluebird, Prunus, 9 In.	127.00
Cake Stand, Maple Leaves, Pink Ground, Etruscan	195.00
Cake Stand, Pond Lily, Three Storks On Base, 9 x 6 In.	305.00
Cake Stand, Water Lily, 8 3/4 In.	259.00
Candlestick, Full Relief Figures Of Girl & Boy, Large Blossoms, 6 3/4 In., Pair	130.00
Celery Tray, Cobalt Blue, 11 In.	145.00
Centerpiece, Serenading Figures In Gondola, Dolphin, Fishnet Base, 18 x 9 x 17 In.	2185.00
Charger, Rape Of Sabine Women, Tin Glaze, Black Crowned M, 24 3/4 In.	1045.00
Cheese Dish, Inverted Acorn Finial, Round Under Tray, 8 x 8 1/4 In.	258.00
Cheese Keeper, Basket Weave, Blackberry, Amber, Green, Blue, 10 1/2 In. *Illus*	880.00
Cheese Keeper, Bird On Branch & Flowers, Cobalt, Cream, Brown, Green, 9 1/2 In.	880.00
Cheese Keeper, Cobalt Fish, Flowers, Seaweed, Cover, Fish Handle, 10 1/2 In.	3300.00
Cheese Keeper, Fish Amid Coral & Seaweed, Cobalt Blue, 10 1/2 In.	3300.00
Cheese Keeper, Lily & Fern, Green, Yellow, Etruscan, 11 In. *Illus*	3850.00
Cheese Keeper, Rope, Leaf, Flowers, Mottled Amber, Green, Brown, 9 1/2 In. *Illus*	605.00
Cheese Keeper, Turquoise Dome Top, Green, Yellow, Cow Handle, 9 In. *Illus*	5775.00
Cheese Keeper, Wild Rose & Treebark, George Jones *Illus*	3850.00
Compote, Begonia Leaf, Yellow Basket, 9 1/4 In.	250.00
Compote, Birds At Fence, 8 In.	200.00
Compote, Maple Leaf, Pink Ground, Etruscan, 10 x 7 1/2 In.	195.00
Compote, Pedestal, Red & Pink Glaze, Cupids & Flowers, 2 Handles, Austria, 13 In.	248.00
Creamer, Beaded Melon	165.00
Creamer, Begonia Leaf, Pewter Top, 3 1/4 In.	190.00
Creamer, Cauliflower	55.00
Creamer, Cobalt Floral, 3 Snail Feet, 5 x 2 3/4 In.	1210.00
Creamer, Goat, 4 1/4 In.	195.00
Creamer, Shell & Coral, 4 In.	300.00
Creamer, Shell, Dolphin Base & Handle, 5 1/2 In.	385.00
Cup & Saucer, Basketry & Bamboo	150.00
Cup & Saucer, Bird & Fan, Turquoise Ground	130.00
Cup & Saucer, Bluebird, Fan, Registry Mark	185.00
Cup & Saucer, Cauliflower, Etruscan	248.00

Majolica, Cheese Keeper, Wild Rose & Treebark, George Jones

Majolica, Dish, Muffin, Cover, Apple Blossoms, Cobalt Blue, 10 1/4 x 5 1/2 In.

Cup & Saucer, Crane & Fan	95.00
Cup & Saucer, Melon	195.00
Cup & Saucer, Pineapple	176.00
Cup & Saucer, Shell & Coral, Rope Handle	230.00
Cup & Saucer, Strawberry	150.00
Cuspidor, Flowers	165.00
Decanter, Figural, Choisy Le Roi, Woman Holding Umbrella, c.1900, 12 3/4 In.	345.00
Dish, Leaf Form, Relief Begonia Flowers, Berries, 10 1/2 In.	150.00
Dish, Muffin, Cover, Apple Blossoms, Cobalt Blue, 10 1/4 x 5 1/2 In. ...... *Illus*	4400.00
Dish, Ruby Luster, Istoriato, Classical Scene, Hercules, Early 20th Century, 15 In.	115.00
Dish, Shells, Encrusted Vegetation, Lobster & Crab, 1900s, 12 1/2 In., Pair	488.00
Figurine, Cat, Sitting, Oval Base, Minton, 13 1/4 In.	3165.00
Gravy Boat, Figural Fish, 5 x 8 In.	935.00
Humidor, Arab, 6 In.	90.00
Humidor, Black Jockey, 5 In.	250.00
Humidor, Black Man's Head, Red Bowtie & Hat, 4 3/4 In.	300.00
Humidor, Clown's Head, 6 In.	70.00
Humidor, Dog, Sitting Up, 6 In.	545.00
Humidor, Gypsy Woman, Green Headdress, 9 In.	140.00
Humidor, Monk's Head, 5 In.	55.00
Inkstand, Minton, Palissy Style, Oval Stand, Applied Lizards, c.1858, 14 1/2 In.	1380.00
Jar, Barrel Form, Relief Leaf Band, 3 3/4 In.	65.00
Jar, Water Lily, Cover, 5 In.	175.00
Jardiniere, Birds In Flight, 10 1/2 x 9 1/2 In.	1870.00
Jardiniere, Deep Blue, Birds, Flowers, George Jones, c.1876, 14 In.	1410.00
Jardiniere, Dragon Handles, 10 x 14 In.	440.00
Jardiniere, Flowers, Oriental Style, 14 In.	170.00
Jardiniere, Pedestal, Lappet, Flowers, Leaf Tip Rim, Blue, Green, Brown, 47 In.	860.00
Jardiniere, Pedestal, Turquoise Glaze, France, c.1880, 70 In.	5700.00
Jardiniere, Planter, Green Leaf & Flowers, 4-Footed, 11 1/2 x 12 In.	575.00
Jardiniere, Relief, Deer, Boar, Goose, Gun, Powder Horn, Oak, Acorns, 14 x 9 1/2 In.	495.00
Jardiniere Stand, Tricornered, 3 Ram's Heads, 3 Hoofed Feet, 42 In.	9900.00
Jug, Baseball & Soccer, Etruscan, 7 3/4 In.	330.00
Match Safe, Stag Beetle Form, Amber Glaze, Signed, 2 1/4 x 5 3/4 In.	300.00
Mirror Frame, Female Figures, Putti, Multichromatic, Minton, c.1870, 29 x 20 In.	49625.00
Mug, Butterfly, Basket Weave, Bamboo	90.00
Mug, Maple Leaf, Twig	55.00
Mug, Oak Leaf, Tree Trunk	55.00
Mug, Puzzle, Grape & Vine, 5 1/2 In.	154.00
Mug, Relief, Art Nouveau Female, Figural, 3 1/2 In.	50.00
Mug, Strawberry	180.00
Mug, Water Lily, Cobalt Blue	175.00
Oyster Plate, 6 Wells, Cobalt Blue, Brown Outlining, Flowers, Minton, 9 In.	2200.00
Oyster Plate, Seaweed, Green & Pink, 10 1/4 In.	400.00
Paperweight, Frog, 2 3/4 In.	358.00
Paperweight, Swan, Etruscan	1430.00
Pedestal, Flower, Leaf Decoration, 47 x 13 x 13 In.	1680.00
Pitcher, Albino Shell, Seaweed, 5 1/2 In.	70.00
Pitcher, Bamboo, Wheat, 8 In.	90.00
Pitcher, Banners, Blue Rose, Pink Interior, 6 In.	220.00
Pitcher, Bird & Flowers, 7 1/2 In.	190.00
Pitcher, Bluebird, Basketry Design, 9 3/4 In.	489.00
Pitcher, Cobalt Blue & Turquoise, Butterfly & Prunus Blossoms, 4 In.	580.00
Pitcher, Cockatoo, Figural, 6 3/4 In.	230.00
Pitcher, Corn, 9 In.	250.00
Pitcher, Dogwood, Light Green Interior, 4 x 5 1/2 In.	165.00
Pitcher, Figural Man, Woman Handle, 12 In.	248.00
Pitcher, Fish, 12 3/4 In.	550.00
Pitcher, Fish, Figural, 11 1/4 In.	288.00
Pitcher, Fish, Fish Handle, Cobalt, Pewter Top, 7 In.	660.00
Pitcher, Flowers, Fern, Blackberry, 7 1/4 In.	80.00
Pitcher, Frog Form, Edward Steele, c.1880, 12 In.	1925.00
Pitcher, Gold Bird On Branch Front & Back, Signed, 6 1/2 In.	175.00

Pitcher, Grape, Treebark Ground, Pewter Top, 6 1/2 In. 130.00
Pitcher, Hanging Game, Fox Handle, Cranberry Glaze Interior, 11 In. 190.00
Pitcher, Heron, Bulrushes, 11 In. 185.00
Pitcher, Heron, Lotus, 8 1/2 In. 145.00
Pitcher, Lily Of The Valley, Red Interior, 6 3/4 In. 120.00
Pitcher, Mulberry, 6 In. 127.00
Pitcher, Oak Leaf, Acorn, Picket Fence, 6 In. 165.00
Pitcher, Owl, Cobalt Blue Handle, 1800s 259.00
Pitcher, Pea Pod, 7 1/4 In. 120.00
Pitcher, Pineapple Form, Green Neck & Handle, 9 In. 165.00
Pitcher, Pineapple, Figural, 6 1/2 In. 185.00
Pitcher, Raised Dairy 1 Side, Fern Other, Weave Ground, Bamboo Handle, 6 In. 180.00
Pitcher, Raised Flower & Leaf, Yellow Ground, Basket Form Foot, Etruscan, 6 1/4 In. ... 90.00
Pitcher, Ram, 8 In. 250.00
Pitcher, Relief, Flowers, Basketry & Bamboo Ground, 9 In. 196.00
Pitcher, Robin, Signed Forester, 9 1/2 In. 120.00
Pitcher, Rose & Basket, 8 3/4 In. 127.00
Pitcher, Seaweed & Shell, Etruscan, Griffen, Smith & Co., 5 3/4 In. 385.00
Pitcher, Sheaf Of Wheat, Figural, 6 In. 175.00
Pitcher, Stork In Marsh, Goose Handle, Cobalt Blue, 9 1/2 In. 550.00
Pitcher, Stork In Marsh, Shorter & Sons, 8 In. 275.00
Pitcher, Syrup, Coral, Pink, Etruscan 525.00
Pitcher, Syrup, Sunflower, Cream Ground, Etruscan 385.00
Pitcher, Water Lily, Yellow Top, 7 In. 110.00
Pitcher, Water, Lilies Of The Valley, 1880s 295.00
Pitcher, Wild Rose, Cobalt Blue, Butterfly Spout, 3 1/2 In. 275.00
Pitcher Set, Barrel, Green, 5 Barrel Shaped Glasses, Japan, 1930s, 6 Piece 35.00
Plant Stand, Sphinx, 41 1/2 In. 440.00
Plaque, Bowl, Figs, Palissy Ware, 7 3/4 In. 575.00
Plaque, Red Cherries & Leaves, Shaded Ground, 12 3/8 In. 235.00
Plate, Blackberry, Basket Weave, 10 In. 95.00
Plate, Chestnut Leaf, Basket Design, 8 In. 90.00
Plate, Daisy Flowers, Green Leaves, Indented Rim, 8 1/4 In. 80.00
Plate, Ecole De Tours, Snake, Lizards, Palmetto Bug, Palissy Ware, 9 In. 460.00
Plate, Flying Stork, White Pebbled Surface, Aqua Ground, Signed, 8 1/2 In. 110.00
Plate, Fresh Asparagus, 9 1/4 In. 138.00
Plate, Girl With Dog, Feeding Cat, Yellow Border, Tan Center, 8 In. 120.00
Plate, Grape Leaf, Grape & Strawberry, Yellow Ground, 9 In. 275.00
Plate, Grape Leaf, Grasshopper, Coiled Larvae, Palissy Ware, 8 3/4 In. 546.00
Plate, Grape Leaf, White Ground, Etruscan, 6 1/4 In. 195.00
Plate, Green & Brown, Yellow, Green & Pink, 8 3/4 In., 3 Piece 137.00
Plate, Leaf & Branch, Pink, Green, 9 In. 60.00
Plate, Leaf, Brown Branch Handle, Etruscan, 11 3/4 In. 192.00
Plate, Mafra, Snake, Toad, Lizard, Beetle, Palissy Ware, 8 1/4 In. 690.00
Plate, Pansy, Blue, Yellow, 6 1/2 In. 80.00
Plate, Pineapple, 9 In. 190.00
Plate, Pond Lily, 8 1/4 In. 110.00
Plate, Quatrefoil, Frogs, Snails, Slugs, Moth, Palissy Ware, Portugal, Late 1800s, 7 3/4 In. ... 750.00
Plate, Raised Under The Sea, Lobster & Clam, Early 20th Century, 13 In. 345.00
Plate, Relief, Knight's Head, Figural Border, 7 3/4 In. 50.00
Plate, Spinach Leaf, Brown, 8 1/2 In. 69.00
Platter, Asparagus & Artichokes, Burgundy & Shades Of Green, 10 1/2 x 13 1/4 In. 360.00
Platter, Basket Weave, Flowers, Cobalt Blue Center, 13 In. 330.00
Platter, Basket Weave, Geranium, Eat Thy Bread With Thankfulness, 12 3/4 In. 440.00
Platter, Begonia Leaf, Yellow Basket, 14 In. 275.00
Platter, Bird & Fan, Bamboo Border, 12 3/4 In. 300.00
Platter, Center Shield, Angel With Banner, Band Of Cherubs, Blue, 19 1/4 In. 980.00
Platter, Classical Urn & Sunflower, 2 Handles, Samuel Lear, 1881, 14 In. 750.00
Platter, Cobalt Blue Fish, Coral, Waves, 13 In. 1095.00
Platter, Corn, 13 In. 546.00
Platter, Deer & Dog, 11 In. 90.00
Platter, Dog & Doghouse, 11 In. 132.00
Platter, Fern, Out-Turned Rim, 2 Fern Leaves Center, June 17, 1876, 13 1/2 x 10 1/2 In. .. 420.00

Platter, Flowers, Cobalt Blue, 13 1/4 In.	431.00
Platter, Leaf & Fern, Lavender Border, 14 In.	330.00
Platter, Leaf & Fern, Pink Border, Mottled Center, 14 In.	275.00
Platter, Mythological Figures On Border, 14 1/2 In.	2530.00
Platter, Napkin, Cobalt Rim, Lavender Fringe, Etruscan, 12 1/2 In.	495.00
Platter, Ocean, 25 1/2 In.	1430.00
Platter, Pond Lily, Brown Ground, 13 In.	440.00
Platter, Tobacco Leaf, Rosette, 12 1/2 In.	250.00
Platter, Urn & Sunflower, Turquoise Border, 15 In.	385.00
Platter, Wild Rose & Rope, Cobalt Blue Center, Twig Handles, 15 1/4 In.	440.00
Salad Set, Bowl, Fork & Spoon Server, 3-D Strawberry	225.00
Salt, Coral, Etruscan	413.00
Salt Dip, Master, Shell, Dolphin Footed, 5 In.	358.00
Sardine Box, Pink Pointed Leaves, Cover, Undertray	2310.00
Sardine Box, Stand, Leaf Borders, Overlapping Fish Cover, 1875, 8 1/2 In.	1092.00
Sauce, Strawberry & Napkin, Pink Ground, 5 1/2 In.	195.00
Serving Dish, Bamboo, Handles, 10 3/4 In.	69.00
Serving Dish, Begonia Leaf, Handles, 7 1/2 In.	69.00
Serving Dish, Flower & Fern, 11 In.	80.00
Serving Dish, Hydrangea, Octagonal, 13 1/2 In.	276.00
Serving Dish, Scallop Shell, Brown, Green, Yellow Glaze, 8 1/4 In.	90.00
Spice Castor, Mouse Nibbling Ear Of Corn, Caldas Da Rainha, Palissy Ware, 5 In.	690.00
Spooner, Water Lily, 5 In.	120.00
Stand, Figural, Blackamoors, Italy, 18th Century, 39 1/2 In.	920.00
Stein, Flowers & Leaves, Inlaid Lid, c.1850, 2 Liter	260.00
Strawberry Server, Birds, Blue Ground, Lozenge Shape, George Jones, c.1875, 11 In.	2070.00
Strawberry Set, Leaves & Blossoms, Heart Shape Tray, Creamer & Sugar, c.1870	1200.00
Sugar, Cauliflower	80.00
Sugar, Shell & Seaweed, Handles, Signed, 3 3/4 In.	110.00
Sugar & Creamer, Pink, Strawberry, Tray	990.00
Tazza, Hummingbird, Prunus Branch, Basket Weave Rim, Trumpet Base, 9 In.	575.00
Tea Set, Blue, Copper Glazes, Winged Dragons, Italy, 7 x 4 In.	316.00
Tea Set, Cauliflower, Etruscan, 3 Piece	495.00
Teapot, Chinaman, Cover, Minton, Marked, c.1874, 5 3/4 In.	1440.00
Teapot, Chrysanthemum Leaf & Flower, 8 1/2 In.	403.00
Teapot, Corn, 7 1/2 In.	375.00
Teapot, Corn, Etruscan, 7 In.	935.00
Teapot, Cover, Coconut, Green Leaf, Brown Ground, c.1875, 10 1/4 In.	405.00
Teapot, Crane, Pussy Willow, 8 1/2 In.	430.00
Teapot, Fan & Scroll, Insect, Pebble Ground, 7 In.	220.00
Teapot, Figural Elephant, Oriental Motif	385.00
Teapot, Pineapple, 5 1/2 In.	275.00
Tile, Molded, Crest, Cattails, Polychrome, Minton & Co., 7 3/4 In.	105.00
Tray, Begonia Leaf, Basketry, 12 In.	220.00
Tray, Begonia, Wicker, Corn, Handles, Etruscan, 11 3/4 In.	935.00
Tray, Butterfly, Wheat, Bamboo, Handles, Turquoise Ground, 13 In.	6050.00
Tray, Dresser, Butterfly & Lily, 11 In.	3300.00
Tray, Eat To Live Not Live To Eat, 13 1/2 In.	316.00
Tray, Fish Shaped, 13 3/4 In.	110.00
Tray, Flowers, 3 Lobes, Butterfly Handle, 11 x 4 1/2 In.	7425.00
Tray, Morning Glory, Handles, 14 In.	220.00
Tray, Parrot On Branch, 10 x 7 In.	330.00
Tray, Pineapple, Pink Center, Round, 11 In.	145.00
Tray, Stag & Dog, Round, 11 In.	220.00
Tray, Turquoise Flowers, 12 In.	330.00
Tray, Water Lily Center, Edge Leaves, Brown Branches Form Handles, 8 x 11 1/4 In.	165.00
Tumbler, Corn Cob, Figural, 3 3/4 In., Pair	90.00
Tureen, Squash, Cover	330.00
Umbrella Stand, Lotus & Water Lilies, Egyptian Craftsmen, 20th Century, 21 1/8 In.	345.00
Urn, Lion's-Head Handles, Landscape, Late 19th Century, 13 3/4 In.	431.00
Vase, Corn, 5 1/2 In.	140.00
Vase, Cover, Bulbous, Bird Head Handles, 19th Century, 19 In.	325.00
Vase, Ecole De Tours, Alligator Handled, Baluster Shape, Palissy Ware, 11 1/2 In.	748.00

Vase, Lily, Etruscan, 3 7/8 In. 605.00
Vase, Pilgrim, Scrolled Shell Handles, Griffins, Masks, Schiller & Sons, 13 5/8 In., Pair . . 750.00
Vase, Pillow, Applied Floral, Mythical Creatures, Figural Handles, France, 13 In. 110.00
Vase, Shell Form Handles, Panels Of Griffins, 1890s, 13 5/8 In., Pair 750.00
Vase, Stork, Yellow, Brown, Blue, 6 In. 210.00
Vase, Twisted Triple Log, 6 3/4 In. 50.00
Vase, Wild Rose, Basket, Triple Hole, Cobalt Blue Accent, 4 3/4 In. 165.00
Wall Pocket, Basket Weave, Fern, Leaf, Cattail, 10 1/2 In. 315.00
Wall Pocket, Mafra, Monkey Climbing, Palm Tree, Palissy Ware, 4 1/4 x 4 1/4 In. 805.00

MALACHITE is a green stone with unusual layers or rings of darker green shades. It is often polished and used for decorative objects. Most malachite comes from Siberia or Australia.

Figure, Fish, Banding Pattern, Dark Green To Light Green, Chinese, 6 1/4 In. 300.00
Figure, Large Foo Dog & 2 Puppies, Stand, Chinese, 2 x 4 In. 750.00
Figure, Woman, Holding Flute, Flowering Robes & Ribbons, Chinese, 7 In. 700.00
Inkwell, Bronze Dore, Crystal Well, Dolphin, Hinged Lid, Square Base, 5 x 5 x 6 In. 728.00
Jewel Keeper, Egg Shape, Bronze Dore, Pedestal, Gold Mounts, 10 1/2 In. 2240.00
Toothpick, Kurt Schlevoght, 1935 . . . . 295.00

MAPS of all types have been collected for centuries. The earliest known printed maps were made in 1478. The first printed street map showed London in 1559. The first road maps for use by drivers of automobiles were made in 1901. Collectors buy maps that were pages of old books, as well as the multifolded road maps popular in this century.

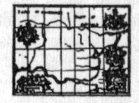

America, Color, Abraham Goos, c.1626, 16 x 20 1/4 In. 5060.00
America, North & South, 1806, 20 3/4 x 33 1/2 In. 440.00
Americas, Engraved Polychrome, Ebony Frame, 1746, 18 x 21 In. 950.00
Amsterdam, Canals, Hand Drawn, Nicholas Vander Geyoe, 1676, 49 x 9 1/2 In. 35.00
Asia, Hand Tinted, Matted, Frame, 1793, 23 1/4 x 19 1/2 In. 200.00
British Isles, 2 Sides, Frame, 1590, 17 1/2 x 21 1/2 In. 756.00
California, Oregon & Washington, Road, Gilmore Oil Co., 8 x 9 In. 95.00
California, Road, Hancock Oil Co., 4 1/2 x 9 3/4 In. 35.00
California, Union Oil Co., 1924, 12 x 9 1/4 In. 253.00
Colonial America, Pen, Colored Pencil, Watercolor, On Paper, 17 x 22 In. 1175.00
Constellations, Southern Circumpolar, Wood Frame, 19 1/8 x 16 1/2 In., Pair 220.00
France, Northern, Matted, Frame, 1940, 32 x 34 3/4 In. 210.00
Globe, Celestial, Brass Meridian Circle, Walnut Stand, 1854, 17 1/2 In. 2990.00
Globe, Mahogany Stand, Merzback & Falk, Brussels, Early 20th Century, 21 In. 1955.00
Globe, Outlined Continents, Red, Green, Brass Axis, Jan Felkl & Son, 13 In. 805.00
Globe, Terrestrial, Beechwood Stand, H.A. Kramers, 1920s, 24 1/2 In. 863.00
Globe, Terrestrial, Black Lacquered Stand, 1840s, 22 In. 345.00
Globe, Terrestrial, Brass Meridian Circle, Oxidized Brass Tripod Stand, 18 1/2 In. 316.00
Globe, Terrestrial, Calibrated Brass Half Disc, Jan Felkl & Son, 12 1/2 In. 805.00
Globe, Terrestrial, Celestial, Spiral Ebony Stands, Button Finials, c.1900, 7 In., Pair 575.00
Globe, Terrestrial, Continental, Ebonized Stand, c.1900, 12 1/4 In. 546.00
Globe, Terrestrial, Cream Sphere, Brass, Iron Axis, Jan Felkl & Son, 23 In. 690.00
Globe, Terrestrial, Ebonized Wooden Stand, J. Forest, 16 x 8 In. 575.00
Globe, Terrestrial, George III, Case, Pocket, Mahogany Stand, Newton, 1817 . . . . 5100.00
Globe, Terrestrial, George III, Tripod Stand, England, c.1900, 36 1/2 In. 1495.00
Globe, Terrestrial, Iron Base, Claw Foot, Rand McNally & Co., 18 In. 784.00
Globe, Terrestrial, Mahogany Floor Stand, Ebonized, Early 20th Century, 38 1/2 In. 575.00
Globe, Terrestrial, Oxidized Tripod Stand, Paw Feet, Hammond, 14 In. 375.00
Globe, Terrestrial, Pavel Rath & Professor A. Krause, 1920s, 29 In. 750.00
Globe, Terrestrial, Pocket, Faux Fishskin Case., J. Newton, 3 In. 4095.00
Globe, Terrestrial, Printed Hour Circle, Cabriole Legs, C.F. Weber, Chicago, 1900, 22 In. . . 1610.00
Globe, Terrestrial, Puzzle, 7 Sections, Plastic, Geographic Educator, c.1927, 6 x 11 In. . . . 688.00
Globe, Terrestrial, Stand, Ludwig Julius Heymann, Leipzig, Germany, 1900, 23 1/2 In. . . . 633.00
Globe, Terrestrial, Tripod Cast Iron Stand, c.1900, 13 3/4 In. 175.00
Globe, Terrestrial, Tripod Stand, Brass Mount, Austro Hungarian, c.1900, 31 x 16 In. 3450.00
Globe, Thread, Brass Pedestal, Clark & Co., London, Late 19th Century, 3 In. 518.00
Globe, Wooden, Lithograph, Maple, Late 19th Century, 17 In. 700.00
Hemisphere, Regency Style, Engraved, Colored, Frame, Early 1800s, 29 x 27 In., 6 Piece 4800.00

Hudson River, Poughkeepsie To Glasgow, Frame, 1862, 39 x 12 In. 259.00
Illinois, Road, $100,000,000 State Bond Issue Road System, Frame, 1923, 36 In. 11.00
Ireland, Baronia Udrone In Comitatu Cathersoughe, Irish, English Seals, 21 x 11 1/4 In. ... 110.00
Lower Mississippi River & New Orleans, I. Tirion, Frame, c.1765, 14 x 18 In. 690.00
Military, United Forces Marches, W.T. Sherman's, 1863-1865, 17 3/4 x 28 5/8 In. 165.00
Mississippi, La Louissane, Place Names, Rivers, Indian Tribes, Frame, 1718, 21 x 28 In. .. 550.00
New World, East Coast, Nova Scotia To Virginia, 18th Century, 15 x 19 In. 3000.00
North & South Carolina, Johnson's, 17 x 23 3/4 In. 280.00
North Dakota, Parco Petroleum Of North Dakota, 12 x 9 In. 50.00
Oklahoma, Road, Phillips 66, 12 x 9 In. 120.00
Pembrokeshire, Copperplate, Hand Colored, John Speed, 1611-1711, 15 x 20 In. 1500.00
United States, Northeast Section, 19th Century, 20 x 28 In. 258.00
Vermont, Hand Colored, Copperplate Engraving, John Roberts, 1795, 27 x 14 In. 1250.00

MARBLE collectors pay highest prices for glass and sulphide marbles. The game of marbles has been popular since the days of the ancient Romans. American children were able to buy marbles by the mid-eighteenth century. Dutch glazed clay marbles were least expensive. Glazed pottery marbles, attributed to the Bennington potteries in Vermont, were of a better quality. Marbles made of pink marble were also available by the 1830s. Glass marbles seem to have been made later. By 1880, Samuel C. Dyke of South Akron, Ohio, was making clay marbles and The National Onyx Marble Company was making marbles of onyx. The Navarre Glass Marble Company of Navarre, Ohio, and M. B. Mishler of Ravenna, Ohio, made the glass marbles. Ohio remained the center of the marble industry, and the Akron-made Akro Agate brand became nationally known. Other pieces made by Akro Agate are listed in this book in the Akro Agate category. Sulphides are glass marbles with frosted white figures in the center.

Candy Stripe, 1 5/8 In. 100.00
Clear, Inlaid Chicken, 1 1/4 In. 48.00
Cloud Type, Indian, Single Pontil, Germany, Late 1800s, 15/16 In. 4085.00
Double Swirl, Blue & White, Gold Stone, Grant Maul, 1 5/8 In. 33.00
Egg Yolk & Oxblood Swirl, Akro Agate, c.1925, 11 11/16 In. 125.00
Glass, Green Galaxy, Peltier Glass Co., 1920s, 7/8 In. 1063.00
Green Galaxy, 1920s, 7/8 In. 1067.00
Latticinio Cone Center, Striped, Green, Pink & Blue, 1 5/8 In. 11.00
Onionskin, Shooter, Red, White, Blue Swirl, Pontil Marks, 1 1/2 In. 80.00
Red, Blue, Yellow & Green, Gold Stone Swirl, Grant Maul, 1 1/4 In. 22.00
Sulphide, Ape, Polished, 1 In. 55.00
Sulphide, Armadillo, Polished, 1 5/8 In. 66.00
Sulphide, Bear, Sitting, 1 3/8 In. 44.00
Sulphide, Bear, Standing, Polished, 1 3/8 In. 55.00
Sulphide, Billy Goat, 2 In. 70.00
Sulphide, Dog, 1 1/2 In. 154.00
Sulphide, Eagle, Resting, Polished, 1 5/8 In. 120.00
Sulphide, Fish, Interior Bubble, 1 1/8 In. 55.00
Sulphide, Frog, Sitting, Bubble Around Figure, 1 3/4 In. 200.00
Sulphide, Girl Sitting In Chair, Bubble Around Figure, 1 9/16 In. 260.00
Sulphide, Goat, Polished, 1 1/2 In. 55.00
Sulphide, Lion, Roaring, Polished, 1 3/4 In. 66.00
Sulphide, Sheep, Reclining, Polished, 1 1/4 In. 88.00
Sulphide, Squirrel Sitting On Hind Legs Holding Nut, 1 1/2 In. 145.00
Sulphide, Squirrel, 1 1/2 In. 55.00
Sulphide, Wild Boar, 1 5/8 In. 55.00

MARBLE CARVINGS, such as large or small figurines, groups of people or animals, and architectural decorations, have been a special art form since the time of the ancient Greeks. Reproductions, especially of large Victorian groups, are being made of a mixture using marble dust. These are very difficult to detect and collectors should be careful. Other carvings are listed under Alabaster.

Baptismal Font, 19th Century, 36 1/2 In. 280.00

Bust, Child Swathed In Blanket, G. Oldofreddi, 26 In. 2645.00
Bust, Child With Kitten, Italy, c.1900, 21 In. 1725.00
Bust, Classical Philosopher, Leone Clerici, 21 In. 3525.00
Bust, Emperor Napoleon I, Black Marble Base, 13 3/4 x 9 x 5 1/2 In. 431.00
Bust, Napoleon, After Canova, Alabaster, 21 In. 3600.00
Bust, Princess, Pendant Necklace, Headwrap, C. Lapins, 1885, 27 In. 5175.00
Bust, Woman With Flowers, Wood Stand, Signed, G. Bessi, 14 3/4 In. 1760.00
Bust, Woman With Hat, White, 17 3/4 In. 715.00
Bust, Woman, Hair Pulled Back In Bun, Late 19th Century, 20 In. 862.00
Bust, Woman, White Marble, Hat, Lace Collar, 25 In. 2530.00
Bust, Young Girl, Looking Right, Purple, White Pedestal, 19 In. 690.00
Bust, Young Woman, Alabaster Pedestal, c.1900, 21 x 9 In. 6600.00
Bust, Young Woman, V-Neck Dress, Wide Belt, White Marble Back, 13 1/2 In. 440.00
Centerpiece, Maid & Horse, Allegorical Swans, Figural Shaft, 1800s, 20 1/2 x 7 In. . . 920.00
Dog, Lying Down, Carved Coat & Tail, Looking Left, 19th Century, 9 x 17 3/8 In. 3055.00
Fountainhead, Lion, Assyrian, 13 x 12 In. 115.00
Gladiator, Green, Lying On Shield, Fluted Column, 1900s, 63 x 33 In. 2875.00
Jardiniere, Louis XVI Style, Gilt Bronze, Copper Liner, 13 1/2 x 18 1/4 x 11 1/2 In. 6000.00
Lion, Crouching On Stone Slab, Signed, Early 1900s, 7 x 18 In. 287.00
Lion, Roaming, Carrara Marble, Rockwork Base, 17th Century, 15 1/2 In. 1840.00
Lion, Waking, Open Mouth, 19 x 18 x 24 In., Pair 4200.00
Obelisk, Band Of Faux Hieroglyphics, Late 19th Century, 22 In., Pair 920.00
Obelisk, Gray & White, 4 Verdigris Bronze Turtle Supports, 24 1/2 In. 430.00
Pedestal, Spiral Entwined Dolphins, Octagonal Base, Green, 42 In. 1035.00
Pedestal, White, Blue Enamel & Gilt, Brass, Ormolu, Classical, 38 1/4 In. 1705.00
Planter, Lobed, Butterfly Handles, Lotus Plant Panels, Oval, 8 1/2 In. 200.00
Plaque, Carved, Relief, Bust Of Woman, c.1910, 12 x 8 In. 175.00
Plaque, Comely Lady, Profile, Signed, Max Klein, 1907, 19 1/2 x 15 In. 290.00
Potpourri, Empire Style, Gilt Bronze, Late 19th Century, 18 1/2 In., Pair 5100.00
Sculpture, Girl, Seated, Crossed Legs, Signed, Volere E Portere, 23 x 11 x 12 In. 4600.00
Silhouette, L. Kopf, Rom, 1869, 14 3/4 In. 550.00
Statue, 2 Cherubs, Signed Pigale, Late 19th Century, 24 In. 4800.00
Statue, 2 Children, Raised On Veined Marble Pedestal, Moreau, 26 In. 9600.00
Statue, Boy Holding Dead Bird, Tear On Cheek, Pedestal Base, 24 In. 4400.00
Statue, Boy Playing Bagpipe, Signed VV, 41 In. 2350.00
Statue, Boy With Birdcage, Signed, T. Pezzica, 18 In. 2160.00
Statue, Cupid, Jug In Left Hand, Right Hand To Lips, 44 In. 1560.00
Statue, Diaphanously Clad Maiden Perched On Leaves, 30 1/2 In. 2875.00
Statue, Foo Dog, 30 In., Pair 1000.00
Statue, Girl Bracing Against Wind, C. Papotti, 1875, 44 In. 7638.00
Statue, Madame Recamier, Raised On Marble Base, 25 In. 1800.00
Statue, Maiden In 19th Century Costume, Holding Book, Oval Base, 29 In. 825.00
Statue, Nude In Chains, Greek Slave, After Hiram Powers, 36 In. 2400.00
Statue, Nude Woman, Reclining, On Boulder, Signed F. Viche, c.1885, 19 x 23 In. 3192.00
Statue, Scythian Slave, Sharpening Knife, 1800s, 21 1/2 x 9 1/2 x 24 In. 2750.00
Statue, Shepherd With Sheep, Raised On Marble Base, 18 In. 1800.00
Statue, Temple Of Vespasian, Italy, 19th Century, 19 1/4 In. 5400.00
Statue, Twig Gatherer, Peasant Girl, Carrying Firewood, Italy, c.1900, 30 In. 1850.00
Statue, Woman, Plinth With Urn, White, Signed, Bazzanti, Florence, 32 In. 2860.00
Statue, Young Maiden, Raised On Pedestal, Signed, Late 19th Century, 11 In. 10200.00
Urn, Cover, Gilt Bronze Mounted, Green, Louis XVI, Early 20th Century, 29 In., Pair . . . 2645.00
Urn, Cover, Gilt Bronze Mounted, Louis XVI, Late 19th Century, 17 In. 3840.00
Urn, Cover, White, 11 In., Pair 412.00
Urn, Domed Cover, White, Tan Striations, Brass Hardware, 15 3/4 In. 165.00

**It is best to wash marble with distilled water. Any trace of acid or
iron in the water will cause deterioration or stains.
Use soft soap, a bit of ammonia, and a plastic container.**

Urn, Gilt Bronze Mounted, Black, Eastlake, Late 19th Century, 16 In., Pair 345.00
Urn, Gilt Bronze Mounted, Rosso Antico, Early 20th Century, 15 3/8 In., Pair 2300.00
Urn, Gilt Bronze Mounted, Rosso Antico, Late 19th Century, 16 1/2 In., Pair 4315.00
Vase, Gilt Bronze, Handles, Lamp Mounted, Rambaud Sculpt. Susse Freres, 18 In. 1265.00
Woman, Powdered Wig, Low Bodice, Turned Socle, France, Late 1700s, 24 1/2 In. 3450.00

MARBLEHEAD Pottery was founded in 1905 by Dr. J. Hall as a rehabil-
itative program for the patients of a Marblehead, Massachusetts, sanitarium. Two years later it was separated from the sanitarium and it
continued operations until 1936. Many of the pieces were decorated
with marine motifs.

Bookends, Multicolored Painted Ship, 6 x 6 In. 3740.00
Bookends, Triangular, Embossed, Sailing Ship, Indigo Ground, Ship Mark, 5 1/2 In. 1840.00
Bowl, Blue Matte Glaze, 5 1/2 In. 320.00
Bowl, Gray Matte Glaze, Marked, 2 In. 230.00
Bowl, Green Speckled Matte Glaze, Squat, 3 1/4 x 5 1/4 In. 520.00
Bowl, Indigo Glaze, Blue Semimatte Interior, 2 1/2 x 6 1/4 In. 635.00
Bowl, Lavender Matte Glaze, 6 In. 265.00
Bowl, Light Rose Matte Glaze, 8 1/2 In. 690.00
Bowl, Lotus Leaf, Speckled Blue Glaze, Speckled Interior, Flared, Mark, 8 1/4 In. 400.00
Bowl, Speckled Blue Green Exterior, Light Celadon Interior, 3 1/2 x 8 In. 600.00
Bowl, Speckled Pink Matte Glaze, Light Speckled Pink Interior, 3 x 8 In. 375.00
Bowl, Yellow Matte Exterior, Teal Matte Interior, Flared Rim, 5 x 8 1/2 In. 450.00
Chamberstick, 3 Handles, Blue Matte Glaze, 5 3/4 x 5 In. 430.00
Chamberstick, Gold, Brown, Yellow Matte Glaze, 4 In. 405.00
Chamberstick, Green Matte Glaze, 7 1/2 In. 920.00
Inkwell, Green Matte Glaze, 3 In. 35.00
Lamp, Blue Matte Glaze, Textured Paper Shade, 23 In. 690.00
Match Holder, Brown, Speckled Green Matte Ground, Abstract, 2 x 2 1/4 In. 865.00
Pitcher, Pinched Waist, Incised Panels, Stylized Flowers, Green, Brown, Marked, 9 In. . . 5750.00
Tile, Blue & White Matte Glazes, Sailing Ship, 6 3/4 x 6 3/4 In. 520.00
Tile, Cream Oatmeal, Blue Matte Glaze, Ship, 4 3/4 In. 350.00
Tile, Flowers In Vase, 4 Colors, Arts & Crafts Dark Oak Frame, Square, 6 In. 2970.00
Tile, House, Trees, Polychrome, Gray Matte Ground, Frame, Square, 6 In. 1725.00
Vase, 4 Groups Of Stylized Leaves & Vines, Green, Brown, 4 1/4 In. 600.00
Vase, 4 Stylized Leafy Green Panels, Gray, Blue Matte Ground, 8 3/4 In. 460.00
Vase, Aqua Blue Mottled Glaze, Cobalt Blue, Black Veining, 8 3/4 x 4 In. 1320.00
Vase, Band Of Grapevines, Signed, 5 1/2 In. 1380.00
Vase, Beaker Shape, Mottled Green Glaze, 6 1/2 In. 460.00
Vase, Black Glaze, Blue Highlights, Chicory Blue Mouth, 5 1/4 x 4 In. 440.00
Vase, Black, Cylinder Shape, 7 1/4 In. 950.00
Vase, Blue Glaze, 7 1/4 In. 2500.00
Vase, Blue Matte Glaze, 3 1/2 In. . . . . .165.00 to 242.00
Vase, Blue Matte Glaze, 5 In. 276.00
Vase, Blue Matte Glaze, 7 1/2 In. 990.00
Vase, Brown Speckled Matte Glaze, Signed, 5 1/2 In. 575.00
Vase, Brown, Speckled Green Matte Ground, Band Of Flowers, Cylindrical, 6 x 3 In. 2760.00
Vase, Carved, Painted Geometric Design, Signed, A.E. Baggs, 4 In. 3738.00
Vase, Chestnut Brown Matte Glaze, Red Clay, 4 3/4 In. 288.00
Vase, Chicory Blue Mottled Glaze, 5 1/2 x 4 In. 770.00
Vase, Cylindrical, Matte Blue Glaze, Signed, 7 1/2 In. 546.00
Vase, Cylindrical, Painted, Stylized Flowers, 4 1/2 In. 748.00
Vase, Dark Gray, Speckled Light Gray Ground, Mistletoe, Oval, 7 x 4 In. 2990.00
Vase, Deep Blue Glaze, Marked, 5 x 4 In. 115.00
Vase, Deep Dove Gray, Cobalt Speckles, 6 x 2 1/2 In. 357.00
Vase, Dove Gray Matte Speckled Glaze, Chicory Interior, 8 3/4 In. 660.00
Vase, Flower Blossoms, Blue, Speckled Gray Ground, 5 1/4 In. 3450.00
Vase, Flowers, Yellow, Blue, Green, Gray, Matte, 3 1/2 x 4 1/2 In. 2310.00
Vase, Flying Goose, Blue, Dove Gray Matte Ground, 3 1/2 In. 2090.00
Vase, Geometric Design, Sage Green Square, Deep Blue, Black Speckles, 4 In. 1045.00
Vase, Gourd Shape, Black Flying Geese, Dark Green Matte Ground, 6 x 5 1/2 In. 2875.00
Vase, Gourd, Deep Caramel Glaze, Ocher Interior, 4 1/2 x 5 1/2 In. 495.00
Vase, Grapes & Leaves, Blue On Speckled Gray Ground, Ship Mark, 3 1/2 In. 2300.00

Vase, Grapes & Leaves, Blue, Green, Brown, Speckled Gray Ground, Marked, 6 1/2 In. . . . 3737.00
Vase, Gray Matte Glaze, 3 1/2 In. . . . . .275.00 to 345.00
Vase, Green Matte Glaze, Brown Incised Geometric Design, 4 In. 4025.00
Vase, Green Matte Glaze, Bulbous, 3 1/2 In. 300.00
Vase, Green Matte Glaze, Cylindrical, 5 1/2 In. 635.00
Vase, Green Matte Ground, Band Of Stylized Palm Fronds, Cylindrical, 8 3/4 In. 5465.00
Vase, Green Mottled Matte Glaze, 7 x 3 1/4 In. 650.00
Vase, Green Mottled Matte Glaze, Red Clay, 11 5/8 In. 1600.00
Vase, Holly, Leaves, Berries, Blue Matte Ground, Cylindrical, 4 1/2 In. 6040.00
Vase, Incised Stylized Flower, Dark Olive Green, Light Green Ground, 10 In. 17250.00
Vase, Lavender Gray Matte Glaze, Signed, 3 1/4 x 5 In. 520.00
Vase, Lavender Matte Glaze, 7 In. 750.00
Vase, Lavender Speckled Matte Glaze, Signed, 5 1/2 In. 490.00
Vase, Lilies, Amber, Brown, Blue, Mustard Ground, Barrel Shape, Hannah Tutt, 4 1/2 In. . . 8625.00
Vase, Mauve Matte Glaze, Cylindrical, 3 1/2 In. 265.00
Vase, Mocha Brown, Lavender, Brown Speckles, 4 1/2 In. 140.00
Vase, Mottled Green & Blue Glaze, Swollen Shoulder, Tapered, c.1920, 2 1/2 In. 115.00
Vase, Multi-Toned Blue Matte Glaze, 3 1/2 In. 310.00
Vase, Multicolored Carved, Painted Ships, 6 In. 1610.00
Vase, Mustard Mottled Glaze, Tan, 3 1/4 In. 350.00
Vase, Pale Ocher Speckled Matte Glaze, Signed, 4 1/2 In. 980.00
Vase, Purple Matte Glaze, 5 1/2 In. 635.00
Vase, Purple, Blue Textured Matte Glaze, 3 1/2 In. 460.00
Vase, Raised Yellow Flower, Blue Center, Green, Blue, Gray Glaze, 3 1/2 In. 2415.00
Vase, Rose Matte Glaze, 3 1/2 In. 160.00
Vase, Speckled Blue Matte Glaze, Impressed Mark, Squat, 3 3/4 In. 460.00
Vase, Speckled Brown Matte Glaze, 5 x 3 1/2 In. 550.00
Vase, Speckled Green Glaze, Bulbous, 3 1/2 In. 950.00
Vase, Speckled Matte Brown Glaze, Paper Label, 4 1/4 In. 520.00
Vase, Speckled Mustard Matte Glaze, Impressed Mark, 1 3/4 x 3 1/2 In. 400.00
Vase, Stick, Lavender Blue, 5 1/2 In. 170.00
Vase, Stylized Flowers, Hanna Tutt, 5 1/2 In. 920.00
Vase, Stylized Leaves, Amber & Brown, Speckled Gray Ground, Ship Mark, 4 1/2 In. 2990.00
Vase, Swollen Shoulder, Gray Matte Glaze, 5 1/2 In. 460.00
Vase, Tapered, Brown Matte, Impressed Mark, 5 1/2 In. 325.00
Vase, Teal, Gray Blue Matte Ground, Egrets In Flight, 6 x 5 1/4 In. 1725.00
Vase, Trees With Broad Leaves & Berries, Hannah Tutt, 7 In. 2530.00
Vase, Trees, Green & Ochre, Gray Ground, Oval, Hannah Tutt, 7 In. 5175.00
Vase, Wall, Light Gray Matte Glaze, Early 20th Century, 8 In. 230.00
Vase, Yellow Matte Glaze, 5 1/2 In. 800.00

MARTIN BROTHERS of Middlesex, England, made Martinware, a salt-
glazed stoneware, between 1873 and 1915. Many figural jugs and
vases were made by the three brothers. Of special interest are the fanciful birds, usually made with removable heads.

Charger, Heraldic, Incised, Signed, 1876, 13 1/4 In., Pair 1200.00
Ewer, Dragon, Incised, Signed, 1893, 9 1/2 In. 4500.00
Figurine, Lion, Signed, 1877, 14 3/8 In., Pair 9600.00
Figurine, Musicians, Lute, Pipes, 1900, 3 5/8 & 4 In. 1800.00
Figurine, Satyr, Wood Base, Signed, 1895, 10 1/8 In. 3300.00
Figurine, Undersea, Grotesque, Monstrous, Signed, 1898 . . . . 8400.00
Jar, Bird, Barrister, Wood Base, 1897, 11 1/2 In. 19150.00
Jar, Figural, Grotesque, Signed, 1890, 7 7/8 In. 7800.00
Jar, Figural, Grotesque, Wood Base, Signed, 1888, 7 1/2 In. 2700.00
Jardiniere, Dragon, Incised, Signed, 1887, 8 5/8 In. 1800.00
Jug, Dragon, Incised, Signed, 1898, 9 In. 2040.00
Jug, Eskimo, Signed, 1910, 12 7/8 In. 5400.00
Jug, Face, 2 Sides, Signed, 1897, 7 3/4 In. 3600.00
Jug, Face, 2 Sides, Signed, 1900, 6 1/2 In. 6000.00
Jug, Face, Signed, 1890, 9 In. 5700.00
Plate, Dragon, Leaves, Incised, Signed, 1886, 10 1/4 In. 3000.00
Spoon Warmer, Figural, Grotesque, Signed, 1882, 6 5/8 In. 11400.00
Spoon Warmer, Figural, Signed, 1890, 4 1/4 In. 5100.00

Vase, Aquatic, Carved, Slip Decorated, 2 Handle, Signed, 1911, 11 1/2 In.	2040.00
Vase, Aquatic, Incised, Signed, 1890, 5 1/2 In.	3300.00
Vase, Aquatic, Incised, Signed, 1890, 8 1/2 In.	3300.00
Vase, Bird, Barrister, Wood Base, 1888, 5 1/2 In.	10800.00
Vase, Bird, Incised, Signed, 1899, 9 In.	1920.00
Vase, Botanical, Incised, Signed, 1891, 7 3/4 In.	2280.00
Vase, Botanical, Incised, Signed, 1892, 9 1/2 In.	600.00
Vase, Clematis, Incised, Signed, 1890, 8 7/8 In.	1440.00
Vase, Dragon, Leaves, Incised, Signed, 1889, 8 3/4 In.	1200.00
Vase, Dragon, Molded, Incised, Signed, 1904, 6 1/2 In.	1320.00
Vase, Dragon, Relief Carved, Signed, 1910, 12 In.	3300.00
Vase, Figural, Grotesque, Wood Base, 1887, 10 7/8 In.	49625.00
Vase, Hunting, 2 Handle, 1879, 13 1/2 In.	1920.00
Vase, Organic, Molded, Incised, Signed, 1902, 9 7/8 In.	1440.00
Wall Pocket, Figural, Grotesque, Signed, 1883, 6 5/8 In.	5100.00

MARY GREGORY is the name used for a type of glass that is easily identified. White figures were painted on clear or colored glass as the decoration. The figures chosen were usually children at play. The first glass known as Mary Gregory was made about 1870. Similar glass is made even today. The traditional story has been that the glass was made at the Sandwich Glass works in Boston by a woman named Mary Gregory. Recent research suggests that it is possible that none was made at Sandwich. In general, all-white figures were used in the United States, tinted faces were probably used in Bohemia, France, Italy, Germany, Switzerland, and England. Children standing, not playing, were pictured after the 1950s.

Biscuit Jar, White Enameled Girl, Seated On Fence, Cranberry, 7 1/4 In.	345.00
Cruet, Ribbed Optic, White Enameled, 8 In.	50.00
Decanter, Victorian Woman, Gold Trimmed Foot, Rim & Stopper, 14 In.	90.00
Ewer, Ribbed Optic, White Enameled, Blue, 8 In.	130.00
Lamp, Facing Pair, Boy & Girl, Frosted Shade, Black Amethyst, 18 1/2 In., Pair	895.00
Lamp, White Enameled Boy & Girl, Frosted Shade, Black Amethyst, 18 1/2 In., Pair	895.00
Mug, Girl, Cranberry, 2 In.	185.00
Mug, White Enameled, Birds, Handle, Blue, 3 7/8 In.	60.00
Pitcher, White Enameled, Green Handle, Lime Green, 12 1/4 In.	245.00
Tumbler, Ribbed Optic, White Enameled, Blue, 6 1/2 x 2 3/4 In.	70.00
Tumbler, Ribbed Optic, White Enameled, Sage Green, 6 5/8 x 2 3/4 In.	25.00
Tumbler, White Enameled, Cowboy On Horse, Green, 3 1/2 x 2 1/8 In.	30.00
Vase, Boy Carrying Tray Of Flowers, Green, 11 1/8 In.	225.00
Vase, Boy, Fancy Outfit, Holding Flower, Ribbed Optic, 9 In.	225.00
Vase, Ribbed Optic, White Enameled, Cranberry, 6 x 3 1/8 In.	90.00
Vase, Sapphire Blue, White Enameled, Boy In Fancy Outfit, 9 In.	225.00
Vase, White Enameled, Black Amethyst, 5 1/2 x 3 In.	50.00
Vase, White Enameled, Young Boy, Holding Flower, Amber, 7 1/4 In.	165.00

MASON'S IRONSTONE was made by the English pottery of Charles J. Mason after 1813. Mason, of Lane Delph, was given a patent for this improved earthenware. He usually called it "Mason's Patent Ironstone China." It resisted chipping and breaking so it became popular for dinnerwares and other table service dishes. Vases and other decorative pieces were also made. The ironstone was decorated with orange, blue, gold, and other colors, often in Japanese inspired designs. The firm had financial difficulties but the molds and the name Mason were used by many owners through the years, including Francis Morley, Taylor Ashworth, George L. Ashworth, and John Shaw. Mason's joined the Wedgwood group in 1973 and the name is still found on dinnerwares.

Bowl, Cereal, Vista, Pink	18.00
Bowl, Vegetable, Round, Stratford, Pink	60.00
Coffeepot, Vista, Pink	125.00
Cup & Saucer, Vista, 4 1/2 x 2 In.	75.00
Dinner Set, Mulberry Transfer, Oriental Design, Service For 10, 45 Piece	415.00
Jar, Apothecary, Flowers, Butterflies, 4 Sides, 4 x 4 x 6 In.	49.00

Plate, Dessert, Scalloped, Oval	195.00
Plate, Dinner, Vista, Pink	24.00
Plate, Salad, Stratford, Pink	15.00
Plate, Scalloped Rim, Center Fruit & Leaf Sprays, c.1890, 10 1/2 In., 6 Piece	505.00
Plate, Soup, 10 In., 7 Piece	1400.00
Platter, Chinese Figures, Cobalt Blue, Red, Gilt Leaves, 14 1/2 In.	1495.00
Platter, Square, 2 Handles, Oriental Scene, Blue Transfer, 10 3/4 In.	95.00
Platter, Vista, Pink, 13 In.	74.00
Saucer, Vista, 7 In.	20.00
Soup, Dish, Imari Palette, Scalloped Rim, c.1849, 10 1/4 In., Pair	310.00
Teapot, 9 1/2 x 7 1/2 x 5 In.	275.00
Teapot, Stratford, Pink	120.00
Tureen, Brown Transfer, Tray, Ladle, Late 19th Century	525.00
Vase, Flag, 11 Openings, Blue Brown Glaze, 1961, 10 x 7 1/2 In.	230.00
Vase, Imari, Bearded Head Under Cornucopia Handle, 1825, 27 In.	6600.00
Wash Set, Imari Style, c.1895, 6 Piece	476.00

MASONIC, see Fraternal category.

MASSIER, a French art pottery, was made by brothers Jerome, Delphin, and Clement Massier in Vallauris and Golfe-Juan, France, in the late nineteenth and early twentieth centuries. It has an iridescent metallic luster glaze that resembles the Weller Sicardo pottery glaze. Most pieces are marked *J. Massier*.

Urn, Tulips, Burgundy, Purple & Green Gold Ground, Handles, 6 3/4 x 3 In.	489.00
Vase, Green Iridescent Glaze, Serpent Handles, Low, 6 3/4 In.	1150.00
Vase, Red & White Glaze, Charcoal Specks, Baluster, 5 1/2 In.	288.00

MATCH HOLDERS were made to hold the large wooden matches that were used in the nineteenth and twentieth centuries for a variety of purposes. The kitchen stove and the fireplace or furnace had to be lit regularly. One type of match holder was made to hang on the wall, another was designed to be kept on a tabletop. Of special interest today are match holders that have advertisements as part of the design.

Alligator, Cast Iron, 8 1/2 In.	126.00
Ashtray, Black Porter Carrying 2 Suitcases, Glass Insert, 8 In.	373.00
Beehive Shape, Raised Bees, Striker, Doulton, 2 1/4 In.	80.00
Black Man Points To Liquor Bottle, Tree Stump Holds Matches, 3 1/2 In.	110.00
Country Kitchen, Cast Iron, Advertising, Coal Scuttle, Wall, 5 1/4 x 4 In.	257.00
De Laval, Separator Shape, Embossed, Tin, 6 In.	126.00
Embossed, Double Pocket, Metal, 6 x 3 In.	30.00
Fatima Cigarettes, Austria, J.R. Gibney, 4 x 3 x 3 1/2 In.	17.00
Fatima Cigarettes, Ceramic, Image Of Cigarettes, 3 In., Pair	75.00
Frog & Shell Shape, Milk Glass, 2 3/4 In.	165.00
Juicyfruit Gum, Tin Lithograph, Striker, 3 3/8 x 5 In.	148.00
Milwaukee Harvester, Wall, 4 7/8 x 3 3/8 In.	185.00
New Process Gas Range, Metal Lithograph, 3 1/2 x 2 1/4 x 1 In.	330.00
Old Judson Whiskey, Hanging, 4 7/8 x 3 3/8 In.	210.00
Ready To Start, Girl Standing Near Trunk, Dog & Umbrella, 5 7/8 In.	50.00
Rooster, Double Pocket, 6 1/4 x 3 In.	30.00
Sharples Cream Separators, Tin Lithograph, 6 7/8 x 2 1/8 In.	600.00
Sharples Tubular Cream Separators, Wall, 6 7/8 In.	297.00
Turtle, Grand Rapids Brass Co., Hinged At Tail, Brass, Striker, 3 x 5 1/4 In.	100.00
Uncle Remus, Copper Striker, Wall, 8 In.	108.00
Unitus Uncle Sam Cigars, Molded Plaster, Hand Painted, 1918, 6 1/2 In.	57.00

MATCH SAFES were designed to be carried in the pocket. Early matches were made with phosphorus and could ignite unexpectedly. The matches were safely stored in the tightly closed container. Match safes were made in sterling silver, plated silver, or other metals. The English call these *vesta boxes*.

Atlantic City, Mother-Of-Pearl, Nickel Plated Metal	65.00
Baby In Shirt, Brass, Back Striker	295.00
Book, Ivory, Sterling Silver, Edge Striker	110.00

Book, Nickel Plated Brass, Yellow Enamel, Edge Striker 65.00
Cat In Hat, Brass, Bottom Striker 295.00
Cork, Brass, Trick Opening Lid, Release Tab 135.00
De Laval, Tin Lithograph, American Art, New York, 1908 .... 420.00
Deer Leg, Wood, Fur, Brass End, Striker On Hoof 135.00
Dragon, Compass, Brass, Bottom Striker 595.00
Flask, Brass, Bottom Striker 130.00
Fox Head, Brass, Glass Eyes, Striker Under Neck 250.00
Golf Motif, Aluminum, Bottom Striker, Scovill Mfg. Co. 310.00
Hunting Motif, Brass, Applied Copper, End Striker 125.00
Indian Scout, Profile, Sterling Silver, Gold Wash Interior 600.00
Indian Scout, Profile, Sterling Silver, Scalloped Edges, Monogram 725.00
Jackknife, 3 Simulated Blades, Nickel Plated Brass 235.00
Laxy Wheel, Celluloid Wrapped, Nickel Plated Brass Ends 225.00
Lithograph On Top, Bottom, Edges, Tin, France 110.00
Los Angeles Brewing Co., Nickel Plated Brass, Bottom Striker 125.00
Moon, Vesta Socket In Mouth, Glass Eyes, Brass 315.00
Mouse, Brass, Glass Eyes, Leather Ears, Tail, Stamped Deponirt 275.00
Pants, I.B. Goltzbach Clothier, Pewter, 1886 .... 145.00
Pig With Moneybag, Little Wadhurst Farm, Nickel Plated Brass 250.00
Ram's Head, Enameled, Hinged Cover, Top Striker, 3 In. 632.00
Rooster Head, Brass, Glass Eyes, Squeeze Beak To Open Lid 295.00
Scottish Thistle, Nickel Plated Brass, Bottom Striker 195.00
Shoe, Aluminum, I. Warren & Son, Heel Striker 145.00
Shoe, Cigar Cutter, Brass 175.00
Stein, Brass, Bottom Striker 175.00
Sterling Silver, Concave Back, Unger 225.00
Sterling Silver, Laughing Buddha, Repousse, Gorham No. 390 .... 820.00
Sterling Silver, Sawtooth Striker, England, 1913, 5/8 In. 125.00
Sterling Silver & Cloisonne Enamel, 4 Flowers, White Beading, c.1900, 1 1/4 In. 138.00
Tiolene Motor Oil, Tin Lithograph, 2 1/4 In. 130.00
Violin, Flat Sides, Nickel Plated Brass, Lid Striker 135.00
Wild Boar, Nickel Plated Brass, Push Button Lid Release 210.00

MATSU-NO-KE was a type of applied decoration for glass patented by Frederick Carder in 1922. There is clear evidence that pieces were made before that date at the Steuben glassworks. Stevens & Williams of England also made an applied decoration by the same name.

Bowl, Reverse Coin Spot, Clear On Amberina, Ruffled Edge, 5 1/2 x 6 In. 168.00
Vase, Frosted Clear Branch, 7 Blossoms, Pale Green Body, 5 1/4 In. 475.00
Vase, White, Rose Cased, Applied Amber Leaves, Handles, 10 In. 378.00

MCCOY pottery was made in Roseville, Ohio. Nelson McCoy and J.W. McCoy established the Nelson McCoy Sanitary and Stoneware Company in Roseville, Ohio, in 1910. The firm made art pottery after 1926. In 1933 it became the Nelson McCoy Pottery Company. Pieces marked *McCoy* were made by the Nelson McCoy Pottery Company. Cookie jars were made from about 1940 until December 1990, when the McCoy factory closed. In 1990 the McCoy mark was put back on pottery by a firm unrelated to the original company. Because there was a company named Brush-McCoy, there is great confusion between Brush and Nelson McCoy pieces. See Brush category for more information.

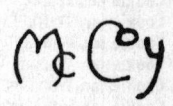

Bowl, Plate & Mug Set, Smiley Face, Child's, Box 85.00
Cookie Jar, Apollo 769.00
Cookie Jar, Apple, Red, Gold Leaf 90.00
Cookie Jar, Asparagus 40.00
Cookie Jar, Bear, Cookie In Vest 65.00
Cookie Jar, Betsy Baker 190.00
Cookie Jar, Bobby Baker .... 10.00 to 45.00
Cookie Jar, Boy On Football 100.00
Cookie Jar, Caboose 165.00
Cookie Jar, Chilly Willy 60.00
Cookie Jar, Chipmunk 90.00

Cookie Jar, Circus Horse, 1962 ....110.00 to 195.00
Cookie Jar, Clown, Bust ....60.00 to 80.00
Cookie Jar, Clown, In Barrel, Yellow 100.00
Cookie Jar, Clyde Dog 90.00
Cookie Jar, Coalby Cat, Gilt Trim 190.00
Cookie Jar, Colonial Fireplace 90.00
Cookie Jar, Cork Lid, Brown & White 100.00
Cookie Jar, Doghouse 180.00
Cookie Jar, Duck On Basketweave 75.00
Cookie Jar, Duck, Yellow 125.00
Cookie Jar, Dutch Boy 45.00
Cookie Jar, Dutch Girl 70.00
Cookie Jar, Dutch Treat Barn 30.00
Cookie Jar, Early American, Frontier Family 45.00
Cookie Jar, Elephant, With Ice Cream Cone 150.00
Cookie Jar, Forbidden Fruit 70.00
Cookie Jar, Fruit In Basket 75.00
Cookie Jar, Granny, White, Red Dots, Glasses 50.00
Cookie Jar, Hobby Horse 50.00
Cookie Jar, Hocus Rabbit, Blue 60.00
Cookie Jar, Indian Dark 350.00
Cookie Jar, Indian, Light ....125.00 to 130.00
Cookie Jar, Kangaroo, Blue 100.00
Cookie Jar, Koala Bear 65.00
Cookie Jar, Lamb On Basketweave 65.00
Cookie Jar, Lemon 60.00
Cookie Jar, Leprechaun 1280.00
Cookie Jar, Lollipop 75.00
Cookie Jar, Lunch Basket 30.00
Cookie Jar, Mac Dog 90.00
Cookie Jar, Mammy, Cookies 90.00
Cookie Jar, Nabisco 60.00
Cookie Jar, Owls, Mr. & Mrs. Owl 60.00
Cookie Jar, Pepper, Green 55.00
Cookie Jar, Picnic Basket 75.00
Cookie Jar, Pig 45.00
Cookie Jar, Quaker Oats 455.00
Cookie Jar, Rag Doll, Raggedy Ann 60.00
Cookie Jar, Rocking Chair, Dalmatians 130.00
Cookie Jar, Sad Clown 80.00
Cookie Jar, Snoopy, On Doghouse 100.00
Cookie Jar, Snow Bear 90.00
Cookie Jar, Spaceship, Friendship 7 ....100.00 to 200.00
Cookie Jar, Teepee ....150.00 to 160.00
Cookie Jar, Traffic Light 40.00
Cookie Jar, Windmill 60.00
Cookie Jar, Wishing Well 65.00
Cookie Jar, Woodsey Owl 385.00
Cookie Jar Set, Nursery Rhymes, 6 Piece 450.00
Ewer, Yellow Glaze, Mark, 1946, 9 In. 125.00
Flower Holder, Fish, Blue, 4 In. 40.00
Mug, Gorilla, 5 In. 15.00
Pitcher, Olympia, Embossed Fruit, 1905, 6 In. 110.00
Planter, Anvil, 9 In. 21.00
Planter, Caterpillar, Floraline, 13 1/2 In. 40.00
Planter, Fish, Multicolor Pastel, 12 In. 870.00
Planter, Leaf Pattern, Green, 3 x 18 In. 35.00
Planter, Pelican, Yellow, 3 In. ....150.00 to 175.00
Planter, Rabbit, On Stump, Gold Trim, 5 1/2 In. 225.00
Planter, Strawberry, 7 In. 45.00
Planter, Uncle Sam, With Eagle, 9 In. 25.00
Pot, Saucer, Basketweave, Yellow, 4 In. 11.00
Scale, Baby, White, 5 x 5 1/2 In. 76.00

Sprinkler, Turtle, Green, 10 x 5 1/2 In.	72.00
Vase, Antigua, White, 1946, 12 1/2 In.	125.00
Vase, Butterfly, 2 Handles, 10 In.	66.00
Vase, Double Bud, Burgundy Glaze, 1940	125.00
Vase, Green Glaze, Aqua Strap, 12 In.	102.00
Vase, Hyacinth, Pink, 8 In.	.91.00 to 130.00
Vase, Matte Blue Glaze, 10 In.	105.00
Wall Pocket, Grapes, 7 In.	165.00
Wall Pocket, Orange, 7 In.	100.00
Wall Pocket, Pear, 7 In.	85.00

MCKEE is a name associated with various glass enterprises in the United States since 1836, including J. & F. McKee (1850), Bryce, McKee & Co. (1850 to 1854), McKee and Brothers (1865), and National Glass Co. (1899). In 1903, the McKee Glass Company was formed in Jeannette, Pennsylvania. It became McKee Division of the Thatcher Glass Co. in 1951 and was bought out by the Jeannette Corporation in 1961. Pressed glass, kitchenwares, and tablewares were produced. Jeannette Corporation closed in the early 1980s. Additional pieces may be included in the Custard Glass category.

Butter, Side Ridges, Top Medallion, Jade Green, 1 1/4 Lb.	215.00
Cake Plate, Quintec, Pedestal, 11 x 4 In.	48.00
Canister, Flour, Chalaine Blue, 7 x 4 In.	445.00
Custard Cup, Metal Rack, 3 In., 5 Piece	275.00
Mixing Bowl, Beater, Jade Green, Child's, 4 1/2 In.	195.00
Punch Bowl, Cups, Rotec, 13 Piece	60.00
Spooner, Eureka, Splint	42.00
Tumbler, Bottoms Down Nude, Leg Handle, Jade Green, 5 1/2 In.	355.00
Vase, 3 Sides, 3 Nudes, Seville Yellow, c.1930, 8 In.	680.00
Water Server, Metal Spout, 11 1/2 x 5 x 4 1/4 In.	265.00
Window Box, Lions, Jade Green, 9 3/4 x 5 3/8 x 3 1/4 In.	152.00

MECHANICAL BANKS are listed in the Bank category.

MEDICAL office furniture, operating tools, microscopes, thermometers, and other paraphernalia used by doctors are included in this category. Veterinary collectibles are also included here. Medicine bottles are listed in the Bottle category. There are related collectibles listed under Dental.

Bag, Doctor's, Leather, 12 1/2 x 18 In.	33.00
Bedpan, Pottery, Black Transfer Inside, 3 1/4 In.	60.00
Bust, Phrenology, Plaster, Late 19th Century	495.00
Cabinet, Apothecary, 5 Drawers, Pine, Bittersweet Paint, New England	995.00
Cabinet, Apothecary, 14 Short Drawers, Each Labeled, Late 19th Century, 33 x 25 In.	1175.00
Cabinet, Apothecary, 18 Small Drawers, 6 Large Drawers, 19th Century	4800.00
Cabinet, Apothecary, 35 Drawers, Brown Stripe Over White, 23 3/4 x 64 In.	5720.00
Cabinet, Apothecary, Grain Painted, 54 x 30 In.	8050.00
Cabinet, Apothecary, Mahogany, Hinged Lid, Lined Interior, 17 Bottles, 10 x 8 In.	690.00

If you have unopened bottles of drugs or other pharmaceuticals, be sure to check for ether or picric acid. These can explode spontaneously and are dangerous to keep.

Medical, Chicken Blinders, Red Lenses, Lifeguard, 2 In.

Cabinet, Apothecary, Painted, Pine, 64 Drawers, Brass Knobs, 1800s, 39 x 43 In.	5135.00
Cabinet, Apothecary, Pine, 2 Over 3 Drawers, Brass Knobs, 14 x 19 3/4 In.	1510.00
Cabinet, Apothecary, Pine, 16 Drawers In 2 Rows, 30 In.	1100.00
Cabinet, Apothecary, Pine, 18 Drawers, Center Cupboard, Open Shelves, 5 1/2 x 3 Ft. . . .	1120.00
Cabinet, Apothecary, Pine, 24 Drawers, Ring Pulls, Partial Labels, 27 1/4 x 47 1/4 In. . . .	3300.00
Cabinet, Apothecary, Pine, 3 Rows Of Drawers, Red Paint, Brass Pull, 30 5/8 In.	1650.00
Cabinet, Apothecary, Pine, Painted, Shelf, Early 19th Century, 32 x 44 x 12 1/2 In.	6600.00
Cabinet, Apothecary, Rosewood, Interior Fitted With Drawers, Chinese, 30 x 28 In.	520.00
Cabinet, Standing On Table Type, Door With Mirror	155.00
Chart, Book, Dr. Minder's Anatomical Manikin For Female Body, 1910, 8 x 19 In.	140.00
Chest, Apothecary, Pine, 18 Drawers, Center Cupboard, Open Shelves, 5 1/2 x 3 Ft.	1120.00
Chicken Blinders, Red Lenses, Lifeguard, 2 In. . . . . *Illus*	12.00
Cup, Bleeder, Tin, 19th Century, 1 1/2 In., Pair	82.00
Display, Bickmore's Gall Cure, Cardboard, Die Cut, 3 Panels, 33 x 22 x 50 In.	517.00
Display, Parke-Davis, Globe, Plastic, 1 Green & 1 Red, Light-Up, 20 In., Pair	90.00
Fleam, Horn Handle, Borwick, 1800	175.00
Globe, Pharmacy, Cast Iron Holder, Chain, 12 x 9 In.	725.00
Hydrometer, 12 1/2 In.	11.00
Inhaler, Dr. Nelson Boots Chemist, England, 1920	110.00
Inhaler, Improved Shelf Crest, Log Shield Transfer	125.00
Lamp, Vapo Cresolene, Box, Dated 1885, 6 1/2 In.	60.00
Medicine Caddy, Mahogany, 2 Doors, Brass, Bottles, 11 x 9 1/2 x 7 In.	1568.00
Mortar & Pestle, Burl, Turned Pestle, 4 1/2 x 6 1/4 In.	220.00
Mortar & Pestle, Iron, 6 3/4 x 10 In.	176.00
Mortar & Pestle, Oak, 9 x 5 In.	46.00
Mortar & Pestle, Porcelain, Coors, 6 1/2 x 4 In.	29.00
Pill Crusher, G.E. Bauer's Ethyl Chloride, Anesthetic Container, 7 1/2 x 1 1/4 In.	17.00
Pill Maker, Pharmacist's, Brass, Walnut, 1870, 16 x 16 In., 2 Piece	52.00
Pitcher, Drug, Tin Glazed, Handle, Italy, 8 1/4 In.	357.00
Skeleton, Anatomically Correct, Medical Plastics Co., 5 Ft.	495.00
Surgeon's Operating Set, Brass Bail Handles, Mahogany Case, c.1860, 6 Piece	3100.00
Syringe, Veterinary, Saxon, Faichney Instrument Corp., With Boxes Of Needles	40.00
Thermometer, Bath, Dr. Forbes, Wooden, Victoria	28.00
Tool, Trephinine Set, Wooden Box, Mid 19th Century	4650.00
Vaporizer, Vapo-Cresoline, Metal Stand, Glass Font, Milk Glass Chimney, Box, c.1900 . .	179.00
Wheelchair, Oak & Cane Seat, Arrow Co. Erie, Pennsylvania	145.00

MEERSCHAUM is a soft white, gray, or cream-colored mineral named magnesium silicate. The name comes from the German word for seafoam, because it was sometimes found floating in the Black Sea and people thought it was petrified seafoam. Pipes and other pieces of carved meerschaum listed here date from the nineteenth century to the present.

Pipe, Black Man Head, Case, 4 1/2 In.	250.00
Pipe, Carved Grapes & Leaves, Amber Stem	70.00
Pipe, Carved Horse, Case, 4 1/4 In.	187.00
Pipe, Dog In Fenced Yard, Cottage, Fitted Brass Lid, 8 In.	250.00
Pipe, Elephant Head, Amber Stem, Case, 2 3/4 In.	190.00
Pipe, Indian Chief Bust, Velvet Lined Case, Late 1800s, 8 1/2 In.	133.00
Pipe, Leda Swan, Amber Stem, Case, 3 In.	225.00
Pipe, Viking Warrior, Amber Stem, Case, 5 In.	255.00
Pipe, Woman, With Dog, Amber Stem, Case, 7 In.	250.00

MEISSEN is a town in Germany where porcelain has been made since 1710. Any china made in the town can be called Meissen, although the famous Meissen factory made the finest porcelains of the area. The crossed swords mark of the great Meissen factory has been copied by many other firms in Germany and other parts of the world. Pieces of Meissen dinnerware in the Onion pattern are listed in their own category in this book.

Beaker, Chrysanthemums, Butterfly, Oriental Style, Crossed Swords, 1824, 3 1/2 In.	250.00
Beaker, Purple Figures Panel, Scroll Handles, Brown Rim, 2 5/8 In.	1200.00
Bowl, Cover, Reticulated Sides, Garlands, Ram's Heads, Round, Marked, 13 In.	2235.00

Box, Hinged Cover, Allegorical Fire Design, 1900, 7 x 11 In. 6000.00
Bust, Child, Girl In Kerchief, Floral Corsage, 20th Century, 6 In. 630.00
Bust, Man, Woman, Scrolling Pillar, Late 19th Century, 8 1/2 In., Pair 325.00
Cachepot, Ladies & Gentlemen Alternating With Scroll Leaf Bands, 4 In., Pair 1840.00
Candelabrum, 3-Light, Gilt Bronze, Woman, Man, 13 In., Pair 460.00
Candlestick, Cobalt Blue, Rococo Design, Gilt, 6 In. 80.00
Centerpiece, Flower Encrusted, Allegorical, Seasons, Stand, 19th Century, 21 3/8 In. 3600.00
Charger, Cobalt Blue Ground, White Enamel, Gilt Rim, Frame, c.1890, 10 In., Pair 5175.00
Clock, Diana The Huntress, Leaf Circular Case, Enameled Dial, 28 In. 7800.00
Clock, Mantel, Crossed Swords, 19 1/2 In. 3000.00
Coffee Service, Enamel, Rose Sprays, Ozier Molded Rim, Early 20th Century, 26 Piece .. 430.00
Cup & Saucer, Continuous River Landscape, Gilt Rims, 1740, 5 1/8 In. 1320.00
Cup & Saucer, Gilt Flowers, Scalloped, Crossed Swords, 1900s, 5 In. 250.00
Dish, Figurine, Male, Female, Holding Basket, Blue Flowers, Gilt, 12 x 7 1/2 In., Pair ... 1528.00
Dish, Flowers, Square Shaped Top, 10 x 10 In. 172.00
Dish, Peony, Gilt Blossom With Scattered Sprays, Handle, 1760, 7 5/8 In., Pair 5700.00
Dish, Red Flying Fox Above Yellow Squirrel, Brown Rim, 7 3/4 In. 5400.00
Dish, Sweetmeat, Figural, Early 20th Century, 12 In. 105.00
Dish, Sweetmeat, Male & Female Figure Reclining Next To Floral Bowl, 13 In. 6600.00
Figurine, Allegorical Figure On Top Of Alligator, Blue Underglaze, 12 In. 4500.00
Figurine, Bacchus, Holding Wineglass, Leaning On Ewer, 9 3/4 In. 645.00
Figurine, Boy & Girl, Picking Grapes, Signed, c.1900, 4 1/4 In., Pair 335.00
Figurine, Boy & Goat, Oval Terrain Base, Early 20th Century, 5 3/4 In. 1035.00
Figurine, Buddha, Nodding, Elaborate Costume, Painted Mark, 5 1/2 In. 1765.00
Figurine, Cat, With Mouse In Mouth, Gilt Edge, Early 20th Century, 7 In. 920.00
Figurine, Child, Feeding Small Dog, 20th Century, 6 1/4 x 3 1/4 In. 1090.00
Figurine, Children, Feeding Fowl, Germany, 20th Century, 5 & 4 5/8 In., Pair 825.00
Figurine, Cockatoo, On Tree Stump, Base Flower & Leaves, 1930s, 14 1/4 In. 2300.00
Figurine, Cupid, With Flower Garland, Painted Mark, 8 In., Pair 2585.00
Figurine, Fantail Turkey, Tan, Brown, Yellow Neck, Crossed Swords, 1800s, 4 1/4 In. ... 400.00
Figurine, Fish Seller, Cap, Hiked Skirt, Holding Fish, Bucket, Signed, c.1750, 7 1/8 In. .. 575.00
Figurine, Gentleman Farmer, Watering Can, Spade, Late 19th Century, 7 1/2 In. 805.00
Figurine, Gentlewoman, Well Dressed, Feathered Muff, Striped Dress, 8 In. 660.00
Figurine, Girl & Satyr, Releasing Dove, Germany, 20th Century, 6 1/2 In. 880.00
Figurine, Ladies, Shawl & Muff, Pedestal, Doll, 19th Century, 8 In., 3 Piece 2640.00
Figurine, Ladies, Sleeping In Chair, Tying Bow On Sheep, 7 In., 19th Century, 2 Piece ... 1560.00
Figurine, Leda & The Swan, Underglaze Blue Crossed Swords, Incised 433, 7 In. 1035.00
Figurine, Man & Woman, Flowers On Base, Signed, Early 20th Century, 8 3/4 In. 476.00
Figurine, Man, Alpine Dancer, Germany, 20th Century, 7 1/4 In. 590.00
Figurine, Man, In Red Robe, Pointed Beard, Flower Strewn Base, 1880s, 6 1/4 In. 1150.00
Figurine, Monkey Band, Painted, Incised Mark, 5 1/2 In., 3 Piece 2530.00
Figurine, Mother & Daughter, Holding Letter & Posy, Gilt Base, 9 In. 1300.00
Figurine, Pagoda, Nodding, Crossed Swords, Incised 154, 5 1/2 In. 2300.00
Figurine, Pastry Seller, Young Woman Wearing Flowered Apron, 1755, 7 3/4 In. 3000.00
Figurine, Putto, Allegorical Of Winter, Fur Lined Cap & Coat, Late 19th Century, 3 1/2 In. 550.00
Figurine, Putto, Gardener, Digging With Spade, Potted Plants, 20th Century, 4 3/4 In. 575.00
Figurine, Putto, Preparing Cup Of Chocolate, Early 20th Century, 4 In. 805.00
Figurine, Sentiment, 18th Century Woman, Birdcage, c.1900, 6 In. 460.00
Figurine, Shepherd & Shepherdess, Holding Hands, Germany, 20th Century, 6 In. 820.00
Figurine, Winged Cupid, Mending Broken Heart, Gilt Edge, 6 3/4 In. 1000.00
Figurine, Woman, Alpine Dancer, Germany, 20th Century, 5 1/2 In. 765.00
Group, 2 Putti Carrying Rabbit, Early 20th Century, 4 1/2 In. 1495.00
Group, 2 Putti Farmers With Plough, Early 20th Century, 6 1/2 In. 635.00
Group, 3 Nude Allegorical Figures, Flanked By Cupid, 1886, 14 In. 6600.00
Group, 3 Soldiers, Blue Underglaze, 20th Century, 7 3/4 In. 1560.00
Group, 3 Warriors & Blackamoor On Back Of Elephant, 15 In. 8400.00
Group, 4 Allegorical Figures, Allegorical Seminude Figure Standing, 1900, 17 In. 4500.00
Group, Allegorical Figure Holding Cornucopia, Seated On Back Of Lion, 9 In. 4200.00
Group, Allegorical Figure Holding Globe, Surrounded By Putti, 7 1/2 In. 3600.00
Group, Allegorical Figure, Seminude, Flanked By Flying Putti, 1900, 20 In. 7200.00
Group, Allegorical, Autumn, 4 Frolicking Putti, Goats, Early 20th Century, 7 3/4 In. 1955.00
Group, Allegorical, Spring & Autumn, Both Seated, Bunch Of Grapes, 1760, 5 In., Pair .. 4500.00
Group, Allegorical, Summer, Girl Playing Lute, Seated Boy, Early 20th Century, 6 1/4 In. 920.00

Group, Allegorical, Winter, 4 Putti, Warming By Fire, Early 20th Century, 6 1/2 In. 2185.00
Group, Apple Pickers, Crossed Swords, 10 1/2 In. 575.00
Group, Capture Of The Tritons, Blue Underglaze, 13 In. ....2400.00 to 3300.00
Group, Children At Various Pursuits, Pressing Grapes, Acier, 1900, 12 In. 4800.00
Group, Children, Dancing In Ring, Late 19th Century, 6 In. 4200.00
Group, Couple, 18th Century Style, 6 In. 200.00
Group, Female Figure, Seated, On Back Of Lion, 19th Century, 12 In. 3900.00
Group, Figures On Rocky Ground, Blue Underglaze, Late 19th Century, 12 In. 2700.00
Group, Girl, With Goat, Painted & Incised Marks, 6 In. 440.00
Group, Lady, Seated Near Tree Writing In Book, Blue Underglaze, 9 In. 5100.00
Group, Man, Presenting Caged Rodent To Gentleman, 1900, 10 In. 3600.00
Group, Oriental Mother, 2 Sons, Flowers Encrusted On Base, 5 1/2 In. 2000.00
Group, Putti With Goat, Early 20th Century, 4 In. 230.00
Group, Silenus Riding Donkey, Flanked By Allegorical Figures, 8 1/4 In. 1440.00
Jug, Pear Shape, Flowering Peony Branches, Turquoise, Blue, 1730, 6 1/8 In. 5700.00
Lamp, 2 Children, Sheaf Of Wheat, Figural, Blue Crossed Swords, 16 In. 140.00
Liquor Barrel, Figural Warrior Top, Battle Scenes, Cherub, Crossed Swords, 17 In. 4025.00
Plate, Floral Spray, Scalloped Edge, Yellow, Red, Blue, Gilt, 9 In., 6 Piece 763.00
Plate, Floral, Fisherfolk By Harbor, Burgundy, Gilt, 9 1/2 In. 470.00
Plate, Ozier Rim, Floral Center, Gilt Accents, c.1895, 9 5/8 In., 8 Piece 460.00
Plate, Transfer Fruit, Signed, 10 1/2 In., 6 Piece 195.00
Pot, Cover, Blue, Green, Turquoise Underglaze, 1730, 4 3/8 In. 3000.00
Saucer, Apollo & Daphne Embracing While Cupid Aims His Arrow, 1760, 6 In. 1920.00
Seagull, White, Max Esser, 20th Century, 16 1/2 In. 900.00
Serving Dish, Geometric, Gold Leaves, Cobalt Blue, Crossed Swords, 9 1/2 x 12 3/4 In. ... 390.00
Snuffbox, Oval, Painted In Brown, Silver Mounted, Cover, 2 3/4 In. 5700.00
Sugar, Cover, Blackamoor, Mid 19th Century, 7 x 6 x 5 1/2 In. 1035.00
Tazza, Swirling Leaves Up To Bowl, Reticulated Sides, Medallion Trim, 9 x 9 In. 330.00
Tea & Coffee Service, Flowers, White Ground, 20th Century, 30 Piece 840.00
Tea & Coffee Service, Purple Indian, Gold Dots, 1900s, 63 Piece 2990.00
Tea Canister, Cover, Chinoiserie Figures, Spray Design, Gilt, 1725, 5 In. 3900.00
Tea Canister, Cover, Turquoise Bamboo, Peony Branches, 1740, 5 1/8 In. 2040.00
Teabowl & Saucer, Hand Painted Flower Sprigs, 19th Century, 4 3/4 In. 57.00
Teapot, Cover, Man, Riding On Back Of Buffalo Conversing With Woman, 4 In. 4500.00
Teapot, Cover, Pomegranate Molded With Trailing Branches, 1730, 4 1/4 In. 1320.00
Teapot, Cover, Quail Beside Blossoming Prunus Tree, 1735, 4 3/8 In. 3000.00
Teapot, Encrusted, Miniature, Round, Leafy S-Scroll Handle, c.1900, 4 1/2 In. 230.00
Teapot, Insects & Flowers, Puce, Marked, 18th Century, 4 In. 2420.00
Tray, Hunting Scene, Hounds Chasing Deer, Gilt Scroll Border, 21 In. 2700.00
Trivet, 5 3/4 In. 115.00
Tureen, Melon, Applied Looped Stalk Handle, Cover, Mid 18th Century, 6 1/4 In. 5100.00
Urn, Coiled Snake & Leaf Handle, Off-White Ground, Pedestal Base, 15 1/4 In. 690.00
Urn, Gilt Flowers, Landscape Reserves, Openwork Top, Signed, 27 In. 345.00
Urn, Reticulated Cover, Wreath Finial, Flowers, Gilt, Handles, Plinth, 11 1/2 x 6 In. 297.00
Vase, Applied Blue Flowers On Vines, Gilt Bronze Base, 7 1/2 In. 633.00
Vase, Basket Weave Design, Applied Flowers, Fruit, Gilt, 16 3/4 In., Pair 5750.00
Vase, Cobalt Blue, Gilt, Double Entwined Snake Handles, 19th Century, Pair 1400.00
Vase, Cobalt Blue, White, Gilt Trim, Handles, Baluster, Marked, 25 In., Pair 3450.00
Vase, Cover, Courting Couples, Eagle Finial, Enamel, Gilt, Augustus Rex, 10 In. 1763.00
Vase, Hunt Scene, Boars, Deer & Dogs, Late 19th Century, 17 In. 3900.00
Vase, Thistle Shape, Gilt Etched Cartouches, Mythological Figures, 24 x 12 In., Pair 1725.00

MERCURY GLASS, or silvered glass, was first made in the 1850s. It lost
favor for a while but became popular again about 1910. It looks like a
piece of silver.

Figurine, Reindeer, Label, Germany, 5 1/2 In., Pair 88.00
Group, Penguin, 2 1/4 In. & 4 In., 3 Piece 104.00
Pitcher, Grapes & Ferns, Applied Clear Handle, Pontil, 6 1/2 In. 175.00
Salt, Grapes & Vine, Engraved, 2 In. 50.00
Vase, Hourglass Shape, Flowers, Leaf, Bird, Gold Interior, 12 In. 255.00
Vase, Oval, Ribbed, Applied Handles, 18 In. 300.00
Vase, Urn Shape, Footed, 14 3/8 In. 235.00

MERRIMAC POTTERY Company was founded by Thomas Nickerson in Newburyport, Massachusetts, in 1902. The company made art pottery, garden pottery, and reproductions of Roman pottery. The pottery burned to the ground in 1908.

Chamberstick, Dark & Light Green Feathered Matte Glaze, 8 1/2 x 5 1/2 In.	690.00
Vase, Globular, Deep Cucumber Green Feathered Design, Hunter Green, 2 3/4 In.	385.00
Vase, Green Matte Glaze, Tapered, 11 1/2 x 5 1/2 In.	920.00
Vase, Teal Green Luster Glaze, Black Shading, 4 1/2 x 5 1/4 In.	1430.00

METTLACH, Germany, is a city where the Villeroy and Boch factories worked. Steins from the firm are marked with the word *Mettlach* or the castle mark. They date from about 1842. *PUG* means painted under glaze. The steins can be dated from the marks on the bottom, which include a date-number code. Other pieces may be listed in the Villeroy & Boch category.

Ashtray, No. 3883, PUG, 6 In.	92.00
Beaker, Gambrinus, Men Drinking, Relief, 6 In.	167.00
Beaker, No. 2327-1014, 1/4 Liter, Munich Child, H. Schlitt, PUG	105.00
Beaker, No. 2327-1140, 1/4 Liter, Men Playing Cards, H. Schlitt, PUG	115.00
Beaker, No. 2327-1200, 1/4 Liter, Nurnberg, PUG	94.00
Beaker, No. 2327-1200, 1/4 Liter, State Of Indiana, PUG	193.00
Beaker, No. 2327-1232, 1/4 Liter, Boy Sitting On Barrel, PUG	210.00
Beaker, No. 2327-1290C, 1/4 Liter, Bavarian Crest, PUG	92.00
Beaker, No. 2327-1290H, 1/4 Liter, Suede, Coat Of Arms, Sweden, PUG	160.00
Beaker, No. 2842-1173, 1/4 Liter, Dwarf, H. Schlitt, PUG	225.00
Beaker, No. 3365, 1/4 Liter, Art Nouveau, Etched	300.00 to 390.00
Boot, No. 225, Character, Platinum, 6 1/2 In.	240.00
Bottle, Lid, Russian Language Design, PUG, 1 Liter	362.00
Bowl, No. 2965III, Art Nouveau, Etched, 7 1/2 In.	288.00
Candlestick, No. 3339, Art Nouveau, Etched, 8 1/4 In., Pair	450.00
Charger, Carved, Painted Horse Portrait, Impressed Mark, 14 In.	173.00
Charger, Carved, Painted Maiden Design, Impressed Mark, 10 1/2 In.	150.00
Charger, Pottery, Landscape & Castle, Marked Neuschwanstein, 14 In.	250.00
Compote, No. 346, Grapevines, Leaves, 9 1/4 x 11 In.	175.00
Cup & Saucer, No. 2962, Secessionist Trees, Blue, Ochre, Ivory, 8 Piece	430.00
Flask, Military Transfer, Soldiers, Canon, 1904-1906, 7 1/2 In.	605.00
Mug, Barrel Form, John Brewing Co., 4 1/4 In.	160.00
Mug, Factory Scene, South Bend Brewing Assoc., 1910s	60.00
Mug, Fauerbach Brewing, Mercury Mark, '96, 4 1/4 In.	740.00
Mug, Hausmann Brewing Co., Mercury Mark, '97, 4 1/4 In.	660.00
Pitcher, No. 1638, Repeating Design, Etched, Glazed Relief, Handle, 5 In.	160.00
Pitcher, No. 6080, Green, 7 1/2 In.	100.00
Planter, No. 2732, 2 Sides, Art Nouveau, Threading, Glazed, Handles, 5 1/2 x 12 1/2 In.	634.00
Plaque, No. 1044, Village At Seashore, Blue, 17 In.	360.00
Plaque, No. 1044-102b, Ducks Flying From Lake, PUG, 12 In.	160.00 to 386.00
Plaque, No. 1044-1122, Girl Feeding Swan, H. Schlitt, PUG, 17 In.	1220.00
Plaque, No. 1044-131, Munster, Freiburg, PUG, 12 In.	242.00
Plaque, No. 1044-133, Einfart In Den Naerofjord, PUG, 14 In.	362.00
Plaque, No. 1044-1352, Heidelberg Castle, PUG, 17 1/2 In.	438.00
Plaque, No. 1044-161, St. Goar, Faint, PUG, 12 In.	69.00
Plaque, No. 1044-162, Niederwalden Kmal, PUG, 14 In.	362.00
Plaque, No. 1044-167a, Castle, PUG, 13 In.	242.00
Plaque, No. 1044-264, Soldier, Woman, 18 In.	468.00
Plaque, No. 1044-485, Castle, PUG, 12 In.	403.00
Plaque, No. 1044-5189, People At Seashore, 17 In.	230.00
Plaque, No. 1044-527, Wirtschaft Zur Treib Am Vierwaldstattersee, PUG, 12 In.	242.00
Plaque, No. 1044-83, Large Bird, Flowers, PUG, 14 In.	362.00
Plaque, No. 1044-9020, Chamois, PUG, 17 In.	483.00
Plaque, No. 1044-9028, Dachshund, PUG, 14 In.	423.00
Plaque, No. 1044-9040, Chillon, PUG, 12 In.	302.00
Plaque, No. 1044-94, Altes Stadtthor Cochem, PUG, 12 In.	156.00

Plaque, No. 1044-97, Ruine Bischofstein Bei Hatzenport, PUG, 12 In. 242.00
Plaque, No. 1365, Castle, Landscape, 17 In. 605.00
Plaque, No. 1617, Figural, Woman With Wings On Branch, 16 In. 1087.00
Plaque, No. 1770, William Tell, Split Apple, Outdoor Scene, 15 In. 415.00
Plaque, No. 2142, Bismarck On Horseback, Etched, 15 1/2 In. 920.00
Plaque, No. 2188, Knight On Horseback, Haus Habsburg, Etched, 17 In. 2995.00
Plaque, No. 2443, Woman With Attendants, Green Ground, Signed, 1898, 19 In. 850.00
Plaque, No. 2550, Bird In Flight With Moonlight, Etched, L. Chevroton, 18 In. 1086.00 to 1148.00
Plaque, No. 2622, Man Holding Beaker, Etched, 7 1/2 In. 207.00
Plaque, No. 2626, Man Drinking, Etched, 7 1/2 In. 217.00
Plaque, No. 2645, Eagles On Mountain Top, 18 In. 2415.00
Plaque, No. 2805, Deer In Forest, Art Nouveau Border, 15 In. 1449.00
Plaque, No. 5038, Cologne City Hall, Delft, 17 In. 420.00
Plaque, No. 5177, Stolzenfels Castle, Blue Delft, 12 In. 132.00
Plaque, No. 7013, Trojan Warriors On Boat, Cream Figures, Signed Stahl, 19 In. 850.00
Plaque, Warrior Scene, Signed Schults, Dated 1910, 14 1/2 In. 750.00
Plaque, Woman Smelling Flowers, Pottery, 20 In. 1150.00
Plate, No. 1082, Geometric Design, Etched, Glazed, 14 In. 345.00
Plate, No. 2096, Secessionist Trees, Blue, Ocher, Ivory, 1900, 8 1/2 In., 8 Piece 430.00
Plate, No. 3096, Secessionist Trees, Blue, Ocher, Ivory, 1900, 7 1/2 In., 6 Piece 403.00
Pokal, No. 168, Drinking Scenes Spiral, Relief, Set On Lid, 20 In. 575.00
Punch Bowl, No. 1888, 6 Liter, Prussian Eagle, Blind Folded Woman Under Handle, Lid . 725.00
Punch Bowl, No. 2087, 8 Liter, Relief Figures Dancing 408.00
Punch Bowl, No. 2234, 6 Liter, Birds Eating Grapes From Vines, Figural Dwarf Lid 495.00
Punch Bowl, No. 2339-1028, 7 1/2 Liter, Dwarfs Harvesting, Pressing Grapes, PUG 495.00
Punch Bowl, No. 2806, 9 1/2 Liter, Bacchus, Floral, Cameo 460.00
Punch Bowl, No. 2814, 7 1/2 Liter, Art Nouveau, Women's Portraits, Etched, Lid 1955.00
Punch Bowl, No. 3037-1315, 9 Liter, Castle Ruins, Dwarf With Wine, PUG, Lid 460.00
Punch Bowl, No. 3037-1348, 6 Liter, Kaiser & Kaiserin, Underplate, PUG 725.00
Punch Bowl, No. 3360, 8 Liter, Art Nouveau, Grapes, Lid, Underplate, Etched, 19 In. . . . 2536.00
Punch Bowl, No. 375, 10 Liter, Figural Relief, Animal Heads, Grapevines, Lid 748.00
Stein, Dance & Celebration, Jokester, 8 1/2 In. 330.00
Stein, No. 202, 1/2 Liter, Choir, Inlaid Lid 206.00
Stein, No. 485, 1/2 Liter, Musicians, People Dancing In Vines, Relief, Inlaid Lid 230.00
Stein, No. 675, 1/2 Liter, Barrel, Figural Inlaid Lid With Drunken Cavalier 288.00
Stein, No. 817, 1/2 Liter, Verse, Flowers 155.00
Stein, No. 1028, 4 Liter, Hay Harvesting Scene, Tree Trunk Ground, Inlaid Lid, 14 In. . . . 316.00
Stein, No. 1053, 1 Liter, Dwarfs Drinking, Etched, Inlaid Lid . . . . .748.00 to 805.00
Stein, No. 1060, 1/2 Liter, Barrel, Figural Inlaid Lid With Fox 403.00
Stein, No. 1120, 3 1/4 Liter, Repeating Design, Mosaic, Inlaid Lid 265.00
Stein, No. 1144, 1/2 Liter, Horse Pulling Wagon, People, Relief, Inlaid Lid 518.00
Stein, No. 1155, 1/2 Liter, Repeating Leaf & Acorn, Inlaid Lid 518.00
Stein, No. 1261, 1/2 Liter, Repeating Floral, Mosiac, Glazed Relief, Matching Lid 350.00
Stein, No. 1266, 1/2 Liter, Men Drinking, Relief, Inlaid Lid 190.00
Stein, No. 1467, 1/2 Liter, Harvest Scene, Relief, Inlaid Lid 240.00
Stein, No. 1494, 5 3/5 Liter, Man Drinking, Seated On Barrel, Etched Pewter Lid 1955.00
Stein, No. 1526, 1 Liter, Munchner Bock Bier Fest, Berliner, Unions Brauerei 316.00
Stein, No. 1526, 1/2 Liter, Crest, Transfer, Enamel, Pewter Lid, c.1907 . . . . 230.00
Stein, No. 1526, 1/2 Liter, Hot Air Balloon, Relief Pewter Lid 748.00
Stein, No. 1526, 1/2 Liter, Man Looking At Moon, Transfer, Enameled, Pewter Lid 210.00
Stein, No. 1526-1110, 1 Liter, Barmaid, Relief, PUG, Pewter Lid 400.00
Stein, No. 1526-587, 1/2 Liter, Cavalier Toasting, Pewter Lid 145.00
Stein, No. 1526-598, 1 Liter, Man Holding Rifle, Pewter Lid, PUG 285.00
Stein, No. 1526-702, 3 Liter, Beer Parade, PUG, Pewter Lid 270.00
Stein, No. 1530-581, 1/2 Liter, Student Smoking Pipe, PUG, Inlaid Lid 405.00
Stein, No. 1645, 1/2 Liter, Man With Guitar, Tapestry, Pewter Lid . . . . .240.00 to 276.00
Stein, No. 1675, 1/2 Liter, Heidelberg Castle, Etched, Inlaid Lid 605.00
Stein, No. 1675, 1/2 Liter, Heidelberg, 500 Year Jublium Plaquard, Etched, Inlaid Lid . . . 725.00
Stein, No. 1734, 1 1/2 Liter, Lovers, C. Warth, Etched, Inlaid Lid . . . . .1150.00 to 1208.00
Stein, No. 1786, 1 Liter, St. Florian Extinguishing Fire, Pewter Lid 1265.00
Stein, No. 1787, 1/2 Liter, Repeating Design, Glazed, Mosaic, Inlaid Lid 430.00
Stein, No. 1796, 1/2 Liter, Cavalier Drinking, Etched, Inlaid Lid 437.00
Stein, No. 1797, 1/2 Liter, 4 Cards, Inlaid Coin Lid 805.00

Stein, No. 1817, 3 Liter, Man & High Wheel Bicycle, Etched, Pewter Lid 2415.00
Stein, No. 1821, 3 1/4 Liter, Man Holding Guitar, Relief, Inlaid Lid 305.00
Stein, No. 1830, 3 Liter, Cavaliers, 4 Sides, Etched, Inlaid Lid 1613.00
Stein, No. 1856, 1/2 Liter, Postman, Inlaid Lid, Silver Plating 1087.00
Stein, No. 1863, 1/2 Liter, Stuttgart, Etched, Inlaid Lid 605.00
Stein, No. 1872, 2 Liter, Woman With Children, Relief, Inlaid Lid 317.00
Stein, No. 1909, 1/2 Liter, Bavaria, Flowers, Hand Painted, Pewter Lid 195.00
Stein, No. 1909, 1/2 Liter, Tapestry, PUG, Pewter Lid, Pewter Hinge 605.00
Stein, No. 1909-702, 1/2 Liter, Beer Parade, PUG, Pewter Lid 289.00
Stein, No. 1909-727, 1/2 Liter, Dwarfs Bowling, PUG, H. Schlitt, Pewter Lid .... 305.00 to 336.00
Stein, No. 1909-943, 1/2 Liter, Knights Taking Barrel From Innkeeper, Pewter Lid 374.00
Stein, No. 1909-983, 1/2 Liter, Falstaff, PUG, Pewter Lid 240.00
Stein, No. 1914, 1/2 Liter, 4F Stein, Bearded Man On Thumb Lift, Etched, Inlaid Lid 575.00
Stein, No. 1932, 1/2 Liter, Cavaliers Toasting, Inlaid Lid 518.00
Stein, No. 1934, 1/2 Liter, Military Uniforms, Inlaid Lid With Eagle 1064.00
Stein, No. 1940, 3 Liter, Keeper Of The Wine Cellar, Etched, Inlaid Lid 1035.00
Stein, No. 1946, 1/2 Liter, Courting Scene, Relief Pewter Lid 472.00
Stein, No. 1995, 1/2 Liter, Musician Drinking, Etched, Inlaid Lid 369.00
Stein, No. 1997, 1/2 Liter, George Ehret, New York Brewer, Etched, PUG .... 136.00 to 385.00
Stein, No. 2001A, 1/2 Liter, Law, Glazed, Hand Painted, Inlaid Lid 845.00
Stein, No. 2001C, 1/2 Liter, Scholars, Glazed, Hand Painted, Inlaid Lid .... 605.00 to 1265.00
Stein, No. 2001D, 1/2 Liter, Mathematics, Glazed, Hand Painted, Inlaid Lid 605.00
Stein, No. 2001I, 1/2 Liter, Theology, Glazed, Hand Painted, Inlaid Lid 890.00
Stein, No. 2002, 1/2 Liter, Munchen Skyline, Etched, Inlaid Lid, Lion Thumblift 346.00
Stein, No. 2007, 1/2 Liter, Black Cat, Etched, Inlaid Lid, F. Stuck 310.00
Stein, No. 2008, 1/2 Liter, Trumpeter On Horse, Etched, Inlaid Lid 725.00
Stein, No. 2024, 1/2 Liter, Berlin Skyline, Etched, Glazed, Inlaid Lid 350.00
Stein, No. 2025, 1/2 Liter, Cherubs, Etched, Inlaid Lid 288.00
Stein, No. 2028, 1/2 Liter, Gasthaus, Inlaid Lid 438.00
Stein, No. 2029, 1/2 Liter, Military Scene, Inlaid Lid 730.00
Stein, No. 2031, 1/2 Liter, Military Scene, Inlaid Lid 966.00
Stein, No. 2050, 1/2 Liter, Wedding, Figural, Slipper Finial, Inlaid Lid 1208.00
Stein, No. 2052, 1/4 Liter, Munich Child, Etched, Inlaid Lid 295.00
Stein, No. 2057, 1/3 Liter, Dancing Scene, Etched, Inlaid Lid 240.00
Stein, No. 2057, Festive Scene, Etched, Inlaid Lid, 1/2 Liter 349.00
Stein, No. 2074, 1/2 Liter, Bird In Cage, Etched, Inlaid Lid 3335.00
Stein, No. 2075, 1/2 Liter, Telegraph, Etched, Glazed, Inlaid Lid .... 1725.00 to 1930.00
Stein, No. 2076, 3 1/4 Liter, Blue, Shield In Each Panel, Relief, Inlaid Lid 290.00
Stein, No. 2083, 1/2 Liter, Boar Hunting Scene, Etched, Inlaid Lid 1225.00
Stein, No. 2083, 1/3 Liter, Boar Hunting Scene, Etched, Inlaid Lid 547.00
Stein, No. 2086, 1/2 Liter, Festive Scene, Relief, Inlaid Lid 230.00
Stein, No. 2089, 1/2 Liter, Winged Barmaid Serving Man, Inlaid Lid 834.00
Stein, No. 2090, 1/2 Liter, Man At Table With Cards, Inlaid Lid, H. Schlitt 427.00
Stein, No. 2090, 1/3 Liter, Man Smoking At Table, Inlaid Lid 90.00
Stein, No. 2091, 1/2 Liter, St. Florian Extinguishing Fire, Etched, Inlaid Lid, H. Schlitt .. 1035.00
Stein, No. 2092, 1/2 Liter, Dwarf Adjusting Clock, Inlaid Lid, H. Schlitt 604.00
Stein, No. 2093, 1/2 Liter, Cards, Etched, Inlaid Lid 575.00
Stein, No. 2100, 1/2 Liter, Germans & Romans, Etched, Inlaid Lid, H. Schlitt .... 805.00 to 933.00
Stein, No. 2104, 1 1/2 Liter, Cavalier Leaning On Staff, Etched, Inlaid Lid 1208.00
Stein, No. 2106, 1/2 Liter, Monkeys In Cage, Figural Monkey Handle, Pewter Lid 1610.00
Stein, No. 2107, 2 1/4 Liter, Gambrinus, Etched, Inlaid Lid, H. Schlitt 1495.00
Stein, No. 2118, 3 Liter, John C. White, White & Crafts, Maltsters, Buffalo, Pewter Lid .. 1237.00
Stein, No. 2140, 1/2 Liter, Lowenbrau Brewery Logo, PUG, Pewter Lid 1323.00
Stein, No. 2140-786, 1/2 Liter, Eisenbahn Regiment No. 2, Pewter Lid 288.00
Stein, No. 2140-840, 1/2 Liter, Infanterie Regiment No. 45, PUG, Relief Pewter Lid 719.00
Stein, No. 2140-941, 1/2 Liter, Beer Barometer, PUG, Pewter Lid 299.00
Stein, No. 2140-942, 1/2 Liter, Night Watchman Meets Rooster, PUG, Pewter Lid 345.00
Stein, No. 2177-1085, 1/4 Liter, Children Having Picnic, Pewter Lid 357.00
Stein, No. 2177-959, 1/4 Liter, Knight Resting, PUG, Pewter Lid 217.00
Stein, No. 2177-960, 1/4 Liter, Jester Playing Mandolin, PUG, Pewter Lid 168.00
Stein, No. 2183-953, 3 1/4 Liter, Dwarfs, PUG, Inlaid Lid 363.00
Stein, No. 2204, 1 Liter, Prussian Eagle 1570.00
Stein, No. 2205, 5 1/4 Liter, Hunters & Diana, Squirrel On Inlaid Lid 1300.00

Stein, No. 2206, 3 Liter, Gasthaus Scene, Etched, Pewter Lid 834.00
Stein, No. 2210, 3 1/4 Liter, Bowling Scene, Relief, Inlaid Lid 362.00
Stein, No. 2223, 5 1/2 Liter, Man On Horse Receiving Drink, Etched, Pewter Lid 2669.00
Stein, No. 2230, 1/2 Liter, Man Drinking With Barmaid, Etched, Inlaid Lid, H. Schlitt ... 513.00
Stein, No. 2235, 1/2 Liter, Barmaid Holding Steins, Etched, Inlaid Lid 661.00
Stein, No. 2255, 1 Liter, Etruscan Wedding, Etched, Inlaid Lid 1086.00
Stein, No. 2282, 1/2 Liter, Men Caught Drinking In Beer Cellar, Etched, Inlaid Lid 540.00 to 589.00
Stein, No. 2324, 1/2 Liter, Early Football Game, Figural Inlaid Lid Of Football 2185.00
Stein, No. 2382, 1 Liter, Thirsty Rider In Cellar, Inlaid Lid 1179.00
Stein, No. 2394, 1/2 Liter, Siegfried Slaying Dragon 345.00
Stein, No. 2401, 1/2 Liter, Tannhauser In The Venusberg, Etched, Inlaid Lid 645.00
Stein, No. 2401, 1 Liter, Tannhauser In The Venusberg, Etched, Inlaid Lid 1380.00
Stein, No. 2402, 1/2 Liter, Courting Of Siegfried, Inlaid Lid 690.00
Stein, No. 2430, Cavalier Drinking, 16 In. 1430.00
Stein, No. 2441, 1/2 Liter, Men Rolling Dice, Music Box Base, Etched, Inlaid Lid 535.00
Stein, No. 2455, 6 4/5 Liter, Lohengrin Wedding, Knight Finial, Pewter Lid 4600.00
Stein, No. 2526, 1/2 Liter, Hunting Scene, Glazed Relief, Creussen, Pewter Lid 1811.00
Stein, No. 2530, 1 Liter, Boar Hunting Scene, Cameo, Inlaid Lid 748.00
Stein, No. 2580, 1 Liter, Castle Scene, Body Forms Tower, Inlaid Lid 1064.00
Stein, No. 2581, 1/2 Liter, Choir, Etched, Inlaid Lid 583.00
Stein, No. 2582, 1 Liter, Jester Performing, Etched, Inlaid Lid, F. Quidenus 1000.00
Stein, No. 2627, 1/2 Liter, Bicycle, Cameo, Inlaid Lid, Stahl 920.00
Stein, No. 2762, 2 Liter, 3 Scenes Of Couples, Grapes, Cameo, Inlaid Lid 1265.00
Stein, No. 2765, 1 Liter, Knight On Horse, Etched, Inlaid Lid, H. Schlitt 1380.00
Stein, No. 2767, 1 Liter, Munich Child With Barrel, Inlaid Lid, H. Schlitt 920.00
Stein, No. 2768, 1/2 Liter, People In Black Forest Attire, Etched, Inlaid Lid 546.00
Stein, No. 2776, 1/2 Liter, Keeper Of Wine Cellar, Etched, Inlaid Lid ....697.00 to 1345.00
Stein, No. 2778, 1 Liter, Carnival, Etched, Inlaid Lid, H. Schlitt 1898.00
Stein, No. 2788-6142, 1/2 Liter, Cavalier Sitting At Table, Rookwood, Pewter Lid 423.00
Stein, No. 2796, 3 Liter, Heidelberg, Etched, Inlaid Lid 532.00
Stein, No. 2800, 1/2 Liter, Art Nouveau Hops, Inlaid Lid 604.00
Stein, No. 2802, 1/2 Liter, Wheat & Heart Design, Art Nouveau, Etched, Inlaid Lid 638.00
Stein, No. 2828, 1/2 Liter, Town Of Wartberg 2173.00
Stein, No. 2833B, 1/2 Liter, Man Sitting Under Tree, Etched, Inlaid Lid 574.00
Stein, No. 2833C, 1/2 Liter, River Scene, Lorelei, Etched 574.00
Stein, No. 2833E, 1/2 Liter, Soldiers, Etched, Inlaid Lid ....483.00 to 600.00
Stein, No. 2888, 1/2 Liter, Three Men Walking, Etched, Inlaid Lid 475.00
Stein, No. 2893-1239, 3 1/4 Liter, Two Young Girls, Chicken, Rooster, PUG, Pewter Lid . 810.00
Stein, No. 2921, 2 4/5 Liter, Campfire, Etched, Inlaid Lid 604.00
Stein, No. 2950, 1 Liter, Bavarian Crest, Cameo, Pewter Lid 546.00
Stein, No. 2957, 1/2 Liter, Bowling Scene, Etched, Inlaid Lid ....492.00 to 518.00
Stein, No. 3008, 1/2 Liter, Man Reading Paper, F. Ringer, Pewter Lid 276.00
Stein, No. 3043, 1/2 Liter, Munchen, Etched, Glazed, Inlaid Lid 1162.00
Stein, No. 3078-403, 1/2 Liter, Wheat, Transfer, Enameled, Bavaria, Pewter Lid 367.00
Stein, No. 3078-421, 1/2 Liter, Floral Wreath, Transfer, Enameled, Bavaria, Inlaid Lid ... 360.00
Stein, No. 3079-404, 1/2 Liter, Repeating Line, Hand Painted, Pewter Lid 360.00
Stein, No. 3079-493, 1/2 Liter, Repeating Design, Bavaria, Pewter Lid 236.00
Stein, No. 3089, 1 Liter, Diogenes, Etched, Inlaid Lid, H. Schlitt 1438.00
Stein, No. 3099, 3 Liter, Diogenes, Etched, Inlaid Lid, H. Schlitt 2415.00
Stein, No. 3136, 1 3/4 Liter, Art Nouveau, Etched, Inlaid Lid 485.00
Stein, No. 3185-1282, 1/2 Liter, Hunters Talking, PUG 150.00
Stein, No. 3185-1359, 1/2 Liter, Hiker Eating Under Tree, PUG, Inlaid Lid 489.00
Stein, No. 3202, 1/2 Liter, Automobile, Etched, Inlaid Lid 575.00
Stein, No. 3251, 1/2 Liter, People Drinking, Etched, Inlaid Lid 574.00
Stein, No. 5189, 1/2 Liter, Man Drinking, Faience, Pewter Lid 375.00
Stein, Regimental, 1/2 Liter, Hand Painted, Pewter Lid 575.00
Stein, Soldier & Train Transfer, Eagle Finial, 10 1/4 In. 605.00
Tankard, Man Drinking At Table, Pewter Lid, 1 Liter 138.00
Tankard, No. 1818, Etched, Drinking Scene, Relief, Pewter Lid 1840.00
Tobacco Jar, No. 2268-1047, Dwarfs Smoking & Mushrooms, PUG, Lid, 7 In. 377.00
Tray, No. 2960, Art Nouveau Design, Etched, 15 In. 513.00
Tray, No. 3363, Art Nouveau Design, Etched, 5 1/4 x 10 In. 390.00
Trivet, No. 3330, Art Nouveau Design, Etched, 3-Footed, 8 In. 380.00

Tumbler, American Eagle Design, Impressed Mark, 5 In., Pair 104.00
Vase, No. 1462, 4 Scenes Of Women, Repeating On 1 Side, 13 In. 230.00
Vase, No. 1579, Repeating Teardrop, Etched, Glazed, 4 1/4 In. 160.00
Vase, No. 1631, Fruit On Branch, Leaves, Etched, 10 1/2 In. 518.00
Vase, No. 1829, Repeating Design, Mosaic, Relief, 9 In., Pair 276.00
Vase, No. 1876, Repeating Design, Etched, Glazed, 6 1/4 In. 259.00
Vase, No. 2209, Siegfried Scenes, Figural Handles, Woman Wearing Helmet, 17 1/2 In. .. 2300.00
Vase, No. 2449, Women, Men Reverse, Cameo, 7 1/2 In. 718.00
Vase, No. 2467, Art Nouveau Flowers, Etched, 4 Handles, 11 3/4 In. 2657.00
Vase, No. 2474, Floral, Art Nouveau, Etched, Stoneware Ring Rim, 2 3/4 In. 345.00
Vase, No. 2902-1014, Munich Child On Globe, PUG, H. Schlitt, 14 In. .... 518.00 to 845.00
Vase, No. 2913, Art Nouveau, Etched, 13 3/4 In. 805.00
Vase, No. 3110, Repeating Design, Relief, 2 1/2 x 4 In. 145.00
Vase, No. 3358, Repeating Design, Etched, 12 1/4 In. 690.00

MILK GLASS was named for its milky white color. It was first made in England during the 1700s. The height of its popularity in the United States was from 1870 to 1880. It is now correct to refer to some colored glass as blue milk glass, black milk glass, etc. Reproductions of milk glass are being made and sold in many stores. Related pieces may be listed in the Cosmos and Westmoreland categories.

Biscuit Jar, Silver Plated Cover, Enameled Flowers, 8 x 5 1/2 In. 112.00
Biscuit Jar, Tree Of Life, Blue Challinor, 7 x 4 1/2 In. 25.00
Biscuit Jar, Tree Of Life, Challinor, 7 x 4 1/2 In. 90.00
Butter, Cover, Tree Of Life, Challinor, 5 1/2 In. 90.00
Dish, Battleship Maine Cover, 4 In. 16.00
Dish, Dog Lying Down Cover, Enameled Gold & Pink, 5 x 5 In. 170.00
Dish, Duck On Nest Cover, Enameled, 4 1/2 In. 35.00
Dish, Fox Cover, Reclining, Oval Lattice Base, August 6, 1889, 6 1/2 In. 165.00
Dish, Hen Cover, Basket Base, Late 19th Century, 8 x 7 x 6 In. 160.00
Dish, Lion Cover, Reclining, Lattice Base, Pat'd 1889, 6 1/2 x 7 1/2 In. 85.00
Dish, Rabbit Cover, Late 19th Century, 4 1/4 x 9 1/2 x 4 In. 69.00
Dish, Retriever Cover, Duck & Leaf, 19th Century, 13 3/8 In. 145.00
Dish, Swan Cover, Open Wings, Basket Weave & Lattice Base, 6 In. 22.00
Dish, Turtle Cover, Scrolled & Beaded Base, 4 1/4 In. .... 60.00 to 77.00
Lamp, Apple Blossom, Enameled Green Bands, Pink Flowers, 7 1/4 In. 90.00
Lamp, Apple Blossom, Enameled Pink Bands, Flowers, Ball Shade, 7 In. 80.00
Lamp, Banquet, Blue Transfer On Font, Ball Shade, 12 1/2 In. 300.00
Lamp, Banquet, Cranberry Shade, White Metal, Brass Finish, Ornate Foot, 16 In. 130.00
Lamp, Enameled Flowers, Reeded Body, 5 1/2 In. 35.00
Lamp, Oil, Geometric, Matching Shade, 6 In. 39.00
Mustard, Bull's Head, 4 1/2 In. 90.00
Pipe, Lowell, Massachusetts 15.00
Platter, Fish, Embossed Bottom, June 4th, 1872, 10 1/4 x 13 3/4 In. 20.00
Punch Cup, Devils Lake, North Dakota 20.00
Sugar Shaker, Acorn, Blue, 5 In. 230.00
Sugar Shaker, Apple Blossom, 4 1/2 In. 160.00
Sugar Shaker, Argus Swirl, Enameled Flowers, 3 In. 100.00
Sugar Shaker, Forget-Me-Not, Blue Challinor, 3 3/4 In. 150.00
Sugar Shaker, Forget-Me-Not, Challinor, 3 3/4 In. 80.00
Sugar Shaker, Forget-Me-Not, Pink Challinor, 3 3/4 In. 190.00
Syrup, Acorn, Blue, 6 1/2 In. 190.00
Syrup, Argus Swirl, Enameled Flowers, 4 1/4 In. 150.00
Syrup, Tree Of Life, Blue Challinor, 6 1/4 In. 140.00
Syrup, Tree Of Life, Challinor, 6 3/4 In. 50.00
Syrup, Tree Of Life, Challinor, 7 In. 30.00
Tumbler, Montezuma, Iowa 20.00

MILLEFIORI means, literally, a thousand flowers. Many small pieces of glass resembling flowers are grouped together to form a design. It is a type of glasswork popular in paperweights and some are listed in that category.

Bowl, Cane Cut Flowers, Silver Flecks, Red Bottom, 14 x 10 x 5 In. 256.00

Compote, Dragon Stem, Gold Flecks, 7 1/4 x 7 1/4 In. 280.00
Cruet, Applied Satin Handle & Stopper, 7 1/2 In. 115.00
Frame, Oval, Flowers, Yellow, Red, Purple, Blue, 3 3/4 x 3 In. 98.00
Lamp, Candle, Mushroom, 2 Piece, 1950s, 13 1/4 In. 568.00
Pitcher, Blue, Olive Green, Purple, Yellow, 2 3/4 In. 88.00
Vase, Blues, Purple, 8 1/2 In. 465.00
Vase, Heart, Circle, Star Canes, 4 In. 75.00
Vase, Multicolored, Urn Shape, 2 Handles, Pontil, 16 1/2 In. 900.00

MINTON china has been made in the Staffordshire region of England from 1793 to the present. The firm became part of the Royal Doulton Tableware Group in 1968, but the wares continued to be marked *Minton*. The word *England* was added in 1891. Minton majolica is listed in this book in the Majolica category.

Candlestick, Hemispheric Base, Squeezebag, Grape Clusters, Blue, Chartreuse, 5 x 5 In. . 230.00
Compote, Agate Body, Cherubs Support, Lovebirds Center, Signed, 10 1/2 In. 2415.00
Cup, 2 Handles, Gilt Flowers, Medallion, Pate-Sur-Pate, Albion Birks, c.1920, 4 1/2 In. ... 705.00
Figurine, Ariadne, Nude Bride Of Bacchus, Reclining On Panther, 1870s, 14 1/2 In. 1610.00
Jardiniere, Blue Willow, 1890s, 10 3/4 In, Pair 1035.00
Paperweight, Maiden Casting Billets Doux To Winds, Pate-Sur-Pate, c.1878, 6 1/2 In. ... 14375.00
Plate, Center Floral Spray, Garland Wreath, Rose Border, c.1891, 8 3/4 In., 8 Piece 225.00
Plate, Dessert, Raised Gilt Matte, Burnished Border, c.1913, 9 In., 25 Piece 20300.00
Plate, Dinner, Armorial, Gilt, White, Early 20th Century, 10 1/4 In., 9 Piece 230.00
Plate, Dinner, Brocade, Floral Spray, Pink Ground, Gilt, 20th Century, 10 5/8 In., 12 Piece 460.00
Plate, Dinner, Raised Gilt Border, Early 20th Century, 10 1/4 In., 18 Pieces 18000.00
Plate, Floral Sprigs, Gilt Trim, Mark, 9 In., 6 Piece 440.00
Plate, Gilt, Cobalt Blue Border, 9 In., 12 Piece 1880.00
Plate, Rose Border, Fruit, Phoenix In Landscape, c.1891, 8 3/4 In. 532.00
Plate, Turquoise Band, Gilt Palmette, Anthemion, 10 1/2 In., 12 Piece 805.00
Vase, Cherubs, Maidens, Cupid, Pate-Sur-Pate, Signed Marc Louis Solon, 18 1/4 In, Pair . 32950.00
Vase, Cover, Medallions, Putti, Pate-Sur-Pate, England, c.1880, 15 1/4 In., Pair 11500.00
Vase, Cuenca, Peacocks, Stenciled, 11 1/2 x 5 1/2 In. 115.00
Vase, Flowers, Blue & White, Green Stems, Handles, Stamped, 11 1/2 x 4 3/4 In. 80.00
Vase, Flying Putti, Cloud Border, Ring Handles, Pate-Sur-Pate, Louis Solon, 12 In., Pair 8056.00
Vase, Secessionist Design, Squeezebag, Pinched Waist, Blue Ground, 10 In. 200.00
Vase, Squeezebag, Black & Green, Raspberry Ground, Stamped, 9 x 5 1/2 In. 145.00
Vase, Squeezebag, Rows Of Circles, Red & Green Ground, 7 1/4 x 5 1/4 In. 175.00
Vase, Turquoise Ground, 2 Handles, Cover, c.1870, 15 1/4 In., Pair 1380.00
Vase, Wreaths, Flowers, Ivory & Green, Sang-De-Boeuf Ground, 12 1/4 In. 750.00

MIRRORS are listed in the Furniture category under Mirror.

MOCHA pottery is an English-made product that was sold in America during the early 1800s. It is a heavy pottery with pale coffee-and-cream coloring. Designs of blue, brown, green, orange, black, or white were added to the pottery and given fanciful names, such as *Tree, Snail Trail,* or *Moss.* Mocha designs are sometimes found on pearlware.

Bowl, Blue, 4 Narrow Dark Brown Bands, Gray Field, 7 1/2 In. 400.00
Bowl, Cat's-Eye, Cover, Hemispherical, Black, White, Gray Field, 6 In. 2530.00
Bowl, Cat's-Eye, White, Ocher, Rust Field, 1820, 4 5/8 In. 575.00
Bowl, Dark Brown Bands, Blue, Brown, White Wavy Field, 7 In. 1380.00
Bowl, Earthworm, Blue, White Looping, Brown Band, Flared Edge, 6 1/4 In. 1320.00
Bowl, Earthworm, Brown, Yellow Ground, 19th Century, 6 1/4 In. 550.00
Bowl, Earthworm, Green Banding, 5 1/2 In. 495.00
Bowl, Earthworm, London Shape, Blue & Brown Bands, 7 1/4 In. 260.00
Bowl, Earthworm, Taupe, Black Band, Black, White, Ocher Field, 1830, 6 1/4 In. 545.00
Bowl, Geometrics, Dot Band, Blue, Brown Ground, Flared Edge, 10 1/4 In. 3410.00
Bowl, Green Glazed Diaper Pattern, Olive, Rust Bands, 10 In. ....*Illus* 1150.00
Bowl, Orange, Blue Band, Black Slip Bands, 1800, 7 1/4 In. 805.00
Bowl, Seaweed, Black, Blue Band, 19th Century, 6 1/4 In. 400.00
Bowl, White Bands, Black Mocha Seaweed, 1795, 7 In. 575.00
Cann & Saucer, Marbled, Ocher, Green, Brown, Impressed Arboras, 5 In. ....*Illus* 403.00
Coffeepot, Seaweed, Brick Red Slip, Black Design, Black Bands, Leaf Handle, 11 1/2 In. 3105.00

Mocha, Mustard Pot, Cover, Seaweed, Orange, Green, Black, 3 7/8 In.; Mocha, Bowl, Green Glazed
Diaper Pattern, Olive, Rust Bands, 10 In.; Mocha, Cann & Saucer, Marbled, Ocher, Green, Brown,
Impressed Arboras, 5 In.; Mocha, Mug, Brown & Black Slip, Vertical Combing, c.1790, 6 1/4 In.; Mocha, Mug,
Black, Ocher, Blue Bands, White Slip Circles, c.1820, 4 3/4 In.; Mocha, Mug, Black, Rust, Blue Bands, Vertical
Diamonds, c.1800, 5 7/8 In.; Mocha, Pepper Pot, Cat's-Eye, Gray & Black Bands, Rust, White, 4 3/4 In.

Container, Seaweed, White Band, Blue Stripes, Pierced Double Handles, 6 3/8 In.	80.00
Creamer, Cat's-Eye, Blue, White, Black, Tan Ground, Cover, 5 1/2 In.	1760.00
Jug, Alternating Black, Brown Slip Bands, Blue, Black, White Cat's-Eyes, 1820	8625.00
Jug, Bands, Wavy Stripes, Undulating Cables, 19th Century, 8 In.	3600.00
Jug, Blue Bands, Pale Yellow Field, Black Mocha Trees, 1790, 8 1/2 In.	8050.00
Jug, Blue, Dark Brown Bands, Gray Field, Handle, 7 3/4 In.	920.00
Jug, Cat's-Eye, Blue & Brown Bands, Baluster Shape, Leaf Handle, 6 1/4 In.	4310.00
Jug, Earthworm, Black, Blue, Green Glaze Roulette Rim, White, 5 7/8 In.	1725.00
Jug, Earthworm, Rust & Brown Bands, Beaded Rows, Baluster Shape, Leaf Handle, 6 In.	3220.00
Jug, Earthworm, White, Rust, Blue, Black Looping, 1830, 4 7/8 In.	5175.00
Jug, Geometrics, Inlaid Black Slip, Rust & Black Bands, Leaf Handle, 6 1/2 In.	3740.00
Jug, Mustard, Rust Band, Green Ground, Black Mocha Trees, 1800, 6 5/8 In.	2645.00
Jug, Ocher, Brown Band, Green Bands, 3 Ocher Bands, 1800, 6 1/2 In.	3737.00
Jug, Seaweed, Black, Blue Bands, 1820, 5 3/4 In.	1840.00
Jug, Seaweed, Cream, Blue, Black Slip Bands, Green Design, Black Seaweed, 3 In.	980.00
Jug, Seaweed, Orange, Black Bands, Black Slip Design, Handle, 7 1/2 In.	3450.00
Mug, Band, Handle With Leaf Center, 2 In.	650.00
Mug, Bands, Black, Ocher & Blue, White Slip Circles, Leaf Handle, 4 3/4 In.	2990.00
Mug, Bands, Rust & Blue, Oval Dot Diamonds Cut Through Black, Leaf Handle, 6 In.	3450.00
Mug, Black, Ocher, Blue Bands, White Slip Circles, c.1820, 4 3/4 In. *Illus*	2990.00
Mug, Black, Rust, Blue Bands, Vertical Diamonds, c.1800, 5 7/8 In. *Illus*	3450.00
Mug, Brown & Black Slip, Vertical Combing, c.1790, 6 1/4 In. *Illus*	3335.00
Mug, Earthworm, Blue, White, 19th Century, 3 In.	250.00
Mug, Geometrics, Rouletted, Brown Bands, Leaf Handle, 5 1/2 In.	170.00
Mug, Geometrics, White, Brown Slip, Caramel Bands, Leaf Handle, 6 In.	2530.00
Mug, Seaweed, Blue, Brown Stripes, White Band, 3 7/8 In.	357.00
Mug, Seaweed, Brown, Blue Band, Cream Ground, 19th Century	315.00
Mug, Seaweed, Bulbous, Applied Handle, 3 1/4 In.	385.00
Mug, Seaweed, Green Reeded Glaze Bands, Black, 1795, 5 1/2 In.	1955.00
Mug, Tree, Black Inlaid Rouletting, Orange & Blue Bands, 2 1/2 In.	546.00
Mustard Pot, Bands, Blue, Black Stripes, Brown, Black, White, Blue, Leaf Handle, 3 In.	1320.00
Mustard Pot, Bands, Orange & Blue, Vertical Ribs, Leaf Handle, Cover, 3 1/2 In.	546.00
Mustard Pot, Bands, Rust & Black, Trees, Leaf Handle, Cover, Ball Top, 3 1/2 In.	865.00
Mustard Pot, Barrel Shape, Bands, Green Reeded, Orange, Black Decoration, Cover, 4 In.	575.00
Mustard Pot, Cover, Seaweed, Orange, Green, Black, 3 7/8 In. *Illus*	575.00
Mustard Pot, Seaweed, Black Stripes, Leaf Handle, 3 3/4 In.	275.00
Pepper Pot, Bands, Alternating Brown & Orange, 4 1/4 In.	1375.00
Pepper Pot, Bands, Black & Brown, White Spread Foot, Baluster Shape, 5 In.	1380.00
Pepper Pot, Cat's-Eye, Black & Gray Bands, Cobalt Crown, Cylindrical, 5 In.	1380.00
Pepper Pot, Cat's-Eye, Gray & Black Bands, Rust, White, 4 3/4 In. *Illus*	1380.00
Pepper Pot, Earthworm, Marbleized, Black Stripes, Wide Blue Band, 4 1/4 In.	550.00
Pepper Pot, Marbleized Brown & White, Satin Top, 3 7/8 In.	470.00
Pepper Pot, Seaweed, Stripes, White Band, 4 1/4 In.	1980.00

Pepper Pot, Shaker Top, Bands, Brown, Green & Blue Body, 4 1/2 In. 1210.00
Pepper Pot, Stripes, Brown & Blue, 5 In. 615.00
Pepper Pot, Stripes, Gray, Black Band, Top Feathering, 4 3/4 In. 1155.00
Pitcher, Bands, Blue, Brown, White Ground, 19th Century, 6 1/4 In. 430.00
Pitcher, Bands, Yellow, Dark Brown, Green, Molded Leaf Handle, 4 3/4 In. 110.00
Pitcher, Earthworm, Brown Zigzag Upper Band, Gray, Tan, Blue, 8 1/4 In. 1540.00
Pitcher, Earthworm, Pale Blue, White Foot, Handle & Spout, 6 In. 360.00
Pitcher, Seaweed, Black, Keg Form, Green Upper Band, 5 3/4 In. 6380.00
Pitcher, Seaweed, Brown Stripes, White Bands, Blue, 6 In. 605.00
Pitcher, Seaweed, Dark Brown Stripes, 8 In. 5720.00
Porringer, Brown Slip Sponging, Reeded Rim, Yellow Glaze, 2 3/4 In. 980.00
Porringer, Stripes, Fans, Green Glazed Reeded Rim, Ocher, Leaf Handle, 3 3/8 In. 6325.00
Pot, Dome Top, Earthworm, Brown, Tan, Gray, Green, 4 1/2 In. 1980.00
Salt, Bands, White & Blue, Footed, 2 1/4 x 3 In. 60.00
Salt, Seaweed, Green, Blue Stripes, White Band, Master, 3 x 2 1/4 In. 770.00
Sugar, Acorn Finial, Seaweed, Green Bands, 4 1/2 In. 2420.00
Tankard, Earthworm, Blue Band, Black Stripes, Molded Leaf Handle, 4 3/4 In. 110.00
Waste Bowl, Earthworm, Brown Stripes, Gray Band, 6 1/2 In. 247.00

MONMOUTH Pottery Company started working in Monmouth, Illinois, in 1892. The pottery made a variety of utilitarian wares. It became part of Western Stoneware Company in 1906. The maple leaf mark was used until 1930. If *Co.* appears as part of the mark, the piece was made before 1906.

Crock, Blue Maple Leaf, Western Stoneware Co., 21 In. 102.00
Jug, Green Splash, Maple Leaf, 3 In. 28.00
Mixing Bowl, Brown, Horizontal Ribbed, Signed 35.00
Mixing Bowl, Yellow, Blue Bank Advertising 40.00
Pot, Floral Band, Brown Glaze, 6 3/4 In. 66.00
Vase, Dark Green Glaze, Stretched Flowers, Paneled, 8 In. 116.00
Vase, Egyptian, Matte Glaze, Glossy Brown Interior, 9 In. 37.00

MONT JOYE, see Mt. Joye category.

MOORCROFT pottery was first made in Burslem, England, in 1913. William Moorcroft had managed the art pottery department for James Macintyre & Company of England from 1898 to 1913. The Moorcroft pottery continues today, although William Moorcroft died in 1945. The earlier wares are similar to the modern ones, but color and marking will help indicate the age.

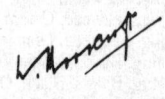

Biscuit Barrel, Moonlit, Trees, Hills, Blue Ground, Electroplated Mounts, 1920 . . . . 3833.00
Biscuit Jar, Pomegranate, Silver Mounted, Lid, Silver Hallmark, Stamped, c.1916 . . . . . . 489.00
Bonbonniere, Poppies, Leaves, White Ground, Signed, c.1902 . . . . 3680.00
Bowl, Blue To Green Glossy Glaze, c.1949, 6 x 12 1/4 In. 288.00
Bowl, Clematis, Green Ground, Stamped, 3 1/2 x 3 1/2 In. 173.00
Bowl, Columbine, Flambe Glaze, Footed, Paper Label, 1 1/2 x 3 1/2 In. 207.00
Bowl, Hibiscus, Green Ground, Stilt-Pulls, Signed, 7 x 5 In. 201.00
Bowl, Pomegranate, Cobalt Blue Ground, Oval, Stamped, Ink Signed, 8 1/2 x 5 In. 690.00
Bowl, Pomegranate, Stamped, 1918-1929, 3 1/4 x 6 1/2 In. 115.00
Bowl, Poppy, Dark Green, Impressed Mark, Facsimile Signature, 4 1/4 x 1 1/4 In. 58.00
Box, Cover, Hibiscus, Green Ground, Stamped, 4 x 5 1/2 In. 115.00
Box, Cover, Oval, Flowers, Green Ground, Impressed Signature, 6 In. 219.00
Box, Poppy, Cobalt Blue, Cylindrical, Cover, Impressed Mark, 3 1/2 In. 633.00
Chalice, Cover, Tulips, Forget-Me-Nots, 2 Handles, Macintyre, c.1908, 8 1/2 In. 3600.00
Cup, Poppy, 2 Handles, Stemmed, Macintyre, c.1903, 7 1/2 In. . . . 4500.00
Ginger Jar, Pomegranates, Leaves, Berries, Mottled Blue Ground, Signed, c.1929, 11 In. . 1955.00
Inkwell, Polychrome Fruit, Mottled Blue Ground, 2 3/4 x 9 In. 431.00
Inkwell, Pomegranate, Mottled Blue Ground, 2 3/4 In. 380.00
Jam Jar, Silver Cover, Pomegranate, Hibiscus, Yellow, Handle, 7 1/2 In. 311.00
Loving Cup, Pomegranate, 2 Handles, Stamped Burslem, 1914-1916, 5 1/2 x 6 In. 1150.00
Pitcher, Cornflower, Scrolling Leaves, Blue Green Ground, Signed, Macintyre, c.1910 . . . 2146.00
Pitcher, Horizontal Banded, Signed, Macintyre, 7 In. 308.00

Pitcher, Pomegranate, Cobalt Blue, Initialed, 5 3/4 In.	403.00
Plate, Toadstools, Blue, Green & Yellow Ground, Signed, Macintyre, c.1904	2146.00
Tea Service, Pomegranate, c.1913, 3 Piece	1560.00
Vase, Anemone, 8 1/2 In.	288.00
Vase, Anemone, Cobalt Blue Ground, Baluster, Stamped, Signed, 9 1/2 In.	1150.00
Vase, Apple, Cobalt Blue Ground, 6 In.	402.00
Vase, Blue & Green Glaze, Landscape, Signed, Macintyre, 12 1/2 In.	6900.00
Vase, Bud, Pomegranate, c.1940, 3 3/4 In.	316.00
Vase, Bulbous, Forest Scene, 10 3/4 x 5 In.	575.00
Vase, Claremont, Macintyre, c.1905, 7 1/2 In.	1320.00
Vase, Cornflower, 13 x 11 In.	3630.00
Vase, Cornflower, 1928, 17 1/4 In.	3600.00
Vase, Cornflower, Blue, Marked, 9 In.	1725.00
Vase, Dalpayrat, Deep Red, Black, Cream, Blue, Light Brown Clay, 8 1/2 In.	550.00
Vase, Double Gourd Shape, Celadon Glossy Glaze, Stamped, 9 1/2 x 5 In.	115.00
Vase, Eventide, Brown Glaze, 5 In.	1100.00
Vase, Eventide, Landscape, c.1920, 7 3/8 In.	2700.00
Vase, Eventide, Tall Trees, Green, Cobalt Blue Ground, Ovoid, Stamped, 15 In.	1840.00
Vase, Fish, 1930s, 20 1/2 In.	2280.00
Vase, Fish, Trumpet, Flambe, Late 1920s, 10 In.	2700.00
Vase, Florian Ware, Tulip, 2 Handles, Macintyre, c.1900, 14 In.	2050.00
Vase, Flowers, Dark Blue Ground, Globular, 7 In., Pair	690.00
Vase, Hibiscus, 9 In.	900.00
Vase, Hibiscus, White Ground, Pear Shaped, Signed, 10 3/4 x 4 3/4 In.	430.00
Vase, Lion's Den, Rampant Lion On Cobalt Blue Ground, 1988, 9 3/4 In.	300.00
Vase, Mixed Flowers, 3 Handles, 1904-1913, 7 3/4 In.	1725.00
Vase, Moonlight Scene, Trees, Mountains, Blue To Turquoise Sky, 16 1/2 In.	5230.00
Vase, Moonlit Blue, Landscape, c.1920, 6 1/2 In.	1495.00
Vase, Orange, Red, Brown, Green Glaze, Landscape, Impressed Mark, 10 In.	21600.00
Vase, Orchid, Cobalt Blue, Impressed Mark, 4 3/4 In.	430.00
Vase, Pansies, Double Handle, Marked, Macintyre, 6 In.	3220.00
Vase, Pansy, Cobalt Blue Ground, Squat, Stamped, Ink Signed, 7 1/4 In.	750.00
Vase, Pansy, Cobalt Blue, Impressed Mark, 2 5/8 In.	230.00
Vase, Peacock Feather, Flambe, 1920s, 8 1/8 In.	3600.00
Vase, Peony Bud, Green Glaze, Burslem, 1916, 8 1/2 In.	1300.00
Vase, Pomegranate, 4 In.	196.00
Vase, Pomegranate, c.1925, 14 7/8 In.	840.00
Vase, Pomegranate, Cobalt Blue Ground, 12 In.	1000.00
Vase, Pomegranate, Cobalt Blue, Open Mouth, Signed, c.1920, 6 1/2 In.	980.00
Vase, Pomegranate, Cobalt Blue, Rolled Rim, Signed, 6 1/8 In.	489.00
Vase, Pomegranate, Deep Cobalt Blue Ground, 8 1/8 In.	500.00
Vase, Pomegranate, Flambe, 1920s, 9 In.	840.00
Vase, Pomegranate, Fruit & Leaves, Cobalt Blue Ground, c.1940, 3 3/4 In.	315.00
Vase, Poppy, Blue & White Blended Ground, Impressed Mark, 2 7/8 In.	105.00
Vase, Poppy, Impressed Mark, Painted Initials, 6 1/8 In.	315.00
Vase, Poppy, Signed, 16 1/2 In.	2420.00
Vase, Spring Flowers, Green Ground, Signed, 7 x 5 In.	400.00
Vase, Toadstool, Mottled Blue Green Ground, Bulbous, Stamped, 4 3/4 x 3 1/2 In.	575.00
Vase, Wisteria, Macintyre, c.1912, 14 3/4 In.	5100.00

MORIAGE is a special type of raised decoration used on some Japanese pottery. Sometimes pieces of clay were shaped by hand and applied to the item; sometimes the clay was squeezed from a tube in the way we apply cake frosting. One type of moriage is called *Dragonware* and is listed under that name.

Box, Floral Clusters, Green Ground, 1940s, 3 1/4 In.	46.00
Candlestick, Red, Blue & Green, White Ground, Green Wreath, 9 1/4 In.	225.00
Chocolate Set, Scale Design, 13 Piece	3250.00
Compote, Green, Marbled Burgundy, Flowers, Nippon, 8 1/2 In.	610.00
Pitcher, Geese, Diving, 10 1/4 In.	103.00
Syrup, Underplate, Oriental Musicians, 5 In.	132.00
Vase, Bulbous, Hand Painted, 5 In.	150.00

Vase, Pink Roses, White Beading, Handles, Nippon, 10 In.	1200.00
Vase, Tree & Mountain Landscape, Handles, 5 1/2 In.	829.00
Vase, Water Birds, Sunset, Turquoise Beading, Serpent Handles, 12 In.	280.00

MOSAIC TILE COMPANY of Zanesville, Ohio, was started by Karl Langerbeck and Herman Mueller in 1894. Many types of plain and ornamental tiles were made until 1959. The company closed in 1967. The company also made some ashtrays, bookends, and related giftwares. Most pieces are marked with the entwined *MTC* monogram.

Figurine, Dog, Sitting, Brown, Ivory Matte Glaze, 9 In.	265.00

MOSER glass is made by Ludwig Moser und Sohne, a Bohemian (Czech) glasshouse founded in 1857. Art Nouveau-type glassware and iridescent glassware were made. The most famous Moser glass is decorated with heavy enameling in gold and bright colors. The firm, Moser Glassworks, is still working in Karlsbad, West Czech Republic. Few pieces of Moser glass are marked.

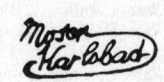

Bowl, Clear, Allover Multicolored Scrolling, Gold Tracery, 4 Reeded Feet, 10 1/2 In.	365.00
Bowl, Enameled Floral, Blue, 3 x 9 In.	175.00
Champagne Flute, Cobalt Blue Cut To Clear, Geometric, 8 In.	746.00
Cheese Dish, White, Gold Trim, 9 3/4 x 9 In.	805.00
Nappy, Pink Opalescent, Leaf Shape, Gold Enameled, 1880s, 6 In.	150.00
Pitcher, Thumbprint, Green & Gold Foliage & Scrolls, Flowers, Amber Handle, 7 In.	425.00
Plate, Clear, Raised Gold Enameled Flowers, 3 1/2 x 4 3/8 In.	400.00
Vase, Alexandrite, Heavy Cutting, Signed, 6 In.	345.00
Vase, Amber, Enameled Design, 9 In.	395.00
Vase, Blue, Gold, Amethyst Bands, 5 3/4 x 6 1/2 In.	345.00
Vase, Clear, Enameled Poppies, Bulbous Body, Narrow Rim, c.1880, 6 1/2 In.	125.00
Vase, Clear, Enameled, Bird, Flowers, Signed, 9 1/2 In.	400.00
Vase, Clear, Enameled, Insects, Flowers, Metal Gargoyle Stand, 12 1/4 In.	500.00
Vase, Clear, Enameled, Jeweled, Elongated Pear Shape, Flared Rim, c.1920, 10 1/2 In.	400.00
Vase, Clear, Inverted Thumbprint, Mother-Of-Pearl, Enameled Fish, 6 1/2 In.	316.00
Vase, Emerald Green Cut To Clear, Flower & Bud, Gold Rim, 4 5/8 In.	415.00
Vase, Frosted Green, Enameled Butterflies, Tall Grasses, Cylindrical, 10 1/2 In.	405.00
Vase, Green Cut To Clear, Flowers, 9 In.	635.00
Vase, Intaglio Cut Floral On Body, Red Flower & Vines, Petals, 6 In.	1230.00
Vase, Marbleized Yellow, 3 Openings, 1880, 9 1/2 In.	795.00
Vase, Shaded Amethyst To Clear, Vertical Ribs, Enameled Pansies, 6 In.	375.00
Vase, Topaz Engraved To Clear, Hunters Under Attack From Rampant Bears, 6 In.	260.00
Water Set, White Enameled, Woman Holding Glass, Signed, 5 Piece	345.00
Wine, Stag & Deer, Forest Scene, Crystal Pedestal, Label, 9 1/2 In.	224.00

MOSS ROSE china was made by many firms from 1808 to 1900. It has a typical moss rose pictured as the design. The plant is not as popular now as it was in Victorian gardens, so the fuzz-covered bud is unfamiliar to most collectors. The dishes were usually decorated with pink and green flowers.

Bowl, Vegetable, Cover, Handles, Rosenthal, 7 1/2 In.	790.00
Bowl, Vegetable, Cover, Heinrich, 9 1/4 In.	120.00
Cake Plate, Royal Albert	55.00
Coffeepot, Heinrich, 6 1/2 In.	175.00
Cup & Saucer, Johann Haviland	20.00
Gravy Boat, Attached Underplate, Rosenthal	375.00
Gravy Boat, Underplate, Johann Haviland	50.00
Plate, Dinner, Johann Haviland	20.00
Plate, Dinner, Royal Albert	85.00
Plate, Shell, Pink Rose, Gold Gilt, Royal Crown Derby, No. 3691, 9 1/2 x 9 1/2 In.	25.00
Platter, Heinrich, 16 1/4 In.	175.00
Platter, Homer Laughlin, Small	30.00
Sugar, Cover, Heinrich	40.00
Sugar, Cover, Royal Albert	135.00
Teapot, Cover, Rosenthal	625.00

MOTHER-OF-PEARL GLASS, or pearl satin glass, was first made in the 1850s in England and in Massachusetts. It was a special type of mold-blown satin glass with air bubbles in the glass, giving it a pearlized color. It has been reproduced. Mother-of-pearl shell objects are listed under Pearl.

Bowl, Diamond-Quilted, 3 Frosted Thorny Feet, 4 7/8 x 6 1/2 In.	325.00
Creamer, Raindrop, Blue Reeded Handle, 4 1/2 x 3 1/8 In.	175.00
Pitcher, Rose To Satin, Floral & Dragonfly, Thorn Handle, Beaded Rim, 8 In.	413.00
Sugar & Creamer, Blue Ribbon, Heart Shape, Satin Handle, 3 In.	325.00
Sugar & Creamer, Heart Form, Frosted Handle, Blue, 2 3/4 In.	325.00
Tumbler, Rainbow Blue & Pink, Thumbprint, Satin, 3 3/4 In.	290.00
Vase, Diamond-Quilted, Ivory Interior, Satin, 6 In.	195.00
Vase, Diamond-Quilted, Shouldered, 6 1/4 In.	364.00
Vase, Green, 5 Pinched Sides, Ruffled Rim, 8 In.	112.00
Vase, Herringbone, White Interior, Frosted Handles, 8 1/2 In.	225.00
Vase, Pink Herringbone, 2 Handles, 8 1/2 In.	225.00
Vase, Pink Herringbone, White Interior, 6 In., Pair	325.00
Vase, Raindrop, Blue, Satin, 5 In., Pair	295.00
Vase, Raindrop, Blue, White Interior, 3-Petal Top, 5 1/2 x 3 1/2 In.	115.00
Vase, Raindrop, White Interior, Fan Form Top, 5 In., Pair	295.00
Vase, Satin, Coralline, Ruffled, Tricorn, Pink Herringbone, 7 In.	345.00
Vase, Trumpet, Diamond-Quilted, Brass Stand, 14 1/2 In.	425.00
Vase, White Interior, Pink Satin Glass, Frosted Handles, 8 1/4 In.	215.00

MOTORCYCLES and motorcycle accessories of all types are being collected today. Examples can be found that date back to the early years of the twentieth century. Toy motorcycles are listed in the Toy category.

Cap, Harley-Davidson, Cotton, Black, Leather Bill, Wings Logo, 8 Panels, 1950s	125.00
Catalog, Emblem Motorcycles, 1912, 16 Pages, 9 1/2 x 7 1/2 In.	330.00
Dirt Bike, Indian, No. 125, 1970s	200.00
Gas Globe, Indian Motorcycle Co., Red & Yellow Glass, 13 1/2 In.	255.00
Instruction Manual, Moto Guzzi, 250 Airone Sport, 1950, 94 Pages, 8 In.	125.00
Jacket, Brown, Belted Waist, Leather, 1940s, Size 38-40	150.00
Jacket, Tan Bodice, Black Sleeves, Zipper, Leather, Bates California, 1960s	300.00
Medal, Race, Reading, Penn., Silver Metal	500.00
Noisemaker, Pictures Indian Motorcycle, Whistles When Twirled On String	80.00
Oil Can, Indian Motorcycles Chain Oil, 4 1/2 In.	300.00
Oil Can, Indian, Contents, 1940s, Qt.	215.00
Patch, BMW Logo, Embroidered, 1960s, 3 In.	40.00
Pin, Indian Motorcycle Convention, 1920s, 1 1/2 x 2 In.	85.00
Pin, Indian, Silver Metal, Hendee Mfg. Co., 3 1/2 In.	180.00
Pin, Isle Of Man Races, Gold Metal, Pearl Wheels, 1950s, 1 1/2 In.	160.00
Postcard, Photo Of Indian Motorcycle Delivering Keen Kutter Tools, 1909	280.00
Poster, Evel Knievel, Snake River Canyon Jump, 1974, 20 x 14 In.	175.00
Poster, Harley-Davidson, Showroom, Mounted On Linen, 1932, 22 x 60 In.	2832.00
Sign, Harley-Davidson, Glass, Hangs On Chain, 21 x 14 In.	545.00
Sign, Koehler Escoffier Motorcycle, Deco Rider, Paris, Frame, 1935, 31 x 45 In.	1265.00

MOUNT WASHINGTON, see Mt. Washington category.

MOVIE memorabilia of all types is collected. Animation Art, Games, Sheet Music, Toys, and some celebrity items are listed in their own sections. Listed here are costumes and paper collectibles. A lobby card is 11 by 14 inches. A set of lobby cards includes seven scene cards and one title card. A one sheet, the standard movie poster, is 27 by 41 inches. A three sheet is 81 by 40 inches. A half sheet is 22 by 28 inches. A window card is made of cardboard, is 14 by 22 inches. An insert is 14 by 36 inches. A herald is a promotional item handed out to patrons. A press book was sent to newspapers and magazines to promote a picture. Press books and/or press kits (with photos) were sent to the media to promote a movie.

Banner, Drive-In, 20,000 Leagues Under Sea, Walt Disney, 1954, 24 x 82 In.	740.00

Banner, Drive-In, House Of Dracula, Lon Chaney, 1950, 24 x 82 In. 340.00
Banner, Drive-In, Isle Of The Dead, Boris Karloff, 1953, 24 x 82 In. 450.00
Banner, Drive-In, The Enforcer, Humphrey Bogart, 1951, 24 x 82 In. 345.00
Book, Music, Sons Of The Pioneers, 18 Songs, 1939 . . . . 18.00
Button, Goodbye Norma Jean, Marilyn Monroe, 3 In. 5.00
Calendar Top, Golden Dreams, Marilyn Monroe, 12 x 16 In. 48.00
Cigar Band, Ken Maynard Western Star First National, 1930s, 7/8 x 2 7/8 In. 14.00
Insert, Rear Window, Paramount, 1952, 14 x 36 In. 200.00
Insert, The Big Shot, Humphrey Bogart, 1942, 14 x 36 In. 542.00
Lobby Card, Headin' Home, Babe Ruth, 1921 . . . . 1497.00
Lobby Card, Mr. Smith Goes To Washington, James Stewart & Jean Arthur, 1939 . . . . 410.00
Lobby Card, Phantom Cowboy, Don Red Barry, Milburn Stone, 1941 . . . . 10.00
Lobby Card, Tarzan & The Amazons, Johnny Weissmuller, 1945 . . . . 415.00
Lobby Card, Vertigo, Paramount, 1958, Insert 259.00
Photograph, Carole Lombard, Signed, Sepia, 5 x 7 In. 350.00
Photograph, Hedy Lamarr, Signed 225.00
Photograph, John Wayne, Black & White, 1930s, 5 x 7 In. 8.00
Photograph, Ken Curtis, Autograph, 1970s, 4 3/4 x 6 3/4 In. 30.00
Photograph, Marilyn Monroe, Black & White, 1963, 8 x 10 In. 8.00
Photograph, Rin Tin Tin, Stamped Name, Ken L Ration, 1931, 5 x 7 In. 24.00
Photograph, Stan Laurel & Oliver Hardy, Signed, Black & White, 8 x 10 In. 900.00
Photograph, Three Stooges, Signed, Sepia, Framed, Early 1950s, 9 3/4 x 11 3/4 In. 1250.00
Pledge Card, Smiley Burnette Fan Club, 1940s, 5 x 7 In. 28.00
Postcard, Luck Cisco Kid, Cesar Romero, 3 1/2 x 5 1/2 In. 8.00
Postcard, The Deputy, Henry Fonda, 1950s, 3 1/2 x 5 1/2 In. 15.00
Poster, A Night At The Opera, Marx Bros., 1935, 1/2 Sheet 2975.00
Poster, Bonnie Scotland, Stan Laurel & Oliver Hardy, 1935, Window Card 575.00
Poster, Bringing Up Father, Jiggs & Maggie, 1946, 3 Sheet 300.00
Poster, Butterfield 8, Elizabeth Taylor, 1960, 1 Sheet 500.00
Poster, Fantasia, 1940, 1/2 Sheet. 675.00
Poster, From Hand To Mouth, Harold Lloyd, 1919, 1 Sheet 1795.00
Poster, Half-Breed, Jack Buetel, Robert Young, 1952, 1 Sheet 15.00
Poster, I Married A Woman, Diana Dors, 1958, 1 Sheet 25.00
Poster, Let's Make Love, Marilyn Monroe & Yves Montand, 1960, 6 Sheet 430.00
Poster, Mademoiselle Fifi, Simone Simon, 1943, 1 Sheet 450.00
Poster, Marihuana, The Devil's Weed, 1935, 1 Sheet 965.00
Poster, Moiseur, Rudolph Valentino, 1924, Window Card 675.00
Poster, Oceans 11, Frank Sinatra, Dean Martin, Sammy Davis Jr., 1960, 1/2 Sheet 915.00
Poster, Pardon Us, Stan Laurel & Oliver Hardy, 1931, 1 Sheet 3827.00
Poster, Psycho, Anthony Perkins & Janet Leigh, 1960, 1/2 Sheet 622.00
Poster, Rebel Without A Cause, James Dean, 1955, 1 Sheet 2779.00
Poster, Road To Zanzibar, Bing Crosby, Bob Hope, Dorothy Lamour, 1941, 1 Sheet 315.00
Poster, Singin' In The Rain, Gene Kelly, Debbie Reynolds, 1952, 1 Sheet 1630.00
Poster, Suzy, Jean Harlow, 1936, 1/2 Sheet 765.00
Poster, Taxi Driver, Robert DeNiro, 1976, 1 Sheet 455.00
Poster, The Ape, Boris Karloff, 1940, 1 Sheet 885.00
Poster, The Birds, Alfred Hitchcock, Universal, 1963, 1 Sheet 230.00
Poster, The Dawn Patrol, Errol Flynn, 1938, Half Sheet 1123.00
Poster, The Gaucho, Douglas Fairbanks, 1927, Window Card 817.00
Poster, The Living Daylights, Timothy Dalton, Color, 1 Sheet 20.00
Poster, The Man Who Shot Liberty Valance, John Wayne, 1962, 6 Sheet 820.00
Poster, The Mighty Barnum, Wallace Beery, 1934, 1 Sheet 550.00
Poster, The Prisoner Of Zenda, Ronald Colman, Madeleine Carroll, 1937, 1 Sheet 2755.00
Poster, The Sheriff Of Fractured Law, Jayne Mansfield, 1959, Insert 15.00
Poster, The Song Of Songs, Marlene Dietrich, 1933, Window Card 900.00
Poster, The Thin Man, William Powell & Myrna Loy, 1934, Window Card 990.00
Poster, They Drive By Night, Humphrey Bogart, 1940, Window Card 575.00
Poster, Winning The West, Richard Arlen, Mary Brian, Re-Issue, 1952, 1 Sheet 15.00
Poster, You Were Never Lovelier, Fred Astaire, Rita Hayworth, 1942, 1 Sheet 675.00
Poster, Young Frankenstein, Mel Brooks, Gene Wilder, 1971, One Sheet 175.00
Press Book, Heart Of The Rockies, Roy Rogers, 8 Pages, 1951, 12 x 18 In. 45.00
Press Book, Man From Oklahoma, Roy Rogers, Black & White, 16 Pages, 1940s 95.00
Press Book, Twilight In The Sierras, Roy Rogers, Gloss Paper, 8 Pages, 12 x 18 In. 70.00

Switch Plate Cover, Steve McQueen On Motorcycle, Kakamamie Co., 1968, 2 x 7 In. 25.00
Tablet, School, Ross Martin, Wild, Wild West TV Series, 1960s, 8 x 10 In. 25.00

MT. JOYE is an enameled cameo glass made in the late nineteenth and twentieth centuries by Saint-Hilaire Touvier de Varraux and Co. of Pantin, France. This same company made De Vez glass. Pieces were usually decorated with enameling. Most pieces are not marked.

Bowl, Green, Purple, Pink Poppies, Gold Leaves, Ruffled Edge, Crimped, 5 x 9 In. 316.00
Vase, Chrysanthemums, Luster Violet Ground, Acid Etched, 4 Sides, 7 1/2 x 3 1/2 In. 345.00
Vase, Enameled Daffodils, Applied Gold Scrolls, On Teal, Sterling Silver Rim, 8 1/4 In. .. 1035.00
Vase, Enameled Lavender Hydrangea, On Frosted Ground, Scalloped Rim, 16 In. 1495.00
Vase, Enameled Orchid, Gold Flowered Tracery At Rim, 11 In. 336.00
Vase, Enameled Violets, Melon Ribbed, On Iridescent Frosted Ground, 15 1/2 In. 865.00
Vase, Enameled, Violets, Gold Leaves, On Green Frosted Ground, Signed, 10 In. 345.00
Vase, Green Irises, Dragonflies, On Frosted Ground, Raised Gold Details, 15 1/2 In. 690.00
Vase, Lily-Of-The-Valley, On Light Yellow Transparent Ground, Paris, 20th Century, 6 In. 200.00
Vase, Maroon Branches & Leaves, Blooming Flower, On Frosted Ground, 12 1/4 In. 308.00
Vase, Trumpet, Burgundy Thistle Petals, Textured Iridescent Honey Ground, 12 In. 575.00

MT. WASHINGTON Glass Works started in 1837 in South Boston, Massachusetts. In 1870 the company moved to New Bedford, Massachusetts. Many types of art glass were made there until 1894, when the company merged with Pairpoint Manufacturing Co. Amberina, Burmese, Crown Milano, Cut Glass, Peachblow, and Royal Flemish are each listed in their own category.

Biscuit Jar, Cover, Enameled Dancing Man & Woman, Gold Scrolls, 6 x 7 In. 400.00
Biscuit Jar, Cover, Enameled Gold Chrysanthemum, Signed, 8 1/2 x 7 In. 1495.00
Biscuit Jar, Enameled Acorn, Oak Leaf, Signed, 9 x 7 In. 430.00
Bride's Bowl, Griffins, Flowers, Yellow, White, 11 1/2 x 9 In. 800.00
Bride's Bowl, Pink On White, Griffins, Ruffled Edge, Silver Plated Holder, 13 In. 1150.00
Celery Dish, Regis, Scalloped Hobstar Foot, 9 1/2 x 4 1/2 In. 950.00
Celery Vase, Pink To Clear, Enameled Birds, Flowers, Silver Plated Holder, 8 In. 489.00
Creamer, Yellow Edge, Piecrust Crimped Edge, 5 In. 485.00
Ewer, Roman Gold, Enameled Gilt Orange Flowering Vine, 7 In. 288.00
Ice Cream Set, Strawberry-Diamond Cutting, 7 Piece 595.00
Pickle Castor, Albertine 2420.00
Pickle Castor, Ribbed, Timothy Canty, Silver Plated Lid, 6 In. 575.00
Salt & Pepper, Yellow To White, Strawberries, Silver Plate Holder 550.00
Saltshaker, Yellow Flowers, Leaves, Metal Chick's Head Cover, 2 3/4 In. ....195.00 to 252.00
Sugar, Melon Ribbed & Shell, Enameled Pansies, Bail Handle, 3 1/2 In. 100.00
Sugar Shaker, Cockle Shell Shape, Flowers On Ribbed Body, 4 In. 5500.00
Sugar Shaker, Fig Shape 1850.00
Sugar Shaker, Melon Ribbed, Flowers, 3 1/4 In. 115.00
Sweetmeat, Cover, Mother-Of-Pearl, Diamond-Quilted, 5 x 4 1/4 In. 402.00
Toothpick, Enameled, Blackberries, Blossoms, Square Rim, Satin, 2 5/8 In. 485.00
Tray, Albertine, Enameled Flowers 800.00
Vase, Dotted Swiss, Satin Pink To White, Applied Clear Edge, 9 1/2 In. 460.00
Vase, Flattened Hobnail, Mother-Of-Pearl Satin, Rolled Inward Rim, 5 3/4 In. 585.00
Vase, Mountains, Light Blue Interior, Overhanging Trees, 6 1/2 In. 550.00
Vase, Pink Swirl, Satin, Ruffled Edge, 10 In. 230.00

MULBERRY ware was made in the Staffordshire district of England from about 1850 to 1860. The dishes were decorated with a reddish brown transfer design, now called *mulberry*. Many of the patterns are similar to those used for flow blue and other Staffordshire transfer wares.

Pitcher, Romantic Scene, Angular Handle, Staffordshire, 1850 .... 359.00

MULLER FRERES, French for Muller Brothers, made cameo and other glass from about 1895 to 1933. Their factory was first located in Luneville, then in nearby Croismare, France. Pieces were usually marked with the company name.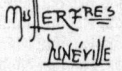

Lamp, Paneled, Etched, Art Deco Design, Wrought Iron Base, Signed, c.1930, 19 In. 1095.00

Sconce, Pink & White, Leaves, Wrought Iron Frame, 17 1/2 In. 1035.00
Vase, Broken Pine, Pine Trees, Silhouetted Against Landscape, Cameo, Signed 4750.00
Vase, Burgundy Flowers, Umber Stems, Leaves, On Pink, Cameo, Signed, 18 1/2 In. 8960.00
Vase, Hillside Of Pines & Spruce Trees, Amber Sky, Cameo, Signed, 9 1/2 In. 4480.00
Vase, Landscape, Wild Boar Scene, Dark Brown, Cameo, Signed, 1910, 15 In. 9600.00
Vase, Mottled Blue & White, Pink, Green, Brown, Flared Rim, Early 1900s, 9 In. 405.00
Vase, Orange & Purple, Oval, Satin, Cameo, Signed, 4 In. 258.00
Vase, Orange, Blue, Cameo, Wrought Iron Floral Base, 24 In. 1150.00
Vase, Pine & Spruce Trees, Lake Scene, Dusk To Sunset, Signed, 12 1/2 In. 3920.00
Vase, Pink Rose, Green Leaves, On Pink, Cylindrical, Cameo, Signed, 10 In. 2875.00
Vase, Poppy Blossoms & Leaves, Cameo, 9 In. 4025.00
Vase, Trees, Distant Forest, On Yellow, Cameo, Signed, 2 3/4 In. 785.00
Vase, Yellow, Red Flowers, Cameo, 8 1/2 In. 805.00

MUNCIE Clay Products Company was established by Charles Benham in Muncie, Indiana, in 1922. The company made pottery for the florist and giftshop trade. The company closed by 1939. Pieces are marked with the name *Muncie* or just with a system of numbers and letters, like *IA*.

MUNCIE

Vase, Blue, Pink Matte Glaze, Handles, 6 In. 138.00
Vase, Orange, Green Mottled Matte Glaze, 8 In. 92.00

MURANO, see Glass-Venetian category.

MUSIC boxes and musical instruments are listed here. Phonograph records, jukeboxes, phonographs, and sheet music are listed in other categories in this book.

Banjo, 4 Strings, Painted, Geometric, Mottled Green Celluloid, Case, 33 1/2 In. 83.00
Banjo, 5 Strings, A.C. Fairbanks, Whyte Ladyie, No. 7, Resonator, Case, 37 In. 4312.00
Banjo, 5 Strings, Fretless, JB Stewart, Big Stone Gap, Va., Pat. Oct. 22-95, 1800s, 35 In. .. 644.00
Banjo, 5 Strings, S.S. Stewart, Pearl Inlay, Case, 1880s 600.00
Bow, Violin, Mother-Of-Pearl, Line Inlay, Case, Germany, 23 1/2 In. 85.00
Box, 3 Bells & Drum, 5 Strikers, Swiss, 1880s, 8 1/2 x 10 1/4 In. 2415.00
Box, A. Perrlet & Co., Geneva, Burl, Inlay, Black Lacquer, 12 Tunes, Swiss, 7 x 27 In. 1120.00
Box, Berliner, Ideal, Sublime Harmonie, Interchangeable Cylinder, Inlaid Case, 8 x 29 In. 2590.00
Box, Capital, 8 Tunes, Oak Case, 19th Century, 15 In. 2300.00
Box, Capitol, Self Playing, Steel Cylinders, 44 Teeth, Oak Case, Picture In Lid, 7 x 15 In. 3450.00
Box, Cylinder, 6 Bells, Swiss, 11 In. 1100.00
Box, Cylinder, Ideal, Soprano Repeater, Floral Inlay, Handle, 8 3/8 x 31 In. 920.00
Box, Cylinder, Inlaid, 6 Bells, 12 Tunes, Rosewood Case, Swiss, 12 x 15 x 26 In. 2240.00
Box, Cylinder, Mahogany Case, Musical Instrument Inlay, 6 Tunes, Swiss, 15 1/2 In. 394.00
Box, Cylinder, Walnut, Ratchet, Swiss, 1890s, 8 x 23 x 9 1/2 In. 488.00
Box, Disc, Impersonator No. 27, 1904 St. Louis Fair Decal, Wood, 4 Discs, 5 x 8 x 7 In. . 460.00
Box, Empress, Mahogany, 60 12-In. Discs, 19th Century, 17 x 10 x 15 In. 2895.00
Box, Floral Inlay, 8 Tunes, 6 Bells, Brass Strikers, Rosewood, Swiss, 22 x 11 In. 2185.00
Box, Herophon, Crank Operates Bellows, Germany, 19th Century, 11 x 19 In. 345.00
Box, Inlaid, Drum, Etched Bells, Castinette, Rosewood Case, 12 Tunes, 10 x 13 x 26 In. ... 3360.00
Box, Inlay, 5 Bells, 8 Tunes, Rosewood Case, Single Comb, 21 x 12 1/2 x 11 In. 920.00
Box, Inlay, Rosewood Case, 8 Tunes, Geneva, 5 1/2 x 20 x 8 3/8 In. 1090.00
Box, Kalliope, 22 Discs, 27-In., Case, Leipzig, Germany, 1890 ....11500.00
Box, Mahogany, Symphonion, Carved, 6 Interchangeable Discs, c.1895, 23 x 20 In. 4480.00
Box, Mermod Freres, Mira, 11 Discs, 10 x 18 In. 2875.00
Box, Mother-Of-Pearl Cartouche, 9 Bells, 2 Tunes, Tune Card, Swiss, 1880s, 24 5/8 In. .. 2645.00
Box, Oak, Carved Pillars, Center Door, Claw Feet, Continental, 30 x 24 In. 575.00
Box, Onyx Lid, Divided Interior, White Metal Base, Table, 4 3/4 x 7 1/4 In. 440.00
Box, Paillard, Cylinder, Interchangeable, Inlaid, Case, 18 x 38 In. 5750.00
Box, Paillard, Swiss, 1883 .... *Illus* 2075.00
Box, Polyphon No. 104, 1900 .... *Illus* 3824.00
Box, Regina, Disc, Birch, Mahogany Finish, Stenciled Design, c.1900, Floor Model 8815.00
Box, Regina, Inlaid, Sarcophagus Top, Mahogany Case, Model No. 55149, 27 Discs 3960.00
Box, Regina, Mahogany Case, Domed Lid, 12 1/4-In. Disc 2070.00
Box, Regina, Mahogany Case, Paneled Lid, 15 1/2-In. Disc, Floor Cabinet, 42 1/2 In. 5460.00
Box, Regina, Mahogany, Casket Lid, Rope Twist, Single Comb, 21 x 19 x 12 In. 2475.00

Music, Box,
Polyphon No.
104, 1900

Music, Box, Paillard, Swiss, 1883

Box, Regina, No. 15, Coin-Operated, Oak Case, 12 1/2 x 22 1/2 In. 4025.00
Box, Singing Bird, Alpine Scene Inside Lid, c.1835, 3 5/8 In. 9600.00
Box, Singing Bird, Alpine Scene, Leather Case, c.1865, 3 7/8 In. 7800.00
Box, Singing Bird, Blue Enameled Body, Feathered Bird, Bun Feet, 1 x 4 In. 750.00
Box, Singing Bird, Blue Panels, Watteauesque Scenes On Case 2875.00
Box, Singing Bird, Enamel Birds & Leaves, Feathered Bird Inside, 4 1/2 In. 4830.00
Box, Singing Bird, Flapping Wings, Tinplate, Germany, 10 In. 200.00
Box, Singing Bird, Fruitwood, Parquetry, Cage, Edwardian, Gilt Metal Mount, Tole, 11 In. 2400.00
Box, Singing Bird, Grapevine On Lid, Floral Bouquet, c.1835, 3 3/4 In. 3600.00
Box, Singing Bird, Silver Plate, Serpentine Front, Sides, Leather Case 805.00
Box, Singing Bird, Silver, Enameled, 18th Century Lovers, Continental 4315.00
Box, Stella, Birch Case, Embossed, Handle, 25 Discs, 19th Century, 24 x 19 x 12 In. 1380.00
Box, Stella, Burled Walnut, Ball & Claw Foot, Table, 20 In. 6900.00
Box, Symphonion, Lithograph, Double Comb, Circassian Walnut, Schutz-Mark, 12 Discs . 1350.00
Box, Tortoiseshell, Painting, Alpine Scene, Key, 3 1/2 x 2 1/4 In. 460.00
Bugle, Brass, Military School, Mid 19th Century, 7 1/2 In. 165.00
Case, Violin, Biedermeier, Fruitwood, Black Piping, Baize, Domed Lid, Brass Handle . . . 560.00
Drum, Bass, Skin Heads, Metal Tension Rods, Painted Red, Wood Stand, 15 1/2 x 29 In. . . 310.00
Drum, Carved Wood, Rawhide Head, African, 20 1/2 In. 115.00
Drum, Parade, Brass Body, Hand-Wrought Iron Fittings, Painted Rim 395.00
Drum, Parade, Skin Heads, Leather Slide Tensions, Rope Tension, 24 x 22 In. 505.00
Drum, Skin Head, Copper Tacked Shell, Brass Mount, 25 1/2 x 26 In. 450.00
Flute, Hayes & Co., Extra C# Foot Joint Roller, Silver, France 460.00
Fork, Tuning, Blacksmith-Made, Pennsylvania, 18th Century 250.00
Harmonica, M. Hohner, Chromonica Model, Professional Model, Case, 7 In. 100.00
Harp, Brass & Hardwood, Fluted Column Support, Carved 4 Toed Feet, 32 x 68 In. 920.00
Harp, George Freemontle, Brass Plate, 67 x 33 In. 950.00
Harp, Sebastian & Erhard Patent Harp No. 552, 68 x 31 In. 505.00
Harp, Sebastian & Pierre Erhard, Bird's-Eye Maple, 7 Pedals, Gargoyle Feet, 70 1/2 In. . . 3585.00
Horn, Concertone, Brass, Copper Band, Leather Travel Case, 7 In. 400.00
Hurdy-Gurdy, Capra, Wagon, Wooden Wheels, Mirror, Sheet Music Inserts, 64 In. 3450.00
Mandolin, Tortoiseshell Guard Plate, Mother-Of-Pearl, Rosewood, Italy, c.1900, 24 In. . . . 78.00
Organ, Band, Military, Wurlitzer, Style 125, 10 Tunes, 44 Note Roll, 65 x 80 In. 7475.00
Organ, Band, Wurlitzer, 52 Wood Pipes, Snare & Bass Drum, Cymbal, Glockenspiel 7150.00
Organ, Pump, Burled Walnut, George Woods & Co., Boston, 48 x 51 x 30 1/2 In. 450.00
Organ, Pump, Empire, Mahogany, Portable, J. Foster, N.H., 32 1/2 x 29 1/2 x 13 1/4 In. . . . 340.00
Organ, Reed, Chicago Cottage, 12 Stops, 2 Sets Of Reeds, c.1894 . . . . 700.00
Organ, Roller, 26 Wood Cobs, Wood Case, 19th Century, 17 In. 490.00
Organ, Roller, Gem, Hand Crank, Stenciled Case, 12 Cobs, Autophone Co., 8 x 14 1/2 In. . 400.00
Organ, Roller, Gem, Table, Hand Crank, Autophone Co., 12 1/2 x 18 In. 400.00
Organ, Roller, Mettez, Wood, Full Size, 26 x 39 In. 917.00
Organ, Street, Hand Crank, Carl Frei 8365.00
Organette, Paper Roll, Turning Crank, Oak Case, Mechanical Orguinette Co., 12 x 9 In. . 345.00
Organette, Perforated Paper Roll, Walnut Case, 26 In. 290.00
Organette, Table, Hand Crank, Walnut, 12 Paper Rolls, 7 x 11 In. 290.00
Piano, Baby Grand, Baldwin, No. 132079 . . . . 2070.00
Piano, Baby Grand, Steinway & Sons, Ebonized, No. 164658 . . . . 8815.00

Piano, Baby Grand, Steinway, Bench, No. 346076 . . . . 5455.00
Piano, Baby Grand, Steinway, Mahogany, No. 285152 . . . . 8050.00
Piano, Baby Grand, Stodart & Co., Square, 36 1/2 x 71 In. 336.00
Piano, Baldwin, Hamilton, Bench, 45 x 57 In. 230.00
Piano, Concert Grand, Chickering, Ebony Case, c.1893, 8 Ft. 9 In. 7840.00
Piano, Grand, Erhard, Carved, Gilded, Amboyna, Burlwood, c.1870, 8 Ft. 6 In. 15525.00
Piano, Grand, Henry Siegling, Rosewood, Cabriole Legs, 19th Century, 6 Ft. 6 In. 700.00
Piano, Grand, Parlor, Parker Piano, Mahogany, Mid 20th Century, 4 Ft. 1840.00
Piano, Grand, Vernis-Martin, Satinwood, Giltwood, 85 Keys 5290.00
Piano, Grand, William Knabe Co., Rosewood, c.1890, 7 Ft. 6 In. 1210.00
Pianoforte, A. Babcock, Rosewood, Brass Inlay, 34 x 68 In. 900.00
Pianoforte, Classical, Brass Inlaid, Mahogany, A. Babcock, Boston, c.1830 . . . . 1955.00
Saxophone, C.C. Conn, Chrome Plated, Velvet Lined Case 290.00
Tambourine, Painted Rawhide, Indians On Horseback, Leslie Cope, 1989, 10 In. 80.00
Trumpet, Olympic, 1984, Los Angeles, Opening Ceremony Official Blessing, Case 2760.00
Ukelin, Manufacturers Advertising Co., Paper Label, Case, 27 1/2 In. 60.00
Violin, A. Monzino & Figli, Maple, Italy, Case 375.00

MZ AUSTRIA is the wording on a mark used by Moritz Zdekauer on porcelains made at his works in Altrolau, Austria, from 1884 to 1909. The mark was changed to MZ Altrolau in 1909, when the firm was purchased by C.M. Hutschenreuther. The firm operated under the name Altrolau Porcelain Factories from 1909 to 1945. It was nationalized after World War II. The pieces were decorated with lavish floral patterns and overglaze gold decoration. Full sets of dishes were made as well as vases, toilet sets, and other wares.

M Z Austria

Biscuit Jar, Flowers, Bulbous, Ribbed, 6 In. 100.00

NAILSEA glass was made in the Bristol district in England from 1788 to 1873. It was made by many different factories, not just the Nailsea Glass House. Many pieces were made with loopings of either white or colored glass as decoration.

Bottle, Bellows, Red & White Loopings, Handles, 1885, 14 1/2 In. 373.00
Bowl, Ruby Ruffled Rim, Amber Collar, 3-Footed, Metal Holder, 6 In. 224.00
Rolling Pin, Blue Aqua, White Loopings, 1880-1910, 18 In. 112.00
Vase, Green, White Looping, Flared, Applied Foot, South Jersey, 1860, 7 1/2 In. 1045.00
Vase, Trumpet, Loopings Blue & White, Ruffled Edge, Metal Holder, 9 In. 140.00
Vase, Trumpet, Opaque White, Blue Looping, Flared, Crimped Rim, 15 1/2 In., Pair 1570.00
Wafer Tray, Blue & White Looping, Flared Rim, Pontil, c.1870-1887, 1 3/4 x 2 1/2 In. 225.00

NAKARA is a trade name for a white glassware made about 1900 by the C. F. Monroe Company of Meriden, Connecticut. It was decorated in pastel colors. The glass was very similar to another glass made by the company called *Wave Crest*. The company closed in 1916. Boxes for use on a dressing table are the most commonly found Nakara pieces. The mark is not found on every piece.

NAKARA

Box, Egret Cover, Enameled, Egrets In Flight With Sunset, Gilt, Pink, Green, 4 1/8 In. . . . 1265.00
Box, Green Crown Mold, Pink & White Roses, Lined, Marked, 8 1/2 In. 1555.00
Jewelry Box, Pink Flowers, Marked, 4 1/4 x 4 1/2 In. 345.00
Pin Tray, Green, Pink Flowers, Silver Plated Hardware, 3 3/4 In. 58.00
Pin Tray, Pink & Green, White Flowers, Metal Ring, Marked, 6 In. 120.00
Trinket Dish, Pink, White Flowers, Footed, Marked, 5 In. 40.00

NANKING is a type of blue-and-white porcelain made in Canton, China, since the late eighteenth century. It is very similar to Canton, which is listed under its own name in this book. Both Nanking and Canton are part of a larger group now called *Chinese export* porcelain. Nanking has a spear-and-post border and may have gold decoration.

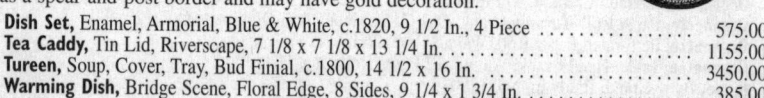

Dish Set, Enamel, Armorial, Blue & White, c.1820, 9 1/2 In., 4 Piece 575.00
Tea Caddy, Tin Lid, Riverscape, 7 1/8 x 7 1/8 x 13 1/4 In. 1155.00
Tureen, Soup, Cover, Tray, Bud Finial, c.1800, 14 1/2 x 16 In. 3450.00
Warming Dish, Bridge Scene, Floral Edge, 8 Sides, 9 1/4 x 1 3/4 In. 385.00

NAPKIN RINGS were in fashion from 1869 to about 1900. They were made of silver, porcelain, wood, and other materials. They are still being made today. The most popular rings with collectors are the silver plated figural examples. Small, realistic figures were made to hold the ring. Good and poor reproductions of the more expensive rings are now being made and collectors must be very careful.

Figural, 2 Standing Bird Supports, Monogram, Silver Plate, 19th Century, 3 In.	97.00
Figural, Angel Blowing Horn, Silver Plate, Simpson, Hall, Miller & Co., 4 x 4 In.	920.00
Figural, Antelope, Ring On Back, Engraved Mary, Flowers, Silver Plate, 3 x 4 In.	82.00
Figural, Box By Bush, Quadruple Plate, Derby Silver, 3 x 2 1/2 In.	575.00
Figural, Cherub, & Bud Vase, Harry To Alice, Silver Plate, 5 1/4 x 4 In.	1035.00
Figural, Dog & Cat, Fighting, Floral Base, Silver Plate, Meriden, 3 1/4 x 3 1/2 In.	690.00
Figural, Dog, Barking, Hunched Forward, Ring On Back, Flowers, Silver Plate, 3 In.	517.00
Figural, Dog, Looking At Frog On Ring, Silver Plate, 2 1/2 x 4 1/2 In.	977.00
Figural, Dog, Sitting, Silver Plate, James Tufts, Boston, 3 1/2 x 4 3/4 In.	1092.00
Figural, Kate Greenaway Figure, Holding Girl, Silver Plate, Reed & Barton, 4 In.	468.00
Figural, Parrot Atop Barrel, Silver Plate, 3 x 3 1/4 In.	345.00
Figural, Parrot, Standing, Base, Silver Plate, Meriden, 4 x 3 1/4 In.	833.00
Figural, Peacock, On Ring, Scroll Base, Silver Plate, 2 1/2 x 3 1/2 In.	402.00
Figural, Sailor Beside Anchor, Geometric, Leaf Shape Feet, Silver Plate, 3 3/4 In.	440.00
Figural, Sailor Pulling Anchor, Bud Vase At Top, Silver Plate, 4 x 5 1/4 In.	1150.00
Figural, Workman With Barrel, Man Hoisting Satchel, Silver Plate, 3 x 4 1/4 In.	632.00
Flower & Leaf Border, Stippled Ground, Russian Silver, 1 1/2 x 2 In.	253.00
Silver Band, Hammered, Oval, Kalo Shop, 3 1/4 x 5/8 In.	95.00
Silver Band, Hammered, Rectangular, Lebolt & Co., 2 1/4 x 5/8 In.	65.00
Silver Band, Hammered, Rectangular, Marshall Field Craft Shop, 3 1/8 In.	85.00

NASH glass was made in Corona, New York, from about 1928 to 1931. A. Douglas Nash bought the Corona glassworks from Louis C. Tiffany in 1928 and founded the A. Douglas Nash Corporation with support from his father, Arthur J. Nash. Arthur had worked at the Webb factory in England and for the Tiffany Glassworks in Corona.

NASH

Plate, Gold Ground, Signed, 9 In.	290.00
Vase, Gold, Iridescent, Ruffed Rim, Disk Base, Inscribed, 9 In.	930.00
Wine, Chintz, Alternating Lavender & Green, Blue Stem, Signed, 6 In.	200.00

NAUTICAL antiques are listed in this category. Any of the many objects that were made or used by the seafaring trade, including ship parts, models, and tools, are included. Other pieces may be found listed under Scrimshaw.

Anchor, Cast Iron, 36 In.	160.00
Anchor, Iron, 28 In.	65.00
Bag, Sail Maker's, Canvas, 30 Tools	250.00
Bell, Ship's, Brass, Engraved Intrepid	800.00
Bell, Ship's, Bronze, Cast Titanic, Manufacturer's Insignia, 7 In.	6000.00
Bell, Ship's, W.T. Garratt & Co., San Francisco, Nickel Plated Bronze, 12 x 10 1/2 In.	345.00
Binnacle, Brass, With Sidelight & Compass, 10 x 12 In.	200.00
Binnacle, Copper & Brass Case, Lionel Compass, Electrified Light, WWII Era	500.00
Binnacle, Yacht, Compass, 2 Side Lanterns, 25 In.	1540.00
Binnacle & Compass, Lionel Corp., Copper & Brass	595.00
Boarding Pike, Iron Head, Wood Shaft, Marked R61, 76 In.	405.00
Box, Sailor's, Inlaid Ivory, c.1850	1250.00
Box, Sewing, Rosewood, Ivory Inlay, Lift-Out Tray With 7 Inlaid Lids, 5 x 13 x 8 In.	345.00
Calipers, G. Ada, S. London, Moon Phases, Brass	9200.00
Canoe, Birch Bark, 12 Ft.	5500.00
Canoe, Restored, 1901, 16 Ft.	4800.00
Canoe Seat, Wicker, Leather Back & Wrapped Legs, Storage Compartment, 17 x 17 In.	138.00
Chest, Campaign, Camphorwood, Brass, 3 Over 3 Drawers, Ball Feet, 42 x 39 In.	3795.00
Chest, Chart, Pine, Green Paint, 7 x 88 x 9 1/2 In.	200.00
Chest, Sea, Painted Inside Lid, Clipper Ship With American Flag	440.00
Chest, Sea, Pine, Dovetailed, Lift Top, Red Paint, 17 1/2 x 48 x 16 1/2 In.	530.00
Chronometer, F.M. Moore, Belfast & Dublin, No. 3780, 1890, 6 1/2 In.	1800.00

Chronometer, H.H. Heinrich, New York, No. 1151, Engraved Vignettes, Eagle, c.1890 ... 1980.00
Chronometer, Joseph Sewell, Liverpool, No. 3321, Mahogany Case, England 9520.00
Chronometer, Morris Tobias, All Keys 2415.00
Chronometer, Morris Tobias, Maker To The Admiralty, London, Double Cased 2415.00
Chronometer, R. Hornby & Son, Liverpool, No. 1353, 1850, 6 3/4 In. 3300.00
Chronometer, Thomas Mercer, 12 Jewels, Silvered Dial, Wind Indicator, St. Albans 935.00
Chronometer, Ulysse Nardin, Wind Indicator, Seconds 198.00
Clock, Chelsea Ship's Bell, Made For Tiffany 1095.00
Clock, Ship's, Brass, L.A. Karcher & Co., Boston, 5 1/2 In. 230.00
Clock, Ship's, Brass, Ship's Wheel Shape, Salem, 5 In. 50.00
Clock, Ship's, Brass, Ship's Wheel Shape, Waterbury, 8 In. 175.00
Clock, Ship's, Dial Marked U.S. Navy, E. Howard & Co., Boston, U.S.A., 7 3/4 In. 805.00
Clock, Ship's, Seth Thomas, Bell Under, Charles L. Hanff, Greenport, N.Y., 1914 ..... 518.00
Clock, Ship's, Seth Thomas, Brass Bell, Silvered Dial, Roman Numerals, 1870, 10 In. ... 1240.00
Clock, Ship's, Seth Thomas, Chrome Plated, 10 1/4 x 7 In. 460.00
Clock, Ship's, Seth Thomas, Wood Back, Brass Case, 8 In. 230.00
Clock, Ship's, U.S. Navy, Chelsea, 7 In. 225.00
Clock & Barometer, Waterbury, Jeweled Movement, Copper, 5 1/2 x 4 In. 475.00
Clock & Barometer/Thermometer, Ship's Wheels, Bronze Base, Ball Feet, 9 x 14 In. ... 550.00
Compass, Ship's, Brass, Dry Card, Robert Merrill, N.Y., Box, Early 19th Century, 7 In. ... 405.00
Compass, Ship's, Friction Fit Cover With Scrimshaw Star, Abalone Inlay, 2 1/4 In. 750.00
Dial, Augsburg, Compass In Base, Hour Ring, Hinged Latitude Scale, Plumb Bob, 9 In. .. 835.00
Diorama, Clipper Ship, Norwegian Flag, Shadowbox Frame, 22 x 4 x 17 In. 82.00
Diorama, Sailing Ship, White Sails, Lighthouse, Gesso Frame, 23 x 32 1/2 In. 1430.00
Figurehead, Male, c.1855, 7 Ft. 2750.00
Figurehead, Sea Horse, 1712, 7 Ft. 1100.00
Figurehead, Woman, Blond Hair Pulled Back, Carved Scrolls, 41 In. x 15 1/2 In. 3525.00
Flask, Navy, Colt, Revolver, 1851 .... 1250.00
Fog Horn, L.D. Lothrup, Gloucester, Mass., Wooden Case, Hand Operated, 1901, 16 In. ... 365.00
Gauge, Determines Strength Of Rope, Boxwood, Brass Sliding Caliper, 6 1/2 x 2 In. 315.00
Gauge, Marking, Cooper's 4025.00
Half-Model, 4-Masted Schooner, Mounted, 6 3/4 x 41 In. 440.00
Half-Model, Fleur De France, Peter Ward, On Mahogany Board, 27 In. 200.00
Half-Model, Penguin, Peter Ward, 8 x 21 In. 345.00
Half-Model, Schooner, Alternating Light & Dark Lifts, Mounted, 10 x 36 In. 1610.00
Half-Model, Stiletto, Peter Ward, On Mahogany Board, 8 5/8 x 33 In. 230.00
Half-Model, US Light Vessel, No. 15, Painted Frame, 12 x 47 1/2 In. 345.00
Harpoon, Wooden Shaft, Whalebone Double Flue, Lanyard Ring, 22 1/2 In. 175.00
Hat, Straw, Lined, Layer Of Tar Cover, 11 1/2 x 10 1/2 In. 4180.00
Helmet, Diving, 3-Light, 3-Bolt, Copper & Brass, Russia 1155.00
Helmet, Diving, A. Schrader Sons, Brooklyn, Brass & Copper, With Original Wrench ... 5000.00
Helmet, Diving, Copper, Brass, Russia, Early 20th Century 1050.00
Knife, Sailor's, Whalebone, Brass Pins, Tortoise Inlay, 6 1/2 In. 130.00
Lamp, Buoy, 360 Degree Ruby Lens, Brass & Copper, 20 In. 605.00
Lamp, Fishing Boat, Oil Burning, Duplex, Red & Green Lens, Early 1900s 175.00
Lamp, Oil, Gimbal, c.1870 .... 525.00
Lamp, Running, Oil Burner, Black Paint 95.00
Lamp, Ship's Running, Brass, Seahorse, 19 In., Pair 230.00
Lamp, Ship's, F.O. Dewey, Boston, Mass., Brass, Early 19th Century, 20 In. 2300.00
Lamp, Ship's, Gimbal, Brass, Reeded Column, Dolphin Mounting Bracket, Globe, 8 In. ... 489.00
Lantern, Brass, Clear Lens, Perko, 17 x 9 1/2 In. 168.00
Lantern, Clear Font, Red Paint, 23 In. 90.00
Lantern, Mast, Fresnel Globe, Early 20th Century, 25 In., Pair 400.00
Lantern, Painted Black, Clear, Ribbed Lens, Nathaniel Tufts, Boston, Mass., 14 In. 220.00
Level, Ship's, L.S. Starrett Co., Athol, Ma., Original Wood Box 58.00
Load Leveling Machine, Ship's, Boosman, Amsterdam, Cased, 7 x 33 1/2 x 20 In. 575.00
Model, 2-Masted Schooner, American, Stephens & Kanau, 25 x 30 In. 460.00
Model, 2-Masted, Magic, America's Cup Yacht, 23 x 27 In. 715.00
Model, 3-Masted Schooner, Amerigo Vespucci, Mahogany Stand, 28 x 40 In. 840.00
Model, 3-Masted Schooner, Atlantic, 58 x 75 In. 2300.00
Model, 3-Masted Schooner, Iron Display Stand, c.1930 .... 1050.00
Model, 3-Masted, Portuguese, Bone, Mounted On Bone Sea, 7 x 5 1/4 In. 99.00
Model, Clipper Ship, American, 5 Carved Men, Mahogany Case, 36 In. 575.00

Model, Clipper Ship, British, Full Sail, Figurehead, Simulated Sea, Case, 24 x 16 In. 330.00
Model, Clipper Ship, Lighting, Copper Sheathing, Mahogany Case, 45 x 63 In. 3680.00
Model, Corsair, Peter Ward, On Mahogany Board, 9 x 33 In. 315.00
Model, Endeavour, 1934 America's Cup Yacht, Planked Deck, 54 x 36 In. 1540.00
Model, Friendship Sloop, Windsong, Benches, Plank On Frame, 72 x 52 In. 2300.00
Model, Harriet Lane, O.C. Becker, Glass & Wood Display Case, 1971, 10 x 18 1/2 In. ...   460.00
Model, Paddlewheel Steamer, Dreamland, Chesapeake Bay, 1940s, 44 x 82 x 23 In. 1200.00
Model, Pinky Sloop, Planked, Silver Lining, 3 Sails, On Wooden Cradle, 37 x 36 x 6 In. .   400.00
Model, Rainbow, 1934 America's Cup, Skylights, Life Boats, 70 x 48 In. 1800.00
Model, Roger B. Taney, Glass & Wood Display Case, O.C. Becker, 14 x 19 In. 290.00
Model, Schooner, America, Full-Rigged, Planked Mahogany Deck, 43 x 49 x 8 In. 2070.00
Model, Schooner, Bluenose, Planked Deck, Brass Trimmed Glass Case, 30 x 37 In. 805.00
Model, Ship, Saga Marastal, Glass & Brass Case & Stand, c.1935, Norway, 58 In. 4315.00
Model, Ship, USS Maine, Plexiglas & Wood Case, 28 x 12 In. 1208.00
Model, Steam Tug Boat, Active, Mahogany & Glass Case, 13 x 17 In. 1207.00
Model, Topaz, Brass & Glass Case, 17 x 24 In. 290.00
Model, Tug, Champion, On Mahogany Board, Glass Case, 12 x 23 In. 630.00
Model, USS Constitution, Cased, 40 x 55 In. 9900.00
Model, USS Constitution, O.C. Becker, Glass & Wood Display Case, 1928, 23 x 34 In. ...   575.00
Model, Whale Ship, Peru, Nantucket, Glass Case, 25 x 28 x 13 In. 1725.00
Model, Whaling Boat, Wood, Textile, Ropes, Tools, Spears, Oars, Glass Case, 20 x 23 In. .   460.00
Navigation Set, Sea Captain's, Brass, Sharkskin Case, 1860s 137.00
Octant, Crichton, Ebony, Ivory, Brass, Box 125.00
Pelorus, Kelvin White, Mahogany Box, c.1940, 7 1/2 In. 950.00
Ruler, Caliper, Stearns & Co., No. 98 1/2, Ivory, 4 Fold, Opens To 12 In. 400.00
Sextant, C. Plath, Hamburg, Metal & Brass, Mahogany Case, 1923 ....   375.00
Sextant, D. McGregor, 5 Colored Lenses, Brass Fittings, Ivory Label, 11 In. 440.00
Sextant, Kelvin & Hughes, Engraved Silver Scale, Wood Case, c.1917, 6 x 6 x 4 In. 300.00
Sextant, Liverpool, Ebony, Ivory, Brass, Oak Box, 4 x 12 x 11 In. 895.00
Sextant, Matsen & Co., England, Brass, Mahogany Case, 11 In. 1008.00
Sextant, N. Beck Pedersen, 2 Eyepieces, 7 Colored Lenses, Handle, 8 3/4 In. 495.00
Sextant, Original Box, Japan, World War II 175.00
Sextant, Pocket, Stanley, London, Brass, Leather Case, c.1890 ....   1375.00
Sextant, Pocket, Stanley, London, Brass, Silver Scale, 1884, 3 1/2 x 4 In. 200.00
Sextant, Spencer Browning & Rust, London, Brass, Early 1800s, 9 1/2 In. 495.00
Shaving Kit, Sea Captain's, Burl Mahogany, Silver Topped Jars, 3 1/2 x 9 1/2 In. 730.00
Ship In Bottle, 3-Masted, American, In Pinch Bottle 66.00
Ship Model, see Nautical, Model.
Sign, Directional, To Life Boats, Brass, 1920s, 4 3/4 x 20 In. 105.00
Sign, Wood, Carved, Boats For Sale & To Rent, Block Letters, Red Ground, 29 x 85 In. ...   800.00
Skiff, Mahogany, Red Paint, White Trim, 2 Oars, 9 Ft. 6 In. 560.00
Skiff, St. Lawrence River, c.1910, 13 Ft. 475.00
Sneak Boat, For Hunting Waterfowl, Kayak Style, Pair 935.00
Sword, Navy, US, Scabbard, 35 In. 80.00
Telegraph, Ship's, Wilcox & Crittenden & Co., Middletown, Conn., Brass, 8 1/4 In. 415.00
Telescope, 2-Draw, Brass, c.1875, 35 In. 259.00
Telescope, Berthiot Opt., Lyon, France, Floor, Brass, 35 In. 288.00
Telescope, Dolland, London, 3-Draw, Wood, Brass Hardware, 13 3/4 In. 140.00
Telescope, Midshipman's, 3-Draw, Wood Covered Barrel, Brass Trim 125.00
Telescope, Midshipman's, 4-Draw, Red Enameled Tube, Brass Trim 100.00
Telescope, Newton & Co. Opticians, London, Table Mount, Brass, 19th Century 1725.00
Telescope, T. Harris & Son, London, Table, Brass, Label, 4 x 30 In. 1783.00
Valentine, Shell, Octagonal, Hinged, To My Darling, 19th Century, 8 1/2 x 17 1/2 In. 4700.00
Wheel, Ship's, Iron Hub, Brass Inlay, 52 In. 520.00
Wheel, Ship's, Oak, Brass Hub, Mounted As Table, Mahogany Base, 60 In. 2070.00
Wheel, Ship's, Oak, Metal Center, 45 In. 192.00

A piece of ribbon can be "pressed" by pulling it across a warm light bulb.

Wheel, Ship's, Teak, Outer Ring, Iron Hub, 51 1/2 In. 230.00
Wheel, Ship's, Walnut, 8 Turned Spokes & Handles, 47 In. 330.00
Whistle, Nickel, 3-Tone, Carry Chain 115.00

NETSUKES are small ivory, wood, metal, or porcelain pieces used as toggles on the end of the cord that held a Japanese money pouch or inro. The earliest date from the sixteenth century. Many are miniature, carved works of art. This category also includes the ojime, the slide or string fastener that was used on the inro cord.

Boxwood, Shoki With Demon 230.00
Brass, Ojime, Seed Shape, Flowers, 19th Century 28.00
Hippo Tooth, 2 Children, Turtle, Treasure Bag, 2 In. 100.00
Hippo Tooth, 2 Figures With Fish, 1 5/8 In. 100.00
Hippo Tooth, 2 Playful Children, 1 1/2 In. 100.00
Hippo Tooth, Buddha, Child, 1 3/4 In. 100.00
Hippo Tooth, Buddha, Child, 2 In. 100.00
Hippo Tooth, Old Man With Staff, Monkey, 2 In. 100.00
Hippo Tooth, Old Man, Child, 1 3/4 In. 100.00
Hippo Tooth, Old Man, Child, Peach, 1 5/8 In. 100.00
Hippo Tooth, Seated Man With Child, 2 3/4 In. 100.00
Inro, 4 Stack, Lacquered, Inlay, Ducks In Flight, 3 1/8 x 1 3/4 In. 145.00
Inro, Gold Lacquered, Hawk On Railing, Gold Ground, Interior Gold Flakes, 3 3/4 In. 4928.00
Inro, Mother-Of-Pearl Inlay, Horn & Ivory, 2 Sections, 19th Century, 4 1/2 In. 4370.00
Ivory, 2 Monkeys On 3 Peaches, 1910, 1 1/2 In. 288.00
Ivory, 2 Oni Bemoaning Loss Of Raiden's Hand, 19th Century 748.00
Ivory, 3 Women With Brocade Ball, Signed Gyokudo, 20th Century 170.00
Ivory, 4 Children Playing In Tub 230.00
Ivory, Bird, Tree Stump, Masaharu, Late 19th Century 259.00
Ivory, Dreaming Figure, Monks At Shrine, Early 20th Century 290.00
Ivory, Entertainer With Monkey, Signed, 20th Century 185.00
Ivory, Fisherman, Children Drawing Up Fishnet, Signed, Late Meiji Period 290.00
Ivory, Frog, Monkey, Japan, Late 19th Century 170.00
Ivory, Ghost Attacking Kneeling Samurai, 18th Century 290.00
Ivory, Monkey In Human Garb Carrying Pole, c.1900 .... 690.00
Ivory, Monkey Trainer, Small Child, Signed 375.00
Ivory, Mother Dog, Pup, Resting, Japan, Late 19th Century, 2 In. 100.00
Ivory, Nesting Crane, Inlaid Eyes, c.1900 .... 230.00
Ivory, Pair Of Chestnuts 115.00
Ivory, Parrot, Perched On Branch, 19th Century 1090.00
Ivory, Pile Of Nuts, Landscape, Signed Gyokuhosai, Late 19th Century 230.00
Ivory, Priest Teaching Oni To Write, Signed, 20th Century 259.00
Ivory, Puppy Seated On Rock, Raised Paw, Signed Rantei Nagai, Late 18th Century 1725.00
Ivory, Rat, Inlaid Eyes, Resting On Coil Of Rope 890.00
Ivory, Red Eyed Rabbit, Woman With Rattle Suckling A Child, Signed, c.1900 .... 230.00
Ivory, Rooster, Signed 230.00
Ivory, Scholar, Rooster, Puppy Attacking Sleeping Devil, Late 19th Century 290.00
Ivory, Shoki, Mythical Chinese Hero, Fighting Devil, Japan, 18th Century 2650.00
Ivory, Snail 170.00
Ivory, Wasp, Gourd, Signed, 2 In. 230.00
Ivory, Woman Beside Sewing Box, Holding Cloth, 19th Century 400.00
Ivory, Woman With Lute Seated On Elephant, Polychrome, Late 19th Century 520.00
Lacquer, Cat, 19th Century 69.00
Ojime, Wood, 2 Rats In Piece Of Fruit, Inlaid Eyes, Signed 69.00
Ojime, Wood, Turtle, Inlaid Eyes, Signed Gyokko 300.00
Okimono, Wood, Shoki, With Oni In Hand, Signed Komin, 9 In. 518.00
Okimono, Wood, Sleeping Monkey, c.1900, 2 1/2 In. 115.00
Sandalwood, Rustic Retreat, Pavilions, Trees, Figures 632.00
Wood, Chinese Lion Guarding Pearl, 18th Century 170.00
Wood, Folded Umbrella, 19th Century 80.00
Wood, Groom Washing Horse In Tub, Signed Sosui, 20th Century 3450.00
Wood, Laughing Man, c.1900 .... 115.00
Wood, Man Standing By Rabbit, 19th Century 115.00
Wood, Octopus, Inlaid Eyes, Japan, Signed 460.00

Wood, Owl Perched On Branch, Inlaid Eyes, Signed, Mitsuhiro, 19th Century 980.00
Wood, Wolf Guarding Decaying Skull, 18th Century 259.00

NEW MARTINSVILLE Glass Manufacturing Company was established
in 1901 in New Martinsville, West Virginia. It was bought and
renamed the Viking Glass Company in 1944. In 1987 Kenneth Dalzell,
former president of Fostoria Glass Company, purchased the factory
and renamed it Dalzell-Viking. Production ceased in 1998.

Figurine, Mama Bear 225.00
Figurine, Piglet, Standing 145.00
Figurine, Seal, Ball On Nose, 7 In. 75.00
Meadow Wreath, Relish, 8 In. 5.00
Moondrops, Candlestick, Ruffled Edge, Cobalt Blue, 2 In. 55.00
Muranese, Bowl, Pink, Gold Iridescent Interior, 5 1/2 In. 99.00
Radiance, Bonbon, Footed, Ruby, 5 1/2 In. 32.00
Radiance, Celery Dish, Cobalt Blue, Pedestal, 10 In. 150.00
Radiance, Cheese & Cracker Set, Ice Blue, 11 In. 195.00
Radiance, Creamer, Amber 11.00
Radiance, Sugar, Ruby 30.00
Radiance, Tumbler, Amber, 9 Oz. 23.00

NEWCOMB Pottery was founded by Ellsworth and William Woodward
at Sophie Newcomb College, New Orleans, Louisiana, in 1895. The
work continued through the 1940s. Pieces of this art pottery are marked
with the printed letters *NC* and often have the incised initials of the
artist as well. Most pieces have a matte glaze and incised decoration.

Bowl, Carved Crocus, Lavender Matte Glaze, 4 Handles, Simpson, 4 1/2 x 5 1/2 In. 3450.00
Bowl, Carved Water Lilies & Leaves, Desiree Roman, 1904, 3 1/4 x 8 1/2 In. 4025.00
Chocolate Pot, Spanish Moss, Annie Simpson 7480.00
Inkwell, Pink Thistles, Green Leaves, Ivory Ground, G.R. Smith, 1902, 2 3/4 x 4 In. 3220.00
Jar, Live Oaks, Spanish Moss, Denim Blue Ground, Matte, A.F. Simpson, 1929, 5 In. 8625.00
Loving Cup, Clover Blossoms, Blue & White, 3 Handles, K. Kopman, 1902, 4 In. 2645.00
Pitcher, Incised Daisies, White, Yellow Stamen, Pale, Cobalt Blue Border 1870.00
Plate, Band Of Carved Flowers, Blue & Green Ground, Henrietta Bailey, 1906, 8 In. 980.00
Tile, Tea, Carved Overlapping Crocuses, Henrietta Bailey, 1915, 5 3/8 In. 1700.00
Tile, Tea, Carved Wild Roses, Anna Frances Simpson, 1916, 5 3/4 In. 1400.00
Vase, Band Of Carved Pink, Green Crocuses, Dark Blue Ground, 4 5/8 In. 1900.00
Vase, Band Of Pink Flowers, Blue Ground, Sadie Irvine, 1927, 6 x 3 In. 1725.00
Vase, Blue, Gray Matte, 4 3/4 In. 430.00
Vase, Carved Catfish, Swimming Through Swirls, Sabina Wells, 1902, 9 3/4 In. 24000.00
Vase, Carved Flowers, Sadie Irvine, 7 1/2 In. 1495.00
Vase, Carved Grapes & Leaves, Medium Blue, Matte, Bulbous, S. Irvine, 1919, 8 In. 5465.00
Vase, Carved Landscape Scene, Moss Laden Oak Trees, Henrietta Bailey, 8 1/2 In. 3105.00
Vase, Carved Live Oaks, Spanish Moss, Blue Ground, Bulbous, S. Irvine, 1929, 5 In. 4315.00
Vase, Carved Palm Trees, Full Moon, Sadie Irvine, 1919, 10 3/4 x 6 1/2 In. 8050.00
Vase, Carved Pine Trees, Full Moon, Henrietta Bailey, 1931, 9 1/4 x 4 In. 8050.00
Vase, Carved Pink & Red Loquat Fruit, Leaves, Sadie Irvine, 1924, 6 1/2 In. 1150.00
Vase, Carved Stylized Blossoms, Allover Lavender Glaze, S. Irvine, 1913, 7 1/4 In. 1725.00
Vase, Carved Willows, Spanish Moss, Full Moon, Blue Ground, Matte, 1928, 6 In. 4600.00
Vase, Carved Wreath Of Pink Trumpet Vines, Blue Ground, A.F. Simpson, 1921, 9 In. . . . 3220.00
Vase, Carved, Painted Landscape, High Glaze, Sadie Irvine, 4 In. 3105.00
Vase, Carved, Painted Orchids, Blue Ground, Egg Shape, H. Bailey, 1917, 14 In. 10350.00
Vase, Carved, Painted, Flowers, Henrietta Bailey, 7 In. 2990.00
Vase, Carved, Painted, Organic, High Glaze, Leona Nicholson, 9 In. 16415.00
Vase, Carved, Pink Flowers, Blue Ground, Bulbous, A.F. Simpson, 1924, 4 1/2 In. 1840.00
Vase, Carved, Pink Japanese Iris, Green Stems, Blossoms At Rim, 4 1/2 In. 3220.00
Vase, Carved, Transitional, Trees, Spanish Moss, Blue, Sadie Irvine, 1914, 8 1/4 In. 5175.00
Vase, Espanol, Blue Green & Pink, Denim Blue Ground, S. Irvine, 1927, 5 1/2 In. 4025.00
Vase, Flower Band At Shoulder, Blue, White, Sadie Irvine, 1925, 3 5/8 In. 1100.00
Vase, Flowers, Blue Design, Blue Body, 4 x 3 1/4 In. 1870.00
Vase, Full Moon Behind Canopy Of Spanish Moss Oak Trees, Smith, 3 3/4 In. 2820.00
Vase, Full Moon Nestled Amidst Spanish Moss Oak Trees, Hunt, 1932, 3 1/2 In. 2585.00
Vase, Full Moon Peeking Behind Canopy Of Spanish Moss Oak Trees, 11 3/8 In. 4115.00

Vase, Geometric, White On Cobalt & Green, Sadie Irvine, 1933, 2 1/4 x 3 In. 1380.00
Vase, Green Geometric Design At Top, Vertical Leaves, Aurelia Arbo, 9 1/4 In. 4600.00
Vase, Iris Design, Green Glaze, Pottery, Hattie Joor, 17 In. 10350.00
Vase, Jonquils, Yellow, Leaves, Blue Ground, Anna F. Simpson, 1908, 9 x 3 In. 6900.00
Vase, Lavender Flowers, 2 1/2 x 3 In. 1870.00
Vase, Light Blue Irises, Green Leaves, Dark Blue Ground, 6 3/4 In. 2645.00
Vase, Live Oak, Spanish Moss, High Glaze, A.F. Simpson, 1926, 4 1/2 In. 3335.00
Vase, Live Oak, Spanish Moss, Moon, Carved, Sadie Irvine, 1932, 3 1/2 x 4 1/2 In. 2645.00
Vase, Live Oaks, Spanish Moss, Bulbous, Anna F. Simpson, 1929, 4 1/2 x 4 1/2 In. 2875.00
Vase, Live Oaks, Spanish Moss, Yellow Sky, Sadie Irvine, 1918, 3 x 3 In. 2415.00
Vase, Magnolia Blossoms, Leaves, Indigo Ground, Leona Nicholson, 1904, 7 1/4 In. 9775.00
Vase, Molded, 4 Large Broad Trees, Hanging Moss, Oak Trees, Meyer, 1923, 6 In. 4115.00
Vase, Morning Glory, Henrietta Bailey, 1913, 9 In. 5000.00
Vase, Moss & Moon Landscape, Dark Green, Anna Simpson, 6 3/4 In. 3450.00
Vase, Moss & Moon Landscape, Sadie Irvine, 5 1/2 In. 2875.00
Vase, Narcissus, Green & Blue Ground, Tapered, A.F. Simpson, 1912, 8 1/2 In. 4315.00
Vase, Oak Trees, Spanish Moss, Blue, Green, Pink Sky, Simpson, 1918, 8 1/2 x 4 In. 5465.00
Vase, Oak Trees, Spanish Moss, Yellow & Red Sky, Sadie Irvine, 1928, 6 1/2 x 3 In. 3738.00
Vase, Painted Landscape, Sadie Irvine, 4 In. 2185.00
Vase, Paperwhites, Green Leaves, Blue Ground, Alma Mason, 1913, 9 x 3 3/4 In. 865.00
Vase, Pinched Waist, Impressed G-12, 4 1/2 In. 920.00
Vase, Red Glaze, Paul Cox, 4 1/2 In. 100.00
Vase, Red Thistles, Blue Green Leaves, Ivory Ground, G.R. Smith, 1902, 4 x 3 1/2 In. . . . 5175.00
Vase, Ribbed, Turquoise Semimatte Glaze, c.1930, 7 x 4 In. 460.00
Vase, Scenic, Pink, Green, Blue, Sadie Irvine, 1919, 3 1/2 In. 1600.00
Vase, Spanish Moss, Full Moon, Blue Ground, Sadie Irvine, 1933, 4 1/2 x 5 1/2 In. 2530.00
Vase, Spanish Moss, Large Oak Trees, Sarah Irvine, 1930, 4 5/8 In. 2820.00
Vase, Spanish Moss, Live Oaks, Full Moon, 11 In. 9775.00
Vase, Spiderwort, Raised Flowers, Soft Yellow, White, Green, 4 5/8 In. 1725.00
Vase, Squat, Carved Blossoms, Lavender Matte Glaze, S. Irvine, 1918, 1 1/2 x 4 In. 980.00
Vase, Stylized Blossoms, Leaves, Blue Ground, Egg Shape, C.M. Chalaron, 1923, 8 In. . . 4315.00
Vase, Stylized Flowers, Elizabeth Villere, 1903, 7 1/2 In. 5500.00
Vase, Tall Pines, Blue Green, Light Green Glaze, A. F. Simpson, 1912, 9 x 4 In. 1840.00

NILOAK Pottery (Kaolin spelled backward) was made at the Hyten
Brothers Pottery in Benton, Arkansas, between 1909 and 1947.
Although the factory did make cast and molded wares, collectors are
most interested in the marbleized art pottery line made of colored
swirls of clay. It was called *Mission Ware.* By 1931 the company made   𝒩𝒾𝓁𝓞𝒜𝒦
castware, and many of these pieces were marked with the name
Hywood.

Ashtray, Marbleized Match Holder, Brown, Orange, Cream, Rim Rest, 2 x 5 In. 440.00
Ashtray, Marbleized, Tan, Brown Swirls, 5 In. 184.00
Bowl, Marbleized, Brown, Blue, Cream, Impressed Mark, 6 In., Pair 69.00
Candlestick, Marbleized, Brown, Blue, Red, Cream, 10 In., Pair 920.00
Ginger Jar, Cover, Marbleized, 8 In. 750.00
Vase, Cover, Marbleized, Light Brown, Tan, Impressed Mark, 4 In. 575.00
Vase, Cover, Marbleized, Mushroom Shape, Brown, Tan, 4 In. 1035.00
Vase, Marbleized, Blue Glaze, Impressed Mark, 12 1/4 In. 750.00
Vase, Marbleized, Blue, 6 1/4 In. 265.00
Vase, Marbleized, Blue, Brown, 6 1/2 In. 165.00
Vase, Marbleized, Blue, Brown, Cream, 6 In. 240.00
Vase, Marbleized, Blue, Brown, Cream, 9 In. 175.00
Vase, Marbleized, Blue, Brown, Cream, Cylindrical, 8 1/4 In. 173.00
Vase, Marbleized, Blue, Brown, Cream, Impressed Mark, 11 3/4 In. 405.00
Vase, Marbleized, Blue, Brown, Cream, Impressed Mark, 3 1/2 In. . . . . .35.00 to 45.00
Vase, Marbleized, Blue, Brown, Cream, Impressed Mark, 4 1/4 In. 1055.00
Vase, Marbleized, Blue, Brown, Cream, Impressed Mark, 9 3/4 In. 299.00
Vase, Marbleized, Blue, Brown, Impressed Mark, 3 1/4 In. 58.00
Vase, Marbleized, Blue, Brown, Rust, Cream, Impressed Mark, 8 1/2 In. 160.00
Vase, Marbleized, Blue, Brown, Rust, Cream, Impressed Mark, 10 1/2 In. 375.00
Vase, Marbleized, Blue, Cream, Red, Brown, Footed, 8 3/8 In. 190.00
Vase, Marbleized, Blue, Light Brown, Cream, Impressed Mark, 10 In. 405.00

Vase, Marbleized, Blue, Red, Brown, Cream, 4 1/2 In. 88.00
Vase, Marbleized, Blue, Tan, Brown, Impressed Mark, 5 1/2 In. 69.00
Vase, Marbleized, Blue, Tan, Impressed Mark, 3 1/2 In. 240.00
Vase, Marbleized, Blue, Tan, Light Tan, Brown, Impressed Mark, 11 In. 489.00
Vase, Marbleized, Bowl, Impressed Mark, 6 3/4 x 3 In. 175.00
Vase, Marbleized, Brown Tones, Light Blue, 9 In. 165.00
Vase, Marbleized, Brown, Blue, Salmon, 12 In. 330.00
Vase, Marbleized, Brown, Ink Stamp, 8 3/4 In. 1095.00
Vase, Marbleized, Brown, Light Tan, Impressed Mark, 6 x 5 In. 265.00
Vase, Marbleized, Brown, Light, Dark, 4 3/8 In. 50.00
Vase, Marbleized, Brown, Light, Dark, Tan, 11 5/8 In. 215.00
Vase, Marbleized, Brown, Red, Cream, Blue, Impressed Mark, 8 1/4 In. 195.00
Vase, Marbleized, Brown, Tan, 3 1/4 In. 105.00
Vase, Marbleized, Brown, Tan, 6 1/2 In. 185.00
Vase, Marbleized, Brown, Tan, 8 1/4 In. ....185.00 to 255.00
Vase, Marbleized, Brown, Tan, Cylindrical, 7 1/4 In. 635.00
Vase, Marbleized, Brown, Tan, Impressed Mark, 4 In. 196.00
Vase, Marbleized, Brown, Tan, Impressed Mark, 4 1/2 In. 90.00
Vase, Marbleized, Brown, Tan, Impressed Mark, 5 In. ....58.00 to 90.00
Vase, Marbleized, Brown, Tan, Impressed Mark, 6 1/4 In. 115.00
Vase, Marbleized, Brown, Tan, Impressed Mark, 7 1/2 In. 185.00
Vase, Marbleized, Brown, Tan, Impressed Mark, 8 In. ....173.00 to 242.00
Vase, Marbleized, Brown, Tan, Light Tan, Cylindrical, Impressed Mark, 10 In. 288.00
Vase, Marbleized, Bulbous, Brown, Blue, Terra-Cotta, Ivory, 10 x 7 1/2 In. 345.00
Vase, Marbleized, Red, Blue, Brown, 10 In. 415.00
Vase, Marbleized, Red, Brown, Cream, Blue Glaze, 10 1/2 In. 299.00
Vase, Marbleized, Red, Green, Blue, Brown, 3 1/4 In. 58.00
Vase, Marbleized, Tan Matte Glaze, 8 1/4 In. 1150.00
Vase, Red, Medium, Dark Brown, Cylindrical, 6 In. 100.00

NIPPON porcelain was made in Japan from 1891 to 1921. *Nippon* is the
Japanese word for *Japan*. A few firms continued to use the word *Nippon*
on ceramics after 1921 as a part of the company name more than as an
identification of the country of origin. More pieces marked Nippon
will be found in the Dragonware, Moriage, and Noritake categories.

Ashtray, Center Scene, Bluebirds, Trees, Enameled Trim On Sides, Green M Wreath, 5 In.   85.00
Ashtray, Owls, Trees, Brown, Green, Round, 2 1/2 x 5 In. 58.00
Bowl, Bachelor Button Flowers, 2 Handles, Footed, Green Mark, 5 5/8 In. 25.00
Bowl, Elk In Field, Nut, Vine Border, Enameled Handles, Footed, Green M Wreath, 9 In. . 310.00
Bowl, Lake Scene, House, Trees, Scalloped Enameled Rim, Blue Mark, 7 3/4 In. 79.00
Chamberstick, House, Lake, Trees, Mountains, Green Wreath Mark, 2 x 4 1/4 In. . .98.00 to 110.00
Charger, Bulldog, Hand Painted, 12 In. 440.00
Chocolate Pot, Gold Beads, Flowers, Gold Handle, 9 1/2 In. 425.00
Chocolate Set, House & Tree, Hand Painted, 8 1/2 In., 4 Piece 45.00
Cup, Flower, Gold Design Interior 50.00
Cup & Saucer, Pink & Purple Flowers, Black Edge, White Beading 40.00
Dish, Pickle, Tab Handles, Center Apple Blossoms, Signed, 8 1/2 In. 65.00
Figurine, Black Man Rides Spotted Alligator, Hand Painted, 5 In. 60.00
Hatpin Holder, Palm Tree Design, Signed, 4 1/2 In. 100.00
Humidor, Oval, Brown Dappled Ground, 3 Geese, Grass, Green M Wreath, 5-In. Diam. . . 422.00
Ringtree, Purple Violets, Green Bands, White Dots, Gold Trim, Marked, 3 1/4 In. 110.00
Salt & Pepper, Little Boy's Head, Tray, Hand Painted ....*Illus* 40.00
Sugar Shaker, Pink Flower Insets, Gold Bands, Handle, Marked, 5 x 3 1/2 In. 95.00
Sugar Shaker, Pink Roses, Green Leaves, Gold Trim, Signed, 4 3/4 In. 135.00
Toothpick, Purple Violets, White Dots, Gold Bands Top & Base, 2 1/4 x 2 In. 95.00
Toothpick, Rose Design, Green Band, Maple Leaf, 2 1/2 In. 60.00
Urn, Inverted Pear Shape, Roses, 8 1/4 In. 115.00
Urn, Pastels, Mountain Lake Scene, Mural, 2 Handles, 13 1/2 In. 1950.00
Vase, Bud, Violet Design, Embossed White Dots, Gold Rim, Square Sides, 6 In. 50.00
Vase, Flowers 1 Side, Sailing Scene On Reverse, Signed, 7 1/2 In. 56.00
Vase, Flowers, Gold Trim, Hand Painted, Green Mark, c.1911, 12 In. 395.00
Vase, Forest, Cabin By River, Green & Brown, Signed, 1892, 12 In. 310.00
Vase, Landscape, Floral, Green Ground, Hand Painted, 10 In. 460.00

Nippon,
Salt & Pepper,
Little Boy's Head,
Tray, Hand Painted

Niloak marbleized pottery can be cleaned by using Softscrub or a similar product and 0000 steel wool. Do not rub too hard.

Vase, Polychrome & Gilt Flowers, 13 x 6 1/2 In.	57.00
Vase, Portrait, Cobalt Blue, 9 In.	725.00
Vase, Ships, Enameled Medallions, Applied Handles, Gold Shoulder, Marked, 8 In.	259.00
Vase, Stylized Tulips, 12 3/4 In.	99.00

NODDERS, also called nodding figures or pagods, are figures with heads and hands that are attached to wires. Any slight movement causes the parts to move up and down. They were made in many countries during the eighteenth, nineteenth, and twentieth centuries. A few Art Deco designs are also known. Copies are being made. A more recent type of nodder is made of papier-mache or plastic. These often represent sports figures or comic characters. Sports nodders are listed in the Sports category.

Andy Gump, Bisque, Germany	100.00
Black Child, Bent Over, Bisque, 5 In.	97.00
Black Girl, Extra Large Head, Composition, Spring Nodding Mechanism, 7 In.	149.00
Black Sailor, Composition, Non-Spring Nodding Mechanism, c.1900, 6 In.	165.00
Charlie Weaver, Holding Letter From Mama, 1960s, 6 1/4 In.	175.00
Chester Gump, Bisque, Germany, 1920s	110.00
Chicken, Papier-Mache & Wood, 7 1/2 In.	104.00
Comic Black Singer, Plays Banjo, Rocks Back & Forth, Spring Legs, 3 1/2 In.	85.00
Cow, Pull Toy, Papier-Mache, 6 3/4 x 7 In.	22.00
Donkey, Felt Covered, Papier-Mache & Wood, 5 x 5 1/2 In.	60.00
Elephant, Papier-Mache, 4 1/2 x 8 1/2 In.	198.00
Goose, Papier-Mache, White, Orange Beak & Feet, 4 1/2 In.	55.00
Happy Hooligan, Composition, 7 In.	110.00
Lion, Papier-Mache, 4 x 8 In.	143.00
Mallard Duck, Mechanical, Composition Body	877.00
Mammy, Smiling, Spoon Rest Body, Spring Mounted Head, 4 1/2 In.	212.00
Man, Holding American Bicentennial Flag, Spring Neck, Papier-Mache, 7 3/4 In.	71.00
Polar Bear, On Hind Legs, Papier-Mache & Wood, 10 In.	715.00
Rabbit, Standing, Spring Neck & Ears, Papier-Mache, 7 1/2 In.	66.00
Santa Claus, Spring Neck, Composition, 6 1/4 In.	192.00
Uncle Walt, Bisque, Germany, 1920s	190.00

NORITAKE porcelain was made in Japan after 1904 by Nippon Toki Kaisha. The best-known Noritake pieces are marked with the M in a wreath for the Morimura Brothers, a New York City distributing company. This mark was used until the early 1950s. There may be some helpful price information in the Nippon category, since prices are comparable. Noritake Azalea is listed in the Azalea category in this book.

Candlestick, Overall Bird On Branch, Blue Ground, Leaf Base, 20th Century, 8 1/4 In.	103.00
Cheese & Cracker, Gold & White	150.00
Flower Blossom, Salt & Pepper, Footed	125.00
Vase, Painted Landscape, Oval, Handles, c.1835, 5 In., Pair	56.00

NORSE Pottery Company started in Edgerton, Wisconsin, in 1903. In 1904 the company moved to Rockford, Illinois. The company made a black pottery, which resembled early bronze relics of the Scandinavian countries. The firm went out of business in 1913.

Humidor, Black Glaze, Turquoise Line Flakes, Marked, 6 1/2 In.	375.00

NORTH DAKOTA SCHOOL OF MINES was established in 1892 at the University of North Dakota. A ceramic course was included and pieces were made from the clays found in the region. Students at the university made pieces from 1909 to 1949. Although very early pieces were marked *U.N.D.*, most pieces were stamped with the full name of the university.

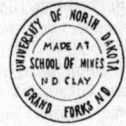

Lamp, Brown, 16 3/4 x 6 3/4 In.	173.00
Plate, Conifer, Flowers, 1931, 7 1/4 In.	400.00
Vase, Black, Blue, Plum, Glossy Glaze, Egg Shape, 8 x 4 In.	345.00
Vase, Blue High Glaze, 3 1/2 In.	115.00
Vase, Blue, Tan Glaze, Signed, Christenson, 4 In.	81.00
Vase, Carved Antelope Heads, Green Matte Glaze, 7 In.	3400.00
Vase, Covered Wagon, Brown Matte Glaze, Ink Mark, 6 1/2 In.	1093.00
Vase, Flowers, Pink High Glaze, 3 In.	518.00
Vase, Green Matte Glaze, 4 In.	173.00
Vase, Green Multicolored Glaze, Signed, J. Schroeder, 2 1/2 In.	66.00
Vase, Incised Narcissus, Umber Matte Glaze, 7 1/2 x 5 1/2 In.	1840.00
Vase, Incised Sheaves Of Wheat, Brown Matte Glaze, 3 In.	450.00
Vase, Mint Green, Sandy Brown Matte Glaze, 3 7/8 In.	425.00
Vase, Multicolored Blue, Green Glaze, 10 In.	413.00
Vase, Multicolored Red Matte Glaze, 4 In.	495.00
Vase, Multicolored, Green Matte Glaze, Incised Pine Trees, 9 In.	6900.00
Vase, Native Indian Designs, Red Ground, Bentonite Clay, 4 In.	173.00
Vase, Prairie Rose Design, 1930, 4 7/8 In.	450.00
Vase, Prairie Rose Design, Green, Gray, Huckfield, 3 5/8 In.	375.00
Vase, Purple, Brown Matte Glaze, Cylindrical, 7 1/2 In.	69.00
Vase, Scenic, Green, Black, Tan, Margaret Cable, 1916, 8 In.	11500.00
Vase, Striated Brown Matte Glaze, 1916, 6 1/8 In.	500.00
Vase, Trees In Silhouette, Amber Ground, 9 In.	3750.00

NORTHWOOD Glass Company was founded by Harry Northwood, a glassmaker who worked for Hobbs, Brockunier and Company, La Belle Glass Company, and Buckeye Glass Company before founding his own firm. He opened one factory in Indiana, Pennsylvania, in 1896, and another in Wheeling, West Virginia, in 1902. Northwood closed when Mr. Northwood died in 1923. Many types of glass were made, including carnival, custard, goofus, and pressed. The underlined N mark was used on some pieces.

Leaf Mold, Creamer, Red Canary Spatter, Satin	250.00
Leaf Mold, Rose Bowl, Red Canary Spatter, Satin	260.00
Leaf Mold, Sugar Shaker, Light Blue, Satin, 4 In.	325.00
Leaf Mold, Sugar Shaker, Lime Green, Satin, 4 In.	550.00
Leaf Mold, Water Set, Red Canary Spatter, Satin	1495.00
Leaf Umbrella, Sugar Shaker, Blue, Satin, 4 1/2 In.	426.00
Leaf Umbrella, Sugar Shaker, Cranberry Spatter, 4 1/2 In.	350.00
Leaf Umbrella, Sugar Shaker, Yellow, 4 1/2 In.	275.00
Memphis, Creamer, Emerald Green, Gold Trim	45.00
Memphis, Sugar, Emerald Green, Gold Trim	60.00
Royal Ivy, Pitcher, Water, Rubina, Applied Clear Handle, 8 1/2 In.	200.00
Wetlands, Cake Plate, 2 Descending Geese, Silver Overlay, 13 1/2 In.	56.00

NU-ART see Imperial category.

NUTCRACKERS of many types have been used through the centuries. At first the nutcracker was probably strong teeth or a hammer. But by the nineteenth century, many elaborate and ingenious types were made. Levers, screws, and hammer adaptations were the most popular. Because nutcrackers are still useful, they are still being made, some in the old styles.

Bear, Glass Eyes, Shaped Base, 7 3/4 In.	165.00
Dog, Bronze, Embossed Flowers & Shells, 5 1/2 x 12 In.	50.00
Dog, Cast Iron, 5 3/4 x 11 In.	34.00
Dog, Full Round, Hair, Molded, Cast Iron, 5 x 4 1/2 In.	294.00

Dog, Porcelain, Black & White, 1900 .... 250.00
Elephant, Cast Iron, Painted, Trunk Handle, 4 x 9 In. 175.00
Elf, Wood, Red Hat, Norwegian 65.00
Girl, Hoop Skirt, Brass, England, 1956 ....300.00 to 350.00
Heart Cutout, Flowers, Brass, 18th Century 695.00
Horse, Bronze Plate, 4 x 7 In. 185.00
Kangaroo, Nestor, England, c.1930, 4 1/2 x 5 1/2 In. 175.00
Lion Head, Swiss, Wooden, Glass Eyes 165.00
Miller Cracker, Aluminum, Ft. Worth, Texas, 1976, 3 x 7 1/2 In. 35.00
Monkey, Glass Eyes, Black Forest 495.00
Moon Man, Hinged Jaw, Wood, 4 x 5 In. 900.00
Parrot, Painted Aluminum 75.00
Punch & Judy, 2 Sides, Brass, England, 4 3/4 In. 75.00
Rabbit Head, Carved Wood, Glass Eyes, 8 In. 125.00
Rocking Horse, Soldier, Painted Wood, German, 1989, 6 1/2 x 7 3/4 In. 65.00
Sailor, Tough Nut, England, c.1897, 4 3/4 x 7 3/4 In. 650.00
Shakespeare, Cottage, Brass, 5 In. 110.00
Skull & Crossbones, Cast Iron, Nickel Plated, England, 1928, 2 x 6 In. 100.00
Skull & Crossbones, England, 1928 .... 200.00
Soldier, Hat, Tricornered, Flag, Erzgebirge, Germany, 5 x 14 In. 135.00
Soldier, Painted, Cast Iron, 1940s, 10 In. 45.00
Soldier, Painted, Red Coat, Wood, Black Forest, Germany, Label GDR, 26 In. ... 50.00
Soldier, Painted, Steinbach, Germany 110.00
Squirrel, Brass, 6 1/8 x 8 1/4 In. 110.00
Squirrel, Bronze, 5 1/2 x 8 In. 200.00
Squirrel, Tail Moves Paws, Nickel Plated, Oval Wooden Base 250.00
Turtle, Painted, Wooden Handle, Iron Screw, 6 x 6 In. 85.00
Uncle Sam, Wooden, Coat Tails Opens Mouth, Taiwan, 1975, 13 3/8 In. 40.00
Whale, Brass, Hand Wrought, 1 1/2 x 6 1/4 In. 125.00

NYMPHENBURG, see Royal Nymphenburg.

OCCUPIED JAPAN was printed on pottery, porcelain, toys, and other goods made during the American occupation of Japan after World War II, from 1945 to 1952. Collectors now search for these pieces. The items were made for export.

Figurine, Geisha Girl, Porcelain, 5 1/2 In. .... *Illus* 20.00
Figurine, Spaniel, In Basket, Hokutosha, 5 In. 35.00
Figurine, Tricycle, Windup, Tinplate, Bell Ringer, 4 1/4 In. 75.00
Salt & Pepper, Chef, At Stove 35.00
Salt & Pepper, Pigs In Poke 25.00
Teapot, Willow, Child's 35.00
Tray, Pin Holder, Hokutosha 25.00

OFFICE TECHNOLOGY includes office equipment and related products, such as adding machines, calculators, and check-writing machines. Typewriters are in their own category in this book.

Adding Machine, 3 Hands, Wooden Case, 8 3/4 In. .... *Illus* 1495.00

Occupied Japan,
Figurine, Geisha Girl,
Porcelain, 5 1/2 In.

Office Technology, Adding Machine,
3 Hands, Wooden Case, 8 3/4 In.

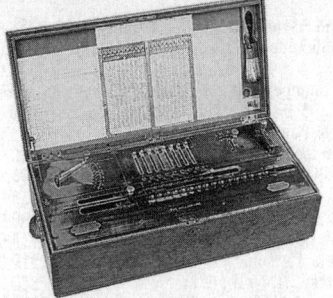

Office Technology, Calculator, Millionaire,
Hans W. Egli, No. 136, 26 In.

Office Technology, Calculator, Thacher,
Keuffel & Esser, Model 4012, 22 1/2 In.

Adding Machine,	Alan Walls, Push Button, 1935	6.00
Book Press,	1880-1900, 9 x 12-In. Plates, 9-In. Wheels	168.00
Calculator,	Alpina, 8-Place Register, Sliding Action, Case, 1960	690.00
Calculator,	Lightning, 7 Dials, Black Metal Case, Box, 1933	57.00
Calculator,	Millionaire, Hans W. Egli, No. 136, 26 In. *Illus*	2990.00
Calculator,	Standard Desk, Nickel Case, 6 Dials, Herbert North Morse	230.00
Calculator,	Thacher, Keuffel & Esser, Model 4012, 22 1/2 In. *Illus*	2530.00
Embosser,	Check, Baby Defiance, 1903	17.00
Mailbox,	Cast Iron, Gilt Lettering, No.2, U.S.A	22.00
Mimeograph,	AB Dick Co., Wood Base, 1910-1920	17.00
Seal,	Corporate, Los Angeles, 1890-1900, 12 x 16 In.	34.00
Telegraph Instrument,	Wood, Iron Base, Receiver & Key, 9 In., 3 Piece	115.00
Ticker Tape Machine,	Edison, Iron Base, 13 1/2 x 8 In.	8050.00
Ticker Tape Machine,	Western Union, Mahogany Pedestal, Floor Model, c.1910	8050.00

OHR pottery was made in Biloxi, Mississippi, from 1883 to 1906 by
George E. Ohr, a true eccentric. The pottery was made of very thin clay
that was twisted, folded, and dented into odd, graceful shapes. Some
pieces were lifelike models of hats, animal heads, or even a potato.
Others were decorated with folded clay *snakes*. Reproductions and
reworked pieces are appearing on the market. These have been
reglazed, or snakes and other embellishments have been added.

Bank,	Brown Luster, Black Mirror Glaze, Acorn Shape, Interior Rattle, 4 x 2 In.	1093.00
Bowl,	Green Mottled Glossy Glaze, Pinched Body, Late 19th Century, 2 5/8 In.	1840.00
Bowl,	Puff Clay, Script Signature, 2 1/4 x 5 1/4 In.	405.00
Bowl,	Spherical, Brown, 2 1/2 x 3 1/2 In.	1760.00
Inkwell,	Panther Head, Cobalt Blue Glaze, Incised Biloxi, 3 1/2 x 3 x 4 1/2 In.	2415.00
Mug,	Joe Jefferson, Dedication, Sheer Olive Glaze, Stamped, 3-18-96, 3 1/4 x 4 1/4 In.	2185.00
Mug,	Puzzle, Green, Brown Glaze, Handle, 3 1/2 In.	750.00
Mug,	Puzzle, Snake Handle, Mottled Brown Gunmetal Glaze, Stamped, 3 1/2 x 5 1/2 In.	1725.00
Pitcher,	Crimped, Tan Bisque, Twisted Side, 3 3/4 x 6 In.	385.00
Pitcher,	Oval, Gunmetal Glaze, Stamped G.E. Ohr, Biloxi, Miss., 4 x 3 3/4 In.	2070.00
Pitcher,	Pinched, 3 Lobed Openings, Speckled Gunmetal Glaze, Handle, 2 1/2 x 4 In.	5465.00
Tyg,	Gunmetal Glaze, Green Luster Drip, 3 Ribbon Handles, Cup Rim, 4 1/2 x 5 In.	5465.00
Vase,	Baluster, Mottled Green Glossy Glaze, Stamped, 4 3/4 x 2 1/4 In.	3105.00
Vase,	Body Twist, Scalloped Rim, Bisque, Footed, Signed, 6 1/4 x 4 In.	4600.00
Vase,	Bottle Shape, Flared Rim, Raspberry, Blue, Green, Mottled Glaze, 2 3/4 In.	3740.00
Vase,	Brown Semimatte Glaze, Speckled, Torn Rim, Squat, 2 1/2 x 4 1/4 In.	865.00
Vase,	Bulbous, Brown, Green, Elephant's Skin Glaze, Signed, 4 x 3 In.	1265.00
Vase,	Bulbous, Red Bisque, Twisted Body, Closed In Rim, Stamped, 3 3/4 x 4 In.	2760.00
Vase,	Crimped, Reticulated Rim, Gunmetal Glaze, Deep Olive Green Accents, 3 In.	1760.00
Vase,	Deep Brown Hunter Green Over Caramel Glaze, 6 1/4 x 3 In.	1430.00
Vase,	Etched, Bisque, Signature, 2 1/2 x 3 In.	520.00
Vase,	Face, Crimped, Alternating With Bulging Circles, 4 x 6 In.	825.00
Vase,	Face, Molded Stylized, Green Flecked Glaze, Gunmetal, Marked, 4 1/2 In.	2820.00
Vase,	Folded Rim, Gunmetal Glaze, Bulbous, Marked, 3 x 3 In.	2530.00

Vase, Gunmetal & Yellow Glaze, Orange Interior, Folded Asymmetric Rim, 5 1/4 In. 3738.00
Vase, Gunmetal Brown Glaze, Straight Sides, Notched Shoulder, Incised Biloxi, 5 1/2 In. . 4025.00
Vase, Hat Shape, Glossy Glaze, 3 In. 4310.00
Vase, Olive Green Semimatte Glaze, Tapering, Footed, Stamped, 4 x 2 1/2 In. 1265.00
Vase, Pinched Waist, Torn Rim, Marbleized, Clear Glaze, 3 1/4 x 3 1/4 In. 750.00
Vase, Raspberry & Amber Glossy Glaze, Squat, Flared & Folded Rim, Stamped, 3 1/4 In. 1955.00
Vase, Speckled Amber, Green, Yellow Luster Glaze, Stamped, 2 x 4 In. 920.00
Vase, Speckled Ocher & Glossy Green Glaze, Squat, Collared Rim, 2 3/4 x 3 In. 1095.00
Vase, Spherical, Deep Khaki Green, Protruding Neck, 3 x 3 1/2 In. 715.00
Vase, Spool, Waisted, Mottled Satin Ocher Green Glaze, Signed, 1898-1902, 6 In. 2990.00
Vase, Tan Bisque, Flared Rim, 4 1/2 x 4 In. 715.00
Vase, Trumpet, Flared Rim, Bulbous, Green Glaze, Black, 3 x 3 In. 2310.00
Vase, Trumpet, Mocha Brown Glaze Body, Metallic Black, 3 1/4 x 2 1/2 In. 880.00
Wall Pocket, Lion Head, Medallion, Glossy Amber Glaze, 4 1/4 In. 2070.00

OLD PARIS, see Paris category.

OLD SLEEPY EYE, see Sleepy Eye category.

OLYMPIC, see Souvenir category.

ONION PATTERN, originally named *bulb pattern*, is a white ware decorated with cobalt blue or pink. Although it is commonly associated
with Meissen, other companies made the pattern in the late nineteenth
and the twentieth centuries. A rare type is called *red bud* because there
are added red accents on the blue-and-white dishes.

Bowl, Blue, Seat Woman Form, Incised Marks, Meissen, 9 1/2 In. 350.00
Bowl, Cover, Scalloped Edges, Scrolled Finial, 2 Handles, Signed, 9 1/2 x 13 In. 110.00
Candelabrum, Blue, 3 Holders, Center Holder, Floral Base, Signed, Meissen, 10 In. 290.00
Plate, Salad, Blue, Meissen, 6 In., 6 Piece 115.00
Platter, Blue, Meissen, 16 1/4 In. 140.00
Tankard, Blue, Crossed Swords, Lid, Meissen, c.1910 .... 488.00
Tureen, Cover, Blue, Oval, Leaf Finial, Rocaille Handles, Meissen, 15 3/4 In. 322.00
Tureen, Serving Platter, Blue, Meissen, Germany, Early 20th Century 747.00

OPALESCENT GLASS is translucent glass that has the tones of the opal
gemstone. It originated in England in the 1870s and is often found in
pressed glassware made in Victorian times. Opalescent glass was first
made in America in 1897 at the Northwood glassworks in Indiana,
Pennsylvania. Some dealers use the terms *opaline* and *opalescent* for
any of these translucent wares. More opalescent pieces may be listed
in Hobnail, Northwood, Pressed Glass, Spanish Lace, and other glass
categories.

Alaska, Berry Bowl, Vaseline, 7 1/4 In. 786.00
Alaska, Creamer, Blue, 3 1/2 In. 30.00
Aztec Medallion Swirl, Syrup, Green, 6 In. 2400.00
Beatty Honeycomb, Sugar Shaker, White, 3 1/2 In. 110.00
Christmas Snowflake, Pitcher, Water, Cranberry, Ribbed 1995.00
Chrysanthemum Base Swirl, Sugar Shaker, Blue, 4 3/4 In. 275.00
Chrysanthemum Base Swirl, Sugar Shaker, Cranberry, 4 3/4 In. 400.00
Chrysanthemum Base Swirl, Sugar Shaker, Cranberry, 5 x 3 1/4 In. 585.00
Coin Spot & Swirl, Syrup, Blue, 6 In. 220.00
Coin Spot & Swirl, Syrup, White, 6 In. 80.00
Drapery, Vase, Blue 5000.00
Hobnail, Bowl, Footed, Vaseline, 2 1/2 In. 75.00
Intaglio, Cruet, White, Stopper, 5 1/2 In. 25.00
Seaweed, Water Set, Blue, 7 Piece 915.00
Swirl, Cruet, Green, Clear Handle, 6 1/2 In. 170.00
Toothpicks are listed in the Toothpick category.

OPALINE, or opal glass, was made in white, green, and other colors.
The glass had a matte surface and a lack of transparency. It was often
gilded or painted. It was a popular mid-nineteenth-century European
glassware.

Bowl, Semitranslucent Rose, Rolled Rim, Polished Pontil, 4 3/4 x 13 1/2 In. 60.00

Compote, Silver Plated Stand, Blue, 6 x 6 In.	165.00
Compote, Underplate, Melon Ribbed, Flower Reserves, 1930s, 11 x 9 1/2 In.	690.00
Compote, Underplate, Melon Ribbed, Gold Band, White, Louis Philippe, 5 x 6 1/2 In.	145.00
Jar, Apothecary, Blue, Semitranslucent, Rough Pontil, 11 3/4 In.	40.00
Jug, Blue, Semitranslucent, Applied Handle, Polished Pontil, 10 1/4 In.	120.00
Puff Box, Cover, Tray, Blue Gray, Applied Medallion, Gold Rim, 6 1/4 x 4 In.	220.00
Punch Bowl, Cover, Ladle, Underplate, Green, Applied Finial, 13 x 10 x 17 In.	120.00
Vase, Campana Form, Gilt Bronze Mount, France, c.1900, 9 In.	299.00
Vase, Enameled Gold & Grisaille, U.S. Capitol View, Urn Shape, Inscribed, 9 1/2 In.	1265.00
Vase, Gold Enameled Flowers & Leaves, 5 1/2 In.	1115.00
Vase, Turquoise Over White, Baluster, France, Mid 19th Century, 14 In., Pair	1380.00
Vase, White, Cream, Birds, Leaves, France, 24 In., Pair	2470.00

OPERA GLASSES are needed because the stage is a long way from some
of the seats at a play or an opera. Mother-of-pearl was a popular decoration on many French glasses.

Black Mother-Of-Pearl, Monogram, Fitted Case, Audemair, 4 1/2 In.	57.00
Enamel, Lavender, Victorian Ladies, Putto, Basse Taille, c.1890, 5 5/8 In.	460.00
Gilt, Black Leather Case, Gentleman's, Belle Epoque, 1900, Pair	403.00
Low Relief, Purple Eyepieces & Handle, Scrollwork, Basse Taille, 4 In.	200.00
Mother-Of-Pearl, Brass Fittings, Iris Paris Handle, 8 1/2 In.	275.00
Pansy Spray, Floral Bouquets In Reserved, Mother-Of-Pearl Eyepiece, 4 1/8 In.	431.00
Silver Painted Ground, Male & Female Musicians, France, 4 1/4 In.	230.00
Whalebone, Brass, 2 1/2 x 4 In.	224.00

ORPHAN ANNIE first appeared in the comics in 1924. The redheaded
girl and her friends have been on the radio and are still on the comic
pages. A Broadway musical show and a movie in the 1980s made
Annie popular again and many toys, dishes, and other memorabilia are
being made.

Ashtray, Figural, Ceramic, White, Orange Accents, Japan, 1 x 4 In.	85.00
Bank, Annie & Sandy, Figural, Ceramic, Knickerbocker, 1982, 3 x 6 1/2 In.	20.00
Book, Comic Strip Reprint, Little Orphan Annie Bucking The World	85.00
Book, Comic, Full Color, Quaker Premium, 1941	40.00
Book, Little Orphan Annie & The Big Town Gunmen, Whitman, 64 Pages	60.00
Doll, Annie, Wood, Joint Held By Elastic, 5 In.	75.00
Doll, Daddy Warbucks, World Of Annie, Knickerbocker, 1982, 6 In.	40.00
Doll, Sandy, Wood, Multiple Joint Held By Elastic, 2 1/4 x 2 1/2 In.	40.00
Figurine, Bisque, Annie, Sandy, Daddy Warbucks, 3 Piece	145.00
Figurine, Sandy, Bisque, Hollow, Japan, 1 1/2 In.	45.00
Game, Rummy Cards, Directions, Whitman Publishing, 1935	65.00
Game, Treasure Hunt, Ovaltine Premium, 1933, 16 1/2 x 11 In.	65.00
Game, Treasure Hunt, Sailboats, 1922, 11 x 16 1/2 In., 4 Piece	175.00
Kit, Limousine, Plastic, Duesenberg, 1929 Model, Box, 6 x 6 1/2 x 16 In.	30.00
Lunch Box, Annie Picture, Vinyl, Red Polka Dot, Aladdin, 7 x 9 In.	28.00
Mask, Paper, Die Cut, Ovaltine Premium, 1933	65.00
Mug, Annie & Sandy, Glass, White, Applied Images In Black & Orange, 3 1/2 In.	15.00
Mug, Ovaltine, Shake-Up, Teal With Red Cap, Beetleware Plastic, 1940s, 4 3/4 In. . .75.00 to 110.00
Plate, Party, Annie & Sandy, Die Cut Cardboard, Square, 1930s, 8 In.	20.00
Stove, Electric, 4 Images Of Annie, Serving Sandy, 3 Opening Doors, Marx, 9 In.	60.00
Toy, Clothespins & Accessories, Transogram, 1938	95.00
Toy, Sandy, Annie Skipping Rope, Dog Walks, Tin, Windup, 5 In.	385.00

ORREFORS Glassworks, located in the Swedish province of Smaaland,
was established in 1898. The company is still making glass for use on
the table or as decorations. There is renewed interest in the glass made
in the modern styles of the 1940s and 1950s. Most vases and decorative pieces are signed with the etched name.

Orrefors

Bowl, Ariel, Rows Of Transparent Green Oval Bubbles, Edvin Ohrstrom, 9 1/2 In.	1035.00
Bowl, Clear Over Blue, Signed, Ingeborg Lunden, 1965, 6 1/2 In.	345.00
Bowl, Fish Graal, Green Fish, Plants, Marked, Edvard Hald, 2 1/4 x 7 5/8 In.	805.00
Decanter, Cut Panels, Pontil, Signed, 10 In.	130.00
Decanter, Ship's, Ball Stopper, Broad Waist, 11 x 7 1/2 In.	200.00

Orrefors, Vase, Fish
Graal, Green
Fish & Seaweed,
Edvard Hald, 6 In.

Old bed linens and tablecloths
that have been stored for a long
time should be soaked in water
for at least 12 hours. This
rehydrates the fibers and loosens
any dirt or leftover soap.

Plate, Yellow, Steel Blue, Signed, Palmquist, 1955, 5 In.	374.00
Punch Set, Flared, Diamond Design, Pinched Cups, Ladle, 18 Piece	230.00
Vase, Ariel, Female Figure & Flowers, Cobalt Blue Layers, Marked, 6 3/8 In.	3335.00
Vase, Blue Lines, Blue On Green, Signed, Palmquist, 6 1/2 In.	403.00
Vase, Clear Over Green, Blue Lines, Signed, Palmquist, 4 1/2 In.	374.00
Vase, Clear Over Green, Smoke, Signed, O.M. Jous, 7 In.	58.00
Vase, Clear Over Red Glass, Marked, 1955, 5 1/2 In.	115.00
Vase, Engraved Girl, Moon & Stars, 4 1/2 In.	198.00
Vase, Engraved Girls Playing Ball, Edvard Hald, 1920, 9 1/4 In.	5400.00
Vase, Engraved Viking Ship, Oval, Karl Rassler, 1951, 7 In.	69.00
Vase, Fish Graal, Green Fish & Seaweed, Edvard Hald, 6 In. .... *Illus*	600.00
Vase, Horizontal Blue, Gray & Orange, Black Bands, Cyrin, 12 x 10 x 6 In.	880.00
Vase, Kraka, Blue, Green, Signed, Sven Palmquist, 1954, 13 1/2 In.	184.00

OTT & BREWER Company operated the Etruria Pottery at Trenton,
New Jersey, from 1871 to 1892. They started making belleek in 1882.
The firm used a variety of marks that incorporated the initials *O & B*.

Basket, Gourd Shape, Scalloped Rim, Branch Handle, Gold Paint, Belleek, 8 x 5 In.	575.00
Cup & Saucer, Gold Paint, Beaded, Turquoise Enameled Rim, Belleek, 6 Piece	144.00
Egg Server, Dolphin Handle, Gold Paint, Bamboo Stalks, 5 x 7 In.	316.00
Honey Pot, Bees, Cattails, Flower, Faux Wood Base, Belleek, 5 x 4 1/2 In.	259.00
Pitcher, Branch Handle, Gold Paint, Wildflowers, Belleek, 10 1/2 x 5 1/2 In.	405.00
Pitcher, Bulbous, Cactus Handle, Bamboo Neck, Gold Paint, Belleek, 8 1/4 x 7 In.	175.00
Pitcher, Gourd Shape, Yellow Lotus, Branch Handle, 9 1/2 x 7 1/2 In.	430.00
Plant Pot, Belleek, Twig Handles, Branches, Flowers, c.1890, 7 1/2 In.	1058.00
Plate, Eggshell, Gold Paint, Flowers, Belleek, 6 1/2 In., 5 Piece	375.00
Plate, Scalloped Rim, Flowers, Belleek, Stamped, 9 In., 4 Piece	405.00
Tea Set, Eggshell, Gold Paint, Cherry Blossom, Butterflies, Belleek, 4 x 6 In., 5 Piece	375.00
Teapot, Applied Branches, Gold Paint, Blue, Pink Flowers, Belleek, 7 x 9 1/2 In.	170.00
Vase, Closed-In Rim, Gold Paint, Daisies, Ivory, Belleek, 6 x 5 In.	175.00

OVERBECK pottery was made by four sisters named Overbeck at a pottery in Cambridge City, Indiana. They started in 1911. They made all
types of vases, each one-of-a-kind. Small, hand-modeled figurines are
the most popular pieces with today's collectors. The factory continued
until 1955, when the last of the four sisters died.

Bowl, Red Clay Glaze, Rust, Maize Interior, Green Matte Drip, 2 3/4 x 5 7/8 In.	230.00
Figurine, Colonial Couple In Blue, Pink Period Dress, 4 1/4 x 4 3/4 In.	400.00
Figurine, Golfer, Purple, Green, White Glossy Glaze, Incised Mark, 4 In.	1095.00
Figurine, Goose, White Glossy Glaze, Yellow Beak & Feet, Incised Mark, 5 1/2 In.	805.00
Vase, Squat, Stylized Art Deco Flowers, Green Matte Glaze, Stamped, 4 x 4 In.	3450.00
Vase, White Matte Glaze, Pink, Blue, Green Incised Flowers, Incised Mark, 10 In.	17250.00

OWENS Pottery was made in Zanesville, Ohio, from 1891 to 1928. The
first art pottery was made after 1896. Utopian Ware, Cyrano, Navarre,
Feroza, and Henri Deux were made. Pieces were usually marked with
a form of the name *Owens*. About 1907, the firm began to make tile
and discontinued the art pottery wares.

Ashtray, Feroza, 5 In.	58.00

Creamer, Utopian, 3 Pulled Feet, 5 3/4 In. 90.00
Humidor, Cover, Utopian 400.00
Jardiniere, Cyrano, Impressed, 7 1/2 In. 160.00
Jug, Utopian, Ear Of Corn, Stamped & Signed, 7 1/2 x 4 3/4 In. 80.00
Lamp Base, Utopian, Pansy Design, Brown Glaze, 10 1/2 In. 69.00
Mug, Painted Flowers, Signed, 1908, 5 In. 35.00
Mug, Utopian, Blackberries, Tot Steele, 4 7/8 In. 80.00
Pitcher, Cherries, Bisque Ground, 7 x 5 In. 175.00
Pitcher, Cyrano, Squat, 6 x 6 In. 115.00
Pitcher, Utopian, Yellow Rose Sprig, 3 1/4 In. 105.00
Plaque, Indian Chief, 11 x 10 In. 173.00
Scent Pot, Lotus, Dogwood Twig, 2 1/4 In. 259.00
Tankard, Cyrano, Stamped, 7 1/2 x 4 1/2 In. 115.00
Tankard, Utopian, Autumn Leaves, 12 1/4 In. 185.00
Tile, Little Bo Peep, Colorful Setting, Mahogany Arts & Crafts Frame, 12 In. 2645.00
Tile, Old Mother Goose, Arts & Crafts Oak Frame, 12 x 12 In. 2300.00
Vase, Feroza, Black Metallic Glaze, Hammered, 7 7/8 In. 100.00
Vase, Feroza, Hammered Surface, 8 1/4 In. 160.00
Vase, Flowers, 6 In. 35.00
Vase, Flowers, Light Tan, 13 5/8 In. 250.00
Vase, Geometric, Green Matte Glaze, 6 In. 375.00
Vase, Green Matte Glaze, 10 1/2 In. 690.00
Vase, Gunmetal, Textured Brown, Green Matte Glaze, 2 Gourds, 4-Footed, 9 In. 978.00
Vase, Incised Dragonflies, Green Matte Glaze, Tapered, Signed, 4 1/4 x 5 1/2 In. 374.00
Vase, Lotus, Berries, Leaves, 6 x 5 In. 288.00
Vase, Lotus, Embossed, Grapes, Glossy Black Ground, 8 3/4 In. 150.00
Vase, Lotus, Silhouette Of Tan Tree, Gray Green Body, 9 1/2 In. 550.00
Vase, Pansy Design, Green, Brown Glaze, Mabel Hall, 11 1/4 In. 185.00
Vase, Pansy Design, Tan High Glaze, 3 3/4 In. 230.00
Vase, Raised Flowers, Handles, 12 In. 138.00
Vase, Reticulated Neck, Greek Key Pattern, Green Matte Glaze, Squat, Stamped, 7 x 8 In. ... 633.00
Vase, Utopian, Beagle Dog Portrait, Oval, 10 1/2 In. 633.00
Vase, Utopian, Bouquet Of Honey Amber Chrysanthemums, 3 3/4 In. 120.00
Vase, Utopian, Flowers, Silver Overlay, Handles, 4 1/2 In. 200.00
Vase, Utopian, Indian Portrait, Bottle Shape, Mary Fauntleroy Stevens, 14 3/4 In. 1495.00
Vase, Utopian, Indian Portrait, Brown Glaze, Signed, 8 3/4 In. 850.00
Vase, Utopian, Pillow, Daisies Painted In Thick Slip, 5 1/4 In. 161.00

OYSTER PLATES were popular from the 1880s. Each course at dinner was served in a special dish. The oyster plate had indentations shaped like oysters. Usually six oysters were held on a plate. There is no greater value to a plate with more oysters, although that myth continues to haunt antiques dealers. There are other plates for shellfish, including cockle plates and whelk plates. The appropriately shaped indentations are part of the design of these dishes.

6 Wells, Fleur-De-Lis, Vein Leaf Shape, Aqua To Rose, 9 1/2 x 8 In. 995.00
Scalloped & Gilt Rim, Poppy Sprays, Limoges, 9 1/4 In., 8 Piece 1495.00
Shell Shape Wells, Scalloped, Enamel Flowers, Fish & Birds, 1860s, 9 7/8 In. 172.00

PADEN CITY Glass Manufacturing Company was established in 1916 at Paden City, West Virginia. The company made more than seventy different colors of glass. The firm closed in 1951. Paden City Pottery is not listed here.

Black Forest, Bowl, 2 Handles, Pink, 8 In. 115.00
Crow's Foot, Bowl, Red, Oval, 9 In. 40.00
Gothic Garden, Bowl, Yellow 550.00
Peacock & Wild Rose, Vase, Pink, 10 In. 175.00

PAINTINGS listed in this book are not works by major artists but rather decorative paintings on ivory, board, or glass that would be of interest to the average collector. Watercolors on paper are listed under Picture. To learn the value of an oil painting by a listed artist you must contact an expert in that area.

Acrylic On Canvas, Florida Scene, T. Daniels, Frame, 23 3/4 x 30 In. 185.00

Oil & Ink On Panel, Studio Interior, Paris, William T. Dannat, Frame, 1882, 7 x 9 In. 6325.00
Oil On Board, 3 Cows, Headed For Pasture, Cottage, Trees, Frame, 15 x 10 In. 220.00
Oil On Board, Abstract, Polychrome, Irving George Lehman, 24 x 29 In. 115.00
Oil On Board, Beach Scene, Matted, Frame, Charles Woodbury, 11 x 14 In. 3300.00
Oil On Board, Boston Street Scene, Anthony Thieme, 11 1/2 x 14 1/2 In. 5750.00
Oil On Board, Bulldog, Sitting, Water Bowl, Oak Frame, 1900, 23 x 18 3/4 In. 385.00
Oil On Board, Cattle In Landscape, 4 1/2 x 6 3/4 In. 635.00
Oil On Board, Cityscape, Mosque, 19th Century, 18 x 22 In. 85.00
Oil On Board, Coastal Scene, Mountains, Boat, P.L. Mueller, 1915, 14 x 17 x 11 In. 190.00
Oil On Board, Cows In Stream, House In Distance, Mountains, Frame, 12 3/4 In. 140.00
Oil On Board, Desert Landscape, Pueblo At Mountain, R.H. Ives, Frame, 14 1/8 x 11 In. . 275.00
Oil On Board, Dock Scene, Frame, 11 x 12 1/2 In. 5225.00
Oil On Board, Fall Landscape, Emma Ruth Burgess, Frame, 12 x 18 In. 460.00
Oil On Board, Folk Art Guinea Cock, In Pumpkin Patch, Frame, 32 x 26 In. 1650.00
Oil On Board, Interior Room Scene, Checker Board Floor, M. Schuibbeo, 13 x 16 In. 770.00
Oil On Board, Landscape, Forest Scene, W.K. Hols, Frame, 23 x 18 1/2 In. 55.00
Oil On Board, Market Day, Lancaster Southern Market, M. Schuibbeo, 15 x 17 In. 440.00
Oil On Board, Mountain Landscape, Continental, Frame, 1800s, 5 x 6 3/4 In. 172.00
Oil On Board, Panoramic Coastal Landscape, R. Huelster, 19 3/4 x 20 3/4 In. 575.00
Oil On Board, Peasants & Cattle Scene, Northeast European School, 14 x 11 In. 115.00
Oil On Board, Sailboat At Anchor, Rudolph Guba, 23 x 27 In. 1095.00
Oil On Board, Shades Of Night, Woman Herding Cattle To Barn, Frame, 14 1/4 x 29 In. . 195.00
Oil On Board, St. Helens From Crow's Nest, W. S. Parrott, 10 x 12 In. 1880.00
Oil On Board, Still Life, Books, Pipe, Quill Pen, M. Schuibbeo, 16 x 12 In. 130.00
Oil On Board, Uncle Tom In The Garden, Clementine Hunter, Signed, 16 x 20 In. 4230.00
Oil On Board, Venetian Canal Scene, Italian School, Monogram, 16 x 11 In. 520.00
Oil On Board, Victorian Woman, Arm On Table, Striped Gray Dress, Frame, 10 x 8 In. . . 230.00
Oil On Board, Village Man, E. Erb, Gilt Frame, 8 1/4 x 8 In. 690.00
Oil On Board, Western Scene, Cowboy Roping Calf, J.G. Storey, Frame, 13 1/2 In. 275.00
Oil On Board, White Horse, Front Of Shed, Thatched Roof, Walnut Frame, 8 1/4 x 10 In. 275.00
Oil On Board, Woman, Brown Hair In Ringlets, Blue Dress, Frame, 1880s, 11 3/8 In. 275.00
Oil On Board, Wooded Lake Scene, Sailboats, Mountains, Frame, 15 5/8 x 20 1/8 In. 275.00
Oil On Board, Young Girl, Brown Hair, Ruffled Dress, 15 1/2 x 12 1/4 In. 7280.00
Oil On Canvas, 3 Chicks, Under Berry Bush, Frame, 11 1/2 x 13 1/2 In. 190.00
Oil On Canvas, 4 Boars, Winter Landscape, W. Franken, 19 x 39 In. 460.00
Oil On Canvas, Abstract Composition, James Bernard Slusser, 1971, 48 In. 230.00
Oil On Canvas, American Indian, Full Headdress, c.1890, 12 x 10 In. 650.00
Oil On Canvas, Autumn Scene, Hillside Into Valley, Frame, 1920s, 20 x 28 In. 140.00
Oil On Canvas, Bark, Charles Edwin, Built By Benjamin W. Pickett, 1856 .... 2585.00
Oil On Canvas, Battle Scene, A. Borris, Frame, 17 x 25 In. 460.00
Oil On Canvas, Bearded Man, Raffaele Frigerio, 18 x 14 In. 645.00
Oil On Canvas, Bentley Tourer, At Speed, 26 x 40 In. 180.00
Oil On Canvas, Billy The Cat, Frame, N.T. Plume, 26 x 20 In. 1045.00
Oil On Canvas, Boat & Fisherman Scene, Crackled, C.P. Appel, 18 x 40 In. 1100.00
Oil On Canvas, Boats In Channel, V. Mirow, Russia, 19th Century, 17 x 28 In. 2450.00
Oil On Canvas, Bobcat, Bushes & Trees, H.B. Dummer, 19 1/2 x 17 1/2 In. 575.00
Oil On Canvas, Bottoms Up, Frame, Waldo Peirce, Autograph, 30 x 22 In. 440.00
Oil On Canvas, Boy At Piano, Pels, Frame, 30 x 16 In. 200.00
Oil On Canvas, Boy In Blue Coat, Frame, 18th Century, 14 x 11 3/4 In. 1725.00
Oil On Canvas, Cabins & Mountain Landscape, Gesso Frame, 17 x 27 1/4 In. 660.00
Oil On Canvas, Cafe Interior, Gabriel Spat, 7 x 10 7/8 In. 2350.00
Oil On Canvas, Calico Kitten, Yarn, Gesso Frame, Signed G.R. 1903, 15 1/2 x 23 1/2 In. . 580.00
Oil On Canvas, Castle Ruins, Peasants, Gesso Frame, 43 3/4 x 36 In. 550.00
Oil On Canvas, Cat, Peeking Out Under Straw Hat, Percy Sanborn, Frame, 9 x 12 In. 3960.00
Oil On Canvas, Cattle Watering, In Mountain, G. Mathieu, 1904, 41 1/2 x 67 1/2 In. 4830.00
Oil On Canvas, Child, Red Dress, Dog, American School, 1800s, 36 x 29 In. 2300.00
Oil On Canvas, Child, Sitting In Windsor Chair, Frame, 17 x 15 In. 495.00
Oil On Canvas, Children, In Barn, Edward Turner, 1800s, 24 x 36 In. 1150.00
Oil On Canvas, Church Scene, Large Steeple, Relined, Frame, Continental, 16 x 19 In. 715.00
Oil On Canvas, Continental City Scape, Andre Gisson, 24 x 12 In. 1150.00
Oil On Canvas, Cottage View, Girl & Horseman, P. Turnkill, 17 1/2 x 23 1/2 In. 630.00
Oil On Canvas, Country House Laundry Day, L.A. Girardot, 12 x 18 In. 2185.00
Oil On Canvas, Deer, Lake At Dawn, Frame, 19th Century, 26 x 36 In. 175.00

Oil On Canvas, Diana Huntress With Hound, Gilt Frame, 19th Century, 40 x 32 In. 3680.00
Oil On Canvas, Edward Lister & Hunt, John Dalby, 8 1/2 x 15 5/8 In. 4800.00
Oil On Canvas, Elk, Moonlit Landscape, Frame, Ockert, 5 x 10 In. 660.00
Oil On Canvas, Encampment Scenes, A.M. Friedlander, Frame, 8 1/4 x 12 1/2 In. 920.00
Oil On Canvas, English Bulldogs, Pair, Samuel Fulton, 14 1/4 x 18 In. 9000.00
Oil On Canvas, European Scene, 2 Men, Distant Castle, Gilt Frame, 14 1/4 x 22 In. 300.00
Oil On Canvas, European Wedding Feast, Gilt Frame, 1883, 37 x 56 In. 920.00
Oil On Canvas, Eve, C. Rothe, 26 x 21 3/4 In. 1000.00
Oil On Canvas, Evening On Milford Fife, P.S. Nisbet, Frame, 20 x 23 1/2 In. 1265.00
Oil On Canvas, Faithful Companion, Henry Chalon, 15 1/4 x 18 1/2 In. 3000.00
Oil On Canvas, Fall Landscape, Frame, R.R. Sitzman, 30 x 40 In. 880.00
Oil On Canvas, Farm Scene, Oxen Pulling Hay Filled Wagon, Frame, 28 x 19 1/2 In. 410.00
Oil On Canvas, Farmyard Idyll, Cart & Draught Horses, E. Claude, 7 1/2 x 13 In. 1840.00
Oil On Canvas, Figures In Wooded Landscape, Robert Ladbrooke, 37 x 48 In. 3645.00
Oil On Canvas, Firefighting Scene, Washington St., Boston, 1872, 30 x 15 1/2 In. 3740.00
Oil On Canvas, Ford, Cecil Arthur Varnon, 25 x 30 In. 6900.00
Oil On Canvas, French Port Scene, Honfleur, 16 x 10 1/2 In. 69.00
Oil On Canvas, Friar On Mountain Path, Frame, A. Pinatta, 28 3/4 x 17 1/2 In. 460.00
Oil On Canvas, Garden Landscape, Figures, Hermann Philips, 30 x 24 In. 4600.00
Oil On Canvas, Gentleman, Frame, 45 x 36 In. 285.00
Oil On Canvas, Gentleman, Tricorner Hat Under Arm, 42 x 36 In. 550.00
Oil On Canvas, George Washington, Frame, 19th Century, 41 1/2 x 29 1/2 In. 5775.00
Oil On Canvas, German City Square, G.J. Buchner, 1926, 21 1/2 x 24 In. 1990.00
Oil On Canvas, Girl Holding Infant, Attillio Simonetti, Frame, 18 1/2 x 14 1/2 In. 920.00
Oil On Canvas, Girl, Ringlets, White & Gray Dress, Frame, 17 x 16 In. 330.00
Oil On Canvas, Girl, Seated At Seaside, British School, 19th Century, 28 x 28 In. 920.00
Oil On Canvas, Gypsy Caravan, George Wright, 12 x 17 In. 6600.00
Oil On Canvas, Harbor Scene, Row Boat & Crew, Frame, 21 1/2 x 14 In. 190.00
Oil On Canvas, Horse Round Up, E. R. Howe, 34 x 58 In. 1175.00
Oil On Canvas, Houses, Red, Orange Roof Lines, Trees, Gate, Frame, 25 1/2 x 21 1/2 In. . 165.00
Oil On Canvas, Hunting Dog, Black Spots, Grouse In Mouth, Field, 22 5/8 x 18 5/8 In. . . 275.00
Oil On Canvas, In The Studio, Juan Duana, 24 x 28 3/4 In. 1530.00
Oil On Canvas, In Times Of Peace, L. Gontier, 19th Century, 24 x 36 In. 1380.00
Oil On Canvas, Interior Scene, Frame, Horvath G.A., 29 1/2 x 39 In. 770.00
Oil On Canvas, Investigating Chicken Coop, M. Bachman, 1889, 18 3/4 x 15 3/4 In. 460.00
Oil On Canvas, Italian Market Scene, Signed, Italy, 19th Century, 15 x 22 In. 1210.00
Oil On Canvas, Italian Plaza, Statues On Street, H. Pelletier, Frame, 1942, 30 x 49 In. . . . 330.00
Oil On Canvas, Jack Russell Terriers, Fannie Moody, 20 x 16 In. 9000.00
Oil On Canvas, Lady, 24 x 20 In. 225.00
Oil On Canvas, Lake & Figures Scene, Hudson River School, 1800s, 13 1/4 x 20 In. 287.00
Oil On Canvas, Landscape, Carriage & Driver, Percy Mills, 1868, 18 x 14 In. 518.00
Oil On Canvas, Landscape, Fisherman, Rowboat, Evan Roland, Frame, 1800s, 24 x 42 In. 715.00
Oil On Canvas, Landscape, Horse In Distance, Frame, 19th Century, 31 x 24 In. 330.00
Oil On Canvas, Landscape, Resting Figures, W. L. Judson, 49 x 30 In. 2240.00
Oil On Canvas, Landscape, Rural, Henry Ward Ranger, 10 x 14 In. 2070.00
Oil On Canvas, Landscape, Sailboat, Mountains, Gesso Frame, 17 1/2 x 24 1/2 In. 165.00
Oil On Canvas, Landscape, Sheep, Signed, Frame, 19th Century, 12 x 18 In. 130.00
Oil On Canvas, Landscape, Summer, Boy Fishing, Jirouch, Frame, 1935, 18 x 26 In. 660.00
Oil On Canvas, Landscape, Summer, Stream, France, 10 x 7 1/2 In. 605.00
Oil On Canvas, Landscape, Sunset, 5 Deer, Setting Sun, Frame, 23 x 31 In. 375.00
Oil On Canvas, Low Tide, Port Clyde, A. Winter, Frame, 16 x 16 In. 5175.00
Oil On Canvas, Madonna & Child, Frame, 13 3/4 x 10 1/2 In. 1610.00
Oil On Canvas, Man & Woman, American School, 1800s, 27 x 22 In., Pair 345.00
Oil On Canvas, Man & Woman, American School, 1800s, 29 x 24 In., Pair 1610.00
Oil On Canvas, Man & Woman, European School, 1800s, 16 x 12 In., Pair 230.00
Oil On Canvas, Man, Edgardo Saporetti, Napoli, c.1885, 21 x 17 In. 920.00
Oil On Canvas, Man, Helmet, Gargoyle Finial, S. Sokolovsky, Frame, 22 x 25 In. 880.00
Oil On Canvas, Man, Jessie Upson, 30 x 24 In. 1265.00
Oil On Canvas, Man, Window Behind, Gold Frame, 30 1/2 x 25 3/4 In. 385.00
Oil On Canvas, Master Of The Hounds, C.A. Varnon, 1918, 20 x 30 In. 7200.00
Oil On Canvas, Mexican Market Scene, Contemporary Gilt Frame, 23 x 26 3/4 In. 110.00
Oil On Canvas, Minding The Children, F.G. Grust, Frame, c.1890, 27 x 32 In. 575.00
Oil On Canvas, Monk With Toothache, Hugo Kotschenreiter, 20 1/2 x 14 In. 3450.00

Oil On Canvas, Monogrammed L.L., Still Life With Flowers, Frame, 21 3/4 x 17 3/4 In. . . . 860.00
Oil On Canvas, Moonlit Mill & Waterfall Scene, Gesso Frame, 22 x 36 In. 110.00
Oil On Canvas, Moorland Loch, Charles Leslie, 1880, 12 x 24 In. 2990.00
Oil On Canvas, Morocco, Richard Newton Jr., 60 1/3 x 48 In. 5290.00
Oil On Canvas, Mother Cat & Kittens, Charles Van Den Eychen, Frame, 18 x 24 In. 6900.00
Oil On Canvas, Mount Hood, Eliza R. Barchus, 12 x 18 In. 4600.00
Oil On Canvas, Mountain Landscape With Stream, A. Calame, 18 1/2 x 26 In. 2300.00
Oil On Canvas, Mrs. James Baille & Daughter, Gainsborough Dupont 9200.00
Oil On Canvas, Mystic Marriage Of St. Catherine, Frame, 1931, 41 x 40 In. 1265.00
Oil On Canvas, Ocean Scene, 2 Sailing Ships, U. Bille, Frame, 24 x 20 In. 110.00
Oil On Canvas, Open Landscape, Native American Hunters, Troy Denton, 24 x 36 In. 1840.00
Oil On Canvas, Paddlewheel Boat, J. Blatter, Frame, Mid 1900s, 13 x 18 in. 330.00
Oil On Canvas, Panoramic River Landscape, Frank E. Jamieson, 30 x 20 In. 35.00
Oil On Canvas, Parisian Street Vendor, A. Boulangier, Paris 54, 11 7/8 x 8 In. 230.00
Oil On Canvas, Park Landscape, Andre Gisson, 24 x 36 In. 2300.00
Oil On Canvas, Parrot Tulip On White, Lowell Nesbitt, 1979, 40 x 40 In. 750.00
Oil On Canvas, Path Through Woods, N. Diaz, 9 1/4 x 10 3/4 In. 3450.00
Oil On Canvas, Portrait, Frederick W. Pelton, Frame, 19th Century, 26 x 21 In. 198.00
Oil On Canvas, Portrait, Sara Dixon, Holding Basket Of Flowers, 32 x 24 In. 9900.00
Oil On Canvas, Racehorse Held By Groom, T.S. Sherwood, 28 x 35 3/4 In. 6600.00
Oil On Canvas, River, 2 Girls, Cattle, Shadowbox Frame, Gilt Liner, 21 x 28 In. 385.00
Oil On Canvas, River, Children Fishing, Girl Washing Clothes, Frame, 37 x 49 1/2 In. 190.00
Oil On Canvas, River, Couple, Bridge, Fisherman, Steamboat, 36 x 22 In. 440.00
Oil On Canvas, River, Elizabeth Barrett, Gilt Frame, 17 x 10 In. 1495.00
Oil On Canvas, River, Mountains, Upper Laitey, Killarney, P. Watts, 1910, 20 x 30 In. 605.00
Oil On Canvas, River, Natives On Raft, Soehady, 27 1/2 x 41 In. 70.00
Oil On Canvas, River, People In Canoe, H.C. Christy, Frame, 15 1/4 x 20 In. 605.00
Oil On Canvas, River, Waterfall, People Fishing, Gilt Lined Frame, 23 x 30 In. 770.00
Oil On Canvas, Santa Barbara, Initialed, Feb. 22, 1941, 14 3/8 x 19 1/4 In. 170.00
Oil On Canvas, Seashore, AHL, Frame, England, 19th Century, 18 x 13 1/2 In. 415.00
Oil On Canvas, Sheep In Barn, Chicken, Frame, 27 3/4 x 33 3/4 In. 140.00
Oil On Canvas, Shepherd Dog, Herding Sheep Down Lane, 27 x 14 In. 630.00
Oil On Canvas, Ship At Sea, H.A. Stark, Frame, 16 x 20 In. 110.00
Oil On Canvas, Shucking Corn, Horvath G.A., Frame, 10 x 15 1/2 In. 525.00
Oil On Canvas, Spaniel In Landscape, Heywood Hardy, 1879, 19 1/2 x 19 1/2 In. 4800.00
Oil On Canvas, Still Life, Basket Of Fruit, Wine Bottle, Candle, Frame, 29 3/4 x 23 1/2 In. 80.00
Oil On Canvas, Still Life, Birds, Fruit & Oysters, Francoide Fabri, 8 x 23 3/4 In. 115.00
Oil On Canvas, Still Life, Bowl, Vase, Bottle & Jar, Loren, 26 1/2 x 38 1/2 In. 55.00
Oil On Canvas, Still Life, Carnations In Pitcher, AC Peck, Frame, 24 x 15 In. 80.00
Oil On Canvas, Still Life, Dahlias, Woven Basket, G. Corbier, Frame, 15 x 21 3/4 In. 1840.00
Oil On Canvas, Still Life, Flowers In Vase, Dutch School, Early 1900s, 27 x 22 In. 460.00
Oil On Canvas, Still Life, Flowers, Countess Tichy, 30 1/8 x 36 1/8 In. 645.00
Oil On Canvas, Still Life, Fruit On Table, Tina Hall, Frame, 1906, 18 1/2 x 25 1/2 In. 275.00
Oil On Canvas, Still Life, Fruit, Cornelius Hankins, 18 x 24 In. 1725.00
Oil On Canvas, Still Life, Geraniums & Lilacs, Baudry, Frame, 1880, 18 1/4 x 23 3/4 In. . 2933.00
Oil On Canvas, Still Life, Pears, Apples, Walnuts, British School, 12 x 18 In. 460.00
Oil On Canvas, Still Life, Violin, Anna Bischof, 36 x 24 In. 170.00
Oil On Canvas, Street Scene, A.M. Guerin, Signed, 13 x 20 In. 290.00
Oil On Canvas, Street Scene, Pestow, 28 1/2 x 17 1/2 In. 330.00
Oil On Canvas, Sunset On The Harbor, Continental, Frame, 1800s, 19 x 31 3/4 In. 460.00
Oil On Canvas, Trophy Of Hunt, Randell Davey, 24 x 18 1/4 In. 2160.00
Oil On Canvas, Troubadour, John Callcott Horsley, 30 x 19 In. 2115.00
Oil On Canvas, Trouville Beach, Francois Gall, 8 3/4 x 10 3/4 In. 3525.00
Oil On Canvas, Umbrella Lady, J.E. Menta, Gilt Frame, 18 x 14 In. 2875.00
Oil On Canvas, Umbrella Man, J.E. Menta, 18 x 14 In. 2875.00
Oil On Canvas, Uncle Sam, Dog Tugging At Heels, R. Gunn, 1986, 24 x 20 In. 1840.00
Oil On Canvas, Venice Morning, Walter F. Lansil, 14 1/2 x 12 1/2 In. 765.00
Oil On Canvas, View Of Rivereaux Abbey, Yorkshire, Methuen, 24 x 37 In. 6000.00
Oil On Canvas, Wake Up, Big Dog, Wake Up, V. De Vos, Frame, 19 x 23 In. 3450.00
Oil On Canvas, Waterfront Scene, Frame, 20th Century, 14 x 14 In. 220.00
Oil On Canvas, Windhover, Brian Coole, 20 3/4 x 28 In. 1595.00
Oil On Canvas, Woman Reading, George Augustus Baker Jr., 13 x 11 In. 1765.00
Oil On Canvas, Woman, Black Dress, Frame, 11 1/2 x 9 1/2 In. 300.00

Oil On Canvas, Woman, Black Dress, Lace Collar, Gilt Frame, 29 1/2 x 23 In. 440.00
Oil On Canvas, Woman, Hudson River Ground, American School, 1800s, 36 x 28 In. 575.00
Oil On Canvas, Woman, Mary Cassatt Style, 1890s, 14 1/4 x 11 In.   440.00
Oil On Canvas, Woman, Red Haired, European School, 1900s, 24 1/2 x 18 In. 575.00
Oil On Canvas, Wooded Country Lane, Jessie Upson, 24 x 18 In.   400.00
Oil On Canvas, Wounded Elk, Stanley Berkeley, 12 1/2 x 20 In.   690.00
Oil On Canvas, Young Man & Woman, Amid Flowers, D.B. Walkley, 27 x 18 In. 3360.00
Oil On Canvas, Young Woman, Marion L. Pooke, Frame, 20 x 16 In. 2200.00
Oil On Canvas, Young Woman, Seated On Empire Sofa, Long Curls, Frame, 38 x 30 In. . .   660.00
Oil On Ivory, Gentleman, 19th Century, 2 3/4 x 2 1/8 In. 440.00
Oil On Ivory, Gentleman, Blue Jacket, 19th Century, 2 1/2 x 2 In. 330.00
Oil On Ivory, Gentleman, Rectangular Frame, 19th Century, 3 x 2 1/4 In. 330.00
Oil On Ivory, Young Boy, Red Book, Oval, 19th Century, 2 7/8 x 2 1/4 In. 495.00
Oil On Ivory, Young Woman, Floral Bonnet & Red Dress, Oval, 1800s, 2 x 1 In. 600.00
Oil On Ivory, Young Woman, Gold Scarf, Oval Frame, 19th Century, 3 x 2 In. 330.00
Oil On Masonite, Artist At Work On Easel On Beach, M. Vautrinot, Frame, 10 1/2 In. . . .   140.00
Oil On Masonite, Friendship Sloop, Vern Broe, Gold Frame, 20 1/2 x 31 1/2 In. 690.00
Oil On Masonite, Large House, Small Trees, Pond & Ducks, Frame, 19 x 28 1/4 In. 110.00
Oil On Masonite, Still Life, Wineglasses, Flowers, Fruit, M. Horn, 16 x 20 In. 259.00
Oil On Masonite, Winter Sunset, W. Morrell, 15 1/2 x 19 1/2 In.   575.00
Oil On Metal, Portrait Of A Young Gentleman, Philadelphia, 12 x 8 1/4 In. 1380.00
Oil On Panel, 2 Men At Table, Examining Letter, T. Rehs, 7 x 5 In. 460.00
Oil On Panel, 3 Men Playing Chess, Continental School, 1800s, 8 x 7 In. 230.00
Oil On Panel, Beach Scene, Women, Continental School, Lenoir, 1900s, 14 x 17 In. 520.00
Oil On Panel, Blond Woman, Off-The-Shoulder Dress, L.R. Ervins, Gilt Frame, 7 In. 140.00
Oil On Panel, Boy Fishing, Smoking Pipe, Pio Ricci, Frame, 10 1/4 x 6 1/4 In. 345.00
Oil On Panel, Coastal Landscape, Sailboats, Hamilor, 17 x 12 In. 145.00
Oil On Panel, Colorado Mountains, A.R. Butler, c.1942, 14 x 10 In. 695.00
Oil On Panel, Continental Street Scene, Early 1900s, 9 x 12 In. 630.00
Oil On Panel, Corralling Sheep, Charles Emile Jacque, 19 3/4 x 22 In. 2350.00
Oil On Panel, European Port Scene With Ships, A. Bradford, 12 x 17 In. 400.00
Oil On Panel, Farmyard Fowl, Rich Barrett, 1804, 13 3/4 x 21 1/2 In. 355.00
Oil On Panel, Figures, Masquerade Ball, Continental School, 1930s, 15 x 19 In. 290.00
Oil On Panel, Journey Across Plains, W.J. Shayer, 1847, 71/4 x 8 3/4 In. 460.00
Oil On Panel, Ladies & Parrot In Landscape, Giltwood Frame, 8 1/2 x 6 1/2 In. 1150.00
Oil On Panel, Landscape, Fence & Dirt Road, Pond & Field, Gilman Bullery, 8 7/8 In. . . .   275.00
Oil On Panel, Man, Signed L.R., Frame, 13 1/4 x 10 1/4 In. 690.00
Oil On Panel, Manayunk, Giovanni De Martino, 12 x 16 In. 920.00
Oil On Panel, Market Scene, Erno Nagy, 1886, 12 x 10 In. 940.00
Oil On Panel, Plowing The Fields, Lee B. Coye, Frame, 1943, 14 x 18 In. 660.00
Oil On Panel, Portrait, General Jeremiah Millay, Frame, 1840s, 30 x 21 In. 550.00
Oil On Panel, Scholar With Books, Miniature, 5 1/2 x 6 1/2 In. 475.00
Oil On Panel, Ship Captain, Hingham, Massachusetts, 27 3/4 x 22 3/4 In. 3900.00
Oil On Panel, Spanish Woman, Pink Dress, Gilt Frame, Lucas, 1800s, 12 In. 330.00
Oil On Panel, Still Life In Studio, Dahlgren, Frame, 18 x 32 In. 465.00
Oil On Panel, Trolley Cars, Pestow, 22 x 25 In. 285.00
Oil On Panel, Woman With Child Under Umbrella, Keny, 8 x 10 In. 90.00
Oil On Panel, Woman With Feather Cap, M. E. Bertschinger, 7 x 5 In. 549.00
Oil On Panel, Young Girl, Continental School, 1800s, 12 x 19 In.   230.00
Oil On Tin, Girl, Sitting Under Tree, White Dress, Oval Frame, 22 1/4 x 18 3/4 In. 550.00
Oil On Tin, Greek Revival House, Fountain, Steeple, Period Gilt Frame, 20 x 28 In. 495.00
On Board, Mountain Cabin, N.A. Knopf, Frame, 16 1/2 x 18 1/4 In. 880.00
On Board, Thatched Roof House, Boat, Anton Melbye, Gesso Frame, 1852, 8 x 12 In. . . .   1760.00
On Faux Ivory, Gainsborough Noblewoman, Feathered Hat, Blue Dress, 2 7/8 In. 275.00
On Ivory, Admiral Dewey, Hero Of Vacite, Naval Uniform, Signed, 7 x 5 In. 630.00
On Ivory, Gentleman, Black Wigged, Lace Collar, Oval Frame, 17th Century, 1 3/4 In. . . .   400.00
On Ivory, Gentleman, Frock Coat, Pin In Neck Scarf, Mutton Chops, 3 x 2 3/4 In. 522.00
On Ivory, Gentleman, Powdered Wig, Oval Giltwood Frame, 1730s, 1 1/8 x 3 3/4 In. 430.00
On Ivory, Girl, White Dress, Red Sash, Kreuze, Ivory Scrimshaw Frame, 3 3/8 In. 330.00
On Ivory, Lady, Blue Gown, Brown Cape, Flowers In Hair, Earrings, 3 1/8 x 2 3/8 In. 530.00
On Ivory, Lady, Facing Left, Necklace, Curly Hair, Gold Frame, 3 1/4 x 2 3/4 In. 1230.00
On Ivory, Lady, Facing Right, Blue Dress, Red Shawl, Brass Frame, 2 1/4 x 1 3/4 In. 335.00
On Ivory, Lady, Lacy Shawl, Pink Gown, Flowers In Hair, Oval Frame, 3 1/2 x 2 7/8 In. . .   730.00

On Ivory, Landscape, People In Front Of Ruins, Wood Frame, 2 9/16 In. 615.00
On Ivory, Memorial, Young Girl, Surround Of Clouds, Pet. Mayr, Frame, 1832, 5 1/2 In. . 400.00
On Ivory, Napoleon, Bone Frame, 3 1/2 x 2 3/4 In. 168.00
On Ivory, Napoleon, I.R. Ines, Square Frame, 1 3/4 x 4 1/4 In. 170.00
On Ivory, Officer, Gold Epaulettes, Breast Star, Frilled Cravat, 3 3/8 x 2 1/2 In. 615.00
On Ivory, Woman By Memorial Urn, Scotland, Late 18th Century, 3 3/8 In. 460.00
On Ivory, Woman, Black Dress, Giltwood Frame, Early 19th Century, 1 1/2 x 3 3/4 In. . . . 230.00
On Ivory, Woman, High Waisted Dress, White Collar, Gold Jewelry, 5 1/4 x 5 1/4 In. 520.00
On Ivory, Woman, Painted Sky Background, Oval Frame, 3 7/8 In. 230.00
On Ivory, Young Beauty, Pearls In Hair, Blue Wrap, J. Isabey, Frame, 4 1/4 In. 1725.00
On Ivory, Young Beauty, Placing Flowers In Vase, Jewels, Wood Frame, 5 3/4 In. 750.00
On Ivory, Young Lady, High Collared Dress, Cloak, Fur Muff, 3 3/8 x 2 1/2 In. 420.00
On Ivory, Young Man, Full Face, Blue Coat With Cape, Silk Ground, Frame, 3 1/8 In. . . . 2350.00
On Ivory, Young Man, Full Face, Blue Coat, White Cravat, Gilt Metal Frame, 2 1/6 In. . . . 730.00
On Ivory, Young Man, Oval Wood Frame, Early 19th Century, 2 3/4 x 4 1/4 In. 115.00
On Ivory, Young Woman In White, Oval Frame, Early 19th Century, 2 5/8 x 4 1/8 In. 172.00
On Ivory, Young Woman, Facing Right, Low-Cut Waisted Dress, Gilt Frame, 2 1/8 In. . . . 616.00
On Kidskin, Woman, Lace Cap, Frame, Continental, Miniature, 2 3/8 x 4 3/8 In. 115.00
On Mattress Ticking, Portrait Of Woman, Black Dress, Ringlets, 30 x 24 In. 1320.00
On Panel, Angels, Archangel, Quatrefoil, Pointed Finials, Italy, 25 x 8 3/4 In., Pair 200.00
On Panel, Arcadian Landscape, Animals, Voysey Style, Frame, England, 21 x 32 In. 690.00
On Porcelain, Plaque, Maiden, Purple Irises, G. Meisel 2590.00
On Tin, Miranda & Her Father, Windswept Coastline, 1880s, 9 7/8 x 8 3/8 In. 230.00
Reverse On Glass, Cottage & Landscape, Black & Gilt Stile Frame, 20 x 10 1/2 In. 165.00
Reverse On Glass, English Coaching Scene, Maple Frame, 12 5/8 x 17 5/8 In. 140.00
Reverse On Glass, Flowers, Butterfly, Pink, Green, Foil, Gold Leaf Frame, 13 x 13 In. 28.00
Reverse On Glass, House, Flanked By Trees, Frame, 18 1/2 x 10 1/2 In. 220.00
Reverse On Glass, Mirror, House & Stream, Mitered Frame, 19 1/2 x 11 1/2 In. 165.00
Reverse On Glass, Patriotic Eagle & Shield, 8 x 10 In. 476.00
Reverse On Glass, Rosiland, Celia, Orlando, Landscape, Giltwood Frame, 12 x 15 In. . . . 575.00
Reverse On Glass, Winter Farm Scene, Home Of Mr. E.R. Jones, Frame, 1881, 22 x 25 In. 770.00
Reverse On Glass, Woman, Karolina, Striped Dress, Shawl, Mahogany Frame, 14 1/2 In. . 410.00
Tempera On Board, Blue Plant, Matted, Frame, Schock, 16 x 13 1/2 In. 30.00
Tempera On Paper, Chinese Female Ancestor, Red Robe, Frame, Mid 1800s, 59 x 40 In. . 6615.00

PAIRPOINT Manufacturing Company started in 1880 in New Bedford, Massachusetts. It soon joined with the glassworks nearby and made glass, silver-plated pieces, and lamps. Reverse-painted glass shades and molded shades known as *puffies* were part of the production until the 1930s. The company reorganized and changed its name several times but is still working today. Items listed here are glass or glass and metal. Silver-plated pieces are listed under Silver Plate.

Biscuit Jar, White Satin, Silver Plated Top & Handle, Arctic Scene, Hand Painted 605.00
Bottle, Cologne, Crystal Body, Matching Stopper, 6 In. 85.00
Compote, Diamond-Quilted, Cut Grape & Leaves, Knop Stem, 8 In. 720.00
Compote, Vaseline Bowl, Controlled Bubble Stem, Clear Foot, 7 1/4 In. 350.00
Condiment Set, Salt, Pepper, Cruet, Burmese, Silver Plated Holder, 10 In. 1495.00
Condiment Set, Salt, Pepper, Mustard, Amberina, Silver Plated Holder, 8 In. 1323.00
Decanter, Nevada Cutting, 12 1/2 In. 375.00
Jewelry Box, Pearl, Sterling Silver Rings, 3 1/2 x 6 In. 490.00
Ladle, Vintage Cutting, Teardrop Handle, Signed, 10 1/2 In. 225.00
Lamp, Bombay Shade, Exotic Birds, Flowers, Lime Green Ground, Signed Base, 18 In. . . 4480.00
Lamp, Bombay Shade, Painted, Woodland Scene, Urn Shape Base, Mahogany, 16 In. 3080.00
Lamp, Carlisle Shade, Corof Scene, Signed, 18 x 22 In. 3220.00
Lamp, Carlisle Shade, Exotic Birds, Flowers, Yellow, Gold Ground, Signed, 18 In. 3640.00
Lamp, Carlisle Shade, Garden Of Allah, Bronze Finish, Signed, 20 x 26 In. 4312.00
Lamp, Directoire Shade, Flower, Black Ground, 16 In. 3360.00
Lamp, Exeter Shade, New England Farm Scene, 22 x 17 1/4 In. 2587.00
Lamp, Exeter Shade, Scrolling Leaves, Signed Base, 17 1/2 In. 2800.00
Lamp, Exeter Shade, Seasons, Urn Shape Base, 19 x 15 In. 3165.00
Lamp, Oil, Pink Outlined Burgundy Tulips, Petal Shape Font, 14 1/2 In. 1540.00
Lamp, Puffy, Amethyst, Orange, Yellow Hollyhocks, Signed, 8 3/4 In. 5750.00
Lamp, Puffy, Butterflies, Pink, Red, Stamped, 20 In. 5750.00

Lamp, Puffy, Flowers, Butterflies & Pond Lilies, Signed, 6 x 11 1/2 In. 4315.00
Lamp, Puffy, Flowers, Butterfly, Gilt Metal Base, 15 1/2 In. 2415.00
Lamp, Puffy, Grape, Purple, Variegated Leaves, Signed Shade & Base, 12 In. 12320.00
Lamp, Puffy, Hummingbird & Roses, Green Top, 22 In. 8625.00
Lamp, Puffy, Mushroom Shape, Poppy, Leaves, Ruby Inserts, Spider Web Support, 20 In. 1430.00
Lamp, Puffy, Pansies, Butterflies, Blue, Violet, Yellow, Silver Plated Base, 9 1/2 x 14 In. . 770.00
Lamp, Puffy, Papillon, Butterfly, Roses Shade, Signed Base, 14 In. 6720.00
Lamp, Puffy, Papillon, Roses & Butterflies Shade, Brass Base, 16 In. 3450.00
Lamp, Puffy, Reverse Painted, Roma Shade, 2 Garlands White Roses, 21 In. 12925.00
Lamp, Puffy, Rose Bonnet, Red Blossoms, Green Leaves, 5 In. 12300.00
Lamp, Puffy, Rose, White Blossoms, Yellow, Pink Highlights, 10 In. 7840.00
Lamp, Puffy, Stratford Shade, Butterscotch Lattice, Yellow, Red Roses, Signed, 14 In. . . . 7840.00
Lamp, Reverse Painted, Forest Scene, Urn Shape Base, Signed 3300.00
Lamp, Reverse Painted, Green Leaf Design, Stylized Border, Matching Base, 15 In. 3360.00
Lamp, Reverse Painted, Urn & Flowers, Signed, No. D 3000, 26 1/2 x 18 In. 3520.00
Paperweight, Purple Flowers, Green Stems, Cut Foot 196.00
Pitcher, Peachblow, Glossy, Applied Blue Handle, Marked, 4 In. 185.00
Plate, Cut, Bishop Hat, Butterfly & Daisy, Hobstar Base, 3 x 15 In. 650.00
Plate, Viscaria Cutting, Flowers & Leaves, 10 In. 195.00
Shade, Dome, Maple Leaf, Reverse Painted, 10 In. 2520.00
Tray, Butterfly & Daisy Cutting, 10 x 6 In. 120.00
Vase, Double, Paperweight, White Draped Loops On Amber Body, 6 1/4 In. 78.00

PALMER COX, BROWNIES, see Brownies category.

PAPER collectibles, including almanacs, catalogs, children's books, some greeting cards, stock certificates, and other paper ephemera, are listed here. Paper calendars are listed separately in the Calendar category. Paper items may be found in many other sections, such as Christmas and Movie.

Baptismal Record, Susanna Kauffeld, Watercolor, Pen & Ink, c.1818, 8 x 9 1/4 In. 3600.00
Birth Certificate & Baptismal, Daniel Ney, 17 x 13 In. 104.00
Birth Record, Elizabeth Riszly, Watercolor, Pen & Ink, c.1820, 9 3/4 x 7 5/8 In. 5100.00
Birth Record, Samuel Compher, Poem, Signed, September 1841 . . . . 165.00
Book, Activity, Bewitched, Screen Gems Inc., 1965, 8 x 11 In., 64 Pages 18.00
Book, Aero Manual, 1909, 1st Edition 69.00
Book, Better Little Book, Kayo, Moon Mullins, One Man Gang, 1939 . . . . *Illus* 40.00
Book, Bewitched Fun & Activity, Color, Screen Gems Inc., 1965, 54 Pages 20.00
Book, Big Little Book, Bonanza, Bubble Gum Kid, 1967, 148 Pages 20.00
Book, Big Little Book, Smokey Bear & The Campers, No. 423, 1971 . . . . 15.00
Book, Ping-Pong, The Game & How To Play It, Arnold Parker, 1902 . . . . 135.00
Booklet, Quaker Meeting House, Preached Sermons, 18th Century 195.00
Bookplate, Elizabeth Ungene, Musical, David Kulp, Bucks County, c.1813, 6 1/4 x 4 In. . 1645.00
Bookplate, John J. Audubon, North American Birds, Bowen, 1840, 11 In., 8 Piece 172.00
Bookplate, Maria Anna Friedrich, Music, Watercolor, Copper Foil, c.1840, 5 x 2 3/4 In. . . 470.00
Bookplate, Peter Fuchs, Watercolor, Ink, c.1790, 4 x 2 5/8 In. 999.00

Never laminate a paper collectible, whether it's a document, photo, letter, press pass, cut autograph, or baseball card. Lamination is permanent, and permanently decreases value.

Paper, Book, Better Little Book, Kayo, Moon Mullins, One Man Gang, 1939

Bookplate, Tulip & Flower, ABC, Hand Colored, Wooden Frame, 1800s, 7 x 5 In. 170.00
Bookplate, Uninscribed, Tulips, Jacob Oberholtzer, c.1880, 6 1/4 x 3 3/4 In. 1528.00
Bookplate, Watercolor, Ink, New Testament, Julianna Miller, c.1824, 6 1/2 x 3 3/4 In. ... 1528.00
Bookplate, Wilhelm Antonius Faber, Scherenschnitten, Bird Of Paradise, 3 x 5 In. 2820.00
Broadside, War Of 1812, 2nd Brigade 1st Division, 1814 .... 373.00
Brochure, Holder, Elevated News-Take One, Brass, 5 1/2 x 15 In. 34.00
Brochure, Holder, Embossed, Cast Aluminum, 4 x 5 1/2 In. 55.00
Catalog, Belleville Threshing Machine, 50 Pages Of Color On Cover, 1917, 9 x 6 In. 69.00
Catalog, Belleville Threshing Machinery, Illustrations, 1898, 9 x 8 In., 18 Pages 138.00
Catalog, Case Machinery, 75th Anniversary, 7 Pages Of Color, 1917, 12 In., 104 Pages ... 143.00
Catalog, Case Threshing Machinery, 88 Pages Of Color, 1915, 9 x 12 In. 138.00
Catalog, F.A.O. Schwarz, Christmas, 1927 .... 110.00
Catalog, Harrison Machine Works, New Jumbo Traction Engine, 1910, 10 x 8 In., Pair ... 115.00
Catalog, Harrison Machine Works, New Jumbo Traction Engine, 1915, 10 x 8 In., Pair ... 126.00
Catalog, Harrison Machine Works, Steam Engine & Thresher On Cover, 26 Pages 103.00
Catalog, Hellers Guide For Ice Cream Makers, 6th Edition, 1918, 154 Pages 115.00
Catalog, Hubbard, Spencer Bartlett & Co., Chicago, 1900, 1550 Pages 126.00
Catalog, Ives Trains, Art Deco Cover, 1930 .... 132.00
Catalog, Kellogg Swim & Dive, 1934, 45 Pages 33.00
Catalog, Moore's, Auto, Toy, 1955, 57 Pages 20.00
Catalog, Otto Young & Co., Chicago, 1884, 285 Pages 172.00
Catalog, Trappers Supplies By Taylor Fur Co., St. Louis, 1927-1928, 50 Pages 92.00
Catalog, Wards, No. 93, 1920 .... 69.00
Catalog, Western Auto, Order Blank & Envelope, 1929, 128 Pages 40.00
Certificate, Wild Bill Hickok Deputy, Hickok Code, Picture, 1955, 8 1/2 x 10 3/4 In. 24.00
Chart, Western Union Maintenance, 1920, 5 x 8 1/2 In., Pair 25.00
Coloring Book, Garrison's Gorilla, Whitman, 1968, 96 Pages 17.00
Dance Card, Bicycle Assoc. Oberhollabrunn 1897 Ball, Brass, Max Jordann, Austria, 4 In. 50.00
Dance Card, Cavalry Cadets School Ball 1893, Enameled Brass, Silk String, 3 1/4 In. ... 50.00
Dance Card, Concordia Ball 1893, Brass, E. Spiegl, Vienna, 4 3/4 In. 28.00
Dance Card, Deutscher Schul-Verein Dance 1890, Silk, Brass Trim, F.W. Papke, 7 1/2 In. . 44.00
Dance Card, Dremsmumfterre Kanzchen 1892 Ball, Figural Doorway, Germany, 3 1/2 In. 133.00
Dance Card, Elite Ball 1902, Brass, Embossed, Mechanical Pencil, Aug. Klein, 2 3/4 In. . 55.00
Dance Card, Elite-Tanzkranzchen 1905 Ball, Velvet & Brass, M. Hinger, Vienna, 3 1/4 In. 39.00
Dance Card, Engraved Ivory, Ivory Tipped Pencil, France, Late 19th Century, 1 3/4 In. ... 50.00
Dance Card, Fachtechnisher Club Ball 1891, Velvet, Embossed Celluloid, Brass Pencil ... 155.00
Dance Card, Humanitarian Society 1897 Ball, Velvet, Brass, Vienna, 3 1/4 In. 55.00
Dance Card, Humanitarian Society Ball 1901, Leather, Celluloid, Ivory Pencil, 9 1/2 In. .. 80.00
Dance Card, Humanitarian Society Club XIV Costume Ball, 1899, Painted Leather, 3 In. . 50.00
Dance Card, JB 1890 Ball, Celluloid, Theyer & Hardtmuth, Vienna, 3 In. 108.00
Dance Card, Joh. Riedls Hausball 1903, Silk, Brass Pencil Holder, Ernst Dohle, 2 1/4 In. . 28.00
Dance Card, Kranzchen Des Wiener Sangerbrund 1906 Ball, Bronze, Vienna, 3 3/4 In. ... 77.00
Dance Card, Lake Geneva Assoc. 1907 Ball, Secessionist, Julius Seitner, Vienna, 3 In. ... 55.00
Dance Card, Purse Shaped, For Kubiceks Shuler-Kranzchen 1891, Richard Golis, 2 1/4 In. 70.00
Dance Card, Train Conductors 1904 Ball, Leather, Brass Trim, Pabel, Vienna, 2 5/8 In. .. 55.00
Dance Card, Train Conductors Benefit 1896 Ball, Velvet, Ignaz Luksch, Vienna, 3 In. 55.00
Dance Card, Vereins Ball 1859, Gold Plated, Carved Ivory, Silver Foil, Mother-Of-Pearl . 411.00
Daybook, Pennsylvania General Store, Commodity & Price Entries, 1817-1818 .... 695.00
Directory, Soo Line Shippers, 4 Color Pages Maps, 1919, 644 Pages 57.00
Document, Land Grant, S. Carolina, 700 Acres, To Frances Young, 1744 .... 364.00
Drawing, Birth, Baptismal, Anna Maria Bordner, Dec. 20, 1835, Angels, 19 x 16 In. 990.00
Family Record, Gardner, Framed, 18th Century, 17 x 13 1/2 In. 144.00
Fare Check, Missouri Pacific, Embossed Aluminum, 1910, 5 1/4 x 3 1/4 In. 34.00
Fraktur, Angels, Birds, Peters, Printed, Frame, c.1851, 17 x 14 In. 155.00
Fraktur, Biblical Figures, Handwritten, Printed, Frame, Harrisburg, 14 3/4 x 10 3/4 In. ... 115.00
Fraktur, Birds & Flowers, Vorschrift, Watercolor, Reeded Frame, 8 1/4 x 10 In. 440.00
Fraktur, Birth & Baptismal, Abraham Zartman, 1822, 15 3/4 x 12 3/4 In. 357.00
Fraktur, Birth & Baptismal, Angles, Noah's Ark, Frame, 1837, 17 1/2 x 14 1/2 In. 165.00
Fraktur, Birth & Baptismal, Anna Eberly, Clock Faces, Frame, 1852, 11 x 9 In. 7150.00
Fraktur, Birth & Baptismal, Charles Long, Softwood Frame, 1878, 19 x 14 3/4 In. 190.00
Fraktur, Birth & Baptismal, Elisabeth Brunner, Softwood Frame, 1837, 15 1/2 x 11 1/2 In. 360.00
Fraktur, Birth & Baptismal, Emma Ennik, 1848, 16 3/4 x 13 1/2 In. 140.00

Fraktur, Birth & Baptismal, English, Cumberland County, Penna., 1828	55.00
Fraktur, Birth & Baptismal, Frederick Krebs, Mirror Image, Parrots, Faces, 13 x 16 In. . . .	1100.00
Fraktur, Birth & Baptismal, Illuminated, Kreider Funk, 1834, 16 x 13 1/4 In.	330.00
Fraktur, Birth & Baptismal, Johanna Zeller, Frame, 1851, 14 3/4 x 11 1/2 In.	220.00
Fraktur, Birth & Baptismal, Lea Loh, Peterman, Born 1824, Baptized 1825, 19 x 16 In. . . .	9350.00
Fraktur, Birth & Baptismal, Lidia Stierle, 1819, 12 x 14 1/2 In.	605.00
Fraktur, Birth & Baptismal, Magelsi Preiss, Center Flowers, Frame, 1798, 14 3/4 x 18 In.	660.00
Fraktur, Birth & Baptismal, Rebecca Luckenbill, Frame, 14 x 12 In.	357.00
Fraktur, Birth & Baptismal, Verses, Parrots On Flowers, Frame, 1831, 11 1/8 x 13 5/8 In.	1980.00
Fraktur, Birth Record, Angel, Rose, Hummingbird, L. Brenemann, 1859, 16 3/4 In.	330.00
Fraktur, Birth Record, Anna Margretha Rappin, Printed & Watercolor, 1785	310.00
Fraktur, Birth Record, Eagle, Angels & Birds, Thomas Koth, Frame, 1791, 16 1/4 x 19 In.	190.00
Fraktur, Birth Record, Heart & Text, Tulips, Berchs County, 1796, 16 3/4 x 20 In.	1595.00
Fraktur, Birth Record, Jacob Dohner, Star Flower Corners, 1806, 8 1/2 x 10 3/8 In.	385.00
Fraktur, Birth Record, Watercolor, Thomas Kern, Heart, Bird, 1834, 10 x 12 In.	2530.00
Fraktur, Bookplate, Elias Krick, Signed Constantin Jacob Deininger, 1844, 5 x 5 In.	1100.00
Fraktur, Carolina Bortz, Black & White Leaves, Rose Vining, 1840, 18 x 15 In.	3190.00
Fraktur, Central Wreath, Angles, Tulips & Roses, Druder, Ohio, 1835, 15 x 17 5/8 In. . . .	660.00
Fraktur, Family Record, George Weiler & Wife Salome, 1793-1831, Frame, 15 x 19 In. . . .	7975.00
Fraktur, Frederich Krebs, Hand Drawn, Parrots, Center Heart, Frame, 1791, 12 x 16 In. . . .	1595.00
Fraktur, Frederich Krebs, King Of Prussia, 19th Century, 15 5/8 x 12 1/2 In.	7200.00
Fraktur, Gerburts Und Tauf, Vining, Birds, Baskets Of Flowers, Frame, 14 1/8 In.	850.00
Fraktur, Penmanship, Marriage Of Heinrich Brubacher To Salme Ever, Frame, 12 7/8 In. .	330.00
Fraktur, Reward Of Merit, 3 Flowers, Pennsylvania, 1800s, 5 x 3 In.	220.00
Fraktur, Tulip Tree, Urn, Checkerboard, Signed John Reist, February 1829, 11 x 16 In. . . .	3300.00
Fraktur, Watercolor, Bird, Maroon Wings, On Branch, John Staves, Frame, 3 x 3 3/4 In. .	190.00
Fraktur, Watercolor, Pen, Ink, Garland, Frame, 15 1/2 x 19 In.	805.00
Fraktur, Watercolor, Valentine Hearts, German Verses, Frame, 14 1/2 x 17 7/8 In.	1980.00
Guide, Travel, Traveler's Guide, 700 Railroad, Canal, Steamboat Routes, 1850	105.00
Indenture, Jeremiah Fargo, Descendent Of Wells Fargo Family, 1813, 19 1/4 x 23 1/2 In. .	90.00
Insurance, Love Stock, Chautaugua Cooperative, Animal Logo, Westfield, N.Y., 1916 . . .	25.00
Insurance Policy, The Ship Sloop Parrot, December 17, 1791, 16 x 12 In.	110.00
License, Liquor, Elf Picture By Still, 1878-1985, 7 x 14 In.	10.00
Magazine, Judge, Puck, 8 Issues, 1890s	375.00
Magazine, Tattler, Vince Edwards & Richard Chamberlain Cover, Dec. 1962	5.00
Magazine, Veteran's World, Vol. 1, No. 3, May, June, 1947	80.00
Magazine Binder, The Winnepeger, Embossed Red Leather, Barrett Bindery, 15 In., Pair .	45.00
Manuscript, Persian, Birds, Fruit, Flowers, Matted, 14 1/8 x 11 5/8 In., Pair	375.00
Manuscript, Persian, Travelers, Flying Dragon, Sage On Rocks, Script, 16 3/8 x 10 1/2 In.	345.00
Menu, Brown Derby, 3377 Wilshire Blvd., Los Angeles, Derby On Cover, 1939	15.00
Merit Award, Tulip, Watercolor, Ink, Henrich Hofenberger, c.1844, 3 7/8 x 3 1/4 In.	646.00
Pamphlet, How To Speak At Union Meetings, UAW-CIO, 4 x 6 In., 23 Pages	20.00
Pinprick, Valentine, Scherenschnitte, Watercolor, Ink, c.1839, 8 1/4 x 8 1/4 In.	590.00
Program, Folies Bergere, California Auditorium, San Francisco, 1939	120.00
Program, Harry Houdini Souvenir Last Tour, 1926	690.00
Reward Of Merit, Floral Front, Annie Mills, 1880s, 3 1/2 x 2 In.	6.00
Show Pass, Buffalo Bill's Wild West Show, William F. Cody, 4 3/4 x 2 1/4 In.	2000.00
Sticker, National Timberwolf Association, 104th Infantry Division, Green & White, 3 In. .	11.00
Stock Certificate, Arkansas Texas Co., Oil & Gas, Green Border, 1920	75.00
Stock Certificate, Atlantic Fire Annihilator Company, 1876, 25 Shares	2450.00
Stock Certificate, Baltimore & Ohio Railroad Co., Small Train, 1843	30.00
Stock Certificate, Colorado Mines, Findley, 1902	15.00
Stock Certificate, Deadwood Gold Mining Co., Nevada, California, 1870s	35.00
Stock Certificate, Durant Motors Inc., Green Overprint, 1929, 100 Shares	150.00
Stock Certificate, Great Cariboo Gold Company, 1908, 15 x 12 1/2 In.	2000.00
Stock Certificate, Ice Service Co., Pine Bluff, Arkansas, 1927-1956	3.00
Stock Certificate, Missouri, Kansas & Texas Railroad Co., Farm & Animals, 1886	25.00
Stock Certificate, Old Mesa Gold Co., Miner 2 Sides, Green Overprint, 1903, 100 Shares	100.00
Stock Certificate, Pyramid Oil Co., Trains Picture, 1920s	2.50
Stock Certificate, Steinway & Sons, American Bank Note Co., 1890s	900.00
Stock Certificate, Tesoro De Sonora Mining Co., Gold Border & Seal, 1906, 30 Shares . .	100.00
Stock Certificate, U.S. Accelerating Steam Navigation Co., 5 Shares	1450.00

Don't store paper collectibles in the trunk or glove compartment of your car. Heat may harm them. If you're on a buying trip, mail paper collectibles to your home or office and avoid exposing them to prolonged heat.

Paper Doll, Cardboard, Crepe Paper Dresses, Hinged Shoulders, Homemade, 3 Piece

PAPER DOLLS were probably inspired by the pantins, or jumping jacks, made in eighteenth-century Europe. By the 1880s, sheets of printed paper dolls and clothes were being made. The first paper doll books were made in the 1920s. Collectors prefer uncut sheets or books or boxed sets of paper dolls. Prices are about half as much if the pages have been cut.

Annie Oakley, Pocket Portfolio, 3 Dolls, Punch-Out Fashions, 1956, 10 x 12	15.00
Archies, Archie, Betty, Veronica, Jughead, Whitman, Uncut, 1969, 6 Pages	18.00
Blondie & Dagwood, Whitman, 1940	15.00
Buffy, Mrs. Beasley, Cardboard, Outfits, 1968, 6 Pages	25.00
Cardboard, Crepe Paper Dresses, Hinged Shoulders, Homemade, 3 Piece ...... *Illus*	50.00
Comic Characters Dolls, Cutout Book, Saalfield, 1930s, Uncut	550.00
Green Acres, Whitman, Copyright 1967	18.00
Hand Drawn, Set Of 4 Dresses, 1810-1840	495.00
Hee-Haw, Columbia Broadcasting, 1971, 8 Pages, Uncut	24.00
Nancy Reagan, 1983, 9 x 12 In.	15.00
Twiggy, Cardboard Punch-Out, Fashion Dresses, Whitman, Minnow Co., Ltd., 1967	30.00
Waltons, 7 Walton Children, Outfits, Whitman, 1975, 8 Pages, Uncut	35.00

PAPERWEIGHTS must have first appeared along with paper in ancient Egypt. Today's collectors search for every type, from the very expensive French weights of the nineteenth century to the modern artist weights or advertising pieces. The glass tops of the paperweights sometimes have been nicked or scratched, and this type of damage can be removed by polishing. Some serious collectors think this type of repair is an alteration and will not buy a repolished weight; others think it is an acceptable technique of restoration that does not change the value. Baccarat paperweights are listed separately under Baccarat.

1000 Bubble Flowerpot, Egg Shape, 3 3/4 x 2 3/16 In.	77.00
Abraham Lincoln, Bronze Finish	55.00
Admiral Dewey, Picture, Star Shape, Sepia	68.00
Advertising, Adlake Centennial, Aluminum, 1857-1957, 5 In.	34.00
Advertising, Atlantic Coast Line, Brass, Embossed, 19th Century, 3 1/4 In.	23.00
Advertising, Bell System, Blue Glass, Bell-Shaped, White Lettering, 3 3/4 In.	210.00
Advertising, Bixbys Santinola, Black Shines Shoes, 1900s, 3 1/4 In.	127.00
Advertising, Lion Oil Co., Brass, Lion On Top, 3 3/4 x 2 3/4 In.	77.00
Advertising, Lion Oil Co., Metal, 3 1/2 In.	88.00
Advertising, Longhorn Cattle, Steer For Iron Mountain Routs, Longhorn Head, 3 In.	190.00
Advertising, National Lead Co., Embossed Dutch Boy Logo, Lead, 1925, 4 In.	5.00
Advertising, Tinactin, Metal, Brass Color, Greek Symbols, 4 1/2 In., Pair	12.00
Advertising, Valvoline Motor Oil, Reverse Graphic Of Container, 4 x 2 1/2 In.	34.00
Ayotte, Butterfly, Blue, Black, Blue Leafy Branches, Yellow Blossoms, 3 In.	690.00
Ayotte, Sparrow, White Crowned, Perched On Green Leafy Branches, 2 3/4 In.	800.00
Ayotte, Thrush, Spray Of Purple Flowers, Green, Yellow Leaves, 2 x 3 3/4 In.	860.00

Bacchus, Chequer, Red, White, 3 1/4 In. 840.00
Banford, Flower Bouquet, Pink, Blue, White Blossoms, 2 3/8 x 2 7/8 In. 630.00
Banford, Fruit, Arrangement Of Pears, Cherries, White Lace Ground, 2 1/2 In. 430.00
Banford, Lily-Of-The-Valley, Cranberry Transparent, Red Ground, 2 x 2 7/8 In. 520.00
Banford, Wheat Flower, Yellow Blossom, Brown Dots On Petals, 2 1/4 x 3 In. 1150.00
Boston & Sandwich, Blue Dahlia On Jasper Ground, 1870 .... 690.00
Boston & Sandwich, Red Double Clematis, White Jasper Ground, 2 3/4 In. 730.00
Clematis, Deep Blue Double Flowers, 6 Leaves, White Latticinio Ground 690.00
Clichy, 5 Pink & Green Roses, Muslin Latticinio Sections 2875.00
Clichy, Central Red Rose, 2 White Roses On Outer Edge 2070.00
Clichy, Concentric, Pastry Mold Cane Rings 400.00
Clichy, Millefiori, Pink, Green Roses, White Muslin, 2 3/16 In. 1320.00
Clichy, Millefiori, Star Shape, Green, Ground, 3 In. 2475.00
Clichy, Mushroom, Concentric Millefiori Canes, Rose Center, Faceted 1495.00
Clichy, Pastry Mold Cane Center, Millefiori Cane, Electric Blue Ground 805.00
Clichy, Rings, Pastry Mold Canes, Latticinio Ground 460.00
Clichy, Swirl Pattern, Opaque Pink, White, Red Ribbons Center Cane 1980.00
Coney & Co., Fire Insurance, Savannah, Georgia, 3 1/4 In. 115.00
Degenhart, Lily, Blue, Cube Shape, 2 1/4 In. 440.00
Degenhart, Ohio With Plaque, 2 x 2 1/2 In. 77.00
Degenhart, Presentation Ebeling Mrs. Louis, Flowers, 1923, 3 1/4 x 2 7/8 In. 77.00
Flowers, Red Blossoms, Green Leaf Stem, Long Island, N.Y., 20th Century, 3 In. 690.00
Frosted Roosevelt Portrait, Metal Rim 130.00
Gentile, Flying Goose, Controlled Bubbles, Concave Base, 3 x 3 1/4 In. ....44.00 to 49.00
Gentile, Old Glory, Flag, 13 Stars, 2 1/2 x 3 1/2 In. 210.00
Gentile, Pull-Up Lily, Bubble Center, Blue Devil's Fire Ground, 2 7/8 x 3 1/8 In. 22.00
Gentile, Snake, Red Forked Tongue, Pebbly Ground, Pontil, 2 3/8 x 3 3/4 In. 330.00
Hansen, Blue Flower, Millefiori Garland, Interior Air Bubbles, 1 1/2 x 2 1/4 In. 77.00
Hansen, Cherries, Yellow Opaque Round, 1 1/2 x 2 In. 99.00
Hansen, Lavender Clematis, Ribbed Petals, Black Opaque Base, 1 3/4 x 2 1/2 In. 176.00
Hansen, Poinsettia, Millefiori Cane Center, Blue Opaque, 1 1/2 x 2 In. 132.00
Home Sweet Home, Frit, Midwest, 2 1/2 x 3 1/4 In. 143.00
Kaziun, Crimped Pink Rose, Pedestal, Signed 575.00
Kaziun, Morning Glory, Signed 690.00
Kaziun, Yellow Cabbage Rose, 3 Millefiori Canes, Signed 460.00
Labino, Green Leaves 2 Sides, Yellow, Trumpet Shape, 2 1/8 x 2 5/8 In. 165.00
Lundberg Studios, School Of Fish, 1976, 3 In. 123.00
McKinley, Cane Top, 4 In. 145.00
Micro Mosaic, Book Form, Roman Ruins, Lapis Lazuli Inlay, c.1890, Italy, 4 1/4 In. 1150.00
Micro Mosaic, Doves Of Pliny, 4 Rounded Venues, Italy, Late 19th Century, 4 1/4 In. 1035.00
Micro Mosaic, Milan Cathedral, Malachite Inlay, Italy, c.1890, 6 In. 1265.00
Micro Mosaic, Scenic Roundel, San Marco, Italy, Late 1800s, 4 In. 978.00
Microcosmic, St. Peter's Plaza Scene, Black Slate, Italy, c.1890, 4 1/2 In. 920.00
Microcosmic, St. Peter's Plaza, 8 Roundels, Roman Scenes, Italy, c.1900, 6 1/4 In. 1610.00
Millefiori, Central Pink, Green, Rose, Star Shaped Canes 2 3/4 In. 1045.00
Millefiori, Pink, Green, Roses, Canes, Clear Ground, 2 7/8 In. 1430.00
Millville, Umbrella, Red, Blue, Green, Yellow, 3 1/8 In. 495.00
Mosser, Ship Plaque, 2 1/2 x 3 1/4 In. 55.00
Murano, Peach On Green Goldstone Base, 2 1/4 x 3 1/4 In. 90.00
New England Glass Co., Double Trefoil Millefiori, White & Blue Canes 430.00
New England Glass Co., Millefiori Canes, Blue & Pink Ring 400.00
New England Glass Co., Millefiori Canes, White Torsade Ring 288.00
New England Glass Co., Millefiori, Canes, Rabbit Silhouettes, 2 1/2 In. 330.00
New England Glass Co., Millefiori, Concentric, White, Red, Blue, Green, 2 1/4 In. 202.00
New England Glass Co., Red Rose, Green Leaves, 3 In. 660.00
Perthshire, Flowers, Dark Green Ground, Signed, 2 1/2 In. 336.00
Perthshire, Millefiori, Concentric, Ribbed Sides, 1 3/8 x 1 3/8 In. 44.00
Perthshire, Millefiori, Flower Canes, Wheel Design, 2 x 3 In. 44.00
Perthshire, Millefiori, Muslin Ground Over Amethyst, Signed, 1972, 2 1/2 In. 392.00
Perthshire, Swan In Bubble, Green Cushion, 2 5/8 x 3 1/8 In. 242.00
Perthshire, Swan On Bubble, 16 Oval Concave Windows, 1 5/8 x 3 1/8 In. 212.00
Perthshire, Swan, Signed, 2 Canes On Wings, 3 In. 532.00

President Dwight D. Eisenhower, Chalkware, Gold, Square, 1956, 2 In. 20.00
President McKinley, Domed, Sepia 52.00
Quilted, Pink Satin, Pontil, Victorian, 3 3/4 x 4 In. 176.00
Ravenna, 2-Tier Lily, Spatter Petals, Bubble Center, 1890, 3 3/4 x 3 3/4 In. 55.00
Rosenfield, Yellow, Orange, Blue, Purple Blossoms, Sand Ground, 2 x 3 1/4 In. 575.00
Salazar, Dragonfly Over Dogwood Branch, Amethyst, 1990, 2 1/2 x 3 In. 357.00
Sandwich, Cobalt Blue Poinsettia, Green Leaves, White Cane 2 5/8 In. 550.00
Smiling Black Boy, Advertisement For Jiffy Self Storing Windows, 4 In. 60.00
Snowdome, Black Man Holds Watermelon, 4 In. 498.00
Souvenir Of Lebanon, Pennsylvania 25.00
St. Claire, Frog, Blue & White Underground, 3 1/4 In. 88.00
St. Louis, 5 Multicolored Turnips, White Latticinio Ground 748.00
St. Louis, Blue Cornflower, Limited Edition, Signed, No. 101/200, Box 230.00
St. Louis, Blue Yellow Pink Central Cane, Blue White Ground, 2 7/8 In. 468.00
St. Louis, Crown, Red, Green, Blue Yellow Twisted Ribbons 1035.00
St. Louis, Dahlia Bouquet, Salmon, Blue Blossoms, France, 1975, 2 1/4 x 3 In. 575.00
St. Louis, Double Clematis, Red, Blue, 5 Sides, Signed, 1975, 3 1/4 In. 392.00
St. Louis, Fruit, 4 Pink To Orange Pears, 4 Red Cherries 2 3/4 In. 1430.00
St. Louis, Gridel Silhouette, Animal, Insect, Stardust Canes, Green Ground 1035.00
St. Louis, Millefiori Mushroom, Signed, c.1960 . . . . 430.00
St. Louis, Pink, White Dahlia, 6 Serrated Blue Leaves, Star Cut Base 2070.00
St. Louis, Poinsettia, Cobalt Blue, 1970, 2 x 3 1/4 In.. . . . . 231.00
St. Louis, Red Double Clematis, Green Leaves, Yellow & Blue Center Cane, 2 1/2 In. 504.00
Stankard, Chokeberry, White Blossoms, Red Berry Cluster, 1976, 2 x 2 7/8 In. 1265.00
Stankard, Flowers, 5-Petal White Blossoms, 1989, 1 1/4 x 3 In. 1610.00
Stankard, Meadowreath, Yellow Flower, Signed, No. 04875, 3 In. 1008.00
Stankard, Wild Rose, Pink Blossom, Leafy Foliage, Late 20th Century, 1 7/8 In. 1265.00
Stankard, Wildflower, White Blossom, Blackberry Clusters, 2 x 3 In. 1840.00
Sulphide, George Washington, Red Ground, Star Cut Base, 3 3/4 In. 69.00
Sulphide, Robert E. Lee, Gray, 1 1/4 x 2 In. 55.00
Tarsitano, Bouquet, Flowers, Buds, Signed, 2 3/4 In. 1064.00
Tarsitano, Faceted Peach On Brown Branch, Green Leaves, 2 x 2 1/2 In. 690.00
Tarsitano, Gray Spider, Red, Orange Back, Sandy Ground, N.Y., 2 3/4 x 3 In. 1380.00
Tarsitano, White Blossom, Brown Stem, Green Leaves, Long Island, N.Y., 2 In. 575.00
Trabucco, Flowers & Fruit, White, Purple Blossoms, 1989, 3 1/4 x 4 In. 747.00
Trabucco, Red Flowers, Pale Pink Blossoms, Green Stems, 1982, 2 In. 402.00
Trubucco, Calla Lily, Red, White, Green, Signed, 1984, 3 In. 560.00
U.S. Glass Co., Oval, Frosted, Woman's Head, Laurel Leaves, Pittsburgh, 4 1/2 In. 78.00
Val St. Lambert, Millefiori Canes, Pink Surround, 1 3/4 x 3 3/4 In. 550.00
Val St. Lambert, Millefiori, Star Pattern, Red, White, Blue, Roses, 3 1/2 In. 468.00
Whitefriars, Concentric Millefiori, Low Dome, 1 1/2 x 3 3/8 In. 198.00
Whitefriars, Millefiori, Blue Lined, Scalloped Edge, White Cane, 3 1/2 In. 468.00
Whitefriars, Red, Blue, Yellow, White, Footed, Rough Pontil, 4 In. 500.00
Whittemore, Pink Pedestal Rose, In Orb, 1 7/8 x 1 7/8 In. 198.00
Ysart, Fantasy Flower, Latticinio, 2 1/2 x 3 In. 495.00
Ysart, Fantasy Flower, Salmon, Green, White, Latticinio Swirled Ground, Signed, 3 In. . . . 785.00
Zimmerman, Fawn In Bubble, Pull-Up Spattered Petals, 3 1/4 x 3 3/4 In. 90.00
Zimmerman, Pull-Up Lily, Green Ground, Satin Bubble, 2 3/4 x 2 7/8 In. 22.00
Zimmerman, Pumpkin, Ribbed, Green Stem, 4 1/2 x 4 In. 44.00

PAPIER-MACHE is made from paper mixed with glue, chalk, and other
ingredients, then molded and baked. It becomes very hard and can be
painted. Boxes, trays, and furniture were made of papier-mache. Some
of the nineteenth-century pieces were decorated with mother-of-pearl.
Papier-mache is still being used to make small toys, figures, candy
containers, boxes, and other giftwares. Furniture made of papier-
mache is listed in the Furniture category.

Buddha, Gilt, Red Painted Base, 20th Century, 20 1/2 In. 110.00
Clown, Roly Poly, Germany, 1920-1930, 7 1/2 In. 115.00
Coaster, Bottle, Lacquered, Pair 460.00
Coaster, Wine, Black, Gilt Painted, 5 In., Pair 550.00
Coaster, Wine, Regency, Circular, Gilt Flowers, 1 3/4 x 5 1/4 In. 259.00

Coaster, Wine, Regency, Gilt Flowers, Leaves, 5 3/8 In. 200.00
Hand Screen, Parcel Gilt, Polychrome, Lacquer, 19th Century, 16 1/4 x 9 3/4 In. 345.00
Poodle, Fur, Seated, Paws Extended Forward, Swivel Head, Curly Tail, c.1910, 18 In. 300.00
Santa Claus, Sitting On Polar Bear, White, Red Trim, c.1920, 9 3/4 x 8 1/2 In. 130.00
Tray, Black Lacquer, Polychrome, Parcel-Gilt Flowers, Serpentine, 15 1/4 In. 230.00
Tray, Oriental Entertainer, Ebonized, Gilt, Polychrome, 19 x 26 1/2 x 20 3/4 In. 865.00
Tray, Oriental Flora, Bamboo Stand, Regency, Black Lacquer, Gilt, 21 In. 1840.00
Tray, Painted, Still Life, Dish Shape, c.1880, 15 x 10 1/4 In. 1645.00
Tray, Parcel Gilt, Russet, Cartouche Shape, Black Lacquered, 22 x 31 3/4 In. 2070.00
Tray, Regency, Black Lacquer, Gilt, Early 19th Century, 19 1/2 x 33 x 24 In. 1095.00
Tray, Stand, Oval, Victorian, 19th Century, 22 x 17 3/4 x 20 1/2 In. 390.00
Tray, Stand, Parcel Gilt, Polychrome, Black Lacquer, 29 1/2 x 23 1/2 x 17 3/4 In. 1610.00
Tray, Stand, Peak & Valley Scroll, Parcel-Gilt, Painted, Dogwood, 19 x 33 In. 1850.00
Tray, Victorian, Black Lacquer, Inlaid, Mid 19th Century, 21 x 30 x 23 3/4 In. 800.00
Tray, Victorian, Serpentine, Painted, Mid 19th Century, 21 x 31 x 22 1/4 In. 1265.00
Wall Decoration, Putti Shape, 43 x 31 x 6 In. 336.00

PARASOL, see Umbrella category.

PARIAN is a fine-grained, hard-paste porcelain named for the marble it
resembles. It was first made in England in 1846 and gained in favor in
the United States about 1860. Figures, tea sets, vases, and other items
were made of Parian at many English and American factories.

Bust, Napoleon, Signed Chaudel, 6 In. 127.00
Bust, Roman Emperor, 12 In. 104.00
Bust, Veiled Woman, Waisted Socle, R. Monti, 1861, 16 In. 2300.00
Dish, Condiment, Shell & Dolphin, 6 x 8 1/2 In. 81.00
Figurine, Boy & Girl, With Goose, 10 1/2 In., Pair 69.00
Figurine, Classical Women, c.1860, 14 In., Pair 235.00
Figurine, Cupid, Sleeping On Pillow, 6 x 11 3/4 In. 440.00
Figurine, Girl, Gathering Wheat, Holding Pot, 21 3/4 In. 660.00
Figurine, Group, Genre Scene, Oval Base, 19th Century, England, 11 In. 206.00
Figurine, Napoleon, Square Base, 10 In. 160.00
Figurine, Nude Woman, Star Drape, Cherub, Oval Base, c.1890, 22 1/2 In. 1035.00
Figurine, Rebekah, Holding Vase, Circular Plinth, 1870s, 19 x 7 In. 863.00
Figurine, Sunshine, Woman, Standing, Hand Over Eyes, Wm. Brodie, 1858, 19 1/2 In. 747.00
Figurine, Uma, The Lion, John Bell Mark, England, 12 5/8 In., Pair 1725.00
Figurine, Woman, Long Dress, Head Piece, S. Terry, 1868, 20 1/2 In. 77.00
Figurine, Woman, Pouring Water, Shell Headdress, Urn, Anchor Mark, c.1890, 30 In. 1150.00
Figurine, Young Hunter, Seated On Rock, Animal Skin Dress, Bow & Arrows, 10 3/4 In. . 93.00
Group, Classically Dressed Couple, In Garden, Oval Base, 8 x 6 3/8 In. 82.00
Jug, Raised Grecian Figures, Roman Columns, Head On Handle, 7 1/2 In. ....165.00 to 175.00

PARIS, Vieux Paris, or Old Paris, is porcelain ware that is known to
have been made in Paris in the eighteenth or early nineteenth century.
These porcelains have no identifying mark but can be recognized by
the whiteness of the porcelain and the lines and decorations. Gold decoration is often used.

Basket, Centerpiece, Anneau D'Or, Reticulated, Footed, Navette Shape, 10 x 15 x 9 In. ... 865.00
Basket, Centerpiece, Gold Ground, Reticulated, Round, Mid 19th Century, 8 1/2 x 9 In. ... 690.00
Basket, Centerpiece, Reticulated, Navette Shape, Kneeling Cherubs, 11 x 12 1/2 x 7 In. ... 4370.00
Basket, Centerpiece, White & Gold, Reticulated, Navette Shape, Putti, 13 x 17 x 9 In. 8050.00
Basket, Centerpiece, White & Gold, Reticulated, Rihouet, Footed, 7 1/2 x 8 1/2 In. 518.00
Basket, Imari Palette, Reticulated, Oval, Mid 19th Century, 7 1/4 x 12 1/2 In. 690.00
Basket, Navette Shape, Gilded Pierced Basket, 10 1/2 x 7 3/4 x 14 In. 2760.00
Basket, Spreading Socle, Square Plinth, 8 3/4 x 9 In. 920.00
Bowl, Flared Wickerwork, Circular Stem, Square Plinth, 1820s, 8 1/2 x 9 1/2 In., Pair 1840.00
Bowl, Integral Base, 4 Gilt Paw Feet, Early 19th Century, 4 5/8 In. 748.00
Bowl, Pierced Basket, Flared Rim, Gilt Square Plinth, 1820s, 8 1/2 x 9 3/4 In. 1380.00
Bowl, Wickerwork, Gilt Outline, Spreading Foot, 7 x 9 In. 175.00
Bowl, Wickerwork, Spreading Foot, Square Plinth, 1850s, 8 x 9 In., Pair 345.00
Bulb Pot, 3 Marys Before Crucified Christ, Footed, Cover, 5 1/2 x 4 In. 635.00

Bulb Pot, Floral Still Life, Gothic Arches, Signed Darte Freres, Gilt Cover, 4 3/4 In., Pair 5750.00
Cachepot, Romantic Landscape, Oval, Cartouche, 19th Century, 7 x 10 3/8 x 5 1/2 In. 420.00
Candlestick, Column Standard, Figure Of Man & Woman, 9 In., Pair 172.00
Coffeepot, Rural Landscape, Italianate, Duck's Head Spout, 10 3/4 In. 375.00
Cologne Bottle, Gothic Spire Shape, Signed, Mid 19th Century, 11 1/2 In., Pair 5290.00
Compote, Bisque, Figural, Basket, Kneeling Putto, Scallop Edge, c.1870, 8 3/4 In. 230.00
Compote, Green Banding On White, Flared, Reticulated Rim, 7 1/2 x 9 In., Pair 1100.00
Cup & Saucer, Allover Gilt, Flowers, Cherubs, Mid 19th Century 490.00
Cup & Saucer, Cobalt Blue Ground, Gilt Guilloche, Flowers, Late 19th Century, 3 x 6 In. . 1095.00
Cup & Saucer, Flowers & Cherub, Allover Gilt, Mid 1800s 490.00
Cup & Saucer, Green Paisley Ground, Edouard Honore, 3 1/2 x 6 1/4 In. 1380.00
Cup & Saucer, Portrait, Louis XVI, France, 3 1/2 x 6 1/2 In. 1495.00
Cup & Saucer, Royal Blue Border, Sepia, 1820s, 3 1/2 In. 865.00
Cup & Saucer, White & Gold, Kihl & Guerhard, 2 3/8 In. 290.00
Cuspidor, Woman's, Moss Rose & Gold, 19th Century 65.00
Dinner Service, Green Border, Botanical Decoration, Gilded, c.1815, 85 Piece 4370.00
Dish, Dessert, Pheasant & Scroll Rim, Fruit Center, Late 19th Century, 11 In., Pair 750.00
Dish, Shell, Cornflower Center, Gilt Bead, Leaf Border, 1795, 9 1/4 In., Pair 360.00
Dish, Shell, Flowers, White, Gold Rim, 11 & 9 In., 2 Piece 127.00
Dish Set, Sweetmeat, Rihouet, White & Gold, 9 x 8 1/2 In., 4 Piece 1265.00
Figure, Allegorical, America, Louis XVI Style, Mid 19th Century, 19 3/4 In. 1725.00
Garniture, Campana Shape, Landscape, Mid 19th Century, 9 In., Pair 520.00
Garniture, Vase, Aqua, Floral Bouquet Roundels, Gilt, Handles, Domed Foot, 3 Piece ... 460.00
Garniture, Vase, Flared, Polychromed Sprays, Mid 19th Century, 9 x 9 x 6 In., Pair 290.00
Garniture, Vase, Schoelcher, Bleu Du Roi & Gold, Campana Shape, 11 3/4 In., Pair 2185.00
Jar, Apothecary, Cylindrical, H. Vignier, Mid 19th Century, 10 1/4 x 5 In. 546.00
Pitcher, Flowers, Gilt Scrolls & Trim, 8 1/2 In. 80.00
Plate, Gilt Bands, Classical Design, Circular, Porcelain, 1 1/4 x 9 1/4 In. 145.00
Plate, Topographical, Chateau De Vincennes, Darte Freres, 8 7/8 In. 690.00
Plate Set, Dessert, Botanical, Gilding, Mid 19th Century, 8 1/2 In., 6 Piece 2530.00
Sauceboat, Cover, Bud Finial, Divided, Undertray, Diamond Borders, 8 x 6 1/2 In. 920.00
Server, Syllabub, Flower Outlines, Gold Rim, White Ground, 2 Tiers, 14 In. 190.00
Stand, Egg, 2 Tiers, Gilt Banded Trays, 12 Footed Cups, 1850s, 12 x 9 In. 750.00
Tankard, Polychromed Reserve, Signed, Early 19th Century, 5 In. 690.00
Tea Set, Classical Maidens, Gilded, Gold Bordered, Reserve, Classical Maidens, 18 Piece 3900.00
Teapot, Central Continuous Reserve, Loop Handle, Gilt Borders, 5 1/2 x 8 In. 90.00
Tureen, Berry Finial Cover, Attached Underplate, Red Floral, Gilt Rim, 9 1/2 x 6 1/2 In. . 80.00
Tureen, Stand, Le Tallec, Oval, 2 Handles, 18th Century Style, 7 3/4 x 10 x 13 3/4 In. 259.00
Urn, Figures, Romantic Scene, Flared Rim, Ovoid Body, Scrolling Handles, 1880s, 11 In. 476.00
Vase, Birds & Flowers, 9 3/4 In., Pair 110.00
Vase, Campana Shape, 2 Handles, Early 19th Century, 8 1/2 In., Pair 230.00
Vase, Cobalt Blue Ground, Swags, Masks, Medallions, Tendrils, 11 x 4 1/2 x 4 1/2 In. 1610.00
Vase, Cornucopia Shape, Scrolling Leaf, Molded Base, 9 In., Pair 470.00
Vase, Flower Reserves, Handles With Gilded Mask, Black Ground, 10 In. 690.00
Vase, Flower Reserves, Loop Handles, 10 1/2 In., Pair 3220.00
Vase, Flower Sprays, White Ground, Gold, Leaf Shape Handle, Flared Rim, 10 In., Pair .. 115.00
Vase, Gilt Mulberry Ground, Floral Reserves, 1840s, 17 3/4 In. 7765.00
Vase, Green Ground, Fashionably Dressed Lady, Signed, T. Leroy, c.1885, 28 3/4 In., Pair 8400.00
Vase, Harbor Scene, Gilt Border, Female Mask Handles, 12 In., Pair 1610.00
Vase, Medici Shape, Flared Rim, Loop Handles, Mask Terminals, 1829, 9 In., Pair 405.00
Vase, Medici Shape, Obverse Figural Reserve, Putto Astride Sphinx, 1815, 10 In. 2300.00
Vase, Neoclassical Style, Gilt, 2 Handles, Mid 19th Century, 12 3/4 In., Pair 865.00
Vase, Painted Flowers, Horn Form, Ending In Griffin, 10 In., Pair 520.00
Vase, Painted Morning Glories, Flared, 20 In., Pair 1265.00
Vase, Pink, Woman, Landscape, Reticulated Neck Bulge, Leaf Handles, 8 1/2 In., Pair ... 400.00
Vase, Putti Figure, Holding Shell, Flowers Reserves, 18 1/2 x 13 x 5 In. 978.00
Vase, Reserve Of Rural Farmhouse Obverse, Courting Couple, 2 Handles, 11 3/8 In. 345.00
Vase, Spill, Barefoot Peasant Girl Standing Beside Tree Trunk, 8 In. 315.00
Vase, Wedding Scenes, Couple Carrying Baby, Griffon Handles, 15 1/2 In. 440.00
Vase, White Heron, Cobalt Blue, 2 3/4 x 5 5/8 In. 465.00
Veilleuse, Cards & Dominoes, Teapot, Stand, Base, Polychrome, 9 x 5 In. 690.00
Veilleuse, Night-Light, Teapot On Top, Landscape, Night Scene Of House, Signed, 9 In. ... 2530.00

Veilleuse, Teapot On Top, Loop Handles, Bird's Head Spout, Flower Bouquets, 9 1/2 In. . 520.00

PATE-DE-VERRE is an ancient technique in which glass is made by blending and refining powdered glass of different colors into molds. The process was revived by French glassmakers, especially Galle, around the end of the nineteenth century.

Ashtray, Relief Portrait, Purple, Signed, 6 1/4 In. 1725.00
Bowl, Blue Poppies, Signed, 3 In. 5460.00
Bowl, Flowers, Blue, Purple, Signed, Decorchement, 5 In. 5460.00
Bowl, Flowers, Cylindrical, Signed, 4 1/2 In. 1265.00
Bowl, Grotesque Masks, Brown, Pink, Decorchement, 5 In. 5460.00
Bowl, Ivy, Green & Purple, Signed, 4 In. 2530.00
Bowl, Orange Berries, Egg Shape, Signed, 2 3/4 In. 2990.00
Bowl, Purple Flowers, On White, Signed, 3 1/2 In. 2070.00
Bowl, Raisins, Grape Clusters, Purple, Magenta, Orange, 1926, 3 In. 4700.00
Bowl, Red Berries On Branches, Ball Shape, Signed, 2 1/2 In. 3220.00
Bowl, Red Flowers, On Purple, Signed, 2 3/4 In. 3450.00
Bowl, Stylized Yellow, Orange, Purple Flowers, Purple Handles, 9 In. 6900.00
Box, Cover, Purple Flowers, Signed, 2 3/4 In. 3450.00
Box, Cover, Stylized Red Flowers, On Yellow, Signed, 3 In. 2300.00
Box, Red Flowers On Cover, Signed, 3 In. 3450.00
Dish, Leaf Shape, 3 Overlapping Grape Leaves, Amber, Green, Purple, 5 In. 575.00
Dish, Lobster Shape, Brown, Initialed, 3 1/2 In. 1265.00
Fig Bowl, Fig Leaves, 2 Lizards, Amber, Purple, Green, 7 5/8 In. 2070.00
Figurine, Bird, Brown, 8 1/2 In. 2200.00
Figurine, Bird, Turquoise, Signed, 3 3/4 In. 460.00
Figurine, Classical Maiden, Holding Vase, Turquoise, Signed, 10 1/4 In. 1725.00
Paperweight, Amethyst Face Of An Infant, 4 1/2 In. 720.00
Paperweight, Brown Fish, On Green, Signed, Decorchement, 4 In. 1610.00
Paperweight, Bumblebee, Signed, 1/2 In. 860.00
Paperweight, Scarabs, Signed, 3 In. 2530.00
Plaque, Egyptian Head, Between Leopards, 13 In. 3220.00
Plaque, Head Of Bacchus, Signed, Despret, 6 3/4 In. 1975.00
Plaque, Male & Female Figures, Below Grapevines, 8 x 11 In. 4840.00
Plaque, Mermaid, 8 1/2 In. 5655.00
Plaque, Mother & Child, Yellow, Green, Round, Signed, B. Chapu, 11 In. 4600.00
Plaque, Nude Female With Birds, 8 In. 3735.00
Plaque, Pegasus, On Rose Ground, 13 In. 760.00
Plaque, Reptile Climbing Tree, 10 In. 2530.00
Plaque, Small Furry Creature, On Fruited Branch, Wood Stand, Signed, 9 In. 4025.00
Plaque, White Centaur, On Rose Ground, 12 3/4 In. 920.00
Vase, Birds On Flowering Branches, Flared, Signed, 6 1/4 In. 4310.00
Vase, Floral Band, 2 Handles, Cylindrical, Signed, 6 In. 1610.00
Vase, Geometric Motifs, Brown & Orange, Signed, 6 1/4 In. 2760.00
Vase, Pink Flowers, On Purple, Oval, Signed, 5 1/2 In. 4840.00
Vase, Pink Thistles, On White, Signed, 6 In. 4885.00
Vase, Stylized Flowers, Square Panels Around Rim, Signed, 8 1/2 In. 6325.00
Vase, Stylized Leaves, Blue & Turquoise, Signed, 6 1/4 In. 4600.00
Wall Pocket, 3 Panels, Stylized Birds In Center, 12 x 16 In. 7475.00

PATE-SUR-PATE means paste on paste. The design was made by painting layers of slip on the ceramic piece until a relief decoration was formed. The method was developed at the Sevres factory in France about 1850. It became even more famous at the English Minton factory about 1870. It has since been used by many potters to make both pottery and porcelain wares.

Bottle, Cherubs, 1 Stoking Fire, 1 Taking Pictures, c.1877, 5 1/2 In., Pair 9775.00
Cup & Saucer, Cupid Playing Pipe, Musical, Medallions, Signed 2300.00
Plaque, Pale Blue, Slip Portraits, Frame, 19th Century, 2 x 3 In., Pair 175.00
Vase, Cupid Walking Tightrope, Gilt Ring Handles, Signed, 7 1/2 In., Pair 2875.00
Vase, Sevres, Geometric Design, Signed, Taxtile Doat, 6 In. 1380.00
Vase, White Slip Cherubs In Flight, Amid Leaves, c.1880, 6 In., Pair 860.00

PAUL REVERE POTTERY was made at several locations in and around Boston, Massachusetts, between 1906 and 1942. The pottery was operated as a settlement house program for teenage girls. Many pieces were signed *S.E.G.* for Saturday Evening Girls. The artists concentrated on children's dishes and tiles. Decorations were outlined in black and filled with color.

Bowl, Ducks, Buttercup Yellow, Brown Feet, 5 x 12 In.	2420.00
Bowl, Flying Goose, Fannie Levine, c.1924, 5 In.	1100.00
Bowl, Powdery Tan, White Glaze, Green, S.E.G., 2 1/2 x 8 In.	360.00
Bowl, Rooster & Chick Design, Yellow Matte Glaze, S.E.G., F. Levine, 1 3/4 In.	1210.00
Bowl, Rooster Extending From Rim Down Body, Fannie Levine, 1926, 2 1/4 In.	1980.00
Bowl, Stylized Tulips, Green Leaves, Ida Goldstein, S.E.G., 1919	3080.00
Creamer, Rabbits In Cabbage, Peering At One Another, S.E.G., T. Block, 3 In.	2090.00
Cup & Saucer, Buttercup Yellow, 2 x 5 1/2 In., Set Of 4	220.00
Jardiniere, White Lotus Blossoms, Yellow Ground, Cuerda Seca, Stamped, 7 x 9 In.	1495.00
Lamp Base, Yellow Glazed, Oval Base, Wooden Base, 18 3/4 In.	230.00
Mug, Rabbit, White, Black, Sage Green Cabbage, 3 3/4 x 4 1/2 In.	990.00
Paperweight, Woman Wearing Nurse's Attire, 2 1/2 x 2 In.	1100.00
Pitcher, Green Glaze, Oval, Applied Handle, 1920, 7 1/8 In.	115.00
Pitcher, Milk, White Tortoise & Hare, Slow But Sure, Blue Ground, Marked, 4 In.	1600.00
Pitcher, Rabbit In Field Of Grass, Fannie Levine, 4 1/4 In.	880.00
Pitcher, Rooster & Chick, Vivid White Glaze, Chicory Blue, S.E.G., 1916, 3 In.	1210.00
Plate, 3 Rabbits Racing, White, 1916, 7 1/2 In.	825.00
Plate, Chicks, c.1911, 6 1/4 In.	935.00
Plate, Cuerda Seca, White Swan, Monogram, S.E.G., c.1919, 8 In.	460.00
Plate, Eate Thy Breade In Joye & Thankfulnesse, Marked, 9 3/4 In.	920.00
Plate, Geese, Water Lilies, Blue, White, Green Matte Ground, 1917, 8 In.	1380.00
Plate, Incised Geese In Mottled Green, Speckled Blue Ground, 1913, 7 5/8 In.	485.00
Plate, Large Ivory Duck Walking Along Hillside, Pale Green Hillside, 7 3/4 In.	1045.00
Plate, Rabbit On Green Hillside, Yellow, Black Bands, Fannie Levine, 1924, 7 In.	715.00
Vase, Lotus, Flowers, Frothy Blue Glaze, S.E.G., 8 3/4 In.	770.00
Vase, Oval, Irises, Cuerda Seca, 1938, 8 3/4 x 4 3/4 In.	5775.00
Vase, Sea Green Matte Glaze, Deep Brown Body, S.E.G., Rose Bacchini, 12 In.	990.00
Vase, Sea Green, Aqua Panels, 1926, 9 x 6 1/2 In.	495.00
Vase, Turquoise, Oval, Cuerda Seca, Oak Leaf & Acorn Band, Marked, 1917, 6 x 4 In.	4025.00

PEACHBLOW glass was made by several factories beginning in the 1880s. New England peachblow is a one-layer glass shading from red to white. Mt. Washington peachblow shades from pink to bluish-white. Hobbs, Brockunier and Company of Wheeling, West Virginia, made coral glass that they marketed as Peach Blow. It shades from yellow to peach and is lined with white glass. Reproductions of all types of peachblow have been made. Related pieces may be listed under Gunderson and Webb Peachblow.

Bowl, Flared, Square, Applied Amber Rim, Wheeling, 9 x 3 3/4 x 8 In.	330.00
Celery Vase, Enameled, Mt. Washington, 6 3/4 In.	375.00
Creamer, Blue Handle, Mt. Washington, 4 In.	896.00
Creamer, Diamond-Quilted, White & Yellow Enameled Flowers, Gold Butterfly, 3 In.	245.00
Cruet, Lapidary Amber Stopper, Wheeling, 6 1/2 In.	270.00
Paperweight, Pear, Applied Green Stem, 3 In.	120.00
Pickle Castor, Silver Plated Top, Raised Diamond Hobnail	1375.00
Pitcher, Amber Handle, Wheeling, 4 1/2 In.	2240.00
Pitcher, Ruffled Edge, Clear Rigaree, 4 1/2 In.	144.00
Pitcher, Square Mouth, New England, 4 1/2 In.	448.00
Pitcher, Tricornered Ruffled Edge, Crystal Handle, 8 In.	225.00
Pitcher, Wheeling Drape, 4 1/2 In.	400.00
Salt Shaker, Bulbous, Metal Cover, 2 3/4 In.	230.00
Sugar, Enameled, Yellow Daisies, 2 3/4 x 4 In.	4200.00
Tumbler, Glossy, 3 1/2 In.	275.00 to 345.00
Tumbler, Wheeling, 3 3/4 In.	115.00
Vase, Amber Rigaree Band Around Collar, Wheeling, 8 1/4 In.	1008.00
Vase, Double Gourd, Mt. Washington, 8 In.	865.00
Vase, Jack-In-The-Pulpit, Glossy, Ruffled Edge, Mt. Washington, 7 3/4 In.	2875.00

Vase, Lily, 6 5/8 x 2 7/8 In.	350.00
Vase, Morgan, Glossy, Griffin Holder, Wheeling, 10 In.	1555.00 to 1980.00
Vase, Morgan, Satin, Griffin Holder, Wheeling, 10 In.	1150.00 to 1438.00
Vase, Pinched Ruffled Edge, 4 5/8 In.	495.00
Vase, Stick, Wheeling	850.00
Vase, Wheeling, Morgan, Yellow To Deep Cranberry, Off White Interior, 8 In.	1155.00

PEANUTS is the title of a comic strip created by cartoonist Charles M. Schulz (1922-2000). The strip, drawn by Schulz from 1950 to 2000, features a group of children, including Charlie Brown and his sister Sally, Lucy Van Pelt and her brother Linus, Peppermint Patty, and Pig Pen, and an imaginative and independent beagle named Snoopy. The Peanuts gang has also been featured in books, television shows, and a Broadway musical.

Bank, Snoopy The Dog, Silver Plated, Coin Trap, 1960	75.00
Book, Suppertime, Suppertime, Snoopy's Habits, 6 x 6 In.	8.00
Brunch Bag, Snoopy, Woodstock, United Features Syndicate, 1950s	30.00
Cookie Jar, Charlie Brown, Benjamin & Medwin	50.00
Cookie Jar, Lucy, Benjamin & Medwin	50.00
Doll, Snoopy Sock It To Me, Vinyl, Boxing Gloves, 1969, 16 1/2 In.	40.00
Jigsaw Puzzle, Lucy, Charlie, Football Game, Milton Bradley, 100 Piece, 7 x 11 In.	10.00
Pencil Case, Snoopy On Doghouse, Vinyl, Zipper, 5 x 8 In.	8.00
Scissors, Snoopy, Hard Plastic, Blades In Mouth, Battery Operated, 2 x 2 x 6 In.	12.00
Telephone, Snoopy & Woodstock, Plastic, Push Button Numbers, 1976, 10 3/4 In.	65.00
Travel Bag, Snoopy, Canvas, Red, Zipper, 14 x 19 1/2 x 4 1/2 In.	15.00

PEARL items listed here are made of the natural mother-of-pearl from shells. Such natural pearl has been used to decorate furniture and small utilitarian objects for centuries. The glassware known as mother-of-pearl is listed by that name. Opera glasses made with natural pearl shell are listed under Opera Glasses.

Card Case, Abalone, Checkered, England, 4 1/8 x 3 1/8 In.	115.00
Jewelry Box, Patchwork Veneer, Amboyna Stars, 3 1/2 x 7 In.	395.00
Nativity Set, Shadow Box Style, Abalone Details, 1930s, 10 x 10 In.	260.00
Needle Case, Gold Trim, Georgian, 2 3/4 In.	70.00
Thread Winder, Knob Corners, England, 1 3/4 In.	60.00

PEARLWARE is an earthenware made by Josiah Wedgwood in 1779. It was copied by other potters in England. Pearlware is only slightly different in color from creamware and for many years collectors have confused the terms. Wedgwood pieces are listed in the Wedgwood category in this book. Most pearlware with mocha designs is listed under Mocha.

Pearl

Bank, Clock, 2 Figures, Dog, c.1820, 9 In.	2115.00
Beaker, Black Slip, Brown Slip Band, 1790, 2 1/2 In.	545.00
Bowl, Blue, Black Wavy Slip Lines, White Field, 1830, 5 3/4 In.	430.00
Bowl, Dark Brown Slip Marble, Blue, Green Glaze Reeded Rim, 1780, 6 5/8 In.	1150.00
Bowl, Dark Brown, Blue Bands, Green Glaze Roulette Rim, 1830, 7 3/4 In.	805.00
Bowl, Tan, Black Border, Tan Field, 1830, 7 In.	750.00
Chamber Pot, Napoleon, Inside Latin Phrase, 2 Loop Handles, Woods, 9 3/8 x 17 In.	1540.00
Charger, Shell Edge, Blossoms, Wreath Interior Border, Scalloped Rim, 13 In.	880.00
Coffeepot, Cover, Agate, Baluster, c.1780, 10 In.	2350.00
Coffeepot, Dome Cover, Acorn Finial, King's Rose, Oyster Pattern, c.1830, 6 1/2 In.	2820.00
Coffeepot, Napoleon On Sled In Russia, Horses, Trees, 12 In.	1095.00
Creamer, Adams Rose	125.00
Creamer, Light Brown Stripes, Yellow Band, Light Brown Leaves	110.00
Creamer, Pineapple & Vase, Brown, Yellow Bands, Ocher, Green	580.00
Cup & Saucer, Figurine, Woman Holding A Bouquet Of Flowers, 4 1/4 In.	110.00
Cup & Saucer, Pineapple & Vase, Ocher, Green, Brown & Yellow Bands	855.00
Ewer, Baluster Shape, Beak Spout, c.1800, 13 1/2 In.	4465.00
Figurine, Child Holding Basket Of Green Grapes, Dark Purple, Yellow Spots, 4 In.	80.00
Figurine, Goat, Late 18th Century, 8 1/2 In.	1295.00
Figurine, Highlander, Portobello, c.1820, 12 1/2 In.	8225.00
Figurine, Jack On Cruise, Yorkshire, c.1815, 9 3/4 In.	590.00

Figurine, Lamb, Reclining, White, Brown Legs, Ears, Light Green Base, 3 x 2 In. 165.00
Figurine, Lion, Hermaphrodite, Ocher, c.1780, 12 In. 4700.00
Figurine, Porcellino, 2 Monkeys, Jay, 1770-1820, 3 7/8 In. 880.00
Figurine, Rooster & Hen, c.1790, Pair 3290.00
Figurine, Stag, Doe, Country Landscape, c.1780, 7 3/4 In., Pair 880.00
Figurine, Summer, Tynside, 1820-1826, 3 7/8 In. 1116.00
Figurine, Tiger, Country Landscape, c.1830, 8 1/4 In. 3055.00
Figurine, Woman & Dolphin, Bear & Sheep, c.1800, 2 5/8 In., Pair 470.00
Flowerpot, Black Slip Checkered Band, Sprigged Swags, 1800, 4 1/2 In. 2185.00
Honey Pot, Cover, Fixed Stand, c.1825, 5 In. 1998.00
Jug, 2 Cobalt Blue Glaze Bands, Orange Field, 1820, 4 3/4 In. 1955.00
Jug, 3 Groups Of Trailed Brown Slip Waves, White Body, Green Glaze, 1835, 6 In. 5460.00
Jug, Apple Green, Purple Slip Band, Black, Gray Accent Bands, 1835, 7 In. 4310.00
Jug, Black, Green Glaze Bands, 1820, 6 In. 3450.00
Jug, Cover, Scroll Handle, Beak Spout, c.1800, 6 In. 825.00
Jug, Tan, Ocher, Black Bands, 1840, 6 3/4 In. 200.00
Mug, Black, Blue, Rust Bands, White Slip Lines, Black Field, 1830, 5 3/4 In. 5750.00
Mug, Black, Ocher, Blue Wavy Slip Lines, Black, Ocher Bands, 1830, 5 1/2 In. 1955.00
Mug, Brown, Blue, Orange, Ocher Field, Reeded Bands, Cobalt Handle, 1820, 3 In. 4310.00
Mug, Circulating Library, Black Transfer, c.1830, 2 3/4 In. 325.00
Mug, Dark Brown, Blue Band, White Slip Dots, 7-Point Stars, 1840, 4 3/4 In. 980.00
Mug, Herringbone Black, Brown Bands, White Field, 1830, 6 In. 2300.00
Pipe, Puzzle, Fable, Yorkshire, Pearlware, c.1800, 8 In. 1410.00
Pipe, Puzzle, Geometric, Leaf Patterns, c.1810, 13 1/4 In. 2820.00
Pitcher, Red Transfer, Drinking Scenes, Verses, Silver Luster On Base, 1809, 6 1/2 In. . . . 1430.00
Plaque, Emblematic, Autumn, Oval, Yorkshire, c.1810, 13 In. 2585.00
Plaque, Judgment Of Paris, Oval, c.1780, 9 In. 2235.00
Plaque, Man, Holding Spade, Woman, Watering Can, Incised WS, 1790, 6 3/8 In. 1440.00
Plaque, Oval, Gretna Green Marriage, c.1815, 10 1/2 In. 410.00
Plaque, Portrait, Catherine The Great, Yorkshire, c.1796, 5 1/4 In. 1000.00
Plaque, Putti, Lion, Oval, c.1810, 8 In. 1000.00
Plaque, Shakespeare Scenes, Yorkshire, Oval, c.1790, 5 1/2 In., Pair 2233.00
Plate, 2 Children About To Touch Beehive, Feather Rim, 5 1/2 In. 390.00
Plate, 3 Gold Flowers, Scalloped Green Border, 8 In. 440.00
Plate, Blue Scalloped Edge, Ocher Sunflower, Flowers, 9 3/4 In. 550.00
Plate, Blue, Shell Edge, Thistles, Flowers, Holly & Berry Interior Border, 5 1/2 In. 470.00
Plate, Central Flower, Embossed Rim, Dark Blue, 5 3/4 In. 135.00
Plate, Double Pansy, Fishscale & Feather Border, Yellow, Blue, Brown, Green, 8 In. 825.00
Plate, Fishscale, Green Feather Border, Double Pansy, Yellow, Blue, Green, 8 In. 825.00
Plate, Fishscale, Green Feather Border, Pansy, Yellow, Blue, Brown, Green, 7 3/4 In. 825.00
Plate, Green, Ocher Vine, c.1775, 8 In., Pair 4700.00
Plate, Lobed, Green, Yellow, Gray Trellis, c.1760 . . . . 1410.00
Plate, Man On Horseback, Sword, Blue & Mustard Sprig Border, 9 1/4 In. 300.00
Plate, Painted Center Flower, Feather Rim, 4 1/2 In. 310.00
Plate, Scalloped Blue Shell Border, Oriental Scene Interior, 9 7/8 In. 330.00
Plate, Scalloped Edge, Green, Ocher Sprig Pattern, Single Flower, Leaves, 8 1/2 In. 580.00
Plate, Scalloped, Blue Embossed Edge, Center Flower, Yellow, Blue, Ocher, 7 3/4 In. . . . 690.00
Plate, Scalloped, Flowers, Blue, Green, Yellow, Ocher, Blue Edge, 7 In. 605.00
Plate, Shell Edge, Blue, Oriental Scene, Pagoda, 9 7/8 In. 330.00
Plate, Shell Edge, Yellow, Orange House, 2 Trees, 4 1/8 In. 715.00
Plate, Silver Luster, Yellow Ground, Greek Key Band, c.1820, 8 3/16 In. 2000.00
Plate, Toddy, c.1800, 4 1/2 In. 75.00
Plate, Young Woman On Shore, Sailboat Background, Feather Rim, 4 1/4 In. 225.00
Plate Set, Silver Luster, Yellow Ground, c.1815, 8 1/4 In., 3 Piece 1600.00
Platter, Blue Oriental Scene, Incised Feather Rim, Oval, 21 x 26 In. 935.00
Platter, Blue Transfer, Printed, Fairmount, Near Philadelphia, c.1830, 21 In. 1840.00
Platter, Undertray, Blue Feather Edge, Child's, 5 3/4 In. 80.00
Pot, Cover, Barrel Form, Blue Band, Black, 1830, 3 5/8 In. 1840.00
Sauceboat, Fox Head, Brown, Swan Handle, c.1795, 6 3/4 In. 1000.00
Sugar, Cover, Swirled Ribs, Sawtooth Edge, Flowers, 8 Sides, 5 x 6 In. 190.00
Sugar, Dark Brown Stripes, Blue, Gold Swags, 5 1/4 x 3 1/2 x 6 In. 385.00
Sugar, Transfer, Archers, Rose Finial 425.00
Teapot, Pink & Green Flowers & Sprigs, 1790, 6 1/2 In. 795.00

Vase, Finger, Raised Flower Borders, Swag, Egg & Dart Border, c.1800, 9 In. 470.00
Vase, Spill, Green Glazed Reeded Bands, Blue Speckled Field, 1790, 4 1/4 In. 575.00
Watch Stand, Tall Case Clock, Children, c.1820, 10 5/8 In. 765.00

PEKING GLASS is a Chinese cameo glass first made popular in the eighteenth century. The Chinese have continued to make this layered glass
in the old manner, and many new pieces are now available that could
confuse the average buyer.

Bottle, Emerald Green, Flowering Branches, Narrow Foot, 19th Century, 7 1/2 In. 172.00
Bowl, Yellow, Carved Taotie Mask, Deep, 1900s, 7 In. 185.00
Bowl, Yellow, Imperial, Bell Shape, 18th Century, 6 1/2 In. 126.00
Vase, Bottle Shape, Chinese Red, White, Fish, Floral, 20th Century, 12 In., Pair 210.00
Vase, Bottle Shape, Ruby, Elongated Neck, 8 1/4 In., Pair 635.00
Vase, Brown, Bulbous, Long Neck, Footed, Early 19th Century, 10 3/4 In. 1150.00
Vase, Green On White, Oriental Scene, 6 1/4 In. 112.00
Vase, Teal Blue, Bulbous, Straight Neck, Mid 19th Century, 10 In. 1150.00
Vase, White, Gingko Leaves, Egrets, 9 In., Pair 170.00

PELOTON glass is a European glass with small threads of colored glass
rolled onto the surface of clear or colored glass. It is sometimes called
spaghetti, or shredded coconut, glass. Most pieces found today were
made in the nineteenth century.

Rose Bowl, Ribbed, White Ground, Pulled Rim, 4 1/4 In. 308.00
Vase, Fan, Pink, Blue, Yellow, White Ground, Applied Clear Foot, Florets, 4 In. 200.00
Vase, Multicolored, Ribbed, Clear Ground, 5 In. 336.00
Vase, Pink, Yellow, Blue, White Ground, Ruffled Edge, 4 3/4 In. 400.00
Vase, White Ground, Ruffled Edge, 6 3/4 In. 140.00

PENS replaced hand-cut quills as writing instruments in 1780 when the
first steel pen point was made in England. But it was 100 years before
the commercial pen was a common item. The fountain pen was
invented in the 1830s but was not made in quantity until the 1880s. All
types of old pens are collected.

PEN, Agate, Pink & Black Stripe, Gold Plated, Lever Filler, Japan . . . . *Illus* 23.00
Autograph, Gold Filled Tip, Yellow & Black, Marbled, Lever Filler 22.00
Avon, Chased Gold Plated & Hard Black Plastic, Lever Filler 11.00
Baker, Black & Cream Marbled, Nickel Plated, Lever Filler . . . . *Illus* 5.00
Carter, 1125, Gold Filled Tip, Orange, Lever Filler 132.00
Century, Black Hard Rubber, Eye Dropper Filler 50.00
Century, Durapoint, Gold Filled Tip, Green, Orange Top Cap, Lever Filler 138.00
Century, Durapoint, Gold Filled Tip, Green, Yellow Marbled Tip, Lever Filler 80.00
Century, Durapoint, Gold Filled Tip, Rosewood, Yellow Cap, Lever Filler 88.00
Columbia Beer, 1960s 10.00
Conklin, Chased Black Hard Rubber, Crescent Filler . . . . .50.00 to 80.00
Conklin, Endura, Gold Filled Tip, Red & Black Rosewood, Lever Filler 50.00
Conklin, Red & Black, Marbled, Self Filler 204.00
Dencraft, Fold Filled Tip, Black & Cream, Marbled, Lever Filler 11.00
Dip, A. Morton, Gold Plated Metal & Wood 11.00
Dip, Aikin Lambert, Gold Plated Metal & Hard Black Plastic 22.00
Dip, Daniel Low, Chased Sterling Silver 33.00
Eagle, Black & Brown, Chased Hard Rubber, Eye Dropper Filler . . . . *Illus* 15.00
Eagle, Never Break, Chased Nickel Plated Metal, Lever Filler 22.00
Eagle, Rosewood, Nickel Plated Tip, Lever Filler . . . . *Illus* 15.00
Float About, Beatles, 4 Lads Float Across Abbey Road 6.00
Float About, F117A Stealth Fighter Flies Over Farmland 3.25
Float About, Flower Blossom Floats In & Out Of Open Hand, Hearts, Blue 3.25
Float About, Horseless Power, Tin Lizzie Passes Storefronts 3.25
Float About, John F. Kennedy In Oval Office, Vertical Action 3.50
Float About, Moon Landing, Neil Armstrong Carries Flag 3.75
Float About, Noah's Ark, Alligators & Sheep Float To Ark 3.25
Float About, Pie Flies Between Three Stooges 3.25
Float About, Save The Planet, Earth Past Eclipsed Moon, Vertical Action 3.25
Float About, Seattle's Best Coffee, Logo Is Brewed In Cup Of Coffee, Red 4.00

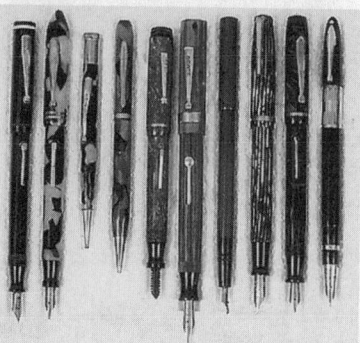

Pen, Eagle, Rosewood, Nickel Plated Tip, Lever Filler; Pen, Baker, Black & Cream Marbled, Nickel Plated, Lever Filler; Pencil, Swallow, Mabie Todd & Co., Black & Cream Marbled, Gold Plated; Pencil, Wearever, Black, Green, Orange Marbled, Nickel Plated; Pen, Gold Bond, Stonite, Green Marbled, Gold Plated, Lever Filler; Pen, Agate, Pink & Black Stripe, Gold Plated, Lever Filler, Japan; Pen, Eagle, Black & Brown, Hard Rubber, Eye Dropper Filler; Pen, Wearever, Silver Pearl Stripes, Gold Filled, Suction Filler; Pen, Wasp, Green & Maroon Swirl, Gold Plated, Lever Filler; Pen, Scheaffer, No. 1250, Black Hard Rubber, Gold Filled

Fountain, Whitney, Wood, Turned, Black Paint, Gilt Metal Nib, 29 x 2 In.	1095.00
Gold Bond, Stonite, Green Marbled, Gold Plated, Lever Filler .... *Illus*	5.00
Heinz, Red Logo, White Ground, Conceal, Reveal, Clicker	5.00
Moore, Gold Filled Mounted, Lever Filler	44.00
Morrison, Tourist, Gold Filled Tip, Black Chased Hard Rubber, Lever Filler	22.00
Morton, Gold Filled Tip, Yellow & Black, Lever Filler	22.00
Parker, Challenger, Gold Plated Tip, Burgundy, Marbled	39.00
Parker, Duofold Jr., Gold Filled Tip, Red Hard Rubber, Button Filler	33.00
Parker, Gold Filled Trim, Black, Touchdown Filler, France	39.00
Parker, Lucky Curve, Gold Filled Trim, Cream Optic, Button Filler, 1911	105.00
Parker, Vacumatic, Gold Filled Trim, Gold Pearl	33.00
Parker, Vacumatic, Gold Filled Trim, Silver Pearl, Plunger Filler	88.00
Remington, Nickel Plated Trim, Yellow, Black, Green, Marbled, Lever Filler	8.50
Ritchie, Gold Filled Tip, Black & Cream, Marbled, Lever Filler	11.00
Salz, Classic, Gold Filled Tip, Black & Cream, Marbled, Lever Filler	44.00
Scheaffer, Black Hard Rubber, Gold Filled, No. 1250 .... *Illus*	5.00
Scheaffer, Feather Touch, Gold Filled Tip, Marine Green Stripes, No. 500	11.00
Scheaffer, Gold Filled Tip, Golden Brown, Radite, Vacuum Filler, No. 875	13.00
Scheaffer, Nostalgia, Silver Overlay On Black, No. 800	236.00
Sunshine Brewing, 1960s	14.00
Traveler, Nickel Plated Trim, Brown & Cream, Marbled, Lever Filler	5.50
Wahl, Gold Filled Mounted, Lever Filler	88.00
Wahl, Signature, Chased Orange Hard Rubber, Lever Filler	66.00
Wasp, Green & Maroon Swirl, Gold Plated, Lever Filler .... *Illus*	10.00
Waterman, Black Hard Rubber, Automatic Self Filler	44.00
Waterman, Desk, Green & Yellow Ripple	121.00
Waterman, Gold Filled Tip, Black Hard Rubber, Lever Filler	25.00
Waterman, Gold Filled Tip, Brown Hard Rubber, Lever Filler	55.00
Waterman, Ideal, Safety, 14S, Gold Plated Trim, Black Chased Hard Rubber	44.00
Waterman, Ripple, Gold Filled Tip, Red & Black, Lever Filler	83.00
Wearever, Silver Pearl Stripes, Gold Filled, Suction Filler .... *Illus*	2.50
Weidlich, Gold Filled Tip, Blue & Black, Marbled, Lever Filler	28.00
Welty Dixie, Gold Plated Trim, Black & Cream, Marbled, Lever Filler	22.00
PEN & PENCIL, Keystone, Black & White Pearl Twist, Lever Filler	20.00
Parker, VP, Black, Gold Filled Metal Top, Pen Jeweled Both Ends, 21 Box	143.00
Scheaffer, Gold Filled Tip, Roseglow Two Tone, Plunger Filler	39.00
Scheaffer, Lifetime, Gold Filled Tip, Green Pearl Stripes	33.00
Wahl, Gold Filled Metal, Lever Filler	95.00
Wahl-Eversharp, Ladies, Gold Filled Metal, Lever Filler	220.00

PENCILS were invented, so it is said, in 1565. The eraser was not added to the pencil until 1858. The automatic pencil was invented in 1863. Collectors today want advertising pencils or automatic pencils of unusual design. Boxes and sharpeners for pencils are also collected. Advertising pencils are listed in the Advertising category. Pencil boxes are listed in the Box category.

PENCIL, Belmont, Gold Filled Tip, Black & Green, Marbled	1.10

If a fountain pen cap or barrel is discolored, the pen has little value.

Before you store an old fountain pen, empty the ink bladder. Wash the bladder out with lukewarm water.

Pencil Sharpener, Turtle, Cast Resin, Painted, 2 In.

Century, 12K Chased Gold Filled Metal	39.00
Century, Gold Filled Tip, Black & Cream, Marbled	50.00
Century, Gold Filled Tip, Green & White	44.00
Century, Gold Filled Tip, Red & Black	39.00
Century, Gold Filled Trim, Blue & Cream, Marbled	44.00
Century, Gold Filled Trim, Green, Marbled, 1926	33.00
Century, Herringbone	39.00
Conklin, Silver Plated Metal, 1920	5.50
Corona, Gold Filled Tip, Black & Cream, Marbled	2.75
Diamond, Gold Plated Tip, Green & Cream	5.50
Gold Bond, Gold Filled Tip, Green Jade	5.50
Gold Filled Mounted, Ivory, Telescoping	33.00
Mechanical, American Pencil Co., Gold Plated Metal, Red Jewel Top	17.00
Mechanical, Whiskey Bottle, Metal, Germany	35.00
Moore, Gold Filled Tip, Red Hard Rubber, 1925	14.00
Moore, Gold Plated Tip, Green & Orange, Marbled	5.50
Parker, Gold Filled Trim, Duofold, Lapis Blue	77.00
Parker, Gold Filled Trim, Red Plastic On Metal	17.00
Parker, Gold Pearl, Gold Filled Tip	5.50
Parker, Nickel Plated Trim, Gray Pearl	12.00
Salz, Gold Filled Tip, Black & Cream, Marbled	4.40
Scheaffer, Gold Filled Trim, Black & Pearl	17.00
Scheaffer, Green Jade	10.00
Swallow, Mabie Todd & Co., Black & Cream Marbled, Gold Plated . . . . *Illus*	7.50
V For Victory, Red, White & Blue, Plastic, Stutz & Sando Co., 4 Unfolds To 6 In., 2 Piece	20.00
Wahl, Eversharp, Chased Gold Filled Metal	6.60
Wearever, Black, Green, Orange Marbled, Nickel Plated . . . . *Illus*	1.00
PENCIL SHARPENER, Black Uncle Sam, Cast Metal, 2 In.	288.00
Car, Die Cast Metal, 1917	6.00
Exaggerated Black Man's Head, Sharpener Is Mouth, 1900s, 1 1/2 In.	108.00
Fiat, Die Cast Metal	5.00
Hodge Steamer, Die Cast Metal	6.00
Pot Metal, Uncle Sam Walking, Eversharp, 1918, 2 x 1 x 3/8 In.	58.00
Roll Royce, 1906 Silver Ghost, Die Cast Metal, Plastic Top	6.00
Stagecoach, Die Cast Metal	6.00
Turtle, Cast Resin, Painted, 2 In. . . . . *Illus*	5.00
Uncle Sam, Painted, Occupied Japan, 1948, 1 7/8 x 1 1/8 In.	138.00

PEPSI-COLA, the drink and the name, was invented in 1898 but was not trademarked until 1903. The logo was changed from an elaborate script to the modern block letters in 1963. Several different logos have been used. Until 1951, the words *Pepsi* and *Cola* were separated by 2 dashes. These bottles are called *double dash*. In 1951 the modern logo with a single hyphen was introduced. All types of advertising memorabilia are collected, and reproductions are being made.

Bank, Inserting Coin Dispenses Soda Into Glass, 1950s, 9 3/4 x 6 3/4 x 5 In.	385.00
Case, Wooden, Anderson Bottling Plant	45.00

Chalkboard, Self-Framed, Tin, 19 1/2 x 30 In.	275.00
Clock, Double Bubbler, Lighted, 15 In.	742.00
Clock, Telechron, Hanging Hole, 1940s, 15 In.	357.00
Cooler, Dual No. 27, 10 Cent, 26 x 52 x 16 In.	330.00
Dispenser, Countertop, Stainless Steel, Side Lettering, 1950s	770.00
Door Pull, Screen Door, 1930s, 12 1/4 In.	375.00
Door Push, Metal & Bakelite, 1930s	193.00
Door Push, Tin, Beveled Border, Canada, 1930s, 13 1/2 In.	495.00 to 985.00
Kick Plate, Enjoy A Pepsi, Porcelain, 29 1/4 In.	214.00
Menu Board, Plastic, Lighted, Metal Rim, 1950s, 12 x 28 In.	440.00
Scorekeeper, Baseball, 2 Sides, Baseball & Football, Cardboard, 1930s, 13 x 30 In.	495.00
Sign, Bottle Cap, Metal, Die Cut, Embossed, Double Dash, 1940s, 13 In.	295.00
Sign, More Bounce To The Ounce, c.1940, 38 x 18 In.	1430.00
Sign, Plastic, Metal Rim, Bottle Cap, Light-Up, 1950s, 16 In.	633.00
Sign, Tin Lithograph, Die Cut Bottle, 1930s, 44 1/2 x 12 In.	688.00
Thermometer, Straw Girl, 7 x 27 In.	743.00
Thermometer, Tin, 1950s, 12 x 7 In.	468.00
Tip Tray, Woman, Victorian Soda Parlor, Tin Lithograph, c.1908, 6 1/8 x 4 3/8 In.	935.00
Tray, Victorian Lady In Bar Room, 1909, 11 1/4 x 13 1/4 In.	2420.00

PERFUME BOTTLES are made of cut glass, pressed glass, art glass, silver, metal, enamel, and even plastic or porcelain. Although the small bottle to hold perfume was first made before the time of ancient Egypt, it is the nineteenth- and twentieth-century examples that interest today's collector. DeVilbiss Company has made atomizers of all types since 1888 but no longer makes the perfume bottle tops so popular with collectors. These were made from 1920 to 1968. The glass bottle may be by any of many manufacturers even if the atomizer is marked *DeVilbiss*. The word *factice*, which often appears in ads, refers to store display bottles. Glass or porcelain examples may be found under the appropriate name such as Lalique, Czechoslovakia, Glass-Bohemian, etc.

Amber Glass, Iridescent, Trumpet Shape, Signed, Steuben, 6 1/2 In.	825.00
Art Glass, Lay Down, Floral & Butterfly, Cameo, England	3250.00
Atomizer, Carved Flowers, Leaves, Cameo, Signed, Galle, 4 In.	1345.00
Black Boy, Painted Glass, Bakelite Hat Cap, Germany, 1930s, 3 In.	208.00
Black Glass, Cut Glass Finials, Atomizer, Covered Box, Austria, 3 Piece	489.00
Blue Aurene, Pedestal, Signed, Steuben, 5 1/2 In.	575.00
Bourjois, Ashes Of Roses, Red Ground, Black Glass Stopper, 1 In.	220.00
Bourjois, Evening In Paris, Brosse & Wheelbarrow, Miniature, 2 1/4 In.	750.00
Bourjois, Evening In Paris, Brosse, Eiffel Tower Box, 3 1/2 In.	375.00
Bourjois, Mais Oui, Brosse, Red Slipper, Miniature, 2 In.	1125.00
Cameo Glass, Purple Flowers, Cylindrical Form, Signed, Galle, 6 In.	460.00
Cameo Glass, Purple Flowers, Purple Ball Stopper, Signed, Galle, 3 3/4 In.	585.00
Cameo Glass, Riverscape, Windmill, Figures, Opaline, Signed, Daum, 4 1/4 In.	1380.00
Cameo Glass, Stylized Flowers, Mottled Purple, Signed, Daum, 3 In.	920.00
Caron, Rose Precieuse, Box, 4 1/4 In.	1050.00
Ciro, Chevalier De La Nuit, 1923, 7 3/4 In.	345.00
Clear Glass, Teardrop Stopper, Signed, Steuben, 7 3/4 In.	785.00
Cologne, Black Amethyst, Gold Trim, Art Deco, Stopper, 5 1/2 In.	175.00
Cologne, Blown, Amberina, Hexagonal, Paneled, Faceted Stopper, c.1970, 8 In.	633.00
Cologne, Blown, Molded, Blue, Opaque, Enamel, Faceted, Hexagonal, Stopper, 4 In.	316.00
Cologne, Blown, Molded, Blue, Ruffled, Flower Stopper, Underplate, 7 1/2 In.	672.00
Cologne, Blown, Molded, Elongated Loop, Hexagonal, Faceted Stopper, 7 In.	460.00
Cologne, Blown, Molded, Faceted, Hexagonal, Stopper, c.1870, 6 1/2 In.	288.00
Cologne, Blue Aurene, Steuben, c.1900, 4 1/2 In.	635.00
Cologne, Extrait D'Eau De Lavender, Sapphire Blue, Conical, Pontil, 6 3/4 In.	550.00
Cologne, Guerlain, Hegemonienne, Pochet Et Du Courval, 9 In.	9004.00
Cologne, Latticinio, Filigree Torsade, Red, White, Gold Enamel, Pontil, France, 5 1/4 In.	784.00
Cologne, Latticinio, Filigree Twist, Red, White, Gold Enamel, Pontil, France, 5 In.	784.00
Cologne, Light Aqua, Barrel, Anchors, Ship, 4 3/8 In. *Illus*	300.00
Cologne, Milk Glass, 5 Vertical Ribs, Label, 1870, 4 3/4 In.	550.00
Cologne, Porcelain, Roses, Gold Ball Stopper, Vienna, 5 1/2 In.	135.00

Cologne, Sapphire Blue, Molded, 6 Panel Ribs, Lip Collar, 1780, 5 In. 316.00
Cologne, St. Clair, 5 Pink Pull-Up Flowers, Green Base, 5 x 3 1/4 In. 145.00
Cologne, White Flowers, Citron Ground, Cameo, England 825.00
Corday, Green Lettering, Stopper, 1/4 Oz. 110.00
Cranberry Glass, Cut & Polished Sides, 8 1/2 In. 66.00
Cranberry Glass, Enameled, Daisy, Gold Leaves & Trim, 3-Petal Mouth, 7 1/4 In. 165.00
Cranberry Glass, Portrait, Young Woman, Gold, 8 3/4 In. 201.00
Cut Crystal, Silver Gilt Cover, London, 1893, 5 In. 259.00
Cut Glass, Blue Tinted, Stopper, Continental, Mid 19th Century, 7 1/4 x 5 In. 403.00
Cut Glass, Emerald Green To Clear, Clear Faceted Stopper, Square, 4 In. 110.00
Cut Glass, Hobstars & Fans, Hoare, 7 In. 595.00
Cut Glass, Silver Sterling Top, Red Jewels, R. Blackinton, 1875, 4 1/2 In. 450.00
Cut Glass, White To Cranberry, 6 3/4 In. 230.00
D'Orsay, Pleats Of A Skirt, Gold Metal Cap, 2 In., 2 Piece 33.00
De Vigney, D'Ou Vient-Il, 3 1/4 In. 5102.00
DeVilbiss, Black Glass Medallion, Amber Glass, 1926, 6 In. 176.00
DeVilbiss, Bullet Shape, Black Glass, Brass Scroll Frame, 1928, 6 In. 365.00
DeVilbiss, Light Amber Iridescent Glass, Metal Neck, Signed, 4 In. 77.00
DeVilbiss, Light Amber Iridescent, Metal Atomizer, Signed, 7 In., Pair 121.00
DeVilbiss, Pale Pink, Black, Orange, Enameled, Metal Atomizer, 9 In. 286.00
DeVilbiss, Roses, Leaves Enamel, Metal Shaker Top, Light Green, 4 In. 66.00
DeVilbiss, Translucent Violet Glass, Gold Metal Atomizer, Signed, 5 In. 44.00
DeVilbiss, White Rabbit 400.00
DeVilbiss, Yellow Satin Glass, Metal Dropper, Yellow Enamel, 9 In. 154.00
Dubarry, Blue Lagoon, Seated Egyptian Woman Stopper, 4 In. 7475.00
Elizabeth Arden, Blue Grass, Christmas Bell, Miniature, 1 3/4 In. 600.00
Elizabeth Arden, It's You, Hand Form, Baccarat, 1937, 8 1/2 In. 460.00
Enameled Glass, Flowers, Signed, Galle, 4 1/2 In. 1495.00
Engraved, Woman On Dolphin, Oval, Paper Label, Orrefors, 6 In., Pair 460.00
Extrait D'Eau De Lavender, Sapphire Blue, Label, 6 Oz. 330.00
Flame Of Glory, Andre Jollivet, Olympic Flame, Frosted Stopper, 2 1/2 In. 435.00
Gelle Freres, Extrait Concentre, M. Depinoix, 3 1/4 In. 180.00
Glass, Silver Overlay, Engraved Scroll, Ball Stopper, S In Cartouche, 4 In. 63.00
Gold Aurene Glass, Melon Ribbed, 5 3/4 x 6 In., Pair 1955.00
Gold Iridescent, Bronze Stopper, Signed, Tiffany, 4 1/4 In. 5175.00
Gold Iridescent, Ribbed, Signed, Tiffany, 6 In. 1380.00
Green Cut To Clear, Silver Top, Stopper, 3 In. 144.00
Guerlain, L'Heure Bleue, R. Noirot, Baccarat, 6 In. 7128.00
Guerlain, Sous Le Vent, Pochet Et Du Courval, Box, 5 In. 1275.00
Guyla, Divin Narcisse, Champagne Flute Shape, c.1926, 5 3/4 In. 460.00
Kazium, Shaded Upright Rose In Stopper, Signed 4 1/2 In. 728.00
Lancome, Magie, Sputnik Presentation, Box, 2 1/2 In. 7503.00
Leaves & Scrollwork, Long Dabber, Marked Sterling, Box, Velvet Lining, 2 In. 120.00
Lentheric, Au Fil De L'Eau, Box, 3 In. 2701.00
Lucian Lelong, Castel, Box, Large 325.00
Mary Chess, Souvenir Di Un Soir, Pulitzer Fountain, 4 3/4 In. .... *Illus* 5175.00

Perfume Bottle, Cologne,
Light Aqua, Barrel,
Anchors,
Ship, 4 3/8 In.

Perfume Bottle,
Mary Chess, Souvenir
Di Un Soir, Pulitzer
Fountain, 4 3/4 In.

Matsu-No-Ke, Amethyst Foot, Signed Steuben, 6 In. 448.00
Monkey, Mohair, Jointed, With Vial & Cork, Schuco 465.00
Owl, Bisque Porcelain, Metal Crown Top, 3 In. 330.00
Pagoda, Cut Glass, Art Deco, Stopper, 8 1/2 x 4 x 2 In. 165.00
Pierrot Form, Bouquet Of Pink Roses, 3 In. 320.00
Porcelain, Gilt Brass Mount, Royal Blue Matte Ground, Spherical, 9 In. 920.00
Roger & Gallet, Bouquet Nouveau, 4 1/4 In. 3752.00
Rosaline Glass, Alabaster Foot, Steuben, 8 1/2 In. 520.00
Rose In Snow, Scent, Stopper 45.00
Sabino, Opalescent, Relief Bathing Women, Art Nouveau, 4 1/4 In. 330.00
Saint-Cyr, Fleches D'Amour, Box, 4 In. 338.00
Sauze, Prestige De Paris, Tolmer, 3 In. 1500.00
Schiaparelli, Miniature, Box, 2 1/2 In. 265.00
Schiaparelli, Shocking You, Metal Cap, Black Pouch, Box, 1 In. 77.00
Schiaparelli, Shocking, Pink Ground Box, Gold Cap, 4 In. 88.00
Silver Gilt Mounted, Cut Glass, Pistol Shape, Early 20th Century, 4 3/4 In. 1380.00
Silver Overlay, Compressed Body, Swirling Flowers, c.1900, 4 1/2 In. 210.00
Turquoise Glass, Yellow, Globe Shape, Signed, Schneider, 2 1/2 In. 410.00
Valreine, Violet, Baccarat, 4 1/4 In. 3750.00
White Friars, Red, White & Blue Concentric Millefiori, 1970, 5 3/4 x 3 1/4 In. 440.00

PETERS & REED Pottery Company of Zanesville, Ohio, was founded by John D. Peters and Adam Reed in 1897. Chromal, Landsun, Montene, Pereco, and Persian are some of the art lines that were made. The company, which became Zane Pottery in 1920 and Gonder Pottery in 1941, closed in 1957. Peters & Reed pottery was unmarked.

Bowl, Brown, Green Matte Glaze, Molded Leaves, Branches, 3 In. 207.00
Bowl, Pereco, Molded Branch, Leaf Design, 3 1/4 x 8 3/8 In. 120.00
Flower Frog, Pereco, Fish, Bronze Patina, 5 In. 110.00
Flower Frog, Pereco, Lily Leaf, 4 In. ....30.00 to 40.00
Jardiniere, Moss Aztec, Rim Poppies, 4 Buttressed Panels, Signed, 9 3/4 In. 460.00
Vase, Green, Brown High Glaze, 8 In. 46.00
Vase, Landsun, 1922, 12 In. 115.00
Vase, Landsun, Autumn Colors, 9 1/2 In. 225.00
Vase, Landsun, Blue, Pale Yellow, 6 In. 140.00
Vase, Landsun, Blue, Tan, 6 1/4 In. 225.00
Vase, Montene, Variegated Greens, Tans, Cream Windows, 4 In. 100.00
Vase, Moss Aztec, Brown Matte Glaze, Leaves & Vines, 18 In. 460.00
Vase, Multicolored Brown High Glaze, 7 In. 46.00
Vase, Sprig Ware, Brown Glaze, c.1910, 5 In. ....40.00 to 46.00
Vase, Stick, Landsun, Blue Speckles, Earthtone, 8 In. 100.00
Vase, Stick, Matte Green, Blue, 10 In. 150.00

PETRUS REGOUT, see Maastricht category.

PEWABIC POTTERY was founded by Mary Chase Perry Stratton in 1903 in Detroit, Michigan. The company made many types of art pottery, including pieces with matte green glaze and an iridescent crystalline glaze. The company continued working until the death of Mary Stratton in 1961. It was reactivated by Michigan State University in 1968.

Ashtray, Gray Over Red Glaze, 4 x 2 1/2 In. 80.00
Bowl, Blue Green Glaze, 10 x 2 1/2 In. 489.00
Bowl, Red, Gold, Blue Metallic Glaze, 3 x 6 1/2 In., 3 Piece 130.00
Candlestick, Blue & Black Glaze, Volcanic Base, Stamp & Paper Label, 12 In. 1035.00
Dish, Burgundy Red Glaze, Vertical Panels Along Perimeter, 5 3/4 In. 165.00
Plate, Luster Red Glaze, Signed Ira, Ella, 7 3/4 In. 230.00
Plate, Rabbits, Trees, Squeezebag Decoration, On Crackled Ivory, Stamped, 10 1/2 In. 2185.00
Tray, Cucumber Crystalline Glaze, 3 Handles, 8 In. 770.00
Tumbler, Early 20th Century, 4 In. 115.00
Vase, Blue Green Glaze, Egg Shape, Factory Mark, 7 1/2 In. 605.00
Vase, Blue Green Iridescent Glaze, 5 In. 835.00
Vase, Blue, Green Metallic Glaze, Broad Shoulder Form, 7 1/2 In. 1725.00

Vase, Blue, Green, Purple Luster Glaze, Bulbous, Flared Rim, Marked, 8 x 8 In. 1150.00
Vase, Carved Geometric Design, Green Matte Glaze, Arts & Crafts, 12 1/2 In. 3850.00
Vase, Deep Tan Glaze, Dark Brown Accents, Blue Base, 8 x 4 In. 300.00
Vase, Gray Flecks, Mustard Glossy Glaze, 1944, 6 1/4 In. 550.00
Vase, Gray Metallic Glaze, Gold, Blue, Round, 5 1/2 In. 825.00
Vase, Large Leaves, Smooth Green Glaze, Signed, 10 In. 4600.00
Vase, Light Green Matte Glaze, Stamped, 5 x 6 1/2 In. 345.00
Vase, Mauve Iridescent Glaze, Marked, 9 x 5 In. 635.00
Vase, Mustard & Lavender Iridized Glaze, Bulbous, Circular Stamp, 6 1/4 x 5 1/2 In. 575.00
Vase, Orange Glaze, Early 20th Century, 4 1/2 In. 345.00
Vase, Persian Blue Glaze Dripping, Bulbous, Gunmetal Base, Paper Label, 5 3/4 In. 920.00
Vase, Purple Luster Glaze, Green Inclusions, 6 1/4 In. 1100.00
Vase, Red, Green, Blue Metallic Glaze, Marked, 5 3/4 In. 1210.00
Vase, Turquoise Glaze, Green, Gold Iridescent Body, Hand Incised, 3 1/2 x 3 1/4 In. 518.00
Vase, Yellow, Blue, Brown Matte Glaze, 4 1/2 In. 230.00

PEWTER is a metal alloy of tin and lead. Some of the pewter made after
1840 has a slightly different composition and is called *Britannia metal*.
This later type of pewter was worked by machine; the earlier pieces
were made by hand. In the 1920s pewter came back into fashion and
pieces were often marked *Genuine Pewter*. Eighteenth-, nineteenth-,
and twentieth-century examples are listed here.

Basin, Edward Danforth, Hartford, 1786-1800, 7 15/16 In. 1450.00
Basin, Frederick Bassett, 18th Century, 6 5/8 In. 450.00
Basin, London, Love Touchmark, c.1800, 11 1/4 x 2 7/8 In. 330.00
Basin, Samuel Hamlin, 7 3/4 In. 1200.00
Basin, Samuel Pierce, Greenfield, Mass., c.1792-1830, 7 15/16 In. 895.00
Basin, T. Danforth, Touchmark, 8 x 2 In. 440.00
Basin, Thomas Badger, c.1815, 9 1/4 In. 1380.00
Basin, Thomas Danforth III, Circular Rampant Lion Touch, c.1777-1782, 8 In. 725.00
Beaker, Boardman & Hart, New York, Banded, 3 3/4 In. 875.00
Beaker, Edward Danforth, Hartford, Conn., 1700s, 5 1/4 In. 3200.00
Beaker, Footed, Handle, 3 1/2 In. 80.00
Biscuit Tin, Archibald Knox, Flower Checkerboard, Square, Liberty, 5 x 5 In. 750.00
Bowl, T. Danforth, Eagle & Star Above Letters, 2 1/2 x 10 In. 690.00
Bowl, Townsend & Compton, London, 8 In. 80.00
Box, Doll Cradle Shape, England, 4 x 4 In. 90.00
Box, Liberty & Co., Wood Liner, Golden Landscape On Lid, 3 1/2 x 6 3/4 In. 996.00
Candleholder, 2-Light, Art Deco, 8 x 5 In., Pair 40.00
Candlestick, Meriden Britannia Mfg., Gadrooned, 9 1/2 In., Pair 350.00
Candlestick, Pricket, Drip Pan, Double Stem, Tripartite Base, 22 3/4 In., Pair 690.00
Candlestick, Push-Up, Beaded, 10 In., Pair 350.00
Candlestick, Wide Capstan Base, Urn Shaped Stem, Tall Socket, 7 1/2 In. 800.00
Canteen, Rum, 2 Porringer Bowls Make Body, 18th Century 495.00
Castor Set, Glass Bottles, Triple Bull's-Eye Pattern, I. Trask, 9 1/2 In., 6 Piece 460.00
Chalice, Boardman, 5 1/4 In. 150.00
Charger, Engraved Tooled Rim, M.F.P., Engraved 1763, 12 1/4 In. 330.00
Charger, I.C. Kraut, Bishop's Hat Form, Triple Reeded Rim, 1600s, 13 1/8 In. 440.00
Charger, John Hoskyn, Single Reeded, c.1750, 18 3/4 In. 400.00
Charger, London Touchmark, Raised Tooled Rim, R.R.S., 20 In. 385.00
Charger, London, c.1800, 13 In. 440.00
Charger, Sailing Ship, Success To The United States, Scotland, c.1800, 16 1/2 In. 440.00
Charger, Stephen Maxwell, Glasgow, Scotland, c.1785, 16 5/8 In. 495.00
Charger, Thomas Badger, Boston, Eagle Touchmark, c.1775, 12 1/8 In. 300.00
Charger, Tooled Edge, C.K., 12 1/2 In. 190.00
Coffee Urn, Oriental Panel Above Spout, Vining At Top, Brass Base, 18 In. 410.00
Coffeepot, Freeman Porter, Bulbous, Dome Lid, Wood Finial, Painted, c.1850, 11 1/4 In. .. 360.00
Coffeepot, Freeman Porter, Lighthouse, Westbrook, Maine, 1835-1865, 10 3/4 In. 675.00
Coffeepot, G. Richardson, Early 19th Century, 10 1/2 In. 290.00
Coffeepot, George Richardson, Cranston, R.I., 9 1/4 In. 575.00
Coffeepot, J. Munson, Lighthouse, Tapering Sides, Scrolled Handle, 1846, 11 In. 605.00
Coffeepot, Lighthouse, Paneled Spout, Scrolled Ear Handle, Wafer Finial, 11 In. 412.00
Coffeepot, Roswell Gleason, Paneled Sides, Enameled Scroll Handle, 13 In. 165.00

Compote, Archibald Knox, Cluthra Green Glass Liner, Liberty, Tudric, Marked, 7 x 8 In. . . 3105.00
Creamer, Sellew 150.00
Cruet, Wine, Amber Glass, Handle, Pedestal, Pewter & Glass Stopper, France, 15 In. 245.00
Cup, Ball Terminal Handle, Footed, Liverpool Stamp, 1/2 Pint 60.00
Cup, Imbibing, Henry Joseph, c.1750 . . . . 750.00
Cup, S-Handle, Footed, 4 In. . . . . 70.00 to 90.00
Dish, Deep, K. Whitehaven, 11 3/4 In. 170.00
Dish, Deep, Thomas Danforth, c.1782, 13 1/4 In. 1035.00
Dish, Deep, William Billings, Providence, R.I., No. 33, 11 3/8 In. 1840.00
Dish, Hammered, Broad Rim, Engraved Wreath, Initials CMS, Touch Marks, 1709, 12 In. 395.00
Dish, Reeded, 18 1/4 In. 500.00
Dish, William Cook, 18 In. 350.00
Figurine, Character, Iron Maiden, Hinged Doors, 4 1/2 In. 145.00
Flagon, Boardman, 12 In. 1000.00
Flagon, Communion, Roswell Gleason, Dorchester, Ma., c.1840, 10 In. 1250.00
Flagon, Cylindrical, Domed Hinged Lid, S-Handle, Boardman & Co., 11 In. 1035.00
Flagon, Eben Smith, Beverly, Ma., 19th Century, 10 3/4 In. 785.00
Flagon, Engraved, Pewter Lid, Crest Finial, Applied Relief Feet, c.1890 . . . . 60.00
Flagon, Figural, Knight, Boar's Head, Shield, Cross Swords, Cherub Heads, 20 In. 605.00
Flagon, Touch Marks, Pewter Lid, Handle 115.00
Flagon, Triple-Tiered Finial, Scroll Handle, Boardman, BX Mark, 12 3/8 In. 2800.00
Flask, Bull's-Eye Decoration, Incised, 4 1/2 In. 99.00
Flask, F. Mendenhall, Embossed, Flowers, Etched Center Medallion, 5 3/4 In. 88.00
Flask, Whiskey, 4 7/8 In. 65.00
Funnel, 3 1/2 In. 30.00
Hair Receptacle, Osiris, Embossed Poppy Pods, Ceramic Lid, 1 3/4 x 5 In. 45.00
Hot Plate, England, 18th Century, 9 1/2 In., Pair 300.00
Ladle, Oval Bowl, 12 In. 60.00
Ladle, Round Bowl, 13 In. 75.00
Lamp, Bull's-Eye, Gleason, 1830-1850, 8 1/2 In. 775.00
Lamp, Capen & Molineux, Acorn Font, Fluid Burners, Snuffer Caps, N.Y., c.1850, 9 In. . . 415.00
Lamp, Paneled Canister Mounted On Wood Base, Initialed, 1812, 23 In., Pair 275.00
Measure, Baluster, Double Volute, Lidless, Pint 150.00
Measure, Domed Lid, 4-Glass Capacity 300.00
Measure, Haystack, Verification, 1/2 Pint 200.00
Measure, John Fasson, Double Volute, Flat Lid, Scroll, London, 18th Century, 1/2 Pt. 535.00
Measure Set, Cylindrical, Applied Molded Lip, Handles, Mid 19th Century, 6 Piece 172.00
Mold, Ice Cream, Dutch Boy & Girl Kissing, 6 1/2 In. 526.00
Mold, Ice Cream, Fireman, Marked S & Co. 340, 5 1/4 In. 185.00
Mold, Ice Cream, Hen On Nest, 3 1/4 In. 27.00
Mold, Ice Cream, Locomotive, 1880s, 8 x 5 In. 3037.00
Mold, Ice Cream, Sitting Rabbit, 3 Parts, 4 Hinges, 8 3/4 x 5 1/4 In. 441.00
Mold, Ice Cream, Tin, Hanging Ring, c.1900, 5 x 3 1/2 In. 195.00
Mug, Acanthus Leaf Handle, England, c.1800 . . . . 225.00
Mug, Joseph Morgan, Straight Sides, Attention Handle, Verification, 1/2 Pt. 50.00
Mug, Samuel Hamlin Jr., Eagle & Anchor Mark, 1801-1840, 5 13/16 In. 3600.00
Mug, Thomas Danforth III, Conn., Qt. 4250.00
Mug, U-Shape, Double C-Handle, Verification, Qt. 100.00
Mug, William Will, Tulip Shape, Qt. 11500.00
Mug, Yates & Birch, Tulip Shape, Verification, Pt. 110.00
Mustard Pot, 3 Legs, No Liner 20.00
Picture Frame, Silver On Pewter, Embossed Satin Pod, Jugendstil, Hallmark, 8 x 6 In. . . . 405.00
Pitcher, Boardman, Pour Spout, Shaped Handle, Hinged Cover, Touchmark, Lion, 8 In. . . . 550.00
Pitcher, France, 1800s, 6 5/8 In. 365.00
Pitcher, Owl Shape, Jade Cabochon Eyes, 8 x 6 1/2 In. 1035.00
Pitcher, Revere Style, Rufus Dunham, Westbrook, Me., c.1855, 6 In. 290.00
Plate, Ashbil Griswold, Meriden, Connecticut, c.1820, 8 In. 220.00
Plate, Boardman, Eagle, Shield, Touchmark, 10 3/4 In. 550.00
Plate, Boardman, Seated Lion, Touchmark, 9 1/4 In. 275.00
Plate, Edward Danforth, c.1786-1800, 7 7/8 In. 595.00
Plate, Edward Danforth, Middletown, Connecticut, c.1789, 8 In. 190.00
Plate, Francis Bassett I, New York City, 1715-1740, 8 1/2 In. 1450.00

Plate, Gersham Jones, Touch Marks, Hallmarks, c.1775 . . . . 550.00
Plate, Hot Water, Henry & Richard Joseph, 8 In. 100.00
Plate, Robert Palethorp Jr., Philadelphia, c.1817-1822, 7 13/16 In. 495.00
Plate, Soup, Thomas & Townsend Compton, Deep, Hammered, c.1802-1814, 8 3/8 In. . . . 240.00
Plate, T&W Willshire, Bristol, England, c.1800, 7 15/16 In., Set Of 4 . . . . 800.00
Plate, T. Danforth, Touchmark, Eagle Over TD, Phila., 7 3/4 In. 300.00
Plate, Thomas Danforth, Taunton, Massachusetts, Norwich, Connecticut, c.1750, 9 In. . . . 250.00
Plate, William Calder, Providence, 7 15/16 In. 475.00
Plate Set, Fasson & Son, London, 1784-1813, 8 15/16, 6 Piece 1150.00
Porringer, Basin Style, Old English Handle, 3 3/4 In. 325.00
Porringer, Boardman, Flat Old English Handle, c.1820, 3 1/4 In. 385.00
Porringer, Boardman, Old English Handle, Beaded Rampant Lion, c.1804, 4 5/16 In. 825.00
Porringer, Conn., 1800s, 4 5/16 In. 425.00
Porringer, Crown Handle, c.1793, 4 1/4 In. 1495.00
Porringer, Crown Handle, Polished, IJ, New England, 4 In. 220.00
Porringer, David Melville, Flower Handle, 5 In. 400.00
Porringer, Geometric Handle, 5 In. 350.00
Porringer, Gershom Jones, Providence, R.I., No. 176, 5 1/2 In. 1840.00
Porringer, Old English Handle, Embossed Bowl, New England, 3 3/8 In. 325.00
Porringer, Old English Handle, Initialed Handle EC, 19th Century, 4 5/8 In. 460.00
Porringer, Openwork Lee Type Handle, Linen Mark Interior, 5 1/2 x 7 3/4 In. 220.00
Porringer, Pierced Heart Handle, Initial R, New England, 19th Century, 3 5/16 In. 295.00
Porringer, Richard Lee, Flower Handle, 2 15/16 In. 385.00
Porringer, Samuel E. Hamlin, Old English Handle, Providence, R.I., 1801-1856, 4 1/4 In. 1125.00
Porringer, TD & SB, Crown Handle, Hartford, Ct., c.1820, 5 In. 985.00
Pot, R. Gleason, Lines Around Body, Enameled Handle & Wafer On Lid, 13 In. 330.00
Salt, Open, Trencher, Brittania Metal, George III, c.1800 . . . . 145.00
Schraubflache, 6 Sides, Smooth Finish, c.1840 . . . . .86.00 to 138.00
Spoon, Hoof Finial, Dutch, c.1650 . . . . 250.00
Sugar, Cover, Boardman, Flattened Ball Shape, Leaves, Scroll Handles, 5 3/4 In. 374.00
Tablespoon, Luther Boardman, East Haddam, Conn., 6 Piece 575.00
Tablespoon Set, William Tutin, W T & Co., Late 18th Century, 8 1/4 In., 8 Piece 375.00
Tankard, Domed Lid, Boardman, Rings Around Base, Eagle Touch, 7 3/4 In. 2860.00
Tankard, Domed Lid, Sir G. Alderson, Double Curved Handle, Side Spout, 6 In. 345.00
Tankard, Double Domed Lid, Henry Will, 6 3/4 In. 12650.00
Tankard, Drinking Scene, Falstaff Design On Lid, Germany, c.1900 . . . . 115.00
Tankard, Edward Ubley, Tulip Form, London, c.1716-1730, 7 1/2 In. 3250.00
Tankard, Henry Will, New York, 1761-1783, 6 1/4 In. 4830.00
Tankard, Richard Yates, Straight Sides, C-Scroll Handle, London, c.1772-1807, 7 3/8 In. . . 1750.00
Tankard, Spiral, Shaped Handle, Ball Thumblift, Cover, 12 1/2 In. 77.00
Tankard, Woman's Bust On Thumblift, Floral Base, Ball Feet, 12 1/2 In. 84.00
Taster, Wine, I.C. Lewis Type, 2 1/4 In. 275.00
Tea Set, Old Colony Pewter, Monogram G, Bakelite, 13 1/2 In., 4 Piece 1150.00
Teapot, A. Porter, Bulbous, Wood & Pewter Finial, Westbrook, Me., c.1835, 12 In. 518.00
Teapot, Allen Porter, Westbrook, Maine, 7 7/8 In. 495.00
Teapot, Broadhead & Co., 9 1/2 In. 35.00
Teapot, Bush & Perkins, Pear Shape, Wooden Handle, 1880s, 6 5/8 In. 862.00
Teapot, Dixon & Son, Oval, Lions Feet, Brightwork 150.00
Teapot, Freeman Porter, No. 1, Black Scroll Handle, Westbrook, Me., 7 In. 345.00
Teapot, G. Richardson, Wooden Wafer Finial Cover, Scrolled Handle, 9 1/2 In. 1330.00
Teapot, H.B. Ward & Co., Black Handle, Wallingford, Ct., 1840s, 6 In. 1553.00
Teapot, H.B. Ward & Co., Black Handle, Wallingford, Ct., 1840s, 11 In. 345.00
Teapot, Israel Trask, Engraved Bands, 11 3/4 In. 1035.00
Teapot, J. Danforth, Ear Handle, Gooseneck & Wood Knop On Finial, 7 In. 440.00
Teapot, James Dixon & Sons, Melon Ribs, Black Wooden Handle, 8 x 9 In. 210.00
Teapot, James Putman, Inverted Mold, Malden, Ma, c.1830-1855, 7 3/4 In. 540.00
Teapot, John Townsend, Queen Anne Style, Wood Handle, c.1748-1801, 6 x 8 In. 3800.00
Teapot, Lighthouse, Freeman Porter, Westbrook, Me., 1840s, 7 1/4 In. 495.00
Teapot, Morey & Ober, Truncated Lighthouse 300.00
Teapot, Roswell Gleason, Spire Finial, Scroll Handle, Dorcester, Ma., c.1850, 7 In. 288.00
Teapot, T.S. Derby, Raised Ring At Shoulder, Enameled Scroll Handle, 9 In. 55.00
Teapot, William Will, Pear Shape, Footed, 6 3/4 In. 23000.00

Tureen, Artichoke Finial, 18th Century 950.00
Tureen, Bombe Shape, Pear, Leaf Cover Finial, Scroll Handles, Leaf Feet, c.1900, 11 In. . 184.00
Urn, Kayserzinn, 3 Handles, Shoulder Leaf & Fruit Band, Art Nouveau, 20 x 9 In. 250.00
Vase, Bud, Secessionist Style, Green Glass Insert, Peacock Feathering, W.M.F., 10 In. ... 863.00
Vase, Gero, Applied Ridges & Dots, Taped Body, Flared Neck, Arts & Crafts, 5 3/4 In. ... 288.00
Vase, Tudric, 4 Handles, Molded, Patina, 3 In., Pair 242.00

PHOENIX BIRD, or Flying Phoenix, is the name given to a blue-and-
white kitchenware popular between 1900 and World War II. A variant
is known as Flying Turkey. Most of this dinnerware was made in Japan
for sale in the dime stores in America. It is still being made.

Dragon, Plate, Signed, 9 1/2 In. 65.00

PHOENIX GLASS Company was founded in 1880 in Pennsylvania. The
firm made commercial products, such as lampshades, bottles, and
glassware. Collectors today are interested in the "Sculptured Artware"
made by the company from the 1930s until the mid-1950s. Some
pieces of Phoenix glass are very similar to those made by the Consolidated Lamp and Glass Company. Phoenix made Reuben Blue, lavender, and yellow pieces. These colors were not used by Consolidated. In
1970 Phoenix became a division of Anchor Hocking, then was sold to
the Newell Group in 1987. The company is still working.

Banana Boat, Diving Girl, Satin, 14 In. 230.00
Lamp, Peacock Feather, Iridescent Blue, Signed, 1979, 20 In. 1008.00
Vase, Blackberry, Purple Wash, 18 1/2 In. 489.00
Vase, Zodiac, Milk Glass, 10 In. 230.00

PHONOGRAPHS, invented by Thomas Edison in 1877, have been made
by many firms. This category also includes other items associated
with the phonograph. Jukeboxes and Records are listed in their own
categories.

Brunswick, Upright, Horn, Oak Case, 45 x 19 In. 200.00
Columbia, Grafonola, A, Carved Griffins, 40 Discs, Mahogany Case, 50 x 23 In. 4600.00
Columbia, Graphophone, Cylinder, Carved Case, c.1898, 12 x 12 In. 690.00
Columbia, Graphophone, Cylinder, Oak Home Grand Cabinet, Brass Horn, 16 In. 6900.00
Columbia, Graphophone, Type Q, Nickel-Plated, Key Wind, Brass Horn, 5 x 8 In. 400.00
Edison, Amberola, Cylinder, Internal Horn, Oak Case, 1909 .... 375.00
Edison, Amberola, Walnut Case, No. SA, Model A, 49 In. 2185.00
Edison, Concert, 5-Inch Mandrel, Triton Motor, 57 In. Brass Horn, Oak Case, 1896 ..... 287.00
Edison, Gem, Brass Horn, Oak Case, 8 x 10 In. ....520.00 to 575.00
Edison, Gem, Model A, Brass Cylinder Horn, Key Wind, 8 x 9 1/2 In. 345.00
Edison, Home, Blue Morning Glory Horn, Adjustable Crane, 12 In. 690.00
Edison, Home, Original Gold, Red Scroll Cover, Oak Case, 30 x 15 1/2 In. ......575.00 to 630.00
Edison, Standard, Banner Front, Brass Bell Horn, 12 x 13 In. 460.00
Edison, Standard, Brass Horn, 12 x 17 In. 750.00
Edison, Standard, Brass Horn, 9 x 12 In. 260.00
Edison, Triumph, Mahogany Horn, Morning Glories Inside & Out, 14 x 18 In. 1150.00
Grafonola, Table, No. 6 Soundbox, Mahogany Case, Columbia 92.00
Gramophone, Maestrophone, Brass Horn 4705.00
Lakeside, U.S. Phonographs For Montgomery Ward, Oak Case, 7 x 13 In. 230.00
Pathe, Upright, Mahogany Case, 43 x 21 In. 230.00
RCA, Dingdong School, 45 RPM 250.00
Silvertone, Sears Roebuck, Vertical, Carved Corner, Walnut Case, 47 In. 375.00
Silvertone, Upright, Oak Case, Volume Control, Sears Roebuck, 42 x 19 In. 715.00
Sonora, Vertical Records, Mahogany Case, 45 x 20 In. 170.00
United Talking Machine Co., Table Top, Oak Case, Internal Horn, 10 x 11 1/2 In. 290.00
Victor, Royal, 7 In. Turntable, Tubular Arm, 21 In. Brass Bell Horn, Oak Case, 1902 .... 660.00
Victor 50, Portable, Stand, Oak Case, Horn In Lid, Nickel Trim, 9 x 12 In. 345.00
Victor V, Mahogany Horn & Case, Early 1900s ....2530.00 to 3920.00
Victrola, Victor, Model XIV, Mahogany, Upright, 45 x 22 1/2 In. 460.00
Victrola, Walnut, Brass Mount, Hinged Cover, Table, Disc, Germany, 7 1/2 x 13 x 12 In. . 460.00
Victrola X, Exhibition Soundbox, Mahogany Cabinet, 42 In. 345.00
Zonophone, Flat Top, Oak Case, Morning Glory Horn, 21 In. 2520.00

Label photographs with the name of the people, place, and date of the event. Do not write on the front of the picture. Do not use a ballpoint pen. Use a graphite pencil or an acid-free label.

Phonograph Needle, Gramophone, His Master's
Voice, Nipper With Phonograph, 1 1/2 In.

PHONOGRAPH NEEDLE CASES of tin are collected today by music and phonograph enthusiasts and advertising addicts. The tins are very small, about 2 inches across, and often have attractive graphic designs lithographed on the top and sides.

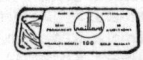

Gramophone, His Master's Voice, Nipper With Phonograph, 1 1/2 In. . . . . *Illus*	12.00
Songster, 100 Loud Tone	28.00
Songster, Soft Tone	28.00
Stars Stripes	150.00

PHOTOGRAPHY items are listed here. The first photograph was a view from a window in France taken in 1826. The commercially successful photograph started with the daguerreotype introduced in 1839. Today all sorts of photographs and photographic equipment are collected. Albums were popular in Victorian times. Cartes de visite, popular after 1854, were mounted on 2 1/2-by-4-inch cardboard. Cabinet cards were introduced in 1866. These were mounted on 4 1/4-by-6 1/2-inch cards. Stereo views are listed under Stereo Card. The cases for daguerreotypes are listed in the Gutta-Percha category. Stereoscopes are listed in their own section.

Album, Celluloid, Teddy Roosevelt, Portrait, Rough Rider Uniform	825.00
Album, Civil War, 23 Soldiers, Officers, Markens Gallery, Frederick, M.D.	2420.00
Album, Gilt Tooled Leather, Aesthetic Style, Last 19th Century, c.1917, 12 1/2 x 10 In. . .	230.00
Album, Velvet, Table Top Stand, 1885-1890	60.00
Albumen, Mardi Gras, New Orleans, S.T. Blessing, 1880s, 3 1/4 x 3 In.	230.00
Albumen, Mauvision Plantation, Amite, Louisiana, Framed, c.1880, 6 x 8 In.	58.00
Albumen, William Frank Doc Carver, Matted, Frame, 23 x 16 In.	6050.00
Ambrotype, Captain Augustin Henry Ravesies, 8th Alabama Infantry, 1/4 Plate	4315.00
Ambrotype, Confederate Drummer Boy	1360.00
Ambrotype, Gentleman Waist Up, Painted Tree Waving In Wind, 1/2 Plate	600.00
Ambrotype, Man, Playing Violin, 1/6 Plate	150.00
Ambrotype, Man, Smoking Cigar, Half Case, 1/6 Plate	55.00
Ambrotype, Mechanic, Man In Top Hat Measuring Cogs, 1/6 Plate	550.00
Ambrotype, Mims & Anderson W. Walker, Law Brigade, Gettysburg, 1/6 Plate	4125.00
Ambrotype, Seated Woman, Brass Frame, 1/4 Plate	290.00
Ambrotype, Woman, Fancy Dress, Holding Book, 3 3/4 x 3 1/2 In.	55.00
Cabinet Card, Abraham Lincoln, 1864	1210.00
Cabinet Card, Annie Oakley, Inscription, Anderson, Indiana, 1901	6325.00
Cabinet Card, Black Face Banjo Player	625.00
Cabinet Card, Boy, Express Tickets, Holding Feather Duster	65.00
Cabinet Card, Butchers	100.00
Cabinet Card, Chief Osage, Drum & Parsons	225.00
Cabinet Card, Farriers, 4 Men Drinking & Holding Horseshoe Tools, Sepia	95.00
Cabinet Card, J.N. Tubbs, Grand Haven, Michigan	75.00
Cabinet Card, Little Girl In Giant Boot, With Dolls, Van Woert, Oneonta, N.Y., 1894	39.00
Cabinet Card, Man With Bicycle	20.00

Cabinet Card, Papoose, Cradle Board, Drum & Parsons 135.00
Cabinet Card, Sitting Bull, Bismark, Dakota, 1885, 7 1/2 x 5 In. 230.00
Cabinet Card, Wild West Show Performer 300.00
Cabinet Card, William McKinley & Garret A. Hobart, Cardboard, 8 x 11 In. 30.00
Camera, Aerial, K-20, 161mm, Kodak Anastigmat Lens 90.00
Camera, AGFA Captain, PB20-JN164, Folding, Box, Instructions 40.00
Camera, Bell & Howell Foton, Cooke Amotal Lens, Original Leather Case 728.00
Camera, Bellows, Gundlach Optical Co., Leather Covered Case, 6 1/2 In. 106.00
Camera, Bellows, Rochester Optical Co., Leather Covered Case, 7 1/2 In. 225.00
Camera, Black Leatherette, Tin, Carrying Case, Japan, 1 3/4 x 2 In. 30.00
Camera, Bolex H 16, Box 446.00
Camera, Campfire Girls, Folding For Vest Pocket, Case 460.00
Camera, Canon AE-1, 35 mm, 3 Lenses, Leather Bag 175.00
Camera, Canon IIB, 50 mm, Serenar Lens, Serial No. 33301 .... 179.00
Camera, Graflex Combat Graphic 45, 127 mm, 4.7 Kodak Lens, Olive Color 420.00
Camera, Graflex Combat Graphic, 2.8 Ektar Lens, Serial No. 477249, 1950 .... 616.00
Camera, Graflex Graphic, No. 0, Zeiss Kodak Anastigmat Lens 110.00
Camera, Graflex, No. 3A, Lens Serial No. 122218 .... 80.00
Camera, Kodak Medalist, 100 mm, 3.5 Ektar Lens, Black Barrel, Leather Case 125.00
Camera, Kodak No. 2 Brownie, Price Tag Says $2.50, 1920s, 6 In. 85.00
Camera, Kodak, 3A Autographic, 110 mm, Leather Case 55.00
Camera, Kodak, 50mm Lens, Leather Body, Brown Leather Snap Case 500.00
Camera, Kodak, Bantam Special, 46 mm, Lens Serial No. 5565 .... 195.00
Camera, Kodak, Brownie, Bakelite, 1950s, 3 1/2 x 3 In. 60.00
Camera, Kodak, Chevron, For 620 Film, 75 mm, Ektar Lens, Leather Case 195.00
Camera, Kodak, No. 2 Stereo, 14 Lenses, Leather Case, 1901-1905 .... 335.00
Camera, Kodak, No. 5 Cartridge, Goerz Lens, Serial No. 150556, Lens Clear 170.00
Camera, Konica, Autoreflex T3, 50 mm, Tan Nikon Gadget Bag, Lens Clear 68.00
Camera, Leica IIIG, Chrome Finish, Eveready Case, Body Cap 800.00
Camera, Leica M3, Leicameter Mc, UV Filter, Leather Case 1200.00
Camera, Leica, IIF, Lens, Chrome, 1956 .... 1150.00
Camera, Leica, IIIG, Lens, Chrome, 1956 .... 980.00
Camera, Leica, M3, Chrome, Case, H.C. Lens, Chrome, 1955 .... 575.00
Camera, Leica, M3, Wide Angle, Viewfinder, Leather Case, Papers 330.00
Camera, Leica, Sekonic Meter, Filters, Meter Case 330.00
Camera, Minolta SR-1, 55 mm, Minolta Auto Rokkor Lens, Leather Case 89.00
Camera, Minolta X570, 55 mm, Strap, Original Black Leather Case 570.00
Camera, Nicca IIIa, Nikkor Lens, Serial No. 41589, Clear Lens, Chrome Finish 280.00
Camera, Nikon F, Wide Angle, Aluminum Case 250.00
Camera, Nikon M, Nikkor Lens, Serial No. 324755, Chrome Finish 1230.00
Camera, Nikon S3, Black, Lens 3737.00
Camera, Nikon S3, Chrome 920.00
Camera, Nikon S4, Lens, Chrome 2990.00
Camera, Photo Vanity Case, Woman's, Hinged Lid With Mirror, 1926 .... 2100.00
Camera, Polaroid 110B, Folding, 127 mm, Rodenstock Lens 335.00
Camera, Realistic Stereo, Viewer, Assorted Slides 80.00
Camera, Robot II, Carl Zeiss Biotar Lens, Leather Case 55.00
Camera, Rochester, Camera Cycle Poco No. 3, Unicum Shutter, 1890 .... 112.00
Camera, Rolleiflex Original, Carl Zeiss 4.5 Lens, Yellow Filter Lid, Leather Case 112.00
Camera, Rolleiflex Standard Tlr, Carl Zeiss 3.5 Lens, Original Lens Cap 70.00
Camera, Stereo, David White, Realist, Case 80.00
Camera, Summaron, Lens, With Caps, Chrome 115.00
Camera, Summicron, Lens, With Caps, Chrome 400.00
Camera, Tripod, Ralph J. Golsen, Mahogany, Single Lens, Extra Tripods, 1800s 260.00
Camera, Voigtlander, Brass, Attached Lens Hood, Serial No. 5804, Brass Lens 280.00
Camera, Zeiss Ikon Contax Lens Serial No. 1429282, Clear Lens 365.00
Camera, Zeiss Ikon Miroflex, Lens Serial No. 569052, Lens Clear, 9 x 12 In. 196.00
Carte De Visite, Admiral Dot, With Companion, Midget 12.00
Carte De Visite, Admiral Dot, With P.T. Barnum's World's Fair, 25 In. 12.00
Carte De Visite, Civil War Soldier, Gangrenous Feet 600.00
Carte De Visite, Colonel Charles Roone, 37th Infantry, 1865 .... 212.00
Carte De Visite, Cut Nose, Murdered 18 Women, 5 Men, Angry Face, c.1862 .... 220.00
Carte De Visite, Drummer Boy With Dog, 1860s 150.00

Carte De Visite, Early Texas Street Scene 220.00
Carte De Visite, Forest City Baseball Team, G.W. Barnes, 10 Vignettes 3600.00
Carte De Visite, General Joseph Knipe, Brady 816.00
Carte De Visite, Georgia Confederate, 2 Tintypes Of Family Women, Child 220.00
Carte De Visite, Hole In Day, Chippewa Chief 260.00
Carte De Visite, Hon. A. Wheeler, Name Printed Below, VP Rutherford B. Hayes 25.00
Carte De Visite, Hon. Schuyler Colfax, Name Printed Below, VP Of U.S. Grant 25.00
Carte De Visite, John L. Burns, Civilian Fighter, Gettysburg, Autographed 1500.00
Carte De Visite, Kitty On Cushion 90.00
Carte De Visite, Little Crow, Sioux Chief, Massacre Of 1852 .... 220.00
Carte De Visite, Little Drummer Boy 140.00
Carte De Visite, Ma-Za-Oo-Nie, Little Bird Hunter 100.00
Carte De Visite, Millie, Christine, Black Siamese Twins, Red Bordered 490.00
Carte De Visite, Mrs. Stephen A. Douglas 28.00
Carte De Visite, Officer At Ease, With Black Servant 820.00
Carte De Visite, Other Day, Rescued 62 Persons From Indian Massacre Of 1862 .... 370.00
Carte De Visite, Robert E. Lee, Autograph 4888.00
Carte De Visite, Schuyler Colfax, Name Printed Below, VP U. Grant, Trimmed 30.00
Carte De Visite, Sport, Uncle Hand's Dog 75.00
Carte De Visite, Spotted Tail, Leader Of Brule Tetons Branch Of Sioux 580.00
Carte De Visite, Tom Thumb, Wife & Child 30.00
Carte De Visite, William Henry Jackson, As Young Man 1330.00
Carte De Visite, Young Girl, White Dress, L. Wright, Providence 3.50
Carte De Visite, Young Man, Arms Folded, A & G Taylor, Manchester 5.00
Carte De Visite, Young Man, W.H. Tipton & Co., Gettysburg 5.00
Carte De Visite, Young Pedestrian, Posed With Medals 90.00
Carte De Visite, Young Woman, 3/4 Profile, W. Usherwood 3.00
Daguerreotype, 2 Women, Capes, 1/6 Plate 75.00
Daguerreotype, Black Canyon Landscape, Gunnison, 1/4 Plate 150.00
Daguerreotype, Boy, Standing, Tinted Shirt, T.S. Jube, 83 Bowery, 1/6 Plate 375.00
Daguerreotype, Buddies From Georgia, 1/6 Plate 750.00
Daguerreotype, Buddies From Pennsylvania, 1/6 Plate 300.00
Daguerreotype, Child In High Chair, McClees & Germon, 1/6 Plate 150.00
Daguerreotype, Choir, Geometric Union Case, 1/6 Plate 3850.00
Daguerreotype, Colorado Homesteaders, Man In Doorway 205.00
Daguerreotype, Covered Wagon, Next To Snowy Field, 1/6 Plate 1400.00
Daguerreotype, Fanny & Edward, Heads Are Turned, 1858, 1/9 Plate 250.00
Daguerreotype, Foppish Young Man, Lock Of Hair Hanging, Plumbe, 1/6 Plate 310.00
Daguerreotype, Helen Farrand, 1st Wife, Ashbel Farrand, Book Case, 1/6 Plate 125.00
Daguerreotype, His Ram, Standing Sideways With Head Turned 1000.00
Daguerreotype, Husband & Wife, 1/6 Plate, Pair 126.00
Daguerreotype, Jefferson Davis, 3/4 Profile, White Mount 190.00
Daguerreotype, Jenny Lind & Husband, Oval 100.00
Daguerreotype, John Kirk, With Book, Pollock Balto, 1/6 Plate 65.00
Daguerreotype, Little Girl Portrait, Gingham Dress, 1/2 Plate 250.00
Daguerreotype, Little Girl, Holding Tinted Flowers, Levi Crowley, 1850 .... 300.00
Daguerreotype, Man Portrait, Plaid Vest, 1/4 Plate 95.00
Daguerreotype, Man Portrait, Plaid Vest, 1/4 Plate, Oversized 140.00
Daguerreotype, Man, Beard, Floral Vest, 1/6 Plate 400.00
Daguerreotype, Man, Goatee, Watch Fob, M. Moses Gallery, Trenton, 1/6 Plate 125.00
Daguerreotype, Man, Holding Book, Little Girl, Half Case, 1/6 Plate 110.00
Daguerreotype, Man, In Suit, 3 x 2 1/2 In. 35.00
Daguerreotype, Man, Pointing Finger To Heaven, Temperance Pledge, 1/6 Plate 2400.00
Daguerreotype, Man, Portrait Of A Gentleman, Sitting, 1841, 1/4 Plate 850.00
Daguerreotype, Man, Strumming His Guitar, Rough Clad, Sitting 225.00
Daguerreotype, Man, Tinted Cheeks, Lawrence, 381 Bway, N.Y., Book Case, 1/6 Plate .. 100.00
Daguerreotype, Man, With White Hyacinth Vase, 1850s 385.00
Daguerreotype, Militia Officer, State Insignia, No. 16, 1/4 Plate 1100.00
Daguerreotype, Ohio Woman Photographer, Portrait Of Girl, Chair 45.00
Daguerreotype, Old Woman, Knitting, 1853, 1/6 Plate 970.00
Daguerreotype, Oliver Wendell Holmes, Standing With Apparatus 325.00
Daguerreotype, Portrait Of A Young Black Woman, Arms Crossed, 1/9 Plate 735.00
Daguerreotype, Portrait Of Woman, Sitting, Full Plate, 1855 .... 300.00

Daguerreotype, Portrait Of Woman, Sitting, Inscribed, 1853, 1/6 Plate 250.00
Daguerreotype, Portrait Of Woman, Sitting, Lace In Her Hair, 1/4 Plate 300.00
Daguerreotype, Post Mortem, Libbie & Austin Dunham, Died 2-22-1852 .... 3850.00
Daguerreotype, Rag Man, Stopped Over Carrying Paper Suitcase 200.00
Daguerreotype, Teenager, Portrait Of Young Girl, Oval, 1/6 Plate 135.00
Daguerreotype, Texas Country String Band, Men Playing Instruments 1400.00
Daguerreotype, Those Devil Eyes, Happy Mom, Possessed Daughter, Half Case 145.00
Daguerreotype, Wiggling Cat, Birch Basket, 1/6 Plate 360.00
Daguerreotype, Woman, Lace Collar & Cuffs, Earrings, 1/6 Plate 40.00
Daguerreotype, Woman, Painting, Landscape In Background, 1/6 Plate 415.00
Daguerreotype, Woman, Seated, Lace Collar & Cuffs, 1/2 Plate 200.00
Daguerreotype, Woman, Spinning, Holding A Brush, 1/6 Plate 1100.00
Daguerreotype, Woman, Tinted Cheeks, Lace Collar, Half Case, 1/6 Plate 85.00
Daguerreotype, Young Cadet, Sitting, In Ornate Chair, S.W. Colton, 1/6 Plate 1000.00
Daguerreotype, Young Girl On Sofa, Newfoundland Dog, 1/4 Plate, 3 1/2 x 5 In. 8740.00
Gelatin Silver Print, Dorothy Lamour, Hurrell, Signed, Numbered, 20 x 24 In. 925.00
Gelatin Silver Print, Douglas Fairbanks, Hurrell, Signed, Numbered, 20 x 24 In. 1060.00
Gelatin Silver Print, Gene Tierney, Hurrell, Signed, Numbered, 11 x 14 In. 660.00
Gelatin Silver Print, Harry Houdini, Portrait, 3 3/4 x 4 3/4 In. 1035.00
Gelatin Silver Print, Humphrey Bogart, Hurrell, Signed, Numbered, 20 x 24 In. 1190.00
Gelatin Silver Print, Joan Crawford, Hurrell, Signed, Numbered, 11 x 14 In. 990.00
Magic Lantern, Brass, 2 Slides, Carrying Case, Germany, 13 1/4 x 10 In. 275.00
Photograph, Arab Musicians, Mosque Courtyard, 11 x 8 1/2 In. 175.00
Photograph, Blackfoot Squaw With Papoose 225.00
Photograph, Blacksmith's Fair Exhibit, Sepia, Card Mount, 1890s, 9 1/2 x 7 1/2 In. .. 150.00
Photograph, Cavalry Encampment, Troutville, Virginia 150.00
Photograph, Chief Rabbit Morris, Holding Sacred Objects 175.00
Photograph, Czar Nicholas II, Family, Debunkine, Frame, 5 1/2 x 3 5/8 In. 259.00
Photograph, Dillinger, Bullet Riddled Body, Chicago Morgue, 1934 .... 300.00
Photograph, E. & H.T. Anthony Factory, Greenwich& King Street 220.00
Photograph, Edison, 8 x 10 In. 800.00
Photograph, Eel River, Humboldt County, California, 12 1/2 x 9 1/2 In. 225.00
Photograph, Harry Houdini, Lowered Into Water Torture Cell, 3 x 2 1/2 In. 1150.00
Photograph, Hunter Group, Sepia, 19th Century, 14 1/2 x 12 In. 375.00
Photograph, Hydraulic Mining, Virginia City, 7 x 9 In. 770.00
Photograph, Kline Circus Midway, Panoramic View, c.1900, 8 x 78 In. 665.00
Photograph, Lincoln, Formal Sitting, 1865 .... 1010.00
Photograph, Lynching Of Leo M. Frank, 1915, 10 x 8 In. 2100.00
Photograph, Major Robertson's Battery Of Horse Artillery, 1862 .... 400.00
Photograph, Marseilles Allee Du Prado, 9 3/4 x 6 1/2 In. 2500.00
Photograph, Mr. & Mrs. Harry Houdini, Restaurant, Beau Rivage, 4 x 5 In. 750.00
Photograph, Of Lake Louise, Original Oak Frame, Early 20th Century, 25 In. 50.00
Photograph, Of Rocky Mountains, Chicago, Matted, Frame, 1910, 53 x 23 In. 920.00
Photograph, Sicilian Street Kids, 6 1/2 x 8 3/4 In. 420.00
Photograph, Slaves Picking Cotton, Heavy Stock, History On Back, 8 x 10 In. 125.00
Photograph, Steam Threshing Machines & Workers, 11 3/4 x 14 In. 35.00
Photograph, Susan B. Anthony, By K. Quinlan, 1899, 19 x 24 In. 396.00
Photograph, Swimmer, Jack Spencer, Gelatin Silver Print, 13 x 13 In. 1250.00
Photograph, Tremont Street, Boston, 7 1/8 x 9 In. 75.00
Photograph, Union Soldier, Standing, Full Dress, E. Kilburn 75.00
Photogravure, German Ostrich Fern, K. Blossfeldt, 7 5/8 x 10 1/8 In. 120.00
Photogravure, Japanese Primrose, K. Blossfeldt, 7 5/8 x 10 1/8 In. 138.00
Photogravure, Lahkedup-Skokomish, E.S. Curtis, c.1912, 8 1/2 x 6 In. 530.00
Photogravure, Weeping Forsythia, K. Blossfeldt, 7 5/8 x 10 1/8 In. 130.00
Projector, Film, Univex, 1950s, 16 mm. 11.00
Projector, Keystone Radiopiction, 10 x 14 x 8 In. 35.00
Projector, Kodascope Model, Eastman Kodak, 1924, 8 mm. 20.00
Projector, Optical, Mahogany 9945.00
Projector, Spinning Disc Projects Shapes On Front, Kindled Candle 9945.00
Stevengraph, John L. Sullivan, Fighting Stance, Original Matte, Frame, 7 x 5 1/2 In. 900.00
Tintype, 2 Men Seated Wearing Hats, 1/9 Plate 400.00
Tintype, 2 Soldiers, One Standing, One Sitting, Brass Frame, 1/4 Plate 345.00
Tintype, 3 Railroad Brakemen, Holding Lanterns, 1880, 1/6 Plate 165.00

Tintype, 10 People Around Buggy, 1/6 Plate 400.00
Tintype, Armed Union Soldier, 1/4 Plate 2070.00
Tintype, Bookbinder, 2 1/4 x 3 1/4 In. 190.00
Tintype, Child, Dotted Dress, Hesler & Erwin, Pat. Feby 19, 1858, 1/4 Plate 205.00
Tintype, Civil War Enlisted Man, Seated, Resting Elbow On Table, 1/6 Plate 385.00
Tintype, Civil War Soldier In Uniform, Union Case, Gold Frame, 1/4 Plate 575.00
Tintype, Civil War Soldier, Seated, Wearing Frock Coat, Forage Cap, 1/6 Plate 250.00
Tintype, Confederate Soldier, Molded Case, 1860s, 1 3/16 x 1 In. 365.00
Tintype, Confederate, Wearing Checked Shirt 110.00
Tintype, Fireman Standing, 3 1/2 x 2 1/4 In. 140.00
Tintype, Gettysburg, 2 Civil War Soldiers Standing, 1/6 Plate, Pair 440.00
Tintype, Man Reads Paper, Black Servant 330.00
Tintype, Man, Blackface, Tambourine & Bones, Uncased 330.00
Tintype, Mill Workers, Women With Shuttles, Scissors, Yarn, 2 1/2 x 3 1/4 In. 149.00
Tintype, Musical Quartet, With Instruments, 2 1/4 x 3 1/4 In. 140.00
Tintype, Painter, Holding Paint Can & Brush, 1/2 Plate 299.00
Tintype, Pastoral, Governess, Baby Carriage, 2 Children 900.00
Tintype, Seated Woman With Dog 200.00
Tintype, Soldier In Military Coat Displaying Bars, Brass Frame, 1/6 Plate 485.00
Tintype, Stagecoach At St. Louis Hotel, Driver At Reins, 1/4 Plate 320.00

PIANO BABY is a collector's term. About 1880, the well-decorated
home had a shawl on the piano. Bisque figures of babies were designed
to help hold the shawl in place. They range in size from 6 to 18 inches.
Most of the figures were made in Germany. Reproductions are being
made. Other piano babies may be listed under manufacturers' names.

Blond Hair, Bisque, c.1910, 13 1/2 In. ....*Illus* 633.00
Boy, Girl, Lying On Back, Reaching For Toes, Gebruder Heubach, 5 1/2 In., Pair 200.00
Crawling, White Outfit, Blue Green Ribbon, Gebruder Heubach, 5 & 4 In., Pair 230.00
Crawling, White Outfit, Blue Ribbon, Sunburst Mark, Gebruder Heubach, 7 In. 175.00
Easter Bunny, Egg, Marked, Gebruder Heubach, 5 1/2 In. 460.00
Girl, Sitting, Blue Flower Dress, 10 x 6 1/2 x 7 In. 250.00
Girl, Sitting, With Hat, 8 x 4 1/2 x 6 In. 140.00
Kneeling, Covering Ears, Naked, Sunburst Mark, Gebruder Heubach, Pair 575.00
Lying On Back, Feet In Air, White Outfit, Green Ribbon, Gebruder Heubach, 7 1/2 In. ... 230.00
Lying On Back, White Outfit, Bonnet, Green Ribbon, Gebruder Heubach 115.00
Sitting, In Tub, Foot To Mouth, Sunburst Mark, Gebruder Heubach, 4 1/2 x 5 1/2 In. 1150.00
Sitting, White Outfit, Green Ribbon, Sunburst Mark, Gebruder Heubach, 7 3/4 In., Pair .. 635.00
Twins, White Outfits, Grass Base, Sunburst Mark, Gebruder Heubach, 4 1/2 x 5 In. 575.00
White Gown, Blue Ribbon, Blond Hair, 3 x 4 1/2 In. 165.00

PICKARD China Company was started in 1898 by Wilder Pickard.
Hand-painted designs were used on china purchased from other
sources. In the 1930s, the company began to make its own china wares
in Chicago, Illinois. The company now makes many types of porcelains, including a successful line of limited edition collector plates.

Bowl, Flower Garden, Hand Painted, Square, Cut Corners, E. Challinor, 8 3/4 In. 795.00
Coffee Service, Flowers, Hand Painted, Edward Challinor, Joseph Simek, c.1938, 15 Piece 500.00
Service Set, 8 Different Hand Painted Scenes, Curtis Marker, 1925-1930, 8 Piece 1995.00

**Never store an old painting on can-
vas flat and face up on a floor. The
paint may crack at the stretcher. A
dog may step on it. Store upright.**

**Never wash, or even wipe, a
watercolor.**

Piano Baby, Blond
Hair, Bisque,
c.1910, 13 1/2 In.

PICTURE FRAMES are listed in this book in the Furniture category under Frame.

PICTURES, silhouettes, and other small decorative objects framed to hang on the wall are listed here. Sandpaper pictures are black and white charcoal drawings done on a special sanded paper. Some other types of pictures are listed in the Print and Painting categories.

Album, Gouache, Punishment, Torture, Chinese, Mid 19th Century, 10 3/4 x 14 1/2 In.	2300.00
Calligraphy, Alphabet, Drawing, I.I.C. Allen, N.Y., Mid 19th Century, 16 1/2 x 13 1/4 In.	118.00
Calligraphy, Alphabet, Drawing, Initials CBR, c.1857, 21 3/4 x 17 In.	294.00
Calligraphy, Bird, Ink, Signed Palmer, Manchester, N. H., 1879, 12 x 15 In.	475.00
Calligraphy, Birds, Drawing, Watercolor, Gilt, Late 19th Century, 2 1/8 x 4 1/2 In.	59.00
Calligraphy, Fanny, American School, Ink On Paper, Mid 19th Century, 13 1/4 x 16 In.	59.00
Calligraphy, Hungarian Lancer, Ink On Paper, Mid 19th Century, 13 1/4 x 15 3/4 In.	59.00
Calligraphy, Penmanship, George D. Griswold, Ink On Paper, c.1862, 14 x 18 1/2 In.	470.00
Calligraphy, Penmanship, Nellie Wilson, Peirce College, c.1891, 13 1/3 x 9 1/2 In.	176.00
Charcoal, Seated Female Figure, Lee Woodward Zeigler, 13 3 /4 x 9 1/4 In.	60.00
Collage, Flowers, Blue Ribbon Tied, Colored Paper Cutouts, Frame, 17 x 14 In.	110.00
Cork, Japanese Scene, Frame, 9 x 17 In. *Illus*	22.00
Crayon & Charcoal, Rutherford Hayes, Bust, Howard Sanden, 1922, 25 x 18 In.	115.00
Crayon & Tempera, Uncle Sam, Pulling Tooth, Boy, Lute Pease, 1941, 15 x 18 In.	230.00
Cutwork, Memorial, Urn, Willows, Mourner, 19th Century, 7 1/2 x 9 1/2 In.	529.00
Diorama, 3-Masted Ship, French Flag, Frame, 10 1/2 x 16 1/2 In.	440.00
Drawing, 2 Women, Dresses, Bird, Flowers, 19th Century, Frame 12 x 13 In.	1045.00
Drawing, Executive Chair, Frank Lloyd Wright, H.C. Price Co., Frame, 22 x 24 In.	1265.00
Drawing, Ink, Cats, Waiting For Cat Dentist, Louis Wain, Frame, 8 x 10 1/4 In.	1320.00
Drawing, Pen & Ink, Church, Cemetery & House, Molded Frame, 9 x 11 1/2 In.	220.00
Drawing, Pencil, Fisherman On Beach, Kees Van Dongen, Holland, 4 x 6 In.	1150.00
Drawing, Pencil, Street Scene, Horse & Wagon, L. Cope, 1966, 11 x 15 In., Pair	275.00
Engraving, 4 Seasons, Colored, Glass Liner, Frame, C.R. Stock, 16 x 33 In., 4 Piece	550.00
Engraving, Battle Of Bunker Hill, June 17th, 1775, Black & White, Frame, 31 x 41 In.	190.00
Engraving, Blue Egyptian Water Lily, Robert John Thornton, c.1804, 22 5/8 x 17 7/8 In.	5100.00
Engraving, Boston, After J.W. Hill, Frame, c.1857, 24 x 34 1/2 In.	1322.00
Engraving, City Of Washington, Bird's-Eye View, After C.H. Andrews, 16 1/2 x 25 In.	865.00
Engraving, Copperplate, Butterflies Suite, Albertus Seba, 18 x 1 1/2 In., 4 Piece	3450.00
Engraving, George Washington Portrait, Gilbert Stuart, 13 1/2 x 11 In.	170.00
Engraving, Hand Colored, Tropical Fish, M.E. Bloch, 18th Century, 9 x 16 In., 6 Piece	2530.00
Engraving, Steel Plate, Hand Colored, Marmosettes, Mid 19th Century, 9 1/4 x 11 1/2 In.	259.00
Engraving, Triumph Of Liberty, J.F. Renault, c.1798, 14 1/2 x 19 5/8 In.	1440.00
Engraving, U.S. Independence, 1876 Centennial, George Stinson, Frame, 31 x 23 In.	86.00
Engraving, View Of Boston, After John Carwitham, c.1764, 12 3/8 x 18 3/8 In.	2400.00
Etching, Coming To The Lake, Signed, Carl Rungius, 8 x 11 In.	5170.00
Etching, Cottage At Top Of Hill, Jacob Van Ruysdael, Frame, 8 x 11 In.	575.00
Etching, On The Skyline, Carl Rungius, Signed, 8 x 11 In.	7150.00
Etching, Young Bull, Carl Rungius, Signed, 8 3/4 x 10 3/4 In.	4620.00
Gouache, Bronze Shield, Frame, Peter Vasseur, 1964, 16 x 13 1/2 In.	467.00
Gouache, Cattle By Stream, Frame, Carl Weber, 18 x 28 In.	660.00
Gouache On Paper, Boys Swimming In Farm Pond, Orville Carroll, Frame, 11 x 31 In.	275.00
Gouache On Paper, Female Dancer, Beatien Yazz, Frame, 10 3/4 x 8 3/4 In.	145.00
Ink & Watercolor, Paper Scroll, Ancestor Portrait, Chinese, 1800s, 42 x 21 3/4 In.	316.00

Picture, Cork, Japanese Scene, Frame, 9 x 17 In.

Spray glass cleaner on a cloth, then wipe the glass on a framed print. Do not spray the glass because the liquid may drip and stain the mat or print.

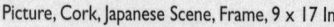

Ink & Watercolor, Paper Scroll, Crane & Flowers, Zou Yi Gui, 1600s, 68 x 18 In. 431.00
Ink & Watercolor, Paper Scroll, Landscape, Lan Ying, 1600s, 62 x 33 In. 2530.00
Ink & Watercolor, Silk & Paper Scrolls, Bird, On Tree, Chinese, 1800s, 37 In., Pair 230.00
Ink & Watercolor, Silk Scroll, Children, Peacocks, Frame, Chinese, 1800s, 15 In., Pair .. 138.00
Ink & Watercolor, Silk Scroll, Figures, Under Pine Trees, Chinese, 1800s, 18 x 11 In. 140.00
Mourning Card, Cutout, Embossed, Mrs. Nancy Holland, 1876, Frame, 12 x 14 1/2 In. .. 55.00
Needlepoint, Christ, Samarian Woman At Well, Frame, 19th Century, 25 1/2 x 20 1/4 In. . 750.00
Needlepoint, Still Life, Fruits, Flowers, 59 x 36 1/4 In. 5100.00
Needlepoint, Young Maiden, Floral Background, Art Nouveau, 20th Century, 20 x 15 In. .. 316.00
Needlepoint & Petit Point, Doll In Ethnic Costume, Brass Frame, 28 x 20 In. 18.00
Needlework, 2 Peacocks, Fruit Tree In Urn, Cherry Frame, 13 x 17 In. 60.00
Needlework, Adam & Eve, Under Tree, Serpent Around Tree, Frame, 10 3/4 x 9 1/2 In. ... 1430.00
Needlework, American Eagle, Banner, Liberty 1776, 15 x 20 In. 80.00
Needlework, Armorial, Mass. Coat Of Arms, Silk On Silk, 19th Century, 19 x 21 3/4 In. . 1880.00
Needlework, Basket Of Flowers, On Mohair, Silver & Black Frame, 19 1/4 x 18 5/8 In. ... 55.00
Needlework, Boy With Lamb, Giltwood Frame, 19th Century, 19 1/2 x 13 In. 400.00
Needlework, Cat, Petit Point Ground, Frame, Late 19th Century, 19 1/4 x 15 3/4 In. 170.00
Needlework, Country Scene, Picnickers, Silk, Watercolor, Frame, 21 1/2 x 25 1/2 In. ... 6038.00
Needlework, Deer Chase, Frame, 26 x 52 In. 58.00
Needlework, Dragon, Metallic Gold Thread, Enameled Frame, 20 1/2 x 20 3/4 In. 160.00
Needlework, Embroidered, Chain Stitch, Sheet Music, Ribbon, Red, Silk, 33 1/4 x 29 In. . 1035.00
Needlework, Embroidered, Red Poppies, Gilt Frame, c.1890, 31 x 28 3/4 In. 460.00
Needlework, Embroidered, Saints, Roundels, Velvet, 17th Century, 34 1/2 x 10 3/4 In. .. 1380.00
Needlework, Fallen Knight, In Woods, Ladies Of Court, Painted Frame, 43 x 58 In. 1430.00
Needlework, Flower Basket, Chenille, Silk, Satin Ground, Frame, 1800s, 18 x 22 In. 2160.00
Needlework, Flower Basket, Silk, Chenille, France, Frame, 1800s, 21 x 23 In. 840.00
Needlework, Flowers In Pedestal Bowl, Chenille & Silk, Frame, 1800s, 15 x 18 In. 2160.00
Needlework, Fruit Basket, George III, Satin Ground, Frame, 1800s, 16 3/4 x 20 In. 2160.00
Needlework, Henrietta Maria Ghengenise, Mrs. Rivardi's Academy, Frame, c.1803 ...... 4315.00
Needlework, Lady, Landscape, Sailing Ship, Silk, Watercolor, c.1811, 23 1/4 x 27 1/2 In. .. 1150.00
Needlework, Landscape, Rider, Horse, Frame, Early 19th Century, 28 1/2 x 24 In. 450.00
Needlework, Leaping Stags & Hounds, Formal Garden, Castle, Moat, 57 1/2 In. 4200.00
Needlework, Memorial, Woman, Cross, Bible, Silk, Chenille, c.1805, 14 x 16 In. 4000.00
Needlework, Memorial, Wool, Linen, Verse, Richmul Greenhalgh, 1839, 27 3/4 x 24 In. ... 529.00
Needlework, Mother, Child, 2 Dogs, Frame, 17 x 14 In. 90.00
Needlework, Mourning, Ink, Silk, Lady, Garden Monument, 19th Century, 7 1/2 x 6 In. .. 118.00
Needlework, Mourning, Washington's Urn, Silk Embroidery, c.1800, 12 x 14 1/2 In. 5100.00
Needlework, Panel, Love Accompanying Age & Beauty, c.1874, 37 x 27 3/4 In. 520.00
Needlework, Portrait Of Dutch Master, Late 19th Century, 32 x 22 In. 175.00
Needlework, Rachel Returning To Father's House, Frame, 1859s, 21 x 17 1/2 In. 260.00
Needlework, Round, Exotic Bird, In & Around Tree, Early 19th Century, 14 3/4 In. 230.00
Needlework, Shepherdess, Man, Playing Flute, Silk, Watercolor, 12 1/2 x 11 3/4 In. 1880.00
Needlework, Silk, Chenille, Watercolor Sky, Seated Girl, Dog, Tree, River, 16 x 15 In. 460.00
Needlework, Silk, Girl, 2 Sheep, Round, Gilt Frame, 14 3/4 In. 470.00
Needlework, Tree, Perched Bird, Ladybug, Metallic Braid Border, Frame, 12 1/2 x 13 In. . 3738.00
Needlework, Watercolor, Family, Oval Giltwood Frame, England, 19 1/4 x 17 1/2 In. 805.00
Needlework, Woman Harvesting Wheat, Late 19th Century, 16 1/2 x 23 3/4 x 20 1/2 In. ... 546.00
Needlework, Women's Shoes, Frame, 17 x 14 In., Pair 115.00
Needlework, Young Woman, Floral Background, 20 x 15 In. 316.00
Pastel, Fruit, Still Life, Frame, Chandler, 16 x 20 In. 286.00
Pastel, Lake Scene, Docked Boat, Trees, Chandler, Frame, 17 x 37 1/2 In. 110.00
Pastel, Landscape, Field Of Trees, Cloudy Day, Initial E, Frame, 9 x 11 In. 165.00
Pen, Ink & Gouache, Cityscape, Matted, Frame, Gerald Garfield, 20 x 28 In. 44.00
Pen, Ink & Gouache, Standing Boy, Matted, Frame, Schock, 20 x 9 In. 11.00
Pen & Ink, Man With Hat, Beard, T.W. Wood, Feb. 15, 1868, Frame, 12 In. 248.00
Pen & Ink, Return Of Jeptha, Fowell School, Philadelphia, c.1800, 16 x 20 In. 4800.00
Pen & Ink, Uncle Sam & Teddy Roosevelt, Matted, C. Nelan, 1901, 18 x 13 In. 460.00
Pen & Ink, Uncle Sam, Between Labor & Capital Fist, J.C. Coy, 1901, 12 x 16 In. 287.00
Pen & Ink, Uncle Sam, Budget Fallout, Matted, F.B. Opper, 1902, 22 x 16 In. 287.00
Pen & Ink, Uncle Sam, Holding Umbrella, Cartoon, Lebertin, 1926, 12 x 9 In. 120.00
Pen & Ink, Uncle Sam, Home From The War, Boots, J.M. Flagg, 1918, 16 x 13 In. 8050.00
Pen & Ink, Uncle Sam, Looking At Political Chestnuts, J.M. Flagg, 1941, 40 x 28 In. 300.00
Pen & Ink, Uncle Sam, Panama Canal, Matted, H.C. Davenport, 1902, 23 x 17 In. 460.00

Pen & Ink, Uncle Sam, Real Estate vs. Monroe Doctrine, J. C. Cory, 16 x 15 In. 287.00
Pen & Ink, Uncle Sam, Thos. B. Reed Bust, Matted, H.D. Murphy, 1902, 18 x 11 In. 230.00
Pencil, Young Woman, Hair Comb, 19th Century, 4 x 3 1/4 In. 220.00
Pinprick, Allegorical, Queen, Cavalry Soldier, Europa, 12 1/4 x 8 5/8 In. 290.00
Scherenschnitte, Cutout, 2 Deer Flanking Urn, Tree Limb Archway, Birds, 7 1/2 x 4 In. . . .   55.00
Scherenschnitte, Cutout, 2 Doves, Tulips, Vine, Leaf, Round, Sawtooth Border, 13 1/4 In. . .   165.00
Scroll On Silk, Noble Woman On Dog, Dragon Reading Scroll, Japan, 15 1/2 x 39 In. . . .   288.00
Scroll On Silk, Seated Buddha On Lotus, 2 Standing Attendants, Japan, 17 x 37 In. 460.00
Silhouette, Black Paper Backing, Gouache, Giltwood Frame, 3 1/2 x 2 1/2 In., Pair 935.00
Silhouette, C.W. Vanfleet, Green, Signed Augustus Day, Frame, 1800s, 5 x 4 In. 1980.00
Silhouette, Cut Initials, Heart, Flowers, Christian Fritz, Bucks Co., Penn., 11 x 9 1/2 In. . .   990.00
Silhouette, Full Figure, Boots & Coat, Thomas Jefferson, 6 1/8 x 4 7/8 In. 190.00
Silhouette, Full Length, Girl, Playing With Toy, Watercolor, Gilt Frame, 8 1/8 x 6 1/4 In. . .   3630.00
Silhouette, Gentleman, 19th Century, 3 5/8 x 2 5/8 In. 300.00
Silhouette, Gentleman, Inked Coat & Hair, Second Cut, Out Behind First, 6 x 5 In. 275.00
Silhouette, Gentleman, Top Hat, Cane, R.M. Wendahack, c.1836, 9 7/8 x 5 1/4 In. 3960.00
Silhouette, Girl, Long Curly Hair, Ruffled Collar, S. Houghton, Frame, 5 3/8 In 250.00
Silhouette, Group, Hollow Cut Over Marbleized Paper, c.1829, 9 3/4 x 13 3/4 In. 1200.00
Silhouette, Horse, Sulky, Man, Dog, White On Black, Frame, L. Hayden, 1870, 6 x 9 In. . .   110.00
Silhouette, Man & Woman, Black Lacquered Frame, 6 1/8 x 5 3/8 In. 250.00
Silhouette, Man & Woman, Hollow Cut, 19th Century, 4 1/4 x 3 In., Pair 1880.00
Silhouette, Man, Auguste Edouart, 1789-1861, 10 1/4 x 6 1/4 In.   120.00
Silhouette, Man, Signed William Y. Haugh, July 16th, 1834, Frame, 5 x 4 In. 1650.00
Silhouette, Woman, Bonnet, Shawl, Gold Ink Detail, Black Frame, 5 1/4 x 4 1/2 In. 220.00
Silhouette, Woman, Braided & Sausage Curled Hair Dog, Gutta Percha Case, 3 7/8 In. . . .   165.00
Silhouette, Woman, Fancy Bonnet With Flower, Black Ink, Gilt Frame, 4 3/4 x 3 3/4 In. . .   605.00
Silhouette, Woman, Hair Comb, Fancy Collar, Brass Fame, 4 1/2 x 5 1/4 In. 440.00
Silhouette, Woman, Hair Tied Up, Mrs. Mary Durnall, 1844, 6 1/2 x 5 1/2 In. 385.00
Silhouette, Young Boy, Inked Hair, Hollow Cut, Oval, Shadowbox Frame, 5 1/2 x 5 In. . . .   190.00
Silhouette, Young Girl, England, c.1860, 7 1/2 x 6 1/4 In. 575.00
Silhouette, Young Man, Gold Painted Liner Frame, 6 x 4 3/4 In. 110.00
Silhouette, Young Man, Kepi, Pen & Ink, W. Becks, Nov. 4, 1956, Frame, 6 x 4 3/4 In. . . .   220.00
Silhouette, Young Man, Wavy Hair, Frock Coat, Black Ink, Reeded Frame, 4 7/8 In. 110.00
Silkwork, Horseback, Angels, Fallen Warriors, Frame, Early 18th Century, 9 x 7 In. 260.00
Theorem, Basket Of Choice Fruit, 16 x 20 In. 3100.00
Theorem, Basket Of Fruit, Gilt Lined Frame, Late 20th Century, 12 1/2 x 15 In. 220.00
Theorem, Basket Of Fruit, Initials J.C., Gilt Frame, 20th Century, 11 x 14 In. 220.00
Theorem, Basket Of Fruit, Initials M.J.B., Mahogany Veneer Frame, 10 3/4 In. 190.00
Theorem, On Paper, Still Life, Fruit Basket, 19th Century, 18 x 15 1/4 In. 6463.00
Theorem, On Velvet, Bouquet, Bird, Early 19th Century, 19 1/2 x 15 7/8 In. 4600.00
Theorem, On Velvet, Early 19th Century, Frame, 19 1/2 x 15 7/8 In. 4600.00
Theorem, On Velvet, Folk Art Rooster, Tulip, David Ellinger, Penn., New Frame, 8 x 9 In.   1045.00
Theorem, On Velvet, Fruit Basket, 19th Century, 18 x 24 In. 805.00
Theorem, On Velvet, Fruit Bowl, Undertray On Marble Slab, 10 1/2 x 14 In. 1265.00
Theorem, On Velvet, Full Basket With Birds, David Ellinger, Frame, 19 x 24 In. 3600.00
Theorem, On Velvet, Spray Of Fruit, American School, 19th Century 805.00
Theorem, On Velvet, Vase Of Flowers, American School, 19th Century 575.00
Theorem, Roses, Verse, Lucien Courier Nash, N.H., Gilt Liner, Frame, 9 x 8 In. 385.00
Theorem, Still Life, Fruit Spilling From Basket, Watercolor, Frame, 7 x 8 In. 690.00
Theorem, Still Life, Fruit, Peaches In White Bowl, 2 Strawberries, Pastel, 14 In. 750.00
Theorem, Urn Of Flowers, Birds & Urn, R.G. Wuerthrich, Gilt Frame, 14 3/8 x 12 7/8 In.   220.00
Tinsel, Lovebirds, On Wreath Of Flowers, Shadow Box Frame, 17 1/2 x 24 In. 385.00
Wallpaper Panel, Ruined Castle, Les Vues De Provence, Walnut Frame, 76 x 36 3/4 In. . . .   1610.00
Watercolor, 3 Masted Schooner, Full Sail, Montague Dawson, 9 1/2 x 14 1/2 In. 9775.00
Watercolor, Abstract, Black, White, Gray, Emlen Etting, 14 1/4 x 20 3/4 In. 290.00
Watercolor, Bamboo Landscape With 7 Figures, Hua Yen, Chinese, 35 1/2 x 62 In. 460.00
Watercolor, Barnyard, Frame, 20th Century, 14 x 20 1/2 In. 66.00
Watercolor, Beach Houses, Robert Fabe, Frame, 15 x 18 In. 55.00
Watercolor, Bird On Branch, Fence, Rocks, Trees, Gilt Frame, 1 1/2 x 9 1/2 In. 1210.00
Watercolor, Black Lab, With Pheasant, Frame, 8 1/2 x 12 1/2 In.   440.00
Watercolor, Butterfly, Alfred Birdsey, 17 x 10 In. 60.00
Watercolor, Caricature Of French Diplomat, C.I. Pon, 18 1/2 x 10 3/8 In. 172.00
Watercolor, Child's Play, Hubert Robert, Frame, c.1780, 7 1/4 x 12 In. 920.00

Watercolor, Church Landscape, Figures, 19th Century, 7 1/2 x 9 1/2 In. 400.00
Watercolor, Daisies, White & Black Frame, 8 3/4 x 9 1/2 In. 330.00
Watercolor, Dove & Flower, David Ellinger, Folk Art Frame, 6 1/2 x 3 1/2 In. 489.00
Watercolor, Doves & Tulips, David Ellinger, Penn.10 x 14 1/2 In. 1840.00
Watercolor, Drawing, Rose & Leaves, Frame, Mid 1800s, 6 x 8 In. 137.00
Watercolor, East India Wharf, 18 1/2 x 11 3/4 In. 850.00
Watercolor, Elephant & Circus Tent, Alfred Birdsey, 25 x 19 In. 69.00
Watercolor, English Country Road, Houses, Church, A. Morris, 10 x 14 1/2 In. 130.00
Watercolor, European Mountain Lake, E.D. Lewis, 1897, 9 1/2 x 21 In. 345.00
Watercolor, Flying Dove, Holding Branch, Ellinger, Sponged Wood Frame, 7 x 7 1/2 In. . . 805.00
Watercolor, Girl, Blue Dress, Holding Doll, Gilt Frame, 8 1/8 x 6 5/8 In. 1155.00
Watercolor, Gouache, Napoleon, Memorial, 19th Century, Giltwood Frame, 7 5/8 x 6 In. . 288.00
Watercolor, Harbor Scene, A. Jankowski, 20th Century, 21 1/4 x 14 1/4 In. 230.00
Watercolor, Hill Town, Matted, Frame, 1950, 14 x 20 In. 110.00
Watercolor, House, Red Roof, Trees, A.J. Knauber, Frame, 22 1/8 x 25 5/8 In. 95.00
Watercolor, Human Hair, Memorial, Oval, 1840, 2 x 2 1/2 In. 1250.00
Watercolor, In Step With The Sycamore, Ted Maddock, 1938, 18 x 23 1/2 In. 80.00
Watercolor, In The Field Near Xochimilco, Charles Culver, 1938, 9 3/4 x 13 3/4 In. 520.00
Watercolor, Ink, Cut Paper, Peacocks & Urn, Early 19th Century, 4 x 6 1/2 In. 1880.00
Watercolor, Ink, Paper, 2 Roosters, Marreyan Rupley, Penn., c.1819, 5 5/8 x 7 1/2 In. . . . 2820.00
Watercolor, Ink, Paper, Bird Of Paradise On Branch, 19th Century, 6 3/4 x 5 1/2 In. 1528.00
Watercolor, Ink, Paper, Bird Of Paradise, Penn., 19th Century, 3 1/4 x 4 7/8 In., Pair 999.00
Watercolor, Ink, Paper, Pair Of Birds, 19th Century, 7 1/4 x 4 3/4 In. 1058.00
Watercolor, Italian Coastal Landscape With Figures, Maria Gianni, 6 x 11 1/2 In. 288.00
Watercolor, Landscape With Cottage, L. Fathers, 1915, 11 x 9 In. 215.00
Watercolor, Lord Morley's Monument, Hingham Church, John Sell, 1817, 10 x 17 In. . . . 125.00
Watercolor, Lumber Schooners At Greenpoint, Reinert, Fred, 14 1/8 In. 168.00
Watercolor, Man Chased By Alligator, 12 3/4 x 10 1/2 In. 1760.00
Watercolor, Man Rowing, 2 Galleons, J. Piesbacch '94, Gilt Frame, 30 x 23 In. 110.00
Watercolor, Morning Light, H. Gasser, Frame, 15 x 22 In. 825.00
Watercolor, Mountain, Children Playing, E. Hargitt, 1856, 9 3/8 x 14 In. 700.00
Watercolor, Navajo, Yeibechai Ceremony, Matted, Framed, 10 x 20 5/8 In. 165.00
Watercolor, Old Lobster House, Shacks, Jackson Grey Storey, Frame, 21 In. 55.00
Watercolor, Pen & Ink On Paper, Bird & Tulips In Pot, Frame, Early 1800s, 6 x 4 In. 5100.00
Watercolor, Pen & Ink On Paper, Portrait, Colonel & Mrs. Fisk, Frame, 1810, 4 x 3 In. . . 7200.00
Watercolor, Pen & Ink, Woman, Silhouette, Rufus Porter, c.1825, 4 1/2 x 3 3/8 In. 9000.00
Watercolor, Phenomena Storm Warnings, Paul Jenkins, 1978, 43 x 31 In. 1440.00
Watercolor, Purple Finches, Signed Naudi, 13 1/4 x 9 In. 170.00
Watercolor, Rainbow Trout, William J. Shaldach, 11 1/2 x 8 1/4 In. 2450.00
Watercolor, River Scene, Trees, J. Wesley Little, Frame, 18 x 20 In. 220.00
Watercolor, Rooster, Tulip, Red, David Y. Ellinger, Penn., Black Frame, 11 1/2 x 15 In. . . 1400.00
Watercolor, Seamen, Frame, Jeff Madden, 10 x 10 3/4 In. 20.00
Watercolor, Seated Female Nude, 23 1/2 x 18 1/2 In. 200.00
Watercolor, Shadows On Building & Sculptures, Miedzblocki, Frame, 20 In. 145.00
Watercolor, St. Laurence Well, John Sell, 1812, 8 7/8 x 12 In. 80.00
Watercolor, Still Life, Apples & Cantaloupe, Pittman, Hobson, 8 3/4 x 11 In. 275.00
Watercolor, Still Life, Flowers, Richard Jerzy, 44 x 31 In. 1035.00
Watercolor, Street Scene, Frame, 19th Century, 13 x 9 In. 112.00
Watercolor, Truck Loading Dock, Brass Plaque, Baker '51, Frame, 32 3/4 In. 80.00
Watercolor, Uncle Sam, Black, Saluting The Flag, J.M. Flagg, 1896, 7 1/2 x 13 In. 575.00
Watercolor, Uncle Sam, I Need You, J.M. Flagg, Frame, 16 x 28 In. 4600.00
Watercolor, Uncle Sam, Integrity-Hones-Service, J.M. Flagg, 1917, 18 x 23 In. 4310.00
Watercolor, Uncle Sam, You Want Me, J.M. Flagg, 1960, 14 x 10 In. 3740.00
Watercolor, Venetian Canal Scene, 8 1/4 x 10 7/8 In. 390.00
Watercolor, Vulcan, Frame, Julius Faysash, 21 1/2 x 25 1/2 In. 935.00
Watercolor, Winter Farm Scene, Hattie K. Brunner, Frame, 8 3/8 x 10 3/8 In. 880.00
Watercolor, Woman With Guitar, Woman With Tambourine, Signed JP, 9 x 7 In. 80.00
Watercolor, Wroxham Church, South Door, John Sell, 1815, 8 3/4 x 12 In. 55.00
Watercolor On Ivory, Charles Et Marie Adelaide De France, Delacroix, 5 x 3 1/2 In. 1090.00
Watercolor On Silk, Woman & 2 Children, Landscape, Setting Sun, Japan, 14 x 37 1/2 In. 230.00
Watercolor On Velvet, Day Lilies & Iris, Canton Bowl, Ellinger, Frame, 16 x 16 In. 2700.00
Wax, Child, Paper Flowers & Braid Of Hair, Shadow Box, Ornate Frame, 1830s 695.00
Wax, Portrait, Woman's Bust, Profile, Black Dress, Shadowbox, Gilt Frame, 14 x 13 In. . . 546.00

PIERCE, see Howard Pierce category.

PILKINGTON Tile and Pottery Company was established in 1892 in England. The company made small pottery wares, like buttons and hatpins, but soon started decorating vases purchased from other potteries. By 1903, the company had discovered an opalescent glaze that became popular on the Lancastrian pottery line. The manufacture of pottery ended in 1937. Pilkington's Tiles Ltd. has worked from 1938 to the present.

Charger, Luster, Richard Joyce, Royal Lancastrian, c.1920, 11 3/4 In.	1920.00
Ginger Jar, Fish, Seaweed, Luster, Richard Joyce, Lancastrian, 1911, 8 3/8 In.	2400.00
Vase, Bulbous, 2 Lizards On Body, Copper Brown Glaze, 4 In.	200.00
Vase, Exotic Birds & Flowers, Blue Ground, Joyce, Royal Lancastrian, 1915, 9 In.	1400.00
Vase, Huntsmen, Bored, Deer, Wolf, Lancastrian, Luster, Richard Joyce, c.1913, 7 1/2 In.	2700.00
Vase, Luster, Trees, Inscription, William S. Mycock, Royal Lancastrian, c.1913, 8 1/8 In.	2040.00
Vase, Stylized Flowers & Leaves, Red Ground, 2 x 2 In.	300.00
Vase, Tapered, Blue Flowers, Green Leaves, High Glaze, Multi-Streaked Body, 4 In.	240.00

PINCUSHION DOLLS are not really dolls and often were not even pincushions. Some collectors use the term *half-doll*. The top half of each doll was made of porcelain. The edge of the half-doll was made with several small holes for thread, and the doll was stitched to a fabric body with a voluminous skirt. The finished figure was used to cover a hot pot of tea, powder box, pincushion, whisk broom, or lamp. They were made in sizes from less than an inch to over 9 inches high. Most date from the early 1900s to the 1950s. Collectors often find just the porcelain doll without the fabric skirt.

Blue Gown, Brunet Finger Curls, 5 In.	32.00
Hands On Heart, Gray Rococo Style Hair, Germany, c.1925, 4 1/4 In.	28.00
Madame Pompadour, 5 1/2 In.	45.00
Marlene Dietrich, Wax, Flirty Pose, Rooted Blond Hair, c.1930, 16 In.	1600.00
Pink & White Fan, Blond, Blue Dress, Left Arm Away From Body, 5 1/2 In.	115.00
Satin Dress, Chalkware	45.00

PINK SLAG pieces are listed in this book in the Slag Glass category.

PIPES have been popular since tobacco was introduced to Europe by Sir Walter Raleigh. Carved wooden, porcelain, ivory, and glass pipes may be listed here. Meerschaum pipes are listed under Meerschaum.

Bellows Form, Oak, England, 18th Century, 5 1/4 In.	250.00
Box, Hanging, Dovetailed Drawer, Brass Ring Pull, 16 3/4 x 6 1/2 In.	440.00
Box, Oak, Incised Fan & Pinwheel	4095.00
Briar, Bulging Eyed Screaming Black Man, Signed, 5 1/2 In.	371.00
Clay, Tavern, Gouda, Holland, PIJP, 16 In.	45.00
Creamware, Briar, Brown Chevron Reserves, Black Ground, Continental, c.1770, 5 In.	881.00
Creamware, Briar, Brown Spiral Stripes, Continental, c.1770, 4 1/8 In.	881.00
Hardwood Mount, Porcelain Bowl, Lady's Portrait, 19th Century, 13 1/2 In.	400.00
Head Of European Sailor, Africa, 8 3/4 In.	115.00
Porcelain, Student, Remembering My University Time In Ilmenau 1918-1919, 3 3/4 In.	137.00
Tongs, Wrought Iron, Ember Tongs, Bowl Scrape, Tobacco Tamp, Pair	1610.00
With Box, Inro, Head Is Box Cover, Man Stretching & Yawning, Japan, 4 x 7 3/4 In.	75.00
Wood, Bowl & Stem Resembles Revolver, 5 In.	95.00
Wood, Carved, Silver Decorated, Hinged Cover, Switzerland	65.00
Wood, Long Nosed Man, Ponytail, Tall Hat, Riding Donkey, Carved, 5 In.	55.00

PISGAH FOREST pottery was made in North Carolina beginning in 1926. The pottery was started by Walter B. Stephen, who had been making pottery in that location since 1914. The pottery continued in operation after his death in 1961. The most famous kinds of Pisgah Forest ware are the cameo type with designs made of raised glaze and the turquoise crackle glaze wares.

Bowl, Chinese Shape, Crackled Blue To Aubergine Glaze, c.1941, 4 1/4 x 6 In.	193.00
Jar, Covered Wagon, Blue, Crackle Glaze, 1938, 6 In.	715.00

Match Safe, Figure At Spinning Wheel, Green, Red Matte Glaze, 3 In. 489.00
Pitcher, Covered Wagon, W.B. Stephen, 5 1/2 In. 440.00
Pitcher, Sea Green Gloss Feldspathic Glaze, Tapered Handle, 8 In. 193.00
Plate, Couple On Horseback With Dog, 1941, 8 3/4 In. 489.00
Urn, Turquoise Semimatte Glaze, c.1929, 7 x 6 In. 104.00
Vase, Baluster Shape, Aubergine Glaze, Crackled Blue Glaze, c.1941, 8 1/4 In. 220.00
Vase, Baluster Shape, Ivory Crystals, Green, Ivory Field, 9 1/2 In. 220.00
Vase, Bulbous, Green Semimatte Exterior, Pink Interior, c.1939, 5 x 6 In. 92.00
Vase, Chinese Shape, Runny Brown Glaze, c.1935, 8 1/2 In. 220.00
Vase, Flared, Swollen Shape, Purple Glaze, Stephen, 9 In. 690.00
Vase, Gray & Ivory Crystalline Glaze, Pink Interior, 6 1/4 x 4 1/2 In. 316.00
Vase, Green, Silver Glaze, Crystals, Embossed Mark, 5 1/2 In. 345.00
Vase, Handles, Indian On Horseback, Buffalo, 3 1/4 In. 518.00
Vase, Indian On Horseback Hunting Bison, Signed, Stephen, 1930, 18 1/2 In. 5750.00
Vase, Ivory & Celadon Crystalline Glaze, Pink Interior, 5 1/4 x 3 1/2 In. 345.00
Vase, Ivory & Umber Crystalline Glaze, Pink Interior, 1950, 7 1/2 x 4 3/4 In. 374.00
Vase, Multitoned Blue, Green Glaze, 1930, 7 3/4 In. 468.00
Vase, Multitoned Brown Glaze, Crystals, Raised Mark, 9 In. 299.00
Vase, People Around Christmas Tree, Red, Blue, Green Glaze, Signed, 8 In. 1840.00
Vase, Persian Blue Crackled Glaze, Raised Mark, 1940, 7 x 4 In. 104.00
Vase, Purple Glaze, Signed, Stephen, 8 3/4 In. 460.00
Vase, Purple, Blue Glaze, 1938, 9 1/2 In. 523.00
Vase, Purple, Blue High Glaze, 6 In., Pair 173.00
Vase, Red, Green Glaze, 3 Handles, 1930, 17 In. 1725.00
Vase, Runny Blue Glaze, Green Field, Pink Interior, Oval, c.1950, 8 In. 468.00
Vase, Squat, Turquoise To Eggplant Crackled Glaze, 3 3/4 x 5 In. 46.00
Vase, White Crystals, Yellow, Blue, Stephen Cameo Long Pine Mark, c.1953, 8 In. 440.00
Vase, White Figures, Green Body, Signed, 13 1/2 In. 1495.00
Vase, Yellow, Gold Brown Ground, Green, Silver Crystals, 1933, 7 In. 4313.00

PLANTERS PEANUTS memorabilia is collected. Planters Nut and
Chocolate Company was started in Wilkes-Barre, Pennsylvania, in
1906. The Mr. Peanut figure was adopted as a trademark in 1916.
National advertising for Planters Peanuts started in 1918. The company was acquired by Standard Brands, Inc., in 1961. Standard Brands
merged with Nabisco in 1981. Some of the Mr. Peanut jars and other
memorabilia have been reproduced and, of course, new items are being
made.

Bank, Hat Reads Mr. Peanut, Turn Hat To Open, 1950s, 8 1/2 x 3 1/2 In. 55.00
Bank, Mr. Peanut, Cast Iron, Planters Peanut Company, 1970s 95.00
Bank, Planters Peanut, Mr. Peanut On Hat, 1950s, 8 x 3 1/2 In. 55.00
Blotter, Mr. Peanut, With Truck, 1930 .... 10.00
Box, Held 5 Cent Sugared Peanut Bags, 1920s, 2 Piece 633.00
Box, Mr. Peanut, Held 24 Packages, Made In Canada, 8 x 6 x 4 1/2 In. 2530.00
Box, Waxy Cardboard, 1920s, 8 x 6 x 4 1/2 In. 2530.00
Clock, Battery Operated, 1970s, 17 1/4 x 12 1/2 In. 450.00
Costume, Mr. Peanut, Figural, Hard Plastic, 21 x 47 In. ....248.00 to 600.00
Doll, Mr. Peanut, Wooden, Jointed, Schoenhut, 8 1/2 In. 195.00
Figure, Mr. Peanut, Cane & Top Hat, Wooden, Jointed, Schoenhut, 8 1/2 In. 287.00
Jar, Cover, Glass, Counter Display, Box, 1971 .... 125.00
Marble Bag, Mr. Peanut, Picture, Contents, 1950s 7.00
Pin, Mr. Peanut, Planters Peanut Co., Wooden, 1 7/8 x 7/8 In. 66.00
Scale, Figural, Mr. Peanut, 1960s-1970s, 44 In. 3165.00
Sign, Trolley Car, 1920s, 11 x 21 In. 1725.00
Tin, Peanut Butter, Mr. Peanut, Girl & Boy Eating Sandwiches, 2 Lb. 440.00
Toy, Walker, Windup, Plastic, 8 1/2 In. 375.00

PLASTIC objects of all types are being collected. Some pieces are listed
in other categories; celluloid is listed in its own category.

Creamer, Florence Pattern, Melamine, Prolon .... *Illus*   5.00
Drinking Straw, Smiling Cowboy, Red, 1950s, 2 3/8 x 2 3/4 .... 14.00
Necklace, Interchangeable Segments With Letters, Pink, Yellow, Green, 1960 ...... *Illus* 10.00
Plate, Daisy Decal, Melmac, Oneida, 7 In. .... *Illus*   8.00

Plastic, Creamer, Florence
Pattern, Melamine, Prolon

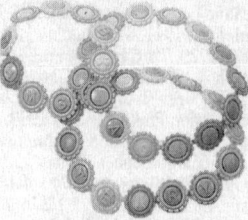

Plastic, Necklace, Interchangeable
Segments With Letters, Pink,
Yellow, Green, 1960

Plastic, Plate, Daisy Decal,
Melmac, Oneida, 7 In.

Plastic, Plate, Fruit In Basket, Decanter,
Melmac, Texas Ware, 10 In.

Plastic, Tray, Gold Threads, Butterfly Decals,
Fiber Glass Strands, 9 x 14 In.

Plate, Fruit In Basket, Decanter, Melmac, Texas Ware, 10 In. .... *Illus*	8.00
Tray, Gold Threads, Butterfly Decals, Fiberglass Strands, 9 x 14 In. .... *Illus*	8.00

PLATED AMBERINA was patented June 15, 1886, by Joseph Locke and made by the New England Glass Company. It is similar in color to amberina, but is characterized by a cream colored or chartreuse lining (never white) and small ridges or ribs on the outside.

Tumbler, Melon Ribbed, 3 3/4 In. 2300.00

PLIQUE-A-JOUR is an enameling process. The enamel is laid between thin raised metal lines and heated. The finished piece has transparent enamel held between the thin metal wires. It is different from cloisonne because it is translucent.

Bowl, Translucent, Red Flowers, Leaves, Rosettes, Russia, 2 1/4 x 5 In. 1035.00
Cigarette Case, Hinged Cover, Flowering Branches, Silver Edges, 3 1/4 In. 345.00
Pin, Blue Gray Enamel, Flowering Vine Design, Sterling Silver, 1910, 2 2/3 In. 862.00

POLITICAL memorabilia of all types, from buttons to banners, is collected. Items related to presidential candidates are the most popular, but collectors also search for material related to state and local offices. Memorabilia related to social causes, minor political parties, and protest movements are also included here. Many reproductions have been made. A jugate is a button with photographs of both the presidential and vice presidential candidates. In this list a button is round, usually with a straight pin or metal tab to secure it to a shirt. A pin is brass, often figural, sometimes attached to a ribbon.

Antenna Attachment, Goldwater, Miller, Plastic, White, Red & Blue Letters, 4 x 9 1/2 In.   17.00
Ashtray, Nixon, Smoked Glass, Square, 1960 .... 17.00
Ashtray, Reagan Republican Dinner, Metal, Huntington, W.V., May 29, 1975 .... 22.00
Ashtray, Willkie, Red, Blue, Milk Glass 25.00
Badge, Ben Butler, Spoon Hanger At Top, 1 1/8 In. 1000.00

Badge, Delegate Bar, Flag Ribbon, Celluloid Uncle Sam & Lady Liberty, 1906, 2 x 6 In. . .   30.00
Badge, Democratic National Convention, 1924 . . . .   235.00
Badge, Harrison & Morton, 1888 . . . .   47.00
Badge, Theodore Roosevelt, Bull Moose, Sepia, Ribbon, Eagle Top, 2 1/4 In. 2640.00
Badge, Washington Inaugural Centennial, Medal Suspended From Pin Bar, 1889 . . . .   125.00
Badge, Willkie For President, White, Blue Letters, Celluloid, 6 In. 218.00
Badge, Win With Wilson, Button Center, 1 1/8 In. 72.00
Bag, I Like Ike, 2 Elephants Facing Each Other, Black & White, Fabric 55.00
Bag, Sports, Jerry Ford Invitational 1984, Golf Tournament, Vinyl, 10 x 21 In. 50.00
Bandanna, Harrison, Tippecanoe & Morton Too, Flag, Silk, 1888, 20 x 20 In. 132.00
Bandanna, Theodore Roosevelt, Moose 135.00
Bandanna, Wendell Willkie, Stars & Stripes, Red, White & Blue, Square, 1940, 22 In. 108.00
Bank, Dime, Woodrow Wilson, Celluloid Buttons Each Side, 2 1/8 In. 1430.00
Bank, JFK Half Dollar, Embossed, Tin, 1960s, 2 1/2 x 2 x 5 In. 15.00
Bank, Mechanical, T. Roosevelt, Game Hunting, Penny Makes Bear Pop Up, 10 In. 1815.00
Bank, Roosevelt, Rough Rider Outfit, Cast Iron 250.00
Banner, Blaine, Logan, Cloth, 1884, 40 x 25 In. 455.00
Banner, Douglas MacArthur Picture, Rayon, 11 1/2 x 17 1/2 In. 10.00
Banner, For Everybody's Needs, Uncle Sam, NRA, 1935, 11 x 30 In. 80.00
Banner, George Washington Campaign, Oil On Canvas, 71 1/2 x 109 1/2 In. 4000.00
Banner, Willkie, Rayon, Metal Hanger, Red, White & Blue, 5 x 6 In. 32.00
Belt Buckle, Harding, Coolidge, Sepia 1999.00
Book, Cartoon, Jerry Brown, 1978, 2 x 11 In. 15.00
Book, The Photographs Of Abraham Lincoln, 1944, 6 1/2 x 9 1/2 In., 72 Pages 95.00
Book, William McKinley, Hardbound, 1902 . . . .   30.00
Booklet, Nixon, Red, White & Blue, 1952, 6 x 9 In. 12.50
Booklet, Robert F. Kennedy For Senator 10.00
Booklet, You Will Decide, Time To Change Horses, Wendell Willkie vs. FDR 57.00
Bookmark, FDR, Aluminum, 2 In. 28.00
Bottle, Roosevelt, Teddy Club Label, Amber Glass, 11 1/2 In. 270.00
Bottle, Whiskey, Grant, c.1890 . . . .   85.00
Bottle Stopper, Charles DeGaulle, Cork, 4 In. 50.00
Bottle Stopper, Jackie Kennedy, Walnut Head, 5 In. 95.00
Bottle Stopper, JFK, 3-D, Wood, Painted Cork, 1962, 3 1/2 In. 48.00
Bottle Stopper, Truman, 4 1/4 In. 85.00
Bowtie, Eisenhower, Ike, '52, Cloth, Clip On 80.00
Box, Cigar, McKinley, Hobart, 8 In. 270.00
Box, Garfield Tea, Laxative & Diuretic, Hewlett, N.Y., 3 3/4 In. . . . . *Illus*   50.00
Brochure, RFK 1968 Campaign, 8 x 10 In., 4 Pages 7.00
Brochure, Yes The People Like Dick Nixon, 8 1/2 x 11 In., 4 Pages 7.00
Brooch, James Madison, Portrait, Glass, 1 1/2 x 1 1/4 In. 1020.00
Buckle, Stephen A. Douglas, Ferrotype 825.00
Bumper Sticker, Another Veteran For Kennedy & Johnson, 1960 . . . .   20.00
Bumper Sticker, J.P. Stevens Boycott, 1977, 3 x 12 In. 12.00
Bumper Sticker, Mike Dukakis For President, 1988, 4 x 15 In. 20.00
Bumper Sticker, Wallace, Red, White & Blue 7.00
Bust, Benjamin Harrison, Frosted Clear Glass On Black Pedestal, 16 1/4 In. 560.00

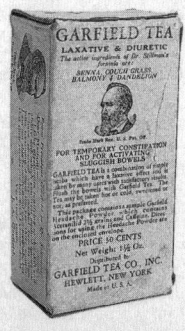

Political, Box, Garfield Tea,
Laxative & Diuretic,
Hewlett, N.Y., 3 3/4 In.

Political, Button,
Billionaires For Bush
(Or Gore), 2 3/8 In.

Bust, Franklin D. Roosevelt, Beer, Prosperity, Painted, Plaster, 14 1/2 In. 1100.00
Bust, General Douglas MacArthur, Gold, Name On Base, Chalkware, 1940s, 11 In. 25.00
Bust, McKinley, Plaster, Black Paint, Turned Wooden Base, 18 1/2 In. 55.00
Bust, President John F. Kennedy, Marble Finish, 1962, 3 x 5 In. 24.00
Button, 1968 Hopefuls, 8 Primary Candidates, 3 1/2 In. 28.00
Button, Adlai & Estes, The Bestest, Winning Team, 4-Leaf Clover, Celluloid, 1956, 3 In. . 634.00
Button, Al Smith, Joe Robinson, Celluloid, 1928, 1 In. 255.00
Button, Alf Landon, Frank Knox, Jugate, In Sunflower, Celluloid, 1936, 1 1/4 In. 3630.00
Button, Alfred E. Smith For President, Picture, 4 In. 15.00
Button, Alton Parker, Henry Davis, Jugate, 1904, 1 1/4 In. 649.00
Button, Archie For President, Black On Yellow, Celluloid, 1972 .... 13.00
Button, Barry Goldwater For Nixon & Lodge, 1964, 1 3/4 In. 255.00
Button, Billionaires For Bush (Or Gore), 2 3/8 In. ....*Illus* 5.00
Button, Black Power, Black, Red Lettering, Late 1960s, 3 1/2 In. 12.00
Button, Bob LaFollette, Teapot Dome, 1920s, 1 In. 4659.00
Button, Boycott Chiquita, Red Line Through Banana, Celluloid, 1 1/2 In. 7.00
Button, Brothers & Sisters Join Our Struggle, United Farm Workers, 1 1/2 In. 26.00
Button, Bryan, A.E. Lee For Governor, Celluloid, 1 1/4 In. 810.00
Button, Bryan, Bennett, West Virginia, 1 1/2 In. 845.00
Button, Bryan, Commoner, 1 1/4 In. 376.00
Button, Bryan, I Gave My Dollar Did You, 1 1/4 In. 106.00
Button, Bull Moose, 1912, 3/4 In. 640.00
Button, Bush, Quayle, Elephant Ears, 1988, 2 1/4 In. 80.00
Button, Carter, Mondale, I Am For Alabama COPE, 2 1/8 In. 696.00
Button, Carter, Mondale, The People's Choice, Caricature, 1976, 2 1/4 In. 339.00
Button, Chavez Si, Teamsters No, Black On Neon Green, Celluloid, 1 1/2 In. 6.00
Button, Cleveland, Shell Frame, Horseshoe Form, 3/4 In. 210.00
Button, Cleveland, Stevenson, Jugate, Tin 35.00
Button, Clinton For President, Picture, Chelsea, Vote For My Daddy, Celluloid, 2 1/4 In. . 385.00
Button, Clinton, Gore, Sign Language, Celluloid, 1996, 2 1/4 In. 98.00
Button, Clothing, Bear & Big Stick, 7/8 In. 30.00
Button, Clothing, Taft, Billy Possum, Gold, 1 1/4 In. 50.00
Button, Clothing, U.S. Grant, Ferrotype, 1 1/8 In. 300.00
Button, Commercial Travelers For Taft, Picture In Suitcase, Celluloid, 1 1/4 In. 1300.00
Button, Cox, Peace Progress Prosperity, 3/4 In., 1920 .... 405.00
Button, Cox-Roosevelt Club, 1 In. 23656.00
Button, D.D. Eisenhower, Railroad Employees Support, 1 1/4 In. 430.00
Button, D.D. Eisenhower, Sign Language, Red, White & Blue, 1/4 In. 339.00
Button, Davis & Bryan, Purple, Celluloid, 7/8 In. 225.00
Button, Deadheads For Dukakis, Skull, Lightning Bolt, Celluloid, 2 1/4 In. 404.00
Button, Draft Eisenhower For President League, Celluloid, 3/4 In. 158.00
Button, Dwight Eisenhower, Happy Birthday Mr. President, Picture, Oval, 7 3/4 In. 116.00
Button, Dwight Eisenhower, Richard Nixon, Red, White, Blue & Black, 3 1/2 In. 275.00
Button, Eisenhower For President, 1956, 9 In. 450.00
Button, Eisenhower, Nixon, Portrait, 3 1/4 In. 399.00
Button, Eisenhower, Nixon, Red, White & Blue, 1956, 9 In. 555.00
Button, End Mass Murder In Vietnam, N.Y., S.F., Psychedelic Design, 1 1/2 In. 42.00
Button, Eugene Debs, Benjamin Hanford, Jugate, Socialist Torch, 1908, 1 1/4 In. 2662.00
Button, FDR, No Third Term, Uncle Sam Center, 1939, 3/4 In. 30.00
Button, FDR, Red, White & Blue, Tues. Nov. 5, 1940 Hanger, Paper On Linen, 3 1/2 In. . 54.00
Button, FDR, You Bet I'm With You, Inauguration, 1933 .... 371.00
Button, Fight Discrimination, Defend Bill Of Rights, Labor Party Emblem, 1948, 1 In. ... 121.00
Button, Ford, Caricature, 1 1/2 In. 1847.00
Button, Ford, Dole, America's Choice, Caricature, 1976, 2 1/4 In. 255.00
Button, Franklin Roosevelt, Wyoming Bucking Cowboy, 2 3/4 In. 670.00
Button, George McGovern For President, 2 Doves Against Flag, Celluloid, 3 In. 483.00
Button, George McGovern For President, Portrait On Flag, 3 In. 92.00
Button, George Washington Inaugural, March 4th, 1789, Brass, Reattached Shank 1100.00
Button, Gerald Ford, Boxing Elephant, Black & Green, Celluloid, 2 1/2 In. 363.00
Button, Get Out Of Vietnam, International Days Of Protect, Oval, 1 1/2 x 2 In. 295.00
Button, Goldwater Vote In '64, Portrait, 3 1/4 In. 101.00
Button, Goldwater, Gold, Black, Red, Black & White Photo, Easel Back, 6 In. 18.00
Button, Harding, Coolidge, Penrose, Trigate, Ribbon, Celluloid, 1920, 1 1/4 In. 5978.00

Button, Harding, Smiling, 1 1/2 In. 754.00
Button, Harding, Smiling, 1920-1924, 1 1/4 In. 454.00
Button, Harry S. Truman For Judge, Sepia, 7/8 In. 3300.00
Button, Harry S. Truman For President, Portrait, Donkeys, 3 1/4 In. 152.00
Button, Harry Truman, Give 'Em Hell, Minnesota, Gold & Purple, 1 1/4 In. 1393.00
Button, Harry Truman, Song Of The Time, Blue & White, 1948, 3 1/2 In. 1906.00
Button, Hawaii For RFK, Celluloid, 1 1/4 In. 1904.00
Button, Henry A. Wallace For President, Portrait, 3 1/4 In. 259.00
Button, Herbert Hoover, Cooper For Governor, 7/8 In. 40.00
Button, HHH, We're For Him, Wobble Eyes, 3 1/2 In. 103.00
Button, Huey Long For President, Black & White, 1934 .... 1599.00
Button, Hughes & Fairbanks, Jugate, 1 In. 68.00
Button, I Have A Dream, Dr. Martin Luther King, 3 1/2 In. 17.00
Button, I Like Bobby Kennedy, Yeah, Yeah, Yeah, 3 1/2 In. 375.00
Button, I'm For Harding, Picture, 3/4 In. 35.00
Button, I'm For Harry Truman, Picture, Celluloid, 1 3/4 In. 3025.00
Button, Ike, Nixon, Lodge, Your First Team Committee, Oval, 2 3/4 In. 1090.00
Button, It's LBJ All The Way, Portrait, Red, White & Blue, Celluloid, 4 In. 12.00
Button, James Cox, Peace, Progress, Prosperity, 1920, 1 1/4 In. 848.00
Button, Jesse Jackson For President, Win Jesse Win, Celluloid, Photo, 1992, 3 In. 20.00
Button, JFK, As He Leads Us Safely Through The Perilous Atomic Age, 1 3/4 In. 1301.00
Button, Jimmy Carter, Walter Mondale, Sample Button By Philips Co., 4 In. 1961.00
Button, Jimmy Hoffa For President, Teamsters, 1950s, 3 1/2 In. 450.00
Button, Joe & I Want Willkie, Joe Lewis Picture 605.00
Button, John Davis For President, Black & White, 1924, 1 1/4 In. 990.00
Button, John W. Davis For Congress, White Ground, Celluloid, 1 1/4 In. 840.00
Button, John W. Davis For President, Black & White, Celluloid, 1 1/4 In. 487.00
Button, John W. Davis, Portrait, 1924, 1 1/4 In. 2795.00
Button, Johnson, Going Up With Lyndon, 2 1/2 In. 466.00
Button, Johnson, Showing Off Vietnam Shape Scar, Cartoon Illustration, Levine, 6 In. 146.00
Button, Keep Dick On The Job, Black & White Photo Inset, 1960s 58.00
Button, Keep The Buses Rolling, Desegregate Boston Schools, Celluloid, 1 3/4 In. 11.00
Button, Landon & Knox, Sunflower Edge, 1936, 1 In. 976.00
Button, Landon Knox Out Roosevelt, Blue, White Letters, Celluloid, 7/8 In. 733.00
Button, LBJ's For LBJ, Red, White & Blue Hearts, 3 In. 17.00
Button, Let Well Enough Alone, Roosevelt, Fairbanks, Dinner Bucket, 1904, 1 1/4 In. 1460.00
Button, March On Boston, Desegregate Schools, Stop Racist Attacks, April 24, 2 1/4 In. .. 20.00
Button, March On Washington, End War In Vietnam, April 17, 1965, 1 1/2 In. 42.00
Button, McGovern, Black & White, Photo, 3 1/2 In. 5.00
Button, McGovern, Skinny Cat, 2 1/4 In. 154.00
Button, McKinley, Do You Smoke, Celluloid, 2 1/8 In. 3634.00
Button, McKinley, Hobart, Jugate, National Wheelman's Club, 1 1/4 In. 293.00
Button, McKinley, Patriotism, Prosperity, Color, Celluloid, 2 1/8 In. 997.00
Button, McKinley, T. Roosevelt, Jugate, Rough Rider Horse, 1 3/4 In. 872.00
Button, Minnesota Truman Club, 1948-1960, 2 1/4 In. 320.00
Button, Minnesota Women For Humphrey, Black, Pink, White, Celluloid, 1954, 2 1/4 In. .. 175.00
Button, MLK, I Have A Dream, Let Freedom Ring, Picture, White On Black, 1 3/4 In. .. 17.00
Button, NASCAR For Bush, Quayle '88, Celluloid, 4 In. 333.00
Button, Nixon, Man Of Steel, 1968, 3 In. 270.00
Button, Parker, Davis, Uncle Sam's White Elephant, 1904, 1 1/4 In. 619.00
Button, Peace In Vietnam, March On Washington, Bring GIs Home, Celluloid, 1 3/4 In. .. 459.00
Button, Phooey On Dewey, 1948, 1 1/4 In. 40.00
Button, Re-Elect Carter-Mondale, Portraits Over Stars, 3 1/4 In. 52.00
Button, Re-Elect Humphrey, P.A.C. 1954, Celluloid, 1 1/4 In. 589.00
Button, Reagan, I Shot J.R., I Despise Bleeding Heart Liberals, Cowboy Portrait, 4 In. .. 168.00
Button, Reagan, Made In Detroit, 1 3/4 In. 441.00
Button, Remember Brownsville, 1906, Discharged Without Honor, 1972, 1 1/4 In. 349.00
Button, Ronald Reagan, Bayou State, Celluloid, 1980, 4 In. 800.00
Button, Roosevelt, Garner, Repeal & Prosperity, Celluloid, 1 1/4 In. 2475.00
Button, Roosevelt, Prosperity, 1932, 7/8 In. 450.00
Button, Roosevelt, Stand Pat, Card Hand, 1 1/4 In. 339.00
Button, Roosevelt, Truman, Picture, 1 1/2 In. 518.00
Button, Roosevelt, Uncle Sam, Welcome, Celluloid, 2 In. 2297.00

Button, Save Our Sons, Stop The War, Blue, Green Flower Silhouette, 1 1/2 In. 39.00
Button, Shirley Chisholm For President, 3/4 In. 3.00
Button, Shoeworkers For Kennedy, Picture, 3 1/2 In. 440.00
Button, Smith, Robinson, Celluloid, Jugate, 7/8 In. 207.00
Button, Socialist Party, Workers Of The World Unite, Hands Shaking, 1904, 3/4 In. 28.00
Button, Stassen Stop Harassin', Orange, Black Letters, Celluloid, 1956, 6 In. 66.00
Button, Steelworkers For Mondale, Ferraro, 3 1/2 In. 198.00
Button, Stevenson, America Needs, For President, 3/4 In. 10.00
Button, Stevenson, Kefauver, Celluloid, 1 In. 20.00
Button, Stevenson, Sparkman, Portrait, 3 1/4 In. 61.00
Button, T. Roosevelt's Return From Africa, Welcome, Uncle Sam, Sunrise, 1 1/4 In. 3515.00
Button, T. Roosevelt, Moose Head, National Progressive Party, Celluloid, Sepia, 2 1/4 In. 4076.00
Button, T. Roosevelt, Progressive Women, Bull Moose Head, Massachusetts, 3/4 In. 1800.00
Button, Taft, Sherman, Our Candidates, Jugate, Flags, Celluloid, 1908, 2 In. 6413.00
Button, Teddy Roosevelt, Bull Moose, 1912, 1 1/4 In. 320.00
Button, Teddy Roosevelt, Fairbanks, Jugate, Multicolored, 1904 . . . . 253.00
Button, Theodore Roosevelt & Charles Fairbanks, Celluloid, 1904, 1 1/4 In. 4290.00
Button, Theodore Roosevelt, Bull Moose Party, Put In Elephant Ears, 1908, 1 1/4 In. 9016.00
Button, Theodore Roosevelt, Down With The Trust, Bull Head Center 217.00
Button, Theodore Roosevelt, Johnson, Missouri State Convention, 1912, 1 1/4 In. 11786.00
Button, Theodore Roosevelt, June 3-4, Brown-Black Sepia, 1 3/4 In. 2200.00
Button, Theodore Roosevelt, Memorial Day 1907, Indianapolis, 2 1/4 In. 956.00
Button, Theodore Roosevelt, Portrait, Welcome Our President, 1 1/4 In. 514.00
Button, Truman & Civil Rights, Blue & White, 1 1/4 In. 1664.00
Button, Truman Minnesota Club, Celluloid, 2 1/4 In. 259.00
Button, Truman, Barkley, Golden Eagle, Inaugural, 2 1/4 In. 1481.00
Button, Truman, Barkley, Red Heart, Inaugural, Illinois Ribbon 1599.00
Button, Truman, Churchill, Westminster College, Fulton, Mo., 1946 . . . . 789.00
Button, Truman, Minnesota Club, 2 1/4 In. 373.00
Button, Truman, Photo Behind The 8 Ball, Lithograph, 1 1/2 In. 11314.00
Button, Ultimate Pollution, Stop The War Machine, Women For Peace, Chicago, 1 1/2 In. 97.00
Button, V For Victory, Celluloid, World War II, 1 In. 14.00
Button, Victory Club, I'm Saving For Defense Savings Bonds, 1 In. 17.00
Button, Vote For Woman Suffrage Nov. 6th, Black On Yellow, Celluloid, 1 1/4 In. 242.00
Button, Vote Republican, For Dewey, Warren, Portrait, 3 1/4 In. 104.00
Button, Vote Socialist, 1920s, 1 In. 15.00
Button, W. Wilson, Jubilee & Ox Roast, Sieholzville, Pa., Dec. 2, 1916, 1 3/4 In. 1120.00
Button, W.H. Taft, Kaiser Wilhelm, Jugate, 6th Annual National German Day, 1 1/4 In. . . 425.00
Button, W.J. Bryan, Adlai Stevenson, Jugate, Cornucopia, 1900, 1 1/4 In. 1078.00
Button, Wallace, LeMay, American Independent Party 1968, 3 1/4 In. 29.00
Button, William Howard Taft, Candidate With Eagle, Outstretched Wings, 1 1/4 In. 2904.00
Button, William Jennings Bryan, First, Last, All The Time, Celluloid, 1908, 4 In. 4100.00
Button, William Jennings Bryan, Full Dinner Pail, Celluloid, 1 1/4 In. 1300.00
Button, William McKinley, Full Dinner Pail, Celluloid, 1 1/4 In. 1300.00
Button, William McKinley, Theodore Roosevelt, Jugate, Musical Notes, 1 3/8 In. 4538.00
Button, Willkie Or Bust, Celluloid, Red, White & Blue, 3 1/2 In. 35.00
Button, Willkie, Don't Be A Jackass Follow The Eagle, 3 1/2 In. 70.00
Button, Wilson, Football Shape, Celluloid, 1 x 7/8 In. 7750.00
Button, Wilson, Man Of The Hour, 1912-1916, 1 3/4 In. 835.00
Button, Wilson, Marshall, Jugate, Flag, Celluloid, 1 1/4 In. 4235.00
Button, Youth International Party, Miami Beach, Stylized Yin-Yang, 1972, 2 In. 75.00
Cane, 45-Star Flag, Noisemaker, 1896, 35 1/4 In. . . . . *Illus* 952.00
Cane, Landon, Knox, Wood, Names On Side, 1936, 31 In. 254.00
Cane, McKinley & Hobart, St. Louis Republican National Convention, 1896 . . . . 843.00
Cane, McKinley, Tin, Hollow Shaft 280.00
Cane, Parade, Cleveland 475.00
Cane, Parade, Gerald Ford, 34 In. 75.00
Cane, Parade, Jimmy Carter, 34 In. 92.00
Cane, Walking Stick, Herbert Hoover, Attached Felt Pennant 150.00
Cane, William Jennings Bryan, 16 To 1, Free Coinage, 1896, 35 In. 165.00
Cane, William McKinley, Bust, Our Next President, 35 In. 165.00
Cane, With Whistle, Patriotism, Protection, Prosperity On Knob, 1896, 33 1/2 In. 200.00
Canteen, Tariff Club, GAR, McKinley, Strap, Spout, E. Liverpool, Ohio, 1888, 8 1/2 In. . 2870.00

Mint, rosemary, lavender, and
thyme will repel moths.
Hang bunches of the herbs
near stored textiles.

Political, Cane, 45-Star
Flag, Noisemaker,
1896, 35 1/4 In.

Card, 10 Protest Commandments Of Spiro Agnew, 1969	24.00
Card, Barry Goldwater, Republican For United States Senator	15.00
Card, Franklin Delano Roosevelt, Wallace Inaugural, 1/20/1941	45.00
Card, Goldwater, Black, White, 8 1/2 x 11 In.	10.00
Card, John F. Kennedy, Youngstown, Oh., 10/9/1980, 4 Page, 5 1/2 x 8 1/2 In.	20.00
Card, Membership, Michigan Democratic Club, President Franklin D. Roosevelt, 1935	20.00
Card, Palm, FDR Picture, Support Roosevelt Democracy, Primary, May 19th, 2 x 4 In.	15.00
Card, President Wilson, Woman Suffrage	25.00
Card, Reagan's Movie Career, 1980	8.50
Cartoon, Roosevelt For 1904, Truman In Jester's Costume, 10 x 13 In.	32.00
Charm, Adlai Stevenson, 1/2 In.	12.00
Cigar, Hughes, 1916	78.00
Cigar Band, Judge Taft, Full Color, Havana, 1920s, 3 In.	12.00
Cigarette Case, Dewey, Elephant, Metal, Burgundy & White, GOP, 1948	35.00 to 61.00
Cigarette Case, Truman, Donkey, Metal, Red & White, Dems, 1948	35.00 to 50.00
Clock, Mantel, Daniel Webster, Reverse On Glass Portrait, 1830	6032.00
Clock, Wall, Re-Elect Clinton, Plastic, Battery Operated, 1996	25.00
Clock, Wall, Spiro Agnew, Caricature, Stars & Arabic Numerals, 9 In.	44.00
Cloth, Wilson Campaign, 1872, 7 x 11 In.	92.00
Cocktail Napkins, The People's Choice Of Course, Elephant Cartoon, Box Of 36	5.00
Creamer, Roosevelt, Fairbanks, Decal, Custard Glass, 4 In.	1540.00
Cup, Anti-LBJ Campaign, Slogan Other Side, Tin, Gold, 19743 1/2 x 5 In.	30.00
Dart Board, Agnew, Black & White Photo, Cardboard, Nose Is Bull's-Eye, 14 In.	28.00
Decal, MacArthur For President, 1952, Red, White & Blue, Wisconsin, 5 x 7 In.	22.00
Decal, We Want Willkie, 1940, 3 1/2 x 9 In.	15.00
Desk Calendar Holder, Eisenhower Photos, Cardboard, c.1956	14.00
Dinner Bucket, Cover, McKinley, Roosevelt, Wooden, 5 3/4 In.	2200.00
Dish, President & Mrs. Nixon, Black, White, Gold Trim, 3 3/4 x 4 3/4 In.	25.00
Dish, President Seal, Gerald R. Ford, Glass, Smoky, Tulsa, April 27, 1974	30.00
Dress, Romney For President, 1968 Convention Hopeful, 33 x 36 In.	50.00
Earrings, Bush, Quayle '92, Plastic	8.00
Earrings, IKE, Rhinestone, 5/8 In.	14.00
Fan, Franklin Delano Roosevelt Picture, Brown, White	38.00
Fan, Reagan, Wooden Handle, 1966	35.00
Ferrotype, Lincoln, 1 3/4 In.	5682.00
Figure, Black Power, Male With Fist In Air, Plaster, 6 1/2 In.	30.00
Figure, Elephant, Land On Roosevelt 1936, Cast Iron, Painted	590.00
Figure, GOP Elephant, Taft, Sherman, Iron, Embossed, 1908, 4 1/2 In.	450.00
Figure, John-John Salutes JFK, Ceramic, 7 In.	65.00
Figure, Presentation, McKinley, California Bear, Gold, Onyx Base, c.1901, 9 1/2 In.	29500.00
Figure, Uncle Sam, Cardboard, Jointed, 1944, 55 x 15 1/4 In.	29.00
Flag, American, 13 Stars, Stripes, Lincoln, Hamilton, Linen, 13 x 18 1/2 In.	11825.00
Flag, Antenna, Kennedy, Johnson, Paper, 1960	11.00
Flag, McKinley, Mechanical	88.00
Flag, Washington Bicentennial, Cloth, Orange, Black, Brown, White, 1932, 7 x 11 In.	38.00
Flyer, Dukakis For President, Perry Square Rally, Erie, Pa., Autograph, 1988, 8 1/2 In.	17.00
Flyer, Gene McCarthy For President Rally, Pittsburgh, 1968, 4 x 11 In.	20.00
Flyer, Join The NAACP, For Civil Rights, 1953 Membership Campaign, 8 1/2 x 11 In.	61.00
Flyer, Ken Keating, Anti-Robert F. Kennedy	7.50

Flyer, Teddy Roosevelt & Woodrow Wilson, In Perfect Agreement, 1918, 8 x 14 In. 25.00
Flyer, Walter Mondale, Geraldine Ferraro, 1984, 5 1/2 x 8 1/2 In. 40.00
Game, Checkers, Harrison, Cleveland, Wood Box, Board, Pieces, 8 1/2 In. 843.00
Game, Teddy Bear, Multicolored, 11 Cards, Box 67.00
Garter Belt, Reagan, Red & White 23.00
Glass, Edith Bunker For Foist Lady, 5 In. 3.00
Glass, Vote To Win In 1960 With Jack Kennedy, Lyndon Johnson, Blue Lettering 80.00
Glass, Willkie Acceptance Speech, Red, White & Blue, 4 1/2 In. 32.00
Gloves, I'm Working For Nixon & Lodge, Yellow Cotton, 1960 .... 30.00
Handkerchief, Bryan, Sure Winner This Time, Donkey In Corners, 1908 .... 694.00
Handkerchief, Cleveland, Thurman 95.00
Handkerchief, Grover Cleveland, Allen G. Thurman, Portraits, 22 x 23 In. 110.00
Handkerchief, Harrison, Morton, Silk 270.00
Handkerchief, We Want Roosevelt, Red, White & Blue, 11 1/2 x 11 3/4 In. 32.00
Hanger, Wall, Franklin Delano Roosevelt, Rayon, Red, White & Blue, 5 x 6 1/2 In. 12.00
Hanger, Wall, General Douglas MacArthur, Wood, Embossed 85.00
Hanger, Wall, Scranton President, Cardboard, String, 7 1/2 In. 10.00
Hat, Boater Type, Humphrey For President Campaign, Styrofoam, 1968, 13 In. 25.00
Hat, Cowboy, LBJ, Picture, Plastic, 1964, 15 In. 30.00
Hat, Golf, Ronald Reagan President, Red, White & Blue 15.00
Hat, Women's, Plastic, John F. Kennedy For President, Gold On Green, 3 In. 50.00
Headband, Next President Goldwater, Cloth, Unopened, 1964, 2 x 10 In. 17.00
Hood Ornament, Gerald Ford On Front Of Edsel, 1976, 2 1/2 In. 254.00
Horn, Parade, Mack & Teddy, Jonnie's Horn, Marion, Ohio, 66 In. 5225.00
Invitation, Lincoln Inauguration, Envelope, March 4, 1861, 10 1/4 x 9 In. 4500.00
Jam Jar, Teddy Roosevelt, Roosevelt Bears Around Jar, Milk Glass 40.00
Jug, Parker, Davis, 1904 Campaign, Miniature 1200.00
Kerchief, Eisenhower The Man, Brown, White, 17 x 18 In. 30.00
Key Chain, Watergate, Celluloid, 2 1/2 In. 31.00
Knife, Jimmy Carter, Mr. Peanut For President, Metal, Plastic, Pocket, 1976, 3 1/2 In. 20.00
Knife, Reagan, Red & White, 1980 .... 22.00
Label, Rosenbergs Must Not Die, Wire Pres. Truman, 6 x 4 In. 73.00
Lantern, Japanese, Grant & Wilson, 1872, 7 In. 245.00
Lantern, McKinley, Hobart, Portraits, Etched Glass 1960.00
Lantern, Willkie, Roosevelt, Dinner Bucket Parade Style, 9 In. 2087.00
License Plate, Al Smith For President, Metal, Raised Letters & Border 66.00
License Plate, Al Smith, White, Green 35.00
License Plate, Anti-Dukakis, Embossed, Red, Blue & White, New Mexico 14.00
License Plate, Anti-LBJ, Cartoon, Metal, Black, Blue, White 32.00
License Plate, Anti-Ronald Reagan, Cartoon, Embossed 22.00
License Plate, George Wallace, Cartoon, Embossed, 1968 .... 32.00
License Plate, Goldwater, Metal, Red Letters On White, 1964 .... 38.00
License Plate, Humphrey, Muskie, Plastic, 6 x 12 In. 24.00
License Plate, John F. Kennedy 163.90
License Plate, McGovern, Peace & Truth, Plastic, Red, White & Blue 8.00
License Plate, Nixon, Agnew, Embossed, Black, White, 1968 .... 35.00
License Plate, Nixon, Agnew, Metal, Red, White & Blue 25.00
License Plate, Nobody For President, Embossed, 1988 .... 20.00
License Plate, Wallace For President, Metal, Portrait, Red, White & Blue 50.00
Light Bulb, Interior Filament Reading Peace & Peace Symbol, 4 In. 68.00
Lighter, Kennedy, Johnson, Red, White & Blue 770.00
Lock, Watch Fob, Taft, Mechanical, 1912 .... 46.00
Match Safe, McKinley, Silvered Brass 182.00
Matchbook, Lyndon B. Johnson With Congressional Candidate Tommy O'Toole 16.00
Matchbook, Wendell Willkie For President Front, Pull For Willkie Back, 2 x 2 1/4 In. ... 14.00
Matchbook, Wendell Willkie, Red, White & Blue 12.00
Matchbox Holder, FDR WWII Quotes, Celluloid Over Metal, 1 x 1 1/2 x 2 1/4 In. 65.00
Medal, Cox, Campaign, Bronze, 1920, 1 1/4 In. 55.00
Medal, Delegate, Democrats, St. Louis, 1916, 1 1/2 In. 48.00
Medal, Harrison, Morton, Eagle At Top, 1 1/8 In. 50.00
Medal, Press, Democratic Convention, Baltimore, Pink Ribbon, 1912, 1 1/2 In. 142.00
Mirror, Ike, Full Color Portrait Under Celluloid, 3 1/2 In. 45.00
Mobile, Campaign, Al Smith, American Liberty, 1928, 9 1/2 In. 190.00

Model Kit, JFK's PT-109, Revell, 1963, 6 1/2 x 13 1/2 x 2 In. 68.00
Mug, Archie Bunker, Build A Better Yesterday With Bunker, 1972, 5 1/2 In. 12.00
Mug, Archie Bunker, Clear Glass, Portrait Of The Stars, 5 In. 12.00
Mug, Cleveland, Stevenson, Ceramic, 1 1/2 In. 160.00
Mug, Eisenhower Portrait, Ceramic, Miniature 40.00
Mug, Franklin Delano Roosevelt, Royal Winton 100.00
Mug, Nixon, Caricature 100.00
Mush Cup, McKinley, Hobart, Purple Transfer, Ironstone 863.00
Mustard, McKinley, Lid, Glass, Embossed 65.00
Mustard, W.J. Bryan, Lid, Glass, Embossed 75.00
Necktie, I Like Ike, 4 Stars, Elephants, White, Blue 45.00
Necktie, I Like Ike, 5 Stars, Embroidered, Red 28.00
Necktie, I Like Ike, Brown, Yellow, Polka Dots 45.00
Necktie, I Like Ike, Burgundy, Blue Letters 45.00
Necktie, Kennedy For President, White, Gray 95.00
Necktie, Landon 50.00
Notepad, Union, Don't Buy Sweat Shop Clothing, Celluloid Cover, 2 1/2 x 4 1/2 In. 65.00
Pamphlet, Pro-Chinese Minority Of California To American President, 1882, 10 Pages .. 187.00
Pamphlet, The Battle Of 1900, Pictures Of McKinley, Bryan, 12 x 18 In. 40.00
Pen, Eisenhower, Be Safe With Ike 22.00
Pen, John F. Kennedy, Signing Federal Airport Act, 1961 .... 4428.00
Pen, LBJ Logo, Facsimile Signature, Black, Plastic, Felt Tip 18.00
Pencil, Adlai Stevenson For President In 1956 .... 35.00
Pencil, Dewey, Warren, Worthy Of The Victory 35.00
Pencil, Estes Kefauver, Democrat Who Wants To Win, 2 1/2 In. 35.00
Pencil, Henry Wallace 40.00
Pencil, Kennedy For President, Orange, Golf Scoring, 3 1/4 In. 14.00
Pencil, Mechanical, Kennedy For President, JFK Portrait, PT 109, Flag 143.00
Pencil, Red, White & Blue, Vote For Eisenhower In '52 .... 35.00
Pencil, Wendell Willkie Is My Man For President 17.00
Pendant, Muskie, Box 12.00
Pennant, 43rd Inauguration, Ike, 1957 .... 52.00
Pennant, Barry Goldwater, Red, White & Blue, 28 1/2 In. 8.50
Pennant, Barry M. Goldwater, Blue, 29 1/2 In. 20.00
Pennant, Eisenhower, Inaugural, Blue, New Mexico, 17 1/2 In. 15.00
Pennant, Franklin Delano Roosevelt, Wallace, Yellow, White, 1941, 9 1/2 In. 58.00
Pennant, George Wallace, Paper, Red White & Blue 15.00
Pennant, Hoover, Inaugural, Blue 75.00
Pennant, Ike, Nixon, Inaugural, Red, 28 1/2 In. 40.00
Pennant, John F. Kennedy, Photograph Of President, Felt, 30 1/2 In. 50.00
Pennant, National Republican Convention, June 21st-28th, Phila., Pa., 1948, 28 In. 22.00
Pennant, Our Next President Hoover, Red, White & Blue 35.00
Pennant, Panama Canal Building, Balboa Heights, Cloth, 36 In. 15.00
Pennant, Republican National Convention, Miami Beach, Fla., 1968, 30 In. 15.00
Pennant, Socialist Party, Emblem, Felt, c.1930, 2 x 5 In. 35.00
Pennant, Teddy Roosevelt, Oil Cloth, 1912 .... 917.00
Pennant, Vote Yes On The Woman Suffrage Amendment, June 5, 1916, 12 x 34 In. 2090.00
Pennant, Votes For Women, 22 In. 586.00
Pennant, Votes For Women, Brown & Black Cloth, 22 In. 587.00
Pennant, Willkie, Felt 138.00
Photograph, Lincoln For President, Cardboard 5750.00
Picture, Alfred E. Smith, Joe T. Robinson, Honest, Able, Fearless, Frame, 1928 .... 295.00
Picture, Horace Greeley, Tintype, Brass Shell 450.00
Picture, Miniature, Douglas MacArthur, Uniform, Gold Trim, 2 1/2 x 2 1/2 In. 35.00
Picture, Progressive Party Presidential Candidate Robert LaFollette, 1908, 4 x 6 In. 50.00
Picture, Zachary Taylor, Reverse On Glass, Framed, 1846, 2 3/4 In. 2662.00
Pillow, Goldwater '64, Cloth, Blue On White, 12 In. 30.00
Pillow Topper, Remember Pearl Harbor, Red, White & Blue, 1940s, 16 x 16 In. 50.00
Pin, Bar, Woodrow Wilson's Signature, Goldtone, 2 1/2 In. 73.00
Pin, Bryan, Little Pinkie, Multicolored 42.00
Pin, Elephant, GOP, Harding, Pewter, 7/8 In. 15.00
Pin, Gold Bug, McKinley 60.00
Pin, It Needs Goldwater, Lyndon Tree, Gold, 3 1/2 In. 425.00

Pin, Lincoln In Star, 1864, 1 1/2 x 1 1/2 In. 4114.00
Pin, McClellan In Star, 1804, 1 1/2 x 1 1/2 In. 609.00
Pin, McKinley, Nailed To McKinley, Nail Form, White Metal, 2 1/2 In. 83.00
Pin, Mondale & Ferraro, Outline Of U.S. Map 6.50
Pin, Name, Truman, Shield Background, 1 In. 590.00
Pin, Press, Mrs. Kennedy Visits India, Enamel, 1962, 1/2 In. 1416.00
Pin, Ribbon, Hughes, Fairbanks, 1 3/4-In. Pin, 4-In. Ribbon 14300.00
Pin, Silver Bug, Bryan 90.00
Pipe, Who Fears To Speak Of Ireland A Nation, Clay, Carved Harp, 5 In. 264.00
Pitcher, George Washington Transfer, Full Color Transfer Of Sailing Ship, 7 In. 3367.00
Pitcher, Grant, Lady Liberty, Stoneware, c.1880, 7 1/2 In. 420.00
Plaque, Mirror, Etched, Eagle & Flag, Ship & Anchor, Remember Pearl Harbor, 1941 ... 50.00
Plate, Andrew Jackson, Brown Rim, Enoch Wood, 7 1/2 In. 990.00
Plate, Campaign Dinner, Landon, 8 In. 423.00
Plate, Eisenhower In Military, Gold, Green, 7 In. 30.00
Plate, Frances Willard, Temperance Leader 20.00
Plate, Franklin Delano Roosevelt Picture, Orange Trim, 9 1/4 In. 45.00
Plate, General & Presidential Candidate Douglas MacArthur, Ceramic, 1940s, 12 In. 27.00
Plate, General Lafayette, Welcome To The Land Of Liberty, Early 19th Century, 6 1/2 In. 1100.00
Plate, JFK & Mrs. Kennedy, Center Full Color Photo, Red Fabric Hanger, 1962, 6 In. ... 12.00
Plate, John Logan, For Vice President With James G. Blaine, Maine, 1884 .... 245.00
Plate, Portrait, Grover Cleveland, Frosted, 1884, 11 In. 225.00
Plate, President & Mrs. Gerald Ford, China, Photo Illustration, 1970s, 9 In. 8.00
Plate, Republican National Convention, Ceramic, White, 1956, 13 In. 24.00
Plate, Roosevelt, Allied Flags Around Border, 10 3/4 In. 22.00
Postcard, Anti-John F. Kennedy Sons Of Business (SOB) Club, We Miss Ike, 1960 ...... 16.00
Postcard, Cartoon Of British Boxer Knocking Out Japanese Boxer, WWII 20.00
Postcard, Hallinan-Bass, Progressive Party, Vote For Peace Candidates, 1952 .... 493.00
Postcard, Michigan Governor & 1964 President Hopeful George Romney 25.00
Postcard, Peace, Progress, Prosperity, Get On Raft With Taft Boys 17.00
Poster, Calvin Coolidge, 21 x 17 In. 20.00
Poster, Carter In Wheat Field, Inspirational Quote, Facsimile Signature, 16 x 20 In. 12.00
Poster, General Douglas MacArthur, Cardboard, 8 x 10 In. 15.00
Poster, George Romney, Romney Gets Results, Vote Republican, 1964, 14 x 19 In. 28.00
Poster, Harding & Coolidge, America Always First, 11 x 16 In. 60.00
Poster, Honoring Clinton, Starring The Four Tops, Fox Theater, Detroit, 1992, 20 x 30 In. 65.00
Poster, I Put Buildings Up, I Can't Keep Up, Cost Of Living, Vote McGovern, 12 x 19 In. 10.00
Poster, Indiana Coat-Tail Poster For Harding & Coolidge, 25 x 38 In. 384.00
Poster, International Workers, Strike Me Red, Cast Of 100 Children, 11 x 15 In. 33.00
Poster, Jimmy Carter, Brown, White, Carter In Wheat Field, Signature, 1976, 16 x 20 In. . 15.00
Poster, Kennedy For President, Black & White Photo, 13 x 18 In. 65.00
Poster, LBJ, In Front Of JFK, Let Us Continue, 12 1/4 x 18 1/2 In. 24.00
Poster, Let McGovern Put The You Back In The USA, 14 x 22 In. 22.00
Poster, Mondale, Ferraro, For The Family Of America, 1984, 17 x 22 In. 29.00
Poster, Nixon, Agnew, Now More Than Ever, 1972, 17 x 24 In. 25.00
Poster, Pride Integrity Gallantry Service, Anti-Police, Late 1960s, 21 x 29 In. 28.00
Poster, Reagan, Let's Make America Great Again, 22 x 32 In. 50.00
Poster, Repeal The Abortion Laws Now, Nov. 20, 1971 March, 10 7/8 x 16 3/4 In. 15.00
Poster, Robert Kennedy, Black & White Photograph, 1968, 23 1/3 x 35 1/2 In. 59.00
Poster, Spiro T. Agnew VP, Black & White Photo, Red Lettering, 1968, 23 x 34 In. 24.00
Poster, Suppose They Gave A War & Nobody Came, Day-Glo, 24 x 30 In. 46.00
Poster, The New Action Army, Recruiting, Fluorescent On Black, 1960s, 21 x 32 In. 45.00
Poster, Truman, Sepia Toned Real Photograph, Facsimile Signature, 1948, 15 x 20 In. ... 79.00
Poster, U.S. Presidents Up Through Incumbent Cleveland, 21 1/2 x 30 In. 106.00
Poster, Vote Dry For Us, Children Waving Flag, 12 x 18 In. 135.00
Poster, Vote For Dewey, Kill The Klan 1684.00
Poster, Wanted, Patty Hearst, Other SLA Members, Pictures, 10 1/2 x 16 In. 55.00
Poster, Welcome President Nixon To Peking, Cardboard, 14 x 20 In. 15.00
Poster, William Jennings Bryan, Liberty Bell, Flags, 1900, 28 x 22 In. 4950.00
Poster, Women's Action, Nov. 16, 1975 Pentagon Gathering, 9 1/2 x 16 5/8 In. 35.00
Print, Anti-Van Buren Cartoon, Whig Magnets Attracted By Pole, J. Childs, 13 x 21 In. ... 375.00
Print, JFK, Full Color, Linen, R. Mondello, 1965, 23 x 34 In. 28.00
Printing Block, Harriman Portrait 40.00

Program, Inaugural, FDR, Garner, Jan. 29, 1937 .... 45.00
Program, Inaugural, Truman, Barkley, 1949 .... 45.00
Program, Memorial Service For Pres. William McKinley, Sept. 19, 1901, 5 x 8 In. 20.00
Rain Bonnet, Barry Goldwater For President, Plastic, Gold Pouch, 1964 .... 15.00
Record, Ronald Reagan, Freedom's Finest Hour, 78 RPM 25.00
Ribbon, Abe Lincoln, For President, Picture, Clean Shaven, 1846, 7 In. 2426.00
Ribbon, Abraham Lincoln, Campaign, Beardless Lincoln, Black On Green Silk, 1860 .... 2530.00
Ribbon, Bryan, Red, White & Blue, Paper Tab 20.00
Ribbon, Democratic Convention Alternate, Baltimore, 1912, 1 1/2 In. 85.00
Ribbon, Dewey Rally, Celluloid, Red, White & Blue, 3 In. 140.00
Ribbon, Franklin D. Roosevelt, Inaugural, 1941, 1 1/4 In. 45.00
Ribbon, Franklin Pierce & William King 1870.00
Ribbon, Hoover, Silk, 2 x 1 1/4 In. 40.00
Ribbon, In Memory Of W.H. Harrison, Silk, Black & White, 1841, 3 x 6 In. 45.00
Ribbon, McKinley Calendar Memorial, Gray, Black Lettering, Silk, 1902, 2 x 6 1/2 In. 30.00
Ribbon, McKinley, Jr., Chairman Invitation Committee, Inauguration 1892 .... 667.00
Ribbon, Nixon, Agnew, White, Blue Lettering, 2 x 7 1/2 In. 10.00
Ribbon, Our Next President, John F. Kennedy, 1 3/4 In. 15.00
Ribbon, Parker, Davis, Democratic Convention, St. Louis, Portraits, 1904, 8 In. 315.00
Ribbon, Pomona Hosts Nixon Kick-Off, Light & Dark Blue, 1952, 1 1/2 x 5 In. 195.00
Ribbon, Presidential Campaign Kick-Off, Eisenhower, Nixon, Sept. 18, 1956, 2 x 6 1/2 In. .. 70.00
Ribbon, Reagan, Red & White, Celluloid Button At Top, 4 In. 38.00
Ribbon, Robert Kennedy, President, 1 1/2 In. 10.00
Ribbon, Roosevelt In Black & Cream Celluloid Button, Welcome, Santa Fe, 8 1/2 In. ... 1043.00
Ribbon, Teddy Roosevelt, Gold & Black, 1904 Fremont, Lincoln Voters Club, 2 x 7 In. ... 90.00
Ribbon, Truman, Cardboard, Blue & White, c.1948, 3 1/4 x 7 3/4 In. 70.00
Ribbon, Welcome Home Dunmore, Hero Of 1919 .... 22.00
Ribbon, Welcome Home Pershing, 1919 .... 35.00
Ribbon, Winfield, Kansas Association Of Soldiers, 1913, 2 1/4 In. 26.00
Roach Clip, Jimmy Carter, Figural, Peanut Character, Plastic, Metal, 1976, 3 In. 39.00
Rosette, Votes For Women, Attached Ribbons, 7 In. 825.00
Ruler, Prohibition Text On Both Sides, Wood, 12 In. 45.00
Salt & Pepper, John F. Kennedy, Rocking Chair, Glazed, 1962, 4 x 2 x 2 In. 49.00
Sash, Goldwater, Rayon, Blue, Yellow, 1964 .... 16.00
Sheet Music, Admiral Dewey's March, 1898 ....20.00 to 25.00
Sheet Music, Believe In Stevenson, 1956 .... 24.00
Sheet Music, Eisenhower, All For The USA, 4 Pages, 9 1/4 x 12 In. 14.00
Sheet Music, Franklin Delano Roosevelt, Nation's Prayer, 1933 .... 28.00
Sheet Music, Harrison's Victory March, 1888 .... 48.00
Sheet Music, Hubert Humphrey March 18.50
Sheet Music, Ike Is On The Tee, Picture Of Eisenhower, Golf Club, 1953 .... 35.00
Sheet Music, John W. Davis 25.00
Sheet Music, League Of Nations March, 1919 .... 28.00
Sheet Music, New Frontier, John F. Kennedy, 1961 .... 22.00
Sheet Music, One World, Inspired By Wendell Willkie's Book, Globe, 1940, 9 x 12 In. 39.00
Sheet Music, Our President, Truman, 1945 .... 40.00
Sheet Music, Roosevelt NRA March Song, 1933 .... 28.00
Sheet Music, Vote On Pennsylvania, 1936 .... 48.00
Sheet Music, With Assassinated President James Garfield, Nation's Tears, Dated 1881 ... 30.00
Shopping Bag, Compliments Jerry Ford Who Works For You In Congress, Paper, Handles 24.00
Shopping Bag, Hubert Humphrey For President, Humphrey's My Bag, 1968, 13 x 16 In. .. 20.00
Shower Head, Richard Nixon, Rubber, Shower Head In Nixon's Mouth, 1988 .... 75.00
Sign, Bryan, Stevenson, Celluloid, 10 In. 7150.00
Sign, Buy Liberty Bonds, Hot Air Balloon, Cardboard, 7 x 14 In. 35.00
Sign, Cartoon, Anti-LBJ, Cardboard 14.00
Sign, Goldwater, Barry Boxed Dolls, Remco, 8 1/2 x 22 In. 38.00
Sign, McKinley, Roosevelt, Celluloid, 10 In. 4125.00
Sign, Paper, V For Victory Logo, Invest, War Bonds, 1940s, 24 x 24 In. 70.00
Sign, Vote Republican, Blue, Silver Reflectors, White Lettering, 2 x 13 In. 5.00
Snuffbox, Henry Clay Picture, Papier-Mache, 3 1/4 In. 4290.00
Snuffbox, Pressed Paper, Rutherford B. Hayes & William A. Wheeler, 3 In. 4125.00
Spoon, Townsend's Plan, Early 1930s 20.00
Stamp, Davis, Bryan, Victory, Red, White & Blue, Square, 1924, 1 1/2 In. 990.00

Statue, Franklin Delano Roosevelt, Metal, 1933, 4 1/2 In. 15.00
Statue, General Pershing, Medals, Shield, Metal, 4 1/2 In. 45.00
Sticker, Kennedy For President, Johnson For Vice President, Shield Shape, Pair 25.00
Sticker, Lapel, Dan Quayle For Senate, Red & White, 3 In. 15.00
Sticker, No Third Term! Democrats For Willkie, Uncle Sam, Thumb's Down 17.00
Sticker, Window, Roosevelt, Garner, Red, White & Blue 9.00
Sticker, Window, Static, Candidate Hubert Humphrey, Some Men Talk About Change ... 18.00
Sticker, Window, Wallace For President, Stand Up For America, 1968 .... 4.00
Stickpin, Bull Moose, Figural 8.00
Stickpin, Hoover, Elephant, Plastic 15.00
Stickpin, Teddy's Big Stick, 7/8 In. 43.00
Stud, Bull Moose, Figure 6.00
Stud, Cox, Rooster, Figural, Pewter, Embossed Name, 7/8 In. ....17.00 to 34.00
Stud, Gold, McKinley, Sound Money 20.00
Stud, Harding, Elephant 22.00
Stud, Hughes, Pewter 17.00
Stud, McKinley, 1/2 In. 15.00
Suspenders, Roosevelt, Red, White & Blue Striped, FDR, Cloth 123.00
Suspenders, Willkie, Red, White & Blue, Cloth 152.00
Swizzle Stick, Elephant, Donkey, c.1968, Pair 10.00
Tab Button, Bryan, Paper 23.00
Teapot, Figural, Reagan, Ceramic, 10 In. 86.00
Textile, Franklin On His 1790 Death, George Washington As President, 27 x 30 In. 3450.00
Thimble, Hoover 9.00
Ticket, Nixon, Agnew Inauguration, Black & White Photos, Seating Information, 1973 ... 7.00
Tie, Let's Back Jack, Dark Blue, White Lettering, Arnel Acetate 48.00
Tie, Roosevelt & Prosperity, For President, FDR's Picture 102.00
Tie, Truman, Woven Face, Capitol Dome, Blue & Tan, 1948 .... 133.00
Tie, USA Likes LBJ, Gray, White Lettering, Arnel Acetate 8.00
Tie, Vote Republican, Purple, White Lettering, Arnel Acetate 5.00
Tie Tack, Initials, I K E, 1/2 x 1/2 In. 5.00
Toby, Jug, Eisenhower, William MacLean, 1956, 3 1/2 In. 35.00
Token, Abraham Lincoln, White Metal, 1 1/2 In 55.00
Token, Arthur, 3/4 In. 25.00
Token, Blaine, Logan, Picture, Sepia, Shield Form, Brass Shell, 1 1/2 In. 225.00
Token, Franklin D. Roosevelt, Garner, Elect The Democratic Party, 3/4 In. 27.00
Token, George Washington, Long Live The President, Shank Back, Copper 1485.00
Token, Grant, 3/4 In. 30.00
Token, Parker & Davis League, Rope Frame, 1 1/4 In. 120.00
Top Hat, Benjamin Harrison, He's All Right, Same Old Hat, Glass, 2 In. 237.00
Tray, Alton B. Parker, Tin Lithograph, Wisconsin Clothier Advertising, Oval, 16 In. 330.00
Tree Ornament, Reagan, Wood, 1984 .... 24.00
Tumbler, Bryan, The People's Choice For 1896-1900, Clear Glass 70.00
Umbrella, McGovern 40.00
Umbrella, McKinley, Hobart, Protection, Sound Money, Pictures, 1896, 33 In. 669.00
View-Master Reel Packet, LBJ Country, 3 Reels, 21 Pictures, 4 1/2 In. 12.00
Waste Can, Agnew, Playing Golf & Tennis, c.1972, 13 x 10 1/2 In. 24.00
Watch Fob, Bryan, Kern 40.00
Watch Fob, Taft, Sherman 35.00
Watch Fob, Theodore Roosevelt, Bronze 22.00
Wristwatch, Spiro Agnew Caricature, c.1972, 1 3/4 In. 34.00

POMONA glass is a clear glass with a soft amber border decorated with
pale blue or rose-colored flowers and leaves. The colors are very, very
pale. The background of the glass is covered with a network of fine
lines. It was made from 1885 to 1888 by the New England Glass Company. First grind was made from April 1885 to June 1886. It was made
by cutting a wax surface on the glass, then dipping it in acid. Second
grind was a less expensive method of acid etching that was developed
later.

Creamer, Blue Cornflower, Amber Rim, Butterfly On Reverse, 4 In. 480.00
Finger Bowl, Blue Cornflower, 2nd Grind, 5 1/4 In. 69.00
Pitcher, Pink, Blue Cornflowers, Leafy Stems, Twisted Rope Handle, 2nd Grind, 7 1/2 In.   252.00

Salt & Pepper, Blue Cornflower, Metal Silver-Plated Holder, 7 1/4 In. 1150.00
Tumbler, Blue Cornflower, 2nd Grind, 3 3/4 In. 100.00

PONTYPOOL, see Tole category.

POPEYE was introduced to the Thimble Theatre comic strip in 1929.
The character became a favorite of readers. In 1932, an animated car-
toon featuring Popeye was made by Paramount Studios. The cartoon
series continued and became even more popular when it was shown on
television starting in the 1950s. The full-length movie with Robin
Williams as Popeye was made in 1980.

Airplane, Crazy Flying Action, Windup, Tin, KFS, 1940, 7 In. 1045.00
Ashtray, Figural, Wimpy, Painted Plaster, c.1940, 7 1/4 In. 120.00
Badge, I'm Keepin' Fit With Popeye, Popeye Making Muscle, c.1950, 3 In. 30.00
Bank, Mechanical, Knockout, Swings Arm, Knocks Over Brutus, Tin, Straits, 4 1/2 In. . . . 1600.00
Bank, Popeye Head, American Bisque . . . . .140.00 to 325.00
Bank, Swee' Pea, Pottery, American Bisque, 6 1/4 In. 525.00
Book, Wonder Book, Popeye Goes On A Picnic, 20 Pages 17.00
Bottle, Soap, Brutus, Vinyl, Colgate Palmolive, 10 In. 25.00
Bowl, Cereal, Popeye & Swee'pea, Royal Tudor Ware 65.00
Chalk Sticks, 6 White, 6 Colored, American Crayon Co., Box, 1953 . . . . 15.00
Cookie Jar, American Bisque 250.00
Cookie Jar, Olive Oyl, American Bisque, 10 1/2 In. 240.00
Cup, China, Popeye & Olive Oyl Taking A Stroll, 2 1/2 In. 40.00
Display, Flashlight, 12 On Board, 1960s 900.00
Doll, Cloth, Straw Stuffed, Posing Wire In Arms & Legs, Japan, 9 In. 165.00
Doll, Eugene The Jeep, Jointed, Wood & Composition, Painted, Decal, 7 In. 605.00
Doll, Jointed, Wood & Composition, Painted, Decal On Shoe, Chein, 13 In. 358.00
Doll, Multiple-Jointed, Held By Elastics, King Features Syndicate, c.1930 . . . . 90.00
Doll, Wood, Multiple-Jointed, Held By Elastics, King Features Syndicate, c.1930 . . . . 90.00
Eggcup, Glazed China, White, Painted, Japan, 2 x 3 In. 95.00
Figure, Articulated, Celluloid, c.1920, 5 3/4 In. 400.00
Figure, Celluloid, Flesh Tone, Painted Outfit, Painted Magenta Cap, Holding Pipe, 4 In. . . . 40.00
Figure, Holding Pipe To Chest, Celluloid, Hollow, 3 1/2 In. 40.00
Figure, Movable Head & Arms, Hard Vinyl, R. Dankin & Co., 8 In. 35.00
Figure, Wimpy, Composition Wood, King Features, 1944, 4 1/2 In. 95.00
Figure Set, Popeye, Olive & Wimpy, Wooden, Jointed, Jaymar, 1930s, 3 Piece 425.00
Game, Standup Targets, Instructions, Parker Bros., Box, 11 x 18 In. 200.00
Game, Wimpy Where Are My Hamburgers, Hasbro, 1965 . . . . 48.00
Glass, Popeye & Eugene The Jeep, Yellow Art, Canada, 1950s, 5 In. 125.00
Glass, Vinyl, Yellow, Blue Ink, 3 x 3 1/2 In. 24.00
Glass, Yellow & Orange Ink, Popeye & Oscar, 2 1/2 x 4 5/8 In. 70.00
Lamp, Desk, White Metal, Idealite Inc., 1935, 11 1/2 In. 86.00
Lamp, Painted, Cast Metal, 11 In. 60.00
Lamp, Vinyl, Hollow, Painted, Combex Of England, King Features Syndicate, 1959 . . . . . 85.00
Lantern, Linemar, Box, 8 In. 695.00
Light Set, Popeye Christmas Tree, Character Type, Royal Electric Co., Box, 16 In. 230.00
Mug, Plastic, Flicker Eye, 1950s, 4 In. 24.00
Night-Light, Tugboat, Popeye, With Torch, Metal, Aerolux Happy Lamp, 7 1/2 In. 201.00
Notebook, 44 Blue Lined Pages, King Features, 1929, 6 3/4 x 8 1/4 In. 35.00
Pencil, Mechanical, Metal Ends, Enamel Barrel, Eagle Pencil Co., 10 1/2 In. 28.00
Pencil Box, Hazel-Maid Bread Premium, 7 1/2 x 17 In. 20.00
Pencil Set, Die Cut Opening, Tin Lithograph Lid, 12 Pencils, Box 55.00
Pillow Cover, Popeye, Olive Oyl, Swee'pea, Linen, Preprinted For Needlework, 1930s . . . 60.00
Poster, Movie, Me Feelins Is Hurt, 1940 . . . . 4070.00
Puppet, Olive Oyl, Gund Kings Feature, 11 In. 45.00
Puzzle, Popeye, Hitting Brutus, Saalfield, 7 3/4 x 9 1/2 In. 95.00
Salt & Pepper, Popeye & Olive Oyl, Vandor 30.00
Soaky, Bluto, Salesman's Sample, Box, 1960s 70.00
Soaky, Popeye, Salesman's Sample, Box, 1960s 50.00
Tablecloth, Checkered, Popeye & Wimpy, Paper, 36 x 72 In. 20.00
Target Board, SS Spinach, Transogram, 1958, 11 1/2 In. 52.00
Thermometer, Wall Plaque, Slotted For Hanging, 4 1/4 x 6 1/2 In. 24.00
Toothbrush Holder, Bisque, Movable Arm, Japan, 4 1/2 In. . . . . .110.00 to 550.00

Toy, Airport, Tin Lithograph, Clockwork, Cardboard Diorama, Marx, 9 In. 1430.00
Toy, Band Wagon Xylophone, Paper Lithograph On Wood, 8 1/2 In. 150.00
Toy, Brutus, Dippy Dumper, Celluloid, Tin Lithograph, Clockwork, Marx, 9 In. 412.00
Toy, Champ, Popeye & Bluto Fight, Tin, Celluloid, Box, KFS, 7 In. . . . . .2090.00 to 4400.00
Toy, Finger Puppet Set, Vinyl, Hollow, Popeye, Olive Oyl, Wimpy, Brutus, Swee'pea, 2 In.   35.00
Toy, Olive Oyl, Pop Up, Push Down, Umbrella, Cloth, Box, Linemar, 7 1/2 In. 908.00
Toy, Popeye Express, Parrot On Wheelbarrow, Tin Lithograph, Clockwork, 8 In. . . .517.00 to 660.00
Toy, Popeye, Carrying 2 Suitcases, Windup, Tin, 8 In. 258.00
Toy, Popeye, Dippy Dumper, Celluloid, Tin Lithograph, Clockwork, Marx, 9 In. 550.00
Toy, Popeye, Drummer, Hand Action, Tin Lithograph, Chein, 7 In. 660.00
Toy, Popeye, Figure Tumbles Down Easel, Wood, 6 x 20 In.   40.00
Toy, Popeye, Grows When Eats Spinach, Box, 1960s, 11 1/2 In. 450.00
Toy, Popeye, Head Goes Up & Down, Celluloid, Painted, Clockwork, Box, Japan, 8 In. . .   880.00
Toy, Popeye, In Barrel, Walking Action, Windup, Tin, Chein, 7 In. 495.00
Toy, Popeye, In Barrel, Windup, Tin, Chein, 1930s, 7 In. . . . . .695.00 to 1495.00
Toy, Popeye, In Rowboat, Pressed Steel, Hoge Mfg., 1935, 14 In. 610.00
Toy, Popeye, On Tricycle, Peddles In Circle, Bell, Tin & Celluloid, Linemar, 4 1/2 In. . . .   440.00
Toy, Popeye, Parrot Cages, Tin, Windup, Chein, 8 1/2 In. . . . . .230.00 to 330.00
Toy, Popeye, Parrot Cages, Tin, Windup, Marx, Box, 1930s 675.00
Toy, Popeye, Patrol Motorcycle, Cast Iron, Hubley, 1930s, 8 1/2 In. 3392.00
Toy, Popeye, Pilot In Airplane, Spinning Action, Chein, 1930, 6 1/2 In. 360.00
Toy, Popeye, Pilot In Airplane, Tin Lithograph, Clockwork, Marx, 8 In. 440.00
Toy, Popeye, Pilot In Airplane, Tin Lithograph, Mechanical, Marx, 9 In. . . . . .585.00 to 725.00
Toy, Popeye, Pop-Up, Boom Boom, Paper Lithograph On Wood, Fisher-Price, 9 1/2 In. . .   225.00
Toy, Popeye, Pop-Up, Push Down, Pipe, Spinach Can, Sign, Box, Linemar, 7 1/2 In. 990.00
Toy, Popeye, Punching Bag, Tin Lithograph, Clockwork, Chein, 7 1/2 In. 550.00
Toy, Popeye, Roller Skater, Holds Spinach Can, Blue Pants, Box, Windup, 7 In.   3630.00 to 4560.00
Toy, Popeye, Roller Skater, Mechanical, Tin Lithograph, Linemar, 5 3/4 In. 825.00
Toy, Popeye, Shooting Basketball, Windup, Linemar 1400.00
Toy, Popeye, Sparkling, Finger-Operated Action, Box, Chein, 5 1/2 In. 460.00
Toy, Popeye, Walking, Tin Lithograph, Chein, 1932, 6 In. . . . . .240.00 to 475.00
Toy, Popeye, Xylophonist, Strikes Notes While Moving, Noma, c.1957, 10 1/2 x 9 In. 175.00
Toy, Sand Set, Pail, Shovel, Character Head Molds, Peer Products Co., c.1960 . . . .   18.00
Toy, Truck, Transit, Linemar, 12 1/2 In. 1195.00
Toy, Wimpy, Celluloid, Windup, Japan, 1930s 230.00
Toy, Wimpy, On Tricycle, Peddles In Circle, Linemar, 4 1/2 In. 918.00
Trinket Box, Popeye & Wimpy, Wood, 1930s 145.00
Wallpaper, Character Repeats, Joliet Wallpaper Mills, King Features, 19 1/4 x 70 1/2 In. .   190.00
Watch, Face On Dial, Arms Shown As Hands, New Haven, Box, 1930s 1265.00

PORCELAIN factories that are well known are listed in this book under
the factory name. This category and the two following list pieces made
by the less well-known factories. Porcelain-Contemporary lists pieces
made by artists working after 1975. Porcelain-Midcentury includes
pieces made from the 1950s to the 1980s.

Abacus, Blue & White, Calligraphy, Chinese, 19th Century, 5 x 13 1/4 x 6 1/4 In. 635.00
Basin, Exotic Birds In Tree Branches, Inside & Out, Fishscale Band, 4 1/2 x 16 3/8 In. 110.00
Basket, Centerpiece, Sitzendorf, Reticulated, Polychrome, Dresden Style, 18 x 13 In. 748.00
Basket, Navette, White, Gold, Royal Blue, Rectangular Plinth, Putto, Paw Feet, 6 1/2 In. .   1610.00
Basket, Potpourri, Cover, Hand Painted, Floral Band, Branch Handle, 4 1/4 In. 460.00
Basket, Reticulated Footed, Square Base, Anneau D'Or, Paris, 9 x 10 In. 405.00
Basket, Turtledove On Cover, Blue Ribbon, Holding Letter, H & S, 7 7/8 In. 300.00
Berry Set, Scenes, Blue To Pink Rims, Mehlem, Bonn, Germany, 5 Piece 100.00
Biscuit Jar, Pink Flowers, Yellow Matte, Gilded Bands, Conch Shell Finial, 7 1/2 In. 35.00
Bowl, Bamboo, Pine & Prunus, Blue, White, Wide Border, Meiji, Japan, 12 In. 230.00
Bowl, Centerpiece, Gilt Bronze Mounted, Sevres Style, Oval, Early 20th Century, 17 In. . .   1955.00
Bowl, English Market Scenes, Grimwades, Royal Winton, 10 1/2 x 8 3/4 In. 50.00
Bowl, Figural, Gilt Decorated, Reticulated, Putti, Early 20th Century, 4 x 8 3/4 In. 575.00
Bowl, Hand Painted Phoenix, Flowers, Gilt, Anchor Mark, France, 11 x 5 In. 360.00
Bowl, Hand Painted, Square, Austria, 10 In. 45.00
Bowl, Man Portrait, Brocade Curtain Border, Blue, White, Meiji, Japan, 11 7/8 In. 290.00
Bowl, Panels, Mandarin Life Scene, Chinese, c.1795, 5 x 11 1/2 In. 2970.00
Bowl, Polychrome, Bell Shape, Passion Flower Design, Yellow Ground, 7 In. 980.00

Bowl, Stand, Gilt Oriental Figures, Pagoda, 1870s, 11 1/4 In. 430.00
Bowl, Stylized Flowers & Dragons, Chinese, K'ang Hai Period, 3 1/8 x 8 1/2 In. 325.00
Box, Blue & White, Scroll Shape, Riverscape, Chinese, c.1900, 7 1/2 x 9 In., Pair 375.00
Box, Gilt Bronze, Continental, Early 20th Century, 6 x 5 1/2 x 5 1/2 In. 1095.00
Box, Sevres Style, Courting Couple Scene, Gilt Metal Mounted, 4 In. 345.00
Box, Sevres Style, Gilt Bronze Mounted, Miniature, Round, Reeded Frame, 6 1/4 In. 1265.00
Brushpot, Deer, Pine Tree, Blue, White, Qing Dynasty, Chinese, 1600-1700, 6 1/4 In. 2185.00
Bust, Children, Girl In Headscarf, Boy In Coronet, 1930s, 9 1/2 In. Pair 316.00
Cachepot, Blue Landscape Scene Reserve, Leaf Rim, 1840s, 9 1/2 In. 7765.00
Cachepot, Eggplant, Enameled Bird, Fruit, Squirrel, Gilt, Paw Feet, Jacob Petit, 7 In. ... 1456.00
Cachepot, Saucer, Blue & White, Deer, Flowers, Hexagonal, c.1900, 10 1/2 x 13 1/2 In. .. 1035.00
Cachepot, Scalloped Rims, Green Dragon, Base Rim, Blue, Orange, 7 1/2 x 8 In. 110.00
Cachepot, Urn Shape, Dried Leaves & Flowers, c.1900, 7 1/2 x 10 1/4 In., Pair 225.00
Candlestick, Putti Seated, Supporting Floral Bobeche, Germany, 1920s, 10 1/4 In., Pair .. 250.00
Centerpiece, Cobalt Blue, Cherubs, Flowers, Reticulated, 13 1/2 In. 336.00
Charger, Polychrome Enamels, Earthquake Fish, Late 19th Century, 3 1/4 x 16 In., Pair .. 805.00
Charger, Shogun & Dragon, Phoenix Scene, Japan, 1840s, 24 In. 1610.00
Charger, Tower & 2 Men, Lattice, Flower Basket Border, Holland, 1790, 15 In. 990.00
Cheese Keeper, Hand Painted, Light Green, Flowers, Gold Accents, C.C. Hulme, c.1901 . 220.00
Chocolate Pot, Floral Bands, Enamel, Green Ground, Gold Outline Leaf, 9 1/2 In. 45.00
Coffee & Tea Service, Chinoiserie, Landscapes, Gilt Border, Late 19th Century, 5 Piece .. 2185.00
Coffeepot, Character, Woman, Holding Coffeepot, Umbrella, Head Is Stopper, 11 In. 159.00
Coffeepot, Pink, Gilt Pyramid In Reserve On Cobalt Ground, Paris, 10 3/4 In. 520.00
Compote, Openwork, Acorn & Oak Leaf Design, Gilding, 2 Handles, 17 In. 525.00
Cup & Saucer, Painted, Scenic, Cerulean Blue Band, Scroll Handle, Paw Feet, 3 5/8 In. .. 1035.00
Cup & Saucer, Tea Leaves Fortune, Paragon ....*Illus* 48.00
Cup & Saucer Set, Continental, Pink Ground, Mid 19th Century, 6 Piece 546.00
Dish, Blue & White, Bird & Peony Design, 18th Century, 5 3/4 In. 115.00
Dish, Heart Shape, Enameled Flowers, Gold, Blue, Pink, Early 19th Century, 11 In., Pair . 258.00
Dish, Hen On Nest Cover, c.1890, 9 1/2 In. 230.00
Dish, Hen Shape, Sitting On Nest, Bisque Body, Early 20th Century, 11 In. 290.00
Dish, Hen Shape, Sitting On Nest, Early 20th Century, 7 1/2 In. 345.00
Dish, Leaf Shape, Flowers, Twisted Handle, Longton Hall, 8 1/2 & 8 3/4 In., Pair 3360.00
Dish, Portrait, Napoleon, Josephine, Frame, R. Sinori, Italy, 4 1/2 In., Pair 77.00
Dish, Swan On Basket Cover, Luster, Enameled, Gilt, 6 x 6 3/8 In. 165.00
Dish, Sweetmeat, Navette Shape, England, Early 19th Century, 12 In., Pair 92.00
Ewer, Stippled Flower Branch, Gilt, Pink & Green Striped Neck, RW, 9 In. 82.00
Figurine, Actors, With Face Masks, Polychrome, Japan, 20th Century, 9 In., Pair 345.00
Figurine, American Eagle, Standing Proudly, Carpie, 16 1/2 In. 200.00
Figurine, Bear, Playing String Bass, Hand Painted, Maker's Stamp, 5 1/8 In. 55.00
Figurine, Boy Blowing Horn, Popov, Russia, c.1830, 6 In. 1093.00
Figurine, Boy In Nightgown, Father's Shoes, Umbrella, 7 1/2 In. 135.00
Figurine, Boy Shearing Sheep, Popov, Russia, c.1840, 4 1/2 In. 920.00
Figurine, Boy, Seated On Tree Trunk, Popov, Russia, c.1830, 4 1/2 In. 413.00
Figurine, Boy, Standing, Holding Lamb Over Shoulders, Popov, Russia, 5 1/2 In. 575.00
Figurine, Bun Merchant, Male, Kornilov, Russia, c.1850, 7 In. 1093.00

Porcelain, Cup & Saucer, Tea Leaves
Fortune, Paragon

Porcelain,
Figurine, Chinese
Man, Imperial,
1780, 8 1/2 In.

Porcelain, Figurine,
Girl, On Tree
Trunk, Marked,
1860, 10 1/4 In.

Porcelain, Figurine,
Peddler, Basket, Backpack,
Popov, Russia, 19th
Century, 8 3/4 In.

Porcelain, Figurine,
Soldier, Russian,
Kuznetsov, 1840,
11 In.

Porcelain, Figurine,
Traveler, Walking Stick,
Popov, 1845,
8 7/8 In.

Porcelain, Figurine,
Woman, Standing,
Kozlov,
7 1/2 In.

Figurine, Cherubs Wrestling With Goat, Flower Base, Metal Plinth, Germany, 15 In. 176.00
Figurine, Chinese Man, Holding Fur Trimmed Hat, Imperial, Russia, c.1780, 8 1/2 In. . . . 5462.00
Figurine, Chinese Man, Imperial, 1780, 8 1/2 In. . . . . *Illus* 5462.00
Figurine, Cobbler, Popov, Russia, 19th Century, 6 1/4 In. 748.00
Figurine, Cockatiels, Blanc De Chine, Giltwood, Germany, Mid 20th Century, 27 In., Pair 1610.00
Figurine, Columbine, Standing, Cape, Mask, Imperial, Russia, c.1840, 5 3/8 In. 1092.00
Figurine, Cossack, Long Coat Off Shoulders, Signed, 19th Century, 7 3/4 In. 1035.00
Figurine, Dancers, Polychrome & Gilt Crinoline Decoration, Germany, 10 In. 173.00
Figurine, Dandy, Meissen-Style, Standing, Flower Garland, Popov, c.1840, 5 7/8 In. 920.00
Figurine, Dog, Seated, Hand Painted, Green Collar, Gilt Bell, Base, 6 3/4 x 7 1/2 In. 275.00
Figurine, Elephant With Young, Bisque, Italy, 15 1/2 x 21 In. 577.00
Figurine, Forester, Carrying Basket, Tools, Kozlov, Russia, c.1825, 6 7/8 In. 1265.00
Figurine, Frog Bandsmen, Playing Instruments, Sitzendorf, c.1900, 5 In., 7 Piece 2160.00
Figurine, Geese, Neck Turned, Rests On Back Feathers, Chinese, 20th Century, 10 1/4 In. 104.00
Figurine, Girl Dancing, Hand On Hip, Kornilov, Russia, c.1850, 7 1/2 In. 546.00
Figurine, Girl, On Tree Trunk, Marked, 1860, 10 1/4 In. . . . . *Illus* 1265.00
Figurine, Hercules, Nemean Lion, Kozlov, Russia, c.1830, 7 1/2 In. 1840.00
Figurine, Hound, Seated, Green Collar, Gilt Bell, 19th Century, 9 In. 470.00
Figurine, Hound, Seated, Mottled Base, Popov, Russia, 19th Century, 8 1/2 In. 633.00
Figurine, Lady Playing Spinet, Wearing Bonnet, Popov, Russia, 19th Century, 7 1/2 In. . . . 1840.00
Figurine, Lion, Oval Base, Jacob Petit, 7 x 10 1/4 In. 1725.00
Figurine, Man & Woman, Colonial Dress, Blue & White, 12 1/2 In., Pair 633.00
Figurine, Man & Woman, Dancers, Rococo Base, Popov, 1840, 5 3/8 In., Pair 1380.00
Figurine, Man In Arabesque Dress, Seated On Tasseled Cushion, 6 In. 1093.00
Figurine, Man, Woman, Meissen-Style, 18th Century Costume, Bower, 12 In., Pair 672.00
Figurine, Monkey Band, Playing Drum, Various Instruments, 4 3/4 In., 5 Piece 632.00
Figurine, Monkey Eating Fruit, Meissen Style, Achille Bloch, Late 1800s, 17 In. 2400.00
Figurine, Monkey, Continental, Late 19th Century, 18 In. 2400.00
Figurine, Officer, Russian, Long Coat, Sword, Kuznetsov, Russia, c.1840, 11 In. 1380.00
Figurine, Papa, Boy, Pink Gown, Father's Shoes, Carrying Umbrella, 7 1/2 In. 135.00
Figurine, Peasant Dancing, Male, Holding Hat Over Head, Kornilov, c.1840, 7 1/2 In. . . . 1035.00
Figurine, Peasants Dancing, Imbibing, Oval Base, Leaves, Gilt, c.1900, 14 1/2 In. 588.00
Figurine, Peddler, Basket, Backpack, Popov, Russia, 19th Century, 8 3/4 In. . . . . *Illus* 1955.00
Figurine, Phoenix Birds, Carved, Serpentine, 19 In. 403.00
Figurine, Priest, Standing, Traditional Costume, Popov, Russia, 19th Century, 7 7/8 In. . . . 1265.00
Figurine, Scribe, Holding Slippers, Basket, Imperial, Russia, Early 1800s, 7 3/4 In. 1840.00
Figurine, Soldier, Dragoon Regiment, Russia, 1820, 7 1/4 In. 1495.00
Figurine, Soldier, Kissing Girlfriend, Germany, 9 In. 184.00
Figurine, Soldier, Russian, Kuznetsov, 1840, 11 In. . . . . *Illus* 1380.00

Figurine, Tea Vendor, Pouring From Kettle, 19th Century, 7 1/4 In. 1825.00
Figurine, Traveler, Bearded, Walking Stick, Popov, Russia, c.1845, 8 7/8 In. 1840.00
Figurine, Traveler, Man Carrying Pitcher, Walking Stick, Popov, Russia, c.1825, 4 In. 632.00
Figurine, Traveler, Walking Stick, Popov, 1845, 8 7/8 In. .... *Illus* 1840.00
Figurine, Troubadour Pirate, Seated, Holding Pistol, Popov, Russia, c.1827, 7 1/4 In. ... 1840.00
Figurine, Woman Seated On Tree Trunk, Basket Of Flowers On Head, c.1860, 10 1/4 In. .. 1265.00
Figurine, Woman Seated, Dog, Kornilov, Russia, Mid 19th Century, 9 1/4 In. 1265.00
Figurine, Woman, Carrying Basket, Kozlov, 18th Century, 7 1/2 In. 805.00
Figurine, Woman, Flower Bouquet & Fan, J.M. Meir, 1914, 12 x 6 1/2 In. 290.00
Figurine, Woman, Long Hair, Diaphanous Wrap, Painted, Wagner, 1900s, 5 In. 138.00
Figurine, Woman, Modeled As Sphinx, Pompadour Hairstyle, Leopard, c.1850, 6 3/4 In. .. 1380.00
Figurine, Woman, Sportsman, Hunting Dogs, Ludwigsburg, c.1770, 9 1/4 In. 9000.00
Figurine, Woman, Standing, Kozlov, 7 1/2 In. .... *Illus* 805.00
Figurine, Young Poacher, Holding Dead Bird, Dog, Popov, 1840, 7 1/4 In. 1092.00
Flowerpot, Saucer, Blue & White, Hexagonal, Landscape Scene, 11 In., Pair 1035.00
Fruit Coolers, Footed, Insert, Bale Handles, Berry Finial, 7 x 7 In., Pair 470.00
Group, Man & Woman, Playing Flute, Greiner & Halzapfel, Signed, 1910, 7 3/4 In. 225.00
Group, Napoleon & Family, Bisque, Playing With Daughter, Gilt Metal, 19 1/2 In. 1725.00
Group, Seated Lady, Gentleman, Fountain, Early 20th Century, 8 1/4 x 7 In. 431.00
Group, Woman, Seated, Playing Cello, 18th Century Clothes, Continental, 10 x 8 In. 145.00
Incense Burner, Basket Weave, Blue Underglaze Flower Sprays, 4 1/4 In. 258.00
Inkstand, Double, Flower Basket Shape, Jacov Petit, 5 x 10 In. 4830.00
Jar, Cover, Potschappel, Flower Encrusted, 2 Handles, 20th Century, 9 1/2 In. 431.00
Jar, Powder Blue, Cover, Oval, 4 Chinese Characters, Late 19th Century, 6 In. 25.00
Jar, Red Flowers, Blue Leaves, Allover Foliage Ground, Teak Lid, 16 In. 110.00
Jar, Temple, Flowers, Fauna, Exotic Birds, Chinese, 20th Century, 12 In., Pair 28.00
Jardinere, Stand, Gray Marbled Ground, England, c.1815, 6 3/4 In. 345.00
Jardiniere, Blue & White, Bronze Mounts, Birds, Flowers, Continental, 21 x 14 In. 518.00
Jardiniere, Blue & White, Cylindrical, Landscape, Late 19th Century, 19 x 23 In. 920.00
Jardiniere, Blue & White, Oval, Flowers, Early 20th Century, 10 1/2 In. 58.00
Jardiniere, Cherry Blossom, Butterfly, Ivory Ground, Wood Stand, 14 In., Pair 720.00
Jardiniere, Cottage Scene, Brass Beaded Rim, Black Ground, 5 1/2 x 7 1/2 x 9 In. 145.00
Jardiniere, Japanese, Polychrome, Applied Handles, 1868-1912, 11 1/2 x 13 3/4 In. 1380.00
Jardiniere, Oriental Decoration, Oval, Cobalt Blue, White Scenes, 23 1/2 x 16 In. 2970.00
Jardiniere, Sevres Type, Ormolu Mounted, c.1900, 11 1/4 In. 1955.00
Kettle, Dresden, Ormolu, Floral Handles, Spout, Rococo Stand, c.1900, 16 In. 764.00
Mustache Cup, 2 Lovers, Women & Man Seated On Grass, Pink Luster, 1887, 3 1/4 In. ... 145.00
Pillow, Blue & White, Rectangular, Foo Lion, Peony Design, 4 1/2 x 2 x 2 1/2 In. 17.00
Pitcher, Gilt, Raised, Gilded Swans, Foliate Design, 6 1/4 In. 400.00
Plaque, 2 Peasant Girls, Resting, Harvest, Cobalt Blue Ground, Signed A.F., 13 In. 805.00
Plaque, Angel Blowing Horn, Gilt Background, Hand Painted, 14 In. 345.00
Plaque, Dark-Haired Beauty, Wreath In Hair, Bare Shoulders, Frame, 5 In. 400.00
Plaque, Dutch Girl, Flowers, Fruit, Painted, 20th Century, 5 x 3 3/4 In. 635.00
Plaque, Flowers & Fruit, Giltwood Frame, 1835, Rectangular, 12 1/2 In. 7600.00
Plaque, Flowers, In Pot, Cherub, Gilt Shadowbox Frame, 19 x 16 1/2 In. 330.00
Plaque, Girl, With Candle, Guten Nacht, Gilt Frame, Germany, Early 1900s, 5 In. 1035.00
Plaque, L'Esilave After Shatillon, Painted, Slave Girl, Dock, Brass Frame, 5 x 4 In. 865.00
Plaque, Madame Dubarry, Continental, Painted, Velvet Lined Frame, 7 1/4 x 5 1/2 In. ... 315.00
Plaque, Madonna Of The Chair, Round, Giltwood Frame, Italy, c.1900, 11 x 11 In. 1410.00
Plaque, Madonna, Gilt Frame Shadow Box, 5 1/2 x 3 In. 1400.00
Plaque, Maiden Feeding Doves, Glass Backing, Giltwood Shadowbox, 13 3/4 In. 1035.00
Plaque, Nude, Forest Scene, F.N. Sutton, 11 x 8 In. 1265.00
Plaque, Woman, Classical Clothes, Wooden Frame, Continental, 6 x 4 1/2 In. 1150.00
Plaque, Woman, Medieval Scarf, Coat, Gold Cross Pendant, Bamboo Frame, 8 3/4 In. ... 110.00
Plate, 2 Men, Drinking Water, Gilt Leaf & Green Borders, Imperial, 9 3/4 In. 747.00
Plate, Cavetto, Medallions, Blue & White, Kraak, Ming Dynasty Wanli, Chinese, 9 In. ... 290.00
Plate, Central Bouquet, Garlands, 20th Century, 9 1/2 In., 6 Piece 315.00
Plate, Continental, Anneau D'Or Buffet Germany, 12 1/2 In., 12 Piece 575.00
Plate, Dinner, Gilt Rimmed, Continental, 20th Century, 10 5/8 In., 20 Piece 575.00
Plate, Gilt Gloria, Belle Epoque Style, Fairies, Germany, 10 3/8 In., 12 Piece 1840.00
Plate, Hirado, Landscape Design, Molded Floral Ground, Late 19th Century, 6 In. 115.00
Plate, Japan Pattern, Lattice Work Border, c.1830, 7 1/2 In., Pair 280.00

Plate, Kakiemon, Chrysanthemums, Floral Festoon, Japan, 1700s, 5 1/2 In. 825.00
Plate, Luncheon, Imperial, Nicholas II, Blue Enamel Band Border, Gilt, c.1900, 9 1/4 In. . . 316.00
Plate, Maiden Holding Flowers, Gilt, Jeweled Border, 9 1/2 In. 2185.00
Plate, Tulips, Bold Flowers, Green, Gold Trim, Square, Royal Winton, 9 3/4 In. 60.00
Plateau, Figural, 2 Dancers, Polychrome, Gilt Crinoline, Germany, 10 In. 172.00
Platter, Oval, Queen, Grimwades, 10 x 7 3/4 In. 25.00
Punch Bowl, Blue & White, 8 Panels, Flowering Trees, Chrysanthemums, 1900s, 14 In. . . 1955.00
Punch Bowl, Central Scenic Panel, Green, Gilded, Austria, 6 1/2 x 14 3/4 In. 605.00
Punch Bowl, Cottage, Bridge, Hand Painted, 6 x 13 1/2 In. 190.00
Punch Bowl, European Men & Women Panels, Wood Base, 7 1/4 x 16 In. 715.00
Punch Bowl, Flowers, Gilt Scrolls, Flowers, Early 20th Century, 12 In. 287.00
Salt, Master, Navette Shape, Footed, Jacob Petit, Mid 19th Century, 5 1/2 x 6 1/2 In. 690.00
Sauceboat, Leaf Form, Insects, Twig Handle, 18th Century, 4 1/4 x 8 1/2 In. 935.00
Shaker, Woman's Face, Headdress & Crown, R In Star, 5 1/4 In. 250.00
Sugar & Creamer, Queen, Grimwades, 4 1/2 In. 40.00
Tea Strainer, Purple Violets, Leaves, White & Tan Ground, Germany, 1 3/4 x 4 In. 125.00
Teapot, 2 Tiers, Upper Strainer, Loop Handle, Upturned Spout, 10 x 7 1/2 In. 259.00
Teapot, Blue & White, Chinese, 19th Century, 5 In. 345.00
Teapot, Gilt Stars, Oval, Griffon Handle, Elephant Head Spout, Old Paris, 9 In. 980.00
Teapot, Trembly Rose Type, Floral, Birds Head Spout, Longton Hall, 5 1/2 In. 7200.00
Teaspoon, Floral, Rococo, Gilt Rim, Bristol A, 1775 . . . . 2900.00
Tete-A-Tete, Alice In Wonderland, Bisque, 20th Century, 5 5/8 In., 3 Piece 690.00
Tray, God & Goddess, Offered Drink By Cherubs, Enamel, Burgundy, 17 In. 646.00
Tray, Vegetable, Blue & White, Floral Borders, Late 18th Century, 17 1/2 In. 1725.00
Tureen, Blue & White, Applied Garlands, Fruit, Leaves, Ladle, Tray, Italy, 9 x 13 1/2 In. . . 66.00
Tureen, Cover, Bird Finial, Cauliflower, Germany, 19th Century, 5 5/8 In. 2280.00
Tureen, Cover, Oval, 2 Handles, Continental, Early 20th Century, 13 3/8 In. 184.00
Tureen, White & Gold, Ram Mask Handles, Round, England, 12 x 7 3/4 In., Pair 2415.00
Umbrella Stand, Blue Gentlemen, Amid Bamboo Stalks, 20th Century, 23 1/2 In. 150.00
Umbrella Stand, Tapering, Flowers & Berries, Austria, 20th Century, 21 1/4 In. 175.00
Urn, Berry Finial Cover, Champleve, Cherub, Landscape, V. Bern, 17 In., Pair 2530.00
Urn, Blue & White, Baluster Shape, Foo Dog Heads, Chinese, 28 In. 1610.00
Urn, Cobalt Blue Glazed, Domed Cover, Scrolled Gilt Handles, Bohemia, 16 In. 175.00
Urn, Cover, Flowers On Sides, Birds' Nest, Butterfly, Spiders, Ring Handles, 15 In., Pair . 1045.00
Urn, Cover, Urn Finial, Green Glaze, Trumpet Foot, Early 20th Century, Bohemia, 26 In. . 400.00
Urn, Figures, Pagodas, Trees, Fisherman, Ear Handles, Cobalt Blue, 22 1/2 In., Pair 220.00
Urn, Louis XVI Style, Gilt Bronze, Chinese, Late 19th Century, Pair 13200.00
Urn, Sevres Type, Ormolu Mounted, Cobalt Blue Glaze, Early 20th Century, 26 3/4 In. . . 3450.00
Vase, 2 Women In Pagoda, Trees, Raised Band At Base, 20th Century, 17 3/4 In. 330.00
Vase, Altar, White & Gold, Elliptical, Cross, Monogram, France, 14 3/4 In. 400.00
Vase, Amber, Gray, Turquoise Glaze, Carved Frogs, 13 1/2 x 11 1/2 In. 230.00
Vase, Art Nouveau, Bust Of Woman, Girandoles, Austria, 15 In. 2585.00
Vase, Baluster, Flared Rim, Bird & Flower Panels, Applied Foo Dog Heads, 14 In. 110.00
Vase, Blue & White, Immortal Garden, Flared Baluster, Ch'ien Lung, 16 3/4 In., Pair 980.00
Vase, Blue, White, Baluster Shape, Waisted Base, Meiji Period, Japan, 9 In. 345.00
Vase, Bottle, Ducks, Waterweeds, Blue & White, Yuan Dynasty, Chinese, 11 1/2 In. 2070.00
Vase, Bottle, Mirror Black, Globular, Low Foot Ring, Kangxi, 10 1/2 In. 690.00
Vase, Bottle, Sang-De-Boeuf, Copper Red Tone, Lamp Mounted, Oval, Chinese, 14 In. . . 460.00
Vase, Bulb, Raised Gold, Floral Reserves, Scrolled Rocaille Feet, Jacob Petit, Paris, 9 In. . 2185.00
Vase, Cherry Blossoms, Flowers, White Ground, Teak Stand, 22 1/4 In. 80.00
Vase, Cover, Blue & White, Baluster Shape, Late 19th Century, 30 In., Pair 1495.00
Vase, Cover, Figural Scenes, Ram's Head Handles, Potschappel, 26 In. 800.00
Vase, Double Gourd Shape, Straw Glaze, Wood Base, c.1820, 18 In. 800.00
Vase, Egrets, Standing In Water, Cylindrical, Tapered, Short Neck, Flared Rim, 12 In. 115.00
Vase, Flared, Scalloped Rim, Baluster Shape Body, Late 19th Century, 24 3/4 In. 179.00
Vase, Louis XVI Style, Ormolu Mount, Blue Glaze, Loop Handles, 1800s, 11 In., Pair . . . 2875.00
Vase, Mermaids, Net Of Fish 1 Side, Swimming Other Side, 11 x 12 In. 742.00
Vase, Napoleon III, Allegorical Reserve, La Peinture, 2 Handles, 23 In. 635.00
Vase, Oriental, Cylindrical, Hand Painted, Character Signature, 5 x 11 In., Pair 60.00
Vase, Painted Riverscape, Oval, Meiji, Japan, 10 In. 290.00
Vase, Pedestal, Hand Painted, Peasant Wedding Couple, Handles, Continental, 11 In. 180.00
Vase, Pierced Oval Rim, Shells, Jacob Petit, 14 1/4 x 6 x 8 1/2 In., Pair 3910.00

Vase, Potpourri, Gilt Bronze Mounted, Sevres Style, Cobalt Blue Ground, 17 In. 3105.00
Vase, Red Glaze Neck, Rose To Celadon, Flambe, Oval, Qing Dynasty, Chinese, 18 In. .. 115.00
Vase, Rococo Style, Jacob Petit, Mid 19th Century, 11 1/2 In. 690.00
Washbowl, Chinese Blue & White, 19th Century, 18 1/2 In. 345.00
Writer's Coupe, Robin's-Egg Blue, Dragon, Fruit, Glazed, Chinese, 19th Century, 5 In. .. 115.00

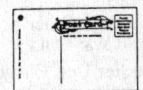

POSTCARDS were first legally permitted in Austria on October 1, 1869. The United States passed postal regulations allowing the card in 1872. Most of the picture postcards collected today date after 1910. The amount of postage can help to date a card. The rates are: 1872 (1 cent), 1917 (2 cents), 1919 (1 cent), 1925 (2 cents), 1928 (1 cent), 1952 (2 cents), 1959 (3 cents), 1963 (4 cents), 1968 (5 cents), 1973 (8 cents), 1975 (7 cents), 1976 (9 cents), 1978 (10 cents), 1981 (12 cents), 1981 (13 cents), 1985 (14 cents), 1988 (15 cents), 1991 (19 cents), 1995 (20 cents).

Alfred E. Neuman, Picture, Mad Magazine, Impko, 1960s, 3 1/2 x 5 1/2 In. 26.00
Ambassador Hotel, Front Of Hotel, Postmarked 6-25-1937 .... 5.00
Brookside Park, View Of Lake, Cleveland, Ohio, 1930s, 3 1/2 x 5 1/2 In. .... *Illus* 3.00
Camp Curry, California, Sierra Club Logo, Buff Color, July 11, 1911 .... 15.00
Catalina Island, Avalon Bay & Casino, 1940 .... 6.00
Coronado Hotel, Smokey Bear Cancellation, 1956 .... 2.00
Cypress Point Golf Course, California, Famous 16th Hole, 1950s 8.00
Eureka Inn, Redwood Area, Linen, c.1940 .... 5.00
Folder, Sandusky, Ohio 50.00
Fordyce Baths, Hot Springs, White Border, c.1930 .... 7.00
GAR Reunion, Photograph 50.00
Gastonia Relief, Food Relief For Strikers, 1929 .... 183.00
Grand Canyon National Park, Guests Arriving, Others On Horseback, c.1912 .... 7.00
Grand Canyon National Park, Hermit's Rest, Fireplace, c.1915 .... 6.00
Harry Houdini, Hamburg-America Liner, SS Imperator, Photograph, Signed 863.00
Harry Houdini, In Chains, Photograph, Campbell-Gray, May, 22, '04, Signed 4140.00
Hearst Ranch, West's Largest Most Popular Dude Ranch, Pleasanton, Ca., 1930 .... 20.00
Hester Street, Active Center Of Jewish Neighborhood, c.1910 .... 18.00
Hollywood Roosevelt Hotel, Night View, Neon Sign, Linen 6.00
Hotel St. Catherine, Catalina Island, Beach At Avalon Bay, Linen 6.00
Hotel St. Catherine, Entrance, 1931 .... 5.00
Hotel Wheeler, People In Front, c.1912 .... 7.00
Illinois Sewing Machine Co., 1915 .... 1.00
Indian 45 Motorcycle, 1941, 3 1/2 x 5 1/2 In. 104.00
Jefferson Hotel, Pine Bluff, Interior Of Women's Parlor, May 1906 .... 6.00
Mad, Alfred E. Neuman, What Me Worry, 1950s 5.00
Old King Cole Bar, St. Regis Hotel, New York, 3 1/2 x 8 1/4 In. 85.00
Paradise Inn, Swimming Pool, c.1930 .... 7.00
Post Office, U.S. Customs House, Cleveland, Ohio, 1930s, 3 1/2 x 5 1/2 In. .... *Illus* 2.00
Rockingham Memorial Hospital, Barrisonburg, Va., Colored Linen, 1940 .... 10.00
Spaniel On Hind Legs, Photograph, York, Pennsylvania 25.00

Postcard, Brookside Park, View Of Lake, Cleveland, Ohio, 1930s, 3 1/2 x 5 1/2 In.

Postcard, Post Office, U.S. Customs House, Cleveland, Ohio, 1930s, 3 1/2 x 5 1/2 In.

Tavern Restaurant, Newark, N.J., 1930s	1.00
Valentine's, Man In Formal, War, Woman Holding Her Heart, Lace, 1910	12.00
Wild Bill Hickok, Guy Madison, Signatures, 1954, 3 x 5 In.	12.00
Wisconsin Logging Scene, 2 Loggers & Oxen, Photograph	14.00

POSTERS have informed the public about news and entertainment events since ancient times. Nineteenth-century advertising or theatrical posters and twentieth-century movie and war posters are of special interest today. The price is determined by the artist, the condition, and the rarity. Other posters may be listed under Movie, Political, and World War I and II.

Anchor Line, Glasgow & New York, Ship Picture, 1930, 40 x 25 In.	1265.00
Ask Alexander, Profile Alexander's Head Form Question Mark, Color, 41 x 27 In.	288.00
Baie Du Mont St. Michel In Avranches, Woman, Scarf, Parasol, A. Bergevin, 43 x 31 In.	2990.00
Boston & Maine Railroad, Revere Beach Sunday, 44 1/8 x 29 1/8 In.	1840.00
Bridlington, Promenade With Families, Couples, Sailors, 1938, 40 x 50 In.	4600.00
British Empire Trophy Race, April 4, 1936, 30 x 20 In.	605.00
Broadway Limited, New York, Philadelphia, Chicago Connections, 1940, 40 x 25 In.	920.00
Brockton Fair, Child Pulled By White Rooster, Matted, c.1910, 22 x 15 In.	316.00
Bruce Springsteen, Ashbury Park, 1971	4680.00
Cannery, San Francisco, Psychedelic, Woman, People In Water, Ducks, 1973, 22 x 28 In.	23.00
Cape Cod, Night & Day Village Picture, Lighthouse, 1945, 42 x 28 In.	1150.00
Chicago, Illinois Central, Lake Michigan Beach, Gold Coast, 39 1/2 x 27 In.	2990.00
Circus, Barnum & Bailey, Strobridge, 29 x 37 In.	925.00
Circus, Christy Bros., Animal Show, Lithograph, Riverside Print Co., Chicago, 38 x 42 In.	550.00
Circus, Ringling Bros. Barnum & Bailey Three Ring Circus, 1926, 25 x 41 In.	1200.00
Eaton's, 3 Fashionable Flappers Around A Statue Of Cupid, L. Caillaud, 47 x 31 In.	3910.00
Enchanted Isle, Martha's Vineyard Picture, 1934, 41 3/4 x 28 1/4 In.	7475.00
End The War Now, New Haven Inaugural Action Committee, 11 x 17 In.	27.00
Erte Alphabet, Silver, Black, White, Female Figure Letters, Frame, 1970s, 36 x 24 In.	55.00
George Vanderbilt Cup, Roosevelt Raceway, October 12th, 1936, Helck, 20 In.	2530.00
Gleneagles, Lover's Gait Golf Course, 1924, 39 1/4 x 59 3/4 In.	9200.00
Grand Prix Of Cuba At Havana, Silk Screen, February 25, 20 x 30 In.	913.00
Have You Had Your Pill Today, Uncle Sam, J.M. Flagg, 1964, 30 x 24 In.	52.00
Hippie, Pop Musical Group, Dave Schiller, 1960s, 21 x 16 In.	115.00
Kar-Mi Performing, Startling Mystery All Time, Selma, 1914, 28 x 41 1/2 In.	400.00
Nantucket, Town & Port View, 1925, 41 3/4 x 28 1/8 In.	6670.00
New York Central, Niagara Falls, Rainbow, 40 1/2 x 26 1/4 In.	2530.00
New York Central Lines, Adirondack Mountains, Lake Placid, 1935, 40 1/2 x 26 1/4 In.	8050.00
Olympic, 1912, Stockholm, Male Figure, O. Hjortzberg, 40 x 29 In.	2530.00
Pennsylvania Railroad, Home For Over Christmas & New Year's, 40 1/4 x 25 1/4 In.	632.00
Red Riding Hood, Pinup Picture, 1929, 20 x 30 In.	18.00
Ringling Bros. & Barnum-Bailey Circus, Lion & Tiger, 1960s, 28 x 43 1/2 In.	230.00
Roberts Circus, Black Man On Donkey, Frame, Donaldson Lithograph Co., 28 x 20 In.	357.00
Rolling Stones, Naked Lady Tour, 1969, 14 x 23 In.	35.00
See Boulder Dam, New York Central, Boulder Dam Route, 41 x 27 1/2 In.	1380.00
Sevilla, Semana Santa, Pablo Sebastian, Roman Scene, 1951, 19 1/2 x 20 In.	45.00
Silverstone, Daily Express Trophy Race, May 7, 1955, 30 x 20 In.	480.00
SS Statendam, Holland America Line, Part Blueprint Of Ship, R. Dirksen, 38 x 24 In.	690.00
Sunbeam Alpine, Car, Teal, Red Interior, Haycock Press, England, c.1960, 30 x 40 In.	1265.00
Swiss Air, Airplane Over Alps, Fisherman In Boat, Herbert Leupin, 1951, 25 x 40 In.	135.00
Transportation Scenes, 1882, 31 x 24 5/8 In.	920.00
Uncle Sam, John Bull, Miss Liberty & Britannia, Frame, Expo 1900, 38 x 27 In.	750.00
Uncle Sam As Forest Ranger, J.M. Flagg, Frame, 1934, 20 x 12 In.	230.00
United Airlines, Chicago, Framed Under Glass, 41 x 26 In.	105.00
United Airlines, New England, Framed Under Glass, 41 x 26 In.	33.00
Vento & Tommy Atkins, Ventriloquist, Holding Dummy, Frame, 1920, 29 x 18 In.	288.00
Virginian Circus, Shrine Circus In Harrisburg Pa., 1960s, 14 x 22 In.	30.00
Weary Willie Walker, Color Lithograph, 19 1/3 x 13 1/4 In.	85.00
Woman's Basketball, Sigil, Brev. Colleg., Washington In., 1911, 14 x 22 In.	270.00
Woodstock Music & Art Fair, Mounted, Framed, 1969, 23 3/4 x 17 3/4 In.	690.00
Yellowstone National Park, Park View, 1904, 29 1/2 x 44 1/2 In.	2530.00
You Can Lick Runaway Prices, Uncle Sam, J.M. Flagg, 1950, 24 x 18 In.	170.00

POTLIDS are just that, lids for pots. Transfer-printed potlids had their heyday from the 1840s to the early 1900s. The English Staffordshire potteries made ceramic containers with decorative lids for bear's grease, shrimp or meat paste, cold cream, and toothpaste. Printed advertising and pictures of historical events, portraits of famous people, or scenic views were designed in black and white or color. Reproductions have been made.

Alexandra Cherry Toothpaste, Pink Ground, 3 1/4 In.	495.00
Atkinsons Bear Grease, 3 1/8 In.	50.00
Bears Grease, 3 In.	385.00
Begging Dog, F & R Pratt, 1870s, 3 In.	120.00
Cattle & Ruins, F & R Pratt, c.1860, 4 1/2 In.	110.00
Chlorine Detergent & Orris Dentifrice, Black Transfer, 3 x 3 In.	825.00
Chlorine Detergent & Orris Dentifrice, Royce & Estery, 2 7/8 In.	220.00
Cold Cream, 1 3/4 In.	137.00
Compound Extract Of Copaiba Cubets & Iron, Cure Gonorrhea, 3 In.	440.00
Crown Perfumery Toothpaste, 3 In.	240.00
Dartmouth Tooth Paste, Dartmouth Castle, 2 1/2 In.	320.00
Dartmouth Tooth Paste, Dartmouth Castle, 3 1/2 In.	240.00
De Courcy's Nerve Destroyer, Black Transfer, 1 In.	89.00
Dr. Allport's Dentifrice For Cleansing & Beautifying Teeth & Gums, 3 3/8 In.	470.00
Dr. E.I. Coxe's Extract Of Copaila Sarsaparilla, 2 7/8 In.	385.00
Dr. Wright's Pearl Ointment, Domed Lid, Pink Transfer, 2 1/4 In.	60.00
Edinburgh Cold Cream, 2 1/4 In.	48.00
French Street Scene, F & R Pratt, c.1860, 4 In.	70.00
Harrogate Cold Cream, Black Transfer, 2 3/4 In.	40.00
Hauling In The Trawl, Pratt Factory, c.1860, 4 In.	70.00
Hull Cold Cream, Holy Trinity Church, 3 1/2 In.	911.00
Hull Skin Ointment, Blue Transfer, Gold Band, 3 1/4 In.	175.00
I See You My Boy, 3 Figures, 1860s, 4 In.	70.00
Imperial Hotel, Hair Dressing, Turkish Baths, Green Transfer, 2 1/2 In.	527.00
Irishman, Man & 2 Women, c.1860, 4 In.	80.00
Jewsbury & Brown Cold Cream, Black Transfer, Blue Border, 2 3/4 In.	200.00
Jules Hauel Perfume, Long Haired Man In Center, 3 1/3 In.	1439.00
Man Of Ross Cold Cream, Black Transfer, 2 3/4 In.	160.00
Otto Of Rose Cold Cream, Gold Band, 2 1/4 In.	48.00
Phalon's Ambrosial Shaving Cream, 3 1/2 In.	130.00
Philadelphia Exhibition, F & R Pratt, 1876, 4 In.	80.00
Prince Consort, F & R Pratt, 4 In.	106.00
Rivals, 2 Men & Wman, c.1860, 4 In.	112.00
Second Appeal, No By Heaven I Exclaimed, 1857, 4 In.	96.00
Shakespeare's House, F & R Pratt, 1850s, 4 In.	47.00
Strasburg, T.J. & J. Mayer, c.1850, 4 In.	80.00
Superior Toothpaste, Green Transfer, 3 In.	103.00
Tam O'Shanter, Cauldon Factory, c.1860, 4 In.	144.00
Thirsty Soldier, Man Seated, 2 Women Standing, c.1870, 4 In.	103.00
Tremeers Cherry Toothpaste, Ink Ground, 2 3/4 In.	128.00
Tunbridge Wells Cold Cream, Black Transfer, 3 In.	32.00
Wolf & Lamb, F & R Pratt, c.1860, 4 In.	64.00
Wright's Gold Medal Shaving Cream, Dog Over Fallen Soldier, 3 1/2 In.	145.00

POTTERY and porcelain are different. Pottery is opaque; you can't see through it. Porcelain is translucent. If you hold a porcelain dish in front of a strong light, you will see the light through the dish. Porcelain is colder to the touch. Pottery is softer and easier to break and will stain more easily because it is porous. Porcelain is thinner, lighter, and more durable. Majolica, faience, and stoneware are all pottery. Additional pieces of pottery are listed in this book in the categories Pottery-Art, Pottery-Contemporary, Pottery-Midcentury, and under the factory name. For information about pottery makers and marks, see *Kovels' Dictionary of Marks—Pottery & Porcelain: 1650–1850* and *Kovels' New Dictionary of Marks—Pottery & Porcelain: 1850 to the Present.*

Bowl, Earthenware, Enameled, Blue, Green, Flowers, Serpents, Lappet Foot, 1800s, 15 In. 316.00

Bowl, Glazed, Flower Shape, White Spot, Black Ground, Henan, 19th Century, 4 1/2 In. ... 58.00
Bowl, Leaves Exterior, Celadon Glaze, Wooden Base, 3 x 5 1/2 In. 358.00
Bowl, Recumbent Lion Finial, Basalt, Neale & Co., 4 1/8 In. 198.00
Bust, Makala, Blackware, Nepal, 18th Century, 3 1/2 In. 115.00
Cachepot, Neoclassical Style, Black, Satin, Pompeian Red, Continental, 8 x 9 In. 144.00
Cake Crock, Flowers & Vines, Blue Accents, Stoneware Lid, 1850s, 6 1/4 In. 715.00
Charger, Adam & Eve, Tin Glazed, Bristol, England, 1750, 13 In. 2860.00
Charger, Flowers, Blue Ground, Persia, 1800s, 11 In. 161.00
Charger, S.E.G., Multitoned, Blue Crystalline Glaze, 12 1/4 In. 276.00
Chicken Waterer, Impressed 1 At Shoulder, Blue Accents At Hole Rim, 1840, 11 In. 413.00
Churn, Double Plume, Fitted, Carved Wood Guide, c.1870, 13 In. 275.00
Churn, Green Ash Glaze, 2 Handles, Impressed 5, Southern, 9 1/2 x 17 In. 110.00
Cream Pot, Swan, Old Scotch, G. Haidle, Union Pottery, Newark, 1871, 9 1/2 In. 1265.00
Creamer, Uncle Sam's Bust, Grimwades, Royal Winton, 1910, 4 3/4 In. 58.00
Crock, Bird, Flack & Van Arsdale, Canada, c.1870, 3 Gal., 10 1/2 In. 688.00
Crock, Budding Flower 2 Sides, Incised, Applied Loop Handles, c.1800, 9 1/4 In. 2420.00
Crock, Earthenware, Oval, 11 In. 80.00
Crock, Standing Horse, Blue Accents, Incised Eye, c.1870, 6 Qt., 8 In. 2640.00
Crock, Starface, 8-Point Star, Detailed Face, Lyons, 5 Gal., 11 1/2 In. 3850.00
Dish, Hen On Nest Cover, 3 Chicks, Cover, Earthenware, Glazed, c.1880, 8 1/2 In. 1265.00
Dish, Hen On Nest Cover, Bisque Body, Natural Glaze, c.1890, 10 1/2 In. 431.00
Figurine, Ao-Kutani, Hotei, Green Kimono, Treasure Sack At Feet, 19th Century, 9 1/2 In. 345.00
Figurine, Blackamoor, Standing, Holding Cushion, Raised Stand, 56 In., Pair 1265.00
Figurine, Cat, Seated, Buff Clay, Brown Glaze, Yellow Spots, 7 1/4 In. 110.00
Figurine, Cat, Seated, Free Standing, Brown Glaze, 11 1/4 In. 935.00
Figurine, Cat, Seated, Molded Yellow, Green, Brown Streaking, 19th Century, 10 In. 5775.00
Figurine, Cat, Standing On Rooftop, White, Green Eyes, Dark Green Rooftop, 16 In. 1320.00
Figurine, Cupid, Holding Bouquet, Impressed & Painted Mark, Austria, 19 In. 460.00
Figurine, Dog, Scotty, Sylvac, No. 1209, 11 In. 103.00
Figurine, Dog, Seated, Unglazed, Brown Glaze On Tail, Ears & Face, Base, 4 1/2 x 3 In. . 467.00
Figurine, Duck, Sylvac, No. 1499, 4 1/2 In. 58.00
Figurine, Gentleman, Blue Frock Coat, Pink Pants, Powdered Wig, 9 1/2 In. 36.00
Figurine, Girl, Holding 2 Baskets, Blue Green, 9 1/2 In. 30.00
Figurine, Lion, Reclining, Glazed, Stamped Moore Ceramics, Uhrichsville, O., 10 x 5 In. . 440.00
Figurine, Peach Of Immortality, Glazed, Chinese, Late 19th Century, 6 In. 230.00
Figurine, Woman, Holding Flower Basket, Hand Painted, Artist Signed, Italy 55.00
Flask, Figural, Monkey On Chamber Pot, Green, Blue Glaze, 5 1/2 In. 121.00
Jar, Canning, 4 Wide Stripes, c.1850, 9 1/2 In. 110.00
Jar, Orange & Brown Splotches, Daubs Over Green Glaze, Flared Rim, Oval, 12 3/4 In. .. 935.00
Jar, Oval, Flying Bird, Tulips, c.1870, 2 Gal., 11 In. 743.00
Jar, Oval, Incised Accents At Shoulder & Handles, Ocher, Boston, c.1800, 15 In. 495.00
Jar, Preserves, Brushed Blue, Double 2's At Ears, Lyons, c.1860, 11 In. 605.00
Jardiniere, Earthenware, England, c.1900, 9 x 9 In. 81.00
Jardiniere, Eskimos In Boat, 7 x 10 In. 345.00
Jardiniere, Pedestal, Flowers, Mottled Glaze, 12 x 29 1/2 In. 172.00
Jug, 3-Petal Leaf, Black, Cobalt Blue, C.E. Pharis & Co., c.1865, 13 1/2 In. 413.00
Jug, Devil Face, Upturned Eyebrows, Chin Whiskers, Shard Teeth, 15 3/4 In. 550.00
Jug, Devil Face, Upturned Eyebrows, Long Chin Whiskers, Shard Teeth, 16 1/2 In. 330.00
Jug, Devil Face, Upturned Eyebrows, Mustache, Chin Whiskers, 15 In. 1210.00
Jug, Double Flowers Over 2, Cobalt Blue, c.1850, 14 In. 468.00
Jug, Ducal, 2-Tone Green, Leaves, Charlotte Rhead, c.1935, 9 3/4 In. 588.00
Jug, Face, Blue, White Eyes, Glossy Glaze, Stamped, B.B. Craig, 5 x 6 In. 81.00
Jug, Face, Grotesque, Brown Mottled Glaze, 2 Pebbled Teeth, Signed, 10 1/2 In. 805.00
Jug, Grotesque, 2 Rows Of Shard Teeth, Double Handles, 16 1/2 In. 275.00
Jug, Stanford, Crimean War Commemorative, Portraits, c.1860, 10 1/2 In. 575.00
Jug, Sunburst, N. Clark Jr. Athens, New York, c.1850, 2 Gal., 14 In. 523.00
Jug, Wedding, Unglazed Orange Black, 2 Spouts, Maude Welch, 1930s, 3 In. 132.00
Jug, Whiskey, Souter Johnnie, Scotland, 11 In. 1200.00
Mug, Raised White Figures, Playing Cricket, Brown, 19th Century, 4 In. 173.00
Panel, Maid Picking Blossom, Earthenware, England, Frame, c.1870, 14 1/4 x 8 3/8 In. .. 7800.00
Pitcher, Blue Glaze, Relief Images Of Birds, Hare, Dogs, Hound Handle, 11 In. 173.00
Pitcher, Blue, Painted Line & Vine Decoration, Pewter Lid, Base Rim, 7 In. 115.00
Pitcher, Flowers, Blue Accents At Handle & Spout, Pennsylvania, c.1860, 10 In. 1815.00

Pitcher, Flowers, Brushed Blue, Shenandoah Valley, c.1850, 3 Gal., 17 In.	1210.00
Pitcher, Goodwin, Red Ground, Native American Figures, 12 In.	86.00
Pitcher, Native American Figure, Red Ground, Goodwin, 13 In.	86.00
Pitcher, Uncle Sam's Bust, Crazing, Grimwades, Royal Winton, 1920, 7 3/4 In.	58.00
Planter, Marguerita, Girl, Basket On Head, Hedi Schoop, 12 1/2 In.	125.00
Planter, Rustic Style, Acorns, Leaves, Deepcar, c.1807, 3 1/2 In.	44.00
Plate, Combware, Yellow, Brown, Slip, New England, Early 19th Century, 11 In.	285.00
Plate, Couple Dancing, Wooden Shoes, 4 Apple Rim, Charles Maillard, c.1920, 13 In.	1250.00
Plate, White Tin Glaze, Painted Cherub, Fluted Rim & Foot, 7 3/4 In.	470.00
Punch Bowl, Floral, Gilt Trim, Crown Derby Type, Japan, 1800s, 12 3/4 In.	750.00
Sugar Shaker, Silver Plated Top, English Village At Top, Band Of Yellow, 6 In.	55.00
Teapot, Bargeware, Teapot Finial, Paste Plaque, Brown Glaze, Flowers, 12 In. ..... *Illus*	330.00
Teapot, Cover, Figural, Wileman & Co., Intarsio Ware, c.1900, 4 1/2 In.	3600.00
Teapot, Oribe, Oval, Stylized Flowers, c.1900, 5 3/4 In.	69.00
Tureen, Cover, Acorn Finial, Underplate, Oval, 2 Handles, Round Foot, 11 3/4 In.	230.00
Tureen, Cover, Lemon Finial, Underplate, Tin Glazed, Oval, Handles, c.1910, 12 x 17 In. .	316.00
Umbrella Stand, Beige, Cylindrical, American, c.1900, 22 x 10 In.	175.00
Umbrella Stand, Geometric Design, Green, Blue Glaze, 19 In.	145.00
Umbrella Stand, Pink Flowers, Scholars Standing Amid Green Leaves, 23 3/4 In.	110.00
Umbrella Stand, Water Lily, Hand Painted, Cylindrical, Early 20th Century	460.00
Vase, 2 Handles, Embossed, Yellow Berries, Green Leaves, Mottled Ground, 11 1/2 x 7 In.	175.00
Vase, Band Of Trees, Mountains, Green Matte Glaze, Signed Ephram, 7 1/4 In.	220.00
Vase, Blue & Yellow Crystalline Drip Glaze, Baluster, Marked, Aultcliffe, 5 1/2 In.	288.00
Vase, Bottle, Flared Neck, Oval, Scheier, 6 x 3 1/2 In.	275.00
Vase, Bretby, Brown, Hunter Green Glaze, 18 1/2 In.	470.00
Vase, Brown Mouth, Rust, Tanraoul Lachanel, 1910, 8 1/2 In.	5100.00
Vase, Bulbous, 2 Buttressed Handles, Medallion, Secession, Austria, 8 1/2 x 4 1/2 In.	259.00
Vase, Bulbous, Green Matte Glaze, Egyptian Potters Band, Dressler, Mark, JBD, 6 1/2 In.	165.00
Vase, Bulbous, Lustered Green, Yellow, Squat, 5 x 5 1/2 In.	460.00
Vase, Bulbous, Pillar Mold, 8 Ribs, Flared Mouth, England, 6 1/2 x 7 In.	55.00
Vase, Burley Winter, Mythological Figures, Mottled, Red, Brown Matte Glaze, 17 In.	460.00
Vase, Cloudburst, Green, Brown, Mottled, 3 x 2 1/8 In.	358.00
Vase, Cylindrical, Tapered, Handle, Blue, Green Glaze, Denby, 9 1/4 In.	45.00
Vase, Earthtone Stripes, Flattened Sides, Toshiko Takaezu, 5 1/2 x 4 3/4 In.	345.00
Vase, Flambe, Hoswon's, England, c.1913, 3 In.	46.00
Vase, Flowers, Peach, Ivory, Gold Trim, Shell Mold, 2 Handles, Austria, 8 In.	40.00
Vase, Hamada, Textured, Cobalt Blue, Gray, Brown, Shoji Hamada, 11 x 4 In.	1320.00
Vase, Magenta, Enamel Flowers, 2 Handles, Gold Trim, Mehlem, Germany, 12 In.	600.00
Vase, Molded Leaf, Green Matte, Arts & Crafts, 8 In.	115.00
Vase, Mulberry Rose, White Ironstone, A.J. Wilkinson, c.1860, 5 In.	55.00
Vase, Multitoned Green Matte Drip Glaze, Double Gourd Shape, Luxembourg, 8 In.	230.00
Vase, Mythological Figures, Relief, Tan, Brown, Green, Dove Handles, 8 In.	63.00
Vase, Panoramic Landscape, Figures, Oval, Early 20th Century, 12 In.	400.00
Vase, Seahorses & Leaves, Red & Crackled Gray, 6 1/4 In.	325.00
Vase, Swirl Design, Incised Mark, Eureka Springs Pottery, 5 1/2 In.	253.00
Wall Pocket, Creamware, Cornucopia, Urn, Scroll Flowers, England, 1800, 7 3/4 In.	441.00

Use denture cleaning tablets to remove a stain from a ceramic teapot. Follow the directions for use with false teeth.

Pottery, Teapot, Bargeware,
Teapot Finial, Paste Plaque,
Brown Glaze, Flowers, 12 In.

Wall Pocket, Fish, Blue, Black, Ceramicraft, 7 1/2 x 7 5/8 In. 35.00
Water Cooler, 3 Flowers, Dotted Tornadoes, Ovoid, W.H. Farrar, 5 Gal., 15 In. 1018.00
Water Cooler, Plume, Cobalt Blue, Double Handle, Satterlee & Mory, 6 Gal., 19 In. 1210.00
Wig Stand, Earthenware, Georgian Style, Brown & Black Glaze, 1900s, 10 1/2 In. 230.00

POTTERY-ART Art pottery was first made in America in Cincinnati, Ohio, during the 1870s. The pieces were hand thrown and hand decorated. The art pottery tradition continued until the 1920s when studio potters began making the more artistic wares. American, English, and Continental art pottery by less well-known makers is listed here. Most makers listed in *Kovels' American Art Pottery,* such as Arequipa, Ohr, Rookwood, Roseville, and Weller, are listed in their own categories in this book. More recent pottery is listed under the name of the maker or in the Pottery category.

Bowl, Crouching Man, Tattooed Face, Red Glaze, Mexico, 2 1/4 In. 27.00
Bowl, Santo Domingo, Rust & Black Geometric, A. Garcia, 4 x 13 In. 74.00
Box, Cover, Blue Around Rim At Top & Base, Rhead, 1 1/2 x 4 1/4 x 5 In. 225.00
Candlestick, Painted, Blue Background, Wardle, 13 1/2 In. 69.00
Figurine, Lion, Reclining, Yellow Glaze Ground, 9 1/4 x 15 In. 1980.00
Figurine, Nude, Kneeling, Looking Into Mirror, 11 1/2 In. 1150.00
Head, Woman With Hat, Wiener Werkstatte, Signed, 9 1/2 In. 4890.00
Inkwell, Reclining Nude Female, In Waves, Signed, France, Early 20th Century, 10 1/2 In. 115.00
Jar, Cover, Yellow & Pink Leaves, Iridized Trim, Rhead, 1940s, 6 1/4 In. 300.00
Jardiniere, Flowers, Trailing, Frederick Hurten Rhead, 6 1/8 In. 500.00
Jardiniere, Stand, Brown & Tan Running Glaze, Paw Feet & Legs, 54 In. 530.00
Planter, Green Matte Glaze, Elks In Wooded Forest Scene, 12 x 15 In. 375.00
Plaque, Scenic, Peasant Walking, Spanish Mission, Frame, Signed Zuloaga, 6 x 8 In. 690.00
Sake Set, Iron Red, Silver, Bottle, Waste Bowl, Cup & Saucer, Japan, 1940s, 11 Piece ... 127.00
Teapot, Green Matte Glaze, University City, 1910, 8 1/2 In. 4025.00
Umbrella Stand, Art Nouveau, Pale Green, E. Muller Type, 1900, 27 x 18 x 12 In. 5700.00
Umbrella Stand, Molded Geometric Design, Green Matte Glaze, 19 In. 545.00
Umbrella Stand, Painted, Water Lilies, Cylindrical, Fire Glazing, 20th Century 460.00
Vase, 3 Dog Scene, 5 1/4 In. 35.00
Vase, Arabesque, Flowers On Gray Ground, Rhead, 7 1/2 In. 210.00
Vase, Blue Floral Design, Gold, University City, 1912, 3 In. 1495.00
Vase, Bottle Shape, Salt Glaze, Incised, Cobalt Blue Poppies, Frackleton, 6 In. 8625.00
Vase, Brown & Green Matte Glaze, Flat Shoulder, Squat, W.J. Walley, 2 1/2 x 5 In. 518.00
Vase, Bulbous, Mottled Green, Black Matte Glaze, 4 Curled Handles, 5 x 5 In. 40.00
Vase, Charcoal Matte Glaze, Turquoise Horses, Germany, Signed, 14 In. 748.00
Vase, Charcoal, Green Matte Glaze, Flared, Zark, 8 In. 1035.00
Vase, Circular Platform Top, 4 Angled Handles, Matte Green Glaze, 11 3/4 In. 110.00
Vase, Cobalt Blue Crystalline Glaze, Spherical, A. Robineau, 3 3/4 x 4 In. 6325.00
Vase, Cylindrical, Closed-In Rim, Squeezebag, Panels, Jervis, Oyster Bay, 5 1/2 x 3 In. .. 400.00
Vase, Double Gourd, Glazed, Dalpayrat ....*Illus* 6325.00
Vase, Dragon Handles, Birds, Flowers, Theodore Deck, 11 In., Pair 2645.00
Vase, Dragon, Purple, Green, Blue Glaze, Burmantoft, Faience, 1880s, 13 1/2 In. 1020.00
Vase, Flared, Gray, Black Textured Glaze, North State Pottery, Sanford, N.C., 7 1/2 In. ... 250.00
Vase, Green Matte Glaze, Molded Vertical Leaves, 7 1/2 In. 431.00
Vase, Green Matte, 3 Handles, 7 x 3 1/2 In. 209.00
Vase, Green Textured Matte Glaze, Swollen Body, 3 Handles, Marlotte, Marked, 9 1/4 In. 402.00
Vase, Landscape Scene, Black Leafless Trees, Bright Orange Sky, Jervis, 5 7/8 In. 440.00 to 550.00
Vase, Light Blue High Glaze, Round, California Faience, 3 3/4 In. 132.00
Vase, Molded Flowers, Purple Glaze, 4 In., Pair 60.00
Vase, Molded Leaves, Multicolored Green, Blue Matte Glaze, Brown, 8 In. 413.00
Vase, Mottled Pink Matte Glaze, Handles, 7 In. 160.00
Vase, Multicolored Blue Glaze, California Faience, 11 In. 231.00
Vase, Multitoned Green Crystalline Drip, Impressed Mark, 7 In. 100.00
Vase, Orange, Yellow Brown, Flame Painted, Bronze Glaze, Marked, Brouwer, 12 In. 8625.00
Vase, Overlapping Leaves, Brown, Green Matte Glaze, 7 3/4 In. 431.00
Vase, Painted, Serpent, Bird, William De Morgan, c.1897, 9 3/8 In. 2400.00
Vase, Pheasant, Red Flowers, Double Handles, Oval, Decoro, 8 1/2 In. 165.00
Vase, Phlox, Honey Bee, Burgundy, Green, Ivory Ground, J. Bennet, 7 1/2 In. 2875.00
Vase, Shouldered, Dark Blue, Red, Charcoal Glaze, 7 In. 403.00

Vase, Tigereye Glaze, Impressed Mark, 9 In. 46.00
Vase, White Slip Design, Limoges Glaze, Blue Ground, M.L. McLaughlin, 1878, 8 In. . . . 750.00

POTTERY-CONTEMPORARY lists pieces made by artists working after 1975.
Disc, Christopher Gustin, 1985, 25 In. 575.00
Pitcher, Devil's Face, Smiling On Reverse, Pablo Picasso, Black, White, 5 In. 805.00
Vase, Blue & Green Hare's-Fur Glaze, Bulbous, Pillin, 6 x 6 In. 489.00
Vase, Blue Glaze, Black Luster, Cabat, 6 x 2 1/2 In. 935.00
Vase, Blue, Green Drip Glaze, Cabat 59, 3 x 2 3/4 In. 250.00
Vase, Bottle, Ridges, Brown, Green Matte Glaze, Laura Andreson, 6 1/2 In. 299.00
Vase, Charcoal Matte Glaze, Black, Cabat, 3 1/2 x 2 In. 302.00
Vase, Cobalt Blue, Periwinkle Purple, Green Drip, Cabat, 2 1/2 x 2 1/2 In. 300.00
Vase, Crackled Oxblood Glaze, Ivory Ground, Stonelain, 11 1/4 x 5 1/4 In. 230.00
Vase, Fish, Speckled Beige, Stoneware, Vivika & Otto Heino, 6 1/2 In. 520.00
Vase, Globular, Emerald Green, Deep Brown Sections, Cabat, 3 x 2 1/4 In. 440.00
Vase, Gourd Shape, Brilliant Aqua Glaze, Charcoal Black, Cabat, 3 3/4 x 2 In. 300.00
Vase, Green, Blue Crystalline Mate, Cabat, 3 In. 240.00
Vase, Lavender Gray Mottled Glaze, Chartreuse Ground, Cabat, 4 1/2 In. 825.00
Vase, Onion Shape, Brown, Tan Vertical Streaks, Black, Cabat, 2 1/3 x 2 In. 275.00
Vase, Onion Shape, Cobalt Blue, Black Sections, Ivory Ground, Cabat, 3 In. 300.00
Vase, Painted, 4 Horses, Pillin, 4 In. 400.00
Vase, Painted, Birds, Pillin, 8 1/2 In. 489.00
Vase, Pear Green, Frosted Ivory, Emerald Green, Cabat, 3 1/2 x 2 1/4 In. 360.00
Vase, Purple Glaze, Black Highlights, Cabat 59, 2 3/4 x 3 In. 660.00
Vase, Spherical, Mustard Yellow Over Yellow Matte Glaze, Cabat, 3 In. 192.00
Vase, Squat, Quatrefoil Lip, Mauve Glaze, Waco, Early 1900s, 4 3/4 In. 77.00
Vase, Teardrop, Green Glaze, Cabat, 4 x 2 1/2 In. 660.00

POTTERY-MIDCENTURY includes pieces made from the 1950s to the 1980s.
Bowl, Blue & White Glaze, Flaring Scheier, 1950s, 3 x 6 1/4 In. 201.00
Bowl, Blue, White & Brown Volcanic Glaze, Footed, Natzler, 6 3/4 In. 1610.00
Bowl, Brown Pattern, Beige Ground, Purple Interior, Heino, 5 1/2 x 7 In. 259.00
Bowl, Green Matte Glaze, Sarong Clad Figure Pedestal, Brayton, 13 x 12 In. 374.00
Bowl, Half Human Half Fish, Mottled Tan, Blue, Green Glaze, Scheier, 1964, 5 In. 518.00
Bowl, High Ends, Scalloped, Splattered Green, Los Angeles Pottery, 13 x 8 In. 32.00
Bowl, Low, Blue Glaze, Purple, Ivory, Natzler, 5 In. 1495.00
Bowl, Periwinkle Glaze, Ivory, Cobalt Blue Speckled, Scheier, 6 In. 440.00
Bowl, Sang Reduction Glaze, Slight Iridescence, Signature, Natzler, 5 In. 1725.00
Bowl, Tan High Glaze, Handles, Scheier, 2 In., Pair 115.00
Bowl, White Faces, Purple Ground, Hemispherical, Scheier, 3 1/2 x 4 3/4 In. 259.00
Bust, Monkey, Cubist Style, Matte Gray, Blue Glaze, Signed Helbo, 7 x 8 In. 345.00
Charger, Woman Holding Child, Cream & Mauve, Round, Scheier, 16 In. 748.00
Dish, 2 Women & Bird, Signed, Pillin, 9 1/2 In. 2070.00
Dish, Scalloped, Turquoise, Cream Inside, La Mirada, No. 206, 8 1/2 x 7 1/2 In. 36.00
Dish, Serving, Orange Splatter, Gold Inside, Maurice Of Calif., 14 x 5 1/2 In. 10.00
Egg Plate, Red, Orange, Vines In Relief, 6 Footed, Treasure Craft, 12 1/2 In. 25.00
Figurine, Boy, Standing, Holding Floral Swag, Weiner Keramik, 18 In. 863.00

Pottery-Art, Vase,
Double Gourd,
Glazed, Dalpayrat

Pottery-Midcentury,
Figurine, Poppet,
Mother In Scarf With
Baby, Poppytrail, 6 In.

Figurine, Poppet, Mother In Scarf With Baby, Poppytrail, 6 In. .... *Illus*   40.00
Jardiniere, Lois Loraine To Sister Rose Gertrude, 1936 ....   69.00
Planter, Bathtub, Flowers On Tub, California Originals, 12 1/4 x 6 3/4 In. 35.00
Planter, Double Cone, LaGarado Tackett, c.1950, 11 1/2 x 20 1/2 In. 5175.00
Planter, Hank, DeLee, 1940s, 7 In. 50.00
Planter, Oriental Boy, Holding 2 Baskets, McCarty Bros., 1944, 8 In. 26.00
Planter, Oriental Girl, Holding Jars, McCarty Bros., c.1948, 8 1/4 In. 28.00
Planter, Sassy Girl, Blue Skirt, Peasant Blouse, 8 Sides, McCarty Bros., 9 In. 95.00
Plaque, 5 Dancers, Original Hanger, Pillin, 15 1/2 In. 3138.00
Plaque, 5 Dancers, Woman & 2 Fish, Signed, Pillin, 4 In. 3220.00
Plaque, Profil De Jacqueline, Faience, Glaze, Painted, Picasso, 1956, 8 In. 2700.00
Plate, Danseuse Moderne, Dancers, Cocktails, V. Schreckengost, 1931, 11 In. 8815.00
Platter, Joueur De Flute, Faience, Glazed, Painted, Pablo Picasso, c.1947, 15 In. 4500.00
Platter, La Danse, Faience, Glaze, Painted, Pablo Picasso, c.1957, 16 In. 2280.00
Platter, La Pique, Faience, Glaze, Painted, Round, Pablo Picasso, c.1950, 15 In. 6000.00
Platter, Poisson Bleu, Faience, Glazed, Painted, Pablo Picasso, c.1953, 5 In. 3000.00
Platter, Visage De Femme, Faience, Glaze, Painted, Pablo Picasso, c.1953, 15 In. 3900.00
Relish, 3 Sections, Chartreuse, Gold Handle, Marcia Of Calif., 11 3/4 In. 25.00
Relish, 4 Sections, Apples, Grapes, Pears In Relief, Treasure Craft, 13 1/2 In. 25.00
Shaker, Avocado Green, Handle, Cheese, Los Angeles Pottery, 6 1/2 In. 10.00
Vase, Bottle Shape, Green, Brown, Yellow Matte, Fantoni, 11 1/2 In. 374.00
Vase, Gray Lava Glaze, Yellow Overflow, Painted Signature, Natzler, 6 In. 5750.00
Vase, Green Flambe Glaze, Worcester State Hospital, W.J. Walley, 3 x 6 In. 345.00
Vase, Green, Blue, Brown Crystalline Glaze, Leaf Handles, Denbac, 10 In. 518.00
Vase, Green, Blue, Tan Crystalline Glaze, Swirled, Handles, Denbac, 11 In. 978.00
Vase, Green, Tan, Ivory Drip Glaze, 5 Openings, Buttresses, Greber, 6 1/2 In. 402.00
Vase, Multitone Brown Glaze, Geometric Design, Peter Voulkos, 5 1/2 In. 2990.00
Vase, Pink, Yellow, Green, Brown Fish, Blue Ground, Flattened, Pillin, 6 In. 640.00
Vase, Primitive Woman Engulfed By Fish, Mocha, Brown, Scheier, 7 In. 660.00
Vase, Stylized Figures, Taupe & Brown, Round Shouldered, Scheier, 9 In. 1035.00
Vase, Stylized Woman, Sgraffito Frieze, Brown Glaze, Scheier, 16 In. 1265.00
Vase, Tan & Brown Matte Glaze, Painted & Incised Fish & Ribs, Heino, 6 In. 572.00
Vase, Tete De Femme Couronnee De Fleurs, Faience, Picasso, c.1954, 9 In. 7200.00
Vase, White, Cutout Design, Arabia, 7 In. 138.00

POWDER FLASKS AND POWDER HORNS were made to hold the gunpowder used in antique firearms. The early examples were made of
horn or wood; later ones were of copper or brass.

POWDER FLASK, Brass, Raised Floral Motif, Elk Head, Marked Hawksley, 19th Century ...   110.00
Horn, Brass Pins, Rings, Dram Graduations, Marked F. Gertner 275.00
Horn, Carved Spout, Animal Head, Metal Ends, Flat, 7 x 3 7/8 In. 143.00
Horn, Engraved Soldier On Horseback, Chasing Stag, 16th Century, 13 In. 750.00
Horn, For Wheel Lock Musket, Flattened, Wood Base Plug, 1600, 7 1/2 In. 725.00
Maple Burl, Early 19th Century 295.00
Scene Of Soldier On Horseback, Chasing Stag, 13 In. 750.00
POWDER HORN, Carved Crosshatched Band, Revolutionary Artillery, Wooden Plug, 14 In.   275.00
Cow Horn, Andrew Dunhamn, Powder Measure, November 1780, 11 In. 5875.00
Engraved Thistles, Scotland, 1700s, 9 In. 110.00
Molded & Carved Cherry Butt, Rattlesnake Carved Screw Tip, York County, 11 In. 1575.00
Rope Stamped Butt, Metal Hand, 13 1/2 In. 143.00
Spring Stopper Mechanism, 11 In. 123.00

PRATT ware means two different things. It was an early Staffordshire
pottery, cream-colored with colored decorations, made by Felix Pratt
during the late eighteenth century. There was also Pratt ware made
with transfer designs during the mid-nineteenth century in Fenton,
England. Reproductions of the transfer-printed Pratt are being made.

PRATT

FENTON

Box, Round, Lid, Scenic, Persuasion, 4 1/4 In. 33.00
Figurine, Hen, Yellow, Blue & Ocher Feathers, Green Base, Staffordshire, 3 1/2 In. 715.00
Figurine, Lion, Standing, Front Paw On Blue Ball, Rectangular Base, c.1815, 4 3/8 In. 2280.00
Figurine, Woman In Robe, Anchor, Blue, Orange, Green, Staffordshire, c.1790, 8 1/2 In. .   165.00
Jar, Battle Of The Nile, 4 1/2 In. Diam. 69.00
Jug, Cover, Figural, Bear, Muzzled, Holding Monkey, Boney's Friend, c.1805, 10 1/4 In. .   8400.00

Pipe, Figural, Multicolored, Mask Heads, Serpent, Hound Stem, Pearlware, c.1800, 9 In. .   288.00
Pitcher, Classical Warrior, Green, Gold, Dark Brown, Cobalt Blue, 5 5/8 In. 660.00
Pitcher, Hunt Scene With Riders & Dogs Chasing Rabbit, Cobalt Blue, Brown, 6 In. 935.00
Pitcher, Tavern Scenes, Foliage Around Base, 9 1/4 In. 275.00
Pitcher, Vine, Hunting Dog Scene, Searching For Bird, 6 3/4 In.   330.00
Plaque, 3 Huntsmen Outside Tavern, Embossed, c.1800, 8 3/4 In. 3300.00
Plate, Poultry Woman, Center Scene, 7 In. 60.00
Sauceboat, Figural, Duck, Ochre & Blue, c.1810, 7 In. 2700.00
Syrup, Seashell Design, Teal, Multicolored, Pewter Top, 7 1/4 In. 55.00

PRESSED GLASS was first made in the United States in the 1820s after the invention of glass pressing machines. Hundreds of patterns of pressed glass were made in complete table settings. Although the Boston and Sandwich Works was the most famous of the pressed glass factories, there were about sixteen other factories making pressed glass from 1830 to 1850, and still more from 1850 to 1900, when pressed glass reached its greatest popularity. It is now being widely reproduced. The pattern names used in this listing are based on the information in the book *Pressed Glass in America* by John and Elizabeth Welker. There may be pieces of pressed glass listed in this book in other categories, such as Lamp, Ruby, Sandwich, and Souvenir.

    100-Leaved Ivy pattern is listed here as Hundred-Leaved Ivy.
    1000-Eye pattern is listed here as Thousand Eye.
    Acanthus pattern is listed here as Ribbed Palm.
    Actress, Goblet, Lotta, 6 1/2 In. 80.00
    Actress, Platter, 7 1/8 x 11 1/4 In. 20.00
    Admiral Dewey pattern is listed here as Spanish American.
    Alba, Shaker, Sugar, Pink Opaque, 4 1/2 In. 190.00
    Alba, Shaker, Sugar, White Opaque, 4 1/2 In. 70.00
    Alhambra, Goblet, 6 1/4 In. 770.00
    Amberette, Goblet, 6 1/2 In. 130.00
    Anchor & Shield, Nappy, 10 1/2 In. 30.00
    Arch, Tumbler, Cobalt Blue, 3 In. 200.00
    Arch, Vase, Canary, Flared, Crimped Rim, 11 1/4 In. 504.00
    Argus, Eggcup 22.00
    Ashburton, Celery Dish, 10 1/2 In. 140.00
    Ashburton, Celery Vase, 9 In. 60.00
    Ashburton, Creamer, Applied Handle, 6 3/4 In. 190.00
    Ashburton, Decanter, Qt., 10 In. 90.00
    Aster & Leaf, Sugar Shaker, Emerald Green, 5 In. 450.00
    Austrian, Cordial, 3 In. 40.00
    Austrian, Wine, Emerald Green, 4 In. 300.00
    Baby Face, Goblet, Engraved Fern & Flower, 6 3/8 In. 210.00
    Baby Thumbprint pattern is listed here as Dakota.
    Banded Portland, Bottle, Water, Maiden's Blush, 8 1/2 In. 110.00
    Banded Portland, Bowl, Maiden's Blush, 2 In. 25.00
    Banded Portland, Goblet, Blue, 5 5/8 In. 50.00
    Banded Portland, Goblet, Yellow, 5 3/4 In. 45.00
    Banded Portland, Puff Box, Cover, Iridescent, 2 1/4 x 2 1/2 In. 40.00
    Banded Portland, Salt & Pepper, Maiden's Blush, 3 x 1 1/4 In. 45.00
    Banded Portland, Toothpick, Maiden's Blush, 2 3/8 In. 30.00
    Banded Worcester, Sugar, Cover, 9 1/4 In. 25.00
    Barberry, Goblet, 5 3/4 In. 20.00
    Barberry, Pitcher, Applied Handle, 9 In. 150.00
    Barley, Spooner 28.00
    Barrel Honeycomb, see also the related pattern Honeycomb.
    Barreled Block pattern is listed here as Red Block.
    Beaded Dewdrop pattern is listed here as Wisconsin.
    Beaded Grape, Cake Stand, 6 1/4 x 8 3/4 In. 170.00
    Beaded Grape, Cake Stand, Emerald Green, 6 1/4 x 9 In. 140.00
    Beaded Grape, Compote, Cover, Emerald Green, 11 x 8 1/2 In. 90.00
    Beaded Grape, Goblet, Emerald Green, 6 1/4 In., 4 Piece 325.00
    Beaded Grape, Pitcher, Emerald Green, Gold Trim, 10 1/4 In. 100.00

Beaded Grape, Tankard, Emerald Green Applied Handle, 10 In. 135.00
Beaded Grape, Wine, Emerald Green, 4 1/8 In., 4 Piece 110.00
Beaded Grape Medallion, Bowl, Cover, Oval, 7 1/8 x 10 1/4 In. 60.00
Bearded Head pattern is listed here as Viking.
Bearded Man pattern is listed here as Queen Anne.
Beehive, Sugar, Cover, Sandwich & Boston Glass, 1830, 8 3/4 In. 5225.00
Beehive & Thistle, Dish, 8 Sides 70.00
Bellflower, Celery Vase, 8 1/4 In. 500.00
Bellflower, Compote, 4 3/4 In. 50.00
Bellflower, Compote, 4 3/4 x 8 In. 56.00
Bellflower, Compote, 8 In. 120.00
Bellflower, Compote, Cover, 8 In. 200.00
Bellflower, Creamer, 7 In. 260.00
Bellflower, Goblet 66.00
Bellflower, Plate, 6 In. 25.00
Bellflower, Tumbler, Water, 3 3/8 In. 90.00
Belmont, Compote, Open, Vaseline, 8 1/2 x 10 3/4 In. 180.00
Bent Buckle pattern is listed here as New Hampshire.
Bigler, Compote, Cover, Double Knop Finial, Baluster Stem, Scalloped, 10 In. 250.00
Bigler, Creamer, Applied Handle, Footed, 6 In. 110.00
Bigler, Vase, Canary, Flared, 9 1/2 In. 518.00
Bigler, Vase, Gauffered Rim, Amethyst, Square Base, 1840-1860, 11 In. 2185.00
Bigler Variant, Goblet, Way Colonial Stem, 5 5/8 In. 70.00
Birch Leaf, Sauce, Vaseline 18.00
Bird & Strawberry, Goblet, 6 1/2 In. 700.00
Bird & Strawberry, Punch Cup, 6 Piece 110.00
Blackberry, Celery Vase, Milk Glass, 6 5/8 In. 25.00
Blackberry, Compote, Cover, Milk Glass, 8 3/4 In. 30.00
Blackberry, Dish, Sweetmeat, Cover, Hollow Stem, Wafer Foot, 7 x 5 1/2 In. 100.00
Bleeding Heart, Cake Stand, 8-Sided Stem, 10 7/8 In. 110.00
Bleeding Heart, Compote, Cover, 8-Sided Stem, 5 3/8 x 10 7/8 In. 60.00
Bleeding Heart, Creamer, Applied Handle 65.00
Bleeding Heart, Goblet, 6 1/4 In. . . . . .40.00 to 45.00
Bleeding Heart, Pitcher, Applied Handle, 8 3/4 In. 180.00
Bleeding Heart, Plate, 4 Egg Depressions, 4 x 7 In. 550.00
Bleeding Heart, Salt, 2 1/4 x 2 7/8 In. 100.00
Bleeding Heart, Tumbler, 3 3/4 In. 110.00
Block & Circle, Goblet, Ruby Stained Stem & Foot, 6 1/4 In. 100.00
Block & Fan pattern is listed here as Romeo.
Block & Fine Cut pattern is listed here as Fine Cut & Block.
Block & Star pattern is listed here as Valencia Waffle.
Block & Thumbprint, Creamer, Applied Handle, 5 1/2 In. 70.00
Bluebird pattern is listed here as Bird & Strawberry.
Bowtie, Butter Chip, 2 3/4 In., 5 Piece 120.00
Bowtie, Goblet, 5 3/4 In. . . . . .60.00 to 70.00
Bradford Blackberry, Compote, 4 x 7 1/2 In. 120.00
Bradford Grape pattern is listed here as Bradford Blackberry.

Pressed Glass, Alhambra

Pressed Glass, Buckle

Pressed Glass, Classic

Broken Column, Wine, 4 In. 100.00
Brooklyn & Giant Prism With Thumbprint Band, Tumbler, Ship's, 4 1/4 In. 150.00
Bryce pattern is listed here as Ribbon Candy.
Bucket pattern is listed here as Oaken Bucket.
Buckle, Sugar 25.00
Bull's-Eye & Cure, Goblet, 5 3/4 In. 90.00
Bull's-Eye & Ellipse, Vase, Emerald Green, Gauffered Rim, 7 1/2 x 3 1/4 In. .....690.00 to 1035.00
Bull's-Eye & Ellipse, Vase, Emerald Green, Gauffered Rim, 9 x 4 In., Pair 4025.00
Bull's-Eye & Ellipse, Vase, Vaseline, Gauffered Rim, 7 3/8 x 3 1/4 In. 230.00
Bull's-Eye & Fleur-De-Lis, Goblet, 6 1/4 In. 150.00
Bull's-Eye & Wishbone, Goblet, 6 1/4 In. 220.00
Butterfly, Tray, 1 1/4 In. 60.00
Cabbage Leaf, Butter, Frosted, 5 x 6 1/2 In. 675.00
Cabbage Rose, Tumbler, 3 3/4 In. 18.00
Cable, Decanter, Bar Lip, Pt., 8 3/4 In. 150.00
California pattern is listed here as Beaded Grape.
Candlestick, Smokey Canary, Petal Socket, Applied By Wafer To Base, 7 In. 670.00
Candlewick as a pressed glass pattern is properly named *Banded Raindrop*. There is also a pattern called *Candlewick*, which has been made by Imperial Glass Corporation since 1936. It is listed in this book in the Imperial Glass category.
Candy Ribbon pattern is listed here as Ribbon Candy.
Cape Cod, Goblet, 5 1/2 In. ....45.00 to 80.00
Carnation, Berry Set, Ruby Stain, 6 Piece 80.00
Centennial, see also the related patterns Liberty Bell, Viking, and Washington Centennial.
Chain With Diamonds pattern is listed here as Washington Centennial.
Chandelier, Goblet, Engraved Fern & Berry, 6 1/4 In. 60.00
Cherry, Sugar, Cover, 7 In. 30.00
Chilson, Goblet, 6 1/2 In. 425.00
Classic, Butter, Cover, Log Feet, 7 x 5 3/4 In. 100.00
Classic, Creamer, Log Feet, 5 3/4 In. 90.00
Classic, Goblet, Frosted, 6 In. 1100.00
Classic, Pitcher, Collared Base, 10 In. 210.00
Cleat, Pitcher, Water, Applied Handle, 10 In. 100.00
Coin Spot pattern is listed in this book in its own category.
Colonial, Sugar, Covered, 7 1/4 In. 60.00
Colonial, Tumbler, Footed, 4 1/8 In. 325.00
Colonial, Tumbler, Whiskey, Applied Handle, 2 3/4 In. 160.00
Columbian Coin, Butter, 4 3/4 x 6 1/2 In. 140.00
Columbian Coin, Goblet, Frosted Coins, 6 In. 100.00
Compact pattern is listed here as Snail.
Cone, Cruet, Pink, Stopper, 5 In. 110.00
Confederacy, Sugar, Cover, 8 1/2 In. 90.00
Cord & Tassel, Barber Bottle, Ceramic Spout, 8 1/4 In. 70.00
Cord & Tassel, Spooner 40.00
Cord & Tassel, Tumbler 45.00
Cosmos pattern is listed in this book as its own category.
Cottage, Cake Stand, 9 In. 60.00
Cottage, Creamer 48.00
Croesus, Tumbler, Amethyst, Gold Trim, 3 3/4 In. 45.00
Crossed Peacock's Feather, Dish, Oval, 2 1/4 In. 45.00
Crown Jewels is a name used for two different patterns listed here as Chandelier.
Cryptic, Goblet, Ruby Stained Blocks, 6 1/2 In. 120.00
Crystal With Honeycomb, Goblet, 6 In. 15.00
Cupid & Venus, Bread Plate, Amber, Tab Handles, 11 3/8 In. 35.00
Cupid & Venus, Pitcher, 7 3/4 In. 25.00
Curling Heart, Bowl, Covered, 7 In. 70.00
Curling Heart, Cake Stand, 6-Sided Knop Stem, 10 1/2 In. 300.00
Curling Heartless, Compote, Pagoda Cover, 10 x 6 3/4 In. 160.00
Curling Heartless, Sugar, Cover, 8 3/4 In. 45.00
Curling Heartless, Sugar, Pagoda Cover, 6 In. 70.00
Cut Log, Cake Stand, 6 x 9 1/2 In. 60.00
Cut Log, Compote, Cover, 12 In. 35.00
Cut Log, Juice, 3 3/8 In. 60.00

Pressed Glass, Deer   Pressed Glass, Double Frosted Ribbon   Pressed Glass, Elephant

Cut Log, Pitcher, Straight Sides, 9 In.	150.00
Cut Log, Pitcher, Straight Sides, 12 1/4 In.	60.00
Cut Log, Vase, Pulled Neck, 16 1/2 In.	40.00
Cut Reverse Ashburton, Goblet, 5 3/4 In.	100.00
Daisy & Button, Cruet, Amber, Stopper, 6 1/4 In.	30.00
Daisy & Button, Novelty, Shoe, Attached Tray, Blue, Pat. 1886	146.00
Daisy & Button, Novelty, Umbrella, Vaseline, Metal Handle, 6 3/4 x 3 In.	450.00
Daisy & Button, Tray, Water, Blue, Tab Handles, 12 In.	90.00
Daisy & Button, Vase, Ruby Stain, 6 In.	130.00
Daisy & Button With Thumbprint Panel, Cake Stand, Amber, 6 1/2 x 10 In.	60.00
Daisy & Button With Thumbprint Panel, Cake Stand, Blue, 6 1/2 x 10 In.	110.00
Daisy & Button With Thumbprint Panel, Compote, Blue, 10 1/2 In.	70.00
Dakota, Cake Basket, Footed, Engraved Fern & Berry, Brittania Handle, 9 3/4 In.	390.00
Dakota, Cake Stand, Engraved Fern & Berry, 6 1/4 x 8 3/8 In.	180.00
Dakota, Compote, Cover, Engraved Fern & Berry, 14 In.	90.00
Dakota, Creamer, Ruby Stain, 4 1/8 In.	290.00
Dakota, Cruet, Amber, Stopper, 8 In.	130.00
Dakota, Finger Bowl, Flared, Engraved Fern & Berry, 3 x 4 1/2 In.	100.00
Dakota, Mug, Ruby Stain, 3 1/2 In.	170.00
Dakota, Pitcher, Slender Tapered, Engraved Fern & Berry, 9 3/4 In.	80.00
Dakota, Pitcher, Slender Tapered, Ruby Stain, 12 3/4 In.	110.00
Dakota, Saltshaker, Engraved Fern & Berry, 3 1/4 In.	60.00
Dakota, Tray, 10 3/4 In.	40.00
Dakota, Tray, 12 7/8 In.	80.00
Dakota, Tumbler, Engraved Fern & Berry	22.00
Dakota, Wine, 4 In.	50.00
Deer, Goblet, Cut Square & Fan Border, 6 1/8 In.	220.00
Deer & Dog, Butter, Pedestal, 8 x 6 1/4 In.	190.00
Deer & Dog, Compote, Cover, 12 In.	330.00
Deer & Dog, Cordial, 3 1/2 In.	140.00
Deer & Pine Tree, Goblet, 6 5/8 In.	80.00
Deer & Pine Tree, Mug, Amber, 2 3/4 In.	45.00
Delaware, Pitcher, Straight Sides, Green, Gold Trim, 9 3/8 In.	70.00
Delaware, Ring Tray, Green, Gold Trim, 3 1/2 x 6 1/2 In.	70.00
Dewey, see also the related pattern Spanish American.	
Dewey, Pitcher, Gridley You May Fire When Ready, Manila, 1898, 9 1/4 In.	156.00
Diamond & Bull's-Eye Band, Goblet, Engraved Berry, Fern, Bellflower, 6 In.	40.00
Diamond & Bull's-Eye Band, Pitcher, Straight Sides, 11 1/2 In.	30.00
Diamond Point, Celery Vase, 9 3/8 In.	60.00
Diamond Point, Jar, Pomade, Cover, 5 1/2 In.	500.00
Diamond Point, Sugar & Creamer, Cover, Applied Handle	90.00
Diamond Point With Panels, Creamer, Applied Handle, 5 1/4 In.	90.00
Diamond Quilted, Plate, Leaf Shape, Amethyst	42.00
Diamond Spearhead, Toothpick, Vaseline	70.00
Diamond Thumbprint, Celery Vase, 9 1/2 In.	100.00
Diamond Thumbprint, Goblet, 6 1/2 In.	750.00
Diamond Thumbprint, Tumbler, Whiskey, 3 In.	160.00

Diamond Thumbprint, Tumbler, Whiskey, Handle, 3 In.	750.00
Dickery Dock, Goblet, 6 1/2 In.	60.00
Divided Diamonds, Goblet, 6 1/4 In.	50.00
Dog Hunting, Pitcher, Light Green, 8 1/2 In.	170.00
Dolphin, Creamer	65.00
Doric pattern is listed here as Feather.	
Double Frosted Ribbon, Compote, Low, 5 3/4 In.	30.00
Double Loop pattern is listed here as Ribbon Candy.	
Double Wedding Ring pattern is listed here as Wedding Ring.	
Dragon, Goblet, 5 3/4 In.	1450.00
E Pluribus Unum pattern is listed here as Emblem.	
Egyptian, Creamer	65.00
Elephant, Goblet, Bar & Oval Border, 6 1/8 In.	990.00
Ellipse & Double Prism, Goblet, 6 1/2 In.	130.00
Emblem, Butter, Cover, 6 In.	210.00
Emerald Green Herringbone, Cake Plate, 6 1/2 x 9 In.	75.00
Empire Colonial, Spooner, Hexagonal Foot, 4 3/4 In.	60.00
Empress, Toothpick	175.00
English Hobnail Cross pattern is listed here as Amberette.	
Esther, Rose Bowl, Amber Stain, 4 In.	60.00
Etched Dakota pattern is listed here as Dakota.	
Eugenie, Celery Vase, 8 In.	50.00
Eugenie, Goblet, 6 In.	90.00
Eureka, Goblet, Floral Engraving, 6 In.	25.00
Excelsior, Candlestick, 8 In., Pair	310.00
Excelsior Variant, Tumbler, Electric Blue, 4 In.	150.00
Excelsior Variant With Double Ring Stem, Wine, 4 1/4 In.	25.00
Fan, Tray, Engraved Floral & Foliate, 10 7/8 In.	3000.00
Fan With Acanthus Leaf, Butter, Cover	65.00
Fan With Diamond pattern is listed here as Shell.	
Fancy Flute, Goblet, 6 5/8 In.	150.00
Feather, Goblet, Amber Stain, 5 3/4 In.	250.00
Fedora Loop, Champagne, 5 In.	15.00
Fine Cut & Block, Goblet, Blue	60.00
Fine Cut & Block, Pitcher, Water, Amber	70.00
Fine Cut & Feather pattern is listed here as Feather.	
Fine Cut & Panel, Sauce, Vaseline	16.00
Fine Rib, Champagne, 5 1/4 In.	80.00
Fine Rib, Compote, High, 7 3/4 In.	50.00
Fine Rib, Compote, High, 8 1/4 In.	150.00
Fine Rib, Wine, 4 In.	50.00
Fine Rib With Cut Ovals, Champagne, 5 1/4 In.	175.00
Fine Rib With Cut Ovals, Goblet, 6 1/4 In.	225.00
Fishscale, Celery Vase	35.00
Fishscale, Compote, Cover, 12 In.	45.00
Fishscale, Goblet, 6 In.	20.00
Fishscale, Pitcher, Water	55.00

Pressed Glass,
Fine Cut & Block

Pressed Glass,
Frosted Dolphin

Fishscale, Salt & Pepper, Undertray 60.00
Fishscale, Scoop 15.00
Fishscale, Tumbler, 3 3/4 In. 45.00
Fishscale, Water Set, Pitcher, Goblets, Tray, 8 Piece 120.00
Flamingo, Goblet, 6 1/4 In. 130.00
Flat Diamond & Panel, Decanter, Pt., 12 1/4 In. 130.00
Flat Diamond & Panel, Eggcup, 4 1/8 In. 230.00
Flat Diamond & Panel, Goblet, 6 1/4 In. 130.00
Fleur-De-Lis & Thistle, Nappy, 10 7/8 In. 50.00
Florida pattern pieces are listed here as Emerald Green Herringbone if made of green glass.
Flower Flange pattern is listed here as Dewey.
Flying Robin pattern is listed here as Hummingbird.
Four Petal, Sugar & Creamer, Cover, 7 In. 50.00
Four Petal, Sugar, Cover, 8 In. 45.00
Four Ring, Pitcher, Milk, 8 1/2 In. 200.00
Four Ring, Pitcher, Water, 9 7/8 In. 225.00
Frosted patterns may also be listed under name of main pattern.
Frosted Crane pattern is listed here as Frosted Stork.
Frosted Deer, Jam Jar, Partridge Finial, Cover, 6 1/2 In. 250.00
Frosted Dog, Bowl, Cover, Dog Finial, Footed, 6 1/2 x 3 1/2 In. 310.00
Frosted Dolphin, Compote, 6 1/2 x 7 1/2 In. 60.00
Frosted Dolphin, Spooner, 6 1/4 In. 100.00
Frosted Eagle, Compote, Cover, 13 x 8 In. 70.00
Frosted Fruit, Pitcher, 9 1/4 In. 210.00
Frosted Leaf, Celery Vase, 9 In. 90.00
Frosted Leaf, Champagne, 5 In. 110.00
Frosted Leaf, Goblet, 5 3/4 In. .... 170.00 to 210.00
Frosted Leaf, Tumbler, Footed, 5 1/4 In. 40.00
Frosted Leaf, Tumbler, Water, 3 1/4 In. 160.00
Frosted Lion, Bread Plate 95.00
Frosted Lion, Celery Vase, Engraved Fern, 8 3/4 In. 45.00
Frosted Lion, Compote, Cover, Rampant Lion Finial, 12 1/2 x 8 In. 100.00
Frosted Lion, Jam Jar, Crouching Lion Finial, 6 3/4 In. 60.00
Frosted Lion, Pitcher, Milk, 7 In. 6000.00
Frosted Lion, Sugar, Cover, Lion Head Finial, Engraved Drape, 8 1/4 In. .. 50.00
Frosted Oak Leaf Band, Spooner 35.00
Frosted Ribbon, Butter, Cover, Footed 55.00
Frosted Roman Key pattern is listed here as Roman Key, Frosted.
Frosted Stork, Sugar, Cover, Stork Finial, 9 In. 575.00
Frosted Thumbprint, Goblet, 5 7/8 In. 425.00
Garden Of Eden, see also the related pattern Lotus & Serpent.
Garfield Drape, Cake Stand, 6 3/4 x 10 In. 70.00
Gargoyle, Goblet, 6 1/4 In. 375.00
Giant Baby Thumbprint, Champagne, 5 In. 120.00
Giant Baby Thumbprint, Wine, 3 3/4 In. 45.00
Giant Bull's-Eye, Compote, Open 45.00
Giant Prism, Champagne, 5 1/2 In. 100.00
Giant Prism With Thumbprint Band, Champagne, 5 In. 220.00
Giant Sawtooth, Goblet, 6 1/4 In. 80.00
Good Luck pattern is listed here as Horseshoe.
Goose Boy, Cake Stand, Frosted Stem & Foot, 7 1/2 x 8 7/8 In. 375.00
Goose Girl, Cake Stand, Frosted Stem & Foot, 7 3/8 x 8 1/2 In. 375.00
Goose Girl, Compote, Frosted Stem & Foot, 8 1/2 x 8 In. 220.00
Gooseberry, Syrup, Applied Handle, Britannia Cover, Dolphin Finial, 8 In. .. 80.00
Gothic, Goblet, Rayed Foot, 6 In. 25.00
Gothic Arch, Celery Vase, 10 1/4 In. 60.00
Gothic Arch, Sugar, Canary, 5 1/4 In. 330.00
Gothic Arch, Sugar, Cover, 5 1/4 In. 80.00
Gothic Arch, Sugar, Cover, Round Foot, 5 1/4 In. 45.00
Gothic Arch, Sugar, Cover, Scalloped Foot, 5 1/2 In. 15.00
Grape, see also the related patterns Beaded Grape, Beaded Grape Medallion, and Magnet & Grape with Frosted Leaf.
Grasshopper, Jam Jar, Engraved Fern, 8 In. 45.00

Pressed Glass,
Horse, Cat & Rabbit

Pressed Glass, Heart in Sand

Greenfield Swirl, Goblet, Vaseline	25.00
Grooved Bigler, Champagne, 5 1/2 In.	50.00
Grooved Bigler, Goblet, 6 3/4 In.	160.00
Hairpin, Goblet, Opalescent Foot, 6 In.	250.00
Hairpin, Tray, Peacock Shape, 8 In.	9750.00
Hamilton With Frosted Leaf, Compote, Cover, 10 1/4 In.	140.00
Hand, Cake Stand, Scalloped Lower Edge, 8 1/2 x 10 1/4 In.	80.00
Harp & Lyre, Spooner, 4 1/2 In.	50.00
Heart & Lyre, Nappy, Underplate, 1 3/4 In.	90.00
Heart In Sand, Water Set, Ruby Stain, 5 Piece	3200.00
Heart With Thumbprint, Compote, Point & Scallop Rim, 8 1/4 x 8 1/2 In.	600.00
Heart With Thumbprint, Cordial, 3 In.	220.00
Heart With Thumbprint, Goblet, Green, Gold Trim	335.00
Heart With Thumbprint, Saltshaker, 2 3/4 In.	80.00
Heart With Thumbprint, Syrup, Britannia Cover, 5 1/2 In.	90.00
Heart With Thumbprint, Tumbler, 3 3/4 In.	70.00
Heart With Thumbprint, Vase, 10 In.	75.00
Heart With Thumbprint, Wine, Green, Gold Trim, 3 7/8 In.	325.00
Hercules Pillar, Goblet, 6 3/4 In.	35.00
Heron, Celery Vase, Needle Etched, 8 1/2 In.	50.00
Herringbone, Cake Stand, Emerald Green, 6 1/2 In.	75.00
Herringbone, Salt & Pepper, Emerald Green, 2 3/4 In.	25.00
Hexagonal Block, Pitcher, Straight Sides, Ruby Stain, 12 1/2 In.	70.00
Hinoto pattern is listed here as Diamond Point with Panels.	
Hobnail pattern is in this book as its own category.	
Holly, Cake Stand, Rope Edge, 6-Sided Wafer Stem, 6 1/8 x 12 3/4 In.	325.00
Holly, Creamer, Applied Handle, 6 In.	150.00 to 160.00
Holly, Eggcup, 3 3/4 In.	80.00
Holly, Goblet, 6 In.	140.00 to 190.00
Holly, Goblet, Slightly Flared Bowl, 5 7/8 In.	160.00 to 190.00
Holly, Pitcher, Applied Handle, 8 1/2 In.	325.00
Holly, Spooner, 5 1/4 In.	60.00 to 70.00
Holly, Sugar, 5 1/4 In.	90.00
Holly, Syrup, Applied Handle, Metal Cover, 6 1/2 In.	210.00
Holly, Tumbler, 3 5/8 In.	150.00
Holly, Tumbler, Footed, 4 7/8 In.	140.00
Holly, Wine, 3 5/8 In.	130.00 to 140.00
Holly Band, Celery Vase, 8 1/4 In.	80.00
Honeycomb, Pitcher, Molded Handle, Engraved Pat 1865, 8 5/8 In.	100.00
Honeycomb, Pitcher, Water, 9 In.	130.00
Honeycomb, Pitcher, Water, 10 1/2 In.	110.00
Honeycomb, Tumbler, Whiskey, Handle, 3 1/4 In.	110.00
Horn Of Plenty, Bowl, Footed, 4 In.	80.00
Horn Of Plenty, Compote, High, 6 1/2 In.	80.00
Horn Of Plenty, Compote, High, 8 1/2 In.	190.00
Horn Of Plenty, Creamer, 5 1/2 In.	340.00
Horn Of Plenty, Creamer, 6 3/4 In.	190.00
Horn Of Plenty, Goblet, 6 In.	120.00
Horn Of Plenty, Spooner, 4 1/2 In.	130.00

Horn Of Plenty, Sugar, 7 1/4 In.	160.00
Horn Of Plenty, Wine, 4 1/2 In.	150.00
Horse, Cat & Rabbit, Goblet, 6 3/8 In.	1209.00
Horseshoe, Spooner	40.00
Horseshoe, Sugar Shaker, Amber, 5 In.	25.00
Horseshoe, Wine, 4 1/8 In.	140.00
Huber, Compote, High, 9 3/4 In.	310.00
Huber, Tumbler, Whiskey, Handle, 2 7/8 In.	30.00
Hummingbird, Goblet, 6 In.	80.00
Hummingbird, Wine, 4 In.	120.00
Hundred-Leaved Ivy, Butter, Cover, 5 1/4 x 6 1/6 In.	25.00
Icicle, Celery Vase, 8 1/2 In.	70.00
Icicle With Chain Band, Goblet, 6 1/4 In.	45.00
Icicle With Chain Band, Goblet, Frosted, 6 1/2 In.	130.00
Icicle With Diamond Bowl, Goblet, 5 3/4 In.	50.00
Iconoclast, Goblet, 6 1/4 In.	50.00
Indiana Swirl pattern is listed here as Feather.	
Industry, Bowl, 11 1/8 In.	120.00
Inverted Diamond & Thumbprint, Spooner, Amethyst, 4 1/2 In.	616.00
Inverted Thumbprint, Cruet, Blue, Floral, Reeded Handle, Stopper, 6 In.	110.00
Inverted Thumbprint, Cruet, Blue, Floral, Reeded Handle, Stopper, 8 In.	80.00
Inverted Thumbprint, Pitcher, Blue, Square Top, Bulbous Base, 8 1/4 In.	125.00
Inverted Thumbprint, Pitcher, Water, Amber, Floral, 8 1/2 In.	150.00
Inverted Thumbprint, Pitcher, Water, Cranberry, Crimped Rim, Handle, 8 In.	160.00
Inverted Thumbprint, Stein, Blue, White Enameled, 5 5/8 x 2 1/4 In.	90.00
Inverted Thumbprint, Sugar Shaker, Cranberry, 4 3/4 In.	210.00 to 225.00
Inverted Thumbprint, Syrup, Apple Green, Tapered, 7 In.	100.00
Inverted Thumbprint, Syrup, Blue, Pinched Base, 6 7/8 In.	30.00
Jacob's Ladder, Goblet, 6 1/4 In.	60.00
Jacobs Ladder, Plate, Tea, 1876, 6 In.	35.00
Jacobs Ladder With Maltese Cross, Relish	20.00
Jewel & Dewdrop, Toothpick	55.00
Jeweled Heart, Berry Bowl, White Opalescent, Ruffled Edge	50.00
Jeweled Heart, Cruet, Apple Green, Stopper, 7 In.	80.00
Jeweled Heart, Sugar Shaker, Blue, 4 3/4 In.	300.00
Jeweled Heart, Sugar Shaker, Gold Trim, 4 1/2 In.	90.00
Jeweled Heart, Syrup, Apple Green, 6 In.	550.00
Jeweled Heart, Syrup, Blue, 5 1/2 In.	700.00
Jumbo, Butter, Cover, Elephant Head Under Each Handle, 7 1/2 x 5 5/8 In.	800.00
Jumbo, Goblet, 6 1/4 In.	775.00 to 1100.00
Jumbo, Spoon Rack, 11 1/2 In.	1150.00
Kansas pattern is listed here as Jewel & Dewdrop.	
King Arthur, Tumbler	15.00
King's Crown, Goblet	13.00
King's Crown, Pitcher, Water, Etched Bird, 7 1/2 In.	310.00
Klondike pattern is listed here as Amberette.	
Knights Of Labor, Mug, 5 3/4 In.	45.00
Lacy, Plate, American Eagle, 8 Sides, 7 In.	180.00
Lacy, Plate, Arch & Checkerboard, Cobalt Blue, Scalloped Edge, 5 1/2 In.	300.00
Lacy, Plate, Basket Of Flowers, 8 Sides, 7 In.	560.00
Lacy, Plate, Beehive, Thistles, 8 Sides, 8 In.	200.00
Lacy, Plate, Paddle-Wheel Steamer, 8 Sides, Midwest, c.1830-1845, 6 In.	1456.00
Lacy, Plate, Peacock Eye & Thistle, 8 In.	135.00
Lacy, Plate, Union, Sailing Ship, Clear, 8 Sides, Midwest, c.1830-1845, 6 In.	1230.00
Laminated Petals, Goblet, 5 3/4 In.	70.00
Lattice & Oval Panels pattern is listed here as Flat Diamond & Panel.	
Leaf & Flower, Pitcher, Amber Stain, Frosted, 12 In.	80.00
Liberty Bell, Salt & Pepper, Metal Lids, Embossed 1776 Liberty 1876, 2 3/4 In.	310.00
Lily-Of-The-Valley, Celery Vase, 8 In.	120.00
Lily-Of-The-Valley, Compote, Cover, 11 x 8 1/2 In.	150.00
Lily-Of-The-Valley, Goblet, 6 In.	100.00
Lily-Of-The-Valley, Pitcher, Applied Handle, 8 5/8 In.	220.00

Pressed Glass, Iconoclast

Pressed Glass, Jumbo

Pressed Glass, Medallion

Lily-Of-The-Valley, Scoop	15.00
Lily-Of-The-Valley, Tumbler, Etched	10.00
Lily-Of-The-Valley, Tumbler, Footed, 5 1/4 In.	110.00
Lily-Of-The-Valley, Wine, 4 In.	170.00
Lincoln Drape, Compote, Low, 5 1/4 In.	50.00 to 60.00
Lincoln Drape, Sugar, 5 5/8 In.	45.00
Lincoln Drape With Tassel, Goblet, 6 In.	210.00
Log Cabin, Compote, Cover, 10 1/2 In.	850.00
Log Cabin, Jam Jar, Vaseline, 6 3/4 In.	2200.00
Log Cabin, Sauce, 4 In.	85.00
Loop, Bowl, Footed, Low, 2 3/4 In.	425.00
Loop, Bowl, Footed, Low, 3 1/4 In.	1050.00
Loop, Dish, Sweetmeat, Cover, 6 1/4 In.	50.00
Loop, Sugar, Footed, 5 3/8 In.	45.00
Loop & Arch, Tumbler, Whiskey, 2 1/4 In.	200.00
Loop & Moose Eye, Champagne, 5 In.	30.00
Loops & Drops pattern is listed here as New Jersey.	
Lorne, Butter, Cover	65.00
Lotus & Serpent, Goblet, 6 In.	260.00
Lotus & Serpent, Pitcher, 8 1/2 In.	100.00
Lyre & Cinquefoil, Dish, Rectangular, 10 3/4 In.	110.00
Madison, Celery Vase, 8 1/2 In.	50.00
Madison, Goblet, 6 In.	275.00
Magnet & Grape With Frosted Leaf, Compote, High, 7 In.	50.00
Magnet & Grape With Frosted Leaf, Compote, Low, 4 3/4 In.	50.00
Magnet & Grape With Frosted Leaf, Straw Dispenser, 21 In.	3250.00
Magnet & Grape With Frosted Leaf & American Shield, Sugar, Cover, 9 In.	800.00
Magnet & Grape With Frosted Leaf, Wine, 4 In.	90.00
Maple Leaf, Berry Bowl, Green	40.00
Maple Leaf, Compote, Green, Gold Trim, 4 3/8 x 4 1/2 In.	140.00
Maple Leaf, Sauce, Vaseline	22.00
Maple Leaf, Sugar & Creamer, Green, Gold Trim, 4 1/2 x 4 1/4 In.	40.00
Marble, Cake Stand, Amethyst, Stepped Domed Base, 6 x 9 In.	90.00
Medallion, Pitcher, Water, Amber	85.00
Medallion Sprig, Syrup, Blue, 8 In.	90.00
Minerva, Creamer	70.00
Minnesota, Pitcher, 8 3/4 In.	45.00
Mirror, Compote, 9 1/2 In.	40.00
Nail, Champagne, Etched Leaf, 4 3/4 In.	45.00
Nail, Goblet, Ruby Stain Above & Below Pattern, 6 1/4 In.	120.00
Nail, Mug, Ruby Stain, 3 5/8 In.	130.00
Nail, Wine, 3 7/8 In.	15.00
Nailhead, Sugar & Creamer	25.00
Nectarine, Nappy, Footed, 3 3/4 In.	90.00
Nestor, Berry Bowl, Blue, White & Gold Enameled, 5 x 8 3/4 In.	50.00

New England Pineapple, Champagne, 5 1/4 In. 250.00
New England Pineapple, Decanter, Pt., 8 1/4 In. 60.00
New England Pineapple, Decanter, Qt., 9 1/2 In. 180.00
New Hampshire, Tumbler 12.00
New Jersey, Toothpick, Gold Trim 65.00
New Jersey, Tumbler 15.00
New Jersey, Wine 40.00
Niagara Falls, Tray, Frosted, 11 1/2 x 16 In. 160.00
Oak Leaf Band With Loops, Goblet, 6 In. 50.00
Oak Wreath, Dish, Sweetmeat, Cover, Rope Band, 7 1/4 x 6 1/8 In. 50.00
Oaken Bucket, Pitcher, Water, Blue 110.00
Old Abe pattern is listed here as Frosted Eagle.
One-Thousand Eye pattern is listed here as Thousand Eye.
Open Rose, Cake Stand, 5 3/4 x 9 1/2 In. 110.00
Open Rose, Goblet, 6 In. 25.00
Open Rose, Pitcher, Applied Handle, 8 In. 190.00
Oval Framed Clover, Tumbler, Footed, 4 1/4 In. 130.00
Ovals With Long Bars, Goblet, 6 3/4 In. 240.00
Paneled 44, Toothpick, Platinum Stain 75.00
Paneled 44, Tumbler, Platinum Stain 20.00
Paneled Fine Tooth, Goblet, 6 1/4 In. 80.00
Paneled Flattened Sawtooth, Goblet, 6 3/4 In. 70.00
Paneled Forget-Me-Not, Butter, Cover 52.00
Paneled Forget-Me-Not, Pitcher, Water 75.00
Paneled Ovals, Sugar Lid, 3 1/2 In. 10.00
Paneled Tulip, Vase, Blue Green, Flared Scalloped, Octagonal Base, 9 1/2 In. 1035.00
Peacock Feathers, Dish, Open Handle, 9 1/2 In. 8400.00
Peacock's Eye pattern is listed here as Peacock Feathers.
Pendleton, Champagne, 5 In. 150.00
Pennsylvania, see also the related pattern Hand.
Persian Rug, Creamer, Adams, 1881, 5 1/2 In. 85.00
Pillar, Bottle, Bitters, 6 3/4 In. 60.00
Pillar, Celery Vase, Scalloped, Stem, 11 3/8 In. 550.00
Pillar & Bull's-Eye pattern is listed here as Thistle.
Pillar Thumbprint, Pitcher, Water, Pink Enameled Flowers, 9 In. 30.00
Pinafore pattern is listed here as Actress.
Pineapple & Gothic Arch, Dish, Rectangular 10 1/2 In. 80.00
Plain Tulip, Goblet, 6 In. 60.00
Plume, Compote, Cover, 12 1/2 x 8 In. 25.00
Plume, Tumbler, 3 7/8 In. 10.00
Pointed Buckle, Goblet, 5 3/4 In. 120.00
Polar Bear, Goblet, Frosted, 6 1/8 In. 170.00
Portland, Salt, Embossed Word Salt In Branches 110.00
Portland With Diamond Point Band pattern is listed here as Banded Portland.
Powder & Shot, Creamer, 5 1/4 In. 90.00

Pressed Glass,
Paneled Forget-Me-Not

Pressed Glass,
Sandwich Star

Pressed Glass,
Shell & Jewel

Prayer Rug pattern is listed here as Horseshoe.

Pressed Block, Finger Bowl, 3 1/8 In.	35.00
Pressed Leaf, Pitcher, Applied Handle, 8 3/4 In.	60.00
Princess Feather Medallion & Basket Of Flowers, Dish, Cover, Oval, 8 3/4 x 10 1/2 In.	6500.00
Prism & Lobular Loops, Goblet, 6 1/2 In.	60.00
Queen Anne, Creamer, 5 In.	85.00
Rebecca At The Well, Compote, Frosted Ribbon Bowl, 12 1/2 x 10 1/2 In.	350.00
Red Block, Butter, Cover, Ruby Stain, 5 x 6 In.	80.00
Red Block, Tumbler	25.00

Reverse 44 pattern is listed here as Paneled 44.

Reverse Torpedo pattern is listed here as Diamond & Bull's-Eye Band.

Ribbed Acorn, Nappy, Cover, Footed, 5 1/2 In.	15.00
Ribbed Grape, Creamer, 5 5/8 In.	110.00
Ribbed Ivy, Bottle, Bitters, 71/4 In.	250.00
Ribbed Ivy, Celery Vase, 7 1/4 In.	700.00
Ribbed Ivy, Compote, High, 7 1/2 In.	160.00
Ribbed Ivy, Compote, Low, 6 1/4 In.	25.00
Ribbed Ivy, Decanter, Cordial 7 1/2 In.	425.00
Ribbed Ivy, Goblet, 6 In.	150.00
Ribbed Ivy, Salt, 2 3/4 In.	110.00
Ribbed Ivy, Sugar, Cover, 5 5/8 In.	150.00
Ribbed Ivy, Tumbler, Whiskey, Handle, 2 3/4 In.	50.00
Ribbed Palm, Celery Vase, 8 7/8 In.	80.00
Ribbed Palm, Compote, High, 10 1/4 In.	400.00
Ribbed Palm, Creamer, 6 1/4 In.	50.00
Ribbon, Bonbon, Cover, 8 x 6 2/3 In.	110.00
Ribbon Candy, Goblet, 5 3/4 In.	50.00 to 70.00
Ribbon Candy, Wine, 3 3/4 In.	50.00
Roman Key, Champagne, 5 In.	50.00
Roman Key, Goblet, 6 In.	35.00
Roman Key, Goblet, Frosted, 6 In.	90.00 to 100.00
Roman Key, Sugar, Cover, Frosted, 9 In.	50.00
Roman Key With Flutes, Goblet, Frosted, 6 In.	60.00
Romeo, Goblet, Ruby Stain, 5 3/4 In.	160.00
Rose In Snow, Plate, Handle, 9 1/2 In.	45.00
Rose Sprig, Gravy Boat, Amber	45.00
Rose Sprig, Gravy Boat, Blue	45.00
Rose Sprig, Pitcher, 7 3/4 In.	60.00
Sandwich Heart-Variant, Sugar, Cover, 8 7/8 In.	250.00
Sandwich Ivy, Compote, 5 3/4 In.	15.00
Sandwich Ivy, Sugar, Footed, 3 1/2 In.	15.00
Sandwich Leaf, Compote, 6 1/8 In.	190.00

Sandwich Loop, see also the related pattern Hairpin.

Sandwich Loop, Decanter, Qt., 9 3/4 In.	60.00
Sandwich Star, Spooner, 5 In.	50.00
Sandwich Vine, Goblet, Gold Trim, 6 1/2 In.	2400.00
Sandwich Vine, Goblet, Hexagonal Foot, 6 3/8 In.	1700.00
Sawtooth, Bottle, Bell Form, 8 1/2 In.	35.00
Sawtooth, Dish, Sweetmeat, Cover, 8 1/2 In.	35.00
Sawtooth, Pitcher, Water, 8 3/8 In.	260.00
Sawtooth, Salt, Cover, 4 7/8 In.	120.00
Sawtooth, Salt, Pedestal, 2 7/8 In.	15.00
Sawtooth, Spooner, Low, 4 1/2 In.	10.00
Scarab, Champagne, Rayed Foot, 5 3/4 In.	200.00
Scarab, Goblet, Rayed Foot, 6 1/4 In.	130.00
Scroll, Compote, Opaque Blue, 7 1/2 x 8 1/4 In.	25.00
Scroll With Cane, Toothpick	45.00
Scroll With Flowers, Pitcher, Water	85.00
Scrolled Eye, Nappy, 10 1/2 In.	40.00
Shell, Dolphin Foot, Compote, 9 x 10 1/2 In.	130.00
Shell & Hairpin, Salt, 1 5/8 In.	90.00
Shell & Jewel, Tumbler	40.00
Shell & Tassel, Bowl, Blue, Oval, Quadruple Plate Holder, 10 3/4 x 9 7/8 In.	475.00

Shell & Tassel, Cake Stand, Square, 4 1/2 x 7 x 7 In. 160.00
Shell & Tassel, Vase, Engraved Leaf & Berry, 7 1/2 In. ....70.00 to 90.00
Shoshone, Cruet, Stopper 55.00
Snail, Biscuit Jar, Cover, 8 1/2 In. 260.00
Snail, Rose Bowl, 5 x 6 In. 30.00
Snail, Spooner, Amethystine 35.00
Spanish American, Pitcher, Cannon Ball, 1900, 9 1/8 In. 135.00
Spanish Coin pattern is listed here as Columbian Coin.
Squirrel, Goblet, 6 In. 875.00
Star & Buckle, Pitcher, Molasses, 7 3/8 In. 50.00
Star & Buckle, Spill, 4 7/8 In. 40.00
Star & Dart, Dish, Sweetmeat, Cover, 6 1/2 In. 25.00
Stars & Bars, Cruet, Amber, Stopper, 7 1/2 In. 90.00
Stedman, Champagne, Rayed Foot, 5 1/4 In. 50.00
Stedman, Goblet, Plain Foot, 6 In. 30.00
Stippled Scroll pattern is listed here as Scroll.
Strawberry, Celery Vase, 8 1/2 In. 100.00
Strawberry, Compote, Cover, Loop & Dart Foot, 10 1/2 x 8 1/4 In. 90.00
Strawberry, Creamer, 5 1/2 In. 30.00
Strawberry, Pitcher, Applied Handle, 9 1/8 In. 230.00
Strawberry, Tumbler, 3 1/2 In. 70.00
Swan, Goblet, Vaseline, 6 In. 80.00
Tackle Block, Goblet, 6 In. 45.00
Tacoma, Dish, Banana Split, Flat 38.00
Teardrop & Diamonds, Goblet, 6 1/4 In. 45.00
Teardrop & Tassel, Cordial, 3 In. 280.00
Teardrop & Tassel, Goblet, 5 3/4 In. 200.00
Thistle, Syrup, Applied Handle, Britannia Cover, 6 1/2 In. 130.00
Thousand Eye, Butter, Cover, Footed 85.00
Thousand Eye, Compote, 8 1/2 x 6 In. 35.00
Thousand Eye, Honey, Cover, 6 1/4 x 8 In. 60.00
Thousand Eye, Pitcher, Britannia Cover, 7 1/4 In. 70.00
Thousand Eye, Platter, 8 x 11 In. 36.00
Thousand Eye, Tumbler, Amber 20.00
Three Face, Celery Vase, Engraved Leaf & Floral Wreath, 9 In. 60.00
Three Face, Champagne, Hollow Stem, 4 x 3 1/2 In. 5000.00
Three Face, Compote, 9 1/2 In. 275.00
Three Face, Goblet, Engraved Rose, 6 3/8 In. 160.00
Three Graces, see also the related pattern Three Face.
Three Printie, Vase, Emerald Green, Gauffered Rim, 9 3/4 x 3 3/4 In. 3680.00
Three Printie, Vase, Light Blue, Gauffered Rim, 9 3/4 In. 1265.00
Three Sisters pattern is listed here as Three Face.
Thumbprint, Bowl, Footed, 4 1/4 In. 146.00
Thumbprint, Compote, Baluster Stem, Scalloped Rim, 9 x 13 5/8 In. 300.00
Thumbprint, Decanter, Canary, Stopper 2050.00
Thumbprint, Salt, Cover, Donut Shape Finial, 4 In. 400.00
Thumbprint & Draped Prism, Goblet, 5 3/8 In 160.00
Tiny Diamond & Prism Band, Goblet, 6 In. 40.00
Torpedo, Goblet, Engraved Fuchsia, 6 1/4 In. 15.00
Tree Of Life, Champagne, 6 1/4 In. 65.00
Tree Of Life, Epergne, Scallop Rim Bowl, 6 Petal Top Vase, 19 x 8 1/8 In. 700.00
Tree Of Life, Goblet, 7 In. 35.00
Tree Of Life, Tumbler, 6 1/8 In. 22.00
Tulip, Vase, Amethyst, Flared Scalloped Rim, Octagonal Foot, 10 x 4 3/8 In. 4600.00
Tulip, Vase, Emerald Green, Flared Scalloped Rim, 10 x 4 1/4 In., Pair 9200.00
Tulip & Sawtooth, Champagne, 5 In. 40.00
Tulip & Sawtooth, Cruet, 8 1/2 In. 80.00
Tulip & Sawtooth, Cruet, Footed, 6 1/4 In. 120.00
Tulip & Sawtooth, Cruet, Footed, 9 1/2 In. 140.00
Tulip & Sawtooth, Decanter, Qt., 14 1/2 In. 120.00
Tulip & Sawtooth, Goblet, 6 1/2 In. 60.00
Tulip & Sawtooth, Jar, Horseradish, Cover, 5 1/2 In. 150.00

Pressed Glass,
Shell, Dolphin Foot

Pressed Glass,
Silver Anniversary

Pressed Glass,
U.S. Coin

Tulip Band, Goblet, 6 1/2 In.	160.00
Twisted Loop, Vase, Amethyst, Gauffered Rim, Faceted Base, 10 In.	3220.00
U.S. Coin, Compote, Frosted Coins, 5 3/4 x 7 1/4 In.	400.00
U.S. Coin, Goblet, Half Dollar, Frosted, 6 7/8 In.	495.00
U.S. Coin, Tray, 7 x 10 In.	230.00
Umbilicated Sawtooth, Goblet, 6 1/4 In.	100.00
Valencia Waffle, Berry Set, Cranberry Stain, 7 Piece	345.00
Valentine, Goblet, 5 3/4 In.	180.00 to 230.00
Valentine, Pitcher, 9 In.	130.00 to 210.00
Victoria, Compote, Cover, Low, 11 3/4 In.	90.00
Victoria, Compote, Low, 7 1/4 In.	60.00
Viking, Bread Tray, Embossed, Give Us This Day Our Daily Bread, 9 x 12 1/2 In.	60.00
Volunteer, Plate, 9 3/8 In.	600.00
Waffle, Celery Vase, 9 In., Pair	100.00
Waffle, Decanter, Canary, Stopper	2200.00
Waffle, Dish, Sweetmeat, Cover, Footed, 5 1/4 In.	25.00
Waffle, Eggcup, 3 5/8 In.	40.00
Waffle, Sugar, Cover, 8 3/4 In.	50.00
Waffle & Thumbprint, Champagne, 5 1/2 In.	90.00
Waffle & Thumbprint, Decanter, 13 In.	4250.00 to 6250.00
Waffle & Thumbprint, Goblet, 6 1/2 In.	40.00 to 90.00
Waffle & Thumbprint, Goblet, 6 In.	600.00
Washington, Goblet, 6 In.	100.00
Washington, Wine, 4 In.	120.00
Washington Centennial, Bread Tray, Embossed, First In War, First In Peace, 8 x 12 In.	60.00
Way Colonial, Champagne, 5 1/2 In.	60.00
Way Colonial, Goblet, 6 In.	50.00
Wedding Bells, Pitcher, Gold Trim, 8 3/8 In.	60.00
Wedding Bells, Wine, Amethyst Stain, 4 1/4 In.	25.00
Wedding Ring, Champagne, 5 In.	80.00
Wedding Ring, Goblet, 6 In.	90.00
Westward Ho, Platter, Frosted Deer Handles, Cabin, Buffalo, 9 x 13 In.	130.00
Westward Ho, Wine, 4 3/8 In.	250.00
Wheat In Shield, Goblet, 6 In.	60.00
Wheat In Shield, Syrup, Applied Handle, Tin Cover, 7 In.	130.00
Wildflower, Cake Stand, Vaseline, 6 x 9 1/2 In.	150.00
Wildflower, Tumbler, Blue	25.00
Wildflower, Tumbler, Green	30.00
Willow Oak, Goblet, 6 In.	12.00
Willow Oak, Tumbler	22.00
Willow Oak, Water Set, Pitcher, Tumblers, Tray, 8 Piece	150.00
Windflower, Pitcher, Applied Handle, 9 In.	140.00
Wisconsin, Cake Stand, 4 1/4 x 8 1/4 In.	40.00
Wisconsin, Wine, 4 In.	70.00

Wooden Pail pattern is listed here as Oaken Bucket.
Zipper Slash, Goblet, Frosted, Amber Stain, 5 3/4 In. 15.00

PRINT, in this listing, means any of many printed images produced on paper by one of the more common methods, such as lithography. The prints listed here are of interest primarily to the antiques collector, not the fine arts collector. Many of these prints were originally part of books. Other prints will be found in the Advertising, Currier & Ives, Movie, and Poster categories.

Al Capone, Smiling, With Cigar, Escorted On Train 100.00
Aldin, Cecil Charles, Dutch Girls, Chromolithograph, Frame, 13 x 39 1/2 In. 489.00
America Forever, Justice & Liberty, Lithograph, Tramp Art Frame, 1917, 31 x 24 In. 495.00

Audubon bird prints were originally issued as part of books printed from 1826 to 1854. They were issued in two sizes, 26 1/2 inches by 39 1/2 inches and 11 inches by 7 inches. The quadrupeds were issued in 28-by-22-inch prints. Later editions of the Audubon books were done in many sizes, and reprints of the books in the original size were also made. The bird pictures have been so popular they have been copied in myriad sizes by both old and new printing methods. This list includes originals and later copies because Audubon prints of all ages are sold in antiques shops.

J.W.Audubon

Audubon, American Crossbill, R. Havell, c.1834, 38 x 25 3/8 In. 4800.00
Audubon, American Goldfinch, Havell & Son, 23 3/4 x 16 In. 2585.00
Audubon, Black Or Surf Duck, R. Havell, 27 x 38 In. 5290.00
Audubon, Canada Lynx, J.T. Bowen, c.1843, 21 5/8 x 27 In. 6000.00
Audubon, Caribou Or American Reindeer, 7 x 10 5/8 In. 110.00
Audubon, Crested Grebe, J. Bien, 26 x 39 In. 2070.00
Audubon, Crested Titmouse, Havell & Son, 23 3/8 x 16 1/4 In. 2350.00
Audubon, Double-Crested Cormorant, No. 52, R. Havell, c.1835 .... 3737.00
Audubon, Great Crested Flycatcher, 28 x 21 In. 230.00
Audubon, Green Black-Capt Flycatcher, R. Havell, c.1830, 39 3/8 x 25 3/8 In. 2280.00
Audubon, Grizzly Bear, J.T. Bowen, c.1848, 21 x 27 1/2 In. 1920.00
Audubon, Jumping Mouse, J.T. Bowen, 28 x 22 In. 489.00
Audubon, Least Bittern, R. Havell, c.1834, 25 3/8 x 38 1/8 In. 3000.00
Audubon, Little Harvest Mouse, J.T. Bowen, 28 x 22 In. 1035.00
Audubon, Little-Chief Hare, Frame, 1846, 21 3/8 x 27 3/8 In. ....330.00 to 550.00
Audubon, Musk-Ox, J.T. Bowen 2185.00
Audubon, Northern Hare, J.T. Bowen, 18 x 26 In. 1495.00
Audubon, Plumed & Thick-Legged Partridge, R. Havell, c.1838, 20 3/4 x 27 In. 3600.00
Audubon, Red-Bellied Squirrel, J.T. Bowen, 26 x 21 In. 2070.00
Audubon, Red-Winged Starling Or Marsh Blackbird, J. Bien, 39 x 26 In. 1093.00
Audubon, Republican Cliff Swallow, R. Havell, c.1837, 38 x 25 In. 1200.00
Audubon, Ruddy Duck, R. Havell, c.1836, 26 x 39 1/4 In. 9600.00
Audubon, Tawny Lemming, J.T. Bowen 460.00
Audubon, Townsend's Rocky Mountain Hare, J.T. Bowen, c.1842, 21 5/8 x 27 In. 3900.00
Audubon, Whip-Poor-Will, 28 x 21 In. 230.00
Audubon, White American Wolf, J.T. Bowen, 7 5/8 x 10 3/8 In. 110.00
Audubon, White-Breasted Black-Capped Nuthatch, R. Havell, c.1832, 38 x 25 5/8 In. 4200.00
Audubon, Winter Wren, Rock Wren, R. Havell, c.1837, 38 x 25 5/8 In. 2040.00
Audubon, Yellow Red-Poll Warbler, R. Havell, 24 x 18 In. 2760.00
Audubon, Yellow-Billed Cuckoo, Lizards, 23 5/8 x 29 3/8 In. 4700.00
Bill, G. & F., Bird's-Eye View Of Mt. Vernon, Gold Repainted Frame, 13 1/2 x 16 3/8 In. .. 165.00
Carruthers, Roy, Standing Man, Seated Woman, Smoking, Signed, 1981, 29 1/2 x 22 In. .. 287.00
Chance Acquaintance, 2 Young Girls, Color, Gilt Frame, 26 x 16 In. 40.00
Cupid Awake/Cupid Asleep, Tinted, Period Frame, 8 x 10 In., Pair 45.00
Eleanor Roosevelt Archive, Showing Her Visiting Squalid Street In San Juan 500.00
Epply, Lorinda, Landscape, Trees, Etching, Frame, 8 x 6 In. 242.00
Fawcett, Male & Female Ptarmigan, Matted, Frame, 11 3/4 x 14 3/4 In. 330.00
Fox, R. Atkinson, Where Nature Beats In Perfect Tune 193.00
Gardiner, H. Marshall, Rainbow Fleet, Nantucket 635.00
Girl, With Dog, Color, Gilt Frame, 29 x 18 In. 45.00

Gutmann, Bessie Pease, Great Love 1155.00
Gutmann, Bessie Pease, Lorelei .... .550.00 to 1760.00

Icart prints were made by Louis Icart, who worked in Paris from 1907
as an employee of a postcard company. He then started printing magazines and fashion brochures. About 1910 he created a series of etchings of fashionably dressed women and he continued to make similar
etchings until he died in 1950. He is well known as a printmaker,
painter, and illustrator. Original etchings are much more expensive
than the later photographic copies.

Icart, Autumn Storm, Etching, 7 x 9 In. 748.00
Icart, Bathers Baigneuses, Signed, Dated 1926, 24 1/2 x 17 In. 690.00
Icart, Cigarette Memories 2970.00
Icart, Coursing II, Etching, 15 x 25 In. 2300.00
Icart, Coursing II, Greyhounds, Girl, Flowing Dress, Frame, Mark, 16 x 26 In. 1430.00
Icart, Early Harvest, Etched, Drypoint, Oval, Signed, 18 7/8 x 15 In. 1725.00
Icart, Le Panier De Pommes, Morris Bendien, Frame, 17 3/4 x 24 In. 303.00
Icart, Partially Clad Woman, On Fur Sofa, Velvet Liner, Frame, Signed, 24 x 29 In. 1320.00
Icart, Seated Female Nude, 8 7/8 x 11 In. 1305.00
Innis, George, Birds In Flight, Frame, 23 x 14 1/2 In. 81.00
Iron Mountain Route, Between St. Louis & Texas On Iron Mountain Route, 1920, 27 In. ... 92.00

Japanese woodblock prints are listed as follows: Print, Japanese, name
of artist, title or description, type, and size. Dealers use the following
terms: Tate-e is a vertical composition. Yoko-e is a horizontal composition. The words Aiban (13 by 9 inches), Chuban (10 by 7 1/2 inches),
Hosoban (13 by 6 inches), Oban (15 by 10 inches), and Koban (7 by 4
inches) denote size. Modern versions of some of these prints have been
made. Other woodblock prints that are not Japanese are listed under
Print, Woodblock.

Japanese, Asano, Drizzling Rain In Nijo Castle, Kyoto, Tate-e 52.00
Japanese, Eizan, Woman In Green Kimono Beside Brown Hibachi, Tate-e 69.00
Japanese, Figures In Rain, Stone Wall, Castle 633.00
Japanese, Folding Album Of Flowers, Late 19th Century, Meiji Period 316.00
Japanese, Hiroshi Yoshida, February Temple, Framed, Tate-e 259.00
Japanese, Hiroshi Yoshida, Large Landscape Of American West 517.00
Japanese, Hiroshi Yoshida, Little Temple Gate, Frame 460.00
Japanese, Hiroshige, Clear Weather After Snow At Kameyama, Yoko-e 489.00
Japanese, Hiroshige, Sakawa River Near Odawara, Yoko-e 144.00
Japanese, Hiroshige, View Of Mount Fuji, Rocky Crags, Yoko-e 633.00
Japanese, Hokusai, Dwarf Sits Beside Stone Rabbit, Surimono, Frame 460.00
Japanese, Kawase Hasui, Beach House, Fukui, 1921, Yoko-e 2875.00
Japanese, Kawase Hasui, Night Scene, Mountain Landscape, Frame, Tate-e 489.00
Japanese, Kawase Hasui, Red Temple In Snow, Frame, Tate-e 1495.00
Japanese, Kawase Hasui, Single Figure With Umbrella Before Pagoda In Snow 460.00
Japanese, Kawase Hasui, Snow Falling On Temple At Night, Frame, Tate-e 1610.00
Japanese, Kawase Hasui, Snow Scene, Pines, River Landscape, Frame 690.00
Japanese, Kawase Hasui, Villagers On Back Street At Night, Tate-e 690.00
Japanese, Kuniyoshi, 19 Seated Warriors, Yellow Ground, 1842 .... 431.00
Japanese, Kuniyoshi, Hundred Poets Series, Woman, Infant & Child By Stream 172.00
Japanese, Kuniyoshi, Lord & His Retainers In Interior, 1840 .... 230.00
Japanese, Kuniyoshi, Tokaido Series, Yoshitsune & Benkei, 1842 .... 172.00
Japanese, Kuniyoshi, Woman Arriving On Barge To Meet Samurai, 1850 .... 316.00
Japanese, Kuniyoshi, Woman Shielding Herself From Falling Snow, Frame, 1842 ...... 345.00
Japanese, Lakeside Landscape, Frame, 1920 .... 949.00
Japanese, Shiro Kasamatsu, Gold Pavilion In Snow, Tate-e 58.00
Japanese, Shiro Kasamatsu, House In Ontake, Woman Under Red Maple Tree 58.00
Japanese, Shiro Kasamatsu, Night Scene, Figure Outside A Shop, Tate-e 69.00
Japanese, Shiro Kasamatsu, Red Lantern, Tate-e 202.00
Japanese, Shiro Kasamatsu, Temple In Rain, Tate-e 138.00
Japanese, Toshihide, Seated Female Figure, Standing Young Girl, 8 1/4 x 12 1/2 In. 287.00
Japanese, Tsuchiya Koitsu, Rain Scene With Temple & Figures, Frame, Tate-e 115.00

Print, Nutting, Sheep At The Temple,
Paestrum, Frame, 1904, 13 x 17 In.

Mold is living and will spread. Keep "foxed" prints away from any others.

Japanese, Yoshitoro, Fireworks At Rygyoku Bridge, 3-Panel	127.00
Japanese, Yoshitoshi, Maiden Under Waterfall On Rocky Ledge	115.00
Johnson, D.H., Making World Safe For Democracy, Uncle Sam, Frame, 19 x 15 In.	287.00
Lithograph, Dictionaire Universelle D'Historie Naturelle, 8 3/4 x 4 3/4 In., Pair	200.00
Lithograph, General View From Brooklyn, Hand Colored, c.1850, 7 3/8 x 11 1/4 In.	720.00
Lithograph, Memorial, Susan Isabella Ligitt, James Baillie Printer, c.1849, 12 1/2 x 9 In.	59.00
Lithograph, New York, & Vicinity, Panorama, Hand Colored, John Bachman, c.1866	9600.00
Max, Peter, Zodiac, 13 1/4 x 21 1/2 In., 12 Piece	298.00
Northwestern 400 Diesel Train, Frame, 20 x 30 In.	172.00

Nutting prints are now popular with collectors. Wallace Nutting is known for his pictures, furniture, and books. Nutting *prints* are actually hand-colored photographs issued from 1900 to 1941. There are over 10,000 different titles. Wallace Nutting furniture is listed in the Furniture category.

Nutting, Autumn Processional, Outdoor Scene, Frame, 9 1/4 x 5 3/4 In.	66.00
Nutting, Gardner Parlor Corner, 7 1/4 x 9 1/4 In.	97.00
Nutting, Little Washerwoman	770.00
Nutting, Sheep At The Temple, Paestrum, Frame, 1904, 13 x 17 In. .... *Illus*	4070.00
Nutting, Wine Carrier	1238.00
Ogden, H.A., American Militia Officers, Gold Frame, 1885, 21 x 18 1/2 In., Pair	77.00

Parrish prints are wanted by collectors. Maxfield Frederick Parrish was an illustrator who lived from 1870 to 1966. He is best known as a designer of magazine covers, posters, calendars, and advertisements.

Parrish, City Of Brass, 3 Horsemen Gazing At City, Frame, c.1905, 13 x 10 3/4 In.	190.00
Parrish, Court Jester, Knave Of Hearts, Seated On Stone, Holding Lute, Frame, 10 3/4 In.	95.00
Parrish, Daubreal, 1923, 18 x 30 In.	805.00
Parrish, Dreaming, 1928, 10 x 18 In.	735.00
Parrish, Garden Of Allah, 1918, 9 x 18 In.	285.00
Parrish, Garden Of Allah, 1918, 15 x 30 In.	375.00
Parrish, Hilltop, 1927, 12 x 20 In.	455.00
Parrish, Jell-O, King & Queen Might Eat, Cardboard, 3-Fold, Frame, 1920s	9900.00
Parrish, Mirror, Lute Players, 1920, 6 x 10 In.	550.00
Parrish, Romance, 1925, 14 x 25 In.	1790.00
Parrish, Spirit Of Transportation, 1923, 16 1/2 x 20 In.	500.00
Parrish, The Rubaiyat, 1917, 7 x 28 1/2 In.	615.00
Parrish, Twilight, Creek, House & Farm, 17 x 13 In.	172.00
Parrish, Violetta & Knave, Golden Garments, Kneeling, Frame, c.1925, 13 x 10 1/2 In.	112.00
Piranesi, Veduta Del Ponte Molle Sul Tevere Due Miglia Lontan Da Roma, 19 x 28 In.	242.00
Remington, Argument With The Town Marshall, c.1941, 15 1/2 x 23 3/4 In.	22.00
Rock Island System, Army & Navy Hospital, Hot Springs, Ark, Oak Frame, 1920, 32 In.	115.00
Senseney, George, Winter Landscape Scene, White Matte, Mahogany Frame, 17 In.	400.00
Sorenson, Landscape Scene, Etching, Frame, 1934, 4 1/2 x 5 3/4 In.	242.00
Sowerby, J., Botanical, Hand-Colored, London, Frame, c.1801, 12 3/4 x 9 In., 4 Piece	165.00

Union Pacific, U.P. Streamlined Train, Frame, 24 x 20 In. 69.00
Warren, Karl, Late Afternoon, Winter Landscape, Turquoise, Black, White, 7 x 12 1/2 In. 58.00
Wilson, Edward A., Pipeline Construction, 1941, 11 x 14 In. 2990.00
Wilson, Edward A., Propeller, 1941, 9 1/2 x 13 In. 1725.00
Wood, Grant, Family Doctor, Hands, With Instruments, 1940, 10 x 11 7/8 In. 5060.00

Woodblock prints that are not in the Japanese tradition are listed here.
Most were made in England and the United States during the Arts
and Crafts period. Japanese woodblock prints are listed under Print,
Japanese.

Woodblock, Babcock, Dean, Birch Trees In Front Of Mountain Range, Oak Frame, 8 In. . 546.00
Woodblock, Babcock, Dean, Woods Of Aspens, Arts & Crafts Oak Frame, 2 1/2 x 4 In. ... 322.00
Woodblock, Baker, Mary F., Young Girl Decorating Vase, Newcomb, Frame, 8 x 5 1/2 In. 2070.00
Woodblock, Bartlett, Charles, Numerous People Among Elaborate Trees, 11 x 7 In. 633.00
Woodblock, Baumann, Gustave, Eagle Ceremony At Tesque Pueblo, 1932, 6 1/2 In. 1100.00
Woodblock, Berry, Carroll Thayer, Between Forest & Sea, Maine Coast, 12 x 9 In. 425.00
Woodblock, Bresslerm-Roth, Norbertine, Angora Cat, White Mat, Frame, Signed, 7 In. .. 424.00
Woodblock, Bridge, Waterway Scene, Arts & Crafts Oak Frame, 10 x 11 1/2 In. 518.00
Woodblock, Dow, Arthur Wesley, Asian Foliage, Arts & Crafts Oak Frame, 6 x 7 In. 863.00
Woodblock, Dow, Arthur Wesley, Book Cover, Modern Art, 16 x 11 In. 1093.00
Woodblock, Dow, Arthur Wesley, Ipswich Press, Marsh Island, c.1901, 3 1/2 x 5 1/2 In. .. 805.00
Woodblock, Dow, Arthur Wesley, Marsh Scene, Arts & Crafts Oak Frame, 5 x 3 In. 1380.00
Woodblock, Dow, Arthur Wesley, Numerous Houses & Trees, Oak Frame, 5 x 4 In. 1380.00
Woodblock, Erickson, Oscar, Winter Nights, Numbered, Frame 489.00
Woodblock, Gardiner, Eliza D., Boy & Cat, Matted, Frame, Signed, 1916, 10 x 7 1/2 In. . 650.00
Woodblock, Gearhart, Francis H., Cliffs Edge, Matted, Frame, 10 x 11 In. 1840.00
Woodblock, Hyde, Helen, 2 Children Bowing To Each Other, Signed, 7 1/2 x 7 In. 425.00
Woodblock, Hyde, Helen, Asian Child, Arts & Crafts Oak Frame, 2 1/4 x 7 1/4 In. 1035.00
Woodblock, Hyde, Helen, Asian Female Holding Baby, Arts & Crafts Oak Frame, 15 In. . 460.00
Woodblock, Hyde, Helen, Asian Female With Infant, Iris Field, 7 1/4 x 15 In. 805.00
Woodblock, Hyde, Helen, Asian Lady With Child, Arts & Crafts Oak Frame, 17 x 4 In. .. 748.00
Woodblock, Hyde, Helen, Child Among Cacti, Oak Frame, 10 1/4 x 3 1/2 In. 403.00
Woodblock, Hyde, Helen, Oriental Scene, Signed, 5 x 9 In. 550.00
Woodblock, Hyde, Helen, Young Asian Female, Oak Frame, 2 1/2 x 7 1/2 In. 575.00
Woodblock, Hyde, Helen, Young Asian Lad Chasing Butterflies, Oak Frame, 1908, 8 In. . 605.00
Woodblock, Jacoulet, Joaquina Et Sa Mere, Young Woman & Her Mother, Near Ocean .. 287.00
Woodblock, Large Bold Pink, White Flowers, Oak Frame, 5 x 6 In. 311.00
Woodblock, Lord, Elyse, Woman & Bird, Matted, Frame, 11 1/2 x 12 In. 299.00
Woodblock, Lum, Bertha, Market Scene, Matted, Frame, Signed, 9 x 10 In. 288.00
Woodblock, Lum, Bertha, Young Asian Female Among Swirling Waves, 2 x 9 In. 460.00
Woodblock, Marcus, Eva Maria, On The Hill, Frame, 9 x 11 1/2 In. 518.00
Woodblock, Matt Helen, Landscape With Mountain In Background, 1909, 4 x 5 In. 805.00
Woodblock, McDonald, Katherine H., Cup Of Gold Flower, Matted, Frame, 10 x 8 In. ... 299.00
Woodblock, Miller, Lilian, Asian Children, Arts & Crafts Oak Frame, 6 x 10 In. 460.00
Woodblock, Miller, Lilian, Oriental Village Scene, Matted, Frame, 1921, 13 x 8 In. 489.00
Woodblock, Norton, Elizabeth, Dog, Matted, Arts & Crafts Oak Frame, 7 1/2 x 6 1/2 In. . 460.00
Woodblock, Norton, Elizabeth, Fishing Boats, Framed, Signed, 1926, 6 x 4 1/4 In. 489.00
Woodblock, Patterson, Margaret, Landscape Scene With Mountains, 10 In. 690.00
Woodblock, Phillips, W. J., Boy Fishing, Signed, Numbered, Matted, Frame, 3 1/2 x 5 In. 600.00
Woodblock, Rice, William S., Trees, Mountain Range, Matted, Frame, 6 x 9 In. 2415.00
Woodblock, Richert, Charles Henry, Boats At Sea, Arts & Crafts Oak Frame, 4 x 5 In. ... 374.00
Woodblock, Richert, Charles Henry, Boats, Arts & Crafts Oak Frame, 4 x 5 In. 546.00
Woodblock, Riviera, Henri, City Harbor Scene, Arts & Crafts Oak Frame, 21 x 33 In. ... 690.00
Woodblock, Schaffer, Rose, Fisherman, Matted, Frame, Signed, Titled, 18 1/2 x 11 In. ... 230.00
Woodblock, Still Life, Poppies, Signed, 12 1/2 x 13 In. 550.00
Woodblock, Stream Running Through Snow, Signed, 6 x 8 In. 345.00
Woodblock, Thompson, A. T., Green, Trees, Book, Oak Frame, Signed, 10 In. 460.00
Woodblock, Trees Swaying In Breeze, Green Ground, Oak Frame, 15 In. 575.00
Woodblock, Tyson, Dorothy, Woman, Cherry Blossoms, Lantern, Signed, 7 3/4 x 5 3/4 In. 250.00
Woodblock, Watson, Ernest, Large Ship At Sea, Airplane Soaring Over Waves, 9 In., Pair 431.00
Woodblock, Whitehead, Buell, Desert Scene, Green, Tan, Arts & Crafts Oak Frame, 18 In. 690.00
Woodcut, Weber, Max, Seated Woman, Nude, 1919, 4 3/8 x 2 In. 1035.00

PURINTON POTTERY COMPANY was incorporated in Wellsville, Ohio, in 1936. The company moved to Shippenville, Pennsylvania, in 1941 and made a variety of hand-painted ceramic wares. By the 1950s Purinton was making dinnerware, souvenirs, cookie jars, and florist wares. The pottery closed in 1959.

Purinton Pottery

Apple, Tumbler, Large	27.00
Heather Plaid, Creamer	18.00
Heather Plaid, Sugar, Cover	20.00
Ivy, Red Blossom, Teapot, 2 Cup, 4 In.	39.00
Ivy, Red Blossom, Tumbler, Juice	25.00
Normandy Plaid, Creamer	18.00
Normandy Plaid, Oil & Vinegar	65.00

PURSES have been recognizable since the eighteenth century, when leather and needlework purses were preferred. Beaded purses became popular in the nineteenth century, went out of style, but are again in use. Mesh purses date from the 1880s and are still being made. How to carry a handkerchief and lipstick is a problem today for every woman, including the Queen of England.

18K Yellow Gold, Hinged Lid, Rope Edge, Link Handle	3450.00
18K Yellow Gold, Leaf Clasp, 115 Small Diamonds, Inside Mirror	4025.00
Alligator, Black, Gilt Brass Mounted, Bary Kieselstein-Cord, 12 1/2 x 12 In.	2760.00
Alligator, Brown, Trapezoidal, Interior Coin Purse, Mark Cross, 1950s	345.00
Alligator, Charcoal, Suede Lined, Shoulder Strap, Barry Kieselstein-Cord, 8 In.	1495.00
Alligator, Ecru, Gilt Brass Mounted, Oval, Handle, Barry Kieselstein-Cord	980.00
Alligator, Taupe, Frog Clasp, Barry Kieselstein-Cord, 8 3/4 x 3 1/2 In.	1840.00
Beaded, Arabesque, Cutout Fringe, Flower Basket Silk Lined, 1920, 9 3/4 x 6 In.	170.00
Beaded, Biblical Scene, Gleaners, Beaded Fringe, Satin, Metal Frame, Strap, 7 3/4 In.	170.00
Beaded, Black Satin, Black Bugle, Seed Beads, Goldtone Frame, Shell Shape, La Regale	27.00
Beaded, Blue Iridescent, Roses, Loop Fringe, Embossed Brass Frame, 8 1/2 In.	200.00
Beaded, Clutch, Gold, Ivory Ground, 1950s	55.00
Beaded, Embroidered, Shoulder Strap, Judith Leiber	750.00
Beaded, Flowers, Paisley, Twisted Loop Ring, Sterling Frame, 8 1/2 x 8 1/2 In.	255.00
Beaded, Geometric, Black & Blue Iridescent, Silver-Plate Filigree, 5 1/2 In.	169.00
Beaded, Gold & Silver, Fishnet Fringe, Gilt Frame, Silk Lined, c.1920, 9 x 5 In.	90.00
Beaded, Leaves, Flowers, Metal Frame, Fringe, c.1920, 10 x 8 In.	80.00
Beaded, Orange, Brown, Silver, Heart Form, Arabesque, Floral Frame, c.1920, 9 x 6 In.	172.00
Beaded, Scenic, Electra Cooley, 1830s	500.00
Beaded, Silver, Horizontal Band, Daisy, Red Silk Lining, Chain Drawstring, 8 x 5 In.	80.00
Beaded, Silver, Peacock, Metal Frame, Tassels, Leather Lined, Fittings, 7 x 6 1/2 In.	172.00
Beaded, Silver, Steel, Flowers, Velvet, Silver Frame, Acorn Clasp, Lined, 9 x 7 In.	218.00
Beaded, Steel, Arabesque, Twisted Loop Fringe, Enamel & Jewel Frame, 8 x 7 In.	322.00
Beaded, Steel, Flowers, Fabric Handle, Metal Frame, Jewel Clasp, Lined, 5 1/2 x 8 In.	34.00
Beaded, Steel, Flowers, Fabric Handle, Silk Lining, 2 Pockets, Fittings, 7 x 9 In.	46.00
Beaded, Steel, Flowers, Wood Frame, Strap, Tassel, Silk Lined, c.1920, 10 x 8 In.	220.00
Beaded, White, Pearlized, Stars Within Stars, Hand Strap, Czechoslovakia, 5 1/2 x 3 In.	25.00
Betty Boop, Kathrine Baumann	635.00
Cat, Black, White Whiskers, Ears & Nose, Green Eyes, Handle, Walnorg	2300.00
Coin, Leather, Tooled, Wiener Werkstatte, Dark Brown, Silk Lining, 3 x 5 In.	405.00
Coin, Suede, Green, Metal Snap Top, Compliments Of First National Bank, 1923	95.00
Crocheted, Miser Bag, Steel Beads, c.1920, 16 In.	115.00
Crocodile, Black, Foldover Flap, Amber Tab, Top Handle, Gucci	920.00
Crystal, Abstract Flowers, Judith Leiber	1380.00
Crystal, Art Deco Style, Black & White, Judith Leiber	1725.00
Crystal, Asparagus, Judith Leiber	2530.00
Crystal, Black & White, Pig, Judith Leiber	1035.00
Crystal, Blue, Gift Box, Judith Leiber	2300.00
Crystal, Blue, Patchwork Cat, Judith Leiber	2185.00
Crystal, Book Bag, Judith Leiber	1840.00
Crystal, Bronze, Violin, Gold Kid Lining, Judith Leiber	2070.00
Crystal, Firecrackers, Judith Leiber	1150.00
Crystal, Flowers, Buddha, Gold & Multicolored, Judith Leiber	1265.00

Crystal, Fruit, Gilt, Judith Leiber 1265.00
Crystal, Gold & Black, Rabbit, Judith Leiber 1610.00
Crystal, Gray, Zebra, Judith Leiber 2070.00
Crystal, Greek Revival, Judith Leiber 1955.00
Crystal, Leopard Pave, Gilt Rope Shoulder Strap, Katherine Baumann, 6 In. 1150.00
Crystal, New Yorker, Judith Leiber 3450.00
Crystal, Pave, Dalmatian Shape, Black & White, Onyx Clasp, Katherine Baumann, 7 In. . 635.00
Crystal, Tomato, Judith Leiber 1265.00
Crystal, Watermelon, Judith Leiber 1495.00
Crystal, White, Flowers, Sack, Judith Leiber 1610.00
Embroidered, Linen, Drawstring, Appliqued, Polychrome, Arts & Crafts, 8 1/2 In., 2 Piece 144.00
Embroidered, Olive, Blue, Peach Flowers, Beads, Brass Frame, Snap Closure 35.00
Fabric, Multicolored Jewel Frame, Lavender & Red, Clutch, Black, Hobe 4025.00
Fabric, Silver, Silver Metal Frame, Clasp, Chain, 7 x 8 In. 20.00
Feather, Pheasant, Plastic Cover, Gold Ball Chain, Pumpkin Satin Interior, Helfts 90.00
Gilt Metal, Flowers, Pate-De-Verre Frame 865.00
Jeweled, Baseball, Kathrine Baumann 575.00
Jeweled, Coca-Cola Bottle, Kathrine Baumann 635.00
Jeweled, Enamel, Jeweled Frame, Clasp & Handle, Silk Lined, c.1920, 8 x 6 In. 210.00
Jeweled, Gold, Taxi, New York, Kathrine Baumann 920.00
Jeweled, Sapphire, Rhinestone, Faux, Clutch, Black, Gilt Frame 2185.00
Leather, Celadon, Alligator Mask Clasp, Barry Kieselstein-Cord, 11 1/2 x 9 1/2 In. 920.00
Leather, Celadon, Cocktail, 2 Gilt Chain Handles, Judith Leiber, 6 In. 375.00
Leather, Ecru Pebble Grained, Shoulder Strap, Barry Kieselstein-Cord, 12 x 12 1/2 In. ... 546.00
Leather, Enamel, Silver Plate Front, Floral Filigree, Mirror, Lined, 6 3/8 In. 515.00
Leather, Navy Bargello, Woven, Shoulder Strap, Barry Kieselstein-Cord, 10 In. 633.00
Lucite, Oval, Clear, Chrome Strap, Brass Tag, Judith Leiber, 3 x 6 In. 310.00
Magazine, Hawaii Scene, Hula Dancers, Singers, Yellow, Red, Green 65.00
Mesh, Blue Stone Cabochon Closure, Pierced, 14K Gold 980.00
Mesh, Indian Symbols On Frame, Chain, Silver, Gorham, 6 1/2 In. 3220.00
Needlepoint, Black Border, Chain, Foldover Clutch, Walborg, 9 x 6 In. 25.00
Panda, Red Vested, Judith Leiber 1380.00
Patchwork, Shoulder Strap, Judith Leiber 865.00
Plastic Laminated Cloth, Automobile Insignia, Ronay, 1950s 500.00
Poodle, Pink, Gray, Rhinestone Eyes, Pegie By The Sea Originals, 1950s, 8 x 10 In. 165.00
Psychedelic, Multicolored, Judith Leiber 978.00
Pug, Gold & Brown, Judith Leiber 1265.00
Rhinestone, Pave, Blue & Charcoal Flowers, Silver Shoulder Strap, Judith Leiber, 5 In. ... 1495.00
Rhinestone, Pave, Red, Blue & Rose Flowers, Gilt Shoulder Strap, Judith Leiber, 6 3/4 In. 1150.00
Silk, Embroidered, Floral & Stripe, Silver Mounted, 6 x 9 In. 84.00
Silver, Copper & Brass Applied Tulip, 6 1/2 x 4 1/4 x 2 1/4 In. 176.00
Silver, Enamel, Lavender Enamel, Leather Lined, Silver Link Chain, EJH, 1938, 4 In. ... 230.00
Snakeskin, Box Shape, Leather Strap Handle 60.00
Sterling Silver, Mesh Link, Geometric Frame, Cord Strap, R. Blackington, 6 In. 230.00
Suede, Black, Paisley Printed, Clutch, Judith Leiber, 8 1/2 In. 690.00
Suede, Carnelian, Plaques, Marcasite Offset, Faille Lined, Suede Strap, 7 x 6 In. 402.00
Titanic, Red, Blue & White, Katherine Baumann, Limited Edition Of 25 .... 2765.00
Tortoiseshell, Silver Inset, Coin, Silver Flowers, 2 1/2 x 2 In. 290.00
Velveteen, Bag, Box, Rigid Gilt Metal Handle, Suitcase Lock, Emilio Pucci, 1960s 345.00
Wallet, Flame Stitch, Pin Flaps, New England, c.1750 .... 595.00
Walnut, Italian, Bucket Shape, Gilt Brass, Arched Handles, Ferragamo, 13 In. 374.00
Wicker, Creel Shape, Cloth Lining, Leather Hinges, Shoulder Strap, 6 x 9 x 7 In. 83.00
Wool, Bag, Blue, Felted Wool, Foldover Flap, Leather Handle, Fendi 230.00

QUEZAL glass was made from 1901 to 1924 by Martin Bach, Sr., in Queens, New York. Other glassware by other firms, such as Loetz, Steuben, and Tiffany, resembles this gold-colored iridescent glass. Martin Bach died in 1921. His son-in-law, Conrad Vahlsling, Jr., went to work at the Lustre Art Company about 1920 and his son, Martin Bach, Jr., worked at the Durand Art Glass division of the Vineland Flint Glass Works after 1924.

Quezal

Bowl, Brown, Iridescent Gold Interior, Ribbed, Signed In Pontil, 10 In. 460.00

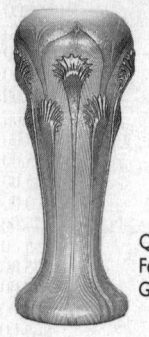

Be sure that any restorer, refinisher, or upholsterer working on your antique is insured. If you are having a piece restored, get a written estimate first.

Quezal, Vase, Combed Green
Feathers, Applied Iridescent
Gold Shells, 10 1/4 In.

Bowl, Iridescent Gold, Blue Highlights, Ruffled Edge, Signed, 6 1/2 In. 360.00
Bowl, Iridescent Orange Pulled Swirls, Footed, Signed, 8 In. 1265.00
Cup & Saucer, Iridescent Gold, Applied Handle, Signed, 2 1/2 In. 360.00
Hanging, Iridescent Gold & Green Pulled Leaves, Signed, 21 In. 6325.00
Lamp, Emerald Green, Gold Leaves Pulled From Base, Opal Shoulder, 14 In. 1840.00
Salt, Iridescent, Gold, Faceted, Marked, 1 1/4 x 2 1/2 In. 375.00
Shade, 2-Tone Iridescent Gold, Molded Flame, 8 In. 750.00
Shade, Colonial Blue Feathers, Amber Tipped, On Pearl, Puffy Shape, Signed, 6 1/2 In. ... 800.00
Shade, Cream & Green Pulled Feathers, On Gold Iridescent, 5 x 2 1/8 In., Pair 345.00
Shade, Cream Pulled Feather, On Gold Iridescent, 5 & 2 In., 2 Piece 550.00
Shade, For Sconce, Gold Iridescent, 5 x 4 In., 4 Piece 430.00
Shade, Gold Iridescent, King Tut, Domed, Signed, 5 3/8 In. 690.00
Shade, Gold Pulled Feathers, Green Tipped, On Opal Ground, Bell Form, 5 In. 259.00
Shade, Gold Pulled Feathers, On Cream, 5 x 2 In., Pair 776.00
Shade, Gold Pulled Feathers, On White Opalescent Glass, 4 5/8 x 2 1/8 In. 145.00
Shade, Green Pulled Feathers, Gold Borders, On White Opalescent, 5 1/2 In., Pair 575.00
Shade, Green Pulled Feathers, Gold Outline, On Cream, 5 1/4 x 2 In., Pair 375.00
Shade, Green, Gold Iridescent Pulled Feather, 5 x 2 1/4 In., Pair 520.00
Shade, Iridescent Gold, Green, Pulled Feather, Ruffled, Flared, 9 In. 3450.00
Shade, Iridescent Gold, White Accents, Reptilian Pattern, 4 3/4 In. 207.00
Shade, Iridescent Opal, Gold Pulled Vines, Green Leaves, Tulip Shape, 5 In. 260.00
Shade, Red Iridescent Ribs, Gold, Blue Highlights, 5 1/2 In., Pair 575.00
Shade, Ribbed, Bell Shape, Gold Iridescent, White Pulled Stripes, 5 In. 520.00
Shade, Silvery Pink & Blue, Flared, 5 3/4 x 4 1/2 In. 110.00
Vase, Agate, Haloed Colors, Cased, 5 1/2 In. 2645.00
Vase, Amber, 5 Pulled Feathers, White Opaque, 6 3/8 In. 920.00
Vase, Blue Iridescent Shoulder, Signed, 7 1/4 In. 950.00
Vase, Blue, Purple, Gold & White, Originally A Lamp Base, 11 1/2 In. 3500.00
Vase, Combed Green Feathers, Applied Iridescent Gold Shells, 10 1/4 In. .... *Illus* 5750.00
Vase, Gold Iridescent, Flared, 1920, 6 In. 3300.00
Vase, Green Iridescent, Oval, Signed, 6 1/2 In. 2115.00
Vase, Green Pulled Feathers, Gold Outline, On White, Crimped Rim, 3 In. 750.00
Vase, Green, Gold Pulled Feathers, Ivory, Gold Interior, Flower Form, Bronze Foot, 17 In. 8625.00
Vase, Iridescent Blue, Green Pulled Feathers, Signed, 7 3/4 In. 980.00
Vase, Iridescent Gold Pulled Swirls, Flared Rim, Urn Shape, 12 In. 290.00
Vase, Iridescent Gold, Applied Threading, Signed, 4 In. 360.00
Vase, Iridescent Gold, Magenta Hues, Tricornered Stretched Rim, 5 1/2 In. 550.00
Vase, Jack-In-The-Pulpit, Green Iridescent, 1920, 12 1/2 In. 8400.00
Vase, Platinized Gold Pulled Feathers, Green Tips, Ivory Shoulder, Gold Interior, 9 1/2 In. 750.00
Vase, Pulled & Hooked, Yellow, Green, Gold, On Ivory, Signed, 8 In. 2300.00
Vase, Pulled Green Feathers, On Gold Iridescent, Flared, 9 1/2 In. 5775.00
Vase, Red, Blue Highlights, On Orange, Signed, 4 In. 1200.00
Vase, Trumpet, Gold Iridescent, 2 Snakes & Foliage, 18 1/2 In. 2070.00
Vase, Trumpet, Gold Iridescent, Wheat Husks, Bronze Mount, 12 3/4 In. 800.00
Vase, Trumpet, Iridescent Gold, Signed, 10 In. 575.00

QUILTS have been made since the seventeenth century. Early textiles were very precious and every scrap was saved to be reused. A quilt is a combination of fabrics joined to a filler and a backing by small stitched designs known as quilting. An appliqued quilt has pieces stitched to the top of a large piece of background fabric. A patchwork, or pieced, quilt is made of many small pieces stitched together. Embroidery can be added to either type.

Amish, Blue Border, Red String Ties, Alternating Squares, Blue, Red, 1905, 60 x 64 In. . . .	910.00
Amish, Bow Tie, Navy Ground, Green Border, 19th Century, 79 1/4 x 68 In.	920.00
Amish, Diamond In The Square, Brown, Green, Purple, Maroon, Black, 74 x 75 In.	420.00
Amish, Diamond In The Square, Frame Mounted, Lancaster, Pa., 80 1/2 x 79 1/2 In.	2235.00
Amish, Diamond In The Square, Wool, Homespun, Lancaster Co., Pa., 78 x 78 In.	1265.00
Amish, Double Diamond, Bars, Cotton, Early 1900s, 41 3/4 x 28 1/2 In.	3290.00
Amish, Four Patch Variation, Wool, Mifflin County, 1920s, 87 x 73 1/4 In.	5875.00
Amish, Lemoyne Star, Cotton, Pennsylvania, Early 20th Century, 31 x 28 1/2 In.	1175.00
Amish, Log Cabin, Polished Cotton, Flowers On Backing, 72 x 77 In.	330.00
Amish, Log Cabin, Wool, Indiana, Early 20th Century, 38 3/4 x 31 3/4 In.	3290.00
Amish, Patchwork, Hexagonal Shapes, Synthetic Upholstery Fabrics, 78 x 46 In.	575.00
Amish, Patchwork, Sunshine & Shadow, Wool, Lancaster, c.1920, 77 x 77 3/4 In.	8815.00
Amish, Sunshine & Shadow, Blue Border, Burgundy Corners, 109 x 93 In.	495.00
Amish, Sunshine & Shadow, Wide Border, White Backing, 72 x 72 In.	825.00
Amish, Tumbling Block, Pieced, Blues, Purples, Cotton, c.1940, 88 x 77 In.	250.00
Amish, Tumbling Block, Red, Green, Aqua, Purple Ground, Cotton, Crib, 39 x 39 In.	235.00
Amish, Windmill Blade, Wool, Red Binding, Flowers & Scroll Back, c.1875, 66 x 77 In. . .	805.00
Appliqued, 3 Tulips, White, Teal Binding, Cora Mack, Marion, Ohio, 1870, 66 x 82 In. . .	770.00
Appliqued, 7-Pointed Stars, Vining Flower Border, 62 x 80 In.	495.00
Appliqued, 8-Pointed Star Medallion, Eagle Corners, Made By Wm. Ney, 73 x 88 In.	412.00
Appliqued, 8-Pointed Star, Surrounded By 5-Pointed Stars, Vine Corners, 81 1/2 x 83 In. .	747.00
Appliqued, 16 Blocks, Tulips, Red, Orange, White Field, Feather Border, 74 x 76 In.	413.00
Appliqued, 16 Floral Wreaths, Border Flowers & 3 Wreaths, Red Binding, 74 x 74 In. . . .	385.00
Appliqued, ABC, Cat, Duck, Ice Cream Cone, Doll, 54 x 36 In.	330.00
Appliqued, Album, 16 Blocks, Red, Yellow, Green Calico, White, 3 Borders, 98 x 98 In. . .	6490.00
Appliqued, Album, 20 Blocks, February 20, 1857, Madison Co., N.C., 92 x 74 In.	1870.00
Appliqued, Album, Embroidered, 12 Blocks, American Flag, 71 1/2 x 97 In.	470.00
Appliqued, Album, Flowers, Wreath, Flowerpot Corner, Red, Yellow, Orange, 80 x 78 In. .	730.00
Appliqued, Album, Red, Green, White, Embroidery, Trapunto Squares, 86 x 84 In.	785.00
Appliqued, American Flag, 48 Stars, 31 1/2 x 19 1/2 In.	632.00
Appliqued, Basket Of Flowers, White, Sawtooth Border, Stretcher Sewn, Crib, 40 x 42 In. .	935.00
Appliqued, Blue & White Baskets, Blue Border, 72 x 75 In.	220.00
Appliqued, Blue On White Ground, Leaf & Band Border, 78 x 80 In.	275.00
Appliqued, Bride's, White On White, Poppy Medallion, Ocean Wave Borders, 74 x 80 In. .	302.00
Appliqued, Camels, Elephants, Red Plaid Flower Squares, 1850, 64 In.	1870.00
Appliqued, Courthouse Steps, Pink Border, Phoebe A. Ubil, 19th Century, 86 x 86 In. . . .	330.00
Appliqued, Dark Red Roses, Yellow Centers, Blue Gray Leaves, 77 x 100 In.	220.00
Appliqued, Diamonds, 4 Floral Medallions, Red, Green, Goldenrod, 84 In.	1210.00
Appliqued, Eagle, From Kit, Centennial, 96 x 75 In.	468.00
Appliqued, Embroidered, 48 States Names & State Flowers, Red, White, Blue, 83 x 90 In. .	1380.00
Appliqued, Embroidered, Dolls, Airplanes, Cats, Dogs, Flowers, Redwork, 60 x 66 1/2 In. .	385.00
Appliqued, Embroidered, Rose Of Sharon Center, Double Medallions, 87 x 87 In.	4115.00
Appliqued, Exotic Birds Drinking From Urns, Hanging From Trees, 94 x 116 In.	1430.00
Appliqued, Figures, Outstretched Arms, North Carolina, Mid 20th Century, 72 x 80 In. . . .	990.00
Appliqued, Flag, 48 Stars, c.1918, 76 x 74 In.	7500.00
Appliqued, Fleur-De-Lis, White Border, 19th Century, 70 x 78 In.	675.00
Appliqued, Flower Medallions, Cotton, Scalloped Border, 88 x 85 In.	1540.00
Appliqued, Flowers, Hand Sewn, Machine Sewn White Edging, 82 x 82 In.	440.00
Appliqued, Friendship, Fruit Basket, Strawberries, Grapes, Flowers, 1849, 96 x 96 In. . . .	448.00
Appliqued, Green, Red, Double Red & White Border, 19th Century, 64 x 64 In.	420.00
Appliqued, Harrison Rose, c.1850, 76 x 76 In.	248.00
Appliqued, Hawaiian, Kahili, Red Flower & Plant Design, White Ground, 80 x 92 In. . . .	4600.00
Appliqued, Lady Of The Lake, 4 Poster, Bedpost Cut, 1800, 68 x 77 In.	500.00
Appliqued, North Carolina Lily, Red, Green Calico, White Ground, c.1879, 81 x 82 In. . . .	468.00
Appliqued, Oak Leaf & Reel, White, Green Reel, Red, Green Leaves, Pa., 42 x 43 In. . . .	358.00

Appliqued, Oak Leaf & Tulip, Flowered Chintz Border, 104 x 96 In. 2495.00
Appliqued, Patchwork, Goose Foot, Red, Green, Printed Ground, 1900, 42 x 42 In. 410.00
Appliqued, Pink, Purple, Orange Tulips, Light Green Binding, 70 x 82 In. 770.00
Appliqued, Pinwheel, Red Calico, White Ground, Leafy Border, 52 x 36 1/2 In. 529.00
Appliqued, Poppy Medallions, White, Tan Border, 79 x 82 In. 1045.00
Appliqued, Princess Feather, Center Orange Star, Red, Green, 79 x 81 In. 275.00
Appliqued, Princess Feather, Red & Green Triangles, Block Border, 78 x 80 In. 660.00
Appliqued, Red & Orange Flowers, Green Leaves, Sawtooth Border, 84 x 86 In. 522.00
Appliqued, Rose & Star, Red, Green, Orange, White Field, West Virginia, 89 x 90 In. 248.00
Appliqued, Spread Eagle Center, Vining Tulips, Red Petal Flowers, c.1930, 82 x 100 In. . . 1375.00
Appliqued, Starburst, Deborah Meserve, 1895, 90 x 88 In. 770.00
Appliqued, Sunbonnet Sue, Red & White, Picket Fence Border, 1800s, 84 x 88 In. 1000.00
Appliqued, Trapunto Grapes, Vining Leaves, Floral Corners, c.1840, 91 x 91 In. 330.00
Appliqued, Tulips, Vining Flowers, Medallion, Eagle, Scalloped Border, 80 x 96 In. 412.00
Appliqued, Turkey Tracks, Blue, White Ground, Floral, Berries, Corner Stars, 84 x 84 In. . 440.00
Appliqued, Urn & Flower, Floral & Bud Border, 78 x 83 In. 3300.00
Appliqued, Whole Cloth, Glazed, Indigo, 5 Panels, Quilting, Wool, c.1790, 48 x 48 In. . . . 5400.00
Chintz, Fruit Panels, Strawberries, Grapes, Olive & Yellow, Unwashed, 100 x 102 In. 220.00
Crazy, Blocks With Fans, Embroidered Accents, 68 x 76 In. 137.00
Crazy, Embroidered, Animals, Girls, Multicolored, Burgundy Velvet Border, 62 x 62 In. . . 605.00
Crazy, Embroidered, Painted, Satin, Silk, Velvet, Rust Velvet Border, 69 x 69 In. 550.00
Crazy, Embroidered, Rust Backing, L.M. Dinhard, Duboistown, Pa., c.1890, 48 x 48 In. . . 196.00
Crazy, Silk, Taffeta, Red, Green, Blue, Feed Sack Backing, 62 x 92 In. 45.00
Patchwork, 4-Point Stars, 3 Band Border, Brick Red, Rose, Natural Ground, 82 x 88 In. . . 412.00
Patchwork, 9 Patch, Chintz Squares & Border, c.1850, 84 x 86 In. 165.00
Patchwork, 9 Patch, Red Grid, Cotton, 20th Century, 75 x 71 In. 230.00
Patchwork, 30 Red Stars, White Ground, Feather Wreath, 83 1/2 x 72 1/2 In. 687.00
Patchwork, 36 Blocks, Wide Brown Border, Dark Blue Binding, Wool, 36 x 36 1/2 In. . . . 165.00
Patchwork, Album, 16 Pattern Blocks, Signed Blocks, Union Forever, 1865, 80 x 80 In. . . 4465.00
Patchwork, Alternating Off White, Multicolored Squares, Red, 81 1/2 x 75 In. 460.00
Patchwork, Bars & Triangles, Maroon & Pumpkin Bar Backing, 88 x 84 In. 190.00
Patchwork, Bars, Scrolled Feather Quilting, Multicolored, Blue Border, 99 x 110 In. 578.00
Patchwork, Basket, Hand Sewn, 19th Century, 75 x 71 In. 168.00
Patchwork, Basket, White Field, Brown Print Border, 42 1/4 x 36 In. 880.00
Patchwork, Basket, White Squares Alternating With Red Squares, 76 x 88 In. 770.00
Patchwork, Baskets In Diamonds, Green Bands, White Ground, 90 x 90 In. 220.00
Patchwork, Blue, White, Betty Wage, England, Midwife, Quilter, 1930, 65 x 79 In. 2295.00
Patchwork, Bow Tie, Red Zigzag Border, Green Sawtooth Edge, 74 x 79 In. 1567.00
Patchwork, Broken Star, 6-Color Star, Sky Blue Ground, N. Carolina, c.1920, 90 x 98 In. . 330.00
Patchwork, Dolly Madison's Workbox, Square & Triangle Block Border, 42 x 42 In. 247.00
Patchwork, Dolly Madison's Workbox, To Louise Phillips, 1854, 64 x 90 In. 165.00
Patchwork, Double Irish Chain, Hand Sewn, White Ground, c.1900, 80 1/2 x 83 In. 336.00
Patchwork, Double Irish Chain, Red, Green, White, York County, c.1858, 82 x 92 In. 578.00
Patchwork, Double Irish Chain, Yellow, Red, Calico, Green Ground, 80 x 80 In. 250.00
Patchwork, Double Wedding Ring, Red Binding, c.1930, 78 x 76 In. 330.00
Patchwork, Dresden Plate, Inverted Scalloped Border, Lavender, 76 x 74 In. 220.00
Patchwork, Drunkard's Path, Pink & Green Calico, Blue Plaid Backing, 70 x 73 In. 138.00
Patchwork, Fan, White Field, Graduated Colors, Sawtooth Border, 87 x 74 In. 415.00
Patchwork, Feathered Star & Medallions, Sawtooth Border, 86 x 86 In. 495.00
Patchwork, Feathered Star, Double Calico Pinks, White Ground, 76 x 80 In. 330.00
Patchwork, Field Of Stars, Scalloped, Sawtooth Borders, Salmon, Lavender, 76 x 62 In. . . 275.00
Patchwork, Fleur-De-Lis Medallions, White Squares, Feathered Medallions, 90 x 94 In. . . 165.00
Patchwork, Flowers, Multicolored Bow Tie Squares, Dark Maroon, 92 x 96 In. 1320.00
Patchwork, Flying Geese, Multicolored Silk Triangles, Blue Bands, 86 x 85 In. 345.00
Patchwork, Friendship, Reds & White On White Ground, 83 x 87 In. 192.00
Patchwork, Grandmother's Fan, Cone Border, 94 x 77 In. 440.00
Patchwork, Grandmother's Flower Garden, c.1920, 94 x 92 In. 165.00
Patchwork, Grandmother's Flower Garden, Calico, Hexagon Pieces, c.1920, 90 x 73 In. . 220.00
Patchwork, Grandmother's Flower Garden, Green Garden Path Binding, 88 x 70 In. 250.00
Patchwork, Grandmother's Flower Garden, Pink, Blue, Gold, Green, 108 x 82 In. 220.00
Patchwork, Green Field, Multicolored Diamond, Feather Border, 74 x 76 In. 90.00
Patchwork, Green, Pink Pinwheels, Pink, Green Double Border, 92 x 93 In. 302.00
Patchwork, Irish Chain, 9 Patch, White, Turkey Red Binding, Grid Quilting, 76 x 80 In. . 140.00

Patchwork, Irish Chain, Navy, Pink, White Ground, Sunflowers, Border, 90 x 90 In. 415.00
Patchwork, Irish Chain, White Ground, Chintz Border, 86 x 88 In. 1650.00
Patchwork, Log Cabin, 12 Blocks, Red, White, Blue, Wool, Crepe, 72 x 70 In. 138.00
Patchwork, Log Cabin, Barn Raising, Blue, Red, White, c.1910, 82 x 80 In. 330.00
Patchwork, Log Cabin, Courthouse Steps, 100 Blocks, Wool, 19th Century, 72 x 73 In. . . 825.00
Patchwork, Log Cabin, Mennonite, Cotton & Wool, Velvet Binding, c.1890, 77 x 68 In. . . 977.00
Patchwork, Log Cabin, Multicolored, Silk, Velvet, 1890 Embroidered Red, 77 x 58 In. . . 750.00
Patchwork, Log Cabin, Printed Cotton, New England, Mid 19th Century, 90 x 88 In. 288.00
Patchwork, Log Cabin, Red, Blue, Yellow, Orange, Purple, Ky., 91 x 100 In. 715.00
Patchwork, Log Cabin, Satin & Cotton, 60 x 70 In. 1300.00
Patchwork, Log Cabin, Sunshine & Shadow, 74 x 72 In. 577.00
Patchwork, Log Cabin, Sunshine & Shadow, Blue, Tan, Pocket Back, 68 x 79 In. 495.00
Patchwork, Log Cabin, Sunshine, Blue, Red, Pink, 71 x 72 In. 495.00
Patchwork, Log Cabin, Wool, Mennonite, Lancaster Co., Pa., c.1880, 82 x 86 In. 770.00
Patchwork, Lone Star, Gray, Red, Green Blue Double Border, c.1920, 82 x 80 In. 385.00
Patchwork, Lone Star, Pink Stripe, Meandering Border, 82 x 82 In. 590.00
Patchwork, Lone Star, Red Backing, 75 x 79 In. 330.00
Patchwork, Lone Star, Yellow, Pink, Lavender, Green, White Ground, 81 x 79 In. 550.00
Patchwork, Mountains, Red, White Print, Pink, Brown Striped Back, 79 x 79 In. 385.00
Patchwork, Old Maid's Puzzle, Calico, Green Border, Red & White Backing, 73 x 73 In. . 578.00
Patchwork, Patriotic, Red, White, Blue, Sawtooth Border, 84 x 84 In. 560.00
Patchwork, Peonies In Baskets, Tulip Swag Border, Red Binding, c.1850, 84 x 84 In. . . . 358.00
Patchwork, Pinwheel Variation, White, Green, Red Calico Border, 17 3/4 x 18 In. 75.00
Patchwork, Pinwheel, Star, Red, Cream, c.1910, 84 x 72 In. 358.00
Patchwork, Princess Feather, Turkey Red & White, Initials, c.1909, 70 x 68 In. 415.00
Patchwork, Quilted Cotton, Blue & White, 1930, 65 x 79 In. 2295.00
Patchwork, Red & White Diamond & Clover Pattern, Bar Border, 83 x 83 In. 275.00
Patchwork, Red, White & Blue Geometric, 17 x 29 In. 110.00
Patchwork, Sawtooth Diamond, Pumpkin Calico, Green Sawtooth Border, 83 x 88 In. . . . 635.00
Patchwork, Schoolhouse, Bowtie, Pinwheels, Calico, Blue Grid, 78 x 78 In. 495.00
Patchwork, Schoolhouse, Hand Sewn, Blue On Red Floral Ground, c.1920, 70 x 69 In. . . 169.00
Patchwork, Star Of Bethlehem, Cotton, Mid 19th Century, 114 1/2 x 115 In. 2070.00
Patchwork, Star Of Bethlehem, Multicolored, White, Swag, Tassel, Sawtooth, 95 x 93 In. 1100.00
Patchwork, Star Of Bethlehem, White, Blue, Green, Star Corners, 1890, 76 x 76 In. 910.00
Patchwork, Star Of East, Brown, Green, Purple, Haverstraw Family, 1840, 98 x 86 In. . . . 990.00
Patchwork, Star, Blue, White, Blue Grid, Red Borders, 73 x 74 In. 468.00
Patchwork, Star, Calico, Yellow, Green, Pink, Sawtooth Border, 66 x 65 In. 120.00
Patchwork, Star, Red & Green 8-Pointed Stars On 30 Panels, 69 x 84 In. 275.00
Patchwork, Star, York Co., Crib, 39 1/2 x 40 3/4 In. 635.00
Patchwork, Triple Irish Chain, Yellow Ground, Leona Baldwin, Ohio, c.1923, 70 x 86 In. 330.00
Patchwork, Turkey Tracks, Red Calico, White, Feather Borders, Hand Sewn, 75 x 75 In. . 330.00
Patchwork, Union Jack, Belongs To Geo. Westley Farlson Jr., 1923, 90 x 67 In. 590.00
Patchwork, Wine Red, White, Cross-Stitched Stars On Blue Square, 1940s, 82 x 54 In. . . 750.00
Patchwork & Appliqued, 9 Flower Medallions, Red, Yellow, Green, 82 x 83 In. 1430.00
Patchwork & Appliqued, Geometric Snowball, Early 20th Century, c.1890, 89 x 78 In. . . 1760.00
Patchwork & Appliqued, Red, Yellow, Brown, Running Vine Border, 76 x 80 In. 308.00
Patchwork & Appliqued, Snowball Block, Calico, Heart Corners, c.1890, 89 x 78 In. 1790.00
Trapunto, Large Vase Of Flowers, Baskets Of Fruit, White, 1852, 73 3/4 x 83 In. 5175.00

QUIMPER pottery has a long history. Tin-glazed, hand-painted pottery has been made in Quimper, France, since the late seventeenth century. The earliest firm, founded in 1685 by Jean Baptiste Bousquet, was known as HB Quimper. Another firm, founded in 1772 by Francois Eloury, was known as Porquier. The third firm, founded by Guillaume Dumaine in 1778, was known as HR or Henriot Quimper. All three firms made similar pottery decorated with designs of Breton peasants and sea and flower motifs. The Eloury (Porquier) and Dumaine (Henriot) firms merged in 1913. Bousquet (HB) merged with the others in 1968. The group was sold to a United States family in 1984. The American holding company is Quimper Faience Inc., located in Stonington, Connecticut. The French firm has been called Societe Nouvelle des Faienceries de Quimper HB Henriot since March 1984.

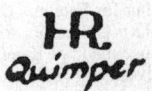

Basket, Man Holding Cane & Pipe, 6 In. 255.00

Box, Figural, Head Cover 165.00
Candlestick, Underglaze Blue, c.1940, 7 7/8 In., Pair 595.00
Clock, Wall, Marked Henriot 65.00
Compote, Flowers, Signed H.R. Quimper, 9 In. 200.00
Eggcup & Saucer, Geometric, Signed H.R. Quimper, 4 1/8 In. 90.00
Figurine, St. Anne, Signed Henriot Quimper, 3 1/2 In. 175.00
Figurine, St. Marie Holding Baby Jesus, 3 1/4 In. 220.00
Inkwell, Lid, Man & Woman Dancing, 2 Wells 225.00
Knife Rest, Flowers, Triangular, Signed A.P., 3 3/8 In., Pair 170.00
Match Holder, Fleur-De-Lis, Footed, Signed H.R., 2 1/2 In. 185.00
Match Holder, Man, 3 In. 127.00
Menu Holder, Fan Form, Man & Woman, Inscribed La Baule, 2 7/8 In. 185.00
Paperweight, Sailing Ship Crest, Octagonal, 3 1/2 In. 150.00
Pitcher, Child Holding Fishing Rod, Cobalt Blue Stripes On Handle, 8 1/2 In. 180.00
Pitcher, Crosshatch, Signed Henriot Quimper, 3 3/4 In. 115.00
Pitcher, Woman, Signed Henriot Quimper, 3 3/4 In. 105.00
Placecard Holder, Fleur-De-Lis Form, 3 3/8 In., Pair 160.00
Plate, Man, Woman, HB, c.1930, 10 1/2 In., Pair 350.00
Plate, Oyster, Majolica 140.00
Plate, Woman Figural Design, Leaf & Berry Border, 9 3/4 In. 316.00
Platter, Peasant Woman, Blue Flowers Border Rim, Oval, Signed, 11 3/4 x 7 3/4 In. 225.00
Platter, Vining Leaf Border, Man In Center, Bag & Walking Stick, 8 1/4 x 11 1/4 In. 80.00
Salt, Double, Egg Form, Goose Head Handle, Signed H.R. Quimper, 3 3/4 In. 220.00
Salt, Double, Shoe, Geometric Floral, Signed H.B., 3 7/8 In. 150.00
Serving Dish, Serving, Woman, Decor-Riche Border, Oval, 14 1/2 In. 405.00
Shoe, Man Figural Design, Signed H.B., 6 1/4 In. 145.00
Shoe, Small Heel, Upturned Toe, No Back 225.00
Shoe, Woman, Flowers, Signed P.B.X., 4 3/4 In. 140.00
Shoe, Woman, Signed H.R. Quimper, 4 1/4 In. 69.00
Snuff Bottle, Shoe, Flower & Berry Design, 4 In., Pair 375.00
Snuff Bottle, Star & Pansy, Ovoid, 3 In. 230.00
Spoon Tray, Leaf Form, Woman, Signed H.R. Quimper, 4 In. 185.00
Sugar, Cover, Man With Cane & Pipe, Flowers, 5 1/2 In. 170.00
Vase, 5 Finger, Quintel, Woman, Egg Basket, Crisscross Band, Orange, Blue, 5 1/4 In. ... 115.00
Vase, Bud, 6 Openings, Man & Woman Scene, Pedestal 750.00
Vase, Flowers, White Ground, Signed, c.1900, 5 x 4 In. 115.00
Vase, High Button Shoe On Platform, Signed H.B. Quimper, 3 1/4 In. 195.00
Wall Pocket, Shoe, Man Figural Design, Flowers, Signed H.B., 8 1/4 In. 175.00
Wall Pocket, Woman Figural Design, Biniou Form, Signed H.R. Quimper, 4 1/8 In. 260.00

RADFORD pottery was made by Alfred Radford in Broadway, Virginia,
Tiffin and Zanesville, Ohio, and Clarksburg, West Virginia, from 1891
until 1912. Jasperware, Ruko, Thera, Radura, and Velvety Art Ware
were made. The jasperware resembles the famous Wedgwood ware of   *RADURA.*
the same name. Another pottery named Radford worked in England
and is not included here.

Pitcher, Jasperware, Tan, Mask Of Bearded Man, Tan, Handle, 9 In. 70.00
Vase, Jasperware, Classical Female Figure In Long Gown, Frolicking, 5 3/4 In. 70.00
Vase, Jasperware, Immortal Driving Chariot Through Clouds, White, 6 7/8 In. 150.00

RADIO broadcast receiving sets were first sold in New York City in
1910. They were used to pick up the experimental broadcasts of the
day. The first commercial radios were made by Westinghouse Com-
pany for listeners of the experimental shows on KDKA Pittsburgh in
1920. Collectors today are interested in all early radios, especially
those made of Bakelite plastic or decorated with blue mirrors. Figural
advertising radios and transistor radios are also collected.

Admiral, Model 5Y22AN, Phonograph, 1952 .... 39.00
Advertising, Heinz Ketchup, Bottle Shape, Battery Operated, 1960s 15.00
Air King, Catalina, Model A-600 Dutchess, Tone Catalin, Green & Yellow, c.1947 ...... 1760.00
Arvin, Model 440T, Midget, Red Metal Case, 1950 .... 44.00
Atwater Kent, Model 45, Metal, Lift-Off Top, Table Model, 1929 .... 540.00
Atwater Kent, Model 47, Speaker, Console, 1929 .... 137.00

Atwater Kent, Model 60, Window Dial, Console, 1929 .... 94.00
Atwater Kent, Model 217, Table, Wood, Cutouts, 1933 .... 300.00
Atwater Kent, Model H, Tin Horn, 14 In. 80.00
Brunswick, Console, 1939, 42 x 23 In. 110.00
Coronado, Model 438190, Table Set, Plastic, Handle, 1946 .... 95.00
Crosley, Model 68TA, Plastic, Boomerang Louvers, 3 Knobs, 1948 .... 65.00
Emerson, Catalin, Model AU190, Tombstone, Marbleized Blue Green, Cloth Grill, 1938 . 12100.00
Emerson, Model 578A, P. Evans, Eames Office Cabinet, c.1946, 10 x 6 x 6 In. 635.00
Emerson, Model 888, Transistor Gift Set, Portable, 1959 .... 65.00
Emerson, Patriot, Model 400, Red, White, Blue, Plastic, 1940 .... 770.00
Emersonette, Midget, Bakelite, 1939 .... 40.00
Empress, Cottage, Ivory, Dark Red & Green Trim, 1946 .... 325.00
Fada, Catalin, Model 53, Yellow, Aqua Inset Grill, Yellow Knobs, c.1938, 6 x 4 x 9 In. .. 5500.00
Fada, Model No. P80, Portable, Maroon, Deco Grill Cutouts, 1947 .... 55.00
Magnavox, Model M-4, Horn Speaker 242.00
Majestic, Model 91, 7 Tubes, Walnut, Console, 1929 .... 55.00
Masterphone, Battery, Walnut, Engraved Face Plate 77.00
Motorola, Model 60-X-2, 1941 .... 65.00
Musicaire, Model MD16, Marbleized, Red 1045.00
Neutrowound, 3 Top Raised Dials, 6 Tubes, Metal, 1926 .... 440.00
Philco, Cathedral, Model 20, Window Dial, Scroll Cutouts, Wood, 1930 .... 198.00
Philco, Cathedral, Model 20B, Walnut Case, Table Model, 1930 .... 165.00
Philco, Model 37-630, Round Front Dial, Wood, Table Model, 1937 .... 88.00
Philco, Model 40-190, Console, Slide Rule Dial, Push Buttons, Wood, 1940, 41 x 29 In. .. 110.00
Philco, Model 86, Hand Painted, Console, c.1928, 38 In. 80.00
Philco, Transitone, Model 42-PT95, Front Plastic Panel, Wood, 1942 .... 50.00
RCA, Model 87X, Wood, 1938 .... 65.00
RCA, Victor, Lowboy Console, Escutcheon, Wood, 1929 .... 135.00
Silvertone, Cathedral, Model 1660, Front Window Dial, Wood, 1935 .... 155.00
Sparton, Bluebird, Mirrored Blue Glass, Chrome Accents, c.1936, 14 1/2 In. 2300.00
Westinghouse, Crystal, Aereola Jr., Mahogany Case, Lift Top, 1922 .... 300.00
Westinghouse, Crystal, Radio & Receiver, Case 110.00
Westinghouse, Model H126, Little Jewel, Refridgerator, Ivory, 1945 .... 120.00
Zenith, Broadcast & Short-Wave Bands, Console Floor Model, 1937 .... 850.00
Zenith, Half Round, Model 6S238, Front Grill, Chairside, 1938 .... 415.00
Zenith, Model 6D2615, Boomerang Dial, Grill, Cutouts, Wood, 1942 .... 100.00
Zenith, Tombstone, Model 6S27, Black Dial, Round, Cloth Grill, Wood, 1935 ..... 305.00

RAILROAD enthusiasts collect any train memorabilia. Everything is
wanted, from oilcans to whole train cars. The Chessie system has a
store that sells many reproductions of their old dinnerware and uniforms.

Agent's Cap, Soo Line, Embossed Marshall Field & Co., Chicago, 7 In. 46.00
Air Horn, Locomotive, Diesel, Cast Aluminum, 25 In. 138.00
Air Horn, Locomotive, Diesel, Cast Iron, 28 In. 138.00
Ashtray, Soo Line, Track, Car Border, Marked, Denver Wright Co., 7 In. 23.00
Ashtray, Southern Railway, Brass, 5 1/4 In., Pair 23.00
Bar Cart, Rolling, Bland, Silver, Metal, Round, 24 x 33 In. 299.00
Bell, Locomotive, Diesel, Bronze, Air Actuated, 12 In. .... 160.00 to 230.00
Board, Railroad Switch Control, Nickel Plate, Wood Case, 32 In. 375.00
Bond, Ohio & Mississippi Railroad, 500 Dollars, 1856 .... 395.00
Book, Tariff, Mobile & Ohio Railroad, Map, 1917, 8 x 11 In., 24 Pages 1.00
Book, Western Pacific Railway, From San Francisco, Illustrated, 1915, Pair 80.00
Bowl, Elgin, Joliet & Eastern Railroad, Stainless Steel, 12 In., Pair 25.00
Bowl, Florida East Coast Railway, Flagler System, Silver, 4 1/2 In., Pair 260.00
Bowl, Hinged Cover, New York Central, Silver, 3 3/4 In. 46.00
Bowl, West Point Route, Silver, Embossed Rim, Reed & Barton, 7 In. 316.00
Box, Flare & Flag, Gulf Mobile & Ohio Railroad, Flag, Fuses, Tin, 30 In. 17.00
Box, Flare, Chicago Rock Island & Pacific Flare, Black Paint, Tin, 13 1/2 In. 60.00
Box, Hinged Cover, Token, Galvanized Tin, Embossed, 5 x 4 1/2 x 4 In. 25.00
Broadside, Chicago, Rock Island & Pacific, Restaurant Cars, 1870, 14 x 22 In. 4255.00
Brochure, Great Northern Railway, Original Illustration, Color, 1920, 9 x 14 In. 316.00
Bucket, Fire, Missouri, Kansas & Texas, Original Red Paint, Embossed, 12 In. 60.00

Cabinet, Ticket, Oak, Locking Tambour Front, Divided Interior, 1905, 29 x 36 x 13 In. .. 373.00
Cabinet, Ticket, Soo Line, Oak, Tambour Slant Front, 1 Drawer, 1915, 21 x 36 In. 460.00
Calendar, Missouri Pacific Lines, Route Of Eagles, Removable Date Cards, 19 x 13 In. .. 172.00
Calendar, Pennsylvania, Paper, Color Photo Of Train Station, 1945, 28 x 29 In. 60.00
Can, Chicago, Milwaukee, St. Paul & Pacific Railroad, Embossed, Tin, 11 In., Gal. 46.00
Can, Kerosene, Chicago & Northwestern, Embossed, 5 Gal., 13 In. 34.00
Can, Kerosene, Chicago & Northwestern, Oxidized Finish, Embossed, Gal., 13 In. 23.00
Can, Northern Pacific Railroad, Galvanized Tin, Embossed, 14 In., 2 Gal. 23.00
Cap, Brakeman's, Open Weave Crown, 6 3/4 In. 35.00
Cap, Brakeman's, Soo Line, Open Weave Crown, Silver Nameplate, Size 7 1/4 In. 185.00
Cap, Conductor's, A.G. Meier & Co., Chicago, 7 1/4 In. 92.00
Cart, Rolling-Bar, Black & Silver Metal, Casters, U-Shaped Top, 1930s, 24 x 33 In. 300.00
Chimes, Dining Car, 4 Tone Bars, Original Striker, Wood Case, 10 1/2 In. 149.00
Clipboard, Soo Line, Locomotive Scene, Embossed, 1960, 8 1/2 In. 11.00
Club, Brakeman's, Marked, Wood, 35 In. 69.00
Coffee Server, Nashville, Chattanooga, St. Louis, Silver, Wood Handle, 32 Oz. 517.00
Coffeepot, Chicago & Eastern Illinois Railroad, Reed & Barton, 10 Oz., 7 In. 264.00
Coffeepot, Cover, Union Pacific, International Silver Co., 32 Oz. 115.00
Coffeepot, Erie Railroad, Silver, 8 Oz., 5 In. 345.00
Creamer, Santa Fe, Atlantic Coast Line, Silver, Pair 23.00
Cuspidor, Missouri Pacific, White Porcelain, Metal, Black Lettering, 7 1/2 In. 149.00
Cuspidor, St. Louis & Southwestern, Brass, Handle, Embossed, 9 In. 126.00
Cuspidor, Texas & Pacific, White, Blue Lettering, 8 In. 258.00
Drawing, Pencil, Steam Engine, NY-NH, A. Kemp, Frame, 10 x 22 1/2 In. 500.00
Glass, New York Central, Enameled, 3 3/4 & 5 In., Pair 11.00
Glass, Pennsylvania Railroad, Brown Locomotive, Enameled, 4 1/2 In., Pair 11.00
Hat, Chicago & Illinois Valley Railroad, Celluloid Tag, 7 In. 57.00
Jug, Baltimore & Ohio, Brown Cone Top, Gal., 11 1/2 In. 201.00
Lamp, Candle, Adlake, Embossed, 19th Century, 10 In. 34.00
Lamp, Car, Brass Wall Mount, 19th Century, 7 In. 805.00
Lamp, Coach, Square Beveled Lenses, Brass, 11 In., Pair 34.00
Lamp, Oil, Signed, 8 In., Pair 495.00
Lantern, Boston & Albany, Fixed Globe, Etched, 1865, 13 In. 258.00
Lantern, Boston & Worchester, Fixed Globe, Etched, 13 In. 661.00
Lantern, Caboose, Fever Hand, 8 In. 30.00
Lantern, Carrying Handles, Red, Green, Tin, Germany 373.00
Lantern, Chicago & Eastern Illinois Railroad, Embossed, 5 1/2 In. 115.00
Lantern, Dietz, New York Central Railroad, Clear Globe, Brass, 15 1/2 In. 69.00
Lantern, Erie Railroad, Embossed, 5 1/2 In. 57.00
Lantern, Fixed Globe, 1860, 13 In. 161.00
Lantern, Minneapolis & St. Louis Railroad, Embossed, Safety First, 5 1/2 In. 149.00
Lantern, Pennsylvania Railroad, Embossed, 5 1/2 In. 57.00
Lantern, Pere Marquette, Embossed, 5 1/2 In. 92.00
Lantern, Signal, 4 Sides, Blue & Amber Lens, Swing Handle, Electrified, Adlake 79.00
License Tag, Corn Belt Route, Tin, 10 In. 103.00
Lock, Belt Line, Brass, Heart Shape, Hansl Mfg. Co. 40.00
Lock, Green Bay & Western, Brass, Heart Shape 138.00
Lock, Gulf Mobil, Steel 46.00
Lock, Illinois Central, Brass, Heart Shape 34.00
Lock, Pennsylvania Line Railroad, Steel 17.00
Lock, Rock Island Lines 103.00
Lock, Soo Line, Brass, 2 Keys 57.00
Lock & Key, M.W. Co., Cast Iron, 3 1/2 x 3 In. 45.00
Lock & Key, Switchman's, Steel & Iron, Rivets, Chain, Yale & Towne Mfg. Co. 100.00
Map, Illinois, Railroad & Routes, Rand McNally, Oak Frame, 1900, 19 x 31 In. 46.00
Map, Iowa, Chicago, Nebraska, J. Sage & Sons, Frame, 1859, 26 x 23 In. 460.00
Map, New England States, Williams Telegraph & Railroad, 1852, 32 x 30 In. 60.00
Medallion, Baltimore & Ohio, Bronze, 100 Years 1827-1927, Original Box, 2 In. 45.00
Medallion, Santa Fe, Brass, Original Box, Pair 11.00
Oiler, Chicago & Alton Railroad, Embossed, Oxidized Finish, 25 In. 57.00
Oiler, Chicago & Alton Railroad, Oxidized Finish, Embossed, 24 In. 35.00
Paperweight, Seaboard Coastline, Original Box 23.00
Paperweight, Steer For The Iron Mountain Route, Longhorn Head, Domed, 3 In. 190.00

Pass, Pullman Car, Mobile & Ohio RR Director R.P. Dow, 1875 & 1876, Pair 80.00
Photograph, Boston & Maine Railroad, B & M Locomotive, Wood Frame, 35 In. 488.00
Photograph, Burlington Missouri River Railroad, Building, Employees, 1882, 14 In. 45.00
Photograph, Chicago & Alton Engine, No. 5, Sepia, 1890, 8 1/2 x 4 1/2 In. 45.00
Photograph, Dells Of Wisconsin, Steamboat Scene, Frame, 28 In. 490.00
Photograph, Denver & Rio Grande Railroad Depot, Original Oak Frame, 33 In. 2645.00
Photograph, Machinist Apprentices On C & A Locomotive, No. 605, 17 x 11 In. 490.00
Photograph, Mt. Hood, Snow Capped, Gifford, Oak Frame, 1920, 22 x 32 In. 215.00
Photograph, Soo Line Engine No. 5000, Silver Gelatin, Frame, No Glass, 22 x 8 In. 400.00
Photograph, Union Pacific Railroad, Yellowstone Falls, Frame, Matted, 13 x 27 In. 90.00
Poster, Contest For Burlington Route Employees, Frame, 14 x 23 In. 69.00
Poster, Cross-Crossings-Cautiously, America Warns You! Chandler, 1936, 14 x 22 In. . . . 345.00
Pot, Cover, New York Central, 5 1/2 In. 34.00
Print, Chicago, Milwaukee & St. Paul Railroad, King Of The Rails, 1916, 49 In. 1840.00
Print, Mail & Express, Crossing Dale Creek Embankment, 1910, 31 1/2 x 27 In. 1265.00
Print, PC & T Railroad, Gilt Gesso Frame, Foliage & Acorns, 16 1/2 x 14 1/2 In. 460.00
Print, Rio Grande Depot, Castle Gate, Utah, Frame, 17 x 19 In. 57.00
Print, Water Lily Bend, Original Oak Frame, 1910, 34 1/2 x 28 1/2 In. 184.00
Schedule, Tariff, New York & Erie, 1852, 18 x 24 In. 143.00
Seal Crimper, Nickel Plate, Handle, Embossed, 7 In. 115.00
Sign, Rockford Railroad Watch, Victorian Couple, Cardboard, 12 x 17 1/2 In. 115.00
Sign, Santa Fe Railroad, Scout, Horse & Cowboy, Porcelain, 40 1/8 x 20 In. 2875.00
Sign, Santa Fe, Black Lettering, Etched, 15 x 2 1/2 In. 57.00
Sign, Soo Line Car, Black Enamel Ground, Cast Aluminum, 16 x 24 In. 1380.00
Sign, Southern Railway, Gold Letters, Dark Glass, 34 x 4 In. 75.00
Sign, Ticket, Standard Accident Insurance Co., Brass, Aluminum, 8 x 5 In., Pair 57.00
Stepladder, Folding, St. L. K & N-W & Mail Car 103, 4 Steps, Wooden 287.00
Stepladder, Southern Pacific Railroad, Cast Iron 250.00
Stepstool, Denver & Rio Grande Railroad, Rubber Feet, No Skid Top, 9 In. 258.00
Stepstool, International & Great Northern, Diamond, Cast Iron, 1894, 32 x 16 In. 115.00
Stepstool, Northern Railroad, Grater Top, Pressed Metal, 11 In. 160.00
Stepstool, NYC & H R Railroad, Wood, Metal Corners, 9 In. 92.00
Stepstool, Pullman, Diamond Top, 2 Handles, Rubber Feet, Cast Metal, 10 In. 170.00
Stepstool, Rock Island Line, Grater Top, Embossed, Pressed Metal, 11 In. 103.00
Stepstool, Wabash Railroad, Wood Top, Embossed, Cast Iron Legs, 11 In. 345.00
Stock Certificate, Dan Patch Electric Line, Frame, 1910, 8 x 14 In. 46.00
Stock Certificate, Penn Street Passenger Railway Co., Graphics, 40 Shares, c.1874 . . . . . 28.00
Stock Certificate, Pleasantville & Ocean City Railroad Co., N.J., 1880 . . . . 275.00
Sugar & Creamer, Ornate, Embossed, Silver, 19th Century, 5 In. 11.00
Switch Plate, Embossed, Brass Impedance Plate, 1914, 16 1/2 x 12 1/2 In. 34.00
Tape Measure, Salt Lake Route, Orange Grove Of Southern Ca., 1 3/4 In. 138.00
Teapot, Missouri Pacific & Iron Mountain, 10 Oz., 4 1/2 In. 230.00
Teapot, Soo Line, Silver, 7 1/2 In., Pair 126.00
Thermos, Pullman, Stanley Vacuum, 11 In., Pair 69.00
Ticket Window, Baltimore & Ohio, Embossed, Walnut Frame, 28 x 33 1/2 In. 690.00
Ticket Window, Soo Line Depot, Wood, Reverse Painted Window, 24 x 35 In. 402.00
Timetable, Chicago, Danville & Vincennes Railroad, Mar. 4, 1877, 17 x 13 In. 46.00
Timetable, Marquett Houghton & Ontonagon RR, Frame, 1875, 13 x 20 In. 46.00
Torch, Alton Railroad, Tin, 9 x 7 1/2 In., Pair 11.00
Torch, Minneapolis, St. Louis, Pacific, Cone Shape, Embossed, 9 1/2 In. 34.00
Transom Window, Amber, Green, Red Leaded Glass, Walnut Frame, 59 x 17 In. 258.00
Tray, Louisville & Nashville, International Silver Co., 12 In., 4 Piece 316.00
Tray, Soo Line, Montana Success, Wood Grain Ground, 10 1/2 x 15 In. 240.00
Tray, Union Pacific System Railroad, International Silver Co., 11 In., 10 Piece 126.00
Triptych, Chicago & Alton Railroad, Women Fencers, Oak Frame, 42 x 27 In. 430.00
Tureen, Sauce, Cover, Chicago Great Western, Silver, Handles, Reed & Barton, 8 In. 126.00
Water Bottle, Pullman, Stanley, 11 In. 34.00

Don't use ammonia on glasses with gold or silver decorations.

RAZORS were used in ancient Egypt and subsequently wherever shaving was in fashion. The metal razor used in America until about 1870 was made in Sheffield, England. After 1870, machine-made hollow-ground razors were made in Germany or America. Plastic or bone handles were popular. The razor was often sold in a set of seven, one for each day of the week. The set was often kept by the barber who shaved the well-to-do man each day in the shop.

Devon Co., Straight, Ivory Celluloid, Ear Of Corn, Germany	95.00
Gem, Man & Baby Shaving, Box, 4 x 2 1/2 In.	120.00
Geneva Cutlery, Straight, Ivory Celluloid Handles, Eagle On Blade	95.00
Myatt, Woman's, Metal Body, Blade, Handle & Head, Leather Pouch, 1 1/4 x 7/8 In.	125.00
Old English Razor, Straight, Oversized Blade, Sheffield	75.00
Rodgers & Sons, Straight, Pearl Handles, England	275.00
Tuckmar Extra-Ober Prima, Straight, Tortoise Celluloid Handles, Germany	60.00
Wade & Butcher, Straight, Horn Handles	85.00
Wostenholm & Son, Straight, Spotted Horn Handles	125.00

REAMERS, or juice squeezers, have been known since 1767, although most of those collected today date from the twentieth century. Figural reamers are among the most prized.

Glass, 3 x 6 In., 2 Piece	55.00
Jadite, 2 1/4 x 7 In.	65.00
Jadite, 2 3/4 x 6 In.	65.00
Jadite, 2 Cup	165.00
Sunkist, Milk Glass, White	95.00

RECORDS have changed size and shape through the years. The cylinder-shaped phonograph record for use with the early Edison models was made about 1889. Disc records were first made by 1894, the double-sided disc by 1904. High-fidelity records were first issued in 1944, the first vinyl disc in 1946, the first stereo record in 1958. The 78 RPM became the standard in 1926 but was discontinued in 1957. In 1932, the first 33 1/3 RPM was made but was not sold commercially until 1948. In 1949, the 45 RPM was introduced. Compact discs became available in the U.S. in 1982 and many companies began phasing out the production of phonograph records.

Edward R. Murrow & Victor Borge, Shulton Label, 1950s, 45 RPM	5.00
Negro Prison Songs, Missisippi State Prison, Tradition Records, 1960s, LP	105.00
Rolling Stones, Emotional Rescue, Signed By Jagger, Richards, Wood, Watts, LP	250.00
The Monkees, Valerie & Tapioca Tundra, Colgems Label, 1960s, 45 RPM	5.00

RED WING Pottery of Red Wing, Minnesota, was a firm started in 1878. The company first made utilitarian pottery. In the 1920s art pottery was made. Many dinner sets and vases were made before the company closed in 1967. Rumrill pottery was made for George Rumrill by the Red Wing Pottery and other firms. It was sold in the 1930s. For more information, see *Kovels' Depression Glass & Dinnerware Price List*.

Art Pottery, Bowl, Nokomis Glaze, Tan, Olive Green, Strap Handles, 3 1/2 x 8 3/4 In.	350.00
Art Pottery, Ewer, Nokomis Glaze, Angular Handle, Blue Ink Stamp, 9 1/4 In.	230.00
Art Pottery, Ewer, Nokomis Glaze, Light Tan, Olive Green, Handle, 9 3/8 In.	375.00
Art Pottery, Figurine, Ram, Salt Glaze, George Hehr, c.1896, 4 1/2 x 3 1/4 In.	825.00
Art Pottery, Vase, Embossed Lions, Mottled Drip Glaze, Green & Beige, Marked, 8 In.	125.00
Art Pottery, Vase, Embossed, Geometric Bands, Textured Body, Ivory, Umber, 22 In.	430.00
Art Pottery, Vase, Green, Brown Metallic Glaze, Buttressed Form, 6 3/4 In.	310.00
Art Pottery, Vase, Nokomis Glaze, Light Tan, Olive Green, 10 1/4 In.	400.00
Art Pottery, Vase, Nokomis Glaze, Light Tan, Olive Green, Blue Circular Mark, 6 1/4 In.	275.00
Art Pottery, Vase, Nokomis Glaze, Light Tan, Olive Green, Blue Circular Mark, 7 3/8 In.	250.00
Bob White, Bowl, Vegetable, Divided, Oval	32.00
Bob White, Creamer	28.00
Bob White, Gravy Boat, Cover	49.00
Bob White, Plate, 6 1/2 In.	8.00
Bob White, Plate, Dinner, 10 1/2 In.	12.00
Bob White, Salt & Pepper, Bird	45.00

Bob White, Soup, Dish	22.00
Bob White, Sugar, Cover	27.50
Churn, Cover, Birchleaf, 8 Gal.	797.00
Cookie Jar, Basket Weave & Morning Glory, Says Put Your Fist In, 7 1/2 In.	625.00
Cookie Jar, Katrina, Dutch Girl	95.00
Cooler, Water, Birchleaf, 5 Gal.	605.00
Cooler, Water, Stoneware, 2 Gal.	1100.00
Jar, Refrigerator, Grayline	467.00
Magnolia, Bowl, Fruit	5.50
Magnolia, Bowl, Serving, 8 In.	20.00
Magnolia, Bread Plate	5.00
Magnolia, Casserole, Cover, Gray Exterior	10.00
Magnolia, Cup & Saucer, Gray Exterior	10.00

REDWARE is a hard, red stoneware that originated in the late 1600s and continues to be made. The term is also used to describe any common clay pottery that is reddish in color.

Bank, Apple, Red & Yellow Glaze, 3 In.	220.00
Bank, Brown Glaze, Tooled Foot, 5 1/2 In.	350.00
Bank, Bulbous, Mottled Glaze, 1870, 4 1/2 In.	825.00
Bank, Cottage, 2-Story, Chimney, Rockingham Type Glaze, 6 In.	190.00
Bank, Dresser Shape, 2 Over 3 Drawers, Yellow Glazed Rosettes, 7 x 4 x 6 3/4 In.	250.00
Bank, Pear, Painted Red & Yellow, 4 In.	305.00
Bank, Round, Molded Finial, Orange Glaze, c.1800	395.00
Basin, Yellow Slip, 13 3/4 In.	605.00
Batter Jug, Albany Slip, 9 In.	65.00
Bottle, Brown Splotches, 5 1/2 In.	357.00
Bowl, Brown Mottled Glaze, Applied Rib Handle, 6 x 3 3/4 In.	220.00
Bowl, Brown Mottled, 19th Century, 1 1/4 x 3 3/4 In.	70.00
Bowl, Glazed, Stamped S. Bell & Son, c.1870, 4 1/2 In.	5700.00
Bowl, Incised Line, Mottled Glaze, 2 3/4 x 6 3/4 In.	176.00
Bowl, Manganese & Copper Oxide Slip, Orange Glaze, 3 3/4 x 12 1/4 In.	2420.00
Bowl, Manganese Decorated, Straight Flared Sides, Splotching, 4 1/2 x 9 3/4 In.	80.00
Bowl, Manganese Mottled Glazing Over Orange Ground, 7 In., Pair	66.00
Bowl, Milk, Brown Glaze, Black Specks, Flared Sides, 9 5/8 x 2 1/2 In.	190.00
Bowl, Milk, Orange Glaze, Applied Handles, 10 x 20 1/2 In.	165.00
Bowl, Mottled Brown Glaze, 2 1/8 x 8 In.	115.00
Bowl, Mottled Brown Glaze, 5 1/8 x 9 3/4 In.	172.00
Bowl, Multiple Bands Of Zigzag & Scalloped Lines, 3 1/4 x 12 In.	660.00
Bowl, Orange & Green Glaze, 4 x 8 1/2 In.	165.00
Bowl, Rolled Upper Rim, Green & Orange Glaze, 2 1/2 x 6 In.	200.00
Bowl, Slip Decorated, Manganese, Copper Oxide Bands, 19th Century, 13 3/4 x 4 In.	1058.00
Bowl, Splayed Edge, Rounded Rim, W. Smith, 3 3/4 x 8 3/4 In.	1485.00
Bowl, Tapering Sides, Flat Bottom, Green & White Slip, 19th Century, 13 1/8 In.	1175.00
Bowl, Unglazed, Impressed, 2, J. Miller, Wheeling, West Virginia, c.1869, 9 x 4 In.	138.00
Bowl, Yellow Slip Double Band, Muted Ground, 19th Century, 13 1/4 In.	940.00
Breast Pump, Manganese Splotching, York Co.	360.00
Butter Mold, Woman Wearing Bonnet, Applied Yellow Glaze, 4 1/2 In.	55.00
Canister, Red Alkaline Glaze, Impressed, All Spice, Pepper, Ginger, Lid, 5 In., 3 Piece	415.00
Chamber Pot, Orange Ground, Handles, 6 x 9 3/4 In.	265.00
Chamber Pot, Ribbed Handle, Glazed, 6 1/4 x 9 In.	60.00
Charger, 2 Soldiers, Titled Shoulder Firelock, Signed, 7-26-78, 12 1/2 In.	80.00
Charger, 2 Unicorns, Coggled Rim, Signed Breininger, 7-17-82, 15 1/2 In.	150.00
Charger, Barnyard Scene, Signed Lester Breininger, 1984, 15 5/8 In.	55.00
Charger, Coggled Rim, 3-Line Slip, 13 In.	605.00
Charger, Coggled Rim, Triple Quill, Yellow Zigzag, 12 1/8 In.	935.00
Charger, Crackle Glaze, Octagonal, Stamped I.T., 12 3/4 In.	190.00
Charger, Deer, Dogs & Horse, Coggled Rim, Signed, 1973, 12 1/4 In.	80.00
Charger, Orange Glaze, Yellow Oak Leaf Slip Design, 2 x 12 x 8 1/2 In.	880.00
Charger, Rooster, Yellow & Green Glaze, Octagonal, Signed Breininger, 14 In.	150.00
Charger, Sgraffito Peacock & Flower, 1793 HR, Yellow Ground, 12 5/8 In.	110.00
Charger, Soldier On Horse, Drawn Sword, Firing Pistol, Coggled Rim, 12 1/2 In.	95.00
Charger, Tulips & Urn, Coggled Rim, Signed, May 20, 1982, 12 1/2 In.	100.00

Coffeepot, Cover, Glaze, Engine Turned, c.1770, 9 1/2 In. 325.00
Coffeepot, Cover, Teapot, Cover, Lighthouse, c.1755 . . . . 7050.00
Colander, Mottled Orange & Green Glaze, Handle, Footed, 4 1/2 x 6 In. 520.00
Creamer, Burnt Orange Glaze, 4 1/2 In. 190.00
Creamer, Glazed, Brown, Applied Handle, 3 x 3 1/2 In. 165.00
Creamer, Molded, Brown, Raised Flowers, Applied Flower Handle, 4 1/2 x 4 In. 385.00
Creamer, New Geneva, Shiny Glaze Flowers, Handle, 4 3/4 In. 605.00
Creamer, Rose & 2 Doves, Panels, Rosette On Curved Handle, 4 3/4 In. 715.00
Creamer, Side Spout, Manganese Glaze, Tubular Handle, 4 1/2 In. 330.00
Creamer, Transparent Black Glaze, Coggled Rim, Mid 1800s 145.00
Crock, Apple Butter, Pitted Glaze, 5 1/2 In. 302.00
Crock, Brown, Green Splotched Glaze, 2 Ear Handles, Ribbed Cover, Button Finial, 6 In. . 374.00
Crock, Crazing Pattern, 2 Incised Lines On Shoulder, 9 7/8 In. 220.00
Crock, Flared Mouthed, Orange & Green, 3 3/4 x 3 1/2 In. 38.00
Crock, Green Glaze, Brown Spots, Raised Ring At Base, Incised Line, 19 In. 137.00
Crock, Ivory Splotches, Incised Lines, 7 1/4 In. 1595.00
Crock, Storage, Flared Rim, Incised Band, Handle, Interior Glaze, 10 x 8 1/2 In. 137.00
Crock, Storage, Interior Glaze, Handle, Signed W. Smith, 7 x 7 1/2 In. 165.00
Crock, Storage, Interior Glaze, Signed John Bell, 10 3/4 x 9 1/2 In. 242.00
Crock, Storage, Manganese Glaze, Signed John Bell, 6 1/2 x 8 1/4 In. 302.00
Cup, Mush, Impressed Sarreguemines, Mocha, Cream, 19th Century, 3 1/2 x 4 1/2 In. 115.00
Cuspidor, Brown Glaze, Beehive Form, 4 1/4 x 7 3/4 In. 57.00
Cuspidor, Mottled Glaze, Cream, Green, Brown, Molded Leaves, Ribbed Top, 4 x 8 In. . . . 95.00
Dish, 3-Line Yellow Slip, Coggled Rim, 5 1/4 In. 990.00
Dish, Black Glaze, Scalloped Rim, 4 3/4 x 4 In. 1100.00
Dish, Loaf, Slip Trailed Bird, Pa., 12 1/2 In. 2588.00
Dish, Loaf, Yellow Slip, Alfred Jones, Mid 19th Century, 10 x 12 1/2 In. 1265.00
Dish, Salt, Flared Mouth, Brown Design, 1 1/2 x 2 1/2 In. 220.00
Eggcup, Green Splotching, Shenandoah Valley, 3 In. 358.00
Figurine, Adam & Eve Under Apple Tree, Allegorical, Late 18th Century, 10 In. 2090.00
Figurine, Bear, Seated, Upright On Haunches, Brown Glazed Body, 4 1/2 In. 7638.00
Figurine, Bear, Standing, Manganese Glaze, 1850-1880, 3 1/2 x 6 In. 6050.00
Figurine, Black Man, Painted Feet, Hands & Head, Mounted On Coconut, 12 In. 1860.00
Figurine, Bulldog, Seated, Hollow Body, 19th Century, 5 3/4 x 5 5/8 In. 385.00
Figurine, Cradle, Dated 1733, 6 3/4 x 8 1/8 In. 411.00
Figurine, Dog, Facial Features, Ringed Collar, Floral Oval Base, 6 1/4 In. 1175.00
Figurine, Dog, Seated, Articulated Ears, Snout & Hair, 19th Century, 4 In. 3055.00
Figurine, Dog, Seated, Brown Glaze, 3 1/2 In. 192.00
Figurine, Dog, Seated, Free Standing Front Legs, 9 1/8 In. 82.00
Figurine, Dog, Seated, Incised Collar & Chain, Van Vorhis, 7 In. 192.00
Figurine, Dog, Seated, Modeled, Slab, Manganese Splotching, Adams Co., 3 1/2 In. 2420.00
Figurine, Dog, Seated, Multicolored Glaze, Stamped Platform Base, 4 In. 1100.00
Figurine, Dog, Standing, Holding Basket, c.1880, 3 3/4 x 4 1/2 In. 990.00
Figurine, Dog, Standing, Upcurled Tail, Rectangular Base, 4 1/4 In. 3955.00
Figurine, Lamb, Reclining, Gold Paint Over White, Hollow, 9 1/2 In. 100.00
Figurine, Lion, Reclining, Sewer Tile Glaze, Wadsworth, 5 3/4 x 9 In. 275.00
Figurine, Log Cabin, White Clip, Round Open Chimney, Windows, Door, 6 1/2 In. 77.00
Figurine, Plume Tail Rooster, R.R. Stahl, 1/4/51, 4 1/4 In. 285.00
Figurine, Rocker, Wing Chair, Scroddleware, Yellow, Tooled Crest, 1862, 8 5/8 In. 440.00
Figurine, Rooster, Incised Detail, Green Running Slip, 15 In. 190.00
Figurine, Seated Cat, R.R. Stahl, 1/9/51, 4 1/4 In. 210.00
Figurine, Young Girl, Seated, Open Book, On Tree Stump, Painted, Molded, 7 1/4 In. 187.00
Flask, Mermaid Form, Tail Curled To Form Handle, Rockingham Glaze, 7 3/4 In., Pair . . . 705.00
Flowerpot, Attached Saucer, Brown Mottled Glaze, Impressed John W. Bell, 5 In. 880.00
Flowerpot, Brown Splotch Glaze, Piecrust Rim, 5 1/4 x 4 3/4 In. 138.00
Flowerpot, Flared Mouth, Mottled Brown & Orange Glaze, 5 1/2 x 5 1/4 In. 140.00
Flowerpot, Impressed Baecher, Winchester, Va., 7 In. 2295.00
Flowerpot, Mottled Orange & Brown Glaze, Flared Mouth, 5 x 5 1/4 In. 155.00
Flowerpot, Saucer Base, Fluted Top, 6 x 7 In. 300.00
Frame, Molded, Octagonal, Manganese Splotching, Stamped W.L., 6 1/2 In. 224.00
Humidor, Acorn, Molded Base, Tree Trunk Feet, 6 In. 265.00
Jar, 2-Tone Glaze, Brown Vertical Bands, Raised Lip, Oval, 5 1/4 x 6 1/4 In. 275.00
Jar, Acorn Shape, Branch Feet, Textured Base, White Band, Green Trim, 4 In. 149.00

Jar, Apple Butter, Brown Splotches, Incised Lines On Shoulder & Handle, 6 In. 115.00
Jar, Applied Reddish Brown Glaze, Wide Mouth, 1/2 Gallon, 8 1/2 In. 44.00
Jar, Black Spots, Raised Rim, Impressed John Bell, Waynesboro, Pa., 1881, 5 In. 330.00
Jar, Brown Daubed Glaze, Oval, Pa., 4 x 4 1/2 In. 190.00
Jar, Brown Glaze, Egg Shape, Ring Foot, Flared Mouth, 12 x 8 In. 250.00
Jar, Brown Running Glaze, Geometric & Star Design, Raised Bands, 8 In. 440.00
Jar, Canning, Coggled Rim, Straight Sides, 5 1/8 In. 660.00
Jar, Cover, Moss Green Body, Brown Specks, 6 3/4 In. 6900.00
Jar, Cover, Mottled Orange & Brown Glaze, Flared Mouth, 7 3/4 x 6 In. 467.00
Jar, Cover, Running Brown Glaze, Egg Shape, Incised Rings, 7 3/8 In. 1650.00
Jar, Cover, Scroddleware, Yellow, Stepped Base, Handles, R. Pollard Bradford, 6 1/8 In. . . 330.00
Jar, Cylindrical, Manganese Streaks, Deep Collar, Incised Lines, 7 1/2 x 6 In. 290.00
Jar, Dark Brown Splotched Glaze, Cylindrical, Flared Mouth, Incised Lines, 8 3/4 In. 690.00
Jar, Daubed Design, Flared Rim, Handles, 19th Century, 11 In. 940.00
Jar, Domed Top, Knop Handle, Hand Holds, Coggled Rim, 19th Century, 11 1/2 In. 590.00
Jar, Flint Glaze, Applied Handles, 10 1/2 In. 125.00
Jar, Lug Handles, Brown Splotches, 19th Century, 10 5/8 In. 460.00
Jar, Mottled Glaze, Cream, Brown, Green, Flared Rim, 5 3/4 x 3 1/2 In. 50.00
Jar, Mottled Green & Orange Glaze, 2 Lines Of Tan Slip At Shoulder, 4 3/4 In. 978.00
Jar, Olive Green, Splotched Brown & Black Glaze, Flared Lip, Sloping Shoulders, 7 In. . . 1495.00
Jar, Peppered Tan Brown Alkaline Glaze, Tooled Rim Accents, c.1835, 9 In. 1980.00
Jar, Running Green, Tan & Brown Glaze, Double Handles, 10 3/4 In. 1320.00
Jar, Storage, Dark Brown Stripes, Pa., 1880-1900, 4 1/2 x 6 1/4 In. 495.00
Jar, Storage, Glazed Interior, Signed John Bell, 7 1/2 In. 220.00
Jar, Storage, Glazed Interior, Signed, J.S. Henne, 6 1/2 In. 275.00
Jar, Storage, Green & Orange Glaze, Molded Rim, 4 3/4 In. 285.00
Jar, Yellow Splotches, Concave Sides, 7 1/8 In. 330.00
Jug, Applied Ear Handle, New England, 6 1/4 In. 287.00
Jug, Brown Glazed, Strap Handle, 5 x 4 x 3 1/4 In. 250.00
Jug, Brushed Dark Brown, Incised Ring, Strap Handle, 6 3/4 In. 385.00
Jug, Dark Brown Applied Alkaline Glaze, c.1820, 1/2 Gal., 8 1/2 In. 66.00
Jug, Double Face, Swirled, 2 Handles, Ivory, Brown, Stamped, B.B. Craig, 11 1/2 x 8 In. . . 1380.00
Jug, Face, Swirl, Brown, Ivory, Blue Eyes, Teeth, Charlie Lisk, 13 x 9 In. 920.00
Jug, Face, Swirl, Gray Green, Ivory, Walter Fleming, 14 x 8 1/2 In. 400.00
Jug, Face, Yellow, Green, Black Glaze, 10 1/2 x 6 In. 58.00
Jug, Grotesque Face, Allover Brown Glaze, Stamped Brown Pottery, 8 In. 1595.00
Jug, Handle, Orange Mottled Manganese Design, John Bell, 9 1/2 In. 3630.00
Jug, Heilbrounier & Co. Of Schenectady, 19th Century, Gal. 138.00
Jug, Mottled Brown & Green Glaze, Flared Mouth, 5 x 4 x 3 In. 60.00
Jug, Reddish Orange Glaze, Green Spots, 8 3/4 In. 496.00
Jug, Yellow Orange Alkaline Glaze, Fitted Stopper, Ribbed Handle, 11 1/2 In. 550.00
Lamp, Grease, Brown Red Glaze, Saucer Base, Oval Font, Strap Handle, 7 In. 300.00
Mold, Fish, Footed, Mottled Glaze, 2 1/2 x 12 In. 550.00
Muffineer, Pear Shape, Footed, Albany Glaze, 5 In. 440.00
Mug, Barrel Form, Green & White Slip-Decorated Flowers, Applied Handle 39.00
Mug, Barrel Shape, Brown Splotches, 2 Horizontal Ribs, 4 1/2 In. 201.00
Mug, Mottled Glaze, Applied Handle, 3 1/4 In. 495.00
Mug, New England, 19th Century 325.00
Mug, Red, Brown Sprinkles, Flared Rim, 5 Horizontal Ribs, Applied Handle, 4 In. 489.00
Mug, Ribbed Handle, Yellow, Brown Drip Glaze, 19th Century, 3 3/4 In. 4312.00
Mustard, Cover, Incised Line, Ear Handle, Barrel Form, 3 1/2 In. 770.00
Newel Post Cap, Bulbous, Raised Spiral Ribs, Green, Brown Glaze, 8 1/2 x 9 1/2 x 4 In. . . 286.00
Pan, Loaf, Coggled Rim, 3-Line Yellow Slip, 9 1/2 x 12 3/4 In. 770.00
Pan, Milk, Interior Glaze 300.00
Pan, Milk, Pouring Spout, Manganese Sponging, 2 Incised Lines, Early 1800s 395.00
Pan, Milk, Tooled Bands, Sponge On Rim & Handle, 5 x 8 1/2 In. 605.00
Pie Plate, 3-Line Yellow Slip, Dots, Coggled Rim, 10 1/4 In. 385.00
Pie Plate, 3-Line Yellow Slip, Wavy Line Clusters, Pennsylvania, Early 1800s, 11 In. 1200.00
Pie Plate, Coggled Rim, 3-Line Yellow Slip, 3 Feathered Lines, 10 1/4 In. 578.00
Pie Plate, Coggled Rim, 3-Line Yellow Slip, 8 In. 990.00
Pie Plate, Coggled Rim, 3-Line Yellow Slip, 10 In. 1045.00
Pie Plate, Coggled Rim, 3-Line Yellow Slip, 10 3/4 In. 605.00
Pie Plate, Coggled Rim, 3-Line Yellow Slip, 11 1/4 In. 935.00

Pie Plate, Coggled Rim, Wavy Lines, Breininger, 1976, 10 3/8 In. 55.00
Pie Plate, Coggled Rim, Wavy Slip Lines, 6 1/2 In. 275.00
Pie Plate, Coggled Rim, Yellow Slip Design, 6 1/4 In. 440.00
Pie Plate, Coggled Rim, Yellow Slip Design, Resembles 4 Double Flags, 9 1/8 In. 385.00
Pie Plate, Coggled Rim, Yellow, Green Slip Design, Wavy Lines, Double Loops, 9 In. 7590.00
Pitcher, Albany Slip, Flint Glaze, 1/2 Gal., 10 1/4 In. 125.00
Pitcher, Applied Ribbed Ear Handle, Brown Splotch, 6 1/2 In. 345.00
Pitcher, Applied Strands Of Clay, Mottled Brown Alkaline Glaze, 1820, 9 1/2 In. 275.00
Pitcher, Brown Splotches, Strap Handle, 5 1/2 In. 137.00
Pitcher, Cover, Orange & Brown Mottled Glaze, Strap Handle, 7 1/2 x 5 In. 577.00
Pitcher, Green & Brown Running Glaze, Yellow Slip Ground, c.1880, 9 1/2 In. 1450.00
Pitcher, Incised Bowtie, Strap Handle, Schofield Pottery, 6 In. 357.00
Pitcher, Mottled Glaze, 7 In. 2035.00
Pitcher, Mottled Glaze, Bulbous, 8 1/2 In. 247.00
Pitcher, Paneled, Raised Ribs & Mask Spout, 7 3/4 In. 220.00
Pitcher, Ring At Neck, Strap Handle, 3 3/8 In. 55.00
Pitcher, Sgraffito Eagle & Liberty Banner, Bulbous, Mottled Glaze, 7 1/2 In. 2310.00
Pitcher, Side Spout, Cover, Green & Orange Blaze, Squat Form, 6 1/4 x 8 1/2 In. 600.00
Pitcher, Spots On Green Ground, Coggled Bands At Top, Handle, 8 In. 935.00
Pitcher, Tankard Shape, Brown, Strap Handle, Carved Wooden Lid, 6 1/4 In. 550.00
Plate, 4 Squiggle Bands, Crossroad Pattern, Crimped Edge, 12 In. 880.00
Plate, Brown & Green Tulip Design, Red Orange Glaze, 8 5/8 In. 5280.00
Plate, Coggled Rim, 3-Line Yellow Slip, 11 In. 385.00
Plate, Coggled Rim, Soldier On Horseback, Sword, Signed, July, 1986, 6 7/8 In. 66.00
Plate, Coggled Rim, Triple Quill Slip, Zigzag, 10 3/4 In. 1210.00
Plate, Coggled Rim, Triple Quill Yellow Slip, 10 In. 520.00
Plate, Coggled Rim, Triple Quill Yellow Slip, Glazed, 10 3/4 In. 220.00
Plate, Coggled Rim, Yellow Slip Waves, Flanked By Flourishes, 11 1/2 In. 825.00
Plate, Flower Form Slip, 7 3/4 In. 770.00
Plate, Inscribed Willoughby Smith Womeldorf, Signed, May 27, 1904, 10 1/4 In. 95.00
Plate, Molded, Orange, Yellow Slip Design, 1 1/2 x 8 1/2 In. 275.00
Plate, Orange Glaze, Coggled Rim, Slip Design Wave, 1 1/4 x 9 1/2 In. 550.00
Plate, Orange Glaze, Coggled Rim, Yellow Zigzag Design, 9 1/4 In. 770.00
Plate, Pie, Coggled Rim, Orange Glaze, Yellow Slip Design, 1 1/4 x 9 3/4 In. 935.00
Plate, Pie, Yellow Glaze, Mottled Brown Wreath Design, 2 x 9 In. 302.00
Plate, Pumpkin Glaze, Brown & Yellow Slip Design, 19th Century, 1 x 6 1/2 In. 935.00
Plate, Slip Design, Oak Leaf, Orange & Yellow, 1 1/4 x 7 3/4 In. 165.00
Plate, Slip Design, Orange & Yellow, Coggled Rim, 1 x 6 1/2 In. 220.00
Plate, Slip Design, Orange & Yellow, Marked H, 1 x 8 In. 360.00
Plate, Slip Design, Yellow & Pumpkin, Coggled Rim, 1 x 9 In. 1100.00
Plate, Slip Design, Yellow, Wavy Line & Dots, Coggled Rim, 9 3/4 In. 748.00
Plate, Thrown, Orange With Coggled Rim, Yellow Floral Slip Design, 1 x 5 In. 220.00
Plate, Yellow Slip, Decorated, Early 19th Century, 10 In, 3 Piece 690.00
Plate, Zigzag, Signed W. Smith, Glazed, 8 1/4 In. 275.00
Platter, Coggled Rim, Sprig Yellow Slip, Glazed, 11 1/2 x 17 In. 605.00
Porringer, Dark Brown Glaze, Horizontal Rib On Shoulder & Handle, 2 1/2 x 4 In. 1725.00
Potty, Manganese Spots, 2 Incised Lines Around The Body, Mid 1800s 245.00
Quill Holder, Lamb Shape, Scroddle Brown, Yellow Glaze, Scroll Work, 1800s, 2 1/4 In. . . 330.00
Rooster, Manganese Glaze, 4 1/4 In. 850.00
Stamp, Rooster Over Tulip, Sunflower On Reverse, Cumberland, Penn., 5 x 3 1/8 In. 275.00
Teapot, Oriental, Lion Finial, Yi Ching Kansu Province, 1800s, 3 1/2 In. 467.00
Teapot, Pagoda Shape, Brown, 7 In. 11.00
Vase, Baluster Form, 3 Handles, Incised Rings, Light Green Slip, 19th Century, 6 1/4 In. . . 1175.00
Vase, Canted Applied Handles, Incised 10, 7 1/2 In. 110.00
Vase, Face, Slip Decorated, Molded Arms, 19th Century, 10 1/2 x 4 3/4 In. 1175.00
Vase, Figural, Tree Stump Shape, Woodpecker, Multiglaze, Green, Brown, Yellow, 4 In. . . 990.00
Vase, Man, Figural, Yellow, Cream, Brown Dabs, Applied Handle, 10 1/2 In. 302.00
Wall Pocket, Birds, Fluted, 8 x 9 1/2 In. 1430.00
Wall Pocket, Embossed Flowers & Foliage, G.S. Freshley, 10 1/2 x 8 1/2 In. 1595.00
Wall Pocket, Yellow & Green Glaze, 9 In. 165.00
Whistle, Bird, Manganese Eyes, Wings 495.00
Whistle, Bird, Seated On Trunk, Cream, Running Brown Glaze, Shenandoah, 9 1/4 In. . . . 330.00
Whistle, Quill Holder Shape, Manganese Sponge Glaze, Mark, 1 3/4 In. 495.00

REGOUT, see Maastricht category.

RICHARD was the mark used on acid-etched cameo glass vases, bowls, night-lights, and lamps made by the Austrian company Loetz after 1918. The pieces were very similar to the other French cameo glasswares made by Daum, Galle, and others.

Vase, Berries & Leaves, Dark Blue, Mottled Blue & Orange Ground, 4 1/4 In.	375.00
Vase, Blue Flowers, Pale Yellow Ground, Signed, 4 1/2 In.	431.00
Vase, Dark Blue Flowers, Red Ground, Flared, Signed, 8 In.	575.00
Vase, Ruins, Farm By Lake, Tree Other Side, Acid Cut, Signed, 8 1/4 In.	595.00

RIDGWAY pottery has been made in the Staffordshire district in England since 1808 by a series of companies with the name Ridgway. The transfer-design dinner sets are the most widely known product. They are still being made. Other pieces of Ridgway are listed under Flow Blue.

Bowl, Boston State House	275.00
Creamer, Uncle Sam's Bust, Ridgway Sterling Pottery, 1792, 3 1/4 In.	120.00
Custard Cup, State House, Boston, Dark Blue, 2 3/4 In.	168.00
Pitcher, Uncle Sam's Bust, Lincoln's Head, 1909, 5 1/8 In.	98.00
Platter, Capitol Washington	1430.00
Platter, Italian Flower Garden, Transfer Printed, 1870s, 22 In.	259.00
Platter, Josephine, Floral Border, 15 In.	85.00
Platter, Pennsylvania Hospital, Philadelphia	1155.00
Platter, Tyrolean, Transfer, Oval, 1870s, 19 In.	345.00
Soup, Dish, Pembroke Hall, Cambridge, 9 3/4 In.	140.00
Soup, Dish, Pembroke Hall, Cambridge, Medium Dark Blue, 10 In.	392.00
Tureen, Sauce, Peaked Cover, Underplate, Flower Sprays, Leaf Handle, 6 3/4 In., Pair	460.00

RIFLES that are firearms are not listed in this book. BB guns and air rifles are listed in the Toy category.

RIVIERA dinnerware was made by the Homer Laughlin Co. of Newell, West Virginia, from 1938 to 1950. The pattern was similar in coloring and in mood to Fiesta and Harlequin. The Riviera plates and cup handles were square. For more information, see *Kovels' Depression Glass & Dinnerware Price List.*

COLONIAL

Blue, Soup, Dish	30.00
Green, Butter, Cover, 1/4 Lb.	95.00
Green, Platter, Closed Handles	28.00
Green, Sugar, Cover	26.00
Green, Teapot, Cover	110.00
Green, Tumbler, Handle	45.00
Green, Tumbler, Juice	40.00
Ivory, Tumbler, Handle	190.00
Red, Creamer	15.00
Red, Salt & Pepper	50.00
Yellow, Batter Jug, Cover, 5 In.	215.00
Yellow, Bowl, 8 1/2 In.	35.00
Yellow, Chop Plate, 13 In.	45.00
Yellow, Cup & Saucer	26.00
Yellow, Soup, Dish	30.00

ROCKINGHAM, in the United States, is a pottery with a brown glaze that resembles tortoiseshell. It was made from 1840 to 1900 by many American potteries. Mottled brown Rockingham wares were first made in England at the Rockingham factory. Other types of ceramics were also made by the English firm. Related pieces may be listed in the Bennington category.

Bowl, 10 1/2 In.	275.00
Coffeepot, Embossed, Rebekah At The Well, 8 In.	104.00
Cuspidor, Shell Pattern, Brown & Blue, 7 1/4 x 3 3/8 In.	60.00
Figurine, Dog, Seated, Chain Along 1 Leg, Rectangular Base, 5 1/2 In.	577.00

Figurine, Dog, Seated, Open Front Legs, Running Brown Glaze, 11 1/2 In. 495.00
Figurine, Dog, Seated, Open Front Legs, Scalloped Base, 10 5/8 In. 330.00
Figurine, Dog, Spaniel, Seated, Embossed, Flower Bands, 14 x 12 In. 743.00
Figurine, Lion, Reclining, Amber Running Glaze, 5 3/4 x 9 1/2 x 4 In. 440.00
Flask, Donut, Fruit Vines, Man With Tankard Neck, Dark Brown Glaze, 8 1/2 In. 165.00
Inkwell, Girl, Reclining On Tree Stump, Hat, 5 In. 192.00
Jar, Storage, Gothic Arched Design, Domed Cover, 8 x 9 In. 660.00
Pitcher, Dog, Open Mouth Spout, 8 5/8 In. . . . . ∴ 165.00
Pitcher, Embossed, Star & Tulip, Bulbous, 8 In. 71.00
Pitcher, Floral Swag, Brown Glaze, 8 1/2 In. 28.00
Pitcher, Octagonal, 9 In. 58.00
Pitcher, Toby, Taking Pinch Of Snuff, Cover, 10 1/4 In. 77.00
Soap Dish, Embossed, Leaf On Rim, 2 x 6 1/4 In. 38.00
Soap Dish, Oval, Ribbed, 2 1/4 x 4 3/4 In. 50.00
Sugar Bowl, Cover, Button Finial, Pedestal Base, 5 1/2 x 5 3/4 In. 220.00
Tea Set, Rococo Style, Enameled Landscape, Buff Band, c.1820, 4 Piece 201.00
Teapot, Rebekah At The Well, Brown Glaze, 8 In. 28.00
Toby Jug, Brown & Blue, High Concave Base, 5 3/4 In. 83.00

ROGERS, see John Rogers category.

ROOKWOOD pottery was made in Cincinnati, Ohio, from 1880 to 1960. All of this art pottery is marked, most with the famous flame mark. The R is reversed and placed back to back with the letter P. Flames surround the letters. After 1900, a Roman numeral was added to the mark to indicate the year. The name and some of the molds were purchased in 1984. A few new pieces were made, but these were glazed in colors not used by the original company.

Ashtray, Blue Matte Crystalline Glaze, 1929, 5 1/8 In. 70.00
Ashtray, Eagle, Embossed, Turquoise High Glaze, 1954, 5 3/8 In. 70.00
Ashtray, Elephant & Man, Mosiac, Blue, Square, 1928, 6 3/8 In. 150.00
Ashtray, Embossed, Yellow Matte Glaze, 1938, 5 3/4 In. 100.00
Ashtray, Frog, Green Matte Glaze, 1933, 3 1/8 In. 900.00
Ashtray, Jet Black Glaze, 1953, 5 1/2 In. 130.00
Ashtray, Organic, Green High Glaze, 1961 . . . . 58.00
Ashtray, Puppies, Perched On Edge, Ivory, 1942, 2 5/8 In., Pair 275.00
Ashtray, Seal, Green, Black Crystalline Matte Glaze, 1929, 3 7/8 In. 325.00
Ashtray, University Of Nebraska Scene, Blue Matte Crystalline Glaze, 7 5/8 In. 90.00
Bookends, Birds, Blue Matte Glaze, 1937, 5 In., Pair 184.00
Bookends, Bloodhound Puppies, Brown Matte, Louise Abel, 1931, 4 3/4 In. 357.00
Bookends, Cat, Green Matte Glaze, 1938, 5 1/4 In. 500.00
Bookends, Crows, Celadon Green High Glaze, McDonald, 1949, 5 In. 150.00
Bookends, Eagle, Black, 1930, 6 1/8 In. 190.00
Bookends, Eagle, Blue Speckled, Over Tan Glaze, Louise Abel, 1934, 6 In. 400.00
Bookends, Elephants, Blue Matte Glaze, 1926, 5 In. 546.00
Bookends, Elephants, Ivory Matte Glaze, 1919 . . . . 219.00
Bookends, Flower Basket, Glossy, Pink, Blue, Green, Yellow, 1927, 6 1/2 In. 173.00
Bookends, Fruit Clusters, Grapes, Cherries, Lemons, 1937, 3 1/8 In. 850.00
Bookends, Leopard, Green High Glaze, McDonald, 1924, 5 In. 748.00
Bookends, Man O War, Cream High Glaze, 1946, 6 1/2 In. 1380.00
Bookends, Panthers, Seated, Green Glossy Glaze, 1949, 6 1/2 In. 287.00
Bookends, Peacocks, Light Blue Matte Glaze, 1926, 4 1/2 In. 489.00
Bookends, Penguins, Blue, Black, Ivory, Gray, 1931, 5 3/4 In. 1200.00
Bookends, Reclining Child On Park Bench, Multitone Blue Matte, 1927, 5 1/2 In. 650.00
Bookends, Rook, Blue Matte Glaze, William McDonald, 1930, 5 In. 403.00
Bookends, Rook, Green Matte Blaze, 1922, 5 1/4 In. 220.00
Bookends, Rook, Green, Ivory Matte Glaze, 1926, 6 In. 805.00
Bookends, Rook, Ivory Matte Glaze, 1943, 5 In. 325.00
Bookends, Rook, Tan Matte Glaze, William McDonald, 1926, 5 1/8 In. 160.00
Bowl, Avocado Green, Footed, No. 1745, 1919, 2 7/8 x 5 1/4 In. 196.00
Bowl, Blue Matte Glaze, Footed, 1921, 3 1/2 In. 120.00
Bowl, Boy Scouts Of America Emblem, Blue High Glaze, 1 In. 70.00
Bowl, Butterflies, Pink, Green Matte Glaze, 1921, 3 In. 90.00

Bowl, Ducks, Molded, Blue Matte Glaze, 1919, 4 1/2 In.	300.00
Bowl, Elephants, Molded, Pink, Green Matte Glaze, Green Interior, 5 In.	400.00
Bowl, Emerald, Embossed, 1931, 6 3/4 In.	130.00
Bowl, Flowers, Cameo Glaze, Scalloped Edge, Grace Young, 9 In.	290.00
Bowl, Flowers, Porcelain Glaze, Elizabeth Barrett, 1944, 8 In.	5500.00
Bowl, Flowers, Purple Matte Glaze, Elizabeth N. Lincoln, 1921, 3 In.	375.00
Bowl, Gourd Shape, Maroon, Green Matte Glaze, 1911, 3 In.	170.00
Bowl, Green Matte Glaze, 1927, 8 In.	240.00
Bowl, Ivory & Yellow Glaze, 1915, 2 1/2 x 5 In.	115.00
Bowl, Ivory High Glaze, Green Aventurine Interior, 6 In.	140.00
Bowl, Ivory Matte Glaze, Turquoise Interior, Molded Flower Frog, 6 In.	865.00
Bowl, Ivory, Water Lily Form, 1933, 4 1/4 x 7 1/4 In.	130.00
Bowl, Leaf & Berry At Rim, Pink Matte Glaze, 1930, 7 1/2 In.	150.00
Bowl, Leaf Shape, Blue High Glaze, 1946, 6 1/2 In.	50.00
Bowl, Leaves & Berries, Embossed, Blue Matte Glaze, 1921, 6 3/4 In.	130.00
Bowl, Light Pink High Glaze, Gray Interior, 1915, 4 1/2 In.	90.00
Bowl, Magnolia Blossoms, Geometric Border, Sara Sax, 1926, 13 In.	1380.00
Bowl, Oval, 2 Figures, Ivory Matte, Louise Abel, c.1927, 7 1/2 x 12 3/4 In.	1150.00
Bowl, Painted Apples, Porcelain Glaze, Arthur Conant, 1919, 3 1/2 In.	500.00
Bowl, Peach, Blue Blossoms, Green Leaves, Burnt Orange, Green Ground, 9 In.	520.00
Bowl, Peacock Feathers, Blue, Brown, Green, 4-Footed, Sara Sax, 1909, 3 x 5 1/2 In.	1495.00
Bowl, Pink, Mint Green Matte Glaze, 3 Handles, 1933, 4 3/8 In.	70.00
Bowl, Plum, Lavender, Cobalt, Curdled Butterfat Glaze, Lorinda Epply, 1926, 3 In.	935.00
Bowl, Salad, Blue Ships, 1924, 5 1/2 In., 6 Piece	700.00
Bowl, Tan Mottled Matte Glaze, 3 Handles, 1912, 6 In.	175.00
Bowl, Tomato Shape, Green Glaze, 1923, 3 1/4 In.	150.00
Bowl, Turquoise, Embossed Flowers, No. 2131, 1915, 2 5/8 x 4 7/8 In.	185.00
Bowl, Wild Roses, Standard Glaze, Albert Valentien, 1887, 4 3/4 In.	400.00
Bowl, Yellow Matte Glaze, 1919, 2 1/2 In.	150.00
Box, Camel, Yellow Matte Glaze, 1931, 5 3/4 In.	2645.00
Box, Cover, Ivory Matte Glaze, 1933, 7 In.	350.00
Box, Cover, Molded Flowers, Ivory Matte Glaze, 1936, 4 x 1 1/2 In.	130.00
Bust, Jacobean Woman, Cream Glaze, No. 2026, 8 1/2 In.	484.00
Bust, Woman, Ivory Matte Glaze, 1928, 7 1/2 In.	5750.00
Candlestick, Elephant, Black High Glaze, Green Interior, 1929, 10 x 5 In., Pair	865.00
Candlestick, Leaves, Brown Matte Glaze, 1921, 7 In., Pair	350.00
Candlestick, Maroon High Glaze, 7 1/2 In., Pair	240.00
Candlestick, Molded Flowers, Green Mottled Glaze, 1921, 1 1/4 In.	115.00
Candlestick, Molded Flowers, Pink Matte Glaze, 1920, 2 In., Pair	120.00
Candlestick, Pale Green, Pink Mottled Glaze, 1919, 4 5/8 In., Pair	160.00
Candlestick, Primrose, Shaded Pink To Green Matte Glaze, 2 x 4 In., Pair	69.00
Candlestick, Yellow Matte Glaze, 1923, 9 1/2 In.	250.00
Coffeepot, Bird Perched On Branch, 1887, 8 1/2 In.	745.00
Compote, Green Matte Glaze, 1905, 7 In.	489.00
Cup, Dogwood Design, Pinched Handle, Cameo, Foertmeyer, 1890, 1 7/8 In.	225.00
Cup & Saucer, Painted Flowers, Mahogany Glaze, Wilcox, 1886, Demitasse	185.00
Dish, Fish Shape, Turquoise Blue Glaze, 5 1/2 In.	80.00
Dish, Moths & Insects, Tan Matte Ground, 1883, 4 1/4 In.	460.00
Ewer, 2 Iris Blossoms, Green, Gold, Brown Glossy Glaze, 1899, 11 3/4 In.	750.00
Ewer, Berries & Holly, Standard Glaze, Elizabeth Lincoln, 1901, 5 1/2 In.	435.00
Ewer, Berries & Leaves, Standard Glaze, Edith Felten, 1899, 7 In.	475.00
Ewer, Butterflies & Leaves, Chocolate Brown Glaze, Daly, 1888, 13 In.	1035.00
Ewer, Flowers & Vines, Standard Glaze With Tiger Eye, Matt Daly, 10 1/4 In.	650.00
Ewer, Flowers, Mahogany Glaze, Red Clay, Sallie Toohey, 1890, 7 In.	880.00
Ewer, Flowers, Standard Glaze, Irene Bishop, 1899, 5 1/2 In.	375.00
Ewer, Flowers, Stylized Daisies, Blue Glaze, Matt Daly, 1888, 10 7/8 In.	1800.00
Ewer, Lily, Brown Glaze, Signed, 1897, 7 1/2 In.	600.00
Ewer, Orchids, Standard Glaze, Silver Floral Overlay, J. Zettel, 1891, 5 1/2 In.	2300.00
Ewer, Orchids, Tiger Eye, Shaded Brown Ground, A. Valentien, 1887, 12 x 5 In.	978.00
Ewer, Painted Cherries, Standard Glaze With Tiger Eye, A.R. Valentien, 18 In.	1900.00
Ewer, Painted Flowers, Applied Silver Overlay, Standard Glaze, 5 1/4 In.	2000.00
Ewer, Pansy Blossoms, Gold, Brown Glaze, Harriet E. Wilcox, 1888, 10 In.	720.00
Ewer, Standard Glaze, Flame Mark, Ed Diers, 1900, 10 In.	575.00

Ewer, Yellow, Green Pansies, Standard Glaze, Valentien, 1891, 5 1/2 In. 865.00
Figurine, Cat, Tan High Glaze, Louise Abel, 6 1/2 In. 235.00
Figurine, Cockatoo, Yellow, Ivory, Green High Glaze, 1944, 9 In. . . . . .430.00 to 520.00
Figurine, Deer, Brown, Red High Glaze, 5 In. 430.00
Figurine, Deer, Ivory High Glaze, Louise Abel, 6 In. 345.00
Figurine, Duck, Blue, Green Matte Glaze, 1929, 2 1/2 In. 207.00
Figurine, Grotesque Face, Brown High Glaze, 1954, 3 In. 92.00
Figurine, Woman & Child, Blue, Ivory High Glaze, 1949, 7 In. 230.00
Figurine, Woman, Long Flowing Hair, Gown, Green, Brown, Rose, 6 In. 2700.00
Flower Frog, Pink High Glaze, 1921, 6 In. 290.00
Ginger Jar, Pink, Green Matte Glaze, 1920, 8 In. 240.00
Humidor, American Indian Portrait, Standard Glaze, Grace Young, 1901, 6 In. 4315.00
Jar, Cover, Blue Matte Mottled Glaze, Ram's Head Handles, 1927, 5 In. 185.00
Jar, Cover, Delicate Flowers On Cover, Pink Glaze, McLaughlin, 1915, 6 In. 1150.00
Jar, Cover, Dome, Oak Leaves, Shouldered, 3 Handles, c.1911 . . . . 495.00
Jar, Cover, Nuts, Dark Green High Glaze, 1949, 5 1/8 In. 170.00
Jar, Incense, Cover, Blue Matte Glaze, 1924, 3 1/2 In. 405.00
Jar, Potpourri, Flowers, Red, Yellow, Green, Blue, Reticulated Lid, L. Epply, 1919, 10 In. . 3220.00
Jar, Scent, Cover, Yellow Matte Glaze, 1924, 4 1/8 In. 225.00
Jar, Scent, Small Flying Sparrows Among Oriental Grasses, Gold, 1886, 7 In. 600.00
Jar, Tea, Cover, Swallows Gliding Through Tall Grasses, Gold, Valentien, 1882, 5 In. 500.00
Jar, Yellow Matte Glaze, 2 Handles, 1935, 3 1/2 In. 130.00
Jardiniere, Light Turquoise, 1917, 5 3/4 In. 150.00
Jardiniere, Lotus Blossoms & Pads, Standard Glaze, Amelia Sprague, 1898, 8 In. 900.00
Jardiniere, Multicolored Brown Chrysanthemums, Deep Yellow, 1886, 8 In. 990.00
Jug, Black Birds Flying, Pine Tree, Gray Ground, Matt Daly, 1886, 9 In. 1100.00
Jug, Classical Figures, White Mottled Glaze, Handle, 1945, 10 3/4 In. 130.00
Jug, Incised Flowers, 2 Handles, H. Wenderoth, 1883, 5 In. 299.00
Jug, Spiders, Bat, Oriental Grasses, Black, Tan, Brown, Nichols, 1882, 10 In. 1495.00
Lamp, Green Matte Glaze Shade, Incised Bronze Base, Fechheimer, 1903, 20 In. 8050.00
Lamp, Multicolored Green Matte Glaze, Serpent Handles, 25 1/2 x 18 In. 6050.00
Lamp, Pink Flowers, Gray, White, Flared, Shirayamadani, 1901, 27 In., Pair 440.00
Letter Holder, Molded, Blue High Glaze, 3 x 4 In. 300.00
Match Holder, Painted Cigarettes, Matches, Holly, Standard Glaze, 2 In. 240.00
Mug, Embossed Owl, Oak Branch, Green Matte Glaze, Flame Mark, 1906, 5 1/2 In. 230.00
Mug, Puzzle, Monk Portrait, Standard Glaze, 1899, 5 In. 635.00
Mug, Raised Corn, Standard Glaze, Josephine Zettel, 1896, 4 1/2 In. 220.00
Paperweight, Cat, Caramel Matte Glaze, Louise Abel, 1946, 6 3/4 In. 1000.00
Paperweight, Double Goose, Ivory Matte Glaze, 1930, 4 In. 200.00
Paperweight, Duck, Ivory, Louise Abel, 1934, 3 3/4 In. 475.00
Paperweight, Duck, Matte Yellow, 1934, 3 7/8 In. 978.00
Paperweight, Duck, White Matte Glaze, 1931, 2 1/8 In. 130.00
Paperweight, Elephant, Cream Matte Glaze, 1934, 3 3/8 In. 290.00
Paperweight, Elephant, Ivory Matte Glaze, McDonald, 1934, 3 1/2 In. 400.00
Paperweight, Goat, Art Deco, Celadon High Glaze, 1945, 6 1/4 In. 175.00
Paperweight, Owl, Beige High Glaze, 1951, 4 1/4 In. 175.00
Paperweight, Reclining Woman, Green High Glaze, Abel, 1927, 4 In. 260.00
Paperweight, Squirrel, Mottled Tan Matte Glaze, Toohey, 1929, 4 In. 70.00
Paperweight, Woman, Yellow High Glaze, 1951, 7 1/2 In. 375.00
Pin Tray, Green High Glaze, 1947, 1 7/8 x 4 3/8 In. 110.00
Pitcher, Daisy, Gold Green, Rust Glaze, Angle Handle, 1892, 4 5/8 In. 430.00
Pitcher, Fuchsia Blossoms, Brown Standard Glaze, 1893, 9 1/2 In. 546.00
Pitcher, Gold, Rust, Green Glaze, Tricorn Rim, Angled Handle, 6 & 2 In., 2 Piece 690.00
Pitcher, Green Leaves, Rust, Brown, Gold, Green Ground, Baker, 1891, 9 In. 345.00
Pitcher, Skeleton With Lamp, Standard Glaze, Shirayamadani, 1900, 9 In. 3450.00
Plaque, Autumnal Scene, Vellum Glaze, E. T. Hurley, 1946, 12 x 14 In. 14950.00
Plaque, Bend Of The River, Vellum Glaze, L. Asbury, c.1916, 9 1/4 x 12 1/4 In. 7188.00
Plaque, Birch Trees Divided By A Stream, Hurley, 1939, 7 In. 5750.00
Plaque, Black Rook Perched On Brown Branch With Leaves, 1904, 5 x 9 In. 6050.00
Plaque, Early Day, Vellum, Frame, Lorinda Epply, 1919, 8 x 5 In. 3220.00
Plaque, End Of The Woods, Trees, Green, Blue, Pink, 1920, 10 x 13 In. 6900.00
Plaque, Evening Cloud, Small Body Of Water, Large Trees, Diers, 12 In. 7000.00
Plaque, Lake Louise, Vellum, Quartersawn Oak Frame, Sara Sax, 1914, 9 x 12 In. 6900.00

Plaque, Landscape, Pastels, E.T. Hurley, 8 1/2 x 11 In. 865.00
Plaque, Moonlit Lake Surrounded By Pine Trees, 1912, 8 In. 3105.00
Plaque, November High, Trees, Mountain, River, E.T. Hurley, 1914, 10 x 12 In. 9000.00
Plaque, Pine Tree, River Landscape, Vellum, Gilded Frame, Lenore Asbury, 11 x 7 In. 6325.00
Plaque, Placid Lake With Dusky Forest, Sallie Coyne, 1923, 4 x 8 In. 4800.00
Plaque, Pond At Sunrise, Reflections, Edward Diers, 1927, 9 x 12 In. 6610.00
Plaque, River Bank, Trees, Blue, Pink, Lavender, E.T. Hurley, 1920, 12 In. 4465.00
Plaque, River Landscape At Sunset, L. Asbury, 1926, 14 1/2 x 9 1/4 In. 9000.00
Plaque, Seascape, 4 Sailing Boats, Vellum Glaze, 1911, 8 x 4 In. 3750.00
Plaque, Songbird In Flight, Sea Green Glaze, A.R. Valentien, Frame, 8 x 10 In. 17000.00
Plaque, Summer Meadow, Vellum Glaze, Ed Diers, 1913, 9 x 14 1/2 In. 6610.00
Plaque, Tranquil River, Blue, Green, Brown, C. Schmidt, 1913, 10 3/4 In. 4465.00
Plaque, Trees & Mountains Along River Bank, 1948, 12 In. 5750.00
Plaque, Trees Along River Bank, Vellum Glaze, Diers, 10 In. 4600.00
Plaque, Venetian Scene, Gondolas In Canal, Vellum Glaze, E.T. Hurley, 10 x 8 In. 5000.00
Plaque, View Of Lake Through Trees, Vellum, 8 x 14 In. 8625.00
Plaque, Vivid Colored Trees, Bushes, Mountains, 1917, 9 In. 7480.00
Plaque, Winding Body Of Water Through Trees, 7 x 9 In. 6050.00
Plaque, Winter Scene, Pine Trees & Mountains, Coyne, 9 x 5 In. 4600.00
Plaque, Winter Sunset, Pine Trees, Mountains, River, S. Coyne, 1924, 8 x 5 In. 6500.00
Plaque, Winter Twilight, Snow & Trees By A Pond, 1919, 8 1/2 x 10 In. 4945.00
Plate, Blue Ship Pattern, 1924, 10 In., 8 Piece 350.00
Plate, Cameo Glaze, Scalloped Edge, Harriet Wilcox, 7 1/2 In. 150.00
Plate, Cherry Blossoms, Cameo Glaze, Scalloped Edge, Sallie Toohey, 8 In. 160.00
Plate, Flowers, Cameo Glaze, Scalloped Edge, Amelia Sprague, 7 1/2 In. 140.00
Platter, Blue Ship Pattern, 14 In. 260.00
Pot, Green, Pink Matte Glaze, 1922, 3 1/2 In. 185.00
Rose Bowl, Inverted Rim, Clover Blossoms, Brown, Gold, Green, 3 x 7 1/4 In. 690.00
Rose Bowl, Yellow Violets, Standard Glaze, Sadie Markland, 1892, 3 In. 1800.00
Sconce, Blue Matte, Arts & Crafts, 1921, 8 1/2 In. 690.00
Smoking Set, Lighter, Ashtray, Birds & Leaves, Porcelain Glaze, 1946, 5 In. 350.00
Stein, Flowers, Cast Relief Pewter Lid, No. 783, 1/2 Liter, 6 1/2 In. 1840.00
Stein, Portrait, Edgar Allen Poe, Frog On A Mushroom Finial, Green, 10 1/4 In. 2415.00
Sugar & Creamer, Blue Ships, Oval Underplate, 1924 .... 475.00
Tankard, Applied Silver Mounts, Sea Green, Handle, Ed Diers, 1900, 9 1/8 In. 9750.00
Tankard, Whimsical Character, Copper Overlay On Lid, Grape Thumblift, 9 In. 8000.00
Teapot, Cover, Jonquils, Aerial Blue, William McDonald, 1896, 4 In. 2000.00
Tile, 3-Masted Ship, Mustard, Purple, Blue, Faience, Arts & Crafts Frame, 8 In. 690.00
Tile, Forest, Sallie Toohey, Frame, c.1904, 8 1/2 x 6 1/2 In. 9200.00
Tile, Frieze, Flowers, Yellow Ground, Red, Purple, Blue, Framed, Each 6 In., 16 Piece 550.00
Tile, Frieze, Fruits, Flowers, Polychrome Matte Glazes, 8 x 6 In., 10 Piece 1725.00
Tile, Frieze, Ship At Sea, Raised Sails, Large Clouds, Frame, 12 x 24 In., 2 Piece 2530.00
Tile, Frieze, Ship On Turbulent Waters, Billowing Clouds, 12 x 36 In., 3 Piece 2185.00
Tile, Geometric Pattern, Olive Pale Green, Light Rose Matte Glaze, Oak Frame, 6 In. 635.00
Tile, Landscape, Frame, Square, 12 In. ....2700.00 to 4025.00
Tile, Perched Bird, Blue, Green, Brown Matte Glaze, Round, 6 In. 635.00
Tile, Portrait, Woman, Iris Glaze, Grace Young, Experimental, Square, 1903, 6 In. 5175.00
Tile, Potter Throwing Vase, Green Matte Glaze, 1935, 3 1/2 In. 130.00
Tile, Seagulls In Flight, Turquoise Matte Sky, 1918, 5 5/8 In. 220.00
Tile, Ship At Sea, Turbulent Water, Billowing Clouds, 12 x 12 In. 1700.00
Tile, Trees, Blue, Green, Tan Matte Glazes, Faience, Frame, Square, 6 In. 3450.00
Tile, Water, Mountains, Arts & Crafts Frame, 12 In. 4900.00
Tray, Frogs, Black Matte Glaze, Turquoise High Glaze, 1945, 4 In. 460.00
Tray, Leaf, Applied Branch, Mushrooms, Copper Overlay, Sea Green Glaze, 7 In. 1600.00
Tray, Molded Cabbage Leaf, Blue High Glaze, 1884, 7 1/2 In. 90.00
Tray, Ring, Rook, Blue Matte Glaze, c.1934, 4 x 6 1/4 In. 345.00
Tray, Sunflowers, Yellow, No. 988, 1905, 5 1/2 In. 290.00
Trivet, Crow, Blue & Ivory Ground, 1929, 5 3/4 In. 575.00
Trivet, Fleur-De-Lis, Cobalt Blue, 1915, 3 3/4 In. 195.00
Trivet, Geometric Pattern, Blue, Ivory Matte Glaze, Square, 4 In. 60.00
Trivet, Grapevine, Blue Matte Glaze, Footed, 1 x 5 1/2 In. 345.00
Trivet, Incised Swirl, Blue, Green High Glaze, 1922, 6 In. 288.00
Trivet, Parrot, Pastel Matte Glaze, 1928, 5 3/4 In. 300.00

Trivet, Parrot, Pink & Purple, 1924, 5 3/4 In. 259.00
Trivet, Peaches, Blue & Green Ground, Footed, 1921, 5 1/2 In. 375.00
Trivet, Purple Grapes, Green Leaves, Footed, 5 1/2 In. 230.00
Vase, 3 Panels, Molded, Light Blue Matte Glaze, 1924, 6 In. 242.00
Vase, Abstract Flowers, Turquoise, Burgundy, Rose, Jens Jensen, 1930, 8 3/8 In. . . 900.00
Vase, Acorns & Leaves, Embossed, Blue Matte Glaze, 1919, 9 In. 605.00
Vase, American Indian, Grace Young, 1898, 11 1/2 In. 20000.00
Vase, American Indian, Pink, No. 2873, 1926, 3 5/8 In. 115.00
Vase, Animals, Art Deco, Elizabeth Barrett, 1944, 4 1/2 In. 1095.00
Vase, Antelope, Stylized, Cream, Brown Drip Glaze, Hentschel, 1931, 5 In. 1095.00
Vase, Apache, No Talq, Standard Glaze, Adeliza Sehon, 1900, 9 In. 4830.00
Vase, Apple Blossoms, Iris Glaze, Constance Baker, 1904, 8 In. 430.00
Vase, Apple Blossoms, Red, Green To Rose Butterfat Ground, E. Lincoln, 1926, 8 x 4 In. . 1265.00
Vase, Apple Blossoms, Shaded Teal, Ivory, Pink Ground, Vellum, Tapered, Asbury, 10 In. . 805.00
Vase, Apples, Red, Incised, Light Green Leaves, Green Matte Glaze, Pons, 7 In. 1840.00
Vase, Attenuated Leaves, Blue Matte Glaze, Tapered Oval Shape, c.1917, 6 In. 430.00
Vase, Bamboo, Purple Mottled Matte Glaze, 1924, 6 1/2 In. 489.00
Vase, Band Of Flowers, Red, Yellow, Green, Amber To Rose Glaze, Todd, 11 x 5 In. 1955.00
Vase, Band Of Stylized Flowers, Purple, Green, Blue Gray, C. Todd, 1914, 8 x 4 1/4 In. . . 865.00
Vase, Band Of Swans, Red Ocher & Green Glaze, W. Hentschel, 1914, 7 x 5 In. 1495.00
Vase, Band Of Trees In Winter Landscape, Shirayamadani, 1912, 9 In. 2415.00
Vase, Bands Of Gold Dividing Frogs & Spiders, Nichols, 1883, 26 In. 4315.00
Vase, Bayberries, Vellum, Lorinda Epply, 1923, 6 1/2 In. 4315.00
Vase, Berried Vines, Scrolled Leaves, Helen Stuntz, 1893, 3 3/4 In. 1000.00
Vase, Berries & Leaves, Multicolored Drip Glaze, 1919, 9 1/2 In. 460.00
Vase, Berries & Leaves, Green Matte Glaze, 1915, 7 In. 605.00
Vase, Berries, Deep Maroon, Green Broad Leaves, Katherine Jones, 1923, 4 In. 880.00
Vase, Berries, Leaves, Iris Glaze, Celadon Ground, Lenore Asbury, 1904, 7 x 6 In. 5465.00
Vase, Birch Trees Along Body Of Water, Vellum Glaze, Hurley, 16 In. 8625.00
Vase, Birch Trees, Autumn Leaves, E.T. Hurley, 1945, 8 In. 9250.00
Vase, Bird In Tall Grasses, Standard Glaze, Shirayamadani, 1895, 9 In. 4315.00
Vase, Bird Perched On Cherry Blossom Branch, M. McDonald, 1928, 5 In. 1760.00
Vase, Bird, Brown, Perched On Brown Branch, 21 7/8 In. 200.00
Vase, Birds In Flight, Cream Matte Glaze, Raised Rim, 8 3/8 In. 200.00
Vase, Birds In Flight, Molded, Ivory Matte Glaze, 1938, 3 In. 90.00
Vase, Birds On Split-Rail Fence, 1909, 13 7/8 In. 9000.00
Vase, Birds, Ivory, Jewel Porcelain, Lorinda Epply, 1928 . . . . 2700.00
Vase, Black Man With Flowing Hair, Leaves, Hentschel, 8 In. 9200.00
Vase, Blossoms, Diamond Shape, c.1913, 9 In. 460.00
Vase, Blossoms, Golden, Lavender Ground, Iris Glaze, O.G. Reed, 1903, 11 3/4 In. 920.00
Vase, Blossoms, Gray & White, Vellum, Bulbous, 1904, 4 x 5 In. 750.00
Vase, Blossoms, Leaves, Pink, Green, Blue, Iris Glaze, Irene Bishop, 1904, 5 x 3 In. 635.00
Vase, Blossoms, Leaves, Purple Butterfat Ground, Oval, c.1919, 10 1/2 x 5 In. 575.00
Vase, Blossoms, Trailing, White, Blue, Curving White Lines, Sara Sax, 1929, 4 In. 700.00
Vase, Blue & Aqua, Upturned Handles, No. 77C, 5 1/2 In. 196.00
Vase, Blue & Green, Pinched Neck, 1910, 6 In. 175.00
Vase, Blue Crystalline Matte Glaze, 1916, 6 In. 115.00
Vase, Blue Crystalline Matte Glaze, 1923, 6 1/2 In. 115.00
Vase, Blue Crystalline Matte Glaze, 1933, 3 1/4 In. 150.00
Vase, Blue Jay & Butterfly, Embossed, Emerald Green, No. 6350, 1945, 4 5/8 In. 150.00
Vase, Blue Matte Glaze, Swollen Shoulder Shape, 1922, 5 1/2 In. 150.00
Vase, Blue Matte Glaze, Yellow Interior, 1924, 5 In. 150.00
Vase, Blue Mottled Matte Glaze, 1929, 4 1/2 In. 140.00
Vase, Blue, Brown Matte Glaze, 1916, 6 1/2 In. 320.00
Vase, Blue, Matte, Tapered, c.1920, 9 3/4 x 4 3/4 In. 460.00
Vase, Blue, Tan Matte Glaze, 1922, 3 In. 185.00
Vase, Blue, Yellow Matte Glaze, 1915, 7 In. 220.00
Vase, Branches, Leaves, Brown, Celadon Matte Ground, Hentschel, 5 x 6 1/2 In. 920.00
Vase, Brown Matte Glaze, 1920, 11 1/4 In. 350.00
Vase, Brown, Mustard Glaze, 1915, 4 1/8 In. 190.00
Vase, Brown, Tan Mottled Glaze, 1927, 8 In. 805.00
Vase, Bud, Blue, Molded Flowers, 1921, 7 5/8 In. 175.00
Vase, Bud, Green, No. 2307, 1930, 7 1/8 In. 160.00

Vase, Bulbous, Mottled Amethyst Glaze, No. 955, 1920, 2 5/8 x 4 3/4 In. 126.00
Vase, Butterflies, Celadon Green, 1952, 4 1/2 In. 225.00
Vase, Calla Lilies, Purple, Light Green Matte Ground, R. Fechheimer, 1905, 12 In. 1725.00
Vase, Carnations, Olive Green, c.1894, 7 x 6 In. 825.00
Vase, Carnations, Orange, Yellow, Standard Glaze, C. Baker, 1895, 11 x 6 In. 1380.00
Vase, Carnations, Standard Glaze, K. Shirayamadani, 1892, 13 In. 1035.00
Vase, Catfish & Seaweed, K. Shirayamadani, 1896, 10 1/2 In. 805.00
Vase, Celadon Green Interior, Ivory Matte Glaze, Handles, 1929, 10 1/2 In. 405.00
Vase, Chartreuse, Cocoa Brown Glaze, No. 925E, 6 1/4 In. 195.00
Vase, Cherries, Gold Rust, Green Glaze, Harriet R. Strafer, 1892, 7 In. 690.00
Vase, Cherries, Leaves, Brown, Anna M. Valentien, c.1892, 7 3/4 x 5 1/2 In. 615.00
Vase, Cherries, Leaves, Olive Green, Deep Yellow, c.1895, 6 x 5 In. 440.00
Vase, Cherries, Leaves, Standard Glaze, Leona Van Briggle, 1900, 7 1/2 In. 978.00
Vase, Cherries, Vellum Glaze, Sallie Coyne, 1908, 8 1/4 In. 800.00
Vase, Cherry Blossom Branches, Taupe Ground, Iris Glaze, Oval, Epply, 1911, 8 1/2 In. . . . 1035.00
Vase, Cherry Blossoms, Blue, Green, Ivory, Vellum Glaze, 9 In. 1380.00
Vase, Cherry Blossoms, Butterfat Ground, Wax Matte, Panels, E. Lincoln, 1922, 6 In. 1265.00
Vase, Cherry Blossoms, Green, Blue Ground, Vellum Glaze, Asbury, 1914, 9 In. 920.00
Vase, Cherry Blossoms, Iris Glaze, Irene Bishop, 1906, 4 In. 1265.00
Vase, Cherry Blossoms, Mauve Ground, Sallie Coyne, 1917, 9 1/2 In. 1265.00
Vase, Cherry Blossoms, Orange, Branches, Yellow Ground, Lenore Asbury, 1924, 5 In. . . . 980.00
Vase, Cherry Blossoms, Orange, Green, Brown Ground, Baluster, 9 1/2 x 3 3/4 In. 230.00
Vase, Cherry Blossoms, Pink, Gray Ground, Sallie Coyne, 1909, 5 In. 520.00
Vase, Cherry Blossoms, Pink, Leaves, Shirayamadani, 1933, 8 1/4 In. 1440.00
Vase, Cherry Blossoms, Vellum Glaze, E.T. Hurley, 1948, 7 In. 1495.00
Vase, Cherry Blossoms, Vellum Glaze, Elizabeth N. Lincoln, 1909, 5 In. 690.00
Vase, Cherry Blossoms, Vellum Glaze, Sallie Coyne, 1912, 6 5/8 In. 650.00
Vase, Cherry Blossoms, White, Deep Blue Leaves, McDonald, 1919, 7 x 3 In. 825.00
Vase, Chestnuts, Mahogany Glaze, Albert Valentien, 1889, 9 7/8 In. 600.00
Vase, Choppy Body Of Water, Gnarled Tree, Arthur Conant, 1919, 18 In. 3800.00
Vase, Chrysanthemum, Polychrome, Lavender, Green, Lincoln, 8 1/2 x 4 3/4 In. 1495.00
Vase, Chrysanthemums, Transparent White, Cobalt Ground, 1893, 14 1/2 In. 8750.00
Vase, Clover Blossoms, White, Pink, Lavender, Carrie Steinle, 1912, 8 In. 715.00
Vase, Cobalt Blue, Magenta, Green Abstracts, Elizabeth Lincoln, 1918, 7 1/4 In. 330.00
Vase, Cobalt Blue, Tie Handle, No. 354, 1922, 3 In. 210.00
Vase, Crane In Flight, Sea Green, Artus Van Briggle, 1896, 5 3/8 In. 7475.00
Vase, Cranes In Flight, Carved, Painted, White, Vellum, 1906, 10 In. 4315.00
Vase, Crocus, Blue, Shaded Celadon Ground, Iris Glaze, Rothenbusch, 1904, 9 1/2 In. 1380.00
Vase, Cyclamen, Deep Red On Soft Red Ground, K. Shirayamadani, 1907, 6 x 3 In. 1725.00
Vase, Daffodils, Elizabeth Lincoln, c.1909, 7 x 4 In. 1045.00
Vase, Daffodils, Mauve, Orchid Matte Ground, Shouldered, J. Harris, 1929, 9 1/2 In. 1150.00
Vase, Daffodils, Standard Glaze, Matt Daly, 1902, 11 1/2 In. 635.00
Vase, Daffodils, White, Yellow, Vellum Glaze, Lorinda Epply, 1907, 7 In. 2070.00
Vase, Daffodils, Yellow, Vellum Glaze, E.T. Hurley, 1942, 3 1/2 In. 1265.00
Vase, Daisies, Blue, Ivory Ground, Vellum, Lorinda Epply, 1902, 6 In. 750.00
Vase, Daisies, Blue, Pink Ground, Ed Diers, 1927, 7 In. 2070.00
Vase, Daisies, Cherry Blossoms, Blue, Gray Ground, 1927, 4 1/2 In. 1150.00
Vase, Daisies, Cobalt Blue, Blue Tinted Glaze, 1927, 7 7/8 In. 3800.00
Vase, Daisies, Orange, Yellow, High Glaze, Kataro Shirayamadani, 1922, 12 In. 7500.00
Vase, Daisies, Stylized, Blue Crystalline Matte Glaze, 1934, 5 1/8 In. 160.00
Vase, Daisies, Stylized, Blue, Brown, Charles Todd, 1914, 5 1/4 x 5 1/4 In. 1265.00
Vase, Daisies, Vellum Glaze, Fred Rothenbusch, 1927, 4 1/4 In. 950.00
Vase, Daisies, White, Shaded Teal To Gray Ground, Katharine Hickman, 1909, 7 In. 1150.00
Vase, Daisies, Yellow, Gray, Cream Ground, Edward Diers, 1903, 7 1/8 In. 1265.00
Vase, Daisy, Incised, Gold Yellow Glaze, Pear Shape, 1885, 9 3/8 In. 315.00
Vase, Dancing Maidens, Plum Glaze, c.1921, 13 1/4 x 6 In. 460.00
Vase, Dandelions, Blue & Mauve Ground, Vellum, Squat, L. Asbury, 1920, 6 1/2 In. 1380.00
Vase, Deep Blue Matte Glaze, 1928, 7 1/2 x 4 In. 290.00
Vase, Deep Purple, Green Matte Glaze, 1909, 5 In. 575.00
Vase, Deep Red Glaze, Green Highlights, Signed, 1910, 12 1/2 x 4 1/2 In. 400.00
Vase, Deer, Leaping, Pink, Green Matte Glaze, 1931, 4 3/8 In. 140.00
Vase, Deer, Stylized, Brown, Cream Ground, Elizabeth Barrett, 1934, 7 In. 1495.00
Vase, Diamonds & Leaves, Blue Crystalline Matte Glaze, 1931, 6 7/8 In. 375.00

Vase, Dogwood Blossoms, Green, Yellow Ground, Vellum, Coyne, 8 In. 1380.00
Vase, Dogwood Blossoms, Red, Jens Jensen, 1930, 3 x 4 In. 546.00
Vase, Dogwood, Green, Vellum Glaze, Edith Noonan, 1909, 6 In. 920.00
Vase, Dogwood, Peach, Green Ground, Vellum, Lenore Asbury, 1911, 9 In 300.00
Vase, Dogwood, Purple, Amber & Blue Matte Glaze, Charles Todd, 1913, 6 x 4 1/2 In. 805.00
Vase, Dogwood, White, Green, Umber & Orange, Shirayamadani, 1889, 14 In. 2185.00
Vase, Dots & Petals, Embossed, Yellow Matte Glaze, Handles, 1926, 6 7/8 In. 275.00
Vase, Dragonflies, Stylized, Embossed, Yellow Matte Glaze, 1922, 6 5/8 In. 375.00
Vase, Ducks Flying Over Cattails, Emerald Green Glaze, 1939, 6 In. 250.00
Vase, Ducks, Molded Band, Rose Matte Glaze, 1921, 2 In. 58.00
Vase, Embossed Panels, Blue Matte Glaze, 1929, 3 3/4 In. 150.00
Vase, Embossed, Sky Blue Crystalline Glaze, 1924, 7 In. 300.00
Vase, Feathers, Abstract, Yellow Glaze, 6 1/4 x 3 In. 375.00
Vase, Fern Cutouts, Green Matte Glaze, Flame Mark, 1909, 3 x 8 In. 575.00
Vase, Fern Fronds, Carved, Green, Blue, Maroon Ground, 1905, 4 1/2 In. 575.00
Vase, Fish, Green Ground, Matt Daly, Flame Mark, 1901, 9 1/2 x 5 In. 7480.00
Vase, Fish, Stylized, Exotic Pastel Seaweed, E.T. Hurley, 1931, 8 7/8 In. 2500.00
Vase, Flower Garlands, Repeating, Stylized, Arthur Conant, 1919, 13 1/2 In. 6000.00
Vase, Flower Petals, Orange, Molded, No. 2088, 51/4 In. 290.00
Vase, Flower Petals, Raised, Emerald Green Matte Glaze, Spearhead Shape, 1925, 4 In. . . 190.00
Vase, Flower Petals, Turquoise, Rose Mottled Matte Glaze, 1918, 5 In. 180.00
Vase, Flower Spray, Irene Bishop, c.1900, 8 1/4 x 4 In. 950.00
Vase, Flowers, Aqua, High Glaze, Kararo Shirayamadini, c.1922, 6 x 3 1/4 In. 1430.00
Vase, Flowers, Band, Blue Interior, Cream, Pink Ground, 1916, 5 In. 920.00
Vase, Flowers, Birds, Stylized, Butterfat, Gray Glaze, Epply, 1929, 11 In. 6250.00
Vase, Flowers, Blue Crystalline Matte Glaze, Buttressed, 1923, 7 1/2 In. 290.00
Vase, Flowers, Blue Glaze, Ovoid, 1946, 9 In. 145.00
Vase, Flowers, Blue Ground, Vellum Glaze, Vera Tischler, 1921, 6 In. 185.00
Vase, Flowers, Blue, Green Mottled Matte Glaze, 1935, 3 1/2 In. 140.00
Vase, Flowers, Blue, Nubian Black Glaze, Sara Sax, 1924, 12 5/8 In. 9750.00
Vase, Flowers, Blue, White, Kataro Shirayamadani, 1925, 8 7/8 In. 2600.00
Vase, Flowers, Blue, Yellow, Green, Red & Blue Ground, C. Todd, 1915, 5 x 5 In. 920.00
Vase, Flowers, Branches, Matte, Katherine Jones, c.1927, 6 1/2 x 3 1/2 In. 660.00
Vase, Flowers, Burgundy, Mottling, Matte, c.1929, 7 1/2 x 4 In. 880.00
Vase, Flowers, Caramel Matte Glaze, 1920, 7 3/4 In. 140.00
Vase, Flowers, Caramel, Green, Russet, Wax Matte Glaze, Chalice Form, Handles, 9 In. . . 2300.00
Vase, Flowers, Carved Abstracts, Deep Mustard, 1928, 6 In. 360.00
Vase, Flowers, Carved, Green Crystalline Glaze, Elizabeth Lincoln, 1922, 9 7/8 In. 550.00
Vase, Flowers, Dark Brown, Sara Sax, 1918, 13 1/8 In. 4500.00
Vase, Flowers, Deep Blue, Leaves, Brown Mottled Glaze, M. McDonald, 1924, 8 In. 990.00
Vase, Flowers, Deer, Ivory Matte Glaze, 1931, 7 1/2 In. 115.00
Vase, Flowers, Deer, Ivory Matte Glaze, 1934, 4 1/2 In. 130.00
Vase, Flowers, E. Lincoln, 1922, 6 1/2 In. 1150.00
Vase, Flowers, Elizabeth Neave Lingenfelter Lincoln, 1901, 6 1/4 In. 490.00
Vase, Flowers, Embossed, Leaves, Pink Matte Glaze, 1931, 3 5/8 In. 130.00
Vase, Flowers, Embossed, Yellow Matte Glaze, 1927, 3 1/8 In. 110.00
Vase, Flowers, Garland, Embossed, Blue Crystalline Matte Glaze, 1923, 7 1/8 In. 325.00
Vase, Flowers, Glazed, Clara Christiana Lindeman, 4 5/8 In. 575.00
Vase, Flowers, Green, Brown, Margaret McDonald, 1933, 8 In. 750.00
Vase, Flowers, Green, White, Blue, Pale Gray Ground, 7 In. 290.00
Vase, Flowers, Heart Shape, Geometric Pattern, Blue, W.E. Hentschel, 1911, 6 1/2 In. 825.00
Vase, Flowers, Horses, Blue & White, Jens Jensen, 1945, 6 1/4 In. 3220.00
Vase, Flowers, Incised Wreath, Cobalt Band, 1914, 4 1/4 In. 500.00
Vase, Flowers, Incised, Elizabeth Lincoln, 1919, 9 3/8 In. 1300.00
Vase, Flowers, Incised, Leaves, Butterflies, Green Glossy Glaze, 11 7/8 In. 230.00
Vase, Flowers, Incised, Standard Glaze, K. Shirayamadani, 1891, 14 In. 1265.00
Vase, Flowers, Iris Glaze, Sara Sax, 1901, 10 In. 4025.00
Vase, Flowers, Lavender, Leaves, Ivory Ground, 1946, 4 In. 600.00
Vase, Flowers, Leaves, Green & Rose, Yellow Ground, Drip Glaze, 1919, 5 In. 805.00
Vase, Flowers, Leaves, Incised, Stylized, Green, Blue Mottled Ground, 1920, 11 In. 1380.00
Vase, Flowers, Leaves, Molded, Multicolored Blue Matte Glaze, 1926, 9 In. 235.00
Vase, Flowers, Leaves, Stylized, Yellow Matte Glaze, 1926, 5 3/4 In. 170.00
Vase, Flowers, Mahogany Glaze, Tiger Eye Glaze, 5 In. 375.00

Vase, Flowers, Mauve Mottled Glaze, 1920, 6 1/2 In. 375.00
Vase, Flowers, Mauve, Green Matte Glaze, 1911, 5 1/2 In. 550.00
Vase, Flowers, Molded, Blue Matte Glaze, 1928, 6 In. 265.00
Vase, Flowers, Molded, Blue Matte Glaze, 1946, 6 1/2 In. 160.00
Vase, Flowers, Molded, Brown Drip Matte Glaze, 1930, 6 In. 160.00
Vase, Flowers, Molded, Green Matte Glaze, 1926, 6 1/4 In. 175.00
Vase, Flowers, Orange, Lime Green Matte Glaze, 1931, 8 1/4 In. 325.00
Vase, Flowers, Pink Ground, Kataro Shirayamadani, 1944, 12 In. 1380.00
Vase, Flowers, Purple, Canary, Magenta Glaze, 1928, 5 1/2 x 3 In. 990.00
Vase, Flowers, Purple, Green Ground, Iris Glaze, Rothenbusch, 1903, 8 In. 1840.00
Vase, Flowers, Red, Green, Blue Leaves, C. Covalenco, 1925, 14 In. 3335.00
Vase, Flowers, Red, Yellow Centers, Blue, Purple Ground, 1922, 7 1/2 In. 920.00
Vase, Flowers, Red, Yellow, Green, Peach Butterfat Ground, Todd, 9 1/2 x 3 3/4 In. 1265.00
Vase, Flowers, Shirayamadani, 1936, 9 1/2 In., Pair 2588.00
Vase, Flowers, Squeezebag, Blue, Yellow, Elizabeth Barrett, 1929, 7 In. 1210.00
Vase, Flowers, Standard Glaze, A.R. Valentien, 1900, 12 In. 405.00
Vase, Flowers, Standard Glaze, Bertha Cranch, 1895, 8 1/2 In. 220.00
Vase, Flowers, Standard Glaze, c.1900, 4 5/8 In. 575.00
Vase, Flowers, Standard Glaze, C.J. Dibowski, 1894, 4 In. 320.00
Vase, Flowers, Standard Glaze, Dibowski, 1895, 4 1/2 In. 265.00
Vase, Flowers, Standard Glaze, Katharine Hickman, 1899, 8 In. 520.00
Vase, Flowers, Standard Glaze, Laura Asbury, 1898, 7 In. 518.00
Vase, Flowers, Standard Glaze, Mary Nourse, 1894, 7 In. 575.00
Vase, Flowers, Stylized, Blue Ground, Jens Jensen, 1914, 6 In. 185.00
Vase, Flowers, Stylized, Blue, Vivid Mustard Ground, Abel, 1922, 6 3/4 In. 1380.00
Vase, Flowers, Stylized, Diagonal Bands, Semimatte Glaze, 13 1/2 In. 1840.00
Vase, Flowers, Stylized, Geometric, Green Ground, 1930, 10 In. 1150.00
Vase, Flowers, Stylized, Gray, Blue, Maroon, White, Vellum, Conant, 1916, 7 x 3 In. 715.00
Vase, Flowers, Stylized, Green Matte Glaze, 1938, 6 In. 275.00
Vase, Flowers, Stylized, Indigo & Caramel Flambe Glaze, Hentschel, 1914, 16 1/2 In. ... 5750.00
Vase, Flowers, Stylized, Leaves, Aqua Matte Glaze, 1932, 5 In. 145.00
Vase, Flowers, Stylized, Purple, Green, Wax Matte Glaze, 1937, 6 In. 1380.00
Vase, Flowers, Tan, Blue Mottled Glaze, Katherine Jones, 1928, 5 1/2 In. 690.00
Vase, Flowers, Vellum Glaze, M.G. Denzler, 1914, 7 1/2 In. 1150.00
Vase, Flowers, Vellum Glaze, Mary Grace Denzler, 1914, 6 In. 520.00
Vase, Flowers, Vines, Blue, Orange Ground, Harriet Wilcox, 1902, 7 In. 8625.00
Vase, Flowers, White, Bands Of Gold, Albert Valentien, 1886, 24 In. 5175.00
Vase, Flowers, White, Purple Ground, Van Horne, 1915, 9 In. 1095.00
Vase, Flowers, Yellow Matte Glaze, 1929, 4 1/2 In. 130.00
Vase, Flowers, Yellow, Green Leaves, Standard Glaze, Caroline Steinle, 1907, 8 In. 1265.00
Vase, Flowers, Yellow, Iris Glaze, Olga Geneva Reed, 1901, 8 1/4 In. 700.00
Vase, Flowers, Yellow, Leaves, c.1893, 7 x 3 1/4 In. 385.00
Vase, Flowers, Yellow, Red & Purple, Pink Ground, J. Jensen, 1929, 9 1/2 In. 1610.00
Vase, Flowers, Yellow, Standard Glaze, Sehon, 1898, 7 In. 400.00
Vase, Fruit, Branches, Magenta, Mottling, Charles Klinger, c.1925, 7 x 3 1/2 In. 715.00
Vase, Fruit, Purple, Yellow, Green, Turquoise Ground, Charles Todd, 14 x 7 1/2 In. 1725.00
Vase, Geese & Ducks, Porcelain Glaze, Arthur Conant, 1920, 19 In. 5750.00
Vase, Geese In Flight, Iris Glaze, E. T. Hurley, 1904, 5 3/4 In. 6325.00
Vase, Geese, White, Purples, Blue Greens, K. Shirayamadani, 1911, 6 1/4 x 3 In. 3335.00
Vase, Geometric Pattern, Blue Matte Glaze, 1913, 4 1/2 In. 520.00
Vase, Geometric Pattern, Blue Matte Glaze, 1922, 5 1/4 In. 175.00
Vase, Geometric Pattern, Blue Matte Glaze, 1928, 5 1/2 In. 90.00
Vase, Geometric Pattern, Celery Green Matte Glaze, 1936, 4 In. 300.00
Vase, Geometric Pattern, Green Matte Glaze, William Hentschel, 1910, 5 In. 1380.00
Vase, Geometric Pattern, Green, Brown Matte Glaze, 1910, 4 1/2 In. 405.00
Vase, Geometric Pattern, Green, Pink Matte Glaze, Fan Shape, 1904, 6 3/4 In. 150.00
Vase, Geometric Pattern, Incised, Green Matte Glaze, 1903, 5 1/4 In. 127.00
Vase, Geometric Pattern, Molded, Blue Matte Glaze, 1937, 6 In. 288.00
Vase, Geometric Pattern, Pink Matte Glaze, 1922, 9 In. 345.00
Vase, Geometric Pattern, Rose, Green Matte Glaze, 1911, 9 In. 990.00
Vase, Geometric Pattern, Tan Mottled Matte Glaze, 1928, 7 In. 196.00
Vase, Geometric Pattern, Thick Blue Matte Glaze, 1913, 8 1/2 In. 865.00
Vase, Glasgow Roses, Burgundy & Teal Glaze, Squat, W. Hentschel, 1910, 4 x 5 1/2 In. ... 805.00

Vase, Gooseberry Branches, Purple, Vermilion, Green, E. Lincoln, 1925, 15 x 6 In. 2760.00
Vase, Grapes, Iris Glaze, Lenore Asbury, 1908, 7 7/8 In. 2415.00
Vase, Grapes, Leaves, Vines, Ed Diers, 1909, 5 7/8 In. 400.00
Vase, Grapes, Leaves, Yellow Ground, E. Barrett, 1924, 8 1/2 In. 865.00
Vase, Grapes, Mottled Green & Red Matte Ground, Ovoid, C. Todd, 1914, 10 In. 978.00
Vase, Grapes, Silver Handle, Silver Stopper, Abel, 1893, 7 1/8 In. 4200.00
Vase, Grapes, Standard Glaze, Laura Lindeman, 1908, 5 In. 220.00
Vase, Gray, Brown, Yellow, Blue, Iris Glaze, Urn Shape, c.1950, 15 3/4 In. 403.00
Vase, Green Ground, Brown & Blue Glaze Dripping From Rim, 10 3/4 In. 750.00
Vase, Green, Brown Matte Glaze, 1910, 2 3/4 In. 290.00
Vase, Green, Maroon Crystalline Glaze, Aqua Glaze Interior, 1921, 13 In. 430.00
Vase, Green, Maroon Mottled Matte Glaze, 1910, 6 In. 690.00
Vase, Green, Multitoned Red Matte Glaze, 1904, 14 In. 1210.00
Vase, Green, Pink Matte Glaze, 1907, 7 In. 100.00
Vase, Green, Pink Matte Glaze, 1925, 5 1/2 In. 230.00
Vase, Green, Pink Matte Glaze, 1929, 7 1/2 In. 275.00
Vase, Green, Pink Matte Glaze, Petal Shape, 1917, 3 1/8 In. 110.00
Vase, Green, Red Matte Glaze, 1906, 5 In. 335.00
Vase, Harbor Scene, 8 Sailboats, Vellum, Schmidt, 1920, 11 In. 2875.00
Vase, Hemlock Flowers, Green Ground, E.T. Hurley, 1934, 5 In. 2415.00
Vase, Holly, Standard Glaze, Butterfly Handle, 1896, 2 In. 345.00
Vase, Holly, Standard Glaze, E. Lincoln, 1899, 5 1/2 In. 635.00
Vase, Holly, Standard Glaze, Sadie Markland, 4 1/2 In. 105.00
Vase, Hyacinths, Purple, K. Shirayamadani, 1939, 8 In. 6050.00
Vase, Hydrangeas, Blue & Green Ground, Iris Glaze, Ed Diers, 1910, 10 x 5 In. 2760.00
Vase, Hydrangeas, Iris Glaze, A.R. Valentien, 1902, 14 In. 8050.00
Vase, Imperial Cranes Standing In Tall Grasses, Vellum Glaze, 1904, 11 In. 2500.00
Vase, Incised Band Of Blossoms, Ocher, Blue, Green, Cylindrical, 1913, 9 In. 605.00
Vase, Iris Blossoms, Purple, Beige Ground, Sara Sax, 1925, 11 1/8 In. 6600.00
Vase, Iris, Black, Cobalt Blue, Schmidt, 1911, 8 In. 11500.00
Vase, Iris, Purple, Green Matte Ground, Albert Pons, 1907, 10 x 5 In. 1610.00
Vase, Iris, Purple, Iris Glaze, Carl Schmidt, 1904, 6 In. 1495.00
Vase, Iris, Purple, White, Constance Baker, 1902, 8 5/8 In. 2100.00
Vase, Irises, Blue, Pale Green Ground, Schmidt, 1906, 10 1/2 In. 8250.00
Vase, Irises, Green, Blue, Yellow, Standard Glaze, Mary Nourse, 1900, 12 In. 860.00
Vase, Irises, Iris Glaze, Carl Schmidt, 1908, 10 1/2 In. 5175.00
Vase, Irises, Iris Glaze, Carl Schmidt, 1909, 8 1/8 In. 6900.00
Vase, Irises, Red & White, Sara Sax, 1926, 16 In. 8250.00
Vase, Irises, White, Blue, Standard Glaze, L. Asbury, 1903, 11 In. 1800.00
Vase, Irises, Yellow, Lavender, Silver Overlay Rim, Valentien, 14 In. 12100.00
Vase, Irises, Yellow, Tan, Cream Ground, Carl Schmidt, 1900, 6 In. 1495.00
Vase, Japanese Iris Blossoms, Iris Glaze, Sallie Coyne, 1907, 8 1/2 x 3 3/4 In. 1495.00
Vase, Japanese Irises, Purple, Pale Green Leaves, Sallie Coyne, 1910, 9 1/2 In. 2300.00
Vase, Japanese Maple Leaves, Stems, Standard Glaze, Steinle, 1900, 6 1/2 In. 600.00
Vase, Jonquils, Green Matte Glaze, Albert Pons, 1907, 8 x 6 In. 1495.00
Vase, Jonquils, Molded, Blue Matte Glaze, 1926, 8 In. 430.00
Vase, Jonquils, White, Shaded Ground, Constance Baker, 1902, 7 1/2 In. 1035.00
Vase, Lake & Trees, Mountains In Background, Rothenbusch, 17 1/2 In. 8625.00
Vase, Landscape Scene, 1914, 8 In. 805.00
Vase, Landscape, Pink Sky, Vellum Glaze, E.T. Hurley, 1943, 9 7/8 In. 5060.00
Vase, Landscape, Pink, Ivory, Aqua, Green, Fred Rothenbusch, c.1916, 8 x 3 1/2 In. 1540.00
Vase, Landscape, Vellum Glaze, F. Rothenbusch, 1918, 15 In. 4750.00
Vase, Large Yellow Full Moon Reflecting Off Water, Coyne, 1910, 9 In. 12000.00
Vase, Leaves & Acorns, Brown, Green, Gold, Rust Glaze, Mary Nourse, 7 1/8 In. 575.00
Vase, Leaves & Acorns, Standard Glaze, Sallie Toohey, 1895, 6 In. 635.00
Vase, Leaves & Berries, Maroon, Gray Matte Glaze, 1922, 7 In. 300.00
Vase, Leaves & Berries, Molded, Aqua Ground, Panels, 1930, 7 1/2 In. 255.00
Vase, Leaves & Berries, Molded, Blue Matte Glaze, 1924, 6 1/2 In. 225.00
Vase, Leaves & Berries, Molded, Tan Matte Glaze, 1935, 3 In. 219.00
Vase, Leaves & Berries, Pink, Green Mottled Matte Glaze, 1919, 11 1/4 In. 400.00
Vase, Leaves & Berries, Standard Glaze, Sprague, 1893, 8 In. 235.00
Vase, Leaves & Berries, Stylized, Ochre Glaze, 1921, 6 In. 325.00

Vase, Leaves & Berries, Yellow Matte Glaze, 1925, 4 3/4 In. 190.00
Vase, Leaves & Flowers, Stylized, Blue, Red, Yellow, Green, Jensen, 1930, 6 1/2 In. 750.00
Vase, Leaves, Blue Matte Crystalline Glaze, Gray Matte Glaze, 1929, 4 In. 325.00
Vase, Leaves, Brown, Blue Gray, Yellow Ground, Jens Jensen, 1928, 6 1/4 In. 1150.00
Vase, Leaves, Brown, Ivory Interior, Kay Ley, 1946, 5 1/2 In. 935.00
Vase, Leaves, Green, Red Matte Glaze, 1912, 12 1/2 In. 1840.00
Vase, Leaves, Molded, Green, Blue Matte Glaze, 1920, 8 In. 415.00
Vase, Leaves, Molded, Rose Matte Glaze, 1920, 6 In. 127.00
Vase, Leaves, Molded, Stylized, 12 In. 546.00
Vase, Leaves, Molded, Vertical, Leaves, Rose Matte Glaze, 6 1/2 In. 358.00
Vase, Leaves, Molded, Vertical, Mauve Matte Glaze, 1912, 6 In. 259.00
Vase, Leaves, Molded, Vertical, Pink, Green Matte Glaze, 1928, 6 In. 175.00
Vase, Leaves, Oak, Shaded Ground, Lenore Asbury, 1905, 7 In. 1437.00
Vase, Leaves, Pink Matte Glaze, 1927, 4 7/8 In. 110.00
Vase, Leaves, Sculpted, Green, Red Matte Glaze, K. Shirayamadani, 1913, 5 1/2 In. 865.00
Vase, Leaves, Stylized, Blue Matte Glaze, 5 1/4 x 4 In. 160.00
Vase, Leaves, Stylized, Blue, Green Crystalline Matte Glaze, 1936, 5 In. 265.00
Vase, Light Green High Glaze, 1904, 3 3/4 In. 100.00
Vase, Lilies Of The Valley, Gold Yellow, Brown Ground, 1891, 6 In. 750.00
Vase, Lilies, Iris Glaze, Irene Bishop, 1906, 6 3/4 In. 345.00
Vase, Lilies, Red, Yellow, Turquoise Ground, E. Lincoln, 1931, 8 3/4 x 6 1/4 In. 1265.00
Vase, Lotus Blossoms, Buds, Blue Slip, William Hentschel, 1925, 11 1/8 In. 700.00
Vase, Lotus Blossoms, Pink Butterfat Ground, Bottle Shape, C.S. Todd, 1920, 6 1/2 In. . . . 690.00
Vase, Lotus Blossoms, White, Iris Glaze, Olga Geneva Reed, 1902, 11 In. 34000.00
Vase, Magnolia Blossoms, Lavender, No.905c, 1905, 9 3/4 In. 4700.00
Vase, Magnolia Blossoms, Purple, Light Green Ground, 1906, 7 In. 4315.00
Vase, Magnolia Branches, Yellow, Cobalt Blue, Louise Abel, 1925, 10 1/2 x 6 1/2 In. 1840.00
Vase, Magnolia, Standard Glaze, Laurence, 1902, 11 In. 920.00
Vase, Magnolia, Turquoise Butterfat Ground, Wax Matte, Jens Jensen, 1934, 6 1/2 In. 1265.00
Vase, Magnolias, Brown, 2-Tone Brown Leaves, Ivory, Jewel Porcelain, Jensen, 10 In. . . . 1870.00
Vase, Magnolias, Mauve & White, Sara Sax, 1905, 9 3/4 In. 5405.00
Vase, Maiden Among Tree & Grasses, Aerial Blue Glaze, Horsfall, 1895, 3 In. 1495.00
Vase, Maple Branch, Green, Shaded Teal To Ivory Ground, Sara Sax, 1906, 6 x 3 In. 1495.00
Vase, Maple Leaves, Dark Brown, Tan, Matt Daly, 1892, 12 1/8 In. 1300.00
Vase, Marine Scene, Pink Shaded To Blue, Vellum, Carl Schmidt, 1922, 7 1/2 In. 2415.00
Vase, Mauve Mottled Drip Glaze, 1907, 4 1/2 In. 430.00
Vase, Mauve To Green Matte Glaze, 3 3/8 x 4 1/4 In. 250.00
Vase, Mint Green Glossy Glaze, Handles, 1923, 4 3/8 In. 130.00
Vase, Mountain Lake, Vellum Glaze, Lenore Asbury, 1912, 11 In. 2300.00
Vase, Mountain Range, Snow Covered, Blue, Iris Glaze, 1911, 14 In. 20000.00
Vase, Multicolored, Blue Matte Glaze, 1924, 8 In. 290.00
Vase, Multicolored, Green Crystalline Matte Glaze, 1927, 4 In. 265.00
Vase, Multicolored, Green Crystalline Matte Glaze, 6 In. 240.00
Vase, Multicolored, Tan Mottled Matte Glaze, Green Interior, 1921, 6 1/2 In. 255.00
Vase, Mushrooms, Standard Glaze, Carl Schmidt, 7 x 3 1/2 In. 1610.00
Vase, Mustard Matte Glaze, 1935, 3 1/2 In. 300.00
Vase, Mustard Matte Glaze, Handles, 1921, 5 1/8 In. 150.00
Vase, Narcissus, Green, Brown Stems, Vellum, Vera Tischler, 6 In. 660.00
Vase, Nasturtium Band, White, Bright Yellow Stamen, Sallie Coyne, 1931, 6 In. 1100.00
Vase, Nasturtium Blossoms, Leaves, Standard Glaze, Lenore Asbury, 1895, 8 In. 1000.00
Vase, Nasturtiums, Encircling Body Below Shoulder, Diers, 1905, 7 7/8 In. 1000.00
Vase, Nasturtiums, Yellow, Iris Glaze, Ed Diers, 1904, 9 7/8 In. 425.00
Vase, Neoclassical Figures, Ivory Matte Glaze, Louise Abel, 1920, 5 In. 240.00
Vase, Nudes, Flowers, Cobalt & Black On Shaded Taupe, Bulbous, Jensen, 1926, 7 In. . . . 3738.00
Vase, Oak Leaves, Embossed, Blue, Green Glaze, 1916, 11 1/2 In. 800.00
Vase, Oblong Panels, Raised Beads, Hunter Green Leaves, 1924, 4 In. 715.00
Vase, Orange Day Lilies, Standard Glaze, Baluster, Sallie Toohey, 1899, 15 x 6 In. 8653.00
Vase, Orchids, Leaves, Pink Shaded To Green, Vellum, Carl Schmidt, 1905, 8 1/2 In. 4025.00
Vase, Orchids, Pink, Blue, Cream, Shirayamadani, 1927, 4 3/4 In. 10000.00
Vase, Palm Frond, Green, Gold, Rust Glaze, Kate C. Matchette, 1893, 8 1/2 In. 517.00
Vase, Pansies, Blue, Cream Ground, Iris Glaze, Baker, 1902, 6 In. 2070.00
Vase, Pansies, Yellow, Brown Accents, Hunter Green, 1894, 6 1/4 x 3 1/2 In. 935.00

Vase, Pansies, Yellow, Sage Green Leaves, Hunter Green, 1907, 5 x 2 In. 715.00
Vase, Peach, Pearl Gray Glossy Glaze, Footed, 1931, 6 In. 275.00
Vase, Peacock Feathers, Blue Glaze, 1923, 9 In. 460.00
Vase, Peacock Feathers, Green Ground, Albert Valentien, 1895, 14 In. 7250.00
Vase, Peonies, White, Green Leaves, 1939, 7 1/4 In. 2600.00
Vase, Peony, Blue, Yellow Double Circle Stamen, Charles Klinger, 1925, 7 In. 825.00
Vase, Picasso Style Painting, Matte, William Hentschel, c.1930, 6 x 5 In. 2640.00
Vase, Pillow, Carnation, Honeysuckle, Gold, Green, Brown Glaze, 1894, 5 x 7 In. 630.00
Vase, Pillow, Fish, Sea Green Glaze, Fred Rothenbusch, 1900, 6 3/4 In. 3450.00
Vase, Pink Matte Glaze, Handles, 1925, 4 In. 175.00
Vase, Pink Mottled Matte Glaze, 1930, 5 In. 105.00
Vase, Pink, Embossed Beading, No. 2762, 1928, 3 3/4 In. 105.00
Vase, Pink, Embossed Diamonds, No. 2870, 1927, 5 In. 115.00
Vase, Pink, Green Matte Glaze, 1922, 5 1/4 In. 185.00
Vase, Pink, Green Matte Glaze, 1930, 7 1/2 In. 210.00
Vase, Pink, Green Matte Glaze, Buttressed, 1916, 6 1/2 In. 345.00
Vase, Pink, Green Matte Glaze, Square Handle, 1921, 4 3/4 In. 150.00
Vase, Pink, Green Matte Mottled Glaze, 1926, 5 In. 115.00
Vase, Poppies, Blue, Iris Glaze, Carl Schmidt, 1908, 9 1/2 In. 7480.00
Vase, Poppies, Forest Green, Sturgis Laurence, 1903, 11 5/8 In. 2000.00
Vase, Poppies, Long Stemmed Navy Blue, Stylized, Spring Green Ground, 9 In. 1880.00
Vase, Poppies, Maroon, Rose Glaze, 1930, 10 3/4 In. 3300.00
Vase, Poppies, Orange, Green, K. Shirayamadani, 1898, 12 3/4 x 7 3/4 In. 1955.00
Vase, Poppies, Orange, Standard Glaze, Constance Baker, 10 1/2 x 5 In. 1380.00
Vase, Poppies, Pink, Green Leaves, Teal, Ivory, Vellum, Ed Diers, c.1927, 11 x 6 In. 719.00
Vase, Poppies, Pink, Green Leaves, Vines, Pink Matte Glaze, 1931, 6 In. 1150.00
Vase, Poppies, Red, Orange, Green, Purple, E. Lincoln, 1922, 10 3/4 x 5 1/2 In. 3335.00
Vase, Poppies, Red, Vellum Glaze, Lenore Asbury, 1905, 12 1/4 In. 1800.00
Vase, Poppies, Stylized, Red, Green, Pink, Green Ground, 1944, 6 1/2 In. 1380.00
Vase, Purple Matte Glaze, Flared Rim, Oval, 1922, 6 In. 260.00
Vase, Rabbits, Running, Pink High Glaze, 1916, 2 3/8 In. 160.00
Vase, Red, Yellow Matte Glaze, 1953, 10 In. 375.00
Vase, River Scene, Green, Blue, Vellum Glaze, 1908, 13 In. 3525.00
Vase, River, Trees, Blue, Ivory, Brown, Vellum Glaze, 1928, 11 In. 2350.00
Vase, Rooks, Molded Band, Ivory, Pink Matte Glaze, 1922, 6 In. 240.00
Vase, Rooks, Molded, Flowers, Multicolored Blue Matte Glaze, 1920, 7 In. 920.00
Vase, Rooks, Molded, Green Matte Glaze, 1927, 5 3/4 In. 518.00
Vase, Rooks, Molded, Green Mottled Matte Glaze, 1917, 6 1/2 In. 375.00
Vase, Rooks, Molded, Pink Matte Glaze, 1919, 6 1/2 In. 400.00
Vase, Rooks, Molded, Purple Matte Glaze, 1922, 5 In. 345.00
Vase, Rooks, Molded, Tan, Green Matte Glaze, 1915, 6 In. 489.00
Vase, Rose Blossoms, Brown, Gold, Teal Glossy Glaze, Perkins, 1899, 5 3/8 In. 690.00
Vase, Rose Blossoms, Green, Gold, Brown Glossy Ground, Angle Handles, 9 3/8 In. 980.00
Vase, Rose Over Green Matte Glaze, Broad Shoulders, 1904, 4 1/2 In. 290.00
Vase, Rose Over Green Matte Glaze, Tapered, 1906, 9 In. 635.00
Vase, Rose, Geometric Pattern On Neck, Green Matte Glaze, 1914, 7 1/8 In. 375.00
Vase, Rose, Multicolored, Brown Crystalline Matte Glaze, 1923, 6 In. 175.00
Vase, Rose, Stylized, Mustard Matte Glaze, 1921, 5 3/4 In. 170.00
Vase, Roses, Cream Ground, Vellum Glaze, Ed Diers, 1905, 6 1/4 In. 865.00
Vase, Roses, Daisies, Leaves, Blue, Orange, Green Ground, 1925, 14 1/2 In. 1610.00
Vase, Roses, Molded, Purple Matte Glaze, 1917, 8 In. 430.00
Vase, Roses, Red, Green, Indigo, Pink To Orange Ground, Jens Jensen, 5 x 5 1/2 In. 1495.00
Vase, Roses, Stylized, Purple Ground, Turquoise Interior, Sax, 1918, 9 In. 4315.00
Vase, Roses, Vellum Glaze, Ed Diers, 1926, 7 In. 1955.00
Vase, Roses, White, Green Stems, Blue Opal Glaze, Wilcox, 1924, 11 In. 2415.00
Vase, Roses, Yellow, Iris Glaze, Ed Diers, 1903, 8 1/2 In. 4025.00
Vase, Salmon, Embossed Flowers, No. 6444, 1959, 5 3/8 In. 150.00
Vase, Salmon, Pink Wild Rose Vellum Glaze, Diers, 1907, 11 In. 1300.00
Vase, Sea Green Glaze, Albert Valentien, 1895, 14 5/8 In. 4600.00
Vase, Silhouette Of Tall Trees In Foreground, Lorinda Epply, 1911, 13 In. 4000.00
Vase, Silhouette Of Tall Trees, Dark Blue, Gray Sky, Albert Valentien, 1905, 12 In. 2600.00
Vase, Silhouette Of Trees, Pink Sky Of Early Evening, Sara Sax, 1911, 10 In. 6750.00

Vase, Sky Blue Glossy Glaze, 1931, 5 3/8 In. 120.00
Vase, Snowdrops, White, Pink & Blue Shaded Ground, Iris Glaze, 1910, 7 In. 1840.00
Vase, Snowy Landscape, Blue Grays, Ed Diers, 1916, 8 1/2 x 5 1/4 In. 3335.00
Vase, Songbird, White, Brown, Black Reeds, Matt Daly, 1885, 10 1/2 In. 980.00
Vase, Speckled Trout, Sea Green, E.T. Hurley, 1903, 8 1/2 In. 9775.00
Vase, Spider Mums, Mauve, 2 Small Birds, Blue, Black Glaze, Epply, 1925, 9 In. 1100.00
Vase, Spiderwort, Purple, Yellow Butterfat Ground, Shirayamadani, 5 x 5 1/2 In. 1265.00
Vase, Spring Trees, Meadows, Small Houses, Rothenbusch, 1926, 11 In. 4000.00
Vase, Squeezebag, Blue Matte Glaze, William Hentschel, 1930, 12 In. 1380.00
Vase, Sunflowers, Yellow, Green Leaves, Vellum Glaze, Lenore Asbury, 1925, 6 In. 1265.00
Vase, Swans Swimming, Vellum Glaze, E.T. Hurley, 1908, 9 3/8 In. 1400.00
Vase, Swans, Burgundy, Aqua Mottled Matte Glaze, 1919, 3 1/2 In. 375.00
Vase, Tan Crystalline Glaze, Paneled, 1922, 6 1/4 In. 275.00
Vase, Tan, Green, Mottled Matte Glaze, 1920, 6 3/4 In. 220.00
Vase, Thistle, Textured, Turquoise, Amber, Purple Ground, E. Lincoln, 10 x 4 1/2 In. 1610.00
Vase, Thistles, Cream, Blue Ground, Iris Glaze, Sara Sax, 1906, 8 In. 2990.00
Vase, Tiger Eye Glaze, 1931, 4 1/4 x 2 1/2 In. 345.00
Vase, Tiger Eye, Cylindrical, c.1897, 8 1/2 x 3 In. 345.00
Vase, Trailing Blossoms, White, Blue, Curving White Lines, Sara Sax, 1913, 9 In. 1500.00
Vase, Tranquil Lake, Late Summer Evening, 1912, 9 1/4 In. 4000.00
Vase, Trees & River At Sunset, Vellum, A. Conant, 1922, 7 In. 1095.00
Vase, Trees After Heavy Snowfall, Coyne, 1916, 10 In. 1300.00
Vase, Trees, Charcoal, Cerulean, McDermott, 1917, 8 In. 1650.00
Vase, Trees, Charcoal, Reflecting Off Body Of Water, 1904, 8 In. 2750.00
Vase, Trees, Green, Brown, Hurley, 1931, 12 In. 5175.00
Vase, Trees, Mountains, Vellum, Ed Diers, 1918, 15 In. 865.00
Vase, Trees, Pastels, Vellum, Sallie Coyne, 1915, 10 In. 920.00
Vase, Trees, River, Blue, Green, Brown, Vellum Glaze, Schmidt, 1917, 11 In. 2820.00
Vase, Trees, Sage Green, Green Grass, Coyne, 1917, 9 In. 1760.00
Vase, Treetops, Green, Smoky Gray Trunks, 1915, 5 x 3 In. 1870.00
Vase, Tulips, Brick Red, Lenore Asbury, 1903, 6 x 5 In. 863.00
Vase, Tulips, Gold, Rust, Green, Brown, Harriet R. Strafer, 1893, 9 In. 805.00
Vase, Tulips, Incised, Pink Glaze, 3 Panels, Sara Sax, 1907, 7 1/2 In. 1380.00
Vase, Tulips, Ivory Body, Deep Blue Glaze, 1938, 11 x 6 In. 1100.00
Vase, Tulips, Leaves, Red, Green, Amber To Blue Ground, E. Lincoln, 1924, 8 x 7 In. 1955.00
Vase, Tulips, Pink, Green Leaves, Harriet Wilcox, 1905, 10 3/8 In. 7750.00
Vase, Tulips, Red, Pale Green Leaves, Black Ground, Diers, 1900, 10 In. 6250.00
Vase, Tulips, Stylized, Turquoise Matte Crystalline Glaze, 1913, 6 5/8 In. 180.00
Vase, Tulips, White, Blue, Ivory Ground, Sara Sax, 1906, 8 1/2 In. 3220.00
Vase, Turquoise High Glaze, 1920, 15 In. 275.00
Vase, Turquoise Mottled Glaze, 1937, 6 1/2 In. 375.00
Vase, Turquoise, No. 826D, Bell Shape, 1918, 6 1/2 In. 138.00
Vase, Turquoise, No. 6767, 1943, 6 1/8 In. 115.00
Vase, Turtles, Standard Glaze, A.R. Valentien, 1885, 11 In. 865.00
Vase, Venetian Harbor Scene, 4 Large Vessels, Carl Schmidt, 1918, 13 1/8 In. 5500.00
Vase, Violets, Embossed, Blue Crystalline Matte Glaze, 1937, 3 3/4 In. 120.00
Vase, Water Lilies Under Waves, William Hentschel, 1914, 8 1/2 x 4 3/4 In. 1610.00
Vase, Water Lilies, Dark Purple, Pink Ground, Coyne, 1924, 13 In. 4950.00
Vase, Water Lilies, Shaded Pink & Green Ground, Iris Glaze, L. Asbury, 11 1/2 In. 690.00
Vase, Water Lilies, Standard Glaze, Lenore Asbury, 1901, 7 In. 235.00
Vase, Wheat, Molded, Mustard Matte Glaze, 1931, 4 1/2 In. 127.00
Vase, Wild Roses, Blue, Green, Vellum Glaze, Ed Diers, 1914, 8 In. 2070.00
Vase, Wild Roses, Green To Brown Matte Glaze, 1912, 10 1/4 x 5 1/4 In. 1035.00
Vase, Wild Roses, Pale Gold, Charcoal Gray Ground, Zettel, 1903, 6 7/8 In. 1500.00
Vase, Wild Roses, Standard Glaze, Anna M. Valentien, 1890, 4 1/4 In. 550.00
Vase, Wild Roses, Stylized, Green, Gunmetal Ground, Hurley, 1925, 16 In. 2990.00
Vase, Wild Roses, Stylized, Matte Glaze, Arts & Crafts, E. Lincoln, 1920, 5 3/4 In. 750.00
Vase, Wisteria, Blue, Green, Ed Diers, 1912, 9 In. 1265.00
Vase, Wisteria, Butterflies, Lenore Asbury, 1920, 14 1/8 In. 23000.00
Vase, Wisteria, Sheer Turquoise Glaze, c.1947, 13 3/4 x 6 In. 345.00
Vase, Wisteria, Stylized, Cascading From Shoulder, Rothenbusch, 1919, 12 In. 700.00
Vase, Wisteria, Vellum, E.T. Hurley, 1928, 8 In. 2070.00

Vase, Yellow Crystalline Glaze, 1934, 3 1/2 In. 130.00
Vase, Yellow Matte Glaze, 3-Footed, 31925, 3 1/4 In. 110.00
Vase, Z Line, Green Matte Glaze, c.1903, 9 1/4 x 3 1/4 In. 175.00
Wall Pocket, Child's Face, Blue, Green Matte, 2 1/2 In. 375.00
Wall Pocket, Cicada, Matte Blue Glaze, 1922, 9 In. 776.00
Wall Pocket, Mottled Green Glaze, 2 Handles, 7 In. 450.00
Wall Pocket, Tan High Glaze, Clotilda Zanetta, 1947, 8 1/2 In. 170.00

RORSTRAND was established near Stockholm, Sweden, in 1726. By the nineteenth century they were making English-style earthenware, bone china, porcelain, ironstone china, and majolica. The company is still working. The three crown mark has been used since 1884.

Teapot, Brown, Celadon Flambe Crystalline Glaze, Gunnar Nylund, 8 1/2 x 7 In. 345.00
Vase, Applied Protruding Petals, Pink, Ivory, Green High Glaze, Marked, 3 1/2 In. 690.00
Vase, Black, Brown Glaze, Carl Harry Stalhane, 1940, 10 In., Pair 920.00
Vase, Blue, Gray, White Glaze, Gunnar Nylund, 1950, 3 1/2 In. 185.00
Vase, Blue, Purple Matte Glaze, Gunnar Nylund, 7 1/2 In. 431.00
Vase, Entwined Branches Terminating With Clusters Of Leaves, Ivory, 18 In. 5290.00
Vase, Floral Top, Pale Blue, Axel Waldmar Lindstrom, 1900, 16 In. 5400.00
Vase, Gray, Brown, Ivory Matte Glaze, Carved Ribs, Incised Mark, 6 1/2 In. 230.00
Vase, Ivory, Green, Blue Crystalline Glaze, Gunnar Nylund, 7 In. 127.00
Vase, Molded Flowers, Pastel Glaze, Mela Anderberg, 10 1/8 In., 3 Piece 1410.00
Vase, Yellow, Blue, Black, Brown Glaze, Carl Harry Stalhane, 1940, 3 In. 185.00

ROSALINE, see Steuben category.

ROSE BOWLS were popular during the 1880s. Rose petals were kept in the open bowl to add fragrance to a room, a popular idea in a time of limited personal hygiene. The glass bowls were made with crimped tops, which kept the petals inside. Many types of Victorian art glass were made into rose bowls.

Cranberry Spatter, Over White, Mica Flecks, 5 1/2 In. 35.00
Inverted Thumbprint, Vaseline, Shaded Rose Top, Hobbs & Brockunier, 4 In. 140.00
Mica Branches, Rose Ground, White Interior, Victorian, 4 1/2 x 6 In. 77.00
White Satin, Shaded Blue Top, Crimped Rim, Pontil, 4 1/2 In. 30.00
White Satin, Shaded Yellow Top, Enameled Pansies, Crimped Rim, 3 1/2 In. 70.00
White Satin, Shaded Yellow, Enameled Apple Blossom Branches, Pontil, 6 In. 200.00
Yellow Satin Ribs, Over White, Tricornered Rim, 3 1/8 In. 130.00

ROSE CANTON china is similar to Rose Mandarin and Rose Medallion, except no people or birds are pictured in the decoration. It was made in China during the nineteenth and twentieth centuries in greens, pinks, and other colors.

Condiment Set, Tray, Square, Footed, 10 1/2 In., 7 Piece 220.00
Dish, Vegetable, Sepia, Square, Cover, Gilt, Peach Finial, 9 1/2 In. 1725.00
Tray, Diamond Shape, Raised Flared Sides, 10 1/2 In. 352.00

ROSE MANDARIN china is similar to Rose Canton and Rose Medallion. If the panels in the design picture only people and not birds, it is called Rose Mandarin.

Bowl, Cover, 2 Handles, Early 19th Century, 6 In. 200.00
Bowl, Fruit, Footed, Oval, 19th Century, 3 7/8 x 15 1/4 x 11 3/8 In. 1092.00
Bowl, Mandarin Scenes Interior & Exterior, 9 1/4 In. 105.00
Bowl, Mandarin Scenes, Rainbow Sides, 3 x 8 3/4 In. 250.00
Bowl, Mandarin Scenes, Reticulated, Orange Peel Glaze, 9 x 10 1/4 In. 440.00
Jardiniere, Polychrome Design, Interior Carp, Signed, 24 x 16 In. 247.00
Mug, Mandarin Scene, Gilt Rim, Intertwined Handle With Leaves, 4 5/8 In. 137.00
Platter, Mandarin Scenes, Gold In Hair, 13 5/8 x 10 1/2 In. 825.00
Platter, Oval, 19th Century, 11 3/4 x 14 1/2 In. 977.00
Platter, Oval, 19th Century, 14 3/4 x 17 1/4 In. 1610.00
Punch Bowl, Basket Of Flowers On Interior, 4 3/4 x 11 In. 588.00
Teapot, 18th Century, 6 1/2 In. 1035.00

Vase, Turquoise, Lamp Mounted, 1780, 12 In., Pair 2160.00
Warming Dish, Round, 19th Century, 10 7/8 In., Pair 805.00

ROSE MEDALLION china was made in China during the nineteenth and
twentieth centuries. It is a distinctive design with four or more panels
of decoration around a central medallion that includes a bird or a
peony. The panels show birds and people. The background is a design
of tree peonies and leaves. Pieces are colored in greens, pinks, and
other colors. It is similar to Rose Canton and Rose Mandarin.

Bowl, 19th Century, 5 7/8 x 14 1/8 In. 1380.00
Bowl, Allover Figures, Green, Orange & Pink, 11 1/2 In. 2415.00
Bowl, Alternating Figural, Bird Reserves, c.1840, 10 In. 920.00
Bowl, Figural Butterfly, Panels, Up-Swept Rim, c.1860, 10 In. 308.00
Bowl, Panels, Bronze Dore Foot, Bronze Handles, 9 1/2 x 10 1/2 In., Pair 1380.00
Bowl, Vegetable, Cover, Pomegranate Finial, 11 1/2 In. 440.00
Bowl, Vegetable, Gilded, Pomegranate Finial, Flared Rim, 10 1/4 In. 28.00
Charger, 13 In. 55.00
Charger, Central Scene, Actors Performing, 19th Century, 15 In. 690.00
Charger, Landscape Panel, Conforming Wood Stand, 23 7/8 In. 200.00
Charger, Mandarin Scenes, 4 Panels, Figures, Birds, Flowers, 12 In. 195.00
Charger, Scenic Panels, Floral Wide Rim, c.1920, 12 In. 275.00
Dish, Mandarin Center, Bird, Butterfly, Flower, c.1830, 8 In. 105.00
Gravy Boat, 19th Century, 8 In. 265.00
Jardiniere, Figural Panels, Hexagonal, 8 In. 518.00
Pitcher, Domestic Scenes, Famille Rose Enamel, Reserves, c.1880, 13 In. 1725.00
Plate Set, Alternating Panels, Central Reserve, Bird, c.1840, 8 1/2 In. 259.00
Platter, Alternating Figural Panels In Garden, Gilt Rim, c.1840, 8 1/2 In. 1120.00
Platter, Enameled Court Figures, Birds, Butterflies, Flowers On Rim, 16 1/2 In. 1150.00
Platter, Flora, Fauna & Court Scenes, Cavetto & Broadwell, Oval, 17 x 15 In. 600.00
Platter, Mandarin Scenes, Birds & Flowers, Orange Peel Glaze, 15 1/8 In. 330.00
Platter, Orange Peel Glaze, Panels, 14 3/4 x 11 3/4 In. 140.00
Platter, Oval, 8 x 11 In. 140.00
Platter, Oval, 11 In. 308.00
Platter, Oval, 13 x 16 In. 495.00
Platter, Oval, 14 3/4 In. 195.00
Platter, Oval, 19th Century, 18 In. 865.00
Platter, Women & Gentlemen, Gilded Rim, 1830s, 16 3/16 In. 1440.00
Punch Bowl, Bronze Mounted, Handles, 4 1/2 x 16 1/2 In. 616.00
Punch Bowl, Court Scenes, Birds, 20th Century, 16 In. 1150.00
Punch Bowl, Daoguang Period, 6 1/8 x 14 7/8 In. 1265.00
Punch Bowl, Domestic Scene, Garden Panels, Carved Wood Stand, 15 1/2 In. 860.00
Punch Bowl, Domestic Scenes, Flower, Panels, Late 19th Century, 5 x 13 In. 635.00
Punch Bowl, Late 19th Century, 14 3/4 In. 575.00
Razor Box, Cover, Rectangular 865.00
Serving Dish, Cover, 9 In. 305.00
Serving Dish, Cover, Flowers, Birds, Scalloped Rim, Fruit Finial, 8 x 6 x 3 In. 165.00
Soap Dish, Lid, Knobbed, Removable Pierced Liner, 3 x 6 7/8 In., 3 Piece 230.00
Tazza, 8 1/2 x 4 In. 440.00
Tea Set, Court Scenes, Flora & Fauna, Teapot, 8 3/4 In., 17 Piece 520.00
Tea Set, Oval Carrying Basket, 19th Century, 6 Piece 259.00
Tea Set, Pear Shape, Bamboo Handles, 6 1/2 In., 3 Piece 358.00
Teapot, Sugar, Early 20th Century, 4 1/4 In. 160.00
Teapot, Twisted Ribbed Body, Handle, 19th Century, 5 In. 690.00
Tray, Square, Flared Sides 210.00
Tureen, Undertray, Bull's Head Cover, 19th Century, 13 x 17 In. 1380.00
Umbrella Stand, Court & Garden Scenes, 27 In. 3700.00
Umbrella Stand, Cylindrical, 24 In. 3335.00
Umbrella Stand, Flowers & Court Scene Reserves, Cylindrical, 23 In. 2485.00
Urn, Birds & Flowers, Panels, Center Figures, c.1860, 15 1/2 In. 620.00
Urn, Cover, Ormolu Mounted, 19th Century, 25 In., Pair 6325.00
Urn, Figures, Birds, Butterflies & Flower Panels, c.1860, 23 3/4 In. 615.00
Vase, Baluster, Salamanders, Foo Dog Handles, 12 In. 330.00

Vase, Bulbous, Tall Tapered Neck, Court Scenes, 13 In., Pair 805.00
Vase, Butterfly, 15 1/2 In. 635.00
Vase, Dragons, Court Life, Foo Dog Handles, Late 19th Century, 24 In. 4370.00
Vase, Dragons, Gilt Foo Dog Handles, Late 19th Century, 24 1/2 In., Pair 1440.00
Vase, Familial Scenes, Butterfly & Flowers, 5 3/4 In. 130.00
Vase, Figure & Bird Panels, Foo Dogs, 11 3/4 In. 250.00
Vase, Flower Sprays, Butterflies, Lamp Mounted, 1800s, 15 1/2 In. 1440.00
Vase, Flowers, 19th Century, 12 3/4 In. 520.00
Vase, Garden Scene, Applied Ho Bird Handles & Dragons, 13 In. 575.00
Vase, Reserves, Butterfly, Hu Shape, c.1840, 15 In. 1495.00
Vase, Scenic Panels, Lion Handles, Late 19th Century, 13 3/4 In. 225.00
Vase, Temple, Gilt Foo Dogs, Salamanders, Baluster Shape, Scalloped Rim, 33 In. 2200.00
Washbowl, People, Birds, Flowers, Butterflies, Bouquets, 5 x 16 1/2 In. 690.00
Water Bottle, Covered, Chinese, 19th Century, 15 1/2 In. 518.00

ROSE O'NEILL, see Kewpie category.

ROSENTHAL porcelain was made at the factory established in Selb, Bavaria, in 1880. The factory is still making fine-quality tablewares and figurines. A series of Christmas plates was made from 1910. Other limited edition plates have been made since 1971.

MARKE
Rosenthal

Bowl, Cobalt Blue, Band Of Silver Stylized Animals, Argenta, 20th Century 635.00
Bust, Faun, Ferdinand Liebermann, c.1930, 16 In. 1380.00
Bust, Satyr Holding Reed Pipes, Surprise Look, Bug On Arm, Gray, Black, White, 16 In. . 3105.00
Dinner Service, Cobalt Blue & Gilt, 48 Piece 1840.00
Figurine, Poodle, Gray, Prof. Karner, 7 1/2 In. 155.00
Figurine, Scalares, Carp Swimming In Seaweed, Signed, c.1937, 15 3/4 In. 315.00
Plaque, Bowl Of Tropical Fruit, Glossy Polychrome Glazes, 13 1/4 x 19 In. 290.00
Teapot, Violet Flowers, Gilt Trim, c.1891-1904, 9 1/2 x 9 In. 145.00
Vase, Applied Copper & Gold, Costumed Woman, 2 Cats On Elephant, 1950, 17 1/2 In. . . 290.00
Vase, Cylinder, Painted, Blue Ground, White, Gold Flower, Feather Leaf, 12 x 3 1/2 In. . . 90.00
Vase, Jean Cocteau, 1952, 8 In. 345.00
Vase, White, Organic Shape, Beaded Rings Around Offset Neck, 5 In. 375.00

ROSEVILLE Pottery Company was organized in Roseville, Ohio, in 1890. Another plant was opened in Zanesville, Ohio, in 1898. Many types of pottery were made until 1954. Early wares include Sgraffito, Olympic, and Rozane. Later lines were often made with molded decorations, especially flowers and fruit. Most pieces are marked *Roseville*. Many reproductions made in China have been offered for sale the past few years.

Roseville
U.S.A.

Apple Blossom, Basket, Blue, Handle, 8 In. 285.00
Apple Blossom, Basket, Blue, Handle, 10 In. . . . . .173.00 to 285.00
Apple Blossom, Basket, Green, 7 3/8 In. 154.00
Apple Blossom, Basket, Hanging, Blue, 8 In. 190.00
Apple Blossom, Basket, Hanging, Green, 8 In. 220.00
Apple Blossom, Basket, Hanging, Pink, 8 In. . . . . .115.00 to 245.00
Apple Blossom, Basket, Pink, 8 In. 150.00
Apple Blossom, Bookends, Green, Pair 198.00
Apple Blossom, Bookends, Pink, Pair 260.00
Apple Blossom, Bowl, Green, Flat Handles, Green, 6 In. 145.00
Apple Blossom, Candlestick, Green, 2 In. 35.00
Apple Blossom, Candlestick, Pink, 2 In. 120.00
Apple Blossom, Console Set, Bowl, 8 In., Candlestick, 2 In., 3 Piece 500.00
Apple Blossom, Console, Green, 14 In. 200.00
Apple Blossom, Ewer, Green, 8 In. 110.00
Apple Blossom, Ewer, Pink, Oval, 8 In. 145.00
Apple Blossom, Jardiniere, Pedestal, Relief, Rose, 11 x 24 In. 635.00
Apple Blossom, Vase, Blue, Squat, Cylindrical Neck, 2 Handles, 6 In. 200.00
Apple Blossom, Vase, Blue, Tapered Cylindrical Body, Flared Foot, 7 In. 130.00
Apple Blossom, Vase, Bud, Green, Flared Foot, 2 Base Handles, Trumpet Shape, 7 In. . . . 306.00
Apple Blossom, Vase, Cornucopia, Green, 6 In., Pair 165.00
Apple Blossom, Vase, Cornucopia, Pink, 6 In. 160.00

Apple Blossom, Vase, Floor, Blue, Oval, 18 In. 355.00
Apple Blossom, Vase, Green, Asymmetrical Rim, Handles, 7 In. 135.00
Apple Blossom, Vase, Green, Squat Base, 10 In. 200.00
Apple Blossom, Vase, Green, Wide Flared Rim & Foot, Oval, 8 In. 185.00
Apple Blossom, Vase, Pink, 2 Handles, Flared Rim, 8 In. 138.00
Apple Blossom, Vase, Pink, Cylindrical, Base Handles, Pink, 10 In. 185.00
Apple Blossom, Wall Pocket, Green, Conical, Handle, 8 In. 225.00
Apple Blossom, Window Box, Blue, 2 Handles, 9 In. 110.00
Apple Blossom, Window Box, Pink, 2 Handles, 2 1/2 x 10 1/2 In. 155.00
Aztec, Pitcher, Blue, 5 1/2 x 7 In. 690.00
Aztec, Vase, Blue, 8 In. 200.00
Baneda, Bowl, Pink, 6 Sides, 3 1/4 x 11 In. 430.00
Baneda, Candlestick, Pink, 5 In., Pair 545.00
Baneda, Console, Green, 12 In. 750.00
Baneda, Jardiniere, Green, 6 In. 750.00
Baneda, Jardiniere, Pink, 12 1/4 x 9 3/4 In. 1610.00
Baneda, Jardiniere, Pink, 9 1/4 x 7 3/4 In. 1035.00
Baneda, Vase, Green, 12 1/4 x 7 1/4 In. 1380.00
Baneda, Vase, Green, 15 In. 3738.00
Baneda, Vase, Green, 5 1/2 x 6 In. 920.00
Baneda, Vase, Green, 6 In. 185.00
Baneda, Vase, Green, 7 In. . . . . .633.00 to 978.00
Baneda, Vase, Green, Collared Rim, 9 In. 1840.00
Baneda, Vase, Green, Globular, 6 1/4 x 6 In. 660.00
Baneda, Vase, Green, Incised Blue Panel, Yellow Flowers, 6 1/4 x 7 1/4 In. 825.00
Baneda, Vase, Pink, 5 1/2 x 4 In. 259.00
Baneda, Vase, Pink, 6 In. 345.00
Baneda, Vase, Pink, Handles, Pink Glaze, Spattered White, 7 1/4 x 7 In. 300.00
Baneda, Vase, Pink, Panel, Blue, Deep Green Leaves, 9 x 5 In. 990.00
Baneda, Vase, Pink, Panel, Curved Deep Green Leaves, Angular Handles, 7 1/4 In. 660.00
Bittersweet, Bookends, Green, Pair 265.00
Bittersweet, Vase, Gray, 10 In. 240.00
Bittersweet, Vase, Yellow, 7 In. 175.00
Blackberry, Basket, 7 In. 1265.00
Blackberry, Bowl, Faceted, 3 1/2 x 10 In. 430.00
Blackberry, Jardiniere, Broad Upper Body, Looped Handles, 6 x 6 In. . . . . .460.00 to 550.00
Blackberry, Vase, 2 Handles, 8 In. . . . . .770.00 to 863.00
Blackberry, Vase, 8 In. 748.00
Blackberry, Vase, Bulbous Berries In Midsection, 5 In. . . . . .316.00 to 440.00
Blackberry, Vase, Bulbous Blackberries, Carved Leaves, Brown, Green, 4 In. 440.00
Blackberry, Vase, Squat, Handles, 4 In. 430.00
Blackberry, Wall Pocket, Cascading Blackberries, Brown, Green Leaves, 7 x 6 In. 660.00
Bleeding Heart, Basket, Green, 8 In. 260.00
Bleeding Heart, Basket, Pink, 8 In. 240.00
Bleeding Heart, Bookends, Blue, Pair 207.00
Bleeding Heart, Cornucopia, Pink, 6 In. 70.00
Bleeding Heart, Jardiniere, Handles, 3 In. 60.00
Bleeding Heart, Vase, Blue, 12 In. . . . . .196.00 to 345.00
Bleeding Heart, Vase, Pink, 6 In. 90.00
Burmese, Candlestick, Black Matte Glaze, 8 In., Pair 160.00
Burmese, Wall Pocket, Green, 7 7/8 In. 140.00
Bushberry, Basket, Blue, 8 In. 230.00
Bushberry, Basket, Blue, 10 In. 288.00
Bushberry, Basket, Brown, 10 In. 290.00
Bushberry, Ewer, c.1948, 15 In. 460.00
Bushberry, Jardiniere, c.1940, 3 x 5 In. 105.00
Bushberry, Vase, c.1940, 8 In. 145.00
Bushberry, Vase, Green, Handles, 12 In. 345.00
Carnelian, Jardiniere, Pedestal, Brown Over White Glaze, Green Patches, 34 In. 1380.00
Carnelian I, Bowl, Green, With Flower Frog, 8 In. 90.00
Carnelian I, Candlestick, Blue, 2 In., Pair 58.00
Carnelian I, Floor Vase, Dark Blue Drip Over Light Blue, 18 In. 290.00
Carnelian I, Vase, Green Drip Over Peach Matte Glaze, 15 In. 805.00

Carnelian I, Wall Pocket, Dark Blue Drip Over Light Blue, 8 In. 210.00
Carnelian II, Urn, Teal & Mauve, 10 x 6 1/2 In. 316.00
Carnelian II, Vase, Blue, Green Mottled Glaze, 15 In. 1095.00
Carnelian II, Vase, Magenta Glaze, Tan Swirls, Gourd Shape, 7 x 5 In. 300.00
Carnelian II, Vase, Mauve, Brown, Ocher, 9 In. 430.00
Carnelian II, Vase, Rose, Green, Orange Matte Glaze, 9 In. 310.00
Cherry Blossom, Jardiniere, Brown, Handles, 5 x 7 In. . . . . .259.00 to 265.00
Cherry Blossom, Vase, Brown, 7 In. 196.00
Cherry Blossom, Vase, Brown, 8 In. 518.00
Cherry Blossom, Vase, Brown, Handles, 5 In. 230.00
Cherry Blossom, Vase, Pink, Blue Glaze, Brown Branches, 7 In. 770.00
Cherry Blossom, Vase, Pink, Dark Green Leaves, Brown Branches, 4 x 5 In. 385.00
Chloron, Lamp, Green Matte Glaze, Looped Handles, 8 1/2 x 4 3/4 In. 360.00
Chloron, Vase, Molded Design, Green Matte Glaze, 8 In. 265.00
Chloron, Vase, Scalloped Rim, 5 In. 275.00
Clematis, Basket, Brown, 7 In. 115.00
Clematis, Bowl, Green, 10 In. 2399.00
Clematis, Candlestick, Green, 5 In., Pair 46.00
Clematis, Cornucopia, Blue, 6 In. 115.00
Clematis, Ewer, Blue, Elongated Spout, 15 In. 400.00
Clematis, Vase, Blue, 5 In. 46.00
Clematis, Vase, Blue, 8 In. 58.00
Clematis, Vase, Blue, 12 In. 374.00
Clematis, Vase, Brown, 8 In. 150.00
Clematis, Vase, Bulbous, Brown, 15 In. 259.00
Clematis, Vase, Green, 14 In. 265.00
Clematis, Vase, Handles, 6 In. 69.00
Clemena, Vase, Tan, Handles, 9 In. 90.00
Columbine, Basket, Blue, 12 In. 315.00
Columbine, Basket, Brown, 7 In. 290.00
Columbine, Basket, Hanging, Blue, 8 In. 150.00
Columbine, Basket, Hanging, Blue, Original Chain, 4 5/8 x 8 1/2 In. 175.00
Columbine, Basket, Pink, 10 In. 575.00
Columbine, Bookends, Planter, Blue, 5 In., Pair 259.00
Columbine, Bookends, Planter, Brown, 5 In. 80.00
Columbine, Vase, Brown, 10 In. 259.00
Columbine, Vase, Pink, Handles, 8 In. 45.00
Corinthian, Bowl, 7 1/2 In. 69.00
Corinthian, Vase, 6 1/2 In. 69.00
Corinthian, Vase, Footed, 7 3/8 In. 175.00
Corinthian, Wall Pocket, 9 1/2 In. 210.00
Cosmos, Vase, Blue, Handles, 5 3/8 In. 90.00
Cosmos, Wall Pocket, Green, 8 In. 460.00
Cosmos, Window Box, Blue, 3 3/4 x 10 1/2 In. 175.00
Creamware, Stein, Knights Of Pythias, 5 In. 80.00
Creamware, Stein, Masonic Temple, Chicago, 4 In. 35.00
Cremona, Vase, Green, Handles, 10 1/2 x 5 3/4 In. 259.00
Dahlrose, Basket, Hanging, Original Chain, 7 1/2 In. 235.00
Dahlrose, Bowl, Flared Rim, 10 In. 275.00
Dahlrose, Bowl, Squat Body, Flared Rim, Angular Handles, 8 In. 210.00
Dahlrose, Candlestick, Angular Handles, 3 In., Pair 135.00
Dahlrose, Vase, 8 In. 310.00
Dahlrose, Vase, Bud, Triple, 6 In. 256.00
Dahlrose, Vase, Footed, Flared Rim, Trumpet Shape, Low Arched Handles, 8 In. 495.00
Dahlrose, Vase, Handles, 12 In. 400.00
Dahlrose, Vase, Pedestal Base, Flared Rim & Foot, Tapered Cylindrical Shape, 16 In. 605.00
Dahlrose, Vase, Pillow, 1924-1928, 6 1/4 x 8 3/8 In. 149.00
Dahlrose, Wall Pocket, Angular Handles, 8 x 6 3/4 In. 330.00
Dahlrose, Wall Pocket, Brown, 10 In. 575.00
Dahlrose, Wall Pocket, Flared Base, Buttress Sides, 8 In. 235.00
Dahlrose, Wall Pocket, Molded Rim, Bullet Shape Body, Angular Handles, 10 In. 315.00
Dawn, Bookends, Green, 5 1/4 x 4 1/4 x 4 1/2 In., Pair 489.00
Dawn, Bookends, Pink, 5 1/4 x 4 1/2 x 4 1/2 In., Pair 575.00

Dawn, Jardiniere, Green, Handles, 6 In. 316.00
Dawn, Vase, Green, 8 In. 105.00
Dawn, Vase, Green, 11 In. 489.00
Dawn, Vase, Pink, 6 In., Pair 405.00
Della Robbia, Dish, Round, Ruth Bare, c.1900, 13 1/2 In. 720.00
Della Robbia, Plaque, Alfred The Great, Harold Steward Rathbone, 1900, 27 x 16 1/2 In. . . 2160.00
Della Robbia, Vase, 2 Handles, Ruth Bare, c.1900, 15 In. 1020.00
Della Robbia, Vase, Stylized White Poppies, Frederick Hurten Rhead, 9 In. 4900.00
Dogwood I, Jardiniere, Tapered Foot, 7 In. 175.00
Dogwood I, Vase, Flared Collar, 8 1/4 In. 150.00
Dogwood I, Vase, Tapered Foot, 9 1/2 In. 290.00
Dogwood I, Wall Pocket, 9 1/2 In. 290.00
Dogwood II, Basket, 5 1/2 In. 160.00
Dogwood II, Jardiniere, 10 x 11 1/2 In. 175.00
Dogwood II, Jardiniere, Pedestal, 30 In. 575.00
Donatello, Ashtray, Columnar Sign, 2 5/8 In. 69.00
Donatello, Basket, Hanging, 5 x 7 1/2 In. 145.00
Donatello, Compote, 4 5/8 In. 58.00
Donatello, Jardiniere, 9 In. 175.00
Donatello, Jardiniere, 10 In. 230.00
Donatello, Jardiniere, Pedestal, 33 In. ....720.00 to 750.00
Donatello, Vase, 14 1/2 In. 253.00
Donatello, Vase, Bell Shape Base, 10 In. 105.00
Donatello, Vase, Double Bud, 4 3/8 In. 69.00
Donatello, Wall Pocket, 12 In. 185.00
Earlam, Umbrella Stand, Flared, 20 In. 5750.00
Earlam, Window Box, Tan Glaze, 15 x 5 In. 520.00
Egypto, Bowl, 3 3/4 x 8 1/2 In. 375.00
Egypto, Ewer, Crimped, Green Crystalline Glaze, 6 1/2 x 7 1/4 In. ....520.00 to 635.00
Egypto, Pitcher, Handle, 5 In. 575.00
Falline, Vase, Blue, Embossed Pea Pod Design, Ivory Accents, Handles, 12 1/2 x 7 In. ... 2090.00
Falline, Vase, Brown, Handles, 6 1/2 In. 635.00
Falline, Vase, Brown, Handles, 9 In. 978.00
Falline, Vase, Green, Blue, Ovoid, Bulbous Neck, Collared Rim, 15 1/2 In. .... *Illus* 4025.00
Ferella, Vase, Beehive Shape, Red, 6 x 7 In. 1265.00
Ferella, Vase, Brown, 5 x 6 3/4 In. ....575.00 to 805.00
Ferella, Vase, Brown, 6 x 4 1/2 In. 430.00
Ferella, Vase, Brown, 10 1/4 x 6 In. 1095.00
Ferella, Vase, Bud, Red, 6 In. 750.00
Ferella, Vase, Dark Rose, 5 In. 235.00
Ferella, Vase, Red, 5 1/4 x 4 1/4 In. 920.00
Ferella, Vase, Red, 8 x 7 1/2 In. 920.00
Florane II, Vase, Green, Tan Interior, 7 In. 115.00
Florane II, Vase, Green, Tan Interior, 8 In. 175.00
Florentine I, Basket, Hanging, Original Chain, 9 In. 115.00
Florentine I, Candlestick, 10 In., Pair 290.00
Florentine I, Wall Pocket, 9 3/4 In. ....115.00 to 195.00
Foxglove, Bowl, Pink, 4 In. 70.00
Foxglove, Bowl, Pink, 6 In. 127.00
Foxglove, Conch Shell, Pink, 6 In. 80.00
Foxglove, Console, Pink, 14 In. 140.00
Foxglove, Ewer, Pink, 6 1/2 In. 207.00
Foxglove, Jardiniere, Pink, 3 In. 23.00
Foxglove, Tray, Pink, 10 In. 70.00
Foxglove, Vase, Bulbous, Green, 12 In. 230.00
Foxglove, Vase, Pink, 4 1/2 In. 184.00
Foxglove, Vase, Pink, 5 In. 60.00
Foxglove, Vase, Pink, 6 In. 90.00
Foxglove, Vase, Pink, 7 In. 105.00
Foxglove, Vase, Pink, 8 In. ....60.00 to 138.00
Foxglove, Vase, Pink, 10 In. 240.00
Foxglove, Vase, Pink, 16 In. 265.00
Foxglove, Wall Pocket, Blue, 8 In. 345.00

Roseville, Falline, Vase, Green,
Blue, Ovoid, Bulbous Neck,
Collared Rim, 15 1/2 In.

Roseville, Futura, Vase, Orange,
Brown, Blue Green, Faceted
Top, Handles, 14 1/2 In.

Roseville, Jonquil, Strawberry Pot,
Attached Underplate,
6 1/4 In.

Foxglove, Wall Pocket, Pink, 8 In.	405.00
Freesia, Basket, Blue, 7 In.	489.00
Freesia, Basket, Blue, 10 In.	219.00
Freesia, Basket, Green, 8 In.	219.00
Freesia, Bowl, Green, 6 In.	90.00
Freesia, Bowl, Green, Handles, 11 In.	35.00
Freesia, Candlestick, Green, 2 In., Pair	69.00
Freesia, Console, Green, 12 In.	58.00
Freesia, Ewer, Brown, 6 In.	50.00
Freesia, Ewer, Green, 6 In.	50.00
Freesia, Flowerpot, Saucer, Green, 8 In.	185.00
Freesia, Vase, Brown, Flared, 16 x 10 In.	410.00
Freesia, Vase, Green, 6 In.	115.00
Freesia, Vase, Green, 8 In.	115.00 to 160.00
Freesia, Vase, Handles, 6 In.	90.00
Freesia, Vase, Purple, Green, Bulbous, Low Handles, c.1945, 7 3/8 In.	115.00
Freesia, Wall Pocket, Brown, 8 In.	175.00
Fuchsia, Bowl, Brown, Green Leaves Along Rim, 4 In.	165.00
Fuchsia, Bowl, Brown, Handles, 5 In.	58.00
Fuchsia, Bowl, Green, Flared, Handles, 6 1/2 In.	144.00
Fuchsia, Bowl, Green, Handles, 4 In.	105.00
Fuchsia, Bowl, Handles, 12 In.	280.00
Fuchsia, Flower Frog, Brown, 4 3/4 In.	60.00
Fuchsia, Jardiniere, Blue, 3 In.	150.00
Fuchsia, Jardiniere, Brown, 3 In.	60.00
Fuchsia, Jardiniere, Brown, 6 3/4 x 9 1/2 In.	200.00
Fuchsia, Vase, Blue, 8 In.	495.00
Fuchsia, Vase, Blue, 15 In.	1695.00
Fuchsia, Vase, Blue, Handles, 15 In.	460.00
Fuchsia, Vase, Blue, Pink Glaze, White Stamen, Green Leaves, 7 x 5 In.	330.00
Fuchsia, Vase, Blue, Pink, White Stamen, 6 x 4 In.	250.00
Fuchsia, Vase, Brown, 5 In.	138.00
Fuchsia, Vase, Brown, Handles, 7 In.	115.00
Fuchsia, Wall Pocket, Brown, 8 In.	375.00
Fujiyama, Vase, Stylized Flowers, Leaves, 10 x 3 In.	633.00
Futura, Bowl, Handles, 7 In.	235.00
Futura, Jardiniere, Brown, Handles, 6 In.	255.00
Futura, Jardiniere, Spade Shape Leaves, 7 x 10 1/2 In.	489.00
Futura, Vase, Blue & Green, Stepped Design, Terra-Cotta, Cone Shape, c.1928, 8 In.	575.00
Futura, Vase, Blue Geometric Design, 3 Sides, 9 1/4 In.	748.00
Futura, Vase, Green & Blue, Green Ground, Geometric, Tapered, Label, c.1928, 6 In.	520.00
Futura, Vase, Green, Balloon Shape, 8 1/2 In.	805.00 to 1265.00
Futura, Vase, Green, Blue Matte Glaze, 4 Sides, 10 In.	750.00

Futura, Vase, Green, Multicolored, 12 In. 920.00
Futura, Vase, Green, Tan Matte Glaze, Handles, 9 In. 1095.00
Futura, Vase, Orange & Blue, 4 Sides, 8 1/4 In. 750.00
Futura, Vase, Orange, Brown, Blue Green, Faceted Top, Handles, 14 1/2 In. .... *Illus* 4312.00
Futura, Vase, Pillow, Blue, 5 1/4 x 6 In. 430.00
Futura, Vase, Pillow, Fir Tree, Orange, Blue, Green, 6 x 9 In. 430.00
Futura, Vase, Pink & Green, Star Shaped, 8 In. 370.00
Futura, Vase, Pink & Tan Matte Glaze, Square Rim, Footed, 1928, 9 In. 650.00
Futura, Vase, Pink, Blue & Green Geometrics At Rim, Twisted, 8 1/4 In. 690.00
Futura, Vase, Pink, Dark Green, 8 In. 430.00
Futura, Vase, Pink, Green, Gray, 8 In. 405.00
Gardenia, Vase, 1940s, 14 In. 300.00
Gardenia, Vase, Brown, Handles, 12 In. 235.00
Gardenia, Vase, Tan, Brown, Handles, 12 In. 80.00
Gardenia, Window Box, Handles, 9 In. 80.00
Holly, Jardiniere, Creamware, c.1940, 6 In. 288.00
Imperial I, Basket, 10 3/4 In. 230.00
Imperial I, Flower Frog, c.1924, 1 1/2 x 3 1/2 In. 25.00
Imperial I, Vase, c.1916, 10 In. 200.00
Imperial I, Vase, Handles, 11 5/8 In. 175.00
Imperial II, Bowl, Orange, 8 1/2 In. 430.00
Imperial II, Bowl, Turquoise Glaze, Yellow Rim, Closed-In Rim, 7 1/4 In. 635.00
Imperial II, Vase, Blue, Green Drip Glaze, 8 1/2 In. 1380.00
Imperial II, Vase, Camel, Brown Matte Glaze, Handles, 8 In. 1095.00
Imperial II, Vase, Embossed, Green & Purple, Collar Rim, 4 1/2 In. 375.00
Imperial II, Vase, Purple & Yellow, Ribbed, 6 1/4 In. 635.00
Iris, Vase, Brown, 10 In. 255.00
Iris, Vase, Bulbous, Brown, 12 In. 316.00
Ixia, Vase, Green, Handles, 7 In., Pair 115.00
Ixia, Vase, Pink, 4 In. 115.00
Jonquil, Crocus Pot, Attached Flower Frog, Underplate, 6 In. 489.00
Jonquil, Jardiniere, 6 3/4 x 7 1/4 In. 290.00
Jonquil, Strawberry Pot, Attached Underplate, 6 1/4 In. .... *Illus* 3105.00
Jonquil, Vase, 3 In. 161.00
Jonquil, Vase, 6 In. 140.00
Jonquil, Vase, Handles, 4 5/8 In. 110.00
Jonquil, Vase, Handles, 7 In. 300.00
Juvenile, Plate, Creamware, 5 Baby Chicks, 7 1/2 In. 58.00
Juvenile, Plate, Rabbit Design, 6 1/2 In. 69.00
Ladyslipper, Vase, Pink Shaded To Blue, Yellow, White Flowers, Experimental, 8 In. *Illus* 4600.00
Laurel, Vase, Green, Collared Rim, 6 In. 345.00
Laurel, Vase, Green, Handles, 6 In. 430.00
Lotus, Vase, Blue, Ivory Vertical Overlapping Leaves, 10 In. 150.00

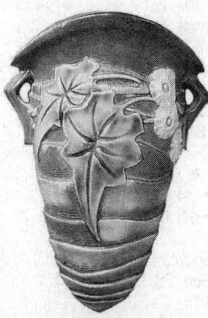

Roseville, Ladyslipper, Vase, Pink Shaded To Blue, Yellow, White Flowers, Experimental, 8 In.

Roseville, Luffa, Wall Pocket, Green, c.1934, 8 1/4 In.

Roseville, Magnolia, Jardiniere, Bulbous, Blue, Handles, 9 In.

Luffa, Bowl, Green, 9 x 4 1/4 In. 185.00
Luffa, Wall Pocket, Brown, 8 1/4 In. 288.00
Luffa, Wall Pocket, Green, c.1934, 8 1/4 In. .... *Illus* 805.00
Magnolia, Basket, Blue, Handles, 8 In. 175.00
Magnolia, Bookends, Blue, 5 1/4 In. 145.00
Magnolia, Cookie Jar, 10 In. 375.00
Magnolia, Jardiniere, Bulbous, Blue, Handles, 9 In. .... *Illus* 4025.00
Magnolia, Pitcher, Blue, Signed, 9 1/2 In. 220.00
Magnolia, Vase, Blue, 16 In. 145.00
Magnolia, Vase, Blue, Flowers, Handles, 14 In. 299.00
Ming Tree, Vase, Green, 14 In. 145.00
Ming Tree, Vase, Green, 15 In. 460.00
Ming Tree, Vase, White, 14 In. 290.00
Ming Tree, Wall Pocket, White, 8 In. 35.00
Monticello, Vase, Aqua, 7 1/2 In. 546.00
Monticello, Vase, Aqua, Handles, 5 1/4 In. 240.00
Morning Glory, Vase, Cream, 4 In. 161.00
Morning Glory, Vase, Cream, Handles, 7 1/4 In. ....185.00 to 196.00
Morning Glory, Vase, Purple, Yellow, Green, Handles, 9 1/2 x 7 1/2 In. 1045.00
Moss, Vase, Black, Blue, Ivory, 8 1/2 x 6 1/2 In. 385.00
Moss, Vase, Brown, Green, Handles, 7 In. 115.00
Moss, Vase, Bulbous, Blue, 12 In. 430.00
Moss, Vase, Pink, 8 In. 290.00
Mostique, Bowl, Yellow Flowers, Enameled, 6 3/4 In. 105.00
Mostique, Jardiniere, Gray, 9 1/2 In. 230.00
Mostique, Jardiniere, Pedestal, Gray, 29 x 13 1/2 In. 920.00
Mostique, Umbrella Stand, Gray, 21 In. 1035.00
Mostique, Vase, Gray, 10 In. 385.00
Normandy, Umbrella Stand, 22 x 10 In. 460.00
Olympic, Vase, Transfer Of Minerva, Hector, Mercury, Marked, 11 3/4 In. 2530.00
Orian, Candlestick, Turquoise, 4 3/4 In., Pair 150.00
Orion, Vase, Raspberry, Green Interior, Handles, 11 x 4 In. 145.00
Panel, Wall Pocket, 3 Black-Eyed Susans, Ivory, Black Stamen, Green, 9 In. 440.00
Peony, Basket, Pink, 8 In. 115.00
Peony, Basket, Pink, Green, 10 In. 210.00
Peony, Basket, Yellow, 4 In. 150.00
Peony, Vase, Pink, Handles, 6 In. 60.00
Persian, Candlestick, Creamware, Stylized Lotus Blossom, 8 3/4 In. 210.00
Pine Cone, Ashtray, Brown, c.1940, 4 1/2 In. 70.00
Pine Cone, Basket, Globular, Blue, Ivory, Branch Handle, 6 In. 385.00
Pine Cone, Bookends, Blue, 4 In. 300.00
Pine Cone, Bowl, Blue, Handles, 6 In. 255.00
Pine Cone, Bowl, Green, Flower Frog, c.1940, 13 x 5 x 3 In. 405.00
Pine Cone, Candelabra, Triple, Brown, 5 1/2 In. 195.00
Pine Cone, Candlestick, Blue, 2 1/2 In. 105.00
Pine Cone, Candlestick, Double, Green, 5 In., Pair 315.00
Pine Cone, Candlestick, Green, 2 5/8 In., Pair 185.00
Pine Cone, Ewer, Blue, Handle, 15 In. 920.00
Pine Cone, Ewer, Brown, Handle, 10 In. 460.00
Pine Cone, Ewer, Green, Twig Handle, 15 5/8 In. 520.00
Pine Cone, Flowerpot, Underplate, Blue, 5 In. 300.00
Pine Cone, Jardiniere, Blue, 3 In. 140.00
Pine Cone, Jardiniere, Blue, 4 1/4 x 6 3/4 In. 200.00
Pine Cone, Jardiniere, Blue, Handles, 4 In. 150.00
Pine Cone, Jardiniere, Blue, Handles, 5 In. 230.00
Pine Cone, Jardiniere, Brown, 4 In. 175.00
Pine Cone, Jardiniere, Brown, Spherical, 4 In. 290.00
Pine Cone, Jardiniere, Pedestal, Green, 28 3/8 In. 1265.00
Pine Cone, Pitcher, Blue, Handle, 7 In. 1210.00
Pine Cone, Planter, Blue, 10 In. 980.00
Pine Cone, Planter, Blue, Side Handle, 5 1/4 x 5 In. 275.00
Pine Cone, Vase, Blue Trumpet, 10 1/2 In. 605.00
Pine Cone, Vase, Blue, 10 In. ....635.00 to 1100.00

Pine Cone, Vase, Blue, 14 In. ....1725.00 to 1840.00
Pine Cone, Vase, Blue, 15 In. 2185.00
Pine Cone, Vase, Blue, 7 1/4 x 3 3/4 In. 605.00
Pine Cone, Vase, Blue, Branch Handles, 6 In. 250.00
Pine Cone, Vase, Blue, Flared, 11 1/2 x 6 In. 750.00
Pine Cone, Vase, Blue, Handles, 7 1/2 In. 290.00
Pine Cone, Vase, Blue, Tapered, 7 x 6 In. 315.00
Pine Cone, Vase, Blue, Trophy Shape, Branch Handles, 10 x 8 In. 715.00
Pine Cone, Vase, Blue, Trumpet, 2 Branch Handles, 10 1/2 In. 605.00
Pine Cone, Vase, Brown, 10 In. 290.00
Pine Cone, Vase, Brown, 18 In. 805.00
Pine Cone, Vase, Brown, 7 1/2 In. 345.00
Pine Cone, Vase, Brown, Angular Branch Handles, 10 1/2 In. 520.00
Pine Cone, Vase, Brown, Footed, 14 In. 690.00
Pine Cone, Vase, Brown, Handles, 7 In. ....105.00 to 230.00
Pine Cone, Vase, Brown, Handles, 14 In. 805.00
Pine Cone, Vase, Brown, Trophy Shape, 6 1/3 In. 165.00
Pine Cone, Vase, Bud, Triple, Brown, 8 1/2 x 4 1/2 In. 430.00
Pine Cone, Vase, Bulbous, Branch Handles, 15 1/2 In. 425.00
Pine Cone, Vase, Green, 6 In. ....160.00 to 185.00
Pine Cone, Vase, Green, 10 In. 265.00
Pine Cone, Vase, Green, 15 In. 1380.00
Pine Cone, Vase, Green, 6 Candleholders, 10 7/8 In. 430.00
Pine Cone, Vase, Pillow, Blue, 12 In. 1840.00
Pine Cone, Vase, Trumpet, Blue, 6 In. 275.00
Pine Cone, Wall Pocket, Green, 9 In. 1035.00
Pine Cone II, Ashtray, Green, 4 3/4 In. 60.00
Pine Cone II, Bookend Planter, Green, 5 3/8 In. 290.00
Pine Cone II, Bowl, Green, Oval, 9 In. 90.00
Pine Cone II, Jardiniere, Pedestal, Green, 28 1/2 In. 1265.00
Pine Cone II, Pitcher, Blue, 7 1/2 In. 920.00
Pine Cone II, Pitcher, Green, Brown, Matte Glaze, Branch Handle, 8 In. 350.00
Pine Cone II, Pitcher, Green, Ice Lip, 9 1/4 In. 490.00
Pine Cone II, Planter, Green, Needle Spray Handle, 7 In. 185.00
Pine Cone II, Tray, Green, Round, Twig Handle, 7 1/2 In. 345.00
Pine Cone II, Vase, Fan, Green, 6 5/8 In. 195.00
Pine Cone II, Vase, Green, 7 In. 210.00
Poppy, Bowl, Gray, 10 In. 104.00
Poppy, Hanging Basket, Gray, Original Chain, 5 1/8 In. 230.00
Poppy, Jardiniere, Handles, 4 In. 69.00
Poppy, Vase, Green, Bulbous, 10 In. 200.00
Poppy, Vase, Pink, 7 In. 175.00
Poppy, Vase, Pink, Handles, 8 In. 80.00
Primrose, Jardiniere, 5 1/2 In. 80.00
Primrose, Vase, Blue, Handles, 8 3/8 In. 150.00
Primrose, Vase, Tan, 9 1/2 In. 127.00
Rosecraft Black, Vase, Handles, 12 In. ....150.00 to 490.00
Rosecraft Panel, Vase, Fan, Brown, 8 1/4 x 5 3/4 In. 575.00
Rosecraft Panel, Vase, Multicolored, 8 In. 265.00
Rosecraft Panel, Vase, Nudes, Handles, 11 1/2 In. 575.00
Rosecraft Panel, Wall Pocket, Brown, 9 1/4 In. 260.00
Rosecraft Panel, Wall Pocket, Nude Figure, Brown, 7 1/4 x 5 In. 550.00
Rosecraft Vintage, Jardiniere, Embossed Grape Cluster, 9 1/4 x 12 In. 460.00
Rosecraft Vintage, Jardiniere, Pedestal, Dark Brown, 30 In. 720.00
Rosecraft Vintage, Vase, Dark Brown, Footed, Embossed Grape Cluster, 7 1/8 In. .. 490.00
Rozane, Ewer, Blackberry Design, Handle, 16 In. 500.00
Rozane, Vase, Carved Fish Design, Multicolored Green Glaze, 10 1/2 In. 2760.00
Rozane, Vase, Painted Flowers, 3-Footed, 7 In. 160.00
Rozane, Vase, Red, Yellow, Carnations, 10 In. 140.00
Rozane Royal, Tankard, Grape, Leaves & Vines, Signed, W. Myers, 10 1/2 In. 375.00
Rozane Royal, Vase, 2 Dogs, Brown High Glaze, Signed, 9 In. 575.00
Rozane Royal, Vase, Blackberry Design, W. Myers, 16 In. 3100.00
Rozane Royal, Vase, Crocus, Signed, 8 7/8 In. 600.00

Rozane Royal, Vase, Dark, Nasturtium Design, Twist Shape, Footed, H. Pillsbury, 8 In. .. 225.00
Rozane Royal, Vase, Dark, Palomino Portrait, Fred Steele, 1905, 14 In. 2500.00
Rozane Royal, Vase, Dark, Red Daisies, 10 In. 140.00
Rozane Royal, Vase, Lily Of The Valley, Corseted, Hester Pillsbury, 10 3/8 In. 115.00
Rozane Royal, Vase, Red Clover Design, Corseted, Minnie Mitchell, 10 3/4 In. 260.00
Rozane Royal, Vase, Red, White Roses, W. Myers, 1905, 14 1/8 In. 3300.00
Savona, Basket, c.1945, 11 1/2 x 12 In. ....258.00 to 290.00
Savona, Wall Pocket, Blue, c.1924-1930, 8 1/4 In. ....*Illus* 635.00
Silhouette, Bowl, Orange 235.00
Silhouette, Vase, Green & White, 7 1/4 In. 345.00
Snowberry, Basket, Brown, Handle, 8 In. ....99.00 to 175.00
Snowberry, Jardiniere, Blue, Pedestal, 8 In. 1300.00
Sunflower, Bowl, Handles, 5 1/4 In. 635.00
Sunflower, Candlestick, 4 1/4 In., Pair 316.00
Sunflower, Jardiniere, Sunflower & Leaf Design, 7 3/4 x 9 In. ....1430.00 to 1650.00
Sunflower, Planter, Hanging, Sunflower Design, Gold Yellow, 5 1/2 In. 1430.00
Sunflower, Vase, 6 x 7 In. 920.00
Sunflower, Vase, 7 1/2 x 4 In. 405.00
Sunflower, Vase, 8 1/2 In. 1495.00
Sunflower, Vase, 10 x 6 In. 2530.00
Sunflower, Vase, Handles, 5 In. 520.00
Sunflower, Vase, Handles, 9 In. 1610.00
Sunflower, Vase, Oval, Handles, c.1930, 5 1/8 In. 550.00
Sunflower, Vase, Yellow Sunflowers, Looped Handles, 6 In. 770.00
Sunflower, Wall Pocket, 2 Yellow Sunflowers In Center, Ocher, Blue, 7 x 6 In. ... 1980.00
Sunflower, Wall Pocket, 8 1/2 In. 1345.00
Teasel, Vase, Aqua, 7 1/4 In. 150.00
Teasel, Vase, Red, 9 In. 80.00
Thorn Apple, Bookends, Blue, 5 1/2 In. ....105.00 to 230.00
Thorn Apple, Wall Pocket, Brown, 8 In. 405.00
Thorn Apple, Wall Pocket, Pink, c.1937, 9 1/4 In. ....*Illus* 575.00
Topeo, Bowl, Red, 3 x 8 In. 115.00
Topeo, Jardiniere, Red, 6 1/2 x 7 In. 260.00
Topeo, Vase, Blue, 6 1/4 x 7 In. 460.00
Topeo, Vase, Blue, 9 1/2 x 5 1/2 In. 750.00
Topeo, Vase, Red, 7 In. 115.00
Topeo, Vase, Red, 8 In. 320.00
Topeo, Vase, Red, 9 1/4 x 6 3/4 In. 290.00
Tourist, Jardiniere, Creamware, 8 In. 2070.00
Tourist, Vase, Creamware, Female Figure, 12 In. 575.00
Tuscany, Vase, Blue, Handles, 9 1/2 x 7 In. 60.00
Utility Ware, Plate, 1915-1930, 12 3/4 In. 35.00
Velmoss, Vase, Pink, Handles, 9 In. 300.00
Velmoss, Wall Pocket, Cast Split Front, 10 7/8 In. 489.00

 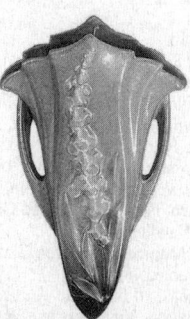 

Roseville, Savona, Wall Pocket, Blue, c.1924-1930, 8 1/4 In.

Roseville, Thorn Apple, Wall Pocket, Pink, c.1937, 9 1/4 In.

Roseville, Wisteria, Vase, Bulbous, Blue, 2 Handles, 15 In.

Velmoss II, Vase, Rose, 5 In. 240.00
Vista, Vase, 14 1/2 x 7 1/2 In. 920.00
Vista, Vase, 15 1/2 In. 635.00
Water Lily, Basket, Hanging, Blue, 5 1/2 x 8 3/4 In. 230.00
Water Lily, Vase, Blue, 9 1/2 In. 207.00
Water Lily, Vase, Blue, Green, 14 In. 400.00
Water Lily, Vase, Blue, Handles, 9 x 3 In. 35.00
White Rose, Basket, Green, 10 In. 316.00
White Rose, Basket, Hanging, Blue, 6 1/2 In. 138.00
White Rose, Basket, Pink, Green, Brown Handle, 6 In. 210.00
White Rose, Bowl, Handles, 9 x 2 1/2 In. 45.00
White Rose, Candlestick, 2 In., Pair 635.00
White Rose, Pitcher, Pink, Green, 7 1/2 In. 150.00
White Rose, Vase, 18 In. 490.00
White Rose, Vase, Blue, Handles, 6 In. 69.00
White Rose, Vase, Blue, Notched Rim, Handles, 7 3/8 In. 127.00
White Rose, Vase, Off-Set Handles In Brown & Green, 7 3/8 In. 127.00
White Rose, Vase, Pillow, Brown, 8 In. 200.00
Wincraft, Ewer, Brown, 8 In. 105.00
Wincraft, Vase, Blue, Yellow, 12 In., Pair 175.00
Windsor, Bowl, Brown, Green, 3 x 10 In. 255.00
Windsor, Console, Brown, 2 3/4 x 12 In. 240.00
Wisteria, Bowl, Brown, Handles, 5 x 6 In. 176.00
Wisteria, Jardiniere, Bulbous, Brown, 5 1/4 x 6 3/4 In. 460.00
Wisteria, Planter, Brown, 4 Sides, 3 1/4 x 12 In. 400.00
Wisteria, Vase, Blue, 4 1/2 x 6 In. 460.00
Wisteria, Vase, Blue, 5 1/8 In. 546.00
Wisteria, Vase, Blue, 8 1/4 x 6 1/4 In. 1495.00
Wisteria, Vase, Blue, 9 x 6 1/2 In. 175.00
Wisteria, Vase, Blue, Closed Rim, 5 1/4 x 6 1/2 In. 518.00
Wisteria, Vase, Blue, Cylindrical, Handles, 10 1/4 x 6 1/4 In. 1380.00
Wisteria, Vase, Blue, Gourd Shape, 7 1/2 x 5 1/2 In. 1095.00
Wisteria, Vase, Blue, Gourd Shape, Handles, 9 1/4 x 7 In. 1725.00
Wisteria, Vase, Blue, Lavender Glaze, Green Leaves, Angular Handles, 4 x 6 In. ... 605.00
Wisteria, Vase, Brown, 6 In. 345.00
Wisteria, Vase, Brown, Bulbous, 7 1/2 x 5 3/4 In. 375.00
Wisteria, Vase, Brown, Handles, 9 1/4 x 5 3/4 In. 635.00
Wisteria, Vase, Bulbous, Blue, 2 Handles, 15 In. .... *Illus* 2588.00
Wisteria, Vase, Tan, 4 In. 345.00
Wisteria, Wall Pocket, Blue, 8 1/2 x 7 In. 1955.00
Woodland, Vase, Flowers, Light Green Leaves, 11 In. 1265.00
Woodland, Vase, Flowers, Signed, 11 In. 690.00
Woodland, Vase, Orange, Green Flowers, Stippled Gray, 8 In. 550.00
Woodland, Vase, White Spiderwort Design, Green, Brown, Twist Shape, 10 3/8 In. ... 950.00
Zephyr Lily, Basket, Hanging, Brown, Original Chain, 5 1/4 In. 58.00
Zephyr Lily, Jardiniere, Pedestal, Brown, 24 1/2 In. 690.00
Zephyr Lily, Vase, Brown, 12 1/2 In. 230.00
Zephyr Lily, Vase, c.1940, 9 1/2 In. 160.00

ROY ROGERS was born in 1911 in Cincinnati, Ohio. In the 1930s, he
made a living as a singer; in 1935, his group started work at a Los
Angeles radio station. He appeared in his first movie in 1937. From
1952 to 1957, he made 101 television shows. The other stars in the
show were his wife, Dale Evans, his horse, Trigger, and his dog, Bullet. Roy Rogers memorabilia is collected, including items from the
Roy Rogers restaurants.

Bandanna, Square, Blue, Red Artwork, Roy, Trigger, Nellybelle, Bullet, Ropes, 18 In. 90.00
Bank, Dale Evans Boot, Fosta, c.1950 .... 20.00
Book Bag, Dale Evans 125.00
Cap Gun, Kilgore Repeater, Metal, White & Silver, 1950s, 8 1/2 In. 90.00
Clock, Alarm, Roy Rogers & Trigger, Galloping, Animated, Ingraham, 4 1/2 In. 290.00
Comic Book, Dell No. 109, 1946 .... 90.00
Comic Book, Dell Vol. 1 No. 18, June 1949 .... 18.00

Comic Book, Matted, Autograph, 11 x 14 In. 200.00
Decals, Roy & Trigger, Die Cut Oilcloth 30.00
Doll, Bobbin Head, 1962 .... 495.00
Guitar, Cardboard, Wood Neck, Nylon Strings, Range Rhythm Toys, 30 In. 95.00
Gun, Signal, Die Cast Metal, Plastic Trigger, Blinks On & Off, 6 In. 95.00
Holder Set, Copper Handle, Schmidt Guns, 10 In. 1200.00
Holster, Simulated Cowhide Leather, Studs, Metal Buckle, 4 1/2 x 8 1/4 In. 60.00
Ink Pad, Branding Set, 1950s, 2 In. 75.00
Lantern, Red & Blue, Yellow Lettering, Tin Lithograph, 7 1/2 In. 55.00
Lunch Box, Saddlebag, Vinyl, Tan, Thermos, 1960, 7 x 9 1/4 x 4 In. 95.00
Lunch Box, Trigger, Metal, Thermos, 1957 .... 115.00
Mug, King Of The Cowboys, Portrait, Plastic, 4 1/4 In. 25.00
Necktie, White, Red Artwork, Metal Loop & Catch Fastener, Child's 70.00
Paper Doll, Roy Rogers, Dale Evans, Punch-Out, Cardboard, Whitman, 1950s, 7 1/2 In. ... 110.00
Photograph, Happy Trails, Cowboy Outfit, Personalized To Sue 75.00
Photograph, Roy, Dale Evans & Gabby Hayes, Matted, Autographed, 11 x 14 In. 230.00
Premium, Calendar, Color Photos, Nestle's Quik, 1960 .... 145.00
Premium, Puzzle, Roy Sitting On Trigger, Post Cereal, 4 x 5 In. 18.00
Premium, Quaker Oats Cereal Container, Figure Of Roy 350.00
Premium, Yellow Trading Stamps, March Of Comics, No. 206, 1960, 5 x 7 In. 20.00
Record Album, Sons Of The Pioneers Cowboy Classics, RCA Victor, 1940s 20.00
Sheet Music, When My Blue Moon Turns To Gold Again, 6 Pages, 9 x 12 In. 25.00
Shirt, Flannel, Roy & Trigger Stitched On Front, Child's 50.00
Souvenir Program, 8 1/2 x 11 In. 35.00
Tie, Painted Rogers & Trigger, 1950s, Child's 125.00
Yo-Yo, Roy Picture, 1950s 13.00

ROYAL BAYREUTH is the name of a factory that was founded in Tettau, Bavaria, in 1794. It has continued to modern times. The marks have changed through the years. A stylized crest, the name *Royal Bayreuth*, and the word *Bavaria* appear in slightly different forms from 1870 to about 1919. Later dishes may include the words *U.S. Zone*, the year of the issue, or the word *Germany* instead of *Bavaria*. Related pieces may be found listed in the Snow Babies and Sunbonnet Babies categories.

Ashtray, Figural Elk, 2 x 6 In. 295.00
Ashtray, Nautilus Shell, 5 In. 108.00
Biscuit Jar, Cover, Grape, Iridescent White, 7 1/2 x 6 In. 170.00
Cake Plate, Wheat Girl 115.00
Coal Scuttle, Cavalier, Musicians, Center Handle, 3 x 2 1/2 In. 55.00
Creamer, Cow, 3 3/4 In. 245.00
Creamer, Dutch Girl & Dog, Blue & Brown, Gold Handle, Marked, 2 3/4 In. 65.00
Creamer, Frog, Early 1900s, 2 1/2 x 5 In. 345.00
Creamer, Grapes, Purple, 3 3/4 x 5 In. 245.00
Creamer, Spiky Shell, 4 1/2 In. 245.00
Creamer, Toasting, Cavaliers, Marked, 3 1/4 In. 35.00
Match Holder, Clown, Hanging, c.1900, 5 In. 495.00
Pitcher, Cards, Devil Handle, 7 In. 690.00
Pitcher, Lobster, c.1900, 6 3/4 In. 545.00
Pitcher, Tapestry, Playful Polar Bears In Arctic Waters, Marked, 7 In. 450.00
Plate, Little Jack Horner, 6 In. 125.00
Sugar & Creamer, Spiky Shell, 4 1/2 & 4 In. 395.00
Sugar & Creamer, Tomato, 3 1/2 & 3 In. 200.00
Vase, Rose Tapestry, 2 Gilt Handles, 5 1/2 In. 200.00
Vase, Rose, Tapestry, White, Pink, Yellow, 4 1/4 In. 12.00

ROYAL BONN is the nineteenth- and twentieth-century trade name for the Bonn China Manufactory. It was established in 1755 in Bonn, Germany. A general line of porcelain was made. Many marks were used, most including the name *Bonn*, the initials *FM*, and a crown.

Charger, Rembrandt, In Armor Center, Blue Floral Border, 19 3/4 In. 275.00
Clock, 4 Pillars, Roses Around Leaves, 10 3/4 In. 391.00
Jar, Domed Cover, Flowers, Gold Rim Base & Finial, 20 1/4 In. 385.00
Plaque, 2 Cows, Porcelain, Blue & White, 7 3/4 x 12 3/4 In. 357.00

Vase, Art Nouveau, Squat, Blue Iris, Black & Green Leaves, Teal Ground, 6 x 6 1/2 In. ... 290.00
Vase, Brass Mounts, Hand Painted, Tapered, Long Handles, 19 In. 720.00
Vase, Bulbous, Painted Landscape, Chickens, Marked, 9 In., Pair 720.00
Vase, Flowers, Gilt, 15 1/2 In. 145.00
Vase, Flowers, Oval Shape, 9 In. 265.00
Vase, Yellow & Pink Roses, Smoky Green To Gray Ground, 14 In. 175.00

ROYAL COPENHAGEN porcelain and pottery have been made in Denmark since 1772. The Christmas plate series started in 1908. The figurines with pale blue and gray glazes have remained popular in this century and are still being made. Many other old and new style porcelains are made today.

Bowl, Flora Danica, 8 3/4 In. 1680.00
Bowl, Flowers & Leaf Design, Off-White Ground, Pierced, Oval, 11 1/2 In. 276.00
Bowl, Fruit, Oval, Flared, Blue Flowers, Leaves, Off-White Ground, 11 1/2 In. 287.00
Cup & Saucer, Flora Danica, Cylindrical, Gold Rim, 2 1/2 In. 575.00
Dinner Service, Blue Fluted, Early 20th Century, 170 Pieces 14400.00
Figurine, Lioness, Tan Glaze, Marked, 6 1/4 x 12 1/4 In. 200.00
Figurine, Maharajah Kissing Nude Woman, Gilt Base, 8 In. 410.00
Figurine, Man With 2 Calves, 9 In. 259.00
Figurine, Nymph & Satyr, Kneeling At Feet, 20th Century, 15 1/4 In. 1090.00
Figurine, Pan Seated On Pedestal With Lizard, 8 1/2 In. 200.00
Figurine, Pan Seated With Frog On Knee, Marked, 4 3/4 In. 127.00
Figurine, Pan With Child, Blanc-De-Chine Glaze, 5 1/2 In. 60.00
Figurine, Peasant Girls, 7 1/2 In. 175.00
Figurine, Sparrows, Marked PH, 2 1/4 In., 1 3/4 In., Pair 175.00
Gravy Boat, Fish, Helmet Shape, Attached Stand, 9 1/2 In. 1680.00
Plate, Christmas, 1987, Bing & Grondahl, Reunion, No. 0142, 8 1/4 In. 25.00
Plate, Fish Border, Each Plate Titled, 9 In., 6 Piece 1760.00
Platter, Fish, 18 1/4 In. 3600.00
Platter, Flora Danica, Flowering Botanical Specimen, 13 1/8 In. 3300.00
Pot De Creme, Flora Danica 748.00
Salt, Open, Flora Danica, 4 1/2 x 3 In. 374.00
Tureen, Cover, Flora Danica, Botanical Specimens, Green, Brown, 14 In. 7200.00
Tureen, Cover, Flora Danica, Handle, 14 1/2 In. 5100.00
Tureen, Cover, Platter, Oval, 2 Handles, 20th Century, 12 3/8 x 16 1/4 In. 316.00
Tureen, Fish, Domed Cover, Painted, Twig Handle, 9 3/8 In. 3000.00
Vase, Art Nouveau, Jenny Meyer, 20 1/2 In. 2970.00
Vase, C. Zernichow, 29 In. 4070.00
Vase, Classical Shape, Pink Rose, Stamp, 9 x 3 1/4 In. 115.00
Vase, Farm House, Landscape, Marked, Denmark, 13 1/4 In. 600.00
Vase, Fishing Boats, Coastal Scene, Egg Shape, Harald Henrickson, 13 In. 600.00
Vase, Flying Bird Over Water, Pastel Blues, 5 1/4 In. 145.00
Vase, Gourd Shape, Fish, Blue Ground, 8 1/2 x 3 1/4 In. 201.00
Vase, Serpents, Stylized Waves, Carl Frederik Lusberg, 10 1/4 x 5 In. 201.00
Wine Cooler, Flora Danica, Oval, Painted, Twig Handles, 6 3/4 In. 2280.00

ROYAL COPLEY china was made by the Spaulding China Company of Sebring, Ohio, from 1939 to 1960. The figural planters and the small figurines, especially those with Art Deco designs, are of great collector interest.

Figurine, Bird, Dove, 4 3/4 In. 33.00
Figurine, Bird, Swallow, Broad Winged, Red & White, 8 In. 99.00
Figurine, Bird, Titmouse, 8 In. 35.00
Figurine, Blackamoor, Princess, 8 In. 40.00
Figurine, Dog, Cocker Spaniel, 6 1/2 In. ....20.00 to 23.00
Figurine, Dog, Puppy, 5 3/4 In. 26.00
Figurine, Dog, Puppy, 6 1/2 In. 29.00
Figurine, Dog, Schnauzer, 6 1/4 In. 36.00
Figurine, Duck, Mallard, 9 In. 35.00
Figurine, Gazelle, 9 In. 35.00
Figurine, Hen & Rooster, 7 In. 122.00
Figurine, Kitten, 8 1/4 In. 42.00

Royal Copley, Planter, Rooster, Marked, 8 In.

The playing surface of phonograph records should never be touched by a bare hand. The records should be stored vertically and packed to prevent warping. Keep away from extremes of heat or cold.

Figurine, Parrot, 8 In.	45.00 to 55.00
Planter, Box, With Bucket, 6 1/4 In.	25.00
Planter, Boy, Leaning On Barrel, 6 In.	22.00
Planter, Boy, Oriental, 6 1/4 In.	18.00
Planter, Deer & Fawn, 9 3/4 In.	50.00
Planter, Dog, Cocker Spaniel, 7 In.	24.00
Planter, Dog, With Mailbox, 8 1/2 In.	35.00
Planter, Duck, 8 In.	38.00
Planter, Duck, Mallard, 9 In.	35.00
Planter, Duck, Old Royal, 5 1/4 x 5 In.	20.00
Planter, Elephant, 7 1/2 In.	30.00
Planter, Girl, Leaning On Barrel, 6 1/4 In.	22.00
Planter, Head Vase, Deer & Fawn, 9 1/4 In.	25.00 to 39.00
Planter, Horse, With Mane, 8 In.	40.00
Planter, Kitten, Yellow, Ball, 5 In.	20.00
Planter, Pouter Pigeons, 6 In.	22.00
Planter, Rooster, Marked, 8 In. .... *Illus*	20.00
String & Scissors Holder, Chick, 5 5/8 x 5 3/8 In.	140.00
Vase, Dogwood, Pink, 9 1/2 In.	18.00
Vase, Dragon, 6 1/2 In.	20.00
Vase, Fish, With Open Mouth, Green & Brown, 9 x 5 In.	29.00
Vase, Gray, Pink, With Black Pillow, 5 1/2 In.	18.00
Vase, Head, India Man, 7 3/4 x 4 1/2 In.	45.00
Vase, Leaf & Steam, Black, 7 3/4 x 4 In.	18.00
Wall Pocket, Blackamoor, 8 In.	45.00
Wall Pocket, Granny, 7 1/2 In.	84.00
Wall Pocket, Pigtail Girl, 6 5/8 In.	35.00
Wall Pocket, Pirate, 8 In.	50.00

ROYAL CROWN DERBY Company, Ltd., was established in England in 1890. There is a complex family tree that includes the Derby, Crown Derby, and Royal Crown Derby porcelains. The Royal Crown Derby mark includes the name and a crown. The words *Made in England* were used after 1921. The company is now a part of Royal Doulton Tableware Ltd.

Animal, Dragon, Squirrel, Dolphin, Bird, 4 Piece	242.00
Animal, Koala Bear, Bird, Tortoise, Penguin, 4 Piece	472.00
Bowl, Vegetable, Cover, Imari Red, Cobalt Blue & Gold, 5 x 11 x 7 1/4 In.	525.00
Cake Server, Porcelain Handle, Imari, 10 In., Pair	230.00
Dessert Service, Imari, Early 20th Century, 12 11/14 x 7 In., 7 Piece	530.00
Dish, Cover, Imari, Dome-Shape Lid, Gilt Handle, c.1900, 8 3/4 In.	530.00
Garniture Vase, Edwardian, Enamel, Gilt, 2 Handles, c.1900, 8 3/4 x 5 1/4 In.	750.00
Plate, Imari, Gilt Trim, 1939, 10 1/2 In., 12 Piece	1035.00
Plate Set, Imari, Cobalt Blue, Red, Gilding, 10 In., 12 Piece	1000.00
Plate Set, Yellow, Parcel Gilt Grapevine Border, 8 In., 8 Piece	960.00
Platter, Imari, Pattern 2451, Red Printed Factory Mark, 1892, 19 1/4 In.	575.00
Tea Set, Blue Flowers, 3 Piece	390.00
Tete-A-Tete, Lily, Cobalt Blue Flowers, Diaperwork, Tray, Teapot, Creamer, Sugar	520.00

Vase, Band Of Beading, Upright Gilt Handles, Foo Dogs, Vines, 1882, 6 1/2 In. 368.00
Vase, Red Ground, Raised Gilding, Flowers & Butterflies, 1888, 6 In. 645.00

ROYAL DOULTON is the name used on Doulton and Company pottery made from 1902 to the present. Doulton and Company of England was founded in 1853. Pieces made before 1902 are listed in this book under Doulton. Royal Doulton collectors search for the out-of-production figurines, character jugs, vases, and series wares. Some vases and animal figurines were made with a special red glaze called flambe. Sung and Chang glazed pieces are rare. The multicolored glaze is very thick and looks as if it were dropped on the clay.

Animal, Cat, Seated, Flambe, 4 1/2 In.	115.00
Animal, Dog Of Fo, Flambe, HN 2957, 5 In.	250.00
Animal, Dog, Airedale Terrier, HN 1024, 4 In.	350.00
Animal, Dog, Alsatian Seated, K 13	125.00
Animal, Dog, Boxer, HN 2643, 6 1/2 In.	225.00
Animal, Dog, Bulldog, Brindle, Small, HN 1044	350.00
Animal, Dog, Bulldog, Union Jack, HN 5913A, 6 1/2 In. .... 1000.00 to 1250.00
Animal, Dog, Bulldog, Union Jack, Small, HN 5913C	350.00
Animal, Dog, Bulldog, White, Fawn Eyes, DA 222	75.00
Animal, Dog, Character, Kitten, Looking Up, HN 2584	125.00
Animal, Dog, Character, Kitten, On Hind Legs, HN 2582	125.00
Animal, Dog, Character, Running, HN 1097	125.00
Animal, Dog, Character, Yawning, HN 1099	125.00
Animal, Dog, Cocker Spaniel Lying In Basket, HN 2585	66.00
Animal, Dog, Cocker Spaniel, Black, White, Miniature, DA 1754B	20.00
Animal, Dog, Cocker Spaniel, HN 1002, 6 1/2 In.	450.00
Animal, Dog, Cocker Spaniel, Seated, L-0A	125.00
Animal, Dog, Cocker Spaniel, With Pheasant, HN 1001, 6 1/2 In.	750.00
Animal, Dog, Cocker Spaniel, With Pheasant, HN 1029, 3 1/2 In.	275.00
Animal, Dog, Collie, HN 1059, 3 1/2 In.	300.00
Animal, Dog, Dachshund, HN 1141, 2 3/4 In.	275.00
Animal, Dog, Dalmatian, HN 1114, 4 1/4 In.	500.00
Animal, Dog, English Setter, HN 1051, 4 In.	300.00
Animal, Dog, English Setter, Pheasant, HN 2529, 8 1/2 In.	700.00
Animal, Dog, Greyhound, HN 1067, 4 1/2 In.	775.00
Animal, Dog, Irish Setter, HN 1056, 4 In.	300.00
Animal, Dog, Pekinese, HN 1012, 3 In.	135.00
Animal, Dog, Scottish Terrier, HN 1019, 3 1/2 In.	900.00
Animal, Dog, Sealyham, Begging, K 3, 2 3/4 In.	150.00
Animal, Dog, Sealyham, HN 1032, 3 In.	450.00
Animal, Dog, Springer Spaniel, HN 2517, 3 3/4 In.	250.00
Animal, Dog, St. Bernard, K 19, 1 1/2 In.	125.00
Animal, Dog, Terrier, Sitting In Basket, Brown Mark, HN 2587, 3 In.	125.00
Animal, Dog, Welsh Corgi, HN 2558, 5 In.	575.00
Animal, Duck, Standing, HN 2591, 2 1/2 In.	150.00
Animal, Kitten, Character, HN 2584, 2 In.	100.00
Animal, Penguin, K 22, 1 3/4 In.	325.00
Animal, Piglet, HN 2648, 2 In.	375.00
Animal, Tiger, HN 1084, 2 In.	800.00
Ann Hathaway's Cottage, 3 1/2 x 7 1/4 In.	957.00
Ash Pot, Farmer John, D 6007	99.00
Ashtray, Match Stand, Dick Turpin, D 5601	150.00
Ashtray, Parson Brown, D 5600 .... 65.00 to 175.00
Bookends, Sea Horse, White Glaze, Marked Carrera, 6 x 4 1/4 x 3 1/2 In.	1000.00
Bowl, Apples, Blossoms, Leaves, D 3176, 4 3/4 x 9 1/2 In.	100.00
Bowl, Dick Swiveller, Octagonal, Dickens, D 2973, 8 1/2 In.	50.00
Bowl, Flower, Warwick Castle, D 4643, 11 In.	30.00
Bowl, Foot, Welsh, Women & Child Walking To Chapel, D 2414, 7 In.	60.00
Bowl, Gnomes, 6 In.	150.00
Bowl, Grapes, Vines, Royal Blue Ground, Pedestal Foot, 7 x 9 In.	500.00
Bowl, Salad, Dutch, Man With Stick & 4 Children, Noke, 8 In.	90.00
Bowl, Series Ware, Royal Mail Coach, 3 3/4 x 8 In.	45.00

Bowl, White Flowers, Cobalt Ground, Cover With Holes, 3 1/4 In. 60.00
Box, Cigarette, Cover, Home Waters, Wooden Pier, Sailboats, D 6434 .... 80.00
Cake Plate, Blue Bird On Branch, Pine Cones, Yellow Trim, 5 1/4 In. 165.00
Candlestick, Incised Stems, Light & Dark Blue Borders, 6 3/4 In., Pair 110.00
Candlestick, Mottled Green, Cobalt Glaze, Diamonds, Vines, 12 In., Pair 325.00
Candlestick, Scroll Borders, Leaves, Mottled Brown Stems, 7 1/2 In., Pair 110.00
Candlestick, Ships, Brown, Rowboats, D 2872, 6 In. 85.00
Candlestick, Under The Greenwood Tree, Alan A Dale, D 7227, 6 1/4 In. 100.00
Candlestick, Ye Canterbury Pilgrims, D 7277, c.1910, 9 In. 295.00

Royal Doulton character jugs depict the head and shoulders of the subject. They are made in four sizes: large, 5 1/4 to 7 inches; small, 3 1/4
to 4 inches; miniature, 2 1/4 to 2 1/2 inches; and tiny, 1 1/4 inches.
Toby jugs portray a seated, full figure.

Character Jug, 'Ard Of 'Earing, Large 2500.00
Character Jug, 'Ard Of 'Earing, Miniature 1100.00
Character Jug, 'Arriet, Small 150.00
Character Jug, 'Arry, Large 175.00
Character Jug, 'Arry, Small 125.00
Character Jug, Alfred Hitchcock, 7 1/2 In. 225.00
Character Jug, Anne Boleyn, Large 175.00
Character Jug, Anne Boleyn, Miniature 20.00
Character Jug, Annie Oakley, Mid Size 150.00
Character Jug, Antony & Cleopatra, Large 175.00
Character Jug, Aramis, Large 44.00
Character Jug, Aramis, Miniature 40.00
Character Jug, Aramis, Small 75.00
Character Jug, Athos, Large 125.00
Character Jug, Athos, Miniature 20.00
Character Jug, Athos, Small 57.00
Character Jug, Auld Mac, Large 120.00
Character Jug, Auld Mac, Small .... .40.00 to 83.00
Character Jug, Bacchus, Large 81.00
Character Jug, Bacchus, Miniature 20.00
Character Jug, Bacchus, Small .... .35.00 to 43.00
Character Jug, Baseball Player, Dark Blue Cap, Small 125.00
Character Jug, Beefeater, Large 145.00
Character Jug, Beefeater, Miniature 20.00
Character Jug, Beefeater, Small .... .30.00 to 65.00
Character Jug, Benjamin Franklin, Small 135.00
Character Jug, Blacksmith, Hammer, Anvil & Pliers Handle, Large ...... .81.00 to 150.00
Character Jug, Blacksmith, Miniature 75.00
Character Jug, Bootmaker, Large 57.00
Character Jug, Bootmaker, Miniature 85.00
Character Jug, Buzfuz, D 5838, Small 91.00
Character Jug, Cap'n Cuttle, Mid Size 180.00
Character Jug, Capt Ahab, Miniature 25.00
Character Jug, Capt Ahab, Small .... .60.00 to 100.00
Character Jug, Capt Henry Morgan, Large 200.00
Character Jug, Capt Henry Morgan, Miniature 20.00
Character Jug, Captain Bligh, Large 200.00
Character Jug, Captain Hook, Crocodile & Clock Handle, Large 750.00
Character Jug, Captain Hook, Crocodile & Silver Hook Handle, Large 240.00
Character Jug, Cavalier, No Goatee, Small 20.00
Character Jug, Cavalier, Small 80.00
Character Jug, Chopin, Large 260.00
Character Jug, Christopher Columbus, Large 160.00
Character Jug, Clark Gable, Large 5000.00
Character Jug, Cyrano De Bergerac, Large 200.00
Character Jug, D'Artagnan, Large 61.00
Character Jug, David Copperfield, Tiny 95.00
Character Jug, Dick Turpin, Miniature 40.00
Character Jug, Dick Whittington, Large 550.00

Character Jug, Don Quixote, Large 150.00
Character Jug, Don Quixote, Miniature 50.00
Character Jug, Don Quixote, Small 80.00
Character Jug, Drake, Large 200.00
Character Jug, Elf, Miniature 125.00
Character Jug, Fagin, Tiny 85.00
Character Jug, Falconer, Large 135.00
Character Jug, Falstaff, Large 44.00
Character Jug, Falstaff, Small 65.00
Character Jug, Farmer John, Large ....67.00 to 200.00
Character Jug, Farmer John, Small 57.00
Character Jug, Fat Boy, Miniature 100.00
Character Jug, Fireman, Large ....57.00 to 250.00
Character Jug, Fortune Teller, 3 3/4 In. 500.00
Character Jug, Fortune Teller, 6 1/2 In. 288.00
Character Jug, Fortune Teller, Tarot Cards Handle, Large 530.00
Character Jug, Fortune Teller, Zodiac Handle, Large 1200.00
Character Jug, Friar Tuck, Large 550.00
Character Jug, Gardener, Large ....170.00 to 200.00
Character Jug, Gardener, Miniature 40.00
Character Jug, Gardener, Small 100.00
Character Jug, Genie, Large 137.00
Character Jug, Geoffrey Chaucer, Large 800.00
Character Jug, George Harrison, Mid Size 275.00
Character Jug, George Washington, Large 225.00
Character Jug, Geronimo, Mid Size 250.00
Character Jug, Gladiator, Large 650.00
Character Jug, Gladiator, Miniature 525.00
Character Jug, Golfer, Large 125.00
Character Jug, Gondolier, Miniature 550.00
Character Jug, Granny Toothless, Large 1100.00
Character Jug, Granny, One Tooth Showing, Large ....39.00 to 125.00
Character Jug, Granny, Small 35.00
Character Jug, Groucho Marx, Large 200.00
Character Jug, Gulliver, Large 950.00
Character Jug, Gulliver, Small 500.00
Character Jug, Hamlet, Large 175.00
Character Jug, Henry VIII, Large ....47.00 to 165.00
Character Jug, Henry VIII, Miniature 35.00
Character Jug, Henry VIII, Small ....30.00 to 68.00
Character Jug, Hiawatha, Never Any Deed Of Daring, 5 In. 55.00
Character Jug, Jane Seymour, Miniature 190.00
Character Jug, Jarge, Small 275.00
Character Jug, Jesse Owens, Large ....170.00 to 225.00
Character Jug, Jester, Small ....50.00 to 135.00
Character Jug, Jimmy Durante 200.00
Character Jug, Jockey, Large 475.00
Character Jug, John Barleycorn Old Lad, Miniature ....20.00 to 40.00
Character Jug, John Barleycorn, Large 85.00
Character Jug, John Barleycorn, Small 57.00
Character Jug, John Doulton, Small ....45.00 to 65.00
Character Jug, John Lennon, Mid Size 300.00
Character Jug, John Peel, Miniature 69.00
Character Jug, John Peel, Small 35.00
Character Jug, Johnny Appleseed, Large 475.00
Character Jug, Juggler, Large 225.00
Character Jug, King Charles I, Large 450.00
Character Jug, King Edward VII, Small 310.00
Character Jug, Lawyer, Large 75.00
Character Jug, Lawyer, Small 70.00
Character Jug, London Bobby, Large 325.00
Character Jug, Long John Silver, Large ....47.00 to 160.00
Character Jug, Long John Silver, Miniature 50.00

Character Jug, Lord Nelson, Large 160.00
Character Jug, Louis Armstrong, Large 300.00
Character Jug, Lumberjack, Large ....48.00 to 150.00
Character Jug, Macbeth, Witches Facing Inward Handle, Large 200.00
Character Jug, Mad Hatter, Small 165.00
Character Jug, Mark Twain, Large ....47.00 to 175.00
Character Jug, Merlin, Large 150.00
Character Jug, Mine Host, D 6513, 2 In. 20.00
Character Jug, Mozart, Large 265.00
Character Jug, Mr. Bumble, Tiny 55.00
Character Jug, Mr. Micawber, Small ....87.00 to 125.00
Character Jug, Mr. Pickwick, Miniature 30.00
Character Jug, Mr. Pickwick, Plain Handle, Small 100.00
Character Jug, Mr. Pickwick, Sam Weller Handle, Small 47.00
Character Jug, Mr. Quaker, Large 900.00
Character Jug, Neptune, Large ....57.00 to 135.00
Character Jug, Neptune, Miniature 40.00
Character Jug, Neptune, Small 43.00
Character Jug, Night Watchman, Miniature 95.00
Character Jug, North American Indian, Large ....83.00 to 150.00
Character Jug, Old Charley, Small 112.00
Character Jug, Old King Cole, Large 325.00
Character Jug, Old King Cole, Small 72.00
Character Jug, Old Salt, Small 90.00
Character Jug, Oliver Twist, Tiny 50.00
Character Jug, Othello, Large ....75.00 to 175.00
Character Jug, Paddy, Miniature 10.00
Character Jug, Paddy, Small 75.00
Character Jug, Parson Brown, Large 185.00
Character Jug, Pearly King, Large 200.00
Character Jug, Pearly Queen, Large 200.00
Character Jug, Pied Piper, Large 47.00
Character Jug, Pied Piper, Miniature 85.00
Character Jug, Piper, Large 158.00
Character Jug, Poacher, Figural Fish Handle, Small 220.00
Character Jug, Poacher, Large 68.00
Character Jug, Porthos, Large 135.00
Character Jug, Porthos, Miniature 20.00
Character Jug, Porthos, Small 47.00
Character Jug, Punch & Judy Man, Large 925.00
Character Jug, Punch & Judy Man, Miniature 600.00
Character Jug, Queen Victoria, Large ....71.00 to 250.00
Character Jug, Regency Beau, Small 1000.00
Character Jug, Ringo Starr, Mid Size 275.00
Character Jug, Rip Van Winkle, Small ....50.00 to 75.00
Character Jug, Robin Hood, Large ....58.00 to 200.00
Character Jug, Robin Hood, Miniature 25.00
Character Jug, Robin Hood, Small 47.00
Character Jug, Robinson Crusoe, Miniature 55.00
Character Jug, Robinson Crusoe, Small 75.00
Character Jug, Romeo, Large 125.00
Character Jug, Sairey Gamp, Large ....50.00 to 80.00
Character Jug, Sairey Gamp, Small 65.00
Character Jug, Sam Johnson, Large 400.00
Character Jug, Sam Weller, Mid Size 30.00
Character Jug, Sam Weller, Miniature 69.00
Character Jug, Sancho Panca, Large 185.00
Character Jug, Sancho Panca, Miniature 25.00
Character Jug, Santa Claus, Large ....70.00 to 163.00
Character Jug, Santa Claus, Miniature 125.00
Character Jug, Scaramouche, Miniature 480.00
Character Jug, Schubert, Large 260.00
Character Jug, Scrooge, Tiny 60.00

Character Jug, Simon The Cellarer, Small	30.00
Character Jug, Simple Simon, Large	750.00
Character Jug, Sir Francis Drake, Large	44.00
Character Jug, Sir Henry Doulton, Large	285.00
Character Jug, Sleuth, Miniature	20.00
Character Jug, Sleuth, Small	30.00
Character Jug, Smuggler, Large	225.00
Character Jug, Snooker Player, Small	100.00
Character Jug, Tam O' Shanter, Miniature	40.00 to 120.00
Character Jug, Tam O' Shanter, Small	70.00 to 75.00
Character Jug, The Gardener, Large	55.00
Character Jug, Toby Philpots, Large	48.00
Character Jug, Toby Philpots, Small	65.00
Character Jug, Tony Weller, Miniature	150.00
Character Jug, Town Crier, Large	225.00
Character Jug, Town Crier, Small	68.00 to 185.00
Character Jug, Trapper, Small	75.00
Character Jug, Ugly Duchess, Small	475.00
Character Jug, Uncle Tom Cobbleigh, Large	500.00
Character Jug, Veteran Motorist, Large	83.00 to 200.00
Character Jug, Veteran Motorist, Miniature	45.00
Character Jug, Vicar Of Bray, Large	325.00
Character Jug, Vice Admiral Lord, Nelson, Large	275.00
Character Jug, Viking, Miniature	225.00
Character Jug, Viking, Small	130.00
Character Jug, W.C. Fields, Large	250.00
Character Jug, Wild Bill Hickock, Mid Size	175.00
Character Jug, William Shakespeare, Large	500.00
Character Jug, Winston Churchill, Large	350.00
Character Jug, Yachtsman, Large	112.00 to 200.00
Character Jug, Yeoman Of The Guard, Large	175.00
Charger, Eagle Clutching Fish, Waves, Sung Flambe, C. Noke, 12 1/2 In.	920.00
Charger, Landscape & Shepherds, 13 In.	88.00
Creamer, Eglington Tournament, c.1905, 4 In.	265.00
Cup, Night Watchman, Series Ware, 2 1/2 In.	16.00
Dish, Fruit, Granville, 5 1/2 In.	10.00
Ewer, Moorish, Incised, Beaded, Medallion, Cobalt, Amber, 5 3/4 In.	230.00
Ewer, Mottled Green, Cobalt Glaze, Outlined Leaves, Beaded Veins, 9 In.	125.00
Figurine, Across The Miles, HN 3934	100.00
Figurine, Affection, HN 2236	104.00
Figurine, Ann Of Cleves, HN 3356	600.00
Figurine, Annabella, HN 1872	1400.00
Figurine, Anne Boleyn, HN 3232	600.00
Figurine, Antoinette, HN 1850	500.00
Figurine, Artful Dodger, HN 546	315.00
Figurine, Ascot, HN 2356	250.00
Figurine, Auctioneer, HN 2988	325.00
Figurine, Autumn Breezes, HN 1911	300.00
Figurine, Autumn Breezes, HN 1934	138.00 to 275.00
Figurine, Autumn Breezes, HN 2147	475.00
Figurine, Autumn, HN 2087	725.00
Figurine, Babie, HN 1679	110.00
Figurine, Baby Bunting, HN 2108	350.00
Figurine, Balinese Dancer, HN 2808	975.00
Figurine, Ballerina, HN 2116	450.00
Figurine, Balloons, HN 3187	500.00
Figurine, Beachcomber, HN 2487	275.00
Figurine, Belle O' The Ball, HN 1997	355.00
Figurine, Belle, HN 2340	69.00
Figurine, Belle, HN 3703	300.00
Figurine, Bess, HN 2002	425.00
Figurine, Bluebeard, HN 2105	675.00
Figurine, Bon Appetit, HN 2444	250.00

Figurine, Bridesmaid, HN 2874 . . . . 90.00
Figurine, Bridget, HN 2070 . . . . 426.00
Figurine, Broken Lance, HN 2041 . . . . 725.00
Figurine, Bumble, M 76 . . . . 315.00
Figurine, Bunnykins, 60th Anniversary Bunnykins, DB 137 . . . . 85.00
Figurine, Bunnykins, Astro Bunnykins Rocket Man, DB 20 . . . . 200.00
Figurine, Bunnykins, Aussie Surfer Bunnykins, DB 133 . . . . 150.00
Figurine, Bunnykins, Billie & Buntie Bunnykins, Sleigh Ride, DB 4, 3 1/2 In. 11.00
Figurine, Bunnykins, Boy Skater Bunnykins, DB 152 . . . . 50.00
Figurine, Bunnykins, Buntie Bunnykins Helping Mother, DB 2 . . . . 85.00
Figurine, Bunnykins, Christmas Surprise, DB 146 . . . . 65.00
Figurine, Bunnykins, Doctor Bunnykins, DB 181 . . . . 50.00
Figurine, Bunnykins, Family Photograph Bunnykins, DB 1 . . . . 165.00
Figurine, Bunnykins, Father Bunnykins, DB 154 . . . . 75.00
Figurine, Bunnykins, Fireman Bunnykins, DB 183 . . . . 95.00
Figurine, Bunnykins, Fisherman Bunnykins, DB 170 . . . . 65.00
Figurine, Bunnykins, Gardener Bunnykins, DB 156 . . . . 50.00
Figurine, Bunnykins, Homerun Bunnykins, DB 43 . . . . 125.00
Figurine, Bunnykins, Mother's Day Bunnykins, DB 155 . . . . 50.00
Figurine, Bunnykins, Mr. Bunnykins Autumn Days, DB 5 . . . . 475.00
Figurine, Bunnykins, Sleepytime Bunnykins, DB 15 . . . . 85.00
Figurine, Bunnykins, Tom Bunnykins, DB 72 . . . . 100.00
Figurine, Bunnykins, Wizard, No. 1888, DB 168, 4 3/4 In. 240.00
Figurine, Buttercup, HN 2309 . . . . 225.00
Figurine, Buttercup, HN 2399 . . . . 275.00
Figurine, Camellia, HN 2222 . . . . 350.00
Figurine, Captain Cuttle, M 77 . . . . 315.00
Figurine, Caroline, HN 3694 . . . . 350.00
Figurine, Carpenter, HN 2678 . . . . 172.00
Figurine, Celeste, HN 2237 . . . . 350.00
Figurine, Cherie, HN 2341 . . . . 92.00
Figurine, Clare, HN 2793 . . . . 275.00
Figurine, Clown, HN 2890 . . . . 300.00
Figurine, Cobbler, HN 1283 . . . . 320.00
Figurine, Cobbler, HN 1706 . . . . 425.00
Figurine, Country Lass, HN 1991 . . . . 225.00
Figurine, Cymbals, HN 2699 . . . . 950.00
Figurine, Daddy's Girl, HN 3435 . . . . 100.00
Figurine, Dancing Years, HN 2235 . . . . 500.00
Figurine, Danielle, HN 3001 . . . . 200.00
Figurine, Darby, HN 2024 . . . . 275.00
Figurine, David Copperfield, M 88 . . . . 125.00
Figurine, Daydreams, HN 1731 . . . . 350.00
Figurine, Debbie, HN 2400 . . . . 135.00
Figurine, Dorothy, HN 3098 . . . . 160.00
Figurine, Elaine, HN 2791 . . . . 425.00
Figurine, Elegance, HN 2264 . . . . 225.00
Figurine, Elfreda, HN 2078 . . . . 975.00
Figurine, Eliza, HN 2543 . . . . 300.00
Figurine, Ellen, HN 4231 . . . . 285.00
Figurine, Emily, HN 3806 . . . . 56.00
Figurine, Enchantment, HN 2178 . . . . 250.00
Figurine, Fagin, M 49, 4 In. 315.00
Figurine, Fair Lady, HN 2193 . . . . .60.00 to 225.00
Figurine, Fair Maiden, HN 2211 . . . . .32.00 to 150.00
Figurine, Falstaff, HN 2054 . . . . .86.00 to 200.00
Figurine, Fat Boy, HN 1893 . . . . 315.00
Figurine, Fat Boy, HN 530 . . . . 55.00
Figurine, Fat Boy, M 44 . . . . 140.00
Figurine, Fiddler, HN 2171 . . . . 1300.00
Figurine, Fleur, HN 2368 . . . . 225.00
Figurine, Flora, HN 2349 . . . . 450.00
Figurine, Flower Seller's Children, HN 1342 . . . . 287.00

Figurine, Flowers For Mother, HN 3454	100.00
Figurine, Flute, HN 2483	1250.00
Figurine, Forty Winks, HN 1974	400.00
Figurine, Gay Morning, HN 2135	450.00
Figurine, Genie, HN 2989	300.00
Figurine, Good Catch, HN 2258	275.00
Figurine, Goody Two Shoes, HN 2037	160.00
Figurine, Gossips, HN 1429	1500.00
Figurine, Grace, HN 2318	235.00
Figurine, Grandma, HN 2052A	550.00
Figurine, Gulliver, HN 3750	57.00
Figurine, Gypsy Dance, HN 2157	1400.00
Figurine, Gypsy Dance, HN 2230	475.00
Figurine, Harmony, HN 2824	325.00
Figurine, Helen Of Troy, HN 2387	1650.00
Figurine, Her Ladyship, HN 1977	500.00
Figurine, Home At Last, HN 3697	150.00
Figurine, Homecoming, HN 3295	300.00
Figurine, Hometime, HN 3685	140.00
Figurine, Innocence, HN 3730	90.00
Figurine, Jacqueline, HN 2001	800.00
Figurine, Jane, HN 3711	300.00
Figurine, Janet, M 69	535.00
Figurine, Janice, HN 2022	700.00
Figurine, Jasmine, HN 1862	546.00
Figurine, Jennifer, HN 3447	450.00
Figurine, Jester, HN 2016	450.00
Figurine, Joan, HN 1422	450.00
Figurine, Jovial Monk, Brown, DB 2144	350.00
Figurine, Julia, HN 2705	225.00
Figurine, Julie, HN 2995	81.00
Figurine, Karen, HN 2388	500.00
Figurine, Kate Hardcastle, HN 2028	316.00
Figurine, Kathleen, HN 2933	184.00
Figurine, Kitty, HN 3876	140.00
Figurine, Lady Charmian, HN 1948	290.00
Figurine, Laird, HN 2361	138.00
Figurine, Lambing Time, HN 1890	325.00
Figurine, Laurianne, HN 2719	225.00
Figurine, Lavinia, HN 1955	150.00
Figurine, Lights Out, HN 2262	350.00
Figurine, Lilac Time, HN 2137	355.00 to 475.00
Figurine, Lily, HN 1798	175.00
Figurine, Lisa, HN 2310	225.00
Figurine, Little Nell, M 51	125.00 to 140.00
Figurine, Lizzie, HN 2749	225.00
Figurine, Lobster Man, HN 2317	250.00
Figurine, Lorraine, HN 3118	300.00
Figurine, Love Letter, HN 2149	625.00
Figurine, Lucy Lockett, HN 485	638.00
Figurine, Lunchtime, HN 2485	275.00
Figurine, Lynne, HN 2329	115.00
Figurine, Marie, HN 1370	100.00
Figurine, Market Day, HN 1991	225.00
Figurine, Mary, HN 2374	400.00
Figurine, Mask Seller, HN 2103	98.00 to 325.00
Figurine, Masquerade, HN 2259	425.00
Figurine, Maytime, HN 2113	425.00
Figurine, Meditation, HN 2330	230.00
Figurine, Melanie, HN 2271	275.00
Figurine, Melissa, HN 2467	138.00
Figurine, Memories, HN 2030	650.00
Figurine, Mendicant, Brown, HN 1365	400.00

Figurine, Mexican Dancer, HN 2866 .... 900.00
Figurine, Milkmaid, HN 2057A 200.00
Figurine, Miranda, HN 3037 .... 300.00
Figurine, Miss Muffit, HN 1936 .... 225.00
Figurine, Mother & Daughter, HN 2841 .... 200.00
Figurine, Mother's Helper, HN 3650 .... 125.00
Figurine, Mrs. Bardell, M 86 .... 315.00
Figurine, My Best Friend, HN 3011 .... 410.00
Figurine, Newsvendor, HN 2891 .... 275.00
Figurine, Nicole, HN 3421 .... 200.00
Figurine, Off To School, HN 3768 .... 200.00
Figurine, Old Balloon Seller, HN 3737 .... 375.00
Figurine, Old Mother Hubbard, HN 2314 .... 550.00
Figurine, Olga, HN 2463 .... 225.00
Figurine, Oliver Twist, M 89 .... 100.00
Figurine, Omar Khayyam, HN 2247 .... 250.00
Figurine, Paisley Shawl, HN 1988 .... 250.00
Figurine, Pantalettes, HN 1362 .... 850.00
Figurine, Pecksniff, HN 535 .... 315.00
Figurine, Peggy, HN 2038 .... 160.00
Figurine, Penny's Worth, HN 2408 .... 127.00
Figurine, Pickwick, HN 529 .... 315.00
Figurine, Picnic, HN 2308 .... 92.00
Figurine, Pied Piper, HN 2102 .... 400.00
Figurine, Piper, HN 2907 .... 196.00
Figurine, Plate, Bunnykins, Game Of Golf, SF 11 .... 250.00
Figurine, Poacher, HN 2043 .... 450.00
Figurine, Pride & Joy, Box, Collectors Club, HN 2945, 7 1/4 In. .... 120.00 to 350.00
Figurine, Primroses, HN 1617 .... 1500.00
Figurine, Prince Of Wales, HN 2884 .... 900.00
Figurine, Professor, HN 2281 .... 250.00
Figurine, Queen Anne, HN 3141 .... 500.00
Figurine, Queen Of Sheba, HN 2328 .... 1600.00
Figurine, Rachel, HN 2936 .... 138.00
Figurine, Rachel, HN 3976 .... 215.00
Figurine, Rag Doll, HN 2142 .... 135.00
Figurine, Rebecca, HN 2805 .... 625.00
Figurine, Rose, HN 1368 .... 100.00
Figurine, Roseanna, HN 1926 .... 650.00
Figurine, Rosemary, HN 3143 .... 275.00
Figurine, Ruth, HN 2799 .... 127.00
Figurine, Sabbath Morn, HN 1982 .... 400.00
Figurine, Sairey Gamp, HN 533 .... 315.00
Figurine, Sara, HN 2265 .... 495.00
Figurine, Scrooge, M 87 .... 125.00
Figurine, Sharon, HN 3047 .... 150.00
Figurine, She Loves Me Not, HN 2045 .... 325.00
Figurine, Simone, HN 2378 .... 64.00
Figurine, Sir Walter Raleigh, HN 2015 .... 1000.00
Figurine, Skater, HN 2117 .... 450.00 to 575.00
Figurine, Sleepy Darling, HN 2953 .... 275.00
Figurine, Soiree, HN 2312 .... 150.00
Figurine, Solitude, HN 2810 .... 325.00
Figurine, Sonia, HN 1692 .... 2000.00
Figurine, Spanish Flamenco Dancer, HN 2831 .... 2000.00
Figurine, Special Friend, HN 3607 .... 120.00
Figurine, Spring Flowers, HN 1807 .... 375.00
Figurine, Spring Morning, HN 1922 .... 315.00 to 400.00
Figurine, Springtime, HN 3033 .... 350.00
Figurine, Stiggins, HN 535 .... 315.00
Figurine, Strolling, HN 3755 .... 250.00
Figurine, Summer Rose, White, Pink Flower, HN 3309 .... 250.00
Figurine, Summertime, HN 3478 .... 350.00

Figurine, Sunday Best, HN 2206 .... 250.00
Figurine, Sunday Best, HN 2698 .... 225.00
Figurine, Sunday Morning, HN 2184 .... 500.00
Figurine, Sunshine Girl, HN 4245 .... 440.00
Figurine, Suzette, HN 1696 .... 1000.00
Figurine, Suzette, HN 2026 .... 525.00
Figurine, Sweet & Twenty, HN 1360 .... 1100.00
Figurine, Sweet Sixteen, HN 2231 .... 450.00
Figurine, T'Zu-Hsi, Empress Dowager, HN 2391 .... 1300.00
Figurine, Take Me Home, HN 3662 .... 250.00
Figurine, Teatime, HN 2255 ....161.00 to 325.00
Figurine, Thanksgiving, HN 2446 .... 225.00
Figurine, The Alchemist, HN 1282 .... 1070.00
Figurine, Tiny Tim, HN 539 ....71.00 to 315.00
Figurine, Top O' The Hill, HN 1834 ....103.00 to 350.00
Figurine, Town Crier, HN 2119 ....127.00 to 400.00
Figurine, Trotty Veck, M 91 .... 315.00
Figurine, Valerie, HN 2107 .... 160.00
Figurine, Vanity, HN 2475 .... 185.00
Figurine, Victorian Lady, HN 728 .... 700.00
Figurine, Violin, HN 2432 .... 1150.00
Figurine, Vivienne, HN 2073 .... 400.00
Figurine, Wedding Vows, Cake Topper, HN 2750 .... 275.00
Figurine, Wendy, HN 2109 .... 100.00
Figurine, What's The Matter? HN 3684 .... 140.00
Figurine, When I Was Young, HN 3457 .... 360.00
Figurine, Winsome, HN 2220 .... 250.00
Figurine, Wintertime, HN 3060 .... 300.00
Figurine, Wistful, HN 2472 .... 350.00
Figurine, Wizard, HN 2877 .... 575.00
Figurine, Zoe, HN 4208 .... 165.00
Flask, Ben Jonson, Dewar's, Signed Noke, 7 In. 152.00
Flask, Bonnie Prince Charlie, Dewar's, 7 In. 71.00
Flask, Falstaff, Kingsware, Flattened, Round, Elongated Handle, 7 1/2 In. 588.00
Flask, Galleon, Kingsware, 7 1/4 In. 4945.00
Flask, George The Guard, Kingsware, Cylindrical, Dewar's Whiskey, 9 3/4 In. 255.00
Flask, Jovial Monk, Kingsware, Pear Shape, Dewar's Scotch, 8 In. 303.00
Flask, Jug, Hogarth, Kingsware, 6 1/2 In. 103.00
Flask, Stopper, Cream Glaze, White, Richard Garbe, c.1934, 13 1/2 In. 3900.00
Flask, Tony Weller, 8 In. 638.00
Flask, Watchman, Dewar's Scotch, 10 1/2 In. 137.00
Humidor, Coaching Days, Man With Trunk, Silver Rim, D 2716 .... 160.00
Jar, Stylized Flowers, Mottled Green, Cover, Flowers, 5 1/2 In. 110.00
Jardinere, Pedestal, No. 8606, Eliza Simmance, 20th Century, 34 1/2 In. 1680.00
Jardiniere, 3 Chrysanthemums, Flowers, Beading, Ruffled Rim, Base, 8 In. 250.00
Jardiniere, Art Nouveau Flowering Vine, Ocher & Blue, Mottled Green, 7 1/2 In. ... 120.00
Jardiniere, Art Nouveau Heart Shaped Flowers, Ruffled Rim, 7 1/2 x 8 1/2 In. ... 120.00
Jardiniere, Children, 7 x 9 In. 247.00
Jardiniere, Pedestal, Stoneware, Flowers, Early 20th Century, 44 3/4 In. 4500.00
Jug, Art Nouveau Medallions, Circles, Mottled Green, 7 1/4 In. 170.00
Jug, Bayeux Tapestry, Death Of Harold, D 2873, 4 3/4 In. 60.00
Jug, Blackjack, 7 3/4 In. 57.00
Jug, Blue Top, Tan Salt Glaze Ground, 6 1/2 In. 42.00
Jug, Blue Willow Pattern, Buff Ground, 7 1/4 In. 80.00
Jug, Brown, White Glaze, Hunting Ware, Greyhound Handle, 6 1/2 In. 25.00
Jug, Chinoiserie Pattern, Pewter Cover, 6 1/2 In. 70.00
Jug, Eglington Tournament, c.1905, 6 In. 315.00
Jug, Galleons, Billowing Sails, Seagulls, D 317, 6 In. 150.00
Jug, Incised Fruits, Tan & Green On White, D 5034, 8 1/2 In. 60.00
Jug, Izaak Walton, Compleat Angler, D 2557, 7 3/4 In. 250.00
Jug, Liquor Container, John Dewar & Sons, Egyptian Style, 5 3/4 In. 71.00
Jug, Memories, Dickens, 4 1/2 In. 207.00
Jug, Memories, Dickens, Kingsware, 5 1/4 In. 35.00

Jug, Mendoza, Kingsware, Boxer, 5 In. 2871.00
Jug, Night Watchman, D 6569, 7 1/4 In. 71.00
Jug, Rip Van Winkle, Much The Flavour Of Excellent Hollands, D 2553, 7 1/4 In. 275.00
Jug, Salt Glaze, Applied Hunt Scenes, Floral Sprays, Hound Handle, 6 1/2 In. 90.00
Jug, Series Ware, Sir Roger De Coverley, Horse & Rider, 6 1/4 In. 16.00
Jug, Series Ware, Toasting Mottoes, Toastmaster, Empty Bag, 6 In. 25.00
Jug, Shells, Green Glaze, Blue Flowers, 8 1/2 x 5 In. 220.00
Jug, Tan Salt Glaze, Hunting Scenes, 6 1/2 In. 16.00
Jug, Toby XX, Man Sitting On Keg, Dark & Light Brown, Variation 2, 10 1/2 In. 650.00
Jug, Turquoise & White Flowers, Mottled Green Border, Handle, Metal Cover, 9 In. 80.00
Jug, Welsh, Woman Leaning On Fence, 2 3/4 In. 160.00
Jug, Welsh, Women & Child Walking To Chapel, 5 3/4 In. 140.00
Jug, Whiskey, Brown, Scotch Whiskey, Tan Salt Glaze, 7 1/2 In. 210.00
Jug, Whiskey, Dewar's Whiskey, Hunting Scene, Tan Salt Glaze, 5 1/4 In. 64.00
Jug, Whiskey, McCallums, Whisky Is Perfection, Blue Body, 5 In. 320.00
Jug, Whiskey, McCallums, Whisky Is Perfection, Green Body, 5 In. 414.00
Jug, Whiskey, Mottled Brown Glaze, 7 1/4 In. 225.00
Jug, Zunday Zmocks, Smiling Man Under Tree, Noke, 5 In. 110.00
Lighter, Lawyer, D 6504, 3 1/2 In. 225.00
Lighter, Long John Silver, D 6386, 3 1/2 In. 225.00
Lighter, Poacher, D 6464, 4 3/4 In. 175.00
Liquor Container, Dewar's Perth Whisky, Tan Salt Glaze, Pistol Shape, 9 1/4 In. 670.00
Loving Cup, King George VI & Queen Elizabeth Coronation, 6 In. 16.00
Matchstriker, Double Face, Green, Brown, Yellow Glaze, 3 In. 200.00
Menu Holder, Organ Grinder, Marked W.G. 14, Early 20th Century, 3 1/2 In. 1920.00
Pin Tray, Nasturtium, D 6235, 4 1/4 x 3 3/4 In. 25.00
Pitcher, Hunting Scene, Light To Dark Brown, 9 1/2 In. 224.00
Plaque, Pembroke Castle, Blue & White, 13 1/2 In. 40.00
Plaque, Pomeroy, Fruit & Flower Border, 13 1/2 In. 70.00
Plaque, Rustic England, Mending Rush Chair, D 5694, 13 1/2 In. 70.00
Plaque, Under The Greenwood Tree, Friar Tuck, Acorn Border, 15 1/4 In. 140.00
Plaque, Warrior, Relief, Cream Terra-Cotta, Irregular Oval, 5 1/4 x 3 In. 525.00
Plaque, Zunday Zmocks, Profiles Of Men, Noke, D 5680, 13 1/2 In. 170.00
Plate, Admiral, D 6278, 10 In. 300.00
Plate, Bookworm, D 3089, 10 In. 300.00
Plate, Bunnykins, Postman Delivering Letters, HW 19 .... 75.00
Plate, Chop, Jackdaw Of Rheims, Bishop, Abbot, Pryor, D 2532, 12 1/2 In. 40.00
Plate, Christmas 1977 .... 85.00
Plate, Doctor, D 6281 .... 300.00
Plate, Dutch, Man With Hands In Pockets, Noke, D 1826, 9 1/2 In. 40.00
Plate, Dutch, Old Man Holding Child's Hand, Noke, 9 1/2 In. 60.00
Plate, Fox-Hunting, Horses Jumping Fence, 10 1/4 In. 65.00
Plate, Gallant Fishers, Perch Or Pike, Noke, D 2704, 9 1/2 In. 110.00
Plate, Gallant Fishers, There Stood My Friend, Noke, D 2704, 8 1/2 In. 85.00
Plate, Gypsies, Man & Family On Donkey, D 3191, 10 1/2 In. 40.00
Plate, Hunter Scene, D 6282 .... 300.00
Plate, Jackdaw Of Rheims, & Off That Terrible Curse He Took, D 2532, 9 1/2 In. 30.00
Plate, Jester, Rack, D 6277, 10 1/2 In. 300.00
Plate, Landscape, Flambe, 10 1/2 In. 80.00
Plate, Mayor, Rack, D 6283, 10 1/2 In. 300.00
Plate, Monks & Mottoes A, Tomorrow Will Be Friday, Noke, D 3429, 10 In. 90.00
Plate, Monks, Cook Inspecting Fish, Noke, D 2385, 10 1/4 In. 80.00
Plate, Parson, D 3303, 10 1/2 In. 300.00
Plate, Queen Of Hearts, 10 1/2 In. 325.00
Plate, Rural England, Bluebell Gatherers, 7 3/4 In. 57.00
Plate, Series Ware, English Cottages, D 3693, 10 In. 20.00
Plate, Series Ware, Landscape Scene, Burslem, D 2550, 10 1/2 In. 9.00
Plate, Series Ware, Rheims, D 2543, 10 In. 39.00
Plate, Shakespeare, Juliet, D 3596, 10 1/4 In. 150.00
Plate, Shakespeare, Romeo, D 3746, 10 1/2 In. 150.00
Plate, Shylock, D 7202, 10 1/2 In. 150.00
Plate, Sir Toby Belch, Noke, 10 1/2 In. 30.00

Plate, Springtime, Old Lady With Basket, Cottage, D 4933, 10 1/4 In.	30.00
Plate, Welsh, Women With Baskets, Lacy Flower Border, Noke, D 3363, 6 1/2 In.	30.00
Plate, Wolsey, D 3596, 10 1/2 In.	150.00
Punch Bowl, Gallant Fishers, Isaak Walton, Compleat Angler	575.00
Relish Tray, Mr. Pickwick, Sam Weller, Dickens E Series, D 5833, 8 3/4 In.	100.00
Soap Dish, Old Gleaners, Series Ware, D 3821, 2 1/4 In.	16.00
Soup, Cream, Underplate, Granville, 4 3/4 In.	25.00
Stein, Woodlands, c.1910, 5 1/2 In.	165.00
Sugar, Old Charlie, D 6012	800.00
Tankard, Shakespeare, Series Ware, Elizabethan Man, D 4750, 5 1/2 In.	44.00
Tankard, Watchman, Series Ware, D 4746, 5 1/2 In.	32.00
Tea Caddy, Old Lady Sipping Tea, Kingsware, 4 1/2 In.	130.00
Tea Set, Night Watchman, 3 Piece, D 3910	175.00
Tea Set, Turquoise Flowers, Mottled Green Shoulders, Buff Body, 3 Piece	300.00
Teapot, Darby & Joan, Self-Pouring, Kingsware, Marked Royles, 8 1/2 In.	800.00
Teapot, Hounds, Stags, Windmill, Salt Glaze, 7 In.	40.00
Teapot, Hunting Scene, Tan Salt Glaze, White, 5 In.	32.00
Teapot, Pink & Blue Flowers, Textured Buff Body, Leaves, 5 1/2 In.	100.00
Tobacco Jar, Dutch, Old Man With 4 Children, D 1836	40.00
Tobacco Jar, Fishermen, 6 1/2 In.	403.00
Toby Jug, Albert Sagger, Potter Doultonville	150.00
Toby Jug, Alderman Mace, Mayor Doultonville	100.00
Toby Jug, Betty Bitters, Doultonville	100.00
Toby Jug, Cap'n Cuttle, Small	250.00
Toby Jug, Capt. Salt, Doultonville	110.00
Toby Jug, Charlie Cheer, The Clown, Doultonville	125.00
Toby Jug, Clown, Medium	200.00
Toby Jug, Falstaff, Large ....48.00 to 58.00
Toby Jug, Falstaff, Small	65.00
Toby Jug, Father Christmas, Small	175.00
Toby Jug, Florist, Flora Fuchsia, Doultonville	150.00
Toby Jug, Happy John, Large	64.00
Toby Jug, Happy John, Small	100.00
Toby Jug, Huntsman, Large	100.00
Toby Jug, Jester, Medium	225.00
Toby Jug, King & Queen Of Diamonds, Small	275.00
Toby Jug, Leprechaun, Medium ....60.00 to 125.00
Toby Jug, Rev. Cassock The Clergyman, Small	100.00
Toby Jug, Sgt. Peeler The Policeman, Small	100.00
Toby Jug, Sir Francis Drake, Large ....80.00 to 175.00
Toby Jug, Town Crier, Medium	60.00
Toby Jug, Vic Schuler, Large	223.00
Toby Jug, Winston Churchill, Large	175.00
Toby Jug, Winston Churchill, Small	100.00
Toothpick, Sairey Gamp, D 6150	600.00
Tray, Dresser, Salmon, Yellow & Magenta Flowers, D 6227, 8 1/2 x 7 1/4 In.	60.00
Tray, Dutch, Octagonal, Old Man & Woman, Noke, D 2606, 11 1/4 x 7 1/4 In.	90.00
Tray, Robin Hood, King Of The Archers, 8 1/4 x 7 1/4 In.	85.00
Tray, Under The Greenwood Tree, Series Ware, D 6341, 11 x 5 3/4 In.	80.00
Trivet, Farm Workers, Silhouette, Man With Lantern, D 3356, 6 1/2 In.	45.00
Trivet, Venetian Canal Scene, D 3039, 6 In.	50.00
Vase, Acanthus Leaves & Pods, Amber & Blue, Flared Rim, Simmance, 16 In.	920.00
Vase, Art Nouveau Flowers, Mottled Green & Ochre, Beading On Base, 3 1/4 In.	45.00
Vase, Art Nouveau Incised Vines, Flowers, Leaves, Mottled Light Green, 7 1/4 In.	130.00
Vase, Art Nouveau Medallions, Flowers, Green & Blue Glaze, 9 In.	305.00
Vase, Arts & Crafts Flowers, Mottled Blue, Mulberry Matte Glaze, 7 In.	110.00
Vase, Beaded Panels, Cobalt & Mustard Flowers, Mottled Blue, 6 1/2 In.	90.00
Vase, Bird On Branch, Stylized White Flowers, Leaves, Brown Overglaze, 11 In.	525.00
Vase, Blacksmith & Child, Brown Ground, 2 Handles, Kingsware, 3 In.	90.00
Vase, Bud, Ball Shape, White Flowering Branches, Holbein Ware, 4 In.	50.00
Vase, Bud, Scroll Medallions, Flowers Green, Brown, Cobalt Glaze, 5 1/2 In.	100.00
Vase, Buff Glaze, Olive Green Band, Flowers, Cylindrical, Tapered, 7 3/4 In.	60.00

Vase, Central Band Of Fruiting Vine, Signed, c.1925, 6 3/8 In. 230.00
Vase, Coaching Days, Man Operating Gate, 4 1/4 In. 80.00
Vase, Cows In Pasture, Scrolls, Flowers, Mottled Blue & Green, 12 In. 575.00
Vase, Dragon, Bird, Stoneware, Francis C. Pope, 1922, 19 1/2 In. 3300.00
Vase, Dutch, Man Talking To 2 Others, Squat, 2 Handles, 2 1/2 In. 60.00
Vase, Eglinton Tournament, Knight With Foot Soldiers, D 2039, 3 3/4 In. 60.00
Vase, Fanling, Sung Flambe Oriental, Stamped, 7 In. 316.00
Vase, Female Heads, Stoneware, No. 354, Eliza Simmance, 1903, 11 1/2 In. 1440.00
Vase, Flambe, Classical Shape, Stamp, 7 x 5 1/2 In. 345.00
Vase, Flambe, Flowers, Silver Overlay, Signed, 7 1/2 In. 644.00
Vase, Flambe, Landscape Scene, 6 In. 200.00
Vase, Flambe, Stick, 5 1/2 In. 46.00
Vase, Flambe, Sung, No. 2692/E, C. Noke, c.1930, 8 3/4 In. 1680.00
Vase, Flambe, Swirling Red, Oval, Stamped, 11 1/4 In. 460.00
Vase, Fox-Hunting Scene, D 5105, 8 In. 140.00
Vase, Glazed Flowers, Leaves, 11 3/4 x 5 In. 358.00
Vase, Incised Cobblestone, Gold Outline, Greek Key Band, 3 1/2 In. 55.00
Vase, Japanese Design, Cylindrical, Tapered, 2 Handles, 6 3/4 In. 60.00
Vase, Landscape With Sheep, 8 1/4 In. 55.00
Vase, Lantao, Chang Glaze, No. 231/250, 6 1/4 x 5 3/4 In. 316.00
Vase, Leaves, White Ground, Stoneware, No. 557, Marshall, 1904, 15 3/8 In. 780.00
Vase, Maple Leaves, Blue Flowers, Stippled Ground, 11 x 4 In., Pair 176.00
Vase, Monk Reading Book, 2 Handles, Kingsware, 12 In. 1600.00
Vase, Mottled Brown, Blue & Pink Flowers, Squat, 4 1/2 In. 105.00
Vase, Mottled Cobalt, Ocher & Cobalt Blue Art Deco Design, Bulbous, 10 In. 90.00
Vase, Mottled Green, Cobalt Blue Grape Clusters, Flared Cobalt Rim, 3 1/2 In. 90.00
Vase, Mottled Green, Flowers, Shells, Leaves, Crimped Rim, 2 Handles, 3 3/4 In. ... 65.00
Vase, Mottled Olive Green, Ochre Glazed Flowers, Tassels, Wide, Flared Rim, 4 In. ... 120.00
Vase, Mottled, Red, Blue, White, Green, Oval, Painted Sung, Artist Mark, 6 3/4 In. ... 374.00
Vase, Pink, Ocher Leaves, Green, Stoneware, No. 283, c.1906, 18 1/2 In. 2160.00
Vase, Ploughing, Ploughman With Horses, D 4934, 2 1/4 In. 40.00
Vase, Salmon, Yellow & Magenta Flowers, Mottled Blue, Flared, D 6227, 8 3/4 In. ... 90.00
Vase, Sir Roger De Coverley, Series Ware, 7 3/4 In. 50.00
Vase, Slaters, Fluted Top, SP 5583 .... 100.00
Vase, Spill, Green, Tan Salt Glaze, 7 3/4 In. 32.00
Vase, Stoneware, No. 585, Frank A. Butler, 1909, 15 In. 3600.00
Vase, Stylized Floral Bouquets, c.1920, 8 3/4 In., Pair 400.00
Vase, Stylized Roses, Stoneware, No. 156, Eliza Simmance, 1910, 12 1/4 In. 480.00
Vase, Sunflower, Blue, Minnie Webb, 8 3/4 x 5 In. 330.00
Vase, Sung, Flambe, Undersea Landscape, C. Noke, F. Allen, c.1930, 9 In. 1680.00
Vase, Titanian, Bird On Branch, White-Throat, H. Allen, 4 x 3 1/2 In. 489.00
Vase, Titanian, Young Mavis, Bird On Branch, Crescent Moon, H. Allen, 10 In. 1035.00
Vase, Tube Lined, Birds, Trees, Stoneware, Early 20th Century, 21 In. 2700.00
Vase, Welsh, Woman With Umbrella, Other Women, 1032A, 7 In. 180.00
Wall Mask, Jester, 11 1/2 In. 415.00
Wall Pocket, Jackdaw Of Rheims Series Ware, D 5772, 7 1/4 x 8 In. 110.00
Waste Bowl, Gnomes, Signed Noke, 5 1/4 In. 200.00

ROYAL DUX is the more common name for the Duxer Porzellanmanu-
faktur, which was founded by E. Eichler in Dux, Bohemia, in 1860. By
the turn of the century, the firm specialized in porcelain statuary and
busts of Art Nouveau–style maidens, large porcelain figures, and
ornate vases with three-dimensional figures climbing on the sides. The
firm is still in business.

Bust, Maiden, Hair & Body Set With Flowers, 21 In. 2185.00
Centerpiece, Women Climbing Seashell, Art Nouveau, 14 x 7 x 10 In. 1568.00
Figurine, 2 Hunting Dogs, Impressed Diamond, Signed, 9 x 15 1/2 In. 275.00
Figurine, Dancing Couple, Mid-Eastern Dress, Cobalt Blue, Gold, Art Deco, 11 1/2 In. 330.00
Figurine, Polar Bear, Pink Triangle Mark, 11 x 13 In. 310.00
Figurine, Russian Wolf Hound, 11 In. 70.00
Group, Hunting Dogs, 7 x 14 In. 250.00
Vase, Woman With Flowing Hair, Marbleized, Iris Design, Signed, 8 In. 110.00

ROYAL FLEMISH glass was made during the late 1880s in New Bedford, Massachusetts, by the Mt. Washington Glass Works. It is a colored satin glass decorated with dark colors and raised gold designs. The glass was patented in 1894. It was supposed to resemble stained glass windows.

Biscuit Jar, Cover, Thistle Design, Signed, 11 In.	920.00
Lamp Font, Shield Design, 4 1/2 x 6 In.	330.00
Vase, 4 Coins, Paneled Background, 7 x 8 In.	6038.00
Vase, Azalea Blossoms, Gold, Silver, Soft Pink, Gold Ground, 13 1/2 x 6 In.	2470.00
Vase, Ducks In Flight, Gold Sunburst, Brown Swirl, Crowned Top, 15 In.	8510.00
Vase, Handle, Raised Gold Body, Crowned Shield, Rampant Lions, 12 In.	1736.00
Vase, Peacock With Jewels, Signed, 13 In.	5750.00
Vase, Stick, 2 Courting Pea Fowls, 4 1/2 In.	1480.00

ROYAL HAEGER, see Haeger category.

ROYAL HICKMAN designed pottery, glass, silver, aluminum, furniture, lamps, and other items. From 1938 to 1944 and again from the 1950s to 1969, he worked for Haeger Potteries. Mr. Hickman operated his own pottery in Tampa, Florida, during the 1940s. He moved to California and worked for Vernon Potteries. The last years of his life he livd in Guadalajara, Mexico, and continued designing for Royal Haeger. Pieces made in his pottery listed here are marked *Royal Hickman, Florida.*

Ashtray, Alligator, 8 In.	185.00
Figurine, Fish, 7 In.	235.00
Figurine, Panther, 8 In.	950.00
Vase, Long Neck, Orange Glaze, 14 In.	15.00
Vase, Swan Shape, 6 In.	295.00
Vase, Urn Shape, Green & Blue, S-Handles, 12 In.	82.00

ROYAL IVY, see Northwood, Royal Ivy

ROYAL NYMPHENBURG is the modern name for the Nymphenburg porcelain factory, which was established at Neudeck-ob-der-Au, Germany, in 1753 and moved to Nymphenburg in 1761. The company is still in existence. Marks include a checkered shield topped by a crown, a crowned *CT* with the year, and a contemporary shield mark on reproductions of eighteenth-century porcelain.

Bowl, Beaded Rim, Center Scenic Roundels, Titled Scenes, 7 3/8 In.	315.00
Figurine, Lady, Kerchief, Maroon Dress, Apron, Signed, 1800, 5 1/4 In.	320.00
Snuffbox, Partially Clothed Woman, Flower Sprays, c.1760, 2 7/8 In.	3600.00
Tankard, Allegorical Female Figure, Charity, Bird On Branch, 9 In.	5700.00
Teapot, Flowers, Gilt Trim, Branch Handle, Gold Rose Finial, 4 x 8 In.	250.00
Vase, Enameled, Continuous Landscape, R. Sieck, 10 1/2 In.	747.00

ROYAL RUDOLSTADT, see Rudolstadt category.

ROYAL VIENNA, see Beehive category.

ROYAL WORCESTER is a name used by collectors. Worcester porcelains were made in Worcester, England, from about 1751. The firm went through many different periods and name changes. It became the Worcester Royal Porcelain Company, Ltd., in 1862. Today collectors call the porcelains made after 1862 *Royal Worcester.* In 1976, the firm merged with W. T. Copeland to become Royal Worcester Spode. Some early products of the factory are listed under Worcester.

Biscuit Jar, Cover, Bamboo, Ivory, Gilt Leaves & Handle, 6 x 7 In.	275.00
Biscuit Jar, Gourd Shape, Flowering Vine, Gilt, c.1889, 7 x 6 1/2 In.	308.00
Candelabra, Boy & Girl Between 2 Branches, Hadley, c.1891, 8 5/8 In., Pair	764.00
Compote, Flower Petal Shape, Flowers, Poppy Pod Base, c.1888, 3 1/2 In.	616.00
Demitasse Set, Geometric, Scrollwork, Jewels, Gilt, Box, c.1926, 2 In., 18 Piece	920.00
Dish, Shell, 3-Footed, Marked, c.1953, 7 1/4 In., Pair	764.00

Ewer, Gilt Handle, Oval Body, Flowers & Gilt, c.1893, 7 3/4 In. 224.00
Figurine, Debutante, White, Green Dress, Brown Jacket, c.1981, 7 1/2 In. 35.00
Figurine, Grandmother's Dress, Fuchsia, Doughty, 6 1/4 In. 55.00
Figurine, Man & Woman Holding Basket, No. 880, c.1882, 10 1/4 In., Pair 470.00
Figurine, Parakeet, Doughty, 6 1/2 In. 110.00
Figurine, Venus, Seated In Shell, 2 Dolphins & Water Plants, 7 1/2 In. 402.00
Figurine, Water Carrier, 1884, 17 In. 412.00
Figurine, Water Carrier, Ivory, Bronze, Hadley, c.1880, 16 1/4 & 17 1/4 In., Pair 705.00
Figurine, Water Carrier, Woman, Flowers, Ivory, Gilt Trim, c.1893, 31 1/2 In. 881.00
Figurine, Woman Standing By Tree, Sir Thomas Brock, c.1917, 24 1/2 In. 940.00
Jug, Basket Weave, Encrusted Gold Leaves, Trim, 1886, 12 1/2 In. 66.00
Jug, Tankard Shape, Elephant Head Handle, Enameled, 1881, 7 5/8 In. 245.00
Lamp Base, Moorish Type Handles, Shipwreck Scene, Electrified, 13 3/4 In. 316.00
Lamp Base, Urn Shape, Flower Sprays, Key Pattern, Pedestal Base, 16 In. 230.00
Nappy, Hand Painted, Floral Sprays, Gilt Rim, Initialed, 1892, 8 In. 175.00
Pie Bird, Blue & White, 2 Piece 155.00
Pitcher, Floral Sprays, Flat Back, Hand Enameled, Signed, 1885, 5 1/2 In. 245.00
Pitcher, Flowers, Gilt Twig Handle, c.1890, 5 1/2 In. 224.00
Pitcher, Flowers, Scalloped Rim, Leaf Spout, Twig Handle, c.1889, 6 In. 476.00
Pitcher, Lion Head Spout, Lion Paw Handle, Gilt Flowers, c.1889, 7 3/4 In. 896.00
Pitcher, Lion Head Spout, Lion Paw Handle, Gilt Rim, 1889, 9 In. 950.00
Pitcher, Mask Spout, 1889, 6 1/4 In. 225.00
Pitcher, Mums, Gilt, Ribbed Handle, c.1888, 5 3/4 In. 55.00
Pitcher, Tiger Lilies, Gilt Accents, Ribbed Handle, c.1890, 6 3/8 In. 55.00
Plate, Flowers, Polychrome, Gilt Rim, Mid 20th Century, 9 1/4 In., 12 Piece 330.00
Plate, Quatrefoil, Painted, Fish, 8 3/4 In., 4 Piece 412.00
Plate, Village Of Tewsbury, Gold Rim, Nicholl, 1953, 10 3/4 In. 225.00
Platter, Wild Game, Pheasants, Bird Handles, c.1899, 17 3/4 In. 499.00
Salt, Master, Dolphin Form 65.00
Sugar, Dolphin Handles, 1893, 3 3/4 x 5 In. 145.00
Teapot, Floral Sprays, Hand Enameled, 1888, 7 In. 195.00
Teapot, Imari, Puce Printed Factory Mark, 6 In. 170.00
Vase, Austria Wild Flowers, Reginald Austin, c.1904, 4 5/8 In. 380.00
Vase, Flowers & Vine, Blue Ground, Gilt Rim, 2 Handles, c.1888, 18 1/4 In. 1176.00
Vase, Gold Coiled Dragon, Open Mouth, 2 Sets Of Feet, 15 x 9 In. 2645.00
Vase, Landscape, Cattle, Garniture, Painted, J. Stinton, Late 1920s, 3 Piece 11400.00
Vase, Scenic Panel, Perched Peacocks, R. Austin, c.1900, 8 1/2 In. 1344.00
Vase, Spill, Group, Majolica, Frog, Monkey, Tortoise, Marked, c.1880, 9 In. 2040.00
Vase, Stick, Floral Spray On Cream Ground, Green Mark, 6 1/2 In. 56.00
Vase, Vibrant Insects, Butterflies & Gilt Branches, 2 Handles, c.1887, 9 In. 476.00

ROYCROFT products were made by the Roycrofter community of East
Aurora, New York, in the late nineteenth and early twentieth centuries.
The community was founded by Elbert Hubbard, famous philosopher,
writer, and artist. The workshops owned by the community made furniture, metalware, leatherwork, embroidery, and jewelry. A printshop
produced many signs, books, and the magazines that promoted the sayings of Elbert Hubbard. Furniture by the Roycroft community is listed
in the Furniture category.

Album, Photo, Leather, Tooled, Signed, Cordova Shops, 12 x 15 In. 430.00
Ashtray, Original Patina, Circular Base, 8 x 29 In. 425.00
Bean Pot, c.1910, 4 1/2 In. 35.00
Book Set, Little Journeys, Elbert Hubbard, Miriam Edition, Leather, c.1903, 27 Piece ... 316.00
Bookends, Copper, Brass Washed, Hammered, Tooled Leather, Deer, 4 1/2 In. 635.00
Bookends, Copper, Hammered, Brass Patina, 5 1/2 In. 275.00
Bookends, Copper, Hammered, Brass Wash, Fleur-De-Lis, 5 x 5 1/4 x 4 In. 230.00
Bookends, Copper, Hammered, Dark Blue Patina, 5 x 3 3/4 In. 395.00
Bookends, Copper, Hammered, Dogwood Design Border, 4 1/2 x 5 x 3 In. 90.00
Bookends, Copper, Hammered, Flowers, Original Patina, 8 1/2 In. 185.00
Bookends, Copper, Hammered, Original Patina, 3 1/4 In. 430.00
Bookends, Copper, Hammered, Original Patina, 4 x 3 1/2 In., Pair 230.00
Bookends, Copper, Hammered, Original Patina, 5 1/2 In. .... 300.00 to 575.00
Bookends, Copper, Hammered, Original Patina, 8 1/2 In. 345.00

Bookends, Rectangular, Riveted Band, Orb Mark, No. 309, 5 1/4 x 4 1/2 In. 200.00
Bowl, Copper, Acid Etched, Silver Wash, 2 1/4 x 4 1/4 In. 144.00
Bowl, Copper, Hammered, 10 1/2 x 4 1/2 In. 1000.00
Bowl, Copper, Hammered, Brass Wash, Polished, 12 x 4 3/4 In. 440.00
Bowl, Copper, Hammered, Original Patina, 2 1/4 In. 288.00
Bowl, Copper, Hammered, Original Patina, 6 1/2 In. 311.00
Bowl, Copper, Hammered, Scroll & Bubble Pattern, Dark Patina, 2 1/2 x 6 1/2 In. 575.00
Bowl, Copper, Hammered, Silver Wash, Acid Etched, 3-Footed, 4 x 10 In. 750.00
Box, Cigarette, Copper, Hammered, Cedar Lining, Hinged Lid, Marked, 2 x 4 x 5 In. 405.00
Box, Copper, Hammered, Brass Wash, Dogwood Design, Hinged Lid, 2 x 7 x 3 1/2 In. . . . 518.00
Box, Copper, Hammered, Sailing Vessel, Medium Brown Patina, 2 1/4 x 5 5/8 In. 850.00
Box, Mahogany, Wrought Copper Strap, Monogram, 10 x 23 x 13 In. 635.00
Box, Stamp, Cover, 3 Sailboats, Green Rolling Hills, Dark Brown Patina, 2 3/4 x 4 In. . . . 695.00
Candlestick, Copper, Hammered, Domed Base, Dark Brown Patina, 6 1/2 In., Pair 875.00
Candlestick, Copper, Hammered, Original Patina, 4 1/2 In., Pair 230.00
Candlestick, Copper, Hammered, Original Patina, 7 1/2 In., Pair 430.00
Candlestick, Copper, Hammered, Thin, Twisted Stem, Circular Base, 13 In., Pair 978.00
Candlestick, Copper, Original Patina, 7 1/2 In., Pair 550.00
Chandelier, 3-Light, Amber Shades, Cutout Hearts, Triangular Base, 11 x 14 In. 1955.00
Frame, Copper, Hammered, Acid Etched, Original Patina, Marked, 12 x 10 In. 575.00
Frame, Copper, Hammered, Brass Patina, 6 1/4 In. 175.00
Frame, Print, The Philistine, Matted, Glass, Frame, 28 x 23 1/2 In. 345.00
Humidor, Copper, Hammered, Brass Wash, Trillium Pattern, Marked, 5 1/2 x 4 1/2 In. . . . 315.00
Inkwell, Copper, Hammered, Original Brass Patina, 4 In. 230.00
Lamp, Copper, Hammered, 4 Riveted Bands, Steuben Shade, Orb & Cross, 15 In. 5750.00
Lamp, Copper, Hammered, Desk, Square Column, Square Base, 14 1/4 In. 2415.00
Lamp, Copper, Hammered, Dome Shade, Riveted Leaf Straps, Marked, 14 1/2 In. 3220.00
Lamp, Copper, Hammered, Helmet Shade, 14 x 5 In. 210.00
Lamp, Copper, Hammered, Steuben Iridescent Glass Shade, Marked, 17 x 10 1/2 In. 3450.00
Letter Holder, Copper, Hammered, Stylized Flowers, Brass Wash, 3 3/4 x 4 3/4 In. 230.00
Mirror, 6 Iron Hooks, Rectangular, Hanging Chains, 30 x 50 In. 2990.00
Pitcher, Copper, Hammered, Silver Wash, Hollow Handle, Flared Spout, 7 1/2 x 9 In. . . . 275.00
Purse, Leather, Tooled, Embossed, Flower, Clasp, Turn-Lock, 2 Mirrors, 9 1/2 x 7 In. . . . 175.00
Sconce, Copper, Fluted Glass Shade, Spiral Mounted, Scalloped Base, 7 In., Pair 690.00
Sconce, Copper, Hammered, Riveted Strap Holder, Impressed Backplate, 10 In., Pair 635.00
Smoking Set, Copper, Hammered, 3 1/2 x 10 In., 3 Piece 290.00
Stand, Little Journeys, Rectangular Top, 2 Shelves, 26 x 14 x 26 In. 980.00
Tray, Copper, Hammered, Brass Wash, Handles, Oval, 22 x 9 1/2 In. 405.00
Tray, Copper, Hammered, Radial, Original Patina, 9 In. 285.00
Tray, Copper, Hammered, Riveted Handles, Circular, 18 1/4 In. 375.00
Vase, Bud, Copper, Hammered, 3 Buttress Form, Tooled, Impressed Mark, 7 In. 1900.00
Vase, Copper, Hammered, American Beauty, Grove Park Inn, 22 x 8 In. 3450.00
Vase, Copper, Hammered, American Beauty, Original Dark Patina, 7 x 2 1/2 In. 1840.00
Vase, Copper, Hammered, Brass Wash, Signed, 4 1/2 In. 400.00
Vase, Copper, Hammered, Buttress, Egyptian, 4 Angular Handles, 7 1/8 In. 5175.00
Vase, Copper, Hammered, Closed In Rim, Original Patina, Marked, 4 1/2 x 2 1/2 In. 405.00
Vase, Copper, Hammered, Cone Shape, 2 Ring Handles, Round Base, 18 In. 4025.00
Vase, Copper, Hammered, Cylindrical, Nickel Silver Overlay Band, 6 1/2 x 3 In. 1035.00
Vase, Copper, Hammered, Dark Patina, Karl Kipp, Hand Wrought, 4 1/16 In. 5460.00
Vase, Copper, Hammered, German Silver Band, Original Patina, Stamped, 6 x 3 In. 1380.00
Vase, Copper, Hammered, Glass Liner, Box, 7 x 3 1/2 In. 345.00
Vase, Copper, Hammered, Heavy Gauge, Brass Patina, 7 1/2 In. 690.00
Vase, Copper, Hammered, Original Dark Brown Patina, 4 3/4 In. 835.00
Vase, Copper, Hammered, Original Dark Brown Patina, 4 3/8 In. 475.00
Vase, Copper, Hammered, Original Patina, 4 1/2 In. 240.00
Vase, Copper, Hammered, Original Patina, 5 In. 320.00
Vase, Copper, Hammered, Original Patina, Handles, 6 In. 715.00
Vase, Copper, Hammered, Signed, 8 1/2 In. 1035.00
Vase, Copper, Hammered, Squat, Original Patina, Orb & Cross Mark, 4 1/4 x 6 1/2 In. . . . 690.00
Vase, Copper, Hammered, Trumpet, Riveted Rim Collar, Applied Handles, 13 1/2 In. 4025.00
Vase, Cylindrical, Rim Border, Dogwood Flowers, Diamonds, Orb Mark, 10 In. 480.00
Vase, Silver Rim, Monogram, 3 1/4 x 3 1/8 In. 121.00
Vase, Silver Wash, Cylindrical, Quatrefoil, Orb & Cross Mark, 5 In. 635.00

Vessel, Bulbous, Hammered, Copper, Orb & Cross, 6 x 5 In.	230.00
Waste Basket, Mahogany Finish, 16 x 13 1/2 In.	1750.00

ROZANE, see Roseville category.

ROZENBURG worked at The Hague, Holland, from 1890 to 1914. The most important pieces were earthenware made in the early twentieth century with pale-colored Art Nouveau designs.

Jar, Dome Cover, Heart Shape, Rooster & Flower, Blue, Gray, Brown, Stamped, 13 In.	489.00
Vase, Purple Blossoms, Green & Cobalt Ground, 10 1/4 x 2 3/4 In.	635.00
Vase, Stylized Tulips, Leaves, Yellow & Green On Cobalt Blue, Bulbous, c.1896, 13 In.	633.00

RRP is the mark used by the firm of Robinson-Ransbottom. It is not a mark of the more famous Roseville Pottery. The Ransbottom brothers started a pottery in 1900 in Ironspot, Ohio. In 1920, they merged with the Robinson Clay Product Company of Akron, Ohio, to become Robinson-Ransbottom. The factory is still working.

Bean Pot, Brown & Mottled Tan Drip Glaze, 6 1/2 In.	7.50
Cookie Jar, Sherrif Pig, 12 In.	90.00
Jardiniere, Embossed Branch, Light Green & Brown Drip Glaze, 7 1/2 In.	55.00
Jardiniere, Embossed Flowers, Brown Drip Glaze, 9 In.	90.00
Mixing Bowl, Embossed Diamond Point Between Ribs, Ivory Glaze, 8 In.	10.00
Pitcher, Brown & Mottled Tan Drip Glaze, 7 1/2 In.	9.00
Pitcher, Brown Drip Glaze, Marked, 21 In.	50.00
Vase, Embossed Art Deco Design, Shaded Brown & Tan Glaze, Handles, 8 In.	45.00
Vase, Embossed Iris & Thistle, Brown & Green Drip Glaze, 14 1/2 In., Pair	185.00

RS GERMANY is part of the wording in marks used by the Tillowitz, Germany, factory of Reinhold Schlegelmilch from 1914 until about 1945. The porcelain was sold decorated and undecorated. The Schlegelmilch families made porcelains marked in many ways. See also ES Germany, RS Poland, RS Prussia, RS Silesia, RS Suhl, and RS Tillowitz.

Bowl, Magnolia Blossoms, 10 In.	85.00
Hatpin Holder, Pink Flowers, 4 1/2 In.	90.00

RS POLAND (German) is a mark used by the Reinhold Schlegelmilch factory at Tillowitz from about 1946 to 1956. After 1956, the factory made porcelain marked PT Poland. This is one of many of the RS marks used. See also ES Germany, RS Germany, RS Prussia, RS Silesia, RS Suhl, and RS Tillowitz.

Sugar & Creamer, Tan & Gold Ground, White & Gold Flowers, 4 1/4 In.	125.00

RS PRUSSIA appears in several marks used on porcelain before 1917. Reinhold Schlegelmilch started his porcelain works in Suhl, Germany, in 1869. See also ES Germany, RS Germany, RS Poland, RS Silesia, RS Suhl, and RS Tillowitz.

Berry Set, Point & Clover, Snowball & Rose Center, Signed	1200.00

RS Prussia, Chocolate Pot, Portrait, Summer Season, Carnation Mold, 10 In.

RS Prussia, Cracker Jar, 5 Portraits, Handles, Lily Mold

Don't use tape on porcelain or
pottery that has overglazed
decorations. Gilding and enamels may
pull off when the tape is removed.
Antiques shops often tape a lid to a
bowl; when you buy, ask the dealer to
remove the tape to be sure no
damage has been done.

RS Prussia, Plate, Melon Eaters, Gold,
Green, Opal, Point & Clover Mold, 8 1/2 In.

Bowl, Bread, Lily, 12 1/2 In.	4000.00
Bowl, Bread, Rose Bud, Wild Flowers, Signed, 14 In.	900.00
Bowl, Carnation, Pink & White Rose, 8 In.	320.00
Bowl, Flowers, Leaves, Pink, White, Lilies Of The Valley, Blue Ground, 10 In.	175.00
Bowl, Iris, Cream Center, Pink Poppy, 10 In.	500.00
Bowl, Leaves, Grapes, 10 1/2 In.	45.00
Bowl, Lebrun II Portrait, Bronze Tiffany Finish Border, 10 1/2 In.	1700.00
Bowl, Lebrun II Portrait, Tapestry Finish, 10 3/4 In.	2100.00
Bowl, Pink & Cream Roses, Iris Variation, 10 In.	600.00
Bowl, Point & Clover, Cobalt Blue, Flowers, 9 1/2 In.	550.00
Bowl, Ribbon & Jewel, Diana The Huntress, 11 In.	2300.00
Bowl, Schooner, Masted, 10 1/2 In.	3700.00
Bowl, Wild Rose, Gold Border, 10 In.	325.00
Cake Plate, Pink Rose, White Border, Artist Klett, 11 In.	400.00
Cake Plate, Swag & Tassel, 10 In.	225.00
Celery Tray, Dice Throwers, Green Trim, 13 1/2 In.	2500.00
Chocolate Pot, Portrait, Summer Season, Carnation Mold, 10 In. .... *Illus*	2800.00
Chocolate Pot, Wild Flowers, Pink & White, 9 In.	1000.00
Clock, Hidden Image, Wild Flowers, 9 In.	1000.00
Clock, Steeple, Flowers, Gold Stencil, 7 1/2 x 7 1/2 In.	300.00
Cracker Jar, 5 Portraits, Handles, Lily Mold .... *Illus*	6400.00
Cracker Jar, Iris, Summer Season Portrait, 6 1/2 In.	2900.00
Cracker Jar, Lily, 5 Portraits	6400.00
Cracker Jar, Wild Flowers, Signed, 7 In.	1200.00
Muffineer, Rose Spray, Daisies, Pink, Orange, Blue To Yellow, White Ground, 4 In.	175.00
Pitcher, Cider, Pink Flowers, Yellow, 6 1/2 In.	225.00
Plaque, Cottage Scene, 7 1/2 In.	550.00
Plate, Melon Eaters, Gold, Green, Opal, Point & Clover Mold, 8 1/2 In. .... *Illus*	1800.00
Plate, Poppy, Wild Flowers, Signed, 9 3/4 In.	170.00
Plate, Wild Flowers, Blue Border, 8 1/2 In., 6 Piece	1250.00
Platter, Leaves, Flowers, Yellow, Blue, Violet, Signed, Crown & Bee Mark, 13 In.	330.00
Spooner, Morning Glory, Yellow & Green, 4 1/4 In.	90.00
Tankard, Flowers, Pink & White, Scrolling, Gold Trim, Open Base, 11 1/2 In.	460.00
Vase, Dice Throwers, Skirted, Opalescent Jewels, 9 In.	1500.00
Vase, Melon Eater, 2 Handles, 6 In.	600.00
Vase, Melon Eater, Front & Back, Jeweled, 7 In.	2350.00
Vase, Pillow, Swan, Handles, Blue Green, 9 1/2 In.	1200.00

RS SILESIA appears on porcelain made at the Reinhold Schlegelmilch
factory in Tillowitz, Germany, from the 1920s to the 1940s. The
Schlegelmilch families made porcelains marked in many ways. See
also ES Germany, RS Germany, RS Poland, RS Prussia, RS Suhl, and
RS Tillowitz.

Candy Dish, Peonies, Turquoise, Gold Trim, Bowtie Shape, Handle, 9 1/2 In.	10.00

RS SUHL is a mark used by the Erdmann Schlegelmilch factory in Suhl, Germany, between 1900 and 1917. The Schlegelmilch families made porcelains in many places. See also ES Germany, RS Germany, RS Poland, RS Prussia, RS Silesia, and RS Tillowitz.

Bowl, Berry, 2 Women & Cherub, 5 In. 500.00

RS TILLOWITZ was marked on porcelain by the Reinhold Schlegelmilch factory at Tillowitz from the 1920s to the 1940s. Table services and ornamental pieces were made. See also ES Germany, RS Germany, RS Poland, RS Prussia, RS Silesia, and RS Suhl.

Ladle, Sauce, Orchid, Gold Trim, 4 3/4 In. 20.00
Plate, Sailboats, Hand Painted Transfer, 7 7/8 In. 125.00
Relish, Poppies, Hand Painted, Oval, 7 7/8 In. 25.00

RUBINA is a glassware that shades from red to clear. It was first made by George Duncan and Sons of Pittsburgh, Pennsylvania, about 1885. This coloring was used on many types of glassware. The pressed glass patterns of Royal Ivy and Royal Oak are listed under Northwood.

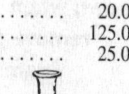

Finger Bowl, Threaded Top Rim, 2 x 4 1/2 In. 85.00
Rose Bowl, Ruffled Edge, Vertical Ribs, 4 1/2 x 5 In. 56.00

RUBINA VERDE is a Victorian glassware that was shaded from red to green. It was first made by Hobbs, Brockunier and Company of Wheeling, West Virginia, about 1890.

Pitcher, Water Set, Inverted Thumbprint, Square Top, 7 1/2 In., 2 Piece 230.00

RUBY GLASS is the dark red color of the precious gemstone known as a *ruby*. It was a popular Victorian color that never went completely out of style. The glass was shaped by many different processes to make many different types of ruby glass. There was a revival of interest in the 1940s when modern-shaped ruby table glassware became fashionable. Sometimes the red color is added to clear glass by a process called flashing or staining. Flashed glass is clear glass dipped in a colored glass, then pressed or cut. Stained glass has color painted on a clear glass. Then it is refired so the stain fuses with the glass. Pieces of glass colored in this way are indicated by the word *stained* in the description. Related items may be found in other categories, such as Cranberry Glass, Pressed Glass, and Souvenir.

Bowl, Reeded & Knopped Cover, Ribbed & Knopped Stem, Footed, 1930s, 9 3/4 In. 460.00
Vase, Hyacinth, Handles, Applied Rigaree, 6 1/2 In. 125.00

RUDOLSTADT was a faience factory in the Thuringia region of Germany from 1720 to about 1791. In 1854, Ernst Bohne began working in the area. From about 1887 to 1918, the New York and Rudolstadt Pottery made decorated porcelain marked with the RW and crown familiar to collectors. This porcelain was imported by Lewis Straus and Sons of New York, which later became Nathan Straus and Sons. The word *Royal* was included in their import mark. Collectors often call it *Royal Rudolstadt*. Most pieces found today were made in the late nineteenth or early twentieth century. Additional pieces may be listed in the Kewpie category.

Chocolate Set, Forgert-Me-Nots, Gold Trim On Cover, Signed, 10 In., 12 Piece 335.00
Chop Plate, Bunches Of Forget-Me-Nots, Green Leaves, Blue Border, 12 3/4 In. 115.00
Figurine, Boy & Girl, Gazing At Chicks, Ernst Bohne Sons, 9 1/2 x 7 In. 295.00
Vase, Flowers, 2 Handles, 13 1/4 In. 192.00
Vase, Green, Bronze Luster Glaze, 4 Organic Handles, Reticulated Shoulder, 9 1/2 In. ... 288.00

RUGS have been used in the American home since the seventeenth century. The oriental rug of that time was often used on a table, not on the floor. Rag rugs, hooked rugs, and braided rugs were made by housewives from scraps of material.

Afghan, Geometric Flowers, Blue Field, Red, Green, White, 2 Ft. 7 In. x 13 Ft. 6 In. 489.00

Afghan, Medallions, Blue, Green, Red Field, 2 Ft. 8 In. x 11 Ft. 489.00
Afghan, Red Ground, Blue, Ivory, Brown Border, 7 Ft. 5 In. x 8 Ft. 6 In. 385.00
Amish, Woven, Multicolored, Felt, 1 Ft. 10 In. x 3 Ft. 9 In. 225.00
Ardebil, 6 Medallions, c.1950, 8 Ft. 10 In. x 5 Ft. 7 In. 505.00
Art Deco, Chinese, Geometric Radiating From Ivory Circle, 11 Ft. 5 In. x 8 Ft. 10 In. 8400.00
Art Deco, Geometric Center Field, Tan, Brown Ground, Border, 8 Ft. 2 In. x 10 Ft. 2 In. .. 784.00
Art Deco, Geometric, Tan Ground, Wool, France, 1930, 8 Ft. 10 In. x 6 Ft. 8 In. 8400.00
Arts & Crafts, Diagonal Design, Flowers, Brown, 6 Ft. 2 In. x 11 Ft. 2 In. 405.00
Aubusson, Flowers, Black, Brown, Off-White, 7 Ft. 5 In. x 9 Ft. 9 In. 575.00
Aubusson, Needlepoint, Black, Browns, Off-White, 7 Ft. 5 In. x 9 Ft. 9 In. 575.00
Aubusson, Tan Ground, Floral Trellising, Center Medallion, 16 x 12 Ft. 3450.00
Bakhtiari, Allover Flowers, Indigo, Brown, Peach, Ivory, 4 Ft. 11 In. x 8 Ft. 3 In. 345.00
Bakhtiari, Birds & Flowers, Ivory Border, 9 Ft. 7 In. x 7 Ft. 275.00
Bakhtiari, Dark Blue Spandrels, Red Ground, Gray Border, 6 Ft. 10 In. x 10 Ft. 825.00
Bakhtiari, Divided Field, Ivory, Red & Brown, Ivory Border, 7 Ft. 3 In. x 11 Ft. 1 In. 275.00
Bakhtiari, Floral Medallion, Ivory, Brick, Blue, Multiple Borders, 6 Ft. 8 In. x 9 Ft. 9 In. . 750.00
Bakhtiari, Flowers, Birds, Trees, Wide Borders, Ivory, Brick, Blue, 5 Ft. 2 In. x 9 Ft. 9 In. 865.00
Bakhtiari, Lobed Diamond Medallion, Vines, Navy, Red, Ivory, 16 Ft. x 12 Ft. 8 In. 5460.00
Bakhtiari, Medallion, Cypress Palmetto, Ivory, Rose, Burgundy, 10 1/6 x 12 1/2 Ft. 1265.00
Bakhtiari, Millefleur Field, Pulled Medallion, Blue Ground, Vine Border, 6 x 5 Ft. 635.00
Bakhtiari, Red Ground, Oval Lobed Medallion, Ivory, Blue, Vine Border, 6 x 4 Ft. 575.00
Bakhtiari, Stylized Flowers, Cream, Blue, Ivory, Rose Ground, 5 Ft. 2 In. x 9 Ft. 9 In. ... 865.00
Bakhtiari, Trees, Flowers, Blue Ground, Multiple Borders, 9 Ft. 10 In. x 14 Ft. 2300.00
Baku, Floral Lozenge Medallions, Blue Field, c.1900, 4 Ft. 1 In. x 3 Ft. 8 In. 300.00
Baluchi, Allover Maroon, Blue, Ivory, Brown, Runner, 3 Ft. 10 In. x 9 Ft. 3 In. 715.00
Baluchi, Flowers, Medallions, Red, Black, White, Wave Border, 7 Ft. 6 In. x 3 Ft. 10 In. . 175.00
Baluchi, Geometric Tiles, Brown, Black, Crimson Ground, 3 Ft. 10 In. x 6 Ft. 4 In. 375.00
Baluchi, Prayer, Tree Of Life, Columns Of Octagons, Camel Field, 4 Ft. 6 In. x 2 Ft. 9 In. 175.00
Baluchi, Red, Brown, Ivory Ground, Blue Borders, 2 Ft. 6 In. x 3 Ft. 9 In. 250.00
Baluchi, Red, Ivory, Navy Grond, Early 20th Century, 3 Ft. 1 In. x 5 Ft. 3 In. 365.00
Baluchi, Tree Of Life, Blues, Ivory, Rose, Rust, Camel, Blue Border, 5 Ft. x 2 Ft. 9 In. ... 520.00
Baluchi, Wool On Cotton, Burgundy Ground, 5 Ft. 1 In. x 2 Ft. 9 In. 196.00
Bidjar, Center Pulled Medallion, Blue Spandrels, Millefleur Field, Red Ground, 7 x 4 Ft. . 460.00
Bidjar, Flowers, Tan Ground, Ivory Border, 10 Ft. 4 In. x 4 Ft. 330.00
Bidjar, Ivory, Blue, Red Field, c.1930, 3 Ft. 8 In. x 6 Ft. 1 In. 560.00
Bidjar, Strawberry Vine & Flower Trellis, Ivory, Palmette Border, 7 Ft. 7 In. x 5 Ft. 1 In. . 7800.00
Bokhara, 5 Alternating Rows, Geometric Shapes, Red Field, 9 x 6 Ft. 460.00
Bokhara, Black & Off-White, Dark Red Ground, Runner, 3 Ft. 3 In. x 10 Ft. 9 In. 175.00
Bokhara, Black Geometric, Cream Ground, Pakistani, 4 x 5 Ft. 115.00
Bokhara, Blue & Ivory, Mauve Ground, Multiple Borders, 4 Ft. x 4 Ft. 10 In. 110.00
Bokhara, Geometric, Red Field, Brown & Off-White Border, 3 Ft. 3 In. x 4 Ft. 4 In. 345.00
Bokhara, Gul Design, Red Ground, 6 Ft. 1 In. x 7 Ft. 9 In. 290.00
Bokhara, Gul Field, Geometric Red Borders, 2 Ft. 8 In. x 2 Ft. 11 In. 345.00
Bokhara, Pink & Blue, Ivory Ground, Multiple Borders, Runner, 3 Ft. 1 In. x 8 Ft. 9 In. ... 140.00
Bokhara, Red Ground, Blue, Teal, Brown, Ivory, 8 Ft. 4 In. x 13 Ft. 4 In. 1100.00
Braided, Dark Blue, Teal, Yellow & Green, Wool, Helen Pool, 3 Ft. 1 In. x 6 Ft. 5 In. 220.00
Braided, Multicolored, Round Corners, Border, 5 Ft. 6 In. x 6 Ft. 5 In. 300.00
Braided, Multicolored, Wool, Helen Pool, 2 Ft. 7 In. x 4 Ft. 1 1/2 In. 55.00
Braided, Oval, Striped, Wool, New Materials, Flax Tied, Helen Pool, 6 Ft. 5 In. x 3 Ft. ... 130.00
Braided, Oval, Wool, Helen Pool, 9 Ft. 6 In. x 14 Ft. 7 In. 550.00
Braided, Oval, Wool, Robin's-Egg-Blue, Helen Pool, 9 Ft. 4 In. x 13 Ft. 8 In. 220.00
Camel Hair, Red, Tan, Center Rosette, 5 Pulled Medallions, Leaf Border, 17 x 3 Ft. 489.00
Caucasian, 6 Square Panels, 3 Floral Borders, 6 Ft. x 5 Ft. 5 In. 770.00
Caucasian, Ivory Ground, Multiple Borders, 6 x 6 Ft. 440.00
Caucasian, Ivory, Light Blue, Green, Tan, Red Ground, 2 Ft. 9 In. x 3 Ft. 4 In. 110.00
Caucasian, Kazak, Diamond Panels, Latch Hook, Ivory, Blue, Brick, 4 Ft. 4 In. x 8 Ft. 1380.00
Caucasian, Kilim, Panels Of Keys, Blue, Ivory, Brick, Diamond Border, 4 Ft. 9 In. x 9 Ft. . 1265.00
Caucasian, Rust Ground, Multiple Borders, 4 Ft. 10 In. x 6 Ft. 1 In. 580.00
Chinese, Blue Flowers, Open Ground, Border, 57 x 39 In. 55.00
Chinese, Blue, Ivory, Peach, Tan, Urns, Flowers, Leaves, Fringe, 2 Ft. 6 In. x 4 Ft. 3 In. .. 165.00
Chinese, Bronze Central Ground, Burgundy, Blue Borders, 6 Ft. 3 In. x 8 Ft. 7 In. 385.00
Chinese, Camel, Flower Sprays In Corners, c.1930, 8 Ft. 8 In. x 11 Ft. 5 In. 220.00
Chinese, Corner Flowers, Yellow, Red, Green, Camel Field, Runner, 2 Ft. x 4 Ft. 11 In. .. 240.00

Antique rugs sometimes get dry rot in the cotton backing. It's an airborne fungus that lives on fibers. The rug will have weak, brittle fibers.

Rug, Chinese, Pagodas, Trees, Great Wall, Multiple Borders, Silk, 8 Ft. 10 In. x 11 Ft. 10 In.

Chinese, Floral Medallion, Spandrels, Blue, Gold, Brown, c.1890, 9 Ft. 9 In. x 6 Ft. 9 In.	1840.00
Chinese, Flowers, Gold Field, Rose Border, 8 Ft. 9 In. x 11 Ft. 6 In.	1093.00
Chinese, Flowers, Gray Field, Burgundy Border, 4 Ft. 10 In. x 7 Ft. 7 In.	115.00
Chinese, Flowers, Green Field, Red, Tan, 5 x 8 Ft.	288.00
Chinese, Flowers, Green, Brown, Purple, Mauve Field, Camel Border, 8 Ft. 10 In. x 12 Ft.	1150.00
Chinese, Flowers, Medallion, Mountains, Clouds, Blue, Ivory, Tan, c.1890, 8 x 5 Ft.	1610.00
Chinese, Flowers, Reds, Blues, Greens, White, Silk, 3 x 5 Ft.	776.00
Chinese, Landscape, Flowering Trees, Birds, Pagoda & Clouds, 6 Ft. 10 In. x 4 Ft.	520.00
Chinese, Landscape, Tan Ground, Blue Border, 3 x 5 Ft.	170.00
Chinese, Multicolored Flowers, Open Rose Ground, 11 Ft. 4 In. x 9 Ft.	825.00
Chinese, Noblemen, Gaming Table, Bat & Clouds, Ivory Ground, 7 Ft. 8 In. x 5 Ft.	1035.00
Chinese, Open Rose Ground, Borders Of Trailing Flowers, 6 Ft. 10 In. x 3 Ft. 11 In.	130.00
Chinese, Oval, Tan, Flowers, Butterflies, Medallion, Blue Borders, 7 Ft. x 10 Ft. 6 In.	550.00
Chinese, Pagodas, Trees, Great Wall, Borders, Silk, 8 Ft. 10 In. x 11 Ft. 10 In. *Illus*	3220.00
Chinese, Peking, Corner Vases, Bird Medallion, Blue, Tan, Brown, White, 3 x 4 Ft.	220.00
Chinese, Pictorial, 3 Women Riding Chariot, Phoenix, Round, 2 Ft. 8 In.	220.00
Chinese, Pictorial, Bearded Monkey, Brown, Tan, White, Round, 3 Ft. 2 In.	140.00
Chinese, Pink, Green & Beige Dragons, Open Blue Ground, Border, 7 Ft. x 4 Ft. 1 In.	130.00
Chinese, Quatrefoil Medallions, Leaves, Blue Field, Tan Border, 6 Ft. 9 In. x 4 Ft.	860.00
Chinese, Red Ground, Center Pot Of Flowers, Blue Borders, 8 x 10 Ft.	330.00
Chinese, Saddle Cover, Blue, Gold, Tan, Brown, Red Ground, 2 Ft. 4 In. x 5 Ft.	330.00
Daghestan, Blossom Filled Trellis, Ivory Field, Geometric Border, 4 Ft. 6 In. x 3 Ft. 7 In.	1800.00
Drugget, Arts & Crafts, Asymmetrical, Purple, Orange, Brown, Oatmeal Ground, 4 x 7 Ft.	403.00
Fereghan, Allover Medallion & Flowers, Blue Gray Ground, 3 Ft. 3 In. x 4 Ft. 10 In.	690.00
Fereghan, Blue Ground, Millefleur Field, 4 Ft. 6 In. x 6 Ft.	435.00
Fereghan, Blue Pendant Medallion, Red Field, Ivory, Blue Border, 10 Ft. x 6 Ft. 9 In.	8800.00
Fereghan, Ivory Lozenge Medallion, Blue Field, c.1900, 14 Ft. 10 In. x 6 Ft. 6 In.	840.00
Gorevan, Brown Ground, Black Border, 7 Ft. 6 In. x 9 Ft. 2 In.	330.00
Gorevan, Ivory Spandrels, Rust Ground, 8 Ft. x 11 Ft. 5 In.	1430.00
Hamadan, Birds, Flowers, Geometrics, Tan Ground, 20th Century, 3 Ft. 7 In. x 8 Ft. 8 In.	310.00
Hamadan, Black Spandrels, Red Ground, 4 Ft. 5 In. x 8 Ft. 4 In.	440.00
Hamadan, Blue & Red, Border, 3 Ft. 5 In. x 6 Ft. 7 In.	412.00
Hamadan, Blue Ground, Red, Ivory Field, c.1920, 3 Ft. 4 In. x 6 Ft. 5 In.	336.00
Hamadan, Brick Red, Dark Blue, Sage, Pink, 8 Ft. 7 In. x 8 Ft. 11 In.	448.00
Hamadan, Herati Design, Dark Red Terra Cotta Field, Blue Border, 6 Ft. 6 In. x 4 Ft. 6 In.	400.00
Hamadan, Ivory Spandrels, Blue Ground, Red & Camel Borders, 4 Ft. 4 In. x 7 Ft.	165.00
Hamadan, Ivory Spandrels, Animals & Birds, Multicolored Borders, 5 Ft. x 10 Ft. 4 In.	440.00
Hamadan, Mauve Center, Red, Blue Borders, 3 Ft. 8 In. x 6 Ft. 1 In.	275.00
Hamadan, Medallion, Rose, Crimson Ground, Multiple Borders, 4 Ft. 2 In. x 7 Ft. 4 In.	375.00
Hamadan, Medallions, Blue, Green, Red Field, Geometric Border, 4 Ft. 5 In. x 7 Ft. 8 In.	345.00
Hamadan, Medallions, Multiple Borders, Ivory, Brick, Blue, 1920s, 5 Ft. x 6 Ft. 9 In.	2070.00
Hamadan, Red Spandrels, Black Medallion, Blue Border, 4 Ft. 6 In. x 6 Ft. 7 In.	330.00
Hamadan, Red, Yellow, Blue, White, Brown Field, Runner, 3 Ft. x 6 Ft. 7 In.	195.00
Hamadan, Spandrels, Mauve Ground, Black Border, 4 Ft. 6 In. x 7 Ft.	250.00
Hamadan, Spandrels, Red Ground, Borders, Runner, 3 Ft. 2 In. x 9 Ft. 10 In.	140.00

Hamadan, Staggered Hexagons, Blues, Red, Brown, Ivory, Camel Field, 6 Ft. 2 In. x 3 Ft.   405.00
Hamadan, Stylized Blue, Brown, Flowers, Faded Red Ground, 6 Ft. 7 In. x 3 Ft. 8 In.   . . .   77.00
Hamadan, Stylized Flowers, Multicolored, Ivory, Red Ground, 4 Ft. 7 In. x 10 Ft. 10 In.   .   575.00
Hereke, Paradise, Silk, Birds, Flowers, Trees, Ivory, Burgundy Ground, 5 Ft. x 8 Ft. 7 In.   .   4675.00
Heriz, 7 Medallions, Rust Field, Blue, Wide Border, Runner, 12 Ft. 3 In. x 4 Ft. 9 In. 920.00
Heriz, Blue Medallion, Red Field, Ivory, Red & Ocher Borders, 8 Ft. 3 In. x 11 Ft. 3 In.   . .   4950.00
Heriz, Burgundy & Ivory Spandrels, Burgundy Ground, 6 Ft. 10 In. x 9 Ft. 6 In. 385.00
Heriz, Center Geometric Medallion, Ivory, Blue, Rust, 10 Ft. 10 In x 8 Ft. 6 In. 1440.00
Heriz, Geometric, Blue, Red, Orange, Ivory Ground, 11 x 14 Ft. 5175.00
Heriz, Herati Field, Star Medallion On Blue, Rust Ground, Romania, c.1950, 18 x 12 Ft.   .   920.00
Heriz, Ivory, Dark Blue, Light Blue, Brick Red Field, 3 Ft. 3 In. x 4 Ft. 5 In. 250.00
Heriz, Medallion, Allover Crimson Flowers, 8 Ft. x 9 Ft. 10 In. 1035.00
Heriz, Medallion, Green, Crimson, Ivory, Floral Ground, Borders, 7 Ft. 6 In. x 9 Ft. 6 In.   .   805.00
Heriz, Medallion, Ivory Spandrels, Brick Ground, Multiple Borders, 9 Ft. 6 In. x 13 Ft.   . .   1380.00
Heriz, Medallion, Multicolored Spandrels, Cartouche & Rosette Border, 10 x 13 Ft. 1380.00
Heriz, Spandrels, Burgundy Ground, 8 Ft. 3 In. x 10 Ft. 8 In. 385.00
Heriz, Star Medallion, Celadon, Ivory Spandrels, Rose Ground, Blue Border, 9 x 13 Ft.   . .   1380.00
Heriz, White, Blue, Rust, 7 Medallions, Rust Field, 3 Borders, 11 Ft. 1 In. x 2 Ft. 10 In.   . .   575.00
Hooked, 2 Apple Trees, 24 x 38 In. 800.00
Hooked, 2 Kissing Horses, Field Of Flowers, Horseshoe Corners, Frame, 31 x 42 In. 3737.00
Hooked, 3 Chickens Design, Geometric Border, 32 x 50 In. 575.00
Hooked, 4 Skiers, Skiing Slopes, William Moore, New Hampshire, 1920, 26 x 114 In.   . . .   750.00
Hooked, 40 Squares, Lighthouse, Ship, Clock, Tan, Browns, 129 x 104 In. 145.00
Hooked, Allover Flowers, Tan Ground, Black Borders, 114 x 161 In. 230.00
Hooked, Amish, Multicolored Circles, Scallops & Sunbursts, Braided Border, 39 x 37 In.   .   2185.00
Hooked, Art Deco, Geometric, Multicolored, Tan & Pink Ground, Runner, 31 x 65 In.   . . .   165.00
Hooked, Basket With Flowers, Corner Scrolls, Multicolored, 18 x 43 In. 220.00
Hooked, Battleship Maine, Havana Harbor, Flowers, Blue & Tan Border, 31 x 61 In. 1785.00
Hooked, Bear, Man In Tree, Cotton, Early 20th Century, 27 3/4 x 43 1/2 In. 635.00
Hooked, Beavers, Stag, Flowers, Leaves, Abstract, Cotton, 20th Century, 93 1/2 x 114 In.   4113.00
Hooked, Bird Gathering Berries, Chain Border, Scrolls, 19th Century, 27 x 38 1/2 In. 3450.00
Hooked, Black Horse, Star & Circle Design, Block Pattern Border, 32 x 51 In. 1155.00
Hooked, Black People Farming, Marked NGS, Multicolored, 33 x 40 In. 280.00
Hooked, Blocks, Cream, Blue, Wool, Flowers, Men, Women, 1930-1940, 143 x 106 In.   . .   2585.00
Hooked, Brown Spotted Terrier, 2 Trees Ground, Black Border, On Frame, 20 x 31 1/2 In.   165.00
Hooked, Brown, White Deer, In Round Medallion, Oak Leaf Borders, 32 x 57 In. 220.00
Hooked, Cat, Self-Satisfied, Gray, Blue Eyes, 28 1/2 x 17 In. 495.00
Hooked, Cats On Rug, Multicolored, Red Border, Marked NGS, 30 x 58 In. 476.00
Hooked, Center Dog, Surrounded By Floral Borders, 19 1/2 x 37 In. 285.00
Hooked, Central Flower Basket, 5 Tulips, Word Welcome, 20th Century, 27 1/2 x 35 In.   . .   588.00
Hooked, Connecting Concentric Circles, Black & Gray Ground, Wool, Cotton, 25 x 40 In.   290.00
Hooked, Country Winter Scene, Horse & Sleigh, Early 20th Century, 35 x 22 In. 1850.00
Hooked, Covered Bridge, Trees, Barn, Dates 1830-1913 In Corner, 40 x 23 1/2 In. 86.00
Hooked, Crowing Roosters, Gray Ground, Rosebud Each Corner, On Frame, 33 x 44 In.   .   1870.00
Hooked, Diamond, Orange & Gray, Brown Ground, Mid 20th Century, 40 1/2 x 32 In.   . . .   747.00
Hooked, Floral Bouquet, Pink, Green, Yellow, Blue, Red, Scalloped Edges, Round, 33 In.   55.00
Hooked, Flower Basket, 26 1/2 x 69 In. 4800.00
Hooked, Flower Tiles, Green Border, c.1930, 67 1/2 x 48 In. 2160.00
Hooked, Flower, Mid 20th Century, 31 x 52 In. 115.00
Hooked, Flowers & Leaves, Tan Ground, Dark Blue Border, 24 x 39 1/2 In. 140.00
Hooked, Flowers, Pear McGowan Design, Mounted, Frame, 36 x 48 In. 425.00
Hooked, Flowers, Yellow Leaves, Pine Cones, Brown, Early 20th Century, 60 x 33 In.   . . .   490.00
Hooked, Flying Dove, Flower & Vine Border, 1887, 25 x 40 In. 5170.00
Hooked, Geometric, 6 Scallop-Edged Diamonds, Maroon Border, 36 x 25 In. 145.00
Hooked, Geometric, Abstracted Zigzag, Hooked Border, Late 19th Century, 36 x 73 In.   . .   3055.00
Hooked, Geometric, Art Deco, Multicolored Ground, Black Border, c.1935, 83 x 53 In.   . .   1380.00
Hooked, Geometric, Black, Multicolored Field, 17 x 53 In. 896.00
Hooked, Geometric, Bow Tie, Random Outlined Panels, Twill Binding, 27 x 44 In. 488.00
Hooked, Geometric, Concentric Stars, Gold & Blue Ground, 20th Century, 36 1/2 x 24 In.   460.00
Hooked, Geometric, Flowers, 62 x 96 In. 920.00
Hooked, Geometric, Multicolored Diagonal Chevrons, 20th Century, 39 1/4 x 26 In. 460.00
Hooked, Geometric, Multicolored Stripes, Green Border, 26 1/4 x 44 In. 80.00
Hooked, Geometric, Random Blocks, Black Outlines, Black & Gray Border, 86 x 53 In.   . .   1380.00

Hooked, Geometric, Red & Black Border, 31 x 55 In. 440.00
Hooked, Geometric, Red, Mauve, Black, Light Blue, Triangle Border, 26 x 46 In. 330.00
Hooked, Geometric, Semi-Circles, Green Stripes, Wool, Frame, 30 1/2 x 60 1/2 In. 880.00
Hooked, Grenfell, Flying Geese, New Moon, Pine Trees, Early 1900s, 2 Ft. 2 In. x 3 Ft. . 1250.00
Hooked, Grenfell, Hen Pintail, 38 x 42 In. 575.00
Hooked, Grenfell, North Star, Fishing Symbols, Dogs, Sled, 25 x 20 In. 1380.00
Hooked, Halloween, Jack-O'-Lantern On Fence, Black Cat, Crescent Moon, 38 3/4 In. 1760.00
Hooked, Hit Or Miss Pattern, Black Borders, Wool, 27 1/2 x 22 12 In. 635.00
Hooked, Horse & Buggy, Flowers Each Corner, Scalloped Borders, 25 1/2 x 47 In. 220.00
Hooked, Horse & Cat, Black, Burgundy Ground, Initialed E. 1943 H, Frame, 23 x 36 In. . 525.00
Hooked, Horse In Pasture, Flowers, Grass, Landscape Ground, 28 1/2 x 36 In. 316.00
Hooked, Horse, Prancing, Black, Border, 36 x 41 1/2 In. 3080.00
Hooked, House, Barn, Fence, Well Sweep, Flower Border, Frame, 32 x 53 In. 748.00
Hooked, House, Red, Blue, Brown, Yellow, Wool, Mounted, 32 3/4 x 34 In. 940.00
Hooked, House, Trees, Mile Point Inscription, Early 20th Century, 30 1/4 x 40 In. 940.00
Hooked, Lamb, Early 20th Century, 24 x 37 In. 660.00
Hooked, Leaves, Pink, Coral, Orange, Natural Ground, Edward Fields, 120 x 150 In. 290.00
Hooked, Log Cabin, Multicolored, Red, Green, Blue, Brown, Wool, 19 1/2 x 28 In. 95.00
Hooked, Man Walking In Village, Tan Ground, Black Border, 35 x 59 In. 2016.00
Hooked, Multicolored Lines, 9-In. Blocks, Black, Brown, 57 x 91 In. ·· 440.00
Hooked, Multicolored Rectangles, Random Border, 35 x 24 1/2 In. 230.00
Hooked, Multicolored Rectangles, Triangular Corner Blocks, 61 1/2 x 30 In. 630.00
Hooked, Oriental Design, Geometric Flowers, Stepped Pyramid Border, 37 x 60 In. 220.00
Hooked, Pink Bird, Center Scrolled Leaves, Frame, 28 x 39 In. 120.00
Hooked, Ponies, Horses Shoes, Wooden Frame, 35 x 44 In. 1275.00
Hooked, Purple Pony, Stars, Tulips, Birds, Multicolored, Frame, 24 x 40 1/2 In. 990.00
Hooked, Rabbit, Red Stars Each Corner, Mounted, 24 x 40 In. 550.00
Hooked, Rag, 40 Dark Blocks, Multicolored Radiating Lines, 36 x 57 In. 190.00
Hooked, Rag, Geometric Crosses At Corners, Striped Squares, 83 x 41 In. 80.00
Hooked, Reclining Dog, Blue, Striped Border, Star Corners, 1880-1900, 24 x 34 In. 12500.00
Hooked, Recumbent Lion, Oval Rope Border, 31 x 60 In. 345.00
Hooked, Red Horse, Black Ground, Olive Green Border, Wooden Frame, 21 x 30 1/2 In. . 8225.00
Hooked, Red, Pink, Yellow, Blue Flowers, Blue, Purple Border, Ivory, 24 x 72 In. 880.00
Hooked, Repeating Concentric Diamonds, Wool, Frame, 19th Century, 7 x 39 1/2 In. 4465.00
Hooked, Rising Sun, Mountains, Deer, Bear & Cubs, 20th Century, 20 1/4 x 36 In. 460.00
Hooked, Rosebuds, Blossoms, Diamond Grid, Green, Pink, Brown, 35 1/2 x 66 3/4 In. 690.00
Hooked, Running Horse, Dated February 14, 1922, 29 x 40 In. 2500.00
Hooked, Scrolls, Leaves, Blue, Green, Yellow, Red, Gray, Brown, Wool, 33 x 62 In. 575.00
Hooked, Shirred, Flower Garden, Multicolored Blossoms, Earth Tone Border, 37 x 66 In. . 489.00
Hooked, Spotted Dog, Pink Flower Border, Red Scrolls, 1920, 40 x 30 In. 150.00
Hooked, Stag & Birds, Blue & Black Ground, Red Floral Border, c.1880, 29 x 55 In. 670.00
Hooked, Step-Down Pattern, Red Center, White Cross, Gray Ground, 22 x 35 1/2 In. 140.00
Hooked, Stripes, Tan Ground, Geometric Borders, Mid 20th Century, 54 1/2 x 31 In. 575.00
Hooked, Tan, Black Striped Cat, Flower, Wool, 19th Century, 17 x 26 3/4 In. 1495.00
Hooked, Thunderbirds, Arrowheads & Triangles, Black On Black Ground, 51 x 33 In. ... 300.00
Hooked, Union Is Strength, Soldier Holding Flag, Wool, Cotton, c.1862, 34 x 43 In. 11163.00
Hooked, Urn Of Flowers, Striped Border, Squares At Corners, Frame, 28 x 40 In. 575.00
Hooked, Water Lily, Red, Blue & Black Ground, 26 x 45 1/2 In. 440.00
Indo-Heriz, Ivory Spandrels, Midnight Blue Border, Red Ground, 5 Ft. 8 In. x 8 Ft. 330.00
Indo-Persian, Allover Flowers, Off-White Ground, Floral Borders, 4 Ft. 2 In. x 6 Ft. 3 In. 260.00
Indo-Persian, Central Medallion, Stylized Flowers, Sawtooth, 11 Ft. 6 In. x 7 Ft. 825.00
Indo-Persian, Off-White Field, Flowers, Borders, Red, Blue, Brown, 4 Ft. x 6 Ft. 3 In. ... 259.00
Indo-Sarouk, Geometric, Red Field, Blue, Green, Floral Border, 2 Ft. 9 In. x 9 Ft. 10 In. . 750.00
Isfahan, Round Medallion, Palmette & Trellising Field, Red Ground, 14 x 10 Ft. 920.00
Karabagh, 3 Joined Hexagonal Medallions, Wine-Red Ground, 9 Ft. 9 In. x 3 Ft. 6 In. ... 489.00
Karabagh, 4 Stars, Red, Orange, Camel, Green, Black, Red Border, c.1890, 8 x 4 Ft. 520.00
Karabagh, Eagle, 3 Sunburst Medallions, Rust Red Field, Ivory Border, 7 Ft. 4 In. x 4 Ft. 920.00
Karabagh, Herati, Blue, Brown, Green, Red, c.1890, 9 Ft. 6 In. x 4 Ft. 10 In. 460.00
Karabagh, Hexagon, Medallion, Herati, Mid 20th Century, 7 Ft. 4 In. x 4 Ft. x 9 In. 690.00
Karabagh, Octagonal Medallions, Inset Cloud Designs, Rust Red Field, 7 Ft. 7 In. x 4 Ft. . 400.00
Karabagh, Paisley, White Ground, Leaf Border, c.1875, 7 Ft. 4 In. x 3 Ft. 6 In. 1176.00
Karabagh, Stepped Diamond Medallions, Leaf & Chalice Border, 7 Ft. 6 In. x 4 Ft. 2 In. . 3000.00
Karaja, Red Ground, Blue Border, 3 Ft. 1 In. x 12 Ft. 7 In. 880.00

Karaja, Reds & Greens, 5 Medallions, Multiple Borders, Wool, 3 Ft. 2 In. x 10 Ft. 8 In. . .	196.00
Kashan, Allover Flowers & Medallions, Off-White Ground, Floral Border, 6 Ft. x 9 Ft. 5 In.	590.00
Kashan, Blue Spandrels, Deep Red Ground, Wide Border, 9 Ft. 8 In. x 12 Ft. 10 In.	1045.00
Kashan, Central Persia, Silk, 3rd Quarter 20th Century, 5 Ft. 8 In. x 4 Ft.	1725.00
Kashan, Flowers, Blues, Greens, Off-White, Red Field, 6 Ft. 5 In. x 10 Ft. 4 In.	520.00
Kashan, Ivory & Spandrels, Burgundy Ground, 8 Ft. 1 In. x 12 Ft. 7 In.	1045.00
Kashan, Overall Flowers, Medallion, Off-White Field, Flower Borders, 6 Ft. x 9 Ft. 5 In. . .	690.00
Kashan, Persian, Rust Ground, Flower Border, 11 x 17 Ft.	2300.00
Kashan, Spandrels, Pink Ground, Purple Border, 9 Ft. 3 In. x 12 Ft. 8 In.	1100.00
Kashan, Star Medallion, Palmette & Trellised Vine Field, Red Ground, 11 Ft. 3 In. x 9 Ft.	1092.00
Kashan, Trees, Birds, Blue Border With Deer & Birds, c.1920, 14 Ft. 2 In. x 10 Ft.	3450.00
Kayseri, West Anatolia, Mercerized Cotton, Mid 20th Century, 7 Ft. 7 In. x 5 Ft. 3 In. . . .	1095.00
Kayseri, West Anatolia, Mercerized Cotton, Mid 20th Century, 9 Ft. 4 In. x 6 Ft. 5 In.	1265.00
Kazak, 2 Medallions, Birds, Brown Field, 3 Ft. 3 In. x 6 Ft. 7 In.	785.00
Kazak, 3 Lesghi Stars, Red, Navy Blue, Ivory, Gold, Brown Field, Ivory Border, 6 x 4 Ft.	635.00
Kazak, Blue & Salmon Spandrels, Reddish Ground, Blue Border, 5 Ft. 3 In. x 5 Ft. 4 In. .	495.00
Kazak, Camel & Ivory, Blue Ground, Red & Blue Border, 3 Ft. 8 In. x 6 Ft. 9 In.	825.00
Kazak, Geometric, Ivory, Brick, Blue, Multiple Borders, 4 Ft. 4 In. x 7 Ft. 10 In.	1380.00
Kazak, Ivory Ground, Red, Blue, Salmon Field, 6 Ft. 6 In. x 9 Ft. 9 In.	560.00
Kazak, Ivory Medallion, Animals, Blue Ground, Geometric Borders, 6 Ft. x 8 Ft. 4 In. . . .	357.00
Kazak, Lori-Pambak, Octagonal Medallion, Flower Heads, Blues, Red Field, 6 x 4 Ft. . . .	690.00
Kazak, Narrow Red Center, Wide Borders, 5 Ft. 9 In. x 6 Ft. 3 In.	190.00
Kazak, Navy, Ivory, Red Field, Red Ground, Early 20th Century, 3 Ft. 5 In. x 5 Ft. 8 In. . .	1344.00
Kazak, Octagonal Medallion, 4 Star-Filled Squares, Blue Green Field, 7 Ft. x 6 Ft. 3 In. . .	865.00
Kazak, Orange & Tan Medallions, Dark Blue Border, Runner, 3 Ft. 4 In. x 8 Ft.	250.00
Kazak, Prayer, Geometric, Figural, Red Field, Border, Red, Blue, Green, 3 Ft. 9 In. x 5 Ft.	775.00
Kazak, Red Ground, Multicolored Borders, 6 Ft. x 6 Ft. 5 In.	385.00
Kazak, Spandrels, Red Ground, Ivory & Blue Borders, 5 Ft. 4 In. x 5 Ft. 9 In.	330.00
Kazvin, Ivory, Blue, Red, 9 Ft. 10 In. x 14 Ft. 8 In.	2475.00
Kazvin, Spandrels, Ivory Ground, Red Border, 8 Ft. 10 In. x 11 Ft. 9 In.	440.00
Keristan, Red, Ivory, Navy Field, Navy Ground, 11 Ft. 3 In. x 20 In.	450.00
Kerman, Allover Flowers Medallions, Tan Ground, Floral Borders, 3 x 4 Ft.	115.00
Kerman, Allover Flowers, Green Ground, Floral Borders, Runner, 2 Ft. 9 In. x 6 Ft. 11 In.	175.00
Kerman, Blue Medallion, Burgundy Cartouche, Ivory Field, 7 Ft. 10 In. x 12 Ft. 7 In.	1980.00
Kerman, Center Medallion, Floral Field, Red Ground, 8 x 5 Ft.	520.00
Kerman, Flowers, Medallion, Tan Field, Red, Blue, Green, Off-White Borders, 3 x 4 Ft. . . .	115.00
Kerman, Flowers, Red, Ivory Ground & Border, 3 Ft. x 4 Ft. 8 In.	275.00
Kerman, Flowers, Reds, Blues, Greens, Off-White Field, 4 Ft. x 7 Ft. 1 In.	490.00
Kerman, Ivory, Navy, Red Field, Red Ground, Late 19th Century, 2 Ft. x 2 Ft. 5 In.	170.00
Kerman, Olive Green, Rust, Beige Ground, 12 Ft. x 8 Ft. 7 In.	600.00
Kerman, Pastel Flowers, Ivory Ground, Blue & Green Border, 11 Ft. 6 In. x 19 Ft. 10 In. . .	880.00
Kerman, Serrated Lobed Diamond Medallion, Blue Field, 12 Ft. 4 In. x 8 Ft. 10 In.	3740.00
Keshan, Star Medallion, Blue Spandrels, Floral Spray Field, Red Ground, 11 x 8 Ft.	1150.00
Keshan, Star Medallion, Palmette & Trellising Field, Blue Ground, 7 Ft. 3 In. x 4 Ft. 6 In.	575.00
Kilim, Turkish, Geometric, Red, Blue, Yellow, Ivory Ground, 4 Ft. 6 In. x 9 Ft. 4 In.	150.00
Kuba, Medallions, Brown Ground, Ivory Border, 3 Ft. x 3 Ft. 9 In.	660.00
Kuba, Stylized Leafy Trellis, Mustard Field, Ivory Star & Bar Border, 4 Ft. x 2 Ft. 8 In. . .	7200.00
Kurdish, Hexagonal Medallions, Diamond Guls, Blue Field, Sunburst Border, 6 x 4 Ft.	2160.00
Kurdish, Ivory Ground & Border, 3 Ft. 8 In. x 5 Ft.	165.00
Lilihan, Red Ground, Blue Border, 9 Ft. 2 In. x 12 Ft. 5 In.	825.00
Lillihan, Diamond Medallions, Red Field, Ivory Floral Border, 4 Ft. 8 In. x 2 Ft. 6 In.	405.00
Lillihan, Open Flowers, Midnight Blue Ground, 2 Ft. 10 In. x 6 Ft. 9 In.	1155.00
Luristan, Column, Rosettes, Octagons, Diamonds, Blue, Ivory Border, 8 Ft. 6 In. x 6 Ft. . .	978.00
Luristan, Ivory Spandrels, Blue Ground, Red, White, Blue Borders, 4 Ft. 9 In. x 7 Ft.	495.00
Mahal, Sunburst Medallion, Red Field, Blue, Beige Shaped Ground, Borders, 21 x 13 Ft. .	3450.00
Malayer, Allover Boteh, Red, Blue, Green, Blue, Floral Border, 4 Ft. 7 In. x 6 Ft. 6 In.	460.00
Malayer, Allover Flowers, Red, Brown, Off-White, Brown, Borders, 4 Ft. 5 In. x 6 Ft. 5 In.	460.00
Malayer, Spandrels, Blue Ground, Ivory Border, Runner, 3 Ft. 7 In. x 9 Ft. 10 In.	220.00
Meshed, Beige Ground, Floral Spray Field, Lobed Medallion, Red Spandrels, 18 x 9 Ft. . .	460.00
Meshed, Purple, Blue Spandrels, Red Ground, Slate Blue Ground, 9 Ft. 6 In. x 12 Ft. 6 In.	715.00
Meshed, Red & Blue Spandrels, Dark Red Ground, Blue Border, 9 Ft. 8 In. x 12 Ft. 10 In.	825.00
Mexican, Geometric, Purple, Green, Beige, Red, Brown, 48 x 77 In.	330.00
Mir, Bright Yellow, Orange, Red, Runner, 3 Ft. 2 In. x 7 Ft.	220.00

Mosul, Midnight Blue Ground, Blue Border, 3 Ft. 5 In. x 6 Ft. 2 In. 220.00
Oriental, Iran, 3 Borders, Brown, Blue, Geometric, Red Ground, 3 Ft. 2 In. x 6 Ft. 250.00
Oushak, Center Medallion, Blue, Orange, Beige Field, 17 Ft. x 10 Ft. 2 In. 7700.00
Penny, Diamond Shape, Multicolored, Felt, Wool, Late 19th Century, 6 Ft. 8 In. x 4 Ft. . . 230.00
Penny, Star Circles, Tear Drop Border, c.1900, 4 Ft. 5 In. x 3 Ft. 3 In. 950.00
Persian, 3 Geometric Medallions, Red, Blue, Multiple Borders, 4 Ft. 2 In. x 7 Ft. 6 In. . . . 431.00
Persian, Allover Flowers, Off-White Ground, Floral Borders, 4 Ft. 10 In. x 7 Ft. 5 In. . . . 1380.00
Persian, Allover Flowers, Red Ground, Border, Runner, 2 Ft. 3 In. x 10 Ft. 5 In. 172.00
Persian, Allover Geometric, Off-White Ground, Borders, Runner, 2 Ft. 6 In. x 11 Ft. 7 In. 488.00
Persian, Allover Herati, Blue Field, Flower & Geometric Borders, 2 Ft. 8 In. x 5 Ft. 201.00
Persian, Allover Herati, Blue Ground, Flowers & Geometric Borders, 2 Ft. 8 In. x 5 Ft. . . 201.00
Persian, Blue Spandrels, Burgundy Ground, Dark Blue Border, 9 Ft. 3 In. x 11 Ft. 7 In. . . 660.00
Persian, Brick Red, Ivory, Blue Field, Navy Ground, Early 20th Century, 4 x 6 Ft. 896.00
Persian, Chevron Panel, Multiple Geometric Borders, 4 Ft. 6 In. x 8 Ft. 4 In. 230.00
Persian, Diamond Medallion, Floral Diamonds On Cobalt, 10 Ft. x 13 Ft. 10 In. 1955.00
Persian, Earth Tones, Red Ground, Gray Border, 4 Ft. 4 In. x 7 Ft. 3 In. 357.00
Persian, Floral Medallions, Ivory Field, Light & Dark Blue Border, 8 Ft. 3 In. x 9 Ft. 2200.00
Persian, Flowers, Spandrels, Ivory Ground, Rust Red Border, 9 Ft. x 12 Ft. 2 In. 1155.00
Persian, Geometric Flowers, Dark Blue Ground, Borders, 3 Ft. 2 In. x 9 Ft. 7 In. 220.00
Persian, Geometric, Spandrels, Red Ground, Dark Blue Border, 4 Ft. 3 In. x 7 Ft. 3 In. . . . 203.00
Persian, Herati, Red, Blue, Ivory, Blue Field, Green Border, 14 Ft. 4 In. x 12 Ft. 1725.00
Persian, Herati, Red, Blue, Rose, Ivory, Green, c.1900, 13 Ft. 10 In. x 9 Ft. 4 In. 2760.00
Persian, Medallions, Animals, Red, Green, Blue Field, 4 Ft. 6 In. x 7 Ft. 3 In. 230.00
Persian, Northwest, Green & Light Blue Guls, Dark Red Ground, 4 Ft. x 5 Ft. 7 In. 345.00
Persian, Northwest, Medallions, Tan Ground, Blue Border, 3 Ft. 5 In. x 10 Ft. 2 In. 250.00
Persian, Red & Gold Medallions, Purple Ground, Red Border, 4 Ft. 4 In. x 10 Ft. 5 In. . . . 385.00
Persian, Red Field, Flowers, Border, Red, Blue, Green, Off-White, 2 Ft. x 10 Ft. 5 In. 175.00
Persian, Red, Ivory, Navy Field, Red Ground, Early 20th Century, 7 Ft. 9 In. x 11 Ft. 1 In. 1120.00
Persian, Rosette Medallion Surrounded By Vines, Blue Field, 12 Ft. 5 In. x 9 Ft. 2530.00
Persian, Rosette Medallion, Spandrels, Blue, Multiple Borders, 17 Ft. 10 In. x 8 Ft. 8 In. . . 3737.00
Portuguese, Vines, Blue, Red, Brown, Green, c.1950, 15 Ft. 6 In. x 12 Ft. 1035.00
Prayer, Belouchi, Mosques, Black Ground, Borders, 2 Ft. 11 In. x 4 Ft. 2 In. 110.00
Prayer, Kazak, Geometric, Blue, Green, White, Red Field, 3 Ft. 9 In. x 5 Ft. 5 In. 776.00
Prayer, Konya, Triple Reserve Mihrab, Hooked Arches, Leaf Border, 5 Ft. 8 In. x 3 Ft. . . . 1800.00
Prayer, Persian, Diamond Center Medallion, Rose Field, Red Ground, 2 Ft. 3 In. x 3 Ft. . . 225.00
Prayer, Persian, Red Field, Mustard Border, 3 Ft. 7 In. x 5 Ft. 6 In. 900.00
Prayer, Shirvan, Ivory Ground, Leaf Border, Late 18th Century, 4 Ft. 3 In. x 3 Ft. 3 In. . . . 730.00
Prayer, Tabriz, Royal Figures In Landscape, Animal Border, 7 Ft. x 4 Ft. 4 In. 2475.00
Prayer, Tribal Style, Red, Ivory, Blue Ground, 5 Ft. 4 In. x 3 Ft. 2 In. 145.00
Prayer, Turkoman, Late 19th Century, 5 Ft. 3 In. x 3 Ft. 11 In. 1008.00
Ryijy, Repeating Spiral Pattern, Blue, Purple, 8 x 11 Ft. 105.00
Sarouk, Allover Floral Sprays, Blossoming Vines, Red Field, 12 Ft. 6 In. x 8 Ft. 9 In. 920.00
Sarouk, Allover Flowers, Red Ground, Border, Mat, 2 Ft. 10 1/2 In. x 2 Ft. 1 1/2 In. 130.00
Sarouk, Allover Flowers, Red Ground, Floral Borders, Mat, 2 Ft. 1 In. x 4 Ft. 175.00
Sarouk, Allover Palmettes, Rosettes, Blossoming Vines, 1920s, 13 Ft. x 9 Ft. 6 In. 2185.00
Sarouk, Allover Palmettes, Vases Of Flowers, Vines, Wine Red Field, 11 Ft. 8 In. x 9 Ft. . . 1955.00
Sarouk, Blue Ground, Burgundy Border, 10 Ft. 8 In. x 13 Ft. 9 In. 1100.00
Sarouk, Blue Medallion, Leaves, Blue Spandrels, Blue Border, 8 Ft. 5 In. x 11 Ft. 4 In. . . 6600.00
Sarouk, Blue, Red, Light Blue, Ivory Ground, 3 Ft. 3 In. x 4 Ft. 10 In. 670.00
Sarouk, Burgundy Ground, Blue Border, 9 Ft. 1 In. x 14 Ft. 3 In. 550.00
Sarouk, Center Floral Spray, Vases, Red Field, Blue Border, 4 Ft. 9 In. x 3 Ft. 3 In. 460.00
Sarouk, Floral Center, Blue, Gold, Green, Red, Blue Border, c.1900, 9 Ft. x 6 Ft. 2 In. . . . 3335.00
Sarouk, Flowers, Allover Red Ground, Mat, 4 Ft. 1 In. x 2 Ft. 45.00
Sarouk, Flowers, Diamonds, Vines, Blue, Tan, Green, Red, Blue, c.1910, 12 x 9 Ft. 4945.00
Sarouk, Flowers, Red Field, 3 Borders, 2 Ft. 5 In. x 2 Ft. 115.00
Sarouk, Flowers, Red Field, Blue Border, 20th Century, 11 Ft. 9 In x 5 Ft. 4 In. 2300.00
Sarouk, Flowers, Vines, Maroon Field, Midnight Blue Border, 11 Ft. 8 In. x 8 Ft. 6 In. . . 1610.00
Sarouk, Ivory Spandrels, Mauve Ground, Blue Border, 4 Ft. 2 In. x 6 Ft. 1 In. 1870.00
Sarouk, Mauve Ground, Blue & Camel Borders, 4 Ft. 1 In. x 6 Ft. 3 In. 1320.00
Sarouk, Navy Field, Brick Red Ground, Ivory, Red Borders, 3 Ft. 5 In. x 5 Ft. 3 In. 900.00
Sarouk, Navy, Ivory, Light Blue Field, Red Ground, 6 Ft. 4 In. x 7 Ft. 10 In. 560.00
Sarouk, Red Abrash Ground, Midnight Blue Border, 9 x 12 Ft. 1100.00
Sarouk, Red Ground, Blue Border, 2 Ft. 2 In. x 6 Ft. 5 In. 300.00

Sarouk, Red Ground, Blue, Ivory Border, 3 Ft. 2 In. x 4 Ft. 8 In.	110.00
Sarouk, Red Ground, Blue, Olive, Gold Borders, 3 Ft. 5 In. x 5 Ft. 2 In.	605.00
Sarouk, Red Ground, Flowers, Multiple Borders, 6 Ft. 10 In. x 5 Ft. 4 In.	575.00
Sarouk, Red Ground, Midnight Blue Ground, 9 x 12 Ft.	3740.00
Sarouk, Wine Ground, Blue Border, 3 Ft. 4 In. x 4 Ft. 8 In.	495.00
Savonnerie, Large Yellow Flowers, Black Ground, 1930, 9 Ft. 9 In. x 5 Ft. 10 In.	8400.00
Sennah, Blue Border, Blue Spandrels, Orange Ground, 3 Ft. 6 In. x 4 Ft. 10 In.	270.00
Serapi, Blue Center Medallion, Ivory Spandrels, Red Border, 10 Ft. x 12 Ft. 9 In.	7150.00
Serapi, Ivory Medallions, Olive Spandrels, Red Ground, 3 Borders, 7 Ft. 10 In. x 9 Ft. . . .	660.00
Serebend, Red Ground, Ivory Border, 3 Ft. x 4 Ft. 8 In.	275.00
Shiraz, People, Animals, Tents, Medallions, Blue Ground, Borders, 5 Ft. 5 In. x 10 Ft. . . .	3960.00
Shiraz, Spandrels, Burgundy Ground, Geometric Border, 5 Ft. 4 In. x 8 Ft. 7 In.	247.00
Shirvan, Allover Animals, Bird & Geometrics, Floral Border, 5 Ft. 7 In. x 6 Ft. 7 In.	290.00
Shirvan, Beige, Center Flowers, Vines & Scrolls, Wool, 20th Century, 3 Ft. x 4 Ft. 8 In. . .	200.00
Shirvan, Olive & Gold, Dark Blue Ground, 3 Ft. 8 In. x 5 Ft. 5 In.	275.00
Tabriz, Allover Flowers, Ivory Field, 12 x 18 Ft.	747.00
Tabriz, Flowers, Off-White Field, Reds, Blues, Greens, Silk, 3 x 5 Ft.	920.00
Tabriz, Flowers, Red Field, Blues, Greens, Off-White, 6 Ft. 9 In. x 10 Ft. 2 In.	460.00
Tabriz, Orange Field, 16 Ft. 2 In. x 9 Ft. 10 1/2 In.	660.00
Tabriz, Red Field, Flowers, Red, Blue, Green, White, Borders, 6 Ft. 9 In. x 10 Ft. 2 In. . . .	460.00
Tabriz, Rows Of Medallions, Red Ground, 5 Ft. 2 In. x 8 Ft. 9 In.	250.00
Tappa, 4 Round Geometric Sections, Round, 2 Ft. 7 In.	225.00
Tekke, 3 Columns, Guls On Rust Red Field, Midnight Border, 5 Ft. 4 In. x 3 Ft. 4 In.	290.00
Tribal, Baluchi, Geometric, Red, Black, Red Ground, 4 Ft. 1 In. x 7 Ft. 7 In.	430.00
Turkish, Allover Animals, Tan Field, Red, Blue, Green, Border, 6 Ft. 9 In. x 9 Ft.	2530.00
Turkish, Animals, Tan Field, Floral Border, 6 Ft. 9 In. x 9 Ft. 4 In.	2530.00
Turkish, Ivory, Red, Navy Field, Red Ground, Early 20th Century, 2 Ft. 10 In. x 11 Ft. . . .	560.00
Turkoman, Gul, Late 19th Century, 4 Ft. 8 In. x 3 Ft. 6 In.	364.00
Uzbekistan, Embroidered, Stars In Circles, Yellow Ground, Silk, 5 Ft. x 3 Ft. 8 In.	3000.00
William Morris, Acanthus Leaves, Stylized Blossoms, Silk, Runner, c.1910, 12 x 3 Ft.	5460.00
Yomud, Turkoman, Latch & Lattice, Crimson Ground, Stepped Borders, 10 x 13 Ft.	1265.00
Yomud, Turkoman, Torba, West Turkestan, Late 19th Century, 1 Ft. 6 In. x 3 Ft. 6 In.	633.00

RUMRILL Pottery was designed by George Rumrill of Little Rock, Arkansas. From 1933 to 1938, it was produced by the Red Wing Pottery of Red Wing, Minnesota. In 1938, production was transferred to the Shawnee Pottery in Zanesville, Ohio. It was moved again in December of 1938 to Florence Pottery Company in Mt. Gilead, Ohio, where Rumrill ware continued to be manufactured until the pottery burned in 1941. It was then produced by Gouda Ceramic Arts in South Zanesville until early 1943.

Vase, 2-Tone Green Matte Glaze, Double Handles, 5 1/2 In.	115.00
Vase, No. 600-8, Sky Blue, 3 Openings, Art Deco, 8 In.	400.00

RUSKIN is a British art pottery of the twentieth century. The Ruskin Pottery was started by William Howson Taylor, and his name was used as the mark until about 1899. The factory, at West Smethwick, Birmingham, England, stopped making new pieces in 1933 but continued to glaze and sell the remaining wares until 1935. The art pottery is noted for its exceptional glazes.

Bowl, Orange Iridescent Glaze, Footed, Stamped, 1920-1935, 2 3/4 x 7 In.	40.00
Vase, Purple, Red, Green Crystalline Glaze, Shouldered Body, Impressed Mark, 4 In.	1150.00

RUSSEL WRIGHT designed dinnerwares in modern shapes for many companies. Iroquois China Company, Harker China Company, Steubenville Pottery, and Justin Tharaud and Sons made dishes marked *Russel Wright*. The Steubenville wares, first made in 1938, are the most common today. Wright was a designer of domestic and industrial wares, including furniture, aluminum, radios, interiors, and glassware. Dinnerwares and other pieces by Wright are listed here. For more information, see *Kovels' Depression Glass & Dinnerware Price List*.

American Modern, Cup, White	8.00
American Modern, Salad Spoon, Granite Gray	48.00

Art Pottery, Bowl, Figured White & Gunmetal Glaze, Irregular Shape, 1946, 13 In. 2070.00
Art Pottery, Bowl, Georgia Brown Glaze, Raymor Turquoise Interior, Marked, 24 In. 2530.00
Art Pottery, Vase, Exterior Bubble White, Georgia Brown Interior, 1946, 9 In. 975.00
Cocktail Set, Shaker, 6 Cups & Tray, Aluminum, 11 1/4 In. 8050.00
Iroquois, Bowl, Cereal, Ice Blue, 5 In. 10.00
Iroquois, Bowl, Cereal, Lemon Yellow 11.00
Iroquois, Bowl, Cereal, Lettuce Green, 5 In. 10.00
Iroquois, Bowl, Fruit, Ripe Apricot, 5 1/2 In. 10.00
Iroquois, Bowl, Fruit, Sugar White, 5 1/2 In. 15.00
Iroquois, Bowl, Gumbo, 2 Handles, Charcoal 55.00
Iroquois, Bowl, Gumbo, 2 Handles, Pink Sherbet 45.00
Iroquois, Bowl, Vegetable, Divided, Avocado Yellow, 10 In. 68.00
Iroquois, Bowl, Vegetable, Divided, Ice Blue, 10 In. ....38.00 to 45.00
Iroquois, Bowl, Vegetable, Open, Avocado Yellow, 10 In. 40.00
Iroquois, Bowl, Vegetable, Open, Nutmeg Brown, 8 In. 22.00
Iroquois, Bowl, Vegetable, Open, Parsley Green, 8 In. 22.00
Iroquois, Carafe, Pink Sherbet 200.00
Iroquois, Casserole, Avocado Yellow, 2 Qt. 30.00
Iroquois, Casserole, Cover, Divided, Avocado Yellow, 10 In. 55.00
Iroquois, Casserole, Cover, Nutmeg Brown, 2 Qt. 65.00
Iroquois, Casserole, Cover, Ripe Apricot, 2 Qt. 65.00
Iroquois, Creamer, Ice Blue 12.00
Iroquois, Creamer, Lemon Yellow 12.00
Iroquois, Cup & Saucer, Avocado Yellow 7.00
Iroquois, Cup & Saucer, Charcoal 16.00
Iroquois, Cup & Saucer, Lettuce Green 8.00
Iroquois, Cup & Saucer, Nutmeg Brown 12.00
Iroquois, Cup & Saucer, Oyster 12.00
Iroquois, Cup & Saucer, Parsley Green 16.00
Iroquois, Cup & Saucer, Pink Sherbet ....7.00 to 14.00
Iroquois, Cup & Saucer, Ripe Apricot 15.00
Iroquois, Cup & Saucer, Sugar White ....16.00 to 18.00
Iroquois, Plate, Avocado Yellow, 7 1/2 In. 5.00
Iroquois, Plate, Avocado Yellow, 9 In. 10.00
Iroquois, Plate, Charcoal, 10 In. 14.00
Iroquois, Plate, Ice Blue, 9 In. 12.00
Iroquois, Plate, Ice Blue, 10 In. 12.00
Iroquois, Plate, Lemon Yellow, 6 In. 4.50
Iroquois, Plate, Lemon Yellow, 7 1/2 In. 10.00
Iroquois, Plate, Lettuce Green, 6 In. 4.50
Iroquois, Plate, Nutmeg Brown, 9 In. 10.00
Iroquois, Plate, Nutmeg Brown, 10 In. 12.00
Iroquois, Plate, Parsley Green, 9 In. 10.00
Iroquois, Plate, Ripe Apricot, 7 1/2 In. 12.00
Iroquois, Plate, Ripe Apricot, 10 In. 15.00
Iroquois, Plate, Sugar White, 7 1/2 In. 12.00
Iroquois, Plate, Sugar White, 10 In. 15.00
Iroquois, Platter, Avocado Yellow, 14 1/2 In. 25.00
Iroquois, Platter, Charcoal, 12 3/4 In. 38.00
Iroquois, Platter, Ice Blue, 12 3/4 In. 28.00
Iroquois, Platter, Ice Blue, 14 1/2 In. 28.00
Iroquois, Platter, Lettuce Green, 12 3/4 In. 22.00
Iroquois, Platter, Pink Sherbet, 14 1/2 In. 28.00
Iroquois, Platter, Ripe Apricot, 13 1/4 In. 25.00
Iroquois, Soup, Cream, Charcoal 60.00
Oceana, Bowl, Wood, Incised Signature, 1938, 13 In. 2530.00

SALOPIAN ware was made by the Caughley factory of England during
the eighteenth century. The early pieces were blue and white with
some colored decorations. Another ware referred to as *Salopian* is a
late nineteenth-century tableware decorated with color transfers.

Salopian

Coffeepot, Oriental Figures, Gazebo, Landscape, Dome Top, 11 In. 990.00
Creamer, Milkmaid, Helmet Form, 3 1/2 In. 495.00

Cup & Saucer, Bird On Branch, Floral Border, Swan Transfer In Cup	470.00
Cup & Saucer, Harvest Scene, Polychrome Floral Border	330.00
Cup & Saucer, Seashell & Coral, Handleless	165.00
Cup & Saucer, Sheep Herder, Cottage & Castle Scene, Flowers	40.00
Cup Plate, Sheep Herding Scene, Cottage, Castle, 4 1/2 In.	330.00
Mug, Lion & Cave, 2 In.	330.00
Pitcher, Oriental Figures, Gazebo, Landscape, 5 1/2 In.	495.00
Plate, Acorn & Leaves, Greek Key Border, 7 1/4 In.	275.00
Plate, Bird, Fruit, Floral Border, Shaped Edge, 7 In.	275.00
Plate, Deer, Floral Border, 7 1/4 In.	140.00
Plate, Stag, Shaped Edge, Floral Border, 7 1/4 In.	303.00
Waste Bowl, Bird, Floral Transfer, Greek Key Border, 3 x 5 1/4 In.	385.00
Waste Bowl, Sheep Herder & Cottage Scene, Floral Border, 3 x 6 1/4 In.	165.00

SALT AND PEPPER SHAKERS in matched sets were first used in the nineteenth century. Collectors are primarily interested in figural examples made after World War I. *Huggers* are pairs of shakers that appear to embrace each other. Many salt and pepper shakers are listed in other categories and can be located through the index at the back of this book.

Alligators, Japan, 3 In.	20.00
Black Baking Women, Bakin' Time, 4 In.	24.00
Brooklyn Dodgers Logo, White, 1950s	455.00
Bugs & Taz, 4 In.	24.00
Bugs Bunny, Smiling, Carrot Right Hand, Yellow Glove Left Hand, 4 1/8 In.	60.00
Esso Gas Pumps	40.00
Fort Pitt Beer, Bottle Shape, Glass, Label .... *Illus*	12.00
Half Disc Shape, Metal, Revere, 1935, 2 In.	748.00
Just Married, 4 In.	24.00
Lookout Mountain, Cylindrical, Logo, 3 In.	16.00
Mammy, 4 1/4 In.	3.00
Mice With Cheese, Japan, 3 In.	20.00
Mobilflame Bottled Gas, Plastic, 2 7/8 In.	105.00
Native & Hippo, Plays Guitar While Riding, 4 In.	.80.00 to 95.00
Opryland Kettles, 3 In.	20.00
Owl, Japan, 4 In.	20.00
Pillsbury Dough Boy, 4 In.	24.00
Pink Panther With Bar Stool, 4 In.	24.00
Rickshaw Hound & Poodle, 4 In.	24.00
Shmoo Couple, Glazed Ceramic, Girl 3/12 In., Boy 4 In.	95.00
Shopper & Credit Card, 4 In.	24.00
Uncle Sam, Bust, Ceramic, Hand Painted, 1920, 2 1/2 x 1 1/2 In.	29.00

Salt & Pepper, Fort Pitt Beer, Bottle Shape, Glass, Label

Salt Glaze, Jug, Gray, Relief Scene, Naomi & Daughter-In-Law, Metal Lid, 10 In.

Salt Glaze, Jug, Ridgway, Tan, Witches, Horseman, Strainer Spout, Metal Lid, 8 1/2 In.

SALT GLAZE has a grayish white surface with a texture like an orange peel. It is a method of decoration that has been used since the eighteenth century. Salt-glazed pieces are still being made.

Canister, Cover, Oak Leaf Design, Blue, 7 In.	88.00
Crock, Butter, Indian Good Luck Sign, Blue, White, 5 1/4 x 7 1/2 In.	55.00
Crock, Incised Bird, Wide Mouth, Sloping Shoulder, 19th Century, 14 In.	470.00
Cuspidor, Blue Sponge, 5 1/2 x 10 In.	60.00
Figurine, Spinario, Naked On Base, Removing Thorn From Foot, c.1760, 4 1/4 In.	2160.00
Jug, Gray, Relief Scene, Naomi & Daughter-In-Law, Metal Lid, 10 In. ....*Illus*	275.00
Jug, Ridgway, Tan, Witches, Horseman, Strainer Spout, Metal Lid, 8 1/2 In. ....*Illus*	275.00
Jug, Stylized Plant Form, Entrail Stem, Branches, Strap Handle, 1860s, 16 1/2 In.	590.00
Mug, Blue Accent Vine Design, Chautauqua, 2 1/2 In.	300.00
Mug, Rochester Brew. Co., Rochester, N.Y., 4 Blue Accent Bands, Handle, 5 In.	165.00
Pitcher, Apricot, Chain Medallion, Leaves, Twigs Roped Handle, Blue, White, 8 In.	132.00
Pitcher, Embossed Grapes, Blue, 9 In.	70.00
Pitcher, Embossed Kissing Dutch Boy & Girl, Windmill Scene, 7 In.	95.00
Pitcher, Fox Hunt Scene, Grapevines, Basket Weave Base, Leaf Handle, 7 1/2 In.	330.00
Pitcher, Indian, War Bonnet Design, Blue, White, Handle, 8 1/4 In.	360.00
Pitcher, Vintage Pattern, Tan, Havelock, 1858, 7 x 7 1/4 In.	90.00
Teapot, Eagle & Lady Liberty, c.1800, 6 In.	990.00

SAMPLERS were made in America from the early 1700s. The best examples were made from 1790 to 1840. Long, narrow samplers are usually older than square ones. Early samplers just had stitching or alphabets. The later examples had numerals, borders, and pictorial decorations. Those with mottoes are mid-Victorian. A revival of interest in the 1930s produced simpler samplers, usually with mottoes.

ABCDE

5 Alphabets, Verse, Plants, Animals, Mary Miles, Aged 12 Years, 12 1/2 x 13 In.	431.00
7 Alphabets, Mary Starbuck, 17 x 13 1/4 In.	4480.00
Allegorical Scene, Sarah S. Paine, Aged 12 Years, Charlestown, 1826, 13 x 18 In.	1380.00
Alphabet, Adam & Eve, Wreath, Angels, Ship, Flowers, ICB 1803, Frame, 14 x 15 In.	800.00
Alphabet, Annie Faulkner, Age 12, Hinderwell School, 1882, Wool On Linen, 7 x 7 In.	100.00
Alphabet, Biblical Verse, Meandering Vine, Julia A. Wysong, 1824, 19 1/4 x 19 1/2 In.	4465.00
Alphabet, Birds, Flowers, Blue, Red, Signed Alice Linfords, 1819, 7 1/2 x 7 1/2 In.	415.00
Alphabet, Caroline Arnold, Age 12, c.1811, Frame, 4 1/2 x 11 1/2 In.	138.00
Alphabet, Clarissa Ramsey Horn, June The 3, 1798, Blue Stitch Border, 19 x 10 In.	175.00
Alphabet, Cross-Stitch, Susan B., July 23, 1823, Frame, 6 x 12 1/4 In.	110.00
Alphabet, Emily Ann Hawley, Mary Balch's School, 1820, 9 1/2 x 7 1/4 In.	1410.00
Alphabet, Flower Basket, 2 Potted Plants, Blue, Yellow, Initials L.D., 12 x 10 1/2 In.	275.00
Alphabet, Flower Baskets, Ocean Wave Border, Hannah S Fitz 1809, 12 x 11 In.	633.00
Alphabet, Flower Border, Early 19th Century, Frame, 16 1/2 x 8 1/2 In.	316.00
Alphabet, Flower Border, Nancy Holman, 1804, 16 1/2 x 16 In.	200.00
Alphabet, Flowers, Vine Border, Wrought By Margaret A Brown, 1828, 16 x 16 In.	460.00
Alphabet, Margaretta Shrom, Age 8, Easton School, 1827, Silk On Linen, 9 1/4 x 9 1/4 In.	365.00
Alphabet, Mary Ann Lewis, Poughkeepsie, 1834, Silk On Linen, 8 1/4 x 12 In.	470.00
Alphabet, Mary Black, Aged 10 Years, Silk Thread, Gilt Frame, 21 x 16 In.	990.00
Alphabet, Numbers, Caroline Robinson's, Frame, 12 x 12 In.	175.00
Alphabet, Numbers, Homespun, Frame, 17 5/8 x 12 7/8 In.	770.00
Alphabet, Picture, House, Lucretia Clark, 11 Yrs. Old, 1804, Frame, 12 x 6 3/4 In.	1430.00
Alphabet, Quaker, Elizabeth Humphreys, Vine, Berry Border, 1836, 14 1/2 x 17 1/4 In.	3290.00
Alphabet, Red, Yellow, Signed Sarah Freeman, 9 1/2 x 6 1/2 In.	110.00
Alphabet, Verse, Betsey Gardner, Aged 10, 1831, Folk Art Frame, 21 1/2 x 11 In.	748.00
Alphabet, Verse, Delia G Chace, Age 10, 1836, Somerset, Mass., 20 1/2 x 20 1/2 In.	2415.00
Alphabet, Verse, Floral, Delaware, Silk On Linen, Frame, 24 1/2 x 20 In.	2300.00
Alphabet, Verse, House, Trees, Ann Calvert, March 2, 1828, Wool, Linen, Pa., 17 x 15 In.	5700.00
Alphabet, Verse, Houses, Pond, Eirene Smith, Aged 14 Yrs., June 18th 1816, 16 x 16 In.	2300.00
Alphabet, Verse, Orchard, Houses, Sophronia Brubank, 1821, 17 x 17 In.	3760.00
Alphabet, Verse, Strawberry Border, Mary Stuart, Her Sampler, 1765, 7 3/4 x 11 In.	690.00
Alphabet, Verse, Virginia Ann Godwin, 1812, 21 x 21 In.	13200.00
Alphabet, Wool On Linen, Harriet Smith, Aged 8, New England, 1830, 11 In.	2115.00
Alphabet & Numbers, Garland Border, Hannah Wingate, Frame, 1841, 17 x 16 In.	1065.00

Alphabet & Numbers, Strawberry Vine, Hester Jane Stacy, Aged 8 Years, 1834, 16 In. 690.00
Alphabets, Animals, Family Register, Melcher Family, 1769 Through 1808, 16 x 17 In. ..   1095.00
Alphabets, Barbara Stubbl, Age 13 Years, 1851, Homespun, Shadowbox, 19 x 15 In. 605.00
Alphabets, Butterflies, Vining Strawberries, Verse, Sarah Stafford, Frame, 14 x 11 In. 330.00
Alphabets, Floral Band, Ann Saunders, Age 12 Years, Born February 9, 1796, 13 x 10 In.   865.00
Alphabets, Floral Band, Vine Border, Amy Lewis's, Ad 1826, Frame, 12 x 15 In. 520.00
Alphabets, Margaret Swayer, Born April 29th, Frame, 1817, 15 1/2 x 17 In. 715.00
Alphabets, Pious Verse, Abigail Haskell, Aged 12 Years 7 Months, 1825, 11 x 16 In. 980.00
Alphabets, Strawberry Border, Homespun, Eunice Huntington, 1790, 19 3/4 In. 740.00
Alphabets, Verse, Plants, Vine, Elvira Ordway Aged 10 Years, 1830, 14 1/2 x 16 1/2 In. ...   1495.00
Alphabets, Verse, Sarah Elizabeth Thurman, Trees, Framed, 1814, 19 x 15 In. 835.00
Ann Murphey, 1825, Silk Floss On Linen, Frame, 18 5/8 x 18 7/8 In. 2090.00
Birds, Fruit Basket, Bumble Bees, House, Pine Trees, Vine & Berry Border, 18 x 18 In. ..   130.00
Brick House, Adam & Eve, Flowers, Trees, Angels, Birds, Eliza Cox, 16 x 19 3/4 In. 3000.00
Butterflies, Bird & Trees, Mary E. Kellom, Age 12, 16 x 17 In. 1035.00
Castle Tower, Man In Boat, Reeded Frame, 7 3/4 x 6 3/4 In. 470.00
Cross-Stitch, Mary Harrop, November 5th 1788, Frame, 19 1/4 x 19 In. 905.00
Dog Under Tree, Verse, Sarah R. McConnell, 1851, Frame, 17 1/2 x 18 1/2 In. 190.00
Doves, Potted Tulip, Margaret Patterson, Aged 8, 1810, Frame, 17 1/4 x 11 3/4 In. 825.00
Edward Samuel Young, Accomac High School, Activities, 1940 ....   295.00
Family Record, Alphabets, Verse, Dates, Anna Clark, July 3 1806, Frame, 12 x 8 In. 575.00
Flowers, Birds, Strawberry Border, Martha Wright Her Work, 22 3/4 x 19 3/4 In. 605.00
Flowers, Harriet Plummer, 1814, Fly Speck Frame, 20 x 19 In. 1456.00
Flowers, Mary Melcher, 1805, Black Stick Frame, 19 x 15 1/2 In. 785.00
Genealogy, Names, Dates, Wrought By Sarah Weld, Aged 13 Years, 1832, 21 x 25 In. 750.00
Hannah Challenor, 1818, Silk On Linen, 23 x 22 1/4 In. 1200.00
House, Flowers, Plants, People, Birds, Basket, Lion, 1807, Frame, 22 1/2 x 19 1/4 In. 850.00
House, Vining Strawberry Border, Cross-Stitch, Elisa Walker, 1819, 16 1/2 In. 2475.00
Institutional Building, Bennette Street Sunday School, Wool, Founded 1801, 14 1/2 In. ..   588.00
Jane Davidson, Work In 10th Year, Vining Border, Frame, 1801, 25 1/2 x 19 1/4 In. 6250.00
Lord's Prayer, Meandering Vines, Fruit, Birds, Hannah Attmore, 1808, 20 x 14 In. 3760.00
Map Of England, Flower Border, Signed Anne Griffiths, c.1810, 15 x 13 In. 220.00
Mary Hafline, 178-, Silk On Linen, 12 1/2 x 12 1/2 In. 6000.00
Mary Roberts, Ten Years Old, Chester County, Urn In Center, Frame 7500.00
Memorial, Grieving Woman, Monument, Trees, Coffin Family, 1800, 19 x 17 In. 1725.00
Memorial, On The Death Of A Parent, Floral Border, Eliza Whitmarsh, 1807, 17 x 24 In. ..   1380.00
Peacock, Strawberry In Mouth, Silk Thread, Strawberry Edge Frame, 10 1/2 In. 990.00
Peacocks, Cottages, Animals, Adam & Eve, Petit Point, Linen, Frame, 20 7/8 In. 2090.00
Pictorial, Schoolhouse, Family Crest, Signed A. Devroe, Frame, c.1795, 15 x 22 In. 360.00
Poem, Figures & Trees, Ann Bould, Her Work, 1804, 17 x 19 In. 1840.00
Poem, Floral, Sarah Ellis Clipston, Northamptonshire, 1812, 20 1/2 x 16 In. 345.00
Prayer, Elizabeth Stansbury, August 18, 1835, 17 3/4 x 17 1/4 In. 6720.00
Religious Verse, Hannah Munro, Aged 8 Years, Butterflies, Birds, Frame, 20 1/2 In. 1980.00
Strawberry Border, Louise Bickley, 13th Year, Silk Floss, 21 3/4 In. 1100.00
Verse, Amelia Edbrook, Wool On Linen, 19th Century, 21 3/4 x 7 3/4 In. 470.00
Verse, Christ On Cross, Geometric Vine Border, Martha Jackman, 1825, 15 x 18 In. 375.00
Verse, Flowers, Hearts, Rebecca Elizabeth Loomer, Born Oct. 8, 1834, 21 x 19 In. 2550.00
Verse, Prayer, 4 Lines, Alphabet, Vine, Flower Border, Mary Ann Joliff, 1837, 12 x 12 In.   965.00
Vining Border, Hannah Stanes, Aged 10 Years, Gilt Lined Frame, 19 x 16 1/2 In. 760.00
White House, Green Windows, Catherine E. Pells, February 20th, A.D. 1840, 19 In. 1100.00
Wool On Linen, Silk, Eleanor R. Conaway, Georgetown, 1847, 12 x 12 In. 140.00

SAMSON and Company, a French firm specializing in the reproduction of collectible wares of many countries and periods, was founded in Paris in the early nineteenth century. Chelsea, Meissen, Famille Verte, and Chinese Export porcelain are some of the wares that have been reproduced by the company. The firm uses a variety of marks on the reproductions. It is still in operation.

Box, Hinged Lid, Figures In Romantic Scenes, 4 3/8 In. 245.00
Figurine, 2 Chinamen, Basket Of Flowers, Tole-Peinte Stems, 14 1/4 In. 5100.00
Plate, Chinese Export Style, Gilt Leaf Border, Painted Center, c.1860, 9 1/4 In., Pair 420.00
Punch Bowl, Armorial, Blue Bands, Gilt, Flowers, Coat Of Arms, c.1890, 11 1/2 In. 540.00

SANDWICH GLASS is any of the myriad types of glass made by the Boston and Sandwich Glass Works in Sandwich, Massachusetts, between 1825 and 1888. It is often very difficult to be sure whether a piece was really made at the Sandwich factory because so many types were made there and similar pieces were made at other glass factories. Additional pieces may be listed under Pressed Glass and in related categories.

Basket, Prunts & Leaves At Reeded Handle, 7 1/2 In.	45.00
Candlestick, Clambroth, Column Shape, Square Base, 19th Century, 9 In.	145.00
Candlestick, Clambroth, Petal & Loop, 6-Sided Foot, 19th Century, 9 In.	115.00
Candlestick, Petal & Loop, Opalescent, 7 In., Pair	575.00
Celery Vase, Amethyst, Paneled Sides, Flared, Scalloped Rim, 10 1/2 In.	1095.00
Cologne, Jade Green, Ribbed Stopper, 5 7/8 In.	300.00
Compote, Loop, c.1845-1860, 6 1/2 In. x 10 In.	200.00
Compote, Loop, Milk Glass, 1850-1870, 8 3/4 In.	335.00
Compote, Paneled Loop, Clambroth, 8 x 9 1/2 In.	900.00
Compote, Roman Rosette, 6 1/4 In.	135.00
Compote, Roman Rosette, Blown Stem, 4 1/4 x 5 1/2 In.	475.00
Creamer, New England Pineapple, 6 1/2 In.	185.00
Decanter, 3-Piece Mold, Diamond Pattern, Fan Shaped Stopper, 8 In.	110.00
Epergne, 1 Horn, Blue, Gold Enameled Dog, 12 In., Pair	290.00
Lamp, Blown, 12 Arched Panels, Scallops, Tin & Cork Burner, 8 In.	880.00
Lamp, Blue Cut To Clear, 17 In.	6050.00
Lamp, Brass, Pewter Collars, Tumbler Base, 12 In., Pair	935.00
Lamp, Clear Font, Brass Collar, Opaque Base, 1876, 5 3/8 In.	155.00
Lamp, Cobalt Blue, Paneled Font, Sandwich Glass, c.1835, 9 1/2 In.	745.00
Lamp, Oil, Frosted Cranberry Cut To Clear	520.00
Lamp, Oil, Inverted Diamond, Thumbprint Fonts, Hexagonal Base, 16 In., Pair	630.00
Lamp, Onion, Reeded Base & Font, 21 In.	7000.00
Lamp, Red Cut To White Cut To Clear, Brass Standard, Marble Base, 10 In.	560.00
Lamp, White Cut To Ruby, Brass Standard, Marble Base, c.1860-1887, 12 In.	500.00
Pitcher, Overshot, Cranberry Stain, Clear Handle, 7 In.	925.00
Pomade Jar, Bear, Black Amethyst, One Cent Tax Stamp, 3 3/4 In.	600.00
Puff Box, Cover, Hobnail, Clambroth, 6 In.	250.00
Salt, 3-Piece Mold, Purple Blue, Rayed Base, 2 1/2 In.	900.00
Salt, Ball & Groove, Flared Petal Rim, Pedestal, 6-Sided Foot, 3 1/4 In.	25.00
Salt, Diamond Diaper, Sunburst, Herringbone Bands, Blue, 2 1/4 In.	550.00
Salt, Morning Glory, Round, Footed, 2 3/4 In.	240.00
Salt Set, New England Pineapple, Flint, 3 Piece	185.00
Spill Holder, Amethyst, Inverted Diamond & Thumbprint, 4 5/8 In.	977.00
Spill Holder, Canary, Inverted Diamond & Thumbprint, 4 5/8 In.	575.00
Spill Holder, Canary, Loop, Ruffled Edge, 5 3/4 In.	575.00
Spill Holder, Cobalt Blue, Loop & Petal, 4 1/2 In.	460.00
Spill Holder, Emerald Green, Swag, 5 In.	575.00
Spill Holder, Fiery Opalescent, Puntie & Ellipse, 5 1/8 In.	1035.00
Spill Holder, Light Green, Multiloop, 4 3/8 In.	290.00
Spill Holder, Milk Glass, Snowflake, 4 3/4 In.	170.00
Spill Holder, Pale Green, Loop & Leaf, 5 In.	460.00
Spill Holder, Sapphire Blue, Swag, 5 In.	345.00
Spill Holder, White Clambroth, Sandwich Star, 5 In.	400.00
Spooner, Star, 5 In., Pair	46.00
Toothpick, Cover, Basket, Clambroth, 4 x 2 1/4 In.	180.00
Tray, Hairpin, Peacock Shape	9750.00
Tumbler, Paneled, Fiery Opalescent, 3 1/2 In.	730.00
Vase, Amethyst, Gauffered Rim, 2 Faceted Tiers, 6-Sided Base, 12 In.	1265.00
Vase, Enameled Flowers, Tan, 10 In., Pair	400.00
Vase, Loop, Amethyst, Gauffered Rim, Octagonal Standard, 10 x 3 In.	2070.00
Vase, Loop, Canary, Gauffered Rim, Hexagonal Foot, Marble Base, 10 x 4 In.	315.00
Vase, Loop, Emerald Green, Gauffered Rim, 6 Elongated Loops, 10 x 4 In.	1610.00
Vase, Trumpet, Jade Green, Applied Molded Rosette, 6 1/4 In.	550.00
Vase, Trumpet, Witch's Ball Cover, Emerald Green, c.1840-1860, 13 1/2 In.	2800.00

SARREGUEMINES is the name of a French town that is used as part of a china mark. Utzschneider and Company, a porcelain factory, made ceramics in Sarreguemines, Lorraine, France, from about 1775. Transfer-printed wares and majolica were made in the nineteenth century. The nineteenth-century pieces, most often found today, usually have colorful transfer-printed decorations showing peasants in local costumes.

Asparagus Set, Bleeding Heart Flowers, Majolica, 15-In. Platter, 7 Piece	250.00
Basket, Grapes, Vine Handle, Majolica, 8 1/2 In.	175.00
Bowl, Fruit, Grapes Cover, Basket Base, Majolica, 3 1/2 x 9 In.	180.00
Oyster Plate, 6 Wells, Scallop-Shaped Wells, Seaweed Border, 9 1/2 In.	100.00
Pitcher, Figural Rooster, Rose, Blue, Ivory, Majolica, 7 1/2 In.	1825.00
Placecard Holder, Shell & Coral, Majolica, 2 1/4 In.	495.00
Planter, Bamboo Stalk Shape, Flower Stem & Leaf Handle, Majolica, 12 In.	365.00
Plate, Grape Leaf Shape, Green, 10 In.	40.00

SASCHA BRASTOFF made decorative accessories, ceramics, enamels on copper, and plastics of his own design. He headed a factory, Sascha Brastoff of California, Inc., in West Los Angeles, from 1953 until about 1973. He died in 1993. Pieces signed with the signature *Sascha Brastoff* were his work and are the most expensive. Other pieces marked *Sascha B.* or with a stamped mark were made by others in his company. Pieces made by Matt Adams after he left the factory are listed here with his name.

Ashtray, Brown, Eggshell, White, Blue & Gold Trim, Signed, 1950s, 6 In.	40.00
Charger, Fruit Still Life Design, Yellow Ground, Signed, 22 In.	280.00
Cigarette Set, Roof Tops, 3 Piece, c.1958	150.00
Dish, Vanity Fair, Pink, Blue Orange Flowers, Black Ground, 9 1/2 x 5 1/2 In.	125.00
Platter, Alaska, Gray Seal, Blue Sky, White Ground, Matt Adams, 13 3/4 x 8 In.	130.00
Vase, Alaska, Blue Igloos, White Ground, Matt Adams, 7 3/4 In.	22.00

SATIN GLASS is a late nineteenth-century art glass. It has a dull finish that is caused by hydrofluoric acid vapor treatment. Satin glass was made in many colors and sometimes has applied decorations. Satin glass is also listed by factory name, such as Webb, or in the Mother-of-Pearl category in this book.

Barber Bottle, Diamond-Quilted, Clear Over Blue, Sheared Lip, 8 In. . . . . *Illus*	110.00
Bowl Set, Rose, Victorian, 19th Century, 3 To 4 1/2 In., 3 Piece	69.00
Ewer, Blue, Diamond-Quilted, Applied Frosted Leaf, Handle, Mid 19th Century, 7 1/2 In.	30.00
Lamp, Green, Brass Base, Victorian, 30 1/2 In.	99.00
Pitcher, Peacock Eye, Blue, Applied Reeded Handle, 7 In.	52.00
Rose Bowl, Apricot To White, Box Pleated Top, Applied Thorn Feet, 6 In.	345.00
Rose Bowl, Blue Stripes, Pinched Sides, 6-Crimp Edge, 3 5/8 In.	150.00
Rose Bowl, Shell & Seaweed, White Interior, 3 1/4 In.	75.00

Satin Glass, Barber Bottle, Diamond-Quilted, Clear Over Blue, Sheared Lip, 8 In.

There is a product called "Peel' in stationery stores that can be used to remove old labels you want to save or old labels that are disfiguring an antique.

Toothpick, Amethyst, Ribbed, Applied Gold Frosted Petal Feet, 4 In. 160.00
Vase, Blue, Egg Shape, Pinched Top, 3 Applied Satin Feet, 5 3/4 In. 259.00
Vase, Bright Lemon Yellow, Pink, Pale Brown, Creamy White Interior, 6 1/2 In. 115.00
Vase, Green, Bottle Shape, Ground Top, 8 In. 98.00
Vase, Herringbone, Melon Ribbed, White Interior, 6 1/2 In., Pair 325.00
Vase, Ivory Over Pink, Trefoil Ruffled Edge, 4 1/2 In., Pair 85.00
Vase, Pastel Yellow, Enameled Amethyst & Gold Flowers, Scalloped, 8 1/2 In. 200.00
Vase, Pink To White, Bulbous, Ground Top, 9 1/2 In. 115.00
Vase, Pink To White, Gold Enameled Dragonfly & Trim, 6 In. 60.00
Vase, Yellow Swirl, Bulbous, Flared, 6 1/2 In. 240.00

SATSUMA is a Japanese pottery with a distinctive creamy beige crackled glaze. Most of the pieces were decorated with blue, red, green,
orange, or gold. Almost all Satsuma found today was made after 1860.
During World War I, Americans could not buy undecorated European
porcelains. Women who liked to make hand painted porcelains at
home began to decorate plain Satsuma. These pieces are known today
as *American Satsuma.*

Bowl, Figural Cartouche, Brocade Ground, Meizan, Meiji 140.00
Bowl, Haloed Figures, Earthenware, Relief, Gold On White Ground, c.1912, 9 5/8 In. 2240.00
Bowl, Interior Figure Riding Sea Monster, Panels Of Cranes In Flight, 6 5/8 In. 345.00
Box, Cover, Allover Multicolored Flowers, Marked, 1 x 3 1/4 In. 275.00
Charger, Center Scene, Peacock Amid Leaves, Early 20th Century, 18 1/4 In. 310.00
Incense Burner, 19th Century, 4 1/2 x 6 3/8 In. 490.00
Incense Burner, Domed Lid, Foo Dog Handles, Figures & Faces, c.1915, 17 In. 560.00
Jar, Cover, Earthenware, Bulbous Base, c.1912, 8 1/2 x 6 In. 840.00
Lamp, 3 Fighting Warriors, Round Shape, Scalloped Band Top, No Shade, 36 In. 110.00
Lamp Base, Satsuma Sits On 3 Feet, Dragon Handles, 26 In. 200.00
Teacup, Ruffled Edge, Red Orange, 2 In. 6.00
Teapot, Bulbous, Red Orange, 9 x 7 1/2 In. 65.00
Teapot, Red Orange, 6 x 7 In. 45.00
Teapot, Strainer, Red Orange, 9 x 6 1/2 In. 45.00
Vase, 100 Rakan, Gold, Brown Cartouche, 4 3/4 In., Pair 145.00
Vase, Bird On Flowering Branch, 6-Footed, Character Signed, 19 1/4 In. 1430.00
Vase, Enameled Flowers, Cobalt Blue Glaze, 20th Century, 5 In., Pair 115.00
Vase, Entwined Dragons, 2 Gate Posts, Brocade, 1911, 25 In. 6900.00
Vase, Figures In Garden Scene, c.1880, 19 1/4 In. 660.00
Vase, Figures In Garden Vignettes, Cobalt Blue Ground, Gilt, Signed, 16 In. 1495.00
Vase, Figures In Interior, Signed, Early 20th Century, 5 In. 115.00
Vase, Figures, Faces, Raised Dragon, Enamel, Rolled Rim, Beading, 1930s, 12 In., Pair .. 450.00
Vase, Flowers, Figures, Earthenware, 35 3/4 In. 490.00
Vase, Flowers, Lavender, Gold Vining, Beading, Oriental Mark, 1900s, 12 1/2 In., Pair ... 165.00
Vase, Gilt & Figural Design, Mounted At Table Lamp, 26 In. 125.00
Vase, Gilt Chrysanthemums, Early 20th Century, 5 3/4 In. 115.00
Vase, Green Shishi Carrying Vase On Back, 1911, 5 3/4 In. 315.00
Vase, Haloed Arhats, Gold Ground, Earthenware, Signed, c.1912, 7 In. 505.00
Vase, Kinkozan, Inverted Pear Shape, Figural Design, Relief Work, 6 In. 2070.00
Vase, Landscape Scene, View Of Fuji & Pavilions, Signed, 1911, 6 1/4 In. 2645.00
Vase, Ornate Brocade, Floral Reserve, Meiji Period, 1911, 9 1/2 In. 630.00
Vase, Overall Floral, Geometric Landscape Panel, 6 In. 290.00
Vase, Panels Of Birds, Flowers, Flying Cranes, Black Ground, Gilded, 25 x 13 In. 605.00
Vase, Pavilions In Garden Settings, Black, Gilt, Signed, 9 1/2 In., Pair 115.00
Vase, Shishi Carrying Vase On Back, 1911, 7 In. 345.00
Vase, Teardrop Shape, Lohan Design, Relief Dragon, c.1900, 6 1/2 In. 290.00
Vase, Wisteria, Earthenware, Classical, Cream Ground, c.1912, 2 1/2 In. 560.00

SATURDAY EVENING GIRLS, see Paul Revere Pottery category.

SCALES have been made to weigh everything from babies to gold. Collectors search for all types. Most popular are small gold dust scales and
special grocery scales.

    Automatic, Bridgeport 600.00
    Balance, Analytical Beam, Glazed Mahogany Case, Lacquer Fittings, 18 In. 172.00

Balance, Analytical Beam, Whitall, Tatum & Co., Glazed Mahogany Case, 16 1/2 In.	172.00
Balance, Apothecary, Henry Troemmer, No. 13, Marble Top, 14 x 4 1/2 x 7 In.	52.00
Balance, Brass, Mahogany Case, Various Weights, Pocket	115.00
Balance, Brass, Warranted Accurate, Mahogany Base, 4 x 8 x 5 In.	112.00
Balance, Christian Becker, Brass Scales, Plated Pans, Celluloid Hardware, Case, 18 In. . . .	330.00
Balance, Cooperative Wholesale, Brass, Weights, Oak Base, England, 26 1/2 x 24 x 12 In.	336.00
Balance, Ebonized Columns, Gilt Flowers, Mid 19th Century, 29 In.	5500.00
Balance, Fairbanks Morris, Wooden Beam, Goldfield, Nev., 1905	112.00
Balance, Fairbanks, Brass, Iron, Shaped Base, Brass Pan, Arm, Fixed Brass Weight	55.00
Balance, Felix, Tin Lithograph, 2 Trays, 7 In.	1430.00
Balance, I. Edwards, N.Y., Blacksmith-Made Iron, Hammered Sheet Brass Pans, c.1750 . .	495.00
Balance, Indian Figure, Horn Holders, 7 1/2 In.	50.00
Balance, Micrometer, Dodge Mfg. Co., Cast Iron, Marble Top, 1903, 17 x 11 In.	230.00
Balance, Troemner, Cast Iron, Black Body, 13 x 28 In.	85.00
Balance, Tubular Brass Standard, Pivoting Brass Arm, Iron, Blue Ceramic Dish, 40 In. . . .	2530.00
Balance, W. & T. Avery, Cast Iron, Brass Bowls, 9 x 14 x 4 In.	140.00
Butcher, Brass Steer Head On Top, Metric Weights, 48 In.	1250.00
Copper, Iron, 4 Weights, 9 x 16 In.	121.00
Fish, La Gleh, Weighs Up To 8 Lbs.	8.00
Gold, Coin, Cherry, Brass Pan, Inlaid Silver Scale, 11 In.	750.00
Hanging, Brass Trim Above Hooks, Wrought Iron, Engraved HAG & Ano 1849, 13 In. . . .	55.00
Hide, 4 x 3 1/2 In.	82.00
Jockey, Toledo Lollipop, White Porcelain, 1 Cent Slot, 71 x 16 In.	840.00
Oak, Brass, Rectangular Oak Base, Brass Bun Feet, England, Late 19th Century, 11 In. . .	345.00
Penny, Watling, Emerald Iron, 5 Cent Horoscope Attachment, 64 In.	230.00
Platform, Buffalo Standard, Wood Case, Late 19th Century	1750.00
Postage, Mordan & Co., Gilt Bronze, 3 Weights, Wedgwood Jasper Base, 6 3/4 x 4 1/2 In.	345.00
Postage, Nolan Scale Co., Boston, Nickel Plated, Square Pan, 1889, 4 1/2 In.	170.00
Shopkeeper's, Countertop, Sliding Weight, Pouring Pan, Toledo Scale Co., 1820	170.00
Steelyard, Weight Balance, 36 In.	70.00
Weighing, Henry Troemner, Brass, 1/8 Oz. To 4 Lb., Walnut Case, 9 x 5 x 5 In.	165.00
Weighing, Royal Crown Cola, Coin-Operated, Plastic Bottle, Hamilton, 1950, 45 In.	2300.00
Weighing, Step On, Joseph Sinel, Steel, Cast Iron, Firm's Mark, 77 In.	3000.00
Weighing, Vendinator, Art Deco, Black & Blue Porcelain, Coin-Operated, 43 In.	60.00

SCHAFER & VATER, makers of small ceramic items, are best known for
their amusing figurals. The factory was located in Volkstedt-Rudolstadt, Germany, from 1890 to 1962. Some pieces are marked with the
crown and R mark, but many are unmarked.

Bottle, Blue Glaze, Marked First Aid	525.00
Bottle, Man, Holding Glass, Finger Pointing, Prosit On Cap, Blue, White, 6 1/4 In.	165.00
Bottle, Rooster, Orange Jacket, Yellow Tie, Tail Stopper, 7 3/4 In.	195.00
Bottle, Rooster, White & Orange Coat, Green Feathers, 5 1/2 In.	150.00
Creamer, Orange & Yellow Robe, Holding White Goose, Pony Tail Handle, 4 In.	125.00
Figurine, Dog, Gold Bee On Tail, Ribbon Around Neck, 3 1/2 x 3 1/2 In.	145.00
Sugar Shaker, Grecian Women On Urns, Green Foliage, 6 1/8 In.	135.00

SCHNEIDER Glassworks was founded in 1913 at Epinay-sur-Seine,
France, by Charles and Ernest Schneider. Art glass was made between
1913 and 1930. The company still produces clear crystal glass.

Bowl, Pale Orange Mottled Leaves, Hanging Flowers, Rolled Inward Rim, 6 3/4 In.	920.00
Bowl, Pink, Line & Circle Decoration, France, 20th Century, 14 In.	290.00
Bowl, Purple To Mottled Orange, Cherries On Wrought Iron Base, 6 1/2 In.	920.00
Bowl, Rose, Purple Foot, Signed, 9 1/4 In.	470.00
Compote, Green Controlled Bubbles, Black Foot, France, 3 1/4 x 8 In.	290.00
Coupe, Orange Shaded To Purple, Signed, 7 1/2 In.	1035.00
Coupe, Shaded Cranberry, Wrought Iron Holder, 8 In.	1035.00
Couple, Lavender, Pink Base, Flared, Signed, 6 1/2 In.	980.00
Goblet, Mottled Orange & Yellow, Signed, 6 1/2 In.	345.00
Vase, Amber Tint, Satin, Etched Overlay, c.1915, 16 In.	2530.00
Vase, Blue, Green, Yellow, Pink, Signed, France, Mid 20th Century, 19 3/4 In.	1840.00
Vase, Burgundy Mottled Flecks, Signed, France, 20th Century, 11 1/2 In.	520.00
Vase, Flecked Tangerine, Purple, Cream, Aubergine Stem & Foot, 7 1/2 In.	1765.00

Vase, Lavender, Orange Handles, Knopped Foot, Signed, 6 1/4 In. 805.00
Vase, Mottled Brown, Stylized Flowers, On Mottled Orange, Signed, c.1925, 8 In. 690.00
Vase, Mottled Pink, Purple & Yellow, Flattened Oval, Signed, 12 1/2 In. 2300.00
Vase, Orange, Mottled Brown, Cameo, Fruit, Footed, Signed, 18 In. 1265.00
Vase, Pale Pink, Etched Textured Surface, Stylized Rays, 1900s, 3 7/8 In. 115.00
Vase, Pillow, Green, Controlled Bubbles, Drip Handles, Black Foot, Signed, 11 x 9 In. ... 1760.00
Vase, Purple, Orange, On Yellow, Goblet Shape, Signed, 16 3/4 In. 1760.00
Vase, Red, Interior Design, Spreading Base, Oval, Signed, 9 In. 1725.00
Vase, Sea Foam, Swirled Ribs, Signed, France, 20th Century, 6 3/4 In. 980.00
Vase, Yellow & Orange Spattered, Clear Ground, Signed, 6 1/2 In. 95.00
Vase, Yellow, Orange, Signed, France, Mid 20th Century, 12 1/2 In. 1150.00

SCIENTIFIC INSTRUMENTS

SCIENTIFIC INSTRUMENTS of all kinds are included in this category. Other categories such as Barometer, Binoculars, Dental, Nautical, Medical, and Thermometer may also price scientific apparatus.

Calculator, Step-Drum, Roll Top, Germany, 1910 .... *Illus* 4916.00
Compass, Dry Card, E.G. Gert & Son, Blue Bowl, Pine Case, 10 In. 520.00
Compass, Dry Card, Wm. Helffrict, Pa., Green Painted Case, 9 1/2 In. 520.00
Compass, Screw Top, 18th Century, 1 1/2 In. 99.00
Compass, Ship's, Brass Binnacle, Domed Top, 10 1/2 In. 170.00
Compass, Surveyor's, E. Suffield, Engraved Silver Dial 3750.00
Compass, Surveyor's, Thomas Whitney, Brass, Pine Case 2105.00
Computer, Mark 3, Germany, 1974 .... 4100.00
Computer, MITS Altair 8800, Personal, Introduced As Kit In 1975 .... 4705.00
Electrostatic Generator, 2 Electrodes At Ends, 16 1/2 In. 440.00
Heliograph, Brass, Fitted Brown Leather Case, Tripod Stand, c.1910 .... 400.00
Hourglass, White Sand Loaded, 13 x 5 1/2 In. 37.00
Hydrometer, Alcohol Testing Kit, I.R.S., Copper, Case, 4 x 10 1/2 x 7 In. 336.00
Magnifying Glass, Asprey, Ivory Handle, Silver Rim, 1930, 12 7/8 In. 630.00
Magnifying Glass, Brass, Ivory Handle, Late 19th Century, 15 1/2 In. 86.00
Magnifying Glass, Circular, Brass Frame, Wooden Handle, 9 1/4 In. 80.00
Magnifying Glass, Dragon & Cord Handle, Cloisonne, 1900s, 13 In. 170.00
Magnifying Glass, Green Jasper Handle, Yellow Trellis, 1870s, 3 3/4 In. 170.00
Magnifying Glass, Horn Frame & Case, 18th Century 135.00
Magnifying Glass, Horn Handle, Stag's Head End, Silver, Mount, 13 In. 335.00
Microscope, Bausch & Lomb, Brass, 11 In. 80.00
Microscope, Bausch & Lomb, Dissecting, Fitted Mahogany Case, 6 In. 230.00
Microscope, Bausch & Lomb, Fitted Mahogany Case, 13 In. 805.00
Microscope, Brass, Black Enamel, 12 In. 287.00
Microscope, Brass, Enameled Steel, 5X & 8X Eyepiece, 14 1/2 In. 275.00
Microscope, Brass, Nickeled Body Tube, Japanned, 13 1/4 In. 1090.00
Microscope, Leitz, Brass, Coarse Micrometer Focusing, 12 1/2 In. 230.00
Microscope, Leitz, Dissecting, Flat Horseshoe Foot, Fitted Case, 6 In. 145.00
Microscope, Nachet, Brass, Fitted Mahogany Case, 11 1/2 In. 258.00
Microscope, Nonpareil, Gundlach, Brass, Black Cast Iron, 12 In. 575.00
Microscope, Society Of Arts, Brass, Fitted Mahogany Case, 13 In. 258.00
Microscope, Spencer, 3 Lenses, Mirror, Wood Case, 11 1/8 In. 110.00
Microscope, Zeiss, Fitted Mahogany Case, 12 In. 630.00
Octant, London, Ebony, With Brass Arm, Ivory Scale, 12 In. 630.00
Sextant, Army Air Force, Bubble, With Accessories, Case, 1943, 12 In. 115.00
Sextant, London, Lattice, Oxidized Brass, Silver Scale, 12 In. 805.00
Surveyor's Tool, Mahogany, 3 Sections, Folding, Victorian, 50 In. 115.00
Telescope, 5 Section, Tabletop Or Floor, Brass, Extended, 44 In. 200.00
Telescope, Astronomer's, Folding Stand, 1920s, 62 1/2 In. 978.00
Telescope, Bardou & Son, Paris, Brass, Rack & Pinion Focusing 3105.00
Telescope, Brass, 2 Draw, Wood Base, Extended 35 In. 150.00
Telescope, Dollond, Single Draw, Mahogany Body Tube, 1800, 26 In. 1380.00
Telescope, Four Draw, Mahogany Body Tube, Lens Cap, 13 1/2 In. 575.00
Telescope, Iron Frame, 75 In. 3450.00
Telescope, J.A. O'Donohoe, England, Brass, Engraved Tube 4200.00
Telescope, Queen & Co., Philadelphia, Brass, 47 1/2 x 4 In. 310.00
Telescope, Ship's, Canvas Covered, 35 In. 165.00

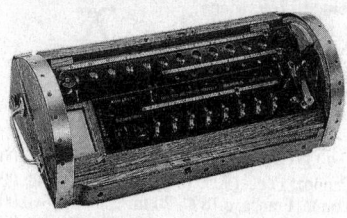

**Your collectibles will live best at
the temperature and humidity
that is comfortable for you. Not
too hot, cold, wet, or dry.**

Scientific Instrument, Calculator, Step-Drum,
Roll Top, Germany, 1910

Telescope, Tabletop, Brass, Signed J. White, Glasgow, Barrel 37 1/2 In. 1035.00
Telescope, Walking Stick, Rosewood Veneer Bottom, 28 3/4 In. 175.00
Tellurium, Germany, 1885 . . . . 3550.00
Transit, Surveyor's, Richard Paten, Glass Lens & Level, 13 1/2 In. 385.00
Wye Level, Surveyor's, A.S. Aloe, Serial No. 8161, Reversible Telescope 750.00

SCRIMSHAW is bone or ivory or whale's teeth carved by sailors and
others for entertainment during the sailing-ship days. Some scrimshaw
was carved as early as 1800. There are modern scrimshanders making
pieces today on bone, ivory, or plastic. Other pieces may be found in
the Ivory and Nautical categories.

Box, Ditty, Whalebone, 4 In. 5175.00
Cribbage Board, Walrus Tusk, X Designs, Vines, c.1900, 20 In. 345.00
Cribbage Board, Whalebone, 2 Mounted Whale Teeth, 11 In. 490.00
Cribbage Board, Wide Mouth Fish, Walrus, Seal On Reverse, Eskimo, 12 In. 750.00
Dipper, Coconut Ladle, Whalebone Handle, 9 3/4 In. 138.00
Dipper, Curved Handle, Ivory, Wood Spacers, Heart Shape Connector 525.00
Dominoes, Ivory, Ebony, Box, 4 x 3 x 2 In. 476.00
Fid, Rope Making Tool, Whalebone, Mother, Daughter, J E, 1884, 10 1/2 In. 825.00
Frame, Walrus Tusk, Mariner's Stars On Each Corner, 7 1/4 x 5 3/8 In. 470.00
Hairpin, Whalebone, 2 Columns, Balls Inside, Red, Blue Designs, 6 1/2 In. 230.00
Pie Crimper, Walrus Ivory Wheel, Handle, 6 In. 330.00
Powder Horn, Eagle, Shield, Man, Animals, Carved Rings, 1856, 8 In. 1430.00
Powder Horn, Mermaid, Double Eagle, John Pendergast, The Elenden, 1831, 14 In. 1980.00
Rolling Pin, Wood, Whale Ivory, Acorn-Form Handles, 17 In. 600.00
Snuffbox, 2 Separate Teeth Hinged Together, 3 3/8 In. 185.00
Snuffbox, Ivory, Cross Hatching, Serrated Edge, Carved Snuff Spoon, 3 3/4 In. 220.00
Swift, Whalebone, Scribed Staves, Cup, Square Stepped Base, 13 1/2 In. 1495.00
Swift, Whalebone, Turned Finial, Animal Head Clamp, Fist Screw, c.1855, 23 In. 11500.00
Swift, Wooden Slats, Whale Ivory Base & Top, Mahogany Box, c.1845, 21 In. 1150.00
Tooth, 2-Masted Ship, Marine Accouterments, 20th Century, 5 In. 288.00
Tooth, Amorous Couple, Woman's Portrait, Pair 4600.00
Tooth, Whale, 3 Sailing Ships, American Flags, 2 Whales, 8 1/2 In. 2128.00
Tooth, Whale, 3-Masted Sailing Ship, Lighthouse, 6 1/2 In. 600.00
Tooth, Whale, Constitution 1 Side, Guerriere Other, Pair 9350.00
Tooth, Whale, Engraved, Lady Wearing Hat With Feathers, 19th Century, 4 1/2 In. 980.00
Tooth, Whale, Engraved, Polychrome, Woman, Vine, Heart, 19th Century, 6 3/8 In. 920.00
Tooth, Whale, Memorial, Tree, Woman, 5 3/8 In. 4025.00
Tooth, Whale, Moby Dick, Capt. Ahab, Pequod In Background, 7 In. 770.00
Tooth, Whale, Ship, American Flag, Lighthouse, Flowers, 7 x 2 1/2 In. 6100.00
Tusk, Man Trapped By Alligator, Large Fish Behind, Belgian Congo, c.1930, 24 1/4 In. . . 169.00
Tusk, Walrus, 14 1/2 In., Pair 2300.00
Tusk, Whaling Ship Mercury 1 Side, Shield, Laurel Other, Tools, 16 In. 550.00
Walking Stick, Turned Whale Ivory Handle, Whale Bone Shaft, 35 In. 865.00
Walking Stick, Whale Ivory Handle, Mahogany Shaft, 35 In. 195.00

SEG, see Paul Revere Pottery category.

SEVRES porcelain has been made in Sevres, France, since 1769. Many copies of the famous ware have been made. The name originally referred to the works of the Royal Porcelain factory. The name now includes any of the wares made in the town of Sevres, France. The entwined lines with a center letter used as the mark is one of the most forged marks in antiques. Be very careful to identify Sevres by quality, not just by mark.

Bowl, Feuille De Choux, Bouquets, Blue, Gilt Leaves, c.1775, 9 1/4 In.	315.00
Bowl, Ormolu, Oval, Couple, Flowers, Gilt, Handles, Trumpet Foot, 1905, 10 x 14 In.	1725.00
Bust, Marie Antoinette, Flowers, Gilt Base, Incised Secomte, France, c.1890, 20 In.	1840.00
Bust, Woman, Hair In Quiver Clip, Holding Sheer Wrap, c.1890, 19 In.	575.00
Casket, Jewelry, Figural Bronze Supports, Painted Cupids, Flower Panels, 5 x 4 x 8 In.	1900.00
Centerpiece Set, Victorian Courting Couple In Courtyard, 4-Footed Holder, 14 1/2 In.	280.00
Cup & Saucer, Couple Playing With Dog, Flower Center, Cup, 5 x 5 5/8 In.	805.00
Cup & Saucer, Courting Couple, Jeweled, Late 1800s, 2 7/8-In. Cup, 5 1/2-In. Saucer	1495.00
Cup & Saucer, Figural Scene, Blue Celeste Ground, Signed	920.00
Cup & Saucer, Flowers, Gilt Frame, Flower Rim On Saucer, 1842, 3 1/8 & 6 In.	1610.00
Cup & Saucer, Rustic Scene, Gilt Yellow Panels, Painted Mark, Large	1725.00
Figurine, Polar Bear, Seated, 1940s, 11 In.	860.00
Garniture Set, Louis XVI, Figural Cupids, Celeste Blue, 2 Urns, 18-In. Clock, 3 Piece	6900.00
Group, Allegorical, Gilt Bronze Base, Late 19th Century, 17 In.	2700.00
Jardiniere, Gold Leaf Rim, Relief Cherubs, Ram's Head 2 Side, 15 In.	740.00
Patch Box, Hinged Lid, Hand Painted Napoleon On Horseback, L.R. Morin, 3 1/4 In.	230.00
Pedestal, Hunt Scene, Gilt, Cobalt Blue Ground, Plinth Base, 46 1/2 In.	9600.00
Pedestal, Napoleon & His Army, Cobalt Blue Border, Square Onyx Base, 41 In.	9000.00
Plaque, Woman, Marie Antoinette In Gown, Giltwood Frame, 10 1/2 x 9 5/8 In.	520.00
Plate, Gilt Band Border, Cobalt Blue Ground, 9 1/2 In.	230.00
Plate, Man & Woman, Flower Panels & Gilding, Pink Border, 9 1/2 In.	302.00
Plate, Portrait, Blue Border, Signed G. Perier, Roi De Rome, 9 In.	110.00
Plate, Portrait, Woman, Blue, White Dress, Bonnet, Blue Rim, Vignettes, France, 9 1/2 In.	115.00
Saucer, Gilt Bronze Mounted, Turquoise Ground, Fluted, Late 19th Century, 5 1/8 In.	345.00
Teapot, Cover, Flower Sprays, Green Ground Border, Gilt Rim, 1760, 4 1/4 In.	3900.00
Trinket Box, Painted Gilt Bellflowers & Roses, 1 1/2 x 3 3/4 x 2 5/8 In.	210.00
Urn, Courting Scene Panel, Cobalt Blue, Gilt, Double Scroll Handles, 20 In.	660.00
Urn, Courting Scenes, Bronze Maiden Handles, Cover, Signed L. Murin, 18 In., Pair	1960.00
Urn, Courting Scenes, Bronze Mounted, Maidenhead Handles, c.1900, 21 In., Pair	3080.00
Urn, Domed Lid, Courting Couple, Cobalt Blue Ground, Leaf Handles, 1900s, 26 In., Pair	9200.00
Urn, Gilt Bronze Mounted, Signed Eug. Carvelle, Landscape, 33 In., Pair	7800.00
Vase, Cover, Lady Lawrence Portrait, Bronze, Gilt, Wagner, 27 1/4 x 6 1/2 In., Pair	5500.00
Vase, Louis XVI, Gilt, Bronze, Flower Reserves, Blue Celeste Ground, 12 In., Pair	3450.00
Vase, Potpourri, Cover, Gilt Bronze Mounted, Early 20th Century, 13 1/2 In.	546.00
Vase, Purple Matte Glaze, Suspended Particles, Shouldered Body, Marked, 10 1/2 In.	920.00
Vase, Tan & Cream Matte Glaze, Melon Ribbed, Signed, Marked, 7 3/4 In.	520.00

SEWER TILE figures were made by workers at the sewer tile and pipe factories in the Ohio area during the late nineteenth and early twentieth centuries. Figurines, small vases, and cemetery vases were favored. Often the finished vase was a piece of the original pipe with added decorations and markings. All types of sewer tile work are now considered folk art by collectors.

Bank, Pig, Mollow, Sewer Tile Base, 10 1/2 In.	550.00
Birdhouse, Conical Roof, Round, Tooled Bark-Like Surface, 7 1/4 In.	250.00
Bottle, Bear, Pocket Watch, Bag, Dark Brown Matte Glaze, Cork, 6 1/4 In.	154.00
Bust, Admiral Dewey, 19th Century	5500.00
Bust, Brown Glaze, Hollow Body, 15 1/2 In.	275.00
Dice, Red Paint, White Pips, 3 1/2 In., Pair	190.00
Figurine, Cat, Reclining, Tooled Eye Lashes, White Blazed Eyes, 9 In.	357.00
Figurine, Cat, Seated, Bushy Tail, White Clay Eyes, 7 1/2 In.	410.00
Figurine, Cat, Seated, Hand Tooled Fur, Translucent Brown Glaze, 7 5/8 In.	520.00
Figurine, Cat, Whimsical, Head Crooked To Side, Curious Look, 13 1/4 In.	660.00
Figurine, Crow, On Stump, Brown Glaze, Initials E.J.E., 9 1/2 In.	1320.00
Figurine, Dog, Collar & Lock, Hollow Body, 11 1/4 In.	495.00
Figurine, Dog, Collie, Brown Glaze, Hollow Body, Rectangular Base, 12 x 11 1/4 In.	935.00

Figurine, Dog, Reclining Mastiff, Indented Chain Collar, 8 In. 220.00
Figurine, Dog, Seated, Collar & Chain, 8 1/4 In. 165.00
Figurine, Dog, Seated, Incised Face, Ears & Paws, 11 1/2 In. 960.00
Figurine, Dog, Seated, Long Hair, Bushy Tail, Pert Ears, 22 x 10 1/2 In. 935.00
Figurine, Dog, Spaniel, Seated, Collar, Superior Uhrichsville, Ohio, Unglazed, 11 In. 660.00
Figurine, Dog, Spaniel, Seated, Incised, Brown Glaze, 1928, 9 1/4 In. 460.00
Figurine, Dog, Spaniel, Seated, Tooled Surface & Collar, Open Legs, 10 1/2 In. 385.00
Figurine, Frog, Incised 1920, 9 3/4 In. 520.00
Figurine, Groundhog, Tooled Features, Marked E.J.E., 8 1/2 In. 1540.00
Figurine, Hippo, Black Glaze On Feet, 23 3/4 x 12 1/2 In. 165.00
Figurine, Horned Owl, On Tree Trunk, E.J.E., Tuscarawas County, Ohio, 14 1/8 In. 2750.00
Figurine, Horned Owl, Orange Glaze, Perched On Pedestal Base, 10 1/2 In. 440.00
Figurine, Horse, No Tail, Brown Glaze, 10 1/4 In. 66.00
Figurine, Lion, Full Mane, Smile, Unglazed, Gold Paint Underside, 10 1/8 x 5 x 7 In. 250.00
Figurine, Lion, Reclining On Base, 3 1/2 x 5 1/2 In. 220.00
Figurine, Lion, Reclining On Logs, Full Mane, 12 1/2 x 6 x 6 1/2 In. 300.00
Figurine, Lion, Reclining, Tooled Ribs, Mane & Tail, Moore Ceramics, 7 1/8 x 11 In. ... 1100.00
Figurine, Lion, Smiling, Curled Tail, Reclining On Base, 6 1/2 x 9 3/4 In. ....715.00 to 825.00
Figurine, Squirrel, Sitting, Large Ears, Shiny Glaze, 11 In. 165.00
Paperweight, Lion Head, Nelsonville Sewer Pipe Co., 3 1/8 In. 165.00
Paperweight, Scowling Face, Metal Specks, 4 In. 80.00
Planter, Medallion, Cambria Co., Blackfork, Ohio, 15 x 10 x 12 In. 385.00
Planter, Strawberry, Multiple Rimmed Holes, 14 x 13 In. 140.00
Planter, Stump, Molded Bark, 3 Limbs, Dark Brown Glaze, 28 x 36 In. 358.00
Planter, Tooled Bark, 4 Branches, 3 Open, 28 1/2 x 17 1/2 In. 165.00
Planter, Tree Trunk, 3 Branches, 28 x 32 In. 330.00
Planter, Tree Trunk, 3 Branches, Tooled Bark, 18 In. 110.00
Planter, Tree Trunk, Cover, Leaves, Acorns, Impressed Mileux, 5 x 7 In. 165.00
Planter, Tree Trunk, Maple Leaves, Fern Fronds, Retriever Finial, 7 x 6 In. 300.00
Plaque, Heron & Water Plants, Maude Perdue, 1890, 11 x 6 1/4 In. 605.00

SEWING equipment of all types is collected, from sewing birds that
held the cloth to tape measures, needle books, and old wooden spools.
Sewing machines are included here. Needlework pictures are listed in
the Picture category.

Basket, Straw, Round, Bakelite Handle 35.00
Bird, Round Cushion, Screw On Clamp, Gilding, Victorian 145.00
Bird, Velvet Pincushions, Silvered Brass, Feb. 15, 1853, 5 In. 145.00
Box, Bentwood, Lid, Spring Latches, Arched Handle, Scandinavian, 5 1/4 x 8 3/4 In. ... 165.00
Box, Blond Tortoiseshell, Blue Moire Lining, Brass Lock, England, 3 x 10 3/4 x 7 In. 595.00
Box, Brown Lacquer, Ivory Fittings, Compartment Tray, Drawer, Chinese, 6 x 14 x 10 In. 865.00
Box, Cherry & Pine, Folding Steel Clamp, Pincushion Top, 5 1/2 x 6 1/2 In. 110.00
Box, Cherry Veneer, Inlaid Band, Dovetailed Drawer, Pincushion Top, 5 x 3 x 2 3/4 In. 302.00
Box, Curly Maple Veneer, Diamond Escutcheon Inlaid, Lift-Out Tray, 3 Sections, 11 In. .. 440.00
Box, Decorated, Hinged Cover, Mirror, Fitted Interior Spool Caddy, Pincushions 99.00
Box, Grain Painted, Flowers, Pin Striping, N.Y., Mid 19th Century 595.00
Box, Lacquered Ground, Foliage Around Pagodas, Lift-Out Tray, Fitted Lower Drawer ... 330.00
Box, Mahogany Flame Veneer Over Pine, Dovetailed Case, Lined Interior, 7 x 12 In. ... 550.00
Box, Mahogany, Lift-Out Tray, Fold Away Handle, Interior Lock, 5 1/8 x 10 1/4 In. 145.00
Box, Marquetry Inlay, Lift-Out Fitted Tray, 19th Century, 7 x 11 3/4 In. 750.00
Box, Needle, Tortoiseshell, Domed, Velvet Lined, Bone Edges, 2 x 5 1/2 In. 230.00
Box, Pine, Slide Lid, Natural, T-Head Nail Corners, Tape Loom 1 End, 14 x 5 x 15 In. ... 1485.00
Box, Rosewood Veneer, Interior Fitted Lift-Out Tray, Sewing Tools, 4 1/2 x 9 3/4 In. 412.00
Box, Rosewood, Hinged Cover, Shield Shape Cartouche, Monogram, 13 x 8 5/8 In. 185.00
Box, Rosewood, Inlaid Parquetry, c.1860, 6 x 12 In. 180.00
Box, Rosewood, Light, Dark Wood Star, Compartments, 6 x 15 1/2 x 11 1/2 In. 825.00
Box, Satinwood, Inlaid Rosewood, Domed Cover, c.1820, 4 x 7 x 4 3/4 In. 633.00
Box, Spool Holder, Alternating Drawers, Revolving Pincushion Top, 8 x 9 In. 520.00
Box, Spool Holder, Revolving, Lower Drawer, Pincushion Top, 10 x 7 In. 300.00
Box, Spool Holder, Wood, 6 1/2 x 5 3/4 In. 137.00
Box, Stepped Hinged Lid, Sarcophagus Form Case, Star, Geometric, 5 3/4 In. 977.00
Box, Tiger Maple, School Girl, Botanical Print On Paper Lining, 1819, 8 x 6 1/2 x 3 In. .. 812.00
Box, Walnut, Mother-Of-Pearl Inlay, Brass, Mirrored Top, Tools, c.1870, 4 1/2 x 7 In. 336.00

Box, Wood, Dovetailed, Raised Panel Top, Red & Yellow, Hinges, Lehnware, 11 In. 2750.00
Cabinet, Mahogany, Lift Top, Cutout Sides, Signed, 28 x 18 In. 400.00
Cabinet, Spool, see Advertising category under Cabinet, Spool.
Cabinet, Stickley Bros., No. 2569, Oak, Drop Leaf, 29 1/2 x 18 1/2 In. 2010.00
Cabinet-On-Stand, Stand, Oriental Landscapes On Doors, Inner Sewing Tools, 54 1/4 In. . 2300.00
Caddy, Mahogany, 2 Tiers, Top Spool Box, Platform, Drawer, c.1840, 7 x 5 1/2 In. 55.00
Caddy, Rotating, Shaped Tiers, Paw Foot Base, Apple Shape Top, Cast Iron, 12 In. 143.00
Caddy, Treen, 3 Graduated Tiers, Yellow, Green & Red, 18 Spool Pegs, Cup Top, 13 In. . . 990.00
Caddy, Walnut, Velvet Pincushion Top, Drawer 110.00
Clamp, Hemming, Ivory, Carved, Inked Tulip Shape Knob, 4 1/2 In. 105.00
Clamp, Pincushion, Wood, White, Yellow Flower Bands, Striping 165.00
Clamp, Winding, Rotating Cage, Carved, Chinese Figures, Landscape, Ivory, 5 3/4 In. . . . 300.00
Clamp, Wooden, Painted, Script Signed, 1832, 5 3/4 In. 385.00
Darner, Egg, Aqua Glass 55.00
Display, Thimble, Sterling Silver, 20th Century, 79 x 9 1/2 x 7 3/4 In. 800.00
Distaff, Yarn Spinner's, Carved, 1772 . . . . 325.00
Embroidery Set, Canvas, Children On Lid, Cardboard, Threads, c.1880 . . . . 225.00
Kit, Bakelite, Iridescent Green, Carved Leaves, Flowers, White, Red, 3 1/4 In., 4 Pieces . . 140.00
Knitting Needle, Carved Hickory, 18th Century, 14 In. 195.00
Machine, Buttonhole, Folding, Metal Base, American Button Hole Machine 250.00
Machine, Salesman Sample, Walnut, Hinged, Cast Iron, Tension Wheel, French, 9 In. 1050.00
Machine, Singer, Featherweight, Black, Gold Stencil, Case, c.1951, Size C 405.00
Machine, Singer, Model 99, Carrying Case, Jan. 20, 1926 . . . . 125.00
Machine, Singer, No. 221-1, Featherweight, Attachments, Case, 1941, 8 1/2 In. 259.00
Machine, Singer, No. 221-K, Featherweight, Attachments, Case, 1940s, 9 In. 200.00
Machine, Soeze, Clamp-On, 1901, Miniature 1900.00
Machine, Stitchwell, Cast Iron, Painted, Wooden Box, Label, 5 x 8 x 3 1/2 In. 896.00
Needle Case, Acme Markets, Cardboard, Blue & White Blimp Shape, 1 Fold 10.00
Needle Case, Army & Navy Heroes Of Our Late War, McKinley, Cardboard, 5 x 2 5/8 In. . . 30.00
Needle Case, Golden Casket, Butterfly, Gilt Brass, Waverly & Son Redditch, 3 In. 121.00
Needle Case, Happy Home, Mother, Daughter, Cardboard, 1950, 6 x 3 1/2 In. 5.00
Needle Case, Manhattan Needle Book, Cardboard, NYC, Indians, 7 Group, 6 1/2 x 4 In. . . 15.00
Needle Case, Oak, 2 Drawers, Watson's Needles, 8 3/8 x 13 In. 225.00
Needle Case, One World, Cardboard, Statue Of Liberty, Threader, 6 3/8 x 3 5/8 In. 10.00
Needle Case, Rocket, Man & Woman Riding, Cardboard, Threader, 6 1/2 x 3 1/2 In. 12.00
Needle Case, Sewing Susan, Cardboard, Foil, Threader, 1 Fold, 1950, 5 7/8 x 3 1/2 In. . . . 10.00
Needle Case, The Favorite, Cardboard, Runners, U.S. Flag, Threader, 6 7/8 x 3 3/4 In. . . . 15.00
Niddy Noddy, Carved On Both Ends 110.00
Niddy Noddy, Hand Reel For Yarn, Walnut, Dated 1798, 14 1/4 x 17 1/2 In. 455.00
Pincushion, Blue & Gold Velvet, Floral, Table Clamp, Round Mirror, 7 1/4 In. 110.00
Pincushion, Clamp, Ball On Barrel Maple Clamp, Iron Screw, Heart End, 9 3/4 In. 165.00
Pincushion, Clamp, Steel, Engraved Flowers, Table Plate, Silk, Velvet, 5 In. 209.00
Pincushion, Clamp, Wood, Blue, White Flowers 275.00
Pincushion, Dove Form, Heart Hanging From Mouth, Glass Base 3850.00
Pincushion, Grinning Mammy, 4 3/4 In. 85.00
Pincushion, Mammy Face, Stuffed Cloth, 1920s, 5 1/2 In. 65.00
Pincushion, Rocking Chair, Red Velvet Seat, 4 1/2 In. 18.00

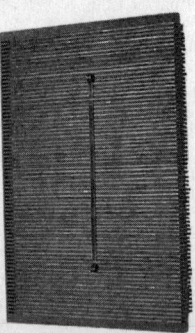

Sewing, Plaiter, Young's
Improved, Abel
Wheeler & Co., Wood,
Tin, 15 In.

Sewing, Sewing Bird, Corduroy
Cushions, Gold Paint, 4 In.

Pincushion, Woven, Embroidered Floral Sprays, Dogs & Birds, Glass Stand, 8 In.	1265.00
Pincushion Dolls are listed in their own category.	
Plaiter, Young's Improved, Abel Wheeler & Co., Wood, Tin, 15 In. .... *Illus*	55.00
Quilt Pattern, S Curve, 7 Conforming Ribs, Tin, Penna., 12 1/2 In.	176.00
Quilting Frame, Mustard Repaint, Shoe Feet, Chamfered, Mortised, 33 x 32 x 93 In.	110.00
Sewing Bird, Corduroy Cushions, Gold Paint, 4 In. .... *Illus*	100.00
Shuttle, Weaving, Wooden, Handmade, Graduated, 6 In. To 12 In., 9 Piece	35.00
Spool Cabinets are in the Advertising category under Cabinet, Spool.	
Spool Chest, Walnut, 3 Drawer, Porcelain Pulls, Open Interior Drawers, 9 x 22 In.	115.00
Spool Holder, Painted, Splayed Legs, Lower Shelf, 16 1/2 x 27 In.	385.00
Stand, Empire, Drop Leaf, Veneered, Faux Drawers Back, Wood Bag	1650.00
Stand, Papier-Mache, Black, Flowers, Hinged Lid, Urn Post, Quatrefoil Base, 30 x 16 In.	978.00
Stand, Sheraton, Black Walnut, 1 Dovetailed Drawer, Pigeon Holes, 20 x 29 In.	1155.00
Swift, Maple & Birch, Iron Table Clamp, 23 In.	110.00
Table, Chinese Export, Gilt, Black Lacquer, Mid 19th Century, 28 x 24 1/2 x 16 1/4 In.	2875.00
Tape Measure, Apple	28.00
Tape Measure, Black Man Smoking, 1900, 1 1/2 In.	23.00
Tape Measure, Black Man Smoking, Cigarette Tape Pull, Celluloid, 1 1/2 In.	213.00
Tape Measure, Dutch Girl, Pedestal, Embossed Sailing Ship, 4 In.	90.00
Tape Measure, Lady, 6 In.	16.00
Tape Measure, Mazda, Parrish Design, 1920, 1 1/2 In.	335.00
Tape Measure, Owl, Metal, Germany	45.00
Tape Measure, Smokes Cigarette Which Is Tape Pull, 1900s, 1 1/2 In.	234.00
Tape Measure, Swordfish	135.00
Tape Measure, Teapot Shape, Brass, On Stand, 1890s, 2 1/4 In.	190.00
Thimble, 10 Panels, Wide Band, Chasing, 14K Gold, Simons, Size 8	88.00
Thimble, Embossed Bottom, Flowers, Leaves, Sterling Silver, 3/4 In.	29.00
Thimble, Gold, 10K, Engraved, Hallmarked, Victorian	125.00
Thimble, Ornate Curlicues, Stylized Flowers, Leaves, Sterling Silver, Mexico, 1 In.	39.00
Thimble Case, Filigree, Loop, Sterling Silver	135.00
Thimble Case, Nut Shape, Chatelaine, Sterling Silver, 1 1/4 In.	66.00
Tray, Silver Plate, Serpentine Border, Handles, Marked W.S. Blackinton, 30 1/2 In.	143.00
Yarn Winder, Mortised Base, Chip Carving, 41 In.	44.00

SHAKER items are characterized by simplicity, functionalism, and orderliness. There were many Shaker communities in America from the eighteenth century to the present day. The religious order made furniture, small wooden pieces, and packaged medicines, herbs, and jellies to sell to *outsiders*. Other useful objects were made for use by members of the community. Shaker furniture is listed in this book in the Furniture category.

Apple Peeler	600.00
Basket, Oval, Splint, Ash Handle, Sabbathday Lake Community, Maine, 11 x 15 In.	316.00
Basket, Pincushion, White Paper Band, Purple Velvet Pincushion, 2 1/2 x 3 In.	1265.00
Basket, Wash, 34 1/2 x 22 x 11 In.	184.00
Basket, Wood Bottom, Slat Sides, Grip, Bail Handle, Wire Rim, Kentucky, 6 x 14 1/2 In.	468.00
Basket, Woven Splint, Square, Bentwood Handles, 4 3/8 x 12 x 12 In.	357.00
Bottle Carrier, Wood, Wire, Rectangular, Swing Handles, Bottles, 3 1/2 x 13 1/2 In.	863.00
Box, 1-Finger, Lid, Copper Tacks, 5 1/8 In.	165.00
Box, 1-Finger, Lid, Oval, Chrome Yellow Paint, 11 1/2 x 3 x 2 1/4 In.	1984.00
Box, 2-Finger, Lid, Copper Tacks, 3 3/8 x 8 3/4 In.	385.00
Box, 2-Finger, Lid, Oval, Yellow Paint, Enfield, Ct. Community, 1 1/4 x 3 3/4 In.	2990.00
Box, 3-Finger, Lid, Copper Tacks, 2 7/8 x 7 3/4 In.	330.00
Box, 3-Finger, Lid, Maple & Pine, Refinished, 12 x 9 x 4 In.	220.00
Box, 3-Finger, Lid, Oval, Copper Tacks, 5 x 7 1/4 x 2 1/2 In.	192.00
Box, 3-Finger, Lid, Oval, Natural, Copper Tacks, 9 7/8 x 3 3/4 In.	110.00
Box, Domed Lid, Pine, Fitted Interior, Till, Lower Drawer, 15 1/4 x 25 1/2 In.	550.00
Box, Lid, Oval, 7 1/4 x 4 3/4 x 2 7/8 In.	137.00
Box, Lid, Oval, Blue Paint, 9 1/2 x 7 x 3 3/4 In.	1485.00
Box, Lid, Oval, Copper Finish, 7 1/4 x 4 5/8 x 2 7/8 In.	110.00
Box, Lid, Oval, Dark Finish, 6 x 3 7/8 x 2 1/2 In.	165.00
Box, Lid, Oval, Dark Green Paint, 6 1/8 x 4 x 2 In.	687.00
Box, Lid, Oval, Green Paint, 5 1/2 x 3 1/2 x 2 1/8 In.	852.00

Box, Lid, Oval, Red Finish, 7 1/2 x 5 1/8 x 2 1/2 In.	300.00
Box, Oval, Cherry Finish, Yellow, 4 1/2 x 3 1/8 x 1 5/8 In.	110.00
Box, Oval, Mellow Natural Finish, 12 x 8 3/4 x 4 3/4 In.	440.00
Box, Overlapping Seams, Copper Tacks, Label On Lid, New Lebanon, 5 3/4 In.	247.00
Box, Pantry, Lid, Maple, Poplar & Pine, Copper Tacks, 10 x 7 x 4 In.	412.00
Box, Sewing, Poplar, Square, Sweetgrass Striping, Lid, Silk Ribbon Hinges, 2 x 4 In.	345.00
Box, Writing, Cherry, Roll Top, Brass Knob On Lid, Enfield, Ct., 3 1/4 x 8 1/2 In.	1495.00
Bucket, Sugar, Bentwood Bands, Wire Bail Handle, 6 1/4 x 6 1/4 In.	80.00
Caddy, Sewing, Pine, Pincushion Top, 3 Tiers, Ivory Thread Holes, 9 x 6 x 9 In.	300.00
Carrier, Bentwood, Copper Tacks, Bentwood Handle, 2 1/4 x 5 1/4 In.	330.00
Carrier, Bentwood, Maple, Pine Base, Bentwood Handle, Copper Tacks, 13 x 9 In.	165.00
Dipper, Wood, Carved, Mid 19th Century, 2 3/4 x 6 1/4 In.	748.00
Feather Duster, Red Leather Collar, Turned Handle, Sabbathday Lake Community, Me.	865.00
Firkin, Blue Paint, Tapered Form, Pine Staves, Ash Bands, Swing Handle, Lid, 20 In.	3163.00
Hanger, Clothes, Painted Yellow, Bow Shape, Signed Daniel Orcutt, 18 1/4 In.	374.00
Pie Peel, Maple, 7 Vertical Wood Strips, Inlaid Horizontal Strip, 17 x 34 In.	748.00
Pincushion, Painted Scenes, Shaker Building, Stock Barn, Red, Dated 1917, 2 In.	175.00
Pincushion, Round, Silk Cover, Wooden Base, Buildings, Red Ribbon, Signed, 1917, 2 In.	173.00
Rack, Herb Drying, Wooden, Early 19th Century, 67 In.	895.00
Sewing Steps, Pine, Washed, Yellow, Signed Olive Hatch, c.1830, 8 x 12 1/2 In.	2530.00
Spool Winder, Flax & Wool, Dual-Purpose, Enfield Colony	495.00
Towel Rack, Swing Arm, Acorn-Knob Rod Pivots, 7 x 18 In.	250.00
Washtub, Pine & Birch, Carved Handles, 4 Overlapping Bands, 20 x 20 In.	1495.00

SHAVING MUGS were popular from 1860 to 1900. Many types were made, including occupational mugs featuring pictures of men's jobs. There were scuttle mugs, silver-plated mugs, glass-lined mugs, and others.

3 Sheep In Field, 1890-1925, 3 3/8 In.	896.00
Advertising, Compliments Season Burmeister, Cast Metal, 1870s, 6 In.	190.00
Bar Scene, A.G. Ferguson, 1925, 4 In.	448.00
Bicycle, 1890-1925, 3 5/8 In.	1344.00
Billiards Table, T & V France, 1925, 3 5/8 In.	896.00
Bird In Flight, Long & Colorful Tail, J.G. Heins, 3 3/4 In.	112.00
Cow, With Calf, 1890-1925, 3 1/2 In.	212.00
Fraternal, American Order Of United Woodmen, c.1890, 3 1/2 In.	182.00
Fraternal, Joint Bakers & O.U. Union Of America, Karl Fischer, Blue Wrap, 4 In.	202.00
Fraternal, Knights Of Golden Eagle, Melvin F. Schrierber, c.1925, 3 5/8 In.	302.00
Fraternal, Knights Of The Maccabee, Emblem, 1925, 3 3/4 In.	156.00
Fraternal, Knights Of The Maccabee, Fred Rogers, c.1890, 3 1/2 In.	466.00
Fraternal, Knights Templar, R.D. Mede, 3 1/2 In.	175.00
Fraternal, Odd Fellows, 3 Link Chain, Initials F.L.T., Crossed Branches, 3 3/4 In.	44.00
Fraternal, Order Of The Moose, Emblem, 1890-1925, 3 3/4 In.	84.00
Fraternal, Redman's Lodge, Herbert Close, c.1890, 3 1/4 In.	253.00
Fraternal, Shriners, Emblem, 1890-1925, 3 7/8 In.	67.00
Fraternal, Shriners, Emblem, S.A. Bowman, 1925, 3 5/8 In.	123.00
Fraternal, Woodmen Of The World, J.A. Gubser, c.1925, 3 7/8 In.	155.00
Horses' Heads, Inside Horseshoe, H.T. Ball, W.G. & Co., France, 3 3/4 In.	202.00
House, 2 People On Front Porch, 1925, 3 In.	1456.00
Indian, Headdress Forming Handle, Pink & Blue Glaze, 3 7/8 In.	110.00
K.G. Carsen, Telephone, Box Of Cigars, 3 5/8 In.	1008.00
Mason, Masons Building Brick Wall, Gold Trim, Ceramic, 3 5/8 x 3 5/8 In.	199.00
Mug Of Beer, 1890-1925, 3 3/8 In.	268.00
Occupational, Anvil, J.J.E., 1890-1925, 3 5/8 In.	179.00
Occupational, Baker, Christ. Schuett, 3 5/8 In.	797.00
Occupational, Baker, Putting Pretzels In Oven, Maroon Wrap, 3 3/8 In.	1112.00
Occupational, Barber, Shop, 5 Customers, 1925, 3 5/8 In.	1344.00
Occupational, Barrel Maker, On His Bench, Harry Hughes, 1925, 3 7/8 In.	1008.00
Occupational, Bartender, Barroom Scene, F.C. Miller, 3 5/8 In.	467.00
Occupational, Bartender, Barroom Scene, J. Wisniewski, 3 3/4 In.	235.00
Occupational, Bartender, Customers Hold Beers, Gold Trim, 3 3/4 In.	180.00
Occupational, Blacksmith, Preparing To Shoe Horse, Porcelain, 4 In.	373.00
Occupational, Blacksmith, Shoeing Horse, 1925, 3 1/2 In.	364.00

Occupational, Blacksmith, Working Anvil, 1925, 3 1/2 In. 168.00
Occupational, Brewmaster & Wooden Keg, 3 1/2 In. 468.00
Occupational, Butcher, Shop, James Forten, 3 1/2 In. 522.00
Occupational, Butcher, Shop, Robert Murray, T. & V. Limoges, 3 5/8 In. 616.00
Occupational, Butcher, Tools, 3 1/2 x 3 1/4 In. 128.00
Occupational, Carpenter, Band Saw, 3 5/8 In. 246.00
Occupational, Carpenter, Tools, Crossed, A. Theusch, MR France, 3 5/8 In. 190.00
Occupational, Carpenter, Working At Bench, A.M. Scott, 3 5/8 In. 728.00
Occupational, Cement Finisher's Tools, Maroon Wrap, C.M. Miller, 3 5/8 In. 157.00
Occupational, Coal Wagon, Horse Drawn, Hand Painted, 3 7/8 In. 1018.00
Occupational, Cobbler, Working At Bench, N.R. Dubreuil, 3 1/2 In. 235.00
Occupational, Cobbler, Working At Bench, Same Almgren, 4 In. 1344.00
Occupational, Dairy Cow, Sad Looking, Gilt, Edgar F. Funk, 3 5/8 In. 392.00
Occupational, Delivery Wagon, Horse Drawn, J.G. Stehman, 1890-1925, 3 In. 1008.00
Occupational, Dentist, Raised Gold Tooth On Front, Marked Limoges, 1925 . . . . 75.00
Occupational, Engine, Standing, T.G. Carothers, 1925, 4 In. 2016.00
Occupational, Farmer, Wheat Field, Cut Wheat Piles, Farmhouse, 4 In. 220.00
Occupational, Fisherman, Whaling Boat, T & V Limoges, 3 5/8 In. 330.00
Occupational, Grocer, Grocery Delivery Vehicle, 3 5/8 In. 232.00
Occupational, Gyroscope, John Bentz, 1925, 3 3/4 In. 201.00
Occupational, Harness Maker, Working At Bench, R.Y. Smith, 3 1/4 In. 123.00
Occupational, Harness Maker, Working At His Bench, 1925, 4 In. 672.00
Occupational, Horse Track, 1925, 3 7/8 In. 1792.00
Occupational, Horseman, Steeplechase Scene, R.G. Boatman, 3 7/8 In. 440.00
Occupational, Iceman, Taking Ice From Wagon, J.F. Hix, T. & V. Limoges, 3 3/4 In. 224.00
Occupational, Locomotive & Tender, Jack Nelson, 1925, 3 5/8 In. 168.00
Occupational, Locomotive Scene, Gilt, Handle, Marked, C.C. Dotson, 3 7/8 In. 460.00
Occupational, Man Standing Next To Standing Engine, 1925, 3 5/8 In. 840.00
Occupational, Man, Delivery, Horse, Wagon, M. Becker, Limoges, 3 5/8 In. 2128.00
Occupational, Man, Driving Horse Drawn Wagon Carrying Barrels, 4 In. 1035.00
Occupational, Man, Driving Horse Drawn Water Tank, Handle, 3 3/4 In. 3910.00
Occupational, Man, Feeding Boiler With Coal, K. Lucas, 4 In. 616.00
Occupational, Man, Horse Drawn Delivery Wagon, 1925, 4 In. 364.00
Occupational, Man, Horse Drawn Wagon, 1925, 3 In. 268.00
Occupational, Man, Motorcar, 1890-1925, 3 7/8 In. 952.00
Occupational, Man, Preparing Food In Bakery Wagon, 3 5/8 In. 41950.00
Occupational, Mason, Trough & Mortar Board, Pink & Gold Bands, 3 7/8 In. 134.00
Occupational, Mayor, Charles E. Jackson, Sepiatone Photo Portrait 855.00
Occupational, Milkman, Delivery Wagon, Milk & Cream, C.C. Phippen, 4 In. 476.00
Occupational, Milkman, Driving Horse Drawn Wagon 700.00
Occupational, Milkman, Driving Milk Wagon, Pure Milk, Martin Meyer, 3 1/2 In. 532.00
Occupational, Milkman, On Milk Wagon, Adolphus Champigney, Limoges, France 810.00
Occupational, Minister, Open Bible, Rev. Thus. Geo. Baxter, 2 In. 385.00
Occupational, Motorcar, R.R. Thibault, 1890-1925, Limoges, 3 5/8 In. 1064.00
Occupational, Musician, Coronet, G.H. Maricle, 1890-1925, 3 7/8 In. 504.00
Occupational, Musician, Violin, George Roehrs, 1925, 4 In. 616.00
Occupational, Pawnbroker, 3 Gold Globes, Isaac Leavy, 1890-1925, 3 3/4 In. 784.00
Occupational, Printer, A.W. St. Jacques, Duplex Press, 3 1/2 In. 1925.00
Occupational, Printing Press, A.L. Halen, 1890-1925, 3 5/8 In. 448.00
Occupational, Printing Press, C.W. Gelpke, 1890-1925, 3 7/8 In. 476.00
Occupational, Railroad, Handcar, John Rice, 3 7/8 In. 952.00
Occupational, Railroad, Red Caboose, J.A. Hager, Gilt, 3 7/8 In. 235.00
Occupational, Red Caboose, Red Lettering, 1890-1925, 3 1/2 In. 364.00
Occupational, Red, White, Blue Shield, American Express, 4 In. 1120.00
Occupational, Sailing Ship, Choppy Water, W.P. Williams, 3 3/4 In. 1232.00
Occupational, Sailing Ship, Gold Trim, 3 5/8 In. 3850.00
Occupational, Sheep Farmer, P.R. Bennett, Gilt, 3 1/2 In. 715.00
Occupational, Steam Engine, 1925, 3 5/8 In. 392.00
Occupational, Steam Fire Engine, Horse Drawn, W.E. Thomas, 1925, 3 5/8 In. 2912.00
Occupational, Steer's Head, Joseph Levy, 1890-1925, 3 3/8 In. 1008.00
Occupational, Stock Broker, Tickertape Machine, Hand Painted, Gold Trim 4180.00
Occupational, Tailor, Cutting Cloth At Bench, A.F. Kreuger, 3 1/2 In. 616.00
Occupational, Tug Boat, Gold Trim, Ceramic, 3 7/8 x 3 3/4 In. 6850.00

Occupational, Undertaker, Horse Drawn Hearse, Gravestones, 3 7/8 In.	1760.00
Occupational, Water Tanker, Man, Horse Drawn Wagon	2400.00
Occupational, Western Union Delivery Man, c.1925, 3 5/8 In.	880.00
Open Roll Top Desk, F.W. Manley, 4 In.	840.00
Owl On Branch, Man In Moon, S.T. Helmick, 3 3/8 In.	224.00
Pink Roses, Grapes, 4 Frames, Gilt, David H. Eppley, 1927, 3 7/8 In.	56.00
Profile Of Pretty Woman, 1925, 3 5/8 In.	201.00
Rooster, J.C. Ritter, 1890-1925, 3 1/2 In.	952.00
Sheaf Of Wheat, P. Germany, P. Eisemann, 3 3/4 In.	392.00
Silhouette, Man & Woman On Park Bench, Moon, W.G. & Co., France, 3 3/4 In.	179.00
Skull & Crossbones, Gold Trim, Ceramic, 3 3/4 x 3 5/8 In.	442.00
Tapered Shape, Huntingware All Around, 5 In.	94.00
Windmill, T.G. Shannon, 1925, 4 In.	952.00
Yellowware, Mr. John Maugham Hewitson, Black Label, 1850, 4 1/4 In.	154.00

SHAWNEE POTTERY was started in Zanesville, Ohio, in 1937. The company made vases, novelty ware, flowerpots, planters, lamps, and cookie jars. Three dinnerware lines were made: Corn, Lobster Ware, and Valencia (a solid color line). White Corn pattern utility pieces were made in 1945. Corn King was made from 1946 to 1954; Corn Queen, with darker green leaves and lighter colored corn, from 1954 to 1961. Shawnee produced pottery for George Rumrill during the late 1930s. The company closed in 1961.

Shawnee
USA

Cookie Jar, Drum Major, 10 In.	160.00
Cookie Jar, Jo-Jo Clown, 9 In.	220.00
Cookie Jar, Muggsy, Gold Trim, 11 1/4 In.	250.00
Cookie Jar, Puss 'n Boots	260.00
Cookie Jar, Sailor Boy, Gold Trim	350.00
Cookie Jar, Smiley Pig, Bank Head	300.00
Cookie Jar, Winking Owl, Gold Trim	110.00
Planter, Stagecoach, Tan, Brown	35.00
Salt & Pepper, Muggsy, Gold Trim, Large	450.00
Salt & Pepper, Muggsy, Gold Trim, Small	150.00
Salt & Pepper, Puss 'n Boots, Gold Trim	50.00
Salt & Pepper, Smiley Pig, Blue Neckerchief	50.00
Salt & Pepper, Smiley Pig, Flower Decal, Gold Trim	110.00
Salt & Pepper, Smiley Pig, Peach Neckerchief	50.00
Salt & Pepper, Smiley Pig, Pink Neckerchief	50.00
Salt & Pepper, Winnie & Smiley Pig, Blue	80.00
Salt & Pepper, Winnie & Smiley Pig, Blue Neckerchief, Pink Collar	100.00
Salt & Pepper, Winnie & Smiley Pig, Blue Neckerchief, Small	40.00
Salt & Pepper, Winnie & Smiley Pig, Pink	30.00

SHEET MUSIC from the past centuries is now collected. The favorites are examples with covers featuring artistic or historic pictures. Early sheet music covers were lithographed, but by the 1900s photographic reproductions were used. The early music was larger than more recent sheets, and you must watch out for examples that were trimmed to fit in a twentieth-century piano bench.

Aba Daba Honeymoon, 2 Weeks With Love, Dick Powell, 1942	12.00
An Old Straw Hat, Shirley Temple, Rebecca Of Sunnybrook Farm, 1938	25.00
Anchors Aweigh, Picture Of FDR, 1936, 9 x 12 In.	40.00
Animal Crackers In My Soup, Curly Top, 1935	18.00
Any Bonds Today, Irving Berlin, 1941	11.00
Buttons & Bows, The Paleface, Bob Hope & Jane Russell, 1948	35.00
Clicquot Fox Trot March, Clicquot Club, Eskimo On Cover, 1926	8.00
Creole Belles, J. Bodewalt Lampe, Oval Photos On Cover, 1901	12.00
Dance Me Loose, Arthur Godfrey, Irwin Powered Music Co., 1951	3.00
Dreaming Out Loud, Lum & Abner & Others On Cover	20.00
God Bless America, Irving Berlin Inc. Music Publishing, New York, 1939	12.00
Good-Bye, France, Irving Berlin, Name Stamp On Front	22.00
Half As Much, Rosemary Clooney, 1951	10.00
Have Yourself A Merry Little Christmas, Judy Garland On Cover, 1944	45.00

How High The Moon, Les Paul, Mary Ford, 1940	15.00
I'm Waiting Just For You, Pat Boone, Picture, 1951	10.00
Liberace Theme, TV Set With Liberace Design On Cover, 9 x 12 In., 2 Pages	8.00
Love's Old Sweet Song, J.L. Molloy, 1911, 13 x 10 In.	35.00
My Heart Tells Me, Betty Grable, Robert Young, 1943	8.00
My Love Song To You, Jackie Gleason, Bob Manning, 1954, 3 Pages	12.00
My One & Only Highland Fling, Fred Astaire & Ginger Rogers, Pictures, 1949	12.00
Precious Little Thing Called Love, The Shopworn Angel, Gary Cooper Cover, 1928	110.00
Roman Lyrics, Geometric Linework, Wood Frame, 17 x 11 1/2 In.	172.00
Sugar Moon, Pat Boone, Picture, 1958	10.00
Thank Your Lucky Stars, Humphrey Bogart, Cantor & Others On Cover	25.00
The Trolley Song, Meet Me In St. Louis, Judy Garland, 1944	12.00
There's A Gold Mine In The Sky, Bing Crosby, Picture, 1937	10.00
There's A Star Spangled Banner Waving Somewhere, Roberts & Darnell, 1942	10.00
When It's Night Time Down In Dixieland, Irving Berlin, 1914	17.00
When Lindy Comes Home, Jugate, Lindbergh & Cohan, 1927, 11 x 17 In.	40.00
World Peace March, J.S. Zamecnik, 11 x 13 3/4 In., 6 Pages	46.00
Yankee Doodle, Howard Pyle Illustrations, Dodd Mead & Co., Book, 1881	57.00
Yo-Ho, Jack Haley & The Wonder Show, Continental Baking Co, 1938	60.00

SHEFFIELD items are listed in the Silver Plate and Silver-English categories.

SHELLEY first appeared on English ceramics about 1912. The Foley China Works started in England in 1860. Joseph Ball Shelley joined the company in 1862 and became a partner in 1872. Percy Shelley joined the firm in 1881. The company went through a series of name changes, and in 1910 the then Foley China Company became Shelley China. In 1929 it became Shelley Potteries. The company was acquired in 1966 by Allied English Potteries, then merged with the Doulton group in 1971. The name *Shelley* was put into use again in 1980. A trio is the name for a cup, saucer, and cake plate set.

Butter, Cover, Maytime Pattern Allover, 5 x 7 In.	295.00
Coffeepot, Wild Flower Pattern, Cambridge Shape	325.00
Cup & Saucer, Chintz, Field Of Daisies, No. 13206, 1949	135.00
Cup & Saucer, Montrose, No. 13554	165.00
Cup & Saucer, Red Daisy Pattern, Queen Anne Shape	165.00
Cup & Saucer, Rose Pansy Forget-Me-Not Pattern, Canterbury Shape	300.00
Eggcup, Double, Regency Pattern, Dainty Shape, 3 3/4 In.	100.00
Mug, Maytime Pattern Allover, 4 1/4 In.	240.00
Sugar & Creamer, Red Daisy Pattern, Queen Anne Shape	165.00
Teapot, Duchess Pattern, Mayfair Shape, 4-6 Cup	365.00
Tidbit, Melody Pattern Allover, Metal Handle, 1 Tier, 8 1/4 In.	165.00
Trio, Archway Of Roses Pattern, Queen Anne Shape	155.00
Trio, Golden Harvest Pattern, Gainsboro Shape	130.00
Trio, Syringa Pattern, Regent Shape	140.00
Vase, Harmony, Green, Yellow, Gray, Orange Rings, 5 In.	150.00

SHIRLEY TEMPLE, the famous movie star, was born in 1928. She made her first movie in 1932. Thousands of items picturing Shirley have been and still are being made. Shirley Temple dolls were first made in 1934 by Ideal Toy Company. Millions of Shirley Temple cobalt blue glass dishes were made by Hazel Atlas Glass Company and U.S. Glass Company from 1934 to 1942. They were given away as premiums for Wheaties and Bisquick. A bowl, mug, and pitcher were made as a breakfast set. Some pieces were decorated with the picture of a very young Shirley, others used a picture of Shirley in her 1936 *Captain January* costume. Although collectors refer to a cobalt creamer, it is actually the 4 1/2-inch-high milk pitcher from the breakfast set. Many of these items are being reproduced today.

Bowl, Cereal, Cobalt Blue	12.00 to 15.00
Doll, Composition, Green Metal Sleep Eyes, Cloth, Mohair Curls, 22 In.	92.00
Doll, Ideal, Composition Head, 6 Upper Teeth, Crazing, 13 In.	500.00
Doll, Ideal, Composition Head, Holding Doll, Pleated Dress, 20 In.	1700.00

Never try to clean a doll with polish or wax. It will put a layer of wax on the surface, making it almost impossible to repaint the doll's face.

Shirley Temple, Doll, Ideal, Vinyl,
5-Piece Body, Rooted Hair,
Sailor Dress, 1957, 15 In.

Doll, Ideal, Composition Head, Sleep Eyes, Open Mouth, Plaid Dress, 13 In.	700.00
Doll, Ideal, Composition Socket Head, Hazel Sleep Eyes, Blond Curls, 18 In.	489.00
Doll, Ideal, Composition, Sleep Eyes, Open Mouth, Jointed Body, 20 In.	500.00
Doll, Ideal, Flirty Sleep Eyes, 6 Teeth, 5-Piece Body, Red & White Dress, 27 In.	550.00
Doll, Ideal, Original Wig & Dress, Box, 1940, 20 In.	1700.00
Doll, Ideal, Rebecca Of Sunnybrook Farm, Plastic, Plaid Dress, 1950, 17 In.	275.00
Doll, Ideal, Socket Head, Flirty Eyes, Seated At Wood Organ, c.1935, 34 In.	4400.00
Doll, Ideal, Vinyl Head, Hazel Eyes, 6 Upper Teeth, Taffeta Slip, Panties, 12 In.	475.00
Doll, Ideal, Vinyl Head, Hazel Sleep Eyes, Open-Close Mouth, 1957, 12 In.	550.00
Doll, Ideal, Vinyl Head, Sleep Eyes, Open-Close Mouth, Rooted Hair, 1957, 12 In.	550.00
Doll, Ideal, Vinyl, 5-Piece Body, Rooted Hair, Sailor Dress, 1957, 15 In. .... *Illus*	180.00
Doll, Ideal, Vinyl, Purple & White Striped Dress, 12 In.	40.00
Doll, Sleep Eyes, Open-Close Mouth, Velvet Dress, Ideal, Box, 1957, 12 In.	230.00
Fan, Cardboard, RC Cola Advertising, 1944	45.00
Mug, Cobalt Blue, 3 3/4 In.	60.00
Pitcher, Cobalt Blue	65.00
Plate, Cobalt Blue, Open Edge, 7 In.	41.00
Sheet Music, On The Good Ship Lollipop, Bright Eyes, 1934	18.00

SHRINER, see Fraternal category.

SILVER DEPOSIT glass was first made during the late nineteenth century. Solid sterling silver is applied to the glass by a chemical method so that a cutout design of silver metal appears against a clear or colored glass. It is sometimes called silver overlay.

Pitcher, Flowers, Vines, 9 3/4 x 9 3/4 x 5 1/2 In.	448.00
Scent Bottle, Silver Overlay, Glass, Engraved, Hinged Cap, 4 1/8 In.	431.00
Vase, Scrolls, Cobalt Blue, 12 x 7 1/4 In., Pair	187.00
Vase, Trumpet Form, Black Glass, Intricate Silver, Leaping Antelope, 13 In.	450.00

SILVER FLATWARE includes many of the current and out-of-production silver and silver-plated flatware patterns made in the past eighty years. Other silver is listed under Silver-American, Silver-English, etc. Most silver flatware sets that are missing a few pieces can be completed through the help of one of the many silver matching services that advertise in many of the national publications.

SILVER FLATWARE, English King, Tiffany & Co., c.1900, 94 Piece	8400.00
Flemish, Sterling, Bagged, Tiffany & Co., 112 Piece	4600.00
Linenfold, Wooden Box, Tiffany & Co., c.1960, 89 Piece	9600.00
Olympian, Tiffany & Co., 106 Piece	7975.00
Saratoga, Tiffany & Co., c.1895, 92 Piece	8400.00
Wave Edge, Tiffany & Co., 60 Piece	9200.00
Winthrop, Original Fitted Box, Tiffany & Co., 130 Piece	880.00
SILVER FLATWARE PLATED, Columbia, Carving Set, Hollow Handle, 1847 Rogers, 3 Piece	110.00
Grosvenor, Punch Ladle, Hollow Handle, Community	95.00
Orange Blossom, Bouillon Spoon, Rogers	8.00
Orange Blossom, Cold Meat Fork, Rogers	22.00

Orange Blossom, Cream Soup Spoon, Rogers 10.00
Orange Blossom, Fruit Knife, Rogers, 6 In. 6.00
Orange Blossom, Grapefruit Spoon, Rogers 5.00
Orange Blossom, Iced Tea Spoon, Rogers 10.00
Orange Blossom, Salad Fork, Rogers 12.00
Vintage, Butter Spreader, 1847 Rogers 14.00
Vintage, Cocktail Fork, 1847 Rogers 14.00
Vintage, Demitasse Spoon, 1847 Rogers 12.00
Vintage, Dinner Fork, 1847 Rogers 8.00
Vintage, Youth Set, Box, 1847 Rogers, 3 Piece 48.00
SILVER FLATWARE STERLING, Acanthus, Butter Spreader, Georg Jensen, 12 Piece 745.00
Acorn, Caviar Set, Horn Faces, Georg Jensen, 7 In., 4 Piece 460.00
Acorn, Cheese Scoop, Georg Jensen, 20th Century 230.00
Art Nouveau, Nut Spoon, Webster Company, 4 3/4 In., Pair 200.00
Avalon, Nut Spoon, Monogram, International, c.1900, 10 1/4 In. 224.00
Blossom, Sauce Ladle, Saart, 20th Century 45.00
Blossom, Spoon Set, Demitasse, Georg Jensen, Copenhagen, 12 Piece 863.00
Cambridge, Carving Set, Gorham, 1899, 3 Piece 80.00
Chantilly, Grapefruit Spoon, Gorham, 20th Century 45.00
Chantilly, Seafood Fork, Monogram, Gorham, 5 1/2 In., 12 Piece 172.00
Chantilly, Sugar Tongs, Gorham, 20th Century 55.00
Corinthian, Mustard Ladle, Gorham 50.00
Empire, Punch Ladle, Whiting, 14 1/2 In. 633.00
Flora Variant, With Lily, Serving Fork, Shiebler, 1889, 10 1/2 In. 400.00
Francis I, Punch Ladle, Hollow Handle, Reed & Barton, 15 1/2 In. 315.00
Francis I, Soup Ladle, Reed & Barton, 11 1/2 In. 345.00
Georgian, Spoon Set, Demitasse, Towle, 8 Piece 140.00
Grand Baroque, Salad Server, Wallace, 1941, 9 1/2 In., Pair 460.00
Grape, Claret Spoon, Twisted Shaft, Dominick & Haff, c.1890 .... 595.00
Hindostanee, Berry Spoon, Gorham 195.00
Hope, Salad Server, Howard Sterling Co., 20th Century, 10 5/8 In., Pair 172.00
Iris, Gravy Ladle, Gilt Bowl, Durgin 650.00
Jac Rose, Ladle, Gorham, c.1885, 12 1/4 In. 259.00
Josephine, Butter Knife, Master, Patent 1855, Gorham 55.00
King Edward, Teaspoon, Gorham Whiting, 1901 .... 66.00
King George, Soup Ladle, Gorham, Late 19th Century, 11 In. 345.00
King I, Salad Fork, Gorham 225.00
Kings, Gravy Ladle, Bigelow, Kennard & Co. 92.00
La Marquise, Teaspoon, Monogram, Reed & Barton, 12 Piece 77.00
Lady Washington, Sugar Spoon, Gorham, 5 3/4 In., Pair 95.00
Les Six Fleurs, Serving Fork, Reed & Barton, c.1901, 10 3/4 In. 690.00
Lily, Asparagus Server, Whiting 70.00
Lily, Cake Slicer, Wedding, Stainless Blade, Whiting, 12 1/2 In. 140.00
Lily, Demitasse Spoon ....40.00 to 50.00
Lily, Fish Fork, Whiting, 7 1/8 In. 100.00
Lily, Five O'Clock Spoon, Monogram, Whiting, 5 3/8 In. 35.00
Lily, Fork, Monogram, Whiting, 6 3/4 In. 90.00
Lily, Fork, Whiting, 6 3/4 In. 90.00
Lily, Gravy Ladle, Shell Bowl, Whiting, 7 In. 220.00
Lily, Gravy Ladle, Whiting, 7 1/8 In. 200.00
Lily, Iced Tea Spoon, Whiting, 8 3/4 In. ....50.00 to 60.00
Lily, Knife, New French, Hollow, Whiting, 9 1/4 In. 70.00
Lily, Macaroni Server 150.00
Lily, Oyster Server, Whiting 140.00
Lily, Pie Server, Whiting, 10 1/4 In. 60.00
Lily, Salad Fork, Whiting, Individual, 6 In. 80.00
Lily, Salad Serving Spoon, Whiting, 11 5/8 In. 130.00
Lily, Soup Spoon, Whiting 80.00
Lily, Strawberry Fork, Whiting, 4 1/4 In. 55.00
Lily, Sugar Tongs, Gorham, 3 5/8 In. 150.00
Lily, Sugar, Shell, Gorham, 5 7/8 In. 70.00
Lily, Tablespoon, Monogram, Whiting, 8 1/4 In. 150.00
Lily, Tablespoon, Pierced, Whiting, 8 1/2 In. 130.00

Lily, Tablespoon, Whiting, 8 1/4 In. 80.00
Lily, Teaspoon, Monogram, Whiting, 4 In. 45.00
Lily, Teaspoon, Whiting, 5 7/8 In. 45.00
Lily Of The Valley, Gravy Ladle, Whiting, 6 1/2 In. 500.00
Lily Of The Valley, Serving Spoon, Whiting, Early 1900s, 8 3/4 In., Pair 518.00
Lily Of The Valley, Soup Spoon, Oval 150.00
Lily Of The Valley, Tablespoon 140.00
Lily Of The Valley, Teaspoon 36.00
Lily Of The Valley, Teaspoon, Five O'Clock, Monogram, Whiting, 5 3/8 In. 40.00
Lily Of The Valley, Teaspoon, Gold Wash, Whiting, 4 3/8 In. 70.00
Lily Of The Valley, Teaspoon, Monogram, Whiting, 4 3/8 In. 60.00
Lily Of The Valley, Teaspoon, Whiting, 5 7/8 In. 45.00
Lotus, Stuffing Spoon, Porter Blanchard, 20th Century, 12 In. 350.00
Love Disarmed, Fish Set, Reed & Barton, 2 Piece 690.00
Love Disarmed, Salad Server, Maiden Handles, Reed & Barton, 11 In., Pair 575.00
Love Disarmed, Salad Server, Reed & Barton, 20th Century, 10 3/4 In., Pair 690.00
Lucerne, Asparagus Fork, Wallace, 20th Century 295.00
Lucerne, Cocktail Fork, Wallace, Monogram, 17 Piece 374.00
Luxembourg, Cheese Scoop, Polychrome Handle, Gorham, 1910, 8 In. 115.00
Madison, Salad Server, Wallace, Pair 61.00
Mayflower, Gravy Ladle, William Gale & Son, 1852 .... 175.00
Medallion, Mustard Ladle, Gorham 175.00
Mythologique, Bouillon Spoon, Gorham, 4 7/8 In., 12 Piece 632.00
Mythologique, Dinner Fork, Gorham, 9 Piece 287.00
Old English, Punch Ladle, Dominick & Haff, 1813, 12 In. 110.00
Old Newbury, Butter Knife, Master, Flat Handle, Towle, 6 7/8 In. 40.00
Old Newbury, Butter Spreader, Flat Handle, Towle, 5 3/4 In. 30.00
Old Newbury, Carving Set, Steak, Towle, 2 Piece 90.00
Old Newbury, Cheese Cleaver, Stainless Blade, Towle, 6 7/8 In. 45.00
Old Newbury, Cocktail Fork, Towle, 5 3/4 In. 25.00
Old Newbury, Cranberry Server, Towle 45.00
Old Newbury, Demitasse Spoon, Towle, 3 7/8 In. 22.00
Old Newbury, Dessert Spoon, Towle, 7 1/8 In. 40.00
Old Newbury, Fish Fork, Stainless Tines, Hollow, Towle, 7 3/8 In. 40.00
Old Newbury, Gravy Ladle, Towle, 6 3/4 In. 90.00
Old Newbury, Iced Tea Spoon, Towle, 7 1/2 In. 40.00
Old Newbury, Knife, French, Hollow, Plated Blade, Towle, 8 7/8 In. 32.00
Old Newbury, Knife, Orange, Towle, 8 In. 85.00
Old Newbury, Pie & Cake Server, Towle 45.00
Old Newbury, Pie Server, Stainless Blade, Towle, 10 7/8 In. 45.00
Old Newbury, Punch Ladle, Towle 60.00
Old Newbury, Soup Spoon, Towle, 6 1/2 In. 40.00
Old Newbury, Steak Knife, Towle 40.00
Old Newbury, Tablespoon, Towle 65.00
Old Newbury, Teaspoon, Towle 22.00
Olive, Gravy Ladle, Pear & Bacall, c.1855 .... 125.00
Olive, Tablespoon, Pierced, Farrington & Hunnewell, c.1855 .... 100.00
Olive, Tablespoon, Tiffany, Young & Ellis, c.1845 .... 115.00
Palm, Gravy Ladle, Gilt Wash Bowl, Gorham 150.00
Persian, Teaspoon Set, Leather Case, 12 Piece 161.00
Poppy, Bonbon Spoon, Paye & Baker 150.00
Poppy, Teaspoon, Gorham, 1902, 9 Piece 121.00
Princess Ingrid, Butter Spreader, Frank Whiting 28.00
Princess Ingrid, Carving Fork, Frank Whiting 50.00
Princess Ingrid, Carving Knife, Frank Whiting, 13 1/2 In. 60.00
Princess Ingrid, Cocktail Fork, Frank Whiting 30.00
Princess Ingrid, Fork, Frank Whiting, 7 1/8 In. 45.00
Princess Ingrid, Gravy Ladle 100.00
Princess Ingrid, Iced Tea Spoon, Frank Whiting, 7 3/8 In. 38.00
Princess Ingrid, Poultry Shears, Frank Whiting, 11 1/2 In. ....150.00 to 160.00
Princess Ingrid, Salad Fork, Frank Whiting, 6 1/4 In 60.00
Princess Ingrid, Sugar Spoon, Frank Whiting, 6 1/8 In. 40.00
Princess Ingrid, Teaspoon, Frank Whiting, 6 1/8 In. 30.00

Pyramid, Carving Set, Georg Jensen 575.00
Raphael, Soup Ladle, Gorham 345.00
Repousse, Berry Spoon, S. Kirk & Son, 9 1/8 In. 105.00
Shell, Ladle, Gorham, 7 In. 84.00
St. Cloud, Server, Obverse & Reverse Design, Monogram, Gorham, 12 In. 632.00
Versailles, Ladle, Gorham, c.1888, 12 3/4 In. 805.00
Versailles, Tomato Server, Gorham, 7 1/2 In. 430.00
William Penn, Tongs, Alvin, 20th Century, 7 In. 200.00

SILVER PLATE is not solid silver. It is a ware made of a metal, such as
nickel or copper, that is covered with a thin coating of silver. The letters *EPNS* are often found on American and English silver-plated
wares. Sheffield is a term with two meanings. Sometimes it refers to
sterling silver made in the town of Sheffield, England. In this section,
Sheffield refers to a type of silver plate, usually English.

Bar, Traveling, Zeppelin Form, Signed, 12 In. 4830.00
Basket, Hinged Handle, Grape & Vine, Pedestal Base, c.1850, 9 1/2 x 23 In. 224.00
Berry Set, 4 Spoon & Grape Shears, Allover Leaf & Chased, Box, 1867, 5 Piece 287.00
Biscuit Barrel, Repousse, Child Riding A Sheep, Acanthus Feet, Flat Hinged Lid, 6 In. 40.00
Biscuit Barrel, Swing Handle, Allover Etched Flowers & Fern Glass, 5 x 7 1/2 In. 69.00
Biscuit Jar, Cannon Finial, Allover Repousse Geometric, 1874, 6 1/2 x 8 In. 345.00
Biscuit Jar, Domed Cover, Floral, Meriden Britannia Co., Late 1800s 200.00
Bowl, Acanthus Leaves, Openwork Sides, Intertwined Grape Vines, 9 x 22 In. 192.00
Bowl, Organically Shaped, Alexander Calder, Stamped Reed & Barton, 3 x 13 1/2 In. 400.00
Bowl, Repousse, Chased Flowers & Leaves, Crest, 7 1/2 x 3 1/4 x 5 1/2 In. 358.00
Bowl, Shallow, Oval, Footed, Elkington, Raised Leaves, England, 13 3/4 In. 345.00
Bowl, Vegetable, Cover, Hot Water Stand, Leaf & Scroll, Wooden Handle, 13 In. 115.00
Bowl, Vegetable, Cover, Leaves, Scroll Borders, Stand, Side Handle, 13 In. 115.00
Bowl, Vegetable, Engraved Scroll, Tray, Dome Lid, Square Handles, Footed, 9 In. 400.00
Box, Casket Form, Domed, 4 x 5 x 3 In. 80.00
Box, Sandwich, Loop Handle, Monogrammed Lid, Case, Gilt Interior, 5 3/4 In. 57.00
Butter, Cover, Cow Finial, Cow Head Handles, Charters & Brother, 5 1/2 In. 425.00
Cake Basket, Grapes, Vine, Swing Handle, Monogram, 1890s, 10 1/4 In. 86.00
Cake Basket, Swing Handle, 9 1/2 x 12 1/2 In. 450.00
Candelabrum is listed in its own category.
Candlesticks are listed in their own category.
Candy Dish, Griffin Supporting Dish On His Nose, 5 x 7 In. 105.00
Carving Set, Image Of Windsor Castle On Blade, Horn Handles, Case, 16 1/2 In. 345.00
Carving Set, Stag Horn Handles, Goat Head, Wreath, Repousse, JR, Sheffield, 3 Piece ... 615.00
Carving Set, Steel Blade, Antler Handle, Sheffield, England, Case, 1900-1902, 5 Piece ... 250.00
Casket, Hinged Lid, Cherubs, Arches, Continental, c.1880, 4 x 5 x 2 1/2 In. 230.00
Centerpiece, Greyhounds, Palm Trees, Scalloped Cut-Glass Bowl, 20 x 12 1/2 In. 1330.00
Centerpiece, Jardiniere, Baluster Gallery, Acanthus Handles, 4 1/2 x 19 1/2 x 13 In. 1610.00
Centerpiece, Mirror In Frame, Coat Of Arms, Vines, Monogram, 18 In. 2185.00
Chafing Dish, Rim Shells, Double Handles, Amber Bakelite, 12 x 18 1/2 In. 330.00
Chalice, Cast Metal, Bear & Cubs Lid, Liner, Hunt Scene, Putti, 1853, 15 In. 345.00
Cheese Scoop, Victorian, Gadrooned Ivory Handle, c.1865, 9 1/2 In. 575.00
Chocolate Pot, Neoclassical, Laurel Rims, Acanthus Design, France, 9 3/4 In. 288.00
Chocolate Pot, Staves Design, Fruitwood Handle, Sheffield, 8 In. 259.00
Cocktail Set, Rooster, Wallace Bros., c.1928, 14 1/2 In., 5 Piece .... *Illus* 13800.00
Cocktail Shaker, Lighthouse Form, Meriden S.P. Co., No. 343, 1920, 13 1/2 In. 4140.00
Cocktail Shaker, Penguin, Napier Co., 1936-1938, 12 In. .... *Illus* 1150.00
Coffee & Tea Set, Bulbous, Spiraled Ribs, 4 Piece 77.00
Coffee & Tea Set, Pattern 5314, Barbour Silver Co., c.1895, 8 Piece 952.00
Coffee & Tea Set, Strasbourg, 10 3/4 In., 5 Piece 560.00
Coffeepot, Cover, Ornate Embossed Handle, Zinc Lining, Copper Bottom, 11 In. 57.00
Coffeepot, Ivory Finial, Allover Chased Flowers, 1879, 9 1/4 In. 115.00
Coffeepot, Tapered Body, Scrolling Leaf, Shell Shapes, Handles, c.1865, 8 1/4 In. 157.00
Compote, Round, Blossom Supports, Tripod Base, Argit, France, 1910, 7 x 9 1/2 In. 115.00
Compote, Squirrel Eating Acorn, Sitting On Branch, Sheffield, USA, 9 x 6 In. 325.00
Condiment Set, 2 Salt Cellars, Glass Lined Bowls, Dolphin Finials, 8 1/4 In. 633.00
Condiment Set, 2 Salts, 2 Mustard Jars, 2 Pepper Castors, 4 Spoons, Mappin & Webb ... 230.00
Condiment Set, Drawer In Base, Compartments Of 3 Bowls, Meriden, 11 x 16 In. 330.00

Silver Plate, Cocktail Set,
Rooster, Wallace Bros.,
c.1928, 14 1/2 In., 5 Piece

Silver Plate, Cocktail
Shaker, Penguin, Napier
Co., 1936-1938, 12 In.

Condiment Set, Jockey's Hat Form, Boot Is Pepper Pot & Mustard, 1900, 5 1/2 In.	230.00
Cover, Entree, Cornish Hen Size, Monogram, 19th Century	195.00
Cover, Entree, Stepped Dome, Beaded Edge, Engraved, France, 10 1/2 In.	400.00
Cover, Meat, Engraved, Gadroon Border, H. Wilkinson & Co., 1836, 14 In.	80.00
Cover, Meat, Leaf Shape Handle, Domed, Early 20th Century, 10 x 14 x 18 1/4 In.	448.00
Cover, Meat, Relief, Floral, Scroll, Chased Heraldic Pattern, Sheffield, 19 x 12 In.	230.00
Cruet Set, 6 Crystal Bottles, Stand, Ball Feet, 8 1/2 In.	115.00
Cruet Set, Empire, Laurel Garlands, 4 Spatulate Feet, France, 9 1/2 x 6 1/2 In.	230.00
Decanter, Liqueur, Barrel, Spigot, Trestle Form Wood Stand, 7 1/2 x 4 1/2 In.	1035.00
Decanter Set, 2 Barrels, On Wagon Form Holder, Glass, England, 16 In.	1265.00
Decanter Set, Cut Crystal, Pierced Stand, Stem Handle, 1930s, 16 In., 3 Piece	785.00
Decanter Stand, Reticulated, Vintage, Sheffield, Mid 19th Century, 14 In.	978.00
Desk Set, Inkwell, Pen Rack, Hunt Design, Edwardian, c.1900	546.00
Dessert Set, Boxed, Mother-Of-Pearl Handles, 1905, 24 Piece	144.00
Dessert Set, Forks, Knives, Mother-Of-Pearl Handles, Box, 1909, 24 Piece	145.00
Dish, 8 Sides, Scalloped Ends, Acanthus Handle & Feet, Dome Lid, 7 x 10 1/2 In.	489.00
Dish, Coquille Shape, Spiraling Feet, Crest, 1 1/2 x 6 1/4 x 5 3/4 In., Pair	288.00
Dish, Entree, Cover, C-Scroll Cartouches, Lion Mask Handles, 1912, 14 In.	977.00
Dish, Entree, Oval, 4 Parts, Paw Feet, Reed & Barton, 10 x 10 1/2 x 13 In., Pair	345.00
Dish, Entree, Rectangular, Scroll Feet, Liner, Early 20th Century, 13 3/8 In., Pair	748.00
Dish, Ferns, Ivory Knob Handle, Floral Garlands Base, Cloven Hoof Feet, 9 In.	440.00
Dish, Gadrooned Rim, Cover, Sheffield, c.1820, 6 1/4 x 9 x 12 In., Pair	920.00
Dish, Sweetmeat, Woven Silver Handle, Cobalt Blue, 8 1/2 In.	165.00
Dish Cross, Cast Shell Terminals, England, 19th Century, 13 1/4 In., Pair	200.00
Egg Warmer, Mother-Of-Pearl Handle On Lid, 4 Holders, 7 In.	190.00
Eggcup Stand, Allover Raised Leaves, Swags, Handle, Ball Foot, 6 Cups, 1884, 8 In.	170.00
Epergne, 4 Arms With Crystal Bowls, Larger Center Bowl, Paw Supports, 12 In.	1725.00
Epergne, 4 Reeded Arms, Scroll Feet, Sheffield, 1840, 14 1/2 x 21 1/2 x 11 In.	3220.00
Epergne, Center Ring Supporting Bowl, Ruffled Rim, 3 Bud Vases, 1890s, 8 1/8 In.	143.00
Epergne, Neoclassical Figural Center, Rococo, Ellis & Co., 1875, 17 x 9 In., Pair	978.00
Epergne, Stem Supports Crystal Bowl, Fluted Base, 1920s, 15 3/4 x 16 In.	1200.00
Ewer, Snake Shape Handle, Oval Shape, 14 In.	1060.00
Fish Knife, Pierced Floral Blade, Smooth Ivory Handle, 12 1/4 In.	55.00
Frame, Circular, Repousse Putti Design, England, 8 x 9 In.	86.00
Grape Scissors, Spiral Handles, Ring Segments, Gilt Leather Case, 1880, Pair	230.00
Gravy Boat, Engraved Scroll Handle, Monogram, c.1860, 5 3/4 In.	374.00
Hatpin, Woman's Head, Flowers Around Rim, 1 1/4 In. Round	75.00
Ice Bucket, Glass Lining, Poole Silver Co., 9 In.	25.00
Ice Water Set, Meriden Britannia Co., Late 19th Century, 9 1/2 In.	316.00
Jardiniere, Swan Shape, Italy, Modern, 16 In., Pair	1150.00
Jewelry Box, Rogers Smith & Co., Flying Bird, Engraved Bertha, 1870s, 5 x 5 In.	560.00
Kettle, Hot Water, Allover Floral & Swag, Burner, Stand, 1875, 9 x 15 1/2 In.	258.00
Kettle, Hot Water, Spirit Burner, Stand, Leaf Chased, Bulbous, 1856, 8 x 16 1/2 In.	290.00
Kettle, Hot Water, Spirit Burner, Stand, Oval, 1909, 12 1/2 x 14 1/2 In.	172.00
Kettle, Spirit Burner, Stand, Bulbous, Flowers, Swing Handle, 1875, 9 x 15 1/2 In.	259.00
Kettle, Stand, Sheffield, Paneled Flowers, Mid 19th Century, 17 x 12 In.	1725.00

Lamp, Glass Shade, Engraved, Flowers, Old Sheffield, c.1900, 20 1/2 In., Pair 345.00
Lazy Susan, Center Soup Tureen, 4 Dishes, Celluloid Handles, 23 1/4 In. 1955.00
Meat Skewer, Raised Shell, c.1884, 14 1/4 In. . . . . .86.00 to 96.00
Mirror, Dressing Table, Round, Hammered, Clarkson, North Allerton, c.1900, 7 In. 115.00
Mirror, Plateau, Flowers & Scroll Edge, Footed, 3 x 12 In. 235.00
Mirror, Plateau, Repousse, 3 Bun Feet, Round, 1857, 14 In. 402.00
Muffin Server, Scallop Shell Shape, Edwardian, c.1900, 10 1/2 x 9 3/4 In., Pair 1035.00
Napkin Rings are listed in their own category.
Pitcher, Wine, Scroll Handle, Cylindrical, Birmingham, 1941, 9 1/2 In. 488.00
Plaque, Adam & Eve, Angel, Garden Of Eden, 1891, 10 1/8 In. 287.00
Plaque, Semi-Nude Woman, Attendants, Repousse Borders, 1876, 20 In. 517.00
Platter, Engraved Stag Head, Oval, c.1900, 22 In. 430.00
Punch Bowl, Scalloped Rim, Cartouches, Lion Head Handles, c.1910, 8 x 13 3/4 In. 123.00
Punch Cup, Lavigne, 1881 Rogers 25.00
Salad Server, Faces, Engraved, Hourglass Shape Handles, 9 1/8 In., Pair 115.00
Salt, Open, Spoon, Elkington, Birmingham Mark, England, c.1905, 4 Piece 431.00
Salver, Beaded Serpentine Rim, Shell Relief, Flowers, Sheffield, EBRS, 11 In. 56.00
Salver, Cast Acanthus Edge, Plateau, Engraved Scrolls, Flowers, 13 3/4 In. 518.00
Salver, Cast Acanthus Rim, Engraved Roses, 3 Cast Applied Feet, 15 3/4 In. 863.00
Salver, Rococo Style, Raised On 4 Shell & Scroll Feet, England, 2 x 16 In. 1380.00
Salver, Shell & Scroll Rim, Acanthus Scrolls, Feet, 1 1/4 x 9 3/4 In. 230.00
Salver, Shell, Scroll Rim, 4 Scrolled Acanthus Feet, Sheffield, 2 1/4 x 23 1/2 In. 1725.00
Salver, Stylized Shell & Scroll, Leaf Border, Paw Feet, Sheffield, 9 1/4 In. 92.00
Samovar, Tea Tray, Over Brass, Embossed, Russia, Late 19th Century, 19 1/2 In. 635.00
Sauceboat, England, Handles, Early 18th Century, 5 1/4 x 5 1/4 x 8 In., Pair 546.00
Serving Dish, Corner Shells & Leaves, Faux Ivory Handles, Signed, 20 1/4 In. 250.00
Serving Dish, Handle, 4 Paw Feet, Cover, Ellis Barker, 13 1/2 x 10 1/2 x 7 1/2 In. 300.00
Serving Dish, Roll Dome Top, Flower Repousse, Footed, Double Insert, 9 x 12 x 9 In. . . . 336.00
Serving Dish, Serpentine Shape, Covered, c.1900, 5 1/2 x 13 x 9 1/2 In. 146.00
Spoon, Souvenir, see Souvenir category.
Stand, Shaving, Round Mirror, Florals, 2 Cups, Early 20th Century, 18 3/4 In. 520.00
Stirrup Cup, Stag's Head Terminal, 8 In. 172.00
Table Ornament, Pheasant, 12 In., Pair 185.00
Tankard, Sheffield Type, Dome Cover, Handle, Marked IG, 9 1/2 In. 57.00
Tea & Coffee Set, Geometric & Floral Chased, Ring Foot, Elkington, 4 Piece 1437.00
Tea & Coffee Set, Joanne, Webster & Wilcox, 14 1/4 x 22 1/2 In., 5 Piece 115.00
Tea & Coffee Set, Ribbed Baluster, Ebonized Handles, Cheltenham & Co. 345.00
Tea Caddy, Engraved, Marked J.D. & S., 5 x 4 1/2 x 3 1/2 In. 168.00
Tea Caddy, Floral Bands, Chased Geometric Border, Lock Lid, Sheffield, 5 1/2 In. 197.00
Tea Set, Medallions, Buildings, Floral Sprays, Grape Leaves, Reed & Barton, 3 Piece . . . 152.00
Tea Set, Paneled Sides, Octagonal Base, Double Handles, 5 Piece 385.00
Tea Set, Paneled Spout, Scrolled Handle, Engraved Bellflowers, 3 Piece 247.00
Tea Set, Swags, Shells & Flowers, Ear Handles, Domed Lids, H.L. & Co., 5 Piece 247.00
Tea Set, Winthrop, Fluted Sides, Budding Flower Finials, Reed & Barton, 6 Piece 495.00
Teapot, Faux Ivory Handle, Plated Stand, Curling Stone Presentation, England 373.00
Teapot, Silver, Dixon & Smith, Goose Neck Spout, Scrolled Wood, 6 In. 330.00
Teapot, Stand, Lobed Sides, Wafer Finial, Scrolled Handle & Spout 247.00
Teapot, Stand, Rococo Scrolls & Shells On Pot, Reeded Legs, 12 1/2 In. 110.00
Teapot, Stand, Shell Feet, Pierced Aprons, Bone Wafer In Handle, 13 3/4 In. 330.00
Teapot, Tapering Fluted Sides, Celluloid Wafer Finial, 6 3/4 In. 110.00
Toast Rack, Cricket Theme, Ring Handle Over Cricket Ball, Late 19th Century, 7 In. 86.00
Toast Rack, Crossed Tennis Rackets, 5 1/4 x 3 1/2 In. 295.00
Toothpick, Kettle, Pig, Acme Silver Plate Co., Boston, 1 3/4 In. 143.00
Tray, Cast Grapevine Border, Handles, Rococo Motifs, England, 29 3/4 x 18 In. 144.00
Tray, Center Crest, Scale & Trellis Cartouches, Circular, Footed, Sheffield, 20 In. 518.00
Tray, Center Eagle, Gadroon Banded Rim, Acanthus Handles, 21 In. 805.00
Tray, Center Etched Leaf, Shell Form Handles, 18 x 29 In. 250.00
Tray, Chased Design, Beaded Scalloped Rim, Handles, Low Feet, 29 In. 84.00
Tray, Floral Shell & Scroll, Circular, Footed, Sheffield, 18 1/4 In. 460.00
Tray, Gadroon Border, 21 3/8 x 16 In. 57.00
Tray, Gadroon Border, Scrolled Leaf Handles, Sheffield, 26 In. 632.00
Tray, Grapevine Rim, Leaf Handles, Sheffield, 1885, 30 3/4 x 21 In. 230.00
Tray, Handles, Gorham, Rhode Island, c.1900, 2 1/2 x 11 3/4 x 16 3/4 In. 1265.00

Tray, Melon, Scalloped Rim & Handles, Oneida, 26 3/4 In. 173.00
Tray, Oval, Convex Rim, Repousse Ferns, Fluted Edge, Fern Handles, 19 x 29 In. 430.00
Tray, Oval, Open Handle, Raised Scroll Border, c.1873, 29 1/4 In. 345.00
Tray, Oval, Straight Edge, Flat Foot, W. Werkstatte, J. Hoffmann, Austria, 1910, 14 In. 805.00
Tray, Pierced Dragons & Flowers Border, Waterfowl On Bank, c.1880, 22 5/8 In. 3900.00
Tray, Scroll & Flowers, Handles, 32 In. 173.00
Tray, Serving, Footed, Pierced Rim, Crown Mark, 30 In. 88.00
Tray, Serving, Rectangular, Applied Grapes, Vines, Leaves On Rim, Handles, 31 In. ... 275.00
Tray, Shaped Rim, Cast & Applied Grape Clusters, Acanthus Handles, 14 x 22 In. 564.00
Tray, Shell & Scroll Rim, Engraved, Acanthus, Cast Applied Feet, Handles, 28 x 18 In. .. 400.00
Tray, Supper, Revolving, Relief, Scroll, Turned Handles, Lehman Bros., 29 x 19 In. 460.00
Tray, Tea, Raised Scroll Borders, Open Handles, Oval, 1873, 29 1/4 In. 345.00
Tray, Vintage Border, Engraved Leaves, 2 Handles, Gorham, 25 1/2 In. 50.00
Tray, Vintage Rim, Double Floral & Acanthus Leaf Handles, Oval, 20 x 29 In. 82.00
Trophy Cup, 1st Annual Horse Show, Handles, Pedestal, Wilcox 200.00
Tureen, Hand Hammered, Basket Weave Border, Bird, Butterfly, Derby Mfg., 10 In. 80.00
Tureen, Revolving, Neoclassical Style, Garland Stand, 9 x 13 x 8 In. 615.00
Tureen, Revolving, Oval, Reed Design, c.1900, 8 1/4 x 13 3/4 x 9 1/4 In. 672.00
Tureen, Revolving, Winged Legs, Paw Feet, Engraved, Flowers, Sheffield, 13 In. 260.00
Tureen, Sauce, Cover, Beaded Edge Body, Ball Feet, George III, 8 1/2 In., Pair 460.00
Tureen, Spherical Body, Domed Lid, 3 Prong Feet, Sheffield, 1900, 6 1/2 In. 430.00
Tureen, Undertray, Gadroon Rim, Acanthus Handles, J. Dixon, c.1840, 16 In. 1495.00
Urn, Coffee, Brass Spout, 2 Large Handles, Domed Lid, 21 In. 385.00
Urn, Coffee, Warmer Base, Leaf Feet, Scrolled Handles, Reed & Barton, 17 In. 275.00
Urn, Hot Water, Georgian Style, Flower, Scroll Relief, 16 In. 402.00
Urn, Hot Water, Georgian Style, Sheffield, 19th Century, Ivory Spigot, 13 1/2 In. 144.00
Urn, Hot Water, Georgian, Relief Flowers & Scroll, 16 In. 400.00
Urn, Repousse Band, Laurel, Marble Plinth, 3rd Republic, France, 16 In., Pair 805.00
Waiter, Old Sheffield Style, Vintage Borders & Footed, Handles, 32 1/2 In. 1380.00
Wall Plaque, Round, Adam & Eve, 1891, 10 1/8 In. 288.00
Wine Caddy, Carriage Shape, Rococo, Flywheel, 8 3/4 x 4 1/4 x 12 1/2 In. 1955.00
Wine Caddy, Double Carriage Shape, Grape Cluster & Vine, 2 Bottles 1210.00
Wine Caddy, Double Carriage Shape, Grape Clusters & Vines, 6 x 19 In. 1232.00
Wine Coaster, Cast & Chased Grapevines, Wooden Base, 8 7/8 In. 82.00
Wine Coaster, Convex Sides, Pierced, Engraved, Palm Fronds, Wood Base, 2 In., Pair ... 430.00
Wine Coaster, Double, 2 Connected Circular Dishes, c.1950, 9 1/2 x 1 1/4 In. 230.00
Wine Coaster, Flowers, 19th Century, 7 In. 57.00
Wine Coaster, Lotus Shape, Flared, Scalloped Rim, England, 2 1/4 x 7 In., Pair 1265.00
Wine Coaster, Openwork, Arched Leaf Decoration, England, 5 In., Pair 160.00
Wine Coaster, Pierced, Grapevines, Gadrooned Rim, 2 3/4 x 5 1/2 In., Pair 430.00
Wine Cooler, Banded, Faux Tortoiseshell Inlay, Lion Handles, England, 7 1/2 In. 633.00
Wine Cooler, Bucket Shape, Handles, Early 20th Century, 8 3/4 In., Pair 805.00
Wine Cooler, Campana Form, Engraved Arms, Leaf Border, c.1805, 9 1/2 In., Pair 3000.00
Wine Cooler, Flared Leaf Rim, Coat Of Arms, Loop Handles, 1930s, 12 In. 316.00
Wine Cooler, Lift-Off Rim, Flower Garland Border, Urn Shape, Branch Handles, 11 In. ... 253.00
Wine Cooler, Relief Flowers & Scroll, Georgian, 9 1/2 In., Pair 920.00
Wine Cooler, Removable Liner, Chantilly, Gorham, 20th Century, 11 1/2 In. 295.00
Wine Cooler, Shaped Leaf Rim, Wood Base, 20th Century, 6 1/2 In., Pair 200.00
Wine Cooler, Shell & Scroll Rim, Cornucopia Handles, Regency, 1820, Pair 2990.00
Wine Cooler, Urn Shape, Lion's Head Handles, Monogram, 9 1/2 x 8 In. 99.00

SILVER, SHEFFIELD, see Silver Plate; Silver-English categories.

SILVER-AMERICAN. American silver is listed here. Coin and sterling silver are included. Most of the sterling silver listed in this book is subdivided by country. There are also other pieces of silver and silver plate listed under special categories, such as Candelabrum, Napkin Ring, Silver Flatware, Silver Plate, Silver-Sterling, and Tiffany Silver. For information about makers and marks, see *Kovels' American Silver Marks: 1650 to the Present.*

SILVER-AMERICAN, Argyll, Gravy, Gadroon Band, Swan Spout, George IV, c.1828, 5 In. 3000.00
Asparagus Dish, Liner, Flowers, Scrolls, Footed, Tiffany & Co., c.1897, 12 3/4 In. 4500.00
Asparagus Dish, Liner, Rococo Style, Tiffany & Co., c.1895, 14 1/4 In. 6600.00

Basket, Leaf, Naturalistic, Copper Fly, Stem Handle, c.1885, 6 1/4 In. 3000.00
Basket, Pierced Rim, Conforming Handle, Early 20th Century, 7 x 4 1/4 In. 168.00
Basket, Pierced, Gorham, 8 1/4 In. 92.00
Basket, Swing Handle, Pierced, Engraved, Meriden Britannia, 10 x 17 In. 546.00
Beaker, Asa Blanchard, 1808, 3 3/8 In. 3910.00
Beaker, Scovil & Co., Cincinnati, Ohio, c.1836, 3 1/2 In. 546.00
Berry Bowl, Floral Side, Textured, Jacobi & Jenkins, 1908, 5 3/4 In., Pair 145.00
Berry Bowl, Floral, Rococo Scroll Borders, Gorham, 1893, 9 x 7 x 3 In., Pair 1795.00
Berry Scoop, Gilt Bowl, Gorham 350.00
Berry Spoon, R. & W. Wilson, Presentation Box, Philadelphia, Pair 975.00
Berry Spoon, Repousse Fruit, Embossed Floral Handle, S. Kirk & Son, 5 1/8 In. 85.00
Bonbon, Quatrefoil Body, Cellini Craft Ltd., Early 20th Century, 7 1/2 In. 345.00
Bowl, 3-Footed, Applied Wire, Frederick J.R. Gyllenberg, 2 3/4 x 5 3/4 In. 495.00
Bowl, 3-Footed, Frederick J.R. Gyllenberg, 1 7/8 x 5 In. 375.00
Bowl, Applied Bands, Robert R. Jarvie, 2 5/8 x 4 3/4 In. 1650.00
Bowl, Applied Wire Rim, Arthur J. Stone, 2 1/8 x 3 7/8 In. 425.00
Bowl, Art Nouveau, Chased Flower Decoration, International Silver Co., 9 In. 374.00
Bowl, Arts & Crafts, Hammered, Copper & Brass Overlay, Gorham, 3 x 8 In. 6325.00
Bowl, Bronze, Swirling Water Form, Gorham Mfg. Co., c.1910, 14 1/4 In. 16450.00
Bowl, Centerpiece, Graff, Washbourne & Dunn, Marked, 12 In. 430.00
Bowl, Centerpiece, Grille, Pierced, Artichoke Finial, Footed, Gorham, c.1930, 9 In. 632.00
Bowl, Centerpiece, Japanese Style, Parcel Gilt, Gorham, c.1872, 13 1/8 In. 14400.00
Bowl, Centerpiece, Lobed Rim, Chased Leaf & Tendrils, M.C. Fina, c.1935, 8 In. 575.00
Bowl, Centerpiece, Old Friend, Oval Serpentine Edge, Repousse, 1900s, 15 1/2 In. 863.00
Bowl, Centerpiece, Pierced, Tiffany & Co., Marked, Numbered, c.1895, 22 In. 11500.00
Bowl, Centerpiece, Scandinavian Style, Hammered, DeMatteo, c.1960, 10 In. 920.00
Bowl, Centerpiece, Strawberry, Fluted Dome, Lebolt & Co., c.1900, 17 In. 2700.00
Bowl, Chased, Scalloped Edge, Dominick & Haff, 9 x 3 In. 400.00
Bowl, Cone Shape, 8 Supports, Black Starr & Gorham, c.1960, 6 In. 310.00
Bowl, Cutout, Reticulated, 2 Handles, Initials, Howard & Co., c.1903, 11 x 8 In. 120.00
Bowl, Detachable Rim, Flowers & Leaves Ground, Welsh & Bro., 9 3/4 In. 2400.00
Bowl, Domed Lid, Steep Sides, Ball Finial, Marked, Woodside, c.1920, 6 1/4 In. 173.00
Bowl, Fluted, Embossed Flowers, Whiting, c.1909, 7 1/8 x 11 In. 145.00
Bowl, Footed, Relief Flowers, Scroll, Mask, Gorham, Early 1900s, 10 1/2 In. 375.00
Bowl, Francis I, Reed & Barton, 8 In. 288.00
Bowl, Francis I, Reed & Barton, c.1951, 11 x 3 In. 467.00
Bowl, Francis I, Scrolled Rim, Fluted, Bunches Of Fruit, Reed & Barton, 11 1/2 In. 400.00
Bowl, Fruit, Flower, Leaf Decoration, Fluted, Gorham, 20th Century, 10 1/4 In. 170.00
Bowl, Fruit, Pierced Rim, Flowers & Scroll Rim, Gorham, 1911, 11 3/8 In. 400.00
Bowl, Fruit, Royal Danish Pattern, Marked, Old Newbury Crafters, 10 1/4 In. 230.00
Bowl, Gadroon Border, Pedestal Base, Gorham, c.1941, 3 x 12 In. 336.00
Bowl, Grape Cluster, Vines, Flaring Shape, Hobstar Cut, Gorham, 12 In. 3820.00
Bowl, Hammered, Flower-Form, J.O.R. Randahl, 3 x 9 1/2 In. 375.00
Bowl, Hand Hammered, 3 Scroll Feet, Gorham, 3 x 12 In. 1790.00
Bowl, Inscribed Award, Gorham, 1964, 5 1/4 x 10 1/4 In. 230.00
Bowl, Martele, Gorham, 9 1/2 In. 5750.00
Bowl, Relief With Roses Border, Whiting, 11 In. 690.00
Bowl, Relief, Floral, Scroll, Mask, Footed, Gorham, 10 1/2 In. 374.00
Bowl, Repousse Borders, Monogram, Gorham, c.1896, 2 1/2 x 16 x 8 In., Pair 1035.00
Bowl, Repousse, Flower Border, S. Kirk & Son Co., c.1918, 3 x 7 1/2 In. 196.00
Bowl, Repousse, Scrolling, Flowers, S. Kirk & Son, 1900s, 1 1/2 x 11 1/2 In. 364.00
Bowl, Ribbed, Flared Rim, Dunkirk, 8 In. 75.00
Bowl, Ribbed, Monogram, Black, Starr & Frost, Late 19th Century, 8 3/8 In. 374.00
Bowl, Ring Foot, Arthur J. Stone, 1 3/4 x 6 1/4 In. 500.00
Bowl, Round, Flared Foot, Square Base, Joseph Lownes, Late 18th Century, 5 In. 1093.00
Bowl, Round, Lobed Shape, Molded Flared Foot, c.1815, 5 5/8 x 7 1/2 In. 430.00
Bowl, Round, Scalloped Edge, Repousse, S. Kirk & Son Co., Early 1900s, 11 In. 276.00
Bowl, Scalloped Edge, Meriden Co., 1903, 2 1/2 x 11 In. 290.00
Bowl, Scalloped Rim, Hammered, Old Newbury Crafters, 3 x 5 1/8 In. 595.00
Bowl, Seafood Salad, Naturalistic, Gorham Mfg. Co., c.1872, 16 In. 8400.00
Bowl, Trompe L'Oeil, Chased, Shells, Crabs, Seaweed, Gorham Mfg. Co., 9 3/8 In. 1610.00
Bowl, Underplate, Floral Repousse Borders, Kirk & Son, 10 x 2 In. 345.00
Bowl, Vegetable, Cover, Oval, Reeded Finial, Gorham, c.1912, 10 1/8 x 7 In. 288.00

Bowl, Windsor Pattern, Reed & Barton, 15 In. 230.00
Bowl & Tray, Hammered, Rectangular, Arts & Crafts, 10 In. 805.00
Box, Coin Silver, Chased Flowers, Flower Finial, 6 1/2 x 4 1/4 In. 1092.00
Box, Presentation, Chase Manhattan Bank, Divided Wood Interior, 1958 .... 80.00
Box, Repousse, Hinged Domed Lid, Footed, Velvet Lining, 7 1/2 x 5 x 4 In. 132.00
Box, Stamp, Hinged Cover, George C. Gebelein, 1 7/8 x 1 1/4 In. 295.00
Box, Stamp, Round, Hinged, Gilt Inside, Enamel Top, Abercrombie & Fitch, 4 In. 310.00
Bread Basket, Reed & Barton, 20th Century, 12 In. 450.00
Bread Tray, Francis I Pattern, Reed & Barton, 7 1/2 x 12 In., Pair 2381.00
Bread Tray, Openwork, J.E. Caldwell & Co., Late 1800s, 14 3/8 x 10 1/4 In. 633.00
Buckle, Shoe, Paste Set, Belonged To George Washington, 1780-1790, 2 3/4 In. 4500.00
Butter, Cover, Coin, Gorham, Dove Finial, 19th Century, 8 1/2 In. 520.00
Butter, Cover, Domed Lid, Reeded Finial, Gorham, c.1876, 6 In. 690.00
Butter, Domed Lid, Gorham, 6 In. 352.00
Butter Knife, Arthur J. Stone, 6 3/8 In., 5 Piece 85.00
Cake Plate, Leaf Band With Mermaids, Whiting, 1908, 12 In. 750.00
Cake Plate, Scrolled Rim, Scroll & Shell Handles, Gorham, 1909, 12 In. 170.00
Candelabrum is listed in its own category.
Candlesticks are listed in their own category.
Cann, Baluster Shape, Molded Foot, Scroll Handle, c.1780, 5 1/4 In. 16450.00
Cann, Engraved Script Monogram, Marked T. Emery, c.1800, 6 In. 1265.00
Cann, Presentation Inscription, Samuel Bartlett, Joseph Loring, c.1780, 6 In. 3900.00
Card Case, Raised, Chased Eagle On Branch, Leonard & Wilson, Phil., 3 1/2 In. ... 1265.00
Carving Set, Steel Blade, Leaf Handles, Jacobi & Jenkins, 1894, 13 In. 115.00
Castor, Ball, Tomkins & Black, Marked, 7 1/2 In. 980.00
Celery Vase, Greek Key Rim Band, Gorham, c.1869, 10 1/2 In. 1610.00
Chalice, Gilt Wash, 3 Bands Of Leaves, International, 7 3/4 In. 170.00
Chalice, Gold Wash, 6 Natural Pearls, 5 Plaques, W.J. Feeley, 9 3/4 In. 1475.00
Cheese Scoop, Gilded Bowl, Towle, 20th Century 175.00
Child's Set, Nursery Rhyme, Lebolt, Old Mother Hubbard, 20th Century, 6 1/2 In. 520.00
Cigarette & Match Holder, Mixed Metal, Gorham Mfg. Co., c.1882, 2 In. 3225.00
Cigarette Case, Flowers, Leaves, Chased Border, Elgin-Am. Mfg. Co. 39.00
Cocktail Shaker, Hammered, Lebolt, Knob Finial, Early 20th Century, 9 1/2 In. 740.00
Coffee Set, Ivory Insulators, Hyman & Co., 3 Piece 1850.00
Coffee Set, Strap Handles, Cellini Craft, 3 Piece 4300.00
Coffeepot, Allcock, Allen & Co., Banner Mark, 10 1/2 In. 518.00
Coffeepot, Domed Lid, Leaf & Tendril Finial, DeMatteo, Demitasse, 7 In. 460.00
Coffeepot, Lighthouse Shape, Ebony Handle, c.1949, Reed & Barton, 10 In. 144.00
Coffeepot, Repousse, S. Kirk & Son, Marked, Numbered, 8 1/4 In. 1035.00
Comb, Bright Cut, Monogram, E. & W. Wilson, 1830s 995.00
Compote, Beaded Rim, Scrolling Leaves, 3 Claw Feet, Gorham, 14 3/8 In. 750.00
Compote, Chrysanthemum, Pierced, Howard & Co., c.1895, 6 3/8 x 14 1/8 In. 1495.00
Compote, Dolphin Pedestal, Shell Shape Bowl, Redlich & Co., 7 1/2 In., Pair 978.00
Compote, Flaring Bowl, Corkscrew Base, Stamped Fisher, 5 1/4 x 6 In. 50.00
Compote, Floral Repousse, Curved Rim, Chased, Stippled, S. Kirk & Son, 9 1/2 In. 385.00
Compote, Francis I, Reed & Barton, c.1952, 5 1/2 x 11 In. 805.00
Compote, Pierced Leaf Rim, Footed, Gorham, c.1898, 9 In., Pair 1265.00
Cream Jug, Coin, Alexander Crouckeshanks, Bulbous, Beaded Rim, Handle, 5 In. 400.00
Cream Jug, Coin, Paul Revere, Helmet Shape, Molded Rim, Early 1800s, 6 3/4 In. 2760.00
Cream Jug, Pear Shape, Scrolled Rim, S Scroll Handle, 3 Legs, Belden, 3 In. 1495.00
Creamer, Baluster Shape, Stepped Foot, Banding, 1843-1848, 8 1/4 In. 460.00
Creamer, Coin, Squat Urn Shape, Gadroon Rim, Scroll Handle, c.1834, 5 1/2 In. 365.00
Creamer, Cut Crystal, Black, Starr & Frost, Dolphin Handle, 1876, 7 In. 560.00
Creamer, Gorham, Repousse 85.00
Creamer, Paul Revere, Jr., Loop Handle, From Shell, Signed, 6 1/2 In. 7200.00
Crumber, Ball, Black & Company 350.00
Crumber, Bright Cut, Flowers, Justis & Armiger, Baltimore, c.1893, 13 1/2 In. 195.00
Cup, Central Shield, Engraved, Lake Scenes, Towns, Marked, 3 3/4 In. 375.00
Cup, Communion, 2 Handles, Urn Shape, Oval Cartouche, c.1810, 6 3/4 In. 8815.00
Cup, Demitasse, Frank W. Whiting, 1900s, 12 Piece 1035.00
Decanter Set, Engraved Glass, Mt. Vernon Silver Co., 1915, 7 1/4 In., 6 Piece 595.00
Demitasse Set, Domed Lid, Leaf Medallions, Bud Finial, T. Starr, 1910s 2070.00
Dessert Spoon, Kings Pattern, Coin, R. & W. Wilson, 7 In., 5 Piece 225.00

Dinner Knife, Stainless Steel Blades, Square Ends, Arthur J. Stone, 9 1/2 In. 90.00
Dish, Alms, Reeded Border, Deep Well, Engraved Rim, c.1805, 10 3/8 In., Pair 7640.00
Dish, Alms, Reeded Border, Engraved Rim, c.1834, 10 1/2 In., Pair 3055.00
Dish, Applied Strapwork Band, R.W. Edwards, 6 In. 335.00
Dish, Canoe Shape, Cast Shell Feet, Gorham Mfg. Co., c.1872, 12 1/2 In. 5288.00
Dish, Entree, Cover, Repousse, S. Kirk & Son, Fox Hunt, Marked, 12 1/4 In. 3220.00
Dish, Round, Rolled Rim, Leaf Form Handles, Hand Wrought, c.1925, 8 In. 161.00
Dish, Shell Shape, Gorham, 9 In. 315.00
Dresser Box, Bud Finial, J.E. Caldwell & Co., Early 1900s, 5 1/8 x 3 3/4 In. 460.00
Dresser Set, Engraved, R. Wallace & Sons, Late 19th Century, 11 Piece 345.00
Dresser Set, Hair Brush, Clothes Brush, Comb, Mirror, Gorham, c.1920, 4 Piece 200.00
Dresser Set, Love's Dream, Unger Brothers, 1890, 3 Piece 850.00
Dresser Set, Repousse, Flowers, S. Kirk & Son, c.1900, 9 1/2 In. 489.00
Ewer, Baluster Shape, Chinese Architecture, Reeded Handle, c.1846, 16 3/4 In. 4700.00
Ewer, Coin, Scrolling Handle, John Kitts, Louisville, KY, c.1838, 9 In. 308.00
Ewer, Waisted Round Base, Grapevine Foot, Branch Handle, c.1852, 13 3/4 In. 1293.00
Fish Servers, Shells, Seaweed, Gorham, Leather Case, c.1885, Pair 13200.00
Fish Set, Fork & Knife, Plated Blade & Tines, Stieff Co., c.1905, 12 1/2 In. 460.00
Fish Set, Pointed Antique, Monogrammed, Dominick & Haff, 10 7/8 In. 402.00
Flask, Glass Lined, Hinged Cap, Monogram S.H.A., Gorham, c.1912, 6 In. 250.00
Flask, Hinged Cap, Lower Grip, Monogram, Reed & Barton, c.1900, 6 In. 225.00
Fork, Kings Pattern, Coin, R. & W. Wilson, 8 In., 6 Piece 360.00
Fork & Spoon, Seafood, Flowerheads, Hourglass Handles, Krider & Biddle 1395.00
Frame, Embossed Flowers & Maiden, Unger Bros., 4 7/8 In. 170.00
Frame, Flower Crest, Rectangular, La Paglia, 8 x 5 In. 1265.00
Goblet, Coin, Beadwork Border, Grape & Vine, Inscribed, c.1856, 5 1/4 In. 280.00
Goblet, Coin, Cartouche, Inscribed, Early 19th Century, 5 1/8 In., Pair 560.00
Goblet, Coin, Wheat Design, Cartouche, Pedestal Base, c.1840, 6 x 5 In. 280.00
Goblet, Flared Base & Rim, Gorham, 6 5/8 In., 8 Piece 660.00
Grape Scissors, Cast Handles, Grapevines, c.1900, 6 1/2 In. 53.00
Grape Scissors, Gorham, Figural, Fox & Grape Handles, 6 3/4 In. 784.00
Ice Cream Fork, Green & Blue Enamel, Wreath, Ribbon, Shiebler, 5 3/4 In. 730.00
Jug, Flowers, Scrolls, Hinged Lid, Kirk, 10 In. 2875.00
Jug, Pineapple Finial, Beaded & Leaf Bands, Durgin, 1920s, 9 1/8 In. 575.00
Jug, Water, Glass Insulated Liner, Mercury Glass Stopper, Gorham, 9 3/4 In. 340.00
Julep Cup, Chicago Silver Co., c.1935, 4 x 3 1/4 In., 6 Piece 1150.00
Julep Cup, Reeded, Monogram, Manchester Silver Co., 3 3/4 In., 8 Piece 467.00
Julep Cup, W. Kendrick, 3 7/8 In. 440.00
Kettle, Stand, Classical Revival, Drum Shape, Gorham, c.1875, 12 3/4 In. 5175.00
Knife Rest, Dachshund, Raised Tail, Gyllenberg & Swanson, 3 1/4 In. 258.00
Ladle, Scalloped, Hand Wrought, Die-Stamped Mark, Kalo Shops, 8 In. 375.00
Loving Cup, Bulbous, Repousse Leaves, Scroll, Howard & Co., c.1905, 10 5/8 In. 3335.00
Loving Cup, Cut Glass Insert, 3 Handles, Tiffany & Co., c.1900, 8 1/2 In. 2585.00
Luncheon Fork, Four-Tined, Arthur J. Stone, 7 1/8 In. 85.00
Meat Dish, Oval, Frank Whiting, 15 1/2 In. 230.00
Mug, Beaded Rim, Scrolling Leaves, Hoyt, Badger & Dillon, 1850s, 4 1/2 In. 57.00
Mug, Engraved, R. & W. Wilson, Child's, 3 3/8 x 2 3/4 In. 118.00
Mug, Footed, Laurel Border, Strawberry Frieze, Leaf Handle, c.1869, 4 3/8 In. 940.00
Mustard Pot, Urn Form, Beaded Trim, Shiebler, 4 3/4 In. 84.00
Napkin Rings are listed in their own category.
Nut Dish, Gold Wash, Whiting Division, Gorham, Chased Floral, Pair 173.00
Nut Dish, Shell Shape, Gorham, 6 Piece 63.00
Nut Set, Horseshoe Shape, Reed & Barton, Early 20th Century, 10 1/4 x 7 3/4 In. 258.00
Olive Fork, Spoon, Double Ended, Gorham, c.1880 .... 374.00
Page Turner, Rabbit Form Handle, Dominick & Haff, 11 1/2 In. 1725.00
Pie Knife, Medallion, Female Bust, Facing Right, 8 1/4 In. 695.00
Pie Server, Cut Leaves, Monogrammed Handle, Crosby & Morse, 10 3/4 In. 144.00
Pitcher, Baluster Form, S-Scroll Handle, S. Kirk & Son, 20th Century, 8 3/4 In. 373.00
Pitcher, Baluster Shape, Dense Flowers, Grapevine Handle, c.1880, 8 3/4 In. 1410.00
Pitcher, Barrel Shape, Hammered Handle, Shreve & Co., 9 1/2 x 8 In. 2300.00
Pitcher, Caldwell & Co., 7 In. 403.00
Pitcher, Cut Glass Body, Honeycomb Pattern, Gorham, 9 3/4 In. 403.00
Pitcher, Ice Water, Stepped Oval Foot, Gorham1912, 10 3/8 In. 690.00

Pitcher, Octagonal, Initial L, Kalo Shops, Engraved Date, 1914, 9 1/2 In. 4310.00
Pitcher, Oval, Hammered, Stamped KALO, 9 x 6 1/2 In. 2415.00
Pitcher, Presentation, Floral Wreath, June 1836, Jones, Lows & Ball, 10 7/8 In. 852.00
Pitcher, Presentation, Scroll Handle, Inscribed, Coin, 8 1/4 In. 302.50
Pitcher, Repousse Floral Swags, Waisted Domed Foot, Shaped Lip, c.1915, 9 In. 748.00
Pitcher, Repousse, Allover Flowers, S. Kirk & Son, 7 1/4 In. . . . . .978.00 to 1725.00
Pitcher, Shield Form Body, Leaf Repousse, Whiting, 11 In. 1250.00
Pitcher, Stepped Foot, Reeded Rim, Front Inscription, c.1855, 11 1/2 In. 488.00
Pitcher, Water, Bulbous, Round Foot, Fisher, Jersey City, N.J., 1900s, 9 In. 315.00
Pitcher, Water, Floral Repousse, Frank W. Smith, 9 1/2 In. 863.00
Pitcher, Water, Japanese Style, Spiral, Insects, Tiffany & Co., c.1880, 7 5/8 In. 14400.00
Pitcher, Water, Large Spout, Scroll Handle, Ivory Ball, c.1825, 6 5/8 In. 6000.00
Pitcher, Water, Naturalistic, R. & W. Wilson, c.1850, 12 1/4 In. 9000.00
Pitcher, Water, Wallace, 9 1/2 In. 288.00
Pitcher, Wide Spout, Semicircular Hollow Handle, Gorham, 7 3/4 In. 2100.00
Plate, Border Of Mixed Flowers, Redlich, 20th Century, 8 1/4 In. 250.00
Plate, Dinner, Chased, Flowers, Leaves, Gorham Mfg. Co., c.1914, 11 3/8 In. 3760.00
Plate, Pierced, Ring Foot, Watson, 10 1/2 In. 150.00
Plate Set, Place, Gadroon Rims, Shells, Tiffany & Co., 20th Century, 10 Piece 7800.00
Platter, Round, Repousse Rim, Banded Laurels, Gorham, 1924, 15 In., Pair 2910.00
Porringer, 2 Handles, Gebelein, 11 In. 259.00
Porringer, Bombe Sides, Domed Center, Elias Pelletreau, c.1790, 4 7/8 In. 7800.00
Porringer, Francis I, Reed & Barton, 4 3/4 In. 330.00
Porringer, Hammered, Handle, Gorham, 1 1/2 x 6 1/4 In. 425.00
Porringer, Keyhole Handle, Monogram, Baldwin Gardiner, c.1825, 8 In. 1175.00
Porringer, Pierced 3-Hole Handle, Engraved, c.1770, 7 1/2 In. 11165.00
Punch Ladle, Bailey, Banks & Biddle 325.00
Salad Fork, Arthur J. Stone, 6 3/4 In. 85.00
Salad Server, Japanese Style, Dragon, Carp, Gorham, c.1884, 11 1/4 In., Pair 3000.00
Salt, Open, Flower Design, Hoof Feet, P.B. Sadtler, 19th Century, Pair 150.00
Salt & Pepper, Floral Repousse, Chased, Footed, S. Kirk & Son, 4 5/8 In. 220.00
Salt & Pepper, Medallion Pattern, Gorham, 6 In., Pair 575.00
Salt Cellar, Repousse, Dominick & Haff, Early 20th Century, 2 1/8 In., Pair 172.00
Salt Dip, Squat, Bulbous, Shaped Rims, Gorham, c.1878, 1 1/2 In. 288.00
Salt Set, Master, Oyster Shell, Shell Spoons, Gold Bowls, Gorham, Box, 2 In. 840.00
Salt Spoon, Kings, Woodbury, Dix & Hartwell, c.1836 . . . . 45.00
Salt Spoon, Master, Gale, Wood & Hughes, 1833 . . . . 35.00
Salver, Floral Band, Foliate Rim, 4 Claw & Ball Feet, S. Kirk, 9 1/2 In. 488.00
Salver, Molded Scroll & Shell, Bands, Gorham, 1905, 22 5/8 In. 4312.00
Salver, Raised On Pierced Foliate Scroll Feet, Marked W. Adams, 13 In. 748.00
Sandwich Tray, Pierced, Fruit Design Rim, Wallace, 14 In. 160.00
Sauce Ladle, 1915, 8 1/2 In. 52.00
Sauceboat, Allcock, Allen & Co., Banner Mark, 5 3/4 In. 288.00
Sauceboat, Flared Rim, Reed Handle, Rim, Cast Handle, Gorham, 8 x 5 1/8 In. 115.00
Server, Buckwheat, Bead, Sailboats On Lake, Wood & Hughes, 8 1/2 In. 695.00
Service Plate Set, Gubernatorial, Flowers, C-Scroll Border, Stieff, 1950s, 12 Piece 8050.00
Serving Dish, Cover, Ram's Head Handles, Gorham, Providence, R.I., c.1875, Pair 3600.00
Serving Fork, Pierced, Engraved Spade, Spatulate Handle, Ivy Leaf, 6 In. 200.00
Serving Spoon, Coin, Bright Cut, Coffin Ends, B. Wenman, 9 In., Pair 110.00
Serving Spoon, Coin, Engraved & Dated 1816, Marked, 16 In. 154.00
Serving Spoon, Repousse, Arts & Crafts, Leaf, Hammered, 10 1/2 In. 218.00
Serving Spoon, Twisted Handle, Scalloped Edge Bowl, Whiting 56.00
Shaker, Pepper, Mushroom Cap, Hammered, John O. Bellis, 2 In., Pair 235.00
Soup Ladle, Chased Leaves, Engraved, A.E. Warner II, c.1870, 10 1/4 x 9 1/4 In. 259.00
Soup Ladle, Engraved B. Pitman, Providence, Early 19th Century 330.00
Soup Ladle, Fiddle Pattern, Initial, Charles A. Burnett, c.1815, 11 7/8 In. 2820.00
Spoon, Coin, Paul Revere, 1785, 9 1/4 In. 3575.00
Spoon, Egg, Gilt Bowl, William Gale & Son, c.1853 . . . . 50.00
Spoon, Shovel Shape, Coin, John Vogler, Salem, N.C., c.1806, 4 1/4 In. 1760.00
Sugar, Lobed Shape, Urn Finial, Engraved, Domed Cover, c.1810, 8 In. 316.00
Sugar, Oval, Gadroon Border, Riggs, c.1819, 4 x 5 x 7 In. 402.00
Sugar, Urn Shape, Beaded Border, Finial, Monogram, Lownes, c.1790, 9 3/8 In. 2280.00
Sugar, Urn Shape, Stepped Round Foot, Domed Cover, c.1830, 9 1/4 In. 431.00

Sugar & Creamer, Bucket Shape, Reeded Loop Handle, Gorham, c.1871 . . . . 575.00
Sugar & Creamer, Flat Strap Handles, Marshall Field Craft Shop, 2 1/2 In. 375.00
Sugar & Creamer, Floral Repousse, Gold Wash Interior, Whiting, c.1888 . . . . 225.00
Sugar Scoop, Bamboo Leaves, Gold Fly, Ginko Branch, Shiebler, 9 In. 2576.00
Sugar Shaker, Flared Reeded Body, Etched Leaves, c.1900, 5 1/2 In. 224.00
Sugar Tongs, Acorn Pincers, Marked P. Garrett, 6 1/2 In. 169.00
Tablespoon, Fiddle Tipped, Pointed Bowl, F.A. Tyler, New Orleans, c.1865, 9 In. 115.00
Tankard, Domed Cover, Engraved, Leaves, Adrian Bancker, c.1730, 7 1/4 In. 6000.00
Tazza, Repousse Border, Monogram, S. Kirk & Son., 7 1/4 x 3 1/4 In. 330.00
Tea & Coffee Set, Beaded Bases, Krider Co., 1880, 11 & 10 & 9 In., 3 Piece 5100.00
Tea & Coffee Set, Bradford, Leaf Knops, Reed & Barton, 5 Piece 1380.00
Tea & Coffee Set, Bulbous, Scrolling, Gorham, c.1887, 6 Piece 3000.00
Tea & Coffee Set, Carved Ebony, Arthur Stone, Gardner, Mass., 9 x 4 x 3 In. 7400.00
Tea & Coffee Set, Coin, Fletcher & Gardiner, 1820, 5 Piece 9520.00
Tea & Coffee Set, Flowers, Leaves & Grape Vines, Peter L. Krider, 5 Piece 3256.00
Tea & Coffee Set, Flowers, Oval Shape, Loring Andrews & Co., 6 Piece 5287.00
Tea & Coffee Set, Greek Key Border, Bailey & Co., c.1860, 4 Piece 3290.00
Tea & Coffee Set, Hampton Court, Footed, Reed & Barton, 5 Piece . . . . .805.00 to 1210.00
Tea & Coffee Set, Hampton Court, Reed & Barton, 1949, 6 Piece 5750.00
Tea & Coffee Set, Leaf Decoration, Flowers, c.1883, 6 Piece 6600.00
Tea & Coffee Set, Leaf Panels, Leaf Handles, Dominick & Haff, 4 Piece 2160.00
Tea & Coffee Set, M. Fred Hirsch Co., New Jersey, 1920-1945, 5 Piece 980.00
Tea & Coffee Set, Octagonal, Tapered, J.E. Caldwell & Co., 6 Piece 1840.00
Tea & Coffee Set, Tray, Maintenon, Gorham, c.1926, 6 Piece 6600.00
Tea Canister, Horizontal Fluting, Domed Lid, Ball Finial, S. Kirk & Son, 4 In. 210.00
Tea Set, Beaded Borders, Monogram, c.1820, 11 1/2 In., 4 Piece 7200.00
Tea Set, Fairfax, Engraving, Monogram, William Durgin, 3 Piece 489.00
Tea Set, Floral Repousse, Monogram, Gorham, 7 1/2-In. Teapot, 3 Piece 489.00
Tea Set, Hepplewhite, Gorham, 1915, 9 Piece 8010.00
Tea Set, Neoclassical, Coin, Harvey Lewis, Philadelphia, c.1820, 8 x 11 In. 2760.00
Tea Set, Paneled Rectangular Shapes, Gorham, Anchor Mark, 4 Piece 440.00
Tea Set, Pitcher, Embossed Ruins, S. Kirk & Son, Late 19th Century, 4 Piece 5400.00
Tea Set, Plymouth, Gorham, Bailey, Banks & Biddle, Federal, Footed, 4 Piece 633.00
Tea Set, Plymouth, Monogram, Gorham, 4 Piece 540.00
Tea Set, Rectangular, Alexander Gordon, c.1800, 7 1/8 In., 3 Piece 3900.00
Tea Set, Tray, Frank M. Whiting & Co., 5 Piece 3000.00
Tea Set, Watson, Exemplar, Black Scroll Handle, Monogram, 4 Piece 633.00
Tea Urn, Foliage Pendants, Persian Decoration, Gorham, Providence, R.I., c.1869 . . . . . . 2400.00
Teapot, Acorn & Branch Finial, Swan Neck Spout, Lincoln & Foss, 9 x 10 x 6 In. 670.00
Teapot, Engraved, Wooden Handle, Daniel Van Voorhis, Marked, 6 3/4 In. 8050.00
Teapot, Pear Shape, Round Foot, Shells, Scrolls, Daniel Parker, c.1760, 8 7/8 In. 14100.00
Teapot, Reed & Barton, Individual 100.00
Teapot, Ribbed Body, Ball Finial, Bird Spout, Wood Handle, S. Kirk, 9 1/2 In. 920.00
Teapot & Coffeepot, Floral Rocaille Band, Scroll Spout, c.1830 . . . . 2820.00
Tongs, Shell Ends, Gale, Wood & Hughes, 6 3/4 In. 150.00
Traveling Case, Gentleman's, Silver Mounted, Cartier, 5 x 1/2 x 1 3/4 In. 635.00
Tray, Canape, Bright Cut Flowers, Cut Jar, International Silver, 12 In. 290.00
Tray, Carmel Pattern, Oval, Cutout Handles, R. Wallace & Sons, c.1912, 22 1/4 In. 1090.00
Tray, Crumbing, Repousse, S. Kirk & Son, 20th Century, 6 3/4 In. 250.00
Tray, Crumbing, Violet, Wallace, 20th Century, 9 x 6 1/2 In. 395.00
Tray, Fluted Sides, Beaded, Arne Myhre, Kalo Shop, 1920, 1/2 x 3 1/4 In. 150.00
Tray, Gadroon Edge, Durham Silver Co., 23 1/2 In. 860.00
Tray, Grape & Vine Border, A.G. Schultz & Co., Monogram, c.1913, 14 In. 1230.00
Tray, Greek Key Border, Porter Blanchard, California, 20th Century, 21 In. 3055.00
Tray, Lily Pad Group, 3 Loop Handles, 9 1/4 In. 489.00
Tray, Medford, Scroll, Festoon, Monogram, Molded Rim, Mauser, 16 x 12 In. 690.00
Tray, Oval, Embossed Reeded Band, Monogram, Gorham, c.1898, 14 x 9 1/2 In. 315.00
Tray, Pierce Work, Floral Border, Fuchs & Beiderhase, Square, 1891, 10 3/4 In. 505.00
Tray, Raised Border, Hammered, Oval, Arthur J. Stone, 3/4 x 12 In. 875.00
Tray, Raised Flower Border, Monogram, Dominick & Haff, 13 1/2 x 9 1/2 In. 545.00
Tray, Rectangular, Waved Rim, Barbour, Early 20th Century, 15 x 12 1/2 In. 2070.00
Tray, Round, Everted Rim, Embossed, Gorham, c.1930, 14 1/4 In. 260.00
Tray, Scroll, Leaves, Cast, Monogram, Oblong, Montgomery Bros., 15 In. 690.00

Trophy, Kennebec Yacht Club, 1906, Clover Handles, Gorham, 9 In. 3740.00
Trophy Cup, Handles, Lid, Urn Finial, E. Caldwell & Co., 15 1/2 x 7 In. 2645.00
Tureen, Repousse Flowers, Scrollwork, Cover, Gorham, 7 1/2 x 14 1/2 In. 980.00
Tureen, Soup, Ivy Border, Geometric Finial, Handle, c.1872, 16 1/2 In. 3900.00
Tureen, Soup, Pedestal Foot, Chased, Flowers, Twig Handles, c.1870, 12 In. 3525.00
Tureen, Vegetable, Cover, Dominick & Haff, N.Y., c.1899, 11 3/4 In., Pair 2350.00
Tureen, Vegetable, Cover, Gorham Mfg. Co., 1863-1867, 14 1/4 In. 3525.00
Vase, Chased Flowers, Barbour Silver Co., 12 3/4 In. 2350.00
Vase, Flared, Wood & Hughes, New York, 9 1/2 In. 546.00
Vase, Hammered, Kalo, Arts & Crafts, 4 1/2 In. 310.00
Vase, Trumpet, Oval Medallions, Chased, Cowell & Hubbard, 21 In. 880.00
Water Set, Pitcher, 2 Goblets & Tray, Jaccard & Co., 1864 . . . . 9900.00
SILVER-ASIAN, Vase, Ivory Tusks, 6 Masks, Part Human, Part Bird Supports, 21 3/4 In., Pair 7200.00
SILVER-AUSTRIAN, Bowl, Stand, Mythological Figure, Cupid, Floral, Enamel, Vienna, 6 In. . 4015.00
Chalice, Jugendstil, Embossed, 3 x 3 1/4 In. 430.00
Snuffbox, Chased Figural Decoration, Oval, 2 1/2 x 2 x 5/8 In. 46.00
Tazza, Openwork Iris, Scroll Base, Bruder Frank, 1900, 11 1/8 In., Pair 3000.00
Tea Caddy, Rectangular, Turned Decoration, Foliate Feet, Rabbit Finial, 6 x 4 In. 575.00
Tray, Art Nouveau, Asymmetrical, c.1922, 16 x 11 3/4 In. 805.00
Tray, Art Nouveau, Scalloped Leaf, Flowers, Stem Handle, c.1922, 13 x 9 In. 978.00
Tray, Tea, Flower Rim Design, Handles, Oval, 29 In. 1955.00
SILVER-AUSTRO-HUNGARIAN, Casket, Bombe Form, Hinged Cover, c.1820, 6 1/2 In. 604.00
Centerpiece, Medallion, Late 19th Century, 15 3/4 x 10 3/8 In. 805.00
Match Holder, Figural, Man Carrying Pails, 19th Century, 5 7/8 In. 316.00
SILVER-BELGIAN, Dish, Oval, Wood Handles, Molded Sides, Marked, Wolfers, 12 3/4 In. . . . 253.00
SILVER-BRAZILIAN, Tea & Coffee Set, Pear Shape, Scrolled Feet, 5 Piece 230.00
SILVER-CANADIAN, Mustard Pot, Flashed Ruby Glass Liner, Edgar Caron, c.1936 . . . . 460.00
SILVER-CHINESE, Basket, Flowers, Berries & Bamboo Panels, W. Hing, 1870s, 10 1/2 In. . . 345.00
Belt, Mother Of Pearl, Quatrefoil Buckle, Embossed Dragons, 27 5/8 In. 173.00
Belt, Round Buckle, Writhing Dragons, Roundels Formed As Coins, 28 In. 170.00
Bottle, Rosewater, Bird Dropper, Chased, Embossed, Knop Stem, 12 1/4 In. 316.00
Bowl, 2 Handles, Stylized Leaves, Goblet Shape, 8 3/4 In. 635.00
Bowl, Chased Side Panels, Birds, Flowers & Carp, 1890s, 13 In. 805.00
Bowl, Chrysanthemums, Flared, Shanghai Canton Luenwo, 8 In. 635.00
Bowl, Flower Form, Chrysanthemums, Herons, Wang Hing, 1911, 11 x 5 1/2 In. 1844.00
Bowl, Greek Key Border, Stylized Sun & Sky, Horn Feet, 9 5/8 x 10 In. 805.00
Bowl, Lobed, Bamboo Shoots, Center Shield, 1840s, 4 1/8 In. 546.00
Bowl, Reticulated, Embossed Dragons, Clouds, c.1900, 8 1/2 In. 1092.50
Bowl, Trophy, 1 Large Dragon, Inscription, 1909, 7 3/8 In. 488.00
Bowl, Woven Wire Lid, Beaded Handles, Teakwood Stand, 7 1/8 In. 862.00
Box, Ch'ang Character, Warrior On Horseback, Hinged Cover, 3 1/2 x 2 3/8 In. 633.00
Box, Lid Scene Of Advancing Army, Animal Cartouche, 1880s, 6 3/4 In. 1265.00
Cocktail Set, Dragon, Bamboo Swing Handle, Mon Enfant, Wang Hing, 7 Piece 490.00
Cocktail Shaker, Flat Lid, Domed Top, Dragon On Stippled Ground, 13 In. 860.00
Compote, Figural, Embossed Leaves, Sunshing, c.1890, 9 3/4 In. 4313.00
Compote, Scalloped Rim, Flowering Tree Stem, W. Hing, 1920s, 7 In. 1090.00
Compote, Vignette Of Figures, Squash Form Handle, WSL, 1870s, 8 1/4 In. 230.00
Condiment Set, Side Prunus Branches, Luenwo, 1870s, 4 Piece 345.00
Cup, Floral Panels, Cartouche, Dragon Handles, Hoaching, Canton, 8 1/2 In. 2415.00
Cup, Shield Cartouche, Bamboo Handles, Domed Foot, 1800s, 9 3/4 In. 575.00
Goblet, Dragons On Bowl, 3 Bamboo Trees Stem, Mark LH., 8 1/8 In. 287.00
Goblet, Embossed Prunus Trees & Birds, Textured Ground, 1800s, 5 7/8 In. 287.00
Goblet, Export, Hung Chong & Co., Early 20th Century, 7 7/8 In. 460.00
Goblet, Panels Of Village Scenes & Birds, 1880s, 7 3/8 In. 920.00
Humidor, Bamboo Design, Rectangular, Stamped Zeewo, 8 In. 1150.00
Humidor, Dragon, Wooden Lined, Rectangular, Nanking Store, 9 In. 2070.00
Parasol Handle, Kaishu Script, Dragon On Knob, 1904, 10 5/8 In. 115.00
Rose Bowl, Kaishu Script Marks, Characters, Early 20th Century, 6 7/8 In. 290.00
Sauceboat, Side Chrysanthemum Blossoms, 1880s, 9 1/8 In. 690.00
Shaving Mug, Brush, Dragon Encircling Body, Samurai Shokai, 4 7/8 In. 287.00
Vase, Allover Embossed Dragons, 3-Footed, Late 1800s, 6 1/8 In., Pair 373.00
Vase, Bamboo & Dragons Rim, Hung Chong, 1930s, 6 1/2 x 8 In. 460.00
Vase, Bud, Engraved Bands, Serpentine Dragons, 6 3/4 In., Pair 546.00

SILVER-COLOMBIAN, Salver, Rococo Style, Autographed Central Section, 17 3/4 In. 374.00
SILVER-CONTINENTAL, Bowl, Basket Weave, Repousse Flowers, 10 In. 470.00
   Bowl, Centerpiece, Glass, Boat Shape, Cupids On Handles, 19 In. 3738.00
   Bowl, Centerpiece, Winged Terms Of Minerva, Lion Masks On Stem, 1860, 21 In. 9600.00
   Bowl, Lobed Sides, Grapevine Design, 11 In., Pair 2530.00
   Box, Cigarette, Rectangular, Chased Ribbing, Marked, c.1920, 7 x 4 In. 300.00
   Box, Hinged Lid, People & Animals In Landscape, 19th Century, 6 1/8 In. 250.00
   Box, Hinged, Chased Design, Late 19th Century, 3/4 x 4 1/4 x 3 In. 280.00
   Box, Patch, Chased Figural Decoration, Oval, 3 1/4 x 2 1/4 x 1 1/2 In. 115.00
   Coffee Set, Yellow Enamel, 3 1/2-In. Coffeepot, Demitasse, 8 Piece 3165.00
   Dish, Convex Dome Lid, Double Handles, 19th Century, 7 1/2 x 8 In. 690.00
   Dish, Cover, Floral Embossed Body, S Scroll Handles, Rectangular, 7 In. 400.00
   Epergne, Cherubs, Eagle Head Handles, GR Hallmark, 12 x 11 1/2 In. 575.00
   Ewer, Caryatid Form Handle, Chased Masque, Late 19th Century, 12 In. 1080.00
   Figurine, Pheasant, Salamander & Turtle At Feet, c.1900, 10 1/2 In. 950.00
   Fork & Spoon, Soldier Fleeing A Woman, 20th Century, 5 7/8 In., Child's 50.00
   Goblet, Cover, Floral Repousse, 14 In. 2530.00
   Jewelry Box, Engraved Decoration, Velvet Lining, Key, 1870s, 4 1/2 x 3 In. 258.00
   Jug, Leaf Bands, Serpent Handle, Spanish, 19th Century, 6 3/4 In. 1090.00
   Liquor Set, 3 Bottles, Etched, Figural Stopper, Pierced Leaf Stand, 14 In. 2300.00
   Nef, Masted Ship Shape, Enamel, Early 20th Century, 21 3/4 In. 3450.00
   Pastry Server, Spade Shape, Wood Handle, Late 18th Century, 14 In. 345.00
   Pitcher, Baluster Form, Molded Rim, H.J. Wilm, c.1935, 6 1/4 In. 140.00
   Pitcher, Water, Oval, Flared Rim, Scroll Handle, Wilkens & Son, c.1920, 9 In. 546.00
   Snuffbox, Carnelian Inset, Gilded Interior, 2 1/2 In. 690.00
   Stirrup Cup, Fox Head, 6 In. 1150.00
   Tea & Coffee Set, Repousse Flowers, 5 Piece 1175.00
   Tray, Rectangular, 4 Bracket Feet, Marked, Koch & Bergfeld, 14 In. 375.00
   Vase, Cylindrical, Chased Band Of Roses, Marked, 12 7/8 In. 310.00
   Vase, Pear Form, Lobed Rim, Mythological Creatures, 1880s, 6 1/4 In. 290.00
   Wine Bottle Holder, Floral Repousse, Tray Base, 7 In. 230.00
SILVER-DANISH, Basket, Swags, Ram's-Head Feet, Liner, Michelsen, 1928, 22 In. 7200.00
   Bell, Dinner, Floral Knop, Georg Jensen, 3 1/2 In. 690.00
   Bowl, Flared Sides, 2 Cast Tendrils, Leaf Handles, Georg Jensen, 3 5/8 In. 240.00
   Bowl, Flared, Open Tripod Base, Georg Jensen, 1950, 15 In. . . . . *Illus* 18400.00
   Bowl, Molded Foot, Scroll Base, Georg Jensen, 1941 . . . . 8400.00
   Bowl, Open Floral Standard, Footed, Georg Jensen, 1974, 7 3/4 x 6 In. 4025.00
   Bowl, Oval Shape, Raised Legs, Leaves, Georg Jensen, 15 1/2 In. 3525.00
   Box, Blossom Feet, Square, Georg Jensen, 5 In. 6800.00
   Box, Fluted Final Cover, Georg Jensen, 1945, 4 1/4 In. 2700.00
   Cocktail Shaker, Ball Finial Cover, Bombe, Handles, Georg Jensen, 10 1/2 In. 2400.00
   Cocktail Shaker, Presentation, Cylindrical Body, Tapered, Engraved, 9 1/4 In. 375.00
   Coffee Set, Blossom, Copenhagen, Georg Jensen, 1945, 3 Piece 3900.00
   Coffee Set, Rectangular Tray, Blossom Pattern, Georg Jensen, 1930, 4 Piece 4200.00
   Coffee Spoon Set, Scroll Pattern, Box, 12 Piece 290.00
   Coffeepot, Pear Shape, Domed Lid, Leaf & Berry Finial, Marked, HR, c.1950, 9 In. 375.00
   Compote, Acanthus Stem, 10-Sided Base, Georg Jensen, No. 181, 4 7/8 In. 460.00
   Compote, Grape Pattern, Circular, Lobed Stem, Georg Jensen, 8 In. 604.00
   Compote, Grape Pattern, Flared, Georg Jensen, Copenhagen, 7 3/8 In. 1725.00
   Compote, Leaf Design, Georg Jensen, 5 x 5 3/4 In. 730.00

Silver-Danish, Bowl, Flared, Open Tripod Base,
Georg Jensen, 1950, 15 In.

**After washing a teapot, dry it as
well as possible. Then put a
sugar cube in the teapot to
absorb the remaining water.**

Compote, Pendant Grape Clusters, Georg Jensen, 7 1/2 In. . . . . .3450.00 to 3735.00
Condiment Set, Acorn, Georg Jensen, Copenhagen, After 1945, 36 Piece 3600.00
Creamer, Oval, Flared Spout, Scroll Handle, Marked, Silverco, 1955, 5 3/8 In. 90.00
Demitasse Set, No. 80, Bulbous, Ebony Bud Finials, Georg Jensen, c.1933, 7 In. 2185.00
Dish, Blossom, Georg Jensen, 8 In. 1955.00
Dish, Round, Tapered, 2 Handles, Rolled Rim, Marked, Georg Jensen, c.1950, 8 In. 196.00
Fork, Hollow Leaf Handle, Georg Jensen, No. 136, Early 20th Century, 5 7/8 In. 170.00
Gravy Boat, Reticulated Standard, Georg Jensen, 6 1/2 In. 2875.00
Humidor, Embossed Band At Base, K. Anderson, Wood Lined, 9 x 5 1/2 In. 630.00
Pillbox, Circular, Flowers, Lozenge Border, Georg Jensen, 3 x 2 In. 220.00
Pillbox, Cover, Floral Repousse Center, Georg Jensen, 2 1/2 In. 253.00
Pitcher, Grape Pattern, Georg Jensen, Copenhagen, Ebony Handle, 8 3/4 In. 8050.00
Punch Bowl, 5 Flared Panels, Stylized Leaves Above Base, Marked, 1918, 11 In. 1840.00
Salver, Scalloped Edge, Leaves, Georg Jensen, 11 1/2 In. 3450.00
Shaker, Cover, Melon Form, Pierced, Ringed Foot, Georg Jensen, 5 1/2 In. 1650.00
Tazza, Grapevine Pattern, Georg Jensen, 1945, 10 1/2 In. 6000.00
Tazza, Pendant Grape Clusters, Flared, Georg Jensen, 5 In. 1610.00
Tea & Coffee Set, Arts & Crafts, Bulbous Bodies, Hammered, 20th Century 1495.00
Tea Set, Ivory Handle, Teapot, Creamer & Covered Sugar, Georg Jensen, 1925 . . . . 5875.00
Tea Strainer & Holder, Georg Jensen, No. 2H, c.1950, 5 3/8 In. 1290.00
Tray, 2 Flared Handles, Shaped Rim, Round, Georg Jensen, 1945, 15 3/8 In. 6600.00
Tray, Blossom Pattern, Oval, Blossom Handles, Georg Jensen, 1926, 14 In. 748.00
Tray, Oval, 2 Strap Handles, Marked, Georg Jensen, La Paglia, c.1950, 10 1/2 In. 460.00
Tray, Round, Hand Hammered, Georg Jensen, 11 3/4 In. 1610.00
Vase, Engraved, David Andersen, 9 In. 605.00
Vial, Scent, Danish Flower On Lid, Cylindrical, Georg Jensen, 3 In. 120.00
Wine Coaster, Grapevine Pattern, Wood Disc, Georg Jensen, 1935, 5 3/4 In. 8400.00
SILVER-DUTCH, Basket, Festoons, Cherub & Bouquet Handle, 1880s, 10 In., Pair 1380.00
Basket, Sweetmeat, Shell & Strapwork Rim, Pendant Handles, 1785, 4 In. 3000.00
Bowl, Ecuelle, Continental,.833, Early 20th Century, 2 7/8 x 9 1/4 In. 345.00
Bowl, Scroll Handles, Pierced Sides, Early 20th Century, 13 5/8 x 8 1/4 In. 230.00
Box, Oval, Cover, Embossed Tavern Scene, Village Scenes, 5 7/8 In. 345.00
Card, Case, Tortoiseshell, Compartments Lined In Rose Silk, 5 1/2 In. 460.00
Cream Jug, Reeded Rim & Handle, Beaded Bands, 19th Century, 4 5/8 In. 290.00
Creamer, Cow, Red Glass Eyes, Raised Tail To Brush Flies, Fly Finial, c.1900, 4 In. 1120.00
Creamer, Flared Lip, Scroll Handle Over Squat Body, 1835, 3 1/2 In. 140.00
Cruet, Frame Formed As Branches, Leaf Capped Handles, 1768, 8 5/8 In. 1800.00
Decanter Set, Rococo Style, 3 Bottles, Etched Lattice, Stoppers, c.1900, 11 In. 400.00
Muffineer, Ship Decoration, 6 In. 184.00
Penknife, Serpent Form, Engraved, Spring Back, c.1750, 4 In. 395.00
Sculpture, Windmill, Movable Blades & Rigging, Marked HH, 10 1/4 In. 633.00
Serving Fork, Scroll Mounted Tines, Intertwined Handle, 19th Century, 12 1/2 In. 520.00
Tea Caddy, Chased Windmill & Sailboat, Stamped Holland, 5 1/2 In. 345.00
Tray, Incurved Angles, Trellis Gallery, Hoop Handles, 1774, 22 5/8 In. 3900.00

SILVER-ENGLISH. English sterling silver is marked with a series of four
or five small hallmarks. The standing lion mark is the most commonly
seen sterling quality mark. The other marks indicate the city of origin,
the maker, and the year of manufacture. These dates can be verified in
many good books on silver.

SILVER-ENGLISH, Apple Corer, Molded, Reeded Band, George III, Early 19th Century, 6 In. . 432.00
Argyll, Gravy Warmer, C. Aldridge, Henry Green, George III, 1773, 6 In. 3600.00
Argyll, Gravy Warmer, Cylindrical Shape, Scrolling Handle, c.1830, 6 x 6 In. 431.00
Ashtray, Round, Rolled Rim, Open Scroll Handle, Cartier, London, 1939 . . . . 90.00
Baby Rattle, Coral Accents, Birmingham, George III, 5 3/4 In. 1265.00
Basket, Sugar, Engraved, Reticulated, Swing Handle, S. Adams, 1768, 4 1/2 In. 315.00
Basket, Sweetmeat, Beading, Grape Bunches, E. Aldridge, 1766, 5 3/4 In. 805.00
Basting Spoon, Rattail Bowls, c.1725, 14 1/2 & 13 1/2 In., Pair 2400.00
Beaker, Embossed Leaves, Masks, Molded Rim, Ball Feet, c.1901, 3 In. 375.00
Berry Spoon, Chased Vermeil Bowl, Monogram, Hallmark, London, c.1811, Pair 105.00
Berry Spoon, Gilt Bowl, Engraved Crests, Robert Rutland, 1810, 8 1/2 In., Pair 145.00
Berry Spoon, Vermeil Bowl, Repousse Handles, Case, W. Sutton, 8 1/2 In., Pair 250.00
Biscuit Barrel, Plated, Engraved Flower Swags, Ball & Claw Feet, 7 1/2 In. 258.00

Bowl, Centerpiece, Victorian, Charles Stuart Harris, Marked, 1890, 8 In. 345.00
Bowl, Centerpiece, Winged Sphinx, Pierced, Liner, Edward Barnard & Sons, 16 In. 3900.00
Bowl, Raised Leaf & Woman's Head, Handle, Footed, Oval, Elkington, 13 3/4 In. 345.00
Bowl, Scrolling Leaves, Lobed, Engraved, Samuel Hood, William III, c.1695, 8 In. 1495.00
Bowl, Shell Form, Ribbed & Fluted, 2-Tailed Dolphin Handle, 1896, 14 In. 3000.00
Box, Biscuit, Hinged Cover, Lion Mask & Ring Handles, Stephen Smith, 8 In. 2700.00
Box, Patch, Engraved Fide Et Virtue, Crest, Man With Scythe, 1863, 3 x 1 In. 315.00
Box, Repousse Bird Decoration, Round, Cover, London, 1892, 3 1/2 In. 175.00
Box, Tobacco, Slip-On Cover, Trotting Stallion, Bald Galloway, 1728, 3 1/2 In. 7200.00
Butter, Applied Border, Cover, Wooden Finial, London, 1911, 7 1/2 In. 316.00
Caddy, Rococo, Charles Stewart Harrison, London, Georgian, c.1780 .... 440.00
Caddy Spoon, King's, Shell Form Bowl, c.1860 .... 150.00
Cake Basket, Gadrooned Rim, Swing Handle, Atkin Brothers, 1899, 11 1/4 In. 805.00
Cake Basket, Swing Handle, Openwork Bands, P. & A. Bateman, 1791, 14 1/8 In. 1035.00
Candelabrum is listed in its own category.
Candlesticks are listed in their own category.
Cann, Chased, Gilded Interior, William Fleming, George I, Marked, 1719, 5 In. 1150.00
Cann, Engraved, Dorothy Grant, Charles II, Marked, 1684, 3 1/8 In. 2760.00
Cann, Engraved, John Kirkup, George III, Marked, 1757, 4 3/4 In. 905.00
Cann, Gilded Interior, Fuller White, George III, Marked, 1762, 4 3/4 In. 460.00
Card Case, Leaves, Monogram, Nathanial Mills, 1851, 4 In. 550.00
Case, Ribbed, Marked M & M Ltd., London, c.1902, 3 1/2 x 3 1/8 In. 56.00
Case, Watch, Cherubs In Cartouches, Leathered Sides, Inner Swiss Watch, 3 3/4 In. 315.00
Cheese Scoop, Wood Handle, Hallmark, George III, c.1800, 9 In. 430.00
Chop Tongs, Engraved Garter & Crest, Henry Chawner, 1795, 9 5/8 In. 400.00
Cigarette Case, Chased Grooves, Engraved, Cartier, London, 1936, 3 x 2 1/2 In. 865.00
Claret Jug, Frosted Glass, Scrolling Leaves, Joseph Angell, 1850, 15 1/4 In. 2400.00
Claret Jug, Hinged Cover, Regimental, Lion, Glass, John Figg, 1867, 12 3/4 In. 4800.00
Coffee Set, Coffeepot, Hot Milk Jug, Lighthouse Form, Ivory Handles, 5 3/4 In. 575.00
Coffeepot, Bands Of Rococo Ornament, Bud Finial, H. Payne, 1750, 10 In. 1920.00
Coffeepot, Spiral Finial, Ivory Handle, W. & J. Priest, 1770, 9 1/2 In. 110.00
Coffeepot, Urn Finial, W. Fountain & D. Pontifex, 1793, 12 1/4 In. 1800.00
Coffeepot, Wicker-Bound Handle, Charles Wright, George III, 1772, 9 3/4 In. 1380.00
Coffeepot, William Shaw & William Priest, George II, c.1752, 9 3/4 In. 1495.00
Condiment Holder, 3 Royal Worcester Inserts, Sheffield, 1895, 6 1/2 In. 345.00
Cream Jug, Ear Handle, Leaf Band, G. Smith & T. Hayter, 1796, 5 3/4 In. 316.00
Creamer, Chased Floral Decoration, 1779, 4 1/2 In. 115.00
Creamer, Etched Floral Band, Peter, Ann & William Bateman, c.1801, 4 7/8 In. 336.00
Creamer, Repousse Scrolls, London Hallmark, William Shaw, 1753, 4 In. 220.00
Creamer, Vase Shape, Architectural Decoration, London, 1782, 4 1/2 In. 920.00
Cruet Set, Navette Shape, 6 Bottles, George III, 9 In. 1265.00
Cup, Cover, Detachable Stand, Monogram, Barnard, George IV, 1909, 20 In. 5700.00
Cup, Cover, Wreath Inscription, Racing Inscription, P. Storr, 1813, 14 3/4 In. 9600.00
Cup, Urn Form, Floral Swag, Acanthus, 2 Handles, Cover, London, 1808, 11 1/2 In. 2300.00
Cup, Wine Tasting, Plain Body, London Marks For 1739, 3 1/4 In. 489.00
Dessert Fork, Enameled Terminals, Liberty & Co., Birmingham, 6 Piece 1100.00
Dessert Knife Set, Hardstone, Gilt Blade, Vines, Francis Higgins, c.1853, 8 In. 690.00
Dessert Set, Fork, Knives, Ivory Handles, Box, Birmingham, 1909, 24 Piece 1725.00
Dinner Fork, Fiddle Pattern, George Adams, c.1854, 7 7/8 In., 9 Piece 375.00
Dish, Entree, Cover, Armorial Crest, William Frisbee, 1804, 10 5/8 In. 748.00
Dish, Entree, Cover, Frosted Glass Liner, Marked Angell & Browne, 1865, 8 3/4 In. 860.00
Dish, Meat, Gadroon Rim, Engraved Arms, G. Wickes, 1739, 15 In. 8400.00
Dish, Parcel Gilt & Niello, Toilet Of Venus, Roman Interior, 1875, 11 1/2 In. 3000.00
Dish, Pierced, Engraved, Burner, Paul Storr, London, 1835 .... 980.00
Dish, Sweetmeat, Openwork Base, George III, 5 x 5 3/4 In., Pair 1095.00
Dish, Venison, Plated Warming Stand, Well & Tree, Engraved Arms, 1806, 25 In. 4800.00
Egg Coddler, Sandglass Timer, John Emes, George III, 1802, 9 3/4 In. 5400.00
Epergne, 5 Baskets, Sheffield, Edwardian, 1905-1906, 9 1/2 In. 3105.00
Epergne, Bacchic Masks, No Glass Bowls, M. Boulton, George III, 1801, 22 In. 8400.00
Ewer, Hinged Cover, Classical, Chariots, E.J. & W. Barnard, 1850, 13 In. 2700.00
Ewer, Urn Shape, Fluted Body, Helmet Spout, Sheffield, c.1810, 14 1/4 In., Pair 4935.00
Ewer, Wine, Frieze Of Figures & Warriors, 1894 Inscription, 14 In. 7800.00
Figurine, Arab & Horse, Palm Tree, Pendant Buds, 1769, 12 In. 6000.00

Fish Knife, Engraved Fish & Eels On Side, G. Adams, 1864, 8 3/4 In. 400.00
Fish Knife, Openwork Blade, Hester Bateman, 1781, 12 1/4 In. 546.00
Fish Service, Faces, Grapes, Ivorine Handles, Brass Mounted Wood Case, 12 Piece 115.00
Fish Service, Fish Design, Case, 2 Piece 420.00
Fish Service, Pierced, Mythological Masks, Dolphin, Fisherman, 14 In., 2 Piece 1060.00
Fish Service, Shell Pattern, 14 Piece 336.00
Fish Service, Tray, Samuel Kirkby & Co., Georgian, Sheffield, c.1815, 8 In., 12 Piece . . . 375.00
Flask, Perfume, Floral & Embossed At Lid, Neck & Base, Monogram, 9 In. 490.00
Flask, Rectangular, Engine-Turned, Hinged Screw Lid, Birmingham, 1939, 4 In. 138.00
Fork Set, Hanoverian Pattern, Boar's Head Crest, 18th Century, 6 Piece 150.00
Frame, Rectangular, Embossed Flowers, 1925, 15 1/4 In. 520.00
Frame, Repousse & Floral Landscape, 12 x 18 In. 375.00
Funnel, Gadroon Pattern, Richard Pargeter Mark, London, c.1780, 6 x 3 3/4 In. 1232.00
Ginger Jar, Cover, Putti, Leaves, R. & S. Garrard, 1890, 18 3/4 In. 4800.00
Gravy Boat, Footed, Bold Rococo Chasing, George III, 1763 . . . . 1100.00
Gravy Boat, Scalloped Rim, Scroll Handle, Sheffield, 1936, 2 7/8 In. 110.00
Kettle, Lampstand, Masks, Raffia Swing Handle, J. Edwards, 1729, 12 In. 5100.00
Kettle, Lampstand, Rococo, 3-Footed, T. Whipham, George II, 1747, 14 5/8 In. 3600.00
Kettle, Lampstand, Swan Neck Spout, Acorn Finial, W. Gamble, 1705, 14 1/4 In. 7200.00
Kettle, Stand, Chinoiserie, Domed Cover, Georgian, c.1790, 16 In. 1840.00
Ladle, Engraved Crest, Wm. Bateman, c.1822 . . . . 422.00
Ladle, Hester Bateman, c.1764, 7 In. 364.00
Ladle, Old English Pattern, Legacy Engraving, Makers Mark, George III, 13 In. 287.00
Ladle, Pierced, Engraved Handle, Hester Bateman 115.00
Marmalade, 2 Repousse Covers, Bamboo, Thomas Orley & Sons, 7 In. 385.00
Marrow Scoop, 1729, 8 3/8 In. 287.00
Marrow Scoop, George II, Hallmark, London, c.1740, 8 3/4 In. 460.00
Marrow Scoop, Victorian, Hallmark, London, c.1896, 9 1/4 In. 201.00
Marrow Spoon, Monogram, Hester Bateman, 1783, 9 3/8 In. 460.00
Miniature, Tea Tables, Chippendale, Goldsmiths & Silversmiths Co., 1908, 4 In. 374.00
Mirror, Dressing Table, Birds In Leaves, Embossed, London, 1898, 16 In. 632.00
Mirror, Hand Beveled Plate, Slender Handle, Sunburst Engine Turning, 12 1/4 In. 143.00
Monteith, Lion Mask & Ring Handles, Birmingham, 1906, 5 3/4 In. 86.00
Muffineer, Domed Lid, Acorn Finials, Pear Shape, A. M. & Co., 1932, 7 3/4 In., Pair . . . 402.00
Muffineer, Mappin & Webb, Sheffield, George VI, c.1946, 7 1/2 In. 402.00
Muffineer, Mordecai Fox, George II, c.1748, 7 1/4 In. 574.00
Mug, Child's, Floral Engraving, Cast Handle, Edward C. Brown, 1871, 3 1/8 In. 375.00
Mug, Scroll Handle, Acanthus Thumb Rest, W. & R. Peaston, 1763, 5 1/4 In. 750.00
Mustard Pot, Flower Repousse, Blossom Finial, Footed, 3 x 3 1/2 In. 252.00
Napkin Rings are listed in their own category.
Nutmeg Grater, Barrel Form, S I Mark, 1796, 1 1/2 In. 518.00
Nutmeg Grater, Birmingham, 1807, 1 3/4 In. 357.00
Nutmeg Grater, Shell Opens To Reveal Grater, H. & T. Birmingham, 2 In. 345.00
Page Turner, Spiraling Gadroon Handle, Ivory Blade, 16 1/2 In. 635.00
Pen Tray, Stamp Box, Arts & Crafts, Turquoise, Enamel, Liberty & Co., Cymric, 1904 . . . 2070.00
Pepper Castor Set, Bulbous, Lion Feet, Elizabeth II, c.1969, 3 1/2 In., 4 Piece 287.00
Pitcher, Animals In Border, Leaves, Monster Head Cover, 1877, 10 1/4 In. 3000.00
Pitcher, Askos-Shape, Winged Figure Base, Handle, William Elliott, 8 5/8 In. 4200.00
Pitcher, Pressed Glass Body, Alligator Skin Finish, Birmingham, 10 1/4 In. 150.00
Plate Set, Dessert, Birds, C.S. Harris & Sons, Edwardian, 1908, 9 3/8 In., 12 Piece 7200.00
Platter, Meat, Engraved Crest Border, W. Fountain, 1805, 22 1/4 In. 3000.00
Presentation Cup, Chased Plinth, Sea Monsters, Sailor Finial, c.1872, 23 In. 10572.00
Punch Bowl, Scrolls, Leaves, Monteith Rim, Monogram, 1887, 13 In. 4800.00
Punch Ladle, Oval 1787 Inset Coin Bowl, George III, 1819, 15 In. 145.00
Punch Strainer, Marked, George III, c.1780, 6 3/8 In. 375.00
Rattle, Coral Handle, Embossed Design, 5 Silver Bells, Whistle, 4 In. 400.00
Rattle, Engraved All Over, 8 Attached Bells, John Robins, c.1796, 6 1/4 In. 805.00
Salad Serving Set, Silver Mounted, Horn, Spoon, Fork, Late 19th Century, 11 In. 518.00
Salt, Bacchic Infants, 2 Sides, Gilt Interior, Footed, John Bodman, 1894, 7 1/2 In. 7800.00
Salt, Circular Swirl, 3 Scroll Legs, Pierced Border, Spoon, Box, 8 Piece 430.00
Salt, Conch Shell Form, 4 Piece 875.00
Salt, Open, Classical, Footed, Gadroon Rim, George III, 1811, 3 1/4 In. 110.00
Salt, Oval, Pierced Rosette Bands, Cobalt Blue Liner, William Abdy, George III, Pair 345.00

Salt, Spool Form, Scroll Thumbpieces, A. Smith, 1899, 3 3/4 In., 4 Piece 2700.00
Salver, 5 Inset Agricultural Medals, John Tuite, George II, 1735, 13 1/2 In. 2040.00
Salver, 12 Sides, 3 Blossom Center, Footed, Marked, Sheffield, 1936, 8 1/4 In. 150.00
Salver, Beaded Edge, Engraved Coat Of Arms, D. & R. Sharp, 1779, 13 1/8 In. 1840.00
Salver, Center Engraved Crest, Scrolling Feet, c.1938, 14 In. 1230.00
Salver, Chippendale, Pad Feet, Georgian, c.1823, 7 1/2 In. 690.00
Salver, Engraved Crest In Floral Wreath, Gadroon Rim, 1770, 12 In. 1920.00
Salver, Floral Fluted Rim, Queen Anne, Sterling Silver, 12 1/4 In. 430.00
Salver, Gadroon Rim, Engraved Lion Crest, Paw Feet, W. Burwash, 1816, 9 In. 1090.00
Salver, Gadroon Rim, Scrolling Leaves, Ebenezer Coker, George III, 1766, 19 In. 4200.00
Salver, Matthew Boulton, Sheffield, Early 19th Century, 13 1/8 x 10 1/4 In. 316.00
Salver, Oval, Beaded Edge, 4 Ball & Claw Feet, Hester Bateman, 1 x 6 1/2 In. 633.00
Salver, Scrolling Feet, Engraved, c.1938, 8 In. 280.00
Salver, Sheffield, I.W.G., Scrolling Legs, 8 In. 215.00
Salver, Shell & Scroll Rim, 3-Footed, W. & R. Peaston, George II, 1757, 14 In. 4500.00
Salver, Shell & Scroll Rim, Contemporary Arms Center, R. Piercy, 1760, 15 In. 4200.00
Sauce Ladle, Fiddle Pattern, Engraved Crest, George IV, c.1827, 7 In. 115.00
Sauce Ladle, Reeded Handle, William Eley, William Fearn, London, 1814, 7 In. 123.00
Sauceboat, Arms In Cartouche, Scroll Handles, I.L.W.V., 8 1/8 In., Pair 5700.00
Sauceboat, Flying Scroll Handles, 3 Shell & Hoof Feet, TE, 1773, 7 1/4 In., Pair 4800.00
Sauceboat, Georgian, Covered, Thomas Daniel, c.1785, 9 5/8 x 4 1/8 x 5 3/4 In. 1090.00
Sauceboat, Loop Handle, Pedestal, Hester Bateman, George III, 1787, 8 In. 1800.00
Sauceboat, Robert Sharp, George III, 1792, 6 1/2 x 10 In., Pair 6900.00
Sauceboat, Scalloped Rim, Open Scroll Handle, 3 Spade Feet, c.1804, 7 3/8 In. 1375.00
Server, Meat, Dome Cover, Warmer Base, Wood Handles, 15 x 21 In. 220.00
Serving Spoon, Allover Fruit & Soldier, Gilt, Elkington, 1892, Pair 316.00
Serving Spoon, Pointed Bowl, Squared Shoulders, Fiddle Handle, 13 In. 368.00
Skewer, Meat, Shell & Thread, William Trailis, George IV, 1827, Pair 460.00
Skewer, Meat, W. Ealy & W. Fearn, 1798, 7 In. 5144.00
Soup Ladle, Onslow, Fluted Bowl, Monogrammed Handle, W. Williams, 1757 .... 402.00
Strainer, Flared Rim, Cast Scrolled Handle, Georgian, c.1766, 4 1/4 In. 258.00
Stuffing Spoon, Engraved Crest, Ann & Peter Bateman, 1792, 11 7/8 In. 260.00
Stuffing Spoon, Engraved Rampant Lion On Handle, York, 11 1/2 In., Pair 275.00
Stuffing Spoon, Exeter, Maker's Mark, George IV, 1828-1829, Pair 690.00
Stuffing Spoon, George IV, Pair 690.00
Stuffing Spoon, Rounded Fiddle End Handle, Monogram, c.1807, 11 3/4 In. 145.00
Stuffing Spoon, Simple Handle, Crest, London, 1807, 11 1/2 In. 125.00
Sugar & Creamer, 8 Sides, Engraved, Hannah Northcote, 1801-02 .... 690.00
Sugar Basket, Swing Handle, Hester Bateman, 1789, 5 1/2 In. 1725.00
Sugar Tongs, Peter & Ann Bateman, c.1798, 5 1/2 In. 170.00
Tablespoon, Fiddle Form, Elkington & Co., Birmingham, 1909 .... 46.00
Tankard, Anno Dom. 1708, Shaped Peak, J. Jackson, 8 1/2 In. 4800.00
Tankard, Crest, Handle, Hallmark, 4 1/4 In. 560.00
Tankard, Domed Cover, Open Thumbpiece, H. Bateman, 1783, 7 7/8 In. 9000.00
Tankard, Engraved Cow Head, Crown Crest, Marked, George III, 7 1/2 In. 1840.00
Tankard, Open Scrollwork Thumbpiece, Engraved N Over Handle, 8 3/4 In. 3900.00
Tankard, William Bellassyse, George I, 1717, 7 1/4 In. 5750.00
Tea & Coffee Set, Floral Finial, Barnard & Sons, 1835, 5 Piece 3800.00
Tea & Coffee Set, Geometric, Flowers, Birmingham Mark, c.1877, 4 Piece 1438.00
Tea Caddy, Birmingham, 1928-29, 4 1/2 x 4 1/2 x 2 3/4 In. 520.00
Tea Caddy, Molded Rim & Base, J. Schofield, 1799, 3 1/8 In. 1265.00
Tea Set, Wooden Handles, G.B. & S., London, c.1912, 3 Piece 170.00
Tea Urn, 4 Pilaster Supports, Paw Feet, Lion Mask, Ring Handles, 1801, 17 In. 5400.00
Teapot, Barrel Form, Ivory Finial, Wood Handle, John Carter, 1789, 5 3/4 In. 860.00
Teapot, Beaded, Crest & Motto Side, Arms Of Lyle, H. Bateman, 1784, 6 In. 3600.00
Teapot, Carved Wood Pineapple Finial, Family Armorial, T.W., George III, 1796 .... 795.00
Teapot, Ivory Handle & Finial, Hester Bateman, Marked, 5 In. 3220.00
Teapot, Wood Handle, Ivory Finial, Phoenix Crest, John Emes, 1804, 6 In. 315.00
Teapot Stand, Engraved, Edward Jay, Beaded, Engraved, c.1783, 6 3/4 x 4 7/8 In. 430.00
Toast Rack, Ball Feet, Scalloped Side, 19th Century, 6 1/2 x 6 3/4 In., Pair 115.00
Toddy Ladle, Fluted Bowl, Wood Handle, P. De Lamerie, George II, 1736, 13 In. 7200.00
Toilet Set, Traveling, C. Rawlings, W. Summers, William IV, 1832, 15-In. Box 6000.00
Tray, Beaded Rim, Acanthus & Bead Handles, J. Bernard, 1874, 30 3/4 In. 5175.00

Tray, Celtic Interlace Border, Snake Handles, Rectangular, 25 In. 2645.00
Tray, Dolphin Heads, 2 Handles, Footed, E. & J. Barnard, 1853, 30 In. 4200.00
Tray, E. & J. Barnard, 4 Scroll Feet, Late 19th Century, 20 1/2 In. 2000.00
Tray, Engraved & Bright Cut, Maxfield & Sons, 1898, 23 1/4 x 15 1/2 In. 2185.00
Tray, Gadroon Sides, Handles, Rectangular, 26 In. 2530.00
Tray, Handles, George III, Marked, 1761, 16 1/4 In. 550.00
Tray, Handles, Sheffield, Edward VII, 1902, 29 1/4 In. 2990.00
Tray, Tea, Interlaced Leaves, Footed, Charles Reily, George Storer, 1850, 31 In. 4800.00
Tray, Victorian, Handles, James Deakin & Sons, 1898, Marked, 32 In. 4830.00
Trophy Cup, Cover, Victorian, Urn Shape, Capstan Base, c.1868, 18 In. 6465.00
Tureen, Cover, Loop Handles, George III, c.1785, 17 1/2 x 8 1/2 x 12 1/2 In. 5750.00
Tureen, Revolving, Engraved, Scroll, Flowers, Handle, Late 19th Century, 13 In. 259.00
Tureen, Sauce, Cover, Bombe, Edward Farrell, George III, 1831, 8 In., Pair 5400.00
Tureen, Soup, Cover, Stand By W. Bond, Dublin, W. Tuite, 1763, 17 1/2 In. 5700.00
Urn, Cover, Floral, Loop Handles, John Schofield, George III, 1784, 16 1/2 In. 2415.00
Urn, Cover, Victorian, 2 Handles, William Sills, c.1900, 14 In. 489.00
Urn, Hot Water, Georgian, Ivory Spigot Handle, Sheffield, 13 1/2 In. 145.00
Urn, Scrolling Handle, Etched Flowers, 1835, 5 1/8 In. 160.00
Urn, Waisted Cover, Urn Finial, George III, c.1781, 21 1/2 In. 5750.00
Vase, Flared Rim, Repousse Flowers & Bow, W. Volund, 14 In., Pair 1840.00
Vase, Pedestal, 2 Handles, Victorian, Warwick, London, 1900, 15 In. 7800.00
Vase, Round, Stepped Pedestal, Weighted, Elkington, 1897 In. 105.00
Vase, Victorian, Henry Stratford, Sheffield, c.1889, 4 1/4 In., Pair 196.00
Waiter, Arms In Ribbon Tied Wreath Of Bellflowers, 1787, 9 In., Pair 4500.00
Waiter, Beaded Rim, 3 Taloned Feet, Martin, Hall & Co., 1874, 8 1/4 In. 650.00
Waiter, Chippendale Rim, Pad Feet, Center Crest, W. Turton, 1772, 6 3/4 In. 490.00
Waiter, Engraved Armorial Crest, Francis Nelme, Marked, George II, 9 7/8 In. 1150.00
Wine Coaster, Shaped Gadroon Border, Openwork Decoration, 5 1/2 In. 195.00
Wine Coaster, Shaped Shell Border, 7 In., Pair 575.00
Wine Coaster, Turned Wood Base, Repousse, 2 x 5 In., Pair 170.00
Wine Coaster, Wooden Base, Pierced Gallery, Henry Lias, 4 7/8 In. 895.00
Wine Cooler, Fluted Body, Gadroon Rim, Collar, Liner, 8 1/2 In., Pair 920.00
Wine Cooler, Square, Bulbous Gadroon Bottom, 2 Ivory Handles, 7 In., Pair 3680.00
Wine Ewer, Gilded Interior, Charles Thomas Fox, 1828, Marked, 10 1/2 In. 1030.00
Wine Harness, King's Pattern, Asprey & Co., c.1926, 8 In. 805.00
SILVER-FINNISH, Vase, Free-Form, Walnut Pedestal Base, Tapio Wirkkala, Signed, 10 1/4 In. 1380.00
SILVER-FRENCH, Berry Spoon, Reticulated, Gilt Bowl, Engraved, Flowers, c.1895, 9 In. 170.00
Bowl, Cover, Stand, Rosette & Palmette Border, Butterfly Finial, 1809, 9 1/4 In. 7800.00
Bowl, Cut Glass Insert, Doves & Cherubs, Hoof Feet, 1869, 15 1/4 In. 4887.00
Bowl, Ecuelle, Cover, Removable Silver Liner, Lebrun, Paris, c.1825, 11 1/8 In. 1840.00
Bowl, Oval, Flowers, Cartouches, Applied Handles, 3 x 4 3/4 x 10 1/4 In. 431.00
Box, Cigarette, Table, Enameled Black Bands, Art Deco, Cartier, 1928, 6 1/2 In. 6000.00
Box, Round, Gilt, Patriotic Scene, Charles Odiot, Paris, 20th Century, 6 1/4 In. 575.00
Chalice, Gilt & Ivory, Hemispherical Bowl & Foot, Jean E. Puiforcat, 6 In. 5400.00
Chalice, Raised Flowers, Religious Medallion, Gold Wash, 8 1/4 x 5 3/4 In. 430.00
Claret Jug, Hinged Cover, Gilt, Thumbpiece, G. Keller, 9 1/4 In., Pair 3300.00
Claret Jug, Spiral Gadrooning, Handle, Shell Shaped Spout, 1880, 11 In. 1610.00
Compact, Figure Of Orion On Back, Constellation, 1920s, 3 1/8 In. 143.00
Cordial Set, Gilt, Tapering, Cylindrical, Monogram, Leather Case, 1 1/2 In., 12 Piece 230.00
Cruet Set, 6 Panel Cut Bottles, Grapevine Base, Feet, Marked Tete-Leroy 176.00
Cup, Wine Tasting, Inset Coin, Chased Vine Decoration, 3 In. 345.00
Cup, Wine Tasting, Plain Body, Marked Marie Colmain A Darvois, 1782, 3 In. 635.00
Cup, Wine Tasting, Ribbed & Grape Decoration, Engraved P. M. Dutour, 2 3/4 In. 375.00
Cup, Wine Tasting, Ribbed, Marked P. Duperrier, 1829, 3 In. 460.00
Dish, First Standard, Square, Curved Corners, c.1900, 1 3/4 x 10 x 10 In. 865.00
Dish, Shallow, Ridged Ebony Stem, Domed Foot, Engraved, Puiforcat, c.1930, 4 In. 630.00
Ewer, Louis XIV, Plumed Head Handles, Tetard Freres, 9 5/8 In., Pair 4500.00
Ewer, Rushes Finial Cover, Pear Shape, 1880, 14 3/4 In. 7800.00
Muffineer, Pear Shape, Pierced Lid, Embossed, Late 19th Century, 7 7/8 In. 374.00
Platter, Meat, Applied Grapevine, Gadrooned Base, Domed Cover, 12 In. 1380.00
Platter, Oval, Curved Ends, Scrolling, A. Avcoc, Paris, c.1900, 19 x 13 1/4 In. 2760.00
Porringer, Scallop Edge, 2 Pierced Repousse Handles, 1899, 2 In. 616.00
Salt, Dolphin & Shell, Gilt Interior, Odiot, Paris, 3 3/8 In., 4 Piece 4500.00

Salt, Double, Tripod Base, Palmette Feet, Hebrew Lettering, 1805, 5 1/4 In., Pair 2400.00
Salt, Master, Restauration, Paris Assay Office, c.1838, 3 1/4 x 2 3/4 In., Pair 865.00
Sandwich Server, Shell & Thread Pattern, Pierced Handle, c.1880, 11 1/4 In. 525.00
Sauceboat, Neoclassical, Oval, Liner, Eagle's Head Handle, 8 x 10 In. 1265.00
Sauceboat, Undertray, Gadroon Rim, Scroll & Leaf Handle, Engraved, 10 In. 1181.00
Sugar, Restauration, Charles Nicolas Odiot, Bulbous, Reeded, 1819-1838, 4 1/2 In. 259.00
Tablespoon, Provincial, Fiddle Shell Pattern, Inscription, c.1770, 7 7/8 In. 1998.00
Tea & Coffee Set, Empire, 8-Sided Tray, Tetard Freres, 5 Piece 2400.00
Tea & Coffee Set, Tapered, 4 Stepped Supports, Ebony Finials, 4 Piece 1725.00
Teapot, Domed Lid, Flower Finial, Wood Handle, Christofle, 9 1/2 In. 170.00
Tray, 6 Sides, First Standard, c.1900, 13 In. 865.00
Tray, Oval, First Standard, c.1900, 17 1/2 In. 1093.00
Tray, Plate, Molded Rim, Double C-Scroll Handles, 20th Century, 25 3/4 In. 316.00
Tray, Rim With Husk, Beaded Bands, Monogram, Cartier, 13 1/8 In. 920.00
Tureen, Leaves, Shells, Covered, Gold Wash, Fleur De Lis Hallmark, 9 x 13 In., Pair 1035.00
Tureen, Soup, Head Of Ceres, Bud Finial, Puiforcat, Early 20th Century, 11 1/2 In. 4800.00
Vase, Louis Philippe, Reticulated, 2 Handles, Footed, 9 1/4 x 6 In. 635.00
Warming Platter, Domed Cover, Reeded, Leaf Scroll Handles, 18 1/2 In. 575.00
SILVER-GERMAN, Beaker, Lobed, Shells, Chased, Gilt Interior, T. Stoer, 1630, 3 1/2 In. 4800.00
Bowl, 6 Sides, 19th Century, 8 1/2 In. 200.00
Bowl, Cast Ram's Heads, Floral Swags, Classical Scene, Cutout Feet, 7 x 17 x 8 In. ... 748.00
Bowl, Centerpiece, Oval, Scroll Handles, 20th Century, 17 In. 1150.00
Bowl, Centerpiece, Rococo Style, Ram's-Head Handles, Early 19th Century, 14 In. 2070.00
Bowl, Fruit, Rococo Style, c.1900, Marked, 11 1/2 In. 345.00
Bowl, Scalloped Edge, Pierced Garlands, 19th Century, 7 In. 431.00
Box, Bombe Shape, Hinged Cover, 19th Century, 7 In. 805.00
Box, Hinged Cover, Repousse Dolphin Scrolls, Gilt Interior, 2 1/4 In. 690.00
Box, Squat, Bulbous, Hinged Cover, Art Deco, c.1930, 4 1/2 In. 288.00
Box, Squat, Hinged, Serpentine Rim, Hammered, Art Deco, 1930, 10 x 4 In. 518.00
Coffee Set, Neoclassical Style, Bulbous, Late 19th Century, 3 Piece 805.00
Coffee Urn, Spirally Lobed & Fluted, 3 Supports, Figural Finial, 1751, 15 3/4 In. 7200.00
Coffeepot, 1920s, 10 1/2 In. 115.00
Creamer, Cow, Tail Raised To Brush Off Fly, Fly Finial, c.1900, 3 1/4 In. 1232.00
Decanter, 6 Cups, Bottle Shape, Stopper, J.D. Schleissner & Son, 19th Century 1265.00
Dish, Sweetmeat, Scalloped Form, Flowers & Leaf, Scroll Handles, 1680, 5 3/8 In. 3000.00
Figurine, Hound Dog, Head Cover, Neresheimer, Hanau, 1898, 12 In. 7800.00
Figurine, Knight & Lady, Armor, Golden Fleece Collar, Lily Scepter, 14 3/4 In. 8400.00
Figurine, Knight, Decorated Armor, Long Sword, Heraldic Shield, 15 3/4 In. 4200.00
Figurine, Knight, Standing, Shield, Sword, Early 20th Century, 11 1/2 In., Pair 4200.00
Kettle, Hot Water, Stand, Burner, 12 1/2 In. 690.00
Pitcher, Cow, Red Glass Eyes, Tail Raised, Cover, 1900, 3 x 4 1/2 In. 1200.00
Punch Bowl, Swirling Ribs,.925 Silver, Early 20th Century, 12 In. 865.00
Sauceboat, Leaves & Cartouche Of Cherubs & Birds, 1880s, 5 3/4 In. 200.00
Sugar Box, Bombe Form, Lockable Cover, Sprays Of Flowers, c.1765, 6 1/2 In. 2400.00
Tea & Coffee Set, Raised Lids, Spiral Reeding, Bud Finials, 20th Century, 10 In. 460.00
Tea Set, Pear Shape, Scroll Feet, 19th Century, 3 Piece 518.00
Vase, Bulbous Inverted Pear Body, Bowknot Design, 3 Rams Heads Legs, c.1900 .... 310.00
Vase, Tapered Oval Body, Beaded Rim, Marked, Wilkens, c.1920, 7 In. 430.00
SILVER-GREEK, Dedicatory Cross, Emeralds, Pearls, Garnets & Coral, 1721, 9 3/4 In. 9000.00
SILVER-IRISH, Bowl, Sloping Flutes, Scrolls & Cherubs' Heads Border, 1906, 12 1/4 In. 3600.00
Coffeepot, Flat Cover, Baroque Cartouche, Tapered Spout, Dublin, 1714, 8 In. 7200.00
Dish, Strawberry, Dolphin, Swan & Heron Surface, J. Pittar, 1750, 6 3/8 In. 1680.00
Gravy Spoon, Engraved Crest, Tipped Fiddle, T. Farnett, 1824, 12 5/8 In. 460.00
Jug, Beer, Pear Shape, Short Spout, Handle, Joseph Jackson, 1785, 10 In. 1800.00
Marrow Scoop, Widened Bowl, Dublin, 8 1/2 In. 435.00
Sauceboat, Beaded Rim, Double Scroll Handle, M. West, Beaded Rim, 1792, 7 In., Pair .. 3300.00
Stuffing Spoon, Widened Bowl, Charles Marsh, 1824, 12 1/4 In. 375.00
Tea Set, Classical, Engraved Family Crest, Waterhouse, Dublin, 5 Piece 450.00
Teaspoon, Monogram, J. Pittar, 1780s, 5 1/2 In., 6 Piece 345.00
Wine Funnel, Engraved Crest, Late 18th Century, 3 3/4 In. 920.00
Wine Funnel, Sterling, Strainer, Dublin, George IV, c.1829, 6 x 3 1/2 In. 805.00
SILVER-ITALIAN, Basket, Modeled Fruit, Mario Buccellati, 20th Century, Round, 12 In. 4800.00
Lamp, Bouillotte, Lotus Finial, Adjustable Knop, 1900, 18 3/4 x 7 In. 2760.00

Lamp, Oil, 4 Candle Arms, Urn Finial, Italy, c.1810, 20 In. 1035.00
SILVER-JAPANESE, Bowl, Dragon, Rolling Waves, Scalloped, Footed, Oval, 1909, 9 x 6 In. .. 2530.00
  Bowl, Footed, 2 Impressed Seal Marks, 6 1/4 x 9 1/8 In. 635.00
  Bowl, Relief Chrysanthemums & Structures, Kaishu, 1920s, 9 5/8 In. 1725.00
  Bowl, Wisteria, Enamel, Meiji, 5 x 9 1/4 In. 1100.00
  Castor, Spice, Pierced Top, Drum Shape, Enameled Dragons, 4 1/4 In. 460.00
  Figurine, 2 Cranes, Bronze Rockery, 10 In. 1265.00
  Kettle, On Stand, Dragon's Head Finial, Early 20th Century, 13 1/2 In. 1840.00
  Vase, Tapered, Engraved Flowering Plant, Short Neck, 20th Century, 8 In. 310.00
  Writing Box, Prunus, Inkstone, Water Dropper, Chrysanthemums, 2 3/4 In. 402.00
SILVER-MEXICAN, Bowl, Flared Rim, Openwork Loop, Beaded Foot, Spratling, c.1950, 4 In. 489.00
  Bowl, Handles, Pedestal, 20th Century, 7 1/4 x 23 1/4 x 8 3/4 In. 1064.00
  Bowl, Petal Shape, Hammered, Linda Plata 925, 8 1/2 x 2 In. 58.00
  Bowl, Raised On Leaf Scrolled Feet, 9 7/8 In., Pair 400.00
  Cheese Knife, Carved Wooden Handle, Spratling, 6 1/2 In. 345.00
  Cheese Knife, Scroll & Line, Ebony Handle, Sterling, Marked, c.1962, 6 1/4 In. 660.00
  Cordial Set, Allover Fluted & Ribbed, Sterling, 12 Piece 345.00
  Dish, Heart Shape, Ortega 35.00
  Ladle, Oval Bowl, Tapered Flowers & Beaded Handle, Ramirez, 11 In. 247.00
  Pitcher, Aztec Sun, Maciel, Cocktail 144.00
  Pitcher, Hand Hammered, Dot Finish, Scroll Handle, 6 In. 201.00
  Tea & Coffee Set, Gourd Form, Scroll Feet, R. Lopez, 20th Century, 7 Piece 980.00
  Tray, Footed, 3 Compartments, Cabriole Legs, 20th Century, 2 3/4 x 19 x 14 In. 560.00
  Tray, Round, Aztec Calendar Design, Sanborn's, 14 In. 115.00
  Tray, Sanborn's, Handles, 23 x 17 In. 633.00
  Tray, Serpentine Flared Border, 20th Century, 17 In. 201.00
SILVER-NORWEGIAN, Dish, Footed, Flared Rim, Fridtjof Morken, Pair 230.00
  Tea & Coffee Set, Embossed Flowers, F. Domaas, 20th Century, 9 7/8 In. 690.00
  Vase, Bud, Elongated, Spreading Foot, Grooved Edge, c.1960, 8 In. 92.00
SILVER-PERUVIAN, Bowl, Scrolled Rim, 4 Hoof Feet, Peru Plate Esterlina, 11 x 2 1/2 In. ... 55.00
  Frame, Embossed, Mounted Hardwood Strut, Marked, 23 1/2 x 16 In. 288.00
SILVER-POLISH, Tankard, Barrel, Putti, John III Sobieski Medallion, J.G. Holl, 1674, 8 In. .. 6600.00
SILVER-PORTUGUESE, Bowl, Handles, Pedro A Batista, 6 3/4 In. 201.00
  Figurine, Swan, Hinged Wings, Articulated Head & Neck, Liner, 15 1/2 In. 4800.00

SILVER-RUSSIAN. Russian silver is marked with the Cyrillic, or Russian, alphabet. The numbers 84, 88, or 91 indicate the silver content. Russian silver may be higher or lower than sterling standard. Other marks indicate maker, assayer, or city of manufacture. Many pieces of silver made in Russia are decorated with enamel. Faberge pieces are listed in their own category.

SILVER-RUSSIAN, Belt, Niello, Buckle, Stylized Leaves, 35 Links, 1900, 32 In. 896.00
  Belt, Niello, Silver Gilt, Rectangular, Bead Panels, Early 20th Century, 29 In. 865.00
  Box, 2 Eagle Heads, Rosette Within Beads On Cover, Animal Feet, 2 1/8 In. 920.00
  Box, Cigar, Parcel Gilt, Trompe L'Oeil With Labels & Wood Graining, 5 1/2 In. 2185.00
  Box, Cigarette, White Stripes On Cover & Sides, Acanthus Leaves, c.1900, 4 In. 7800.00
  Box, Cloisonne, Floral, Oval, 4 1/2 In. 3450.00
  Box, Gilt & Enamel, 3 Ball Feet, G. Sbitnev, c.1906, 1 3/4 In. 115.00
  Box, Repousse Bugs, Flowers, Twig Handle, Cover, Signed Khlebnikov, 4 x 4 In. 2590.00
  Buckle, Flowers & Leaves, 2 Cathedrals, Dagger Form Clasp, c.1900, 2 3/4 In. 690.00
  Buckle, Stippled Gold Ground, Dagger Form Clasp, Kokoshnik, c.1900, 2 3/4 In. 345.00
  Cigar Case, Cover, Niello, Horses & Wagon, Geometric Borders, 1879, 5 In. 390.00
  Cigarette Case, Cover, Niello, Winter Palace Scene, Moscow, 1871, 5 In. 420.00
  Cigarette Case, Enamel, Owls, 4 1/4 x 3 1/4 x 1/2 In. 2875.00
  Cigarette Case, Enameled, Sixth Artel, Moscow, c.1910, 4 1/4 In. 2185.00
  Cigarette Case, Gilt & Cloisonne, Blue Enamel Ground, Moscow, c.1896, 3 1/4 In. 690.00
  Cigarette Case, Russian Tobacco Labels, Gilt Interior, Moscow, 1887, 3 x 2 In. 1725.00
  Cigarette Case, Troika Scene, Foliage, Moscow, Dated 1885, 4 1/2 In. 450.00
  Cigarette Case, Trompe L'Oeil, Basket Weave, Moscow, 1889, 4 In. 450.00
  Cup, Gilt, Enameled Flowers, 3 Handles, Ovchinnikov, 1900, 2 3/4 In. 5400.00
  Cup, Kiddush, Engraved Scenes, Monogram, HE, 1882, 5 5/8 In., Pair 345.00
  Dish, Presentation, Double Headed Imperial Eagle, Copper, Foliage, 10 In. 450.00
  Drink Set, Etched Architectural Scenes, Tray, 1882, 8 Piece 560.00

Fish Fork, 1800s, 6 In., Pair	230.00
Fork Set, Rounded Shoulders, 84 Zolotniki, St. Petersburg, c.1880, 8 In.	400.00
Frame, Apricot Ground, Pierced Border, Wood Back, c.1900, 19 3/4 In.	9600.00
Kovsh, Foliage & Pink Flowers, Cream & Red Ground, F. Ruckert, 1900, 4 1/2 In.	1150.00
Kovsh, Gilt, Enameled Stylized Leaves, Circle Border, Handle, 1900, 7 1/2 In.	3600.00
Kovsh, Imperial Crown Interior, Foliage On Handle, 1834, 15 1/2 In.	3000.00
Kovsh, Leaves & Cyrillic Rim, Engraved Handle & Face, BC, 1854, 8 In.	805.00
Kovsh, Silver Gilt Interior, Embossed, Melon & Flowers, P. Sazikov, c.1856, 8 In.	1610.00
Ornament, Cap, Double Headed Eagle, Shield Of Peter The Great, 1903, 2 1/2 In.	400.00
Paperweight, Lizard, Green Stone Eyes, Red Stone Tail Top, 1 x 4 In.	225.00
Plaque, Embossed Scene, Crucifix, Men, Women, God In Cloud, 12 x 10 In.	605.00
Plate, Colored Leaves & Flowers, SB Monogram, c.1900, 5 In.	400.00
Sugar & Creamer, Cover, Floral Design, Pedestal Foot, 1896, 4 1/2 In.	448.00
Sugar Sifter, Dots Within Border Of Blue Enamel, I. Khlebnikov, 1900, 4 3/4 In.	115.00
Tankard, Engraved, Bird, Flowers, Russian Mark AN 84, 8 In.	690.00
Tankard, Gilt, Embossed, Chased, Landscape, Hunter Finial, Marked, 9 1/2 In.	3220.00
Tea Strainer, Handle Within Border Of Enamel, I. Khlebnikov, c.1910, 5 In.	630.00
Teapot, Lion Mask On Spout, Foliage On Handle, Flower Finial, 7 1/2 In.	950.00
Teaspoon, Enamel, Late 19th Century, 12 Piece	690.00
Teaspoon, St. George Slaying Dragon Finial, A. Kuzmitchev, c.1897, 4 1/2 In.	170.00
Teaspoon, Standing Teddy Bear Handle, Enameled, 5 5/8 In.	170.00
Vase, Geometric Flower Ornament, V. Savinkov, c.1891, 3 In.	460.00
Vase, Tapered, Cylindrical, Band Of Lozenges, Marked, Zolotnik, c.1910, 13 In.	489.00
SILVER-SPANISH, Bowl, Everted Upturned Rim, 18th Century, 15 1/2 x 10 3/8 In.	1150.00
Dish, Chased Birds & Animals, Flowers, Domed Center, 1750s, 16 3/4 In.	7800.00

SILVER-STERLING. Sterling silver is made with 925 parts silver out of 1,000 parts of metal. The word *sterling* is a quality guarantee used in the United States after about 1860. The word was used much earlier in England and Ireland. Pieces listed here are not identified by country. Other pieces of sterling quality silver are listed under Silver-American, Silver-English, etc.

SILVER-STERLING, Basket, Glass Lined, Double Handle, Early 20th Century, 3 x 4 1/2 In.	146.00
Bonbon, Hammered Body, Pierced Flower Handles, Cellini Craft, 8 In.	345.00
Book Cover, Cherubs, Guest Register, Brooklands, 1930s, 8 1/2 x 11 In.	201.00
Bowl, Hammered, Footed, Arthur Stone, 1907, 2 x 4 1/2 In.	520.00
Bowl, Hand Hammered, Footed, 5 x 3 In.	144.00
Bowl, Lobed, Hammered Surface, Rolled Rim, Arts & Crafts, c.1915, 7 1/4 In.	242.00
Bowl, Openwork Flower Rim, Lobed Sides, Monogram, Simons Bro., 10 1/2 In.	287.00
Bowl, Vegetable, Octagonal, Detachable Handle On Cover, 1918, 10 In., Pair	1750.00
Box, Enamel, Silver Gilt Interior, 3 3/8 x 2 3/4 In.	373.00
Box, Wax Stamp, Flower Garlands, Gold Wash Divided Interior, 1 1/8 x 5 3/4 In.	385.00
Brush & Mirror Set, Arts & Crafts, Hammered, Embossed Flower, 9 1/2 In.	489.00
Cake Stand, 3 Tiers, Center Looped Handle, Pierced Rims, c.1900, 16 x 11 In.	1232.00
Candelabrum is listed in its own category.	
Candlesticks are listed in their own category.	
Cann, Honeycomb, Middle Diamond Panels, Birds, Insects Rim, 3 1/2 In.	385.00
Card Case, Relief, Man Playing Mandolin, Mother, Daughter, Trees, Hallmark	275.00
Chalice, Cross Finial, Overall Floral & Grape, Gold Wash, Benziger, 13 1/2 In.	750.00
Cigarette Case, 3 Geese In Flight Over Marsh, Silver Gilt Interior, 5 x 8 In.	805.00
Cigarette Case, Hunter & Dog With Bird In Flight, Silver Gilt Interior, 6 In.	545.00
Cigarette Case, Jumping Sailfish In Sea, Silver Gilt Interior, 5 3/4 x 3 In.	690.00 to 747.00
Coffee Set, Art Deco, Coffeepot, Teapot, Creamer, Sugar, Whiting Mfg. Co., 1923	850.00
Coffee Set, Pendant Flower Blossoms, Scrolled Handles, 3 Piece	805.00
Compote, Oak Leaves, Acorns, Lion Heads, Round Base, Leaf, Bead, 9 1/2 x 9 1/4 In.	920.00
Compote, Pierced, Scroll Feet, Theodor Starr, Early 20th Century, 3 5/8 x 9 In.	230.00
Cordial, Marked Y.T.K., 5 In., 12 Piece	335.00
Cup, Scalloped Feet, Overlapping Handle, Gilt Interior, 3 1/4 In.	690.00
Cup, Squat Cylindrical Shape, Flared, Hammered, Arts & Crafts, c.1903, 4 1/4 In.	460.00
Decanter, Pheasant Shape, Hinged Wings, 6 x 13 1/2 In., Pair	605.00
Decanter, Star, Trellis Pattern, Spherical Stopper, Scrolls, 10 1/4 x 5 x 4 In.	405.00
Decanter Frame, Basket Weave, 8 1/2 In.	190.00
Dish, Lobed, Repousse, Chased Floral Swags, Reticulated Rim, 12 In.	275.00

Dish, Oval, Reticulated Sides, Putti, Hallmark, c.1905, 3 1/2 x 6 x 8 1/2 In. 460.00
Dish, Pierced Palm Fronds Border, Footed, Glass Insert, 3 1/2 x 2 1/8 In. 220.00
Dish, Shell Shape, c.1935, 12 In. 375.00
Document Clip, Eagle Atop Shield, Shreve, Crump & Low, Boston, 4 x 5 In. 405.00
Dresser Bottle, Cut Crystal, Trumpet Shape Body, 7 1/2 In. 215.00
Dresser Set, Engraved Caliphs Of Cairo, 1940s, 3 Piece 200.00
Epergne, Basket Rim, Scroll Rim, Husk Pattern Sides, 10 x 7 1/8 In. 1840.00
Fork & Spoon Set, Napoleon & Josephine, Rampant Lion & Crown 220.00
Frame, Arts & Crafts, Hammered, Embossed Daisies, Hallmark, 9 x 6 In. 748.00
Frame, Chased Bird & Flower Decoration, 19 x 15 In. 520.00
Frame, Cherub, Blue Basalt Panel, Bust Portrait, Greek Warrior, 1895, 4 x 3 1/4 In. 80.00
Frame, Photograph, Rectangular, Repousse, Reed & Ribbon, 9 x 7 In. 175.00
Funnel, Wine, Fluted Bowl, Pierced Strainer, Shell Form Clip, c.1836, 5 1/2 In. 1456.00
Goblet Set, Water, Flared Bowl, Simple Stem, 6 Piece 785.00
Ladle, Engraved, Coconut Shell Shape, Wood Handle, 15 In. 345.00
Ladle, Victorian, 1846, 13 1/4 In. 172.00
Letter Opener, Fire Opal Inset, Sunflower Border, 8 1/4 In. 112.00
Letter Opener, Pierced, Hearts, 3-Leaf Clover, Dragon, 9 1/4 In. 259.00
Menorah, Birds, Branches, 1920s, 10 In. 410.00
Mirror, Dressing Table, Cartouche Scene, Embossed, 1900, 15 1/2 x 11 In. 920.00
Mirror, Repousse Scroll, Courting Couple, Landscape, 19 1/2 x 13 1/4 In. 1093.00
Mustard Pot, Leaf Thumbpiece, Cobalt Blue Liner 135.00
Mustard Pot, Squat, Urn Shape, Hinged Cover, Handle, c.1837, 3 1/4 In. 202.00
Napkin Rings are listed in their own category.
Pipe Tray, 8 Sides, Concave, Beaded Corners, Palmette Baluster, Match Safe, 7 In. 230.00
Pitcher, Urn Form, Scrolling Handle, Monogram E, Early 1900s, 9 1/2 In. 475.00
Pitcher, Water, Classical Shape, Flowers, Vine, c.1930, 3 1/2 Pt., 9 In. 310.00
Pitcher, Water, Urn Shape, Geometric Handle, Early 20th Century, 8 In. 475.00
Plaque, Medieval Folklore, Castle, Velvet Cover, 10 1/4 x 7 5/8 In., Pair 495.00
Plate, Bread & Butter, Monogram, 6 3/8 In. 72.00
Pot, Demitasse, Turkish Style, Bulbous, Reeded Ball Lid, c.1891, 8 1/4 In. 748.00
Salad Servers, Hammered, Monogram, Impressed, 1900s, 9 In. 173.00
Salt & Pepper, Embossed Floral, Leaf & Scroll, Soppini, 7 1/4 In. 99.00
Shoehorn, Tongue Form Body, c.1875, 5 1/4 In. 134.00
Spade, Pitchfork, Filmore, Miniature, 4 x 3/4 In. 56.00
Spoon, Souvenir, see Souvenir category.
Sugar Castor, Scroll Repousse, Loring & Andrews, 6 3/4 In. 259.00
Sugar Tongs, George III, Acorn Bowl, Tapered Handles, c.1790, 5 1/2 In., Pair 105.00
Tazza, Leaf Decoration, Trumpet Feet, Early 20th Century, 6 3/4 x 2 1/2 In., Pair 258.00
Tea & Coffee Set, Black Resin Finials & Handles, Impressed 950, 5 Piece 800.00
Tea & Coffee Set, Blossom Design, Ivory Handles, Jensen Style, 1900s, 7 Piece 2415.00
Tea & Coffee Set, Georgian Style, Monogram, 5 Piece 460.00
Tea & Coffee Set, Gourd Shape, Blossom Finials, Jensen Style, 7 Piece 3450.00
Tea Set, Ribbed, Embossed Ribbons, Squared Handles, Acorn Finials, 5 Piece 935.00
Tea Set, Ribbed, R W & S, 3 Piece 390.00
Tong Set, Elongated Handle, Monogram, Early 19th Century, 4 Piece 110.00
Tray, Edwardian, Rectangular, Gadroon Border, Handle, 2 x 16 1/2 x 29 3/4 In. 2530.00
Tray, Smoking, Attached Lighter, 14 x 10 In. 290.00
Vanity Jar, Pressed Glass, Victorian, Charles May, c.1899, 6 x 3 In., Pair 1150.00
Vanity Jar, Silver Mounted, Pressed Glass, Hinged Cover, 4 1/2 x 3 1/2 In., Pair 290.00
Vase, Baluster, Cushion Foot, Flaring Neck, Engraved, Art Nouveau, 1900, 10 In. 980.00
Vase, Basket Form, Hinged Handle, Pierced Turned Rim, 1920s, 15 In. 365.00
Vase, Bud, Cobalt Blue Glass Insert, c.1900, 8 In. 375.00
Vase, Trumpet, Weighted, Chased Flowers, 18 In. 210.00
Vase, Urn Shape, Flowers, Scrolling, Engraved, Weighted Base, 12 x 4 1/2 In. 475.00
Wine, Beaded Trim, Marked Y.T.K., 6 1/4 In., 12 Piece 670.00
Wine Coaster, Dutch Genre Scenes, Felt Liner, 5 1/8 In. 105.00
Wine Coaster, Flowers & Leaf, Scroll & Berry Design, 1873, 7 1/2 In. 730.00
Wine Cooler, Relief, Embossed, Grape Clusters, Wood Footed Base, 3 x 7 In., Pair 1125.00
Youth Set, Monogrammed Jane, W.B. Kerr, 1915, 6 Piece 675.00
SILVER-SWEDISH, Box, Square, Hinged, Commemorative Medal, Marked, Erik Fleming, 6 In. 460.00
Dish, Rolled Rim, 2 Chased Anthemion Handles, K. Anderson, 1930, 14 In. 195.00

SILVER-TURKISH, Console, Scroll Handles, Woman's Head Finial, Flowers, 7 x 15 x 5 In. ... 690.00
  Tray, Raised Floral Repousse, Vine Handles, Border, 21 x 12 In. 690.00
  Tray, Rectangular, Raised Floral Repousse, Mavlana, 20 x 11 In. 865.00
  Vase, Gilt, Tulip Shape, Applied Flowers, Footed, 19th Century, 7 1/2 In. 1955.00

SINCLAIRE cut glass was made by H.P. Sinclaire and Company of
Corning, New York, between 1905 and 1929. He cut glass made at
other factories until 1920. Pieces were made of crystal as well as
amber, blue, green, or ruby glass. Only a small percentage of Sinclaire
glass is marked with the S in a wreath.
  Compote, Twist Stem, Blue, 6 x 7 1/4 In. 56.00
  Tea Set, Globular Teapot, Cover, 5 Mugs, Engraved Scrolled Floral Vines, 6 Piece 2090.00

SKIING, see Sports category.

SLAG GLASS resembles a marble cake. It can be streaked with different
colors. There were many types made from about 1880. Caramel slag is
the incorrect name for Chocolate glass. Pink slag was an American
Victorian product made by Harry Barstow and Thomas E.A. Dugan at
Indiana, Pennsylvania. Purple and blue slag were made in American
and English factories. Red slag is a very late Victorian and twentieth-
century glass. Other colors are known but are of less importance to the
collector. New versions of chocolate glass and colored slag glass are
being made.
  Blue, Bowl, Hobstar, Kanawha, 6 3/4 In. 45.00
  Blue, Tumbler, England, 4 3/8 In. 30.00
  Caramel slag is listed in the Chocolate Glass category.
  Light Green, Saltshaker, Melon Ribbed, Paneled Neck, 3 1/2 In. 70.00
  Pink, Tumbler, Inverted Fan & Feather, 4 In. 150.00
  Pink, Water Set, Inverted Fan & Feather, 5 Piece 5000.00
  Purple, Bowl, Open Edge, Basket Weave, Sowerby 125.00
  Red, Orange, Ashtray, Macbeth-Evans, 4 3/4 In. 115.00
  Yellow, Orange, Coaster & Ashtray, Vidrio, 6 In. 20.00

SLEEPY EYE collectors look for anything bearing the image of the nineteenth-century Indian chief with the drooping eyelid. The Sleepy Eye
Milling Co., Sleepy Eye, Minnesota, used his portrait in advertising
from 1883 to 1921. It offered many premiums, including stoneware
and pottery steins, crocks, bowls, mugs, and pitchers, all decorated
with the famous profile of the Indian. The popular pottery was made
by Western Stoneware, Weir Pottery Company, and other companies
long after the flour mill went out of business in 1921. Reproductions
of the pitchers are being made today. The original pitchers came in
only five sizes: 4 inches, 5 1/4 inches, 6 1/2 inches, 8 inches, and 9
inches. The Sleepy Eye image was also used by companies unrelated
to the flour mill.
  Lemonade Set, No. 5 Pitcher, 6 Tall Mugs 1875.00
  Mug, Green, Cream, Tan, c.1910, 4 1/2 In. 86.00
  Mug, Short 45.00
  Mug, Yellow & Blue 800.00
  Pitcher, No. 3, Blue & Gray, Circle Mark, 6 1/2 In. 900.00
  Pitcher, No. 4, Black & Gold, 8 In. 2500.00
  Pitcher, No. 4, Blue Scalloped Rim, Weir, 8 In. 750.00
  Pitcher, No. 5, Brown & Yellow, 9 In. 3600.00
  Pitcher, No. 5, Dark Blue, Indian & Teepees, 9 In. 255.00
  Pitcher, Standing Indian, Light Blue, Gray, 8 1/2 In. 1075.00
  Stein, All Brown, 7 3/4 In. 675.00
  Stein, Blue & White, 7 3/4 In. ....175.00 to 330.00
  Stein, Light Brown & White, 7 3/4 In. 925.00
  Sugar & Creamer, 3 1/4 In. 400.00
  Teapot, Brown, Decal 575.00
  Thermometer 800.00

Vase, Cattail, All Brown, 8 1/2 In. 2300.00
Vase, Cattail, All White, 8 1/2 In. 7000.00
Vase, Cattail, Dragonfly, Frog, 8 1/2 In. 305.00

SLOT MACHINES are included in the Coin-Operated Machine category.

SMITH BROTHERS glass was made after 1878. Alfred and Harry Smith had worked for the Mt. Washington Glass Company in New Bedford, Massachusetts, for seven years before going into their own shop. They made many pieces with enamel decoration.

Smith Bros. Co.

Bowl, Multicolored Flowers, Yellow Rim, White Dots, 2 3/8 x 2 3/4 In. 100.00
Bowl, Multicolored Pansy Design, Blue Rim, White Dots, 2 1/2 x 2 3/4 In. 110.00
Cracker Jar, Gold Flowers, Embossed Balled Lid, 9 1/2 In. 390.00
Cracker Jar, Melon Ribbed, Applied Gold Flowers & Child, Burmese, 9 1/2 In. 290.00
Jar, Potpourri, Silver Plated Cover & Insert, Hand Painted Yellow Rose 470.00
Sugar & Creamer, Melon Rib, Gold Prunus Blossom, Silver Plated Hardware 270.00
Sugar & Creamer, Sunflower, Portrait Of Man, Marked, 3 1/2 x 3 1/4 In. 403.00
Sugar Shaker, Ribbed, Enameled, Flowers, Silver Plated Top, 6 In. 290.00
Vase, Daisies, Signed, 5 1/2 In. 120.00
Vase, Double Canteen, Painted, Burmese, Wisteria, Columns, Boats, Signed, 7 In. 145.00

SNOW BABIES, made from bisque and spattered with glitter sand, were first manufactured in 1864 by Hertwig and Company of Thuringia. Other German and Japanese companies copied the Hertwig designs. Originally, Snow Babies were made of candy and used as Christmas decorations. There are also Snow Babies tablewares made by Royal Bayreuth. Copies of the small Snow Babies figurines are being made today and can easily confuse the collector.

Candy Box, 4 Teeth, Faux Hands In Muff, c.1900, 12 In. 950.00
Figurine, 3 Babies Sitting On Sled, Germany, 1910, 3 In. 300.00
Figurine, Baby Playing Drum, U.S. Zone, Germany, 2 In. 75.00
Figurine, Baby With Skis, Polar Bear Nipping Butt, Germany, 1 3/4 In. 240.00
Pin Box, Cover, Babies Sledding, Royal Bayreuth, 5 1/4 In. 260.00
Plate, Babies On Ice, One Falling Down, Royal Bayreuth, 6 1/4 In. 185.00

SNUFF BOTTLES are listed in the Bottle category.

SNUFFBOXES held snuff. Taking snuff was popular long before cigarettes became available. The gentleman or lady would take a small pinch of the ground tobacco or snuff in the fingers, then sniff it and sneeze. Snuffboxes were made of many materials, including gold, silver, enameled metal, and wood. Most snuffboxes date from the late eighteenth or early nineteenth centuries.

Agate, Gold Mounted, Bowfront, Germany, Late 18th Century, 3 In. 1840.00
Brass, Gilded, Thomas Jefferson, England, c.1807 .... 4400.00
Burlwood, Ivory Portrait, Young Woman, Tortoiseshell Lined, c.1820, 3 3/8 In. 488.75
Carved Horn, Boot Shape, Oval Lid, 2 1/2 In. 140.00
Enamel, Brass, 19th Century, 2 In. 170.00
Enamel, Figures In Country Landscape, Metal Mounts, Battersea, c.1760, 2 1/2 In. 360.00
Enamel, Green, Pink Flowers, Brass, France, 19th Century, 2 In. 170.00
Enamel, Spray Of Flowers On Lid, Scrolls On Sides, c.1835, 3 3/4 In. 3600.00
Enamel, Transfer, Landscape, Oval, Battersea, c.1760, 1 1/8 x 2 1/2 x 1 1/2 In. 365.00
Gold, Enamel, Harvest Trophy Cover, Flower Sides, Geneva, 1825, 2 7/8 In. 4200.00
Gold, Indian Woman Portrait Cover, Continental, 1900, 2 3/4 In. Diam. 1800.00
Horn, 19 Separate Sections, Rocker Shape Bottom, c.1850, 2 1/2 x 1 3/4 In. 170.00
Horn, Intricate Dark Inlay On White Bone Field, Inlaid Lid, 3 3/4 x 1 1/2 In. 190.00
Horn, Tortoise Border, 13 Diamond Shapes, G. Lockwood, 3 1/4 x 1 3/8 In. 240.00
Mahogany, Scenic Cover, Painted, Riverside Town, Mountains, Rectangular, 3 1/8 In. 90.00
Papier-Mache, Black, Inlaid Mother-Of-Pearl, Hinged Lid, 1 1/2 x 4 x 2 1/2 In. 70.00
Papier-Mache, Lacquer, Pewter Inlay, Scotland, 1700s, 1 3/4 x 1 1/4 x 3/4 In. 195.00
Papier-Mache, Paper Transfer, Family Scene, Man, Bundle Of Wood, Round, 3 1/2 In. 110.00
Papier-Mache, Paper Transfer, Soldier Homecoming Scene, Mark, Round, 3 1/2 In. 110.00
Papier-Mache, Paper Transfer, Victorian Girl, Yellow Background, Round, 2 3/4 In. 110.00
Pewter, Horse On Lid, 1860s, 2 1/2 x 1 1/2 In. 30.00

Porcelain, Landscape, Couple In 18th Century Dress, Germany, 19th Century, 3 In. 200.00
Pressed Wood, Uncle Sam, John Bull, Birchbark, 1876, 2 3/4 x 1 1/4 x 7/8 In. 345.00
Silver, Racing & Hunting Scene, Fitted Case, England, 1929, 3 In. 460.00
Silver, Rectangular, Leaf Design, Continental, 1 7/8 In. 46.00
Sterling Silver, Mocha Agate, Gilded, John Carman, London, c.1755, 2 1/2 In. 920.00
Sterling Silver, Oval, Hinged Lid, c.1876, 1 x 3 1/2 x 2 1/2 In. 179.00
Tortoiseshell, Copper Beading, Mt. Vesuvius On Lid, 1 x 3 In. 300.00
Tortoiseshell, Copper Inlay Of Hearts & Winged Lion, 1 x 2 1/4 In. 80.00
Tortoiseshell Front & Back, 18th Century Boy & Girl, Book Form, 3 3/8 In. 316.00

SOAPSTONE is a mineral that was used for foot warmers or griddles
because of its heat-retaining properties. Soapstone was carved into figurines and bowls in many countries in the nineteenth and twentieth
centuries. Most of the soapstone seen today is from China or Japan. It
is still being carved in the old styles.

Figurine, Foo Dog, Engraved Block, 7 In., Pair 90.00
Figurine, Hsi Wang, On Lion's Back, 19th Century, 11 3/4 In. 315.00
Figurine, Servant, Kneeling Before Woman, Holding Fan, 3 In. 115.00
Indian Head, Early 19th Century, 9 In. 395.00

SOFT PASTE is a name for a type of pottery. Although it looks very
much like porcelain, it is a chemically different material. Most of the
soft-paste wares were made in the early nineteenth century. Other
pieces may be listed under Gaudy Dutch or Leeds.

Bowl, Basket Of Strawberries, Roses, Red, Green, Pink, Yellow Border, 8 1/4 In. 880.00
Creamer, Molded Face Of Bearded Man, Brown Rim Stripe, 4 1/2 In. 220.00
Gravy Boat, Ladle & Underplate, Green Foliage, Berries, 8 3/8 x 10 1/2 In. 410.00
Pepper Pot, Cobalt Blue Scalloped Line & Feather, 4 1/2 In. 360.00
Pitcher, 2 Black Transfers, Hunters, Horse & Dog, Silver Luster Neck, 7 5/8 In. 440.00
Pitcher, 2 Transfer Scenes, 1 Masonic, 1 Sailor & Sweetheart, Verse, 8 1/2 In. 550.00
Pitcher, Dark Red King's Rose, Blue, Yellow Flowers, Green Leaves, 5 5/8 In. 220.00
Pitcher, Grapevines & Shells, Pink Reserves Each Side, Leaf Handle, 6 In. 99.00
Pitcher, Long Eliza, Pagoda & Garden, John Saunders, 1804, 8 1/2 In. 440.00
Pitcher, Red Transfer, Coat Of Arms, 2 Figures, Royal Shepherds, 4 3/4 In. 190.00
Pitcher, Triple Embossed Joker Face, 6 x 5 3/4 In. 300.00
Plate, Floral Center, Grapevine Border, Dark Purple, Green, Yellow, 8 7/8 In. 110.00
Plate, Green, Yellow Pineapple, Blue, Gold Leaf Border, 6 1/2 In. 550.00
Plate, King's Rose, 6 In. 80.00
Plate, King's Rose, 8 In. 185.00
Plate, King's Rose, 10 In. 190.00
Sugar, Strawberry, Ring Handles, Brown Stripes, Yellow Seeds, Berry Finial, 5 1/4 In. 220.00
Teapot, Gaudy Flowers, Leaf Handle, Beehive Finial, 7 1/8 In. 360.00
Teapot, Strawberry, Raised Design, Gadrooning, Leaf Handle, Berry Finial, Lid, 6 3/8 In. .. 440.00
Waste Bowl, Oriental Panels Of Outdoor Scenes, Blue Dots, 3 x 6 In. 300.00

SOUVENIRS of a trip—what could be more fun? Our ancestors enjoyed
the same thing and souvenirs were made for almost every location.
Most of the souvenir pottery and porcelain pieces of the nineteenth
century were made in England or Germany, even if the picture showed
a North American scene. In the twentieth century, the souvenir china
business seems to have gone to the manufacturers in Japan, Taiwan,
Hong Kong, England, and America. Another popular souvenir item is
the souvenir spoon, made of sterling or silver plate. These are usually
made in the country pictured on the spoon. Related pieces may be
found in the Coronation and World's Fair categories.

Ashtray, Blue Hole, Castalia, Ohio, Tin 15.00
Ashtray, Hotel Mapes, 2 Cowboys, Silkscreen 28.00
Ashtray, Olympic, 1928, Amsterdam, Glass, Amber, Octagonal, 6 1/2 In. 253.00
Ashtray, Reno, Nevada, Primadonna, Amber, Silkscreen, Cabaret Girl, Glass 6.00
Badge, Olympic, 1940, Tokyo, Silvered, Colored Enameled, Green Moire Rosette 2530.00
Ball, Olympic, 1968, Mexico City, Porcelain, Soccer, Brazilian Champions, 5 1/2 In. 242.00
Book, Olympic, 2000, Sydney, Olympic Torch Relay, 9 x 11 In., 146 Pages 115.00
Bracelet, Olympic, 1956, Melbourne, Gilt, Color Enameled, Rings, 8 3/8 In. .... *Illus* 230.00

Souvenir, Bracelet, Olympic, 1956, Melbourne,
Gilt, Color Enameled, Rings, 8 3/8 In.

Souvenir, Pennant, West Virginia,
Frontiersman, Orange Felt, 7 3/4 In.

Souvenir, Pennant, Alabama, View Of Capital,
Four Color Picture, Blue Flannel, 26 1/4 In.

Souvenir, Plate,
Minnesota, Land
Of 10, 000 Lakes,
Porcelain, 5 In.

Brochure, Olympic, 1960, Rome, Closing Ceremony Rules, Regulations, 5 1/2 x 8 1/2 In. ... 115.00
Cigarette Case, Olympic, 1964, Tokyo, Silvered, Rings, 6 1/2 x 3 In. 196.00
Creamer, Atlantic City, New Jersey Glass, Ruby Stain, 1923 .... 30.00
Creamer, Green Mills Gardens Park, Illinois, Custard Glass 35.00
Cup, Atlantic City, New Jersey Glass, Ruby Stain, 1899 .... 40.00
Cup, Custard, Elk's Carnival, Hancock, Michigan, 1902 .... 60.00
Cup, Savin Rock Park, Connecticut, Glass, Ruby Stain 45.00
Diploma, Olympic, 1944, London, Lists U.S. Athletes, 16 1/2 x 14 1/4 In. 360.00
Dish, Royal Canadian Mounted Police On Horseback, 1950s, 7 In. 10.00
Emblem, Red, Chinese-Burma, Flying Tiger, Shield Shape, Black 110.00
Flag Holder, Uncle Sam Standing, Porcelain, God Bless America, Troy, N.Y., 1976, 15 In. 11.00
Goblet, Huntington, Indiana, Glass, Ruby Stain 30.00
Handkerchief, Remember The Maine, Uncle Sam, White Silk, Frame, 18 1/2 In. 287.00
Hatchet, Milk Glass, Pen Mar Park, Pennsylvania 50.00
Hatchet, Wood, Ottawa Fair, Montreal, Canada 15.00
Jewelry Box, Niagara Falls, New York, Glass, Green 25.00
Kettle, Niagara Falls, New York, Glass, Green 20.00
Lighter, Olympic, 1964, Tokyo, Silvered, Color Rings, Japanese Legend On Back 173.00
Match Holder, Aurora, Indiana, The Plucky City 30.00
Medal, Olympic, 1920, Antwerp, Bronze 414.00
Medal, Olympic, 1988, Calgary, Mayor's Presentation, Gold Plated, Case, Brochure 184.00
Mortar & Pestle, Jamaica, West Indies, Wood, 3 x 5 1/2 In. 5.75
Mortar & Pestle, Terra-Cotta, Says Spain, 5 1/2 x 3 1/2 In. 11.00
Mug, Brown, Incised Uncle Tom's Cabin, Paint Lick, Ky., Applied Strap Handle, 4 1/2 In. 60.00
Mug, Cedar Point, Ohio, Glass, Clear 35.00
Pennant, Alabama, View Of Capital, Four Color Picture, Blue Flannel, 26 1/4 In. .... *Illus* 20.00
Pennant, Cedar Point, Ohio 20.00
Pennant, Minneapolis, Minnesota, Felt, Colored Feathers, 1950, 17 In. 20.00
Pennant, Oglebay Park, Wheeling, West Virginia 15.00
Pennant, West Virginia, Frontiersman, Orange Felt, 7 3/4 In. .... *Illus* 20.00
Pillow Case, Musicians & Dancer Scene, 1950s, 19 In. 20.00
Pin, Olympic, 1956, Melbourne, Kenya Team Pin, Multicolored 276.00
Pin, Uncle Sam, Celluloid, Hand Painted, Spanish American War, 1898, 2 5/8 In. 52.00
Pipe, Cadillac, Michigan, Glass, Orange 15.00
Pitcher, Atlantic City, New Jersey, Custard Glass, 8 In. 255.00
Pitcher, Revere Beach Park, Massachusetts, Glass, Ruby Stain, 1909, 8 In. 150.00

Plate, Minnesota, Land Of 10,000 Lakes, Porcelain, 5 In. .... *Illus*   8.00
Pocket Knife, Olympic, 1936, Berlin, Steel, Color Rings, Brown Suede Pouch 173.00
Poster Set, Olympic, 1980, Moscow, Stiff Paper, Color Folder, 9 x 13 In., 37 Piece 173.00
Program, Olympic, 1924, Paris, July 7, Daily, Javelin Thrower On Cover, 9 x 11 In. 201.00
Punch Cup, Port Huron, Michigan, Glass, Ruby Stain 40.00
Scarf, Olympic, 1968, Grenoble, Silk, Winter Events, Pierre Ambrogiani, 33 x 33 In. 201.00
Shot Glass, Durand, Michigan, Glass, Ruby Flash 35.00
Spoon, Barcelona Crest 8.00
Spoon, Berlin Crest, Brandenburger Tor, Silver Plate 12.00
Spoon, Bruxellus Top St. George Crest 12.00
Spoon, Daffodil, Holland, Brecks, Silver Plate 12.00
Spoon, Denver, Bronze, Die Cut Miner Holding Pick & Nugget 75.00
Spoon, Dome & VW Cathedral Crest, Koln 18.00
Spoon, Hamburg Crest, Silver Plate 12.00
Spoon, Moederdag, Holland, 1971 ....   12.00
Spoon, Mother's Day, England, 1973 ....   10.00
Spoon, Padova Crest, Silver Plate 6.00
Spoon, Silver Plate, 5,000,000,000 For Defense, Banner Handle, Feb. 15, 1898, 4 In. ...   57.00
Spoon, Sterling Silver, Alaska, Totem Pole Stem, Bowl Miner Panning Gold, 3 5/8 In. ...   45.00
Spoon, Sterling Silver, Colonel Davenport's Home, Arsenal Island 85.00
Spoon, Sterling Silver, Colorado Burro, Floral Stem 49.00
Spoon, Sterling Silver, Flatiron Building, New York 30.00
Spoon, Sterling Silver, Fort Worth 30.00
Spoon, Sterling Silver, Grand Canyon, Chief On Stem, Indian & Horse On Bowl, 6 In. ...   90.00
Spoon, Sterling Silver, Grand Canyon, Indian Chief, Gold Wash Bowl, 6 In. 120.00
Spoon, Sterling Silver, Mexican Cowboy, Embossed Stem Front & Back 70.00
Spoon, Sterling Silver, Milwaukee, Flowered Stem, Gold Wash Bowl, Engraved Aces ...   75.00
Spoon, Sterling Silver, Montana Cowboy On Steed, 5 3/8 In. 80.00
Spoon, Sterling Silver, Montana Cowboy, Miner, Indian Symbols 60.00
Spoon, Sterling Silver, Phoenix, Flowered Stem, 4 Aces Enameled In Bowl, 5 1/8 In. 250.00
Spoon, Sterling Silver, S. Dakota Seal, Stem Enameled, Bowl Engraved 110.00
Spoon, Sterling Silver, Texas Cowboy, State Symbols, Star, Longhorn, 5 3/4 In. 70.00
Spoon, Sterling Silver, Twin Falls, Idaho 30.00
Spoon, Sterling Silver, Uncle Sam On Handle, 1898 In Bowl, 6 In. 150.00
Spoon, Sterling Silver, Uncle Sam On Handle, 1898, 4 In. 69.00
Spoon, Sterling Silver, View Of Rookwood Pottery Building, Cincinnati, Ohio, 5 3/8 In. .   374.00
Spoon, Sterling Silver, West Point Cadet, 4 1/8 In. 85.00
Spoon, Sterling Silver, Williamsport, Indiana 30.00
Spoon, Sterling Silver, Wyoming Cowboy Lassoing Steer, Bear, Elk, Bison, 5 7/8 In. 80.00
Stein, Florida, Alligator Handle, Pewter Lid, 4 In. 218.00
Sword, Milk Glass, Atlantic City, New Jersey 20.00
Ticket, Fats Domino Concert, Loyola Field House, Unused, April 1956, 90 Piece 1265.00
Ticket, Olympic, 1980, Lake Placid, Closing Ceremony, Pair 115.00
Vase, Cedar Point, Ohio, Ruby Stain, 1907 ....   100.00
Vase, Missaukee Park, Lake City, Michigan, Ruby Stain 40.00

SPANGLE GLASS is multicolored glass made from odds and ends of colored glass rods. It includes metallic flakes of mica covered with gold,
silver, nickel, or copper. Spangle glass is usually cased with a thin
layer of clear glass over the multicolored layer. Similar glass is listed
in the Vasa Murrhina category.

Basket, Blue Over White, Spangle Panels, Looped Thorn Handle, 8 In. 190.00
Basket, Red Over White, Spangled Interior, Twisted Handle, 10 In. 190.00
Tumble-Up, Carafe, Tumbler, Pink To White, Mica Flecks, 7 1/4 In. 173.00
Vase, Double Gourd, Maroon Spatter, Gold Spangles, Glossy, 10 1/2 In., Pair 173.00

SPANISH LACE is a type of Victorian glass that has a white lace design.
Blue, yellow, cranberry, or clear glass was made with this distinctive
white pattern. It was made in England and the United States after 1885.
Copies are being made.

Sugar Shaker, Cranberry, 4 1/2 In. 325.00
Sugar Shaker, Vaseline, 4 1/2 In. 275.00
Sugar Shaker, White, 4 1/2 In. 110.00

Spatter Glass, Barber Bottle, Blue & Oxblood
Spatter, 1885-1925, 11 In.

Spatter Glass, Barber Bottle, Pink,
Yellow & Green Spatter, 11 In.

Spatter Glass, Barber Bottle, White, Yellow-Green
& Red Spatter, Zigzag Ribbing, 11 In.

SPATTER GLASS is a multicolored glass made from many small pieces of different colored glass. It is sometimes called *End-of-Day* glass. It is still being made.

Barber Bottle, Blue & Oxblood Spatter, 1885-1925, 11 In. .... *Illus*	231.00
Barber Bottle, Pink, Yellow & Green Spatter, 11 In. .... *Illus*	440.00
Barber Bottle, White, Yellow-Green & Red Spatter, Zigzag Ribbing, 11 In. .... *Illus*	231.00
Bowl, Amethyst, Multicolored Flowers & Butterfly, Ruffled Edge, 8 3/4 In.	700.00
Pitcher, Sapphire Blue, White Spatter, 8 Sides, Clear Applied Handle, 8 1/4 In.	175.00
Pitcher, White Spatter, Clear Handle, 8 1/2 In.	175.00
Vase, Basket Weave, Blues, Pinks, White, Tortoise, Ruffled Edge, 9 In.	80.00

SPATTERWARE is the creamware or soft paste dinnerware decorated with colored spatter designs. The earliest pieces were made in the late eighteenth century, but most of the spatterware found today was made from about 1800 to 1850, or it is a form of kitchen crockery with added spatter designs, made in the late nineteenth and twentieth centuries. The early spatterware was made in the Staffordshire district of England for sale in America. The later kitchen type is an American product.

Bowl, Bull's-Eye, Rainbow, Purple & Black, 10 1/2 In.	5500.00
Bowl, Sugar, Cover, Pinwheel, Blue, 4 In.	135.00
Bowl, Vegetable, Red & Green Stripes, Tulip, Rainbow, 8 Sides, 6 x 8 In.	2530.00
Bowl, Vegetable, Shell Finial Cover, Rainbow, 8 Sides, Footed, 10 1/4 x 8 In.	2200.00
Charger, Bull's-Eye, Red Leaf & Cut Sponge Blossoms, c.1840, 14 1/2 In.	600.00
Coffeepot, Tulip, Yellow, Red Flowers, Green Leaves, 9 In.	18700.00
Creamer, 3-Petal Flower, Paneled, Red, Blue, 5 1/2 In.	605.00
Creamer, 3-Petal Flower, Red, Blue, 5 1/2 In.	605.00
Creamer, 4-Petal Flower, Blue, Green Leaves, 3 5/8 In.	440.00
Creamer, Cockscomb, Blue, Red, Green, 5 In.	850.00
Creamer, Flowers, Yellow, Mulberry & Green, 5 1/2 In.	5500.00
Creamer, Fort, Blue, Yellow, Black & Red, 4 1/2 In.	220.00
Creamer, Fort, Brown, Paneled, Yellow, Red, 5 1/2 In.	825.00
Creamer, Fort, Green Trees, Blue, Gray, Brown, 4 In.	250.00
Creamer, Morning Glory, Blue, Green, Red Border, 3 3/4 In.	2750.00
Creamer, Peafowl, On Green Branch, Deep Yellow, Molded Leaf Handle, 3 1/2 In.	4125.00
Creamer, Peafowl, Rainbow Thumbprint, Red, Blue, Green, 4 In.	1650.00
Creamer, Peafowl, Red, Green, Blue, 5 5/8 In.	770.00
Creamer, Rainbow, Bulbous, 4 1/2 In.	1760.00
Creamer, Rose, Red, Green, Brown, Black, 3 1/2 In.	660.00
Creamer, School House, Blue, Green Tree, Brown Ground, Red Border, 3 3/4 In.	525.00
Creamer, Thistle, Red, Green, 6 In.	935.00
Creamer, Tulip, Red, Green, Blue, Handle, 4 1/2 In.	577.00
Cup, Flower, Brown, Blue, Teardrop Shaped Petals, Red Sprigs	220.00
Cup & Saucer, 4-Petal Blue Flower, Red Border, 6 x 2 3/4 In.	385.00
Cup & Saucer, 4-Petal Flowers, Blue & Red, Handleless	300.00
Cup & Saucer, 6-Point Star, Impressed R	1210.00
Cup & Saucer, 6-Point Star, Red, Mustard, Green, Blue	910.00

Cup & Saucer, Acorn, Yellow, Blue Border, 6 x 3 3/4 In.	770.00
Cup & Saucer, Bull's-Eye, Red & Blue, Handleless	605.00
Cup & Saucer, Christmas Balls, Green, Red, Yellow Border	1045.00 to 3960.00
Cup & Saucer, Cluster Of Buds, Red Buds, Green Leaves	385.00
Cup & Saucer, Cockscomb, Green, Blue Flower, Yellow Leaves	1155.00
Cup & Saucer, Crisscross, Red, Blue, Green, Handleless	3520.00
Cup & Saucer, Dahlia, Blue, Handleless	165.00 to 220.00
Cup & Saucer, Deer, Blue Border	1815.00 to 3000.00
Cup & Saucer, Drape, Red, Yellow, Blue Flower, Handleless	9075.00
Cup & Saucer, Eagle & Shield, Blue Transfer, Double Sided	522.00
Cup & Saucer, Fish, Red, Green & Brown, Handleless	27500.00
Cup & Saucer, Military Scene, Black Transfer, Blue	495.00
Cup & Saucer, Morning Glory, Yellow, Handleless	990.00
Cup & Saucer, Open Body Peafowl, Red, Yellow Wavy Lines, Handleless	412.00
Cup & Saucer, Parrot, Red & Green	850.00
Cup & Saucer, Peafowl, Blue, Green, Red, Marked, 5 7/8 x 2 1/2 x 4 In.	660.00
Cup & Saucer, Peafowl, Blue, Green, Yellow, Handleless	55.00
Cup & Saucer, Peafowl, Blue, Yellow & Green, Red Border	165.00
Cup & Saucer, Peafowl, Blue, Yellow, Red, Handleless	715.00
Cup & Saucer, Peafowl, Green, Blue, Red, Child's	578.00
Cup & Saucer, Peafowl, Light Red, Yellow, Blue, Green Spatter Tree Branch	330.00
Cup & Saucer, Peafowl, Red Border	3190.00
Cup & Saucer, Peafowl, Red, Yellow, Blue, Handleless	302.00
Cup & Saucer, Pomegranate, Dark Blue, Green, Red, Yellow Dots	797.00
Cup & Saucer, Rainbow	2500.00
Cup & Saucer, Rainbow, Black & Purple, Child's	990.00
Cup & Saucer, Rainbow, Blue Interior, Handleless, Oversize	1100.00
Cup & Saucer, Red & Blue Design, Handleless, Child's	85.00
Cup & Saucer, Rooster, Yellow, Blue & Red	1265.00
Cup & Saucer, Rose, Red, Green Leaves	880.00
Cup & Saucer, Rose, Red, Green Leaves, Purple & Blue	275.00
Cup & Saucer, Rose, Red, Green, Blue Border, Handleless	137.00
Cup & Saucer, Rose, Red, Leaves, 6 x 2 1/2 x 4 In.	440.00
Cup & Saucer, School House, Blue Roof, Yellow Door, Red	1017.00
Cup & Saucer, School House, Blue, Handleless	1595.00
Cup & Saucer, School House, Green, Red, Handleless	2750.00
Cup & Saucer, School House, Red & Brown, Green Border, Handleless	1870.00
Cup & Saucer, School House, Red House & Roof, Green Tree & Ground	5610.00
Cup & Saucer, School House, Red Roof, Green Tree	1045.00
Cup & Saucer, Spray, Red, Blue, Green Leaves, Light Brown, Handleless	385.00
Cup & Saucer, Thistle	1700.00
Cup & Saucer, Thistle, Green Leaves	3630.00
Cup & Saucer, Thistle, Red & Yellow Rainbow, Handleless	1540.00
Cup & Saucer, Thistle, Red, Yellow, Green, Handleless	2530.00
Cup & Saucer, Thistle, Yellow	1955.00
Cup & Saucer, Thistle, Yellow Border	1020.00
Cup & Saucer, Thistle, Yellow, Red Flower, Green Leaves, Handleless	2090.00
Cup & Saucer, Tulip, Blue, Handleless	990.00
Cup & Saucer, Tulip, Blue, Red, Yellow, Handleless	110.00
Cup & Saucer, Tulip, Memorial, Green Leaves, Blue	1760.00
Cup & Saucer, Tulip, Red, Green Leaves, Red Sponge	440.00
Cup & Saucer, Tulip, Red, Green, Handleless	1760.00
Cup & Saucer, Tulip, Red, Purple, Yellow, Handleless	770.00
Cup & Saucer, Tulip, Red, Yellow, Green Leaves, Handleless	3190.00
Cup & Saucer, Tulip, Red, Yellow, Green, Blue, Handleless	192.00
Cup & Saucer, Yellow & Black, Handleless	3850.00
Figurine, Tall Case Clock, Red, Blue, Yellow, Green, 4 3/4 In.	415.00
Mug, Peafowl, Red, Blue, Green, Loop Handle, Straight Sided, 2 1/2 In.	880.00
Mug, Rainbow, Purple & Blue Vertical Stripes, Handle Leaf Ends, 2 3/4 In.	935.00
Pitcher, Acorn, Yellow, Teal Green, Green, Dark Brown Leaves, Purple, 8 In.	3630.00
Pitcher, Arabian Knights, 2 Red Transfers, Blue Border, 7 3/4 In.	250.00
Pitcher, Drape, Blue, Rim, Handle, 6 3/4 In.	440.00
Pitcher, Parrot, Blue, Red & Green, 6 5/8 In.	3410.00

Pitcher, Peafowl, Blue, Green, Brown, Red, 5 3/4 In. 415.00
Pitcher, Peafowl, Double Sided Peafowl, Red, 8 In. 1650.00
Pitcher, Peafowl, Red, Blue, Green, 8 Sides, 11 In. 1100.00
Pitcher, Rainbow, Green, Yellow, Black, Blue, Red, 7 In. 9900.00
Pitcher, Rainbow, Paneled Red & Green, Embossed Shell, 6 1/2 In. 1925.00
Pitcher, Rainbow, Purple & Black, Paneled, Molded Fan Under Spout, 6 1/2 In. 2640.00
Pitcher, Rose, Red, Green Leaves, Blue, Handle, 7 3/8 In. 1430.00
Pitcher, Tulip, Deep Yellow, Red & Green, Paneled, 6 3/8 In. 4675.00
Pitcher, Water, Floral, Blue, Red & Green, Bulbous, 10 In. 1980.00
Plate, 6-Point Star, Blue Border, 9 1/2 In. 1070.00
Plate, 13-Point Star, Blue, Paneled Rim, 9 1/2 In., Pair 250.00
Plate, Acorn, Brown, Teal Caps, Leaves, Purple, 9 3/8 In. 880.00
Plate, Acorn, Purple, Brown, Teal, 6 1/4 In. 1870.00
Plate, Blue, Paneled, Rose & Green Leaves, Paper Label, c.1851, 8 1/4 In. 415.00
Plate, Bull's-Eye, Purple & Black, Rainbow Border, 9 1/2 In. 1925.00
Plate, Bull's-Eye, Purple & Blue, Rainbow Border, 8 3/8 In. 385.00
Plate, Bull's-Eye, Rainbow Border, 8 1/4 In. 935.00
Plate, Bull's-Eye, Rainbow, 8 1/2 In. 825.00
Plate, Bull's-Eye, Rainbow, Red & Green, 6 In. 990.00
Plate, Cluster Of Buds, Red Buds, Blue, 9 5/8 In. 1320.00
Plate, Columbine With Rosebud & Thistle, Daisy Border, Red Stripes, 9 3/4 In. ... 250.00 to 330.00
Plate, Crisscross Strawberry Thumbprint, Blue, 9 1/4 In. 4950.00
Plate, Daffodil, Blue, Paneled Red Flower, Blue Buds, Leaves, Blue Border, 8 1/2 In. ... 740.00
Plate, Daffodil, Blue, Red, Blue Buds, Green Leaves, Blue Border, 8 1/2 In. 1210.00
Plate, Dahlia, Blue, 8 1/4 In. 305.00
Plate, Dahlia, Paneled, Red & Blue, Green Sprigs, 8 1/4 In. 880.00
Plate, Dahlia, Red & Green, Blue Border, 8 3/8 In. 330.00
Plate, Festoon, Red & Green Sprig, Red & Blue, 8 3/8 In. 3630.00
Plate, Flowers, Blue, Red Rose, Pearl Stoneware, PW & Co., 8 1/2 In. 250.00
Plate, Flowers, Red, Blue, Green, Red Border, 8 3/4 In. 110.00
Plate, Flying Eagle, Brown Transfer, Blue, 8 1/4 In. 380.00
Plate, Fort, Paneled, 9 3/4 In. 1430.00
Plate, Pansy, Red Bow Border, Blue Stripes, 10 In. 265.00
Plate, Peafowl, Blue, Green, Red, Black Branch, Blue Border, 8 1/2 In. 145.00
Plate, Peafowl, Blue, Molded Feather Edge, Label, 8 1/2 In. 687.00
Plate, Peafowl, Blue, Red, Mustard & Green, Black Branch, Blue Border, 9 In. ... 900.00
Plate, Peafowl, Blue, Red, Mustard, Green, 9 3/4 In. .... 580.00 to 660.00
Plate, Peafowl, Blue, Yellow & Green, Red, 9 3/4 In. 1265.00
Plate, Peafowl, Blue, Yellow & Red, Blue, Feather Edge, 9 1/2 In. 825.00
Plate, Peafowl, Dark Blue, Green, Dark Brown, 8 5/8 In. 715.00
Plate, Peafowl, Green, Blue, Yellow, Black Branch, 9 In. 550.00
Plate, Peafowl, J. Heath On Reverse, 9 1/2 In. 1650.00
Plate, Peafowl, Red, Blue, Yellow & Green, 8 1/4 In. 990.00
Plate, Peafowl, Red, Blue, Yellow, Green, 8 3/4 In. 550.00
Plate, Peafowl, Red, Yellow, Green Long Tail, Blue, Ground, 9 1/2 In. 770.00
Plate, Peafowl, Red, Yellow, Green, 7 1/2 In. 110.00
Plate, Peafowl, Yellow & Red, Blue, Black Branch, 9 5/8 In. 1100.00
Plate, Primrose, Red, Green, Yellow, Blue Border, 8 1/4 In. 55.00
Plate, Purple, Yellow, Viola, Red Stripes, Green Double Loop Border, 9 In. 49.00
Plate, Rainbow Border, 8 5/8 In. 3520.00
Plate, Rainbow Border, Red, Blue, 8 1/2 In. 770.00
Plate, Rainbow, Blue, Yellow Leaves, 9 1/8 In. 4400.00
Plate, Rainbow, Paneled Red & Green, 9 1/4 In. 303.00
Plate, Rainbow, Red, Blue & Yellow Border, 8 3/4 In. 1320.00
Plate, Rainbow, Red, Yellow, Blue, Dinner 4500.00
Plate, Rainbow, Stripes, Paneled Border, 8 1/2 In. 2640.00
Plate, Red, Blue, Green Border, Scalloped Edge, 10 1/2 In. 385.00
Plate, Red, Green Flower, Blue Border, 8 1/2 In. 137.00
Plate, Rose, Red, Paneled, Green Leaves, 1 Blue Bud, 10 1/2 In. 742.00
Plate, Rosebud & Thistle, Purple Daisy Border, Red Stripes, 9 3/4 In. 330.00
Plate, School House, Red Border, 9 1/2 In. 5500.00
Plate, School House, Red, Blue, Green, Brown, 8 1/4 In. 3190.00
Plate, School House, Red, Brown & Green Tree, 8 3/8 In. 2750.00

Plate, School House, Red, Brown, Green, 9 1/4 In. 4400.00
Plate, Soup, Rainbow, Red, Green, Yellow Stripes, Blue Border, 8 3/4 In. 165.00
Plate, Thistle, Deep Yellow, Red & Green, 8 3/8 In. 1540.00
Plate, Thistle, Red & Green, Yellow Paneled Edge, Crazing, 9 3/4 In. 3960.00
Plate, Thistle, Red, 9 3/8 In. 302.00
Plate, Toddy, 8-Point Star Border, Red Stripes, 5 3/4 In. 330.00
Plate, Toddy, Pansy, Blue Bow Border, Red Stripes, 5 1/2 In. 220.00
Plate, Tree, Paneled, 8 In. 1925.00
Plate, Tulip, 3 Colors, Green Leaves, 8 1/4 In. 110.00
Plate, Tulip, Blue, Paneled Border, 7 1/4 In. 825.00
Plate, Tulip, Blue, Red Flowers, Green Leaves, Rainbow Border, 7 In. 1760.00
Plate, Tulip, Green & Red, Paneled, 8 5/8 In. 2900.00
Plate, Tulip, Red & Yellow Flowers, Blue, 9 3/4 In. 360.00
Plate, Tulip, Red Flower, Green Leaves, 7 7/8 In. 2530.00
Plate, Tulips, Paneled, Blue, 9 1/2 In. 440.00
Plate, Umbrella Flower, Mulberry, Blue Buds, Green Leaves, 8 1/4 In. 2975.00
Plate, White Shield, Blue Stripes, Red Stars, 9 1/4 In. 1155.00
Plate Set, 6-Point Star Border, 8 3/4 In., 3 Piece 2090.00
Platter, Flowers, Red, Blue, Green Leaves, 10 3/4 In. 137.00
Platter, Peafowl, Red, Blue, Dark Brown, Red, 8 1/4 x 10 3/4 In. 600.00
Platter, Rainbow, Blue & Green, 3 1/2 x 4 1/2 In. 880.00
Platter, Tulip, Red & Blue, Rainbow Border, 8 Sides, 9 1/2 x 12 1/2 In. 4620.00
Platter, Tulip, Red, Blue, Green, Black Leaves, 10 1/2 x 13 3/4 In. 4510.00
Platter, Well, Cluster Of Buds, Burgundy, Green, White Ground, 12 x 15 3/4 In. 1045.00
Platter, White Center Panel, Light Blue Border, 12 3/8 x 15 7/8 In. 220.00
Saltshaker, Blue, Footed, 2 In. 27.00
Soup, Dish, Dahlia, Blue, Red, Green Sprigs, 10 1/4 In. 1650.00
Soup, Dish, Paneled, Blue, 10 1/2 In. 165.00
Soup, Dish, Peafowl, On Branch, Red, Green Leaves, 8 5/8 In. 2200.00
Soup, Dish, Peafowl, Paneled Edge, 10 1/2 In. 880.00
Soup, Dish, Rainbow, Purple & Black, 10 1/2 In. 6325.00
Sugar, Cover, Blue, Shell Form Handles, 3 3/4 In. 1100.00
Sugar, Cover, Fort, Gray, Brown, Red, Green, Blue Border, 4 1/4 In. 190.00
Sugar, Cover, Hex Sign, Floral Finial, Green, 5 In. 110.00
Sugar, Cover, Parrot, Blue, Paneled, Handles, 7 1/4 In. 220.00
Sugar, Cover, Peafowl, Green, Bulbous, 5 In. 605.00
Sugar, Cover, Rainbow, Purple & Black Stripes, 4 1/4 x 3 7/8 In. 55.00
Sugar, Cover, Rainbow, Red & Blue 1375.00
Sugar, Cover, Rose, Blue, Green Leaves, Red, 4 1/4 In. 275.00
Sugar, Cover, Rose, Blue, Red Flower, Green Leaves, 7 1/2 In. 440.00
Sugar, Cover, Rose, Red, 2 Relief Handles, Ring & Shell, 5 1/2 In. 440.00
Sugar, Cover, Roseate, Red Rays On Blue Center, 4 1/4 In. 165.00
Sugar, Cover, Star, Red, Blue Double Sided Star, 4 1/4 In. 300.00
Sugar, Cover, Thistle, Rainbow, Yellow & Blue Stripes, Oval, 4 3/4 x 5 1/4 In. 3740.00
Sugar, Cover, Tulip, Red, Green Leaves, Blue, 4 1/2 In. 495.00
Sugar, Loop, Red Finial & Handles, 3 Color, 7 1/2 In. 5060.00
Sugar, Rainbow, Paneled Shoulders, Stripes, 5 3/8 In. 660.00
Sugar, School House, Red, Green Trees & Grass, Blue, 5 3/4 In. 715.00
Teapot, 8-Point Star, Floral Finial, Blue, 5 1/2 In. 1375.00
Teapot, Castle, Green & Black Trees, Blue, 5 1/2 In. 1155.00
Teapot, Cockscomb, Red, Green, 6 5/8 In. 550.00
Teapot, Green, Yellow, Purple Loops, Black Spots, Handle, 5 In. 5060.00
Teapot, Hex Sign, Blue, Floral Finial, 7 In. 220.00
Teapot, Peafowl, Blue, Paneled, Molded Arches Shoulder, 8 5/8 In. 990.00
Teapot, Peafowl, On Branch, Green Thumbprint, 6 1/2 In. 1870.00
Teapot, Peafowl, Red, Scroll Handle, 9 In. 1980.00
Teapot, Rainbow, Red, Blue, Molded Arch Design On Shoulder & Spout, 9 1/4 In. 550.00
Teapot, Red Band Around Middle, 8 1/4 In. 110.00
Washbowl, Tulip, Red Blossoms, 4 1/2 x 14 In. 1210.00
Waste Bowl, Fort, Brown, Red, Black, 6 1/4 x 3 1/2 In. 190.00
Waste Bowl, Peafowl, Blue, Red, Green, Yellow, 2 3/4 x 6 3/4 In. 4470.00
Waste Bowl, Peafowl, Double Bulbous, Red, 3 x 5 3/4 In. 1375.00

Spelter, Pipe Holder,
Hobo's Boot, 3 1/2 In.

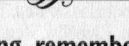

**When moving, remember there
is no coverage for breakage if
the items are not packed
by the shipper.**

SPELTER is a synonym for a zinc alloy. Figurines, candlesticks, and other pieces were made of spelter and given a bronze or painted finish. The metal has been used since about the 1860s to make statues, tablewares, and lamps that resemble bronze. Spelter is soft and breaks easily. To test for spelter, scratch the base of the piece. Bronze is solid; spelter will show a silvery scratch.

Figurine, Maiden With Bird, French Foundry Mark, 20 In.	280.00
Figurine, Maiden With Flower Basket, Bouquetiere, Bronze Finish, Wood Base, 22 In.	310.00
Figurine, Man Reading Book, Seated, 3 1/2 In.	49.00
Figurine, Oriental Woman Holding Floral Bells, 7 1/2 In.	66.00
Figurine, Young Harvester, Standing, Scythe In Hand, Brown Patina, 27 In.	805.00
Group, Elephants, Graduated, 14 In., 5 Piece	99.00
Incense Burner, Figural, Woman Holding Vase, France, 7 In.	45.00
Jewelry Box, Art Nouveau, Gilt Copper, Winged Fairy, Monogram, 1903, 10 x 7 In.	430.00
Lamp, Conquistador, With Lance, Converted From Gas, Glass Shade, Bronze, 28 In.	195.00
Lamp, Girl With Doll, Boy With Accordion, 6-Sided Green Glass Shade, Germany, Pair	960.00
Pipe Holder, Hobo's Boot, 3 1/2 In. ....*Illus*	50.00

SPINNING WHEELS in the corner have been symbols of earlier times for the past 100 years. Although spinning wheels date back to medieval days, the ones found today are rarely more than 200 years old. Because the style of the spinning wheel changed very little, it is often impossible to place an exact date on a wheel.

Flax Wheel, Turned, Gouge Decoration, Initials, Penna.	55.00
Flax Wheel, Hardwoods, 1 Treadle, Double Flyers With Bobbins, 45 In.	247.00
Folk Art, Signed NC Saxony, Inlaid Base	495.00
Walnut, Ivory Knopped Mechanism, Flower Carved Wheel, 19th Century, 44 In.	630.00
Yellow Pine & Oak, 64 x 64 In.	280.00

SPODE pottery, porcelain, and bone china were made by the Stoke-on-Trent factory of England founded by Josiah Spode about 1770. The firm became Copeland and Garrett from 1833 to 1847, then W.T. Copeland or W.T. Copeland and Sons until 1976. It then became Royal Worcester Spode Ltd. The word *Spode* appears on many pieces made by the factories. Most collectors include all the wares under the more familiar name of Spode. Porcelains may be listed in this book by the name that appears on the piece. Related pieces may be listed under Copeland, Copeland Spode, and Royal Worcester.

Bowl, Imari Style, Stoneware, Footed, Gilt Trim, Marked, 1800s, 14 3/4 x 10 3/4 In.	525.00
Bowl, Vegetable, Cover, Blue, Italy	65.00
Condiment Set, Camilla, Lazy Susan Base, 4 Bowls, Center Bowl, Cover, 11 1/2 x 21 In.	440.00
Dinner Service, Blanche De Chine, Yellow, Pink, Blue, 152 Piece	1645.00
Plate, Common Wolf Trap, 8 1/4 In.	336.00
Platter, Basket Ware, Oval, c.1810, 11 In.	403.00
Platter, Dooreahs Leading Out Dogs, Blue, White, Well & Tree, 18 3/4 x 14 3/4 In.	660.00
Platter, Shooting A Leopard, Oriental Sports Series, Blue, White, 15 3/4 x 20 1/2 In.	2100.00
Platter, Shooting At Edge Of Jungle, 14 3/4 In.	2240.00
Tea & Coffee Service, Blue & White, Fitzhugh	460.00
Tea Set, Blue Willow, Burns' Quotation, Tiffany & Co., Late 19th Century, 21 In., 17 Piece	920.00
Tea Set, Jasperware, White Hunting Scene, Blue Ground, 5 1/4 In., 3 Piece	172.00
Tureen, Hog At Bay, Handle, 10 1/2 x 15 x 8 1/2 In.	3575.00
Tureen, Sauce, Underplate, Cobalt Blue & White, Gold Trim, 6 1/2 x 5 In.	295.00

Tureen, Vegetable, Blue & White Transfer Print, Rural Landscape, Figures, 17 In. 1725.00

SPONGEWARE is very similar to spatterware in appearance. The designs were applied to the ceramics by daubing the color on with a sponge or cloth. Many collectors do not differentiate between spongeware and spatterware and use the names interchangeably. Modern pottery is being made to resemble the old spongeware, but careful examination will show it is new.

Bank, Pig, Blue, Cream, Top Coin Slot, 5 1/2 In.	154.00
Bean Pot, Cover, Blue & White, Handle, 6 1/2 In.	120.00
Bowl, Blue, White, 2 x 4 1/2 In.	120.00
Bowl, Blue, White, 4 Blue Accent Bands, 3 1/4 x 7 3/4 In.	165.00
Bowl, Blue, White, Deep Blue Base, 4 x 11 In.	155.00
Bowl, Blue, White, Flared Rim, 13 In.	195.00
Bowl, Blue, White, Ribbed Exterior, 1 1/8 x 2 3/4 In.	715.00
Bowl, Blue, White, Ribs, Flared Rim, 4 x 10 1/4 In.	200.00
Bowl, Blue, White, Wide Flattened Rim, 3 1/4 x 9 In.	145.00
Bowl, Blue, White, Wide Flattened Rim, 4 x 11 In.	180.00
Bowl, Dark Navy Blue & White, 3 1/4 x 6 3/4 In.	66.00
Bowl, Domed Lid, Flat Finial, Blue, White, Flat Rim, 5 1/2 x 10 1/2 In.	200.00
Bowl, Molded Ribbed Sides, Flared Rim, 4 x 10 In.	200.00
Chamber Pot, Blue, White, Applied Handle, 1 1/2 x 2 1/2 In.	415.00
Creamer, Blue, White, Cream, Handle, 4 1/2 In.	176.00
Creamer, Cow, Brown Sponge Painting, 4 1/2 x 6 1/2 In.	400.00
Crock, Butter, Blue, White, Oval Dotted Outline, Butter, 5 3/4 x 9 In.	230.00
Cup, Purple, Black, Interior Bull's-Eye Design	330.00
Cup & Saucer, Blue, Handleless	45.00
Cup & Saucer, Handleless, Blue, Red Flower	220.00
Cup & Saucer, Handleless, Green, Peafowl	220.00
Cup & Saucer, Purple, Handleless	140.00
Cup & Saucer, Red, Handleless, Demitasse	28.00
Cup & Saucer, Red, Peafowl, Handleless	385.00
Cuspidor, Blue, White, 1 7/8 x 2 3/4 In.	745.00
Cuspidor, Blue, White, 2 x 5 In.	45.00
Cuspidor, Blue, White, Blue Accent Band, 4 x 6 1/2 In.	60.00
Mixing Bowl, Blue, White, Flared Rim, White Band, 6 1/4 x 14 In.	400.00
Mixing Bowl, Embossed Heart Design, 1910, 12 In.	350.00
Pitcher, Blue, White, 8 1/2 In.	250.00
Pitcher, Blue, White, 8 Sides, Stylized Rectangular Handle, 12 In.	130.00
Pitcher, Blue, White, Allover Chicken Wire, Handle, 9 In.	525.00
Pitcher, Blue, White, Blue Rim, 6 1/2 In.	155.00
Pitcher, Blue, White, Blue Rose Design, Handle, 9 In.	99.00
Pitcher, Blue, White, Blue Wild Rose Design, Handle, 9 In.	412.00
Pitcher, Blue, White, Handle, 6 3/4 In.	165.00
Pitcher, Blue, White, Handle, 9 3/4 In.	360.00
Pitcher, Blue, White, Straight Sides, 8 1/2 In.	259.00
Pitcher, Cobalt Blue, White, Circular Pattern, 8 3/4 In.	460.00
Pitcher, Dark Navy Blue, White, Bulbous Base, 9 In.	385.00
Pitcher, Tapering At Top, Handle, 8 7/8 In.	385.00
Plate, Blue, Ironstone, 7 1/4 In.	49.00
Plate, Blue, Peafowl, 9 1/4 In.	275.00
Plate, Blue, Red Flower, 8 1/2 In.	250.00
Plate, Blue, Rose Design, 8 1/2 In.	250.00
Plate, Green, Shell Edge, Yellow, Blue, Brown Peafowl Border, 8 In.	715.00
Plate, Red, Yellow, Green Tulip Center, Blue Sponge Border, 8 3/4 In.	80.00
Plate, Tulip, Blue, Red & Yellow Flower, Green Leaves, 8 3/4 In.	165.00
Platter, Blue, Flow Blue Rim, 7 7/8 x 11 3/4 In.	300.00
Platter, Blue, White, 16 In.	230.00
Platter, Scalloped, Oval, 10 x 13 1/2 In.	385.00
Salt, 3 Colors	225.00
Soap Dish, Flared Rim, 2 x 5 1/2 In.	80.00
Sugar, Blue, 5 In.	110.00
Sugar, Blue, Red Flower, 3 In.	93.00

Sugar, Cover, Blue, Peafowl, 6 In. 580.00
Sugar, Cover, Purple, 4 1/2 In. 140.00
Sugar, Cover, Tulip, Red, Green, 5 1/2 In. 110.00
Sugar, Green, Blue & Brown, Embossed Mask Handles, 4 In. 60.00
Tray, Blue, Buff Ground, Scalloped, 9 1/4 In. 55.00
Water Cooler, Dark Blue, Brass Tap, Straight Sides, Ears, Domed Lid, 14 In. 310.00

SPORTS equipment, sporting goods, brochures, and related items are
listed here. Items are listed by sport. Other categories of interest are
Bicycle, Card, Fishing, Sword, Toy, and Trap.

Auto Racing, Glass, Indianapolis Speedway, Tony Hulman Autograph, 1964, 5 In. 15.00
Baseball, Bag, Equipment, Joe DiMaggio, N.Y. Yankees, Green Canvas, 1940 .... 350.00
Baseball, Ball, Autographed, Babe Ruth & Lou Gehrig Signed 5245.00
Baseball, Ball, Autographed, N.Y. Yankees, Babe Ruth, Lou Gehrig, 28 Others, c.1935 ... 2500.00
Baseball, Ball, Autographed, New York Yankees, 19 Players, 1934 .... 4189.00
Baseball, Ball, Autographed, Pittsburgh Pirates, 25 Signatures, 1947 .... 275.00
Baseball, Ball, Autographed, Ty Cobb 9900.00
Baseball, Banner, Philadephia Phillies, 1915 .... 4290.00
Baseball, Bat, Autographed, 37 Players, 1961 New York Yankees, Hillerich & Bradsby ... 1290.00
Baseball, Bat, Autographed, 500 Home-Run Club, Mantle, Williams, Hank Aaron Model . 1375.00
Baseball, Bat, Autographed, Don Larsen, 1961-1962 .... 2839.00
Baseball, Bat, Autographed, George Brett Model, Louisville Slugger Replica, 16 In. 18.00
Baseball, Bat, Autographed, Mickey Mantle 4478.00
Baseball, Bat, Autographed, Mike Piazza, Dodgers & Mets 2619.00
Baseball, Bat, Autographed, Pete Rose, Louisville Slugger, Game Used, 1964 .... 2420.00
Baseball, Bat, Autographed, Willie Mays, Adirondack, Game Used, 1958-1960 .... 7506.00
Baseball, Booklets, How To, Full Color, 16 Pages, 1965, 3 1/2 x 4 3/4 In., 12 Piece 40.00
Baseball, Brooch, Chicago White Sox, Margaret Dykes Center Initials 985.00
Baseball, Button, Go Mets, Celluloid, Black & White, Early 1970s, 3 1/2 In. 8.00
Baseball, Button, Minnesota Twins, 1987 Western Div. Champions, Celluloid, 3 1/2 In. ... 8.00
Baseball, Button, The Amazing Mets, Celluloid, Orange & Blue, 1969, 3 1/2 In. 5.00
Baseball, Cuff Links, Angels All Star Game, Anaheim Stadium, Enameled, 1967 .... 95.00
Baseball, Display, Roberto Clemente, Batting Action, 23 1/2 x 33 In. 95.00
Baseball, Dixie Cup Lid, Bob Feller, Large 75.00
Baseball, Figure, Jim Busby, Plastic, Robert Gould Inc., 1955, 2 1/2 In. 18.00
Baseball, Figure, Junior League, China, Hollow, 1960s, 1 1/2 x 2 x 5 In. 35.00
Baseball, Figure, Nellie Fox, Hartland Plastics, 7 In. 155.00
Baseball, Figure, Whitey Ford, Hartland Plastics, 4 1/2 x 6 x 9 1/2 In. 65.00
Baseball, Figure, Yogi Berra, Hartland Plastics, 6 1/2 In. 95.00
Baseball, Glass, Cincinnati Reds, Team Of The '70s, Stir Rods, Glass, 5 1/2 In., 8 Piece .. 32.00
Baseball, Glass, Pittsburgh Pirates, 1971 World Champions, Plastic, Clear, 3 In., 4 Piece . 24.00
Baseball, Glove, Autographed, Sammy Sosa 2984.00
Baseball, Golf Bag, Autographed, Joe DiMaggio 1250.00
Baseball, Invitation, Opening Day Game, Comiskey Park, February 15, 1910, Envelope .. 6345.00
Baseball, Jersey & Pants, Tommy Thomas, White Sox, 1926 .... 3499.00
Baseball, Jersey, George Kell, Boston Red Sox, Flannel, 1953 .... 500.00
Baseball, Jersey, Home, Earle Mack, Philadelphia Athletics 8800.00
Baseball, Jersey, Reggie Jackson, Autographed, Oakland A's, No. 9, Green, Knit, Size 44 . 2500.00
Baseball, Jersey, Road, Bill White, Philadelphia Phillies, 1969 .... 2200.00
Baseball, Jersey, San Francisco Giants, 1986 .... 1938.00
Baseball, Jersey, Vince Castino, Chicago White Sox, No. 14, 1945 .... 4957.00
Baseball, Life Magazine Cover, August 1, 1949, Photo Joe DiMaggio, Autographed 225.00
Baseball, Megaphone, Popcorn Box, N.Y. Yankees, 1960, 10 In. 8.00
Baseball, Nodder, Detroit Tiger, c.1961, Box, 6 1/2 In. 145.00
Baseball, Nodder, Philadelphia Phillies, Black Face, Porcelain 1870.00
Baseball, Nodder, Roberto Clemente, Pittsburgh Pirates, Early 1960s 3616.00
Baseball, Nodder, Roger Maris, N.Y. Yankees, Mr. Home Run, 1960 .... 845.00
Baseball, Pen & Pencil, Louisville Slugger Bats, Plastic, Yellow, 5 1/2 In. 20.00
Baseball, Pen, Mets Bat, Red Emblem, Plastic, Ivory, Late 1960s, 5 3/4 In. 8.00
Baseball, Pennant, Cleveland Indians, American League Champions, 1920, 25 In. 4608.00
Baseball, Pennant, New York Yankees, Uncle Sam, Felt, 1940, 8 x 26 In. 29.00
Baseball, Pennant, World Tour, Christy Mathewson, White Sox & Giants, 1913-14, 29 In. 2197.00
Baseball, Photograph, Babe Ruth, Autographed, Black & White, 7 1/2 x 9 In. 2500.00

Baseball, Photograph, Babe Ruth, Autographed, Blue Ink, Sepia, 3 1/2 x 5 1/4 In. 2000.00
Baseball, Photograph, Babe Ruth, Autographed, Sepia, 7 x 9 In. 5768.00
Baseball, Photograph, Connie Mack, Mid-Career, Black & White, 6 1/2 x 8 1/2 In. 95.00
Baseball, Photograph, Derek Jeter, Autographed 400.00
Baseball, Photograph, Dick Williams, Autographed, Early 1970s, 8 x 10 In. 14.00
Baseball, Photograph, Ebbets Field, From Brooklyn Dodgers Hall Of Fame, 1957 . . . . 1000.00
Baseball, Photograph, Hank Greenberg, Autographed 500.00
Baseball, Photograph, Joe DiMaggio, Autographed, Color, Matted, 8 x 10 In. 249.00
Baseball, Photograph, Lou Gehrig, Autographed, Black Fountain Pen 9935.00
Baseball, Photograph, Mickey Mantle & Joe DiMaggio, Black & White, 1951 . . . . 475.00
Baseball, Photograph, Mickey Mantle & Ted Williams, Black & White, 16 x 20 In. 425.00
Baseball, Photograph, Mickey Mantle, Autographed, 14 x 22 In. 100.00
Baseball, Photograph, Mickey Mantle, Autographed, Color, 8 x 10 In. 129.00
Baseball, Photograph, Roger Maris, N.Y. Blue Suit, Autographed, Matted, 3 x 10 In. 429.00
Baseball, Photograph, Ted Williams, Autographed, Black & White, 21 x 25 In. 275.00
Baseball, Photograph, Walter Johnson, Autographed 750.00
Baseball, Postage Stamp, Mickey Mantle, 1961 . . . . 100.00
Baseball, Poster, Frank Robinson, Batting Action, Full Color, 24 x 36 1/2 In. 14.00
Baseball, Poster, Joe DiMaggio Kissing His Bat, Autographed, Black & White, 15 x 18 In. 175.00
Baseball, Press Pin, 1946 World Series, Boston Red Sox, 2 Red Socks 572.00
Baseball, Press Pin, St. Louis Cardinals, 1942, 2 In. 2200.00
Baseball, Program, 1944 World Series, St. Louis, 9 x 12 In. 125.00
Baseball, Program, 1966 World Series, Dodgers-Orioles, 8 1/2 x 11 In. 18.00
Baseball, Ring, Paul Blair, 1970 World Series, Baltimore Orioles 4675.00
Baseball, Rug, Cleveland Indians, Chenille, Foam Gripper Pad, 24 In. 12.00
Baseball, Seat, Fenway Park, Red Arm Rails, Number 4 On Back Slat 2750.00
Baseball, Sheet Music, Oh You, Babe Ruth, 1921 World Series Song, Photo Of Babe 730.00
Baseball, Sign, Reggie Jackson, Rawlings Balls & Gloves, 9 1/2 x 10 In. 18.00
Baseball, Stock Certificate, American League Baseball Co., St. Louis Browns, 1936 . . . . . 575.00
Baseball, Ticket, 1938, World Series, Game 3, Yankee Stadium 940.00
Baseball, Vase, Almendares, Applied Scorpion, Letter A, Cuban Team, Pottery, 8 In. . *Illus* 110.00
Baseball, Visor, Boston Red Sox, Cardboard, Die Cut, 7 x 10 1/2 In. 5.00
Baseball, Yearbook, Detroit Tigers, 1981 . . . . 6.00
Basketball, Action Figure, Dr. J, Julius Erving, Photo, Biography, Box, 9 1/2 In. 78.00
Basketball, Bag, Garment, Wilt Chamberlain Stitched One Side, No. 13 One Side 150.00
Basketball, Ball, Autographed, New York Knicks, 14 Signatures, 1973 . . . . 500.00
Basketball, Basketball, Autographed, Dennis Rodman 75.00
Basketball, Jersey, Grant Hill, Autographed, Detroit Pistons, Champions 94/95, Size 48 . . 1500.00
Basketball, Jersey, Michael Jordan, Autographed, No. 23, Red Mesh, 1992, Size 46 . . . . . 9000.00
Basketball, John Havlicek, Celtics, Road Jersey, 1970s 4700.00
Basketball, Nodder, Seattle Supersonic, Painted Composition, 1970s, 7 In. 24.00
Basketball, Pencil Holder, Ceramic, Dribbler & Ball, 4 1/4 x 5 1/2 In. 38.00
Basketball, Photograph, Kobe Bryant, Autographed, 20 x 24 In. 125.00
Basketball, Photograph, Magic Johnson, Autographed, Color, 8 x 10 In. 30.00
Basketball, Photograph, Michael Jordan, Autographed With 15 Celebrities, 8 1/2 x 11 In. . 375.00
Basketball, Photograph, New York Knicks, Autographed, 7 Signatures, 1973 . . . . 225.00
Basketball, Photograph, Wilt Chamberlain & Bill Russell, Autographed, 28 x 32 In. 750.00
Billiards, Ball Rack, Autographed, Willie Mosconi 900.00
Bobsled, Wood, Wrought Iron Runners, Stenciled, Fleetwing, Marked 84, 84 In. 990.00
Bowling, Ashtray, Figural Caricature Bowler, Gutter Gus, c.1950, 3/4 x 4 1/2 x 6 In. 45.00
Boxing, Belt, All America Amateur Championship, Gold Plated, Center Diamond 2250.00
Boxing, Belt, Irish American International Featherweight, Gold Plated, 1930s 2250.00
Boxing, Brochure, Rocky Marciano Training Camps, Biography, 8 Pages, 5 1/2 x 8 1/2 In. 35.00
Boxing, Button, Holmes, Ali, The Last Hurrah, Celluloid, c.1980, 4 In. 25.00
Boxing, Button, Joe Lewis, Full Figure, Fighting Stance, Celluloid, 1 3/4 In. 28.00
Boxing, Cassius Clay, Stubless Ticket, Golden Gloves Finals, 1959 . . . . 185.00
Boxing, Handbill, John L. Sullivan, Partnership, Circus, John B. Doris, 1888, 20 x 10 In. . 195.00
Boxing, Pennant, Frazier-Ali Fight, March 1971, 8 x 21 In. 48.00
Boxing, Photograph, Jack Dempsey, U.S. Army Signal Corps, 1944, 8 1/4 x 10 In. 17.00
Boxing, Photograph, Larry Holmes, Autographed, 6 x 9 In. 25.00
Boxing, Photograph, Marvelous Marvin Hagler, Autographed, 1980s, 8 1/2 x 11 In. 45.00
Boxing, Photograph, Rocky Marciano, Autographed, 3 x 5 1/2 In. 150.00
Boxing, Photograph, Sugar Ray Robinson, Championship, March 1958, 8 x 10 In. 15.00

Sports, Baseball, Vase,
Almendares, Applied
Scorpion, Letter
A, Cuban Team,
Pottery, 8 In.

Sports, Football, Tie Tack, NFL,
Progressive Insurance Co., Enamel, 1 1/2 In.

Football, Action Figure, O.J. Simpson, Bills Uniform, Biography, Box, 9 1/2 In. 48.00
Football, Alarm Clock, Houston Oilers, Metal, Windup, Lafayette Watch Co., 4 x 6 x 2 In.   20.00
Football, Ball, Autographed, Chicago Bears Team, 1964 . . . .   932.00
Football, Bank, Philadelphia Eagles, Ceramic, White Football, 4 x 7 In. 24.00
Football, Button, Pittsburgh Steelers, Super Bowl X, 1976 . . . .   7.00
Football, Helmet, Earl Campbell, Houston Oilers, Game Worn 4441.00
Football, Helmet, Leather, c.1900 . . . . 1264.00
Football, Nodder, Chicago Bears, Wooden Base, c.1961, 6 In. 50.00
Football, Pencil Case, NFL, Vinyl, Zippered, Light Blue, 5 x 8 In. 8.00
Football, Pennant, Philadelphia Eagles, Green, White & Silver, Felt, 29 In. 4.00
Football, Photograph, Johnny Unitas, Autographed, 1960s, 8 x 10 1/2 In. 24.00
Football, Photograph, Miami Dolphins, Super Bowl Team, 1972, 21 x 23 In. 275.00
Football, Photograph, New York Giants, Autographed, 1937 . . . .   275.00
Football, Photograph, St. Louis Cardinals, Grand Old Ball, 1944 . . . .   275.00
Football, Print, Vince Lombardi Tribute, George Loh Drawing, 1970s, 7 3/4 x 11 In. 9.00
Football, Tie Tack, NFL, Progressive Insurance Co., Enamel, 1 1/2 In. . . . . *Illus*   50.00
Golf, Ashtray, Arnold Palmer, Good Golf Is A State Of Mind, Ceramic, 7 x 1 In. 20.00
Golf, Club, Aim Rite, Wood Shaft, Leather Grips, Jock Hutchinson 175.00
Golf, Club, Hudson Bay Company, Left Handed 132.00
Golf, Club, Hudson Bay Company, Right Handed 121.00
Golf, Club, Stainless Steel Head, Hickory Shaft, Cochrane's Ltd., Edinburgh, Scotland . . .   805.00
Golf, Photograph, Arnold Palmer & Jackie Gleason, Autographed, Framed, 23 x 28 In. . . .   897.00
Golf, Photograph, Bobby Jones, Autographed, Blue Lettering, 1930 . . . . 2000.00
Golf, Photograph, Dave Chappel, 36th Annual Bob Hope Chrysler Classic, 12 x 15 In. . . .   300.00
Golf, Spoon, Sterling, Victorian Woman Golfing, 3 7/8 In. 204.00
Hockey, Glass, Philadelphia Flyers Stanley Cup Champions, 1974-1975, 5 3/4 In. 20.00
Hockey, Jersey, Wayne Gretzky, Autographed, Rangers, No. 9 . . . .   375.00
Hockey, Nodder, Toronto Maple Leafs, Painted Composition, 4 3/4 In. 48.00
Hockey, Stick, Goalie, Terry Sawchuck, Detroit Red Wings, Game Used, 1950s 3540.00
Horse Racing, Glass, Kentucky Derby, 1945 . . . .   280.00
Horse Racing, Glass, Kentucky Derby, 1950 . . . .   260.00
Horse Racing, Glass, Kentucky Derby, 1951 . . . .   375.00
Horse Racing, Glass, Kentucky Derby, 1959, 5 1/2 In. 48.00
Horse Racing, Glass, Kentucky Derby, 1978, 5 3/8 In. 5.00
Horse Racing, Glass, Kentucky Derby, Jockey On Horse, Blue, 1976 . . . .   8.00
Horse Racing, Snowdome, Jockey On Horse, 3 x 4 In. 18.00
Hunting, License, Button, Dixie Seal & Stamp Co., 1935-1936 . . . .   708.00
Hunting, Light, Coon Hunting, Mounts On Head, Winchester 40.00
Hunting, Shot Shells, Mallard, Sears, 12 Gauge, Box, Contents 33.00
Hunting, Sign, Dupont Gun Powder, Tin, Self-Framed, Grandfather, Grandson, 33 x 23 In. 1150.00
Hunting, Vest, Shooter's, Winchester, Pockets 35.00
Pool, Table, Renaissance Revival, Rosewood, Lion Head Medallions, 33 x 55 x 101 In. . . 10640.00
Pool, Table, Rosewood, Reeded Legs, Brunswick-Balke-Collender Co., 59 x 34 x 109 In. . . 6160.00
Skating, Ice Skates, Leather, Carrying Bag, 1900 . . . .   135.00
Skating, Ice Skates, Painted Wood, Brass, Steel, Leather Strap, Heel Spike, 12 In. 605.00
Skating, Ice Skates, Winchester, With Key, 12 1/2 In. 70.00
Skating, Ice Skates, Wooden 40.00

Skating, Ice Skates, Wooden Soles, Iron Blades, Front Curls, Leather Straps, 12 3/4 In. . .	165.00
Skating, Roller Skates, Aluminum & Copper, Ball Bearing, Marx, Box, 1950s	125.00
Skating, Roller Skates, Extra Ankle Pads, No. 3831, Winchester, 1925	65.00
Skiing, Skis, Maple, Davis Binding, Leather Straps, Original Decal, 64 In.	220.00
Snooker, Rack, Triangular Oak Case, Brass Handle, 22 Balls, 17 In.	750.00
Snowshoes, Leather Bindings, Decal, Bastien Brothers, Village Huron, Que., 16 x 42 In. .	85.00
Snowshoes, Leather Bindings, Marked, US AF & H CO, No. 0126, 57 In., Pair	195.00
Soccer, Photograph, Pele, Autographed, Black, White, 9 1/2 x 12 1/2 In.	150.00
Surfing, Surfboard, Hollow, Molded Tom Blake Fin, 1940s, 12 Ft.	7200.00
Surfing, Surfboard, Hollow, Red Paint, Pops Inscription, 1940s, 12 Ft.	3000.00
Surfing, Surfboard, Hollow, Redwood, 1940s	5000.00
Surfing, Surfboard, Pacific Systems Homes, Swastika, 1930s, 11 Ft.	18200.00
Surfing, Surfboard, Velzy First, Foam, Redwood Stringers, 1948, 12 Ft.	600.00
Tennis, Photograph, Arthur Ashe, Autographed, Magazine Page, Early 1970s, 8 x 11 In. . .	40.00
Toboggan, Worthington	225.00
Weightlifting, Badge, 1947 World's Championship, 2 x 5 1/4 In.	8.00
Weightlifting, Medal, Bob Hoffman, 1936, 1 1/2 In.	24.00

STAFFORDSHIRE, England, has been a district making pottery and porcelain since the 1700s. Hundreds of kilns are still working in the area. Thousands of types of pottery and porcelain have been made in the many factories that worked and still work in the area. Some of the most famous factories have been listed separately, such as Adams, Davenport, Ridgway, Rowland & Marsellus, Royal Doulton, Royal Worcester, Spode, Wedgwood, and others. Some Staffordshire pieces are listed under categories like Fairing, Flow Blue, Mulberry, Shaving Mug, etc.

Basket, Undertray, Trentham Hall, Double Handles, 10 1/2 In.	1456.00
Basket, Yellow Ground, Leaf Molded, c.1820, 10 17/8 In.	2585.00
Bowl, Pains Hill Surrey, R. Hall, 9 In.	405.00
Bowl, Romantic Scene, Boatmen On Lake, Scalloped, 4 1/8 x 9 In.	495.00
Bowl, Vegetable, Explorer, Eskimos Building Igloo, Black Transfer, 11 x 2 In.	935.00
Bowl, Vegetable, Underplate, Shepherds, Waterfall, Blue, Riley's, 11 x 3 1/4 In.	467.00
Bowl, Yellow Flowers, Late 1800s, 12 In.	245.00
Bust, George Washington, Pink Jacket, Porcelain, Plinth, 7 1/2 x 5 In.	265.00
Bust, George Washington, Wig, Blue Coat, Vest, Black Neck Scarf, 8 1/4 In.	190.00
Charger, Lake George, Stepped Frame Rim, Blue, Transfer, Oval, 16 x 12 1/2 In.	1175.00
Cheese Dish, Undertray, Figural, Cow's Head, Pink Luster, 7 x 9 In.	260.00
Coffeepot, Cover, Classical Subjects, Swan Finial, 1830s, 10 1/4 In.	258.00
Coffeepot, Dome Lid, Acorn Finial, Floral, Blue, Scroll Handle, Ribbed Spout, 11 1/2 In. .	440.00
Coffeepot, George Washington	770.00
Coffeepot, Lafayette At Franklin's Tomb, Blue, 8 3/4 In.	550.00
Coffeepot, Spring, Bulbous, Shaped Spout & Handle, 10 1/2 In.	22.00
Creamer, Catskill Mountains Hudson River	495.00
Creamer, Cow, Black & White, 6 1/2 In.	127.00
Creamer, Cow, Cover, Pottery, Overglaze, Enamel, Mid 19th Century, 6 1/2 In.	52.00
Creamer, Fisherman, Canary, Black Transfer, Black Stripes, 5 1/2 In.	385.00
Creamer, Strawberry & Rose Design, Scroll Handle, Scalloped, 4 1/2 In.	80.00
Cup, Glazed, Brown, Green, Blue Enamel, 2 Handles, c.1780, 4 3/8 In.	175.00
Cup, Invalid, Leaf & Fruit, Blue Transfer, Cylindrical Spout, Splashguard, 2 1/2 In.	300.00
Cup, Yellow Ground, 2 Handles, Inverted Bell Shape, c.1810, 5 1/4 In.	590.00
Cup & Saucer, American Flag, Red & Blue Striped Border, Handleless	145.00
Cup & Saucer, Cabbage Rose	275.00
Cup & Saucer, Floral Design, Blue, Dark Green, Gold	250.00
Cup & Saucer, Lafayette At Franklin's Tomb, Handleless, Enoch Wood & Sons	275.00
Cup & Saucer, Landing Of General Lafayette, Blue, Handleless, Signed	525.00
Cup Plate, Cadmus, Blue, 3 5/8 In.	195.00
Cup Plate, Castle Garden Battery, Blue, Impressed Wood, 3 5/8 In.	248.00
Custard Cup, Cover, Stand, Pink Luster, Rectangular, c.1810, 3 11/16 In.	3525.00
Dish, Hen On Basket Cover, 6 x 8 In.	357.00
Dish, Hen On Nest Cover, Bisque, Polychrome, 8 In.	310.00
Dish, Hen On Nest Cover, Brown, Orange & Pink, Yellow Basket, 10 1/2 x 8 In.	470.00
Dish, Hen On Nest Cover, Glazed, 7 1/2 x 9 In.	330.00

Dish, Hen On Nest Cover, Matte, 7 3/4 x 9 In. 1980.00
Dish, Vegetable, Cover, Fruit, Blue Transfer, Square, 9 In. 1840.00
Dish, Vegetable, Cover, Ship Of The Line In The Downs, Shell Border, 6 x 9 In. 1380.00
Figurine, 2 Lovers, Under Bower, 10 1/2 In. 127.00
Figurine, 2 Spaniels On Cask, Flat Back, 19th Century, 8 1/4 In. 750.00
Figurine, Barefoot Girl, In Wingback Chair, Red Plaid Dress, 3 3/8 In. 410.00
Figurine, Benjamin Franklin, Dark Blue Coat & Vest, 14 1/2 In. 990.00
Figurine, Boy, Reading From Open Book, 6 1/2 In. 290.00
Figurine, Cat, With Boot, 4 3/4 In. 80.00
Figurine, Cherub, Holding Flower Basket, Garland In Hair, 1840, 5 In. 335.00
Figurine, Courting Couple, On Couch, 6 1/2 In. 46.00
Figurine, Cradle, Canary, Molded, Zigzag Lines, 4 1/2 x 2 1/4 In. 410.00
Figurine, Dog, Black & Gray, Hollow Body, 11 1/4 In., Pair 550.00
Figurine, Dog, Black Muzzle, Yellow Eyes, Copper Luster Collar, 6 In., Pair 110.00
Figurine, Dog, Jackfield Spaniel, England, c.1865, 12 In. 850.00
Figurine, Dog, Pomeranian, Ribbons, c.1900, 8 In., Pair 520.00
Figurine, Dog, Poodle, c.1865, Miniature 250.00
Figurine, Dog, Poodle, On Clock, c.1865 .... 695.00
Figurine, Dog, Seated, Black Muzzle, Gilt Collar, Sanded Coat, 4 1/2 In. 80.00
Figurine, Dog, Seated, White Coat, Black Muzzle, Glass Eyes, 11 1/4 In., Pair 275.00
Figurine, Dog, Spaniel, c.1865, Miniature 285.00
Figurine, Dog, Spaniel, Flat Back, Mid 19th Century, 12 In., Pair 400.00
Figurine, Dog, Spaniel, Seated, Gilt Trim, 19th Century, 12 1/2 In., Pair 489.00
Figurine, Dog, Spaniel, Seated, Orange Nose, Yellow Eyes, 8 1/2 In., Pair 190.00
Figurine, Dog, Spaniel, Seated, Padlocked Collar, Chain, 20th Century, 12 In., Pair 4020.00
Figurine, Dog, Spaniel, Seated, Painted Face, Gold Trim, 12 1/2 In., Pair 365.00
Figurine, Dog, Spaniel, Seated, Red & White, Cobalt Blue Base, 8 In., Pair 2640.00
Figurine, Dog, Spaniel, Seated, Red Spots, Silver Luster Chain, 6 In., Pair 220.00
Figurine, Dog, Spaniel, Seated, White, Black Muzzle, Chain Loop, 1860, 10 In., Pair 900.00
Figurine, Dog, Spaniel, Standing, Brown, Glass Eyes, 10 x 14 In. 250.00
Figurine, Dog, Spaniel, With Flower Basket, c.1855, 7 1/2 In. 950.00
Figurine, Dog, Spaniel, Yellow Basket Of Flowers, 8 1/8 In. 550.00
Figurine, Dog, Spaniels On Barrel, c.1865, Miniature 395.00
Figurine, Dog, Whippet, Standing, Rabbit In Mouth, 7 1/2 In., Pair 209.00
Figurine, Dog, White Painted Face, Gilt Accent, 10 In. 250.00
Figurine, Dog, White, Black Nose, Glass Eyes, 12 3/4 In., Pair 495.00
Figurine, Dog, White, Black Nose, Luster Trim, 10 x 8 In., Pair 395.00
Figurine, Equestrian Scottish Hunter, Slain Stag, 14 1/2 In., Pair 730.00
Figurine, Girl, Holding Flowers In Her Apron, 6 1/4 In. 69.00
Figurine, Girl, Riding Goat, c.1860, Miniature 395.00
Figurine, Lamb, Lying, Early 19th Century, 4 1/2 x 6 1/4 In. 160.00
Figurine, Lion, c.1860, Miniature 395.00
Figurine, Lion, Glass Eyes, Lancaster & Sons, Hanley, England, 1940, Pair 650.00
Figurine, Lion, Glass Eyes, Orange Brown Glaze, 9 3/4 x 13 In., Pair 300.00
Figurine, Lion, Lying, Amber Glass Eyes, Late 19th Century, 9 x 12 In., Pair 430.00
Figurine, Lion, Lying, Crossed Paws, Green Glass Eyes, Orange Glaze, 10 In. 358.00
Figurine, Little Red Riding Hood, 5 1/2 In. 58.00
Figurine, Little Red Riding Hood, c.1865 .... 395.00
Figurine, Napoleon, Standing, Blue Coat, 5 In. 45.00
Figurine, Ram, Sanded Coat, Gray Horns, Hollow Trunk, 5 1/2 In. 190.00
Figurine, Rebecca, 14 1/2 In. 95.00
Figurine, Royal Princess, With Sheep, 1860 .... 450.00
Figurine, Scotsman, In Kilt, With Dog, c.1865, 14 1/2 In. 420.00
Figurine, Scottish Woman, Holding Riding Crop, 12 In. 365.00
Figurine, Shakespeare, Leaning On Books, Pedestal, 18 In. ....440.00 to 900.00
Figurine, Shakespeare, Mounted As Lamp, 19th Century, 18 In. 345.00
Figurine, Sheep & Goat, Lying, Rockwood Base, c.1783, 7 1/4 In., Pair 7638.00
Figurine, Venus, Dolphin At Foot, Seashells On Base, c.1830, 9 1/2 In. 258.00
Figurine, Woman, Reading Book, c.1825, 7 In. 375.00
Figurine, Zebra, Standing On Grassy Ground, Pottery, 5 In. 224.00
Footbath, Boating Scenes, Blue Transfer, Open Handles, 8 1/2 x 21 x 14 In. 825.00
Footbath, Flowers, Landscapes, Ruins, Dark Blue Underglaze, 1816-1836 .... 3220.00
Gravy Boat, Underplate, States, Blue, Signed 1760.00

Group, Cow & Maid, 7 In. 635.00
Group, Eva & Uncle Tom, 8 1/4 In. 468.00
Group, Horse & Rider, Green Blanket, Yellow Hat On Man, 9 1/4 x 9 In. 229.00
Group, Lions, Lying, Brown, White, Glass Eyes, Black Trim, 8 1/2 x 8 In. 345.00
Group, Man & Woman, Seated Under Arbor, 14 1/4 In. 275.00
Group, Mother Goose, Astride Goose, Late 19th Century, 7 In. 129.00
Group, Prince & Princess, Standing, Arm In Arm, Full Figure, 16 In. 275.00
Group, Scottish Couple, Man Carrying Basket, Woman In Pink Dress, 14 In. 140.00
Group, Spotted Cow & Calf, Standing By Stream, 5 1/2 In. 150.00
Group, Welsh Shepherds, Man & Woman, 2 Sheep, Both Sides, 14 In. 385.00
Group, Whimsy, Brick Courtyard, Gate, Tree, Snake, Sheep, 8 1/2 x 8 In. 290.00
Group, Woman, Seated On Horseback, Attendant, 19th Century, 13 x 8 In. 200.00
Hatpin Holder, Blue & Gold, 1900 .... 22.00
Hatpin Holder, Pink Flowers, 1900 .... 22.00
Hutch, Watch, 3 Foxes, 1 Holding Bird, Grape, 8 1/8 In. 550.00
Jar, Cover, Bear, Pig, Salt Glazed, Mid 18th Century, 8 In. 3600.00
Jug, Cover, Cream, Pear Shape, 3 Paw Feet, c.1800, 5 In. 175.00
Jug, Famous Naval Heroes, 8 1/2 In. 1780.00
Jug, Milk, Flower Molded, Serpentine, Eagle, Yellow Ground, c.1815, 7 1/2 In. 1175.00
Jug, Presented By Alfred Meakin, Tunstall, England, 29 1/2 In. 5175.00
Mug, 3 Men Drinking, Front & Back, Frog Inside, Crawling Up Side, 5 1/4 In. 225.00
Mug, Biblical, They That Seek Me Early Shall Find Me, c.1850, 2 5/8 In. 180.00
Mug, Billy Button, Man Riding Horse Backward, 2 5/8 In. 121.00
Mug, Drinking Scene, 3 People, Grapevine, Scroll Handle, 5 1/4 In. 165.00
Mug, Going To Market & Fishing, Black Transfer Scene, 1840, 2 5/8 In. 235.00
Mug, Present For A Good Boy, Canary Yellow, Red Transfer, Child's, 2 1/2 In. 460.00
Mug, Strawberry Design, Canary, Silver Luster Stripes, Child's, 2 1/2 In. 578.00
Pastille Burner, Castle Shape, Early 19th Century, 4 1/2 In., Pair 860.00
Pastille Burner, Cottage, Mid 19th Century 225.00
Pastille Burner, Samuel Alcock, c.1835 .... 2850.00
Pipe, Snake, Coiled, Pottery, Enamel, 19th Century, 7 1/2 In. 350.00
Pitcher, Abraham Lincoln, Malice Toward None, Oval Portraits, 8 1/2 In. 990.00
Pitcher, Bell Flower Design, Cream, Red, Blue & Green, Bulbous, 5 1/2 In. 50.00
Pitcher, Blue & White, Mayer, 6 In. 259.00
Pitcher, Boston State House, New York City Hall, Medallion Sides, 6 3/8 In. 935.00
Pitcher, Floral, Bridge, Green, Pink & Copper Luster, 4 1/2 In. 66.00
Pitcher, Girl, Picking Flowers, Boy, Robbing Nest, Blue Transfer, 5 1/2 In. 495.00
Pitcher, Naval War Heroes, Lakeside Monument, 5 7/8 In. 660.00
Pitcher, New York City Hall, New York Insane Asylum, 6 7/8 In. 1430.00
Pitcher, Romantic Scene, Deer & Ruins, Floral Handle, 8 1/2 In. 275.00
Pitcher, Water, Rebecca At The Well, Blue Transfer, 8 1/2 In. 1155.00
Pitcher, World's Only Corn Palace, Mitchell, S.D., Purple, 5 1/2 In. 140.00
Plate, Baltimore Exchange, Blue, 10 In. 385.00
Plate, Bird, Flowers & Bug, Give Us This Day Our Daily Bread, 12 x 9 In. 135.00
Plate, Boating Scene, Cottage, Castle, Blue Transfer, 9 3/4 In. 66.00
Plate, Boston State House, 7 3/8 In. ....*Illus* 192.00
Plate, Boston State House, Blue, White, John Rodgers & Son, 1842, 14 x 19 In. 1495.00
Plate, Boston State House, Floral Border, Enoch Wood, 9 3/4 In. 110.00
Plate, City Hall, New York, Blue, 9 3/4 In. 300.00
Plate, Coaching Stages, Charles Dickens, W.H. Grindley, 10 In. 30.00
Plate, Commodore MacDonnough's Victory, Shell Border Series, 10 In. 460.00
Plate, Eagle Scene, Blue Transfer, 1831, 8 3/4 In. 170.00
Plate, Fall Of Montmorenci Near Quebec, E Pluribus Unum, 9 1/8 In. 250.00
Plate, Flowers, Wavy Lines, Brown Transfer, 6 5/8 In. 55.00
Plate, Hobart Town, Blue, Impressed Rosette, 9 In. 385.00
Plate, Lafayette At Washington's Tomb, Blue, 10 In. 990.00
Plate, Lafayette, Nation's Guest & Our Country Is Glory, Blue, Round 1950.00
Plate, Landing Of The Fathers At Plymouth, Dec. 22, 1620, Burslem, 8 1/2 In. 345.00
Plate, Landing Of The Pilgrims, Ships In Medallions, Enoch Wood, 10 1/4 In. 385.00
Plate, Lion Center, Surrounded By Deer, Goats & Zebras, 10 1/4 In. 385.00
Plate, Luscombe, Devonshire, Reticulated Border, R. Hall, 12 In. 460.00
Plate, Nahant Hotel, Near Boston, Spread Eagle Border Series, 8 1/4 In. 600.00
Plate, New York City Hall, American Scenery Series, Brown & White, 8 In. 130.00

Staffordshire, Plate,
Boston State House,
7 3/8 In.

Staffordshire, Platter, Capitol,
Washington, Beauties Of
America, 15 1/2 x 20 1/2 In.

Staffordshire, Platter,
Niagara Falls, From The
American Side, 15 In.

Plate, Park Theatre, New York, Blue, 10 In.	330.00
Plate, Philadelphia Library, Beauties Of America, 19th Century, 8 In.	430.00
Plate, Regents Park, London, Blue Transfer, 6 In.	120.00
Plate, Shannon, Shell Border, Blue Transfer, Enoch Wood & Sons, 1846, 10 In.	345.00
Plate, St. Paul's Church, New York, Blue, 6 1/4 In.	275.00
Plate, State House, Philadelphia, 1776, Royal Cauldon, 11 In.	95.00
Plate, States, 3-Story Building, Observatory, Blue, 10 In.	330.00
Plate, Table Rock, Niagara, Impressed Enoch Wood, 9 1/4 In.	440.00
Plate, Union Line, Shell Border, 10 1/4 In.	690.00
Plate, Upper Ferry Bridge Over The River Schuylkill, 8 3/4 In.	360.00
Plate, Windsor Castle, 9 x 7 1/2 In.	160.00
Plate, Winter View Of Pittsfield, Mass., Blue, Signed, 8 In.	360.00
Plate, Wistow Hall, Leicestershire, Lake, 2 Women, 8 3/4 In.	137.00
Plate Set, Rural Scenes, Brown, Goodridge, 19th Century, 6 3/4 In., 9 Piece	310.00
Platter, Blue, 8 Sides, Friburg G. Phillips, 18 x 14 In.	200.00
Platter, Blue, Mayer, 15 In.	200.00
Platter, Brown Sponged, Scalloped Rim, 1780s, 15 In.	1090.00
Platter, Capitol, Washington, Beauties Of America, 15 1/2 x 20 1/2 In. . . . . *Illus*	5280.00
Platter, Castle Scene, Dark Blue Transfer, Acanthus Leaf Rim, 11 3/4 x 15 In.	440.00
Platter, Classical Urn, Light Blue Transfer, Vine & Berry Border, 8 Sides, 20 In.	145.00
Platter, Diorama View Of Houghton Conquest House, 16 3/4 In.	880.00
Platter, East View Of La Grange, The Residence Of The Marquis Lafayette, 10 In.	385.00
Platter, Elkin Knight, Canton Views, Blue, 19 x 20 1/2 In.	750.00
Platter, Fairmont, Near Philadelphia, Blue Transfer Print, Joseph Stubbs, c.1830	1840.00
Platter, Flower Filled Urns, Enamel, Imari Palette	150.00
Platter, Lake George, State Of New York, Blue Transfer, 1846, 13 x 16 1/2 In.	1840.00
Platter, Niagara Falls, From The American Side, 15 In. . . . . *Illus*	2200.00
Platter, Palace Of St. Germain, Picturesque Scenery, Dark Blue Transfer, 19 In.	440.00
Platter, Rural Landscape, Sheep, House, Floral Border, Blue, 18 1/2 In.	520.00
Platter, Sandusky, Harbor View, Floral Border, Blue, 16 1/2 In.	4620.00
Platter, Sheltered Peasants, Blue, Fruit & Floral Border, 14 1/2 x 19 In.	770.00
Platter, Turkey, 2 Birds, Red, Floral Border, Burslem, 17 1/4 x 21 1/4 In.	110.00
Platter, Upper Ferry Bridge Over The River Schuylkill, 18 In.	1650.00
Platter, Well & Tree, Black & White Landscape, J. Carr & Co., 9 1/2 In.	345.00
Platter, Wharf, Baltimore, Green Transfer, Flower Border, T. Godwin, c.1840	430.00
Punch Pot, Stoneware, Red, Crabstock Spout & Handle	2500.00
Sauceboat, Enamel Leaves & Berries, 3 Lion Mask Feet, Oval, 7 In.	2645.00
Saucer, George Washington Standing At His Tomb, Scroll In Hand, Wood, 6 In.	140.00
Saucer, Lafayette At Franklin's Tomb, Wood & Son, 5 3/4 In.	247.00
Serving Dish, Cover, Blue & White, 9 1/4 In.	230.00
Shelf, Bracket, Figural, Doe Head, 19th Century, 11 x 7 1/2 x 7 In.	345.00
Shelf, Bracket, Figural, Horse Head, 19th Century, 11 x 7 1/2 x 7 In.	175.00
Soup, Dish, American Villa, Blue, Signed, 10 In.	220.00
Soup, Dish, Bird Dog & Hunter, Blue Transfer, Wood & Sons, 10 In.	630.00
Sugar, Commodore MacDonnough's Victory, Enoch Wood	630.00
Sugar, Cover, Acorn Finial, Castle Scene, Canary, Black, 2 Ring Handles, 6 1/8 In.	220.00
Sugar, Cover, Lafayette At Franklin's Tomb, Blue, 6 1/2 In.	660.00

Sugar, Cover, Sower, Red Transfer, 5 1/2 In. 104.00
Sugar, Deer, Floral Finial, Blue, Scrolled Handles, 5 3/4 In. 715.00
Tea Canister, 5 Dot Clusters, Stoneware, Salt Glaze, c.1760, 3 1/4 In. 355.00
Tea Set, Child's, Greek Key Border, 13 Piece 200.00
Tea Set, Flowers, Blue Transfer, Nesting Bird, 9 1/2 In. Teapot, 3 Piece 605.00
Tea Set, Washington Standing At His Tomb, Scroll In Hand, Enoch Wood, 5 Piece 2750.00
Teabowl & Saucer, Lafayette At Washington's Tomb, Scroll In Hand, 6 In. 750.00
Teapot, Cover, Agate Pectin Shell, c.1740, 6 In. 7050.00
Teapot, Cover, Leaves, Shells, Stoneware, Salt Glaze, 3-Footed, c.1760, 4 In. 705.00
Teapot, Cover, Lion Mask & Paw Feet, Globular, c.1775, 4 In. 375.00
Teapot, Cover, Pineapple, Yellow, Green, c.1765, 5 3/4 In. 8815.00
Teapot, Cover, Prussian Eagle, Vignettes, Stoneware, Salt Glaze, c.1760, 3 1/2 In. 2000.00
Teapot, Cover, Redware, White Leaves & Berries, Globular, c.1740, 3 1/2 In. 1295.00
Teapot, Flowers & Urn, American Eagle With Shield, 6 1/2 In. 660.00
Teapot, Lafayette At Franklin's Tomb, 8 1/2 In. 1495.00
Teapot, Molded Floral Finial, Man Fishing, Blue Transfer, 7 1/2 In. 465.00
Teapot, Musical Family, Canary, Black Transfer & Stripes, Flared Rim, 5 1/8 In. 495.00
Teapot, Red Transfer, Sower, 7 1/2 In. 60.00
Teapot, Redware, Boy In Tree, Serpent Handle, Leaf Spout, 8 Sides, 1755, 4 In. 750.00
Teapot, Riverside Estate, Sailboat, Shells, Dark Blue 935.00
Teapot, Scratch Blue Flowers, c.1760, 4 In. 170.00
Toby Jugs are listed in their own category.
Tureen, Cover, Underplate, Man, Woman, Lake, Brown, 1795, 13 In. 275.00
Tureen, Fisherman's Hut, Blue Transfer, Applied Handle, 15 x 5 3/4 In. 415.00
Vase, Figural, Little Red Riding Hood, Fox, Tree Trunk, 15 1/4 In. 605.00
Wall, Pocket, Satyr Head, Dolphin Head, Stoneware, Salt Glaze, c.1760, 5 5/8 In. 353.00
Wall Pocket, Cornucopia, Landscape, Stoneware, Salt Glaze, c.1760, 7 1/4 In. 1116.00
Warming Dish, Wild Rose, Blue Transfer, Mid 19th Century, 9 3/4 In. 170.00
Wash Pitcher, Brown, White, 19th Century, 10 In. 546.00
Waste Bowl, Sower, Red Transfer, 3 In. 231.00

STANGL Pottery traces its history back to the Fulper Pottery of New Jersey. In 1910, Johann Martin Stangl started working at Fulper. He left to work at Haeger Pottery from 1915 to 1920. Stangl returned to Fulper Pottery in 1920, became president in 1926, and changed the company name to Stangl Pottery in 1929. Stangl acquired the firm in 1930. The pottery is known for dinnerware and a line of bird figurines. Martin Stangl died in 1972, and the pottery was sold to Frank Wheaton, Jr., of Wheaton Industries. Production continued until 1978, when Pfaltzgraff Pottery purchased the right to the Stangl trademark, and the remaining inventory was liquidated. A single bird figurine is identified by a number. Figurines made up of two birds are identified by a number followed by the letter "D" indicating "Double."

ABC, Cup, Child's 65.00
Aztec, Bowl, Cereal, 5 1/2 In. 11.00
Aztec, Bowl, Fruit, 5 1/2 In. 8.00
Aztec, Cup 6.00
Aztec, Plate, Dinner, 10 In. 10.00
Aztec, Plate, Salad, 8 In. 7.50
Bird, Bluejay, No. 3715 .... 110.00
Bird, Red-Headed Woodpeckers, Double, No. 3752D. 110.00
Bittersweet, Coffeepot 75.00
Garland, Bowl, Fruit, 5 1/2 In. 8.50
Garland, Bowl, Salad, 12 In. 45.00
Garland, Bowl, Vegetable, 8 In. 25.00
Garland, Bread Tray 18.00
Garland, Casserole, Cover, 8 In. 40.00
Garland, Casserole, Cover, Individual 32.00
Garland, Coffeepot 68.00
Garland, Cup & Saucer 12.50
Garland, Plate, 6 In. 6.00
Garland, Plate, 8 In. .... 9.00 to 10.00

Garland, Plate, 10 In. 13.00
Garland, Soup, Lug, 5 1/2 In. 14.00
Golden Harvest, Console 20.00
Little Boy Blue, Bowl, Child's 85.00
Lyric, Coffee Server 78.00
Magnolia, Bowl, Vegetable, Round, 8 In. 25.00
Magnolia, Coffeepot, Individual 98.00
Magnolia, Cup 9.00
Magnolia, Plate, 8 In. 12.00
Magnolia, Plate, 10 In. 18.00
Magnolia, Salt & Pepper 25.00
Mealtime Special, Dish, Divided, Child's 115.00
Orchard Song, Coffeepot 72.00
Orchard Song, Cup & Saucer 10.00
Orchard Song, Plate, 6 In. 4.00
Orchard Song, Plate, 10 In. 10.00
Orchard Song, Soup, Dish 10.00
Our Barnyard Friends, Dish, Divided, Child's 110.00
Prelude, Cup & Saucer 10.00
Prelude, Plate, 8 In. 9.00
Prelude, Sugar, Cover 18.00
Sailfish, Ashtray 68.00
Thistle, Casserole, Cover, Individual 35.00
Thistle, Salt & Pepper 18.00
Vase, Satin White, 5 1/2 In. 35.00
Vase, Terra Rose, Green, Pink Interior, 7 1/2 In. .... *Illus* 75.00

STAR TREK and STAR WARS collectibles are included here. The television series *Star Trek* ran from 1966 through 1969. The TV show *Next Generation,* a sequel, ran from 1987 to 1994. The first Star Trek movie was released in 1979 and 8 others followed, the most recent in 1999. The movie *Star Wars* opened in 1977 and sequels and prequels were released in 1980, 1983, and 1999. Other science fiction and fantasy collectibles can be found under Batman, Buck Rogers, Captain Marvel, Flash Gordon, Superman, Movie, and Toy.

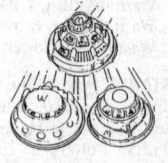

STAR TREK, Book, Enterprise Logs, First 8 Issues, Gold Key Comics, Soft Cover, 224 Pages   17.00
Book, Stories, Game Board, Puzzles, Annual, 1978, 7 3/4 x 10 3/4 In., 64 Pages 12.00
Bracelet, Navigation, Blue, Plastic, Paper Scene, Stickers, McDonald's Premium 20.00
Card, Birthday, Captain Kirk On Front, Punch-Out Kirk Inside To Assemble 12.00
Coloring Book, Mr. Spock On Cover, Saalfield Publishing, 1975, 62 Pages 8.00
Comic Book, Dark Traveler, No. 6, Color, 1971, 3 x 6 In., 24 Pages 15.00
Comic Book, Psycho Crystals & A Bomb In Time, Whitman, 1978, 7 x 10 In. 5.00
Communicator, Blue Plastic, Metal Antenna, Battery Operated, 1 x 2 1/2 x 6 In., Pair ... 20.00
Figure, Captain Kirk, Posable, Costumed, Mego Corp., 1979 .... 40.00
Figure, Miniatures, Wrath Of Kahn, 25 mm Lead Scale, Set No. 2, Box 17.00
Game, Board, Ideal, For Paramount Pictures, 1967 .... 95.00
Game, Board, Star Fleet, McDonald's Meal Premium, 1979 .... 20.00
Ink Stamp, Figural, Canadian, 4 Piece 20.00
Iron-On, Captain Kirk & Star Trek Emblem, Glitter, McDonald's Premium 20.00
Ring, Blue, Plastic, Secret Compartment, McDonald's Premium 20.00
Water Pistol, Hand Phaser, Raised Logo On Grip, Color Control Sticker 18.00
STAR WARS, Bank, Darth Vader, Glazed Ceramic, 6 x 6 1/2 x 6 In. 28.00
Cookie Jar, Darth Vader, C-3PO, R2-D2, Glazed Ceramic, Cover, 4 1/4 x 9 x 10 1/2 In. .. 90.00
Doll, Boba Fett, Box, 12 In. 1495.00
Doll, Stormtrooper, Box, 12 In. 365.00
Figure, 4-LOM, Revenge Of The Jedi, Bug-Eyes, Kenner, 3 1/4 In. 95.00
Figure, Anakin Skywalker, Posable, Kenner, 3 3/4 In. 25.00
Figure, AT-AT Driver, Return Of The Jedi, Palitoy, On Card 125.00
Figure, Battle Droid, Theed, On Card 3.00
Figure, Ben Kenobi, Star Wars, On Card, 3 3/4 In. 425.00
Figure, C-3PO, Empire Strikes Back, Removable Limbs, On Card, 3 3/4 In. 130.00
Figure, Cloud Car Pilot, Empire Strikes Back, On Card, 3 3/4 In. 100.00
Figure, Darth Vader, Return Of The Jedi, On Card 100.00

Figure, Darth Vader, Star Wars, 3 3/4 In. 15.00
Figure, Darth Vader, Star Wars, On Card, 3 3/4 In. 575.00
Figure, Ewok, Teebo, Return Of The Jedi, On Card, Canada 45.00
Figure, Ewok, Wicket, Return Of The Jedi, 3 3/4 In. 20.00
Figure, Han Solo, Large Head, Star Wars, 3 3/4 In. 20.00
Figure, Han Solo, Large Head, Star Wars, On Card, Unpunched, 3 3/4 In. 1995.00
Figure, Jawa, Return Of The Jedi, On Card 125.00
Figure, Luke Skywalker, Star Wars, 3 3/4 In. 45.00
Figure, Luke Skywalker, Star Wars, On Card, Taiwan, 3 3/4 In. 995.00
Figure, Luke Skywalker, X-Wing Pilot, Star Wars, On Card 350.00
Figure, Princess Leia, Bespin, Empire Strikes Back, On Card 275.00
Figure, Princess Leia, Combat Poncho, Return Of The Jedi, 3 3/4 In. 30.00
Figure, Princess Leia, Hoth, Empire Strikes Back, On Card 180.00
Figure, Princess Leia, Organa, Empire Strikes Back, On Card 225.00
Figure, Princess Leia, Star Wars, On Card, 3 3/4 In. 700.00
Figure, R2-D2, Empire Strikes Back, On Card 135.00
Figure, Stormtrooper, Return Of The Jedi, On Card 100.00
Figure, Stormtrooper, Star Wars, 3 3/4 In. 15.00
Figure, Yoda, Brown Snake, Empire Strikes Back 45.00
Figure, Yoda, Brown Snake, Empire Strikes Back, On Card 375.00
Figure, Yoda, Orange Snake, Empire Strikes Back, On Card, Canada 225.00
Model Kit, Jedi, Posable, Assembled, 8 In. 15.00
Playset, Jabba The Hutt, Movable Figure, Platform With Prison Gates, 1983 .... 35.00
Socks, Chewbacca, Nylon, Polyester, 20 In., Pair 18.00
Toothbrush, Character Portraits, Clear Plastic Handle, Battery, Kenner 25.00
Toy, Interceptor, Light, Battle Sound, Pop-Off Panels, Battery, Plastic 65.00
Toy, Jedi Speeder Bike, Return Of The Jedi, Box, 1983 .... 46.00
Toy, X-Wing Fighter, Battle Sound, Movable Landing Gear, 12 x 23 1/2 x 5 In. 90.00

STEINS have been used by beer and ale drinkers for over 500 years. They have been made of ivory, porcelain, stoneware, faience, silver, pewter, wood, or glass in sizes up to nine gallons. Although some were made by Mettlach, Meissen, Capo-di-Monte, and other famous factories, most were made by less important German potteries. The words *Geschutz* or *Musterschutz* on a stein are the German words for *patented* or *registered design*, not company names. Steins are still being made in the old styles. Lithophane steins may be found in the Lithophane category.

Anheuser-Busch, Americano, Ceramarte, 1/2 Liter 360.00
Anheuser-Busch, Brew House Tower Clock, 1/2 Liter 399.00
Anheuser-Busch, Bud Man, Hollow Head, 1/2 Liter 425.00
Anheuser-Busch, City Scenes, 1/2 Liter 230.00
Anheuser-Busch, City Series, Frankfurt, Ceramarte, 1/2 Liter 240.00
Anheuser-Busch, City Series, Heidelberg, Ceramarte, 1/2 Liter 265.00
Anheuser-Busch, City Series, Munchen, Ceramarte, 1/2 Liter 265.00
Anheuser-Busch, Das Festhaus, Busch Gardens, 1/2 Liter 146.00
Anheuser-Busch, Delft, Ceramarte, 1/2 Liter 300.00
Anheuser-Busch, Katakombe, Blue Background, Ceramarte, 1/2 Liter .... 113.00 to 182.00
Anheuser-Busch, Old Country, Busch Gardens, Williamsburg, Ceramarte, 1/2 Liter 45.00
Anheuser-Busch, Old Country, Oktoberfest, Ceramarte, 1/2 Liter 362.00
Bicycle, Breaking From Ride, Budapest Bicycle Club, Pottery, Pewter Lid, 1893, 1/2 Liter ... 145.00
Bicycle, Man Riding Standard Bicycle, Pewter, Relief Pewter Lid, 1/2 Liter 345.00
Bicycle, Man, High Wheel Bicycle, Vorwarts Lubeck Bicycle Club, Pewter Lid, 1/2 Liter . 750.00
Bicycle, Woman, Riding, White Enamel, Blown Glass, Prism Inlaid Lid, 1/3 Liter 315.00
Brewery, Angustinerbrau Munchen, Stoneware, Transfer, Enameled, Pewter Lid, 1/2 Liter ... 138.00
Brewery, Brauerei Zum Munchner Kindl, Transfer, Enameled, Pewter Lid, Logo, 1/4 Liter ... 362.00
Brewery, Erste Kulmbacher, Stoneware, Pewter Lid, Engraved Logo, 1 Liter 250.00
Brewery, Frankenbrau Bamberg Bayern, Pottery, Pewter Lid, Logo, 1/3 Liter 210.00
Brewery, Hacker-Brau Munchen, Enameled, Pottery, Pewter Lid, Relief, Logo, 1/2 Liter .. 375.00
Brewery, Hirschbraukeller, Stoneware, Pewter Lid, 1 Liter 440.00
Brewery, Lowenbrau Keller, Enameled, Pewter Lid, 1 Liter 544.00
Brewery, Lowenbrau Munchen, Transfer, Enameled, Engraved Pewter Lid, Logo, 1/2 Liter . 133.00
Brewery, Petzbrau Kulmbach, Transfer, Enameled, Stoneware, Pewter Lid, 1/4 Liter 362.00

Brewery, Purity Law, Porcelain, Copper Plated Lid, 1/2 Liter 84.00
Brewery, Salmenbrau Rheinfelden 1799-1899, Pottery, Pewter Lid, Relief, Logo, 1/2 Liter   425.00
Brewery, Unions Brau Munchen, Enameled, Pottery, Pewter Lid, Engraved, 1/2 Liter 665.00
Brewery, Zacherlbrau Munchen, Enameled, Pewter Lid, Relief, Logo, 1/2 Liter 575.00
Buildings, 2 Panels, Faience, Pewter Lid, c.1790, 8 3/4 In., 1 Liter 645.00
Cavaliers, Drinking, 1/2 Liter 135.00
Character, Alligator, Porcelain, Inlaid Lid, E. Bohne & Sons, 1/2 Liter 755.00
Character, Artillery Shell, Stoneware, Stoneware Lid, 1/2 Liter 280.00
Character, Bismark Radish, Porcelain, Inlaid Lid, Schierholz, 1/2 Liter 368.00
Character, Bowling Ball, Porcelain, Inlaid Lid, Thumblift, Schierholz, 1/2 Liter 360.00
Character, Bowling Pin, Pottery, Inlaid Lid, 15 1/2 In., 1 3/4 Liter 550.00
Character, Bull, Pottery, Pottery Lid, 1/2 Liter 950.00
Character, Devil, Porcelain, E. Bohne Soehne, Inlaid Lid, 1/2 Liter 575.00
Character, Diana & Hunter, Etched, Pottery, Inlaid Lid, Gerz, 1/4 Liter 130.00
Character, Football, Pennant With Initials MTHS, Pottery, Lid, 1/2 Liter 386.00
Character, Four Men Under Umbrella, Porcelain, Pewter Lid, Schierholz, 1/2 Liter 965.00
Character, Fraternity Frogs Dueling At Lake, Pottery, Figural Finial, 1/2 Liter 767.00
Character, Happy Radish, Porcelain, Inlaid Lid, Schierholz, 1/2 Liter 260.00
Character, Hunters, Figural Inlaid Cover, Drinking Cavalier, Regensburg, 1 Liter 250.00
Character, Knight, Stoneware, Relief, Inlaid Lid, Dumler & Breiden, 1/2 Liter 430.00
Character, Monkey, Sitting On Music Box Base, Pottery, Lid, 1/2 Liter 288.00
Character, Munich Child, Stoneware, Enameled, Pewter Lid, Sarreguemines, 1/2 Liter ... 150.00
Character, Owl, Porcelain, Porcelain Lid, Schierholz, 1/2 Liter 1340.00
Character, Owl, Pottery, Inlaid Lid, 1/2 Liter 288.00
Character, Pixie, Porcelain, Porcelain Lid, Schierholz, 1/2 Liter 865.00
Character, Prussian Eagle With Crown, Pottery, Relief, Pewter Lid, 1 Liter 489.00
Character, Sad Radish, Porcelain, Inlaid Lid, Schierholz, 1/2 Liter 360.00
Character, Soldier, Porcelain, Inlaid Lid, 1/2 Liter 460.00
Character, Story Of German Michael, Pewter, Pewter Lid, 1871, 1/2 Liter 905.00
Character, Tower, Pottery, Pewter Lid, 1/2 Liter 755.00
Character, Woman Holding Umbrella, Pottery, Pottery Lid, 1/2 Liter 725.00
Character, Woman, Pottery, Inlaid Lid, Diesinger, 1/2 Liter 405.00
Child Scene, Glass, Pink, Ribbed, Pewter Overlay, Pewter Lid, 1/2 Liter 324.00
Deer Running In Forest, Faience, Pewter Base Ring & Lid, Austria, c.1790, 1/2 Liter .. 1150.00
Double Headed Eagle, Crest, Ceramic, Pewter Lid, Hafner, Germany, 1833, 1 Liter 1095.00
Drinking Scene, Pottery, Etched, Pewter Lid, 1/2 Liter 125.00
Dwarf Reading Book, Stoneware, Transfer, Enameled, Pewter Lid, 1874, 1 Liter 375.00
Dwarfs, Carrying Grapes, Turning Wine Press, Pottery, Etched, Inlaid Lid, 1/3 Liter .. 136.00
Dwarfs, Walking Through Village, Pottery, Pewter Lid, Hauber & Reuther, 2 Liter 605.00
End Of Day Glass, Multicolored Interior Layer, Pewter Lid, 1/2 Liter 978.00
Figure & House, Twig Form Handle, Early 20th Century, 14 In. 90.00
Flowers, 3 Panels, Faience, Hand Painted, Pewter Lid, 1 Liter 150.00
Flowers, 4 Sides, Pottery, Relief, Pewter Lid, Diesinger, 20 In., 4 Liter 760.00
Fraternity Student, Pipes, Beer Steins, Pottery, Transfer, Enameled, 1/2 Liter 185.00
Frauenkirche Tower, Porcelain, Inlaid Lid, Martin Pauson, 1 Liter 1610.00
Gass Beery, Blue To Clear Threaded, Pewter Hinged Top & Top, Clear Handle, 7 5/8 In. .. 165.00
Gasthaus, Falstaff, Relief Pewter Lid, Bock Thumblift, 1 Liter 175.00
Gasthaus, Glass, Amber, Hand Painted, Pewter Base Ring, Pewter Lid, 1/2 Liter 485.00
Gasthaus, People Dancing, Transfer, Enameled, Pewter Lid, Victoria, Austria, 1/2 Liter .. 240.00
Glass, Amber, Enameled Leaf, Mold Blown, Inlaid Lid, 1/2 Liter 345.00
Glass, Boot, Color, Chimney Sweep, Transfer, Enameled, 1/2 Liter 127.00
Glass, Drunken Man, Cut Design, Porcelain Inlaid Lid, 1/2 Liter 524.00
Glass, Goat, 7 In. 210.00
Hearts, Flowers, Milk Glass, Enameled, Pewter Base & Lid, c.1800, 1/2 Liter 1200.00
Heidelberg University, 500 Anniversary, Heidelberg Castle, Majolica, 1/2 Liter 425.00
Horse, Leaping, Hannoversch Munden, Faience, Pewter Lid, Tool Cut, 8 1/2 In., 1 Liter .. 755.00
Horses, In Stable, Dogs, Pottery, Inlaid Lid, Signed, R. Decker, 1/2 Liter 318.00
Hunter, Rabbit, Dwarf, Mice, Pottery, Relief Pewter Lid, Hauber & Reuther, 1/2 Liter ... 460.00
Interior Man With Pipe, Women Peeling Apples, Branch Handle, 9 1/8 In. 140.00
Jockey, Glass, Fluted, Glass Inlaid Lid With Jockey Cap, 1/3 Liter 345.00
Knight, Horse, Standing At Stream, Pottery, Etched, Inlaid Lid, Marzi & Remy, 1/2 Liter . 345.00
Leaves, Berries, Glass, Amber, White, Purple, Enameled, Pewter Lid, 16 1/2 In. 145.00
Lohengrin Opera, Pottery, Pewter Lid, Hauber & Reuther, 1/2 Liter 460.00

Man, Red Jacket, Transfer, Enameled, Speckled Ground, Pewter Lid, Franz Ringer, 1 Liter 460.00
Man & Woman, Holding Hands, Pottery, Pewter Lid, Marked, Thewalt Paulus, 1/2 Liter . . 105.00
Man Playing Flute, Whites, New York, 2 Liter 198.00
Medieval Scene, Text, German, Ceramic, Pewter Lid, Early 20th Century, 11 1/2 In. 224.00
Medieval Scenes, Text, German, Ceramic, Figural Finials, 20th Century, 13 In., Pair 112.00
Men Bowling, Pottery, Pewter Lid, Hauber & Reuther, 1/2 Liter 375.00
Men Drinking, Whites, New York, Stoneware, Relief, Blue, Silver Plate Lid, 1/3 Liter . . . 100.00
Men On Horseback, Pottery, Etched, Pewter Lid, Marzi & Remy, 1/2 Liter 240.00
Mettlach steins are listed in the Mettlach category.
Military, Infantry & Target Shooting, Pottery, Figural Pewter Lid, Helmet Finial, 1/2 Liter 365.00
Military, Knight With Large Shield, Pewter Lid, 1/2 Liter 105.00
Military, Medic, Red Cross On Flags, Stoneware, Pewter Lid, 1/2 Liter 400.00
Military, Photograph, Young Boy, Inscription, Fritz Newburger, 1933, 1/2 Liter 725.00
Military, Signal Battalion, Boeblingen, Germany, Pewter Lid, 1 1/3 Liter 145.00
Military, Soldiers & Children Charging Woman Cooking, Pottery, Pewter Lid, 1 Liter 290.00
Military, Soldiers Changing Guardhouse Post Duty, Art Nouveau Pewter Lid, 1/2 Liter . . . 265.00
Military, Weihnachten 1931, Pottery, Flat Metal Lid, Germany, 1/2 Liter 290.00
Military, World War I Scene, Stoneware, Transfer, Enamel, Pewter Lid, c.1916, 1/2 Liter . 260.00
Monks, Transfer, Enameled, Pewter Lid, 2 Liters 145.00
Munich Child, Porcelain, Inlaid Lid, 6 1/2 In., 1/4 Liter 175.00
Munich Child, Stoneware, Transfer, Enameled, Pewter Lid, F. Ringer, 1/2 Liter 430.00
Munich Child, Stoneware, Transfer, Enamel, Pewter Lid, 1/4 Liter 115.00
Musicians, Pottery, Etched, JWR, Inlaid Lid, 1/2 Liter 115.00
Nun, Realistic Faces, Pewter Rim & Thumb Rest, Lithophane Bottom, 6 5/8 In., Pr. 250.00
Occupational, Cabinetmaker, Large Scene, Pewter Lid, 1/2 Liter 270.00
Occupational, Carpenter, 3 Scenes, Porcelain, Transfer, Enameled, Pewter Lid, 1/2 Liter . 375.00
Occupational, Cheese Maker, House, Cows, Mountains, Porcelain, Pewter Lid, 1/2 Liter . 390.00
Occupational, Chicken Breeding, Porcelain, Transfer, Enameled, Pewter Lid, 1/2 Liter . . . 725.00
Occupational, Chimney Sweep, 2 Large Scenes, Pewter Lid, 1/2 Liter 575.00
Occupational, Fireman With Trucks, 3 Scenes, Stoneware, Pewter Lid, 1926, 1/2 Liter . . . 390.00
Occupational, Fireman, 4T Turner Logo, Munich Child, Hunting Equipment, 1 Liter 415.00
Occupational, Fireman, Pewter Lid, 1/2 Liter 90.00
Occupational, Fireman, Pottery, Hand Painted, Roster, Pewter Lid, 1 Liter 345.00
Occupational, Firemen, Stoneware, Enameled, Pewter Lid, Relief Munchen, 1 Liter 385.00
Occupational, Furniture Maker, Porcelain, Transfer, Enameled, Pewter Lid, 1/2 Liter 489.00
Occupational, Locksmith, Porcelain, Transfer, Enameled, Pewter Lid, 1/2 Liter 345.00
Occupational, Post & Telegraph, Pottery, Relief, Pewter Lid, Eagle Thumblift, 1/2 Liter . . 546.00
Occupational, Streetcar Driver, Glass, Engraved, Pewter Lid, 1891-1916, 1/2 Liter 340.00
Occupational, Wagon Builder, Pewter Lid, 1/2 Liter 460.00
Oriental Scene, Glass, Tan, Enameled, Inlaid Lid, c.1870, 1/3 Liter 127.00
People Drinking, Pottery, Etched, Relief, Inlaid Lid, 1/2 Liter 60.00
Pewter, Glass, Continental, Domed Pewter Lid, Late 19th Century, 4 1/2 In. 60.00
Pewter, Ram's Head Around Sides, Hinge Top Lid, Amber, France, 15 1/4 In. 445.00
Regimental, 2 Sided, Roster, Lion Thumblift, 5 Liter, 9 1/4 In. 485.00
Regimental, 2-Sided, Farmer, 10 Comp., 5 Bayr., Inftr. Regt. Bamberg 1893-95, 1/2 Liter 235.00
Regimental, 2-Sided, Porcelain, Eagle Thumblift, Mainz, c.1903, 10 1/2 In., 1/2 Liter 485.00
Regimental, 2-Sided, Porcelain, Roster, Eagle Thumblift, 11 In., 1/2 Liter 368.00
Regimental, 2-Sided, Porcelain, Roster, Griffin Thumblift, 1905-07, 12 In., 1/2 Liter 430.00
Regimental, 2-Sided, Pottery, Roster, Eagle Thumblift, c.1913, 15 In., 1 Liter 835.00
Regimental, 2-Sided, Rgt 7, Saarbrucken, Porcelain, Eagle Thumblift, 1897, 1/2 Liter . . . 405.00
Regimental, 2-Sided, Roster, Lion Thumblift, Ulan Sack, c.1901, 11 1/2 In., 1/2 Liter 575.00
Regimental, 2-Sided, Target Shooting, Eagle Thumblift, Soldier Finial, 11 In., 1/2 Liter . . 483.00
Regimental, 4-Sided, Bamberg, Porcelain, Roster, Bavarian Thumblift, Helmet Lid, 10 In. 1020.00
Regimental, 4-Sided, Horse Grooming, Pottery, Eagle Thumblift, c.1912, 15 In. 966.00
Regimental, 4-Sided, Infantry, Porcelain, Roster, Lion Thumblift, 11 3/4 In., 1/2 Liter . . . 357.00
Regimental, 4-Sided, Rgt. 3, Augsburg, Stoneware, Roster, 1909, 1/2 Liter 485.00
Regimental, 4-Sided, Rgt. 5, Esc Munchen, Porcelain, 1898, 1/2 Liter 725.00
Regimental, 4-Sided, Roster, Sachsen Thumblift, Otto Hankel, c.1900, 12 In., 1/2 Liter . . 1751.00
Regimental, 4-Sided, Roster, Wurttemberg, Germany, c.1914, 12 In., 1/2 Liter 470.00
Regimental, Anheuser-Busch Brewing Assoc., 1/2 Liter 2246.00
Regimental, Boxer Aufstand China, Ships, Harbor, Wall Of China, Roster, 8 In., 1/2 Liter 5555.00
Regimental, Esk. Drag. Regt., No. 14, Colmar 1908-1911, Glass, 6 3/4 In., 1/4 Liter 455.00
Regimental, Infanterie Leib Regiment, Stoneware, Transfer, Enameled, 1 Liter 275.00

Regimental, Third Reich, Artillery, Abt. Art. Regt. 173, Frankreich, 1939, 1/2 Liter 276.00
Regimental, Third Reich, Iron Cross, Swastika, Tomaschow, Maz Polen, 1939, 1/2 Liter .   276.00
Regimental, Third Reich, Unteroffiziercorps, Der Minenwerfer Kompanie, 1/2 Liter 460.00
Royal Vienna, Woman Near Fence, Flowers, Green, Porcelain, Inlaid Lid, 1/2 Liter 2215.00
Scene, Relief, Porcelain, Figural Boar Finial, Capo-Di-Monte, 1/2 Liter 185.00
SCI Convention, New York City, Stoneware Lid, Ceramarte, 1974, 1/2 Liter 170.00
Shooting Festival, Transfer, Enameled, Elk Relief, Target Thumblift, c.1927, 1 Liter 480.00
Silver, Heart Initial, Repeating Design, Gold Washed Interior, 7 1/2 In. 1208.00
Smiling Mikado, 1/2 Liter 405.00
Spa, Buildings, Glass, Enameled, White, Yellow, Gold, 1/3 Liter 725.00
Stags Fighting, Glass, Fluted, Enameled, Pewter Lid, 1/2 Liter 150.00
Stoneware, Fuingen, Pewter Lid, Closed Hinged, c.1800, 1 Liter 151.00
Stoneware, Repeating Design, Paul Wynand, R. Merkelbach Grenzhausen, 2 Liter 725.00
Stoneware, Repeating Design, R. Merkelbach Grenzhausen, Pewter Lid, 3 Liter 725.00
Stoneware, Repeating Relief Design, Inlaid Lid, 1 1/2 Liter 127.00
Stoneware, VIII Deutches Sangerbundesfest Nurnberg 1912, Pewter Lid, 1/2 Liter 240.00
Student Society, Stoneware, Munich Child On Lid, Dated 1901, 1 Liter 483.00
Tankard, City, Naval Scenes, Pottery, Transfer, Enameled, 1/2 Liter 115.00
Tankard, Glass, Pink Interior, Cut Design, Silver Mount, Glass Inlay Lid, 1/2 Liter 690.00
Tankard, Tin, Heart Shape Finial, Applied Handle, Spade Shape, Hinged Cover, 13 In. 55.00
Tower, Stoneware, Blue & Purple Salt Glaze, Pewter Lid, 1/2 Liter 690.00
Trumpeter Of Sackingen, Glass, Transfer, Enameled, Pewter Lid, 1/2 Liter 275.00
Trumpeter Of Sackingen, Tan, Brown, Green, Relief, Pewter Lid, 1 1/2 Liter 100.00
Warriors, Around Campfire, Stoneware, Pewter Lid, Marzi & Remy, 1/2 Liter 238.00
Wood, Carved Body, Wood Handle, Wood Lid, c.1820, 1 Liter 2300.00

STEREO CARDS that were made for stereoscope viewers became popular after 1840. Two almost identical pictures were mounted on a stiff
cardboard backing so that, when viewed through a stereoscope, a
three-dimensional picture could be seen. Value is determined by maker
and by subject. These cards were made in quantity through the 1930s.

9 Bar Harbor, Maine Views, 1901 ....   90.00
Ault, Colorado, Cripple Creek Labor Violence, E.A. Dickerson, Ohio 190.00
Big Freighter, Ca., Covered Wagon Drawn By 8 Pairs Of Horses, Stonecypher, Neb. 50.00
Black Hawk, Colorado, View Of Mining Town, Tan Mount, 6 x 8 1/2 In. 530.00
Booker T. Washington, Presko Binocular Co., Chicago, 1912 ....   135.00
Boston Street Scene, Apartments For Rent, Upper Stories, 13 1/2 x 10 1/8 In. 270.00
Brigham Young's Party, Celebration Of Utah Central 10th, Yellow Mount 300.00
British Isles, 400, G.W. Wilson, London 805.00
Chief Geronimo, Standing, Holding A Small Bow & Arrow, 5 x 3 1/2 In. 440.00
China Town, Monterey, Shantytown With Several Figures At Left, 4 x 8 In. 180.00
Civil War, New York Harbor, 74 Gun Vessel, Brooklyn Navy Yard, 1868 ....   70.00
Civil War, Panorama Theater, Arlington Grove, June 10, 1862 ....   350.00
Dreaming, Old Man With Gouty Foot Dozing, Girl Reading 125.00
Early Salt Lake City Views, Storefront Of Zion's Cooperative Store, Carter 220.00
Egyptian, Eastern Series, 100 ....   260.00
Firemen Parade, Broadway, Approaching Square, Large Crowd 65.00
Fulton Ferry, Omnibuses, South Ferry, N.Y.C. 66.00
Georgia Gold Mine, Dahlonega Gold Mines, Black Man Up On Pipe 75.00
Geronimo & Camp, C.S. Fly, Tombstone, 1886 ....   2000.00
Graf Zeppelin, Lakehurst 28 ....   45.00
Main St., Monterey, Ca., Various Establishments Including Bakery, 7 1/2 In. 225.00
Montana Views, Virginia City, Overview Of Town, Savage & Ottinger 825.00
More Savage, Cottonwood Lake, Man In Boat, Savage & Ottinger, Green Mount 100.00
New York State, 350, Niagara Falls, Hudson River 1150.00
Pennsylvania, 300, Pike County 5750.00
Railroad & Survey, Engine 11 BCR, Bitter Creek, Tan Mounts 290.00
Salt Lake Street Scene, Front Of Establishments 120.00
Savage Out Camping, Camping Out, Get Up Boys, Savage & Ottinger, 1870, Pair 280.00
Slapping Her Awake, Movement, Man Slapping Older Woman 60.00
Western United States, 350 ....   1610.00
World In The Stereoscope, Hart & Anderson, N.Y., 1872 ....   103.00

STEREOSCOPE were used for viewing stereo cards. The hand viewer was invented by Oliver Wendell Holmes, although more complicated table models were used before his was produced in 1859. Do not confuse the stereoscope with the stereopticon, a magic lantern that used glass slides.

Brewster, Mahogany, Hinged Hood	200.00
Brewster, Mahogany, Serpentine Body, Hinged Hood, Ground Glass	90.00
Brewster, Painted Black, Hinged Hood, Binocular Eyepieces, Ground Glass	60.00
Brewster, Walnut, Hinged Hood, London	258.00
Brewster, Walnut, Serpentine Body, Hinged Hood, Ground Glass . . . . .375.00 to 400.00
Brewster, Walnut, Serpentine Case	375.00
Hinged Hood, Focusing Eyepieces, Walnut Pedestal, 20 In.	520.00
Holmes-Bates, Nickel, Swiveling Electric Lamp, Telescoping Stand, White	200.00
Mahogany, Tin, With Cards, 3 1/2 x 12 In.	170.00
Negretti & Zambra, Rack For 50 Cards, Walnut Pedestal, 21 1/2 In.	430.00
Rowsell, Mahogany, Hinged Hood, Binocular Eyepieces, 21 In.	860.00
Scissors Type, No Eye Shield	60.00
Stand, Rosewood, Viewer, Revolving Racks, Cards, Restored, Victorian	770.00
Underwood & Underwood, Oak & Brass, 1881 & 1901, 11 In.	75.00

STERLING SILVER, see Silver-Sterling category.

STEUBEN glass was made at the Steuben Glass Works of Corning, New York. The factory, founded by Frederick Carder and T.G. Hawkes, Sr., was purchased by the Corning Glass Company. They continued to make glass called *Steuben*. Many types of art glass were made at Steuben. The firm is still making exceptional quality glass but it is clear, modern-style glass. Additional pieces may be found in the Aurene, Cluthra, and perfume bottle categories.

Ashtray, Blue Calcite, Applied Twisted Ring Handle, Carder, 1929, 1 x 3 3/4 In.	575.00
Basket, Pomona Green, Looped Lattice, 20th Century, 4 1/2 In.	287.00
Bowl, 4 Scrolled Feet, Signed, 10 3/4 x 4 In.	300.00
Bowl, Blue Calcite, 14 In.	510.00
Bowl, Calcite, Gold Aurene Interior, Low, 10 1/2 In.	315.00
Bowl, Calcite, Gold Aurene, Ribbed, 4 3/4 In.	275.00
Bowl, Calyx Shape, Oval, Solid Foot, 1962, 3 x 9 In.	230.00
Bowl, Flared Rim, Signed, 4 x 9 1/2 In.	615.00
Bowl, Floret, No. 8059, Donald Pollard, 1954, 3 x 7 3/4 In. . . . . .86.00 to 201.00
Bowl, Gold Calcite, Inverted Rim, Early 20th Century, 8 3/8 In.	316.00
Bowl, Green To White, Acid Stamp & Mark, 4 3/4 In.	635.00
Bowl, Green, Amber, Flared, 6 Sides, 7 In.	325.00
Bowl, Grotesque, Ivory, 8 Folds, 1930, 8 3/4 x 12 In.	860.00
Bowl, Grotesque, Ivory, 8 Folds, Black Footed, 8 1/8 x 6 In.	750.00
Bowl, Iridescent Gold To Blue, 6 In.	230.00
Bowl, Light Blue Jade, 1925, 6 In.	805.00
Bowl, Light Blue Jade, Applied Alabaster Foot, 1925, 3 x 9 In.	750.00
Bowl, Low Footed, John Dreves, No. 7909, 1942, 10 3/4 x 4 In.	290.00
Bowl, Rosaline, Alabaster Base, 3 3/4 x 12 In.	240.00
Bowl, Sunflower, Signed, Eric Hilton, 1986, 10 In.	170.00
Candlestick, 2-Light, Oriental, Green Jade Cup, Alabaster Body, 10 1/4 In., Pair 8000.00 to 8960.00
Candlestick, 2-Light, Scroll Supports, Orb Finial, Engraved, 6 3/4 x 8 In.	775.00
Candlestick, Applied Black Cabochons, Pair	2530.00
Candlestick, Aurene, Gold, Twist Stem, Pair	1980.00
Candlestick, Black Edges, Applied Threading In Cup, Twisted Stem, 12 In.	2576.00
Candlestick, Celeste Blue Foot & Cup, Clear Stem, 10 1/4 In., Pair	450.00
Candlestick, Celeste Blue, Pale Green, Domed Foot, 20th Century, 6 1/2 In.	290.00
Candlestick, Controlled Bubbles, Random Reeding On Cup, Footed, Signed, 5 In., Pair . .	340.00
Candlestick, Disk Foot, Balastered Stem, 4 Cabochons At Center, Signed, 3 3/4 In., Pair .	560.00
Candlestick, Green Glass, Pontil, Carder, N.Y., 20th Century, 10 In.	115.00
Candlestick, Green Jade, Alabaster, Floral, 15 1/2 x 6 In.	290.00
Candlestick, Green, Amber, Acid Stamp Mark, 12 In., Pair	750.00
Candlestick, Pomona Green, Signed, 12 In., Pair	560.00

Candlestick, Ribbed Stem, Wide Foot, Clear Double Wafer, 10 In., Pair 560.00
Candlestick, Rope Twist, Signed, 8 1/4 In., Pair 145.00
Candlestick, Rosaline, Alabaster Foot, Finger Handle, Paper Label, 4 In. 700.00
Candlestick, Rosaline, Alabaster Foot, Signed R Carder, 3 3/4 In., Pair 505.00
Candlestick, Ruby Foot & Holder, Clear Stem, Signed, 7 In. 390.00
Candlestick, Twist Stem, Aurene, Signed, Pair 2016.00
Candlestick, Verre De Soie, Circular Foot, Turned Stem, 3 3/4 In. 345.00
Candlestick, Verre De Soie, Half Twist Stem, 10 In., Pair 489.00
Candy Dish, Cover, Ram's Head Finial, c.1940, 6 1/2 In. 435.00
Centerpiece, Aurene, Gold, 3 1/2 x 12 1/4 In. 290.00
Centerpiece, Calcite, Gold Aurene Interior, c.1920, 3 x 10 1/2 In. 690.00
Centerpiece, Dolphin & Wave Finial, Applied Wave Design Base, Inscribed, 12 In. 690.00
Cocktail Shaker, Signed, David Hill, 1950, 7 1/2 In. 520.00
Compote, Ashtray, Ruffled Edge, Blue, 4 & 6 In., 2 Piece 230.00
Compote, Celeste Blue, Amber Disk Foot, Carder, 6 In. 230.00
Compote, Celeste Blue, Flared, Signed, 9 In. 750.00
Compote, Celeste Blue, Swirl Prunts, Disk Foot, Signed, 7 In. 520.00
Compote, Cover, Alabaster Foot & Finial, 10 1/4 In. 225.00
Compote, Domed Cover, Pear Finial, Carder, 9 3/4 In. 460.00
Compote, Green Jade, Alabaster Foot, 6 In. 120.00
Compote, Horizontal Ribs, Black Edge, 4 Black Cabochons, 10 1/4 In. 560.00
Compote, Ruffled Edge, Alabaster, Signed 3200.00
Compote, Topaz, Rolled Rim, Carder, 8 x 8 3/8 In. 260.00
Cordial, Clear Cased Rosaline Bowl, Opaline Stem, 5 1/8 In. 55.00
Cuspidor, Woman's, Calcite, Blue Aurene Interior, 3 x 6 In. 495.00
Decanter, Stopper, Teardrop Shape, Trapped Bubble Base, Signed, 10 1/2 In. ...... 95.00 to 105.00
Dish, Mayonnaise, Amethyst, Apple Shape, 5 1/2 In. 60.00
Dish, Olive, Signed, 6 In. 170.00
Figurine, Arctic Fisherman, James Houston, c.1970, 6 1/2 In. 3450.00
Figurine, Beaver, Transparent Pink Eyes, Signed, Late 20th Century, 6 1/4 In. 860.00
Figurine, Dinosaur, Signed, 12 3/4 In. 1840.00
Figurine, Donkey, Standing, Signed, 10 1/2 In. 975.00
Figurine, Dove, On Stainless Steel Stand, Signed, 12 1/8 In. 630.00
Figurine, Eagle, On Ball, Donald Pollard, 1975, 12 x 5 3/4 In. 375.00
Figurine, Giraffe, Dome Base, Signed, 15 In. 1840.00
Figurine, Owl, c.1940, 5 1/4 In. 375.00
Figurine, Porpoise, 3 Sizes, Lloyd Atkins, 1960-1970, 3 Piece 1375.00
Figurine, Seal, Resting On Flippers, 8 1/2 In. 375.00
Figurine, Snail, Signed, 3 5/8 In. 115.00
Figurine, Squirrel, Signed, 4 1/8 In. ....345.00 to 460.00
Figurine, Walrus, Silver Tusks, Signed, 7 1/4 In. 1380.00
Figurine, Wolf, 5 In. 315.00
Goblet, Black Glass, Ivory, Carder, 4 3/4 In., Pair 517.00
Goblet, Green Threaded Design, Signed, 9 In. 517.00
Lamp, Desk, Bronze, Hammered, Iridescent Glass Shade, Adjustable, 20 In. 865.00
Lamp, Iridescent, Domed Shade, Glass Base, 13 x 20 In. 2240.00
Lamp, Tyrian Glass, Gilt Metal, Opaque Green To Purple, 1916, 21 1/2 x 12 In. 8400.00
Paperweight, Sphere Of Randomly Engraved Hearts, 2 1/2 In. 115.00

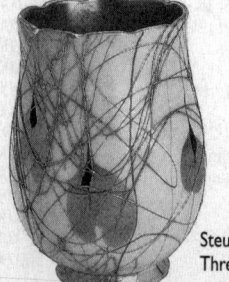

Use coasters under glasses and flower vases on marble-topped tables. Marble can stain easily.

Steuben, Shade, Calcite, Pulled Leaves, Threading, Gold Aurene Interior, 5 In.

Parfait, Oriental Poppy, Pink, White Opalescent Ribs, Applied Green Foot, 6 In. 489.00
Pitcher, Clear, Elongated Flared Rim, Egg Shape, Signed, c.1950, 10 1/2 In. 255.00
Shade, Calcite, Pulled Leaves, Threading, Gold Aurene Interior, 5 In. . . . . *Illus* 275.00
Sherbet, Underplate, Gold Aurene, Calcite Interior, 4 1/4 x 6 In. 280.00
Sugar & Creamer, Celeste Blue, Handles, Carder, 20th Century, 4 1/2 x 3 3/4 In. 185.00
Sugar & Creamer, Clear, Signed John Dreves, 1950-1960, 3 1/4 In. 270.00
Urn, Rosaline, Alabaster, 14 In. 450.00
Vase, Alabaster, Gold Aurene Pulled Vines, 6 1/4 In. 635.00
Vase, Amber, Pedestal Foot, Signed, 14 1/2 In. 440.00
Vase, Black Reeding, Acid Stamp Mark, 6 3/4 x 7 1/2 In. 230.00
Vase, Blue Ground, Green, Aqua Squiggles, Iridescent Neck, 7 1/2 In. 17360.00
Vase, Bud, Clear, Controlled Bubble Base, Signed Robert Browning, 8 In. 210.00
Vase, Bud, Trumpet, Controlled Bubble Base, Signed, 8 1/2 In. 69.00
Vase, Calcite, Ruffled Edge, Blue Interior, Footed, 6 1/4 In. 1035.00
Vase, Celeste Blue, Controlled Bubbles, Threaded Rim, 6 1/4 In. 168.00
Vase, Cintra, Mottled Yellow, Rolled Rim, Signed, 7 3/4 In. 900.00
Vase, Cintra, Rose, Signed, 6 1/4 x 8 In. 1440.00
Vase, Clear, Black Reeding, Acid Stamp Mark, 6 3/4 x 7 1/2 In. 230.00
Vase, Diamond-Quilted, Amethyst, Silver Mica Flecks, 8 In. 660.00
Vase, Diamond-Quilted, Green Reeding, Signed, 11 3/4 In. 805.00
Vase, Diamond-Quilted, Pink Reeded Rim, Signed, 6 In. 105.00
Vase, Fan, Clear, Controlled Bubbles, Signed, 9 In. 225.00
Vase, Fan, Green Jade, Alabaster, Optic Ribbed, Signed, 8 1/2 In. 490.00
Vase, Fan, Spanish Green, Optic Ribbed, Carder, 20th Century, 8 1/4 In. . . . . 170.00 to 225.00
Vase, Gold Aurene, Millefiori Design 3740.00
Vase, Green Etched Glass, Purple, 7 1/2 & 11 In., Pair 690.00
Vase, Green Jade, Applied Alabaster Lion Masks, Leafy Metal Base, 11 1/2 In. 805.00
Vase, Green Jade, Carder, 1930s, 5 1/2 In. 345.00
Vase, Grotesque, Ivory, Signed, 6 1/4 x 12 In. 230.00
Vase, Grotesque, Ruby Rim, Signed, 5 3/4 In. 785.00
Vase, Iridescent Swirls, Blue, Gold, 9 1/2 In. 115.00
Vase, Ivory, Flared Rim, Carder, 1935, 9 1/4 In. 575.00
Vase, Ivory, Prong, Applied Star, Carder, 1933, 8 1/2 In. 430.00
Vase, Jack-In-The-Pulpit, Calcite, c.1900, 6 3/4 In. 375.00
Vase, Light Blue Jade, Alabaster Foot, 5 In. 95.00
Vase, Matsu-No-Ke, Green Jade, Cameo, Egg Shape 1500.00
Vase, Moss Agate, Multicolored Swirls, 10 1/2 In. 7015.00
Vase, Oriental, 2 Crested Birds, Branch, Green Jade, Alabaster, Cameo, 9 1/4 In. 1035.00
Vase, Oriental, Birds, Green, Jade, Alabaster, Cameo, Carder, 9 In. 2070.00
Vase, Oriental, Green Jade, Alabaster, Stylized Floral Cameo, 8 1/4 In. 450.00
Vase, Oriental, Pine Tree, Clouds, Green Jade, Cameo, 7 1/8 x 8 In. 1725.00
Vase, Pink Reeded Neck, Signed, 2 1/2 x 2 1/2 In. 715.00
Vase, Pomona Green, Rolled Rim, Footed, Signed, 11 x 8 1/2 In. 450.00
Vase, Rosaline, 2-Ball Alabaster Foot, Signed, 8 1/2 In. 950.00
Vase, Silverina, Air Trapped Silver Mica, Flared Rim, 12 1/2 In. 505.00
Vase, Spiral, No. 8058, Donald Pollard, 1955, 6 1/4 In. 170.00
Vase, Teardrop, Amethyst Mouth, Signed, 10 1/2 In. 170.00
Vase, Topaz, Rolled Rim, Signed, 8 5/8 & 6 1/4 In. 370.00
Vase, Tree Trunk, Green Jade, 3 Prongs, Alabaster Foot, 6 1/4 In. 785.00
Vase, Tree Trunk, Green Jade, 3 Prongs, Alabaster Pod Base, 10 In. 1095.00
Vase, Tree Trunks, Blue Aurene, Signed, 6 1/4 In. 1400.00
Vase, Trumpet, Clear, Tapered Center, Flared Base, Applied Swirl, 11 1/2 In. 220.00
Vase, Wisteria, Spiral Optic Ribs, Domed Base, Carder, 9 1/8 In. 630.00

STEVENS & WILLIAMS of Stourbridge, England, made many types of
glass, including layered, etched, cameo, and art glass, between the
1830s and 1930s. Some pieces are signed *S & W*. Many pieces are decorated with flowers, leaves, and other designs based on nature.

Bowl, Yellow Jade, Alabaster Foot, 3 1/4 x 3 3/4 In. 95.00
Cologne, Intaglio, 5 In. 2470.00
Creamer, Applied Strawberry, Leafy Stem, Amber Rim & Handle, 4 3/4 In. 280.00
Finger Bowl, Underplate, Intaglio Cut Grapes & Leaves, 6 1/2 In. 295.00
Finger Bowl, Underplate, Intaglio Cut Grapes & Leaves, Satin, 4 3/4 In. 245.00

Pitcher, Opal & Yellow Prunts, Ruby Threads, John Northwood, 9 In. 730.00
Rose Bowl, Osiris, Pulled Feather, John Northwood 1750.00
Vase, Apricot, Alabaster Foot, Rolled Rim, 11 3/4 In. 225.00
Vase, Aqua Blue Over White, Applied Flowers, Leaves, 8 In. 300.00
Vase, Birds, Geometric Intaglio Cutting, 12 In. 980.00
Vase, Deep Purple, Yellow, Flower Blossom Rim, 10 1/8 In. 10350.00
Vase, Diagonally Swirled Air Trapped Design, 7 1/4 In. 336.00
Vase, Lacy Intaglio Cutting, White Lining, Ruffled Edge, 4 1/4 In. 195.00
Vase, Opal Over Ruby, Applied Amber Crest, 3 Leaf Feet, 6 1/2 In. 400.00
Vase, Peachblow, Applied Fruit & Leaves, Pair 2000.00
Vase, Pink Intaglio Cutting, Yellow Interior, Square Bulbous, 4 In. 210.00
Vase, White Nasturtiums, On Raspberry, Gourd Shape, Cameo, 10 In. 2420.00

STIEGEL TYPE glass is listed here. It is almost impossible to be sure a piece was actually made by Stiegel, so the knowing collector refers to this glass as *Stiegel type*. Henry William Stiegel, a colorful immigrant to the colonies, started his first factory in Pennsylvania in 1763. He remained in business until 1774. Glassware was made in a style popular in Europe at that time and was similar to the glass of many other makers. It was made of clear or colored glass and was decorated with enamel colors, mold blown designs, or etching.

Bottle, Clear, Enameled, Flowers, Rectangular, Chamfered Corners, 1770, 4 5/8 In. 259.00
Bottle, Clear, Enameled, Flowers, Rectangular, Chamfered Corners, 1770, 6 1/8 In. 259.00
Bottle, Woman, Heart, Verse, 1/2 Post Neck, Pewter Collar, Enamel Case, 4 7/8 In. 193.00
Bowl, Expanded Diamond, Amethyst, 1810, 4 1/2 In. 1275.00
Creamer, 20 Ogees, Cobalt Blue, Applied Handle, Pontil, 4 In. 190.00
Salt, Expanded Diamond, 2 3/4 In. 330.00
Salt, Sapphire Blue, Double Ogee Bowl, Applied Foot, Pontil, 2 7/8 In. 550.00
Salt, Sapphire Blue, Expanded Diamond, 2 3/4 In. 715.00
Sugar, Dahlia Cover, Cobalt Blue, 16 Diamonds, Pontil, 6 3/4 In. 4840.00
Sugar, Diamond, Cobalt Blue, Flat Foot, Pontil, 4 In. 672.00
Tumbler, Flowers, Red, Blue, Green, White & Yellow, 3 1/2 In. 110.00
Vase, Urn Shape, Flared Turn Down Rim, Pontil, 1820, 8 1/4 In. 605.00

STONE includes those articles made of stones not listed elsewhere in this book. Micro mosaics (small decorative designs made by setting pieces of stone into a pattern), urns, vases, and other pieces made of natural stones are listed here. Alabaster, Jade, Malachite, Marble, and Soapstone are in their own categories. Stoneware is pottery and is listed in the Stoneware category.

Figure, Buddha, Seated, White, Black Inclusions In 2 Dragons, China, Agate, 2 3/4 In. ... 400.00
Figure, Chinese Cabbage, White & Light Green, Jadeite, Chinese, 4 1/2 In. 500.00
Figure, Clouds, 4 Bats & Chinese Characters On Coin, 3 Colors, Stand, China, Agate 400.00
Figure, Deer Under Peach Tree, Turquoise, 2 7/8 In. 150.00
Figure, Dolphins, Playing In Waves, Ruby & Zoisite, Chinese, 2 3/4 In. 500.00
Figure, Fish, Lapis, White Mottled, Gold Pyrite Flecks, Chinese, 5 1/4 In. 200.00
Figure, Frog, Ruby & Zoisite, Chinese, 3 1/2 In. 600.00

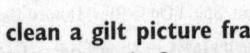

To clean a gilt picture frame, first boil 3 onions in 2 cups of water, then dampen a soft cloth with the cooled water and rub the frame.

Stone, Plaque, Micro Mosaic, Women, Courtyard,
Italy, Frame, 1800s, 7 1/2 x 10 1/2 In.

Figure, Goldfish, Labradorite, Blue Sheen, Chinese, 5 In. 200.00
Figure, Meijin, Gray, Standing Holding A Basket, Agate, c.1900, 7 In. 57.00
Figure, Mythical Dragon Horse, Kneeling, Chewing Sacred Fungi, Lapis, Chinese, 7 In. .. 1250.00
Figure, Seated Woman With Child, Turquoise, 2 3/4 In. 150.00
Flask, Moon, Flowers, Scrolling Leaves, Blue & White, Chinese, 1700s, 13 In. 978.00
Jadeite, Bowl, Carved, Lotus Shape, 2 Handles, Cover, Carved Wooden Stand, 10 In. 3300.00
Plaque, Carved Birds & Flowers, Amber, 19th Century, 2 1/4 In., Pair 160.00
Plaque, Micro Mosaic, Capriccio Amidst Ruins, Gilt Metal Frame, Italy, 1 7/8 In. 1610.00
Plaque, Micro Mosaic, Doves Of Pliny, Serpentine Shape, Italy, 1900s, 5 3/4 In. 402.00
Plaque, Micro Mosaic, Women, Courtyard, Italy, Frame, 1800s, 7 1/2 x 10 1/2 In. .. *Illus* 21850.00
Plaque, Pietra Dura, Trompe L'Oeil, Shells, Rose, Figs, Insects, c.1900, 22 x 20 In. 3335.00
Vase, Cover, Phoenix Bird Shape, Tigereye, Light & Dark Brown, Chinese, 7 3/4 In. 500.00
Vase, Cover, Phoenix Bird, Dragon, Tigereye, Chinese, 7 1/4 In. 700.00

STONEWARE is a coarse, glazed, and fired potter's ceramic that is used to make crocks, jugs, bowls, etc. It is often decorated with cobalt blue decorations. In the nineteenth and early twentieth centuries, potters often decorated crocks with blue numbers indicating the size of the container. A "2" meant 2 gallons. Stoneware is still being made.

Bank, Church, Albany Glaze Exterior, 1900, 3 1/2 In. 145.00
Bank, Floral Salt Glaze Design, Slot In Base, Handle, 19th Century, 4 In. 896.00
Bank, Jug Form, Handle, Miniature, 4 1/8 In. 3495.00
Bean Pot, Cover, Boston Baked Beans, Children Eating Beans, Handle, 9 3/4 In. 300.00
Bean Pot, Cover, Spirit Of Bunker Hill, Blue Accents, 7 1/2 In. 300.00
Bean Pot, E. Swasey, Portland, Me., Miniature, 2 1/2 In. 149.00
Bottle, Cuba Rum, Brown Alkaline Glaze, Paper Label, 1933, 7 In. 55.00
Bottle, Figural, Woman, Dress, Hat, Salt Glaze, Blue Slip, Mark 26, Germany, 14 In. 55.00
Bottle, Impressed, Blue Accents, Handle, J. Cochranes, Rochester, c.1860, 8 In. 330.00
Bottle, Oval, Small Opening, Mahogany Matte Glaze, Heino, 14 x 8 1/2 In. 690.00
Bottle, Pinch, Mirror Black Glaze, Smithfield Pottery, c.1935, 8 7/8 In. 44.00
Bottle, Shaped Lip, Tapered Shoulder, c.1850, 8 1/2 In. 560.00
Bottle, Snakes & Frogs, Woman, Snake Handles & Stopper, 16 1/2 In. 660.00
Bowl, Blue Green Matte Glaze, Antonio Prieto, 3 x 7 1/4 In. 200.00
Bowl, Cameo, Westward Ho, Covered Wagon, Glaze, Mark, c.1952, 5 x 11 In. 2200.00
Bowl, Crackle Glaze, Red, Green, Chrysanthemums, Japanese Studio, c.1900, 8 1/4 In. 200.00
Bowl, Heavy Band Rim, Alkaline Glaze, c.1900, 6 1/4 In. 3064.00
Bowl, Milk, S.H. Sonner, Strasburg, Va., 1, Shenandoah, 10 1/2 x 4 3/4 In. 330.00
Bowl, White, Rust, Semimatte Glaze, Textured, Warren MacKenzie, 5 1/2 x 15 In. 575.00
Butter, Cover, Molded Scenes, Hunters, Trees & Deer, 9 In. 385.00
Canning Jar, Albany Slip, Late 1800s 55.00
Casserole, Orange Gloss Glaze, Flat Handles, Flat Lid, Acorn Finial, Ben Owen, 4 x 8 In. . 88.00
Chamberstick, Olive Gloss Glaze, Stylized Cord Handle, J.F. Meaders, 6 1/4 In. 110.00
Chicken Waterer, Brushed Cobalt Blue Leaves & Finial, 8 In. 360.00
Chicken Waterer, Cobalt Blue Flowers, Knob Top, Late 1800s, 12 In. 4290.00
Churn, American, 1860, 2 Gal., 12 3/4 In. 520.00
Churn, Black & Brown Glaze, Oval, Handles, Lid With Dasher, 15 In. 110.00
Churn, Blue Flowers, Oval, Handles, Raised Lip, 16 1/2 In. 190.00
Churn, Blue Tulips, Leaves & Accents, No. 3, Hamilton & Jones, 14 x 8 1/2 In. 990.00
Churn, Cobalt Blue Star Face, Snowflake Accents, Jordan, 1850, 2 Gal. .... *Illus* 9075.00
Churn, Cobalt Blue Stencils, 2 Ear Handles, Williams & Reppert, 3 Gal. 365.00
Churn, Cobalt Blue Tulip, Impressed 3 On Side, Applied Handles, Oval, 14 1/2 In. 165.00
Churn, Dotted Quail & Jack-In-The-Pulpit, J. Burger Jr., c.1885, 4 Gal. 5500.00
Churn, Dotted Quail, Perched On Branch, c.1870, 4 Gal. 3520.00
Churn, Impressed 5 On Lid & Body, Edgefield, 17 In. 110.00
Churn, Incised Cobalt Blue Beaver Tail Bird, c.1890, 17 3/8 In. 530.00
Churn, Large Wreath, 1883, 4 Gal. 520.00
Churn, N. Clark, Cobalt Blue Foliage, Double Handles, 13 In. 220.00
Churn, Salt Glaze, Cobalt Blue Bird On Branch, Handles, Fancher & Durkee, 21 3/8 In. .. 1840.00
Churn, Salt Glaze, Cobalt Blue Flower Basket, Lug Handles, 17 1/2 In. 1090.00
Cistern, Cover, Bear Baiting, Nottingham, Mid 18th Century, 11 In. 3525.00
Coffeepot, Olive Satin Glaze, Flattened Handle, Extended Spout, M.L. Owens, 9 In. 275.00
Crock, 2 Handles, Incised Floral & Leaves, Paul Cushman, c.1810, 7 3/4 x 7 In. 495.00
Crock, 3 Sprays Of Flowers & Leaf, John Bell, Gal., 9 1/4 In. 880.00

Stoneware, Churn, Cobalt Blue
Star Face, Snowflake Accents,
Jordan, 1850, 2 Gal.

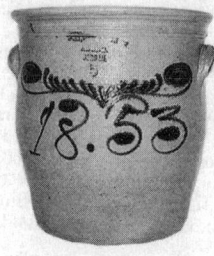

Stoneware, Crock, Cobalt
Blue 1853, Antler Shape
Accent, J. McBirney, 5 Gal.

Stoneware, Crock, Cobalt
Blue Bird In Nest With Eggs,
A.K. Ballard, 1870, 6 Gal.

Crock, 8 Vertical Lines, Flared Rim, Handles, J.M. Pruden, Elizabeth, N.J., 13 1/2 In. 80.00
Crock, Bird On Stump, Lug Handles, Evan R. Jones, 3 Gal. 850.00
Crock, Bird Resting On Branch, Applied Handles, White's, Utica, 3 Gal., 11 In. 415.00
Crock, Blue Fantail Bird In Leaves & 3, Ear Handles, White's, 10 1/2 In. 770.00
Crock, Blue Flower, Bullard & Scott, Cambridge, Mass., 3 Gal. 395.00
Crock, Blue Flowers, Oval, Cowden & Wilcox, Harrisburg, Pa., No. 4, 13 1/4 In. 300.00
Crock, Blue Grape Hyacinth, Bowden & Wilcox, 7 7/8 In. 300.00
Crock, Blue Leaves, Stylized Hearts, Double Handles, Impressed 3, 9 1/2 In. 190.00
Crock, Blue Lettering, Down On The Farm, C.W. Rodefer Co., Shadyside, Ohio, 6 In. ... 140.00
Crock, Blue Slip Tulips, Ear Handles, 7 x 9 In. 300.00
Crock, Blue Stenciled Eagle, T.F. Reppert, Greensboro, Pa., 8 Gal., 20 In. 1760.00
Crock, Blue, Shenfelder, Reading, Penna., 6 1/4 x 6 1/4 In. 195.00
Crock, Brushed Bird Perched On Stump, J.A. & C. Underwood, 12 1/2 In. 355.00
Crock, Brushed Cobalt Blue 5, 2 Handles, 13 x 11 1/2 In. 55.00
Crock, Brushed Cobalt Blue Flower & 3, Hall & Thomas, 12 In. 550.00
Crock, Brushed Cobalt Blue Tulip & 4, Burger & Co., Double Handles, 11 1/4 In. 300.00
Crock, Brushed Cobalt Blue Tulips Both Sides, Double Ear Handles, 11 In. 110.00
Crock, Brushed Flowers, Lug Handles, J.B. Leathers, 4 Gal. 2420.00
Crock, Bunch Of Grapes, Double Handles, Flared Rim, 11 In. 275.00
Crock, Butter, Brown & White, Blue Stencil, Bell Seed Co., Manlius, N.Y., 3 1/4 In. 99.00
Crock, Butter, Brushed Leaf Band All Around, Blue On Lid, Gal. 688.00
Crock, Butter, Cobalt Blue Flowers, Applied Ears, Marked R.C.R. Phila., c.1900 .... 330.00
Crock, Butter, Cobalt Blue Stripes, Raised Rim, 6 3/4 x 4 In. 300.00
Crock, Butter, Graduated Blue Line Around Rim, Double Handles, 8 1/4 x 4 In. 415.00
Crock, Cake, Cloud Design, Cobalt Blue, 8 1/2 In. 120.00
Crock, Cake, Cobalt Blue, Leaves, Applied Handles, 5 x 8 In. 305.00
Crock, Cobalt Blue 1853, Antler Shape Accent, J. McBirney, 5 Gal. .... *Illus* 3410.00
Crock, Cobalt Blue 3-Part Tulip & 2, Shoulder Rings, 13 In. 300.00
Crock, Cobalt Blue 5-Petal Flower, Double Handles, A.O. Whittemore, 7 3/4 In. 110.00
Crock, Cobalt Blue Bird In Nest With Eggs, A.K. Ballard, 1870, 6 Gal. .... *Illus* 5170.00
Crock, Cobalt Blue Bird, Flower, 19th Century, 4 Gal., 11 1/4 In. 400.00
Crock, Cobalt Blue Bird, Impressed 2, 9 1/4 In. 190.00
Crock, Cobalt Blue Bird, On Branch, Long Tail, White's Utica 2, Handles, 10 1/2 In. 467.00
Crock, Cobalt Blue Bird, Ottman Bros., Double Handles, 12 In. 190.00
Crock, Cobalt Blue Bird, Ottman Bros., Fort Edward, N.Y., Double Handles, 11 In. 220.00
Crock, Cobalt Blue Brushed Bird, On Branch, New York Stoneware Co., 7 1/2 In. 470.00
Crock, Cobalt Blue Cornucopia & 2, Incised Line Under Lip, 9 1/2 x 9 1/2 In. 1045.00
Crock, Cobalt Blue Curlicues, Narrow Base, Wide Rim, Crow's Feet, 9 1/4 In. 80.00
Crock, Cobalt Blue Dog Head & 2, 2 Incised Lines, 9 x 10 In. 440.00
Crock, Cobalt Blue Dotted Duck In Wreath, M.W. Woodruff, 1870, 6 Gal. .... *Illus* 6050.00
Crock, Cobalt Blue Dotted Tornado, W.H. Farrar, Geddes, N.Y., 1860, 16 In. ...... *Illus* 1815.00
Crock, Cobalt Blue Flourished & 8, Label, Williams & Reppert, 8 Gal., 19 3/4 In. 300.00
Crock, Cobalt Blue Flower & 2, Label, Harrington & Burger, Wood Lid, 11 In. 495.00
Crock, Cobalt Blue Flower Basket, Applied Ears, J.A. & C.W. Underwood, N.Y., 6 Gal. ... 3025.00

Crock, Cobalt Blue Flower Design, Double Handles, 9 In. 110.00
Crock, Cobalt Blue Flower, Crosshatch Center, A.O. Whitmore, 1870, 5 Gal. . . . . . . *Illus* 2310.00
Crock, Cobalt Blue Flower, Oval, 2 Handles, 4 Gal., 14 3/4 In. 978.00
Crock, Cobalt Blue Flowers Under Signature, Haxstun & Co., No. 2, 9 1/4 In. 190.00
Crock, Cobalt Blue Flowers, 2 Handles, Haxstun & Co., Fort Edward, N.Y., 4, 11 1/4 In. . . 330.00
Crock, Cobalt Blue Flowers, 2 Handles, Ottman Bros., Fort Edward, N.Y., 11 1/2 In. 259.00
Crock, Cobalt Blue Flowers, 2 Loop Handles, C-Shape Handle, Wide Spout, 7 1/2 x 10 In. 405.00
Crock, Cobalt Blue Flowers, Applied Double Handles, 10 In. 410.00
Crock, Cobalt Blue Flowers, D.P. Shenfelder, Reading, Pa., Late 1800s, 6 Gal., 16 In. 220.00
Crock, Cobalt Blue Flowers, Ear Handles, M. & T. Miller, 4 Gal., 12 3/4 In. 1155.00
Crock, Cobalt Blue Flowers, Leaves, Applied Handles, 12 1/2 In. 187.00
Crock, Cobalt Blue Flowers, Leaves, Applied Handles, Stamped, R.C.R. Phila. 220.00
Crock, Cobalt Blue Flowers, Leaves, Oval, Handles, 15 1/2 In. 415.00
Crock, Cobalt Blue Freehand Design, Flowering Plant On Side, No. 4, 11 3/4 In. 165.00
Crock, Cobalt Blue Incised Bird, C. Hart & Son, Sherbourne, c.1880, 9 In. 900.00
Crock, Cobalt Blue Leaf & 5, Norton, Bennington, Vt., Handles, 12 1/2 In. 385.00
Crock, Cobalt Blue Leaf, 3 Handles, E. & L.P. Norton, Bennington, Vt., 10 1/4 In. 165.00
Crock, Cobalt Blue Peafowl, Applied Ears, Impressed White's, Utica, 9 1/2 In. 1155.00
Crock, Cobalt Blue Pony, Somerset, New Jersey, 4 Gal. 3450.00
Crock, Cobalt Blue Prancing Horse, C.W. Braun, Buffalo, N.Y., c.1870, 3 Gal. 11550.00
Crock, Cobalt Blue Running Bird & 4, Double Handles, Whites, Utica, 11 1/2 In. 990.00
Crock, Cobalt Blue Slip Flower & Handle, Salt Glaze, Cowden & Wilcox, 1875, 9 3/8 In. . 255.00
Crock, Cobalt Blue Stencil, Tapered Sides, Gal. 110.00
Crock, Cobalt Blue Stylized Flowers, Double Handles, 10 In. 330.00
Crock, Cobalt Blue Swans, Impressed, 12 Rings, Barrel Shape, 16 In. 616.00
Crock, Cobalt Blue Tulip, Double Handles, E. Fowler, 5, 15 3/4 In. 1210.00
Crock, Cobalt Blue Tulip, Straight Side, Handles, Evan R. Jones, 2 Gal., 9 x 10 In. 195.00
Crock, Cobalt Blue Tulips, C.C. Thorp, 6 Gal., 16 In. 220.00
Crock, Cobalt Blue Tulips, Flared Lip, Tapered Sides, Gal. 165.00
Crock, Cobalt Blue Tulips, Leaves, Handles, Oval, 4 Gal., 15 1/2 In. 633.00
Crock, Cobalt Blue Turkey, 4 Gal. 9000.00
Crock, Cobalt Blue Turkey, Freehand, Stamped 4, 4 Gal. 9000.00
Crock, Cobalt Blue Turkey, In Tree, Applied Double Handles, 14 x 17 1/2 In. 3410.00
Crock, Cobalt Blue Wreath, 11 1/4 In. 110.00
Crock, Cobalt Blue, 2 Ear Handles, Impressed N. Clark & Co. Lyons, 2, 9 x 10 1/4 In. . . . 300.00
Crock, Cobalt Blue, Impressed, Egg Shape, Raised Rim, 2 Handles, 12 1/2 In. 605.00
Crock, Cobalt Blue, Parallel Lines, 8 In. 198.00
Crock, Cobalt Blue, Salt Glaze, Applied Handles, c.1847, 9 In. 805.00
Crock, Cobalt Blue, Tulips, 2 Handles, Damson, 5 3/4 In. 5060.00
Crock, Cover, Blue Design, White, Applied Handles, 9 1/4 x 5 1/2 In. 165.00
Crock, Cover, Cobalt Blue Flowers, Applied Handles, Shenfelder, Reading, 5 Gal., 13 In. . 385.00
Crock, Cover, Cobalt Blue Freehand Design, Incised Lines Around, 7 1/2 x 4 3/4 In. 220.00
Crock, Cover, Cobalt Blue Leaves Around Finial, Applied Handles, Round, 10 x 6 In. 220.00
Crock, Cover, Flowers, Ballard Brothers, Double Handles, 11 1/2 In. 250.00

Stoneware, Crock, Cobalt Blue
Dotted Duck In Wreath,
M.W. Woodruff, 1870, 6 Gal.

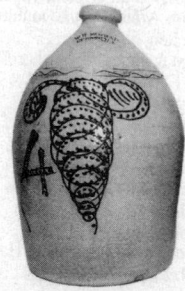
Stoneware, Crock, Cobalt Blue
Dotted Tornado, W.H. Farrar,
Geddes, N.Y., 1860, 16 In.

Stoneware, Crock, Cobalt Blue
Flower, Crosshatch Center, A.O.
Whitmore, 1870, 5 Gal.

Stoneware, Crock, Horse, C.W. Braun, Buffalo, N.Y., 1870, 3 Gal., 10 In.

Stoneware, Crock, Instruments, Flowers, J. & E. Norton, Bennington, Vt., 1855, 5 Gal., 14 In.

Stoneware, Crock, J. McBirney & Sons, Jordan, Large 1853, Oval, 5 Gal., 13 In.

Crock, Cover, Incised, Cobalt Blue Flowers, Flared Neck, 2 Handles, 2, 8 x 10 In. 385.00
Crock, Cover, Stylized Flowers, Flared Rim, Handles, New York Stoneware Co., 13 In. .. 385.00
Crock, Cream, Blue, E. Swasey & Co., Portland, Me. 690.00
Crock, Cream, Cobalt Blue Letters, Geo. W. Helme, Cor. Water & Pine St., N.Y., 13 In. .. 616.00
Crock, Eagle, Stars, Handle, T.F. Reppert Eagle Pottery, 21 x 12 In. 2875.00
Crock, Edmunds & Co., Cobalt Blue, 19th Century, 2 Gal., 11 1/2 In. 184.00
Crock, Fat Bird On Branch, Haxstun & Co., 4 Gal. 550.00
Crock, Fat Songbird On Branch, Ear Handles, E.B. Norton Sons, 7 1/4 In. 302.00
Crock, Flower & Leaf, Lug Handles, Cowden & Wilcox, 5 Gal. 3300.00
Crock, Flower Bud, Ear Handles, 1896, 2 Gal., 8 1/2 In. 880.00
Crock, Flower, E. & L.P. Norton, Bennington, Vermont, 6 Gal. 795.00
Crock, Flower, Flared, Double Handles, 8 3/4 In. 275.00
Crock, Freehand Design, Double Handles, N.G. Hormell, Ohio 4, 15 In. 550.00
Crock, Freehand Flowers, Cobalt Blue Slip, J. Weaver, 16 In. 1800.00
Crock, Horse, C.W. Braun, Buffalo, N.Y., 1870, 3 Gal., 10 In. .... *Illus* 11550.00
Crock, Incised Armstrong & Wentworth, Norwich, 2 Gal., 11 In. 525.00
Crock, Incised Swan, Medsford, McFeat & Swan Ship Grocers, c.1850, 7 1/2 In. 225.00
Crock, Instruments, Flowers, J. & E. Norton, Bennington, Vt., 1855, 5 Gal., 14 In. .. *Illus* 7500.00
Crock, J. McBirney & Sons, Jordan, Large 1853, Oval, 5 Gal., 13 In. .... *Illus* 3410.00
Crock, John D. Heatwole, Rockingham County, 1851 .... 5000.00
Crock, Large Triple Fern, Burger & Co., c.1877, 5 Gal. 522.00
Crock, Long Tail Bird, Dotted Plume, New York Stoneware, c.1880, 5 Gal. 412.00
Crock, Oval, Lug Handles, Cowden & Wilcox, 5 Gal. 3300.00
Crock, Raised Rings Top & Bottom, Incised Flowers, Handles, 8 In. 165.00
Crock, Salt Glaze, Cobalt Blue Scrolled Swag, 2 Applied Handles, C. Crolius, N.Y., 11 In. 1610.00
Crock, Signature & Star, T. Harringron, 5 Gal. 3850.00
Crock, Spray Of Flowers, Straight Sides, Applied Handles, 4 Gal., 16 In. 635.00
Crock, Stenciled Eagle, Banner, Number 12-In. Wreath, 12 Gal., 19 1/2 In. 210.00
Crock, Stenciled Eagle, On Shield, Dots Around Rim, Double Handles, 15 In. 2310.00
Crock, Stenciled Tiger, F.T. Wright & Son, 5 Gal. 110.00
Crock, Storage, Blue Stencil, Hamilton & Jones, Greensboro, Pa., 9 3/4 In. 220.00
Crock, Stylized Flower, Ear Handles, F. Woodworth, 9 1/4 x 9 3/4 In. 100.00
Crock, Swan & States, Stonington, Oval, 7 1/2 In. 380.00
Crock, Tulip Design, Incised Bands, Handles, 9 1/2 In. 300.00
Crock, Tulip, Stamped, Cowden & Wilcox, 9 1/4 In. 660.00
Crock, Tyler & Co., c.1860, 3 Gal. 2970.00
Cuspidor, Butterfly & Shield, Blue & White 160.00
Dispenser, Wine-Dip, 5 Cents, 8 x 10 In. 99.00
Figurine, Horse & Rider, Partially Glazed Tan, 16 1/2 In. 3335.00
Figurine, Pig, Albany Glaze, Impressed Facial Features & Hair, 3 1/2 x 7 In. 385.00
Flask, Dark Brown Glaze, c.1850, 6 1/2 In. 135.00
Flask, Salt Glaze, Flat, c.1810, 7 1/2 In. 209.00
Flask, Trees, Brushed Blue, 2 Sides, Incised Reeds At Neck, c.1810, 6 1/2 In. 2530.00
Foot Warmer, Blue & White, Logan Pottery Co., Logan, Ohio 80.00
Foot Warmer, Cobalt Blue Design, Sloped, Handle, Hot Water Opening, 4 x 7 In. 910.00

Jar, 2 Bands & Slash Marks, Double Handles, Joseph G. Baynham, c.1890, 11 1/2 In. 200.00
Jar, 4 Cut Bands, Double Handles, Sylvanus L. Hortsoe, c.1850, 16 In. 500.00
Jar, 5 Dots, 2 Reverse Cs & X, Out-Turned Rim, 2 Handles, 16 In. 1008.00
Jar, Albany Slip Glaze, Double Handles, c.1920, 12 1/4 In. 146.00
Jar, Alkaline Glaze, Double Handles, Nelson Bass, c.1880, 12 In. 310.00
Jar, Blue Bands At Shoulder, Mouth & Waist, New Geneva, 9 1/2 In. 2750.00
Jar, Blue Design, Samuel Cooper, Gal., 9 1/2 In. 795.00
Jar, Blue Stenciled, No. 2, Jas. Hamilton & Co., 11 3/4 In. 300.00
Jar, Canning, Blue Slip Lines, Tooled Line At Shoulder, 6 1/2 In. 275.00
Jar, Canning, Cobalt Blue Leaf, Flared Mouth, Incised & Raised Bands, 8 1/2 In. 250.00
Jar, Canning, Cobalt Blue Stripe 1 Side, Raised Rings, 8 1/8 In. 190.00
Jar, Canning, Cobalt Blue Tulips, Birds, T.F. Reppert, Greensboro, Pa., 9 7/8 In. 165.00
Jar, Canning, Dotted Bird On Thistle Flower, W.H. Farrar, 4 Gal. 1650.00
Jar, Canning, Flared Rim, Sloped Shoulder, Jesse P. Bodie, c.1870, 11 1/2 In. 250.00
Jar, Canning, Flopped Shoulder, William F. Hahn, c.1870, 9 In. 260.00
Jar, Canning, Rounded Rim, Oval Body, Base Stamped Y, c.1830, 7 3/4 In. 615.00
Jar, Canning, Tooled Lines, Stenciled Cobalt Blue Urn Of Flowers, 6 1/2 In. 300.00
Jar, Canning, Wax Sealer Rim, Cobalt Blue Text, Early 20th Century, 6 1/2 In. 56.00
Jar, Cobalt Blue Flowers Both Sides, Impressed 2, 12 In. 190.00
Jar, Cobalt Blue Flowers, Applied Ears, Incised Bands, 13 In. 300.00
Jar, Cobalt Blue Grapevine, Leaves, Oval, Lug Handles, Jas. Hamilton & Co., 23 In. 978.00
Jar, Cobalt Blue Swirled Leaves, 8 1/2 In. 230.00
Jar, Cobalt Blue, Leaf Design, 8 3/4 In. 50.00
Jar, Cobalt Blue, Man In The Moon, Applied Ears, Cowden & Wilcox, c.1870, 3 Gal. 5225.00
Jar, Cover, Albany Slip Glaze, Handle On Lid, c.1920, 8 In. 146.00
Jar, Cover, Bristol Glaze, Standard Ink Co., Buffalo, N.Y., 1890, Qt., 5 1/2 In. 80.00
Jar, Cover, Brown & Amber Glaze, Textured, Karen Karnes, 11 1/4 x 8 1/2 In. 375.00
Jar, Cover, Brown, Blue, Gray, Amber Glaze, Shoulder Knobs, McKinnell, 16 x 10 1/2 In. 175.00
Jar, Cover, Cobalt Blue Lovebirds, G.S. Guy & Co., Fort Edward, N.Y., 17 In. 2970.00
Jar, Cover, White, Semimatte Glaze, Random Strokes, Faceted Middle, MacKenzie, 8 In. . 431.00
Jar, Cream, Impressed M & T Miller, Newport, Pa., 4 Gal. 2450.00
Jar, Dotted Bird On Branch, Large Flower, W.H. Farrar, c.1850, 3 Gal. 580.00
Jar, Double Ear Handles, 2 Shoulder Slashes, Lewis Miles, c.1850, 13 In. 1732.00
Jar, Double Rounded Handle, Ridge At Shoulder, B.F. Landrum Sr., c.1840, 15 In. 1560.00
Jar, Eagle Stencil, 4 Gal. 1500.00
Jar, Flared Neck, Cylindrical Body, J.P. Bodie, c.1875, 7 1/2 In. 340.00
Jar, Flared Rim, 1 Handle, W.F. Hahn, c.1870, 11 In. 336.00
Jar, Impressed Hugh Smith & Co., 3 Gal. 2200.00
Jar, Incised Leaves & 4 Tigers, China, 23 x 19 In. 770.00
Jar, Leaf Shoulder Design, Leaves, Grapes, Cobalt Blue, 10 1/2 In. 70.00
Jar, Leaves, Cobalt Blue, 1 Gal., 10 In. 70.00
Jar, Out-Turned & Flared Rim, Marked No. 4, Joseph G. Baynham, c.1900 . . . . 336.00
Jar, Out-Turned Rim, Double Ear Handles, Dave Edgefield, c.1850, 13 1/2 In. 2575.00
Jar, Out-Turned Rim, Marked 3, Double Handles, Daniel Seagle, c.1860, 15 In. 2350.00
Jar, Oyster, E. Swasey & Co., Portland, Me. 165.00
Jar, Oyster, Pine Tree, E. Swasey, 5 In. 240.00
Jar, Piano, Slip Glaze, Hand Built, Elizabeth Fritsch, c.1978, 6 3/4 In. 2700.00
Jar, Rolled Rim, Dragons, Yellow On Brown, Chinese, c.1860, 27 In. 532.00
Jar, Soda, Salt Glaze, Fly Ash Greens, Chocolate, Incised Lines, C. Webster, 9 In. 121.00
Jar, Stylized Leaf, No. 2., Steven Bell, 11 1/4 In. 440.00
Jar, Tulip Design, Freehand Lines, Signed Hamilton Jones, 12 In. 248.00
Jar, Unglazed Exterior, Matte Interior, Karen Karnes, Signed, 1964, 6 1/2 In. 200.00
Jardiniere, Ribbed Body, Speckled Matte Glaze, Len Ferguson, 10 1/2 x 14 1/2 In. 4600.00
Jug, 2, Salt Glaze, A.G. Smalley, 128 Hanover St., Boston, 2 Gal., 14 In. 82.00
Jug, 2, Strap Handle, Julius Norton, Bennington, Oval, 13 1/2 In. 249.00
Jug, 4 Cut Designs, Strap Handle, Thumb Print At Base, c.1860, 14 In. 213.00
Jug, Albany Slip Glaze, Spout, E. & L.P. Norton, 9 x 8 In. 275.00
Jug, Albany Slip, Base Handle, Spout Other Side, Iron Bail, Walnut Handle, 11 1/2 In. . . . 82.00
Jug, Alkaline Glaze, 2 Handles, Thomas Chandler, c.1850, 17 In. 1232.00
Jug, Batter, Blue Flowers & Accents, Bail Handle, Cowden & Wilcox, 8 1/4 In. 1650.00
Jug, Batter, Blue Foliage, Wood & Steel Handles, Cowden & Wilcox, 9 1/4 In. 880.00
Jug, Batter, Flowers Under Signature & Spout, Cowden & Wilcox, 9 3/8 In. 770.00
Jug, Batter, Spout Cover, No. 4, Bird, Cobalt Blue, Bail Handle, Wood Grip, 4 Gal., 10 In. 880.00

Jug, Beehive, Flag, Acher Edgar & Co., Yonkers, N.Y., 1862, Gal., 10 In. .... *Illus* 5500.00
Jug, Bird & Flowers, Signature, Wh. Farrar, c.1850, 2 Gal. 700.00
Jug, Bird On Branch, White & Wood, Binghamton, N.Y. 2, 2 Gal. 440.00
Jug, Bird On Plume, White's, c.1865, 2 Gal. 1320.00
Jug, Black Green Gloss Streaks Over Gray Glaze, Thin Flat Handle, 14 1/2 In. 935.00
Jug, Block Letters, Cobalt Blue Flowers, 2, Lehman & Rudinger, 12 In. 522.00
Jug, Blue & White, Allover Sponged, Strap Handle, 11 In. 220.00
Jug, Blue Dotted Tornado, W. H. Farrar, Geddes, N.Y., 1860, 4 Gal., 16 In. .... *Illus* 1815.00
Jug, Blue Flower, Sipe, Nichols & Co., Williamsport, Pa., Strap Handle, 11 In. 192.00
Jug, Blue Flowers, Impressed, Ottman Bros., Fort Edward, N.Y., 2 .... 275.00
Jug, Blue Flowers, P.V. Vidvard & Son, 1879, 11 1/4 In. 990.00
Jug, Blue Leaf, Impressed H.H. Schieffelin, Druggist, Gal., 11 1/4 In. 190.00
Jug, Blue Slip Tulips, Cortland, 11 In. 192.00
Jug, Blue Stencil, Horkeimer Bro's, Wheeling, W.V., 2 Gal., 15 In. 140.00
Jug, Bone Though Nose, Ceramic Eyes & Teeth, L. Meaders, 10 1/2 In. 6820.00
Jug, Brown Flowers, Oval, Handle, Lyman & Clark, Gardiner, 13 In. 690.00
Jug, Brown Gloss Slip Glaze, Orange Yellow Specks, W.J. Gordy, 3 1/4 In. 22.00
Jug, Brushed Cobalt Blue Flower & 3, Oval, Handle, 14 3/4 In. 360.00
Jug, Brushed Zinnias, Leaves & 2, Strap Handle, W.H. Farrar & Co., 13 3/4 In. 550.00
Jug, Buggy, Flattened Shoulder, Handle, Shaw Creek, c.1850, 8 In. 480.00
Jug, Cobalt Blue Design & 2, With Halo & Wings, 13 In. 55.00
Jug, Cobalt Blue Double Flower & 4, Higgins & Co., Ohio, 15 1/2 In. 770.00
Jug, Cobalt Blue Fern Wreath, John Burger, Rochester, N.Y, 19th Century, 2 Gal. 475.00
Jug, Cobalt Blue Flower, Applied Strap Handle, Impressed Harrisburg, 12 In. 1210.00
Jug, Cobalt Blue Flower, Cowden & Wilcox, Harrisburg 2, 14 1/2 In. 250.00
Jug, Cobalt Blue Flower, Strap Handle, Cowden & Wilcox, Harrisburg, Pa., 2 Gal. 580.00
Jug, Cobalt Blue Flower, Strap Handle, Presentation, Miniature, 3 1/2 In. 4125.00
Jug, Cobalt Blue Flowers & 2, Bulbous Shape, 2 Gal. 495.00
Jug, Cobalt Blue Flowers & 3, Handle, E.L. & P. Norton, Bennington, Vt., 15 1/2 In. 360.00
Jug, Cobalt Blue Flowers, D.P. Shenfelder, 2 Gal., 13 In. 935.00
Jug, Cobalt Blue Flowers, Marked Charlestown, 2 Gal. 290.00
Jug, Cobalt Blue Folk-Type Leaf & 2, Strap Handle, West Troy Pottery, 14 In. 140.00
Jug, Cobalt Blue Freehand, Strap Handle, L. Fischer & Bro., Jersey City, N.J., 14 In. 105.00
Jug, Cobalt Blue Incised Bird, 14 1/2 In. 3000.00
Jug, Cobalt Blue Incised Flowers, Oval, Handle, c.1820, 13 1/2 In. 1570.00
Jug, Cobalt Blue Leaf Design, Applied Double Handles, 9 7/8 In. 385.00
Jug, Cobalt Blue Leaf, Strap Handle, E. & L.P. Norton, Bennington, Vt., 11 1/2 In. 250.00
Jug, Cobalt Blue Lettering, Strap Handle, John Conton, 3, 17 In. 300.00
Jug, Cobalt Blue Man In Moon, Cowden & Wilcox, Harrisburg, Pa., 2 Gal., 13 In. 6040.00
Jug, Cobalt Blue Slip Horse, W. Hart, Ogdensburgh, 5 Gal., 18 In. 2650.00
Jug, Cobalt Blue Slip Over Letters, Tooled Ribs At Neck & Bottom, Handle, 15 3/8 In. 785.00
Jug, Cobalt Blue Slip, John Horting, 142 N. Queen Street, Lancaster, Pa., Gal. 2200.00
Jug, Cobalt Blue Spiral Design & 2, Burger & Lang, Rochester, N.Y., 1800s, 2 Gal. 275.00
Jug, Cobalt Blue Stripe, Strap Handle, Goodwin & Webster, Hartford, 1800s, 14 In. 190.00
Jug, Cobalt Blue Stylized Bird, Handle, New York Stoneware, Fort Edward, 11 In. 165.00
Jug, Cobalt Blue Tulip, Applied Strap Handle, 10 3/4 In. 770.00
Jug, Cobalt Blue Tulip, Impressed 3, Strap Handle, Oval, 16 In. 190.00
Jug, Cobalt Blue Tulip, Oval, Handle, M.B. Sherwood, Buffalo, N.Y., 15 1/2 In. 165.00

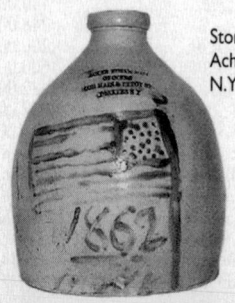

Stoneware, Jug, Beehive, Flag,
Acher Edgar & Co., Yonkers,
N.Y., 1862, Gal., 10 In.

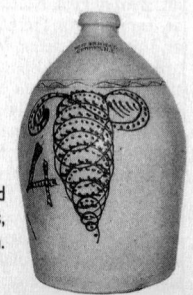

Stoneware, Jug, Blue Dotted
Tornado, W. H. Farrar, Geddes,
N.Y., 1860, 4 Gal., 16 In.

Jug, Cobalt Blue Writing, Flared Spout, Strap Handle, Evan R. Jones, 11 In. 80.00
Jug, Cobalt Blue, Applied Strap Handle, John Patrick, Wheeling, W.V., 9 In. 220.00
Jug, Cobalt Blue, High Glaze, Laubach's, Northampton, Pa., 13 3/4 In. 70.00
Jug, Cobalt Blue, Leafy Floral Blossom Design, 1858-1865, 3 Gal., 15 1/2 In. 460.00
Jug, Cobalt Blue, Peacock, Salt Glaze, Continental, 19th Century, 4 7/8 In. 860.00
Jug, Cobalt Blue, Tulip, Egg Shape, Strap Handle, Wood Stopper, 3 Gal., 17 In. 470.00
Jug, Double Banded Mouth, Strap Handle, B.F. Landrum, c.1840, 13 1/2 In. 1345.00
Jug, E. Swasey, Portland, Me., 3 In. 175.00
Jug, Elongated Mouth, 1 Strap Handle, Stamped 3, c.1875, 16 In. 420.00
Jug, Face, 4 Teeth, Green Matte Alkaline Glaze, Lanier Meaders, c.1990, 10 x 8 In. 1380.00
Jug, Face, 7 Teeth, Squat, Handle, Lanier Meaders, c.1990, 8 1/4 x 8 In. 2300.00
Jug, Face, Black Rust Gloss Glaze, Tongue Sticking Out, M. Rogers, c.1900, 11 In. 110.00
Jug, Face, Brown Running Glaze, Lanier Meaders, c.1990, 10 x 8 In. 1150.00
Jug, Face, Bulging Eyes, Amber Drips, Brown Ground, Archie Teague, 9 1/2 x 5 In. 520.00
Jug, Face, Chocolate Gloss Slip Glaze, Protruding Features, C. Ferguson, c.1902, 7 In. . . . 1485.00
Jug, Face, Devil, Applied Ears, Horns, Strap Handle, 12 In. 1210.00
Jug, Face, Double, Devil, Incised Moustache, Bulging Eyes, Olive Gloss Glaze, 14 In. . . . 415.00
Jug, Face, Double, Grotesque, Good & Evil, Strap Handles, Vicki Miller, '98, 9 1/8 In. . . . 165.00
Jug, Face, Elongated Neck, Alkaline Glaze, B.B. Craig, 20th Century, 12 1/2 In. 440.00
Jug, Face, Grotesque, Mossy Creek Monster, No. 15, Handles, 1992, 11 1/4 In. 410.00
Jug, Face, Grotesque, Reggie Meaders, Square, 8 3/4 In. 275.00
Jug, Face, Grotesque, Straw Gloss Glaze, Foot Resembling Neck, J.B. Hamilton, 10 In. . . 116.00
Jug, Face, Handles, Glossy Green Glaze, Crocker Brothers, c.1992, 11 1/2 x 7 In. 315.00
Jug, Face, Protruding Facial Features, Shard Teeth, Brown Glaze, 6 1/2 In. 1150.00
Jug, Face, Raised Eye Sockets & Mouth, Rock Teeth, L. Meaders, 9 1/2 In. 7260.00
Jug, Flared Neck, Strap Handle, Stamped V, c.1880, 12 In. 535.00
Jug, Flower, Cobalt Blue, Stamp, H. Heilbronner Schenectady, 4 Gal., 18 1/2 In. 525.00
Jug, Flowers, Haxstun, N.Y., 2 Gal. 225.00
Jug, Glossy Salt Glaze, Rolled Rim, Elongated Flat Handle, W.H. Hancock, 7 1/2 In. 1155.00
Jug, Grape & Leaf Stencil, James Hamilton & Co., Greensboro, Pa., Gal., 15 In. 300.00
Jug, Gray, Cobalt Blue Decoration, Marked James Hamilton, Greensboro, Pa., Gal. 315.00
Jug, Green Ash Glaze Extends To Above Base, Strap Handle, 15 In. 55.00
Jug, M.L. Bamman, Our Grocer, Mid 19th Century, 13 In. 520.00
Jug, Medicinal Use, A. Moll Grocer, Co., St. Louis, Mo. 140.00
Jug, Merchant's, Flared Mouth, 1 Handle, Stamped 3, c.1880, 17 In. 450.00
Jug, Molasses, Marked Swaseyware, Portland, Me. 325.00
Jug, Olive Gloss Alkaline Glaze, Straight Sides, Round Shoulders, Flat Flared Rim, 9 In. . . 468.00
Jug, Osage Rub For The Hair & Head, Bristol Glaze, Bail Handle, Utica, N.Y., 9 In. 385.00
Jug, Out-Turned Mouth, Handle, B.F. Landrum Site, c.1870, 13 In. 425.00
Jug, Paddle-Tail Bird On Floral Branch, White & Son, Utica, N.Y., 2 Gal., 14 In. 1320.00
Jug, Plaquard In Center, Bartman, Germany, c.1580, 9 In. 677.00
Jug, Ring, Salt Glaze, 9 x 10 In. 250.00
Jug, Rounded Shoulder, Cylindrical Body, William Hahn, c.1890, 14 1/4 In. 335.00
Jug, Salt Glaze, Handle, Incised Handwritten H. William, Utica, 1864, 5 3/4 In. 560.00
Jug, Salt Glaze, Oval, L. Norton & Son, Bennington, Vt., c.1838, 2 Gal., 13 1/2 In. 860.00
Jug, Shaped Lip, H.F. Reinhart, 6 1/2 In. 535.00
Jug, Shaped Mouth & Neck, Shaped Handle, Inscribed 2, c.1900, 14 In. 135.00
Jug, Shaped Spout, Handle, Stork Landrum, c.1860, 10 1/4 In. 195.00
Jug, Strap Handle, Signature, Dixon Bros., Commercial Wharf, 12 In. 140.00
Jug, Stripes, J.E. Howson, Wine & Spirit Merchant, 12 1/2 In. 55.00
Jug, Stylized Flowers, Cobalt Blue, Fort Edward, N.Y., 1885, 5 Gal., 19 1/2 In. 920.00
Jug, Syrup, Olive Gloss Glaze, Green Matte Drip, Raised Ridge Handle, 15 In. 110.00
Jug, Tapered Body, Handle, Shaped Neck, Shaw Creek, c.1850, 9 3/4 In. 290.00
Jug, Tapering Shoulder, J.A. Bishop, 2, c.1900, 14 In. 56.00
Jug, Tin Lid, Batter, Bail Handle, Oval, 11 In. 467.00
Jug, Tulip & 2, Applied Handle, 14 1/2 In. 110.00
Jug, Whiskey, Applied Handle, Alkaline Glaze, Cheever Meaders, Late 1960s, 7 1/2 In. . . 550.00
Jug, Wide Mouth, Strap Handle, Catawba Valley, c.1875, 14 1/2 In. 179.00
Loving Cup, Brown, Salt Glaze, Hunt Scene In Relief, 6 3/4 In. 55.00
Milk Pan, Cobalt Blue 3-Leaf Clover, 9 1/2 In. 110.00
Milk Pan, Cobalt Blue Flowers, 11 1/2 In. 95.00
Milk Pan, Cobalt Blue Swag Design, 8 1/2 In. 195.00
Milk Pan, Double Ridge Rim, Handle, Edgefield Area, c.1880, 5 3/4 In. 560.00

Milk Pan, Tapered Body, Handle, c.1860, 6 In. 530.00
Mug, Cider, Cobalt Blue, Coggled Banding, 19th Century, 9 1/2 In. 250.00
Pail, Butter, Allover Flowers & Leaves, Tin Lid, Cowden & Wilcox, 1 1/2 Gal. 4180.00
Pansy Pot, Green Feldspathic Glaze, 12 Pierced Holes, E. Harwell, 1941, 3 1/2 In. 99.00
Paperweight, Lion, Recumbent, Oval Base, Manganese Splotching, 6 In. 165.00
Pitcher, Blue & White Sponge Painted, Molded Rings, 9 In. 385.00
Pitcher, Blue Accent Vine Design, Tooled Diamond, Bristol Glaze, 8 1/2 In. 250.00
Pitcher, Blue Bands At Shoulder & Base, Pewter Lid, Thumb Latch, 9 3/8 In. 1210.00
Pitcher, Blue Dove, Norton, 9 In. 1495.00
Pitcher, Blue Leaves, 1 1/2 With Medallion, 12 1/4 In. 550.00
Pitcher, Blue Slip Dab Design, Shaped Spout, 1 1/2 Gal., 10 In. 137.00
Pitcher, Blue Slip Flowers, Bulbous, 11 In. 1430.00
Pitcher, Cobalt Blue Around Lettering, Strap Handle, G.M. Mowbry, 13 1/4 In. 140.00
Pitcher, Cobalt Blue Brushed V Flowers, Lines At Neck, 9 In. 1100.00
Pitcher, Cobalt Blue Decoration, Applied Handle, 10 In. 70.00
Pitcher, Cobalt Blue Flower, Impressed I Am Dry, Strap Handle, 1800s, 9 In. 2420.00
Pitcher, Cobalt Blue Flowering Plants, 10 1/2 In. 410.00
Pitcher, Cobalt Blue Flowers On Front & Neck, Strap Handle, 11 In. 300.00
Pitcher, Cobalt Blue Flowers, Uneven Rim, Handle, c.1870, 12 1/2 In. 1120.00
Pitcher, Cobalt Blue Plants On Front, Line Around Spout & Handle, 10 5/8 In. 880.00
Pitcher, Cobalt Blue Slip, Flowers & Scrolled Leaves, Gal., 11 In. 440.00
Pitcher, Cobalt Blue Tulip, Applied Strap Handle, 9 1/4 In. 360.00
Pitcher, Cobalt Blue Tulips, Strap Handle, Pennsylvania, 1800s, 7 In. 2420.00
Pitcher, Cobalt Blue, Flower Sprays, Light Blue Glaze, 8 3/4 In. 155.00
Pitcher, Elongated Neck Forms Spout, 2 Bands, Handle, c.1830, 10 3/4 In. 1344.00
Pitcher, Elongated Neck, Shaped Spout, Handle, Jessie Bodie, 10 3/4 In. 750.00
Pitcher, Fern Leaf Designs, 5 Qt. 1950.00
Pitcher, Flared Rim, Spout & Handle, J.W. Seagler, c.1880, 8 1/4 In. 170.00
Pitcher, Milk, Cobalt Blue Floral Slip, Bulbous, 7 1/4 In. 2750.00
Pitcher, Milk, Dark Blue, Egg Shape Base, Raised Foot, Applied Handle, Rim Lines, 8 In. ... 440.00
Pitcher, Milk, Green Glaze, Embossed Design, 7 In. 35.00
Pitcher, Oval, S.I. Pewtress, New Haven, Ct., 11 In. 310.00
Pitcher, Pear & Freehand Cobalt Blue Detail, Strap Handle, Raised Rings Top, 14 1/4 In. .. 110.00
Pitcher, Pickles & Vinegars, Spout, Bristol Glaze, Handle, 1900, 6 3/4 In. 110.00
Pitcher, Pickles & Vinegars, Spout, Handle, Bristol Glaze, 1900, 7 3/4 In. 110.00
Pitcher, Polka Dot Flowers, Cobalt Blue, Raised Rime, 10 In. 605.00
Pitcher, Relief, Rose, Daisy, Mottled Gray, Hand Inscribed Anna V. Stief, 7 In. 745.00
Pitcher, Salt Glaze, Incised Poinsettia Blossom, Bird, Dots, C. Webster, 1850s, 5 In. .. 9350.00
Pitcher, Slip Design, J. Burger, Rochester, N.Y., Gal., 11 In. 440.00
Pitcher, Spray Of Flowers, Cobalt Blue, 9 1/4 In. 385.00
Pitcher, Stenciled, A.P. Donaghho, Parkersburg, W. Va., 10 In. 740.00
Pitcher, White, Blue Flowers On Each Side, 7 In. 145.00
Pitcher & Bowl, Sponge Design, Stripe At Center, 12 In. & 15 In. 275.00
Punch Bowl, Bardwell's Root Beer, Stars, Garlands, 9 3/4 x 19 1/2 In. 2300.00
Puzzle Jug, Brown Glaze, Relief Scenes, Men Smoking, England, Late 19th Century 210.00
Stein, Double Headed Eagle, Crown & Floral, Pewter Lid, 2 1/2 Liter, 14 In. 1330.00
Stein, Hunter With Rifle, Scene Of Woman On Reverse, Pewter Lid, 2 1/2 Liter 485.00
Tankard, Lid, Sachsen Crest, Flowers, Pewter Mounts, Altenburg, 18th Century 1955.00
Tankard, Salt Glaze, England, 5 1/2 In. 715.00
Tea Set, Mirror Black Lead Glaze, Cord Handles, Ben Owen, 1930s, 9 Piece 550.00
Teabowl, Leaves, Brown Glossy Glaze, Footed, Norman Arsenault, 3 x 4 In. 145.00
Teapot, E. Swasey, Portland, Me., 3 In. 125.00
Teapot, Spongeware, Red Flower, Leaves, Octagonal, 9 1/2 x 9 x 5 1/2 In. 525.00
Tureen, Dome Lid, Yellow Gloss Clear Glaze, 2 Squared Handles, B. Owen, 9 In. 300.00
Urn, Orange Glaze, Blue Splotches, Arched Shoulders, 3 Handles, D.Z. Craven, 6 1/2 In. .. 880.00
Vase, Applied Grapevine Cameo, Green Matte Field, Mark, c.1960, 6 3/4 In. 990.00
Vase, Black Over Green Gloss Glaze, Oval, Footed, Indented Base, W. Cole, 6 3/8 In. 300.00
Vase, Browns, Dead-Matte Glaze, Textured, Warren MacKenzie, 13 1/4 In. 690.00
Vase, Bulbous, Cream Matte Glaze, Highlights, Royal Crown, 7 1/2 x 8 1/2 In. 145.00
Vase, Bulbous, Fine Purple, Black Semimatte Glaze, O.L. Batchelder, 5 x 4 1/2 In. 750.00
Vase, Caramel, Gray, Dead-Matte Glaze, Faceted, Warren MacKenzie, 11 1/4 In. 375.00
Vase, Colonial Cream Glaze, Oval Shoulders, 2 Braided Cord Handles, 23 1/2 In. 605.00

Vase, Flaring, Green Rutile Glaze, Royal Crown, 10 1/4 x 7 In. 170.00
Vase, Flaring, Volcanic Blue Glaze, Signed, 5 x 8 In. 4225.00
Vase, Gloss & Matte Greens & Yellow, Streaked Orange Brown, 2 Handles, 16 In. 605.00
Vase, Handles, Oval, Mottled Olive Alkaline Glaze, Cheever Meaders, c.1966, 8 1/4 In. . . 358.00
Vase, Mint Over Dark Green Glaze, Red, 2 Handles, Defined Foot, J.H. Owen, 7 In. 468.00
Vase, Orange Gloss Glaze, Oval, Jonah Owens, c.1925, 6 7/8 In. 305.00
Vase, Oval, Glass Runs, Lug Handles, Amber Matte Glaze, Bill Ray Hussey, 14 1/4 In. . . . 300.00
Vase, Swirlware, Salt Glaze, Jonah Owens, c.1925, 6 1/4 In. 495.00
Vase, Turquoise Satin Glaze, Incised Lines On Shoulders, 2 Ring Handles, 17 3/4 In. 145.00
Water Cooler, 3 Colors, Columbus Landing, White's 4730.00
Water Cooler, Blue Bird On Branch, 2 Handles, Bulbous, 19th Century, 16 In. 1540.00
Water Cooler, Chicken Pecking Ear Of Corn, New York Co., 19 1/2 In. 2750.00
Water Cooler, Cobalt Blue Flower, Applied Ears, Cylindrical, 13 In. 2640.00
Water Cooler, Cobalt Blue Incised 5, Flowers, 3 Bands, 5 Gal., 17 In. 560.00
Water Cooler, Cover, Blue & Gray Bristol Glaze, Robinson, c.1880, 3 Gal. 300.00
Water Cooler, Cream, Cobalt Blue Bands, Bands Of Leaves, c.1875, 12 1/2 In. 475.00
Water Cooler, Double Handles, Satterlee & Mory, c.1870, 6 Gal. 1210.00
Water Cooler, Flowers, Leaves, Applied Handles, Blue Squiggle, 3 Gal., 15 In. 550.00
Water Cooler, Impressed Shepard Jr., Double Flower, No. 5, 18 In. 165.00
Water Cooler, Incised Bands, Blue Flowers, Wooden Spout, 11 x 14 In. 440.00
Water Cooler, Relief Design, Columbus Holding Flag, Ships, Blue, Carmel Slip, 22 In. . . . 4730.00
Wine Cooler, Brown Tin Glaze, Herald Crest, Grapes, Cork Lining, Hole Top, 10 1/2 In. . . 70.00

STORE fixtures, cases, cutters, and other items that have no advertising
as part of the decoration are listed here. Most items found in an old
store are listed in the Advertising category in this book.

Bin, Nail, Oak, Pine, 8 Sides, 40 Drawers, Porcelain Pulls, Revolving, 1900s, 35 x 23 In. . . 476.00
Bin, Tea, Countertop, Hinged Lid, c.1910, 12 1/4 x 15 In. 530.00
Cabinet, 21 Small Drawers, 2 Glazed Doors, 4 Large Drawers, 18 x 29 x 13 In. 1125.00
Cabinet, Haberdasher's, Walnut, Ornate Carved, 16 Drawers, Victorian, 36 x 17 x 62 In. . . 1840.00
Cabinet, Nuts & Bolts, 8 Sides, 72 Drawers, Porcelain Pulls, 43 x 21 In. 1207.00
Cabinet, Pine, Gold Lettering On 32 Drawers, 14 x 35 1/4 In. 1320.00
Cabinet, Pine, Hardware, Octagonal Top, 80 Drawers, Porcelain Pulls, 45 x 28 In. 1625.00
Cabinet, Ribbon Display, Oak, 24 Shelves, Exposition Showcase Co., 49 x 22 x 27 In. . . . 1610.00
Cabinet, Ship's Cabinetmaker, Walnut, 72 3/4 In. 2590.00
Cabinet, Watchmaker, 120 Drawers, 69 x 4 1/2 x 54 In. 7800.00
Case, Display, 2 Shelves Over Sliding Doors, Chrome Pulls, Bentwood Legs, 52 3/4 In. . . . 515.00
Case, Display, Countertop, Slant Front, Brass Thumblatch Opens To Mirror, 3 x 2 In. 110.00
Case, Display, Jewelry, Oak, Slant Front, Decal, 12 1/2 x 12 1/2 In. 575.00
Case, Display, Metal Tubing, 1 Glass Shelf, Back Opens, Mirrored, 13 1/2 x 26 In. 357.00
Case, Display, Oak, 2 Sections, Mirrored Doors, c.1900, 42 x 120 x 27 In. 690.00
Change Maker, Brandt Automatic Cashier, Pat. Dec. 27, 1921, 9 x 11 x 14 In. 80.00
Coffee Grinders are listed in their own category.
Counter, Pine Base, Yellow Paint, Double Front Panel, Line Carving, 71 3/4 In. 495.00
Counter, Pine, Red, White, Blue Paint, c.1890, 8 Ft. 1650.00
Counter, Seed Bin, Oak, 15 Glass Display Frames, 96 In. 1600.00
Counter, Seeds & Beans, Oak, 4 Tilt Drawers, 1890, 71 x 37 x 23 In. 1265.00
Counter, Tiled Checkerboard, Base Tiles, 1910, 35 1/2 x 97 In. 3740.00
Dispenser, Syrup, Rattan Over Glass, Porcelain Vase, Briet-Paris, 18 x 6 1/2 In. 345.00
Display, 4 Show Globes, Apothecary, Liquid Filled, Light-Up, Base, 1900, 16 In. 3450.00
Display, Gum, Rotating, 5 Columns, Painted, Glass, 14 1/2 In. 172.00
Display, Jar, Apothecary, Globe, Hanging, Brass Plated, Chains, Round, 12 1/2 In. 360.00
Display, Jar, Apothecary, Pointed Stopper, Pear Shape, 33 In. 600.00
Display, Jar, Apothecary, Stacking, 3 Sections For Colored Water, 26 In., 4 Piece . .420.00 to 480.00
Display, Jar, Candy, Cover, Swirl Foot & Neck, 12 3/4 In. 115.00
Display, Jar, Candy, Pointed Cover, Teardrop, 1950s, 13 In. 28.00
Display, Jar, Globe, Apothecary, Hanging, Acorn Glass, Iron, Whitall Tatum, 24 In. 750.00
Display, Jar, Globe, Apothecary, Hanging, Brass Plated, Whitall Tatum, 21 In. . . . .750.00 to 960.00
Display, Mortar & Pestle, Black Glazed, Gilt, Gilman Brother Inc., 15 x 12 In. 120.00
Display, Mortar & Pestle, Ceramic, White Glazed, Gilt, 5 3/4 x 6 3/4 In. 50.00
Display, Rack, Sporting Goods Store, Hartford, Ct., c.1880 . . . . 1500.00
Popcorn Machine, Manley, Red Panels, 3 Sides, 1940s, 36 x 32 x 22 In. 230.00

Seed Counter, Oak, Display Front, Back Drawers, Brass Pulls, 8 Ft. 2 In. 2400.00
Showcase, Oak, 8 Glass Cabinet Doors, Drawers, 15 In. 5900.00
Stool, Bar Or Ice Cream Parlor, Half-Ring Step, Upholstered Seat, 1900s, 6 Piece 1900.00
Strawholder, Brass Lid, Paneled Glass, 11 In. 90.00
Strawholder, Copper Lid, Glass, Flared Base, Pat. Jan. 16, 1912, 12 In. 230.00
Strawholder, Lid, Paneled Glass, Oversized Base, 11 1/2 In. 48.00
Table, Soda Fountain, Iron, Glass Display Top, 4 Swing Out Round Seats, 26 x 32 In. . . . 1610.00

STOVES have been used in America for heating since the eighteenth
century and for cooking since the nineteenth century. Most types of
wood, coal, gas, kerosene, and even some electric stoves are collected.

Caboose, Square Footprint, Hamilton, Ohio, c.1905, 27 x 23 In. 415.00
Cook, Baking Oven, Iron, Victorian, 29 In. 785.00
Door, Latch In Back, Cow's Head Front, 2 Projecting Hoofs, Cast Iron, 11 x 22 In. 1175.00
Heating, Wood, Iron, Embossed Colebrook Furnace, Flowers, 23 x 13 x 20 1/2 In. 110.00
Parlor, 3-Story House, Mansard Roof, 42 In. 5600.00
Parlor, Cast Iron, Emerich & Pinger, No. 12, 56 In. 412.00
Parlor, Oakdale Crawford, Restored, 1890 . . . . 900.00
Parlor, S Fire Box, Gothic Designs, Stylized Urns & Torches, Wager, 1853, 38 In. 1175.00
Potbelly, Cast Iron, Athens Stove Works 100.00
Potbelly, Spark, Cast Iron 295.00

SUMIDA is a Japanese pottery that was made from about 1895 to 1941.
Pieces are usually everyday objects—vases, jardinieres, bowls,
teapots, and decorative tiles. Most pieces have a very heavy orange-
red, blue, brown, black, green, purple, or off-white glaze, with raised
three-dimensional figures as decorations. The unglazed part is painted
red, green, black, or orange. Sumida was called *Korean Pottery* or *Poo
Ware* in the past.

Vase, Bisque Figures, Orange Ground, Early 20th Century, 11 In. 115.00
Vase, Rakan, With Incense Burner, Signed, Early 20th Century, 9 1/4 In. 230.00

SUNBONNET BABIES were first introduced in 1900 in the book *The*
Sunbonnet Babies. The stories were by Eulalie Osgood Grover, illus-
trated by Bertha Corbett. The children's faces were completely hidden
by the sunbonnets. The children had been pictured in black and white
before this time, but the color pictures in the book were immediately
successful. The Royal Bayreuth China Company made a full line of
children's dishes decorated with the Sunbonnet Babies. Some Sunbonnet Babies plates have been reproduced, but are clearly marked.

Doorstop, Cast Iron, Painted, Orange, Yellow, Red, Black, Raised 72, 6 In. 115.00
Hair Receiver 325.00

SUNDERLAND luster is a name given to a special type of pink luster made
by Leeds, Newcastle, and other English firms during the nineteenth
century. The luster glaze is metallic and glossy and appears to have
bubbles in it. Other pieces of luster are listed in the Luster category.

Cup & Saucer, Luster 115.00
Jug, Poem, Sailor's Tear & Peace & Plenty, Mariner Compass, 9 In. 715.00
Mug, Cast Iron, Bridge View, Interior Frog, E & C. England, 4 3/4 x 3 1/2 In. 300.00
Pitcher, Hunt Scenes, Pink Luster, Leaf Spout, Basket Weave Base, 5 7/8 In. 330.00
Pitcher, Masonic Arms & Symbols, Pink Luster, 1823, 10 1/8 In. 1210.00
Pitcher, Pink Luster, Farmer's Arms, Masonic Symbols, 6 1/2 In. 385.00
Pitcher, Pink Luster, Four Ways Inn, 4 In. 58.00
Pitcher, Pink Luster, Queen's Roses, 3 Ships, Verse, Satyr Head Spout, 8 1/2 In. 1320.00
Pitcher, Pink Luster, Ship & Poem, Polychrome, 7 In. 1650.00
Pitcher, Pink Luster, Wear Bridge & Poems, Anna Clard, April 16, 1818, 7 In. 1485.00
Pitcher, Red Transfer Of Ship, 2 Sailors, Verse, Hand Painted Enamel, 8 In. 770.00
Plaque, Pink Luster, Flying Cloud, Boston, 7 x 8 In. 660.00
Plaque, Pink Luster, Prepare To Meet Thy God, Polychrome, 8 x 9 In. 580.00
Plaque, Pink Luster, Thou God Seest Me, Dixon Co., 7 x 8 In. 330.00
Plate, Transferware, Brigantine, 10 In. 560.00
Pot, Center Floral Band, Flowers, Pink Luster, 10 1/2 In. 780.00

SUPERMAN was created by two seventeen-year-olds in 1938. The first issue of *Action* comics had the strip. Superman remains popular and became the hero of a radio show in 1940, cartoons in the 1940s, a television series, and several major movies.

Blanket, Child's, Man Of Steel Pictured	460.00
Book, Paperback, Strip Reprints From 1950s, 160 Pages, 4 1/4 x 7 1/2 In.	12.00
Cake Decorations, Superman, Buildings, 6 Piece	10.00
Catalog, Superman At The Gilbert Hall Of Science, 5 1/2 x 8 1/2 In.	60.00
Charm, Sterling Silver, Dell Weston Company, 1947, 2 In.	505.00
Coloring Book, World Without Water, Whitman, 1980, 8 x 10 In.	5.00
Comic Book, Tim Store, Christmas Cover, 1942	400.00
Comic Book, Tim Store, July 1947	200.00
Figurine, Plaster, Painted, Hollow, c.1940, 4 1/2 x 5 x 15 In.	215.00
Game, Flying Bingo, 12 x 12 x 1/2 In.	20.00
Game, Spin Cycle Series, Pressman Toy Co., 1967, 10 1/4 x 15 3/4 x 1/2 In.	60.00
Game, Superman III, Parker Bros., 1982, 9 x 17 x 1/2 In.	15.00
Glass, Superman In Action, Saving Bus, Pulling Chariot, Rescuing Man, 5 3/4 In.	24.00
Magazine, Tim Stamp Album Issue, Sept. 1945, 16 Pages, 5 1/2 x 8 In.	95.00
Mirror, Chromed Metal Frame, Superman Breaking Chains, 9 1/4 x 12 1/4 In.	24.00
Patch, Junior Olympics, Linen, 5 Sides, Red, White, Blue, Yellow, 1972, 4 In.	12.00
Playsuit, Outfit, Box, 10 1/4 x 13 x 2 In.	165.00
Soaky, No Cape, 1970s	25.00
Thermos, Red Cup, Canada, 8 In.	40.00
Tin, Fiftieth Birthday Commemorative, 9 In.	12.00
Towel, Beach, 1970s	25.00
Toy, Back A Whack, Paddle With Cord & Ball, 5 x 10 x 3/4 In.	15.00
Toy, Peel-Off Cards, Set Of 99, Puzzle On Reverse, 2 x 3 In.	12.00
Toy, Swim Fins, Rubber, Blue, Red, 7 In.	18.00
Wallpaper, 6 Different Illustrations, 21 In. Wide	24.00
Watch, Pocket, Superman Cruising Skyline Of Metropolis, Bradley, 1959	1079.00

SUSIE COOPER began as a designer in 1925 working for the English firm A.E. Gray & Company. In 1932 she formed Susie Cooper Pottery, Ltd. In 1950 it became Susie Cooper China, Ltd., and the company made china and earthenware. In 1966 it was acquired by Josiah Wedgwood & Sons, Ltd. The name Susie Cooper appears with the company names on many pieces of ceramics.

Bowl, Blue Rings, 10 In.	45.00
Bowl, Longleaf, 7 1/2 In.	60.00
Coffee Set, Tiger Lily, Kestrel Shape, 15 Piece	750.00
Coffeepot, Patricia Rose, Kestrel Shape, 7 1/2 In.	550.00
Cup & Saucer, Crescent Sgraffito, After Dinner	70.00
Cup & Saucer, Dresden Spray	85.00
Cup & Saucer, Printemps	80.00
Gravy Boat, Underplate, Swansea Spray	75.00
Pitcher, Milk, Dresden Spray, 4 1/2 In.	95.00
Pitcher, Milk, Red Band, 4 In.	80.00
Plate, Patricia Rose, Pink Border, 10 In.	75.00
Platter, Leaping Deer, 16 In.	95.00
Soup, Cream, Underplate, Tiger Lily, Handles	55.00
Sugar, Tiger Lily, 3 1/2 In.	60.00
Tea Set, Cream, Blue & Black Bands, Porcelain, Marked	520.00
Tea Set, Glaze, 17 Piece	110.00
Tureen, Cover, Dresden Spray, Kestrel Shape, 8 In.	125.00

SWANKYSWIGS are small drinking glasses. In 1933, the Kraft Food Company began to market cheese spreads in these decorated, reusable glass tumblers. They were discontinued from 1941 to 1946, then made again from 1947 to 1958. Then plain glasses were used for most of the cheese, although a few special decorated Swankyswigs have been made since that time. A complete list of prices can be found in *Kovels' Depression Glass & Dinnerware Price List*.

Band No. 2, Red & Black, 5 In.	10.00

Band No. 3, Blue & White, 3 3/8 In.	4.00
Bustlin' Betsy, Red, 3 3/4 In.	6.00
Kiddie Kup, Little Jack Horner, Frosted, 4 1/2 In.	15.00
Kiddie Kup, Red, Bicycle, Children, Animals, Plastic Lid, 4 1/2 In.	10.00
Posy Tulip No. I, Blue, 3 1/2 In.	4.00
Posy Tulip No. I, Green, 3 1/2 In.	4.00

SWORDS of all types that are of interest to collectors are listed here. The military dress sword with elaborate handle is probably the most wanted. Be sure to display swords in a safe way, out of reach of children.

Artillery, Germany, Officer's, Iron Scabbard, Wire Wrap Composition Grip, 34 In.	450.00
Bayonet, Krag, 1899, 11 3/4 In.	80.00
Briquet, France, Naval, Knuckle Bow, Brass Hilt, 1790, 23 In.	925.00
Cavalry, Bavaria, Officer's, Broad, Iron Hilt, Wrapped Leather Grip, 1826, 32 In.	575.00
Cutlass, Curved Broad, Ribbed Cast Iron Grip, 1810, 24 In.	1250.00
Cutlass, Navy, U.S.M., Curved, 2-Piece Wood Scale Grips, Leather Scabbard, 18 In.	175.00
Cutlass, War Of 1815, Broad Fullered Blade, Brass Hilt, Stirrup Form Guard, 23 3/4 In.	475.00
Dagger, Ivory Handle, Silver Plated Mounts, Tibetan, 15 1/2 In.	431.00
Dress, Lodge, Ivory Handle, Engraved Blade, Leather Case, Chrome & Enamel Scabbard .	40.00
England, Steel Hilt, Silver Wire & Tape Wrap Grip, 1750, 33 In.	2850.00
Field & Staff, Officer's, Shark Grip, Wire Wrap, Floral & Eagle Hilt, 1860, 29-In. Blade .	325.00
Foot Officer, Brass Helmet, Leather & Wire Wrapped Handle, 41 1/2 In.	330.00
Infantry, England, Officer's, Dumbbell Blade, Leather Scabbard, 1895, 32 1/2 In.	575.00
Infantry, Germany, Officer's, Wire Wrapped Sharkskin Grip, 1861, 32 1/4 In.	525.00
Katana, Japanese, Brown Lacquer Saya-Blade, 1800s, 28 1/2 In.	2130.00
Katana, Japanese, Iron Mokko Form Isuba, Black Lacquer Saya-Blade, 1800s, 25 In.	1006.00
Machete, Collins No. 127, Leather Grip, Brass Fittings, Embossed Scabbard	250.00
Rapier, Spain, Cup Hilt, Iron, Pommel & Silver Wire Wrapped Grip, 1650, 37 In.	2495.00
Saber, Artillery, Brass, 1-Branch Hilt, Scabbard, Model 1840, 1861, 39 In.	522.00
Saber, Cavalry, Brass Hilt, Leather Grip, 1840, 36-In. Blade	650.00
Saber, Georgian, Officer's, Leather Scabbard, Henry Osborn, c.1808, 36 1/4 In.	448.00
Saber, Japanese Army, Parade, Horn Grip, Curved Blade, 1873, 37 1/2 In.	252.00
Saber, Mexican War, Confederate, D-Hilt, Civil War	6050.00
Saber, Poland, Cavalry, Curved Narrow Fullered S.E. Blade, Iron Ferrule, 1770, 31 In.	1650.00
Saber, U.S. Cavalry, Brass Hilt, Leather Grip Bound In Brass Wire, 42 1/4 In.	550.00
Samurai, Scabbard Painted Green, Wooden Handle	40.00
Stick, Germany, Stepped Cane Shaft, Cane Root Cluster Curved Handle, 1850	495.00
Tsuba, Iron, Hokei Shape, Gold Inlaid Dragonfly, c.1800, 3 1/4 In.	635.00
Tsuba, Iron, Nade Gaku Hokei, Inlaid, Landscape, Flowers, Vines, 18th Century, 2 1/2 In.	160.00
Tsuba, Iron, Shin No Maru-Gata, Engraved Shou Design, Moriyoshi, 18th Century, 3 In. .	430.00
Tsuba, Iron, Shin No Maru-Gata, Sukashi Paulownia Design, 18th Century, 3 1/4 In.	635.00

TEA CADDY is the name for a small box made to hold tea leaves. In the eighteenth century, tea was very expensive and it was stored under lock and key. The first tea caddies were made with locks. By the nineteenth century, tea was more plentiful and the tea caddy was larger. Often there were two sections, one for green tea, one for black tea.

Apple Form, 19th Century, 5 In.	220.00
Applewood, Hinged Lid, Conforming Body, 5 3/4 In.	67.00
Brass, Floral & Swag Engraved Around Body, c.1780	450.00
Brass, Plaques, Cupids, Faces, Musical Instruments On Lid, Oak, 7 x 10 In.	345.00
Burl, Chenille Lining, Ringed Lion Masks, Ivory Compartment Finials, 6 x 9 x 5 In.	1150.00
Burl, Inlaid Stripes, Ivory Escutcheon, Brass Claw Feet & Ring Handles, 8 x 12 In.	1380.00
Burl Walnut, Brass Mounted, Double, England, c.1840, 5 7/8 x 9 7/8 x 5 3/4 In.	672.00
Burl Walnut, Brass Mounted, Mid 19th Century, 5 3/4 x 9 x 5 1/2 In.	460.00
Burl Walnut, Dome Top, Hinged, England, c.1850, 5 x 6 1/4 x 3 7/8 In.	560.00
Cherry Veneer, Brass Hinges, 4 3/4 x 3 3/8 x 4 3/4 In.	715.00
Chrome Cover, Art Deco Style, Pottery, 5 In.	28.00
Fruitwood, Apple Form, Late 18th Century	1960.00
Fruitwood, Apple Shape, Silver Foil Interior, George III, 1800, 4 1/4 In.	7800.00
Fruitwood, Pyriform, Late 18th Century	5600.00

Glass, Green, Pewter Rim, Cover, Embossed, Leaves, Finial Top, 3 Cabochons, 6 In. 1095.00
Ivory, Oval, Diamond Quilted, Flowers, Silver Plate Mount, Beaded, 5 1/2 In. 1345.00
Ivory, Silver Plate Mount, Hinged, Leaf Finial, Beaded Rim, 4 1/4 In. 460.00
Ivory Panel, Flowers & Foliage, Japan Ground, 4 1/8 In. 2530.00
Kingwood, 8-Sided Lid, Ivory Finial Interior, George III, 4 3/4 x 5 1/2 x 4 In. 635.00
Kingwood, Brass Strung, Regency, Sarcophagus, Gilt Paw Feet, 7 x 9 x 5 3/4 In. 690.00
Lacquer, Black, Chinese Export, Hinged Cover, Late 18th Century, 5 1/4 x 10 x 8 In. 288.00
Lacquer, Japan, Late 19th Century, 5 x 7 3/4 x 4 1/4 In. 690.00
Mahogany, 2 Compartments, Beveled Top, Canted Sides, Bun Feet, 13 x 7 1/2 In. 808.00
Mahogany, Brass Drop Bail Handle, Divided, Bracket Feet, c.1820, 6 1/2 x 9 14 In. 225.00
Mahogany, Brass Lion Head Handles, Divided Interior, c.1810, 7 x 8 1/2 In. 616.00
Mahogany, Casket Form, Divided Interior, Button Handles, Bun Feet, 7 x 13 In. 420.00
Mahogany, Chippendale, Tole Canisters, England, c.1780 .... 725.00
Mahogany, Coffin Shape, Inlaid Satinwood, 8 1/2 x 10 1/4 x 6 1/2 In. 250.00
Mahogany, Coffin Shape, Silver Mounts, Ball Feet, 5 1/2 x 7 x 4 In. 750.00
Mahogany, Divided Interior, Original Brass Bail Handle, 10 7/8 x 6 x 6 1/2 In. 440.00
Mahogany, Domed Lid, Fitted Interiors, Bun Feet, 7 1/2 x 10 In. 365.00
Mahogany, Double, Banded, Inlaid, 8 Sides, George III, 5 x 8 1/2 x 5 1/2 In. 460.00
Mahogany, Federal, Inlaid Pinwheels, 2 Compartments, Brass Ball Feet, 7 x 11 In. 3760.00
Mahogany, Hinged Lid, Brass Bail Handle, George IV, c.1820, 9 1/4 x 5 3/4 In. 310.00
Mahogany, Inlaid, 2-Lid Compartment, Ivory Pulls, 6 x 13 x 6 In. 520.00
Mahogany, Inlaid, 3 Compartments, Rectangular, Regency, c.1815, 6 x 9 1/2 x 5 In. 730.00
Mahogany, Inlaid, Coffin Shape Lid, 2 Lead Caddies, Center Well, c.1850, 13 x 6 In. 250.00
Mahogany, Inlaid, Double, Coffin Shape, Cover, Regency, 7 1/4 x 12 x 6 1/2 In. 420.00
Mahogany, Inlaid, Oval Lid, Patera, George IV, 19th Century, 4 x 5 x 3 In. 635.00
Mahogany, Inlaid, Rectangular, Hinged Lid, George III, c.1800, 4 1/2 x 3 5/8 In. 730.00
Mahogany, Ivory Escutcheon & Handle, Late 18th Century, 6 1/2 x 4 In. 287.00
Mahogany, Marquetry Inlay On Lid, Inverted Teardrop Shape, 1780s, 4 1/4 In. 920.00
Mahogany, Rectangular, Enamel, Brass Inlay, France, 6 1/2 In. 375.00
Mahogany, Rectangular, Hinged Lid, Bail Handle, Satinwood Cartouche, 12 x 7 In. 115.00
Mahogany, Regency, Sarcophagus, Divided Interior, 6 1/4 x 11 1/2 x 5 3/4 In. 290.00
Mahogany, Rococo Scroll & Leaf Carving, Bombe Sides, Divided Interior, 9 In. 250.00
Mahogany, Sarcophagus Shape, 2 Lid Compartments, George III, 7 In. 750.00
Mahogany, Scalloped Base, Rococo Leaf & Scrollwork, 3 Compartments, 9 3/4 In. 110.00
Mahogany, Triple Tin Interior, Brass Hardware, 5 1/4 x 8 3/4 In. 140.00
Mahogany Veneer, 3 Faux Drawers, 4 Turned Ball Feet, Early 19th Century 980.00
Mahogany Veneer, Central Paterae, Banding, String Inlay, 5 1/4 x 4 1/4 In. 430.00
Mahogany Veneer, Exotic Wood, Leaves, Floral Reserves, 5 x 6 3/4 x 3 5/8 In. 1840.00
Mahogany Veneer, Flowers, Leaves Oval Reserve, Early 19th Century, 4 1/2 In. 520.00
Mahogany Veneer, Silver Engraved Handle, Frost Homestead, Durham, N.H., 1700s 575.00
Mahogany Veneer, Silver Painted Interior, Fitted Lock, England, 12 x 5 x 7 In. 335.00
Maple, Regency, Sarcophagus, Divided Interior, 8 x 8 1/2 x 5 In. 633.00
Milk Glass, Blue Green, Opalescent, Metal Cap, Russian Label, 5 In. 110.00
Mother-Of-Pearl, Angled Lid, 2 Compartments, Bun Feet, 4 1/2 x 4 1/4 x 7 In. 2116.00
Mother-Of-Pearl, Diamond Pattern, Interior Lid, 19th Century, 4 x 5 1/4 x 3 1/2 In. 635.00
Mother-Of-Pearl, Inlaid, Papier Mache, c.1840, 5 3/4 x 9 1/4 x 6 3/8 In. 345.00
Mulberry Wood, Rosewood Crossbanding, Brass Footed, George II, 1750, 5 x 7 In. 2280.00
Oak, Walnut, Burl Veneer, Copper Liner, Continental, Queen Anne, 12 x 12 x 20 In. 550.00
Olive Wood Veneer, Dome Top, 2 Interior Sections, Pewter Mixing Bowl, 6 1/2 In. 250.00
Porcelain, Enameled Flowers, Armorial, 3 Sides, Faux Oriental Mark, 5 1/8 In. 165.00
Regency, Rolled Paper, Scrolls, Cut, Shuttle-Shape, Polychrome Bone, 5 x 7 5/8 In. 1840.00
Rosewood, Brass Inlaid Flowers, 4 x 6 x 4 1/2 In. 476.00
Rosewood, Carved, 2 Compartments, Bun Feet, Regency, Mid 19th Century 450.00
Rosewood, Continental, Various Geometric Design, 5 x 7 1/4 x 3 3/4 In. 1840.00
Rosewood, Lion Head Handles, Brass Paw Feet, England, c.1850, 12 x 6 1/2 In. 420.00
Rosewood, Mahogany, Coffin Shape, 2 Compartments, Glass Insert, Gilt Paw Feet, 1830 . 670.00
Rosewood, Mother-Of-Pearl Escutcheon, Early 19th Century, 12 1/2 x 6 x 7 In. 345.00
Rosewood, Mother-Of-Pearl Escutcheon, Handles, England, 1800s, 12 x 6 In. 345.00
Rosewood, Mother-Of-Pearl, Hinged Cover, c.1860, 7 1/2 x 9 1/2 x 6 In. 390.00
Rosewood, Sarcophagus Shape, 2 Foil Lined Wells, Mixing Bowl, 6 1/4 In. 290.00
Rosewood, Sarcophagus Shape, 2 Lidded Sections, Pendant Handles, 6 x 8 x 5 In. 460.00
Rosewood, Sarcophagus Shape, Brass Inlay, Lion Handles, Regency, 12 x 8 In. 2100.00

Rosewood, Sarcophagus Shape, Divided Compartment, Regency, 6 x 8 x 5 In. 489.00
Rosewood, Sarcophagus, Ivory Escutcheon, Bronze Paw Feet, Regency, 8 x 12 In. 575.00
Rosewood, Satinwood Stringing, Regency, Early 19th Century, 7 1/2 x 12 x 6 In. 575.00
Rosewood, Silver Foil Inlay, Double, Bun Feet, 6 x 9 In. 448.00
Rosewood Veneer, Line Inlay, Keyhole Escutcheon, 4 1/2 x 4 5/8 In. 165.00
Satinwood, Burl Walnut Inlay, Ivory Shield Key Escutcheon, George III, 5 x 9 In. 920.00
Satinwood, Double, Crossbanded, George IV, 4 3/4 x 8 x 4 1/2 In. 460.00
Satinwood, Double, Top Medallion, Ivory Finials, 5 In. 1380.00
Satinwood, Inlaid Borders & Panels, Silver Ring Pull, Quilted Lid, 6 x 12 In. 1380.00
Satinwood, Mahogany, 2 Inlaid Panels To Front, Inlaid Top, 4 1/2 x 7 In. 115.00
Satinwood, Rectangular Hinged Top, Divided Compartment, George III, 4 In. 1035.00
Satinwood, Rosewood Banded, Dome Lid, Trunk Shape, 5 3/4 x 10 x 5 1/2 In. 550.00
Silver, Repousse, European, 4 1/2 x 2 1/2 In. 345.00
Stoneware, Salt Glaze, Applied Decoration, Pewter Lid, Late 1700s, 5 In. 295.00
Teak, Beveled Lid, Moon Brasses, Iron Handle Either Side, Oriental, 6 3/4 In. 385.00
Tole, Band At Top, Colored Flowers, Red Ground, 4 1/8 In. 495.00
Tole, Red Acorn Design, Black Ground, 6 In. 495.00
Tortoiseshell, 2 Square Covers, Bone Footed, England, 3 3/4 x 6 1/2 x 9 In. 2760.00
Tortoiseshell, Abalone, Mother-Of-Pearl, 2 Covers, Anglo-Dutch, 4 x 5 x 3 In. 1380.00
Tortoiseshell, Bombe Form, Silver Plate Cartouche On Lid, 2 Sections, 5 5/8 In. 1495.00
Tortoiseshell, Bone, Double, Mid 19th Century, 4 1/4 x 6 x 3 3/4 In. 2070.00
Tortoiseshell, Footed Blown Mixing Bowl, Ivory Escutcheon, 6 x 11 x 5 In. 2185.00
Tortoiseshell, Ivory & Silver Bands, 2 Compartments, Bun Feet, Regency, 6 x 7 In. 2760.00
Tortoiseshell, Silver Inlaid, Regency, Domed Lid, Early 19th Century, 5 x 7 x 3 3/4 In. .. 3910.00
Tortoiseshell, Silver Mounted, Edwardian, c.1907, 4 5/8 In. 1265.00
Turtleback Form, Engraved Tea Roses & Pansies, Silver Plate, 4 1/4 In. 230.00
Walnut, 2 Interior Compartments, Central Well, Ivory Escutcheon, 12 x 6 1/4 In. 460.00
Walnut, Shield Design, 2 Compartments, Bone Pull, 8 1/4 x 5 1/2 In. 220.00
Wood, Double, Coffin Shape Lid, Divided Interior With Covers, 7 1/4 x 10 1/2 In. 252.00
Wood, Double, Covered Interior, Ring Handle, 1820s, 6 1/8 x 8 In. 392.00
Wood, Double, Reserves Of Marquetry Seashells On Lid, Ivory Finials, 1870s, 5 In. 1093.00
Wood, Line & Star Medallion, 3 Sections, Center For Mixing Bowl, 6 x 12 In. 1320.00
Wood, Man Standing On Sleigh, 3 Horses, Tinned Interior, Russian, 5 7/8 In. 170.00
Wood, Scallop Rim, Engraved Both Sides, Arms & Crest, Urn Finial, 1791, 5 1/4 In. 3000.00

TEA LEAF IRONSTONE dishes are named for their decorations. There
was a superstition that it was lucky if a whole tea leaf unfolded at the
bottom of your cup. This idea was translated into the pattern of dishes
known as *tea leaf.* By 1850, at least twelve English factories were
making this pattern, and by the 1870s, it was a popular pattern in many
countries. The tea leaf was always a luster glaze on early wares,
although now some pieces are made with a brown tea leaf.

Bowl, Vegetable, Cover, Davenport 150.00
Bowl, Vegetable, Cover, L & P 220.00
Bowl, Vegetable, Cover, Meakin 120.00
Bowl, Vegetable, Cover, Shaw 110.00
Bowl, Vegetable, Cover, Wedgwood ....80.00 to 115.00
Butter, Cover, Liner, Copper Trim, Mellor Taylor, 3 Piece 60.00
Butter, Cover, Liner, Copper Trim, Morning Glory, 3 Piece 2100.00
Butter, Cover, Liner, Copper Trim, Morning Glory, Portland Style, 3 Piece 875.00
Butter, Meakin, 2 Piece ....70.00 to 90.00
Cake Stand, Red Cliff 135.00
Coffeepot, Meakin 60.00
Coffeepot, T. Furnival 100.00
Creamer, East End, Child's 95.00
Creamer, Mayer 100.00
Creamer, Meakin 160.00
Creamer, Teaberry, Clementson ....225.00 to 300.00
Creamer, Wedgwood 100.00
Cup, Handleless, J. Furnival 100.00
Cup & Saucer, Teaberry, Clementson 80.00
Cup & Saucer, Wilkinson 50.00

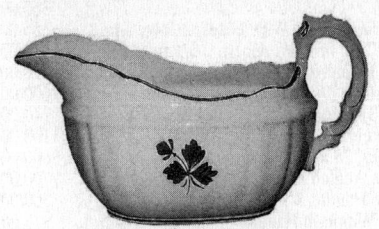

Tea Leaf Ironstone, Gravy Boat, Chelsea Style

Tea Leaf Ironstone, Teapot, Bordered Fuchsia, Shaw

Dish, Honey, Copper Trim, Shaw . . . . .65.00 to 170.00
Eggcup, Copper Trim, Adams 250.00
Gravy Boat, Ceres, Copper Trim, Elsmore & Forster 450.00
Gravy Boat, Chelsea Style . . . . *Illus*   60.00
Gravy Boat, Copper Trim, Shaw . . . . .30.00 to 75.00
Gravy Boat, Grindley 130.00
Gravy Boat, Mayer 180.00
Gravy Boat, Wedgwood 80.00
Jug, Milk, Copper Trim, Meakin 60.00
Ladle, Copper Trim, Sayres, 9 In. 120.00
Pickle, Copper Trim, Shaw 65.00
Pickle, Mayer 200.00
Pitcher, Milk, Burgess 90.00
Pitcher, Milk, Copper Trim, Grindley 40.00
Posset Cup, Chinese, Shaw 325.00
Relish, Copper Trim, Shaw 275.00
Shaving Mug, Copper Trim, Shaw 225.00
Shaving Mug, Furnival 275.00
Soap Dish, Copper Trim, Sayres, 3 Piece 110.00
Soap Dish, Copper Trim, Shaw, 3 Piece 275.00
Soap Dish, Wedgwood, 3 Piece 180.00
Sugar, Cochran 425.00
Sugar, Grindley 25.00
Sugar, Meakin 45.00
Sugar, Teaberry, Clementson . . . . .220.00 to 325.00
Sugar, Walley 1025.00
Teapot, Bordered Fuchsia, Shaw . . . . *Illus*   700.00
Teapot, East End, Child's 200.00
Teapot, Mayer 60.00
Teapot, Shaw 80.00
Tureen, Sauce, Cover, Meakin, 3 Piece 80.00
Tureen, Sauce, Cover, Red Cliff, 4 Piece 225.00
Tureen, Sauce, Cover, Walley, 3 Piece 140.00
Tureen, Sauce, Cover, Wilkinson, 4 Piece 350.00
Tureen, Soup, Cover, Lily-Of-The-Valley, 4 Piece 1000.00
Tureen, Soup, Cover, Shaw, 4 Piece 1000.00
Wash Basin, Clementson 85.00

TECO is the mark used on the art pottery line made by the American Terra Cotta and Ceramic Company of Terra Cotta and Chicago, Illinois. The company was an offshoot of the firm founded by William D. Gates in 1881. The Teco line was first made in 1885 but was not sold commercially until 1902. It continued in production until 1922. Over 500 designs were made in a variety of colors, shapes, and glazes. The company closed in 1930.

    Bowl, Emerald Green Glaze, Charcoaling, 1 7/8 x 6 7/8 In. 200.00

Bowl, Green Matte Glaze, 2 1/8 x 9 1/8 In. 300.00
Bowl, No. 80, Flower, Green Matte Glaze, Squat, Flared Rim, W.D. Gates, 2 3/4 x 7 In. .. 355.00
Bowl, No. 317, Flower, Green Matte Glaze, Fluted Top, Fritz W. Albert, 2 3/4 In. 1880.00
Bowl, No. 400, Roman Salad, Green Glaze, 4 Feet Extend To Rim, Holmes Smith, 6 In. .. 3290.00
Candlestick, Green Matte Glaze, Floral, Fritz W. Albert, 9 1/2 In. 600.00
Cigar Holder, Cover, No. 355, Green Matte Glaze, Horizontal Ribs, Button Top, 7 In. 940.00
Ewer, Green Matte Glaze, Organic Form, Impressed Mark, 9 In. 1100.00
Jardiniere, Green Matte Glaze, 4 Buttressed Handles, 28 x 20 In. 13800.00
Mug, No. 168, Green Matte Glaze, Horizontal Ribs, Angled Hande, W.D. Gates, 4 In. 700.00
Pitcher, Antique Verde Green, Crimped, Body Side Handle, 4 x 4 3/4 In. 300.00
Pitcher, Art Nouveau, Green Matte Glaze, Double Whiplash Handle, Stamped, 9 x 5 In. . 978.00
Pitcher, Dark Brown Crystalline Glaze, 4 In. 375.00
Pitcher, Dark Brown Glaze, Handles, 4 In. 575.00
Pitcher, Sheer Green & Brown Glaze, Embossed Stylized Leaves, 3 1/4 x 4 In. 400.00
Poster, Showing Pieces Of Teco, Frame, 1989, 23 1/2 x 16 In. 196.00
Vase, Antique Verde Green Glaze, 2 Body Handles, 9 x 5 In. 1430.00
Vase, Antique Verde Green Glaze, Bulbous, 2 3/4 x 2 1/2 In. 495.00
Vase, Blue Matte Glaze, William Gates, 9 1/2 In. 385.00
Vase, Brown To Gunmetal Crystalline Glaze, 4 1/2 In. 475.00
Vase, Bud, Brown Matte Glaze, Bulbous, Stamped, 3 3/4 x 3 1/4 In. 460.00
Vase, Cream Matte Glaze, Gunmetal, Green, Leaves, Flowers, 8 In. 605.00
Vase, Curdled Green Matte Glaze, Charcoaling, Gourd Shape, 15 1/2 x 7 1/2 In. 1840.00
Vase, Gray Matte Glaze, 4 Cutout Handles, William Gates, 8 In. 2990.00
Vase, Gray Matte Glaze, Cylindrical, 6 In. 690.00
Vase, Green Glaze, Gray Speckles, Stamped, 4 1/2 x 3 1/2 In. 550.00
Vase, Green Matte Glaze, 2 Buttressed Handles, William Gates, 7 1/2 In. 195.00
Vase, Green Matte Glaze, 3-Footed, Fritz Albert, 4 In. 500.00
Vase, Green Matte Glaze, 3-Footed, Impressed Mark, 4 In. 500.00
Vase, Green Matte Glaze, 4 Buttresses, Impressed Mark, 6 1/2 In. 1265.00
Vase, Green Matte Glaze, 4 Lobed Buttresses, Foot Ring, Squat, 5 3/4 x 9 3/4 In. 1150.00
Vase, Green Matte Glaze, 6 In. 635.00
Vase, Green Matte Glaze, 8 1/2 In. 2415.00
Vase, Green Matte Glaze, Beaker Form, 7 x 5 1/2 In. 1725.00
Vase, Green Matte Glaze, Buttressed Form, William Gates, 6 1/2 In. 865.00
Vase, Green Matte Glaze, Charcoaling, 2 Open Buttressed Handles, 5 1/2 x 8 In. 1955.00
Vase, Green Matte Glaze, Charcoaling, 4 Buttressed Handles, Double Gourd Form, 7 In. . 4600.00
Vase, Green Matte Glaze, Charcoaling, 4 Whiplash Handles, Corseted, 12 x 5 In. 980.00
Vase, Green Matte Glaze, Charcoaling, Bulbous, 6 x 5 1/2 In. 635.00
Vase, Green Matte Glaze, Charcoaling, Clay Body, Fritz W. Albert, 13 In. 1035.00
Vase, Green Matte Glaze, Charcoaling, Cylindrical, 4 Cutouts, Fritz W. Albert, 14 In. 12650.00
Vase, Green Matte Glaze, Charcoaling, Embossed Leaves & Daffodils, Oval, 9 x 4 1/2 In. . 976.00
Vase, Green Matte Glaze, Charcoaling, Flared Rim, William Gates, 11 1/2 In. 1100.00
Vase, Green Matte Glaze, Charcoaling, Tapered Form, Flared Rim, Marked, 11 In. 1100.00
Vase, Green Matte Glaze, Collar Rim, Bulbous, 7 x 7 In. 2070.00
Vase, Green Matte Glaze, Double Gourd Form, 4 Buttressed Handles, W.B. Mundie, 7 In. . 4315.00
Vase, Green Matte Glaze, Gourd Form, 7 In. 715.00
Vase, Green Matte Glaze, Handle, William Gates, Impressed Mark, 9 In. 1100.00
Vase, Green Matte Glaze, Handles, Fritz W. Albert, 9 1/2 In. 1320.00
Vase, Green Matte Glaze, Handles, N. Forrester, 8 1/2 In. 1265.00
Vase, Green Matte Glaze, Handles, Signed, 3 3/4 In. 630.00
Vase, Green Matte Glaze, Handles, William Gates, 4 In. 1130.00
Vase, Green Matte Glaze, Horizontal Ribs, 3 Handles, William Gates, 6 1/2 In. 2100.00
Vase, Green Matte Glaze, Molded Leaves, Water Lily Blossoms, William J. Dodd, 10 In. .. 5750.00
Vase, Green Matte Glaze, Narrow Neck, Spherical, Stamped, 4 1/2 x 4 1/2 In. 690.00
Vase, Green Matte Glaze, Raised Leaves & Berries, Signed, 2 1/4 In. 690.00
Vase, Green Matte Glaze, Signed, 5 x 5 3/4 In. 630.00
Vase, Green Matte Glaze, Spherical, 3 1/4 x 3 3/4 In. 450.00
Vase, Green Matte Glaze, William Gates, 5 1/4 In. 360.00
Vase, Green Matte Glaze, William Gates, 8 In. 6325.00
Vase, Green, Cut Back Design, 4 Pierced Handles, Harold Hals, 13 In. 69000.00
Vase, Light Blue Glaze, Dark Blue Spots, Tan, Blue, Green Glaze, Handles, 20 In. 99.00
Vase, Light Green, 2 5/8 x 7 In. 275.00

Vase, Light Mocha Matte Glaze, Lavender, Spherical Base, 5 3/4 x 4 1/2 In. 715.00
Vase, Lime Green Matte Glaze, Bulbous, Squat, Marked, 4 1/2 In. 1095.00
Vase, No. 60B, Green Matte Glaze, Overlapping Leaf Blades, Flared Mouth, 8 3/4 In. . . . 2115.00
Vase, No. 71, Green Matte Glaze, Flared Rim, Hugh M.G. Garden, 20 In. 5290.00
Vase, No. 89, Green Matte Glaze, 4 Long Sinewy Handles, William J. Dodd, 12 In. 2820.00
Vase, No. 120, Green Matte Glaze, Cylindrical, Tapered, Fritz W. Albert, 13 1/4 In. 1410.00
Vase, No. 198, Green Matte Glaze, Squat Base, Cylindrical Neck, 7 In. 1060.00
Vase, No. 260, Green Matte Glaze, 4 Buttressed Lobes, Flared Base, 13 1/2 In. 2820.00
Vase, No. 269, Green Matte Glaze, 4 Handles, Shoulder To Rim, W.B. Mundie, 11 In. . . . 1528.00
Vase, No. 297, Green Matte Glaze, Grecian Form, 2 Buttressed Lobes, 1910, 5 1/2 In. . . . 1410.00
Vase, Periwinkle Blue Glaze, White, Blue Glaze, Tiny Handle At Neck, 4 3/4 x 4 In. 470.00
Vase, Purple Blue Matte Glaze, Flattened Base, Long Flared Neck, Marked, 5 1/2 In. 635.00
Vase, Ribbed Body, Squat Base, Stamped, 5 x 3 3/4 In. 520.00
Wall Pocket, Molded Vertical Leaf, 14 In. 805.00

TEDDY BEARS were named for a president of the United States. The
first teddy bear was a cuddly toy said to be inspired by a hunting trip
made by Teddy Roosevelt in 1902. Morris and Rose Michtom started
selling their stuffed bears as *teddy bears* and the name stayed. The
Michtoms founded the Ideal Novelty and Toy Company. The German
version of the teddy bear was made about the same time by the Steiff
Company. There are many types of teddy bears and all are collected.
The old ones are being reproduced. Other bears are listed in the Toy
section.

Farnell's Alpha Toys, Mohair, Brown, Swivel Head, Amber Glass Eyes, 1935, 19 In. 550.00
Ideal, Mohair, Honey Beige, Articulated Limbs, Amber Eyes, 1920s, 30 In. 275.00
Mohair, Articulated, Embroidered Mouth, Glass Eyes, Black Pupils, 16 In. 65.00
Mohair, Brown, Ride-On, Embroidered, Button Eyes, Wood Wheels, c.1930, 13 In. 375.00
Mohair, Cinnamon, Open Felt Mouth, Swivel Head, Excelsior Stuffing, 22 In. 155.00
Mohair, Ginger, Embroidered, Jointed, Glass Eyes, c.1920, 30 In. 430.00
Mohair, Gold, Swivel Head, Excelsior Stuffing, Glass Eyes, Felt Pads, 15 In. 145.00
Mohair, Yellow, Movable Arms & Legs, Glass Eyes, 16 In. 345.00
Mohair, Yellow, Movable Limbs, 22 In. 260.00
Musical, Mohair, Pink, Curly, Embroidered, Cream Felt Pads, c.1920, 26 In. 690.00
Schuco, Mohair, White, Jointed, Embroidered, Glass Eyes, 3 3/4 In. 259.00
Schuco, Musical, Yes-No, Mohair, Shaved Muzzle, Crystal Eyes, 1950s, 20 In. 1700.00
Schuco, Yes-No, Shaved Muzzle, Jointed Long Arms, Movable Tail, c.1930, 21 In. 1400.00
Steiff, Beige, Jointed, 2 Tags, Booklet, 5 1/2 In. 55.00
Steiff, Christmas, Mohair, Santa Suit, Boots, Toys, Button Eyes, Felt Pads, 1970, 14 In. . . 100.00
Steiff, Growler, Ivory Knit Sweater, Western Germany, Tag, 12 In. 55.00
Steiff, Light Blond, Jointed, Leather Muzzle, Embroidered, c.1908, 13 In. 1955.00
Steiff, Light Brown, Brass Button In Ear, Yellow Cloth Tag, 10 1/2 In. 60.00
Steiff, Mohair, Black Steel Eyes, Excelsior Stuffing, Embroidered, c.1905, 4 In. 750.00
Steiff, Mohair, Blond, Embroidered Nose, Black Steel Eyes, c.1905, 8 In. 690.00
Steiff, Mohair, Blond, Embroidered, Brown Claws, Cream Pads, 1910, 9 1/2 In. 635.00
Steiff, Mohair, Blond, Long Snout, Black Shoebutton Eyes, 1915, 13 In. 300.00
Steiff, Mohair, Caramel, Swivel Head, Glass Eyes, 5-Piece Body, 11 In. 230.00
Steiff, Mohair, Cinnamon, Swivel Head, Elongated Arms, Button Eyes, 19 In. 2100.00
Steiff, Mohair, Gold, Embroidered, Jointed, Tan Pads, Ear Button, c.1905, 15 1/2 In. 1840.00
Steiff, Mohair, Gold, Jointed, Embroidered Features, Steel Eyes, 1905, 6 In. 2225.00
Steiff, Mohair, Gold, Jointed, Embroidered Nose, Mouth, Claws, 10 In. 430.00
Steiff, Mohair, Gray, Plush, Brass Button In Ear, White Tag, Articulated, 12 In. 130.00
Steiff, Mohair, Gray, West Germany, Box, 11 1/2 In. 70.00
Steiff, Mohair, Swivel Head, Pointy Nose, Blue Eyes, c.1925, 17 In. 650.00
Steiff, Mohair, Tan, Jointed, Ginger Felt Pads, Embroidered, c.1930, 12 In. 490.00
Steiff, Mohair, White, Plush, Jointed, Embroidered, Steel Eyes, 3 3/4 In. 230.00
Steiff, Mohair, Yellow, Curly, Embroidered, Jointed, Tan Felt Pads, Ear Button, 20 In. . . . 4025.00
Steiff, Mohair, Yellow, Embroidered, Glass Eyes, Jointed, Ear Button, c.1950, 12 In. 545.00
Steiff, Mohair, Yellow, Plush, Blue Collar, Silvertone Ear Button, 16 In. 1500.00
Winnie The Pooh, Squeaker, Plush, Gold, Swivel Head, Glass Eyes, Long Arms, 14 In. . . 645.00
Yes-No, Plush, Gold, Embroidered Muzzle, Glass Eyes, 5 1/2 In. 240.00

TELEPHONES are wanted by collectors if the phones are old enough or unusual enough. The first telephone may have been made in Havana, Cuba, in 1849, but it was not patented. The first publicly demonstrated phone was used in Frankfurt, Germany, in 1860. The phone made by Alexander Graham Bell was shown at the Centennial Exhibition in Philadelphia in 1876, but it was not until 1877 that the first private phones were installed. Collectors today want all types of old phones, phone parts, and advertising. Even recent figural phones are popular.

American Electric Co., Wall, Oak Case, Bracket Shelf, Nickel Plated Collar, 23 In.	330.00
Art Deco, Walnut Case, Crank, c.1930	88.00
Candlestick, Brass, Dated Dec. 21, 1920, 12 1/2 In.	300.00
De-Luxe, Norway, 1885	9832.00
Eiffel, Payphone, 1975	425.00
European Style, Cream, Gold Trim, Korea	48.00
Illinois Electric Co., Oak, Wall, 1901, 11 x 7 x 7 In.	112.00
Kellogg, Wall, Oak, A.K.S. & S. Co., No. 5812-MX, 32 In.	187.00
Kellogg, Wall, Working, 1925	250.00
Monophone, Cradle, Bakelite	110.00
North Electric Co., Wall, Oak Case, Bracket Shelf, Cleveland, O., 27 In.	303.00
Oak, Bakelite Earpiece, 8 x 3 x 2 In.	56.00
Old Western Electric, Candlestick, 12 x 7 x 7 In.	84.00
Propriete De Letat, Table Top, Mahogany Case, c.1935	66.00
Sign, Bell System, Public Telephone, Metal, 12 x 12 x 2 In.	11.00
Sign, Bell Telephone Of Canada, Porcelain, 1950s, Square, 10 1/2 In.	220.00
Sign, New Jersey Bell Telephone Co., Dark Brown, Porcelain, Flange, 19 In.	30.00
Sign, Western Union Telephone, Ask Operator For Your Telegram, Flange, 19 In.	240.00
Stromberg Carlson, Candlestick, Drilled For Lamp, Plastic Mouth, Earpiece	55.00
Stromberg Carlson, Wall, Oak Case, Rotary Dial, Battery Box, 32 1/2 In.	165.00
Toy, Truck, Bell, Cast Iron, Red, Hollow, USA, 10 In.	385.00
Toy, Truck, Bell, Cast Iron, Rubber Tires, Hubley, 4 In.	165.00 to 200.00
Toy, Truck, Maintenance, Accessories In Factory Paper, Buddy L, Box, 16 In.	770.00
Vought Magnetic, Wall, Refinished, 1890	375.00
Wall, Oak Case, Cast Iron Bracket, Bottom Hinged Shelf, 30 In.	138.00
Wall, Oak Case, Fold Down Shelf, 26 In.	165.00
Wall, Oak, Lower Slanted Shelf, Marked 354 At Mouthpiece	33.00
Western Electric, Bell Systems, Desk, Bakelite, 4-Prong Outlet, Attached Plug	125.00
Western Electric, Candlestick, Brass, 1913	140.00
Western Electric, Candlestick, No. 929, 12 x 7 x 5 1/4 In.	110.00
Western Electric, Cradle, Model B1	88.00
Western Electric, Crank, Wall, c.1914	80.00
Western Electric, Train Yard, Brass, c.1920	130.00
Western Electric, Wall, 1317-P, Oak Case, July 17, 1894, 20 1/2 In.	300.00
White Co., Sound Box, 18 x 11 x 5 In.	336.00

TEPLITZ refers to art pottery manufactured by a number of companies in the Teplitz-Turn area of Bohemia during the late nineteenth and early twentieth centuries. Two of these companies were the Alexandra Works and The Amphora Porcelain Works, run by Reissner, Stellmacher, and Kessel. Ernst Wahliss, connected with the RS & K wares, started his own factory after 1900.

Basket, Bedouin Woman, Stellmacher, Amphora, 1900-1917, 6 3/4 x 5 1/4 In.	395.00
Basket, Cuerda Seca, Butterfly, Flowers, Leaves, Pink Ground, Amphora, 4 1/2 x 5 In.	104.00
Candlestick, Kneeling Camel Figure, Amphora, 1920s, 6 x 3 1/2 In.	265.00
Ewer, Animal, Floral Body, Turtle Footed, Stellmacher, Amphora, 9 In.	695.00
Figurine, Monkey, Seated, Amphora, 10 In.	1035.00
Jug, Egyptian Figures, Medallions, Blue Matte Glaze, Amphora, Czechoslovakia, 14 In.	288.00
Lamp, Basket Urn, Blue Grapes, Green & Gold Vining, No Shade, Amphora, 36 In.	330.00
Vase, 2 Handles, Enameled Flowers, Brown Ground, Amphora, 5 3/4 x 3 In.	35.00
Vase, 3-Dimensional Bird Posed Against Tree, Iridescent Blue & Silver Glaze, 16 In.	1840.00
Vase, Blue & Green Glaze, Allover Ivy, Tendril Handles, Marked, Paul Dachel, 6 In.	1035.00
Vase, Blue, Yellow Enamel, 4 Spouts & Handles, Orb Top, Flared Base, Amphora, 14 In.	690.00
Vase, Cattle & Herdsman, Amphora, 1940s, 19 In.	1495.00
Vase, Egyptian Design, Amphora, 1920s, 19 1/2 In.	975.00

Vase, Elephant Head Handles, Gold Highlights, Matte & Gloss Glazes, Amphora, 20 In. . . . 2875.00
Vase, Embossed Red Poppies, Applied Stems, Amphora, Austria, 11 1/4 In. 690.00
Vase, Enameled, Chicken, Floral Bouquet, Tan Matte Glaze, White Overglaze, 8 In. 230.00
Vase, Enameled, Faux Jewels, Roses, Butterfly, Amphora, 7 1/2 In. 173.00
Vase, Enameled, Multicolored Flowers, Tan Glaze, Amphora, Czechoslovakia, 8 In. 127.00
Vase, Geometric Cutout Design, 2 Handles, Paul Dachal, 15 1/2 In. 2300.00
Vase, Ivory & Gold Glaze, Organic Shape, Molded Leaf & Stem Handle, Stamped, 6 In. . 431.00
Vase, Molded Cutout Design, Green, Gold Vertical Panels, Multi Gray Tones, 9 In. 311.00
Vase, Orange Poppies, 2 Handles, 16 x 8 1/2 In. 880.00
Vase, Raised Flowers, 3 Bats, Brown, Green Matte Glaze, 14 1/2 In. 690.00
Vase, Raised, Swirling Design, Green Ground, Amphora, 9 1/2 In. 875.00
Vase, Round Gilt Design, Jewels, Footed, Oval, Amphora, Impressed Mark, 10 In., Pair . . 1955.00
Vase, Trailing Opalescent Slip, Wavy, Straight & Webbed Pattern, Faux Jewels, 8 1/4 In. . 1150.00
Vase, Twisted Handles, Amphora, 1900, 5 1/4 In. 245.00

TERRA-COTTA is a special type of pottery. It ranges from pale orange to
dark reddish-brown in color. The color comes from the clay, which is
fired but not always glazed in the finished piece.

Bowl, Woman, Toreador, Polychrome Glazes, Matte White Exterior, Signed, 12 In. 460.00
Bust, Girl, Jeune Fille On Brass Plate, Au Raisin, Marble, Truex Lian, Paris, 19 In. 1100.00
Figure, Putto, Seated On Grassy Mound, Beside Urn, Louis XVI Style, 15 In. 575.00
Figurine, French Clown, Gilt, Base, Signed T.H. Cartier, Early 20th Century, 9 In. 230.00
Figurine, Man, Kneeling, Wearing Loin Cloth, Shackles, Darcy Paris, Merval, 22 In. 575.00
Figurine, Seated Nude, Hands On Head, 1930s, 14 1/4 x 13 1/2 In. 33.00
Figurine, Spaniel, Cast Composition, Italy, 20th Century, 13 In. 575.00
Figurine, Virgin Mary, Painted Bun Hair, Original Silk Gown, Sandles, 17 In. 250.00
Figurine, Wolfhound, White Crackle Glaze, 41 In. 402.00
Figurine, Woman, With Child, Herman Kahler, K. Nielson, 14 x 4 In. 175.00
Frieze, Architectural, Snarling Lion, Late 1800s, 18 In. 460.00
Medallion, Bas Relief, Classical, Castor & Pollux, Brown Glaze, Italy, 23 x 4 In. 504.00
Plaque, Victory In Chariot, 2 Horses, F. Almenraeder, 1832, 15 1/2 x 23 In. 247.00
Sculpture, Pheasants, F. Foucher, 25 In. 448.00
Tub, Tree, Citron Glaze, Applied Fleur-De-Lis, Round, c.1900, 32 x 30 In., Pair 3220.00

TEXTILES listed here include many types of printed fabrics and table
and household linens. Some other textiles will be found under Clothing, Coverlet, Quilt, Rug, etc.

Apron, Full, Embroidered Butterflies, 2 Pockets, 24 1/2 x 33 1/4 In. 4.00
Bedspread, Candlewick, Embroidered, Basket, Willows, Lucy Tilson, 1844, 95 x 100 In. . 110.00
Bedspread, Chenille, Alice In Wonderland, White, Twin Size, 72 x 84 In., Pair 100.00
Bedspread, Chenille, Joe Lewis & Boxing Glove Pictures 2500.00
Bedspread, Chenille, Pink, Yellow & Blue Flowers, White Ground, 86 x 108 In. 200.00
Bedspread, Cotton, Cowboys, American Indians, Branding Iron Symbols, 84 x 78 In. 316.00
Bedspread, Crocheted, Cherub & Flower Field, Cotton Backing, 82 x 72 In. 132.00
Bedspread, Crocheted, Ecru, 94 x 120 In. 66.00
Bedspread, Crocheted, Lime Green & Salmon, White, 96 x 84 In. 30.00
Bedspread, Crocheted, Pinwheel Pattern, Ice Blue Satin Back, Sham, 70 x 70 In. 66.00
Bedspread, Satin, Red, Green, Gold, Florals, Cherubs, Braids, Tassels, 56 x 180 In. 588.00
Bedspread, Wool, Blue & Brown Stripes, Cream Ground, 72 x 88 In. 173.00
Bell Pull, Needlepoint, Cornucopia & Flowers, Crystal Pendant, Brass Mount, 65 In. 308.00
Bell Pull, Needlepoint, Roses, Leaves, Gray Beads, Gilt Frame, 47 x 6 1/2 In. 28.00
Bell Pull, Petit Point, Flowers, Rose, Gold Ground, 46 x 58 In., Pair 173.00
Blanket, Buggy, Striped & Geometric, Metal Loops, 20th Century, 81 1/2 x 76 In. 316.00
Blanket, Mexican, Rio Grande, Diamonds, Striped Bands At Ends, Fringe, 83 x 50 In. . . . 385.00
Blanket, Tan Squares, Iacobacci Wool, 57 x 78 In. 224.00
Blanket, Wool, Blue Plaid, 2 Piece, Extra Piece For Between Bed Posts, 95 x 95 In. 302.00
Blanket, Wool, Blue, Pink Stripes, 107 x 83 In. 95.00
Blanket, Wool, Checks Alternating With Geometric Bands, 62 x 56 In. 230.00
Blanket, Wool, Crewelwork, Embroidery, Yellow, Red Floral, 69 x 76 In. 248.00
Blanket, Wool, Hudson's Bay, 4 Colors, Striped, 82 x 62 In. 57.00
Blanket, Wool, Pictorial, Reversible, Happy Hunting Ground, 1920s, 73 x 60 In. 747.00
Blanket, Wool, Stripes, White Triangles, Dots & Curlicues, 58 1/2 x 79 1/2 In. 316.00
Blanket, Wool, Woven, Geometric, Red & Blue, 57 x 93 In. 28.00

Textile, Handkerchief, Cotton,
Early Biplane With Spectators,
Frame, 11 1/4 In.

Textile, Pillow, Linen, Embroidered,
Stylized Flowers, White,
Yellow, 14 x 17 1/2 In.

Textile, Runner, Embroidered,
Coneflowers, Amber, Oatmeal
Ground, 53 x 19 1/2 In.

Blanket, Woven Diamonds, Multicolored, c.1925, 58 x 67 In.	230.00
Cloth, Cotton, Painted, Flowering Tree, Birds, Frame, Early Persian, 42 x 34 In.	336.00
Counterpane, Homespun, Tan, Pulled Loops, Trees, Fleur-De-Lis, Star, 84 x 100 In.	110.00
Curtain, Fortuni, Ivory Ground, Red Border, Bead Trim, 52 1/2 x 20 1/2 In., Pair	92.00
Curtain, Glass Beads, Ending In Faceted Ruby Beads, Wood Hanger, 33 x 49 1/2 In.	247.00
Dresser Scarf, Linen, Embroidered, Flowers, Red, Blue, Lavender, 40 x 20 In.	24.00
Feed Bag, Stenciled, Black, Eagle Over Date, No. 8, John Bamberger, c.1833, 52 x 19 In.	240.00
Flag, American, 13 Stars, 25 x 42 In.	300.00
Flag, American, 13 Stars, 58 x 105 In.	1265.00
Flag, American, 13 Stars, Brass Grommets, 1884, 36 x 62 In.	1155.00
Flag, American, 13 Stars, Hand Sewn Silk, 15 x 21 In.	316.00
Flag, American, 30 Stars, Frame	395.00
Flag, American, 38 Stars, Silk, For President, J.G. Blaine & J.A. Logan, 1884, 15 x 23 In.	5775.00
Flag, American, 45 Stars, c.1900	500.00
Flag, American, 46 Stars, 1910-1912	120.00
Flag, Ferrari, Red Cloth, Prancing Horse Logo, 48 x 72 In.	145.00
Flag, Jaguar, Red Logo, Red & White Lettering, 36 x 48 In.	220.00
Handkerchief, Commemorating Nansen's Expedition To North Pole, 1893-96, Map	150.00
Handkerchief, Cotton, Early Biplane With Spectators, Frame, 11 1/4 In. .... *Illus*	50.00
Handkerchief, Love Of Truth, Mark The Boy, Frame, 12 3/4 x 12 3/4 In.	385.00
Handkerchief, Running Gingerbread Black Boy	15.00
Mat, Table, Braided, Bands, Tan, Black, Green, Orange, 14 x 9 1/4 In.	165.00
Napkin, Linen, Off-White, Crocheted On Edges & 1 Corner, 13 1/2 x 13 1/2 In., 6 Piece	15.00
Napkin, Matching Place Mats, Linen & Lace, Star Flowers, 12 x 16 In., 8 Piece	55.00
Obi, Silk, Gold Threaded	70.00
Panel, Aubusson, Pair Of Putti Holding Garland, Center Urn, 31 x 97 In.	2760.00
Panel, Check & Rectangular, Alexander Girard, 25 1/2 x 54 1/2 In., Pair	520.00
Panel, Crocodile, Dragon, Seahorses, Deer, Birds, Kanatang District, 49 x 112 In.	860.00
Panel, Ikat, Dancers, Habab Motifs, Sumbawa, 19th Century, 44 1/2 x 104 In.	170.00
Panel, Ikat, Deer, Horses, Birds, Sumbawa, 19th Century, 62 x 92 In.	690.00
Panel, Printed Cotton, Quilted, George Washington, Shield, 19th Century, 22 x 16 In.	575.00
Panel, Silk, Dragons, Branches, Chinese, 42 x 6 In., Pair	230.00
Panel, Silk, Embroidered, Birds, Flowers, Fringe, Chinese, 20th Century, 106 x 69 1/2 In.	805.00
Panel, Silk, Needlework, Scenes Of Women & Men With Animals, Floral Frame, 31 In.	360.00
Panel, Silk, Red, Embroidered, Chinese Imperial Dragon, c.1880, 37 x 36 1/2 In.	1120.00
Panel, Wallpaper, Various Classical Motifs, Fanned Floral Border, 96 1/2 In.	7200.00
Pillow, Gros & Petit Point, Louis XIV Style, Elephant, Ram, Fringe, 23 In., Pair	978.00
Pillow, Leaf Design, Red, Brown, Green, Beige Ground, Ruffle, Arts & Crafts, 21 x 19 In.	115.00
Pillow, Linen, Embroidered, Stylized Flowers, White, Yellow, 14 x 17 1/2 In. ...... *Illus*	288.00
Pillow, Printed Silk, Brocade & Velvet, Kitten's Head, Fringe, 14 1/2 In.	105.00
Pillow, Sampler, God Bless America, Uncle Sam, Crocheted Edge, 1930, 13 x 17 In.	60.00
Pillow, Silk, Green, On Beige Linen, Ovals & Crescents, Arts & Crafts, 23 x 21 In.	115.00
Pillow, Sofa, Gros & Petit Point, Fringe, 17th Century Style, 22 In., Pair	460.00
Pillow, Stylized Flowers, Gold & Red, Beige Ground, Arts & Crafts, 20 x 20 In.	316.00
Pillow, Stylized Poppies, Orange & Green On Beige Linen, 16 x 23 In.	374.00
Pillow, U.S. Flag Forms Pocket On Bottom, Uncle Sam, Purple, 1918, 14 x 10 In.	11.00
Pillow, Velvet, Beadwork, White, Gray, Pink, Blue Floral Scene, 14 x 15 In.	200.00
Pillow Set, Tapestry, 2 Square, 1 Rectangle, Fringe, 20th Century, 21 x 24 In., 3 Piece	1265.00

Pillow Set, Tapestry, Aubusson, Landscape, Late 19th Century, 13 x 11 In., 4 Piece 1495.00
Pillowcase, Embroidered, Gold Threads, Alexandra Deodorovna Monogram, c.1900 ..... 4500.00
Runner, Embroidered, Coneflowers, Amber, Oatmeal Ground, 53 x 19 1/2 In. ...... *Illus* 115.00
Runner, Linen, Embroidered, Irises, Arts & Crafts, 47 x 19 In. 145.00
Runner, Silk, 9 Dragons, Sea Waves, Green Ground, Chinese, 15 1/2 x 69 In. 300.00
Runner, Table, Linen, Cutwork, White, 40 x 14 In. 12.00
Shawl, Piano, Ivory Silk, Multicolored Flowers, Fringe, Early 20th Century, 60 x 60 In. ... 288.00
Shawl, Piano, Silk, Black, Embroidered, Cream & Pastel Flowers, Fringe, 52 x 46 In. 430.00
Shawl, Piano, Silk, Black, Large & Small Peonies, Flowers, Knotted Fringe, 52 x 52 In. ... 1380.00
Shawl, Piano, Silk, Embroidered Flowers, Pink, Red, Fuchsia, Purple & Teal, 1935 ..... 275.00
Shawl, Piano, Silk, Embroidered, Flowering Vines, Butterflies, Fringe, 60 x 60 In. 748.00
Tablecloth, Art Deco, Embroidered, Multicolored Flowers, Fringe, Round, 35 In. 546.00
Tablecloth, Checkerboard Pattern, Alexander Girard For H. Miller, 1961, 54 x 56 In. 489.00
Tablecloth, Cotton, Round, Embroidered, Ribbons, Crocheted Edge, Arts & Crafts, 41 In. 92.00
Tablecloth, Crewelwork, American Eagle, Emblem, Crocheted Border, 1900, 37 x 29 In. . 690.00
Tablecloth, Cut Out & Embroidered Designs On Corners, Edges, Ecru, 34 x 33 1/2 In. ... 30.00
Tablecloth, Fanciful Animals, Bouquets, 12 Napkins, Milanese Lace, 124 x 65 In. 3163.00
Tablecloth, Lace, Inset Linen Panels, Embroidered, Drawn Work, Ecru, 68 x 102 In. 220.00
Tablecloth, Linen & Lace, Drawn Work Grid, Bands Of Milanese Lace, 144 x 62 In. 1395.00
Tablecloth, Linen, Embroidered Scottie Dogs With Cards, Card Table, 31 1/2 x 27 In. 20.00
Tablecloth, Linen, Embroidered, Crocheted Fringe, Arts & Crafts, 35 x 51 In., 2 Piece ... 145.00
Tablecloth, Linen, Hand Woven, The Popular Shop, McHugh Furniture Co., 72 In. Square 115.00
Tablecloth, Linen, Silver Cutwork, Needlework Center Square & Edges, 34 x 31 In...... 45.00
Tablecloth, Runner, Embroidered, Flowers, Red, Blue, Yellow, On Buff Linen, 53 x 19 In. 405.00
Tablecloth, Silk Pongee, Dragons, Japan, Early 1900s, 96 x 63 In. 168.00
Tapestry, 3 Girls, Young Man, Flower & Scroll Corners, 83 x 61 1/2 In. 412.00
Tapestry, Aubusson, Dog, Landscape, Gilt Wood Frame, 34 x 36 In. 940.00
Tapestry, Central Medallion, Roses, Tan, Urns Of Flowers, Rose Border, 26 x 68 In. 55.00
Tapestry, Continental, Birds, Landscape, Early 20th Century, 66 3/4 x 62 1/2 In. 400.00
Tapestry, Courting Couple, Landscape, Ribbon Guilloche, 18th Century, 70 x 58 In. 3737.00
Tapestry, Diana & Consorts Hunting Stag, Distant Town, Muslin Back, 90 x 77 In. 4025.00
Tapestry, Figural Abstracts, Blue, Brown, Rust, Beige, Joan Miro, 66 x 35 In. 920.00
Tapestry, Floral Center, Scrolled Leaf Border, Mauve, Pink, Black Ground, 35 x 60 In. .. 55.00
Tapestry, Floral Panels & Border, Black Ground, 45 x 74 In. 330.00
Tapestry, Fruit Garlands, Green, Burgundy Ground, Tan Serrated Borders, 30 x 102 In. .. 195.00
Tapestry, Jean Picart Le Doux, La Lyre Au Matin, Sun Centered By Tree, 42 1/2 x 69 In. . 865.00
Tapestry, Landscape, Floral Border, Flemish, 72 x 84 In. 3220.00
Tapestry, Needlepoint, Pink, Red & White Roses, Burgundy Ground, Green Border, 37 In. 305.00
Tapestry, Needlework, Crucifixion Of Jesus, Frame, 23 1/2 x 20 1/8 In. 225.00
Tapestry, Pale Blue, Pink & Green Rose Lattice, 30 x 72 In. 275.00
Tapestry, Panel, Cherubs, Flowers, Landscape, Double Border, 81 x 15 3/4 In. 1293.00
Tapestry, Pink Roses, Medallion, Dusty Pink Ground, Tan Border, 72 x 108 In. 195.00
Tapestry, Silk, Embroidered, World Map, Ink, 17 1/2 x 23 3/4 In. 840.00
Tapestry, Woodland Scene, Tree, 2 Birds, Floral Border, Hanging Rod, 84 x 60 In. 605.00
Towel, Show, Geometric Design, Blue, Dark Pink, Susanna Johnson, 1839, 14 x 40 In. ... 190.00
Towel, Show, Petit Point, 3 Flowering Trees Top, Signed M.H.L.H., 1864, 21 1/2 x 17 In. . 250.00
Towel, Show, Urns Of Flowers, Heart Shape, Betz Huhn, 1808, 19 x 62 In. 250.00
Towel, Show, Urns Of Flowers, Pink, Blue, Elisabeth Schli, 1810, 15 x 54 In. 440.00
Wall Hanging, Geometric, Black, White, Orange, Crimson, Morocco, 66 x 110 In. 80.00
Wall Hanging, Silk, Embroidered, 3 Happy Gods Scene, Pine Tree, White, 46 x 34 In. 275.00
Wall Hanging, Silk, Embroidered, 5 Foo Dogs, Streamers, Green Ground, 38 x 22 In. 75.00
Wall Hanging, Silk, Embroidered, 9 Pink Fish, Teal Ground, Chinese, 27 x 38 In. 150.00
Wall Hanging, Silk, Embroidered, 18 White Cranes, Black Ground, Chinese, 31 x 57 In. . 250.00
Wall Hanging, Silk, Embroidered, Dragon & Phoenix Design, Chinese, 17 1/2 x 37 In. 75.00
Wall Hanging, Silk, Embroidered, Dragon, Clouds, Gold Ground, Chinese, 15 x 20 In. .. 50.00
Wall Hanging, Silk, Embroidered, Jurojin, With Stag, Red Ground, Chinese, 32 x 21 In. .. 100.00
Wall Hanging, Silk, Embroidered, Turtles, Tree, Shore, Blue Ground, Chinese, 31 x 22 In. 75.00

THERMOMETER is a name that comes from the Greek word for heat.
The thermometer was invented in 1731 to measure the temperature of
either water or air. All kinds of thermometers are collected, but those
with advertising messages are the most popular.

Alka-Seltzer, Degrees In Celsius, Spanish Text, 12 In. 275.00

Allstate Battery, Dial, 16 In.	60.00
Atlas Perma-Guard, Metal, 24 x 8 In.	35.00
Atlas Wiper Blades, 8 x 14 1/4 In.	110.00
Auto Supply, Auto & Large Tire, 6 x 14 3/4 In.	110.00
B-1 Lemon-Lime, Tin, 16 3/8 x 4 5/8 In.	66.00
Biltrite Heels & Soles, Metal, Stamped, 6 x 14 In.	185.00
Briggs Dairy Milk, 1930s, 14 x 38 In.	635.00
Camel Cigarette, Red, Embossed Cigarette Pack, Long Cigarette, Tin, 6 x 13 In.	100.00
Candy, Engraved Scale, From 40 To 380 Degrees, Copper, 13 1/2 In.	40.00
Carter's Little Liver Pills, Porcelain, Blackbird Top	6750.00
Doan's Pills, Help Your Kidneys! For Backache & Bladder, White, 24 x 6 In.	195.00
Dr Pepper, Box, Tin, 7 1/4 x 26 3/4 In.	231.00
Dr Pepper, Good For Life, 17 1/4 x 5 1/4 In.	180.00
Dr Pepper, Hot Or Cold, Aluminum, 12 1/4 In.	110.00
Dr Pepper, Hot Or Cold, Tin, 26 5/8 In.	155.00
Dr Pepper, Tin Lithograph, 6 1/4 x 16 1/4 In.	260.00
Dupont, Cutlery By Remington, Porcelain, 8 x 38 In.	231.00
Engraved Brass Gauge, Bowed Glass Front, J. McAllister, 17 1/2 In.	1100.00
Ex-Lax, Chocolate Laxative, Porcelain, 36 1/4 In.	275.00
Ex-Lax, Keep Regular, Porcelain, 36 1/4 x 8 1/4 In.	155.00
Ex-Lax, Millions Prefer, Porcelain, 1940s, 8 x 36 In.	275.00
Fleet-Wing, Red Lettering, Yellow Ground, 6 3/8 x 2 In.	110.00
Fulmen Battery, Metal, 27 1/4 x 7 1/4 In.	35.00
Glass Vial In Arched Frame, Malachite Veneered Marble Base, Bronze, 11 In.	460.00
Gothick, Ivory Scale, Calibrated In Fahrenheit, Stepped Plinth, 1828, 9 In.	750.00
Henry & Sons, Frank Fuhr, Wood, 6 x 24 & 4 x 15 In., Pair	33.00
J.L. Taylor, Wood, Side Scale Measuring Person's Height, 22 x 7 In.	50.00
Mail Pouch, Tin Lithograph, 3 x 9 In.	165.00
Marathon, Ohio Oil Co., 16 In.	35.00
Marlboro Tobacco, 1950, 7 x 14 In.	11.00
Mission Orange, Naturally Good Emblem, Tin, 17 x 4 1/2 In.	550.00
Mobil, Socony Vacuum At Top, Frame, Metal, 35 3/4 x 8 x 3/4 In.	250.00
Mowrer's Milk, Celluloid, Care Instructions, 6 1/4 In.	70.00
Neuweiler's Ale & Beer, Glass Cover, Labels On Bottles, 1940s, 12 In.	165.00
NuGrape Soda, Bottle Shape, Tin Lithograph, Hole, 5 x 17 In.	150.00
NuGrape Soda, Tin, 16 x 6 3/4 In.	130.00
Ohio Coal Co., Painted Wood, 14 3/4 In.	100.00
Old Dutch Beer, Wood, 1930s, 15 x 4 In.	22.00
Prestone Anti-Freeze, Porcelain, Dial, 10 In.	190.00
RCA Victor Radio, Nipper Dog, Porcelain, 39 In.	440.00
Red Crown Gasoline, Porcelain, Frame, 19 1/2 x 73 In.	1495.00
Royal Crown Cola, Soda Bottle, 13 1/2 In.	110.00
Royal Crown Cola, Tin, Box, 13 1/2 In.	90.00
Royal Crown Cola, Yellow Thermometer, 25 3/4 x 9 3/4 In.	95.00
Snow Bird Cigars, Wood, Allen & Dunning Co., Patterson, N.J.	275.00
Standard Oil, White Ground, 11 1/2 x 3 In.	45.00
Sun Drop, Original Ohio Jumbo Dial, Metal, Plastic, 12 1/4 In.	45.00
Texaco, White Ground, Metal, 6 1/4 In.	100.00
United Motors, Wood, 15 x 4 In.	170.00
Van Voorhies Saddlery, Wood, 1920, 21 x 5 In.	450.00
Veedol, White Ground, 35 1/2 x 11 1/2 In.	200.00
Wall, Giltwood, Calibrated Scale, Louis XVI, Molded Frame, 31 x 9 In.	1840.00
Whistle, Sparkling Orange Refreshment, Dial, 12 In.	120.00
Whistle, Thirsty? Just..., Round, 12 In.	410.00
White Rose Gasoline, Hanging, Cardboard, 7 x 5 In.	85.00
Willard Batteries, Free Check Here, Dial, 16 In.	60.00
Winston Cigarette, Tin, Yellow, Circular, 8 3/4 In.	146.00

TIFFANY is a name that appears on items made by Louis Comfort Tiffany, the American glass designer who worked from about 1879 to 1933. His work included iridescent glass, Art Nouveau styles of design, and original contemporary styles. He was also noted for stained glass windows, unusual lamps, bronze work, pottery, and sil-

Louis C. Tiffany

ver. Other types of Tiffany are listed under Tiffany Glass, Tiffany Gold, Tiffany Pottery, or Tiffany Silver. The famous Tiffany lamps are listed in this section. Tiffany jewelry is listed in the jewelry and wristwatch categories. Some Tiffany Studio desk sets have matching clocks. They are listed here. Clocks made by Tiffany & Co. are listed in the Clock category. Reproductions of some types of Tiffany are being made.

Ashtray, Match Safe, Spanish, Bronze, Gold Dore, 8-Sided Tray, Signed, 4 1/2 x 4 In. . . .	750.00
Ashtray, Match Safe, Venetian, Sculptured Minks, Bronze, Gold Dore, 5 In.	450.00
Ashtray Set, Nested, Bronze, Gold Dore, Ruffled Edge, 2 3/4 To 4 1/2 In., 4 Piece	300.00
Bell, Desk, Bronze, Raised Flowers, Leaf Designs, Impressed, 1900s, 2 3/4 In.	748.00
Bill File, Bookmark, Bronze, Gold Dore, 8 Sides, 3 3/4 x 6 1/2 In.	650.00
Bill File, Graduate, Bronze, Gold Dore, 8 Sides, Curved Spindle, Signed	450.00
Bill File, Pine Needle, Green Slag Glass, Curved Spindle, Signed, 7 1/2 In.	750.00
Blotter, Abalone, Bronze, Gold Dore, Knob Handle, Signed	350.00
Blotter, Graduate, Bronze, Gold Dore, Signed, 6 x 3 In., Pair	135.00
Blotter, Louis XVI, Bronze, Gold Dore, Knob Handle, Signed, 5 1/2 x 2 3/4 In.	300.00
Blotter, Ninth Century, Blue & Green Jewels, Bronze, Gold Dore, 5 1/2 x 3 In.	450.00
Blotter Ends, Abalone, Bronze, Gold Dore, Signed, 12 x 2 1/4 In., Pair	350.00
Blotter Ends, Abalone, Bronze, Gold Dore, Signed, 4 Piece	450.00
Blotter Ends, Adam, Bronze, Signed, 12 1/4 x 2 1/4 In., Pair	200.00
Blotter Ends, Adam, Bronze, Signed, 19 x 1 1/4 In., Pair	200.00
Blotter Ends, Bookmark, Bronze, Gold Dore, Signed, 12 x 2 In., Pair	250.00
Blotter Ends, Graduate, Bronze, Gold Dore, Signed, 19 x 2 1/4 In., Pair	150.00
Blotter Ends, Spanish, Bronze, Gold Dore, Signed, 19 x 2 In., Pair	600.00
Blotter Ends, Zodiac, Bronze, Gold Dore, Signed, 12 x 2 In., Pair	250.00
Blotter Ends, Zodiac, Bronze, Gold Dore, Signed, 19 x 2 In., Pair	250.00
Book Rack, Grapevine, Green Slag Glass, Signed, 14 In., Extends To 23 In. . . . .2000.00 to	2500.00
Bookends, Adam, Scroll At Border, Ribbon & Sunburst Center, Signed, 43 In.	1200.00
Bookends, Figures Of Saints Under Arches, Peacocks, Signed, 6 1/8 x 4 1/2 In.	330.00
Bookends, Graduate, Bronze, Gold Dore, Signed, 5 x 5 3/4 In.	750.00
Bookends, Grapevine, Amber Slag Glass, Bronze, Gold Dore, 5 1/2 In., Pair	1500.00
Bookends, Ninth Century, Jewels & Enamel, 5 Center Roundels, Line Design, Signed . . .	1500.00
Bookends, Shield & Scroll, Bronze, c.1922, 7 In.	650.00
Bookends, Venetian, Bronze, Gold Dore, Signed, 5 x 6 In., Pair . . . . .1200.00 to	1500.00
Bookends, Zodiac, Bronze, Brown & Green Patina, Signed, 6 x 4 3/4 In.	489.00
Bowl, Star & Lattice Rim, Bronze, No. 1707, 9 In.	230.00
Box, Card, Hinged Cover, Pine Needle, Bronze, Green Slag Glass, 2 Sections, 3 x 4 In. . .	1500.00
Box, Cover, Enamel, Blue, Gold, Silver, Footed, Bronze, No. 257, 3 3/4 x 3 3/4 x 2 1/2 In.	860.00
Box, Cover, Enamel, Bronze, Footed, 6 x 3 1/2 In.	1512.00
Box, Cover, Grapevine, Green & Blue Slag Glass, Bronze, Brown Patina, 3 x 8 In.	2300.00
Box, Glove, Cover, Grapevine, Bronze, Beaded, Signed, 13 1/4 In.	2700.00
Box, Grapevine, Hinged Cover, Slag Glass, Bronze, Signed, 3 1/4 In.	1500.00
Box, Hinged Cover, 4 Ball Feet, Bronze, Enameled Border, Signed, 5 x 6 In.	1200.00
Box, Hinged Cover, Adam, Bronze, Gold Dore, Signed, 5 x 3 3/4 x 1 3/4 In.	750.00
Box, Hinged Cover, Adam, Front Ribbon, Wreath & Urn, Bronze, Signed, 3 3/4 x 5 In. . . .	750.00
Box, Hinged Cover, Bookmark, Bronze, Gold Dore, Cedar Lining, Signed, 6 x 5 3/4 In. . .	1200.00
Box, Hinged Cover, Bronze, Enameled Floral, Green & Yellow Ground, Signed	950.00
Box, Hinged Cover, Chest Style, Ball Feet, Bronze, Gold Dore, Signed, 3 3/4 x 3 In.	2500.00
Box, Hinged Cover, Enameled, Monogram, Ball Feet, Bronze, 3 3/4 x 3 3/4 x 2 1/2 In. . . .	862.00
Box, Hinged Cover, Graduate, Bronze, Gold Dore, Signed, 5 1/2 x 3 1/2 x 1 In.	450.00
Box, Hinged Cover, Spanish, Bronze, Gold Dore, Signed, 5 x 3 x 2 In.	900.00
Box, Hinged Cover, Zodiac, Bronze, Signed, No. 811, 3 x 6 1/4 In.	750.00
Box, Jewel, Hinged Cover, Abalone, Bronze, Tray, Sections, Signed, 6 1/2 x 4 In.	1500.00
Box, Jewel, Hinged Cover, Chinese, Velvet Lining, 10 x 5 x 2 1/2 In.	1000.00
Box, Jewel, Hinged Cover, Grapevine, Amber Slag Glass, Bronze, Signed, 6 x 4 x 3 In. . .	1500.00
Box, Letter, Zodiac, Bronze, Signed, 6 1/4 x 9 1/2 x 2 1/4 In.	495.00
Box, Pine Needle, Green Slag Glass, Bronze, 2 1/4 x 6 1/2 x 4 In.	978.00
Box, Stamp, Cover, Zodiac, Line Design, Tray, 3 Sections, 4 x 3 In.	550.00
Box, Stamp, Cover, Zodiac, Tray, 3 Sections, Signed, 3 3/4 x 2 1/4 In.	500.00
Box, Stamp, Grapevine, Amber Slag Glass, Bronze, Gold Dore, Tray, 3 Sections, 4 x 2 In.	550.00
Box, Stamp, Hinged Cover, Abalone, Bronze, Gold Dore, Tray, 3 Sections, Signed	550.00
Box, Stamp, Hinged Cover, Zodiac, 3 Sections, Signed, 3 3/4 In.	550.00

If your electric clock stops, turn it upside down for a day.
The oil inside may flow into the gears and the clock may
start working again.

Box, Stamp, Hinged Cover, Zodiac, Tray, 3 Sections, Signed, 3 3/4 x 2 1/4 In.	550.00
Box, Stamp, Venetian, Border Of Sculpted Minks, Signed, 2 x 4 In.	650.00
Box, Twine, Hinged Cover, Grapevine, Amber Slag Glass, Bronze, 6 Sides, 3 1/4 x 4 In.	1500.00
Candelabrum, 2-Light, Bronze, Green & Gold Iridescent Glass Jewels, Signed, 9 In.	2760.00
Candelabrum, 4-Light, Blown Glass Inserts, Jewels, Signed, 12 In.	2070.00
Candelabrum, 4-Light, Glass Inserts, Bronze, Signed, 11 In.	3220.00
Candle Lamp, Twisted Ribbed Body, Glass Cup, Ruffled Shade, Signed, 12 In., Pair	3500.00
Candlestick, 2-Light, Adjustable Root Base, Snuffer, 1920, 23 In.	8400.00
Candlestick, 3-Light, Branches, 3 Feet, Snuffer, Bronze, Signed, 9 In., Pair	4500.00
Candlestick, 4 Curved & Ribbed Supports, Bobeche, Bronze, Gold Dore, Signed, Pair	2500.00
Candlestick, Bronze, Apple Green Glass Insert, 3 Feet, Round Base, 7 1/2 x 9 In.	4500.00
Candlestick, Bronze, Favrile Glass, Tripod Base, 8 In., Pair	8040.00
Candlestick, Bronze, Green Glass Insert, Bobeche, Signed, 18 1/2 In.	2000.00
Candlestick, Bulbous Cup, Branch Support, Leaf-Shaped Base, Stamped, 7 1/2 In.	1840.00
Candlestick, Enameled, Alternating Abstract Flowers, Copper, 2 5/8 In., Pair	1410.00
Candlestick, Purple Enameled, Disc Base, Handle, Bronze, Gold Dore, 3 1/2 In., Pair	1500.00
Candlestick, Stick Body, Green Glass Blown Through Openings, Bronze, Signed, 20 In.	2000.00
Cane, Beryl Handle, Gold, Pale Green, Blue Color, Marked, 1910, 35 1/2 In.	2900.00
Cane, Silver Eagle, Horn Ferrule, Marked, 1900, 1 3/4 x 2 2/3 x 35 In.	7000.00
Chandelier, Turtleback Tile, Bronze, Brown Patina, Favrile, 1899-1920, 18 1/2 In.	16800.00
Cigar Lighter, Aladdin Lamp Shape, Snuffer On Chain On Top, Bronze, Signed	1500.00
Clock, Desk, Adam, Bronze, Gold Dore, 8 Sides, Signed, 4 x 4 1/4 x 2 In.	1800.00
Clock, Heraldic, Enameled, Bronze, Gold Dore, 1918, 8 In.	6600.00
Compote, Peacock Eyes & Trailings Around, Bronze, Gold Dore, Signed, 8 x 4 In.	550.00
Compote, Raised Florets Border, Red Jeweled, Bronze, Gold Dore, Signed, 10 x 2 1/2 In.	1200.00
Cordial Set, Iridescent Gold, Pinched, Decanter, Stopper, Cordials, 7 Piece	3162.00
Daily Memoranda, Venetian, Chain Link, Arms, Bronze, Gold Dore, Signed, 6 x 5 x 4 In.	1200.00
Daily Memoranda, Zodiac, 2 Curved Arms, Bronze, Signed, 6 x 4 x 2 In.	850.00
Desk Set, Abalone, Mother-Of-Pearl, Bronze, Gold Dore, c.1920, 9 Piece	5376.00
Desk Set, Art Nouveau, Bronze, 8 Piece	2310.00
Desk Set, Bookmark, Bronze, Gold Dore, Signed, 5 Piece	2070.00
Desk Set, Zodiac, Inkwell, Blotter Ends, Pen Tray, Blotter, Bronze, Signed	1250.00
Dish, Mint, Bronze, Gold Dore, Gold Favrile Glass Insert, Signed, 5 In.	550.00
Dish, Open Bronze Border, Center Well, Enameled, Signed, 8 In.	1500.00
Dresser Set, Ivory, 5 Piece	695.00
Figurine, Bronze, Bull, Pestered By Dog, Head Lowered, Marked, 5 x 8 3/8 In.	575.00
Flower Arranger, 5 Glass Tube Holders, Center Handle, Bronze, Gold Dore, 8 x 4 In.	2500.00
Frame, Adam, Bronze, Gold Dore, Signed, 9 x 12 In.	1800.00
Frame, Bronze, Brown Patina, Favrile, 1928, 10 5/8 x 7 In.	8400.00
Frame, Chinese, Bronze, Easel, Signed, 8 3/4 x 7 1/4 In.	950.00
Frame, Graduate, Bronze, Gold Dore, Easel, Signed, 6 1/2 x 5 3/4 In.	650.00
Frame, Grapevine, Bronze, Glass, Easel, 12 x 14 In.	3500.00
Frame, Grapevine, Green Slag Glass, Bronze, 6 1/2 x 7 In.	1725.00
Frame, Heraldic, Arms & Armor, Bronze, Gold Dore, Easel, Signed, 10 x 12 In.	1500.00
Frame, Ninth Century, Jeweled, Bronze, Gold Dore, 8 x 6 1/2 In.	2500.00
Frame, Pine Needle, Amber Slag Glass, Bronze, Gold Dore, Signed, 11 1/2 x 9 1/3 In.	2000.00
Frame, Pine Needle, Green Slag Glass, Bronze, Signed, 9 x 7 1/2 In.	2000.00
Frame, Pine Needle, Opalescent Glass, Silver Plate, Easel, 7 5/8 x 6 1/2 In.	525.00
Frame, Spanish, Bronze, Gold Dore, Signed, 5 x 5 1/2 In.	2200.00
Frame, Venetian, Bronze, Gold Dore, Signed, 9 x 12 In.	2000.00
Glue Pot, Grapevine, Cover, Attached Brush, Bronze, Signed, 3 In.	550.00

Humidor, Bronze Cover & Lined, Gold Favrile, Green Leaf & Vine Side, 9 1/2 In. 2500.00
Humidor, Cover, Grapevine, Green Slag Glass, Bronze, Gold Dore, 6 1/2 In. 815.00
Humidor, Grapevine, Amber Slag Glass, Bronze, Signed 3000.00
Humidor, Nautical, Shell & Barnacle, Bronze, Brown Patina, 1899-1918, 2 3/4 In. 6600.00
Inkwell, Abalone, Bronze, Curved Spindle, Signed, 3 1/2 x 3 1/2 In. 750.00
Inkwell, Bookmark, Bronze, Gold Dore, Glass Insert, Square, Signed, 3 x 2 1/2 In. 500.00
Inkwell, Cover, Green Glass, Blown Into Frame, Bronze, Signed 3500.00
Inkwell, Favrile, Bronze, Pine Needle Pattern, 7 In. 460.00
Inkwell, Grapevine, Green Slag Glass, Bronze, Signed, 3 1/4 In. 270.00
Inkwell, Hinged Cover, Abalone, Bronze, Gold Dore, Insert, Signed, 3 1/2 x 3 1/2 In. 750.00
Inkwell, Hinged Cover, Adam, Bronze, Gold Dore, Oval, Signed, 4 x 3 x 2 1/2 In. 550.00
Inkwell, Hinged Cover, Bookmark, Bronze, Gold Dore, 8 Sides, 4 1/2 x 2 1/2 In. 750.00
Inkwell, Hinged Cover, Bronze, Gold Dore, Blue Jewels, Square, 4 x 3 1/2 In. 750.00
Inkwell, Hinged Cover, Graduate, Bronze, Gold Dore, Insert, Square, Signed, 4 x 2 In. ... 450.00
Inkwell, Hinged Cover, Grapevine, Green Slag Glass, Bronze, Round, 7 In. 1800.00
Inkwell, Hinged Cover, Zodiac, Bronze, Gold Dore, 6 Sides, Glass Insert, 6 1/2 x 4 In. ... 750.00
Inkwell, Spanish, Bronze, Signed, 4 1/2 In. 2200.00
Inkwell, Venetian, Sculptured Minks, Bronze, Gold Dore, 8 Sides, Signed, 3 x 3 In. 650.00
Jar, Applied Silver Metal, Dragonfly, Ivory, Cover, 3 1/2 In. 2630.00
Jar, Favrile Glass, Enameled Cover, Signed 2240.00
Jar, Grapevine, Bronze, Signed, 2 1/4 x 2 1/4 In. 225.00
Lamp, 3-Light, Green Opalescent Glass, Leaded, Bronze Base, 21 1/2 In. 14375.00
Lamp, 3-Light, Lily, Bronze, Brown Patina, Signed, Favrile, 5 In. 6720.00
Lamp, 3-Light, Lily, Bronze, Gold Dore, Hook Support, Signed, 16 In. 3920.00
Lamp, 3-Light, White, Opalescent, Shades, Flared, Bronze, Fluted Base, 17 x 11 In. 3220.00
Lamp, 3-Part Gold Amber Glass Screen Shade, Bronze, Urn Shape, Signed, 16 1/2 In. ... 3000.00
Lamp, 10-Light, Lily, Lily Pad Base, Bronze, Gold, Signed, 21 In. 6460.00
Lamp, 10-Light, Lily, Upswept Stems, Assorted Shades, Signed, c.1920, 21 In. 7250.00
Lamp, Abalone Discs Set In Circle, Bronze, 8-Sided Base, Desk, 9 In. 4000.00
Lamp, Acorn, Amber, White Leaves On Meandering Vine, Bronze, Favrile, 57 3/4 In. 9775.00
Lamp, Acorn, Domed Shade, Mottled Orange, Bronze Base, 29 In. .... *Illus* 19950.00
Lamp, Apple Blossom, Pink, White, Signed Base, 10 In. 39200.00
Lamp, Arabesque, Bronze, Gold Dore Shade, Favrile, 1899-1920, 14 3/4 In. 5700.00
Lamp, Arabian, Conical Shade, Carmel, Gold Iridescent Zipper Pattern, Favrile, 15 In. ... 5000.00
Lamp, Arabian, Zipper Shade, Glass Base, Favrile, 15 In. 5000.00
Lamp, Band Of Water Lilies Shade, Green Geometric, Bronze, 27 In. 4935.00
Lamp, Bronze, Adjustable, Dark Brown Patina, Favrile, 1899-1918, 18 In. 3600.00
Lamp, Brown Glass, Bronze, Signed, Favrile, Desk, 15 In. 3450.00
Lamp, Carved Green Leaves, Vines, Gold Iridescent, Favrile, 15 1/2 In. 8625.00
Lamp, Daffodil, Orange Yellow Segments, Leaded Glass, Bronze, 1922, 22 In. 27600.00
Lamp, Damascene, Brown Glass, Bronze Base, 14 1/2 In. 6325.00
Lamp, Damascene, Cobalt Blue Glass, Bronze, Favrile, 14 1/2 In. 8050.00
Lamp, Damascene, Ribbed Shade, Bronze, Gold Dore, Lotus Buds Stem, Signed, 55 In. ... 9625.00
Lamp, Dogwood, Signed Shade & Base, 16 In. 35840.00
Lamp, Domed Shade, Geometric, Mottled Green, Opalescent, Bronze Base, 22 In. 11500.00
Lamp, Fabrique Glass, Bronze Base, Harp Support, Signed, 19 1/2 In. 6000.00
Lamp, Fabrique Glass, Green, Favrile, Bronze, Harp, 19 1/2 In. 6000.00
Lamp, Fleur-De-Lis, Leaded, Bronze, Gold Dore, c.1910, 21 1/8 In. 14100.00
Lamp, Geometric, Green To White Panels, Double Circle Column Base, 21 In. ...... *Illus* 10350.00
Lamp, Gold & Pink Iridescent, Signed, Desk, 17 1/2 In. 1495.00
Lamp, Gold Iridescent Shade, Adjustable, Bronze, Signed, Desk, 19 In. 4000.00
Lamp, Grapevine, Bell Shape, Slag Glass, Stick Body, Signed, 13 1/2 In. 4000.00
Lamp, Grapevine, Green Slag Glass, Bronze, Harp Support, Desk, 13 1/2 In. 4000.00
Lamp, Greek Key, Domed Shade, Urn Base, Quatrefoil Foot, Bronze, 11 1/2 x 7 In. 865.00
Lamp, Greek Key, Leaded, Green & Yellow, Bronze, c.1910, 28 1/4 In. 18800.00
Lamp, Green Iridescent Shade, 4-Footed Base, Favrile, Signed, 7 x 19 In. 5600.00
Lamp, Green Pulled-Feather Shade, Harp Support, Round Base, Signed, 14 1/2 In. 5290.00
Lamp, Green, Ribbed, Gold Pulled Zipper, Glass Base, Favrile, 13 1/2 In. 4315.00
Lamp, Hanging, 5 Green Turtlebacks, Bronze Body, 23 x 7 1/2 In. 9200.00
Lamp, Hanging, Light Amber, Violet Glass, Green & Brown Patina, Favrile, 41 In. 6325.00
Lamp, Jonquil, Green Leaves, Violet Ground, Bronze Base, Signed, 18 In. 30800.00
Lamp, Leaf & Vine Leaded Shade, Green Glass, Blown Into Etched Bronze Base, 20 In. . 18400.00

Tiffany, Lamp, Acorn, Domed
Shade, Mottled Orange,
Bronze Base, 29 In.

Tiffany, Lamp, Geometric, Green To
White Panels, Double Circle
Column Base, 21 In.

Tiffany, Lamp, Pomegranate,
Leaded, Bronze Base,
Adjustable, 20 In.

Lamp, Linenfold, Bronze, Gold Dore, Signed, 16 In. 16800.00
Lamp, Linenfold, Opalescent, Acid Etched, Signed, 14 In. 7280.00
Lamp, Mosque, Bronze, Gold Dore Finial, 8-Sided Shade, Wooden Base, 8 1/2 In. 2800.00
Lamp, Pine Needle, Conical Shade, Green Slag Glass, Bronze, 18 In. 4000.00
Lamp, Pine Needle, Green Slag Glass, Harp Support, Signed, Desk, 18 In. 4000.00
Lamp, Pomegranate, Leaded, Bronze Base, Adjustable, 20 In. . . . . *Illus* 18400.00
Lamp, Shell-Form Shade, Green, White, Raised Leaf Design, 1892, 12 In. 8625.00
Lamp, Student, 2 Arms, Iridescent Shade, Favrile, Signed, 8 In. 5600.00
Lamp, Student, Damascene, Bronze Base, Favrile, 2 Arms, Signed, 16 In. 4600.00
Lamp, Tulip, Leaded, Amber, White, Blue, Green, 1906, 21 x 16 In. 21850.00
Lamp, Tulips, Green Slag Glass, Bronze, Flared, Fluted Base, 28 x 20 In. 4900.00
Lamp, Turtleback, Blue, Purple, Cabochons, Signed, 8 x 15 In. 8400.00
Lamp, Turtleback, Domed Shade, Rippled Glass, 16 In. 19600.00
Lamp, Venetian, Bronze, Desk, 14 In. 1495.00
Lamp, Vine Border, Leaded, Yellow Glass, Bronze, c.1910, 57 In. 12925.00
Lamp, Weight-Balance, Bronze, Green & Brown Patina, Favrile, 1918, 15 In. 7800.00
Lamp, Zodiac, Turtleback Tile, Bronze, Favrile, 14 1/4 In. 7800.00
Lamp Base, Abstract Scrolling Teardrops, 24 7/8 In. 6465.00
Lamp Base, Abstract Scrolls, Reticulated, 19 1/4 In. 6465.00
Lamp Base, Baluster Shape, Intaglio, Bronze, Gold Dore, 20 In. 2185.00
Lamp Base, Geometric Design, Cylindrical Standard, 27 In. 4700.00
Lamp Base, Pine Needle, Bronze, Brown Patina, 1899-1920, 21 In. 4500.00
Lamp Base, Turtleback Tile, Adjustable, Bronze, Green, Brown Patina, Favrile, 13 In. . . . 4800.00
Lamp Shade, Peacock Feathers, Leaded, Bronze Panel, 1905, 16 In. 7640.00
Lamp Shade, Pulled Vertical Lines, Favrile, 12 In. 6440.00
Letter Holder, Bookmark, Bronze, Gold Dore, Signed, 6 x 4 1/2 x 2 3/4 In. 750.00
Letter Holder, Graduate, Bronze, Gold Dore, 2 Sections, Signed, 6 1/4 x 5 x 2 1/2 In. . . . 500.00
Letter Holder, Grapevine, Verdigris Patina, Signed, 6 1/4 x 10 In. 690.00
Letter Holder, Venetian, Bronze, Gold Dore, Enameled, Ball Feet, Signed, 6 x 3 x 3 In. . . 900.00
Letter Opener, Adam, Bronze, Gold Dore, Curved Handle, Signed, 9 In. 350.00
Letter Opener, Chinese, Bronze, Gold Dore, Signed, 11 In. 250.00
Letter Opener, Grapevine, Amber Slag Glass, Bronze, Gold Dore, Signed, 9 1/4 In. 550.00
Letter Opener, Pine Needle, Bronze, Gold Dore, Signed, 7 In. 550.00
Letter Opener, Zodiac, Bronze, Gold Dore, Signed, 10 1/2 In. 250.00
Letter Rack, Adam, Bronze, Gold Dore, 2 Sections, 9 1/4 x 2 1/4 x 6 In. 700.00
Letter Rack, Grapevine, Green Slag Glass, Bronze, 3 Sections, 12 x 8 x 3 1/2 In. 1700.00
Letter Rack, Ninth Century, Bronze, Gold Dore, Jeweled, 10 x 6 x 2 1/2 In. 1200.00
Letter Rack, Pine Needle, Green Slag Glass, Bronze, 3 Sections, 12 x 8 x 3 1/2 In. 1800.00
Letter Rack, Spanish, Bronze, Gold Dore, 2 Sections, Signed, 10 x 8 x 3 In. 1500.00
Letter Rack, Zodiac, Bronze, Gold Dore, 2 Sections, Signed, 9 1/2 In. 750.00
Magnifying Glass, Abalone, Bronze, Shell Discs, Signed, 8 7/8 In. 315.00

Magnifying Glass, Adam, Beaded Edge, Signed, 8 1/4 In. 1500.00
Magnifying Glass, Bookmark, Bronze, Gold Dore, Signed, 8 3/4 In. 1500.00
Magnifying Glass, Graduate, Bronze, Gold Dore, Signed, 8 3/4 In. 1500.00
Magnifying Glass, Rosette Pattern, Bronze, Gold Dore, Signed, 9 In. 750.00
Magnifying Glass, Venetian, Bronze, Gold Dore, Signed, 9 In. 1500.00
Magnifying Glass, Zodiac, Signed, 8 3/4 In. 1500.00
Mirror, Hand, Grapevine, Amber Slag Glass, Bronze, Gold Dore, Signed, 7 1/2 In. 1800.00
Note Pad Holder, Bookmark, Bronze, Gold Dore, Wood Backing, Signed, 4 x 8 1/2 In. .. 550.00
Note Pad Holder, Hinged Cover, Abalone, Bronze, Gold Dore, Signed, 4 3/4 x 7 1/2 In. . 550.00
Note Pad Holder, Ninth Century, Bronze, Gold Dore, Green & Blue Jewels, Signed 650.00
Note Pad Holder, Spanish, Bronze, Gold Dore, Signed, 4 1/2 x 7 1/2 In. 650.00
Nut Dish, Iridescent Gold, Signed, 1 1/8 x 2 3/4 In. 300.00
Paper & Pen Tray, Gilded Sterling, Art Deco, Signed, 1 x 9 x 7 In. 635.00
Paper Clip, Grapevine, Amber Slag Glass, Bronze, Signed, 2 x 3 3/4 In. 450.00
Paper Clip, Pine Needle, Green Slag Glass, Bronze, Signed, 2 1/2 x 3 In. 450.00
Paper Clip, Venetian, Bronze, 3 3/8 In. 315.00
Paper Clip, Zodiac, Bronze, Gold Dore, Signed, 2 1/2 x 3/4 In. 450.00
Paper Rack, Chinese, Bronze, Intaglio Finish, 1920, 8 x 12 x 3 3/8 In. 3600.00
Paperweight, Art Nouveau, Green Glass, Silver Line Design, Bronze, Favrile, 3 x 1/2 In. .. 3500.00
Paperweight, Bulldog, Bronze, Signed, 1 1/4 x 2 In. 550.00
Paperweight, Commemorative, Signed, Dinner March, 1905, 3 1/2 In. 550.00
Paperweight, Dog's Head, Bronze, Verdigris Patina, Signed, 2 1/2 x 3 1/4 In. 690.00
Paperweight, Grapevine, Amber Slag Glass, Bronze, Gold Dore, Handle, 3 1/2 In. 450.00
Paperweight, Lion, Bronze, Signed, 3 1/2 In. 635.00
Paperweight, Owl, Bronze, 3 In. 805.00
Paperweight, Pine Needle, Green Slag Glass, Bronze, Knob Top, Signed, 3 1/2 In. 450.00
Pen Brush, Ninth Century, Bronze, Gold Dore, Blue & Green Jewels, Square, 2 3/4 In. .. 550.00
Pen Tray, Abalone, 3 Sections, Ball Feet, Signed, 8 1/2 x 2 1/2 In. 300.00
Pen Tray, Adam, Bronze, 3 Sections, Signed, 9 1/4 x 2 3/4 In. 250.00
Pen Tray, Graduate, Bronze, Gold Dore, 3 Sections, 4 Ball Feet, Signed 125.00
Pen Tray, Grapevine, Green Slag Glass, Bronze, Ball Feet, Signed, No. 845, 3 x 2 In. 330.00
Pen Tray, Louis XVI, Bronze, Gold Dore, Ribbed Handle, Signed, 8 3/4 x 3 1/2 In. 300.00
Pen Tray, Ninth Century, Bronze, Gold Dore, Jewels, Signed, 3 1/4 x 9 3/4 In. 450.00
Pen Tray, Spanish, Gold Dore, Signed, 9 3/4 In. 500.00
Pen Tray, Zodiac, Bronze, Gold Dore, Signed, 3 x 9 3/4 In. 250.00
Pitcher, Green Pulled Leaf & Vine, Applied Handle, N.Y., 5 1/4 In. 1840.00
Planter, Geometric, Bronze, Gold Dore, Liner, 8 1/2 x 2 1/2 In. 650.00
Planter, Grapevine, Amber Slag Glass, Bronze, Gold Dore, Signed, 10 1/2 In. 2500.00
Plaque, Dragonfly, Blue Green, Leaded, Bronze Filigree Wings, 10 x 6 1/2 In. 3500.00
Plate, Enameled Gold, Copper, Bronze, 8 1/4 In. 400.00
Plate, Iridescent Pink & White, Pedestal Foot, Signed, No. 1681, 6 1/2 In. 230.00
Plate, Ivory Iridescent Center, Blue Pulled Peacock Feather Rim, Signed, 7 In. 550.00
Salt, Master, Blue, Favrile, Signed LCT No. 20, 1 1/8 x 2 3/4 In. 200.00
Scale, Postage, Bookmark, Blue Enamel, Bronze, Gold Dore, Signed 1500.00
Scale, Postage, Grapevine, Green Slag Glass, Bronze, Signed, 3 x 3 In. 1500.00
Scale, Postage, Inlaid Abalone Leaves & Flowers, Bronze, Signed 1500.00
Scale, Postage, Pine Needle, Amber Slag Glass, Signed, 3 1/2 In. 1200.00
Scale, Postage, Pine Needle, Green Slag Glass, Bronze, Signed, 1 1/2 x 3 x 3 In. 1500.00
Scale, Postage, Zodiac, Signed, 1 1/2 x 3 x 3 1/4 In. 1200.00
Scissors, Linear Design, Bronze, Gold Dore, Signed, 9 In. 750.00
Scissors & Letter Opener, Chinese, Box, Signed, 10 3/4 In. 2300.00
Sconce, 3 Turtleback Tiles, Copper, Natural Patina, 4 x 9 1/2 x 4 In., Pair 800.00
Sconce, Amber Turtleback, Yellow Slag Glass, Bronze, Gold Dore Arm, 9 1/2 In., Pair ... 9200.00
Smoking Stand, Bronze, Gold Dore, Green Enameled, Stick Body, Signed, 25 In. 1800.00
Sword, Engraved Blade, Scabbard, Stamped Tiffany 1863 .... 500.00
Thermometer, Byzantine, Bronze, Beaded Center, Easel, Signed 2000.00
Thermometer, Grapevine, Bronze, Green Slag Glass, Easel Style, 8 1/4 x 3 3/4 In. 1800.00
Tray, Abalone Disks On Border, Bronze, Gold Dore, Signed, 14 In. 750.00
Tray, Bronze, Round, Signed, 13 3/4 In. ....120.00 to 230.00
Tray, Enameled Flower & Leaf, Bronze, Gold Dore, 2 Handles, Round, Signed, 8 1/4 In. .. 550.00
Tray, Raised Edge, Bronze, Gold Dore, 9 In. 175.00
Tray, Venetian, 2 Sections, Sculptured Minks, Signed, 10 In. 350.00

Vase, Bud, Pineapples, Round Base, Bronze, Signed 259.00
Vase, Patinated Bronze, Favrile, c.1928, 14 1/2 In. 2645.00
Vase, Pulled Green Feathers, Gold Iridescent, Signed, 12 In. 1093.00
Vase, Shell Handles, Curled To Top, Pedestal Base, Signed, 6 1/2 In. ....1800.00 to 2500.00
Vase, Trumpet, Bronze, Gold Dore, Iridescent, Signed, 12 1/2 In. 1840.00
Vase, Trumpet, Pulled Feather Glass, Artichoke Support, Bronze, Favrile, 9 In. ... 1500.00
TIFFANY GLASS, Bonbon, Green, Flared, Gold Flat Base, Signed, Favrile, 5 1/4 x 2 3/4 In. ... 650.00
  Bowl, Alternating Opalescent Bands, Intaglio Butterfly, Signed, 10 In. 900.00
  Bowl, Amber Iridescent, Interior Cut Ivy, Scalloped, Favrile, 10 In. 1035.00
  Bowl, Aqua Pastel, Optic Ribs, Favrile, 2 1/4 x 9 3/4 In. 1035.00
  Bowl, Blue Rim, Opalescent Optic Laurel Leaves, Signed, 2 x 6 1/4 In. 950.00
  Bowl, Butterfly, Blue Iridescent, 10 Vertical Ribs, Signed, 9 3/4 x 3 3/4 In. 690.00
  Bowl, Electric Blue Rim, Opalescent Light Blue Optic Pattern, 6 1/4 In. 950.00
  Bowl, Etched Scroll Band, Flower Frog, Low, Signed, 9 In. 170.00
  Bowl, Flared, Gold, Ruffled Edge, Etched, Favrile, 2 1/2x 6 In. 345.00
  Bowl, Flower, 6 Green Lily Pads, Center Flower Holder, Signed, 11 1/2 In. 3500.00
  Bowl, Flowers, Gold Iridescent, Pulled Heart & Vine, 10 1/2 In. 920.00
  Bowl, Gold Iridescent, Diagonally Ribbed, Crimped Top, Signed, 6 1/2 In. 500.00
  Bowl, Gold Iridescent, Favrile, 9 x 1 1/2 In. 480.00
  Bowl, Gold Iridescent, Favrile, c.1900, 3 1/2 x 8 1/4 In. 748.00
  Bowl, Gold Iridescent, Onion Skin, Repeating Leaves, Favrile, 1925, 2 1/4 In. 690.00
  Bowl, Gold Iridescent, Ribbed Body, Ruffled Edge, Favrile, 3 x 7 1/2 In. 490.00
  Bowl, Gold Iridescent, Ribbed, Wavy Rim, Favrile, Signed, 3 x 7 In. 805.00
  Bowl, Gold Iridescent, Rolled Rim, Pedestal, Underplate, Signed, Favrile, 5 1/4 In. 750.00
  Bowl, Gold Iridescent, Ruffled, Underplate, Violet Tones, Signed, Favrile, 6 In., Pair 750.00
  Bowl, Gold Iridescent, Scalloped, Ribbed, Signed, 3 x 4 In. 630.00
  Bowl, Gold, 8-Ribbed Body, Ruffled Edge, Favrile, 2 3/8 x 4 1/2 x 6 1/4 In. 920.00
  Bowl, Gold, Blue Green, Violet Iridescent, Favrile, 3 x 13 1/2 In. 2415.00
  Bowl, Gold, Handkerchief Rim, Favrile, 7 1/2 In. 1540.00
  Bowl, Honeycomb Optic, Blue, Footed, Signed, Paper Label, 8 1/4 x 2 1/8 In. 520.00
  Bowl, Incised Branches, Leaves, Gold, Pink Iridescent, Signed, Favrile, 10 In. 920.00
Candlestick, Blue Ribbed Body, Flared Foot, Signed, Favrile, 12 In. 1840.00
Candlestick, Gold Iridescent, Ribbed Sticks, Favrile, 10 3/4 In., Pair 1880.00
Candlestick, Twisted Ribbed Body, Silver & Blue Tones, 5 1/4 In., Pair 1200.00
Charger, Pulled Feathers, Burgundy, Gray, Gold Opalescent, Favrile, 18 In. 4700.00
Compote, Blue, Favrile, 3 1/8 x 11 3/4 In. 805.00
Compote, Blue, Intaglio, 8 In. 1100.00
Compote, Blue, Light Green Iridescent, Ruffled Rim, Favrile, 4 In. 460.00
Compote, Chinese Gold, Red Highlights, Ruffled Edge, Pedestal, Signed, Favrile, 6 In. ... 900.00
Compote, Diamond Optic, Pink Foot, Stretch Edge, Signed, 8 In. 1500.00
Compote, Double Ribbed Body, Scalloped, Short Pedestal, Signed, 3 3/4 In. 750.00
Compote, Flower Form, Scalloped, Ribbed, Signed, 6 In. 1065.00
Compote, Pigtail Punts On Foot & Bowl, Signed, 3 1/2 In. 728.00
Cordial, Favrile, Flared Rim, Stem, Pink Accents, Marked, 4 3/4 In. 360.00
Cordial, Gold Iridescent, 4 Pinched Sides, Signed, 2 In. 245.00
Dish, Blue Favrile, Ruffled Rim, Round, Inscribed, 1 1/2 x 5 In. 485.00
Dish, Blue Iridescent, Blue Violet Disk Base, Favrile, 1 3/4 x 4 In. 290.00
Dish, Medallion, World War I Victory, Gold, Amber, Favrile, 1918, 4 3/4 In. 460.00
Finger Bowl, Gold Iridescent, Ruffled Edge, Signed, 6 1/4 x 4 1/2 In. 750.00
Finger Bowl, Underplate, Gold Favrile, Ruffled Edge 725.00
Finger Bowl, Underplate, Gold Iridescent, Ruffled Edge, 6 x 4 1/2 In. 720.00
Flask, Perfume, Favrile, Bulbous, Etched, 7 1/2 x 3 In. 920.00
Goblet, Cordial, Favrile, Pastel, 1918-1928, 6 3/8 In., 6 Piece 8400.00
Goblet, Twist Stem, Signed, 7 1/4 In. 450.00
Goblet, Water, Favrile, Pastel, 1918-1928, 8 1/2 In., 6 Piece 7200.00
Goblet, Wine, Favrile, Pastel, 1918-1928, 7 7/8 In., 6 Piece 7800.00
Nut Dish, Flaring Rim, Gold Ribbed Body, Signed, 3 In. 225.00
Panel, Amber Iridescent, Craqueleur Surface, Ebonized, Giltwood Frame, 10 1/2 In. 690.00
Paperweight, Swirl Curves Around Center, Silver Line, 8 1/2 In. 3500.00
Pitcher, Purple & White, Signed, Paper Label, 4 In. 850.00
Plate, Paperweight, Swirls, Clear, Favrile, 1899-1920, 6 In. 2400.00
Plate, Pulled Leaves, Shaded Blue, Signed, Favrile, 10 1/2 In. 490.00
Punch Cup, Gold Iridescent, Applied Pods & Vines, Handle, 3 1/4 In. 750.00

Salt, Elephant, Diagonal Curled Ribs, Gold Iridescent, Signed, 1 1/2 In. 1200.00
Salt, Gold Iridescent, 4 Feet, Signed, 2 1/4 In. 201.00
Salt, Gold Iridescent, Swollen Forms, Zigzag Border, Favrile, Signed, 2 3/8 In. 920.00
Salt, Pods & Trailing Vines, 1 1/4 x 2 1/4 In. 550.00
Salt, Ribbed, Stand-Up Collar, Signed, 1 1/2 x 2 1/4 In. 350.00
Salt, Twisted Prunts All Around, Signed, 1 1/4 x 2 In. 350.00
Scarab, Red Iridescent, Favrile, 5/8 x 3/8 In. 150.00
Shade, Amber Iridescent, Cylindrical, Signed, Favrile, 8 1/4 In. 390.00
Sherbet, Gold Iridescent, Signed, 3 1/2 x 4 3/4 In. 230.00
Tile, Gold Iridescent, Blue Highlights, Diamond Shape, 3 1/4 In. 120.00
Tile, Red & Yellow Swirl Finish, Raised Curves, Square, 4 In. 250.00
Tile, Red & Yellow Swirl, Square, 4 In. 250.00
Tile, Slag, Impressioned Shell, Raised Rim, Square, 3 In. 140.00
Tile, Swirl Finish, Embossed Curves, Red & Yellow, Square, 4 In. 250.00
Toothpick, Gold Iridescent, Blue & Pink Highlights, Pinched Sides, Signed, 2 In. .190.00 to 385.00
Tumbler, 8 Pigtail Punts, Scalloped Foot, Signed 560.00
Tumbler, Gold Iridescent, Signed, Favrile 325.00
Tumbler, Whiskey, Pinched, Gold Iridescent, Blue & Silver, Favrile, 1 1/2 In. 235.00
Vase, 10 Vertical Ribs, Gold Glaze, Signed, Favrile, 12 x 5 1/4 In. 1725.00
Vase, Amber Iridescent, Green Heart Shaped Leaves, Oval, Favrile, 1919, 9 In. 995.00
Vase, Amber Iridescent, Pulled Trailings, Green Leaves, Favrile, 6 3/4 In. 1495.00
Vase, Blue Iridescent, Signed, Favrile, 9 In. 1438.00
Vase, Bright Green Star-Shaped Flowers, Pale Green Vines, Favrile, 7 x 4 1/2 In. 1897.00
Vase, Cameo, Silver Mounted, Grapes, Favrile, 14 1/2 In. ....*Illus* 23000.00
Vase, Cobalt Blue, Variegated Green & Gray Leaves, Favrile, 2 In. 3105.00
Vase, Cypriote, Favrile, 4 3/4 In. 8700.00
Vase, Cypriote, Swollen Body, Long Neck, Signed, Favrile, 10 1/2 In. 21850.00
Vase, Daffodil, Gold Iridescent, Domed Ribbed Circular Base, Signed, 15 In. 6830.00
Vase, Flower Form, Gold Iridescent, 5-Fold, Pedestal, Favrile, 5 1/2 In. 1800.00
Vase, Flower Form, Green Pulled Feather Stem, Gold Foot, Signed, 14 1/4 In. 9775.00
Vase, Flower Form, Green Pulled Heart & Vine, Gold Iridescent, Signed, 6 1/4 In. 2125.00
Vase, Flower Form, Green Pulled Heart & Vine, Gold Iridescent, Signed, 9 In. 3450.00
Vase, Flower Form, Pale Yellow, Favrile, 1918, 13 1/4 In. 4800.00
Vase, Flower Form, White, Green Leaves Base, Cameo, 1909, 5 1/4 In. 7200.00
Vase, Gold Favrile, Ruffled, Slight Ribbed Body, Signed, 18 x 3 In. 2500.00
Vase, Gold Iridescent Pulled Feathers, Dichroic Yellow Ground, 11 5/8 In. 1495.00
Vase, Gold Iridescent, Amber, Ruffled Edge, Footed, Early 20th Century, 4 In. 460.00
Vase, Gold Iridescent, Bulbous, Medial Pulled Green Waves, Signed, 2 1/2 In. 1265.00
Vase, Gold Iridescent, Experimental, Applied Button Pontil, 5 1/4 In. ....*Illus* 800.00
Vase, Gold Iridescent, Favrile, 11 3/4 In. ....750.00 to 863.00
Vase, Gold Iridescent, Favrile, 8 In. 2185.00
Vase, Gold Iridescent, Flared Base, Favrile, No. 1974, 12 In. 2185.00
Vase, Gold Iridescent, Flared, Favrile, 17 1/2 In. 1500.00
Vase, Gold Iridescent, Flower Form, Ruffled Edge, Disk Base, Signed, 5 In. 500.00
Vase, Gold Iridescent, Green Highlights, Gourd Shape, Signed, 5 1/4 In. 1495.00
Vase, Gold Iridescent, Green Pulled Feathers, Signed, 25 In. 3565.00

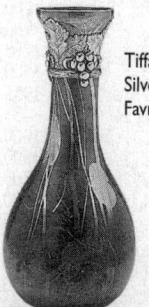

Tiffany Glass, Vase, Cameo,
Silver Mounted, Grapes,
Favrile, 14 1/2 In.

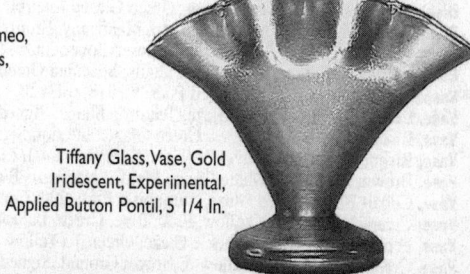

Tiffany Glass, Vase, Gold
Iridescent, Experimental,
Applied Button Pontil, 5 1/4 In.

Vase, Gold Iridescent, Green Pulled Heart & Vine, Signed, 8 3/4 In. 3360.00
Vase, Gold Iridescent, Green Pulled Leaves, Bud, Bronze Mount, 16 In. 920.00
Vase, Gold Iridescent, Oval, Signed, 13 In. 2000.00
Vase, Gold Iridescent, Pale Amber, Green Heart Shaped Leaves, 3 1/2 x 3 In. 2070.00
Vase, Gold Iridescent, Pulled Green Leaf, Signed, 1915, 7 3/4 In. 3220.00
Vase, Gold Iridescent, Pulled Leaf & Vine, Green, Brown, 4 In. 1035.00
Vase, Gold Iridescent, Purple Punts, Bulbous, Favrile, 7 In. 1500.00
Vase, Gold Iridescent, Ribbed, Dimpled Body, Flared, Signed, Favrile, 4 In. 750.00
Vase, Gold Iridescent, Ruffled Edge, Disk Base, Favrile, 5 3/4 In. 2070.00
Vase, Gold Iridescent, Signed, 3 1/2 In. 560.00
Vase, Gold Iridescent, Signed, 7 In. 560.00
Vase, Gold Iridescent, Violet & Blue, 6-Sided Rim, Signed, Favrile, 6 3/4 In. 800.00
Vase, Gold, Flower Form, Pulled Feather Stem, Triangular 6160.00
Vase, Green Iridescent, Blue Pulled Feathers & Swirls, Signed, 10 In. 3720.00
Vase, Green Pulled Feathers, Yellow Ground, Bronze Base, Signed, 15 In. 2875.00
Vase, Green Pulled Leaves & Trailing Vines, Gold Iridescent, Favrile, 6 1/2 In. 4935.00
Vase, Jack-In-The-Pulpit, Favrile, Gold Iridescent, 19 3/4 In. 5288.00
Vase, Paperweight, Amber, Star Millefiori, Trailings, Green Leaves, Favrile, 6 In. 5750.00
Vase, Paperweight, Millefiori, Green Iridescent Vines, Gold Iridescent, Favrile, 9 In. 2115.00
Vase, Paperweight, Pink & White Petals, Tapered, Signed, 3 3/4 In. 1725.00
Vase, Paperweight, Yellow Flowers, Blue Stems, Green Leaves, 5 3/4 In. 4900.00
Vase, Peacock Blue, 5-Fold, Pedestal, Signed, Favrile, 7 3/4 In. 2500.00
Vase, Peacock Blue, Gourd Shape, Signed, 1 1/4 In. 1200.00
Vase, Peacock Blue, Green Pulled Leaves & Vines, Bronze Mount, 4 x 6 In. 2500.00
Vase, Pulled Feathers, Tipped In Gold, Opal Ground, Signed, 2 3/8 In. 1345.00
Vase, Pulled Green Leaves, Amber, Gold Cupped Base, Favrile, 11 In. 8050.00
Vase, Pulled Leaf & Vine, Green, Signed, Favrile, 3 1/2 In. 1380.00
Vase, Tel El Amarna, Gold, Blue Top & Base, Favrile, 1904, 6 In. 6600.00
Vase, Topaz Iridescent, Gold, Plum, Green Pulled Feathers, Favrile, 6 In. 2820.00
Vase, Trumpet, Gold Iridescent, Favrile, 11 In. 1370.00
Vase, Trumpet, Gold Iridescent, Green Pulled Leaves, 13 5/8 In. 920.00
Vase, Trumpet, Gold Iridescent, Ruffled Edge, 6 1/4 In. 632.00
Vase, Trumpet, Pulled Green & Gold Iridescent Feathers, Impressed, 14 In. 485.00
Vase, Trumpet, Yellow Stripe, Signed, 9 3/4 In. 1410.00
Vase, Turquoise, Oval Shape, Signed, Favrile, 4 3/4 In. 825.00
Vase, Upright Scroll Handles, Band Of Palmettes, c.1905, 20 In. 5980.00
Vase, Urn, Blue, 2 Shell Handles, Pedestal, Favrile, 6 1/2 x 5 In. 1500.00
Vase, Violet & Green, 10 Trailing Gold & Green Prunts, Favrile, 10 1/2 In. 402.00
Vase, White Flowers, Deep Green, Small Mouth, Cameo, 8 In. 6600.00
Vase, White Iridescent, Gold Pulled Feathers, 12 In. 1897.00
Vase, White Pulled Feathers, Cupped Rim, 10 3/4 In. 16075.00
Vase, Yellow, Brown Leaves, Oval, Cameo, Paper Label, 6 3/4 In. 550.00
Vase, Yellow, Green Shades, Favrile, 17 In. 1528.00
Wine, Opalescent Bowl, Iridescent Stem, Signed & Numbered, 7 1/2 In., Pair 1500.00
TIFFANY GOLD, Cigarette Case, Ribbed, 14K Yellow Gold, Rectangular 675.00
Shoehorn, 18K Yellow Gold, Tiffany & Co., No. 19506 & 403M, 7 1/2 In. 747.00
TIFFANY POTTERY, Bowl, Bisque, Embossed Seaweed, Fish, Green Glaze Interior, 4 x 7 In. . . 2070.00
Bowl, Bisque, Speckled Green Glazed Interior, Artichoke Shape, 6 x 5 1/4 In. 1265.00
Bowl, Fish & Shell, Black, Green, Brown Glaze, Green Interior, Signed, 6 x 3 In. 200.00
Dish, Bisque, Raised Carved Leaves, Green Glazed Interior, 4 1/2 x 3 In. 950.00
Dish, Coupe, Volcanic White Matte Drip, Mahogany, Bronze Glazes, 4 x 3 In. 1265.00
Ginger Jar, Cover, Leaves & Vines, Berries, Allover Glaze, Signed, 9 x 5 In. 3500.00
Pitcher, Bisque, Embossed Leaves, Cattails, Speckled Green Interior, 12 In. 1955.00
Vase, Baluster Shape, Leaves, Seed Pods, c.1918, 6 1/4 In. 431.00
Vase, Berry Branches, Cream Glaze, Teardrop Shape, Signed, 7 3/4 In. 1060.00
Vase, Bisque, Blossoms & Vines, Green Glazed Interior, Signed, 13 1/4 In. 1800.00
Vase, Bisque, Interlaced Leaves & Vines, Signed, 4 x 4 1/2 In. 2500.00
Vase, Brown, Blue, Gray Matte Glaze, Molded Narcissus Blossoms, Signed, 14 In. 4600.00
Vase, Cobalt Blue Mottled Glaze, Turquoise, Early 20th Century, 12 3/4 In. 1955.00
Vase, Cream Matte Glaze, Yellow, Pink, Blue, Green, Baluster, Signed, 21 In. 6610.00
Vase, Fern Tendrils, Green Crackle Glaze, Green To Yellow Interior, 10 In. 3500.00
Vase, Green Leaf, Mottled Yellow & Brown Ground, Signed, 3 1/4 x 4 1/4 In. 3500.00
Vase, Green Matte Glaze, Signed, 1904-1910, 10 In. 6600.00

Vase, Hanging Pods Center, Leaves Top, Blue Green Glazed, 6 1/2 x 4 In. 2000.00
Vase, Ivory, Heart-Shaped Chartreuse Leaves, Moss Green, 5 3/8 In. 11750.00
Vase, Mustard, Burgundy, Moss Green, Chartreuse Swirls, Favrile, 5 1/2 In. 16450.00
Vase, Purple Magnolias Blossoms, Green Leaves, Pendant Vines, 12 1/4 In. 11163.00
Vase, Raised Blossoms & Vines, Border, Green Glazed Interior, Signed, 14 In. 2000.00
Vase, Yellow, Gray, Green Agate Design, Light Green Ground, Signed, 7 1/2 In. 8050.00
TIFFANY SILVER, Asparagus Tongs, Palm Pattern, 4 3/4 In., 6 Piece 740.00
Basket, Sugar, Footed, Sterling, Georgian Style, c.1900, 3 1/4 x 4 In. 90.00
Berry Spoon, English King, Shaped Bowl, Monogram On Handle, 9 1/4 In. 575.00
Berry Spoon, Richelieu, Conch Shape Bowl, 9 1/2 In. 550.00
Bowl, Centerpiece, Scroll Feet, Buds, Leaves, Grapevine, 1878-1891, 10 3/4 In. 9400.00
Bowl, Chrysanthemums, 9 In. 470.00
Bowl, Draped Bead Garlands, Repousse, c.1876, 9 1/4 In. 715.00
Bowl, Flower Form, Sterling, 6 In. 325.00
Bowl, Flowers & Leaf Band, Leaf Handles, Flower Holder, 1883, 12 1/2 In. 2760.00
Bowl, Leaf Shape, Leaf Handle, 10 1/2 In. . . . . .315.00 to 430.00
Bowl, Pierced Rim, Blackberries & Scrolls, 1902, 10 1/4 In. 1150.00
Bowl, Reeded Sides, Banding, Arts & Crafts Style, 1947-1956, 9 1/4 In. 2300.00
Bowl, Reeded Sides, Fruit Bands, Arts & Crafts, 1943-1945, 9 1/4 In. 1725.00
Bowl, Revere Style, 5-Line Chased Midsection, 5 1/2 x 3 In. 109.00
Butter, Domed Cover, Chased, Flower Finial, c.1855, 5 3/8 x 5 3/4 In. 785.00
Candelabrum, 3-Light, Shells, Scrolls & Leaves, Monogram, 18 x 15 In., Pair 660.00
Candelabrum, Neoclassical Style, Embossed Urn, Convertible, c.1940, 16 7/8 In. 6325.00
Candlestick, Bone Pattern, Weighted, Elsa Peretti, 1978, 15 In., Pair 3000.00
Centerpiece, Flared, Shaped Foot, Art Deco Monogram, 1925, 15 3/8 In. 5400.00
Centerpiece, Flower Frog, Sterling Silver, 1910, 3 1/2 x 17 In. 3165.00
Chafing Dish, Fluted Dome Lid, Loop Finial, Oval, c.1902, 11 1/4 x 8 1/2 In. 1380.00
Cocktail Fork Set, Palm Pattern, Gilt Bowl, 6 1/4 In., 12 Piece 1035.00
Cocktail Set, Shaker, Goblets, 1930, 13 Piece 4800.00
Coffee Set, Octagonal, Wooden Handle, Sterling, c.1969, 11 1/2 In., 3 Piece 1095.00
Compote, Scalloped Shell Border, Repousse Band, Early 20th Century, 5 x 9 1/4 In. 950.00
Compote, Scrolled Handles, Birds At Top, Monogram, 1870s, 9 1/8 In. 1610.00
Condiment Set, Pepperettes, Salt Cellars, Salt Spoons, Fiddle, Sterling, 36 Piece 865.00
Crumber, Outcurved Rim, Wide Gadroons, 8 3/4 x 6 1/4 In. 575.00
Dish, Ovoid, Pierced, Scrolled Handle, 4 Ball Feet, Stamped, 10 1/2 In. 650.00
Dish, Pierced & Scrolled Handle, Ball Feet, Oval, Art Deco, Stamped, 10 1/2 In. 750.00
Dish, Scrolls, Shell, Florals, 1902, 11 3/4 In. 4025.00
Dish, Square Cut Corners, Deep Well, Square, 7 In. 20.00
Dish, Square, Radiating Ribbing, Monogram, c.1889, 9 1/2 In. 635.00
Dish, Wavy Edge, Branch-Like Wire Handle, Oblong, 4 1/2 In., Pair 310.00
Dressing Set, Foliate Strapwork, Monogram, c.1920, 12 Piece 2700.00
Fish Set, Broom Corn Pattern, 12 In. 1200.00
Frame, Gilt, Rectangular, 20th Century, 15 x 12 In. 460.00
Frame, Sterling Silver, No. 16542, 8 3/4 x 5 1/4 In. 200.00
Goblet, Paneled Bowl, Flared Rim, White Rim & Foot, Signed, 8 5/8 In. 715.00
Jar, Condiment, Cover, Apple Shape, Stem & Leaf Finial, 20th Century, 4 3/8 In. 430.00
Jigger, 2-Cone Shape, Connected At Tapered Point, 4 5/8 In. 240.00
Jug, Water, Molded Rim, Ear Handle, Geometric Bands, 7 1/4 In. 1610.00
Ladle, Relief, Avian, Floral, Late 19th Century 719.00
Loving Cup, 3 Ear Handles, Monogram, Sterling, Early 20th Century, 9 1/4 In. 750.00
Mug, Beaded Band, Engraved, 1854-1865, 4 1/8 In. 431.00
Pastry Server, Tiffany & Co., Patented 1902 . . . . 990.00
Pitcher, Cover, Beaker, Japanese Style, Branch, Berry, c.1885 . . . . 9600.00
Plate, Scalloped Rim, Open Strapwork Cavetto, 10 1/2 In. 935.00
Plate, Serving, Monogrammed Center, Reticulated, 1927, 10 1/2 In. 460.00
Platter, Meat, Leaf & Scroll, Turned Out Rim, Reeded, 1893, 18 1/2 x 14 1/4 In. 2760.00
Platter, Round, Wide Molded Edge, Marked, 12 1/2 In. 690.00
Porringer, Bulbous, Molded Rim, Scroll Handle, Monogram, 1902-1907, 5 In. 375.00
Porringer, Little Tom Tucker's Dog Molded Band, Sterling, 1907-1947, 4 1/2 In. 460.00
Presentation Cup, 3 Handles, Paw Feet, c.1900, 11 3/8 In. 7200.00
Punch Bowl, Trophy, Pendant Ring Handles, Inscription, c.1910, 16 1/4 x 9 In. 9400.00
Punch Ladle, Vine, Heart Shape Bowl, Monogram, c.1872, 11 1/2 In. 670.00
Salad Server, Gilt Face, Wave Edge, 1884-1891, 10 1/8 In., Pair 862.00

Salad Serving Set, Florentine, Sterling, Spoon, Fork, 10 In. 1380.00
Salad Set, Tomato Vine, Sterling, 2 Piece 690.00
Salt & Pepper, Cubic Rectangle, Pierced Top, Marked Tiffany & Co., 1 1/4 In. 185.00
Salver, Engraved Zigzag Rim, Cornucopia Feet, Sterling, c.1879, 1 x 10 In. 1265.00
Sandwich Server, Scallop Shell, Flower, C-Scroll Rim, 1892-1902, 18 3/4 In. 4465.00
Sandwich Tongs, Grape Vine, Monogram, 1902, 7 5/8 In. 1495.00
Sauceboat, Gadrooned Rim, Scrolled Handle, Shell & Scroll Feet, 5 x 4 x 8 1/2 In. 1035.00
Serving Dish, Trefoil Body, 3 Ball Feet, Shallow, 7 In. 265.00
Serving Spoon, Cranberry, Fruit Basket Pattern, 1909, 9 In. 225.00
Serving Spoon, Strawberry Pattern 460.00
Soup Ladle, Chrysanthemum, Monogram, 1875, 13 In. 1840.00
Soup Ladle, Chrysanthemum, Monogram, c.1890, 12 1/4 In. 1780.00
Spoon, After Dinner, Floral Finial, Flowers, 4 1/8 In., 6 Piece 360.00
Spoon, Berry, Blackberry, 9 1/2 In. 1550.00
Spoon, Demitasse, Gilt Bowls, 4 In., 6 Piece 345.00
Stand, Flower Swag, 3 1/2 In., Pair 2643.00
Sugar & Creamer, Engraved Bodies, Swallows & Ivy, Gilt Interior, 1870, 7 In. 1265.00
Sugar Sifter, Palm Pattern, c.1907 .... 325.00
Tazza, Chrysanthemum Pattern, Pedestal Foot, 9 In., Pair ....5640.00 to 7475.00
Tazza, Scalloped Rims, Flowers, Paw Feet, c.1890, 9 3/4 In., Pair 3300.00
Tea & Coffee Set, Beaded Borders, John C. Moore, c.1865, 6 Piece 5700.00
Tea & Coffee Set, Persian Style, Foliage, Ornamental Bands, c.1876, 6 Piece 5400.00
Tea & Coffee Set, Swirling Flowers, Ferns, 1891-1902, 3 Piece 1880.00
Tea & Coffee Set, Urn Shape, Domed Cover, Urn Finial, 10 1/4 In., 3 Piece 2415.00
Tea Caddy, 3 1/2 x 2 1/2 In. 201.00
Tea Set, Chrysanthemum Pattern, c.1902, 3 Piece 4465.00
Tea Strainer, 2 Handles, 5 1/4 In. 250.00
Tea Tray, Chrysanthemum, Monogram, 1875-1891, 27 7/8 x 17 7/8 In. 18400.00
Tray, Pierced Leaves, Mazarin, Rectangular, 12 1/2 In. 2875.00
Tray, Round, Sterling, 13 In. 345.00
Tray, Shaped Rim, Raised Sides, Monogram Center, Oval, 1907, 18 x 13 3/8 In. 1380.00
Tureen, Cover, Greek Key Borders, John C. Moore, 15 1/2 In. 4800.00
Tureen, Domed Cover, Chrysanthemum Loop Finial, 2 Handles, Footed, 1883, 11 In. 9200.00
Vase, Basket Shape, Engraved Leaf, c.1930, 10 In., Pair 1250.00
Vase, Basket Shape, Loop Handle, Liner, c.1930, 10 x 8 1/4 x 4 3/4 In. 1400.00
Vase, Trumpet, Engraved, 20 In. 2875.00
Watering Can, Curved Handle, Upswept Elongated Spout, c.1890, 8 1/4 In. 14100.00

TIFFIN Glass Company of Tiffin, Ohio, was a subsidiary of the United
States Glass Co. of Pittsburgh, Pennsylvania, in 1892. The U.S. Glass
Co. went bankrupt in 1963, and the Tiffin plant employees purchased
the building and the inventory. They continued running it from 1963 to
1966, when it was sold to Continental Can Company. In 1969, it was
sold to Interpace, and in 1980, it was closed. The black satin glass,
made from 1923 to 1926, and the stemware of the last twenty years are
the best-known products.

Brocade, Candlestick, Black, 8 In. 250.00
Byzantine, Goblet, Water, 9 In. 28.00
Byzantine, Parfait, 7 In. 34.00
Colonial, Candy Jar, Ground Lid, 11 1/2 In. 345.00
Columbia, Candy Jar, Slip Fit Cover, 15 In. 115.00
Columbia, Candy Jar, Swirled Cover, Cylinder, 13 In. 460.00
Columbia Egyptian, Candy Jar, Slip Fit Cover, 1950s, 9 1/2 In. 11.00
Dakota, Candy Jar, Slip Fit Cover, Cylinder, 1950s, 18 In. 172.00
Dakota, Candy Jar, Slip Fit Cover, Footed, 1950s, 24 In. 287.00
Flanders, Vase, Footed, Pink, 8 In. 350.00
Fuchsia, Cordial, 1 Oz. 60.00
King's Crown, Bowl, Cranberry Stain, 4 In. 17.00
King's Crown, Bowl, Salad, 9 1/4 In. 75.00
King's Crown, Compote, Ruby Stain, 7 1/4 In. 25.00
King's Crown, Goblet, Cranberry Stain, 5 1/2 In. 17.00
King's Crown, Plate, Dinner, Cranberry Stain, 10 In. 30.00
King's Crown, Sugar & Creamer 25.00

King's Crown, Sugar & Creamer, Ruby Stain	65.00
No. 66, Console Set, Frosted Blue, Footed, Flared Sides, Twisted Candlesticks, 3 Piece	82.00

TILES have been used in most countries of the world as a sturdy building material for floors, roofs, fireplace surrounds, and surface toppings. Many of the American tiles are listed in this book under the factory name.

Children, Among Roses, Square, 6 In., 11 Piece	385.00
Flowers, California Faience, 5 1/4 In.	173.00
Frieze, Elk, Encaustic, Mueller, 6 In., 16 Piece	115.00
Goat Eating Grapes From Vine, Arts & Crafts, Polychrome, 5 x 5 In.	690.00
Indian Princess, 9 x 3 1/2 In.	260.00
Landscape, Thatched Roof Cottage, Footbridge, Frame, Claycraft, 6 x 12 In.	1610.00
New York Cityscape, Walnut Frame, Harris Strong, 11 3/4 In.	600.00
Parrots, On Flowering Branches, Clay, Crackling, 7 x 7 In., 2 Piece	137.00
Peter, Peter, Pumpkin Eater, Dark Mahogany Frame, Square, 8 In.	1495.00
Puce, Center Flower Basket, Stylized Corner Blooms, c.1740, 5 x 5 In.	165.00
Qajar Pottery, Biblical Scenes, Hebrew Lettering, Late 19th Century, 13 x 9 In.	1560.00
Raised & Painted Mission Scene, Arts & Crafts Frame, Claycraft, 7 1/4 x 15 1/2 In.	1150.00
Tan, Green, Blue Matte Glaze, Oak Frame, Arts & Crafts, 5 1/2 x 3 1/2 In.	299.00
Urn, Lemons, Tiger Lilies, Fireplace Framed, Late 19th Century, 37 1/2 x 9 1/2 In.	1035.00

TINWARE containers for household use have been made in America since the seventeenth century. The first tin utensils were brought from Europe, but by 1798, tin plate was imported and local tinsmiths made the wares. Painted tin is called tole and is listed separately. Some tin kitchen items may be found listed under Kitchen. The lithographed tin containers used to hold food and tobacco are listed in the Advertising category under Tin.

Canister, Yellow Brush Strokes, Bail Handle, Green Leaf Band, Red Cherries, 6 In.	3737.00
Coffeepot, Applied Strap, Wood Finial, Cone Shape, 19th Century, 11 In.	770.00
Coffeepot, Dome Lid, Brass Finial, Punched Wrigglework, Urn, Tulips, 11 In.	1595.00
Coffeepot, Dome Lid, Gooseneck Spout, 19th Century, 11 In.	110.00
Figure, Man, Top Hat, Articulated, Blue Paint, 12 In.	415.00
Foot Warmer, Birch, Punched Design, Removable Tray, Bail Handle, 9 x 7 1/2 x 6 In.	165.00
Foot Warmer, Pierced Hearts, Wood, Bail Handle, Oval	605.00
Foot Warmer, Pierced, Wood, Heart Decoration, 6 In.	160.00
Foot Warmer, Punched, Heart Designs, Wooden Frame, Wire Bail, 7 1/2 x 9 x 5 3/4 In.	190.00
Jardiniere, Turkey Shape, Early 20th Century, 19 1/2 In.	400.00
Mirror, Side Candle Sconces, Mexico, c.1880	425.00
Mold, Candle, 3 Tube, Applied Handle, 10 In.	143.00
Mold, Candle, 4 Tube, Folded Edge, Applied Handle, 10 In.	93.00
Mold, Candle, 4 Tube, Splayed Top, Platform Base, 3 x 3 In.	410.00
Mold, Candle, 5 Tube, Folded Edge Handle, Reinforcing Band, Platform Base, 4 3/4 In.	440.00
Mold, Candle, 12 Tube, Applied Handle, 10 3/4 In.	140.00
Mold, Candle, 12 Tube, Pine, Dovetailed Ends, Square Nails, 17 1/4 x 15 In.	690.00
Mold, Candle, 12 Tube, Pine, Rose & Square Head Nails, 14 1/2 x 23 3/4 In.	410.00
Mold, Candle, 12 Tube, Swivel Hanging Ring, 11 3/4 x 9 In.	440.00
Mold, Candle, 24 Tube, 2 Handles, 20 1/2 x 11 In.	80.00
Mold, Candle, 24 Tube, Double Handles, 10 x 10 In.	220.00
Mold, Heart, Punched Flower Design Base, Applied Handle, Footed, 4 1/2 x 3 1/8 In.	385.00
Mold, Ribbed Sides, Loop Handle, Cover, 6 1/2 In.	11.00
Mold, Tool, Light, Loom, Twisted Hanger, Hook & Candle Socket, Wrought Iron, 15 In.	165.00
Suit Of Armor, Chest Protector, Hip Shields, Gloves, Helmet, Joust Rod, Base, 74 In.	1045.00
Tray, Peacock, Hand Painted, 18 1/2 x 25 In.	275.00
Tray, Peacock, On Fountain, Scrolled Rim, Alligatored, 25 x 33 In.	330.00

TOBACCO CUTTERS may be listed in either the Advertising or Store categories.

TOBACCO JAR collectors search for those made in odd shapes and colors. Because tobacco needs special conditions of humidity and air, it has been stored in special containers since the eighteenth century.

3 Black Poker Players, Cards & Dice On Top, 1880s, 10 In.	1285.00

4 Indians, Lid Of 5th Indian, Wood, 9 1/2 In. 345.00

Arab Boy, Turban & Scarf, Green Stripes, Earrings, 5 In. 175.00

Barrel, Brass, England, Late 18th Century, 4 In. 295.00

Bermudian Man, Cheroot In Teeth, Bisque, Painted, 1900s, 8 In. 375.00

Bisque, Character, Painted, Black Man, Pork Pie Cap, 20th Century, 5 1/2 In. 290.00

Black Dandy Sits On Havana Cigar, Box, 8 In. 385.00

Black Mariners, Bisque, 1880s, 7 1/2 In. 540.00

Black Minstrel Pops Out Of Barrel, 1890s, 8 In. 540.00

Boy Cleans Doghouse, Roof Top, Terra-Cotta, 1880, 8 In. 760.00

Boy In Barrel, Terra-Cotta, 7 1/4 In. 240.00

Boy's Head Pops Out Of Barrel, Terra-Cotta, 1880s, 8 In. 175.00

Cigarette Holder, Boy On Sled, Terra-Cotta, Marked BB 55008, Austria, 6 3/4 In. 425.00

Devil, Pottery, 6 1/2 In. 195.00

Dog, Glass Eyes, Majolica, 5 In. 200.00

Dog, Wearing Hat, Terra-Cotta, 8 1/2 In. 600.00

Elephant With Driver, Terra-Cotta, 8 In. 215.00

Franz Josef, Marked Bernhard Bloch, No. 8339, Terra-Cotta, 9 1/2 In. 600.00

Girl With Headdress, Marked Wm. Schiller & Sohn, No. 18, Terra-Cotta, 8 In. 375.00

Gypsy Woman, Terra-Cotta, 10 In. 480.00

Hoof Form, Silver Plate Mounts & Cover, 7 1/2 In. 258.00

Man In Barrel, Terra-Cotta, 6 1/2 In. 300.00

Man Seated In Chair, Pipe, Smoking Robe, Figural, Ceramic, 19th Century, 9 In. 345.00

Man Seated On Barrel, Marked Wm. Schiller & Sohn, No. 8296, Terra-Cotta, 12 In. 580.00

Man With Cigars, Terra-Cotta, 9 In. 100.00

Mixture Pipe Tobacco Inscribed On Leaves, 7 1/2 In. 135.00

Native America Indian, Terra-Cotta, 6 1/4 In. 200.00

Prince Of Wales Crest, Octagonal, Fitted Lid, Head Finial, Footed, 1825, 4 x 5 In. 330.00

Seated Black Woman Holding Dog, Bisque, Pottery, 8 In. 605.00

Smiling Black Boy, 1880s, 5 3/4 In. 537.00

Woman, With Broom, Key, Terra-Cotta, Marked, JM 3673 Austria, 9 In. 605.00

TOBY JUG is the name of a very special form of pitcher. It is shaped like the full figure of a man or woman. A pitcher that shows just the top half of a person is not correctly called a toby. More examples of toby jugs can be found under Royal Doulton and other factory names.

Admiral Rodney, White Ware, Hilltop Pottery, 1792, 4 5/16 x 4 7/8 In. 250.00

Blue Willow Coat, Gray Hair, Orange Vest, Yellow Knickers, Staffordshire 700.00

Cobalt Blue, Copper Luster, 5 1/2 In. 86.00

Figure Holding Pipe, Success To Our Wooden Walls, Staffordshire, 10 1/4 In. 977.00

Hearty Good Fellow, c.1800, 10 1/2 In. 1645.00

Hearty Good Fellow, c.1815, 8 1/2 In. 2820.00

King & Queen Of Clubs, Small 275.00

King & Queen Of Hearts, Small 275.00

King & Queen Of Spades, Small 275.00

Man, Black Coat, Yellow Hat, Brown Pants, 1850s, 9 1/4 In. 139.00

Man On A Barrel, c.1790, 9 1/2 In. 4935.00

Pratt Type, Frock Coat, c.1800, 9 1/4 In. 2235.00

Sailor, On Sea Chest, Pearlware, c.1790, 11 1/2 In. 2820.00

Squire, Pearlware, c.1795, 11 In. 4700.00

Thin Man, Creamware, c.1780, 9 1/4 In. 6465.00

TOLE is painted tin. It is sometimes called *japanned ware, pontypool,* or *toleware.* Most nineteenth-century tole is painted with an orange-red or black background and multicolored decorations. Many recent versions of toleware are made and sold. Related items may be listed in the Tinware category.

Box, Black, Yellow Scrollwork, Loop Handle, 1860, 3 x 4 3/4 In. 575.00

Box, Candle, Red & Yellow Grained, Flowers, Hanging, Cylindrical, 14 3/8 In. 900.00

Box, Coal, Dog's Head On Cover, Victorian, 20 In. 140.00

Box, Deed, Red Flowers, Berries Front, Scrollwork Lid, Tin Hasp, Wire Handle, 9 3/8 In. .. 440.00

Box, Deed, Starflowers On Lid, Red Acorns, Wire Handle, 7 7/8 In. 660.00

Box, Deed, White Swags On Front & Sides, Petaled Flowers, Leaves, Brass Handle, 8 In. .. 440.00

Box, Document, Brass Handle, Scrolled Hasp, Ribbon Borders, 6 1/2 x 9 1/4 In. 880.00

Box, Document, Dome Top, Red, Pink & Green Flowers, 8 x 4 x 4 In. 190.00
Box, Document, Red & Green Flowers, Yellow Lines, 4 1/8 x 2 1/4 x 2 7/8 In. 165.00
Box, Dome Top, Brown, Red Draped Swags, Yellow Leaves, 11 x 6 1/4 In. 990.00
Box, Dome Top, Cherry, Leaves, Yellow Highlights, 2 x 3 x 2 In. 250.00
Box, Dome Top, Green Painted Flowers, Black Ground, 19th Century, 4 1/2 x 8 1/4 In. . . . 2000.00
Box, Dome Top, Original Dark Brown, White Band, Green Leaves, Red Cherries, 6 x 4 In. 660.00
Box, Dome Top, Pomegranate, Yellow Zigzag, 6 x 9 x 4 3/4 In. 770.00
Bread Basket, Berry, Flowers & Foliage, Yellow Border, 8 x 12 3/4 In. 3300.00
Bucket, Red Paint, Decorated, Tapered Cone Shape, 19th Century, 2 1/2 In. 1880.00
Coffeepot, Black Ground, Red, Yellow Flowers, Tapered Cone Shape, 10 3/4 x 6 1/4 In. . . 4115.00
Coffeepot, Black, Painted Fruit, Flowers, Tapered Body, Strap Handle, Hinged Lid, 9 In. . 590.00
Coffeepot, Circle Each Side, Flowers, Tulip, Stylized Leaves Base, 10 1/4 In. 1210.00
Coffeepot, Dome Top, Flowers, Leaf At Base, Brass Finial, 10 1/2 In. 1100.00
Coffeepot, Dome Top, Gooseneck Spout, Scroll Handle, Tulip & Leaves, 10 1/4 In. 1210.00
Coffeepot, Dome Top, Strap Handle, Arched Spout, 19th Century, 10 1/2 In. 4465.00
Coffeepot, Flowers, Red & Yellow, c.1840 . . . . 4700.00
Coffeepot, Painted, Urn Form, Oval Base, Loop Handle & Spout, Brass Finial, 10 3/4 In. . 375.00
Coffeepot, Red Flower, Black Ground, Applied Handle, 9 x 5 x 4 In. 55.00
Coffeepot, Red Flowers, Yellow Scrollwork, 19th Century, 10 In. 315.00
Coffeepot, Straight Spout, C-Scroll Handle, Hinged Lid, 2 Flowers Oval Panels, 8 3/4 In. . 6050.00
Jardiniere, Painted Oval Tub, Oriental Landscapes, Brass, Paw Feet, 28 1/2 x 17 3/4 In. . . 5060.00
Jardiniere, Regency, Lacquer, Oriental Scenes, Pierced Brass Gallery, Paw Feet, 31 In. . . . 920.00
Lamp, Circular Top, Molded Base, Black, Gilt Flowers, Napoleon III, 63 x 13 In. 920.00
Lamp, Empire, Deep Green Shade, Bands Of Leaves, Octagonal Plinth, 21 In. 1265.00
Lamp, Flowering Rose Branches, Forest Green, White Marble Base, 1820s, 26 1/2 In. 2760.00
Lamp, Venetian Lantern Form, Brass Plated Tin Base, 18th Century, 15 1/4 In. 230.00
Lavabo, Faux Spout, Urn Form, Wooden Finial, Eagles Within Wreaths, 26 x 20 1/2 In. . . 920.00
Light, Double Arms, Candle Shape, Prisms, Glass Bead Strings, Marble Base, Pair 145.00
Mug, Black, 4 Red Apples, Yellow Foliage, 4 3/4 In., Pair 390.00
Mug, Pomegranate, Applied Strap Handle, Flared Base, 6 In. 7150.00
Mug, Red, Yellow & Green Design, Black Ground, Applied Strap Handle, 5 x 4 In. 220.00
Tea Caddy, Red, Yellow & Green Apples, Black Ground, 7 x 4 In. 275.00
Tea Caddy, Stylized Flowers & Leaf, 4 1/4 In. 2430.00
Tea Canister, Cylinder, Red Ground, Brown & Yellow, 4 1/2 x 3 1/2 x 2 3/4 In. 360.00
Tea Canister, Red & Black Ground, Yellow, Red & Blue Design, 8 x 5 In. 770.00
Teapot, Yellow Ground, Red, Blue, Green, Flowers & Leaf, 2 1/2 In. 1210.00
Topiary, Painted Fruit, 58 In. 3160.00
Tray, 8 Spherical Scenes, Myths, Athena On Center Painted Mustard, Oval, 32 x 24 In. . . . 1175.00
Tray, 16 Fretwork Sides, 19th Century, 25 In. 1150.00
Tray, Apple, Pomegranate, Yellow & Green Trailing Leaf Border, 12 1/2 x 8 In. 415.00
Tray, Apple, Red & Yellow Rim, Center Flowers, 13 3/4 x 8 1/2 In. 770.00
Tray, Apple, Red, Yellow, Polychrome Leaf On Band, Rolled Edges, 12 3/4 x 8 In. 220.00
Tray, Band Of Scrolled Leaves, Brass Handles, Gilt, Black, 31 In. 860.00
Tray, Bird Perched On Flower Filled Vase, Wood Stand, Victorian, 20 x 25 In. 920.00
Tray, Bucolic Landscape, Figures In Leisure Activities, Bamboo Stand, 22 x 30 1/4 In. . . . 3450.00
Tray, Coffin Form, 8 Flared Sides, Gypsum, Red, Yellow, 8 3/4 x 6 In. 75.00
Tray, Family, House, Ship, Flower Border, Black Ground, 21 x 28 In. 145.00
Tray, Flower Sprays Surrounding Central Pattern, 2 Carrying Handles, 21 x 20 In. 980.00
Tray, Fruit & Flower, Black & Gray Ground, 12 x 8 1/2 In. 440.00
Tray, Fruit & Flowers, Crystalized Center, 2 1/2 x 12 x 7 In. 2200.00
Tray, Fruiting Grapevines, Raised Sided, Round, Early 20th Century, 15 1/4 In. 58.00
Tray, Gilt Figures In Palace, Boats On Shore, Clouds Border, 1870s, 30 3/4 x 24 3/4 In. . . 920.00
Tray, Greek Key Border, Faux Bamboo Stand, Gilt Accents, 19 1/2 x 32 In. 1600.00
Tray, Handled Gallery, Scrolling Flat Leaves Rim, Eagles In Wreath, 1840s, 26 In. 920.00
Tray, Ivory Band, Red Fruit & Flowers, Green Leaves, Octagonal, 5 3/4 x 8 1/2 In. 220.00
Tray, Jungle Scene, Multicolored, Ebonized Stand, Gilt, 19th Century, 21 x 30 1/2 x 22 In. 575.00
Tray, Landscape, Lovers, England, Late 19th Century, 30 x 24 In. 345.00
Tray, Octagonal, Black Ground, Central Gilt Decoration, Girl, Statue, 26 In. 288.00
Tray, Peacock In Center, Floral Border, Scalloped Rim, 29 x 22 1/2 In. 302.00
Tray, Red Berries, Tan & Teal Leaves, Yellow Band, 6 x 8 3/4 In. 220.00
Tray, Red Chinoiserie, 3 Pagodas In Wooded Landscape, Red Ground, 25 1/2 x 19 1/2 In. . 345.00
Tray, Red Flowers, Green, Yellow Leaves, Canted Corner, 8 x 12 In. 275.00
Tray, Regency, Black Lacquer, Early 19th Century, 21 x 26 x 21 In. 575.00

Tray, Regency, Black Lacquer, Gilt Stars Overall, Rounded Corners, 29 x 23 In. 460.0

Tray, Regency, Ebonized, Serpentine, Gilt, Flowers, 21 x 27 1/2 x 22 In. 1380.0

Tray, Restauration, Oval, Raised Gallery, Greek Key Border, Vase, 20 x 24 x 18 1/2 In. . . . 1438.0

Tray, Serpentine, Raised Edge, Bamboo Stand, Gilt, 21 x 32 1/2 x 24 1/2 In. 1150.0

Tray, Stand, Flowers & Exotic Birds, Green, Serpentine, Victorian, 24 x 31 1/2 In. 2400.0

Tray, Stenciled Swallow On Flowering Branch, 20 1/2 x 26 In. 104.0

Tray, Stenciled, Pheasant, Pagoda, Flowered Flared Rim, Flying Birds, 22 x 16 In. 77.0

Tray, Tiger In Landscape, Floral Border, Cutout Hand Holds, 19th Century, 22 In. 3290.0

Tray, Wavy Line, Center Design, Oval, 6 7/8 In. 1760.0

Tray, Yellow Ground, Chinoiserie Decoration, 31 x 22 In. 288.0

Tray, Yellow Leaves, Red, Alligatored, 8 Sides, 5 7/8 x 8 7/8 In. 412.0

Tray Set, Oval, Black, Gold, Graduated, 29 In. 805.0

Urn, Chestnut, Red Paint, Regency, Ring Handles, Cover, Early 19th Century, 12 In., Pair 805.0

Waiter, Japanese Style, Parcel Gilt, Silvered, Black, Rectangular, Stand, 30 x 22 3/4 In. . . 1380.0

Waiter, Lady-Of-Fashion In Park, Flower Heads, 1820s, 30 x 2 1/2 In. 1035.0

TOM MIX was born in 1880 and died in 1940. He was the hero of over 100 silent movies from 1910 to 1929, and 25 sound films from 1929 to 1935. There was a Ralston Tom Mix radio show from 1933 to 1950, but the original Tom Mix was not in the show. Tom Mix comics were published from 1942 to 1953.

Badge, Doby County Sheriff, Folder & Envelope 95.0

Bathrobe, Youth, Flannel, Tom Mix Patch, Drawstring Waist, c.1945 . . . . 95.0

Book, Dust Jacket, By Olive Mix, 1957 . . . . 95.0

Book, The Rider Of Death Valley, Hardcover, Copyright 1934, 154 Pages 38.0

Book, The Texas Bad Man, Film Scenes, Hardcover, Copyright 1934, 156 Pages 75.0

Coloring Book, Straight Shooter, c.1950, 8 1/2 x 11 In., 8 Pages 30.0

Comic Book, No. 9, March 1942 . . . . 120.0

Figure, Horse Tony, Plaster, 4 3/4 x 4 3/4 In. 135.0

Flip Booklet, Ideal Moving Pictures, Stapled Tablet, Stiff Paper, 1 1/2 x 1 3/4 In. 60.0

Label, Cigar Box, Color Lithograph, 1933, 4 1/4 x 5 1/4 In. 28.0

Magnet Ring, Brass, Silver Magnet Ring, 1947 . . . . 125.0

Movie, Ransomed, Film For Toy Projector, 8 mm, Box, c.1940 . . . . 20.0

Paper Doll, Movie Outfits Sheet, 1930s, 9 x 13 In. Sheets, 6 1/2-In. Doll 48.0

Pencil Case, Cardboard, Snap Fastener Lid, Rodeo Art, 1 1/4 x 6 x 8 1/2 In. 95.0

Periscope, Ralston Premium, 1939 . . . . 60.0

Poster, Tom Mix Safety Story, Late 1940s, 17 x 22 In. 35.0

Program, Circus Souvenir, Black & White, 1931 Season, 32 Pages 50.0

Sign, Radio Program, Ralston Ad, c.1933, 14 1/4 x 23 1/2 In. 125.0

Siren Ring, Brass, 1944 . . . . 110.0

Spurs, Ralston Premium, 1935, 3 1/2 x 4 1/2 In. 75.0

Theater Flyer, The Lucky Horseshoe, Cast Member Photos, 9 x 12 In. 25.0

Wrapper, Chewing Gum, Save 75 & Get A Deputy Ring 125.0

TOOLS of all sorts are listed here, but most are related to industry. Other tools may be found listed under Iron, Kitchen, Tinware, and Wooden.

Adze, Head, Shipwright's, Mathieson, 1901 . . . . 99.00

Anvil, Eagle Mark, Clark Fisher, 37 Lbs. 125.00

Awl, Sheffield, Marked Deer Leg Bone, Fur Trade, 6 In. 180.00

Ax, Battle, Steel Blade, Calligraphic, Inlaid Silver & Brass, 18th Century, 29 1/2 In. 747.00

Ax, Fireman's, Strapped, 1890 . . . . 49.00

Ax, Head, 1897 . . . . 455.00

Ax, Hewing, Broad Blade, Star On Blade, Maria Rast In Circle, Wood Handle, 12 In. 275.00

Ax, Sorby, 6 In. 35.00

Ax, Sugar, Scalloped Sides Of Blade, Wood Handle, 1740s 265.00

Ax, Sugar, Wood, Wrought Iron, Carved Handle, Articulated Crescent Blade, 12 x 8 In. . . . 4400.00

Ax, Sugar, Wrought Iron Head, Turned Maple Handle, 18th Century 495.00

Ax, Wing, Buzzard, Forged, 7 3/4 x 13 1/2 In. 45.00

Ax Blade, Bronze, Socket-Type, Dragon Relief, Borneo, 19th Century, 4 1/2 In. 173.00

Barrel Tap, Bronze, Crown-Form Handle, England, c.1500 . . . . 250.00

Bevel, Butt Locking, St. Johnsbury Tool Co., I.J. Robinson Pat. June 14, 1879, 9 In. 650.00

Bevel, With Level, L.D. Howard, Cast Bronze, Pat. Nov. 5, 1867, 8 In. 385.00

Bin, Amish, Grain Painted, Canted Front, 49 x 33 x 22 In. 975.00

Bit, Wood, Irwin, No. 21, Adjustable To 3-In. Swing 27.00
Blade Set, Stanley, No. 465, 11 Piece 110.00
Block, Violin Maker's, Stanley, No. 100 1/2 . . . . 135.00
Book Press, Cast Iron, Castle Series, Brass Trim, Oval Nameplate 595.00
Box, Carpenter's, Lift Top, Copper Hinges, Reinforced Corners, 2 Drawers 275.00
Box, Carpenter's, Maple, Butternut, Hickory, Vertical Slats, Interior Drawers, Cover 650.00
Box, Cobbler's, Wood, Shoe Repair Tools, 1890, 28 x 16 x 12 In. 28.00
Box, Wooden, Green Paint, 2 Lift-Out Trays, 10 1/2 x 22 x 12 1/12 In. 165.00
Brace, Wooden, George Wheatcroft, Newark, New Jersey, c.1850 . . . . 375.00
Broadax, Hand Carved Handle, 13-In. Wide Blade 35.00
Caliper, Iron, 19 In. 45.00
Caliper, Log, D.P. Sanborn, 45 In. 100.00
Caliper, Lumber, 19th Century 1950.00
Caliper, Micrometer, Brown & Sharpe, No. 102, Ratchet Stop 45.00
Caliper, Sawyer, Outside Spring, Stamped 25.00
Caliper, Toolmaker's, Brown & Sharpe, No. 82, Inside Spring, 2 In. 15.00
Caliper Set, Brown & Sharpe, 18 3/4 In. 70.00
Cane Cutter, Wrought Iron, Brass, Turned Walnut Handle, 12 x 3 3/4 x 6 In. 220.00
Catalog, Stanley Tools, No. 34, Dated 7-1-26, 192 Pages 50.00
Chest, Black Over Red Flame Grain, Painted, 9 Interior Drawers, 22 1/4 x 45 1/4 In. 110.00
Chest, Cabinetmaker, Wood, Handmade, E.F.P., Texas, c.1890, 35 x 21 x 20 In. 1075.00
Chest, Pine, Maple, Inlaid Interior Of Lid, J. Bernatchez, 1895, 28 1/4 x 40 1/2 In. 3200.00
Chest, Pine, Painted Interior Scene, c.1848, 42 x 25 x 23 3/4 In. 4950.00
Chest, Wood, Painted, Dovetailed, 2 Slide Till Compartments, Tools 285.00
Chisel, Mortise, T.H. Witherby, 17 1/4 In. 95.00
Chisel Set, Buck Brothers, 8 Piece 500.00
Chisel Set, Everlast, Stanley, No. R50, Black Rubber Handles 700.00
Chisel Set, P.S. & W., 8 Piece 375.00
Cigar Box Opener, 6 1/2 In. 22.00
Clockmaker's, Drill, Turret Clock, Fitted Box, Senkspiel 45.00
Clockmaker's, Rounding Off, Brass, Oak Base, 19th Century, Switzerland 275.00
Combination, Level, Bevel, Rule, Stephens Co., Boxwood, Brass, Pat. Jan. 12, 1858 . . . . 175.00
Curler, Hair, Ringlette, Electric, Walnut Case 90.00
Divider, Pfleghar & Schollhorn & Co., Pat. Jan. 9, 1866, 6 3/4 In. 65.00
Dowel Jig, Stanley, No. 59, 6 Guides, Instructions, Box 35.00
Dowel Jig, Stanley, No. 77, 5 Cutters, Boxes 1000.00
Draw Knife, Folding, Wilkinson 65.00
Drill, Breast 100.00
Fork, Hay, Signed, W. Bleistein, 94 In. 192.00
Gauge, 2 Dials, Brass, 6 In. 40.00
Gauge, 2 Dials, Obverse & Reverse, Cast Iron Frame, Ashton, 400 Lb., 10 In. 520.00
Gauge, Brake, Westinghouse, 140 Lb., 6 1/2 In. 35.00
Gauge, Brass, Westinghouse, 160 Lb., 6 In. 60.00
Gauge, Depth, Stanley, No. 49 . . . . 20.00
Gauge, Locomotive Stoker Co., Brass, Pittsburgh, Pa., 250 Lb., 6 In. 80.00
Gauge, Surface, Starrett No. 52, Black Japanned, 1st Model, c.1881 . . . . 150.00
Gauge, Thickness, Brown & Sharpe No. 646, 6 Blades, 2 13/16 In. 12.00
Gauge, Vacuum, Westinghouse, Brass, 30 Lb., 7 1/2 In. 35.00
Grabber, Can, Spring Action, Oak, Cast Iron, 55 In. 40.00
Grain Measure, 3 Woven Lapped Fingers, Applied Rim, Incised Initials HG, 8 x 16 In. 290.00
Hammer, Coppersmiths', Hickory Shaft, 1910 . . . . 115.00
Hay Fork, Wooden, 5 Tines 60.00
Hay Spear, Trigger Mechanism, Marked Nellis H201 . . . . 28.00
Hinge, Spring Loaded, Brass, 18 Lb., 15 In., Pair 69.00
Jack, Conestoga Wagon, 1803, 18 In. 295.00
Jack, Conestoga Wagon, 25 1/2 x 8 1/2 In. 385.00
Lathe, South Bend, On Factory Cabinet, 10 In. 750.00
Leather Splitter, Aaron Crawford, c.1850 . . . . 65.00
Level, Hall & Knapp, New Britain, Ct., 1853-1857, 20 3/4 In. 155.00
Level, Line, Brass, Original Wood Box, 19th Century, 20 In. 575.00
Level, Lufkin, No. 2062 . . . . 85.00
Level, Stanley, No. 36G, Box, 12 In. 60.00
Level, Stratton Bros., Mahogany, Brass Bound, 30 In. 78.00

Level, Winchester, 18 In. 65.00
Level, Wooden, Keen Kutter, Pat'd 5-8-06, Stamped Brass Plate 20.00
Magnifier, Lace Maker's, Glass Globe Hangs From Stand, Box, 34 In. 57.00
Mallet, 4 Sides, Burl Head, Paneled Curly Maple Handle, 11 1/4 In. 110.00
Mallet, Keen Kutter, Wooden 25.00
Miter Box & Saw, Stanley, No. 358 .... 750.00
Mold, Bullet,.30-.30, Ideal Mfg. Co., Conn. 40.00
Mold, Bullet,.44 WCF, Pat. 1874, 8 In. 55.00
Mold, Bullet, Brass, Turned Wooden Handles, Stamped 32, 5 1/8 In. 95.00
Mold, Glove, Rubber, Porcelain, Mayer China, Beaver Falls 35.00
Monkey Wrench, Side Grips, Winchester, No. 00, Coes Type, 6 1/2 In. 110.00
Nippers, Wire, Starrett, 2 Cuts Spring Wire 30.00
Padlock, Miller, 2 1/8 x 3 In. 17.00
Pipe Wrench, Cochtan, Model 1910, Patd. 1908, 18 In. 25.00
Pipe Wrench, Winchester, Patent 1922, Black Japanning 110.00
Pitchfork, 3 Prongs, Signed, M.B. Young, 66 In. 121.00
Plane, Bed Rock, Jointer, Type 7, c.1923 .... 179.00
Plane, Bed Rock, Stanley, No. 605, Type 6A, 1922 .... 135.00
Plane, Bed Rock, Stanley, No. 607C, Type 7, Iron Trademark 135.00
Plane, Block, Birmingham, 5 1/4 In., 1 5/16-In. Wide Blade 115.00
Plane, Block, Reversible, Stanley, No. 131 .... 180.00
Plane, Block, Squirrel Tailed, Stanley, No. 9 3/4, Sweetheart Logo 295.00
Plane, Block, Stanley, No. 60 1/2, 1930-40 .... 24.00
Plane, Block, Stanley, No. 140 .... 115.00
Plane, Bossing, Panel Raising, Frans Moret, Holland, 1759 .... 142.00
Plane, Cabinetmaker's, Stanley 97 .... 500.00
Plane, Carriage, Squirrel Tail, Mockridge & Francis 175.00
Plane, Combination, Stanley, No. 45, With Set Of Cutters, Homemade Box 150.00
Plane, Corebox, Stanley, No. 57, 1 Set Of Extension Wings 175.00
Plane, Crown Molding, Stamped, Marley, c.1825 .... 525.00
Plane, Dado, Stanley, No. 39, 3/8 In. 126.00
Plane, F.C. Brandt 1500.00
Plane, Fillister, Fruitwood, 1868, 4 1/2 In. 140.00
Plane, Fore, Stanley, No. 6C, Notched Logo, Black Handles, WWII Model 65.00
Plane, J. Opping 1600.00
Plane, Jack, Stanley, No. 5 1/4 .... 40.00
Plane, Keen Kutter, Symbol 40.00
Plane, Low Angle, Stanley, No. 62, SW Logo 415.00
Plane, Millers Patent, Type 3A, 2 Fences 3500.00
Plane, Miter, Bird's-Eye Maple Handle, J. Hering & Sons, 7 In. 295.00
Plane, Miter, English, J. Herring & Sons, Bird's-Eye Maple, 7 In. 295.00
Plane, Plow, Applewood, H. Chapin No. 239-1/2 .... 325.00
Plane, Plow, Boxwood, Arrowmamett Works 150.00
Plane, Rabbet & Block, Stanley, No. 140 .... 115.00
Plane, Rabbet, English, Marples & Son, Iron, 1 3/8 x 8 In. 295.00
Plane, Rabbet, Stamped W.C. Bacon 1888 .... 650.00
Plane, Rabbet, Stanley, No. 45, Book 265.00
Plane, Rabbet, Stanley, No. 98, With Fence 170.00
Plane, Rabbet, Stanley, No. 181, Type 1, Japanned 50.00
Plane, Rabbet, Stanley, No. 182, S.R. & L. Logo, Japanned 40.00
Plane, Rabbet, Stanley, No. 182, Type 1, Japanned 65.00
Plane, Rabbet, Stanley, No. 190, Type 1, Japanned 65.00
Plane, Rabbet, Stanley, No. 191, S.R. & L. Logo, Japanned 50.00
Plane, Rabbet, Stanley, No. 191, SW Logo, Pat. 6-7-10 .... 77.00
Plane, Sargent, No. 3408, Circular T.M. Length 8 In. 300.00
Plane, Sash, A & E Baldwin, New York 50.00
Plane, Scraper, Cabinet, Stanley, No. 112, Sweetheart Logo On Blade 215.00
Plane, Scraper, Veneer, Stanley, No. 12, Sweetheart Logo On Blade 65.00
Plane, Smoothing, Stanley, No. 2, V Logo 225.00
Plane, Smoothing, Stanley, No. 3, 1892 Patent Date On Blade 45.00
Plane, Smoothing, Stanley, No. 35, Type 8, 1888 .... 24.00
Plane, Smoothing, Stanley, No. 122, Liberty Bell, 1886-88 .... 49.00
Plane, Stanley, No. 45, Box 150.00

Plane, Steel Blade, Brass Thumb Screw, Edw. Preston, 16 In. 110.00
Plane, Tongue, John Stall, Philadelphia, Late 1700s 30.00
Plane Blade Set, Stanley, No. 444 .... 85.00
Pliers, Fencing, Winchester, No. 2116, Combination Pliers, Wire Cutters, 8 1/2 In. 45.00
Pliers, Round Nose, Pexto, No. 250, 5 1/4 In. 20.00
Pliers, Winchester No. 2109, 10 In. 35.00
Plumb Bob, Brass, Steel, 19th Century, 8 1/4 In. 35.00
Plumb Bob, General, No. 800, Solid Brass, Original Container, 12 Oz. 25.00
Rein Rounder, Harness Maker's, Joseph English, Tool.C.1842 .... 75.00
Releading, Winchester, 1894, 7 1/2 In. 95.00
Riveting Tool, Ginn Wall Of S.F., Cast Iron 39.00
Router, Double Pistol, Mockridge & Francis 425.00
Rule, Caliper, Lufkin, No. 014, 4 In. 15.00
Rule, Caliper, Lufkin, No. 372, 2-Fold 20.00
Rule, Folding, Flower Petals At Hinge, 13 1/8 In. 60.00
Rule, Folding, Stanley, No. 36, With Caliper 65.00
Rule, Folding, Stanley, No. 62-1/2, 2 Ft. 50.00
Rule, Marswells, No. 81, Brass Bound 20.00
Rule, Stanley, No. 816, Zigzag, On Card 50.00
Saw, Tenon, Brass, Handle, Alex Mathieson, 19th Century, 10 In. 65.00
Scissors, Bench, Broom Maker 45.00
Scissors, Sheffield, Hudson Bay Company, 19th Century, 9 1/2 In. 50.00
Scraper Blades, Stanley, No. 80 .... 6.00
Screwdriver, Winchester, Hardwood Handle, 7 In. 45.00
Shovel, Tapered, Flared Shovel Head, Iron, Round Handle, 19th Century, 30 x 4 In. 55.00
Slide Rule, Tavella Sales Co., New York, Original Pouch, Copyright 1939, 4 In. 55.00
Spokeshave, Millers Falls, No. 11884, Pat. 30.00
Spokeshave, Stanley, No. 52 .... 17.00
Square, Eagle, South Shaftsbury, No. 14, Vermont Trademark 45.00
Stay Chains, Conestoga Wagon, Forged, 28 1/2 In. 330.00
Swift, Cooper's, 4-In. Blade 95.00
T-Square, Starrett No. 163, Draftsman's, Aluminum Head, 30-In. Blade 75.00
Tobacco Cutting Block, Receptacle For Chopped Tobacco, 5 1/2 In. 350.00
Tongs, Pipe, Wrought Iron, 18th Century, 19 1/2 In. 1450.00
Trammel, Starrett No. 50A, Adjustable, 3-In. Points 35.00
Trough, Iron, 4 Wooden Legs, Painted, Aaron Wissler Brunnerville Foundry, 29 x 26 In. .. 80.00
Turnscrew, For Rope Bed, 18 1/2 In. 154.00
Utility Carrier, Walnut, Dovetailed, Brass Handle 155.00
Vise, Blacksmith 150.00
Watchmaker's, Screwdriver, Tweezer, File, Scale, Case Opener, Mirror, Gauge 35.00
Water Pump, Dempster Of Nebraska, Cast Iron, Black, Gilt Lettering, 1 1/2 In. 28.00
Wheel, Steam Engine, Firehouse Type, Brass Cap, Steel Band, Red, Black, 55 In., Pair ... 220.00
Wheelbarrow, Elm & Maple, Shaped Handles, 1 Wheel, 15 1/2 x 46 1/4 In. 805.00
Wheelbarrow, Painted, Red, Stencil, Jackson Manufacturing Co., Harrisburg, Penn. 195.00
Wick Trimmer, Scissors, Tole Tray, Gold Stenciled Border, Apples & Strawberries, 10 In. 140.00
Wire Nippers, Starrett 30.00
Wrench, Angle, Mephisto, June 23, 1914, 8 In. 85.00
Wrench, Pipe, Winchester, 10 1/2 In. 72.00
Wrench, Universal, 5 In. 55.00
Yarn Winder, Brass, F.A. Leigh & Co., Boston, Mass. 795.00
Yoke, Ox, Wooden, Painted, Yellow, 34 In. 34.00

TOOTHPICK HOLDERS are sometimes called *toothpicks* by collectors.
The variously shaped containers used to hold small wooden toothpicks
are made of glass, china, or metal. Most of the toothpick holders are
Victorian. Additional items may be found in other categories, such as
Bisque, Silver Plate, Slag Glass, etc.

Alligator, Clear, 3 In. 120.00
Beaded Rope Panel, Clear 45.00
Beatty Rib, Blue Opalescent, 1 7/8 In. 90.00
Bull, Figural, 5 Silver Toothpicks Fit In Hole, LSG, Sterling Silver, 3 7/8 In. 220.00
Button Arches, Unadilla, Nebraska, Opalescent 58.00
Buzz Star, Clear 40.00

Daisy & Button, Blue, 1 7/8 In. 50.00
Daisy & Button, Blue, 3 3/8 In. 60.00
Daisy & Button, Kitten On Pillow, Vaseline, 3 1/2 In. 130.00
Daisy & Button, Vaseline, Square, 2 In. 25.00
Delaware, Green, Gold Trim, 2 1/2 In. 30.00
Diamond Spearhead, Vaseline 65.00
Dog With Top Hat, Blue, 3 1/2 In. 80.00
Enameled Brown Sailboats, Satin, C. Vessiere, Nancy, 1 7/8 In. 165.00
Esther, Green, Gold Trim, Riverside Glass Works, 2 1/2 In. 40.00
Falcon Strawberry, Clear 50.00
Florette, Pink Opaque, 2 In. 30.00
Flower & Pleat, Satin 115.00
Frog & Shell, Blue, 2 1/2 In. 70.00
Gonterman Swirl, Adonis, Amber, Footed, 2 1/2 In. 140.00
Inverted Fan & Feather 550.00
Iris With Meander, Green Opalescent 95.00
Jenkin's Grape, Clear 50.00
Minnesota, 3 Handles, Gold Trim, Crystal 125.00
Peacock, Green, Oval, Footed, 2 1/2 In. 110.00
Prince Of Wales, Plumes, Clear 135.00
Priscilla, Crystal 150.00
Rabbit, Basket On Back, Clear, 3 3/8 In. 100.00
Reverse Swirl, Opalescent 225.00
Rooster Head, Blue, 2 1/2 In. 130.00
Ruby Stain, Hot Springs, Arkansas, 1893 .... 20.00
Ruby Stain, Jacksonville, Florida, 1987 .... 30.00
Shell & Seaweed, Pink Cased 185.00
Spearpoint Band, Ruby Stain, 2 3/8 In. 40.00
Victoria, Filigree Cage, Clear 150.00
Wreath & Shell, Blue Opalescent 310.00

TORQUAY is the name given to ceramics by several potteries working near Torquay, England, from 1870 until 1962. Until about 1900, the potteries used local red clay to make classical-style art pottery vases and figurines. Then they turned to making souvenir wares. Items were dipped in colored slip and decorated with painted slip and sgraffito designs. They often had mottoes or proverbs, and scenes of cottages, ships, birds, or flowers. The *Scandy* design was a symmetrical arrangement of brushstrokes and spots done in colored slips. Potteries included Watcombe Pottery (1870–1962); Torquay Terra-Cotta Company (1875–1905); Aller Vale (1881–1924); Torquay Pottery (1908–1940); and Longpark (1883–1957).

TORQUAY

Ashtray, Cottage, Motto Ware, Better To Smoke Here Than Hereafter, 3 1/4 x 5 1/4 In. 45.00
Berry Bowl, Pigeon Blood, Large 195.00
Berry Bowl, Pigeon Blood, Small 50.00
Chamberstick, Motto Ware, Many Are Called But Few Get Up, 3 1/4 In. 65.00
Chamberstick, Scandia, Motto Ware, Dinna Licht Ye Can'le Bouth Ends, 5 1/4 In. 85.00
Chamberstick, Ship, Motto Ware, Guid Nicht An Joy Be Wi Ye, 4 1/4 In. 85.00
Creamer, Coreopsis 125.00
Creamer, Cottage, Motto Ware, Help Yourself To Milk, 3 3/4 In. 65.00
Creamer, Cottage, Motto Ware, Isle Of Wight Back, 3 3/4 In. 75.00
Creamer, Cottage, Motto Ware, Take A Little Milk, 3 x 3 1/4 In. 55.00
Cup & Saucer, Cottage, Motto Ware, Have Another Cup Full, 3 In. 65.00
Cup & Saucer, Cottage, Motto Ware, Think & Be Thankful, 2 5/8 x 3 1/2 In. 65.00
Cup & Saucer, Motto Ware, Black Cockerel, 2 1/2 In. 75.00
Eggcup, Motto Ware, Say Little Bit Think Much, 1 3/4 x 2 3/4 In. 70.00
Hair Receiver, Cover, Motto Ware, Keep Me On The Dressing Table, 3 1/2 x 3 1/2 In. 20.00
Inkwell, Scandy, Motto Ware, 2 x 2 3/4 In. 75.00
Jam Jar, Cottage, Motto Ware, 4 x 3 1/2 In. 55.00
Jam Jar, Cottage, Motto Ware, Go Aisy Wi It Now, 4 1/4 x 3 1/4 In. 65.00
Jam Jar, Cottage, Motto, Help Yourself & Don't Be Shy, 4 In. 65.00
Mug, Cottage, Motto Ware, Have A Little Drink, 2 3/4 In. 55.00
Mustard, Cottage, Motto Ware, I Improve Everything, 2 3/4 x 2 1/2 In. 55.00

Pitcher, Cottage, Motto Ware, Help Yourself, Don't Be Shy, 5 1/4 In. 95.00
Pitcher, Cottage, Motto Ware, If You Can't Be Easy..., 5 1/4 In. 110.00
Pitcher, Motto Ware, Say Well Is Good Do Well Is Better, 4 x 4 In. 125.00
Pitcher, Motto Ware, Stratford On Avon, Help Yourself, Don't Be Shy, 5 1/4 In. 95.00
Plate, Cottage, Motto Ware, To Thine Own Self Be True, 6 1/2 In. 45.00
Sugar, Cottage, Motto Ware, Take A Little Sugar, 3 x 3 1/4 In. 55.00
Sugar, Motto Ware, Black Cockerel, 3 3/4 In. 75.00
Sugar & Creamer, Cottage, Fresh From The Dairy, On Creamer, 2 1/2 In. 75.00

TORTOISESHELL is the shell of the tortoise. It has been used as inlay
and to make small decorative objects since the seventeenth century.
Some species of tortoise are now on the endangered species list, and
old and new objects made from these shells cannot be sold legally.

Box, Domed Lid, Concave Frieze, Ivory Button Feet, Continental, 2 x 4 In. 750.00
Box, Domed Lid, Serpentine Frieze, Ivory Bun Feet, 2 x 4 1/2 x 3 In. 750.00
Box, Fitted Lid, Polychrome, Ivory, Lady, Attendant, 19th Century, 3 In. 635.00
Box, Mother-Of-Pearl Banded Cover, Ivory Footed, England, 1 1/2 x 3 x 2 In. 375.00
Box, Razor, Gold Mounted, 4 Ivorine Straight Razors, c.1905, 7 x 3 x 1 3/4 In. 1150.00
Card Case, Blond Figured, Mid 19th Century, 4 x 2 3/4 In. 200.00
Card Case, Gold Inlay, Initialed Plaque, Victorian, 2 3/4 x 4 1/4 In. 345.00
Card Case, Silver Inlay, Urns, Flowers, Victorian, c.1870, 4 1/4 x 3 1/8 In. 200.00
Coffer, Brass Bound, Rectangular, Cover, Continental, 19th Century, 6 x 9 In. 5290.00
Coffer, Concave Sides, Bun Feet, 1 1/2 x 5 1/2 x 3 3/4 In. 575.00
Desk Set, Brass Inlay, 5 Piece 1680.00
Etui, Gilt Metal, Continental, Round, Engraved Strapwork, 19th Century, 4 In. 1090.00
Etui, Inlaid, 19th Century, 2 3/4 In., 5 1/2 In., 2 Piece 460.00
Jewelry Box, Engraved Bone, 6 Sides, Violets Panel, Dutch, 2 3/4 x 3 1/2 In. 520.00
Tea Box, Domed Lid, Georgian, Ivory Banded, Silver Mounted, 6 x 7 x 3 1/2 In. 3910.00
Tea Box, Georgian, Brass Footed, Oblong, 3 Compartments, 5 x 11 1/2 x 5 In. 2070.00
Tea Box, Georgian, Ivory Banded, Serpentine Front, 3 1/2 x 5 3/4 x 3 1/2 In. 2530.00
Tea Caddy, Hinged Cover, 2 Interior Compartments, 6 x 8 x 5 In. 1495.00
Vase, Honey Amber, Amethyst Rim, Clear Footed, 2 3/8 x 2 In. 190.00

TOY collectors have special clubs, magazines, and shows. Toys are
designed to entice children, and today they have attracted new interest
among adults who are still children at heart. All types of toys are collected. Tin toys, iron toys, battery operated toys, and many others are
collected by specialists. Dolls, Games, Teddy Bears, and Bicycles are
listed in their own categories. Other toys may be found under company
or celebrity names.

ABC's, 21 Cardboard Letter & Picture Discs, Wood Canister, Royal 230.00
Acrobat, Balloonist, Painted Tin, Spring Motor, c.1910, 14 In. 1700.00
Acrobat, Henry, On Metal Trapeze, Windup, 1930s 385.00
Acrobat, Swinging, Carved Torso, Man, Top Hat, Moustache, 4 Wheels, Wood, 10 1/2 In. 50.00
Acrobat, Trapeze, Tin Lithograph, Wyandotte, 9 In. 50.00
Action Figure, Alan Verdon, Planet Of The Apes, Vinyl, 1974, 8 In. 36.00
Action Figure, Bionic Woman, Beauty Salon, Universal City Studios Inc., 1976 . . . . 40.00
Action Figure, Ultraman, Movable Arms, Waist, Red, Silver, Hard Vinyl, Bandai, 6 In. . . . 10.00
Action Figure, Zira, Planet Of The Apes, Vinyl, 1974, 8 In. 30.00
Air-E-Go-Round, Tin, Finger-Powered, 4 Planes, Reeves, Box, 9 3/4 In. 315.00
Airplane, Air Canada, Battery Operated, Stop & Go, Up & Down, 13-In. Wingspan 195.00
Airplane, Air Canada, Tin, Friction, Japan, 17 In. 120.00
Airplane, Air Tower, Windup, Tin Lithograph, Cragston 195.00
Airplane, Army, Windup, Tin, Marx, 7 x 8 x 3 1/2 In. 145.00
Airplane, Biplane, World War I Sopwith Camel, Tin, Kingsbury, 12 x 16 In. 450.00
Airplane, Biplane, Wright Brothers, Tin, Brass Plated, Pilot, J.Ph. Meier, c.1910, 3 In. . . . 600.00
Airplane, Blue, Yellow, Rubber Wheels, Hubley 125.00
Airplane, Bomber, Tin Lithograph, Camouflage Paint, Mechanical, Marx, 18 1/2 In. 275.00
Airplane, Cast Iron, Embossed Champion On Wings, Army Air Corps, 4 1/2 In. 85.00
Airplane, Cast Iron, Wheels, 1930s, 3 1/4 In. 110.00
Airplane, China Clipper, 4-Engine Prop, Pressed Steel, Wyandotte 275.00
Airplane, China Clipper, Chein, 10 1/2 x 11 In. 955.00
Airplane, Civilian Bomber, Clockwork, Tin Lithograph, 2 Lead Cap Bombs 3630.00

Airplane, Dive Bomber, Fireball, Continental Super Flyer, Balsawood, Box, c.1949 ..... 135.00
Airplane, Enola Gay, 4-Engine Prop, Super Fortress, Aluminum, 12 x 16 In. 650.00
Airplane, Flying Tiger, Cargo, Tail Section Opens, Tin, Plastic, Battery, 1960s, 14 1/2 In. . 295.00
Airplane, Friction, Pressed Steel, Red, White, Blue, Gray, Kingsbury, 20 x 18 In. 650.00
Airplane, Friction, Pressed Steel, Rubber Wheels, Red & Yellow, Turner, 28 x 24 In. 750.00
Airplane, Heinkel, Nazi Bomber, Box, 1930s 485.00
Airplane, Heinkel, Nazi Fighter, Box, 1930s 485.00
Airplane, Huckleberry Hound, Pilots WWII Plane, Prop Spins, Linemar, Box, 9 In. 1540.00
Airplane, Lucky Boy, Cast Iron, 9-In. Wingspan 80.00
Airplane, Military, Personnel Carrier, Driver, Tin Lithograph, Windup, Prewar, 12 In. 875.00
Airplane, Monoplane, Decal, Buddy L, 10 In. 695.00
Airplane, Monoplane, Military Green, Tin, Windup, Chein, c.1924, 6 1/2 In. 135.00
Airplane, Northwest Airlines, Friction, Japan, 10-In. Wingspan 275.00
Airplane, Painted Cast Iron, Aluminum, Clacker, Propellers, Pull Toy, 17 In. 2800.00
Airplane, Painted Pressed Steel, Decals, Keystone, 23-In.Wingspan 400.00
Airplane, Pan American, DC-6, Friction, Tin Lithograph, Japan, 1950s, 11 1/2 In. 250.00
Airplane, Pan American, Metal Props Spin, Activated By Tires, Japan, 1950s, 11 In. 545.00
Airplane, Prop, NX130, Pressed Steel, Steelcraft, 22 In. 230.00
Airplane, Propeller, Friction, Linemar, Box 125.00
Airplane, Rollover, Tin, Continental 750.00
Airplane, Rollover, Tin, Marx 225.00
Airplane, Silver, Red Paint, Retractable Landing Gear, Die Cast, Hubley 110.00
Airplane, Sit-N-Ride, Keystone, 24 In. 2420.00
Airplane, Spirit Of America, Tin, Windup, Marx, 1930, 7-In. Wingspan 440.00
Airplane, Spirit Of St. Louis, 2 Extra Engines, Metalcraft 275.00
Airplane, Spirit Of St. Louis, Lindy Embossed On Wings, Cast Iron, 4 In. ....125.00 to 150.00
Airplane, Spirit Of St. Louis, Painted Cast Iron, Lindy, 13-In.Wingspan 1200.00
Airplane, Spirit Of St. Louis, United, Pressed Steel, Electric, 22 In. 1610.00
Airplane, TCA, Tin, Friction, Japan, 1956, 13-In. Wingspan 275.00
Airplane, Transport, Painted Pressed Steel, Buddy L, 6-In. Wingspan 250.00
Airplane, Transport, Pressed Steel, 4 Engines, Buddy L, Box, 27 In. 1650.00
Airplane, Tri-Motor, Cast Iron, Hubley, 1920s, 17-In. Wingspan 3080.00
Airplane, Trimotor Ju-52, Clockwork Powered, Marklin ....1225.00 to 2465.00
Airplane, TWA, Boeing 727, Jet Engine Makes Noise, Box, 10 In. 79.00
Airplane, TWA, Douglas, Twin Prop, Red, Blue, Tin Lithograph, Friction, 1940s, 10 In. ... 250.00
Airplane, Twin Prop, Wood, Green, Red, Wyandotte 300.00
Airplane, UX-166, Painted Cast Iron, Wheels, Propeller, Hubley, 6 In. 130.00
Airplane, Vacation Land Ride, Tin Lithograph, Mechanical, Yone, Japan, 5 1/2 In. 70.00
Airport, 6 Tootsietoy Planes, Radio, Electric, Beacon Light, Marx, 11 x 7 In. 920.00
Alabama Coon Jigger, Tin Lithograph, Painted, Lehmann, 1912, 10 In. ....345.00 to 460.00
Alligator, Paper, 10 Linked Sections, Tin Bracket, Wood Wheels, Wilder Mfg., 17 x 4 In. . 200.00
Ambulance, 1959 Ford, Box, Toy Master, 7 1/2 In. 125.00
Ambulance, Hillclimber, Pressed Steel, Black, Gold Details, 11 In. 250.00
Ambulance, Military, Pressed Steel, Metalcraft, 1930s 450.00
Ambulance, Painted Tin, Friction, Composition Driver, Germany, 11 In. 275.00
Amos, Sparkler, Tin Lithograph, Lever Action, Glass Eyes, Germany, 4 In. 420.00
Amos 'n' Andy, Walker, Tin, Windup, Marx, 1920, 11 1/2 In. 920.00
Animal Express, 3 Coal Cars, Each Marked Bunny Express, Marx, c.1930, 4 In. 935.00
Anticraft Jeep, Army, Driver & Rear Gunner, 1950s 189.00
Aquaplane, Pilot, Helmet, Prop Spins, Passengers, Lithograph, Chein, 9 In. 330.00
Aquaplane, Windup, Chein, Box, 1930s 550.00
Armoire, Doll's, Mahogany, Lift Top, 2 Doors, Base Drawer, Fretwork Crown, 11 x 7 In. . 144.00
Astro Base Space Explorer, Spaceman, Missile, Plastic, Remote Control, Ideal, 20 In. ... 235.00
Astronaut, Moon Man, Walker, Head Moves, Plastic, Box, 1960, 6 In. 275.00
B.O. Plenty, Walker, Windup, Marx 225.00
Baby, Crying, Windup, Celluloid, Japan, 6 In. 57.00
Baking Set, Sunny Suzy, Glass, Wolverine Supply, 14 Piece 95.00
Ballerina, Tin Lithograph, Gyro Operated, Marx, 6 In. 225.00
Balloon Vendor, Monkey Swings, Tin Lithograph, Arm & Eyes Move, 6 1/2 In. 400.00
Banana Joe, Watch Him Go, Tin, Windup, England, Box, 1950s 325.00
Banana Man, Black, Carries Bananas, Windup, Distler, 1920s 900.00
Barney Google, Rides Sparkplug, Tin Lithograph, Clockwork, Nifty, 1920s, 7 In. .330.00 to 975.00
Barney Rubble, Rides Tricycle, Windup, Linemar, Original Box 495.00

Barney Rubble, Windup, Tin, Marx, 3 1/2 In. 195.00
Bartender, Black, Red Coat, With Martini Shaker & Glass, Electric, 12 x 5 In. 11.00
Baseball Batter, Inflatable, Vinyl, 1970s, 8 x 12-In. Envelope 8.00
Be-Bop, Jivin' Jigger, Black Figure, Plastic, Tin Base, On-Off Switch, Marx, 10 In. 195.00
Bears are also listed in the Teddy Bears category.
Bear, Balloon Blowing, Battery Operated, Alps, 1950s 175.00
Bear, Cloth Dressed, Glass Eyes, Red Mouth, Paper Collar, Wheels, Pull Toy, 7 1/4 In. . . . 137.00
Bear, Drummer, Windup, Alps, Japan, Box 125.00
Bear, Jumping Rope, Tin Lithograph, Mechanical, Germany, 4 1/2 In. 40.00
Bear, On Scooter, Red Tin, Spring Motor, Plush Bear, 1950, 6 In. 115.00
Bear, On Wheels, Brown Mohair, Black Bead Eyes, Ear Button, Steiff, 5 1/4 x 6 1/2 In. . . 137.00
Bear, Picnic, Battery Operated, Japan, Box, 1950s 195.00
Bear, Playing Accordion, Tin, Japan, 1950s, 11 1/2 In. 495.00
Bear, Polar, Fishing, Battery Operated, Japan, Box, 1950s, 11 In. 245.00
Bear, Riding Rocking Horse, Wearing Cap, Pants, Windup, Japan, 1950s 75.00
Bear, Shoemaker, Windup, TN Co., Japan, Box 135.00
Bear, Sleeping Baby, Battery Operated, Linemar, Box, 1950s 465.00
Bear, Smoking, Lighted Pipe, Japan, 1950s 145.00
Bear, With Lawn Mower, Tin Lithograph, Cloth Dressed, Mechanical, Japan, 7 In. 100.00
Bear Circus Trainer, Squeeze Toy, Hand Painted 475.00
Bed, Doll's, Brass, 18 x 28 In. 195.00
Bed, Doll's, Brass, 34 In. 45.00
Bed, Doll's, Brass, Mattress, Quilt, Grandmother's Flower Garden Pattern, 29 1/2 In. 45.00
Bed, Doll's, Renaissance Revival, Walnut, Mattress, 19th Century, 24 x 35 x 17 In. 144.00
Bed, Doll's, Walnut, Carved Shaped Headboard, Tulip Footboard, 14 In. 25.00
Bee, Tin, Windup, Marx, 1950s, 5 1/2 In. 95.00
Beetle, Crawling, Windup, Tin Lithograph, Lehmann, Box, 4 1/2 In. 1000.00
Bell Ringer, Banana Boys Seesaw, Cast Iron, c.1905, 6 In. 360.00
Bell Ringer, Camel With Rider, Tin, Painted, Bergmann, 9 In. 5320.00
Bell Ringer, Cart, Horses, Prancing, On Platform, Pull, Cast Iron, c.1895, 6 1/2 In. 1320.00
Bell Ringer, Cart, Pig, Clown Driver, Cast Iron, Gong Bell Mfg., c.1905, 6 1/2 In. 480.00
Bell Ringer, Cart, Swing, Blue, Gold Accents, Cast Iron, c.1890, 9 x 9 1/2 In. 1800.00
Bell Ringer, Centennial, 1776-1876, Cast Iron, Gong Bell Mfg., c.1876, 8 In. 3900.00
Bell Ringer, Chaplin & Mammy, Painted, Cast Iron & Strap Metal, Watrous, 10 In. 410.00
Bell Ringer, Cinderella's Chariot, Gray Horse, Cast Iron, J. & E. Stevens, c.1890, 9 In. 480.00
Bell Ringer, Clown, Painted, Cast Iron & Steel, Watrous, 6 In. 248.00
Bell Ringer, Elephant, 3 Clappers, Tin, c.1880, 9 In. 1920.00
Bell Ringer, Goat, Tin, c.1885, 9 In. 1320.00
Bell Ringer, Goose & Rider, Cast Iron, Gong Bell Mfg., c.1900, 7 In. 1680.00
Bell Ringer, Horse, Tin, Yellow & Orange, Cast Iron Wheels, 7 In. 275.00
Bell Ringer, Jonah & The Whale, Cast Iron, N.N. Hill Brass Co., c.1890, 5 1/2 In. 4200.00
Bell Ringer, Kicking Mule, Cast Iron, Gong Bell Mfg., 8 In. 960.00
Bell Ringer, Landing Of Columbus, Boat, Wheels, Gong Bell, Iron, Gold Finish, 7 In. 345.00
Bell Ringer, Monkey & Coconut, Log, Cast Iron, N.N. Hill Brass Co., c.1905, 6 In. 1560.00
Bell Ringer, Monkey, Running, Holding Bell, Gong Bell Mfg., c.1905, 6 In. 1440.00
Bell Ringer, Pig, Clown Rider, Cast Iron, Gong Bell Mfg., c.1900, 6 In. 840.00
Bell Ringer, Pony & Carriage, Boy Driver, Cast Iron, Gong Bell Mfg., c.1905, 6 1/2 In. . . . 480.00
Bell Ringer, Poodle, Clown Holding Leash, Gong Bell Mfg., c.1890, 8 In. 2280.00
Bell Ringer, Tandem Bicycle, Tin, Painted, Clockwork, 8 In. 5040.00
Bell Ringer, Teddy Bear, Double Clappers, Cast Iron, Gong Bell Mfg., c.1910, 7 1/2 In. . . . 2040.00
Bell Ringer, Teeter-Totter, Boy, Girl, Iron, Nickel Plate, Gong Bell Mfg., c.1875, 7 In. 3600.00
Bell Ringer, Tramp, Alternating Clappers, Cast Iron, Gong Bell Mfg., c.1905, 6 In. 360.00
Bell Ringer, Trick Elephant, Cast Iron, Gong Bell Mfg. Co., 7 3/4 In. 1344.00
Bell Ringer, Trick Pony, Cast Iron, Gong Bell Mfg., c.1903, 8 In. 1560.00
Bell Ringer, Washerwoman, Washtub, Seated Child, Cast Iron, Ives, c.1885, 7 1/2 In. 8400.00
Bell Ringer, Young America, Cast Iron, Gong Bell Mfg., c.1876, 6 In. 1440.00
Bench, Doll's, Modern, Metal & Wooden 13.00
Bench, Doll's, Tree-Branch Style, Woven Seat, 5 1/2 In. 7.50
Bench-Table, Doll's, Blue Paint 20.00
Bicycles that are large enough to ride are listed in their own category.
Billiard Player, Tin, Windup, Germany, 1920s, 6 In. . . . . .210.00 to 242.00
Billiard Table, Mechanical, Tin Lithograph, Ranger Toy, 14 1/2 In. 280.00
Bird, Musical, Tin Lithograph, Mechanical, Kohler, Germany, 7 1/2 In. 30.00

Bird, Pecking, Reticulated, Wood, 13 In. 71.00
Bird, Pip-Squeak, In Cage, Papier-Mache, 6 1/4 In. 330.00
Bird, Pip-Squeak, Yellow, Papier-Mache, 5 1/2 In. 275.00
Blocks, Captain Kangaroo, Wood, Red, Pull Toy, Holgate Toys, 1950s 25.00
Blocks, Nesting, Mother Hubbard's, 10 Cubes, Chromolithographic Scenes, 1889, 7 In. .. 2875.00
Blocks, Pictures Of 6 Different Farm Animals, Hinged Box, 7 1/4 x 5 1/2 In. 70.00
Blondie's Peg Set, Box, 1934, 13 x 9 In. 165.00
Boat, 2 Masts, 4 Life Boats, Flags, Prop Spins, Tin, Windup, Germany, 20 In. 770.00
Boat, 2 Smokestacks, Flag Pole, Lifeboats, Catwalk, Tin, Windup, Fleischmann, 18 In. .. 690.00
Boat, Armada, 10 Boats, Painted Tin, Mechanical, Articulated Movement, Bing, 27 In. 400.00
Boat, Battleship B2, Painted Tin, Steel, Mechanical, Orkin, 38 In. 5000.00
Boat, Battleship, 3 Stacks, Turrets, Cream, Yellow, Blue, Cast Iron, Dent, c.1905, 20 In. ... 1800.00
Boat, Battleship, Painted Steel, Clockwork, Instructions, Sutcliffe, Box, 12 In. 88.00
Boat, Battleship, Red, Silver, Blue Decks, Windup, Tin, Japan, Bandai, 1960s, 15 In. 195.00
Boat, Battleship, USS New York, Clockwork, Searchlights, Davits, Anchors, Orkin, 25 In. 400.00
Boat, Battleship, Windup, Orbor, Germany, 11 1/2 In. 965.00
Boat, Battleship, Wisconsin, Tin, Friction, Box, 1950s, 14 In. 495.00
Boat, Cabin Cruiser, Multicolor, Electric Motor, Ito, Box, 12 In. 230.00
Boat, Cabin Cruiser, Outboard Motor, Roof Lights, Battery Operated, Linemar, 13 In. ... 797.00
Boat, Carrier, Half Track, 10 Composition Soldiers, Elastolin 2875.00
Boat, Cream Top, Off-White Sides, Red Hull, 2 Men, Front Cockpit, Windshield, Lionel . 690.00
Boat, Enclosed Teak Deck, Green Hull, 2 Men, Back Cockpit, Long Key, Stand, Lionel .. 935.00
Boat, Gun, Painted Tin, Mechanical, Carette, Germany, 18 1/2 In. 850.00
Boat, Gun, Windup, Wood, Italy, 14 1/2 In. 150.00
Boat, Hurricane Speed, Tin Lithograph, Plastic Driver, Mechanical, Germany, 8 In. 35.00
Boat, Launch, Steam Power, Zinc Hull, Brass Boiler, Bow Gun, Radiguet, 1890, 16 In. ... 850.00
Boat, Marine Crew, 8 Oars, On Wheels, Iron, U.S. Hardware Co., 14 In. 5925.00
Boat, Miss America, Wood, Steel, Mengel, 1930, 18 1/2 In. 230.00
Boat, Ocean Liner, 2 Stacks, Twin Screw Engine, Dual Clockwork, Liberty, 27 In. 385.00
Boat, Ocean Liner, Painted Tin, Mechanical, Ives, 13 In. 1050.00
Boat, Ocean Liner, Painted, Tin Lithograph, Clockwork, Bing, 6 1/2 In. 230.00
Boat, Ocean Liner, Pressed Steel, Friction, Red & White, Hillclimber, 1920s 250.00
Boat, Ocean Liner, SS United States, Box 495.00
Boat, Ocean Liner, Tin Lithograph, Flywheel Motor, Germany, Box, 8 In. 460.00
Boat, Paddlewheel, Adirondack, White, Yellow, Rocker Arm, Iron, Dent, c.1905, 15 In. .. 1680.00
Boat, Paddlewheel, Natchez, 60 In. 5500.00
Boat, Patrol, Windup, Marusan, Box, 11 In. 395.00
Boat, Pond, 2-Masted, Gaff Rigged Sail, 2 Jibs, 48 Star U.S. Flag, 48 In. 975.00
Boat, Racing, 12 Cylinders, Tin, Windup, Marx, 1940s, 16 In. 400.00
Boat, River, Carette, 15 In. 3895.00
Boat, River, Queen Mary, Smoke Out Of Stack, Passengers, 13 In. 715.00
Boat, Riverboat, Great Swanee, Tin Lithograph, Plastic Cylinders, Friction, 10 1/2 In. ... 150.00
Boat, Riverboat, Side-Wheel, Tin, Spring Motor, Smoke Key, Carette, c.1900, 8 In. 150.00
Boat, Sail, Peggy Ann, Tin Lithograph, Wood Mast, Cloth Sails, Chein, 12 In. 35.00
Boat, Sail, Racing, Wood, Mast Sails, Keystone, Box, 1940s, 19 1/2 In. 90.00
Boat, Single Stack, Windup, Tin, U.S. Zone, Germany 60.00
Boat, Speedboat, Cast Iron, Williams, 4 3/4 In. 275.00
Boat, Speedboat, Inboard, Box, 1950 .... 200.00
Boat, Speedboat, Miss America, Wood Hull, Brass Propeller & Rudder, Mengel, 14 In. .. 75.00
Boat, Speedboat, Tin Lithograph, Clockwork, Lindstrom, 14 In. 187.00
Boat, Steam Launch, Little Pet, Brass, Motor, Propeller, Union Toy, Box, 1885, 12 In. ... 3105.00
Boat, Steam, Atlantic, Tin, Painted, Stenciled Name, Althof, Bergman & Co., 9 3/4 In. ... 6500.00
Boat, Steam, Single Screw, Alcohol Burner, Steerable, Painted, Tin, Zinc, c.1888, 11 In. .. 1300.00
Boat, Submarine, Sea Wolf, Battery Operated, Submersible, Tin, 1950s, 12 In. 495.00
Boat, Submarine, Wood & Metal, Rubber-Band Propulsion, Kingsbury, 13 In. 80.00
Boat, Tanker, Oil, Painted Tin, Clockwork 742.00
Boat, Torpedo, Crank, Friction, Marusan, Box, 11 In. 395.00
Boat, Torpedo, Prop Spins, Engine Noise, Deck Guns, Tin, 11 1/2 In. 285.00
Boat, Windup, Black, Red, White, Tin, U.S. Zone, Germany, 14 In. 69.00
Boat, Windup, Orkin Craft 2950.00
Bobo The Magician, Tin Lithograph, Mechanical, Disappearing Rabbit, 8 In. 95.00
Book, Speaking, Chromolithographed Plates, 9 String-Operated Sounds, Germany 115.00
Bookcase, Doll's, Mahogany, French Books, Glass Door, c.1860, 14 In. 2000.00

Bowl & Pitcher, Doll's, Ironstone 36.00
Bowler, Andy Mill, Sand, Wolverine, 1919, 20 In. 145.00
Box, Fire Alarm, Pressed Steel, Battery Operated, Gong Bell Mfg. Co., 12 In. 143.00
Box, Fire Station, Kingsbury, 9 x 11 In. 675.00
Boxer, Black, Strikes Punching Bag, Bakelite, Tin, Windup, France 375.00
Boxers, Slugger Champions, Tin Lithograph, Windup, Box, 4 x 4 In. 460.00
Boxers In Ring, Rap & Tap, Windup, Strauss, 1920s 450.00
Boxing Gloves, Joe Palooka, Joe Silk-Screened On Each, Harvey Comics, Boy's, 2 Pair .. 220.00
Boy, Naughty, Painted, Tin, Lehmann, Early 20th Century, 5 In. 750.00
Boy, On Handcar, Circular Track, Celluloid & Tin, Clockwork, Japan, 4 1/2 In. 220.00
Boy, On Sled, Flywheel Mechanism, Pressed Steel, 9 In. 600.00
Boy, On Sled, Windup, Germany, 9 1/2 In. 450.00
Boy, On Trike, Celluloid, Tin Lithograph, Clockwork, Kiddy, Tokyo, Japan, 5 1/2 In. 248.00
Boy, On Trike, Windup, Celluloid, Tin, Occupied Japan, 5 In. 34.00
Boy, Peddles 4-Wheel Cart, Lehmann, 1912 .... 395.00
Boy, Plays Banjo, Sways Back & Forth, Tin, Celluloid, Windup, 1920s, 10 In. 250.00
Boy, Riding Bicycle, Kiddy Cyclist, Windup, Red, Blue, White Stripe Shirt, 1941, 9 In. .. 201.00
Boy, With Suitcase, Celluloid, Tin Lithograph, Mechanical, Japan, 8 In. 225.00
Boy, With Suitcase, Celluloid, Tin, Occupied Japan, 4 1/2 In. 46.00
Brontosaurus, Mohair, Yellow, Green, Black Googly Glass Eyes, Steiff, 1960s, 12 1/2 In. 230.00
Bubble Set, Wonder, Box, 1930s, 6 x 6 In. 45.00
Bugs Bunny, Dressed As Uncle Sam, Rubber, Jointed, R. Dakin & Co., 1975, 8 5/8 In. 28.00
Builder Set, Electric, Electrocraft, Box 250.00
Bulldozer, Caterpillar, Painted Cast Iron, Metal Treads, Decal, Arcade, 8 In. 750.00
Bulldozer, Diesel, Painted Cast Iron, Rubber Treads, Arcade, 7 1/2 In. 500.00
Bureau, Doll's, Mahogany Veneer, Empire, Sleigh Front, 2 Over 3 Drawers, 9 x 9 In. 115.00
Bus, Animal, Red, White, Green, 1960s, 10 1/4 In. 135.00
Bus, Animal, Red, Yellow, Blue, Ichiko, 1970s, 12 In. 85.00
Bus, Battery Operated, Door Opens, NGS, Japan, 1950, 20 1/2 In. 275.00
Bus, Camping, Battery Operated, Red & Blue, Ichiko, 1960s, 10 In. 375.00
Bus, Climber, Red, Gold Stripes, Hill, 12 x 7 In. 230.00
Bus, Clutch Mechanism, Rotates Or Lifts, Tin Lithograph, Wolverine, 17 In. 27.00
Bus, Double-Decker, Blue, Gold Stripes, Driver, Cast Iron, Arcade, 7 3/4 x 3 In. 490.00
Bus, Double-Decker, Cast Iron, Red & Green, Driver, Kenton, 10 In. 300.00
Bus, Double-Decker, Driver, Tin Lithograph, Clockwork, Sliding Rear Door, Orobr, 8 In. .. 605.00
Bus, Double-Decker, Interstate, Tin Lithograph, Mechanical, Strauss, 10 1/2 In. 300.00
Bus, Double-Decker, Painted Cast Iron, Decal, Arcade, 8 In. 300.00
Bus, Double-Decker, Windup, Tin Lithograph, 11 In. 240.00
Bus, Double-Decker, Windup, Tin Lithograph, Paya, 9 In. 520.00
Bus, Double-Decker, Windup, Tri-Ang, England, 1950s, 7 1/2 In. 145.00
Bus, Dream, Box, 9 In. 275.00
Bus, Excursion, Bonnet, Japan, 9 1/2 In. 1250.00
Bus, Greyhound Coast-To-Coast, Packard, Lid Opens, Working Steering, Keystone, 27 In. . 687.00
Bus, Greyhound, Clockwork Motor, Ringing Bell, Stoplight, Buddy L, Box, 16 In. 770.00
Bus, Greyhound, Friction, Yonezawa, 17 x 7 In. 950.00
Bus, Greyhound, Great Lakes Exposition 1936, Cast Iron, Rubber Wheels, Arcade, 11 In. .. 625.00
Bus, Greyhound, Scenic Cruiser, White, Blue, Bell Plastics, 18 In. 275.00
Bus, Greyhound, Tin, Windup, Cream, Blue, Kingsbury, 18 In. 450.00
Bus, Greyhound, Windup Motor, Buddy L, Box, 16 1/2 In. 275.00
Bus, Jackie Gleason, Honeymooners, Tin, 1955, 14 In. 350.00
Bus, Lakeshore Lines, Safety Coach, Painted Cast Iron, Fageol, 12 In. 750.00
Bus, Motorbus, Pressed Steel, Buddy L, 1925, 29 In. 2070.00
Bus, Original Orange Paint, Cast Iron, Fageol, 12 In. 316.00
Bus, Rapid Transit Co., People In Windows, Windup, Marx 95.00
Bus, Scenic Cruiser, Tin, Friction, K.T.S., 10 1/2 In. 135.00
Bus, School, VW, Red & Yellow, Ichiko, 1970s, 12 In. 85.00
Bus, School, Yellow, Lithographed Seats, Friction, Japan, Box, 10 In. 375.00
Bus, Seeing New York, Mamma Katzenjammer, Others, 5 Passengers, Kenton 3220.00
Bus, Silver, Cutout Roof, Side, 2 Open Doors, Japan, 1950s, 13 In. 395.00
Bus, Sonicon, Japan, 1950s, 14 1/2 In. 345.00
Bus, Space Sightseeing, Bump & Go Action, Lights, Space Sound, Box, 8 x 12 In. 745.00
Bus, Space, Battery Operated, Lighted Cockpit, Engine, Directional Control, 1950s, 14 In. 1200.00
Bus, Tin Lithograph, Mystery Motor, Wolverine, 14 In. 220.00

Bus, Tin, Silver, Box, MSK, Japan, 13 In. 375.00
Bus, Trailways, White, Red Trim, PMC, 1951, 18 In. 285.00
Bus, Trailways, White, Red, Silver, 1960s, 10 In. 185.00
Bus, Yellow, Flat Nose, Japan, 1950s, 11 In. 120.00
Butcher, In Cart, Pulled By Pig, Windup, Stocke, 1915 .... 650.00
Butter & Egg Man, Tin Lithograph, Windup, 8 In. 575.00
Buzzy Bee, String Antenna, Yellow Wings, Pull Toy, Fisher-Price, 6 x 5 1/2 In. 44.00
Cab, Hansom, Hillclimber, Pressed Steel & Wood, 2 Figures, 11 In. 412.00
Cab, Li-La Hansom, Blue, Lehmann, 1933 .... 1795.00
Cable Car, Passengers, Crank Mechanism, Box, Lehmann, 1928 .... 475.00
Cable Car, San Francisco, Friction Motor, Powell & Madison Streets, 6 1/2 In. 75.00
Cabriolet, Double-Sided, Yellow Stripe, Facing Seats, Sunshade, Doors Open, Tin, 25 In. .. 3200.00
Calliope, Circus, Bell Rings, Cast Iron, Steel, Royal, Hubley, c.1922, 16 In. 3000.00
Canister Set, Doll's, Porcelain, Iridescent, White, Covers, Germany, c.1910, 15 Piece ... 345.00
Cannibal, Head Jumps Around, Plastic, Windup, Daishia, Box, 2 1/2 In. 45.00
Cannon, Barrels & Wheels, Cast Iron, Carbide, 14 In. 80.00
Cannon, Brass & Wood, 25 In. 470.00
Cannon, Field, Wood Firing Pin, Treaded Wheels, Carlin, 15 In. 120.00
Cannon, Quad Pompom Guns, Battery Operated, Remote, Suzuki & Edwards, 12 1/2 In. .. 375.00
Cannon, Twin Pompom, Antiaircraft, Tin Lithograph & Plastic, Marx, Box, c.1961 ...... 200.00
Cap Bomb, Yellow Kid, Cap In Mouth, Cast Iron, 1898, 1 1/2 In. ....185.00 to 200.00
Cap Gun, 2 Boys On Hands & Knees, Single Shot Between Heads, Cast Iron 1250.00
Cap Gun, Boys Brigade, Model A, FA Requath Co., Payton, Ohio 120.00
Cap Gun, Corporal, 9 In. 55.00
Cap Gun, Dyna-Mite, Silver Metal, Celluloid Panel, Nichols, Texas, 3 In. .... *Illus*   50.00
Cap Gun, Lasso 'em Bill, Long Brass Barrel, Accepts Bullets, Kenton, 1923, 9 In. 250.00
Cap Gun, Mare's Laig, Miniature Rifle, Wanted Dead Or Alive, TV Series, Marx, 5 1/2 In. .. 35.00
Cap Gun, Niggerhead, 1887, 4 1/2 In. 1873.00
Cap Gun, Plastic Grips, Daisy, 9 1/2 In., Pair 60.00
Cap Gun, Pluck, Military Flap Style, Leather Holster 75.00
Cap Gun, Senator, 7 In. 50.00
Cap Gun, Trooper Safety, Long Barrel, Cast Iron, Thatched Grip, Logo, c.1920, 10 In. ... 200.00
Cap Gun, Wild West, 11 1/2 In. 135.00
Cap Guns, Holster Set, Deputy Dawg, Hubley, Brown Leather, 2 1/2 x 5 1/2 In. 70.00
Captain Video, Punch Out Figures & Badge, Lido, Box, 1950s 2456.00
Car, African Safari, Plastic Rhinoceros, Corgi, 3 3/4 In. 220.00
Car, Air Flow, Painted Cast Iron, Nickel Grill, Battery Headlights, Hubley, 8 In. 600.00
Car, Andy Gump, Original Paint, Cast Iron, Arcade, 7 In. 1725.00
Car, Armored, Pressed Steel, Friction, Clark, 10 1/2 In. 330.00
Car, Army Command, Soldier, Tin, Friction, Light, Marx, 1950, 20 In. 500.00
Car, Auto Onkel, Windup, Lehmann, 5 In. 57.00
Car, Blondie's Jalopy, Tin Lithograph, Mechanical, Marx, 16 In. 1050.00
Car, BMW Turbo, Automatic, Bump & Go, Taiyo, Box, 9 In. 440.00
Car, Bobby, Crazy, Metal Crank, Japan, 1950s 295.00
Car, Buick Convertible, Disappearing Headlights, Wood, Buddy L, 18 In. 825.00
Car, Buick, Estate Wagon, Blue & Red, Bandai, 1963, 8 In. 85.00
Car, Buick, Marlines, Battery Operated, Green, Marx, 7 In. 69.00
Car, Buick, Station Wagon, Luggage Rack, Headlights, Wood, Buddy L, 17 1/2 In. 3520.00
Car, Builder, Pressed Steel, Original Box, Structo, 15 1/2 In. 1150.00
Car, Bumper, Carnival, Battery Operated, Jouets, Box For Cars, 1950s, 10 x 20 In. 2250.00
Car, Bumper, Carnival, Dodgem, Windup, Irwin Toy Co., Box 245.00

Battery-operated toys should be run regularly to keep the parts working. Remove batteries if storing the toy.

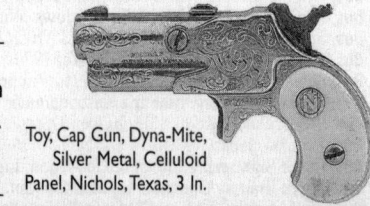

Toy, Cap Gun, Dyna-Mite, Silver Metal, Celluloid Panel, Nichols, Texas, 3 In.

Car, Bumper, Metal, Windup, Canada, 1930s, 6 1/2 In. 120.00
Car, Cadillac, 1951 Model, 2 Doors, Friction, Red Interior, 11 In. 75.00
Car, Cadillac, 1952 Model, Convertible, Robin's-Egg Blue, Friction, 11 1/2 In. 600.00
Car, Cadillac, 1959 Model, Sedan, Huge Rear Fins, Friction, Bandai, 11 In. 225.00
Car, Cadillac, 1961 Model, Tin Lithograph, Friction, Trunk Opens, Japan, 17 In. 475.00
Car, Cadillac, 1965 Model, Blue, Friction, TN Japan, 25 In. 835.00
Car, Cadillac, 1965 Model, Red, Friction, TN Japan, 25 In. 885.00
Car, Cadillac, 1968 Model, Convertible, Shifting Gear, Battery Operated, 10 1/2 In. 200.00
Car, Cadillac, Convertible, Tin Lithograph, Alps, Japan, 11 1/2 In. 195.00
Car, Cadillac, Coupe, Driver, Windup, Marx, 1930s, 11 In. 450.00
Car, Cadillac, El Dorado, 1967 Model, Friction, Ichiko, 28 In. 885.00
Car, Cadillac, Eldorado, Tin, Friction, Japan, 28 In. 495.00
Car, Cadillac, Lapin Plastic, U.S.A., 1950s, 8 1/2 In. 75.00
Car, Cadillac, Metal, Battery Operated, Korea, 13 In. 295.00
Car, Cadillac, Moving Windshield Wipers, Battery Operated, Bandai, 10 In. 225.00
Car, Cadillac, Remote Control Steering, Joustra, Box, 12 1/2 In. 300.00
Car, Cadillac, Sedan, Friction, 2 Rearview Mirrors, Bandai, 13 In. 250.00
Car, Cadillac, Woodie, Toy Town Estate, Rear Doors Open, Wyandotte, 1941, 20 In. 98.00
Car, Carette 50, 4 Riders, Tin Lithograph, Clockwork, Rubber Tires, c.1906, 8 In. 2860.00
Car, Chevrolet Van, Jewel Tea Decal, Green, Pale Green, 1960s, 11 In. 95.00
Car, Chevrolet, 1927 Model, Cast Iron, Black, Gray, Ironman's, 8 In. 495.00
Car, Chevrolet, Impala, Friction, Japan, c.1959, 11 1/2 In. 395.00
Car, Chrysler, Air-Flow, Battery-Operated Headlights, Music Box, Kingsbury, 14 In. 3150.00
Car, Citroen, 1960s, 12 In. 425.00
Car, Citroen, 2CV, Japan, Box, 8 In. 685.00
Car, Constructor, G.P. Type, Cream, Red, Meccano Ltd., 9 1/2 In. 550.00
Car, Convertible, Wood, Painted, Buddy L, 19 In. 1000.00
Car, Corvette, Stingray, Friction, Japan, 8 1/4 In. 245.00
Car, Corvette, Stingray, Sports Coupe, Tin, Red, Headlights, Ichida, Box, 12 In. 440.00
Car, Coupe, Pressed Steel, Clockwork, Metal Hubs, Kingsbury, 9 In. 70.00
Car, Coupe, Pressed Steel, Friction, Schieble, 18 In. 159.00
Car, Coupe, Pressed Steel, Original Paint, 8 In. 143.00
Car, Coupe, Soft Top, Buddy L 1600.00
Car, Coupe, Steel, Clockwork, Electric Headlights, Radio, Vienna Waltz, Kingsbury, 13 In. 990.00
Car, Coupe, Tin, Windup, Red & Cream, Wells, 1933, 8 1/2 In. 120.00
Car, Crash, Motorcycle, White Tires, Red, Cast Iron 109.00
Car, Crazy, Jolly Joe, Tin Lithograph, Clockwork, Marx, 6 In. 385.00
Car, Crazy, Milton Berle, On Trunk, Marx, c.1956, 6 In. 425.00
Car, Crazy, Milton Berle, Windup, Marx, Original Box 550.00
Car, Delivery, Painted Pressed Steel, Buddy L, 12 In. 525.00
Car, Edsel, Citation, Friction, Japan, 13 In. 950.00
Car, Edsel, Ford On Side, Japan, 1958, 9 In. 475.00
Car, Edsel, Tin, Friction, Japan, Box, 1958, 7 1/2 In. 475.00
Car, Examico 4001, Windshield, Schuco, U.S. Zone, Germany 50.00
Car, Fire Chief, Friction Motor & Siren, Wood, Buddy L, 18 1/2 In. 2310.00
Car, Fire Chief, Friction, Japan, 1962, 10 In. 145.00
Car, Fire Chief, Pressed Steel, Battery Operated, Girard, 14 In. 172.00
Car, Fire Chief, Pressed Steel, Windup, Original Paint, Electric Headlights, Hoge, 14 In. ... 373.00
Car, Fire Chief, Tin Lithograph, Mechanical, Courtland, 7 In. 55.00
Car, Fire Chief, Tin Lithograph, Mechanical, Siren, Marx, 11 In. 110.00
Car, Fire Department, Japan, Box, 1930s 75.00
Car, Flintstones, Barney In Stone Age Car, Tin, Friction, Hanna-Barbera, Marx 495.00
Car, Ford Roadster, Painted Tin, Mechanical, Bing, 6 1/2 In. 750.00
Car, Ford, 1920s Model T, Flivver Coupe, Aluminum Spoke Wheels, Buddy L, 11 In. 4070.00
Car, Ford, 1955 Model, Japan, 15 In. 395.00
Car, Ford, Black, Cast Iron, Arcade, 6 1/2 In. 450.00
Car, Ford, Bronco, Red, Black Interior, Movable Windshield, Ny-Lint, 1960, 5 x 10 1/2 In. 15.00
Car, Ford, Center Door, Cast Iron, Arcade, 6 1/4 In. 325.00
Car, Ford, Coupe, Cast Iron, Dent, 6 In. 450.00
Car, Ford, Jalopy, Tin, Windup, Cast Iron Wheels, Marx, 7 In. 235.00
Car, Ford, Model A, Coupe, Cast Iron, Red, Rumble Seat, Arcade, 5 In. 173.00
Car, Ford, Model T, Center Door, 12 In. 635.00
Car, Ford, Model T, Coupe, Black, Dent, 6 In. 325.00

Car, Ford, Model T, Litho Driver, Painted, Running Board, Windup, Tin, Bing, 6 1/4 In. . . .   330.00
Car, Ford, Mustang, Die Cast, Jeweled Headlights, Doors Open, Dinky Toys, 4 1/4 In. 35.00
Car, Ford, Skyline, Battery Operated, Japan, Box, 1958, 9 In. 295.00
Car, Ford, Sunliner, 1960 Model, Visors Over Windshield, Yonezawa, 10 In. 632.00
Car, Ford, With Dog, Metal, Friction, Japan, 8 In. 475.00
Car, General Motors, Convertible, TN, 1950s, 9 1/2 In. 235.00
Car, Graham, Town Car, Tootsietoy 135.00
Car, Grandpa Figure Driving, Litho, Marked E.T. Co., Japan, 5 1/2 In. 220.00
Car, Hillclimber, Pressed Steel, Painted, Flywheel Drive, Cast Iron Man, Girl, 8 In. 460.00
Car, Hot Race, Tin, 2 Race Cars, Technofix, 23 1/2 x 11 1/2 In. 225.00
Car, Hot Rod Dog, Masuya, Box, 9 In. 125.00
Car, Hot Rod, Metal, Die Cast, Renwall, 7 In. 95.00
Car, Hudson, Friction, Tin, Japan, 1950s, 6 In. 495.00
Car, Ice Cream Vendor, Tin Lithograph, Courtland, 6 1/2 In. 160.00
Car, Ito, Driver, Windup, Lehmann, 1914 . . . .   485.00
Car, Jaguar, Blue, 1960s, 9 In. 575.00
Car, Jaguar, Mark II, Convertible, Black With Black Interior, 8 In. 195.00
Car, Jaguar, Metal, Friction, Japan, 1950s, 7 1/2 In. 195.00
Car, Jalopy, Driver, Friction, Tin, Linemar Comics, 5 In. 150.00
Car, Jeep, Military, Tonka, Box, 1964, 10 1/2 In. 145.00
Car, Jeepster, Painted Cast Metal, All Toy, 15 In. 800.00
Car, Joy Rider, Jalopy, Rider's Head Spins, Marx, Prewar, 7 1/2 In. 145.00
Car, LaSalle, Sedan, Wood Red Wheels, White Tires, Hubley, 1939 . . . .   295.00
Car, Lightning Hot-Rod, Battery Operated, Japan, Box 475.00
Car, Limousine, Baron, Cream, Blue, Germany, 13 In. 225.00
Car, Limousine, Battery Operated Headlights, Windup, C.C. & G.P., 10 1/4 In. 315.00
Car, Limousine, Carette, 12 In. 3695.00
Car, Limousine, Ebo Motor, Tin, Painted, 10 In. 1650.00
Car, Limousine, Fisher, Tin, 10 In. 1375.00
Car, Limousine, Tin Lithograph, Black, Driver, Red Trim, Clockwork, c.1910, 16 In. 3360.00
Car, Limousine, Tin Lithograph, Doors Open, Driver, Carette, Germany, 14 In. 900.00
Car, Limousine, Tin Lithograph, Mechanical, Driver, Doors Open, Germany, 11 In. 1500.00
Car, Limousine, Tin, Windup, Gray, Carette, 1908, 12 In. 3000.00
Car, Lincoln Continental, 1958 Model, Convertible, Light Green, Tin, 11 1/2 In. 400.00
Car, Lincoln Continental, Die Cast Metal, Hood & Trunk Open, Dinky Toys, 5 In. 50.00
Car, Lincoln Continental, Mark III, Friction, Tin, Bandai, 12 In.   220.00
Car, Lincoln, Sedan, Pressed Steel, Original Paint, 26 In. 6325.00
Car, M.G., Die Cast, Doepke, U.S.A., 15 In. 295.00
Car, M.P., Moving Gun, Friction, Tin, Japan, 5 1/2 In. 95.00
Car, Mercedes, 220, 4 Door Sedan, Gray, 9 In. 175.00
Car, Mercedes, 360SL Convertible, Friction, Blue, Japan, Box, 8 In. 275.00
Car, Mercedes, 600 Sedan, Tin, Black, Japan, Box, 1950s, 10 In.   450.00
Car, Mercedes, Gull Wing, Tootsietoy, 7 In. 302.00
Car, Mercedes, Metal, Friction, Germany, 1950, 7 1/2 In. 275.00
Car, Mercedes, Space Robot Patrol, Tin, Asahitoy, Box, 8 In. 2090.00
Car, Mercedes, SSK Black Prince, Black, 1930s, 11 In. 1500.00
Car, Mercedes, Stunt Car, Battery Operated, Tin Lithograph, 3 x 7 x 2 In. 75.00
Car, Mercury, 1954 Model, Whitewall Tires, Rock Valley, 9 1/2 In. 1240.00
Car, Mercury, Auto-Trailer, Man & Woman, Rear Doors Open, Tin, 13 In. 670.00
Car, Mercury, Pulls Trailer, Prop Spins, Japan, 1950s, 12 1/2 In.   198.00
Car, MG, Tin, Friction, Open Top, Japan, 1950, 7 1/2 In. 475.00
Car, Old Time, Driver With Cap, Coat, Tin, 1950s 120.00
Car, Old Time, Shaking, Tin, Red, Headlights, Battery Operated, Box 145.00
Car, Packard, 1937 Model, Maroon & Cream, 24 In. 2300.00
Car, Pat & Patachon, Hinged Top, Driver & Passenger, Germany 4950.00
Car, Peugeot, Victoria Coupe, Red, Tan, Whitewalls, Tin, France, 1930s, 14 1/2 In. 1800.00
Car, Phaeton, 4 Doors Open, Side Mount Tire, Goggled Chauffeur, Tin, Windup, 6 In. . . .   435.00
Car, Phaeton, Double, Folding Top, Clockwork Mechanism, Tin Passenger, Driver, 12 In. .   2860.00
Car, Phaeton, Goggled Chauffeur, 4 Doors, Tin, Windup, Orobr, 6 In. 150.00
Car, Phaeton, Oilcloth Cover, Clockwork, Tin Driver, Carette, 12 In. 2860.00
Car, Phaeton, Open, Pewter, Brass, Brake, Lamps, Rubber Tires, Germany, 8 1/2 In. 950.00
Car, Phaeton, Pinard, Silk Upholstery, Windup, Brass, Wood, 1903, 11 x 6 x 5 1/2 In. 3200.00
Car, Phaeton, Silver, Pressed Steel, Clockwork, Driver, Bell Ringing, Kingsbury, 10 In. . . .   470.00

Car, Plastic, Battery Operated, Remco, 19 In. 175.00
Car, Plymouth, Convertible, Tin Lithograph, Friction, Boat & Trailer, Japan, 23 In. 700.00
Car, Police, Cadillac, Metal, Friction, Japan, 1965, 25 In. 495.00
Car, Police, Friction, Tin Lithograph, Japan, Box 250.00
Car, Police, Moving Gun, Friction, Tin, 1950s, 7 In. 120.00
Car, Racing, 2 Seats, Driver, Crank, Tin Lithograph, Clockwork Motor, 1908, 8 3/4 In. 1650.00
Car, Racing, Acrobat Car, Windup, Tin, Occupied Japan, 5 In. 60.00
Car, Racing, Agajanian Special, No. 98, Tin Lithograph, Friction, Yone, Japan, 19 In. 3520.00
Car, Racing, Atom Jet Speedster, Low Slung, Japan 2970.00
Car, Racing, Atom, Tin, No. 153, Japan 1980.00
Car, Racing, Austin, Original Rubber Tires, Cast Iron, 3 3/4 In. 105.00
Car, Racing, Battery Operated, Door Opens, Japan, 11 In. 375.00
Car, Racing, Boat Rail, Driver, Windup, Tin, 6 In. 222.00
Car, Racing, Electro Special, No. 21, Checkered Flag, Yone, Japan 1155.00
Car, Racing, Ferrari, Plastic, Friction Mechanism, 2 1/2 x 5 1/2 x 1/2 In. 12.00
Car, Racing, Ford, GT, Die Cast Metal, Opening Hood & Trunk, Dinky Toys, 3 3/4 In. 35.00
Car, Racing, Golden Arrow, Steel, Spring Motor, Rubber Tires, Kingsbury, 19 1/2 In. 316.00
Car, Racing, Golden Jet, Tin Lithograph, Friction, Bandai, 12 1/2 In. 275.00
Car, Racing, Jaguar, Box, 8 In. 375.00
Car, Racing, Midget, Yonezawa, Box, 7 In. 3200.00
Car, Racing, No. 5, White & Black, Marx 89.00
Car, Racing, Pressed Steel, Clockwork, Headlamps, Wilkens, 8 1/2 In. 187.00
Car, Racing, Red Devil, No. 5, Cast Iron, Hubley, 1920s, 9 1/2 In. 880.00
Car, Racing, Schuco, Box, 4 In. 80.00
Car, Racing, Speedway, Mechanical, Marx, Box 99.00
Car, Racing, Tin Lithograph, Clockwork, Marx, 6 1/2 In. 275.00
Car, Racing, Windup, Red, White, Rubber Wheels, Built-In Key, 4 x 9 1/2 x 2 1/2 In. 18.00
Car, Racing, With Driver, Boat-Tail Type, Cast Iron, Hubley, 6 3/4 In. 250.00
Car, Rambler Wagon, Trailer Hitch, Green & White, Bandai, 1960s, 12 In. 145.00
Car, Renault, Coupe, Painted Tin, Mechanical, France, 11 1/2 In. 300.00
Car, Renault, Roadster, Maroon, Black, Windup, Tin, C.I.J., France, c.1933, 13 In. 1700.00
Car, Roadster, Brown & Green, Steel, Clockwork, Steel Wheels, Kingsbury, 12 1/2 In. 3630.00
Car, Roadster, Cast Iron Driver, Friction, Republic, 11 In. 250.00
Car, Roadster, Delage, JEP, Box 2640.00
Car, Roadster, Flivver, Paint, Red Spoke Wheels, Pressed Steel, Buddy L, 11 In. ...460.00 to 535.00
Car, Roadster, Friction, Tin Driver, Schieble, 12 1/2 In. 132.00
Car, Roadster, Open Coupe, Spare Tire On Trunk, Mettoy, 1930s, 8 In. 250.00
Car, Roadster, Painted Pressed Steel, Friction, Cast Iron Driver, Schieble, 11 1/2 In. 192.00
Car, Roadster, Pressed Steel, Clockwork, Electric Headlights, Kingsbury, 12 1/2 In. 852.00
Car, Roadster, Pressed Steel, Friction, 18 1/2 In. 357.00
Car, Roadster, Pressed Steel, Friction, Cast Iron Driver, Clark, 11 In. 297.00
Car, Roadster, Pressed Steel, Friction, Rubber Tires, 13 In. 341.00
Car, Roadster, Pressed Steel, Schieble, 18 In. 430.00
Car, Roadster, Pressed Steel, Windup, Republic 290.00
Car, Roadster, Rumble Seat, Driver, Orange, Cast Iron, Kilgore, 7 1/2 In. 550.00
Car, Roadster, Rumble Seat, Painted Cast Iron, Reo, 9 In. 925.00
Car, Rubberneck Ducky Farm, Pulling Red Wagon, Express, Driven By Duck 295.00
Car, Sedan, 4 Doors, Windup, Orobr, 1920s, 6 In. 350.00
Car, Sedan, Cast Iron, Arcade, 4 3/4 In. 149.00
Car, Sedan, City Meat Market, Windup, Courtland, c.1940, 7 1/2 In. 250.00
Car, Sedan, Classic 1930 Deluxe Package, Iron, 2-Tone Green, 11 1/2 In. 950.00
Car, Sedan, Model T, Garage, Tin, No Rear Wheels, Bing, 6 1/2 In. 115.00
Car, Sedan, Original Paint, Cast Iron, Arcade, 3 3/4 In. 145.00
Car, Sedan, Painted Tin, Mechanical, Doors Open, 6 1/2 In. 185.00
Car, Sedan, Penny, Tin, Germany, 4 1/4 In. 430.00
Car, Sedan, Skyroof, Pressed Steel, Clockwork, Solid Rubber Tires, Kingsbury, 14 In. ... 1100.00
Car, Sonny Peter, Boy Driver, Balloon, Tin, Windup, Marked West Germany, 5 1/2 In. ... 180.00
Car, Space Explorer, Bump & Go, Astronaut Driver, Crank Friction Motor, KO, Japan ... 295.00
Car, Space Patrol, Flashing Lights, Battery Operated, Japan, Box, 12 In. 1650.00
Car, Space, Robby The Robot Driver, Battery Operated, Nomura, Japan 3170.00
Car, Speedster, Cast Iron, 4 In. 46.00
Car, Speedster, Friction, 2 Cast Iron Figures, Schieble, 11 In. 253.00
Car, Station Wagon, Battery Operated, Wagon & Boat, Box, 5 In. 325.00

Car, Stunt, Rolls Over, Stops, Helmeted Driver, Japan, Box, 7 In. 137.00
Car, Surrey Rider, Battery Operated, Illco, 1970s, 4 x 10 x 5 1/2 In. 24.00
Car, Tin, Tipp, 1930, 12 In. 2495.00
Car, Tin, Windup, Steerable Front Wheels, Doors Open, 12 x 5 3/4 In. 690.00
Car, Tom & Jerry, Battery Operated, Box, 12 In. 495.00
Car, Torpedo, Tin Lithograph, Mechanical, Delage-Jep, France, Box, 13 In. 2400.00
Car, Touring, 1920s Style, Yellow, Tin, Lenox, Germany, 7 1/2 In. 695.00
Car, Touring, 2 Riders, 2 Seats, Tin Lithograph, Clockwork, Gunthermann, 6 In. 522.00
Car, Touring, Chrome Spoke Wheels, Spare, Cast Iron, 7 In. 690.00
Car, Touring, Driver, Hand Enameled, Clockwork, Rubber Tires, Bing, 8 In. 2310.00
Car, Touring, Driver, Tin Lithograph, Clockwork, Gunthermann, 7 In. 358.00
Car, Touring, Heavy Tin, Spoke Wheels, Green, 13 In. 410.00
Car, Touring, Hillclimber, Friction, 2 Cast Iron Figures, 7 In. 440.00
Car, Touring, Lithograph, 4 People, Rubber Tires, 8 In. 3472.00
Car, Touring, Orange, Black, Tin, Windup, Bing, 6 In. 200.00
Car, Touring, Penny, Tin, Germany 316.00
Car, Touring, Pressed Steel, Friction, Driver, Steering Wheel, Clark, 10 1/2 In. 360.00
Car, Touring, Pressed Steel, Wood, Clark, 10 1/4 In. 345.00
Car, Touring, Renault, Embossed, Tin Lithograph, Driver, Side Lamps, Fischer, 8 In. 742.00
Car, Touring, Tin, Clockwork, 4 Figures, Carette, 8 1/4 In. 2860.00
Car, Touring, Tin, Germany, 6 In. 230.00
Car, Town, Driver, Tin Lithograph, Friction, G & K, 5 In. 358.00
Car, Tut Tut, Man In Horseless Carriage, Windup, Lehmann 950.00
Car, Uncle Wiggly, Tin Lithograph, Clockwork, Marx, 7 In. 660.00
Car, Volkswagen, Visible Engine, Battery Operated, Tin, Japan, Box, 1960s, 8 In. 210.00
Car, Volvo, 444, Windup, Brio, Sweden, 1960s, 10 In. 985.00
Car, Whoopee, College Sayings On Car, Spinning Head, Windup, Marx, 7 1/2 In. 115.00
Car, Whoopee, Sheriff Sam, Tin & Plastic, Windup, Marx 275.00
Car, Windup, Tin, Germany, Early 20th Century, 5 1/2 In. 400.00
Car, Winnebago, Pressed Steel, Hard Plastic, Green, White, Tonka, 8 x 22 1/2 x 10 1/2 In. 65.00
Car, Yellow Metal Spoke Wheels, Cast Iron, 5 1/8 In. 55.00
Carousel, Children On 4 Horses, Windup, 1900, 11 In. 950.00
Carousel, Horses, Unicorns, Dogs, Lions, Fringed Canopy, Hand Crank 160.00
Carousel, Swans & Airplane, Windup, Wyandotte, 6 In. 375.00
Carriage, Black Paint, Wood, Folding Hood, 3 Yellow Wheels, 1880s Style, 28 In. 110.00
Carriage, Cabriolet, Horse, Driver, 2 Passengers, Cast Iron, Kenton, c.1905, 15 1/2 In. . . . 4500.00
Carriage, Doll's, Baby Penny, Cloth Cover, Germany 17.00
Carriage, Doll's, Nickel Plated Wheels, Handle & Canopy, Cast Iron, Hubley, 5 1/4 In. . . . 345.00
Carriage, Doll's, Paint, Wood, 4 Wheels, Black Accents, Leatherette Surrey Top, 29 In. . . 80.00
Carriage, Doll's, Streamline, Frankonia 695.00
Carriage, Doll's, Tin, Children Playing, Collapsible Cloth Hood, Long Handle, 11 In. 110.00
Carriage, Doll's, White Wicker, Pulled By Wood Pony, 1870s 5800.00
Carriage, Doll's, Wicker, Clamshell Hood, Heywood Wakefield, 28 x 30 In. 144.00
Carriage, Doll's, Wicker, Natural, Wood Spoke Wheels, Parasol, 28 x 30 In. 230.00
Carriage, Doll's, Wicker, Wood, Upholstered Seat, 26 x 42 In. 58.00
Carriage, Doll's, Wicker, Wood, White, Red Painted Wheels, Turned Handle, 20 x 24 In. . 60.00
Carriage, Doll's, Wood, Brown Paint, Gold Stencils, 3 Wheels, c.1870, 25 x 31 In. 290.00
Carriage, Fire Chief, Horse-Drawn, Removable Driver, Cast Iron, 15 In. 1540.00
Carriage, Gig, Open, Lady's, Horse, Driver, Black, Cast Iron, Shimer, c.1890, 10 In. 1920.00
Carriage, Gig, Stanhope, Cast Iron, Hubley, 1906, 12 In. 1320.00
Carriage, Hansom Cab, Cast Iron, Pratt & Letchworth, c.1890, 11 In. 1080.00
Carriage, Hansom Cab, Walking Horse, Cast Iron, Ives, c.1893, 19 In. 8400.00
Carriage, Horse, Painted, Tin, c.1880, 14 In. 600.00
Carriage, Horseless, Cast Iron Wheels, Driver, Shield, Sheet Metal & Wood, 7 1/2 In. . . . 250.00
Carriage, Phaeton, Horse, Driver, Cast Iron, Pressed Steel, Wilkins, c.1900, 15 In. 1560.00
Carriage, Plated Wheels & Handle, Cast Iron, Kilgore, c.1930, 5 In. 250.00
Carriage, Spoke Wheels, Wooden Carriage, 2 Bench Seats, Saddle, Wood, Pull Toy, 18 In. 1150.00
Carriage, Surrey, 2 Horses, Driver, Lady Passenger, Cast Iron, 11 In. 69.00
Carriage, Surrey, Doll's, Paint, Wood Wheels, Platform Top, Fringe, 1870, 28 x 32 In. . . . 175.00
Carriage, Surrey, One Seat, Cast Iron, Pratt & Letchworth, c.1895, 15 In. 1440.00
Carriage, Surrey, Pulled By Horse, Driver, Passenger, Removable Seat, Dent, 1910, 11 In. . 795.00
Cart, Chester Gump, Original Paint, Cast Iron, Arcade, 7 1/2 In. 400.00
Cart, Chick, Chirping, Articulated Tail, Beak, Holly Leaves, Pull, Cast Iron, c.1890, 5 In. . 3600.00

Cart, Coal, Cast Iron, Says Coal On Side, Kenton, 1930s, 4 1/4-In. Wheels 95.00
Cart, Coal, Pulled By Mule, Driver In Seat, Dent, 1900s, 13 1/2 In. 1000.00
Cart, Dare Devil, Bucking Cowboy, Kicking Zebra, Tin Lithograph, Lehmann, 7 In. 550.00
Cart, Dray, Stake, 2 Black Horses, Cast Iron, Wood, Shimer, c.1900, 26 In. . 840.00
Cart, Horse Drawn, Pulling Covered Wagon, Cast Wheels, Tin Horse, 7 1/2 In. 90.00
Cart, Horse, White, Galloping, Standing Figure, Red, Cast Iron, Carpenter, c.1885, 10 In. . 600.00
Cart, Oxen, Black, Red Trim, Tip, Welker & Crosby, c.1882, 11 In. 720.00
Cart, Pedal, Name Toby Stenciled On Seat Back, 1860s 1095.00
Cart, Pine, 2 Seater, High Wheel, Steel Spoke Wheels, Flip Seat, 36 In. 330.00
Cart, Pony, Black, Cast Iron, Gold Details, Red Wheels, 1 Horse & Driver, Wilkins, 10 In. 425.00
Cart, Sam The City Gardner, With Tools, Windup, Marx, Box 350.00
Cart, Work Horse, Tin Lithograph, Mechanical, Marx, 9 1/2 In. 40.00
Cash Register, Asten, Box, 5 In. 45.00
Cash Register, Money, Receipt Roll, Buddy L, Late 1930s, 10 x 13 In. 770.00
Casper The Friendly Ghost, Vinyl, White, Orange, Plastic Bag, 6 1/2 In. 60.00
Cat, Felix, Button Sew-On Cards, 1959, 7 x 7 1/2 In. 75.00
Cat, Felix, Jointed, Black & White, Leather Ears, Composition, Schoenhut, 8 1/4 In. . *Illus* 358.00
Cat, Felix, On Scooter, Tin Lithograph, Clockwork, Gunthermann For Nifty, 7 In. 770.00
Cat, Felix, Painted, Applied Letters, Chalkware, Red, 13 1/2 In. 605.00
Cat, Felix, Squeak, In Sealed Bag, Irwin, c.1950, 6 1/4 In. 180.00
Cat, Felix, Walking, Tin, Painted, Clockwork, Gunthermann, 6 1/2 In. 358.00
Cat, Mohair, Plush, Recumbent, Excelsior Stuffing, Embroidered, c.1910, 13 In. 200.00
Cat, Papier-Mache, Fur Covered, Upright, Glass Eyes, Lorgnette, Paper Fan, 12 In. 700.00
Cat, Pip-Squeak, Papier-Mache, 3 In. 960.00
Cat, With Ball, Windup, Chein, 1930s 125.00
Catcher, New York Yankees, Celluloid, Occupied Japan, 5 In. 34.00
Cement Mixer, Model, Doepke, 15 In. 230.00
Chair, Doll's, Adirondack, Rush Seat, Old Finish, 12 In. 132.00
Chair, Doll's, Gold Paint, Wooden, Youth Style, Caved Spindles, Ball Accents, 26 In. 15.00
Chair, Doll's, Spindle Back 20.00
Chair, Rocking, Doll's, Oak, Cane Seat & Back, 17 In. 50.00
Charleston Trio, Black Dancer, Boy & Dog, Battery Operated, Box Stage, 1921, 9 1/2 In. 900.00
Charley Weaver, Bartender, Battery, 1962 .... 375.00
Child, On Horseback, Paper Covered Wood & Tin, Push Toy, 7 1/2 x 8 In. 385.00
Child, Swinging, Wooden Platform, Wire Frame, Gibbs, 8 1/2 In. 143.00
Chinese Children, Laundry Tub & Washboard, Chein, 1920s, 2 Piece 195.00
Chuggy, Pop-Up, Fisher-Price, 1950s 200.00
Circus, Chipper Field, No. 200, Trailer, Crane Truck, Land Rover, Cage, Corgi, 4 Piece .. 475.00
Circus, Ring-A-Ling, Ringmaster Center, 4 Animals, Marx, 7 1/2 In. 520.00
Circus, Tin Lithograph, Bear Rings Bell, Seal's Ball Moves, Pull Toy, 10 In. 130.00
Circus Chariot, 3 Horses, Red & Gold Design, Musicians, Lion's Head, Hubley, 10 1/2 In. 950.00
Circus Chariot, Clown, Cast Iron, Painted, 3 Horses, Hubley, 10 In. 1000.00
Circus Chariot, Red, Gold, Yellow Wheels, 3 Horses, Woman Driver, Hubley, 10 1/2 In. . 950.00
Circus Wagon, Cage, Polar Bear, Cast Iron, Pressed Steel, Royal, Hubley, c.1920, 16 In. ... 1680.00
Circus Wagon, Cage, Rhino, Cast Iron, Pressed Steel, Royal, Hubley, c.1920, 16 In. 2400.00
Circus Wagon, Overland, Cage, Pulled By 2 Horses, Driver, Painted, Cast Iron, 14 In. 275.00
Circus Wagon, Overland, Drivers, Bear, Iron, Kenton, 1930s, 14 In. ....565.00 to 695.00

Toy, Cat, Felix, Jointed,
Black & White, Leather Ears,
Composition, Schoenhut, 8 1/4 In.

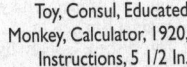

Toy, Consul, Educated
Monkey, Calculator, 1920,
Instructions, 5 1/2 In.

Clown, 2 On Teeter-Totter, Windup 1695.00
Clown, Bimbo, Drumming, Battery Operated, Box 475.00
Clown, Black, Plays Cymbals & Drum, Windup, 1930s, 4 1/4 In. 385.00
Clown, Blinky, Battery Operated, Japan, 11 In. 475.00
Clown, Bobo, Juggling, Tin, Windup, TPS, 5 1/2 In. 936.00
Clown, Bozo, Vinyl, Windup, Dances, Vibrates, Die Cut Box, 4 1/2 In. 55.00
Clown, Cart, Donkey, Tin, Windup, Lehmann, 7 1/2 In. 115.00
Clown, Charlie Drumming, Celluloid Face, Nose Lights, Alps, Box, 10 In. 175.00
Clown, Donkey, Celluloid, Tin Lithograph, Tin Wheels, Clockwork, Japan, Box, 5 In. 248.00
Clown, Drumming, Windup, Japan, 1950s, 7 In. 95.00
Clown, Moves Back & Forth On Donkey, Windup, Gama, Germany, 1930 .... 450.00
Clown, On Roller Skates, Windup, TPS, Box 425.00
Clown, Peddles Unicycle All Directions, Moving Arms, All Tin, Ahi, 6 In. 247.00
Clown, Poodle Jumping Through Hoop, Windup, Tin 325.00
Clown, Riding Unicycle, Sitting, Back & Forth, Peco, Spain, 8 In. 85.00
Clown, Roly Poly, Composition, Brilliant Colors, Musical Base, 10 In. .... 95.00 to 155.00
Clown, Violinist, Windup, Japan, 1950s, 9 In. 295.00
Clown, Windup, Tin, Japan, 6 1/2 In. 75.00
Clown & Darkey, Cast Aluminum, Nickel Plate Gong Bells, Painted, Pull Toy, 3 1/2 In. . . 1500.00
Coach, Doll's, Gilded Wood, Cloth, Lanterns, 3 Dolls, Horse, France, 40 x 16 In. 1250.00
Colorforms, Battlestar Galactica, 13 Punch Out Stand-Ups, 2 Sheets Magic Transfers 12.00
Colorforms, E.T. Dress-Up Set, Board, 24 Plastic Stick-On Pieces 15.00
Concrete, Mixer, Buddy L, 9 1/2 In. 373.00
Construction Set, Clockwork Platform, Graphics Of Race Cars, 6 1/2 x 8 In. 412.00
Consul, Educated Monkey, Calculator, 1920, Instructions, 5 1/2 In. .... *Illus* 259.00
Couch, Doll's, Cast Iron, Arcade, 4 x 8 In. 460.00
Couch, Fainting, Doll's, Red Velvet, Yellow Floral, 17 In. 40.00
Cow, Composition, Brown & White, Glass Eyes, Iron Wheels, Cow Moos, Pull Toy, 8 In. . 338.00
Cow, Holstein, Steer, Black & White Plush, Felt Ears, Glass Eyes, 10 x 15 1/2 In. 220.00
Cow, Wooden Horns, Moos, Tin Wheels, Wooden Base, Pull Toy, Germany, 11 In. 365.00
Cowboy, Galloping Horse, Tin Lithograph, Mechanical, Rocks, Haji, Japan, 7 1/2 In. 35.00
Cowboy, Gun Toting, Fighting Zebra, Tin, Windup, Lehmann, Box, 7 1/2 In. 150.00
Cowboy, Range Rider, Moving Lasso, Gun On Arm, Pinto Horse, Windup, Marx, 9 1/2 In. . 330.00
Cowboy, Whoopee, Windup, Marx, 8 In. 150.00
Cowboy, With Lasso, Windup, Tin, Germany, 6 In. 172.00
Cradle, Doll's, Bleuette, Cardboard, Children, Geese, Flowers, Directions, 1930s, 12 In. .. 225.00
Cradle, Doll's, Pine, Hooded, Square & T-Head Nails, Rockers, 13 x 15 In. 140.00
Cradle, Doll's, Tin, Yellow Flowers, Green Leaves, Bird On Foot, 14 3/4 x 21 1/4 In. 550.00
Crane, 2007, Finger Wheel, Clamp, Doepke 250.00
Crane, Mechanical, Buddy L, Original Box, 24 In. 495.00
Cream Separator, McCormick Deering, Cast Iron, Arcade, 4 7/8 In. 316.00
Creeple Peeple Thingmaker, Electric Unit, 5 Molds, Plastigoop, Mattel, 1964 .... 58.00
Crocodile, Chomping, Tin Lithograph, 1920s, 15 In. 300.00
Crocodile, Crawls, Mouth Opens, Windup, Lehmann 370.00
Cupboard, Doll's, Oak, Spindled Design, With Child's Pewter Tea Set, Victorian, England .. 172.00
Cyclist, Circus, High Wheel Cycle, Bell, TPS, 1956 .... 495.00
Cyclist, Kiddy, Bell Ringing, Tin Lithograph, Unique Art, 1930s, 9 In. .... 150.00 to 475.00
Cyclist, Red Suit, Blue Shoes, 1930, 9 In. 172.00
Dachshund, Moving Head & Tail, Carved & Painted, Pull Toy, 7 x 4 3/4 In. 1725.00
Dagwood, Walker, Celluloid, Clockwork, Japan, 5 In. 138.00
Dancer, Black, Brass Bells, Windup, Mahogany Base, 1800s, 7 In. 2127.00
Dancer, Jackie, Hornpipe, On Boat, Strauss, 1920s 485.00
Dancer, Suspended From Metal Rod, Jumping Board, c.1900, 11 1/2 In. 252.00
Dancer, Tango, Windup, Tin, Gunthermann .... 1150.00 to 1265.00
Dancer, Webb's Jubilee, Jointed Wood, Spring Motor, Walnut Base, 1870, 8 In. 1150.00
Dapper Dan, Coon Jigger, Tin, Windup, Marx, 10 1/2 In. 1090.00
Dennis The Menace, Plays London Bridge Falling Down On Xylophone, Sears, 9 In. 250.00
Diesel Roller, Aveling Barford, With Flat Trailer, Dinky Toys, 1950s 60.00
Digger, Giant Dandy, Buddy L, Original Box, 24 In. 633.00
Dinosaur, T-Rex, Plush, Mohair, Airbrushed, Googly Eyes, Steiff, 1960s, 17 In. 230.00
Dinosaur, T-Rex, Tysus, Mohair, Tan, Googly Eyes, Jointed Arms, Steiff, 8 In. 200.00
Dog, Bonzo The Educated Barking Dog, Windup, Wags Tail, Nods Head, Box 150.00
Dog, Bulldog, Bully, On Wheels, Swivel Head, Button, Voice, Steiff, 1910 .... 1000.00

Toy, Dollhouse,
2 Rooms, Wood,
Keyhole Gable,
Dormer, Chimney,
Bliss, 16 x 10 x 7 In.

Toy, Dollhouse,
4 Rooms,
Balcony, Wood
Frame, Glass
Windows,
22 x 71 x 9 In.

Dog, Bulldog, Growler, Leather Collar, Wheeled Feet, Hinged Mouth, 1890, 18 In. 1350.00
Dog, Bulldog, Growler, Papier-Mache, Wheels, Straw Mane, Leather Collar, 1900, 22 In. . . 3300.00
Dog, Bulldog, Musical, Battery Operated, Japan 495.00
Dog, Bulldog, Papier-Mache, Flocked, Glass Eyes, Pull Along, France, c.1890, 17 In. 1600.00
Dog, Foxy Fido, Paul S. Jones Co., Brockton, Mass., Original Box, 1925, 8 In. 143.00
Dog, Platform, Rider, Jockey Habit, Brown, Red, Yellow, Tin, U.S.A., c.1880, 9 1/2 In. . . 1920.00
Dog, Playing, Windup, Tin, Celluloid, Occupied Japan, 4 In. 25.00
Dog, Wooden Wheels, Stuffed, Brown & White, Steiff, c.1920 . . . . 950.00
Dolls are listed in their own category.
Dollhouse, 2 Rooms Each Floor, Peaked Roof, Chimney, 19th Century, 43 1/2 In. 4465.00
Dollhouse, 2 Rooms, Cottage, Front Porch, Window Boxes, Electrified, Schoenhut 415.00
Dollhouse, 2 Rooms, Wood, Keyhole Gable, Dormer, Chimney, Bliss, 16 x 10 x 7 In. *Illus* 2300.00
Dollhouse, 2 Rooms, Wood, Porch Each Floor, Glass Windows, Gottschalk, 1902, 18 In. . . 1500.00
Dollhouse, 4 Rooms, Balcony, Wood Frame, Glass Windows, 22 x 71 x 9 In. . . . . . . *Illus* 1210.00
Dollhouse, 6 Rooms, English Stockbroker's Tudor, Garage, 24 x 27 x 17 In. . . . . *Illus* 220.00
Dollhouse, 13 Rooms, Electrified, Auto Switches, 41 x 53 In. 460.00
Dollhouse, 2 Story, 2 Rooms, Blue Roof, 2 Porches, Moritz Gottschalk, 18 In. 2500.00
Dollhouse, 2 Story, Blue Roof, Lithograph Paper, Attic Gable Dormer, c.1910, 18 x 12 In. 1200.00
Dollhouse, 2 Story, Clock Tower, Turrets, Stained Glass, Fireplaces, 45 x 26 x 15 In. 8000.00
Dollhouse, 2 Story, Cottage, Wood, Front Porch, Windows, Side Door, 1900-1920, 20 In. . 8500.00
Dollhouse, 2 Story, Folding, Steeped Roof, France, c.1890, 11 1/2 x 8 x 7 In. 900.00
Dollhouse, 2 Story, Lithographed, Porch, Stairs, Schoenhut, 1920, 27 x 23 x 23 In. 2400.00
Dollhouse, 2 Story, Recessed Facade, Cardboard, Gottschalk, 1912, 26 x 30 x 14 In. 2300.00
Dollhouse, 3 Story, Double Elevator, Electricity, Gottschalk, c.1914, 43 x 35 x 14 In. 7250.00
Dollhouse, 3 Story, Mansion, Gutter Style, Side Balconies, c.1890, 28 x 22 x 17 In. 6250.00
Dollhouse, 3 Story, Orphanage, Roof Garden, Double Chimney, Balcony, 52 x 23 x 10 In. 9400.00
Dollhouse, 3 Story, Painted Faux Stone Finish, Interior Staircase, 52 x 46 x 19 In. 4000.00
Dollhouse, Bedroom, Glass Front, 2 Windows, Needlepoint Rug, 25 x 31 In. 4000.00
Dollhouse, Blue Roof, Paper, Elevator, Electricity, Gottschalk, c.1900, 23 x 13 x 10 In. . . 3600.00
Dollhouse, Cottage, Gabled Windows, Window Box, Porch, Gottschalk, c.1921 . . . . 1050.00
Dollhouse, Cottage, Painted Wood, Lift-Off Roof, Lace Curtains, c.1900, 11 x 20 1/4 In. . 495.00
Dollhouse, Dining Room, Newlyweds, Marx, Original Box 258.00
Dollhouse, Duplex, Yard, Steeped Blue Roof, Barn Roofline, c.1910, 16 x 19 x 9 In. 2000.00

Allergic to dust and dust mites? Put old stuffed animals in a sealed plastic bag, then put the bag in the freezer for 24 hours. The temperature will kill the dust mites and the eggs.

Toy, Dollhouse, 6 Rooms, English Stockbroker's
Tudor, Garage, 24 x 27 x 17 In.

Dollhouse, Gable, Turret, Awnings, Balcony, Elevator, Electricity, c.1900, 16 x 10 In. 6750.00
Dollhouse, Garden House, Elaborate Trellis, Bird Bath, Gottschalk, c.1915, 12 x 18 x 9 In. 1300.00
Dollhouse, Georgian Style, Polychrome, Wood, Paperboard, Decorated, 28 x 33 x 16 In. . 1035.00
Dollhouse, Greenhouse Windows, Brass Railing, Bell, Christian Hacker, 31 x 30 x 21 In. . 5000.00
Dollhouse, Kitchen, Faux Marble Sink, Lithograph Floor, Tiles, c.1890, 17 x 32 x 14 In. . 1500.00
Dollhouse, Kitchen, Newlyweds, Marx, Original Box 258.00
Dollhouse, Kitchen, Tin, Accessories, 14 In. 200.00
Dollhouse, Kitchen, Wood, Wallpaper, Cabinets, Doll, Accessories, Germany, 22 x 29 In. . 1380.00
Dollhouse, Knusperhaus, Germany, Box, 1920s, 11 In. 895.00
Dollhouse, Library, Newlyweds, Lithographed, Red Bookcase, Table, Marx 200.00
Dollhouse, Milliner's Shop, Paper Floor, Walls, Gottschalk, c.1912, 8 x 19 x 8 In. 1300.00
Dollhouse, Schoolroom, Stairs, Washroom, Furniture, 6 Dolls, 1920, 12 x 25 x 12 In. . . . 4400.00
Dollhouse, Seaside Residence, Gables, Chimney, Balcony, Bliss, c.1901, 20 x 18 x 10 In. 1600.00
Dollhouse Furniture, Armoire, Buffet, Sewing Table, Chairs, Oak, Schneegas, c.1895 . . . 425.00
Dollhouse Furniture, Bed, Four-Poster, Mahogany, Canopy, Finials, 20th Century 145.00
Dollhouse Furniture, Bed, Oak, Images Of Baby Dolls Headboard, 15 x 16 In. 230.00
Dollhouse Furniture, Bedroom Set, Newlyweds, Original Box, Marx 258.00
Dollhouse Furniture, Chair Set, Cast Iron, Lattice Seat, Stevens, 1870s, 2 1/2 In., 3 Piece 200.00
Dollhouse Furniture, Cradle, Cheese-Cutter Rockers, Cherry, 11 x 19 In. 80.00
Dollhouse Furniture, Crib, Poplar, Shaped Rockers, Headboard, 11 x 16 1/2 In. 302.00
Dollhouse Furniture, Kitchen Sink, Original Paint, Cast Iron, Arcade, 5 7/8 In. 80.00
Dollhouse Furniture, Porch Set, Pressed Cardboard, Woven Wicker, c.1915, 4 Piece 375.00
Dollhouse Furniture, Salon Chair, Gold Leaf Finish, Silk Upholstery, c.1870, 10 In. 175.00
Dollhouse Furniture, Set, Ebony Painted Finish, Lithographed, c.1885, 10 Piece 1000.00
Dollhouse Furniture, Table, Tortoise & Bronze, Florals, Label, 3 In. 550.00
Dollhouse Furniture, Tub, Sink & Toilet, Arcade, 1920s 575.00
Dollhouse Furniture, Tub, Sink & Toilet, China, Japan, Box, 1930s, 3 x 3 In. 35.00
Donkey, Floppy Ears, Stuffed, Red Saddle Blanket, Cast Iron Wheels, Steiff, c.1913 . . . . . 1100.00
Donkey, Wood, Yarn Mane, Leather Harness & Saddle, Pull Toy, 1910, 10 In. 1300.00
Donkey, Wooden Wheels, Papier-Mache, Pull Toy, 7 1/4 x 7 1/4 In. 104.00
Donkey Cart, Tin Lithograph, Mechanical, Marx, 8 In. 60.00
Dray, Iron Horses, Pressed Steel, Clockwork, Iron Driver, Wilkens, 17 In. 74.00
Dray, Spring Driven, Pressed Steel, Iron Driver, Wilkens, 9 In. 165.00
Dresser, Doll's, Oak, 4 Drawers, Mirror, 1890s 175.00
Dresser, Doll's, Poplar, Wire Nail Construction, Mirror, 2 Drawers, 16 x 9 1/2 In. 110.00
Drugstore, Home Town, Marx, Original Box 290.00
Drum, 7 Different Black Children, Rubber Top & Bottom, Carry Lanyard 110.00
Drum Major, Googly Eyes, Tin, Marx, 9 In. 85.00
Drum Major, Windup, Tin, Wolverine, 15 In. 325.00
Drummer, Beats Drum, Slaps Cymbals, Tin Lithograph, Clockwork, Chein, 9 In. 275.00
Drummer, George The Drummer Boy, Crashes Cymbals, Marx, 1930s 160.00
Drummer, Windup, Tin, Linemar, 1961 . . . . 400.00
Dry Sink, Doll's, Open Well, 1 Drawer, Grained Surface, c.1880, 21 3/4 In. 1980.00
Duck, Papier-Mache, Wood, Painted, Pull Toy 785.00
Duck, Strolling, Wings Flap, Windup, Celluloid, Japan, Box 225.00
Dutch Boy & Girl, On Wheeled Platform, Automated, Celluloid, Composition, 11 1/2 In. . 275.00
Dwarf, Puck, Felt, Glass Eyes, Jointed, Stitched Feathers, Mohair Beard, Hat, 1914, 8 In. . 290.00
Easy-Bake Oven, Pans, Kenner, Box, 1970 . . . . 55.00
Electric Motor, 6 Volt, England, 1930 . . . . 95.00
Elephant, Circus, Howdah On Back, Advances & Circles, Windup, Tin, 7 1/2 In. 385.00
Elephant, Circus, Sheet Iron, Head Moves Up & Down, 20th Century, 6 1/2 x 10 In. 650.00
Elephant, Circus, Windup, Tinplate, Japan, Box 215.00
Elephant, Circus, With Whirligig, Balances Ball, Plays Banjo, Windup, Music, 1920s . . . 250.00
Elephant, Gray, Pull Toy, Steiff, 6 x 6 In. 80.00
Elephant, Riding, Felt Blankets, Button Eyes, Cast Iron Wheels, Steiff, c.1920, 38 In. . . . 3300.00
Elephant, Rocking, Painted Papier-Mache 2800.00
Elephant, Teeter Ball, Multiple Actions, Windup, Germany, U.S. Zone, Box, 9 In. 375.00
Elephant, White, Trunk Up, Steiff 26.00
Erector Set, Gilbert, No. 7, Builds Steam Shovel, Wooden Box 395.00
Erie Power Shovel, Classic Construction, No. 88B, Yellow, Maroon, Green, 1993, 12 In. . 1950.00
Etagere, Doll's, Walnut, 3 Shelves, Bronze Finial, c.1875, 16 In. 300.00
Fan, Whizzer, Mechanical, Red, Blue, Plastic, Irwin, Box, 7 In 75.00
Farm Set, Elastolin Type, Cottage, Barn, Stables, Shed, Animals, Platform, 22 x 19 In. . . . 195.00

Farm Set, Stock, Wood Barn, Removable Roof, 6 Pairs Animals, Roosevelt, 19 1/2 In. 345.00
Farm Truck, John's Farm, Battery Operated, Cheeping Chickens, Japan, 1950s, 10 In. 195.00
Fawn, Silvertone Button, Steiff, 5 In. 70.00
Ferdinand The Bull, Marx, Box 495.00
Ferdinand The Bull, Windup, Head Moves, Tail Spins, All Tin, Linemar 250.00
Ferris Wheel, Hercules, Tin, Spring Motor, Bell, Chein, Box, 16 1/2 In. 460.00
Ferris Wheel, Passenger, Clockwork, Pressed Steel, Yellow Cast Iron Seat, 1905, 17 In. .. 2185.00
Ferris Wheel, Tin Lithograph, Clockwork, Chein, Box, 16 In. 302.00
Ferry, Bump & Go, Smokestack Lights, Train Noise, Battery Operated, 14 In. 120.00
Fire House, General Alarm, Marx, Box 1650.00
Fire House, Home Town, Marx 430.00
Fire Patrol, Ladder, Fireman, Steel, Windup, Water Cans, Marx, Box, 1930, 14 In. 1760.00
Fire Pumper, 2 Horses, 2 Figures, Black, Gold, Cast Iron, Ives, c.1895, 16 1/2 In. 2700.00
Fire Pumper, 2 Horses, Cast Iron, Painted, 22 In. 1230.00
Fire Pumper, 3 Horses, 2 Firemen, Dent, 1907, 21 1/2 In. 1395.00
Fire Pumper, 3 Horses, Black, Yellow Paint Steamer, Cast Iron, 10 In. 115.00
Fire Pumper, 3 Horses, Boiler, Cast Iron, 11 1/2 In. 350.00
Fire Pumper, 3 Horses, Cast Iron, Dent, c.1910, 22 In. 4500.00
Fire Pumper, 3 Horses, Cast Iron, Wilkens, 15 In. 175.00
Fire Pumper, 3 Horses, Driver, Cast Iron, 13 1/2 In. 110.00
Fire Pumper, 3 Horses, Painted, Cast Iron, Dent, 21 In. 520.00
Fire Pumper, 3 Horses, Pressed Steel, Wood Bell Ringer, Wilkins Kingsbury, 18 In. 3375.00
Fire Pumper, Aerial Ladder, Pressed Steel, Friction, Tuner, 13 In. 470.00
Fire Pumper, Aluminum Disk Wheels, Nickel Plated Boiler, Buddy L, 1920, 24 In. 1100.00
Fire Pumper, Black, Green & Gold Trim, Wilkins, 1888, 25 In. 10200.00
Fire Pumper, Cast Iron, Hubley, 13 In. 345.00
Fire Pumper, Driver, Cast Iron, Hubley, 13 1/2 In. 850.00
Fire Pumper, Hand Drawn, Brass, Nickel Plate, Weeden, c.1910, 19 In. 1920.00
Fire Pumper, Hillclimber, Pressed Steel, Friction, Cast Iron Driver, 11 In. ....330.00 to 495.00
Fire Pumper, Live Steam, Cast Iron, Tin, Painted, 10 In. 1232.00
Fire Pumper, Packard, Rubber Tires, Keystone, 33 In. 605.00
Fire Pumper, Painted Pressed Steel, Buddy L, 23 1/2 In. 950.00
Fire Pumper, Pressed Steel, Buddy L 630.00
Fire Pumper, Pressed Steel, Clockwork, Iron Driver, Wilkens, 9 1/4 In. 175.00
Fire Pumper, Pressed Steel, Friction, Clark, 14 1/2 In. 240.00
Fire Pumper, Pressed Steel, Push Toy, Schieble, 19 1/2 In. 360.00
Fire Pumper, Pressed Steel, Turner, 15 In. 145.00
Fire Pumper, Rubber Tires, Nickel Grill, Hubley, 8 1/4 In. 90.00
Fire Pumper, Steam, Pressed Steel, Wood, No Driver, Clark, 10 1/2 In. 316.00
Fire Station, 2 Engines, 50 In. 225.00
Fire Station, Aerial Ladder, Pressed Steel, Clockwork, Driver, Kingsbury, 19 In. 2200.00
Fire Station, Car, Truck, Motorcycle, Airplane, Plastic, Hubley, Box, 1950, 12 In. 385.00
Fire Station, Pumper, Tin Lithograph, Bell Rings, Kingsbury, 13 In. 800.00
Fire Station, Toytown, Tin, Wyandotte, 6 1/2 x 8 1/2 In. 195.00
Fire Truck, 3 Aerial Ladders, Painted, Buddy L, 29 1/2 In. 633.00
Fire Truck, Aerial Ladder, Aluminum Wheels, Buddy L, 1920s, 39 In. 1760.00
Fire Truck, Aerial Ladder, Clockwork, Pressed Steel, Kingsbury, 34 In. 2530.00
Fire Truck, Aerial Ladder, Hillclimber, Painted Wood & Steel, Friction, 18 In. 300.00
Fire Truck, Aerial Ladder, Nickel Plated, Rear Bell, Kingsbury, 36 In. 7709.00
Fire Truck, Aerial Ladder, Nickel Wheels, Buddy L, 39 In. 770.00
Fire Truck, Aerial Ladder, Painted Pressed Steel, Keystone, 31 In. 500.00
Fire Truck, Aerial Ladder, Pressed Steel, Friction, 2 Iron Figures, Clark, 19 In. .... 330.00 to 522.00
Fire Truck, Chemical, 2-Tone Slant Design, Hand-Crank Siren, Buddy L, 1949, 25 In. ... 850.00
Fire Truck, Chemical, Clockwork, 2 Ladders, Pressed Steel, Kingsbury, 14 In. 440.00
Fire Truck, Chemical, Ladders, Pump & Siren, Buddy L, Box, 24 In. 1370.00
Fire Truck, Chemical, Pressed Steel, Friction, Republic, 12 In. 120.00
Fire Truck, Chemical, Siren, Buddy L, Box, 1940s, 22 In. 440.00
Fire Truck, Courtland Fire Patrol No. 2, U.S.A., 8 1/2 In. 75.00
Fire Truck, Extension Ladder, 4 Firemen, Windup, Germany, 1930s, 9 1/2 In. 275.00
Fire Truck, Extension Ladder, Pressed Steel, Friction, Schieble, 20 In. 360.00
Fire Truck, Extension Ladder, Rider, Hand-Crank Siren, Buddy L, 1949, 32 1/2 In. 1000.00
Fire Truck, Extension Ladder, Sit & Ride, Siren, Buddy L, Box, 30 In. 470.00
Fire Truck, Fire Tower, Ladders, Keystone, 1920s, 34 In. 1100.00

Fire Truck, Hook & Ladder, Aluminum Wheels, Hose & Nozzle, Buddy L, 28 In 1210.00
Fire Truck, Ladder & Hose Reel, 3 Firemen, Citroen, 1930s, 18 In. 715.00
Fire Truck, Ladder, 5 Riders, Embossed, Tin Lithograph, Clockwork, Distler, 4 In. 385.00
Fire Truck, Ladder, Buddy L, Box, 1930s, 21 1/2 In. 770.00
Fire Truck, Ladder, Hillclimber, Metal, Rear Flywheel Driven, Schieble, 1911, 21 In. 700.00
Fire Truck, Ladder, Hillclimber, White Pressed Steel, Flywheel Drive, 21 In. 375.00
Fire Truck, Ladder, Metal, Motorized, Tools, Accessories, 53 In. 2645.00
Fire Truck, Ladder, Painted Pressed Steel, Friction, Tin Driver, Turner, 13 In. 250.00
Fire Truck, Ladder, Painted, Cast Iron, Hubley, 23 1/2 In. 1870.00
Fire Truck, Ladder, Pressed Steel, Friction, Cast Iron Driver, Green, Clark, 10 In. 110.00
Fire Truck, Ladder, Pressed Steel, Friction, Tin Driver, Schieble, 11 In. 132.00
Fire Truck, Ladder, Steel, Friction Drive, 3 Wood Ladders, Tin Driver, Schieble, 21 In. ... 220.00
Fire Truck, Ladders, Driver, Rubber Tires, Ringing Bell, Cast Iron, Kilgore, 14 In. 800.00
Fire Truck, Packard, Hose & Ladder, Steerable Front, Brass Nozzle, Keystone, 28 In. 460.00
Fire Truck, Packard, Ladder, Pressed Steel, Winch, Keystone, 30 In. 748.00
Fire Truck, Pig, Friction, Japan, 7 In. 175.00
Fire Truck, Pressed Steel, Original Paint, American National, 27 In. 1380.00
Fire Truck, Pressed Steel, Tin Driver, Friction, Republic, 18 In. 170.00
Fire Truck, Red, Blue Fenders, Silver Detail, Cast Iron, Kenton, 22 In. 100.00
Fire Truck, Ride-On, Keystone, 27 In. 170.00
Fire Truck, Sit & Ride, Marx, Box, 32 In. 4400.00
Fire Truck, Structo, 30 In. 375.00
Fire Truck, Tin Lithograph, Friction, Siren, Japan, 17 In. 250.00
Fire Truck, Tin Lithograph, Red, Ladder, Blue Uniform, England, 1930, 15 In. 125.00
Fire Truck, Tin, Rock & Graner, Germany, 1895 .... *Illus* 3280.00
Fire Truck, Water Tower, Aluminum Wheels, Hydraulic, Pump, Buddy L, 1920s, 41 In. .. 3300.00
Fire Truck, Water Tower, Cast Iron, Factory Sample Tag, Dent, c.1925, 12 1/2 In. 5700.00
Fire Truck, Water Tower, Hydraulic, Pump, Buddy L, 1920s, 41 In. 2530.00
Fire Truck, Water Tower, Hydraulic, Pump, Buddy L, 1920s, 46 In. 4180.00
Fire Truck, Water Tower, Pressed Steel, Friction, Schieble, 11 In. 145.00
Fire Truck, Water Tower, Pressed Steel, Friction, Tin Driver, Clark, 19 In. 230.00
Fire Truck, Water Tower, Pressed Steel, Original Decals, Buddy L, 33 In. 2760.00
Fire Truck, Water, Sit & Ride, Non-Electric Headlights, Buddy L, 1933, 41 In. 3630.00
Fire Wagon, Chief's, Cast Iron, Hubley, c.1900, 13 1/4 In. 1560.00
Fire Wagon, Hook & Ladder, 2 Horses, Cast Iron, Painted, Ives, 25 In. 2015.00
Fire Wagon, Hook & Ladder, 3 Horses, 2 Firemen, Open, White, Ladder, Cast Iron, 30 In. 6030.00
Fire Wagon, Hook & Ladder, 3 Horses, Bell, Harris, c.1905, 30 In. 3000.00
Fire Wagon, Hook & Ladder, 3 Horses, Cast Iron, Dent, c.1910, 31 In. 7200.00
Fire Wagon, Hose Reel, 2 Horses, Driver, Late 19th Century, 19 In. 490.00
Fire Wagon, Hose Reel, 3 Horses, Cast Iron, Painted 1232.00
Fire Wagon, Hose Reel, Driver, Articulated, Cast Iron, Welker & Crosby, c.1885, 14 In. .. 3000.00
Fire Wagon, Hose Reel, White & 2 Black Horses, Driver, Fireman, Dent, c.1910, 23 In. .. 5700.00
Fire Wagon, Hose Reel, White Horse, Bell, Driver, Pratt & Letchworth, c.1885, 14 1/2 In. 2700.00
Fire Wagon, Iron Horses & Driver, Pressed Steel, Wilkens, 17 In. 220.00
Fire Wagon, Ladder, 2 Horses, Firemen On Front & Back, Iron, 14 1/2 In. 60.00
Fire Wagon, Patrol, 2 Horses, Driver, Blue, Gold, Cast Iron, Carpenter, c.1885, 17 In. ... 4200.00
Fire Wagon, Patrol, Phoenix, Horses, Ives, 1893, 20 1/2 In. 2395.00
Fire Wagon, Water Tower, 3 Horses, Aerial, Cast Iron, Dent, c.1910, 23 x 30 In. 3600.00
Fireman, Climbing Ladder, Tin Lithograph & Plastic, Marx 215.00

Fisher-Price toys were made of wood from 1931 to 1950. Some plastic was used in the 1950s. By 1964 the toys were almost entirely plastic.

Toy, Fire Truck, Tin, Rock & Graner, Germany, 1895

Fireman, Climbing Ladder, Windup, Tin, Marx, 23 In. 170.00
Fireman, Climbing, Windup, Lithograph, Marx, 9 In. 786.00
Fish, Celluloid, Hinged Mouth, Gobbles Smaller Fish, Marked Rico, c.1940, 6 In. 80.00
Fish, Tropical, Bump & Go As Fish Moves, Japan, 8 In. 495.00
Flip A Ring, Flub-A-Dub, 6 1/2 x 12 In. 75.00
Flying Saucer, Battery Operated, Bump & Go Action, Noise, K.O., Japan 225.00
Flying Saucer, Friction, 2 Spacemen, MT Japan, 1950s, 5 1/2 In. 145.00
Flying Saucer, Sparking, Jako, Box 350.00
Flying Saucer, X1, Lights, Nomura, Box 115.00
Food Packages, Doll Size, Cardboard, Tin, 1930s & 1940s, 8 Piece 500.00
Football Player, Cast Iron, Red & Yellow, Kicking Leg, Sliding Ball Holder, 8 In. 200.00
Football Player, Original Paint, Cast Iron, Steel, 8 x 7 In. 115.00
Fox, Goose In Basket, Schuco 865.00
Frankenstein Monster, Battery Operated, Tin Lithograph, 1950, 12 In. 900.00
Frog Racer, Tin, Windup, Boat Rail Racer, Rubber Tires, Jep France, 14 1/2 In. 435.00
G.I. Joe, Action Pilot, Painted Hair, Orange Jumpsuit, Dog Tags, Box 350.00
G.I. Joe, Action Sailor, Painted Brown Hair, Denim Work Shirt, Navy Blue Pants, Box ... 450.00
G.I. Joe, Action Soldier, Join The G.I. Joe Club, Black Box 1800.00
G.I. Joe, Adventurer, Black 1300.00
G.I. Joe, Air Security, Black AS Radio, Blue AS Helmet, Ammo Pouches 4200.00
G.I. Joe, Battle Tank, Motorized, Box, 1982 .... 175.00
G.I. Joe, British Commando, With American G.I. Joe, Box 4250.00
G.I. Joe, Cobra Commander, Figure, On Card, 1987 .... 60.00
G.I. Joe, Crash Crew Fire Truck, Water Pump, Hose & Nozzle, Jacket 1950.00
G.I. Joe, Green Beret, Uniform, Plastic Beret, 1966 .... 175.00
G.I. Joe, Lady Jaye, Figure, On Card, 1985 .... 185.00
G.I. Joe, Marine Jungle Fighter, Accessories 1650.00
G.I. Joe, Phantom X-19 Stealth Fighter, Box, 1988 .... 295.00
G.I. Joe, Rock & Roll, Figure, 1982 .... 20.00
G.I. Joe, Snake Eyes, With Wolf, Figure, On Card, 1985 .... 375.00
G.I. Joe, State Trooper 600.00
G.I. Joe, Storm Shadow, Figure, On Card, 1984 .... 395.00
Games are listed in their own category.
Garage, 2 Cars, Racer & Town, Clockwork Mechanism, Bing, 6 x 8 In. 220.00
Garage, Cars, Tin, Windup, Schuco, 5 Piece 450.00
Garage, Tin, Bing, 3 x 6 In. 30.00
Gas Pump, Original Paint, Cast Iron, Arcade, 4 1/4 In. 145.00
Gas Pump, Pressed Steel, Gong Bell Co., 13 In. 316.00
Gas Pump Set, Tin Lithograph, Battery-Powered Lights, Marx, 9 1/4 In. 440.00
Giraffe, Ball Playing, T.P.S., Box, 1950s, 8 1/2 In. 295.00
Giraffe, Ivory Mohair, Orange Spots, Glass Eyes, Ear Button, Steiff, 13 1/4 In. 55.00
Giraffe, Mechanical, Seated, Bouncing Ball On Wire, Moving Feet, Tin, Linemar, 9 In. 600.00
Girl, Horse & Cart, Bisque Doll, Mechanical, Pull Toy, Roullet & Decamps, 15 In. 2200.00
Girl, Make-Up, Celluloid, Windup, Occupied Japan, Box 495.00
Girl, Playing Violin, Windup, Celluloid, Occupied Japan, 6 In. 46.00
Girl, Windup, Tin, Lindstrom, 8 In. 140.00
Gnome, On Egg, With Rabbit, Tin, Penny Toy, 3 In. 1760.00
Gondola, Cast Wheels, Clockwork, Passengers Moving, Hubley, 1905, 20 x 11 In. ... 13800.00
Grasshopper, Painted Cast Iron, Aluminum, Wheels, Hubley, 10 In. 600.00
Grocery Store, Boxes, Doors Open, Children Shopping, Awning, Tin, 1930s, 13 In. 490.00
Grocery Store, Home Town, Marx, Original Box 260.00
Guitar, Tin, Nomura, Box, 28 In. 475.00
Gun, Automatic, Sparking, Marx, Box 89.00
Gun, Buffalo Bill, Cast Iron, Nickel Plated, J. & E. Stevens, 8 In. 330.00
Gun, Clicker, Bamboo, Wood Crank, Japan, 8 In. 18.00
Gun, Clicker, Holster, Tin Lithograph, Trigger Guards, Barrels, 1950s 65.00
Gun, Coast Defense, Baldwin Toy Co., Box 150.00
Gun, Cork, Metal, Holster 60.00
Gun, Flying Saucer, Red & Yellow Plastic, Launches 3 Flying Tops, 1950s 35.00
Gun, Pop, Image Of Buck Rogers, Daisy, 1930s, 9 1/2 In. 220.00
Gun, Pop, Sparks Fly Out Of Barrel, Marx, Box, c.1930, 23 In. 150.00
Gun, Rapid Fire, Painted Cast Metal, Brass Barrel, Smith, 14 1/2 In. 310.00
Gun, Six Shooter, Plastic, Ideal, Box, 1950s, 9 In. 20.00

Gun, Sonic Ray, Rotating Color Wheel & Sound, 1950, 7 1/2 In. 95.00
Gun, Space Outlaw Atomic, Planets Embossed Grip, England, Box, 1950s, 10 In. 295.00
Gun, Squirt, Space, Bicycle Attachment, Hard Plastic, Plug On Top, 1 x 3 1/2 x 9 1/2 In. . . 30.00
Gun, Sub-Machine, Pull Back Bolt Action, Pulsating Muzzle, Marx, 1959, 18 In. 125.00
Gun, Waste Space, Launches 4 Darts, Viewing Lens, Plastic, Vinyl Belt, Knickerbocker . . 75.00
Gyroplane, Cast Iron, White Rubber Tires, Nickel Plated Wheels, Hubley, 1930, 4 1/2 In. . 350.00
Ham & Sam, Ham Plays Piano, Rocks, Sam Plays Banjo, Dances, 1921, 7 1/2 In. . . .696.00 to 790.00
Ham & Sam, Tin Lithograph, Windup, Doing Cakewalk, 1921, 6 1/2 In. . . . . .630.00 to 935.00
Hand Car, Barney Rubble & Fred Flintstone, Plastic, Windup, 5 In. 165.00
Hansom Cab, Driver In Back, Top Hat, Pratt & Letchworth, 1888, 13 In. 1950.00
Happy Hooligan, Drum Head, Tin Lithograph, Hand Operated, Kiddies Metal Toy, 10 In. 935.00
Happy Hooligan, Riding Cart, Mule, Cast Iron, Rubber Neck Nodder, Hubley 450.00
Happy Joe, Turn Crank & Happy Joe Dances, Penny Toy, c.1910, 3 1/4 In. 260.00
Harold Lloyd, Walker, Changing Face Mechanism, Tin, Windup, 11 In. 240.00
Helicopter, Emergency, Japan, Box, 1960s 45.00
Helicopter, M*A*S*H, Action Figure Of Hawkeye, Tri-Star International, 1982 . . . . 35.00
Helicopter, Moon Patrol, Lever Lifts Helicopter, NASA Emblem, Marx, Box, 10 In. 150.00
Henry, Acrobat, Celluloid, Wire Swing, Clockwork, Japan, 6 In. 330.00
Hey-Hey Chicken Snatcher, Tin, Windup, 8 1/2 In. 920.00
Hoky Poky, Tin Lithograph, Mechanical, Wyandotte, 6 In. 100.00
Holiday Camp 304, Windup, Technofix, West Germany, Box, 28 In. 475.00
Holster, Bat Masterson, Vinyl, Black, 1960, 4 x 7 1/2 In. 35.00
Holster, Double, Pony Boy, Brown, White, Silver Rivets, Esquire Novelty Co., 1944 . . . . 75.00
Holster & Strap, Police Chief, Leather, Wyandotte, No Gun, Box, 1940s, 7 x 10 In. 75.00
Horse, Black Hide Covered, Harness, Platform, Wheels, 7 x 7 In. 145.00
Horse, Bucking Bronco, Pinto, Riding, Wood, Muslin Blanket, 20th Century, 38 3/8 In. . . 316.00
Horse, Cloth, Saddle, Stirrups, Platform, Cast Iron Wheels, Pull Toy, Germany, 15 In. . . . 546.00
Horse, Faux Leather Harness & Saddle, Wheeled Platform, Pull Toy, c.1900, 9 In. 700.00
Horse, Flat, Leather Harness, Wood Platform, Pull Toy, 1880, 9 In. 325.00
Horse, Gray & Cream, Leather Straps & Stirrups & Ears, Burlap Cover, Pull Toy, 24 In. . . 110.00
Horse, Gray, Carved, Prancing, Wood Platform, Iron Wheels, Pull Toy, 9 1/2 In. 115.00
Horse, Hide Covered, Prancing, Collar & Bridle, Blinders, Pull Toy, 17 In. 395.00
Horse, Hillclimber, Drive Wheel In Back, Sheet Metal, Heads Moves Up & Down, 10 In. 200.00
Horse, Horsehair Mane, Tail, Swing Base, Wood, Carved, Painted, c.1900, 41 In. 750.00
Horse, Horsehair Tail, Leather Saddle, Swing Base, Wood, 14 x 56 In. 960.00
Horse, Horsehide Over Straw-Stuffed Frame, Harness, Platform, Wheels, 41 In. 460.00
Horse, Jumping, Papier-Mache, Wood, Painted, Squeak, 5 x 5 In. 1230.00
Horse, Leather Harness & Saddle, Cast Iron Wheels, Pull Toy, c.1880, 18 In. 700.00
Horse, Leather Saddle, Painted, Cast Iron, Marked Ft. Riley, 7 1/2 In. 220.00
Horse, Papier-Mache & Wood, Pull Toy, 10 x 8 3/4 In. 130.00
Horse, Papier-Mache & Wood, Tin Wheels, Pull Toy, 13 In. 440.00
Horse, Platform, Iron Back Wheels, Wood Front Wheels, Pull Toy, 32 x 35 In. 330.00
Horse, Rocking, Boy Cowboy Rider, Windup, Japan, 1950s 120.00
Horse, Rocking, Brass Eyes, Scrolled Rockers, 19th Century, 20 x 41 In. 1530.00
Horse, Rocking, Derby Rider, Paper Horse, Tin, Bowed Wood, Gibbs, c.1911, 9 In. 1000.00
Horse, Rocking, Papier-Mache & Wood, 7 1/4 x 7 3/4 In. 130.00
Horse, Rocking, Wood, Painted, Stirrups, Saddle, 63 In. 1495.00
Horse, Silk, Brown Eyes, Brown Felt Hooves, Airbrushed Face, Pink Ears, Steiff, 10 In. . . 75.00
Horse, Silver Bells, Flannel Over Wood, Late 19th Century, 3 In. 325.00
Horse, Tin Wheels, Felt Covered Papier-Mache & Wood, Pull Toy, 13 x 13 3/4 In. 265.00
Horse, Wheels, Red Saddle, Leather Ears, c.1930, 20 x 21 In. 225.00
Horse, Wood, Dapple Gray, Leather Saddle, Horsehair, 38 x 32 1/2 x 12 1/2 In. 1650.00
Horse, Wood, Horsehide Ears, Mane, Tail, Glass Eyes, Leather Saddle, Base, 29 x 28 In. . 495.00
Horse & Carriage, Composition, Horse, Rider, Spring Motor, 2 Wheels, Germany, 6 In. . . 175.00
Horse & Wagon, 2 Horses, Black & White, Green Wagon, Kenton, 14 1/2 In. 275.00
Horse & Wagon, 2 Horses, Driver, Tin, Painted, 12 In. 3360.00
Horse & Wagon, 2 Horses, Tin, Plastic, Panel Wagon, Marx, Box, 8 1/2 In. 90.00
Horse & Wagon, 2 Horses, Windup, Tin Lithograph, Driver, Marx, 13 1/4 In. 250.00
Horse & Wagon, 3 Horses, Driver, Barrel, Transfer, Green, Red, Iron, Dent, c.1910, 19 In. 5400.00
Horse & Wagon, Black Driver, 2 Pigs, Cast Iron, 6 In. 250.00
Horse & Wagon, Black Driver, Red, Yellow, Cast Iron, 14 In. 950.00
Horse & Wagon, Driver, Cast Iron, Arcade, 1940, 11 In. 850.00
Horse & Wagon, Farm, Windup, Wolverine, 10 In. 180.00

Horse & Wagon, Red & Blue Paint, Pull Toy, Germany, c.1910 .... 750.00
Horse & Wagon, Victor No. 33, Black Horse, Cast Iron, Ives, c.1890, 9 1/2 In. 2400.00
Horse & Wagon, Windup Horse, Tin, Marx 120.00
Hula Dancer, Black, Windup, Celluloid, Occupied Japan, 6 In. 80.00
Humphrey Mobile, Rolls, Waves Arms & Legs, Tin Lithograph, Wyandote, 7 In. . .420.00 to 747.00
Ice Cream Vendor, Windup, Tin, Built-In Key, Celluloid, Japan, 1940s, 3 x 3 1/2 x 4 In. . . . 65.00
Icebox, Alaska, Arcade, 7 1/2 x 5 3/4 In. 235.00
Icebox, Mary Lu, Tin Over Galvanized Steel, 3 Doors, Latch & Hinge, J.C. Penney, 12 In. 225.00
Indian Picture Craft Kit, 3 Teepee Cutouts, 1934 .... 5.00
Ironing Board, Little Bo Peep, Iron, Tin Lithograph, Wolverine, 1950s 50.00
Jazz Musician, Regent Petrol, Accordion Player In Tuxedo, 4 In. 77.00
Jazzbo Jim, Jigs On Cabin, Holding Banjo, Unique Art, Box, 10 In. .... .695.00 to 852.00
Jeep, American Airlines, Japan, Friction, 10 In. 95.00
Jeep, Army Anti-Aircraft, Driver & Rear Gunner, 1950s 190.00
Jeep, Friction, Tin, K.O., Japan, Box, 1950s, 11 1/2 In. 295.00
Jeep, Jumpin' Jeep, Soldiers, Tin Lithograph, Clockwork, Marx, Box, 6 In. .... .198.00 to 220.00
Jeep, King Star, Tin Lithograph, Male Lion On Roof, Rubber Tires, Hadson, 4 In. 40.00
Jeep, Police, Driver, Bell, 1960s, 8 In. 165.00
Jeep, U.S. Army, Searchlite Trailer, Steel, Marx, 22 In. 400.00
Jeep, Willys Station Wagon, Cast Metal, Painted, 1949, 14 1/2 In. 1375.00
Jeep, Willys, Movable Windshield, Marx, Box, 11 In. 195.00
Jeep, Willys, Searchlight, Trailer, Battery Powered, Instructions, Box, 24 In. 360.00
Jigger, Black, Tin, Mechanical, Lever Action, Wyandotte, 6 1/2 In. 86.00
Jockey, On Horse, Barclay, 1930s 40.00
Jockey, On Horse, Tin, Wheeled, 5-In. Platform 250.00
Joe Penner, Carrying Ducks, Tin, Windup, Tipping Hat, Smoking, 8 In. .... .250.00 to 500.00
Jolly Jumper, Paper On Wood, Plastic Feet, Croak Sound, Fisher-Price, 4 1/2 x 6 In. . *Illus* 66.00
Joy Rider, Tin Lithograph, Humorous Slogans, Erratic Action, Marx, 7 In. 405.00
Katzenjammer, Comic Character, Cast Iron, Mechanical, 3 1/2 In. 40.00
Kazoo, Woody Woodpecker, Kellogg's Cereal Premium, 6 1/2 In. 25.00
Kennel Frolics, Celluloid, Dog On Rod Chases Cat Back & Forth, Tin, Windup, Japan . . . 275.00
Kitchen Set, Pretty Maid, Tin Lithograph, Complete With Smalls, c.1953 .... 450.00
Komikal Kop, Beat It, Tin, Windup, Marx, 1930, 8 In. 750.00
Lamb, Curly, Looped Fabric, Excelsior Stuffing, Shoebutton Eyes, Felt Ears, c.1900, 8 In. 86.00
Lamb, Red Painted Ribbon, Yellow Bell, Wood Base, Tin, Germany, 5 3/4 x 6 In. 247.00
Lamb, White Paint, Black Feet, Pull Toy, 3 x 4 1/4 In. 385.00
Lamb, White Wool Coat, Leather Ears, Pink Ribbon, 6 x 5 3/4 In. 110.00
Lamb, White Wool Coat, Long Tail, Red Paper Collar, Brass Bell, 4 3/4 x 5 In. 110.00
Lamb, Wood Base, Leather Ears, Black Paint Legs & Face, Ribbon With Bell, 8 1/2 In. . . . 137.00
Lawn Mower, Reel Type, Green, Red Decals, Webb, 27 In. 495.00
Li'l Abner Dogpatch Band, Piano, Tin Litho., Clockwork, Unique Art, 1945, 9 In. .460.00 to 495.00
Lincoln Logs, Logs In 8-Wheeled Wagon, Set No. 83-6, Paperwork, Halsam 12.00
Lincoln Tunnel, Tin Lithograph, Clockwork, Unique Art, 1930s, 24 In. .... .300.00 to 450.00
Lion, Roaring, Windup, Alps, Occupied Japan, Box, 1940s, 7 1/2 In. 150.00
Lion Tamer, Schoenhut 225.00
Little Snoopy, Pull Toy, Fisher-Price, 1968 .... 50.00
Locomotive, Riding, Ringing Bell, Black & Red, Keystone, 22 1/2 In. 285.00
Locomotive, Windup, Brass Fixtures, Mechanism Connects Drive Wheels, 10 In. 460.00
Loop-A-Loop, Rocking Action, Wheels, Windup, Tin Litho, Wolverine, 19 In. 500.00
Lop-Ear Louie, Fisher-Price, 1934 .... 385.00
Maggie & Jiggs, Windup, Platform, Runs Back & Forth, Einfalt, Germany, 1920 .... 1050.00
Magic Bubble Pipe, Giant Bubbles, 2 Pipe Set, 1950s, 14 In. 18.00
Mail Cart, Black Driver, Ostrich, Lead Fly Wheel, Mechanical, Lehmann, 1889 .... 850.00
Main Street, Windup, Tin, Marx, 24 In. 172.00
Mammy, Sweeping, Windup, Lindstrom, 8 In. 575.00
Man, Black, On Rocking Chair, Clockwork, Mouth Opens & Closes, 1900 .... 1975.00
Man, Great Billiard Champion, Table, Tin, Windup, K.I. Co., Box, 6 In. 630.00
Man From U.N.C.L.E., Coloring Set, Foto Fantstiks, 1965 .... 25.00
Maxi The Mole, With Shovel, Steiff, 2 Tags, 4 1/2 In. 30.00
Meat Market, Home Town, Marx, Original Box 345.00
Megaphone, S.W.A.T., On Card, 1975, 7 In. 55.00
Merry-Go-Round, Horses, Internal Bells, Tin Lithograph, Clockwork, Box, 11 In. 660.00
Merry-Go-Round, Metal, Friction, Unique Art, 1950s, 10 In. 395.00

Merry-Go-Round, Tin Lithograph, Spring Mechanism, Wolverine, 12 In. 275.00
Merrymakers Band, 4 Mice, Piano, Tin Lithograph, Clockwork, Marx, 9 In. 660.00
Mickey Mouse-Like, Wood, Flexible Arms, Legs, Tail, Performo Toy, 5 In. 85.00
Microscope, Space Patrol, Metallic Green, Black, Adjustable Lens, JVZ Co., 1950s 65.00
Millinery Shop, Contents, Mirror Back, Shelves, Hat Boxes, Flapper Girl, 1890, 32 In. . . . 2900.00
Minstrel, Black, Dances, Holding Accordion, Windup, 1920s 850.00
Minstrel, On Sax, Bangs Drum, Hits Cymbal, Tin, Mechanical, Pull String, 5 In. 405.00
Missile Carrier, Steel, Adjustable, Buddy L, Box, 1958, 15 1/2 In. 375.00
Model, Steam Engine, Marklin, No. 8, 1950 . . . . 1480.00
Model Kit, Airplane, Marklin Constructor, Assembled, 48-In. Wingspan 820.00
Model Kit, Blue Knight Of Milan, Aurora 20.00
Model Kit, Car, Mustang, Box 40.00
Model Kit, Russia's First Spacecraft, Vostok, Gray Plastic, Revell, Box 20.00
Monkey, Acrobatic Marvel, Rocking Platform, Windup, Marx, Box 275.00
Monkey, Baseball Player, Tin Lithograph, Mechanical, Japan, 7 1/2 In. 60.00
Monkey, Batter, Box, Japan 850.00
Monkey, Bear, Jumping Rope, Assahi, Original Box, 5 1/2 x 2 1/4 In. 70.00
Monkey, Bubble Blowing, Battery Operated, Solution, Alps, Box . . . . .80.00 to 150.00
Monkey, Catcher, Japan, Box 1250.00
Monkey, Climbing Palm Tree, Tin Lithograph, 1950s, 18 In. 185.00
Monkey, Crawling, Dress, Pantaloons, Rubber Band Mechanism, Ives, c.1893, 5 1/2 In. . . 1440.00
Monkey, Dancing With Mouse, Schuco 365.00
Monkey, Dog Chases Monkey Up Tree, Friction, Masudaya, Box, 1965 . . . . 425.00
Monkey, Fiddler, Hat Tippers, Mechanical, Cloth-Covered Steel, 1940s, 4 1/2 In. 200.00
Monkey, Jocko, Climbing, Tin Lithograph, Linemar, Box, 5 1/2 In. . . . . .29.00 to 100.00
Monkey, Jocko, Drinking, Battery Operated, Linemar, Japan, Box, 1950s, 9 In. 175.00
Monkey, Lawn Mowing, Windup, Japan, 1950s 296.00
Monkey, Mohair, Glass Eyes, Felt Mask Face, Felt Hands & Feet, c.1940, 18 In. 325.00
Monkey, Mohair, Moves Head, Straw Stuffed, Glass Eyes, Felt Outfit, 9 In. . . . . . .80.00 to 180.00
Monkey, On Motorcycle, Tin Lithograph, Clockwork, Gama, Box, 7 In. 577.00
Monkey, Playing Banjo, Celluloid, Occupied Japan, 8 In. 35.00
Monkey, Rock & Roll, Alps, Box 425.00
Monorail, Tin, Japan, 1950s, 16 In. 95.00
Motorbike, Delivery, RSA, Spain, 1922 . . . . 3004.00
Motorcycle, Arnold 995.00
Motorcycle, Arnold Mac 700, Rider, Tin Lithograph, 1950s, 7 1/2 In. 1400.00
Motorcycle, Autocycle, Windup, Tin, Occupied Japan, 5 In. 345.00
Motorcycle, Camouflage, Tin Lithograph, Clockwork, Sparking Gun, 5 In. 88.00
Motorcycle, Cast Iron, Champ, 7 In. 450.00
Motorcycle, Cast Iron, Green, Hubley, 6 1/2 In. 375.00
Motorcycle, Champion, Cast Iron, Rubber Wheels, 7 In. 220.00
Motorcycle, Champion, Police, Blue Paint, Rubber Tires, Cast Iron, Hubley, 9 In. 145.00
Motorcycle, Champion, Police, Blue, White Tires, Cast Iron, 7 In. 288.00
Motorcycle, Condor, Metal, Windup, Tin Lithograph, I.Y., Japan, Box, 11 In. 2970.00
Motorcycle, Crash Car, White Rubber Tires, Wooden Rims, Cast Iron, Hubley, 4 x 2 In. . . 143.00
Motorcycle, Davidson, Tin Lithograph, Friction, I.Y. Metal Toys, Japan, 15 In. 3400.00
Motorcycle, Embossed, Tin Lithograph, Inertia Drive, Kellermann, 3 3/4 In. 935.00
Motorcycle, Friction, Tin Lithograph, Japan 400.00
Motorcycle, Harley-Davidson, Cast Iron, Spoke Wheels, Decal, Hubley, 8 In. 412.00
Motorcycle, Harley-Davidson, Mailman, Parcel Post, Cast Iron, Hubley, c.1928 . . . . 1560.00
Motorcycle, Harley-Davidson, N.Y., 15 In. 242.00
Motorcycle, Harley-Davidson, Orange, Gold Letters, Cast Iron, Hubley, 6 1/8 In. 230.00
Motorcycle, Harley-Davidson, Original Paint, Cast Iron, Hubley, 5 1/2 In. 316.00
Motorcycle, Harley-Davidson, Sidecar, Policeman, Cast Iron, Hubley, 5 In. 450.00
Motorcycle, Harley-Davidson, Sidecar, Spoke Wheels, Letters On Gas Tank, Hubley, 6 In. 275.00
Motorcycle, Hillclimber, Tin Rider, Technofix, c.1949, 7 In. 295.00
Motorcycle, Indian, Orange Paint, Rubber Tires, Cast Iron, Hubley, 6 x 3 1/2 In. 316.00
Motorcycle, Indian, Sidecar, Cop Rider, Painted, Decals, Hubley, 9 In. 1450.00
Motorcycle, Indian, Traffic, Painted Cast Iron, Rubber Wheels, Hubley, 9 In. 575.00
Motorcycle, Military, Camouflage Painted, Rider, Gun, Metal, Japan, 1950s, 5 1/4 In. 295.00
Motorcycle, Motodrill, Schuco, Box, 5 In. 675.00
Motorcycle, Original Paint, Cast Iron, Hubley, 4 1/4 In. 280.00
Motorcycle, Parcel Post, 3 Wheels, Door Opens, Rider, Cast Iron, 9 12 In. 2420.00

Toy, Jolly Jumper, Paper On Wood, Plastic Feet, Croak Sound, Fisher-Price, 4 1/2 x 6 In.

Toy, Omnibus, Tin, Painted, Embossed, Field & Francis, 21 In.

Motorcycle, Patrol, Green, Uniformed Rider, Rubber Tires, Cast Iron, 6 1/2 In.	258.00
Motorcycle, Police Patrol, Battery Operated, Japan, 1950s, 10 In.	235.00
Motorcycle, Police Squad, Siren Noise, Sparking Headlight, Marx, 8 1/2 In.	1072.00
Motorcycle, Police, Sidecar, Painted Cast Iron, Hubley, 8 1/2 In.	500.00
Motorcycle, Police, Sidecar, Sparking Gun, Tin Lithograph, Clockwork, Levy, 4 In.	330.00
Motorcycle, Police, Steering Mechanism, Lehmann, 5 In.	489.00
Motorcycle, Police, Tin, Friction, Japan, Box, 1960s, 9 In.	120.00
Motorcycle, Police, With Siren, Marx, 1936, 8 1/4 In.	195.00
Motorcycle, Policeman Riding, Cast Iron, Champion, A.C. Williams, 7 In.	245.00
Motorcycle, Rider, Cast Iron, Champion, 1930s, 5 In.	235.00
Motorcycle, Sidecar, Cast Iron, Hubley, 8 1/2 In.	488.00
Motorcycle, Socius, Rider & Passenger, Tin, Kellerman, Repro Box, 6 In.	795.00
Motorcycle, Tin, Spring Motor, No. G.E. 258, Technofix, c.1950, 7 In.	145.00
Motorcycle, U.S. Airmail, Indian, Painted Cast Iron, 9 1/2 In.	1400.00
Mr. & Mrs. Potato Head, Family, Baby With Stroller, General Mills Premium, 1952	335.00
Mr. Dan, The Hot Dog Eating Man, Eats Hog Dog, Wipes Face, Tin Lithograph, 7 In.	150.00
Mr. Fox, The Magician, Bubble Blowing, Tin & Cloth, Battery Operated, 9 1/2 In.	120.00
Mule, Jenny The Balking Mule, Spring Motor, Bearded Rider, Oats Pail, Strauss, 9 1/2 In.	345.00
Mule, Windup, Tin, Cart, Farmer Driver, 3 x 8 x 4 3/4 In.	85.00
Musicians, Windup, Tin Lithograph, Schuco, Pair	295.00
Mystery Alpine Express, Metal, Windup, 1950s, 10 1/2 x 14 1/2 In.	295.00
Mystery Police, Travels In Circle, Arms Steer, Light On Hood, Tin, Japan, 9 1/2 In.	190.00
Newsboy, Rings Bell, Waves Paper, Celluloid Head, Tin Lithograph, Japan, 6 In.	220.00
Noah's Ark, Leather Hinges, Pine, 18 Animals, Noah & Wife, Miniature	410.00
Noah's Ark, Wood, Painted, 30 Figures, 14 x 7 x 5 In.	1250.00
Noah's Ark, Wood, Painted, Lift-Off Roof, Hinged Ramp, Pull Toy	320.00
Noah's Ark, Wood, Painted, Orange Roof, Hull, 20 Figures, 17 In.	546.00
Noah's Ark, Wood, Painted, Red Roof, Green Base, Cloth Hinged Roof, 11 1/4 In.	176.00
Oliver Hardy, Windup, Tin, Plastic, Zorita Co., 9 In.	165.00
Omnibus, Tin, Painted, Embossed, Field & Francis, 21 In.	*Illus* 43000.00
One Man Band, Tin Lithograph, Windup, Harold Lloyd, 7 1/4 In.	3520.00
Operation Airlift, Tin Lithograph, Plastic Airplanes, Automatic Toy Co., 10 In.	120.00
Owl, Silvertone Button, Felt Extremities, Steiff, 4 In.	55.00
Oxen & Wagon, Log Wagon Bed, Man In Seat, Hubley, 1900s, 15 1/2 In.	1795.00
Paddle Wheel, Tin, Painted, Up & Down Pistons, Pull Toy, Daisy, 14 In.	5600.00
Pail, 2 Kittens Playing In Fish Bowl, Tin, 2 In.	20.00
Pail, 3 Cheers Of Red, White & Blue, Tin, T. Cohn Inc.	90.00
Pail, Baby Tigers At Play, Tin, Ohio Art, 1960s	20.00
Pail, Boy & Girl Water Skiing, Tin, Ohio Art	27.00
Pail, Boy & Girl, Dog On Beach, Tin, Eagle Toys Ltd.	50.00
Pail, Children Playing On Beach, Tin	50.00
Pail, Children With Balloons, Tin, Chein	20.00
Pail, Clowns, Tin, Ohio Art, 1940s	75.00
Pail, Couple, Canoeing & Fishing Scene, Lithographed, Tin, General Steel Wares, 11 In.	60.00
Pail, Dutch Kids Playing By Water, Tin, J. Chein & Co.	54.00
Pail, Easter, Swing Handle, Lid, Chick In Egg, Rabbit Policeman, Ducks, Deco, 4 1/2 In.	79.00
Pail, Good Girl, Hearts, Bird & Leaves, Painted Wood, 3 1/2 x 4 1/2 In.	3520.00
Pail, Tin, Little Girl, Good Luck, Yellow, Red, Cover, Wire Bail Handle, Lithograph	310.00
Pail, Wolf & Pig Fishing, Tin	75.00
Paint Set, Mork & Mindy, 3 Different Sets, Craftmaster, Copyright 1979	18.00 to 20.00

Parrot, Pip-Squeak, Spring Head, Felt, 8 1/2 In. 104.00
Parrot, Plastic Tail Feathers, Yellow Beak & Wings, Pull Toy, Fisher-Price, 6 x 5 1/2 In. . 72.00
Parrot, Pretty Peggy, Battery Operated, TN, Japan, Box, 1950s 465.00
Peacock, Tail Fans Out, Walks, Windup, Alps 145.00
Pedal Car, 2-Tone Blue, Red, Steelcraft, 1939, 42 In. 2750.00
Pedal Car, 3 Wheels, 34 In. 2500.00
Pedal Car, Airplane, Commando Air, Bi-Wing, Gendron, 36-In. Wingspan 7700.00
Pedal Car, Airplane, Murray, 47 In. 600.00
Pedal Car, Buick, Roadster, Spoke Wheels, Sidway-Topliff Co., 1929, 52 In. 4220.00
Pedal Car, Chevrolet Bel Air, 1955 Model, Trunk Opens, Padded Seat, Chain Drive, 1958 1700.00
Pedal Car, Chevrolet, Grille, Artillery Wheels, Headlight Pod, Steelcraft, 1930s, 38 In. ... 605.00
Pedal Car, Chevy Roadster, Spare Tire, Chrome Hood Ornament, Jet Flow Drive, 35 In. ... 402.00
Pedal Car, Chrysler, Air Flow, Hood Ornament, Windshield & Horn, Steelcraft, 46 In. ... 1760.00
Pedal Car, Chrysler, Blue, White, Spoked Wheels, Steelcraft, 1941, 39 In. 1980.00
Pedal Car, Chrysler, Fire Chief's, Red & White, Bumpers, Bell, Steelcraft, 1941, 39 In. . 1760.00
Pedal Car, Chrysler, Maroon, White Wheels, Steelcraft, 1946, 37 In. ....1045.00 to 1870.00
Pedal Car, Chrysler, Nickel Plated Grill, Spare, Steelcraft, 48 In. 4950.00
Pedal Car, Chrysler, Windshield, Headlight Pod, Steelcraft, 1941, 37 In. 2200.00
Pedal Car, Columbia 6, Gendron, 50 In. 23100.00
Pedal Car, Fire Truck, Red, Yellow Lining, Pressed Steel, Ladder, Crank, 1910, 80 In. ... 3000.00
Pedal Car, Franklin, Electric Headlights, Running Board, Trunk, Steelcraft, 54 In. 5170.00
Pedal Car, Horse Head, 3 Wheels, Spoke Tires, Flat Wooden Seat, Original Paint, 34 In. .. 2500.00
Pedal Car, Kidillac, Accessories, Garton, 1950, 48 In. 495.00
Pedal Car, Mack Dump Truck, Playboy Trucking Co., Steelcraft, 48 In. 3850.00
Pedal Car, Marmon, Embossed Body Lines, Steelcraft, 48 In. 5220.00
Pedal Car, Oldsmobile, Fire Chief's, Bumper, Bell, Wheel, Steelcraft, 1939, 41 In. 1430.00
Pedal Car, Oldsmobile, Green & White, 1939, 39 In. 2310.00
Pedal Car, Oldsmobile, Red, White, Headlights, Windshield, Steelcraft, 1939, 42 In. 2640.00
Pedal Car, Packard, 2-Tone Green, Red Wheels, Gendron, 54 In. 7700.00
Pedal Car, Packard, Shifting Knob, Blue & Yellow Stripes, American National, 1932 .... 6200.00
Pedal Car, Packard, Stone Guard, Balloon Wheels, American National, 1920s, 45 In. 2530.00
Pedal Car, Painted Graphics, National, 48 In. 9900.00
Pedal Car, Pioneer Willys Knight, Wood-Spoke Wheels, Fenders, Gendron, 1920s, 48 In. .. 7700.00
Pedal Car, Pontiac, Blue, Spoked Steering Wheel, Steelcraft, 1941, 37 In. 1320.00
Pedal Car, Pontiac, Green, Spoked Steering Wheel, Steelcraft, 1941, 37 In. 660.00
Pedal Car, Pontiac, Maroon, White, Hood Ornament, 3 Spokes, Steelcraft, 1941, 36 In. .. 605.00
Pedal Car, Pontiac, Station Wagon, Silver Rail, Maroon & White, 1941 .... 1600.00
Pedal Car, Pressed Steel, Chrome Steering Wheel & Mascot, Purple Paint, 46 In. 402.00
Pedal Car, Streamliner, Windshield, Steelcraft, 1937, 40 In. 1870.00
Pedal Car, Studebaker, Hood Ornament, Spotlight, American National, 54 In. 9900.00
Pedal Car, Studebaker, Lark, Checker Cab, Toll Bridge Free, Chrome Hubcaps, 35 In. ... 258.00
Pedal Car, Supersonic Jet, Medium Blue &silver, Maroon Stripes, Chain Drive, 1950s ... 2150.00
Pedal Car, Tow Truck, Texaco 3277.00
Pedal Car, Train, Locomotive, Ride-On, Erie, Steerable Front, Ringing Bell, 29 In. 330.00
Pedal Car, Wood & Steel, American National, 36 In. 2145.00
Pee-Wee Herman, Scooter, Helmet, Herman Toys Inc., 1988, 10 In. 35.00
Pelican, Plastic Bill & Feet, Paper Over Wood, Pull Toy, Fisher-Price, 8 x 9 In. 50.00
Pencil Tablet, Bullwinkle, Rocky, Fish Underwater, Ruled Pages, 8 x 10 In. 18.00
Pepper The Frog, Rubber, Squeeze, Box, c.1940, 4 3/4 x 7 1/4 x 2 In. 60.00
Periscope, Cardboard Tube, Plastic Ends, Ralston, 1960s, 17 1/2 In. 24.00
Petro Pumps, Oil Bin Set, No. 49, Dinky Toys, Box, 1935 .... 225.00
Piano, Baby Grand, White Paint, Stool, Eli Deluxe Mellowtone, Pa., 19 In. 40.00
Piano, Doll's, Wooden, Harmony, 6 1/2 In. 25.00
Piano, Grand, Internal Xylophone, Bliss, 16 In. 115.00
Piano, Stool, Original Paint, Cast Iron, Arcade 258.00
Piano, Upright, Frincken, 19th Century 560.00
Pig, Beige Flannel, Papier-Mache, Wood Legs, Glass Eyes, Felt Ears, c.1900, 5 1/2 In. ... 403.00
Pig, Happy, With Key, Tin, Chein & Co., 4 3/4 In. 54.00
Pig, Pink, Silvertone Button, Steiff, 4 1/2 In. 60.00
Pig, Running, Mechanical, Tin, Painted, Germany, 5 In. 275.00
Pig, Violinist, Schuco, Box 575.00
Pigeon, Squeak, Windup, Tin, Bavaria, 8 In. 110.00
Planet Of The Apes, Adventure Set, Box 375.00

Planet Of The Apes, Dr. Zanis, Battery Operated, Box 375.00
Plate Set, Alphabet, Children's, Tin, c.1900, 9 Piece 140.00
Play Set, Circus, Clowns, Elephant, Accessories, Delvan, Box, c.1947, 23 x 15 In. 468.00
Playland Sky Ride, Tin Lithograph, Plastic, Mechanical, Yone, Japan, 5 1/2 In. 80.00
Plow, 2 Gang, Cast Iron, Arcade 215.00
Plow, 2 Gang, Hubley 100.00
Pogo Stick, Hoppy The Hopparoo, Flintstones, 1965 . . . . 300.00
Police Station, Home Town, Original Box . . . . .315.00 to 475.00
Policeman, Drunk, Windup, Celluloid, Occupied Japan, 6 In. 100.00
Policeman, State Trooper, Windup, Tin Lithograph, Marx, 1950s, 8 1/2 In. 275.00
Policeman, Stop & Go Sign, Tin Lithograph, Lever Action, USA, 5 1/2 In. 210.00
Policeman, Stop & Go, Safety First, Bell, Celluloid, Tin Litho., Clockwork, Japan, 12 In. . 410.00
Poodle, Jointed Legs, Mohair, Steiff 110.00
Poodle, Mimi, With Bone, Plush, Battery Operated, Nomura, Box 40.00
Poodle, Snobby, Mohair, Button Nose, Glass Eyes, Jointed Head, Legs, Steiff, 8 In. 80.00
Pool Player, 2 Men Alternate Shooting, Tin Lithograph, Clockwork, Wyandotte, 14 In. . . . 440.00
Pool Player, Penny, Tin, Germany, 1920s, 14 In. . . . . .145.00 to 185.00
Porky Pig, With Parasol, Tin Lithograph, Mechanical, Parasol Turns, Marx, 8 In. . .400.00 to 525.00
Porter, Luggage Cart, Windup, Tin Lithograph, 6 1/2 In. 265.00
Porter, With Suitcase, Windup, Occupied Japan 295.00
Powerful Katrinka, Lifts Jimmy Into Wheelbarrow, Windup, Tin, 1920s . . . . . . .1150.00 to 1500.00
Printing Press, Instruction, Printer Journal, Superior, No. 8401, 1946 . . . . 95.00
Projector, Movie, Edison, Mechanical, Box, 11 x 16 In. 55.00
Puss-In-Boots, Mohair, Gray, Plush, Glass Eyes, Jointed, Velvet Boots, c.1912, 11 In. . . . 1093.00
Quilt, Doll's, Star Pattern 35.00
Rabbit, Brown Mohair, Standing, White Shirt, Lederhosen, Glass Eyes, Steiff, 28 In. 140.00
Rabbit, Brown Velvet, Glass Eyes, Metal Spoke Wheels, Pull Toy, 5 1/2 x 7 In. 280.00
Rabbit, Easter, Delivery Cycle, Push Toy, Wyandotte, 1930s 225.00
Rabbit, Hopping, Windup, Chein, 1920s 225.00
Rabbit, Pull & Push Toy, Metro Toy Co., Box 95.00
Rabbit, Pushing Egg, Chein 150.00
Rabbit, Pushing Wagon, Chein 150.00
Rabbits, Running, Push Toy, 34 In. 425.00
Radar Scope, Space Scout, Battery, Tin, Plastic, TV In Chest, Box, 1960s, 9 1/2 In. 285.00
Railcar, Riding, Passenger Seat, Red, Black Paint, Keystone, 1920, 24 In. 315.00
Railway Express, Ride-On, Steerable Front, Sliding Cargo Doors, 23 In. 400.00
Ram, Gilt Horns, Blue Glass Eyes, Papier-Mache, Pull Toy, 16 In. 2650.00
Record Player, Victrola, Tin Lithograph, Germany, 1920s, 5 1/2 In. 210.00
Ring, Spider Woman, Raised Image In Black 20.00
Road Grader, Driver, Cast Iron, Red, Kenton, 7 1/2 In. 225.00
Road Roller, Galion Master, Cast Iron, Nickel Wheels, Wood Roller, Kenton, 5 In. 85.00
Road Roller, Painted Cast Iron, Hubley, 15 In. 600.00
Robot, Action, Plastic, Japan, Box, 10 In. 395.00
Robot, Anime, Superhero, Tin Lithograph, Composition Head, Japan, Box, 1960s, 8 In. . . 800.00
Robot, Blockhead, Action Antenna, Arms, Head, Lights, Yoshiya Chief, c.1959, 11 In. . . . 1300.00
Robot, Change Man, Tin, Battery Operated, 1960s, 11 1/2 In. 4400.00
Robot, Deep Sea, Walks, Rifle, Oxygen Hoses, Windup, Tin, ANJ, 8 In. 1870.00
Robot, Electric, Lightning Bolt On Chest, Brown, Red, Plastic, Marx, 1950s, 14 1/2 In. . . 200.00
Robot, Laughing, Plastic, Japan, Box, 13 In. 595.00
Robot, Lost In Space, Battery Operated, Remco, 14 In. 650.00
Robot, Machine Man, Gang Of 5, Battery Operated, 15 In. . . . . *Illus* 38125.00
Robot, Mr. Atomic, Tin, Battery Operated, Cragstan, Box, 1950s, 11 In. 630.00
Robot, Mr. Mercury, Gold Body, Gray Legs, Red Helmet & Battery Pack, Marx, 13 In. . . 200.00
Robot, Mr. Mercury, Tin Body, Plastic Arms, Battery Operated, Linemar, 13 1/2 In. 345.00
Robot, Planet, Tin, Battery Operated, Remote Control, 9 1/2 In. 330.00
Robot, Radar, Battery Operated, Box, 1950s, 9 In. 1320.00
Robot, Robert, Battery Operated, Talks & Walks, Ideal, Box, 1950s, 13 In. 236.00
Robot, Skirt, Action Head, Eyes, Arms, Tin Lithograph, Yonezowa, c.1964, 10 3/4 In. . . . 1900.00
Robot, Space Explorer, Boy Face, Action, Sparks, Windup, Tin Litho., Yonezawa, 10 In. . 2500.00
Robot, Space Trooper, Tin Lithograph, Windup, Hall, 1965, 6 3/4 In. 700.00
Robot, Space Trooper, Windup, Tin Lithograph, Helmet, Space Rifle, Haji, c.1955, 7 In. . 1100.00
Robot, Spaceman, Mechanical, Walking, Box, 1950s 1200.00
Robot, Spaceman, Porthole, Walks, Laser Rifle, Battery Box, Linemar, 1950s, 8 In. 3500.00

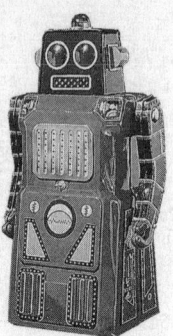

Toy, Robot, Machine Man, Gang
Of 5, Battery Operated, 15 In.

Toy, Robot, Television,
Windup, Box, 1955, 8 In.

Toy, Robot, Train, Giant Sonic, Gang
Of 5, 1955, 15 1/2 In.

Robot, Spaceman, Smoking, Tin, Battery Operated, Linemar, Box, 1950s, 12 In. 1650.00 to 2200.00
Robot, Sparky, Walking Action, Tin, Windup, Box, 8 In. . . . . .695.00 to 742.00
Robot, Television, Windup, Box, 1955, 8 In. . . . . *Illus* 24900.00
Robot, Tin, Plastic, Battery, Walks, Arms Swing, Lights Up, Japan, 1960s, 4 x 5 x 11 In. . . 345.00
Robot, Train, Giant Sonic, Gang Of 5, 1955, 15 1/2 In. *Illus* 6600.00
Robot, Walks, Bump & Go Action, Electrons Spin Light, Tin, Battery Operated, 11 In. . . . 2860.00
Robot, Walks, Stops, Head Opens Up Like Flower, Radar Screen, Japan, Box, 12 1/2 In. . 2090.00
Robot, Zoomer, Walks As Eyes Light, Holding Wrench, Battery Operated, Japan, 8 In. . . . 1480.00
Rocket, Fighter, Tin, Windup, Marx, 1930s 225.00
Rocket Ranger, Windup, Post War 255.00
Rocket Ride, Passengers, Moves Around Tower, Windup, Chein, 18 In. . . . . .575.00 to 750.00
Rocket Ship, Apollo, Spaceman, Tin Litho., Pop-Up Action, Japan, Box, 1960s, 16 In. . . . 160.00
Rocket Ship, Space Cruiser X300, Japan, 1955 . . . . *Illus* 9600.00
Rocky, Battery Operated, 1960s 175.00
Roll About, 4 Steel Wheels, Wood Platform, Pole Handle, Henley, Richmond, Ind., 1913 . 4000.00
Roller Coaster, Tin, Spring Motor, 2 Cars, Bell, Chein, Box, 19 1/2 In. 375.00
Row Cycle, Gear Drive, Pump-Handle Steering, 48 In. 990.00
Sailboat, Pond, Wooden, Blue Hull, Stand, 40 In. 375.00
Sambo & Donkey, Painted Wood, Original Pull Cord, Hustler Toys, 12 In. 237.00
Sand, Dancing Lady, Articulated Paper Figure, Glazed Front, France, 1860s, 6 In. 230.00
Sand Loader, Automatic, Chein, Box, 1930s, 10 In. 500.00
Sand Loader, Pressed Steel, Original Paint, Buddy L, 20 In. 460.00
Sand Mill, Yankee, Uncle Sam, Wood, Metal, 1944, 17 1/2 x 11 In. 201.00
Scale, Cast Iron, Weights, Miniature 175.00
Scale, Counter, Cast Iron, Toledo, Arcade, 5 In. 86.00
Schoolroom, Lilliput Poopchen Teacher, Pupils, Desks, Chalkboards, Cloth & Wire, 1950 115.00
Scoop-N-Dump, Hydraulic Action, Buddy L, 26 In. 715.00
Scooter, Black, Orange, Pressed Steel, 1940s 66.00
Scooter, Foot Brake, 1920s, 38 In. 120.00
Scooter, Ice Cream, Windup, Tin Lithograph, Vendor Rings Bell, 1915, 6 1/2 In. 475.00
Scooter, With Girl, Metal, Windup, USA, 1930, 7 In. 295.00
Scraper, Heilner 2011, Doepke 195.00
Service Station, Pressed Steel, Wood, Gibbs, 1920, 15 In. 375.00
Service Station, Roadside Rest, Battery Lights, Tin Lithograph, Marx, 14 x 10 In. 440.00

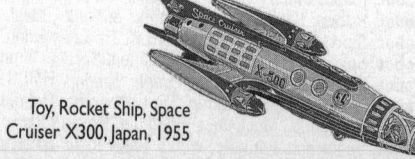

**To loosen a rusted metal
part on a toy or tool, try
soaking it in Coca-Cola.**

Toy, Rocket Ship, Space
Cruiser X300, Japan, 1955

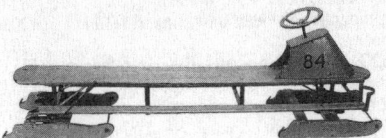

Toy, Sled, Fleetwing Bob, Wrought Iron Runners,
Cast Iron Wheel, Orange Stripes, 84 In.

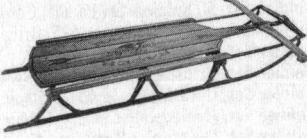

Toy, Sled, Flexible Flyer, Racer, Wood, Metal
Runners, Logo Decal, 56 In.

Service Station, Texaco, Accessories & Auto, Buddy L, Box, 10 x 18 In.	1430.00
Sewing Kit, Board, La Petite Industrie Peliere, Bead Stringing, Box, c.1895, 12 x 11 In.	700.00
Sewing Machine, Ornate Scrolled Pinstriping, Cast Iron, Germany, 1890, 9 In.	105.00
Sewing Machine, Singer, c.1920, 7 In.	88.00
Sewing Machine, Singer, Hand Operated, Cast Iron, 6 In.	160.00
Sewing Machine, Stitchwell, Decals, Box, 6 x 9 In.	332.00
Sewing Machine, Tin, Germany, 1920, 8 In.	161.00
Sewing Outfit Set, Jean Darling, Bisque, Hal Roach, Our Gang, Box, 1936, 17 x 13 In.	200.00
Shooting Gallery, Ducks, Rabbits, Geese, Marx, Box, 1950s, 28 x 14 In.	400.00
Sideboard, Doll's, Oak, Mirror, 2 Drawers & Doors, Shelf Sides, 1900s, 24 x 33 x 10 In.	515.00
Sir Gordon, Gold Knight, With Bravo The Armored Horse Set, Marx	70.00
Skeleton, Sam The Strolling, Windup, Tin, Mikuni, Japan, 1960s, 2 x 4 x 5 1/4 In.	190.00
Sketch Set, Venom Comic Book, 4 Piece	175.00
Ski Jump Ride, Tin Lithograph, Clockwork, Chein, Box, 18 In.	520.00
Skip Rope Animals, Tin, Windup, TPS, Japan	155.00
Slate, School, Wooden Frame, 19th Century	22.00
Sled, 3 Stenciled Curved Runners, Blue Painted Seat, Red Pinstripe, Flowers, 27 x 9 In.	2015.00
Sled, Doll's, Pine, Curved Metal Runners, Yellow Poinsettia, 17 In.	550.00
Sled, Firefly, No. 8G, Stenciled Holly, Wood, Metal Runners, 26 In.	94.00
Sled, Fleetwing Bob, Wrought Iron Runners, Cast Iron Wheel, Orange Stripes, 84 In. *Illus*	990.00
Sled, Fleetwood, Red Paint, Salesman's Sample, 18 1/2 In.	580.00
Sled, Flexible Flyer, Racer, Wood, Metal Runners, Logo Decal, 56 In. *Illus*	138.00
Sled, Folding, L.L. Bean, Open 50 x 17 In.	140.00
Sled, Hickory, Steel Runners, Paint, White Trim, Stenciled Letters, 14 x 33 x 8 1/2 In.	275.00
Sled, Iron Runners, Red Paint, White Stripes, U.S.A., 1888, 46 1/2 x 11 In.	175.00
Sled, Lake Scene Medallions, Black, White, Red, Gold, 38 x 11 3/4 x 12 1/2 In.	578.00
Sled, Oak, Hickory Runners, Flowers On Center, Stenciled Fleur-De-Lis, 30 3/4 In.	520.00
Sled, Painted Bird, Stenciled Decoration, Marked Almy B&W, Salem, Mass., 32 In.	950.00
Sled, Pine, Turned Braces, Running Horse Stencil, Red Paint, Child's, 31 3/4 In.	205.00
Sled, Push, Wood, Painted, Stenciled, Cast Iron Swan Heads, 50 In. *Illus*	605.00
Sled, Royal Racer, Wooden, Steel, 1950s, 22 x 54 In.	100.00
Sled, Stenciled Runners, Metal Steering Bar, Nov. 20, 1894, Salesman Sample	2015.00
Sled, Victor, Eagle & Shield, Iron Runners & Hand Holds, Pine, 6 1/2 x 46 1/2 In.	3450.00
Sled, Wood, Curved Iron Runners, 16 1/4 x 33 x 12 1/4 In.	770.00
Sled, Wood, Green Paint, Iron Runners, Bentwood Seat, Arrow Front, 32 x 16 1/2 x 16 In.	495.00
Sled, Wood, Green Paint, Red Frame, Brush Christmas Tree, Handle, 23 In.	110.00
Sled, Wood, Metal Sheathed Wood Runners, Cast Iron Swan Heads, 33 In. *Illus*	300.00
Sleigh, 2 Horses, Green, Gold, Pratt & Letchworth Figure, Iron, Hubley, c.1905, 15 In.	2160.00
Snake Charmer, Battery Operated, Box	650.00
Snowmobile, Battery Operated, Japan, Box, 1950s, 7 1/2 In.	595.00
Soldier, Crawling, Tin Lithograph, Mechanical, Ohio Art, 7 In.	35.00

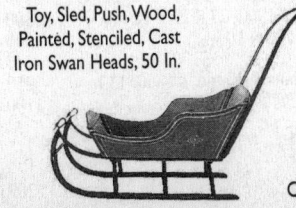

Toy, Sled, Push, Wood,
Painted, Stenciled, Cast
Iron Swan Heads, 50 In.

Toy, Sled, Wood, Metal
Sheathed Wood Runners,
Cast Iron Swan Heads, 33 In.

Soldier, Honorable Corps Of Gentlemen Of Arms, Sentry, Lead, 4 1/2 In., Pair 85.00
Soldier Set, 50 Soldiers On Parade, Cardboard Lithograph, Wooden Base, Box, 6 1/2 In. . . 120.00
Soldier Set, Abyssinian, No. 1425, Britains, 8 Piece 80.00
Soldier Set, Aviator, Dispatcher, Cook, Operator, Gas Mask, Typewriter, Barclay, 6 Piece . 175.00
Soldier Set, British RAF, Marching, Swords, 6 Piece 150.00
Soldier Set, Coldstream Guards, Britains, Box, 24 Piece 750.00
Soldier Set, Confederate Cavalry, Britains, Box, 1960, 14 1/2 In. 175.00
Soldier Set, Devonshire Regiment, No. 110, Marching, Boer War, Britains, 1930, 8 Piece . 475.00
Soldier Set, Flag Bearer, Drummer, Drum Major, Bugler, French Horn, Fife, Barclay 90.00
Soldier Set, Forward March, Cardboard, Paper Lithograph, Field Pieces, Box, 10 x 13 In. . 60.00
Soldier Set, French Army Zouaves, No. 142, Charging, Britains, 7 Piece 160.00
Soldier Set, Gloucestershire Regiment, No.2089, Marching, Britains, 1954, 8 Piece 250.00
Soldier Set, Gordon Highlanders Firing, Service Dress, Britains, c.1940, 16 Piece 600.00
Soldier Set, Gordon Highlanders, No. 77, Marching At Slope, Britains, 6 Piece 130.00
Soldier Set, Imperial Russian Cossacks, No. 136, Mounted At Gallop, Britains, 5 Piece . . 130.00
Soldier Set, Red Army, No. 2032, Marching, Britains, Box, 8 Piece 175.00
Soldier Set, Royal Air Force, No. 2011, Blue Service Uniforms, Britains, 22 Piece 750.00
Soldier Set, Royal Dublin, Marching At Trail, Khaki Dress, Pith Helmets, 1910, 8 Piece . 650.00
Soldier Set, Royal Marines, No. 1264, Marching & Running, 16 Piece 160.00
Soldier Set, Russian Infantry, Marching At Trail, Green Uniforms, Britains, 8 Piece 550.00
Soldier Set, Shoots Wooden Bullets, Tin Lithograph Figures, Box, 13 In. 275.00
Soldier Set, Tin, Searchlite Vehicle, 6 British Soldiers, Elastolin, 13 1/2 In. 3750.00
Soldier Set, Welsh Guard, No. 2108, Marching, Drums & Fifes, Britains, 1960, 12 Piece . 700.00
Space Capsule, Battery Operated, Box 325.00
Space Jet, Battery Operated, Tin Lithograph, Flashing Lights, Bandai, 10 In. 750.00
Space Ranger, Y-36, Tin Lithograph, Japan, Box, 1950s, 6 3/4 In. 385.00
Space Tank, Robot, Windup, Camera Dome, KO, Japan, 1950s 335.00
Space Trip Station, Battery Operated, Lithograph, Yonezawa, 1950s, 14 In. 635.00
Spaceship, Tin, Japan, Box, 8 In. 195.00
Spic & Span, The Hams What Am, Mechanical 495.00
Spooky Shapes Maker, Franken Berry Cereal, 1970s 12.00
Spreader, Manure, Original Paint, John Deere, Cast Iron, 10 In. 1090.00
Sputnik, Tin, Box 90.00
Squirrel On Treadmill, Tin, Windup, K-Japan, 1950s 195.00
Stagecoach, Tin, 2 Horses, Northwest Products, 11 1/2 In. 365.00
Steam Cylinder, Nickel Plated Brass, W.H. Wigmore, 1899, 6 In. 100.00
Steam Engine, Cast Iron Base, Juls Walbrecht, Germany, 1900, 10 In. 490.00
Steam Engine, Cast Iron, Brass, Red 84.00
Steam Engine, Weeden Electric, Iron Base, 1920, 7 In. 140.00
Steam Engine, Weeden Electric, Iron Base, 1930, 6 In. 60.00
Steam Launch, Vertical Boiler, Rudder, Canopy, Twin Benches, Schoenner, 21 In. 325.00
Steam Shovel, General, Cast Iron, Hubley, 8 1/2 In. 450.00
Steam Shovel, Marion, 1920-1930 . . . . 455.00
Steam Shovel, Pressed Steel, Buddy L, 1920 . . . . 315.00
Steam Shovel, Pressed Steel, Original Paint, Structo, 12 In. 115.00
Steam Shovel, Pressed Steel, Structo, 4 1/4 x 12 x 10 In. 95.00
Steam Shovel, Ride-On, Painted Pressed Steel, Keystone, 20 In. 110.00
Steamroller, Cast Iron, Orange, Hubley, 7 3/4 In. 210.00
Steamroller, Original Paint, Pressed Steel, Keystone, 1920, 20 In. 230.00
Steamroller, Tin, Mechanical, Lindstrom, 11 In. 95.00
Steamroller 60, Ride-On, Pressed Steel, Keystone, 19 In. 259.00
Stegosaurus, Plush, Mohair, Airbrushed, Backbone, Googly Eyes, Steiff, 1960s, 12 In. . . 230.00
Stork, Glass Eyes, Metal Feet, Celluloid Beak, White, Black Felt, Steiff, 1940s, 6 In. . . . 100.00
Stove, Cook, 4 Range Covers, Side Door, Shelf, Cast Iron, 13 In. 115.00
Stove, Cook, Buck's Junior 2, Sample, Pots, Kettles, Poker, c.1900, 27 x 22 x 12 In. 3300.00
Stove, Cook, Buck's No. 4, Nickel Plate, Enamel, Iron, 13 x 15 x 10 In. 4000.00
Stove, Cook, Eagle, Cast Iron, 9 In. 145.00
Stove, Cook, Graduated Burners, 5 Oven Doors, 13 Brass Pans & Kettle, c.1880, 13 In. . . 950.00
Stove, Cook, Jewel Range Jr., Cast Iron, Black Enamel, 15 3/4 x 18 x 9 In. 1100.00
Stove, Cook, Little Cook, Electric, Burner, Oven 22.00
Stove, Cook, Qualified Range Co., Sheet, Cast Metal, 21 x 13 x 9 In. 715.00
Stove, Cook, Rival, Cast Iron, Pans & Food, 4 1/2 x 7 In. . . . . *Illus* 175.00
Stove, Cook, Royal Esther, Cast Iron, Accessories, Mt. Penn Stove Works, 18 In. 209.00

Toy, Stove, Cook, Rival, Cast Iron, Pans & Food, 4 1/2 x 7 In.

Toy, Teddy Zilo, Paper, Wood, Plays Xylophone, Fisher-Price, 1948, 11 x 9 In.

Stove, Cook, Tin, Brass Doors, Nickel Top, Marklin, 1900, 8 1/2 x 11 In.	1200.00
Stove, Cook, Tin, Kettle, Pans, Accessories, Germany, 20th Century	785.00
Stove, Cook, Tin, U.S. Zone, Germany, 11 Piece	375.00
Street Sweeper, Tin, Windup, Ny-Lint, 8 In.	180.00
Streetcar, Cast Metal, O Gauge, Flywheel Drive, Inertia Mechanism, 11 1/2 In.	220.00
Streetcar, Tin Lithograph, Bell Ringing Mechanism, Wolverine, 13 1/2 In.	165.00
Streetcar, Track, Trolley Pulls, Electric Powered, Box, 11 In.	250.00
Stroller, Doll's, Wicker, Wood & Iron, 27 In.	145.00
Strutting Sam, Black Dancer On Tub, Battery Operated	325.00
Submarine, U.S., Tin, Spring Motor, 1950, Arnold, 12 In.	460.00
Submarine Set, Navy, Tootsietoy, Box, 8 x 11 1/2 In., 6 Piece	275.00
Subway Express, Train Travels Around Station, Windup, Marx, c.1950, 9 1/2 In.	400.00
Suitcase, Doll's, Jack & Jill Jungle Jinks, Metal, California Perfume Co., 6 x 3 3/4 In.	75.00
Sulky Cart, Original Paint, Cast Iron, Kenton, 8 1/4 In.	170.00
Suzy Bouncing Ball, Windup, Tin Lithograph, Japan, Box	250.00
Swan, Chariot, Girl Sitting In Seashell, Cast Iron, J. & E. Stevens, c.1891, 9 In.	5700.00
Swan, Signet, Windup, Tin, Occupied Japan, 5 In.	126.00
Tank, 65-5-M, German, Windup, Gescha, Box	350.00
Tank, Army, Mystery & Shooting Action, Battery Operated, Tin, Japan, 1950, 7 In.	185.00
Tank, E-12 Army, Marx	350.00
Tank, Fighting, Climbing, Plastic Wheels, Windup, Marx, 1951, 5 1/4 In.	225.00
Tank, Mars Planet Patrol, Windup, Marx, 1940s, 10 In.	435.00
Tank, Patton, Tin	35.00
Tank, Remote Control, Removable Metal Barrel, Plastic	35.00
Tank, Soldier Popping Out With Gun, Windup, Marx, 10 In.	295.00
Tank, Tin Lithograph, Windup, Rubber Treads, Marx, 9 3/4 In.	130.00
Tank, Turnover, Jetson, Rosie Robot Underneath Turns Tank Over, Marx, Box, 4 In.	925.00
Tank, Windup, Tin, Germany, 6 1/2 In.	35.00
Tank, Windup, White Rubber Treads, Gama, 3 In.	95.00
Tank, World War I, Tin, Windup, Rolls Forward, Firing Gun, Soldier, Marx, 10 In.	150.00
Taxi, Amos 'n' Andy, Fresh Air, Tin Lithograph, Windup, Marx, 8 In.	400.00 to 660.00
Taxi, Amos 'n' Andy, Windup, Marx, Original Box, 1930s	1350.00
Taxi, Cadillac, 1914 Model, Hubley, 7 In.	145.00
Taxi, Checker Cab, Driver, Passengers, Sign On Top, Tin, 6 In.	365.00
Taxi, Checker Cab, Tin Lithograph, Windup, 6 In.	80.00
Taxi, Painted Pressed Steel, Friction, Tin Driver, Republic, 10 1/2 In.	203.00
Taxi, Tin Lithograph, Clockwork, Driver, Side Lamps, G & K, 6 1/2 In.	2970.00
Taxi, Touring, Friction, Red, JBN Laudolette	350.00
Taxi, Tricky, Windup, Tin Lithograph, Marx, 1940s	66.00
Taxi, Wacky Taxi Co., Tin Lithograph, Friction, Marx, 7 1/2 In.	160.00
Taxi, Yellow Cab, Nickel Plated Driver, Orange, Black, Cast Iron, Arcade, c.1924, 9 In.	1560.00
Taxi, Yellow Cab, Orange, Black, Cast Iron, Kenton, c.1925, 7 1/2 In.	1320.00
Taxi, Yellow Cab, Painted Cast Iron, Arcade, 8 In.	1050.00
Tea Set, Bunny, Service For 4, Tray, Chein	125.00
Tea Set, Crown Fairy, Porcelain, Blue & Yellow Raised Flowers, Germany, Box, 10 Piece	90.00
Tea Set, E.T., White Plastic, 5 Different Scenes, 20 Piece	18.00
Teddy Bears are also listed in the Teddy Bear category.	
Teddy Bear, Bell Ringer, Original Paint, Cast Iron, 5 3/4 In.	430.00

Teddy Bear, On Wheels, Rubber Rims, Floss Nose & Mouth, Leather Collar, 14 x 19 In. . 425.00
Teddy Zilo, Paper, Wood, Plays Xylophone, Fisher-Price, 1948, 11 x 9 In. . . . . *Illus* 85.00
Teeter-Totter, Plastic, Windup, Red & Yellow, 1950, 7 In. 75.00
Telephone, Wall Phone, Battery Operated, S.B. Co., Box, 1920s, 6 1/2 x 14 In. 65.00
Thresher, McCormick Deering, Cast Iron, Arcade 795.00
Tidy Tim, Keep Your City Spick & Span, Tin Lithograph, Clockwork, Marx, 9 1/2 In. . . . 632.00
Tidy Tim, Sanitation Worker, Tin Lithograph, Clockwork Motor, Marx, 9 In. 115.00
Tigrett, Educational Building, Paper, Wood Dowels, Box 8.00
Toaster, Sunnie Miss, Tin Lithograph, Ohio Art, 1960s 18.00
Toaster, Tin, Working Spring, Japan 45.00
Tombo, Alabama Coon Jigger, Performs Jig On Stage, Strauss, Box, 10 In. 1045.00
Tombo, Alabama Coon Jigger, Tin, Windup, Strauss, 1910, 10 In. 392.00
Tool Box, Tools, Miscellaneous Parts, Tool List, Buddy L, 11 x 23 In. 3520.00
Toonerville Trolley, Cast Iron, Green, Maroon & Orange, Dent, Repro Box, 1924, 4 1/2 In. 795.00
Toonerville Trolley, Figure On Platform Moves, Fischer, 1922 . . . . 850.00
Toonerville Trolley, On Track, Tin Lithograph, Clockwork, Nifty, 5 1/2 In. 550.00
Topper, Trash Can, Amusement Park, Clown's Face, Cone Shaped Hat, 25 x 17 In. 570.00
Tractor, Adams Grader 12006, Orange, Doepke 150.00
Tractor, Allis Chambers, Arcade, 1941, 6 1/2 In. 375.00
Tractor, Auto Builder, Pressed Steel, Clockwork, Structo, 11 1/2 In. 154.00
Tractor, Cast Iron, Rubber Wheels, Arcade, 12 In. 240.00
Tractor, Caterpillar, Pressed Steel, Clockwork, Little Jim Decal, Kingsbury, 7 1/2 In. 93.00
Tractor, Caterpillar, Pressed Steel, Windup, Structo, 8 1/2 In. 287.00
Tractor, Climbing, Highboy, Red, Yellow, Windup, Tin Lithograph, Marx, Box, 8 1/2 In. . 450.00
Tractor, Die Cast, Hubley, 1950s, 9 In. 175.00
Tractor, Disc Harrow, Massey Harris, Dinky Toys, 1950s 65.00
Tractor, Earth Mover & Grader, Mechanical, Marx, Box 245.00
Tractor, Fordson, Gray, Red Wheels, 1928 . . . . 125.00
Tractor, Grader, Driver, Silver & Red, Tin Lithograph, Marx, Box, 10 1/2 In. 225.00
Tractor, Grader, Windup, Driver, Orange & Yellow, Tin Lithograph, Marx 235.00
Tractor, Hay Rake, Cast Iron Driver, 1930s, 12 1/2 In. 145.00
Tractor, John Deere, Green & Yellow, Metal Wheels, 1960 . . . . 150.00
Tractor, John Deere, Row Crop, Green & Yellow, Closed Flywheel, 1947 . . . . 175.00
Tractor, Little Logging, USA, Box, 1920 . . . . 375.00
Tractor, Metal, Windup, England, 1950s, 8 1/2 In. 95.00
Tractor, Muir-Hill, Dumper, Yellow & Red, Dinky Toys 49.00
Tractor, Painted Cast Iron, Rubber Wheels, Driver, Arcade, 7 1/2 In. 250.00
Tractor, Pressed Steel, Clockwork, Solid Rubber Wheels, Kingsbury, 20 In. 100.00
Tractor, Pressed Steel, Structo, 9 In. 143.00
Tractor, Windup, Tin, Yellow, Marx, Box 195.00
Trailor, Sears, Friction, Japan, Box, 15 In. 325.00
Train, American Flyer, Bluebird, Engine & 3 Passenger Coaches, No. 3115 . . . . 385.00
Train, American Flyer, Burlington Zephyr, Locomotive, 2 Cars, O Gauge 145.00
Train, American Flyer, Engine, 2 Passenger Cars, Freight Car, Caboose, Track 127.00
Train, American Flyer, Hiawatha Streamline, 1930s, 5 Piece 795.00
Train, American Flyer, Milwaukee Hiawatha, Windup, 1936, 5 Piece 495.00
Train, American Flyer, O Gauge, 1920s, 9 Piece 825.00
Train, Arcade, Railplane, Pullman, Cast Iron, Articulated, 16 In. 60.00
Train, Arcade, Railplane, Pullman, Painted Cast Iron, Rubber Tire Wheels, 5 In. 80.00
Train, Battery, Tin Litho, Porter, Luggage, Standard Gauge, Japan, Box, 7 x 8 In. 400.00
Train, Bing, Locomotive, No. 2550, Tin Lithograph, 4 Piece 2860.00
Train, Buddy L, Industrial, Engine, Wrecking Car, 3 Box Cars, 8 In. 5170.00
Train, Buddy L, Industrial, Locomotive, 4 Cars, Track, 7 1/2 In. 1155.00
Train, Caboose, Painted Cast Iron, Marked L.S. & M.S., Kenton, 7 In. 132.00
Train, Canadian Pacific, Montclair Pullman, 7 Piece 299.00
Train, Carpenter, Steam Locomotive, 3 Gondolas, Caboose, Cast Iron, c.1885, 24 In. 720.00
Train, Carpenter, Wood Smoking Mechanism, Cast Iron, Brass, c.1890, 20 In. 960.00
Train, Circus, Locomotive & Tender, 4 Cages, 2 Tractors, Caboose, 5 Piece 495.00
Train, Circus, Wooden, 4 Piece 39.00
Train, Engine & Caboose, Giant, Friction, Japan, 16 In. 75.00
Train, Engine, Attached Tender, Black, Gold, Pullman Cars, Cast Iron, 18 In., 5 Piece 176.00
Train, Hafner, Freight, Clockwork Engine, Tender & 3 Cars 209.00
Train, Hafner, Overland Flyer, Clockwork Engine, Tender, 2 Cars 187.00

Train, Hafner, Sunshine Special, Clockwork Engine, Tender, 2 Cars 120.00
Train, Harris, 4-2-0 Locomotive, Tender, Baggage, Coach, Cast Iron, 39 In. 1440.00
Train, Horney Meccano, English Locomotive, Coal Tender, Cars, Windup, Tin, 22 In. 400.00
Train, Ives, Buffet Car, Parlor Car, Observation Car, Standard Gauge 345.00
Train, Ives, Empire Express, No. 5 Engine, Cast Iron, Windup, Tin Passenger Cars 88.00
Train, Ives, Locomotive, 2-2-0, Tender, Cast Iron, Clockwork, c.1890, 12 In. 1320.00
Train, Joyline Coaches, Green, Orange, Drop Couplers, 3 Piece 79.00
Train, Karl Bub, Freight, Lithographed, Clockwork Locomotive, O Gauge, 5 Piece 295.00
Train, Kenton, Passenger, Pennsylvania Lines, Electro-Oxidized Finish, 5 Piece 220.00
Train, Lionel, Engine, Boxes, 2 Controllers, Whistle Controller, Switches, No. 249E 550.00
Train, Lionel, Engine, Lehigh Valley Gondola, Caboose, Transformer, Track 120.00
Train, Lionel, Engine, No. 380, 2 No. 337 Pullmans, No. 338 Observation Car, 4 Piece ... 275.00
Train, Lionel, Engine, Tender, 5 Freight Cars, Crane 660.00
Train, Lionel, Freight, No. 1664, Engine, Tender, 4 Cars 93.00
Train, Lionel, Green Body, Cream Seats, Red Roof, 2 7/8-In. Gauge 356.00
Train, Lionel, Locomotive & Pullmans, No. 380E 3135.00
Train, Lionel, Locomotive, 2 Pullmans, Observation Car, Orange, 4 Piece 2750.00
Train, Lionel, Peacock, No. 10E Engine, Pullman, Railway Mail, Observation, 5 Piece ... 305.00
Train, Lionel, Pink, Yellow, Blue, Purple, No. 1587S, 8 Piece 1155.00
Train, Lionel, Steamer, Tender, Brass Dome, Copper Handrails, 1930s 850.00
Train, Lionel, Trainmaster, Jersey Central Lines, No. 2341, Orange, Blue Strip, Blue Top . 1155.00
Train, Locomotive, Tall Stack, 4-4-0, Carpenter, Black, Gold, Red, Iron, c.1885, 12 In. ... 480.00
Train, Marklin, Locomotive & Tender, Black & Red 295.00
Train, Marklin, Magnetic-Dynamo, Locomotive & Tender, No. D1021/3393, 2 Piece 4070.00
Train, Marx, Streamliner, Coaches, Coaches Buffet, 2 Piece 279.00
Train, Moon Mullins, Original Tracks 750.00
Train, Pratt & Letchworth, Empire State Express, Central & Hudson River, Cast Iron 6325.00
Train, Railbus, Tin, Pale Green, ML, France, 1930, 6 In. 195.00
Train, Skip, Tin, 24 In., 4 Piece 325.00
Train, Smith-Miller, Boxcar, Orange Enamel Lettering, Pressed Metal, 1950, 33 In. 977.00
Train, Streamline Express, Silver & Red, Friction, c.1950, 13 In. 125.00
Train, Super Electric Locomotive, Tin Lithograph, Friction, Japan, 18 In. 160.00
Train, Tyco, Petticoat Junction, 1960 .... 300.00
Train, Unique Art, Freight, Engine, Tender & 4 Cars 110.00
Train, Unique Art, Hobo, On Top Of Moving Train, Dog Bites Seat, 1930s 650.00
Train, Weeden Dart, Locomotive, Steam, 0-4-0, Tender, c.1890, 22 In. 600.00
Train Accessory, American Flyer, Crossing Lights & Shanty, S Gauge 69.00
Train Accessory, American Flyer, Operating Crossing Signal, Light Post, O Gauge 115.00
Train Accessory, Arcade, Highway Sign, U.S. 30, Cast Iron, Yellow Paint, 3 3/4 In. 65.00
Train Accessory, Bing, Station House, Tin Lithograph, 4 Opening Doors, 8 In. 100.00
Train Accessory, Bing, Station, Tin 350.00
Train Accessory, Freight Station, Original Box, 1950-1953 .... 100.00
Train Accessory, Lionel, Automatic Gateman, O Gauge, Original Box, 1937-1942 .... 46.00
Train Accessory, Lionel, Landscaped Plot, No. 195, 3 Houses 3300.00
Train Accessory, Lionel, Operating Crane, O Gauge 60.00
Train Accessory, Lionel, Operating Lascule Bridge, O Gauge, 1942 .... 149.00
Train Accessory, Lionel, Operating Oil Derrick, Red Base, O Gauge, 1950-1954 .... 195.00
Train Accessory, Lionel, Signal Bridge, O Gauge, Original Box 69.00
Train Accessory, Lionel, Station, No. 134, Box 467.00
Train Accessory, Lionel, Station, Swing Doors, Illuminated, Tin, Box, 13 1/2 x 9 1/4 In. ... 154.00
Train Accessory, Lionel, Switch Signal Tower, No. 437, 10 In. 143.00
Train Accessory, Marklin, Bridge Set, Span, Approaches, Signs, Arches, Poles, I Gauge ... 2070.00
Train Accessory, Marklin, Crossing Guard House, Tin, German 375.00
Train Accessory, Marklin, Crossing, Level, Pressure Operated, I Gauge, 13 3/4 In. 175.00
Train Accessory, Marklin, Goods Station, No. 2047, c.1906, 14 3/4 In. 4600.00
Train Accessory, Marklin, Lamp, Street 396.00
Train Accessory, Marklin, Passenger Gate, Destination Flags, 10 1/2 In. 1980.00
Train Accessory, Marklin, Railroad Station, No. 1040 .... 665.00
Train Accessory, Marklin, Railroad Station, No. 2350 .... 1265.00
Train Accessory, Marklin, Railroad Station, Tin, 4 Doors, Furnished, Electric Lights, 13 In. . 4620.00
Train Accessory, Marx, Station, Yellow, Red Roof, O Gauge 28.00
Train Accessory, Mystic, Train Station, Tin Plate 150.00
Train Accessory, Signal Tower, Orange Trim, Box 825.00

Train Accessory, Ticket Office, Tin Lithograph, 7 x 11 1/2 In. 71.00
Train Accessory, Train Shed, Painted Tin, Corrugated Roof, Sign Board, 16 In. 740.00
Train Car, American Flyer, Tank, O Gauge 46.00
Train Car, Arcade, Engine, Nickel Plated Cast Iron, Merchant's Dispatch, 2 Doors, Box .. 88.00
Train Car, Bing, Peerless Tank Line Car, Gray, Silver Letters, I Gauge, 11 In. 288.00
Train Car, Buddy L, Bottom Dump Car, 22 In. 3960.00
Train Car, Buddy L, Boxcar, Opening Side Doors, 21 In. 633.00
Train Car, Buddy L, Boxcar, Outdoor, Open Top, 1925, 3 1/4 In. 575.00
Train Car, Buddy L, Boxcar, Tank, Painted Pressed Steel, Red, 17 1/4 In. ....425.00 to 625.00
Train Car, Buddy L, Cattle Car, 21 In. 660.00
Train Car, Buddy L, Coal Car, 22 In. 2750.00
Train Car, Buddy L, Engine & Tender, 41 In. 2970.00
Train Car, Buddy L, Flat Car, 10 Wood Stakes, Order Cards, Box, 23 In. 3740.00
Train Car, Buddy L, Flat Car, 21 In. 715.00
Train Car, Buddy L, Locomotive & Tender, 1925 .... 747.00
Train Car, Buddy L, Locomotive, Copper Plated, Display, 26 In. 2310.00
Train Car, Buddy L, Locomotive, Wrecking Crane, 1925 .... 747.00
Train Car, Buddy L, Ore Car, Side Dumping Action, 12 In. 5500.00
Train Car, Buddy L, Sand & Gravel Car, 22 In. 3300.00
Train Car, Buddy L, Service Lift, Box 50.00
Train Car, Buddy L, Stock Car, Opening Side Doors, 22 In. 1210.00
Train Car, Buddy L, Tank Car, Yellow, 19 1/2 In. 1100.00
Train Car, Dent, Engine & Tender, Cast Iron, Tender Marked P.R.R. Co., 14 In. 145.00
Train Car, Girard, Hand Car, Windup, Tin Lithograph, 5 1/2 x 6 In. 66.00
Train Car, Ideal, Stock, Horses, Articulated, Yellow, Red, Cast Iron, Tin, c.1895, 14 In. 720.00
Train Car, Lionel, Boxcar, Blue Feather, Box 143.00
Train Car, Lionel, Boxcar, No. 1814, Orange & Red 4620.00
Train Car, Lionel, Caboose, No. 517 .... 44.00
Train Car, Lionel, Caboose, No. 2957, Tuscan Red, Semiscale 523.00
Train Car, Lionel, Cattle Car, Operating, With Platform, O Gauge, Original Box 100.00
Train Car, Lionel, Crane Car, No. 219 .... 176.00
Train Car, Lionel, Crane, Bucyrus Erie, O Gauge, Original Box, 1946 .... 69.00
Train Car, Lionel, Floodlight, Nickel Lights 193.00
Train Car, Lionel, Hand Car, Chickmobile, Peter Rabbit, Tin, Clockwork, 10 In. 440.00
Train Car, Lionel, Hand Car, Motorized, O Gauge, Original Box, 1962 .... 290.00
Train Car, Lionel, Locomotive & Tender, No. 484, Rock Island 165.00
Train Car, Lionel, Maintenance Car, Motorized, Bridge, O Gauge, 1962 .... 200.00
Train Car, Lionel, Refrigerator, No. 814R, White & Red 5390.00
Train Car, Lionel, Refrigerator, O Gauge, Santa Fe, Original Box, 1954 .... 34.00
Train Car, Lionel, Shell Tanker, Black, Box 303.00
Train Car, Lionel, Shell Tanker, Red 1320.00
Train Car, Lionel, Steam Locomotive, No. 6-8215, Original Box 154.00
Train Car, Lionel, Stock Car, No. 813, Red, Black Anodized Trim 6600.00
Train Car, Lionel, Sunoco Tanker, Gray Tank, Black Base 44.00
Train Car, Lionel, Tank, Water, O Gauge, Silver, Original Box, 1932 .... 80.00
Train Car, Lionel, Tanker, Box 935.00
Train Car, Lionel, Traveling Aquarium, Gold Lettering, Box 220.00
Train Car, Locomotive, Tin, Wood, Clockwork, c.1870, 10 In. 900.00
Train Car, Marklin, Baggage Truck, 5 In. 176.00
Train Car, Marklin, Cattle Car, Brown, Black Roof, I Gauge, 10 In. 748.00
Train Car, Marx, Auto Transport, No. 1220, Box 350.00
Train Car, Marx, Hand Car, Moon Mullins & Kayo, Windup, 1930s 525.00
Train Car, Pratt & Letchworth, Engine & Tender, Cast Iron Engine, Steel Tender, 15 In. ... 135.00
Train Car, Weeden, Locomotive, Live Steam, Original Decal & Burner, 12 In. 165.00
Train Car, Welker & Crosby, Locomotive, Cast Iron & Wood, Boiler, Patent '85, 12 In. ... 880.00
Train Set, American Flyer, Cast Iron, Original Box, 13 Piece 1265.00
Train Set, Bing, Der Fliegende, No. 2550, Hamburger, Box 420.00
Train Set, Bing, NYC Steeplecab Locomotive, Uphill Tracks, No. 3238, Miniature, Box .. 3410.00
Train Set, Ives, Clockwork, Engine Tender, Track, 1 Car, Cast Iron, No. 1, Original Box . 185.00
Train Set, Lincoln Log Railway, Box 75.00
Train Set, Lionel, Chugger Conversion Locomotive, 3 Red Cars, No. 241E, Box 4280.00
Train Set, Lionel, No. 134, Engine, 3 Box Cars, O Gauge, Box, 1926 .... 1070.00
Train Set, Lionel, Virginian Diesel, No. 2322, Yellow, Blue Stripe, Original Box 468.00

Train Set, Marx, Clockwork Engine, Tender, Track, Original Box, 3 Piece 115.00
Train Set, Marx, Commodore Vanderbilt, Transformer, 6 Cars, Boxes 66.00
Train Set, Marx, Empire Express, Tin Lithograph, Clockwork, Tracks, Box, 14 1/2 In. . . . 220.00
Train Set, Marx, Freight, Plastic, Windup, Box, 1950s, 21 In., 5 Piece 95.00
Train Set, Marx, New York City, Transformer, Tracks, No. 8994, Box, 6 Piece 225.00
Train Set, Marx, Scenic Express, Signals, 3 Trains, Box, c.1951 . . . . 350.00
Train Set, Marx, Streamline, No. 397 Engine, 4 Sections Track, 6 Cars, Box 99.00
Train Set, Mohave, Passenger, No. 253 . . . . 220.00
Train Set, Union Pacific, Panama Locomotive, 2 Dumping Cars, Wood, 1877, 16 In. 1610.00
Train Set, Zeuke-Bahnen, T-48, Marked Berlin-Erfurt, Boxes, 4 Piece 105.00
Treasure Chest, Inserts, Dent, Box, 7 x 13 In. 95.00
Tree, Walking, Whistling, Marx, 14 In. 1250.00
Tricycle, Horse, Glass Eyes, Suede Saddle, Chain Driven, Jugnet, 33 In. 805.00
Tricycle, Rocking Horse 385.00
Tricycle, Windup, Tin, Green & Red, 1940s, Japan, 2 x 4 1/4 x 2 1/2 In. 28.00
Trolley, Black Horse, Red Trolley, Broadway Car Line, Cast Iron, Wilkins, 19 In. 1000.00
Trolley, Broadway & 4th Ave., 2 Horses, Tin, Painted, 15 1/2 In. 7560.00
Trolley, Broadway Car Lines, Stencil, Horse, Black, Red, Iron, Wilkins, c.1895, 18 In. . . . 3900.00
Trolley, Broadway, Tin Lithograph, Floor Toy, Chein, 8 In. 145.00
Trolley, Cast Iron Wheels, Movable Seats, Tin, Pull Toy, Pre-1900 . . . . 69.00
Trolley, City Hall, Heavy Steel, Clockwork, Orange, Converse, 16 In. 520.00
Trolley, Clockwork, Motorman, Richter, Germany, 1908, 10 In. 550.00
Trolley, Embossed Electric Railway, Carlisle 960.00
Trolley, Friction, Dark Red & Green, Schieble, 1906, 15 In. 550.00
Trolley, Hillclimber, Pressed Steel, Flywheel Drive, Open Sides, 13 1/2 In. 230.00
Trolley, Hillclimber, Summer, Heavy Tin, Inertia Mechanism, 13 1/2 In. 410.00
Trolley, Hillclimber, Tin, Inertia Mechanism, Silhouette Of 7 Children, Red, 14 1/2 In. . . . 155.00
Trolley, Hillclimber, Tin, Inertia Mechanism, Silhouette Of 8 Children, Green, 13 In. 120.00
Trolley, Horse, City Passenger, Tin, Hull & Stafford, USA, c.1880, 15 In. 1080.00
Trolley, No. 50, Reversing Mechanism, Tin, Clockwork, 4 1/2 In. 275.00
Trolley, No. 520, Tin Lithograph, Clockwork, Painted Roof, Glazed Windows, 10 In. 357.00
Trolley, Orange, Kingsbury, 1930, 14 In. 550.00
Trolley, Painted, Early 20th Century, 11 x 7 1/2 x 25 1/2 In. 1380.00
Trolley, Pay As You Enter, Pressed Steel, Yellow, 23 In. 220.00
Trolley, Pressed Steel, Red & Yellow, Kingsbury, 16 In. 350.00
Trolley, Saratoga, Chein, 1920, 8 1/2 In. 95.00
Trolley, Tin Lithograph, Clockwork Engine Reversing Mechanism, Bing, 8 In. 522.00
Trolley, Tin Lithograph, Clockwork Propels Car & Rings Bell, Walbert, 13 In. 286.00
Trolley, Tin Lithograph, Clockwork, Glass Windows, Motorman, Gunthermann, 10 1/2 In. 990.00
Trolley, Tin Lithograph, Clockwork, Orobr, Stamped Germany, 10 In. 410.00
Trolley, Tin Lithograph, Friction, Bell Ringer, 9 1/2 In. 350.00
Trolley, Tin, USA, 1930, 14 In. 245.00
Trolley, Tin, Windup, Richter, 1910, 6 In. 395.00
Trolley, Windup, Gunthermann, 1930s, 12 In. 395.00
Trolley, Windup, Lithographed, Gunthermann, c.1927, 8 In. 435.00
Trolley, Yellow & Red, Schieble, 21 In. 395.00
Trooper, U.S. Parachute, Raggy Doodle, Cloth, Painted Features, 7 In. 110.00
Truck, ABC Freight Forwarding, Pressed Steel, Box, 11 1/2 In. . . . . Illus 200.00
Truck, Acme Van, Steel Lithograph, Marx, 1950s, 25 In. 550.00
Truck, Alfa Romeo Ferrari Team, Grand Prix, Tripoli, Yellow, Carlos Briani, Box, 1936 . . 330.00
Truck, Apple, Friction, 6 1/2 In. 95.00
Truck, Arctic Ice Cream, Cast Iron 1250.00
Truck, Army Carrier, Painted Steel, Wood, Decal, Smith-Miller, 20 In. 575.00
Truck, Army Engineer's, Windup, Marx, Box 295.00
Truck, Army Transport, International, Trailer, Canvas Cover, Buddy L, Box, 1930s, 33 In. 1100.00
Truck, Army Troop Transport, Tin Lithograph, Marx, 8 In. 100.00
Truck, Army, Olive Green, Pressed Steel, Canvas Cover, Marx, 18 1/2 In. 120.00
Truck, Artillery, Pressed Steel, Clockwork, Solid Rubber Tires, Kingsbury, 15 In. 70.00
Truck, Baggage, Accessory Ladder, Buddy L, Box, 18 In. 715.00
Truck, Bekins, Moving Van, Friction Cab, 3 Opening Doors, GMC, 25 In 275.00
Truck, Breyers Ice Cream, Cast Iron, 8 1/2 In. 1760.00
Truck, Brinks, GMC, Automatic Burglar Alarm, Buddy L, 15 In. 330.00
Truck, Brinks, GMC, Automatic Burglar Alarm, Rear Door Lock, Figures, Box, 15 In. . . . 1595.00

Toy, Truck, ABC Freight
Forwarding, Pressed
Steel, Box, 11 1/2 In.

Toy, Truck, Express,
Headlights, Rubber Tires,
Doors Open, Buddy L, 25 In.

Truck, Cannon, Olive, Pressed Steel, Battery, Electronic, No. 2400, Ny-Lint, 23 In. 125.00
Truck, Car Carrier, 4 Model A Fords, Arcade, 1931, 24 In. 985.00
Truck, Car Carrier, Cars, Marx, Box, 14 In. 250.00
Truck, Car Carrier, Metal, 14 Plastic & Tin Cars, Japan, 1950, 17 In. 245.00
Truck, Car Carrier, Orange, 6 Cars, Smith-Miller, 38 In. 1650.00
Truck, Car Carrier, Painted Cast Iron, A. C. Williams, 12 1/2 In. 275.00
Truck, Car Carrier, Pressed Steel, 4 Cars, Canada, 1950s 395.00
Truck, Car Carrier, Pressed Steel, Marx, 1930s, 6 Piece 595.00
Truck, Car Carrier, Red, Gray Paint, Windup, Red Wheels, Copper, Marx, 1935, 22 In. 2012.00
Truck, Car Carrier, Red, Light Blue, Tail Ramps, Tin, Friction, 16 1/2 In. 160.00
Truck, Car Carrier, Turnpike, 9 Cars, Sears, Japan, 1950s 595.00
Truck, Carnation Milk, Pressed Steel, Tonka, USA, 1950s, 10 In. 295.00
Truck, Cast Iron, Arcade, 1930s, 4 In. 75.00
Truck, Cattle, Plastic & Metal, Marx, 1950s, 14 In. 100.00
Truck, Cement Mixer, Cast Iron, Jaeger 895.00
Truck, Cement Mixer, Cast Iron, Kenton, c.1940, 9 1/4 In. 2280.00
Truck, Cement Mixer, Rotating, Diesel Truck, Shioji, Box, 1960s, 14 In. 300.00
Truck, Chad Valley Co., Tin, Windup, Balloon Tires, 10 In. 990.00
Truck, Circus, Friction, Japan, 1960, 8 In. 95.00
Truck, Circus, Overland, Driver, Cast Iron, Kenton, 9 In. 1250.00
Truck, Circus, Pinder, 1960s, 13 In., 2 Piece 350.00
Truck, Circus, Pressed Steel, Embossed Tin, Animals, Buddy L, 25 1/2 In. 160.00
Truck, City Dray, Baggage Cart, Green & Yellow, Buddy L, Box, 1930s, 21 In. ..1760.00 to 2970.00
Truck, City, Cast Iron, Harris, c.1903, 15 In. 5400.00
Truck, Coal, Dump, Red & Gray, Marx, Box, 21 In. ....275.00 to 375.00
Truck, Coal, Pressed Steel, Side Chute Doors, Buddy L, 25 In. 1095.00
Truck, Crane, Chipperfield Circus, Red & Blue, Corgi ....110.00 to 120.00
Truck, Delivery, Fanny Farmer Candies, Cardboard, Wood Wheels, 1930s, 9 1/2 In. 225.00
Truck, Delivery, Open, Pressed Steel, Clockwork, Bell Underneath, Kingsbury, 9 1/2 In. .. 176.00
Truck, Delivery, Pressed Steel, Friction, Cast Iron Driver, Blue, Clark, 10 In. 330.00
Truck, Delivery, Pressed Steel, Painted Blue, Flywheel Drive, D.P. Clark, 11 In. 200.00
Truck, Delivery, Sheet Metal, Bon Ton, 13 In. 770.00
Truck, Deutsche Reichspost, Tin, Windup, Red, Marklin, Germany 995.00
Truck, Ditcher, Buckeye, Painted Cast Iron, Chain Driven, Kenton, 9 In. 425.00
Truck, Ditcher, International, Yellow, Ertl 69.00
Truck, Dowel Logs, Held By Removable Chains, Flag On End, Hubley, Box, 18 In. 325.00
Truck, Dump, Buddy L, 17 In. 375.00
Truck, Dump, Cast Iron Driver, Windup, Pressed Steel, Kingsbury, 1920s, 9 In. 250.00
Truck, Dump, Cast Iron, Red & Gray, Arcade, 10 1/2 In. 585.00
Truck, Dump, Chain, Aluminum Disc Wheels, Buddy L, 5 In. 575.00
Truck, Dump, Drive Crank Action, Steerable Front, Buddy L, 24 In. 860.00
Truck, Dump, Ford, Black, Pressed Steel, Open Cab, Bed, Buddy L, 11 In. 1100.00
Truck, Dump, Ford, Painted, Ny-Lint, Box, 1959, 13 1/2 In. 140.00
Truck, Dump, Ford, Tin, S & E, 16 In. 175.00
Truck, Dump, Ford, Trailer, Arcade, 1930, 13 In. 895.00
Truck, Dump, Front Loader, Red & Yellow, Tin, Marx, 14 In. 110.00
Truck, Dump, Front Self Loader, Wyandotte, 1949, 12 1/2 In. 185.00
Truck, Dump, Gold Trim Radiator, Steering Wheel, Kingsbury, 15 In. 200.00
Truck, Dump, Hercules Mack, Tin Lithograph, Chein, 20 In. 225.00
Truck, Dump, Hi-Mac, Military, Windup, Marx, 11 In. 350.00

If you want to keep your collections free from harm, always clean and dust them yourself.

Toy, Truck, Dump, Red & Green,
Matchbox, Lesney, England, No. 2, 1 5/8 In.

Truck, Dump, Hydraulic, Buddy L, 1930s, 22 In.	295.00
Truck, Dump, Hydraulic, Pressed Steel, Buddy L, 24 In.	375.00
Truck, Dump, International, Buddy L, 24 In.	675.00
Truck, Dump, International, Tin, Side Mirrors, Plated Grill, 1951, 23 In.	895.00
Truck, Dump, Junior, Pressed Steel, Electric Lights, Decal, Buddy L, 20 1/2 In.	275.00
Truck, Dump, Lights, Battery Operated, Japan, 1950, 11 In.	195.00
Truck, Dump, Load, Pressed Steel, Tin, Lever Action, Marx, 26 In.	330.00
Truck, Dump, Mack, Bulldog Style, Steelcraft, 48 In.	1265.00
Truck, Dump, Mack, Cast Iron, Green Body, Red Bed, Rubber Tires, 7 In.	225.00
Truck, Dump, Mack, Yellow, Green, Tootsietoy, 5 1/2 In.	55.00
Truck, Dump, Pressed Steel, Clockwork, Kingsbury, 8 3/4 In.	230.00
Truck, Dump, Pressed Steel, Clockwork, Tailgate Chain, Kingsbury, 13 1/2 In.	330.00
Truck, Dump, Pressed Steel, Crank & Chain Action, Decal, Buddy L, 24 In.	520.00
Truck, Dump, Pressed Steel, Winch, Buddy L, 25 In.	431.00
Truck, Dump, Red & Green, Matchbox, Lesney, England, No. 2, 1 5/8 In. .... *Illus*	85.00
Truck, Dump, Sand & Stone, Buddy L, Box, 14 1/2 In.	550.00
Truck, Dump, Scoop, Buddy L, Original Box, 18 In. ....360.00 to 495.00	
Truck, Dump, Side, Steel, Blue, Red, 9 1/2 In.	195.00
Truck, Dump, Studebaker, Red & Green, Hubley, 7 In.	285.00
Truck, Dump, Sturditoy Construction Co., 27 In.	605.00
Truck, Dump, Tin Lithograph, Lumar, c.1941, 12 In.	165.00
Truck, Esso Oil, Trojan, Meccano, Dinky Toys	125.00
Truck, Express Line, Pressed Steel, Buddy L, 25 In. ....520.00 to 630.00	
Truck, Express, Headlights, Rubber Tires, Doors Open, Buddy L, 25 In. .... *Illus* 33000.00	
Truck, Express, Painted Pressed Steel, Friction, Tin Driver, Schieble, 10 In.	330.00
Truck, Farm Supplies, Buddy L, Original Box, 1940s, 21 In.	880.00
Truck, Fast Freight Express, Coast To Coast, Red, Yellow, Tin	20.00
Truck, Firestone Service, Jack, Tools & Toolbox, Buddy L, Box, 25 In.	7700.00
Truck, Flat Bed, Railing, Tin, England, 1950s, 9 In., 2 Piece	110.00
Truck, Ford, Wooden, Stenciled Sides, Wood Wheels, Steering Wheel, 10 In.	33.00
Truck, Freight, Sunshine Fruit Growers, Tin Lithograph, 13 1/2 In. ....*Illus*	150.00
Truck, Fuel, Pressed Steel, Wyandotte, 10 1/2 In.	95.00
Truck, Gasoline, Cast Iron, 7 In., 2 Piece	195.00
Truck, Green Giant, Pressed Steel, Tonka, 22 In.	210.00
Truck, Hathaway's Bread & Cake Co., Black & White, Cast Iron, Arcade, 9 In.	1900.00
Truck, Highway Maintenance, Cement Mixer, Loading Ramp, Buddy L, 1950s, 21 In.	1980.00
Truck, Highway Maintenance, Fixed Bed, Compressor, Buddy L, Box, 13 1/2 In.	770.00
Truck, Hillclimber, Fire Ladder, Sheet Metal, 3 Ladders, Flywheel, Schieble, 1911, 21 In.	700.00
Truck, Hollywood Film, Ad Light, Red Cab, Battery, Searchlight, Smith-Miller, 18 In.	1300.00
Truck, Horse Van, Pressed Steel, 2 Plastic Horses, Tonka, 13 In.	150.00
Truck, Ice Cream, Friction, Tin Lithograph, Japan, 1960s, 6 In.	125.00
Truck, Ice, International, Canvas Cover, Tongs, Buddy L, Box, 1938, 28 In.	15920.00
Truck, Ice, Red, Cast Iron, Arcade, 7 In.	350.00
Truck, Jaeger Cement Mixer, Painted Cast Iron, Chain Driven Mixer, Kenton, 9 In.	1400.00
Truck, Jewel Tea, Pressed Steel, Tonka, 24 In.	400.00
Truck, Junior Dairy, Painted Pressed Steel, Buddy L, 24 In.	1800.00
Truck, Kraft Cheese, Painted Metal, Smith-Miller, 14 In.	450.00
Truck, Krug's Bakery, Pressed Steel, Painted, Metalcraft, 11 1/2 In.	130.00
Truck, Libby's Coast To Coast Tractor Trailer, Die Cast, Label, Tootsietoy, 9 1/2 In.	240.00

Truck, Livestock, Pressed Steel, Tonka, 22 In. 120.00

Truck, Log, Electric Headlight, 2 Logs, Wood, Buddy L, 26 In. 1100.00

Truck, Long Haulage, Windup, Driver, Tin Lithograph, 10 In. 340.00

Truck, Lorry, Army, Searchlight, 3 Soldiers, Windup, Wells, Box, 1940s, 9 In. 550.00

Truck, Lorry, Drop Side, Plastic Trailer, Milk Churns, Corgi, Box, 4 Piece 200.00

Truck, Lorry, Military, Searchlight, Windup, England, Box, 9 1/2 In. 150.00

Truck, Lumber, Painted Metal, Smith-Miller, 19 1/2 In. 450.00

Truck, Mack, Panel, Cast Iron, Champion, c.1930, 7 5/8 In. 900.00

Truck, Mail, Painted Pressed Steel, Sturditoy, 26 In. ....2900.00 to 3200.00

Truck, Mail, Painted, Steel, Clockwork, Cast Iron Driver, Kingsbury, 7 In. 220.00

Truck, Mail, Pressed Steel, Friction, Schieble, 11 1/2 In. 385.00

Truck, Mail, Steel, Marx, Box 325.00

Truck, Mail, Van Trailer, Pressed Steel, Marx, Box, 25 In. 450.00

Truck, Military, Bulldog Mack Front, Cloth Cover, Chein, 19 In. 130.00

Truck, Milk & Cream, Cast Iron, Rubber Tires, Raised Letters, 3 3/4 In. 360.00

Truck, Milk, Milk Bottle & Holder, Marx, Box, 4 x 11 In. 185.00

Truck, Milk, Opening Side Doors, Milk Cartons, Wood, Buddy L, 12 1/2 In. 1870.00

Truck, Minic Dust Car, Windup, Tin, England, 5 In. 92.00

Truck, Missile Carrier, Buddy L, 1958, 16 In. 450.00

Truck, Mobile Gas, Friction, Tin, Box, 15 In. 1155.00

Truck, Mounted Crane, Lithograph, Bandai, Box, 15 In. 450.00

Truck, Moving Van, Allied Van Lines, Folding Rear Gate, Furniture, Box, 1930s, 30 In. ... 6820.00

Truck, Moving Van, Allied Van Lines, Friction, Tin Lithograph Trailer, 1 x 3 1/2 x 2 In. .. 20.00

Truck, Moving Van, Allied Van Lines, Japan, 1950s, 13 In. 225.00

Truck, Moving Van, Allied Van Lines, Painted Pressed Steel, Buddy L, 30 In. 900.00

Truck, Moving Van, Big Load Van, Mack, C Scale, Tin Litho., Clockwork, Marx, 13 In. .. 385.00

Truck, Moving Van, Lumar Van Lines, Red Cab, Marx, Box, 19 In. 450.00

Truck, Moving Van, North American Van Lines, Metal, Windup, Marx, 13 1/2 In. 195.00

Truck, Moving Van, United Van Lines, Pressed Steel, Tonka, 24 In. 1050.00

Truck, Moving Van, Wood, Painted, Buddy L, 27 1/2 In. 240.00

Truck, Oil, Dan-Dee, Tin Lithograph, Clockwork, Chein, Box, 8 1/2 In. 1650.00

Truck, Oil, Pressed Steel, Buddy L 520.00

Truck, Parcel Post Special Delivery, Tin, Orange, Spring Motor, Strauss, 6 1/2 In. 300.00

Truck, Patrol, Painted Pressed Steel, Friction, Schieble, 11 In. 190.00

Truck, Pickup, Ford, Model T, Painted Cast Iron, Arcade, 8 1/2 In. 425.00

Truck, Pickup, Ford, U Haul, With Trailer, Ny-Lint, Box, 24 1/2 In. 260.00

Truck, Pickup, Horse Trailer, Tonka, Box, 14 In. 225.00

Truck, Pickup, Pressed Steel, Friction, Schieble, 19 In. 440.00

Truck, Plastic, Friction, Box, 1950s, 15 In. 95.00

Truck, Police Patrol, Cast Iron, 1 Passenger, Kenton, 5 1/2 In. 120.00

Truck, Police Patrol, Hillclimber, Pressed Steel, Friction, 2 Figures, 9 In. 250.00

Truck, Police Patrol, Painted Steel, Decals, Keystone, 27 In. 2310.00

Truck, Police Patrol, Pressed Steel, Friction, Cast Iron Driver, Clark, 14 In. 203.00

Truck, Police Patrol, Pressed Steel, Rubber Tires, Keystone, 27 In. 2310.00

Truck, Poultry, Hubley, Box, 1950s 175.00

Truck, Pressed Steel, Friction, Green & Gold, Hillclimber, 1920s 250.00

Truck, Pressed Steel, Structo, 1950s, 18 In. 145.00

Truck, Railway Express, Milk & Ice Cream, Decals, Pressed Steel, Buddy L, 22 In. 650.00

Truck, Railway Express, Pressed Steel, Tin Lithograph, Marx, 20 In. 600.00

Truck, Riecks Ice Cream, Pressed Steel, Steelcraft, 1933, 22 In. 395.00

Truck, Sanitation, Pressed Steel, Tin Lithograph, Marx, 13 1/4 In. 150.00

Truck, Searchlight, Pressed Steel, Buddy L, 15 In. 150.00

Truck, Silver Streak, Painted Metal, Smith-Miller, 23 1/2 In. 200.00

Truck, Silver Streak, Plastic, Windup, Aurora, 1950s, 13 In. 95.00

Truck, Sit-N-Ride, Decals, Keystone, 24 In. 1430.00

Truck, Sprite Boy, Pressed Steel, Marx, 1940s, 21 In. 450.00

Truck, Stake, Arcade, 6 In. 90.00

Truck, Stake, Blue Cab, Red Bed, Marx, 1930s, 13 1/2 In. 230.00

Truck, Stake, Mack, Cast Iron, Marked Champion, Rubber Tires, 7 1/2 In. 985.00

Truck, Stake, Motor Driven, Steel, Clockwork, Rubber Tires, Kingsbury, 15 1/2 In. 7700.00

Truck, Stake, Rubber Tires, Separate Grill, Cast Iron, 4 In. 140.00

Truck, Stake, Steel, Clockwork, Metal Wheels, Rubber Tires, Kingsbury, 10 1/2 In. 250.00

Truck, Tanker, Mack, Hess, Gasoline, Red Funnel, Hong Kong, Marx, 1964 .... 395.00

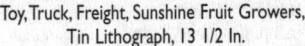

Toy, Truck, Freight, Sunshine Fruit Growers,
Tin Lithograph, 13 1/2 In.

Toy, Van, Indian Motorcycle, Say It With
Flowers, Cast Iron, Hubley, 10 3/4 In.

Truck, Tanker, Pressed Steel, Green & Blue Paint, Red Wheels, Buddy L	745.00
Truck, Tanker, Red Decal, Buddy L, 1925, 3 1/4 In.	575.00
Truck, Texaco Fire, Pressed Steel, Aluminum, Buddy L, 25 In.	130.00
Truck, Tow, Cast Iron, Arcade, 5 7/8 In.	172.00
Truck, Tow, Crank On Side, Rubber Tires, Pressed Steel, Structo, 12 x 4 1/2 In.	70.00
Truck, Tow, Emergency, Buddy L, Box, 14 1/2 In.	350.00
Truck, Tow, Hercules, Tin Lithograph, Chein, 18 In.	750.00
Truck, Tow, International Wrecker Towing Service, Buddy L, Box, 1952, 27 In.	1100.00
Truck, Tow, Japan, 1950s, 8 In.	120.00
Truck, Tow, Marx, 9 In.	495.00
Truck, Tow, Original Paint, No Driver, Cast Iron, Arcade, 8 1/2 In.	747.00
Truck, Tow, Original Paint, Rubber Tires, Arcade, 5 1/2 In.	172.00
Truck, Tow, Packard, Pressed Steel, Decals, Keystone, 27 In.	900.00
Truck, Tow, Pressed Steel, Clockwork, Metal Wheels, Kingsbury, 11 In.	302.00
Truck, Tow, Pressed Steel, Friction, Battery Searchlight, 8 In.	150.00
Truck, Tow, Pressed Steel, Friction, Schieble, 19 1/2 In.	580.00
Truck, Tow, Turnpike, Metal, Japan, Box, 1950s, 11 In.	295.00
Truck, Tow, Wooden Wheels, 3 Colors, Pressed Steel, Buddy L, 1940s, 19 1/2 In.	300.00
Truck, Tow, Wooden, Painted, Buddy L, 18 In.	185.00
Truck, Trailer, Windup Grader, Driver, Steel, Marx, Box	375.00
Truck, Transport, Airplane, Tin, Japan, 1950s, 13 In.	275.00
Truck, Transport, Cattle, Removable Racks & Tailgate, Buddy L, Box, 15 In.	770.00
Truck, Transport, Die Cast, Dinky Toys, England, 17 In., 2 Piece	175.00
Truck, Troop Carrier, Tin Lithograph, Canvas Cover, Marx, 20 1/2 In.	170.00
Truck, Utility, Lifting Mechanism, Plastic Poles, Lumar, 19 In.	144.00
Truck, Water Sprinkler, Tin Lithograph, Driver, Strauss, 11 In.	800.00 to 1265.00
Truck, Water Tower, Painted Pressed Steel, Brass Handrails, Buddy L, 39 In.	2200.00
Truck, Windup, Tin, Wyandotte, 9 x 5 x 7 In.	22.00
Truck, Wrigley's Gum, Semitrailer, Railroad Express Agency, Buddy L, 1935, 23 In.	1095.00
Trunk, Doll's, Dome Top, Paper Trim, Lid Compartments, Clothes, 14 x 18 x 12 In.	978.00
Trunk, Doll's, Dome Top, Wooden, Paper Interior, 19 3/4 x 9 3/4 x 10 3/4 In.	285.00
Trunk, Doll's, Leather, Bentwood, Clasp, Hutchinson, Colorado Spgs., c.1890, 18 In.	325.00
Trunk, Doll's, Metal, Wood, Dome Top, Strapping, Clothing, Interior Tray, 14 x 10 1/2 In.	250.00
Trunk, Doll's, Wooden, Metal Trim	50.00
Tunnel, Lincoln, From N.Y. To N.J., Unique Arts, 1920s	349.00
Typewriter, Types Capital & Small Letters, Red Metal, Berwin, 1930s, 12 x 12 x 8 In.	80.00
Uncle Sam, Bicycle Act, Mechanical, American Flyer, 1915, 20 1/2 x 17 x 3 In.	1150.00
Uncle Sam, Dancing, Wooden, Metal, Dances When Board Snapped, 1885, 15 x 28 In.	1955.00
Uncle Sam, Eagle Chariot, Star Spangled, Cast Iron, Kenton, c.1911, 12 In.	4200.00
Uncle Sam, On Bicycle, Gravity Toy, Gilbert, 1920s, 8 x 7 In.	460.00
Van, Indian Motorcycle, Say It With Flowers, Cast Iron, Hubley, 10 3/4 In. ...... *Illus* 1	26750.00
Velocipede, Boy Rider, Painted, Stenciled, Clockwork, Stevens & Brown, c.1880, 12 In.	2280.00
Velocipede, Girl Rider, Papier-Mache, Cloth, Cast Iron, Clockwork, c.1870, 11 1/2 In.	4500.00
Velocipede, Horse Drawn, Hide Covered, Glass Eyes, Wood Cart, Wicker Basket, 57 In.	715.00
Vendor, Ice Cream, Windup, Japan, Box, 1950s	275.00
View-Master, E.T., Gift Set, Unit & 3 Reels, 1982	18.00
Village, School, Church, Fire Station, Studio, Houses, Figures, Built-Rite Toys, 1900	75.00
Violin, Tin, 10 1/2 In.	175.00
Wagon, 2 Horses, Driver In Seat, Sack, Pratt & Letchworth, 1893, 17 1/2 In.	3500.00

Wagon, Chester Gump, Cast Iron, 7 1/2 In. 200.00
Wagon, Circus, Royal Band, Cast Iron, 4 Hoses, 8 Musicians & Driver, Hubley, 22 In. 2240.00
Wagon, Coal, 1 Horse, Driver, Hubley, 1906, 15 1/2 In. 995.00
Wagon, Coal, Driver & Shovel, Hubley, 1915, 12 In. 525.00
Wagon, Coal, Original Driver & Shovel, Hubley, 1915, 4 1/2 In. 250.00
Wagon, Doll's, American Company Express, Paper On Wood, Oak Handle, 17 In. 402.00
Wagon, Doll's, Push, Blue & Red Paint, 31 In. 795.00
Wagon, Dray, Balancing, Horse, Cast Iron, Ives, c.1893, 15 In. 2280.00
Wagon, Dray, Open Seat, Driver, Cast Iron, Harris Co., 13 In. 860.00
Wagon, Eclipse, Roller Bearing, c.1890 .... 525.00
Wagon, Farm, Ox Team, Driver, Cast Iron, Dent, c.1905, 15 1/2 In. 1800.00
Wagon, Grocery, Plaque At Side, Groceries, Tin, Windup, Kingsbury, 8 In. 60.00
Wagon, Harrisburg Telegraph, Newsboy, Painted, Rubber Tires 413.00
Wagon, Hygeta Ice, Moving Horses, Driver, Red Lettering & Wheels 2310.00
Wagon, Ice, Driver, 2 Horses, Orange, Red, Cast Iron, 9 1/2 In. 300.00
Wagon, Ice, Polar, Black Horse, Orange, Red, Cast Iron, Kenton, c.1905, 13 1/4 In. 1800.00
Wagon, Mail, Tin Lithograph, 18 In. 605.00
Wagon, Milk, Alderne Dairy, Wood, Pulled By Fabric-Covered Horse, Schoenhut 2530.00
Wagon, Milk, Horse Drawn, Tin, Marx, 1930s, 10 In. .... 235.00 to 295.00
Wagon, Milk, Red, Wooden, 8-Spoke Wheels 1100.00
Wagon, Milk, Ride-On, Wood Horse, Leather Harness, Golden Pasture Farm, 31 In. 1440.00
Wagon, Milk, Tin Lithograph, Converse, 7 1/2 In. 425.00
Wagon, Milk, Toytown, Dappled Horse, Tin Lithograph, Windup, Marx, 10 In. .... 140.00 to 180.00
Wagon, Painted, Stencil, Dives, Pomeroy & Stewart, Pull Toy, c.1915, 9 In. 745.00
Wagon, Police, Happy Patrol, 2 Black Horses, 3 Figures, Kenton, c.1905, 19 In. 3000.00
Wagon, Police, Happy Patrol, Cast Iron, Horse Drawn, Kenton, c.1911, 19 In. 1960.00
Wagon, Police, Patrol, Cast Iron, Horses, Police Figures, Ideal, 21 In. 575.00
Wagon, Sand & Gravel, 2 Horses, Mechanical Floor-Dumping Action, Hubley, 14 In. 100.00
Wagon, Show, 2 Spotted Mares, 4 Bay Mares, Leather Harness, 60 In. 650.00
Walker, Choo-Choo Cherry, Funny Face Drink Mix, Plastic Weight, Premium, 1971, 3 In. .. 12.00
Wallet, Barbie, Vinyl, Barbie Figures, Comb, Nail File, Photo Holders, Mirror, 1961 .... 90.00
Wash Set, Doll's, Enameled Tin, Violet Design, Gilt Edging, Red Box, c.1910, 8 In. 325.00
Washing Set, Sunny Monday, Ironing Board, Wash Tub, Parker Bros., Box 400.00
Western Frontier Set, Auburn, Box, 1950-1960, 18 x 12 In. 225.00
Western Sheriff, White Horse, Black Hat, 4 Guns, Hartland Plastics, 7 In. 40.00
Whirligig, Boswell Bros., Groceries & Dry Goods, Polychrome, Painted, Wood 575.00
Woman, Churning, Bends At Waist, Clockwork, Ives, c.1880, 11 In. 5100.00
Workers, Sawing Top Of Bench, Windup, 1920s 290.00
Workman, At Grindstone, Tin, 1930, 4 1/2 In. 34.00
Yo-Yo, Beech-Nut Candy, White 40.00
Zeppelin, Barn & Landing Pad, Cast Iron, Green 200.00
Zeppelin, Pony Blimp, Cast Iron, 6 In. 350.00
Zeppelin, Pressed Steel, Windup, Moving Propellers, Marklin, 17 In. 1350.00
Zeppelin, Tin, Propellers Spin When Pulled, Pull Toy, 28 In. 375.00
Zeppelin, Wheels, Cast Iron, 5 In. 250.00
Zigzag, Tin Lithograph, Red, White, Blue, Spring Motor, Black & White Riders, 5 In. ... 1300.00
Zilotone, Pressed Steel, Spring Motor, Xylophone, Clown, 3 Song Cans, Wolverine, 7 In. . 400.00
Zoo Pavilion, Elastolin Type, Animals, Keeper, Stickers, Austria, 14 x 17 x 8 In. 330.00

TRAMP ART is a form of folk art made since the Civil War. It is usually
made from chip-carved cigar boxes. Examples range from small boxes
and picture frames to full-sized pieces of furniture.

Birdhouse, Indian, Hatchet In Hand, Knife In Other, 3 Windows, 19 x 20 In. 1430.00
Box, Chip Carved Stepped Pyramid, Lift Lid, 4 1/2 x 10 1/2 x 8 1/2 In. 275.00
Box, Floral Print Cloth, Brass Trim, Lion Head Lid, Lined Interior, 10 1/2 In. 190.00
Box, Handle Shaped Hinged Lid, Red, 6 1/2 x 14 1/2 In. 259.00
Box, Hearts & Geometric Design, 7 1/4 x 12 1/2 In. 140.00
Box, Letter, Horses, Fish, Leaf, Wall Mount, 18 x 13 In. 308.00
Box, Nickel Plated Handle, Lid Escutcheon, Lion's Head Ring Pulls, 1885, 5 3/4 In. 220.00
Box, Pine, Graduated Sections, Brass Feet, Embossed 1897 C.R., 13 x 9 In. 55.00
Box, Pine, Stepped, Brass Double Handles, Lid Mirror, Lined, 13 1/2 In. 165.00
Box, Rectangles & Squares, Carved Hearts & Teardrops On Cover, 7 x 10 1/2 In. 165.00
Box, Red & Black, Pedestal, c.1900, 11 x 9 1/2 x 8 In. 395.00

Box, Sewing, 2 Drawers, 1914-1916, 8 1/2 x 11 x 6 1/2 In. 1350.00
Box, Sewing, Notched Edges, Drawer, Interior Pincushion, Lift Lid, 1898, 7 1/2 In. 220.00
Box, Sewing, Padded Velvet Inset On Cover, Early 20th Century, 14 x 9 x 8 In. 374.00
Box, Stand, Stacked, Chip Carved Decoration, Lift Top, 30 1/2 x 21 1/2 x 16 In. 660.00
Box, Triangular Side Panels, Diamond On Lid, Lion Head Ring, Lock, 3 1/2 x 6 In. 126.00
Box, Triangular Stepped, Concentric Squares On Front, 5 1/2 x 11 3/4 In. 55.00
Box, Uncle Sam, Brother Can You Spare A Dime, Troy, N.Y., 1990, 20 x 14 In. 345.00
Cabinet, Hanging, Figures On 2 Pierced Doors, 19 x 11 1/2 In. 175.00
Case, 3 Drawers, Mirror On Shaped Supports, Geometric Designs, 67 x 39 1/2 In. 8050.00
Chair, Doll's, Puzzlework, Arched Crest, Incised Foliage, 14 1/2 x 11 In. 345.00
Chest, 2 Drawers, Chip Carved Border, Marked Minnie, 6 1/2 x 7 x 4 1/2 In. 360.00
Church, Steeple, Flowerpot Cutouts, Fence, 20 x 17 In. 1955.00
Cupboard, Pine, 2 Sections, Chip Carved Panels, 67 x 28 x 13 In. 1320.00
Display Case, Castle Shape, Door, Drawer, 1870s 695.00
Dresser Box, Hinged Lid, Mirror, 7 1/2 x 7 1/2 x 10 In. 495.00
Frame, 2 Interior Bands, Diamonds, Molded Liner, 29 x 25 In. 770.00
Frame, 3-Step, Indian Beadwork, Blower, Geometric, Symbols, 8 1/2 x 11 1/8 In. 690.00
Frame, Flower Petal Corners, Late 19th Century, 9 x 7 1/2 In. 1250.00
Frame, Heart Corners, Rectangular, Stepped, Mirror, 24 x 19 1/2 In. 440.00
Frame, Stepped Pyramid, Notched Edges, Print Titled Playing Cook, 5 1/2 x 7 In. 125.00
House, 2-Story, Carved Tiles On Roof, Interior Poems, 13 3/4 x 13 3/4 In. 8800.00
House, Colonial, 2 Story, Side Porches, 3 Chimneys, Doors Open, 11 x 11 In. 302.00
Jewelry Box, Lid, Chip Carved Geometric Decoration, 5 1/2 x 10 1/2 x 6 1/2 In. 275.00
Jewelry Box, Pincushion Top, Lined Interior, Mirror On Lid, Lock, 5 1/4 x 9 3/4 In. 140.00
Match Safe, Star Shaped Back, Philip Weingard, 1904, 11 x 7 In. 69.00
Mirror, Chip Carved Frame, Scrolled Sides, Stacked Pyramid, 35 x 23 x 2 1/2 In. 880.00
Mirror, Chip Carved Stepped Pyramids, Laminated Back, 35 x 31 In. 440.00
Mirror, Stepped Diamond & Teardrop, Alligatored Red & Black Paint, 17 x 26 In. 660.00
Mirror, Yellow Paint, Pierced Crest, Love Birds, Deer, c.1911, 36 x 17 3/8 x 6 In. 2990.00
Planter, Window, Arched Gateway, Picket Fencing, 16 1/2 x 20 In. 137.00
Secretary, Drop Front, Carved, Pierced Tin Top & Bottom 9000.00
Trinket Box, Cherry & Vine, Red & Green Paint, 3 3/4 x 29 1/2 x 5 In. 112.00
Umbrella Stand, 2 Holders, 4 Short Drawers, Angled Feet, Painted, 26 1/2 x 30 In. 633.00
Wall Pocket, Arched Back Set With Stars, 8 x 4 1/2 In. 431.00
Wall Pocket, Heart Shape, Mirror, Applied Hearts, 31 x 17 1/2 In. 1265.00

TRAPS for animals may be handmade. One of the most unusual is the
mousetrap made so that when the mouse entered the trap, it was hit on
the head with a mallet. Other traps were commercially manufactured
and often are marked with the name of the manufacturer. Many traps
were designed to be as humane as possible, and they would trap the
live animal so it could be released in the woods.

Bear, LR On Springs, 41 1/2 In. 247.00
Beaver, Hand Forged, 12 In. 66.00
Double Spring, Chain, 19 1/2 In. 120.00
Forged, Single Spring, Made Into Double Spring, 21 In. 35.00
Forged, Teeth, 16 1/2 In. 77.00
Newhouse No. 4, Oneida Community 22.00
Sing Spring, Forged, Chain, Ideal & IV, 22 In. 385.00
Single Long Spring, No. 1, Oneida Community, 8 1/2 In. 14.00
Wolf, Double Spring, Hand Forged, 33 In. 165.00

TREEN, see Wooden category.

TRENCH ART is a form of folk art made by soldiers. Metal casings from
bullets and mortar shells were cut and decorated to form useful objects,
such as vases.

Belt, Buttons From Enemy Soldiers, Leather, Marked HH & 1918 .... 225.00
Candlestick, From German Officer's Sword Hilt, Lion's Head Pommel, Pair 350.00
Cigarette Lighter, Gun, Brass, World War II, 4 1/4 In. 200.00
Knife, Shell Casing Handle, Engraved Nude & Sicily 1944, 9 In. 80.00
Lamp Base, Cannon Shell, Monogram A.E.F., 13 1/2 In. 150.00
Ring, Etched 1947 & Korea, 6-Pointed Star & Rising Sun 25.00

Vase, Cannon Shell, Hammered Holly Branch, World War II	150.00
Vase, Drape Design, Pair	125.00

TRIVETS are now used to hold hot dishes. Most trivets of the late nineteenth and early twentieth centuries were made to hold hot irons. Iron
or brass reproductions are being made of many of the old styles.

Aluminum, Griswold, 4 Indentations Making 4 Button Legs, 8 In. Diameter	20.00
Brass, Footman, Eagle, Wooden Handle, 8 3/4 x 16 In.	168.00
Brass, Lyre Shape, Floral Center, Wood Handle, Iron Base, 3 Legs, Snake Feet, 13 x 5 In.	110.00
Cast Iron, Compliments Toledo Stove & Iron, Copper Washed, 7 1/2 In.	173.00
Cast Iron, Tulips, Intertwined Handle, Initialed WBR	55.00
Fleur-De-Lis, Trefoil Cutout, 3-Footed, Swan Tavern, 10 In.	27.00
Forged Copper, Heart Shape, Wood Handle, 18th Century, 12 In.	224.00
Geometric Design, Bulbed Shaft, 3-Footed, Black Paint, 19th Century, 11 3/4 In.	258.00
Heart Shape, Iron, 3 Peg Feet, 8 1/2 x 4 1/2 In.	165.00
Heart Shape, Iron, Footed, 2 x 7 In.	143.00
Heart Shape, Pencil Legs, 1 3/8 x 6 3/4 In.	522.00
Heart Shape, Wrought Iron, 3 Riveted Feet	143.00
Phoenix Bird, Forged Iron, Brass, Reticulated, 9 x 16 x 12 In.	392.00
Star, Iron	40.00
Triangular, Handle, Center Rams Horn Support, Punch Design, Iron, Peg Feet, 11 x 6 In.	250.00
Wood, Brass, Iron, Cut Brass Top, Wood Handle, Hearth, 14 x 6 x 13 In., Pair	460.00
Wood, Shaped Apron, Cutout Feet, Square Nails, Alligatored Varnish, Hearth, 5 x 9 In.	385.00
Wrought Iron, Twisted Pot Handle, 5 1/4 x 7 1/4 In.	56.00

TRUNKS of many types were made. The nineteenth-century sea chest
was often handmade of unpainted wood. Brass-fitted camphorwood
chests were brought back from the Orient. Leather-covered trunks
were popular from the late eighteenth to mid-nineteenth centuries. By
1895, trunks were covered with canvas or decorated sheet metal.
Embossed metal coverings were used from 1870 to 1910. By 1925,
trunks were covered with vulcanized fiber or undecorated metal.

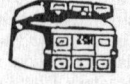

Black Stenciled Landscapes, On Stand, Paper Label, 24 1/2 x 37 In., Pair	4200.00
Brass, Repousse, Domestic Life Scenes, Foliate Border, Dutch, 18 x 26 x 17 In.	365.00
Brass Tacks For Hex Signs, Leather Cover, 18 In.	4450.00
Camphorwood, Brass Bound, Brass Handles, 33 x 16 x 15 In.	259.00
Camphorwood, Carved, Landscape & Figures, 21 x 41 x 21 In.	300.00
Camphorwood, Leather Cover, Brass Tack Design, Bail Handles, Chinese Export, 25 In.	495.00
Camphorwood, Leather Cover, Floral Borders, Brass Tacks, Chinese Export, 19 1/2 In.	385.00
Camphorwood, Leather Covered, Chinese Export, 13 x 30 1/2 In.	990.00
Camphorwood, Leather, Brass Tacks, Side Handles, Escutcheons, c.1890, 25 x 13 x 10 In.	489.00
Dome Top, Bail Handle On Top, Painted, Sponged, Green, Gold, Black, 8 x 7 In.	110.00
Dome Top, Bird, Flowers & Leaves, Tin Hinges & Hasp, Early 19th Century, 5 x 12 In.	2090.00
Dome Top, Hide Covered, Brass Tacks, Marked W.H.W., 19 1/2 x 10 x 8 In.	83.00
Dome Top, Inlaid Bone Panels, Silver Plated Strips, Lined Interior, 13 1/2 x 16 In.	110.00
Dome Top, Painted Stenciled Design, 19th Century, 20 x 10 In.	875.00
Dome Top, Pine, Black Painted Metal, 14 1/2 x 28 In.	115.00
Dome Top, Pine, Dovetailed, Original Red Grained Paint, 32 x 20 In.	385.00
Dome Top, Red Polka Dot Panels, 42 1/2 x 20 x 17 In.	165.00
Dome Top, Red, Blue, Mustard Wallpaper, Flowers, Bentwood Handles, 14 In.	165.00
Dome Top, Softwood, Painted, Scrolled Leaves, Basket, Drapery, 19th Century, 24 In.	230.00
Dome Top, Yellow & Brown Sponge Grain, Green Interior, Heart Handles, 30 x 20 In.	770.00
Foot Locker, C.E. Hackenburg, 1st Nebraska Co., Spanish American War	110.00
Leather Covered, Black, Tooled Design, Metal Strap, Brass Tacks, Civil War, 13 x 28 In.	60.00
Louis Vuitton, Box, Hat, Canvas, Leather Trim, Strap Handle, Padded Interior, 1950s	863.00
Louis Vuitton, Case, Luncheon, Stainless Steel Thermos, Sandwich Box, 11 1/2 In.	2530.00
Louis Vuitton, Foot Locker, Leather Trim, Wood Bands, Wheels, 1930s, 43 In.	3450.00
Louis Vuitton, Garment Bag	345.00
Louis Vuitton, Hat Case, 20 x 17 1/2 In.	2587.00
Louis Vuitton, Steamer, Rectangular, Red, Black Monogram, 22 x 43 x 22 1/4 In.	3680.00
Louis Vuitton, Steamer, Rectangular, Yellow Monogram, 22 x 22 1/2 In.	3680.00
Louis Vuitton, Steamer, Rectangular, Yellow Monogram, 25 3/4 x 43 1/2 x 21 In.	3220.00
Louis Vuitton, Stripped Canvas, Fabric Lined, 4 Trays, Late 19th Century, 27 1/2 In.	1630.00

Louis Vuitton, Suitcase, Brown, 2 Piece 476.00
Louis Vuitton, Suitcase, Canvas, Leather Trim, Brass Locks, Top Tray, 19 1/2 x 9 In. 1035.00
Louis Vuitton, Suitcase, Canvas, Leather Trim, Monogram, Brass Corners & Lock, 27 In. .. 1095.00
Louis Vuitton, Suitcase, Leather Trim, Brass Corners, Lock & Fittings, 1930s, 22 In. 1265.00
Louis Vuitton, Suitcase, Leather Trim, Canvas Interior, Top Tray, 31 1/2 In. 1150.00
Louis Vuitton, Suitcase, Leather, Brassbound, 9 x 28 In. 632.00
Louis Vuitton, Suitcase, Monogrammed Canvas, Leather Trim, Brass Lock, 29 1/2 In. ... 575.00
Louis Vuitton, Suitcase, Monogrammed Canvas, Leather Trim, Brass Locks, 16 x 24 In. .. 575.00
Louis Vuitton, Suitcase, Monogrammed Canvas, Leather Trim, Paper Label, 24 In. 980.00
Louis Vuitton, Suitcase, Tan, Customized Lock Plate, 1930s, 32 In. 1610.00
Louis Vuitton, Suitcase, Vertical, 21 x 8 1/2 x 24 In. 290.00
Louis Vultton, Suitcase, Zippered Lid, Buckle Straps, 12 x 22 x 8 In. 415.00
Louis Vuitton, Wardrobe, Hanging, Monogrammed Canvas, Leather Trim, 44 In. 3220.00
Louis Vuitton, Wardrobe, Leather Trim, Brass Corners & Locks, Rods, Hangers, 45 In. ... 3740.00
Oriental, Dovetailed, Mother-Of-Pearl Inlay, Wrought Iron Handles, 31 x 15 In. 110.00
Oriental, Painted, Red, Flowers, Iron Escutcheon, 52 1/2 x 18 x 24 3/4 In. 215.00
Pine, Unicorn & Tulip Panels, Star On Dome Top, 25 1/2 x 40 In. 825.00
Rawhide, Brass Tacks, Original Lining, Maker's Logo, Early 1800s, 27 x 13 x 10 3/4 In. . . 165.00
Sailor's, Cherrywood, Inset Tray, Sailor In Full Dress On Inner Lid, 1850s 650.00
Tacks, Marbled Paper Lining, 21 x 11 x 10 In. 27.00
Trinket, Baird, Tulip & Floral, Late 18th Century, 5 x 13 3/4 In. 880.00
Wood, Wrought Iron Bands & Trim, 2 Bale Handles, Brass Hasp, 26 1/2 x 31 In. 137.00

TUTHILL Cut Glass Company of Middletown, New York, worked from
1902 to 1923. Of special interest are the finely cut pieces of stemware
and tableware.

Cake Stand, Vintage, 8 In. 1750.00
Dish, Oval, Signed, 9 1/4 In. 450.00

TYPEWRITER collectors divide typewriters into two main classifica-
tions: the index machine, which has a pointer and a dial for letter selection, and the keyboard machine, most commonly seen today. The first
successful typewriter was made by Sholes and Glidden in 1874.

Corona, Model 3, Pat. July 20, 1917, 10 1/2 x 6 x 10 In. 29.00
Edison-Mimeograph Typewriter No. I, 1894 .... *Illus* 12300.00
Oliver, No. 3, Visible 165.00
Oliver, No. A5, Visible, c.1900 .... 45.00
Royal, Portable, Self-Contained Case, Complete 52.00
Sholes & Glidden, 1873 .... *Illus* 33500.00
Tin, Carter's Ink Co., Green, Brown Lady In Cameo Frame 4.00

TYPEWRITER RIBBON TINS are now being collected. The lithographed
tin containers have been used since the 1870s. Most popular with collectors are tins with pictorial graphics.

A & W 3R, Orange & Black Diamonds 33.00
A. P. Little, Red, Black Child, Square, 2 5/8 In. 100.00
Advocate, Red & Black, Lion 27.00
Aladdin, Purple & Cream, Genie 125.00
Aladdin, Red, Magic Lamp 30.00
Allied Flagship, Sail Boat 6.00

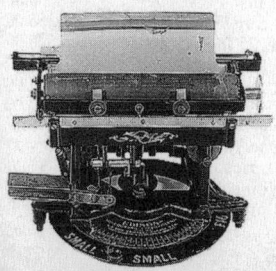

Typewriter, Edison-
Mimeograph Typewriter
No. I, 1894

Typewriter, Sholes &
Glidden, 1873

Beauvais National, Teal, Eagle 187.00
Benjamin Franklin Brand, Green, Portrait Of Benjamin Franklin 50.00
Blue, Seagull On Reeds 12.00
Blue, Secretary Silhouette ....18.00 to 36.00
Carters Ink Co., Green, Brown Lady, Cameo Frame 4.00
Crowfoot, Red, Black Crow 70.00
Deluxe Clean Type, Red, Star, Red Parrot 40.00
Duchess Excellence, Green, Lady In Gold Ball Gown 32.00
Duro Flex, Blue & Red, White Ribbon 30.00
Gibraltar, Mountain, Sun & Water 30.00
Green Buccaneer, Green, Pirate 10.00
Guardian, Blue, Airplanes 14.00
HCS Brand, Red, Gold Lilies On The Left 21.00
Horse Jumping 10.00
IBM, Green, Electronic Typewriter 32.00
Ideal Nylon, Flowers On Edge 3.00
Indiana, Red, American Indian 98.00
International Telephone, Green, Center Graphic 152.00
Invincible, Red, Silk Feather 10.00
Kabella Brand, Black Bell 39.00
Kwill, Red Logo, Decorative Metal 34.00
Old Colony, Green 18.00
Old Dutch, Blue, Dutch Scene 32.00
Old English, Winter Scene, Stage Coach, 4 Horses, 6 Men 30.00
Old Town, Blue, Old Brooklyn Bridge 20.00
Panama Bronze, Blue, Gold Land, Airplane In Corner 15.00
Panama Commercial Brand, Brown & White, Land 77.00
Perfect, Black & White Design 39.00
Pigeon Brand, Black, Pigeon 13.00
Queen's, Gray, Boy With Balloons 200.00
Satin Finish, Red & Black, Black Boy 40.00
Silk Gauze, Curled Up Dragon 18.00
Tagger, Yellow 30.00
Varsity Roytype Silver, Scottish Terrier, Black 50.00

UHL pottery was made in Evansville, Indiana, in 1854. The pottery
moved to Huntingburg, Indiana, in 1908. Stoneware and glazed pottery
were made until the mid-1940s.

Jug, Christmas, 1930 .... 875.00
Jug, Christmas, 1941 .... 250.00
Jug, Commemorative, 1991 .... 125.00
Jug, Commemorative, 1994 .... 90.00
Jug, Commemorative, 2000 .... 100.00
Pitcher, Maple Leaves On Sides, Oval Bottom, Straight Neck, Handle, 9 1/2 In. ... 165.00

UMBRELLA collectors like rain or shine. The first known umbrella was
owned by King Louis XIII of France in 1637. The earliest umbrellas
were sunshades, not designed to be used in the rain. The umbrella was
embellished and redesigned many times. In 1852, the fluted steel rib
style was developed, and it has remained the most useful style.

Gold Plated, Engraved Vertical Bands, Mother-Of-Pearl Band, 31 In. 230.00
Ivory, 2 Bands Of Silver Gilt Wire, Leather Wrist Strap, Carved Acorn, 36 In. .. 258.00
Parasol, Black Lace, Butterfly & Flowers, Carved Looped Handle, 35 In. 825.00
Parasol, Black Lace, Daisy Design, White Silk Lining, Wooden Handle, 32 1/2 In. ... 55.00
Parasol, Edwardian, Gold, Ivory, Handle, c.1905, 11 In. 138.00
Sterling Silver & Ivory, Handle, Cavorting Elephants, Black Silk, 11 In. 373.00

UNION PORCELAIN WORKS was established at Greenpoint, New York,
in 1848 by Charles Cartlidge. The company went through a series of
ownership changes and finally closed in the early 1900s. The company
made a fine quality white porcelain that was often decorated in clear,
bright colors.

Oyster Plate, Shell Shape, Assortment Of Shells, c.1881, 8 1/2 In. 5175.00

Plate, Shellfish, Clamshell Form, Briggs, Boston, 8 1/2 In., Set Of 11 .... 2640.00
Tazza, Ribbon Border, Gilt Trim, Marked, c.1876, 6 3/4 In. 176.00

UNIVERSITY OF NORTH DAKOTA, see North Dakota School of Mines category.

VAL ST. LAMBERT Cristalleries of Belgium was founded by Messieurs
Kemlin and Lelievre in 1825. The company is still in operation. All
types of table glassware and decorative glassware have been made.   *Val St Lambert*
Pieces are often decorated with cut designs.

Figurine, Crucifixion, 13 3/4 x 6 1/2 x 2 3/4 In. 110.00
Plate, Van Dyck, Intaglio Portrait, Etched, 1969, 8 In. 25.00
Plate, Van Gogh, Intaglio Portrait, Etched, 1969, 8 In. 25.00
Vase, Romeo, Pink, Handles, Remnant Label 249.00

VALLERYSTHAL Glassworks was founded in 1836 in Lorraine, France.
In 1854, the firm became Klenglin et Cie. It made table and decorative
glass, opaline, cameo, and art glass. A line of covered, pressed glass
animal dishes was made in the nineteenth century. The firm is still
working.

Vase, Leaves & Flowers, Cameo Foot Washed In Gold, Signed, 5 3/4 In. 2240.00

VAN BRIGGLE pottery was made by Artus Van Briggle in Colorado
Springs, Colorado, after 1901. Van Briggle had been a decorator at
Rookwood Pottery of Cincinnati, Ohio. He died in 1904. His wares
usually had modeled relief decorations and a soft, dull glaze. The pottery is still working and still making some of the original designs.

Bowl, Acorns, Leaves, Oval Shape, Purple Matte Glaze, Blue Veins, c.1940, 6 1/4 In. 374.00
Bowl, Dragonfly, Closed In Rim, 4 Dragonflies On Rim, 1922, 2 x 8 3/4 In. 345.00
Bowl, Flower Frog, Dragonflies, Frogs, Shaded Turquoise Matte Glaze, 8 In. .....259.00 to 302.00
Bowl, Indian Woman Grinding Corn, Turquoise Glaze, 5 1/2 x 5 In. ....135.00 to 173.00
Bowl, Leaf Band, Green Matte Glaze, 2 1/2 x 6 In. 345.00
Bowl, Leaves, Spade Shape, Brown Matte Glaze, 1903, 4 3/4 x 3 1/4 In. 1380.00
Flower Frog, Light Brown, 2 1/2 x 5 1/2 In. 120.00
Plate, Poppy Blossom, Leaves, Green Matte Glaze, 1903, 8 1/2 In. 1265.00
Sconce, Celtic Design, Cobalt, Turquoise Matte Glaze, Electrified, 7 1/4 x 6 In. 288.00
Vase, Alternating Leaves, Mulberry Brown Glaze, 1920, 4 1/4 In. 200.00
Vase, Aqua Matte Glaze, Squat, Marked, 5 1/4 x 6 1/2 In. 632.00
Vase, Arrowroot Leaves, Purple, Rose Matte Glaze, Collared Rim, 17 x 12 In. 3220.00
Vase, Bird-Of-Paradise, Tiger Eye, Walnut Glaze, 1897, 6 1/2 In. 3200.00
Vase, Blue Black Glaze, Leaf Shape, Anna Van Briggle, 6 x 4 In. 86.00
Vase, Blue Green Matte Crystalline Glaze, 1906, 8 x 5 In. 805.00
Vase, Blue Matte Glaze, 1905, 5 In. 460.00
Vase, Blue Matte Glaze, Buttressed Handles, Closed Mouth, 8 1/2 x 7 In. 880.00
Vase, Blue Matte Glaze, Trefoils, Bulbous, 7 1/2 x 6 In. 460.00
Vase, Blue To Aqua Ground, Waisted Neck, Tapering Body, 6 3/4 In. 103.00
Vase, Blue, Maroon Matte Glaze, Handles, 1930s, 2 1/4 In. 11.00
Vase, Broad Carved Leaves, Purple, Yellow Matte Glaze, 1906, 8 In. 1760.00
Vase, Broad Foot, Turquoise Glaze, Strap Handles, Cylindrical Shape, 1920s, 5 In. 345.00
Vase, Bud, Blue, Green Matte Glaze, Squat, 5 x 3 1/2 In. 489.00
Vase, Bud, Leaves, Green Matte Glaze, Bottle Shape, c.1904, 4 1/2 x 3 1/2 In. 805.00
Vase, Climbing For Honey, Blue & Turquoise Matte Glaze, 1920s, 16 x 5 1/2 In. 3220.00
Vase, Clover, Mulberry Blue Glaze, 6 x 2 5/8 In. 190.00
Vase, Cornflowers, Aqua Blue Matte Glaze, Signed, 12 In. 805.00
Vase, Crocus, Green Matte Glaze, Marked, 1903, 7 1/2 In. 4025.00
Vase, Daisies, Broad Leaves, Blue Matte Glaze, 2 Handles, Tapered, 9 In. 175.00
Vase, Daisies, Turquoise Matte Glaze, Elongated Oval, 10 x 3 1/2 In. 2070.00
Vase, Deer Scene, Green, Blue Matte Glaze, Post 1930s, 9 In. 58.00
Vase, Flowers On Neck, Purple Matte Glaze, 3 3/4 In. 220.00
Vase, Flowers, Blue Matte Glaze, 1907-1912, 10 In. 978.00
Vase, Flowers, Blue, Purple Glaze, c.1916, 6 3/4 x 3 In. 345.00
Vase, Flowers, Broad Leaves, Blue, Aqua Matte Glaze, 4 x 3 In. 192.00
Vase, Flowers, Buff Clay, Brown & Celadon Matte Glaze, 6 1/2 x 3 3/4 In. 1840.00
Vase, Flowers, Deep Plum Maroon Matte Glaze, Gourd Shape, 6 x 2 In. 165.00

Vase, Flowers, Leaves Design, Brown Matte Glaze, 1920s, 17 In. 495.00
Vase, Flowers, Walnut Brown Matte Glaze, 1905, 6 1/2 In. 920.00
Vase, Green, Gray Mottled Matte Glaze, 1906, 7 In. 1430.00
Vase, Iris, Broad Leaves, Turquoise, Blue & Green Matte Glaze, 16 1/2 x 8 1/2 In. 7480.00
Vase, Leaves, Blue, Aqua Mottled Matte Glaze, Post 1930s, 3 In. 115.00
Vase, Leaves, Cream, White Matte Glaze, Post 1930s, 4 In. 11.00
Vase, Leaves, Persian Rose Matte Glaze, Tapered Rim, 4 1/2 x 5 In. 373.00
Vase, Leaves, Red, Blue Matte Glaze, c.1920, 7 1/2 In. 299.00
Vase, Leaves, Teal & Red Matte Glaze, Bottle Shape, 1904, 8 1/2 x 5 1/2 In. 3220.00
Vase, Leaves, Turquoise Semi Matte Glaze, 1908-1911, 5 x 3 1/2 In. 518.00
Vase, Leaves, Vertical Long Stem, Mauve Matte Glaze, 6 In. 2420.00
Vase, Lorelei, Burgundy, Deep Blue Matte Glaze, 1920-1930, 10 1/2 In. 1210.00
Vase, Mustard & Blue Matte Glaze, Bulbous, Tapered Neck, 1914, 8 1/2 In. 460.00
Vase, Oak, Acorn, Green, Burgundy Matte Glaze, 1916, 3 3/4 x 5 1/2 In. 518.00
Vase, Pink Matte Glaze, 2 Lower Handles, Marked, 1904, 13 In. 3450.00
Vase, Poppy Pods, Burgundy Matte Glaze, Incised, Squat, 1906, 3 1/2 x 6 In. 1150.00
Vase, Poppy Pods, Leaves, Tapered Shoulder, Turquoise Matte Glaze, 10 x 7 1/4 In. 4025.00
Vase, Quatrefoil, Green Matte Glaze, 1908-1911, 3 1/4 x 3 In. 460.00
Vase, Raised Leaves, Handles, Marked, 9 In. 460.00
Vase, Red To Teal Matte Glaze, Corseted Shoulder, 1906, 11 1/4 x 5 In. 1955.00
Vase, Rose, Green Matte Glaze, Marked, 1905, 7 In. 286.00
Vase, Tapered Shoulder, Poppy Pods, Turquoise Matte Glaze, 10 x 7 1/4 In. 4025.00
Vase, Teal Matte Glaze, Sloping Shoulder, 1905, 9 3/4 x 4 1/4 In. 920.00
Vase, Thistles, Green Crystalline Glaze, Incised, c.1910, 10 x 4 In. 1265.00
Vase, Trillium, Molded, Persian Rose Matte Glaze, Handle, Oval, 1904, 12 x 5 1/4 In. ... 6900.00
Vase, Trillium, Teal Matte Glaze, Bottle Shape, 1906, 5 x 3 3/4 In. 1093.00
Vase, Vertical Leaves, Mottled Mauve Matte Glaze, 1912, 6 1/2 In. 1430.00
Vase, Woman In Diaphanous Gown, Purple Matte Glaze, 1898, 13 In. 52500.00

VASA MURRHINA is the name of a glassware made by the Vasa Murrhina Art Glass Company of Sandwich, Massachusetts, about 1884.
The glassware was transparent and was embedded with small pieces of
colored glass and metallic flakes. The mica flakes were coated with silver, gold, copper, or nickel. Some of the pieces were cased. The same
type of glass was made in England. Collectors often confuse Vasa
Murrhina glass with aventurine, spatter, or spangle glass. There is
uncertainty about what actually was made by the Vasa Murrhina factory. Related pieces may be listed under Spangle Glass.

Basket, White & Gold Over Blue, Silver Mica Flakes, 11 1/4 x 8 In. 245.00
Vase, Alternating Pink & Green, Gold Mica, 6 3/4 In. 85.00

VASELINE GLASS is a greenish-yellow glassware resembling petroleum
jelly. Some vaseline glass is still being made in old and new styles.
Pressed glass of the 1870s was often made of vaseline-colored glass.
Additional pieces of vaseline glass may also be listed under Pressed
Glass in this book.

Bowl, Opalescent, 3 Piece, Mold, Rigaree Trim, 2 1/2 x 5 In. 75.00
Candleholder, 6 Sides, 5 1/2 In. 115.00
Candlestick, 5 1/2 In. 35.00
Candlestick, Dolphin Single Step, 10 3/8 In., Pair 750.00
Candy Dish, Opalescent, 6 Pointed Star, 5 In. 35.00
Creamer, Owl, Figural, Tree Bark Handle, 3 3/4 In. 60.00

**Bright sunlight will damage antiques by fading colors
or drying wood. There are several brands of film that can
be applied to your window to cut UV rays, heat, and glare.
3M and Vista window film are the best known.**

Decanter, 8-Sided Neck, Cut Stars, Arches, Diamonds, Hollow Stopper, 13 3/4 In. 180.00
Epergne, 5 Horns, Opalescent, Ribbed, Ribbon Rigaree On Each Horn, 20 In. 1350.00
Salt, Rose Sprig, Sleigh Shape, 2 x 3 In. 130.00
Smoke Bell, Opalescent, Fluted & Ruffled Edge, Loop Handle, 8 1/2 In. 121.00
Tumbler, Daisy & Button 15.00
Vase, Gauffered Rim, Stepped 6-Sided Base, 1850-1880, 11 x 3 3/4 In. 977.00
Whimsy, Lady Caroline, 3 Opalescent Handles, 3 3/4 In. 85.00

VENETIAN GLASS, see Glass-Venetian category.

VERLYS glass was made in France after 1931. It was made in the United
States from 1935 to 1951. The glass is either blown or molded. The
American glass is signed with a diamond-point-scratched name, but
the French pieces are marked with a molded signature. The designs
resemble those used by Lalique.

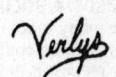

Bowl, Kingfisher, Signed, 13 3/4 In. 70.00
Bowl, Poissons, Fish, 2 Handles, Oval, Opalescent, Marked, 19 3/4 In. 357.00
Bowl, Poppy, Topaz, 14 In. 140.00
Vase, Mandarin, 5 x 9 1/4 In. 275.00

VERNON KILNS was the name used by Vernon Potteries, Ltd. The company, which started in 1931 in Vernon, California, made dinnerware
and figurines until it went out of business in 1958. The molds were
bought by Metlox and they continued to make some patterns. Collectors search for the brightly colored dinnerware and the pieces designed
by Rockwell Kent, Walt Disney, and Don Blanding. For more information, see *Kovels' Depression Glass & Dinnerware Price List*.

Brown Eyed Susan, Cup & Saucer 10.00
Brown Eyed Susan, Plate, 6 1/2 In. 3.50
Brown Eyed Susan, Sauceboat 20.00
Lei Lane, Dinner Set, 108 Piece 2310.00
Organdie, Casserole, Cover 45.00
Organdie, Chop Plate, 12 In. 29.00
Organdie, Cup & Saucer 8.00
Organdie, Pitcher, Milk 19.00
Organdie, Plate, 7 1/2 In. 8.00
Organdie, Plate, 9 1/2 In. 10.00
Organdie, Platter, 12 1/2 In. 24.00
Organdie, Tumbler 22.00
Organdy, Mug 20.00
Penguin, Decanter, Figural, Black & White, 9 1/2 In. 66.00
Raffia, Creamer 5.00
Raffia, Cup & Saucer 7.00
Raffia, Sugar, Cover 8.00
Shadow Leaf, Pitcher, Qt. 24.00
Tam O'Shanter, Bowl, Salad, Bowl, Deep 15.00
Tam O'Shanter, Butter Pat, 2 1/2 In. 16.00

VERRE DE SOIE glass was first made by Frederick Carder at the
Steuben Glass Works from about 1905 to 1930. It is an iridescent glass
of soft white or very, very pale green. The name means *glass of silk*,
and it does resemble silk. Other factories have made verre de soie, and
some of the English examples were made of different colors. Verre de
soie is an art glass and is not related to the iridescent, pressed, white
carnival glass mistakenly called by its name. Related pieces may be
found in the Steuben category.

Cruet, Engraved Garland & Cornflowers, Steuben, 7 In. 140.00
Perfume, Stick, Engraved, Wreath Base, Sterling Silver Top, 6 In. 170.00
Perfume Bottle, Flame Stopper, Steuben, 4 1/2 In. 448.00
Salt, Ruffled Top, 4 Applied Feet, 3 3/4 In. 120.00
Vase, Stump, 3 Openings, 6 In. 660.00

VIENNA, see Beehive category.

VIENNA ART plates are round metal serving trays produced at the turn of the century. The designs, copied from Royal Vienna porcelain plates, usually featured a portrait of a woman encircled by a wide, ornate border. Many were used as advertising or promotional items and were produced in Coshocton, Ohio, by J.F. Meeks Tuscarora Advertising Co. and H.D. Beach's Standard Advertising Co.

Plate, Cherubs In Clouds, Cobalt Blue Rim, Gold Highlights, 6 1/2 In., Pair	105.00
Plate, Square, 16 x 2 3/4 In.	240.00
Vase, Portrait, Seminude, Urn Shape, 3 Lion-Mask Feet, Hoofs, Triangular, 7 1/4 In.	575.00

VILLEROY & BOCH Pottery of Mettlach was founded in 1836. The firm made many types of wares, including the famous Mettlach steins. Collectors can be confused because although Villeroy & Boch made most of its pieces in the city of Mettlach, Germany, they also had factories in other locations. The dating code impressed on the bottom of most pieces makes it possible to determine the age of the piece. Additional items, including steins and earthenware pieces marked with the famous castle mark or the word *Mettlach,* may be found in the Mettlach category.

Beaker, Dresden, Jockey On Horseback, 1/4 Liter	300.00
Charger, Dutch Scene, Cows, Windmill, Blue, White, 1885-1905, 17 5/8 In.	165.00
Punch Set, Elf Festivities, Handle On Covered Bowl, 12 Cups	600.00
Tureen, Wallerfangen, 16 In.	650.00
Vase, Green Crystalline Matte Glaze, 12 5/8 In.	700.00

VOLKSTEDT was a soft-paste porcelain factory started in 1760 by Georg Heinrich Macheleid at Volkstedt, Thuringia. Volkstedt-Rudolstadt was a porcelain factory started at Volkstedt-Rudolstadt by Beyer and Bock in 1890. Most pieces seen in shops today are from the later factory.

Figure Set, Monkey Band, 18th Century Uniforms, Instruments, 5 1/2 In., 6 Piece	883.00

WADE pottery is made by the Wade Group of Potteries started in 1810 near Burslem, England. Several potteries merged to become George Wade & Son, Ltd. early in the twentieth century, and other potteries have been added through the years. The best-known Wade pieces are the small figurines given away with Red Rose Tea and other promotional items. The Disney figures are listed in this book in the Disneyana category.

c. 1936+

Figurine, Badger, 4 1/4 In.	32.00
Figurine, Circus Lion, 1 1/2 In.	3.00
Figurine, Circus Poodle, 1 5/8 In.	3.00
Figurine, Circus Seal, 1 5/8 In.	3.00
Figurine, Dog, Brown Spaniel, 3 1/4 In.	25.00
Figurine, Hawk, 1 1/4 In.	3.00
Figurine, Owl, 1 3/4 In.	3.00
Figurine, Polar Bear, White, 1 In.	5.00
Figurine, Scamp, 1 1/2 In.	8.00
Figurine, Sea Turtle, 1 1/8 In.	3.00
Figurine, Tiger, 1 1/8 In.	3.00
Figurine, Walrus, Gray, 7/8 In.	3.00
Figurine, Whale, Gray Humpback, 3/4 In.	5.00
Figurine, Wolf, 1 3/4 In.	3.00
Jug, Copper Lustre, 6 1/2 In.	11.00
Mug, Churchill, Roll Out The Barrel, 5 1/2 In.	48.00

WALLACE NUTTING photographs are listed under Print, Nutting. His reproduction furniture is listed under Furniture.

WALRATH was a potter who worked in New York City; Rochester, New York; and at the Newcomb Pottery in New Orleans, Louisiana. Frederick Walrath died in 1920. Pieces listed here are from his Rochester period.

Walrath
Pottery

Pitcher, Cider, Matte Glaze, Yellow Fruit, Green Leaves, Brown Ground, 5 x 7 In.	1495.00

WALT DISNEY, see Disneyana category.

WALTER, see A. Walter category.

WARWICK china was made in Wheeling, West Virginia, in a pottery working from 1887 to 1951. Many pieces were made with hand painted or decal decorations. The most familiar Warwick has a shaded brown background. The name *Warwick* is part of the mark and sometimes the mysterious word *IOGA* is also included.

Bowl, Painted Pink, Purple & Blue Flowers, Swirled Edge, Handles, 8 In.	35.00
Gravy Boat, Silver Moon Pattern	25.00
Pitcher, Colored Floral Transfer Print, Gold Trim, White, 1893-1898, 11 1/2 In.	100.00
Pitcher, Straight Sides, White, Angular Handle, Ironstone, 7 1/4 In.	125.00
Plate, Indian Portrait, Shaded Brown Ground, IOGA, In.	85.00
Plate, Spring Flowers, Gold Trim, 1930s-1940s, 9 3/4 In.	15.00
Vase, Campana Form, Entwined Handles, Portrait Busts Side, Late 19th Century, 14 In.	575.00
Vase, Floral Cartouche, Black Ground, Gold Trim, Handles, 9 3/4 In.	250.00
Vase, Portrait Of Woman, Shaded Brown Ground, IOGA, 1920s, 15 In.	500.00

WATCH pockets held the pocket watch that was important in Victorian times because it was not until World War I that the wristwatch was used. All types of watches are collected: silver, gold, or plated. Watches are arranged by company name or by style. Pocket watches are listed here; wristwatches are a separate category.

22 Rubies, 14 Diamonds, 14K Pink Gold	517.00
A. Lange & Sohne, White Enamel Dial, 14K Gold, 1900	2400.00
American Watch Co., Hunting Case, 18K Yellow Gold, Pocket, 1877	615.00
Aquimac A Paris, Gold, White Enamel Dial, Blue Enamel Cover, Gilt Stars, 1800	2040.00
Boucheron, Silver Matte Dial, Baton Numerals, Molded Case, 18K Gold, 1915	1560.00
Buhre, Button Chronograph, White Enamel Dial, 14K Gold, 1910	5100.00
C.H. Meylan, Brassus, Hunting Case, Minute Repeater, 32 Jewel, 18K Gold, Size 18	3300.00
Character, Little Black Sambo, Chrome Case, Pocket, c.1948	70.00
Charles Oudin, White Enamel Dial, Roman Numerals, Gold Fittings, 18K Gold, 1830	5040.00
Chevalier, Gold, Blue Enamel Case, Bezel Set With Pearls, Diamond Monogram, 1790	3000.00
Chronograph, Open Face, Black Numerals, Continental, 19th Century	213.00
Chronograph, Roman Numerals, 14K Gold, Pocket	375.00
Chronograph, White Enamel Dial, Pocket, 18K Gold	1265.00
Chronograph, White Enamel Dial, Roman Numerals, Heraldic Shield, 1900	1800.00
E. Howard, Hunting Case, Enamel Face, Second Hand, Engraved, Patent 1868, 2 1/4 In.	140.00
E. Howard, Open Face, 23 Jewel, 14K Yellow Gold, Model 1907, c.1912	600.00
E. Howard, Series 0, Open Face, Jeweled Banking Pins, 5 Positions, c.1912	440.00
E. Mathey Trist, Minute Repeater, 25 Jewel, 14K, Open Face, Size 16	1760.00
Ekegren, Hunting Case, Moon Phase, Calendar, 18K Gold, Porcelain Dial, Signed	4180.00
Elgin, Hunting Case, 14K Gold, Double Case	325.00
Elgin, Hunting Case, 17 Jewel, 14K Gold, Multicolored, Diamond, Size 18	880.00
Elgin, Hunting Case, Marked Fahys 14K Monarch, Model 2, c.1895	80.00
Elgin, Illinois Ramona, 20 Year Hunting Case, Model 2, 15 Jewel, Roman Dial	90.00
Elgin, Open Face, 17 Jewel, Silverine Case, Roman Dial, Sunk Seconds, Pocket	45.00
Elgin, Woman's, Open Porcelain Face, Blue Numbers, Sub Dial, 15 Jewel, 14K Gold	110.00
Fusee Movement, Reverse Painted, Tortoiseshell, Plique Case, Pocket, 1 1/2 x 2 3/4 In.	488.00
Hamilton, Cover, Center Diamond, Square Cut Diamond Melee	4600.00
Hamilton, Crescent 25 Year, Engraved, Open Face Case, Sunk Seconds, c.1908	120.00
Hamilton, G.C.T., 22 Jewel, Black Dial, Keystone Base Metal Case, Open Face, c.1946	300.00
Hamilton, Motor Barrell 950, Railroad Dial, Engraved, 14K, Chain, Case, Pat. 5-22-26	615.00
Hamilton, No. 992, 21 Jewel, Railway Special Dial, Size 16	550.00
Hamilton, Railroad, 21 Jewel, c.1913	270.00
Hamilton, Silvertone Dial, 14K Gold Face Case, 17 Jewel, Chased Rim	66.00
Hamilton, Wadsworth, Gold Fill, Pentagon Case, Chased Edge, 17 Jewel, c.1938	66.00
Hamilton, Yellow Gold Fill, Engraved, Sub Seconds, 17 Jewel	90.00
Hunting Case, Chronograph, Enamel Dial, Jeweled Nickel Movement, 14K Gold	488.00
Hunting Case, Gold, White Enamel Dial, Roman Numerals, Pocket, 18K Gold	430.00 to 490.00
Hunting Case, Pink Matte Dial, Gemstones Between Arabic Numerals, Pocket, 1880	2160.00
Hunting Case, Romeo Chambert, 18K Gold, Push Jump Sweep, 1875, Size 16	1540.00

Illinois, Keystone 25 Year Case, Chased Rim, Gilt Numerals, 19 Jewel, c.1923 .... 55.00
Illinois, Wadsworth, Open Face, Engraved Medallion, Chased, 17 Jewel, Sunk Seconds .. 44.00
Jaeger LeCoultre, Champagne Matte Dial, Octagonal Case, 18K Gold, 1990 .... 2160.00
Jules Jurgensen, Open Face, White Enamel Dial, Roman Numerals, 18K Pink Gold 3900.00
Key Wind, 6 Jewel, 18K Gold Case, 1830 .... 395.00
Key Wind, Open Face, Washington Capital Engraved On Back, Gold Chain, England 1175.00
Lapel, Silver Sterling, Gold Wash, 7 Jewel 35.00
LePhare, Days Of Week, Months Of Year, Moon Phase, 14K Yellow Gold 2700.00
Lewis Samuel, White Enamel Dial, Roman Numerals, Parlor Scene, Liverpool, 1830 .... 8400.00
Liberty & Co., Frame, Pewter, Enamel, Pocket, 3 3/4 In. 800.00
Longines, 17 Jewel, Gold Filled Case, Size 12 .... 325.00
Longines, Chronograph, White Enamel Dial, Roman Numerals, 18K Gold, 1910 3840.00 to 4200.00
Lord Elgin, Open Face Case, 10K Gold Filled, 21 Jewel, Pocket, c.1925 .... 145.00
M.J. Tobias, Open Face, Key Wind, Scene Of Fisherman Near Village, Yellow Gold Case . 220.00
Monnier, Hunting Case, Chronograph, 14K White Gold, Diamonds, No. 20775 .... 1210.00
Musical, White Enamel Dial, Gilt Cuvette, 1820 .... 4800.00
New Era, Philadelphia, Silveroid, 2-Tone Dial, Pink Center, Outer Ring 45.00
New York Standard, Hunting Case, Engraved Leaves, Gold Face 45.00
Omega, Open Face, Champagne Matte Dial, Enamel Case, 1920 .... 2160.00
Omega, Woman's, Silver Matte Dial, 17 Jewel, 18K White Gold, Baton Numerals 3300.00
Open Face, 14K Gold, Engraved Medallion, Silvered Dial, Applied Numerals, Pocket ... 165.00
Open Face, Grizzly Bear On Back, Nickel Finish, Size 14, 1 3/4-In. Diam. 300.00
Open Face, White Enamel Dial, Roman Numerals, 18K Gold, 1890 .... 4200.00
Open Face, Woman's, White Enamel Dial, Rose Cut Diamond, 1900 .... 3600.00
Patek Philippe, 20 Jewel, 18K Gold, Black Matte Dial, Baton Numerals, 1971 .... 2400.00
Patek Philippe, Hunting Case, 18K Gold, Black Roman Numerals, Leather Box 1150.00
Patek Philippe, Open Face, Champagne Matte Dial, 31 Jewel, 18K Gold 5400.00
Patek Philippe, Open Face, White Enamel Dial, 18K Gold, 1900 .... 9600.00
Patek Philippe, Open Face, White Enamel Dial, 18K Gold, 1912 .... 2040.00
Patek Philippe, Open Face, White Enamel Dial, Roman Numerals, 18K Gold, 1912 ..... 3600.00
Patek Philippe, Open Face, White Enamel Dial, Roman Numerals, 18K, 1905 ..2400.00 to 2880.00
Patek Philippe, Open Face, White Enamel Dial, Roman Numerals, Gold Cuvette 1200.00
Patek Philippe, Open Face, White Enamel Dial, Roman Numerals, Signed, 1910 .... 2700.00
Patek Philippe, Regulator, Champagne Matte Dial, Arabic & Baton Numerals, 1937 .... 1680.00
Patek Philippe, Sapphire Set Crown, Sapphire Numerals, 18 Jewel, 18K Gold 4500.00
Patek Philippe, White Enamel Dial, 18K Gold, 1905 .... 1800.00
Patek Philippe, White Enamel Dial, Blue Enamel Roman Numerals, 1890 .... 6600.00
Patek Philippe, White Enamel Dial, Roman Numerals, Gold Cuvette, 18K Gold, 1910 ... 3900.00
Patek Phillipe, Roy, Open Face, 20 Jewel, Brequet Style Hands, Monograph, c.1899 .... 1815.00
Pendant, Leroy & Fils, White Enamel Dial, Diamonds Set In Flower Head Shape, 1900 . 2400.00
Pendant, Open Face, Dust & Outer Cover, 18K Gold, Enamel Anemone, Art Nouveau .. 400.00
Pendant, Woman's, Gold, Open Face, Roman Numerals, Flowers, 13 Rose Cut Diamonds 260.00
Repeater, Hunting Case, Second Hand Dial, Stop Watch 1322.00
Repeater, White Enamel Dial, Black Roman Numerals, Russian Hallmarks, Size 18 ..... 345.00
Rockford, Open Face, Indicator, 21 Jewel, 14K Gold, Bridge Movement, Size 16 ...... 2400.00
Seth Thomas, Hunting Case, 18K Yellow Gold, American Shield, Stars, Stripes, Pocket .. 575.00
Sterling Silver, Hunting Scene, Repousse, Roman Figures, Tortoiseshell Case, c.1780 .... 920.00
Tavannes, Purse, Sterling Silver, 2 Hinged Doors, Square Watch, Art Deco, 1930 .... 230.00
Tiffany & Co., Demi Hunting, Sterling Silver, Japanese Style Flowers. 350.00
Time King, New Columbia Watch Co., Monogram, Shield On Sides, Chain, 14 In. 2645.00
Ullman, Diamond, Concealed Face, 17 Jewel, Raised Leaf Form, c.1960, 6 1/4 In. 400.00
Ulysse Nardin, Open Face, Chronograph, 18K Gold, 1900 .... 3000.00
Ulysse Nardin, Open Face, Cronometro Medical, Roman Numerals, Pulsemeter, 1900 ... 1560.00
Vacheron & Constantin, Hunting Case, Bas Relief Sunset Over Lily Pad, 1910, Pocket .. 2040.00
Vacheron & Constantin, Open Face, Silver Matte Dial, Sapphire Numerals, 1930 .... 5100.00
Vacheron & Constantin, Open Face, White Enamel Dial, Roman Numerals, 1920 .... 3000.00
Vacheron & Constantin, Silver Matte Dial, 15 Jewel, Signed, 1930 .... 3900.00
Vacheron & Constantin, Silver Matte Dial, 17 Jewel, Circular Case, 1960 .... 3300.00
Vacheron & Constantin, White Enamel Dial, 18K Gold, 1910 .... 1800.00
Vanguard, Open Face, 23 Jewel, 10K Yellow Gold, Lever Set, 6 Positions, c.1930 ...... 670.00
Waltham, 7 Jewel, Coin Silver Case, 1888, Size 18 .... 175.00
Waltham, A.W.W. Co., Model 1894, Open Face, Plain Keystone, 17 Jewel, c.1921 ...... 55.00
Waltham, Cowboy Design, High Relief, 14K Gold Case, White Enamel Dial 750.00

Waltham, Crescent St., Model 1908, Open Case, Keystone Victory, 21 Jewel 175.00
Waltham, Ellery, Hunting Case, Leaf & Shield Engraving, Yellow Gold Fill, Model 1873 . 70.00
Waltham, Enamel Dial, Cowboy On Cover, 14K Gold Case, Pocket 750.00
Waltham, Engraved Case, Yellow Gold, Gold Filled Chain, Yellow Gold Fob 165.00
Waltham, Hunting Case, 14K Gold, Blue Enamel Vine, Flower, Diamonds, Bow Pin 1257.00
Waltham, Hunting Case, 14K Gold, Jeweled Nickel Movement, Gold & Heart Slide 170.00
Waltham, Hunting Case, Engraved Shield On Cover, Cowboy On Back, 15 Jewel 750.00
Waltham, Hunting Case, P.S. Bartlett, Model 1879, Engraved, 14K Gold, Sunk Seconds .. 275.00
Waltham, Hunting Case, Riverside, 17 Jewel, 14K Gold, Size 0, S#12050383 .... 880.00
Waltham, Keystone Engraved Gold Filled Case, Enamel Dial, Chain 110.00
Waltham, Octagonal, 14K Gold Case, Size 12 .... 350.00
Waltham, Open Face, Engraved Case, Birds, Leaves, 17 Jewel, 14K White Gold Chain .. 330.00
Waltham, Open Face, White Enamel Dial, Gold Filled Chain, 17 Jewel 145.00
Waltham, Premier Colonial, Keystone Premier Metal Case, 9 Jewel 35.00
Waltham, Riverside Maximus, Open Face, 23 Jewel, 14K Gold, Chased Rim, c.1901 .... 965.00
Waltham, Woman's, Tricolor, Enameled Porcelain Face, 14K Gold Chain, c.1901 ...... 495.00
White Enamel Dial, Black Roman Numerals, 14K Gold, Pocket 575.00
Wittnauer, Platinum, Diamond, Emerald, Sapphire, Amethyst, Oval Face 1150.00
Wm. Keales, White Enamel Dial, Ruby Eyed Swan, London, 1790 .... 3000.00
Woman's, Audemars Piguet, Blue Matte Dial, 17 Jewel, 18K White Gold, 1975 ...... 3720.00
Woman's, Silver Matte Dial, Blue Translucent Enamel 1200.00
Yellow Gold Chain, Double Locket, Tassel, 2 Slides, Geometric Enamel 460.00

WATCH FOBS were worn on watch chains. They were popular during
Victorian times and after. Many styles, especially advertising designs,
are still made today.

5 & Day's Big Five, Union Made Overalls & Shirts, Celluloid, 1 1/2 In. 65.00
Anheuser-Busch, Cardboard, Gold, Diamond & Ruby, Pendant, 1 1/2 In. 1035.00
Black Cat, Inlaid Cloisonne Porcelain, Ullman-Einstein Co., 1 3/4 In. 165.00
Bust Of Woman, Whip Co., Silvered, Scalloped Edges, c.1900 .... 95.00
C.H. Schoellkopf Saddlery, Elephant, Saddled, Leather, 2 3/8 In. 75.00
California Historical Assn., Gold Filled, Inset California Bear, 7/8 In. 90.00
California Oil Fields, Brass & Cloisonne, Christmas Souvenir, 1916, 1 3/8 In. 12.00
Canoe & Crossed Paddles, Eustis On Side Of Canoe, Red Ground, High Relief 99.00
Caterpillar Tractor Co., 1970s 9.00
Cowboy & Bronco, Los Angeles, Gilt Finish, 1915 .... 160.00
Dead Shot Gunpowder, Transparent Enamel, Duck On Front, 1 5/8 x 1 1/8 In. 578.00
Echo Springs Rye Whiskey, Silver Plated, Scalloped Edges 75.00
Fisk Tires, Multicolored, Cloisonne, Enamel, 2 x 1 3/8 In. 853.00
Hammer & Anvil, Circular Plinth, 14K Gold, c.1875 .... 345.00
Heavyweight Boxing, 2 Boxers In Ring, Bronze, Gilt Finish, 1923 .... 150.00
Hollinger Mines, Enamel 150.00
Horse Collar, Tom Padgitt Co., Leather 145.00
John Hoberg Co., Tissue Paper, Cherubs & Toilet Paper, Cloisonne 110.00
Kansas City Annual Meeting 1921, Southwestern Lumbermen's Assoc., Key Shape 75.00
Keystone Lumber Co., Elephant, Carrying Wood, Die Cut 75.00
Magnolia Gasoline, Motor Oil, Cloisonne, 1 5/8 In. 242.00
Montana Sheriff, 5-Pointed Star, Compliments Of Nominee For Sheriff, 1908 .... 290.00
Old Timers Cowboys Reunion Assoc., Enamel, Scalloped Edges 225.00
Pendant, Brass Heart, Feather Strap, Lima, Ohio, 1933, 4 3/4 In. 65.00
Pine Tree Mfg. Co., Swan Swimming In River, Oval, White Metal 75.00
Pioneer Bottling Works, Coca-Lula, Soda Case, Metal 88.00
Railroad Crossing Sign, Safety First, Brass 50.00
Red Diamond Overalls, St. Louis, Man With Oil Can, Celluloid 85.00
Texaco Petroleum Products, Metal, Embossed, 1 9/16 x 1 1/4 In. 198.00
Wedgwood, Cameo, 14K Gold, Flowers, Classical Man, Laurel Leaf Frame 575.00

WATERFORD type glass resembles the famous glass made from 1783 to
1851 in the Waterford Glass Works in Ireland. It is a clear glass that
was often decorated by cutting. Modern glass is being made again in
Waterford, Ireland, and is marketed under the name *Waterford*.

Champagne, Powerscourt, Acid Stamp Mark, 5 1/2 In., 6 Piece 302.00
Claret, Powerscourt, Acid Stamp Mark, 7 In., 12 Piece 545.00

Decanter, Cut, Spherical, Lapidary-Cut, Stopper, Signed, Acid Stamp Mark, 8 3/8 In.	465.00
Goblet, Powerscourt, Acid Stamp Mark, 7 3/4 In., 12 Piece	544.00
Sherry, Glengariff, 5 In., 6 Piece	160.00
Vase, Diamond & Scalloped Rim, Acid Stamp Mark, 9 3/4 In.	410.00
Vase, Diamond Block, Marked, 8 1/2 x 5 1/4 In.	56.00
Vase, Marquis, 10 In.	49.00

WAVE CREST glass is an opaque white glassware manufactured by the Pairpoint Manufacturing Company of New Bedford, Massachusetts, and some French factories. It was decorated by the C.F. Monroe Company of Meriden, Connecticut. The glass was painted in pastel colors and decorated with flowers. The name *Wave Crest* was used after 1898.

WAVE CREST WARE

Bowl, Helmschmied Swirl, Floral, Metal Rim & Feet, 8 In.	100.00
Box, Cigar, Pink Enameled Flowers, Gold Stems, Word Cigars, Signed, 6 1/4 In.	1000.00
Box, Collars & Cuffs, Egg Crate Shape, Enameled, Flowers, Gold Words, 5 1/2 x 7 In. . . .	785.00
Box, Collars & Cuffs, Opal Body, Enameled Flowers & Words, Signed, 6 1/2 x 7 In.	1400.00
Box, Helmschmied Swirl, Floral, Blue & Brown, Satin Lining, Label, 5 1/2 In.	175.00
Cigar Holder, Flowers & Scrolling, 4-Footed Base, 2-Handled Rim, Signed, 4 In.	250.00
Cracker Jar, Cover, Daisies Transfer, Light Blue, White, 8 In. . . . . .100.00 to 160.00
Cracker Jar, Melon Ribbed, Silver Plated Trim, Bail Handle, 8 In.	280.00
Cracker Jar, Metal Cover, Pink Blossoms & Green Leaves Transfer, 11 In.	315.00
Cracker Jar, Multicolored Flowers, Bail Handle, 8 1/2 x 4 1/2 In.	375.00
Creamer, Floral Transfer, Pink, White, Spiral Handle, 2 1/2 In.	30.00
Creamer, Helmschmied Swirl, Rose Transfer, Silver Plated Mount, 3 1/2 In.	90.00
Dresser Box, Baroque Shell, Daisy, Sage Green, 3 1/4 x 5 1/2 In.	325.00
Dresser Box, Dresser, Helmschmied Swirl, Flower Sprays, Leafy Stems, 4 1/4 x 6 In. . . .	900.00
Dresser Box, Helmschmied Swirl, Enameled Flowers, 2 7/8 x 4 1/2 In. . . . . .240.00 to 260.00
Dresser Box, Helmschmied Swirl, Flower Sprays, Turquoise Body	336.00
Dresser Box, Rococo Daisies & Berries, Cream Swirl, Lined, 8 x 7 In.	1230.00
Dresser Tray, Swing Mirror, Flowers, On Pink, 2 Arms, 7 3/4 x 7 In.	730.00
Fernery, Egg Crate Shape, Enameled, Flowers, Metal Mount, 6 1/2 In.	175.00
Glove Box, Rococo, White Daisies, Opal Scrolling, Blue Ground, 10 x 5 In.	2015.00
Letter Holder, Egg Crate Shape, Ferns, Metal Mount, 6 x 4 1/2 In.	345.00
Pin Tray, Helmschmied Swirl, Enameled Flowers, 1 5/8 x 4 1/2 In.	80.00
Salt, Blue Daisies, Pair	195.00
Sugar, Cover, Cupid Transfer Design, Spiral Bail Handle, 3 In.	50.00
Sugar & Creamer, Cover, Light Blue, White, Cupid Transfer Design, Handles, 3 In.	110.00
Sugar & Creamer, White Daisies On Stems, Metal Mounts, 4 1/4 x 5 1/2 In.	280.00
Sugar Shaker, Japanese Style, 3 In.	430.00
Vase, Blue Flowers, Gilded Metal Rim, Handles & Base, 7 In.	385.00
Vase, Pink Flowers, Rosy Opal Body, Ormolu Collar & Handles, Signed, 6 In.	450.00
Vase, Shasta Daisies, Mauve Ground, Rose Tracery, Dots, 4-Footed, Signed, 11 In.	2240.00

WEAPONS listed here include instruments of combat other than guns, knives, rifles, or swords. Firearms are not listed in this book. Knives and Swords are listed in their own categories.

Dagger, Hunting, Stag Horn Handle, Post-Nazi Era, 10-In. Blade	460.00
Dagger, Northwest Coast, 20 In.	66.00
Gunpowder Tester, Wooden Handle, 18th Century	350.00
Handcuffs, Working Key, 2 Swivel Links, H & R Arms Co.	175.00
Harpoon Arrow, 6 1/2-In. Point, 36 In.	83.00
Iron Knuckles, Boxer Patent, Pyramid Points On Loops, Brown Metal	290.00
Iron Knuckles, Raised Bumps Over Loops, Crown Opening, Palm Rest	75.00
Nightstick, Rosewood, Lathe Turned Handle, Loop At Grip With Tassels, 23 In.	110.00
Saber, Calvary, Brass Hilt, Leather Grip, Stamped 1864, 41 1/4 In.	220.00

WEATHER VANES were used in seventeenth-century Boston. The direction of the wind was an indication of coming weather, important to the seafaring and farming communities. By the mid-nineteenth century, commercial weather vanes were made of metal. Today's collectors often consider weather vanes to be examples of folk art, even though they may not have been handmade.

Arrow, 6-Point Stars, Trio Of Circles, 19 x 54 In.	3220.00

Arrow, Banner, Scroll Design, Red, Orange Paint, Bullet Hole, 32 In. 165.00
Arrow, Banner, Scrollwork, Verdigris, Ball & Spire Finial, Copper, 21 x 48 In. 2415.00
Arrow, Bannerette, Cut Out Scrollwork, Verdigris, Black Stand, Copper, 17 x 24 In. 633.00
Arrow, Copper, Zinc Center, 9 1/2 x 56 1/2 In. 2530.00
Arrow, Eagle, Spread Wings, On Ball, Copper, Stand, 19 x 18 In. 1265.00
Arrow, Eagle, Spread Wings, On Ball, Copper, Wood Stand, 29 x 25 In. 1955.00
Arrow, Eagle, Spread Wings, On Ball, Directional, Gilt On Copper, 61 x 50 In. 1960.00
Arrow, Eagle, Spread Wings, On Ball, Gold Repaint, New Steel Stand, 26 In. 825.00
Arrow, Eagle, Verdigris, Beige Paint, Copper, Cast Zinc, Gilt, 41 x 28 In. 6500.00
Arrow, Iron, c.1870, 30 In. 2000.00
Arrow, Old Green Paint, Gilt, Iron, 39 In. 935.00
Arrow, Wood, Mounted, Cast Iron Hardware, 12 x 32 In. 860.00
Banner, Blossoms, Pierced Letter C, Gilt, Ball Finials, Stand, Copper, 26 x 28 In. 3738.00
Banner, Flowers, Black Enameled Stand, 25 1/2 x 26 In. 2860.00
Banner, Scrolled, Ball Finial, Corrugated Tail, Iron, Copper, Cutout, 37 1/2 In. 1610.00
Banner, Scrollwork, Pierced, Cruciform Tail, Copper, Zinc Arrow, 22 x 40 In. 2185.00
Bannerette, 4 Prong Lightning Rod Finial, Sheet Copper, Figure In Canoe, 82 In. 4465.00
Bannerette, Church, Paddlewheel Tail, J. Howard, Zinc & Copper, 23 1/2 In. 2115.00
Bannerette, Copper, Lightning Rod, Iron, Lead, Early 19th Century, 4 1/2 In. 3290.00
Bannerette, Double Lyre, 4 Copper Leaves Arrow Point, 1880s, 34 x 47 In. 6463.00
Bannerette, Finial Above Pierced Copper Banner, J. Howard, 54 x 59 In. 3055.00
Bannerette, Lyre Form Body, Tulip Form Tail, Arrow, Sheet Copper, 19 1/2 In. 2233.00
Bannerette, Scrolled Tail, Iron Lightening Rod, Copper & Zinc, 47 In. 5640.00
Bull, Adjustable Bracket, Copper & Zinc, J. Howard, Mid 19th Century, 12 In. 1645.00
Bull, Swelled Body, Iron Head, Cushing & White, Late 19th Century, 16 1/2 In. 8225.00
Car, Hollow, Open Buggy, Man At Wheel, Copper, Iron & Tube Arrow, 22 In. 172.00
Church, Horizontal Scrolls, 3 Ball Finials, Gilded Zinc, Iron, 55 x 72 In. 8050.00
Cod, Molded, Gilded, Round, Molded Scales, Marble Eyes, 17 1/2 x 39 x 5 In. 18800.00
Cow, Copper, Stand, 19th Century, 23 3/4 x 33 1/4 In. 9200.00
Cow, Wood, Carved, Painted, Cast Iron Horns, Ears, Eyes, 48 3/4 In. 1410.00
Dog, Labrador, Black Paint, Sheet Metal, 20 x 20 In. 106.00
Dog, Silhouette, Copper Directionals, Verdigris Surface, 26 3/8 x 17 5/8 In. 690.00
Eagle, Ball & Arrow Directionals, Copper, 63 x 29 In. 784.00
Eagle, On Globe, Directional Arrow, Blown Copper, 17 x 19 In. 440.00
Eagle, Spread Wings, Molded & Gilt Copper, 33 In. 920.00
Eagle, Spread Wings, Molded, Copper, Late 19th Century, 22 x 25 x 25 In. 5875.00
Eagle, Verdigris, Full-Bodied, 20th Century, 68 In. 747.00
Fire Engine, Horse Drawn, Fireman Driving, Sheet Iron, 36 1/2 x 14 1/2 In. 450.00
Fish, Half Body, Cast Iron, 23 3/4 x 11 In. 1265.00
Gamecock, Profile, Sheet Copper, Cushing & White, 19th Century, 18 3/4 In. 4700.00
Horse, Articulated Body & Tail, Cushing & White, Late 1800s, 12 x 26 In. 3525.00
Horse, Gold Paint, Copper, Gilt, c.1880, 23 x 15 x 3 In. 2850.00
Horse, Hackney, Gilt Over Yellow Paint, Stand, Copper, Zinc Head, 22 5/8 x 32 In. 4888.00
Horse, Hollow, Copper Body & Legs, Zinc Fore Part 4480.00
Horse, Leaping, Original Gilt, Brown, Gold Paint, Copper, 1860, 16 1/2 In. 21850.00
Horse, Prancing, Molded Zinc, Sheet Copper, 25 x 26 1/2 In. 8400.00
Horse, Prancing, On Center Bar, Riveted, Sheet Metal, 26 x 19 1/2 In. 195.00
Horse, Rearing, Front Legs Kicking, Molded, Gilt, Copper, Stand, 25 x 36 x 5 In. 8815.00
Horse, Rider, Silhouette Form, Soldier, Leading Troops To Battle, 20 In. 4113.00
Horse, Running, 2 Bullet Holes, Verdigris, Copper, Cast Iron Head, 17 1/2 x 29 In. 825.00
Horse, Running, Abstract Shape, Molded Man, Late 19th Century, 18 x 4 x 31 In. 6465.00
Horse, Running, Abstract, Suggested Mane, Modern Base, 22 1/2 x 41 x 5 In. 1765.00
Horse, Running, Copper, Zinc, Dexter, L.W. Cushing, Late 19th Century, 16 x 31 In. 2300.00
Horse, Running, Full-Bodied, Copper, 17 x 23 In. 1650.00
Horse, Running, Full-Bodied, Verdigris Surface, Copper, 15 x 27 In. 1495.00
Horse, Running, Gilt Zinc, 19th Century, 15 x 23 In. 1380.00
Horse, Running, Green Patina, Copper, Cast Iron Head, 28 In. 2013.00
Horse, Running, Hollow Zinc, Rod & Directionals, 53 1/2 In. 935.00
Horse, Running, Molded, Articulated Features, Copper, 26 1/2 x 20 In. 4700.00
Horse, Running, Mountain Boy, J. Fiske, Verdigris, Zinc, Copper, 19 x 34 In. 4370.00
Horse, Running, Pulling Sulky & Driver, Molded, Gilded, 25 3/4 x 46 1/4 x 5 In. 14100.00
Horse, Running, Rod Support, Molded Copper, A.L. Jewell, 12 x 25 In. 8813.00
Horse, Running, Sheet Iron, Black Metal Stand, 18 x 26 1/2 In. 862.00

Horse, Running, Sheet Metal Mane & Tail, Hole Eyes, A.L. Jewell, 18 1/2 In. 6465.00
Horse, Running, Silhouette, 4 Sections, Sheet Tin, 24 x 45 1/4 In. 1763.00
Horse, Running, Verdigris Patina, Gilt, Stand, Copper, Zinc Head, 18 x 26 In. 2300.00
Horse, Standing, Man On Horseback, Arm Raised, Sheet Steel, 20 x 19 In. 1430.00
Horse, Trotting, Articulated Features, Applied Sheet Mane, Copper, 18 x 30 In. 4115.00
Horse, Trotting, Copper, Zinc, L.W. Cushing, 18 1/4 x 31 In. 1955.00
Horse, Trotting, Gilt Metal, Early 20th Century, 14 1/2 x 27 In. 747.00
Horse, Trotting, Sheet Metal Mane, Copper, Comb & Waddle, 18 1/4 x 30 In. 4110.00
Horse, Trotting, Sheet Metal, 19th Century, 16 1/2 x 33 1/2 In. 400.00
Horse, Walking, Painted, Sheet Iron, Stand, Late 19th Century, 25 x 32 x 5 In. 1410.00
Horse & Rider, Copper Flowing Mane, Cushing & White, 1888, 16 x 27 1/2 In. 9400.00
Horse & Rider, Copper, A.L. Jewell & Co., 19th Century, 28 1/4 x 27 1/2 In. 19550.00
Horse & Rider, Painted, Red, c.1880, 28 x 53 In. 15500.00
Locomotive, Painted, Iron 1550.00
Pig, Creamy White, Gilt, With Stand, Copper, 19th Century, 15 1/2 x 23 In. 10925.00
Ram, Swell Bodied, Repousse Wool, Copper, Mid 19th Century, 19 x 27 1/2 In. 10200.00
Rider, Sulky, Full Bodied, Copper, Zinc, Late 19th Century, 17 1/2 x 33 x 9 1/2 In. 4025.00
Rooster, Arrow, Gilt Surface, 24 x 30 In. 3165.00
Rooster, Ball, Directionals, Wooden Post, Copper, 22 x 19 In. 5345.00
Rooster, Black Paint, Cast, Early 19th Century, 33 3/4 x 16 1/2 In. 1610.00
Rooster, Cast Iron, Gold Paint, Late 19th Century, 24 1/2 x 24 x 6 In. 3525.00
Rooster, Crowing, Sheet Iron, 19 1/2 x 33 3/4 In. 605.00
Rooster, Cubist Form, Copper, Painted, Early 20th Century, 19 x 27 1/2 In. 8400.00
Rooster, Cutout Comb, Wattle, Tail, Verdigris Patina, Copper, 21 3/4 x 16 In. 860.00
Rooster, Directional Arrow, Iron Shaft, Bullet Holes, Blown Copper, 74 x 31 In. 385.00
Rooster, Directional, Marked James, Cast Iron, Steel & Zinc, 23 x 32 In. 330.00
Rooster, Full-Bodied, Copper, Wooden Base, 2 x 19 In. 3410.00
Rooster, Full-Bodied, Gilt Copper, 19th Century, 22 x 18 In. 2875.00
Rooster, Hummer, Cast Iron, Elgin Wind Power & Pump Co., Ill., 17 x 16 In. 1265.00
Rooster, Iron Directional Arrow, Steel, Copper Tube, Cherry Base, 9 1/2 x 22 In. 140.00
Rooster, Molded, Abstract Feathers, Copper, 19th Century, 51 x 41 x 15 In. 19975.00
Rooster, Mounted On Brass Handle, Sheet Iron, 25 In. 660.00
Rooster, Stylized Comb, Wattle, Talon, Pendant Rod, Zinc & Copper, 22 In. 3325.00
Rooster, Tail On Spurred Feet, Copper & Zinc, J.W. Fiske, 23 x 21 In. 4110.00
Rooster, Weathered White & Red Paint, Sheet Iron, 22 1/4 x 21 1/4 In. 805.00
Scroll & Arrow, A.O. Co., Copper, American Optical Co., 46 x 75 In. 3100.00
Shaped Comb, Above Groove & Punch Tail, J. Howard, 12 x 12 1/2 In. 8225.00
Shovel, Red Paint, Sphere Finial, Cast Iron, Late 19th Century, 29 x 42 x 6 In. 7638.00
Soldier, Lighting Cannon, Flat Figures, Painted, 21 x 14 In. 6325.00
Soldier, Uniformed, Cannonballs Behind 9500.00
Star Finial, Pyramid Form, Early 20th Century, 41 In. 820.00
Steer, Allover Verdigris Patina, Gilt, Copper, 13 1/2 x 25 In. 6325.00
Steer, Copper & Zinc, Cushing & White, Late 19th Century, 15 1/4 x 25 1/4 In. 9400.00
Swan, Verdigris Patina, Copper, Cast Iron, Late 19th Century, 37 x 29 In. 9700.00
Tennis Player, Female, Full-Bodied, Zinc, 29 In. 8800.00
Whale, Pulling Chase Boat, Folk Art, Black Paint, Wooden 4950.00
Whirligig, African American Man & Woman, Washing Clothes, 26 1/2 In. 1075.00
Whirligig, Man, Pot Belly, Hooked Nose, Pointed Chin, Paddle Arms, 12 In. 3300.00

WEBB glass is made by Thomas Webb & Sons of Ambelcot, England.
Many types of art and cameo glass were made by them during the Victorian era. Production ceased by 1991, and the factory was demolished
in 1995. Webb Burmese and Webb Peachblow are special colored
glasswares of the Victorian era. They are listed at the end of this section. Glassware that is not Burmese or Peachblow is included here.

Webb

Dish, Gold Prunus Blossoms, Gold Butterfly, White Interior, Yellow, 2 1/8 x 5 1/4 In. 245.00
Dish, Yellow, Carlton Ware, Potpourri Jar, Cover, Oriental Scene, Marked, 9 3/4 In. 395.00
Perfume Bottle, Amber Cut To Yellow Flowering Branches, Silver Screw On Cap, 5 In. . 1205.00
Sand Shaker, For Drying Ink 1050.00
Vase, Alternating Blue & Pastel, Vertical Lines, White Cased, Signed, 5 In. 280.00
Vase, Black, Enameled, Birds, Flowers, Butterflies, Signed, 1870, 10 1/2 In. 495.00
Vase, Blue, Green, Brown, Flower Blossoms, Cameo, Thomas Webb & Sons, 10 5/8 In. . . 5060.00
Vase, Bottle, Satin Glass, Cream Lining, 4 1/2 x 9 In. 375.00

Vase, Bottle, Satin, Rose Shaded To Green, Cream Lining, 9 x 4 1/2 In. 375.00
Vase, Cameo, 3 Color, Squat, 2 1/2 In. 1650.00
Vase, Cameo, Green Amber Glass, White Opaque, Gentian Blossoms, 4 3/4 In. 1150.00
Vase, Cameo, Ivory, Trumpet Floral, Signed, 6 1/2 In. 1540.00
Vase, Cameo, Leaves, Griffin Heads, Brown, Handles, Thomas Webb, 7 1/2 In. 4880.00
Vase, Cameo, White Floral, Blue Ground, 4 In. 1480.00
Vase, Cameo, White Flowers, Soft Blue Ground, 7 In. 1080.00
Vase, Cameo, White Leaves, Blue Aqua Ground, Signed, 1900, 9 In. 3300.00
Vase, Chartreuse Glass, Clematis Blossom On Budding Vine, Cameo, 9 In. 1265.00
Vase, Double Gourd, Floral Cutting, Peachblow, 9 In. 3300.00
Vase, Fireglow, Enameled Gold Bird, 1880s, 9 1/2 x 4 1/2 In. 265.00
Vase, Frosted Blue Flowers, Butterfly On Reverse, Signed, 5 In. 1960.00
Vase, Fuchsia & Butterflies, White Over Citrine, 1880s, 6 1/4 In. 800.00
Vase, Mirror Finish, Bulbous Shoulder, 6 1/2 In. 310.00
Vase, Sapphire Blue, White Columbine Leaves, Butterfly On Reverse Side, 8 In. 2700.00
Vase, Stick, Bulbous, Signed, 5 In. 1260.00
Vase, Tortoiseshell, Enameled, 1880s, 8 1/4 In. 525.00
Vase, Trumpet Flowers On Leafy Vines, Signed, 6 1/2 In. 1560.00
Vase, White & Red, Yellow Ground, Flowers, Butterfly, Signed, 3 1/4 In. 1840.00
Vase, White Wisteria Design, Butterfly, Yellow, Signed, 7 1/2 In. 420.00
Vase, White, Citron Yellow, Signed, 4 In. 480.00

WEBB BURMESE is a colored Victorian glass made by Thomas Webb
& Sons of Stourbridge, England, from 1886.

Creamer, Enameled Acorns, Oak Branches, Ruffled Top, 3 In. 335.00
Creamer, Enameled Red Flowers & Buds, Leafy Stem, 5-Sided Rim, 3 In. 195.00
Epergne, Enameled Flowers, 9 1/2 In. 1265.00
Rose Bowl, Enameled Holly Berries, Flowers, Buds, Stems, 6-Sided Rim, 3 1/2 In. 535.00
Vase, Enameled Flower Sprays, Leaf Stems, Signed, 9 3/4 In. 1065.00
Vase, Enameled Flowers, Leaves, 6-Sided Top, 3 1/8 In. 325.00

WEBB PEACHBLOW is a colored Victorian glass made by Thomas
Webb & Sons of Stourbridge, England, from 1885.

Vase, Gold Enameled Flowers, Black Leafy Stems, Gold Rim, 7 1/4 In. 728.00
Vase, Gold Enameled Leafy Branch, 11 1/4 In. 224.00
Vase, Gray Flowers, Gold Leafy Stems, 5 In. 190.00
Vase, Silver Enameled Flowers, Gold Stems & Leaves, 5 1/8 x 3 3/8 In. 275.00

WEDGWOOD, one of the world's most successful potteries, was
founded by Josiah Wedgwood, who was considered a cripple by his
brother and was forbidden to work at the family business. The pottery
was established in England in 1759. A large variety of wares has been
made, including the well-known jasperware, basalt, creamware, and
even a limited amount of porcelain. There are two kinds of jasperware.
One is made from two colors of clay, the other is made from one color
of clay with a color dip to create the contrast in design. The firm is still
in business. Other Wedgwood pieces may be listed under Flow Blue,
Majolica, Tea Leaf Ironstone or in other porcelain categories.

WEDGWOOD

Basket, Candy, Creamware, Lattice, Scroll To Foot Rim, c.1780, 6 1/2 x 8 In. 1850.00
Basket, Fruit, Basket Weave Center, Oval, Stand, Marked, c.1900, 8 1/2 In., 2 Piece 380.00
Biscuit Barrel, Faux Onyx Glaze, Silver Plated Mounts, Blue Interior, 5 1/4 In. 450.00
Biscuit Barrel, Jasperware, Cameo, c.1900, 6 In. 259.00
Biscuit Jar, Cover, Jasper Dip, Classical Figures, Handle, Mark, c.1900, 6 In. 590.00
Biscuit Jar, Cover, Jasper Dip, Classical Relief, Handle, Tricolor, c.1900, 5 1/4 In. 705.00
Biscuit Jar, Greek Key Band, Apollo & Muses, Silver Plated Lid & Base, 6 1/4 In. 360.00
Biscuit Jar, Silver Plated Cover, Rims & Handle, c.1900, 6 1/4 In. 115.00
Biscuit Jar, White Figures, Silver Plated Rim, Handle & Cover, 5 1/4 In. 375.00
Bottle, Barber, Cover, Jasper Dip, Tricolor, Blue Ground, c.1870, 10 3/4 In., Pair 2070.00
Bottle, Barber, Jasperware, Tricolor, Green Medallions, White, 9 3/4 In. 550.00
Bottle, Cover, Jasper Dip, Classical Medallions, Tricolor, c.1870, 10 1/4 In. 2235.00
Bough Pot, Cover, Jasperware, 3 Wells, Late 18th Century, 4 5/8 In., 5 In., Pair 1765.00
Bough Pot, Cover, Pearlware, Buff, Fluting, Banded Relief, 18th Century, 11 1/4 In. 880.00
Bough Pot, Jasper Dip, Blue, Oval, Applied Figures, Late 18th Century, 11 1/8 In. 1840.00

Bowl, Banded Laurel Border, White Figural, Dancing Hours, 1957, 10 In. 690.00
Bowl, Butterfly Luster, Mottled Yellow Pearl, Orange Luster Interior, 3 1/2 x 9 In. 1695.00
Bowl, Chicks On Basket Cover, Creamware, Glazed, 7 3/4 x 5 1/4 In. 300.00
Bowl, Cover, Queen's Ware, Iron Red, Black Border, Stand, 6 1/8 In., Pair 57.00
Bowl, Cover, Queen's Ware, Pierced, Molded, Flowers, Marked, 8 1/4 In. 380.00
Bowl, Creamware, Overall Brown Floral, Cream Ground, 19th Century, 7 In. 170.00
Bowl, Dragon Luster, 8 Sides 725.00
Bowl, Dragon Luster, Flared Rim, Red, Blue, Lavender Luster Interior, 3 x 7 In. 1295.00
Bowl, Dragon Luster, Mottled Green, Aqua Mother-Of-Pearl Interior, 4 1/2 x 2 1/2 In. 575.00
Bowl, Fairyland Luster, Red, Mother-Of-Pearl Interior, Footed, 5 1/2 x 8 3/4 In. 3450.00
Bowl, Fish Luster, Octagon, Blue, Marked, c.1920, 6 In. 999.00
Bowl, Harvard, Red, Print, Marked, c.1936, 12 3/8 In. 295.00
Bowl, Hummingbird Luster, Green, Aqua Mother-Of-Pearl, 3 1/2 x 8 In. 1795.00
Bowl, Jasperware, Blue Ground, 20th Century, 4 1/4 x 8 1/4 In. 125.00
Bowl, Punch, Queen's Ware, 3-Footed, Molded Dogs, Marked, c.1880, 4 5/8 In. 1058.00
Bowl, Salad, Silver Plated Rim, Black Figures, c.1930, 7 7/8 In. 1035.00
Bowl, Silver Plated Mounts, 4-Footed, 2 Handles, c.1865, 13 1/2 In. 1610.00
Bowl, Terra-Cotta Jasperware, Applied White Classical Relief, Footed, c.1959, 7 7/8 In. . . 230.00
Box, Cover, Sardine, Majolica, Boat Shape, c.1886, 10 1/8 In. 600.00
Box, Cupids & Woman On Top, Cupids & Roses At Base, 1 3/4 x 3 In. 165.00
Box, Roses On Lid, Cupids & Woman On Top, Cupids At Base, 1 3/4 x 3 In. 150.00
Bulb Pot, Cover, Blue Glaze, Stand, Marked, c.1872, 11 1/4 In. 880.00
Bust, Ariadne, Black Basalt, Waisted Circular Socle, England, c.1900, 3 7/8 In. 470.00
Bust, Mercury, Black Basalt, Waisted Circular Socle, England, c.1900, 4 3/8 In. 590.00
Bust, Minerva & Man, Black Basalt, c.1900, 2 3/8 & 2 1/4 In., Pair 705.00
Bust, Shakespeare, Black Basalt, Waisted Circular Socle, c.1900, 4 In. 470.00
Candleholder, Jasperware, Blue & White, 3 3/4 In., Pair 100.00
Candlestick, Jasper Dip, Applied Medallions, Black, Late 1800s, 5 1/2 In., Pair 1090.00
Candlestick, Jasperware, Mounted Ormolu, White Classical Relief, c.1900, 11 In., Pair . . . 1116.00
Candlestick, Jasperware, Yellow, Black Classical Figures, c.1930, 7 1/2 In., Pair 980.00
Candlestick, White Figures, Arabesque Floral Border, Signed, 5 In., Pair 375.00
Cheese Dish, Jasper Dip Dark Blue, 19th Century, 11 1/8 In. 705.00
Cheese Dome, Cover, Underplate, Jasperware, Early 19th Century, 10 1/2 x 12 1/2 In. . . . 460.00
Clock, Mantle, Jasperware, Blue, Mounted Ormolu, Columns, c.1900, 11 In. 1175.00
Compote, Queen's Ware, Shell, Landscape, Emile Lessore, c.1860, 6 3/4 In. 470.00
Creamer, Lilac & Green Medallion Drops, Grapevine Festoons, 1890s, 3 In. 980.00
Creamer, Silver Luster, Mulberry Ferrara Transfer, Sailing Vessels, Venice, 4 1/4 In. 154.00
Crocus Pot, Stand, Black Basalt, Hedgehog, 19th Century, 10 In. 1410.00
Cup, Fairyland Luster, Leapfrogging Elves, Boston, Marked, c.1920, 4 In. 705.00
Cup & Saucer, Jasperware, Tricolor, White Body, Green & Lilac Relief, 5 1/4 In. 1090.00
Decanter, Sherry, Figural, Mid 20th Century, 10 In. 20.00
Desk, Writing, Jasperware, Light Blue, 5 Plaques, Classical Relief, c.1900, 11 1/2 In. 1645.00
Dessert Stand, Basket Weave, Ribbon Border, c.1971, 9 1/4 In. 375.00
Dinner Service, Queen's Ware, Porcelain, 174 Piece 1840.00
Dish, Fruit, Majolica, Foot, 19th Century, 9 In. 995.00
Dish, Queen's Ware, Scalloped Rim, Emile Lessore, c.1870, 11 1/2 In. 865.00
Ewer, Jasperware, Blue, Boys, Floral Borders, Mark, 18th Century 11 5/8 In. 1175.00
Figurine, Bear, Black Basalt, Ernest Light, c.1915, 2 1/2 In. 410.00
Figurine, Bridal Group, Gray, Tan, Marked, Arnold Machin, c.1959, 10 1/4 In. 1295.00
Figurine, Duiker Lying, Cream Glaze, Skeaping, c.1925, 6 1/4 In. 120.00
Figurine, Elephant, Black Basalt, Glass Eyes, White Tusks, c.1915, 3 1/2 In. 646.00
Figurine, Figure Of Hope, Pearlware, Enameled, Marked, c.1800, 7 1/4 In. 265.00
Figurine, Group On Square Plinth, Enameled, Marked, c.1800, 8 1/2 In. 499.00
Figurine, Kingfisher, Black Basalt, Glass Eyes, Ernest Light, c.1915, 7 1/2 In. 470.00
Figurine, Raven, Black Basalt, Glass Eyes, Ernest Light, c.1915, 4 In. 529.00
Figurine, Sea Lion, Moonstone Glaze, Skeaping, c.1925, 8 In. 295.00
Figurine, Sleeping Boy, Stoneware, White, England, c.1820, 5 1/4 In. 470.00
Figurine, Tiger & Buck, Moonstone Glaze, Skeaping, c.1925, 13 1/4 In. 176.00
Figurine, Voltaire, Standing On Base, Queen's Ware, c.1900, 13 1/4 In. 355.00
Flowerpot, Jasper Dip, Dark Blue, Classical Relief, 19th Century, 6 3/4 In., Pair 385.00
Ginger Jar, Blue Windmill, Clarice Cliff, 9 In. 495.00
Jam Pot, Jasperware, Silver Plated Cover, Grecian Women Around Base, 4 In. 125.00
Jar, Cover, Classical Figures, c.1871, 6 3/8 In. 520.00

Some tea and coffee stains on dishes can be removed by rubbing them with damp baking soda.

Wedgwood, Plate, Wellesley College, Munger Hall, 1946, 10 1/2 In.

Jardiniere, Dragon Luster, Powder Blue Glaze, 9 x 12 In.	1695.00
Jardiniere, Jasper Dip, Blue, White Classical Muses, Marked, 9 In.	440.00
Jardiniere, Jasper Dip, Classical Muses, Marked, 19th Century, 8 In., Pair	910.00
Jardiniere, Jasper Dip, Green, 6 Classical Figures, Lion's Head On Swags, 9 x 10 In.	415.00
Jardiniere, Majolica, Dark Blue, Portraits, Floral Festoons, Marked, c.1871, 13 In.	1058.00
Jug, Blue, Flowers, Harry Barnard, c.1900, 12 In.	825.00
Jug, Cover, Caneware, Allover Engine Turned, Marked, 19th Century, 7 In.	825.00
Jug, Jasper Dip, Crimson, Applied Relief, Rope Twist Handle, c.1920, 6 1/2 In.	1725.00
Jug, Jasper Dip, Crimson, White Classical Relief, Marked, 5 3/4 In.	940.00
Jug, Jasperware, Crimson, c.1920, 5 5/8 In.	1035.00
Jug, Majolica, Caterer, Jewel, Banded Motto Relief, Marked, c.1874, 6 3/4 In.	175.00
Jug, Queen's Ware, Portrait Of Longfellow On 1 Side, Verse Other, c.1880, 6 1/2 In.	260.00
Jug, Tricolor, Lilac Ram's Heads, Floral Festoons, Band Of Oak Leaves, 6 In.	980.00
Lamp, Earthenware, Buff, Enameled, 2 Sides, Peacock, Marked, c.1878, 11 In.	355.00
Lamp Base, Jasperware, Dark Blue, Sill Vase Form, White Figures, 7 In.	290.00
Match Holder, Jasper Dip, Green, White, Classical & Floral Relief, 3 3/4 In.	75.00
Medallion Set, Black Basalt, Self-Framed, Roman Portraits, 2 x 2 3/4 In., 6 Piece	315.00
Mustard Pot, Jasper Dip, Yellow, Black Fruiting, Lion Mask, Marked, c.1930, 4 In.	235.00
Necklace, Jasper Dip, Beaded, Blue, Applied White Leaves, 19th Century, 11 3/4 In.	978.00
Perfume Bottle, Jasperware, Blue, White Figures, Late 18th Century, 4 In.	690.00
Pie Dish, Cover, Game, Caneware, Early 19th Century, 12 1/2 In.	460.00
Pie Dish, Cover, Game, Molded Relief, Grape Vine, Rabbit Finial, c.1863, 6 3/4 In.	440.00
Pitcher, Flowers & Gilt, Off-White Ground, 7 In.	60.00
Pitcher, Twisted Handle, Grapevine Border, Mythological Scenes, 1890, 8 1/4 In.	389.00
Planter, Tile, Iron Frame, Transfers, Helen J.A. Miles, c.1877, 7 1/2 In.	558.00
Plaque, Black Basalt, Oval, Bacchanalian Boy, Marked, c.1900, 7 1/4 In.	470.00
Plaque, Black Basalt, Oval, Female Figure, Marked, 19th Century, 8 3/4 In.	645.00
Plaque, Fairyland Luster, Elves In Pine Tree, Marked, c.1920, 7 5/8 x 10 In.	3290.00
Plaque, Jasper Dip, Yellow, Green, Classical Relief, c.1900, Marked, 2 1/2 x 7 In.	499.00
Plaque, Jasperware, Black, Applied White Relief, Rectangular, 6 x 14 1/2 In., Pair	3450.00
Plaque, Jasperware, Blue, Applied White Relief, Seascape, Framed, 1800s, 22 x 14 In.	520.00
Plaque, Jasperware, Green, Relief Figures, Giltwood Frame, 6 3/4 x 15 1/2 In., Pair	400.00
Plaque, Jasperware, Medusa, Oval, White Mask Head, Marked, 19th Century, 9 3/4 In.	705.00
Plaque, Jasperware, White Classical Figures, Oval, 19th Century, 2 x 4 In., 4 Piece	355.00
Plaque, Queen's Ware, Blue, Cupid & Psyche, Marked, c.1863, 7 1/2 x 13 In.	1295.00
Plaque, Rosso Antico, Marriage Of Cupid & Psyche, Marked, c.1900, 3 x 4 In.	825.00
Plate, Charnwood, 10 3/4 In.	28.00
Plate, Fairyland Luster, Imps On A Bridge, Floral, Fruit, Leaves, c.1920, 10 1/2 In.	8225.00
Plate, Majolica, Center Leaves On Basket Weave Ground, 7 7/8 In.	522.00
Plate, Silver Resist, Fruit Basket, Flowers, c.1930, 10 3/4 In.	40.00
Plate, Soup, Pearlware, Chrysanthemum	295.00
Plate, Soup, Queen's Ware, Crest, Enameled, Marked, c.1900, 9 5/8 In., 4 Piece	235.00
Plate, Wellesley College, Munger Hall, 1946, 10 1/2 In.	Illus 85.00
Plate, Yellow Ground, Reticulated, Mythological Scene, c.1780, 9 3/8 In.	1058.00
Plate Set, Luncheon, Flowers, Diamond Folded Borders, Etruria, 8 7/8 In., 12 Piece	275.00
Plate Set, Queen's Ware Series, Industrial, Claire Leighton, 10 1/2 In., 12 Piece	1095.00
Platter, Charnwood, 13 1/2 In.	105.00
Platter, Fallow Deer, Oval, Floral Border, Marked, c.1915, 18 1/2 In.	440.00
Platter, Ironstone, Blue Design, Off-White Ground, 18 In.	170.00
Platter, Pearlware, Chrysanthemum	395.00
Platter, Pearlware, Well & Tree	595.00

Potpourri, Cover, 3 Dolphin Supports, Dolphin Feet, Early 19th Century, 5 In. 750.00
Potpourri, Cover, First Period, Bone China, Puce Enamel Landscape, c.1815, 3 5/8 In. 1150.00
Potpourri, Muses Over Musical Symbols, c.1862, 10 3/4 In. 3737.00
Potpourri, Pierced Cover, Applied Black Basalt, Dolphin Feet, 5 In. 865.00
Sconce, Cornucopia, Cream Glaze, Raised Decoration, Pair 57.00
Sconce, Wall, Jasperware, Light Blue, Medallions, Classical Relief, c.1900, 10 In., Pair . . .   470.00
Soup, Cream, Underplate, Charnwood, 2 1/4 x 4 1/2 In. 35.00
Sphinx, Seated, Basalt, Gilt, Rectangular Plinths, Hieroglyphs, c.1978, 8 3/4 In., Pair 2530.00
Tea Infuser, Cover, Pearlware, Scrolled, Gilt, Spigot, Beane's, c.1891, 12 1/4 In. 825.00
Tea Service, Liberty, U.S. Shield, Allies Flags, War Relief Fund, c.1917, 18 Piece 920.00
Tea Set, Black Basalt, Silver Shape, Figures, 19th Century, c.1900, 3 Piece 999.00
Tea Set, Blue Scrolls, Ribbed Body, 7 Piece 168.00
Tea Set, Jasper Dip, Light Green, Applied Classical Relief, c.1900, 3 Piece 145.00
Tea Set, Jasperware, Blue, Early 19th Century, 3 Piece 345.00
Tea Set, Jasperware, Blue, White Classical Figures, 7-In. Teapot, 3 Piece 99.00
Tea Set, Jasperware, Royal Blue, Queen Elizabeth II Coronation, c.1953, 3 Piece 230.00
Tea Set, Jasperware, Tricolor, Green, Lilac, White, Applied Leaves, 20th Century, 3 Piece   2185.00
Teapot, Cover, Caneware, Oval, Enameled, Neal & Co., c.1790, 8 1/2 In. 560.00
Teapot, Cover, Queen's Ware, Daisy Makeig-Jones, c.1913, Marked, 4 1/4 In. 765.00
Teapot, Cover, Queen's Ware, Globular, Floral, David Rhodes, c.1775, 4 1/2 In. 1765.00
Teapot, Cover, Rosso Antico, Gilt, Enameled, Flowers, 19th Century, 2 1/4 In. 825.00
Teapot, Creamware, Black Transfer, Hunt Scene, Flowers On Lid, Spout, 7 In. 690.00
Teapot, Jasperware, Blue, Salt Glaze, c.1820, 6 In. 468.00
Tile, Printed Years, 1905, 1911, 1914, 1917, Signed, 3 1/4 x 4 3/4 In. 145.00
Tiles, 12 Months, Blue, Helen J.A. Miles, 19th Century, 6 x 6 In. 765.00
Tureen, Cover, Pearlware, Stand, Pink Enamel, Marked, c.1875, 6 In. 294.00
Tureen, Cover, Stand, Queen's Ware, Impressed Mark, c.1900, 13 1/4 In. 705.00
Tureen, Cover, Stand, Yellow Ground, Bracket Handles, c.1800, 7 In. 1295.00
Tureen, Vegetable, Cover, Queen's Ware, Crest, Marked, c.1900, 9 1/2 In. 295.00
Urn, Black Basalt, Ebonized Base, 38 In., Pair 6600.00
Urn, Jasperware, Light Blue, White Muse Figures, Upturned Loop Handles, 12 In., Pair . .   1150.00
Vase, Bottle Shape, Enameled, Gilt, Bird, Branch, Marked, c.1885, 9 3/4 In. 265.00
Vase, Caneware, Bamboo, Enameled, Marked, c.1900, 10 3/4 In. 2115.00
Vase, Cherubs, Black, Representing 4 Seasons, Signed, c.1930, 4 3/4 In., Pair 860.00
Vase, Cover, Center Arabesque Flowers, Leaf Border, Signed, 8 1/4 In., Pair 2530.00
Vase, Cover, Classical Figures, Green Flowers Ground, Bronzed, Gilt, 9 3/4 In. 2875.00
Vase, Cover, Classical Medallion Between Swags, Mid 19th Century, 9 In. 860.00
Vase, Cover, Dancing Hours, Leaf Border, Late 19th Century, 9 1/2 In. 805.00
Vase, Cover, Gilt Dragon, 20th Century, 9 1/2 In. 705.00
Vase, Cover, Jasper Dip, Dancing Hours, Bacchus Head Handles, c.1900, 7 1/2 In. 999.00
Vase, Cover, Jasper Dip, Green, Classical Medallions, 11 In. 705.00
Vase, Cover, Jasper Dip, Scrolled Ribbons, Fruiting Vines, Marked, c.1900, 8 3/4 In. 1410.00
Vase, Cover, Jasper Dip, Tricolor, Applied White Classical Relief, 12 1/4 In. 1610.00
Vase, Cover, Jasper Dip, Tricolor, Applied White Relief, Lilac Ground, 8 1/4 In. 1725.00
Vase, Cover, Jasperware, Black, Classical Medallions, 2 Handles, Marked, c.1900, 9 In. . . .   999.00
Vase, Cover, Jasperware, Black, Leaves, Scrolled Handles, Signed, 1959, 10 1/2 In. 1150.00
Vase, Cover, Jasperware, Blue, White Sprigging, Winged Maiden, Lamp Mount, 14 In. 518.00
Vase, Cover, Jasperware, Handles, Ram's Head, Marked, 19th Century, 7 In. 646.00
Vase, Cover, Jasperware, Tricolor, White Body, Lilac & Green Relief, 11 1/4 In. 5750.00
Vase, Cover, Jasperware, Tripod, Floral Borders, Lion Masks, Marked, c.1900, 8 1/4 In. . .   2235.00
Vase, Cover, Victoria Ware, Salmon, Trophies, Floral Swags, Marked, c.1900, 9 In. 825.00
Vase, Dancing Hour Figures, Bacchus Head Handles, c.1830, 7 3/8 In. 690.00
Vase, Dragon Luster, Blue, c.1920, 11 3/4 In. 705.00
Vase, Earthenware, Buff, Millicent Taplin, c.1925, 8 3/4 In. 880.00
Vase, Fairyland Luster, Sycamore Tree With Mythical Bird, c.1920, 8 1/2 In. 3290.00
Vase, Flaring, Ribbed, Matte Yellow Glaze, Circular Ink Stamp, 7 1/2 x 5 1/2 In. 575.00
Vase, Golcondaware, Raised Gold Paste, Flowers, Marsden, 1878, 7 In. 325.00
Vase, Hummingbird Luster, Mottled Blue, Orange Luster Interior, 11 1/2 In. 1795.00
Vase, Hummingbird Luster, Orange Interior, 6 Birds, 7 1/2 In. 1400.00
Vase, Ivory, Gilt, Silver, Leaves, Berries, 2 Handles, Marked, c.1885, 8 3/4 In. 295.00
Vase, Jasper Dip, Black, Applied Acanthus, Bell Flowers, Band, 19th Century, 7 1/4 In. . .   805.00
Vase, Jasper Dip, Black, Applied Relief Muses, Mid 19th Century, 11 In. 920.00
Vase, Jasper Dip, Black, Applied Striping, Bands, c.1956, 8 In., Pair 865.00

Vase, Jasper Dip, Blue, Classical Woman, 6 1/2 In., Pair	110.00
Vase, Jasper Dip, Floral, Marked, c.1930, 6 5/8 In., Pair	1295.00
Vase, Jasper Dip, Tricolor, Dancing Figures, Marked, 19th Century, 6 3/4 In.	765.00
Vase, Jasper Dip, Yellow, Trumpet, Black Fruiting, Marked, c.1930, 9 1/2 In., Pair	529.00
Vase, Jasperware, Caryatid Corners, Figures, Urns, Mounted, 18th Century, 9 In.	1058.00
Vase, Jasperware, Green, Upturned Loop Handles, Applied White Relief, Cover, 12 In.	1035.00
Vase, Jasperware, Mustard Yellow, Black Jasper Relief, 1929-1933, 5 1/8 In.	325.00
Vase, Jasperware, Portland, 6 In.	350.00
Vase, Jasperware, Tricolor, Blue Ground, Lilac Medallions, 10 5/8 In., Pair	4600.00
Vase, Mother-Of-Pearl Interior, Gilt Tree Bark, Cherubs In Garden, 9 In.	2070.00
Vase, Portland, Black, Classical Relief, Marked, c.1900, 5 In.	355.00
Vase, Portrait, White, Gilt Trim, Signed, Late 19th Century, 5 In., Pair	1150.00
Vase, Queen's Ware, Cylindrical, Fruit, Flowers, c.1860, 7 3/4 In.	235.00
Vase, Queen's Ware, Embossed, Fluting, Blue Fruit Bands, c.1942, 13 In.	170.00
Vase, Ribbed, Flaring, Butter Yellow, Ink Stamp, 7 1/2 In.	575.00
Vase, Spill, Jasper Dip, Yellow, Applied White Figures, Early 20th Century, 2 3/8 In.	288.00
Vase, Trophy, Jasperware, Black, Classical Relief, Floral Band, c.1900, 14 1/2 In.	880.00
Vase, Trumpet Form, Band Of Fruiting Grapevines, c.1942, 13 In.	170.00
Vase, Victoria Ware, Deep Teal, Red Ground, Gilt Trim, Handles, 6 1/4 x 7 In., Pair	345.00
Wall Pocket, Moonlight Luster, Shell, Pierced Lid, c.1810, 9 3/4 In.	1295.00

WELLER pottery was first made in 1872 in Fultonham, Ohio. The firm moved to Zanesville, Ohio, in 1882. Art wares were introduced in 1893. Hundreds of lines of pottery were produced, including Louwelsa, Eocean, Dickens Ware, and Sicardo, before the pottery closed in 1948.

LOUWELSA

WELLER

Ardsley, Vase, Cattails, Water Lilies, Flaring, 9 x 3 3/4 In.	345.00
Art Nouveau, Vase, Yellow Flowers, Silver Overlay, Cylindrical, 10 In.	2500.00
Athens, Vase, Mermaids Riding A Piscine Chariot, Black, 9 1/2 In.	325.00
Aurelian, Ewer, Burnt Orange Carnations, 11 1/2 x 4 3/4 In.	635.00
Aurelian, Jardiniere, Pedestal, Dogwood Design, Dark Brown, Yellow, 45 1/4 In.	2400.00
Aurelian, Jardiniere, Pedestal, Grapes & Leaves, 37 In.	3200.00
Aurelian, Jardiniere, Pedestal, Wild Roses, Jonquils, Twist Form, 37 1/2 In.	1380.00
Aurelian, Jardiniere, Yellow Iris, 10 1/2 x 13 In.	175.00
Aurelian, Mug, Blackberry Design, Minnie Mitchell, Ribbed, 6 1/4 In.	175.00
Aurelian, Mug, Corn In Husk, Painted In Heavy Slip, Frank Ferrell, 5 3/4 In.	175.00
Aurelian, Plaque, Apples, Frank Ferrell, 16 1/2 x 10 7/8 In.	520.00
Aurelian, Umbrella Stand, Brown & Green Leaves, Hand Painted, 24 In.	1500.00
Aurelian, Vase, Grapes, Eugene Roberts, c.1900, 10 3/4 In.	1035.00
Aurelian, Vase, Twist, Daffodils, Marked, 11 3/8 In.	650.00
Baldin, Vase, Apples, Stems, Leaves, 6 3/4 In.	175.00
Barcelona, Vase, Stylized Flowers, Paper Label, 11 x 6 1/2 In.	345.00
Bedford, Umbrella Stand, Green Matte Glaze, Tulips, 20 x 11 In.	690.00
Blo' Red, Vase, Gourd, 7 3/4 In.	40.00
Blue Drapery, Candlestick, 9 x 4 1/2 In., Pair	80.00
Blue Drapery, Jardiniere, Pedestal, 11 In., 18-In. Pedestal	635.00
Blue Ware, Jardiniere, Pedestal, Embossed, Grotesque Masks, 32 In.	800.00
Blue Ware, Vase, 2 Classic Figures, Embossed, Blue Matte Glaze, 10 In.	350.00
Blue Ware, Vase, Classic Figure, Stylized Tree, Blue Matte Glaze, 7 In.	150.00
Bonito, Bowl, Flowers, Multicolored Band, Cream Ground, 3 5/8 In.	70.00
Bonito, Vase, Blue Flowers, Bent Loop Handles, 5 7/8 In.	100.00
Bonito, Vase, Blue, Russet Flowers, Trailing Leaf Design, 4 5/8 In.	90.00
Bonito, Vase, Pansy & Bleeding Heart Bouquet, 11 3/4 In.	150.00
Bonito, Vase, Stylized Daisies, Flowers, Cream Ground, 9 1/4 In.	150.00
Burntwood, Vase, 3 Magi Scene, 9 In.	225.00
Burntwood, Vase, Egyptian Figures, Columns, Paper Label, 9 1/2 x 4 In.	290.00
Burntwood, Vase, Grapes, Vines, Tapering, Stamped, 8 1/2 x 4 In.	90.00
Burntwood, Vase, Morning Glories, Bulbous, 8 1/2 x 6 In.	115.00
Cameo, Jardiniere, Polychrome Jewels, Green To Lavender Ground, 7 1/2 x 10 In.	175.00
Cameo Jewell, Umbrella Stand, Ladies, Flowers, Glazed Jewels, c.1915, 22 In.	345.00 to 690.00
Chase, Vase, White Molded Rider On Horseback, Dark Blue Ground, 10 1/4 In.	180.00
Chengtu, Vase, Chinese Red Glaze, 8 1/4 In.	30.00
Clarmont, Candlestick, 2 Handles, 8 In.	90.00

Clarmont, Vase, Beehive, 6 In. 80.00
Clarmont, Vase, Bronze, Column, 7 In. 90.00
Clarmont, Vase, Bronze, Column, 10 In. 140.00
Classic, Wall Pocket, Blue Matte Glaze, 6 1/2 In. 45.00
Claywood, Bowl, Ducks, Bulbous, 2 x 3 In. 90.00
Claywood, Bowl, Fish, 2 x 3 In. 80.00
Claywood, Vase, Butterflies, Bulbous, 3 x 3 1/4 In. 105.00
Cookie Jar, Mammy, Marked, 11 1/2 x 7 In. ....1650.00 to 1725.00
Coppertone, Console, Flower Frog, Matte Glaze, Incised Mark, 3 x 12 In. ...300.00 to 545.00
Coppertone, Console, Frog Perched By Water Lily, Green, Brown Glaze, 2 x 10 1/2 In. ... 805.00
Coppertone, Console, Green, Brown Matte Glaze, 3 x 11 In. 175.00
Coppertone, Figurine, Frog On Lotus Blossom, Marked, 3 3/4 In. 140.00
Coppertone, Figurine, Frog, Green & Tan, Signed, 4 In. 325.00
Coppertone, Figurine, Frog, Green, Tan, Brown, Black Matte Glaze, 2 In. 300.00
Coppertone, Tray, Frog, Lily Pads, Green Semigloss Glaze, Ink Stamp, c.1925, 15 In. ... 635.00
Coppertone, Vase, Brown, Green Matte Glaze, 2 Handles, 8 In. 405.00
Coppertone, Vase, Dark Brown, Copper, Green Matte Glaze, 6 In. 345.00
Coppertone, Vase, Deep Brown, Green Matte Glaze, Flared, 8 1/2 In. 400.00
Coppertone, Vase, Green Matte Glaze, 2 Handles, 8 x 9 In. 517.00
Coppertone, Vase, Green, Brown Matte Glaze, 6 1/2 In. ....115.00 to 230.00
Coppertone, Vase, Green, Brown Matte Glaze, 11 In. 430.00
Coppertone, Vase, Green, Brown Matte Glaze, 15 In. 748.00
Coppertone, Vase, Green, Brown Matte Glaze, 2 Closed Handles, Round, 9 In. 160.00
Coppertone, Vase, Green, Brown Matte Glaze, 2 Handles, 15 In. 1095.00
Coppertone, Vase, Green, Brown Matte Glaze, Tapered, Marked, 6 In. ....160.00 to 345.00
Coppertone, Vase, Green, Copper Matte Glaze, 8 In. 265.00
Coppertone, Vase, Green, Copper Matte Glaze, 2 Handles, 18 1/2 In. 575.00
Coppertone, Vase, Mottled Green, Brown Mottle Glaze, 2 Handles, 11 In. ....520.00 to 575.00
Cornish, Vase, Applied Leaves, Blue Ground, 7 1/2 In. 1720.00
Cretone, Vase, Brown Glaze Deer, Cream Body, 6 3/4 In. 1500.00
Cretone, Vase, Stylized Flowers, Leaves, Deer, Dark Green Glaze, 5 5/8 In. 375.00
Dickens Ware, Jardiniere, Chickadee Perched On Hibiscus Bush, 9 In. 475.00
Dickens Ware, Jardiniere, Solitary Spotted Yellow Lilly, 12 1/2 In. 550.00
Dickens Ware, Jug, Whiskey, Leafy Ear Of Corn, 6 In. 170.00
Dickens Ware, Mug, Fruit Design, Silver Bands At Rim, Base, 6 In. 46.00
Dickens Ware, Tankard, Fierce Toothy Dragon, 13 1/2 In. 225.00
Dickens Ware, Tobacco Jar, Turk, 7 1/4 x 6 1/2 In. 345.00
Dickens Ware, Vase, Marching Soldiers Scene, Impressed Mark, 20 In. 575.00
Dickens Ware, Vase, Upward Growing Vines 3 Sides, Signed, 11 3/4 In. 375.00
Dickens Ware I, Mug, Incised With Smartly Dressed Father Seated With Son, 5 In. 225.00
Dickens Ware I, Vase, Lotus Design, Black, 12 1/4 In. 400.00
Dickens Ware I, Vase, Small Yellow Flowers, Cobalt Blue Ground, 5 1/2 In. 400.00
Dickens Ware II, Bowl, Raised Painted Leaf Design, Blue High Glaze, 4 In. 90.00
Dickens Ware II, Vase, Black Heart Indian Chief Portrait, 1905 .... 2700.00
Dickens Ware II, Vase, Incised Monk Design, 3 Sides, 6 3/4 In. 210.00
Dickens Ware II, Vase, Incised Venetian Scene, C.A. Dusenbery, 17 In. 1150.00
Dickens Ware II, Vase, Portrait Of Monk, 6 3/8 In. 120.00
Eocean, Jardiniere, Pedestal, Grapes, Signed, Eugene Roberts, 36 In. 3100.00
Eocean, Jardiniere, Roses, 8 In. 115.00
Eocean, Pitcher, Mary L. Pierce, 6 1/2 In. 375.00
Eocean, Tankard, Red Cherries, Leafy Vine, 12 1/4 In. 750.00
Eocean, Vase, Iris, Bearded, Magenta, Blue, Forest Green Ground, 12 In. 1900.00
Eocean, Vase, Painted Iris, Green Glaze, Signed, Burgess, 11 In. 3165.00
Eocean, Vase, Pink Cherries, Footed, 8 In., Pair 170.00
Eocean, Vase, Pink Rose Design, William H. Stemm, 6 3/8 In. 650.00
Eocean, Vase, Pink, White Tiger Lily Design, 16 1/4 In. 3000.00
Eocean, Vase, Pink, White Tulips, Salmon Ground, 12 In. 750.00
Eocean, Vase, Red Poppies, Green Ground, 9 1/2 x 4 In. 195.00
Eocean, Vase, Stargazer Lilies Blooming On Stalks, Orchid, Cream, 20 1/4 In. 1100.00
Eocean, Vase, Water Lily Design, Green Slip On 1 Side, 14 In. 2800.00
Eocean, Vase, White Daffodil Design, Sage, Taupe Ground, 10 In. 1100.00
Eocean, Vase, Wild Pink Rose Design, 7 1/4 In. 80.00
Eocean, Vase, Yellow, White Roses, Signed, 8 1/2 In. 90.00

Etna, Bowl, Ruby Phlox, Entwined Branch Handles, Signed, 4 1/2 In. 215.00
Etna, Jardiniere, Embossed Thistles, 10 In. 300.00
Etna, Jardiniere, Embossed, Pink & Gray Roses, 8 1/2 In. 130.00
Etna, Jardiniere, Red Flowers, 8 1/2 In. 115.00
Etna, Mug, Hearty Cluster Of Grapes, Signed, 5 1/2 In. . . . . .115.00 to 150.00
Etna, Pitcher, Ruby, Pink Peonies, 10 1/2 In. 140.00
Etna, Vase, Embossed Pink Apple Blossoms, Signed, 7 In. 160.00
Etna, Vase, Embossed Poppies, Gray Ground, Signed, 10 1/4 In. 250.00
Etna, Vase, Pink Grapes, Marked 15 In. 375.00
Flemish, Fountain, Fishing Boy, 20 x 7 1/2 In. 2415.00
Flemish, Jardiniere, Parrots, Chrysanthemums, 10 1/2 x 15 In. 980.00
Flemish, Jardiniere, Pedestal, Molded Parrots, 32 In. 1725.00
Flemish, Pedestal, Hyacinth Macaw, Cockatoo, Magnolias, 21 3/8 In. 460.00
Flemish, Vase, Red Flowers, Green Vines, Brown Matte Glaze, 12 1/4 In. 750.00
Flemish, Wall Pocket, Roses, 6 3/4 x 3 In. 115.00
Floretta, Mug, Pink Flower, 2 Buds, Handle, 5 1/8 In. 60.00
Floretta, Vase, Dark Brown, Black, 2 Handles At Neck, 7 1/4 In. 90.00
Forest, Jardiniere, Pedestal, 28 In. 1150.00
Forest, Vase, Woodland Scene, Brown & Green Matte Glaze, Cylindrical, c.1920, 8 In. . . 230.00
Fudzi, Vase, Sunflowers, Orange Shaded To Blue Base, Corseted, 8 1/2 x 3 3/4 In. 805.00
Glendale, Candlestick, Birds & Nests Design, 2 1/8 In., Pair 90.00
Glendale, Vase, Bird, Hovering Over Nest, Cattails, 13 In. 2200.00
Glendale, Vase, Blue Bird, Sitting On Nest, Surrounded By Reeds, 4 In. 375.00
Greora, Vase, Black, Green, Terra Cotta, Textured Glaze, 7 3/4 In. 160.00
Greora, Vase, Embossed, Floral Band At Shoulder, 9 x 4 In. 175.00
Greora, Vase, Stylized Flowers Around Center, Flared Rim, 5 x 4 In. 60.00
Hudson, Bowl, Daisy Design, 3 Footed, Signed, 11 1/2 In. 35.00
Hudson, Vase, Birch Trees, Lake, Mountain, Hester Pillsbury, Signed, 12 x 7 In. 5460.00
Hudson, Vase, Blue Berries, Branch, Leaves, Gray Ground, 8 1/2 In. 250.00
Hudson, Vase, Blue Iris, Sarah Timberlake, 8 3/8 In. 1100.00
Hudson, Vase, Blue Morning Glories, Gray, Blue Ground, Signed, 10 In. . . . . . . .690.00 to 978.00
Hudson, Vase, Daffodils, 9 In. 290.00
Hudson, Vase, Daisies Around Shoulder, Marked, 6 5/8 In. 450.00
Hudson, Vase, Dogwood Branches, Pale Blue, 2 Handles, Naomi Walch, 6 1/2 In. 200.00
Hudson, Vase, Floral, 10 1/2 In. 220.00
Hudson, Vase, Forget-Me-Nots On Bed Of Leaves, 5 3/4 In. 225.00
Hudson, Vase, Iris Blossom & Bud, Dorothy England, 8 1/4 In. 865.00
Hudson, Vase, Iris, Purple, Tear Drop Shape, 11 1/2 x 6 In. 690.00
Hudson, Vase, Irises, Purple, 9 3/4 In. 1400.00
Hudson, Vase, Lily Of The Valley, Sarah Timberlake, 8 3/4 In. 650.00
Hudson, Vase, Monarch Butterfly, On Pinecone, Mae Timberlake, 3 1/2 In. 1700.00
Hudson, Vase, Nasturtiums, Pink, 4 1/2 In. 170.00
Hudson, Vase, Nasturtiums, Pink, Green Pods, Hester Pillsbury, 9 1/2 In. 600.00
Hudson, Vase, Octagonal, Roses Painted Around Rim, 7 In. 400.00
Hudson, Vase, Orchids In Pink Outline, Claude Leffler, 9 5/8 In. 1600.00
Hudson, Vase, Painted Flowers, Brown Background, Bulbous, 6 In. 175.00
Hudson, Vase, Painted Flowers, Signed, McLaughlin, 12 In. 2530.00
Hudson, Vase, Painted Lotus Blossoms, Leaves, Buds, Gourd Shape, 9 1/2 In. 200.00
Hudson, Vase, Painted, Wisteria, Blue, Green Ground, Tapered, 9 1/2 In. 335.00
Hudson, Vase, Pine Tree, Landscape, Shades Of Gray, Hester Pillsbury, 7 x 5 1/4 In. 3740.00
Hudson, Vase, Pink Buds, Branches, Yellow, Rose Ground, 5 1/2 In. 325.00
Hudson, Vase, Poppies, 11 In. 485.00
Hudson, Vase, Ruby, Yellow Mums, L. Morris, 8 3/4 In. 1100.00
Hudson, Vase, Salmon Roses Painted On Shoulder, 8 1/2 In. 290.00
Hudson, Vase, Water Lilies, Shaded Gray Ground, 8 x 6 In. 315.00
Hudson, Vase, White Blossoms, Leaves, Sarah Reid McLaughlin, 2 Handles, 10 In. 690.00
Hudson, Vase, Wisteria Pods, Vines, Foliage, L. Morris, 7 1/2 In. 920.00
Hudson, Vase, Yellow Poppies, California State Flower, Hester Pillsbury, 9 3/4 In. 2415.00
Hudson, Vase, Yellow, White Roses, Powder Blue, 2 Handles, 5 3/8 In. 180.00
Hunter, Vase, Flying Duck, 7 In. 430.00
Hunter, Vase, Incised Duck Design, 5 In. 400.00
Hunter, Vase, Pillow, Butterflies, Artist Initials, 5 1/4 x 4 1/2 In. 400.00
Ivory, Jardiniere, Pedestal, Applied Rose Garlands, 35 5/8 In. 690.00

Jap Birdimal, Pedestal, Trees Framing Coastal Hamlet, 20 In. 325.00
Jap Birdimal, Tea Set, Indigo Squeezebag, Windmills, Teal Ground, 3 Piece 1035.00
Jap Birdimal, Vase, Geisha, Green Glaze, 9 1/4 In. 600.00
Jap Birdimal, Vase, White Geese, 10 In. 375.00
Kenova, Bowl, 4 Applied Dragonflies, 3 1/4 x 5 1/4 In. 1300.00
Kenova, Vase, Applied Fiddlehead Ferns, 8 1/2 In. 900.00
Kenova, Vase, Red, Green Wild Roses, Tan Ground, 5 7/8 In. 425.00
Klyro, Candlestick, Pyramid, Raised Flowers, Vine, Brown, Impressed, 9 3/8 In., Pair 145.00
Klyro, Vase, Raised Flowers, Green Matte Glaze, Pink, Brown Flowers, 1920s, 7 In. 200.00
Knifewood, Bowl, Swans, Trees, 3 x 5 In. 345.00
Lamar, Vase, Pine Trees, Red Glaze, Paper Label, 8 1/4 x 4 In. 489.00
LaSa, Lamp, Palm Tree, Design, Signed, 13 In. 290.00
LaSa, Vase, Lake, Tall Trees, Hills, Trumpet Form, 12 1/4 In. 230.00
LaSa, Vase, Landscape, John Lessell, 10 In. ....500.00 to 650.00
LaSa, Vase, Pine Tree, Lake Landscape, Pyramidal Shape, Marked, 6 1/4 x 1 3/4 In. 259.00
Lonhuda, Ewer, Flowering Blackberry Blossoms, Foliage, S. Reed McLaughlin, 13 In. 290.00
Lonhuda, Lamp, Flowers, c.1892, 20 1/2 In. 495.00
Louella, Vase, Flowers, Ribbed, Taupe Ground, 4 3/4 In. 110.00
Louwelsa, Ewer, Blackberry Design, Signed, 7 In. 140.00
Louwelsa, Ewer, Spray Of Roses, M. Hurst, 11 In. 375.00
Louwelsa, Jug, Whiskey, Dark Brown, Handle, 6 1/2 In. 110.00
Louwelsa, Mug, Gooseberries, Leaves, Artist Initials, 6 1/4 x 5 1/2 In. 115.00
Louwelsa, Mug, Monk, Levi Burgess, 5 3/4 In. 545.00
Louwelsa, Pitcher, Indian Head, 12 1/2 In. 1495.00
Louwelsa, Vase, Arabian Sheik, 2 Angled Handles, 9 1/2 In. 635.00
Louwelsa, Vase, Bud, Dark Brown, Red Blossom, 5 In. ....130.00 to 140.00
Louwelsa, Vase, Creeper Design, Dark Brown, Trumpet Shape, 6 5/8 In. 130.00
Louwelsa, Vase, Dog Portrait, Brown Glaze, 2 Handles, 11 1/2 In. 920.00
Louwelsa, Vase, Flowers, Brown, Light Tan, 6 In. 225.00
Louwelsa, Vase, Grapes, Stems, Frank Ferrell, 14 1/4 In. 575.00
Louwelsa, Vase, Indian Portrait, Brown Glaze, Signed, 12 In. 600.00
Louwelsa, Vase, Pansy Design, 3 x 5 1/2 In. 80.00
Louwelsa, Vase, Pillow, Brown, 4 In. 100.00
Louwelsa, Vase, Pillow, Canine Profile, Wearing Wide Collar, 10 1/4 In. 500.00
Louwelsa, Vase, Red Grapes, Vines, 20 In. 2100.00
Louwelsa, Vase, Russet, Yellow Nasturtium, 12 5/8 In. 225.00
Louwelsa, Vase, Saint Bernard, Elizabeth Blake, Signed, 9 1/2 x 5 3/4 In. 920.00
Louwelsa, Vase, Square, Buttercup, 9 In. 185.00
Louwelsa, Vase, Stick, 2 Carnations, 10 In. 225.00
Marvo, Jardiniere, Pedestal, Fern & Leaves Design, Green, Brown Matte Glaze, 26 In. 750.00
Marvo, Umbrella Stand, Ferns & Leaves, Embossed, 19 5/8 In. 450.00
Marvo, Vase, Ferns, Cattails, Flared, 9 In. 225.00
Minerva, Vase, Horse & Rider, 5 5/8 In. 180.00
Muskota, Figurine, Dogs, Red Retrievers, On Point, 6 7/8 In. 805.00
Muskota, Flower Frog, Fisher Boy, 6 7/8 In. 185.00
Muskota, Flower Frog, Girl With Watering Can, 6 3/4 In. 315.00
Muskota, Flower Frog, Newt On Lily Pad, 4 1/2 In. 140.00
Muskota, Flower Frog, Nude On Rock, 7 1/2 In. ....460.00 to 490.00
Muskota, Flower Frog, Snapping Turtle, 4 1/2 x 10 In. 275.00
Muskota, Powder Jar, Southern Belle, Yellow Hoop Skirt, 7 In. 180.00
Muskota, Vase, Double, Gate With Pots & Cats, 7 1/2 In. 1150.00
Muskota, Vase, Molded Fish Design, 5 In. 240.00
Noval, Bowl, White Body, Cluster Of Red Fruit, Black Bands, 3 1/2 x 9 1/2 In. 50.00
Noval, Candlestick, Apple & Blueberry Design, Black Trim, 9 1/2 In., Pair 120.00
Orris, Bowl, Molded Leaf Design, Footed, 3 x 9 1/4 In. 150.00
Patricia, Planter, Swan, Matte Green Glaze, 3 1/2 In. 2900.00
Raceme, Vase, Squeezebag, Blue, White, 5 x 5 1/2 In. 275.00
Rochelle, Vase, Yellow Roses, Hester Pillsbury, 10 In. 375.00
Roma, Jardiniere, Pedestal, Molded Flowers, 26 In. 300.00
Roma, Vase, Incised Flowers, White Body, 8 3/4 In. 80.00
Roma, Vase, Tapered, 8 3/4 In. 140.00
Rosemont, Vase, Blue Jay On Branch, Black Gloss Glaze, 10 x 5 In. 345.00
Sabrinian, Vase, Pillow, Shell Design, 2 Seahorse Handles, 7 In. 770.00

Sabrinian, Vase, Shell Design, 2 Seahorse Handles, 12 x 4 In.	1320.00
Sicardo, Bowl, Leaves, Green, Gold, Burgundy Ground, 2 Handles, Signed, 2 x 4 1/4 In.	690.00
Sicardo, Candlestick, Scattered Stylized Florets, 8 1/4 In.	1265.00
Sicardo, Vase, Berry & Leaf Design, Blue, Gold Iridescent, Signed, 9 In.	860.00
Sicardo, Vase, Berry & Leaf Design, Blue, Gray Iridescent Ground, Signed, 5 In.	630.00
Sicardo, Vase, Berry & Leaf Design, Blue, Green Iridescent, Signed, 9 3/4 In.	1000.00
Sicardo, Vase, Berry & Leaf Design, Green, Gold, Blue, 5 1/4 In.	690.00
Sicardo, Vase, Carnation Blossoms, Loose Petals, 13 5/8 In.	600.00
Sicardo, Vase, Dandelion Leaves, Citron Flowers, Signed, 17 3/4 In.	2070.00
Sicardo, Vase, Fantasy Spider Mums, 7 1/2 In.	850.00
Sicardo, Vase, Flowers, Dark Brown, 2 Handles, 6 In.	920.00
Sicardo, Vase, Gold Cornflowers, Burgundy Ground, 2 Handles, Signed, 7 1/4 x 8 1/2 In.	2185.00
Sicardo, Vase, Gold Dandelion Leaves, Purple Iridescent Glaze, Signed, 5 x 3 1/4 In.	400.00
Sicardo, Vase, Gold, Amethyst Iridescent, Signed, 5 In.	980.00
Sicardo, Vase, Green, Gold Iridescent, Signed, 4 1/2 In.	520.00
Sicardo, Vase, Green, Purple Glaze, Signed, 9 1/4 In.	460.00
Sicardo, Vase, Holly Sprigs & Berries, Olive Green, Signed, 5 In.	345.00
Sicardo, Vase, Honeysuckle Blossom Sprigs, Signed, 4 1/8 In.	200.00
Sicardo, Vase, Large Exotic Flowers, Scrolling Leaves, Cylindrical, Signed, 9 In.	195.00
Sicardo, Vase, Morning Glory Vines, Blooms, Signed, 7 1/8 In.	750.00
Sicardo, Vase, Peacock Feathers, Spider, Mums, 15 In.	4450.00
Sicardo, Vase, Shamrock Design, Signed, 4 1/8 In.	425.00
Sicardo, Vase, Spider Mum Blossoms, Leafy Stems, 7 1/8 In.	300.00
Sicardo, Vase, Stylized Flowers, Multicolored Iridescent, 12 In.	1300.00
Sicardo, Vase, Vine & Flower, Signed, J.W. Sicard, c.1907, 6 1/2 x 8 1/2 In.	1540.00
Sicardo, Wall Plaque, Whimsical Wide Eyes Fish Peering At Viewer, 10 1/2 In.	2200.00
Silvertone, Console, Flower Frog, Cast Rose Branch, 3 1/2 x 12 In.	230.00
Silvertone, Vase, Flowers, 2 Handles, Signed, 10 In.	325.00
Silvertone, Vase, Spring Jonquils, 7 3/4 In.	250.00
Souevo, Bowl, 4 Indian Designs At Mid-Body, White Ground, Cream, Rust, 3 1/2 In.	80.00
Souevo, Vase, White Base, Red, Black Rim, 6 In.	110.00
Stellar, Vase, Black, White Stars, 6 1/8 In.	375.00
Stellar, Vase, White Stars, Blue, Hester Pillsbury, Initialed, 6 In.	690.00
Turada, Lamp Base, Oil, Squeezebag, Olive Ground, Brass Font, 7 1/4 x 11 In.	920.00
Turada, Mug, Twisted Handle, 6 x 4 1/2 In.	58.00
Turada, Potpourri, Cover, Black Filigree, Dark Brown Base, 4 In.	200.00 to 275.00
Turada, Tobacco Jar, 5 1/2 In.	425.00
Turkis, Vase, Bronze, 2 Handles, 6 1/4 In.	110.00
Velvetone, Vase, Green, Orange, Yellow, Matte Glaze, Mottled, Handle, 11 In.	690.00
Warwick, Vase, Circular, Stamped, 7 x 7 In.	200.00
Warwick, Vase, Copper, Handle, 9 3/4 In.	70.00
Warwick, Wall Pocket, Marked, Foil Label, 11 In.	290.00
Woodcraft, Bowl, Squirrels, 3 1/2 x 6 In.	175.00
Woodcraft, Planter, Center Twig Handle, Stump Feet, Log Shape, 9 1/2 In.	80.00
Woodcraft, Planter, Flower Frog, Foxes, 6 x 8 In.	345.00
Woodcraft, Vase, Apple Tree Trunk Shape, 7 3/4 In.	100.00
Woodcraft, Vase, Bud, Fruit Trees, 7 In.	120.00
Woodcraft, Vase, Fruit Tree, 6 3/4 In.	130.00
Woodcraft, Vase, Red Crab Apple Blossom Design, 10 In.	200.00
Woodcraft, Wall Pocket, Squirrel, 9 1/2 In.	175.00
Woodcraft, Wall Pocket, Wolf, 10 1/2 x 6 In.	230.00
Zona, Jardiniere, 11 x 8 1/2 In.	58.00
Zona, Pitcher, Kingfisher, Cattails, 9 x 9 In.	230.00

WESTMORELAND GLASS was made by the Westmoreland Glass Company of Grapeville, Pennsylvania, from 1890 to 1984. They made clear and colored glass of many varieties, such as milk glass, pressed glass, and slag glass.

3 Fruits, Punch Set, 11 Piece	110.00
Cat On Sailor Cover, Dish, Lace, Glass Eyes, Green, Slag Glass, 5 x 8 x 6 1/2 In.	340.00
Checkboard, Water Set, Ice Blue, 5 Piece	66.00
Cherry, Biscuit Jar, Milk Glass, 8 In.	22.00
Compote, Lotus, Pink	80.00

Della Robbia, Compote, Footed, 8 x 7 3/4 In. 265.00
Della Robbia, Pitcher, Water 550.00
Dolphin & Shell, Compote, Black Amethyst 40.00
Figurine, Bulldog, Vaseline 68.00
Mary Gregory, Vase, Greek Lady, Black Amethyst, 7 1/4 In. 115.00
Old Quilt, Banana Boat 105.00
Paneled Grape, Canister, Milk Glass, 11 In. 255.00
Paneled Grape, Decanter Set, 6 Piece 155.00
Paneled Grape, Dresser Set, 6 Piece 150.00
Paneled Grape, Epergne, 2 Piece 200.00
Paneled Grape, Torte Plate, 1776, 14 In. 305.00
Paneled Grape, Wall Pocket 115.00
Pillow & Sunburst, Butter, Cover, Gold, Patent Date 75.00
Princess Feather, Pitcher, Water 102.00
Roses & Bows, Basket, Handle, Crimped Rim, Ball Shape, 1976, 5 In. 245.00
Roses & Bows, Water Set, Milk Glass, 10 In., 3 Piece 81.00
Shells & Dolphins, Compote, Satin Amethyst 120.00
Standing Eagle, Doorstop 102.00
Wakefield, Bowl, Ruffled Edge, 11 In. 66.00

WHEATLEY Pottery was established in 1880. Thomas J. Wheatley had worked in Cincinnati, Ohio, with the founders of the art pottery movement, including M. Louise McLaughlin of the Rookwood Pottery. Wheatley Pottery was purchased by the Cambridge Tile Manufacturing Company in 1927.

Jar, Sand, Feathered Green Matte Glaze, Grape Leaves, Vines, 24 x 15 In. 2410.00
Jardiniere, 4 Buttresses In Feathered Matte Green Glaze, No. 663, 7 x 9 In. 920.00
Vase, 4 Buttresses Joined At Base, Copper Tube, 11 x 8 1/2 In. 575.00
Vase, Applied Ceramic Frog & Cattails, Fragile Blossoms, 1881, 8 1/2 In. 1500.00
Vase, Bouquet Of Field Daisies, Blue Flowers, Gray Ground, 1881, 5 In. 200.00
Vase, Bulbous, Ribbed Neck, Green Matte Glaze, 3 Handles, 9 1/4 x 7 1/2 In. 633.00
Vase, Bulbous, Stylized Flowers, Green Matte Glaze, 5 1/2 x 5 3/4 In. 230.00
Vase, Charcoal Green Matte Glaze, 4 Rim Buttresses, 11 1/2 In. 1380.00
Vase, Curdled Green Glaze, Embossed, Leaves, 3 Buttressed Legs, 12 x 10 1/2 In. 2070.00
Vase, Cylindrical, Embossed Palette, Green Matte Glaze, 11 x 7 In. 201.00
Vase, Embossed Ferns, Dark Green Matte Glaze, 12 1/2 In. 3100.00
Vase, Embossed Flowers, Blue Matte Glaze, 12 1/4 In. 1800.00
Vase, Feathery Green Matte Glaze, 3 Climbing Lizards, Bulbous, 12 x 6 3/4 In. 1380.00
Vase, Green Matte Feathered Glaze, Horizontal Ridges, 11 1/4 x 6 In. 575.00
Vase, Green Matte Glaze, Embossed Symbols, Incised, 4 Cube Handles, 17 x 11 In. 920.00
Vase, Molded, Thistles, High Relief, Green Matte Glaze, 12 x 7 In. 805.00
Vase, Ocher Matte Glaze, Embossed Leaves & Buds, 4 Buttressed Feet, Marked, 10 In. .. 1150.00
Vase, Painted Flowers, Multicolored Brown, Ivory Ground, 1880, 8 In. 235.00
Vase, Poppy Pods, Frothy Green Matte Glaze, Split Bamboo Shade, 23 x 14 In. 1380.00
Vase, Squat, Embossed, Leaves, Quatrefoil, Green Matte Glaze, 4 x 6 1/2 In. 288.00
Vase, Stylized Flowers, Tooled Leaves, Green Matte Glaze, Squat, Incised, 10 1/4 In. 1095.00
Vase, Water Lily Pads, Buds, Green Matte Glaze, 21 x 10 1/2 In. 805.00

WHIELDON was an English potter who worked alone and with Josiah Wedgwood in eighteenth-century England. Whieldon made many pieces in natural shapes, like cauliflowers or cabbages.

Plate, Almona, 8 Sides, Exotic Bird 60.00
Plate, Tortoiseshell Glaze, 8 Sides, 10 1/2 In. 110.00
Plate, Tortoiseshell Glaze, Brown Sponge, Blue, Green Spots, 9 3/8 In. 495.00
Plate Set, Mid 18th Century, 4 Piece 2350.00

WILLETS Manufacturing Company of Trenton, New Jersey, began work in 1879. The company made Belleek in the late 1880s and 1890s in shapes similar to those used by the Irish Belleek factory. They stopped working about 1912. A variety of marks were used, all including the name Willets.

Bowl, Blossom Interior, Oranges On Band, Signed, 8 1/2 In. 230.00
Pitcher, Shell Form, 7 1/2 x 8 1/2 In. 275.00

WILLOW pattern has been made in England since 1780. The pattern has been copied by factories in many countries, including Germany, Japan, and the United States. It is still being made. Willow was named for a pattern that pictures a bridge, birds, willow trees, and a Chinese landscape. Most pieces are blue and white.

Bowl, Churchill, England, 9 In.	58.00
Bowl, Deep, 4 3/4 In.	19.00
Bowl, Soup, Coupe, 7 In.	19.00
Plate, 6 In.	6.00
Plate, Burleigh Ware, England, 1890, 6 In.	35.00
Platter, 18 3/4 x 14 3/4 In.	200.00
Platter, Blue Transfer Printed Mark, 15 3/4 x 12 1/2 In.	145.00
Platter, Egg Shape, J. & M.P. Bell, Glasgow, Mid 19th Century, 16 x 13 1/4 In.	144.00
Platter, Floral Rim, Chinese, 19th Century, 18 x 15 In.	288.00
Platter, Rectangular, 19th Century, 17 1/2 In.	201.00
Platter, Roasted Meats, Staffordshire, Mid 19th Century, 17 1/2 In., Pair	520.00
Sauce, 4 1/2 x 10 In.	110.00
Saucer	3.50
Soup, Dish, Rim	16.00
Toaster, Porcelain, 1928	2300.00
Tureen, Cover, Underplate, Ladle, 10 In.	50.00

WINDOW glass that was stained and beveled was popular for houses during the late nineteenth and early twentieth centuries. The old windows became popular with collectors in the 1970s; today, old and new examples are seen.

Barroom, Etched Whiskeys, Brass Rail, Mahogany Frame, 56 x 29 In.	316.00
Beveled, Etched, Frosted Center Panels, Pine Frame, 30 1/4 x 8 In.	190.00
Interlocking Arches & Trefoils, Cast Iron, 43 x 17 In., Pair	405.00
Leaded, Arts & Crafts, Flowers & Grapes, 39 x 19 In.	175.00
Leaded, Arts & Crafts, House & Mill Scene, Frame, 36 x 19 In.	12.00
Leaded, Arts & Crafts, Scene Of Woman In Landscape With Houses, Frame, 30 In.	460.00
Leaded, Gilt Bull's-Eye, Colorless Center, Beveled Diamonds, 19 1/4 In.	1035.00
Leaded, Maine Coastal Scene, Cathedral Studio, 50 1/2 x 94 1/2 In.	2590.00
Leaded, Portrait, Flowers, Porthole Type Border, John LaFarge, 14 x 14 1/2 In.	9350.00
Leaded, Prairie School Design, Arts & Crafts Oak Frame, 16 3/4 x 46 1/2 In., Pair	1380.00
Leaded, Prairie School, Geometric, Frosted, Hammered Field, 16 x 59 In.	185.00
Leaded, Prairie School, Hammered Amber, Green, 16 x 48 In.	1380.00
Leaded Glass, Scottish Rose, Textured Field, Arts & Crafts, 16 x 9 In.	900.00
Stained Glass, 1 With Crown, Other With Crest, Oval, 16 x 13 In., Pair	460.00
Stained Glass, American Indian Dancers, Landscape, Wewell, 2 Piece, 18 x 23 In.	230.00
Stained Glass, Geometric & Flowers, 37 x 20 In.	110.00
Stained Glass, Half Round, Caramel Glass Center, Leaves Each Side, 31 x 69 In., Pair	935.00
Stained Glass, Judaic, 1900s, 45 x 39 In.	2300.00
Stained Glass, Leaded, Arched Inter Panel, Henry VIII, c.1860, 34 1/4 x 36 3/4 In.	475.00
Stained Glass, Leaded, Art Deco Style, No Frame, Early 1900s, 13 1/2 x 19 1/2 In.	115.00
Stained Glass, Leaded, Figure Of Henry VIII, Arched Inner Panel, 34 1/4 x 36 3/34 In.	335.00
Stained Glass, Leaded, Flowers, Victorian, 48 x 42 In.	990.00
Stained Glass, Leaded, Geometric & Swag, 15 1/2 x 36 1/2 In.	280.00
Stained Glass, Leaded, Geometric, 15 1/2 x 37 In.	140.00
Stained Glass, Leaded, Geometric, 16 3/4 x 25 3/4 In., Pair	195.00
Stained Glass, Leaded, Geometric, 21 x 23 In.	115.00
Stained Glass, Leaded, Geometric, 39 1/2 x 23 1/4 In., Pair	170.00
Stained Glass, Leaded, Geometric, 47 x 22 In.	170.00
Stained Glass, Leaded, Geometric, Flowers, 18 1/2 x 18 In.	224.00
Stained Glass, Leaded, Geometric, 27 x 12 In.	170.00
Stained Glass, Leaded, Geometric, Purple Shell Center Panel, 17 x 15 1/2 In., Pair	250.00
Stained Glass, Seated Women, Pond, Layered Enamel, Rippled, 74 x 44 1/2 In.	15680.00
Stained Glass, Star, Border, Bible & Cross Windows, Victorian, 59 & 54 In., 3 Piece	1100.00
Stained Glass, Victorian Style, Amethyst, Amber, Late 19th Century, 16 x 34 In.	3734.00
Stained Glass, Water Lilies, Frame, 23 1/2 x 44 1/2 In.	600.00
Transom, Reverse Glass Decal, Apothecary Mortar & Pestle, 60 x 15 In.	460.00
Transom, Sunflower, Wood, Carved, Painted White, Center Rosette, 18 x 50 In.	1380.00

WOOD CARVINGS and wooden pieces are listed separately in this book. Many of the wood carvings are figurines or statues. There are also wooden pieces found in other categories, such as Kitchen.

Adam & Eve, Apple Tree, Snake, M. Morose, Frame, 19 1/2 x 22 1/2 In.	550.00
Allegorical Figure, Elongated Arms, Bowl Over Head, Ivory, Japan, 21 In.	290.00
Amish Couple, Beard On Man, Bonnet On Woman, 5 1/2 In.	80.00
Angel, Outstretched Arms & Wings, Flowing Robes, 29 1/2 x 23 x 11 In.	2346.00
Angel, Tyrolean, Painted, 18th Century, 35 In.	4315.00
Angels, Giltwood, Gesso, Kneeling, Silver Accent, c.1800, 22 x 23 In., Pair	6038.00
Bamboo, 2 Boys On Water Buffalo, c.1900, 8 In.	30.00
Bear, Cub, Glass Eyes, c.1885, 8 1/2 In.	785.00
Bear, Standing, Salmon In Mouth, 11 x 17 In.	980.00
Bear, Walking, Glass Eyes, Switzerland, c.1910, 4 3/4 x 8 In.	195.00
Big Horn Sheep, 1 Foot Raised, Yellow Horns, Tail & Nose, 10 1/2 In.	220.00
Billy Goat, Whimsical, Life Size, Standing, 20th Century, 37 1/2 x 35 In.	460.00
Bird, Common Tern, Miniature, Oval Base, James Lapham, Dennisport, Mass.	140.00
Bison, Bull, Detailed Hide, 10 x 13 1/2 In.	830.00
Blackamoor, 1 Holding 2 Sconces, Other With Basket, 25 & 14 3/4 In., Pair	3360.00
Blackamoor, Gesso, Polychrome, Molded Base, 20th Century, 54 1/2 In.	530.00
Blackamoor, Standing, Holding Urn On Head, Black Paint, Italy, 48 In., Pair	3740.00
Boat, Dragon Shape, Warriors, 19 1/2 In.	495.00
Bodhisattva, Seated, White Floral Headdress, Ming Dynasty, Chinese, 38 In.	1495.00
Bodhisattva, Standing, Draped Robes, Red, Gold Lacquer, Chinese, 11 2/3 In.	290.00
Boy On Water Buffalo, Teak, Wooden Teeth, Brass Eyes, 6 x 10 3/4 In.	110.00
Brown Bear, On All Fours, Brown Paint, 10 3/4 x 20 1/2 In.	120.00
Buddha, Gold Paint, Dark Patina, 24 1/2 In.	385.00
Bust, Store Display, Articulated Nose, Eyes & Mouth, 19th Century, 17 In.	1880.00
Bust, Victorian Woman, Ruffled Collar, Carved From Log, Old Paint, 18 1/4 In.	80.00
Calico Cat, Seated, Curled Tail, Yellow Eyes, J. Siloski, c.1960, 14 1/2 In.	660.00
Card Holder, Figural, Uncle Sam, Holding Red Tray, Painted, 1976, 13 x 4 In.	17.00
Carp, Bamboo Pole, Chain, 59 1/2 In.	82.00
Cat, 3 Kittens, Jade Eyes, Mother-Of-Pearl Plaque, Signed Tomotada, 9 In.	546.00
Cherub Face, Curly Locks, Outstretched Wings, 47 1/2 x 11 In.	1150.00
Cherubs, Pair Of Wings Below, Brown Wash, Rustic, 17 1/2 In.	192.00
Circus Wagon, Painted, Decorated, Barred Cage, 1930s, 16 x 22 x 13 1/2 In.	2585.00
Clock, Hunter, Walnut, Switzerland, c.1870, 30 x 30 x 14 In.	5750.00
Colonial Boy, Pine, Polychrome, Period Costume, c.1800, 16 1/2 In.	16000.00
Cow & Calf, Suckling, Full-Bodied, 19th Century, 6 1/4 In.	1998.00
Cowboy, Bowlegged, Chaps Over Blue Pants, Vest, 6 1/2 In.	330.00
Cowboy & Indian, Painted, 20th Century, 15 3/4 x 16 1/2 x 16 1/2 In., Pair	920.00
Crucifix, Polychrome & Gilt, Spanish Colonial, 1830s, 27 In.	1800.00
Dancing Couple, Jacques Adnet, France, 12 7/8 In.	9600.00
Decanter Set Holder, Black Forest, Bear, Glass Eyes, Branch Glass Holders, 18 In.	1288.00
Der Wildemann, Crouching, Draped, Gilt Paint, Continental, 28 In., Pair	1380.00
Devil, After Giambolgna's Il Diavolina, Fruitwood, Florence, 32 In.	460.00
Dog, Boxer, Seated, Pert Ears, Small White Spots, 11 1/2 In.	580.00
Dog, Seated, Painted, Signed W.F. Maddox, Milton, 11 3/4 x 5 x 6 In.	1998.00
Dogs, Foo, Flower In Paw, Black Mane & Tail, Puppy, 20th Century, 16 1/2 In.	1375.00
Donkey, In Corral, Split Rail Fence, 9 1/2 x 8 1/2 In.	93.00
Eagle, Half Round, Articulated Feathers, Features, Shield, Stars, Painted, 44 In.	5640.00
Eagle, Half Round, Spread Wing, Articulated Features, Glass Eyes, 25 In.	235.00
Eagle, Live & Let Live Banner, Painted, 20th Century, 72 In.	2645.00
Eagle, Pilot House, Pine, Gilt, Iron Wing Support Strap, c.1870, 30 x 15 In.	7600.00
Eagle, Shield, Crossed Flags, Painted, Early 20th Century, 9 1/2 x 27 3/4 In.	3220.00
Eagle, Spread Wings, 12 x 22-In. Wingspan	1925.00
Eagle, Spread Wings, Brown & Red Paint, Late 19th Century, 34 x 52 In.	6500.00
Eagle, Spread Wings, Carved, Painted, Wilhelm Schimmel, c.1890, 15 x 24 In.	28200.00
Eagle, Spread Wings, Courthouse, Standing On Rocky Plinth, 1920s, 46 In.	5875.00
Eagle, Spread Wings, Don't Give Up The Ship, Late 19th Century, 7 1/2 x 26 In.	35250.00
Eagle, Spread Wings, Facing Right, 13 1/2 In.	730.00
Eagle, Spread Wings, Facing Right, Clutching Shield, Painted, 20 x 41 x 6 1/4 In.	1645.00
Eagle, Spread Wings, Ocher Talons & Beak, H. Winter, 10 1/2 In.	880.00

Eagle, Spread Wings, On Orb, Gesso, Gilt, Mahogany Stand, 17 x 19 In. 2070.00
Eagle, Spread Wings, On Orb, Marble Base, 11 x 14 x 8 In. 825.00
Eagle, Spread Wings, On Orb, Weathered 6325.00
Eagle, Spread Wings, On Rock, Painted, Brown, Black, White, 34 x 40 x 31 In. 1725.00
Eagle, Spread Wings, Open Beak, Flag Shield, Painted, J. Bellamy, 26 In. 1440.00
Eagle, Spread Wings, Perched On Rocks, 19th Century, 27 3/4 In. 5400.00
Eagle, Spread Wings, Pilot House, Rocky Plinth, 23 x 31 In. 6465.00
Eagle, Spread Wings, Red, Green & Black, Wilhelm Schimmel, 7 x 12 In. 5875.00
Elderly Russian Jewish Couple, Book With Star Of David, 9 1/2 In. 440.00
Elephant, 2 Riders, Howdah, India, 15 x 11 In. 115.00
Elk, American, Stained Pine, Head Raised, 19th Century, 14 x 20 In. 8400.00
Finial, Pine, Flame Top, Fluted Urn, Stepped Plinth, c.1800, 24 In., Pair 5400.00
Finial, Urn Shape, Spiral Reeding, Knop, Fluted, Relief Cartouches, 20 In., Pair 430.00
George Washington, On Horseback, Pine, Henry Blade, 13 1/4 x 12 3/4 In. 6600.00
Grapes, Winery Sign, Painted, Green, Wrought Iron Hanger, c.1880, 20 x 13 In. 8500.00
Gull In Flight, Red & Yellow Beak & Feet, 14 In. 110.00
Head, Bearded Man, 1 Piece Wood, 19th Century 995.00
Head Rest, Curved Top & Supports, Flared Feet, South Pacific, 17 In. 2760.00
Hen, Rebar Legs, Painted Wood Base, 17 3/4 In. 580.00
Herman The Lion, Brush Whiskers, Fur Mane, Felt Ears, 1901, 9 3/4 In. 1495.00
Heron, White Body, Green, Red & Black Wings, 24 1/2 In. 2420.00
Horse, Hair Mane & Tail, Leather Ears, Glass Eyes, Gray Sponge, 22 In. 440.00
Horse & Rider, Leather Tack, Fred H. Foote, 6 3/4 In. 110.00
Humidor, Mahogany Top Hat, Austria, 1880s, 7 1/2 In. 505.00
Indian, Polychrome, Full Headdress, 7 x 2 In. 2850.00
Indian Man & Woman, Mahogany, 19th Century, 11 In. 275.00
Kingfisher, Standing, On Mound, Elmer Crowell, Mass., Late 1900s 6465.00
Lazy Susan, Fruitwood, Waste Not, Want Not, Staff Of Life, 19th Century, 17 In. 345.00
Lion, Crouched, Polychrome, c.1890, 8 x 4 1/2 In. 495.00
Lion, Oak, Forepaws Rest On Sphere, c.1900, 12 1/4 x 14 1/2 In., Pair 330.00
Man, Coat, Vest, Top Hat, Cane, White, Black, Brown, Pink, Blue, Varnish, 18 In. 605.00
Man & Woman, Cathedral Steps, Hand Out, R. Moroder, 31 x 24 3/4 In. 230.00
Man Worshipping, Wearing Robe, Gesso, Gilt, Applied Glass, 10 In. 55.00
Measuring Stick, Seated Figure, Borneo, 19th Century, 20 In. 259.00
Melon, Realistic Paint, Signed S. Hensal, 6 In. 165.00
Merganser, Painted, Early 20th Century, 6 1/2 x 5 3/4 x 15 1/2 In. 3760.00
Neptune, Fruitwood, Continental, 18th Century, 36 In. 920.00
Newel Post, Chestnut, Gent's Head, c.1890, 12 1/2 x 3 3/4 In. 450.00
Nude Man In Top Hat, Seated On Coiled Snake, 15 In. 7505.00
Nutcracker, Fruitwood, Head Of Soldier, Swiss, 20th Century, 8 1/2 In. 345.00
Panel, Circus Wagon, Painted, Lion, c.1875, 30 x 74 1/2 x 2 1/2 In. 2300.00
Panel, Pierced Center, Pagoda, Fish, Molded Frame, Mortised, 18 x 33 In. 100.00
Panels, Giltwood, Continental, 26 x 32 1/2 In., Pair 1380.00
Parrot, Long Tail, Green Body, Black Wings, Wire Legs, 17 x 21 In. 110.00
Peacock, Fanned Tail, Blue Body, Green Tail, Tack Eyes, P. Tyson, 9 In. 660.00
Peasant Man & Woman, Wood, Bone, 11 In., Pair 190.00
Penguin, Signed, F. Finney19 1/2 In. 364.00
Pig, Drinking, On Green Stool, Smoking Cigar, 1920s, 9 In. 3525.00
Pigeon, Raised Wings, Wire Legs On Green Stand, J.W. Kuisst, 5 1/4 x 10 In. 240.00
Pilgrims, Cherry Wood, 19th Century, 10 1/4 In. 2310.00
Pitcher, Water, Revolutionary War, 10 1/4 x 6 In. 176.00
Plaque, Mahogany, Eagle, Spread Wings, Applied Flags, 6 x 33 In. 690.00
Plaque Set, Teak, Figures, Trees, Pagoda, Asian, 13 1/4 x 12 In. 110.00
Pole Finial, Parcel Gilt, Painted, Mounted As Lamps, Neoclassical, 13 1/2 In., Pair 575.00
Policeman, Whirligig, Holding Billy Club, c.1920, 12 In. 1750.00
Puffin, Standing Upright On Rocky Crag, 23 In. 100.00
Putti, Continental, Stained Walnut, 18th Century, 34 In., Pair 1495.00
Putti, Gesso, Raised Hand, Glass Eyes, Gilt Pedestal, Ball Feet, c.1900, 13 In. 690.00
Robin, Black & Orange Body, Metal Beaded Eyes, Wire Legs, 3 3/4 In. 190.00
Roman Warrior, Walnut, Continental, Early 20th Century, 42 In. 1090.00
Santos, Hat, Metal Star, Blue Garments, Sheet Metal Wings, 13 1/4 In. 2645.00
Sculpture, Foo Dog, Pearl, Mounted, Converted To Lamp, Chinese, 28 In. 316.00
Selection, Festival Of Dead, Articulated Arms, Mexico 345.00

Shelf, Pipe, Chamois Head, Glass Eyes, 5 Cutouts For Pipes, c.1910, 7 x 9 1/2 In. 356.00
Shepherd Carrying Lamb, Tin Flag, Cross Finial, 8 1/2 In. 190.00
Shorebird, Peep, Painted, Sanderling, 8 x 7 1/2 In. 1955.00
Sleepy Joe Estes, Black Man, Foam Hair, 11 1/2 In. 385.00
Snake, Diamondback Rattler, Sand Background, 35 1/2 In. 55.00
Soldiers, Stag, Lion Head, Eagles, John F. Cathcart, 1883, 49 x 26 In. 5500.00
Spaniel, Reclining, Alert Face, Black Paint, 8 5/8 In. 300.00
Sparrow, Painted, Signed, Joseph A. Moyer, 1946, 6 In. 1430.00
Staff Head, Crosier, Fruitwood, Acanthus, Fluted Stem, 18th Century, 10 1/4 In. 86.00
Stag, Brown Body, Cream Underside, Black Rack &, Hooves, 23 3/4 In. 850.00
Tantalus, Walnut, Cherubs, Claw Feet, Fruit Basket Pediment, 18 x 13 x 18 In. 3416.00
Terrier, Seated, 9 5/8 In. 250.00
Thermometer, Deer, Glass Eyes, Switzerland, c.1910, 10 1/2 In. 145.00
Trout, Pine, Painted, Gold, Screw Mounts, Maine, c.1880, 29 x 8 1/2 x 1 In., Pair 2700.00
Tug Boat, Red & Black Hull, White Top Side, Buoys, Coiled Rope In Bow, 18 1/4 In. ... 330.00
Uncle Sam, Holding Flag, On Big Wheeled Cast Iron Bicycle, 52 In. 1800.00
Vase, Mountain Goat, Flowers, Switzerland, c.1910, 6 In. 115.00
Venetian Gondolier, Blackamoor, Gesso, Polychrome, Late 1800s, 78 In. 1725.00
Virgin Mary, Painted Hair, Jointed Body, Original Clothes, 19 In. 2050.00
Wall Pocket, Hunter's Weapon, Hanging Bird & Deer, 9 1/2 x 5 1/2 In. 235.00
Watch Hutch, Bone Inlay, House Form, Set Windows, Base Drawer, c.1800 .... 5800.00
Watch Safe, Eagle Form, Central Clock, Stained, Mid 19th Century, 11 x 7 In. 3750.00
Whimsy, Man's Head On One End With Elongated Leg, 9 1/4 x 14 In. 518.00
Whimsy, Sailor's, Rectangle, Woman, Umbrella, Snake, 19th Century, 11 1/2 In. 175.00
Wild Boar, Standing, Rocks, Signed Ed. R. Blatter, Switzerland, c.1910, 6 x 5 In. 138.00

WOODEN wares were used in all parts of the home. Wood was used for many containers and tools. Small wooden pieces are called *treenware* in England, but the term woodenware is more common in the United States. Additional pieces may be found in the Advertising, Kitchen, and Tool categories.

Alphabet, Cutout Letters, Red, Blue, Green, Yellow, Early 1900s, 1 7/8 In., 26 Piece 110.00
Artist's Model, Articulated Joints, 15 3/4 In. 220.00
Barrel, Storage, Oak, Metal Band, Cover, 17 1/2 x 14 In. 44.00
Barrel, Syrup, Painted Blue Staves, Orange Iron Bands, 35 x 31 1/2 In. 725.00
Basket, Corn, 10 x 24 x 17 In. 200.00
Bin, Grain, Poplar Boards, Slant Front, Iron Hinges, 39 x 49 1/2 In. 357.00
Birdhouse, Cottage, Painted, Early 20th Century, 21 1/2 x 16 x 17 1/2 In. 431.00
Book, Trick Pop-Up, Lift Top, Hinged Snake, Painted, Brown, 5 1/2 In. 22.00
Bootjack, English Oak, Brass Mounted Hinge, 31 x 15 x 21 In. 728.00
Bowl, Ash, Burl, Scrubbed Interior, Raised Rim, Footed, 11 1/4 x 4 In. 550.00
Bowl, Ash, Burl, Thinly Turned, Incised Exterior Rings, c.1830, 19 x 4 3/4 In. 4850.00
Bowl, Birch, Lathe Turned, James Prestini, c.1933, 6 x 10 In. 1955.00
Bowl, Bird's-Eye Maple, Oval, 3 1/2 x 10 1/4 In. 220.00
Bowl, Burl, Carved Handles Under Rim, Oval, c.1800, 6 1/2 x 22 1/2 In. 2530.00
Bowl, Burl, Curved Sides, Footed, New England, 18th Century, 5 1/4 In. 950.00
Bowl, Burl, Flared Rim, Footed, Treen, 19th Century, 5 x 10 1/4 In. 880.00
Bowl, Burl, Hand Hewn, Oblong, Dry Scrubbed, Irregular Rim, 15 1/2 x 13 x 5 In. 605.00
Bowl, Burl, New England, 18th Century, 4 3/4 In. 850.00
Bowl, Chopping, Painted Blue, Mid 19th Century, 5 x 10 1/4 In. 1090.00
Bowl, Hand Carved, Handles, Stand, 19th Century, Oversized, 48 x 19 x 6 In. 90.00
Bowl, Hand Hewn, Oval At Rim Tapering To Round Base, 4 1/4 x 15 In. 2090.00
Bowl, High Sides, Hand Hewn, Oval, 6 x 17 1/2 In. 440.00
Bowl, Incised Line On Body, Spiral Carved Grooves At Rim, Turned Foot, 11 3/8 In. ... 1430.00
Bowl, Maple, Filled With Carved Fruit, 11 In. 495.00
Bowl, Maple, Raised Rim, Stained Exterior, 6 3/8 x 19 1/2 In. 470.00
Bowl, Peaseware, Swing Handle, Lid, Treen, 19th Century, 6 1/4 In. 1250.00
Bowl, Stave Construction, 15 Sections, Circular Rings, Twisted Wire Bands, 22 In. 275.00
Bowl, Tiger Maple, 13 In. 595.00
Bowl, Yellow Paint, Treen, 19 x 21 In. 880.00
Bucket, Bentwood, Interlocking Bands, Wooden Pegs, Gray Paint, 11 In. 550.00
Bucket, Buttonhole Hickory Bands, 18th Century, 10 In. 295.00
Bucket, Cover, 2 Metal Bands, Wire Bail Handle, 9 1/2 x 10 1/4 In. 66.00

Bucket, Cover, Stave Construction, Brass Bands, Old Gray Paint, 4 3/4 x 3 7/8 In. 220.00
Bucket, Cover, Stave Construction, Swing Handle, Painted Blue, 12 x 12 In. 300.00
Bucket, Hanging, Staved Construction, 5 Bands, Painted, Hanging Hole, 8 x 13 In. 690.00
Bucket, Stave Construction, Tapered Sides, 3 Bands, 15 1/2 x 14 1/2 In. 248.00
Bucket, Stave Construction, Wooden Bands, Bentwood Swivel Handle, 12 1/4 In. 550.00
Bucket, Sugar, Red Paint, Copper Tacks, Wooden Pegs, Wire Bail Handle, 7 3/4 In. 550.00
Bucket, Sugar, Stave Construction, 1 Black & 1 Metal Band, Red Lid, 10 In. 385.00
Bucket, Sugar, Stave Construction, 3 Iron Bands, Bail Handle, Lehnware, 7 In. 880.00
Bucket, Sugar, Steel Tacks, Bentwood Handle, c.1889, 14 In. 440.00
Bucket, Water, Iron Bands, Bail Handle, Wood Stand, 19th Century, 25 In. 920.00
Bucket, Water, Iron Bands, Fittings, Wood Yoke Handle, Chinese, 19th Century, 24 1/2 In. 635.00
Canteen, Buttonhole Hickory Bands, Revolutionary War, 6 3/8 In. 495.00
Canteen, Red Paint, 2 Bands, New England, Early 19th Century, 6 1/4 x 10 1/2 In. 316.00
Canteen, Stave Construction, Barrel Form, 6 Lapped Staves, Initials D.P., 1815, 8 In. ... 346.00
Canteen, Stave Construction, Flat Base, Arched Sides, 8 1/4 x 9 In. 440.00
Carrier, Bentwood, Cover, Hickory, Pine, Brown Refinish, Arched Handle, 9 1/2 x 10 In. . 385.00
Comb, Apple Wood, Fan Carved, New England, 18th Century, 4 1/2 In. 550.00
Compote, Cover, Pedestal, Wafer & Ring, Treen, 5 1/4 x 7 7/8 In. 140.00
Cup, Cover, Saffron, Cream, Red, Yellow, Green, Black Knob, Lehnware, 6 In. 550.00
Cup, Cover, Saffron, Pink, Red, White, Green, Turned Foot, Lehnware, 6 In. 165.00
Cup & Saucer, Salmon Ground, Painted Sprig, Flower Decal, Lehnware 300.00
Cup & Saucer, Salmon Ground, Red, White & Green Leaves, Flower Decal, Lehnware ... 935.00
Dish, Laminated, Light & Dark Layers, Oval, Tapio Wirkala, 1 1/2 x 7 In. 920.00
Doorknocker, Dog's Head, Resting On Front Paws, 6 1/2 In. 275.00
Drying Rack, Blue, Folding, 3 Sections, 2 Crossarms Each, Mortised, 37 x 28 In. 340.00
Eggcup, Concentric Ring, Footed Base, Strawberry Design, Lehnware, 2 In. 1485.00
Eggcup, Cream, Red, Blue, Green Flowers, Turned Foot, Signed, Joseph Lehn, 2 1/4 In. .. 2310.00
Eggcup, Red & Black Bands, Blue Ground, Strawberry Design, Lehnware, 2 In. 2750.00
Eggcup, Red, Yellow, Lehnware, Pennsylvania, c.1870, 2 3/4 In., 6 Piece 3300.00
Eggcup, Turned, Salmon Ground, Painted Sprig, Flower Decal, Joseph Lehn, 3 1/2 In. ... 770.00
Firkin, Painted, Blue, Fingered Lap Bands, Swing Handle, 9 In. 290.00
Firkin, Painted, Yellow, Fingered Lap Bands, Wire & Wood Bail Handle, 7 1/2 x 7 In. ... 200.00
Firkin, Slanted Sides, Stave Construction, Bentwood Laced Bands, 6 x 6 3/4 In. 412.00
Firkin, Staved, Brass Bands, Bail Handle, Stamped R.C.M., c.1890, 8 3/4 x 10 In. 450.00
Flower Press, Rosewood, Reverse Painting, Victorian, 8 1/2 x 4 1/2 In. 365.00
Fruit Press, Ram Form, 15 In. 60.00
Goblet, Black, Green & Red Bands, Pink Ground, Tulip, Lehnware, 3 In. 2860.00
Grain Holder, Oak, Wall Mount, 8 x 20 1/2 x 14 In. 175.00
Jar, Cover, Brown Graining, Sponged Tree, 8 x 6 In. 385.00
Jar, Cover, Salmon, Stripes, Strawberries, M.M. Grubaker Lititz, Pa., 1865, 4 5/8 In. 220.00
Jar, Cover, Turned Pedestal Base & Finial, 5 3/4 In. 50.00
Jar, Poplar, Red Over Mustard In Arches, Rings On Base & Top, Domed Lid 1760.00
Jar, Saffron, Flowers, Peach, Pedestal, Strawberries On Cover, Lehnware, 4 3/4 In. 660.00
Letter Holder, Mounted, Rosewood, Birds Eye Maple, Art Deco, 5 1/2 x 10 x 5 1/2 In. ... 28.00
Mirror, Hand, Pine, Original Red Paint & Glass, Hanging Hook, 12 In. 850.00
Mortar & Pestle, Ash, Burl, Rough Interior, Turned Pestle, 5 x 6 1/2 In. 220.00
Mortar & Pestle, Treen, Graining, 6 x 5 1/2 In. 95.00
Mortar & Pestle, Turned Base, 19th Century, 8 In. 115.00
Mug, Burl, One Piece, New England, c.1800 .... 1400.00
Noah's Ark, Pine, Painted, Germany, Late 19th Century, 5 x 3 1/2 x 12 In., 46 Piece 860.00
Paddle, Butter, Curly Maple, Curved Handle, Hook End, 10 1/2 In. 250.00
Penguin, Spread Wings, Black & White, On White Block Simulation Ice, 16 In. 460.00
Pitcher, Oak, Stave Construction, Iron, 19th Century, 15 In. 430.00
Planter, Trough, Green, Yellow Legs, 14 1/2 x 19 1/2 In. 825.00
Plaque, Bass, Carved In Relief, Painted, Mounted On Oval Board, 15 x 28 In. 1955.00
Plate Rack, Pine, 3 Shelves, Belgium, 1940s, 31 x 68 x 4 In. 1600.00
Powder Keg, 1860s, 11 x 6 In. 70.00
Rolling Pin, Walnut, Pennsylvania, Mid 18th Century, 16 In. 325.00
Salt, Master, Black & Red Bands, Red, Green & Yellow Strawberry, Lehnware, 2 3/4 In. .. 1980.00
Salt, Master, Blue, Yellow Interior, Red & Green Base, Footed, Joseph Lehn, 2 3/4 In. 580.00
Shield, Patriotic, Red, White, Blue, Patina, American Flag, 13 Stars, 34 1/2 x 30 In. 440.00
Sign, Don't Spit On The Floor, White Letters, Black Ground, 2 Sides, 12 x 13 In. 2415.00
Sign, Post Office & Store Across The Bridge, Painted, 19th Century, 10 1/4 x 39 In. 1092.00

Sock Stretcher, Tiger Maple, 19th Century, Child's 250.00
Stand, Hat, Tiger Maple, 19th Century, 12 In. 325.00
Strainer, Cheese, Mortise & Peg Base, Attached Basket, 12 Spindles, 8 7/8 In. 190.00
Sugar, Cover, Apple On Pedestal, Flowers, Lehnware, 4 In. 1155.00
Tray, Cutlery, 10 Assorted Wooden Kitchen Implements, 19th Century 140.00
Tray, Fruitwood, Inlaid Sailboats, Pierced Handles, Signed, Galle, 1900s, 16 x 24 In. 2300.00
Trencher, Hand Hewn, Painted, Scrubbed Interior, Hanging Hole, 20 x 10 1/2 x 3 1/2 In. .. 468.00
Trencher, Salmon Paint, Geometric Design Base, Treen 330.00
Tub, Grained, Brown Over Yellow, White Interior, Steel Bands, 11 x 6 1/2 In. 275.00
Watch Hutch, Carved, Columns, Leaves, Sunburst, Opening For Watch, Painted, 13 In. ... 165.00

WORCESTER porcelains were made in Worcester, England, from 1751.
The firm went through many name changes and eventually, in 1862,
became The Royal Worcester Porcelain Company Ltd. Collectors
often refer to *Dr. Wall*, Barr, *Flight*, and other names that indicate time
periods or artists at the factory. It became part of Royal Worcester
Spode Ltd. in 1976. Related pieces may be found in the Royal Worcester category.

Basket, Chestnut, Inside Floral Sprays, Outside Flower Heads, Twig Handle, 10 1/8 In. ... 1200.00
Basket, Cobalt Blue Rim, Overlapping Twig Handle, Doe & Rogers, 1830, 3 3/4 In. 632.00
Basket, Earl Manvers Pattern, Pierced Rim, C-Scroll Handles, 1780, 10 5/8 In. 5520.00
Basket, Pinecone Pattern, Blue, White, Scalloped, Round, 1775, 7 1/4 In., Pair 1200.00
Bowl, Blue Flowers & Butterfly, Signed, 18th Century, 5 1/2 In. 172.00
Bowl, Imari Style, Paneled Fan Designs, Chinese Marks, 18th Century, 8 7/8 In. 201.00
Coffeepot, Cover, Cobalt Blue Flowers, Leaves, 18th Century, 9 1/2 In. 230.00
Creamer, Butterfly, In Flowers, Blue & White, Blue Crescent Mark, 3 1/2 x 2 1/2 In. 196.00
Dessert Service, Chinese Flowers & Fence, Cinnabar, 8 1/4-In. Plate, 11 Piece 5750.00
Dish, Leaf Shape, Landscape Center, Floral Sprays, 1765, 13 3/4 & 14 In., Pair 9000.00
Dish, Molded Leaf, Floral Sprays, Butterflies, Late 18th Century, 12 5/8 In. 230.00
Drain Dish, Flowers, Dr. Wall, 18th Century, 7 3/4 In. 315.00
Mug, Butterfly, Bird, In Garden, Blue & White, Blue Crescent Mark, 5 x 3 1/2 In. 728.00
Mug, King George II, Black Transfer, Signed RH, 1760, 3 1/2 In. 2160.00
Mug, King Of Prussia, 1760, 3 3/8 In. 780.00
Mug, King Of Prussia, Fame Blowing 2 Trumpets, R. Hancock, 1760, 4 3/8 In. 720.00
Mug, William Pit Portrait, Minerva & Fame Blowing Trumpet, 1760, 3 3/8 In. 2400.00
Plate, Blind Earl, Budding Rose Sprig, Gilt Scalloped, 1770, 7 3/4 In., Pair 1440.00
Plate, Dessert, Earl Manvers Pattern, 1780, 8 3/8 In., Pair 2640.00
Plate, Red Border, Framed Floral Cartouches, Ribbon Banner, c.1840, 10 In. 1725.00
Plate, Thumb & Finger, c.1815, 7 1/4 In., Pair 1175.00
Teabowl, Sauce Dish, Flowers, Stand, Dr. Wall, 18th Century, 1 3/4 x 4 3/4 In. 173.00
Tea Caddy, Blue Flowers, Tombstone Shape, 4 1/4 x 2 3/4 x 2 In. 110.00
Tea Caddy, Flowers, Dr. Wall, 4 1/4 In. 145.00
Tureen, Cover, Quail, Nesting In Oval Basket, 1760, 6 1/2 In. 4800.00

WORLD WAR I and World War II souvenirs are collected today. Be
careful not to store anything that includes live ammunition. Your local
police will tell you how to dispose of the explosives. See also Sword
and Trench Art.

WORLD WAR I, Banner, Welcoming Home Veterans, Red, White, Blue, 11 x 16 1/2 In. 85.00
Bond, Before Sunset, Buy U.S. Government Bond, E. DeLand, 1917, 30 x 20 In. 440.00
Bond Poster, USA Bonds Third Loan Campaign, Charles Leydendecker 259.00
Flag, Red Cross Week, 10 1/2 x 11 1/2 In. 14.00
Flag Holder, Figural, Uncle Sam, Plaster, F.W. Eichorn, 1917, 12 5/8 In. 58.00
Helmet, Doughboy Type, Metal 50.00
Needle Book, Army & Navy, Battleship Iowa, 2 3/4 x 5 In. ....*Illus* 6.00
Pennant, World War Service, Felt, Sheer Fabric Flag Stitched On, 22 1/2 x 67 In. 18.00
Poster, 4th Liberty Loan, Flag Design, 19 1/2 x 27 In. 18.00
Poster, Aviation Examining Board, Cleveland, J. Paul Verreel, 1917, 42 x 25 In. 1100.00
Poster, Beware, Wrath, Patient Man, Uncle Sam, J.M. Flagg, 1918, 30 x 20 In. 720.00
Poster, Care For Her Through YWCA, Woman, In Front Of V, A. Treidler, 40 x 30 In. 1705.00
Poster, Help Him To Help Us, Uncle Sam, American Red Cross, Flagg, 1918, 33 x 23 In. .. 460.00
Poster, I Am Telling You, Uncle Sam, W.S.S., J.M. Flagg, 1917, 30 x 20 In. 575.00
Poster, Joan Of Arc Picture, U.S. Treasury Bonds, 30 x 40 1/2 In. 200.00

World War I, Needle Book, Army &
Navy, Battleship Iowa, 2 3/4 x 5 In.

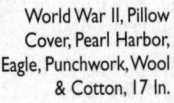

World War II, Pillow
Cover, Pearl Harbor,
Eagle, Punchwork, Wool
& Cotton, 17 In.

Poster, Liberty Bonds, Lincoln Profile Portrait, 20 x 30 In.	28.00
Poster, Miss Liberty, Victory Gardens Help Hungry, J.M. Flagg, 1918, 33 x 21 In.	780.00
Poster, Our Daddy Is Fighting At The Front For You, 30 x 20 In.	330.00
Poster, Parliamentary Recruiting Committee, Britain, 50 x 40 In.	172.00
Poster, Soldier Silhouette, Kidnapping Girl, Remember Belgium, 30 x 20 In.	55.00
Poster, Third Liberty Loan, Little Girl, Blond Hair, Frame, 38 3/4 x 28 1/4 In.	220.00
Poster, United We Serve, Red, White & Blue Borders, Tan Ground, 30 x 20 In.	55.00
Poster, War Garden Commission, Farmer, Hoe, Maginel W. Enright, 29 x 22 In.	412.00
Poster, War Gardens Over The Top, Maginel Wright Enright, 29 2/3 x 22 1/3 In.	275.00
Poster, YMCA Workers, Lend Your Strength To Red Triangle, Gilt Spear, 27 x 20 In.	110.00
WORLD WAR II, 3 Flying Models Kit, Spotter & Material, Paper Planes, 1944, 9 x 12 In.	29.00
Armband, Nazi	85.00
Ashtray, Anti Mussolini, Vulture On Tree Limb	95.00
Ashtray, Aviation Engineers, Hexagonal, Chinese, 5 1/2 In.	17.00
Bank, Figural, Bomb, Plaster, Victory Slogans, 3 x 7 1/2 In.	95.00
Bank, Figural, Drill Sergeant, Plaster, Painted, 12 In.	24.00
Banner, Cloth, String, Red, White, Blue	32.00
Banner, Son In Service, Star In Center, Gold Fringe Trim, 8 1/2 x 11 In.	39.00
Banner, War Worker, Cloth, Gold Fringe, 8 x 11 In.	18.00
Banner, Welcome Home, Cloth, Eagle, Fringe, 8 x 12 In.	18.00
Beanie, Child's, Patriotic Slogans, Remember Pearl Harbor	55.00
Brochure, Ravaged Earth, Early Anti-Japan Film, 9 x 12 In.	48.00
Brooch, Statue Of Liberty, Remember Pearl Harbor On Banner, Preview Creations	75.00
Clock, God Bless America, Die Cut, Tin Lithograph, 5 x 7 1/4 In.	48.00
Coloring Book, Marines In Action, 11 x 13 In.	38.00
Game, Keeping America On The Job, Dexterity Puzzle, Celluloid, Red, White, Blue	65.00
Glass, Medical Corp, Gold Trim, Messinger 4 3/4 In.	25.00
Glass, Pinup Girl, Gold Trim, Messinger, 4 3/4 In.	25.00
Key Chain, Bakelite, Remember Pearl Harbor, 1 In.	15.00
Machete, Marine, Horn Grips, Plastic Scabbard, 1945	85.00
Matchbook, United We Stand, Uncle Sam Stretching Across USA, 3 x 4 In.	18.00
Notebook, V For Victory Calendar Meter Reading Plan, Conserve Rubber, 1944	29.00
Paperweight, Remember Pearl Harbor, Ship, Plane, December 7, 1941, 3 1/2 In.	35.00
Patch, Patriotism, Felt, Red, White & Blue, 7 In.	12.00
Patch, War Production Soldier, Home Front Worker, Fabric, Wings, 3 1/4 x 7 1/2 In.	48.00
Pencil Box, V For Victory, Cardboard, Snap Fastener, Early 1940s, 1 x 5 x 8 In.	65.00
Pennant, Armed Forces, Felt, Black, Yellow, Pin-Back, 9 x 22 In.	45.00
Pennant, Remember Pearl Harbor, Blue, White	30.00
Pennant, US Army, Fort McClellan, Felt, Purple, White, 11 1/2 x 29 1/2 In.	18.00
Photo Album, South Pacific Region, Green, 360 Photos	179.00
Photograph, 82nd Seabees Reunion, 1957, 5 x 36 In.	11.00
Picture, US Navy Ship Leaving N.Y. With Torpedo Bombers, 1941, 6 x 8 In.	69.00
Pillow Cover, Pearl Harbor, Eagle, Punchwork, Wool & Cotton, 17 In. *Illus*	85.00
Pin, V For Victory Shield, On Card, Unused Order Form, Metal Arts Jewelry, 1940s	25.00
Pin, Winston Churchill, Plaster, Painted, Cigar In Mouth, 1 3/4 x 2 1/4 In.	95.00
Poster, 4 Freedoms, U.S. Treasury, Norman Rockwell, 16 x 12 3/4 In.	170.00
Poster, Adolf Hitler, Mein Kamph, Picture, Book, 1930s, 13 x 20 In.	35.00
Poster, Anti Runaway Prices, Uncle Sam, 1940s, 16 1/4 x 22 1/2 In.	65.00
Poster, Buy U.S. Defense Bonds & Stamps, Uncle Sam, Gruen Watches, 1941	258.00
Poster, Coast Guard Spars Recruitment, 28 x 42 In.	38.00

Poster, Fuel Conservation, Chamberlain Metal Weather Strip Co., 17 1/4 x 22 In.	40.00
Poster, I Want You, Uncle Sam, With F.D.R., J.M. Flagg, 1939, 24 x 18 In.	603.00
Poster, I'm Counting On You!, Uncle Sam, Tom Helguera, 1943, 28 x 20 In.	109.00
Poster, Let 'm Have It, Buy Bonds, 10 1/4 x 14 In.	130.00
Poster, Talk Can Kill, Buy Bonds, Black & White, 17 1/4 x 23 In.	30.00
Poster, Uncle Sam, Red Cross Nurse, J.M. Flagg, Frame, 1943, 20 x 13 In.	175.00
Poster, United China Relief, Uncle Sam, People, J.M. Flagg, 1938, 42 x 28 In.	287.00
Poster, Yours For Victory, Uncle Sam, E.H. Baker, 20 1/2 x 14 In.	170.00
Print, Keep 'em Flying, Flag, Capitol, Frame, 6 x 8 In.	18.00
Radio, German Armed Forces, 1944	5227.00
Sheet Music, Army Air Corps, 1942, 9 x 12 In.	8.00
Sheet Music, The Marines Hymn, 1945, 9 x 12 In.	5.00
Sheet Music, To My Darling, 1943, 9 x 12 In.	5.00
Sheet Music, Vict'ry Polka, 1943, 9 x 12 In.	5.00
Tablecloth, Army Air Forces, Nylon, Gray, Fringe, Logo, Flags, 38 x 38 In.	39.00
Toy, Junior Ranger Anti-Aircraft Gun, Box, 10 x 13 1/2 In.	135.00
Whistle, V For Victory Logo, Morse Code, Plastic, 1940s, 2 1/4 In.	25.00

WORLD'S FAIR souvenirs from all of the fairs are collected. The first fair was the Great Exhibition of 1851 in London. Some other important exhibitions and fairs include Philadelphia, 1876 (Centennial); Chicago, 1893 (World's Columbian); Buffalo, 1901 (Pan-American); St. Louis, 1904 (Louisiana Purchase); San Francisco, 1915 (Panama-Pacific); Philadelphia, 1926 (Sesquicentennial); Chicago, 1933 (Century of Progress); Cleveland, 1936 (Great Lakes); San Francisco, 1939 (Golden Gate International); New York, 1939 (World of Tomorrow); Seattle, 1962 (Century 21); New York, 1964; Montreal, 1967; New Orleans, 1984; Tsukuba, Japan, 1985; Vancouver, B.C., 1986; Brisbane, Australia, 1988; Seville, Spain, 1992; and Genoa, Italy, 1992; Seoul, Korea, 1993; and Lisbon, Portugal, 1998. Memorabilia of fairs include directories, pictures, fabrics, ceramics, etc. Memorabilia from other similar celebrations may be listed in the Souvenir category.

Apron, 1962, Seattle, Fabric, Ties, Come To The Fair, 35 In.	75.00
Ashtray, 1964, New York, Glass, Clear, Unisphere & Fountains, 6 x 6 x 1 1/2 In.	20.00
Ashtray, 1964, New York, John F. Kennedy Inset, Smoked Glass, 4 x 5 In.	30.00
Bank, 1934, Chicago, Tin Can, Slot Top, 3 1/2 In.	40.00
Beer Mug, 1964, New York, Glazed Ceramic, Cobalt Blue, 3 1/2 x 6 In.	20.00
Beer Mug, 1982, Knoxville, Ceramic, Logo, 5 In.	8.50
Book, 1939, New York, Official, Pictures & Summary, 144 Pages	85.00
Boot, 1982, Knoxville, Ceramic, Cream Color, Logo, 6 In.	18.00
Calendar, 1962, Seattle, Linen, 30 x 15 1/4 In.	38.00
Candy Dish, 1962, Seattle, White China, Heart Shape, 6 x 6 In.	15.00
Cigarette Snuffer, 1962, Seattle, Blue Plastic, Magnetic Base, 3 1/2 In.	25.00
Clip, 1904, St. Louis, Holds Paper, Steer For The Iron Mountain Route RR	150.00
Clock, 1934, Chicago, Circular, Burlwood, Electric, Herman Miller, 9 x 6 x 3 In.	2300.00
Coaster, 1964, New York, Plastic & Tin, 3 1/4 In., 6 Piece	20.00
Cocktail Shaker, 1939, New York, Shake A Leg, Glass, Chromium, Etched, 15 In.	5290.00
Comb, 1939, New York, Plastic, Ivory, Matching Case	30.00
Compact, 1933, Chicago, Silvered Brass, Enameled, 1 3/4 x 2 3/8 In.	20.00
Decanter, 1962, Seattle, Jim Beam, Space Needle Shape, 13 1/2 In.	65.00
Dish, 1904, St. Louis, Festival Hall & Cascade Gardens, Open Weave Rim, 7 1/4 In.	15.00
Earrings, 1962, Seattle, Cooper, Token Shape, Screw On, Pair	20.00
Figure, 1939, New York, Trylon & Perisphere, Bakelite, Butterscotch, 1 x 2 x 3 In.	60.00
Flag, 1968, San Antonio, Orange, White Plastic Pole, 7 1/2 x 11 In.	18.00
Folder, 1934, Chicago, Seagrams Whiskey Drink Recipe, 7 x 11 In.	10.00
Glasses, 1962, Seattle, White, 4 Different Attractions, 6 1/2 In.	12.00
Handkerchief, 1939, New York, Sheer, White, Lime Green & Yellow, 12 x 12 In.	12.00
Jack Knife, 1982, Knoxville, Double Blade, Red On Yellow, Coca-Cola Logo, 3 1/2 In.	15.00
Letter Holder, 1962, Seattle, Brass Clip, 1 x 2 1/4 x 3 1/2 In.	10.00
Letter Opener, 1939, New York, Metal Blade, Copper Luster, 6 1/4 In.	20.00
Match Safe, 1904, St. Louis, Brass, Flag, Louisiana Purchase, 1 1/2 x 2 1/2 x 3/8 In.	38.00
Memo Booklet, 1904, St. Louis, Ivory White, Celluloid Cover, 2 1/2 x 4 3/4 In.	45.00
Money Clip, 1904, St. Louis, Route, Spring Clip To Hold Notes, Celluloid, 1 3/4 In.	150.00

Don't store fabrics in cedar chests, cardboard boxes, or plastic. The fabrics will yellow and may mildew. Use archival boxes.

World's Fair, Scarf, 1939, New York, Nylon, 18 In.

Mug, 1893, Chicago, Stoneware, Gray, Cobalt Incised Letters, 5 In.	202.00
Mug, 1904, St. Louis, Palace Of Electricity, Bronze, 6 In.	103.00
Mug, 1934, Chicago, A Century Of Progress, Ceramic, Green Glaze, 1939, 6 1/2 In.	20.00
Mug, 1962, Seattle, Porcelain, Portrait, Official Visitor, Rosella, 4 1/2 In.	50.00
Paperweight, 1984, New Orleans, Die Cast Metal, Mascot Pelican, 6 In.	20.00
Parasol, 1933, Chicago, Rice Paper, Balsa Wood Struts, Bamboo Shaft & Handle	38.00
Pencil, 1939, New York, Cane On Top, Removable Pennant On Shaft	24.00
Pennant, 1933, Chicago, Felt, Blue, White Inscriptions, 5 1/2 x 18 In.	15.00
Pillow Cover, 1939, New York, Gloss Fabric, 2 In. Tassels, 16 x 16 1/2 In.	35.00
Pin, 1904, St. Louis, Steer For The Iron Mountain Route RR, Celluloid, 1 1/4 In.	65.00
Plaque, 1939, New York, Potter At His Wheel, Turquoise Glaze, Stamped, 7 In.	46.00
Postcard, 1964, New York, Equitable Life Insurance Pavillion	.75
Poster, 1933, Chicago, Red Ground, Yellow Building, 40 1/2 x 27 1/2 In.	4830.00
Poster, 1939, New York, New York Central, Route To World's Fair, 41 x 27 In.	4140.00
Poster, 1939, New York, United Air Lines, Golden Gate Bridge, 19 1/4 x 15 1/2 In.	920.00
Poster, 1940, New York, Peace & Freedom, Fountains, Lawns, Trees, 30 x 20 In.	575.00
Program, 1940, New York, Billy Rose's Aquacade, 9 x 12 In.	15.00
Ribbon, 1893, Chicago, Landing Of Columbus, 2 1/2 x 6 In.	30.00
Salt & Pepper, 1933, Chicago, Silver Plate, Embossed Logo, Twist-Off Tops, 5 In.	32.00
Salt & Pepper, 1983, New Orleans, Porcelain	15.00
Scarf, 1939, New York, Nylon, 18 In. *Illus*	22.50
Scarf, 1962, Seattle, Rayon, Space Age, Space Needle Towers, 30 x 30 In.	40.00
Sombrero, 1933, Chicago, Felt, Black, Gold Trim, Cord, Balls, 7 1/2 In.	30.00
Souvenir Spoon, 1933, Chicago, Metal, Scalloped, Rope Twist Handle, 5 1/2 In.	25.00
Spoon, 1893, Chicago, Sterling, 4 1/4 In.	15.00
Spoon, 1893, Columbian Exposition, 4 1/4 In.	40.00
Spoon, 1962, Seattle, Demitasse, Silver Plate, Die Cut, 4 1/4 In.	18.00
Table Lighter, 1933, Chicago, White Metal, Camel Shape, 3 In.	35.00
Thermometer, 1964, New York, Wood Plaque, 3/8 x 4 1/4 x 6 1/2 In.	12.00
Tie Clasp, 1934, Chicago, Wire Frame, Blue & Silver Logo	25.00
Tin, 1903, St. Louis, Blanke's Coffee, Fairgrounds, 10 5/8 x 3 1/4 In.	1870.00
Tin, 1904, St. Louis, World's Fair Tea, Tetley Tea, East India Building, 4 x 2 1/2 In.	53.00
Toy, 1933, Chicago, Bus, Cast Iron, Arcade, 5 1/2 In.	93.00
Toy, 1933, Chicago, Bus, Greyhound, Painted, Arcade, 10 1/2 In.	600.00
Toy, 1939, New York, Bus, Greyhound, Cast Iron, Arcade, 7 In.	250.00
Toy, 1939, New York, Bus, Greyhound, Decals, Nickel Plated, Arcade, 10 1/2 In.	220.00
Tray, 1933, Chicago, Aerial View, 7 x 10 x 1/2 In.	35.00
Tray, 1964, New York, Round, Metal	18.00 to 25.00
Tray, 1982, Knoxville, Enjoy Coca-Cola At The Fair, 12 In.	18.00
Tumbler, 1962, Seattle, Glass, Painted, Red Space Needle	15.00
Vase, 1893, Chicago, Columbian Exposition, Amberina, 7 1/2 In.	57.00
Vase, 1893, Chicago, Golden Rod, Pale Blue Flowers, Smith Brothers, 6 In.	287.00
Vase, 1893, Chicago, Palace Of Fine Arts, Peachblow Glass, 10 In.	172.00

WRISTWATCHES came into use during World War I. Wristwatches are listed here by manufacturer or as advertising or character watches. Pocket watches are listed in the Watch category.

Audemars Piguet, 18 Jewel, White Gold Bezel, Sapphire Markers, Baton Numerals, 1949	4800.00
Audemars Piguet, Woman's, Bracelet, 18 Jewel, Silver Matte Dial, 18K Gold	3000.00

Audemars Piguet, Woman's, Bracelet, White Matte Dial, Baton Numerals, Case, 1990 ... 2400.00
Audemars Piguet, Woman's, Pink Gold, Square Dial, Silver Matte, Baton Numerals, 1943 1920.00
Baume & Mercier, Conforming Strap, Florentine Finish, 17 Jewel 375.00
Benrus, Sunburst Dial, Yellow Gold Filled Case ...., 135.00
Black Dial, Gold Roman Numerals, Stainless Steel, 18K Gold 430.00
Breitling, Navitimer, Chronograph, 17 Jewel, Black Matte Dial, 1950 .... 1800.00
Cariole, Woman's, Date Window, Flex Band, Hong Kong, 1 In. 20.00
Cartier, Cream Matte Dial, Roman Numerals, Leather Box, 18K Gold, 1990 .... 5400.00
Cartier, Rectangular Dial, Diamond Back Winder, Platinum, 1927 .... 9200.00
Cartier, Rectangular Ivorytone Metal Dial, 18K Gold, 1927 .... 6325.00
Cartier, Vendome, 17 Jewel, White Dial, Roman Numerals, Circular Molded Case 1680.00
Cartier, White Matte Dial, 17 Jewel, Roman Numerals, 18K Gold, 1980 .... 4200.00
Cartier, White Matte Dial, 17 Jewel, Santos Case, 18K Gold, 1980 .... 2400.00
Cartier, White Matte Dial, Roman Numerals, 18K Gold, 1972 ....10200.00
Cartier, White Matte Dial, Roman Numerals, Molded Square Case, 18K Gold, 1970 ..... 3000.00
Cartier, White Matte Dial, Roman Numerals, Water Resistant Case, 1990 .... 3600.00
Cartier, Woman's, Cream Dial, Roman Numerals, 75 Diamonds, 18K Gold, 1990 ...... 7200.00
Character, 3 Little Pigs, Wolf's Eyes Move, Ingersoll, 1934, 2 In. 1025.00
Character, Cool Cat, Red Leather Strap, Gold Accents, Metal Case, 1 1/4 In. 125.00
Character, E.T., Metal Case, Blue Vinyl Straps 45.00
Character, It's Bugs Bunny Time, Chrome, Red Vinyl Band, Box, 1 1/8 In. 65.00
Character, Smitty, Instructions, Box, New Haven, Child's, 1930s 400.00
Character, Tom Corbett, Space Cadet, Space Ship On Band, Box, Ingraham, 1950 ...... 1540.00
Character, Woody Woodpecker, Ingram, 1950, 7 1/4 In. 310.00
Chopard, Woman's, Bracelet, 17 Jewel, Textured Champagne Dial, 18K Gold, 1985 .... 5100.00
Chopard, Woman's, Bracelet, Champagne Matte Dial, 6-Sided Case, 18K Gold, 1985 ... 2700.00
Chopard, Woman's, Bracelet, Champagne Matte Dial, 8-Sided Case, 18K Gold, 1990 ... 2700.00
Chopard, Woman's, Bracelet, Gilt Dial, Diamond Gilt 8-Sided Case, 18K Gold, 1900 .... 3900.00
Chopard, Woman's, Mother-Of-Pearl Dial, 17 Jewel, 18K White Gold, Signed, 1985 .... 3240.00
Chopard, Woman's, Silver Matte Dial, 17 Jewel, 18K White Gold, 1980 .... 6600.00
Corum, 17 Jewel, Manual Wind, 155 Diamonds Around Movement, c.1950 .... 8960.00
Corum, Skeletonized, Single Bridge, Sapphire Crystals, 18K Gold, Signed, 1985 .... 5100.00
E. Huguenin, Art Deco, Platinum, Diamonds, 18K Gold Case, Signed, Tiffany & Co. 2070.00
Enamel Dial, Crocodile Band, 14K Yellow Gold, Tiffany & Co., c.1950 .... 840.00
Eska, Silver Matte Dial, 17 Jewel, Roman Numerals, 18K Gold, Signed, 1970 .... 1800.00
Fleury, Chronograph, White Enamel Dial, Roman Numerals, 18K Gold, 1900 .... 2700.00
Floral Enameled Face, 17 Jewel, Cover & Band, Russia 260.00
Geneve, Woman's, Bracelet, Diamond Numerals, Grain Finish, 18K Gold, 1970 .... 2400.00
Gilbert, Western Saddle, Plastic, Brown, Silver Studs, 1960, 2 x 2 1/2 In. 45.00
Girard Perregaux, 17 Jewel, 14K Gold, Ivorytone Dial, Rectangular, 7 1/2 In. 630.00
Gruen, 15 Jewel, 2 Silver Matte Dials, Baton Numerals, Stepped Sides, 1935 .... 2700.00
Hamilton, Electric, Partial Engine Turned Face, Leather Strap, 1960s 100.00
Hamilton, Rutledge, 18K White Gold, 19 Jewel, c.1937, 8 3/4 In. 1530.00
Hamilton, Woman's, 17 Jewel, 14K White Gold & Platinum Bracelet, 44 Diamonds 1840.00
Hamilton, Woman's, 17 Jewel, Platinum, Diamonds Around Bracelet Band 3335.00
Hamilton, Woman's, Diamond, Platinum, 14K White Gold, Open Face Bracelet 1840.00
Jaeger LeCoultre, Bracelet, Woman's, Silver Matte Dial, Baton Numerals, 18K Gold 1680.00
Kingston, 14K Yellow Gold, Enamel Face, Radium Numerals 575.00
LeCoultre, 18K Pink Gold, Silver Matte Dial, Calendar, Moon Phases, 1955 .... 2760.00
LeCoultre, Memovox, Black Matte Dial, Arabic, Baton Numerals, Self-Winding, 1955 ... 3000.00
LeCoultre, Mystery Dial, 17 Jewel, Fabric Strap 750.00
LeCoultre, Woman's, 18K Pink Gold Mesh Bracelet, Heart Of Diamonds, 1945 .... 2700.00
Longines, Chronograph, Silver Matte Dial, 18K Gold, 1950 .... 4500.00
Longines, Open Face, Gold Filled Case By Wadsworth, Tiffany, Early 20th Century 210.00
Lucien Picard, Gold Tone Dial, Applied Marks, Mesh Band, Rectangular, 14K Gold 300.00
Marso, Woman's, 18K Gold, 3 Diamonds, Link Band, French Stamp, 7 In. 200.00
Minerva, Chronograph, Gold, Pink Dial, Circular Case, 18K Gold, 1950 .... 1920.00
Movado, Chronograph, 17 Jewel, Cushion Shape Case, Subsidiary Dials, 1930 .... 4200.00
Omega, Constellation, 24 Jewel, Champagne Matte Dial, 1980 .... 2040.00
Oval Dial, 22 Round Cut Diamonds, 14K Yellow Gold 345.00
Palais Royal, Woman's, Square Dial, H-Shape Links, Sapphires, Diamonds, Art Deco 3300.00
Patek Philippe, 18 Jewel, Black Matte Dial, Faceted Baton Numeral, 1950 .... 7200.00
Patek Philippe, 18 Jewel, Platinum, Silver Matte Dial, Mesh Bracelet, 1925 .... 5400.00

Patek Philippe, 18K Pink Gold, Square Case, Arabic & Baton Numerals, 1946 . . . . 4500.00
Patek Philippe, Black Matte Dial, Baton Numerals, 18K Gold, 1950 . . . . 4200.00
Patek Philippe, Charcoal Matte Dial, 18 Jewel, White Roman Numerals, 18K Gold 5100.00
Patek Philippe, Military, White Enamel Dial, 18K Gold, 1915 . . . . 7800.00
Patek Philippe, Pink Matte Dial, 18 Jewel, Baton Numerals, 18K Gold, 1940 . . . . 3600.00
Patek Philippe, Pink Matte Dial, 20 Jewel, Arabic & Baton Numerals, 1943 . . . . 46750.00
Patek Philippe, Pink Matte Dial, Arabic & Disc Numerals, 18K Pink Gold 10200.00
Patek Philippe, Pink Matte Dial, Baton Numerals, 18 Jewel, 18K Gold 5700.00
Patek Philippe, Pink Matte Dial, Roman Numerals, Signed, 18K Gold, 1940 . . . . 8400.00
Patek Philippe, Silver Matte Dial, 18 Jewel, 18K Gold, 1935 . . . . 5100.00
Patek Philippe, Silver Matte Dial, 18 Jewel, Rectangular Case, 1925 . . . . 5400.00
Patek Philippe, Silver Matte Dial, 18 Jewel, Rectangular, Signed, 1925 . . . . 6120.00
Patek Philippe, Silver Matte Dial, Arabic & Baton Numerals, 18K Gold, 1950 . . . . 5400.00
Patek Philippe, Silver Matte Dial, Baguette Cut Diamond Numerals, 1945 . . . . 16800.00
Patek Philippe, Silver Matte Dial, Baton & Dot Numerals, 18K Gold, 1950 . . . . 9000.00
Patek Philippe, Silver Matte Dial, Baton Numerals, 18K Gold, Signed, 1935 . . . . 7200.00
Patek Philippe, Silver Matte Dial, Baton Numerals, 18K Pink Gold, 1955 . . . . 8280.00
Patek Philippe, Silver Matte Dial, Baton Numerals, Circular Case, 1950 . . . . 6000.00
Patek Philippe, Silver Matte Dial, Roman & Baton Numerals, 18K Gold, 1945 . . . . 4200.00
Patek Philippe, Silver Matte Dial, Roman & Baton Numerals, 18K Gold, 1948 . . . . 5400.00
Patek Philippe, Silver Matte Dial, Roman Numerals, 18K Gold, 1945 . . . . 13800.00
Patek Philippe, Silver Matte Dial, Signed, 18K Gold, 1927 . . . . 9000.00
Patek Philippe, Silver Matte Dial, Signed, 1920, 18K Gold 4500.00
Patek Philippe, Square White Dial, Abstract Design, 18K Gold, 1950 . . . . 1380.00
Patek Philippe, White Enamel Dial, Roman Numerals, Case, 18K Gold, 1920 . . . . 3900.00
Patek Philippe, Woman's, Diamonds, Blue Matte Dial, 20 Jewel, Diamond Numerals . . . 7200.00
Patek Philippe, Woman's, Rectangular Dial, Caliber Cut Sapphires, Diamonds, 1922 . . . . 7640.00
Piaget, 18K White Gold, Silvered Textured Dial, 44 Single Cut Diamonds, 1960 . . . . 3900.00
Piaget, Black Banded Dial, Circular Water Resistant Case, 18K Gold, 1985 . . . . 1680.00
Piaget, Polo, Quartz Movement, 18K Gold 6750.00
Piaget, Woman's, 18K White Gold, Quartz Movement, Oval, Mesh Band, 6 3/8 In. 1495.00
Piaget, Woman's, Black Banded Dial, Water Resistant Case, 18K Gold, 1985 . . . . 1320.00
Piaget, Woman's, Bracelet, Diamond, 18 Jewel, Silver Matte Dial, 18K Gold 5100.00
Piaget, Woman's, Bracelet, Silver Matte Dial, Baton Numerals, 18K White Gold 2160.00
Retro, Woman's, Square Rubies, Diamonds, 14K Gold Bracelet, Paul Ditisheim, 6 In. . . . 690.00
Rolex, Blue Guilloche Enamel, 15 Ruby Nickel Movement, 9K Gold, Leather Strap 980.00
Rolex, Bracelet, Woman's, Silver Matte Dial, 18K Pink Gold, 1945 . . . . 1680.00
Rolex, Bracelet, Woman's, Silver Matte Dial, Baton Numerals, 18K Pink Gold, 1950 . . . . 1440.00
Rolex, Oyster Extra Prima, 15 Jewel, Octagonal Face, Coin Edge Bezel, 1928 . . . . 2280.00
Rolex, Oyster Perpetual, 18K Pink Gold, Black Matte Dial, Bombe Case, 1950 . . . . 3900.00
Rolex, Oyster Perpetual, Black Dial, Arabic & Roman Numerals, 18K Gold, 1945 . . . . . . 8400.00
Rolex, Oyster Perpetual, Black Matte Dial, 26 Jewel, Baton Numerals, 1977 . . . . 6000.00
Rolex, Oyster Perpetual, Black Matte Dial, Arabic & Roman Numerals, 1950 . . . . 2160.00
Rolex, Oyster Perpetual, Black Matte Dial, Luminescent Baton Numerals, 1970 . . . . 6600.00
Rolex, Oyster Perpetual, Bracelet, Silver Matte Dial, 18K Gold 6300.00
Rolex, Oyster Perpetual, Calendar, Silver Matte Dial, 26 Jewel, 18K Gold, 1958 . . . . 3600.00
Rolex, Oyster Perpetual, Champagne Matte Dial, Baton Numerals, 18K Gold 3300.00
Rolex, Oyster Perpetual, Silver Matte Dial, 26 Jewel, Screw Down Case, 1978 . . . . 2700.00
Rolex, Oyster Perpetual, Silver Matte Dial, 27 Jewel, Baton Numerals, 1980 . . . . 1800.00
Rolex, Oyster Perpetual, Silver Matte Dial, Arabic & Baton Numerals, 1945 . . . . 4500.00
Rolex, Oyster Perpetual, Submariner, 26 Jewel, Black Matte Dial, 1969 . . . . 3000.00
Rolex, Oyster Perpetual, Submariner, Black Dial, Abstract Numerals, Stainless Steel 1840.00
Rolex, Oyster Perpetual, Woman's, Black Matte Dial, 28 Jewel, 18K Gold, 1982 . . . . 5400.00
Rolex, Oyster Perpetual, Woman's, Blue Matte Dial, 28 Jewel, 18K Gold, 1979 . . . . 4800.00
Rolex, Oyster Precision, King Of Wings, Stainless Steel, Black Dial, 1944 . . . . 4500.00
Rolex, Oyster, Chronograph, Silver Matte Dial, Gilt Numerals, 17 Jewel, 1945 . . . . 4800.00
Rolex, Prince, 2-Tone Gold, Nickel Lever Movement, 2 Dials, 1929 . . . . 5400.00
Rolex, Princess Oysterdate, Woman's, Ivorytone Dial, Tudor Band, Stainless Steel 320.00
Rolex, Silver Matte Dial, 15 Jewel, 18K Gold, 1920 . . . . 1800.00
Rolex, Silver Matte Dial, Dot, Baton Numerals, 17 Jewel, 18K Gold, 1945 . . . . 3600.00
Rolex, Silver Matte Dial, Roman Numerals, Pink Gold Bezel, 17 Jewel, 1945 . . . . 3000.00
Rolex, Silver Matte Dial, Triangular Numerals, Signed, 1945 . . . . 3000.00
Rolex, Woman's, 18 Jewel, Flanked By Diamonds, Gold Filled Band, 1950s 950.00

Rolex, Woman's, Bracelet, Silver Matte Dial, Faceted Baton Numerals, 18K Gold	3600.00
Rolex, Woman's, Pave Diamond Dial, Sapphire Numerals, 18K Gold, 1978	7200.00
Rolex, Woman's, Pink Matte Dial, 4 Rows Of Diamonds, 18K Gold, Curved Bars, 1950	1920.00
Sunburst Dial, Luminous Numbers & Hands, Silver Case	300.00
Tissot, Woman's, Polychrome Map, Star Numerals, Link Bracelet, 1950 ......2400.00 to	3000.00
Universal Geneve, Black Matte Dial, Arabic & Baton Numerals, 18K Pink Gold	3000.00
Universal Geneve, Chronograph, Silver Matte 24-Hour Dial, 1950	16800.00
Universal Geneve, Tachometer, Silver Matte Dial, Baton Numerals, 18K Gold, 1950	1440.00
Vacheron & Constantin, Black Matte Dial, Arabic & Disc Numerals, 17 Jewel, 1940	1560.00
Vacheron & Constantin, Pink Matte Dial, Arabic & Baton Numerals, 17 Jewel	2160.00
Vacheron & Constantin, Silver Matte Dial, 17 Jewel, 18K Gold, 1945	3000.00
Vacheron & Constantin, Silver Matte Dial, 17 Jewel, 18K Gold, 1965	2280.00
Vacheron & Constantin, Silver Matte Dial, 18 Jewel, 18K Gold, 1955	2760.00
Vacheron & Constantin, Silver Matte Dial, Roman & Baton Numerals, 1935	2700.00
Vacheron & Constantin, Woman's, Bracelet, Ivory Dial, 36 Jewel, 18K Gold, 1940	2880.00
Waltham, White Metal Dial, Black Numerals	345.00
Wittnauer, 17 Jewel, Gold Filled Band, 14K Gold Case, Woman's	66.00
Woman's, 19 Jewel, 18K Gold, Stone Winder, Gold Link Band, Art Deco, Tiffany & Co.	290.00
Woman's, 22 Diamonds, White Gold Rope Bracelet, 10 Diamonds, 1955	1680.00
Woman's, Diamond Bezel, Ruby, Gold Mesh Strap, 14K Gold	3450.00
Woman's, Diamond, Sapphire, Cultured Pearl, 18K Yellow Gold, Bracelet	920.00
Woman's, Filigreed Chain Mesh Band, Bueche Girod, 18K Yellow Gold	980.00
Woman's, Goldtone Round Dial, Integral Mesh Bracelet, 18K Gold	575.00
Woman's, Platinum, Oval Case, Square Dial, Diamonds, Onyx, Mesh Strap, Art Deco	825.00
Woman's, Rectangular Dial, 17 Jewel	690.00
Woman's, Rectangular White Dial, Black	690.00
Woman's, Square Ivorytone Dial	920.00
Woman's, Textured Mesh Bracelet, Rectangular Dial, 17 Jewel, 14K Gold	230.00
Woman's, White Metal Dial, 6 1/2 In.	1150.00
Woman's, White Metal Dial, Black Numerals, 7 3/4 In.	373.00
Woman's, White Metal Dial, Black Numerals, Cobalt Blue Case	145.00
Woman's, White Metal Dial, Roman Numerals, 14K Gold	145.00

YELLOWWARE is a heavy earthenware made of a yellowish clay. It varies in color from light yellow to orange-yellow. Many nineteenth- and twentieth-century kitchen bowls and jugs were made of yellowware. It was made in England and in the United States. Another form of pottery that is sometimes classed as yellowware is listed in this book in the Mocha category.

Baker, Dark Rockingham Glaze On Interior, 1870, 9 x 12 In.	125.00
Baker, Woodland, Mottled Green & Brown Glaze, Applied Handles, 9 1/2 In.	39.00
Bank, Cottage Building, Rockingham Glaze, 2 3/4 x 2 5/8 In.	175.00
Bank, Pig, Brown Green, Pierced Eyes, 2 x 3 In.	250.00
Bank, Pig, Molded Shape, Cream, Brown Mottled Glaze, 3 1/4 x 5 In.	70.00
Bank, Pig, Running Brown Glaze, 6 1/2 x 4 In.	165.00
Bowl, 2 Slip White Accent Strips, 2 Brown Strips, 2 3/4 x 5 In.	45.00
Bowl, 2 Wide White Bands, 6 x 13 In.	165.00
Bowl, 3 Brown Accent Bands, 3 1/4 x 7 In.	22.00
Bowl, 3 Brown Bands, 5 x 2 3/4 In.	65.00
Bowl, Chicken Wire Sponge Design In Rust & Green, Warm Yellow, 10 1/2 In.	215.00
Bowl, Low, Sunburst Type Design, Rockingham Glaze, 8 In.	120.00
Bowl, Nesting, Center Brown Slip Band, 2 Brown Pinstripes, Flower Panels	285.00
Bowl, Oblong Paneled, Applied Handles, Rockingham Glaze, 4 1/4 x 7 3/4 In.	55.00
Bowl, Orange, Blue, Black Bands, Cable Pattern, Rolled Foot, 7 1/4 In.	690.00
Bowl, Pitcher, Blue Sponging, Gilded Rim	80.00
Bowl, Pour Spout, Paneled Sides, 14 1/2 In.	130.00
Bowl, Vegetable, Flared Edge, Rockingham Glaze, 12 3/4 In.	70.00
Bowl, Wide White Slip, Rust Bands, 12 x 6 In.	225.00
Casserole, Brown & Green Sponged, Cover, 8 1/4 x 5 In.	195.00
Crock, Open, Straight Sides, Applied Ear Handles, Rockingham Glaze, 6 3/4 x 8 In.	70.00
Crock, White Slip Band, Thin Brown Slip Bands, Cover, 5 In.	210.00
Cuspidor, Paneled, Rockingham Glaze, 3 1/4 x 6 3/4 In.	28.00
Custard, Green & Rust Sponged, c.1890, 3 3/4 x 2 In.	115.00

Figurine, Dog, Seated, Brown Running Glaze, Molded Shell Base, 10 In.	1485.00
Figurine, Dog, Spaniel, Seated, Rockingham Glaze, Shaped Base, 10 1/2 In.	330.00
Figurine, Lion, Molded, Hollow, Manganese Splotched, Stamped Star Base, 4 1/8 In.	365.00
Figurine, Spaniel, Seated, Manganese Splotches, 2 1/2 In.	220.00
Figurine, Spaniel, Seated, Rockingham Glaze, c.1850, 12 In.	275.00
Figurines, Ram, Spring Putto, Man, 1800-1820, 4 In., 3 Piece	700.00
Funnel, Rockingham Glaze, 6 3/8 In.	85.00
Humidor, Ribbed, Embossed Chain Link Bands, Cover, Branch, Oak Leaves, 5 3/4 In.	165.00
Jar, 3 Blue Bands, Relief, Spices, Reeded Relief Base, 3 1/2 In.	187.00
Jar, Milk Can Shape, Manganese Glaze, Molded Handles, 3 In.	33.00
Measure, Incised Groove Around Top, 2 In.	66.00
Mixing Bowl, Brown Slip Bands, Snowflake Design, 8 In.	33.00
Mixing Bowl, Green, 10 1/2 In.	225.00
Mixing Bowl, Nested, Brown, White Banding, 5 Piece	198.00
Mixing Bowl, Running Brown Glaze, Impressed Signature, 4 1/4 x 12 In.	358.00
Mug, Applied Ear Handle, Straight Sides, Rockingham Glaze	55.00
Mug, Flared Top, Rockingham Glaze, 3 1/4 In.	27.00
Mug, Slip Brown & Black Bands, Combed Vertically, Leaf Handle, 1790, 6 1/4 In.	3335.00
Mug, Soda Fountain, Cylindrical, Tall, 5 1/2 In.	22.00
Mug, Swirl Comb, Brown, Orange, Tan, White, 6 In.	5775.00
Nappy, Applied Copper Luster, Floral, 1860, 2 3/4 x 9 1/2 In.	275.00
Nappy, Recessed Bottom Resulting In Feet, 3 Pontils, 13 x 3 1/2 In.	265.00
Paperweight, Fawn, Recumbent, Manganese Splotching, Oval Base, Rushmore, 4 In.	155.00
Pie Plate, Colander, 10 In.	210.00
Pie Plate, Woodland, Green, Brown Splotched Glaze, 10 In.	110.00
Pitcher, Barrel Form, Brown & Green Sponged, c.1915, 7 1/2 In.	255.00
Pitcher, Bowl, Blue Sponging, Sponge Gilded Rims, 2 1/2 x 6 1/2 In.	55.00
Pitcher, Mottled Glaze, 4 1/2 In.	33.00
Pitcher, Paneled Scroll Design, Rockingham Glaze, 7 1/2 In.	33.00
Pitcher, Toby Character, Rockingham Glaze, 9 1/4 In.	110.00
Planter, Reticulated, Oval, Latticework, Flowers, 5 x 11 x 6 In., Pair	1380.00
Plate, Flared Edge, Rockingham Glaze, 11 In.	85.00
Punch Pot, Cover, Scroll Handle, Spout, Copper Pink Luster, c.1820, 8 5/8 In.	1410.00
Salt, Hanging, Chicken Wire Sponge In Brown & Green, Lid, 6 x 5 1/4 In.	450.00
Salt, Master, Footed, Brown Band, 2 x 3 In.	198.00
Salt & Pepper, Brown & Green Sponged, Morton Pottery Co., 4 3/4 In.	775.00
Soap Dish, Rectangular, Footed, Canted Corners, Rockingham Glaze, 3 3/4 x 5 In.	220.00
Sugar, Cover, Bulbous Form, Rockingham Glaze, 5 1/4 In.	60.00
Teapot, Applied Brown Green Sponged Glaze, Lid, 5 In.	110.00
Teapot, Confetti, Embossed Berry Rim, Acorn Finial, 5 In.	2530.00
Tureen, Raspberry Swirl, c.1830, 6 1/2 x 5 In.	950.00
Vase, Polychrome, Sanded, Flared, 4 1/2 In.	1320.00
Vase, Scroddled Glaze, Mid 1800s	175.00
Washboard, Cobalt Blue Glaze, Wood Frame, 1870, 24 x 13 In.	1595.00
Washboard, Mottled Rockingham Glaze, Wood Frame, c.1880, 5 x 12 In.	605.00

ZANE Pottery was founded in 1921 by Adam Reed and Harry McClelland in South Zanesville, Ohio, at the old Peters and Reed Building. Zane pottery is very similar to Peters and Reed pottery, but it is usually marked. The factory was sold in 1941 to Lawton Gonder.

Lamp, Multicolored Green Glaze, Black High Glaze, 14 In.	288.00
Vase, Blue, Green, Tan, 8 In.	92.00
Vase, Bulbous, Painted Landscape, Red, Blue, Brown, Yellow, 6 In.	288.00
Vase, Green, Yellow, Blue, Brown, 12 In.	161.00
Vase, Shadow Ware, Flared Rim, Deep Blue, Blue, 8 In.	400.00
Vase, Shadow Ware, Gourd Shape, Blue, Light Blue, 5 1/8 In.	325.00
Vase, Shadow Ware, Rolled Rim, Blue, Light Blue, 8 7/8 In.	450.00

ZANESVILLE Art Pottery was founded in 1900 by David Schmidt in Zanesville, Ohio. The firm made faience umbrella stands, jardinieres, and pedestals. The company closed in 1962. Many pieces are marked with just the words *La Moro*.

LA MORO

Bowl, Green, 4 Squares, Abstract Design In Relief, Squat, Impressed, c.1915, 7 In.	230.00

Vase, Flowers, Dark Brown, La Moro, 7 1/2 In. 110.00
Vase, Flowers, Dark Olive Green, La Moro, 7 1/3 In. 130.00

ZSOLNAY pottery was made in Hungary after 1862 and was characterized by Persian, Art Nouveau, or Hungarian motifs. A series of new
Zsolnay figurines with green-gold luster finish is available in many
shops today. Early Zsolnay was not marked, but by 1878 the tower
trademark was used.

Bowl, Stylized Flowers, Iridescent, 7 1/2 In. 690.00
Charger, Folklore Design, Blue Glaze, Enameled, 1875, 15 In. 595.00
Ewer, Openwork Flowers, Gilt, 11 In. 170.00
Figurine, Nude Woman, Iridescent Blue & Green Glaze, Stamped, 1900s, 5 1/2 x 9 In. ... 460.00
Umbrella Stand, Dark Purple Iridescent, 1900, 25 3/4 In. 14400.00
Vase, Copper, Green & Cobalt Blue, Iridescent, Label, 10 1/2 In. 405.00
Vase, Dancing Maiden Scene, Burnt Orange Iridescent, 12 1/2 In. 3738.00
Vase, Gold Iridescent Design, Signed, 13 In. 1090.00
Vase, Gold, Marbleized, 1900, 6 5/8 In. 295.00
Vase, Handles, Pink, Yellow, Blue, Gold Trim, 1885-1887, 8 x 4 1/2 In. 275.00
Vase, Iridescent Gold, Blue & Pink Berry Vines, 2 Handles, Stamped Medallion, 11 In. .. 1430.00
Vase, Mermaid & Meriman Clasping Hands, Green Metallic Glaze, 4 In. 2115.00
Vase, Red, Yellow, Gold Metallic Glaze, 6 Carved Exotic Birds, Impressed Mark, 10 In. ... 6900.00

INDEX

This index is computer-generated, making it as complete as possible. References in uppercase type are category listings. Those in lowercase letters refer to additional pages where pieces can be found. There is also an internal cross-referencing system used in the main part of the book, so if you look for a Kewpie doll in the Doll category, you will be told it is in its own category. There is additional information at the end of many paragraphs about where to find prices of pieces similar to yours.

KOVELS' DEPRESSION GLASS & DINNERWARE

PRICE LIST · 7TH EDITION

LEARN FROM AMERICA'S ANTIQUES EXPERTS!

- *More than 8,000 actual appraiser-approved prices*

- *More than 200 Depression glass patterns,*
  with photos and line drawings

- *Ceramic dinnerware patterns from the 1920s to the 1980s—*
  the patterns seen most often at shops and flea markets

- *Prices and histories of collectible plastic dinnerware—*
  included here for the first time

- *Special sixteen-page full-color report*

- *Factory histories, makers, dates, and marks*

256 PAGES, PAPERBACK, $16.00 · ISBN: 0-609-80640-8

KOVELS'
BOTTLES
PRICE LIST · 12TH EDITION

THE INDISPENSABLE BOTTLES PRICE LIST

- *More than 12,000 actual appraiser-approved prices*

- *Identifies bottles made from the 1700s to the 1990s*

- *Hundreds of bottles pictured in black-and-white and color*

- *Sixteen-page full-color report, featuring collectible plain and fancy bottles*

- *Easy-to-use picture dictionary of bottle shapes, closures, and bottoms*

288 PAGES, PAPERBACK, $16.00 · ISBN: 0-609-80623-8

KOVELS' LIBRARY

The authorities on antiques and collectibles in this country" —*Los Angeles Times*

0-609-80757-9

0-609-80982-2

0-517-58840-4

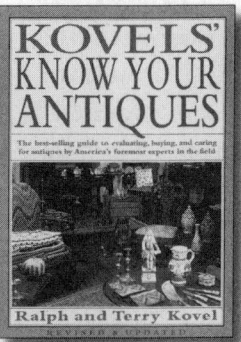

0-517-57806-9

0-517-80640-8

0-609-80623-8

0-517-70137-5

0-517-55914-5

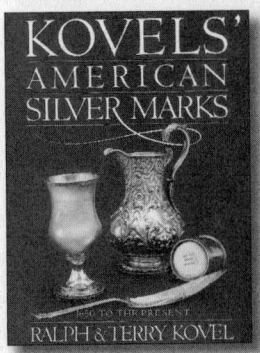

0-517-56882-9

AVAILABLE WHEREVER BOOKS ARE SOLD

K O V E L S

SEND ORDERS & INQUIRIES TO:
CROWN PUBLISHERS
c/o RANDOM HOUSE, 400 HAHN ROAD,
WESTMINSTER, MD 21157
ATTN: ORDER DEPARTMENT

SALES & TITLE INFORMATION:
1-800-733-3000

FOR ORDER ENTRY:
FAX# **1-800-659-2436**

WEBSITE: WWW.RANDOMHOUSE.CO

NAME _____

ADDRESS _____

CITY & STATE_____ ZIP_____

Please send me the following books:

ITEM NO.	QTY.	TITLE	PRICE	TOT
0-609-80982-2	___	Kovels' Antiques & Collectibles Price List —*current edition*	PAPER $16.95	___
0-517-70137-5	___	Dictionary of Marks—Pottery and Porcelain	HARDCOVER $17.00	___
0-517-55914-5	___	Kovels' New Dictionary of Marks	HARDCOVER $19.00	___
0-517-56882-9	___	Kovels' American Silver Marks	HARDCOVER $40.00	___
0-609-80757-9	___	Kovels' Bid, Buy, and Sell Online	PAPER $14.00	___
0-609-80623-8	___	Kovels' Bottles Price List—*current edition*	PAPER $16.00	___
0-609-80640-8	___	Kovels' Depression Glass & Dinnerware Price List —*current edition*	PAPER $16.00	___
0-517-57806-9	___	Kovels' Know Your Antiques, Revised and Updated	PAPER $17.00	___
0-517-58840-4	___	Kovels' Know Your Collectibles Updated	PAPER $16.00	___
0-517-88381-3	___	Kovels' Quick Tips: 799 Helpful Hints on How to Care for Your Collectibles	PAPER $12.00	___
0-609-80417-0	___	Kovels' Yellow Pages: A Collector's Directory of Names, Addresses, Telephone and Fax Numbers, E-Mail, and Internet Addresses to Make Selling, Fixing, and Pricing Your Antiques and Collectibles Easy	PAPER $18.00	___

___ TOTAL ITEMS

TOTAL RETAIL VALUE ___

CHECK OR MONEY ORDER ENCLOSED
MADE PAYABLE TO CROWN PUBLISHERS
or telephone 1-800-733-3000 (No cash or stamps, please)

CHARGE: ☐ Master Card ☐ Visa ☐ American Express
Account Number (include all digits) Expires: MO.___ YR.___

_____

_____

....
Signature

Shipping & Handling
Charge (per order) $5.

Please add applicable
sales tax.   ___

TOTAL AMOUNT DUE   ___

**PRICES SUBJECT TO CHANG
WITHOUT NOTICE.**

If a more recent edition of a pric
has been published at the same
it will be sent instead of the old ed

Thank you for your order